DICTIONARY

OF

NATIONAL BIOGRAPHY

1951–1960

THE

DICTIONARY

OF

NATIONAL BIOGRAPHY

———

1951–1960

v. 27

EDITED BY

E. T. WILLIAMS

AND

HELEN M. PALMER

With an Index covering the years 1901–1960
in one alphabetical series

OXFORD UNIVERSITY PRESS

1971

Oxford University Press, Ely House, London W. 1

GLASGOW NEW YORK TORONTO MELBOURNE WELLINGTON
CAPE TOWN SALISBURY IBADAN NAIROBI DAR ES SALAAM LUSAKA ADDIS ABABA
BOMBAY CALCUTTA MADRAS KARACHI LAHORE DACCA
KUALA LUMPUR SINGAPORE HONG KONG TOKYO

PRINTED IN GREAT BRITAIN

PREFATORY NOTE

THE notices in this Supplement describe the lives of men and women who for a significant period of their careers were British subjects and died between 1 January 1951 and 31 December 1960. The earliest born was John Scott Lidgett, the Methodist, in 1854 during the Crimean war; the most recent, J. M. Hawthorn, the racing motorist, was born in 1929, the year in which the second Labour Government took office. Many lived to a great age: some fifty worthies lived into their nineties; two were centenarians, both Fellows of the Royal Society, H. N. Ridley, the botanist, and James Swinburne, a pioneer of plastics. Many of our number were born abroad; some, of course, in India or the colonies; more than thirty came to this country as refugees from Hitler's or earlier continental tyrannies. One is impressed by how many there were—some sixty of all those included—who lost their father when very young. Some scarcely knew a father at all; some, indeed, who he may have been. Much was owed to mothers. Nearly all of the men and women recorded here died in peace, if some in pain; but too many, and they include the three youngest, Hawthorn, Dennis Brain, and Michael Ventris, were killed as a result of road accidents. Some took their own lives; some died of drink; four were assassinated; and one was murdered.

They were subjects of King George VI whose own life is recorded here, with that of his mother Queen Mary; Cromer and Clarendon, his lord chamberlains; Hardinge, one of his secretaries; Dunhill, Smart, and Horder, his surgeon, manipulative surgeon, and physician respectively; Arnold Bax, the Master of his Musick; Edmund Dulac, the designer of the postage stamps which bore his image; and one of the first recipients of the award which the King himself initiated, Henry Blogg, G.C.

If this volume follows the pattern of its immediate predecessor, it differs in three obvious regards. Nobody was killed in battle; there are more scientists and engineers to be discovered here; and there are more women. If some spent serene lives of service and fulfilment or found a serenity in their beliefs, it is evident that for many others life was marked by struggle and difficulty, not only because of two world wars. To help to edit these brief biographies of 760 men and women—who come together here only because they are chosen from amongst those who died in the first decade of the second half of our century—is to become increasingly aware, in the thousand or so pages which follow, of the virtues and defects of obstinacy, conviction, prejudice, or determination; and to be reinforced in the humility of one's admiration for courage, genius, sacrifice, or sheer hard work. If times were difficult, so sometimes were people. If there were storms, there was no shortage of petrels: Hilaire Belloc or Wyndham Lewis, for example; Bishop Barnes or Gilbert Harding; Ernest Benn who refused to complete his census form. Inevitably, there are conflicts and controversies to be recorded here, and *causes célèbres*: Henry Harrison champions Parnell; Gertrude Tuckwell fights for Dilke's good name; Bodkin and Humphreys appear for the prosecution, Serjeant Sullivan and J. H. Morgan for the defence, in the Casement trial. Frederick Maurice challenges Lloyd George's veracity. Marie Stopes and Halliday Sutherland argue the question of birth control; Christabel Pankhurst and Annie Kenney fight for women's suffrage; Elizabeth Kenny urges her methods of treating polio on a reluctant medical profession; Ernest Bevin challenges A. L. Bowley on what a docker needs to eat; D. R. Jardine ruffles Anglo-Australian relations in the row about 'bodyline' bowling. The Duchess of Atholl supports one side in the Spanish civil war, Roy Campbell the other. Hoare, Simon, and Halifax favour one approach in foreign policy in the thirties: Duff Cooper and Vansittart disagree. Trenchard and Sykes are in conflict from the early days of the first war, Lindemann and Tizard before the outbreak of the second.

Clearly, there are divisive matters too, as well as temperaments: two wars, most obviously, and how best to avoid or to win them; poverty; industrial relations; the role of women; Ireland; India; 'Appeasement'; Palestine; 'Apartheid'. There are dreamers of dreams, some realized. Chaim Weizmann and Selig Brodetsky work untiringly for the Zionist movement and live to see the foundation of Israel. D. S. Senanayake and Liaqat Ali Khan finally obtain the independence of Ceylon and Pakistan; Malan and Strijdom relentlessly pursue their Afrikaner goal in South Africa. It is a far cry from the hopes of the *Round Table* group, such as Dougal Malcolm or Lionel Curtis who had served under Milner, to the secession of another South African republic from British allegiance, in this instance from that Commonwealth of Nations which had been accorded their separate but shared recognition at the peace conference in 1919 which so many recorded here—and notably W. M. Hughes—had attended in their varying capacities; and which in the Statute of Westminster barely a dozen years later had seemed in the coinage of Edward Harding and Maurice Gwyer to have elicited a formula flexible enough to link without shackling; and was to survive another world war. Most disappointing of all was the failure of the League of Nations, both the first and last secretary-general of which, Eric Drummond and Sean Lester, are described in this volume, with Lord Robert Cecil, Gilbert Murray, Maxwell Garnett, Alfred Zimmern, and Harold Butler, the second director of the International Labour Office.

If nobody included in this Supplement was killed in battle, there was nobody whose life war did not affect. The King himself had served at

Prefatory Note

Jutland where Dreyer was Jellicoe's flag captain and Forbes his flag commander in the *Iron Duke*, and Cowan flag captain in the *Princess Royal*. We note Gordon Campbell and his Q-ships, Evans of the *Broke*, Carpenter in command of the *Vindictive* at Zeebrugge where he won the V.C. and Hilton Young lost an arm; and Reginald Tyrwhitt who, commanding the Harwich Force throughout, took the first ships into action on 5 August 1914 and the first U-boat surrenders in the November when the war ended. Those who served on the western front include two of Haig's intimate staff, Kiggell and Davidson, and two of his corps commanders, Ivor Maxse and Charles Fergusson. There too were Trenchard and Brooke-Popham laying the foundations of the Royal Air Force. Many had a share in the evolution of the tank: Ernest Swinton, Murray Sueter, Tennyson-d'Eyncourt, W. G. Wilson among them. Arden-Close furnished the maps, W. H. Mills the photographic plates, P. F. B. Bennett the aeromagnetos, Bruce Bairnsfather and Ian Hay the lighter relief, Muirhead Bone, Eric Kennington, and others the artistic, and eventually J. E. Edmonds the not undisputed historical, record. Farther afield than Flanders, Birdwood and Godley were at Gallipoli, Cassels at Sharqat, Ironside at Archangel. The increasing application of science and engineering to warfare may be noted in the contributions of G. M. Bennett, M. Copisarow, F. G. Donnan, H. A. Humphrey, P. V. Hunter, Mouat Jones, or O. J. Silberrad; and the involvement of business men in the notices of Maclay as shipping controller, Waley Cohen as petroleum adviser, or, at the new Air Ministry, William Weir who later, with Balfour and Lithgow, was to devise shadow factories against the coming of renewed hostilities. At home on leave there was a welcome, for some, from Rosa Lewis at the Cavendish, or an evening in the theatre with George Robey and Violet Loraine, with Jack Buchanan, or with José Collins in Frederick Lonsdale's *The Maid of the Mountains*.

The cause of women was perhaps one of the few to achieve its assured victory when the war ended, not only by reason of the organization of V.A.D.s and W.R.N.S. by Katharine Furse, but through the work of those who toiled in munitions and other factories with remarkable leadership from such women as Hilda Martindale, Violet Markham, Lilian Barker, or Margaret Bondfield who in 1924 was to become the first woman Cabinet minister. Between the wars two strongly independent papers—to Left and Right—were controlled by women: *Time and Tide* by Lady Rhondda and the *National Review* by Lady Milner. Rose Macaulay was coming to the fore as a novelist, Maude Royden as a preacher. Caroline Haslett founded the Electrical Association for Women; Lady Bailey was popularizing aviation; Winifred Cullis became the first woman professor in a British medical school; medical men like Victor Bonney, Dick-Read, Gilliatt, and Munro Kerr were making life easier for women. Constance Spry was turning flower arrangement into an art and a profession; Margery Fry was urging penal reform and helping to organize higher education; and far away in Central Asia Mildred Cable and the two French sisters were following the desert trade routes in pursuit of their missionary vocation. The advent of the second war brought their journeys, as so much else, to an end, and overshadowed Evelyn Lowe's chairmanship of the L.C.C.

And so it became time for Vera Laughton Mathews to revive the W.R.N.S. and Lady Denman to evolve the Land Army. Ernest Bevin took over the Ministry of Labour, with Godfrey Ince at his side. Hudson was at the Ministry of Agriculture, Llewellin eventually at the Ministry of Food, and Andrew Duncan at the Ministry of Supply where he was aided by men like Garner, Claude Gibb, Lennard-Jones, Guy, Lithgow, and Cecil Weir. C. D. Howe organized the Canadian arsenal. Richard Hopkins was still at the Treasury when John Anderson, the greatest administrator of his time, became chancellor of the Exchequer. At sea the Western Approaches were guarded in turn by Percy Noble and Max Horton; Bowhill's Coastal Command tracked down and helped to sink the *Bismarck*; Burnett's cruisers sent the *Scharnhorst* to her destruction on one of his many Arctic convoys; Agnew in the *Aurora* was in the Mediterranean where, like McGrigor and Arthur Power, he played his part in the invasion of Sicily and Italy. Before that could happen Morshead's Ninth Australians had held Tobruk and later the right flank at Alamein. In Whitehall, Charles Lambe was director of naval planning and Ronald Weeks, a Territorial soldier, deputy chief of the imperial general staff. Roderic Hill organized defence against flying bombs, as, earlier, William Paterson and Stradling had devised air-raid shelters; and Richard Fairey aircraft such as the Swordfish which helped to cripple the Italian fleet at Taranto. F. B. Halford, who had redesigned the engine of the D.H. 4 in the first war, now designed the Goblin engine for the first British jet propulsion aircraft to fly. For the invasion of Normandy, Alexander Gibb, W. T. Halcrow, and Oscar Faber helped to provide the Mulberry harbour; Bassett-Lowke the models; A. C. Hartley the pipelines under the ocean. In Normandy itself and beyond Percy Hobart's 79th Armoured Division deployed further mechanical ingenuity. If in the first war the signal British contributions to warfare had been the tank and the aeroplane, in the second they were radar and in the earlier stages of what became an atomic bomb. Tizard, Wimperis, Wilfrid Freeman, and Raymund Hart had their share in the development of radar; F. E. Simon and F. A. Paneth were among those scientists born in a foreign land whose researches helped eventually to develop the bomb which brought a long war to its controversial conclusion. While scientists like Lindemann and Tizard disagreed about the effectiveness of allied bombing strategy, and Bishop Bell condemned it, we recognize how devastatingly changed

Prefatory Note

warfare's dimension had come to be since that first raid by Verdon-Roe's Avro 504s on the Zeppelin sheds at Friedrichshafen on 21 November 1914.

In the first war Plimmer studied foodstuffs at the War Office and Charles Martin advanced the study of nutrition while in Lemnos; in the second war Martin helped to devise the national loaf; Drummond was at the Ministry of Food as scientific adviser and Mellanby in the Medical Research Council was concerning himself with wartime diet. Harold Gillies's pioneering of plastic surgery in the first war was renewed, with him, in the second by his cousin Archibald McIndoe. Gordon-Taylor's surgical skill served the army in the first war, the navy in the second. We remember with gratitude the advance surgical teams created by Hugh Cairns for the western desert; or the blood transfusion services organized by Lionel Whitby and T. B. Davie; the research on insecticides of P. A. Buxton, which resulted in the introduction of D.D.T. urged by Ian Heilbron, or of Tattersfield who developed pyrethrum. Alexander Fleming's discovery of penicillin ushered in the antibiotic era; and the realm of chemotherapy was explored by Harold King, by Otto Rosenheim, and by A. J. Ewins who with his collaborators gave us 'M & B 693'.

It was a changed, shrinking world into which men stepped in the demobilization suits from Montague Burton's factories. The second world war ended with the first real taste of power by a Labour Government. Clement Attlee and some others of his Cabinet contribute to this Supplement; some are included in it: Stafford Cripps, chancellor of the Exchequer; Ernest Bevin and Aneurin Bevan; Jowitt, the lord chancellor; Addison, the leader in the Lords; Shepherd his whip there; George Tomlinson, a minister of education, and William Whiteley, chief whip in the Commons, both to remind us of the strong links between trade-unionism and Methodism. The Bank of England was nationalized with Catto as its governor; Cable and Wireless with Angwin as its chairman. The National Coal Board was set up with Hubert Houldsworth and Arthur Street upon its directorate; the National Assistance Board with George Buchanan. Aneurin Bevan with William Douglas at his right hand brought the National Health Service into existence with the help of Webb-Johnson and Boldero. The railways, which had been served in their day by executives such as Sam Fay, Ralph Wedgwood, and Felix Pole, engineers like Lemon, and trade-unionists like A. G. Walkden, came into the nationalized orbit. And the Government decided to benefit from the earlier organization of Wallace Akers and John Anderson by calling on the services of engineers like Claude Gibb in the creation of Harwell and Calder Hall to harness nuclear energy for peaceful uses.

The Indian and the colonial empires were coming to their close. King George VI was the last Emperor, Edwina Mountbatten the last vicereine, of India. Aspects of the Indian story may be perceived in this volume in the lives of the Aga Khan, Ambedkar, Wedgwood Benn, Cripps, Halifax, Hoare, Simon, Findlater Stewart, Rowlands, or L. S. Amery. No longer may we expect viceroys like Linlithgow who could

ERRATUM

Page x, line 7, *for* Ronald *read* Reginald

.... to be recorded too in the sciences and in engineering. Take, for readiest example, the five scientific Nobel prizemen included here: Fleming; Frederick Soddy, who coined the term 'isotope'; O. W. Richardson the word 'thermion'; C. T. R. Wilson who devised the cloud chamber; and Charles Scott Sherrington, 'the philosopher of the nervous system'. Other scientists have furnished their personal labels: in the Chapman theory of detonation, Dakin's solution, the Evershed and the Townsend effects, the Lennard-Jones formula, the Richardson number, the Saha equation, or the Whittaker integral. Some will be remembered by their inventions: the Martel box girder bridge, the Michell thrust-block, the Denny–Brown stabilizer, the Twyman–Green optical interferometer, the Hartley hoister, or the Humphrey gas pump. In the evolution of the motor-car we notice Wilson's gearbox; Egerton's investigation of 'knock'; Tizard's and Pye's work on the internal combustion engine financed by Waley Cohen; du Cros's development of the pneumatic tyre; Bennett's magnetos; or Woollard's application of automation to the industry. The resultant traffic led to the Belisha beacon. In agriculture we remark the revolution brought about by Harry Ferguson's tractors; and indoors a domestic revolution due to H. C. Booth's invention, as early as 1901, of the vacuum cleaner. Turing and Hartree helped to bring us into the age of the computer. Small wonder that in this volume we record Holmyard and Singer producing their *History of Technology*.

Significant names emerge too in humane scholarship and the arts. G. E. Moore, Wittgenstein (whose *Tractatus* C. K. Ogden translated), and J. L. Austin altered our ways of going about philosophy; L. B. Namier our ways of writing history; O. G. S. Crawford, Childe, J. L. Myres, Woolley, and Ventris our study of the more distant past; Bowley and Yule our approach to statistics; William Craigie our lexicography. The days and ways of Max Beerbohm seem far removed from Malcolm Lowry's; those of Edward Marsh's 'Georgians', such as Frances Cornford or even Walter de la Mare, remote from those of Dylan Thomas. E. C. Bentley devised a rival method of writing biography and a novel approach to detective fiction which Dorothy Sayers was to bring, some held, into the field of literature; and Ronald Knox, another writer of detective stories, produced a new translation of the Bible.

Prefatory Note

There were changes too in journalism. Belloc's *Eye-Witness* and Squire's and then Scott-James's *London Mercury* have not survived. The *Athenaeum*, edited by Middleton Murry, merges with the *Nation*, edited for a time by Hubert Henderson, but soon to unite with the *New Statesman* of which Ernest Simon had been a founder and Desmond MacCarthy an original member and to which H. N. Brailsford, G. D. H. Cole, and Aylmer Vallance were also to contribute. Seton-Watson wrote for the *Spectator*, of which Beach Thomas was the annalist, and Wilson Harris for long the editor. F. W. Hirst edited *The Economist*, Wadsworth the *Manchester Guardian*; and Wickham Steed and W. F. Casey *The Times*, of which Charles Morgan was for long the dramatic critic; and for twenty-five years Dean Inge wrote a weekly article in the *Evening Standard*. Eric Parker edited the *Field*, C. G. Grey the *Aeroplane*, Malan *Die Burger*. The *Daily Telegraph* was taken over by Camrose and Iliffe; and one recalls pleasurable weekends in the thirties with Astor's *Observer* or more especially the *Sunday Times*, edited by W. W. Hadley, when Ernest Newman, MacCarthy, and G. M. Young were contributors, to be joined later by R. C. K. Ensor. In more specialized fields L. P. Jacks's editorship of the *Hibbert Journal* goes back as far as its foundation in 1902 and Richard Gregory joined *Nature* as early as 1893.

W. J. Macqueen-Pope and John Parker were noteworthy chroniclers of the theatre, which was enlivened by impresarios like C. B. Cochran and André Charlot and enhanced significantly by Ashley Dukes at the Mercury, Lennox Robinson at the Abbey in Dublin, William Armstrong at Liverpool, and by Komisarjevsky's revolutionary seasons at Stratford. Three notable landmarks in the profession were the encharting of R.A.D.A. under the direction of Kenneth Barnes; the foundation of the British Drama League by Geoffrey Whitworth; and the formation of Equity of which Godfrey Tearle was first president. If the days of the actor-manager seemed perhaps to be on the wane, the public were coming to associate performers with the plays of certain writers: Lillah McCarthy with Shaw's, Hilda Trevelyan with Barrie's, Gertrude Lawrence with Noël Coward's, Robert Donat with James Bridie's, maybe, or Ivor Novello with his own. But they would see their favourites more often on the screen: the silent film, to the accompaniment of Ketèlbey's music, had by now given way to the lavish productions of Alexander Korda. Meanwhile, at Sadler's Wells, British ballet has been greatly enriched by the musical directorship of Constant Lambert as has the whole field of music by the work of Vaughan Williams. To hear a recording of the voice of Kathleen Ferrier is sadly to observe that all the work in the field of cancer research and surgery—by men like Gask, Kennaway, Robert Muir, Rock Carling, W. C. M. Lewis, or Holburt Waring—has not so far found a certain cure.

Prefatory Note

Some of our subjects have been recorded for us too by portrait painters such as Birley, Codner, or Henry Lamb. To mention artists is but to return to dreams and difficulties: Matthew Smith becomes a painter despite intense parental disapproval; Stanley Spencer pursues his vision of heaven in the village streets of Cookham; Munnings loses an eye when he is twenty but he goes on painting; and Epstein is the centre of controversy, not least over his sculptural work for the architect C. H. Holden to whom we owe the university of London complex. Giles Gilbert Scott, by contrast, was in the family tradition and no more than twenty-two when he entered the winning design for the Anglican cathedral at Liverpool. In London, Battersea power-station, Waterloo Bridge, and the rebuilt House of Commons, with engineering by Faber, are all his, while the planning for post-war London was stimulated by Patrick Abercrombie. Places come to have their particular association in sport as well as architecture: Wembley, developed by Elvin, where Charles Buchan and Alex James played association football; Twickenham typified by Adrian Stoop and where Barrington-Ward the surgeon played in the first rugby international match there; Scarborough where Leveson Gower presided annually over its cricket festival; or the Oval where George Hirst and Gilbert Jessop batted memorably in 1902; Wimbledon where Mrs. Lambert Chambers played lawn tennis; Henley recalled for us by Harcourt Gold.

Many we meet here took their recreation in climbing, especially in the Alps, of which Geoffrey Winthrop Young was an accomplished recorder too. Some explored virtually unknown regions: St. John Philby, for example, in Central Arabia; or geologists like Lees in search of the oil which mechanization was increasingly requiring. Kingdon-Ward brought back for English gardens plants which he had collected wandering in India, Burma, China, and Tibet. Of those struggles which did not avail two especially are once again recalled here: the Everest expedition, later described by David Pye, which E. F. Norton came to lead in 1924; and the story of the world's worst journey which Apsley Cherry-Garrard was to tell of Scott's last expedition in which he, Evans, and Murray Levick all took part. Polar exploration came to be more scientifically organized, more mechanically assisted, as the expeditions of Douglas Mawson and Hubert Wilkins were to demonstrate; yet Augustine Courtauld was to show how one man could brave an Arctic winter alone.

Endurance has been well matched by enterprise. Of institutions with which we have grown familiar one may notice in browsing through this volume that the year 1903, to take but one example, saw the launching of the Workers' Educational Association by Albert Mansbridge; the opening at Bedford of Margaret Stansfeld's Physical Training College; the first welcome by Francis Wylie of a Rhodes scholar to Oxford; the establishment, with much collaboration, of the National Art-

Prefatory Note

Collections Fund by Robert Witt; a new constitution of the British Medical Association which Alfred Cox was soon to operate; the recommendation of a school medical service, in which Janet Campbell was to serve. Tissington Tatlow became general secretary of the Student Christian Movement; C. B. Fry played a memorable innings at Lord's; Charles Peers was appointed architectural editor of the *Victoria County Histories*; and Bethune-Baker editor of the *Journal of Theological Studies*.

Other disparate but familiar institutions glimpsed in this Supplement include the Agricultural Research Council with Dampier as its first secretary; the Anglo American Corporation of South Africa which Ernest Oppenheimer effected in 1917; the Church Assembly to which Lord Hugh Cecil and Philip Baker Wilbraham dedicated so much of their devotion; the British Postgraduate Medical School at Hammersmith which the Athlone committee initiated, Gask helped to plan, and where Grey Turner was first director of surgery; the Heritage Craft Schools founded by Dame Grace Kimmins; the British Communist Party of which Pollitt was a founder-member in 1920 and later general secretary; the Council for the Preservation of Rural England, fostered by planners like Pepler and Abercrombie; the Royal Institute of British Architects to which MacAlister gave his service; the Fabian Society with which E. R. Pease and G. D. H. Cole were long associated; the Family Planning Association of which Lady Denman was first chairman; James Caird's gift of the National Maritime Museum; Robinson in the Forestry Commission; the Pilgrim Trust of which the first secretary was Thomas Jones, later to follow Macmillan as chairman; the British Academy which Frederic Kenyon had a hand in founding and of which he compiled the early history; the series of Nuffield benefactions which Goodenough steered so skilfully, and notably here Nuffield College of which Harold Butler and Henry Clay were early wardens. The list of public school headmasters like Cyril Alington, Frank Fletcher, Spencer Leeson, and Cyril Norwood is joined by J. F. Roxburgh who invented Stowe; and Roedean appears in the life of a judge, Paul Lawrence, who helped to found and sustain this public school for girls. Christine Burrows was involved in the foundation of two colleges for women at Oxford; Kenneth Vickers devotedly built up what is now the university of Southampton; and after the second war came new schools in Hertfordshire designed by Aslin; and a new university college in Staffordshire, here commemorated in the lives of its first three principals: A. D. Lindsay, John Lennard-Jones, and George Barnes to whom we were indebted also for the Third Programme and the expansion of television. Overseas, Thomas Taylor was establishing the university of the West Indies at Mona, whilst at home Arthur Trueman was amongst those guiding the post-war work of the University Grants Committee.

Prefatory Note

As well as novelty and upheaval there were continuities. The inclusion of more scientists in this Supplement is by no means the sole explanation why no fewer than fifty of the worthies recorded here were members in their day of Trinity College, Cambridge. If much was changing, one may perceive a core of stability also: reflected in the monarchy and in religious leaders like Archbishop Garbett or Cardinal Griffin and those many others who chose to pursue religion, justice, scholarship, the public service, or diverse other avocations with dedication and without flamboyance. These may be quietly seen here too.

We are most grateful for permission to quote to: Messrs. Cassell & Co. (from volume iv of *The Second World War* by Winston S. Churchill); Messrs. Collins (from *Triumph in the West* by Arthur Bryant and from *The Private Papers of Hore-Belisha* edited by R. J. Minney); Messrs. Curtis Brown (from *Present Indicative* by Noël Coward); Messrs. Faber and Faber (from Walter de la Mare's poem 'The Bottle' in his *Collected Poems*); and Messrs. Michael Joseph (from *I'm on a See-Saw* by Vivian Ellis).

Contributors have been most kind both in consenting to prepare their notices and in settling with us what is printed here. We are sorry that they have had to wait so long to see it. For more than a hundred, alas, it is too late. Many of them have been most generous, in addition, with the counsel we have sought from them. We are very grateful to them all. We have continued the practice of inviting to contribute when possible those who knew the subjects personally. We have tried to check the facts; their opinions are their own. We do not necessarily share them.

In the acknowledgements which follow we have not thanked contributors individually but we would like to express gratitude for advice from: Sir George Abell; Sir Thomas Armstrong; Mr. Michael Ayrton; Professor R. P. Bell; Dr. T. S. R. Boase; the late Sir Alexander Cadogan; Mr. D. N. Chester; Sir George Clark; Lord Cohen of Birkenhead; Dr. Alexander Cooke; Professor R. M. Crawford; Mr. G. R. Crone; Professor Rupert Cross; Mr. R. H. S. Crossman; Lord Devlin; Sir Ralph Furse; the late Mr. A. D. Garson; Professor J. A. Gibson; Lord Gladwyn; Mr. Strathearn Gordon; the late Lord Hailey; Sir Arnold Hall; Sir Keith Hancock; Sir William Hayter; Professor D. W. Holder; Professor A. M. Keppel-Jones; Mr. J. F. Kerslake; Mr. R. B. McCallum; Air Vice-Marshal W. F. MacNeece Foster; Professor Arthur J. Marder; Sir David Martin; Mr. R. W. Mason; Sir Penderel Moon; the late Professor C. L. Mowat; the late Sir Archibald Nye; Sir George Pickering; Captain Stephen Roskill; Professor J. A. Steers; Lord Strang; the late Lord Tedder; Professor L. M. Thompson. The Editor would like to mention two friends who have sustained him particularly: Sir Harold Hartley, doyen of the Royal Society, and Sir Kenneth Wheare, the president of the British Academy.

Prefatory Note

This volume would not have appeared even now but for the continued devotion of Miss Helen M. Palmer, the assistant editor. Since she has undertaken by far the heaviest load from beginning to end, it would be wholly inappropriate were her name not to appear, with a most grateful editor's, on the title-page. He is indeed deeply indebted to her. We would wish to acknowledge too, especially on her behalf, the most willing assistance of the staffs of the Bodleian and its associated libraries. Finally, we would like to thank the Oxford University Press and in it especially Mr. C. H. Roberts, the secretary to the Delegates, and Mr. D. M. Davin, the Oxford publisher.

E. T. W.

Rhodes House, Oxford
October 1970

LIST OF CONTRIBUTORS

†ABEL, Deryck:
  Benn.
ABERCONWAY, Charles Melville McLaren, Baron:
  McLaren (Aberconway).
†ABERDARE, Clarence Napier Bruce, Baron:
  Latham.
†ADCOCK, Sir Frank Ezra:
  Tarn.
AITKEN, Adam Jack:
  Craigie (W. A.).
†ALLEN, Sir Carleton Kemp:
  Wylie.
ALLEN, Sir Roger:
  Peterson.
ALLEN, Sir Roy George Douglas:
  Bowley.
ALLEN, Victor Leonard:
  Deakin.
ALLSOPP, Cecil Benjamin:
  Twyman.
†ALTHAM, Harry Surtees:
  Fry (C. B.).
ANDREWS, Sir (William) Linton:
  Clarke (T.); Cummings; Wadsworth.
ANGLE, Aidan:
  Carlyle.
†ARBERRY, Arthur John:
  Thomas (F. W.).
ASHTON-GWATKIN, Frank Trelawny Arthur:
  Wellesley.
ATKINSON, William Christopher:
  Peers (E. A.).
†ATTLEE, Clement Richard Attlee, Earl:
  Whiteley.

BABINGTON SMITH, Constance:
  Macaulay.
†BAILEY, Cyril:
  Fletcher (F.).
BAILEY, Stanley John:
  Winfield.
BAKER, George:
  Hambourg.
BAKER, Sir John Fleetwood:
  Inglis.
BALFOUR, Sir John:
  Campbell (R. H.).
BARCLAY-SMITH, (Ida) Phyllis:
  Kinnear.
BARNABY, Kenneth Cloves:
  Tennyson-d'Eyncourt.
BARNETT, Correlli Douglas:
  Davidson; Kiggell; Maxse.
BARRY, Frederick Donal:
  Atkinson.
†BARRY, Sir Gerald Reid:
  Cruikshank; Vallance.
BATEY, Charles Edward:
  Johnson (J. de M.).
BATTLE, Richard John Vulliamy:
  Gillies; McIndoe.

BAWDEN, Sir Frederick Charles:
  Goodey.
BAWN, Cecil Edwin Henry:
  Garner; Lewis (W. C. M.).
†BELL, Sir Harold Idris:
  Kenyon.
BELLASIS, Margaret Rosa:
  Arlen; Farnol; Mercer (Dornford Yates).
BENNET-CLARK, Thomas Archibald:
  Dixon.
BENTLEY, Nicolas Clerihew:
  Bairnsfather; Freedman.
BERTRAM, (Cyril) Anthony (George):
  Lewis (P. W.).
†BILSLAND, Alexander Steven Bilsland, Baron:
  Colville (Clydesmuir); Denny; Weir (C. M.).
†BLAIKLEY, Ernest:
  Codner.
BLAKE, Robert Norman William:
  Lindemann (Cherwell); Sykes.
BLAND, Sir (George) Nevile (Maltby):
  Vansittart.
BLUNDELL, Sir Michael:
  Scott, Montagu-Douglas-.
BLUNDEN, Edmund Charles:
  Squire.
BLUNT, Sir Anthony Frederick:
  Antal.
BOARDMAN, John:
  Myres.
BOWDEN, Ruth Elizabeth Mary:
  Cullis.
BOWEN, Edmund John:
  Chapman (D. L.).
†BOYD, James Dixon:
  Duckworth.
BOYLE, David Hugh Montgomerie:
  Cornwallis.
†BRAIN, Walter Russell Brain, Baron:
  Boldero.
†BRAMBELL, Francis William Rogers:
  Gatenby.
†BRAND, Robert Henry Brand, Baron:
  Curtis; Kindersley.
BRIGGS, Asa:
  Cole.
BROCK, Michael George:
  Ensor.
BROCKLEHURST, Robert James:
  Kent.
BROCKWAY, Archibald Fenner Brockway, Baron:
  Buchanan (G.).
BROGAN, Sir Denis William:
  Harding (G. C.).
BROOKE, John:
  Namier.
BROOKS, Peter Wright:
  Scott-Paine.
BROWN, Ivor John Carnegie:
  Ashwell; Donat; Robey.

List of Contributors

BROWN, Sir James Raitt:
  Wilbraham.
BROWN, John:
  Bell (T.).
BRUNNER, Dorothea Elizabeth Brunner, Lady:
  Denman.
BRYAN, Sir Andrew Meikle:
  Redmayne.
†BURN, William Laurence:
  Percy.
BURNET, Sir (Frank) Macfarlane:
  Ross.
BURTON, Hester:
  Kenney.
†BUTLER, Arthur Stanley George:
  Scott.
BUTLER, Ruth Florence:
  Burrows.
BUTTER, Peter Herbert:
  Muir (E.).

CADE, Sir Stanford:
  Carling.
CAIRNS, Julia (Mrs. Paul Davidson):
  Spry.
CALDER-MARSHALL, Arthur:
  Lowry.
CALLOW, Robert Kenneth:
  Rosenheim.
†CAMERON, Sir Roy:
  Muir (R.).
CAMPBELL-JOHNSON, Alan:
  Mountbatten.
CAROE, Sir Olaf Kirkpatrick:
  Bajpai.
CARR, Frank George Griffith:
  Caird.
CARR, Samuel:
  Batsford.
CASLON, Clifford:
  Forbes.
CATLIN, Sir George Edward Gordon:
  Barker (E.).
CECIL, Lord (Edward Christian) David (Gascoyne):
  Asquith; Beerbohm.
CECIL, Robert:
  Clark Kerr (Inverchapel).
CHADWICK, Henry:
  Bethune-Baker.
CHADWICK, John:
  Ventris.
CHALMERS, William Scott:
  Horton.
CHAPMAN, Frederick Spencer:
  Courtauld.
CHARLES, Sir John Alexander:
  Spence.
CHARLES, Robert Lonsdale:
  Brangwyn; John.
†CHERRY, Sir Thomas MacFarland:
  Michell.
CHICK, Dame Harriette:
  Martin (C. J.).
CHILD, Clifton James:
  Peterson.

CHOPRA, Iqbal Chand:
  Williamson.
†CHRISTIAN, Garth Hood:
  Massingham.
CHRISTIE, John Traill:
  Bailey (C.).
CHURCH, Richard Thomas:
  De la Mare.
CITRINE, Walter McLennan Citrine, Baron:
  Haslett; Pugh.
CLARK, Sir Wilfrid Edward Le Gros:
  Jones (F. W.); Keith.
CLARKE, Arthur Wellesley:
  Burnett.
CLAUSON, Sir Gerard Leslie Makins:
  Shuckburgh.
CLEGG, Hugh Anthony:
  Cox.
†CLIFFORD, Hon. Sir Bede Edmund Hugh:
  Cambridge (Athlone).
COLE, Dame Margaret Isabel:
  Pease.
COOK, Arthur Herbert:
  Heilbron.
COOTE, Sir Colin Reith:
  Elliot; Milner.
COURATIN, Arthur Hubert:
  Dix.
COWPER, Francis Henry:
  Greene; Humphreys; Lawrence (P. O.); Sullivan.
†COX, Leslie Reginald:
  Arkell; Woods.
COX, Sir Trenchard:
  Maclagan.
†CRASTER, Sir (Herbert Henry) Edmund:
  Salter.
CRIPPS, John Stafford:
  Orwin; Parker (E.).
CRISP, Leslie Finlay:
  Chifley.
CROOKSHANK, Henry:
  Fermor.
CRUICKSHANK, Robert:
  Fleming (A.).
CUMBERLEGE, Geoffrey Fenwick Jocelyn:
  Corbett.

DAICHES, David:
  Grierson.
†DALE, Sir Henry Hallett:
  Dakin; Ewins; Hill (L. E.); Kellaway.
DANIEL, Glyn Edmund:
  Crawford.
DARLINGTON, William Aubrey:
  Banks; Lane; Loraine; Tearle.
†DARWIN, Sir Charles Galton:
  Hartree.
DAVIES, Aneirin Talfan:
  Thomas (D. M.).
DAVIN, Winifred Kathleen:
  Cary.
DAVIS, Sidney George:
  Geddes.
DAVIS, Sydney Charles Houghton:
  Cobb.
DAVIS, Sir William Wellclose:
  Lambe.

List of Contributors

DEAN, Basil:
Henson.

†DEBENHAM, Sir Piers Kenrick, Bart.:
Henderson.

DEL MAR, Norman Rene:
Brain.

DE NORMANN, Sir Eric:
Hicks.

DENT, Alan Holmes:
Lawrence (G.); Macqueen-Pope; Millar.

†DERRY, Cyril:
Bassett-Lowke.

DICKINSON, John Compton:
Thompson (A. H.).

DICKSON, (Horatio Henry) Lovat:
Hilton.

DODDS, Sir James Leishman:
Craigie (R. L.).

DONNISON, Frank Siegfried Vernon:
Mason-MacFarlane.

†DOUGLAS OF KIRTLESIDE, William Sholto
Douglas, Baron:
Freeman.

DOUGLAS-HOME, Hon. William:
Matthews.

DOW, George:
Fay; Wedgwood.

DRAKE, John Collard Bernard:
Chatterjee.

DUDLEY, Norman Alfred:
Bennett (Bennett of Edgbaston); Woollard.

DUKE-ELDER, Sir Stewart:
Parsons.

†EADY, Sir (Crawfurd) Wilfrid Griffin:
Hopkins.

EDGCUMBE, John Aubrey Pearce:
Clark.

EDWARDS, Joseph:
Walton.

†ELLIS, Lionel Frederic:
Deedes.

ELLIS, Vivian:
Cochran.

ELWES, Simon:
Lonsdale.

ENGEL DE JANOSI, Alfred Hans:
Townsend.

†EVERSHED, Francis Raymond Evershed,
Baron:
Somervell.

FALCON, Norman Leslie:
Lees.

FALLS, Cyril Bentham:
Cassels; Edmonds.

FARR, Dennis:
Lamb.

†FAY, Gerard:
Robinson (E. S. L.).

†FELLOWES, Sir Edward Abdy:
Brown (Ruffside).

FERNALD, John Bailey:
Barnes (K. R.).

FIELD, John William:
Watson.

FITZHERBERT, Cuthbert:
Goodenough.

†FLECK, Alexander Fleck, Baron:
Akers; Soddy.

FOOT, Michael Richard Daniell:
Cope.

FORD, Brinsley:
Oppé.

FORD, Sir Edward William Spencer:
Villiers (Clarendon).

FORGE, Andrew Murray:
Bomberg.

FORSEY, George Frank:
Vickers.

FOSTER, Edward Waddington:
Richardson (O. W.).

†FRANCIS-WILLIAMS, Edward Francis Williams, Baron:
Bevin.

†FRASER, Sir Francis Richard:
Dunhill.

FRASER, Peter Marshall:
Last.

†FREETH, Francis Arthur:
Donnan; Swinburne.

FROSTICK, John Michael Lawrence:
Hawthorn.

FRYBERG, Sir Abraham:
Kenny.

FULFORD, Roger Thomas Baldwin:
Hirst (F. W.); Housman; Pankhurst.

FULLMAN, Molina:
Jowitt.

FULTON, Alexander Strathern:
Barnett.

FULTON, John Scott Fulton, Baron:
Duncan.

GALBRAITH, Vivian Hunter:
Sumner.

GARDNER, Arthur Duncan:
Whitby.

†GARDNER, William Henry:
Campbell (I. R. D.).

GARRARD, Lancelot Austin:
Jacks.

GARROD, Lawrence Paul:
Gordon.

GARRY, Robert Campbell:
Cathcart.

GARSON, Noel George:
Pirow; Strijdom.

†GAVIN, Sir William:
Hudson.

GAYE, Freda:
Parker (J.).

GEDDES, Hon. David Campbell:
Geddes.

GIELGUD, Val Henry:
Neilson.

GILLESPIE, William Hewitt:
Jones (A. E.).

†GILLIAM, Laurence Duval:
Barnes (G. R.).

GOLD, Ernest:
Richardson (L. F.).

GOLDIE, Grace Wyndham:
Armstrong.

GOODALL, Norman:
Mathews (B. J.).

List of Contributors

GOODHART, Arthur Lehman:
Asquith (Asquith of Bishopstone).

GOODMAN, Stanley:
Foot.

†GOODMAN, Sir Victor Martin Reeves:
Badeley.

GOODWIN, Albert:
Thompson (J. M.).

GOPAL, Sarvepalli:
Rau.

GORDON, Isabella:
Calman.

GORE, John Francis:
Baring (Cromer); Queen Mary; Ponsonby (Bessborough); Wigram.

GOSSE, Richard Fraser:
Duff.

†GRAAFF-HUNTER, James de:
Arden-Close.

GRAHAM, Roger:
Meighen.

GRAND, Keith Walter Chamberlain:
Pole.

GRAY, Sir James:
Bidder.

†GREGORY, Sir Theodore Emanuel:
Oppenheimer.

GRIFFITHS, Sir Percival Joseph:
Liaqat Ali Khan.

GRIMSDITCH, Herbert Borthwick:
Berry (Camrose); Connard; Fyfe; Grahame-White; Heal; Iliffe; Reed.

GUEST, Christopher William Graham Guest, Lord:
Macmillan.

GUILLEBAUD, Claude William:
Hitchcock.

GURNEY, Oliver Robert:
Garstang.

†GYDE, Edward Arnold:
Young (F. B.).

HADDOW, Sir Alexander:
Kennaway.

HADFIELD, John Charles Heywood:
Gibbings.

†HAINES, Frederick Merlin:
Fritsch.

HALE, (Charles) Leslie:
Benn (Stansgate).

†HALL, Wilfrid John:
Marshall (G. A. K.).

†HALLIDAY, Sir William Reginald:
Dawkins.

†HAMILTON, Mary Agnes:
Bondfield.

HAMILTON-EDWARDS, Gerald Kenneth Savery:
Carpenter; de Chair; du Cros; Lithgow; Weir (Inverforth).

HAMPSHIRE, Arthur Cecil:
Campbell (G.).

HAMSON, Charles John:
Lauterpacht.

HANBURY, Harold Greville:
Porter.

HANKEY, Robert Maurice Alers Hankey, Baron:
Kennard.

HARDY, Peter:
Sarkar.

HARGREAVES, Frederick James:
Evershed.

HARINGTON, Sir Charles Robert:
King.

HARRISON, John Richard:
Faber.

HART, Herbert Lionel Adolphus:
Austin.

HART-DAVIS, Sir Rupert Charles:
Cape; House.

HARTLEY, Sir Harold:
Gregory; Jones (B. M.); Lemon; Raikes; Sidgwick; Tizard.

†HARVEY OF TASBURGH, Oliver Charles Harvey, Baron:
Mendl.

†HASSALL, Christopher Vernon:
Marsh.

HAVERGAL, Henry MacLeod:
Finzi; Quilter.

HAYES, Kevin Henry Joseph O'Connell:
Bonham-Carter.

HAYLOCK, Edward Fowles:
Nicholson.

HAZELL, James Temple:
Hunter.

HEATON, Herbert:
Lipson.

HECKSTALL-SMITH, Hugh William:
Roxburgh.

†HENDERSON, Mary Isobel:
Murray.

HENDERSON, Roy Galbraith:
Ferrier.

HERBAGE, Julian Livingston-:
Bax.

HEUSTON, Robert Francis Vere:
Simon (J. A.).

†HEVESY, George:
Paneth.

HILDRED, Sir William Percival:
Bowhill.

HILL, (John Edward) Christopher:
Lindsay (Lindsay of Birker).

†HILL, Richard Hamilton:
Gower, Leveson.

HINDLE, Edward:
Kerr (J. G.).

HINTON OF BANKSIDE, Christopher Hinton, Baron:
Gibb (C. D.).

HODGE, Sir William Vallance Douglas:
Baker.

HODGKIN, Thomas Lionel:
Fry (S. M.).

HODSON, Francis Lord Charlton Hodson, Baron:
Singleton.

HODSON, Henry Vincent:
Hadley.

HOGARTH, Margaret Cameron:
Campbell (J. M.).

List of Contributors

HOLFORD, William Graham Holford, Baron:
Abercrombie.
HOLLIS, (Maurice) Christopher:
Brown (W. J.); Knox (R. A.).
HOLT, Richard:
Lindrum.
HONORÉ, Antony Maurice:
Lee.
HOOPER, Howard Owen:
Rowlands; Weeks.
HOPE-SIMPSON, John Frederic:
Tansley.
HOUGHTON, (Arthur Leslie Noel) Douglas:
White.
†HOWARD, George Wren:
Simon (O. J.).
HOWES, Frank Stewart:
Newman; Vaughan Williams.
HUDSON, Derek:
Blackwood; Harris (H. W.); Sadleir; Stacpoole; Strong; Thomas (W. B.); Tomlinson (H. M.).
HUMPHREYS, (Travers) Christmas:
Bodkin; Leyel.
HURST, Harold Edwin:
MacDonald.
HUTTON, Charles William:
Holden.

INNES, Fergus Munro:
Khan Sahib.
IRVINE, John Graham Gerard Charles:
Comper.

†JACKSON OF BURNLEY, Willis Jackson, Baron:
Fleming (A. P. M.).
†JAMES, Sir Frederick Ernest:
Dadabhoy; Ismail.
JAMES, Robert Vidal Rhodes:
Birdwood.
JAMES, William Owen:
Keeble.
JARVIS, William Arthur Walter:
Sorabji.
JASPER, Ronald Claud Dudley:
Bell (G. K. A.).
JEFFRIES, Sir Charles Joseph:
Bell (H. H. J.); Shiels; Stanley.
JEWKES, John:
Clay.
JEWKES, Sylvia:
Clay.
JOHNSTON, Muir:
Booth.
†JOHNSTON, Thomas:
Kirkwood.
JOHNSTONE, Kenneth Roy:
Kelly.
†JONES, Sir Lawrence Evelyn, Bart.:
Young (G. M.).
JONES, Martin:
Stapledon.

†KABIR, Humayun Zahiruddin Amir:
Azad.
KARMEL, David:
Burton.

KEETON, George Williams:
Morgan (J. H.).
†KEITH OF AVONHOLM, James Keith, Baron:
Cooper.
KELF-COHEN, Reuben:
Street.
KELLY, Sir Gerald Festus:
Munnings.
KEMP, Eric Waldram:
Kirk.
KEMP, Peter Kemp:
Dreyer; Noble; Power; Sueter; Tyrwhitt.
†KENNEDY, Sir John Noble:
Anderson (K. A. N.); Maurice.
KENT, Sir Harold Simcox:
Ram.
KEOGH, Eustace Graham:
Blamey; Morshead.
KERRISON, Oscar Carl:
Paterson.
KEYNES, Sir Geoffrey Langdon:
Cornford.
KIMMINS, Sir Brian Charles Hannam:
Kimmins.
KLINCK, Carl Frederick:
Service.
†KNOX, Edmund George Valpy:
Milne.
KOTHARI, Daulat Singh:
Meghnad Saha.
KURTI, Nicholas:
Simon (F. E.).

LAITHWAITE, Sir (John) Gilbert:
Aga Khan; Hope (Linlithgow); Stewart (S. F.).
†LANG, Herbert Raphael:
Whipple.
LAUWERYS, Joseph Albert:
Clarke (F.).
LAVER, James:
Bone (M. and S.); Gooden; Hardie; McBey; Spare.
LAWRENCE, Harry Gordon:
Malan.
LAWSON, Frederick Henry:
Jolowicz; Wolff; Zulueta.
LEGERTON, Harold John Webb:
Martin (H. H.).
LEIGH-PEMBERTON, John:
Birley.
LEJEUNE, Anthony (E. A. Thompson):
Hastings; Thomas (Rhondda).
LESLIE, Sir (John Randolph) Shane, Bart.:
Noyes.
LEWIS, Eiluned:
Morgan (C. L.).
LEWIS, Jonathan Tudor Stafford:
Llewellin.
†LIDDELL HART, Sir Basil Henry:
Brown (J.); Burnett-Stuart; Hore-Belisha; Lindsay; Martel; Stirling; Swinton.
LINKLATER, Eric Robert Russell:
Mavor (James Bridie).
LIVERMORE, Harold Victor:
Prestage.
†LLOYD, Roger Bradshaigh:
Garbett.

†LLOYD, Sir Thomas Ingram Kynaston:
  Chancellor.
†LONGFORD, Edward Arthur Henry Paken-
  ham, Earl of:
  Plunkett (Dunsany).
LONGFORD, Francis Aungier Pakenham,
  Earl of:
  Shepherd.
†LONGSTAFF, Tom George:
  Norton.
LOVE, Robert John McNeill:
  Barrington-Ward.
†LOVEDAY, Alexander:
  Butler (H. B.).
LOVELL, Reginald:
  Minett.
LOW, David Morrice:
  Douglas (G. N.).
†LOWERY, Harry:
  Paget.
LOWNDES, John:
  Plimmer.
LUBBOCK, Mark Hugh:
  Ketèlbey.
†LUKE, Sir Harry Charles:
  Storrs.
LUNN, Sir Arnold Henry Moore:
  Young (G. W.).
LYONS, Francis Stewart Leland:
  Harrison.

MACDERMOTT, John Clarke MacDermott,
  Baron:
  Andrews.
McDOUALL, Robin (Robert Ninian Huddle-
  stone Pennington):
  Lewis (R.).
MACGIBBON, James:
  MacCarthy; Pollitt; Stopes.
MACGIBBON, Jean:
  Klein.
MACHTIG, Sir Eric Gustav:
  Harding (E. J.).
MACKENZIE, Chalmers Jack:
  Howe.
MACKENZIE, Kenneth Roderick:
  Campion.
†McKIE, Douglas:
  Taylor (F. S.).
MACLAGAN, Michael:
  Bruce (Aberdare).
MACLEOD, Roderick:
  Ironside.
McNAIR, Arnold Duncan McNair, Baron:
  Gutteridge.
MACPHERSON, Crawford Brough:
  Douglas (C. H.).
†MACQUEEN-POPE, Walter James:
  Novello; Tilley.
MALLABY, Sir (Howard) George (Charles):
  Garrod.
MALLOWAN, Sir Max Edgar Lucien:
  Woolley.
MANN, Frederick George:
  Mills.
†MARKHAM, Violet Rosa (Mrs. Carruthers):
  Tuckwell.

MARQUARD, Leopold:
  Davie.
MARSHALL, Norman:
  Komisarjevsky.
MARTIN, Sir Alec:
  Witt.
†MARTIN, (Basil) Kingsley:
  Brailsford.
†MARTIN, Hugh:
  Tatlow.
†MARYON-WILSON, Sir (George) Percy
  (Maryon), Bart.:
  Royden.
†MASCHWITZ, Eric:
  Charlot.
MASEFIELD, Peter Gordon:
  Grey.
†MATHEWS, Dame Vera Laughton:
  Furse.
MATTHEWS, Walter Robert:
  Inge.
MELVILLE, Sir Harry Work:
  Evans.
MERRITT, John:
  Pearce.
†METHVEN, John Cecil Wilson:
  East.
MIDDLETON, Michael:
  Minton.
MILLER, Albert Arthur:
  Wilson (W. G.).
MILTON, Sir Frank:
  Harris (P. A.).
MINNEY, Rubeigh James:
  Frankau.
MOFFAT, Rennie John:
  Houldsworth.
MOIR, John Chassar:
  Kerr (J. M. M.).
MONCRIEFF, Sir Alan Aird:
  Hutchison.
†MOORE, Sir Henry Monck-Mason:
  Gurney; Senanayake.
MORAES, Frank:
  Ambedkar.
MORRAH, Dermot Michael Macgregor:
  Malcolm.
†MORRISON OF LAMBETH, Herbert Stanley
  Morrison, Baron:
  Lowe.
MORRISON, Samuel:
  Aslin.
MOTT, Sir Nevill Francis:
  Lennard-Jones.
MOTT-RADCLYFFE, Sir Charles Edward:
  Hoare (Templewood).
MOULT, Thomas:
  Coppard; Phillpotts.
MULLINS, Claud:
  Page.
MUNRO, Mary:
  Lenox-Conyngham.
MURRAY, Patrick:
  Beith (Ian Hay).
MYNORS, Sir Humphrey Charles Basker-
  ville, Bart.:
  Catto.

NAPIER, Hon. Sir Albert Edward Alexander:
Schuster.
NEVINSON, John Lea:
Marillier.
NEWITT, Dudley Maurice:
Egerton.
NEWSOME, Noel Francis:
Ferguson.
NICHOLL, Angus Dacres:
Agnew.
NICKALLS, Guy Oliver:
Gold.
†NICOLSON, Hon. Sir Harold George:
Cooper (Norwich).
†NOCK, Arthur Darby:
Cook.
NOEL-BAKER, Philip John:
Cecil.
NORRINGTON, Sir Arthur Lionel Pugh:
Milford.
†NOSWORTHY, Sir Richard Lysle:
Crowe.
NOWELL-SMITH, Simon Harcourt:
Fox-Strangways (Ilchester).

OAKESHOTT, Walter Fraser:
Leeson.
†OLIPHANT, Sir Lancelot:
Clerk.
OPIE, Iona:
Fyleman.
O'REGAN, John William Hamilton:
Caldecott.
†ORWIN, Charles Stewart:
Mansbridge.
OSBORN, Sir Frederic James:
Pepler.
OVEREND, William George:
Wardlaw.

PALMER, Helen Maud:
Bevan; Blogg; Boothman; Dampier; King George VI; Hardinge; Livingstone; Turing.
PALMER, John Wood:
Ginner.
PALMER, Joseph Mansergh:
Mathews (V. L.).
†PANIKKAR, Kavalam Madhava:
Bhopal.
PARKER, Henry Michael Denne:
Ince.
PARKES, James William:
Brodetsky.
PARRY, John Horace:
Taylor (T. W. J.).
PAYNE, Edward Raymond:
Gere.
PAYNE, Ernest Alexander:
Aubrey.
PEEL, Sir John Harold:
Gilliatt.
PENFIELD, Wilder Graves:
Sherrington.
PERKINS, John Frederick:
Perkins.
PETERKIN, Norman:
Foss.

†PHELAN, Edward Joseph:
Lester.
PHEMISTER, James:
McLintock.
PICKERSGILL, John Whitney:
Claxton.
PIGGOTT, Stuart:
Childe.
PING, Aubrey Charles:
Walkden.
†PIPPARD, Alfred John Sutton:
Gibb (A.); Stradling.
†PLATT, Benjamin Stanley:
Mellanby.
PLATT, Robert Platt, Baron:
Hall.
PLATT, William James:
Cable; French (E. F. and F. L.).
†POPHAM, Arthur Ewart:
Hind.
POTTER, Charles:
Tattersfield.
POWELL, Lawrence Fitzroy:
Chapman (R. W.).
†POWICKE, Sir (Frederick) Maurice:
Webb.
PRICE, Sir Archibald Grenfell:
Mawson.
PRICE, Morgan Philips:
Trevelyan (C. P.).
PRIESTLEY, Sir Raymond Edward:
Levick.
PRITCHARD, Sir Fred Eills:
Lynskey.
†PRITCHARD, John Laurence:
Fairey; Halford; Verdon-Roe.
PUGH, Sir William John:
Trueman.

†RADLEY, Sir (William) Gordon:
Angwin.
RANDALL, Sir Alec Walter George:
Palairet.
RATCLIFFE, John Ashworth:
Eckersley.
†RAWLINSON, Alfred Edward John:
Barnes (E. W.).
READER, William Joseph:
Weir (W. D.).
REDMAN, Roderick Oliver:
Stratton.
†REES, Sir Richard Lodowick Edward Montagu, Bart.:
Murry.
REESE, Max Meredith:
Buchan; Hirst (G. H.); James; Jardine; Jessop.
REEVES, Joseph:
McCabe.
RENNELL, Francis James Rennell Rodd, Baron:
Smith (Bicester).
RHODES, Philip:
Dick-Read.
RICHARDS, Denis George:
Hill (R. M.).
RICHARDSON, Sir Ralph David:
Korda.

List of Contributors

RICHES, Sir Eric William:
Webb-Johnson.

RILEY, Norman Denbigh:
Jordan.

†ROBBINS, Alan Pitt:
Casey; Steed.

ROBBINS, Brian Gordon:
Guy.

ROBERTS, Arthur Loten:
Smith (E. W.).

ROBERTS, Harold:
Lidgett.

ROBERTS, Harold Vernon Molesworth:
Fletcher (B. F.).

ROBERTS, Michael Rookherst:
Hobart.

†ROBERTS, Sir Sydney Castle:
Bentley; Butler (M. S. D.).

ROBERTSON, Sir James Wilson:
Wingate.

ROBINS, Robert Henry:
Firth (J. R.).

ROBINSON, Edward Austin Gossage:
Pigou.

ROBINSON, Sir Robert:
Copisarow; Simonsen.

ROCHE, Hon. Thomas Gabriel:
Holmes; Roche.

ROGERS, David MacGregor:
Perrins.

ROLO, Paul Jacques Victor:
Russell (T. W.).

†ROQUES, Frederick William:
Bonney.

ROSE, Kenneth Vivian:
*Cecil (Quickswood); Grigg (Altrincham);
Princess Marie Louise; Thomas (Cilcen-
nin); Wood (Halifax).*

ROSS, Angus:
Godley.

ROSS, Sir James Paterson, Bart.:
Gask.

ROTHENSTEIN, Elizabeth Kennard Whitting-
ton Rothenstein, Lady:
Spencer (S.).

†ROTTER, Godfrey:
Silberrad.

ROUSE, Edward Clive:
Tristram.

ROUTH, Charles Richard Nairne:
Alington.

ROWAN, Frederick Claude:
Bandaranaike.

†ROWLEY, Harold Henry:
Manson.

RUGGLES-BRISE, Sir John Archibald, Bart.:
Bathurst (Bledisloe).

†RUNGE, Sir Peter Francis:
Lyle.

RUPP, Ernest Gordon:
Workman.

RUSSELL, Dorothy Stuart:
Turnbull.

RUSSELL, John:
Smith (M. A. B.).

RUSSELL, Peter Edward Lionel Russell:
Entwistle.

RUSSELL, William Ritchie:
Cairns.

RYAN, Alfred Patrick:
Amery; Norway (Nevil Shute).

†SACKVILLE-WEST, Hon. Victoria Mary (Lady
Nicolson):
Wellesley (Wellington).

SADLER, Donald Harry:
Jones (H. S.).

SALISBURY, Sir Edward James:
Oliver; Ridley.

SALTER, James Arthur Salter, Baron:
*Anderson (Waverley); Drummond (Perth);
Maclay; Zimmern.*

SAMUELS, Sir Alexander:
Bressey.

SAUNDERS, Sir Owen Alfred:
Pye.

SAW, Ruth Lydia:
Joad.

SAWER, Geoffrey:
Hore-Ruthven (Gowrie); Hughes.

SCANLAN, James Donald, Archbishop of
Glasgow (R.C.):
Brown (W. F.).

SCHOLDERER, (Julius) Victor:
Thomas (H.).

SCOTT, Sir David John Montagu Douglas:
Hodgson; Knox (G. G.).

†SCOTT, Sir Harold Richard:
Barker (L. C.).

SCOTT, Joseph William:
Ogden.

SCOTT-KILVERT, Ian Stanley:
Scott-James.

SEARLE, Humphrey:
Dent; Lambert (C.).

SEAVER, George:
Cherry-Garrard.

SEDDON, Richard Harding:
Epstein.

SERBY, John Edward:
Perring; Wimperis.

SHAKESPEARE, Sir Geoffrey Hithersay,
Bart.:
Lambert (G.); Stewart (P. M.).

SHARP, Evelyn Adelaide Sharp, Baroness:
Douglas (W. S.); Martindale.

SHAW, Albert Thompson:
Atkins.

SHAW, Harold Watkins:
Fellowes.

SHAW, James Byam:
Dodgson; Gibson.

SHEPPARD, Percival Albert:
Walker (G. T.).

SHOCK, Maurice:
Addison.

SILLERY, Anthony:
Tshekedi Khama.

†SIMEY, Thomas Spensley Simey, Baron:
Rowntree.

SIMON, John Gilbert Simon, Viscount:
Anderson (A. G.).

SIMONDS, Gavin Turnbull Simonds, Viscount:
Maugham.

List of Contributors

SINCLAIR, Hugh Macdonald:
  Drummond; McCarrison.
†SLADE, Roland Edgar:
  Humphrey.
SMITH, Arthur Lionel Forster:
  Tallents.
SMITH, Isobel Agnes:
  McKenzie.
SMITH, Kenneth Manley:
  Salaman.
SMITH, Walter Campbell:
  Spencer (L. J.).
SMYTH, Sir John George, Bart.:
  Chambers (D. K.).
SNOW, Philip Albert:
  Buck; Grimble.
SORSBY, Arnold:
  Edridge-Green.
SPRAGG, Cyril Douglas:
  MacAlister.
†STEED, Henry Wickham:
  Seton-Watson.
STEIN, Leonard Jacques:
  Weizmann.
†STEVEN, Henry Marshall:
  Robinson (R. L.).
STEWART, John Innes Mackintosh:
  Sayers.
STEWART, Oliver:
  Bailey (M.); Mollison.
STOCKS, Mary Danvers Stocks, Baroness:
  Simon (Simon of Wythenshawe); Stewart-Murray (Atholl).
STONE, (Alan) Reynolds:
  Raverat.
STOWERS, Arthur:
  Dickinson.
STREAT, Sir (Edward) Raymond:
  Chapman (S. J.).
†STRONG, Leonard Alfred George:
  Vachell.
SUMMERSON, Sir John Newenham:
  Goodhart-Rendel.
SUTHERLAND, David Macbeth:
  Watt.
SUTTON, Sir (Oliver) Graham:
  Johnson (N. K.).
SWAN, Robert Arthur:
  Wilkins.
SYKES, Christopher Hugh:
  Hoare; Mann.

TAIT, Sir Victor Hubert:
  Hart.
TAPLIN, Walter:
  Craig; Firth (W. J.); Larke.
TAYLOR, Cyril:
  Downey.
TAYLOR, Sir George:
  Kingdon-Ward.
TEALE, Godfrey Benjamin:
  McGrigor.
TEMPLE, George:
  Whittaker.
†THOMAS, Alan Ernest Wentworth:
  Garnett.
THOMAS, Sir Ben Bowen:
  Jones (T.).

THOMAS, Edgar:
  Ashby.
†THOMAS, Hugh Hamshaw:
  Arber.
THOMAS, Ruth Rees:
  Fox.
†THURSFIELD, Henry George:
  Cowan; Evans (Mountevans).
TIBBOTT, Gildas:
  Davies.
†TITCHMARSH, Edward Charles:
  Jeffery.
TRAILL, David:
  Irvine.
TREWIN, John Courtenay:
  Collins; Dukes; McCarthy; Trevelyan (H.); Whitworth.
TUCKER, William Eldon:
  Smart.
†TURNER, George Charlewood:
  Norwood.
TWEEDSMUIR, Susan Charlotte Buchan, Lady:
  Markham.

UNDERWOOD, Edgar Ashworth:
  Singer.

VEALE, Sir Douglas:
  Goodenough; Gwyer.
VENABLES, Cedric:
  Stoop.
VIVIAN, Arthur Cecil:
  Hartley.

WAIN, Ralph Louis:
  Bennett.
WAKELEY, Sir Cecil Pembrey Grey, Bart.:
  Gordon-Taylor; Turner; Waring.
WALDOCK, Sir (Claud) Humphrey (Meredith):
  Brierly.
WALTON, Mary:
  Balfour (Riverdale).
WARD, John Owen:
  Scholes.
WARDLAW, Claude Wilson:
  Lang.
WATSON, David Meredith Seares:
  Broom.
WELLS, William:
  Burrell.
WESTAWAY, Katharine Mary:
  Stansfeld.
WHEARE, Sir Kenneth Clinton:
  Coupland.
WHEELER, Sir Charles Thomas:
  Ledward.
WHEELER, Sir (Robert Eric) Mortimer:
  Marshall (J. H.); Peers (C. R.).
WHEELER-BENNETT, Sir John Wheeler:
  Alexandra (Princess Arthur of Connaught); Fergusson.
†WHITAKER, Sir (Frederick) Arthur:
  Halcrow.
WHITE, James:
  Hone; Yeats.

List of Contributors

WHITE, Terence de Vere:
Gogarty.

WHITELEY, Derek Pepys:
Buchanan (W. J.).

WHITTET, George Sorley:
Kennington.

WHITTICK, Arnold:
Mendelsohn.

WIGGLESWORTH, Sir Vincent Brian:
Buxton.

WILENSKI, Reginald Howard:
Dulac.

WILLIAMS, David:
Boswell.

WILLIAMS, Edgar Trevor:
Whitehead; Young (G. M.).

†WILLIAMS, Sir (Evan) Owen:
Elvin.

WILLIAMS, Sir Griffith Goodland:
Tomlinson (G.).

WILLIAMS, John Hargreaves Harley:
Sutherland; Young (R. A.).

WILLIAMS, Trevor Illtyd:
Holmyard.

WILLIAMS-ELLIS, Clough:
Elkan.

WILSON, Sir (Archibald) Duncan:
Peake.

†WILSON, Frank Percy:
Chambers (E. K.); Greg.

†WILSON, Sir (James) Steuart:
Boughton.

WILSON, John Graham:
Wilson (C. T. R.).

WIMPENNY, Ronald Stenning:
Russell (E. S.).

WINGATE, Sir Ronald Evelyn Leslie, Bart.:
Jarvis; Philby.

†WINTER, Carl:
Clarke (L. C. G.).

†WISEMAN, Herbert Victor:
Greenwood.

WISKEMANN, Elizabeth Meta:
Voigt.

WITTS, Leslie John:
Horder.

WOODALL, Mary:
Walker (E.).

WOODRUFF, (John) Douglas:
Belloc; Bracken.

WOODS, Oliver Frederick John Bradley:
Astor.

†WOOLF, Leonard Sidney:
Moore.

WORLOCK, Derek John Harford, Bishop of Portsmouth (R.C.):
Griffin.

†WORTHINGTON, Sir (John) Hubert:
Green.

WRIGHT, Georg Henrik von:
Wittgenstein.

WRIGHT, Kenneth Anthony:
Coates.

WYATT, Woodrow Lyle:
Cripps.

WYKEHAM, Sir Peter Guy:
Brooke-Popham; Trenchard.

YATES, Frank:
Yule.

YOUNG, Wayland Hilton (Baron Kennet):
Young (Kennet).

YOUNGER, Hon. Kenneth Gilmour:
McNeil.

DICTIONARY

OF

NATIONAL BIOGRAPHY

(TWENTIETH CENTURY)

PERSONS WHO DIED 1951–1960

ABERCONWAY, second BARON (1879–1953), industrialist. [See McLAREN, HENRY DUNCAN.]

ABERCROMBIE, SIR (LESLIE) PATRICK (1879–1957), architect and professor of town planning, was born 6 June 1879 at the Manor House, Ashton-upon-Mersey, the seventh of nine children of William Abercrombie, stockbroker, a Fifeshire man, by his Yorkshire wife, Sarah Ann Heron. Patrick's junior by some eighteen months was his brother Lascelles Abercrombie, the poet [q.v.]. The family later moved to Brooklands, in Cheshire; and it was in Chester, the county town so often quoted in Abercrombie's lectures on town planning, that in 1920 he became a partner in the architectural firm of Lockwood, Abercrombie, and Saxon. Meanwhile, after going to Uppingham, he had been articled to Charles Heathcote, a Manchester architect, then to (Sir) Arnold Thornely's firm in Liverpool. The Cunarders in those days embarked their passengers at Prince's landing stage and the great joy of coming into Liverpool from the Cheshire side was the crossing by ferryboat from Birkenhead, where Abercrombie had his lodgings. This daily journey and the walking excursions in the other direction, across the Dee into Wales, must have made permanent impressions of town and suburb, industry and the countryside, on his perceptive eye and retentive mind; and it was on the ferryboat that he met and fell in love with Emilia Maud, schoolgirl daughter of Robert Gordon, whom he subsequently married (1909). She bore him a daughter and a son, Neil, who afterwards became town planning commissioner in Tasmania; her death in 1942 was a most grievous loss.

Abercrombie's first academic post was that of assistant lecturer in architecture and instructor for architectural students in drawing at the university of Liverpool. He was himself a draughtsman out of the ordinary. He wrote, until the end of his life, an elegant Italian hand, lettered his own maps and geological sections, and made clear and distinctive drawings of joinery, the façades of buildings, bird's-eye views of towns and features in landscape—of which he had an intuitive as well as a self-disciplined understanding. This post in the School of Architecture, beginning to flourish under the presiding genius of (Sir) C. H. Reilly [q.v.], he held from 1907 to 1909. He was then appointed to the research fellowship in town planning and civic design, newly endowed by W. H. Lever (later Viscount Leverhulme, q.v.), along with the publication of the *Town Planning Review*, of which Abercrombie was the first editor, and the inauguration of the Lever professorship to which S. D. Adshead [q.v.] was appointed. Abercrombie doubled the role of research fellow under Adshead with that of lecturer in building construction and Gothic architecture under Reilly, who naturally reserved to himself the more important lectures on classical architecture.

This was a time of great activity in civic survey, town planning, and housing. The Housing, Town Planning, etc. Act of 1909 first gave statutory recognition to the process of planning the use of land. At the big town planning conference in London in 1910, Abercrombie acted as one of the secretary-reporters. Soon after, he began a series of analytical and descriptive reports on the growth and condition of Paris, Vienna, Berlin, Brussels, Karlsruhe, and other European cities and contributed to the first World Congress of Cities at Ghent in 1913. The title of Abercrombie's thesis, for which he gained distinction in the final professional examinations of the Royal Institute of British Architects in 1915, was 'Three Capital Cities'; and although he became a fellow of the R.I.B.A. in 1925, and vice-president in 1937–9, and maintained an interest as well as a skill in architectural design throughout his working life, he never undertook a major building commission as sole executive architect. But his energy and resourcefulness as writer, editor, illustrator, teacher, and student of cities were prodigious.

The outbreak of war in 1914 put an end to European travel, but he managed to visit Dublin to take part in an open international competition for the replanning of the city. Despite the war the judging went forward, and in 1916 Abercrombie and his associates, Sydney and Arthur Kelly, were awarded first prize. *Dublin of the Future: the new town plan* was not, in fact, published until 1922; the proposals were not adopted for another sixteen years; and the amending report and 'sketch development plan' did not come out until 1941. Nevertheless the skill and originality of his competition entry made an immediate impression.

In 1915 Adshead was appointed to the chair of town planning at University College, London, and Abercrombie at the age of thirty-six became professor of civic design at Liverpool, a post he held for twenty years until in 1935 he succeeded Adshead in London. The advisory reports and plans which he prepared during these twenty years, sometimes on his own and sometimes jointly, are legion. This was his period of discovery in England and Wales, in which he depicted landscapes and townscapes, analysed the form and extent of urban growth, and became involved in the consequences of industrial development. At Dormanstown, for example, he was responsible with Adshead and Stanley Ramsey for the design of this new industrial settlement, with its early attempt to combine standard houses in a varied layout; and for the Doncaster coalfield he formulated in 1922, on the satellite principle, the first regional scheme in this country to be consciously planned as such. This was followed by a study of Deeside in 1923 and of the East Kent coalfield in 1925. Of the older industrial towns themselves one of his most interesting reports was on Sheffield where he made his civic survey in 1924 and the embracing regional plan in 1931.

The impact of growth on the countryside could not fail to engage his mind and trouble his vision of an orderly Britain. Reports on the Thames Valley (1929), Cumberland (1932), the Wye Valley and East Suffolk (1935) show a growing concern with the legislative and administrative means necessary to canalize and control development. Already in 1926, during his term of office as president of the Town Planning Institute, he had published a tract for the times called *The Preservation of Rural England*. This led directly to the establishment of the Council for the Preservation of Rural England of which Abercrombie was honorary secretary and later executive chairman. He often said that preservation for its own sake was never his aim, but that a country so rich and varied in its landscape and in its traditions could not afford to rely on official regulation only, but should cultivate an informed and vigilant body of opinion of a voluntary kind. Thus he campaigned for the Green Belt around London, not only in theory but in practice and in detail. In all this Abercrombie was the link between the enlightened amateur of the nineteenth century and the professional expert of the twentieth.

Looking through some thirty pre-war reports, all delightfully presented but now largely superseded and dust-laden, one is made aware of Abercrombie's immense industry and fertility; but also of the fact that although they were persuasive, and beginning to be influential, they were not yet backed by administrative power or by economic incentives. Nevertheless, if any one man had a truly synoptic view of the physical planning problems of the British Isles, that man was Abercrombie; and it was this endowment which he brought to the royal commission on the distribution of the industrial population, appointed in 1937 under the chairmanship of Sir Anderson Montague-Barlow. Abercrombie's quick mind and wide experience helped to make the minutes of evidence illuminating and the recommendations of more lasting value than usual. His additional minority report made a permanent contribution to the development of British planning machinery.

The Barlow report appeared after the war of 1939–45 had begun and it threw into lurid relief the hazards of industrial and urban concentration which the commission had been assessing. The challenge to the future which this created, coupled with the desire to maintain civilian morale in the face of destruction by bombing, caused early in the war a concern with the principles of post-war reconstruction. In April 1941 Lord Reith, as minister of works and buildings, by agreement with the London County Council, appointed Abercrombie, in association with J. H. Forshaw, the L.C.C. architect, to prepare a plan for post-war rebuilding over the whole area of the county of London. Fifteen months later Lord Reith's successor, Lord Portal [q.v.], announced that consideration was to be given to the planning of the area surrounding the county. Abercrombie was again called on to undertake this very considerable task, assisted by a team of younger men from the staff of what was about to become the Ministry of Town and Country Planning.

These two reports, the *County of London Plan* (1943) and the *Greater London Plan* (1944), were the most comprehensive, the most far-reaching and the most effective of Abercrombie's career. Undertaken in conditions of emergency, and in a spirit almost of bravado, the plans could not be profound as social or economic studies. But they matched the needs of the time, and provided a usable framework for post-war development policy, including the launching of the New Towns programme in 1946. Abercrombie made many other plans after the war, notably for Plymouth, Hull, Edinburgh, the Clyde region, and the West Midlands. And he made many reports abroad, not only in countries such as Ceylon and Israel where he had worked before, but in Malta, Ethiopia, Cyprus, and Hong Kong, where the reputation of his London plans had run ahead of him, for by this time he was an international figure. He had retired from his London chair in 1946; and his students were scattered all over the world, many in posts he had helped to create. It was typical of him that he should devote so much time in his later years to yet another voluntary and unpaid post, new in its conception but this time international in scope, the *Union Internationale des Architectes*, established by means of conferences in London and Brussels in 1947 and 1948. It was due mainly to Abercrombie's energy and tact that constitutional teething troubles were overcome, that the U.S.S.R. and Yugoslavia supported the Union, along with the U.S.A., the South American republics, and all the countries of western Europe. He was president from 1951 to 1956, succeeding Auguste Perret; and confessed to a friend that these were the most taxing years of his life.

Sir Frederic Osborn, a lifelong colleague in the town and country planning movement, remarked of Abercrombie that 'he never began to ossify mentally'. Certainly,

his quick enthusiasm, his characteristic high-pitched laugh, the pace at which he lectured and the speed at which he took a point at a public meeting, did not appear to have slowed down at all over the fifty years of his professional life. Yet he never sought the limelight, was generous to students and colleagues, and wore his honours lightly. Knighted in 1945, he was also an officer of the Order of the Crown in Belgium, of the Legion of Honour in France, and an honorary graduate of the universities of London, Melbourne, and Liverpool. Among many other awards he received the royal gold medal for architecture in 1946, and the gold medal of the American Institute of Architects in 1949. He never really retired, saying that he could not afford to, but in fact it was not in his nature; and he died in harness, with projects and reports as widely different as the precincts of Winchester Cathedral and the revision of his plan for Addis Ababa still receiving his unflagging attention. He died 23 March 1957 at his house at Aston Tirrold in Berkshire and was buried at Rhoscolyn in Anglesey, a countryside which he loved and had laboured to preserve.

[Private information; personal knowledge.]
HOLFORD.

ABERDARE, third BARON (1885–1957), athlete. [See BRUCE, CLARENCE NAPIER.]

ABUL KALAM AZAD, MAULANA (1888–1958), Indian minister of education. [See AZAD.]

ADDISON, CHRISTOPHER, first VISCOUNT ADDISON (1869–1951), statesman, was born at Hogsthorpe, Lincolnshire, 19 June 1869. His father, Robert Addison, came of a line of yeomen who had farmed in the vicinity of Hogsthorpe for generations. In 1861 he had married Susan, daughter of Charles Fanthorpe, a customs official in Newcastle. There were twelve children of the marriage of whom seven survived; Christopher was the youngest of three boys.

Brought up on a farm, Addison retained throughout his life a taste for country ways. But it was so clear at an early age that he possessed exceptional abilities that it was decided he should receive an education beyond that customary in the neighbourhood for a farmer's son. At thirteen he was sent to Trinity College,

Harrogate, and later, in conditions of considerable financial stringency, he went to the medical school at Sheffield and thence to St. Bartholomew's. He specialized in anatomy and, soon after qualifying in 1892, returned to Sheffield to teach. In 1897 he was appointed professor of anatomy in the University College of Sheffield, leaving in 1901 to become a lecturer in anatomy at the Charing Cross Hospital in London. During these years he taught, researched, published, and administered with the energy and enthusiasm which were later to characterize his political activities. He published several works on anatomy, delivered the Hunterian lectures, edited the *Quarterly Medical Journal*, and, as a result of one piece of research, gave his name to a part of the human body, the Addison plane.

In 1902 he married Isobel Mackinnon, daughter of Archibald Gray who had made a considerable fortune in trade with India. They were to have three sons (one of whom died in early childhood) and two daughters. The money which his wife brought to the marriage made it possible for Addison to think seriously of a political career. In 1907 he was adopted as a Liberal candidate for the Hoxton division of Shoreditch.

His decision to abandon medicine and enter politics was taken at a time of political ferment. The Liberal upsurge which culminated in the victory at the election of 1906 appeared to open up totally new prospects for radical reform. Addison's own interests were in matters of health and social welfare. His general political outlook was that of a typical Radical. He was well read in John Stuart Mill [q.v.], was in favour of Home Rule, and supported the nationalization of land. But what had moved him to enter politics was the plight of the poor which he had witnessed as a doctor, their chronic state of undernourishment, the lack of adequate medical attention when they were ill, the miserable and overcrowded conditions in which so many of them lived.

Addison entered the Commons at the first election of 1910 and, astonishingly for a man with no connections and little skill as an orator, had made his mark in not much more than a year. His chance came with the national health insurance bill of 1911. His special knowledge made him an invaluable member of the group of politicians and civil servants around Lloyd George which was responsible for the measure. Addison helped with the drafting of amendments, served as a link with the doctors, and worked indefatigably in the lobbies. It was the sort of work for which he had entered politics and for which, within the Liberal Party, he was uniquely fitted.

During these months he fell under the spell of Lloyd George. It was the making of an association which was to shape his whole political future. Lloyd George, a politician to his finger tips, had popular appeal, a subtlety of approach to difficult issues, an ability to charm and manage men, qualities which Addison almost totally lacked. But Addison's own skills were not inconsiderable, especially as they were complementary. He had a capacity, unusual in politicians, for mastering technical problems, his appetite for work was inexhaustible, and he was to prove himself a sound and thorough administrator. Moreover, he was content to be a subordinate since he was almost without the kind of political ambition and competitiveness which Lloyd George himself possessed in such abundance. Believing that Lloyd George shared his aims and that he was the only man in politics capable of achieving them, Addison was to serve him with total loyalty.

At the outbreak of war in 1914 Addison was still a backbencher, although since 1911 he had been much involved as Lloyd George's aide in a number of schemes for the expansion of welfare services. He was appointed parliamentary secretary to the Board of Education in August 1914; then, when a ministry of munitions was set up with Lloyd George at its head in May 1915, Addison joined him. His post was that of parliamentary secretary, but to him Lloyd George assigned the main responsibility for organizing from scratch a ministry which, in the range of its personnel and the scope of its functions, had no precedent. It came into existence at a time of crisis when the traditional methods of supplying the army had proved incapable of meeting the demands generated by modern war. By the application of new techniques, soon to be labelled 'war socialism', a transformation was wrought in the British economy. Production soared, private industry was brought under a system of control and supervision, the Government itself built and operated factories on an enormous scale. In all this, Addison was invaluable, undertaking much of the detailed ministerial work which Lloyd George was only too happy to delegate. Perhaps Addison's largest contribution was to work out a costing system for munitions which by the end of the war had saved the country an estimated £440 million. He was sworn of the Privy Council in June 1916.

In July Lloyd George left munitions to become secretary for war, but Addison remained absolutely his man. In the ministerial crisis of December his canvass of Liberal members of Parliament was of key importance. The assurance that many Liberals would be willing to support Lloyd George if he could form a government enabled Lloyd George to demonstrate not only that he could muster sufficient support to maintain himself in office, but that he was the only man who could do so.

Addison's reward was the Ministry of Munitions which by now exercised control over almost every aspect of war production. But in July 1917 he left to become minister of reconstruction. He went with some reluctance, but Lloyd George was anxious to replace him by (Sir) Winston Churchill and had taken pains to weaken Addison's position by some characteristically devious activities during an engineers' strike in June. Addison, however, was soon enthusiastic about his new task: reconstruction not only offered a chance to plan the transition of the economy from war to peace, but also to produce longer-term schemes for social reform. Once again he threw himself into the organization of a new ministry. Committees in abundance were set to work to draw up blueprints for the future.

As the war drew to a close, Addison began to realize that most of his hopes were to be dashed. His capacity to influence policy had always derived from his relationship with Lloyd George. He had neither party support nor political backing of his own. To the public at large he was still 'Dr. Addison', remote and almost unknown. By 1918 he was no longer as close to Lloyd George as before. The prime minister was preoccupied with more pressing problems than reconstruction and on matter after matter Addison found himself unable to get a decision.

From the general wreck of reconstruction, however, Addison's favourite scheme, the establishment of a ministry of health, was salvaged. He became president of the Local Government Board in January 1919 and then introduced a bill to establish a ministry of health, becoming the first minister himself in June. He had always been attracted by the opportunities

offered by the consolidation of all health questions in one ministry, but in 1919 the first priority was to devise ways of implementing the pledge of 'Homes fit for heroes' which had been so loosely given at the election of 1918. Before the war the provision of housing for the working classes had been left almost completely to private builders and Addison knew from the start that the situation required a solution such as had been imposed by the Ministry of Munitions in 1915. But he had no control over prices and raw materials and no power to direct capital or labour from inessential work to housing. Houses could be built only by stimulating the local authorities to build them. The Housing, Town Planning, etc. Act of 1919 (usually called the Addison Act) provided that local authorities should build a virtually unlimited number of houses, that their rents should be controlled at a low level, and that the Government would meet, by subsidy, any loss beyond that which could be covered by a penny local rate. During the next three years the State built or financed well over 200,000 houses but, in conditions of post-war boom, the cost was tremendous. There was an outcry among many of the Conservative supporters of the coalition and, in April 1921, Lloyd George decided to let them have Addison's head. Addison kicked his heels until July as minister without portfolio and then, his housing policy having been torn to shreds, left the Government.

There was some force in Lloyd George's complaint that Addison regarded himself 'as a martyr to the cause of public health' and refused to understand that not even the prime minister had any hope of stemming the tide running in favour of economy and against extravagance. But Addison could see only the betrayal of the promises that had been made to the homeless and the slum dwellers. It was for him a period of deep bitterness and frustration. His attachment to Lloyd George had long since cut him off from the main body of Liberals so that, after a defeat at the election of 1922, it was almost inevitable that he should turn to the Labour Party. His experience of the post-war coalition had persuaded him that the Labour Party offered the sole hope of achieving the social reforms on which his heart was set and, as he reflected on the lessons to be drawn from his years at munitions and reconstruction, he became convinced that socialist forms of control were not only socially desirable but could also be considerably more efficient than the methods of traditional capitalism.

Addison failed to get back to the Commons at the election of 1924 when he stood for Hammersmith South, and these years were mainly devoted to writing. He gave his version of the housing controversy in *The Betrayal of the Slums* (1922) and this was followed by *Politics from Within* (2 vols., 1924) and *Practical Socialism* (2 vols., 1926). In 1929 he was returned for Swindon and was appointed parliamentary secretary to the Ministry of Agriculture in the second Labour Government, succeeding Lord Noel-Buxton [q.v.] as minister in June 1930. In a Cabinet which contained few energetic figures Addison was quickly ready with a major legislative programme for agriculture. Then came a stroke of fortune. Because Addison's parliamentary secretary was in the Lords, it was agreed that he would need help with piloting what were certain to be extremely controversial measures through the Commons. C. R. (later Earl) Attlee, who had recently succeeded Sir Oswald Mosley as chancellor of the Duchy of Lancaster, was assigned the task. He was deeply impressed by Addison's ability to master a subject and by the skill with which he ran his department and managed both his own party and the Opposition in standing committee.

In major political matters, Addison was on the outer fringe of the Cabinet. But when the financial crisis which destroyed the Government came to a head on 23 August 1931 he stood with those who opposed MacDonald and Snowden on cuts in unemployment benefit, the only middle-class member of the Cabinet to do so. Loss of office was followed, at the election in October, by loss of his seat in the Commons. He regained it at a by-election in 1934 only to be defeated at the election of 1935. His wife had died in the previous year.

In May 1937, powerfully persuaded by Attlee, he was created a baron. Later in the same year he married (Beatrice) Dorothy, daughter of Frederick Percy Low, a solicitor. He continued to be an active writer and publicist, his most important books of these years being *Four and a Half Years* (2 vols., 1934) and *A Policy for British Agriculture* (1939). In 1940 he became leader of the Labour peers, but the war afforded no outlet for his talents more considerable than the chairmanship of the Buckinghamshire war agricultural executive committee.

But, after the Labour victory at the election of 1945, Attlee appointed him leader of the House of Lords. He was then seventy-six, yet he was still in the Attlee government when it fell in October 1951, having held meanwhile the posts of secretary of state for dominion affairs (1945–7), lord privy seal (1947–51), paymaster-general (1948–9), and lord president of the Council (1951). Throughout this period if his administrative responsibilities had been small, in the Lords he faced a task which tested his skill to the utmost. He was responsible, in the face of an overwhelming Conservative majority, for the passage of a large and far-reaching legislative programme. He managed the Lords superbly, greatly aided by the fact that Lord Salisbury, with whom he struck up a remarkable understanding, was leader of the Conservative peers. To explain Addison's success, Attlee was wont to quote what a Conservative whip had said of him in 1931, 'How can we oppose this man? He is so decent.' No doubt deeper political consideration than this lay at the root of the decision of the Conservative peers to make sparing use of their strength after the débâcle of 1945, but Addison's persuasiveness did much to reconcile them to their lot.

As an elder statesman with no political ambitions of his own, he was of great value to Attlee in the Cabinet. His advice was listened to and he could always be relied upon for help in dealing with 'difficult people like Aneurin Bevan'. Attlee, who rarely allowed personal and political relationships to come into contact, had a great admiration and affection for Addison and turned to him constantly as friend and adviser.

Addison was advanced to a viscountcy in 1945 and created K.G. in 1946. He died 11 December 1951 at his home at Radnage in Buckinghamshire, and was succeeded by his eldest son, Christopher (born 1904). His career had been one of the most unusual of his time. Not entering the Commons until he was forty, he was, apart from Lloyd George, the only man to hold office continuously from 1914 to 1921. Then, his career seemingly in ruins, he had to wait until he was seventy-six for a second chance. His responsibilities in the Attlee government were general and legislative, but few politicians of the second rank can match his record of innovation in the earlier part of his career. Before 1914 he helped to work out the details of a new medical and welfare system. During the war of 1914–18 he played a large part in initiating the methods of 'war socialism' which began the conversion of individualist capitalism to the collectivism of a later age. The Ministry of Health was his personal creation and, in spite of the circumstances of his political fall, it was Addison who more than any other man transformed the housing of the working classes from a capitalist enterprise into a social service. The setting up of the research councils for medicine, science and industry, and agriculture was largely due to his energy and determination.

Attlee wrote of him, 'Patience, friendliness, common sense—these were his virtues—nobody wanted to quarrel when Addison was around. He made it seem wrong.' But Addison's career was based on more than these personal qualities. He represented the idealist and humanitarian tradition in British politics and part of his importance is that he emphasized the chain of continuity which linked the Labour Party to a Radical past. But he was at his best in office, loyal to colleagues, active in innovation, sage in council, and skilled in administration.

[Addison's own writings; R. J. Minney, *Viscount Addison: Leader of the Lords*, 1958; *Observer*, 7 February 1960; private information.]   Maurice Shock.

AGA KHAN, AGA SULTAN Sir MOHAMMED SHAH (1877–1957), third holder of the title Aga Khan (bestowed on his grandfather by the British Government), 48th head of the Ismaili sect of the Shiah Moslem community, and a member of the ruling Kajar dynasty in Persia, was born in Karachi 2 November 1877. Son of Aga Khan II, he succeeded his father in 1885. His mother, Lady Ali Shah, a former Persian princess, and a woman of character and vision, alive to the importance of the role, political and religious, which her son would have to fill, brought him up with a care, skill, and judgement for which he always remained grateful.

He assumed the active administration of the Imamate in 1893, in his sixteenth year. His eleven to twelve million followers, scattered over India, Burma, the Middle East, and Africa, looked to him not only as their spiritual leader, but for the resolution of their temporal problems. So early as 1893 he instructed his followers in Bombay to keep out of communal rioting; in 1901 he applied spiritual sanctions to Ismailis who had made murderous attacks on Sunnis; he consistently urged his followers to identify themselves, in manners, language, and customs, with the countries in which they lived. There were occasions when his liberal and moderate attitude failed to carry his community with him, as in 1901, when the Isma Asri sect broke away, and again during the Balkan wars (1912–13) and the Khilafat agitation (1919–21). But his was a restraining influence and broadly speaking the community responded to his lead over political issues. His spiritual influence remained unshaken, even after old age and ill health had reduced his political importance.

The Aga Khan was chosen in 1897 by the Moslems of Western India to convey to the viceroy their greetings to the Queen Empress on her diamond jubilee. In 1898 he began a lifelong series of visits to Europe, Africa, Asia, and America and was received at Windsor by Queen Victoria.

In 1902 Lord Curzon [q.v.] nominated him to the viceroy's legislative council, on which he served for two years, declining a second term. He used the opportunity to urge the claims of a Moslem university at Aligarh, to which he had lent substantial financial support.

The Aga Khan had throughout maintained the friendliest of relations with the Indian Congress leaders, and particularly with G. K. Gokhale. He had spared no pains to maintain communal unity, to integrate Moslem political feeling with the Congress Party, and so to present a united front, with constitutional advance as its objective, to the British Government. He had, too, done his best to reduce the communal antagonisms which derived from the partition of Bengal of 1905. But by 1906, now established as a political force, and as the recognized leader and spokesman of the Indian Moslems as a whole, he began to conclude that Congress would prove incapable of representing Indian Moslem feeling: 'already that artificial unity which the British Raj had imposed from without was cracking'; 'our only hope lay along the lines of independent organization and action'.

In that year he led a delegation to Lord Minto [q.v.] which urged the case for increased Moslem participation in the political life of the country and pressed that they should be regarded as a nation within a nation, with rights and obligations safeguarded by statute, with adequate and separate representations both in local bodies and on legislative councils, and with a separate communal franchise and electoral roll. Lord Minto's reply was reassuring.

Later in 1906 the All-India Moslem League was founded, and the Aga Khan was elected its first president, an office which he held until 1912. He lent his active support to the Morley–Minto reforms of 1909, but intercommunal feeling continued to grow, despite the cancellation of the partition of Bengal.

On the outbreak of war in 1914 the Aga Khan, who had exercised a restraining influence on Indian Moslem opinion during the Balkan wars of 1912–13, was in Zanzibar. He at once volunteered his services and instructed his followers to render all possible support. He was advised that he could help best in the diplomatic field. His endeavours to promote Turkish neutrality failed, but when Turkey joined the Central Powers and by declaring a *jehad* or holy war created a difficult situation for Indian and other Moslems, he unhesitatingly and successfully urged on them full co-operation with the Allies. In 1915 he was entrusted with a mission of major importance to Egypt, the effect of which was to reassure Egyptian opinion and to secure the internal stability of the country, with the invaluable consequent assistance to the Allies of a strategically placed and dependable base.

On his return to England in September 1914 the Aga Khan had again met Gokhale, and with him strove to compose a memorandum on Indian constitutional progress representing their joint views on the establishment of federation in India as a step towards self-government. Early in 1915 Gokhale died, addressing his political testament to the Aga Khan, and not to M. K. Gandhi [q.v.] or any Hindu leader, for publication two years later, by when he hoped the war would be over and India capable of working out her own destiny. The testament was duly published, with a further plea by the Aga Khan that after the war East Africa might be reserved for Indian colonization in recognition of India's services. But it was overtaken by events which led to the Montagu–Chelmsford reforms of 1919.

Ill health prevented the Aga Khan from taking the part he would have wished in these developments. But his enforced leisure resulted in 1918 in his *India in Transition*, dedicated to his mother, a thoughtful and closely argued study which attracted much attention. He reminded the British of their grant of full self-government to South Africa, and urged the case for the sharing of power in India, and for a widely based South Asian Federation of which an India ultimately self-governing must be the centre and pivot.

After the war the Aga Khan was active in pressing on the Allies the long-term importance of the question of the Caliphate, and of a policy towards Turkey which should be practical as well as temperate, just, and equitable. Strongly as his own sympathies lay with Turkey, he was a realist and restraining influence on Moslems in India, and as such sharply criticized by many members of his community during the Khilafat agitation in which the Ali brothers had the active support of Gandhi and the Congress.

By 1924 difficulties in Kenya between the British settlers on the one hand, and the British Government and the local Indian interests on the other, resulted in a committee of inquiry under (Sir) John Hope Simpson. The Aga Khan, who had declined the chairmanship, was a member, and the committee's report proposed compromises, more particularly over Indian immigration into East Africa, and the reservation of certain districts in the coastal lowlands which were of much importance to India.

From 1924 to 1928 the Aga Khan spent 'a period devoted almost exclusively to my own personal and private life'.

At the end of 1928 an All-Indian Moslem conference met at Delhi under his chairmanship to formulate Moslem opinion in view of the commission under Sir John (later Viscount) Simon [q.v.] on India's constitutional future. Its unanimous conclusions, the more significant in that they had the support of M. A. Jinnah [q.v.], remained the guiding light for the Moslem community in all subsequent discussions. They contemplated a federal system with complete autonomy and residuary powers vested in the constituent states: took note that the right of Moslems to elect their representatives in the various Indian legislatures was now the law of the land, of which they could not be deprived without their consent: and stipulated that in the provinces in which Moslems constituted a minority they should have a representation in no case less than that already enjoyed: and that they must have their due share in the central and provincial cabinets.

The Simon report of 1930 was followed

by the three Round Table conferences of 1930–32. The Aga Khan was elected chairman of the British-India delegation and throughout played a material part in the discussions. At all times alive to the importance of compromise, and of adapting communal claims to the interests of India as a whole, he made an important contribution to securing a unanimous report from the joint select committee (1933–4) presided over by Lord Linlithgow [q.v.] which resulted in the Government of India Act of 1935. But he failed to secure Congress acceptance of a joint memorandum, with the drafting of which he was closely concerned, embodying a united demand on behalf of all communities covering almost every important political point in issue, which sought to ensure continuity in the process of the further transfer of responsibility, and which, in his judgement, would have immensely simplified all future constitutional progress.

With the passing of the Government of India Act he ceased for the time actively to concern himself with Indian constitutional advance. But his high standing, religious and political, his extensive travels and wide contacts, his fluency in the principal European languages, and his independence of outlook, had made him increasingly a figure not merely of Indian and Commonwealth but of international importance, and from 1932 he was for some years prominent in the League of Nations. He was a representative of India at the world disarmament conference at Geneva in 1932, was leader of the Indian delegation to the League of Nations Assembly in 1932 and 1934–7, and in 1937 president of the Assembly. It was while president that he visited Hitler. He subsequently lent his fullest support to the Munich settlement, suggesting in a much criticized article in *The Times* that the Führer should be taken at his word, and questioning whether he had really meant what he had said in *Mein Kampf*.

On the outbreak of war in 1939 the Aga Khan was in Europe. He at once issued a manifesto urging his followers to give the fullest support to Britain. In the winter of 1939–40 he visited India, when he persistently restated British war aims, and endeavoured to act as an intermediary with Reza Shah of Persia. He led a deputation to the viceroy on behalf of Indians in South Africa, and endeavoured, unsuccessfully, by discussion with the Nawab of Bhopal [q.v.] and Gandhi, to bring about mutual understanding between the Indian parties for the prosecution of the war. He returned to Europe in April 1940, and on the fall of France withdrew to Switzerland, where he remained under medical treatment, barred from political activity, until the end of the war. The criticism which his inactivity provoked took perhaps insufficient account of his serious and continued ill health.

He returned to India in 1946 to find that, while his influence remained unshaken with his own community, which celebrated his diamond jubilee in India and East Africa in 1946, the Moslem political leadership had passed decisively to Jinnah, to whom he was to pay a generous tribute in his *Memoirs*. After partition in 1947 the Aga Khan ceased to be an active participant in Indian politics.

Ill health in his later years greatly reduced his activity, but he maintained the closest touch with the Ismaili community, and continued to travel extensively. In 1949 he took up Persian citizenship, while remaining a British subject. His platinum jubilee was celebrated in Karachi in February 1954. In that year he published his *Memoirs*.

Throughout his life he was keenly interested in horse-racing, and his scientific concern with bloodstock and breeding methods had a material effect on English horse-breeding. Coming to the English turf after 1918, he won the Queen Mary Stakes at Ascot in 1922 (Cos) and had thereafter a record of outstanding distinction, winning, in addition to many minor successes, the Derby in 1930 (Blenheim); the Two Thousand Guineas, Derby, and St. Leger (the triple crown) with Bahram in 1935; and the Derby again in 1936 (Mahmoud), 1948 (My Love), and 1952 (Tulyar). In 1954 he finally disposed of his studs.

Shrewd, active, a connoisseur of the arts, a good scholar, a citizen of the world, an experienced and courageous politician, a hardworking religious leader alive to the importance of the education and physical fitness of his community, with great material resources, he was for long a major figure in Indian politics, and in his time, helped by his broadminded and constructive approach and his instinct for compromise, he gave service of great value to his community and to the Commonwealth.

The Aga Khan was married in 1896 to a cousin in her teens, Shahzadi Begum. There was no issue, and the marriage was dissolved. In 1908 he married, in Cairo, by Moslem rites, an Italian lady, Teresa Magliano, by whom he had a son who died in infancy, and Aly Khan.

The Begum died in 1926. In 1929 he married Andrée Carron, by whom he had one son, Sadruddin. This union having been dissolved by divorce in the Geneva civil courts in 1943 (the Aga Khan being awarded custody of the son), he married in 1945 Yvette Larbousse, who survived him, and to whose devoted care in old age and illness he owed much.

In 1898 Queen Victoria had personally invested him with the K.C.I.E. He was appointed G.C.I.E. (1902), G.C.S.I. (1911), G.C.V.O. (1923), and G.C.M.G. (1955), thus receiving his last decoration from Queen Elizabeth. He held also the Brilliant Star of Zanzibar 1st Class (1900) and (1901) the Royal Prussian Order of the Crown, 1st Class (which he returned on the outbreak of war in 1914).

In 1934 he was sworn of the Privy Council, the first Indian, other than members of the Judicial Committee, to receive this honour. He was an honorary LL.D. of Cambridge (1911). In 1916, an honour which he particularly valued, King George V gave him a salute of eleven guns, and the rank and precedence for life of a first-class ruling chief of the Bombay Presidency.

The Aga Khan died at Versoix, near Geneva, 11 July 1957, and is buried at Aswan. He nominated as his successor as Aga Khan IV his grandson Karim (born 1936), elder son of Aly Khan.

The Begum Aga Khan has two portraits by Van Dongen; Princess Andrée Aga Khan has one by Sir Oswald Birley and another by Edmond Souza; Prince Sadruddin Aga Khan has one by John Berwick.

[The Aga Khan, *Memoirs*, 1954; Stanley Jackson, *The Aga Khan*, 1952; H. J. Greenwall, *The Aga Khan*, 1952; personal knowledge.]   GILBERT LAITHWAITE.

AGNEW, SIR WILLIAM GLADSTONE (1898–1960), vice-admiral, was born in London 2 December 1898, the fifth son of Charles Morland Agnew, art dealer, and his wife, Evelyn Mary, daughter of William Naylor, and grandson of Sir William Agnew [q.v.]. He joined the Royal Navy in September 1911 and was at Dartmouth when war broke out in 1914. He was sent to sea as a midshipman, serving in the battleships *Glory* and *Royal Oak* and in the destroyer *Skilful*. After the war his appointments included the royal yacht

and in 1924 he went to the *Excellent*, the gunnery school at Portsmouth, to qualify as a specialist in gunnery. During these years he played rugby football regularly for the navy as well as cricket, hockey, and tennis.

Agnew's first ship as a specialist officer was the cruiser *Durban* and in 1931 he was appointed gunnery officer of the battleship *Queen Elizabeth*, flagship of the Mediterranean Fleet. He was promoted commander in 1932 and captain in 1937.

On the outbreak of war in 1939 he was given command of the armed merchant cruiser *Corfu* and in October 1940 was transferred to the cruiser *Aurora*. It was the start of a period in which his name and that of his ship became world-famous. In the summer of 1941 the *Aurora* had a share in the sinking of a German cruiser, a destroyer, and two supply ships. Then in the autumn Agnew was sent to the Mediterranean as the senior officer of Force K, consisting of the *Aurora*, her sister ship the *Penelope*, and the destroyers *Lance* and *Lively*. This move was quickly justified. On the night of 8 November, Force K intercepted a strongly escorted enemy supply convoy of seven ships bound for North Africa. Agnew had made carefully thought-out plans for just such an encounter and had discussed his tactics in detail with the other commanding officers. As a result he was able to stalk the convoy undetected and took the enemy completely by surprise. All the supply ships and one of their escorting destroyers were sunk without so much as a scratch on Force K. As he left his ship on return to harbour to report to the vice-admiral, Malta, Agnew was spontaneously cheered by the officers and men of the *Penelope*— a rare tribute. A great leader, he was at the same time the most likeable and modest of men. For his services in this action he was appointed C.B. (1941).

Further sorties by Force K led to the sinking of three fuel tankers. All these successes created a critical fuel situation for the German Air Force in North Africa and had an important effect on Axis plans. In December the *Aurora* struck a mine but Agnew got her safely back to England after temporary repairs in Malta and she soon returned to the thick of the fighting. At the end of 1942 the *Aurora* formed part of the naval force in Operation Torch, the allied invasion of North Africa, and from then on was constantly in action, attacking enemy warships and convoys and fighting off enemy air attacks. It was a tribute to Agnew and the *Aurora* that the ship was chosen to carry King George VI from Tripoli to Malta for the royal visit to the island in June 1943. For this service the King appointed Agnew C.V.O.

The *Aurora* played a full part in the allied invasions of Italy and Sicily, carrying out a great many bombardments in support of the landings. In October, however, she was severely damaged in an air attack in the Eastern Mediterranean. Agnew took his damaged ship into Alexandria whence he was ordered home to take command of the *Excellent*. He had been appointed to the D.S.O. in April 1943 and subsequently received a bar (1944).

After the war, in March 1946, Agnew was appointed to command the battleship *Vanguard*. He was promoted rear-admiral in January 1947 and remained in command for the royal visit to South Africa. On conclusion of the tour he was promoted K.C.V.O. In August 1947 Agnew was appointed director of personal services at the Admiralty, where he remained until October 1949. In January 1950 he retired from the navy at his own request, and later in the year was promoted to vice-admiral on the retired list.

For the next three years Agnew was the general secretary of the National Playing Fields Association. By his drive, inspiration, and sheer hard work he put it on its feet again after its lapse during the war and re-established its effectiveness throughout the country. In 1953 he turned his energies to the work of local government. He also took a lead in the Christian Stewardship campaign in his local parish. In the midst of these many and varied activities he died suddenly at his home in Alverstoke 12 July 1960.

In 1930 Agnew married Patricia Caroline, daughter of Colonel Alfred William Bewley, C.M.G.; they had no children.

[Private information; personal knowledge.]
A. D. NICHOLL.

AKERS, SIR WALLACE ALAN (1888–1954), chemist, was born at Walthamstow 9 September 1888, the son of Charles Akers, a chartered accountant, and his wife, Mary Ethelreda Brown. He was the second child in a family of five, and the middle of three brothers. He was educated at Bexhill-on-Sea and at Aldenham School. From there he went to Christ Church, Oxford, where he studied chemistry and obtained first class honours in 1909. He took a prominent part in rowing and was in his college boat which won the Grand

Challenge cup at Henley in 1908 and the Visitors' Challenge cup in 1909.

In 1911 Akers joined Brunner Mond & Co. in Cheshire where apart from a brief spell in the research laboratory he was occupied with process work for its development and better understanding. He was by training a physical chemist—one of the first Oxford produced—and the type of work he had in Cheshire suited him very well.

In 1924 he went for some three years to the Far East in the employment of the Borneo Company, Ltd. Meanwhile, Imperial Chemical Industries had been formed in 1926 and in 1928 he returned to London to work in close conjunction with Colonel George Paton Pollitt who was then I.C.I.'s technical director. This work gave Akers wide experience in many branches of chemical technology and so in 1931, when a process of decentralization was put into effect throughout I.C.I., Akers was made responsible for their Billingham activities. These were essentially concerned with high pressure techniques using hydrogen. Ammonia synthesis was a major interest at this time.

In his period of responsibility at Billingham much prominence was given to the possibility of an industry based on the hydrogenation of coal and its derivatives to yield various oil products and it was under his general direction that the important experiment of treating something of the order of 450T per day of coal (designed to produce of the order of 100,000T per year of petrol) was inaugurated, to be continued until the unexpected economic conditions consequent on the war inevitably brought it to a conclusion.

When he returned to I.C.I. headquarters in 1937 Akers worked with (Sir) Holbrook Gaskell mainly in connection with the enormous wartime factory expansion programme. In 1939 he was appointed an executive manager, in 1941 a director, and in 1944 director responsible for research. He held that position until his retirement from the company in 1953.

In 1941 Akers was seconded to a special section of the Department of Scientific and Industrial Research to be director, under the general guidance of Sir John Anderson (later Viscount Waverley, q.v.) as lord president of the Council, for all the British contribution to the development of atomic energy. Lord Waverley wrote: 'Experience showed clearly that no better selection could have been made. His wide knowledge, unbounded energy, even temper, and absolute integrity fitted him admirably for a task which called for ingenuity, tact, and organizing ability of a high order. He had not only to co-ordinate the activities of scientists of the greatest eminence here and abroad, but also to conduct negotiations of great delicacy in both the United States and Canada. His services were recognized by the award of a C.B.E. in 1944 and a knighthood in 1946.'

In 1946 Akers reverted whole time to his position on the board of I.C.I. In carrying out his responsibilities as research director he made it the outstanding feature of his work to be a guiding inspiration and not in any sense an instructor. He never interfered in the detailed work of the research staff working in the decentralized divisions. The broad way in which he interpreted his duties enabled him to concentrate some of his activities so that they had far-reaching influences. Thus he was instrumental in establishing a series of I.C.I. research fellowships which have sponsored research activities in many universities. He was a guiding inspiration in securing the publication of *Endeavour* to fill a unique place among regular scientific publications. He was also largely responsible for setting up in 1946 near Welwyn a central research laboratory to study problems not directly the concern of any of the decentralized divisions. It was fittingly renamed the Akers Research Laboratory after his death.

Akers was a most clubbable man. For many years he resided in the Royal Thames Yacht Club where he delighted in having friends and acquaintances to dine. If he could do a friend a service he did it thoroughly, to the smallest detail. A hard worker, he readily occupied himself reading and writing to the small hours. Outside professional affairs his interests were in music and art, but a reputation as a good pianist was brought to an end by an accident to his hand. His interest in the arts was acknowledged by his appointment as a member of the scientific advisory committee, and subsequently a trustee, of the National Gallery.

He received the honorary degree of D.Sc. from Durham (1949) and of D.C.L. from Oxford (1952) and was elected F.R.S. in 1952. He was treasurer of the Chemical Society from 1948 until 1954.

His friends looked upon him as a confirmed bachelor and were surprised when in 1953 he married Mademoiselle Berna-

dette La Marre. After he died at Alton, Hampshire, 1 November 1954, his widow returned to France where she survived him by nearly six years.

[*Manchester Guardian* and *The Times*, 2 November 1954; Lord Waverley and Sir Alexander Fleck in *Biographical Memoirs of Fellows of the Royal Society*, vol. i, 1955; private information; personal knowledge.]

FLECK.

ALEXANDRA VICTORIA ALBERTA EDWINA LOUISE DUFF, PRINCESS ARTHUR OF CONNAUGHT, DUCHESS OF FIFE (1891–1959), elder daughter of the first Duke of Fife and of Princess Louise [q.v.], eldest daughter of the then Prince of Wales, was born at Mar Lodge, Braemar, 17 May 1891. Her father, the sixth Earl of Fife, who bore titles in the peerages of both the United Kingdom and Ireland, had been created a duke by Queen Victoria on the occasion of his marriage with the Queen's granddaughter in 1889; but a new creation was made in 1900 whereby the succession might pass to his daughters, the second of whom, the Lady Maud, was born in 1893. In 1905 King Edward VII created his eldest daughter Princess Royal and granted her two children the style and title of Princess and Highness, with precedence after members of the royal family styled Royal Highness.

In December 1911, Princess Alexandra set out with her parents and sister for their fourth winter in Egypt. In the early hours of 13 December, their ship, the P. & O. liner *Delhi*, ran ashore off Cape Spartel, on the coast of Spanish Morocco. Boats from the *Duke of Edinburgh* put off to the rescue, but many passengers, including the Duke of Fife's party, were completely submerged and greatly buffeted by the waves before reaching shore. Wet through and in piercing cold, they struggled through a gale of wind and rain to Cape Spartel lighthouse, where they were revived; but they did not reach the British legation at Tangier until six o'clock in the evening, after a ten-mile ride on muleback. After a few days' rest the party returned to Gibraltar and thence proceeded to Egypt and the Sudan. On 19 January the Duke of Fife contracted a chill which developed into pleurisy and pneumonia; he died at Aswan, 29 January 1912, aged sixty-two. His titles, other than those of the creation of 1900, became either extinct or dormant, but Princess Alexandra succeeded him as Duchess of Fife and Countess of Macduff.

In July of the following year came the announcement of the engagement of the Duchess of Fife to her cousin Prince Arthur [q.v.], the only son of the Duke of Connaught [q.v.] and Princess Louise of Prussia. They were married in the Chapel Royal, St. James's, 15 October 1913, and on 9 August 1914 was born their only child, Alastair Arthur, who bore the title of Earl of Macduff.

The war of 1914–18 gave to Princess Arthur of Connaught the opportunity to embrace a vocation of nursing in which she subsequently made a highly successful career. In 1915 she joined the staff of St. Mary's Hospital, Paddington, as a full-time nurse and worked untiringly in this capacity until the armistice. After the war she continued her training at St. Mary's, becoming a state registered nurse in 1919 and being awarded a first prize for a paper on eclampsia (convulsions in late pregnancy). She also served in Queen Charlotte's Hospital where she specialized in gynaecology, receiving a certificate of merit. Throughout these years Princess Arthur increasingly impressed her superiors by her technical skill and practical efficiency.

When in 1920 Prince Arthur of Connaught was appointed governor-general of the Union of South Africa, Princess Arthur ably seconded him and shared his popularity. Her tact and friendliness made her many friends among the South Africans, who also greatly admired the interest which she displayed in hospitals, child welfare, and maternity work throughout the Union. To these subjects she brought her exceptional personal knowledge and experience, which enabled her to make many effective and valuable suggestions.

On her return to London (1923) Princess Arthur resumed her nursing career at the University College Hospital, where she was known as 'Nurse Marjorie', and at Charing Cross Hospital. At this time she was specializing in surgery, proving herself a competent, dependable, and imperturbable theatre sister, who was capable of performing minor operations herself and of instructing juniors in their duties. Her services to the nursing profession were recognized in July 1925, when she was awarded the badge of the Royal Red Cross.

The outbreak of war in 1939 afforded Princess Arthur further scope for her nursing abilities. She refused the offer of a post as matron of a hospital in the country, preferring to become sister-in-charge of the casualty clearing station of the 2nd London General Hospital. Shortly thereafter, however, she opened the Fife Nursing Home in Bentinck Street which she personally equipped, financed, and administered as matron for ten years with great competence.

The death of her husband in 1938 was followed by that of her father-in-law, the Duke of Connaught, in 1942. He was succeeded by his grandson, Alastair, but little more than a year later the young Duke, who had seen service in Egypt as a subaltern in the Scots Greys, died of pneumonia in Ottawa, 26 April 1943.

Princess Arthur served as a counsellor of state during King George VI's absences abroad in 1939, 1943, and 1944. She was appointed colonel-in-chief of the Royal Army Pay Corps in 1939 and was also president and later patron of the Royal British Nurses' Association (of which she held the honorary diploma) and patron of the Plaistow Maternity Hospital. In 1949 the multiple-rheumatoid-arthritis, from which Princess Arthur had suffered for many years, rendered her completely crippled and necessitated the closing of her nursing-home. She retired to her house in Regent's Park where she wrote for private circulation two autobiographical fragments in a vivid and entertaining style: *A Nurse's Story* (1955) and *Egypt and Khartum* (1956), in which she gave a graphic account of the wreck of the *Delhi*; she was engaged on a further volume on big-game hunting in South Africa when she died at her London home, 26 February 1959. At her special request she was cremated, her ashes being laid in the chapel of Mar Lodge. The dukedom of Fife devolved upon her nephew, Lord Carnegie, the son of her sister, who had married the eleventh Earl of Southesk in 1923 and died in 1945.

[Private information; personal knowledge.]
JOHN WHEELER-BENNETT.

ALINGTON, CYRIL ARGENTINE (1872–1955), headmaster and dean, was born in Ipswich 22 October 1872, the second son of the Rev. Henry Giles Alington, an inspector of schools, and his wife, Jane Margaret Booth. He went with classical scholarships to Marlborough where he was in the cricket eleven and to Trinity College, Oxford. A first class in honour moderations (1893) and in *literae humaniores* (1895) was followed by his election at the second attempt to a fellowship at All Souls in November 1896. In that year he had returned as sixth-form master to Marlborough. He was ordained deacon (1899) and priest (1901) and in the former year moved to Eton where in 1904 he became master in College. In the nine years between 1899 and 1908 he was 'the most alive and brilliant of the younger masters—the best preacher, the most entertaining division master, the most inspiring tutor'. In 1908 he was appointed headmaster of Shrewsbury School and in January 1917 he succeeded his brother-in-law, Edward Lyttelton (whose biography he subsequently wrote for this Dictionary), as headmaster of Eton. He retired in 1933 and until 1951 was dean of Durham.

Alington was endowed with almost every gift to ensure a successful career. Extraordinarily handsome, especially in later years when robed and in the pulpit, he never failed to impress the boys at Shrewsbury and Eton. As a young man he was a very successful cricketer and for years afterwards he maintained a high standard as a player of fives and rackets. He was never quite a first-class classical scholar, nor was he looked upon as a profound theologian. He possessed a wide and extraordinarily retentive memory which enabled him to produce the apt quotation for any occasion. He was a most facile and brilliant versifier and he composed some admirable hymns. He was greatly interested in political history and wrote some historical works which are lively, readable, and often illuminating. Probably the best is *Twenty Years*, a study of the party system, 1815–1835 (1921). He also wrote a number of detective stories and other novels: clever, witty, but quickly perishable. All these varied publications bear witness to the incredible speed at which his mind, his imagination and his pen worked and which characterized also the brilliance of his conversation. In everyday life, at the dinner table, in after-dinner talk, it was possible, especially for a stranger, to write Alington off as a brilliant but facile and ungenuine man. But his ephemeral books and pyrotechnic conversation served as a safety-valve for the volcanic energy of his mind and for the depth of his very real emotions.

Undoubtedly his greatness lay in his genius for teaching, especially for teaching religion as distinct from theology. In *A Dean's Apology* (1952) Alington quotes Bishop Creighton [q.v.] as saying 'the

function of a teacher is to be an intellectual mustard plaster'. This function he carried out to the full. He was probably a better teacher of the ordinary boy than of the first-class scholar. His teaching was at first a bewildering, exhausting, and always an exciting and rewarding experience for those boys who had ears to hear; and it was Alington's triumph that the deaf were made to hear. He was not concerned with imparting information but with bringing boys' minds alive.

In the pulpit Alington was much nearer to the mind of the public-school boy than was any other preacher of his time. His series of Shrewsbury and Eton *Fables* provided a wholly new approach to illustrating in modern idiom the fundamental Christian doctrine. His addresses to boys and also to masters and their families during Holy Week were without doubt his greatest contribution to the religious education of the young.

Alington always had a tremendous zest for living. Probably he was most serenely happy during his years in College, where he produced one of the most brilliant generation of scholars Eton had ever known; and at Shrewsbury where the time had come for new men and new measures and he gave himself wholly to the task of putting the school back on the map. He returned to Eton to triumph over the difficulties of the war years. To each successive stage of his life he brought the same infectious enthusiasm, the same kindness and capacity for friendship, so that the care he lavished on beautifying the site at Shrewsbury was easily transferred to the cathedral at Durham, and the affection which he had for the boys at Eton and Shrewsbury was equally displayed to the miners of Durham. He was blessed with the most perfect family life in which his wife played at least half the main part. The deaths in his lifetime of two of their six children were bitter blows, but they were met with a fortitude made possible only by their invincible belief in the Christian religion.

In 1904 Alington married Hester Margaret, daughter of the fourth Lord Lyttelton [q.v.]. She was appointed C.B.E. in 1949 and died in 1958. They had two sons and four daughters. The elder son, Giles, became dean and senior tutor of University College, Oxford, and died in 1956; he was a much loved man, of wit, wisdom, and compassion. The second son was killed at Salerno in 1943. The eldest daughter died at the age of thirty. The three other daughters became the wives respectively of (Sir) Alec Douglas-Home, (Sir) Roger Mynors, and the Rev. John Wilkes, warden of Radley College (1937–54).

Alington proceeded D.D., Oxford, in 1917 and received an honorary D.C.L., Durham, in 1937. He was elected an honorary fellow of Trinity in 1926 and was chaplain to the King in 1921–33. He died at Treago, Herefordshire, 16 May 1955. A portrait by G. Fiddes Watt is in the possession of the family, and a drawing by Francis Dodd is at Eton.

[C. A. Alington, *A Dean's Apology*, 1952; *Eton College Chronicle*, 27 May 1955; private information; personal knowledge.]

C. R. N. ROUTH.

ALTRINCHAM, first BARON (1879–1955), administrator and politician. [See GRIGG, EDWARD WILLIAM MACLEAY.]

AMBEDKAR, BHIMRAO RAMJI (1891–1956), Indian statesman, was born at Mhow in Central India 14 April 1891, the youngest of the fourteen children of Ramji Maloji Sakpal, a subedar-major in the British Indian Army and headmaster in a military school, and his wife, Bhimabai Murbadkar. When the boy was barely two his father retired and settled first at Dapoli, then at Satara, where he attended the high school. His family were Untouchables, belonging to the community of Mahars who though of lowly caste are reputed to be a spirited and sensitive people from whom the Bombay Army obtained its earliest recruits. The indignities, humiliations, and hardships to which he was subjected stirred in this proud, intelligent, and sensitive boy a bitter resentment which lingered with him to the end. From a teacher who showed him kindness he adopted the surname Ambedkar.

He next attended Elphinstone High School in Bombay and later Elphinstone College with financial help from the Maharaja Gaekwar of Baroda [q.v.]. He graduated in 1912 and in the following year went with a scholarship from the Maharaja to Columbia University, New York, graduating in 1915 with a thesis on 'Ancient Indian Commerce'. Proceeding to London he joined the London School of Economics and was admitted to Gray's Inn. His scholarship expired in 1917 and unable to afford further studies he returned to India where the terms of his scholarship required him to enter the service of Baroda State. Although a junior administrative officer he found himself as an Untouchable treated with contempt by clerks and office boys, unable to obtain accommodation, and even denied food.

Consequently Ambedkar left Baroda State in disgust and in November 1918 managed to secure a job as lecturer in political economy at Sydenham College, Bombay. Two years later he returned to England where he was called to the bar in 1922 and obtained his M.Sc. (1921) and his D.Sc., London, in 1923 for a thesis, subsequently published, on 'The Problem of the Rupee'. After a brief stay at the university of Bonn he returned to India in April 1923 and started legal practice in Bombay. In his professional career he was again handicapped by the fact of being an Untouchable; and his intellectual arrogance did little to further his popularity. He was a better jurist than lawyer, combining a combative manner with massive scholarship which he flourished rather ponderously. He was less impressive as an advocate in court than as a politician on a platform.

Ambedkar soon began to organize the Untouchables and to make them politically conscious of their lack of status. In 1924 he founded the Society for the Welfare of Outcastes and three years later the British Government nominated him as a representative of the Untouchables to the Bombay legislative council. It was the beginning of his political career. He soon grew to be a prominent figure on public platforms, became a professor of the Government Law College, Bombay (1928), and not long after was appointed by the Government to the Bombay committee which on a provincial basis assisted the reforms commission headed by Sir John (later Viscount) Simon [q.v.].

In September 1930 Ambedkar was officially invited to attend the Indian Round Table conference in London as a representative of the so-called Depressed Classes. His appointment marked a milestone in the socio-political struggle of the Untouchables, for never before had they been consulted in framing the future of India. Ambedkar became an all-India figure. He used this vantage-point successfully to question with blunt and militant doggedness the claim of M. K. Gandhi [q.v.] to represent all India, including the Untouchables. The inability of the Congress Party to reach a Hindu–Moslem settlement at the second Round Table conference led the British Government to announce its own communal award which treated the Untouchables as politically separate from the Hindus. Gandhi, then in prison, launched on a protest fast which led ultimately to negotiations with Ambedkar culminating in the Poona Pact of 1932 which conceded far more parliamentary representations to the Untouchables than they had been allotted under the British award. It was the price which Congress had to pay to keep the Untouchables within the Hindu fold.

Ambedkar's attitude to the Congress Party and particularly to the caste Hindus thereafter grew increasingly bitter and demanding. In 1935 he first announced his intention to convert the Depressed Classes to some other religion. In 1945 he founded the People's Education Society which was devoted primarily to their educational uplift. In the meantime, on the declaration of war in 1939 Ambedkar opposed the claim of Congress to speak on behalf of the country and drew politically nearer to M. A. Jinnah [q.v.] and the Moslem League in their opposition to what both characterized as Hindu chauvinism. In 1940 Ambedkar published *Thoughts on Pakistan* which though critical of some aspects of Jinnah's thinking was not hostile to the idea of Pakistan. When in 1942 Lord Linlithgow [q.v.] decided to expand his Executive Council, Ambedkar was invited to join it as the member in charge of labour.

As independence drew near Ambedkar turned his attention and energies to the constructive constitutional tasks for which he was well equipped by training and temperament. He became a member of the Constituent Assembly in 1946 and figured prominently and to much positive purpose in its deliberations. His interest in and knowledge of constitutional law inevitably marked him as one of the principal architects of independent India's constitution. Poetic justice and natural aptitude combined to enable this distinguished Untouchable leader to introduce, as law minister of the first government of free India, the draft constitution in the Constituent Assembly on 4 November 1948. Ambedkar also contributed to the drafting of the Hindu code bill, in the process earning, not without some irony, the accolade of 'a modern Manu' after the celebrated Hindu lawgiver. On 27 September 1951 he resigned from Jawaharlal Nehru's government, thereby abruptly ending an association wherein neither he nor the Congress Party was uniformly at ease.

Ill health hampered the tempo of his normal activities and his last days were occupied with the thought of embracing Buddhism which he did, with many of his followers, at a ceremony in Nagpur in October 1956. In November he attended the fourth conference of the World Fellowship of Buddhists at Katmandu, Nepal. It was his last public appearance. He died in his sleep on the night of 5–6 December 1956 at Delhi.

Ambedkar was twice married: first, in 1908 to Ramabai (died 1935), daughter of Bhiku Walangkar, a railway porter at Dapoli. They had four sons and one daughter. In 1948 he married Sharda Kabir, a Saraswat Brahmin by caste and a doctor by profession. They had no children.

[Dhananjay Keer, *Dr. Ambedkar, Life and Mission*, 1954.]   FRANK MORAES.

AMERY, LEOPOLD CHARLES MAURICE STENNETT (1873–1955), statesman and journalist, was born 22 November 1873 at Gorakhpur in the then North-Western Provinces of India, the eldest of the three sons of Charles Frederick Amery, of the Indian Forest Department, and his wife, Elizabeth Leitner. His father came of an ancient Devon family. His mother was a Hungarian who had left after the unsuccessful revolution of 1848, her widowed mother marrying in Constantinople Dr. J. M. Leitner, a British subject of Austrian origin who was a medical missionary. She was brought to London in 1861 at the age of eighteen. When Amery was three she was left almost penniless when her husband threw up his job and went off to America leaving her no alternative but to divorce him. She contrived to obtain a good education for her sons and it was to her that Amery owed an inherited gift for languages and an early background of historical and political knowledge.

In 1887, two terms ahead of (Sir) Winston Churchill, Amery went to Harrow where he won a number of scholarships; a 'pocket Hercules', he represented the school at gymnastics. He went as an exhibitioner to Balliol College, Oxford, where he took firsts in classical moderations (1894) and *literae humaniores* (1896), was *proxime accessit* to the Craven scholar (1894), and won his half-blue as a cross-country runner. He was awarded the Ouseley scholarship in Turkish by the Imperial Institute in 1895. After one unsuccessful attempt, he was elected a fellow of All Souls for history in 1897, his friend John (later Viscount) Simon [q.v.] becoming law fellow at the same election. Between the two examinations Amery had his first glimpse of public life by acting as private secretary to Leonard Courtney (later Lord Courtney of Penwith, q.v.), the blind Liberal statesman.

At the end of his first term at All Souls, Amery telegraphed to C. P. Scott [q.v.], editor of the *Manchester Guardian*, offering to visit the Near East. A midnight interview resulted in a cheque for £100 and a free hand to write on whatever interested him from Vienna to Constantinople. He had already travelled in the Balkans and knew at various levels of proficiency French, German, Italian, Turkish, Magyar, Serbian, Bulgarian, and Sanskrit. His special qualifications as a journalist were noted by the correspondent of *The Times* in Vienna and this led to an appointment in 1899 as assistant to (Sir) Valentine Chirol [q.v.], its foreign editor. He remained on the staff of *The Times* for the next ten years, writing leading articles, relieving the Berlin correspondent, and carrying out general editorial duties.

The South African war gave him experiences which had a lasting effect on his political creed. Falling under the spell of Sir Alfred (later Viscount) Milner [q.v.], he became a passionate advocate of British imperialism. Having made friends among the Boers before the outbreak of war, he recognized their sturdy qualities, yet had no doubts that Joseph Chamberlain [q.v.] was in the right and Kruger the aggressor. Organizing the war correspondents of *The Times* and serving at the front, he added greatly to his professional reputation. He might have been taken prisoner with Churchill had he not stayed in the tent they shared when Churchill went out to catch the armoured train which the enemy intercepted.

Returning to London after a year in South Africa, Amery edited and wrote much of *The Times* history of the war which ran to seven volumes and occupied him, intermittently, until 1909. He was able to persuade All Souls, his 'wider family' with which he maintained a lifelong connection, to endow a chair of military history at Oxford; and he was equally successful in his suggestion to Alfred Beit [q.v.] that he should endow a chair of colonial history.

Called to the bar in 1902 by the Inner Temple, Amery continued to be active in daily journalism but became more and more drawn into extreme right-wing politics. He advocated army reform and national service and was Chamberlain's loyal disciple on the tariff reform and free-trade issue. Lord Northcliffe [q.v.] offered him the editorship of the *Observer* in 1908, and wanted him to succeed G. E. Buckle [q.v.] in the editorial chair of *The Times* in 1912. But by then Amery had turned to politics, and he supported Geoffrey Robinson (later Dawson, q.v.) as candidate for the editorship. After failing in four attempts to enter Parliament, Amery was returned unopposed in 1911 as member for South Birmingham (later named Sparkbrook) and held the seat until 1945.

Once in the House of Commons, Amery threw himself with zest into opposing the Liberal Government. He sided with the 'Diehard' Conservatives, the 'Last Ditchers' who thought the Lords should insist upon their amendments to the Parliament bill despite Asquith's threat to create sufficient peers to obtain its passage. This cause lost, the Irish Home Rule crisis gave full rein to his delight in battle. He visited Ireland early in 1912 and in six weeks wrote seventeen articles for the *Morning Post*, reprinted as *The Case Against Home Rule*. As the Government's difficulties mounted, after the Curragh incident, so did Amery's spirits. The harrying of ministers on the Irish question, he recalled in later years, 'afforded splendid hunting—or perhaps dentistry might be a more appropriate word . . . I thoroughly enjoyed the hunt myself . . .'. By contrast, his service on the select committee on the Marconi contract in 1912–13 was 'the most unpleasant and exasperating experience' of his political life.

During the war of 1914–18 Amery helped to organize the earliest recruiting drives; then saw service as an intelligence officer in Flanders, the Balkans, Gallipoli, and Salonika. He was in the *Caledonian* when she was torpedoed by a submarine in the Mediterranean and escaped by concealing his small body in the stern sheets of an open boat afterwards picked up by a hospital ship. In 1916 Milner took Amery into the cabinet secretariat as one of two political secretaries, the other being Sir Mark Sykes [q.v.]. This brought him into close contact with the inner workings of the Imperial War Cabinet and the Supreme War Council at Versailles.

When Milner went to the Colonial Office in 1919 he chose Amery as his parliamentary under-secretary, a post he held until 1921 when he became parliamentary and financial secretary to the Admiralty. He was sworn of the Privy Council in the following year. Although he admired Lloyd George's 'imagination and driving power' Amery became convinced that the coalition was a menace by reason of the ascendancy of Churchill with his free-trade convictions. The return of the Conservatives in 1922 brought Amery promotion as first lord of the Admiralty. His defence of the navy against the Geddes economies was vigorous and adroit and made him a controversial figure in the eyes of the public. He stood up for the admirals in their stubborn attempt to regain control of their own air service. He claimed some share in the suggestion of Baldwin in preference to Lord Curzon [q.v.] as prime minister when Bonar Law resigned and he was in the forefront of Baldwin's unsuccessful appeal to the country over a tariff policy in 1923. In the new Conservative ministry of 1924, after the downfall of Labour, Amery became colonial secretary: the office which most attracted him. His faith in Britain's imperial destiny sprang from his loyalty to Milner and Chamberlain and to the convictions he had formed by extensive travel in the Empire. For the next five years he played a leading part in the revolution which transformed the Empire into an association of independent partner states linked by the Crown. His whole-hogging advocacy of closer economic relations between the British member countries led to clashes with colleagues, especially with Churchill, whose appointment to the Treasury he considered disastrous. Desiring passionately to have the Conservative Government go all the way with him over tariffs and preference, Amery saw in Churchill the incarnation of those nineteenth-century political and economic habits of thought whose dead hand had, in his view, frustrated Chamberlain's grand plan. Amery always maintained that failure to put his imperial creed into practice in the twenties led to industrial woes and to the working classes being won over to the illusion that socialism was the remedy. Nemesis, he reflected, had overtaken the impenitent free trader Churchill when the country rejected him in 1945. Zeal amounting to bigotry on this issue did not prevent Amery from keeping on friendly personal terms with his colleagues, including Churchill. Often a lone wolf in urging the adoption of measures which had no chance of attracting majority opinion even inside his own party, he never grew embittered and continued to

enjoy social life in wide political, intellectual, and business circles, where he was always a welcome figure.

He got the new office of secretary of state for dominion affairs created in 1925 and held it jointly with the colonial secretaryship until 1929. Baulked of imperial preference he set up, in the face of strong Whitehall opposition, an Empire Marketing Board with an annual grant of a million pounds and (Sir) Stephen Tallents [q.v.] as its secretary to promote the sales of empire produce in Great Britain. This body gave a great impetus to team work in agricultural scientific research on an empire-wide scale. The imperial conference of 1926 brought the definition of dominion status later enshrined in the Statute of Westminster. In 1927-8 Amery visited all the dominions in a single tour which took him away from London for six months and in the course of which he made nearly 300 speeches. This experience gave a fresh impetus to his urge for imperial preference. But the general election of 1929 put Labour in and Amery characteristically blew away the cobwebs by a holiday in Canada, where he made the first ascent of Mount Amery, a 10,940-feet peak in the Rockies which had already been named after him.

In the 'national' Government of 1931 Baldwin was unable to obtain a place for Amery who was thought too uncompromising. Throughout the thirties he made himself heard as an independent-minded critic of successive ministries on economic and foreign policy issues. Baldwin did not go far enough for him over the safeguarding of industries; in *Empire and Prosperity* (1930) and *The Forward View* (1935) and other writings Amery continued to be an undaunted advocate of his central creed. This was far from absorbing all his energies. He attacked disarmament and the conception of a League of Nations with power to coerce as 'imaginary imperial robes'. Unmoved by the clamour against the Hoare–Laval pact over Abyssinia, he defended it as a common-sense agreement. While seeing the weakness of the Munich settlement his first-hand knowledge of Central European affairs held him back from being a root-and-branch critic of the Government. Gradually his pleas for an agreed national policy gained him the ear of the House. His finest parliamentary hour came in May 1940 when in a peroration, pointing directly at the prime minister, Chamberlain, he quoted Cromwell's words when turning out the Long

Parliament: 'You have sat too long here for any good you have been doing. Depart, I say, and let us have done with you. In the name of God, go.'

On the formation of the Churchill ministry Amery hoped to be put in charge of defence or economic policy but loyally accepted the India Office, although feeling that he was being side-tracked. In the event he had his hands full, working to bring India into free and equal partnership within the Commonwealth; he had to face the pacifist Congress, influenced by M. K. Gandhi [q.v.]; the failure of the mission under Sir Stafford Cripps [q.v.] in 1942; the 'quit India' movement; and the Bengal famine of 1943–4. Amery's influence had helped to carry the Government of India Act of 1935 which Churchill had opposed and the latter's continued reluctance to allow any fundamental change made in the Raj added to Amery's burdens. But Indian affairs were not an all-absorbing task: he found time to send letters and memoranda to his colleagues on a diversity of subjects. These interventions were not always welcome.

Amery was appointed C.H. in 1945. He lost his seat at the Labour victory in that year and did not stand again. But the last ten years of his life were spent with unflagging industry, in public life, and as an author. The three volumes of *My Political Life* (1953–5), going from his birth to 1940, all written, without undue modesty, in his seventies, are a vivid historical chronicle as well as a testimony of faith.

Amery was a very short, wiry man; an athlete who kept up his prowess as a mountaineer into advanced age. A dull, prosy speaker unless aroused by indignation, he might have been prime minister, it was said, had he been half a head taller and his speeches half an hour shorter. His table talk brought out his broad range of learning, his knowledge of men and places, his wit and kindly humanity. While he told a good story his eyes twinkled impishly from behind old-fashioned glasses. His delight in strenuous escape from Westminster shines through *Days of Fresh Air* (1939) and *In the Rain and the Sun* (1946). Pleasure in re-reading the classics, above all the *Odyssey* and Horace, stayed with him to the end. So did his remarkable proficiency in many modern languages. He had been in his time president of the Classical Association, the Alpine Club, and the Ski Club of Great Britain, and was elected an honorary fellow of Balliol in 1946. A founder of the Empire (later

Commonwealth) Parliamentary Association, he served it in one capacity or another for over twenty-five years.

In 1910 Amery married Adeliza Florence ('Bryddie'), daughter of John Hamar Greenwood, of Whitby, Ontario, and sister of Hamar (later Viscount) Greenwood [q.v.]. There were two sons. The elder, John, was executed in 1945 for treason. He had formed the belief that Communism was the great menace and, spending the war in Germany and occupied Europe, had sought to enlist British prisoners of war or internees to fight against Russia but not against Britain. The younger son, Harold Julian Amery, after a distinguished war career, entered politics, married a daughter of Harold Macmillan, and was secretary of state for air (1960–62) and minister of aviation (1962–4).

Amery died in London 16 September 1955. A portrait by (Sir) James Gunn is in the National Portrait Gallery; and by Simon Elwes at Rhodes House, Oxford. Amery had been a Rhodes trustee from 1919 and was senior trustee from 1933.

[Amery's own writings; private information; personal knowledge.]   A. P. RYAN.

ANDERSON, SIR ALAN GARRETT (1877–1952), shipowner and public servant, was born in London 9 March 1877, the only son of James George Skelton Anderson and his wife, Elizabeth Garrett Anderson [q.v.], the first woman to qualify as a doctor in Great Britain. The family came from Aberdeen where they had been shipowners and traders since the seventeenth century. Anderson's great-uncle, James, had established a branch of the business in London, and it was here that his father was engaged.

Anderson was a scholar of Eton and of Trinity College, Oxford, of which he later became an honorary fellow. On leaving the university he entered the family business, Anderson, Anderson & Co., joint founders and joint managers of the Orient Line. They subsequently amalgamated with their partners as Anderson, Green & Co. and later became associated with the wider shipping businesses controlled by the first Earl of Inchcape [q.v.]. Anderson then became one of Inchcape's most valued colleagues and a director of the P. & O. Company.

It did not take Anderson long to establish his reputation in the world of shipping. He brought to the business a powerful intellect and an immense capacity for work. But beyond that he understood and loved ships, and maintained throughout his life the closest ties of friendship with those who served afloat. Brought up in his mother's home town, Aldeburgh, he early became a keen sailor; this gave him added interest in his contacts with the captains and officers of the Orient Line, and they in turn understood and trusted him.

In 1923 Anderson was vice-president of the Chamber of Shipping, becoming president in the following year. He was also, from 1927 to his death, one of the British directors of the Suez Canal Company. It is interesting to find him in 1952 giving serious consideration to the future administration of the Canal when ownership reverted to Egypt, and suggesting lines of a possible understanding with Egypt in advance of the crisis which he foresaw.

Although shipping was Anderson's first love, he had wide interests in other fields. In 1911 he was elected a director of the Midland Railway Company, and so continued when the company was absorbed in the London, Midland, and Scottish Railway. This was the start of a long association with railway administration, culminating in his appointment as chairman of the Railway Executive Committee and controller of railways during the war years from 1941 to 1945.

Long before this, Anderson had performed valuable public work in other spheres. During the war of 1914-18 he served in various capacities under Walter (later Viscount) Runciman [q.v.], the president of the Board of Trade, and then in 1916 was appointed vice-chairman of the royal commission on wheat supplies and chairman of the Wheat Executive which controlled the supply of grain to the western Allies. In 1917 he was a member of Balfour's mission to the United States, and played a part in setting up the machinery for the control of wheat in North America. His success in this field led to his appointment in 1938 as chairman of the cereals advisory committee, and later, on the outbreak of war in 1939, as chairman of the Cereals Control Board —a post he relinquished on becoming controller of railways.

After returning from the United States in 1917 he left the Wheat Commission and was appointed controller in the Admiralty, responsible for the supply of ships and equipment for both the Royal and Merchant navies. So far as the Royal Navy was concerned, this had previously and has since always been undertaken by one of the sea lords. Anderson displayed, in difficult circumstances, his remarkable ability of getting on with other people, and his skill in guiding a team with tact and firmness. In this, as always, he made valuable use of a sense of humour, with which he was able to break down formidable barriers.

His wide experience led, in 1918, to his being invited to join the court of the Bank of England, and he was chosen as deputy governor in 1925-6. In 1935, against his natural inclination, he was persuaded by Montagu (later Lord) Norman [q.v.] and others to enter Parliament as one of the representatives of the City of London. Accustomed as he was to reach decisions after calm reflection and carefully reasoned argument, he did not find the atmosphere of the House of Commons much to his liking, but his knowledge and experience of business and finance ensured him an attentive hearing. He gave up his seat in 1940 to make way for Sir Andrew Duncan [q.v.] who had just been appointed president of the Board of Trade, and thereafter devoted all his energies to his wartime tasks.

When Anderson was rising to a position of influence in the British shipping industry, it was still dominated, like most industries, by men brought up in the traditions of rugged individualism. This was his own background, but well in advance of most of his contemporaries he saw the need for international co-operation and vigorously espoused the cause of the International Chamber of Commerce, in the development of which he played an outstanding part, serving successively as vice-president, president, and honorary life president.

His firm belief in the need for economic co-operation between nations led Anderson inevitably to the view that co-operation over a wider field, especially between the industrially developed nations of western Europe, must be sought. He accordingly gave strong support to the moves initiated in 1948 towards some form of political unity in Europe. In his last major contribution to the deliberations of the International Chamber of Commerce, at its Lisbon conference in the summer of 1951, he outlined his beliefs and called for a readiness among business men to support organic change in Europe. 'For thirty years we have framed liberal resolutions pointing the road to prosperity and peace; for thirty years national divisions, hopes, and jealousies have blocked the road to progress. Shall we be "minding our business" if we do not make sure that the public know how much of their poverty, of their fear, of their danger, they owe to frontiers and sovereignties?'

Perhaps the most striking thing about this many-sided man was the thoroughness with which he was prepared to probe in depth any matter he took up. His mother's influence had naturally led him to interest himself in hospitals, and he threw himself energetically into problems of hospital management, and finally found, in this sphere, the activity which, of all others, captivated his interest and enthusiasm. This lay in the establishment of the Hospital Saving Association. The idea was not his; but it was his own determination which transformed it into a valuable and successful social organization.

Anderson was appointed K.B.E. in 1917 and G.B.E. in 1934. In spite of all his many interests, he could always find time for relaxation, especially yachting, was a delightful host and companion, and the father of a strongly united family. He married in 1903 Muriel Ivy, daughter of G. W. Duncan, of Richmond, Surrey. They had two sons both of whom became prominent in the shipping world and two daughters. He died in London 4 May 1952.

A bronze bust by W. A. Verbon is at the headquarters of the Hospital Saving Association. Another cast is at his old home, Notgrove Manor, near Cheltenham.

[Private information; personal knowledge.]
SIMON.

ANDERSON, JOHN, first Viscount Waverley (1882–1958), administrator and statesman, was born in Edinburgh 8 July 1882, the only surviving son of David Alexander Pearson Anderson, fancy stationer, and his wife, Janet Kilgour, daughter of Charles Briglemen, of Edinburgh. He was educated at George Watson's College and Edinburgh University, where in 1903 he graduated B.Sc., with special distinction in mathematics, natural philosophy, and chemistry, and M.A. with first class honours in mathematics and natural philosophy. He then spent a year at Leipzig making a special study of uranium. The combination of the humanities and science in his education noticeably affected his attitude to the problems which later confronted him and added to the value of his contribution to their solution.

In 1905, after winning the first place in the Civil Service examination of that year, he entered the Colonial Office where he served as secretary to committees on Nigerian lands (1908) and West African currency (1911–12). In 1912 he transferred to the National Health Insurance Commission of which Sir Robert Morant [q.v.] was chairman and of which in 1913 Anderson became secretary. The creation of the new health insurance system confronted the Civil Service with a greater task than any it had previously undertaken, and some of the best civil servants, like Anderson, were hastily recruited from a number of different departments. It was a great opportunity both to reveal and to develop personal ability. Anderson's own distinctive qualities were already evident: the poise and *gravitas* which inspired confidence in the fairness and soundness of his decisions; the depth and range of his knowledge; his transparent integrity of character and intellectual objectivity.

In 1917 he became secretary of the Ministry of Shipping under Sir Joseph (later Lord) Maclay [q.v.]; and in dealing with shipowners he showed again that to an exceptional extent he was able to impress and guide men of widely differing experience. In March 1919 he was appointed additional secretary to the Local Government Board, and when in July the new Ministry of Health absorbed both that office and the work of the Insurance Commission, he became its second secretary. In October of the same year he became chairman of the Board of Inland Revenue but in 1920 went to Ireland as joint under-secretary, with Sir Hamar (later Viscount) Greenwood [q.v.] as chief secretary, during the critical and dangerous period of the 'Black and Tans'. In 1922 he succeeded Sir Edward Troup as permanent under-secretary at the Home Office where he remained for ten years and matured his purely administrative qualities—a readiness to delegate, an unflurried and objective judgement on issues of policy—together with an air of somewhat pontifical authority. In 1924–5 he was chairman of a sub-committee of the Committee of Imperial Defence on air-raid precautions whose recommendations were the basis of the measures adopted in 1939. A more immediate task was his chairmanship in 1925–6 of the committee controlling preparations for the emergency of a general strike. In Whitehall he was by now 'among the giants'.

In 1932 Anderson went to India as

governor of Bengal at a time of especial difficulty and danger. His life was twice attempted and in each case he narrowly escaped death. There again he showed that rare combination of physical with moral courage which enabled him, whatever the personal risk and violent opposition involved, to carry on his task, undeflected and unperturbed. The respect which he won helped to end the terrorism and he proceeded with the social and economic measures which the condition of the province made urgently necessary. There were serious financial difficulties and much sickness, poverty, and distress, aggravated at the time by the world-wide fall in agricultural prices. Among the steps he took was the establishment in small industries of many of the *détenus* of the terrorist period, and the creation of an industrial credit corporation. After a considerable success with these reforms he carried through the transition from dyarchy to full provincial authority; and his normal five-year term of office was extended by six months to enable him to supervise its completion.

Returning to England, he was elected to the House of Commons in February 1938 as an independent nationalist for the Scottish Universities which he represented until the abolition of the university seats in 1950. In May–July 1938 he was chairman of a committee inquiring into problems of evacuation and at the time of the Munich crisis he was regional commissioner for London and the Home Counties. In November 1938 he accepted office under Neville Chamberlain as lord privy seal, with special responsibility for manpower and civil defence. He then invited his old friend (Sir) William Paterson [q.v.], the Scottish engineer, to design what was, with some modification, to become known as the 'Anderson shelter'. In September 1939 he became home secretary and minister of home security. He was responsible for the arrangements for evacuation, the internment of aliens, and in general for many of the measures involved in the transition from peace to war. The rapid improvement, and indeed transformation, of civil defence, in which he was assisted by the work of the unofficial Air Raid Defence League, was due to his drive and administrative ability.

Anderson entered the War Cabinet as lord president of the Council in October 1940 and thenceforward had an over-all responsibility for the organization of the country's civilian and economic resources

for total war. By adaptation and co-ordination he was mainly responsible for the efficiency of the machine of civil administration and thus enabled the prime minister to devote himself more exclusively to military problems. He also took charge of much secret work, for which his scientific training helped him. This included work on the atomic bomb and the use of atomic energy, with which he continued to be concerned after the war as chairman of the advisory committee on atomic energy (1945–8) and of the committee which led to the establishment of the Atomic Energy Authority in 1954. In 1943 he became chancellor of the Exchequer and remained in office until the fall of (Sir) Winston Churchill in July 1945. Earlier in the year, on the eve of his departure for the Yalta conference, Churchill had advised the King to send for Anderson as prime minister should he and Anthony Eden (later Earl of Avon) perish on their journey. Anderson's work during the war was of outstanding importance but little known except to his colleagues in the Cabinet and others who worked with and under him in Whitehall. Although recognized later in the official history of the war (e.g. W. K. Hancock and M. M. Gowing, *British War Economy*, 1949), it has perhaps never been appreciated adequately by the general public.

Throughout his political career Anderson continued to be an independent without membership of any of the political parties. When he joined the Chamberlain government it was for a war task and in the subsequent Churchill government he had, of course, Labour as well as Conservative colleagues. Nevertheless the Labour members regarded him as aligned with the Conservatives and probably resented his attitude more because he was not a member of the Conservative Party but an independent university member. This led to what was probably the most wounding personal experience in his career. Shortly after he had been raised to the peerage as Viscount Waverley in 1952, his appointment was announced as chairman of the royal commission on taxation of profits and incomes, for which his experience so well qualified him. He was subjected to bitter and sustained attack from the Labour benches as not being sufficiently impartial, and after a protest against the 'wholly unjustified personal aspersions', he resigned. Thereafter his political interventions were comparatively infrequent and his main activity was in business and in many forms of unofficial public work.

Anderson became chairman of the Port of London Authority in 1946 and was associated with a number of other organizations including the Canadian Pacific Railway, Imperial Chemical Industries, and the Hudson's Bay Company. He took a leading part in the foundation of the Royal Institute of Public Administration of which he became president; and when he gave the Romanes lecture at Oxford in 1946 he chose as his subject 'The Machinery of Government'. In this, as the main lesson he had learnt from personal experience, he emphasized the need for improving the machinery for making a reality of the collective responsibility of the Cabinet, especially through a permanent but flexible system of cabinet committees, and the reinforcement of the cabinet secretariat by the addition of technical sections. He undertook a number of public tasks such as that of presiding over the committee on the export of works of art (1950–52) and over the committee of inquiry after the floods of 1953. And in this late period of his life he entered a new field as patron of the arts, becoming chairman of the Covent Garden Opera Trust in succession to Lord Keynes [q.v.]. With devoted industry he took a leading part in the development of both the opera and the ballet.

The range of Waverley's career—official, proconsular, ministerial—was perhaps unique. He was great both as an administrator and as a minister, but it was his quality as an administrator which was dominant. He was, in the general judgement of Whitehall, the greatest administrator of his time, perhaps of any time in the country's history. Many qualities contributed to this: a shrewd and mature judgement, a capacious and retentive memory and an exceptional capacity for hard work which put at his service the precedents of past experience without impairing a flexible adjustment to new conditions. He wrote sparingly and rather than impose detailed instructions encouraged those under him to come to him for counsel. In dealing with his vast responsibilities during the second war, instead of creating a large new office of his own, he preferred to use fully, while retaining his own effective decision and control, both the other agencies of the Government and the experience and skill to be found in the great business organizations. With this administrative technique

there was always a willingness to accept personal responsibility, however onerous, as well as the exceptional combination of physical and moral courage which has already been remarked.

He was not equally great as a parliamentarian. For an official helping a minister to decide between alternative policies, or for a minister taking the decision, an objective analysis of the reasons for and against is desirable. But in Parliament a member or a minister is an advocate. He needs to win the interest of the House (and for this wit, lightness of touch, and occasional felicity of phrasing are a great help), then to present convincingly the policy on which he has decided. Anderson was listened to with respect, and there were often at the core of what he said new facts or arguments hitherto unappreciated and, when realized, convincing. But they were sometimes made less effective by a wider exposition more appropriate to a judge than to an advocate. In general his speeches were impressive because they reflected and recalled the reputation which he had won in Whitehall rather than in Westminster.

Anderson never courted, indeed seemed rather to shun, publicity; and he had no urge to write. His published work comprises little more than a few articles in the press. He left no books or autobiographical memoirs. His physical characteristics, presence, and manner were appropriate to his qualities and attainments. Anderson's seriousness of manner sometimes for a time disguised, but did not long conceal, a rather pawky humour, a rich humanity, and a capacity for friendship.

He received a number of honorary doctorates and foreign decorations and was elected F.R.S. in 1945 after his work on atomic research. He was appointed C.B. (1918), K.C.B. (1919), G.C.B. (1923), G.C.I.E. (1932), and G.C.S.I. (1937). He was sworn of the Privy Council (Ireland, 1920, United Kingdom, 1938); and the Order of Merit was conferred on him during his last illness, a few weeks before he died in London 4 January 1958.

Anderson married first, in 1907, Christina (died 1920), daughter of Andrew Mackenzie, commercial traveller, of Edinburgh, by whom he had one son, a doctor, David Alastair Pearson (born 1911), who succeeded him, and one daughter, Mary Mackenzie, who became director of the Women's Royal Army Corps in 1967; secondly, in 1941, Ava, daughter of the late

John Edward Courtenay Bodley, historian, and widow of Ralph Follett Wigram, of the Foreign Office.

A bust of Anderson by (Sir) Jacob Epstein was commissioned during the war for the Imperial War Museum; a later cast is in the village church of Westdean, Sussex, in the yard of which he is buried.

[*The Times*, 6 January 1958; Sir John W. Wheeler-Bennett, *John Anderson, Viscount Waverley*, 1962; private information; personal knowledge.]   SALTER.

ANDERSON, SIR KENNETH ARTHUR NOEL (1891–1959), general, was born at Dhazwar, Madras, 25 December 1891, the only son of (Sir) Arthur Robert Anderson, railway engineer, and his wife, Gertrude, daughter of J. D. Fraser, of Tiverton. He was educated at Charterhouse and the Royal Military College, Sandhurst, from which he was commissioned in 1911 in the Seaforth Highlanders. In the war of 1914–18 he served on the western front, was awarded the M.C., and was seriously wounded. Later he took part in Allenby's campaign in Palestine.

Between the wars he graduated at the Staff College, and in 1930 he commanded the 2nd Seaforths in operations on the North-West Frontier and was mentioned in dispatches.

In the war of 1939–45 Anderson's first active service was as commander of the 11th Infantry brigade during the withdrawal to Dunkirk; in the final stages of the evacuation he took over the command of the 3rd division from General Montgomery (later Viscount Montgomery of Alamein).

Becoming a major-general he spent the next two years in the Home Forces, commanding in succession the 1st division, VIII Corps, II Corps, and the Eastern Command.

In the autumn of 1942 he was nominated to command the Eastern Task Force which was being prepared for the landings in French North Africa. These took place successfully on 8 November 1942, and three days later Anderson took over the command of the First British Army, which consisted at first of only four brigades, and of the II United States Corps; the XIX French Corps came under his orders a little later. His mission was to dash eastwards from Algiers as rapidly as possible in an effort to secure Tunis over 500 miles away. As there had been no assault landing east of Algiers, it was doubtful from the first that Tunis could

be reached before it had been reinforced by the Germans. French co-operation was not at first forthcoming, the American troops were new, communications through the mountainous country were sparse, and there was a shortage of motor transport and of aircraft. Yet another handicap was the supreme commander (General Eisenhower)'s lack of experience in the field and his preoccupation with political rather than military matters. By 28 November, Anderson reached a point only twelve miles short of Tunis, having overcome slight German resistance, which he first encountered near Bône. He undertook an assault on 22 December, but was held up by torrential rain. The attack then had to be postponed until the spring, since it had become clear that much larger forces would be required and a more deliberate operation planned. Strong German forces were pouring into Tunisia by sea and air as well as by land from Rommel's army as it withdrew before Montgomery's victorious advance from Alamein.

The winter was spent in reorganizing and reinforcing the allied forces and in repelling German counter-attacks, the most serious of which penetrated the line at the Kasserine Pass. In February the 18th Army Group headquarters was set up under General Sir Harold Alexander (later Earl Alexander of Tunis) to co-ordinate the operations of all the ground forces. He moved round powerful reinforcements from the Eighth Army and resumed the offensive at the end of March. After some clearing-up operations the final attack was launched on 6 May.

Pressure was applied along the whole front of the Axis, now about 130 miles in length. Then a concentrated attack was made under Anderson's command, up the Mejerda Valley direct on Tunis, supported by intense bombing and by the fire of over a thousand guns. Two infantry divisions broke through on a frontage of three thousand yards. These were followed by two armoured divisions which occupied Tunis on the following day. A quarter of a million men, of whom 125,000 were German, laid down their arms in unconditional surrender. The allied casualties were fewer than 2,000 men.

After Tunis, Anderson was given command of the Second Army which was preparing for the landing in Normandy, but a few months later, not long after Montgomery's arrival to command 21st Army Group for the invasion, Anderson was transferred to the Eastern Command and replaced by General (Sir) Miles Dempsey. This was, of course, a sad disappointment for Anderson. His last military appointment was the East African Command (1945–6). He was appointed C.B. in 1940, K.C.B. in 1943, and promoted general in 1949.

From 1947 until 1952 Anderson was governor of Gibraltar. His term of office was marked by considerable improvements in the housing conditions of the population and by the introduction of far-reaching constitutional and administrative reforms, including the establishment of a legislative council.

Anderson was a courageous, competent, energetic commander, with a high sense of duty and an abundance of common sense. He could be forceful and frank, almost to the point of rudeness, in argument, but his shy, reserved manner made him a difficult person to know well and he lacked those characteristics which catch the public eye.

His later years were saddened by illness and by personal tragedy. His only son was killed in action in Malaya in 1949 and his daughter died a few years later. He had married in 1918 Kathleen Lorna Mary, daughter of Sir Reginald Gamble, comptroller and auditor-general in India. Anderson died in Gibraltar 29 April 1959. A drawing by S. Morse Brown is in the Imperial War Museum.

[*The Times*, 30 April 1959; Earl Alexander of Tunis, *Memoirs 1940–1945*, 1962; Dwight D. Eisenhower, *Crusade in Europe*, 1948; official dispatches; private information; personal knowledge.]   JOHN KENNEDY.

ANDREWS, SIR JAMES, baronet (1877–1951), lord chief justice of Northern Ireland, was born in Comber, county Down, 3 January 1877, the third son of Thomas Andrews, flax spinner, of Ardara, Comber, by his wife, Eliza, daughter of James Alexander Pirrie and sister of William James, Viscount Pirrie [q.v.]. Thomas Andrews was president of the Ulster Liberal Unionist Association from 1892 and was sworn of the Privy Council of Ireland in 1903. James Andrews was a brother of Thomas Andrews, shipbuilder, who perished in the *Titanic* disaster in 1912, and of John Miller Andrews, prime minister of Northern Ireland, 1940–43. He was educated at the Royal Academical Institution, Belfast, and then at Stephen's Green School, Dublin. At Trinity College, Dublin, he had a distinguished career,

becoming a senior exhibitioner (1897), a prizeman in civil and international law (1898), and graduating in 1899 with honours in ethics and logics. He was also gold medallist and auditor of the College Historical Society.

Although his family was closely associated with the shipbuilding and linen industries, Andrews's decision to read for the bar was no break with family tradition since his uncle, William Drennan Andrews (1832–1924), had a distinguished career in Dublin as a barrister and then as a judge. At King's Inns, Dublin, James Andrews proved himself an industrious student; in 1900 he was called to the Irish bar and joined what was then the north-east circuit. He built up a lucrative practice and soon established himself as a sound lawyer and a shrewd and capable advocate. In 1918 he took silk; in 1920 he was elected a bencher of King's Inns; and in 1921 he was appointed a lord justice of appeal in the new Supreme Court of Northern Ireland set up under the Government of Ireland Act, 1920. In 1924 he was sworn of the Privy Council of Northern Ireland. In 1926, on its foundation, he was made a bencher of the Inn of Court of Northern Ireland, and in 1928 he was appointed deputy-lieutenant for county Down. In 1937 he succeeded Sir Willeim Moore as lord chief justice, an office which he adorned until his death at Comber 18 February 1951. In 1938 an honorary LL.D. from his old university reflected the general satisfaction with which this appointment had been received, and in 1942 he was created a baronet.

Throughout his career on the bench Andrews maintained the firm grasp of legal principles which he had gained as a student and at the bar. This, together with an alert intelligence, a marked capacity for taking pains to master the facts of a case, and the ability to express himself simply and clearly, made him a competent and businesslike judge. But his undoubted success also owed much to the quality of his character and his constant anxiety to do justly and love mercy. Although firm in his rulings and capable of rebuking error, the essential kindness of his nature was never obscured. His patience and care were matched by a courtesy which was the same for all, from the humblest to the greatest, from the rawest junior to the most experienced silk. He did not often show the exasperation which all judges must feel on occasion, and when he did he was not given to sarcasm. Whatever their disappointment, those who lost before him as a trial judge seldom left his court with a sense of grievance or injustice, for he had the natural gift of presiding in a manner which was manifestly fair.

Andrews's interests were not confined to the law. The cause of higher education was also close to his heart and he was an active member of the senate of the Queen's University of Belfast and of many of its committees from 1924 and a pro-chancellor from 1929. During the war of 1939–45 he devoted himself to promoting the savings movement in Northern Ireland and was chairman and later president of the Ulster Savings Committee.

Physically, Andrews was a tall man of dignified appearance. He had a pleasant speaking voice and spoke fluently and well; he had a good command of language, a sense of the appropriate, and a sincerity which informed all he said. He liked the open air and enjoyed shooting and golf. But perhaps his keenest outdoor pleasure was sailing on Strangford Lough or promoting the fortunes of the North Down Cricket Club either as an enthusiastic spectator or on the field, for in his day he was an enterprising batsman and in 1904–7 captained the first eleven. While holding in private as in public life to the highest standards, he remained the most companionable and approachable of men, with few enemies and many friends. He enjoyed the support and encouragement of a very happy marriage, having in 1922 married Jane Lawson (died 1964), daughter of Joseph Ormrod, of Bolton, and widow of Captain Cyril Gerald Haselden, R.E. They had no children.

No portrait of Andrews exists but there is an excellent photograph of him in robes in the Royal Courts of Justice, Belfast.

[Private information; personal knowledge.]
MacDermott.

ANGWIN, Sir (ARTHUR) STANLEY (1883–1959), engineer, was born in Penzance 11 December 1883, the son of the Rev. George William Angwin, nonconformist minister, and his wife, Lucinda Cambellock. Change of circuit brought the family nearer London and Angwin went to school in Chatham and Rochester. He obtained a Whitworth exhibition and studied engineering at East London (later Queen Mary) College, obtaining his B.Sc. (Eng.) in 1907. His first practical experience was with Yarrow & Co., shipbuilders on the Clyde, but when still in his early twenties he entered the Post Office engineering department. He was sent back to Glasgow where he was engaged in telephone installation work. While in Scotland he raised the Lowland Division Telegraph Company of the Territorial Army which was mobilized in 1914 as the 52nd Divisional Signal Company. Angwin commanded it in Gallipoli, Egypt, Palestine, and France and was appointed to the D.S.O., awarded the M.C., and five times mentioned in dispatches. After the war he commanded the 44th (H.C.) Divisional Signals and subsequently retained a close association with Army Signals for many years.

Angwin's identification with radio began after the war. His seniors in the Post Office recognized that they had a young engineer with knowledge of mechanical, civil, and electrical engineering and used his ability to the full in the design and construction of the large radio stations at Leafield, Cairo, and Rugby. It was during this period that Angwin began his association with other radio engineers in the Post Office, such as (Sir) George Lee, Edward Shaughnessy, and (Sir) Archibald Gill. Together they built up the reputation of the engineering department's radio branch. Angwin took charge of it in 1928 and under his leadership they went on to develop the shortwave radio installations which gave Great Britain a predominating position in world telephony.

In 1932 Angwin became assistant engineer-in-chief, in 1935 deputy, and in 1939, three months before the outbreak of war, engineer-in-chief. He was responsible for maintaining Post Office communications throughout the period of bombing. Furthermore his wide knowledge of military requirements enabled him to be of exceptional assistance to the fighting Services: he knew and helped to find the kind of equipment and the kind of engineers they needed. During these years of strain, which must have taxed a constitution at no times robust, those who were close to him never once saw him rattled. He continued to study calmly each problem submitted to him and, having done so, made his decision.

Angwin's service in the Post Office was always in a technical capacity, but as engineer-in-chief he was also an assistant director-general and as such played an important part in shaping Post Office policies. It was his association and friendship with Sir Raymond Birchall, who later became director-general, and others which did much to draw together the administrative and engineering sides of the Post Office.

Early in 1945 Angwin accompanied Lord Reith on a tour to discuss with Commonwealth governments the future of the then privately owned Cable and Wireless Company. The trip was extremely arduous and involved 44,000 miles' flying in six weeks. The Government took over the company on 1 January 1947 and Angwin then retired from the Post Office to become its chairman. He had the difficult task of merging a private enterprise into a government-owned organization, but his understanding of the feelings of the staff did much to ease their resentment. He remained chairman until 1951 when, following Lord Reith's resignation, he was unanimously invited by all the Commonwealth governments concerned to become chairman of the Commonwealth Telecommunications Board. For the next five years he filled this office with distinction and did much to further Commonwealth co-operation in all spheres of telecommunications. In 1954 he headed a delegation of the Board to Australia and New Zealand. This was his last major overseas task and in 1956 he felt obliged to retire owing to ill health.

Angwin was widely known in international circles. He made his name as chairman at the Telecommunications Conference at Madrid in 1932. Thereafter he represented the United Kingdom at international conferences at Lucerne, Lisbon, Bucharest, Cairo, Montreux, Bermuda, Moscow, and Atlantic City. His abilities as a chairman were outstanding. Despite the rival or vested interests with which delegates came to a meeting—and these were many when frequency allocations were under discussion—they went away feeling that his judgements had been fair. At home he was chairman of the Radio Research Board in 1947–52 and was also very much in demand for government and official committees, among them the first (1934) and subsequent committees on television, in the development of which he was keenly interested.

Angwin was always interested in the education of young engineers and for some years was a member of the board of studies of the university of London. He was a member of council of the Institution of Civil Engineers and of the Institution of Electrical Engineers. In the latter he was chairman of the wireless section (1931–2), vice-president (1939–42), president (1943–

4), and was awarded the Faraday medal (1953) and made an honorary member (1956). Other honours included a fellowship of his old college, and the honorary degree of D.Sc. (Eng.) from London (1953). He was knighted in 1941, appointed K.B.E. in 1945 and K.C.M.G. in 1957, and was awarded the Haakon VII cross of freedom for services to Norway in 1939–45.

A great engineer, who did much to advance telecommunications, Angwin also held posts of high administrative responsibility. He had the rare gift of being able to inspire a team to work harmoniously together and his staff always remembered him with affection. His counsel and kindly wisdom helped many of them round difficult corners.

In 1921 Angwin married Dorothy Gladys, daughter of Walter H. Back, of Exeter. There were three sons and a daughter of the marriage and they were an exceptionally united family. Lady Angwin did much to support her husband on his travels when, as chairman of the Commonwealth Telecommunications Board, he visited various Commonwealth countries.

Angwin died at his home at Welwyn Garden City 21 April 1959.

[*The Times*, 22 April 1959; *Journal* of the Institution of Electrical Engineers, June 1959; Post Office and Telecommunications Board records; personal knowledge.]

GORDON RADLEY.

ANTAL, FREDERICK (1887–1954), art historian, was born in Budapest 21 December 1887, the only child of Alajos Antal, M.D., and his wife, Sofia Gerstl. He first studied at the university of his native city, where he graduated as a doctor of law, but later he went to Vienna to study art history under Max Dvořák, for whom he wrote a thesis on French painting of the neo-classical and early romantic periods. From 1914 to 1919 he worked in the print room of the Museum of Fine Arts at Budapest where, with Professor Johannes Wilde, he catalogued the collection of drawings. In 1917–18 he was sent to Udine by the Austro-Hungarian Government to look after the works of art in Italian territory occupied by the Austro-Hungarian army. In 1919 at the time of the Communist regime he was commissioned to make a record of paintings by Old Masters and the nineteenth-century French painters in private collections which had been confiscated by the State, and he organized a remarkable exhibition of them in Budapest. After the collapse of the Communist regime he left Hungary, going for a short time to Florence and Vienna before settling in Berlin in 1922. In 1933 he came to England where he lived for the remainder of his life, becoming a naturalized citizen in 1946.

In Berlin, Antal devoted himself primarily to the study of sixteenth-century Italian and Flemish painting and was one of those who first clarified the meaning of the word Mannerism. He was deeply interested in the method of art history and was one of the founders of the *Kritische Berichte*, a short-lived journal which was mainly devoted to the critical examination of the literature of art history. In this and in other periodicals he published a series of important articles devoted to the stylistic examination of Mannerist painting.

At the same time he was working on what was to be the major undertaking of his life, a history of Florentine painting of the sixteenth century. The text of this was finished in the late twenties, but Antal decided not to publish it for two reasons. First, he had become increasingly interested in the Marxist interpretation of history and its application to his own special field of art history, and as a result he felt that he must master the social and economic history of Florence before he could write a full history of Florentine art. Secondly, he realized that the crucial revolution in the development of Florentine art had occurred in the late fourteenth and fifteenth centuries, and that, in order to see the later history of Florentine art in correct perspective, it was essential to begin with an account of the earlier period, particularly since he saw Florentine Mannerism as in some ways a revival of late Gothic art. By 1933 he had finished the draft of the first volume dealing with the period up to about 1430, and he spent much of his first years in England reworking it and collaborating with various English art historians in the difficult task of translating it. Publication was held up owing to the war, and the book appeared in 1948 under the title *Florentine Painting and its Social Background. The Bourgeois Republic before Cosimo de' Medici's Advent to Power*. This work constituted a major contribution to knowledge of the early Renaissance, but it was also intended as a demonstration of how the Marxist interpretation of history could be applied to the arts. Its importance is widely recognized and it has been published in a number of languages, but it has been attacked by some critics as being over-rigid in its attempt to link artistic phenomena with social and economic causes.

During the war Antal devoted much time to the study of Italian sixteenth-century drawings in the Royal Library at Windsor Castle, the results of his research being incorporated in the catalogue published in 1949 by A. E. Popham and Johannes Wilde.

In his last years Antal returned to his early interest in the eighteenth century and in 1956 published a volume of studies on Fuseli and his contemporaries, in which he analysed brilliantly the connections between the art of Fuseli and sixteenth-century Mannerism. Even more important was his study of Hogarth, who fascinated him as an expression of English middle-class morality and culture. In his book on this artist, which was not published until 1962, after his death, his methods were applied more flexibly and more subtly than in his book on Florentine painting.

Many of Antal's most original ideas were published in the form of articles. The most important of these were republished in 1966 in a volume entitled *Classicism and Romanticism, with Other Studies in Art History*. This volume included his 'Remarks on the method of art history' which is a statement of his own credo.

Antal never held a regular teaching post in England, although he occasionally lectured at the Courtauld Institute of Art in the university of London; but he exerted considerable influence on a small group of students, to whom his enthusiasm and his astonishing range of knowledge were an inspiration.

In 1936 Antal married Evelyn Foster, daughter of the late Rev. Thomas Foster Edwards, Presbyterian minister. Three previous marriages had been dissolved. He had one son by his third marriage. Antal died in London 4 April 1954.

[Private information; personal knowledge.]
ANTHONY BLUNT.

ARBER, AGNES (1879–1960), botanist, was born in London 23 February 1879, the eldest child of Henry Robert Robertson, an artist who during most of his life worked at Steele's Studios, Haverstock Hill. Her mother, Agnes Lucy Turner, was descended from Robert Chamberlain [q.v.], of Worcester, and related to two fellows of the Royal Society, John Davidson and George Fownes [qq.v.].

Her brother, Donald Struan Robertson, became regius professor of Greek at Cambridge (1928–50), and a sister, Janet, a portrait painter.

Agnes Robertson received early drawing lessons from her father, and her mother gave her an interest in plants. From the age of eight she was a pupil at the North London Collegiate School for Girls. She obtained an entrance scholarship to University College, London, where she came under the stimulating influence of F. W. Oliver [q.v.]. Having taken her B.Sc. with first class honours (1899), she proceeded with an entrance scholarship to Newnham College, Cambridge, where she obtained first classes in both parts of the natural sciences tripos (1901–2), in part i adding chemistry and physics to her study of botany and geology.

On leaving Cambridge she became research assistant to Ethel Sargant in whose private laboratory at Reigate she learnt the technique of the study of anatomy by serial sections. Miss Sargant had established a reputation as a plant-anatomist, especially for her work on seedling structure. From 1903 to 1908 Agnes Robertson held the Quain studentship in biology and in 1908–9 a lectureship in botany at University College, London, and devoted much attention to the Gymnosperms, including a valuable study of the seed of the fossil form *Mitrospermum compressum* and a detailed study of the palaeozoic cone genus *Lepidostrobus*.

In 1909 she married Edward Alexander Newell Arber (1870–1918), elder son of Edward Arber [q.v.] and university demonstrator in palaeobotany at Cambridge; he was responsible for the collections of fossil plants in the Sedgwick Museum, Cambridge, and published many papers on palaeobotany, and books on fossil plants, alpine plants, and coast scenery. They had one daughter who became a geologist.

Until 1927 Agnes Arber carried on research work at the Balfour laboratory which then belonged to Newnham. Thereafter she worked in a room fitted up as a laboratory in her private house. She was almost continuously concerned in research on plant anatomy. *Water-plants: a Study of Aquatic Angiosperms* (1920) dealt mainly with both the morphology and the biology of species common in Britain, illustrated with many beautiful original drawings by the author. It was accompanied by a series of papers mainly on the structure and morphology

of monocotyledonous plants. In 1925 a book on the *Monocotyledons: a Morphological Study* reviewed the vegetative structure seen in the group, and examined the conclusions drawn from comparative anatomical study. A second volume was *Gramineae* (1934) which showed the similarities and differences in structure in this group of organisms of considerable economic importance. The interpretation of the many facts of structure which she recorded and the discussions which she initiated about their significance, added considerably to the material bearing on the origin and evolution of species, as understood at that time. The value placed on her work was shown by her election as a corresponding member of the Botanical Society of America, by the award of the gold medal of the Linnean Society of London (1948), and by her election as F.R.S. (1946).

The history and philosophy of botany were among the chief interests of Mrs. Arber throughout her life. Her first and most widely read book was *Herbals, their Origin and Evolution*, an account of the printed works on plants which appeared between 1470 and 1670, with biographical notes on their authors and typical reproductions of their illustrations. First published in 1912, it soon became the standard work on the subject; a second enlarged edition appeared in 1938. She made other important contributions to the history of botany, especially in connection with Nehemiah Grew [q.v.].

During her anatomical and comparative studies she turned her attention to the botanical work of Goethe and to the philosophy of biology which he introduced, publishing *Goethe's Botany* as a number of *Chronica Botanica* (1946). This eventually led to her important study on *The Natural Philosophy of Plant Form* (1950) which distinguishes between a relationship based on objective relationship due to descent from a common ancestor and a resemblance due to similarities in form or structure without any genetic relationship. This distinction is one of the most important and fundamental in comparative biology. Other studies of a philosophical nature were the outcome of a long series of observations on plant structures reviewed from a critical standpoint. *The Mind and the Eye, a Study of the Biologist's Standpoint* (1954) outlines the stages through which the biologist passes on the road towards reality. She read deeply in philosophy, being especially influenced by

Spinoza, and the outcome of her contemplation was *The Manifold and the One*, a philosophical essay published in 1957. She died in Cambridge 22 March 1960 and was buried in the churchyard at Girton.

[H. Hamshaw Thomas in *Biographical Memoirs of Fellows of the Royal Society*, vol. vi, 1960; *The Times*, 24 March 1960; *Taxon*, vol. ix, No. 9, 1960.]   H. HAMSHAW THOMAS.

ARDEN-CLOSE, SIR CHARLES FREDERICK (1865–1952), geographer, was born 10 August 1865 at St. Saviour's, Jersey, the eldest son of Captain (later Major-General) Frederick Close, R.A., by his second wife, Lydia Ann Stevens. He changed his name to Arden-Close by deed poll in 1938. He was educated at Thompson's School, Jersey, and at a crammer's, passing second into the Royal Military Academy, Woolwich, in 1882. In 1884 he passed out first, with the Pollock memorial medal, was commissioned in the Royal Engineers, and joined the School of Military Engineering, Chatham. After a year (1886) in Gibraltar he was first attached to and later commanded the balloon section at Chatham (1887–8). He was next posted to India where he served one year on battery construction, Hooghly defences, and then four years (1889–93) with the Survey of India, engaged in topographic work in Upper Burma and geodetic triangulation on the Mandalay primary series (Toungoo–Katha) and the Mong Hsat secondary series up to the Siam border.

Returning to Chatham at his own request, he was sent in the next year (1895) to West Africa to survey the boundary between the Niger Coast Protectorate and the German Cameroons. On his return he was appointed to the Ordnance Survey and in 1898, at the age of thirty-three, was made British commissioner to delimit the frontier of British Central Africa and Northern Rhodesia with German East Africa for over two hundred miles between lakes Nyasa and Tanganyika. Before leaving England he had an interview with Cecil Rhodes [q.v.]; and subsequently there was collaboration with (Sir) David Gill [q.v.], H.M. astronomer at the Cape, in relation to longitude fixation of points on the German frontier. He was appointed C.M.G. in 1899. Next year he led a small survey detachment for the South African war, for which practically no maps existed, but developed enteric and was invalided home. In 1902–5 he was chief instructor in surveying at Chatham. There he intro-

duced new methods and wrote a *Text Book of Topographical and Geographical Surveying* (1905) which remained the standard work for the next half-century.

Thus by 1905 Close had very wide practical experience of surveying, both geodetic and topographic, in three continents, as well as first-hand knowledge of international boundary surveys and settlements. In that year he became head of the geographical section, general staff, at the War Office, of which a major concern was overseas maps. He pressed, with success, for the formation of the colonial survey committee and for surveying in British colonies. An even wider project was the Carte Internationale du Monde au Millionième—first proposed in 1891 and exhaustively discussed later but with little progress. With support from the War and Foreign Offices, Close arranged an international conference at the Foreign Office in 1909, attended by delegates of the great powers, at which concrete proposals were made. The large number of maps on this system now in existence is a glowing tribute to Close's driving power.

In 1911 Close became director-general of the Ordnance Survey which he found 'rather out of touch with the scientific world'. He proceeded with a second geodetic levelling of the United Kingdom and directed the creation of 'fundamental points' 'likely to last for hundreds of years', as well as three mean-sea level tidal stations—at Dunbar, Newlyn, and Felixstowe, of which the second remains in operation. Close also secured the appointment of two advisers, one scientific and one archaeological; the one-inch map of the United Kingdom was redesigned; and a map of Roman Britain was published. In 1914 he delivered the Halley lecture at Oxford which was incorporated in his 'Notes on the Geodesy of the British Isles' (O.S. Prof. Pap.No. 3).

During the war of 1914–18 32 million maps were printed by the Ordnance Survey for the armies in France and elsewhere. Close, who had been promoted major (1901), lieutenant-colonel (1908), and colonel (1912), periodically visited the western front. After the war various committees produced recommendations for drastic cuts which Close had the unpleasant task of implementing until his retirement in 1922. His record of *The Early Years of the Ordnance Survey* appeared in 1926.

In the many productive years still before him Close devoted himself mainly to work

on geographical and kindred matters.
He served on the council of the Royal
Geographical Society (1904–40), was
Victoria gold medallist (1927), and president (1927–30). He was chairman of the
National Committee for Geography and
general secretary of the International
Union of Geography, becoming president
in 1934–8. He was chairman of the Palestine Exploration Fund (1930–45) and
president of the Hampshire Field Club
(1929–32 and 1935–6). In 1927, when
president of the Geographical Association,
he addressed that body on 'Population
and Migration'. His broad open mind
found interest in social problems concerning population and age of marriage. His
paper 'Our Crowded Island' in which
matters relating to over-population are
considered may be found in the *Eugenics
Review* for April 1948. He was president of
the International Union for the Scientific
Investigation of Population Problems in
1931–7.

Close was elected F.R.S. in 1919; received an honorary Sc.D. from Cambridge
(1928); and was an honorary member of
the Russian, German, Belgian, Dutch,
Spanish, and Swiss geographical societies.
He was appointed C.B. in 1916 and K.B.E.
in 1918; was an officer of the Order of
Leopold, and a member of the Afghan
Order of Astaur.

In 1913 Close married Gladys Violet
(died 1953), daughter of the late Theodore
Henry Perceval, sometime of the India
Office. They had one daughter and two
sons, the younger of whom died in 1943 as
a Japanese prisoner of war on the Burma–
Siam railway. Arden-Close died at Winchester 19 December 1952.

[J. de Graaff-Hunter in *Obituary Notices of
Fellows of the Royal Society*, No. 22, November
1953; *Geographical Journal*, June and September 1953; *Eugenics Review*, April 1953;
Royal Engineers Journal, March 1953; *The
Times*, 22 December 1952; private information; personal knowledge.]

J. DE GRAAFF-HUNTER.

ARKELL, WILLIAM JOSCELYN
(1904–1958), geologist, was born in
Highworth, Wiltshire, 9 June 1904, the
youngest of a family of seven of James
Arkell, brewer, and his wife, a talented
artist, Laura Jane, daughter of Augustus
William Rixon, a London solicitor. From
an early age Arkell displayed a keen interest in natural history, explored the
countryside, and collected insects, plants,
and fossils. At Wellington College, Berk-

shire, he was an enthusiastic member
of the school natural history society. At
New College, Oxford, he decided to make
geology and palaeontology his special subjects, receiving much encouragement from
W. J. Sollas [q.v.], then professor of
geology. In 1925 he gained the only first
class honours of his year in geology and
a few months later was awarded the
Burdett-Coutts scholarship, which opened
the way for research in his chosen field. In
1929–33 he was lecturer in geology at New
College, an appointment which enabled
him to devote most of his time to research,
and thereafter he held senior research
fellowships: at New College (1933–40)
and at Trinity College, Cambridge (1947–
58). He received the D.Sc. degree of the
university of Oxford in 1934.

Arkell's name will long be associated
with the study of the rocks of the Jurassic
system and their fossils. His earliest work
was on the Corallian beds of Oxfordshire
and neighbouring counties and his first
paper, which dealt with certain fossil bivalve molluscs from these strata, appeared
in 1926. It was the forerunner of his
voluminous *Monograph of British Corallian Lamellibranchia*, published by the
Palaeontographical Society in 1929–37.
His first stratigraphical paper, dealing
with the Corallian rocks of the area just
mentioned, was published in 1927 in the
Philosophical Transactions of the Royal
Society. It was soon followed by contributions on the Cornbrash (with J. A. Douglas) and on the Great Oolite. At the same
time, he was also working industriously at
the literature, and his *Jurassic System in
Great Britain* appeared in 1933. A great
work of major importance and an amazing
achievement for a man still in his twenties, it presented a critical and exhaustive
survey of information scattered in hundreds of memoirs and papers. It immediately gained for its author an
international reputation.

While continuing with stratigraphical
researches in a number of areas in southern
England, Arkell now also took up the
study of ammonites as being most usefully
applicable to problems of Jurassic correlation. His *Monograph on the Ammonites of
the English Corallian Beds* was published
by the Palaeontographical Society in
1935–48, while publication by the same
society of his *Monograph of the English
Bathonian Ammonites*, begun in 1951, was
completed posthumously towards the end
of 1958. Shorter papers dealt with ammonites from the Oxford and Kimmeridge

Clays of England and with several collections from overseas. He was also responsible for the sections on Jurassic ammonites in Part L (1957) of the *Treatise on Invertebrate Paleontology* (ed. R. C. Moore). Arkell's *Geology of Oxford* appeared in 1947 and his *Jurassic Geology of the World* in 1956. The latter, his second major stratigraphical work, was not only an able and critical digest of a very extensive literature, but also embodied much original information. It became a standard work of reference throughout the world and a translation has been published in Russia.

Arkell's interests were by no means confined to his Jurassic studies. For four winter seasons (1926–30) he accompanied Dr. K. S. Sandford on a survey of traces of Palaeolithic man in Egypt organized by the Oriental Institute of the university of Chicago. Four notable monographs under their joint authorship (1929–39) were the outcome of this work and occasional papers on palaeoliths and Pleistocene chronology appeared from Arkell's pen even later in life. Tectonic problems also attracted him, and among his papers on this subject was one on Mesozoic and Cainozoic folding in England read at the International Geological Congress in Washington when he visited America in 1933. Topographical names and local dialects interested him considerably. Place-names in Wiltshire, Dorset, and Gloucestershire formed the subject of papers in 1940–42 and in 1953 he published (with S. I. Tomkeieff) a work entitled *English Rock Terms, Chiefly as Used by Miners and Quarrymen*. He was an authority on building stones and his *Oxford Stone* appeared in 1947. An artist of no mean ability, he not only drew many of the illustrations for his various works, but painted in water colours as a hobby.

Elected F.R.S. in 1947, Arkell was awarded the Mary Clark Thompson gold medal of the National Academy of Sciences of America in 1944, the Lyell medal of the Geological Society of London in 1949, and the von Buch medal of the German Geological Society in 1953. He was also an honorary member or correspondent of several foreign learned societies.

Tall, robust in appearance, and fair-haired, Arkell was somewhat reserved and aloof in manner, but was nevertheless very approachable and always ready to help younger workers. He had a strong inclination to participate in controversies (particularly in print), but bore no malice towards those with whom he disagreed. Less strong physically than he appeared, he did not recover completely from a wartime illness after work in London as a temporary civil servant (1941–3), and at the Sedgwick Museum in Cambridge he was allotted a downstairs room to save fatigue. A stroke in 1956 left him partially paralysed and he died in Cambridge 18 April 1958. He was survived by his wife, Ruby Lilian, daughter of S. R. S. Percival, of Boscombe, Hampshire, whom he had married in 1929, and by his three sons.

[L. R. Cox in *Biographical Memoirs of Fellows of the Royal Society*, vol. iv, 1958; *Proceedings* of the Dorset Natural History Society, 1959; personal knowledge.]

L. R. Cox.

ARLEN, MICHAEL (1895–1956), novelist, began life as Dikran Kouyoumdjian, son of an Armenian merchant, Sarkis Kouyoumdjian. He was born at Rustchuk in Bulgaria 16 November 1895, and with an elder brother was educated at Malvern College. In 1922 he was naturalized in the name under which he had begun to publish novels and short stories. With these he was soon to achieve considerable, if temporary, fame. His first novel, *The London Venture*, was published in 1920 on the recommendation of (Sir) Edmund Gosse [q.v.]. Surprisingly George Moore [q.v.] was his early model; but his mannered and ornamented style had certainly a reminiscent tang of the nineties. Three more books in the next three years established him on the literary scene, and in 1924 came *The Green Hat* which was acclaimed, attacked, parodied, and read, to the most fabulous degree of best-sellerdom; and made him a comfortable small fortune. It was a romance suited to its decade—cynical, sophisticated, yet sentimental, highly coloured, and glittering. If the colours have now faded, and the glitter seems mostly tarnished tinsel, the book cast a spell in its day and influenced many young writers. The character of the heroine, Iris Storm, that wanton of quality, 'shameless, shameful lady', gallantly crashing to her death in her great yellow Hispano-Suiza—'for Purity'—set a new fashion in fatal charmers; and the pictures of London café society were exact as glossy photographs. 'The Loyalty'—recognizable as the Embassy Club, at which the smartest people, including young princes, then danced to the blues —was depicted almost table by table, with a mixture of mockery and romanticism which delighted those who read of themselves.

Perhaps because he was a foreigner, who while mingling among them viewed them from outside, Michael Arlen had free licence to mock these people. Rather as English society had petted the young Disraeli, it forgave Arlen his cleverness and his exuberant elegance. Even when poor and struggling this young man had contrived to be elegant; and in prosperity, it was said that his white waistcoat always seemed to be whiter than anybody else's; but Arlen himself was forestallingly ready to disarm criticism—describing himself as 'Every other inch a gentleman', 'The one the Turks forgot', or 'A Case of Pernicious Armenia'. His wit not being above the heads of his fashionable hearers, they found him the best of company; moreover, he was a man of whom his friends spoke with lasting regard.

Arlen took a hand in several plays, published collections of his short stories and, among further novels, *Lily Christine* (1929), *Men Dislike Women* (1931), *Hell! said the Duchess* (1934), and finally *Flying Dutchman* (1939). All had the professional touch of the born story-teller; but he never believed himself an important writer, and in after years steadily declined to have his 'rubbishy' best-sellers reprinted. His gains were well invested; and when he was happily married in 1928 to Atalanta, daughter of Count Mercati, they presently settled in the south of France. They had one son and one daughter. At the outbreak of war in 1939 Arlen returned to England to offer his services and was injured in the bombing of the city which had formed a background to his most successful fictions. The world of which he had written was destroyed in the flames of that bombing; but it can still be resurrected from his pages; and his name, whenever remembered, connected with that coign of Mayfair, that 'collection of lively odours' called Shepherd's Market. Eventually settling in New York he died there 23 June 1956.

[*The Times*, 25 June 1956; private information.] M. BELLASIS.

ARMSTRONG, WILLIAM (1882–1952), actor and producer, eldest son of John Armstrong and his wife, Annie Tait, was born in Edinburgh 30 November 1882. His father, a grocer who forgave too many debts to be prosperous, brought William up to be proud of an ancestry which included many schoolmasters and ministers, to be a devout Baptist and a crusading teetotaller, singing

When the wine around you is passing, Have courage, my boy, to say 'No',

at Band of Hope concerts. He never forgot his Edinburgh background and, since he was a brilliant raconteur, his stories of Edinburgh life; of his experiences as a conductor of Polytechnic tours; and of theatrical personalities—notably Mrs. Patrick Campbell [q.v.]—were a delight to his friends and, when broadcast, to wider audiences.

He was educated at Heriot's School but left at fourteen. His main interest was music and he wanted to be a schoolmaster. Helped by the Carnegie Trust, he was enrolled as a student in the faculty of music at Edinburgh University; but, as always, his interest was in performance not theory and, although he passed his first professional examination for the degree of Mus.B., the purely theoretical study of music chilled him and he turned to the theatre. He joined an amateur dramatic society; frequented the sixpenny gallery at the Lyceum to see Sir Henry Irving and (Sir) Herbert Beerbohm Tree, and (Dame) Ellen Terry [qq.v.]; and founded the Edinburgh University Dramatic Club with (Sir) J. M. Barrie [q.v.] as president. By the time he was twenty-six he had started his career as a professional actor with (Sir) Frank Benson [q.v.], playing Jamy in *Henry V* at the Stratford Memorial Theatre. He was tall, willowy, with reddish fair hair and a Scottish accent; shy but with a gift of humour which won him friends. He interested G. B. Shaw [q.v.], who wrote the one-act play *The Music Cure* for him and Madge McIntosh. He acted innumerable parts with reasonable success, and was for two years a member of the Glasgow Repertory Theatre.

His connection with Liverpool began in 1914 when he became a member of the 'Commonwealth', an experiment which kept the Repertory Theatre alive during the early war years. He was remembered; and when, in 1922, a permanent producer was needed, he was offered the post. From 1922 as producer, and from 1923 to 1944 as a director as well as producer, he ran what was undoubtedly the most successful repertory theatre in the country. From his Liverpool base he had a great influence upon the English theatre. Under him, the Liverpool Repertory Theatre certainly did not become, as had been hoped, the centre of a new school of dramatic writing; but, at a time when English playwrights had ceased to be inspired by the energies of Shaw, Galsworthy, and Granville-Barker [qq.v.] and were seeking new forms amid the drawing-room dramas of (Sir) Noël Coward, Somerset Maugham, and Frederick Lonsdale [q.v.], Liverpool became a great school of acting. Players, later well known and even famous, grew up under him, (Sir) Michael Redgrave, Rex Harrison, Diana Wynyard, Marjorie Fielding, Robert Donat [q.v.], Wyndham Goldie, Cecil Parker, Harry Andrews, and Alan Webb among them. He was not intellectual in his approach and never forced his own interpretation of a play upon his company; he rather seemed to feel for the tone, the pace, and the style which was developing. Generous, emotional, easily moved by pathos and by beauty, he demanded, and recognized, sensibility in his actors; but his irrepressible humour made him detect instantly, with destroying laughter, a false note. His musical background affected his work; he listened for the harmonies in a play, rather than analysed it, and changed moves and intonations because they were discordant rather than because they did not fit into a preconceived pattern. His informality, his wit, his appreciation of youth, made young actors and actresses flock to Liverpool where they flowered under his willingness to develop their talents rather than force them into a mould. They left with an unforgettable training in a flexible, sensitive style of acting which could never be forced or heavy-handed.

He made the Repertory Theatre a powerful influence in Liverpool life and, although the laddie from Edinburgh had become a sophisticated and even flamboyant man of the theatre, he never lost his shrewd hold on those financial realities which reassured his fellow directors, many of them Liverpool business men. He gave the Shute lectures on 'The Art of the Theatre' at the university of Liverpool in 1928: was made an honorary M.A. by the university in 1930, and was appointed C.B.E. in 1951 for services to the Liverpool and Birmingham repertory theatres. He left Liverpool in 1944; directed many plays in London and was assistant director to Sir Barry Jackson at the Birmingham Repertory Theatre in 1945–7. He died, unmarried, at his home near Birmingham

5 October 1952. A portrait of him by Wilhem Kaufman hangs in the Walker Art Gallery, Liverpool.

[Grace Wyndham Goldie, *The Liverpool Repertory Theatre*, 1935; *Who's Who in the Theatre*; private information; personal knowledge.]   GRACE WYNDHAM GOLDIE.

ARTHUR OF CONNAUGHT, PRINCESS (1891–1959). [See ALEXANDRA VICTORIA ALBERTA EDWINA LOUISE DUFF.]

ASHBY, ARTHUR WILFRED (1886–1953), agricultural economist, was born in the Warwickshire village of Tysoe, 19 August 1886, the eldest of eight children of Joseph Ashby and his wife and cousin, Hannah Ashby. His father was a remarkable man whose life, as told by his daughter, is the classic story of the articulate village leader of the second half of the nineteenth century for whom religion, farming, and politics were the stuff of life. Leaving the village school a little before his twelfth birthday, young Ashby spent the next eleven years helping his father in the multifarious duties of small farmer, self-taught surveyor, Methodist lay-preacher, poor-law guardian, organizer of village clubs, and local agent for the Liberal Party. This apprenticeship to a robust heritage laid the foundation for Ashby's lifelong study of rural society.

His orderly studies started in 1909 when he went to Ruskin College, Oxford, with a Charles Buxton scholarship. There he took the diploma (with distinction) in economics and political science and wrote his contribution on the administration of the poor law (1912) for *Oxford Studies in Social and Legal History* edited by (Sir) Paul Vinogradoff [q.v.]. In 1912 the Board of Agriculture awarded him the first of its scholarships in agricultural economics. This took him in turn to the newly founded Institute for Research in Agricultural Economics at Oxford and to the university of Wisconsin where he was honorary fellow in political science.

In 1915 he returned to the Oxford Institute to study the history of allotments and smallholdings; his book (1917) on this topic has not been superseded. From 1917 to 1919 he was seconded to the Board of Agriculture where he had a big share in shaping the first Agricultural Wages Board and in the work of the food production department. Back at the Institute he was senior research assistant until, in 1924, he went to Aberystwyth as head of the new department of agricultural economics in the University College of Wales. His work there was recognized by his elevation in 1929 to the first professorship in agricultural economics in this country. It was entirely fitting that, in 1946, he should return to the Institute at Oxford to succeed C. S. Orwin [q.v.] as director, the post he held until his retirement in 1952.

Ashby was a prominent member of the small group who were pioneers in the study of agricultural economics as a subject in its own right. It was his efforts which led, in the face of considerable opposition, to the formation in 1926 of the Agricultural Economics Society, of which he was twice president. He was also a founder-member and, from 1949 to 1952, a vice-president of the International Conference of Agricultural Economists. Through his contributions to teaching, to research, and to policy over a period of forty years he made a decisive and enduring impact on the development of his chosen subject.

His undoubted greatness as a teacher was given full scope with his translation to Aberystwyth. His deliberate manner of speaking coupled with his tall and dignified presence was always calculated to command full attention; but it needed the encouragement of sympathetic Welsh farmer-audiences to mould the halting lecturer of earlier years into the familiar platform figure who spoke with such confidence and authority. On returning to Oxford in 1946 he used his twenty years' experience in Wales to give a new emphasis to the teaching side of the work of the Institute. Both at Aberystwyth and at Oxford he attracted students from all over the world. Having himself been denied the educational advantages which usually lead to an academic career, he was particularly sympathetic to overseas students; when he visited India in 1949 to advise on the development of agricultural economics it gave him great pleasure to be greeted by old pupils.

He was equally gifted as a director of research, for he was indefatigable both as instigator of original work and as supervisor of advanced studies. He was himself a prolific contributor to the literature of his subject. His writings are scattered in many journals and a selected list representative of their wide range is given in the *Journal of Agricultural Economics*, vol. xii, 1956. Many of his most stimulating contributions were made, however, in extempore discussions at conferences and meetings. Some of the best of these contributions will be found fully indexed in the *Journal of Proceedings* of the Agricultural Economics Society and in the *Proceedings* of the International Conference of Agricultural Economists, which also contain some of his more important papers.

Ashby's background meant that to him agricultural economics could never be an arid exercise. Hence his untiring work on the many official and voluntary bodies on which he served from 1919 onwards. Three of these are worth special mention because they concerned causes in which he had a special interest. First, his membership of several important marketing committees in the inter-war years gave him the chance to propagate his profound belief in the efficacy of co-operation. His knowledge of milk marketing was probably unequalled and, in the background, he played a big part in designing the Milk Marketing Board for England and Wales. Secondly, as an appointed member of the Agricultural Wages Board from 1924 onwards he was able to use his influence in the furtherance of good relations between master and man on the farm. Finally, he welcomed the opportunity which service on the awarding committee for scholarships to the sons and daughters of rural workers gave him to express his lifelong interest in the education of country children.

Throughout his life Ashby remained true to his radical-reformist upbringing. In politics he was a supporter of the Labour Party, yet successive Labour governments failed effectively to utilize his unrivalled knowledge of the problems facing British agriculture.

Ashby was a shy, reserved person with a touch of the suspicious caution of the typical countryman. In academic circles he was never entirely at ease and he never rid himself completely of a certain nervous tension in public, characteristics which led him, on occasion, to do less than justice to himself. But he was essentially a kind and friendly man, always generous with his help to those, especially young people, who sought it. His sense of humour was of the quiet kind; he loved to hear a good story and to chuckle loudly at one of his own.

In 1923 Ashby received the honorary degree of M.A. from the university of Oxford (and M.A. by decree in 1946) and he was elected a fellow of Lincoln College in 1947. He was appointed C.B.E. in 1946.

A justice of the peace, he sat on the bench both in Cardiganshire (1940–46) and in Oxfordshire (1946–53). He became a foreign member of the Royal Swedish Academy of Agriculture (1951) and a member of the Scientific Agricultural Society of Finland (1953).

A commemorative portrait by Percy Horton (1953) hangs in the Institute for Research in Agricultural Economics at Oxford.

In 1922 Ashby married Rhoda, daughter of John Dean Bland. They had one son who also became an agricultural economist. Ashby died in Oxford 9 September 1953.

[*The Times*, 11 September 1953; *Countryman*, Winter 1953; *Journal of Agricultural Economics*, vol. xii, 1956; M. K. Ashby, *Joseph Ashby of Tysoe 1859–1919*, 1961; private information; personal knowledge.]

EDGAR THOMAS.

ASHWELL, LENA MARGARET (1872–1957), actress, was born 28 September 1872 on board the training ship *Wellesley*, moored in the Tyne, the daughter of Captain Charles Ashwell Botelar Pocock and his wife, Sarah Margaret Stevens. Nicholas Pocock [q.v.], the marine painter, was her great-uncle and Roger Pocock, the traveller and founder of the Legion of Frontiersmen, her brother. Her father was then in charge of the lads sent to the *Wellesley* for entry to a maritime life. A deeply religious man, he later took deacon's orders in the Church of England. He was the owner of some property but this was lost by bad investment; the family moved to Canada and Lena Pocock, who was to use her father's second name on the stage, was educated at Bishop Strachan's School for Young Ladies in Toronto and also at the university. Owing to her proficiency in music she was then sent to study at the Lausanne Conservatoire and later attended the Royal Academy of Music in London. It was hoped that she would have a career as a singer, but her voice did not develop as expected. (Dame) Ellen Terry [q.v.], who came to examine the elocution class, was impressed by the vivid feeling as well as good diction displayed and wisely advised her to concentrate on becoming an actress.

There was no easy start or swift promotion, but in 1892 Lena Ashwell was touring with (Sir) George Alexander [q.v.], taking a small part in *Lady Windermere's Fan*. In 1895 she realized the highest ambition of all aspiring actresses at that time and played for Sir Henry Irving [q.v.] at the Lyceum, as Elaine in *King Arthur*. In 1896 she returned to take the part of the Prince of Wales in *Richard III*. G. B. Shaw [q.v.], then dramatic critic of the *Saturday Review*, found her performance in the former play to be 'weak, timid, subordinate' with her voice 'a squawl', but in the latter he thought she had 'developed precipitously' and now possessed 'authority and assurance as one of the younger generation knocking vigorously at the door'. The door was decisively opened when in 1900 she was chosen to play Mrs. Dane in *Mrs. Dane's Defence* by Henry Arthur Jones [q.v.] under (Sir) Charles Wyndham [q.v.] at Wyndham's Theatre. Both play and player had a notable success.

With the status of a leading actress she went in 1903 to (Sir) Herbert Beerbohm Tree [q.v.] in a dramatized version of Tolstoy's *Resurrection* and was much admired both in this and in *The Darling of the Gods* in the same year. She won further tribute in another play of Russian life, *Leah Kleschna*, in 1905. She next had her first experience of management at the Savoy Theatre in 1906, appearing as Ninon de l'Enclos in *The Bond of Ninon*; this was not successful and a visit to America also proved disappointing. But she had backing for a new and memorable venture, the reopening in 1907 of the Great Queen Street Theatre under the new name of the Kingsway with a distinguished company in a series of contemporary plays. Lena Ashwell modernized the decoration of the house, chose plays outside the west-end routine, and made this small playhouse, on the eastern fringe of the theatre area, a centre of intelligent drama. The adventure had its risks since the theatre was in a side street and somewhat remote, but it was gallantly sustained.

Opening with *Irene Wycherley*, Lena Ashwell, who had the powerful aid of Norman McKinnel, secured an immediate success in a play of great emotional force. She followed it with a piece about shopgirl life, *Diana of Dobson's*, by Cicely Hamilton, later a prominent champion of women's causes in whose work for women's franchise Lena Ashwell actively joined. Plays about working-class conditions were then unusual but it made its impact. The productions following proved less attractive and the Kingsway venture had to be given up. Lena Ashwell returned there in 1915 to play Margaret Knox, the defiant young feminist, in Shaw's *Fanny's First Play*.

She had inherited religious faith and was always ready to back a good cause. In 1912 she helped to found the Three Arts Club as a centre where young women working in the arts, especially on the stage, could live, as well as meet, comfortably and economically. When the war continued she engaged herself in an enterprise which took all her time, the provision of concerts and later on dramatic performances for the troops at the front. Thus she anticipated the work of E.N.S.A. in the second war. At first the effort had to be privately financed and to this end £100,000 was raised. By the time of the armistice there were twenty-five companies in the field. For her pioneering work she was appointed O.B.E. in 1917.

When peace came she determined to provide the suburbs with a somewhat similar service. With the remnant of the Concert Fund she founded the Once-a-Week Players, later known as the Lena Ashwell Players, and with the aid of the London mayors obtained the right to act in town halls and public baths at a nominal fee. Excellent work was done, not only for the public who could see work of quality, Shakespeare as well as the plays of the leading contemporary authors, at prices ranging from sixpence to half a crown, but also for young actors and actresses seeking opportunity. Many players who subsequently reached the front rank had precious experience in this exhausting but stimulating work which involved continual rehearsal of new pieces by day and journeys to fit up stages in the suburbs, some quite distant, by night. Central premises were established in 1924 at the Century Theatre. Unfortunately there was financial stringency after the general strike of 1926 and a serious influenza epidemic; but the venture might have survived had there been any escape, for such work of civic value, from the entertainment duty. 'During the season 1926–7', Lena Ashwell recorded, 'for entertaining 174,000 people, we were taxed £2,683.6.8.' The experiment ended in 1929.

Lena Ashwell did not thereafter return to the stage. She had overcome many difficulties. Her features were not those of the conventional stage beauty and she entered the profession with no friends in it to help her. But from the time of *Mrs. Dane's Defence* she was much in demand for roles where intensity of feeling was necessary: she could play light comedy

with a sure technique, but it was in the portrayal of suffering that she was essentially herself. Her personality was invigorating to any company with which she played or which she organized. Her sphere of activities was centred on the stage, but not confined to it. She was an able writer, recording her war work in *Modern Troubadours* (1922) and telling her own life story in *Myself a Player* (1936).

After a most unhappy first marriage to the actor Arthur Wyndham Playfair (1869–1918) she married in 1908 (Sir) Henry John Forbes Simson (died 1932), a brilliant surgeon who had qualified in Edinburgh and who rose to a high place in London, specializing in maternity cases and serving the royal family in that capacity. This union was one of entire happiness. Lena Ashwell had no children and died in London 13 March 1957.

[Her own writings; private information; personal knowledge.]   IVOR BROWN.

ASLIN, CHARLES HERBERT (1893–1959), architect, was born in Sheffield 15 December 1893, the younger of two sons of Arthur William and Louisa Aslin. His parents, both north-country people, came from Lincolnshire and Derbyshire. By the time Aslin was born his father was foreman in a Sheffield steelworks and Aslin was a Yorkshireman by birth and adoption. He received his early education at Sheffield Central School and later at Sheffield University. At the outbreak of war in 1914 he immediately volunteered for the infantry but was rejected because of defective vision. After a period in the Army Pay Corps and the Oxford and Bucks. Light Infantry he was commissioned in the Royal Artillery in 1916. Holding the rank of captain he served with a field regiment on the western front until 1919.

Before enlisting Aslin had passed the final examination of the Royal Institute of British Architects and in 1920 he was admitted an associate, becoming a fellow in 1932. After service on the staff of the city architect of Sheffield he was appointed in 1922 architect to the borough engineer of Rotherham where he designed the new municipal offices. During the following years he lectured at Sheffield University, became an associate of the Institution of Civil Engineers, and in 1926 was appointed deputy county architect of Hampshire. In 1929 he became the borough architect of Derby where he first demonstrated the talent which was later to carry him to the top of his profession. Apart from more orthodox schemes he was responsible for the complete re-development of the central areas of the town including new municipal offices, police courts, bus station, covered markets, and riverside gardens. Common as this kind of work later became, it was then a pioneer task.

When in 1945 Aslin became county architect to Hertfordshire it was clear to him that the Education Act of 1944 would create a national demand for new school building far in excess of the capacity of the traditional building industry, depleted moreover by wartime requirements; committed to essential tasks of repairing war damage, providing new houses to cater for the shift in population, and at grips with the problems of New Town construction. In no part of the country were these problems more acute than in Hertfordshire and Aslin determined on the bold course of developing prefabricated construction which would make extensive use of factory capacity and so relieve the strain on the traditional industry. He was fortunate in the encouragement and co-operation of the county council and its associated chief officials; nevertheless the responsibility was his and the enterprise was regarded by many in the profession as daring to the point of foolhardiness.

Aslin's vision was completely justified and the system proved remarkably successful. The Hertfordshire schools became places of pilgrimage by architects from all over the world. Existing values were challenged; new technical and administrative procedures were adopted; and a new aesthetic evolved using space, light, and colour to create an entirely new kind of environment. When in 1955 his hundredth school was opened by the minister of education Aslin's approach had been completely vindicated and his methods had been adopted by leading authorities throughout the country. Aslin, an outstanding team leader, collected on his staff some of the brightest young men of the day. His judgement in their selection, the encouragement he gave them, and his generous acknowledgement of their contribution to the task were part of his strength. Jobs in his office were amongst the most sought after in the country.

Although Aslin will be remembered primarily for his contribution in this field,

it did not represent his total effort. From 1941 to 1943 he was president of the Notts., Derby, and Lincoln Society of Architects and was their representative on the council of the R.I.B.A. He continued to do valuable committee work at the R.I.B.A. in particular as chairman of the official architects committee on which he helped to heal the breach developing between architects in private practice and those in salaried posts who were justifiably dissatisfied with their conditions of service. In 1945 he was elected in his own right to the council of the R.I.B.A. and in 1954–6 was president. His presidency coincided with the end of building licensing when the industry was in a more confident and optimistic mood than for many years past. In his presidential address he spoke of the need to study the structure of the profession, to make it more efficient and to equip it to give better service to the client and the public at large. His ideas introduced a period of reform which began to bear more fruit as time passed. Appointed C.B.E. in 1951, Aslin was an associate of the Institution of Structural Engineers, a member of the Royal Society of Arts, honorary fellow of the American Institute of Architects, and R.I.B.A. bronze medallist (1951).

Always respected for his kindness and wisdom, Aslin made friends easily and amongst his wide circle was equally at ease with people of widely differing age, background, race, and temperament. Coupled with his charm he retained a native north-country shrewdness and strength enabling him to adopt a firm stand when serious issues were at stake. Above all he detested pomposity or pretension. During the whole of his career he was supported and encouraged by his wife without whom, as he freely acknowledged, he could not have developed anything like his full potential. The help and hospitality which were extended to all with whom they came in contact were remarkable. Aslin led too full a life to have much time for hobbies. Nevertheless, he played a good game of tennis, was interested in cricket, and a keen devotee of the theatre, particularly Shakespeare. He was an expert photographer, an indefatigable reader over a wide field of literature, and supporter of numerous societies. He did a great deal during the second war to foster Anglo-Polish relations. Brought up as a strict nonconformist, he embraced the Church of England. Although never sanctimonious he was a staunch member of that Church and a man of sincere religious principles.

Aslin had a narrow escape from death during a visit to Staffordshire in 1955 on R.I.B.A. business when his bedroom filled with gas owing to a fractured main. He was seriously ill and it is doubtful whether he ever completely recovered his previous robust health. He retired in 1958 and died in Hertford 18 April 1959.

In 1920 Aslin married Ethel Fawcett Armitage, also of Sheffield; they had one daughter. His portrait, by Allan Gwynne-Jones, may be seen at the headquarters of the Royal Institute of British Architects.

[Private information; personal knowledge.]
S. MORRISON.

ASQUITH, LADY CYNTHIA MARY EVELYN (1887–1960), writer, eldest daughter of Lord Elcho, later the eleventh Earl of Wemyss, and his wife, Mary Constance, daughter of Percy Scawen Wyndham, was born 27 September 1887 at Clouds, East Knoyle, Wiltshire. Her childhood was unusually happy, spent amid an intelligent and affectionate family and in a home which was one of the most brilliant social centres of the age. Her mother was a leading figure in that circle called 'The Souls' which included among others Curzon, Balfour, her brother, George Wyndham, and Margot Tennant [qq.v.] and which was celebrated as uniting the attractions of intellect and of fashion. In 1910 Cynthia Charteris married Herbert, the second son of H. H. Asquith, later first Earl of Oxford and Asquith [q.v.], the Liberal leader, by whom she had three sons.

After 1914 Lady Cynthia's life was darkened by trouble. She lost two of her brothers, to whom she was devoted, in the war. Further, now that Herbert Asquith was in the army, he was unable to support his family. Lady Cynthia in 1918 accepted an appointment as private secretary to Sir J. M. Barrie [q.v.]. She soon became responsible for running his whole social and domestic life. She went on with this until his death, for Asquith returned from the war with his health too much weakened to take up regular work. She also added to her income by freelance writing. During the next thirty years her publications included anthologies of ghost stories and children's tales, biographies of the Duchess of York (1928) and Princess Elizabeth and Princess Margaret (1937); two novels, The Spring House (1936) and One Sparkling Wave (1943), and a book

of short stories What Dreams May Come (1951).

Barrie died in 1937 leaving her heir to the greater part of his fortune and the Asquiths left London to live first at Sullington in Sussex and afterwards at Bath where Herbert Asquith died in 1947. Lady Cynthia later returned to London. Meanwhile a play of hers about the Tolstoys, entitled No Heaven for Me, had been produced at the Little Theatre, Bristol, in 1947. She published three volumes of reminiscences, Haply I May Remember (1950), Remember and Be Glad (1952), and Portrait of Barrie (1954). A life of Countess Tolstoy, entitled Married to Tolstoy, was published posthumously in 1960 and Lady Cynthia's Diaries (1915–18) in 1968.

Lady Cynthia was a competent writer and her reminiscences, in particular, were an agreeable contribution to contemporary social history. But it was in the sphere of private life that her nature fulfilled itself. Here she was revealed as one of the most interesting and fascinating women of her time. Hauntingly beautiful with a tall, graceful figure, magnolia-white skin, and slanting, elfin glance, her appearance was the true image of a personality at once intimate and mysterious, romantic and ironical, whose conversation was remarkable alike for its poetic sensibility and its infectious unpredictable humour. Further, she had a talent for friendship, more especially with writers and artists, which she assiduously cultivated all her life; with the result that she was a close friend of some of the most distinguished men of the day, including D. H. Lawrence, Sir Desmond MacCarthy, Walter de la Mare, Sir Walter Raleigh, Rex Whistler [qq.v.], L. P. Hartley, and Augustus John. She was never the mistress of a salon, still less a lion huntress: it was unobtrusively in the tête-à-tête interview and the private correspondence that her friendships flourished. They were singularly lasting and untroubled, for Lady Cynthia's character was faithful, discreet, even-tempered, and unpossessive. Although too intelligent to be unaware of her own attractions, she was also too wise to presume upon them. She died in Oxford 31 March 1960.

There is a drawing of her as a child by Burne-Jones in the possession of her family and as a girl by Sargent; also paintings by Augustus John (in the National Gallery of Canada), Ambrose McEvoy, Tonks, and others.

[Personal knowledge.] DAVID CECIL.

ASQUITH, CYRIL, BARON ASQUITH OF
BISHOPSTONE (1890–1954), judge, was
born at Eton House, in what used to be
John Street, Hampstead, 5 February
1890. He was the fourth son and the
youngest of the five children of Herbert
Henry Asquith, later first Earl of Oxford
and Asquith [q.v.], by his first wife, Helen
Melland, daughter of a distinguished
Manchester physician. The daughter became Lady Violet Bonham Carter in 1915
and was created a life peeress in 1964.
Their mother's death in 1891 may have
contributed to the shyness which affected
'Cys', as he was always known to his
friends, throughout his life. From Summer Fields, Oxford, Asquith went as a
scholar to Winchester where he was a
notable player of football. Like his father
and his brother Raymond, he became
a foundation scholar of Balliol College,
Oxford, where he obtained first classes in
classical moderations (1911) and *literae
humaniores* (1913), and won the Hertford,
Craven, and Ireland scholarships. He then
became an Eldon scholar and was elected
a fellow of Magdalen College in 1913. His
reserve kept him from taking the same
active part in college and university
affairs as had his brothers Raymond and
Herbert who had both been president of
the Union. When the war began he immediately volunteered in the Queen's
Westminster Rifles, later being promoted
captain. From 1916 to 1918 he was employed in the Ministry of Munitions.

In 1920 Asquith was called to the bar
by the Inner Temple and became a pupil
in the chambers of W. A. (later Earl)
Jowitt [q.v.], a choice of considerable
significance later in Asquith's career. His
main practice was in the common law
courts. It is surprising that, with his many
qualities, he was not more successful, yet
his father had also been slow in acquiring
a practice. From 1925 to 1938 Asquith was
assistant reader in common law to the
Council of Legal Education. Throughout
his life he showed great interest in the
academic side of the law. He seemed to be
more concerned with legal questions than
with questions of fact. If he found some
difficulty in understanding the ordinary
man, it did not arise from any sense of
class distinction. In 1936 he took silk and
in 1937 he was made recorder of Salisbury
where he obtained useful experience in the
trial of criminal cases.

In 1938 Asquith was appointed a judge
of the King's Bench division (with the
customary knighthood) by the lord chan-

cellor, Lord Maugham [q.v.]. The appointment caused some surprise at the bar,
for his practice had been a comparatively
limited one; but this lack of experience
did not prove a handicap. It was said that
the lord chief justice, Lord Hewart [q.v.],
had felt that he had not been shown sufficient respect in being consulted regarding
Asquith's appointment, and that for this
reason he assigned him to try a number of
notorious criminal cases at the Old Bailey
where an error would have had an unfortunate effect on Asquith's reputation.
It was, however, in the trial of criminal
cases that Asquith proved particularly
successful, because his clarity of expression and his skill in explaining the law
when charging a jury were of special
value. There was some complaint that
he was over-merciful in sentencing the
guilty, but this did not bother him.

In 1946 he was appointed a lord justice
of appeal by C. R. (later Earl) Attlee on
Jowitt's recommendation, and was sworn
of the Privy Council. His knowledge of the
law, coupled with his delightful literary
quotations and his flashes of humour,
gave distinction to his judgements. Of
these, perhaps the most frequently quoted
are *Victoria Laundry (Windsor) Ltd.* v.
Newman Industries Ltd., [1949] 2 K.B.
528, in which he stated the law concerning
the measure of damages on the breach of
a contract; *Thurogood* v. *Van Den Berghs
& Jurgens*, [1951] 2 K.B. 537, on the
measure of damages in tort; and *Candler*
v. *Crane, Christmas & Co.*, [1951] 2 K.B.
164, in which he replied to his friend Lord
Denning's remark that 'there were the
timorous souls who were fearful of allowing a new cause of action' by saying 'If
this relegates me to the company of
"timorous souls", I must face that consequence with such fortitude as I can command.'

In 1951 Asquith became a lord of appeal
in ordinary, with a life peerage, again
on Jowitt's recommendation. It was remarked that 'the higher he went the better
he became'. He held this post for only
three years before he died, but during that
time he gave a number of judgements of
great interest. In *Bank of New South
Wales* v. *Laing*, [1954] A.C. 135, he delivered the decision of the Judicial Committee of the Privy Council on a difficult
procedural point concerning the onus of
proof in an *indebitatus assumpsit* count.
His two dissenting judgements in *King*
v. *King*, [1953] A.C. 124, and in *Stapley*
v. *Gypsum Mines Ltd.*, [1953] A.C. 663,

illustrate the clarity and liveliness of his style.

The most remarkable moment in Asquith's life came in October 1951 when (Sir) Winston Churchill offered him the lord chancellorship. He refused it, to the deep disappointment of the few persons who had heard about the offer, and Asquith himself never referred to it again. The offer was unexpected, since Asquith had no political experience which would have aided him in presiding in the House of Lords as a legislative body. Perhaps Churchill's choice was influenced in part by the fact that Asquith was the son of the prime minister under whom he had first served in the Cabinet; it may also have been due in part to the fact that they were fellow members of The Other Club, where they often met at dinner, and where Churchill had an opportunity to judge Asquith's brilliance of mind. But Asquith was far too high-minded to accept a post which he felt he was not strong enough physically to perform adequately. In a letter to his son-in-law (Sir) John Stephenson he insisted that Churchill 'mustn't be saddled with a lame duck on the Woolsack'.

Apart from his judicial career, Asquith filled a number of posts of importance. He became a member of the lord chancellor's Law Revision Committee in 1934. He was the high court judge attached to the General Claims Tribunal (1939) and he was chairman for six months in 1940 of the advisory committee on aliens. He was chairman of the commission on higher education in the colonies, 1943–4, and chairman of the royal commission on equal pay for equal work, 1944–6. This particularly onerous assignment gave rise to some complaints concerning the length of time that the commission sat, but the report when finally issued justified the work done in preparing it.

Asquith must have been one of the major contributors to The Times in the number of letters he wrote to it and in the unsigned leaders. They varied from extreme seriousness to delightful humour. Most of the leaders concerned possible reforms in the law and dealt with such subjects as 'The Cost of Litigation', 'Reforming the Law', 'The Legal Machine', and 'The Law relating to Married Women'.

Asquith's publications included Trade Union Law for Laymen (1927) which achieved a popular success; Versions from 'A Shropshire Lad' (1930), a translation into Latin of poems by A. E. Housman

[q.v.] which was less popular but received the approval of his former Balliol tutor, Cyril Bailey [q.v.]; and in 1932 with J. A. Spender [q.v.] the life of his father. About half the first volume, which deals with his father's early and family life, was written by Asquith, and a smaller part of the second volume; they would probably have been more successful if he had written the whole of them.

His conversation and his writings have been described as showing 'the same deliberation, dry humour and careful choice of words that marked his father's style'. Cyril Asquith was himself an illustration of his father's famous remark concerning 'the effortless superiority of Balliol men'. Like his father he was elected an honorary fellow of the college.

In 1918 Asquith married Anne Stephanie (died 1964), daughter of (Sir) Adrian Donald Wilde Pollock, chamberlain of the City of London; they had two sons and two daughters. He died in London 24 August 1954.

A portrait by Honor Earl is in the possession of the family.

[Private information; personal knowledge.]
A. L. GOODHART.

ASTOR, WALDORF, second VISCOUNT ASTOR (1879–1952), public servant, was born in New York 19 May 1879, the elder son of William Waldorf (later first Viscount) Astor, who settled in England in 1889 and was naturalized ten years later, and his wife, Mary Dahlgren Paul, of Philadelphia. He had a distinguished career at Eton where he won the Prince Consort's first French prize (1897), was captain of the boats (1898), and one of the editors of the Eton College Chronicle. He went on to New College, Oxford, where he obtained a fourth class in history (1902) and represented the university at polo, steeplechasing, and sabres.

In 1906 Astor married Mrs. Nancy Witcher Shaw (died 1964), daughter of Chiswell Dabney Langhorne, of Virginia. She was one of the sisters whose grace and beauty were made famous by the artist Charles Dana Gibson who was himself married to one of them. His father gave them as a wedding present his house Cliveden, built by Sir Charles Barry [q.v.] in 1850, overlooking the Thames.

After a defeat in January 1910 Astor entered Parliament in December as a Unionist member for Plymouth. In the following year, 1911, his father bought the Sunday newspaper, the Observer, from

Lord Northcliffe [q.v.]. Since his father lived mainly in Italy, Astor, as the man on the spot, became in many ways the *de facto* proprietor, especially in matters relating to editorial policy. A close political co-operation with the editor, J. L. Garvin [q.v.], developed. Ownership of the paper enhanced Astor's influence as a young Tory member of Parliament. In other ways, too, he widened his influence. He was a prominent member of the Round Table group concerned with the advancement of imperial unity which included his brother-in-law Lord Brand; and Lionel Curtis, Philip Kerr (later Marquess of Lothian), and Edward Grigg (later Lord Altrincham) [qq.v.]. These remained his friends and political associates for many years.

In 1914, because of poor health contracted as a young man, he was unable to join the armed forces and served as an inspector of ordnance factories for which he was mentioned in dispatches. His political career prospered. He became successively parliamentary private secretary to the prime minister, Lloyd George (1917), parliamentary secretary to the Ministry of Food (1918) and to the Ministry of Health (1919–21). Meanwhile in 1916 his father was created a baron and in 1917 a viscount, and on his death in 1919 Astor had to resign his seat. He endeavoured to decline the title in order to remain in the House of Commons, but this proved to be legally impossible. His wife stood for the Sutton division of Plymouth in his stead and was elected, and thereby became the first woman to take her seat in the British Parliament, thus beginning a career which was to make her one of the most widely known public figures in Britain.

Although after a few years Astor gave up political office, he did not give up his political interests but pursued them through other channels. He remained proprietor of the *Observer*. He was an original member of the Royal Institute of International Affairs (Chatham House) and served as chairman of its study groups committee and later as chairman of council (1935–49). He was an active supporter of the League of Nations, and was a British delegate to the Assembly in 1931. He developed his lifelong special interest in agriculture. He was the joint author with Keith Murray (later Lord Murray of Newhaven) of *Land and Life* (1932). In the following year, also with Murray, he published *The Planning of Agriculture* and in 1938 *British Agriculture* to which

B. Seebohm Rowntree [q.v.] and others contributed. After the war, with Rowntree, he published *Mixed Farming and Muddled Thinking* (1946). In 1936 Astor became chairman of the joint committee of agricultural, economic, and health experts appointed by the League of Nations, the progenitor of the subsequent United Nations Food and Agricultural Organization.

Cliveden, situated conveniently halfway between Oxford and London, was a week-end rendezvous for politicians, journalists, and dons. In the late thirties those who regularly gathered there as the guests of the Astors became popularly known as the 'Cliveden set'. They included the prime minister, Neville Chamberlain, the editor of *The Times*, Geoffrey Dawson [q.v.], and Lord Lothian who was later ambassador in Washington. They were the people who believed, in varying degrees, in the general thesis that a second world war could be averted by making restitution to Hitler's Germany for the disabilities laid upon her by the treaty of Versailles. The opponents of this policy of 'appeasement' as it came to be known claimed that members of this group, meeting as they did regularly at Cliveden, were exercising an undue and even unconstitutional influence on foreign policy. As those who met regularly at Cliveden were people holding key positions of power in the country it was natural that they influenced policy, but their conduct was neither unconstitutional nor unprecedented in English history. Nevertheless in 1938 Astor felt it necessary to rebut the charges in a letter to *The Times*.

While engaged in these wider activities, Astor did not neglect Plymouth, for which his wife remained the sitting member until 1945. He built a housing estate there which bore his name. He founded Virginia House as a social centre for women and girls: besides playing fields, an institute and a university hall of residence. After the war of 1939–45, during which Plymouth was severely damaged by bombing he played a leading part in planning its reconstruction. He was made an honorary freeman of the city in 1936 and was lord mayor in 1939–44.

In 1942 Astor parted company with Garvin. During the latter years of the partnership there had been mounting difficulties. Garvin had been editor of the *Observer* for over thirty years and Astor was looking to the succession. There was an open breach when Garvin wrote an article in the *Observer* dealing with the higher direction of the war; his views were in direct opposition to Astor's. The tribunal which existed to adjudicate on the relations between them decided against Garvin. In 1945 Astor set up a trust, which was to own all the shares in the *Observer* and to devote the income to charitable purposes, chiefly connected with newspapers or journalism.

One of Astor's abiding interests throughout his life was his racing stable. While at Oxford he bought the mare Conjure, and later Popinjay and Maid of the Mist. From these brood mares and their stock were bred the winners of eleven classic races. His horses ran second in the Derby five times, but he never succeeded in winning it. The building up of one of the best-known studs in the country from scratch was his personal consideration, the fruit of much study and care.

Born to great wealth and the first of his line to be brought up in England from an early age, Astor devoted his energies to public service, without asking or expecting reward or recognition. He was a good, modest, and dedicated man, who in the public eye was inevitably overshadowed by the powerful and vivid personality of his wife. In agriculture he possessed especial expertise and his views were ahead of his time. He was a committee man, rather than an individualist, and for this reason his influence on affairs was not always easy to trace. One result, as in the case of the 'Cliveden set' myth, was that responsibility was sometimes attributed to him for views or actions which he would not necessarily have agreed with in their entirety, particularly in their more extreme expressions. In youth an outstanding games player and sportsman, he was addicted to country pursuits, but ill health put a limit on his activity. Like his wife, he was a Christian Scientist.

Astor died at Cliveden 30 September 1952 and was succeeded by his eldest son, William Waldorf (1907–66). His second son, David Astor, became editor of the *Observer* in 1948. He had two other sons, both of whom served as members of Parliament, and a daughter (the Countess of Ancaster).

A portrait of Astor by (Sir) James Gunn hangs in the Astor Room in Chatham House. Another, in lord mayor's robes, by the same artist hangs in the Astor Room at the Guildhall, Plymouth, and a copy of this, in ordinary dress, is in the boardroom of the *Observer*. A portrait by P. A.

de László is at Cliveden which in 1942 was handed over to the National Trust.

[*The Times*, 1 October 1952; Michael Astor, *Tribal Feeling*, 1963; Alfred M. Gollin, *The Observer and J. L. Garvin, 1908–14*, 1960; private information.]   OLIVER WOODS.

ATHLONE, EARL OF (1874–1957). [See CAMBRIDGE, ALEXANDER AUGUSTUS FREDERICK WILLIAM ALFRED GEORGE.]

ATHOLL, DUCHESS OF (1874–1960), public servant. [See STEWART-MURRAY, KATHARINE MARJORY.]

ATKINS, SIR IVOR ALGERNON (1869–1953), organist and choirmaster, the fifth child and third son of Frederick Pyke Atkins, professor of music and for many years organist of St. John's, Cardiff, by his wife, Harriet Maria Rogers, was born 29 November 1869 at Llandaff. He was educated privately before passing into the hands of Charles Lee Williams at Llandaff Cathedral. In 1885 he became pupil-assistant to George Robertson Sinclair and served in that capacity at the cathedrals of Truro and (from 1890) at Hereford. In 1892 he matriculated, through the Queen's College, Oxford, as a non-resident musical scholar, and was admitted to the degree of bachelor of music. Thus qualified, he was appointed, in 1893, organist of Ludlow parish church. There he enlarged his experience, and in 1897 he was appointed organist at Worcester Cathedral, a post carrying with it the duty of conducting the triennial festival of the Three Choirs.

At first conditions at Worcester were not easy. His taste was offended by the facile music which bulked large in the repertory. And it was not until the Edwardian decade was drawing to its close that Atkins's views prevailed. Then, in his zeal for reform, he discarded much Victorian music and by 1930 had revived the works of his Tudor predecessors, Thomas Tomkins [q.v.] and Nathaniel Patrick. He also showed proofs of his scholarship by reviving the use of portions of the thirteenth-century *Worcester Antiphonar* and producing for the Worcestershire Historical Society an account of the early organists of Worcester Cathedral (1918); by a preface to *Worcester Mediaeval Harmony* (1928), and (with Neil R. Ker) the *Catalogus Librorum Manuscriptorum Bibliothecae Wigorniensis 1622–23* (1944).

Atkins was cathedral librarian for twenty years (1933–53) and was elected F.S.A. in 1921.

He was an excellent organist but his daily work did not involve the regular exercise of a conductor's skill. During his first festival in 1899 his conducting was criticized adversely; notwithstanding, from 1902 onwards his great powers of organization and all-round musicianship carried him through. His greatest service to the festival, enlarging the repertory, was the fruit of broad musical sympathies. In 1902, while the repercussions of the secession of John Henry Newman [q.v.], were still felt, his courageous introduction of *The Dream of Gerontius* was the beginning of the close association of (Sir) Edward Elgar [q.v.] with the Three Choirs. In the same year he gave a first festival commission to (Sir) Walford Davies [q.v.], thus inaugurating the enterprising policy with regard to new works which distinguished all his programmes.

Atkins's love of Bach was supreme. He produced a valuable edition of the *Orgelbüchlein* (1916) and, with Elgar, prepared an edition of the *St. Matthew Passion* (1911), and established that work as a regular feature of the festival. He also edited the *St. John Passion* (1929), Brahms's *Requiem* (1947), and the *Worcester Psalter* (1948). Although not ambitious as a composer, he produced a cantata, 'Hymn of Faith' (1905), and several anthems, services, and songs.

In 1914 the declaration of war led to a break in the sequence of the festivals which lasted for six years. Many influential persons felt that it would be impossible to revive them. But in 1920 Atkins undertook the immense task. The revived festival at Worcester was almost entirely his own creation and its success brought the honour of knighthood in the following year.

Thereafter, until he conducted his last festival at Worcester in 1948, his life was uneventful and his employment never varied. At Easter 1950 he retired.

Atkins became an honorary R.A.M. in 1910; doctor of music in 1920; a fellow of St. Michael's College, Tenbury Wells, in 1921. He was president of the Royal College of Organists in 1934–6.

In 1899 Atkins married Katharine May Dorothea, daughter of the Rev. Edward Butler, of Llangoed Castle, and had one son. Atkins died at Worcester 26 November 1953. Lady Atkins, who was prominent in the life of the city and the first woman to become high sheriff of Worcester, died in 1954.

[Watkins Shaw, *The Three Choirs Festival*, 1954; *Grove's Dictionary of Music and Musicians*; *Berrow's Worcester Journal*, passim; personal knowledge.]   A. T. SHAW.

ATKINSON, SIR EDWARD HALE TINDAL (1878–1957), lawyer, was born in Beckenham 19 September 1878, the only son of Henry Tindal Atkinson, county court judge, by his wife, Marion Amy Lewin, and grandson of Henry Tindal Atkinson, serjeant-at-law. (Sir) Edward Tindal Atkinson, his uncle, became chancellor of the county palatine of Durham; all were members of the Middle Temple. Atkinson was educated at Harrow and at Trinity College, Oxford, where he lodged in the Garden Quad., and was known to his friends as 'Tatters'. He obtained a third in classical honour moderations (1899) and a second in modern history (1901). Inevitably, he joined the Middle Temple; he was called in 1902. He practised in chambers and joined the South-Eastern circuit and the Herts. and Essex sessions. The greater part of his practice consisted of rating and local government work and to a lesser degree taxation, fields in which he built up a substantial practice.

Atkinson was elected to the Bar Council in 1913 and served until 1921. His practice was interrupted by the war when he enlisted in 1917 as a lieutenant in the Royal Naval Volunteer Reserve and was transferred as a captain to the Royal Air Force in 1918, being promoted major in 1919. He went to Paris as legal adviser to the air section of the British delegation at the peace conference and became British secretary to the International Air Commission. For his work he was appointed C.B.E. and received the French Legion of Honour.

Returning to his chambers in 1920 he soon built up a substantial practice again. In 1928–30 he was an additional member of the Bar Council. In 1929 he followed in his father's footsteps as a bencher of the Middle Temple; and in the same year he was appointed the first recorder of Southend-on-Sea. In March 1930 he was appointed director of public prosecutions, somewhat unexpectedly and very much to his own surprise. Invited to visit the Home Office to discuss 'a certain matter', he went convinced that he had made some fearful blunder as recorder; when it was suggested that he should become director he refused to believe it, walked out of the room, and had to be fetched back.

Once in the director's chair, Atkinson displayed his extraordinary grip of law. His experience of criminal practice was limited and at almost a moment's notice he was now called upon to devote his days exclusively to the criminal law. He knew none of his staff and few of the counsel engaged in that type of work. His predecessor, Sir Archibald Bodkin [q.v.], one of the most experienced criminal lawyers in the country, was a difficult man to follow. But Atkinson soon showed that his knowledge of criminal law was considerably greater than was at first thought. During his first two years he was haunted by the fear that he was not making a success of his appointment; later he described this period as the most unpleasant of his life. His doubts disappeared as his experience widened, particularly after he was appointed K.C.B. in 1932. Soon he became involved in the preparation of possible wartime legislation. The defence regulations in use throughout and subsequent to the war were in no small measure the result of his advice. During the war he was deeply involved in many serious and important cases including, of course, all the spy cases. He expressed personal sympathy for enemy nationals who were caught but had no patience with British subjects who assisted the enemy.

Atkinson was a modest man with a quiet sense of humour who treated his staff with a rather shy courtesy. He was an excellent example of a gentle man: he never lost his temper or raised his voice; he was polite and considerate; he was also extremely generous, but this he was at great pains to conceal. To a member of his department who had suffered a great disappointment he gave a cheque, pointing out that it was post-dated by ten days, because he was satisfied that if the recipient was going to mention the matter he would do so within that period, whereupon the cheque would be stopped.

When Atkinson had time to consider a legal problem in detail he could write an opinion which was a masterpiece of clarity. But when he was expected to give a 'snap' judgement he often had to alter it on reconsideration. He was most reluctant to express such an opinion unless specifically asked and in that event his advice was sometimes at fault because of his uncertainty. He retired in 1944 and in the following year was appointed chairman of the central price regulation committee which was set up under the Prices of Goods Act, 1939. It was the duty of this committee to advise the Board of Trade on orders to be made under the Act and to supervise the enforcement of the provisions of the 1919 Act and the orders made thereunder. His advice and experience on the enforcement of price control legislation were invaluable. Here again his shyness and reluctance to express anything other than a carefully considered opinion made his work in negotiating fair prices with trade associations more arduous than was necessary. He remained chairman of the committee until it was dissolved in April 1953.

In 1948 Atkinson exceeded the records of his father and grandfather and followed his uncle by becoming treasurer of his Inn; he has the distinction—with two other treasurers—of having his initials carved in the stonework of the entrance of the Middle Temple hall to commemorate the fact that all three held office during the period of post-war restoration.

Atkinson died in Windsor, after an accident, 26 December 1957. He was unmarried.

[Private information; personal knowledge.]
F. D. BARRY.

AUBREY, MELBOURN EVANS (1885–1957), Baptist minister, the eldest child of the Rev. Edwin Aubrey by his wife, Elizabeth Jane Evans, was born in the Rhondda 21 April 1885. His father was then pastor of Zion Baptist church, Pentre, and subsequently ministered in Abercarn, Glasgow, and Merthyr Tydfil. Aubrey's boyhood was therefore set amid changing scenes. He early heard the call to the Christian ministry and, after proving himself an able student at Cardiff Baptist College, went on in 1908 to Mansfield College, Oxford, where A. M. Fairbairn [q.v.] was nearing the end of his principalship. In 1911 Aubrey was ordained to the ministry at Victoria Road church, Leicester, as assistant to P. T. Thomson, a man of great ability and charm, who became his lifelong friend. After only eighteen months there he was persuaded to undertake the pastorate of the historic Baptist church in St. Andrew's Street, Cambridge, to which Robert Robinson and Robert Hall [qq.v.] at one time ministered. Aubrey's gifts as a preacher and speaker matured quickly and in spite of the difficulties brought by the war of 1914–18 he drew large congregations, which included many students and others connected with the university. T. R. Glover [q.v.], of St. John's College, became a deacon of the church and Aubrey was one of the first consulted about the addresses which became *The Jesus of History* (1917).

In 1925, after twelve happy years in Cambridge, Aubrey was chosen to succeed J. H. Shakespeare as secretary of the Baptist Union of Great Britain and Ireland. He faced no easy task for Shakespeare's health had given way some time before and the mind of the denomination was confused and uncertain as a result of sharp differences of opinion on Church union. The first annual assembly for which Aubrey was responsible coincided with the general strike. His immediate task was the raising of a ministerial superannuation fund of £300,000. Thereafter he had to guide the Baptist denomination during the economic, constitutional, and international crises which preceded the second world war, a period when almost all the British Churches suffered severe losses from their membership. But he was a man of courage, wisdom, and resource, deeply devoted to his task, and his powers of leadership were soon recognized beyond the borders of his own denomination. In 1936 he was appointed moderator of the Federal Council of the Evangelical Free Churches and in 1937 he was made a C.H.

Aubrey was closely involved in the ecumenical movement and in 1937 was a prominent figure at the Oxford conference on Church, Community, and State and the Edinburgh Faith and Order conference. As a member of the Committee of Fourteen, he helped to draft the constitution of the World Council of Churches. During the war years of 1939–45 his steadiness and faith proved an inspiration to his colleagues at the Baptist Church House and to the churches in all parts of the country. He took a close interest in the work of Baptist and Congregational chaplains and during a visit to the Mediterranean and the Near East he interviewed many servicemen whose thoughts were turning to the ministry. He had been appointed chairman of the Churches' Committee for Christian Reconstruction in Europe and was one of the first British churchmen to visit Germany at the close of hostilities. In 1947 he was appointed a member of the royal commission on the press and in the same year, during a visit to Canada and the United States, received an honorary LL.D. from McMaster University and an honorary D.C.L. from

Acadia University. From 1948 to 1950 he was a vice-president of the British Council of Churches, in the formation of which he had taken a deep interest. From 1948 to 1954 he served on the central committee of the World Council of Churches. For twenty-seven years he was a member of the executive of the Baptist World Alliance.

These manifold activities did not deflect Aubrey from his constant concern for the spiritual welfare of the Baptist churches and the needs of ministers in this country. In his personality strength, spiritual passion, and tenderness were blended. He was gifted both as a preacher and as an administrator and, without ever concealing his own convictions, successfully held together the diverse elements in the Baptist denomination during a period of no little difficulty. His services gained for him widespread confidence and gratitude, and on the eve of his retirement he was unanimously called to the presidency of the Baptist Union for 1950–51. There followed further visits to the United States, where a number of members of his family had settled, including his brother, Dr. Edwin Ewart Aubrey, one time president of Crozer Seminary.

Aubrey married in 1912 Edith Maria, daughter of Joseph G. Moore, a furniture dealer, of Watford, and by her had one son and one daughter. He died in Godalming 18 October 1957. A portrait by Frank O. Salisbury hangs in the library of the Baptist Church House, London.

[E. A. Payne, *The Baptist Union: A Short History*, 1959; personal knowledge.]

E. A. PAYNE.

AUSTIN, JOHN LANGSHAW (1911–1960), philosopher, was born in Lancaster 28 March 1911, the second son of Geoffrey Langshaw Austin, architect, of St. Andrews, and his wife, Mary Bowes-Wilson. He was educated at Shrewsbury School and Balliol College, Oxford, of which he was a classical scholar, winning the Gaisford prize (1931) and obtaining first classes in honour moderations (1931) and *literae humaniores* (1933). He was a fellow of All Souls (1933), fellow and tutor in philosophy of Magdalen (1935), and from 1952 White's professor of moral philosophy and fellow of Corpus Christi. He was junior proctor in 1949–50 and was appointed a delegate of the Oxford University Press in 1952, serving as chairman of its finance committee from 1957 until his death. In 1955 he delivered the William James lectures at

Harvard University and in 1958 was visiting professor at the university of California in Berkeley. He was elected F.B.A. in 1958 and was president of the Aristotelian Society in 1956–7. During the war of 1939–45 he served in the Intelligence Corps, from 1944 in S.H.A.E.F., reaching the rank of lieutenant-colonel. In 1945 he was appointed O.B.E., received the croix de guerre, and was made an officer of the Legion of Merit.

When war broke out in 1939 Austin had taught philosophy for only four years and had published only one philosophical paper ('Are there *a priori* Concepts?', 1939), but his power, originality, and critical acumen were already respected by his contemporaries and by many of his seniors. From 1946 when he returned to Oxford until his death at the age of forty-eight, his was the most powerful single influence on the development of philosophy in Oxford. It was also widely felt in the universities of America and the Commonwealth. He was a gifted teacher and his lectures and classes were eagerly attended; but his influence was perhaps most seminally exercised in regular informal meetings for philosophical discussion attended by a varying group of philosophy dons. He regarded discussion not only as the best but as an indispensable instrument of progress in philosophy; and though he was utterly without pomp or pretension his intellectual power, serene lucidity, and astringent wit conferred on him a natural authority in any gathering of philosophers. He believed that by such co-operative discussion, conducted with sufficient care for detail, step-by-step progress could be made and recordable solutions of philosophical problems reached.

Austin believed that philosophers had altogether underestimated the subtlety and complexity of ordinary language and neglected the important distinctions incorporated in it; and he thought it one of the main tasks of philosophy to bring these to light by patient and minute inquiries conducted without theoretical preconceptions. Much philosophical discussion, e.g. of the problems of perception, was, in his view, condemned to end in inconclusiveness, irrelevance, or incoherence because it was conducted in a technical classificatory language such as that of 'sense datum' and 'material object' which had been hastily and uncritically adopted and had obscured vital differences in the phenomena which were the subject of conflicting theories. A new start was required in which expressions such as 'looks', 'seems', 'appears', 'illusion', 'delusion' were carefully discriminated, and (in his words) 'a sharpened awareness' obtained both of these expressions and the facts to which they refer. Such a new start Austin made in his lectures on perception given under the title (a characteristic joke) of 'Sense and Sensibilia'. The reconstruction of these lectures made by G. J. Warnock from Austin's notes was published under the same title in 1962.

Much of Austin's work was destructively critical and the object of his criticism was often some technical term which he thought too coarse-grained to be fit for use in philosophy. But he was not solely concerned to criticize nor was he in the least averse from the introduction of technical classificatory terms in order to exhibit important features of language previously neglected. His most constructive work in fact made much use of these in a systematic classification of 'speech acts' outlined in his William James lectures and published posthumously in 1962 under the title of *How to do Things with Words*. Here Austin reconsidered with impressive detachment a distinction which he himself had earlier introduced ('Other Minds', 1946) between statements susceptible of assessment as true or false ('constatives') and a class of utterances not so assessed which he termed 'performative' because they are best understood as the performance of an action by the use of words (such as 'I hereby bequeath'). Austin's further examination of this distinction led him to absorb the performative aspect of language into a general classificatory theory exhibiting the various senses and ways in which in saying something we are also doing something else. This theory is likely to illumine many different philosophical problems.

Austin himself published only seven papers and these together with three previously unpublished essays were posthumously published under the title of *Philosophical Papers* in 1961. Two of these, 'Ifs and Cans' (1956) and 'A Plea for Excuses' (1956), contain his important and widely discussed contributions to the philosophical study of human action, responsibility, and freedom. He was also a talented classical scholar and in earlier years frequently lectured on philosophical problems in Plato and Aristotle.

Austin was a skilled and devoted administrator whose services were much valued for the same qualities of inventiveness, acumen, and integrity which distinguished his philosophical work. He was often reserved in manner and on occasions formidable. But he had great natural courtesy, gaiety, and charm, and much manifest benevolence, especially for his pupils. His intellectual daring, power, and wit made his company a constant source of pleasure as well as of instruction.

In 1941 Austin married Jean, daughter of the late C. R. V. Coutts, actuary, by whom he had two sons and two daughters. He died in Oxford 8 February 1960.

[*Times Literary Supplement*, 9 February 1962; G. J. Warnock in *Proceedings* of the British Academy, vol. xlix, 1963; private information; personal knowledge.]

H. L. A. HART.

AZAD, MAULANA ABUL KALAM (1888–1958), Indian minister of education, whose original name was Ahmad, was born at Mecca 11 November 1888, in an Indian family of scholars, several of whom had held high position under the Mogul emperors. His father, Maulana Khairuddin, had migrated to Mecca, where he married the daughter of Sheikh Mohammed Zaher who was a well-known scholar of Medina, and himself became well known throughout the Islamic world after an Arabic work of his in ten volumes was published in Egypt. When Ahmad was two years old his father returned to India and settled in Calcutta where before his death in 1909 he had attracted many disciples throughout India. Ahmad, who had two sisters and one brother older to him and a younger sister, was taught at home according to the traditional system of education for orthodox Moslems in India. He was taught first Persian, then Arabic. Then came philosophy, geometry, arithmetic, algebra, and Islamic theology. He completed his studies at the unusually early age of sixteen and soon afterwards adopted Abul Kalam Azad as his pen name. In view of his learning and scholarship he was acclaimed as a Maulana (Teacher), by which name he became known throughout India and beyond.

It was about this time that Maulana Azad came across the writings of Sir Syed Ahmed Khan and was greatly impressed by his views on modern education and his interpretation of the Koran. He decided to study English and this led to an intellectual crisis. Born in an orthodox family where traditions were accepted without question, Maulana Azad became a rebel and sought to find out the truth for himself. The differences among the sects of Moslems increased his scepticism. The impact of western ideas also led him to political activity. Believing that literature and philosophy can flourish only in an atmosphere of freedom, he was attracted by the revolutionary movement sweeping through Bengal after the partition of 1905 and joined one of the revolutionary groups. He regarded it as one of his first tasks to draw Moslems into the Indian political struggle. When he was about twenty he toured extensively in the Middle East, and these travels strengthened his conviction that independence was necessary not only for the sake of India but also for the liberation of the whole of western Asia.

In June 1912 Maulana Azad started *Al Hilal*, a weekly paper in Urdu which marks the turning-point in the history of Urdu journalism which hitherto had had hardly any influence on public opinion. The vigour of his political views and the power of his style led to an unprecedented success for the journal. He had already been recognized as a promising poet, but even before he went abroad he had decided that he must devote himself to political and religious writing. In fact he achieved a fusion between the poet's passion and the scholar's erudition, so that his style set a new model for Urdu prose. All his writings were marked by a strong note of nationalism and created a revolutionary stir among the masses. Maulana Azad had accepted Sir Syed's educational programme but in *Al Hilal* he challenged his political policies. The Government was disturbed by the success of *Al Hilal* and in 1915 confiscated its press. Maulana Azad then started a new journal called *Al Balagh*. The Government retorted by externing him from Calcutta in April 1916 and soon after interned him at Ranchi. He was released in January 1920. In this period he wrote his *Tazkirah*, a new style of writing which introduced belles-lettres into Urdu literature, and he also prepared the first draft of his famous translation, with commentary, of the Koran. Unfortunately the manuscript was lost through the action of the police and he had to undertake the work afresh after release. He had planned to complete the work in three volumes and follow it by a critical study, but owing to the uncertainties of political life he was able to publish only two volumes. Nevertheless, many scholars regard it as the most important commentary written on the Koran in the last three hundred years. It has since been translated into English.

Soon after his release Maulana Azad went to Delhi and became one of the leading figures in the non-co-operation movement launched by M. K. Gandhi [q.v.]. He was again imprisoned. After his release in January 1923 he was elected president of the special session of the Congress held at Delhi in September. He was then thirty-five, the youngest man to be elected to this office. Thereafter his life centred round the Indian political struggle. He took part in the civil disobedience movement of 1930, was imprisoned, but released in 1934. When, after the elections of 1937, Congress decided to accept office in the provinces, it was decided that there should be a small parliamentary board of three to supervise the work of the provincial Congress ministries. Maulana Azad was one of the members and placed in charge of parliamentary affairs in Bengal, Bihar, United Provinces, Punjab, Sind, and the North-West Frontier Province. Soon after the outbreak of war in 1939 Congress ministers in the provinces resigned and Congress leaders, including Maulana Azad, were again arrested. In 1940 he was elected president of Congress for the second time and held that office until June 1946, the longest period that anyone had held that office continuously; but much of this period was passed in jail. With Gandhi and other leaders he was arrested in August 1942 immediately after the Congress had passed the 'quit India' resolution. He remained in the Ahmednagar Fort jail until June 1945. There he wrote *Ghubar-i-Khatir*, which contains some of the most exquisite personal essays in Urdu or any other Indian language.

Maulana Azad was the chief spokesman of Congress during the mission under Sir Stafford Cripps [q.v.] in 1942, the Simla conference convened by Lord Wavell [q.v.] in 1945, and the more successful cabinet mission under Lord Pethick-Lawrence in 1946. In spite of requests from many quarters he did not join the provisional government in September 1946, but later became education minister of India in January 1947. There were many suggestions of some other portfolio, but he considered education to be the most important instrument for nation-building after the attainment of independence in August 1947. Accordingly, he held this office until his death at Delhi 22 February 1958, and was the chief archi-

tect of the educational policy of new India.

Maulana Azad was an intellectual in politics who sought to judge everything in the light of reason. Trained in traditional oriental learning, he welcomed the knowledge of science and technology contributed by the West. He was mainly responsible for sponsoring a *History of Philosophy: Eastern & Western* (2 vols., 1952–3) and was the founder-president of the Indian Council for Cultural Relations, which has a portrait of him by K. K. Hebbar. Another by the same artist is in the Central Hall of Parliament and the Delhi corporation has one by Satish Gujral.

Maulana Azad married Zuleikha Begum (died 1944), the daughter of a government official; they had one son who died young.

[Private information; personal knowledge.]
HUMAYUN KABIR.

BADELEY, HENRY JOHN FANSHAWE, BARON BADELEY (1874–1951), clerk of the Parliaments and engraver, was born at Elswick, Newcastle upon Tyne, 27 June 1874, the elder child and only son of Captain Henry Badeley, of Guy Harlings, Chelmsford, and his wife, Blanche, daughter of Christian Augustus Henry Allhusen, of Elswick Hall, and of Stoke Court, Stoke Poges. He was educated at Radley College and Trinity College, Oxford, of which in 1948 he became an honorary fellow. Here his small energetic figure, which changed but little throughout his life, marked him for athletics, and in the years 1895 to 1897 he was chosen to represent his university in the quarter mile against Cambridge. Rowing also became one of Badeley's accomplishments, although golf remained his favourite form of relaxation.

In 1897 Badeley won first place in a Civil Service competition for a clerkship in the Parliament Office, and in that year began a career remarkable for its loyalty to, and affection for, the institution which he served. He eagerly threw himself into his official life and, when not employed on his routine work, was often found helping the lord chancellor's secretaries, and building an interest in matters parliamentary, legal, and heraldic. It was in the last of these interests that Badeley first made his mark.

After studying under (Sir) Frank Short [q.v.] at the Royal College of Art, Badeley was elected an associate of the Royal Society of Painter-Etchers and Engravers, and was almost at once appointed honorary

secretary (1911–21). In 1914 he was elected
a fellow and exhibited regularly until his
death. His combined interest in heraldry
and line-engraving turned his talent for
the latter towards the engraving of bookplates. His work in this field became
widely known and he executed commissions for a large number of individuals and
institutions, which included plates for the
library of the House of Lords.

In 1919 Badeley became principal clerk
of the Judicial Office and judicial taxing
officer of the House of Lords. Here his
energy and capacity for making personal
contacts soon enabled him to break
through formalities, and he became the
adviser both of the lord chancellor of the
day and of the law lords as well as of all
those members of the legal profession
whose business brought them to the
House.

The turning-point of Badeley's career
came in 1930 when he was appointed clerk
assistant of the Parliaments, while retaining the principal judicial clerkship.
This was the first known promotion to the
Table of the House of Lords from the staff
of the Parliament Office, and opened for
Badeley himself and for his successors
an avenue to the top of their profession.
Badeley strode this avenue in four years,
and in 1934 became clerk of the Parliaments. He was clearly suited for this
office, although his qualifications differed
somewhat from those of his predecessors.
His strength lay in the force of his personality, coupled with a quick intelligence
and a broad practical knowledge of parliamentary affairs.

Badeley was appointed K.C.B. in 1935.
He had also been made C.B.E. in 1920 for
his work as county director of auxiliary
hospitals and voluntary aid detachments
in the county of London (1917–19).
From 1919 to 1923 he was president of
the county of London branch of the
British Red Cross Society.

On reaching the age of seventy in 1944,
Badeley was due to retire but the House
had no wish to lose such a valuable servant whose vigour was in no way
diminished, and Badeley was granted by
the Crown an extension of five years.
When this final term of service was completed he was created (1949) a member of
the House he had served so well, with the
title of Baron Badeley, of Badley, in the
county of Suffolk.

The position he had attained in the
parliamentary world may perhaps best be
summarized in the words of the Marquess
of Salisbury on the occasion of Badeley's
retirement: 'In an age when a great many
things have altered, he has appeared to
be the one unchanging element, and that
shrewd, kindly face has seemed as much a
part of the House of Lords as the Table at
which he sat. But for the fact that he did
not technically qualify, I think he might
certainly have been described as the
Father of the House.'

Badeley died in London 27 September
1951. He was unmarried and the peerage
became extinct.

[Private information; personal knowledge.]
VICTOR GOODMAN.

BAILEY, CYRIL (1871–1957), classical
scholar, was born in Kensington 13 April
1871, the eldest son of Alfred Bailey,
barrister-at-law and some time Stowell
law fellow of University College, Oxford,
and his wife, Fanny Margaret, eldest
daughter of George Coles, of the firm of
Warne & Co., rubber merchants. He was
educated at St. Paul's, where he was captain of the school in 1888–90. Going up to
Balliol as a scholar in 1890, he was among
the outstanding classics of his generation, obtaining the Hertford scholarship
and a Craven scholarship (1891) and first
classes in honour moderations (1892) and
literae humaniores (1894). He was, besides, a good cricketer and a notable actor;
in later years he did much to encourage
and inspire Oxford Greek plays. His love
of walking and mountaineering, begun as
an undergraduate, remained with him for
the rest of his active life, and he was for
many years a member of the Alpine Club.
From 1894 he was classical fellow and
tutor of Exeter College until his election in
1902 to a fellowship at Balliol where he
remained for nearly forty years. He retired in 1939 but returned during the war.

Bailey was wholly devoted to Balliol
and might well have expected to succeed
A. L. Smith [q.v.] as master; but it was
as a superb classical teacher that he was
remembered by many generations of
pupils, by no means all of them first-class
men. Humane but exacting, and, if necessary, faithful in rebuke, he not only left
them with a taste for good literature, but
loved to share with them his vacations and
his own varied interests. They drew on
him for counsel in after life, and many felt
that a return to Oxford was not complete
without a journey to East Hanney where
Bailey lived during his last years. He had
no great inclination for university busi-

ness, but he was a strong, if unobtrusive, force in the university. Anyone, young or old, who was interested in Oxford music or Oxford philanthropy or the progress of women's education was sure to find Cyril Bailey near the centre of things. An enthusiastic member of the Bach Choir, he became its president, and wrote a vivid memoir of Sir Hugh Allen [q.v.]. He was a devoted supporter of the Balliol Boys' Club. From 1921 to 1939 he was chairman of the council of Lady Margaret Hall on which he served from 1915 until 1953.

An elegant classical composer, especially in Latin, Bailey's venerable appearance, mellow voice, and touches of scholarly humour, concise and not too recondite, qualified him perfectly for the post of public orator which he held from 1932 to 1939; his long service as a delegate of the University Press was a testimony to his wise and discriminating scholarship; for many years he gave the benefit of his advice to the projected Oxford Latin Dictionary. He was an admirable and popular lecturer, alike on Cicero and Aristophanes, but a chance request while he was a young fellow of Exeter to lecture on Lucretius was the starting-point for what proved to be his lifelong study. He published the Oxford Text of Lucretius in 1900 (2nd ed. 1922) and in 1947 produced his *magnum opus*, a text with full commentary and translation. Neither in his powers as a textual critic, nor in his knowledge of early Latin, is he to be compared to a Lachmann or a Munro. Indeed in these respects the work was already done. But as an expert in the background of Lucretius' thought, as a sympathetic interpreter of his ideas and a sensitive expositor of his argument, Bailey produced an edition which will stand for many generations and is indispensable to any study of the poet.

His Lucretian studies led him to the adjacent but more arid field in which he published *Epicurus* (1926) and *The Greek Atomists and Epicurus* (1928). From Lucretius there began also his study of Roman religion in general. Here he was the heir to Warde Fowler [q.v.] whom he greatly admired, and on this subject he published, besides many articles and reviews, a volume of Sather lectures *Phases in the Religion of Ancient Rome* (1932) and *Religion in Virgil* (1935). On a more popular level he contributed to *The Legacy of Rome* (1923) of which he was the editor. He projected an edition of Ovid's *Fasti* but did not proceed with it in view of the forthcoming edition by Sir James Frazer [q.v.].

Bailey deserves to be remembered not only as a scholar and teacher, but as a great Oxford personality whose prime virtues were his humanity, his modesty, and his power of friendship. He had entered Balliol in the reign of Benjamin Jowett [q.v.] and throughout the years he kept alive what was best in the Jowett tradition by his personal and affectionate interest in individual Balliol men, whether or not they were classics, an interest which extended to men from other colleges if they happened to be his pupils. These friendships he kept in repair if possible by meeting; if not, by faithful and assiduous correspondence which was always full of good humour and good judgement.

Balliol meant to Bailey far more than any given generation of undergraduates. It meant the whole community of Balliol men spread over the world, and he had an astonishingly accurate memory for their achievements and personalities, well-known or unknown, as was evident from a speech which he made at a dinner to celebrate his eightieth birthday, when he spoke of representative figures from five decades of Balliol history as intimately as though the men had just gone down. Indeed, his interest in them began before they came up. As an examiner and a frequent visitor to schools, he kept in touch with potential Balliol scholars and their teachers. Few dons were better known to the fraternity of schoolmasters, and for many years he was chairman of the annual conference known as 'Dons and Beaks'. They admired the unassuming modesty of so eminent a scholar and the Christian faith which was transparently the foundation of his ideas and ideals. He was heard in later life to regret, half-humorously perhaps, that he had allowed this gift for friendship to rob him of time which he might have devoted to pure scholarship, but those who knew him best would maintain that the loss (if loss it was, for he was by any standard a fine scholar) was far less than the gain.

Bailey was an honorary fellow of Balliol and of Lady Margaret Hall and received honorary degrees from Oxford, Durham, Wales, Glasgow, and California. He was elected F.B.A. in 1933, was president of the Classical Association in 1934, and was appointed C.B.E. in 1939. He was elected a governor of St. Paul's School in 1901 and for over fifty years was a moving spirit of that body. He was a member of the council of Marlborough College from 1932 to 1945. During the first war he worked in the Ministry of Munitions and in the second he was an ideal member of the conscientious objectors tribunal.

Bailey married in 1912 Gemma, youngest daughter of Mandell Creighton [q.v.], by whom he had three daughters and one son. He died at East Hanney 5 December 1957. There is a drawing of Cyril Bailey in chalk by Sir William Rothenstein and an etching by Andrew Freeth, both in Balliol; the latter may seem to Bailey's friends the better likeness of the two.

[*Balliol College Record*, 1958; personal knowledge.]   J. T. CHRISTIE.

BAILEY, MARY, LADY BAILEY (1890–1960), airwoman, was born in London 1 December 1890, the only daughter of the fifth Lord Rossmore, of Monaghan, and his wife, Mittie Naylor. In 1911 she married Sir Abe Bailey [q.v.] by whom she had two sons and three daughters.

Lady Bailey learnt to fly in Moth light aeroplanes at the London Aeroplane Club at Stag Lane in 1926 and took her pilot's licence in 1927. She was the first woman to fly across the Irish Sea, and in July 1927, with Mrs. Geoffrey de Havilland, in a Moth, she climbed to over 17,280 feet, the greatest height to which any woman had flown in a light aeroplane.

On 9 March 1928 Lady Bailey set off alone from Croydon in a Cirrus-engined de Havilland Moth to fly to Cape Town to meet her husband. She was thirty-eight and the mother of five children. Her action emphasized the increasing independence of women and at the same time directed public attention to the practical transport capabilities of the light aeroplane. By the almost casual manner in which she undertook long and difficult flights she showed that light aeroplanes could be used for personal travel in all parts of the world and this gave a wider popularity to personal aviation. In her flight to the Cape she suffered set-backs which would have deterred anyone less determined. A month after her departure, at Tabora, her aeroplane was badly damaged when she landed in turbulent conditions and a replacement had to be sent to her. Travelling southward from Cairo, through Malakal, Kisumu, Tabora, and Johannesburg, she reached the Cape 30 April 1928 and decided to make the

return flight. Soon after starting her aircraft was again damaged; but repairs were completed and she restarted from Broken Hill on 21 September 1928. Flying westwards through Kano and Dakar and then north along the French Aéropostale route, she reached Croydon on 16 January 1929. In an aeroplane with a top speed of less than 100 miles an hour, she had completed 18,000 miles in the air. It was for this flight that she was awarded the Britannia Trophy in 1930. She was appointed D.B.E. in the same year for her services to aviation.

Lady Bailey took part in many sporting and competitive flying events. She entered for the King's Cup air race in 1927, 1929, and 1930, the last, which was won by Miss Winifred Brown, attracting over a hundred entries. She flew in the international challenge competition round Europe in 1929 and 1930. Some of her exploits occurred when she was still an inexperienced pilot and her remarkable will power and courage were the determining factors in her success. But she worked hard to develop her piloting technique and took a course of instruction in instrument flying and obtained a certificate of proficiency.

She died at her home at Kenilworth, near Cape Town, 29 August 1960.

[*The Times*, 30 August 1960; Sir Geoffrey de Havilland, *Sky Fever*, 1961; Terence Boughton, *The Story of the British Light Aeroplane*, 1963; *Royal Aero Club Gazette*, November 1963; *Who's Who in British Aviation*, 1935; private information.]
    OLIVER STEWART.

BAIRNSFATHER, CHARLES BRUCE (1888–1959), cartoonist, was born at Murree, India, 9 July 1888, the son of Lieutenant (later Major) Thomas Henry Bairnsfather. His mother's maiden name was Every. He was educated at the United Services College, Westward Ho! Having chosen the army as his profession he served for a time with the Royal Warwickshire Regiment but soon decided to abandon a military career and take up art. He became a student, under Charles van Havermaet, at an art school run by John Hassall [q.v.], but was not long in arriving at the conclusion that he was no more likely to be successful as an artist than as a soldier. He therefore gave up studying art, although continuing to draw in his spare time, and became apprenticed to a firm of electrical engineers, Spensers, Ltd., at Stratford on Avon. In due course he was appointed one of their representatives and travelled widely on the firm's behalf. At the same time, he kept up his drawing and also became an amateur comedian.

On the outbreak of war in August 1914 he rejoined his regiment and in the following November went out to the 1st battalion in France. In July 1915 he was promoted captain. During the same year the first of his cartoons depicting life at the front appeared in the *Bystander*. Seven collections of these were subsequently published under the title 'Fragments from France' and achieved an enormous popularity. His two famous characters were Old Bill, a blob-nosed, middle-aged cockney with a walrus moustache, and Bert, a gormless youth with a cigarette dangling permanently from his lips. Best remembered of his cartoons was that of two men immured in a shell-hole at the height of a barrage with the caption 'Well, if you knows of a better 'ole, go to it' (*Bystander*, 24 November 1915) which became a wartime catchword.

Bairnsfather continued to serve in France until December 1916 when he joined the intelligence department of the War Office as an officer-cartoonist and was sent to various fronts. He also wrote sketches of life in the trenches for a revue at the London Hippodrome, and for another produced by André Charlot [q.v.] at the Comedy Theatre, as well as a play (in collaboration), *The Better 'Ole*, produced by (Sir) C. B. Cochran [q.v.] at the Oxford Theatre in 1917.

So far as any marked influence is discernible in Bairnsfather's work as a draughtsman—his style though commonplace was paradoxically distinctive, in that it was unmistakably his own—it would seem to be that of the comic magazines of the period, and in particular the work of Tom Brown in the *Sketch*, of whose fruitier characters Old Bill might be claimed as a distant connection by reason of the exaggerated emphasis placed upon physical features. Bairnsfather's drawing in its coarse and facile way was sound and his observation of externals accurate, but there was little attempt at subtlety either in his humour or in his technique. The immense popularity of his cartoons must be attributed partly to the conditions of the period; anyone who could extract humour from the grim realities of trench warfare could not fail to be regarded in some degree as a comic genius. The appeal of his cartoons was not only in their topicality but in the simplicity of his ideas: *Bert* to *Old Bill*, apropos a gigantic shell-hole in the middle of the wall: 'What made that 'ole ?' *Bill*: 'Mice.'

In exploiting such humour as was to be found in the tensions, the grievances, and the frustrations of the period Bairnsfather was at his best, giving succinct expression to the universal determination to 'grin and bear it'. With the return to peacetime conditions, however, attitudes changed and the appeal of this particular vein of humour declined. He drew for the *Passing Show* and the *Bystander* in England, for *Life*, the *New Yorker*, and *Judge* in the United States, but his cartoons never achieved the same popularity. He spent his time in both America and England, lecturing, drawing, writing, and appearing in music-halls. He also wrote the synopsis for a film made in Canada called *Carry on, Sergeant*. In 1942–4 he was attached as an official cartoonist to the United States Army in Europe.

In 1921 Bairnsfather married Cecilia Agnes (died 1966), daughter of the late William Bruton, of Sydney, Australia, and formerly the wife of the Hon. Michael Scott. They had one daughter. He died in Worcester 29 September 1959.

[Bruce Bairnsfather, *Wide Canvas*, 1939; private information.]   Nicolas Bentley.

BAJPAI, Sir GIRJA SHANKAR (1891–1954), Indian statesman, was born in Lucknow 3 April 1891, the second of three sons of Rai Bahadur (Sir) Seetla Prasad Bajpai and his wife, Rukmini, daughter of Pandit Uma Charan Shukla. His father, the scion of a conservative Brahmin family, who became chief justice of Jaipur, Rajputana, was knighted in 1939 and died in 1947. Educated at the Muir Central College, Allahabad, and at Merton College, Oxford, where he obtained a second class in modern history in 1914, Bajpai in the same year entered the Indian Civil Service, in which he was perhaps the most brilliant younger Indian member during the period between the wars. Almost the whole of his career during the British period was passed in secretariat appointments, or representing India in various posts in the Commonwealth and at Round Table conferences. This part of his life attained its peak in his appointment as member of Council for the education department in 1940, and in 1941 as the first agent-general for India in the United States, a post which he held for six years, laying the foundations for the Indian

Embassy set up when India attained independence in 1947.

During the British period it was Bajpai's fortune to serve at a time when, with the advance towards independence, there came within the reach of able Indians new and challenging opportunities for proving their worth both in administration at the top and as spokesmen in the central legislature. To this, towards the end, was added the responsibility for the conduct of India's relations overseas, not only in parts of the Commonwealth where Indian expatriates resided, but, in Bajpai's case, in America. In all these fields he showed himself to be a fine craftsman. He was immensely industrious; he was a good orator, skilled in repartee and debate, in which he had to match men of the calibre of Bhulabhai Desai and M. A. Jinnah [q.v.]; and he was possessed of those qualities of persistence and persuasion associated with the successful diplomatist. In Washington he impressed Roosevelt and was at pains to correct many of the more naïve American opinions on the realities of the British relationship with India; he was able to show that in dealing from Delhi with the problems of Indians overseas it was easier to negotiate with the British than it was later with the independent governments.

Bajpai's career won its crown with independence in 1947. The new India had not unnaturally inherited prejudices against the Indian Civil Service, and for a period he seemed to meet with a studied lack of courtesy and consideration. This he bore with unfailing dignity, and it was not long before his merit was recognized by Jawaharlal Nehru. Late in 1947 he was appointed secretary-general, the post at the head of the Indian Ministry of External Affairs recognized as parallel with the Treasury secretaryship in Britain. In this office he was associated with, and influenced, many decisions of high policy.

In Bajpai the Commonwealth had a doughty champion, and the reality of the Commonwealth bond between India and Britain in all probability owed more to his steady counsel behind the scenes than to the decisions of statesmen. Above all he stood for that synthesis of eastern and western values which is the most profound result of Britain's association with India. The last appointment of an outstanding career was in 1952 to the governorship of Bombay, in some ways the most dignified post in India. In 1953 he represented India at the Geneva United Nations talks on Kashmir. He died in Bombay, in harness, 5 December 1954, full of honours, a great Indian who cared deeply for the British heritage. He was appointed C.B.E. in 1922, C.I.E. in 1926, K.B.E. in 1935, and K.C.S.I. in 1943.

Outwardly Bajpai seemed a little austere and aloof. He was fond of reading, and in the Indian manner cultivated an air of detachment designed to ensure a privacy which he prized. In his lighter moments he turned to things of beauty, in particular carpets, paintings, and flowers —he loved roses and cultivated fine varieties in his garden. He was devoted to Persian poetry. Born to the gracious way of living, with all his elegant manners and his courtesy he had a Puckish streak and liked both to poke fun yet be willing to be its object. He liked to tell against himself of his encounter with a Washington policeman when he crossed the road against the lights: 'You had better have my name, I am Sir Girja Shankar Bajpai.' 'You may be meat-pie or pork-pie, or any other sort of pie', replied the policeman, 'but you'll be mince-pie next time!'

In 1911 Bajpai married Rajni, daughter of R. A. Misra, a Brahmin lady of Cawnpore, by whom he had three sons and four daughters.

[Private information; personal knowledge.]
OLAF CAROE.

BAKER, HENRY FREDERICK (1866–1956), mathematician, was born in Cambridge 3 July 1866, the son of Henry Baker, a domestic butler, and his wife, Sarah Ann Britham. After attending various small schools he entered the Perse School, Cambridge. He was awarded a sizarship at St. John's College, Cambridge, in the summer of 1883, but remained at school in order to prepare for the entrance scholarship examination to be held in the following December. He was successful in being elected to a foundation scholarship and began residence in October 1884. In 1887 he was bracketed senior wrangler with three others, and in the following year he was placed in the first division of the first class in part ii of the mathematical tripos. He was elected into a fellowship of St. John's College in 1888 and remained a fellow for nearly sixty-eight years. In 1889 he was awarded a Smith's prize and in the next year he was appointed a college lecturer.

Baker spent the whole of his working life in Cambridge, first as a college lecturer, then as a university lecturer (1895–1914), holding the special Cayley lectureship (1903–14), and finally as Lowndean professor of astronomy and geometry (1914–36). He was elected F.R.S. in 1898 and received the Sylvester medal in 1910. He was awarded the De Morgan medal of the London Mathematical Society in 1905 and was president of the society in 1910 and 1911. In 1923 the university of Edinburgh conferred on him the honorary degree of LL.D. and in 1943 the Royal Society of Edinburgh made him an honorary fellow.

Baker's whole life was devoted to the service of mathematics, by his erudition, by his own research, and by his power to communicate his enthusiasm to his pupils. His researches covered a wide range of subjects, but chronologically they fall into two distinct periods. In the earlier period, which lasted until about 1911 or 1912, Baker's main interest was in the theory of algebraic functions and related topics. But his work on this often had a bearing on other branches of pure mathematics, to which he made useful contributions from time to time. Subjects on which he wrote included invariant theory, differential equations, and Lie groups; moreover his work on algebraic functions led him, after the turn of the century, to consider wider problems in the theory of functions, including functions of several complex variables. While many of Baker's papers were noteworthy in their day, it was his two books, *Abel's Theorem and the Allied Theory, including Theta Functions* (1897) and *Multiply Periodic Functions* (1907), which were his most lasting contributions to mathematics during this first period.

Some of the problems which Baker was considering when he wrote his *Multiply Periodic Functions* led him to take an interest in geometry; on the one hand, he came to read T. Reye's *Geometrie der Lage*, on the other, he came in contact with the work of the Italian school of geometers on the theory of surfaces. These subjects fascinated him, and he soon began to write on them. He made the work of the Italian geometers the subject of his presidential address to the London Mathematical Society in 1911 which became one of the classic surveys of the subject, and he was soon recognized as a leader of British geometers. On the death of the Lowndean professor, Sir Robert Ball [q.v.], in November 1913, Baker was the obvious choice of those electors to the

chair who wished to appoint a geometer. It was, however, contested by other electors who wished to continue the astronomical traditions of the chair. The appointment passed to the chancellor, who selected Baker. Baker had no intention, however, of neglecting that part of his responsibilities which related to astronomy, and for many years he lectured with considerable success on gravitational astronomy and wrote some useful papers on this subject. But for the rest of his life his real love was geometry, and for over twenty years he taught and wrote on it, and it is indeed for the work done as a professor that he will best be remembered. His own contributions are summed up in a treatise of six volumes, entitled *Principles of Geometry* (1922–33). He continued working on geometry after his retirement and published his last paper when he was eighty-six.

Baker's standing as a mathematician has to be judged against the background of the mathematical traditions in the university. He early came under the influence of Arthur Cayley [q.v.] and from him derived his concern with algebraic manipulations. But Cayley was an old man and pure mathematics in Cambridge had little in common with the exciting things which were going on in the subject on the Continent. A. R. Forsyth [q.v.] who succeeded Cayley as professor in 1895 strove hard to bring the continental ideas into Cambridge, but was not himself able to assimilate the continental standards of rigour. Baker, who learned much during some visits which he paid to Göttingen as a young man, was a better mathematician than Forsyth, and was thoroughly at home with continental ideas, but his early training led him to prefer the objectives of the older Cambridge mathematicians, using the new ideas primarily as tools. The result was that he was little affected by the revolution brought about amongst the Cambridge mathematical analysts by G. H. Hardy [q.v.] in the first decade of the twentieth century. During this period Baker's position was essentially that of one of the leaders of the older generation.

When he changed his interests to geometry, Baker again came to the subject at an awkward stage. In spite of the great advances which the Italians had achieved in the theory of surfaces, it was already apparent that their methods were not proving adequate, and indeed the proofs of a number of the most important

Baker, H. F.   D.N.B. 1951–1960

theorems had already been shown to be faulty. Baker did not invent any new methods and his work was largely devoted to examining the difficulties and to using algebraic methods of the type used years before by Cayley to examine special cases; this he did extremely well, but his work served to make it still clearer that radical changes in approach were necessary before real progress could be made. In projective geometry the situation was different. There were no structural problems, and each individual problem was an end in itself. It was here that Baker was at his best; for at heart he believed that the object of mathematics was to solve special problems completely, basic principles and general theories being of less interest to him. The fact that Baker did not achieve any major break-through was to a large degree due to his native modesty; he had an admiration amounting to veneration for the great masters of mathematics, and he could not imagine that he could ever take his place beside them.

While Baker's original contributions to mathematics were considerable, his forte lay in expounding the work of others and in inspiring the younger generation of geometers. In this last he was conspicuously successful. Between 1920 and 1936 he attracted around him a large following of young and enthusiastic geometers, many of whom subsequently achieved high positions. An important feature of the school he founded was his Saturday afternoon seminar or 'tea-party', one of the earliest seminars held in Cambridge. This was the focus of the great activity in geometry which he stirred up, and was the essential key to his success.

In appearance Baker was a heavily built man, with a thick moustache. This made him rather formidable to strangers and as he was also very shy some found him difficult to approach at first. But once the barriers were broken down his pupils found him less awe-inspiring, although they always treated him with great respect. The protocol at his 'tea-parties' was strict, and a pupil could not stay away without an acceptable excuse; but provided the rules were obeyed the atmosphere was extremely friendly.

In 1893 Baker married Lily Isabella Homfield, daughter of O. C. Klopp, of Putney, formerly of Leer, Germany. She died in 1903, leaving two sons. In 1913 Baker married Muriel Irene Woodyard, of Norfolk, by whom he had a daughter. When Baker died in Cambridge 17 March

1956 his widow survived him by only a few months.

[*The Times*, 19 March 1956; W. V. D. Hodge in *Biographical Memoirs of Fellows of the Royal Society*, vol. ii, 1956; autobiographical notes; personal knowledge.]

W. V. D. HODGE.

BAKER, JAMES FRANKLIN BETHUNE- (1861–1951), professor of divinity. [See BETHUNE-BAKER.]

BALFOUR, ARTHUR, first BARON RIVERDALE (1873–1957), industrialist, was, by his own account, born in London 9 January 1873, the elder of the two sons of Herbert Balfour. The birth was not registered. He finished his education in 1887–9 at Ashville College, Harrogate, and was afterwards employed in the office of Seebohm and Dieckstahl, of Sheffield, a firm which sold crucible steel all over Europe. Balfour went to the United States for a few years to enlarge his experience, and did well; he thus began early the interest in overseas trade for which he and his firm became famous. He returned to Sheffield in 1897, and in 1899, when the firm became a limited company, he was appointed managing director, taking over also the work of local vice-consul for Denmark. In the same year Balfour married Frances Josephine (died 1960), daughter of Charles Henry Bingham, a partner in the silver and electro-plating firm of Walker and Hall. He chose a world tour for his honeymoon, opening new branches for his firm.

The company was then a considerable producer of rifles, interested in obtaining overseas markets for rifle parts steels; but at this time it was one of the first two in Sheffield to develop high speed steel, and in 1901 Balfour negotiated with American researchers to launch this product. The company prospered, establishing a research laboratory in 1905 and selling in the United States considerable quantities of tool steels. The engineers' tool department established in 1910 became the most considerable of the company's activities. The name of the firm was changed in 1915 to Arthur Balfour & Co., Ltd.

From 1911 when he was the master cutler, honours and interests came to Balfour yearly. He chaired a committee to deal with the new national insurance in Sheffield in 1912; he was a member of the royal commission on railways in 1913, and in 1914 became a member of the advisory committee on war munitions and of

56

the industry advisory committee to the Treasury, on which he served until 1918. In 1915 he was made consul for Belgium, and undertook much work for the 9,000 Belgians who were given asylum in his district. He was a member of the man-power committee, the Advisory Council for Scientific and Industrial Research (of which he was chairman in 1937–46), the engineering industries committee, and the committee on commercial and industrial policy after the war under Lord Balfour of Burleigh [q.v.]. On a visit to Italy he had a long talk on the prospect of her entry into the war with the prime minister, Salandra, who thought his country unable to stand a long war. Only Great Britain, he remarked, could go to war for a right and just cause and stay in the war to the end.

During the period of reconstruction Balfour served on the coal industry commission (1919) and the therm charges committee (1922–3), and on the advisory councils of the Post Office, the Board of Trade, and the Department of Overseas Trade, as well as on the safeguarding of industries permanent panel. He was British delegate to the international conference on customs and other formalities in 1923. In the same year he was appointed K.B.E. and was a member of the government committee appointed to draw up the agenda for the Imperial Conference.

He was chairman, appointed in 1924, of the industry and trade commission which produced its important reports in six volumes up to 1929. He was a British delegate in preparing for and at the League of Nations economic conference of 1927. And in October 1930, as a member of the Economic Advisory Council, he wrote to the prime minister prophesying the severity of the approaching 'slump' in terms which shook both the Cabinet and the King, who considered him 'of almost unique experience'. An address which he gave to a meeting of business men in Sheffield in 1932 outlined his recipe for recovery; he was a shrewd if orthodox economist, with staunch faith in retrenchment and a wholesome hatred of inflation. In this, as in many spheres, his personal opinions were those which so often go with the political temperament of the Conservative.

He continued to serve, often as chairman, on innumerable committees and advisory bodies right up to the threshold of war. His last direct service to the Government was to lead the commission which went to Canada in 1939 to negotiate the scheme for training Royal Air Force pilots there, a difficult assignment successfully carried out. In 1942 he was promoted G.B.E. He had been created a baronet in 1929, and raised to the peerage as Baron Riverdale, of Sheffield, in 1935. He took the title from his home, Riverdale Grange, on the wooded slopes of western Sheffield. In 1921 he had headed a deputation to the United States on behalf of Sheffield firms to put their case to the Senate finance committee against certain sections of the Fordney tariff, and was instrumental in obtaining some modifications. In the midst of all the travel and work of national importance during the thirty years when he was a favourite of successive Governments, this energetic man was chairman and managing director of Arthur Balfour & Co., Ltd., of C. Meadows & Co., Sheffield, and of High Speed Alloys, Ltd., of Widnes, and a director of six other companies, besides serving on several Sheffield trade bodies, as a justice of the peace, and, for a short time, on the city council. In the words of another Sheffield business man: 'He was a great Sheffielder, and was always pushing Sheffield.' The university of Sheffield conferred on him the honorary degree of LL.D. in 1934.

Riverdale was continuously successful in promoting overseas trade both in his own business and as a national policy; he was a colleague of every economic expert of his day; but the reason why he achieved a general reputation as a necessary source of advice is not for brief description. He had a firm grasp of fact and a direct and courageous line of thought and conduct. He was always interested in the matter in hand and not in its effect on himself. He never consciously sought honours, and only incidentally sought wealth. He has been described as 'a big man, without conceit, willing to listen to humbler men' and 'a man of outstanding mental ability'. This ability was not of the intellectual order; it was a matter of practical grasp and judgement. He never put things off; he never took the easy things first. Added to boundless health and energy, these gifts enabled him to get through far more than a lifetime's work and to take more right decisions than would seem possible at such a speed of working.

Personally he was a jovial man, who loved fun, lived simply, and was easy and affectionate with his family. He died in Sheffield 7 July 1957, and was cremated.

His elder son, Robert Arthur (born 1901), succeeded to the title and as head of the business; he had another son, and three daughters.

A portrait by Harold Knight is in the possession of the family. A portrait in the board-room at Arthur Balfour & Co., Ltd., presented by Belgian war refugees in recognition of his work for them, is by an unknown Belgian painter. There is another portrait, unsigned, in the possession of the company, given to them by the directors of the Telegraph Construction Company.

[*The Times* and *Sheffield Telegraph*, 8 July 1957; private information.] MARY WALTON.

BANDARANAIKE, SOLOMON WEST RIDGEWAY DIAS (1899-1959), fourth prime minister of Ceylon, was born at the family home, Horagolla, Veyangoda, 8 January 1899, the only son of (Sir) Solomon Dias Bandaranaike and his wife, Daisy Ezline, daughter of (Sir) Solomon Christoffel Obeyesekera. One of his godfathers was Sir Joseph West Ridgeway [q.v.], the governor of the colony. As Maha Mudaliyar and aide-de-camp to no fewer than eight governors over a period of thirty-two years his father was the principal Sinhalese confidant and dignitary in a governor's personal entourage. He was also in his own right a leading member of Sinhalese society, a landowner, a patron of the turf, and a pillar of the Anglican Church.

In this setting of affluence, authority, and high social status Bandaranaike grew up, with a Cambridge graduate for tutor for four years before he went at sixteen to St. Thomas's College, Colombo. It was the first time 'Sonny' had left his father's supervision. He went on to Christ Church, Oxford, where he obtained a second class in classical honour moderations in 1921 and in 1923 a third in jurisprudence to which he had changed as unlikely 'to cause too great a strain on my time or energy'. It was not until November 1921 that he spoke at the Union and was reported by *Isis* to have made the best speech of the evening. Thereafter he spoke frequently and was recognized as a brilliant debater with an outstanding command of English. In Michaelmas term 1923 he served as secretary and in Trinity term 1924 as junior treasurer. His lack of success in contesting the presidency in 1924 he attributed to the determination of life members, who did not normally exercise their right to vote, to prevent the

election of a president who was not white. Whether or not he was right in this belief it had some influence on his future career. He went down, was called to the bar, and in 1925 returned to Ceylon to practise as an advocate.

In a series of entertaining and sensitive articles in the early thirties Bandaranaike nevertheless wrote without rancour of the problems of an Asian undergraduate at Oxford and of the awakening of his political consciousness. Lingering on Magdalen bridge on his last afternoon in a mood of somewhat uncharacteristic sentimentality he contrasted the mellowness of the English scene with the disease and poverty of his own country: 'Oxford had revealed to me my life's mission and Oxford was the dearer to me because she had taught me to love my country better.'

At a by-election in 1927 to the Colombo municipal council Bandaranaike defeated the most influential trade-union leader of the time. In the same year he was elected secretary of the Ceylon National Congress, the spearhead of agitation for constitutional reforms. When the Donoughmore constitution of 1931 introduced adult suffrage and a measure of self-government Bandaranaike was elected unopposed and was thereafter continuously a member of the legislature. In 1936 he became minister of local administration. Although the constitution did not encourage the development of the party system certain alignments became manifest. Bandaranaike became a Buddhist: there was an irresistible appeal to his mentality in its doctrine that man must work out his own salvation and was not dependent upon a God whose favour must be sought and wrath appeased. An ardent nationalist, in 1937 he formed the Sinhala Mahasabha to represent Buddhist Sinhalese interests. When in 1947 Ceylon became fully self governing this party joined the Ceylon National Congress to form the United National Party which at the ensuing election emerged the largest party and formed the government under D. S. Senanayake [q.v.] with Bandaranaike as minister of health and local government.

Although Bandaranaike was an outstanding debater and speaker and an energetic minister he invariably had an unfavourable press; this he felt to be inspired by his colleagues who were irritated by the continued existence of the Sinhala Mahasabha which Bandaranaike used as his personal political platform. He complained that he was being used and a the same time discredited. He became increasingly disenchanted with the United National Party, not only because he was not in accord with the party's policies but also because he felt himself excluded from the inner councils of the prime minister and believed that he was being edged out of his position as heir apparent to Senanayake. In 1951 he resigned from the party and on joining the Opposition dissolved the Sinhala Mahasabha and formed the Sri Lanka Freedom Party (S.L.F.P.) to enable members of other communities to join him. Although in the election of 1952 his party obtained very few seats they sufficed to make him leader of the Opposition.

Bandaranaike was not slow to realize that the role of friend of the underprivileged in which he had cast himself offered his party the greatest opportunity to develop what he regarded as his progressive policies. The peasants were asking what independence had done for them; the Buddhists felt they had received too little recognition after centuries of alien rule; a multiplicity of parties had no chance of defeating the United National Party. Bandaranaike offered a government of the People or the 'Masses', with a programme including the adoption of Sinhalese as the sole official language, a special status for Buddhism, the termination of British military bases, and the nationalization of certain key sectors of the economy including the transport services, a principal source of financial support to the U.N.P. In addition he established the Mahajana Eksath Peramuna (The Peoples United Front) comprising his own S.L.F.P. party with three other groups of the Left and entered into a no-contest pact with the Marxist and Communist parties. At the 1956 election he secured an astounding victory with 51 seats; the U.N.P., partly through the ineptitude of their campaign, retained but eight.

The victory was unexpected not only by the country but by Bandaranaike himself who had no capable and experienced politicians from whom to choose his government, in which he included two left-wing Marxists, an uneasy association which ended with the latter's being forced to resign in the spring of 1959. Bandaranaike became the victim of the manifesto on which his party had been elected. The People's Government became a government not of the people but by the people and he could not control the ex-

tremists. He was slow to recognize the communal and religious conflicts and antagonisms which his policies had unleashed or the consequences of the indiscipline which they induced. In 1958 there were widespread communal disturbances with much loss of life which created a wide gulf between the majority Sinhalese and the minority Tamils and resulted in a rather tardy declaration of a state of emergency.

Some of Bandaranaike's Buddhist supporters were angered by his failure to implement pre-election promises and a group of them, headed by a small but influential section of the Buddhist clergy, realized that they could not win his backing to serve their own personal ambitions. On 25 September 1959 he was attacked by a Buddhist monk in his own house where each morning he was accustomed to receive people with grievances or requests. He died the following day.

His death cast a long shadow over the public life of Ceylon and lost to his country a man of outstanding intellectual gifts, culture, and sincerity of purpose who was moving towards more practical policies whilst preserving what he considered to be the requirements of social justice. He had a sharp mind and a biting tongue which estranged him from many—yet he was a generous political opponent and, unlike many of his contemporaries, did not bear grudges. He was a keen, useful tennis player, bred greyhounds, wrote some short stories, and enjoyed both bridge and billiards.

In 1940 Bandaranaike married Sirimavo, daughter of Barnes Ratwatte Dissawa, a Kandyan chief; they had a son and two daughters.

The tragic death of Bandaranaike immediately cast him in the role of martyr. At the general election of 1960 his widow, helped by and making full use of the mounting wave of popular sympathy, led the S.L.F.P. to victory with a convincing majority and herself became prime minister.

There is a portrait of Bandaranaike at the Oxford Union.

[S. W. R. D. Bandaranaike, *Speeches and Writings*, Ceylon, 1963, and *Towards a New Era*, Ceylon, 1961; *Ceylon Causerie Platé Ltd.*, Ceylon, 1933–5; W. Howard Wriggins, *Ceylon—Dilemmas of a New Nation*, Princeton, 1960; Sir Solomon D. Bandaranaike, *Remembered Yesterdays*, 1929; Christopher Hollis, *The Oxford Union*, 1965; personal knowledge.]   F. C. ROWAN.

BANKS, LESLIE JAMES (1890–1952), actor, was born 9 June 1890 in West Derby, Lancashire, son of George Banks, general merchant, and his wife, Emily Dalby. He won a classical scholarship at Glenalmond and then went on to Keble College, Oxford, again as a classical scholar. He made his first professional appearance on the stage in 1911 at the town hall, Brechin, as old Gobbo in *The Merchant of Venice* with the company of (Sir) Frank Benson [q.v.]. He remained with Benson until the following year, when he went on tour with (Sir) George Dance's company in *The Hope*, a racing melodrama from Drury Lane. He then joined H. V. Esmond [q.v.] and Eva Moore in a tour of the United States and Canada, making his first New York appearance in a small part in Esmond's comedy *Eliza Comes to Stay*. Returning to London, he made his west-end début at the Vaudeville, in May 1914, in a play called *The Dangerous Age*.

The war cut short his career just as it was beginning to show promise. He served in the Essex Regiment, receiving a disfiguring wound in the face which might have driven a less firm character to seek some less public profession. Banks never allowed it to deter him and when he started again after the war he found that it did not handicap him. A month after the armistice he made a fresh start under (Sir) Nigel Playfair [q.v.] at the Lyric, Hammersmith; from there he went to the Birmingham Repertory Theatre under (Sir) Barry Jackson, and in 1919–20 played leads in the repertory company of Lena Ashwell [q.v.]. A Shaw season at the Everyman, Hampstead, followed early in 1921, and in May of the same year he had his first important part in a successful west-end play, as Archie Beal in *If* by Lord Dunsany [q.v.] at the Ambassadors.

In little more than two years he had established himself in the good opinion of most of the managements in London who could be relied on to show discrimination in their choice of plays and players, and this at a time when the disillusion consequent on the war had forced down the standard of public taste to a depressingly low level. Because he was so much in demand, he was free to pick what plays he acted in; and to study the long list of parts he played is to realize what care he took to avoid claptrap or rubbish. To see Leslie Banks's name on a playbill or in a theatre programme was to be given a virtual guarantee that the play had merit.

He was an actor of very wide range and as his services were constantly in demand in films as well as on the stage he was able to avoid being stereotyped. No better evidence of this need be asked for than the fact that in a season of repertory at the Haymarket, October 1944–June 1945, he played Lord Porteous in *The Circle*, Tattle in *Love for Love*, Claudius in *Hamlet*, Bottom in *A Midsummer Night's Dream*, and Antonio Bologna in *The Duchess of Malfi*; and that he played such disparate leading roles as those in *Goodbye Mr. Chips* (1938) and *Life with Father* (1947). Among the many films in which he appeared may be mentioned such Hitchcock productions as *The Man Who Knew Too Much* and *Jamaica Inn*. Banks belonged to that stalwart type of actor which, ranking as leading man rather than popular star, is able for that very reason to reach a pitch of distinction in his career which many stars miss.

One of the most variously talented and deeply respected figures on the British stage of his time, no man in private life ever looked or behaved less like the popular conception of a stage player. He showed no trace of that exhibitionism, that desire to be noticed, which is the motivating force with many actors of every degree of distinction. 'He remained through all his success', said A. A. Milne [q.v.], 'the man next door, a good neighbour and a good friend.' Yet the serene integrity of his nature did not interfere with his versatility as an artist. He was able to understand and play with sympathy a character with whom it seemed he could have nothing at all in common. As Gerald Coates in *Grand National Night* at the Apollo in 1946 his besetting fault, which brought him to ruin, was a streak of wild recklessness. It was unthinkable that Leslie Banks in his own person could ever yield to such weakness; and yet it seemed inevitable that the man on the stage, undoubtedly and without disguise Leslie Banks, should be brought low by a fatal flaw in his character.

In 1915 Banks married Gwendoline Haldane, daughter of Edwin Thomas Unwin; they had three daughters. He was appointed C.B.E. in 1950 and died in London 21 April 1952.

A portrait by W. R. Sickert of Leslie Banks as Petruchio with Dame Edith Evans as Katharine is in the Bradford City Art Gallery.

[*Who's Who in the Theatre*; private information; personal knowledge.] W. A. DARLINGTON.

BARING, ROWLAND THOMAS, second EARL OF CROMER (1877–1953), lord chamberlain to the household, 1922–38, elder son of Evelyn Baring, later first Earl of Cromer [q.v.], by his first marriage, to Ethel Stanley, second daughter of Sir Rowland Stanley Errington, eleventh baronet, was born 29 November 1877 at Cairo. A bad attack of typhoid contracted in Egypt in his boyhood affected his health all his life. His mother died when he was nearly twenty-one, but the influence of her noble character helped to mould his own and remained potent throughout his career. He was educated at Eton where he made many friends, but left early by his father's wish, without particular distinction in scholarship or games, in order to learn foreign languages. His knowledge of French was unusually good in an Englishman. In 1900 he entered the Diplomatic Service, serving as third and second secretary between 1902 and 1906 at Cairo, Tehran, and St. Petersburg. He then transferred to the Foreign Office and acted as private secretary to successive permanent under-secretaries of state between 1907 and 1911 when he resigned the service.

In 1913 Lord Errington, as he then was, became a managing director of Baring Brothers and in a short time acquired a useful knowledge of finance. In 1914 he joined the Grenadier Guards, serving in the special reserve until 1920. In 1915 he became aide-de-camp to successive viceroys of India (Lord Hardinge of Penshurst and Lord Chelmsford, qq.v.). The following year he was appointed assistant private secretary and equerry to King George V. In 1917 he succeeded his father as second Earl of Cromer. He acted as chief of staff to the Duke of Connaught [q.v.] during his visit to India (1920–21) and to the Prince of Wales during his Indian tour (1921–2) when his knowledge of India proved of great service.

In 1922 Cromer was appointed lord chamberlain to the household, a post which he held with distinction under three sovereigns until 1938 when he became a permanent lord-in-waiting. Apprehension about the status of the monarchy during the war, despite the devotion to duty of the King and Queen, had been expressed in 1918, notably by Cromer himself and by Lord Esher [q.v.]. This disquiet was soon dissipated but Cromer never forgot the need for the monarchy to adjust itself to the post-war social revolution. By his tact and imperturbability and his liberal and

shrewd interpretation of his diverse functions he gave general satisfaction and very little cause for offence, according to the same serious but always sympathetic attention to his social as to his political functions. Probably his work as censor of plays interested him most. He came to know a great deal about the theatre, and in this contentious field his tact and sympathy earned the respect and gratitude of dramatists and actors. In his administration and reformation of royal household affairs his business experience stood him in good stead. A sense of humour lightened the burden of his responsibilities, if on social occasions his determination to keep inviolable the confidences of his office sometimes kept it in check. Throughout his term of office he enjoyed the complete confidence and true friendship of the three sovereigns he served.

Cromer was of middle height and slim build. Never robust, he enjoyed shooting and riding but his favourite recreations were reading, family golf, and gardening. A chief virtue of his character was an endearing modesty, to which were added shrewd common sense, great tact, imperturbability and moral courage, and a farsighted liberalism of outlook. He was devoted to children, and young people were always at ease in his company. He devoted much time and trouble to the Cheyne Hospital for children, and was president of the National Hospital for Chest Diseases. At various times he was a British Government director of the Suez Canal Company, a director of the P. & O. and the B.I. steam navigation companies and various banking and insurance concerns. He was not a rich man, and these City interests were of importance to him since the office of lord chamberlain carried no pension rights. In 1934–5 he was president of the M.C.C. He received many high British honours and a variety of foreign Orders. He was sworn of the Privy Council in 1922 and rose to the rank of grand cross in the Orders of the Bath, the Indian Empire, and the Victorian, and received the Victorian Chain in 1935.

In 1908 Cromer married Lady Ruby Florence Mary Elliot, daughter of the fourth Earl of Minto [q.v.] by whom he had a son and two daughters. Lady Cromer was of constant help to him in his career and his family life was ideal. Some of their happiest days were spent at a modest estate he acquired in Somerset. Cromer died rather suddenly 13 May 1953 in London and was succeeded by his only son, George Rowland Stanley (born 1918), who was governor of the Bank of England in 1961–6.

A portrait of Cromer by P. A. de Lásló is in family possession.

[John W. Wheeler-Bennett, *King George VI*, 1958; John Gore, *King George V*, 1941; H.R.H. the Duke of Windsor, *A King's Story*, 1951; private information.]   JOHN GORE.

BARKER, SIR ERNEST (1874–1960), scholar, was born at Woodley, Cheshire, 23 September 1874, the eldest of the seven children of George Barker and his wife, Elizabeth Pollitt. His father had been a miner but was then working on the farm belonging to his wife's family. Ernest Barker owed a vast debt to the energy and sober ambition of his mother; to the accident that he was tutored, mainly as pace-maker to another boy, for a scholarship to Manchester Grammar School by an imaginative village schoolmaster; and to the high standards of scholarship of Manchester Grammar School itself. On these matters Barker comments in the pamphlet which expresses much of his personal philosophy, 'The Father of the Man', reprinted in his autobiographical *Age and Youth* (1953).

A classical scholar of Balliol College, Oxford, Barker obtained first classes in honour moderations (1895), *literae humaniores* (1897), and modern history (1898); and a Craven scholarship in 1895. He was a classical fellow at Merton (1898–1905); lecturer in modern history at Wadham (1899–1909); fellow and lecturer at St. John's (1909–13); and fellow and tutor of New College (1913–20). In 1920 he left Oxford to become principal of King's College, London. Although his years there were those of much interest in the university's development, thanks to the politics of administration they were not perhaps personally his happiest. In January 1928 he moved to Cambridge as first professor of political science and fellow of Peterhouse. He retired from the chair in 1939, becoming an honorary fellow of Peterhouse, as he had been of Merton since 1931.

Barker will probably be remembered as a tutor and man of character, emphatically 'a character' in the Oxford tradition; as a polymath scholar; and as a political philosopher and first holder of a distinguished chair of political science. The first element enters profoundly into his matured philosophy as a moralist. He himself described as his 'golden year' that of 1919–20 when the young, but unusually mature, men had just returned to New College from the war; for him they were all Rupert Brookes *redivivi*. Even in an age accustomed to undepartmentalized and humane learning, he was conspicuous in that he could pass with equal felicity from classical studies to medieval history and, then, to political theory. Not a Bentley, or a Stubbs, or a Max Weber, he could yet move with familiarity in all their fields—perhaps least in that of Weber. In later life an Anglican, he owed much to his nonconformist (Congregationalist) and Liberal background; but the staunch individualism which he derived therefrom was tempered by his classical and medieval studies. He appreciated to the full Aristotle's doctrine of the welfare state, 'the *polis* continues in being for the sake of the good life'; and he remained a lifelong friend of the Co-operative Movement, the Workers' Educational Association, and of the National Council of Social Service.

Among his most valuable services, as a political theorist, were his translations from the great German writers, Otto von Gierke—here adding to the work of F. W. Maitland [q.v.]—and Ernst Troeltsch, although his most brilliant writings were perhaps his early *Political Thought of Plato and Aristotle* (1906) which he later intended to rewrite in two volumes on *Greek Political Theory* of which only one, *Plato and his Predecessors* (1918), was completed; and his brief Home University Library *Political Thought in England from Herbert Spencer to Today* (1915; revised ed. 1947). His stress, in his own life, upon personal character naturally led on to an interest in and stress upon national character, a subject upon which he gave the Stevenson lectures at Glasgow in 1925–6. They were published under the title *National Character* (1927; 4th and revised ed. 1948); and later he wrote *Britain and the British People* (1942; revised ed. 1955) and edited a symposium, *The Character of England* (1947). Barker's thought on the theme crystallized in one of the most characteristic books that he wrote, *Traditions of Civility* (1948), in which he was able to expound the guiding creed of a humanist with all the authority of an historian of wide range as well as a classical scholar. His two books, *Reflections on Government* (1942) and *Principles of Social and Political Theory* (1951), based on his earlier academic lectures and displaying the knowledgeableness which one would expect of him, are sound but on the whole conventional expositions of their subject.

It was characteristic of Barker that, as with his students in personal relations so with their academic ideas, he was happy to stir thought and even to encourage innovations, but—being a cautious man, emotionally conservative if culturally liberal—he was disinclined to commit himself to any final judgement on their value. It was consistent with his temper that, in his last years, instead of summarizing some particular political theory (although guiltless of that contempt for theory which has occasionally been fashionable), he preferred to fill in gaps in scholarship, not covered by the great work of Sir R. W. and A. J. Carlyle [qq.v.] by surveying Hellenic, Patristic, and Byzantine political thought, in his *From Alexander to Constantine* (1956) and in his *Social and Political Thought in Byzantium* (1957). He was perhaps happiest when 'dividing the swift mind' in discussing medieval history with, for example, the headmaster of Ampleforth.

Possibly one of the most important movements in political thought in western Europe and America in this century has been the emergence of Pluralism, with its immense repercussions on current views of the State and Society, and with its repudiation of 'monistic' or centralizing theories, especially in German thought since Hegel and including, in some aspects, Marx. This theory in no small part traces from the historical work of von Gierke, of which Maitland and Barker himself were the leading expositors in the English language. Barker was the contemporary of J. N. Figgis and G. D. H. Cole and the tutor of H. J. Laski [qq.v.]. He assiduously called attention to the new ideas, although with especial reservations about Laski. Some writers were prepared to acclaim him as 'the godfather of modern Pluralism', but such an honour he modestly and characteristically disclaimed. His important article 'The Discredited State' (February 1915 in the Oxford *Political Quarterly*) expressed interest but was critical of the theory. The historical arguments he could appreciate; but of the conclusions he fought shy. He had an aversion from theories which he regarded as not quite sound, and the necessary crudity and one-sidedness of the pioneer did not come naturally to him. He wore his great erudition easily, but it inhibited violent new departures.

When Barker was appointed to the chair of political science at Cambridge some thought that this might herald a renaissance of a subject which, in England, had been neglected since the days of Sir J. R. Seeley and Henry Sidgwick [qq.v.] and the eclipse of the Utilitarian School. Barker, however, was content to accommodate his chair to the mood of the history faculty in Cambridge to which it was attached, although he records in his autobiography his shy embarrassment at finding himself, as a polymath, in the society of historical specialists. He was by nature a great Oxford tutor and he carried this mood over to Cambridge, where he was at his happiest discussing ideas with the young men. Although he showed curiosity about psychology he did not affirm, with Lord Bryce [q.v.], that politics, as a study, was based on it or follow up the contemporary and fascinating initiative given by Graham Wallas [q.v.]. He remained the philosopher-historian (as distinct from being any 'philosopher of history'), outlining his theory of tradition, and endeavouring to reconcile English individualism in the style of J. S. Mill [q.v.] and even of the earlier Puritans with his strong 'sense for the community' which he believed that Laski lacked.

Barker's large, lanky figure and broad Manchester accent were of the material of which anecdote is made. Together with natural dignity he had that individual personality which is vital in university life and he occupied for thirty and more years a prominent position in the English academic world. He was chairman of the drafting committee of the Hadow report on *The Education of the Adolescent* (1927); presided over the education section of the British Association meeting in Toronto in 1924; was visiting professor at Amherst College, Massachusetts (1920), and Lowell lecturer in Boston (1929). It was characteristic that, already retired, he was prepared, as the contribution of a good European, to accept an invitation from Cologne where he went as professor of political science in 1947–8 and was awarded the Verdienstkreuz. He was one of the chief contributors to the Oxford volume, *Why We are at War: Great Britain's Case* (1914), examining the origins of the first war; in the second he was chairman of a wartime books commission under the Conference of Allied Ministers of Education, president of its history committee, and one of the editors of *The European Inheritance* (1954). His career was a protest against excessive departmentalism in learning; and his reputation finally is that of an eminent humanist, leaving his impress upon generations of students in three major universities.

Barker received a number of honorary doctorates and foreign decorations, was elected F.B.A. in 1947, and knighted in 1944. In 1900 he married Emily Isabel (died 1924), daughter of the Rev. Richard Salkeld, vicar of St. Mark's, Dukinfield, by whom he had one son and two daughters; in 1927 he married Olivia Stuart, daughter of John Stuart Horner, of Mells, a Balliol man and director of an engineering firm, by whom he had one son and one daughter. Barker died in Cambridge 17 February 1960.

Drawings by Mrs. Campbell Dodgson and John Mansbridge are in the possession of the family.

[Sir Ernest Barker, *Age and Youth*, 1953; G. E. G. Catlin in *Proceedings* of the British Academy, vol. xlvi, 1960; private information; personal knowledge.]

GEORGE E. GORDON CATLIN.

BARKER, DAME LILIAN CHARLOTTE (1874–1955), first woman assistant prison commissioner, was born in Islington 21 February 1874, the fifth of seven children and youngest daughter of James Barker, tobacconist, and his wife, Caroline Williams. Educated at the local elementary school, she was trained at Whitelands College, Chelsea, and began her career as a teacher in elementary schools under the London County Council. After a break of seven years to nurse her invalid mother she resumed her teaching. Her success, first with a class of boys and later with a group of difficult girls, showed her to be of exceptional ability, and led to her appointment in 1913 as principal of the Council's Women's Institute which from 1914 was in Cosway Street, Marylebone.

The outbreak of war interrupted her career and in 1915 she was appointed the first commandant of the Women's Legion cookery section in which she did valuable work in training cooks for the army. Later in 1915 she became lady superintendent at Woolwich Arsenal where her talent for dealing with people first found full scope. She was responsible eventually for the welfare of some 30,000 women in an organization where women had never before been employed. She set up canteens, first-aid posts, cloakrooms, and rest rooms. Not content with her official tasks, she went on to organize outside recreation,

sick visiting, convalescent and holiday homes, and the care of unmarried mothers and their babies; for all of which she raised the necessary private funds. Her services were recognized by her appointment as C.B.E. in 1917.

In 1919 she joined the training department of the Ministry of Labour; then in 1920 became executive officer of the Central Committee on Women's Training and Employment to administer a sum of £600,000 for the training and maintenance of women who had suffered from the economic effects of the war. In 1923 she became governor of the Borstal Institution for Girls at Aylesbury. Borstal training for girls had at that time fallen seriously behind that for boys, and the prison commissioners were fortunate to attract the services of one who had already made a position for herself in social and educational work. Although acceptance meant a considerable loss of salary she realized the importance of the post and agreed to undertake it on being assured of a free hand by the commissioners.

Up to that time Aylesbury as an institution housing about a hundred of the worst girl offenders between the ages of sixteen and twenty-one had been run on lines which differed little from the conventional prison regime of the previous century, and the results were not encouraging. Lilian Barker brought a new spirit. She realized that the will to lead a good and useful life is never manifest in the unhappy and unfulfilled, and at once set to work to humanize the treatment of her girls. Print dresses replaced the old prison clothes, cells were transformed into pleasantly furnished rooms with comfortable beds, meals became appetizing, and organized games and a swimming pool were introduced. Even more important was her own personal influence.

Short and stocky, with iron-grey hair cut short under a pork-pie hat, and almost always dressed in a tweed suit of severe cut, her somewhat mannish appearance was emphasized by a deep voice and a manner which could be very direct and even brusque. Beneath this rather uncompromising exterior was concealed a deep humanity, supported by a firm Christian faith and a will to comfort and help anyone in trouble. Her laugh was full and infectious, her humour dry but penetrating; her bright eyes could flash with fun as well as anger. Her nightly talks to her girls over a cigarette were one of the secrets of her success. But any who tried to kick over the traces found an iron hand in the velvet glove. Her punishments were imaginative if unconventional and designed to fit the crime: the girl who in a fit of temper tore her blankets into strips was made to sew them up and sleep under the resulting exiguous covering. It was not long before Lilian Barker won the respect and affection of her difficult charges, yet there was never any doubt that at Aylesbury discipline was maintained. Long after they had left she continued to receive a voluminous fan mail from her old girls and to take an interest in their weddings and their children.

In 1935 Lilian Barker was invited to become the first woman assistant commissioner of prisons, and, although it cost her a great deal to leave Aylesbury, she responded at once to this call to wider service. She became responsible for all women's prisons in England and Wales, and, by arrangement with the prison department there, also in Scotland. Under her guidance improvements were made in the clothing and feeding of women prisoners, and she was immersed in plans for the creation of a new prison for women outside London when the outbreak of war in 1939 brought this and other developments in which she was interested to an end. She retired in 1943 and was appointed D.B.E. in 1944. She continued to live at her cottage at Wendover Dean and to maintain a lively interest in affairs until her death, 21 May 1955, while on holiday at Hallsands, Devon.

[*The Times*, 23 May 1955; *Observer*, 29 May 1955; *Annual Report* of the Prison Commissioners, 1955; Elizabeth Gore, *The Better Fight*, 1965; private information; personal knowledge.]   HAROLD SCOTT.

BARNES, ERNEST WILLIAM (1874–1953), bishop of Birmingham, was born 1 April 1874 in Altrincham, Cheshire, the eldest of the four sons of John Starkie Barnes and his wife, Jane Elizabeth Kerry, of Charlbury, Oxfordshire. An elementary schoolteacher, J. S. Barnes was appointed headmaster of a school in Birmingham, so that the son's boyhood was spent in the city which was later to know him as bishop. Educated at King Edward's School (the school of Westcott, Lightfoot, and Benson, qq.v.), Barnes went up to Cambridge as a scholar of Trinity College in 1893 and in 1896 was bracketed second wrangler. In 1897 he became president of the Union and was

placed in the first division of the first class in part ii of the mathematical tripos. In the following year he was first Smith's prizeman and was elected a fellow of his college, becoming assistant lecturer in 1902, junior dean in 1906–8, and tutor from 1908 to 1915. In 1909 he was elected F.R.S.

Barnes's relations with his Cambridge colleagues were not always harmonious. A shy man, who was yet conscious of unusual powers, he could be arrogant in controversy and did not shrink from declaring his views. In particular, the strong pacifist principles of which the outbreak of war in 1914 found him an ardent champion failed to endear him to the more bellicose of his colleagues at Trinity. It is said that Barnes, whose father was a Baptist, was a professed atheist when he first went up to Cambridge but as an undergraduate experienced a conversion to Christianity. In 1902 he was made deacon and in 1903 was ordained priest. In 1915–19 he was master of the Temple; in 1918 he was made canon of Westminster; and in 1924 Ramsay MacDonald nominated him bishop of Birmingham.

A broad churchman, whose training at Cambridge had been primarily mathematical, Barnes conceived it to be his mission and duty to urge the necessity of substituting a world outlook based on the natural sciences for the traditionally scriptural outlook characteristic of Christian theology. He preached what came to be known as 'gorilla' sermons, supporting the evolutionary theory of man's biological descent from some creature akin to the apes. He showed himself negatively hostile towards all forms of the doctrine of the Real Presence of Christ in the Eucharist; sacramentalism, as understood by Anglican churchmen not only of the Anglo-Catholic school but of other schools as well, was outside his purview. The essence of Christianity, as he understood it and as he practised it, was to be found in a personal discipleship of the Jesus of the Gospels, and in the acceptance of an ethic based on the Sermon on the Mount. His congregation at the Temple, during his mastership, he believed to consist of 'wistful agnostics' in need of the spiritual diet of somewhat self-conscious modernism which he provided.

It is indeed probable that it was during this period that Barnes's best work as a preacher was done. There was a challenging incisiveness about his utterances, and an evident, if somewhat naïve, intellectual honesty, which his congregation of able lawyers could appreciate; nor at this stage does controversy of a public kind appear to have arisen, although at the Temple as in Cambridge there were those who shook their heads at Barnes's pacifism. The canonry of Westminster gave him a wider audience, and by the time of his appointment to Birmingham he had already become something of a controversial figure. His opinions were by now well known. His 'gorilla' sermons were generally held to be unnecessary since the theory of evolution had long ceased to be a matter of dispute among educated churchmen. But his attacks upon the doctrine of the Real Presence caused pain and distress to many and were widely resented.

The Birmingham diocese to which he went in 1924 was largely high church in tone and there were plenty of parishes in which the accustomed usages were not such as the bishop approved. In 1925 trouble threatened by reason of his refusal to institute a patron's nominee to a vacant benefice unless he agreed in advance to discontinue the practice of reservation which had been customary in the parish. The incumbent designate preferred to withdraw; the next candidate gave the assurance although it went beyond anything the bishop was legally entitled to demand.

In September 1927 the bishop preached a vigorous 'gorilla' sermon in Westminster Abbey, and in Birmingham a fortnight later delivered an address on sacramental teaching which contained a provocative onslaught upon the doctrine of the Real Presence. A public protest was made ten days later in St. Paul's Cathedral, where the bishop was about to preach, by a London incumbent who appeared with a large body of laymen and, denouncing the bishop as a heretic, demanded that the bishop of London should inhibit him from preaching in his diocese and that the archbishop of the province should arrange for his trial. The bishop took the unusual course of addressing an open letter to Archbishop Davidson [q.v.] in which he complained of the disturbance and, defending his position, remarked that no one should drive him to Tennessee or to Rome. The archbishop published a courteous reply, assuring the bishop that no one in England desired to lead or to drive him to either, dismissing the evolutionary sermons as of little importance, but criticizing, as being

needlessly wounding, what the bishop had said about sacramentalism. Before the end of the year the bishop published, in reply to his critics, a book giving a positive account of his beliefs, bearing the title *Should Such a Faith Offend?*, which had the effect of causing the controversy to die down for a time.

In 1929 there occurred a renewed instance of the bishop's refusal to institute to a benefice the nominee of the patrons unless promises were made which went beyond those required by law. The patrons in this case included the bishop of Truro and the controversy went on for eighteen months. In the end the patrons obtained from a judge of the High Court a writ of mandamus directed to the archbishop of Canterbury enjoining him to license a fit person to the benefice. Archbishop Lang [q.v.] admitted the patrons' original nominee.

The course of the war of 1939-45 saw Barnes involved in a controversy with the makers of cement. At a public meeting in Birmingham in November 1940 concerned with the provision of air-raid shelters, he had attacked the Cement Makers' Federation as a ring of monopolists holding up the supply of cement at a time of great public need in the interests of their own private profit. The bishop was sued for slander. He did not appear in court, although he was represented by counsel. The cement companies were awarded £1,600 damages. It was an index of the respect, and even affection, in which Barnes was by this time held that the money was raised by lay friends in the diocese. The bishop in a speech in the House of Lords in June 1941 returned undaunted to the attack, maintaining that a cement ring did exist, that it was contrary to the public interest, and that big business was using libel and slander actions to suppress criticism.

In 1947 Barnes entered the lists as a theological author, his book, *The Rise of Christianity*, arousing fierce opposition. History cannot be written without presuppositions, and the bishop's presuppositions precluded the recognition of miracles. In his reconstruction of the beginnings of Christianity he relied too exclusively upon the conclusions of a limited number of scholars whose tendency was to date the New Testament writings impossibly late. The outraged orthodox demanded his condemnation. Under great pressure to take action of some kind, but unwilling to prosecute,

Archbishop Fisher, in a presidential address to Convocation, after expressing deep appreciation of the bishop's Christian character and of the sincerity of his aims, delivered a strong and damaging criticism of his book and of certain of its presuppositions, and cautioned readers against accepting its claim to be an adequate and impartial setting forth of the truth. While declaring that he 'would have no trial in this matter', he went on to say: 'If his views were mine, I should not feel that I could still hold episcopal office in the Church.' The hint was ignored by Barnes who made in the House of Bishops a personal statement which their lordships did not discuss. Action parallel with that of the archbishop of Canterbury having been taken also in York Convocation by Archbishop Garbett [q.v.], the matter was allowed to drop.

The external record of recurring crises and controversies by which his tenure of the see of Birmingham was marked exhibits Barnes as a very unusual type of prelate: a stormy petrel of the episcopate. Yet there is another side to the story. Thorny and unbending in controversy, and indifferent to the exasperation roused by his utterances, he was none the less personally charming and manifestly a man of the highest character and purpose. He had made initial mistakes, but in the later phases of his episcopate he appreciably mellowed. He had either worn down opposition or had reached a tacit *modus vivendi* with his opponents. His was a complicated and many-sided character; he could be shy and awkward, but he was inwardly eager for friendship and capable of great personal kindness. The story is told that a young Anglo-Catholic curate who went to tea with him returned from the encounter remarking: 'I do not know whether I agree with him, but I know he is a saint.' By all but a few of the laity of his diocese he was held in the highest honour and admired as a man of inflexible courage. The administrative side of a bishop's work was admittedly not congenial to him, but during his time at Birmingham a considerable number of new churches were built and consecrated, and new parishes were formed to meet changing conditions. He resigned his see in May 1953 and died on 29 November of the same year at his home at Hurstpierpoint in Sussex.

Barnes was a fellow of King's College, London (1919), Gifford lecturer at Aberdeen (1926–8), and received the honorary degrees of D.D. from Aberdeen (1925) and Edinburgh (1927), and LL.D. from Glasgow (1926).

In 1916 Barnes married Adelaide Caroline Theresa (died 1963), daughter of Sir Adolphus Ward [q.v.], master of Peterhouse, Cambridge; there were two sons of the marriage. A bronze plaque of Barnes by David Wynne is in Birmingham Cathedral.

[*The Times*, 30 November 1953; *Chronicle of Convocation*, 1947; Sir Edmund Whittaker in *Obituary Notices of Fellows of the Royal Society*, vol. ix, 1954; G. K. A. Bell, *Randall Davidson*, 1935; private information; personal knowledge.]   A. E. J. RAWLINSON.

BARNES, SIR GEORGE REGINALD (1904–1960), broadcasting director and college principal, was born in Byfleet 13 September 1904, the son of Sir Hugh Shakespear Barnes, lieutenant-governor of Burma, and his second wife, Edith Helen, sister of (Sir) Kenneth Barnes and Irene and Violet Vanbrugh [qq.v.]. Educated at the Royal Naval Colleges at Osborne and Dartmouth, he was ultimately rejected for the navy because of his eyesight. But his interest in naval affairs never diminished, however varied and strong his other interests. With Commander J. H. Owen he published in 1932–8 four volumes of the private papers of the fourth Earl of Sandwich [q.v.] and he always cherished the dream of finding time to write a study of the British navy in the early nineteenth century.

From Dartmouth he went to King's College, Cambridge, where he obtained a second class in part i of the historical tripos (1924) and a first in part ii (1925). There was some expectation that he would try for the Foreign Office but the pull of the navy proved too strong and he returned to Dartmouth for three years (1927–30) as an assistant master. In 1930 he went as assistant secretary to the Cambridge University Press where he developed 'a fine taste and a good judgement in the economics as well as the aesthetics of the trade', and revised the *Hand-List of Cambridge Books* extending it to 1800.

In 1935 Barnes joined the British Broadcasting Corporation where his strong social conscience gave an educational impetus to his work. He believed that public taste needs guiding: that it should be led, not followed. Coupled with this belief was his sense of responsibility towards listener minorities and the complex needs of each individual listener. In 1941 he was

67

appointed director of talks in succession to Sir Richard Maconachie under whom he had worked since Maconachie joined the Corporation in 1937; in 1945 he became Maconachie's assistant controller of talks. In that year he made his first visit to the United States from which he returned with his horizons widened and with a final access of assurance which never deserted him.

When the Third Programme was established in 1946 Barnes was the obvious choice to give the idea practical form. He aimed at the highest standards in both programme and performance: 'We shall live or die by the amount we are prepared to experiment... We will experiment with new forms of radio, new writers, new performers, and new presentations.' His own lifelong devotion to music found scope which he described as 'vast and even thrilling' in the Third Programme's long-term plan to give the finest available performances of music of every style and epoch, with special emphasis on rarely heard works of interest and beauty. Comparably large in conception was the great series of programmes on the 'Ideas and Beliefs of the Victorians' (1948).

In 1948 Barnes joined the B.B.C.'s board of management as director of the spoken word and in October 1950 he was appointed to the newly created post of director of television. The B.B.C.'s five-year plan to expand and develop its television service, giving priority to 'coverage', had been under way for a year. New transmitters were opened at Sutton Coldfield (1949) and Holme Moss (1951) and the Lime Grove studios were taken over early in 1950. But the service was still based on Alexandra Palace and 'for two nightmare years', as Barnes later recorded in the *B.B.C. Quarterly* (Summer 1954), 'every piece of scenery and every property for the half-dozen different productions each day had to be transported twenty-four miles'. It was not until 1954 that concentration at Shepherds Bush was achieved.

The enormous increase in range which B.B.C. television obtained during the six years of Barnes's directorship is reflected in an increase in licences from 343,882 (1950) to 5,739,593 (1956). Among the many new ventures were the first experimental schools television programmes (May 1952); the televising of the coronation of Queen Elizabeth II (June 1953); the first large-scale Eurovision link-up of eight countries (June 1954); the inaugura-

tion of a daily 'News and Newsreel' (July 1954); and ceaseless experiment with colour television (the first colour television outside broadcast, transmitted on closed circuit to the Children's Hospital, Great Ormond Street, was of the coronation). In October 1953 on a visit to Lime Grove studios the Queen knighted Barnes with a sword which had been smuggled in from Buckingham Palace.

In 1955 the Independent Television Authority began commercial television. In the previous year Barnes had stressed the necessity of a second channel for the B.B.C. to provide a planned alternative programme in order to cater for the varying tastes of its public; in 1956 he emphasized the need to maintain high standards and avoid the exclusive pursuit of mass popularity: 'The audience figures that are being bandied about in the fine shouting-war that is going on are not a criterion of excellence. To seek success in popularity alone is a trivial use of a great invention. Mass without mind always comes a cropper...'.

In 1956 Barnes became principal of the University College of North Staffordshire which had been unfortunate in the death of its first two principals (Lord Lindsay of Birker and Sir John Lennard-Jones, qq.v.) within a few years of their appointment. A similar fate was to strike Barnes who died at Keele, 22 September 1960, after no more than four years of stimulating service to the new foundation. A memorial fund was devoted to the development and teaching of music in the university which Barnes had done much to improve. His concern was ever with quality, whether in music, the visual arts, or human relationships. From a wide circle of friends he entertained at Keele distinguished writers, politicians, painters, and scholars, whose visits greatly enriched the life of a small and relatively isolated university; and by his own diligence in accepting public engagements he sought in his turn to make Keele more widely known. A frail-looking man, he possessed great resilience and inner strength, nourished by his deep concern for the life of the chapel. His naval training imbued him with a sense of service and he devoted all his energy and practical idealism to the furtherance of the things of the mind and of the spirit which he valued.

At one time or another Barnes served on many bodies concerned with the interests he had at heart. They included the council of the Royal College of Art, the British Film Institute, the Standing Commission on Museums and Galleries, the Council of Industrial Design, the Wedgwood Society (formed early in 1955 with Barnes as first chairman), the British Pottery Manufacturers' Federation, and the committee appointed in January 1958 by the Gulbenkian Foundation to inquire into the needs of the arts in Britain. He received an honorary D.C.L. from Durham in 1956.

In 1927 Barnes married Dorothy Anne, daughter of Henry Bond, master of Trinity Hall, Cambridge (1919–29); they had one son.

[Private information; personal knowledge.]
LAURENCE GILLIAM.

BARNES, SIR KENNETH RALPH (1878–1957), principal of the Royal Academy of Dramatic Art, was the youngest son of the Rev. Reginald Henry Barnes, vicar of Heavitree, Devonshire, prebendary of Exeter Cathedral. He was born at the vicarage 11 September 1878, the youngest of a family of six. His mother, Frances Mary Emily Nation, had a natural but unfulfilled talent for acting and encouraged the dramatic spirit in her children; this flourished in two of Barnes's sisters, Violet and Irene Vanbrugh [qq.v.]. In Kenneth a natural interest in the drama was matched by a bias towards the climate of simple piety and conventional religious faith into which he was born. His father died when he was still a boy and his upbringing owed much to the influence of his mother and sisters; the latter, in particular, had a considerable influence on his life and subsequent career.

He was educated at Westminster School but left when not yet seventeen to pay an extended visit to a sister who had recently married the British resident in Kashmir and who was to be the mother of Sir G. R. Barnes (see above). There began the familiarity with the personalities of English ruling society which was to assume importance when his ambitions became more clearly defined. After three years at Christ Church, Oxford, he was still uncertain what his calling should be. At one time he had almost been persuaded to follow his father's profession, but a desire for variety and dislike of a predictable future led him, after a short period as a clerk in the Land Registry, towards freelance journalism. This gave him opportunity for travel, for many acquaintanceships, and for frequent visits to the theatre, a world open to him through the success of his sisters. The

editor of the *Daily Mirror* soon commissioned him to write criticisms of plays; the *Standard* and, later, *The Times* also engaged him from time to time to write on theatrical matters. In 1907 he toured Canada with a party of journalists for the *Westminster Gazette* and the next two years were spent in journalism, in writing two one-act plays, and in translating Hervieu's *Connais-Toi* which was presented, as *Glass Houses*, at the Globe Theatre in 1910.

His opportunity came in 1909 when George Bancroft, the administrator of the Academy of Dramatic Art founded by (Sir) Herbert Beerbohm Tree [q.v.] in 1904, invited him for an interview at 62 Gower Street. The Academy was neither very flourishing nor, in the opinion of many of the theatrical profession, very necessary. Yet certain distinguished men of the theatre whom Tree had gathered into a governing body obstinately believed in its value. It could not pay a large salary and Bancroft was giving up his post. Barnes was engaged as principal of 'ADA', as it was flippantly called, at a salary of £250 per annum.

From the beginning the new principal was in conflict. He was himself no actor. Actors were customarily trained in the rough school of the companies of the actor-managers. The tradition had lasted since Burbage, and it seemed to many members of the profession that there was no need for the academic aura which Barnes seemed to be striving to give to their calling. Time, however, was on the principal's side: the actor-managers were dying out and in their place were avowed business men who had neither the intention nor the ability to train young performers. The number of students attracted to ADA increased steadily and it seemed that a dramatic school was after all a welcome institution.

After serving with the Hampshire Regiment during the war years, in India, the Middle East, and Siberia, Barnes returned to Gower Street in 1919 to face a series of formidable tasks. He brought to them a sense of high duty and dedication and qualities of indefatigable tenacity, courage, and simple faith. By persistent begging for the cause of his heart he found space and money for the Academy to expand. A student theatre in Malet Street, started before the war, was completed in 1921; and the modern building in Gower Street in 1931. No sooner was the theatre destroyed in 1941 than plans were worked out for its replacement by something better. The Vanbrugh Theatre, named after his sisters, for which he successfully launched a mass appeal for £78,000, was opened in 1954, the year before his retirement.

Barnes wanted more than imposing buildings and prosperity for his Academy. He wanted official recognition of his institution and of the art of acting. Through his continued efforts the Academy received a royal charter and became the Royal Academy of Dramatic Art in 1920. The Treasury accorded it a grant-in-aid in 1924; and the Inland Revenue recognized it as a charity, with consequent exemption from income-tax, in 1926. In 1930, after taking seven legal actions, he obtained from the quarter-sessions a decision of historic significance. This was that acting was henceforth to be classed as a fine art in company with literature, painting, sculpture, architecture, and music. It was characteristic of Barnes's thrift that this decision was obtained in pursuance of a claim for the Academy to be exempted from the burden of the general rate. So successful were the principal's financial methods in general that by the time of his retirement he had steered the Academy at last into a position of complete economic security.

The success of his life-work was the reward, he would have said, of many years of single-minded devotion to a worthy cause under the blessing of God. He was a kindly man who, when faced with controversy in matters of religion or art, accepted naturally the views of the Church of England and conservative opinion. Without his faith in what were for him eternal values, it is doubtful whether his achievements would have been possible. He believed firmly that the theatre could serve towards the spiritual betterment of man; more firmly still he believed in the theatre's importance as a part of society, and he was well placed to guide his students towards achieving the necessary social graces. Instruction in the artistic and technical problems of acting was a matter for his staff. Sometimes the charge of snobbery was laid at his door; and it was true that he sometimes failed to recognize talent when it was concealed beneath an uncouth or provincial exterior. Matters of social distinction had importance for him, if only because he had to rely so often for help to the Academy on the generosity of titled people. The social aspirations which he had for his institu-

tion and for its products were greatly aided by his happy and successful marriage in 1925 to Daphne, daughter of Sir Richard James Graham, fourth baronet, of Netherby, Cumberland. They had one son.

Barnes was knighted in 1938 and died at Kingston Gorse, Sussex, 16 October 1957. A bust in bronze by Clemence Dane was placed in the entrance hall of the Royal Academy of Dramatic Art in Gower Street.

[Sir Kenneth Barnes, *Welcome, Good Friends*, 1958; private information; personal knowledge.]   JOHN FERNALD.

BARNETT, LIONEL DAVID (1871–1960), orientalist, was born in Liverpool 21 October 1871, the eldest son of Baron Barnett, banker, by his wife, Adelaide Cowan. He was educated at the High School, Institute, and University College, Liverpool. He went up to Trinity College, Cambridge, in 1892 and was elected a scholar in 1893. He was Sir William Browne's medallist (Greek ode, 1893, 1894, 1896; Greek epigram, 1893); gained a first class (division 1) in part i of the classical tripos in 1894 and was elected Craven scholar the same year. In 1896 he was awarded a first class, with special distinction in language, in part ii of the classical tripos, together with the Chancellor's medal. He was appointed Craven student in 1897 and in 1900 the university of Manchester conferred on him the degree of Litt.D. He studied Sanskrit at Cambridge and Halle.

In 1899 Barnett joined the staff of the British Museum as assistant keeper in the department of oriental printed books and manuscripts and after only nine years was promoted keeper of the department in succession to Sir Robert Douglas. To the duties of this post, its functions officially defined as 'to conserve, augment and catalogue the collections', he brought a remarkable threefold equipment of fine scholarship, administrative ability, and business acumen which resulted in the museum's store of oriental manuscripts and books being enormously enriched during his twenty-eight years of office. The vast range of his erudition in the cultures of both East and West was probably unique in the museum's history. He compiled a monumental series of no fewer than ten descriptive catalogues of oriental printed books in the Indo-Aryan and Dravidian languages, covering Sanskrit, Pali, Prakrit, Kannada, Badaga, Kurg,

Tamil, Telugu, Burmese, Hindi, Bihari, Pahari, Panjabi, Saurashtra, and other dialects, large quarto volumes containing in all some 8,000 columns of text.

Library administration and bibliography on this massive scale were only a part of his many-sided activity. From 1906 to 1917 he held the professorship of Sanskrit at University College, London. When the university's School of Oriental Studies was founded he was included on its staff as lecturer in Sanskrit (1917–48); lecturer in ancient Indian history and epigraphy (1922–48); and librarian (1940–47). When he retired from the School in 1948 a special volume of its *Bulletin* was published in his honour. He was elected F.B.A. in 1936 and appointed C.B. in 1937. A prominent figure in the Royal Asiatic Society, he was at various times a member of council and vice-president, its honorary librarian from 1939 onwards, and was awarded its gold medal in 1950.

The Greek and Latin classics were Barnett's first love and throughout life his prodigious memory was stored with them. For the benefit of the young student and the cultured lay public he published between 1900 and 1904 a succession of useful volumes, some translated from the German, on classical history and literature. Thereafter the works he produced, as separate books or as monographs in learned periodicals, dealt almost entirely with Indological subjects: *The Antagaḍa-dasāo, etc.*, translated from the Prakrit (1907); *The Paramarthasara* (text and translation, 1910); *Lallā-vākyāni*, edited and translated (with Sir George Grierson, q.v., 1920). While studies such as these appeal mainly to the specialist, he also aimed, and with remarkable success, to interest a wider audience in India's history and culture with *Antiquities of India* (1913) and a number of works, mostly translations from the Sanskrit, published in 'The Wisdom of the East' series and elsewhere, such as *The Bhagavadgītā* (1905); *Brahma-knowledge* (1907); *The Heart of India* (1908); *The Golden Town, etc.* (1909); *The Path of Light* (1909; 2nd ed. 1947); *Hindu Gods and Heroes* (1922). His numerous contributions to learned journals embraced Indian history, epigraphy, folk-lore, drama, philology, and also Tibetan texts. He even published translations of Spanish documents relating to the history of the Jewish community of which he was a faithful and active member, holding several of its honorary offices.

His encyclopedic learning was carried with effortless ease and with never a trace of ostentation; indeed, he was only too prone to over-estimate the intelligence and erudition of others. This natural humility and his countless unobtrusive kindnesses, especially towards younger scholars, drew to him the affection of a host of friends. Although little given to outdoor recreation he enjoyed constant good health, until suddenly in 1932 his eyesight gave way under the intense strain of years, one eye becoming permanently useless and the sight of the other impaired. This grievous blow did not deter him, after a brief convalescence, from pressing on with fruitful academic work both in the study and in the lecture-room. In 1948 when he retired from his university duties he might reasonably have sought an easier life after half a century of ceaseless industry, but hearing that his old department at the British Museum from which he had retired in 1936 was in sore straits for staff, he offered his services as an assistant keeper and for the last twelve years of his life the museum once more profited from his vast knowledge and experience. A fortnight before his death in London, 28 January 1960, the Asiatic Society of Calcutta awarded him the Sir William Jones gold medal.

In 1901 Barnett married Blanche Esther (died 1955), daughter of the Rev. B. Berliner, minister of the St. John's Wood synagogue. They had a daughter and a son, Richard David Barnett, who in 1955 became keeper of the department of western Asiatic antiquities in the British Museum.

[Bibliography of the published writings of Dr. L. D. Barnett, by Edith M. White, in the *Bulletin* of the School of Oriental and African Studies, vol. xii, 1948; A. L. Basham in *Proceedings* of the British Academy, vol. xlvi, 1960; *The Times*, 29 January 1960; private information; personal knowledge.]

A. S. FULTON.

BARRINGTON-WARD, SIR LANCE-LOT EDWARD (1884–1953), surgeon, was born at Worcester 4 July 1884, the second son of Mark James Barrington-Ward, inspector of schools, later rector of Duloe in Cornwall and an honorary canon of Truro Cathedral, and his wife, Caroline Pearson. Barrington-Ward's four brothers all distinguished themselves in their various professions, one of them, R. M. Barrington-Ward [q.v.], becoming editor of *The Times*. Barrington-Ward entered

Westminster School as a classical scholar, but owing to ill health he was transferred to Bromsgrove in his native county where he was restored to vigorous health and gained a classical exhibition at Worcester College, Oxford. Throughout his life his classical education was in evidence by his masterly command of word and phrase. He decided, however, upon medicine as his career and entered Edinburgh University where he qualified with second class honours in 1908 and was captain of the university rugby fifteen. Although light of build for a forward, he was awarded four English international caps and had the distinction of playing against Wales in the first international match played on the new ground at Twickenham. His other interest in sport was boxing, and he represented his university as a middle-weight.

Barrington-Ward passed the Edinburgh Fellowship examination in 1910 and the English Fellowship two years later after studying for this at the Middlesex Hospital. In 1913 he returned to Edinburgh to obtain the degree of Ch.M. and was awarded the much coveted Chiene medal for outstanding ability. His London career in surgery began with his appointment in 1910 as a resident at Great Ormond Street Hospital for Sick Children, where he had the good fortune of assisting two of the leading children's surgeons of the day—George E. Waugh and (Sir) Thomas Fairbank. He continued his work at this hospital as medical superintendent, and was appointed to the consulting staff in 1914. Immediately after the outbreak of war later in that year he volunteered to go to the Balkans as surgeon-in-chief of No. 2 Serbian Relief Fund Hospital, with the honorary rank of lieutenant-colonel. He was awarded the grand cross of the Order of St. Olave and St. Sava.

While still a young man Barrington-Ward's skill as a surgeon was widely recognized. He was much sought after by private patients and operated on several members of the royal family. In 1935 he was appointed K.C.V.O. and two years later he was made surgeon to His Majesty's household. In 1952 he was invited to become an extra-surgeon to the Queen.

His experience in children's surgery is recorded in numerous articles which he published in various journals and a standard textbook entitled *Abdominal Surgery of Children* (1928). In 1952 he delivered a Hunterian lecture at the Royal College of Surgeons on 'Swellings of the neck in children' and the council minutes record that the attendance was 175, a striking tribute to the reputation of the lecturer.

In addition to his work at Great Ormond Street, Barrington-Ward was on the staff of the Wood Green and Royal Northern hospitals. At the last he eventually became senior surgeon. To his colleagues there he suggested that they should co-operate in producing a textbook of operative surgery in which each member of the staff, many of whom were well-known authors, dealt with his own speciality. *Royal Northern Operative Surgery* was published in 1939 under his editorship and proved a notable addition to the literature of British surgery.

Barrington-Ward's success as a surgeon was not only due to his clinical judgement and technical skill: he was a most gentle and sympathetic surgeon and had the enviable knack of obtaining the confidence of children who were his patients. Handsome and debonair in appearance, kindly and courteous in manner, he invited confidences and inspired instinctive trust. The numerous medical colleagues (and their families) who sought his advice were an indication of the high esteem in which he was held. In the operating theatre he showed punctilious courtesy to all the staff including the most junior nurse, and in consequence the atmosphere was never tense. One gained the impression that he considered temperamental outbursts on the part of the surgeon to be the result of either bad manners or poor surgery. His critical mind and sound judgement were invaluable in committee work and most helpful in maintaining good relations between medical and lay bodies.

Barrington-Ward was twice married: first, in 1917 to Dorothy Anne, second daughter of T. W. Miles, of Caragh, county Kerry, who did much charitable work for hospitals with which her husband was connected and also for the Peter Pan League. She died in 1935, leaving three daughters. Barrington-Ward married secondly, in 1941, Catherine Wilhelmina, only daughter of E. G. Reuter, of Harrogate; they had one son.

Barrington-Ward enjoyed welcoming his friends to his happy and charming country home, Hawkedon House, near Bury St. Edmunds. He was knowledgeable enough about agriculture to be elected president of the Suffolk Agricultural Association. Unfortunately he was not long spared to enjoy the retirement to which he had been looking forward, for despite undergoing drastic surgery he died at his home 17 November 1953. A bust by June Barrington-Ward was shown at the Society of Portrait Sculptors exhibition in 1959.

[*The Times*, 18 November 1953; *British Medical Journal*, 28 November and 12 December 1953; *Lancet*, 28 November 1953; private information; personal knowledge.]
              McNEILL LOVE.

BASSETT-LOWKE,   WENMAN JOSEPH (1877–1953), model maker, was born in Northampton 27 December 1877, the eldest son of Joseph Thomas Lowke, and his wife, Eliza Goodman. After leaving school he worked with his father in the firm of J. T. Lowke & Sons, engineers and boiler makers, of Northampton, founded as Bassett & Sons by his grandfather in 1859. It was while working for his father that, with Harry Franklin as cashier, he founded the firm of Bassett-Lowke, Ltd., a small mail-order business selling components for model engines. At the Paris exhibition of 1900 he met Stephen Bing of Nuremberg, chairman of a toy-making firm, who agreed to manufacture for him and to specialize in O-gauge steam engines of British railway design, more closely to scale than any previous production.

By the outbreak of war in 1914, works and offices were functioning in Northampton and shops had been opened in London, Manchester, and Edinburgh. The shop at High Holborn, London, became a centre of attraction to boys of all ages and its catalogues are greatly treasured. After the war the firm not only manufactured scale model toys but also entered the business of making all types of exhibition models. The results of his firm's endeavours can be seen in the windows of many steamship companies, in museums, as well as in the playrooms of countless private homes. His customers, said the *Daily Mail*, 'ranged from small boys to oriental princes, from millionaires to kings'.

In warfare as in peaceful industry, models play an important part, and Bassett-Lowke was always equal to the calls made upon him by the armed Services, in particular those for the Normandy invasion of 1944. Plans and models of Mulberry harbours, landing-craft, pontoons, block-ships, Bailey bridges, and unit construction bridges were all made in Northampton. As a result, Combined Operations headquarters were said to have had the most up-to-date fleet of models of landing ships and equipment in the world.

Bassett-Lowke travelled extensively in Europe and America and often lectured and broadcast on models, railways, and ships. In 1948 there appeared the fourteenth edition of *The Model Railway Handbook* which he had edited since 1906. He was joint author of *Ships and Men* (1946) and of two Puffin books, *Waterways of the World* (1944) and *Marvellous Models* (1945). He also produced the Penguin *Book of Trains* (1941) and the Puffin book *Locomotives* (1947).

Bassett-Lowke was a member of the Institution of Locomotive Engineers, a fellow of the Royal Society of Arts, a founder-member of the Design and Industries Association, and a member of the Town and Country Planning Association. In Northampton he was a founder-member of the Rotary Club and founder-director of the repertory theatre. For several years he did much useful work on the town council; was finally an alderman; and in 1948 was asked to become mayor but was unable to accept. He brought Northampton into prominence through his modern architectural ideas, some of which were strikingly embodied in his own home.

A disciple of Fabianism before he entered into the wider sphere of socialism and Labour politics, Bassett-Lowke was a friend of G. B. Shaw [q.v.] who used to stay with him when he visited Northampton. Declining an invitation in his eighty-seventh year Shaw wrote: 'I am too damned old to go summer schooling nowadays. . . . I forget everything now in ten minutes but not the happy days at Northampton. Dotty and doddering but still able to write a bit.'

In 1917 Bassett-Lowke married Florence, third daughter of Charles Jones, of Crockett and Jones, shoe manufacturers, of Northampton, and niece of (Sir) James Crockett; there were no children. He died in Northampton 21 October 1953. A portrait by J. A. A. Berrie hangs in the Northampton offices.

[*Northampton Independent*, 23 October 1953; private information; personal knowledge.]   CYRIL DERRY.

BATHURST, CHARLES, first VISCOUNT BLEDISLOE (1867–1958), agriculturist and public servant, was born at Lydney, Gloucestershire, 21 September 1867, the second son of Charles Bathurst, of Lydney Park, and his wife, Mary Elizabeth, only daughter of Lieutenant-Colonel Thomas

Pasley Hay. Educated at Sherborne, Eton, and University College, Oxford, he obtained third classes in classical honour moderations (1888) and jurisprudence (1890). In 1935 he was made an honorary fellow of his college and received an honorary D.C.L.

In 1892 Bathurst was called to the bar by the Inner Temple but from 1893 until 1896 he studied at the Royal Agricultural College, Cirencester, where he obtained his diploma, was Ducie gold medallist, edited the college journal, and helped in the compilation of the students' register. His interest in the college was enduring; he was chairman of its governors in 1919-25 and for over fifty years was active in its cause. In 1950 a college hostel was named after him. It became customary for the estate management students to visit his estate from time to time to study its organization and his farming—he was famous for his herd of Red Poll cattle and the excellent fruit he grew in his orchards.

Meantime Bathurst practised as a Chancery barrister and conveyancer, until 1910 when he became Conservative member of Parliament for the South or Wilton division of Wiltshire. But his lifelong preoccupation was essentially agriculture. A founder-member of the Central Land Association, as it was originally called, Bathurst was its first honorary secretary from 1907 to 1909. In 1921-2 he was its president and in 1922 gave his celebrated address as president of the agricultural section of the British Association in which he criticized the unbusinesslike attitude of some landowners. He fathered the modern concept of landownership as a profession useful to the community, demanding specialized training to meet changed conditions. On these matters he had deep convictions: that agricultural landowners should continue to give constructive leadership to the industry and help to apply the latest scientific methods to its problems; that the C.L.A. should remain a rural organization and never join forces with urban landowners (it was renamed the Country Landowners' Association); that the growth of owner-occupation brought a beneficial infusion of new blood to landownership. He regarded the agricultural depression of the twenties and thirties as a challenge to farmers' enterprise and ingenuity and always kept up to date in the application of the latest scientific methods to running his own estate.

In 1916-17 Bathurst was parliamentary secretary to the Ministry of Food and at the same time chairman of the Federation of County Agricultural Executive Committees. In 1917-19 he was chairman of the royal commission on sugar supplies and director of sugar distribution. He was appointed K.B.E. in 1917 and created a baron in the following year. In 1924, now Lord Bledisloe, he became parliamentary secretary to the Ministry of Agriculture and in 1926 was sworn of the Privy Council. In the next year he was chairman of the royal commission on land drainage in England and Wales and of the imperial agricultural research conference. He resigned office in 1928 when he became chairman of the Imperial Grassland Association.

In 1930 Bledisloe was appointed governor-general of New Zealand, a country to which he took much that appealed to its people: a knowledge of farming; an eye for an animal; a gift of extensive oratory; the charm of a typical aristocrat of the 'old country'. Among the highlights of a most successful term of office was his gift to New Zealand of the historic site where the treaty of Waitangi was signed. The years of his administration were happy ones on both sides. On its conclusion in 1935 he was created a viscount; he had been appointed G.C.M.G. in 1930.

There were few countries Bledisloe did not visit on tours of agricultural investigation or other missions. In 1938 he was chairman of the royal commission on the closer union of the Rhodesias and Nyasaland. In early 1947 he carried out a goodwill visit to Australia and New Zealand and in 1948 made another to South Africa and Southern Rhodesia, both on behalf of the Royal Agricultural Society of England of which he had been president in 1946. He held office at one time or another in all the important agricultural societies of the country and in such other varied fields as the National Council of Social Service, the Empire Day Movement, and the Museums Association. In 1949 he was president of the second international congress of crop protection. He was an honorary D.Sc. (and pro-chancellor) of Bristol University and LL.D. of Edinburgh. For many years he was a verderer of the Forest of Dean and he was active in all local affairs. His benefactions locally were most generous. Deeply religious and a man of culture, he combined breadth of sympathy with a high sense of public duty, but probably the services he rendered to his well-loved

Lydney and Aylburton and the Forest of Dean gave him the most pleasure.

In 1898 Bathurst married Bertha Susan Lopes, youngest daughter of the first Baron Ludlow [q.v.]; they had two sons and a daughter. His wife died in 1926 and Bledisloe married in 1928 Alina Kate Elaine (died 1956), daughter of the first and last Baron Glantawe and widow of Thomas Cooper-Smith. There were no children of this marriage. Bledisloe died at his home at Lydney 3 July 1958 and was succeeded by his elder son, Benjamin Ludlow (born 1899).

[*Country Landowner*, August 1958; private information.]   JOHN RUGGLES-BRISE.

BATSFORD, HARRY (1880–1951), publisher, bookseller, and author, was born in London 18 April 1880, the only son of Henry George Batsford, publisher, who died two years later, by his wife, Matilda, daughter of William Ward. He was educated at Henley House School, Kilburn, where he was taught for a time by H. G. Wells [q.v.] and at the City of London School. In 1897 he entered the family bookselling and publishing business which had been founded fifty-four years earlier by his grandfather, Bradley Thomas Batsford. In 1917 he succeeded his uncle, Herbert Batsford, as chairman and managing director of B. T. Batsford, Ltd., and he remained in that position until his death.

In 1926 Batsford's work as a publisher of books on the technique and history of architecture was recognized by his election as an honorary associate of the Royal Institute of British Architects. In the early thirties, responding to economic pressure and changing taste, Batsford widened the scope of his firm's activities: he initiated more than one series of books, fully illustrated by photographs, on the architecture and topography of Britain, which gave the term 'a Batsford book' a recognized significance. These series, of which the best known were the 'British Heritage' and the 'Face of Britain', introduced to a new and wider public the beauties of Britain's landscape and ancient buildings and were not without influence in helping to preserve both from destruction. Batsford himself wrote, sometimes pseudonymously, or in collaboration with Charles Daniel Fry, a number of works, among them *Homes and Gardens of England* (1932), *The Landscape of England* (as Charles Bradley Ford, 1933), *The*

Cathedrals of England (1934), and *The English Cottage* (1938).

The more important part of Batsford's work and influence, however, was indirect, in the books which he stimulated others to write. Most of those whose works were published by his firm during more than half a century gladly acknowledged the help and stimulus which he gave them from a mind fully and variously stored. Among the authors whose work he published were Katharine Esdaile and H. J. Massingham [qq.v.], Margaret Jourdain, (Sir) Sacheverell Sitwell, (Sir) A. E. Richardson, and John Russell, who recorded (*Architectural Review*, April 1952) that of Batsford's 'passion for architecture there could never be any doubt; and in this, as in everything else, his inclination was always to put aside what was notorious and large in favour of what was plain, inviolate and true'.

In himself Batsford was vital, generous, and individualistic. He loved England and knew the country and its antiquities with exceptional intimacy, but he also felt himself a citizen of the world and had travelled enthusiastically in Europe and America. Apart from architecture, he had a keen amateur's knowledge of subjects as diverse as astronomy, natural history, geology, railway locomotives, and watches. He had a great fondness for animals, particularly for cats, for whose welfare he left a special legacy when he died in London 20 December 1951.

In 1928 Batsford married Rose Verene (died 1930), daughter of François André Sennwald, of Chaux de Milieux, Neuchâtel, Switzerland; there were no children. A portrait of Batsford by John Berry is in the possession of the firm.

[*The Times*, 21 December 1951; Hector Bolitho, *A Batsford Century*, 1943; personal knowledge.]   SAMUEL CARR.

BAX, SIR ARNOLD EDWARD TREVOR (1883–1953), composer, eldest son of Alfred Ridley Bax and his wife, Charlotte Ellen Lea, was born in Streatham 8 November 1883. His father, a man of independent means, was a fellow of the Society of Antiquaries and a regular subscriber to the Saturday concerts of Sir August Manns [q.v.] at the Crystal Palace. Clifford Bax, the author and playwright, was a younger brother. According to Bax's autobiographical *Farewell, my Youth* (1943) he could not remember the time when he was not able to read music at the piano 'with the same unthinking ease with which a man reads a book'. His early education was private, and in 1898 he became a student of the Hampstead Conservatoire, then in the charge of Cecil Sharp [q.v.]. Even in youth, however, Bax was not interested in English folksong, and two years later he entered the Royal Academy of Music, studying composition with Frederick Corder and pianoforte with Tobias Matthay. He won the Battison Haynes prize for composition in 1902, and in the following year, which saw his first public appearance in St. James's Hall as a composer, he was awarded the Macfarren scholarship for composition, which he held until he left the Academy in 1905. He distinguished himself also by winning the Charles Lucas medal for composition and the Walter Macfarren prize for piano playing. In addition to these achievements he was considered unique in his ability to read complex modern scores at the piano. Later he was to be elected an associate (1910) and a fellow (1921) of the Academy.

A formative influence during his early years was his private study of scores by Wagner, Strauss, and Debussy, whose music was then largely frowned on in academic circles. On leaving the Academy he twice visited Dresden, where he heard the original production of Strauss's *Salome*. But already another influence had entered his life. In 1902 he had come across 'The Wanderings of Oisin' by W. B. Yeats [q.v.] and in his own words, 'in a moment the Celt within me stood revealed'. For a time, indeed, he adopted a dual personality, and published three books of tales as 'Dermot O'Byrne'. Musically, also, he deliberately adopted a Celtic idiom to free himself from the influence of Wagner and Strauss, and in the tone-poem *In the Faëry Hills*, first given at a promenade concert in 1910, he employed what he described as 'figures and melodies of a definitely Celtic curve'. A visit to Russia in the same year also contributed to Bax's formulative musical experiences, providing material for, amongst other works, the First Piano Sonata.

The orchestral tone-poems were the first of Bax's works to attract attention, and *The Garden of Fand* (1916) is perhaps the most immediately appealing of them. No less important, however, are the later *Tintagel* and *November Woods* (both 1917) and *The Tale the Pine Trees Knew* (1931). None of these later works is based on Celtic subjects, and indeed this influence

almost completely disappeared from his music in the twenties. Colin Scott-Sutherland has listed the following among the inspirational origins of Bax's music— Wagner, Strauss, Yeats, Swinburne, Shelley, Grieg, the Icelandic sagas, the pre-Raphaelites, Finland, the seascapes of the North. The turning-point from the Celtic to the Nordic was possibly the Symphonic Variations for Piano and Orchestra (1917) written for Harriet Cohen, and it is significant that *Winter Legends*, composed for the same pianist thirteen years later, should have a Nordic and not a Celtic setting.

The music critic Edwin Evans, writing about Bax's music in 1919, described it as containing two complementary and compensatory qualities—robustness and wistfulness. The first he regarded as responsible for the elements of structure and inventiveness, while the second provided the music with its chromatic character: 'to be wistful and at the same time robust is a combination of qualities that falls to few'. Although none of the symphonies had then been produced, Evans had already observed in Bax's music the emergence of a more abstract, austere art; 'the harmony has become more incidental to the polyphonic interest'. As if to prove the rightness of Evans's judgement, Bax composed the unaccompanied motet *Mater ora Filium* (1921), an exercise in pure polyphony which undoubtedly prepared him for the seven symphonies (1922-39) upon which his ultimate reputation rests.

The symphonies may be divided into two groups, the first three and the last three, with the Fourth Symphony, written in both Donegal and Inverness-shire, forming an extrovert interlude between these largely introspective works. Together with the symphonies must be considered the two important works for piano and orchestra already mentioned, the Cello Concerto (1932), which Bax considered one of his finest works, and the Violin Concerto (1937-8) distinguished both for its geniality and for its inventive musical structure.

Bax's orchestral virtuosity was equalled in the chamber music field, and his output of some thirty works includes several unusual instrumental combinations, such as the Nonet for string quartet, double-bass, flute, clarinet, oboe, and harp. The harp, indeed, is an instrument much exploited by Bax, as is the viola. The piano music, which includes four solo sonatas, is important, and there is much fine choral music and also many songs of character. Bax also composed ballet and film music, his principal works in these fields being the ballet *The Truth about the Russian Dancers* (1920), written in collaboration with Karsavina and Sir J. M. Barrie [q.v.], and the film *Malta, G.C.* (1943). Like his contemporary John Ireland, he never showed any interest in opera.

Bax described himself as a 'brazen Romantic'. His life was conditioned both by literature and by nature: he was remarkably well read, and was never happier than when contemplating the ever-changing panorama of nature. Naturally such a man avoided public occasions whenever possible, and though he could mix easily with country people he had an almost claustrophobic distaste for urban society. The only time he could be seen in a crowd was at Lord's, for he was an enthusiastic lover of cricket.

In 1911 he married Elsita Luisa, a concert pianist, daughter of Carlos Sobrino, the Spanish pianist; they had one son and one daughter. Bax's increasing reputation as a composer brought him many honours, including a knighthood in 1937. He received honorary doctorates of music from Oxford (1934), Durham (1935), and the National University of Ireland (1947). In the last year of his life he was appointed K.C.V.O.

Possessing private means, Bax never needed to seek a musical appointment, which indeed would not have suited his temperament; when in 1942 he accepted the post of Master of the King's Musick, he did not overburden royal ears with occasional compositions. He probably found it embarrassing to 'shuffle around in knee-breeches', as he once put it, but he was a man who realized both the responsibility of the artist and the dignity of the composer.

He died in Cork 3 October 1953, on the day after he had taken part in the university's autumn music examinations. A memorial room dedicated to his memory has been created in Cork University which includes a death mask, his compositions, including some manuscripts, and the books he wrote as Dermot O'Byrne. A portrait, by Vera Bax, is on permanent loan to the Royal Academy of Music, and a drawing by Powys Evans is in the National Portrait Gallery.

[Sir Arnold Bax, *Farewell, my Youth*, 1943; R. H. Hull, *A Handbook on Arnold Bax's Symphonies*, 1932; Edwin Evans in *Musical Times*, March and April 1919; *Grove's Dictionary of Music and Musicians*; private information; personal knowledge.]

Julian Herbage.

BEERBOHM, Sir HENRY MAXIMILIAN (MAX) (1872–1956), author and cartoonist, was born in London 24 August 1872, the youngest child of Julius Ewald Beerbohm, a man of good Baltic family who had settled in England as a corn merchant, and of his second wife, Eliza Draper. Max Beerbohm was educated at a preparatory school in Orme Square, at Charterhouse, and at Merton College, Oxford. Gifted and precocious, by the time he left Oxford Beerbohm was already an accomplished personality, delicately dandified in looks and manner, and a detached, ironical observer of the human comedy. In 1893 he met young (Sir) William Rothenstein [q.v.] who, struck by his talent as a cartoonist, introduced him to the literary and aesthetic circle in London which revolved round the Bodley Head and whose most famous member was Aubrey Beardsley [q.v.]. By this time Max was also friendly with Oscar Wilde [q.v.]. He contributed 'A Defence of Cosmetics' to the first number of the *Yellow Book* in 1894; this had the distinction of being attacked angrily in *Punch*. In 1895, after going down from Oxford, Beerbohm made a short visit to the United States as secretary to his half-brother (Sir) Herbert Beerbohm Tree [q.v.], the actor. During this journey Max became engaged to Grace Conover, a member of Tree's company. He then settled in London, living with his sisters and widowed mother, drawing and writing: he contributed to various periodicals, notably the *Yellow Book*, the *Savoy*, and to the *Daily Mail*. In 1898 he succeeded G. B. Shaw [q.v.] as dramatic critic for the *Saturday Review*, a post which he held for twelve years. For the rest he occupied himself in social life, artistic and fashionable, where he was much in demand as a charming and witty talker. He became a friend of various distinguished persons including Henry James, Swinburne, Meredith, Conder, G. K. Chesterton [qq.v.], Gordon Craig, and, later, (Sir) Desmond MacCarthy [q.v.]. *The Works of Max Beerbohm*, a volume of essays, appeared in 1896, followed by *The Happy Hypocrite* (1897), *More* (1899), *Yet Again* (1909), and three volumes of drawings: *Caricatures of Twenty-five Gentlemen* (1896), *The Poets' Corner* (1904), and *A Book of Caricatures* (1907).

Meanwhile his love life followed an

uncertain course. His engagement with Miss Conover ended in 1903 to be followed by a brief engagement to the well-known actress Constance Collier. She broke it off and a few months later Max began a romantic friendship with yet another actress, Florence Kahn, an American known for her performances in the plays of Ibsen. In 1910 he married her. Partly because they were poor and Italy was cheap, partly because Max had grown tired of the pressure of London social life, they retired to Rapallo which was to be Beerbohm's main home for the rest of his life. In 1911 Max published his prose fantasy *Zuleika Dobson*; in 1912 *A Christmas Garland*, a book of parodies; in 1911 the cartoons *The Second Childhood of John Bull*; in 1913 *Fifty Caricatures*. But his life was passed mainly in humorous and leisurely contemplation, only interrupted by an occasional visit to England to superintend an exhibition of his drawings. In 1915, however, too keenly concerned for his country's fate in the war to stay abroad, he returned to England. Here he remained until 1919. During this period he produced *Seven Men* (1919), much of the work embodied in *And Even Now* (1920), and a memorial volume (1920) to his half-brother Herbert. His drawings were published in *A Survey* (1921); *Rossetti and his Circle* (1922); *Things New and Old* (1923); *Observations* (1925); and *Heroes and Heroines of Bitter Sweet* (1931). A selection of his dramatic criticisms entitled *Around Theatres* appeared in two volumes in 1924.

Two exhibitions, in 1921 and 1923, met with a more mixed reception than hitherto. His caricatures of Labour in 1921 led left-wing critics to rebuke him as a reactionary, whereas in 1923 his caricatures of royalty made Conservative writers attack him as an iconoclast. Amused but unwilling to cause scandal, Beerbohm agreed to withdraw some of the royal caricatures. Meanwhile, back in Italy, he had settled down into his old routine. *A Variety of Things*, his last volume of essays, appeared in 1928. Failing energy combined with a rigidly high standard of performance to make him write very little: and for the most part he set up as a figure from the past, happily resigned to the fact that his day was done. He continued now and again to visit London, notably in 1930 (when he was awarded an honorary LL.D. at Edinburgh), and in 1935 when his wife made a return to the stage in *Peer Gynt* at the Old Vic. In 1935 he was persuaded to broadcast on the subject of 'London Revisited'. He applied himself to the task with his usual high standard of perfection as regards both the text and the performance, with the result that in this wholly modern medium he made an extraordinary success. During the rest of his life he gave occasional broadcasts, some of which were published in *Mainly on the Air* in 1946. An enlarged edition appeared in 1957, after his death. He was knighted in 1939 and made an honorary D.Litt. of Oxford and an honorary fellow of Merton in 1942. The outbreak of war in 1939 had again kept the Beerbohms in England: but they returned to Italy in 1947. In 1951 Florence Beerbohm died. For the rest of his life Beerbohm was looked after by Elisabeth Jungmann (died 1959), an old friend of himself and his wife, although many years younger than either of them. Beerbohm married her in 1956; a few weeks later, 20 May 1956, he died in Rapallo. His ashes were placed in the crypt of St. Paul's Cathedral, where there is a memorial tablet. He had no children.

Max's character was unique and paradoxical: at once friendly and detached, childlike and prudent, sensible and fantastic. But he was much loved: for beneath his dandy's mask he hid a modest, honourable, and affectionate nature and an easy agreeability, enlivened by the play of a whimsical fancy and a demure, impish humour. The work mirrored the man. He aspired only to entertain; but it was entertainment of classical quality: the expression of a distinguished highly cultivated intelligence and an unfailing sense of style. He was a shrewd if not a profound critic and the best essayist, parodist, and cartoonist of his age. His satire was ruthless and urbane, the manifestation of a civilized and independent conservatism, repelled alike by the work of Kipling and of Wells [qq.v.]. Meanwhile, in his masterpieces, *Zuleika Dobson* and *Seven Men*, he discovered an original form of ironical fantasy. The blend of aesthete and comedian in him gave his work a double charm: it is at once exquisitely pretty and exquisitely comic.

A portrait of Beerbohm by J.-E. Blanche is on loan from the Ashmolean Museum to Merton College where there is also a portrait statuette by Lady Kennet and a drawing by Rothenstein; another drawing by Rothenstein is in the Manchester City Art Gallery; the National Portrait Gallery has a portrait by Sir William Nicholson, pencil drawings by R. G. Eves and Rothenstein, and a lithograph by C. H.

Shannon; a portrait in oils by Eves is in the Tate Gallery.

[A. E. Gallatin and L. M. Oliver, *A Bibliography of the Works of Max Beerbohm*, 1952; J. G. Riewald, *Sir Max Beerbohm*, The Hague, 1953; David Cecil, *Max*, 1964; private information; personal knowledge.]

DAVID CECIL.

BEITH, JOHN HAY (1876–1952), writer under the pseudonym of IAN HAY, was born 17 April 1876 in Manchester, the third son and sixth child of John Alexander Beith, a cotton merchant prominent in the public life of the city, and his wife, Janet, daughter of David Fleming, also a merchant in Manchester. He was the grandson of Alexander Beith [q.v.], one of the founders of the Free Church of Scotland in 1843, and his background was passionately old-style Scottish. From Fettes he went to St. John's College, Cambridge, where he obtained a second class in part i of the classical tripos (1898) and distinguished himself at rowing; later, 'large oars' were to garnish his house. He showed early interest in writing and the theatre, submitting 'pars' to the popular press, and haunting country-houses devoted to amateur theatricals.

In 1901 Beith was a junior master at Fettes before returning to Cambridge for a short period to study science. In 1902 as a junior science master he joined Durham School where he worked supremely hard; he coached the rugby teams and river crews and did house tutoring. A charming companion, with a developed social sense, he was extremely popular. Although not in the plot, Durham featured in one of his best books, *Housemaster* (1936).

In 1906 Beith returned to Fettes. Whilst sharing largely in school life, reviving the debating society, fostering school and house concerts, and helping to form the O.T.C., he spent most of his leisure writing, curiously usually in cynosural spots. He was a resourceful if unconventional teacher—lessons on compound interest might wander into New York's finances and end by stabilizing the national debt, but he knew public-school boys instinctively and enjoyed schoolmastering. When in 1912 he left Fettes to make writing his career his decision was generally regretted, perhaps even eventually by himself.

Beith's first novel, *Pip* (1907), coloured by early Manchester schooldays, had been a best-seller and had been followed by other equally light and humorous novels, among them *The Right Stuff* (1908)

and *A Man's Man* (1909). With the publication in 1914 of *A Knight on Wheels* and his *Lighter Side of School Life* which owes much to Fettes, his career as a writer was assured. His humour, family gift for story telling, shrewd observation, sentimentality, and truly 'English' grace of sympathetically conveying eccentric characters perfectly suited the age.

In the war of 1914–18 Beith served first with the Argyll and Sutherland Highlanders, then transferred to the Machine Gun Corps. He reached the rank of captain in 1915 and major in 1918 and was mentioned in dispatches and awarded the M.C. in 1916. In the meantime his most famous book, *The First Hundred Thousand*, had been published in 1915. Written in billets at home and in France, it was effective beyond its apparent literary stature, especially in America, then isolated by war conditions from British thought. It was followed by *Carrying On* (1917) and *The Last Million* (1918). Earlier employed in recruiting, Beith spent 1916–18 in America with the information bureau of the British War Mission where his energy and success were rewarded by a C.B.E. (1918).

In 1919 Beith took up the theatre, living from then on in London, absorbed in its social and theatrical life. He was particularly successful in translating his own novels into plays, among them *A Safety Match* (1921), *Housemaster* (1936), and, perhaps his most successful play, *Tilly of Bloomsbury* (1919, based on his novel *Happy-go-Lucky*, 1913). This has considerable merit and largely through his skill in making small parts interesting has remained an amateurs' favourite. Despite the cynicism and vulgarity of the age, his wit, romanticism, decorous mind, and exceptional theatrical sense kept his plays popular. He proved an excellent collaborator with other writers, among them Anthony Armstrong (*Orders are Orders*, 1932); Guy Bolton (*A Song of Sixpence*, 1930); (Sir) Seymour Hicks (q.v., *Good Luck*, 1923); Stephen (later Lord) King-Hall (*The Middle Watch*, 1929, and others); A. E. W. Mason (q.v., *A Present from Margate*, 1933); L. du Garde Peach (*The White Sheep of the Family*, 1951); and P. G. Wodehouse (*A Damsel in Distress*, 1928, *Leave it to Psmith*, 1930, and others).

Although Beith's gay theatrical flair was unfaltering, through some curious change in emphasis his later novels never achieved his pre-war success. He eventually failed to adjust and his last works were considered failures. *The King's Service* (1938), an informal history of the army, may have helped him to the directorship of War Office public relations (1938–41) and the rank of major-general, but this and the war cut him off from his public. His tribute to Malta, *The Unconquered Isle* (1943), an attempt at a second *Hundred Thousand*, misjudged the mood of a people who with their own experience of bombing resented his cheerful glossing.

On the lapse of his directorship Beith returned to work in America. After 1945 he wrote semi-official histories, deemed failures, though none is bad; his one serious, and inexplicable, play, *Hattie Stowe* (1947), about Harriet Beecher Stowe, failed, possibly only through an over-large cast.

Beith had apparently enjoyed his London years. He travelled, was chairman of the Society of Authors (1921–4, 1935–9), a member of the council of the League of British Dramatists from 1933, and president of the Dramatists Club from 1937. He was an officer of the Order of St. John of Jerusalem, for long a governor of Guy's Hospital, and gave his services also to St. Dunstan's. A very fine bow shot he was a member of the Queen's Body Guard for Scotland, the Royal Company of Archers, a history of which he wrote in 1951. He was noted for charm, striking personality, equable temperament, after-dinner speeches, and personal austerity. Some observers, however, thought they detected an inner unhappiness; perhaps his essential Calvinism evoked a sense of regret discernible in his own reported remark, bitter though humorously offered, that all his life he had lived on his wits.

In 1915 Beith married Helen Margaret, only daughter of the late Peter Alexander Speirs, of Polmont Park, Stirlingshire; they had no children. He died near Petersfield 22 September 1952. There is a portrait at the Garrick Club by T. C. Dugdale.

[*The Times* and *Scotsman*, 23 September 1952; *The Fettesian*, December 1952; *Fifty Years of Fettes, 1870–1920*, 1931; private information; personal knowledge.]

PATRICK MURRAY.

BELISHA, (ISAAC) LESLIE HORE-, BARON HORE-BELISHA (1893–1957), politician. [See HORE-BELISHA.]

BELL, GEORGE KENNEDY ALLEN (1883–1958), bishop of Chichester, was born at Hayling Island 4 February 1883, the eldest of the five sons and seven children of the Rev. James Allen Bell and his wife, Sarah Georgina, daughter of John George Megaw, merchant banker, of Upper Norwood, London. His father, then the incumbent of Hayling Island, finally became canon residentiary of Norwich Cathedral in 1918. Bell was educated at Westminster School and Christ Church, Oxford, where he obtained a first in classical moderations (1903) and a second in *literae humaniores* (1905). At Oxford he established a reputation as a poet, winning the Newdigate prize in 1904 and becoming general editor of the *Golden Anthologies* of verse while still an undergraduate. After a year at Wells theological college he was ordained deacon in 1907 (priest in 1908) to a curacy of Leeds parish church under Samuel Bickersteth. Here he developed a keen interest in social affairs and began a lifelong connection with Albert Mansbridge [q.v.] and the Workers' Educational Association. This interest developed further after 1910 when he returned to Christ Church as tutor and lecturer (1910) and student (1911). It brought him into close contact with such kindred spirits as Scott Holland and William Temple [qq.v.] and he played a leading part in the establishment of university settlements in London and in the industrial north.

At the outbreak of war in 1914 Bell accepted, although not without some hesitation, the invitation of Archbishop Davidson (whose notice he later contributed to this Dictionary) to become one of his domestic chaplains, thereby inaugurating a long and fruitful partnership. Thanks to an unusual combination of affairs both civil and ecclesiastical, arising primarily from the war and its aftermath, Bell became the linchpin of Lambeth administration, and the accomplished intermediary between the archbishop and a host of leaders in Church and State both at home and abroad. His introduction to the ecumenical movement took place in 1919, when he attended the first post-war meeting of the World Alliance for International Friendship through the Churches in Holland, as a member of the British delegation. Here he first met Archbishop Söderblom of Sweden and heard him propound the then apparently utopian plan for a permanent Ecumenical Council of the Christian Churches. In the following year, when he acted as assistant secretary of the Lambeth Conference, Bell was largely responsible for the initiation of the private discussions which resulted in the issue of the Appeal to all Christian People. It was obvious that his preferment could not long be delayed, and in 1924 he was appointed dean of Canterbury at the early age of forty-one—Ramsay MacDonald's first important ecclesiastical appointment.

His tenure of the deanery (1924–9) was marked by vast changes in the life of the cathedral. The Chapter Office was reorganized, the Friends of the Cathedral were instituted, visitors' fees were abolished, pilgrimages were encouraged, services were broadcast regularly, and non-Anglicans were invited to preach. The most remarkable of Bell's ventures was the production of John Masefield's *The Coming of Christ* in 1928, the first dramatic performance in an English cathedral since the Middle Ages. This set the pattern for a succession of productions in which he still took an interest even after he had left Canterbury. It was, for example, at his instigation that T. S. Eliot wrote *Murder in the Cathedral* for the Canterbury Festival in 1935; and this achievement was followed by other new plays from Charles Williams, Dorothy L. Sayers [qq.v.], Christopher Hassall, and Christopher Fry.

Bell adopted a similar forward-looking policy when he became bishop of Chichester in 1929. His willingness to try new methods of evangelism was evinced by a series of appointments at the time quite unique in the Church of England: a director of religious drama, a liturgical missioner, a bishop's chaplain for schools, and a canon teacher. He continued his pioneer work of encouraging the arts, and he firmly believed that the artist should be given freedom to respond to his own vision. This principle was clearly enunciated in his famous judgement on the Goring case in 1954, when he granted a faculty for a mural painting by Hans Feibusch depicting Christ in Glory despite the objections of the advisory committee to the preliminary drawings.

Before moving to Chichester, Bell had already established himself as one of the leaders of the Life and Work movement. He had been one of the small group responsible for drafting the *Message* of its first conference at Stockholm in 1925, which affirmed the duty of all Churches to apply the Gospel to every sphere of human life. As chairman of the council from 1932 to 1934 and as chairman of the administrative committee from 1934 to 1938 his guidance not only brought the movement safely through a period of crisis, but also gave it purpose and a policy. Nothing indicated this more clearly than his attitude to the Church conflict in Nazi Germany. He firmly supported the Confessional Church in its struggle for freedom. During the war of 1939–45 his consistent refusal to identify the German people as a whole with National Socialism and his courageous condemnation of the indiscriminate allied bombing of German cities despite considerable adverse criticism undoubtedly contributed to the disregard of his strong claims to succeed William Temple as archbishop of Canterbury in 1944. His work in re-establishing fellowship between the German Church and other Churches after the war was a major contribution to the success of the first meeting of the World Council of Churches in 1948, when the Life and Work and the Faith and Order movements joined forces. He was the first chairman of its central committee from 1948 to 1954, and honorary president from 1954 until his death. Official recognition of his work in the cause of Anglo-German understanding came in 1958 when the Federal German Republic awarded him the grand cross of the Order of Merit.

Bell's great moral courage in consistently proclaiming the Christian truth as he saw it, however unpopular it might be, was matched by his passionate concern for the individual. His definition of the task confronting the World Council of Churches in 1953 indicated this clearly: 'The World Council of Churches stands before the nations, and before the United Nations, as a world-wide fellowship appealing for an end of hatred and suspicion and war, declaring that the world of nations is one single family and that all are responsible for their neighbour's welfare.' In 1936 he had sponsored a National Christian Appeal for Refugees from Germany from which there resulted—again with his help —an International Christian Committee for German Refugees. He was also chairman of the Church of England committee for non-Aryan Christians, and chairman of the Famine Relief Committee, while after the war he took the lead in mobilizing the British Churches to help with the work of reconstruction in Europe. Nor was all this work undertaken at the committee level; he took a personal interest in a phenomenal number of cases. In 1947 the International Hebrew Christian Alliance invited him to accept honorary membership in recognition of his services to Jewish Christians throughout the world.

Bell's devotion to Christian unity was also manifest in a number of other ways. A firm believer in personal contacts, his visits to other Churches were extensive. He shared with A. C. Headlam [q.v.], bishop of Gloucester, the responsibility of urging upon the Church of England the need for a Council on Foreign Relations, and he succeeded Headlam as its chairman from 1945 to 1958. He was a strong supporter of the Church of South India, which was created in 1947; he was joint-chairman of the Anglican–Methodist conversations in this country which began in 1956; and he wrote a number of books to further the cause of unity—four volumes of *Documents on Christian Unity* (1924–58), *Christian Unity, the Anglican Position* (1948), and *The Kingship of Christ* (1954). Two other of his literary works deserve mention. The first is his two-volume biography of *Randall Davidson* (1935) which presented not only a vivid, lifelike portrait of the archbishop but also an authoritative history of the Church of England during the first three decades of the twentieth century, and has been justifiably acclaimed as the finest of modern ecclesiastical biographies. The second is *Christianity and World Order* (1940) which argued that the Christian religion provided the only solution to the bankruptcy of common social purpose in the twentieth century: it was a pioneer work—the first theological book to be written specifically as a paperback—and over eighty thousand copies were sold in three years.

Throughout his life Bell's interests covered an astonishingly wide field. He was closely concerned with the problems of Church–State relations, and he was an active member of the Archbishops' Commission on Church and State appointed in 1930. He firmly supported the Establishment, but he was also convinced that the Church should have freedom to deal with matters of worship and doctrine—a principle for which he fought strenuously but unsuccessfully throughout his episcopate. His early interest in social affairs never waned, he was a keen supporter of the trade-union movement, and he was well versed in the intricacies of international politics. From 1923 he was a member of the Royal Institute of International Affairs. It must not be thought, however, that he neglected his diocese. Chichester was given the major portion of his time

and energy, and he proved himself to be an excellent administrator and a devoted pastor. His knowledge of the parishes and their clergy and people was profound, and he excelled at personal contacts. His effectiveness in so many fields was due to a strong constitution, tremendous energy, and a retentive mind. Until the last year of his life he was never seriously ill, despite the fact that he had few relaxations except reading and poetry: and he always retained a youthful appearance, his almost cherubic countenance being dominated by large, prominent, clear blue eyes.

He resigned from the see of Chichester 31 January 1958, and a few weeks later suffered a stroke while attending a session of the Anglican–Methodist conversations at Oxford. He recovered sufficiently, however, to attend the Lambeth Conference in July and August, and a meeting of the executive of the World Council of Churches in Denmark immediately afterwards. Here, at the tenth anniversary of the inauguration of the Council, he preached his last sermon. He died at Canterbury 3 October 1958.

He married in 1918 Henrietta Millicent Grace (died 1968), eldest daughter of the late Canon R. J. Livingstone and sister of (Sir) Richard Livingstone [q.v.]. There were no children. There are four portraits of Bell: by Sir William Coldstream in the Tate Gallery, by A. R. Middleton Todd at Chichester, by P. A. de László and by Eric Kennington at Canterbury.

[*The Times*, 4 October 1958; R. C. D. Jasper, *George Bell, Bishop of Chichester*, 1967; Bell private papers; private information.]　　　　R. C. D. JASPER.

BELL, SIR HENRY HESKETH JOUDOU (1864–1952), colonial administrator, was born 17 December 1864. Beyond indications that he was born in the West Indies, was the eldest son of Henry A. J. Bell, and was educated in Brussels and Paris, information regarding his parentage and upbringing is lacking. Any informality in his education did not prevent him from becoming a highly distinguished public servant, a writer and artist of considerable merit, and a recognized authority on the subject of witchcraft.

In 1882 he was appointed a clerk in the office of the governor of Barbados and the Windward Islands, and in the following year he was transferred to Grenada. He became established as a regular colonial civil servant, and in 1890 was moved by the Colonial Office to the Gold Coast, where he served for four years. He was then promoted to be receiver-general and treasurer of the Bahamas, where he gained a varied and useful experience of colonial administration and politics, and became known to the Colonial Office as a promising young man.

In 1899 he applied for the administratorship of Seychelles, and although he was not successful, he was shortly afterwards offered the administratorship of St. Kitts–Nevis. This he accepted, but later agreed to go to Dominica instead. His energetic work in this small independent command attracted the notice of the colonial secretary, Joseph Chamberlain [q.v.], and marked him out for further promotion.

In 1906 Bell became commissioner for the Uganda Protectorate, responsibility for which had just been transferred from the Foreign Office to the Colonial Office. He could not refuse so fine an opportunity, but it was with real regret and some apprehension about the future that he parted company with the West Indies.

His four years in Uganda (the title of his office being changed to governor in 1907) proved to be fruitful and rewarding. He found the country in the grip of an epidemic of sleeping sickness which called out his powers of vigorous administration and of improvisation with very limited financial resources. He conceived many plans for the development of the country, and the cotton-growing industry, so important to the future prosperity of Uganda, may fairly be considered as a monument to his period of office and to what Lord Elgin [q.v.], as secretary of state, described as his system of benevolent despotism.

Colonial Office practice normally limited the term of governorship to four or five years, and in 1909 Bell was moved to Northern Nigeria, which he governed until it was amalgamated with the South under Sir Frederick (later Lord) Lugard [q.v.]. His work there was largely concerned with the economic development of the region and the opening up of communications. In 1912 he was posted to the governorship of the Leeward Islands and in 1916 he went on his last governorship, Mauritius. This colony was particularly congenial to him, in view of his partly French background. He enjoyed the comparatively sophisticated social life of the island, and frankly relished the prestige and glamour attached to the office and person of a colonial governor in those days. But in Mauritius, as elsewhere, his main interest was in development. One of his notable achievements was the building up, by placing an export duty on sugar during years of prosperity, of a reserve fund which was to prove of great value when the price of the colony's principal commodity declined. He also did much for the housing and welfare of the poorer members of the population.

After his retirement in 1924, Bell went to live in Cannes, but he continued to take an active interest in colonial affairs, and in 1926 he made a tour of Java and French Indo-China, producing, as a result, a valuable study of foreign colonial administration in the Far East which was awarded the gold medal of the Royal Empire Society. He also undertook a business mission to what was then the new country of Yugoslavia.

Bell wrote well, and took much trouble over his official dispatches, considering, perhaps with justice, that this was the way to ensure their full consideration in the Colonial Office. His published works, including *Glimpses of a Governor's Life* (1946) and *Witches and Fishes* (1948), are readable, instructive, and informed by a strong sense of humour.

Bell was appointed C.M.G. in 1903, promoted to K.C.M.G. in 1908, and to G.C.M.G. in 1925.

During the war of 1939–45 Bell returned to the Bahamas. Although he never made a home in England, he visited London frequently, and it was there that he died 1 August 1952. His last years were saddened by increasing deficiency of eyesight. He was unmarried.

A portrait by P. A. de László was included in the collection of governors' portraits at the official residence of the governor of Mauritius.

[*The Times*, 5 and 14 August 1952; private information.]   CHARLES JEFFRIES.

BELL, SIR THOMAS (1865–1952), shipbuilder, was born at Sirsawa, India, 21 December 1865, the son of Imrie Bell, a consulting engineer well known as a designer of lighthouses, and his wife, Jane Walker, of Edinburgh. His early education took him to King's College School, London, and in 1880 he entered the Royal Naval Engineering College, Devonport, from which he graduated in 1886 with the full qualifications of an engineer officer. To his regret, he was prevented from following that career because of his eyesight.

Instead he joined the engineering design staff at the Clydebank Engineering & Shipbuilding Yard, then owned by James and George Thomson, where his promotion was rapid and his experience embraced both office and workshop positions of responsibility. When the firm was acquired by John Brown & Co., Ltd., in 1899 Bell was appointed engineering manager and his ability was recognized by his new principals when, in 1903, he was appointed a local director. In 1909 he took control as director in charge, later to be known as managing director.

Bell was tall of stature, grave in demeanour, and his strength of character was evident to all who met him. He was a strict disciplinarian, not least with himself, yet withal mindful of the needs and interests of all who served under him, as was best shown by his untiring efforts to end the period of unemployment for the workpeople of Clydebank in the critical years of the suspension of the construction of the *Queen Mary* in 1932–4.

His breadth of outlook made him alert to the many technical developments in his professional field and he applied himself with vigour to keeping the Clydebank firm in the forefront of these advances. Bell undertook his management duties when the steam turbine was appearing in the field of marine propulsion. Clydebank built an experimental set, subsequently fitted in the Clyde passenger ferry *Atalanta*, and went on to install turbines in the *Carmania*, Cunard's first venture of this kind, and the prototype for the quadruple screw machinery of the *Lusitania*. The performance of this machinery was the subject of a paper presented in 1908 by Bell to the Institution of Naval Architects. This early application to the development of turbine machinery was carried a stage further in the building of the *Aquitania*, which, leaving Clydebank in 1913, had a remarkable career of thirty-seven years of service to her owners and the nation. The production of turbine machinery for merchant ships under Bell's guidance reached its climax in the propelling plant of the *Queen Mary* launched in 1934.

Similar progress was achieved in the field of naval machinery. The first Brown-Curtis turbines were fitted in the cruiser *Bristol*. The first naval installation of geared turbines was in the *Repulse*, to be followed by the powerful machinery for the *Hood*, the world's largest warship of her day. The Admiralty sought Bell's assistance in 1917 as deputy controller of dockyards and war shipbuilding. In that year he was appointed K.B.E.

Bell's record of devoted work at Clydebank was matched by the service he rendered in many other spheres. He was a member of the Institution of Engineers and Shipbuilders in Scotland for 65 years; of the Institution of Naval Architects for 49 years, including 36 as vice-president and honorary vice-president; and of the Institution of Civil Engineers for 48 years. He was a senior liveryman of the Worshipful Company of Shipwrights. In Lloyd's Register of Shipping his counsel was valued in both the technical and general committees of which he was a member.

In 1935 Bell retired from the position of managing director of Clydebank but continued in office as a director of John Brown & Co., Ltd., until 1946.

In addition to his professional work, Bell interested himself in the public life of Clydebank. He was an active member and benefactor of St. Columba's Episcopal church. Early in the century he founded the Clydebank Nursing Association, and in 1914 established for it a residential home in which he and his wife took a keen interest in subsequent years. After his retirement from executive duties in 1935, he became district commissioner of the Boy Scouts in the Clydebank area, and in 1947 was elected honorary president of the Dunbartonshire Association, to the affairs of which he had given very vigorous support. As a young man he was a keen gymnast; in later years his recreations were golf and gardening.

In 1900 Bell married Helen (died 1926), daughter of Malcolm Macdonald, a Scottish wool merchant; they had two daughters, one of whom died in childhood. Bell died at Helensburgh 9 January 1952.

[Private information; personal knowledge.]
                                    JOHN BROWN.

BELLOC, JOSEPH HILAIRE PIERRE RENÉ (1870–1953), poet and author, was born at St. Cloud near Paris 27 July 1870 at the outbreak of the Franco-Prussian war. He was of curiously mixed descent; the Bellocs were a Nantes family engaged in the sugar trade with the French West Indies, with a tradition of having come from the South. Belloc's grandfather, after whom he was named Hilaire, was a painter of some note of the school of Delacroix, and some of his pictures were hung in the Louvre. He married Louise, the daughter of a Colonel Swanton, of an

Irish family which settled in France in the eighteenth century. Their son Louis married an English wife, Bessie Rayner Parkes. She was, through her mother, a great-granddaughter of Joseph Priestley [q.v.]; her father was Joseph Parkes [q.v.], a Birmingham Unitarian, the historian of the Chancery bar, and one of the founders of the Reform Club. She had become a Catholic before her marriage and lived much with her French relations. But when her husband died in 1872 she brought her young daughter, afterwards to be the well-known authoress Mrs. Belloc Lowndes, and her son to London. Having rashly entrusted a lodger who worked on the Stock Exchange with much of her capital, she found herself suddenly reduced to near-poverty, and in 1878 retired to Slindon in Sussex.

Here Belloc, in a boyhood full of open-air life, learning to tramp the downs, to sail and ride, acquired a lifelong devotion to the country of the South Downs. But he was equally at home in France where the summers were regularly spent at St. Cloud. At the age of ten he was sent with the help of relatives to Cardinal Newman's Oratory School at Edgbaston, Birmingham. There he acted with verve in the Latin plays which the Cardinal himself liked to direct, and won a good number of prizes without showing particular promise as a scholar. He left the school just before his seventeenth birthday, and was very unsettled, with many false starts, including a period at the Collège Stanislas in Paris with a view to entering the French navy. He threw himself into the London dock strike of 1889 and acquired some first-hand knowledge of the east end to give body to his radicalism. His sister, who was two years older, was already making her first steps towards journalism and authorship, working for W. T. Stead [q.v.] of the *Pall Mall Gazette*. Stead was prevailed upon to advance a small sum to enable Belloc to travel about France on the new invention, the bicycle, and write some impressions. This was the beginning of the kind of writing about places and men in which Belloc was later to show himself pre-eminent.

His next wanderings took him farther afield, to the United States which he traversed largely on foot, earning his food and lodging at farms by sketches which he made. The purpose of his journey was romantic and practical. He reached California in quest of the girl with whom he had fallen in love at sight in London and

who was later to become his wife. She was Elodie Agnes, daughter of the late Joseph Smethwick Hogan, of Napa, California, of Irish Catholic origin.

Still unsettled at twenty-one, Belloc decided to perform his military service as the French citizen which he was, and he served for ten months in the French artillery at Toul. His sister had by then become engaged to Frederic Lowndes, and by their generosity Belloc was enabled to contemplate going to Oxford. After his being refused at one or two colleges, Jowett's Balliol accepted him, and he went up in Hilary term in 1893. He soon justified the college authorities by winning a Brackenbury history scholarship, which was duly followed by a first in history in 1895, but this was the least part of the great impression he made on Oxford. After the lonely boyhood of the only son of an impoverished widow, he rejoiced in the wide companionship, and made many lifelong friends. He was a resounding success at the Oxford Union, where he was contemporary and often matched with the future Earl of Birkenhead [q.v.] and where he became president in 1895. He was older than most of his companions and with a much wider experience, bursting with energy and zest for physical and mental activity. He championed unfamiliar and rarely combined enthusiasms: for the France of the Revolution, and for the anti-Dreyfusards, with a stout allegiance to the Roman Church which became more marked after his marriage.

Being anxious to marry without further delay, he wanted to become a history tutor in an Oxford college and stayed on after graduation in the unfulfilled hope of such an appointment. He married his wife in California (1896) and brought her back to Holywell Street, Oxford, where he lived by taking pupils, giving university extension lectures mainly in the north of England, and writing books. To these years belong his first book of poems, *Verses and Sonnets* (1896) which fell quite flat, and *The Bad Child's Book of Beasts* (1896) which with three or four successors in the same triumphant vein first made him known to a wider world.

In 1897 he contributed 'The Liberal Tradition' to *Essays in Liberalism* by Six Oxford Men, and after the publication of his *Danton* in 1899 he left Oxford for Chelsea and Fleet Street. Here he immediately made his mark. On the *Speaker*, a Liberal weekly edited by his Oxford contemporary J. L. Hammond [q.v.], he threw himself into the opposition to the South African war, and at this time he met G. K. Chesterton [q.v.] and his younger brother Cecil. Together they brought something new into Liberal journalism, particularly through the columns of the *Daily News*. They developed a high-spirited and stingingly satirical attack on the Edwardian plutocracy and its great South African connection. This was carried on by Belloc through a succession of novels, *Emmanuel Burden* (1904), *Mr. Clutterbuck's Election* (1908), *Pongo and the Bull* (1910), and half a dozen more. Belloc may be said to have derived equally clearly and strongly from his two grandfathers. The French painter made him an artist. Although his Belloc grandmother, too, was a writer of some note, it was from his grandfather that Belloc inherited a particular gift for describing, as well as for sketching, scenery, and the eye for places and people which marks the most famous of his books, *The Path to Rome* (1902), written when he was thirty-one. It followed an historical study of *Paris* (1900) and a serious *Robespierre* (1901); and it was this Belloc, the man of letters, who was offered and accepted the literary editorship (1906–10) of the *Morning Post*, without having the least sympathy with the politics of that paper.

From his Birmingham Radical grandfather he inherited a preoccupation with public life, and a reforming zeal against corruption which led him to seek naturalization (1902) and adoption as a parliamentary candidate. He was returned for South Salford in the Liberal landslide of 1906 and sat in Parliament for five years without allowing his membership to diminish an extraordinary literary output. Three or four books a year flowed from his pen, not only essays contributed originally to the *Morning Post* and other journals, but full-length works like his *Marie Antoinette* (1909), his political novels, and topographical works like *The Historic Thames* (1907) and *The Pyrenees* (1909). At this time he bought a small house with a mill and some land six miles south of Horsham, and this became his home for nearly forty years.

One of Belloc's professed objects in seeking election to Parliament had been to secure an audit of the party accounts, and he was soon a problem to his own party leaders. For his part, he found in Parliament the corroboration of what he had already been asserting: that the party struggle was largely unreal, the government of England being carried on by an understanding between the two front benches to maintain the system. Although party funds were not forthcoming for his campaign in the first election of 1910, he held the seat. But he was not happy in Parliament, and a single phrase in a speech on the Address in February 1910, in which he spoke of 'the modern Anglo-Judaic plutocracy under which we live', did him immense harm. When a second election followed in the same year, he declined the expense of a further campaign and left the House. Immediately afterwards he published in collaboration with Cecil Chesterton *The Party System* (1911), describing as a corrupt collusion what was more generally regarded as proofs of English moderation and common sense and of a recognition that the English parliamentary system presupposed a large measure of common ground between the political parties.

Belloc founded his own journal the *Eye-Witness* in 1911 which in 1912 fastened on the disclosures that some of the Liberal ministers had bought American Marconi shares at a time when the Government was giving a Post Office contract to the English Marconi Company. In this campaign, as in others, Cecil Chesterton, who had succeeded Belloc as editor after a year, took the lead in vehemence and invective, until he was convicted of criminal libel. But he continued to edit the paper, now called the *New Witness*, in a way which often distressed Belloc who had more critical standards of proof, but who stood loyally by his friends.

Belloc had by this time three sons and two daughters at or approaching school age and in addition to his unremunerative and often misdirected writing on public questions had his living to make by writing. He accepted great numbers of publisher's commissions, one of them, for an American publisher, the completion of Lingard's *History of England*, carrying it from 1689 to 1910 (1915). His reaction to Lloyd George's Insurance Act was *The Servile State* (1912) which predicted the steady diminution of personal liberty among the mass of the people, who would exchange freedom for a measure of security.

Then in 1914 came a shattering blow with the death in her early forties of his dearly loved wife, and it may be said that Belloc was never the same man again, that the black he habitually wore and the mourning paper he always used were the outward signs of an inward tragic grief. When war broke out a few months later, Belloc found a new outlet for his energies and gifts as an expounder to the general public of the strategy of the war. He lectured up and down the country with diagram lantern slides, heartened his listeners with estimates of the rate of attrition of the German forces, and carried a weekly journal, *Land and Water*, to a six-figure circulation by an exhaustive military commentary which he kept up week by week to the very end of the war. In 1915–16 he was Lees Knowles lecturer in military history at Trinity College, Cambridge. Belloc had good contacts, particularly with the French general staff, and his analyses and predictions, while in general over-optimistic, were seriously informed as well as singularly lucid, and may be said to have been at the level of the professional staff thinking of the time. He made very considerable sums, but invested his savings in France and lost very heavily through the devaluation of the franc.

The end of the war found him a man of fifty with a family still to educate, although he had lost his eldest son in the war, and there began twenty years of unremitting literary labour which carried the total of his books to well over a hundred. They were of uneven quality; all had a distinction and power, but in general it must be recognized that only a few of this second period are equal in literary merit to the extraordinary galaxy of his works written before 1914. Mention should be made of one of them, *Europe and the Faith* (1920), based on lectures given to a London historical society of his co-religionists during the war years. It illustrates what may be called the classic French thesis against the Germans, about the dark ages: that the society of the Roman Empire was not replaced from outside but transformed itself, taking in new blood but maintaining the continuity of Latin civilization, with the Catholic Church as its inspiration and guide. The conclusion was twofold: that Europe is nothing without the Faith and would perish without it, but equally that the Church is the creation of Europe. There were here ideas as unfamiliar as they were controversial, not only to the general public but also to Belloc's own co-religionists who were more concerned to emphasize the universal character of the Church in the twentieth century than its

historical origin in the Roman world. When Belloc wrote 'Europe' the reader can often substitute 'Gaul' or 'France'. He had little feeling for the Europe which was not Latin. But the book marked the change which the years and bereavement had wrought in Belloc: he devoted his pen increasingly through the twenties and thirties to the Catholic cause. He embarked on a large-scale *History of England*, projected in four volumes (1925–31), but the fourth volume ended in 1612. A shorter one-volume history (1934) covered the whole range, while separate biographies of Wolsey (1930) and Cranmer (1931), Charles I (1933), Cromwell (1934), and Charles II (*The Last Rally*, 1940), and James II (1928) gave him further occasion to elaborate his guiding ideas on the English Reformation as a movement of the rich against the poor, ideas which he had found in Cobbett and espoused at Oxford.

From time to time Belloc showed that his old virtuosity as a writer of comic verse or deliberately mannered prose, as in *Belinda* (1928), was as great as ever, and he continued to travel from the Baltic to the Holy Land for the topographical works which he wrote so well. He engaged in controversy with H. G. Wells, Dean Inge, and Dr. Coulton [qq.v.]. He wrote studies of the Jews (1922), of America (*The Contrast*, 1923), and delivered the Taylorian lecture at Oxford 'On Translation' (1931). He helped G. K. Chesterton who carried on Cecil Chesterton's old paper, renamed *G.K.'s Weekly*, until his own death in 1936 when Belloc himself edited it for a time. He was a man of quite exceptional stamina and power of sustained application who would on occasion dictate as much as ten or twelve thousand words in a long morning's work before meeting to relax with companions over wine. He wrote with a continual sense of the urgency of earning money as each decade increased the difficulty for the serious author who made no appeal to the woman reader and could not write popular fiction. He remained in many ways severely Victorian, particularly in his dislike of personal publicity, and the nearest he could ever be persuaded towards writing an autobiography was *The Cruise of the 'Nona'* (1925) which remains in many ways next to his poetry his most personal memorial but is characteristic by its reticence. He always wrote in the sense of Newman's dictum to writers—aim at things; and though his essays are full of personal experience, they are the experiences of an impersonal 'I'. The last thing he ever dreamt of doing was what he described in the dedicatory ode to an early Oxford *jeu d'esprit*, *Lambkin's Remains* (1900), as turning 'a lax and fluent pen to talking of my private friends'. Yet as a poet, and it was as a poet he most wished to be remembered, his gift was the lyric gift for the expression of deeply felt personal emotion, for love poetry, and in such a work as *An Heroic Poem in Praise of Wine* (1932) there are sudden personal touches of a kind from which he would always have shrunk in prose.

Belloc was a man tenacious of his friendships, with deep and strong feelings, who had the unhappiness to lose by death the majority of his contemporary friends. But he also had the gift of making new ones from younger generations. He inspired affection and even devotion. Strongly as he had written against the plutocracy, holding up to admiration the yeoman and the peasant farmer, he acquired at Oxford and maintained a fondness for birth and great houses and established position, and he had a growing distaste in practice for the kind of roystering public-house life which his early writing had invested with so much authority and romance for many of his younger disciples. Few men with such literary gifts can have held the calling of letters in less regard, though if he had been endowed with private means he would still have written copiously from a combative sense of duty and of the obligation laid on every man to proclaim the truth as far as he can see it. Even those who most strongly disagreed with his general conclusions respected his immense integrity, that of a man who never stopped to think what it was politic to write, but only what was the truth to be stated.

Belloc used to speak slightingly of 'books about books', found reviewing difficult, grew more and more addicted to talking of writing as a trade, and one of the least satisfactory of trades because there was little or no relation between the merit of the work done, the time and pains involved in doing it, and the financial reward. Throughout most of his life, he always had plenty of other things he wanted to do, and felt the constraint of having to write so much in order to keep for himself and his family a reasonable standard of comfort. The life of the countryside, activities like the bottling of wine on a large scale, constant travel, particularly in the French countryside, these, with his boat and his country-house visits, provided the relaxation of a life otherwise filled with determined work. In the second half of his life those who knew him best were increasingly glad that he had so much work that he had to do, because he was inclined to melancholy, restless and never anywhere for very long. Although he became increasingly pessimistic in his prognostications, and maintained in all their severity the judgements he had formed early in life about the quality of English public life and the social evolution that was going on, he was never out of the country for very long. His longest absences were to lecture, reluctantly and from a strictly business point of view, in the United States. Naturally a man of extreme courtesy, of an old-fashioned sort, he could also be brusque and difficult with the importunate strangers and with the editors and publishers whom his fame attracted.

Belloc suffered increasingly from insomnia in middle life, and his health deteriorated when he was seventy. The fall of France in 1940 was something he felt very deeply, after he had for fifty years proclaimed the military and civic virtues of his father's country. In 1941 his youngest son died on service with the Royal Marines. In the next year Belloc suffered a stroke which impaired his memory so that he became progressively incapable from then onwards of sustained intellectual work and the last twelve years of his life were a sad period of failing powers. But he bore his afflictions with fortitude and resignation, and never wholly lost the high spirits which had marked his prime. In the month of his eighty-third birthday a fall in his study in front of the fire caused burns and shock which ended in his death in hospital in Guildford 17 July 1953. He was buried at West Grinstead next to his wife and youngest son. Of his seven grandchildren two have entered religion.

Belloc received the honorary degree of LL.D. from Glasgow in 1920. He refused the honorary fellowship offered to him by Balliol when he was over eighty; and declined the C.H. in 1943. He was three times painted by his friend (Sir) James Gunn: in a full-length portrait which shows him in later middle age, a commanding figure in a black cape; and one seated, in old age after he had grown a beard. This second portrait now hangs in the Oxford Union. There is also a striking likeness of him in the same artist's conversation piece which shows him with Chesterton and Maurice Baring [q.v.]. This hangs in the National Portrait Gallery, where there is also a chalk drawing by Daphne Pollen and a sketch by an unknown artist. A lithograph by (Sir) William Rothenstein was reproduced in *Oxford Characters* (1896) and a sketch by Eric Gill in *Testimony to Hilaire Belloc* (1956).

[Robert Speaight, *Life of Hilaire Belloc*, 1957, and (ed.) *Letters from Hilaire Belloc*, 1958; J. B. Morton, *Hilaire Belloc, a Memoir*, 1955; Eleanor and Reginald Jebb, *Testimony to Hilaire Belloc*, 1956; Mrs. Belloc Lowndes, '*I, too, have lived in Arcadia*', 1941, and *Where Love and Friendship Dwelt*, 1943; G. K. Chesterton, 'Portrait of a Friend', chapter in *Autobiography*, 1936; C. Creighton Mandell and Edward Shanks, *Hilaire Belloc*, 1916; Patrick Cahill, *The English First Editions of Hilaire Belloc*, listing 153 separate publications, 1953; private information; personal knowledge.]   DOUGLAS WOODRUFF.

BENN, SIR ERNEST JOHN PICK-STONE, second baronet, of Old Knoll, Lewisham (1875–1954), publisher, economist, and individualist, was born in Hackney, London, 25 June 1875, the eldest son of (Sir) John Williams Benn, later publisher, Liberal member of Parliament, leader of the Progressive Party in, and sometime chairman of, the London County Council, and first baronet, by his wife, Elizabeth, daughter of John Pickstone, of Hyde, Cheshire. Viscount Stansgate, of whom a notice appears below, was a younger brother. Ernest Benn was educated at the Lycée Condorcet, Paris, and the Central Foundation School, Cowper Street, City Road. In 1891 he joined the firm of Benn Brothers, Ltd., founded in 1880 to publish the *Cabinet Maker*. This journal, declared the father, 'was the cornerstone, but the bricks for the House that Benn built have been collected and well and truly laid by my eldest son'. By the turn of the century Ernest Benn had taken effective control; during the next thirteen years the business developed at a rapid tempo; the *Hardware Trade Journal* and other trade papers were acquired; others were newly launched. He succeeded his father in 1922 and in the next year founded the book publishing company of Ernest Benn, Ltd., introducing in the late twenties the Augustan Poets and Benn's Sixpenny Library as the precursors of the paperback. Erecting Bouverie House, he 'put the trade press into its proper place in the heart of Fleet Street'.

In 1927 Ernest Benn sponsored what became the Boys' Hostels Association, of which the Prince of Wales became patron, to provide residential clubs for homeless boys in the metropolis. He was president of the National Advertising Benevolent Society (1928), the Readers' Pensions Committee (1933), the Royal Commercial Travellers' Schools (1935), and the Advertising Association (1935). In 1932 he became high sheriff of the county of London. From 1934 until 1949 he was chairman of the United Kingdom Provident Institution.

In the war Benn familiarized himself with the ways of Whitehall, serving first at the Ministry of Munitions and later at the Ministry of Reconstruction, being appointed C.B.E. in 1918. At this time he advocated collaboration between Government and business to win the coming trade war, expounding these plans in his first three books. After this relatively brief period, and a five-week visit to the United States in 1921, he repudiated his earlier mild collectivism and embraced a full-blooded individualism.

Benn's classic, *Confessions of a Capitalist* (1925), illustrating the individualist theme by the story of the foundation of a trade-periodical empire, exemplified his rich intellectual and spiritual qualities. Among them were courage, application, relentless energy tempered by kindliness, and an engaging frankness and directness which at once shocked and charmed. His writings displayed a French wit, reminiscent of Bastiat, but with a taste of London salt. His public philosophy was an austere Victorian *laisser-faire*; his private conduct was inspired by the generous dictates of his warm humanity.

From 1925 Individualism was the very kernel of Ernest Benn's life. To him the State was the acme of immorality, the individual good, the collective evil. Faith and works were the individual's province. 'It was easy to mock his views', declared *The Times*, 'for he knew no middle way and was often exaggerated in the emphasis of his warnings. . . . He was the spokesman of no interest but of an idea—of one aspect of liberalism which not even a collectivist society, if it wishes to remain free, dare ignore.' In 1926, with Sir Hugh Bell, he founded the Individualist Bookshop, whose luncheons were to form the model for the Foyle literary luncheons. The launching of the Individualist movement thrust him at the very centre of a campaign which was not to cease until his death. Throughout 1931, as leader of the Friends of Economy, he concentrated his fire primarily on swollen state expenditures. 'One of my glorious failures' was Benn's foundation and editorship of the *Independent* (1933-5). Between 1916 and 1953 he wrote some twenty books, supplementing them between 1941 and 1948 with eleven pamphlets. Although the wartime and post-war pamphlets published in the 'Liberty Library' series of the Society of Individualists were primarily tracts for the times, the argument of some enjoys a broader currency. In 1941 Benn initiated the most powerfully sustained campaign of his life—a crusade in defence of personal and civil liberty, the rule of law and the free market, coupled with resistance to bureaucratic controls and to every project for a state-planned economy. All this was characteristically heralded by two Benn pamphlets, *The Political Method* and *The Profit Motive*. He took the leading part, with Sir Frederic Hamilton, (Sir) Carleton Allen, Lord Leverhulme, Collin Brooks, and F. W. Hirst [q.v.], in drafting in August 1942 a Manifesto on British Liberty and in founding in November 1942 the Society of Individualists. As president of the society, which was to become a model for Antipodean and Canadian sister-societies and for thirty branches at home, Benn undertook the task of furnishing, as he termed it, 'the pabulum', writing libertarian feature articles for scores of newspapers and journals at home and overseas, and contributing for many years his regular weekly 'Murmurings of an Individualist' to *Truth* during the editorship of Collin Brooks.

In 1951 came Benn's census protest. He embellished his census form with the words: 'In view of the critical state of the national economy, I must refuse to take any part in this unnecessary waste of manpower, money, paper and print.' He was fined five pounds and two guineas costs.

In the free-trade general election of 1923, Benn was sounded on behalf of four constituencies as a Liberal candidate. He declined. In 1929 he broke with the Liberal leaders over the *Yellow Book* programme. In 1935 a technicality brought to naught an attempt to secure him as Conservative candidate for East Surrey. This did not perturb him. He preferred his own Individualist banner, 'The State the

Enemy', to any party standard. He was, too, a lifelong free-trader and a zealous Cobdenite. His life and career demonstrated, as the *Sunday Times* said, 'what can be done with an idea when exploited to the full by a latter-day Hampden'. The net result of the influence of Benn and his fellow libertarians was that, by 1960, liberty was fashionable once again.

In 1903 Benn married Gwendoline Dorothy (died 1966), daughter of Frederick May Andrews, of Edgbaston, Birmingham; they had three sons and two daughters. On 17 January 1954 Benn died at Oxted, Surrey, where he had lived since 1913, and was succeeded in the baronetcy by his eldest son, John Andrews (born 1904). A portrait of Sir Ernest Benn by Sir William Orpen hangs in the boardroom at Bouverie House, Fleet Street; a sketch of him at the age of thirty, by Edward Grindlay, forms the frontispiece to Benn's *Happier Days*.

[*The Times*, 18, 21, 23, and 29 January 1954; Sir Ernest Benn, *The Confessions of a Capitalist*, 1925, *The Letters of an Individualist to 'The Times', 1921-1926*, 1927, *Happier Days*, 1949, and other writings; A. G. Gardiner, *John Benn and the Progressive Movement*, 1925; Deryck Abel, *Ernest Benn: Counsel for Liberty*, 1960; *Freedom First*, Spring 1960; private information; personal knowledge.]   DERYCK ABEL.

BENN, WILLIAM WEDGWOOD, first VISCOUNT STANSGATE (1877-1960), parliamentarian, was born 10 May 1877 at Hackney, the younger brother of (Sir) Ernest Benn, a notice of whom appears above. He was educated at the Lycée Condorcet, Paris, and at University College, London, where he obtained a first in French (1898) and later became a fellow (1918). He worked for some years in his father's publishing business. Deeply influenced by social conditions in the east end of London, associated with the London Progressive Party, a lifelong radical nonconformist, Benn was soon adopted as Liberal candidate for his father's former seat of St. George's, becoming member at the general election of 1906. He gained experience at the Treasury, Board of Education, and Admiralty as parliamentary private secretary to Reginald McKenna [q.v.]; retaining his seat at both general elections in 1910 he became a junior lord of the Treasury and thereafter a full-time and singularly active politician. In 1912 he was a successful organizer of relief of suffering during the dock strike and two years later, when war broke out, he became chairman of the organizing committee of the National Relief Fund.

In October when over two million pounds had already been raised, he resigned to respond to the inner call for more personal service. Despite his short stature, Benn secured a commission in the Middlesex Yeomanry, and took part in the fierce fighting on the heights above Suvla Bay, in the Gallipoli campaign. He next became an observer with the Royal Naval Air Service and personally participated in the pinpoint bombing of the Baghdad Railway, was rescued from a sinking aeroplane in the Mediterranean, and was in an improvised aircraft carrier sunk by shore batteries at Castelorizo. He commanded a party of French sailors in guerrilla activities against the Turks, served in authorized privateering in the Red Sea, and returned to England to qualify as a pilot.

Refusing the office of chief whip from the hand of Lloyd George, Benn returned to service in Italy and was eventually seconded to the Italian Army to organize and participate in the first parachute landing of a secret-service agent behind the enemy lines. He was twice mentioned in dispatches, appointed to the D.S.O., awarded the D.F.C., was made a chevalier of the Legion of Honour, received the croix de guerre, the Italian war cross, and the Italian bronze medal for valour.

At the general election of 1918, his former constituency having been redistributed, Benn was returned as member for Leith, a seat which he held, through three more general elections, for nine years of intense parliamentary activity. He and Lord Winterton, in the judgement of Lord Halifax [q.v.], were 'two of the best parliamentarians of my time in the House'. A supporter of Asquith just this side of idolatry Benn chafed under the leadership of Lloyd George, and finding himself increasingly voting with the Labour Party, applied for membership in 1927 and resigned his seat.

He was returned at a by-election in the following year as member for North Aberdeen, and, holding this seat in the general election of 1929, became secretary of state for India with a seat in the Cabinet, and was sworn of the Privy Council.

Benn occupied this high, but exposed, position for the next two years under fairly constant attack. The controversial political trial at Meerut, authorized by his predecessor, was about to commence. The report of the Indian statutory commission under Sir John (later Viscount) Simon [q.v.] was in course of preparation and was published in June 1930. Meantime Benn authorized the viceroy, in 1929, to make the historic declaration that the legitimate goal of Indian aspirations was dominion status. Simon's concurrence was not obtained. In a short but bitter parliamentary debate Benn defended his action with courage and when Lloyd George denounced him as a 'pocket edition of Moses' retorted 'But I never worshipped the golden calf.' In 1930 the Indian leader M. K. Gandhi [q.v.] initiated a successful campaign of civil disobedience, directed against the salt tax, and Benn ultimately felt compelled to order his arrest. Gandhi was released next year for talks with the viceroy which resulted in the Delhi Pact, but by the time he arrived in London for the second Round Table conference, Benn was out of office. On the formation of the 'national' Government Benn had remained loyal to the Labour Party, was decisively defeated at the ensuing general election, and was again defeated in 1935 as a candidate for Dudley.

The period of enforced parliamentary inactivity was used to make, with his wife, a journey round the world by almost every known means of transport, an extensive visit to the United States being continued via the Far East, Japan, Mongolia, Siberia, and Moscow.

At a by-election in 1937 Benn was returned as member for the Gorton division of Manchester. On the outbreak of war in 1939 he enlisted as a pilot officer in the Royal Air Force, rising to the rank of air commodore, being again mentioned in dispatches, and though officially grounded was known to have taken part in air operations. In January 1942 he was called to the House of Lords as first Viscount Stansgate, the peerage being expressly granted to strengthen Labour representation in the Upper House. In 1943–4 he was vice-president of the Allied Control Commission in Italy.

In the Labour Government of 1945 Stansgate became secretary of state for air. In 1946 he was entrusted by the foreign secretary, Ernest Bevin [q.v.], with the conduct in Cairo of the abortive negotiations for a revision of the Anglo-Egyptian Treaty. Late in 1946, on a minor reconstruction of the Government, he resigned his office at the Air Ministry. In 1947, at the age of seventy,

Stansgate became president of the Inter-Parliamentary Union, and held this position for ten years with universal esteem. In the House of Lords he became the authentic voice of liberalism. His persistence might cause temporary annoyance and once Lord Hailsham (later Mr. Quintin Hogg) carried a motion that 'the noble lord be no longer heard', but Stansgate's patent sincerity, his complete freedom from malice, his natural modesty of manner, made many admirers and no enemies. His perpetual effervescence, his buoyancy, his wit, conveyed an impression of the gay cavalier; but 'Wedgy Benn' was really the happy warrior, a man of profound ethical conviction, with a great love for his fellow men.

Stansgate was taken ill in the Palace of Westminster whilst waiting to speak. He had closed the previous day's debate with an appeal for understanding of the problems of India. He was taken to hospital where he died 17 November 1960.

Benn married in 1920 Margaret Eadie, daughter of Daniel Turner Holmes, Liberal member for Govan, Lanark, from 1911 to 1918. There were four sons of the marriage of whom the youngest died at birth. The eldest, a flight lieutenant, was awarded the D.F.C., and died in 1944 of injuries received in action. His second son, Anthony Neil Wedgwood (born 1925), sought to renounce the succession, was held to be disqualified from the Commons, headed the poll at the ensuing by-election, was again ruled disqualified and continued the struggle until, following the report of a select committee of the Lords and Commons, the law was changed in 1963 and having renounced his peerage he was again returned for Bristol and took his seat. He became postmaster-general in the Labour Government of 1964 and minister of technology in 1966. The viscountcy remained in abeyance.

[W. W. Benn, *In the Side Shows*, 1919; W. W. and Margaret Benn, *Beckoning Horizon*, 1935; *The Times*, 18 November 1960; personal knowledge.]　　LESLIE HALE.

BENNETT, GEORGE MACDONALD (1892–1959), chemist, was born in Lincoln 25 October 1892, the third of a family of two sons and one daughter. He was named after George MacDonald [q.v.], a friend of his father, the Rev. John Ebenezer Bennett. His mother was Hannah Martha, daughter of William Grange, a farmer in Hertfordshire. For a number of years Bennett's father had been a schoolteacher

at Tring and later in Peckham Rye, but he subsequently became a Baptist minister at Lincoln. In 1893 he moved to a living in Hackney but six years later had to resign owing to ill health. Thereafter he ran a private boarding-school at Clacton-on-Sea, together with Harold Picton who had previously been a pupil of (Sir) William Ramsay [q.v.] at University College, London. Picton was responsible for science teaching and took charge of the school when J. E. Bennett died in 1906.

Bennett was a pupil in the school for ten years and under Picton's influence developed a liking for chemistry which decided him to take it up as a career. He obtained a London University exhibition in 1909 and entered East London (later Queen Mary) College as an internal student, subsequently obtaining a scholarship in chemistry. In 1911 he took the B.A. degree externally in French, Latin, physics, and chemistry, and in the following year he was awarded first class honours in chemistry. He then began research in organic chemistry but in 1913 he obtained an open exhibition at St. John's College, Cambridge, becoming a foundation scholar and taking a first class in part i of the natural sciences tripos in following year. In 1915, when he obtained a first class in chemistry in part ii, he became a research assistant to (Sir) William Pope [q.v.] with whom, and with C. S. Gibson, he made notable contributions in the field of explosives and war gases. He was a fellow of St. John's from 1917 until 1923.

In 1918 Bennett left Cambridge to take up a post in industry, but he was not particularly happy there and in 1921 he became a senior demonstrator in the chemistry department of Guy's Hospital medical school. In 1924 he became lecturer in organic chemistry in the university of Sheffield where he built up an enthusiastic team of research and in 1931 was appointed to the Firth chair of chemistry. During the next seven years at Sheffield notable contributions to research were made and all those who were fortunate enough to work under Bennett's guidance derived much inspiration.

In 1938 Bennett became professor of organic chemistry at King's College, London, and was in charge of the chemistry department when the college was evacuated to Bristol at the outbreak of war in 1939. There, in addition to his teaching and administrative duties, he made studies on the mechanism of aromatic nitration which were of great importance in relation to the development of explosives. King's College returned to London in 1943 but in 1945 Bennett left academic work to become the government chemist. Here he found much administrative work. He also served on numerous government and other committees but he maintained a close contact with the academic world through the university of London, the Chemical Society, and the Royal Society. He was also concerned in the development of new experimental techniques such as X-ray diffraction and gas chromatography.

Bennett obtained the degrees of Ph.D. (London, 1924) and Sc.D. (Cantab., 1932). He was elected a fellow of Queen Mary College in 1939 and F.R.S. in 1947. In 1948 he was appointed C.B. He gave generously of his time in the service of chemistry, being a member of the council of the Chemical Society (1929–32), honorary secretary (1939–46), and vice-president (1948–51); he was a member of the council of the Royal Institute of Chemistry (1949–51) and vice-president (1951–3). He was also a member of the council of the Faraday Society (1946–8) and honorary secretary of the Chemical Council (1945–51).

Bennett was reserved in nature but could show tremendous enthusiasm and excitement when research investigations were going well. In all his dealings with students he was strictly honest and only the hard worker would get his fullest support. He was a prolific reader but his main interest was always chemistry and apart from walking he had few outdoor activities. He was in every sense a true scientist, scrupulous and conscientious, and a good and inspiring teacher. His contributions to chemical knowledge ranged over a wide field and he was author or joint author of some ninety publications, most of which appeared in the *Journal* of the Chemical Society.

He suffered a severe heart attack in 1953 after which he did little beyond his official duties at the Government Laboratory. In 1918 he married Doris, daughter of James Laycock, M.P.S., of Fulham, and when she died in 1958 he felt this severely. They had no children and when Bennett himself died in London, after a further heart attack, 9 February 1959, he left the bulk of his estate to Dr. Barnardo's Homes.

[*The Times*, 11 February 1959; R. D. Haworth in *Biographical Memoirs of Fellows of the Royal Society*, vol. v, 1959; personal knowledge.]   R. L. WAIN.

BENNETT, PETER FREDERICK BLAKER, BARON BENNETT OF EDGBASTON (1880–1957), industrialist, was born at Dartford, Kent, 16 April 1880, the eldest son of Frederick Charles Bennett, a carpenter and sometime organizing secretary for the Y.M.C.A., and his wife, Annie Eliza Blaker. The family moved to Birmingham when he was twelve and he was educated at King Edward's School, Five Ways, Birmingham. His lifelong connection with the motor industry began in 1903 when he joined the Electrical Ignition Company. Four years later, when sales manager, he left the firm and entered into partnership with James Albert Thomson, founding a small concern in Birmingham known as Thomson Bennett, Ltd. When the company, employing only a hundred or so, moved to a new site, a furniture van sufficed to transfer all the machinery. In December 1914, on the initiative of Harry Lucas, the company was amalgamated with Joseph Lucas, Ltd., to promote the manufacture of combined ignition and lighting systems for cars, tanks, and aircraft. At that time the company employed some four thousand workers; by 1939 there were thirty thousand. This success was due largely to the technical vision of Bennett and the commercial ability of his joint managing director, Oliver Lucas, both of whom provided the necessary drive and sense of purpose. When the latter died in 1948 Bennett became chairman and managing director of the Joseph Lucas group of companies.

Considerable difficulties were encountered during the critical period of the war of 1914–18 principally because the manufacture of magnetos and other components was a German monopoly. Bennett was appointed chairman of the Aero Magneto Manufacturers Association and of the British Ignition Apparatus Association—both newly sponsored by the Admiralty. In the inter-war years Bennett was a member of the British trade deputation to Virginia in 1930 and represented the British motor industry at the Ottawa conference of 1932, the year in which he was president of the Birmingham chamber of commerce. He was president of the Society of Motor Manufacturers and Traders in 1935–6 and president of the Federation of British Industries in 1938–9.

From 1938 until the outbreak of war in the following year Bennett was a member of the prime minister's panel of industrial advisers. In 1939–40 he was director-general of tanks and transport at the Ministry of Supply and from 1940 to 1941 director-general of emergency services organization at the Ministry of Aircraft Production. In 1941–4 he was chairman of the Automatic Gun Board. He was also honorary colonel of the 9th battalion Royal Warwickshire Regiment.

In 1940 Bennett entered Parliament as member for the Edgbaston division of Birmingham in succession to Neville Chamberlain. Although formerly a Liberal he held his seat as a Conservative and retained it until 1953, serving as parliamentary secretary to the Ministry of Labour in 1951–2. He was knighted in 1941 and raised to the peerage in 1953.

Brought up as a Methodist, Bennett was a religious man and a teetotaller and as a young man was a superintendent of Sunday schools in Acocks Green. He was president of the Birmingham Y.M.C.A. and of the Birmingham General Dispensary and a county commissioner of the Boy Scout movement to which he gave lifelong support. He endowed a social centre for a large new housing area in Kingstanding and was a generous benefactor of various Midlands institutions, including the Y.M.C.A. for which he provided funds for the concert hall which bears his name.

In the field of education, he was a governor of the university of Birmingham which in 1950 conferred on him an honorary LL.D. and he established a scholarship fund to enable unsponsored students to attend the university's postgraduate course in engineering production under the Lucas professor of engineering production. The Lucas chair had been endowed a few years earlier by his company as a result of the efforts and advice of Bennett and his deputy (Sir) Bertram Waring who was later to succeed him as chairman of his company.

Throughout his life Bennett maintained a keen interest in sporting activities, playing rugby football in his younger days and continuing to play golf and tennis in his later years. He was also particularly fond of walking. He took a lively interest in cricket and derived much satisfaction from his election as president of the Warwickshire County Cricket Club in 1955.

In 1905 Bennett married Agnes, daughter of Joseph Palmer, who survived him and who had a distinguished record in social service and to whom he looked for guidance and encouragement throughout

his long career. Of exceptional wisdom and strong character, Bennett was always honest, fair, and often generous in his dealings. He had no children and the title became extinct when he died at his home at Four Oaks, Warwickshire, 27 September 1957. A portrait by (Sir) James Gunn is in the possession of the Joseph Lucas Company, Ltd.

[Private information; personal knowledge.]

N. A. DUDLEY.

BENTLEY, EDMUND CLERIHEW (1875–1956), writer, was born in London 10 July 1875, the eldest son of John Edmund Bentley, a civil servant in the Queen's Bench office, and his wife, Margaret Richardson Clerihew. He was a boy at St. Paul's School in the great days of Frederick Walker [q.v.] and there his lifelong friendship with G. K. Chesterton [q.v.] was formed. He was a member of the history eighth, newly created by Walker, and won a history exhibition at Merton College, Oxford. He fell in love with the college at once and never fell out of it. Furthermore, he quickly and gratefully absorbed the spirit of Oxford. At the Union he was an effective debater in a quiet and scholarly style and became president in 1898. F. E. Smith (afterwards Earl of Birkenhead, q.v.), then a recent ex-president, was still a prominent figure at debates, and when he became a fellow of Merton gave Bentley much friendly counsel, including the advice to disregard the practice of a candidate not voting for himself at a presidential election. John (later Viscount) Simon, F. W. Hirst, and John Buchan (later Lord Tweedsmuir) [qq.v.] were also among his friends; he knew Hilaire Belloc [q.v.] slightly, but it was not until later that he became intimate with him. His interests during his Oxford years were far from being confined to political and intellectual discussion. He was captain of the Merton boat club and remained a faithful apologist of the rowing man. Regretfully he gave up rowing in his fourth year in order to work for his degree and the great disappointment of his life was his failure in 1898 to obtain a first in history.

In 1898 he went down from Oxford and read for the bar. He did well in his examinations at the Inner Temple, became a pupil in (Sir) William Hansell's chamber in 1900, and was called in 1902. One of his closest friends recorded that Bentley had all the qualifications of a successful barrister except the legal mind. On the other hand he had from his schooldays onwards been active with his pen. At St. Paul's he had been a contributor to the *Debater*, founded by his friend, Lucian Oldershaw; at Oxford he had written regularly for the *Isis* and for the *J.C.R.*, the magazine in which Belloc's *Lambkin's Remains* first appeared. While still in chambers he wrote light verse for *Punch* under the critical eye of (Sir) Owen Seaman [q.v.], and by the end of 1899 he was a regular contributor to the *Speaker*, the Liberal weekly edited by J. L. Hammond [q.v.]. For that paper he wrote many reviews and took some satisfaction in being the first critic to recognize the quality of Ernest Bramah's *The Wallet of Kai Lung*. In 1901 his forthcoming marriage was one of the reasons which led to his decision to be a journalist by profession and to join the staff of the *Daily News*. The editor was Rudolph Chambers Lehmann, a good Liberal, a strong opponent of the South African war, and a great oarsman. Thus Bentley felt thoroughly at home in his new work and with his new colleagues, among whom were Herbert Paul, H. W. Massingham [qq.v.], and Harold Spender. Lehmann was succeeded by A. G. Gardiner [q.v.] under whom Bentley in due course became deputy editor. In that capacity he was faced at times with critical decisions and he confessed that he enjoyed the experience. When the *Daily News* was amalgamated with the *Morning Leader*, Bentley felt that he was no longer in sympathy with the more violent tendencies of Liberal journalism and in 1912 he joined the *Daily Telegraph* with which he remained for twenty-two years.

Had Bentley confined his activities to leading articles, his name, like that of many eminent journalists, might well have been little known and gradually forgotten. In fact, his name is linked with two highly individual achievements: he added a new word to the language and he wrote what was described as the best detective novel of the century.

As he sat in the science class at St. Paul's at the age of sixteen, the following lines came into his head:

> Sir Humphrey Davy
> Abominated gravy.
> He lived in the odium
> Of having discovered Sodium.

Such was the beginning of what Chesterton called the 'severe and stately form of free verse known as the Clerihew'. Sir Humphry soon had a number of companions and their lives were entered into a notebook with appropriate sketches by Chesterton. Bentley chose to drop his surname for the occasion and *Biography for Beginners* by E. Clerihew, with illustrations by G.K.C., was published in 1905. The book did not have an immediate success, but in Bentley's own words, 'in course of time it seemed to find its way into the hands of connoisseurs of idiocy everywhere'. *More Biography* followed in 1929; *Baseless Biography*, with illustrations by the author's son, Nicolas, in 1939; finally *Clerihews Complete* appeared in 1951.

It was in 1910 that Bentley meditated upon a new kind of detective story. Like all boys of his generation he had revelled in the Sherlock Holmes series; but Holmes's eccentricities and his reputed infallibility irritated him and he conceived the notion of a detective's convincing solution being proved wrong in the end. The result of his meditation was *Trent's Last Case*, published as one of Nelson's two-shilling novels in 1913. It was a best-seller immediately and unlike some other best-sellers it remains very much alive—in many languages—after fifty years. Amid the torrential output of detective stories in that period, it still holds its distinctive place. What Trent deduced was true, but it was not the whole truth, and the complete revelation is reserved, with effective artistry, for the last chapter.

Although he never wholly recovered from the 'shame and disappointment' of his second class at Oxford, Bentley was happy in, and proud of, his profession as a journalist. When war broke out in 1939 he returned to the *Daily Telegraph*; but the worlds that he loved best—Oxford in the nineties and pre-1914 Fleet Street—had vanished and he recalled them nostalgically in *Those Days* (1940).

In 1902 Bentley married Violet Alice Mary (died 1949), fourth daughter of General Neil Edmonstone Boileau, late of the Bengal Staff Corps. They had one daughter and two sons, of whom the younger, Nicolas (who contributes to this Supplement), has illustrated his father's, and many other, books. Bentley died in London 30 March 1956. A life-size charcoal head by H. G. Riviere is in the possession of the family.

[E. C. Bentley, *Those Days*, 1940; Nicolas Bentley, *A Version of the Truth*, 1960.]

S. C. ROBERTS.

BERRY, WILLIAM EWERT, first VIS-COUNT CAMROSE (1879–1954), newspaper proprietor, was born at Merthyr Tydfil 23 June 1879, the second of the three sons, all to be raised to the peerage, of Alderman John Mathias Berry, estate agent, by his wife, Mary Ann, daughter of Thomas Rowe, of Pembroke Dock. At the age of fourteen he was given his opportunity as a cub journalist on the *Merthyr Times* by W. W. Hadley [q.v.]. After working on other South Wales papers he moved to London in 1898 and became a reporter on the *Investors' Guardian* at thirty-five shillings a week. This post did not last long, and three months of unemployment was a chastening experience which Berry was never to forget in his subsequent dealings with staff. He next became a reporter on the Commercial Press Association but in 1901 adventurously launched a paper of his own, the *Advertising World*, the pioneer journal in that field. His only capital was a hundred pounds lent by his elder brother (Henry) Seymour (later Lord Buckland), a coadjutor of D. A. Thomas (later Viscount Rhondda, q.v.) in various coal and steel enterprises. Berry was editor, sub-editor, advertisement canvasser and copy-writer, and layout man. He is reputed to have written every word of the first issue. He lived frugally, worked long hours, and walked to his office from his lodgings in Forest Gate. Before long he was able to bring his brother (James) Gomer (later Viscount Kemsley) from Wales to operate on the business side. It was a most friendly partnership, unclouded by any disagreement. In their bachelor days they shared a flat at Arundel Street, Strand; and until 1936 they had a joint banking account, on which either could draw without consulting the other. By 1905 they were in a position to sell the *Advertising World* at an excellent price. They bought a publishing business and started sundry periodicals, notably in 1909 *Boxing* (of which William was a devotee). Their interests widened rapidly but they were always discerning in their acquisitions.

A major operation was the purchase in 1915 of the *Sunday Times* which William Berry happily supervised as editor-in-chief for twenty-two years, taking a keen personal interest in its progress and nursing its circulation against that of its rival, the *Observer*. At the time of the purchase the *Observer* sold about 200,000 weekly and the *Sunday Times* fewer than 50,000; by 1949 the respective figures were 384,001 and 568,346.

In 1919 the brothers acquired the St.

Clement's Press, with which went the *Financial Times*. Berry remained chairman of this paper until it passed into the ownership of the *Financial News* in 1945. In these post-war years the activities of the Berrys took on an ever-increasing momentum, and important acquisitions were the Weldon's group, Kelly's Directories, and the *Graphic* publications. In 1921 William Berry became a baronet.

The year 1924 saw the foundation of Allied Newspapers (later Kemsley Newspapers), controlled by the Berry brothers and Sir E. M. (later Lord) Iliffe [q.v.]. The purpose of this group was to take over most of the Hulton papers from Lord Rothermere [q.v.]. These included the *Daily Dispatch*, the *Manchester Evening Chronicle*, and the *Sunday Chronicle*. During the years up to 1928 Allied Newspapers further acquired papers in Glasgow, Sheffield, Newcastle, Middlesbrough, and Aberdeen. They also bought the *Daily Sketch* and *Illustrated Sunday Herald* from Rothermere's Daily Mail Trust. In Cardiff, where they already held the *Western Mail* and the *Evening Express*, they acquired the *South Wales Daily News* and the *South Wales Echo*, merging the two morning and the two evening papers.

Newspapers apart, the group's biggest purchase was made in 1926: the Amalgamated Press from the executors of Lord Northcliffe [q.v.]. This great concern comprised a large number of non-political periodicals, ranging from *Woman's Journal* to children's comic sheets. It included a powerful encyclopedia and book section which had been built up under Northcliffe's aegis chiefly by (Sir) John Hammerton and Arthur Mee [q.v.]. There were also printing works at Blackfriars and Gravesend and the Imperial Paper Mills, also at Gravesend. In 1927 paper supplies were further augmented by the acquisition of Edward Lloyd, Ltd., one of the largest mills in the world.

The vast publishing enterprise which had been built up lacked only one element to make it complete—the possession of a first-rate serious London daily newspaper. When in 1927 Lord Burnham [q.v.], chief proprietor of the *Daily Telegraph*, was appointed to the Indian statutory commission at a time when the paper was in urgent need of modernization, he approached the Berry–Iliffe group, and the sale was quickly arranged. The new owners took over on 1 January 1928; Burnham's nephew G. E. F. Lawson (later fourth Lord Burnham) remained as manager and subsequently became managing director (1945–61).

The Berry brothers now controlled two national, one specialized, and six provincial, morning papers; eight provincial evenings; eight provincial weeklies; and about seventy periodicals. No attempt was made to dictate or alter the politics of any of these papers.

William Berry, raised to the peerage in 1929 as Baron Camrose, gradually carried out necessary changes in the type and format of the *Daily Telegraph*. On 1 December 1930 he reduced the price from 2*d*. to 1*d*. and the circulation virtually doubled itself in one day to 200,000. While the more popular sheets were vying with one another to attract readers by free insurance and gift schemes, the *Daily Telegraph*, eschewing such adventitious aids and preserving its dignity of approach and presentation, slowly but steadily increased its readership, and by 1939 the figure exceeded 750,000. In 1937 it had absorbed the right-wing Conservative *Morning Post*, most of whose 100,000 readers went with it. In 1949 the circulation was given as 1,015,514.

The long and close association between Camrose, Kemsley, and Iliffe was amicably dissolved in 1937, chiefly because each had a growing family, and it was felt expedient to split the holdings. Camrose took the *Daily Telegraph*, the Amalgamated Press, and the *Financial Times*. In 1941 he was advanced to a viscountcy.

For a few weeks in 1939 Camrose was controller of press relations in the Ministry of Information where he effected a reduction over 30 per cent in the number of responsible officials and then retired, 'having organized myself out of a job'.

Camrose had a high conception of the professional journalistic function, and disliked vulgar sensationalism. He took great care in the selection of authoritative contributors. He required distinction in English style and was a connoisseur of typography and layout. Worlds away from the conventional picture of the ruthless newspaper proprietor, he treated his staff with courtesy and solicitude and he kept many of them over long periods of years. It was characteristic that he should resist the Fleet Street trend towards young staffs, preferring to make the fullest use of older men of long service and experience.

Distinguished in bearing and dress, and a gifted after-dinner speaker, Camrose was punctilious in his habits, accessible,

genial, good-tempered, with a lively sense of humour. In financial matters he was strictly honourable. His self-confidence was tempered by good judgement and prudence. He had no political ambitions and had no liking for controversy, but he always knew his mind about public affairs. Brought up a Liberal, he became a convinced Conservative of the centre. Although a warm admirer of Neville Chamberlain, he broke with him on his Munich policy. On that, as on most other questions, he was a firm supporter of (Sir) Winston Churchill and one of his closest friends.

Camrose was interested in motoring and yachting. In early years he was a keen rider but gave this up after sustaining severe injuries when thrown in 1926. It was as the result of a riding accident that his brother, Lord Buckland, died in 1928. Camrose and Kemsley acquired from their brother some steel and coal holdings, but this was after their establishment as newspaper owners, and both lost money in preventing the closure of some collieries near Merthyr Tydfil.

In 1905 Berry married Mary Agnes (died 1962), eldest daughter of Thomas Corns, of Bolton Street, London, W. 1, by whom he had four sons and four daughters. His eldest son, John Seymour (born 1909), who succeeded to the title when Camrose died in Southampton 15 June 1954, became deputy chairman of the *Daily Telegraph*; the second son (William) Michael, became its editor-in-chief, and a life peer (Baron Hartwell) in 1968. In 1958 they disposed of the Amalgamated Press to Cecil H. King of Daily Mirror Holdings, who renamed the group Fleetway Publications, Ltd. A portrait in oils of Camrose by Maurice Codner is in the offices of the *Daily Telegraph*; and a memorial tablet by Sir Albert Richardson in the crypt of St. Paul's Cathedral.

[*Daily Telegraph, Manchester Guardian*, and *The Times*, 16 June 1954; *Sunday Times*, 20 June 1954; Bernard Falk, *Five Years Dead*, 1937; Viscount Camrose, *British Newspapers and their Controllers*, 1947; *Report* of the Royal Commission on the Press, 1947–9, 1949; private information.]

HERBERT B. GRIMSDITCH.

BESSBOROUGH, ninth EARL OF (1880–1956), governor-general of Canada. [See PONSONBY, VERE BRABAZON.]

BETHUNE-BAKER, JAMES FRANKLIN (1861–1951), professor of divinity, was born 23 August 1861 in Birmingham, the third son of Alfred Baker, surgeon, by his wife Emmeline Bethune, daughter of George Armitage. Charles and Franklin Baker [qq.v.] were his uncles and his aunt was the mother of Archbishop E. W. Benson [q.v.]. In 1884 Baker assumed the additional name of Bethune. He was educated at King Edward's School, Birmingham, whence he gained a classical scholarship at Pembroke College, Cambridge. In 1884 he took a first class in part i, in 1885 a third class in part ii of the classical tripos; in 1886 a first class in part ii of the theological tripos. In 1886 he won the George Williams prize and submitted an unsuccessful (and so unpublished) essay for the Burney prize in which his later modernist theology is clearly foreshadowed; in 1887 he submitted a successful essay on 'The Influence of Christianity on War', and in the following year won the Norrisian prize. In 1886 he returned to teach at King Edward's School; and in 1888, although an anxious request for reassurance of his orthodoxy came from the dean of Pembroke, E. J. Heriz Smith, he was ordained deacon, accepting a title at St. George's, Edgbaston. He was ordained priest in the next year and in 1891 was elected into a fellowship at Pembroke which he retained until his death. He was also made dean, an office to which in 1906 he was not reappointed in consequence of complaints concerning his attitude to biblical criticism. Thereafter, although continuing to attend college chapel regularly, he never again felt confident to preach there, except on the occasion of a memorial service for his friend A. J. Mason whose notice he contributed to this Dictionary.

Bethune-Baker proceeded B.D. in 1901 and D.D. in 1912. His scholarly reputation was established by The Meaning of Homoousios in the Constantinopolitan Creed (1901) and his Introduction to the Early History of Christian Doctrine (1903) which became a standard textbook. Through the Archbishop's Mission to Assyrian Christians a copy of a Syriac manuscript containing the Bazaar of Heraclides by Nestorius came into his hands; with the aid of a translation by Dom Richard Hugh Connolly (whose name did not appear on account of the papal antimodernist decrees of 1907) he wrote Nestorius and his Teaching (1908), claiming that Nestorius did not hold the doctrines attributed to him and was wrongly condemned by the Ecumenical Council of

Ephesus, 431. In 1911 he succeeded W. R. Inge [q.v.] as Lady Margaret's professor. Except for his time-absorbing work as editor of the Journal of Theological Studies (1903–35) by which he guided and maintained the standards of British theology for a generation, his interest now turned from personal contributions to learning and was more devoted to teaching in Cambridge and to the advancement of liberal Christianity. In 1913–14 he became involved in the controversy concerning clerical orthodoxy in the Church of England. His open letter to Charles Gore [q.v.], The Miracle of Christianity (1914), pleads for the logical consequences of the liberal view of the Bible adopted by Gore himself in Lux Mundi (1889). This avowal of sympathy with 'the critical school' led his friend Bishop J. R. Harmer of Rochester to request his resignation from the office of examining chaplain which he had held since 1905; believing that hope lay only in the coexistence of conservative and modernist views he refused and Harmer (who did not share this belief) relieved him of his post. The claim that the Anglican principle of comprehensiveness extended not only to the unity of Catholic and Protestant but also to that of conservative and modernist he later expounded in Unity and Truth in the Church of England (1934). His dogmatic beliefs are best seen in The Faith of the Apostles' Creed (1918) and in a collection of essays, published at the suggestion of (Sir) S. C. Roberts, The Way of Modernism (1927). He advocated an evolutionary, immanentist approach to the Incarnation and free inquiry in historical criticism, rejecting as irreligious the view that the Virgin Birth and the Resurrection are truths to be accepted on supernatural authority by all believers. He lacked the philosophical equipment to make these writings wholly successful, but their subject-matter was his deepest concern. He was examining chaplain (1924–35) to Bishop E. W. Barnes [q.v.] of whose Rise of Christianity (1947) he disapproved. He was elected F.B.A. in 1924 and resigned his professorship in 1935. He took part in college meetings almost until the end of his life and still drove his car in his eighty-ninth year.

In the teaching of theology at Cambridge Bethune-Baker played a leading part, encouraging in his pupils an attitude of detachment and impartiality. In 1922 he founded the Cambridge D Society for the discussion of philosophical and systematic theology. He had a keenly critical mind, a strong, sometimes obstinate personality, and a satirical tongue which enjoyed opposition and in some induced alarm. He had also a capacity for deep and generous friendship, and above all a profound concern for the presentation of the faith in a form tenable to the modern mind.

Bethune-Baker married in 1891 Ethel (died 1949), daughter of Furneaux Jordan, surgeon, of Birmingham, by whom he had one son who died as a schoolboy at Marlborough. Bethune-Baker died in Cambridge 13 January 1951. A pencil drawing by Randolph Schwabe is in the Cambridge Divinity School.

[H. E. Wynn, Bishop of Ely, in *Proceedings* of the British Academy, vol. xxxix, 1953; *The Times*, 15 January 1951; *Cambridge Review*, 5 May 1951; W. N. Pittenger, 'The Christian Apologetic of James Franklin Bethune-Baker', in *Anglican Theological Review*, vol. xxxvii, 1955; private information.]

H. CHADWICK.

BEVAN, ANEURIN (1897–1960), politician, was born 15 November 1897 in Tredegar, Monmouthshire, the sixth of the ten children, seven of whom survived, of David Bevan and his wife, Phoebe, daughter of John Prothero, blacksmith. David Bevan was a miner, a Baptist, a regular reader of Blatchford's *Clarion*, a lover of music and of books: a gentle, romantic man who had more cultural influence on his son than the elementary school in which Bevan was a rebellious pupil and acquired little but the ability to read. A stammer which he later persevered to overcome probably had some part in his hatred of school; his immense desire for knowledge had hardly developed when at thirteen he left; thereafter he had to educate himself. The Workmen's Library was well stocked with 'the orthodox economists and philosophers, and the Marxist source books'. But it was not in Nye Bevan's undisciplined temperament to become a Communist. Until the failure of the general strike of 1926 he believed that industrial action would bring the workers to the promised land of which he dreamed as he roamed the Welsh mountains, disputed with his friends, or declaimed the poetry which he loved.

Meantime Bevan had gone into the pits. He became an expert collier and almost equally expert at making trouble for his employers: by 1916 he was chairman of his lodge. He was exempt from military service on account of an eye disease and became well known in Tredegar and beyond for his opposition to what he considered a capitalist war. In 1919 the South Wales Miners' Federation sent him to the Central Labour College in London for two years which were probably not quite the waste of time he thought them: his horizons widened and his debating skill improved.

Bevan returned in 1921 to Tredegar and his conflict with the owners who had resumed control of the mines after the war, despite the Sankey recommendation of nationalization. It was not perhaps surprising that Bevan could find no work. His meagre unemployment benefit was stopped when his sister began to earn, and when his father fell ill with the chest disease which was to kill him he received no sickness benefit until his son fought the case. Bevan's enforced familiarity with the intricacies of sickness and unemployment benefit was at the disposal of all who cared to consult him. To keep his position in the mining industry he worked for some months as a checkweighman until the pit closed down and he was once more on the dole. Then in 1926 he became disputes agent for his lodge at a salary of £5 a week. In the long conflict with the owners in that year he showed himself an efficient organizer of relief; made fighting speeches at special national conferences of the Miners' Federation in July and October; yet a month later opposed Arthur Horner by recommending negotiation before the drift back to work should bring about the disintegration of the Federation.

In the following year the local guardians who were deemed to have been too generous with poor relief were replaced by commissioners: 'a new race of robbers' whom Bevan never forgot or forgave. He realized now that power to redress the miseries of the unemployed in the South Wales coalfield must come through political action. Already a member since 1922 of the Tredegar urban district council, in 1928 he was elected to the Monmouthshire county council and in 1929 was returned to Parliament as Labour member for Ebbw Vale, a seat which he retained until his death. For all his turbulence, his highly independent outlook, his criticism of his own leaders, Bevan remained to the last convinced that only through Parliament and the Labour Party could he achieve his aims.

Throughout the early thirties unemployment was a major issue on which Bevan had plenty to say and he soon became known in Parliament as an attacking speaker of considerable if erratic brilliance, marred by a vituperative inability to keep his temper. He was prominent in opposing non-intervention in the Spanish civil war, and as foreign affairs became of increasing concern found himself allied with Sir Stafford Cripps [q.v.] whom he supported in his unity campaign of 1937 and as a founder of and regular contributor to *Tribune*, which he was himself to edit in 1942-5. Early in 1939 he was expelled from the Labour Party for supporting Cripps in his Popular Front campaign, but he was readmitted in December.

The outbreak of war meanwhile had brought Bevan new fields of discontent. His opposition to the Government throughout the war earned him notoriety and suspicion and Churchill's description of him as 'a squalid nuisance' probably reflected the opinion of the man in the street. Yet his complaints had some basis: Churchill, he maintained, was conducting a one-man government; furthermore, was no strategist. Bevan pressed for an early second front; and later mistrusted the 'Big Three' conferences as ignoring the claims of lesser countries and preventing the post-war development of a western Europe strong enough to stand between the opposing American and Soviet powers. He came into conflict with Ernest Bevin [q.v.] over his treatment of the coalmining industry, and in 1944 was nearly expelled again from the Labour Party for his violent opposition to a regulation imposing penalties for incitement to unofficial strike action in essential industries: 'the disfranchisement of the individual'. He was asked for, and gave, a written assurance that he would abide by standing orders. At the Labour Party conference of December 1944 he was elected for the first time to the national executive; and in the Labour Government of the following year C. R. (later Earl) Attlee made him minister of health and housing. He was then sworn of the Privy Council.

The National Health Service Act of 1946 provided free medical and dental care for all who cared to avail themselves of it and in the event ninety-five per cent of the nation did. The scheme derived from a number of sources but Bevan included such daring ideas as the nationalization of the hospitals, to be run by regional boards, and the abolition of the sale of general practices. The service was to be financed from general taxation.

There followed two years of negotiation with the doctors before the scheme came into effect in 1948. The battle was fought on the grand scale. Yet Bevan displayed more patience and flexibility than were usually at his command in bringing to a successful outcome a cause which was very dear to his heart and was certainly his finest achievement. He was ably assisted by his permanent secretary, Sir William Douglas [q.v.]. With the minister of national insurance Bevan was also responsible for the National Assistance Act of 1948 which completed the break-up of the Poor Law and introduced a comprehensive scheme of assistance and welfare services. Housing he tackled with schemes for the repair of war damage, for prefabricated houses, and for large subsidies to local authorities to enable them to provide houses to rent to people in the lower income groups.

For all his achievement, Bevan was still an uncertain asset to his party. He was apt to get carried away by his own rhetoric: his 'lower than vermin' onslaught on the Tories in July 1948 did him more harm than it did the Tories who were estimated by Harold Laski [q.v.], no friend of Bevan, to have gained some two million votes thereby. It was seized upon by the British press, still smarting from Bevan's attack upon it as 'the most prostituted in the world'. With his own Government Bevan was increasingly out of sympathy, mainly over armaments expenditure and Ernest Bevin's policy of alliance with the United States and the containment of Russia. It was unfortunate that Cripps, to whom Bevan was much attached and who could exercise a moderating influence upon him, fell ill and resigned in October 1950. In January 1951 Bevan moved to the Ministry of Labour, only to resign in April when he came into conflict with Hugh Gaitskell over the latter's proposal to introduce certain charges into the health service. Harold Wilson and John Freeman also resigned: the armament programme, it was thought, would impoverish the country. In the election of constituency members to the national executive in October Bevan headed the poll, with Mrs. Barbara Castle second and two other supporters gaining places: a shift of opinion within the Labour Party noted perhaps by the electorate which returned the Conservatives to power at the general election later in the month.

For the remainder of his life Bevan was

in opposition. *In Place of Fear* (1952), his only book, set out his belief in democratic socialism 'based on the conviction that free men can use free institutions to solve the social and economic problems of the day, if they are given a chance to do so'. He deplored American foreign policy and discounted Russia's military aims. For a time it seemed that Bevan would bring about a split in his own party by the growth of the 'Bevanite' group within it. At the Labour Party conference of 1952 six Bevanites were elected to the national executive with Bevan again at the head of the poll. But at a subsequent meeting of the parliamentary Labour Party in October Attlee successfully moved a resolution calling for the abandonment of all unofficial groups within the party. The Bevanites protestingly complied, but the philosophy of 'Bevanism' remained. At the ensuing annual elections of the parliamentary party Bevan unsuccessfully challenged Herbert Morrison (later Lord Morrison of Lambeth) for the deputy leadership; but he was elected to the shadow Cabinet. This position he resigned in April 1954 when he attacked Attlee's approval of S.E.A.T.O. In the summer he went with Attlee in a Labour Party delegation to Russia and Red China. But in March 1955 he was again defying his leader in the House: this time over the use of nuclear weapons in the event of hostilities, even if not used by the aggressor. The party whip was withdrawn and his expulsion from the Labour Party sought, but again Bevan gave an assurance of conformity. Once again a general election was in sight and again Labour lost. When Attlee resigned in December, Bevan unsuccessfully challenged Gaitskell for the leadership, although he outstripped Morrison; then he stood for the deputy leadership, only to be defeated by James Griffiths. But in October 1956, by a narrow majority over George Brown, he attained the post of party treasurer which he had failed to wrest from Gaitskell in the two preceding years.

In Gaitskell's shadow Cabinet Bevan was entrusted with first colonial, then foreign, affairs: an attempt to close the ranks in which Bevan saw that he must co-operate if Labour were to return to power, even if he regarded Gaitskell as 'a desiccated calculating machine'. On colonial problems, Malta, Cyprus, Kenya, and during the Suez crisis, Bevan spoke with skill and moderation for the Opposition. Although he urged the banning, by

agreement with Russia and America, of nuclear and hydrogen bomb tests, at the party conference of 1957 he helped to defeat a motion demanding that Britain should make a unilateral renunciation of such bombs, saying that it would send a British foreign secretary naked into the conference chamber. His standing within his party became more secure and in October 1959 he was elected unopposed as deputy leader of the parliamentary party; he continued as party treasurer. His speeches had become persuasive rather than aggressive, but were delivered with all the old felicity which, despite the hatred and fear he could engender, had made him generally considered the best speaker, after Churchill, to be heard in the House. If a touch of melancholy was to be detected now, it might be attributed to the trend of international affairs and to the decline of his own physical powers. After some months of illness he died at his home at Chesham, Buckinghamshire, 6 July 1960.

With Bevan's passing some of the colour and much of the passion went out of politics. He fought vehemently, with deadly invective, but with gaiety and wit as well, for his beliefs. Not everybody shared them, least of all within his own party where he was strongly opposed by the trade-unionists. He was essentially an original—complex, baffling, and infuriating, especially when he gave way to indolence or showed a tendency to disappear at times of crisis; but the sincerity and stature of the man were not in doubt. If on occasions he could be a menace to, he also vitalized, the Labour Party and enlarged and influenced its thinking. He was sustained throughout by Jennie Lee, herself a staunch left-wing member of the Labour Party, later to hold office, whom he married in 1934; they had no children. Art, literature, and music, as well as politics, contributed to the richness of the domestic life which they enjoyed, for preference in the country. Bevan always hated London and indeed would personally have fitted better into a more exotic background than the British, although politically he would have been unlikely to survive. A large man whose thatch of black hair silvered elegantly early, he was immensely alive, exercising a personal magnetism which made it difficult even for those who most detested his views to resist his charm. The very large congregation which attended the memorial service in Westminster Abbey was a tribute to the affection and respect in which he had come to be held.

[Aneurin Bevan, *In Place of Fear*, 1952; Jennie Lee, *This Great Journey*, 1963; Michael Foot, *Aneurin Bevan*, vol. i, 1897–1945, 1962; Vincent Brome, *Aneurin Bevan*, 1953; Mark M. Krug, *Aneurin Bevan: Cautious Rebel*, 1961; Francis Williams (with Earl Attlee), *A Prime Minister Remembers*, 1961; *The Times*, 7 July 1960; private information.]

HELEN M. PALMER.

BEVIN, ERNEST (1881–1951), trade-union leader and statesman, was born 7 March 1881 in the small Somerset village of Winsford on the edge of Exmoor, the illegitimate son of a forty-year-old village midwife named Mercy Bevin who had separated from her husband, William Bevin, some years before and at the time of Ernest's birth described herself as a widow. It was a period of acute rural depression and she sometimes found it difficult to keep a roof over her family's head. She worked as a domestic help on local farms and in the village public house as well as village midwife, but was several times forced to apply for parish relief. She died after months of illness when Ernest, youngest of her six sons, was eight. He never knew who his father was. After his mother's death Bevin was given a home by his half-sister Mary and at the age of eleven, after reaching Standard IV at the Hayward Boys' School in Crediton and getting his labour certificate, was found work as a farm boy at a wage of 6s. 6d. a quarter, living in. He could read, write, and do simple arithmetic. That was the end of his formal education.

Although in some ways he remained a countryman all his life, Bevin had no liking for farm life and when he was thirteen he joined two of his brothers who had found casual work in Bristol. A succession of blind-alley jobs followed. He was kitchen boy at a cheap eating-house, a van boy, a page boy at a restaurant, conductor on the horse trams, until in 1901 he became van driver with a mineral water firm. He was soon earning 25s. a week in wages and commission which he later increased to nearly £2 by working longer hours and extending his round. Although he was an unskilled man this put him on the level of a skilled artisan in regular employment and he seemed perfectly content to remain at this level. In other ways, also, the job suited him. Once he had climbed on his two-horse dray at six o'clock in the morning he was on his own

in the open air for the rest of the day, a tough, barrel-chested figure of a man, well able to look after himself in a fight or an argument. From the comparative security of this employment Bevin in his early twenties began his lifelong partnership with Florence Anne Townley (died 1968), the daughter of a wine taster at a Bristol wine merchants; they had one daughter.

Bevin had a hard boyhood and youth. He was often hungry, and later claimed that he sometimes had to steal for food. But his struggles left no personal scars and their importance lay far more in their representative than in their personal quality: they gave him a permanent sense of identification with all those others in the working class whose experience had been much the same. He had many of the qualities of a captain of industry. But unlike many self-made men of the Victorian age he never had any wish to climb out of his own class. He preferred, instead, to help it to rise and to rise with it.

His mother, who had been the one sure centre of affection in his early life, had been a keen Chapel woman, a Methodist when Methodism was as much a social as a religious creed, a vehicle of dissent against the massed forces of Church, State, and landlord. Bevin turned naturally to the Chapel in Bristol. He joined the Manor Hall Baptist Mission and had some thought of becoming a minister or even a missionary. He attended the Quaker Adult School and other discussion and study classes and as with many other early labour and trade-union leaders non-conformity provided the nursery of political action and the bridge to socialism. His interests turned gradually from Chapel to politics: he joined the Bristol Socialist Society, affiliated to the Social Democratic Federation, and became an active speaker and organizer in its ranks, and, after 1908, in the Right to Work movement which developed as a result of mounting unemployment. In November of that year he led a procession of 400 unemployed men into morning service at the cathedral to draw attention to their plight. In 1909 he was defeated as a socialist candidate for the city council. In June 1910 a strike at Avonmouth which later spread to the whole of the Bristol docks pushed Bevin in a new direction. Most of the dockers were organized in the Dock, Wharf, Riverside and General Workers' Union. The carters, many of whom worked out of the docks, were unorganized. However, they could not escape the implications of the dockers' struggle, especially when attempts were made to use them as strike breakers to load and unload ships at the docks. Harry Orbell, a local organizer of the Dockers' Union (later its national organizer), who knew of Bevin's activities in the Right to Work committee, persuaded him to bring the carters together. A carmen's branch of the Dockers' Union, with Bevin as its chairman, was formed in August 1910, and Bevin, although he could not know it, pre-pared to enter upon his kingdom. In the spring of 1911 he climbed down from his mineral water van for the last time and became a full-time official of the Dockers' Union.

The union had been born out of the great London dock strike of 1889 led by Ben Tillett, Tom Mann, and John Burns [qq.v.]. Bevin's contribution to the trade-union movement was something very dif-ferent from the passion and demagogy of a man such as Tillett. He brought it massive self-confidence, great negotiating ability, and a conviction of the need for centralized authority. None of these qualities had shown themselves in Bevin earlier: they grew out of his first years as a trade-union official when the failure of a series of dockers' and seamen's strikes called by the loosely organized Transport Workers' Federation forced him to go back to the grass roots of trade-union organization. As he stumped Wales and the west country trying to rebuild the branches he learnt the vital importance of carrying the rank and file with him in every decision. He absorbed also another lesson which remained with him through-out his trade-union life: that numerical strength without central authority is illusory.

By 1913 he had become an assistant national organizer and in 1914 one of the union's three national organizers. Because of his direct personal links with the local secretaries and branch officials and their personal loyalty to himself he held the most important strings of union power in his hands. To him trade-unionism was essentially an instrument to enable workers to meet employers as equals in the negotiating chamber. But because he learned his business of leadership when conciliation was out of fashion on both sides, his public character had a curious duality. Capable of great suppleness in negotiation and sensitive to the mutual interests which made industrial co-opera-tion desirable, he presented in public an image which was dogmatic, overbearing,

uncompromising, and egotistical. In negotiation he was a realist who under-stood the need for compromise. On the public platform he permitted himself every licence of venom, innuendo, and the grossest partiality.

This duality of posture stood him in good stead. Among the rank and file it gave him a reputation for left-wing icono-clasm, valuable to those who wish to push their way to the front in the Labour move-ment, while in private negotiations his realism won many practical advantages for his members. Both sides of this per-sonality were evident during the war of 1914–18. He had no doubt where the sentiments of the great mass of the workers lay and spat scorn on the pacifism of the politicians of the Independent Labour Party. But he found it possible to be equally contemptuous of trade-union leaders like Arthur Henderson and J. R. Clynes [qq.v.] who 'betrayed their class' by joining a Lloyd George government, while he himself took an active and force-ful part in the work of joint committees to secure the efficient use of manpower.

In 1915 for the first time Bevin was a delegate of his union at the Trades Union Congress and in the winter of 1915–16 he went as a fraternal delegate to the annual convention of the American Federation of Labor. It was his first journey abroad and his visit broadened his outlook and stimu-lated his imagination. In the summer of 1916 he was elected to the executive coun-cil of the Transport Workers' Federation. When the war ended Bevin had become an important trade-union official of the second rank. He was one of his union's permanent delegates to the Trades Union Congress and Labour Party conferences and its representative on close to a dozen committees set up by the ministries of Labour and Reconstruction. Moreover, without ever loosening his strong emo-tional link with the rank and file he had become a disciplined administrator with a remarkable talent for absorbing docu-ments and sifting evidence.

In the general election of 1918 Bevin was defeated as the Labour candidate for Central Bristol. In 1920 he became assis-tant general secretary of his union. In that year he became a national figure for the first time, as the 'Dockers' K.C.' when he persuaded the dockers instead of striking to submit a claim for 16s. a day to a court of inquiry under the new Industrial Courts Act. He won their case by brilliant ad-vocacy, at one stage producing before the court a number of plates on which were set out the derisory scraps of food on which dockers would have to move seventy-one tons of wheat a day on their backs if the court accepted as adequate the family budgets advanced by the employers supported by the professional witness of (Sir) A. L. Bowley [q.v.]. Bevin's national status was confirmed by his leadership in the Council of Action which successfully boycotted the sending of arms to Poland for use against the Russian revolutionary armies.

The collapse of the Triple Alliance of miners, railwaymen, and transport workers on Black Friday, 15 April 1921, endorsed all Bevin's earlier suspicions of the fragility of alliances without central command. He was already engaged on the complex and often tortuous negotiations designed to replace the Transport Workers' Federation with its loose alliance of autonomous unions by a compact structure of which his own union should be the centre. The Transport and General Workers' Union which merged fourteen unions with a combined membership of 300,000 came into being on 1 January 1922 with Bevin as general secretary. It was a monolithic achievement ruthlessly secured. Tillett, nominally Bevin's superior in the hierarchy of the Dockers' Union, was swept aside and turned into an ineffectual pensioner after being allowed to believe almost to the very end that he would be president of the new organization, although Bevin had decided at an early stage that he would have to be sacrificed in a deal with one of the other unions. The withdrawal of the union from the Transport Workers' Federation brought about the disappearance of the latter, a blow from which its secretary Robert Williams never recovered. The fate of neither man moved Bevin to any compunction any more than did that of George Lansbury [q.v.] when years later Bevin used all the force he could command to destroy Lansbury's influence in the Labour movement over the issue of sanctions against Italy over Abyssinia.

Had Bevin turned to Communism in the twenties as some militant trade-unionists were tempted to, the history of British Labour might have taken a different course. But for all his ruthlessness and concern for power Bevin could never have been a Marxist and was indeed to become British Communism's most implacable enemy. He never lost the saving grace of human involvement. When he talked of the working class as 'my people' he did not think of an economic class, the proletariat, but of individual men and women who seemed to him the salt of the earth. To him the trade-union movement was not a tool to be used in the pursuit of an ideology. It was the living embodiment of the best hopes and truest comradeship of ordinary men and women who had given him their trust and to whom he had given his loyalty, and he was only happy when he could feel he was referring back to them. Thus the constitution of the Transport Workers' Union with almost as many checks and balances as the American Constitution which he much admired was meticulously designed to create a chain of command going right back to the individual members in the branches, while providing for a national leadership with power to act decisively at times of crisis. It was in some ways a cumbersome constitution and more democratic in theory than in practice, for it required an active participation which only a minority was ready to give. At the beginning it drew its strength much more from Bevin's own character than from any formal safeguards. But it stood the test of time.

The pattern of union advance on which Bevin had set his hopes was interrupted by the general strike of 1926. The failure of that strike, in which Bevin's working-class loyalties were deeply committed but which ran counter to his strongest convictions about the proper use of industrial power, confirmed him in his belief that industrial animosities, if allowed to continue at their former level, must prove self-destructive to both sides and that the best hope of advance for the workers lay in negotiation from strength rather than in industrial conflict. The number of unions absorbed by his union had reached 22 by the end of 1923. By the end of 1926 this had been increased to 27. In 1929 the hundred-thousand-strong Workers' Union was added. From this powerful base Bevin, a member of the general council of the T.U.C. since 1925, set himself to secure a change in the whole climate of industrial relations.

In this he had the strong support of Walter (later Lord) Citrine, the general secretary of the T.U.C. These two were cast in very different moulds and there was little personal sympathy between them. But they saw industrial problems in the same terms and together helped to bring about a decisive shift towards industrial conciliation, beginning with the

Mond–Turner talks in 1928. It was in this year that Transport House was opened, as the headquarters not only of Bevin's union but of the T.U.C. and the Labour Party, and an example of Bevin's imaginative thinking.

Bevin was also branching out in other directions. He travelled abroad as a trade-union delegate to international conferences and to the I.L.O. and began to take a perceptive interest in foreign affairs. He became a member of the Macmillan committee on finance and industry appointed by the MacDonald government and with J. M. (later Lord) Keynes [q.v.] as a fellow member he acquired a shrewd —and highly critical—understanding of the operations of international finance and the working of the gold standard. He was a member of the Economic Advisory Council and of the T.U.C. economic committee. He was instrumental in turning the *Daily Herald*, founded by Lansbury, subsequently owned by the trade unions, but too much of a narrowly based official organ, into a successful popular newspaper under the joint ownership of the T.U.C. and Odhams Press. Although still suspicious of politicians and declining in November 1930 an invitation to go to the House of Lords, he began to play a much more active political role, especially after Ramsay MacDonald, whom he had never trusted, became the head of a 'national' government and Labour suffered the electoral disasters of 1931. Bevin himself was defeated at Gateshead. He was among the first to recognize the threat of Nazism and among the most powerful opponents of pacifism in the Labour Party, urging the case for rearmament at Labour conference after conference and at the meetings of the National Council of Labour. In 1936–7 he was chairman of the T.U.C. In 1938 he made a tour round the world and the knowledge which he gained of Canada, Australia, and New Zealand inspired him with the idea of the British Commonwealth as the nucleus of a new League of Nations with an economic basis.

Bevin was now generally accepted as one of the most powerful of Labour leaders not only on the industrial but also on the political side. Although his power came in part from the size of the block vote he commanded at Labour Party conferences it derived even more from the natural authority of his personality. He was not by any standard a great orator but his utterances had a raw strength which compelled conviction. The very clumsiness of his sentences, his contempt for syntax and the niceties of pronunciation, the harshness of his voice and the powerful emphasis of his gestures seemed when he was speaking to a mass audience to make him the embodiment of all natural and unlettered men drawing upon wells of experience unknown to the more literate. To watch him advance to the rostrum on such occasions in his thick-soled boots with his customary rolling walk and hear him begin to speak after a long slow look around his audience which seemed to say, 'now you are going to hear one of yourselves', was to be brought up against something resembling a force of nature: implacable, confident, yet often lit by flashes of imagination which outspanned and transcended the ordinary limitations of debate. There was, of course, a good deal of the actor in all this; and he had an actor's sense of occasion and timing. But what counted most in the end was the hard content of what he had to say. It was the broad and penetrating sweep of his judgement and the force of his personality which gave him his great influence, no less than the proven strength of his position as a trade-union leader.

All these qualities converged when in May 1940 Bevin became wartime minister of labour and national service. He was member of Parliament for Central Wandsworth (1940–50) and East Woolwich (1950–51) but he was never wholly at home in the House of Commons. He came to it too late. He was nearly sixty when he entered it as a minister—and from a background to decision-making very different from that of political debate. But his impact upon the War Cabinet, which he entered in October 1940, was, as the *Manchester Guardian* reported, 'as decisive for the ends he set himself as was that of Winston Churchill as war-time Prime Minister'. Nor would many of those in a position to assess what he accomplished dissent from the *Guardian*'s further judgement that 'the work he did in mobilising the manpower and the industrial resources of the country could have been done with equal efficiency, sure judgment and resolute purpose by no other man'. The eight months which preceded the Churchill administration had been for Bevin, as for many others, a period of frustration, anxiety, and suspicion. He had always distrusted Chamberlain, and his animosity, which had long roots in the past, was confirmed by what seemed to him

Chamberlain's failure to understand the spirit in which the majority of the British people had gone to war and his patronizing attitude to the trade unions. The only minister with whom he found it possible to establish friendly relations during this period was, to his surprise, Churchill. There was long political enmity between them but this was submerged in their appreciation of each other's understanding of the need for total war.

Despite the shortage of armaments and equipment of all kinds there were more than a million workers unemployed in April 1940. When Bevin became minister of labour and national service he claimed responsibility for all manpower and labour questions, including the right to examine the use made of labour and if necessary withdraw it. He was given, although he did not ask for it, power to conscript and direct labour, and for some time was criticized for his reluctance to use this power. He believed that compulsion hastily used would produce grievance which could lead to bad workmanship and he preferred to wait until the necessity for compulsion was fully accepted by the working class. To obtain the support of both sides of industry he called a meeting of the National Joint Advisory Council of sixty industrialists and trade-union leaders and asked them to appoint a committee of seven trade-union leaders and seven employers to advise on all problems arising from the legislation which had given effect to his powers—greater than those ever previously vested in any man in peace or war. On the same day he met the Engineering and Allied Employers' Federation, the Amalgamated Engineering Union, and the two big general workers unions and began negotiating agreements permitting the breakdown of skilled jobs in factories and the introduction of large numbers of unskilled and semi-skilled workers, including women. This he followed with the appointment of a Labour Supply Board —two trade-unionists, two managers— which until March 1941 met daily under his chairmanship to see that labour was made available wherever it was needed. Subsequently (Sir) Godfrey Ince [q.v.] was director-general of manpower. Bevin also set up a factory and welfare division of the Ministry under Ince which concerned itself not only with working conditions but with the living conditions, feeding arrangements, and leisure of the workers.

Within a week Bevin had transformed the whole industrial atmosphere. His reputation as a wartime minister of labour does not, however, rest solely or even primarily on the speed with which he acted, although this made a substantial contribution to industrial morale. There was no aspect of industrial affairs he did not touch upon. By the middle of 1943 he had so organized the mobilization of labour that there had been an expansion of three and three-quarter million in four years of those serving in the armed forces, civil defence, or industry. The armed forces had increased by nearly four million and the munitions industries by two; there had been a transfer of more than three and a quarter million workers from the less essential industries. This vast disruption of the ordinary life of the community was carried through not only with a speed and efficiency completely unmatched in any of the dictatorships, but with a remarkable lack of industrial trouble. The time lost by industrial stoppages was eventually reduced to rather less than one hour per worker per year. The elaborate organization he built was always touched with humanity. When there were criticisms of the call-up of women who had never done outside work in their lives he could snap, 'It never hurt anyone to work'; but when there were complaints of absenteeism because girls stayed home from the factories when their sweethearts were on leave from the forces, he retorted, 'That's not absenteeism, that's human nature'; and he saw to it that there was a proper system of leave in all factories for such occasions. To him the workers were 'my people'. To them he was 'Ernie' and he knew by instinct what their reactions would be to the demands placed on them. He made some mistakes, among them the too hurried withdrawal of labour from the mines after the fall of France which the later direction of 'Bevin boys' underground did little to correct, although it was dear to his heart because he hoped it would not only ease an emergency but help to break down class barriers. Yet when the scale of his activities is taken into account, the proportion of failures was amazingly small.

These activities were, of course, directed first and foremost to winning the war. But he was also determined to establish a new framework of co-operation in industry and permanently raise the status of the industrial and agricultural worker. 'They used to say Gladstone was at the Treasury from 1860 to 1930', he said jokingly. 'I'm going to be at the Ministry of Labour from 1940 to 1990.' The long-term impact of his policies may in the end be seen in the acceptance of joint machinery for industrial relations by both sides of industry. The efficiency and fairness of the demobilization procedures at the end of the war and the avoidance of the economic dislocation and industrial strife that had followed the war of 1914–18 were a tribute to his foresight. At the end of May 1945 Churchill offered Bevin the C.H. for his 'remarkable work at the Ministry of Labour', but this Bevin declined saying that he desired no special honours for doing his job, like thousands of others, in the interests of the nation.

Bevin had come to be regarded as one of the most helpful members of the Government, not only by reason of his work as minister of labour but as a leading member of the lord president's committee on the civilian and economic resources of the country, as chairman of the Production Executive, and as a member of many other committees. In the last two years of the war, as his own departmental pressures decreased, he had applied himself vigorously to questions of post-war reconstruction such as ways of implementing the Beveridge report and he had strongly supported the Education Act of 1944. He was also deeply interested in international relationships and had become a close student of the foreign telegrams which flowed across his ministerial desk. His first ambition when Labour won its victory at the polls in 1945 was, however, for the Treasury. He had greatly developed the interest in monetary and economic policy he had first acquired as a member of the Macmillan committee, and was full of ideas for making the Treasury a much more creative force in the national economic life. Attlee considered offering Bevin the chancellorship and Hugh (later Lord) Dalton the Foreign Office; indeed he actually discussed this with both of them. Further thought over a solitary lunch persuaded him, however, that Bevin would be better at the Foreign Office for two reasons. The first and most important was that Attlee had become convinced that with the end of the war in Europe, Soviet Russia would become tough, aggressive, and unco-operative and that Bevin was temperamentally the more suited of the two to meet this situation and also more likely by reason of his standing in the Labour movement to carry the party with him in doing so. The second

was that he had decided to invite Herbert Morrison (later Lord Morrison of Lambeth) to be lord president of the Council and leader of the House of Commons with a general oversight of home affairs and thought it better in view of the personal antipathy between Bevin and Morrison—particularly on Bevin's side—to keep the two apart.

It was, therefore, Bevin who accompanied Attlee to the adjourned Potsdam conference as foreign secretary. There, according to James Byrnes the United States secretary of state, the first impact he made was 'so aggressive that both the President and I wondered how we would get along with this new Foreign Secretary'. However, it did not take Byrnes long in his own words 'to learn to respect highly his fine mind, his forthrightness, his candour and his scrupulous regard for a promise'.

In the Foreign Office itself there were many who at first feared that they had been given into the untutored hands of a clumsy Visigoth. These anxieties departed as they got to know him. In the Office itself he became one of the most admired and best loved of foreign secretaries—a response to his humanity and his loyalty to and concern for his staff touchingly demonstrated on his seventieth birthday when every member of the Foreign Office from the permanent under-secretary to the messengers and junior typists each contributed sixpence—the dockers' tanner—to give him a birthday party to which much to his joy they all came, an event unique in Foreign Office history.

But although he sought advice from his permanent officials he made his own decisions and formed his own policy: there was never a man less run by his department. He had hoped and had publicly declared at the pre-election Labour Party conference that in dealing with Russia it would be possible for 'Left to speak to Left'. He even hoped that there might be some residue of gratitude for his part in preventing the sending of arms to aid the anti-Bolshevik forces at the end of the first world war. He proved mistaken in both beliefs as Attlee—more shrewd in his judgement of Soviet ambitions—had from the first assumed would be the case. Nine months of arduous negotiations on peace treaties with Italy and the German satellite countries and for a more permanent settlement with Germany than had been reached at Potsdam convinced Bevin that although broad agreement between Britain and the United States was possible on most matters despite differences in detail, Russia saw in European disorder the best opportunity for ideological and territorial expansion. He believed that behind this lay suspicions of western motives and fears of capitalist attacks that had a certain historical justification and tried to allay them in a personal meeting with Stalin in Moscow by offering to extend the wartime Anglo-Russian Treaty into a fifty-year alliance. But although Stalin at first expressed some interest every effort to negotiate such a treaty failed and Bevin found himself increasingly forced to the opinion that Stalin was determined to exploit Britain's post-war weakness and American preoccupation with domestic problems to expand Communist power right across Europe.

The extent to which Britain was at this time the primary and for long periods the sole target of Soviet attack both at the United Nations and in Turkey, the Dardanelles, Northern Persia, Greece, Trieste, and in the Middle East has often been forgotten. But it forced Bevin to concentrate all the power he could command on confining Soviet expansion until America could be persuaded to commit her weight in the political and ideological struggle. His forces were small. Indeed, along with the wartime prestige Britain still enjoyed they rested very largely on Bevin's own character and his refusal to admit even to himself how slight was his freedom of manœuvre. He was urged by many on the democratic Left, hostile to what they regarded as his too great dependence on America, to seek to build a 'third force' of western European powers standing apart from and between the great power blocs of the United States and the U.S.S.R. and acting as a counter-balance to both. For a time he was drawn to the idea. It fitted in with many of his socialist conceptions. But the socialist idealist was over-ruled by the trade-union realist. He remembered the collapse of the paper forces of the Transport Workers' Federation and the Triple Alliance and came to the conclusion that however numerically impressive it might seem on paper a third power would lack both the cohesion and the resources to fill the power gap. In any event the American presence in Europe was already a fact and as such was capable ultimately, if properly deployed, of restoring in a way nothing else would the balance of power jeopardized by British weakness and Soviet ambition. For the

time being, however, American public opinion was still resistant to the idea of any further involvement in Europe. Moreover a sizeable official opinion inclined to Harry Hopkins's view that no basic conflict existed between Russian and American interests and to Admiral Leahy's much-canvassed judgement that Britain was 'prostrate economically' and 'relatively impotent militarily' and that the Soviet Union must therefore be accepted by the United States as the 'unquestioned, all powerful influence in Europe'.

In these circumstances Bevin saw his responsibility as that of holding the line until such time as the United States could be awakened by a clear issue to the real situation, fully knowing that it was a gamble in which time and his own resources were running out. In February 1947 he judged the time and the issue had arrived in Greece where for two years of civil war Britain had accepted alone the responsibility for meeting and holding Communist pressure. Now as mounting pressure coincided with the first signs, as he judged, of American disillusionment with Russia he instructed the British ambassador to deliver a memorandum to General Marshall, the secretary of state, informing him that Britain's economic position would no longer allow her to act as the main reserve of economic and military support for Greece or Turkey and that if America agreed that their freedom from Soviet control was essential to western security she must be prepared to step in. The immediate effect of this memorandum on American official opinion was of shock and anger. But sixteen days later came the 'Truman doctrine' declaring security throughout the whole of the eastern Mediterranean to be an American interest. Judged by the developing consequences of this doctrine Bevin's carefully timed stroke can be seen as one of the most decisive diplomatic acts in modern history.

Satisfied that the inevitable British withdrawal from areas of traditional British influence would no longer leave a power vacuum which could tempt the Soviet to dangerous adventures, Bevin turned his attention to building a pattern of European alliances which would enable western Europe to play its full part in western security. The treaty of Dunkirk with France (March 1947) was the first substantial brick in this structure. It was followed a year later by a treaty of mutual assistance binding together Britain, France, Belgium, Holland, and Luxembourg. The shock to American opinion of the Communist coup in Czechoslovakia in 1948 enabled Bevin to achieve his larger purpose of widening this alliance into a North Atlantic Treaty of which the United States and Canada would be a part. The treaty was signed 4 April 1949.

The creation of N.A.T.O. came as the climax of Bevin's efforts. But it was not his only achievement. More than any man —including even Marshall himself—he was responsible for the development of Marshall Aid to Europe. When Marshall made his Harvard speech in June 1947 suggesting that if the European nations would organize themselves for mutual help American economic aid for reconstruction might be forthcoming he had, as he subsequently stated, no clear plan in mind; and indeed nearly three weeks later the U.S. secretary to the Treasury was still denying that the speech had any special significance. It was Bevin's response which brought the speech to life—within a matter of hours he had not only cabled Britain's appreciation of the offer and readiness to take it up but had set in motion the machinery necessary to create the Organization for European Economic Co-operation. He hoped it would be possible to bring the U.S.S.R. and satellites in too and with Marshall's agreement invited Molotov to meet the French foreign minister and himself in Paris to discuss their participation. Although Molotov came, the talks were without result; not for lack of trying on Bevin's part.

It can be argued that in doing everything he could to bring America into Europe Bevin helped to make inevitable the division between East and West. But this division was not of his making. It was a fact of Soviet immediate post-war policy to which he had to reconcile himself and was nowhere more apparent than in Germany whose problems occupied so much of Bevin's time. The alternative to American co-operation in Europe was Soviet hegemony over most of the Continent and having once convinced himself that this was the major post-war danger he played his cards with stubborn skill, although his hand was weak and he knew that he would be bitterly attacked by many on his own side. The objectives he set himself he achieved, even if he was never able 'to go down to Victoria Station and take a ticket to where the hell I like without a passport'.

Nor was he always so successful elsewhere. He hoped to bring both stability and economic progress to the Middle East. One of his first policy declarations when he went to the Foreign Office was a memorandum declaring Britain's interest to be peasants not pashas. But Britain no longer had the economic strength to prime the pumps for the reconstruction policies he dreamed of and he himself underestimated the forces of revolutionary nationalism that the war had helped to set in motion in the Arab world. Sometimes he seemed too ready to dismiss those who would not fit into his larger plans as no better than break-away unions. He was essentially a pragmatist and pragmatism was not enough, although it is difficult to see what else he could have done with the resources he had. He tried desperately hard to find a Palestine solution acceptable to both Jews and Arabs. He failed partly because he underestimated the passions on both sides and partly because his efforts, although supported by the U.S. State Department, were continually undermined by the pressures of American domestic policy on the President. He did not hide his anger, believing—perhaps optimistically—that with American backing he might have achieved an agreement which would have met the reasonable claims of Jewry without permanently antagonizing their Arab neighbours and have enabled Jewish skill and intelligence to assist in raising the level of life throughout the Middle East. Failure was, perhaps, inevitable. It was in the end sharpened by his impatience in handing over the problem to the United Nations and pulling out the British administration when a decision was imposed which he thought to be wrong.

Looking at the whole field of foreign affairs his total achievement must, despite his failures, be judged remarkable and Bevin himself a great foreign secretary. He was moreover the strong man of the Government and Attlee's closest and most loyal associate with a powerful voice in all major decisions. Bevin had three careers: trade-union leader; wartime Labour minister; foreign secretary. He was nearly sixty when he embarked on the second and entered the House of Commons for the first time; and only six years short of his death when he went to the Foreign Office. To each he brought integrity, loyalty, and a powerful and imaginative mind. In each his impact was massive and creative. He grew with each demand made upon him and in whatever situation he found himself had in the highest degree that quality which Goethe once thought was to be noted in the English: 'The courage they have to be that which Nature made them.' 'A turn-up in a million' was Bevin's own description of himself.

In March 1951 Bevin became lord privy seal but his health was rapidly declining and he died in London 14 April 1951. His ashes were buried in Westminster Abbey.

Bevin was sworn of the Privy Council in 1940, elected an honorary fellow of Magdalen College, Oxford, in 1946, and received honorary degrees from Cambridge and Bristol. Busts by E. Whitney Smith went to Transport House, the Ministry of Labour, and the Foreign Office; by Sir Jacob Epstein to the Tate Gallery; the National Portrait Gallery has a portrait by T. C. Dugdale.

[Francis Williams, *Ernest Bevin*, 1952; Alan Bullock, *The Life and Times of Ernest Bevin*, 2 vols., 1960–67; personal knowledge.]

FRANCIS-WILLIAMS.

BHOPAL, HAMIDULLAH, NAWAB OF (1894–1960), the third son of Her Highness Nawab Sultan Jehan, the Begum regnant of that state and her consort Ali Ahmed Khan, was born at Bhopal 9 September 1894. He was educated as a commoner at the Mahommedan Anglo-Oriental College at Aligarh, the centre of Islamic feeling in India, and obtained his B.A. (1915) from the Allahabad University to which the college was then affiliated. During his time at Aligarh (1911–15) the temper of that institution was undergoing a very radical change. A wave of pan-Islamism following the Tripolitan and the Balkan wars had begun to influence the younger generation towards an attitude of criticism of British policies, primarily in respect of Islam. There was also a noticeable growth of national feeling. At the university, Hamidullah Khan came under these influences and all through his life these contradictory tendencies were strongly marked in him. At Aligarh he also came into contact with leading public men, especially among the Moslems, and with them he remained on terms of friendship throughout his life.

On return to the state he was employed in administration in various capacities under his mother, notably as chief secretary (1916–22) and as minister of law and justice (1922–6). When Hamidullah Khan's elder brothers died, Lord Birkenhead [q.v.], overriding the decision of the Government in Delhi, declared him heir-apparent in preference to the children of the elder brothers. This was in strict accordance with Moslem law. Soon afterwards his mother abdicated and Hamidullah Khan assumed full ruling powers over his state (1926).

From the very first, Hamidullah took a deep interest in the political evolution of princely India. In view of the rapid growth of the national movement, the ruling princes, organized under a Chamber of Princes, were then seeking to have their rights defined and strengthened. These claims were being pressed under the leadership of the Standing Committee of Princes to which Nawab Hamidullah was elected in the first year of his rule. He occupied that position almost continuously to the end of the British power in India. As a leading member of the princely order he was an unbending champion of the treaty rights of the princes and argued strongly for a rigid limitation of the Crown's powers of paramountcy, and for the recognition of the claim that the relationship of the princes was with the Crown of England and not with the Government of India. Although a staunch champion of the sovereign rights of princes, Nawab Hamidullah was realist enough to recognize that a machinery of co-operation with British India had of necessity to be evolved if the princely states were to survive. He was, therefore, nominated by the Chamber of Princes as one of its delegates to the Round Table conference, convened in London in 1930 to discuss the problem of Indian self-government, where he played a notable part in persuading the rulers of states to accept the principle of federal union with British India. In the committee presided over by Lord Sankey [q.v.] which was entrusted with the working out of the details of federal structure, Hamidullah was one of the most constructive spokesmen of the princes. As chancellor of the Chamber of Princes (1931–2) he exercised a leadership in the negotiations which safeguarded the rights of the princes in the federal constitution. His close association with the political leaders of British India enabled him to present the case of the states in a manner acceptable to national sentiment.

The growth of the Moslem League under M. A. Jinnah [q.v.], the demand for the partition of India and the creation of a separate state of Pakistan placed him in a very awkward dilemma. The original solution of federal union seemed no longer possible and he along with some other princes put forward the idea of a division of India into three areas

Hindustan, Pakistan, and Rajasthan— the last being itself a confederation of princely states bound to the other two in matters connected with defence, foreign policy, and transport. He fought for this idea to the very end. As chancellor of the Chamber of Princes, elected a second time in 1944, he was able to exert considerable pressure on the Government in the political discussions which ended only with the independence of India in 1947. In the negotiations with Sir Stafford Cripps [q.v.] (1942) and with the cabinet mission (1946) he was one of the leading spokesmen of the princely states. When independence came, like the majority of his brother princes, he surrendered his state voluntarily to the Indian Union. From 1947, until he died at Bhopal 4 February 1960, he lived a retired life interesting himself mainly in agriculture.

Nawab Hamidullah, like his mother before him, was deeply attached to the British royal family with whom he maintained close connection until the time of India's independence. As a younger son he was attached to the staff of the Prince of Wales when he visited India in 1921. He was appointed C.S.I. (1921), C.V.O. (1922), G.C.I.E. (1929), and G.C.S.I. (1932). During the war of 1939–45 his unremitting efforts to keep up the loyalty of the Moslems to the allied cause and his own sacrifices brought him the rank of honorary air vice-marshal in the Indian Air Force and honorary major-general in the Indian Army.

Nawab Hamidullah was one of the best-known all-round sportsmen in India. He excelled in cricket, squash, hockey, and other games, but it was as a polo player that he was internationally known. He was one of the most outstanding players of his time and he kept up the game almost to the end.

The Nawab married in 1905 the Princess Shah Bano Maimoona Sultan Begum, the daughter of Shahzada Humayun, the great-grandson of Shah Shuja, King of Afghanistan. By her he had three daughters, the first, Gauhar-i-Taj (Begum Kurwai), opted for Pakistan and thereby lost her claim to succeed to the title. The second daughter, Princess Mehr Taj, married the Nawab of Pataudi, the Oxford and test cricketer who died in 1952. She succeeded on the death of her father to the title and dignity of the Nawab Begum of Bhopal.

[Publications of the former state of Bhopal; personal knowledge.]   K. M. PANIKKAR.

BICESTER, first BARON (1867–1956), banker. [See SMITH, VIVIAN HUGH.]

BIDDER, GEORGE PARKER (1863–1953), marine biologist, was born in London 21 May 1863, the son of George Parker Bidder, barrister, later a Q.C. and bencher of Lincoln's Inn, and grandson of George Parker Bidder [q.v.], the calculating phenomenon among whose engineering works are the London Victoria Docks. His mother was Anna, daughter of John Robinson McClean, M.P., F.R.S. Bidder was educated at Harrow and after working at University College, London, under (Sir) Ray Lankester [q.v.] entered Trinity College, Cambridge, where he obtained a first class in part i (1884) and a second in part ii (1886) of the natural sciences tripos. He next spent a considerable amount of his time at the Stazione Zoologica at Naples and at the laboratory of the Marine Biological Association at Plymouth, where he quickly established his reputation as a leading authority on sponges. To this group he devoted most of his scientific energy for the rest of his life; he was the author of many scientific papers and edited Vosmaer's posthumous *Bibliography of Sponges* (1928). Important as these papers were, Bidder's most valuable contributions to biology arose from an intense desire to promote the interests of science and from the business experience gained as managing director (1897–1908) and later as chairman (1915–19) of the Cannock Chase Colliery Company, for he applied this experience wholeheartedly to the welfare of biological projects. He purchased a trawler and placed it at the disposal of the Marine Biological Association in order to carry out fishery research in the North Sea; with the proceeds of its subsequent sale he endowed a Ray Lankester research studentship at Plymouth. By other equally timely gifts and loans he enabled the laboratories at Naples and Plymouth to survive very critical periods in their history and ensured the continuity of publication of two very important biological journals: *The Quarterly Journal of Microscopical Science* and the *Journal of Experimental Biology*. He had an outstanding ability to give financial advice and help at the right time and in the right way.

Bidder's work on sponges won him the degree of Sc.D. from Cambridge in 1916. He served on the council of the Plymouth laboratory from 1899 until shortly before his death. He was president of the Marine Biological Association (1939-45) and of the zoology section of the British Association at Leeds in 1927. He took a very active part in the work of the Linnean Society, being vice-president in 1924 and 1931, and zoological secretary in 1928-31. His period of office as president of the Marine Biological Association covered a period of intense air raids; his imperturbability during a particularly unpleasant incident made him an almost legendary figure.

Although in latter years he enjoyed reasonably robust health, at least fifteen years of his life were marred by illness. He developed phthisis as a young man and later took an active interest in, and was a founder-member of, the Papworth Hospital. As he grew older he became more and more nocturnal in habit. He rose about tea time and worked far into the night. It is generally believed that his purchase of Parker's Hotel in Naples was prompted by his dislike of being roused at conventional hours. He was a Liberal in politics and for many years helped in the organization of the party in Cambridge.

In 1899 Bidder married Marion (died 1932), daughter of George Greenwood; they had two daughters. Bidder died in Cambridge 31 December 1953. There are portraits by R. G. Eves in the possession of the family and of the Marine Biological Association at Plymouth.

[Private information; personal knowledge.]
JAMES GRAY.

BIRDWOOD, WILLIAM RIDDELL, first BARON BIRDWOOD (1865-1951), field-marshal, was born at Kirkee, India, 13 September 1865, the second son of Herbert Mills Birdwood [q.v.], under-secretary to the Government of Bombay, later a high court judge, and his wife, Edith Marion Sidonie, daughter of Surgeon-Major Elijah George Halhed Impey, of the Bombay Horse Artillery. All five sons were to serve the army in India.

Educated at Clifton College, Birdwood obtained a commission in the 4th battalion, Royal Scots Fusiliers, in 1883. He entered the Royal Military College, Sandhurst, but as a result of the Penjdeh incident of 1885 he was gazetted earlier than he expected to the 12th Lancers and embarked for India in that year; he transferred to the 11th Bengal Lancers at the end of 1886. He first saw active service in the Black Mountain expedition in 1891; and acquitted himself well in the Tirah

expedition in 1897. In 1893-8 he was adjutant of the Viceroy's Body Guard.

Promoted captain in 1896, Birdwood went in November 1899 to South Africa as a special service officer and was appointed to the staff of the Natal mounted brigade commanded by Lord Dundonald [q.v.]. He took part in the battle of Colenso and in the further campaigns to relieve Ladysmith; was later wounded; and five times mentioned in dispatches. When the Natal Force was broken up towards the end of 1900 Birdwood became deputy assistant adjutant-general to Lord Kitchener [q.v.] and on the conclusion of the South African war accompanied him to India as his assistant military secretary (1902-4) and military secretary (1905-9). Birdwood's relationship with Kitchener was one of the decisive elements in his career: 'we seemed to take to each other at once, and for the next nine years [1900-1909] I was scarcely ever away from him.'

Birdwood was promoted colonel in 1905 and in 1908 was chief staff officer to Sir James Willcocks [q.v.] in the Mohmand Field Force. He was appointed to the D.S.O., mentioned in dispatches, and appointed C.I.E. He became brigadier-general in 1909 and major-general in 1911. From 1909 to 1912 he was in command of the Kohat independent brigade. In 1912, after a short period as quartermaster-general, he became secretary to the Government of India in the army department and a member of the governor-general's legislative council. He was thus called upon to play an important part in the dispatch of the Indian Army units to France, Egypt, and Mesopotamia after the outbreak of war in 1914. In December he was given command of the new Australian and New Zealand contingents being sent to Egypt, with corps commander status and the rank of lieutenant-general.

Birdwood at once discerned the outstanding quality of the independent and ardent young Anzacs. He built up an excellent staff and training was put in hand. The original intention was to send the troops to France after training but they were destined for an earlier and more spectacular initiation. A few days after Admiral Carden [q.v.] opened the naval assault on the Dardanelles on 19 February 1915, Birdwood was instructed by Kitchener, now secretary of state for war, to proceed to the Dardanelles and to report back. Birdwood was at once impressed by the difficulties of a purely naval attack and reported in this sense at a time when (Sir) Winston Churchill was urging Kitchener to send the 29th division to the Eastern Mediterranean theatre 'to support our diplomacy'. Kitchener at this stage was vacillating, but some Anzac units and others of the Royal Naval Division were sent to the island of Lemnos where Admiral Wemyss [q.v.] was endeavouring to create an advanced supply base with no staff and hardly any facilities. It was Kitchener's intention that Birdwood should command any military force that might be needed; but his decision on 10 March to send the 29th division was one of the factors which resulted in the appointment of Sir Ian Hamilton [q.v.] to take command of what was to be called the Mediterranean Expeditionary Force. One consequence of this decision was that the preparatory work done by Birdwood's staff was largely negatived. Hamilton's failure to bring Birdwood's staff into his planning and the extent to which he ignored his administrative staff were factors which caused friction.

After the failure of the naval attack of 18 March and the decision taken jointly on 22 March and without reference to London by Hamilton and Carden's successor Admiral De Robeck [q.v.] to deliver a combined naval and military attack as soon as Hamilton's force had been reorganized, Birdwood was strongly opposed to any landings on the Helles beaches of the Gallipoli Peninsula (which he had previously favoured) as the vital element of surprise had been lost. In this he was strongly supported by (Sir) Aylmer Hunter-Weston (29th division), (Sir) Archibald Paris (Royal Naval Division), and Sir John Maxwell (G.O.C. Egypt) [qq.v.]. Hamilton stuck firmly to the plan to land the 29th division at Helles and rejected Birdwood's arguments for a landing on the Asiatic shore of the Dardanelles.

The role of the Anzac Corps was to land on the peninsula at a point just north of the conspicuous promontory of Gaba Tepe on the western shore of the Gallipoli Peninsula and advance eastwards to the eminence of Mal Tepe, thus cutting off the Turkish forces opposed to the 29th division at Helles. Birdwood determined to land his covering force at first light, with no preliminary naval bombardment, in order to achieve the maximum of surprise. The combined assault took place on Sunday, 25 April. The Anzac covering force, for reasons which have never been satisfactorily explained, landed in some con-

fusion well to the north of Gaba Tepe in a small bay subsequently known as Anzac Cove. In spite of this initial error, the surprise was almost complete and some units penetrated deep inland against hastily gathered Turkish resistance. The momentum of the advance was not maintained. Colonel Mustapha Kemal, commanding the Turkish 19th division at Boghali, engaged all available forces. The steep cliffs and precipitous gullies above Anzac Cove became the scenes of fierce and unco-ordinated fighting throughout the day. By evening a thin drizzle was falling on the exhausted dominion troops, Anzac Cove was the scene of serious congestion and confusion, and the ground secured was in fact a small perimeter which penetrated inland barely a thousand yards in places. In these depressing circumstances, Birdwood's divisional commanders urged him to recommend evacuation. Against his own inclinations Birdwood did so. In the general confusion the message was not addressed to anyone and it was only by chance that Hamilton received it. His reply was a firm order to hold on.

For six months the Anzacs defended their wretched, tiny, and arid fragment of coast, overlooked by the enemy and constantly exposed to his fire. Intense heat and disease subsequently added to the already severe burdens of the resolute dominion troops. Birdwood may be faulted for certain aspects of his handling of Anzac operations, and particularly for the failures of the night attacks of 2–3 May and for the heroic but poorly commanded attempt to seize the Sari Bair heights on 6–9 August. He may also be criticized for failing to appreciate until too late the debilitating effects of sickness on the Anzac troops which played a significant part in the failure of the August attacks. But in defence his confident and determined example and bearing fully merited the tribute of Hamilton that he was 'the soul of Anzac'.

Birdwood was one of the very few British commanders to leave Gallipoli with an increased reputation. In one respect he was fortunate. The failure of the IX Corps under Sir Frederick Stopford [q.v.] at Suvla on 6–9 August obscured the errors of Birdwood and (Sir) Alexander Godley [q.v.] at Anzac, both then and later. When, following Hamilton's recall in October, Sir Charles Monro [q.v.] recommended evacuation, Kitchener wanted to appoint Birdwood in his stead. Birdwood, greatly to his credit, protested and the proposal was shelved. It was ironic that Birdwood, the only senior commander initially opposed to evacuation (he subsequently agreed that the decision was right), should eventually be in executive command of the evacuation, as commander of the Dardanelles Army under Monro, when the Cabinet decided upon it. This brilliantly successful operation in December 1915 and January 1916 rightly increased his already high reputation.

After the death of Sir William Bridges [q.v.] at Anzac in May 1915, Birdwood had been made responsible to the Australian minister of defence for administration in addition to his responsibility to the War Office for the conduct of military operations. It was largely due to Birdwood that this arrangement worked so well.

At the end of March 1916 the two Anzac Corps embarked for France, the first under Birdwood's command. In November 1917 it was renamed the Australian Corps and comprised the five Australian divisions in France. In May 1918 Birdwood took command of the Fifth Army. He was promoted general in 1917 and after the war was awarded £10,000 and created a baronet (1919).

Birdwood had proved himself a brave and resolute soldier and keenly alive to the importance of personal relations. But the failings demonstrated in attack on Gallipoli were also evident in France. As was written after his death 'he remained a "character", a virile personality rather than a master of war'. His unconcealed eagerness for personal recognition was one facet of his character which some found unattractive. If not in the first he was high in the second rank of British commanders in the war of 1914–18.

After the war Birdwood commanded the Northern Army in India (1920–24) and in 1925 was preferred to Sir Claud Jacob [q.v.] as commander-in-chief. He was promoted field-marshal at the same time. He was a good commander-in-chief with a deep and sympathetic knowledge of the country and its peoples.

The one position Birdwood coveted but did not attain was the governor-generalship of Australia. On his retirement from India in 1930 he was elected, somewhat unexpectedly, to the mastership of Peterhouse, Cambridge, an office which he exercised with manifest enjoyment until 1938. In 1935 he was appointed captain of Deal Castle and in 1938 was created Baron Birdwood, of Anzac and Totnes. He had been appointed C.B. (1911), K.C.B.

(1917), and G.C.B. (1923); K.C.S.I. (1915) and G.C.S.I. (1930); K.C.M.G. (1914) and G.C.M.G. (1919); and G.C.V.O. (1937). His long and distinguished life, darkened in later years by failing eyesight, ended on 17 May 1951 when he died at Hampton Court Palace.

Birdwood married in 1894 Janetta Hope Gonville (died 1947), daughter of Sir Benjamin Parnell Bromhead, fourth baronet. It was a very happy marriage. They had two daughters and a son, Christopher Bromhead (1899–1962), who succeeded to the title.

The Imperial War Museum has portraits by Alfred Hayward and Francis Dodd, a pencil and water-colour 'General Birdwood returning to his headquarters' by Sir William Orpen, and a bust by Sigismund de Strobl; Birdwood is included in the group 'Some General Officers of the Great War' by J. S. Sargent in the National Portrait Gallery where there is also a drawing by Sargent.

[The Birdwood papers (Australian War Memorial, Canberra); Lord Birdwood, *Khaki and Gown*, 1941, and *In My Time*, 1945; C. F. Aspinall-Oglander, (Official) *History of the Great War. Military Operations, Gallipoli*, 2 vols., 1929–32; C. E. W. Bean, *Official History of Australia in the War*, 6 vols., 1921–42; R. R. James, *Gallipoli*, 1965; *The Times*, 18, 22, 25, and 30 May 1951; private information.]

ROBERT RHODES JAMES.

BIRLEY, SIR OSWALD HORNBY JOSEPH (1880–1952), painter, was born 31 March 1880 at Auckland, New Zealand, the son of Hugh Francis Birley, of St. Asaph, North Wales, and his wife, Elizabeth, daughter of George McCorquodale, of Newton-le-Willows, who were at that time engaged upon a world tour. Oswald was their only child and his father, a man of volatile and artistic temperament, was determined to ensure the development of his son's talent which had shown itself at an early age. He was educated at Harrow and then, in 1897, was taken by his father to Dresden, Munich, and Florence. In 1898 he went up to Trinity College, Cambridge, moving on to Paris in 1901 where he studied under Marcel Baschet at Julian's and exhibited regularly at the Salon until 1904. In 1905 he visited Madrid, staying there for a year and executing a remarkable series of copies from Velazquez; it was perhaps this more than any other influence which presented him with an ideal and formulated his style.

From 1906 he was working in London, rapidly establishing a reputation as a portrait painter in an era which included Sargent, Orpen, Nicholson, McEvoy, and Lavery [qq.v.]. He exhibited at the Royal Academy and at the Modern Society of Portrait Painters, and from time to time continued to exhibit at the Salon and elsewhere.

At the outbreak of war in 1914 he enlisted in the Royal Fusiliers with whom he served until 1915 when he was transferred to the Intelligence Corps, flying as an observer with the Royal Flying Corps. He became a captain in 1916; received the M.C. in 1917; and returned to civil life in 1919.

In 1921 he married Rhoda Vava Mary, daughter of Robert Lecky Pike, of Kilnock, county Carlow (they had one daughter and one son), and the following year moved into 62 Wellington Road, St. John's Wood, which had been built for him to the design of Clough Williams-Ellis. From here he set out on a series of painting travels which, besides Europe, included visits to America (1922 and subsequently), Mexico in 1926, where he painted President Calles; India (1927), and Siam, painting the King and Queen, in 1929. During this period he received his first royal commission, a portrait of King George V for the National Museum of Wales (1928); and thereafter he was to paint virtually every member of the royal family. He continued to exhibit, chiefly with the Royal Society of Portrait Painters, of which he was for some years vice-president.

In 1943, while serving with the Sussex Home Guard, he lost the sight of an eye in an accident when a weapon exploded. Typically he uttered no word of complaint and started to paint again, adapting himself with great patience to the new type of vision. He painted most of the statesmen and military leaders of the war, particularly a series for the Royal Naval College, Greenwich, of King George VI and his admirals, and four portraits of (Sir) Winston Churchill. After the war he made other visits to America in 1949 and 1950; but he was no longer young or robust and certainly took on more work than was good for him.

Birley was knighted in 1949. In 1951 an exhibition of his work, ranging over half a century, was held at the Royal Institute Galleries which revealed remarkably the record he had made of the personalities of his time, almost always faithful likenesses

and of a consistently high quality, while the landscape and subject pictures demonstrated his versatility and breadth of interest. A year later, after a final visit to America and a long period of increasingly poor health, he died at his London home 6 May 1952. He is buried in the country churchyard at West Dean near his Sussex home of Charleston Manor.

Exceptionally handsome, with very well-shaped head and hands, Oswald Birley had immense charm of manner devoid of all affectation or conceit. He was a delightful companion who did most things well and gracefully—he spoke perfect French and was a first-rate shot. He had an enormous circle of friends, most of whom had been his sitters, and not least among them were those who worked for him or with him. He was much more than a 'society' or 'boardroom' painter—apart from royalty and the court circle he had painted American millionaires and Indian beggars, soldiers and artists, statesmen and dancers, children and viceroys, all of them with insight and sympathy and, as he said himself, with the intention not of flattery but of paying a compliment. His work is to be found in the National Portrait and many other galleries and there is a self-portrait (1915) in the Musée de Luxembourg, Paris.

[Personal knowledge.]

JOHN LEIGH-PEMBERTON.

BLACKWOOD, ALGERNON HENRY (1869–1951), author, was born at Shooters Hill, Kent, 14 March 1869, the second son of (Sir) Stevenson Arthur Blackwood, who became secretary to the Post Office, and his wife, Harriet Sydney, daughter of Conway R. Dobbs, of Castle Dobbs, county Antrim, Ireland, and widow of George, sixth Duke of Manchester. He was educated at a school of the Moravian Brotherhood in the Black Forest, and at Wellington College and Edinburgh University. His father, in his youth a man of fashion known as 'Beauty Blackwood', underwent a sudden conversion and became a leading speaker and writer in the evangelical movement. Although Algernon may have inherited something of his father's religious and emotional temperament, and more of his mother's innate wisdom, he did not follow the path of Christian evangelism, but at seventeen began a study of the eastern religions which, with his deep love of nature, became leading influences in his life.

At twenty he was sent out to Toronto

with a small allowance and for the next ten years he lived a perilous existence in Canada and the United States, during which he tried many occupations, touching the depths of poverty and despair before he found work as a reporter on the New York *Sun* and later on the *New York Times*. He described these years in a vivid autobiography *Episodes before Thirty* (1923) which was included by Jonathan Cape [q.v.] in his Travellers' Library as *Adventures before Thirty* (1934).

On his return to England, Blackwood was at first employed in the dried milk business, but he had been in the habit of writing tales for his own pleasure, and after the encouragement of the publisher Eveleigh Nash had led to the appearance of his first book of stories, *The Empty House* (1906), he soon decided to devote himself entirely to authorship, for which his American experience had provided much curious material. From the first he was preoccupied with the supernatural, but before long he extended his range from the macabre 'ghost stories' strictly so-called, as exemplified in *John Silence* (1908, a collection of cases involving a psychologist-detective of that name), to more ambitious full-length novels of fancy and fantasy. Several of these disclosed his interest in the child mind, notably *Jimbo* (1909), *The Human Chord* (1910), and *A Prisoner in Fairyland* (1913) which he dramatized with Violet Pearn as *The Starlight Express* (1915) and for which Sir Edward Elgar [q.v.] composed music. Among his more powerful and persuasive mystical conceptions was *The Centaur* (1911), in which an Irish traveller feels the call of the *Urwelt* and has a vision in the Caucasus of the morning of the world; while there is an impressive strain of poetic feeling in *Pan's Garden* (1912), a volume of nature stories. *Dudley and Gilderoy* (1929), the story of a cat and a parrot, showed more of the light touch and sense of humour which he always had at his command.

In his later years two comprehensive anthologies of Blackwood's stories were published, *The Tales of Algernon Blackwood* (1938) and *Tales of the Uncanny and Supernatural* (1949). Altogether Blackwood published more than thirty books. His craftsmanship, gift of narrative, original turn of mind, and genuine poetic and imaginative force, make him an author to be remembered with respect. Perhaps it was only in some of his short stories that he was entirely successful artistically, for

a certain diffuse and nebulous quality hampered the novels; nor, on the whole, did he receive the financial return which he deserved. But towards the close of his life, from 1947 onwards, he came into his own as a performer on television, where his strongly marked features and distinguished presence enhanced the effectiveness of his story-telling. He received the Television Society's medal in 1948 and in 1949 he was appointed C.B.E. for his services to literature.

Personally, Blackwood, although convivial, was a strongly independent, deeply thoughtful character, whose philosophical detachment did not prevent him from winning the warm affection of many friends. Tall and active, he spent much of his time in Europe, especially in Switzerland, and was a fine skier and a believer in the open-air life.

Blackwood died in London 10 December 1951. He was unmarried. Portraits by John Flanagan and Herbert Gurschner and a pencil drawing by Walter Tittle are privately owned.

[*The Times*, 11 December 1951; *Essays and Studies*, 1961; private information.]

DEREK HUDSON.

BLAMEY, SIR THOMAS ALBERT (1884–1951), field-marshal, was born 24 January 1884 at Lake Albert, near Wagga Wagga, New South Wales, the seventh child and fourth son of Richard Blamey, drover and farmer, by his wife, Margaret Murray. Blamey was educated at the Wagga Wagga superior public school. In 1899 he was appointed a pupil teacher in the New South Wales education department, and began teaching at the Lake Albert public school. In 1901 he was transferred to the South Wagga school where he became an officer in the school cadet corps. In 1903 he went to Western Australia where he secured an appointment as assistant teacher in the Fremantle boys' school. In 1906 he won by competitive examination a commission in the administrative and instructional staff of the Australian Army and was appointed staff officer (cadets) in the state of Victoria.

In 1910 Blamey was promoted captain and in the following year he won by competitive examination the place reserved for Australian regular officers at the Staff College, Quetta. On graduation from the college in December 1913, he served in regimental and staff postings with the Indian Army before sailing for the United

Kingdom for further experience with the British Army. He was promoted major in July 1914. When war broke out he was appointed general staff officer (intelligence) on the headquarters of the 1st Australian division and joined that formation in Egypt in December.

After three months' service in the Gallipoli campaign, Blamey was appointed assistant adjutant and quartermaster-general of the 2nd Australian division, and soon after the Australian Imperial Force was transferred to France he became the division's senior general staff officer. During the campaigns on the western front he served in various staff appointments, with brief periods in command of an infantry battalion and a brigade until, in May 1918, he became brigadier, general staff, of the Australian Corps.

After the war Blamey became in succession director of military operations at army headquarters, colonel, general staff, at the Australian high commissioner's office in London, and deputy chief of the Australian general staff. In 1925 the Victorian government offered him the post of chief commissioner of police. Blamey accepted, resigned his regular commission, and took up the appointment on 1 September.

The force had recently been shaken by a mutiny staged in protest against poor rates of pay and conditions of service. In energetically undertaking the task of restoring morale and efficiency, Blamey introduced many reforms, including an orderly system of promotion. Unfortunately the manner in which he handled some demonstrations by the unemployed during the economic depression brought him into disfavour with powerful political elements. In May 1936 a senior police officer was severely wounded in circumstances which reflected little credit on the force. Blamey vainly endeavoured to conceal the truth, and in the political storm which followed he was forced to resign.

On his resignation from the regular army, Blamey had been granted a commission in the Citizen Forces and he commanded the 3rd division from 1931 to 1937. Soon after war broke out in 1939 he was promoted lieutenant-general and given command of the Australian Army Corps raised for service in the Middle East.

Blamey commanded the Australian Corps during the latter portion of the first Libyan campaign and the Anzac Corps during the brief campaign in Greece. He was then appointed deputy commander-in-chief, Middle East, but retained his office of commander of the Australian troops in that theatre.

After Japan entered the war in December 1941, Blamey was recalled to Australia and appointed commander-in-chief of the Australian Army. The Australian war effort had so far been concentrated chiefly on the maintenance of the formations serving overseas and the forces in Australia were ill equipped, ill trained, and badly organized. With the Japanese advancing through the northern approaches, Blamey was faced with the formidable task of rapidly expanding the army and bringing it to a state of war efficiency. In executing this task, he brilliantly demonstrated his talents as a military organizer and administrator.

Blamey was also the commander of Allied Land Forces under General Douglas MacArthur, the allied commander-in-chief, South-West Pacific, and it was on orders from him that Blamey assumed personal command of the allied land forces in New Guinea on 23 September 1942. However, soon after the recapture of Buna in January 1943, he returned to his Australian army headquarters on the mainland. In subsequent operations, MacArthur avoided the difficult issue of Blamey's dual roles by appointing task force commanders operating directly under his own command. Blamey's appointment of commander of Allied Land Forces became purely nominal, although he was given the direction of the Australian mopping-up operations in New Guinea and the Solomons.

At the conclusion of hostilities, Blamey retired from the army and took up business pursuits. But his name was restored to the active list shortly before his promotion to field-marshal in 1950. It has been remarked that the heaviest handicap of so gifted a soldier was 'not his private life but the fact that it fell so far short of being private'.

Blamey was appointed to the D.S.O. in 1917, C.M.G. in 1918, C.B. in 1919, and knighted in 1935. He was advanced to K.C.B. in 1942 and G.B.E. in 1943, and held a number of foreign decorations.

He married first, in 1908, Minnie (died 1935), daughter of Edwin Millard, of Melbourne, by whom he had two sons; secondly, in 1939, Olga, daughter of Henry Farnsworth, of Melbourne.

Blamey died in Melbourne 27 May 1951. A portrait by Ivor Hele is in the Australian War Memorial and a statue by Raymond

Ewers is at the approach to Government House, Melbourne.

[Australian War Memorial records; *Australia in the War of 1939–45*, Series 1 (Army), vols. i–vii, ed. Gavin Long, 1952–63; John Hetherington, *Blamey*, 1954; personal knowledge.]   E. G. KEOGH.

BLEDISLOE, first VISCOUNT (1867–1958), agriculturist and public servant. [See BATHURST, CHARLES.]

BLOGG, HENRY GEORGE (1876–1954), coxswain of Cromer lifeboat, son of Ellen Blogg, was born in Cromer 6 February 1876. He was educated at the Goldsmiths' School where he proved quick at learning and revealed an unusually retentive memory. He took no part in games, was unsuccessful in defending himself against bullying, and never learnt to swim. When nearly twelve he began life as a longshore fisherman. In 1894 he joined the Cromer lifeboat crew, becoming second coxswain in 1902, and coxswain in 1909. His record of service was unique and when he retired in 1947 Cromer's had long been the most famous of all lifeboats and Blogg himself an international character. A silent, reticent man who neither smoked nor drank, he had a quiet kindliness and humour and remarkable qualities of personality and endurance. He inspired complete confidence in his lifeboat crew who knew him as a superb seaman: quick and resolute in decision, unerring in judgement, fearless before danger.

During Blogg's fifty-three years with Cromer lifeboats 873 lives were saved and he was thrice awarded the gold medal of the Royal National Life-boat Institution. The first of these he received for the rescue in 1917 of 11 men from the Swedish steamer *Fernebo*. His crew of ageing men had already been at sea for several hours and had taken 16 men from a Greek steamer *Pyrin*. When the call to the *Fernebo* came it proved impossible to launch the lifeboat against the mountainous seas. A second attempt was made after darkness fell, but when the boat was halfway to the wreck she was hit by a tremendous sea and losing several oars was forced back to the shore. Undaunted, Blogg seized his moment to make yet another attempt: which proved successful.

By 1927, when Blogg received his second gold medal (for the rescue of 15 men from the Dutch tanker *Georgia* after 20 hours at sea), he was using a motor-lifeboat and the difficulties of launching had been over-

come by the building of a slipway. In 1941 he was awarded his third gold medal and also the British Empire medal for the rescue of 88 men from six steamers in convoy. He was four times awarded the Life-boat Institution's silver medal, for the rescue of: 30 men from the Italian steamer *Monte Nevoso* (1932); 2 from the barge *Sepoy* of Dover (1933); 29 from the Greek steamer *Mount Ida* (1939); and 44 from the steamer *English Trader* (1941). He received the Empire gallantry medal in 1924 and was decorated with the George Cross in 1941; in 1948 the new Cromer lifeboat was named the *Henry Blogg*.

In 1901 Blogg married Annie Elizabeth (died 1950), daughter of Henry Brackenbury, fisherman, of Cromer. Their only son died in infancy and their only daughter in her twenties. Blogg died in Cromer 13 June 1954. A portrait by T. C. Dugdale hangs in Life-boat House, Grosvenor Gardens, London; and there is a bronze bust by James Woodford on the east cliff at Cromer. The Imperial War Museum has a pastel by William Dring.

[*The Life-boat*, September 1954; *Year Book* of the Royal National Life-boat Institution for 1955; Cyril Jolly, *Henry Blogg of Cromer*, 1958; private information.]   HELEN M. PALMER.

BODKIN, SIR ARCHIBALD HENRY (1862–1957), lawyer, was born in Highgate 1 April 1862, the youngest of the eight children of William Peter Bodkin and his wife, Elisabeth, daughter of William Clowser, of Hampstead. He came of a line of lawyers: his grandfather was (Sir) William Henry Bodkin [q.v.], chairman of Middlesex quarter-sessions and a prolific writer on criminal law, and his father was for forty-four years chairman of the Highgate bench. There were plans after 'Archie' left Highgate School to send him to South Africa to join one of his brothers on a farm, and he actually spent a year on a farm at Barnsley; but the boy's interests were already fixed on the criminal bar, and when the South Africa scheme fell through he was without delay entered at the Inner Temple. He was called in 1885, and became a pupil of E. T. E. Besley, then the busiest junior of the day, where he was later joined by (Sir) Travers Humphreys [q.v.].

From the first Bodkin was a tremendous worker, meticulous in detail, and specializing in drafting indictments which, before the passing of the Indictments Act of 1915, was a highly technical accomplishment. His style, as a prosecuting advocate, at North London and Middlesex sessions and at the Old Bailey, was early formed. Simple and direct in manner, he scorned the dramatic mannerisms popular in his day, and although possessed of a bubbling if somewhat heavy sense of humour, never allowed it to get out of hand. He relied on accurate and detailed knowledge of the facts and law contained in his brief, and a strong mind directed to the task in hand: the conviction of the accused. Yet, powerful advocate that he became, he never pressed a case beyond its merits, and in a period when for some counsel to prosecute meant to persecute, he was a pioneer, with Travers Humphreys, of a style which aimed to 'kill with fairness', however powerful the attack might be.

Bodkin's innate ability and sheer hard work were early recognized. He took few and short holidays, and save for a game of billiards allowed himself few other interests than the law. And the law for him meant criminal prosecutions, for his defence briefs were rare. He built up a large licensing practice, but as brewster sessions, when most of the work was done, were then held in August, these briefs did not clash with his work at the Old Bailey. He was already saving money, and in 1891, only six years after call, was able to marry Maud Beatrice, daughter of the Rev. Robert Wheler Bush, rector of St. Alphage, London Wall, a marriage of great contentment which ended only with his death.

In 1892 Bodkin was appointed junior Treasury counsel at the Old Bailey, and rapidly built up a reputation which he shared with (Sir) Horace Avory [q.v.], (Sir) Charles Gill, and (Sir) Richard Muir as one of the four leading criminal advocates of the day. In 1908 he was appointed senior Treasury counsel. By now he had joined the chambers of his uncle, Sir Harry Poland [q.v.], at 5 Paper Buildings, and in time became head of them. In 1901 he succeeded Poland as recorder of Dover, and although he had to resign in 1920 on becoming director of public prosecutions, he was reappointed in 1931 and only resigned at the age of eighty-five in 1947.

Tall and lean of build—he was a considerable athlete as a young man—he had a magnificent physique, and although well able to afford it never drove a car. He preferred to walk long distances from court to court, and at an advanced age was quite content with public transport.

In the war of 1914–18 Bodkin was largely concerned with the prosecution of spies, where his knowledge of the law, great industry, and ability to marshal and direct a mass of deadly detail were of the greatest value. He was responsible for the prosecution of Lody, and built up the complex case against Sir Roger Casement [q.v.] for the attorney-general. Perhaps his greatest murder prosecution was that known as the 'Brides in the Bath' (G. J. Smith) in 1915, in which he called 112 witnesses for the Crown.

In the troubled post-war period it was essential to appoint a strong man to succeed Sir Charles Mathews [q.v.] as director of public prosecutions and in 1920 Bodkin began the most strenuous ten years of his life. He would personally examine some 2,000 sets of papers a year, and here his industry was at times a defect, for he was unwilling to delegate responsibility. Day after day he would be first at his office at Richmond Terrace, personally drafting indictments which should have been left to junior Treasury counsel, and always taking work home at the weekend. Here, too, his understanding of contemporary thought and habit may have been narrowed by the limited range of his own private life. Famous cases to which he gave the whole of his attention included those arising from the I.R.A. troubles in Ireland, the prosecution of Horatio Bottomley [q.v.]; of Armstrong, Mason, Vaquier, Mahon, Thorne, and Browne and Kennedy for murder, and of Clarence Hatry and his associates. The prosecution of the acting editor of the *Workers' Weekly* (1924) brought him as near as he ever came to politics when the withdrawal of the 'Campbell case' at the orders of the attorney-general (Sir Patrick Hastings, q.v.) brought down the Government of the day. The inquiry ordered by Parliament in 1928 to consider the behaviour of the police, and incidentally of the director of public prosecutions, after the dismissal of a charge against Miss Savidge and Sir Leo Chiozza Money for an alleged offence in Hyde Park, was the sole occasion when Bodkin's conduct of his office was in any way impugned, and he came out of the ordeal entirely exonerated from any blame.

Bodkin was knighted in 1917 and appointed K.C.B. in 1924. In 1930 he resigned and went to live in Sidmouth where he became a noted gardener. He soon, however, found new employment in the field of criminal law as chairman of Devon quarter-sessions, where he sat until 1947.

As a judge he loved a legal argument, and insisted, with some pedantry, on the meticulous proof of every fact in dispute. With failing powers he finally relinquished his various appointments and retired to live with his wife and son at Rogate, Sussex. There, at the age of ninety-five, a wealthy man from the savings of his hard-earned income, he died on the last day of 1957.

[Robert Jackson, *Case for the Prosecution*, 1962; Douglas G. Browne, *Sir Travers Humphreys*, 1960; private information; personal knowledge.]   CHRISTMAS HUMPHREYS.

BOLDERO, SIR HAROLD ESMOND ARNISON (1889–1960), physician and medical administrator, was born in Maida Vale 20 August 1889, the elder son of John Boldero, company director, and his wife, Clara Arnison, of Penrith, Cumberland. Boldero was educated at Charterhouse and Trinity College, Oxford, where he obtained a third class in physiology in 1912. He was an outstanding athlete, representing Oxford in the 440 yards in 1911, and then as a hockey player. At the Middlesex Hospital he continued to play hockey and gained a reputation and international representation as a fast and clever centre-half. Having qualified M.R.C.S., L.R.C.P. in 1915, he served in France as a regimental medical officer in a field ambulance and as a deputy assistant director of medical services, and was twice mentioned in dispatches. He returned to the Middlesex in 1919 and took his Oxford B.M., B.Ch. (1920) and D.M. (1925). While holding junior posts at the Middlesex, he became interested in paediatrics and after a period as clinical assistant at the Hospital for Sick Children, Great Ormond Street, in 1921, he was appointed to the staff of the Evelina Hospital for Children (1921–34), and in 1922 was elected an assistant physician to the Middlesex Hospital where in those days the junior physician looked after the children. This appealed to Boldero who had a flair for dealing with children and appeared to be able to enter into their way of thinking.

In 1934 Boldero became dean of the Middlesex Hospital medical school, an appointment which largely determined his subsequent career. He proved a most able administrator and served the hospital with distinction as dean until he retired in 1954. He was at first concerned with the better integration of clinical medicine, teaching, and research, and was responsible, with

A. E. (later Lord) Webb-Johnson [q.v.], for the concept of the Courtauld research wards to which patients were admitted for investigation under the joint care of a member of the staff of the hospital and a professor of one of the basic sciences in the school. As soon as the hospital building was completed, he drew up plans for the rebuilding of the medical school, but only the first phase, an administrative block, could be completed before the outbreak of war in 1939. Boldero, like other medical deans, had been involved in plans for the continuation of the work of the school and hospital in the event of war, and he now became a sector officer in the Emergency Medical Service. He kept the school together without interruption of teaching through two evacuations, to Bristol and Leeds, and, when the hospital was damaged, he was responsible for getting repairs and rebuilding carried out so that the medical staff returned to a hospital ready not only to carry on, but, as it rapidly turned out, to expand. Boldero's work as an educationist included membership of the senate of the university of London, and he was chairman for many years of its board of advanced medical studies.

The war also saw the beginning of a new phase in Boldero's career. Sir Charles Wilson (later Lord Moran) became president of the Royal College of Physicians of London in 1941, and, looking for a capable administrator to help in the work of the College, chose Boldero, who had been elected F.R.C.P. in 1933, first as treasurer (1941), then as registrar, a post which he occupied from 1942 until his death. Consequently Boldero became closely involved in the development of British medicine during the planning and establishment of the National Health Service. He represented the College in the negotiations between the medical profession and the Government, which eventuated in the National Health Service Act, and he continued to do so on the Joint Consultants' Committee which was subsequently accepted by the Ministry of Health as the spokesman of the consultants' interests. There were stormy times when disputes between the profession and the Government on questions of remuneration led to threats of withdrawal from the Service. Boldero was by nature conservative and strongly attached to traditional ideas and practices, but he recognized the need for change and saw that on the whole more was to be gained from co-operation with the Government than from merely negative opposition. His counsel in committee was always shrewd and often quietly humorous. He helped to maintain the influence of the College and gave wise guidance to the profession in difficult times. He spoke also as a man with much practical experience since he was a member of the North-West Metropolitan Regional Hospital Board and of the council of the Medical Protection Society. He also served on the General Medical Council. For six years before his death he was chairman of the council of the Chartered Society of Physiotherapy. He was knighted in 1950.

In 1917 Boldero married Margery Florence (died 1950), elder daughter of Arthur Tempest Blakiston Dunn, the founder and later headmaster of Ludgrove preparatory school, Barnet, and also a well-known international amateur footballer. They had two sons. Boldero died in London 30 November 1960. His portrait, painted by Harold Knight in 1957, is in the Middlesex Hospital and a copy is in the Royal College of Physicians.

[*British Medical Journal*, 10 December 1960; private information; personal knowledge.] BRAIN.

BOMBERG, DAVID GARSHEN (1890–1957), painter, was born in Birmingham 5 December 1890, the fifth child of Abraham Bomberg, leatherworker, an emigrant from Warsaw in the eighties, and his wife, Rebecca Klein; the family moved to Whitechapel in 1895. Apprenticed to a trade lithographer, Bomberg broke his indentures in 1908 to devote all his time to art. He studied for two years at evening classes at the City and Guilds Institute and at Westminster under W. R. Sickert [q.v.]. In 1911–13 he was a full-time student at the Slade School, winning a prize for drawing in his second year. His work at this time revealed a knowledge and understanding of advanced continental art, particularly cubism and futurism. While still a student he was in touch with the circle of Wyndham Lewis [q.v.]. In 1913 he visited Paris and met Picasso, Modigliani, and Kisling, and in the same year was a founder-member of the London Group. Among the pictures exhibited at his first one-man exhibition at the Chenil Galleries in 1914 was his 'Ju-Jitzu', now in the Tate Gallery.

In 1915 Bomberg enlisted and served in France with the Royal Engineers. In 1918 he was commissioned by the Canadian Government to contribute to the Canadian War Memorial; his 'The Canadian Tunnelling Company—Sappers at Work' is now in the National Gallery at Ottawa, and a study for it is in the Tate. In 1923 Bomberg went to Palestine and painted commissions for the Zionist Organization. He worked for six months in isolation at Petra (paintings in the Manchester and Birmingham city art galleries). He returned to London in 1927 and in the following year exhibited his work at the Leicester Galleries. He travelled to Toledo (1929), Morocco and the Aegean (1930), the Soviet Union (1933), and in 1934–5 returned to Spain, visiting Cuenca, Ronda, and Linares. In 1935–45 he was based in London, making occasional expeditions to the country. His travels were resumed in 1948 when he went to Cyprus (paintings in Liverpool and Southampton art galleries), and in 1953 he visited Paris, Chartres, and Vézelay. He returned to Ronda in February 1954, intending to stay for several years, but became ill in May 1956 and returned to England where he died in London 19 August 1957.

Although in his youth Bomberg received critical attention, he was generally neglected and died in obscure poverty. It was only when the Arts Council organized a retrospective exhibition in 1958 that the richness and originality of his work were recognized outside the small circle of his admirers. Fuller recognition came in 1967 with an exhibition at the Tate Gallery. In temperament he was intractable and uncompromising and never capable of concessions which might have eased his path. A prolific painter, he dedicated his life to his work. By 1945 he was convinced that recognition was not forthcoming and began to attach increasing importance to teaching. Classes held at the Borough Polytechnic attracted a nucleus of talented students who identified themselves with his viewpoint. The Borough Group (active in 1947–9), founded by Clifford Holden, organized exhibitions to several of which Bomberg contributed. A similar group called the Borough Bottega was active in 1953–5.

The importance of Bomberg's contribution lay in his profound understanding of the art of the past, his independence from critical orthodoxies and fashions, and the single-minded intensity of his work. From quasi-abstract beginnings he evolved a monumental and painterly figurative style, first adumbrated in the early twenties, set aside in favour of a more limited topographical approach in Palestine, and returned to and developed with increasing mastery after his first visit to Spain. His work was founded on a highly personal philosophy of art which owed much to the writings of Bishop Berkeley [q.v.]. His usual subjects were landscapes, still-life, and the human head. He was a magnificent draughtsman, and his work was distinguished by its firm structure and a sonority of colour unique in English painting. A selection from the extensive manuscripts left by him was published in the review *X*, June 1960.

Small in stature, alert and vigorous, Bomberg's appearance is recorded in an early portrait by Gerald Summers, also in numerous self-portraits, in the possession of the family. There is also a self-portrait in the Slade Collection.

In 1915 Bomberg married Alice, daughter of John Burton Mayes. The marriage was subsequently dissolved and he married a fellow painter, Lilian, daughter of Oliver Oswald Holt; they had one daughter.

[*Catalogues* of the Arts Council (1958) and Marlborough Fine Art (1964) exhibitions; private information; personal knowledge.]

ANDREW FORGE.

BONDFIELD, MARGARET GRACE (1873–1953), trade-union leader and first British woman cabinet minister, was born at Furnham, near Chard, Somerset, the tenth of the eleven children of William Bondfield and his wife, Ann, daughter of George Taylor, a Wesleyan Methodist minister. Her father, who came of yeoman stock with long traditions in the west, was a foreman lace worker with a talent for invention which he failed to exploit financially so that the closing of the firm for which he had worked for forty years left the family in straitened circumstances. Nevertheless both he and his vital energetic wife opened wide windows for their children, for they were spiritually minded persons, devout nonconformists, with strong Radical interests. 'Maggie' was happy at home, but her schooling was brief: she was teaching in the boys' school at thirteen; at fourteen she was an apprentice in a draper's shop in Brighton. She was 'a thoroughly smart business young person' said the testimonial which she took with her to London five years later. After three months' search she found work, but the conditions roused her to rebellion. Shop assistants had then to live in; the statutory maximum of 74 hours was regularly exceeded; her earnings were between £15 and £25 a year. When she learned of

the formation of the National Union of Shop Assistants, she joined it and threw herself ardently into its work, attended conferences and made her mark. For the union journal she wrote lively pieces under the pen-name Grace Dare. For the Women's Industrial Council she undertook a two-year survey, obtaining work in various shops on a descending scale as her references grew shorter. While thus ruining her own chances of advancement she obtained valuable first-hand evidence of the conditions which she sought to remedy.

All this time Margaret Bondfield was cultivating the habit of making clear decisions, was reading widely, and meeting people like the Dilkes, Shaw, and the Webbs [qq.v.]. She joined the Independent Labour Party and shared platforms with Keir Hardie, John Burns, George Lansbury, Ramsay MacDonald [qq.v.], and other leaders. In 1898 she became assistant secretary of her union ('I learnt to smoke in self-defence, as the men's pipes were awful') and in the following year she was the sole woman delegate to the Trades Union Congress where her speech made a great impression. Small in stature, with dark hair, wide brows, and bright dark eyes, she reminded her hearers of a courageous robin as, in her clear, resonant, musical voice, she told them that the unions must get together for political action if they were to achieve their larger aims. The long struggle for a Shop Hours Act confirmed this view. So did her close friendship with Mary Macarthur [q.v.] who joined her union and whom she proposed to the Dilkes and Gertrude Tuckwell [q.v.] as secretary of the Women's Trade Union League. She helped Mary Macarthur to found the National Federation of Women Workers (1906), became its assistant secretary in 1915, and on Mary's death (1921) and the amalgamation of the federation with the National Union of General and Municipal Workers, herself became chief woman officer of that union.

In the meantime she had resigned her post with the shop assistants' union in 1908 to work in a wider field, lecturing for the Independent Labour Party, on the executive of which she served from 1913 until 1921. She worked also for the Women's Labour League of which she was for a time organizing secretary, and for the Women's Co-operative Guild; for the latter's notable report on maternity she was largely responsible. Her mind was always her own, and, unlike many of her Labour colleagues, she opposed the limited bill for female emancipation and stood four-square for adult suffrage. On this she and Mary Macarthur fought not as feminists but as socialists. While holding staunchly to the view that war in 1914 was unjust and unnecessary, Margaret Bondfield worked mainly on the industrial side. She was a member of the Central Committee on Women's Training and Employment and was in the forefront of the fight for proper conditions for women war workers. In 1918 she was at last elected directly to the Parliamentary Committee of the Trades Union Congress and went as its delegate next year to the congress of the American Federation of Labor. In that year also she was a delegate to the Socialist International Conference at Berne and at the International Labour Conference in Washington. In 1920 she went with the British Labour delegation to Russia and in 1923 she became the first woman chairman of the Trades Union Congress.

All this led naturally to parliamentary candidature. She was unsuccessful at Northampton in 1920 and again in 1922 but she captured the seat for Labour in 1923. On occasion an electrifying speaker who could wave the fiery torch as can few, her maiden speech in the House was not a complete success, perhaps because it was the first intellectual speech from a woman' which the House had heard. Her next, from the Treasury bench, was much better: she was made parliamentary secretary to the Ministry of Labour as soon as her party took office in 1924 and by the end of that brief troubled session she had established herself with the House; with her department she never had any difficulty; and she did good work for the International Labour Organization. In the 'Red Letter' election Northampton turned her down; two years later (1926) she got back at a by-election in Wallsend. She received some criticism from Labour for signing the unanimous report of the Blanesburgh committee on unemployment insurance in 1927 and still more in 1929 when as minister of labour in MacDonald's second administration she introduced an unemployment insurance bill as unsatisfactory to her extreme left wing for not going far enough as it was to the Tory opposition for going too far. Nevertheless she conducted it to the statute book with a competence worthy of the first British woman cabinet minister and the first woman to be sworn of the Privy Council.

When cuts in unemployment benefit were proposed among the measures to meet the financial crisis of 1931 Margaret Bondfield together with most of the Cabinet declined to join the consequent 'national' government. She lost her seat in the election and she was defeated again at Wallsend in 1935. She was then adopted as Labour candidate for Reading but resigned when the outbreak of war postponed an election.

In the meantime she had continued her trade-union work, retiring in 1938. From 1939 she was an active vice-president of the National Council of Social Service and as chairman of the Women's Group on Public Welfare until 1949 she directed valuable research and practical social work. Her reaction to the war was entirely different from that in 1914, and between 1941 and 1943 she lectured for the Government in the United States and Canada. Failing health did not diminish her keen interest in public affairs or her enjoyment of her small house and garden in the country where friends found her as alert in mind as ever. She was sustained, as always, by the strong Christian faith which had ever been the mainspring of her disinterested service and glowing serenity. Her autobiography, characteristically entitled *A Life's Work* (1949), is concerned mainly with the causes for which she worked; its extreme modesty underrates both the influence and the impact on others of the vivid and transparently honest personality of a woman who had remarkable qualities of mind and character. She was appointed C.H. in 1948 and received the honorary degree of LL.D. from Bristol University in 1929 and the freedom of Chard in 1930. She died, unmarried, at Sanderstead, Surrey, 16 June 1953.

A miniature by W. M. Knight (1937) is in the National Portrait Gallery, and a black chalk drawing by Colin Gill is in the Manchester City Art Gallery.

[M. G. Bondfield, *A Life's Work*, 1949; M. A. Hamilton, *Margaret Bondfield*, 1924; personal knowledge.] M. A. HAMILTON.

BONE, Sir MUIRHEAD (1876–1953), water-colour painter and etcher, was born in Glasgow 23 March 1876, the fourth of eight children of the journalist David Drummond Bone and his wife, Elizabeth Millar Crawford. His elder brothers were James Bone, who became London editor of the *Manchester Guardian*, and Sir David Bone, commodore of the Anchor Line and writer on life at sea. Muirhead

Bone early showed a talent for drawing and studied first at the Glasgow School of Art evening school while serving his apprenticeship as an architect. This double training not only inspired him to depict the streets of his native town with meticulous realism but left a permanent mark on his art. Finding little support in Glasgow he set up as an art master at Ayr, his father's birthplace. No pupils came and in 1901 he moved to London.

He had already produced more than a hundred plates: figure subjects, portraits, landscapes, scenes in the dockyards of the Clyde. His first London plate was of 'Belgrave Hospital, Kennington', designed by his friend Charles Holden [q.v.], and represented a brick building in course of construction, with the scaffolding still standing round it. Soon after, in 1903, came the unfinished drypoint of 'London Bridge'; unfinished because a policeman moved the artist on, but enough had been done to show the first span of the bridge with the scaffolding erected for widening. Both these plates reflect the mind of the architect, an almost mathematical feeling for strains and stresses, far removed from the sketchiness of etchers working in the tradition of Sir Seymour Haden [q.v.]. Bone preferred the drypoint to the etching needle, and this lent a certain precision to his work and sometimes almost assimilated it to the art of the line-engraver.

Bone despised the protection of steel facing and, as drypoint soon wears out, the editions of his plates were necessarily small. However, he soon began to obtain recognition and made a resolute, and ultimately successful, attempt to widen his scope. His first landscapes were not very accomplished, but very soon, at Winchester, at Cambridge, and among the villages of Sussex, he was once more able to subdue his subject matter. In the drypoint of the 'Old and New Gaiety Theatres' he returned to his first love, and in the same year (1904) he indulged in a perfect orgy, in the plate called 'Building'. In this the planks and poles of the scaffolding, as well as the cords and pulleys, are lingered over with the most loving care. There exist of this plate three trial proofs and no fewer than nine published states showing the trouble which the artist must have taken to obtain the effect he desired. Then, as if to prevent himself from hardening into a specialist, Bone produced a whole series of portraits, and after these came the work which many regard as his masterpiece, 'Ayr Prison'.

Increasing success enabled Bone to travel abroad, and he lived for some year in Italy and Spain. Yet he brought to both countries the same austerity of outlook The grandiose and the picturesque were alike foreign to his temperament, and h could write of Florence that there wa nothing left for an artist: 'Every cat in th world had been there and the plate had been licked clean.'

After the outbreak of war in 1914 he wa the first official artist to be appointed, and the masterly lithographs which resulted were published in two volumes by the Wa Office, under the title of *The Western Front* (1917), with a text by C. E. Montagu [q.v.]. It was largely owing to Bone' energy and his generous enthusiasm fo the work of other artists that the Imperia War Museum was established. In the wa of 1939–45 he was the doyen of the wa artists.

He was a trustee of the National Gallery and the Tate; an honorary LL.D. of St Andrews, Liverpool, and Glasgow, an D.Litt. of Oxford; and honorary R.S.A He was knighted in 1937. He died in Oxfor 21 October 1953. There is a memoria tablet in the crypt of St. Paul's Cathedra

In 1903 Bone married Gertrude Helen Dodd (died 1962), the writer and sister o Francis Dodd [q.v.], one of the best por trait etchers then working in England Among his most successful plates is hi portrait of Muirhead Bone. Bone had tw sons: Gavin, fellow and tutor of St. John' College, Oxford, who died in 1942, an Stephen, a notice of whom appears below

There is an etched self-portrait and i the possession of the family there is a bus by Sir Jacob Epstein. The National Por trait Gallery has a drawing by Sir Stanle Spencer and another by Francis Dodd.

[*The Times*, 23 October 1953; *Graphische Künste*, 1906; *Print Collectors' Quarterly*, vo ix, 1922; Campbell Dodgson, *Etchings an Drypoints by Muirhead Bone*, 1909; G. Bie man, 'Der Schotte Muirhead Bone', *Kuns welt*, 1912; *Drawings and Dry Points by S Muirhead Bone*, Arts Council, 1955; person knowledge.]   JAMES LAVE

BONE, STEPHEN (1904–1958), painte and art critic, elder son of (Sir) Muirhea Bone, a notice of whom appears abov was born at Chiswick 13 November 190 inheriting from both his parents a stron artistic tradition. He began to draw i infancy and while a schoolboy at Bedal had a water-colour accepted by the Ne English Art Club. After leaving school i

920 he travelled with his father all over
Europe and in 1922 went to the Slade
School under Henry Tonks [q.v.]. His professional career began with wood-engraved
book illustrations, for which he won a gold
medal at the Paris International Exhibition in 1925.

Wood-engraving and water-colour were
followed by oil paintings, including some
murals. It was perhaps in oil landscape
that he found himself most completely,
generally choosing his subjects from
ordinary scenes not beautiful in themselves.

He was an inveterate traveller and he
was much appreciated abroad, especially
in Sweden where one of the biggest exhibitions of his work was held at the Galerie
Moderne in 1937. He exhibited also in
London, Glasgow, Dundee, and Oxford.
He was a member of the New English
Art Club and showed work frequently at
the Royal Academy.

In later years he was widely known for
his art criticism in the *Manchester Guardian*, and as a broadcaster on art subjects.
He was an official naval artist in the war
1939–45. In 1929 he married Mary,
daughter of S. D. Adshead [q.v.], architect
and town planner; they had two sons and
a daughter. He died in London 15 September 1958. Glasgow City Art Gallery has
a pencil self-portrait.

[*The Times*, 16 September 1958; personal
knowledge.]   JAMES LAVER.

BONHAM-CARTER, SIR EDGAR (1870–
1956), jurist and administrator, was born
in London 2 April 1870, the fifth of the
seven sons of Henry Bonham-Carter,
barrister and managing director of the
Guardian Assurance Company, and his
wife, Sibella Charlotte, daughter of George
Warde Norman [q.v.], a director of the
Bank of England. Florence Nightingale
[q.v.] was a relative, and took great
interest in his early career. General Sir
Charles Bonham-Carter and Sir Maurice
Bonham Carter were among his brothers.
He was educated at Clifton College, to
which his loyalty was lifelong: he was
vice-chairman of its council in 1934–46.
At New College, Oxford, he obtained
second class honours in jurisprudence in
1892, and played rugby football as a forward for the university and for England.
He read law with Edward Beaumont, and
was called to the bar by Lincoln's Inn in
1895.

In 1899, after the conquest of the Sudan,
he was chosen by Lord Cromer [q.v.] at

the age of twenty-nine to devise and set
on foot a complete system of civil and
criminal law in the Sudan where no legal
system existed. He became judicial adviser, later legal secretary and a member
of the governor-general's council: the only
senior civilian member of a military administration. His success was immediate
and brilliant. In the year of his appointment he introduced a simplified version of
the Indian penal and criminal procedure
codes; his modification of the Indian law
of murder and homicide was considered by
most Sudan judges an improvement on the
original. In 1900 there followed a simple
code of civil procedure, derived from the
Indian: substantive law being based on the
English common law, Sudan statute, and
(particularly as to land) local customary
law. He rescued Mohammedan law courts
from decay, and gave them a solid organization under an ordinance promulgated in
1902. These codes established a complete
system of courts with appropriate jurisdiction, and he followed up his acts as a
lawgiver by years of guidance, firm but
courteous and patient, of the British,
Egyptian, and Sudanese officers and magistrates who then staffed the courts. The law
so declared and administered was understood by the people, by the early amateur
magistracy, and later by the professional
judges; to the ordinary Sudanese his work
seemed the embodiment of justice; the
structure was maintained after the independence of the Sudan.

In 1917 Bonham-Carter became senior
judicial officer in Baghdad and in 1919
judicial adviser in Mesopotamia, then
freed from Turkish rule. There his task
was different, for the Ottoman law existed
in the vilayets; he laid no foundations, but
built up and modernized what he found,
and established a system of courts under
judges with professional qualifications,
and a competent clerical staff. He founded
a School of Law; established the machinery
of justice; and drafted a great deal of the
necessary legislation himself. In the face
of the political ferment engendered by an
ardent nationalism which accompanied
the transition from subjection to freedom,
by the sympathy and trust which he inspired he set up a soundly based Iraqi
judicial system under Iraqi judges which
survived the transition from mandate to
treaty, and finally to complete independence. Nuri Said called him the father and
founder of the legal system in the country;
Gertrude Bell [q.v.] wrote of him as the
wisest of men.

In 1921 Bonham-Carter left the Middle East to begin a new phase of public work at home, which continued until his death, in spite of increasing lameness in his later years. From 1922 to 1925 he represented North-East Bethnal Green as a Liberal member of the London County Council, and became the council's representative on the governing body of the School of Oriental and African Studies, to which he was regularly reappointed until his resignation in 1945. With the decline in Liberal fortunes, he did not sit again, but an interest in housing and planning remained with him. He was chairman of the National Housing and Town Planning Council from 1940 until 1942; and remained a member of the council of the Town and Country Planning Association until his death. From 1927 to 1950 he was a member of the executive committee of the National Trust, and also of its finance and general purposes committee; and he gave long service to the Commons, Open Spaces and Footpaths Preservation Society. From the twenties he had been interested in the work of First Garden City Ltd. in developing the garden city at Letchworth; and in 1929–39 he was a chairman in whom there was complete confidence. His vision and understanding of educational matters as a governor of Letchworth Grammar School won the admiration of his colleagues. At his death he was the last surviving founder-member of the Gordon Memorial and Kitchener School Trusts.

From the thirties he was closely associated with the British School of Archaeology in Iraq, towards the foundation of which Gertrude Bell had left a legacy. The friendship and respect which had grown up between Gertrude Bell and Bonham-Carter during his years in Iraq impelled him, with his wife, to throw himself into the task of raising by public subscription a sufficient fund to realize the project. In 1932 the School was launched with adequate finances, and with Bonham-Carter as the first chairman of the executive committee, an office which he held until 1950, when he yielded to eighty years and impaired health, but remained a member until his death. From 1953 he was president of the North-East Hampshire Agricultural Association.

He was distinguished in appearance, and was remarkable for his courtesy. Although not a fluent speaker, he impressed all who knew him with the great range of his knowledge, his gentle wisdom, his solicitude for those with or for whom h[e] worked, and his moral strength, touche[d] with a delicate humour.

In 1916 he was awarded the Order [of] the Nile, first class; he was appointe[d] C.M.G. in 1909, C.I.E. in 1919, an[d] K.C.M.G. in 1920. In 1926 he marrie[d] Charlotte Helen, daughter of Colonel Wi[l]liam Lewis Kinloch Ogilvy, 60th Rifles; they had no children. He died at his wife['s] estate, Binsted Wyck, Alton, Hampshir[e] 24 April 1956.

[*The Times*, 25 April 1956; private in[in]formation; personal knowledge.]

KEVIN O'C. HAYE[S]

BONNEY, (WILLIAM FRANCIS) VI[C]TOR (1872–1953), gynaecologist, w[as] born in Chelsea 17 December 1872, t[he] son of William Augustus Bonney, surgeo[n], and his wife, Anna Maria Alice Polixi[n] Poulain. Educated privately, he qualifi[ed] in 1896 from Middlesex Hospital with t[he] M.B., B.S. (London) and proceeded to h[is] M.D. (1898), M.S. and F.R.C.S. (189[9]) and B.Sc., with first class honours (190[4]). In 1903 he was appointed obstetric tut[or] to Middlesex Hospital and concomitant[ly] held a research post. In 1908 he w[as] elected to the honorary staff as assista[nt] gynaecological surgeon and in 1930 [he] succeeded Sir Comyns Berkeley as seni[or] gynaecological surgeon. He also gave [his] services to the Chelsea Hospital f[or] Women, the Royal Masonic Hospital, t[he] Miller Hospital, and Queen Alexandr[a] Military Hospital, and was visiting gyn[ae]cologist to the British Postgradu[ate] Medical School. He retired from hospi[tal] practice in 1937.

When Bonney was appointed to t[he] Middlesex, gynaecology was professiona[lly] regarded askance, even though it form[ed] a third part of the qualifying examinati[on] for medical students. With his acute sur[gi]cal acumen Bonney was not slow [to] recognize that the true position of [the] gynaecologist should be co-equal with [his] surgical colleagues and he devoted all [his] great energy towards this end, rais[ing] gynaecology from its medical obscur[ity] into the important position it came to h[ave] as a major branch of surgery. He was [a] pioneer of the operation of myomecto[my] i.e. the removal of fibroid tumours fr[om] the womb without the removal of [the] womb itself; and with Berkeley he [at]tended and perfected the operation [for] cancer of the neck of the womb. He [de]vised a superb operative technique wh[ich] has been emulated by countless pu[pils]

He was a stimulating and invigorating teacher with the kindest of dispositions. He could be a severe critic; but always of the method, never of the man. He was a loyal and true colleague, who was never heard to speak ill of anybody.

A prolific writer, Bonney wrote many of his books with Sir Comyns Berkeley; the best known is *A Textbook of Gynaecological Surgery* which was first published in 1911 and reached a sixth edition in 1952. The illustrations in Bonney's books, drawn by himself, point to the artist in him, as do his water-colours. Like other ready writers he was an avid reader. A great admirer as well as a friend of Rudyard Kipling [q.v.], Bonney became vice-president of the Kipling Society. In early days a useful tennis player, in later life he became a keen fisherman, owning a long stretch of water on the River Wye.

Bonney's spiritual home was the Royal College of Surgeons where he was the first gynaecologist to secure a seat by open election on the council, on which he served for twenty years; he was three times Hunterian lecturer, Bradshaw lecturer (1934), and Hunterian orator (1943). In 1946 he was elected an honorary fellow of the Royal College of Obstetricians and Gynaecologists, and he was the first gynaecologist to be elected an honorary fellow of the Royal Australasian College of Surgeons (1928).

In 1905 Bonney married Annie, daughter of Dr. James Appleyard, of Tasmania; they had no children. He died in London July 1953. A portrait by Sir Oswald Birley is at the Royal College of Surgeons.

[Private information; personal knowledge.]
FREDERICK W. ROQUES.

BOOTH, HUBERT CECIL (1871–1955), engineer, was born 4 July 1871 in Gloucester, the sixth child of Abraham Booth, timber importer, by his wife, Elizabeth Ann Watts. Educated at the College School, Gloucester, and at Gloucester County School, he entered the City and Guilds Central Institution (later the City and Guilds College) in 1889 where he took a three-year course in civil and mechanical engineering. He obtained the associate-ship of the City and Guilds Institute, having distinguished himself in his academic studies. He became an associate member and later member of the Institution of Civil Engineers and was elected a fellow of the City and Guilds Institute.

Booth's first employment was with Maudslay, Sons & Field, then the leading marine engine builders in the country, where he was first employed as a draughtsman attached to a group designing the engines for two new battleships for the Royal Navy. In 1894 he was chosen by W. B. Bassett (a director of Maudslays who had floated a company for the construction and operation of 'Great Wheels') to assist with the correction of faulty techniques which had complicated the erection of the 'Great Wheel' then being built at Earl's Court. He was then commissioned by Bassett to design, plan, and control the erection of three similar structures at Blackpool, Vienna, and Paris. The Paris example was 300 feet in diameter and remained a familiar landmark until it was dismantled in the twenties. The 'Great Wheel' in Vienna continued to be much patronized. The interest of these three huge wheels designed by Booth between the age of 24 and 26 lies in their being the first major structures into which a degree of flexibility was deliberately introduced in a mathematically controlled manner. This resulted in notable economies, the principles governing their design being fundamentally identical with those upon which the design of modern long-span suspension bridges is based.

In 1901 Booth started his own business in London as a consulting engineer. He continued in active practice for the next forty years, apart from a break in 1902–3 when he took complete charge of the erection of Connel Ferry Bridge over Loch Etive. At that time the bridge was about one-quarter built and running badly behind schedule. He returned to London when this task had been successfully completed.

In 1901 Booth invented, perfected, and named the first vacuum cleaner, and it is in this connection that he is most widely remembered. In that year he founded the British Vacuum Cleaner Company which was registered in 1903 and of which he continued as chairman until his retirement at the age of eighty-one in 1952, having seen the industry which he brought into being grow to world-wide proportions. He was particularly interested in the industrial possibilities of the process and was responsible for much of the basic experimental work needed for the successful development of the large installations such as those forming a familiar and vital part of the equipment of modern coal-fired generating stations. Although he regarded the domestic electric cleaner as a mere toy, he derived a deep satisfaction from the invention of a process which, apart from its labour-saving characteristics, has led to an incalculable improvement in the hygiene of nearly every civilized home.

Booth was gifted with a remarkable insight into the elements of any technological or intellectual problem he was called on to solve, and he was meticulous in his attention to detail. Consequently his work, much of it original, was rarely susceptible of improvement save through the development of improved manufacturing techniques. His personal qualities of charm and integrity won him the affection and respect of a wide circle of friends in all walks of life. When young he was a keen amateur boxer. In later years his recreations lay in the field of philosophical speculation of an intuitive but realistic kind and in good talk generally.

In 1903 Booth married Charlotte Mary (died 1948), eldest daughter of Francis Tring Pearce, of Gloucester, by whom he had two sons. He died in Croydon 14 January 1955. A portrait by David Jagger is in the possession of the family.

[Private information; personal knowledge.]
MUIR JOHNSTON.

BOOTHMAN, SIR JOHN NELSON (1901–1957), air chief marshal, was born in Wembley, Middlesex, 19 February 1901, the son of Thomas John Boothman, railway clerk, and his wife, Mary Burgess. He was educated at Harrow County School which he left to become a voluntary motor driver with the French Red Cross, serving in Salonika in 1918 and being awarded the croix de guerre.

In 1921 Boothman was commissioned in the Royal Air Force and became a flying instructor before serving for two years (1926–8) in Iraq. There followed special training in high-speed flight and in 1931 it was Boothman who piloted the Supermarine S.6.B. which won the Schneider Trophy outright for Great Britain. He was awarded the A.F.C. The next four years were spent on flying duties with the performance testing squadron at the Aeroplane and Armament Experimental Establishment.

After graduating from the R.A.F. Staff College in 1935 Boothman spent three years on air staff duties. When war broke out in 1939 he was in command of No. 44 Squadron but moved in December to fighter, and in 1940 to bomber, operations duties. For a time in 1941 he commanded the base at Waddington and after a couple of months on special duties in

Washington returned to command at Finningley. In 1942–3 he was working on operational requirements at the Air Ministry and from June 1943 commanded No. 106 Wing (later Group) at Benson which was engaged on the photographic reconnaissance vital for the landings in Normandy. In July 1944 Boothman was appointed to command the Aeroplane and Armament Experimental Establishment but in the following year he was moved to the Air Ministry as assistant chief of air staff (technical requirements), an important post for the post-war development of the Royal Air Force, in which he remained until 1948.

Boothman went next to the Iraq Command until 1950 when he became controller of supplies (air) in the Ministry of Supply at a time of rapid expansion in face of the threat of war. To this exacting task he brought a wide experience, a lively intelligence, and a pleasant personality which made him an agreeable as well as a calmly efficient colleague. Coastal Command, his last appointment (1953–6), he held concurrently with the N.A.T.O. appointments of air commander-in-chief Channel Command, and air commander-in-chief, Eastern Atlantic Area. He was promoted air marshal in 1952 and air chief marshal in 1954.

Boothman was a natural pilot and throughout his Service career was fascinated by the art of flying. In his higher appointments he would escape from his chair in the Ministry whenever possible to fly off, perhaps to North Africa, in a Spitfire or a Mosquito; or to try out some new development such as the gas turbine or the tricycle undercarriage. He got the feel of a new aircraft immediately. Although he was by no means unsociable he seemed to have few interests outside the Service. He was scornful of what he regarded as the games fetish and did not consider strenuous exercise essential for physical fitness.

In 1922 Boothman married Gertrude daughter of Hubert Andrews. His only child, a son, followed him into the R.A.F. and both were invested with the D.F.C. on the same day in 1945. The son was killed in a flying accident in the following year.

Boothman was appointed C.B. (1944), K.B.E. (1951), and K.C.B. (1954), received the American D.F.C., and was commander of the Legion of Merit. He died in London 29 December 1957.

[Private information.] HELEN M. PALMER

BOSWELL, PERCY GEORGE HAM-
NALL (1886–1960), geologist, was born
at Woodbridge, Suffolk, 7 August 1886,
the second son of George James Boswell,
master printer, of Ipswich, by his wife,
Mary Elizabeth Marshall, of Tasmania.
Nurtured strictly in a Victorian household
on English grammar and punctuation,
Charles Dickens and the Bible, Boswell
soon acquired a disciplined mind and a
flair for lucid writing. As a youth in the
higher grade school at Ipswich his interest
in geology was kindled by fossil collecting
in the near-by fossiliferous crag and Chalk
pits and by poring over displays in the
local museum. Rather than join the
family's printing business he left home
and became first a pupil teacher, later
(1905–12) a science instructor at the
Technical School at Ipswich.

While still in his teens he became a
founder-member of the Ipswich and District Field Club, though his early geological pursuits were carried out mostly in
solitude, and often continued far into the
night. Unfortunately, excessive zeal took
its toll, for at the age of eighteen he developed choroiditis in both eyes and was
virtually blind for several months, his
right eye being so irreparably damaged
that he never regained stereoscopic vision.
Providentially, at about this time, his zest
for geology was further stimulated by the
contagious enthusiasm of George Slater,
a schoolmaster from the north country,
who was destined to remain a lifelong
friend and mentor.

In 1911 Boswell obtained his London
B.Sc. and in 1912, at the comparatively
advanced age of twenty-six, entered the
Imperial College to study under W. W.
Watts, and to continue his researches on
the Pliocene-Pleistocene succession in
East Anglia, the zoning of the Chalk, and
the inter-relation between the culture
stages of Early Man and successive phases
of the Glacial Period. These investigations
were recognized by the Geological Society's
bestowal of the Daniel Pidgeon Fund in
1914, and the Wollaston Fund in 1917, and
by the award of the degree of D.Sc. by the
university of London in 1916.

It was the dearth of fossils in the Tertiary rocks of the London Basin which
prompted Boswell's prescient concept of
using their detrital mineral assemblages
for purposes of stratigraphic correlation.
This led him naturally to acquire an unrivalled knowledge of the mineralogy of
a wide range of British rocks, and to
specialize on the qualitative and quantita-

tive aspects of sedimentary petrology,
later to prove so helpful in deciphering the
palaeogeography, tectonics, and climatic
conditions of past epochs. These pioneer
investigations were turned to vital use
during the war of 1914–18, when as geological adviser to the Ministry of Munitions
he discovered much-needed domestic resources of glass-, foundry-, and furnace-
sands. He was appointed O.B.E. in 1918.

During his tenure of the newly founded
George Herdman chair of geology at
Liverpool (1917–30), he inspired an enthusiastic band of students to engage on
researches on the volcanic rocks of Snowdonia and the Lake District, the Silurian
and Carboniferous strata of North Wales,
and the Triassic and Pleistocene deposits
of the Liverpool district, besides embark-
ing on his own protracted studies on the
stratigraphy and tectonics of the Silurian
rocks of the Denbighshire moors.

Always keenly alive to the applications
of geology to civil engineering, he contributed valuable advice during the planning
and construction of the Mersey road
tunnel and on the silting of the Mersey
estuary, besides acting for long as a consultant to various water undertakings,
notably the Metropolitan Water Board.
He was an exemplary expert witness, for
he had a lucid and incisive mind coupled
with an ability to present evidence with
persuasive clarity.

In 1930 he succeeded his old master,
Watts, as professor of geology at Imperial
College, but owing to the ill health, mainly
bronchitis and asthma, which had scourged
him since childhood he was compelled to
resign in 1938. Nevertheless, during this
period he extended his studies of the
Silurian rocks of North Wales, published
his classic volume *On the Mineralogy of
the Sedimentary Rocks* (1933), and visited
East Africa to adjudicate on disputed
evidence concerning the age of skeletal
remains of Early Man.

After retirement, he continued to work
until 1953 on the Denbighshire moors and
as a consultant in engineering geology;
thereafter, though gravely incapacitated
in his declining years, he still wrote a number of papers on thixotropy and cognate
subjects, together with a final book of
essays on *Muddy Sediments* published
posthumously (1961).

Boswell's flair for administration and
organization found expression not only in
university affairs, but also in the offices of
secretary (1932–4) and president (1940–
41) of the Geological Society of London,

from whom he received the Bigsby medal (1929); president of the Liverpool Geological Society (1921–3) and of the Prehistoric Society (1936); and in the posts of general secretary (1931–5), general treasurer (1935–43), and president of the geology section (1932) of the British Association. He was elected F.R.S. in 1931 and was honorary member of numerous scientific societies at home and abroad.

His scientific writings, embodied in more than a hundred publications, may be epitomized under the headings of East Anglian stratigraphy, the geological relationships of Early Man, the stratigraphy and tectonics of the Silurian rocks of Denbighshire, the economic and engineering applications of geology, and perhaps especially the petrology and physical characters of sedimentary rocks.

A member of the Alpine Club, he often found refreshing relaxation among the mountains of Snowdonia and the Swiss Alps. Of medium height and somewhat lean features, he had a ready twinkle, was ever friendly and encouraging to amateur and professional geologists alike, and took immense pride in the accomplishments of his students. His recreations were recorded in *Who's Who* as 'letter-writing and raising professors'. He married in 1939 Hope, daughter of William Blount Dobell, coal merchant; she was a sister of Clifford Dobell, F.R.S., and an 'adopted daughter' of Sir Basil Mott [q.v.]. They had no children. After Boswell's death at Ruthin Castle Clinic in North Wales 22 December 1960, his ashes were scattered on the headland of Great Orme.

[*The Times*, 23 December 1960; G. H. Mitchell in *Biographical Memoirs of Fellows of the Royal Society*, vol. vii, 1961; private information; personal knowledge.]

DAVID WILLIAMS.

BOUGHTON, RUTLAND (1878–1960), composer, was born in Aylesbury 23 January 1878, the eldest child of William Rutland Boughton, grocer, and his wife, Grace Martha Bishop. He was educated at the Aylesbury Endowed School, and throughout his childhood his mother encouraged his obvious devotion to music. Before his fourteenth year he conceived a cycle of music dramas on the life of Jesus, to be enacted by soloists with the choir of the local Sacred Harmonic Society grouped round three sides of a raised platform. This conception of choral drama was his unique contribution to English music. He had never been in a theatre, but he had seen at the seaside a concert party on a raised platform, had been given Shakespeare's plays as a school prize, and had heard oratorio. It also enabled him to write music on Sunday without offending the family conscience. In the same year, 1892, he was apprenticed to the concert agency of Cecil Barth. His employer was lenient to his shortcomings and generous with material and artistic help.

In 1898 he was accepted by (Sir) Charles Stanford [q.v.] at the Royal College of Music. His formal education had been scanty, but his musical experience, obtained in complete isolation, was already greater than that of his fellow students, and perhaps of his teachers. This self-education did not, unfortunately, at any time include self-criticism.

In 1901 he left the College as the fund raised for his studies was exhausted. He failed as a music journalist, and, nearing starvation, accompanied singing lessons for David Ffrangcon Davies and filled in wind parts on the harmonium in the pit of the Haymarket Theatre.

Nevertheless, in 1903 he married Florence Hobley. In 1905 (Sir) Granville Bantock [q.v.] offered him a post in the Midland Institute in Birmingham, where he was greatly influenced by the activities of Bishop Gore [q.v.] and Father Adderley.

In 1907 Boughton met Reginald Buckley, poet and journalist, who had vague ideas, born of Wagnerian influences, of a music drama of the Arthurian legend. Boughton had also visualized such a scheme in his childhood's *Jesus* drama. Together in 1911 they produced a booklet *Music-Drama of the Future*. Boughton's essay, though naïve and high-flown in language, urged his point that 'the Wagnerian drama lacks just that channel of musical expression which is absolutely necessary to the English people', namely choral singing.

At that moment, Boughton's personal life became complicated. His marriage was ended in 1910 by a deed of separation —divorce was beyond his means—and he joined his life with that of Christina Walshe, an art student in Birmingham who was a member of Boughton's Literary and Musical Fellowship. Christina's home background had been as strict as Boughton's own, but their ideas of 'social freedom' were alike. Local scandals and reproaches were inevitable and they left Birmingham, but Boughton's complete candour overcame many objections. H

had the capacity for demanding and retaining the support of many distinguished
friends, among them G. B. Shaw [q.v.].

In the spring of 1913 Buckley and
Boughton settled on Glastonbury as the
Bayreuth of their new Arthurian enterprise. The first performance of the first
Glastonbury Festival was held on 5
August 1914, the war taking precedence
by twenty-four hours. The annual festival
was suspended after 1916 when Boughton
was called up, to become ultimately band-
master in the Royal Flying Corps of which
(Sir) Walford Davies [q.v.] had been
appointed director of music. The festivals
were resumed in 1919.

In 1921 (Sir) Barry Jackson put on
Boughton's *The Immortal Hour*, an opera
based on the Celtic drama by Fiona Macleod [q.v.], and first performed at Glastonbury in 1914, at his repertory theatre in
Birmingham. Encouraged by its success,
he offered a London production, to which
Boughton agreed unwillingly, as he
thought the sophistication of a normal
theatre would destroy its magic. In fact, it
ran from October 1922 for 216 performances and was revived in 1923, 1926, and
1932, making a total of some 500 performances in London alone. This work and
Bethlehem (1915), based on the Coventry
mystery, represent the only marketable
successes of Boughton's music.

Two other works achieved a temporary
success: a translation of *Alkestis* by Gilbert Murray [q.v.] in 1922 and *Queen of
Cornwall* (1924) by Thomas Hardy [q.v.],
both produced at Glastonbury. These two
works may be said to reflect Boughton's
domestic problems which in 1923 culminated in the rupture of his union with
Christina and an alliance with Kathleen
Davis, a senior pupil at his new school at
Glastonbury.

In 1926 Glastonbury was finally abandoned, both as a festival and as a home,
and the family settled at Kilcote, near
Gloucester, Boughton working a small-
holding with some success and deeply
absorbed in composition. He was granted
Civil List pension in 1938 under the
newly established rules enabling 'men of
genuine distinction to continue their work
without the haunting fear of immediate
penury'.

Boughton's political and personal creed
governed his life and influenced his music,
which tempts the reader to marvel at its
naïvety, from which, however, it derives
its peculiar strength. He wrote in all
forms, but more than half his output

remained in manuscript, deposited in the
British Museum. His literary remains,
other than the libretti of the music
dramas, are contained in two propaganda
pamphlets of 1911 and two full-scale
books on music: *Bach* (1907, revised ed.
1930) and *The Reality of Music* (1934).
The journalistic articles have not been
collected.

Boughton died in London 25 January
1960. His portrait (1911) by Christina
Walshe became the possession of his son-
in-law Christopher Ede, husband of Joy
Boughton (died 1963), oboist, who alone of
his children (three sons and five daughters)
made a name for herself in music.

[Michael Hurd, *Immortal Hour*, 1962; personal knowledge.]   STEUART WILSON.

BOWHILL, SIR FREDERICK WIL-
LIAM (1880–1960), air chief marshal, was
born 1 September 1880 at Morar Gwalior,
India, son of James Henry Bowhill, then
a captain in the 62nd Foot, and his wife,
Mary Noël Carter. Educated at Blackheath School and in the training ship
Worcester, he went to sea in the Merchant
Service for sixteen years and left with a
certificate as extra master square rigged.
He was attached to the Royal Naval
Reserve and went through a course of
flying instruction in 1912 as lieutenant
R.N.R. Not infrequently he crash-landed
on sewage-farms which, despite obvious
disadvantages, had the great merit, as
he said, of being soft to land on. He was
posted to the *Actaeon* and in 1913 went
to the Central Flying School and obtained
his Royal Aero Club certificate. In April
he was appointed flying officer, Royal
Flying Corps, Naval Wing. As flight
lieutenant he was placed in command of
the *Empress* and engaged on raids against
enemy submarine bases, until in 1915 he
was appointed to the air department of
the Admiralty. He became squadron commander and was sent to Mesopotamia to
assist the Tigris Corps in the attempt
to relieve the force under (Sir) Charles
Townshend [q.v.] besieged in Kut, and
was engaged in various air/sea hostilities
for which he was appointed in 1918 to
the D.S.O. In that year, as wing commander, he took command of the seaplane station at Felixstowe, went next
to Killingholme, fighting Zeppelins off the
Humber, and thence to the Mediterranean
to command the Sixty-second Wing where
he gained a bar to his D.S.O. In 1919 he
was chief staff officer to an R.A.F. detachment fighting the 'Mad Mullah' in

Bowhill

Somaliland and was appointed C.M.G.; and after a spell on technical staff duties was posted in 1921 for three years with Coastal Area as group captain. As chief staff officer, Middle East Area, he saw service in Egypt and Iraq. In 1928 he became air commodore and in 1929–31 was director of organization and staff duties at the Air Ministry. In 1931, as air vice-marshal, he became air officer commanding Fighting Area, Air Defence of Great Britain. In 1933 he became a member of the Air Council (as air member for personnel), being appointed C.B. in 1935, and promoted K.C.B. in 1936 the year in which he became air marshal.

In August 1937 Bowhill became head of Coastal Command, a post he held until 1941, in which year he was appointed G.B.E., having been promoted air chief marshal in 1939. Before the outbreak of war Bowhill worked on a system of plotting aircraft movements and of controlling aircraft from the ground which was developed to a high pitch of efficiency in the Battle of Britain. He also advocated the use of barrage balloons to float over large cities as protection against low level attack, an idea adopted on a large scale during the war. Further, he was one of the officers responsible for the development of the Women's Auxiliary Air Force. In 1940 his command located the German blockade runner *Altmark* which had captive British seamen aboard and made possible their release by the follow-up action of the *Cossack* in Josing Fjord.

The greatest exploit of Coastal Command was the destruction of the German battleship, the *Bismarck*, in May 1941. After sinking the *Hood* in Denmark Sound the *Bismarck* proceeded to get lost by the Home Fleet and it was a matter of psychology to guess where she might be heading. Bowhill, with insufficient aircraft to cope with every possible manœuvre, guessed that the *Bismarck* would be ordered to make for the French coast and he sent his Catalinas there to welcome her. One of them came out of the cloud right over the *Bismarck* and she was sunk when the Royal Navy closed in.

Bowhill was already under orders to go to Canada to organize the R.A.F. Ferry Command, set up because Britain's desperate need of aircraft had outgrown the voluntary organization established the previous year by a group of Montreal business men. It was a delicate task to take over from a dedicated voluntary civilian effort and create a para-military organization; but Bowhill achieved the translation with diplomacy and sheer sincerity. He made good friends with the Atfero Group and he and his wife became very popular and highly regarded in Montreal. Dorval airport was taken over for Ferry Command operations as St. Hubert was wanted for training and military purposes. Bowhill remained head of the Ferrying Organization until 1943, then became air officer commanding-in-chief, Transport Command, until 1945, four years after the normal age for retirement. His services were then sought by the Ministry of Civil Aviation; and he returned to Montreal for another two years as British member on the council of the provisional International Civil Aviation Organization. In 1946 he returned to England and was chief aeronautical adviser to the Ministry of Civil Aviation until 1957. He was elected master of the Master Mariners Company and entertained with naval bonhomie in the ward room of the *Wellington* on the Thames. He was also a younger brother of Trinity House, two appointments which linked back a dedicated air leader to his early love of the sea.

During his colourful career he was a first on unique occasions—the first airman to fly a plane off the deck of a ship; whilst in command of the *Empress* the first to make an air attack on a naval fleet; the first high ranking officer to cut off a seaman's leg on board ship. Bowhill was a commander of the American Legion of Merit and received a number of other foreign decorations.

He was spare and compact in figure with hair which gave him the nickname of 'Ginger' or 'Ginge' to his intimates. His tremendous eyebrows were a literally outstanding characteristic, a daunting feature of his leadership. He addressed all men by their surnames and never hesitated to tell them to take running jumps at themselves. Behind this façade he was kindly, humorous, decisive, a good mixer, and a diplomat through sheer straightforwardness and honesty.

He married in 1932 Dorothy (died 1966), daughter of R. H. Arlingham-Davies, of Crickhowell, South Wales, and widow of Wing Commander A. B. Gaskell. A squadron officer in the W.A.A.F., she was on Bowhill's staff in Montreal, saluted him punctiliously, played a hard game of tennis with him, was a gracious hostess and a good friend and companion for Ginge. Two portraits of Bowhill were painted by Sir Oswald Birley and one by Richard Jack. A drawing by Sir William Rothenstein is reproduced in *Men of the R.A.F.* (1942). Bowhill died in London 12 March 1960.

[*The Times* and *Montreal Star*, 14 March 1960; A. O. Pollard, *Leaders of the Royal Air Force*, 1940; personal knowledge.]
WILLIAM P. HILDRED.

BOWLEY, SIR ARTHUR LYON (1869–1957), statistician, was born in Bristol 6 November 1869, the son of the Rev. James William Lyon Bowley, vicar of St. Philip and St. Jacob, and his wife, Maria Johnson. Bowley spent nine years at Christ's Hospital which left a lasting impression on him; later in his life he served as a governor for more than ten years. He went to Trinity College, Cambridge, with a major scholarship in mathematics; was bracketed tenth wrangler in 1891, and later obtained both the Cobden and the Adam Smith prizes. He was awarded the Sc.D. by his university in 1913.

On leaving Cambridge Bowley seemed destined to teach mathematics in schools and he was on the staff, briefly at Brighton College, then at St. John's School, Leatherhead, until 1899. Fortunately for his career he had been in contact with Alfred Marshall [q.v.] and others active at Cambridge in developing the social sciences. He was much concerned both with the refinements of economic analysis and with the investigation of solutions to problems of social reform. He published in 1893 his Cobden prize essay, on England's foreign trade in the nineteenth century. Somewhat later he began an extensive series of research projects, mainly in collaboration with G. H. Wood, on the relationship between movements in wages and prices, and he read his first paper to the Royal Statistical Society early in 1895. He published many further papers on this subject, all of them put together with great historical and statistical care.

These interests outside his teaching duties led, in 1895, to a complete and permanent change in Bowley's career. In that year Sidney Webb [q.v.] and others founded the London School of Economics and assembled a small staff of part-time experts to begin teaching in the autumn. On the basis of his current research work, and on the recommendation of Marshall, Bowley was chosen to take charge of the teaching of statistics. He gave his first lecture on statistics at the School in October 1895 and continued to teach there without interruption for more than forty years. He was never a socialist in Webb's sense but, as a good liberal, he found the senior common-room a congenial and stimulating background to his activities in teaching, research, and public service.

It was, however, some years before he became a full-time member of the staff of the London School of Economics. The focus of his work was increasingly at the School, but for more than twenty years his main source of income was elsewhere. He held appointments at the University College at Reading from 1900 to 1919: as lecturer in mathematics (1900–7), in economics (1913–19), and professor in both subjects (1907–13). Meanwhile, at the School, he became part-time reader in statistics in 1908 and was given the title of professor in 1915. But it was only in 1919 that the university of London created a full-time chair in statistics, tenable at the London School of Economics, of which Bowley became the first occupant. Although he retired from the chair in 1936, he continued many of his activities both at the School and elsewhere until the early fifties. He acted as director of the Oxford University Institute of Statistics during the war years (1940–44) and received an honorary D.Litt. in 1943. He was elected F.B.A. in 1922, appointed C.B.E. in 1937, and knighted in 1950.

As a mathematician Bowley was competent but rather old-fashioned. He published relatively little which was original in mathematical statistics, rather more on mathematical economics and econometrics. He was one of the founders of the international Econometric Society in 1933 and he served later as its president. However, first and foremost Bowley was a practitioner in applied statistics and he took the whole of the social sciences as his field. He was highly regarded by official statisticians but it was unfortunately not the custom in Bowley's day for the British Government to call upon outside experts for advice. Undoubtedly British official statistics in the twenties and thirties would have advanced more rapidly, particularly in the use of sampling techniques, if Bowley had had more to do with them. He exercised his main influence therefore through his teaching and research work on the one hand and his extensive contacts in international circles on the other. And he was called upon as an expert witness in cases such as the inquiry into dockers' wages (1920) which earned Ernest

Bevin [q.v.] the title of the 'Dockers' K.C.'

Two of Bowley's pioneer activities were in the economic field. One comprised a number of studies on the definition and measurement of national income which occupied his attention, on and off, for more than twenty years before the first official estimates were made under the guidance of Lord Keynes [q.v.], during the war of 1939-45. Without Bowley's careful and precise work and the more adventurous studies undertaken independently by Colin Clark the official computations would scarcely have been possible. His other pioneer activity in this field was with the London and Cambridge Economic Service, the first venture of this kind in Britain, a private undertaking financed by subscriptions from the outset in 1923. Bowley was the first editor and he served in this capacity continuously until 1945, remaining a regular contributor until 1953. His editorship was characterized both by the skill with which he pulled together the various views of economists in his own succinct assessment of the current economic position as published in the Bulletins of the Service, and by the statistical techniques he used in designing economic series and in devising ways of presenting them. He showed how economic analysis depends on long runs of comparable series, presented in graphical form (e.g. by the use of ratio scales) and adjusted where necessary for seasonal variation.

The major contribution which Bowley made—and it was one of the utmost importance to statistics—lay in the development of sampling techniques in their application to social studies. This was a major concern to him for most of his active life, both in his own researches and in discussions among statisticians at the international level. While Bowley was forming his own ideas in the nineties, official statisticians from all over the world were engaged in a continuing debate on sampling, the 'representative method' as it was then called. A. N. Kiaer (1838-1919), the head of the Norwegian statistical service for many years, led the case for sampling at sessions of the International Statistical Institute from 1895 (Berne) to 1901 (Budapest). He was supported by C. D. Wright of the U.S. Department of Labor, and then by Bowley himself. Between them they won over the reluctant body of official statisticians in general.

Bowley explored for himself, and largely for the first time, the appropriate design of sample surveys, the proper formulation of sampling precision, and the ways of interpreting the results in their application. He devised and conducted sample surveys of working-class households in four English towns and, in presenting the results in 1915 in a volume of elegant simplicity (*Livelihood and Poverty*, with A. R. Burnett-Hurst), he was far ahead of his time both in explaining the methods used and in formulating the precision of the results. He distinguished four sources of error: incorrect information, loose definitions, bias in selection of samples, and calculable errors of sampling. He may not have been entirely correct in his use of what is now known as cluster sampling, but what he wrote in 1915 would for the most part be readily accepted today.

It was natural that Bowley should become the dominant member of the committee set up in 1924 by the International Statistical Institute to report on the representative method. At the 1925 session (Rome), Bowley's influence was clearly visible in the main recommendation of the committee that 'the investigation should be so arranged wherever possible as to allow of a mathematical statement of the precision of the results, and that with these results should be given an indication of the extent of the error to which they are liable', and in the technical appendix on the measurement of precisions which accompanied the report. Bowley continued to practise what he preached and he himself regarded as his most important work his contribution to the *New Survey of London Life and Labour* conducted in the period 1930-35.

Bowley was effective, if rather dour, on committees and he held many high offices in the British Association, the Royal Statistical Society, the Royal Economic Society, and the International Statistical Institute. He was shy and retiring, never happier than when talking quietly to his research students or playing Bach with his family. He was respected by all his colleagues and students but intimate with few. One of his close friendships was with the distinguished economist Edwin Cannan [q.v.] who shared his enthusiasm for cycling. Sometimes they were joined by F. Y. Edgeworth [q.v.] who was apt to continue discussions of abstract economics even on his bicycle. On one occasion Cannan is reported to have said: 'Bowley, let us go a little faster; Edgeworth cannot talk mathematics at more than eight miles an hour.'

Bowley's published work was very extensive. A fairly complete list of his publications is to be found in the *Journal of the Royal Statistical Society*, part 2, 1957.

In 1904 Bowley married Julia, daughter of Thomas Hilliam, land agent; they had three daughters, one of whom, Marian Bowley, became professor of political economy at University College, London. Bowley died at Haslemere 21 January 1957. A portrait by Stella Bowen (1936) is owned by the London School of Economics.

[Private information; personal knowledge.]
R. G. D. ALLEN.

BRACKEN, BRENDAN RENDALL, VISCOUNT BRACKEN (1901–1958), politician and publisher, was born at Templemore, county Tipperary, 15 February 1901, the younger son of J. K. Bracken, of Ardlaugh House, Kilmallock, and Templemore, county Tipperary, a builder and monumental mason, and one of the leading spirits in reviving the Gaelic games at Thurles. Brendan lost his father when he was very young and his mother moved to Dublin, where he attended the Christian Brothers' School. But she found him hard to manage, and sent him to the Jesuit College, Mungret, near Limerick, from which he ran away, about the time of his fifteenth birthday. His mother then shipped him to Australia in 1916, although she had no connections there except a priest, brother of the Patrick Laffan, a builder, whom she was soon afterwards to marry as her second husband.

Bracken was put on a sheep station in New South Wales, but soon displeased his employer by his addiction to reading instead of sheep tending. The Brigidin nuns near by at Echuca were kind to him, and let him read the books in the convent library. But he had an unhappy time until he made his way to Sydney. There he sought more congenial work, offering himself to the Christian Brothers as a teacher, and obtaining employment on the diocesan newspaper, to secure advertisements. From this precarious life he made his way back to Ireland in 1919, after the war had ended. He found that his mother had married Laffan and he was not wanted at home, but that he had a small legacy of a few hundred pounds. With this he made his way for the first time to England. It was the time of the Black and Tans, but

he represented himself not as coming from Ireland, or as a Catholic, and of a strongly nationalist family, but from Australia, where, he said, his parents had perished in a bush fire.

He applied to various public schools, and had the good fortune to secure admittance to Sedbergh, where he was one day to become chairman of the board of governors. He was nineteen but represented himself as sixteen. He stipulated what subjects he wished to study—history and languages—and paid his own fees in advance. But his money ran out after two terms, and he then secured teaching posts, first in Liverpool, then in a preparatory school at Bishop's Stortford. This second move had the great advantage of bringing him near London. He made the acquaintance of J. L. Garvin [q.v.] who introduced him to Oliver Locker-Lampson, then the owner of the *Empire Review*, for which Bracken undertook to gain subscriptions. It was about this time that he met (Sir) Winston Churchill, to whom he was to attach himself for the rest of his life. Garvin recommended him and he worked for Churchill in his unsuccessful election campaign at Leicester (1923), and in the by-election for the Abbey division of Westminster (1924), and those who were with him remember him as a colourful figure, tall, red-haired, vigorous, with a great power of invective.

The turning-point of his fortunes came in 1924 when he met the head of the publishers Eyre & Spottiswoode, Major Crosthwaite Eyre, a retired Indian Army officer who had married Miss Eyre and was looking for young talent. He recruited Bracken to help with an illustrated monthly of which Hilaire Belloc [q.v.] was the editor. From this small beginning, Bracken emerged in 1925 as a director of the firm, and proved himself full of ideas and drive, with an excellent business judgement. He persuaded Eyre & Spottiswoode to acquire the *Financial News*, to give him a share of the equity, and to let him run it. This was the first of a number of successful newspaper and periodical enterprises. He founded the *Banker*, a handsomely produced monthly, and, as editor, used his position to secure the entrée to City institutions. He acquired the particular friendship of Sir Henry Strakosch [q.v.], with whom in 1929 he joined in the control of *The Economist* with a special constitution guaranteeing the editor's independence. He acquired control of the *Investors Chronicle* and the *Practitioner*, an old-established medical journal. All these prospered, but it was the *Financial News* which established him, and enabled him to secure adoption, with the support of Churchill, then chancellor of the Exchequer, as Conservative candidate for North Paddington, for which he was duly returned in 1929. In the Parliaments of the thirties he made himself, in Stanley Baldwin's phrase, 'the faithful Chela' of Winston Churchill, in those years in which Churchill was not only out of office but very much out of favour with the Conservative Party. Bracken, like Churchill, was a staunch imperialist, opposing the government of India bill, and the foreign policy pursued by Baldwin and Chamberlain.

When on the declaration of war Churchill was called to office at the Admiralty, Bracken went with him as his parliamentary private secretary; and when, in May 1940, Churchill formed his own wartime coalition government, he brought Bracken with him, still as his P.P.S., to No. 10. Bracken, who was sworn of the Privy Council in June, asked for nothing higher than, as he put it, 'to stand round and collect the coats'; but he was in his element at the centre of power throughout the war, one of the two or three men closest to Churchill, sitting up with him in the small hours, and living at 10 Downing Street or its annex. He went out of his way to ease Churchill's burdens and to take the strain from 'the Boss' as he genially called his master. The extent of his influence cannot easily be estimated, but certainly he prompted many of Churchill's appointments, and the disposal of patronage, not excluding appointments in the Church of England which interested him more than they did the prime minister. He had a wide knowledge of English journalism, and particularly cultivated the Commonwealth and American correspondents whose goodwill was so important to Britain at that time. This paved the way for his appointment as minister of information in 1941, a post in which he won golden opinions from Fleet Street for his direct and informal manner. He was fortunate to come to the Ministry when it was beginning to settle down after an uncertain start. He was one of the three political chiefs of the Political Warfare Executive. He deserves great credit for the vitality and imagination which he brought to the Ministry and for lifting it out of the disregard into which it had fallen. At the end of the war Bracken was made first lord of the Admiralty in

Churchill's caretaker government; and when he lost his seat in the general election of 1945, he was promptly found the safest of seats at Bournemouth.

He pursued his business interests as thoroughly as ever, and became chairman of the amalgamated *Financial Times* and *Financial News*, and contributed for many years every Monday a weekly column under the pen-name 'Observer' on 'Men and Matters' in the City. After his death the new offices of the paper were named in his honour Bracken House. He founded *History Today* as a monthly periodical under the wing of the *Financial Times*. His friend Strakosch had arranged for him to become his successor as chairman of the Union Corporation, a large mining and financial house operating in South Africa, and he did so in 1945. When Churchill returned to power in 1951, Bracken declined office in the Government, but in 1952 accepted a viscountcy, although he never took his seat in the House of Lords. In his later years he became increasingly interested in public schools: Trinity College, Glenalmond, and Ampleforth, as well as his old school Sedbergh for which he built a fine school library, to which he bequeathed his own excellent collection of books on English literary and political history of the last two centuries.

He was a man of much architectural and artistic taste, who formed close friendships with the leading figures in the world of architecture and art, and was instrumental in many good aesthetic causes. He avoided publicity, especially for his benefactions. In the last ten years of his life his health deteriorated and he spent long periods abroad. Finally he developed cancer of the throat which he faced with great fortitude, until he died in London 8 August 1958. Such a volume of tributes was paid to him by contemporaries of distinction that they were collected in a book. But he ordered all their papers to be destroyed, so that there should be no biography.

There is an old Irish proverb 'From the fury of the Brackens, good Lord deliver us' and Brendan Bracken, inexhaustibl voluble, was an overpowering figure, wh stormed his way to commercial and politi cal success. Arriving with neither con nection nor wealth, he established himse before he was thirty as a well-place director and member of Parliament, im posing himself at his own valuation. H was impervious to rebuffs, and he dis regarded the conventions: arriving a parties to which he had not been invited, or changing his place at the dinner table to talk to those to whom he wished to talk. If these habits made him many enemies, there was also about him a warm-heartedness, a generosity, an imaginative sympathy, and a readiness to take trouble over individuals, however lowly placed, which won him a great deal of affection. He was a gifted phrase-maker, a ceaseless talker, with unlimited powers of invention, but also with an immense range of information, not always exact, but always delivered with an extreme self-assurance, very galling to those who knew better but lacked his overriding personality. He never married, and bequeathed a large part of his wealth, proved at over £145,000, to Churchill College, Cambridge, where there is a charcoal drawing by Robert Lutyens in the Bracken Library. There is a bust by Uli Nimptsch at Bracken House.

There are many references to Bracken in works on Churchill, notably Lord Moran's *Winston Churchill: The Struggle for Survival, 1940–65* (1966).

[Private and family information; personal knowledge.]   DOUGLAS WOODRUFF.

BRAILSFORD, HENRY NOEL (1873–1958), journalist, was born at Mirfield, Yorkshire, 25 December 1873, the only son of the Rev. Edward John Brailsford, a Wesleyan minister, by his wife, Clara Pooley. He had one younger sister, Mabel, author of *A Tale of Two Brothers* (1954), a biography of the Wesleys. Brailsford's character and career were much influenced by early conflict with his Puritan father who permitted him after early education at George Watson's College, Edinburgh, and Dundee High School, to take up a scholarship at Glasgow University on condition that he did not shave and wore a costume of his father's design—knickerbockers, a tam o'shanter, and an Eton collar. Although Brailsford quickly rebelled against this attempt to mark him out from his fellows, the incident typified for him the authoritarian rule which he was to spend his life combating. It no doubt contributed to the extreme sensitivity and morbid self-consciousness with which he was afflicted throughout his career.

At Glasgow Brailsford made friends with such contemporaries as John Buchan (later Lord Tweedsmuir, q.v.), A. MacCallum Scott, James and (Sir) Muirhead Bone [q.v.], and A. H. Charteris, later

professor of international law at Sydney. His many academic distinctions included medals for moral philosophy and Greek. Gilbert Murray [q.v.] spoke of him as the best Greek pupil he had ever had. Under the terms of his scholarship Brailsford studied at Balliol and Berlin where he learnt to speak fluent German and formed a high opinion of German culture at that period. After taking his degree in 1894 with first class honours in logic and moral philosophy and a second class in Greek and Latin, he taught philosophy for a year as assistant to Robert Adamson [q.v.]. (He received an honorary LL.D. from the university in 1944.) In 1897 he joined as a volunteer to fight in the Greek war of independence. He came away with a loathing of war and a poor opinion of Greek truthfulness. The novel which he wrote on his return, *The Broom of the War-God* (1898), attracted the attention of C. P. Scott [q.v.] who engaged him as special correspondent to report for the *Manchester Guardian* in Crete and the Balkans. He spent the winter of 1903–4, after the Bulgarian rising, working for the British relief fund in the Balkans, and served afterwards on a commission of inquiry into Balkan atrocities.

Brailsford was convinced by the thesis of his friend, J. A. Hobson [q.v.], that war in this epoch is the result of the economic rivalry of the great Powers—a thesis which was accepted and developed by Lenin whom Brailsford met in England early in the century. Two later books, *Olives of Endless Age* (1928) and *Property or Peace?* (1934) further expanded his view of the relation of capitalism and war. The most important of his books on this topic was *The War of Steel and Gold* (1914) which at once became a socialist classic. Early in the war he was closely associated with the founders of the Union of Democratic Control; they included Arthur Ponsonby (later Lord Ponsonby of Shulbrede), G. Lowes Dickinson, Ramsay MacDonald, Philip (later Viscount) Snowden [qq.v.], (Sir) Norman Angell, and Bertrand (later Earl) Russell, and others who played leading roles in the socialist and peace movements. From the beginning of the war they attacked 'secret diplomacy' and worked for a negotiated peace and a permanent organization to end the 'international anarchy'. One of Brailsford's pamphlets *Belgium and 'The Scrap of Paper'* (1915) was confiscated by the War Office. His *A League of Nations* (1917) long lay on Woodrow Wilson's desk.

He stood unsuccessfully as a Labour candidate for Montrose Burghs in 1918.

Immediately after the war Brailsford travelled through devastated Europe; he wrote bitterly attacking the hunger blockade whose effects in Hungary, Austria, and Germany he described, and he became one of the foremost critics of the Versailles Treaty. He was one of the first western journalists to visit Soviet Russia. He learnt Russian before he went and in two books described his experiences: *The Russian Workers' Republic* (1921) and *How the Soviets Work* (New York, 1928). He found as much reason for hope in this early phase of socialist enthusiasm as he later found to lament and attack under Stalinism. Amongst other causes which won his ardent support were the women's suffrage movement, in which he played a leading role as founder and secretary of the Conciliation Committee, and the struggle for colonial independence, especially in India. Indian freedom became one of his life's passions. He became a trusted friend of M. K. Gandhi [q.v.] and Jawaharlal Nehru, and after visiting the country wrote *Rebel India* (1931) and twelve years later *Subject India* (1943).

Brailsford wrote regularly for the Radical *Nation* from its foundation in 1907 until 1923 when the paper passed out of the hands of his friend H. W. Massingham [q.v.]. From 1922 to 1926 he edited the *New Leader*, the organ of the Independent Labour Party which he had joined in 1907. He made it the most distinguished socialist paper in England and it had an immense effect on the thought of the post-war generation. His writing team included G. B. Shaw, H. G. Wells [qq.v.], E. M. Forster, and indeed many of the literary pundits of that period. The paper dealt with books and the arts as well as with politics, and it was in collaborating with Clare Leighton, the artist, that he formed the most important friendship of his life. The owners thought that he appealed too little to 'the masses' and complained of the deficit although he had reduced it to small dimensions by cutting his own salary to a bare living wage and writing most of the paper himself. In this period he summarized his left-wing, but anti-communist, socialism in a book *Socialism for To-day* (1925). In the thirties he joined the staff of the *New Statesman and Nation* where he remained as chief leader-writer until 1946. In the twenties he had denounced Versailles and supported the case for German equality, but after Hitler's accession to power his talents were devoted to informing public opinion about the menace of fascism in Germany, Italy, and Spain. He was no less a critic of Stalinism and was denounced by the Communists. When he retired from journalism in 1946 he returned to his historical interests. His two books in the Home University Library, *Shelley, Godwin, and their Circle* (1913) and *Voltaire* (1935), were both accepted as minor classics. After several years of research at the British Museum he spent the last period of his life writing a history of *The Levellers* which, completed by another hand, was published posthumously in 1961.

Brailsford must rank as one of the most eminent of British journalists. His style broke through his anonymity. He was of all men the most disinterested. He never asked, or received, a wage which would have satisfied a run-of-the-road reporter in Fleet Street, and when a rich admirer offered to settle on him a sum of money which would have made him financially independent for life, he refused on the ground that it might sap his intellectual integrity. With H. W. Nevinson (whose notice he contributed to this Dictionary) he threw up his post on the *Daily News* for which he was a leader-writer, in 1909, in protest against the Liberal Government's harsh treatment of suffragettes in prison for their activities. In his personal relations he suffered from a proud reserve which repelled advances from all but a very few friends. He was animated by a passionate love of freedom. He might have been writing of himself when he said that Edmund Burke had 'a nerve that beat with maddening sensitivity at the sight of human suffering'. He had an intimate relation with birds and animals which, in the case of cats, included an apparently magnetic power of calling them to him from a considerable distance without any audible summons. His greatest personal pleasure was in classical music. Perhaps the most mature and perfect expression of his philosophy is to be found in a pamphlet *All Souls' Day* reprinted from the *New Statesman and Nation* during the worst days of the second war. Inspired by Brahms's *Requiem*, he wrote, in language which none who read it would forget, of the meaning of the Communion of Saints to those who, like himself, could not accept any of the orthodox tenets of Christianity.

In 1898 Brailsford married Jane Mal-loch, of Paisley (died 1937). In 1943 he married Eva Maria Perlmann. He had no children. He died in London 23 March 1958. A portrait by Clare Leighton is in the possession of the family.

[Private information; personal knowledge.]
KINGSLEY MARTIN.

BRAIN, DENNIS (1921–1957), virtuoso horn-player, was born in London 17 May 1921. Educated at St. Paul's School and the Royal Academy of Music, he was the younger son of Aubrey Harold Brain (1893–1955), who was the principal horn of the B.B.C. Symphony Orchestra from its foundation until 1945. His mother, Marion Beeley, was at one time a Covent Garden singer.

Dennis Brain was the third generation of a distinguished family of horn-players, his grandfather and uncle (Alfred Brain) having also made notable careers, the latter in the United States. His brother Leonard became one of the most prominent oboe and cor anglais players in London of his day.

Dennis Brain's career began during the war which he spent as principal horn in the Royal Air Force Central Band and Orchestra, and he became widely known as a soloist immediately upon demobilization in 1946. A number of important works were composed especially for him, notably by Benjamin Britten and Paul Hindemith.

Brain's playing was characterized by a remarkably natural facility and unthinking assurance. It seemed as if the pitfalls of this notoriously unreliable instrument simply never occurred to him, and he executed perfectly passages of hair-raising difficulty in the manner born. He was, to use his own phrase, 'game for anything', while his infectious grin and abrupt bellowing laugh typified a character which never lost an endearing schoolboy ingenuousness and enthusiasm. He was entirely unspoilt by the success which came to him during his latter years and he was as much universally loved in the profession as admired by the musical world.

He was short, and somewhat stocky in appearance, but with great energy and agility. He became very fond of contract bridge, but his abiding interest was in motor-cars of which he had a considerable knowledge and experience. He was in the habit of driving to and from engagements in a single journey, no matter what distance, and it was this which cost him his life. He met with a fatal accident returning to London in the small hours from an Edinburgh Festival concert, 1 September 1957.

His death came at a time of gradually increasing restlessness. A musician of broad interests and culture (he was also an accomplished organist), his profound artistry needed a greater outlet than the limited repertoire of the horn could supply. He had begun a number of ambitious ventures to supplement his normal activities as soloist and orchestral musician, such as a wind ensemble and even a small chamber orchestra which he was beginning to conduct, although he had previously been doubtful of his potential in this direction.

He was an inveterate lover of the country and even entertained wistful dreams of an eventual retirement, perhaps as a chicken farmer. This basic simplicity of outlook may indeed hold the key to his entire character and to the charm and humility of his essentially natural personality.

He married in 1945 Yvonne, a pianist, whom he met at the Royal Academy of Music, daughter of Edward Ralph Coles, bank accountant, of Petersfield, Hampshire; they had a son and daughter.

[Private information; personal knowledge.]
NORMAN DEL MAR.

BRANGWYN, SIR FRANK (FRANÇOIS GUILLAUME) (1867–1956), artist, was born in Bruges 13 May 1867, of Welsh Roman Catholic parentage. His mother was Eleanor Griffiths, of Brecon. His father, William Curtis Brangwyn, was a church architect who had moved to Bruges for economy and there ran a workshop for ecclesiastical furnishings. Brangwyn was their third child and eldest of four sons. The family returned to London in 1875.

Brangwyn received little formal education. He was taken up by A. H. Mackmurdo and Harold Rathbone, who set him to draw in the South Kensington Museum, and was employed for about two years (c. 1882–4) in the workshop of William Morris [q.v.]. Mackmurdo's interest and friendship were lifelong. Other early supporters were Selwyn Image [q.v.] and Harriet Barnett.

Leaving Morris, Brangwyn spent his time in precarious independence in London, and in roaming the country and seaports sketching. His first Academy picture, 'A bit on the Esk, near Whitby', was shown in 1885. In 1888 a backer, Frederick Mills, financed a trip to Cornwall, and in the following years Brangwyn travelled extensively on commission, in Europe, the Near East, and South Africa. These were his *Wanderjahre*, during which he stored up impressions which were to last a lifetime. Meanwhile his work was beginning to attract attention. In 1894 he won a medal at the Chicago exhibition; the next year the French Government bought one of his pictures; and by 1896 he was earning over £400 a year. In this year he married Lucy Ray, a nurse, settled in Hammersmith, and, as he said, began to 'paint big'. A temporary move to Ditchling during the war of 1914-18 was followed after the death of his wife in 1924 by permanent residence there.

Brangwyn had grown up into a world of artistic ferment: he was a near-contemporary of Lautrec, Ensor, Aubrey Beardsley [q.v.], and Klimt. His tutelage to Morris and his friendship with Mackmurdo launched him into the international style of *art nouveau*, and commissions from the Parisian dealer S. Bing brought him to the very centre of that movement. True to the ideals of its adherents, he designed all kinds of decorative arts, including complete rooms. An exhibition of objects made to his designs, held in London in 1930, included furniture, textiles, ceramics, metalwork, jewellery, and glass.

From the start, Brangwyn's pictures were marked by their freshness and virility. His earliest works were painted in the low tones of J. A. McN. Whistler [q.v.]. A sketching-journey to Spain with Arthur Melville [q.v.] in 1891 produced an explosion of colour which announced the maturity of his style. Bright colour and bravura in handling of the medium were typical of the revolutionary artists of the time, and to these elements Brangwyn added sheer largeness. Another lifelong characteristic, due to natural sympathy and the circumstances of his upbringing, was his preoccupation with the working classes and their labours. Brangwyn was a prolific worker, in etching and lithography as well as in oils and water-colours. His great gifts of draughtsmanship and composition were used with a prodigality which sometimes amounted to recklessness: but he was always capable of producing work which was sensitive and deeply felt, as his etching 'The Afflicted' (1931) and his drawings of the life of St. Francis (1947, Ashmolean Museum, Oxford) reveal.

For thirty years of his life Brangwyn was mainly occupied, however, with the execution of large murals, the activity in which he particularly excelled and for which he became best known. In England the most accessible of these are in Skinners' Hall, London. The panels there are, as it happens, the earliest and the latest of his surviving works on this scale (1902 and 1937). They show that he moved from a three-dimensional style of Venetian richness to one which was flatter and placed greater reliance on vivid local colour. Other notable commissions were for the chapel of Christ's Hospital, Horsham (1913-23), the Panama Pacific International Exposition, San Francisco (1914), the Missouri State Capitol (1915), the *Empress of Britain* (1930), and the Rockefeller Center, New York (1930-34). Brangwyn's *maximum opus* in mural decoration was the series of 'British Empire' panels which were commissioned in 1925 by Lord Iveagh [q.v.] as a war memorial for the House of Lords. The rejection of the work by the Lords became something of a *cause célèbre*, and the panels finally went to Swansea where the new Guildhall was specially adapted to accommodate them.

Brangwyn was an active member of the Society of British Artists and many other academies and art societies at home and abroad. He was elected A.R.A. in 1904 and R.A. in 1919. In 1924 a large exhibition of his work was opened by the prime minister, Ramsay MacDonald. He was knighted in 1941 and in 1952 the Royal Academy paid him the unprecedented honour of a retrospective exhibition within in his own lifetime.

Brangwyn enjoyed wide fame abroad, where he was for long considered the outstanding British artist of his day. He received high honours in France, Holland and Italy, including the commission for a self-portrait for the Uffizi. Bruges made him an honorary citizen, in return for the gift of a large collection of his work which is housed in a special Brangwyn Museum (1936). Similar gifts were made to Orange (with the work of his friend Albert de Belleroche, 1947), and to the William Morris house, Walthamstow (1936), and his work is represented in virtually every major art gallery and print room in the world.

At home the panache of his work cast its spell over many, who did not hesitate to compare him with the greatest decorative artists of the past; nor was the artist unwilling to assume the mantle of an Old Master. Other critics convicted his work of empty rhetoric. But Brangwyn's latter neglect in some quarters seems as mistaken as his excessive praise in others. His was a majestic and insubordinate nature. He was of stocky build; from middle age he inclined to ill health and finally became something of a recluse. He died at Ditchling 11 June 1956. He had no children.

There are portraits of Brangwyn at the National Portrait Gallery (by Phil May and A. H. Knighton-Hammond), the National Museum of Wales (by Augustus John, Powys Evans, and Albert Toft), the William Morris Museum, Walthamstow (by John and Toft), and the Ferens Art Gallery, Hull (by J. Kerr-Lawson and A. Sava Botzaris). The artist made numerous slight self-portraits in pen and ink of an illustrational character, and a self-portrait in oils was in the collection of Count W. de Belleroche.

[*The Times*, 13 June 1956; W. Shaw-Sparrow, *Frank Brangwyn and his work*, 1910; P. Macer-Wright, *Brangwyn, A Study of Genius at Close Quarters*, 1940; W. de Belleroche, *Brangwyn Talks*, 1944; C. G. E. Bunt, *The Water-Colours of Sir Frank Brangwyn*, 1958; V. Galloway, *The Oils & Murals of Sir Frank Brangwyn*, 1962.] R. L. Charles.

BRESSEY, Sir CHARLES HERBERT (1874–1951), civil engineer, was born at Wanstead, Essex, 3 January 1874, the son of John Thomas Bressey, architect, and his wife, Mary Elizabeth Farrow. He was educated at Forest School, Walthamstow, also in Bremen and Rouen, and then practised as an architect. During the war of 1914–18 he served in France and Flanders as lieutenant-colonel in the Royal Engineers, was appointed O.B.E., and made a chevalier of the Legion of Honour. In the war of 1939–45 he was a battalion commander in the Essex Home Guard and an army welfare officer.

After the war of 1914–18 he served for a short time as a member of the Inter-Allied Commission, Rhine Province Communications. On the formation of the Ministry of Transport in 1919 he became the first divisional road engineer (London). Sir Henry Maybury [q.v.] was director-general with J. S. Killick as deputy director-general and chief engineer. On Killick's retirement in 1921 Bressey succeeded as chief engineer, the post of deputy director-general being abolished. When Maybury retired at the end of 1928 he was in turn succeeded by Bressey. The post of director-general was abolished and Bressey retained the title of chief engineer.

In this post he remained until he retired in January 1935.

A sound practical engineer, Bressey had the misfortune, perhaps, to be overshadowed by Maybury's brilliance. He is probably best remembered for his work on the Highway Development Survey of Greater London, of which he was engineer in charge in 1935–8, following his retirement from the Ministry. The Survey, intended to determine highway requirements for the next thirty years, was ordered by Leslie (later Lord) Hore-Belisha [q.v.], the minister of transport. Sir Edwin Lutyens [q.v.] was appointed as consultant to help Bressey in his task. Bressey's first step was to tour the Continent, visiting in particular Dresden, Prague, Budapest, Copenhagen, and Oslo. The report of his Survey was issued in 1938 and novel features were the techniques used in its preparation—aerial surveys and aerial photography to bring maps up to date quickly, journey time-studies to measure delays, and an origin and destination survey of traffic to the docks. The report was well received but, owing to the outbreak of war in the following year, no action was taken to implement its recommendations. The report included references to such schemes as the duplication of the Thames tunnels, the north and south orbital roads, the City loop way, the improvement to the dock approaches, and major motorways radiating from the metropolis. Towards the end of the thirty-year period which the Survey was to serve, many of the schemes had only recently been completed or were still under construction, and it is interesting to recall Bressey's closing paragraph: 'So imperative, however, is the need of prompt action that Londoners would be better advised to embark immediately upon useful schemes, admittedly imperfect, rather than wait for the emergence of some faultless ideal which will have ceased to be attainable long before it has received approval.'

During a very active life Bressey was a president of the Chartered Surveyors' Institution and of the Junior Institution of Engineers by whom he was specially remembered as the president who maintained his active interest in the Institution long after his retirement. He was chairman of the Road Engineering Industry Committee and of the British Standards Institution and an honorary member of the Institution of Royal Engineers. He was also a member of the Town Planning Institute and the Institutions of Municipal and of Highway Engineers. He was appointed C.B.E. (1924), C.B. (1930), and knighted in 1935. He was awarded the honorary degree of D.Sc. (Eng.) by London University in 1938.

In 1902 Bressey married Lily Margaret Francis, daughter of Francis Charles Hill, merchant, of Wanstead; they had two sons. He died in Sawbridgeworth 14 April 1951.

[*Journal* of the Institution of Highway Engineers, July 1951; official records; private information.] ALEX SAMUELS.

BRIDIE, JAMES (pseudonym), playwright. [See MAVOR, OSBORNE HENRY.]

BRIERLY, JAMES LESLIE (1881–1955), international lawyer, was born in Huddersfield 9 September 1881, the eldest son of Sydney Herbert Brierly, woollen manufacturer, by his wife, Emily Sykes. He was educated at Charterhouse; then as a scholar of Brasenose College, Oxford, where he gained a first in classical moderations (1902), a second in *literae humaniores* (1904), and a first in jurisprudence (1905), and won a senior Hulme scholarship. In 1906 he gained a certificate of honour in the final examinations for the bar and a prize fellowship at All Souls College. The following year he was called to the bar at Lincoln's Inn, and entered the chambers of F. H. (later Viscount) Maugham [q.v.]. In 1913 he was elected to a fellowship in law at Trinity College, Oxford, but in 1914 he joined the Wiltshire Regiment as a second lieutenant. He served in the adjutant-general's department in the War Office, then as D.A.A.G. with the Army of the Black Sea, reached the rank of brevet major, and was appointed O.B.E. (1919).

In 1920 Brierly was appointed professor of law at Manchester where he played a valuable part in restarting the law faculty. In 1922, on the death of Sir Erle Richards, he was elected Chichele professor of international law and diplomacy at Oxford, and returned to All Souls. His inaugural lecture, published in the *British Year Book of International Law* for 1924, was devoted to 'The shortcomings of international law'. In this lecture, characteristic of his whole approach to international law, he examined the stresses to which the legal system is subject in the international community by reason of the absence of adequate procedures for bringing about peaceful change.

Brierly's best-known work, *The Law of Nations*, was written for 'students and laymen anxious to learn something of the part played by law in the relations between States'. First published in 1928, it set out with admirable clarity and precision the main principles of the law of peace. In its own genre it was a masterpiece, which won wide popularity, being translated into four foreign languages. It showed that Brierly possessed in high degree the qualities of judgement, vision, and scholarship which would have enabled him to write a work of major importance. But this was not forthcoming, for, firstrate technician though he was, the absorbing interest of international law for him was the role which it could play in promoting international peace and human welfare rather than its detailed rules. The lectures given by him at the Hague Academy in the same year, and published in volume 23 of the *Recueil des cours* under the title 'Le fondement du caractère obligatoire du droit international', contain a brilliantly clear study of the different theories concerning the basis of the obligatory force of international law. He pointed out the damaging effect of some traditional postulates such as the doctrine of the fundamental rights of States, questioning their absolute validity and advocating that relief from them should be sought in a resurgence of natural law. A second course of lectures, given in 1936 and published in volume 58 of the *Recueil des cours* under the title 'Règles générales du droit de la paix', was based on his *Law of Nations* but was more critical and reflective. His last book, *The Outlook for International Law*, written in 1944, when people tended to regard international law as a bankrupt system, seeks to draw up a balance sheet of the values and limitations of law in the relations between sovereign States, and contains a penetrating analysis of the problems arising from the so called 'vital interests' of States. Brierly also published numerous articles in learned journals, several appearing in the *British Year Book of International Law*, of which he was editor from 1929 to 1936. Twenty-eight of these articles, covering a large variety of topics, were reprinted together with his first Hague lectures, in a posthumous volume entitled *The Basis of Obligation in International Law* (1958). In addition, he was responsible for the scholarly translation of Zouche's *Juris et Judicii Fecialis Explicatio*, published in the Carnegie series of Classics of International Law. And he joined with Sir John Miles in editing several editions of Ansoon *Contract*, and in compiling a case-book on that branch of English law.

After retiring from his Oxford chair in 1947 Brierly was Montague Burton professor of international relations at Edinburgh (1948–51). His contribution was not confined to the academic field. He was a member of the League of Nations committees on the codification of international law and on the port of Danzig. During the Italo-Abyssinian dispute he acted as legal adviser to the Emperor of Abyssinia, accompanying him in 1938 to the critical session of the League Assembly. In 1948 he was elected an original member of the United Nations International Law Commission, being its rapporteur for the law of treaties in 1949–50 and chairman of the commission in 1951.

Brierly also had a high sense of social obligation which led him to undertake many public duties in his own country. At Oxford he served on the university's council and chest and in 1923–50 was a delegate of the University Press. Taking a keen interest in the emancipation of women, he served on the councils of Somerville and St. Hilda's colleges. A justice of the peace for the city from 1932 to 1955 he discharged his duties with ability and humanity. He was chairman of the Oxford court of referees, of the national service hardship committee, and of four local trade boards, and a member of the Agricultural Wages Board. He served on a number of government committees, including, during the war of 1939–45, the advisory committee established under Defence Regulation 18B. He was appointed C.B.E. in 1946. His deep humanity also led him to many acts of kindness to those in misfortune. Many a refugee from the two world wars, from the Spanish civil war, and from Hitler, found in him an unselfish friend ready to give them personal help and to work in their interest.

Brierly was a D.C.L. of Oxford (1931), and honorary doctorates were conferred upon him by the universities of Oslo (1946), Chicago (1948), and Manchester (1953). In 1929 he was elected an associate of the Institute of International Law and in 1937 full member.

In 1920 he married Ada Ellen (died 1966), who was the daughter of John Christopher Foreman, merchant, and was twice mentioned in dispatches when serving as a nurse with the Army of the Black Sea in 1919. They had one son. Brierly died in Oxford 20 December 1955.

[*The Times, Manchester Guardian*, and *Oxford Mail*, 22 December 1955; *British Year Book of International Law*, vol. xxxii, 1955–6; private information.] HUMPHREY WALDOCK.

BRODETSKY, SELIG (1888–1954), mathematician and Zionist leader, was born 10 February 1888 at Olviopol, a small town in the Ukraine a hundred miles north of Odessa, the second son among the fifteen children of Akiva Brodetsky by his wife, Ada Prober. The family emigrated in 1893 and settled in the east end of London. Brodetsky received the normal education of a poor Russian-Jewish immigrant, for his father's only employment was as beadle of a small east-end synagogue. At a time when this immigration was being seriously criticized and had, in fact, been limited by recent parliamentary action, the boy caused an almost national sensation by being placed first of all England in the Cambridge junior local examinations in 1905, and by winning a mathematical scholarship to Trinity College, Cambridge. In 1908 he was bracketed as senior wrangler. From Cambridge he went with the Isaac Newton studentship to Leipzig and took his Ph.D. in mathematical astronomy. In 1914 he became lecturer in applied mathematics at Bristol University.

He had already established the pattern of dividing his time between serious academic work and equally serious work for the Jewish community and especially for the Zionist movement. At Cambridge he had been warden of the synagogue maintained by Jewish undergraduates, and secretary of the Zionist Society. At Leipzig he had been president of the Zionist Student Union. At Bristol he gave every week-end to travelling and speaking for the Zionist cause. In spite of this additional interest, and of a heavy academic schedule, he found time to do war work in the field of optical research.

In 1919 Brodetsky moved from Bristol to Leeds, becoming professor in 1924 and in 1946 head of the mathematics department. He continued to give his week-ends to his Jewish interests, but was still able in 1927 to publish a life of Sir Isaac Newton, and to take a prominent part in the foundation of the Association of University Teachers, of which he was the second president. In 1928 he became a member of the World Zionist Executive and head of its political department in London. In 1940 he also became president of the Board of Deputies of British Jews, the lay head of Anglo-Jewry. The position had hitherto been confined to old-established families, and the Board had resisted any close association with Zionism. His election was the outcome of organized pressure which resulted in a Zionist majority among its members. But he presided over a divided community, some of whose breaches he could not heal, possibly because he lived his life and formed his judgements at a speed which left little opportunity for the slow workings of negotiation and diplomacy. During the war of 1939–45 he undertook research in aeronautics, and was concerned with the establishment of the corps of air cadets.

In 1948 he retired with the title of emeritus professor and in the same year followed Chaim Weizmann [q.v.] as president of the Zionist Federation of Great Britain and Ireland. In May 1949 he was elected president of the Hebrew University at Jerusalem. It had been going through a difficult period and the emergence of the State of Israel had added to its problems. The presidency had become semi-honorific under his predecessor, but Brodetsky had no use for honorary offices. The reform of the university administration, however, involved controversies which sapped his strength, and he was compelled by ill health to resign in 1952. He never fully recovered his health and died in London 18 May 1954.

In 1919 Brodetsky married Mania, daughter of Paul Berenblum, and had one son and one daughter. There is an oil-painting by Jacob Kramer in the possession of the family who also have a copy of a bust by Mrs. L. Kagan-Rustchuk. A bronze bust by Sir Jacob Epstein was to go eventually to the Hebrew University at Jerusalem.

[*Jewish Chronicle*, 21 May 1954; personal knowledge.]   JAMES PARKES.

BROOKE-POPHAM, SIR (HENRY) ROBERT (MOORE) (1878–1953), air chief marshal, was born at Mendlesham, Hartismere, Suffolk, 18 September 1878, son of Henry Brooke, a country gentleman of Wetheringsett Manor, Suffolk, and his wife, Dulcibella, daughter of the Rev. Robert Moore. From Haileybury he entered the Royal Military College, Sandhurst, graduated in May 1898, and was gazetted to the Oxfordshire Light Infantry as a second lieutenant. At first he showed no special vocation for the profession of arms, but after a year or two of regimental duty discovered a lively ability

and a natural bent for soldiering, and his promotion to captain in 1904, and entry to the Staff College in 1910, both demonstrated a mental standard well above average. His other advantages were a tall sparse figure with a strong physique, somewhat austere good looks, and an outstanding capacity for application and hard work. In 1904 by royal warrant he assumed the additional surname of Popham, the name of an ancestor whom he greatly admired.

Only two years after the first air crossing of the Channel, Brooke-Popham learned to fly at the Bristol School at Brooklands, under the system by which the army repaid the cost of private tuition. His certificate was No. 108, dated July 1911. His early start made him a pioneer of Service aviation, and his first flight preceded by a year that of the future Lord Trenchard [q.v.]. For a few months Brooke-Popham soldiered on with his regiment, but in 1912 he transferred to the Air Battalion, Royal Engineers, which had an aeroplane and a balloon company. He commanded the former and when the Air Battalion became the Royal Flying Corps in May 1912 had command of No. 3 Squadron, which had seven different types of aircraft, and began training reconnaissance crews.

On the outbreak of war in 1914 Brooke-Popham went to France as a staff officer in the H.Q. of the British Expeditionary Force. Appointed deputy assistant adjutant and quartermaster-general, he was responsible for the administrative and technical support of the Royal Flying Corps squadrons in France. He quickly came to understand the importance of the new air weapon to armies in the field, and so to criticize the lack of adequate air support to the B.E.F. In 1915 he formed No. 3 Wing (1 and 4 Squadrons) at St Omer, and controlled its operations at the battle of Neuve Chapelle. For this he was appointed to the D.S.O. He was already too senior an officer to take part in serious operational flying, and he had little active experience of air fighting. He compensated for this with a ferocious energy and industry, and had no hesitation in taking short cuts and unorthodox steps to achieve his ends. He became deputy adjutant and quartermaster-general in March 1916 with the temporary rank of brigadier-general.

After seeing the Royal Flying Corps through their worst battles, to a final position where they dominated the western front, he was summoned in April 1917 to the air staff of the newly created Air Ministry. In addition to French and Russian awards he received the C.M.G. and A.F.C. (1918) and C.B. (1919). Brooke-Popham had by now a considerable reputation for administration and procurement of equipment and he was consequently made controller of aircraft production, and in 1919 transferred permanently to the new Royal Air Force, with the rank of air commodore. After a spell as director of research (1920–21) he became, in 1921, the first commandant of the newly created R.A.F. Staff College. He grasped the opportunity, during the five years in which he was commandant, to pioneer thinking in another element of war. Despite his reputation, he had no dramatic background of air fighting to lend him prestige with his pupils, and his dour public manner did not bring him easy popularity. His universal nickname was 'Brookham', no more than a convenient, if later an affectionate, contraction. But if his manner was sober, his results were excellent. He was promoted air vice-marshal in 1924.

In 1926, in the formation of the Air Defence of Great Britain, he became air officer commanding Fighting Area, creating the acoustic listening chain of huge concrete mirrors which antedated radar. He was promoted K.C.B. in 1927 and in 1928 became air officer commanding in Iraq; when no high commissioner was in office he filled that post also.

In 1931 he was promoted to air marshal and became the first Royal Air Force officer to be appointed commandant of the Imperial Defence College, and followed this by two years as commander-in-chief of Air Defence of Great Britain. In 1935 he became inspector-general, was appointed G.C.V.O., and promoted to air chief marshal. With the onset of the Italo-Abyssinian crisis, he was sent to Cairo as air commander-in-chief Middle East. His immediate concern was the danger of air attack from the Regia Aeronautica, but when this abated he returned to England. In 1937 he retired to become governor and commander-in-chief Kenya, to which he brought first-class qualities of administration and diplomacy. But when war broke out in 1939 he rejoined the Royal Air Force, becoming head of the training mission which went first to Canada to lay the foundations of the Commonwealth Air Training Scheme for aircrew, and then to South Africa. Up to this time Brooke-Popham's life

and career had been that of a successful and distinguished officer and a devoted public servant, whose performance of duty, though seldom newsworthy, had been conducted according to the highest professional traditions. With his appointment in October 1940 as commander-in-chief Far East he was suddenly, at the age of sixty-two, thrust upon the stage of history.

It was a daunting prospect for a man of any age. He was appointed to a joint command, the first R.A.F. officer ever to hold such a post, in an increasingly dangerous situation. The command organization he was called upon to operate was new and basically unsound. Although he was nominally responsible for defence matters in Singapore, Malaya, Burma, and Hong Kong, the naval units in these waters were not under his command but controlled by their own naval commander-in-chief, reporting directly to London. The civil officials in his area continued to serve their own ministers in Whitehall, and that with little sense of urgency. They co-operated reluctantly with the military authority of the commander-in-chief.

Brooke-Popham knew that time was short. In fact he had only thirteen months before Japan was to strike. The defences of Singapore had been built against a threat expected to come from the sea. Thus the plan itself was faulty, but due to Middle East priorities, even the minimum defence forces planned were lacking. He was particularly weak in the air. For a year he struggled to improve the defences, to make his command system work properly, to win his reinforcements from a home government hard pressed and beset by conflicting priorities. In such a situation he was bound to make enemies.

As the scene darkened around him, and Japan established sea and air bases in southern Indo-China, he faced the first important decision of the subsequent campaign: whether or not to push his units forward into Thailand where the Japanese were expected to land, so violating a neutral country, but gaining a far better defensive position. Duff Cooper (later Viscount Norwich, q.v.) had arrived in September 1941 as a special cabinet envoy, further eroding the position of the commander-in-chief. Brooke-Popham urged that he should move into Thailand, but he received permission from London only at the eleventh hour, hedged with many conditions. It came too late for forward defence, and the disastrous war with

Japan began in December 1941 with this among many other handicaps. The second fatal blow to British hopes was the sinking of the *Prince of Wales* and *Repulse* by Japanese aircraft. It was the direct consequence of the shortage of aircraft, particularly modern fighters, against which Brooke-Popham had railed for thirteen long months.

All the ingredients of complete disaster were present, and he had been able to do little to change the course of events. His replacement with a younger man had been agreed in London before the Japanese war began, but Whitehall decided that it was unwise to make a change at so critical a time. At this point, however, he fell victim to the stresses of the previous twelve months, in which land, sea, and civil chiefs had all played their part. Duff Cooper pressed for his replacement. The Cabinet agreed, and he handed over to Sir Henry Pownall on 27 December 1941, at the height of the battle for Malaya.

His return to England, closely followed by the collapse of the Allies in the Far East and the surrender of Singapore, could not fail to be connected in the public mind. He left the active list once more in May 1942, suffering some hasty public attacks as the chief architect of the British defeats in South East Asia. He continued to give service where he could, as president of N.A.A.F.I. and inspector-general of the Air Training Corps, until 1945, living afterwards in retirement.

Brooke-Popham was a fine administrator, and therein lay his greatest value to the Royal Air Force. While having no profound understanding of flying itself, he foresaw the importance of aviation in war. His cautious, reserved, dreamy though somewhat cold personality made him an intellectual rather than an inspirational leader. An able and sometimes brilliant professional officer, and a talented amateur diplomat, it was tragic for him that after his active career should have ended his reputation became closely linked with the greatest calamity ever to strike British arms. This was evidently unjust, since he was allowed neither the time nor the power to solve a problem already beyond solution.

In 1926 he married Opal Mary, second daughter of Edgar Hugonin; they had a son and a daughter. He died in Halton Hospital 20 October 1953. There is a portrait by T. C. Dugdale in the Imperial War Museum.

[S. Woodburn Kirby, (Official History) *The War Against Japan*, vol. i, 1957; Sir Walter Raleigh and H. A. Jones, (Official History) *The War in the Air*, 6 vols., 1922–37; *The Times*, 21 October 1953; *Aeroplane*, 30 October 1953; private information.]   PETER WYKEHAM.

BROOM, ROBERT (1866–1951), palaeontologist, was born in Paisley, Scotland, 30 November 1866, the third child of John Broom, designer of calico prints and shawls, and his wife, Agnes Hunter Shearer. Educated at Hutcheson's Grammar School, Glasgow, he became laboratory assistant to John Ferguson, professor of chemistry, while also attending classes at the university. He qualified M.B., C.M. in 1889, having taken his B.Sc. in 1887. In 1892 he went to Australia where he practised medicine and wrote a series of papers on marsupial anatomy. In 1897 he moved to South Africa and set up in practice first in Port Nolloth, then Port Elizabeth, then Pearston, a fossiliferous but poor district where he first collected Karroo fossils, making several important finds which he immediately described. Finding that medicine interfered with palaeontology he accepted in 1903 the professorship of zoology and geology in Victoria College, Stellenbosch, where he was a brilliant lecturer and attracted large classes.

In 1910, having resigned his chair, he visited London to see fossil material in the British Museum and went on to New York to see comparable material from Texas; he then published 'A comparison of the Permian Reptiles of North America with those of South Africa' (*Bull. Amer. Mus. Nat. Hist.*, 28, 197–234). He resumed medical practice in South Africa but returned to London early in 1914 and when war broke out was working in the Ear, Nose, and Throat Hospital. In 1915 he joined the Royal Army Medical Corps but his age prevented him from serving abroad. He therefore retired after a year and returned to South Africa, eventually settling in practice at Douglas in the Transvaal. There he turned his attention to anthropology, especially to the relationships of the men who lived in South Africa before the incoming of whites and kaffirs.

In 1928 Broom sold his practice and visited England and the United States but eventually once more resumed medical practice in South Africa. In 1934 J. C. Smuts [q.v.] appointed him curator of fossil vertebrates in the Transvaal Museum. He was then eight years beyond the normal age of retirement. In two years he increased the collection of fossil reptiles, adding twenty-six new genera and forty-six new species, mainly found by himself.

The discovery and description by Professor Raymond Dart of the Taungs skull had much interested Broom who in 1936 decided to explore caves at Sterkfontein. There he found a cave commercially exploited which contained fossil bones, including the second skull of an Australopithecine. This find was followed by others, all recorded in short notes, largely letters to *Nature*, but in 1946, with G. W. H. Schepers, Broom described the mode of occurrence and the structure of the Australopithecines in a special volume *The South African Fossil Ape-Men*. Part . *Transv. Mus. Mem.* No. 2, pp. 7–144). In 1950 he published *Finding the Missing Link*. He continued to work on Australopithecines until his death, usually in association with J. T. Robinson, but he still retained his interest in the Karroo fauna, publishing with M. George two papers in 1950.

In all, Broom published over 400 papers. His work was revolutionary in that it gave the first intelligible and accurate accounts of the structure of Permian reptiles from America as well as South Africa, and discussion of their relationships. The work on the manlike apes was of similar quality. It covered the field of fact by accurate descriptions, and it established the zoological position of the animals in relation to the known, living great apes and to man, represented not only by living races but also by fossil forms such s Neanderthal man and *Pithecanthropus*. All Broom's scientific work was intensely personal; in method, in outlook, in its general character, and in the form of its publication it can be recognized immediately and is unlike that of anyone se. Broom's work depended on certain personal qualities. He was an extraordinarily accurate observer and very quick, both mentally and physically. He also had a truly remarkable memory. He himself said that he was always a evolutionist but not a Darwinian. He never accepted natural selection as an effective mechanism, preferring some marckian explanation.

Broom had other interests than science; he played his part in public affairs and was several times mayor of Douglas. As a medical man he was successful, 'devoted keeping his patients in good health rather than making a great fortune by unnecessary operations'. He experimented not very successfully with both water and oil painting and always drew the illustrations to his papers himself, using a pencil with the greatest ease and accuracy. He collected Old Masters and spent much time hunting for Dutch pictures in the small auction rooms in London.

Broom was appointed Croonian lecturer to the Royal Society in 1913, elected F.R.S. in 1920, and awarded a Royal medal in 1928. He received a number of honorary doctorates and was a foreign member of the Royal Academy of Science of Sweden and of many other societies throughout the world. The National Academy of Sciences, Washington, awarded him the Elliot medal and the Geological Society of London its Wollaston medal. A volume of essays by his friends was published in commemoration of his eightieth birthday and a bronze bust of Broom by Elsa Djomba was placed by the South African Government in the entrance hall of the National Museum in Pretoria and unveiled in Broom's presence by Smuts on 31 October 1941.

In 1893 Broom married Mary Braid Baillie; they had three adopted children. He died at Pretoria 6 April 1951.

[D. M. S. Watson in *Obituary Notices of Fellows of the Royal Society*, No. 21, November 1952; personal knowledge.] D. M. S. WATSON.

BROWN, DOUGLAS CLIFTON, VISCOUNT RUFFSIDE (1879–1958), Speaker of the House of Commons, was born 16 August 1879 at Holmbush, Horsham, the fourth surviving son of Colonel James Clifton Brown, member of Parliament for Horsham, and his wife, Amelia, daughter of Charles Rowe, of Elm House, Liverpool. Educated at Eton and Trinity College, Cambridge, where he graduated in 1901, he was commissioned into the Lancashire Royal Garrison Artillery (Militia) (1900), transferred to the 1st King's Dragoon Guards (1902), became captain (1908), transferred to the special reserve (1910), served in France and Belgium (1914–18), and was promoted major (1919). In December 1910 Clifton Brown had unsuccessfully contested St. George-in-the-East and in the general election of 1918 he was returned as a Coalition Unionist for the Hexham division of Northumberland. With the exception of the period November 1923 to October 1924, he held this seat as a Unionist or as Speaker until he retired from the House of Commons in 1951. He continued in the Yeomanry, commanding the Northumberland Hussars in 1925-9. In 1920-22 he was parliamentary private secretary to Ian Macpherson (later Lord Strathcarron, q.v.), then minister of pensions.

In 1937 he was nominated a member of the chairmen's panel, presiding over standing committees and serving from time to time as temporary chairman of committees of the whole House. On 9 November 1938 he was elected deputy chairman of ways and means. In 1941 he was sworn of the Privy Council and in January 1943 was elected chairman of ways and means. Following the death, in office, of the Speaker, E. A. FitzRoy [q.v.], Clifton Brown was elected Speaker on 9 March 1943. The House of Commons had then been in existence for nearly eight years under Mr. Speaker FitzRoy's somewhat authoritarian sway and as, so long as the war continued, domestic politics were in abeyance, procedural problems did not trouble the new Speaker. The assault by V.1 and V.2 bombs raised fresh questions of safety with which Clifton Brown was well fitted to deal, for since 1941 he had been chairman of the defence committee of the Palace of Westminster.

With the war in Europe over, party politics were resumed and in the general election of 1945 the Labour Party was returned with a huge majority. Following the precedents of 1895 and 1906 Clifton Brown was unanimously re-elected Speaker on 1 August 1945. Conditions were very different from those in the previous House: there were many new members, party political warfare had been resumed with great bitterness and, smarting from an unexpected defeat, the Opposition were in no mood to accept in silence rulings contrary to their views. To reimpose the sort of discipline which had existed under FitzRoy would have meant a struggle in which it was by no means certain that the Speaker would have commanded the support of the House and which would have been quite contrary to Clifton Brown's temperament. So, where his predecessors had relied upon authority, Brown relied on good humour, patience, and his patent wish to help members to the utmost of his ability. Although successful to a point, the Speaker's willingness to listen to representations on his rulings was often much abused and the time of the House wasted. Still, that he was unanimously elected for the third time in the Parliament which met on 1 March

1950 was a tribute to his popularity. With the Government's majority of only six, the political struggle was sterner than at any time since 1914. Inevitably these conditions imposed a heavy burden on the Speaker with long hours of sitting and perpetual procedural wrangles. Although Clifton Brown continued to act with the most conscientious impartiality, the circumstances were peculiarly distasteful to a man of his peace-loving temperament and moderate views, and it was no surprise when in 1951 he announced that he would not seek re-election at the coming general election. The House had been fortunate in having a Speaker of so equable a temperament to guide it through the post-war years with their almost revolutionary changes in the economic and social conditions of the country. It was even more fortunate in having a Speaker whose modest but dignified demeanour combined with a charming personality made him an outstanding representative of the House of Commons at a time when it was universally regarded as a symbol of ordered freedom and when its Speaker was called upon to represent it at many diverse functions in this country and overseas.

Clifton Brown paid formal visits abroad to Caen on the anniversary of D-Day; to Nuremberg during the war criminals trial to Paris as the guest of M. Herriot, then president of the French National Assembly, who had previously been officially entertained at Westminster; to Rome and to Copenhagen; in this country he visited the General Assembly in Edinburgh. There were also occasions of more domestic interest. No one who heard the simple but most moving speech when he relit the lantern in Big Ben could doubt his intense love for the House of Commons and its traditions, while the two proudest moments of his life were when he led the Commons to St. Margaret's to return thanks for victory in Europe, and when he first took his seat in the Chair of the rebuilt House of Commons and subsequently led a procession of the Speakers of the Commonwealth into Westminster Hall to present an address to the King. He held honorary degrees from Durham, Cambridge, and Caen, received the grand cross of the Legion of Honour, and was created Viscount Ruffside in 1951.

Clifton Brown married in 1907 Violet Cicely Kathleen, daughter of Frederic Eustace Arbuthnott Wollaston, of Shenton Hall, Nuneaton. They had one daughter who married Sir Harry Hylton-Foster

Speaker of the House of Commons from 1959 until his death in 1965, and who was created a life peeress in the same year (1965). Ruffside died at Northwood, Middlesex, 5 May 1958. A portrait by Sir William Hutchison is in Speaker's House, Palace of Westminster.

[Journals of the House of Commons; Philip Laundy, *The Office of Speaker*, 1964; private information; personal knowledge.]

E. FELLOWES.

BROWN, SIR JOHN (1880–1958), lieutenant-general, Territorial Army, was born in Northampton 10 February 1880, the elder son of John Brown, a clicker, later a licensed victualler and an alderman, and his wife, Kate Davis Allen. He was educated at Magdalen College School, Brackley. Entering the architectural profession, he qualified as an associate of the Royal Institute of British Architects in 1921 and became a fellow in 1930. For many years he was in practice in Northampton and London in partnership with A. E. Henson. But the distinction he gained as an architect was much exceeded by his career as a citizen soldier.

Entering the 1st Volunteer battalion, the Northamptonshire Regiment, in 1901, he continued in it when it became the 4th (Territorial Force) battalion of that regiment, and with it went out to the Dardanelles in 1915 where he took part in the August landing at Suvla Bay. He served with the battalion in the Palestine campaign and subsequently rose to command it. He made such a mark that in 1924 he was given command of the 162nd (East Midland) Infantry brigade which soon became the best-known formation in the Territorial Army. In the army manœuvres of 1925 it represented the citizen force with distinction. Brown became the foremost figure and most dynamic leader in the Territorial Army during years when its strength and efficiency were declining, and by his power of generating enthusiasm he created a local revival which had a far-reaching effect. It was a period when even the nominal strength of many battalions barely exceeded 400, of whom only about half could be induced to attend the annual camp, despite describing it as largely a 'free seaside holiday'. But 'John Brown's Brigade' brought 85 per cent to camp. Its outstanding battalion was the 4th Northamptons which repeatedly brought more than 600 (90 per cent). Brown promised them no easy time but plenty of real training for war and he took care to make it continually interesting and exciting.

Prior to the annual camp many of the officers and N.C.O.s attended as many as thirty week-end tactical exercises in the year. In camp, petty restrictions, 'bull', and fatigues were cut to a minimum. But the men were kept so active during the day and so well entertained in the evenings that few wanted to go out of camp. The standard of tactical training was higher than in most regular battalions and some discerning regular officers brought their N.C.O.s to watch. Brown created the feeling that service in such an élite was a distinction to be sought, so that there was a waiting list to join and local pride was such that crowds in Northampton turned out to cheer when the local battalion set out for camp.

The divisional commander, Sir John Duncan, a regular soldier and tactical enthusiast, recommended Brown as his successor. This would have fulfilled the promise made when the Territorial Force was created in 1907 that citizen soldiers should be eligible for general officers' appointments. But the recommendation was turned down on the score that it would diminish, if only by one, the number of major-generals' jobs available for regulars. So Brown's services were lost to the army in 1928 when he was in the prime of life.

But in 1930 he was elected chairman of the British Legion and held that position for four years, during which he carried out several needed reforms and dealt with a number of awkward internal problems effectively and tactfully, in his inimitable manner. He had a way of talking bluntly as plain John Brown, with frequent dropping of aitches, but he was shrewdly skilled in handling all kinds and degrees of men.

In 1937 Leslie (later Lord) Hore-Belisha [q.v.] became secretary of state for war and his programme of reforms included the long-overdue fulfilment of the promise made by Lord Haldane [q.v.]. John Brown, now too old for active command, was made deputy director-general of the Territorial Army. He thus became the first Territorial to become a major-general as well as the first to be given a high position in the War Office and the chance to guide the treatment of the Territorial Army's special problems.

He got on so well with the higher regular soldiers that two years later, after the outbreak of war, he was promoted to lieutenant-general and made deputy adjutant-general (T), while in 1940 he became director-general of the Territorial Army and inspector-general welfare and education in the War Office, dual posts which he held until retirement in 1941.

Brown was appointed to the D.S.O. in 1918; he was appointed C.B.E. (1923), C.B. (1926), and K.C.B. (1934). He was twice master of the worshipful company of Pattenmakers.

In 1904 Brown married Annie Maria, daughter of Francis Tonsley, confectioner and alderman, of Northampton; they had two sons. Brown died in Northampton 4 April 1958.

[Private information; personal knowledge.]
B. H. LIDDELL HART.

BROWN, WILLIAM FRANCIS (1862–1951), Roman Catholic bishop, was born in Park Place House, Dundee, 3 May 1862, the third of the four sons and six children of Andrew Brown of Lochton House, Inchture, Perthshire, who was the grandson of James Brown of Cononsyth, pioneer of the flax-spinning industry in Dundee. His mother was Fanny Mary, daughter of Major James Wemyss of Carriston, of the Royal Scots Greys, who is the central figure in the famous painting 'Scotland for Ever!' by Lady Butler [q.v.].

Brown attended the High School, Dundee, Trinity College, Glenalmond, and University College School, London. His parents were Episcopalians but within eight years of his mother's becoming a Roman Catholic in 1873 the entire family was of the same faith. Brown's own reception in 1880 turned his thoughts from the forestry service in India to the priesthood. He went to the short-lived Catholic University established in Kensington by Cardinal Manning [q.v.], entered St. Thomas's Seminary, Hammersmith, as a student for the diocese of Westminster in 1882, and, having changed to the diocese of Southwark, was ordained priest in 1886. He was appointed curate to the Sacred Heart church, Camberwell, until in 1892 he became priest-in-charge of a new district formed by detaching part of the area between Lambeth Bridge and Battersea, Clapham and Camberwell, until then served from St. George's Cathedral. This was to become the parish of St. Anne's, Vauxhall, where Brown spent the rest of his life as parish priest, and from which the prospect of high ecclesiastical office in his native Scotland and still less the intensive bombing of the war years could not separate him. That was where his heart lay, and his unceasing perambulation of his parish made him one of the best-known personalities in South London, and inspired his zeal for social reform long before such a tendency ceased to be regarded as dangerous or at least eccentric.

To a parish priest whose children were the apple of his eye, education became an all-consuming interest. In 1896 Brown became secretary of the diocesan association set up in Southwark to administer the grants to voluntary schools. He had already stood unsuccessfully in 1894 as a Catholic candidate for the London School Board to which he was elected in 1897. Two years later his motion that the Board should seek powers to feed undernourished children was defeated, but in the end the necessary legislation was promoted and a start was made with what has become an accepted part of the school system. By the time the Board came to an end in 1904 Brown was recognized as an expert on educational questions who was frequently consulted by (Sir) Robert Morant [q.v.] over the Act of 1902 and its implementation as well as the subsequent Liberal attempts to amend it. In recognition of his work he was appointed protonotary apostolic in 1907.

Ten years later he was the obvious choice of the Holy See as apostolic visitor to Scotland at a critical period in the history of the Catholic Church in that country. The phenomenal growth of the Catholic population in the industrial areas had thrown an impossible burden on the financial resources of a Church faced with the responsibility of providing both schools and teachers. A new education bill was mooted. One solution was to absorb Catholics into a national system of education without prejudice to their principles. The times were propitious. The Catholic population had done its bit in the war effort. The Irish Nationalist Party, from its peculiar point of vantage, came to the aid of its Catholic brethren, themselves mostly of Irish origin. By the exercise of Brown's consummate skill in controlling a team which at times made heavy demands on his reserves of patience and tact, and indeed his physical endurance, the bill became the historic Education (Scotland) Act, 1918. Brown refused the offer of a Scottish archbishopric, but it gave him enormous pleasure that, by a remarkably apt coincidence, the very house in which he was born eventually became part of the first Catholic junior secondary school in Dundee. In the diocese of Southwark he was consecrated auxiliary bishop (with the titular see of Pella) in 1924. He had been vicar-general since 1904 and provost of the chapter since 1916.

Brown was a stocky, virile figure with a rugged beetle-browed face. Tough, but by no means rough, he was very far from being the proud prelate so dear to the imagination of some of his fellow countrymen. Like so many of them, too, he was austere in his habits, and knew the value of money, especially when it was not his own. The fine church of St. Anne which he built was cleared of debt in time to be consecrated in 1911 on the twenty-fifth anniversary of his ordination. He never lost his Scots accent and retained to his dying day the liveliest interest in men and affairs. He could have escaped notice at a meeting of the General Assembly. Church House, the Law Courts, and even the Old Bailey were not unknown to him. His sole publication was a long-contemplated volume of reminiscences, *Through Windows of Memory* (1946). This slim volume, introduced by Sir Shane Leslie, gives a rapid sketch of his life with its catholic interests and varied contacts. The photograph which provides the frontispiece does not belie its subject. Brown died in Southwark 16 December 1951.

[W. F. Brown, *Through Windows of Memory*, 1946; *Burke's Landed Gentry*, 1952; *Tablet*, 22 December 1951; personal knowledge.]

J. D. SCANLAN.

BROWN, WILLIAM JOHN (1894–1960), union leader and member of Parliament, was born in Battersea 13 September 1894, the second son of Joseph Morris Brown, plumber, and his wife, Rosina Spicer. He was educated at an elementary school in Margate and for three years, with a scholarship, at Sir Roger Manwood's Grammar School, Sandwich. After a few months in the City he became in 1910 a boy clerk in the Civil Service; in June 1912 he passed the assistant clerk's examination and transferred from the Savings Bank to the Office of Works. In November 1912 he caused a sensation by giving evidence on behalf of the boy clerks before the royal commission on the Civil Service. His complaint was that boy clerks were liable to discharge at eighteen and he created such an impression that the commission accepted his views and successfully recommended the abolition of the boy clerk system.

In 1919 Brown left the Civil Service to become general secretary of what became, largely through his efforts, the Civil Service Clerical Association. The notion of a unionized Civil Service was at that time by no means universally accepted in Conservative circles, and Brown fought a continuing fight with the Government, especially the Conservative Government of 1922–3.

Defeated as a Labour candidate at Uxbridge in 1922 and at West Wolverhampton in 1923 and 1924, Brown was elected for the latter constituency in 1929. He soon found himself at odds with his party, criticizing it in particular for the alleged ineffectiveness of its attack on unemployment; for a time he was in sympathy with Sir Oswald Mosley who resigned from the Government in May 1930. Brown refused the Labour whip in March 1931 but decided not to align himself with Mosley's New Party and at the election in October stood independently as a Labour candidate. He lost his seat; was defeated again in 1935; but returned in 1942 at a by-election as independent member for Rugby. Owing to the wartime party truce the official parties did not run candidates against one another. Rugby had been a Conservative seat and Labour therefore did not oppose. The National Labour organization made it markedly clear that they gave Brown no support, for over the years he had been increasingly outspoken in his criticism of the alleged tyranny of trade unions and excesses of socialist discipline. On the other hand the local Labour Party supported him. At the general election of 1945 both the Conservative and the Socialist parties ran candidates against him. Brown headed the poll with a majority of over a thousand over the Conservative. In the Parliament of 1945 independent members were few and far between and with the passing of the death sentence on the university constituencies an independent member who could win a normal constituency became something of a marked man. There was a natural interest in the speeches of one whose opinions did not fall into either of the regular party patterns, and Brown was never diffident about giving his. He was a speaker to whom words came easily and who emphasized them with an almost acrobatic abundance of gesture and grimace. When he spoke on Civil Service matters he spoke with authority. He applied to all problems healthy moral terms of reference and was always the defender of liberty against its attackers and a vigorous battler against Communists whether in Russia or in England. On such topics he was always worth hearing. But sometimes he embarked upon historical disquisitions where it was not very clear that he knew enough of his subject to justify him in so confidently giving his opinion.

After 1942 Brown resigned the general secretaryship of the Civil Service Clerical Association and became its parliamentary secretary. But his vigorous criticism of the Labour Government after 1945 was not to the liking of some of the members of the Association who attempted, as he alleged, to control his activities. He raised the matter in 1947 as a breach of privilege but his complaint was not upheld by the Committee of Privileges.

Independent of both the main parties, Brown in the 1945–50 Parliament directed the main volume of his attack upon the Socialists—if only because it was they who were in power. As a result there were many Conservatives who thought it foolish to run a Conservative candidate against him in his Rugby constituency in the 1950 election. However, in defiance of advice from the Central Office the local Conservatives insisted on doing so. The result was that on a split vote the Labour candidate won the seat. At the election of 1951 at West Fulham Brown came second to Dr. (later Baroness) Summerskill in a three-cornered fight.

Although he was never a man who took kindly to party discipline, Brown had always a great love for the House of Commons and believed firmly in the virtues of an idealized somewhat less disciplined House of Commons whose pattern was laid up in heaven and which differed somewhat from the House which he actually knew. He made himself a considerable master of procedure and wrote an interesting handbook, called *Everybody's Guide to Parliament* (1945). He was as fluent with the pen as with the tongue and wrote a number of books, mostly of a semi-autobiographical, semi-didactic nature. For his habit was to put his arguments in a personal form and there was something of the preacher in his make up. He was hostile to any challenge to fundamental moral values and he was an eloquent and edifying advocate of the copybook maxims. For a time he wrote frequently for the Beaverbrook press and later contributed a weekly column of pungent meditations on the passing scene to *Time and Tide* under the pen-name of

Diogenes. But during the last decade of his life he became known principally as a broadcaster and television performer, appearing frequently on the programme 'Free Speech'. He died at his home in Belsize Park 3 October 1960.

In 1917 Brown married Mabel, daughter of Harry Prickett, solicitors' clerk, of Anerley; they had two sons and one daughter.

[W. J. Brown, *So Far . . .*, 1943; private information; personal knowledge.]
CHRISTOPHER HOLLIS.

BRUCE, CLARENCE NAPIER, third BARON ABERDARE (1885–1957), athlete, was born in London 2 August 1885. He was the second son of Henry Campbell Bruce, later second baron, and grandson of Henry Austin Bruce, home secretary and first baron [q.v.]. His mother, Constance Mary Beckett, was a granddaughter of J. S. Copley, Lord Lyndhurst [q.v.]. Bruce was educated at Winchester, where he was in the cricket eleven and was captain of rackets in 1903 and 1904, and at New College. At Oxford he represented the university at cricket in 1907 and 1908 (when he scored 46 for the winning side) and also at golf, rackets, and tennis, at which he won the silver racket in 1907. He gained third class honours in modern history in 1908. In 1911 he was called to the bar by the Inner Temple, and in the following year married Margaret Bethune, only daughter of Adam Black. By her, who died in 1950, he had two sons and two daughters. Bruce was already a notable player of games, but the full extent of his talents did not become apparent until after the war. Between 1914 and 1919 he served with the Glamorgan Yeomanry, with the 2nd Life Guards, on the staff of the 61st division, and with the Guards Machine Gun Regiment. He retired with the rank of captain; the death in action of his elder brother in 1914 left him heir to the title.

From 1919 he began to play cricket for Middlesex, which he had represented twice in 1908. One of his best years was 192? when he scored 527 runs in nineteen appearances. On 23 June, at Nottingham his county were set 502 runs to win in the fourth innings, and achieved that total: Hendren and Bruce added 154 together 95 minutes, and Bruce finished with 103 his name; *Wisden* justly describes this one of the great matches in the history Middlesex cricket. His last game for the county was in 1929.

Bruce was a good golfer and competent at all ball games, but he excelled at the two great indoor court games, rackets and tennis. At rackets he was the amateur champion in 1922 and 1931 and was ten times winner of the doubles with different partners. His finest achievement was to become open champion of the British Isles in 1932 by defeating J. C. F. Simpson. Although the loser was the best receiver of service playing, Aberdare's service was devastating and his court craft superb. He was the singles champion of Canada in 1928 and 1930 and won the doubles in Canada and the United States (with H. W. Leatham) in the latter year.

He was tennis champion of the United States in 1930, and of England in 1932 and 1938; he also won the M.C.C. gold or silver prize every year from 1930 to 1937. Here too his superb fitness assisted him and he was a master tactician. In 1938 he defeated L. Lees, champion for five years and a younger man, in the semi-final 3–2, after being two sets down. His service was always accurate (although he eschewed the American variety) and his attack on the dedans deadly. In the final he won easily, finishing with a spectacular winning gallery shot. In France he won the Coupe de Paris six times. At doubles he had a happy knack of bringing out the best in his partners.

After his succession to the barony in 1929 he played an increasing part in public life. From 1931 to 1946 he was a member of the Miners' Welfare Committee, an appointment reflecting the long connection between his family and the South Wales coal field. He took a great interest in youth welfare and was treasurer of the National Association of Boys' Clubs in 1935 and chairman from 1943 until his death. Another lifelong interest was the Queen's Institute of District Nursing of which he became chairman in 1944. In February 1937 Oliver Stanley [q.v.] announced the creation of a new National Advisory Council on Physical Training of which Aberdare was chairman until 1939. Aberdare was an admirable choice; he was good in the chair, unruffled and modest, while his reputation brought in money and support. In a speech in 1938 he declared that his great ideal was to give everyone 'a chance of making the human body a fit instrument for the human soul'. In that year he himself was amateur tennis champion, and in 1939, at the age of forty-three and partnered by his son, he gained the final of the doubles at rackets.

In Wales he continued the family interest in the university (of which his grandfather was the first chancellor) as president of the Welsh National School of Medicine; he received an honorary LL.D. in 1953. In 1948 he became prior of the Welsh Priory of St. John of Jerusalem, and was a knight of the order which he had long aided. He spoke in the House of Lords on the subjects dear to his heart; in 1944 he twice voiced the claims of youth in the debates on the education bill, and at the end of the same year urged that youth club leaders be not forgotten in the demobilization programme. During the war of 1939–45 he served in the Home Guard; he was honorary colonel of the 77th (later renumbered 282nd) (Welsh) Heavy A.A. brigade. He was appointed C.B.E. in 1949 and promoted G.B.E. in 1954.

In 1931 Aberdare had joined the executive committee of the International Olympics. He attended the games at Los Angeles in 1932, Berlin in 1936, and after the war in London (1948), Helsinki (1952), and Melbourne (1956). In September 1957 he married, secondly, Grizelda Harriet Violet Finetta Georgiana, daughter of Dudley Francis Amelius Hervey, C.M.G.; returning with her from an Olympic meeting in Sofia, he was killed in a car accident in Yugoslavia 4 October 1957. He was succeeded by his elder son, Morys George Lyndhurst (born 1919).

With E. B. Noel, he was the author of an admirable work on *First Steps to Rackets* (1926) and he edited the Lonsdale Library volume on *Rackets, Squash Rackets, Tennis, Fives and Badminton* (1933). He contributed the notice of Peter Latham to this Supplement.

There is a portrait by Flora Lion in the National Museum of Wales, Cardiff.

[*The Times*, 5, 10, 11, and 14 October 1957; private information.]   MICHAEL MACLAGAN.

BUCHAN, CHARLES MURRAY (1891–1960), footballer and journalist, was born 22 September 1891 at Plumstead, the son of William Buchan, blacksmith at the Royal Arsenal, and his wife, Jane Murray. When playing football as a boy for Woolwich Polytechnic, and later for Plumstead, he was noticed by Arsenal, a first division club, and in 1909 he signed for them as an amateur. But after four games with the reserve side he left them because they would not meet a modest claim for 11s. expenses, and for the rest of that season he played for Northfleet in the Kent League.

Buchan was then studying to be a teacher and had no intention of becoming a professional footballer. In 1910, however, he was persuaded to join Leyton, a club in the Southern League, at £3 a week. He was quickly seen to be an inside-forward of unusual promise and in March 1911 he was transferred to Sunderland, which that year finished third in the first division. The transfer fee was £1,200, at that time a large sum for an unproved player of only nineteen. Buchan remained with Sunderland until 1925. Within a year of joining them he played for the Football League against the Scottish League, and he was an English reserve in the international at Hampden Park. In 1912–13, playing mostly at inside-right, he scored 31 goals for Sunderland when they came very close to the 'double' event of League and Cup. They won the League by four points but were beaten 1–0 by Aston Villa in the Cup final at Crystal Palace. In this season Buchan won his first international cap, scoring England's goal in a 2–1 defeat by Ireland.

In the first post-war season he combined teaching with football, and in 1920 he started a business in Sunderland as a sports outfitter. He was by now captain of the club, and in 1922–3, when they came second, his total of 30 goals was the highest in the first division. In 1924 he received the last of his six English caps when he played against Scotland in the first international at Wembley.

At the end of the 1924–5 season Buchan moved to Arsenal, where Herbert Chapman was just starting a triumphant reign as manager. The transfer arrangement was an unusual one, Sunderland being paid £2,000 plus a further £100 for each goal Buchan scored in his first season. He scored 21. He was captain of Arsenal for three years, scoring 49 goals in 102 League games. His transfer was something of a gamble since he was nearly thirty-four, but Chapman needed a man of personality and experience as a foundation for the team he was determined to build. In their many tactical discussions they evolved the Arsenal system of 'defence in depth', with a midfield link to collect the ball out of defence and initiate an attack in a couple of direct moves. In Buchan's first season Arsenal rose to second in the League, so far the highest position attained by any southern club. The next year (1927) they were in the final of the Cup, losing 1–0 to Cardiff City, and they reached the semi-final in the year after that. When Buchan retired in 1928 the foundations had been truly laid for Arsenal's remarkable success in the following decade.

Buchan himself started a new career as a journalist. For some years he had been contributing articles to newspapers, and he now became leading sports writer on the *Daily News*, later the *News Chronicle*. In 1951 he founded his own magazine, *Charles Buchan's Football Monthly*. He was also a radio commentator, and he continued to write and to broadcast until his sudden death while on holiday with his wife near Monte Carlo, 25 June 1960.

On and off the field Buchan was the ideal professional footballer. Technically he was a player of outstanding gifts. He stood over six feet, and his long legs and willowy frame gave him an awkward, even clumsy appearance. But he was so fit that he never missed more than an occasional week's football through injury. He was unsurpassable in the air, and on the ground his close dribbling and superb control were matched by a powerful and accurate shot. He would have played for England more often had the selectors not thought him too clever for the rest of the team. He thought deeply about the rights and status of the player, and by his own modest and sportsmanlike demeanour he brought dignity to his profession.

As a writer his comments were informed and kindly. Although he could be forthright when occasion demanded, he disliked sensationalism of any kind, and his readers could depend on him for expert analysis untouched by personalities or gossip. Over the air his informal approach and homely voice won him thousands of friends among a generation which had never seen him play.

In the war of 1914–18 Buchan enlisted in the Coldstream Guards. He served in France as a sergeant from 1916 to 1918, coming unharmed through the Somme, Cambrai, and Passchendaele, and winning the M.M. He was then commissioned in the Sherwood Foresters, but the war ended before he could return to the front.

As a cricketer he played in a few matches for Durham, and he was a good enough golfer to take part in the amateur championship.

In 1914 Buchan married Ellen Robson, by whom he had a son and a daughter.

[Charles Buchan, *A Lifetime in Football*, 1955; Bernard Joy, *Forward, Arsenal!*, *History of the Arsenal Football Club*, 1952.

M. M. REES

BUCHANAN, GEORGE (1890-1955), politician, was born 30 November 1890 in Naburn Street, Gorbals, then a residential suburb but later the most drab and impoverished district of Glasgow. His own experience of poverty and the influence of his parents led him to dedicate his life to the service of the poor. His father, George Buchanan, came from Kilberry, Argyllshire, a joiner by trade, a Radical in politics. His mother, Ann MacKay, was born in Creich, Sutherlandshire, in a poor croft to which her family had been driven at the 'clearances' from 'Bonnie Strath Naver'. With this background it was not surprising that they should turn to the Independent Labour Party after settling in Gorbals.

Buchanan was educated at near-by Camden Street school and afterwards at evening classes. His parents somehow contrived to send a brother and sister to the university, but savings for this purpose were not available for George. He played a percussion instrument in the local Boys' Brigade band, joined the Rechabites, played junior football, and danced. During school holidays he helped the family exchequer by taking jobs as a boy messenger, for a time with the *Scotsman* in Edinburgh. His parents apprenticed him for five years as an engineers' patternmaker. At sixteen he joined both his trade union and the Independent Labour Party. Before he was twenty he had made a reputation as a street-corner speaker. His big frame, shock of red hair, and his rugged, passionate oratory, linked closely to the daily life of the people, dominated ever-growing crowds. In 1918 he was elected to the Glasgow city council. Outside his working hours all his time was devoted to championship of the poorest among his fellow workers. He made himself a master of the regulations relating to pensions and benefits, and morning after morning at tribunals represented the disabled, the unemployed, and the sick. He was active in the United Patternmakers' union, of which he was destined to be president in 1932-48.

In 1922 Buchanan became member of Parliament for Gorbals. He was one of the group of Clydeside rebels, led by James Maxton [q.v.] who impressed but often shocked Parliament by the manner in which they urged the claims of their impoverished constituents. Buchanan was bitter in language; he cared little for parliamentary etiquette; he was several times suspended. His style of speech broke

all the traditions of the House; it was almost a personal conversation with the Speaker, so Scottish that many members could not follow him. 'Whom do you think I met on the road from Kilmarnock last nicht?', he would ask. 'Archie Henderson. Ye dinna ken Archie, Mr. Speaker, but all Gorbals ken him.' He would then tell Mr. Speaker how Archie Henderson had walked all the way from Glasgow to Kilmarnock and back again in the vain search for work.

In 1924 Buchanan married a Glasgow girl, Annie McNee. They made their home in Gorbals, among the people they knew, not in London where Buchanan always felt an alien. He would travel north each Friday, returning to Westminster on Monday. In London he shared lodgings with Maxton and the Rev. Campbell Stephen, another outspoken member of the Clydeside group. Stephen did the cooking, Maxton made the beds, and Buchanan swept the floors.

During the Labour Government of 1929-31 Buchanan was a fierce critic of Ramsay MacDonald's policy. He was incensed by the Anomalies Act which imposed restriction on unemployment benefits and by the appointment of the commission under Sir George (later Lord) May [q.v.] whose recommendations of cuts brought about the end of the Government and MacDonald's decision to head a coalition 'national' Government. The following year the I.L.P. disaffiliated from the Labour Party and, with Maxton, Stephen, and John McGovern, Buchanan formed an independent socialist group in Parliament. But he was never happy about this decision. Almost simultaneously he was elected chairman of his trade union which was affiliated to the Labour Party. He believed in the unity of the working-class movement and hoped that the split would be temporary. When under Maxton's influence the I.L.P. moved towards further isolation, he rejoined the Labour Party just before the outbreak of war in 1939.

As the Labour Party emerged from opposition to the responsibility of the prospects of renewed government, Buchanan adjusted himself increasingly to the temper of the House. He won respect by his knowledge of pension problems. In 1934 he had been offered a post as a member of the statutory committee established by the new Unemployment Act. The salary was £2,000 a year and he was a poor man; but he had refused the offer because he did not wish to desert the people of Gorbals or his trade-union and political activities. During the war he concentrated on what he termed 'the home front', claiming the status for workers which he felt their contribution to the national effort deserved. With the Labour victory at the end of the war came the first invitations to accept office. C. R. (later Earl) Attlee was astonished when Buchanan preferred the post of joint under-secretary for Scotland to that of minister of national insurance. Buchanan had proved himself a master of the complexities and anomalies of insurance benefits, but his impelling thought now was the need to sweep away the appalling slum conditions of Gorbals, and he initiated rehousing whilst at the Scottish Office. Two years later (1947) he became minister of pensions and won general recognition for the kindliness and wisdom with which he directed administration. He brought to the problem of cases of hardship among ex-servicemen and women all the sympathy which he had shown for the destitute of Gorbals.

In 1948 the 'rebel' of Gorbals was sworn of the Privy Council, but his first concern was still for the poor and a few months later he was appointed chairman of the newly created National Assistance Board. This necessitated his resignation from the House of Commons; he did so to serve those to whom he had dedicated all his endeavours: the poorest of the population. During the five years' term of his chairmanship he initiated the Board in the spirit of human sympathy which set the tradition of its later administration. When his period of office ended in 1953 he continued to serve as a member of the Board. He died in Glasgow 28 June 1955. He had no children. What his successor, Sir Geoffrey Hutchinson, said of him may be accepted as a portrait of his life: 'He has left behind him at the National Assistance Board an immense tribute to his public service, kindliness, and generosity of temperament, which have made him loved by all.'

[Private information; personal knowledge.]
                                   BROCKWAY.

BUCHANAN, WALTER JOHN (JACK) (1890-1957), actor and theatre manager, was born 2 April 1890 at Helensburgh, near Glasgow, the son of Walter John Buchanan, auctioneer, and his wife, Patricia Purves McWatt. Educated at Glasgow Academy, he spoke of becoming a barrister, but his heart was set on the

stage from the first, and particularly he saw himself as a comedian, although he feared his height might militate against this ambition.

After a brief spell in the family business, Buchanan appeared first on the professional stage at the Edinburgh Empire in 1911, billed as 'Chump Buchanan, patter comedian', 'Chump' being a sobriquet from his schooldays. Northern provincial music-halls at this period were a tough training-ground for the stage aspirant, and in his later years of prosperity Buchanan would relate his hard experiences 'on the halls' when his efforts to entertain were vociferously rejected. But in his own words, something personal came through at last when he obtained material which suited him.

On 7 September 1912 he made his first appearance in London, at the Apollo Theatre, in a comic opera called The Grass Widows, and during 1913 and 1914 he appeared and understudied in revues at the Empire Theatre, Leicester Square. Rejected by the army—at no time in his life was his health robust—during 1915 and 1916 he came into prominence playing the George Grossmith [q.v.] part on tour in To-night's the Night; and in 1917 he succeeded Jack Hulbert, acting, singing, and dancing in the revue Bubbly presented by André Charlot [q.v.] at the Comedy Theatre. Other wartime revues followed and Jack Buchanan soon established himself on the west-end light musical stage as a comedian of talent and promise.

In October 1921 he enhanced his reputation in another Charlot revue, A to Z, which he played the lead, produced the sketches, and staged the musical numbers. In December 1922 he appeared for the first time under his own management Battling Butler at the New Oxford Theatre and at the end of the following year went to America, opening in New York at the Times Square Theatre (with Gertrude Lawrence [q.v.] and Beatrice Lillie) André Charlot's Revue of 1924 in which scored a great personal success. This was the first of many visits to New York, a he remained throughout his subsequent career as acceptable to audiences there in Great Britain.

In May 1924 came Toni at the Shaftesbury Theatre, London, and thenceforth regularly long intervals until 1943 he was to present, produce, and play the leading part in a succession of musical comedies through all of which he sang and danced and joked his nonchalant way with seemingly lazy but most accomplished grace. Everything he did on the stage bore the stamp of his personality and was done with an effect of consummate ease, yet without casualness. The hunched shoulders, the sidelong smile, the husky audible diseur's voice, the quick light step across the stage on the ball of his feet, and the loose lithe limbs weaving themselves into easy rhythmical patterns in his step-dances, all were characteristic. Of the long series mention may be made of *Sunny* (1926), *That's a Good Girl* (1928), and *Stand up and Sing* (of which he was part-author, 1931), all at the Hippodrome.

There was some truth in the statement made after his death that Buchanan was the last of the 'Knuts'. With dark wavy hair, fine eyes, and a tip-tilted nose, he was attractive rather than good-looking, but his very tall slim figure well set off the faultless cut of his clothes, and he was re-garded as something of an *arbiter elegan-iarum* by a generation which admired, if it could not emulate, the sartorial perfec-tion of the white tie, white waistcoat, and tails which were his stage emblem. (He was the first to adopt, *circa* 1924, the later prevailing fashion of a double-breasted dinner jacket.) But if he remained the dandy, his innate modesty and humour steadfastly resisted his becoming at any time a matinée idol, a role which some of his more fervent admirers would have assigned him. He was first billed as a comedian, and as a comedian he himself would have preferred to remain and be remembered. He used to say that nature gave him long legs and a croak, but the long legs enhanced the pleasure of watch-ing the timing and gymnastic of his tap-dancing, and the croak was curiously tune-ful. With his quiet unforced technique, no one knew better how to put across the words and music of a song with charm and effect.

In June 1944 at the Savoy Theatre Buchanan broke new ground when he appeared in a straight part, that of Lord Dilling in an Edwardian version of *The Last of Mrs. Cheyney* by Frederick Lons-dale [q.v.]. The light charm of Buchanan's Dilling bore little relation to the amoral character which Lonsdale drew and Sir Gerald du Maurier [q.v.] had portrayed in 1925, but the performance confirmed what many had long suspected, that Buchanan as a comedy actor of the first rank, with split-second sense in the handling of lines, and an unaffected ease of manner. These qualities were borne out in subse-quent straight parts which he played dur-ing the last years of his career.

In 1951 on the sudden death of Ivor Novello [q.v.] Buchanan succeeded to the part of Nikki, written by Novello for his own production of *King's Rhapsody* at the Palace Theatre. This was a courageous and as it proved fully justified venture, but the role of romantic hero was not per-haps entirely congenial to his personality.

Buchanan acted fairly regularly in films after 1925, many of them rather makeshift versions of his musical comedy successes. Special mention should be made of *Monte Carlo* (1931) directed by Ernst Lubitsch; *Good Night, Vienna* (1932); *Break the News* (1938), directed by René Clair, in which he appeared with Maurice Chevalier; *The Band Waggon* (1954), in which, besides singing and dancing with Fred Astaire, he caricatured the actor-manager-producer in the grand manner of a former day; and finally, *The Diary of Major Thompson*, re-leased after his death, a film adaptation of Pierre Daninos's best-seller, in which he acceptably portrayed the French concep-tion of the conventional Englishman.

Among his fellow players Buchanan's encouragement of talent, his quixotic generosity, and his loyalty became some-thing of a theatrical legend. Throughout most of his career he had extensive theatre business interests. He financed the build-ing of the Leicester Square Theatre, and at the time of his death had control of the Garrick Theatre and the King's Theatre, Hammersmith. He was also an early speculator in television.

In 1915 Buchanan married an actress vocalist, Drageva, daughter of the late Drago Dragev Sava, merchant. The mar-riage was dissolved. In 1949 he married Susan Bassett, of Maryland and New York. There were no children. He died in London 20 October 1957.

There were drawings of Buchanan in *Punch* by W. K. Haselden (21 May 1924), J. H. Dowd (1 June 1938), and G. L. Stampa (24 October 1945).

[*The Times*, 21 October 1957; private in-formation; personal knowledge.]

D. PEPYS WHITELEY.

BUCK, SIR PETER HENRY (1880–1951), ethnologist and politician, often known by his Maori name, Te Rangi Hiroa, was born at Urenui in the province of Taranaki, New Zealand, 15 August 1880. He was the son of an Irish father, William Henry Buck, of Galway, and a Maori mother, Rina. His mother died when he was very young and he was brought up by Ngarongo-ki-tua, a chieftainess of the Ngati-Mutunga tribe of North Taranaki. Educated at Urenui School, Te Aute College, and Otago Medical School, he was both university and amateur long jump champion of New Zealand in 1904. His first post after qualifying in that year was as house surgeon at Dunedin Hospital. In the following year he was appointed a medical officer of health to the Maoris and so began his attachment in a direct capacity to the Maori people which was to last until 1927. In 1909 he was elected to Parliament and in 1912 for a brief period he was the representative of the Maori race in the New Zealand Cabinet.

In 1914 Buck joined the New Zealand expeditionary force as a medical officer; he served in Egypt, France, Belgium, Malta, and at Gallipoli; commanded a Maori battalion; was appointed to the D.S.O. (1917), and twice mentioned in dispatches. From 1919 to 1927 he was director of Maori hygiene, his last medical post and his last real connection with the people among whom he had been brought up. With his professional reputation at its highest peak in his own country, he looked away from it and outside New Zealand, but at the time with the intention of returning. Apart from one or two short visits he never did return. From 1927 until the end of his life he was first a lecturer at the Bernice Pouahi Bishop Museum in Hawaii which contains the finest collection of Pacific material in the world; from 1932 visiting professor of anthropology at Yale University; and from 1936 until his death director of the Bishop Museum.

In the last twenty years of his life Buck became known the world over as the authority on Polynesian material culture, a very wide and diversified subject spread over thousands of sea miles. His interest had been stimulated by early associations with two other eminent Maori politicians, Sir Apirana Ngata and Sir Maui Pomare. The three of them had felt that it was time for Maoris to contribute to the scientific work on their own race, to which previously only Europeans had devoted time and energy. Pomare adopted mythology, Ngata poetry, and Buck the physical and material culture of his people. It was as a result of their consortium that Buck's first ethnological paper, 'The Maori Art of Weaving' (Dominion Museum, 1908), was published. This was later elaborated

in *Evolution of Maori Clothing* (Polynesian Society, 1926), by which time Buck had begun to orientate his research outside his own people, the better to trace their origins in, or connections with, the Polynesia beyond the horizon. In 1927 he brought out *The Material Culture of the Cook Islands (Aitutaki)* (Board of Maori Ethnological Research).

Once he had left New Zealand there followed in rapid succession works of the highest scientific value. Under the auspices of the Bishop Museum he published works on Samoan (1930) and Kapingamarangi (1947) material culture; on the ethnology of Tongareva (1932), of Manihiki and Rakahanga (1932), and of Mangareva (1938); on the arts and crafts of the Cook Islands (1944) and of Hawaii (1957); on Mangaian Society (1934) and on *Explorers of the Pacific* (1953). Other works included *Regional Diversity in the Elaboration of Sorcery in Polynesia* (Yale, 1936), *Vikings of the Sunrise* (U.S.A., 1938), *Anthropology and Religion* (Yale, 1939), *Introduction to Polynesian Anthropology* (1945), *The Coming of the Maori* (New Zealand Department of Internal Affairs, 1949), and also many papers to learned societies.

In all these the keen, analytical quality of mind was conspicuous. Buck eschewed conjecture which he could not support at least most of the way with positive fact. But he was not rigid and unimaginative. As the first ethnologist to have the opportunity to survey the whole of Polynesia with thoroughness and skilled assistance he was able to draw conclusions on a broad scale. Nobody had a wider knowledge in so much detail of the scattered pockets of Polynesian culture; the only areas in which he had not carried out field research were the Tongan and Lau groups. It enabled him, as in *Vikings of the Sunrise*, to communicate in popular form an unparalleled collation of facts and findings on Polynesian voyages, customs, and the peopling of the island groups. The very range of his profound studies, the sweep of vision, covered thousands of Pacific miles as far north as Hawaii and as far south as New Zealand. As he himself said, he was born in South Polynesia, lived much of the time in North Polynesia, and did the bulk of his field work in West and East Polynesia, an unrivalled breadth of scientific experience of that part of Oceania. Further, as he himself freely stated, his mixed blood, far from retarding him afforded perspective, breadth of contact, energy, and ambition. Even so, as a half aste child, Buck had to study intensively to know Maori custom so well and to become so rich in expressing the language. Binominal and bilingual, he readily claimed that his mother's blood enabled him to appreciate the Polynesian culture while his father's speech enabled him to interpret it to the world.

There was widespread recognition of his outstanding ethnological talent. His honorary degrees included the D.Sc. (New Zealand, Yale, and Rochester) and D.Litt. (Hawaii). The Royal Anthropological Institute awarded him the Rivers memorial medal for his cultural and physical anthropological work. He was the first Maori to be a fellow of the Royal Society of New Zealand. In 1946 he was appointed K.C.M.G. on the nomination of the New Zealand Government; and from the King of Sweden he received the Royal Order of the North Star.

With all his distinction Buck was reflective, modest, and genial. Like most of his race, he was a powerful orator and physically sturdy. He had a considerable capacity for work and application. The Bishop Museum's fame had been long established before his directorship, but in guiding its distinguished research he enriched it with his own indigenous stature and productivity, his prolific and clearly reasoned probings into the problems of Polynesia. At first doubtful about leaving the Maori people, he ultimately acknowledged that he could have made his contribution to their history only by leaving them.

In 1905 Buck married Margaret Wilson Milton, a chieftainess of the Ngapuhi tribe and widow of a political colleague. They had no children. He died in Honolulu December 1951. A painting by Madge Tennant and a drawing by Eleanor Beckman are in the Bishop Museum.

[Private information; personal knowledge.]
                    PHILIP SNOW.

BURNETT, SIR ROBERT LINDSAY (1887–1959), admiral, was born at Old Deer, Aberdeenshire, 22 July 1887, the fourth son of John Alexander Burnett, of Kemnay, Aberdeenshire, by his wife, Charlotte Susan, daughter of Arthur Forbes Gordon, of Rayne, Aberdeenshire. Sir Charles Burnett [q.v.] was an elder brother. At the early age of seven he announced his intention of joining the navy, and after education at Bedford school and Eastman's he entered the Britannia in 1903. His academic progress was undistinguished, but he showed great promise as an all-round athlete, and after reaching the rank of lieutenant in 1910 he qualified as a physical training instructor. In the ensuing eight years he served mainly in small ships, saw action in the Heligoland Bight and at the Dogger Bank engagement, gained his first command (a torpedo boat) in 1915, and subsequently went on to command destroyers with the Grand Fleet until 1918.

With subsequently only one break of two years in command of a sloop on the South Africa station, Burnett was continually employed until 1928 in physical training appointments, being promoted commander in 1923 while acting as secretary to the sports control board. He did much in this period towards reorganizing the physical training branch of the navy. He himself also won the sabre championship at the Royal Tournament and became a qualified referee for association and rugby football, hockey, water polo, and boxing. In addition, he developed his admirable bent as a producer of amateur theatricals.

Burnett gained his second selective promotion, to captain, in December 1930 at the conclusion of a successful commission as executive officer of the *Rodney*. In the ensuing eleven years in that rank he commanded a destroyer flotilla on the China station, did two years as the director of physical training and sports, commanded the cruiser flagship of the South African squadron, and finally was appointed commodore of the Royal Naval Barracks at Chatham in 1939, where he had the arduous task of mobilizing the personnel of the east country manning port for war.

Although Burnett himself had more than once in his time as a captain expressed surprise at his progressive promotions, his superiors fully appreciated his zeal, energy, and ability, and after only eighteen months at Chatham he was specially promoted to the acting rank of rear-admiral in November 1940 (confirmed two months later) on appointment as flag officer of the Home Fleet minelaying squadron engaged on the hazardous task of laying the deep minefield in northern waters. On completion of this task in 1942 he became flag officer, Home Fleet destroyer flotillas, and a year later flag officer, tenth cruiser squadron, continuing in this appointment on promotion to vice-admiral (1943) until he left the Fleet in mid-1944 to become the commander-in-chief, South Atlantic, responsible for the security of the sea route round the Cape.

It was especially during those fateful years 1941 to 1944 when a hard-pressed Royal Navy faced its greatest challenge that Burnett rendered outstanding service and played a leading part in the saga of the Arctic convoys, when the enemy could choose its own time and place at which to bring superior force to bear upon the lifeline to Russia. These circumstances called for the physical endurance, capable leadership, and readiness to fight back whatever the odds which Burnett notably possessed. His indomitable spirit and simple philosophy of immediate aggressive tactics inspired others and gained for him the trust and loyalty of those who served under him in the course of these exhausting operations to reach North Russia and return.

There were occasions on which his determination was particularly put to the test. In September 1942 he fought a convoy of forty ships through in the face of four days of sustained submarine and massed air attack for a loss of thirteen merchantmen, and then saw the returning empty convoy back. On New Year's Eve 1942, in the Barents Sea, his covering force of two cruisers finally managed to reach another convoy with such an offensive impact that the greatly superior enemy surface force retired in disorder and the merchant ships reached port unscathed. On Boxing Day a year later, off North Cape, again in midwinter, he so skilfully handled his covering force of three cruisers that the *Scharnhorst* was twice forced to turn back from the convoy without achieving any success, and was finally delivered up to destruction by the commander-in-chief's flagship.

Burnett was promoted admiral in 1946 and in the following year took up his last appointment, the Plymouth command, which he held for three years, being placed on the retired list in May 1950. He was subsequently chairman of the White Fish Authority for four years.

Throughout his service Burnett was sustained by a firm religious belief from which he got much help and comfort, and he expected others to try and measure up to his own high moral standards and example of officer-like behaviour and appearance. He loved the navy, was easily moved to emotion, and was a first-class speaker in a manner which carried conviction.

He died suddenly in London 2 July 1959, his wife, Ethel Constance, the daughter of R. H. Shaw, whom he married in 1915, surviving him. They had no children.

During his career he was successively appointed O.B.E. (1925), C.B. (1942), to the D.S.O. (1943), K.B.E. (1944), K.C.B. and C. St. J. (1945), and G.B.E. (1950). He received an honorary LL.D. from Aberdeen (1944) and high orders from the Soviet Union, Greece, and the Netherlands.

His portrait in oils by Edward Roworth is in the possession of the National Maritime Museum, Greenwich, and there is a pastel by William Dring in the Imperial War Museum.

[S. W. Roskill, (Official History) *The War at Sea, 1939–45*, 3 vols., 1954–61; private information; personal knowledge.]

A. W. CLARKE

BURNETT-STUART, SIR JOHN THEODOSIUS (1875–1958), general, was born in Cirencester 14 March 1875, the eldest of four sons of Eustace Robertson Burnett-Stuart, of Dens and Crichie, county Aberdeen, and his wife, Carlotta Jane, daughter of J. Lambert, of Cottingham, Yorkshire. Educated at Repton and the Royal Military College, Sandhurst, he received his commission in the Rifle Brigade in 1895 and served with the Tochi Field Force on the North-West Frontier of India (1897–8) and then in the South African war (1899–1902), where he earned a mention in dispatches and was appointed to the D.S.O. Subsequently, as a captain he served with the 4th battalion of his regiment in Egypt, and graduated at the Staff College in 1904. He was then posted to the War Office in the directorate of military operations, and in 1910 was seconded to the New Zealand military forces as director of organization. Returning home in 1912 he was appointed instructor G.S.O. 2 at the Staff College, Camberley from September 1913 to 4 August 1914, the last course before war broke out.

After holding several staff appointments in France he was promoted brigadier-general and made B.G.G.S. of VII Corps under Sir Thomas Snow [q.v.] in February 1916. In the Cambrai battle of November 1917 the VII Corps was on the flank of the main attack and played no part in the assault. But Burnett-Stuart gave repeated warnings that a German counter-offensive was being mounted—warnings which were unfortunately disregarded by the higher command. Thus the German counter stroke attained a great initial surprise and success, penetrating deeply into the sector held by the VII Corps, but was eventually brought to a halt by the well-directed defence.

In December 1917 Burnett-Stuart was promoted major-general and made deputy adjutant-general at G.H.Q., a post which he held until the end of the war. In 1920 he was sent to India to command the Madras district, and thus had to deal with the Malabar rising of 1921, but in 1922 he was brought back to fill the key post of director of military operations and intelligence in the War Office.

In 1926 he was given command of the 3rd division in the Southern Command, and A. P. (later Earl) Wavell [q.v.] was selected as his G.S.O. 1. In 1927 the first Experimental Mechanized Force was assembled on Salisbury Plain and placed under the higher direction of Burnett-Stuart. He criticized the motley components of the force and pointed out that the infantry would not be capable of keeping pace with the rest of the force in battle unless they were mounted in armoured cross-country vehicles. He also urged that 'enthusiastic experts and visionaries' should be brought in to aid in the new experiments, saying: it doesn't matter how wild their views are if only they have a touch of the divine fire. will supply the common sense of advanced middle age.'

Unfortunately he did not fill his own prescription, and had an early disagreement with Colonel (later Major-General) J. F. C. Fuller who had been chosen to command the new force. This led to the appointment of a new commander who was much less progressive, and Burnett-Stuart himself came to be increasingly disappointed with the methods by which the force was trained.

When on the staff in France he had been very sceptical about the value of tanks, but in the post-war years he changed his views, although still inclined to be excessively critical of their defects and variable in his views. On the other hand he also failed to see eye to eye with his commander-in-chief, Sir Archibald Montgomery-Massingberd [q.v.], who was much more conservative.

From 1931 to 1934 Burnett-Stuart commanded the British troops in Egypt and there became a supporter and advocate of the possibilities of using mechanized forces in desert warfare. He was promoted general in 1934 and in that year he returned home to the Southern Command, holding that post until April 1938 when he was succeeded by his former staff officer, Wavell. That was Burnett-Stuart's last appointment before retirement, but he had been very near to the highest appointment in the army. When Montgomery-Massingberd retired in April 1936 Burnett-Stuart was a leading and certainly the most brilliant candidate for the succession. But he had clashed too often with Montgomery-Massingberd to have a chance of being recommended as his successor by the outgoing chief of the imperial general staff.

'Jock' Stuart, as he was generally known in the army, was a man of sparkling mind, lively imagination, and long if variable vision. He had an impish turn of humour, which handicapped his progress but together with his informality of manner made him much beloved by his subordinates. Although he could be devastating in criticism and witticism, he was remarkably free from malice. He was appointed C.B. (1917), K.C.B. (1932), and G.C.B. (1937), C.M.G. (1916), and K.B.E. (1923).

In 1904 he married Nina, only daughter of Major A. A. C. Hibbert Nelson; they had one son and two daughters. He died at Avington Park near Winchester 6 October 1958. A portrait by Dennis Styles is in the possession of the family.

[B. H. Liddell Hart, *The Tanks*, vol. i, 1959; personal knowledge.]

B. H. LIDDELL HART.

BURRELL, SIR WILLIAM (1861–1958), art collector, was born in Glasgow 9 July 1861, the third son of William Burrell, a shipowner, and his wife, Isabella Duncan Guthrie, and grandson of George Burrell, the founder of the shipping firm later known as Burrell & Son which Burrell joined at the age of fifteen. In 1877 one of the firm's ships salvaged Cleopatra's Needle which had been lost in the Bay of Biscay on its passage to England. For many years Burrell managed the family business in conjunction with his eldest brother, and the firm greatly prospered under his vigorous direction, reaching its peak activity in 1915 when it owned thirty ships all of over four thousand gross tonnage. Burrell, however, determined to devote the remainder of his long life to art and by 1917, when he was fifty-six, almost the entire fleet had been sold.

Burrell's interest in art had shown itself, he used to recall, as a boy when, to his father's annoyance, he had used his pocket money to buy not a cricket bat but a picture. Realizing that it was not very good he had later sold it to buy a better one. By 1901 he was already the owner of a considerable collection, not only of pictures (including works by Géricault, Daumier, and Manet), but of tapestries, stained-glass, Iranian carpets, furniture, metalwork, and carvings in wood and ivory. In that year he lent over 160 works of art to the International Exhibition in Glasgow for which he was an active committee member.

At this time his interests were by no means confined to shipping and art. He served in the corporation of Glasgow as a representative of the tenth ward (1899–1906) and became convener of a sub-committee on uninhabitable houses, back lands, and underground dwellings, retiring, it is said, because the policy of slum clearance he advocated was not considered acceptable. Until 1906 he also acted as consul at Glasgow for Austria-Hungary.

In 1916 Burrell acquired Hutton Castle near Berwick-on-Tweed, previously the home of Lord Tweedmouth who had largely rebuilt and added to the ancient castle. Burrell made further additions to the structure and entirely remodelled the interior. He and his wife went to reside there about ten years later, by which time the castle was sumptuously furnished throughout with works of art, many of which were built into the fabric of the rooms. As the collection continued to grow it soon outstripped the accommodation available in the castle and for many years much of it was widely dispersed on loan to many different art galleries, museums, and cathedrals, including the national galleries of Scotland, England, and Wales. In 1925 Burrell presented over sixty paintings and drawings to the Glasgow Art Gallery, and for several years a large number of his pictures were on loan to the Tate Gallery. Donations were also made to other galleries.

The great collection which Burrell presented to the city of Glasgow in 1944, and to which he added lavishly every year until the end of his life, may be summarized under the following heads: (1) the art of ancient civilizations, including Sumerian, Egyptian, Greek, and Roman antiquities; (2) oriental art of the Far and Near East including Chinese pottery, bronzes, and jades, and Iranian carpets, pottery, and metalwork; (3) European art of the medieval and post-medieval periods including tapestries, stained-glass, furniture, stone, wood, and ivory carvings,

embroideries and lace, pottery, arms and armour, glassware, treen, silver and metalware; (4) between seven and eight hundred paintings, drawings, and engravings, chiefly by European artists of the fifteenth to the nineteenth centuries; the collection also includes the largest single assemblage of works (132) by Joseph Crawhall (1861–1913), a large number of drawings by Phil May [q.v.], and a quantity of Japanese prints.

Burrell's most abiding interest was probably centred in the art of the later Middle Ages and Renaissance, and the collection of Franco-Flemish, German, Swiss, and English tapestries of the fourteenth to sixteenth centuries has been considered the finest of its kind, while that of English, French, German, Dutch, and Swiss stained and painted glass of the twelfth to seventeenth centuries is ever more extensive and hardly less remarkable. Largest of all is the collection of Chinese pottery and porcelain which comprises a magnificent range of wares dating from the earliest known neolithic vessel to the brilliantly enamelled vessels and figures of the reign of K'ang Hsi (1662–1722). The furniture, silver, and needlework is chiefly English of the sixteenth and seventeenth centuries.

Beginning in 1911 the twenty-eight notebooks in which Burrell recorded his acquisitions and payments continue in unbroken sequence until a few months prior to his death. They show that for almost half a century he was spending on an average at least £20,000 a year on acquiring works of art. After 6 April 1944 when the collection as it then stood became the property of Glasgow, he continued to acquire on an equally grand or even grander scale. The year 1948, when he spent over £60,000, probably represents his highest expenditure in any one year with the exception of 1936 when he spent almost £80,000.

To his great gift to Glasgow Burrell added the sum of £450,000 to build a new museum to house the collection in an area of the Scottish countryside not less than sixteen miles from the centre of the city and within four miles of Killearn. This condition proved difficult to honour, and apart from the selections on permanent or changing display in the municipal art gallery and museum at Kelvingrove, the collection remained in store. The exhibition of the tapestries and other textiles in Glasgow is precluded by their susceptibility to damage in polluted air. But

966 Pollok House and Estate on the
outhern outskirts of the city were pre-
ented to Glasgow, and it was proposed to
rect a museum for the Burrell Collection
n the estate.

Like many wealthy men, Burrell was of
eserved character, and in the midst of the
eautiful objects which filled his home,
e led a comparatively frugal existence.
tarting as a private collector, he became,
uring thirty or more years, a collector for
osterity rather than for himself, but in
oite of its size he always preserved a keen
itellectual and artistic interest in his col-
ction, about which he had read widely
nd for the details of which he had an
xcellent memory. By nature he was
early attracted by vigour of form and
olour rather than by elegance, and as a
onsequence the collection is rich in works
? the sixteenth and seventeenth cen-
iries, but deficient in those of the eigh-
enth. Numbering about eight thousand
ojects and valued at almost two million
ounds, the collection was probably one of
ie largest ever assembled by one man,
id certainly the largest given to a
inicipality.

For many years Burrell was a trustee of
e Tate Gallery and from 1923 to 1946 of
e National Gallery of Scotland. He was
ighted in 1927 for his services to art;
eived the freedom of the city of Glas-
w in 1944, and the St. Mungo prize in
46.

In 1901 Burrell married Constance Mary
ockhart (died 1961), daughter of James
ockhart Mitchell, merchant; they had
e daughter. He died at Hutton Castle 29
arch 1958.

[The Times and Glasgow Herald, 31 March
58; D. S. Leslie, Notes on Hutton Parish,
34; private information; personal know-
ge.]   W. WELLS.

JRROWS,   CHRISTINE   MARY
JIZABETH (1872–1959), principal suc-
sively of St. Hilda's Hall (later College)
l the Oxford Home-Students (later St.
ne's College), was born in Chipping
rton, Oxfordshire, 4 January 1872, the
y and posthumous child of Henry
rker Burrows, a partner in the firm of
agton's Breweries, Maidenhead, and of
wife, Esther Elizabeth Bliss. Her child-
od was spent among her Bliss relations
family long connected with the wool-
industry of Chipping Norton. Educated
t at Cheltenham Ladies' College, under
redoubtable foundress, Dorothea Beale
.], she proceeded in 1891 to Lady

Margaret Hall, Oxford, to read modern
history. At the end of her second year she
was summoned to assist her mother, just
appointed principal of St. Hilda's Hall, a
new foundation conceived by Miss Beale
as an Oxford extension of Cheltenham
College.

Though Miss Burrows always preserved
a warm affection for the first of her three
Oxford 'colleges' and for its brilliant head,
Dame Elizabeth Wordsworth [q.v.], it was
to St. Hilda's that, from the date of her
migration, she gave her fullest devotion.
As 'senior student', despite the claims of
her own studies, she was of the greatest
service to her mother, who was new to
Oxford traditions. In 1894 she obtained a
second class and was appointed tutor in
modern history and in 1896 she became
vice-principal of the Hall. It was due to
her ability, as both teacher and administrator, that St. Hilda's—for some time
small in numbers—was before long accepted on equal terms among the other
women's foundations. In 1910 she succeeded her mother as principal, and
directed the fortunes of St. Hilda's
through a period of steady growth and
distinction—set back by the war of 1914–
18 but sharing in the general 'enfranchise-
ment' of women which followed. At school
and college she had come under the
influence of pioneers in women's education and of notable men teachers who gave
time to set the new movement on its way.
Her generation produced many of the
tutors and administrators who guided
women's education until the final granting
of Oxford degrees to women in 1920.

In July 1919, however, she retired from
St. Hilda's in order to live with her
mother, whose health was failing. But in
1921 she resumed academic work as principal of the Oxford Home-Students—a post
which could be combined with residence in
her own home with Mrs. Burrows. To this
new and exacting work she gave the utmost of her mature powers. The Society of
Oxford Home-Students had been fostered
from small beginnings by its first principal,
Mrs. Bertha Johnson. It was large in
numbers, vital in spirit, proud of, if somewhat sensitive about, its own peculiarities.
It had no real constitution, and no real
buildings—the students living mainly in
their own homes or in other private
houses. It was poor financially, and had
no regular system of payment for its
tutors. Shortly after the admission of
women to the university, a delegacy for
home-students was set up, including *ex*

163

officio the vice-chancellor, the proctors, and the principal, who thus acquired full university status. (The degree of M.A. was also conferred upon her by decree.) Thanks to prolonged effort on the part of this delegacy, both the financial and the educational sides of the Society were placed on a more secure basis. The building-up of a strong tutorial staff with definite powers and duties owed much to Miss Burrows's personal experience and initiative.

Perhaps the most striking features of her principalship were her strong interest in study and teaching and her pastoral care for individuals. Skill, humour, and patience were required to handle the new relation of girl undergraduates to the discipline of the proctors—the latter almost nervously vigilant over the women whose quiet 'coexistence' had been ignored by the university until it admitted them to full membership. If this discipline was sometimes irksome to high-spirited post-war young women, its acceptance was assured by the kindness and good sense with which it was administered by Miss Burrows; while every year brought out more clearly her own high standard of life and her grasp of the principles which should govern women in the new careers opening before them.

The eight years of her second principalship were thus not as creative as those at St. Hilda's. It was not pioneer work which was needed, but the capacity to adapt and consolidate. The whole was quiet and unspectacular, with one notable exception. In 1928 came the offer of the benefaction which has since contributed to the emergence of the Society into St. Anne's College. Made at first rather fumblingly by a generous but inexperienced benefactress (Mrs. Amy Hartland), the offer called for tact and courtesy on the part of the beneficiaries. In this Miss Burrows played a valuable part, although the moment for action had not arrived when the increasing pull of family duty caused her to tender her resignation in 1929.

Notable as having twice been a college principal and having twice resigned for purely unselfish reasons, Christine Burrows was even more notable to her friends for her tireless kindness and courtesy and for her life of humility, faith, and sheer goodness. She continued to live in Oxford for the last thirty years of her life, quietly devoting herself to movements for the development of women's powers and usefulness. A member of the Archbishops' commission on the place of women in the

Church, she signed the report but neve wavered in the hope that the ordination o women would come in due time. She wa an active member of the English-Speakin Union and of the Oxford branch of th British Federation of University Women and was an incomparable guide to Oxford delighting to explain its history an treasures to visitors from overseas an especially to soldiers in wartime. She wa an honorary fellow of both St. Hilda's an St. Anne's, and gave faithful service to th senior members' associations of St. Hilda and Cheltenham colleges, besides keepin in touch personally with large numbers (ex-pupils and students. She contribute a full and careful article on St. Hilda College to the *Victoria County History* Oxfordshire (vol. iii, 1954).

Christine Burrows died in Oxford September 1959. A crayon drawing b Leslie Brooke (1919) and an oil-portra by Catherine Ouless (1928) are possesse by St. Hilda's and St. Anne's owns chalk portrait by Jane de Glehn (1929).

[*The Times*, 11 September 1959; *St. Hild College Chronicle*, 1959–60; *The Ship* (Ye Book of St. Anne's College), 1959; R. Butler, *History of St. Anne's College*, 195 personal knowledge.]   RUTH F. BUTLE

BURTON, SIR MONTAGUE MAURIC (1885–1952), multiple tailor, was born Jewish parentage, 15 August 1885, Kurkel, Lithuania, the only son of Charl Judah Burton, bookseller, by his wi Rachel Edith Ashe. Having received early education in the country of his birt he came alone to England in 1900, t proud possessor of £100, given to him a wealthy aunt. Soon after his arrival took to the road as a commercial travell He was later employed as a salesman a tailor's shop and, in 1903, at t early age of eighteen, he commenc business on his own account as a gene outfitter in Chesterfield where he trad as the Castle Clothing Co. in the sale men's, women's, and children's wear.

Burton was a man of immense ener and great imagination which he so turned to the creation of what was to come the largest men's clothing organi tion in the world. His primary aim v to attract the masses by offering th well-made clothes of good quality at cheapest possible prices and he caus something of a sensation by opening number of men's tailor shops in the no of England—there were five by 191 where suits or overcoats made to meas were all sold at the fixed price of 30s. His headquarters were in Sheffield, to which orders from the other four shops were posted; every Sunday Burton took the orders to Leeds where he bought the cloth and linings and arranged for one of the many master tailors there to make up the garments. In order to reduce the cost of making the clothes he decided to become his own master tailor and in 1913 acquired his first factory where he employed approximately fifty workers. In the next two years he made enormous strides and by 1915 he had opened a new factory in Leeds where he employed five hundred people.

The war years saw most of the production harnessed to the manufacture of uniforms but by 1920 Burton had so reestablished his business that he had opened four additional factories making clothes for his retail shops which by this time numbered no fewer than two hundred. He decided that the time had come to eliminate the middle man and buy yarn direct from the spinner and make his own arrangements to have it woven to his designs. Some years later his mills not only made a great deal of cloth, but linings, facings, and buttons were also manufactured on his own premises. When the business became a public company in 1929 with a capital of four million pounds, the number of shops had grown to four hundred. By 1939 the company was employing some twenty thousand men and women in the factories and an additional four thousand in the retail shops. At the time of his death the number of shops had grown to over six hundred and he was well on the way to his life's ambition of having a thousand Burton shops in Great Britain. A quarter of all the uniforms provided in this country in the war of 1939–45 were made by his company, as were a third of the clothes issued on demobilization.

Although Burton constantly sought new ways of reducing expenses he always maintained that low wages were a false economy and from 1921 he was able to claim that he paid the highest wages in the tailoring trade in Europe. He insisted on working conditions of the highest possible standard. When he entered the industry conditions were appalling: long hours, pitifully low wages, and workrooms which defied description. Burton may be numbered among the great pioneers in the field of industrial welfare. In the twenties he equipped his factories with canteens

—the principal factory in Leeds can accommodate eight thousand at one sitting—the services of doctors, dentists, opticians, and even chiropodists, sports fields, and indeed, a savings bank which paid interest at five per cent. In addition he encouraged the foundation of dramatic and operatic societies.

Throughout his life Burton had a passion for peace—peace in industry and peace between nations. He believed that all industrial disputes should be the subject of compulsory arbitration. He was a firm supporter of organized labour and very much in favour of collective bargaining. During the fifty years in which he was in business he experienced only two strikes in his factory—the first in 1927 and the second in 1936 whilst he was in the Philippines. The latter, which lasted three weeks, was in respect of a claim for an increase of one halfpenny per garment by a group of twenty employees out of a total of ten thousand in the factory, and there is little doubt that had Burton been in England it would never have taken place.

Burton endowed a number of chairs and lectureships in industrial relations in the universities, and not unnaturally his first choice was Leeds, where a chair was established in 1929. It was followed by one at Cardiff in the same year and another at Cambridge in 1930. He also endowed chairs in international relations in Jerusalem (1929), Oxford (1930), and Edinburgh (1948), and public lectureships at Nottingham (1930) and Leeds (1942). In 1936 he gave financial support to a chair in international relations at London University which was named after him. It had originally been established in 1923 by means of five-year grants renewed by the trustees of Sir Ernest Cassel [q.v.]. Burton was immensely interested in the League of Nations and unsuccessfully tried to ensure that the appointment of this professor should be made in consultation with the president and chairman of the League. In 1922 he had founded a branch of the League of Nations Union for his employees in Leeds and regular monthly luncheon meetings were held at which members of both Houses of Parliament and other prominent persons were invited to speak. This branch, which in 1945 was absorbed by the United Nations Association, was and remained the largest in the country.

Deeply interested in peoples and countries, Burton had an insatiable thirst for travel. In 1930 he was invited to be the chairman of the Industrial Welfare Society delegation to the United States and Canada and in 1936 he was the delegate of the Leeds Incorporated Chamber of Commerce at the Federation of Commonwealth and British Empire Chambers of Commerce at Wellington, New Zealand. He went round the world four times and was immensely impressed by much that he saw. Not unnaturally he was attracted in 1943 to the concept of a world federation of nations initiated by the British Commonwealth and the United States. He was a Liberal and envisaged a world state where there would be free trade, one language, and one currency, compulsory industrial arbitration, and a tribunal to decide inter-federal disputes whose decisions could if necessary be implemented by a federal force.

He published two volumes of diaries, in the form of letters written to his daughter whilst he was travelling, entitled *Globe Girdling* (1936–8), and was delighted when he was elected a member of the P.E.N. Club in 1944. He was a voracious reader, particularly of the classics; another relaxation was family bridge. A man of simple tastes, he was almost a teetotaller and a non-smoker, with an intense dislike of all forms of gambling. He had a passion for fresh air and exercise and every morning at half-past eight he played nine holes of golf before he started a long day's work which often ended in the early hours of the following morning. When he was at sea he would walk three miles round the ship twice a day. For very many years he conducted his business from the library in his house, keeping in touch with the departments by private line. In order to spend the maximum time in the open air he had telephone points on the roof so that he and his secretaries might work there in reasonably fine weather.

Burton was a member of the council of the university of Leeds from 1929 and received the honorary degree of LL.D. in 1944, the year in which he endowed there a lectureship in modern and medieval Hebrew. Although he sat regularly as a justice of the peace for the city of Leeds from 1924 he took little or no part in public life. None the less in 1930 he received an invitation from representatives of all the political parties to be lord mayor of Leeds, although he was not even a member of the city council. In 1931 he was knighted for his services to industrial relationships.

A humble and self-effacing man Burton disliked any kind of ostentation or personal publicity. Although in fifty years he had seen his business grow from one shop to over six hundred, he never seemed to learn the lesson of delegation. The result was that he carried the whole burden of his vast organization on his own shoulders until the very moment of his death, which took place in Leeds, 21 September 1952, while he was addressing a gathering of his staff.

In 1909 Burton married Sophia Amelia (died 1957), daughter of Maurice Marks, dealer in antiques and furniture in Worksop. They had one daughter and three sons. A portrait by Reginald G. Lewi hangs in the board-room at Leeds.

[Private information.]   DAVID KARMEL

BUTLER, SIR HAROLD BERESFORI (1883–1951), public servant, was born in Oxford 6 October 1883, the elder son of Alfred Joshua Butler, the Coptic scholar by his wife, Constance Mary Heywood, a granddaughter of Marcus G. Beresfor [q.v.], archbishop of Armagh. The academic atmosphere in which Butler was brought up profoundly influenced both his personality and his career. He was a scholar of Eton and a Brackenbur scholar and Jenkyns exhibitioner c Balliol College, Oxford. After obtaining first class in *literae humaniores* he was elected a fellow of All Souls in 1905.

Butler's early ambition was to enter the Foreign Office and after a year at A Souls he went to Germany and Franc where he obtained a knowledge of the languages and an insight into the characteristics of the peoples which later prove of great value to him. There were, however, no vacancies in the Foreign Offic and Butler entered the Local Governmen Board in 1907, transferring to the Hom Office in the following year. In 1910 he ha his first experience of international wor as secretary to the British delegation the conference on aerial navigation. A though he was a captain in the Inns Court O.T.C., Butler was refused pe mission to join the forces on the outbrea of war. His section of the Home Offic concerned with blockade measures, wa ultimately merged with the correspondi section of the Foreign Office as the Forei Trade Department, of which he becam secretary in 1916. A year later he w transferred to the newly created Minist of Labour. While still keeping in tou with his old chief (Sir) Malcolm De vingne [q.v.] at the Home Office, prepared with the help of Edward Phela who later like Butler became director of the International Labour Office, a programme for the labour section of the peace conference which with little change of substance became the constitution of the International Labour Organization.

After the adoption by the conference of the labour section of the treaty, Butler was appointed secretary of the organizing committee of the first Labour Conference and later secretary-general of the Conference. The first of these two positions involved the elaboration of the principles on which a conference including representatives of governments, employers, and workers should be conducted, a task for which there were no precedents. The proposals submitted to the Conference have in the main been applied ever since.

The Conference met in difficult circumstances as not only had the Organization neither funds nor staff, but the American Government, on whose invitation it took place in Washington, failed to ratify the peace treaty and was unable to send an official delegation. It was largely owing to Butler's diplomatic and administrative skill that the Conference not only achieved its purpose but also laid the foundations for all subsequent conferences. Although there were obvious objections to men of the same nationality holding the senior posts in both the League of Nations (of which Sir Eric Drummond, later the Earl of Perth [q.v.], was the first secretary-general) and the International Labour Office, Butler missed being elected provisional director of the Office by a narrow margin; he was subsequently appointed deputy director by Albert Thomas, under whom he served with devoted loyalty. As deputy he was responsible for administration and finance and was able to build up an efficient international staff and to counteract any tendency to over-centralization.

Butler succeeded Thomas as director in 1932 in the depths of the depression which made international co-operation increasingly difficult. Nevertheless, during his six years as director he developed the office along lines which later proved to have been well chosen. His first concern was to induce America to join the organization, which she did in 1934. Believing that the centre of gravity of the world was shifting away from Europe, Butler travelled widely himself, sent his staff to give technical advice to overseas governments, established an overseas section of the Office and in 1934 induced

the Conference to enlarge the governing body so that seven non-European countries were among the sixteen governments represented. He also initiated regional conferences in the belief that many of the problems with which the Office had to deal were of regional rather than universal significance. He made one other major contribution to the policy of the Office by insisting that it should pay attention to the economic conditions which lay behind the social problems with which it was immediately concerned.

In 1938 Butler resigned and shortly afterwards accepted the post of first warden of Nuffield College, Oxford. Although he seemed eminently qualified for this position owing to his academic training, his exceptional knowledge of social problems throughout the world, and his wide acquaintance with leaders of industry and labour, he never had any real opportunity to put his qualifications to the test. He only assumed his functions at the beginning of 1939 and immediately on the outbreak of war was appointed southern regional commissioner for civil defence. He could do little more during his short period at Nuffield than think out plans for the future.

While engaged on his war work he found time to write the first of his three books, *The Lost Peace* (1941). This was followed in 1947 by *Peace or Power* and in 1950 by *Confident Morning*, the first volume of an uncompleted autobiography.

In 1942 Butler went to Washington to take charge of the British Information Service with the diplomatic rank of minister, a position in which his capacity to write, his objectivity, and wide knowledge of the political world stood him in good stead. After his retirement in 1946 he took an active part in the movement for closer European co-operation.

Butler had an ardent belief in the International Labour Organization and in the need for international co-operation, and it was in endeavouring to give reality to this belief that he found his greatest satisfaction. He had, however, few illusions about the pace at which the world would evolve towards a world society. He was a man of vision, but not a visionary; a conservative with strong labour sympathies and a man of deep-rooted principles.

In 1910 Butler married Olive, daughter of Samuel Abraham Walker Waters, assistant inspector-general of the Royal Irish Constabulary, of Stillorgan, county Dublin. His wife aided him greatly in the social side of his official duties. They had one daughter and two sons; the younger, R. D'O. Butler, also became a fellow of All Souls, and editor of *Documents on British Foreign Policy*. Butler was appointed C.B. in 1919 and K.C.M.G. in 1946. There is a portrait of him by Frank Eastman in Nuffield College which is an exceptionally good likeness. He died in Reading 26 March 1951.

[*International Labour Review*, April 1951; Sir Harold Butler, *Confident Morning*, 1950; *The Times*, 28 March 1951; private information; personal knowledge.]   A. LOVEDAY.

BUTLER, SIR MONTAGU SHERARD DAWES (1873–1952), Indian administrator and master of Pembroke College, Cambridge, born in Harrow 19 May 1873, was the third son of Spencer Perceval Butler, barrister, of Lincoln's Inn, later conveyancing counsel to the High Court of Justice and the Office of Works, by his wife, Mary, only child of the Rev. Nicholas Kendall, of Bodmin. He belonged to a family famous in the annals of Cambridge scholarship. His grandfather, George Butler [q.v.], had been senior wrangler in 1794 and afterwards headmaster of Harrow and dean of Peterborough; his uncle, Henry Montagu Butler [q.v.], was senior classic in 1855 and afterwards headmaster of Harrow and master of Trinity. A. G. Butler and George Butler (died 1890) [qq.v.] were also uncles; Sir S. H. Butler and Sir G. G. G. Butler [qq.v.] were brothers.

Montagu Butler was at school at Haileybury and was admitted to Pembroke College, Cambridge, in 1891. There he lived a full life: he gained first classes in both parts of the classical tripos (1894–5) with distinction in the second part; he was president of the Union, coxswain of the college boat, and one of the founders of the May week ball. Elected into a fellowship in 1895, he nevertheless decided, after long talks with his tutor, Leonard Whibley [q.v.], to enter the public service and in the following year he was awarded the Bhaunagar medal, given to the candidate standing highest on the examination list for the Indian Civil Service.

Late in 1896 he was sent out to the Punjab, where his administrative ability was quickly recognized. He was settlement officer of the Kotah State in 1904–9 and in 1912–15 was joint secretary of the royal commission on the public services in India. During the war of 1914–18, when he was deputy commissioner of Attock, he

was active in the recruitment drive for the Indian Army in the Punjab. In 1921, the period of the Montagu–Chelmsford reforms, he became president of the legislative council of the province. In the next year he was appointed secretary to the Government of India in the department of education, health, and lands, and in 1924 he was made president of the Council of State.

In the following year he was transferred to Nagpur as governor of the Central Provinces and had to face the many problems created by the non-co-operation movement. Throughout his career, and whatever his job, Butler aimed always at government by agreement and would exercise infinite patience in the reconciliation of opposing views. He drove a wedge into the phalanx of non-co-operation by appointing a Swarajist leader as home member and succeeded in bringing other non-co-operators into responsible posts. During his second term of office as governor he was confronted by a revival of civil disobedience and endeavoured, wherever possible, to deal with offenders under the ordinary law, without invoking the aid of the special powers given by the Government of India.

Butler's consistent record of work for the welfare of India was recognized by the award of the C.I.E. (1909), C.V.O. (1911), C.B. (1916), C.B.E. (1919), and a knighthood and the K.C.S.I. (1924). In 1933 he resigned to become lieutenant-governor of the Isle of Man. To the problems of that island he applied, without delay, the same energy, thoroughness, and tact that he had displayed in the Central Provinces. His insistence on a balanced budget provoked some preliminary opposition, but it was not long before his measures of reform were accepted as sound and beneficent. He was happy enough during his four years at Douglas, but of his many appointments none gave him such intense pleasure as his election to the mastership of Pembroke in 1937. Through all his time in India his love of the college had remained constant. He had been made an honorary fellow in 1925 and had sent both his sons there. When he returned himself, he was far from regarding the mastership as a provision of leisure for a retired public servant. Pembroke was only just beginning to recover from a series of disastrous losses in 1935, and, in particular, Butler set about reorganizing its finances *con amore*. He was too wise, after an absence of forty years, to interfere unduly in matters purely scholastic policy; but the university and the borough (as it then was) were quick to utilize his administrative capacities and experience and he willingly accepted invitations to serve on the borough council as well as on the council of the senate and the financial board of the university.

The outbreak of war upset many of his plans for the college, but it served to intensify rather than to diminish his activity. Shortly after his election to the mayoralty of Cambridge in November 1941, he insisted on making a tour of A.R.P. posts in the blackout and was knocked over by an ambulance. His injuries were severe; but when he recovered he had no hesitation in accepting the prolongation of his mayoralty for another year. Similarly, he was delighted when the college extended his tenure of the mastership to the statutory limit. He retired in 1948, but even then retained his seat on the borough council as an alderman, for public service was not only his occupation, but his hobby. He died suddenly in Cambridge 7 November 1952.

In all his varied work, Butler was greatly fortified by his marriage in 1901 to Anne Gertrude (died 1953), daughter of George Smith, C.I.E., and sister of Sir George Adam Smith [q.v.]. She was a woman of great charm and a hostess of exceptional grace and skill. There were two sons and two daughters of the marriage, the elder son being R. A. Butler (later Lord Butler of Saffron Walden), in whose achievements his parents, who lived to see him become chancellor of the exchequer, took great pride. He became master of Trinity College, Cambridge, in 1965. The younger son, J. P. (Jock) Butler, who had entered upon a career of public service in the Home Office, was killed in 1943, almost immediately after being commissioned in the Royal Air Force.

A drawing of Montagu Butler by Francis Dodd hangs in the parlour of Pembroke College.

[*The Times*, 8 November 1952; personal knowledge.]   S. C. ROBERTS.

BUXTON, PATRICK ALFRED (1892–1955), medical entomologist, was born in London 24 March 1892, the eldest of three children of Alfred Fowell Buxton, banker and chairman (1916–17) of the London County Council, by his wife, Violet, daughter of the Very Rev. Thomas William Drake-Blake [q.v.]. His forebears had been prominent in business, philanthropy, and social reform, among them his great-grandfather Sir Thomas Fowell Buxton, the philanthropist, and Sydney Charles, Earl Buxton [qq.v.].

After undistinguished and somewhat unhappy schooldays at Rugby, lightened only by his consuming interest in natural history, Buxton entered Trinity College, Cambridge, graduated with first class honours in both parts of the natural sciences tripos (1914–15), and in 1916 was elected into a college fellowship on a piece of undergraduate research completed in difficult wartime conditions. He qualified in medicine from St. George's Hospital in 1917, took up a commission in the Royal Army Medical Corps, and was posted to Mesopotamia and north-west Persia, where he devoted as much time as possible to natural history. In 1921 he was appointed entomologist to the medical department in Palestine; then from 1923 to 1926 he led a research expedition, on filariasis in Samoa, on behalf of the London School of Tropical Medicine. On his return to London in 1926, Buxton was appointed head of the department of entomology in the new London School of Hygiene and Tropical Medicine, becoming professor in the university of London in 1933, where he remained until his death.

Buxton was one of the most widely travelled biologists of his time. He was by profession a medical entomologist, but as soon as he attained a position of influence at the London School of Hygiene and Tropical Medicine he gave a new direction to his subject by insisting on the necessity for basing applied entomology on a scientific understanding of the physiology of insects. By his own researches in this field, and by his example and the appointments and opportunities which he secured for others, he did much to spread these ideas. In his own hands they made their impact on the study of mosquitoes and filariasis in the South Pacific, of plague fleas in Palestine, of the tsetse fly in Nigeria, of the human louse in many parts of the world. On the outbreak of war in 1939 Buxton concentrated all his energies on the improvement of insect control in the armed forces and in civilian life under wartime conditions. He established close relations with the Service medical departments and organized series of lectures to nurses and shelter marshals. He played an influential part on the many official committees dealing with insecticide research and development. His own work on improved methods for dealing with the louse problem prepared the way for the early exploitation of the new insecticide DDT.

Although his scientific publications covered a wide field of anthropology, applied (medical) entomology, and insect physiology, his real flair and his chief distinction lay in his contributions to natural history. His experiences in north-west Persia and in Palestine during and after the first war led to the publication of what he himself called that 'vigorous young man's book' on *Animal Life in Deserts* (1923). This attractive work has become a classic; reprinted in 1955 it has been continuously in demand for half a century. During the expedition to Samoa he and his colleague G. H. E. Hopkins made exhaustive collections of the insect fauna of the island, which formed the basis of the *Insects of Samoa* published by the British Museum in 1927–35. During the thirties Buxton was working on a text-book of medical entomology, one chapter of which developed into a very useful war-time book on *The Louse* (1939). The section on the tsetse flies grew until it formed Buxton's *magnum opus*, *The Natural History of Tsetse Flies* (1955).

Buxton had a strong and distinctive personality. Completely honest, considerate, and helpful to others, and with a quick wit and a lively sense of humour, he yet had an ironic and somewhat sarcastic manner which could strongly antagonize those who did not see beyond it. His interests were at once broad and narrow. He was intensely interested in all sides of the natural history of plants and animals, in geography, meteorology, and in the life of primitive peoples and their languages, and he was an enthusiastic and esoteric gardener. All this was combined with a dislike of music, of poetry and philosophy, and a curious lack of interest in scientific generalizations. He had a fine command of English and wrote in a lucid unaffected style; and he was equally effective as a speaker, with a vivid descriptive power and a way of presenting even familiar matters in a new light.

Buxton was elected F.R.S. in 1943; was twice president of the Royal Entomological Society of London (1942–3 and 1953–5); was awarded the Mary Kingsley medal of the Liverpool School of Tropical Medicine in 1949 and the gold medal of the Linnean Society in 1953. He was appointed C.M.G. in 1947.

In 1917 he married Muryell Gladys, daughter of the Rev. William Talbo Rice, vicar of St. Paul's, Onslow Squar (1919–35). They had two sons and fou daughters. The second son, Andrew, wh bore a strong resemblance to his fathe alone took up a career in science and wa making a promising start as a medica entomologist in Central Africa when h was struck down by poliomyelitis and die three years before the death of his fathe which took place at Gerrards Cross 1 December 1955.

[V. B. Wigglesworth in *Biographic Memoirs of Fellows of the Royal Society*, vol. 1956; private information; personal know ledge.]   V. B. Wigglesworth

CABLE, (ALICE) MILDRED (187 1952), missionary, was born in Guildfo 21 February 1878, the daughter of Jol Cable, master draper, and his wife, Eli Kindred. Educated at Guildford Hi School, from her early days she felt a mi sionary vocation, and with a view to joi ing the China Inland Mission she follow a course of medical studies in Londo Learning that China might be closed f lowing the Boxer rising of 1900 she l England to work in Shansi province whe in 1902 she joined Evangeline Fren [q.v.], already a seasoned missionary w had almost lost her life in the rising. Hwochow they were engaged in edu tional work for girls and were later join by Francesca French [q.v.]. The lives the 'trio' were henceforth so closely lated that it is almost impossible separate their individual stories. Th venture at Hwochow prospered and t school of a dozen illiterate girls became large institution graded from kindergart to teacher training.

In 1923, however, the trio at their o request were permitted by the China land Mission to obey a call which over years had become increasingly insiste Henceforth they were together to foll the desert trade routes in order to take Gospel to the scattered oases of the G To and fro they trekked by cart, by car and on foot across the desert, visiting bazaars and oases of Central Asia, me ing people of many races and differ tongues. The trio themselves spoke Chin and Turki languages, and for fifteen ye they travelled, considering it a prim duty that 'if no more could be done these people, certainly no less was o to them than to place a Gospel in e man's hand written in his mother-tong Local people learned to love them. N lems respected them for what Mildred Cable once called 'the combination of our grey hairs, celibate state, and pilgrim life'.

They were not only missionaries but explorers. Each time they returned to England on leave, scientific societies and universities invited them to lecture, for they had gathered a great deal of unique interest to the geographer, the archaeologist, and the philologist. They were jointly awarded the Livingstone medal of the Royal Scottish Geographical Society in 1943 and Mildred Cable was awarded the Lawrence memorial medal for 1942 by the Royal Central Asian Society. Moreover, in the unsettled state of China at that time there was peril and danger for the traveler. But the trio was a unique partnership in faith and achievement, in courage and endurance, and their names became known throughout the Christian world. From their experiences they reported amongst other things that 'the Bible Society took on an importance which we could never have realized so long as we lived amongst people all of whom spoke one language'. With further political changes taking place in Central Asia, they had to leave their pioneering work and they returned home shortly before the outbreak of war in 1939. Mildred Cable and Francesca French joined the Bible Society Committee and did extensive voluntary deputation work in Britain. For the next twelve years they toured the towns and cities of Britain, speaking at conferences, public meetings, eventually building up the women's work of the Bible Society. By their broadcasts, but principally by their books and meetings, they touched the imagination of post-war Britain. They travelled also to India, Australia, New Zealand, and later South America, visiting and advocating the aims of the spread of the Christian gospel. In all this lifetime of activity Mildred Cable manifested great gifts of leadership and keen insight into missionary strategy. She was a forceful speaker and shared both platform and authorship with Francesca French. Together they published some twenty books, amongst which the best known are *Through Jade Gate and Central Asia* (1927), *Something Happened* (1933), *Desert Journal* (1934), *The Gobi Desert* (1942), *China: Her Life and Her People* (1946), and *Journey with a Purpose* (1950).

Mildred Cable died in London 30 April 1952. A portrait by E. O. Fearnley-Whittingstall is at the headquarters of the British and Foreign Bible Society.

[W. J. Platt, *Three Women*, 1964; private information; personal knowledge.]

W. J. PLATT.

CAIRD, SIR JAMES, baronet, of Glenfarquhar, county Kincardine (1864–1954), shipowner and a founder of the National Maritime Museum, was born in Glasgow 2 January 1864, the elder son in a family of six of James Caird, lawyer, by his wife, Mary Ann Hutcheson. Educated at Glasgow Academy, he joined the firm of William Graham & Co., East India merchants, in 1878. Eleven years later he went to London and in 1890 joined Turnbull, Martin & Co., managers of the Scottish Shire Line of steamships. By hard work and enterprise he prospered, and in twelve months was made manager. By 1903 he was sole partner and owner of the Scottish Shire Line, and in co-operation with the Houlder and Federal lines he opened up the trade between the west coast of England and the Antipodes. Early in 1916 he started a new shipyard at Chepstow to build standard ships quickly where enemy attacks could not interfere with production. Overcoming immense difficulties, the venture succeeded so well that in 1917 the Government stepped in and bought out Caird and his associates. Foreseeing the slump in shipping which would follow the end of the war Caird in the same year sold to the Clan Line his interest in the Shire Line and Turnbull, Martin & Co. He remained a director of some twenty-five companies connected with shipping, shipbuilding, ship repairing and allied industries, as well as being chairman of the Smithfield and Argentine Meat Company, in which he held a large block of founders' shares.

By now Caird was a comparatively rich man and from the early twenties he devoted a large part of his fortune to preserving British naval and shipping memorials, to which he became passionately devoted. It was he who provided most of the money needed to repair and restore H.M.S. *Victory* with an initial sum of £50,000 to start the work and a further £15,000 to enable it to continue. In 1927 steps were being taken to found a national museum of the sea, a venture to which Caird gave his wholehearted and energetic support. Under the chairmanship of the seventh Earl Stanhope and in association with the Society for Nautical Research, with its honorary secretary (Sir) Geoffrey Callender [q.v.], a board of trustees, of whom Caird was one, was set up to found the new museum. The realization of this project became possible when the Royal Hospital School moved to Holbrook and the old school buildings at Greenwich, including the Queen's House, became vacant. Caird then guaranteed to meet the whole cost (amounting eventually to over £80,000) of converting the buildings. In addition, he began purchasing every available collection or individual item of maritime historical interest. Thus the Macpherson collection of sea pictures and the *Mercury* collection of ships' models were secured, and to these he added his own collections. During the second reading of the national maritime museum bill in the House of Commons in June 1934 it was stated that the collections Caird had already offered to the nation were worth more than £300,000.

The new museum was opened by King George VI in April 1937 and Caird continued his never-flagging interest and support. In all, including the Caird Fund which he set up to provide an endowment income to finance purchases, he gave more than a million and a quarter pounds to the museum. To the last, when he became too ill to take an active part, he continued to shower his gifts upon it, filling with treasures the spacious galleries which bear his name. Nor were the museum and H.M.S. *Victory* alone in benefiting from his generosity. The historic 74-gun ship-of-the-line H.M.S. *Implacable* was also saved by him in the years between the wars. To museums and art galleries in his native Scotland he was a generous benefactor; and in the war of 1939–45 he provided the cost of a complete ambulance unit. To his parish church, St. Mary's, Wimbledon, his gifts included a house for the curate and money for the new church spire.

Caird was stocky in stature, tough and wiry, with immense energy, a shrewd expression, a merry twinkle in his eye, and a delightful Scots voice. He was the kindliest of men, generous almost to a fault, but never making a show of his benefactions, shrouding his greatest gifts in secrecy, and never seeking any reward. He nevertheless loved to drive a hard bargain and could not bear to be 'had'; but he was always scrupulously fair and often gave more than was asked when he thought the seller might be in need, or even that a dealer was not taking sufficient profit.

Until his illness in 1949 Caird continued to attend his office in the City daily. He was extremely alert and had an excellent memory. He celebrated his eightieth birthday at his home in Scotland by bringing down a 'royal' after a long day's stalk which many a younger man would have given up. It was this wonderful vitality and his simple way of living which endeared him so much to all around him at Glenfarquhar, Fordoun, where he dispensed quiet yet generous hospitality in which gillies, keepers, shepherds, and guests shared alike.

In 1928 Caird was created a baronet and after the opening of the new museum in 1937 Neville Chamberlain wanted to submit his name for a peerage, but Caird refused, saying that he did not want reward for what he had done for and given to the nation.

Caird married in 1894 Henrietta Ann (died 1953), daughter of William Henry Stephens, architect, of Ardshane, Holywood, county Down. They had one daughter but no son and on Caird's death at his home in Wimbledon, 27 September 195[ ] the baronetcy became extinct. A bust b[y] Sir William Reid Dick is in the Nation[al] Maritime Museum.

James Caird is not to be confused with another philanthropist, Sir James K[ ] Caird (1837–1916), who helped to finan[ce] the Shackleton expedition of 1914–16.

[*Syren and Shipping*, 4 September 1946 a[nd] 6 October 1954; private information; person[al] knowledge.]　　　　FRANK G. G. CA[ ]

CAIRNS, SIR HUGH WILLIAM BEL[L] (1896–1952), neurosurgeon, was born [at] Port Pirie, South Australia, 26 June 18[ ] the only son of William Cairns, a Sco[ts] man who worked in the timber indust[ry] and his wife, Amy Florence Bell. He w[as] educated at Adelaide High School a[nd] University where, returning from milit[ary] service, he qualified M.B., B.S. in 1917; [he] became a captain in the Australian Ar[my] Medical Corps and served in Fran[ce.] Elected a Rhodes scholar in 1917, he w[ent] into residence at Balliol in 1919, stud[ied] physiology, demonstrated anatomy, [and] rowed, getting his blue in the Oxford c[rew] of 1920. He then trained in the Lon[don] Hospital as a house-surgeon and hou[se] physician and remained as a surgeon as[sis-] tant. He was elected F.R.C.S. in 1921 a[nd] was Hunterian professor in 1926. A Roc[ke-] feller travelling fellowship took him [in] 1926–7 to Boston to work with Har[vey] Cushing, and he then made the courage[ous] decision to seek a career in neurosurger[y in] London.

Returning to the London Hosp[ital] Cairns by 1932 had established the ne[uro-] surgical unit which was his sp[ecial] ambition, and here he had some valuable colleagues in George Riddoch, Russell (later Lord) Brain, H. M. Turnbull [q.v.], and Dorothy Russell. He was one of a handful of British surgeons who brought a new surgical technique to Britain from Cushing in Boston, and his special report on Cushing's cases was published by the Medical Research Council in 1929; his further report in 1936 was outstanding. With Sir Geoffrey Jefferson at Manchester and Professor N. M. Dott at Edinburgh, Cairns helped to form a school of British neurological surgery which became second to none.

By 1930 Cairns was beginning to think of a special medical centre for clinicians where there were good opportunities for research, and he felt that it should be in Oxford. After six years of planning Lord Nuffield endowed a medical research school there and in 1937 Cairns became the first professor of surgery and a fellow of Balliol. But the war came in 1939 and Cairns directed nearly all his efforts towards establishing a really good neurosurgical service for the army, to which he was consultant neurosurgeon with the rank of brigadier. With (Sir) Charles Symonds he organized a special hospital for head injuries which from 1940 to 1945 occupied the premises of St. Hugh's College, Oxford. He was involved in such developments as the establishment of well-equipped mobile surgical units, the introduction of the compulsory wearing of helmets by army motor-cyclists, and the first trials of penicillin in the field.

After the war Cairns returned with enthusiasm to the task of developing the clinical side of the Oxford medical school. Many new developments arose from his far-sighted ideas and his vigorous initiative. His early death at the height of his powers was a disaster to Oxford medicine for it happened at a particularly sensitive stage of post-war planning for which his leadership would have been invaluable. He was a stimulating companion, and was always searching for new ideas. Although not particularly original, he was an enthusiastic supporter of research and an excellent judge of men; many of the world's leading neurosurgeons were trained by him. He himself had been the first surgeon in England to remove a pineal tumour; and towards the end of his life he was greatly interested in the alleviation of mental disease by surgery. He wrote over a hundred papers for medical and neurological journals, a list of which appears in

Sir Geoffrey Jefferson's memoir. Cairns was Sims Commonwealth professor (1947–8); president of the Society of Neurological Surgeons (1946–8); Victor Horsley lecturer (1949); and was appointed K.B.E. in 1946.

'Hugo' Cairns was tall and handsome with a keen but engaging and friendly manner. He applied intense concentration to all he did and even played tennis as though his life depended on it. Yet he preferred his household and his amusements to remain entirely simple; many of his juniors will remember visits to Wytham Woods with enormous saws and axes. Here his fine physique dominated the scene and he soon exhausted his companions. He was devoted to music and was often obliged to restrain his inclination to become absorbed in it.

In 1921 Cairns married Barbara Forster, youngest daughter of A. L. Smith [q.v.], master of Balliol; they had two sons and two daughters. Cairns died in Oxford 18 July 1952.

[Sir Geoffrey Jefferson, 'Memories of Hugh Cairns', *Journal of Neurology, Neurosurgery and Psychiatry*, vol. xxii, No. 3, August 1959; private information; personal knowledge.]

W. RITCHIE RUSSELL.

CALDECOTT, SIR ANDREW (1884–1951), colonial governor, was born at Boxley, Kent, 26 October 1884, the eldest son of the Rev. Andrew Caldecott by his wife, Isobel, daughter of the Rev. Stenning Johnson. He was educated at Uppingham and at Exeter College, Oxford, of which he was a scholar and later (1948) an honorary fellow. He was awarded a third class in classical honour moderations and, in 1907, a second class in *literae humaniores*. In that year he joined the Malayan Civil Service; after holding various posts he was appointed in 1923 Malayan commissioner for the Wembley exhibition of the following year. After serving successively as resident in Negri Sembilan, Perak, and Selangor, he was promoted to be chief secretary, Federated Malay States, in 1931, and in 1933 colonial secretary of the Straits Settlements. In 1934 he acted as officer administering the government, Straits Settlements, and high commissioner for the Malay States. The sympathy and understanding which accompanied his great administrative ability, and his wise and tactful handling of racial issues, earned him a respect and popularity rarely equalled.

In 1935 Caldecott was appointed governor of Hong Kong where he was equally popular, and strong representations were made for him to remain when in 1937 he was offered the governorship of Ceylon. Caldecott was clearly sent to Ceylon to smooth the way for further advance at a time when agitation for constitutional reform was intense. In November 1937 he was instructed to sound opinion and to recommend amendments to the constitution. His 'Reforms Despatch' of June 1938 was written with a vigour and directness unusual in official documents: it led to prolonged discussion in the State Council, but to no general agreement, the basic difficulty, as always, being the question of minority representation. The outbreak of war halted consideration of constitutional advance, but Caldecott was convinced that if Ceylon's war effort were to be maintained a positive approach was required. On his recommendation the British Government in 1941, and again in 1943, promised a commission on constitutional reform as soon as the war ended; and a commission was in fact appointed in 1944, the year in which Caldecott retired.

In the meantime he set himself out to be a constitutional governor, an objective misunderstood by certain sections of the European community which failed to see, with his clarity, that early self-government was inevitable. His aims were more clearly appreciated by the local politicians, such as D. S. Senanayake [q.v.], and he soon earned their respect and confidence. That Ceylon remained stable during the critical war years was largely due to his leadership. The sudden appointment, after the fall of Malaya, of Admiral Sir Geoffrey Layton as commander-in-chief in place of the governor nearly led to Caldecott's resignation; happily this step was not taken and the two men, temperamentally so different, worked harmoniously together to the great benefit of Ceylon.

A brilliant, far-sighted administrator, but withal warm-hearted and with a quick intelligence tempered by a human sympathy and understanding, Caldecott was ideally suited for the task of helping to transform empire into commonwealth. Ceylon owed to him much of her trouble-free progress towards the independence which she attained in 1948. Artistically gifted, Caldecott painted, was a skilled pianist, had a happy talent for light verse, and in his Malayan days wrote several witty burlesques; he published two books of uneasy stories: *Not Exactly Ghosts* (1947) and *Fires Burn Blue* (1948).

Caldecott was appointed C.B.E. (1926), C.M.G. (1932), was knighted in 1935, and appointed K.C.M.G. (1937) and G.C.M.G. (1941). He was made a knight of grace of St. John of Jerusalem in 1936 and was awarded the Silver Wolf in 1943 for his services to scouting. He was twice married: first, in 1918, to Olive Mary (died 1943), daughter of John Robert Innes, of the Malayan Civil Service, by whom he had a daughter and a son; secondly, in 1946, to Evelyn May, widow of Dr. J. Robertson and daughter of Canon H. Palmer.

Caldecott died 14 July 1951 at his home at Itchenor, Sussex. An unconventional portrait by David Paynter, the Ceylon artist, was presented by Caldecott to Queen's House, Colombo; a portrait by John Napper is in the possession of his son. A memorial window, commissioned by his widow, is in Itchenor church.

[*The Times*, 16 July 1951; *Ceylon Daily News*, 16 July 1951; *British Malaya*, August 1951; private information; personal knowledge.]   JOHN O'REGAN

CALMAN, WILLIAM THOMAS (1871–1952), zoologist, was born in Dundee 29 December 1871, the only son and elder child of Thomas Calman, music teacher and his wife, Agnes Beatts Maclean. His father's people were chiefly ship masters or shipbuilders who a generation or two back came from the Anstruther district of Fife. Thomas Calman was blind from childhood and died when his son was six years old. A timid lad with no aptitude for games, Calman became an ardent amateur microscopist and student of pond life while still at high school, where his scientific interests, like those of Alex McKenzie [q.v.], were encouraged by Frank Young. At sixteen Calman was apprenticed to an insurance company but was advised four years later that his stammer unfitted him for the work. Meanwhile he had become an active member of the Dundee Working Men's Field Club and joined the Dundee Naturalists' Society over which he was to preside in 1944. There he met the young professor of natural history at Dundee, (Sir) D'Arcy Wentworth Thompson (whose notice he was subsequently to contribute to this Dictionary), whose timely offer of a job as laboratory assistant was eagerly accepted since it enabled Calman to attend classes without payment of fees. He graduated B.Sc. with distinction in botany, physiology, and zoology in 1895. He also found time to learn several foreign languages and assisted with the classification of a large and varied assortment of animals obtained from all parts of the world for the departmental museum. He became interested chiefly, though by no means exclusively, in the crustaceans and published several scientific papers. One of these, which was soon to become a classic, was read before the Royal Society of Edinburgh just before he graduated. He was next appointed assistant lecturer and demonstrator in the natural history department, a post he held until 1903, obtaining his D.Sc. in 1900. He was an excellent teacher and during Thompson's absences abroad was responsible for all the work of the department. In later years he served as external examiner to many universities.

An invitation in 1901 to write the Crustacea volume for *A Treatise on Zoology* edited by (Sir) Ray Lankester [q.v.] marked another turning-point in his career. In 1903 he accepted a temporary post at the British Museum (Natural History) and the following year he was placed in charge of the Crustacea and Pycnogonida. In addition to his official duties he compiled the Arachnida and Crustacea parts of the *Zoological Record* for many years. In 1921, the year in which he was elected F.R.S., he became deputy keeper of the department of zoology, and in 1927 he succeeded Tate Regan [q.v.] as keeper, a post which he held until his retirement in 1936.

As a museum curator Calman kept the collections under his care in excellent order with the minimum of cataloguing and indexing. From 1904 onwards, until administrative duties claimed most of his time, he produced a steady stream of scientific papers of the highest order and became the leading carcinologist of his time. To a remarkably retentive memory was added a gift for winnowing the significant from masses of detail. The *Treatise* volume, which specialists regard as his masterpiece, was published in 1909 and is still the best introduction to the subject. Much of interest which was unsuited to a textbook was included in his more popular book, *The Life of Crustacea* (1911). In 1920 he prepared a report on marine boring animals injurious to submerged structures for a committee of the Institution of Civil Engineers.

Calman took a prominent part in scientific activities outside the museum. He was a member of the board of studies in London University and served on the

council of the Royal Society from 1933 to 1935. He was president of the Quekett Microscopical Club (1927–9) and of the zoology section at the Bristol meeting of the British Association in 1930. As secretary of the Ray Society (1919–46) he edited the Monographs. He was zoological secretary of the Linnean Society (1923–8), president (1934–7), and received its gold medal (1949). He was appointed C.B. in 1935 and received an honorary LL.D. of St. Andrews and an honorary F.R.S. Edinburgh in 1937.

In 1906 Calman married Alice Jean, daughter of James Donaldson, timber merchant, of Tayport, Fife. She was one of the first women graduates in medicine of St. Andrews and in due course their son and daughter both entered the medical profession.

Somewhat below average height, Calman was a rather sedate, modest, kind, and sociable man, with a delightful sense of humour. His early appreciation of English literature gave him an unusual command of words and purity of style which were enhanced by the slight hesitancy of speech which replaced his stammer. He was impatient with inaccuracy in any form and as editor and administrator he set a very high standard. But this was no more than he always demanded of himself and his strictness was tempered by his kindly common sense. If he sometimes treated his younger colleagues with benign ferocity he taught them many things besides zoology.

Three years after his retirement Calman moved to Tayport and during the war years he was a part-time lecturer in zoology at St. Andrews and Dundee. A series of lectures delivered to his students on *The Classification of Animals* was published in 1949. Following a serious illness he returned to London and died at Coulsdon, Surrey, 29 September 1952. A portrait by (Sir) W. T. Monnington is in the possession of the family.

[H. Graham Cannon in *Obituary Notices of Fellows of the Royal Society*, No. 22, November 1953; *Proceedings* of the Linnean Society, Session 165, June 1954; *Nature*, 8 November 1952; private information; personal knowledge.]   ISABELLA GORDON.

CAMBRIDGE, ALEXANDER AUGUSTUS FREDERICK WILLIAM ALFRED GEORGE, EARL OF ATHLONE (1874–1957), was born at Kensington Palace 14 April 1874, the third son of Princess Mary Adelaide and the Duke of Teck, and brother of the future Queen Mary, a notice of whom appears in this Supplement. Originally styled His Serene Highness, Prince Alexander of Teck, he was known to his family as 'Alge'. In 1917 in accordance with policy he relinquished his titles and the name of Teck and took the family name of Cambridge and the title of Earl of Athlone. Although his new name and titles had hereditary associations he and many others regarded these changes as unnecessary and even undignified.

The Prince was educated at Eton and Sandhurst, was commissioned second lieutenant in the 7th Hussars in 1894, joined his regiment in India, and thereafter received his promotion in the normal way. He served in the Matabele war of 1896–7 and was mentioned in dispatches. He transferred to the Inniskilling Dragoons in order to be able to serve in the South African war during which he was mentioned again in dispatches and appointed to the D.S.O. He was spoken of as a capable and enterprising officer and a cheerful comrade, ever willing to endure and to share with his troopers the discomforts of a nomad campaign.

In 1904 the Prince married Princess Alice Mary Victoria Augusta Pauline, daughter of Queen Victoria's fourth son, the Duke of Albany [q.v.]. On this occasion he was appointed G.C.V.O. Their first child, May Helen Emma, was born in 1906; in the following year they had a son, Rupert Alexander George Augustus, later Viscount Trematon. A second son, Maurice Francis George, died in 1910 before he was six months old.

The Prince joined the Royal Horse Guards in 1904. In 1911, at the request of King George V, he transferred to the 2nd Life Guards with the rank of major. At the coronation he was appointed G.C.B. In 1914 he was nominated governor-general of Canada but did not take up the appointment owing to the outbreak of war in which he served as lieutenant-colonel in the Life Guards. Later he joined the staff as G.S.O. 2 and was attached to the British military mission to the Belgian Army. He was promoted G.S.O. 1 with the rank of brigadier-general in 1915 and received Belgian, French, and Russian decorations. He was twice mentioned in dispatches and in 1918 he joined the general headquarters staff.

After the war Athlone retired from the army and took an active interest in national and social work. A man of compassion, he was especially attracted to the work of institutions connected with the relief of human suffering. He had been chairman of the Middlesex Hospital since 1910 and in 1921 the minister of health appointed him chairman of a committee composed of the foremost doctors and surgeons of the day to investigate the needs of medical practitioners. Under his enthusiastic guidance the 'Athlone committee' produced a comprehensive report which recommended the appropriation of substantial sums from public funds to finance the establishment of a post graduate medical school (to be associated with the university of London and existing medical institutions) to promote post graduate instruction and medical research. The work thus initiated by the Athlone committee was carried on by committees presided over by Neville Chamberlain and Arthur Greenwood [qq.v.]. The Post graduate School, subsequently attached to the Hammersmith Hospital, became one of the most famous institutions of its kind. Athlone took a special interest and pride in the school which he frequently visited in later years.

Athlone was closely identified also with the promotion of education. He was chancellor of the university of London (1932–55), taking office at a difficult time in the development of the university under its new statutes. He was an honorary bencher of the Middle Temple, a fellow of the Royal Society, vice-president of the Royal Academy of Music, an honorary fellow of the Royal College of Surgeons, and knight grand cross of the Order of St. John of Jerusalem.

In 1923 Athlone was appointed governor-general of the Union and high commissioner for South Africa, being appointed G.C.M.G. and promoted to the rank of major-general. He arrived in South Africa in time to open Parliament in January 1924. Shortly afterwards J. B. M. Hertzog [q.v.] succeeded J. C. Smuts [q.v.] as prime minister. A difficult period followed. Racial feeling between British and Afrikaners was inflamed by a Nationalist proposal to adopt a new flag for the Union omitting anything symbolic of the British connection. Athlone worked quietly behind the scenes to secure the inclusion of a Union Jack in the white central panel. His speech at the unveiling of this compromise flag in Cape Town did much to soothe and reconcile animosities. His frequent tours in the provinces enhanced his prestige and popularity among all sections of the community and much to bring the two white races closer together. His patience, courtesy, and tact won the trust and esteem of the political leaders of all parties. He was appointed K.G. in 1928 in recognition of his services and his term of office was extended at the request of the Government. The death of their son, Viscount Trematon, as the result of a motor accident in France in April 1928 was a cruel and shattering blow to the Athlones. The expressions of sympathy they received from all over Southern Africa revealed a depth of affectionate sympathy and personal regard which must have robbed their sorrow of some of its bitterness.

At the conclusion of his very successful term of office, Athlone was sworn of the Privy Council in 1931 and appointed governor and constable of Windsor Castle. He and Princess Alice took up residence at Brantridge Park and afterwards transferred to Kensington Palace which they decorated with trophies of their big-game hunting expeditions and paintings of African landscapes by local artists whom they had patronized and encouraged during their tour of duty. They continued their interest in South African affairs and personalities and resumed their social activities in England. Queen Mary and her brother had always been close companions and regular correspondents. After the King recovered from his serious illness he expressed the wish that Lord Athlone should, for family reasons, remain in England.

In 1940, King George VI showed his uncle a telegram from W. L. Mackenzie King [q.v.] asking if he might submit Athlone's name for the governor-generalship of Canada. Greatly as he appreciated the compliment, Athlone thought a younger man should be appointed, but the King persuaded him to accept for a period of two years. In the event he served the full term of five years. He entered upon his new duties with his usual enthusiasm and took a keen interest in efforts to establish in the dominion various military training schemes and factories for the production of war materials. He travelled extensively in all seasons of the year to attend troop reviews and encourage munition workers. In addition he and Princess Alice were always ready to entertain members of official missions, including those of President Roosevelt and (Sir) Winston Churchill, and they offered open hospitality to royalties and other distinguished exiles from allied countries under German oc-

cupation. Although Athlone had occasional differences with Mackenzie King, he had a natural gift for getting on with people and their personal relations always remained very friendly. His unsuccessful efforts to reconcile differences between the prime minister and his defence minister, J. L. Ralston [q.v.], were a disappointment to him.

In August 1944, on the twenty-fifth anniversary of his leadership of his party, Mackenzie King wrote to the governor-general that he was 'particularly happy that the last four years, the most eventful of all, should have been shared with Your Excellency in the administration of Canada's war effort, and that throughout every day of that time I should have had the constant and helpful co-operation of Your Excellency and Princess Alice.' Later the prime minister wrote: 'Your years here, as Representative of the King, have strengthened the country's attachment to the Crown. I doubt if that attachment were ever stronger than it is today.'

Those who knew Athlone intimately and worked with him would agree that kindness was his outstanding characteristic. Yet, like many kind people, he had a quick temper which subsided as rapidly as it flared up. His military training had endowed him with an eye for detail and a keen perception of the manners and peculiarities of others upon which he liked to exercise his quizzical sense of humour. He gave the impression that he modelled his conduct on the precepts of Polonius—especially those relating to manners and deportment. His dress was meticulous but never 'expressed in fancy'. He had an exact sense of symmetry and tidiness and would often adjust ornaments and pictures. His memory for names and faces was quite extraordinary and he was a good judge of character. In public affairs he was tolerant and strove to induce others to modify fixed or extreme opinions before giving expression to his own. His natural tact and intellectual modesty enabled him to impress his counsel upon ministers without provoking opposition or appearing to intrude upon their constitutional prerogatives. His command over the loyalty and affection of his staff was exceptional and he delighted in renewing friendships with them in after years. At the conclusion of his term of office in Canada in 1946 he and Princess Alice made time to stay in Trinidad with their former secretary in South Africa. On his return to England Athlone resumed his interest in national affairs. In 1936 he had been appointed grand master of the Order of St. Michael and St. George, an order associated especially with the dominions, colonial, and foreign services. In that office he presided over the last tributes paid to many of Britain's most distinguished sons. On his death at Kensington Palace, 16 January 1957, he received in his turn the homage of members of the order who, like himself, had faithfully and diligently served their country. The peerage became extinct.

At Kensington Palace there is a portrait of Athlone by H. de T. Glazebrook and a conversation piece with Princess Alice by Norman Hepple. At Government House, Ottawa, there is a portrait by Henry Carr; the university of London has a portrait by Augustus John and the Middlesex Hospital (at Athlone House, Kenwood, Hampstead Lane) one by Francis Hodge. At the Vintners' Hall there is a portrait by (Sir) James Gunn.

[Private information; personal knowledge; *For My Grandchildren*, Some reminiscences of Her Royal Highness Princess Alice, Countess of Athlone, 1966.]   BEDE CLIFFORD.

CAMPBELL, GORDON (1886–1953), vice-admiral, was born at Upper Norwood, London, 6 January 1886, ninth son and thirteenth of the sixteen children of Colonel Frederick Campbell, C.B., V.D., J.P., by his wife, Emilie, daughter of Donald Maclaine of Lochbuie. Educated at Dulwich College, he passed into the *Britannia* as a naval cadet in 1900. He was promoted lieutenant in 1907 and at the outbreak of war in 1914 he was commanding a destroyer on Channel escort duties.

Early in 1915 as part of the anti-submarine measures a number of tramp steamers were converted into decoy ships with naval crews and concealed guns. Campbell volunteered for these 'mystery' or Q-ships, and became the most brilliant exponent of this hazardous form of warfare. To outward appearance harmless merchantmen, the Q-ships offered themselves as targets in U-boat infested waters. After their existence became known and enemy submarine captains more wary, Campbell deliberately allowed his vessel to be torpedoed, remaining on board with his hidden gunners, after part of the crew had 'abandoned ship', waiting for the submarine to close her victim. Using these tactics he sank three of the eleven German submarines destroyed by Q-ships, for

which actions he won the V.C., was appointed to the D.S.O. with two bars, and attained promotion to captain in 1917 at the early age of thirty-one. He also received the thanks of the War Cabinet, was awarded the croix de guerre, and appointed officer of the Legion of Honour. More than seventy decorations, including four Victoria Crosses, were awarded to officers and men of the three Q-ships he commanded

His last Q-ship action typified the outstanding courage of Campbell and the crews he inspired. On 8 August 1917 his decoy ship *Dunraven* was attacked with gunfire by a surfaced U-boat which started a fierce fire on board. After torpedoing the *Dunraven* the submarine continued to shell her while Campbell and his gunners remained at their posts in the burning vessel, with ammunition exploding about them, waiting for the U-boat to come within range, but she finally made off without doing so. Later the *Dunraven* sank while in tow.

After the loss of the *Dunraven* Campbell served as flag captain to the commander-in-chief, Coast of Ireland Patrol, in charge of all anti-submarine operations in the Irish Sea.

After the war Campbell commanded successively the cadet training cruiser *Cumberland*, the boys' training establishment *Impregnable*, and subsequently served as captain in charge of Simonstown dockyard. In 1920 in recognition of his distinguished war service he was elected younger brother of Trinity House. His last seagoing appointment was in command of the battle cruiser *Tiger* from 1925 to 1927. In April 1928 he was retired rear-admiral, his indifferent medical record since the end of the war undoubtedly contributing to this early retirement. He was promoted vice-admiral on the retired list in 1932.

Campbell then turned to writing and lecturing. His first book *My Mystery Ships* (1928) told the story of his exploits in Q-ships, and he delivered many lectures on the subject in this country, Canada, and the United States, proving a fluent and popular speaker. His autobiography *Number Thirteen* appeared in 1932; between 1933 and 1938 he produced a number of other works, mostly short historical accounts of various sea actions, also adventure stories for boys; and (with I. O. Evans) he published a textbook of flags (1950).

When the 'national' Government was formed to deal with the economic crisis

931, Campbell, although not politically minded, decided to stand as a National candidate for Burnley where he sensationally defeated the Labour member rthur Henderson [q.v.], former foreign ecretary. A staunch supporter of Baldwin nd the League of Nations, he was popular ith his constituents and spoke often in ne House. In the general election of 1935 e stood again as Liberal-National candiate but was defeated by the Labour ntender.

At the outbreak of war in 1939 Campll was specially commissioned by (Sir) Vinston Churchill to requisition and fit ut a number of decoy merchantmen with ne object of repeating the earlier *ruse de terre* of the Q-ships. Although under his rection the vessels were well armed and rilliantly disguised they met with no ccess, and after a few months the scheme as abandoned. Campbell was then apinted resident naval officer, Padstow, sponsible for naval defences in that area. appearance the traditional bluff, ruddyced sailor, he nevertheless continued be dogged by ill health aggravated the strain of his Q-ship experiences, d was finally forced to retire from active val service in 1943.

In 1911 he married Mary Jeanne, ughter of Henry V. S. Davids, of Hillier use, Guildford; they had one son and e daughter. Campbell died at Isleworth, ddlesex, 3 October 1953. A charcoal d water-colour by Francis Dodd is in e Imperial War Museum.

Gordon Campbell, *Number Thirteen*, 1932; vate information.]   A. CECIL HAMPSHIRE.

MPBELL, (IGNATIUS) ROYSTON NNACHIE (1901–1957), poet and nslator, known as ROY CAMPBELL, was n in Durban, Natal, 2 October 1901, grandson of a Scots settler and the rth child of Dr. Samuel George Camp- by his wife, Margaret, daughter of nes Dunnachie, of Glenboig, Lanark- re, who had married Jean Hendry of glesham. Educated at Durban High ool, and in a family of soldiers, farmers ninistrators, naturalists, hunters, letes, and verse-writers, Campbell uired early that lifelong passion for animals, poetry, physical prowess, a blunt outspokenness which gave ur range and verve to all his writings.

t fifteen he ran away from school to his brothers in the war, but was ped and brought back to his lessons. t to Oxford in 1919, he failed to master Greek for university entrance: 'university lectures', he told his father, 'interfere very much with my work'—which was versewriting stimulated by avid readings in Nietzsche, Darwin, and the English Elizabethan and Romantic poets. Holidays spent in wandering through France and along the Mediterranean coast in search of the sun, odd jobs, and adventure alternated with periods in bohemian London. Among his early fruitful contacts were (Sir) William Walton, the Sitwells, Wyndham Lewis [q.v.] (many of whose 'blasting and bombardiering' attitudes he adopted), and T. W. Earp, who deserves credit for weaning Campbell from Tennysonian pastiche and arousing his enthusiasm for the French Symbolist poets. In 1922 he married without parental consent and forfeited, for a time, the generous parental allowance.

While living in a small converted stable on the coast of North Wales, Campbell completed his first long poem, *The Flaming Terrapin* (1924), a humanistic allegory on the rejuvenation of man, projected in episodes and images of such flamboyant splendour that the work justly made him famous. Returning to Natal, he started, with William Plomer and Laurens van der Post, a monthly review called *Voorslag* (*Whiplash*), but after two numbers he resigned and returned to England. Beneath the romantic idealism of the *Terrapin* was a promising vein of Byronic satire. This was now opened up with skill and malice in *The Wayzgoose* (1928), a hilarious lampoon, in rhyming couplets, on the cultural limitations of South Africa. But he soon found that the cults and coteries of literary Bloomsbury were as little to his taste as the 'shop-keeping mentality' of Durban; so off he trekked again with his family, this time, in 1928, to the genial warmth of Martigues in maritime Provence. There he lived strenuously as a poet, bon-vivant, casual fisherman, and amateur athlete. The physical activities for which he achieved some local reputation were the dangerous sports of waterjousting, steer-throwing, and snatching the cocarde from between the horns of cows and young bulls in the small arenas of Istres and Fos sur Mer.

Both South Africa and the Midi contributed motives to the passion and luminosity of his first book of lyrics, *Adamastor* (1930), and to the less important *Poems* (Paris) of the same year. Such pieces as 'Tristan da Cunha', 'The Albatross', 'The Zulu Girl', 'The Serf',

'The Palm', 'To a Pet Cobra', and 'Horses on the Camargue' went far beyond Campbell's modest claim to have 'added a few solar colours to English poetry'. Borrowings from Kuhlemann, Mistral, Valéry, and Baudelaire were transmuted into a wholly individual style characterized by firmness of outline, copiousness of images, resonance of tone, symbolic overtones, wit, irony, and a superb mastery of rhyme and versification. This success was quickly followed by his best satire, *The Georgiad* (1931), a comic fantasy which pilloried brilliantly, if somewhat vindictively, the moral and aesthetic follies of Georgian 'Bloomsburies'; it also set deep the foundations of an unpopularity which was exacerbated by the reactionary opinions, and the bark-if-not-bite of fascist attitudes, in his first autobiography, *Broken Record* (1934). Yet in this book he writes with such charm and panache on the wild life of Africa and the carefree life of a 'useless poet' that one forgives or accepts his gasconading and swashbuckling and enjoys (with reservations) his confessedly Münchausen-like anecdotes.

Before leaving France for Spain in 1933, Campbell, always a great *aficionado* and frequenter of the *manades*, published *Taurine Provence* (1932), a book on bull-fighting, and a third book of lyrics, *Flowering Reeds* (1933), which contains the well known 'Choosing a Mast' and 'The Gum Trees' and reveals a new classical restraint and brooding tenderness.

In 1935 the Campbells were received into the Roman Catholic Church and shortly afterwards settled in Toledo. By temperament the poet was aristocratic and traditionalist, and although always a good mixer with peasants, gipsies, fishermen, and door-keepers, he had little sympathy with popular humanitarian movements; hence he watched with distaste the growing revolutionary forces in Spain. At considerable risk he sheltered priests and hid the Carmelite archives in his own house; but on being caught in the bombardment of Toledo he and his family were evacuated to England, where he saw the publication and virtual boycotting of his most religious, subtle, and intensely Spanish book of original poems, *Mithraic Emblems* (1936). Early in 1937 he returned to Spain as war correspondent of the *Tablet*, saw some fighting on the Madrid front, sustained an injury to his left hip, and soon retired to Portugal, where he wrote his longest and least disciplined poem, the virulent anti-Red, pro-Franco *Flowering Rifle* (1939) which horrified the English liberal press.

On returning from Italy to Spain at the end of the civil war, Campbell revised his opinion of the Axis powers. Pulled by old loyalties, and now eager to fight for the democratic principles which he never ceased to criticize, he returned to England, and after launching a popular selection of his best poems, *Sons of the Mistral* (1941), he enlisted as a private in the Intelligence Corps. Later, as a sergeant he commanded Askari coast-watchers in East Africa; but owing to chronic osteo arthritis in his injured left hip he was discharged as unfit in 1944. Back in London, he was a talks producer in the B.B.C. from 1946 to 1949, and in the former year published *Talking Bronco*, a piquant mixture of pure poems, like 'Dreaming Spires' and 'The Skull in the Desert', and with near-libellous attacks on the left-wing poets.

His three years as joint-editor of *Catacomb*, a right-wing periodical, initiated his last productive period: *Collected Poems* (1949; vol. ii, 1957); *Light on a Dark Horse* (1951), his racy and at times *ben trovato* recension of his life-story and legend up to 1935; *Lorca* (1952), a critical study with translations; *The Mamba's Precipice* (1953), a boy's tale of adventure in Natal. His masterly translations from Spanish, French, and Portuguese include *Poems of St. John of the Cross* (1951) awarded the Foyle poetry prize; Baudelaire's *Les Fleurs du Mal* (1952); *Six Spanish Plays* (ed. Bentley, New York 1959), the five translated by Campbell having been produced on the Third Programme; Calderón's *The Surgeon of His Honour* (University of Wisconsin, 1960) two Portuguese novels by Eça de Queiroz —*Cousin Bazilio* (1953) and *The City and the Mountains* (1955); *Poemas Imperfeitos* by J. Paço d'Arcos, englished as *Nostalgia* (1960). In the third volume of his *Collected Poems* (1960) there are fine renderings of Camões, Lorca, Horace, etc. Although not an exact scholar Campbell was a born poet. 'He was an amazing linguist' said T. S. Eliot, 'and certainly no one can have equalled his translations of John of the Cross and Rimbaud's *Bateau Ivre*.'

In 1952 Campbell made his last move to Portugal. In the many lectures which he gave in England, Spain, and on two visits to America, he read and discussed his poems in his unpolished accent, and gaily attacked the obscure, 'cross-word happy' poets (some of whom he had actually punched) and the 'parasitical growths' of modern analytical criticism. The climax of his career came in 1954, when he flew to the university of Natal to receive the honorary degree of D.Litt. On his return to Sintra he wrote his last prose work, *Portugal* (1957). There again we find the great zest for life, the fighting spirit, the passion for heroism and dynamic beauty, the extrovert impatience with doubts and hesitations and the fundamentally pious man's love of earth and of simple agrarian or equestrian peoples; there are also the occasional exaggerations, credulities, prejudices, and tall stories given as fact, which mar the literary quality but not necessarily the readability of his prose. Fortunately his best poetry is quite free from these blemishes.

On 23 April 1957 Campbell was killed outright in a car-crash near Setubal, Portugal, and was buried in the San Pedro cemetery near Sintra. His marriage to Mary Margaret, daughter of Walter Chancellor Garman, a Wednesbury doctor, and sister of the second wife of Sir Jacob Epstein [q.v.], was a very happy one. He was unswervingly devoted to his 'Mary' and their two daughters, and often said that but for his wife's faith in him and her loyal support he would never have achieved success as a writer.

Six foot two, handsome, with remarkable eyes and every inch a poet, the young South African in a typical broad-brimmed hat was painted by Augustus John (*c.* 1924) and the portrait now hangs in the Pittsburgh Art Gallery.

[Campbell's autobiographies and unpublished remains; private information; personal knowledge.]   W. H. GARDNER.

CAMPBELL, DAME JANET MARY (1877–1954), medical officer, was born in Brighton 5 March 1877, the daughter of George Campbell, bank manager, and his wife, Mary Letitia Rowe. She attended Brighton High School and later went to Germany for some months where she acquired a good knowledge of the language which served her when she attended a postgraduate course in Vienna.

After graduating M.B. London in 1901 at the London School of Medicine for Women, she took her M.D. and M.S. degrees in 1904 and 1905, a remarkable achievement. There followed house appointments at the Royal Free Hospital followed by the position of senior medical officer at the Belgrave Hospital for Chil-

dren, a post eagerly sought by women graduates, since at that time it was one of the few London hospitals to employ them.

Janet Campbell was a member of the Medical Women's Federation, eventually becoming its president. At one time she was closely associated with Dartford Physical Training College, first as honorary secretary and afterwards for a time as chairman.

As a result of the South African war public interest in the problem of national physique had been aroused and under the Education Act of 1902 school medical officers were appointed by some education authorities. An interdepartmental committee appointed in 1903 recommended, after extensive inquiries, among other measures the introduction of systematic medical inspection of children in elementary schools which now forms an integral part of every modern system of education.

In 1904 Janet Campbell became an assistant school medical officer in the London School Medical Service where she came under the stimulating influence of James Kerr, the 'father' of school hygiene and the author of *The Fundamentals of School Health* (1926). From there in 1907 she joined the Board of Education as its first full-time woman medical officer.

The high rate of infant mortality was giving concern to the public and to local authorities, and in 1919, when the Ministry of Health made its appearance with Sir George Newman [q.v.] as chief medical officer, Janet Campbell was appointed senior medical officer in charge of maternity and child welfare. At the same time she retained her connection with the Board of Education as chief woman adviser. She gave her time and her energies wholeheartedly to the organization of a vigorous and progressive scheme for the welfare of mothers and children.

During the war of 1914–18 in addition to her specialized work her services were at the disposal of government and international committees. She was a medical member of the War Cabinet committee on women in industry and afterwards served on the health committee of the League of Nations.

In 1917 she wrote a valuable and influential report for the Carnegie United Kingdom Trust on physical welfare of mothers and children. She also produced official reports on the recruitment and training of midwives and on the teaching of obstetrics and gynaecology in medical schools.

In 1924 her well-known report on maternal mortality was published. She was appointed D.B.E. and Durham University made her an honorary doctor of hygiene in the same year. Her reports from 1923 to 1932 on the protection of motherhood, on neonatal and infant mortality, and on the maternity services have all of them had an important influence on administrative reforms and have helped in large part to reduce the mortality and morbidity rate of women and children.

In 1934 she married Michael Heseltine (died 1952), registrar of the General Medical Council, and under Civil Service rules she had to give up her office.

Her influence on the public health services of the whole country as they affected women and children was profound. She was the great pioneer of maternity and child welfare services and as such was universally acknowledged. It was not only the charming and rather diffident manner of this tall good-looking, well-dressed woman which attracted the admiration and respect of those who came into contact with her. Her clear-thinking brain and her sound knowledge of her subject enabled her to grasp essentials quickly so that her wise, considered opinion and advice were sought by local authorities, medical officers, and hospitals throughout the country and by organizations far beyond the confines of the United Kingdom.

Dame Janet was a very good horsewoman and riding gave her special pleasure as did walking and physical exercise which probably accounted for her upright carriage. Gardening was a favourite hobby and when she lived outside London she grew a wonderful display of roses. She had always taken a keen interest in current affairs and in politics of the day and was a justice of the peace for Surrey and also for Gloucestershire. She loved a good play and up to the end she kept her interest in modern literature and the world around her. She died 27 September 1954 in Chelsea where she lived with her two cousins after a long and painful illness spent in a nursing-home in London.

[*British Medical Journal* and *Lancet*, 9 October 1954; private information; personal knowledge.]　　MARGARET HOGARTH.

CAMPBELL, SIR RONALD HUGH (1883–1953), diplomatist, was born in London 27 September 1883, the eldest son of Sir Francis Alexander Campbell, assistant under-secretary of state for foreign

affairs from 1902 to 1911, and his wife, Dora Edith, daughter of Hugh Hammersley, banker. Campbell was educated at Haileybury and in 1907 passed a competitive examination and was appointed a clerk in the Foreign Office. In 1910 he accompanied Sir Arthur Paget on a special embassy to the courts of Munich, Stuttgart, and Sofia to announce the accession of King George V. In the following year he was in attendance on the representative of Venezuela at the coronation. From 1913 to 1919 he was private secretary to the permanent under-secretary and in 1919–20 to Lord Curzon [q.v.], then acting secretary of state. He was appointed C.M.G. in 1917. Having risen by 1928 to be a counsellor in the Foreign office, he was in 1929 appointed envoy extraordinary and minister plenipotentiary in Paris where he often acted as chargé d'affaires. Speaking French to perfection, he made many friends in official circles and proved himself a shrewd observer and an able negotiator. He was appointed minister to Belgrade in 1935 and K.C.M.G. in 1936. His lucid and well-balanced dispatches revealed an exceptional insight into the shifting pattern of Yugoslavia's foreign policy, subjected as it then was to mounting Nazi-Fascist pressures.

In July 1939 Campbell was promoted to be ambassador at Paris as successor to Sir Eric Phipps [q.v.]. He was sworn of the Privy Council and took up his new appointment in early November. Calm, unruffled, as impeccable in his skill at unravelling knotty problems as in his personal appearance, endowed with the sturdiest common sense, an infinite capacity for taking pains, and a pawky sense of humour, this unassuming and gently persuasive Scot soon found his qualities as a diplomatist put to the severest test. When the Germans invaded France, he took part on 11 June 1940 in the exodus of her government from Paris first to Tours and three days later to Bordeaux. In intensely trying conditions he exerted himself without intermission to prevail on the French political leaders to transfer at least the nucleus of a government overseas and to place their fleet beyond the range of Axis interference. After the signature of an armistice between the Pétain government and the Germans had made it useless for him to remain at Bordeaux, he embarked for England on the evening of 22 June. On his return home his zeal and courage were recognized by the award of the

G.C.M.G. In November 1940 he was appointed ambassador to Lisbon.

In mid-December 1941 Anglo-Portuguese relations came near to breaking-point as a result of the unannounced entry of Australian and Dutch troops into Portuguese Timor to protect the defenceless colony from invasion by the Japanese. Campbell's dogged resourcefulness prevented the crisis from adverse development: his masterly telegrams reinforced by a visit to London brought about an agreement that the troops would be withdrawn as soon as Portuguese arrived to replace them. Although the Japanese seized the island before this arrangement could be completed, Dr. Salazar paid warm tribute to the British Government for its helpful attitude. In the summer of 1943 Campbell received the emissaries of Marshal Badoglio when they arrived in Lisbon to sue for an armistice. In the same year he presided over the delicate negotiations which led to the grant of facilities in the Azores to the allied forces. His unremitting efforts were successful in securing for Britain the lion's share of Portugal's vital supplies of wolfram. In 1945 his superbly handled mission in Portugal came to an end and he went into retirement. He died at Lymington 15 November 1953.

It was appropriate that a man of Campbell's exemplary patience should have been an expert angler and that, with his keen eye for precise detail, he also excelled as a skilled cabinet-maker. The last years of his life were clouded by the death in 1949 of his charming and vivacious wife, Helen, daughter of Richard Graham, whom he had married in 1908. He was also predeceased by his only daughter. His only son, Robin, who survived him, had been severely wounded in the attempt to kidnap Rommel during the North Africa campaign.

[*The Times*, 17 November 1953; personal knowledge.]   JOHN BALFOUR.

CAMPION, GILBERT FRANCIS MONTRIOU, BARON CAMPION (1882–1958), clerk of the House of Commons, was born at Simla 11 May 1882, the eldest son of John Montriou Campion, later chief engineer, Punjab, in the public works department of India, by his wife, Grace Hannah, daughter of Abraham Collis Anderson, of county Kilkenny. He was educated at Bedford School and won a classical scholarship to Hertford College, Oxford, where he gained first class

honours in both classical moderations (1903) and *literae humaniores* (1905). In 1906 he took the Civil Service examination but decided to accept the nomination of Sir Courtenay Ilbert [q.v.] for a clerkship in the House of Commons.

Campion's interest in comparative procedure was early shown when he and his colleague, W. P. Johnston, suggested to Ilbert that they should visit the principal countries in Europe and gather information about their parliamentary systems. The results of their investigations were placed at the disposal of the select committee on procedure, 1914, and appended to their minutes of evidence. On the outbreak of war Campion joined the army and became a captain in the Army Service Corps. He was invalided home from France and in 1917 was appointed secretary to the conference on the reform of the second chamber presided over by Lord Bryce [q.v.] who warmly commended Campion's wide knowledge of parliamentary institutions at home and abroad. In 1919 Campion was appointed secretary to the conference on devolution presided over by Speaker Lowther [q.v.]. The scheme of regional grand councils proposed by Lowther is believed to have been substantially Campion's work.

In 1921 Campion became second clerk assistant, and in 1929, the year before his promotion to clerk assistant, he published *An Introduction to the Procedure of the House of Commons*, which was conceived originally as a manual of first-aid for members but was in fact a complete account of the procedure of the House. In 1937 he succeeded Sir Horace Dawkins as clerk of the House and when war broke out in 1939 he was responsible for administering the arrangements for meeting in Church House and the procedural innovations required by security.

The publication in 1946 of the fourteenth edition of Sir T. Erskine May [q.v.] on *Parliamentary Practice* marked the end of twelve years' labour and established Campion's reputation as a master of parliamentary procedure. This massive work was rearranged and largely rewritten under his editorship. New sections on the use and control of parliamentary time, on financial procedure, and on privilege bore the mark of Campion's powers of analysis and exposition. An historical introduction which he had hoped to expand into a separate volume outlined briefly the results of modern research.

In 1945 Campion was invited to submit

a comprehensive scheme of reform to the select committee on procedure. Although his more radical proposals for relieving the House of legislative detail and for improving its control of expenditure and delegated legislation were rejected, his suggestions for reorganizing the business of supply were adopted. These changes with others made on the initiative of the Government were incorporated in the fifteenth edition of Erskine May (1950), edited by Campion with the assistance of (Sir) T. G. B. Cocks.

After the war the movement towards self-government in the colonies stimulated the demand for information and guidance from the mother Parliament. Although Campion's plan for the regular interchange of clerks was never put into operation, he authorized the first official visits of a clerk to Commonwealth legislatures.

In July 1948 Campion retired, and his outstanding services to the Commons were recognized in tributes from Herbert Morrison (later Lord Morrison of Lambeth), the leader of the House, and (Sir) Winston Churchill on behalf of the Opposition. The following month he set out on an official tour of Commonwealth Parliaments in the course of which he visited Ceylon, Australia, New Zealand, South Africa, Rhodesia, Nyasaland, Kenya, and the Sudan. In 1949 he made a similar visit to the legislatures of Canada. Owing to ill health he was never able to write the book which would have contained the results of these investigations, but some impressions of the earlier tour were contributed at intervals to the *Sunday Times*.

On his return from these travels Campion was appointed the first clerk of the Consultative Assembly of the Council of Europe, which met at Strasbourg. The difficulties and weaknesses of this novel experiment in European co-operation were discussed by Campion in articles contributed to the *Sunday Times* (30 July 1950) and *The Times* (13 November 1950). His early interest in comparative procedure had come to fruition in 1946 when he was elected president of the autonomous section of secretaries-general of the Inter-Parliamentary Union. On his initiative the material was collected for the handbook of *European Parliamentary Procedure*, which he compiled jointly with D. W. S. Lidderdale and published in 1953.

Campion ranks with the greatest of his predecessors at the Table of the House. By temperament a scholar and somewhat

shy in his dealings with people, he had a humanity and sense of humour which made him much more than the pre-eminent practitioner of his profession. His power of analysis and lucid expression made him the ideal expositor of the intricacies of procedure; his grasp of principle combined with his wide knowledge of historical precedent and contemporary parallel gave to his views on the British parliamentary system a unique authority.

He was appointed C.B. in 1932, K.C.B. in 1938, G.C.B. in 1948, and was raised to the peerage in 1950. Hertford College made him an honorary fellow in 1946 and the university of Oxford conferred on him an honorary D.C.L. in 1950. He was a keen golfer and in 1948 won the parliamentary golf handicap.

In 1920 Campion married Hilda Mary, daughter of the late William Alfred Spafford, principal of the Darlington training college for women teachers. There were no children. Campion died at his home at Abinger Hammer, near Dorking, 6 April 1958.

[*The Times*, 7 April 1958; private information; personal knowledge.]

K. R. MACKENZIE

CAMROSE, first VISCOUNT (1879–1954), newspaper proprietor. [See BERRY, WILLIAM EWERT.]

CAPE, HERBERT JONATHAN (1879–1960), publisher, was born in London 15 November 1879, the youngest of the seven children of Jonathan Cape, builder's clerk of Cumbrian origin, and his wife, Caroline Page. He received little formal education, and at the age of sixteen he started his career as an errand-boy for Hatchard's bookshop in Piccadilly, at a wage of twelve shillings a week. Four years later, in 1899, he joined the English house of the American publishers Harper & Brothers, where he worked as a travelling salesman, first in the provinces and later in London. In 1904 he moved to the English publisher Gerald Duckworth as London traveller, and later became manager.

In the war of 1914–18 Cape served in the Royal Army Ordnance Corps, where he reached the rank of captain. After the war he returned to Duckworth, but early in 1920 he went as manager to the Medici Society: its chief products were colour reproductions of paintings, with some book-publishing on the side. There he met George Wren Howard, fourteen years junior, who after taking a degree at Cambridge had fought in the war and was now learning the business. Cape quickly saw that Howard had a fine sense of design in book-production, as well as a good business head; the two became friends and allies. After some months they decided that there was no future for them where they were, and that they had better start a new firm of their own. Howard managed to borrow his share of their exiguous starting-capital from his father; Cape with no such resource was compelled to look elsewhere. All the time he had been with Duckworth the firm's most profitable author had been Elinor Glyn [q.v.], and Cape had always advocated cheap editions of her books, which Duckworth had steadfastly refused to issue. Cape persuaded Duckworth to lease him the 'shilling rights' of Elinor Glyn's books, which he republished under the imprint of Page & Co.: the profits of this venture helped to provide Cape with his share of the necessary capital.

One thing more was needful: a literary adviser, and for this they engaged Edward Garnett (husband of Constance Garnett, q.v.), the ablest and most influential publisher's reader of recent time, whom Cape had known at Duckworth's. He stayed with Cape until his death in 1937, and it was largely his literary judgement, coupled with Howard's production, which gained the new firm its outstanding reputation for quality during the next two decades.

The firm of Jonathan Cape opened its doors at 11 Gower Street, Bloomsbury, on January 1921, and its first publication was a reissue of *Travels in Arabia Deserta* by C. M. Doughty [q.v.], originally issued 1888 with no success. This new edition, two volumes at the huge price of nine guineas, seemed so risky that it was initially issued jointly with the Medici Society. But its success was prompt and substantial, and long before its appearance had won the new firm one of its strongest supporters. Knowing that T. E. Lawrence [q.v.] was interested in the book, they persuaded him to write a long introduction for nothing. This eventually led to the firm's publishing Lawrence's *Revolt in the Desert* (1927), *Seven Pillars of Wisdom* (1935), and *The Mint* (1955).

The firm quickly came to the fore. In 1922 Cape purchased the business of A. C. Field, a small publisher of independence and judgement, thus adding the works of Samuel Butler and W. H. Davies [qq.v.] his growing list.

Cape was almost the first English publisher to visit the United States in search of books and authors: hitherto the traffic had been mostly in the opposite direction: and very soon he was the English publisher of three future Nobel prize-winners (Sinclair Lewis, Ernest Hemingway, and Eugene O'Neill), as well as H. L. Mencken, Sherwood Anderson, Louis Bromfield, and Dorothy Canfield. Later Robert Frost was added to the list.

In 1925 the firm moved to its lasting home at 30 Bedford Square, from which in due course appeared the first, and most of the subsequent, works of H. E. Bates, Duff Cooper [q.v.], Ian and Peter Fleming, Eric Linklater, J. E. Neale, (Dame) C. V. Wedgwood, and many others. The children's books of Hugh Lofting and Arthur Ransome were perennially successful, and when Cape heard that Stanley Baldwin was planning to speak at the Royal Literary Fund dinner about *Precious Bane* by Mary Webb [q.v.], which Cape had published, he speedily bought the rights of her earlier books from their original publishers and reissued them in an immensely popular collected edition. Cape's many cheap series, of which the Travellers' Library was the most prominent, set a new standard of quality and appearance, and held the field until the arrival of paperbacks.

Cape knew his own limitations and stuck to what he knew: general publishing and high quality books (never attempting to enter the educational, technical, or specialist markets, of which he was ignorant), and his standard remained unusually high. In this he was helped, first by Edward Garnett, and later by the diverse talents of Hamish Miles, David Garnett, Guy Chapman, J. E. Neale, (Dame) C. V. Wedgwood, Daniel George, and William Plomer.

Cape was a tall, handsome man of commanding stature. He was an extremely hard worker, always keeping the same hours as the most junior member of his staff. By some he was considered a hard man, and he was certainly a shrewd one, but he had a humorous as well as a sentimental side and could sometimes be prevailed upon. He seldom became close personal friends with his authors, but they respected his integrity and admired his thorough knowledge of publishing, realizing also that he undoubtedly possessed that mysterious 'flair' which is worth more to a publisher than an expensive education. Except for reading, and the governorship of Frensham Heights, the co-educational school, he had no other interests. Publishing was his life, and he worked at it until his dying day.

Cape was three times married and three times a widower. In 1907 he married Edith Louisa Creak (died 1919), by whom he had two daughters. Secondly, he married in 1927 Olive Vida James (died 1931), daughter of Maurice George Blackmon; they had a son and a daughter. Thirdly, in 1941 he married Kathleen Webb (died 1953), daughter of Philip Wilson; they had one son. Cape died suddenly in his London flat 10 February 1960. An oil-painting of him by Colin Colahan hangs in the firm's office in Bedford Square.

[Private information; personal knowledge.]
RUPERT HART-DAVIS.

CARLING, SIR ERNEST ROCK (1877–1960), surgeon and pioneer in radio-therapy, was born in Guildford, Surrey, 6 March 1877, the third son of Francis Rees Carling, master ironmonger, and his wife, Lydia Colebrook. He was educated at the Royal Grammar School, Guildford, and King's College, London, and received his medical education at the Westminster Hospital medical school which he joined at the age of eighteen and of which in due course he became dean. His medical training was interrupted by service in the South African war with the Imperial Yeomanry Field Hospital as a surgical dresser to his chief, Charles Stonham, Westminster's senior surgeon.

Carling qualified M.R.C.S., L.R.C.P. in 1901. Early in his university studies he showed both brilliance and versatility by being awarded a gold medal and exhibition in pharmacology and therapeutics, and a further gold medal and scholarship in obstetrics and gynaecology in the final M.B. which he took in 1902, followed by his B.S. in 1903 and F.R.C.S. in 1904. After graduation he held appointments at his own hospital, first in the pathology department, then as surgical registrar, to be followed by his appointment to the honorary consulting staff as assistant surgeon (1906), surgeon (1919), and honorary consulting surgeon on his retirement from the active staff in 1942.

Carling was a general surgeon of more than average ability and before the days of specialization an orthopaedic surgeon of considerable skill. In addition to the Westminster he served the Seamen's Hospital, Greenwich, the Peace Memorial Hospital, Watford, the Chislehurst Hospi-

tal, and the King Edward VII Convalescent Home for Officers at Osborne. As a member of the Territorial Army he was mobilized on the outbreak of war in 1914 and served as captain in the Royal Army Medical Corps with the 4th London Hospital and later in France and Flanders.

In many aspects of medical thinking and practice Carling was ahead of his time. The planning in almost every detail of the new Westminster Hospital, medical school, and nurses home in St. John's Gardens was as much his as the architect's and he spent almost five years to see the completion of the building in the spring of 1939. As a teacher 'Rocky' Carling was best at the bedside and in the operating theatre—gentle, careful, logical, courageous and determined despite the frailty of his appearance. But his interest in and service to medical education were much more widespread: he remained a member of the academic council of the Westminster medical school until the end of his days. For many years he was a member of the faculty of medicine and of the board of advanced medical studies of the university of London, and a member, for a time chairman, of the court of examiners at the Royal College of Surgeons. He was in demand as an examiner in the universities of London, Edinburgh, and Sheffield, and in the Faculty of Radiology. He took a genuine and wide interest in benevolent activities related to his profession: as a member of council of the Royal Medical Benevolent Fund, treasurer of the Society for the Relief of Widows and Orphans of Medical Men, a trustee, and chairman of the medical advisory committee, of the Nuffield Provincial Hospitals Trust, and president of the Medical Protection Society.

Carling's interest in the use of radium in the treatment of cancer dated from 1920 when in company with some of his junior colleagues he visited the Fondation Curie in Paris and the radium institutes in Brussels and Stockholm. It was Carling's foresight which enabled the hospital to open the Radium Annex in Fitzjohn's Avenue, Hampstead, later to be the foundation of the well-equipped and modern radiotherapy department in the new hospital. He designed, and with the help of physicists built, the first early models of mass radium units. His interest in radiation was modern in its outlook and he recognized from the early years that the application of the use of X-rays and radium in medicine needed the special knowledge of physicists to achieve precision, accuracy, and safety.

This scientific approach opened for him the door to a second profession which he embraced with enthusiasm and which occupied most of his time after his retirement from active surgical practice. It shows the character of his intellect which led him to the membership of the National Radium Commission and the Atomic Energy Commission, the chairmanship of the International Commission of Radiological Protection; the membership and for a time chairmanship of the standing advisory committee on cancer and radiotherapy of the Ministry of Health. This second career was to him more rewarding and to the country of greater benefit than even his earlier surgical achievements. His specialized knowledge resulted in his appointment as consultant adviser to the Home Office and to the Ministry of Labour, as expert adviser to the World Health Organization, and member of the Medical Research Council. His ever young and unbiased attitude to scientific progress and the changes in the times he lived made him the obvious choice as chairman of the advisory committee on medical nomenclature.

Carling was knighted in 1944, made an honorary fellow of the Faculty of Radiology, received an honorary LL.D. from Queen's University, Belfast, and was elected a fellow of the Royal College of Physicians.

His chief recreation in his early years was travel and visiting art museums, especially in Italy where for a time he had a small house which he used as a retreat from his many commitments. He was a great conversationalist and a lover of books, mostly on scientific subjects.

In 1901 Carling married Edith Petra (died 1959), daughter of the Rev. Edward Ennis Rock, vicar of Sutton, Woodbridge, Suffolk, and had two sons. He died at his home in London 15 July 1960. The Nuffield Provincial Hospitals Trust funded a Sir Ernest Rock Carling memorial in the form of an annual fellowship. There is a portrait by A. C. Davidson-Houston in the offices of the Medical Protection Society and in the Westminster Hospital; also a bust outside one of the hospital wards named after him.

[*British Medical Journal*, 23 July and 6 August 1960; *Lancet*, 23 July 1960; *The Times*, July 1960; private information; personal knowledge.]

STANFORD CADE.

CARLYLE, BENJAMIN FEARNLEY, DOM AELRED (1874–1955), founder of the Benedictine community of Prinknash Abbey, Gloucestershire, was born in Sheffield 7 February 1874, the elder son and first of the six children of James Fearnley Carlyle and his wife, Anna Maria Champion Kelly, of Yealmpton, Devon. He was named after his grandfather, the Rev. Benjamin Fearnley Carlyle, who had been vicar of Badgeworth, Gloucestershire. In 1885 his father, a civil engineer, was appointed locomotive superintendent of the Buenos Aires and Rosario Railway, and the family moved to the Argentine. Carlyle with his younger brother was sent back to England to school, and was at Blundell's until his father's death in 1890. The family then settled at Newton Abbot where Carlyle attended the College until he passed his pre-medical examinations. He next spent four years as a medical student at St. Bartholomew's Hospital. During that time he was clothed as a Benedictine oblate (1893), taking the name of Aelred, and, encouraged by Archbishop Frederick Temple [q.v.], began the work of founding a religious community of men to revive in the Church of England the ancient Benedictine rule. In 1896 he abandoned his medical studies and went to live in the Isle of Dogs where the Priory soon became the centre both of a monastic life and of work among the poor of London's east end.

In May 1902, when the young community was eventually established at Painsthorpe Hall in Yorkshire, lent them by Lord Halifax [q.v.], Aelred's election as abbot was approved by the same archbishop; and in November 1904, with letters of authorization from W. D. Maclagan [q.v.], archbishop of York, he received Anglican orders in America from Dr. Grafton, bishop of Fond-du-Lac, Wisconsin.

On 18 October 1906 abbot and community took possession of the island of Caldey off Tenby, on the Pembrokeshire coast. With its ancient buildings, natural beauty, and long monastic history, Caldey became increasingly a focus of interest for Anglo-Catholics; but although controversy had no part in the life of the community, developments in the Church of England were watched with some misgivings, and by 1912 doubts had arisen upon the relation of the community to the Anglican Church and of that Church to the rest of the Catholic world. It became clear to the abbot and most of the community that they must make their submission to the 'Church that is in communion with Peter', and on 5 March 1913 they were received into the Roman Catholic Church. The next day they were given canonical status as oblates of the Benedictine Abbey of Maredsous, in Belgium, where Aelred went to serve his novitiate. He made his solemn profession there before Abbot Columba Marmion on 29 June 1914, and on 5 July was ordained priest by the bishop of Namur. On 10 August he was installed at Caldey by the bishop of Menevia, from whom he received the abbatial blessing on 18 October 1914.

The war years were difficult for a community already deeply in debt through the abbot's grandiose building schemes. He made 'begging tours' of the United States and Jamaica in 1917–18 and of Brazil, the Argentine, and Chile in 1920–21. His health, however, had begun to cause some disquiet. In 1921 he resigned his abbacy and, accompanied by one of the older members of the community, sailed for British Columbia whence he had received an urgent appeal for men to work in the mission fields. He was invited by the archbishop of Vancouver to make his headquarters on the shores of the Okanagan Lake where, during the next nine years, he gained valuable experience in the ways of Western Canada. In 1930 he was given care of souls in the mining district of Princeton, but in 1933 he journeyed to Spain to test his possible vocation at the Carthusian monastery of Miraflores, near Burgos. Before long it was agreed that the greater usefulness of this dynamic but restless and erratic priest lay in the West where the clergy were so few; so he returned to his former territories and to the missions along the Pacific coast.

Incardinated into the diocese of Vancouver in 1936 he now entered upon what was probably the most fruitful period of his life. To the chaplaincy of St. Vincent's Home in Vancouver and to the Apostleship of the Sea was added the care of the prisoners in Oakalla, the provincial jail. It was there above all that his wide experience and deep, compassionate knowledge of human nature, salted with his quiet wisdom and swift humour, enabled him to bring hope and courage to those who most needed help on the road to rehabilitation. His after-care of prisoners, as friend of the friendless, won the highest regard from the bench and bar of British Columbia. It was in recognition of this

work especially that he was presented with the freedom of the city of Vancouver at the public farewell ceremony before he left for home in May 1951 to pass the late evening of his life with his brethren. He renewed his solemn vows as a Benedictine monk in 1953; died 14 October 1955 at Corston, near Bath; and was buried in the abbey of Prinknash whither the community had moved in 1928.

Carlyle's principal writings appeared for many years in 'The Abbot's Letter' in *Pax*, the community quarterly; his exposition of 'Our Purpose and Method' written in Anglican days, was considered by the abbot primate of the order one of the best things written on the Benedictine ideal. Voluminous diaries and a vast number of letters remained to be edited.

[Peter F. Anson, *Abbot Extraordinary* (in which is reproduced a drawing by Gregory Brown), 1958; community archives; personal knowledge.] AIDAN ANGLE

CARPENTER, ALFRED FRANCIS BLAKENEY (1881–1955), vice-admiral was born at Barnes, Surrey, 17 September 1881, the only son of Lieutenant (later Captain) Alfred Carpenter, R.N., by his first wife, Henrietta, daughter of G. A. F. Shadwell. His father in 1876 received the Albert medal and the Royal Humane Society bronze medal for rescuing a man overboard while serving in the *Challenger* and while in command of the Marine Survey of India, at the time of the Burmese war, was among the first naval officers to be appointed to the D.S.O. His grandfather, Commander Charles Carpenter, in 1814 assisted in the capture after a long chase of the American privateer *Rattlesnake*. His uncle was the writer Edward Carpenter [q.v.].

On leaving his preparatory school Carpenter entered the Royal Navy as a cadet in 1897. The following year as a midshipman he saw service in Crete during the massacres, and in 1900 he was with the naval brigade landed during the Boxer rising in China. After promotion in 1903 to lieutenant he specialized in navigation becoming a lieutenant-commander in 1911. In the year preceding the war he gained experience in staff duties on a war staff course and received the thanks of the Admiralty for various inventions of a specialized nature. In the same year he was awarded the silver medal of the Royal Humane Society for saving life at sea.

The outbreak of war in 1914 found him

in the *Iron Duke* on the staff of Sir John (later Earl) Jellicoe [q.v.], but in November 1915, after his promotion to commander, he was appointed navigating commander in the *Emperor of India*. In 1917 Roger (later Lord) Keyes [q.v.] was appointed director of plans at the Admiralty and Carpenter, who had been Keyes's navigating lieutenant in the *Venus*, successfully begged to be taken on his staff. There he was engaged in the secret plans for attacking Zeebrugge and Ostend with the purpose of blocking the exits from the submarine and destroyer bases. Keyes in his *Naval Memoirs* writes: 'Commander Carpenter's gift for going into the minutest details with the most meticulous care, greatly assisted me in preparing a detailed plan, and orders, which embodied the work of several officers.'

In selecting Carpenter for the command of the *Vindictive* Keyes knew he was choosing a man familiar with all the main phases of the operation. The whole conception of the attack on Zeebrugge and Ostend had the spirit and elements of the cut-and-thrust raids of Drake and Hawkins. The chance of favouring winds and currents coinciding with the eve of St. George's day 1918 gave the expedition an additional romantic appeal. To Keyes's signal 'St. George for England' Carpenter replied 'May we give the Dragon's tail a damned good twist'.

Carpenter had been promoted to acting captain for the expedition but his duties were confined to the command of the ship and Acting-Captain H. C. Halahan, who as senior to him, was in command of the landing force designed for attacking the Mole at Zeebrugge, partly to divert attention from the block ships and partly to destroy enemy armament. Carpenter's part in bringing the *Vindictive* alongside the Mole was vital to the success of the operation and his achievement in doing so is not to be underrated even though he brought her 340 yards beyond her planned position and thus out of reach of her primary object: the guns which commanded the approach to the harbour. It was characteristic that Carpenter freely admitted this error was entirely his, explaining that it was due to the great difficulty in recognizing the objects on the Mole amidst the shell and smoke flare. Keyes, in his first dispatch, paid tribute to Carpenter's personal share in the attack, pointing out that, from all reports he had, Carpenter's 'calm composure when

navigating mined waters and bringing his ship alongside the Mole in darkness, and his great bravery when the ship came under heavy fire, did much to encourage similar behaviour on the part of the crew, and thereby contributed greatly to the success of the operation'. His skill in bringing his ship away after the action was also highly praiseworthy.

Carpenter, as the senior surviving officer, was asked by Keyes to make recommendations for conspicuous gallantry, but he replied that he felt it would be invidious to select individuals where everyone had acted so splendidly. Nor would he take part in the ballot which was then arranged for an officer and rating for the V.C. in accordance with Rule 13. In this ballot, in which officers could only be elected by officers, Carpenter received one more vote than Commander (Sir) Harold Campbell of the *Daffodil* and was thus awarded the cross. He was immediately confirmed in his promotion to captain and later received the croix de guerre with palm and was made an officer of the Legion of Honour. His detailed account of *The Blocking of Zeebrugge* was published in 1921.

After Zeebrugge Carpenter was sent on a lecture tour of Canada and the United States (1918–19) and on his return, after a brief time in the naval intelligence department, on 1 October 1919 he was given command of a war course at Cambridge for naval officers. In 1921 he took over the command of the light cruiser *Carysfort* and in October 1923 was given charge of the senior officers technical course at Portsmouth. From February 1924 to September 1926 he held the triple post of captain of the dockyard, deputy superintendent, and King's harbour master at Chatham. After a period on special duty at the Admiralty he was given command of the *Benbow* in August 1927, transferring to the *Marlborough* the following May. He was promoted rear-admiral in August 1929, at a time when opportunities for employment in flag rank were limited, and placed on the retired list, on which he was promoted vice-admiral in 1934.

During his retirement Carpenter interested himself in the Merchant Navy, particularly in the training of its junior officers and cadets. He introduced the idea of a training ship, the *St. Briavels*, in which they could have practical experience in handling, manœuvring, and mooring ships, which was necessarily in the hands of senior officers on actual voyages. During the war he commanded the 17th Gloucestershire battalion of the Home Guard from 1940 to 1944. He was appointed a deputy-lieutenant for Gloucestershire in 1946. He died at his home in St. Briavels, Gloucestershire, 27 December 1955.

Lean and ascetic in appearance, Carpenter, brought up in the traditions of the navy, although somewhat conventional in his outlook, embodied many of the highest qualities of the best type of naval officer. Disciplined in mind, courageous and calm in action, energetic and inspiring as a leader and generous in his praise for subordinates, he also possessed an unusual gift for the mastery of detail and exactness in planning.

He married in 1903 Maud (died 1923), daughter of the Rev. Stafford Tordiffe, rector of Staplegrove, Somerset, by whom he had a daughter. He married secondly, in 1927, Hilda Margaret Alison, daughter of Dr. W. Chearnley Smith.

His portrait, painted in 1918 by Sir A. S. Cope, is in the National Portrait Gallery.

[*The Times*, 28 December 1955 and 4 January 1956; A. F. B. Carpenter, *The Blocking of Zeebrugge*, 1921; Sir Roger Keyes, *Naval Memoirs, 1916–18*, 1935; *Ostend and Zeebrugge, April 23; May 10, 1918. The Dispatches of Vice-Admiral Sir Roger Keyes . . . and other narratives of the operations*, ed. C. Sanford Terry, 1919; Sir Henry Newbolt, (Official) *History of the Great War. Naval Operations*, vol. v, 1931; private information.]
G. K. S. HAMILTON-EDWARDS.

CARTER, SIR EDGAR BONHAM-(1870–1956), jurist and administrator. [See BONHAM-CARTER.]

CARY, ARTHUR JOYCE LUNEL (1888–1957), author, was born in Londonderry, Ireland, 7 December 1888, the elder son of Arthur Pitt Chambers Cary and his first wife, Charlotte Louisa, daughter of James Joyce, bank manager, of Londonderry. The Ulster branch of the Cary family was founded by a grandson of Sir Robert Cary of Clovelly Court, Devonshire, George Cary, who went to Ireland in Chichester's administration, became recorder of Derry in 1613, married a sister of Sir Tristram Beresford, bart., built himself a handsome house, Redcastle near Derry, and established a family which was to live the life of Ascendancy landowners in beautiful Inishowen between Lough Swilly and Lough Foyle for 300 years. Joyce Cary's grandfather, Arthur Lunel Cary of Castlecary, lost his estate as

an indirect result of the Land Act of 1881. But already the pattern of life had changed: some of the family had acquired professions, some had emigrated—to Illinois, to Canada, to Australia—and one, Dr. Tristram Cary, had established himself in London. This pattern repeated itself in the next generation: one son to Canada, one to the United States, while two sons—of whom one was Joyce Cary's father—and four of their sisters lived mainly in or near London.

Joyce Cary's father trained and practised as an engineer in England. He lived in London with his wife and two sons, first at Nunhead and later in the Kitto Road. Charlotte Cary died in 1898 when Joyce was nine. Shortly afterwards the family moved to Gunnersbury, Middlesex, where Dr. Tristram Cary's home was a centre of intense, affectionate family life for his nephews and nieces and their children, described by Joyce Cary in a piece called 'Cromwell House' (*New Yorker*, 3 November 1956). There was still a close bond with Ireland, endless talk of the past, and frequent visits: the boys went every summer for their long holidays. When Joyce went to his Cary grandmother he would read omnivorously and dream of the past evoked for him by family portraits and by the stories the country people loved to tell him of his people. But when his grandmother Joyce took a holiday house for all her grandchildren, he with his many cousins would range about the countryside and picnic and bathe and sail. His autobiographical novel *A House of Children* (1941) is a radiant evocation of such a summer. He gained from his Irish experience not only the setting and characters for this novel and for *Castle Corner* (1938) but also a sense of history and tradition alive with the conflicts of religion and politics; a realization of the random injustice of life, from his family vicissitudes; and a deep affection for simple people together with an awareness that dignity is not a class prerogative.

He went to Hurstleigh preparatory school in Tunbridge Wells, then to Clifton College. Fifty years later he recalled, with not uncritical gratitude, two Clifton masters: one, who could communicate his profound love of Shakespeare, another who gave Cary the run of his library and encouraged him to write. At Clifton, Cary met (Sir) William Heneage Ogilvie who was to become not only a lifelong friend but also his brother-in-law.

Sir Frederick Wolff Ogilvie [q.v.] was a younger brother.)

A talent for drawing and painting ran through the Cary family—there are several sketches of Joyce as child and adolescent by his father and by his father's sister, Hessie. Cary resolved to become a painter, and at seventeen, having inherited from his grandmother Helen Joyce property which provided him with about £300 a year, he studied art at Edinburgh, where he spent 1907–9, with occasional visits to Paris. His Edinburgh teacher, devoted to classical art, laid great emphasis on the study of anatomy and drawing; the young Cary accepted that formal skills could be acquired in Edinburgh, but Paris of the Post-Impressionists provided the excitement of creative art.

During his last year at Edinburgh, dissatisfied with his painting, and feeling that this was not the medium in which he could best express himself, Cary turned his thoughts to writing. (A volume of his juvenilia, entitled *Verse* by Arthur Cary, was printed by Robert Grant in Edinburgh in 1908.) But all his life the visual arts remained a constant source of interest and pleasure. Moreover, when he came to write his novels he worked like a painter in that he planned out a rough design for the whole and then lavished his days on any parts of it, not in sequence, but turning happily at will from work on section 10 to section 3, and so on. He came, too, to value his careful training in anatomy and drawing not only for having strengthened his sense of structure and form but also for having made him aware of the sheer hard work involved in acquiring skill in any art.

He next went up to Trinity College, Oxford, ostensibly to read law (in which he got a fourth in 1912) but in practice to spend his time reading widely, writing, arguing and discussing, forming friendships and intellectual interests. Religion and philosophy now assumed an importance for him which they never lost. During his third year he shared digs in Holywell with Middleton Murry [q.v.], who has described Joyce as carpeting the floor with poems in the making. Paris during the vacations for talk and friendship was an extension of Oxford, but for intellectual and artistic excitement unique as always. During his final year he met his friend's sister, Gertrude Margaret Ogilvie, who was to become his wife in 1916 and his devoted love until her death in 1949. After Oxford, years of varied and active experience followed. During the Balkan wars (1912–13) he served as a medical orderly in the British Red Cross attached to the Montenegrin army during two campaigns, an experience recorded and illustrated in his posthumously published *Memoir of the Bobotes* (1964). Dr. Martin Leake, V.C., has attested that Cary 'went into a burning magazine at Antivari at great risk to his own life and helped to rescue two men'. Cary then spent a few months working with Sir Horace Plunkett [q.v.] for the Irish Agricultural Organization Society before joining the Nigerian political service in late 1913. Apart from home leaves, he remained in West Africa from May 1914 until 1920; but part of 1915–17 was spent in military service with the Nigerian Regiment in the Cameroons campaign during which he received a slight wound in an engagement on Mount Mora. After his marriage a long sequence of letters to his wife in England records his daily life in Borgu in vivid detail. The Nigerian experience was to provide the themes and settings for his four African novels: *Aissa Saved* (1932); *An American Visitor* (1933); *The African Witch* (1936); *Mister Johnson* (1939); for an unpublished play, *The King is Dead, Long Live the King*; and for several short stories. It is also the basis of two of his political treatises, *The Case for African Freedom* (1941) and *Britain and West Africa* (1946).

In 1920 Cary left the Nigerian service, and he and his wife settled in Oxford at 12 Parks Road, where they continued for the rest of their lives. Family life with his wife and four sons provided him with joy and anxiety—joy particularly in his wife's love and loyal encouragement, anxiety mainly about his work. His wife's devotion to music gave her an understanding of his stubborn pursuit of his own art, writing. This she needed, for although he had published (under the pseudonym Thomas Joyce) several short stories during and shortly after his African sojourn, he now found himself unable to write the novel he wanted to. He later said that at this time he had not yet arrived at a coherent view of reality and therefore the novel he was engaged on had no form. 'I simply lost control of it.' Ten years were to pass in intensive reading and writing, formulating questions and seeking answers to them, before his creative energies were freed. From then on he wrote easily and quickly, producing after 1932 sixteen novels, many short stories (*Spring Song and other stories*, 1960), and two long poems,

Marching Soldier (1945) and *The Drunken Sailor* (1947), as well as treatises, auto-biographical pieces, and essays.

The African novels were succeeded by *Charley is my Darling* (1940), whose characters are wartime evacuee children from London. After this sympathetic study of the have-nots, he wrote the novel based on his own childhood, *A House of Children* (James Tait Black memorial prize). The two childhood novels are in some sense paralleled by two novels in which the theme is the nature of woman, constant in changing circumstances: *The Moonlight* (1946) and *A Fearful Joy* (1949).

The overriding theme of the novels is man's freedom to shape his idea of the world and so to create his own life: 'from chaos man makes his world'. The main opposition is between the traditional and conserving on the one hand and the dynamic and creative on the other. All the novels are set within the same period, roughly from the end of the nineteenth century up to the second world war years, a period which Cary described as a pro-gress into liberty; he measured freedom of the mind by its ability to accept new truth, and the liberty a society affords not merely by absence of restraint but also by the positive opportunities for freedom it offers in terms of standards of living and education. Each novel is set firmly in its social and historical context of rapidly changing events, of societies in confronta-tion. All are suffused with the joy of living and all embody Cary's belief that beauty, art, loyalty are as indestructible as life itself. Few twentieth-century novelists have presented such a range of characters—politicians and preachers, artists and witches, lawyers and delinquent children. The novels focus on those areas of life where the creative impulse has most range and potential: art, politics, and religion.

Thus the most complex works, the two trilogies, are concerned, the one with art (*Herself Surprised, To Be a Pilgrim, The Horse's Mouth*, 1941–4) and the other with politics (*Prisoner of Grace, Except the Lord, Not Honour More*, 1952–5). A third trilogy was projected, with religion as its centre, but when in 1956 Joyce Cary realized that he could not live long enough to write it, he settled for treating the theme in a single volume, the unfinished, posthumously published novel, *The Cap-tive and the Free* (1959).

Cary was technically inventive and in-genious, and nowhere more than in his trilogies. He said that he devised this form

'to show three characters, not only in themselves, but as seen by others. The object was to get a three-dimensiona depth and force of character. One charac ter was to speak in each book and describe the other two as seen by that person'. The form affords rich opportunity for irony in the divergence between objective truth and the subjective view; between officia record and actual event; and mos notably between how a character see himself and how others see him. By the way in which he selects and interpret events, each narrator reveals his own view of reality. It is no accident that the writer who devised this subtle form en titled his aesthetic credo *Art and Realit* (Clark lectures, 1956).

The novels express his own idea of life and its joyful variety. *Art and Realit* derived inextricably both from his ex perience as novelist and from his percep tion of life's meaning as he conveyed it in his novels and in his own gay, courageou living until the day of his death, in Oxford, 29 March 1957.

A portrait in oils by Eric Kenningto is in the possession of the family; self-portrait (etching) is in the Nationa Portrait Gallery. Joyce Cary's manuscript and papers are in the Cary Collectio presented to the Bodleian Library Oxford, by James M. Osborn.

[Andrew Wright, *Joyce Cary*, 1958; M. M Mahood, *Joyce Cary's Africa*, 1964; Lione Stevenson, 'Joyce Cary and the Anglo-Iris Tradition', in *Modern Fiction Studies* (Purdu University, Lafayette, Indiana), vol. ix, No. 3 Autumn 1963; unpublished letters and papers personal knowledge.]   WINIFRED DAVIN

CASEY, WILLIAM FRANCIS (1884 1957), editor of *The Times*, was born in Cape Town 2 May 1884, the son of Patrick Joseph Casey, theatre proprietor, o Glenageary, county Dublin. He was edu cated in Ireland at Castleknock Colleg and Trinity College, Dublin, of which in later life he was an honorary LL.D. Of restless disposition, he found it difficult t decide upon a career and spent two year reading medicine before turning to law; he was called to the Irish bar in 1909. Hi thoughts, however, were drawn toward the theatre and, while reading for the bar he became interested in the work of the Abbey Theatre when the directors in cluded W. B. Yeats and Lady Gregor [qq.v.]. He worked for a time on th business side and he would sum up thi period as 'One year, one brief, one guinea'

In 1908 two of his plays, *The Suburban Groove* and *The Man Who Missed the Tide*, were produced at the Abbey Theatre and since they had a fair measure of success he decided to try his luck in London. He brought with him a letter to (Sir) Bruce Richmond, editor of *The Times Literary Supplement*. They took to each other at once and it was agreed that Casey should review for the Supplement.

Shortly before the outbreak of war in 1914 Casey was offered a post as a sub-editor in the sporting department of *The Times* and thereafter until his retirement he was a permanent member of the staff. He served as a foreign sub-editor and his lively interest led to his posting to Washington in 1919, then to Paris in the following year. A valuable asset was his ability to make friends quickly wherever he might be. To colleagues who visited him overseas he proved an ideal host and he would provide a mine of local information otherwise unobtainable in a short visit. A witty talker and an eager listener, he always managed, although a tremendously hard worker for his paper, to find time to analyse the international situation for a friend.

Casey returned to London in 1923 as chief foreign sub-editor, one of the most arduous and anxious positions on the paper. He held it until 1928 and revealed his versatility in the general strike of 1926 when both the proprietors and the editorial staff of *The Times* were determined that the motto of the paper should be business as usual'. Afterwards a souvenir volume, *Strike Nights in Printing House Square*, was printed for private record. One of its pictures bore the caption 'amateurs in the foundry' and showed Casey and Captain Shaw, the chairman's secretary, hard at work on a mechanical process, as 'the champion pair of matrix moulders'.

In 1928 Casey was promoted to the foreign leader-writing staff. He attended many of the Geneva sessions of the League of Nations, following events with sympathy towards French rather than German aspirations. The *History of 'The Times'* asserts that Casey was a francophil so 'knew that his judgement on foreign matters carried little weight'. On the retirement of Geoffrey Dawson [q.v.] in 1941, the new editor, R. M. Barrington-Ward [q.v.], appointed Casey his deputy; a selection welcomed by the staff, partly because of his determination not to be made such a prisoner of Printing House Square as many of his predecessors. He was a member of many clubs and he would declare that if he could squeeze in a game of billiards in his dinner break, work went much more easily on his return. Barrington-Ward's health was deteriorating and his death in 1948 threw the burden of the editorship on to Casey's shoulders sooner than he had expected. He did not flinch, although his colleagues realized that the strain was too heavy. He had a streak of obstinacy difficult to break down and, a decision taken, it was well-nigh impossible to move him. Yet most of the decisions which he took proved sound in the long run and no member of his staff ever felt that he had not had a fair chance to put his views. No editor was better loved.

Until his retirement in 1952 Casey continued to keep in touch with national and international affairs, to study the welfare of his staff, and to distribute necessary praise or blame.

Casey died in London 20 April 1957. He married in 1914 Amy Gertrude Pearson-Gee, a widow, daughter of the late Henry Willmott; they had no children.

There is a drawing of Casey by Cuthbert Orde in the possession of *The Times*.

[*History of 'The Times'*, vol. iv, part ii, 1921 to 1948, 1952; *Strike Nights in Printing House Square*, printed for private record, 1926; personal knowledge.]   A. P. ROBBINS.

CASSELS, SIR ROBERT ARCHIBALD (1876–1959), general, was born at Bandora, near Bombay, 15 March 1876, the son of John Andrew Cassels, merchant, and his wife, Helen, daughter of Thomas White. He was educated at Sedbergh and the Royal Military College, Sandhurst, was commissioned in 1896 and went out to India in the following year, eventually joining the 32nd Lancers in 1901. He acted as aide-de-camp to his divisional commander (1906–7), was brigade-major (1909–11), and G.S.O. 2 (1911–13). In 1915 he became deputy adjutant-general at the headquarters of the force, the nucleus of which had landed in Mesopotamia late in 1914. Before the end of 1915, however, he went to the appointment of G.S.O. 1 with the 3rd Indian Army Corps, moving to the 14th division in May 1916. By August 1917 he had served in the same capacity with the small Cavalry division and as brigadier-general, general staff, of the expeditionary force. When in early April 1917 Sir Stanley Maude [q.v.] advanced north astride the Tigris, Cassels manœuvred with masterly skill on the left flank, and on 22 April at Istabulat was sharply engaged.

By now regarded as a coming man, Cassels took command of the 11th Cavalry brigade in November 1917. When his great opportunity came in the final offensive of 1918 he revealed himself as an even more outstanding cavalry leader than his promise had foretold. His orders were to reach with his brigade the Little Zab twenty-five miles above its junction with the Tigris. He marched 77 miles in 39 hours, but unexpectedly found the Turks holding the ford for which he was making in a strength of about a thousand. None the less, he decided to cross, managing to do so by another ford about a mile downstream. Ismael Hakki, his flank turned, skilfully crossed to the right bank of the Tigris and broke up his floating bridge. On 25 October the brigade received orders to cross the river next day above Sharqat and cut off the enemy. Cassels decided he must find a ford near Huwaish, but had to go farther north before one was discovered, all three channels of which were highly dangerous. Most of the horses had to swim; Cassels led the way and rode at a gallop to Huwaish. He had ordered another regiment to join him, but the ford could not be crossed in darkness, so that he was isolated and in considerable danger. He estimated the Turkish force nearest to him, two and a half miles south of Huwaish, at four hundred or more. Early on the 27th he took the bold decision to attack, mainly to disguise his weakness. The action disclosed the Turkish strength to be between eight hundred and a thousand. Cassels therefore drew back and dug in. The Turkish main body facing the infantry under Sir A. S. Cobbe [q.v.] was doing the same thing at Sharqat. In the early hours of 28 October Cassels was reinforced by an infantry brigade which had marched 33 miles to join him, and he felt emboldened to try a bluff. A considerable force of the enemy was moving towards him from the south and he sent the 7th Hussars, less two squadrons, to meet it. A brilliant dismounted attack drove the enemy back, and though they came on again and forced the Hussars to retire, they showed no further signs of attacking. The brigade suffered about a hundred casualties and lost many more horses. In the course of the action the 7th Cavalry brigade arrived, and a few more reinforcements came up later. On the 29th the 13th Hussars carried out a dashing attack, first galloping into dead ground

unscathed, then dismounting, swarming up a height known as Cemetery Hill, driving off the Turks, and taking 730 prisoners. The 29th October was the day of the battle of Sharqat. How great was the part played by Cassels is made clear by the fact that, although the British infantry attack was repulsed, nevertheless next morning white flags fluttered all down the Turkish line.

Cassels next led his forces north to occupy Mosul, but could not induce the Turks to abandon the place until they received the terms of the armistice. He was appointed C.B. and to the D.S.O. in 1918 and promoted major-general in 1919. In June of that year serious unrest in southern Kurdistan disturbed the tribes north and north-east of the Mosul vilayet. His commander, Sir Theodore Fraser, being absent, Cassels took immediate steps to prevent the spread of the rebellion. He acted with his usual vigour, with the consequence that after some months of fighting the Kurds had been so handled that they scarcely stirred in the subsequent general Arab revolt.

Cassels was cavalry adviser in India (1920–23), commandant of the Peshawar district (1923–7), and adjutant-general in India (1928–30), being promoted lieutenant-general in 1927 and general in 1929. He next held the Indian Northern Command (1930–34) in the course of which he became colonel of the 7th Light Cavalry. (He was appointed colonel of his regiment, which had become the 13th (D.C.O.) Lancers, in 1939.) In 1935 came his final promotion to commander-in-chief of the Army of India and member of the executive council of the governor-general an appointment lasting until 1941 when he went on retired pay. Within a few weeks of taking over Cassels had to face one of the familiar troubles on the North-West Frontier. Afridi bands, set in motion by the 'Red Shirt' movement, which in its turn was coached by Russian agents penetrated to Peshawar, and one Indian battalion refused duty. Cassels speedily restored order. Later he undertook the building of a series of blockhouses across a plain which actually lay outside the administrative borders of India. The creation of these defences brought another threat of frontier war but this he succeeded in averting.

The outbreak of war in 1939 brought a host of problems, foremost among them the expansion of the Indian Army, which grew with a rapidity so great that it far outstripped the available equipment. One of the strategic factors he had already anticipated when in May 1936 he had been directed to examine road and rail facilities for moving a division to the Burma frontier and its maintenance there. He estimated that the programme would take eight years, or five if sole reliance were placed in a road from Manipur. He was eager to go ahead at once, but this project was not accepted. Many officers of promise served under Cassels, but the protégé who seemed to excel them all was Sir) Claude Auchinleck, a close friend to whom he acted to some extent as mentor and who served with him in Mesopotamia and on his staff in India. Auchinleck, who was to succeed him as commander-in-chief, or his part thought Cassels had certain of the characteristics of Rommel.

Cassels was appointed K.C.B. in 1927, .C.B. in 1933, and G.C.S.I. in 1940. After his retirement he went to live at opthorne, in Sussex, where he took a prominent and useful part in local affairs. There he died 23 December 1959. By his marriage in 1904 to Florence Emily, daughter of Lieutenant-Colonel Halkett Jackson, he left one son, General Sir (A.) James (H.) Cassels, chief of the general staff, Ministry of Defence, 1965–8. Cassels was always very uncommunicative about his military experiences and never spoke of them even to his son. His greatest assets were his determination and his *coup eil* on the battlefield. He was prepared gamble, as he did at Sharqat, and gambling boldly and skilfully is proverbially a necessity for the successful leader, but he did not make a single mistake in that campaign and was never abandoned fortune. His sense of duty and probity equalled his extreme modesty.

F. J. Moberly, (Official History) *The Campaign in Mesopotamia, 1914–18*, vols. iii and iv, 1925–7; E. W. C. Sandes, *The Indian Sappers and Miners*, 1948; Compton Mackenzie, *Eastern Epic*, vol. i, 1951; private information; personal knowledge.]

CYRIL FALLS.

CATHCART, EDWARD PROVAN (1877–1954), physiologist, was born 18 July 1877 in Ayr, Scotland, the son of Edward Moore Cathcart, merchant, and his wife, Margaret Miller. His father died at an early age, leaving the mother with three small children of whom Edward, the first, was only nine. He was on the classical side in Ayr Academy and graduated B. from the university of Glasgow in 0 with the intention of specializing in

gynaecology. In the next year, however, he went to Munich to study bacteriology, but, instead, fell under the spell of Carl Voit, the foremost authority on human metabolism; he also studied chemical pathology with E. L. Salkowski in Berlin.

Returning to Britain, Cathcart spent three years (1902–5) in the Lister Institute as assistant to S. G. Hedin. For his work on enzyme activity and in bacteriology Cathcart received the M.D. of Glasgow (1904) with honours and a Bellahouston gold medal. In 1906 he was appointed to the Grieve lectureship in physiological chemistry in Glasgow which he held until 1915. These years in Glasgow were fruitful. He received the degree of D.Sc. (1908) for a classical study of human starvation and in 1912 published his *Physiology of Protein Metabolism*. In 1908 he spent five months in Ivan Pavlov's laboratory in St. Petersburg and in 1912 a year with F. G. Benedict at the Carnegie Institution in Boston. With Benedict Cathcart embarked on his second major scientific preoccupation, the factors which affect the expenditure of energy by human beings. This interest he turned to good account in the war of 1914–18 and later in the industrial field. The studies on the expenditure of energy in marching and in the carrying of loads laid the foundation of much of modern applied physiology.

In 1915 Cathcart became professor of physiology in the London Hospital medical school but gave much of his time to war service, first in anti-gas duties, then as lieutenant-colonel, Army Medical Services, engaged on special work in connection with the feeding of the army. In 1919 he returned finally to Glasgow to the new Gardiner chair of physiological chemistry; in 1928 he transferred to the regius chair of physiology, a transfer which did no violence to his interests which continued to be centred on the human scene. Indeed, in his later years he was out of sympathy with much conventional physiological experimentation on animals.

Cathcart became increasingly interested in the dietary habits of people. Between 1924 and 1940 he sponsored the publication by the Medical Research Council, on which he served, of no fewer than five reports based on dietary studies in different parts of Great Britain. He served also on the Agricultural Research Council. A more intimate relationship with agriculture was established when he fostered the early development of the Hannah Dairy Research Institute close to Ayr. From his appointment to the Industrial Fatigue (later Health) Research Board came two major studies, on the physique of women (1928) and men (1935) in industry. Cathcart spoke with authority on industrial problems. He had no sympathy with the sentimental attitudes of the political Left; nor did he approve the growing managerial tendency to regard human beings as robots. He published *The Human Factor in Industry* in 1928; and he would have viewed critically the development of automation. He had no use for leisure: the prime need for man, in his view, was work which furnished creative satisfaction.

In 1933 Cathcart was appointed to the Scottish health services committee. This 'Cathcart committee' published one of the most complete official surveys of the country's health services and gave information of value in the framing of the National Health Service. From 1933 to 1945 Cathcart represented his university on the General Medical Council; and he served as assessor of the senate on the court of the university. Tasks such as these inevitably weaned him from the teaching and research laboratories; yet, to the day when he retired, in 1947, he shouldered, in traditional Scots fashion, with satisfaction and even with enjoyment, the responsibility for the majority of the lectures to the elementary medical class in physiology.

Cathcart was elected F.R.S. in 1920 and F.R.S.E. in 1932. In 1924 he was appointed C.B.E. He received the honorary degree of LL.D. from St. Andrews in 1928 and Glasgow in 1948.

Cathcart could have come from nowhere save the south-west of Scotland. He was tall, dark-haired, and swarthy, yet with light steel-grey eyes. A portrait in oils 'Study in Scarlet' by Norah N. Gray shows him as his pupils remember him in his active heyday and hangs in the Institute of Physiology of the university of Glasgow. His voice was deep and resonant and made no concession to his sojourns in England. He was far from glib but on occasion aroused deep emotion and enthusiasm in his undergraduate audiences. Physically he was remarkably fit until struck down with coronary thrombosis at the age of seventy. Yet he played no games and had little interest in sport; by contrast, he had a most sincere appreciation of the arts, above all of literature and of the theatre; he loved good talk, sometimes physiological 'shop', more often not. He attended the university chapel regu-

larly; he was a friend and admirer of J. S. Haldane [q.v.] with whose philosophical outlook he had sympathy.

In 1913 Cathcart married Gertrude Dorman, daughter of Henry Bostock, a boot and shoe manufacturer in Stafford. She graduated in science, then in medicine, at Glasgow; and their three daughters all graduated in medicine from the same university. Cathcart died in Glasgow 18 February 1954.

[G. M. Wishart in *Obituary Notices of Fellows of the Royal Society*, vol. ix, 1954; personal knowledge.]   R. C. GARRY.

CATTO, THOMAS SIVEWRIGHT, first BARON CATTO (1879–1959), governor of the Bank of England, was the fifth son and seventh child of William Catto, shipwright, of Peterhead, and his wife, Isabella, daughter of William Yule, sea captain. He was born 15 March 1879 at Newcastle upon Tyne, whither his father had moved with his young family in search of more steady employment; but within a year his father died, and the family returned to Peterhead. Catto went to Peterhead Academy, but after a move back to Newcastle he won a scholarship to Heaton School (Rutherford College), and at the age of fifteen entered the office of the Gordon Steam Shipping Co. In the evenings he taught himself shorthand and when the office acquired a typewriter, he learned to pick the lock on it and practised when others had gone home

Although by 1898 his wages had risen from 4s. to 10s. a week, Catto sought wider opportunities; through a newspaper advertisement he obtained the post of secretary to W. H. Stuart, managing partner of F. A. Mattievich & Co. of Batoum, at a salary of £8 a month. He sailed from Cardiff, barely nineteen, with a small trunk, a bicycle, £3 in cash, and the full support of his mother, to whom he owed so much. For six years he worked in Batoum and Baku, learned to speak Russian, and on his twenty-first birthday was made office manager. While working for Stuart he met Vivian Hugh Smith, the banker, who later became Lord Bicester [q.v.], a connection of the utmost importance in later years.

Among other friends made in Baku was David Forbes, junior, a Scottish merchant whose business was soon to be absorbed in MacAndrews & Forbes, Russian and Near Eastern merchants with headquarters in the United States. In 1904 Catto was offered the management of their new

European selling agency and, with Stuart's goodwill, found himself at the age of twenty-four organizing an office in London. He became a member of the Baltic Exchange and learnt London ways of merchanting and the chartering of ships; but after two years he returned to the Near East as second-in-command to Forbes in Smyrna, a post entailing much travel in the Near and Middle East. In 1909 he was transferred to the New York office, becoming a vice-president. America was to be his home for the next eleven years.

When war broke out in August 1914, Catto happened to be in England. His lack of inches prevented military service, and on the introduction of Vivian Smith he was soon employed in the organization of transporting supplies to Russia. From 1915 to 1917 he was British Admiralty representative on the Russian commission to the United States. When Russia collapsed he transferred to the British food mission in the United States, and in 1918 he became chairman of the allied provisions commission and head of the British Ministry of Food in the U.S.A. and Canada. In 1918 he was appointed C.B.E.; in 1919 a commander of the Order of Leopold of Belgium; and in 1921 a baronet for public services particularly in connection with the transport of food and munitions from the United States to Great Britain and allied countries'.

Catto never returned, as he had intended, to MacAndrews & Forbes. In 1917 Vivian Smith's firm, Morgan, Grenfell & Co., had acquired a predominating share in Andrew Yule & Co., of Calcutta, and its associated business, George Yule & Co., of London, the great Indian commercial empire built by Sir David Yule whom Catto was invited to succeed. He had married in 1910 and with a young family had no mind to take up residence in India; but what decided him was that his mother's name was Yule, although no relationship was ever established. The position of head of Andrew Yule & Co. which he assumed in 1919 gave Catto abundant opportunities for playing an active part in financial and economic affairs in India, although he did not seek formal appointments such as the presidency of the Bengal Chamber of Commerce. He served as a member of the Indian Government (Inchcape) retrenchment committee in 1922–3, and of the United Kingdom committee on coaling in 1926. In 1928 he became a partner in Morgan, Grenfell & Co. and retired

from India, although retaining a keen interest in its problems. He remained chairman of Andrew Yule & Co. and of the London business, which became Yule, Catto & Co., until 1940.

Established in London, Catto became a director of the Royal Exchange Assurance Corporation, the Mercantile Bank of India, and other companies; one of his important tasks was to act with Sir Ernest Harvey in reordering the affairs of the Royal Mail and Elder Dempster shipping companies, an unpaid post to which he was drafted by Montagu (later Lord) Norman [q.v.], the governor of the Bank of England. In 1936 he was created a baron, taking his territorial title from Cairncatto, a farm which he had purchased in Buchan whence his forebears had come.

In April 1940 Catto was elected a director of the Bank of England, but a fortnight later succeeded Lord Woolton as director-general of equipment and stores at the Ministry of Supply. In the following July he moved to the newly created post of financial adviser to the Treasury, full-time and unpaid, and resigned his directorship of the Bank. The title had no precise significance. The expert team of civil servants at the Treasury was being augmented by a wealth of outside talent, economists and others, among whom the outstanding personality was J. M. (later Lord) Keynes [q.v.]. In this galaxy Catto represented commercial and banking experience; he and Keynes, hitherto strangers, saw things from a very different standpoint, made great friends, and became the 'Catto and Doggo' of the popular press.

By the close of 1943 it was evident that illness had ended Montagu Norman's long reign at the Bank of England; in April 1944 Catto was elected to succeed him and released from his position at the Treasury. Although he was singularly well equipped by his merchant banking knowledge and by his recent experience in Whitehall to occupy the middle position which the Bank holds between Government and City, this was a considerable burden to assume at the age of sixty-five. Moreover the job was not at all defined: his predecessor had been in office for twenty-four years, during which he had transformed the organization and outlook of the Bank; so that even in normal times to succeed him would have been difficult enough.

Catto relied on the team which he inherited and did not seek to make substantial changes. He occupied himself with the main questions likely to arise in the post-war period, notably in the field of industrial finance, where he was much concerned with the establishment of the Finance Corporation for Industry and the Industrial and Commercial Finance Corporation. But he had been in office little more than a year when a Labour Government was returned, pledged to an early nationalization of the Bank of England and ready to introduce new measures of control over the banking system as a whole; and it is with the working out of these ideas that his name, as governor, will be principally associated. He accepted that the Bank had already been converted *de facto* into a public institution, aligning its monetary policy with the general economic policy of the government of the day and no longer seeking to provide for its private stockholders more than a constant dividend. Accordingly there was nothing in the proposal for public ownership which need diminish the utility or standing of the Bank provided its independence in thought and work was fully safeguarded. Similarly, he did not oppose the provision of a new measure of control over the banking system, provided that it was general in character and operated on the initiative of the Bank.

He judged correctly the strength of his position if he did not come out in active opposition to the general policy. As a result the Bank was taken into public ownership with the minimum public controversy and the maximum retention of operational independence. Catto came under criticism at the time, but his judgement was later vindicated. He accepted appointment as the first governor under the new regime in March 1946, and served until February 1949 on the eve of his seventieth birthday. He received the honorary degree of LL.D. from Manchester in 1945 and was sworn of the Privy Council in 1947.

In retirement Catto served as chairman in 1950–52 of a committee to report on the practicability of determining the financial and economic relations between Scotland and the rest of the United Kingdom. Scottish matters indeed, and particularly those of the county of Aberdeen, were a lifelong concern. In addition to the farm of Cairncatto he bought the House of Schivas not far away; and after his return from India devoted much care to restoring its ancient fabric and filling it with beautiful things. No honour pleased him more than to become in August 1957 the first freeman of Peterhead.

In appearance Catto was very short of stature, with a fresh complexion and clear blue eyes. His open countenance and quiet manner perhaps tended to conceal his shrewdness and skill as a negotiator, so well displayed while he was governor of the Bank of England. He not only took his opportunities as they offered but prepared himself in advance for what might present itself. If there was occasion for controversy he avoided a head-on collision and used his nimble mind and good judgement of personality to carry his objective without sacrificing any point of importance. As the head of a large organization he imposed his will with courtesy and with a considerable feeling for the welfare of those under him.

By the course of his career Catto formed a unique bridge between the pre-1914 world in which British merchants were responsible for the commerce of strange parts of the world and the post-1945 world of international economic and financial problems of the utmost complexity. He was in the neighbourhood when the Baghdad railway was projected and when oil was discovered in Persia; he was still actively interested in economic development, although from a very different viewpoint, when the International Bank for Reconstruction and Development was getting under way. He was also a leading example of the Scottish boy of comparatively humble origin who rose to the top rank in the City of London through a combination of innate qualities and of grasping opportunities whenever they offered.

Catto married in 1910, at Smyrna, Gladys Forbes, daughter of Stephen Gordon, a partner in MacAndrews & Forbes there and a native of Elgin in Morayshire. They had one son, Stephen Gordon (born 1923), a partner in Morgan, Grenfell & Co., who succeeded to the title; and three daughters, the eldest of whom, Isabel, was elected in 1955 president of the World Y.W.C.A. Catto died at his house in Holmbury St. Mary, Surrey, 23 August 1959.

A portrait by David Alison, painted during Catto's governorship, is at the Bank of England; another, painted in 1952 by (Sir) James Gunn, is with Morgan, Grenfell & Co. Portraits by each of these artists and also by Arthur Pan are in the possession of the family.

[Private information; personal knowledge.

H. C. B. MYNORS

CECIL, EDGAR ALGERNON ROBERT GASCOYNE-, VISCOUNT CECIL OF CHELWOOD

CECIL, EDGAR ALGERNON ROBERT GASCOYNE-, VISCOUNT CECIL OF CHELWOOD (1864–1958), a creator of the League of Nations, was born in London 14 September 1864. He was the third son of Lord Robert Arthur Talbot Gascoyne-Cecil, later third Marquess of Salisbury [q.v.], and one of five distinguished brothers; a notice of the youngest appears below.

His upbringing, mainly at Hatfield, was happy and religious, among a united family in which the affection and authority of his parents were unquestioned. Owing to his father's view that children should not leave home until they had been confirmed, he was taught by tutors until he went as an Oppidan to Eton where he became known for progressive views, passed the necessary examinations, and was head of his house. At University College, Oxford, he obtained a second class in law (1886), played real tennis for the university, but found his main activities among friends, the Canning Club, and the presidency of the Union. He was called to the bar by the Inner Temple in 1887 and until his election to the House of Commons practised mostly at the parliamentary bar. He took silk in 1899, became a bencher in 1910, and was chairman of the Hertfordshire quarter-sessions (1911–20).

In 1906 Lord Robert Cecil was elected Conservative member of Parliament for East Marylebone. A moderate free trader and a keen supporter of women's suffrage, he had doubts even at this time whether he would not be happier on the 'other side'. He broke with his party in 1910 and in that year unsuccessfully contested Blackburn and North Cambridgeshire as an independent Conservative. In 1911 he was elected for the Hitchin division of Hertfordshire which he represented until 1923 when he was created Viscount Cecil of Chelwood.

After the outbreak of war in 1914, being over military age, he worked at first with the Red Cross, organizing the wounded and missing department. But he was soon called to government office as parliamentary under-secretary for foreign affairs and minister of blockade (1916–18). He was sworn of the Privy Council in 1915 and in 1918–19 was assistant secretary of state for foreign affairs. Balfour, the foreign secretary, was often away, leaving Cecil in charge of the Foreign Office and its spokesman in the Cabinet.

Lord Robert Cecil was not only shocked by the bloodshed and horror of the war but felt that 'the worst part of it is that it seems to herald an era of destruction. No one can yet estimate the moral injury that it has wrought'. He turned his thoughts to what was to become his life work, the creation of opinion in favour of the abolition of war and armaments. In September 1916 he circulated a memorandum to the Cabinet making proposals for the avoidance of future wars, in which the broad principle was that no country should resort to arms until its grievance had been submitted to an international conference or tribunal; if this obligation came to be violated, sanctions were to follow, first by blockade, then, if necessary, by military force. This paper was criticized in the Foreign Office; nevertheless, owing to his persistence, it led to the appointment of a committee under Sir W. G. F. (later Lord) Phillimore [q.v.] which, with Lord Robert Cecil's memorandum as the basis of its work, produced the first draft of what became the Covenant of the League of Nations.

From this time forward, the maintenance of peace through the League of Nations, collective security, and disarmament absorbed all his time and thoughts. In 1919 he went to Paris where he dominated the debates of the conference commission on the League presided over by President Wilson. No one who was present in the commission could doubt that but for the patient and inspired persuasion of Lord Robert Cecil there might have been no Covenant at all. With the help of Dr. Nansen of Norway, he persuaded the 'neutral' nations to join the League; without them it must have failed.

In the first three Assemblies of the League (1920–22) Lord Robert Cecil, who had resigned from the Government over the Welsh Church disestablishment, was appointed by J. C. Smuts [q.v.] as a delegate for South Africa. With Nansen, Newton Rowell of Canada, Branting of Sweden, Hymans of Belgium, Motta of Switzerland, and others, he transformed what might have been a disordered diplomatic gathering into a well-organized parliamentary institution which grew rapidly in strength. He persuaded his colleagues that all the meetings of the Assembly and of its committees and of the Council should be held in public. He was a firm believer in the value of public international debate, saying that 'publicity is the life-blood of the League'; and he set a standard of courtesy and candour which made this new practice a decided success. It was proved time after time that when private negotiations had failed, public discussion brought a settlement. A notable example was the admission of Germany to the League in 1926. Sir Austen Chamberlain [q.v.] did serious harm in a promising situation by trying to revert to power-politics and to what Geneva called 'hotel bedroom diplomacy'. Cecil was left to clear up the mess, which he did successfully—and in public.

In 1923 Baldwin became prime minister, Lord Curzon [q.v.] his foreign secretary, and Lord Robert Cecil, as lord privy seal, was put in charge of League affairs. He was thus able to do excellent work in the League Council. He had already played a leading part in drafting the statute of the Permanent Court of International Justice; he now secured agreement on the reference to that court of important minority questions, a valuable precedent which led to the effective application of the whole minority protection system; in many contentious matters—the Saar, Danzig, mandates, the traffic in drugs, Nansen's refugee work—he successfully brought the principles of the Covenant to life.

His first major crisis, and his first major conflict with Curzon and his other cabinet colleagues, arose out of the seizure by Mussolini, 31 August 1923, of the Greek island of Corfu in reprisal for the murder of Italian officers on Greek territory. The Greek Government unfortunately telegraphed both to the League Council and to the Allied Conference of Ambassadors in Paris, promising both bodies to accept their decision. Cecil, Nansen, and Branting rallied the Assembly in support of Greece, and the Council drew up a proposed settlement, providing for the evacuation of Corfu by the Italians and reference to the Permanent Court of the question of compensation by Greece. The ambassadors at first agreed, but later decided that Greece must pay the full indemnity demanded by Mussolini.

Baldwin, when he formed his second Government in 1924, at first proposed to leave Cecil out. It was only under the urgent persuasion of Sir Eric Drummond (later the Earl of Perth, q.v.), the secretary-general of the League, that Baldwin changed his mind and made Cecil chancellor of the Duchy of Lancaster, in charge of League affairs. Cecil was soon again at variance with his colleagues, this time over the Geneva Protocol which had been prepared by the delegates of the Labour Government and which Baldwin's Cabinet opposed. The Protocol would have given the Permanent Court compulsory jurisdiction in cases which could be settled by law; it would have organized collective security under the League, and brought an early conference on disarmament. Although Cecil proposed amendments which he hoped would make it acceptable, the Cabinet finally rejected the Protocol. This was a grave shock to League supporters all over the world and in the light of subsequent events a tragic mistake.

Cecil himself believed that 'the nations must either learn to disarm or perish'. In 1926 he was sent as delegate to the preparatory disarmament commission and in 1927 to the Coolidge conference in Geneva on naval disarmament. President Coolidge was proposing large reductions of cruiser, destroyer, and submarine strength, with a ratio of 5:5:3 for Britain, the United States, and Japan. Cecil and W. C. (later Viscount) Bridgeman, the first lord of the Admiralty, who was with him, favoured acceptance; the Cabinet would not agree to parity with America; Cecil resigned, broke with his party, and never again held government office.

He did not regret his resignation. When in 1928 the Baldwin government made a strong attack on the League budget, the purpose being to save Britain £6,000, it seemed to him the final proof that his former colleagues would never understand the importance of the League, or its chance of success.

Fortunately this was not the end of his work for the League. When the second Labour Government came into power in 1929 Arthur Henderson [q.v.] gave Cecil a room and a staff in the Foreign Office and made him chairman of a departmental committee on League affairs, deputy leader of the Assembly delegations, and once again British representative on the preparatory disarmament commission. The two men worked in great harmony and achieved excellent results, including the adhesion of all the Commonwealth countries to the Optional Clause (accepting compulsory jurisdiction) of the statute of the Permanent Court, the preparation of a draft disarmament convention, and the fixing of a date for the general disarmament conference. Before the conference met the Labour Government had resigned, but Henderson remained president and in that capacity arranged for Cecil and others to address the conference on behalf of various private organizations

Cecil spoke on behalf of the International Federation of League of Nations Societies of which he was president; he put forward the doctrine of 'qualitative disarmament', i.e. the abolition of weapons which assist aggressive attack, a principle ultimately accepted by almost every government represented in the conference. In June 1932 President Hoover based upon it a bold and comprehensive plan which was welcomed with enthusiasm by Germany, Italy, Russia, and all the smaller and middle powers. Many of the British Cabinet, including Baldwin and Sir John (later Viscount) Simon [q.v.], the foreign secretary, wanted to accept it; but by a small majority they were defeated and the British delegation played the principal role in killing the Hoover Plan. The disarmament conference failed and the League disintegrated.

Cecil hoped to save the League by organizing public opinion which, thanks to his efforts, amongst others, overwhelmingly supported the League in Britain and in many other countries. He was president of the League of Nations Union from 1923 to 1945 and in 1934-5 organized the peace ballot. In spite of bitter attacks the ballot became a massive demonstration of deep-rooted public feeling. In a vote of over eleven and a half million over 90 per cent were in favour of the League, disarmament, and the abolition of private manufacture of armaments; over 80 per cent for the abolition of national air forces; over 85 per cent for economic sanctions, and 74 per cent of those who answered the question for military sanctions. This result had a profound effect on both the Government and the public. At one time during the Abyssinian crisis it seemed possible that the League might yet be saved; when eventually the Covenant pledges were betrayed and Mussolini was allowed to occupy Addis Ababa, there was no doubt that the outcome was deeply repugnant to British feeling. It is now generally recognized that Cecil was right: that only strong international institutions funded on world law could save mankind.

After the second war Cecil went as British delegate to Geneva for the closing session of the League. 'The League is dead', he said, 'long live the UN.' Even in the crisis of 1941 when Britain stood alone, he wrote on the title-page of a copy of his book about the League 'Le jour viendra'. He was never personally embittered and it was this faith in the ultimate triumph of his cause which sustained him through so many years of disappointment and frustration.

Cecil was chancellor of the university of Birmingham (1918-44) and rector of Aberdeen (1924-7) and received a number of honorary degrees. He was visitor of St. Hugh's College, Oxford, and honorary fellow of University College. He was awarded the Woodrow Wilson peace prize in 1924 and the Nobel peace prize in 1937, and was appointed C.H. in 1956.

In 1889 he married Lady Eleanor Lambton, daughter of the second Earl of Durham. It was a long and happy, though childless, marriage. Lady Cecil was a woman of great intellectual power who ardently shared her husband's views and was a tower of strength to him, particularly at the crises of his career. In 1900 they built a house, Gale, at Chelwood Gate in Sussex, which was their home for the rest of their lives. He died in Tunbridge Wells, 24 November 1958, survived for only a few months by his widow.

Cecil was very tall, and the impression of his height was undiminished by a pronounced stoop. His mobile features, noble forehead, and fearless searching eyes conveyed a feeling of great intellectual penetration and moral power. He could draw immense audiences in any country which he visited, and they always found his wide knowledge and complete candour most persuasive. He cared nothing for the honours and trappings of public life, and was modest to a fault about his own position and achievements. He was an insatiable reader, who knew the works of Jane Austen almost by heart. A portrait by P. A. de László is at London University Hall and a smaller version at Hatfield; others by John Mansbridge and Sir William Orpen are in the National Portrait Gallery. The Royal Institute of International Affairs has a bust by Siegfried Charoux.

[Viscount Cecil of Chelwood, *A Great Experiment*, 1941, and *All the Way*, 1949; private information; personal knowledge.]

PHILIP NOEL-BAKER.

CECIL, HUGH RICHARD HEATHCOTE GASCOYNE-, BARON QUICKSWOOD (1869-1956), politician and provost of Eton, was born at Hatfield 14 October 1869, the fifth and youngest son of the third Marquess of Salisbury [q.v.]. Educated at Eton and University College, Oxford, he laid the foundation of a life devoted to Anglican principles and

Conservative politics in a family circle and historic house consecrated to both. Tradition has it that before he was seven he had indicted his nurse as a Socinian and admitted that for long he himself had not been quite orthodox.

Equipped with a first class in modern history and a prize fellowship at Hertford (1891), he prepared to take holy orders like his brother William, later bishop of Exeter. Instead he was persuaded to become assistant private secretary to his father, who simultaneously held the offices of prime minister and foreign secretary. This apprenticeship led in 1895 to his election as Conservative member of Parliament for Greenwich, a seat he held until his advocacy of free trade helped to ensure his defeat in the general election of 1906. Religion, nevertheless, remained the mainspring of his life; and even had the tenacity of his Conservative beliefs not deterred him from crossing the floor of the House in the wake of his lifelong friend (Sir) Winston Churchill, the strength of nonconformity in the Liberal Party would no less surely have repelled him from so drastic a change of political faith. So his allegiance rested with the Tories and in 1910 he secured a congenial seat as burgess for the university of Oxford which he retained until 1937. He received an honorary D.C.L. (1924) and was an honorary fellow of Hertford, Keble, and New colleges.

Cecil was perhaps the most accomplished classical orator of his generation. He was handicapped by a frail physique, restless mannerisms, and a voice pitched too high for sonority. But Lord Curzon [q.v.], himself a majestic exponent of the art of eloquence, was not alone in holding that Cecil's words combined 'the charm of music with the rapture of the seer'. His most memorable speeches were delivered during debates on the education bill in 1902 and on the Welsh Church bill in 1913. The intensity of his beliefs sometimes provoked him to less edifying interventions and the hysterical animosity which he and his friends bore against Asquith for daring to lay hands on the constitution in the Parliament bill of 1911 earned them the style of 'Hughligans'.

Although well past the age of forty and never in robust health, Cecil joined the Royal Flying Corps in 1915. His intrepid manœuvres while learning to fly eventually brought him his pilot's wings—on condition that he never again made a solo flight. In 1918 he was sworn of the Privy Council, an exceptional honour

for a back-bench parliamentarian whose independence of mind and reverence for individual liberty unfitted him for the discipline of office.

During the years between the wars his interest was captured increasingly by the Church Assembly, which he had helped to create. As in the Commons, he relished an arena where Christian principles as he saw them could be defended by forensic logic and an artful grasp of procedure. In 1927, however, and again in 1928 he unexpectedly failed to persuade the Commons to accept the revised Prayer Book. Too often in controversy he spoke with the tongue of an ecclesiastical lawyer, not of an angel. The subtle magic of his eloquence fascinated as of old but did not convince; and many who thought themselves no less loyal churchmen than Cecil found his interpretation of Christian doctrine so rigid as almost to exclude the charity of Christ. In 1933–4 he exercised his authority in Anglican affairs by successfully challenging the right of a bishop (A. A. David, q.v.) to admit Unitarian ministers to the pulpit of a cathedral. A later demand that the Church Assembly should pass a measure prohibiting the use of the marriage service to all divorced persons was overwhelmingly rejected.

In 1936 he was appointed provost of Eton in succession to M. R. James [q.v.]. He delighted in the services in college chapel and as its ordinary would preface his sermons with the words, 'I speak as a layman to laymen without the authority of the priesthood', then go on to be very authoritative indeed. His tall swaying figure surmounted by a green eyeshade, his incisive and often provocative commentary on biblical texts, and his oblique anti-clericalism will all be remembered. So too will his destructive *obiter dicta* on talks to the boys by distinguished visitors. 'I hope I am not boring you', one of them said nervously in the middle of an address. 'Not yet', the provost replied with a tigerish smile. He regarded the war as a vulgar intrusion on well-established routine and scorned to abandon his habit of dining in knee-breeches. As chairman of the governing body he amused some of his colleagues and exasperated others by insisting that under its statutes Eton was responsible only for educating the boys, not for providing air-raid shelters for their protection. The relentless analysis of a medieval schoolman to which he subjected human problems was not always appreciated. But fellows, masters, and boys alike loved him for the ingenuity of his fancy and the felicity of his phrase.

'Linky' Cecil, who had been best man at Churchill's wedding in 1908, was touched when in 1941 the prime minister recommended him for a peerage. He took the title Baron Quickswood but did not often speak in the Lords. Three years later he retired from Eton. 'I go to Bournemouth in lieu of Paradise', he told the assembled school, and there he bore the growing infirmities of age with cheerful courage. His last act before he died there, 10 December 1956, was to dictate a characteristic letter in support of the local Conservative member of Parliament whose political opinions he had not always shared but whose freedom of action he felt to be intolerably threatened by pressure from the constituency association.

Although Cecil never married and had no house of his own until appointed to Eton, he enjoyed unbroken domestic happiness. For most of his life he lived at Hatfield in rooms set aside for his private use. He took his meals, however, with the rest of the family, who readily forgave his unpunctuality in return for the sustained conviviality of his talk. At night he would retire early to read and to meditate. Unhappily he committed little to print except a small volume entitled *Conservatism*, published in the Home University Library in 1912 and embodying a personal creed which remained unchanged to the end of his days. Pageantry and ceremonial appealed to him as reminders of the past. To aesthetic experience, however, he was immune and when a friend once drew his attention to a glorious sunset he replied, 'Yes, extremely tasteful'. Until well into middle age he was an occasional but adventurous rider to hounds. A portrait by Sargent is at Hatfield and another by P. A. de László at Church House, Westminster.

[*Eton College Chronicle*, 7 February 1957; private information.]   KENNETH ROSE.

CHAMBERS, DOROTHEA KATHARINE (1878–1960), lawn tennis champion, was born in Ealing 3 September 1878, the second daughter of the Rev. Henry Charles Douglass, vicar of St. Matthew's Church, Ealing Common, and his wife, Ora Collick. In 1907 she married Robert Lambert Chambers, merchant, of Ealing, whom she had two sons. She learnt her own tennis at Princess Helena College, Ealing, and at the Ealing Lawn Tennis Club and became a most formidable and determined player, generally considered to be one of the top half-dozen women in the history of the game. Tall, lean, and always superbly fit, she was indeed very hard to beat. Her game, based on steady and accurate driving on either wing, was utterly sound and was backed by generalship and tactics of a high order. Few players have been able to induce such a feeling of hopelessness in their opponents as she did; she had a long string of victories in many tournaments, and won the Olympic ladies gold medal in 1908. Between 1903 and 1914 she won the Wimbledon singles title seven times and lost only once to a British player, in 1908 to Mrs. Sterry who herself won Wimbledon five times. It must be remembered, however, that prior to 1922 the holder did not have to play through the championships but only to defend the title in the challenge round. Winning in 1903, 1904, and 1906, Miss Douglass lost in 1905 and 1907 to the young American girl, Miss May Sutton. In 1909 she did not compete as she was having a baby. But in 1910 and 1911 she was back again and won both times with the utmost ease. In the latter year the winner of the All Comers could not win one game from her in the challenge round. By this time she was probably at her peak; her game contained no weak point at all; and she was acknowledged to be the best woman player in the world. In 1912 she did not defend her title as she was having her second child. In 1913 she won her sixth Wimbledon singles title without losing a set. The holder, Mrs. Larcombe, was compelled to withdraw as she was hit in the eye by a ball in the final of the mixed doubles and put out of action for several weeks. In 1914 Mrs. Larcombe challenged Mrs. Lambert Chambers. The centre court at the old Wimbledon in Worple Road was like a furnace. Both players were completely exhausted after two very hard-fought sets, each of which was won by Mrs. Lambert Chambers to give her her seventh and last Wimbledon singles title. This stood as a record until it was beaten by Mrs. Helen Wills-Moody in 1938.

The real drama in Mrs. Lambert Chambers's career came in 1919 when she defended her title against the challenge of the twenty-year-old Suzanne Lenglen. From the moment the French girl appeared at Wimbledon crowds flocked to see her play. Mrs. Larcombe, the 1912 champion, could only get three games from her, and Miss K. McKane (later

Mrs. Godfree), the most promising young British player, only one. Only Miss Elizabeth Ryan really tested her. A huge crowd assembled to see her meet Mrs. Lambert Chambers on the second Friday of Wimbledon. But it rained heavily all day and no play was possible. When the players came on to court next day King George V, Queen Mary, and Princess Mary were in the royal box. It was very hot and the playing conditions were perfect. Mlle Lenglen's wonderful play throughout the tournament, together with her twenty years' advantage in age, had made her a firm favourite. The only concession Mrs. Lambert Chambers had made to the passing of time since 1903 was that her long-sleeved blouse was open at the neck and her long skirt just a trifle shorter.

Although the French girl eventually won the first set 10–8, the older player counterattacked strongly and won the second set 6–4. In the final set Mlle Lenglen led 4–1, but Mrs. Chambers, playing with the utmost determination, caught up and led 6–5 and 40–15—and had two points for the match. Keeping her nerves under wonderful control Mlle Lenglen launched a do-or-die attack at the net and went out at 9–7 to win a brilliant and memorable victory in one of the finest women's matches ever seen at Wimbledon.

The indomitable Mrs. Lambert Chambers came back again next year to gain her revenge. She beat Mrs. Mallory, the new American champion, for the loss of only three games, and easily defeated the formidable Miss Elizabeth Ryan in the final of the All Comers. But Mlle Lenglen, now almost invincible, overwhelmed her challenger 6–3, 6–0. This was the last singles match Mrs. Lambert Chambers ever played at Wimbledon. In December 1922 she was the first woman to be elected a councillor of the Lawn Tennis Association.

Although the Wightman Cup series between the women of America and the women of Britain only started in 1923, twenty years after Mrs. Lambert Chambers had won her first singles title at Wimbledon, she was invited to captain Britain's team in the 1925 match, which was played at Forest Hills, New York. She won her single against Miss E. Goss 7–5, 3–6, 6–1, and, partnered by Miss Harvey, also won her double against Mrs. Mallory and Mrs. Bundy. These two victories enabled Britain to win the tie by four matches to three. Bearing in mind that she was then forty-six, this was

one of Mrs. Lambert Chambers's finest achievements. She made her last appearance in the Wightman Cup in 1926. In 1928 she turned professional and ceased to be a member of the All England Lawn Tennis Club. But after the war she was re-elected and thenceforward every year, until her death in London, 7 January 1960, she was always to be seen in the members' stand at the championships. She published a book on *Lawn Tennis for Ladies* in 1910.

[Private information; personal knowledge.]
                                   J. G. SMYTH.

CHAMBERS, SIR EDMUND KER-CHEVER (1866–1954), historian of the English stage and civil servant, born at West Ilsley, Berkshire, 16 March 1866, was the son of the Rev. William Chambers, curate, and sometime fellow of Worcester College, Oxford, and his wife, Anna Heathcote, daughter of the late Thomas Kerchever Arnold [q.v.], fellow of Trinity College, Cambridge. From Marlborough he proceeded to Corpus Christi College, Oxford, as a classical scholar, took firsts in honour moderations (1887) and *literae humaniores* (1889), and in 1891 won the Chancellor's English essay prize with an essay on literary forgeries. He was disappointed of a fellowship, but before he left Oxford in 1892 for the Education Department he had already acquired a bent for English studies and produced an edition of *Richard II* (1891). Henceforth he became a notable example of a man who followed two careers, both with distinction.

His duties in the Education Department were not at first onerous, but from 1903 he became a valued lieutenant of (Sir) Robert Morant [q.v.], permanent secretary to the newly constituted Board of Education. Anonymity is the principle of the British Civil Service, yet it is clear that in a period when the whole educational system was being transformed Chambers's contribution was important, especially as it related to day continuation schools and adult education. The day continuation schools were victims of the economies associated with the name of Sir Eric Geddes [q.v.], but the Workers' Educational Association and other promoters of adult education were well aware of the debt of gratitude they owed to Chambers. He rose to be second secretary (1921), but perhaps by reason of his unaccommodating manner with deputations he was not offered the post of permanent secretary, and he resigned in 1926.

During his years as a civil servant he did much higher journalism and edited many editions of the English classics, especially Shakespeare. He was first president of the Malone Society (1906–39) and contributed to its *Collections* valuable papers on dramatic records. Among the best of his many *opuscula* is the anthology of *Early English Lyrics* (1907), chosen by him and Frank Sidgwick, which has introduced many readers to the beauties of medieval lyric. Also compiled with taste and learning is *The Oxford Book of Sixteenth Century Verse* (1932). His interest in Arthurian studies dated from his undergraduate days. More than once he wrote about Malory (e.g. an English Association pamphlet, 1922), and his *Arthur of Britain* (1927) is a synthesis and reassessment solidly based on the available evidence.

From the time Chambers left Oxford he was working at 'a little book about Shakespeare and the conditions, literary and dramatic, under which he wrote'. This 'little book' grew into the two volumes on *The Mediaeval Stage* (1903), the four volumes on *The Elizabethan Stage* (1923), and the two volumes on *Shakespeare* (1930), the works by which he will be chiefly remembered. That a busy civil servant should have been able to complete such substantial works of scholarship points to great powers of application, exceptional quickness of mind and pen, and a natural gift for organization.

A master of dramatic history, he made no attempt in these works to evaluate plays as literature. He was convinced that any history of drama which does not confine itself solely to the analysis of genius must start from a study of the social and economic facts upon which the drama rested, and these facts he presented with a fullness and accuracy not approached before. In *The Mediaeval Stage* the only well-trodden ground was the Interlude; minstrelsy and folk-drama and to some extent on the liturgical and miracle plays, is is pioneer work. *The Elizabethan Stage* more a work of consolidation than discovery, for he had little time to search for the information which lay dormant in the Public Record Office and elsewhere, but even so his originality appears again and again in the acuteness with which he balances complicated evidence. In weighing evidence he was as much a master as in assembling and ordering it. The measure of his achievement is estimated if we compare this work with the only two

extensive chronicles of the stage before his —those of Collier and Fleay [qq.v.].

His *Shakespeare*, completed in his days of leisure, is carefully composed and designed to scale. While aesthetic judgements must enter into a discussion of authorship, chronology, and so on, they are subordinated to the main purpose, a consideration of all the material facts and problems. Here is the same grasp of all relevant evidence, the same lucidity in a prose that achieves a good expository level and sometimes rises into a controlled eloquence, and a caution which Sir Walter Greg [q.v.] described as 'monumental'. He never forgot the distinction between a demonstrated truth and a plausible supposition, and his sardonic wit made short work of implausible suppositions.

After his *Shakespeare* he did not abandon Elizabethan studies (*Sir Thomas Wyatt and Some Collected Studies*, 1933, and *Shakespearean Gleanings*, 1944) but in his biographies of Coleridge (1938) and Matthew Arnold (1947) he turned also to the romantic poetry which persisted down to his own day and of which his own verses are late examples (*Carmina Argentea*, privately printed, 1918). To the merits of eighteenth-century and contemporary poetry he was blind: he called himself 'an impenitent Victorian'. After his retirement he lived at Eynsham near Oxford, and there wrote a life of *Sir Henry Lee* (1936), the ranger of Woodstock, and *Eynsham under the Monks* (Oxfordshire Record Society, 1936), his one work on medieval local history. In his *English Literature at the Close of the Middle Ages* (1945), a contribution to the *Oxford History of English Literature*, he returned, not wholly successfully, to subjects which he had once adorned: medieval drama and lyric, the ballad and folk-poetry, Malory. In 1938 he moved from Eynsham to Beer in Devonshire, where he died 21 January 1954.

Chambers's services to education and scholarship earned him many honours: he received the honorary degree of D.Litt. from Durham (1922) and Oxford (1939), and his election to an honorary fellowship at Corpus (1934) gave him great pleasure. He was elected F.B.A. in 1924 and appointed C.B. in 1912 and K.B.E. in 1925.

In 1893 Chambers married Eleanor Christabel (Nora), daughter of John Davison Bowman, late of the Exchequer and Audit Office. To her he dedicated his three major works. There were no children.

Chambers, E. K.   D.N.B. 1951–1960

A drawing by Sir William Rothenstein is in the National Portrait Gallery.

[F. P. and J. Dover Wilson in *Proceedings* of the British Academy, vol. xlii, 1956; private papers now in the Bodleian Library; personal knowledge.]   F. P. WILSON.

CHANCELLOR, SIR JOHN ROBERT (1870–1952), soldier and administrator, was born in Edinburgh 20 October 1870, the second son of Edward Chancellor, writer to the signet, and his wife, Anne Helen, daughter of John Robert Todd, also a writer to the signet. He was educated at Blair Lodge, Polmont, and the Royal Military Academy, Woolwich, and was commissioned in the Royal Engineers in 1890. After a period of duty at home he served in India with the Dongola (1896) and the Tirah (1897–8) expeditions, and in the latter his courage and initiative earned him a mention in dispatches and appointment to the D.S.O. (1898). Back in England, Chancellor attended the Staff College and in 1904 was appointed assistant military secretary to the Committee of Imperial Defence. He showed such administrative ability and sound judgement that in 1906 he was made secretary of the Colonial Defence Committee. He was promoted major in 1910. It was a tribute to Chancellor's qualities that, at the age of forty, a soldier with no experience of colonial administration, he was appointed to the important governorship of Mauritius where his term of office (1911–16) was still recalled, with admiration, more than thirty years later, by some who by then were leading personalities in the island. His success was rewarded by appointment to the governorship of Trinidad and Tobago (1916–21) and thereafter to the first governorship of Southern Rhodesia. This had to wait until 1923, when the territory was taken over from the Chartered Company, and during the interval he served as a principal assistant secretary to the Committee of Imperial Defence. He had been promoted lieutenant-colonel in 1918.

Chancellor's term in Southern Rhodesia (1923–8) more than justified his reputation as a capable and progressive administrator. The constitution which he helped to establish proved more durable than many such instruments and he firmly opposed any suggestion for the introduction of extreme forms of segregation. The ability which he showed in handling local politicians and in guiding the management of affairs led to his selection for the difficult appointment of high commissioner for Palestine and Trans-Jordan (1928–31) where he succeeded Lord Plumer [q.v.] whose term of office had been noteworthy for its freedom from those serious disturbances so unhappily frequent during the British administration of Palestine. This tranquillity and reasons of economy led to the withdrawal of the British military garrison from Palestine and to the reduction and reorganization of the police force. In consequence the civil power was without military aid when in August 1929, following incidents at, and in connection with, the Wailing Wall at Jerusalem, Arab attacks were made on Jews in several large towns in Palestine. Chancellor was then on leave and, although the parliamentary commission of inquiry under Sir Walter Shaw, reporting in March 1930, found no serious fault with the governmental handling of the riots, there were some in Palestine who felt that events might have taken a very different course had Chancellor been in the country. The principal recommendation of the Shaw commission was that the British Government should issue a statement of policy defining clearly and positively the meaning which they attached to certain passages in the mandate and should make it plain that they intended to give full effect to the policy thus defined. That recommendation was, almost certainly, influenced by Chancellor's views and he must have been well satisfied when, after further investigations, including land and immigration problems by Sir John Hope Simpson, the Government issued a statement on policy in October 1930 which went to what Chancellor undoubtedly regarded as the root of the Palestine problem. When in February 1931 the white paper was in effect reinterpreted by Ramsay MacDonald in a statement to Chaim Weizmann [q.v.], Chancellor's faith in government policy in Palestine was badly shaken and his disappointment was made evident in his speech at a farewell banquet in Jerusalem when he said: 'I came hoping to increase the country's prosperity and happiness. I am leaving with my ambition unfulfilled. Conditions were against me.'

Chancellor, though over sixty, now embarked on a third career, serving as chairman or member of a number of governmental committees; on bodies such as the Royal Geographical, Royal Empire, and Royal African societies; and as a director of various companies.

Although not tall, he was impressive

alike in appearance, in his carriage, and in the good taste with which he always dressed. He did not make friends quickly or easily but to his subordinates he showed a courtesy which commanded their devotion and, once his confidence had been won, his charm and sympathy made him excellent company. He held strong views on many issues of policy but after his retirement from Palestine he scrupulously avoided public controversy.

Chancellor was appointed C.M.G. (1909), K.C.M.G. (1913), G.C.M.G. (1922), G.C.V.O. (1925), and G.B.E. (1947). In 1903 he married Elsie, daughter of George Rodie Thompson, a barrister, of Lynwood, Ascot. He had one daughter (the wife of Air Chief Marshal Sir William Elliot) and two sons, the elder of whom, Sir Christopher Chancellor, was for seventeen years head of Reuters and in 1962 became the chairman of the Bowater Paper Corporation and its associated companies.

Chancellor died 31 July 1952 at Shieldhill, Lanarkshire, an estate which his family had owned for nearly eight hundred years. A portrait of him by a South African painter, Frank Wiles, was hung in the Legislative Assembly Building in Salisbury, Rhodesia.

[*The Times*, 2 August 1952; *Royal Engineers Journal*, December 1952; private information; personal knowledge.]   T. I. K. LLOYD.

CHAPMAN, DAVID LEONARD (1869–1958), chemist, the eldest son of David Chapman, merchant, who later became a builder in Manchester, and his wife, Maria Wells, was born in Wells, Norfolk, 6 December 1869. Sir Sydney Chapman (a notice of whom appears below) was his younger brother. From Manchester Grammar School he won an open exhibition to Christ Church, Oxford, and took the final honour school of natural science chemistry (first class, 1893), then in physics (second class, 1894). After a short period as science master at Giggleswick school he was appointed (1897) to the chemistry staff at Manchester University. In 1907 Jesus College, Oxford, which had just equipped itself with a large college laboratory, elected him fellow and tutor to take charge of the science teaching. This laboratory, the last to be run by an Oxford college, remained open until Chapman's retirement in 1944. He was elected F.R.S. in 1913; acted as senior proctor, served university boards and committees, and was vice-principal of his college in 1926–44. As a tutor Chapman was devoted to his pupils, as they were to him. Research, however, was his real interest, and this he pursued over a long period of years, assisted by his wife and his young chemistry graduates. His approach to research problems was cautious, critical, thorough, and penetrating, relying for inspiration and technique very little on the work of others. Because his standards of proof were very high he was not disposed to accept readily fresh outlooks put forward by newcomers to his subject, although he never rejected them outright. The problem which occupied him for the longest period was the mechanism of the photochemical combination of hydrogen and chlorine, which turned out to be an extraordinarily difficult one to handle. Chapman established that minute traces of impurities were the cause of the apparently capricious behaviour of the reaction. He also found that under certain conditions the reaction rate was proportional to the square root of the light intensity, as in the allied reaction between hydrogen and bromine. In such reactions, if the light is interrupted by a rotating sector, the measured rate varies with the sector frequency, and Chapman was the first to work out and use the theory of this effect to measure the 'mean life' of a reaction intermediate. The method has since been much used by others.

Chapman's most recognized contribution to science was embodied in his first paper, published in 1899, which was the earliest sound theoretical treatment of detonation. Applying an equation derived by Riemann relating the movement of gas to the pressures and densities in front of and behind the detonation wave front, he made the assumption that the limiting velocity is that corresponding to the condition of maximum entropy, and was thereby enabled to calculate detonation velocities in gas mixtures in a most successful manner. His name is now attached to his theoretical method, which is basic in detonation studies.

Although reserved in manner, and somewhat of a recluse in his scientific work, Chapman could demonstrate an informal but effective administrative ability when he so wished. When estates bursar of the college for some years, his way of visiting tenant farmers in Yorkshire on his bicycle, calling at the back door, rather roughly dressed, sometimes led to momentary misunderstandings, but matters were soon put right. His outdoor hobbies were golf and cycling; when he gave these up he continued to be an active walker until the age of eighty-two.

Chapman married in 1918 Muriel Catherine Canning, eldest daughter of the Rev. Samuel Holmes, rector of Braunston, Northamptonshire; they had one daughter. He died in Oxford 17 January 1958.

[E. J. Bowen in *Biographical Memoirs of Fellows of the Royal Society*, vol. iv, 1958; personal knowledge.]   E. J. BOWEN.

CHAPMAN, ROBERT WILLIAM (1881–1960), scholar and university publisher, was born at Eskbank near Dalkeith, Perthshire, 5 October 1881, the youngest of the six children of the Rev. Edward Whitaker Chapman, Episcopalian vicar of Birnam, Dunkeld, Perthshire (1871–7), and secretary and treasurer of the Representative Church Council of the Scottish Episcopal Church, Edinburgh, and his wife, Hannah Margaret Cannon, of a Yorkshire family, who settled near Dundee after her husband's death in 1884. Chapman attended the High School, Dundee, then went with a bursary to St. Andrews, where he obtained first class honours in classics. With the Guthrie and Adam de Brome scholarships he proceeded to Oriel College, Oxford, where he won the Gaisford prize for Greek prose (1903) and was awarded a first class in classical moderations (1904) and in *literae humaniores* (1906).

In 1906 Chapman was appointed assistant secretary to the secretary to the delegates of the Clarendon Press, Charles Cannan (whose notice he contributed to this Dictionary). On the outbreak of war in 1914 he was given a commission in the Royal Garrison Artillery and served in Salonica. Returning to Oxford he succeeded to the secretaryship in January 1920 after Cannan's death. He followed Cannan's *Catalogue of the Oxford University Press* (1916) with the complementary *Account of the Oxford University Press 1468–1921* (1922; 2nd ed. 1926) in which he described the more important books published by the Press, some in progress, in which he had a share, especially the Oxford English Texts and the *Oxford English Dictionary* (completed in 1928) and its *Supplement* (1933), to which he freely contributed. His early interest in lexicography, which was also shown in the revised edition of Liddell and Scott, finally published in 1940, remained throughout his life.

When on active service Chapman wrote a series of essays, *Portrait of a Scholar*

(1920), among them one on 'The textual criticism of English classics' which contains the injunction 'To restore, and maintain in its integrity the text of our great writers is a pious duty'; this duty he observed throughout his life and he demanded its observance by others in editions promoted or controlled by him. The English authors he loved and studied most were Jane Austen and Samuel Johnson and it is on his editions of their works that his fame will rest. As early as 1912 he had planned with Katharine Marion Metcalfe an edition of Jane Austen's novels and this was completed by himself, with her assistance, in five volumes in 1923. Of the text it was authoritatively stated that 'All the persons and events of her novels were present to him with such distinctness and precision that he could detect the small misprints which had long passed muster, and the bigger blunders which had been dismissed or ignored as beyond cure.' This edition was judiciously annotated and accompanied by numerous appendixes of great importance. It was followed by six volumes of juvenilia and minor works and two editions of letters, *The Five Letters of Jane Austen to her Niece* (1924) and *Jane Austen's Letters to her Sister Cassandra and Others* (2 vols., 1932), the only complete edition of her letters, lavishly illustrated. Chapman completed his work on Jane Austen with his edition of J. E. Austen-Leigh's *Memoir* (1926), *Jane Austen: Facts and Problems*, the Clark lectures given in 1948 at Trinity College, Cambridge (Oxford, 1948), and *Jane Austen: a Critical Bibliography* (1953; corrected ed. 1955).

Very early in his career Chapman laid the foundations of his belief that Johnson was one of the first writers of modern times and one of the greatest of Englishmen. He read and studied in Macedonia Boswell's *Life of Johnson* and planned and in a great part executed there an edition of Boswell's *Tour to the Hebrides* and Johnson's *Journey to the Western Islands* which were published together in 1924 in an edition in which the texts were, for the first time, established by scholarly collation and emendation. Chapman had already come to the conclusion that the editions of Boswell's *Life* and Johnson's *Letters* by Birkbeck Hill [q.v.] should be revised and re-edited. The great edition of Boswell's *Life* and *Tour to the Hebrides* (1887) was found on examination to be textually inaccurate and factually inadequate. L. F. Powell was commissioned to undertake the revision: Chapman, in addition to reading the proofs, assisted materially by editing Boswell's *Note Book 1776–77* 1925), *Johnson and Boswell Revised by Themselves and Others* (1928), and *Papers Written by Dr. Johnson and Dr. Dodd, 1777* 1926). Chapman himself undertook the new edition of the letters. He made unusual efforts to obtain new letters and was remarkably successful. His prime aim was to furnish an accurate text and therefore he made a close study of Johnson's difficult handwriting. The indexes, of which there are seven, are very full and are arranged with great skill. This edition, *The Letters of Samuel Johnson with Mrs. Thrale's Genuine Letters to Him*, was published in three volumes in 1952 and is Chapman's greatest contribution to Johnsonian scholarship. In *Johnson, Boswell and Mrs. Piozzi: a Suppressed Passage Restored* (1929) Chapman exposed Mrs. Thrale's editorial malpractices. He also, still in the Birkbeck Hill tradition, produced in 1927 an edition of *Rasselas* of which the text does not need to be recollated.

Chapman was well aware of the need for systematic study of the canon of Johnson's writings. The pioneer *Bibliography* of W. P. Courtney, seen through the press by D. Nichol Smith in 1915, was reissued with the support of Chapman in 1925; it added and described numerous facsimiles, it made no addition to the canon. This was done when 'Johnsonian Bibliography: Supplement to Courtney' by Chapman with the collaboration of Allen T. Hazen was published by the Oxford Bibliographical Society (vol. v, 1940). This provisional supplement added twenty-two pieces to the canon, some of the rarer of which were published by Chapman as soon as they were found. Chapman was an ardent bibliographer. He wrote one important book, *Cancels* (1930), and many articles on bibliography and kindred subjects such as typography, binding, the book-trade (including the long article 'Authors and Booksellers' in vol. ii of A. S. Turberville's *Johnson's England*, 1933), and contributed to its terminology. He freely shared his knowledge with R. B. McKerrow [q.v.], whose *Introduction to Bibliography*, a standard manual, was published by the Clarendon Press in 1927. Chapman was taken seriously ill in 1942 and compelled to resign the secretaryship of the Press. He retired to Barton near Oxford and devoted himself mainly to the completion of his edition of Johnson's letters. An essayist and reviewer of rare distinction, he had an innate feeling for language and always wrote with gracious learning and wit. As a reviewer he was generally kindly but could be severe when occasion required. *Johnsonian and Other Essays and Reviews* (1953), written over the years 1921–49, includes such notable writings as the James Bryce lecture on lexicography and the last of his S.P.E. tracts, *Retrospect*, the obituary notice of a famous society. The reprint of the Oxford Standard Authors edition of Boswell's *Life of Johnson* (1953) was not edited by him, but he added very greatly to its value and importance by supplying translations of the numerous Latin and Greek quotations. The last work to be edited by him was *Selections from Samuel Johnson* (1955), an anthology designed to do justice to Johnson's thought.

In person Chapman was tall and lean, with a distinct stoop when walking, and he was a tireless walker. He never rode a horse, drove a car, or rode a motor-cycle, but was seldom parted from his bicycle clips. His bicycle was famous and he indicated to other road-users with unmistakable elaboration the way he intended to go. He never used a typewriter or wrote with a fountain-pen. He wrote rapidly: what he wrote was not always legible, even to his secretaries, his close friends, or the printer: on one occasion at least it caused serious error. But if his writing was sometimes a torment, his voice was always a joy. He deplored slovenly speech; his own was clear, with every syllable distinctly and naturally uttered; it bore no trace of his northern origin. He believed in reading aloud: 'Our noblest prose, like Shakespeare's verse, demands the tribute of utterance.' In addition to a small but notable collection of books, he collected silver spoons, and, as a minor hobby, abbreviations. He had in 1910 collaborated with his friend George Gordon (whose notice he contributed to this Dictionary) in collecting examples of modern jargon which were pilloried in the *Oxford Magazine*. His tracts for the Society of Pure English, *Names, Designations and Appellations* (1936) and *Adjectives from Proper Names* (1939), could only have been compiled from hundreds of examples collected over a period of years. He was aided by a very good memory. He was remarkable for the ingenuity of devices not only in the making of a book but in affairs of life. His efforts to roll a cigarette were persistent but unsuccessful.

Chapman, R. W.

The honorary degree of D.Litt. was conferred on Chapman by Oxford in 1928 for his part in the production of the *Oxford English Dictionary* and St. Andrews conferred the honorary LL.D. on him in 1933; he was elected a fellow of Magdalen College, Oxford, in 1931, and F.B.A. in 1949, and appointed C.B.E. in 1955.

Chapman married in 1913 Katharine Marion, daughter of Arthur Wharton Metcalfe, a Somerset engineer. After obtaining a first class in the honour school of English language and literature (1910) she had moved from Lady Margaret Hall to Somerville as assistant English tutor. They had three sons and one daughter. Chapman died in Oxford 20 April 1960.

[*The Times*, 22 April 1960; Margaret Lane in *The Times Literary Supplement*, 6 August 1954; Sir S. C. Roberts in *Essays and Studies*, 1961; Mary Lascelles in *Proceedings* of the British Academy, vol. xlvii, 1961; private information; personal knowledge.]

L. F. POWELL.

CHAPMAN, SIR SYDNEY JOHN (1871–1951), economist and civil servant, was born at Wells, Norfolk, 20 April 1871, the second son of David Chapman, merchant, and his wife, Maria Wells. A notice of his elder brother, D. L. Chapman, appears above. The family moved to Manchester where Chapman was educated at the Grammar School and the Owens College. He graduated B.A. (London) in 1891 and after a spell as a schoolmaster went to Trinity College, Cambridge, turning first to philosophy and then to economics, abandoning about this time his earlier idea of taking holy orders. Alfred Marshall [q.v.], especially, inspired him to choose economics as his future field. Chapman obtained first classes in both parts of the moral sciences tripos (1897–8), and the Cobden and Adam Smith prizes. He then became Jevons research student at the Owens College, Manchester, before being appointed as a lecturer to University College, Cardiff, to inaugurate the teaching of economics there.

Within two years (1901) Chapman was back in Manchester as Stanley Jevons professor of political economy at Victoria University. His youth, brilliance, and persuasive charm combined to make important impressions. A paper read to the Manchester Statistical Society 'On Education for Business and Public Life' in 1902 foreshadowed his success a year or two later in securing the institution of a faculty of commerce and administration in the university. In 1904 his *Lancashire Cotton Industry* demonstrated his knack for getting access to detailed information from business men as much as his talents as an economic historian. His honours school of economics and political science soon began to register successes, and among the many brilliant postgraduate students he attracted were F. J. Marquis (subsequently the Earl of Woolton) and T. S. Ashton, later professor at the London School of Economics. Chapman's vitality and charm exerted a powerful influence on his students: his gifts were probably never more evident than in his verbal teaching to small groups. In 1904–14 he published three volumes on *Work and Wages* as a continuation of the inquiry by Lord Brassey [q.v.] whose collaboration and friendship he greatly valued. His *Outlines of Political Economy* appeared in 1911 and he was a frequent contributor to the *Economic Journal* and the proceedings of the Royal and the Manchester statistical societies. His writing was elegant but compressed with deep thought and, in contrast with the more ready comprehensibility of his verbal communications in lectures and seminars, it proved heavy going for the uninitiated.

Chapman was the youngest of a brilliant group in Manchester which included Rutherford, Samuel Alexander, Tout, Tait, and Elliot Smith [qq.v.]. His own view was that Manchester must become an independent instead of a federal university and in due course Liverpool, Leeds, and Sheffield left the parent federation. There were those elsewhere who said that Manchester itself at that time was 'mad on research', thereby intending disparagement, but Chapman saw no reason to heed such criticism and himself initiated research work in industry by his advanced students, relying on his aptitude for personal contacts to secure opportunities for them. In 1909, still under forty, he was president of the economics section of the British Association at its meeting in Canada. Four years later he accepted an invitation to act as chairman of a commission set up by the South African Government to investigate economic and labour problems.

The outbreak of war in 1914 found Chapman at the height of his powers as an economist and at the head of an ever more flourishing faculty in Manchester. But in the spring of 1915 the Board of Trade secured him, first for four days a week but soon full time, to have charge of investiga-

ions into industry as a basis for the
measures necessary to mobilize production
for the war effort. Whitehall soon formed
the highest opinion not only of his
analytical powers and his resourcefulness
in ideas but also of his ability to get along
with all manner of people, not least with
men of business. Early in 1918 he was
invited to join the Civil Service to fill a
new post at the Board of Trade, and with
the encouragement of Sir Albert Stanley
(later Lord Ashfield, q.v.), the president
of the Board of Trade, and after some
heartache he severed his connection with
the university of Manchester. By August
1919 he was joint permanent secretary of
the Board; and by 1 March 1920 the
single head of the department. He remained in this post for seven years,
serving four markedly dissimilar presidents: Sir Robert (later Viscount) Horne,
Stanley Baldwin [qq.v.], Sir Philip Lloyd-
Greame (afterwards the Earl of Swinton),
and Sidney Webb (later Lord Passfield,
q.v.), and enjoying particularly happy
personal relations with them all.

Chapman was involved in all the post-
war difficulties of the Board. Outwardly
serene and unflurried, nevertheless he had
to carry an immense load of work. Reconstruction involved many controversial
measures, notably the Safeguarding of
Industries Act. Lloyd George chose to
commit himself and the country to advocating a world economic conference
at Genoa. Chapman was responsible for
preparing the economic section and participated at the highest official levels in
complicated and, in the result, unfruitful
negotiations at Genoa and The Hague,
especially with the Russians, before they
surprised the world by their separate
agreement with Germany.

Chapman had followed Sir Hubert
Llewellyn Smith [q.v.] as permanent secretary to the Board of Trade and in 1927 he
followed him again in the post of chief
economic adviser to the Government. The
holder of this appointment was expected
to occupy himself largely in acting as
British representative at various conferences and committees of the League of
Nations. At that time it still seemed
legitimate to hope that patient and persistent work by the economic section of the
League might lead to international agreements which would release a wave of
progress and expansion in international
trade. As an outstanding negotiator and
draftsman Chapman was a prominent
member of the team of internationally

minded politicians and civil servants who
maintained their patient efforts through
many frustrations. The work appealed to
his idealism and to his fondness for intellectual challenge and contact with sharp
minds.

In 1932 the British Government reacted
to the economic crisis with a resort to
tariff protection, and by a dramatic reversal of functions Chapman was called
upon to devote his talents to making a
pattern of import duties which would
serve the true interests of an economy still
primarily dependent on export trade. Sir
George (later Lord) May [q.v.] was made
chairman of the Import Duties Advisory
Committee, with Chapman and Sir Allan
Powell [q.v.] as the other two members.
Chapman's understanding of theoretical
economics was now coupled with much
knowledge of industry, wide trust and
respect from business men, and much
experience of the administrative machine
and of foreign tariffs and tariff negotiation, and he made major contributions to
the work of the committee.

Chapman had just retired at the age of
sixty-eight when war broke out in 1939.
He returned to administrative work as
chairman of the arc lamp carbon pool and
as controller of matches and was able to
make some reassuring comparisons between the efficacy of the organization of
economic controls in the two wars. He was
also vice-chairman of the Central Price
Regulation Committee.

Simple and natural in manner, immensely attractive in a quiet way in conversation, always encouraging to younger
men, learned but athletic and companionable, Chapman continued in governmental
circles to draw to himself the affection
and respect which students and colleagues
had given him at Manchester. A rather
cautious common sense in detail markedly
tempered both his idealism and the pro-
gressiveness of his abstract thought. He
had a flair for seeing practicable ways
through difficult situations, though at
times his endless patience and smoothness
may have slightly exasperated the more
thrustful among his colleagues. He was
appointed C.B.E. (1917), C.B. (1919), and
promoted K.C.B. (1920).

Chapman married in 1903 Mabel
Gwendoline (died 1958), daughter of
Thomas Henry Mordey, shipowner, of
Newport, Monmouthshire; they had two
sons and a daughter. He died 29 August
1951 at his home in Ware, Hertfordshire.

[*The Times* and *Manchester Guardian*, 31

August 1951; private information; personal knowledge.]   E. RAYMOND STREAT.

CHARLOT, ANDRÉ EUGENE MAURICE (1882–1956), showman, was born in Paris 26 July 1882, the son of Jules Charles Maurice Charlot and his wife, Jeanne Sargine Battu. His father, the director of several Parisian theatres, among them the Athenée, Palais Royal, and Comédie Royale, was the son of Auguste Charlot, winner in 1850 of the first *grand prix de Rome* to have been awarded for music. André Charlot was educated at the Lycée Condorcet and then entered the Conservatoire de Paris (class of musical composition) which he soon left to become secretary to the manager of the Palais Royal. After acting as administrator of the Théâtre des Ambassadeurs, Femina, Folies-Bergère, Alcazar, and other houses, he opened in 1910 a theatrical agency of his own, from which he came to London in July 1912 as joint manager of the Alhambra.

For twenty years Charlot's name was associated with revue, a form of entertainment which he was one of the first to introduce from France, in rivalry with (Sir) C. B. Cochran [q.v.]. Endowed with an almost feminine artistic taste and a shrewd eye for theatrical talent on the performing side, he produced between 1915 and 1935 thirty-six revues in the west end of London, the most memorable being *5064 Gerrard* (1915), *Some* (1916), *Buzz-Buzz* (1918), *Jumble Sale* (1920), *Pot Luck* and *A to Z* (1921), *Charlot's Revue*, 1924–5, *Charlot's Show of 1926*, *Charlot's Masquerade* (1930), and *Charlot's Char-a-Bang!* (1935). His *London Calling* (1923) was noteworthy as marking the début as a revue writer of (Sir) Noël Coward who as the result of personal encouragement by Charlot went on to make his name as playwright and performer in the London theatre.

Apart from revue Charlot interested himself in light comedy, farce, and the musical play, most notably perhaps the production in 1930 of *Wonder Bar* in which the theatre audience was embodied in the action of the story. In 1922 he was the London pioneer of the restaurant 'floor-show' with his presentation of 'The Midnight Follies' at the Hotel Metropole. He was the first magnate of the London theatre to recognize the potentialities of broadcasting, associating himself actively with the production of almost fifty 'Charlot's Hour' programmes for the B.B.C.

In 1937 London saw virtually the last of André Charlot; he left for California in the belief that his future lay with talking pictures rather than with the living theatre. His decision was not a particularly happy one; after a period as technical adviser to the Paramount Picture Corporation he more or less vanished from the Hollywood scene, apart from some personal appearances as a screen actor and his production at the El Capitan Theatre of *The Charlot Revue of 1940* in aid of British war relief.

Tall, slim, and spectacled, André Charlot was one of the personalities of his time. Usually with a topcoat slung over his shoulders, he moved through his little empire with the assurance of a Caesar who expected the impossible to happen at his command. When things went wrong, he had the habit of taking to his bed and remaining there, unshaven, until they were put right for him. For this he had the excuse of being a diabetic, although not to any serious degree. The financial ability which had distinguished him as a manager of theatres seemed to desert him when he turned producer; his fine taste and perfectionism often landed him in money troubles. It was difficult, however, for the most hard-faced of creditors not to succumb to the siren song of his beguiling personality.

Charlot was naturalized a British subject in 1922. He married Florence Gladman and had one son and one daughter. He died in Hollywood 20 May 1956.

[Private information; personal knowledge.
    ERIC MASCHWITZ

CHATTERJEE, SIR ATUL CHANDRA (1874–1955), Indian civil servant, was born at Malda in Lower Bengal 24 November 1874. He was the fourth son and sixth child of Rai Saheb Hem Chandra Chatterjee of Santipur, an engineer employed in the Bengal Public Works Department and his wife, Srimati Nistarini Debi. After early attendance at various primary schools in the province he was sent to Hare School, Calcutta, and at the age of fourteen passed the matriculation examination of the Presidency College, Calcutta, obtaining a small entrance scholarship. After graduating B.A. in 1892 Chatterjee received an enhanced government scholarship, and the following year was selected for a Government of India scholarship tenable in England and entered King's College, Cambridge, in October 1893. He was awarded an exhibition in 1894. After obtaining a second class in the history tripos of 1895, Chatterjee sat for the Indian Civil Service open examination of 1896 and headed the list of successful candidates. During his probationary year at Cambridge he won the Bhaunagar medal. In India he was posted to the United Provinces and for the next nine years was employed in district administration in the successive grades of assistant, joint, and district magistrate. A period of special duty, during which he conducted a comprehensive survey and produced a report on the industries of his province, was followed in 1912 by his appointment as registrar of Co-operative Credit Societies. In 1917 Sir James (later Lord) Meston [q.v.] selected him for the post of revenue secretary in his government and this was followed in 1919 by his appointment to the highly responsible post of chief secretary under Sir Harcourt Butler [q.v.].

Chatterjee's first appearance as a representative of his country abroad also marked the beginning of his work in a field in which he was subsequently to render conspicuous service. In 1919 he was sent to Washington as representative of India at the first International Labour Conference, and attendance at the Geneva conference of 1921 was followed by his appointment as secretary to the Government of India in the newly constituted department of Industries, then in the charge of Sir Thomas Holland [q.v.]. Later, in 1923, Chatterjee himself became a member of the viceroy's council responsible for the department, and to his untiring efforts in this field were largely due the initiation and progress of labour legislation from 1922 onwards remarked in the report (Cmd. 3883, 1931) of the royal commission on labour in India. When the office of high commissioner for India in London fell vacant towards the end of 1924 Chatterjee was offered the appointment by the viceroy, Lord Reading [q.v.], and accepted it, not without considerable regret at the severance which it involved from his chosen work in India. He was appointed K.C.I.E. (1925). His wide administrative experience and intellectual gifts combined with ready adaptability to new demands and surroundings made him an admirable choice for the post at a difficult point in its history.

After taking up office in London, Chatterjee was soon faced with the necessity to provide more spacious and dignified accommodation for the Indian Government's representative in London, and on his own initiative India House in Aldwych was built to the design of Sir Herbert Baker [q.v.] and formally opened by King George V in the summer of 1930. Chatterjee, the first high commissioner to occupy the building, was appointed K.C.S.I. With location in London came enlarged and extended facilities in the international field. Chatterjee represented India for six consecutive annual sessions of the International Labour Conference from 1924 and again in 1933. He was a member of the governing body of the International Labour Office for five years (1926–31), was vice-president in 1932, and president the following year. In 1927 he was accorded the signal honour of election by a unanimous vote as president of the tenth International Labour Conference. At the conclusion Albert Thomas, the director of the International Labour Office, paid a notable tribute to 'his perfect impartiality, his great authority, his serenity and the wonderful quickness he had shown in imparting and explaining the decisions of the Conference'. Chatterjee also served from 1925 to 1931 as a member of the Imperial Economic Committee. He was a representative of India at the League of Nations Assembly in 1925 and led the International Labour Office delegation to the abortive world economic conference of 1933. He served the League as vice-president of the consultative economic committee, and as a member of the permanent central opium board and of the allocations committee. He was Indian delegate to the London naval conference of 1930. In the inter-imperial field confidence in his diplomatic gifts was marked by his appointment to lead the Indian delegation to the Ottawa conference of 1932. In the following year Chatterjee was promoted G.C.I.E. In the meantime his term of office as high commissioner having ended in 1931 he was offered by the secretary of state for India, and accepted, appointment to the India Council for the statutory period of five years. His last appointment, in 1942, was as adviser to the secretary of state, which he held until 1947 when India became independent.

Chatterjee served on the council of the Royal Society of Arts for twenty years and was its chairman in 1939–40, the first Indian to hold this position. He was for many years vice-chairman of the council of the East India Association and was also a member of the council of the Royal Asiatic Society. His intellectual interests covered a wide range with a predominating historical bent exemplified by his authorship, jointly with his Indian Civil Service colleague, W. H. Moreland, of *A Short History of India* published in 1936 and brought up to date in three subsequent editions. He was also the author of *The New India* (1948). He was a fellow of the university of Allahabad (1908) and an honorary LL.D. of Edinburgh (1931).

Chatterjee was a great servant of India, who, while avoiding political controversy, lost no opportunity of advancing his country's interests in the international field. In his public appearances he eschewed rhetoric, impressing his audience by his sincerity and obvious mastery of his subject. In private a man of simple tastes and abstemious habit he had a great capacity for friendship and, while shrewd in his estimation of character, was never harsh in his judgements. He died 8 September 1955 at Bexhill-on-Sea.

Chatterjee married first, in 1897, Vina Mookerjee (died 1905), by whom he had two daughters. Secondly, in 1924 he married Gladys Mary Broughton, formerly of the Indian Educational Service and adviser to the Government of India on questions affecting the welfare of women and children. She was the daughter of Captain William Barnard Broughton, Dorsetshire Regiment. She was called to the bar in 1933 and died in 1969.

[*The Times*, 9 September 1955; Record of Proceedings: Tenth Session, International Labour Conference, 1927; *Journal* of the Royal Society of Arts, 29 November 1940; family records; personal knowledge.]

J. C. B. DRAKE.

CHERRY - GARRARD, APSLEY GEORGE BENET (1886–1959), polar explorer, the only son of Major-General Apsley Cherry-Garrard, C.B., was born in Bedford 2 January 1886. His father was said by Lord Wolseley [q.v.] to be 'the bravest man I have ever seen'. Soon after marriage late in life to Evelyn Edith, daughter of Henry Wilson Sharpin, this distinguished soldier inherited from his elder brother the Cherry estate of Denford Park, Berkshire, and in 1892 that of his mother's family also, Lamer Park, Hertfordshire, with the added name and arms of Garrard. He leased Denford and made Lamer his residence; it became to his son the dearest place on earth. Shortsightedness handicapped the boy in games at his preparatory school and at Winchester, where he was lonely. But at

Oxford he found congenial friends and interests as well as a sport to which bad eyesight was no bar: he helped the Christ Church eight to win the Grand Challenge Cup at Henley in 1908; in the same year he obtained a third class in modern history.

On his father's death in 1907 he found himself the heir to a double fortune, and two years later went for a cruise round the world on cargo boats. Hearing when at Brisbane that Captain R. F. Scott [q.v.] proposed a second expedition to the Antarctic in 1910, he wrote to Dr. E. A. Wilson [q.v.], whom he had met previously at a shooting party in Scotland, volunteering his services. In an expedition every member of which was a specialist he was accepted by Scott on Wilson's recommendation alone and duly enlisted as 'assistant zoologist'. Yet from the outset despite his youth and inexperience he won the affectionate regard of his more seasoned comrades, and before the close of the expedition had more major sledge-journeys to his credit than any other surviving member.

On the Depôt Journey to lay stores at stages along the southern route, as far as to One Ton Depôt 140 miles from base, Cherry-Garrard was warmly commended by Scott for his efficiency and unselfishness as a sledger and tent-mate. In the comparative comfort of life at the base he edited the *South Polar Times*, a unique periodical afterwards reproduced in facsimile. Wilson chose Bowers and Cherry-Garrard—'the pick of the sledging element (Scott)—as his companions for a Winter Journey in 1911 to the Emperor Penguin rookery at Cape Crozier, an exploit which is still without parallel in the annals of polar exploration. On their return five weeks later Scott described their journey as 'the hardest that has ever been made —a phrase which later suggested to Cherry-Garrard the title of his narrative of the fortunes of the whole expedition: *The Worst Journey in the World* (1922). But the Winter Journey was the climacteric of it for him, so much so that even the outward marches of the great Southern Journey, despite their gruelling nature were a picnic by comparison. He accompanied the polar party as far as the summit of the Beardmore Glacier whence he was sent back, because of his youth, with the first of the two supporting parties Early in March 1912 he set out alone with dog-teams and a Russian dog-driver to speed the return of the polar party

Having reached One Ton Depôt on the night of the 3rd, the date approximately timed for their arrival, he was beset by a four days' blizzard which prevented movement, but stayed on until there remained only just enough dog-food for return. Although his decision to return was the only possible one, he never ceased to reproach himself afterwards for not having attempted the impossible. He was a member of the search party eight months later which found the bodies of Scott, Wilson, and Bowers, who had died within only eleven miles of One Ton Depôt; and learned of the heroic self-sacrifice of L. E. G. Oates [q.v.] a few marches behind, and of Petty Officer Evans's earlier collapse below the Beardmore Glacier. It was at Cherry-Garrard's suggestion that the last line of Tennyson's *Ulysses* was inscribed on the cross surmounting the cairn of snow which covered them, as well as the epitaph commemorating Oates.

The rest of Cherry-Garrard's life was anticlimax. He commanded a squadron of armoured cars in Flanders from 1914 until invalided out two years later, and during a long convalescence wrote *The Worst Journey*, a classic of Antarctic literature. Years later he also wrote introductions to biographies of Wilson and Bowers. He cultivated friendships with men of letters, including Shaw, Wells, and Bennett; and with men of action, especially Mallory of Everest and Lawrence of Arabia. To the latter he paid tribute in the symposium *T. E. Lawrence by his Friends* (1937).

In 1939 Cherry-Garrard married Angela, daughter of Kenneth Turner, of Ipswich. 1947 income-tax demands and ill health obliged him to sell Lamer, which was demolished, and he exchanged its spacious demesne for the confines of a London flat. Many years of intermittent illness terminated with his death in London 18 May 1959. A lifelike statuette of him in polar clothing, executed by Ivor Roberts-Jones and erected by his widow, stands in the south transept of Wheathampstead parish church among other Garrard memorials.

[*The Times*, 19 May 1959; *Scott's Last Expedition*, ed. L. Huxley, 1913; Introduction to the 1965 edition of *The Worst Journey the World*; personal knowledge.]

GEORGE SEAVER.

CHERWELL, VISCOUNT (1886–1957), scientist and politician. [See LINDEMANN, FREDERICK ALEXANDER.]

CHIFLEY, JOSEPH BENEDICT (1885–1951), Australian prime minister, was born at Bathurst, New South Wales, 22 September 1885, the eldest of three sons of Irish-Australian and Irish immigrant parents, Patrick Chifley, a blacksmith, and his wife, Mary Anne Corrigan. He had scanty formal schooling but, before and after joining the New South Wales railways as a shop-boy in 1903, educated himself assiduously for years at night-school, and through the Workers' Educational Association and the Railways Institute. He rose to full driver's rank in 1914 and subsequently also gave instruction in his craft. A local and state trade-union officer (while still working as a driver), he appeared repeatedly as expert witness or advocate in industrial arbitration proceedings. In 1917, as a prominent leader of his union, he was dismissed from the railway service following the failure of a bitter and far-reaching strike in New South Wales industry. On appeal, he was reinstated to a junior rating, with loss of superannuation and seniority rights. His union had been decimated, and was deregistered by the State Industrial Court. He was one of a handful of men who worked unrelentingly for years to rebuild the union and restore the strikers' former positions. In 1920 he was one of the founders of the nationwide Australian Federated Union of Locomotive Enginemen, with access to the Commonwealth Arbitration Court. But not until the return of a Labour government in New South Wales in 1925 were the pre-1917 seniority and other rights of the strikers regained.

In 1922 Chifley followed his father as a director of the Bathurst District Hospital and of a local daily newspaper the Bathurst *National Advocate*. Amongst many other local public activities, he was from 1933 to 1947 a member (and for several years president) of the Abercrombie Shire Council.

In 1922 and again in 1924 Chifley failed to win selection as Labour candidate for the local seat in the New South Wales legislative assembly. In 1925, as Labour candidate for the federal seat of Macquarie (which included Bathurst), Chifley ran the sitting government member to within 903 votes. In 1928 he won Macquarie by 3,578 votes. In 1929 he held it by 12,078 votes when the House of Representatives was dissolved and a Labour Government under J. H. Scullin was swept into office. With only 7 of the 36 seats in the Senate and confronted by the mounting misery and turmoil of the depression, the Labour Party was soon split by frustration and dissension inside and outside Parliament. Early in 1931 the Cabinet suffered defections to right and left. On 2 March Chifley was elected to one of the vacancies and served as minister for defence and minister assisting the treasurer, E. G. Theodore. At the end of March the New South Wales state branch under J. T. Lang who had been at logger-heads with Scullin was expelled from the Australian Labour Party but retained considerable popular support. In November the Government was defeated by the defection of Lang sympathizers in the House of Representatives. Theodore, Chifley, and most other New South Wales members who had remained loyal to the federal Labour Party lost their seats at the December elections (Chifley by only 456 votes) which resulted in a landslide against Labour.

From 1931 until 1940, Chifley's bids to re-enter parliamentary life failed. He gave years of leadership to the struggle in New South Wales to reunite the Labour factions and to oust Lang (which was achieved in 1939-40). In 1936-7 Chifley served on the royal commission on banking, recommending bank nationalization in a minority report. Following the outbreak of war in 1939 the non-Labour Government of (Sir) R. G. Menzies appointed Chifley a member of the Capital Issues Advisory Board, director of labour supply in the Department of Munitions, and a member of other wartime bodies. In September 1940, however, Chifley regained the Macquarie seat and was elected to the Opposition front bench, although by arrangement between the parties he continued in some of his advisory posts.

In October 1941 when Labour under John Curtin [q.v.] took over the government, Chifley took office as third-ranking minister, with the Treasury portfolio (which he held continuously until December 1949), membership of the War Cabinet and the production executive of Cabinet, and also (December 1942-February 1945) the additional portfolio of minister for post-war reconstruction. Curtin increasingly relied on Chifley as his 'home front' and House of Representatives aide and as his closest confidant.

As treasurer, Chifley pushed taxation to new levels, while filling loans of unprecedented proportions several times a year. He imposed stringent controls on credit, prices, and consumption, achieving by 1943 comprehensive stabilization and rationing schemes which afforded 'fair

shares' while releasing a maximum of food and supplies to Britain and her allies and holding cost-of-living figures stationary until the war was won. With the 'uniform taxation' legislation of 1942 he permanently reinforced Commonwealth financial ascendancy by establishing a federal monopoly of direct taxation. By wartime regulation, followed by legislation in 1945 he expanded the central-banking and other functions of the Commonwealth Bank, reformed its direction, and brought other banks under stricter central bank and governmental control.

Despite the Government's failure in the years 1942-4 to win approval for wider constitutional powers for the federal Parliament, Chifley prepared a wide range of measures for demobilization and re-establishment of ex-servicemen and women and war-workers, land settlement housing, social security and health service extensions upon an entirely new financial basis, grants to universities and scholarships for their students, disposal of wool and other surplus stocks, national development works, and the use or disposal of government munition factories and surplus construction equipment. These were applied with a high degree of timeliness and success. In his dual wartime ministerial capacities he was also the key man behind Australian participation in international planning of mutual aid relief, food and agriculture, monetary stabilization, full employment, and increased world trade.

On 30 April 1945 Chifley became acting prime minister and on 12 July, following Curtin's death, prime minister. It thus fell to his lot to represent Australia at two historic prime ministers' conference in London—that of 1946 which made a crucial review of the British Commonwealth's changed strategic and economic requirements and that of 1949 which thrashed out a basis for retaining republican India as a full partner. He was a unvarnished, practical British Commonwealth man. Between 1945 and 1949 during the absence of colleagues overseas he acted as minister for external affairs for a total of some seventeen months and minister for defence for a shorter period Chifley displayed a high order of statesmanship in leading the nation and, no least, his own party to the acceptance of new and uncomfortable facts of international life facing Australia in the field of collective security, world economic arrangements, and the emergent Asia. I all this his hand was strengthened by the convincing vote of confidence his Government was given in the general elections of 1946.

At home, as treasurer as well as prime minister, Chifley carried on his battle for economic stability with high success until his failure in May 1948 to carry a constitutional amendment allowing the federal Parliament to maintain essential economic controls beyond the life of the wartime defence powers; but even then he did not give up the struggle. He was also a firm believer in a large public sector of the economy. He was the leading spirit behind the measures for nationalizing internal and external airlines, banking, stevedoring, telecommunications, for the close public control of coal-mining and broadcasting, or the public development of hydro-electric power, atomic energy, coastal shipping, aluminium production, whaling, and television, for the advance planning of massive national development works by the Australian National Works Council which he created in 1943), and for the reorganization and expansion of the Commonwealth's scientific and industrial research organizations. His was the decisive role in the founding of the Australian National University and the inauguration of the huge Snowy Mountains Hydro-Electricity Scheme. Although the courts ruled nationalization of internal airlines and banking unconstitutional, the Chifley government created a public airline (Trans-Australia Airlines) to compete with private lines and expanded the Commonwealth Bank.

Opposed by the British Medical Association in Australia, Chifley failed to complete his design for non-contributory national health services. In the field of industrial arbitration and conciliation, however, he was successful in reforming the existing institutions on a basis better adapted to cope with the industrial unrest during the post-war transition, unrest greatly aggravated by Communist leadership of some of the largest industrial unions. Chifley insisted on sustaining civil liberties in the industrial field but he provided procedures enabling unionists to overcome Communist 'rigging' of union ballots. His government enlarged the membership of both houses of the national Parliament in 1948 to represent more adequately the growing electorate.

After the 1947 bank nationalization attempt, Chifley's opponents redoubled their efforts to overthrow his Government.

All sectional grievances were vigorously exploited; the Opposition attacked particularly Chifley's economic controls, retained in the post-war years to sustain stability at home and the hard-pressed British food standards and sterling area balances abroad. A severe coalminers' strike in the summer of 1949 made for temporary public hardships. In the December general elections, Opposition promises to end petrol-rationing and extend child endowment (with which Chifley refused to compete) probably proved decisive. A Liberal–Country Party composite Government took office under Menzies. Labour, however, held a majority in the Senate.

As leader of the Opposition (1950–51), Chifley determinedly fought some of the methods provided for in a bill for the suppression of Communism in the trade unions and elsewhere. After he had gained some important concessions from Menzies, the federal executive of the Labour Party, against his advice, called a halt to further opposition which might bring about an early double-dissolution of Parliament on the Communist issue. But Chifley's deputy, H. V. Evatt, on behalf of some of the unions, fought the Communist Party Dissolution Act in the High Court and succeeded in having it declared unconstitutional. A deadlock at that time (March 1951) between House and Senate over a bill to undo parts of Chifley's 1945 banking reforms provided the Government with the opportunity to dissolve both houses and fight an election mainly on the Communist issue. At the end of November 1950 Chifley had suffered a heart seizure which had required three months' rest. But he now campaigned doggedly throughout Australia to the limit of his strength. In April 1951 the Menzies government was returned with a majority in the Senate and a reduced majority in the House. Chifley was re-elected unopposed as leader of the Labour opposition. But on 13 June, while working in his hotel room in Canberra, he suffered a second stroke and died without regaining consciousness.

Chifley was a man of fine presence, naturally shy, yet warm, outgoing, and quietly humorous. He was a most capable and successful negotiator and a tremendous desk-worker for whom his Civil Service officers had unstinted admiration. A much-loved party colleague, with the confidence also of his opponents, he was a very successful parliamentary manager. He was not an orator and a chronic throat condition over the last twenty years of his life detracted from the attractiveness of his otherwise persuasive debating powers. He had (except over Menzies' anti-Communist measures) an extraordinarily complete command of his party inside and outside Parliament—no Labour prime minister has rivalled his sustained command of his followers. He was a typical Australian Labour amalgam of radical, socialist, and conservative.

In 1914 Chifley, a Roman Catholic, married, in the Presbyterian Church, Elizabeth Gibson (died 1962), daughter of George McKenzie, a fellow engine-driver. Although this affected Chifley's standing in his own Church, he never ceased to attend its services regularly. There were no children of the marriage.

Chifley was sworn of the Privy Council in 1946. He was accorded a state funeral and was buried in the Bathurst cemetery, where a memorial has been raised over his grave by the Labour Party. He could never take seriously the making of time for an official portrait painter. A disappointing portrait, posthumously painted from photographs, by A. D. Colquhoun hangs in the King's Hall of Parliament House, Canberra, and another by R. Campbell in the Council Chamber at Bathurst.

[L. F. Crisp, *Ben Chifley*, 1961; private information; personal knowledge.]

L. F. CRISP.

CHILDE, VERE GORDON (1892–1957), prehistorian, was born in Sydney, New South Wales, 14 April 1892, the son of the Rev. Stephen Henry Childe, rector of St. Thomas's, and his wife, Harriet Eliza, daughter of Alexander Gordon, barrister at law, of England. He was educated at the Church of England Grammar School and the university of Sydney where he obtained the Cooper graduate scholarship in classics in 1914. At the Queen's College, Oxford, he obtained a B.Litt. (1916) under the supervision of Sir Arthur Evans and (Sir) J. L. Myres [qq.v.] and a first class in *literae humaniores* (1917). In 1920–21 he was private secretary to the premier of New South Wales, but he left this post for a period of travel in Eastern and Central Europe to study at first hand the prehistoric archaeology of these areas. He returned to England in 1922, was librarian to the Royal Anthropological Institute in London (1925–7), and in 1925 published his first major book, *The Dawn of European Civilization*. In 1927 he was

appointed to the newly founded Abercromby chair of prehistoric archaeology in the university of Edinburgh, remaining until 1946, when he took over the dual post of professor of prehistoric European archaeology and director of the Institute of Archaeology in the university of London, from which he retired in 1956.

During his tenure of these two chairs Childe established himself as a prehistorian of international status, receiving honorary degrees from American and European universities and (posthumously) from the university of Edinburgh. He was elected F.B.A. in 1940. His first book was issued in successive revised editions up to a sixth edition in 1957; *The Aryans* (1926), *The Danube in Prehistory* (1929), *The Prehistory of Scotland* (1935), *New Light on the Most Ancient East* (final ed. 1952), *Prehistoric Communities of the British Isles* (1940), and *Prehistoric Migrations in Europe* (1950) were all major landmarks in the technical literature of prehistory. In a series of publications addressed to a more general public, notably *Man Makes Himself* (1936) and *What Happened in History* (1942), he was instrumental in spreading to a wide circle of readers a knowledge of the evidence of archaeology for social and technological evolution.

Childe, as became apparent in his final publications, pursued a consistent intellectual course throughout his studies. Beginning as a classic, he had started by investigating the possible archaeological contexts for the dispersal of languages within the Indo-European group. This necessitated an assessment of the relations between Europe and the Orient in prehistory, and in such an assessment an assured chronological scheme for all the areas under review was obviously of paramount importance. Side by side with this came the recognition that archaeological sites and objects were to be interpreted as the fossil remains of human behaviour, and that through them the prehistorian should be able to perceive the nameless communities and societies which were responsible for these surviving elements of material culture. To define these societies in time and space, and to study their interaction and succession, both in the non-literate context of prehistory and in their relationships with the ancient historical civilizations, was then the task of the prehistorian.

Following on this, Childe sought to investigate what had appeared to him from the beginning a challenging phenomenon—'the foundation of European Civilization as a peculiar and individual manifestation of the human spirit'. From the twenties onward his main work was directed to the elucidation of this problem, and in his quest he found it necessary to establish a series of postulates and to provide the technical evidence upon which they were based. The latter was presented in his successive works of magisterial synthesis which for his fellow scholars formed the main content of his unique achievement, and the question of relative and absolute chronology so essential for his thesis was argued and reargued here and in papers in technical journals. Interpretation of this mass of material in terms of prehistory could be obtained only within the framework of a conceptual model of the past within which archaeological evidence could play a significant part, and in search of a valid model Childe not unnaturally experimented with Marxist theories of social evolution among others. Concerned essentially with material culture, he necessarily devised schemes based on materialistic philosophies and constructed an evolutionary–technological model of the past within which to order his observations. It was the past as viewed in terms of this model which he presented to the readers of his more popular books; and in his posthumous *Prehistory of European Society* (1958) the essential character of prehistoric Europe, so long sought, is presented largely in terms of the freedom of the technologist in contrast to his bondage within an oriental autocracy.

Childe was a lonely figure, a dedicated scholar difficult to know and by his own awkward shyness rendered almost unapproachable save on the most formal terms. Tall, ungainly, and ugly, eccentric in dress and often abrupt in manner, the generous, kindly, rather naïve person hidden behind the curious and often alarming *persona* was known to few. He was not a good teacher, and undergraduate audiences could make little of the mass of recondite learning which was presented to them; but with senior students and junior fellow scholars he was unsparingly generous of his immense intellectual stores. He founded no school by direct tuition in either of the two universities in which he taught, but his indirect influence on the study of British and indeed European prehistory was enormous. He demonstrated that the prehistory of the British Isles was meaningless unless considered as part of that of Europe, and indeed of the Old World; he taught the lesson of the irrelevance of local studies everywhere unless seen within the context of a greater whole. His own range of knowledge and his linguistic ability enabled him to master Old World prehistory from the beginnings of agriculture to the early first millennium B.C. in a manner incredible in one individual, and perhaps, with the increasing complexity of the subject, hardly possible again. Nevertheless the approach he advocated and practised, even if the theoretical models within which he saw fit to interpret his material may be found unacceptable, will continue to provide future scholars with the essential bases for a sound discipline.

Childe, who was unmarried, met his death accidentally while walking in the Blue Mountains during a visit to his native Australia, 19 October 1957.

[Stuart Piggott in *Proceedings* of the British Academy, vol. xliv, 1958; private information; personal knowledge.]

STUART PIGGOTT.

CILCENNIN, VISCOUNT (1903–1960), politician. [See THOMAS, JAMES PURDON LEWES.]

CLARENDON, sixth EARL OF (1877–1955), public servant. [See VILLIERS, GEORGE HERBERT HYDE.]

CLARK, SIR WILLIAM HENRY (1876–1952), civil servant, was born 1 January 1876 in Cambridge where his father, John Willis Clark [q.v.], was superintendent of the museum of zoology and later registrary of the university. He won a scholarship to Eton and later at Trinity College, Cambridge, where in 1897 he achieved a good first class in part i of the classical tripos. In the following year he sat for the Civil Service and taking a high position was appointed in 1899 to the Board of Trade. He made his mark early in the public service as secretary to the special mission which went in 1901–2 to negotiate a commercial treaty with China after the Boxer rising. In 1903 he was appointed C.M.G., an unprecedented honour for so young a civil servant. In that year he was made secretary to the royal commission which, because of unfortunate happenings during the South African war, was set up to consider the supply of food and raw material in time of war. The commission's work lasted until 1905. From 1906 to 1908

Clark served as private secretary to the president of the Board of Trade, Lloyd George, and for a short time to (Sir) Winston Churchill, until in 1908 Lloyd George, who had become chancellor of the Exchequer, arranged for Clark's transfer to the Treasury to serve him again as private secretary.

Considerable criticism greeted Clark's appointment in 1910 as member for commerce and industry in the executive council of the viceroy of India, criticism grounded on his youth and inexperience of India. But from the outset Clark displayed unusual mastery of his task, and he was appointed C.S.I. in 1911 and K.C.S.I. in 1915.

In 1916 Clark returned to England, reverted to the Board of Trade, and was made head of the commercial intelligence department which needed invigoration and increased staff. Clark's recommendations were taken into full consideration by the Government in its planning both to restore the channels of export trade, still disrupted by war, and to help British exporters against increasing overseas competition. The outcome was the establishment in 1917 of the Department of Overseas Trade of which Clark was the obvious choice for comptroller-general.

For the selection of staff for headquarters and for many newly created posts overseas, in Commonwealth and foreign countries, Clark was largely responsible; greatly to his credit, this new department soon won wide acceptance among British exporters as one which could give them valued help. Among activities which he initiated were the British Industries Fair which became an annual event; British participation in important international exhibitions; and the occasional organization overseas of a purely United Kingdom trade fair. He instituted the systematic publication of economic and commercial reports about numerous overseas markets and arranged for the department's overseas representatives to be available, when on home leave, to interview and advise exporters. The department was also largely responsible for organizing the British Empire exhibition at Wembley in 1924–5.

Clark remained comptroller-general until 1928. As an outcome of the definition of dominion status accepted at the imperial conference of 1926 it was decided that the United Kingdom should be represented by a high commissioner in each dominion which, in turn, should appoint a high

commissioner in London. Clark was the first high commissioner to be appointed to Canada, in 1928; one of his first actions was to appoint the Department of Overseas Trade's senior trade commissioner in Canada as economic adviser on his staff. This gave the high commissioner the opportunity of maintaining close touch with economic and commercial conditions in Canada involving any Anglo-Canadian problem. At the same time, and of equal importance, it invested the trade commissioner with a quasi-diplomatic recognition not previously enjoyed which made it easier for him to contact Canadian government departments as well as official and semi-official organizations. This precedent was shortly followed by all other United Kingdom high commissioners.

Appointed K.C.M.G. in 1930, Clark remained in Canada until 1934 when he was appointed high commissioner in the Union of South Africa and simultaneously high commissioner for Basutoland, the Bechuanaland Protectorate, and Swaziland, a post calling for the exercise of considerable diplomatic skill. Throughout his service in the Union he remained a popular and much respected representative. The year 1937 saw him promoted G.C.M.G. and his return to England followed in 1939 when he became chairman of the Imperial Shipping Committee. He retired from public service in 1940, but in 1946 readily accepted an invitation from the Dominions Office to visit its overseas posts and to make such recommendations in their respect as his experience might suggest. He continued in retirement his great interest in the Royal Empire (later Commonwealth) Society of which at one time he was chairman of the council. Here and with many other bodies he was in great demand as a very amusing speaker.

Tall and spare of build, Clark had a distinguished bearing. His blue eyes were ever ready to sparkle with fun. He combined with an unfailing sense of humour and an old-world charm great tact, imperturbability and, in important issues, determination. These qualities and his patent integrity served him well throughout his public life. No contemporary, and certainly no civil servant, did more than he for his country's export trade, the importance of which was, for many years, never far from his thoughts.

In 1909 Clark married Anne Elizabeth (died 1946), daughter of William Thomas Monsell and widow of William Bennett Pike, barrister. They had one son and two daughters. Clark died in Cambridge 22 November 1952.

[Private information; personal knowledge.]
J. A. P. EDGCUMBE.

CLARK KERR, ARCHIBALD JOHN KERR, BARON INVERCHAPEL (1882–1951), diplomatist, was born 17 March 1882 near Sydney, Australia, the fifth son of John Kerr Clark of Crossbasket, Hamilton, Lanarkshire, and his wife, Kate Louisa, daughter of Sir John Struan Robertson. Both sides of his family were linked with the west of Scotland and, after acquiring family property at Inverchapel on the shores of Loch Eck in Argyll, he later took the additional surname of Kerr. He was educated at Bath College and Heidelberg University before becoming an attaché in the diplomatic service in 1905. After filling various posts overseas, he was transferred to the Foreign Office in 1916. Two years later his request to be released for active service was finally granted and he enlisted as a private in the Scots Guards. He returned to diplomacy after the war and in 1925 became minister to Guatemala. Three years later he was transferred to Santiago, where he met and in 1929 married a beautiful Chilean girl of nineteen, Maria Teresa Diaz Salas. The marriage was childless. There followed nearly four years (1931–5) in Stockholm, at the end of which he was promoted ambassador, appointed K.C.M.G., and assigned to Baghdad (1935).

There had so far been nothing remarkable about his career; but his appointment in 1938 to be ambassador in China and the distinction with which he discharged his duties there placed him at a stride among the leading diplomatists of his day. The post required not only negotiating skill but physical courage; his predecessor, Sir Hughe Knatchbull-Hugessen, had been seriously injured in an attack on his car by low-flying Japanese aircraft. Clark Kerr and his Soviet colleague were the only members of the diplomatic corps to remain in Chungking in spite of the bombing and so earn the respect of the Chinese. He needed every bit he had; whilst British sympathies were with Generalissimo Chiang Kai-shek, it was not possible to help him openly for fear of provoking Japan into declaring war. Even after Pearl Harbour (December 1941) resources were so stretched that little could be done beyond providing goods. Clark Kerr did much by his bearing and fortitude to convince the Chinese of Britain's ultimate intention and capacity to aid them. He established a close personal relationship with Chiang Kai-shek, whilst observing without illusion the corruption of the regime and the growing estrangement between Kuomintang and the Chinese Communists. Shortly before he left Chungking in February 1942 he was promoted G.C.M.G., and awarded the Order of the Brilliant Jade by Chiang Kai-shek.

Clark Kerr had been selected for an equally exacting post, attached to an ally whose sufferings were also terrible and whose faith that these were being loyally shared on other fronts needed constant reassurance. When he succeeded Sir Stafford Cripps [q.v.] in Moscow in March 1942, he went with a warm recommendation to Stalin from (Sir) Winston Churchill, who described him as 'a personal friend of mine of many years' standing'. In August, when the diplomatic corps was still at Kuibyshev, he joined Churchill in Moscow for the first of the prime minister's confrontations with Stalin. In addition to subsequent conferences in Moscow, Clark Kerr took part in the tripartite conferences with Roosevelt at Tehran (1943) and Yalta (February 1945) and also in the last of the great wartime meetings at Potsdam (July 1945). He was sworn of the Privy Council in 1944. Shortly before Clark Kerr left in January 1946 the new foreign secretary, Ernest Bevin [q.v.], visited Moscow and the two men took an instant liking to one another.

Clark Kerr's ability to work with Stalin stood him in good stead in the early part of his mission, when the Russians were waiting with increasing impatience for the western Allies to open a second front in France. Later he was much preoccupied with the hostile attitude of Stalin and Molotov towards the London Poles. These difficult and often acrimonious negotiations came to nothing; but mutual respect remained. When Clark Kerr finally left Moscow, Stalin gave him lavish presents and also showed his esteem in a more unusual way by yielding to Clark Kerr's request for an exit visa for a young Russian, a former employee at the British embassy, who was in serious trouble with the Soviet authorities.

In January 1946 Clark Kerr went for four months as special ambassador to the Netherlands East Indies, where the Indonesian nationalists were exploiting the aftermath of war to achieve their independence. He could accomplish little in so short a time, beyond providing a first-hand account of a confused situation, before taking up his new post at Washington in May 1946. He had in the meantime been raised to the peerage as Baron Inverchapel, of Loch Eck in the county of Argyll.

Inverchapel's last diplomatic appointment proved something of an anticlimax. The grand alliance against Germany and Japan, to which he had made a significant contribution, was rapidly disintegrating. The note of the coming decade had been struck by Churchill's speech at Fulton two months before Inverchapel arrived at his new post. Peace had also transformed the content of the diplomacy to which the war had accustomed him. He was no orator and was wearied by the round of public appearance to which a British ambassador at Washington is exposed. Britain's first Labour Government for fourteen years, of which he was a firm supporter, was viewed with some suspicion in American financial circles; he was much concerned with problems arising from the weakness of sterling. Confidence was gradually restored, however, and in June 1947 his good friend Secretary of State George Marshall delivered at Harvard the historic speech which launched the European recovery programme.

Inverchapel's life in Washington was gladdened by reunion with his wife, who had left him during his service in Chungking. He was suffering, however, from an enlarged heart and in March 1948 resigned his post. He was happy to retire to Scotland and, describing himself simply as a farmer, spent his last years at Inverchapel. He died at Greenock 5 July 1951. His executors were astonished to find among his possessions an unlicensed tommy-gun which had been presented to him by Stalin.

Inverchapel was never a diplomatist in the tradition made familiar by comic dramatists; he throve upon the unusual stresses of war and much preferred the company of unconventional people to that of diplomatic colleagues. At the height of his powers he showed exceptional ability to win the confidence of the wartime leaders and this enabled him in posts of high importance to give good service to his country. A portrait of Inverchapel in middle life, painted by Glyn Philpot, is in the possession of the family.

[*The Times*, 6 and 14 July 1951; private information; personal knowledge.]

R. CECIL.

CLARKE, SIR FRED (1880-1952), educationist, the son of William Clark, a farm bailiff, and his wife, Annie Figg, was born at High Coggs, Witney, 2 August 1880 Educated at an Oxford elementary school where he became a pupil teacher, he attended classes at Oxford Technical College. His ability earned him a Queen's scholarship which enabled him to study at Oxford under the delegacy of non-collegiate students. He obtained a first in modern history in 1903. This, together with his experience of elementary teaching, led to his appointment as senior master of method at the Diocesan Training College, York: he remained a devout practising member of the Church of England all his life. In 1906 he became the first professor of education at Hartley University College, Southampton, and composed a very original *School History of Hampshire* (1909). In it can be discerned many of the ideas which underlie his theory of education: that a society is an historical process and that the lives of the common people are its substance; that education is the socialization of the young by active participation in cultural activity; that education is one aspect of society; that politics are inseparable from education.

The growth of his political and philosophical ideas tempted him, in 1911, to accept the professorship of education at the South African College, afterwards the university of Cape Town: the situation there was a challenge and an opportunity. Among his friends was J. C. Smuts [q.v.] many of whose ideas he shared although he had reservations, especially about Holism. His own philosophy, although influenced by Dewey, Hoernlé, and Hocking, was chiefly derived from Bernard Bosanquet [q.v.]: he went so far as to say he would like to work out the implications for education of the general idealist position expounded by Bosanquet. This is the position taken in his *Foundations of History-Teaching* (1929).

In South Africa his influence went far beyond the university. He played a prominent part in teachers' organizations and worked too for the Department of Labour, helping to establish Juvenile Affairs Boards which dealt with apprenticeships and education for industry He led the South African delegation to the Geneva International Labour Conference in 1925. In 1923 he collected some of his writings for the *Cape Times* and the educational press and published them under the title of *Essays in the Politics of*

Education. Frequent visits to Britain and membership of the Round Table led to a friendship with John Dove [q.v.] and to contacts with Lord Lothian and Lord Eustace Percy [qq.v.] as well as with educationists like (Sir) Percy Nunn and L. P. Jacks [qq.v.]. In 1929 he accepted the chair of education at McGill University, Montreal. In part the reason for the change was his interest in Quebec, a plural society like Cape Province; but it was mainly his deep disillusionment with South African politics. In 1935, after an extensive tour of universities in Canada, New Zealand, and Australia, he came to London as adviser to overseas students at the Institute of Education where he succeeded Nunn as director in 1936. His intense activity led to a breakdown and he spent a whole year in a nursing home. Recovery was complete and he resumed full activity in the autumn of 1938. He saw the coming war as a period of trial for the democratic nations and pinned his faith to education. He defended this view at an international conference, August 1939, at Columbia University, when he was awarded an honorary degree.

The war excited and stimulated Clarke immensely. The Institute of Education was evacuated to Nottingham and from there he led a campaign to promote fundamental reforms. His *Education and Social Change* (1940) expressed his conviction that sociology could give valuable insights into what was needed. It strengthened his close friendship with Karl Mannheim, whom he persuaded to join his staff at the Institute. As in South Africa, his public work grew in importance. He was a member of the McNair committee on the supply, recruitment, and training of teachers and youth leaders whose report gives clear evidence of his influence, especially in its insistence that teacher training is properly a concern of universities. Clarke also served on numerous British Council and Colonial Office committees concerned with education. A long pamphlet on *The Study of Education in England* (1943) stressed the imperative need for research and led to the organization of the National Foundation for Educational Research. His many services were recognized by the award of a knighthood in 1943.

Clarke retired from the directorship of the Institute of Education in 1945 and after a visit to Basutoland became educational adviser and research officer to the National Union of Teachers. In addition he took up his old post as adviser to overseas students in the Institute, many of them senior officials and university teachers. In 1948 he published his *Freedom in the Educative Society* which sums up his philosophy and his experience. He did not write many books. His influence was exercised chiefly through papers and talks, often at a personal level. He commanded respect by his unequalled sensitiveness to the nature of educational problems and by his flair for formulating principles. He evoked affection by his sincerity and simplicity. He gave a new sociological orientation to educational theory and promoted the development of comparative education.

In 1907 Clarke married Edith Annie, daughter of William Gillams, of Oxford. He was always deeply attached to his family and to his five daughters; his home was a perennial source of refreshment and happiness. He died suddenly, but peacefully, in the midst of what was perhaps the most fruitful and happy time of his life, in London, 6 January 1952. The Institute of Education has a portrait by Raymond Coxon.

[Private information; personal knowledge.]
J. A. LAUWERYS.

CLARKE, LOUIS COLVILLE GRAY (1881–1960), connoisseur, collector, and museum director, was born in Croydon 2 May 1881, the tenth son and youngest of the fourteen children of Stephenson Clarke, coal factor, by his wife, Agnes Maria Bridger. He was educated privately and at Trinity Hall, Cambridge, where he read history and graduated in 1903. The family fortune, assisted by a long minority and his wise sense of money values, sufficed to provide a large income even for its youngest member. While still an undergraduate Clarke travelled widely in Europe, forming the taste and developing the interests, both aesthetic and scientific, which were to distinguish his life. A confirmed bachelor with a zest for travel and an initial bias towards anthropological and archaeological studies, he made a long journey to Central America, Mexico, Chile, and Peru in 1906, and in 1910 the first of two visits to Ethiopia, where he spent some months in Addis Ababa.

At home in London, where he had already begun to collect works of art, he formed an enduring friendship with Augustus John, of whose slighter oil-paintings he bought a few and of whose best drawings he gradually acquired a considerable collection. A pencil portrait of Clarke by John, drawn in 1915 at Berkeley House, Hay Hill, Mayfair, is in the Fitzwilliam Museum, and a somewhat later portrait in oils, also by John, is at Trinity Hall. Clarke saw front-line service in the war of 1914–18, but his physical strength being unequal to the rigours of military life, he was before long invalided out. In 1919 he matriculated as a candidate for the diploma in anthropology at Exeter College, Oxford, attracted by the opportunity of studying under R. R. Marett, Arthur Thomson, and Henry Balfour [qq.v.]. Balfour was his tutor in archaeology and technology; under his guidance Clarke did valuable work as a volunteer in the Pitt Rivers Museum, of which he remained a benefactor throughout his life.

In 1922 Clarke was elected to succeed Baron Anatole von Hügel as curator of the University Museum of Archaeology and Ethnology at Cambridge. The appointment, made it is believed at the instance of Sir William Ridgeway [q.v.], then Disney professor of archaeology, if somewhat unexpected, was soon fully justified by the quality of Clarke's work both in Cambridge and abroad. In 1923 he took part in important excavations at Kechipaun, New Mexico. Endowed with winning social gifts and a prodigious memory, manifested for example in a mass of information about genealogy, Clarke was able in the years between the two wars to renew the friendships he had made in his youth with members of the great Austro-Hungarian families, when he took part in excavations at Toszeg and elsewhere in Hungary on several occasions in the twenties. To the growth of what has become the faculty of archaeology and anthropology, Clarke made a notable contribution by methodically building up and rearranging the collections of his museum, by reconciling conflicting academic interests, and by financing out of his own resources much excavation abroad and other work in Cambridge. A portrait of Clarke in coloured chalks by P. A. de László, 1927, is in the Museum of Archaeology and Ethnology. He was elected a fellow of Trinity Hall in 1929, and was a much-loved member of that high table for the rest of his life. His easy manners and hospitable nature endeared him to a wide circle of friends of every age and of many nationalities.

In 1937, when Sir Sydney Cockerell retired after thirty years as director of the Fitzwilliam Museum, Clarke was chosen to succeed him. It was a measure of his gifts and trained experience in dealing with every kind of antiquity and work of art that he was able at once to make himself at home in his new post. Under Cockerell the collections and building had alike been greatly extended, and the Fitzwilliam had acquired, through his energetic and skilful direction, much of the atmosphere of a private mansion which, as a public building, is its distinguishing characteristic. Clarke unfortunately had only a short time to impress his particular personal taste, which was more distinguished than Cockerell's, upon the museum and its collections, before the onset of war in 1939 compelled him to remove its contents to places of safety, some far from Cambridge. With what remained, supplemented by loans, he kept interest in the arts in Cambridge alive during the war by arranging more than forty temporary exhibitions in the museum. Himself the owner of a precious collection of maiolica, porcelain, furniture, silver, objects of vertu, paintings and drawings (some of the latter collected by his brother, Charles Clarke, who bequeathed them to him in 1935), he used the Fitzwilliam's negligible purchase fund most advantageously during these years when prices were low, to add to its collections. These purchases were notably supplemented by his own generosity as a donor, and by the benefactions he obtained for the museum. Between 1937 and 1960 he presented more than 2,700 works of art, including nearly 2,000 engravings of various kinds. When he retired in 19-- he was appointed honorary keeper of the prints, an appointment which, like his honorary keepership of the American collections in the Museum of Archaeology, retained until his death in Cambridge December 1960. The university conferred upon him the honorary degree of LL.-- in 1959. He bequeathed the bulk of his collections to the university, mainly for the benefit of the Fitzwilliam.

A man of slight build, and birdlike rapidity of mind and utterance as well as of bodily movement, Clarke possessed a quite extraordinary degree an intuitive understanding, fortified by extensive knowledge, of every kind of art. He had neither the patience nor the methodical habit of thought, nor did he feel the need to submit himself to the drudgery of serious writing. He produced only a few short articles. His bust in bronze by (Sir) Jacob Epstein was presented to

useum by the Friends of the Fitzwilliam
n 1951. He was a member of the Order of
Merit of Hungary, and an honorary fellow
f the Society of Archaeological and
Historical Arts of Hungary.

[*The Times*, 15 December 1960 and 2
anuary 1961; *Cambridge Review*, 29 April
961; *Man*, 1961, article 220; *Fitzwilliam
Museum Annual Report*, 1961; *Apollo*, July
962; private information; personal know-
dge.]   CARL WINTER.

CLARKE, THOMAS (1884–1957), jour-
alist, author, and broadcaster, was born
t Bolton 6 June 1884, the youngest child
f five sons and three daughters of Joseph
larke, who worked for an insurance
ompany, by his wife, Martha Marsh.
om Clarke went to Clarence Street higher
rade school, forerunner of the Bolton
ounty Grammar School. After contribut-
g to the *Northern Weekly*, a Bolton
aper, he won a year's scholarship at
uskin Hall, where Dennis Hird guided
d sharpened his intellectual zest.
arke's second venture in journalism was
the *Lewisham Journal*, at £1 a week.
e learned quickly and in 1903 he went at
e age of nineteen to the *South China
orning Post*, Hong Kong, to find himlf close to world-shaking events. He
ted as correspondent of the *Daily Mail*
d *Chicago Tribune* in French Indo-
ina, and, always eager to see as much
the world as he could, visited China,
pan, Korea, and Russia, including
beria. When the Russo-Japanese war
ded he returned home and became a
cial writer for the *Daily Dispatch* and
anchester Evening Chronicle. An article
the flying meeting at Blackpool in 1909
lped to win for him promotion to the
ndon news editorship of the *Daily
etch*.

n 1911 Clarke joined the foreign staff of
: *Daily Mail*. This was followed by ser-
e as night news editor from 1914 until
: end of 1916. On his return from mili-
y service he was made news editor by
rd Northcliffe [q.v.] who presently sent
m to the United States and Canada to
dy newspaper methods. Clarke studied
chief's methods and character just
eenly. Northcliffe said, 'What I want
ry morning in the paper, Tom, is
ething new and strange.' Clarke de-
d many talking-points (Northcliffe's
ression) for a mass public, obtained
ch exclusive news, and excelled in
uring the element of surprise. In the
ds of a colleague, F. G. Prince-White,

he was the spirit of news-editorial efficiency personified.

After Northcliffe's death Clarke, on the
invitation of (Sir) Keith Murdoch, went to
Australia and became assistant editor of
the *Melbourne Herald* from 1923 to 1926.
Some of his experiences were related in
Marriage at 6 a.m. (1934). He returned to
London to be managing editor of the
Daily News in 1926 and, on its merging
with a rival, editor and director of the
News Chronicle until 1933. Then, owing to
a divergence of views from colleagues on
the board, whose different sections of
Liberalism he found it hard to reconcile,
he resigned. He turned to freelance work,
in the course of which he visited Finland.
A spell as adviser to *Berlingske Tidende*,
Copenhagen, in 1934, was followed by a
tour with the Australian cricket team in
England for the *Daily Mail*. In 1935 he
became a stimulating director of practical
journalism at London University. When
war broke out in 1939 he became deputy
director of the news division of the
Ministry of Information, but gave up this
work in 1940 because of his wife's ill
health which called for rest in the deep
countryside.

Next he joined (Sir) Edward Hulton in
the development of a chain of specialized
news agencies set up with a parent company under the title of Britanova. Part of
his work was to establish in South America,
with headquarters at Buenos Aires, a news
service for many influential papers south
of Panama. He returned to London to
assume editorial direction and broadcast
a weekly newsletter from London in the
B.B.C. Latin-American service from 1942
to 1948. One product of his South American experiences was *The Word of an
Englishman* (1943).

Clarke, who often worked almost to
the point of exhaustion, collapsed while
broadcasting in the final stage of the war.
He told the story of his illness and temporary recovery in *Living Happily with a
'Heart'* (1954), in which he strongly recommended what he called Doctor Country
as the best physician for coronary thrombosis. He died at Colchester 18 June 1957.

With his brisk manner, friendly brown
eyes, very dark hair, which he kept all
his life, and what a friend described as
a Lancashire-Irish glow, Clarke was not
only handsome but had a confident, con-
fidence-inspiring personality. His reputation in journalism as one of Northcliffe's
young men spread to wider circles when
he wrote *My Northcliffe Diary* (1931).

He addressed himself to a more ambitious theme, what he termed an intimate study of press power, in *Northcliffe in History* (1950). This did justice to Northcliffe's journalistic acumen, but some critics held that its analysis of Northcliffe's political influence showed too much hero-worship. Other books Clarke wrote were *Brian* (1936), the story of his much-loved younger son who died of meningitis at the age of nine; *Round the World with Tom Clarke* (1937); *My Lloyd George Diary* (1939); and *The Devonshire Club* (1944), the history of one of his favourite London resorts for meeting friends.

Clarke was twice married, first in 1910 to Elizabeth Naylor, only daughter of Richard Waddington, J.P., of Bolton, schoolmaster and educational publisher and for a time member of the Bolton town council. There were two sons and one daughter of this marriage, which was dissolved. In 1952 Clarke married Sheila Irene Emily, former wife of Edward Cyril Castle and daughter of the late Harry Samuel Green, who had been a coastguard officer.

[Private information; personal knowledge.]
LINTON ANDREWS.

CLAXTON, BROOKE (1898-1960), Canadian politician, was born at Montreal, Canada, 23 August 1898, the only child of Albert George Brooke Claxton, barrister, by his wife, Blanche Lovat Simpson. He was educated at Lower Canada College and McGill University. Although his education was interrupted by war service he was a brilliant student who received a B.C.L. with honours before his twenty-third birthday and was called to the Quebec bar in the same year (1921). Later in life, when minister of national defence, Claxton recalled with pride that he had served in the ranks of the Royal Canadian Artillery and had won the D.C.M. while a battery sergeant-major.

Claxton entered his father's firm in 1921 and specialized in insurance law. He was active in community life, a generous and discerning patron of the arts, and an active and influential member of the Canadian Institute of International Affairs, the Canadian Radio League, and many other national organizations. He served as associate professor of commercial law at McGill University from 1930 to 1944.

Claxton was first elected to Parliament for the St. Lawrence–St. George riding of Montreal in the wartime election of 1940.

He was re-elected in 1945, 1949, and 195[] as a Liberal. In 1943 he was appointe[] parliamentary assistant to the prim[] minister, W. L. Mackenzie King [q.v.], i[] his capacity as president of the Priv[] Council. Late in 1944 he became minist[] of the newly created Department [] National Health and Welfare in t[] Mackenzie King Cabinet, and he w[] closely associated with the establishme[] of family allowances. From 1946 to 19[] he was minister of national defence in t[] Cabinets of Mackenzie King and Louis [] St. Laurent and was thus primarily r[] sponsible for building up the milita[] strength of Canada to meet commitmen[] to N.A.T.O. and in the Korean w[] He travelled widely inside and outsi[] Canada and took a deep personal intere[] in the welfare of the men and women in t[] Services.

Claxton was one of the Canadian sign[] tories in 1948 of the terms of union [] Canada with Newfoundland; and [] 1943-54 he represented Canada abroad [] many conferences including U.N.R.R.[] the peace conference in Paris (1946); t[] International Labour Conference in Au[] ralia; the United Nations; and the Nor[] Atlantic Council.

He was a prodigious worker and [] addition to his heavy duties as a par[] mentarian and a cabinet minister with [] exceptionally exacting portfolio, he fou[] time to supervise the activities of [] National Liberal Federation and to tak[] detailed interest in the organization [] the Liberal Party throughout the count[] As parliamentary assistant to Macker[] King, he provided many of the ideas, [] did most of the preparatory work [] the post-war programme of the Lib[] Government which helped to ensure [] party twenty-two unbroken years [] office. His original and inventive m[] developed more political and social ini[] tives than any other Canadian of [] generation and his unflagging ene[] carried most of them to fruition. [] voluntary retirement from the St. Lau[] government in 1954 left a great gap [] Canadian public life and coincided wi[] decline in the momentum of poli[] action of the Government which was [] entirely accidental.

On his retirement from public [] Claxton became vice-president and [] in Canada of the Metropolitan Life [] surance Company of New York, a c[] pany with which he and his father [] been associated as legal counsel for n[]

years before 1940. He threw himself into business with his customary energy and effectiveness, but, by 1957, he clearly needed more than business to occupy him fully. In that year the Government established the Canada Council, a munificent public foundation for the promotion of the arts and the encouragement of higher education, of which Claxton became the first chairman. To this spare-time activity he gave a degree of time and attention which few men can give to their principal occupation. The outstanding success of the work of the Council and its public acceptance both owe a great deal to his indefatigable efforts.

In 1959 Claxton, who had always enjoyed good and apparently indestructible health, was stricken by an illness which was prolonged and very painful, but which he bore with great patience and fortitude. He died in Ottawa 13 June 1960.

During his lifetime Claxton had many honours conferred upon him, including a special commemoratory medal (1946) and an air medal (1954) from the French Government; the highest award of the Greek Red Cross; the Western Hemisphere Commercial Arbitration Award; and honorary degrees from many universities, of which the first came in 1950 from his own university, McGill. He was the author of many pamphlets, articles, and reviews.

Claxton married in 1925 Helen Galt, daughter of John G. Savage, of Westmount, Quebec, and had two sons and one daughter. A portrait by Lilias T. Newton is in the possession of the family.

[Private information; personal knowledge.]
J. W. PICKERSGILL.

CLAY, SIR HENRY (1883–1954), economist, was the third son and fourth child of James Henry Clay and his wife, Elizabeth Ulmer, of Bradford. He was born, 9 May 1883, in Germany where his father, a woollen manufacturer, had formed the firm of Goetz, Clay, & Co., near München-Gladbach, a partnership lasting for eight years before the parents returned to Yorkshire with their two girls and four boys. Henry Clay went to Bradford Grammar School which he left as head boy to go as a scholar to University College, Oxford, in 1902.

Disappointed of his immediate hopes of an academic career because of his second class in literae humaniores (1906), Clay became, first, secretary to a London charity organization, then, for two years,

warden of a settlement in Sheffield. Between 1909 and 1917 he lectured for the Workers' Educational Association under the university extension scheme, an experience leading to the writing of *Economics: An Introduction for the General Reader* (1916; 2nd ed. 1942), a book which had great success, especially in Great Britain and the United States, and which, by reason of its lucidity and the homeliness of its examples, broadened public interest in economic matters.

During the latter part of the war Clay worked in the Ministry of Labour. From 1919 to 1921 he was a fellow of New College, Oxford, and a special correspondent on industrial relations to the New York *Evening Post*. During his first visit to America in 1921 he made close friendships with some outstanding young economists, especially Lewis Douglas and Walter Stewart, which he maintained throughout his life. In 1922 he became the Stanley Jevons professor of political economy and it has been said that the best crop of students ever produced by the economics department of the university of Manchester was during Clay's tenure of the chair. In 1925 he went to South Africa as a member of the economic and wage commission and was largely responsible for the subsequent report. In 1927 he asked to exchange his chair for the new professorship of social economics established through the munificence of E. D. Simon (later Lord Simon of Wythenshawe, q.v.): a post relieving Clay of administrative duties which did not interest him. He was never happy with large groups or in the public lecture. He perceived that applied economics could be strengthened by closer regular contacts between economists and business men and he instituted his Manchester Thursday lunches as a successful pioneering effort. Meanwhile he was able to give fuller play to his 'itch to write'. His capacity for the swift but polished production of a balanced treatment of the economic issues of the day was something of a marvel even to the seasoned staff of the *Manchester Guardian* for which Clay wrote regularly. There was also a steady stream of reviews and longer articles in the learned journals. Clay was not a foremost economic theorist; indeed, he often expressed doubts about the value of much of the theorizing then in fashion. He was a tool-user rather than a tool-designer—and frequently impatient of the tools provided. Representative of this phase are *The Post-War Unemployment*

227

Problem (1929) and *The Problem of Industrial Relations* (1929).

In 1930 Clay resigned his chair to join the Bank of England: in the first instance as adviser to the newly established Securities Management Trust. In 1930–31 he was a member of the royal commission on unemployment insurance. In 1933 he went with Sir Otto Niemeyer to the Argentine to advise on the organization of its banking system. Henry Clay's shrewd advice and his knack of getting on with people, especially with Montagu (later Lord) Norman (whose notice he contributed to this Dictionary), led to his appointment in the same year as economic adviser to the governor of the Bank of England. Temperamentally Clay and Norman were poles apart: the governor a prima donna, Clay gentle, scholarly, sensitive, and undogmatic. Yet in many ways their views ran parallel and Clay's pragmatic capacity for swift and clear draftsmanship must have been a godsend to Norman whose inadequacy in expression was in sharp contrast to his considerable powers of thought and decision. They shared the opinion that, necessary as was a proper financial and monetary framework, financial ingenuity by Governments could do little to raise standards of living which would be determined by good organization, hard thinking, and hard work. If both men underestimated the value of the ideas which J. M. (later Lord) Keynes [q.v.] was then disseminating, they shared the anxiety that policies of full employment carried with them the constant dangers of inflation. Clay pleaded for a reduction in government expenditure, the balancing of budgets, and the retention of the gold standard. He believed with Norman that a stable exchange was possible only if British export industries could be made more efficient; that the best way of salvaging them was by drastic rationalization; and that the Bank should support by financing, as well as investigating and sponsoring, schemes of amalgamation and re-equipment.

With Lord Stamp [q.v.], Clay was one of the most active in the establishment (1938) of the National Institute of Economic and Social Research and he guided its research as chairman of its council (1940–49) and later president (1949–52). On the outbreak of war Stamp was called upon by the Government to produce a broad survey of national economic resources and Clay and (Sir) Hubert Henderson [q.v.] were his chief assistants in an

organization which became the forerunner of the economic section and the Central Statistical Office in the Cabinet Secretariat. After Stamp was killed in an air-raid in 1941, Clay went to the Board of Trade as economic adviser and later to the Ministry of War Transport.

In 1944 Clay left Whitehall to become the second warden of Nuffield College, Oxford, where he took particular pleasure in the appointment of visiting fellows chosen for their practical experience in the professions, industry, or commerce. Clay was successful in gaining the confidence of Lord Nuffield who was not at that stage entirely happy about the development of his benefaction. The foundation-stone of the permanent building was not laid until 1949 just before Clay retired; his success as warden, especially with those small groups with which he was always happiest, was despite the temporary and limited premises in which the college was forced to operate.

Clay had been knighted in 1946 and on his retirement from the wardenship of Nuffield he continued to enjoy a busy life. He became part-time economic adviser to Unilever; he pursued his work on a biography of Lord Norman and he was actively engaged in the collection and editing of Sir Hubert Henderson's papers. Clay's writings from his first and famous book in 1916 to the papers he finished at his death show the main line of his thinking unbroken. Private enterprise, he believed was the most efficient method of producing goods. He was a Gladstonian Liberal who, whilst recognizing that he was living in the twentieth century, felt that the liberty of the individual would be endangered by the continued growth of government economic activities. Clay's friendliness and the complete absence of stridency in whatever he said or wrote tended to conceal the strength of his convictions. His views diverged from the main stream of contemporary Liberal economic thought in at least two ways: his doubts about the practical results of Keynes's views on full employment and more especially of the views of some of Keynes's disciples; secondly, concerning industrial monopoly. Clay was not prepared to agree that a competitive system would inevitably degenerate into monopoly unless safeguarded by the State; anti-monopoly legislation in his view was unnecessary, inexpedient, and inequitable.

Clay's greatest joys were found in the family circle. In 1910 he had married

Gladys, the eldest daughter of Arthur Priestman, a worsted manufacturer, of Bradford, by whom he had three sons and a daughter. Clay had a passion for sailing and the whole family would be taken, first on the Broads; later, on more venturesome journeys on the high seas. Outside this intimate family group was a vast circle of friends drawn by the charm of his wife and by Henry Clay's own kindness, modesty, and most entertaining conversational gifts. Although in later years he became something of a man of affairs, he retained the habits and enthusiasms of the scholar; nor might he be mistaken for anything else. Outside economics, Clay was especially interested in architecture, painting, and music. He could never resist a second-hand bookshelf and he collected a large library which included many bargains. His personal needs reflected his solid Yorkshire upbringing and Henry Clay was the most economical of men. His first wife died in 1941. In 1951 he married Rosalind, widow of E. Murray Wrong (the son of G. M. Wrong, q.v.) and daughter of A. L. Smith [q.v.], sometime master of Balliol. They spent three extremely happy years together before his death, 30 July 1954, as a result of a street accident in Holland where he had gone to join his children for a North Sea trip in the family yacht.

There is a drawing at Nuffield College by Kenneth Knowles.

[Private information; personal knowledge.]
JOHN JEWKES.
SYLVIA JEWKES.

CLERK, SIR GEORGE RUSSELL (1874–1951), diplomatist, was born in India 29 November 1874, the only child of (General Sir) Godfrey Clerk, later commandant of the Rifle Brigade and groom-in-waiting to Queen Victoria and King Edward VII, and his wife, Alice Mary, daughter of William Edward Frere, of the Bombay Civil Service. He was educated at Eton and New College, Oxford, where he obtained a third class in *literae humaniores* (1897), and after studying foreign languages abroad passed into the Foreign Office in 1898. In 1903–7 he served at his own request as assistant in the British Agency in Abyssinia, where he gained much useful experience, and a knowledge of Amharic, while in charge of the mission for long periods. His next post abroad was in 1910 when he went as first secretary to the embassy in Constantinople where in his spare time he learnt Turkish. He rejoined the Foreign Office in 1912 and in

the next year attended the fifth international congress for the suppression of the white slave traffic. In October 1913 he was promoted to be a senior clerk.

Appointed head of the new war department of the Foreign Office in 1914, Clerk had in a measure greatness thrust upon him and was enabled to get to know countless foreigners who in normal times would have dealt with under-secretaries. In January 1917 he attended the Rome conference where the principal Allies examined the military situation in Salonica and Macedonia and planned the military and naval campaigns for 1917. Thence he went with Lord Milner [q.v.] on his mission to Russia on the eve of the revolution. In 1919 he was private secretary to Lord Curzon [q.v.], but with three senior under-secretaries absent in Paris he was in practice under-secretary. In September of that year he was appointed the first British minister to the newly created Czechoslovak republic. But before going to Prague he was sent as representative of the Supreme Council at the Paris peace conference to Bucharest where the outlook was menacing since the Romanians by invading Hungary and occupying Budapest were in head-on collision with the Council. Clerk's immediate task was to secure Romania's evacuation of Hungary, the immediate cessation of all requisitioning there, the jettisoning of her claim to the whole of the Banat, and co-operation with the Allies in restoring order and responsible government. M. Bratiano, the Romanian negotiator, while agreeable in his talks with Clerk, gave vent to his anger with the Allies over partitioning the Banat and any treaty about minority rights in Romania. Clerk returned to Paris where he expressed his opinion that the Romanian evacuation of Budapest might well endanger public order. After new elections in Romania, however, and an ultimatum by the Supreme Council, the rejection of which would have isolated their country, the Romanians capitulated and signed the minorities treaty. Clerk's mission to Budapest in October–December of the same year was far more fruitful. His objective was to secure order in the Hungarian chaos after months of Bolshevism and Romanian occupation, and to induce the Hungarians to form a government which the *Entente* could recognize so that peace negotiations might continue. All this Clerk obtained by a display of tact, sympathy, firmness, and patience which entitled him to the gratitude not only of Hungary but of Europe itself, and earned him the expression of M. Clemenceau's 'entire satisfaction with the remarkable success of your mission'.

In 1926 Clerk succeeded Sir Ronald Lindsay [q.v.] as ambassador to Turkey and was sworn of the Privy Council. Relations with Britain were far from good since the Nationalist Party had not forgotten Britain's moral support of the Greek invasion of Anatolia in 1919. But Clerk soon established personal friendship with Mustapha Kemal and was not long in allaying all suspicion and gaining the confidence of the Turkish Government. His appointment to Brussels in October 1933 caused much disappointment to Turkish officialdom and the British colony. In April 1934, to Clerk's amazement and delight, he was transferred to Paris. To follow Lord Tyrrell [q.v.] was far from easy; but he rose to the occasion. The Italo-Abyssinian war, the Spanish civil war, violation of the Treaty of Versailles, all called for exceptional qualities, and Clerk's ability and tact responded admirably. His obvious affection for France and his well-known conviction that Anglo-French ties of cordial friendship were vital made his departure on his retirement in 1937 a matter of keen regret. He was intensely pleased by a farewell message from the secretary of state, Anthony Eden (later the Earl of Avon), which paid tribute to the success of his mission in Paris and to his long years of meritorious service.

Clerk must have seemed to any writer or caricaturist the *beau idéal* of diplomatists. Tall, thin, with a good figure, always faultlessly dressed, with his eye-glass so much a part of him that it needed no ribbon, he would be noticeable in any gathering, and if addressed would at once put the stranger at ease by his welcoming smile. Tactful and sympathetic, he was an able negotiator. Always adhering to his own carefully considered opinion, he was yet able to settle many difficult and dangerous questions by his understanding nature which was neither grasping nor hectoring. His main relaxations were stalking and shooting, fly-fishing and yachting; he also played bridge. These pastimes were never allowed to interfere with his official duties; but he set great store by them, being convinced that they enabled him to have unusually close relations with the local authorities and diplomatic colleagues.

Clerk was appointed C.M.G. (1908), K.C.M.G. (1917), G.C.M.G. (1929), and C.B. (1914). He was a vice-president of the Royal Geographical Society, an honorary fellow of New College, and received a number of foreign decorations.

In 1908 he married Janet Muriel, daughter of Edward Robson Whitwell, of Yarmon-Tees, Yorkshire; they had no children. He died in London 18 June 1951.

[*The Times*, 20 June 1951; private information; personal knowledge.]

LANCELOT OLIPHANT.

CLOSE, SIR CHARLES FREDERICK ARDEN- (1865–1952), geographer. [See ARDEN-CLOSE.]

CLUNIES ROSS, SIR IAN (1899–1959), veterinary scientist and scientific administrator. [See ROSS.]

CLYDESMUIR, first BARON (1894–1954), public servant. [See COLVILLE, DAVID JOHN.]

COATES, ERIC (1886–1957), composer, was born 27 August 1886 in Hucknall, Nottinghamshire, the younger son and youngest of the five children of William Harrison Coates, a skilled surgeon and a notable personality greatly loved by the mainly mining community. From him Eric inherited his lifelong interest in photography and his aesthetic appreciation. His mother, Mary Jane Gwyn Blower, herself an artistic amateur singer and pianist, contributed the Welsh strain responsible largely for the musicality which showed itself at an early age. He demanded his first violin when only six; by the age of thirteen his attainments warranted lessons from Georg Ellenberger in Nottingham. Later, to complete an amateur ensemble, he took up the viola. He had been intended for a commercial career but in 1906 his parents reluctantly allowed him to enter the Royal Academy of Music where Sir Alexander Mackenzie [q.v.], on hearing his settings of poems by Robert Burns, assigned him to Frederick Corder for composition as his first study and to Lionel Tertis for viola. Many evenings became occupied in playing in various London theatres where he gained experience of practical orchestration and skilful arranging which later stood him in good stead as a composer. This led to engagements to play under (Sir) Thomas Beecham; and from 1910 for nine years he was successively sub-principal, then principal, viola in the Queen's Hall Orchestra under Sir Henry Wood [q.v.]. While still a student he had toured South Africa as viola in the Hambourg String Quartet which added much chamber music to his repertoire while releasing him from the drudgery of the theatre pit which aggravated the neuritis increasingly troubling his left arm.

Coates's first real song hit, 'Stonecracker John', appeared in 1909 and the orchestral *Miniature Suite* was launched by Wood at the promenade concerts in 1911. In 1919, having established himself as a successful composer of songs and of excellent light music in the line of Sir Arthur Sullivan and (Sir) Edward German [q.v.], he gave up playing; but he often conducted his works in Scarborough, Hastings, and other resorts which then boasted orchestras of considerable size, as well as in London and Bournemouth. Attractive and popular though his music was proving, it was the selection by the British Broadcasting Corporation of Knightsbridge March' from the *London Suite* to usher in 'In Town Tonight' in 1933 which suddenly made people conscious of Coates as a composer of exhilarating marches. His wartime 'Calling all Workers' had a similar and lasting success. The romantic serenade 'By the Sleepy Lagoon' written in 1930 achieved widespread popularity in the United States in the late thirties and subsequently in Britain and all over the world.

Although a lover of the peace and quiet of the country, Eric Coates found London with its ceaseless bustle of activity a more congenial place in which to compose. He was a first-class craftsman. Characteristic of his music are its freshness, melodiousness, gaiety, charm, and infectious rhythm. While it has an English flavour its language is so universal that it is popular in every country where western music is heard. He introduced the syncopation of modern jazz into many works which are thus very effective when played by large dance-type orchestras. His personal charm and humour were known to a vast public before whom, in concerts or on radio or television, he conducted his music in many countries in Europe and the Americas. That he received no official recognition would not have worried him for he was busy encouraging and helping younger talent. He was a founder-member and director of the Performing Right Society

of which in post-war years he proved to be an able and diplomatic delegate at international conferences as well as a conscientious member of its board.

In his autobiography, *Suite in Four Movements* (1953), Coates tells his personal love story: in 1911 he met a young fellow student, Phyllis, daughter of Francis Black, R.B.A., who was later to become a successful actress; it was a case of love at first sight. Two years later, parental objections overcome, they married and so began a partnership which lasted until he died in London 21 December 1957. Their only child, Austin, for whom the 'Three Bears' fantasy was written, became a successful writer.

[Private information; personal knowledge.]
KENNETH WRIGHT.

COBB, JOHN RHODES (1899-1952), racing motorist, was born at Hackbridge, Surrey, 2 December 1899, the youngest son of Rhodes Cobb, fur broker, and his wife, Florence Goad. He was educated at Eton and Trinity Hall, Cambridge, and went into his father's business with the fur trade which took him at intervals to Russia. Since his home was at Esher, no great distance from Brooklands, his interest in car racing began at a very early age and developed gradually into a determination to drive the fastest cars available. When the opportunity occurred it was typical that he drove a monstrous pre-war Fiat, which was not only very fast but none too easy to handle, instead of the smaller cars with which most drivers begin. John Cobb was a big man and it was in keeping that he was at his best with very large cars.

After his first race in 1925 Cobb progressed rapidly, and having acquired another big car, built by Delage, he achieved part of his ambition by breaking the outer circuit lap record at Brooklands in 1929 with an average of 132·11 m.p.h. To this record he clung with admirable tenacity. Time after time a rival bettered the figures; time after time Cobb did better still. When the Delage could go no faster Reid A. Railton designed the even larger Napier–Railton and with this Cobb achieved the lap records of 139·71 m.p.h. and 140·93 m.p.h., both in 1934, and, in 1935, 143·44 m.p.h. He also broke many world records including those for twelve and twenty-four hours and crowned his success by winning the 500-mile race at Brooklands in 1935 and 1937 with the same car.

The summit of Cobb's ambition was reached when, with a twin-engined car specially designed by Railton, he broke the world's land-speed record at Bonneville salt flats in 1938 at 350·2 m.p.h., in 1939 at 369·74 m.p.h., and in 1947 at 394·2 m.p.h. During the two runs necessary for the last record one was timed at over 400 m.p.h. For his achievements Cobb was awarded the Segrave Trophy for 1947 and the British Racing Drivers' Club gold star in 1935 and 1937.

Cobb had always taken an interest in flying and during the war of 1939–45 he served in the Royal Air Force and Air Transport Auxiliary. He later turned to high-speed motor boats and attempted to raise the water-speed record to 200 m.p.h. On 29 September 1952 he had reached that speed on Loch Ness when his boat submerged and disintegrated and he was killed. Possessed of courage and skill beyond the ordinary, he had never allowed his success and its attendant publicity to spoil a friendly and lovable character.

Cobb married first, in 1947, Elizabeth Mitchell-Smith (died 1948); secondly, in 1950, Vera Henderson. There were no children.

[S. C. H. Davis, *The John Cobb Story*, 1953; personal knowledge.]   S. C. H. Davis.

COCHRAN, Sir CHARLES BLAKE (1872–1951), showman, was born 25 September 1872 in Brighton. It was probably his sense of showmanship which caused him to claim Lindfield, Sussex, where he spent many early holidays with his grandfather, as his birthplace. His father, James Elphinstone Cochran, was a tea merchant and a keen theatre- and race-goer. His mother, Matilda Walton, daughter of a Merchant Navy officer, was the widow of a Mr. Arnold by the time she was twenty-one. She lived to be ninety. By her first marriage she had one son, and by her second nine children, of whom Charles was the fourth.

Cochran was educated at Brighton Grammar School where, on his first day, he met Aubrey Beardsley [q.v.], with whom he came to share a study. Later, through Aubrey's sister, Mabel, Cochran met the *Yellow Book* circle including Walter Sickert, (Sir) Max Beerbohm, (Sir) William Rothenstein [qq.v.], Ernest Dowson, and others. But all this was after a lapse of years. In 1891 he went to New York. Cochran had always been a worshipper of the stars of the stage and circus. Money meant nothing to him—then or at any

other time. It was as an actor that he hoped to make his name. In this he was unsuccessful, so much so that the Chicago World Fair found him selling fountain pens. Eventually, he managed to secure a part with the actor-manager Richard Mansfield, who told him that he would never be a good actor, but, sensing his managerial ability, made Cochran his private secretary. Through this association came much experience and many stage contacts.

After some time Cochran quarrelled with Mansfield and in partnership with E. J. Henley opened a school of acting in New York. In 1897 he made his first production, Ibsen's *John Gabriel Borkman*. In the same year Cochran returned to London, working as a journalist and developing his natural flair for publicity. But the theatre won, as always, and seeing a production of *Cyrano de Bergerac* in Paris, he conceived the idea of Mansfield playing it in New York. This was one of the earliest instances of Cochran's ability to star an actor in the right vehicle. The quarrel was quickly made up, and Cochran returned to the States as Mansfield's manager.

Yet again Cochran preferred to stand on his own feet. Returning once more to London, he set up as a theatrical agent, earning gradual success as a promoter of boxing and wrestling matches and outstanding music-hall acts such as Houdini the escapist and the great wrestler Georges Hackenschmidt, whom he matched at Olympia in 1904 against Ahmed Madrali, the 'Terrible Turk'. His first London production, a farce called *Sporting Simpson* at the Royalty Theatre in 1902, was a failure; so was his second attempt at the same theatre, *Lyre and Lancet*. By 1903 he had been made bankrupt for the first time, from which position he was quickly extricated by Hackenschmidt. Cochran's instinct for entertainment now induced him to promote all kinds of ventures, from pygmies to roller-skating (which became a craze from 1909 until the outbreak of war), as well as circuses at Earl's Court and Olympia in 1912–13. His greatest production of those years was Max Reinhardt's *The Miracle* which opened at Olympia Christmas Eve, 1911. This tremendous spectacle was not the immediate success it should have been until Lord Northcliffe [q.v.] hammered it home every day in the *Daily Mail*. From that time on the eulogies Cochran received from the Northliffe press were offset by his more critical reception by other popular newspapers.

From boxing, roller-skating, and spectacle, Cochran turned to revue, still a novelty during the war years. Beginning in a small way with *Odds and Ends* (1914) at the Ambassadors Theatre, which introduced Alice Delysia to London audiences, he continued at the Empire with Irving Berlin's *Watch Your Step* (1915). As an antidote, he produced two sociological plays by Brieux, *Damaged Goods* (1917) and *The Three Daughters of M. Dupont* (1917). In 1917, at the Oxford Theatre, he put on *The Better 'Ole*, the farce by Bruce Bairnsfather [q.v.], which attained a run of 811 performances, exceeded only by *Bless the Bride* in 1947–9, Cochran's longest run. Both shows started slowly and built up. In 1918 Cochran decorated and reopened the London Pavilion, with *As You Were*, followed during the ensuing decade by a whole string of successful revues, including *London, Paris and New York* (1920); *Fun of the Fayre* (1921); *Dover Street to Dixie* (1923), featuring the American singer Florence Mills; *One Dam Thing After Another* (1927), with a score by Rodgers and Hart; and *Cochran's 1930 Revue*, with many members of the lately defunct Diaghilev ballet. Between these activities, Cochran presented *The League of Notions*, a revue introducing the Dolly Sisters at the New Oxford Theatre in 1921. The decorating of the theatre alone cost £10,000 of his own money. The sumptuous *Mayfair and Montmartre* (1922), a revue containing a sketch debunking the dramatic critics, who resented it, showed losses amounting to £20,000. In order to recoup, he put on six successful American productions in 1923—including Eugene O'Neill's *Anna Christie*—none of which was particularly successful in London. In 1925 Cochran was made bankrupt for the second time. Such was his personal magnetism that both Alice Delysia and the Dolly Sisters offered to sell their jewels in order to save him.

Prior to this Cochran had given London Sarah Bernhardt's last season, at the Prince's Theatre; Eleanora Duse at the New Oxford; Sacha Guitry in the evenings and Sacha Guitry in the evenings at the New Oxford; two Chaliapin appearances at the Albert Hall; the Chauve Souris company at the Pavilion, a season of Diaghilev ballet at the Prince's, in which Stravinsky's music met much critical disapproval. In boxing, he promoted the Wells–Beckett and the

Beckett–Carpentier fights at the Holborn Stadium (1919), and preliminary negotiations for the famous Carpentier–Dempsey fight (1921). Disgusted by the crookedness of boxing promotion and after an unfortunate rodeo season at Wembley (1924), and an equally unprofitable presentation of Suzanne Lenglen in tennis exhibitions all over the country, Cochran in future confined himself, more or less, to the stage. His enthusiasms were easily aroused, but once damped, nothing could rekindle them.

Discharged from bankruptcy, penniless but ebullient, Cochran wrote his first book of memoirs, *The Secrets of a Showman* (1925). With the proceeds, a cabaret at the Trocadero, and backing which was never lacking, Cochran began his association with (Sir) Noël Coward with *On With The Dance* (1925) at the London Pavilion (the first show to feature 'Mr. Cochran's Young Ladies'). Then came their brilliant partnership in *This Year of Grace* (1928) and *Bitter Sweet* (1929). In 1930 came *Private Lives*, with Noël Coward and Gertrude Lawrence [q.v.] in the leads, and in the same year New York saw all three shows. The climax of this association was reached in 1931 with *Cavalcade* at Drury Lane. Meanwhile Cochran had presented a Pirandello season; Sean O'Casey's *The Silver Tassie* (1929); the Lunts in a play called *Caprice* (1929) at the St. James's; the revue *Wake up and Dream* (1929) which also went to America; and *Evergreen* (1930), with Jessie Matthews, and the first use of a revolving stage in London.

Next came Cochran's association and friendship with (Sir) A. P. Herbert, beginning in 1932 with the production of *Helen* at the Adelphi, with Evelyn Laye in the title role, (Sir) George Robey [q.v.], and superb décor by Oliver Messel. Five other shows in that season alone were *Dinner at Eight*, *The Cat and the Fiddle*, *Words and Music*, the Sacha Guitry season, and a revival of *The Miracle*, with Lady Diana Cooper as the Madonna. The year 1933 saw Elisabeth Bergner in *Escape Me Never* and Cole Porter's *Nymph Errant*; 1934, Coward's *Conversation Piece*, the revue *Streamline*, the end of the London Pavilion as a theatre and the break with Coward, both bitter blows.

Then came the lean years. *The Boy David* (1936), Barrie's last play, with Elisabeth Bergner, was not a success. Nor, in 1937, were the coronation revue, *Home and Beauty*, and Lehár's *Paganini*, with

Richard Tauber. A trip to America proved financially abortive. His wartime shows did not fare well. Frank Collins, his stage director for twenty-eight years, took a job with E.N.S.A. Cochran wrote more books of reminiscence: his usual practice when things were at a low ebb. He and his wife faced the London blitz from a furnished flat in St. James's Court. Crippled by arthritis, he was full of plans for the future. Gone were the house in Montagu Street, the crowds of hangers-on, the Impressionist pictures (bought long before Impressionism was fashionable), the butler and the exquisite china; but he remained the *grand seigneur*, investing a sugarless bun with jam while his wife apologized for the tea cups.

After the war Cochran staged his last great come-back. In 1946, with some money for a film of his life which, characteristically, was never made, he commissioned Sir A. P. Herbert and Vivian Ellis to write the light opera *Big Ben*. The opening night at the Adelphi was attended by the Princess Elizabeth, the prime minister and half the Cabinet, in fact by everyone except the inspiration of it all who lay desperately ill at his flat. A fortnight after the removal of a kidney, still in bed, weak but ever courageous, he commissioned *Bless the Bride* by the same team for the same theatre. By 1947 he had a partner, Lord Vivian. 'My enthusiasm over *Bless the Bride* mounts hourly—I have a terrific hunch', wrote Cochran, after a famous actress and an equally well-known producer had utterly condemned it. That is a measure of the man's dogged enthusiasm at the age of seventy-four. His faith was rewarded by a run of 886 performances which would have been even longer had not Cochran, always impatient to produce something new, withdrawn *Bless the Bride* to make way for *Tough at the Top* in 1949. This, the last of his big spectacular shows, was a failure.

Cochran was at various times the chairman and managing director of the Palace Theatre, manager of the Royal Albert Hall, president of the Actors' Benevolent Fund, and a governor of the Shakespeare Memorial theatre. He was knighted in 1948 and appointed a chevalier of the Legion of Honour in 1950. In appearance rubicund but urbane, he was always immaculately dressed. He usually wore a trilby hat at an angle. In later years he sported a monocle and, of necessity, a walking-stick. Somewhat awesome to

meet, he disarmed the timid by his courteous manner. He always answered letters. He was calm in a crisis and seldom raised his voice. He was nothing if not generous and like most of his friends a *bon viveur*. When things were good, he resembled a rooster; when bad, a benign bishop. At one time he used a rooster as a monogram. His friends called him 'Cockie', his enemies a snob, but he himself preferred to be known as 'C.B.' He was an authority on art and all things beautiful, including the feminine. Without any great musical training he possessed a natural musical appreciation; but he had a limited sense of humour and his productions, always appealing to the eye and ear, were somewhat weak in comedy. By contrast, Lady Cochran was a well-known wit. In a runaway marriage in 1903 Cochran married Evelyn Alice (died 1960), daughter of the late Charles Robert Dade, captain in the Merchant Service. There were no children.

Unable, owing to his crippled condition to turn off the hot tap, Cochran was scalded in his bath and died in London a week later, 31 January 1951. His vitality in spite of his arthritis, was so great, his personality so vivid, that it seemed impossible he could be dead. The press, the B.B.C., and all the celebrities of the stage paid him tremendous tributes. He expressly asked that there should be no memorial service. 'Everything', he would say, 'is a nine days' wonder'. But in the words of W. Macqueen-Pope [q.v.] 'the last link with the golden Edwardian era has been snapped'. With the passing of Cochran, the English theatre lost much of its taste and most of its willingness to elevate as well as entertain the public. The things he created were of their nature transient—a roller-skating craze, the golden age of boxing and wrestling, seasons of acting and ballet which brought the London stage into touch with the best of European art; but the sponsorship of talent in authorship, acting, singing, and dancing added lustre to the theatrical scene, even if it did not always profit his managerial pocket.

A bust of Cochran by Peter Lambda was placed in the foyer of the Adelphi Theatre and there is a memorial panel in St. Paul's church, Covent Garden. The National Portrait Gallery has a drawing by Powys Evans, and a drawing by Wyndham Lewis is included in his *Thirty Personalities and a Self-Portrait*, 1932.

[Charles B. Cochran, *The Secrets of a Showman*, 1925, *I Had Almost Forgotten . . .*, 1 ock-a-Doodle-Do, 1941, *Showman Looks On*, 945; Charles Graves, *The Cochran Story*, 951; Vivian Ellis, *I'm on a See-Saw*, 1953; ersonal knowledge.]   VIVIAN ELLIS.

ODNER, MAURICE FREDERICK 888–1958), painter, was born in Stoke ewington 27 September 1888, the son of William Squires Codner, iron merchant, nd his wife, Ada Mary Payne. Educated t the Stationers' Company School and he Colchester School of Art, Codner be- ame widely known for his portraits in ls of distinguished men and women. hese were exhibited principally at the oyal Society of Portrait Painters, of hich he was a member and the honorary cretary, but also at the Royal Academy nd many galleries at home and abroad. is work was always notable for its sin- rity. He was singularly modest about its erits and in occasional moods of depres- on would regard his portraits merely as way of making a living; but at the same ne he always threw himself whole- artedly into his painting and took his ork in every field very seriously. Codner had many successes. His por- ait of King George VI in field-marshal's iform and Garter robes as captain- neral of the Honourable Artillery mpany (Armoury House), executed in 51, was notable and was the last por- ait painted of the King. His portrait of een Elizabeth the Queen Mother (1952) n the silver medal of the Paris Salon 54) where his portrait of Sir George oadbridge in his coronation robes had eived an honourable mention in 1938. Codner was not a great draughtsman; deed, he appeared to take little pleasure the use of pencil or pen. Like most hionable portrait painters, he was beset the need to produce a result which uld be, in a measure, flattering, with t quality of 'swagger' achieved by Van ck, Reynolds, Gainsborough, and the hteenth-century portrait painters, and thermore satisfying to the require- nts of his patrons, their friends, and the re critical judges of art, including him- . Thus official robes, ceremonial uni- n, and theatrical costumes were of the atest assistance to him, for he enjoyed icting decorative dress. His portraits e pre-eminently what are called good nesses, a superficial representation of ures being more in demand than a etrating analysis of character. In this vas extremely successful and his work especially in demand for the board-

rooms of business men and company directors.

Others among his sitters were Gwilym Lloyd-George (afterwards Viscount Ten- by) (1955), Sir Albert Richardson (1956), and among theatrical personalities Sir Seymour Hicks [q.v.], Athene Seyler, Evelyn Laye, and Leslie Henson [q.v.] in the character of Samuel Pepys.

It was, however, with his landscapes that Codner felt that he had more freedom and expressed himself more happily. These were the productions of his holidays and leisure hours, and they were exhibited regularly at the Royal Society of Painters in Oils, the Royal Institute, the New English Art Club, and elsewhere. He had a special delight in subjects which included trees and moving water and he liked to depict snow scenes, his work being con- siderably influenced by the example of his friend Sir Alfred Munnings [q.v.]. This open-air sketching was his great relaxa- tion, as was the pleasure he took in riding and his love of horses. During the war of 1914–18 he served in France in the Royal North Devon Hussars, but life in the army did not greatly appeal to him.

In appearance Codner was, on formal occasions, extremely well groomed; tall, slim, with a neatly trimmed beard and moustache, closely cut hair, and a rather pronounced nose, he had the distinguished air of the prosperous and successful artist. In his studio, at his ease, he often pre- ferred an old cardigan carelessly worn over a pair of shabby trousers. His manners were gentle and he had considerable charm to which was added a streak of melan- choly. This is not to say that he was un- able to enjoy laughter and broad jokes on occasion. He read much in Shakespeare and was devoted to Surtees, but he was not otherwise a great reader. He enjoyed the company of his fellow men and women, being essentially warm-hearted, but a certain reserve or perhaps shyness prevented him from having many inti- mates. He was a member of the Arts Club and of the Garrick Club. His portrait by R. G. Eves (in the possession of Codner's family) shows a man of somewhat pic- turesque appearance and something about the pose reveals his love of the theatre.

Codner's studio, which adjoined his small house in the Hampstead Garden Suburb, was a comfortable and workman- like place, well adapted to his various sitters. In the latter years of his life he added an ante-room in which was hung a selection of his paintings. This and his little garden full of roses and trees were his pride and an interest which he did not long enjoy, for he died in London 10 March 1958. He was buried at Dedham, Essex, in his much-beloved Constable country.

In 1913 Codner married Eleanor Marion, daughter of Thomas Fairfield, a captain in the mercantile marine. They had one son, John Whitlock Codner, who also became an artist.

[Private information; personal knowledge.]
ERNEST BLAIKLEY.

COHEN, SIR ROBERT WALEY (1877–1952), industrialist, was born in London 8 September 1877, the second son of Nathaniel Louis Cohen, a leading figure in the City, and his wife, Julia, daughter of Jacob Waley [q.v.]. The family, long leaders of the Anglo-Jewish community with connections extending from Sir Moses Montefiore [q.v.] to the Rothschilds, traced itself back to seventeenth-century Holland. A sister, Dorothea, married Charles Singer [q.v.]. In the Jewish House at Clifton, Cohen early showed his interest in chemistry and mathematics. With a science scholarship he proceeded to Emmanuel College, Cambridge, where he obtained second classes in both parts of the natural sciences tripos (1898–1900), with an interlude of a year for a trip round the world. A period in Berlin, between school and university, confirmed his attachment to music and science. As one of the leading amateur cellists in the country he played in the same quartet for forty years.

Although wealthy, his family believed that all should be profitably engaged. After Cambridge, Waley Cohen worked on unpaid research in the Meteorological Office. Aroused by family reproaches and helped by his future wife he drafted an advertisement seeking industrial employment. Henri Deterding of the Royal Dutch oil company sent the sole reply, but meanwhile his father had spoken to Sir Marcus Samuel (later Viscount Bearsted, q.v.) of the rival Shell company.

When Waley Cohen joined Shell in 1901 the company was scarcely five years old. At first he was unpaid but by 1904, aged twenty-six, his salary was £2,000. His independence established, he married his kinswoman, Alice Violet, daughter of Henry Edward Beddington, in that year and went on a long working tour in India and the East, challenging the dominance of Rockefeller interests, particularly in oriental markets. He was given massive

authority and operated with marke[d] success.

Two years later as the sole Shell del[e]gate, he negotiated the merger with t[he] redoubtable Royal Dutch group of co[m]panies, tackling the whole force of t[he] Dutch leaders: in the upshot Deterdi[ng] became managing director with Wal[ey] Cohen as his chief assistant. Out of t[he] combine grew one of the world's greate[st] industrial groups, but the union was n[ot] easy. Shell played from a position [of] weakness and legal complexities we[re] innumerable. Only Waley Cohen's cou[ra]geous suggestion that both sides sho[uld] employ the same lawyers made progre[ss] possible. So respected were his powe[rs] and integrity that his nomination to t[he] board of the joint operating compan[y] came not from Shell but from the Ro[yal] Dutch.

In dealing with Borneo oil, for the fi[rst] time in the oil industry Waley Cohen h[ad] petroleum subjected to scientific analy[sis,] with the discovery that what was co[n]sidered an inferior product had [many] chemical compounds in a single distilla[te] including toluol, the essential element [of] T.N.T. The Admiralty rejected the proc[ess] and a factory was consequently erected [at] Rotterdam. When the explosives posit[ion] presented perilous shortages during [the] war of 1914–18, Waley Cohen organi[zed] the transport of the complete factory [to] the United Kingdom. Samuel had ea[rlier] attempted to persuade conservative na[val] experts to transfer from coal to oil. Wh[en] war came, Waley Cohen, under his lea[der]ship, saw that notwithstanding damag[e] the company's prosperity, their great a[nd] widely distributed oil resources were [at] the country's disposal; Cohen him[self] became petroleum adviser to the A[rmy] Council. He was appointed K.B.E. in 1[9..] but the significance of his services has p[er]haps not been generally recognized.

Whereas Waley Cohen's main ener[gies] lay in the oil companies, he had m[any] other interests. In 1928 he purchased [the] Exmoor estate of Honeymead, and at [the] age of fifty-two gave up his directio[n of] Shell, though remaining on various boa[rds.] In the early years a country pleasa[nce] Honeymead became a centre of ex[peri]mental agriculture during the wa[r of] 1939–45, showing that the derelict [and] difficult acres of Exmoor could y[ield] vastly increased food supplies.

When his life seemed to be mo[ving] towards semi-retirement, there cam[e a] challenging opportunity. In 1929 W[aley]

Cohen accepted the chairmanship of African and Eastern, an independent concern operating in West Africa with heavy losses. The rival Niger Company, bought by Lord Leverhulme [q.v.] in 1920 and reorganized by (Sir) D'Arcy Cooper [q.v.], was also operating at a huge loss. Waley Cohen from the first worked for amalgamation and the United Africa Company was formed in 1929. But he had entered unfamiliar territories in which business methods differed widely from that personal control which he had maintained in his association with Samuel. The depression was approaching and many unpopular decisions had to be made, while the pressure of work led him to appear remote and domineering. He failed to achieve the success which he had attained in the oil world, and he resigned in 1931. Yet the principles on which he worked (as distinct from individual decisions in which he may have been at fault) were sound, and ultimately the companies combined successfully to become the leading trading group in West Africa.

Once he had established himself and his family as he thought fit, he lost interest in the mere accumulation of wealth. Other activities, voluntary and charitable, occupied a considerable part of his life. His impact on the popular imagination might have been greater had they been less diverse. He was the acknowledged head of Anglo-Jewry in a way that no successor could be, and as such played the leading role in almost every aspect of the affairs of the Jewish community in Britain. He was for nearly forty years the chief figure of the United Synagogue and died in office as its president. Zionism he opposed as conflicting with his conception of the Anglo-Jewish community as Englishmen of Jewish faith. Yet through the Palestine Corporation, largely his personal creation, he strove for the greatest economic development of the country, and its achievements were a major practical contribution to the establishment of Israel as a prosperous modern State.

His old school, Clifton, owed much to him, as also did University College, London, especially in the war years when the college was nearly destroyed by enemy attack: in these difficult times he always kept in view the possibilities of post-war development. In Cambridge his father had been the prime mover in establishing the appointments Board and he carried on this conception as the pioneer in bringing university men into industry. The con-

tinuing relationship between Cambridge and Shell was largely his creation.

Waley Cohen's large stature, massive proportions, and strong features constituted him a formidable person. Those who knew him in his prime speak of a dominating personality with a tendency to sweep aside all objections to his plans. Yet on the rare occasions when opposition was successful he bore no malice. His commanding authority was coupled in due time with an unaffected kindliness to the benefit of his fellow men and of his country.

Waley Cohen had two sons and one daughter. His elder son, Sir Bernard Waley-Cohen, followed the tradition of social service and at an early age became lord mayor of London. An unusually happy marriage ended when Waley Cohen's wife died as a result of a motor accident in Palestine in 1935 when Waley Cohen himself was seriously injured. He continued his activities to the last few months of life with an increasing emphasis on his charitable and educational attachments, notably in the Sir William Ramsay centenary appeal at University College, London, and in the work of the Council of Christians and Jews, one of the many bodies which he had played a prominent part in founding. He died in London 27 November 1952. A portrait by Joseph Oppenheimer is in the possession of the family.

[Robert Henriques, *Sir Robert Waley Cohen*, 1966; private information.]

COLE, GEORGE DOUGLAS HOWARD (1889–1959), university teacher, writer, and socialist, was born in Cambridge 25 September 1889, the son of George Cole, a jeweller who later moved to Ealing and became a surveyor, and his wife, Jessie Knowles. He was educated at St. Paul's School and Balliol College, Oxford, and proceeded by way of firsts in honour moderations (1910) and *literae humaniores* (1912) to a prize fellowship at Magdalen in the latter year. Even as an undergraduate, when contemporaries noted his 'dark, dynamic presence', he was keenly interested in socialism, which he had accepted as a 'way of life' in 1906. In 1908 he joined the Oxford Fabian Society and went on to edit a red-covered magazine, the *Oxford Reformer*. The Fabian Society and the Independent Labour Party were the two socialist bodies which drew him into active agitation outside the universities, although he worked closely for a

time with the Social Democratic Federation while living in Newcastle upon Tyne
in 1913–14. During the years of bitter
industrial unrest between 1911 and 1914
Cole was strongly critical of the infant
Labour Party for its 'close entanglement'
with the Liberals and became a vigorous
and persuasive advocate of guild socialism:
the establishment of 'workers' control' in
industry through self-governing guilds
based on industrial trade unions. His lucid
mind and his skill in amassing and
interpreting facts were as important as his
passionate convictions and his strong sense
of social purpose in ensuring that even
during his twenties he was a prominent
intellectual figure in what he and his
friends thought of as 'the movement'.
Indeed, by the time he first published his
widely read book The World of Labour in
1913 he had introduced a new note of
rebellion and independence into the affairs
of the Fabian Society, to the executive
of which he was elected in April 1914.
'Socialism', he wrote in 1913, 'will triumph
over Social Reform only as its exponents
learn both to think and to feel—and to do
both at once.' Critical of the 'bureaucratic' approach of Sidney and Beatrice
Webb [qq.v.] and quite uninterested in
the company of either professional politicians or civil servants, Cole turned to
trade-unionists, emphasizing the importance of ideas in 'the movement' and of
the necessity to unleash creative energies
'from below'.

After quarrelling with the Fabian 'old
guard', he resigned from the society and
the executive in June 1915, while retaining his connection through the Fabian
Research Department which he had joined
in May 1913 and of which he became
honorary secretary in 1916. This body
accumulated and diffused a vast quantity
of information about labour and industry.
It also brought together a remarkable
group of young socialists in an atmosphere
of lively and enthusiastic commitment. In
August 1918 Cole married one of the team,
Margaret Isabel, daughter of J. P. Postgate [q.v.]; they had one son and two
daughters. The Coles were to be associated
in many socialist causes, although, as they
both stressed, they did not constitute in
any sense a new 'partnership' on Webbian
lines. In 1915 Cole had become unpaid
research adviser to the Amalgamated
Society of Engineers, a post of influence
which was without precedent in the
history of British trade-unionism: advice
on wages, prices, and 'dilution' of labour

under the existing wartime Treasury
Agreements and Munitions of War Act
brought Cole into touch not only with
trade-union leaders but with shop steward
and union rank-and-file. He was to refe
to his experience in his book Trad
Unionism and Munitions (1923) which
along with his Self-Government in Industr
(1917), Guild Socialism Re-stated (1920)
and Workshop Organization (1923), gives
clear idea of his thinking at this time
expressed, too, in the National Guild
League, founded in 1915. In 1918 th
name Fabian Research Department wa
changed to Labour Research Department
and a year later the Labour Party, with
new constitution, appointed Cole its firs
secretary for research. He was also secre
tary of the workers' side of the Nation
Industrial Conference which first met i
February 1919. In March he and h
chairman, Arthur Henderson [q.v.
drafted a 'Memorandum on the Cause
and Remedies for Labour Unrest' whic
referred to the 'desire to substitute
democratic system of public ownershi
and production for use with an increasir
element of control by the organize
workers themselves for the existing cap
talist organization of industry'.

As an organized movement, howeve
guild socialism did not survive the Ru
sian Revolution of 1917 and the eme
gence of the British Communist Par
after 1920. Cole was never tempted to jo
the Communist Party, although he alwa
insisted that his loyalty to socialism too
precedence over his loyalty to the Labo
Party. He did his best to bring differe
kinds of socialism together, and support
international efforts to build bridg
between communist and social democra
movements. He wrote later, in his aut
biographical introduction to volume
(1958) of his massive history of Socia
Thought, that 'my attitude was basica
pluralistic and libertarian and I was
pelled by the Bolsheviks' conception o
social philosophy based on rigidly det
minist principles and involving the
questionable class-correctness of a sing
unified body of doctrine, regardless
considerations of time and place.' Wh
writing and lecturing sympathetica
about the Russian Revolution and
consequences—directing attention p
ticularly to the 'lessons' of Russian pl
ning after the British economic a
political crisis of 1931 (see his Pract
Economics, 1937)—he was never will
to suspend his own independence

judgement. In 1924 he resigned from his honorary secretaryship of the Labour Research Department which passed under full Communist control. Margaret, a paid official, resigned a year later, when Cole became university reader in economics at Oxford and a fellow of University College. He was to remain closely connected with Oxford for the rest of his life, although after 1929 the Coles maintained a house in London.

In the meantime, however, he had worked since 1921 as the first full-time tutorial class tutor in the university of London, a strategic position in the adult education movement. He made a valuable contribution to the organization and life of the Workers' Educational Association and founded the professional Tutors' Association. When he took up his new post in Oxford, he continued and extended his adult education work while helping to shape Oxford University's own activities in this field. He was, indeed, a conscientious and inspiring teacher, both in the class-room and through his books, and he never wavered in his belief that adult education was a necessary instrument both of working-class emancipation and of social change. It was characteristic, again, of his distaste for indoctrination that he chose to work through the 'non-party political' W.E.A. His wide range of intellectual and cultural interests—he published a life of Cobbett in 1924 and of Owen a year later —found expression in this context, although the move to Oxford in no sense implied, as Beatrice Webb feared, an abandonment of his more immediate socialist interests. Almost immediately after his arrival there he began to invite undergraduates of radical and socialist leanings to his house for informal weekly discussions. The 'Cole Group', as it was eventually called, became something of an Oxford institution for the rest of Cole's life and had a considerable influence on men of different gifts and philosophies who subsequently played an active part in national life: it attracted such men as Colin Clark, (Sir) John Betjeman, W. H. Auden, Hugh Gaitskell, John Parker, Evan Durbin, and Michael Stewart. There was ample room in the 'Group' for the most free and comprehensive discussion, with Cole himself stimulating and inspiring the best in its members. Some of them were drawn very early in the life of the 'Group' into helping trade-unionists in the general strike of 1926 through a university strike committee.

Cole's Oxford readership was in economics, although he often used to say and write that orthodox economists did not regard him as one of their number. He owed much to J. A. Hobson [q.v.] and something to Marx (he published *What Marx Really Meant* in 1934), but his strength lay not in theory but in his willingness, always within a socialist framework, to devote vast energy to the current problems of economic organization. In 1929 he published *The Next Ten Years in British Social and Economic Policy*, in which he argued, in a year when the Labour Party came back into power, that 'Pre-war Socialism could afford to seek after perfection because it was not in a hurry: post-war Socialism needs practical results.' In his preface he thanked the Webbs for 'suggestions for its improvement' while the work was in progress. By this time his differences with the Webbs had been smoothed over, and he had rejoined the Fabian Society in 1928. He became a member of the Economic Advisory Council set up by Ramsay MacDonald in January 1930, and in the same year became prospective Labour candidate for the King's Norton division of Birmingham. He was also a founder in 1930 of the Society for Socialist Inquiry and Propaganda, with initials pronounced 'zip' and Ernest Bevin [q.v.] as chairman, which grew out of a number of week-end meetings at Easton Lodge, a property belonging to the Countess of Warwick [q.v.]; and a few months later in March and April 1931 of the New Fabian Research Bureau, with C. R. (later Earl) Attlee as chairman, Cole as secretary, and Gaitskell as assistant secretary. These bodies survived the fall of the Labour Government, although the former—to Bevin's anger—was subsumed in the Socialist League in 1932. Although thereafter Bevin complained of socialist intellectuals, Cole's own intellectual position was stronger after August 1931 than it had been before. He was secretary of the New Fabian Research Bureau until 1935 and chairman from 1937 to 1939. In the latter year it amalgamated with the Fabian Society with a revised constitution. Of the revived Fabian Society Cole was chairman in 1939–46 and 1948–50 and president from 1952 until his death.

The collapse of the Labour Party in 1931 led to a long period of rethinking about politics and economics in which Cole, mainly through his writings, played a prominent part. By now, indeed, he had established his reputation as the most prolific of all British writers on socialism. The list of his publications continued to grow until it filled more than a column of *Who's Who*, and alongside his economic writings there was a regular flow of books on social theory and labour history, on both of which subjects and also on a course called 'labour movements' he lectured at Oxford. *The Common People*, which he wrote with R. W. Postgate in 1938, was outstanding amongst his publications on popular social history— to be followed by *British Working Class Politics, 1832–1914* (1941), *Chartist Portraits* (1941), and *Attempts at General Union* (1953), the last two of which were more scholarly in context and tone. *The Condition of Britain*, which he wrote with his wife and which appeared in 1937, is a valuable example of the kind of tidily organized and socially pointed survey which he liked to produce and which he knew would be very widely used. Indeed, the survey method was to appeal to him more and more in the next phase of his life.

During the thirties Cole was reaching a wide audience, not only through his books —among which *The Intelligent Man's Guide Through World Chaos* (1932) and *The Intelligent Man's Review of Europe To-day* (1933, with Margaret) were part of a characteristic pattern of the thirties— but through his articles, particularly, but far from exclusively, those in the *New Statesman*. He had written for the *Nation* before 1914 and for the *New Statesman* from 1918 onwards—being considered for the editorship of the latter in 1930. He became a director in 1947 and chairman of the board in 1956. It was in the pages of the *New Statesman*, and on the lecture platform, that he attacked the inability of the Government to cope with unemployment—he had demanded a 'national labour corps' in 1930—claimed that capitalism was 'on trial', pressed for more planning, questioned the prospects of the Labour Party as it was then constituted, welcomed—without fully appreciating— the significance of the *General Theory* of J. M. (later Lord) Keynes [q.v.] ('Mr. Keynes Beats the Band'), and welcoming —without fully supporting—the objects of Roosevelt's New Deal. He was opposed to Fascism and Nazism from the start, but extremely suspicious of a 'capitalist government' rearming in order to wage what in fact might be an 'imperialist war'. This approach led him into a number of

attempts, none of them very hopeful, to secure a 'Popular Front' in Britain, and he was even prepared to push into the background some of his basic distaste for British Liberalism and Liberals in the process.

The volume of Cole's writing was influenced not only by the state of his opinions but by the state of his health. In 1931 he was found to be suffering from diabetes, a complaint which often prevented him from living as he would have liked. When his physical activities were necessarily curtailed, 'he began', as his wife put it, 'to write faster and faster, and longer and more complicated books'. He also took to writing detective novels with his wife and between 1923 and 1942 published twenty-nine of them along with four volumes of short detective stories. Ill health dogged him also during the war when he was compelled, at a critical moment of its history, to be away from the recently founded Nuffield College, of which he had become one of the first faculty fellows in May 1939.

He was asked in June 1940 to assist Sir William (later Lord) Beveridge at the Ministry of Labour in a rapid inquiry into manpower and war production, and this led directly to his becoming chairman and director, early in 1941, of the Nuffield College Social Reconstruction Survey, which was launched in November 1940. During the next three years the Survey did much useful work—with a small Treasury subsidy—in producing local and national surveys on demographic, economic, and social problems, some of which were of direct use to government departments, most of which remained unpublished. In June 1942 Cole was appointed sub-warden of the still embryonic Nuffield College, and he was mainly responsible for the wartime Nuffield Conferences which brought together academics, politicians, civil servants, trade-unionists, and others. The withdrawal of government financial support for the Survey was one of a number of difficulties the college faced at this time, and after a period of illness Cole resigned his sub-wardenship in September 1943, his directorship of the Survey in January 1944, and his faculty fellowship in the following March. 'I can only say most sincerely', one of his ex-colleagues wrote to him in May 1944, 'that as a believer in the purposes of Nuffield College I greatly regret you will no longer be there to provide your drive, inspiration, sense of reality and unique power of pulling together a

agged discussion. This is not meant to
e an exhaustive list of your virtues.'

Cole nevertheless remained as active in
Oxford as he had been before 1939, and in
1944 he was appointed Chichele professor
f social and political theory, which car-
ied with it a fellowship in All Souls. He
ter resumed his connection with Nuffield
nd was made an honorary fellow both of
University College and of Balliol. He was
lso a member of the standing committee
f the Institute of Statistics, an academic
dviser to Ruskin College, and an inde-
tigable spokesman of the Delegacy for
ocial Training. During the last years of
is Oxford life he became doyen of P.P.E.,
eing one of the few remaining Oxford
ons to concern himself with the full
inity of politics, economics, and philo-
ophy, not to speak of history and litera-
re. He also encouraged the development
' the study of sociology and of industrial
lations. His writings continued to record
e diversity of his interests. In 1946 he
blished *A Century of Co-operation*; in
e next year both a little book on Samuel
utler and *The Intelligent Man's Guide to*
e *Post-War World*; and in 1956 his *Post-*
ar Condition of Britain. In 1953 the first
lume of his history of *Socialist Thought*
peared. His lectures covered as wide a
riety of themes as his books, and for a
ne (see his *Local and Regional Govern-*
ent, 1947) he took particular interest in
cal and regional government and schemes
r future reform which would foster the
nse of local community. His attitude to
ommunity' was somewhat similar to his
titude to 'workers' control'. He de-
anded a sense of spontaneous involve-
ent and the energy which he believed
nt with it to make any kind of formal
achinery work. 'If socialization is to
vance much further', he wrote in 1958,
is necessary . . . to give the workers an
creased sense of participation.' The same
ed, he believed, existed in politics,
ere neither organizational reforms nor
extension of 'ameliorative' social ser-
es went far enough to satisfy him.
lf-government' had to be applied to
ry aspect of social organization and
every level, with 'face-to-face groups'
ally important if 'Socialist planning'
s to be reconciled with 'personal free-
m' and democracy was to be made 'real
face of the need for large-scale organiza-
n and control'.

Cole stood unsuccessfully as a candidate
one of the two Oxford University seats
1945—he did not seek official Labour

Party endorsement—and polled 3,414
votes. The 'Cole Group' thrived during
the post-war period, with the domestic
problems of the Labour Government and
the causes and remedies of international
tension receiving equal attention. Cole's
freedom from 'Lib–Lab' attitudes made
him interested in much that was happening outside Britain in very different kinds
of societies and sympathetic to different
approaches to socialism. In his public
writings and lectures he objected to the
Anglo-American loan, argued strongly
after 1945 in favour of a 'third force' in
Europe, was opposed to the Korean war,
and dissatisfied with the British foreign
policy both before and after the Labour
Government fell from power. At the same
time, he recognized realistically that 'substantial gains in real wages and very great
developments of the social services can be
achieved within a predominantly capitalist
order'. Any rethinking about socialism
had to begin there. In 'An Open Letter to
Members from the chairman' in the first
number of the *Fabian Journal* (May 1950)
he stressed that 'we do our best to prevent
them [dogmas] from becoming our masters
by questioning them constantly and refusing to write more than the barest
minimum of them into our constitution. . . .
We duly revere our founders; but we by
no means take what they said as gospel . . .'.

When Cole retired from his chair in
Oxford in 1957—he accepted a research
fellowship at Nuffield College—a number
of Cole's colleagues and friends prepared a
volume of essays in his honour which it
was designed to present to him on his
seventieth birthday. He died, however, 14
January 1959, in London, before the book
appeared. His colleagues and friends paid
particular tribute to his exceptional qualities as a teacher, and this is perhaps how
he would most like to have been remembered—cool and lucid in his exposition,
warm, passionate, even volcanic, in his
feelings—not believing in God but believing in goodness, drawn to satire as much
as to exposition, and, as Margaret Cole
wrote, by inclination 'a strong Tory in
everything but politics'.

[Margaret Cole, *Growing Up Into Revolu-*
tion, 1949, and *The Story of Fabian Socialism*,
1961; Recollections in *Essays in Labour*
History, ed. A. Briggs and J. Saville, 1960;
personal knowledge.]   ASA BRIGGS.

COLLINS, JOSEPHINE (JOSÉ) (1887–
1958), actress and singer, was born 23

May 1887 at Whitechapel, London, the illegitimate daughter of Joseph Van den Berg, professor of music, and Lottie Collins, actress, singer, and dancer. Lottie Collins, whose parents died in her early childhood, was a flamboyantly successful music-hall artist who popularized the song, 'Ta-ra-ra Boom-de-ay', which she had heard first in America and then introduced to London at the Tivoli music-hall in the Strand during October 1891, accompanied by her own dance. One of José Collins's earliest remembrances was of imitating this at a tea-party at home. The girl had successively two stepfathers, the first Stephen Patrick Cooney, the second James W. Tate (died 1922), a fluent composer of light music. In the haphazard early chapters of her autobiography, a good-natured book not very helpful to the researcher, José Collins put forward the date of her birth to May 1893 as 'Josephine Charlotte Cooney', and the place to Salford.

The facts of her life become clearer once she has made her professional stage début. She appeared at a Glasgow music-hall with (Sir) Harry Lauder [q.v.], illustrating his song, 'I love a lassie', by doing 'a toe-dance in a tartan frock and glengarry' as the 'little Scottish bluebell'. Soon after this, at the age of seventeen, then with a contralto voice and already with a strikingly confident stage presence, she was engaged in a touring company of *A Chinese Honeymoon* and later took the leading part of Mrs. Pineapple: in her book she speaks of herself as 'fourteen and a half and the baby of the company'. At Christmas 1905 she was back with Lauder in a Glasgow pantomime *Aladdin*. Some highly variegated years followed, on the music-halls, in touring companies, and in pantomime; and in 1911, not long after her first marriage to an actor, Leslie Chatfield, she went out boldly to the United States without a contract. There she established herself so firmly in New York as a singer in operetta and in revue (she was in the Ziegfeld Follies for some time) that she did not return to London until 1916. She was then summoned back to appear at Daly's in a musical comedy, *The Happy Day*, written by (Sir) Seymour Hicks [q.v.] with music by Sidney Jones [q.v.] and Paul A. Rubens. Although she had not the leading part in *The Happy Day*, within a year (1917) she was Teresa in *The Maid of the Mountains*, an operetta with book by Frederick Lonsdale [q.v.] and music by Harold Fraser-Simson and

her stepfather J. W. Tate, which ran a[t] Daly's for more than three years: in al[l] 1,352 performances. It grew quickly int[o] one of the favourite London plays of th[e] war: soldiers on leave crowded to see Jos[é] Collins, and her song, 'Love will find a way['] was heard everywhere. Towards the end o[f] her life, when she had realized she coul[d] never be a leading player again, somebod[y] at a film studio asked her to telephon[e]. When she did so, hoping for work, sh[e] was told that they were filming a story [of] the war of 1914–18, with one scene lai[d] in a star's dressing-room. 'Can you po[s]sibly lend us one of your pictures to han[g] on the wall ?'

For the next decade José Collins woul[d] be, in effect, upon the wall of every lov[er] of musical comedy. Invariably an attach[-] ing actress, she took the stage with th[e] spirit and confidence which her moth[er] had used on the music-halls. Her stro[ng] bravura performances, her sleek bla[ck] hair, her Spanish-Jewish aspect, her te[m]pestuous personality, and the clear, tr[ue] warmth of her voice which had develop[ed] into a soprano, were famous far beyo[nd] the circle of the west end. Unluckily h[er] success as Teresa limited her to the sa[me] kind of good-hearted romantic flouri[sh] and such parts could not go on indefinite[ly].

She followed *The Maid of the Mounta[ins]* by a similar part, Dolores in *The Southe[rn] Maid* (1920). Thence, still at Daly's, s[he] went on (1921) to Sybil Renaud in *Sy[bil]*. Ultimately she left Daly's after a quar[rel] with James White, the financier fr[om] Rochdale who had bought the theat[re] and who had entered her dressing-ro[om] uninvited, with a party of friends. H[ot] tempered, she was the first to rese[nt] any slight or any attempt to les[sen] her privileges. She moved across, und[er] Robert Evett's management, to [the] Gaiety Theatre where for a time she c[on]tinued her successes in such different pa[rts] (all with the Collins family likeness) [as] Vera in *The Last Waltz* (1922), the na[me] part in *Catherine* (1923), and Nell Gwy[n] in *Our Nell* (1924), the last of thes[e a] typically generous portrait in an und[is]tinguished piece by L. N. Parker [q.v.] and Reginald Arkell to music by Ha[rold] Fraser-Simson and Ivor Novello [q.v.].

At length, with the rapid failure [of] *Frasquita* (1925) at the Prince's Thea[tre,] a piece, to music by Franz Lehar, in wh[ich] she had invested much capital, she [met] professional tragedy. Though she tou[red] various variety theatres in Britain and [the] United States, and took part in the b[

and stormy run of the revue *Whitebirds* at His Majesty's (1927), she declined to plays and characters unworthy of her once dominant position. Eventually her intermittent stage work ceased altogether. Her second marriage which, like her first, was dissolved, had been in 1920 to Lord Robert Edward Innes-Ker; she married in 1935, as her third husband, Dr. Gerald Baeyertz Kirkland. During the war of 1939–45, when her husband served as a major in the Royal Army Medical Corps, she trained as a nurse in order to work voluntarily at the hospitals where he was stationed. During her later years of happy marriage she mellowed into a calm, philosophic woman who accepted with equanimity the change in her career from a public figure to quiet domestic life in suburban Essex. She died in an Epping hospital 6 December 1958. She had no children.

[*The Times*, 8 December 1958; José Collins, *The Maid of the Mountains: Her Story*, 1932; *Who's Who in the Theatre*; personal knowledge.]   J. C. TREWIN.

COLVILLE, DAVID JOHN, first BARON CLYDESMUIR (1894–1954), public servant, was born at Motherwell House, Lanarkshire, 13 February 1894, the only son of John Colville, of Cleland, M.P. for North-east Lanark (1895–1901), and his wife, Christian Downie. He was the grandson of David Colville, founder of the great steel enterprise which became Colvilles, Ltd. His only sister, Christian, married (Sir) Alexander Erskine-Hill, who became first baronet and was M.P. for North Edinburgh (1935–45).

Colville was educated at Charterhouse and Trinity College, Cambridge, where he obtained a third class in part i of the historical tripos in 1914. At the outbreak of war in 1914 he was mobilized with the 1 battalion, the Cameronians (Scottish Rifles), and served as captain in France, where he was thrice wounded. When the Territorial Army was re-formed after the war he rejoined his old battalion which he eventually commanded, retiring in 1936. He was honorary colonel from 1941 until 46. From the date when he received his commission before the first war John Colville took the deepest interest in the Territorial Army. At the time of his death he was chairman of the council of the Territorial and Auxiliary Forces Associations. He was also an officer in the Royal Company of Archers.

In 1919 Colville became a member of Lanarkshire County Council on which he served until 1925. He was unsuccessful in contesting for Parliament the Motherwell division in the National Liberal interest in 1922 and North Midlothian for the Conservatives in January 1929 but was returned for that constituency at the general election a few months later, a notable victory when the tide was running against his party. He was secretary to the Department of Overseas Trade (1931–5) when he took a special interest in the British Industries Fair and led several trade missions overseas; parliamentary under-secretary of state for Scotland (1935–6); financial secretary to the Treasury (1936–8); and in 1938–40 secretary of state for Scotland when he was very much concerned in all the work involved in placing Scotland on a war footing. In 1940 on the creation of the coalition Government, he was one of those who had to make way. He immediately undertook other war work and was colonel on the staff at Lowland District and Scottish Command, as G.S.O. 1, Home Guard, 1940–42.

In 1943 he was appointed governor of Bombay where he remained until 1948. The great ability and success with which he discharged the very exacting duties of governor in time of war may be judged by the fact that at four periods in 1945–7 he acted as viceroy. By his personality, shrewdness, humanity, and human interest, he won the confidence and indeed the affection of all races and types of people with whom he had to deal. He could be firm when necessary, but he was always fair. He was appointed G.C.I.E. in 1943 and later his wife received the Order of the Crown of India and the Kaisar-i-Hind gold medal. The position he had won was demonstrated when he and his wife returned on a visit to Bombay as private citizens a few years before his death.

In 1936 Colville was sworn of the Privy Council and in 1948 he was created a baron and took the title Lord Clydesmuir, of Braidwood. He attended the House of Lords regularly, speaking particularly on Scottish and Commonwealth affairs, and was vice-chairman of the Commonwealth Parliamentary Association. In the same year he joined the board of Colvilles, Ltd., with which he had been associated since his return from the first war. In 1952 he was appointed lord-lieutenant of Lanarkshire. He was for some years (1950–54) a governor of the B.B.C. and was chairman of the national broadcasting council for Scotland in 1953–4.

Clydesmuir's recreations were shooting, deerstalking, fishing, and yachting. In his yacht *Iolanthe* he spent many holidays with his family and friends around the Western Isles of Scotland. He was very musical and it was a delight to hear him play the organ in the music-room at Braidwood. He had great charm of manner, an abounding sense of humour, and a gift for friendship.

In 1915 Colville married Agnes Anne, elder daughter of Sir William Bilsland, baronet; they had two daughters and one son, Ronald John Bilsland (born 1917), who succeeded him when he died at Braidwood 31 October 1954. A posthumous portrait, by Stanley Cursiter, is at Braidwood.

[Private information; personal knowledge.]
BILSLAND.

COMPER, SIR (JOHN) NINIAN (1864–1960), church architect, was born in Aberdeen 10 June 1864, the eldest of the five children of the Rev. John Comper, rector of St. John's episcopal church, and his wife, Ellen, daughter of John Taylor, merchant, of Hull. His father was one of the most advanced priests in the Anglo-Catholic revival in Scotland. A friend of Bishop A. P. Forbes of Brechin and of John Mason Neale [qq.v.], he invited the latter to become the godfather of his eldest son. It was natural therefore that a fervent and advanced Anglo-Catholicism should be the dominant influence in Comper's life. In later years the 'Anglo-' came to mean less and less to him, and he would affect not to recognize any difference between the Anglican and Roman Churches, maintaining that through the work of St. Pius X, to whom he had a special devotion, the two communions were already, if secretly, united. After rather unhappy schooldays at Glenalmond, Comper spent a year at Ruskin's art school in Oxford, before going to London where he was articled to C. E. Kempe, and later to G. F. Bodley and T. Garner [qq.v.]. Bodley he always regarded as his master, and like him always steadfastly opposed the system of qualifying examinations for architects and architectural schools: in *Who's Who* he described himself as 'architect (not registered)'.

With the exception of the Welsh war memorial in Cardiff (1928), all Comper's work was ecclesiastical. His first independent building was a chapel added to his father's church of St. Margaret of Scot-

land, Aberdeen, in 1889. This was followed two years later by conventual buildings near by in the same city, which set the fashion, destined to become the *sine qua non* of successful Anglican convents, of a Comper chapel. One of his last works was the great window in Westminster Hall (1952). In the course of seventy years he built fifteen churches, restored and decorated scores, and designed vestments, banners, and windows in places as far apart as China, North America, France, India, and South Africa; in England there can hardly be a rural deanery without some example of his sensitive, expensive and unmistakable workmanship, which is to be found also in churches of the Roman communion, among them Downside Abbey.

The last rose of the summer of the Gothic revival, Comper was no mere revivalist. His understanding of the purpose of a church was far in advance of any other architect in that tradition. He has been claimed as the greatest church furnisher since Wren. But if he was primarily a decorator rather than a architect, his decorative art was never for art's sake, but for the sake of the function for which he held a church exists, as a roof over an altar. Believing this, he built from the altar outwards, personally designing every detail of the furnishing, leaving nothing—not even the candles—to the repository. While bitterly opposed to 'modernism', he nevertheless anticipated by many years the aims of the *avant-garde*: for example in his use of free standing altars, of pure white interiors and strong clear colours—especially the typical Comper rose and green, and the combination of gilding, blue, and white.

His early work was strictly medieval inspiration. Long hours of poring over illuminations in the British Museum resulted in a paper on 'The English Altar and its Surroundings' read to the Society of St. Osmund in 1893 and later to the St. Paul's Ecclesiological Society. It was included in *Some Principles and Services of the Prayer Book Historically Considered* (1899) edited by John Wickham Legg [q.v.] and marked the first time in the history of the Gothic revival that the altar was taken seriously and not treated as 'a sideboard or a mantelpiece' as described Bodley's series of ledges and gradines.

At St. Wilfrid's, Cantley, in 1893 Comper erected an altar with riddel posts the first of that succession of 'box-be

English altars whose use by inferior artists he came to deplore. In 1892 he installed a hanging pyx in St. Matthew's, Westminster (since removed), thus leading to a development in the practice of reservation in the Church. St. Matthew's was the first of many examples of the hanging pyx, of which the most elaborate was the nine-foot silver *turris* at All Saints', Margaret Street, and the most successful that in the Grosvenor Chapel.

The finest example of Comper's first medieval manner is the church of St. Cyprian, Clarence Gate (1903). His second style dated from about 1904. Visits to the Mediterranean revealed to him, with all the force of a conversion, the debt owed by all Christian art to Greece. Thereafter he avoided the medieval Christ typified by the crucifix in favour of the beardless, virile Christ in Glory of the *Majestas*; where before he had sought for 'unity in beauty by exclusion' of all not in period he now found a deeper 'unity by inclusion'. This was expressed in an uninhibited mingling of classical, gothic, baroque, and even saracenic motifs. This eclecticism can be seen at Wimborne St. Giles, where in 1910 he restored a classical church with perpendicular decorations and a mannerist Jacobean screen ; or—most notably —at his *chef d'œuvre*, St. Mary's, Wellingborough (1904–40), where a perpendicular nave, middle-gothic side chapel, Spanish screens, and classical baldachino, combine brilliantly in one harmonious riot of colour and gilding. In his last period he grew more and more to see the importance of a free-standing altar, usually covered by a ciborium, as in the All Saints' Convent chapel at London Colney, at Pusey House, Oxford, or St. Philip's, Cosham, and by an uncumbered, translucent background to his windows.

Comper's few writings are important monuments of ecclesiology. Besides his essay on the English altar which was reissued in a revised form in 1933, he wrote only three pamphlets: *The Reasonableness of the Ornaments Rubric* (1897), *Of the Atmosphere of a Church* (1947), and *Of the Christian Altar and the Buildings Which Contain It* (1950). They reveal an understanding of the function of the church which puts Comper in a different class from any of his predecessors since Pugin. Holding (and expressing) his strong views with an airy disregard for whatever did not agree with them, possessing a perfectionist sensibility and a disconcertingly teasing sense of humour, Comper in his

prime was a somewhat formidable figure. The only portrait of him (which he disliked) was painted at this time by his cousin Beatrice Bright and is in the possession of the family. But in his later years he mellowed into a youthful and upright nonagenarian, with a perfectly trimmed goatee and gold-rimmed spectacles, courtly manners, and a voice whose exquisite modulations carried with it overtones of the distant days, of which he would talk with relish, when he dined with Beardsley, heard the news of Rossetti's death at Alfred Gurney's table, or engaged in sympathetic discourse with Swinburne's sister, Isabel.

In 1890 Comper married Grace Bucknall (died 1933) ; they had four sons, the eldest of whom became an architect, and two daughters. In 1891 he entered into partnership with his brother-in-law, William Bucknall, and afterwards successively with the latter's son and grandson. He was knighted in 1950.

In 1912 Comper moved into The Priory, Beulah Hill, a stuccoed 'gothick' house near Sydenham, where he lived until his death 22 December 1960. His ashes were buried beneath the windows of his design in Westminster Abbey where he had been responsible also for the Warriors' chapel.

[*The Times*, 23 December 1960; *Times Literary Supplement*, 27 April 1951; *Church Times*, 13 January 1950; *Pax*, November 1937; John Betjeman in *Architectural Review*, February 1939; Peter F. Anson, *Fashions in Church Furnishings*, 1960; private information; personal knowledge.]   GERARD IRVINE.

CONNARD, PHILIP (1875–1958), painter, was born at Southport 24 March 1875, the son of David Connard, house-painter, by his wife, Ellen Lunt. After a modicum of elementary schooling he went into his father's trade. But, having wider ambitions, he attended evening classes and eventually won a National School scholarship in textile designing which took him to South Kensington. With a prize of £100 he went next to Paris where he hoped for a two-year training as a painter. His funds proving insufficient he returned after a few months to London where he succeeded in finding some jobs as an illustrator and soon afterwards became a master at the Lambeth School of Art.

Meanwhile he had begun to submit work to open exhibitions. Some contributions to the New English Art Club caught the eyes of Henry Tonks and P. Wilson Steer [qq.v.] who supported his application for club membership which was duly accorded. For a while he retained his Lambeth post, but he gradually produced more and more of his own work, chiefly as a decorative painter, and before long he was able to abandon teaching and live by independent practice. His next line of work was portraiture, and he joined the National Portrait Society. His portraits, though sound, were not especially distinguished; until the thirties his chief reputation derived from romantic and decorative landscapes in oils. In his early decorative period Connard produced highly stylized compositions which might contain Harlequins, pierrettes, and the like, or very often birds, which he loved dearly. These, though often adapted to decorative uses, were based on careful naturalistic sketches which he made at the Zoo.

As time went on, Connard was asked to carry out sundry important decorative commissions, which included admirable murals in the royal Doll's House room at Windsor. He painted two panels for the main ballroom at Delhi, and for the liner *Queen Mary* he executed a decorative panel 26 feet by 14 feet on the subject of 'England'. Public authorities began to take notice of him and his work is to be seen at the Tate Gallery, the Luxembourg, and many other public galleries. There are also more than forty of his works in the Imperial War Museum. During the war of 1914–18 he served in the Royal Field Artillery as a captain, but was invalided out and became an official artist to the Royal Navy.

As he approached his middle years, Connard began to use water-colours, in which he may be thought to have attained his highest distinction, for a natural good taste and a delicacy of touch and feeling made his work highly ethereal with a subtle apprehension of atmosphere. He became an associate member of the Royal Society of Painters in Water Colours and was quickly promoted to full membership (1934). His dealings with the Royal Academy were unusual in that he submitted no work there until he was admitted as an associate in 1918. Thereafter he showed regularly every year and was promoted R.A. in 1925.

In later life Connard went to live at Richmond, where he had a house overlooking the Thames, and there he painted many riverside scenes which were unlike his earlier works, being far more realistic in style. Connard never allowed himself

to become set in any artistic rut, nor was he a disciple of Post-Impressionism or kindred theories. He was most versatile and all his work had a characteristic 'handwriting'. He was appointed C.V.O. in 1950.

Connard was a man of equable and pleasant disposition though on certain issues his friends were apt to find him obstinate and pig-headed. He was a faithful member of the Arts Club, where he often forgathered with such special cronies as Sir William Orpen and F. Derwent Wood [qq.v.]. An excellent raconteur, he could set the table in a roar with his Lancashire stories.

He was twice married: first, in 1904, to Mary (died 1927), daughter of Archdeacon Daniel Collyer, by whom he had two daughters; secondly, in 1933, to Georgina Yorke, of Twickenham, who figured in many of his later interior paintings. He died at Twickenham 8 December 1958. A pencil drawing by George Lambert became the property of a daughter.

[*Studio*, June 1923; *The Times*, 9 December 1958; private information.]
HERBERT B. GRIMSDITCH

CONYNGHAM, SIR GERALD PONSONBY LENOX- (1866–1956), geodesist [See LENOX-CONYNGHAM.]

COOK, ARTHUR BERNARD (1868–1952), classical scholar and archaeologist was born in Hampstead 22 October 1868 the son of William Henry Cook, M.D., and his wife, Harriet Bickersteth, of a family which produced several noted evangelical figures, including her brother, Edward Henry Bickersteth [q.v.], who became bishop of Exeter. Cook's younger brothers (Sir) Albert Ruskin Cook and John Howard Cook, both became medical missionaries in Uganda. A scholar of St. Paul's School in a brilliant period and of Trinity College, Cambridge, Cook obtained first classes in both parts of the classical tripos (1889–91), won the Craven scholarship and the Chancellor's medal for English verse in 1889, the Chancellor's first medal for classics (1891), and the Members' prize for Latin essay (1892). From 1893 to 1899 he was a fellow of Trinity; Queens' College then elected him lecturer in classics in 1900, a fellow three years later, and in 1935 vice-president. From 1893 he was professor of Greek at Bedford College, London, until in 1907 he became reader in classical archaeology at

Cambridge. He proceeded Litt.D. in 1926 and in 1931 became the first holder of the Laurence chair of classical archaeology from which he retired in 1934. He was elected F.B.A. in 1941, and he was a foreign member of the American Philosophical Society and the German Archaeological Institute.

On men reading classics in Trinity in Cook's time Henry Jackson [q.v.] exercised a remarkable and richly merited influence, and it was no accident that Cook's first book was The Metaphysical Basis of Plato's Ethics (1895). But there were other forces to influence him in his formative years. There was the archaeological teaching of J. H. Middleton [q.v.] and Charles Waldstein (later Sir Charles Walston) to whom Cook did justice in his wise and delightful inaugural lecture, 'The Rise and Progress of Classical Archaeology' 1931): Middleton clearly meant much to him. There was comparative philology, then obligatory for all who took the classical tripos. There was also (Sir) James Frazer [q.v.], not teaching but present and working in the full enthusiasm of the movement of thought to which (Sir) E. B. Tylor and William Robertson Smith [q.v.] had given so powerful an impulse. In England as elsewhere the history of religion then excited interest as perhaps never before or since. Cook's deep and continuing evangelical piety predisposed him towards thought on these things, without alienating him from those who shared his interest but not his beliefs.

As early as 1894 Cook published his 'Animal Worship in the Mycenaean Age' (Journal of Hellenic Studies), soon followed by 'The Bee in Greek Mythology' (ibid., 1895) and other papers, among which that on 'Greek Votive Offerings' (Folk-Lore, 1903) is notable. Cook did not restrict his range of interests. As a young man he planned to edit Theocritus and with his friend Peter Giles [q.v.] did a considerable amount of preliminary work now lodged in the university library. The Classical Review contains his highly original and stimulating papers on 'Associated Reminiscences' (1901) and 'Unconscious Iterations' (1902); a quarter of a century later he served as general editor for Methuen's Handbooks of Archaeology. But Cook's real vocation was the study of ancient religion and in particular of the sky-god Zeus. A series of papers in the Classical Review between 1902 and 1906 and another in Folk-Lore between 1903 and 1907 were the fore-

runners of his monumental Zeus, A Study in Ancient Religion (3 vols., 1914, 1925, and 1940). This shows a fabulous command of every kind of material which could be brought to bear on the subject—ancient literature, monumental evidence, the Near Eastern background, and folk-lore and folk-ways from all parts, all presented with supreme accuracy and so indexed as to be instantly available. Zeus would be indispensable to students in many fields even if every single conclusion of its author were rejected. Perhaps no one has equalled Cook in his ability to present the views of others with generous fairness and to state objections to his own; no one has surpassed him in awareness of the fact that the ancients took their gods seriously. He constantly brought forth new data and parallels and suggestive ideas, and his sheer knowledge of the works of ancient art was so wide and thorough that his lack of aesthetic taste hardly affected his powers of interpreting and illustrating them. On the other hand, his sense of historical criticism and chronological stratification was weak: he drew confident inferences for early times from very late writers, and he never appreciated Wissowa's fundamental discovery of the contrast between the religious heritages of Rome and Greece.

Cook could not, like his friend Frazer, live a life of pure research, and he probably would not have wished to do so. He was an admirable lecturer, always clear, thorough, and entertaining, and he was supremely helpful to younger men, whether undergraduates or colleagues. Anyone who came to consult him was sure to go away with 'a pocket of references' and a sense of encouragement. His weight of learning was never oppressive and was accompanied by a warm friendliness, a joy in living, and a puckish humour which went with the twinkle of his keen eyes. He had a superb assemblage of books and coins and other objects of art, nearly all put together to serve the studies to which he gave his life. His natural instinct for collecting extended to the maintenance of a scrapbook for tales of the uncanny and of extrasensory perception. He never seemed pressed for time and knew how to relax in talk or tennis or travel; his spare, wiry physique appeared to sustain with ease his long labours. He bore ill health in his closing years with serene courage and without losing his old gaiety. Almost his last words before his death, as the opening verses of the 121st psalm were read to him, were 'that is a mistranslation'. He died in Cambridge 26 April 1952.

In 1894 Cook married Emily (died 1943), daughter of George Thomas Maddox, of Hampstead. They had one daughter, and a son who died in infancy.

A portrait of Cook by Trevor Haddon is at Queens' College.

[*The Times*, 28 April 1952; Charles Seltman in *Proceedings* of the British Academy, vol. xxxviii, 1952; personal knowledge.]

A. D. NOCK.

COOPER, ALFRED DUFF, first VIS-COUNT NORWICH (1890–1954), politician, diplomatist, and author, was born at 9 Henrietta Street, Cavendish Square, London, 22 February 1890, the fourth child and only son of (Sir) Alfred Cooper by his wife, Lady Agnes Cecil Emmeline Duff, sister of the first Duke of Fife. His father, who came of a family long established in Norwich, was a popular and successful London surgeon. His mother had been twice previously married. While still a child he acquired from his sisters a love of poetry, a gift for memorizing, and the habit of declamation. He was educated at Eton where he achieved no special prominence and after a year abroad went up in 1908 to New College, Oxford.

His mother by then had retired into secluded widowhood and his three sisters had married. His Eton friend, John Manners, introduced him to Clovelly Court, near Bideford, where he stayed every summer from 1908 to 1914, and where he met the more gifted and vigorous of his contemporaries. They cured him of a tendency to dilettantism and aroused in him the ambition to secure the richest prizes which life had to offer. This ambition was not, it is true, very apparent during his first two years at Oxford. He made a few pugnacious speeches in the Union, profited much from the guidance of his tutor, H. A. L. Fisher [q.v.], but in the end obtained only second class honours in history (1911).

After two years spent mainly in Hanover and Paris he passed into the Foreign Office in October 1913. Many of his dearest friends, including John Manners, were killed during the early stages of the war and it irked him to be tied to a civilian job. In July 1917 he obtained his release from the Foreign Office and, after a period of training, joined the 3rd battalion of the Grenadier Guards in time for the offensive. On 21 August 1918, in the Battle of Albert, known as 'the battle of

the mist', he led his platoon with such skill and gallantry that he was cited in dispatches for 'splendid leading' and was appointed to the D.S.O. On demobilization he returned to the Foreign Office.

In 1919 he married Lady Diana Olivia Winifred Maud Manners, daughter of the eighth Duke of Rutland, and one of the most beautiful women of her time. In her he found a dazzling and valiant companion, who watched over him with intelligent devotion until his death. At their house at 90 Gower Street, where they lived for seventeen years, they would entertain the survivors of his own generation together with some of their older friends, such as Augustine Birrell, Edwin Montagu, Maurice Baring, Hilaire Belloc [qq.v.], Lord Beaverbrook, and (Sir) Winston Churchill. Duff Cooper's ambition to enter Parliament was stimulated by these associations and by the fact that, on being appointed private secretary to the parliamentary under-secretary in February 1922, he was regularly attending debates in the House of Commons. The difficulty was finance. In 1923, however, Lady Diana obtained a rewarding contract to play the leading part in *The Miracle* in New York. On 31 July 1924 Duff Cooper, who had never been a natural civil servant, resigned from the Foreign Office and in October of that year he was elected Conservative member of Parliament for Oldham. On 15 December he delivered an impressive maiden speech which immediately placed him in the forefront of the back-benchers. In January 1928 he was appointed financial secretary to the War Office, but lost his seat in the general election of 1929. He was consoled by the birth of his son, John Julius, on 15 September 1929. He devoted the leisure to working on his biography of *Talleyrand* which, when published in 1932, earned universal acclaim.

In March 1931 a by-election occurred in the St. George's division of Westminster. Certain Conservatives, with the encouragement and support of Lord Rothermere [q.v.] and Lord Beaverbrook, decided to put up an independent candidate as a protest against Baldwin's leadership of the party. Duff Cooper volunteered to stand as the official Conservative. After a spirited campaign, which attracted much public attention, he won by 5,710 votes and retained the seat until he resigned it in 1945. In September 1931 he resumed his former post as financial secretary to the War Office; in June 1934 he was promoted to financial secretary to the Treasury; in November 1935 he became secretary of state for war and a privy counsellor.

During the abdication crisis in 1936 Duff Cooper was one of the two cabinet ministers whom, with Baldwin's approval, King Edward VIII consulted. Realizing that His Majesty's resolve could not be shaken, Duff Cooper begged him to postpone his marriage for a year and meanwhile to be crowned. The King felt it would be wrong to go through so solemn a ceremony as the coronation without letting his ultimate intentions be known: this advice he therefore rejected.

In May 1937, when Chamberlain succeeded Baldwin as prime minister, Duff Cooper was, to his surprise and pleasure, offered the post of first lord of the admiralty. Meanwhile he had been able to complete his life of *Haig*, undertaken at the request of the executors, in two volumes (1935–6). Duff Cooper enjoyed being first lord. He got on well with the naval staff, he grappled with the problem of the Fleet Air Arm, and he strove to put the navy in readiness for a war which he saw to be inevitable. Chamberlain, with whom he was never on terms of ease or confidence, did not support these endeavours. Duff Cooper, having abandoned his initial trust in the League of Nations, had fallen back on the two classic principles that Great Britain must be the natural' enemy of any power seeking to dominate the Continent, and that it was a mistake to have more than one major enemy at a time. Thus, although he was not opposed to an agreement with Italy, he was convinced that any compromise with Hitler would prove unworkable. When, therefore, the Czechoslovak crisis rose in the autumn of 1938, he found himself at variance with Chamberlain and the majority of his colleagues. It was with difficulty that he obtained their approval of the mobilization of the Fleet which took place on 28 September. When three days later Chamberlain returned from Munich, bringing with him the terms of his agreement with Hitler, Duff Cooper was unable to share the general relief and jubilation. On 3 October, in a speech which shocked the country and profoundly impressed the House of Commons, he demonstrated that the Munich agreement was meaningless and dishonourable. Even among those who were most pained by his opinion there was admiration for his moral courage.

Immediately on his resignation he accepted an offer from Lord Beaverbrook to write a weekly article for the *Evening Standard*. Although he did not always share the political views of Lord Beaverbrook, he was accorded complete independence on the condition that the editor need not publish, although he must pay for, any article of which he disapproved. The winter of 1939–40 was devoted to an extended lecture tour in the United States. When in May 1940 (Sir) Winston Churchill succeeded Chamberlain, Duff Cooper was given the post of minister of information. On 26 June 1940 after the fall of France, he flew with Lord Gort [q.v.] on a forlorn hope to Rabat with the intention of establishing contact with those French ministers, such as Georges Mandel, who were credited with the wish to continue resistance in North Africa. The French authorities had orders to prevent any such meeting, if necessary by force: Duff Cooper returned to London with his mission unaccomplished. In July 1941 he left the Ministry of Information with a sigh of relief and became chancellor of the Duchy of Lancaster. In August he left for the Far East on behalf of the War Cabinet to examine and report on the arrangements for consultation and co-ordination between the various British authorities, military, administrative and political, in those regions. After Pearl Harbour he was appointed resident cabinet minister at Singapore and authorized to form a War Council, but the appointment of' Sir A. P. (later Earl) Wavell [q.v.] as supreme commander very shortly afterwards made his post redundant. He arrived in England in February 1942 to find that his name had been associated with responsibility for the Singapore collapse. He consoled himself for this unfairness by working hard as chairman, from June, of the cabinet committee on security and by writing a romantic study of King David (1943).

In January 1944 he arrived at Algiers as British representative with the French Committee of National Liberation established in North Africa under General de Gaulle. In September 1944 his mission moved to Paris and on 18 November he presented his letters of credence as British ambassador. During their three years' residence at the embassy Duff Cooper and Lady Diana sought by their tact and hospitality to heal the wounds left by the war and the aftermath of Vichy. Duff Cooper's aim had always been to secure a treaty of alliance: at first his efforts were hampered by the incompatibility existing between de Gaulle and Churchill: it was not until March 1947 that the treaty was finally signed by Bidault and Ernest Bevin [q.v.] at Dunkirk. When, at the end of 1947, he lost his post as ambassador he had the satisfaction of knowing that the main purposes of his mission had been achieved. He was appointed G.C.M.G. in 1948 and raised to the peerage as Viscount Norwich, of Aldwick, in 1952.

The remainder of his life after his retirement was devoted to literature and to entertaining his friends at his house at Vineuil near Chantilly. His ingenious fantasy *Sergeant Shakespeare* as well as a selection from his poems were published in 1949. In 1950 came his novel *Operation Heartbreak*. His remarkable autobiography *Old Men Forget* appeared in 1953. A few weeks later, on 1 January 1954, he died when on a voyage to the West Indies. His body was landed at Vigo and buried at Belvoir Castle, the home of his wife's family.

Duff Cooper possessed a striking personality. Although too reserved to win popularity, and too proud to court it, he influenced his contemporaries by the force of his courage, the vigour of his principles, and the distinction of his mind, his manners, and his discourses. He was choleric in argument and pugnacious in debate; yet in his later manhood he was never, as some imagined, a fanatical conservative, since he regarded as 'barbarians' all extremists, whether of the Right or the Left. Although his political ambitions waned in middle life, he never lost his zest for literature, travel, conversation, shooting, wine, and the society of gifted and beautiful women. 'Life has been good to me', he wrote in the last paragraph of his autobiography, 'and I am grateful.'

He was succeeded by his son John Julius (born 1929) who entered the Foreign Service and resigned in 1964. A portrait of Duff Cooper by Sir John Lavery, painted in 1919, is at the Château de St. Firmin, Vineuil, Oise. There is a memorial tablet in the crypt of St. Paul's Cathedral.

[Duff Cooper, *Old Men Forget*, 1953; Diana Cooper, *The Rainbow Comes and Goes*, 1958, *The Light of Common Day*, 1959, and *Trumpets from the Steep*, 1960; private information; personal knowledge.]   HAROLD NICOLSON.

COOPER, THOMAS MACKAY, BARON COOPER OF CULROSS (1892–1955), lord justice-general of Scotland, was born in Edinburgh 24 September 1892, the elder son by a second marriage of John Aitken Cooper, burgh engineer of Edinburgh with Margaret Mackay, from Dunnet. His father, who came from Culross, died when Tom Cooper was eight. At nine he entered George Watson's College and left at sixteen, dux of the school, medallist in English, Latin, and Greek, with second place in mathematics and winner of the North American prize for dynamics and chemistry. He passed to Edinburgh University, taking first place in its open bursary list, and graduated M.A. with first class honours in classics (1912) and LL.B. with distinction (1914). For a time during the war he worked in the War Trade Department in London and for his services was appointed O.B.E. in 1920.

Cooper had passed advocate in 1915 and returning to the bar in 1919 made rapid progress. He had the advantage through a maternal uncle, of valuable legal connections, but he had also gifts of advocacy and a knowledge of many technical subjects which pointed to an assured forensic career. He took silk in 1927. After eight years of large senior practice he was elected Conservative member for West Edinburgh in May 1935 and appointed solicitor-general for Scotland. In October of the same year he became lord advocate and was sworn of the Privy Council. He proved himself to be one of the most efficient and popular lord advocates, it is said, that Scotland had ever had. In June 1941 he succeeded Lord Aitchison [q.v.] as lord justice-clerk with the judicial title of Lord Cooper, and in January 1947 he became lord justice general and lord president of the Court of Session. Serious illness overtook him in the late summer of 1954 and he resigned office in December. He had received his barony in June 1954, but, because of illness, he was never able to take part in the business of the Upper House, his sole appearance there being the occasion of his introduction undertaken with great difficulty in March 1955.

Cooper had a well-equipped legal mind. His judgements were vigorous, penetrating, and lucid. As a lawyer he will stand favourable comparison with the most eminent of his predecessors. He was a steadfast supporter of the principles of Scots law, frequently commenting on the unfortunate intrusion into these principles of English legal conceptions and precedents. Perhaps the most publicized of his judgements was that, given shortly before he retired, in an action challeng-

he adoption for Scotland of the numeral I in the title of Queen Elizabeth (*MacCormick v. H.M. Advocate*, 1953 S.C. 396). Though the action failed on certain preminary pleas, Lord Cooper took occasion to criticize the English principle of the sovereignty of Parliament in relation to the Treaty of Union between Scotland and England.

He was active in the formation in 1934 of the Stair Society to study and advance the history of Scots law, and made a number of contributions to its publications, the chief being *Regiam Majestatem* (1947). Independently of the society he published a 1944 *Select Scottish Cases of the Thirteenth Century*. A member of the Scottish History Society from 1934, he gave, as its president (1946–9), four addresses which he published under the title of *Supra repidam* (1951), claiming them to be merely addresses by an amateur to specialists on their own subject. It has been said that his keen perception as an historian is best seen in these addresses. Numerous other addresses and contributions to periodicals, collected in *Selected Papers, 1922–1954*, published by his brother in 1957 after his death, show his breadth of view and width of learning, as also the spirit of a reformer. He was an original member of the Scottish committee on the *History of Parliament* and latterly chairman of its executive committee until his death. When a judge he was called on to be chairman of a number of government committees on Scottish problems; the most important, on hydroelectric development in Scotland (1941–), resulted in the setting up of the North of Scotland Hydro-Electric Board. He was a trustee of the National Galleries of Scotland from 1947, for a short time (1946–9) chairman of the Ancient Monuments Board for Scotland, and, as lord president, trustee *ex officio* of the National Library of Scotland.

Cooper was a man of restless energy, great industry, keen intellect, and a rapid worker. He had a scientific bent of mind, with the genius for the practical application of his knowledge. He was a fellow of the Royal Society of Edinburgh and its vice-president (1945–8), a fellow of the Society of Antiquaries (Scotland), a fellow of the Royal Astronomical Society, and a member of the Astronomical Society of Edinburgh which lent him a telescope which he had erected in his garden. Essentially a friendly man, Cooper was nevertheless shy, not a man of the world

or socially inclined, although drawn to men with whom he could converse on a basis of common understanding. He was happy with very young children, whom he would amuse with drawings and stories, but his interest in them evaporated when they left childhood. He loved animals and never failed to hold converse with a cat. He had some interest in music and art, taught himself to play the piano and organ, and engaged in sketching. He was devoted to his mother with whom he made his home for substantially the whole of his life, surviving her by less than four years. He died in Edinburgh, unmarried, 15 July 1955.

Cooper was an honorary LL.D. of Edinburgh, Glasgow, and St. Andrews, and received an honorary doctorate of Paris University, a signal honour for a Scottish judge. He was an honorary master of the bench of the Middle Temple and honorary member of the Society of Public Teachers of Law, of the Institution of Municipal Engineers, and of the Edinburgh Merchant Company.

A posthumous portrait of Cooper in his robes as lord justice-general, by Sir William Hutchison, hangs in Parliament House, Edinburgh.

[Lord Cooper of Culross, *Selected Papers, 1922–1954*, ed. James M. Cooper, 1957; *Scotsman*, 16 July 1955; *Scots Law Times*, 30 July 1955; private information; personal knowledge.]   KEITH OF AVONHOLM.

COPE, SIR ALFRED WILLIAM (1877–1954), civil servant, was born near Kennington Oval 14 January 1877, the eldest of the eleven children of Alfred Cope, bottle merchant, and his wife, Margaret Elizabeth Dallimore. Familiar friends called him Andy. He entered government service as a boy clerk; joined the detective branch of the department of customs and excise in 1896; and was made a preventive inspector in 1908. His energy and intelligence soon made him head of the branch in London, and he spent ten adventurous years pursuing smugglers and illicit distillers, especially in dockland. In 1919 he was transferred to the Ministry of Pensions as second secretary. The Ministry was paralysed by overwork when he arrived. He effected a substantial office reorganization, chiefly by drastic cuts in the staff, and thus attracted Lloyd George's attention.

In the summer of 1920 Cope went to Dublin as one of the two new assistant under-secretaries under Sir John Anderson (later Viscount Waverley, q.v.), the other being (Sir) Mark (Grant-) Sturgis. Cope was also the last clerk of the Irish Privy Council. Ostensibly his task was to preserve civil order through the Royal Irish Constabulary; in fact he had already been charged by Lloyd George with the task of sounding out Sinn Fein opinion about the possibilities of a truce in the Anglo-Irish war. He was thoroughly used to irregular negotiations, unavowable activities, and unconventional approaches; his social origins made him uncomfortable in the official round trodden by his predecessors and contemporaries in Dublin Castle, and helped him to move easily far outside it. Moreover he was as brave as he was quick-witted. His courage never failed him, although he sometimes appeared irritable or despondent. After several false starts, he secured the confidence of the principal Irish revolutionary leaders, Michael Collins, Arthur Griffith [qq.v.] and Eamon de Valera, in his own good faith, while remaining perfectly loyal to the Crown. It was he who brought de Valera and Sir James Craig (later Viscount Craigavon, q.v.) into touch, and he played a major part in securing the truce of 11 July 1921. After the signature of the treaty in December he remained in Dublin until October 1922 to supervise the disbanding of the Royal Irish Constabulary and generally to wind up British administration. His relations with the Irish leaders continued to provide useful intelligence for Downing Street. He was appointed C.B. in 1920 and promoted K.C.B. in October 1922.

For two years Cope was secretary of the National Liberal Party, but he found close co-operation with Lloyd George impossible, and abandoned politics altogether. From 1925 to 1935 he was, at the nomination of Sir Alfred Mond (later Lord Melchett, q.v.), managing director of Amalgamated Anthracite Collieries, Ltd., a post which made further demands on his courage and diplomatic skill; in it he welded several small pits into an economically viable whole. In 1935 he retired to Seaford on the Sussex coast, where he played some part in local politics. He rejoined Anderson for a few months at the beginning of the war of 1939–45, but was persuaded again to retire. He died at Seaford 13 May 1954.

[Sir John W. Wheeler-Bennett, *John Anderson, Viscount Waverley*, 1962; *The Times*, 14 May and 8 June 1954; private information.]
                                   M. R. D. Foot.

COPISAROW, MAURICE (1889–1959 chemist, was born at Biruch in Russia, August 1889, the son of Conan and Sara Copisarow. His father was a milita: secretary. After emigrating to Englar Copisarow was taken under the wing Chaim Weizmann [q.v.], later first pres dent of Israel and then a lecturer chemistry at the university of Manchester Copisarow obtained his M.Sc. in 1914 a was trained in research methods Weizmann. A joint paper published 1915 dealt with new phthalides of t benzene, naphthalene, and carbaz series. He was naturalized in that year.

Copisarow's originality was ea evinced; even from 1914 he publish papers mostly without collaborators, ve occasionally with a junior colleague. first his work was in the field of synthe organic chemistry, for example on n applications of the Friedel Craft reactic but even in the early years he develop wider interests and these gradually a sorbed his whole attention. In 1914 wrote on the structure and mode of oxic tion of carbon, and this led to a series memoirs on the subject of allotropy.

He was Dalton research scholar (191 16), honorary research fellow (1916–1 and in 1925 obtained his D.Sc. The nec sity to eke out meagre resources co pelled him to accept a variety of tas which interfered with the smooth cou of his scientific development. He work as temporary demonstrator in chemistry department, and on behalf the research committee of the Ro Society, and for the Department Scientific and Industrial Research a the Ministry of Munitions. In the sumr of 1915 he was sent by Professor H. Dixon, certainly on the nomination Weizmann, to organize the analyti section of the newly installed trinit toluene plant at the government factory Gorton. He soon found the Woolw Arsenal specifications to be quite adequate, limited as they were to conditions of nitration and a few test the product. New problems were purification of T.N.T.; the action alkalis thereon; the related question inherent acidity; the utilization of rapi accumulating residues. These led to tensive research, partly published *Chemical News*, but the most signific paper was held back until after armistice, at the express wish of L Moulton [q.v.]. This work was ins mental in substituting steam treatmen

rude T.N.T. for the very dangerous alkali
vash. Copisarow also showed how to
tilize the waste products, a great hazard
n account of their instability, by con-
ersion into gelatinous dynamite, chloro-
icrin, and khaki dyes.

During three years' work with the
linistry of Munitions, Copisarow was on
he so-called coaltar chemical testing
taff, stationed at Manchester University.
n 1919–22 he was on the research staff of
ritish Dyestuffs Corporation. One sub-
ct of a patent in the dyestuff field was
n the industrial production of carbazole
s a base for Hydron Blue. This was
cquired by Levinstein, Ltd. He also
eveloped a continuous process for the
onversion of toluene and the xylenes to
enzene.

As early as 1917 Copisarow's eyesight
gan to fail and the deterioration was
oubtless accelerated by contact with
ich toxic materials as phosgene, chloro-
crin, and T.N.T. He had eight unsuccess-
l eye operations; and lost the sight of
th eyes shortly after 1925. Owing to this
d general bad health he had no employ-
ent after 1922. Between 1925 and 1927
had several major operations for
stric and duodenal troubles and was
tificially fed for a period of six months.
is indomitable character was clearly dis-
ayed in these extremely adverse circum-
ances. Never disposing of ample means,
en in the war, he first of all set to work
th his wife to establish a successful
siness connected with furs; then set up
laboratory in his attic and wrote a
ies of papers on the most varied topics,
of which are characterized by the
hest originality and many of which
uld be profitably reread. After 1932 the
ect of the slump in trade compelled the
pisarows to realize and utilize all their
all means, to resort to mortgages and
rrowing on life policies. Nevertheless
y managed to bring up and educate
eir two children.

Among the more important topics which
gaged Copisarow's interest in his later
ars was, first, the mode of synthesis of
rble and alabaster. He provided evi-
nce which justified the replacement of
igneous theory of Sir James Hall
v.] by a new hydrothermal conception
the formation of marble. He also
eloped his ideas on rock formation
other directions. He wrote on the
alescence of Silicic Acid Gels', 'Silica
the Liesegang Phenomenon', and 'The
ucture of Hyalite and Opal'. Secondly,

he wrote on the fundamentals of periodicity and the co-ordination of physical and
chemical periodic structures; thirdly, on
mineral arborial growth: its range and
bearing on the form of organic structures.
Fourthly, he studied the biochemical
causes of malignant growth and possible
control of carcinoma. Much of this activity
was of a theoretical nature and was published in the Edinburgh Medical Journal.
After reading one of his reviews Lord
Webb-Johnson [q.v.] commented: 'The
production of such a comprehensive review and the sound judgment that pervades the whole presentation is really a
most remarkable piece of work. I am
astounded that an unsighted man has
been able to accomplish it.' Copisarow
was very interested in enzymes and wrote
about their action in relation to malignant
growth and also in relation to radiation
and to influenza and other viruses.

Among many agricultural topics which
he studied were the preservation of fruit
and vegetables, natural and artificial
fertilizers, destruction of bracken; and a
method for making new materials from
woody and other cellulosic starting-
points. Finally, an essay on the ancient
Egyptian, Greek, and Hebrew concepts
of the Red Sea, published in Vetus Testa-
mentum, showed that Copisarow's erudition was not entirely confined to scientific
matters.

In the tragic circumstances of his later
life it was impossible to bring much of this
work to full fruition, but his papers teem
with original ideas. Physical infirmity
deprived the world of the full development of his undoubted genius.

In 1919 Copisarow married Eda Cohen,
of Manchester. They had a daughter and
a son, Alcon Charles Copisarow, who in
1964–6 was chief scientific officer of the
Ministry of Technology. Copisarow died in
Manchester 13 April 1959.

[Private information; personal knowledge.]
R. ROBINSON.

COPPARD, ALFRED EDGAR (1878–
1957), story-writer and poet, was born
at Folkestone 4 January 1878, the eldest
of a family of four, the others being sisters.
His father, George Coppard, was a journeyman tailor, and his mother, Emily
Alma Southwell, had been a housemaid.
They were 'shockingly poor', although as
Coppard was to recall in his unfinished
autobiography, published posthumously,
the two rooms comprising their home were
'snug enough'. The father was a lover of

flowers, birds, and the open air: sometimes on Sundays 'he would hoist me on
to his shoulders and take me for a bit of a
ramble'. But it was not until they moved
to Brighton, when the boy was five, that
their fortunes improved sufficiently for
them to live for the first time as sole
tenants of a house. Ill health terminated
the boy's schooling at nine, but it was his
father's death which then made it necessary for him to go out to work. A vendor
of paraffin and firewood employed him to
call 'oil, oil' in his shrill voice along street
after shabby street. By the time he was
twenty he had worked for an auctioneer,
a cheesemonger, a soap-agent, and a
carrier. He next spent several years in the
office of an engineering firm, and then in
1907 moved to Oxford as confidential
clerk in the Eagle Ironworks.

It was on the first of April 1919 that
Coppard gave up his business occupation
and began full-time as a professional
writer. ' "All Fools" Day was truly the
congenial date of it', he recalled, for he
had saved only fifty pounds and, moreover, he was married. Indeed, his office
colleagues thought he was 'daft'. Nevertheless, many years later he was honoured
by his old firm, which showed great pride
in his literary achievement.

His early enthusiasm for reading and
study had not lessened while he was still
a clerk, and he gained sufficient success as
a spare-time athlete to use the prize-
money to buy books and shape himself for
his literary vocation. He appreciated the
atmosphere of Oxford where he 'was fired,
though not by any more worthy muse than
the spirit of rivalry'. He had tried himself
out in writing and received some editorial
encouragement here and there. The deep
impression made on his creative mind by
Chekhov, Maupassant, Thomas Hardy,
and Katherine Mansfield—also Henry
James as a short-story-writer—had already determined him to concentrate on
their particular literary form. But in his
first three months as a free lance he sold
only 'one little tale, one little poem, and
received twenty rejections'. It was therefore a timely relief and encouragement
when an American periodical paid him
fifty pounds for a story of a few thousand
words.

In 1921 his first collection, *Adam and
Eve and Pinch Me*, was published by the
young owner of the Golden Cockerel Press
who had been impressed by Coppard's
early efforts. This volume was the forerunner of a lengthy series of collected short

stories. The characteristic and wholl[y]
individual level was maintained throughout his career, and the praise bestowed o[n]
him at the beginning by Ford Madox For[d]
[q.v.] might have been applied to eac[h]
volume, for it was only rarely and brief[ly]
that his work fell from its high standard[.]
'He is almost the first English prose
writer to get into English prose th[e]
peculiar quality of English lyric poetry—
the fancy, the turn of the imagination, th[e]
wisdom . . . and the beauty of the grea[t]
lyricists.' Apparent in everything Coppar[d]
wrote was a deep love of all human life
but his unique creations revealed [a]
whimsical preference for the misfit an[d]
the underdog. His detestation of injustic[e]
and cruelty caused him dismay, notabl[y]
when a friend planned to attend a bu[ll]
fight while visiting Spain; and he becam[e]
prominent in the peace movement.

Coppard ranks with Katherine Man[s]-
field [q.v.] in contemporary literatu[re]
although his simplicity and utter lack [of]
sophistication recall an older poet of h[is]
time, W. H. Davies [q.v.]. Indeed, poetr[y]
as well as prose occupied him from the ou[t]-
set, and *Hips and Haws*, the first of fi[ve]
volumes of lyrics, came out in the sam[e]
year as his second book of stories, *Clorind[a]
Walks in Heaven* (1922). Between 19[22]
and 1951 hardly a year passed without [a]
publication bearing the imprint A.
Coppard: *Fishmonger's Fiddle* (192[5],
Silver Circus (1928), *Nixey's Harlequ[in]*
(1931), *Crotty Shinkwin* (1932), and *Du[nky]
Fitlow* (1933) are examples of the tit[les]
he invented for what proved to be h[is]
best successes. *You Never Know Do Yo[u]*
(1939) renewed an old literary fashion [of]
exclamatory titles, and later *It's Me,
Lord!* was the title given to the first part [of]
his autobiography, published a few mont[hs]
after his death in London 13 January 19[57].

His closing years were heartened by t[he]
Book of the Month Club of Ameri[ca]
which issued his *Selected Tales* (1946) to [a]
vast membership, the first occasion [on]
which it had made a work of this kind [its]
leading choice. The undergraduates [of]
Oxford paid him tribute with a celeb[ra]-
tion of his seventy-fifth birthday, atten[ded]
by many distinguished personages, [in]-
cluding Sir Maurice Bowra the vi[ce]-
chancellor.

Coppard married first, in 1905, [to]
Annie, daughter of Albert Richards[on],
plumber, of Brighton. After her death [he]
married Winifred May, daughter of [the]
late Dirk de Kok, solicitor, of So[uth]
Africa; they had a son and a daughter

His many friends remember best his twinkling eyes and a face suggesting the kindest laughter. His last home, at Duton Hill, Dunmow, Essex, delighted him, with its encircling trees, and the birds so tame that he would pretend to be cross with them whenever they became too obtrusive. He was a football follower, and when his favourite soccer club went through a bad spell his friends were amused to receive plaintive postcards asking 'What's the matter with Chelsea?' He spent a term on a rural council, and shared his wife's enthusiasm when she was appointed assistant county medical officer in mid-Essex. She died in 1969, having become popular on television in frank discussions of family problems.

A portrait in oils of Coppard, painted in Walberswick by Tom Van Oss, is in the possession of the family. There is also a woodcut by Robert Gibbings.

[A. E. Coppard, *It's Me, O Lord!*, 1957; private information; personal knowledge.]

THOMAS MOULT.

CORBETT, EDWARD JAMES (JIM) (1875–1955), destroyer of man-eating tigers, naturalist, and author, was born at Naini Tal, India, 25 July 1875, the eighth child of Christopher William Corbett, a soldier, and his wife, Mary Jane, widow of Charles Doyle. Blessed with exceptional eyesight, hearing, and powers of observation, at the age of four or five he was spending nights alone in the jungle learning the cries, calls, and songs of beasts and birds and observing their movements and habits. His early schooling was given him by his mother and half-sister Mary, both women of sterling character. Religious and intelligent, they pervaded the family life with a spirit of service, courage, and cheerfulness, qualities which Jim richly inherited. Later at a preparatory school and at St. Joseph's College, Naini Tal, he excelled in games and popularity if not in scholarship. In 1895 he entered the service of the Bengal and North Western Railway as inspector of fuel at Mankapur and his success led to his transfer, as transshipment inspector, to take over the contract for the supply and employment of the large labour force at Mokameh Ghat, Bengal, at the crossing of the Ganges river. In a recruiting campaign in the war 1914–18 he helped to raise from Kumaon a force of over 5,000 and himself captain took 500 to France in 1917. He brought 499 back the next year and resettled them in their Kumaon villages.

With characteristic generosity he gave the whole of his war bonus to the building of a soldiers' canteen. He served as a major in the Waziristan campaign from 1919 to 1921.

A legacy of house property at Naini Tal enabled Corbett to give up his railway contract and devote his time to the welfare of the people of Kumaon. He and his sisters had a surgery at their house where sick and injured could be treated. Adjoining their winter home at Kaladhungi in the foothills was the dilapidated and almost forsaken village of Choti Haldwani. This Corbett bought and resettled, paying all the villagers' taxes up to 1960.

Corbett was a deadly shot and an expert fisherman. In his later life he preferred to photograph rather than shoot big game. Many thousand feet of film bear witness to his courage and patience. For example, for four months he daily called up tiger, finally succeeding in obtaining a long sequence of six superb specimens, of which the nearest was eight and the farthest thirty feet from his camera. No more remarkable records of wild life in India exist and these are deposited in the British Museum (Natural History). In 1907 Corbett was called on to shoot his first two man-eaters, the Champawat tiger and the Panar leopard. He shot his last of ten man-eaters in 1938. He maintained that no tiger or leopard was by nature a man-eater but that the animal became one through an injury's preventing it from pursuing its normal prey. The thrilling accounts of the destruction of these man-eaters which had taken the lives of nearly 1,500 Indians have been beautifully and modestly given in his three books: *The Man-Eaters of Kumaon* (1946), *The Man-Eating Leopard of Rudraprayag* (1948), and *The Temple Tiger* (1954). Wiry and fit, Corbett was able to endure the terrific hardships which these errands of mercy imposed: consecutive days without sleep and food and many long nights sitting cramped over a kill and always in danger. His courage and determination became proverbial and brought him the deepest affection and even worship of the people. Tall, slim, and blue-eyed, he was an extremely attractive man, notable for his modesty, kindness, and generosity, and beloved by all from viceroys to the humblest peasant.

Although sixty-four, Corbett begged to serve in the war, and from 1940 to 1942 he was deputy military vice-president of district soldiers boards. He recruited 1,400 men from Kumaon for a civil pioneer corps. Despite a serious illness in 1944 he was made lieutenant-colonel and trained men for jungle warfare in Burma.

In 1947 Corbett, who was unmarried, and his devoted sister Margaret (who died in 1963) decided to leave India and settle at Nyeri, Kenya, in the house built by Lord Baden-Powell [q.v.] and where he had died. Corbett was made an honorary game warden and devoted much time to filming wild life and to writing. In addition to the works already mentioned he published *My India* (1952), largely auto-biographical; *Jungle Lore* (1953); and *Tree Tops* (1955), an account of the visit of the Princess Elizabeth and the Duke of Edinburgh to the hotel in the tree tops near Nyeri. Of his books in English well over a million had been sold by 1957 and translations in eighteen languages had been published.

Corbett received the Volunteer decoration (1920), the Kaisar-i-Hind gold medal (1928), the O.B.E. (1942), and the C.I.E. (1946). He was granted in India the free-dom of the forests, a privilege only given once previously; and in 1957 the Indian Government decided that a game sanc-tuary established in Garhwal in 1935 should henceforth be known as the Cor-bett National Park 'in memory of one who had dedicated his life to the service of the simple hill folks of Kumaon'. Corbett died at Nyeri 19 April 1955, and lies in the same cemetery as Baden-Powell. A minia-ture by Violet Butler is in the possession of Corbett's family.

[Corbett's own writings; private informa-tion; personal knowledge.]

GEOFFREY CUMBERLEGE.

CORNFORD, FRANCES CROFTS (1886–1960), poet, was born in Cambridge 30 March 1886, the only child of (Sir) Francis Darwin [q.v.] by his second wife, Ellen Wordsworth Crofts, a great-niece of the poet and a lecturer at Newnham Col-lege. Her father, then lecturer in botany, was the third son of Charles Darwin [q.v.], whom he had helped with his biological researches. Frances was half-sister to the writer and golfing expert, Bernard Darwin, the only child of her father's first mar-riage. Her education was private, and during her childhood her chief associates were her cousins, the children of George and Horace Darwin [qq.v.]. Her mother died when she was seventeen; her father then moved their home for a short time to London, but soon returned to Cambridge

where Frances passed most of the rest o her life.

In the summer of 1908 members o the Cambridge Marlowe Dramatic Societ were arranging a performance of *Comus* a part of a Milton tercentenary celebratio at Christ's College. Francis Macdonal Cornford [q.v.], a fellow of Trinity an afterwards professor of ancient philosoph in the university, had been cast for th part of Comus. Frances Darwin wa brought in to help with the production an one direct consequence was that she an Francis Cornford were married in 190 Their home at Conduit Head off th Madingley Road soon became a meetin place for artists and men of letters such a Will Rothenstein, Eric Gill, Lowes Dicki son [qq.v.], Bertrand Russell, and o casional visitors such as Rabindranat Tagore [q.v.]. The Cornfords had fi children. The eldest son, John, showe great promise but having joined th International Brigade in the Spanish civ war was killed in battle. Their second so Christopher, became an artist and in 19 was appointed the first dean of the Roy College of Art in London.

Frances Darwin, with intellect a artistic sensibility strongly represented her forebears, started writing poetry sixteen and subsequently published sufficient body of poetry to entitle her a distinguished place among the min poets of the 'Georgian' period and lat years. Rupert Brooke [q.v.] was o of her closest friends and she was alwa eager to profit by criticism from him a others. She acknowledged much help her later years from another poet, Christ pher Hassall, and from Sir Edward Mar [q.v.]; she was herself always ready to gi help of the same kind to younger write One of her early books was a 'moralit play, *Death and the Princess* (1912). 1954 her volume of *Collected Poems* w the official 'choice' of the Poetry Bo Society and in 1959 she was awarded t Queen's medal for poetry. Her work ow little to the new fashions set by Eliot a Pound and was unpretentious, the poe usually being short, often scarcely m than epigrams. Her aim was to expr only what she truly felt, and she was a to catch and fix with economy of wo her passing emotions or moments experience realized with visual acuity a often with quiet humour. She also tr her hand with some success at ve translations, publishing *Poems from Russian* (1943, helped by Esther Sa nan), and a selection from the French of Aragon (1950). Her first book, *Poems*, published in 1910, already exhibited her chief characteristics as a poet, though she acquired later more skill in versification and a wider range of subject. Three of her books were decorated with woodcuts by her cousin, Gwen Raverat [q.v.], and one had cuts by Eric Gill.

Frances Cornford was of medium height and of brown complexion with dark hair and eyes. Her appearance was striking and attractive rather than beautiful, her attractions being increased by her gentle friendliness, her amusing conversation, and her wish to enter with warmth and imagination into the feelings and emotions of her many friends. In the ordinary affairs of life she was endearingly vague and unpractical, with an extraordinary capacity for mislaying her possessions. Her sensitive nature led to her suffering from several periods of deep depression, the first one following the shock of her mother's death. Each time, however, she made a good, though slow, recovery and she lived to the age of seventy-four, dying of heart failure in Cambridge 19 August 1960. She had not been christened as a child and was brought up without religion. As Gwen Raverat related in *Period Piece* (1952), Frances began to suffer at an early age from doubts, and long before her death had accepted with deep conviction the faith of the Church of England.

[Private information; personal knowledge.]
GEOFFREY KEYNES.

CORNWALLIS, SIR KINAHAN (1883–1959), administrator and diplomat, was born in New York 19 February 1883, the son of Kinahan Cornwallis, journalist and writer, and his wife, Elizabeth Chapman, of Hartford, Connecticut. Educated at Haileybury and University College, Oxford, where he studied jurisprudence (obtaining a second class in 1905) and arabic, he first became known to a wider public as an athlete, representing Oxford against Cambridge at athletics for four consecutive years, and was president (1904–6). On leaving Oxford he joined the Sudan Civil Service in 1906. After service in Khartoum and Kassala, his exceptional ability was recognized by the Egyptian Government who first borrowed him in 1912 for service in the Ministry of Finance, and then made him a permanent member of their Civil Service to which he belonged for the whole of his career, being seconded at different times to the Army, the Foreign Office, and the Iraq Government.

On the outbreak of war in 1914 (Sir) Gilbert Clayton [q.v.] at G.H.Q. Intelligence had Cornwallis commissioned in the Egyptian Army and took him into his own office; in 1915 he became a member of the Arab Bureau where D. G. Hogarth [q.v.] was then the director. A year later he was sent by Clayton with Hogarth and (Sir) Ronald Storrs [q.v.] to Jedda in order to obtain King Husain's approval of the Arab revolt in which T. E. Lawrence [q.v.] played a famous part.

During 1916–18 Cornwallis's service was almost entirely with the army, as assistant chief political officer to the expeditionary force. He succeeded Hogarth as director of the Arab Bureau (1916), became a lieutenant-colonel, was appointed to the D.S.O. (1917), and C.B.E. (1919), before proceeding to Syria with the Emir Feisal, who had served closely with him in matters concerning the Arab revolt from 1917 onwards.

Cornwallis returned to Cairo in the autumn of 1919, and actively continued the direction of the Arab Bureau until the winter of 1920 when he was seconded to the Middle East department of the Foreign Office in London.

Lawrence described Cornwallis in his *Seven Pillars of Wisdom* as being at this stage of his career 'a man rude to look upon, but apparently forged from one of those incredible metals with a melting point of thousands of degrees. So he could remain for months hotter than other men's white-heat, and yet look cold and hard.' Indeed, as many others have said of him, his Olympian height, big nose, piercing blue eyes, and slow gruff voice allied to a quiet manner, were most impressive. With it all, he inspired trust and confidence at all levels, among all classes, and with all colours, while his kindness, courteousness, and innate leadership evoked the loyalty of all those who served him.

May 1921 saw Cornwallis attached once more to the Emir Feisal who, after the Syrian province was placed under French military mandate, was offered and accepted the newly created throne of Iraq at Baghdad, and especially asked for Cornwallis to accompany him on his journey by sea from Jedda to Basra.

This attachment of Cornwallis was originally suggested by (Sir) Winston Churchill (then at the Colonial Office) to be for at least three months; it lasted for fourteen years, during which he remained permanently in Baghdad at the Ministry of Interior and as personal adviser to King Feisal. While the British mandate operated he worked untiringly to bring about the conclusion of the treaty of 1930, which gave independence to Iraq with strong conditions about the continuing alliance with England. Cornwallis's great influence with the tribes and ruling members of the Iraq Government enabled him to carry on the Iraqi Civil Service originated by Sir Arnold Wilson [q.v.], assisted by a core of the specially selected British political officers combined to train the Iraqis themselves for their duties when independence became possible.

Gertrude Bell [q.v.] wrote of Cornwallis then as a 'tower of strength and wisdom'; others, as one of the makers of the Iraq nation. Perhaps no other Englishman could have maintained the precarious balance at that period between the Iraqi Government and the British authorities, besides retaining throughout the unswerving confidence of King Feisal.

After the signing of the treaty, Cornwallis continued at Baghdad to supervise the workings of the new State, but King Feisal died in 1933 and was succeeded by his young and inexperienced son, Ghazi. He and his rather wilder counsellors decided that they could do without an 'elder statesman', so Cornwallis was asked in May 1935 to retire, the offer being softened by the conferment of the Order of Rafidain (first class) as a special mark of the country's appreciation of his long and devoted service. The amazing demonstration at the airport when he was leaving for England provided a proof (if proof were needed) of his unchallenged prestige, and of the affection and esteem in which he was held by all classes. During these years a C.M.G. in 1926, a knighthood in 1929, and a K.C.M.G. in 1933 underlined the recognition he received from Britain.

The outbreak of war in 1939 found Cornwallis in the Middle East division of the Ministry of Information. In February 1941 he was nominated ambassador in Baghdad where it was felt that his influence might help in a country whose attitude was becoming increasingly pro-Axis. On 2 April a rebel 'national government of defence' took over; Rashid Ali, a former prime minister anxious to co-operate with the Axis, was reinstated; the regent had fled the country. Cornwallis arrived in Baghdad absolutely opposed to

recognizing Rashid Ali to whom on the 16th he conveyed the information that under the terms of the treaty, troops from India would be arriving in Basra on the 18th en route for Palestine. The rebel government's hostility to the presence of these troops and the prospect of more culminated in a threat to the R.A.F aerodrome at Habbaniya and the investment of the embassy itself. Before communication was cut off Cornwalli approved an R.A.F. attack on the Iraqi at Habbaniya which was successfully begun on 2 May. Freya Stark, one of the beleaguered staff, in her book *East is West* (1945), brilliantly describes the ensuing month, during which Cornwallis stood out as the guiding influence. Fortunately the Germans afforded the rebels little help and the news of the slowly advancing relief force put renewed courage into the British in their unpleasant vigil in the embassy. On 31 May an armistice was signed; the regent was reinstated and a new government took office. When the mayor and two officers had come to surrender the city, they asked that the independence of the country might still be respected. Cornwallis, towering down on them from his great height, replied: 'Many years ago I fought, together with King Feisal the lamented who was my friend, for the freeing of the Arabs, and together we built up the Kingdom of Iraq. And do you think that I would willingly see destroyed what I have helped to build?'

Iraq thereafter observed the terms of the treaty with Britain and gave considerable help to the Allies. Cornwallis who was advanced to G.C.M.G. in 1944 remained as ambassador until 1945 generating confidence, a tower of strength amidst the many wartime problems. Returning to England he continued at the Foreign Office for some time as chairman of the Middle East committee, and then in 1946 went with Lord Stansgate [q.v.] to Cairo on the commission to discuss a new Egyptian treaty; but ill health beset him, and he retired altogether in that year.

In 1911 he married Gertrude Dorothy daughter of (Sir) Albert Edward Bowen later first baronet; they had two sons and one daughter. The marriage was dissolved and in 1937 he married Madge, daughter of Harry Ralph Clark, of Lymington. He died at his home in North Warnborough Hampshire, 3 June 1959.

[Private information; personal knowledge
DAVID BOYL

COUPLAND, SIR REGINALD (1884–1952), historian of the British Empire and Commonwealth, was born in London 2 August 1884, the second son of Sidney Coupland, physician, and his wife, Bessie Potter. He was educated at Winchester and New College, Oxford, where he obtained a second class in classical honour moderations in 1905 and a first class in *literae humaniores* in 1907. In the same year he was elected to a fellowship and lectureship in ancient history at Trinity College, Oxford, and seemed destined to pursue a career as a college tutor in the subject. His future was changed, however, by his coming under the strong influence of Lionel Curtis [q.v.] who persuaded him that his duty lay in the study not of ancient empires but of the modern British empire. Coupland was elected to succeed him as Beit lecturer in colonial history at Oxford in 1913, and set about learning his new subject. He resigned his fellowship at Trinity in 1914. When the Beit professorship of colonial history at Oxford became vacant in 1920 by the resignation of H. E. Egerton (whose notice he contributed to this Dictionary), Coupland was elected to it and held it until his resignation in 1948.

His tenure of the chair was marked by a steady output of books, beginning in 1923 with *Wilberforce*, a biography of distinction, which was followed in fairly quick succession by *The Quebec Act* (1925), *Raffles* (1926, a short biographical sketch of Sir Stamford Raffles, q.v.), and *The American Revolution and the British Empire* (1930), a book criticized by some Canadian and American scholars for its interpretation of the consequences upon imperial policy of the loss of the American colonies. Meanwhile in 1928 with *Kirk on the Zambesi* he had published a first book in a field in which it may be said that his best original work in imperial history was undertaken: the history of East Africa. This was followed by *East Africa and its Invaders* (1938), *The Exploitation of East Africa* (1939), and *Livingstone's Last Journey* (1945).

Along with his historical studies of the empire, Coupland maintained a keen interest in its current political problems, particularly in regard to India in which his interest was first given opportunity for practical expression when he was appointed in 1923 a member of the royal commission on the superior civil services in India which visited the country under the chairmanship of Lord Lee of Fareham [q.v.]. Coupland devoted most of the years of the war of 1939–45 to the study of India, visiting the country twice, and having the fortune to be attached in 1942 to the mission to India of Sir Stafford Cripps [q.v.], concerning which he published a short and interesting sketch, *The Cripps Mission* (1942). His major contributions to the study of Indian politics were published at this time: *The Indian Problem 1833–1935* (1942), *Indian Politics 1936–1942* (1943) in which there is to be found the first serious treatment in English of the idea of Pakistan, *The Future of India* (1943), and *India, a Re-statement* (1945). His other principal excursion into current politics was his appointment to membership of the royal commission on Palestine of 1936–7, set up under the chairmanship of Lord Peel [q.v.] which recommended the partition of the country. Coupland had considerable influence upon the deliberations of the commission and its report owed much, in substance and in style, to his mind and pen.

No account of Coupland's life and work at Oxford in the years between 1919 and 1939 would be complete without a reference to his part in fostering and in effect running the Ralegh Club, an undergraduate society whose members were chosen from the United Kingdom and other countries of the Commonwealth and which met on Sunday evenings in Rhodes House to hear and to discuss talks on imperial problems by visiting speakers. That the Ralegh Club could command such a galaxy of distinguished speakers from all over the world and that it could attract to its membership so many of the lively and influential undergraduates of the time was due almost entirely to Coupland's enthusiasm and energy, and, not least, to the high regard in which he was held in imperial circles both at home and overseas.

In the years after 1945 Coupland found himself drawn strongly to the study of nationalism in the Commonwealth, a subject which had necessarily engaged his attention to some extent in his early studies of the Quebec Act and of the American revolution and in his later studies of India. He projected a series of volumes on this theme, but failing health prevented him from completing (and then only with difficulty) more than one volume, *Welsh and Scottish Nationalism*, the text of which he handed to his publisher on the day before he died. The book, which deals with much little-known material, was published posthumously in 1954.

Coupland was an eloquent lecturer; he wrote good English, so good indeed that many scholars of duller style failed to realize the depth and solidity of his learning. Though he was not active in university politics, he played his full part in the work of the faculty boards of modern history and of social studies. He was one of the original founders of the honour school of philosophy, politics, and economics at Oxford in the years after the first world war, and he was associated also with the early years of Nuffield College, of which he was a professorial fellow from 1939 to 1950. His chair carried with it a professorial fellowship at All Souls College which he valued highly. He was in many ways an old-fashioned liberal imperialist, an idealist about the Empire, which was indeed the ruling passion and interest of his life. He was a most friendly and generous teacher; a lively and amusing talker; and a man of integrity. For his services on the Lee commission he was appointed C.I.E. in 1928. In 1944 he was appointed K.C.M.G. His distinction as an historian was recognized by an honorary D.Litt. from Durham (1938), and by election to a fellowship of the British Academy in 1948. He died suddenly on 6 November 1952, as he embarked at Southampton on a voyage to South Africa. He was unmarried. A drawing of him by Miss F. A. de Biden Footner hangs in the community centre at Wootton, the Berkshire village in which he lived for over thirty years, occupying a house named Wootton Ridge, on the southern slopes of Boar's Hill, with a splendid view to the Berkshire Downs and the Vale of White Horse.

[*The Times*, 7 November 1952; Jack Simmons in *Proceedings* of the British Academy, vol. xlv, 1959; personal knowledge.]

K. C. WHEARE.

COURTAULD, AUGUSTINE (1904–1959), Arctic explorer, was born 26 August 1904 at Bocking, Braintree, Essex, the eldest child of Samuel Augustine Courtauld, a director of the family firm, and his wife, Edith Anne (Edian), daughter of Walter Venning Lister. He was a cousin of Samuel Courtauld [q.v.]. He was educated at Charterhouse and Trinity College, Cambridge, where he read engineering and geography and graduated in 1926. In that year he joined (Sir) James Wordie's summer expedition to East

Greenland, and the next ten years of h[is] life were closely connected with this au[s]tere and beautiful country.

In 1927 he visited the Sahara wit[h] Francis Rodd (later Lord Rennell) an[d] Peter Rodd, but he returned to Greenlan[d] to accompany Wordie again in the sum[mer] of 1929 when he was one of the par[ty] which reached the summit of Peterman[n] Peak, 9,300 feet, then the highest know[n] point in the Arctic. In 1930–31 'Augus[tine]' Courtauld was a member of the Briti[sh] Arctic Air Route Expedition led by 'Gin[o]' Watkins [q.v.] which spent a year in Ea[st] Greenland investigating the possibility [of] an air route across the ice-cap to Canad[a]. An essential part of the meteorologic[al] programme was the establishment of t[he] ice-cap station some 140 miles nor[th]west of the base camp and 8,500 fe[et] above sea level, and its maintenan[ce] throughout the year by two men w[ho] would be relieved at approximate[ly] monthly intervals by dog sledge or a[ir]craft. As winter approached, weather co[n]ditions were so severe that a par[ty] including Courtauld, took six weeks [to] reach the ice-cap station from the ba[se] camp, and it became clear that it would [be] many months before it could be reliev[ed] again. All present, including the expe[di]tion doctor, strongly advised abandon[ing] the station as there was not enough f[ood] for two men to be left in safety; [but] Courtauld, who had already achieve[d a] reputation for self-sufficiency, persua[ded] the others to allow him to man the stat[ion] alone, and he was left there on 5 Dece[m]ber 1930. A relief party reached [the] vicinity of the station late in March 1[931] but, owing to appalling weather co[ndi]tions, they were unable to find it. On [the] return of the party with this alarm[ing] news, Watkins, with two companions, [left] the base camp and on 5 May located [the] ice-cap station although it was comple[tely] submerged in snow. Courtauld, [who] had spent five months alone, part [of] the time imprisoned beneath the s[now] and in darkness, was sane, unpertur[bed] and cheerful. He characteristically w[rote] of this episode that his main aim had [been] 'to dispel the strange ideas of danger [and] risk in leaving a man in such a situati[on]'. In 1932 he was awarded the Polar m[edal] by King George V.

In the summer of 1935 Courta[uld] organized an expedition to East Gr[een]land to map and climb a range of m[oun]tains which had been distantly sighted [and] photographed from an aircraft by [the]

Watkins. These proved to be the highest in the Arctic and were named the Watkins Range.

In 1932 Courtauld bought a 22-ton gaffrigged yawl which he named *Duet*. During his ice-cap vigil he had designed a yacht and *Duet* most closely resembled the boat of his dreams. Between 1932 and 1955 he made twenty-five passages of over 100 miles including several ocean races. As a seaman he was fearless and undefeated; and frequently frightened his friends.

Courtauld served through the war of 1939–45 in the Royal Naval Volunteer Reserve, first in naval intelligence, later in M.T.B.s and other craft. It is surprising that such an experienced yachtsman and a man of such proved resource should not have risen beyond the rank of lieutenant, but he was too self-effacing and too much of an individualist to take kindly to what he considered to be unnecessary regulations and restrictions, and he frequently found himself at loggerheads with authority.

After the war he devoted his unusual gifts to local government and community service, particularly those concerned with young people and the sea. He served on Essex County Council in 1945–55, became J.P. and D.L. in 1946 and high sheriff of Essex in 1953. He was a governor of Felsted School, chairman of Essex Association of Boys' Clubs, president of the Cruising Association, and vice-president of the Royal National Life-boat Institution. He served three times on the council of the Royal Geographical Society and was honorary secretary in 1948–51.

In 1953 he was found to be suffering from disseminated sclerosis and from then until he died in hospital in London 3 March 1959 he became increasingly an invalid, but with characteristic fortitude he continued to attend official and social occasions, even when confined to an invalid chair. Because of his illness his autobiography *Man the Ropes* (1957) is disappointing, but his polar anthology *From the Ends of the Earth* (1958) was the result of a lifetime's discriminating and recondite reading. He had the rare courage and single-mindedness to ignore the trammels of inherited wealth and the pressures of social life among those who did not measure up to his own standards of integrity. His disregard of the normal pressures of society sometimes gave the impression almost of perversity until one realized it was the element of intellectual honesty combined with extraordinary modesty and boyish enthusiasm which endeared him to all his friends.

In 1932 Courtauld married Mollie, elder daughter of Frank Douglas Montgomerie, land agent; they had four sons and two daughters. In October 1959 his widow married R. A. Butler (later Lord Butler of Saffron Walden).

[F. Spencer Chapman, *Northern Lights*, 1932; Augustine Courtauld, *Man the Ropes*, 1957; private information; personal knowledge.]   F. SPENCER CHAPMAN.

COWAN, SIR WALTER HENRY, baronet, of the Baltic and of Bilton (1871–1956), admiral, was born 11 June 1871 at Crickhowell, Breconshire, the eldest son of Walter Frederick James Cowan who settled after retirement from the Royal Welch Fusiliers with the rank of major at Alveston, Warwickshire. His mother was Frances Anne, daughter of Henry John Lucas, physician, of Crickhowell. Although he had never been to school, Cowan passed into the navy in 1884, in the same term as David (later Earl) Beatty [q.v.], with whom, two years later, he joined the *Alexandra*, flagship in the Mediterranean of the Duke of Edinburgh [q.v.]. Invalided after less than a year, he returned home, but eventually rejoined the *Alexandra*. She came home in 1889, and Cowan was appointed to the *Volage* in the training squadron where he was promoted sub-lieutenant in 1890. Appointed to the *Boadicea*, flagship on the East Indies station, he took passage in the *Plassy*, a gunboat which was being delivered to the Royal Indian Marine. The *Plassy* took four months to reach Bombay, being nearly lost in a Bay of Biscay storm. Promoted lieutenant in 1892, Cowan was appointed first lieutenant of the gunboat *Redbreast* whence, after about a year, he was invalided again, this time with dysentery. On recovery, he applied for the west coast of Africa, then a very unhealthy station but with the attraction for Cowan that it offered a better chance of active service in one or other of the many punitive expeditions.

He was appointed (1894) to the small cruiser *Barrosa*, in which he was to serve for three and a half years. He assisted in refloating the French gunboat *Ardent* which had grounded 170 miles up the Niger river and soon afterwards was landed with the punitive expedition against Nimbi. After three months at the Cape the *Barrosa* was due for a turn of duty on the east coast where Cowan at once came in for the Mwele expedition, followed by a number of smaller expeditions from individual ships. The *Barrosa*'s next visit to the west coast was just in time for the Benin expedition (1897) in which Cowan had control of the carriers. For the third time he was awarded the general Africa medal, this time with the Benin clasp.

His next appointment was to the *Boxer*, destroyer, in the Mediterranean, which he commanded for a bare six months before being transferred to 'Nile Service', in which he commanded the river gunboat *Sultan*. In her he took part in the battle of Omdurman (1898), after which all the gunboats were ordered to Fashoda, where a French force under Marchand had arrived via Central Africa. The task of dealing with the French devolved almost completely upon Cowan who had the satisfaction of seeing them depart for home via Abyssinia. Cowan was left in command of all the gunboats, all the other naval officers returning to England. He had over a year more in Egypt and was aide-de-camp to Sir Reginald Wingate [q.v.] in the pursuit of the Khalifa in 1899. When Lord Kitchener [q.v.] left for South Africa Cowan gained his permission to accompany him. His status was afterwards regularized by his appointment as Kitchener's aide-de-camp and the whole of 1900 was spent in the field. He returned to England with Lord Roberts [q.v.], to whose staff he had just transferred, to be greeted coldly at the Admiralty for having gone to South Africa without their lordships' permission and for having been over two years away from sea service. Yet he was appointed to the *Prince George* as first lieutenant and, in June 1901, promoted commander at the age of thirty, with only $8\frac{1}{2}$ years' service as lieutenant.

He was then appointed to command the *Falcon*, destroyer, as second-in-command of the Devonport destroyers under Roger (later Lord) Keyes [q.v.]. He had several different ships in the next two years, at the end of which, having built up a great reputation as a destroyer officer, he moved up to succeed Keyes in command, transferring in 1905, at the end of his time, to the scout *Skirmisher*, in which he was promoted captain (1906). He was then appointed to the *Sapphire* (1907) and in 1908 took command of the destroyers attached to the Channel Fleet. Then, after a year in the Reserve Fleet, he took command of a new light cruiser, the *Gloucester* (1910), for two years, taking no leave at

all in the first so that he might have plenty in the second—for hunting, always a passion with him. He got plenty of it in his next job, two years as chief of staff to (Sir) John De Robeck [q.v.], the admiral of patrols, who was just as keen.

When war broke out in 1914 Cowan was in command of the *Zealandia*, but he was not happy in a slow ship. In less than six months, however, he went to the *Princess Royal* as flag captain to (Sir) Osmond Brock [q.v.], an appointment after his own heart, for the battle cruisers were certain to be in the forefront of any action. Yet he had to wait for almost eighteen months before it came. In the battle of Jutland (31 May 1916), the *Princess Royal* was severely damaged and had over a hundred casualties. It took some two months to repair her, during which Cowan paid a visit to the British front in France. In June 1917 he was made commodore of the first light cruiser squadron. His ships were constantly at sea and Cowan with them, to his great delight, for if one were damaged and out of action he could always shift his flag to another. On one occasion they went right into the Heligoland Bight in the attempt to join action with a German light cruiser squadron chasing it to within sight of Heligoland. In 1918 he was promoted rear-admiral and remained in his command, but there was little more activity for the remainder of the war.

In January 1919 Cowan and his squadron were sent to the Baltic, where the situation was extraordinarily involved. His task, as soon appeared, was to hold the ring for Finland and the Baltic States against the Bolsheviks, while keeping the Germans, still armed, to the terms of the armistice. In this he was ably assisted ashore by (Sir) Stephen Tallents [q.v.]. His command lasted until the end of 1919 and he left only when the Russians were sealed up in Kronstadt by ice. Six months later he returned for the plebiscite in Danzig and then relinquished his command.

In 1921 he was appointed to command the battle cruiser squadron, consisting only of the *Hood* and *Repulse*. The high light of the period was a visit to Brazil in 1922 during the international exhibition where they created a great impression, for the battle cruisers had never been smarter or more efficient. Two years' unemployment followed, in the course of which he was promoted vice-admiral (1923), after which he held the Scottish command (1925–6). Before this was over he accepted with alacrity the America and West Indies command (1926–8). It was a peacetime cruise, with his flag first in the *Calcutta*, then in the *Despatch*; but it concluded with a characteristic success, the salving of the *Dauntless* which had grounded in the entrance to Halifax harbour. Cowan was promoted admiral in 1927, appointed first and principal naval aide-de-camp to the King in 1930, and retired from the active list in 1931.

He then became assistant secretary to the Warwickshire Hounds; but on the outbreak of war in 1939 it was more than he could bear not to be in it. Eventually he was allowed to serve in the rank of commander and was appointed to the commandos under his old friend and chief, Roger Keyes. In due course he found himself in Egypt and served with the commandos in their various activities in North Africa. Finally, when his unit was disbanded, he attached himself to the 18th King Edward VII's Own Cavalry, an Indian regiment. He served with them in all their operations in the Western Desert until he was taken prisoner on 27 May 1942 at Bir Hacheim, fighting an Italian tank crew single-handed, armed only with a revolver. He was repatriated in 1943 and, reappointed to the Commandos, headed for Italy, where he took part in many operations against the Dalmatian Islands. For these services in 1944 he was awarded a bar to the D.S.O. which he had won in 1898. By this time he was seventy-three and beginning to feel the strain. He returned to England, where an inspection of a Royal Marine Commando about to go overseas was his last service. In 1945 he reverted to the retired list. One more distinction, a very welcome one, was his: on November 1946 he was appointed honorary colonel, the 18th King Edward VII's Own Cavalry, whom he visited in India in 1947. He retired once more to Kineton, and died in hospital in Leamington, 14 February 1956. In spite of his unequalled record of active service he had never even been wounded. He was appointed M.V.O. in 1904, C.B. in 1916, K.C.B. in 1919, and created a baronet in 1921.

Cowan married in 1901 Catherine Eleanor Millicent (died 1934), daughter of Digby Cayley, of Brompton-by-Sawdon, Yorkshire; they had one daughter. Portraits by L. Campbell Taylor and Rodrigo Moynihan are in the Imperial War Museum. Cowan is also included in the group 'Some Sea Officers of the War of

1914–18' by Sir A. S. Cope in the National Portrait Gallery.

[Lionel Dawson, *Sound of the Guns*, 1949; private information; personal knowledge.]

H. G. THURSFIELD.

COX, ALFRED (1866–1954), general practitioner and medical secretary of the British Medical Association, was born 5 May 1866 at Middlesbrough, the second son in the family of eight children of Thomas Benjamin Cox, a boilersmith, and his wife, Dinah Sanderson Skilbeck, a blacksmith's daughter. Shortly after Alfred's birth they moved to Darlington, where at the age of fourteen he was made a monitor of his board-school as a step to becoming a pupil-teacher. This was not a success, and at the age of seventeen he began to study for the Civil Service lower division, work he continued while staying in Carlisle as assistant to an insurance agent. It was there that a doctor visiting the house persuaded him to become a dispenser-assistant, a mode of entry to the medical profession later forbidden by the General Medical Council. Cox gained a good deal of experience in midwifery, moved to Stockton-on-Tees, later to Haydon Bridge, where he had more time for study, and finally to Newcastle upon Tyne, where he received free board and lodging and £1 a month from the general practitioner for whom he worked. In this somewhat precarious life Cox managed to matriculate at Edinburgh and on his twenty-first birthday entered the university of Durham College of Medicine at Newcastle—still earning his keep as a dispenser-assistant. He qualified M.B., B.S. in 1891 and immediately entered general practice in Gateshead.

Cox's long years of penurious drudgery probably stimulated his interest in medical politics and the reform of his profession. He played an active part in municipal politics in Gateshead, and was elected to its council. With the rector of Gateshead he joined forces in a campaign for slum clearance. Cox formed the Gateshead Medical Association, and tried to reform club practice and the methods used by Friendly Societies in appointing doctors for their members. He was active in forming in other towns in the north various medical societies for discussing medico-political and medico-ethical matters, an expression of dissatisfaction with the British Medical Association. A conference held by the Medical Guild of Manchester in May 1900 brought this dissatisfaction into the open, and the possibility of forming a new organization was debated. It was Cox who carried the day with a motion which gave the B.M.A. a chance to reform itself, and the result of this was the setting up in the same year of the committee which brought in the new constitution of the B.M.A., which to all intents and purposes remained unchanged until the reforms adopted in 1966.

Sidney and Beatrice Webb [qq.v.] described the constitution of 1903 as a model of democratic organization. The culminating structure of this was the Representative Body, which at the annual representative meeting laid down the policy of the B.M.A. Cox was a representative from the beginning and the first honorary secretary of the Gateshead Division, which replaced the Gateshead Medical Association he had formed. Four years after qualification he had been elected a member of the B.M.A.'s Central Council. When the appointment of medical secretary to the B.M.A. was being considered Cox was canvassed as a likely candidate, but he withdrew in favour of (Sir) James Smith Whitaker, who was appointed in 1902. In 1908 Cox became deputy secretary and gave up practice. When Smith Whitaker took office as deputy chairman of the National Health Insurance Commission in 1911, Cox succeeded him, being formally appointed medical secretary of the B.M.A. in 1912, retiring in 1932, the year of the Association's centenary. The introduction of National Health Insurance by Lloyd George was accompanied by a bitter struggle between the B.M.A. and the Government, and Smith Whitaker's decision to leave the B.M.A. at the height of this was the subject of much criticism. But Cox at the time, and in the years to come, never ceased to defend his action.

During the war of 1914-18 Cox acted as secretary of the Central Medical War Committee set up to organize the supply of doctors to the armed forces. For this he was appointed O.B.E. The war over, much of his work as secretary of the B.M.A. was concerned with negotiations between the medical profession and the Ministry of Health, and with the administration of a professional organization which over the years grew in numbers and strength. As ambassador for the B.M.A. he was successful in securing the allegiance to the home organization of doctors in Canada and South Africa. In both countries there had been branches of the B.M.A. and separate medical associations as well. When he died the Canadian Medical Association and the South African Medical Association had become affiliated to the B.M.A. Another successful attempt to cement friendship among doctors of different countries was the formation in 1925 of the Association Professionnelle Internationale des Médecins (A.P.I.M.), Cox being one of the founders and also one of its most enthusiastic supporters. After the end of the war of 1939-45 the A.P.I.M. was merged into a bigger organization, the World Medical Association.

Cox devoted the whole of his life to the welfare and interests of his profession and in the British Medical Association found a powerful instrument to that end. Early in his career he had been a member of the Independent Labour Party, being greatly influenced by Keir Hardie [q.v.]. But in the end he became disillusioned with socialism and socialist policy. 'The end of it all', he wrote in his autobiography, 'seems inevitably to be the authoritarian State.'

Under a rather stern exterior Cox had a warm and generous heart which kept him free from the envies and jealousies which so often beset professional life. He was incapable of meanness, and never missed an opportunity of encouraging younger colleagues with a friendly word in season. He was a man of great integrity, and to the end of his long life kept his friendships in constant repair and his interest undimmed. His one great sorrow was the death of his wife in 1927. She was Florence Amelia, daughter of Thomas Cheesman, iron merchant, of Newcastle upon Tyne and they were married in 1894. There were no children.

Cox received the honorary LL.D. of the university of Manitoba in 1930 and the honorary M.A. of Durham in 1921. The B.M.A. awarded him its gold medal in 1931. He died in Brighton 31 August 1954.

A portrait by Sir A. S. Cope is in B.M.A. House, Tavistock Square, London.

[*British Medical Journal*, 4 and 11 September 1954; *Lancet*, 11 September 1954; 'General Practice Fifty Years Ago' by Alfred Cox in *British Medical Journal*, 7 January 1950; Alfred Cox, *Among the Doctors*, 1950; Ernest Muirhead Little, *History of the British Medical Association*, 1932; personal knowledge.]   H. A. CLEGG

CRAIG, SIR JOHN (1874-1957), steel-master, was born at Clydesdale, New Stevenston, 11 December 1874, the fourth on of Thomas Craig, a heater at David Colville's Dalzell ironworks, Motherwell, by his wife, Elizabeth Wilson. He was educated at Dalziel public school, Motherwell, and in 1888 went to work as an office boy with his father's employers. From the start he showed the qualities which eventually took him to the head of the company, in which he spent his whole life. He was industrious, shrewd, willing to accept responsibility, not afraid of the calculated risk, and completely single-minded in his devotion to Colvilles.

Promotion came to Craig regularly within what was, for the first twenty-eight years of his career, simply a good, well-run, medium-sized business producing open-hearth steel. He became Colvilles's representative at the Royal Exchange, Glasgow, in 1895. His responsibilities within the firm were much increased on the death of John Colville, the chairman, in 1899; he became a director in 1910 and chairman and managing director in 1916. The year 1916 was the turning-point in the history of the firm. The expansion which was then gathering momentum was to a great extent due to war demands for steel and to governmental pressure for the consolidation of the Scottish steel industry into larger and more efficient units. But Craig had made up his own mind that expansion was the right policy. He had played a leading part in the acquisition of a controlling interest in the Fullwood Foundry Co., Ltd., in 1915, and the purchase of the Clydebridge and Glengarnock works was being negotiated when he took over as chairman in 1916, on the death of both David and Archibald Colville, the sons of the founder.

Craig's energy, his foresight, and his skill as a negotiator were exercised in an industry which both exacted and gave scope for them. A major movement towards integration in British industry was in progress at the point of time at which full power came into his hands. He thus went straight forward at the head of a vigorously expanding business. Having reorganized Colvilles's recent acquisitions of Clydebridge and Glengarnock and set on foot two new steelworks, he turned his attention to the question of coal supplies for the growing enterprise, completing in 1917 the purchase of the colliery undertakings of Archibald Russell. The structure of integration was further extended, forward in 1919 into sheet making, alloy steel and steel castings, and backward in 1920 into limestone quarrying.

The strong financial link between Colvilles and the Belfast shipbuilding company of Harland and Wolff, Ltd., was made by Craig in 1919–20.

When the post-war boom broke in 1921 Craig had to deploy still further powers of industrial leadership—tenacity, long foresight, and conservative finance. During the depression in the steel industry which continued until the thirties he kept his works efficient, even though production never came near their capacity of over 800,000 ingot tons per annum. A saying of his, revealing of his habitual optimism and willingness to take calculated risks, was— 'If you go down in a slump, make sure you go down with first-class equipment.' On the financial side he avoided the writing down of capital to which many other steel companies had to resort. Consequently Colvilles found itself poised for a second phase of expansion in the thirties. In 1930 a long series of mergers and acquisitions began; the public company of Colvilles, Ltd., was formed in 1934; and a new point of balance was reached in 1937, by which time the group had a capacity of over 1,100,000 tons of ingots. Craig took the crucial decision to build an integrated steelworks on the Clyde. Clyde Ironworks was completely reconstructed, and the link was made with the Clydebridge steel furnaces by a bridge carrying molten iron across the Clyde itself. Thus Craig took still farther in the war of 1939–45 the movement of consolidation and expansion which he had begun in the first war. The enlargement and modernization of Colvilles's equipment continued during and after the war. In 1956 he retired from the office of chairman and was then appointed honorary president of the company.

The life of John Craig and the development of the steel enterprise of Colvilles are inseparable. His entire working life of nearly seventy years was spent in that one business, forty of them as its chairman. He played a leading part in the affairs of the steel industry as a whole. He was a member of the original council of the National Federation of Iron and Steel Manufacturers, founded in 1918, and became its third president in 1922. He was president of the Iron and Steel Institute in 1940–42, a member of the executive committee of the British Iron and Steel Federation, and a director of the British Iron and Steel Corporation. Virtually his only outside interests were his family, the Church of Scotland, and the Y.M.C.A., with which he had been actively associated at Motherwell since 1897, being the chairman of the Scottish National Council in 1927 and president in 1944.

Craig married in 1901 Jessie, daughter of John Sommerville, shovel plater; they had three daughters and two sons, the elder of whom became a director of Colvilles, Ltd., and the younger secretary of the company. Craig was appointed C.B.E. in 1918 and knighted in 1943. He became a justice of the peace in the county of Lanarkshire in 1919 and deputy-lieutenant of the county in 1934. The honorary degree of LL.D. was conferred upon him by Glasgow University in 1951. He died at his home, Cambusnethan Priory, Wishaw, 1 February 1957. There is a bronze portrait bust by Sir Jacob Epstein at the Craig Home, Skelmorlie, Ayrshire.

[*Glasgow Herald, Scotsman,* and *The Times,* 2 February 1957; *Engineer,* 8 February 1957; J. C. Carr and W. Taplin, *History of the British Steel Industry,* 1962; private information.]
WALTER TAPLIN.

CRAIGIE, SIR ROBERT LESLIE (1883–1959), diplomatist, was born in Southsea 6 December 1883, the only son of Commander (later Admiral) Robert William Craigie and his wife, Henrietta Isabella Dinnis. He was educated at Heidelberg, passed into the Foreign Office in 1907, and served in Berne, Sofia, and Washington as well as on international conferences in London and abroad before resuming duties in the Foreign Office in 1924. Promoted counsellor in 1928 and an assistant under-secretary in 1935, he took part in the negotiation of the London naval treaty of 1930 and the Anglo-German agreement of 1935.

Discontent at the limitations of Japanese naval strength, enforced under the treaty of 1930, gave those in Japan who advocated a forward expansionist policy the opportunity to regain power. The following year saw the start of Japanese aggression in Manchuria and China. From then onwards, from time to time for the next ten years, the problem for successive British Governments and for their representatives in the Far East was, whether, how, and when to stop Japan.

In September 1937 Craigie, appointed by Neville Chamberlain, arrived in Japan as ambassador in succession to Sir Robert Clive [q.v.] who had maintained a firm front in the face of Japanese aggression and anti-British tactics in China. But with Chamberlain as prime minister British foreign policy began to change in the Far East as in Europe. Craigie reached Tokyo shortly after Japanese aircraft had attacked and wounded the British ambassador to China, Sir Hughe Knatchbull-Hugessen, while he was travelling in a motor-car from Nanking to Shanghai. This was not an auspicious beginning to Craigie's embassy, as the Japanese Government apologized only after considerable pressure, and Anglo-Japanese relations continued to deteriorate. Craigie was convinced that the only hope of peace lay through timely concessions to Japanese pressure. This view, which was based on the presence of moderate elements in Japan, was not shared by Eden, Roosevelt, or Churchill. Temporarily Craigie's efforts to improve Anglo-Japanese relations were successful, but the sympathy of British opinion with China in its defence against Japanese aggression and the consequent anti-British propaganda spread by the young officers in the Japanese naval and military services were too strong for the moderate civilian elements whom he had so assiduously cultivated.

In July 1940 the British Government approved the temporary cessation of supplies through Burma to China. Nevertheless, the Japanese continued the aggressive anti-British and anti-American policy which led finally in December 1941 to the attack on Pearl Harbour, the crippling of the United States Pacific Fleet, and the declaration of war on Britain. Craigie had no doubts about Japan's willingness and ability to fight, but his warnings were ignored in London and Singapore, where those with long experience of Japan were regarded, in general, as too pro-Japanese to be taken seriously. It has been suggested that war with Japan might have been avoided had the British and United States Governments not been convinced, in spite of the warnings of their representatives in Tokyo, that Japan would never dare to attack them. But some at least among British professional diplomatists and historians agree that in view of British military weakness in 1937 and 1938, of the collapse of France in 1940, and of the conclusion of the Tripartite Pact between Germany, Italy, and Japan in September of the same year, a policy of concessions to Japan in the hope of strengthening the moderates and liberals who undoubtedly existed there, as against the extremists in the Services, was the only one which offered any prospect of success.

After seven months of internment Craigie and his staff were allowed to return to the United Kingdom. From 1945 to 1948 he was British representative on the United Nations war crimes commission and in 1949 on the Geneva conference for the protection of the victims of war. He was appointed C.M.G. (1929), K.C.M.G. (1936), G.C.M.G. (1941), C.B. (1930), and was sworn of the Privy Council in 1937.

He married in 1918 Pleasant (died 1956), daughter of Pleasant A. Stovall of Savannah, Georgia, then United States minister at Berne; they had one son. Craigie died at Winchester 16 May 1959.

[Sir Robert Craigie, *Behind the Japanese Mask*, 1946; S. Woodburn Kirby, (Official History) *The War Against Japan*, vol. i, 1957; The Earl of Avon, *Facing the Dictators*, 1962; *The Times*, 18 May 1959; Joseph Grew, *Turbulent Era*, 2 vols., 1953; F. C. Jones, *Japan's New Order in East Asia*, 1954; personal knowledge.]
J. L. DODDS.

CRAIGIE, SIR WILLIAM ALEXANDER (1867–1957), lexicographer and philologist, was born in Dundee 13 August 1867, the youngest son of James Craigie, jobbing gardener, and his wife, Christina Low. His native speech was thus the lowland Scots of Angus, and during his childhood he learned some Gaelic from his maternal grandfather and later his eldest brother. About the age of twelve he began reading the early Scottish writers. From the headmaster of his school, the West End Academy, Dundee, he gained a knowledge of phonetics. While attending St. Andrews University, where he graduated with honours in classics and philosophy in 1888, he also found time to learn German and French and began studying Danish and Icelandic. In his final session he carried out the research on the university library's manuscript of the early Scots Wyntoun's *Chronicle* which enabled him to demonstrate conclusively the relationships of the several versions of this work. With a Guthrie scholarship he proceeded to Balliol College, Oxford, and thence, after one term, to Oriel as a bible clerk. Apart from the work of his regular curriculum which led to firsts in both honour moderations (1890) and *literae humaniores* (1892), he continued his private study of Scandinavian, attended lectures on Celtic, and began producing articles on these subjects for Scottish journals. The winter of 1892–3 he spent in Copenhagen, where he studied Icelandic manuscripts and learned modern Ice-

landic from Icelandic friends. From 1893 to 1897 he was assistant to the professor of Latin at St. Andrews. In his spare time he continued his writing of articles, produced his valuable *Primer of Burns* (1896), and contributed translations from Icelandic and Danish to the *Fairy Books* and *Dreams and Ghosts* of Andrew Lang [q.v.] as well as his own *Scandinavian Folk-lore* (1896).

In 1897 Craigie accepted an unexpected invitation to join the staff of the Philological Society's *New English Dictionary* in Oxford. In 1901 he was appointed co-editor with (Sir) James A. H. Murray and Henry Bradley [qq.v.]. Thereafter he continued to work on the Dictionary until the completion of its *Supplement* in 1933, producing the letters N, Q, R, U, and V, Si–Sq, and Wo–Wy, amounting to nearly a fifth of the main work, and about a third of the *Supplement*.

Along with his daily stint of seven and a half hours of lexicography, which was far from using up all his energy or exhausting his zest for work, Craigie kept alive all his old interests. In 1904 he was appointed Taylorian lecturer in the Scandinavian languages at Oxford and in 1916 he became Rawlinson and Bosworth professor of Anglo-Saxon. In 1921 he began seriously to collect material for his projected dictionary of Older Scottish, and when in 1925 he removed to the university of Chicago, as professor of English, in order that he might edit a *Dictionary of American English*, he was for some years occupied simultaneously with three major dictionaries, yet still turning out a steady flow of other writings.

In 1936 Craigie resigned his Chicago chair and settled at Christmas Common, Watlington, on the Chiltern Hills. He now gave most of his time to the *Dictionary of the Older Scottish Tongue*, which he carried to the end of the letter I in 1955, when he was eighty-seven, before handing over to his successor. He had also continued to contribute to the American dictionary until its completion in 1944. After the war he produced his *Specimens of Icelandic Rímur* (3 vols., 1952), a masterly survey of a field of Icelandic literature in which his erudition and discernment were unrivalled, and a supplement (1957) to the *Icelandic Dictionary* of G. Vígfússon [q.v.].

Craigie's remarkable knowledge of many languages was perfected, and friendships with the scholars of other countries cemented, in the course of the travels on which he and his wife spent all their vacations, visiting all the countries of northern

Craigie, W. A.

Europe and in 1921 going round the world. In this way he became one of the most widely known of the scholars of his generation; and the quietly dignified, rather reserved, yet unfailingly kindly and companionable personality of this tiny Scotsman, with his modest tastes and tidy habits, and his fellow-feeling for simple folk and small nations, made him one of the best loved. These travels included four visits to Iceland where he was revered by the whole nation.

Craigie was the ablest and most productive lexicographer of his time and was universally recognized as the supreme master of the art and techniques of dictionary making. Yet in addition to his major works he contrived also to produce, almost entirely in his spare time, an astonishing number of other, smaller-scale but authoritative writings over a wide range of provinces of specialist philology, notably on Older Scottish and on English philology of every period. Over the whole extent of Icelandic literature, ancient and modern, he gained a greater mastery than perhaps any non-Icelander had ever done, and wrote valuably on scaldic verse and on the sagas as well as on his beloved *rímur*. These writings and others on Frisian and on Gaelic display his characteristic virtues of clarity, brevity, and directness, and his acute and perceptive observation of philological facts and details.

His published work was only part of the vast service he rendered to scholarship. He gave a new impetus to Old Norse and Anglo-Saxon studies in Oxford and later in Chicago. Throughout his career he was active in initiating and encouraging new scholarly enterprises. Out of his plan for 'completing the record of English' by means of the 'period dictionaries', which he launched in 1919, were born the great historical dictionaries which followed the *New English*, among them his own American and Scottish dictionaries. His lifelong interest in Frisian and the enthusiastic support which he gave to the Frisian scholars in their attempt to re-establish their language, they recognized by making him one of the two original honorary members of the Frisian Academy on its foundation in 1938. His sponsorship, and the active leadership which he provided in partnership with Professor M. K. Pope, brought about the foundation in 1938 of the Anglo-Norman Text Society and as its president he fostered this society's project (initiated in 1947) for an Anglo-Norman

dictionary. His suggestion and encouragement led likewise to the founding of the Icelandic Rímur Society in 1947. He served for long periods as president or council-member of a number of other famous learned societies in England and in Scotland. All his great academic prestige and his extensive range of contacts he placed at the service of these and other good causes of learning.

Craigie possessed an amazingly retentive memory and an ability to grasp at sight the essence of a problem and to marshal facts and arguments with great speed. Even so, his erudition, and his prodigious output, he achieved only by utilizing his time to the utmost, working methodically for most of each day and evening throughout his long life. Yet he was always accessible and ungrudging of his time to others. To the numerous authors of scholarly works who sought it he gave encouragement, fruitful advice and abundant practical help.

The many honours awarded Craigie included honorary degrees from St. Andrews (1907), Calcutta (1921), Oxford (1928), Cambridge (1928), Michigan (1929), Wisconsin (1932), and Iceland (1946); knighthood in 1928 on completion of the *New English Dictionary*, an honorary fellowship of Oriel in the same year, and fellowship of the British Academy in 1931. The Icelanders' appreciation of his friendship and his service to their literature was shown in many different ways, including a knighthood (1925) and a knight commandership (1930) of the Order of the Icelandic Falcon. In 1952 his eighty-fifth birthday was honoured by a gathering held at Oriel College, Oxford, when he was presented with a commemorative memoir and list of his publications and his portrait by Harold Speed which now hangs in the college.

In 1897 Craigie married Jessie Kinmond (died 1947), daughter of William Hutchen, tailor and clothier, of Dundee, on whose loving care and companionship he depended greatly. They had no children. He died at Watlington 2 September 1957.

[J. M. Wyllie in *Proceedings* of the British Academy, vol. xlvii, 1961; *A Memoir and List of the Published Writings of Sir William A. Craigie*, 1952; *Scottish Historical Review*, vol. xxxii, 1953; *The Times*, 3 and 9 September 1957; private information; personal knowledge.]   A. J. AITKEN

CRAWFORD, OSBERT GUY STANHOPE (1886–1957), archaeologist, w

born 28 October 1886 at Breech Candy, Bombay, where his father, Charles Edward Gordon Crawford, was an Indian Civil Servant; he was later a judge at Ratnagiri. His mother, Alice Luscombe Mackenzie, died a few days after his birth; his father in 1894. He was brought up by two of his father's unmarried sisters, first in London, then in Hampshire, near Newbury. He went to school at Park House, Reading, then Marlborough, where he did not enjoy himself, on one occasion running away. He wrote of his schooldays: 'I was far less unhappy in the prison-camp at Holzminden than I was at Marlborough.' Despite this, it was his membership of the Marlborough natural history society and its archaeological section which first encouraged his interest in the countryside and its antiquities.

Crawford went up to Keble College, Oxford, where he obtained a third class in honour moderations (1907), began reading for *literae humaniores*, but changed to the diploma in geography. 'Going from Greats to Geography', he wrote, 'was like leaving the parlour for the basement; one lost caste but one did see life.' He rowed for his college and was captain of boats in his last year. He graduated in 1910 and was offered by A. J. Herbertson the post of junior demonstrator in the school of geography which he held until the end of 1911. At Oxford (Sir) J. L. Myres, R. R. Marett, (Sir) Arthur Evans [qq.v.], and Herbertson were the main formative influences; outside, H. J. E. Peake [q.v.] and J. P. Williams-Freeman (whose notice Crawford later contributed to this Dictionary). In 1913 he set out on a three-year expedition to Easter Island led by Mr. and Mrs. Scoresby Routledge, but quarrelled with them and left the ship at St. Vincent. In the same year he joined the excavation staff of (Sir) Henry Wellcome [q.v.] in the Sudan, working at Jebel Moya and Abu Geili. Crawford always retained an interest in the Sudan, and particularly the Fungs, publishing in 1951 *The Fung Kingdom of Sennar*.

In 1914 he excavated (with E. A. Hooton) an unchambered long barrow on Vexcombe Down, and was digging when war broke out. He enlisted in the London Scottish, went to France in November 1914, transferred in 1915 to Maps, Third Army, and in 1917 to the Royal Flying Corps as an observer. He was taken prisoner in February 1918. In October 1920 Sir Charles (Arden-) Close [q.v.] appointed him the first holder of the post

of archaeology officer in the Ordnance Survey which he held until his retirement in 1946. His job was the revision and compilation of the Ordnance Survey maps from the point of view of archaeological information; but, in addition to this work on the standard topographical maps, he started a special survey of megalithic monuments, and a series of period maps beginning with the *Map of Roman Britain* (1924). His megalithic surveys led him to write *The Long Barrows of the Cotswolds* (1925). One of his many ideas was to publish geographical memoirs for the Ordnance Survey sheets, but this did not get beyond the first memoir, *The Andover District* (1922), which he wrote himself.

In and out of his professional occupation and throughout his life he was a field archaeologist *par excellence* in the sense defined by Williams-Freeman in his *Field Archaeology as Illustrated by Hampshire* (1915): his prime interest was the face of the countryside in its archaeological aspects. He summarized his ideas on this subject in *Field Archaeology* (1932) and *Archaeology in the Field* (1953). A keen and very gifted photographer, he took panorama photographs in the war of 1914–18, and soon realized the value of air photography to archaeologists and historians. After the war he was a pioneer in the development of the civilian use of air photography, writing *Air Survey and Archaeology* (1924), *Air Photography for Archaeologists* (1929), and, with Alexander Keiller, *Wessex from the Air* (1928).

Crawford was particularly anxious to interest others in man's remote past and his archaeological remains, and to relate these studies to the whole general study of mankind. *Man and his Past* (1921) sets out his credo in these matters. In 1927 he founded *Antiquity: a Quarterly Review of Archaeology* which he edited for thirty years until his death. It was, and remained, the only independent archaeological journal in the world. In *Antiquity* he was able to publish many air photographs, articles on archaeology from all parts of the world, and examples of modern folk-culture and the culture of modern primitive peoples to illumine the mute documents of the past. A man of strong character, likes and dislikes, prejudices and enthusiasms, he found in the editorial columns of his journal a place to vent his views to the delight and fury of a wide circle of readers.

He was elected F.B.A. in 1947; appointed C.B.E. in 1950; received the

Victoria medal of the Royal Geographical Society in 1940 and honorary degrees from Cambridge (1952) and Southampton (1955). He was president of the Prehistoric Society in 1938, and a member of the Royal Commission on Ancient and Historical Monuments in England from 1939 to 1946. He was an enthusiastic and untiring traveller; his last two books, *Castles and Churches in the Middle Nile Region* (1953) and *The Eye Goddess* (1957), reflect the width of his interests. He was presented with a *Festschrift* in 1951; edited by W. F. Grimes it was entitled *Aspects of Archaeology in Britain and Beyond*, and contained an account of his career by his former teacher, Sir J. L. Myres, entitled 'The Man and his Past'. The foreword to this volume opens with the sentence 'No single scholar has done more than O. G. S. Crawford to place the study of the remoter past, and of the past of Britain in particular, on the secure and sound basis upon which it now rests.' Crawford was one of the handful of British archaeologists—Sir Cyril Fox, Sir Mortimer Wheeler, Sir Thomas Kendrick— who revolutionized and revivified British archaeology in the decade after 1918.

In 1955 Crawford published *Said and Done*, a vivacious and amusing autobiography in which the man's character comes clearly through. A bachelor, he lived with a housekeeper and his cats at Nursling; one of his last acts was to give a broadcast on 'The Language of Cats'. He died in his sleep at Nursling on the night of 28–29 November 1957. He did not suffer fools gladly but had a great capacity for friendship, a genuine delight in encouraging and helping young archaeologists, and an infectious enthusiasm for anyone who shared his interest in air photographs and field archaeology or his belief that archaeology, properly studied as a branch of world history and anthropology, was one of the most important subjects. To old and young alike, friends and foes, he was known as Ogs or Uncle Ogs.

His large collection of photographs is at the Ashmolean Museum, Oxford, and his papers are in the Bodleian Library.

[O. G. S. Crawford, *Said and Done*, 1955; *Antiquity*, March 1958; Grahame Clark in *Proceedings* of the British Academy, vol. xliv, 1958; private information; personal knowledge.]   G. E. DANIEL.

CRIPPS, SIR (RICHARD) STAFFORD (1889–1952), statesman and lawyer, was born at Elm Park Gardens, London, 24 April 1889, the fifth child and fourth son of Charles Alfred Cripps (later first Lord Parmoor, q.v.), and his wife, Theresa Potter. His mother, whose sister Beatrice became Mrs. Sidney Webb [q.v.], died when Stafford Cripps was four. Yet her influence remained with him all his life. In a remarkable letter left for her husband when she realized death was imminent she wrote, 'I should like the children brought up as much as possible in the country, and to be educated much in the same style as their father was. I should like their living to be of the simplest without reference to show or other follies. I should like them trained to be undogmatic and unsectarian Christians, charitable to all churches and sects studying the precepts and actions of Christ as their example, taking their religious inspiration directly from the spirit of the New Testament.'

This charge the father faithfully carried out as well as the further precept, 'You will teach my children to love only what is true, and ever to seek further truth, and make it known to others, whatever career they may choose.' All his life Stafford Cripps was never consciously to depart from these standards. From his father's side came a bent towards public service for its own sake. It was always strongly reinforced by powerful but simple religious beliefs. The combination of Potter and Cripps blood merged in Stafford Cripps to produce the highest possible ideals in personal and public life.

Cripps showed early brilliance. The papers which won him from Winchester a natural science scholarship to New College, Oxford, in 1907 were so remarkable that the professor of chemistry at University College, London, Sir William Ramsay [q.v.], who had been asked to scrutinize, persuaded Cripps to prefer the better equipped laboratories at University College. This resulted in Cripps being part author of a paper on the properties of the inert gas xenon which was read before the Royal Society when he was twenty-two. Undoubtedly he could have become an eminent chemist. But the legal and political pulls in his family, which echoed his own inclinations, drew him to the bar, to which he was called by the Middle Temple in 1913.

Medically unfit for the army, for which he volunteered after the outbreak of war in 1914, Cripps worked as a lorry driver for the Red Cross. After a year, because of his knowledge of chemistry, he was recalled from France to work in munitions. As assistant superintendent of the explosives factory at Queensferry he learned and contributed much. Through his gift for administration and capacity to work long hours and master intricate problems he made Queensferry the most efficient of all the munitions factories. It was largely because of the reputation he won there that (Sir) Winston Churchill appointed him minister of aircraft production in the war of 1939–45.

The work at Queensferry was hard. It was made harder by Cripps's zeal and energy. His inherent ill health grew far worse and he was never again to be fully fit. By the end of the war the doctors had despaired of conventional remedies. This prompted Cripps to turn to nature cures, vegetarianism, teetotalism, and the like. By such means he effected a considerable improvement in his health. What others often put down to crankiness was the product of trial and error in an attempt to ease his chronic physical disabilities. He went to bed early and was usually at work by six in the morning or before. This gave him half a day's advantage over his rivals and colleagues in any field throughout his life: one of the reasons for his rapid progress at the bar. But his successes did not come from energy and long hours alone; he had one of the most acute minds of his generation. He could rapidly comprehend complicated matters so that within a few hours he would understand almost as much of them as the experts. His clarity of thought enabled him to set out any proposition with striking lucidity and logic.

Four years after his return to the bar in 1919 Cripps appeared for the Duff Development Company against the Colonial Office. His mastery of constitutional law, his ability to confound expert witnesses from their own writings, and his success in making the Colonial Office pay £387,000 established him in the legal profession as almost unbeatable when it came to digesting masses of complicated documents and evidence. Not only the defeated Colonial Office, but other important authorities and institutions, began to seek his aid; and his reputation advanced rapidly particularly in patent and compensation cases. When he appeared for the London County Council before the Railway Rates Tribunal in a matter which lasted from May 1924 to October 1926, his comprehensive understanding of the 39,000 questions put to expert witnesses on highly techni-

cal matters enormously impressed Herbert Morrison (later Lord Morrison of Lambeth) and formed in his mind the aim to persuade Cripps to join the Labour Party. In 1927 Cripps became the youngest K.C. But his enthusiasms outside his practice were not yet attracted to politics. Instead he spent much time on 'the World Alliance to promote international friendship through the Churches', of which he was for six years treasurer. By 1929 Cripps with his characteristic impatience had become bored by the lack of results achieved.

In that year his father and Sidney Webb [q.v.], his uncle by marriage, were both members of Ramsay MacDonald's Cabinet but it was as much due to Morrison's influence as to his family's that Cripps joined the Labour Party. In 1930 he became solicitor-general and was knighted, and in January 1931 he was elected Labour member for East Bristol. When the 'national' Government was formed in 1931 MacDonald asked him to continue as solicitor-general. Cripps at the time was in a sanatorium at Baden. His delay in replying led to speculation that he was going to accept and there may have been some hesitation in Cripps's mind. In the event he declined and rapidly hurled himself with the same missionary enthusiasm that he had devoted to the World Alliance into propagating socialism. From being not even a member of the Labour Party a few years earlier, he shot right through it in terms of ideals and policies and almost out the other side. Morrison was astonished by the extremism of his protégé. Always irritated by delays, Cripps's logical mind concluded that if socialism were the right answer to economic and social problems it had better be brought in at once, lock, stock, and barrel, with barely a transitional period. He was a leading member of the Socialist League, a militant group within the Labour Party. Among other things he proposed the abolition of the House of Lords, the introduction of a dictatorial Emergency Powers Act to forestall sabotage by financial interests in the event of another Labour Government and, in 1934, he remarked 'there is no doubt we shall have to overcome opposition from Buckingham Palace'. This last observation produced alarmed disclaimers from the Labour leaders but in the public mind Cripps was confirmed as an out-and-out revolutionary while becoming a hero to Labour Party militants of the left wing.

It was not surprising that with his temperament he found the Labour Party in Parliament and outside an ineffectual organization. In 1936 he was a prime mover of the United Front designed to combine the Labour Party, the Communists, and the Independent Labour Party, and radicals in the Liberal Party into one organization. A new journal, *Tribune*, was launched in 1937 to further the cause. Shocked at his willingness to work with Communists the Labour Party executive declared that any member who appeared on the same platform as a Communist or a member of the I.L.P. would be automatically expelled. Despite various protests from Cripps this decision was upheld by the 1937 annual conference which at the same time re-elected Cripps to the national executive.

In the autumn of 1938 Cripps began to advocate an even wider grouping to remove Neville Chamberlain's government from office. This was a Popular Front which was to include Conservatives as well. When he proclaimed his programme for a Popular Front campaign and refused to withdraw it at the request of the national executive he was expelled from the Labour Party in January 1939. He was not readmitted until 1945. During this period considerable criticism was levelled at him by trade-unionists and other sober Labour Party stalwarts on the grounds that he abused his privilege of a rich man by spending considerable sums on internal propaganda in the Labour Party which were denied to the ordinary person. There was also complaint that he professed extreme socialism to assuage his own feelings of guilt at being richer than others, to the detriment of the Labour Party. At the same time Cripps was winning many friends. His handling of the inquiry into the Gresford Colliery disaster of 1934, in which he appeared without fee for the North Wales Miners' Federation, endeared him for ever to the miners, who were prepared to forgive what they regarded as his eccentricities. He had, too, a peculiar gift for inspiring loyalty in those younger than himself. The public picture of a Robespierre was belied by the private charm and kindliness. Nor, apart from his enforced carefulness in diet, did he live in any particular discomfort. He had an agreeable country house and farm and did not wear a hair shirt. Nor was he a non-smoker.

Just after the war broke out in 1939 Cripps embarked on a world tour with some assistance from Lord Halifax [q.v.], then foreign secretary, who admired his honesty of purpose. This journey was of great importance to his future career. He visited India for the first time and was attracted by its people and leaders and infused with a desire to promote Indian independence and to help solve India's problems. He also visited Moscow and formed the view that it was possible to prevent Germany and the Soviet Union actually becoming major allies despite the non-aggression pact of August 1939. On his return to England he urged on all and sundry the need to try and draw Russia away from Germany. Churchill, who had just taken over as prime minister, was so taken by his arguments that he promptly sent him as ambassador to Moscow where Cripps arrived in June 1940.

He remained for nearly two years in Russia where he suffered considerable disillusion; in this he was not alone. Whatever outbursts he had allowed himself he was always a firm believer in the democratic processes and it was a surprise to him to find that the Soviet leaders paid no more regard to a socialist believer in democracy than to a capitalist. It was impossible for him to form any special relationship and he was often not only frustrated but irritated by the long months of idle helplessness. He could not claim to have advanced Anglo-Russian friendship at all up to the time of the German invasion of Russia on 22 June 1941—when Cripps happened to be in London, where he was sworn of the Privy Council. He immediately went back to Moscow and organized the pact of mutual assistance signed on 12 July 1941. When he returned to Britain in the following January he found that he had acquired an unexpected and barely deserved aura of success: the public enthusiasm for the new Russian ally had washed over on to Cripps. The remarkable broadcast which he made when he finally returned from Moscow confirmed this feeling and made him such a popular figure that there was even some talk of his being a potential replacement for the prime minister.

Churchill made him leader of the House of Commons as well as giving him a seat in the War Cabinet as lord privy seal in the month after he returned from Russia. Perhaps for the same reason Churchill allowed him to go on a one-man mission to India in an attempt to secure Indian support for the war with a promise of full self-government after it ended. L. S. Amery [q.v.], secr tary of state for India, subsequently remarked that it was thought better that Cripps should fail than that he should. Cripps very nearly succeeded and remained always convinced that it was M. K. Gandhi [q.v.], who sabotaged the hopes of success, after taking no part in the official discussions himself. Consequently Cripps put the utmost emphasis on Gandhi's being completely involved in any future discussions.

The failure in India produced a fall in popular esteem, and there were differences of opinion with Churchill which brought Cripps near to resignation. He relinquished the leadership of the House and left the War Cabinet in November 1942, to become minister of aircraft production, a post in which he was extremely successful, until the German war ended in 1945. That probably prompted C. R. (later Earl) Attlee to make him president of the Board of Trade in the post-war Labour Government. With his usual long working days and grasp of detail Cripps crashed into Britain's economic problems. He saw clearly what would have to be done and that it would be unpopular. He endeavoured to alleviate the unpopularity by making regular and clear expositions of the country's need to increase exports and production. Nobody at that time could compare with him in his ability to force the House of Commons and the nation to listen to dry unpalatable economic facts and to be moved by his presentation of them, although he never had any gift for literary phraseology or oratorical language.

Cripps went with two other cabinet ministers on the cabinet mission to India in 1946. He was the mission's directing force, working with all his powers of persuasion and energy to bring Congress and the Moslem League to agreement. The cabinet mission plan, with all its complicated essentials drafted by Cripps himself in one morning before breakfast, was the basis of all subsequent political discussion. That it failed was due to Congress withdrawing its initial acceptance although the Moslem League had agreed to it. Yet Cripps's knowledge of the situation and perseverance did much to bring both sides to a realization of Britain's determination to withdraw and to the necessity which lay upon them of coming to terms.

In October 1947 Cripps, who had begun to dominate the home economic front, was appointed minister for economic affairs.

When, in a few weeks' time, Hugh (later Lord) Dalton was forced to resign as the result of a budget indiscretion, Cripps was the natural successor as chancellor of the Exchequer. With things going from bad to worse as a backwash of the war, Cripps instituted in the beginning of 1948 a voluntary wage freeze. Without legislation to back him, by his mental, almost spiritual, force and the strength of his moral integrity, he compelled the trade-union leaders to comply. He promised them that he would likewise make private industry accept a dividend limitation and in 1949 he was able to announce that 93 per cent of business firms had not only agreed to hold their dividends but were in fact doing so. Cripps held the front for two years with no better weapon than the strength of his personality. During this period he probably had more power over the economy than any other single minister before. Despite his efforts, in September 1949 he was obliged to announce the devaluation of the pound. When he explained his reasons to Churchill, then leader of the Opposition, immediately before the announcement, the wartime leader complimented him on his courage and congratulated him for doing exactly the right thing. Cripps was the more distressed, therefore, when Churchill in the House of Commons and elsewhere pointed to Cripps's earlier statements that there was no intention to devalue the pound and said that he could no longer be trusted as chancellor and should resign. To Churchill this was the small change of politics. To Cripps, who believed passionately in truth, it was grievous abuse and later that year he declined to accept an honorary degree from the hands of Churchill as chancellor of Bristol University. Cripps was able to demonstrate that there was no intention to devalue at the time he had made his various disclaiming statements. It was only the suddenly worsening dollar crisis that had forced the measure on him.

Cripps's frail constitution was now letting him down more and more frequently. In the summer of 1950 he was compelled to go for medical treatment to Switzerland. On 20 October 1950 he resigned in a state of almost complete exhaustion. Held so high in the world's regard it was strange, though touching, that he was hurt by the omission of King George VI to offer him one word of thanks for the work he had done when he tendered his resignation. But Cripps had established a firm place in the regard of his countrymen who trusted him because they believed that his clearly expressed Christian principles were not a sham but a reality which moved into every action and word. Although he acquired the sobriquet 'Austerity Cripps', because he was obliged to make the nation tighten its belt in order to survive the arduous post-war years, it was soon realized that he never believed in austerity for austerity's sake and that his toughness had been right and justified.

In October 1951 Cripps returned from Switzerland to his home in the Cotswolds but at the beginning of 1952 he had once more to go back to Switzerland where there was a recurrence of the spinal infection which finally killed him on 21 April 1952, three days before his sixty-third birthday. His ashes were buried in the Cotswold village of Sapperton.

For the whole of his public life Cripps leant heavily on his wife, Isobel, daughter of Commander Harold William Swithinbank, of Denham Court, Bucks., whom he married in 1911. She was appointed G.B.E. in 1946. She shared with Cripps the same simple Christian faith and was always at his side wherever he went. Without her help his health would have been even worse than it was throughout his life and undoubtedly he would have done far less work. Her creation of a happy home atmosphere was more important to him, in constant need of rest from the exactions he placed upon himself, than for most men in public life. They had three daughters and one son, John Cripps, who contributes two notices to this Supplement.

Cripps was a fellow of University College, London (1930), rector of Aberdeen University (1942–5), and was elected F.R.S. in 1948. He was appointed C.H. in 1951.

A bust by Siegfried Charoux is in the possession of the family; another by (Sir) Jacob Epstein is in St. Paul's Cathedral.

[Colin Cooke, *The Life of Richard Stafford Cripps*, 1957; Eric Estorick, *Stafford Cripps*, 1949; private information; personal knowledge.]   WOODROW WYATT.

CROMER, second EARL OF (1877–1953), lord chamberlain to the household. [See BARING, ROWLAND THOMAS.]

CROWE, SIR EDWARD THOMAS FREDERICK (1877–1960), public servant, was born at Zante in the Ionian Islands 20 August 1877, the son of Alfred Louis Crowe, who later became vice-consul for the island, and his wife, Matilda Fortunata Barff. He was sent to England for his education at Bedford Grammar School and in 1897 was appointed a student interpreter in Japan. During the Russo-Japanese war he was in charge of the consulate at Tamsui, Taipeh, then a Japanese possession, where his ability attracted attention at Tokyo, and in 1906 he was appointed to the legation as commercial attaché. In 1918, after the creation in London of the Department of Overseas Trade and the commercial diplomatic service, he was confirmed as the first commercial counsellor to the new embassy at Tokyo, and he held that post until 1924 when he was recalled to London to serve in the department as director of the foreign division. Four years later he was promoted head of the department as comptroller-general. He never returned to the Far East, but his admiration and affection for the Japanese people remained a feature of his life. For seven years he was vice-president of the Japan Society in London, the Japanese ambassador being traditionally its president, and he took an active part in its work, on the council and at its lectures. After the war of 1939–45 he led a movement for the submission of a petition for clemency to the war crimes tribunal at Tokyo for Mamoru Shigemitsu the former ambassador in London. Crowe was later decorated with the Japanese Order (first class) of the Sacred Treasure.

Crowe's nine years as comptroller general in London marked the period of widest influence for the short-lived Department of Overseas Trade. He brought to the post a practical and sympathetic experience of the problems facing exporters to overseas markets and he was endowed with a boundless energy, an inquisitive mind, and a remarkable capacity for holding men and winning their confidence. Not content with the current administrative duties of his office he had to know intimately each member of his staff, at home or overseas; he was in personal contact with the leaders in banking, industry, and commerce in London, and he was repeatedly taking the initiative to visit the great centres of industry in the provinces and to address the chambers of commerce. The legend of the apathy or indifference of government departments to the difficulties of exporters was exploded. Above all, he strove for the expansion of the annual British Industries Fair which reached its international prestige

tige mainly through his exertions. For nine years he was vice-president of the International Exhibitions Bureau at Paris, and vice-president of the board of governors of the Imperial Institute.

In 1937, although at the height of his mental vigour, Crowe reached retiring age. He was elected to the boards of a number of companies and became an ardent supporter of the Royal Society of Arts, serving as vice-president (1937–60), president (1942–3), and chairman of the council (1941–3). He identified himself particularly with the society's work for the education of young people and for sixteen years was chairman of its examination committee. Among the government committees on which he served was that under Lord Fleming [q.v.] on public schools (1942–4).

Crowe was one whose character found its happier development only after his release from the ties of official life. He was not a scholar and he disliked being alone; his delight was in the human touch, in meeting men and women and drawing them to him. He had an easy and graceful facility for public speaking, enjoyed abundant health and appeared to be incapable of fatigue. At the launching of a Mansion House appeal, at the inauguration of some social movement, as a platform speaker, he was always ready to play his part, with his infective zest for life. In his old age, with his mass of white hair, his monocle, and his blue beret, he was a familiar and popular figure. He was appointed C.M.G. in 1911, knighted in 1922, and advanced to K.C.M.G. in 1930.

In 1901 Crowe married Eleanor (died 1947), daughter of William Hyde Lay, who had been British consul at Chefoo. They had one daughter and two sons, one of whom, Sir Colin Crowe, became chief of administration of the diplomatic service in 1965 and British high commissioner in Canada in 1968. Crowe died 8 March 1960 at his son's house in Cairo where he was then chargé d'affaires.

[Foreign Office records; *Journal* of the Royal Society of Arts, April 1960; personal knowledge.]   R. L. NOSWORTHY.

CRUIKSHANK, ROBERT JAMES (1898–1956), journalist, the son of Robert James Cruikshank, a coffee-house keeper, and his wife, Ellen Batcheldor, was born in Kensington 19 April 1898. Although his father was an Ulsterman, 'Robin' Cruikshank, who had little formal education, started his journalistic life as a reporter

on the *Bournemouth Guardian*, whence he rapidly graduated to London. After service in the war of 1914–18, he joined the staff of the *Daily News* in 1919 and remained with that organization for the rest of his life. With his gifted and fluent style he quickly made his mark and started to move up the ladder. In 1919 he was sent to Prague to report the founding of the Czechoslovak republic; his dispatches at once established him as a foreign correspondent of singular promise. Thereafter it was in this field that his most sustained and notable journalistic achievements were to lie. By 1924 he had risen to the post of diplomatic correspondent of the *Daily News* and four years later he was given the important and responsible assignment of representing the paper (which by then had absorbed the *Westminster Gazette*) in New York.

In this position, which he held for the next eight years, Cruikshank made a reputation as one of the top-ranking British correspondents in America, both by the knowledge and sympathetic understanding of America and Americans which he soon acquired and by the vividness and dependability of his reporting. It was once said of him by an American that he 'came to know Americans better than they knew themselves'. This may have been so, but in the course of his life he was to have the opportunity of doing as much as any journalist of his generation in making England and the English known and understood by Americans. He loved England, and was widely and sometimes unexpectedly read in its literature, with a special bias in favour of the Victorians.

In 1936 when the post of managing editor of the *Star* became vacant Cruikshank was invited to return to England to take it up. He was appointed a director of the *Star*, the evening stable companion of the *Daily News* which in the interval had become the *News Chronicle*. The same year marked the publication of his novel *The Double Quest* in which he wittily exploited his knowledge of the contrasts and comparisons between the British and American cultures.

It was not surprising that after the outbreak of war Cruikshank's wide knowledge of the American press and pressmen, combined with his general journalistic talent and his gift for getting on with all manner of people, should have resulted in his being appointed in 1941 director of the American division at the Ministry of Information. This entailed his absence from the editorial chair of the *Star* for the rest of the war. He was also in 1941–2 deputy director-general of the British Information Services in the United States. This second Anglo-American period, with its combination of journalism and diplomacy, probably marked the peak of his professional achievement. He was appointed C.M.G. in 1945 and, the war over, returned to become, as it were, one of the senior statesmen of the *Daily News* organization, being appointed a director of *Daily News*, Ltd. (the parent company), and of the *News Chronicle*, Ltd.

Cruikshank was now taking an active part in the editorial and general direction of both newspapers and seemed destined for the highest positions. It was thus a natural move, when (Sir) Gerald Barry resigned from the editorship of the *News Chronicle* at the end of 1947, that Cruikshank should succeed him. It is questionable whether his talent lay chiefly in the direction of editorship—he was happier and more at ease writing himself than directing others to write—and it seemed that the burdens of editorship lay rather heavily upon him. By 1954 his health had begun to show signs of deterioration which affected his grip on day-to-day control and by the end of the year he found it necessary to resign. His death in London 14 May 1956 at the comparatively early age of fifty-eight cut short a career which held promise of even greater achievement, in which the writing of more books would surely have played a part.

Cruikshank loved writing and seemed to have been born with an easy and ebullient style. His book *Roaring Century*, written in 1946 to mark the centenary of the *News Chronicle*, gave a good example of his rich appreciation of Victorian Britain. Characteristically he waived his royalties in it in favour of the Printers' Pension Fund. Shortly afterwards he wrote *Charles Dickens and Early Victorian England* (1949) and in 1951 *The Moods of London*. As a man, he was gay, gentle, and generous, and the fluency and wit of his conversation made him a delightful and stimulating companion in any company. Success and popularity did nothing to spoil a character which was essentially sensitive, modest, and understanding of others. His other great loves besides journalism and literature were music and the theatre: from 1947 to 1955 he was a governor of the Old Vic, and at one time he was among the sponsors of the London Philharmonic Orchestra.

In 1939 Cruikshank married Margaret Adele MacKnight, herself a gifted journalist, whom he had met in New York. I was a particularly happy marriage which gave him much strength and support They had two daughters. A portrait b William Evans was exhibited at the Roya Society of Portrait Painters in 1964.

[Private information; personal knowledge.
                                        GERALD BARRY

CULLIS, WINIFRED CLARA (1875 1956), physiologist, younger daughter an fifth of the six children of Frederick Joh Cullis, surveyor and civil engineer to th Gloucester Dock Company, by his wife Louisa, daughter of John Corbett, wa born 2 June 1875 in Tuffley, South Ham let, Gloucester. Despite three centuries i the county, the family moved to Birming ham in 1880 for better educational facil ties. Winifred Cullis was a lively, cor siderate, and generous child who learnt s quickly that her older brother Cuthbe lost half his fee for teaching her to rea At the King Edward VI High School fc Girls she was outstanding academically athletic, musical, popular, and know for her beautiful speaking voice. Sh specialized in science, attending Maso College for practical classes in physics an physiology.

She entered Newnham College, Can bridge, as Sidgwick scholar in 1896, takin a second in both parts of the natur sciences tripos (1899–1900). She took h M.A. in 1927. As an undergraduate sh worked under J. N. Langley and (Si F. G. Hopkins [qq.v.] whom she held i affectionate regard. She was elected a associate of Newnham College (1919–3 and president of the College Roll (1952–5

In 1901 she assisted T. G. Brodie in th research laboratories of the Royal Co leges of Surgeons and Physicians ar gained teaching experience as a part-tim instructor in elementary science in private school for girls. Later that ye she was appointed demonstrator physiology at the London (Royal Fr Hospital) School of Medicine for Wome Langley had supported her applicatio writing of her sound qualifications, ha and judicious work, independent though accuracy, and skill. She was appointed c lecturer with Brodie, 1903–8; part-tin lecturer and head of department, 190 whole-time lecturer and head of depar ment, 1912, loyally serving the school ar hospital until her death.

Amongst those with whom she pu

lished papers were W. E. Dixon and W. D. Halliburton [qq.v.], and she also wrote *The Body and Its Health* (with M. Bond, 1935) and *Your Body and the Way It Works* (1949). The university of London in 1908 awarded her the degree of D.Sc. for her work on the isolated mammalian heart and frog kidney, and conferred the titles of reader (1912) and professor of physiology (1920) upon her. In 1926 she became the first holder of the Jex-Blake chair of physiology, retiring with the title of professor emeritus in 1941. She taught some 1,600 medical students with lucidity and disarming simplicity of exposition, a robust sense of humour and endearing enthusiasm. Her integrity, warmth, and charm made her teaching memorable. Always nervous beforehand, she sounded at ease whether lecturing to students, broadcasting, or addressing an audience in the Albert Hall. These gifts lost her a very promising career in research but extended her influence to national and international affairs.

On the death of Brodie in 1916 Winifred Cullis was invited to replace him at Toronto until a successor was appointed. In 1919 she lectured to troops in Gibraltar and Malta for the Colonial Office and was appointed O.B.E., being promoted C.B.E. in 1929. In 1940–41 she travelled over 10,000 miles lecturing on wartime Britain in the Far East, Antipodes, and the United States. In 1941–3 she was head of the women's section of the British Information Services in New York; and she lectured, mainly to the Royal Air Force, in the Middle East in 1944–5.

This intense activity after retirement reflected lifelong interests in promoting international understanding and general and health education for adults and children by lecturing, broadcasting, use of films, and serving on committees responsible for curricula. She was a co-founder of the British and International Federations of University Women, being president of each successively (1925–9, 1929–32). She was deputy chairman of the English-speaking Union and chairman of its educational and universities sections. In these and the scholarship selection committees her judgement, humanity, and breadth of outlook were invaluable.

She was never a militant feminist but sought the emancipation of both sexes. She derived kindly amusement from the threatened resignation of demonstrators at Mason College who declared biology unfit study for a girl; and from her relega-tion to the galleries of Cambridge lecture theatres and her subjection to much passive and some active professional resistance from male colleagues. She received several honorary degrees and was proud of being the first woman member of the Physiological Society; the second to be appointed to a British university chair and the first in a medical school; the guest of the South Australian Government at the centenary celebrations (1936); and the only woman delegate to the silver jubilee of the Indian Science Congress in Calcutta (1937–8).

Her tact, regard for others, persuasive common sense, good humour and wit, made her an admirable committee woman and a formidable opponent. Apart from university, hospital, and medical school committees, she served on the council of the National Institute of Industrial Psychology, the Fatigue Research Board of the Medical Research Council, the Home Office committee on the two-shift system for women and young persons, the British Association and Trades Union Congress committee on scientific planning of industry, the Central Council of Recreative Physical Training, the governing body of the Royal Academy of Dancing; and she was chairman of the governing body of Chelsea Polytechnic and a director of *Time and Tide*. To all these she gave unstinting support and yet found time, as she recorded, for recreation by reading and cross-stitch.

Winifred Cullis was handsome, well built, and well dressed. Although lacking classical beauty, her features were noble, her blue eyes kindly and shrewd. She was high principled but tolerant. The gift of setting children and adults at ease stemmed from serenity, warmth, gaiety, and a regal memory for names. Apparently tireless, her health was indifferent and she slept little. But, as Dr. Edith Batho recorded, 'a wide generosity of temper and unusual mental and physical vigour carried her to an enviable old age and neither she nor her friends had to lament any diminution in her magnificent personality'. Like her brothers, Professors Cuthbert and Charles Cullis, she was a beloved teacher. She was active to the day of her death in London 13 November 1956.

A portrait by Alice Burton is in Crosby Hall, Chelsea, London, and one by P. Dodd is in the Royal Free Hospital School of Medicine.

[*The Times*, 15 November 1956; *British Medical Journal* and *Lancet*, 24 November

1956; *University Women's Review*, vol. xlvii, 1957; *Journal* of the Medical Women's Federation, vol. xxxix, 1957; *Newsletter* of the International Federation of University Women, vol. xiii, 1957; private information; personal knowledge.] RUTH E. M. BOWDEN.

CUMMINGS, ARTHUR JOHN (1882–1957), journalist and author, was born at Barnstaple 22 May 1882, the third child and eldest of three sons of John Cummings, North Devon representative of the *Devon and Exeter Gazette*, by his wife, Maria Elizabeth Richards. B. F. Cummings [q.v.] was his youngest brother. Arthur Cummings went to Rock Park School, Barnstaple, and at his closing speech day was described by his headmaster as *facile princeps*. As a schoolboy he came under the long-lasting influence of Philip Ernest Richards, then an Oxford undergraduate, who after some years in the Unitarian ministry became professor of English in Lahore where he died in 1920; he helped to mould Cummings's judgement of men, books, and ethics. Cummings hoped to study law at Oxford, but this ambition met with disappointment when his father, a Tory journalist of high reputation, especially as a columnist, who presided over a stimulating family life and trained his sons well, broke down in health. Cummings then joined the *Devon and Exeter Gazette* and was entrusted with more than a beginner's routine tasks. He wrote musical notices (he played the violin), leading articles, and even stock market comments. From Devon he moved to the *Rochdale Observer* and thence to the reporting staff of the *Sheffield Telegraph*, for which he not only did vivid descriptive work but also wrote essays in the manner of his lifelong hero, Hazlitt. He moved from Sheffield to the *Yorkshire Post* at Leeds not long before the outbreak of war in 1914. He served in many actions on the western front in the 4th West Riding (Howitzer) brigade, R.F.A., W.R. Territorials, and became a captain. After the war he became an assistant editor of the *Yorkshire Post* but although he did first-rate work for that sturdy Conservative organ his heart was not in its more Conservative politics.

In 1920 Cummings eagerly accepted an invitation to be an assistant editor of the *Daily News* (later the *News Chronicle*), the start of what proved to be thirty-five years' service for that paper. There a trenchant radicalism and campaigning zest found the scope he longed for. He became deputy editor and then political

editor. In the thirties his reputation became international. He sent penetratingly interpretative reports from the economic conference at Ottawa in 1932 and severely criticized the Government for the economic arrangements which were made at the conference. In 1933 he described the Reichstag fire trial in dispatches imbued with a burning hatred of injustice. He made an even deeper impression by the convictions he expressed when reporting in the paper and in a book the trial at Moscow of the British engineers in 1933. The book was hailed as a masterpiece in the literature of great trials. In depicting the Russian political background Cummings deplored the narrow-mindedness and cruelty of dictatorship. He abominated Communism as an ideology.

His foreign correspondence in 1933 won Cummings a Selfridge award. More important was the close, compulsive, and often hostile attention which politicians of more than the Left now paid to all that he wrote. By the late thirties he had become perhaps the best-read political commentator in Britain. His twice weekly 'Spotlight on Politics' achieved a success like that of leading American columnists, but unlike their work it appeared in one newspaper alone.

Cummings had his intimates in political life, among them Lloyd George and Lord Beaverbrook; but he was more of a desk man and a thinker and far less of a peripatetic Autolycus than most journalists who concentrate on political trends. He could have joined the Beaverbrook press on more generous terms than the *New Chronicle* afforded, but his loyalty to the Liberal paper matched and indeed arose from his devotion to its uncompromising creed. He crusaded with heart and soul for radicalism. Opposition steeled his nerve and made his phrases more deadly. He despised any truckling to dictatorship, saw the perils in Hitlerism, accused the British Government of failure to construct adequate defences at home and adequate alliances abroad (such as an alliance with Russia), and was among the foremost in rallying the Left against both appeasement and tyranny.

The Institute of Journalists elected Cummings president for 1952–3. In his presidential address (1953) he gave stout encouragement to the Press Council which had started work that year. The press he said, 'has now an authoritative voice which cannot with impunity be disregarded'. He deplored the increasing parliamentary tendency to raise questions of privilege and foresaw growing difficulties for legitimate press criticism. He retired from the *News Chronicle* in 1955.

Cummings's lucid, analytical mind found expression in eager conversation, never mere gossip, with intimate friends, and a literary style sometimes graceful and persuasive, more often stern and constructively argumentative, never clamorous. A man of strong moral and intellectual fibre, who enjoyed life and said he wanted to live for ever, he might have been described as a cheerful Puritan. His books included *The Moscow Trial* (1933), *The Press and a Changing Civilisation* (1936), and *This England* (1945).

In 1908 Cummings married Lilian, daughter of John Boreham, of Sheffield, who died seven months later of peritonitis. In 1915 he married an artist, Nora, daughter of Arthur Suddards, bank inspector, of Leeds. They had a son, Michael, a political cartoonist, and a daughter, Jean, a journalist. He died in London 4 July 1957.

A lifesize portrait in oils of Cummings by Nora Cummings is in the possession of the family.

[*The Times* and *News Chronicle*, 6 July 1957; private information; personal knowledge.] LINTON ANDREWS.

CURTIS, LIONEL GEORGE (1872–1955), public servant, was born at Coddington, Ledbury, 7 March 1872, the youngest of the four children of the rector, the Rev. George James Curtis, and his wife, Frances Carr. He was educated at the Wells House, Malvern Wells, at Haileybury, and at New College, Oxford, where he obtained third classes in classical honour moderations (1893) and *literae humaniores* (1895). On leaving Oxford he became secretary first to L. H. Courtney later Lord Courtney of Penwith, q.v.), then to Lord Welby [q.v.] who was mainly engaged in work on the London County Council. Twice during this time Curtis set himself to gain practical experience of the working of the Poor Law by assuming the character of a tramp, begging his bread along the high roads, and sleeping at night in workhouses. During these years he also studied law and was later (1902) called to the bar by the Inner Temple.

In 1899 he and his New College friend, Lionel Hichens [q.v.], enlisted as privates in the City Imperial Volunteers, and went off to the South African war. In 1900 he acted as secretary to Sir Alfred (later Viscount) Milner [q.v.] who in the next year

set him to work on a plan for the new Johannesburg municipality and shortly afterwards appointed him town clerk. Curtis gave an account of his experiences in his book *With Milner in South Africa* (1951). In 1903 he left Johannesburg for Pretoria to become an assistant colonial secretary in order to organize municipal government throughout the Transvaal.

After the departure of Milner in 1905 and the arrival of Lord Selborne [q.v.] as high commissioner and governor, 'Milner's kindergarten', headed by Curtis, set themselves to prepare a formal memorandum showing the imperative need for uniting the four South African colonies. This memorandum, written mainly by Curtis, was adopted by Selborne and submitted by him formally in 1907 to all the South African governments, including the new responsible governments of the Transvaal and Orange River Colony. It was accepted by them as the basis for discussion at a national convention. Curtis then resigned from government service in order to create 'closer union' societies throughout South Africa.

In 1909 the Union constitution was completed and Curtis returned to England together with some others of the 'kindergarten'. With his friends he founded the *Round Table*, a quarterly review, of which Philip Kerr (later the Marquess of Lothian, q.v.) became the first editor, to advocate the federation of the self-governing countries of the 'British Commonwealth', thus introducing this name for the first time. For a short time in 1912 Curtis was Beit lecturer on colonial history at Oxford but between the years 1911 and 1916 he devoted himself mainly to a study of the closer union of the British Commonwealth, travelling extensively through the Commonwealth and forming Round Table groups. In 1916 he published two reports: *The Problem of the Commonwealth* and *The Commonwealth of Nations*.

In 1916 and 1917 he took a prominent part in India in discussions relating to the progress of that country towards self-government. His activities and the Montagu–Chelmsford reforms led him to publish a book entitled *Dyarchy* (1920) which also contained his 'Letters to the People of India'. In 1918 Lord Robert Cecil (later Viscount Cecil of Chelwood, q.v.) appointed Curtis a member of the League of Nations section of the British delegation at the Paris peace conference. During this work Curtis initiated plans for the creation of an Institute of

International Affairs, and it was through his efforts in 1920–21 that the (Royal) Institute of International Affairs in London (Chatham House) was founded and endowed.

Curtis was appointed a research fellow of All Souls College, Oxford, in 1921. In the same year he was invited by Lloyd George to take part in the negotiations for an Irish treaty, acting as his adviser and as a secretary, with Thomas Jones [q.v.], to the British delegation at the Irish conference. He assisted in framing the Irish constitution and remained, until October 1924, 'adviser to the Colonial Office on Irish affairs'.

In the ten years between 1924 and 1934 Curtis was engaged mainly in writing his book, *Civitas Dei*, which was published in three volumes over the years 1934–7, and in which he set forth his gospel of Commonwealth, and indeed world, unity under free and democratic institutions. During the war of 1939–45 Curtis, who was then living at Kidlington, took an active part in the foreign research and press service housed at Balliol College, in writing numerous pamphlets, and forming study groups of men and women in the armed Services at Oxford. To the end of his life, as he showed during this period, he had the power to exercise decisive and lasting influence on the young. Among those who admired him, and whom he greatly admired, were T. E. Lawrence [q.v.] and Helmuth von Moltke, the young German patriot done to death by Hitler. Curtis continued publication of further pamphlets after the war. Among other causes which in his time he helped to bring to fruition by his energy were the founding of the Oxford Society and of the Oxford Preservation Trust, as well as the preservation of the Wytham estate for the university.

It was as a man of action and an enthusiast who exercised a compelling influence over others that Curtis was remarkable, rather than as a professional historian—which he never claimed to be. He held no important position and was not well known to the general public, yet his influence was great: in the creation of the Union of South Africa, in the progress of India towards self-government, and in the Irish treaty. 'Possessed by a burning zeal for causes which he thought worthy, he would throw himself into them with complete self-abandonment, with a commanding vigour which pressed into the service the best energies of his friends whether they would or no, and without

thought of recognition either of his efforts or of theirs. In the result his objects were apt to be achieved, while the prime motive force which had produced their achievement remained unknown to the world.' (*Round Table*, March 1956). It was because of his burning zeal for the causes on which he set his heart that his 'kindergarten' friends likened him to Isaiah and nicknamed him 'the prophet'. At times some of his colleagues wilted under the strain, but whether they agreed with him or not they remained his devoted friends.

Curtis received honorary degrees from the universities of Melbourne and Cologne, and was made a C.H. in 1949. He married in 1920 Gladys Edna (Pat), youngest daughter of the late Prebendary Percy Richard Scott, of Tiverton. They had no children. He died at Kidlington, Oxford, 24 November 1955. A portrait by Sir Oswald Birley is at the Royal Institute of International Affairs; another, by Maurice Greiffenhagen, is at Prior Croft, Camberley. A drawing by Augustus John is in the possession of the family.

[Private information; personal knowledge.
BRAND
[Arnold J. Toynbee, *Acquaintances*, 1967.

DADABHOY, SIR MANECKJI BYRAMJI (1865–1953), Indian lawyer, industrialist, and parliamentarian, was born in Bombay 30 July 1865. He came of a much respected Parsi family, the second son of Khan Bahadur Byramji Dadabhoy J.P., registrar of joint stock companies and assurances. He was educated in Bombay at the Fort and Proprietary High School, a well-known institution of its time, then at St. Xavier's College from which he graduated. In 1884 he went to England, was admitted to the Middle Temple, and in 1887 called to the bar. On his return to India he began to practise at the Bombay high court and at an unusually early age was elected a member of the Bombay municipal corporation. In 1888 he was made a justice of the peace. In 1890 he moved to Nagpur and enrolled as an advocate at the court of the judicial commissioner of the Central Provinces. He was appointed manager of Raja Bahadur Laxman Rao Bhonsle's estate in Nagpur and negotiated the partition of that estate between the Raja Bahadur and his brother. For this he received a fee which in those days was regarded as a record and the case brought him prominence in his profession. He was elected to the Nagpur municipal corporation and served the body for forty years (1890–1930). In 1896 he was appointed government advocate. He found time to write commentaries on the Central Provinces Tenancy Acts of 1888 and 1898 which became standard works. He was retained by the G.I.P. Railway in connection with the development of their communications in the Central Provinces, and was also associated with the activities of a wealthy Marwari business house in Ahmedabad.

So Dadabhoy moved more and more into the industrial and public life of his province. Through partnership in a mining syndicate, he had a share in the development of the considerable mineral resources of the Central Provinces. He was director of a number of textile mills, founded and was managing director of the Nagpur Electric Light and Power Company, and was managing proprietor of several collieries and other industrial concerns. His interests and ability brought him leadership in the Indian industrial community as a whole. In 1907 he presided at the Central Provinces and Berar industrial conference, and in 1911 he was elected president of the All-India industrial conference in Calcutta. Throughout his public career he took a keen practical, and urgent interest in the industrialization of India. He was recognized as an authority on the economic life of the country and served on a number of commissions dealing with finance and economics, including the Indian fiscal commission (1921–2) and the royal commission on Indian currency and finance (1925–6). From 1920 to 1932 he was a governor of the Imperial Bank of India.

Dadabhoy's long experience of municipal politics served him well when he entered the wider parliamentary field in 1908, on his nomination to the governor-general's legislative council of which he was subsequently an elected member. He soon established a prominent position as a forceful, independent, and constructive critic of the Government of India. In 1921 he was elected to the Council of State to which he was subsequently nominated in 1926, 1931, and 1937, and of which he became president in 1932. He filled this post with distinction and general acceptance until 1946, when the Constituent Assembly was established to draw up a constitution for the independent India which was to come into being in 1947.

Dadabhoy was short of stature, and this often left the members of the Council of State in some doubt whether their presi-

dent was standing up or sitting down—a dilemma which gave him much amusement. If short, he was sturdy and robust, and gave the impression of great physical strength. He had an agile mind, shrewd judgement, great tact, and a rare capacity for making friends. Although a strong nationalist and a frequent and candid critic of the Government, he was a profound believer in the value of Indo-British partnership and friendship to the Commonwealth and to the world. This conviction was the keynote of his public and parliamentary career and the theme of his outspoken and constructive contribution to the second session of the Round Table conference in London in 1931 which he attended as a delegate. It was also the basis of his conduct during his years as president of the Council of State where, throughout some of the stormiest periods in India's political history, he succeeded in exercising his authority and influence with the general support of all parties in the house.

Dadabhoy was gregarious, cosmopolitan, and hospitable. He was an expert in the arts of 'winning friends and influencing people' of all communities and races. In the United Kingdom he entertained lavishly at Kingsnympton Hall, on Kingston Hill, Surrey. He was a generous host at his spacious house in Nagpur, and at the many social clubs of which he was a member, in Bombay, Delhi, Simla, and Calcutta. Sometimes his hospitality had a political purpose; often there was no other aim than the enjoyment of entertaining friends. Whatever the occasion, his generosity was overflowing.

For his services in India Dadabhoy was appointed C.I.E. (1911), K.C.I.E. (1925), K.C.S.I. (1936), and knighted (1921). In 1884 he married Bai Jerbanoo, second daughter of Khan Bahadur Dadabhoy Pallonji, by whom he had two daughters. He died in Nagpur 14 December 1953.

[*The Times* and *Times of India*, 15 December 1953; *Hitavada of Nagpur*, 16 December 1953; private information; personal knowledge.]   FREDERICK JAMES.

DAKIN, HENRY DRYSDALE (1880–1952), biochemist, was born in Hampstead 12 March 1880, the youngest of a family of five sons and three daughters. His father, Thomas Burns Dakin, was then the owner of a sugar refinery in London, but later acquired an iron and steel business in Leeds, and moved there with his family in 1893. His mother was Sophia Stevens.

Dakin, after a brief period at the Merchant Taylors' School, then in London, was, therefore, removed at the age of thirteen to the Leeds Modern School. When, later, the school moved and was organized in four houses, each named after a distinguished former pupil, one of these was named 'Dakin House'. It would appear, however, that Dakin left school before the age for a university course; for he had served as an apprentice to the Leeds city analyst, T. Fairley, before he entered, in 1898, what was then the Yorkshire College, Leeds. In later years he recalled this early and strict scientific discipline of an analyst's laboratory as valuable training for his lifelong devotion to the then newly emergent science of biochemistry.

Dakin's course for the B.Sc. brought him at once into contact with Julius B. Cohen, then the lecturer in organic chemistry at the Yorkshire College. It was with Cohen that Dakin began to acquire his lasting interest in the optical activity of organic compounds, its influence on their biological activities, or on their acceptability as nutrients. His specially vivid interest in the selective action of a natural enzyme, on one component of a racemic compound, led Cohen to give him the nickname 'Zyme', which his friends were to use as a familiar mode of address for the rest of his life.

After obtaining his B.Sc. in 1901 from the Victoria University of Manchester, and a further year with Cohen as his personal assistant and demonstrator, Dakin was awarded a research exhibition by the 1851 Commissioners, and worked with it at the Jenner (later the Lister) Institute, under S. G. Hedin; at Heidelberg, with A. Kossel; and for a final period again at the Lister Institute. These researches covered enzymatic actions on proteins and, selectively, on racemic esters of mandelic acid; on arginase and protamines; and on the synthesis of the hormone adrenaline and related active bases.

At that juncture Christian A. Herter of New York was inquiring in London for somebody with suitable scientific and personal qualifications for an appointment with him, in a private laboratory for biochemical researches which he had installed, and fully equipped, on two upper floors of his Madison Avenue mansion. Dakin accepted this unusual opportunity, for which, indeed, he had unique qualifications; and, in the event, he was to spend the rest of his working life in developing its special possibilities. Its conditions ac-

centuated in him an inborn shrinking from any kind of publicity, which prevented him from taking part in any open meeting discussion, or ceremony. He was elected F.R.S. in 1917 but an invitation to deliver the Croonian lecture was met by a penitent refusal; and the award to him of its Davy medal (1941) was accepted only because, in wartime conditions, it could be presented in his own library. Congenial colleagues, however, were always welcomed to free and lively discussions of researches, in private. Dakin had, indeed, a genius for quietly intimate friendships. Meanwhile publications of his own important researches in biochemistry were issuing in a steady stream from the Herter Laboratory.

After Herter died in 1910 his widow, Mrs. Susan Dows Herter, was eager to maintain the laboratory, with Dakin thenceforward in sole charge of its uses. In 1916 their personal devotion was confirmed by their marriage. Dakin, though chronically unfit for active service, had hastened to Britain to offer his service for any national purpose. He eventually found opportunity for researches on the antiseptic treatment of wounds, and became an active advocate and exponent of the use of a buffered hypochlorite solution. This he used to great purpose in the *Aquitania* (then serving as a hospital ship for the Dardanelles) after having arranged for the installation of an electrolytic tank with which an unlimited supply of the hypochlorite solution—'Dakin's Solution' —could be made from sea water.

The Dakins moved later from Madison Avenue to a house and estate at Scarborough-on-Hudson, some thirty miles up-river from New York. There the laboratory was reinstated in a special building, and Dakin continued his researches, with their characteristic, unhurried perfection, almost until his death 10 February 1952, a year after that of his wife. They had no children. He had received honorary doctorates from Leeds, Yale, and Heidelberg.

[Sir Percival Hartley in *Obituary Notices of Fellows of the Royal Society*, No. 21, November 1952; private information; personal knowledge.]   H. H. DALE

DAMPIER, SIR WILLIAM CECIL DAMPIER (1867–1952), formerly WHETHAM, scientist and agriculturist, was born in South Hampstead, London, 27 December 1867, the only son (he had one sister) of Charles Langley Whetham, manufacturer nd his wife, Mary Ann, daughter of Thomas Dampier, glove manufacturer, of Yeovil. A shy boy, of indifferent health, he was educated for the most part privately. Becoming interested in science, he entered Trinity College, Cambridge, where he was awarded an exhibition and a scholarship in his second and third years. He obtained first classes in both parts of the natural sciences tripos (1888–9), was Coutts Trotter student (1889), and Clerk Maxwell scholar (1893). Influenced by Sir) J. J. Thomson [q.v.] he undertook research at the Cavendish Laboratory which earned him a college fellowship in 1891. He was a college lecturer (1895–1922), tutor (1907–13), senior tutor (1913–7), and remained a fellow for the rest of his life, an active member of the finance and estates committees and an ardent supporter of the Cambridge Preservation Society. He represented the university on the governing body of Winchester College (1917–47) but an attempt in 1918 to represent Cambridge University in Parliament as an independent Conservative proved unsuccessful.

In 1901 Whetham was elected F.R.S. for his electrolytic experiments and in the following year he published a treatise on the *Theory of Solution* which was for some time the standard textbook. College duties and other pursuits, however, gradually diverted him from research; but he retained an interest in the work of other scientists, contributing several notices to this Dictionary and publishing *The Recent Development of Physical Science* (1904) and *History of Science* (1929), both of which went into a number of editions.

In 1897 Whetham married Catherine Durning, daughter of Robert Durning Holt, shipowner, of Liverpool. They had one son and five daughters, two of whom became scientific research workers. Whetham and his wife meantime had become absorbed in the history of his forebears, among whom were Thomas and William Dampier [qq.v.], bishop and buccaneer respectively; they published a biography of the Roundhead Colonel Nathaniel Whetham in 1907. Led on to a general study of heredity and its influence in society, they wrote next *The Family and the Nation* (1909) and *Heredity and Society* (1912).

After inheriting the Dampier family property in 1916 Whetham farmed the land on the Hilfield estate in Dorset between 1918 and 1926. He specialized in the making of cheese and took part in the investigation of the possibilities of extracting lactose from whey. So he came to his last and abiding interest in agricultural economics. He was co-opted a member of council of the Royal Agricultural Society in 1921, received its gold medal in 1936, and became a vice-president in 1948. In 1925–42 he was a member of the Agricultural Wages Board; in 1933–51 a development commissioner; and in 1938–9 chairman of the land settlement committee. He was chairman of the Ministry of Agriculture machinery testing committee (1925–33) and of the committee for the preservation of grass and other fodder crops (1933–9), and acting chairman of the Rural Industries Bureau (1939–45). In 1931 he was knighted for his services to agriculture, and changed his name to Dampier. In the same year he became first secretary of the Agricultural Research Council which he was able to establish on sound lines with freedom to engage directly in research before resigning in 1935 when he felt the technical side of the work had gone beyond his range of knowledge. He remained a member of the Council until 1945 and served on many of its committees. A shrewd and kindly man who found his long life 'interesting and amusing', he was always willing to give his services in the public welfare. He died in Cambridge 11 December 1952, a few months after his wife. A portrait by George J. Coates is reproduced in Dampier's autobiography.

[*The Times*, 12 and 18 December 1952, and 23 January 1953; Sir William Dampier, *Cambridge and Elsewhere*, 1950; Sir Geoffrey Taylor and E. H. E. Havelock in *Obituary Notices of Fellows of the Royal Society*, vol. ix, 1954; private information.]

HELEN M. PALMER.

DAVIDSON, SIR JOHN HUMPHREY (1876–1954), major-general, was born in Mauritius 24 July 1876, the son of George Walter Davidson, merchant, and his wife, Johanna Smith Humphrey. Educated at Harrow and the Royal Military College, Sandhurst, he joined the King's Royal Rifle Corps and spent the first three years of his career (1896–9) in Mauritius with the 1st battalion. Moving to South Africa, the battalion was badly mauled at Talana in the action in which Sir William Penn Symons [q.v.] was killed, as well as Davidson's colonel and four other officers of his battalion. He went on to see action at the relief of Ladysmith and in the Transvaal with Sir Redvers Buller [q.v.].

He later took part in various sweeps after elusive Boers. He was appointed to the D.S.O. (1900), mentioned in dispatches, and promoted captain (1901).

After service in Malta and with the International Force in Crete, Davidson entered the Staff College by nomination at the end of 1905. It was the time of the reforms of R. B. (later Viscount) Haldane [q.v.] when the British Army began to prepare itself for modern continental war amid an organizational and intellectual renaissance which gave Davidson an opportunity of displaying talents as a staff officer. In 1908–10 he was G.S.O. 3 to the military training directorate of the new general staff; he returned to field duties as brigade-major in the 5th Infantry brigade at Aldershot (1910–12). From 1912 to 1914 he was instructor at the Staff College in training and tactics and also in general staff duties; but he had little experience of staff work with large formations in the field.

In 1914, now a major, Davidson became G.S.O. 2 (Intelligence) to the III Corps on mobilization, and took part in the retreat from Mons, the battles of the Marne and Aisne, and round Armentières. War brought unlooked-for opportunities and responsibilities: in December 1914 Davidson was lent to I Corps for special duties in connection with the delicate operation of relieving the exhausted Indian Corps in the water-logged valley of the Lys in the face of very active and aggressive German forces. During the relief, which lasted ten days, Davidson had to report every night to Sir Douglas (later Earl) Haig [q.v.] who asked for him as operations officer when First Army was formed under his command. In this capacity, as temporary colonel, Davidson took part in the battle of Neuve Chapelle (March 1915), the British Army's first set-piece offensive on the western front.

When Haig became commander-in-chief in December 1915, Davidson at the age of thirty-nine took over the key post of director of military operations to the British Armies in France. Thereafter he was associated with all Haig's tragedies and triumphs until the end of the war. With Sir Launcelot Kiggell [q.v.], chief of the general staff, and John Charteris, director of military intelligence, Davidson formed Haig's intimate entourage, and shared in and helped to form the mental climate in which Haig lived. No more than Kiggell had Davidson the weight of seniority and experience to enable him

strongly to question Haig's ideas and assumptions, or counterbalance Charteris' optimism. To a degree that it is not now possible to estimate, Davidson must be accorded responsibility for the tactical and organizational decisions which led to the British failure and heavy loss at the opening of the battle of the Somme.

In the spring and summer of 191 Davidson had his part in the confused conceptions which underlay British planning for the Passchendaele offensive. He accepted the offensive's distant objectives including clearing the Belgian coast, but his mind had not moved forward to the idea of deep, fluid penetration by groups of all arms already adopted by the German Army. Tanks he thought had no place in the first assault on the enemy's line, but only in the later stages of the battle. Neither Davidson nor his chief appeared to see the discrepancy between the ambitious objectives of the offensive and the limited nature of the tactical system and of the human and material resources. Davidson also shared the responsibility for the instructions given to Sir Hubert Gough, in command of the Fifth Army before the German offensive in March 1918. He recommended the preparation of strong rearward positions on the Somme and before Peronne, although he should have known that Gough had been given no labour for the task. Nor did he visit Gough during the battle.

It was not really until the summer of 1918 after the successes of the German spring offensives that the British Army abandoned the conception of the limited advance in line to a fixed linear objective after long preparatory bombardment. Nevertheless Davidson escaped the mounting outside criticism of G.H.Q. which cost Kiggell and Charteris their posts at the end of 1917 and he remained with Haig during the succession of British victories which followed 8 August 1918 to the end of the war. He was appointed C.B. in 1917 K.C.M.G. in 1919, and promoted major-general in 1918.

In that year he was elected to Parliament as Conservative member for the Fareham division of Hampshire which he represented until 1931. He retired from the army in 1922. He was a member of the army committee of the House of Commons and took a continued and far-sighted interest in defence questions. Yet his eulogy, *Haig: Master of the Field* (1953) revealed no great change in his appreciation of G.H.Q.'s conduct of the battle n France. He was chairman of the select committee on the training and employment of ex-servicemen and of the King's Roll National Council, and president of the Union Jack Club. He also held a number of directorships, including Vickers, and was chairman of the Bank of Australia (1937–49).

In 1905 Davidson married Margaret, daughter of John Peter Grant, of Rothiemurchus, Inverness-shire; they had one daughter. He died at Glack, Daviot, Aberdeenshire, 11 December 1954.

[John Terraine, *Douglas Haig, the Educated Soldier*, 1963; *The Private Papers of Douglas Haig, 1914–1919*, ed. Robert Blake, 1952.]
CORRELLI BARNETT.

DAVIE, THOMAS BENJAMIN (1895–1955), pathologist, teacher, vice-chancellor, was born at Prieska, Cape Colony, 23 November 1895, the fifth child and third son of Thomas Benjamin Davie, law agent, who came from Inverness in Scotland, and his wife, Caroline Charlotte Halliday. He was educated at government schools and at the university of Stellenbosch where he graduated with honours in science (1914) and took a teachers' diploma (1916). He taught in a secondary school for a short period before joining the Royal Flying Corps in which he became a lieutenant in 1918. He returned to South Africa in 1919 and taught science at various boys' schools in the Transvaal. In 1921 he married Vera Catherine, daughter of the Rev. Thomas Roper, a Wesleyan minister, by whom he had one daughter who died in infancy.

Tom Davie had, to all appearances, settled down to a career of schoolmastering for which he had exceptional gifts; but the course of his career was altered by the outbreak of the so-called Rand revolution in 1922. When the Government appealed for volunteers to restore order, he joined the Transvaal Scottish Regiment and, during the course of the disturbances, was wounded in the thigh. It was while convalescing in hospital that he decided to take up medicine, and in 1924 he and his wife went to the university of Liverpool where he had an academic career of unusual brilliance. As an undergraduate he won the Banks, Torr, Holt, and Kanthack medals, the Holt fellowship, the gold medal in public health, the silver medal in forensic medicine, a university scholarship in medicine, an exhibition in surgery, and, in his final year, the Owen T. Williams prize. He qualified in 1928 with first class honours and in the following year

was appointed to a junior lectureship in pathology. In 1931 he took the M.R.C.P. (London), and the M.D. (Liverpool) with a thesis on the production of antibodies. He became pathologist to Walton Hospital in the same year and in 1933 returned to the university of Liverpool as senior lecturer in pathology, a position which he held until 1935 when he was appointed to the chair of pathology at the university of Bristol. In 1938 he succeeded his former chief, Professor J. H. Dible, in the George Holt chair of pathology at Liverpool and collaborated with him in writing a *Textbook of Pathology* (1939).

Until the outbreak of war Davie's abilities were concentrated on the teaching of medicine, at which he excelled. The war brought out latent organizing and administrative qualities. He was responsible for establishing the first blood-bank in Liverpool and played a large part in organizing the blood-transfusion services under the Ministry of Health. He was elected F.R.C.P. (London) in 1940, and was awarded the United States medal of freedom (1947) for services to American hospitals in Great Britain. In 1945 he was appointed professor of applied pathology and became the first full-time dean of the medical faculty at Liverpool.

Three years later (1948) Davie became principal and vice-chancellor of the university of Cape Town. South Africa was in the throes of post-war reconstruction, her problems of readjustment aggravated by political and racial tensions which pervaded all aspects of national life, including the universities. The Nationalist Party which was returned to power in the general election of 1948 had actively opposed South Africa's participation in the war; it was avowedly republican; and it had been elected on the platform of apartheid between white and non-white South Africans. With none of these policies was Davie in sympathy; but it was in regard to the last that he came into conflict with government policy as head of a university which—like all South African universities—drew a large portion of its revenue from the State. Already in 1948 there were indications that the new Government was determined to compel universities to follow the official apartheid policy and to accept dictation from the State in what had traditionally been matters for the universities to decide for themselves. The university of Cape Town, whose policy had always been to admit all races, was particularly affected.

Davie was admirably equipped for the task which lay before him. He had an established reputation as a scientist and one of the foremost teachers of medicine in Britain, a member of learned societies devoted to the advancement of knowledge, and imbued with the great traditions of university education. Moreover, as a South African who spoke English and Afrikaans with equal ease, he had a deep knowledge of the problems of his country. To great intellectual qualities was added a personality which impressed itself on all who worked with him. He was a large man with big features which radiated friendliness and confidence. He had a gift for lucid and rational exposition; he expressed his opinions forcefully and with an enthusiasm which lit up his face; and it was clear to all who heard him that his opinions and enthusiasm were backed by intimate knowledge and great experience. Whether he was conducting post-mortems at Liverpool, or explaining the intricate details of a staffing or financial matter to his council at Cape Town, or addressing undergraduates on the ideals of a university, or leading a deputation to a minister of state—there was always the same dispassionate search for truth and forthright statement of principle which commanded deep respect. His immense vitality infected all with whom he came in contact, and not even the rheumatoid arthritis which he contracted soon after his return to South Africa and which grew progressively worse could subdue his spirit.

Davie was a great university principal. His first duty was to the university of Cape Town, and the development of that university under his wise and energetic leadership bears witness to his remarkable abilities. But his influence was felt far beyond its confines. At a critical time in the history of his country he led and inspired those who believed in the freedom of the university to determine for itself, on academic grounds, 'who may teach, what may be taught, how it shall be taught, and who may be admitted to study'.

In 1948 Cambridge conferred on Davie the honorary degree of LL.D.; and in 1955 the universities of Oxford, Liverpool, and Natal offered him honorary degrees which his death in London, 14 December 1955, prevented him from receiving. A bronze head by I. Mitford-Barberton is in the university of Cape Town.

[*British Medical Journal*, 24 December 1955; *Journal of Pathology and Bacteriology*, vol. lxxii, No. 2, 1956; University of Liverpool *Recorder*, No. 10, January 1956; private information; personal knowledge.]

L. MARQUARD

DAVIES, SIR WILLIAM (LLEWELYN) (1887-1952), librarian, was born at Plas Gwyn schoolhouse, near Pwllheli, 1 October 1887, the third child and younger son of William Davies by his wife, Jane Evans, both natives of Llanafan, Cardiganshire. His father, formerly the Earl of Lisburne's gamekeeper, was then similarly employed at Broom Hall, near Pwllheli but entered the service of (Sir Arthur Osmond Williams, of Castell Deudraeth when his son was five years old. Davie was educated at Portmadoc County School and the University College of Wales Aberystwyth, graduating B.A. (1909) with honours in Welsh and M.A. (1912) by virtue of a dissertation on a group of sixteenth- and seventeenth-century Ardudwy poets. He held various teaching appointments until the beginning of 1917 after which he served in the Royal Garrison Artillery and later as a commissioned officer in the Army Education Service.

In 1919 Davies was appointed first assistant librarian under (Sir) John Ballinger at the young National Library of Wales at Aberystwyth. When Ballinger retired in 1930 Davies succeeded him as chief librarian, a position which he held until his death. He continued the work so successfully begun, of building up in Wales a national library which would rank among the great libraries of the world. His experience as Ballinger's deputy, his interest in Welsh history and literature, his bilingualism, his zeal and enthusiasm, together served him in good stead. Endowed with exceptional organizing ability, he was a hard and conscientious worker who was never satisfied with inferior standards.

Davies was convinced from the outset that one of the library's most important functions was to collect and preserve the mass of manuscript and documentary material relating to Wales which was scattered (often in a state of neglect) throughout the Principality and farther afield—the raw material needed by historians. His task was made easier by the changing economic conditions which brought about the disintegration of large estates and the vacating of old country houses. The list of individual owners, institutions, and official bodies who responded to his diplomatic persuasion to transfer their records to the library, either absolutely or on permanent loan, is a notable one. Of the approximately three and a half million documents housed in the library when Davies died all but 200,000 or so were acquired during his period of administration. Collection and preservation, however, were not enough; adequate steps had to be taken to make the records available to researchers without undue delay. This was achieved by substituting handy, typewritten, brief-entry schedules and handlists for printed detailed calendars, and by the compilation of subject-indexes. Equally anxious to persuade other authorities to preserve the records in their custody, he urged the various county councils of Wales to establish records committees and he gave to municipal, ecclesiastical, and other bodies and to individuals valuable advice and practical assistance. He kept the library in close touch with other institutions with similar aims through his membership of the Historical Manuscripts Commission, the Society of Antiquaries, the executive committee of the Council for the Preservation of Business Archives, and the British Records Association, of which he was a vice-president representing the interests of Wales.

The preservation of records was only part of Davies's conspicuous service to Welsh culture. He was responsible for organizing the lending of books to adult study classes throughout Wales, for operating in eleven counties the Regional Libraries Scheme for Wales and Monmouthshire, and for the selection, acquisition, and distribution of books for patients in the sanatoria of Wales. During the war of 1939–45 he established a national committee to provide Welsh books for men and women serving in the forces. He missed no opportunity, through lectures, broadcast talks, and publications, of bringing the library into closer contact with the Welsh people. In 1937 he published *The National Library of Wales: Survey of its History, its Contents, and Activities*, whilst two years later he launched *The National Library of Wales Journal* which he edited for fourteen years. For varying periods he was honorary editor of the journals of the Welsh Bibliographical Society, the Cardiganshire Antiquarian Society, and the Merioneth Historical and Record Society; was also associate editor of *Y Bywgraffiadur Cymreig*, the Welsh biographical dictionary published in 1953 by the

Honourable Society of Cymmrodorion. A member of numerous academic and other cultural bodies, he was a leading spirit in every organization promoting the intellectual life of the Principality. He was knighted in 1944 and received the honorary degree of LL.D. from the university of Wales in 1951. In the year of his death he was high sheriff of Merioneth.

Davies married in 1914 Gwen, daughter of Dewi Llewelyn, grocer and baker, of Pontypridd, and afterwards adopted the additional name of Llewelyn. There was one daughter. He died at Aberystwyth, 11 November 1952, and his ashes were scattered in the grounds of the library.

[*The Times*, 12 November 1952; private information; personal knowledge.]

GILDAS TIBBOTT.

DAWKINS, RICHARD McGILLIVRAY (1871–1955), scholar, was born 24 October 1871 at Surbiton, Surrey, the eldest child of Richard Dawkins, captain in the Royal Navy, and his wife, Mary Louisa, daughter of Simon McGillivray and granddaughter of Sir John Easthope [q.v.]. In 1878 his father retired with the rank of rear-admiral and made his home at Stoke Gabriel near Totnes. Dawkins received his schooling at Totnes Grammar School and Marlborough College. He was an awkward, ungainly and short-sighted boy with a dislike for all forms of organized games which he retained throughout his life: his schooldays were unhappy, nor did he achieve any distinction in the classroom. He did, however, acquire a taste for botany which enriched his later life. From school he went to King's College, London, to train as an electrical engineer. In 1892, before completing his course, he became apprenticed to a firm of electrical engineers at Chelmsford. He did not find engineering congenial and these years in lonely lodgings were not happy. As the result of a temporary interest in theosophy, he characteristically determined to teach himself Sanskrit; he continued to read Greek and Latin classics, learned a good deal of Italian and some German and even started upon Icelandic, Irish, and Finnish. After the death of his father in 1896 and that of his mother in the following year a small legacy enabled him to forsake his profession and enter Emmanuel College, Cambridge, in 1898 at the age of twenty-six. He was a self-taught scholar without the customary grooming in Latin and Greek, but he was fortunate to find himself in the hands of Peter Giles (whose notice he subsequently contributed to this Dictionary) and James Adam [q.v.]. In 1899 the college gave him a scholarship, in 1901 he was placed in the third division of the first class of part i of the classical tripos, in 1902 he obtained a first class with distinction in part ii, and an honourable mention in the examination for the Chancellor's medals, and a Craven studentship. In 1904 he became a fellow (and in 1922 an honorary fellow) of Emmanuel College.

As Craven student he entered the British School of Archaeology at Athens of which he became director in 1906. His personal interests were primarily philological and any time which could be spared from other duties was spent in travel and the study of Greek dialects. Of this period of his life there were two outstanding achievements. The first was the excavation of the shrine of Artemis Orthia at Sparta, which, apart from its exciting results, set a new standard in methods of excavation. The second was the book *Modern Greek in Asia Minor* (1916), a study of the curious dialects of Greek spoken by the inhabitants of the Cappadocian plateau. In 1914 Dawkins resigned the directorship of the British School at Athens; a very substantial legacy from his mother's cousin, J. A. Doyle [q.v.] who died in 1907, had given him financial independence. From 1916 to 1919 he served in Crete as an intelligence officer, with the rank of temporary lieutenant, R.N.V.R.

In 1920 Dawkins was appointed to the Bywater and Sotheby chair of Byzantine and modern Greek in the university of Oxford and in 1922 Exeter College made him a fellow. His major work during his tenure of the chair was a translation with commentary of the medieval Cypriot *Chronicle of Makhairas* (2 vols., 1932) which records the history of the Lusignan dynasty between 1359 and 1432. In 1939 when he retired under the age limit Exeter College made him an honorary fellow with rooms in college. To the end of his life he kept his zest and interest in young people and he was to generations of Oxford undergraduates a source of real education. Except for music, for which he had no ear, his tastes were catholic: he knew about plants, pictures, and European literature. As a critic, whether of books or men, he was positive and to the end of his long life, though always intolerant of humbug, enviably receptive to new ideas. He had a wide linguistic knowledge and could talk

French, Italian, and modern Greek a rapidly as natives. He knew most parts o the Mediterranean including North Afric and had an unrivalled knowledge at firs hand of the Greek-speaking peoples fror Pontus in the east to Calabria in the wes' In this last period of his life he turned hi attention to the subject matter of folk tales which he had earlier taken down a texts for philological purposes. In 195 he published *Forty-five Stories from th Dodekanese* from manuscripts which ha been presented by W. H. D. Rouse [q.v to the university of Cambridge. This wa followed by *Modern Greek Folktales* (195: and *More Greek Folktales* (1955), the impo tance of which was due to the examina tion of the relative popularity of and th changes undergone by types of Indo European folktales in a definite an exceptionally well-recorded area. In 194 he broke his thigh; this did not diminis his incessant industry. Articles and re views continued to pour out from h somewhat erratic typewriter and h rooms remained a focus of hospitalit for promising young men and congeni seniors. Himself an original he like originals. His taste in men as in books w catholic. By no means all his friends wer academical and his range of acquaintanc extended from Norman Douglas [q.v.], whom in 1933 he published a percepti study, to the egregious Baron Corv Dawkins fell down dead in an Oxfo street on 4 May 1955. He never marrie He was elected F.B.A. in 1933, proceede D.Litt. at Oxford in 1942, and was a honorary D.Phil. of the universities Athens (1937) and Thessalonica (1951). pencil drawing of him by Henry Lamb at Exeter College, Oxford; an oil-paintir by William Roberts is the property Professor Nevill Coghill. Autobiographic notes by Dawkins have been deposite in the Taylor Institution. A lively accou of Dawkins appears in Osbert Lancaste *With an Eye to the Future* (1967).

[R. J. H. Jenkins in *Proceedings* of t British Academy, vol. xli, 1955; persor knowledge.]   W. R. HALLIDA

DEAKIN, ARTHUR (1890–1955), trad union leader, was born at Sutton Coldfiel Warwickshire, 11 November 1890, the so of a domestic servant, Annie Deakin. the age of ten he moved with his moth and stepfather to Dowlais in South Wal where he started to work for the ste firm, Guest, Keen, and Nettlefolds, at t age of thirteen, for four shillings a wee

He joined the National Union of Gas Workers and came under the influence of Keir Hardie [q.v.], then member of Parliament for Merthyr Tydfil of which Dowlais was a part. In 1910 Deakin moved to Shotton in North Wales and took a job with another steel firm as a roll turner. For a brief spell he was a member of the Amalgamated Society of Engineers but in 1911 he moved over to the expanding, heterogeneous Dock, Wharf, Riverside, and General Workers' Union which gave ample scope to his incipient qualities of leadership. Within three years he was an active lay member and in 1919 he became a full-time official of the union. Until that year he belonged also to the small British Roll Turners' Society of which for a brief period he was general secretary. When in 1922 the Dockers' Union became part of the Transport and General Workers' Union, Deakin became assistant district secretary for the North Wales area where the high unemployment of the next ten years strongly conditioned his subsequent attitudes and responses. In 1919 he became an alderman of the Flintshire County Council and in 1932 its chairman.

In 1932 Deakin moved to London where until 1935 he was national secretary of the General Workers' trade group of the Transport and General Workers' Union. He toured the country examining the problems of his group and so impressed Ernest Bevin [q.v.], the general secretary of the union, with his organizing ability that in 1935 he was appointed assistant general secretary. He worked closely with Bevin through a difficult time for the union, for in 1938 some of its members seceded to form a union for busmen; and Bevin himself was showing signs of strain from overwork.

When in 1940 (Sir) Winston Churchill invited Bevin to become minister of labour in the wartime coalition Government, Deakin took Bevin's place in the union and continued as acting general secretary until Bevin retired from union office in March 1946, when Deakin was elected general secretary in his place, with a majority of 59,105 votes over the combined votes of the other five candidates.

Although from 1940 until 1946 Deakin was the formal head of his union, the largest in Britain and one of the largest in the world, his work was done in the shadow of Bevin whose reputation among the ordinary members was almost legendary and who never effectively relinquished his control of union activities. Deakin himself was essentially a Bevin creation and perhaps the most loyal supporter of a man upon whom he modelled himself to the extent of copying some of his public mannerisms. On the General Council of the Trades Union Congress where he took Bevin's place, he was a useful but not an influential member. The Council had been dominated by Bevin and its general secretary, Sir Walter (later Lord) Citrine; with Bevin's departure Citrine remained firmly in control, unaffected by Deakin's presence. Deakin became a member of the Government's War Transport Council and of the committee established to advise the Production Executive. In one respect he achieved notoriety during the war. When he visited Sweden in 1943 as a fraternal delegate to the Congress of the Swedish Transport Workers' Union he conferred with a Finnish trade-union leader on the possibilities of negotiating a peace treaty; for this he received much adverse publicity.

A new phase in Deakin's career began in 1946 when he became leader of his union in his own right. After the resignation of Citrine from the Trades Union Congress and a period of uncertainty in the leadership of the movement, the position gradually clarified and settled and by 1948 Deakin had emerged as the most dominant figure in British trade-unionism and an influential one also in the international movement. He retained his trade-union and political influence until his death which took place on 1 May 1955 while he was addressing a May Day rally in Leicester.

Like so many men who find themselves thrust into positions of power and responsibility, Deakin developed to meet the situation. People who knew him under Bevin could never have imagined his filling the role which he subsequently attained in post-war Britain. A Labour Government was in office and the country faced extreme economic difficulties. Both factors demanded that trade unions break with their traditional attitudes. They required a close collaboration with the Government and the acceptance of attitudes about productivity and profits which unions had traditionally rejected. After an initial hesitation, Deakin gave the Government his unconditional support. He urged unions to try to increase productivity and advocated a policy of wage restraint. He possessed a deep loyalty to the labour movement which was epitomized for him by the Labour Government. In his eagerness to support the Government he stifled much useful criticism of its activities, for he disliked anything which could be misconstrued by the general public or used for political purposes. He was more than an advocate. As far as he could he applied the policy of wage restraint in his own union and incurred the displeasure of some of his more militant members. But if he thought his policy was right no amount of criticism would deter him. At times he risked the unity of his organization and faced large-scale unofficial strikes rather than make expedient concessions. No Government could have had a more loyal supporter.

Deakin travelled widely as a member of the international committee of the Trades Union Congress and as the most prominent representative of his own union. He was a member of the executive board of the World Federation of Trade Unions and did much to heal the breach between its Communist and non-Communist members. During his tenure as chairman of the board, however, he led a walkout of the non-Communist delegates and helped to form the International Confederation of Free Trade Unions in 1949. Thereafter he became uncompromisingly anti-Communist in his attitude towards foreign affairs, national domestic affairs, and the running of his own union which in 1949 he persuaded to ban Communists from holding office.

The attitude of Deakin towards Communists was in part a reflection of his attitude towards opposition. He believed in the sanctity of majority decisions and was intolerant of those who opposed them. He attacked minorities in his union and in the Labour Party with invective and organizational measures. He would defy procedures and conventions to get his own way and was often accused by his antagonists of being a dictator. By his public manner, outspoken, brusque, and intolerant, and by his manner of handling internal union affairs, he lent support to the accusation. The administrative problems of his union increased as it expanded from 743,349 members in 1940 to 1,305,456 in 1955 and by and large Deakin coped with them. But he possessed a vital reluctance to delegate authority and maintained a strict control over even the smallest administrative detail in his union's head office. He would sometimes speak on behalf of his union without consulting the general executive council

which constitutionally controlled him. Deakin believed in positive leadership. 'I cannot and will not be a cipher', he told his members. Yet all the time he was aware of the source of his power and always made sure that on the major issues he had the majority of his ordinary members behind him. He was sentimental about his relations with the lay members of his union. Nothing hurt him more than the suggestion that he was out of touch with them. A cartoon which depicted him with his head in the clouds caused him considerable anger. He did much to improve contacts between officials and lay members and saw the development of educational provisions within the union as a means to this end. His union introduced pioneering training schemes for shop stewards and branch officials and under his guidance the education department became large and influential.

The public image of Deakin lent itself to caricature. He dressed flamboyantly, smoked large cigars, and courted publicity. But in essential ways both the public image and the caricatures gave a misleading impression. Deakin was modest and shy. He lived quietly and modestly in a small semi-detached house in a north London suburb where his evenings, when free from union business, were spent at home with his wife. He did not drink alcohol and was a member of the Primitive Methodist Church. He did not make friends easily and found communication on an individual level difficult. But those with whom he had a close relationship came from various walks of life and different political affiliations. In this respect he was paradoxical. He tended to be distrustful of Labour Party politicians and his personal relations with them were uneasy, whereas he could get on very well with self-made employers and with Conservative politicians. Thus he found it easy to make the transition from a Labour to a Conservative Government in 1951. But he never transferred his distrust of Labour politicians to the party itself and he disapproved of those trade-union leaders who moved into industrial management.

Deakin was often accused of seeking honours, yet he twice refused a knighthood. He was appointed C.B.E. in 1943 and C.H. in 1949, and was sworn of the Privy Council in 1954; these he regarded as honours to the labour movement rather than to himself.

In 1914 Deakin married Annie, daughter of Robert George, of Connah's Quay, Flintshire; they had two sons.

[*The Times*, 2 May 1955; V. L. Allen, *Trade Union Leadership*, 1957; personal knowledge.]

V. L. ALLEN.

DE CHAIR, SIR DUDLEY RAWSON STRATFORD (1864–1958), admiral, was born at Lennoxville, Canada, 30 August 1864, eldest son of Dudley Raikes de Chair, of French Huguenot descent, by his wife, Frances Emily, eldest daughter of Christopher Rawson, of The Hurst, Walton-on-Thames, Surrey. His parents returned to England in 1870 and in 1878 he joined the *Britannia* where Prince Edward and Prince George were also cadets.

As a midshipman de Chair attracted national attention through being captured by some of the Egyptian cavalry of Arabi Pasha when alone on a special mission. He was released after six weeks when Cairo was taken and was later selected by Sir Garnet (later Viscount) Wolseley [q.v.] to take the dispatches to Alexandria.

With the exception of a short period as torpedo lieutenant in the flagship *Royal Sovereign* (1893–4), he served as an instructor in the *Vernon*, the torpedo school at Portsmouth, from 1892 until his promotion to commander in 1897. In that year he was appointed commander in the flagship of his uncle, Sir Harry H. Rawson [q.v.], at the Cape station. In 1899 he became commander in the *Majestic*, in which ship he remained until his promotion to captain in 1902.

In that year he was appointed naval attaché at Washington, where his next three years were spent. Returning to sea-going duties, he next commanded successively the cruisers *Bacchante* and *Cochrane*. In 1908 he was brought into contact with Sir John (later Earl) Jellicoe [q.v.], then controller of the navy, serving as his assistant controller until 1911. After a further spell of sea time as captain of the *Colossus* he returned to the Admiralty on promotion to flag rank in 1912 and on 1 March 1913 he succeeded David (later Earl) Beatty [q.v.] as naval secretary to the first lord, (Sir) Winston Churchill. He had met Churchill previously and had been impressed with his charm of manner and keen interest in naval affairs. But although Churchill had selected de Chair for his appointment, the latter was not as happy in it as Beatty had been. He found Churchill's ebullient zest and headstrong, sometimes impetuous, methods disturbing and had not the great wealth which

Beatty had enjoyed to live fully in the circles which his chief frequented. In June 1914 he became admiral of the training squadron and at the outbreak of war he was moved to the cruiser *Crescent* in command of the tenth cruiser squadron.

The particular task of this squadron was the patrol of the North Sea from the Shetlands to the Norwegian coast as a blockade to Germany, and in his command of this task force until March 1916 de Chair made an important contribution towards the winning of the war. Due to his efficient organization the number of ships which slipped through was negligible and as the war progressed the effect of the blockade became more apparent. For his services de Chair was appointed K.C.B. in 1916.

De Chair relinquished his command to take up a post under the Foreign Office as naval adviser to the Ministry of Blockade. His experience made him eminently suitable for this work, as A. J. Balfour explained to him, but de Chair, as he revealed in his autobiography, was 'almost heartbroken' at giving up his command and active naval service. However he found the minister, Lord Robert Cecil (later Viscount Cecil of Chelwood, q.v.), sympathetic and understanding.

De Chair's valuable work in this appointment continued until September 1917, when he was given command of the third battle squadron, stationed in the Channel, with the task of attacking the German High Seas Fleet, should it come out. That it never did was frustrating and disappointing to him, and he was further dismayed to learn of the dismissal of Jellicoe as first sea lord in December. When his successor, Sir R. E. (later Lord Wester) Wemyss [q.v.], asked de Chair to accept a post on the Board of Admiralty, he refused outright, telling Wemyss that he could not do so as he 'felt so keenly the disgraceful manner in which Jellicoe had been treated'. This outspokenness did de Chair no good and shortly afterwards he was relieved of his command and placed on half pay. He had been promoted vice-admiral in 1917. In July 1918 he was appointed admiral commanding Coastguard and Reserves; in 1920 he was promoted admiral; and in 1921–3 he was president of the inter-allied commission on enemy warships, and was then placed on the retired list.

The same year he was appointed governor of New South Wales, where he remained until 1930. During his term his determination and strength of character were fully tested in the political crisis of 1926, when the Labour premier, J. T. Lang, introduced a bill to abolish the legislative council, the state's second chamber. De Chair agreed to appoint 25 new Labour members to the council, but when the bill was defeated by 47 votes to 41 he refused to appoint more. This led to strong attacks on his action by the Labour Party and to an examination of the powers of the state governors in Australia.

After his retirement de Chair lived mainly in London. He served in the Home Guard from 1940 to 1942. He died at his home in Rottingdean 17 August 1958 and, after cremation, his ashes were scattered, in accordance with his wishes, in the English Channel from the *Hardy*.

In addition to the K.C.B., de Chair was appointed K.C.M.G. (1933), received the D.S.M. (U.S.A.), and was a commander of the Legion of Honour. McGill University conferred on him an honorary LL.D.

Possessing much personal charm, de Chair was a man of great loyalty and integrity, direct in his manner and at times somewhat inflexible. As a leader some found him uninspiring, but Jellicoe termed him 'a very first-rate sea officer suited to any command afloat'. De Chair followed a code of ethics which frequently worked to his personal disadvantage and like Jellicoe, whom he greatly admired, he never allowed his judgement to be affected by personal considerations and never courted publicity.

He married in 1903 Enid (died 1966), third daughter of Henry William Struben, of Transvaal, South Africa, by whom he had two sons and a daughter. The elder son, Henry Graham Dudley de Chair, became a commander in the Royal Navy; the younger, Somerset Struben de Chair, author of *The Golden Carpet* and other works, was for twelve years a member of Parliament.

An oil-painting of de Chair as a rear-admiral by Marshall Sprink is in the family possession, and a drawing by Francis Dodd is in the Imperial War Museum.

[*The Times*, 19 August 1958; Sir Julian S. Corbett, (Official) *History of the Great War. Naval Operations*, vols. i and iii, 1920–23; Viscount Jellicoe, *The Grand Fleet 1914–1916*, 1919; Sir Dudley de Chair, *The Sea is Strong*, 1961; Arthur J. Marder, *From the Dreadnought to Scapa Flow*, vol. ii, 1965; *Burke's Landed Gentry*, 1965; private information.]

G. K. S. HAMILTON-EDWARDS.

DEEDES, SIR WYNDHAM HENRY (1883–1956), soldier and social worker, was born in London 10 March 1883, th younger son of Colonel Herbert Georg Deedes, of Sandling Park and Saltwoo Castle, then serving as assistant under secretary at the War Office, and his wife Rose Eleanor, daughter of Major-Genera Lousada Barrow, of the Madras Sta Corps. Educated at Eton, he was commis sioned in the King's Royal Rifle Corps i 1901, served in the South African wa then in Bermuda, and in Ireland where h was aide-de-camp to the general com manding. In 1908 he went with hi battalion to Malta and served as a aide-de-camp to the governor, Sir Harr Grant.

Deedes was a remarkable man whos army career was unusual. Most of his tim in South Africa had been spent on garriso duty of a small blockhouse where he ha time for much reading and to teach hin self German. He found peace-time soldie ing unsatisfactory, for while he had n personal ambition, he was hungry for wor which would more fully tax his menta and physical energy. In Malta he learn Turkish and in 1910 he was seconded fc employment with the Turkish *gendarmer* which because of Turkish misgovernmen was at that time under a measure c supervision by European powers. Deede was put in sole charge of an area of Nort Africa four times the size of France an he set to work with astonishing energy-training recruits, establishing addition posts, and improving discipline by frequen visits of inspection. His quiet assuranc sense of justice, obvious integrity, an untiring energy, won the admiration an respect of his district and of the remot government he represented. After tw years he was moved to Smyrna where h was largely responsible for the relief an resettlement of refugees and displace population resulting from the dismembe ment of the Turkish empire. He had bee made inspector under the Turkish Minist of the Interior in 1914 when he was recalle to England on the outbreak of war wi Germany.

Promoted lieutenant in 1906, captain i 1914, major in 1916, brevet lieutenan colonel in 1917, and temporary brigadie general in 1918, Deedes served throughou the war, first on Turkish intelligence a the War Office, next on the intelligen staff of the Gallipoli campaign, then charge of Eastern Mediterranean intel gence in Cairo. In 1918–19 he was milita attaché at Constantinople. He was a pointed to the D.S.O. in 1916 and C.M.(

in 1919. In 1919 he was seconded to the Foreign Office for work in Egypt; in 1920 to the Colonial Office for service in Palestine. Sir Herbert (later Viscount) Samuel, appointed to administer the British mandate, records in his memoirs that he had asked for Deedes as his civil secretary not only because he was by profession a soldier of great administrative capacity, but because 'there was in him a strong strain of idealism which drew him powerfully to the Holy Land'. Nevertheless Deedes accepted the appointment reluctantly and on the understanding that it would be for only a few years, for he was now thirty-seven and had been away from England since he was eighteen. He longed to escape from foreign intrigue and power rivalry and to take up social service at home. But he was deeply interested in both the Arab desire for freedom from foreign rule and the Jewish claim on Palestine as a national home. The establishment of an administration acceptable alike to Jew and Arab was an appealing but difficult task. Deedes's personal contribution to its realization was thus expressed in a leading Arab newspaper: 'Every element in the country, as far as we can observe, seems to think that he is their friend. Perhaps his is the secret of the matter. For in truth he sincerely loves and works for all.'

After he had served for three years in Jerusalem and had been knighted in 1921 Deedes suddenly resigned in seeming contradiction to the selfless ideal which he had exemplified. But he was troubled by the gulf which separated him as chief secretary from humble people; he had no interest in material advantages, and the trappings of office and authority seemed only a hindrance to spiritual life. He had always practised stern self-denial and cultivated the great grace of humility and he argued that there were plenty of abler men to replace him. He transferred to the Highland Light Infantry in 1923 and in the same year retired with the rank of colonel and honorary rank of brigadier-general. He never married, and putting off his uniform, he went to live in the east end of London where he was soon recognized as the friend of everyone working for a good cause. His humility and sympathy with others in need were reflected in charming manners and invariable courtesy. He had three other interests outside Bethnal Green: the Zionist movement for which he spoke at meetings throughout England and in many other countries; a Turkish Centre

in London which he helped to found, the translation of Turkish novels and, for twenty-five years, regular broadcasts to the Turkish; and the National Council of Social Service whose aim, the development of co-operative service for the development of 'the good life', matched his own. He was Labour member of the London County Council for North-East Bethnal Green from 1941 until 1946 and a member of the education committee. As chief air raid warden of Bethnal Green in the war he visited all his posts every night and it was then that his health began to give way. After several major operations he was obliged to retire from London in 1950 and by his own choice lived at Hythe near his old home in the single bed-sitting room of a humble lodging, writing in the morning and visiting the old or sick each afternoon. He died in London 2 September 1956.

[John Presland, *Deedes Bey*, 1942; Viscount Samuel, *Memoirs*, 1945; *Memories of Sir Wyndham Deedes*, ed. E. Elath, N. Bentwich, and Doris May, 1958; private information; personal knowledge.]   L. F. ELLIS.

DE LA MARE, WALTER JOHN (1873–1956), poet, novelist, and anthologist, was born 25 April 1873 at Charlton, Kent, the sixth child of James Edward de la Mare, an official in the Bank of England, and his wife, Lucy Sophia Browning. He was educated at St. Paul's Cathedral Choristers' School, where he edited the school magazine, and then entered the service of the Anglo-American Oil Company for which he worked until 1908. He began his literary career with *Songs of Childhood* (1902), followed by the vast *opus* of poems, stories, novels, books for children, and anthologies, all marked by an individual genius which was quickly recognized.

His first prose book, *Henry Brocken* (1904), is a romance using famous figures from the literatures of Europe. It sets the perspective line of all his subsequent work. The background of his view of life was to remain fixed in the world of books. If incongruity threatened, then life had to be refashioned by fantasy to fit that background, whether it was the life of children or adults. Thus, the strange adaptations of fact in *The Return* (1910), *The Three Mulla-Mulgars* (1910), and *Memoirs of a Midget* (1921).

The book which carried his poetry to a wide public was *The Listeners* (1912). Even more popular, perhaps, was the book of poems for children *Peacock Pie*

(1913). *Come Hither*, an anthology (1923), finally established his fame as a writer for children. His two most characteristic anthologies, both enriched by long introductions, are *Behold, This Dreamer* (1939) and *Love* (1943). His most sustained poem, a synopsis of his philosophy of life, and a final revelation of his temperament, is *The Traveller* (1946).

Within his own universe de la Mare was a highly complicated organism, compounded of subtly articulated nervous tensions which made his contacts with the outside world oblique, tentative, sometimes even bizarre. His first book, *Songs of Childhood*, was published under the pseudonym of Walter Ramal, an adaptation of de la Mare read in a mirror. Again, in one of his most characteristic prose books, *The Return*, the central figure looks at himself in the mirror, about to shave, and there sees a face only dimly, historically, resembling his own. This horrifying experience was not horrifying to de la Mare; his nature accepted it welcomingly. It was as though he were endowed with several extra sets of eyes, which he was able to set out in strategic positions to get a many-intelligenced view of any given situation, mood, fear, or passion, person, or place. And it was his multiplied curiosity which did the work in the making of a story or a poem, just as it controlled his conversations with fellow mortals.

In his conversation, the climate of discussion began to resemble that of his poetry. Oblique lights shot across the familiar scene, and what was normally visible became an obscured form gradually filling up with horror, while the vacant lots of the commonplace became peopled with dancing shadows which grew more and more concrete and plausible. Size, form, time, and place intervolved, and the de la Marian universe was all around the visitor: strange, thwart, more yet less than human, full of contradictions that resolved with lightning speed into a weird symbolism of desperate faith. For that is what he moved towards, all his life. He was beset by these damaging queries; he could not refrain from the destructive questioning. But out of the breakages resulting from this passionate, devout scepticism, he contrived (and with a childlike simplicity) to build up the poetry which irradiated all his work.

The nature and texture of that poetry are as interwoven as are the meaning and the strange phrasing in the most charac-teristic of Shakespeare's dialogue; completely a unit as organism, yet more and more miraculous and incredible the more it is analysed. De la Mare's use of poetic inversion, for example, is in itself a study which baffles the critic. It was partly involuntary, because he could not keep himself from this ingrained gesture of turning to the mirror to look out on life in reflection, in opposites, and above all in that weird silence which pervades all reflection. Although he wrote vastly, and usually anonymously, as a critic, he never hesitated to say that he could not be certain how his own work was done, how the moonlight (another reflection) became the chief illuminant of his field of vision. He knew the craft of the poet, and was jealous in the care and use of the medium, the unruly flock of words. In a letter in 1945, he said: 'I often wonder how many people really understand the language. Not a great number, I fancy. There are many good reasons for liking and delighting in poetry, if reasons they can be called; but *the* reason—one could not define it—but that once realized all else is only addendas.'

His was a mind, a personality, which loved dangerous living. He would not be content to bask by the fireside of accepted values. The certainties of life must always be opened, disrupted by him in his almost irresponsible inquisitiveness. In the most ordinary and innocuous of things and events he saw a force which was always a threat. Atomic fission was his daily practice. He drew again and again towards the brink of the abyss which most people ignored or denied, and there he stood fascinated, wondering what might be the result if a mortal defied this pervasive latency.

Any old object would serve towards this perilous adventure: a candle-end, a scarecrow, a snatch of mist, a trail of bindweed. The smallest thing was a key into the humming power-house of the Mystery. In the poem called 'The Bottle' he sums up this attitude, as he describes it,

> Of green and hexagonal glass,
>   With sharp, fluted sides—
> Vaguely transparent these walls,
>   Wherein motionless hides
> A simple so potent it can
>   To oblivion lull
> The weary, the racked, the bereaved,
>   The miserable.

And he applies to himself, and the ever questing consciousness within him, th

efficacy of the drug in that bottle to reveal
the answer,

Wicket out into the dark
   That swings but one way;
Infinite hush in an ocean of silence
   Aeons away—
Thou forsaken!—even thou!—
   The dread good-bye;
The abandoned, the thronged, the watched,
   the unshared—
   Awaiting me—I!

That may be the way into a fuller understanding of this poet and his work; the
realization that always he dallied with
danger, was obsessed with the curiosity of
what might happen if he should dissociate
his material world from its physical
coherence and set free the forces which so
restrained it.

De la Mare received honorary degrees
from the universities of Oxford, Cambridge, London, St. Andrews, and Bristol,
and was an honorary fellow of Keble College, Oxford. In 1948 he was appointed
C.H. and in 1953 O.M.

In 1899 he married Constance Elfrida
(died 1943), daughter of Alfred William
Ingpen and sister of Roger Ingpen who
married Walter de la Mare's sister. He had
two daughters and two sons, the elder
of whom, Richard, became chairman of
Faber & Faber, Ltd., the publishers of the
definitive edition of his father's works.

A drawing of de la Mare by Augustus
John was first in the possession of Lady
Cynthia Asquith. Of several drawings by
Sir William Rothenstein, one is reproduced in *Twenty-Four Portraits* (second
series, 1923) and another in *Twelve Portraits* (1929). A chalk drawing of Walter
de la Mare in bed by H. A. Freeth was
exhibited at the Royal Academy in 1958;
and a death mask was made by his family
for presentation to the National Portrait Gallery which also has a drawing
by Rothenstein and another by Augustus
John.

Walter de la Mare died at Twickenham,
Middlesex, 22 June 1956. His ashes are
buried in the crypt of St. Paul's Cathedral
where there is a memorial plaque.

[Private information; personal knowledge.]
RICHARD CHURCH.

DENMAN, GERTRUDE MARY, LADY
DENMAN (1884–1954), public servant, was
born in London 7 November 1884, the
second of the four children and only
daughter of W. D. Pearson (afterwards
first Viscount Cowdray, q.v.). Her parents
travelled extensively, leaving her for long

periods in the care of often uncongenial
governesses with only the company of
her brothers in the holidays. She always
maintained that she educated herself by
wide reading, especially of books on economics and philosophy in her father's
library. The independence of mind fostered
by her somewhat isolated childhood gave
her a detachment of outlook which remained a characteristic throughout life.
These formative years also developed a
natural shyness which she never allowed
to limit her activities and which she nearly
always overcame by sheer hard work,
enthusiasm, and concentration. Born to
great wealth, she believed from an early
age that the only justification of such an
inheritance was service to, and thought
for, the community. Her father's vitality
in his engineering work and the courage
and equanimity with which he approached
heavy tasks and responsibilities made a
deep impression on her. When she was
quite young her letters to him showed a
mature grasp of his many undertakings.

In 1903 she married the third Baron
Denman and the one son and one daughter of the marriage were born before she
was twenty-three. She acquitted herself
with distinction as the very young wife of
a governor-general when her husband took
up that appointment in Australia in 1911.
She had already been a member of the
executive committee of the Women's
National Liberal Federation (1909–10)
and later became director of S. Pearson
& Son, Ltd., and of the Westminster
Press, Ltd.

In the autumn of 1916 Lady Denman
became chairman of the sub-committee
of the Agricultural Organization Society
which, on the suggestion of Mrs. Alfred
Watt (M. R. Watt, q.v.), had undertaken
to found Women's Institutes of which
there were by this time twenty-four.
When the institutes (then 137) transferred
to the Board of Agriculture in 1917 she
became assistant director of the women's
branch of the food production department. She insisted that the institutes
must be self-governing and on the formation at the same time of the National
Federation of Women's Institutes she was
elected chairman. She held that office
until 1946, retiring at her own wish to
make way for a younger chairman. Personally without ambition, she was eager
for the success of the movement, seeing
in it a great opportunity for democratic
training in citizenship for countrywomen,
for widening their knowledge and for

improving their standards of life. The institutes and their remarkable achievements are the fruit of her talent for administration, her foresight, and the principles of good procedure on which she based their early organization. When she died there were over 8,000 institutes with a membership of 450,000. The Women's Institute residential college, founded in 1948 at Marcham, near Abingdon, Berkshire, was called Denman College in recognition of her services.

In 1930 Lady Denman helped to found and became chairman of the National Birth Control (later Family Planning) Association, an office which she still held at the time of her death. That parents should be given the means to plan their families so that all children of a marriage would be wanted and welcomed seemed to her right and natural. Her acute sympathy for overburdened mothers spurred her to champion a cause which needed great courage and forthrightness.

Lady Denman was chairman of the Cowdray Club for Nurses and Professional Women (1932-53). Always an enthusiastic games player, she was president of the Ladies' Golf Union (1932-8). She was a member of the executive committee of the Land Settlement Association (1934-9), and in 1938 became a trustee of the Carnegie United Kingdom Trust.

In 1939 Lady Denman became director of the Women's Land Army. From the first she realized that there would be many obstacles to be overcome and her powers of leadership were greatly needed to reconcile conflicting demands. She brought to the task initiative, resource, and good sense, always seeing the work of the Land Army in relation to the needs of the nation at war. Nevertheless, she waged her own battles on its behalf with the various Ministries concerned, holding out for conditions of employment which have been of lasting benefit to agricultural workers as a whole. When in 1945 the Government failed to award the Land Army grants, gratuities, and other benefits which it accorded to women in the civil defence and armed services, she resigned in protest.

Lady Denman's public work carries its own memorial in thousands of villages and homes throughout the land. As a chairman she excelled, her impartiality, quick understanding, and sense of humour enabling her to handle with success any meeting, however large or difficult. She could be formidable in opposition—which she enjoyed—but was fair and generous to those who differed from her. Her own transparent honesty banished pretence pomposity, or meanness. Underlying the outstanding ability for organization, the penetrating eye in committee, the often gloriously caustic comment, the intolerance of self-seeking, moral cowardice or foolishness, there was deep affection for those whose cause she championed, for succeeding generations of her own family for her many friends whom she delighted to welcome at her home in Sussex, and especially for young people. She was greatly loved both by her family and friends for her courageous and generous spirit, her unfailing kindness to them, and the humour and joy of life which made everything done in her company a delight.

In 1920 Lady Denman was appointed C.B.E., in 1933 D.B.E., and in 195_ G.B.E. Her death in London, 2 June 1954 was followed within the month by that of her husband.

A portrait (1933) of Lady Denman by E. Hodgkin is at Knepp Castle and another (1951) by Anthony Devas is at Denman College. A third by (Sir) William Nicholson (1909) is privately owned.

[*The Times*, 3, 4, 8, and 14 June 1954 Inez Jenkins, *The History of the Women's Institute Movement of England and Wales*, 1953 Gervas Huxley, *Lady Denman, G.B.E.*, 1961 private information; personal knowledge.]

ELIZABETH BRUNNER

DENNY, SIR MAURICE EDWARD, second baronet, of Dumbarton (1886-1955), engineer and shipbuilder, was born at Dumbarton 11 February 1886, the eldest son of (Sir) Archibald Denny, late first baronet, a notice of whom he contributed to this Dictionary and whom he succeeded in 1936. He was educated at Tonbridge School and spent two years in Switzerland and one in Germany at the universities of Lausanne and Heidelberg before proceeding to America where he spent four years at the Massachusetts Institute of Technology where he graduated with a first class in naval architecture.

On returning home he entered the firm of William Denny & Brothers, shipbuilders, of Dumbarton, of which his grandfather Peter Denny was one of the founders. Later he spent a year in the drawing office of William Doxford & Sons, Ltd., Sunderland. On returning to Dumbarton he joined the staff at the Denny yard, becoming a partner in 191_ When the family business became limited company in 1918 Denny was appointed a director. He was elected vice-chairman in 1920, and in 1922 he suc-ceeded his uncle, Colonel John M. Denny, as chairman. He held that office until 1952 when he retired and became president.

In the war of 1914–18 Denny was an officer in the Machine Gun Corps and served in France; but, on account of the pressure on shipbuilding and the position he had attained in the industry, he was recalled. He became deputy director of design under the controller-general for merchant shipbuilding at the Admiralty and was appointed C.B.E. in 1918.

After the war Denny was keen to apply his scientific brain and well-trained mind to the many shipbuilding problems. But there was a deep depression in world trade and his technical interests had to some extent to take second place because of the need for rigid economies. He piloted his company successfully through these diffi-cult years and enhanced its great reputa-tion, particularly in the construction of fast cross-Channel ships with turbine propulsion. He made a lasting contribution to the progress of the industry, particularly in promoting research. In his approach to all problems, technical and commercial, he was actuated by a meticulous integrity, which was the outstanding quality of his character.

Denny was chairman of the Shipbuilding Conference in 1940. He was instrumen-tal in the foundation of the British Ship-building Research Association in which he was chairman of the research board from its inception until his death. It was largely due to his driving force that the Lucy Ashton trials to measure the power and speed of ships were carried through with such rapidity and success. The modifica-tion of this ship, fitted with four jet engines, permitted full-scale self-propelled experiments from which useful hydro-dynamic data resulted.

The firm had one of the earliest experi-ment tanks in their yard, and Denny carried out many experiments, inter alia two types of torsion meters which were known as the Denny–Johnstone and Denny–Edgcumbe. With (Sir) William Wallace of Brown Brothers he collaborated in the design of the Denny–Brown stabi-lizer, used in ships all over the world. Among many appointments, Denny was chairman of the technical committee of the British Corporation Register of Ship-ping and Aircraft for many years before its amalgamation with Lloyd's Register;

president of the Clyde Shipbuilders' Association; and president of the Ship-building Employers' Federation. He was a valued supporter of many of the profes-sional institutions and notably president in 1935 of the Institute of Marine En-gineers, as his father and grandfather had been. He was a director of the Union Bank of Scotland, of Guest, Keen, and Nettlefolds, of several shipping companies, and of Lloyds British Testing Company. For many years he was chairman of the Air Registration Board which he helped to found.

Denny was appointed K.B.E. in 1946 for his work in the war of 1939–45, during which his firm launched 12 destroyers, 10 sloops, 2 merchant aircraft carriers, and 10 other vessels for the Royal Navy. He re-ceived an honorary LL.D. from Glasgow in 1949.

Denny found his recreation in country life—he was a golfer, a keen gardener, an ornithologist of wide knowledge with an almost complete egg collection of birds of the British Isles. In ship model-making he was a skilled craftsman and he presented to the Science Museum, South Kensington, a perfect model of the Cutty Sark made by his own hands—a model of a famous Denny ship. He had a strong personality and his wit and friendship were enjoyed by a host of friends.

In 1916 Denny married Marjorie, daughter of William Royse Lysaght, steelmaker, of Castleford, Chepstow, Mon-mouthshire; they had two sons and two daughters. The elder son, Alistair Maurice Archibald (born 1922), succeeded to the baronetcy when Denny died at Drymen, Stirlingshire, 2 February 1955. A portrait by David Ewart is in the Denny collection at the National Maritime Museum and a copy is in the possession of the family.

[Private information; personal knowledge.]
BILSLAND.

DENT, EDWARD JOSEPH (1876–1957), musical scholar, was born at Rib-ston Hall, Yorkshire, 16 July 1876, the fourth and youngest son of John Dent Dent, barrister and for many years a member of Parliament, and his wife, Mary Hebden, daughter of John Woodall, of Scar-borough. A scholar of Eton and King's College, Cambridge, Dent obtained a third class in part i of the classical tripos in 1898. He had studied music at Eton under C. H. Lloyd, and at Cambridge, where he was a pupil of Charles Wood and (Sir) Charles Stanford [qq.v.], he obtained his

Mus.B. in 1899. In 1902-8 he was a fellow of King's College and lectured on the history of music, also teaching harmony, counterpoint, and composition. In 1926 he was appointed to the professorship of music in the university, a post which he held until 1941. During this period he reorganized the teaching of music on a broader basis, as not only the prerogative of organists and organ scholars but of those who were interested in all branches of music. His interests were numerous: at first he made a number of researches into seventeenth- and eighteenth-century Italian opera, a subject considerably neglected at that time, and published articles on it in the *Encyclopædia Britannica*, the second edition of *Grove's Dictionary of Music and Musicians*, and the *Riemann-Festschrift* of 1909. He also published a book on Alessandro Scarlatti in 1905 and another on Mozart's operas in 1913 (2nd, revised, edition 1947). He made new translations of Mozart's *Figaro*, *Don Giovanni*, and *The Magic Flute* and supervised a celebrated student production of the last-named at Cambridge in 1911. His later translations included several of Verdi's operas, Berlioz's *Les Troyens*, Beethoven's *Fidelio*, and other works. He also edited and produced many works of Purcell at Cambridge, the Old Vic, the Glastonbury Festival, and elsewhere, and made a new edition of his *Dido and Aeneas* for Hamburg in 1924 which was also produced at Münster in 1926 and Stuttgart in 1927.

In 1919 Dent became the music critic of the *Athenaeum* and he was also active in the formation of the British Music Society. But he remained essentially international in outlook and it was due to him that the International Festival of Contemporary Chamber Music, held in 1922 at Salzburg, developed into the International Society for Contemporary Music, a body which has branches in many countries and gives annual festivals of modern music. He became its first president, a post he held until 1938 and again in 1945-7. He also served on the board of directors of Sadler's Wells Theatre, of which he became a governor. When the Covent Garden Opera Trust was set up in 1946 he became one of the directors and showed a very active interest in the presentation of opera of all kinds in English.

Dent wrote articles on modern English music for Adler's *Handbuch der Musikgeschichte* and on 'Social Aspects of Music in the Middle Ages' for the 1929 edition of the *Oxford History of Music*. Later h served on the editorial board of the *Ne Oxford History of Music*. He was a honorary doctor of music of Oxford (1932) Harvard (1936), and Cambridge (1947) He was also, in 1953, one of the first tw musicians to be elected F.B.A. His othe books included *Foundations of Englis Opera* (1928) and a masterly biograph of Ferruccio Busoni (1933), a compose whom he knew well as a personal frienc His writings included many articles, fore words to books, and programme notes.

Dent composed a small number c original works, of which the most impor tant are a set of polyphonic motets. H also made an arrangement of the *Beggar Opera* which is much more faithful to th original than the well-known version b Frederic Austin—in fact Dent remove the preludes and codas to the songs whic Austin had added unnecessarily. He als made a practical version of one of th earliest oratorios, the sacred drama *L Rappresentazione di Anima e di Corpo c* Cavalieri, c. 1550-1602. The first pe formance of this work was given in 160 in Rome; the next recorded stage perfo mance took place in 1949, given by th Girton Musical Society of Cambridge fro Dent's edition. In 1950 Dent became th first president of the newly formed Lis: Society.

Dent was a man of immense knowledg and wide interests, but his personality w. not in the least academic in the conve tional sense. He inspired his pupils ar widened their range of vision, and he al possessed a mordant (but never crue sense of humour which enabled him puncture many inflated reputations. president of the International Society f Contemporary Music his good sense e abled him to prevent the society bei split apart by warring factions. (His a count of the early days of the societ 'Looking Backward', published in *Mu Today*, 1949, is a comic masterpiece.) H scholarship was always a living activit he was always interested in promoting li performances of the music he was inte ested in, not merely writing articles abo it in learned journals. He revived a gre deal of early music at a time when t vogue for it was not nearly as marked it later became, because he felt that th music was worth performing in the mode age for its own sake, not merely as a m ter of academic interest. At the same tir he kept a keen interest in modern develc ments, and if he did not always relish t nore extreme experiments of the *avant-arde*, he was always willing to let young nusicians have their say and to judge them y results. Thus he became a universally oved and respected figure, because it was elt that his judgements were entirely bjective and based on knowledge and xperience: even his best friends could be he target of his witty but sarcastic tongue ' he felt that their work was below what hey should have been able to achieve. He eft his mark behind in many fields of music, ot only in Cambridge, but in the whole nternational scene.

Dent, who was unmarried, died in ondon 22 August 1957. A portrait by awrence Gowing is at King's College, ambridge, and the Fitzwilliam Museum as drawings by Sydney Waterlow and dmond Kapp.

[*Grove's Dictionary of Music and Musicians*; ersonal knowledge.]   HUMPHREY SEARLE.

'EYNCOURT, SIR EUSTACE HENRY VILLIAM TENNYSON-, first baronet 868–1951), naval architect. [See TENNY-N-D'EYNCOURT.]

ICK-READ, GRANTLY (1890–1959), ostetrician and advocate of natural hildbirth, was born at Beccles, Suffolk, 5 January 1890, the son of Robert John ead, a flour miller of Norwich, and his ife, Frances Maria Sayer, of the White ouse, Thurlton, Norfolk, which had been the family since 1704. Dick Read (the yphen was not assumed until towards the d of his life) was the sixth of seven ildren and the second of three brothers. e went from Bishop's Stortford College St. John's College, Cambridge, where he as a sufficiently good soccer player to be nsidered for the university team, but d not gain a blue. After obtaining a ird class in part i of the natural sciences ipos in 1911 he became a clinical medical udent at the London Hospital where he me under the influence of (Sir) Eardley olland, one of the outstanding obstetri-ns and gynaecologists of his day. He came Holland's house-officer and in aling with problems of safe operative livery of women must have witnessed ostetric events which a later generation uld consider appalling.

Dick Read qualified in 1914, and after ar service in Gallipoli and France and a ell as resident accoucheur at the London ospital went into practice, first at East-urne, then in Woking, with consulting oms in Harley Street. It was in Woking

that he first began the writings which were ultimately to bring him fame, the best known being *Natural Childbirth* (1933) and *Revelation of Childbirth* (1942), in later editions entitled *Childbirth Without Fear*.

A big man with a commanding presence and handsome appearance, Dick Read had a voice of resonant, sonorous quality which made it almost hypnotic, and his vivid and compelling personality was used to good effect for the benefit of his patients and to convey his ideas to audiences to whom he lectured with consummate ease and skill. His passionate interest and enthusiasm for his main subject were always in evidence and he travelled far and wide, especially in Africa (he prac-tised in Johannesburg in 1949–53), gathering material relevant to his beliefs.

Over the years his opinions about natural childbirth developed, but by 1955 may perhaps be crystallized in his own words (*British Obstetric and Gynaecological Practice*, ed. Sir Eardley Holland): 'The psychosomatic approach to childbirth is not new, inasmuch as many of the writers of the past drew attention to the influence of the mind of a woman upon the course of her labour. . . . This approach to child-birth and the belief that healthy natural functions should not be attended by pain or danger became firmly established in my mind over forty years ago.' His ideas might be summed up in his phrase: the 'fear-tension-pain' syndrome. This implies that fear of childbirth, and especially fear in labour, causes general muscular tension and also tension in the uterine cervix, both of which increase the sensation of pain. To diminish the pain of labour it is therefore essential to cast out fear. This may be done by educating women about all that childbirth entails during preg-nancy, labour, the puerperium and after. This can be aided by teaching women during pregnancy how to control their voluntary muscles at will, especially by relaxing them, and by teaching them how to co-operate with the uterine contrac-tions of labour, which cannot be fully controlled voluntarily.

Thousands of women have benefited from the teachings of Dick Read and he has influenced the practice of obstetrics in all countries where it has been possible to apply his methods or some modification of them, although his disciples have been unable to maintain the original purity of the doctrine. In his time Dick Read was disappointed that his ideas did not immediately gain recognition in more conservative medical practice, but since his time there has been an increasing awareness of the importance of psychological factors in childbearing women and for this he is still in large measure responsible. This is a fine and enduring monument although the arguments will continue about how psychosomatic methods in childbirth should be used, how intensively they should be applied, and exactly how they affect the physiology of body-mind relationships.

In 1921 Dick Read married Dorothea, daughter of Neville Cannon, flour miller, of Bexley, Kent; there were two sons and two daughters. The marriage was dissolved in 1952 and he married in that year Mrs. Jessica Bennett, daughter of Leigh Cosart Winters, a business man of world-wide interests. There were no children. Dick-Read died 11 June 1959 at Wroxham, near Norwich.

[Private information.]   PHILIP RHODES.

DICKINSON, HENRY WINRAM (1870–1952), historian of engineering and technology, was born at Ulverston, Lancashire, 28 August 1870, the eldest son of John Dickinson, general manager and secretary of the North Lonsdale Iron and Steel Co., Ltd., by his wife, Margaret Anne Winram. From Ulverston Victoria Grammar School he went to Manchester Grammar School with a foundation scholarship. After a two years' engineering course at the Owens College, Manchester, and four years' apprenticeship (1888–92) at the Parkhead Steel Works of William Beardmore & Co., Ltd., Glasgow, he became a draughtsman at the Glasgow Iron and Steel Company's Wishaw works and then assistant engineer at the Frodingham Iron and Steel Company.

Dickinson's career was settled at twenty-five when in 1895 he was appointed by open competition junior assistant in the Science Department, South Kensington Museum, London, which became the Science Museum in 1909. Promoted assistant keeper in the machinery division in 1900 he was, in addition, made secretary to the advisory council in 1914. From 1915 to 1918 he was secretary of the munitions inventions panel at the Ministry of Munitions. Returning to the Science Museum, he was promoted in 1924 keeper of mechanical engineering, taking charge of numerous industrial collections, including motive power. He supervised the erection of the original Newcomen type and Watt beam engines and many other historical

exhibits in the museum's new eastern block, opened by King George V in 1928 and was responsible for the transfer, from Handsworth to South Kensington, and arrangement of the contents of Watt's garret workshop.

Dickinson represented the Board of Education in 1919 on the memorial committee to commemorate at Birmingham the centenary of the death of James Watt [q.v.]. Resulting from this, Dickinson and other engineers founded in 1920 the Newcomen Society for the Study of the History of Engineering and Technology named after Thomas Newcomen (1663–1729, q.v.) of Dartmouth, maker of the first successful steam engine using a piston in a cylinder. Dickinson was honorary secretary until 1951, except for two years (1932–4) when he was president. As sole editor of the *Transactions* until 1950, he set a very high standard and the first twenty-five volumes are a lasting memorial of his devoted work. He was made secretary emeritus in 1951 for his very distinguished services in guiding the society for over thirty years, including the critical war period. Having retired from the Science Museum in 1930, his main interest during his remaining years was the Newcomen Society. During his career he presented twenty-three papers to it, and two to the Institution of Mechanical Engineers of which he was a member for over fifty years.

He was the British Government's representative at the opening of the Deutsches Museum, Munich, 1925; he served as president of the Croydon and Purley natural history and scientific societies, besides being a vice-president of the Cornish Engines Preservation Society. He made two lecture tours in the United States, in 1923 and 1938, and received the honorary degree of Eng.D. from Lehigh University, Pennsylvania.

Dickinson was the author of definitive books on his favourite subjects: biographies of *Robert Fulton* (1913), *John Wilkinson* (1914), *James Watt* (1936), and *Matthew Boulton* (1937); the two memorial volumes *James Watt and the Steam Engine* (with Rhys Jenkins, 1927) and *Richard Trevithick* (with Arthur Titley, 1934); also *A Short History of the Steam Engine* (1939). His series of articles in the *Engineer* during 1948 was republished after his death as memorial volume entitled *Water Supply of Greater London* (1954).

By his industrious researches and enthusiasm, tempered with sound judgement,

Dickinson made a valuable contribution to establishing the history of technology on a firm basis and was one of the leading authorities on the evolution and application of steam power in the industrial revolution. He inspired others by his example and advice to undertake similar research. He lived modestly and was a lucid author and speaker, his knowledge being based on observation, systematic reading, travel, and the material in the Science Museum for which he wrote several official catalogues. To perpetuate his memory, the Newcomen Society founded in 1954 the Dickinson biennial memorial lecture; the series was inaugurated by Charles Singer [q.v.] who received the first Dickinson memorial medal. In 1956 the Newcomen Society in North America, inspired by Dr. Charles Penrose, senior vice-president, erected a memorial tablet to Dickinson at the Thomas Newcomen Library, West Chester, Pennsylvania.

Dickinson married first, in 1897, Edith (died 1937), youngest daughter of Richard Emerson, schoolmaster, of Dunsforth, Yorkshire. They had one son, Henry Douglas Dickinson, professor of economics at Bristol, 1951–64, who died in 1969. Secondly, Dickinson married in 1939 Elsa Lees, eldest daughter of Frank Walker Burgan, railway traffic agent, of Saltburn-by-the-Sea, Yorkshire. He died at his home in Purley, Surrey, 21 February 1952.

[*Engineer* and *Engineering*, 29 February 1952; Newcomen Society's *Transactions*, vol. xxviii, 1956, and vol. xxix, 1958; private information; personal knowledge.]

ARTHUR STOWERS.

DIX, GEORGE EGLINGTON ALSTON, DOM GREGORY (1901–1952), monk of Nashdom Abbey, was born at Woolwich 4 October 1901, the elder son of George Henry Dix who later took orders and became first principal of the College of St. Mark and St. John, Chelsea, by his wife, Mary Jane, daughter of James Eteson Walker, of Preston. As a King's scholar of Westminster School, Dix already showed an interest, inherited from his father, in both English literature and theology, and displayed such remarkable talent as an actor that at one time he thought seriously of making his career upon the stage. As an exhibitioner of Merton College, Oxford, he rowed the college eight, and cut a well-known figure in a somewhat flamboyant period of university life. In 1923 he obtained a second class in modern history

and was appointed lecturer at Keble College.

After a year at Wells Theological College he was ordained deacon in 1924 and priest in 1925. In 1926 he left Keble and joined the Anglican Benedictine community at Pershore, taking the name of Gregory. He was sent to West Africa, but in 1929 was invalided home, and thought to be incapable of further active work. He spent the next seven years at Nashdom, laying the foundation of his later scholarship by continuous reading. His health improved, he re-entered the novitiate in 1936, took solemn vows in 1940, became prior of Nashdom Abbey in 1948 and held office until his death. In 1946 he was elected proctor in convocation by the clergy of the diocese of Oxford, and maintained in the lower house the same stand in connection with the South India scheme as maintained in the upper house by K. E. Kirk [q.v.], bishop of Oxford. Dom Gregory was not only an ally in ecclesiastical matters, but also a close personal friend of Kirk's, and greatly influenced his thought in certain fields. He received the degrees of B.D. and D.D. from the university of Oxford in 1949. He was taken ill while lecturing in America in 1950, and after a brief recovery returned to England and died at Nashdom 11 May 1952.

Although primarily an historian, Dom Gregory's main contribution to scholarship lay in the field of liturgy. His edition of *The Apostolic Tradition* of St. Hippolytus (1937) provided the scholar with easy access to an indispensable text. His largest work, *The Shape of the Liturgy* (1945), gave to the general reader the results of two generations of specialist work, and set out Dom Gregory's own contribution to liturgical study. Written in a lively and imaginative style, and often from a provocative point of view, it has been responsible for arousing widespread interest in liturgy both at home and abroad.

Dom Gregory was always interested in people, and took immense pains with them. One of his friends wrote: 'I have never known anyone who gave himself so wholeheartedly to every relationship of heart and mind, or who remained so much himself in such bewildering variety: we've seldom seen him the same for an hour at once, and yet each manifestation couldn't have been anyone but him.' He was an acute ecclesiastical politician, a brilliant pamphleteer, a superb raconteur. Possessing a great gift of self-dramatization he could act himself into any part he chose;

but underneath he remained a spiritual person.

[Private information; personal knowledge.]
A. H. COURATIN.

DIXON, HENRY HORATIO (1869–1953), professor of botany, was born in Dublin 19 May 1869, the son of George Dixon, the owner of a soap works who had scientific interests and whose brother, Robert Vickers Dixon, had been Erasmus Smith's professor of natural philosophy in Trinity College, Dublin, and became archdeacon of Armagh. Two years later George Dixon died and his nine children were brought up by their mother, Rebecca, daughter of George Yeates, of Dublin, whose family were scientific instrument makers. Of Dixon's six brothers, one became a chief inspector of technical schools, one a barrister, and two held university chairs: in engineering and anatomy. Dixon followed his brothers to Rathmines School and entered Trinity College with an exhibition. He obtained a classical scholarship in 1890 but changed to natural science in which he obtained a senior moderatorship in 1891. After working in Bonn under Eduard Strasburger he returned in 1894 to Trinity College as assistant to E. P. Wright [q.v.] whom he succeeded in the university chair of botany in 1904. In 1906 he became director of the botanic garden; in 1910 keeper of the herbarium; and in 1922 professor of plant biology in Trinity College.

Two of the major fields of work at Bonn were the studies, then in their infancy, of nuclear division and of transpiration and ascent of sap. The significance of reduction division (meiosis) was just being recognized in the Strasburger school. Dixon himself in a paper communicated to the Royal Irish Academy in 1895 gave probably the first expression of the view that bivalents owed their appearance to the approach together of chromosomes rather than splitting of some structure. Dixon often spoke of conditions in Strasburger's laboratory where a great part of the cytological studies was based on hand sections. He maintained his interests in cytology and a collection of his sections of endosperm made in Bonn were in good condition in the School of Botany in 1926. These had suggested the idea of a mitotic hormone to Dixon as they appeared to show waves of nuclear division. Sections showed a zone of prophases, followed by zones of metaphases, anaphases, and telophases. This must have been one of the first demonstrations of synchronous cell divisions and the importance of their synchronous nature was fully recognized. Photographs of these sections made about 1892 were published by the Royal Dublin Society in 1946.

More important, however, was Dixon's work on transpiration and water relation of plants. This also stemmed from his association with Strasburger who in 1890–93 published work on channels of transport of sap. Dixon, however, made the striking advances in association with his great friend John Joly (whose notice he subsequently contributed to this Dictionary), a physicist of very wide interests and distinction. Dixon's observations of Strasburger's experiment demonstrating ascent of sap up killed sections of trees posed the problem of possible physical mechanisms. Dixon and Joly provided the solution in their classic paper published by the Royal Society of London in 1895 in which they established the role of cohesion of water as an essential factor in plant water relations. This first paper was followed by many studies by Dixon of tensile strength of water and of sap containing gases in solution. Then followed series of studies by Dixon with W. R. G. Atkins on osmotic pressures in plant cells. Further studies concerned the resistance to flow of sap presented by the channels of transport and its relation to the detailed structure of wood.

In his presidential address to the botany section of the British Association (1922) he put forward the view that rates of transport of sugar were such that the channel of transport could not possibly be the phloem but must be the xylem. But Dixon's former student, T. G. Mason working on the subject of transport of sugar in yams and later in cotton, showed that the phloem was responsible for the transport and that what Dixon regarded as an impossibly fast rate of movement did occur. The mechanism remained to be elucidated.

Dixon was full of ideas, some of them terrifying, as when he measured hydrostatic pressures in leaf cells by compressing leafy shoots in glass containers which occasionally blew up. He grew seedlings in sterile culture in 1892, some thirty years before this became a fashionable research procedure. He published in 1902 the compensated manometric technique for study of respiration and photosynthesis in plants which was subsequently much extended by others. In the very different field of taxonomy, he developed 'keys' for the recognition of timbers, especially mahogany, and worked on the experimental taxonomy of some of the saxifrages of county Kerry. His publications included *Transpiration and the Ascent of Sap in Plants* (1914) and *Practical Plant Biology* (1922).

The School of Botany in Trinity College, Dublin, was Dixon's creation. Provided by the generosity of Viscount (later the Earl of) Iveagh [q.v.], the building and laboratory, opened in 1907, were Dixon's design and the School and the activities within it were an expression of his orderly and very active nature. His critical and at the same time cordial and delightful personality pervaded it. Visitors came from all over the world and left enriched with many an idea from Dixon's fertile mind and with an enhanced opinion of the scientific contributions made in Dublin.

Dixon, who retired from his chair in 1949, served in many public capacities. He was a commissioner of Irish Lights; a trustee of the National Library of Ireland; and a member of the council of the International Institute of Agriculture. He was elected F.R.S. in 1908 and was Croonian lecturer in 1937; was awarded the Boyle medal (1916) of the Royal Dublin Society over which he later presided; and was an honorary fellow of Trinity College. He was a visiting professor to the university of California in 1927 and was an honorary life member of the American Society of Plant Physiologists.

In 1907 Dixon married Dorothea Mary, daughter of Sir John Franks, secretary of the Irish Land Commission. They had three sons all of whom maintained the tradition of academic distinction, one as a neurologist, and two as biochemists and fellows of King's College, Cambridge.

Dixon died in Dublin 20 December 1953.

[W. R. G. Atkins in *Obituary Notices of Fellows of the Royal Society*, vol. ix, 1954; private information; personal knowledge.]

T. A. BENNET-CLARK.

DODGSON, FRANCES CATHARINE (1883–1954), artist, was born 15 December 1883 at Oxford, the eldest daughter of the Rev. W. A. Spooner [q.v.], afterwards warden of New College, Oxford, by his wife, Frances Wycliffe, daughter of Harvey Goodwin [q.v.], bishop of Carlisle. At the age of fifteen she studied drawing at the Ruskin School at Oxford, and later attended the Royal Academy Schools

and (for a short period) the Slade School. In 1913 she married Campbell Dodgson [q.v.], keeper of prints and drawings in the British Museum, and from that time until her husband's retirement in 1932 she was chiefly occupied with social and domestic duties in her house in Montagu Square, and found little time for drawing or painting. An oil-painting by her, a portrait of Dean Inge (q.v., whose wife was her first cousin), was exhibited at the Royal Academy in 1923; but it was not until the middle of the thirties that Catharine Dodgson began again to indulge her artistic inclinations, and it was from then onwards that most of her surviving work was produced. She then abandoned painting in oils, and her favourite medium, in which she achieved considerable success, was drawing in pen or black or red chalk, with transparent washes of pale brown, often on coloured paper and heightened with white.

Between 1933 and 1945 she exhibited about a dozen portrait-drawings at the Royal Academy, including those of her husband (1933, now in the British Museum), of Dean Inge (1934, the property of Mr. Craufurd Inge), and of Sir Thomas Barlow (q.v., 1936, the property of Miss Helen Barlow). She had a real flair for catching a likeness, her portrait-drawings were in great demand, and she could have had many more commissions than she had time or inclination to carry out. She remained in the best sense an amateur; she was too conscientious to enjoy a commission for its own sake, and she lacked the self-confidence which enables a professional portrait painter to impose his personality on a subject in which he is not particularly interested. Her best portraits, therefore, were those of her own family, of intimate friends, or of children.

A visit with her husband to Würzburg, and the charming gardens of Veitshöchheim, provided a new source of inspiration, with equally successful results; and excellent examples of her elegant drawings of German rococo sculpture, made on this occasion, are now in the Ashmolean Museum at Oxford and in various private collections. In the same vein she drew the busts of Sir Christopher Wren by Edward Pierce (Ashmolean) and Charles II by Honoré Pelle in the Victoria and Albert Museum. She also produced some drawings of dancers in the Covent Garden Opera in the same medium, and, towards the end of the war of 1939–45, some sketches of Regent's Park, rather more

elaborate in colour, and remarkable for
their lightness and deftness of touch.

Her husband's illness a year or two
before his death in 1948 affected her own
health very seriously, and she hardly drew
again; she died in London 30 April 1954.
Two exhibitions of her drawings were held
at Colnaghi's in Bond Street, in the autumn
of 1936 and in the spring of 1939, and both
were warmly praised by the critics. She
was modest to a fault, and was inclined
to attribute this success to the writers'
friendship with her husband, who was of
course widely known and respected in
artistic circles. But few seemed to share
this view, least of all Campbell Dodgson
himself, who was genuinely proud of her
achievements. A loan exhibition in her
memory was held in the same gallery after
her death, October–November 1954.

[Private information; personal knowledge.]
                    J. BYAM SHAW.

DONAT, (FRIEDERICH) ROBERT
(1905–1958), actor, the fourth and youngest
son of Ernst Emil Donat, civil engineer
of Polish origin, and his wife, Rose
Alice Green, was born at Withington,
Manchester, 18 March 1905. He went to
the Central School, Manchester, and later
took a stage-training under James Bernard of the same city. In 1924 he joined
Sir Frank Benson [q.v.] whose company
was not then so constantly on tour as it
had been; thus Donat could alternate
continuing membership with seasons in
provincial repertory. This was well-varied
and helpful schooling: the Shakespearian
apprenticeship was valuable, for among
Donat's enduring distinctions was the
purity of his diction and the beauty of his
voice. He worked for a while with Alfred
Wareing whose repertory seasons at the
Theatre Royal, Huddersfield, had unusual ambition and quality. In 1928 he
began a year at the Playhouse in Liverpool and this was followed by important
work at Terence Gray's Festival Theatre
in Cambridge where plays by Euripides,
Pirandello, Sheridan, and Shakespeare
gave him opportunities to experiment in a
range of widely different and challenging
leading roles.

He made his mark decisively in London in 1931 when he created the part
of Gideon Sarn in a dramatization of
Precious Bane by Mary Webb [q.v.]. His
handsome features and beautiful delivery,
together with the equipment of technique
acquired in his repertory years, promised
promotion to the front rank and there was

confirmation of his powers in the Malvern
Festival of 1931. Again at Malvern, in
1933, he played the two Camerons in
A Sleeping Clergyman by James Bridie
[q.v.]; the piece was transferred to Lon
don and had a long run at the Piccadilly
Theatre. Donat's performance of the two
roles, the dying consumptive and his so
the brilliant doctor, was memorable and
repeated in a revival of 1947. To the
simulation of a man with lung-trouble he
brought his own knowledge of pain, for he
was himself a sufferer from asthma and hi
later career was much impeded by illness

His success carried him to importan
film work, especially with (Sir) Alexande
Korda [q.v.] who was then recruiting re
markable casts from the leading player
of the living stage. His notable appearance
were in The Private Life of Henry VII
(in which Charles Laughton played th
king), The Ghost Goes West, and as anothe
Scottish doctor, Andrew Manson, in
screen-version of A. J. Cronin's Th
Citadel. Perhaps his most widely ap
preciated film-role was that of Mr. Chips
the ageing schoolmaster well known t
readers of the novel by James Hilton [q.v.

Donat continued to mingle screen-wor
with important returns to the stage, tak
ing on the cares and risks of managemen
at the Queen's Theatre in 1936 when h
presented J. L. Hodson's Red Nigh
During the war he gave vigour and volum
to the eloquence of Captain Shotover i
a revival of Shaw's Heartbreak Hou
(1943). At the Westminster Theatre i
1945 he was much liked in a plebeia
comedy part in The Cure for Love b
Walter Greenwood. His last venture as
manager was at the Aldwych Theatre i
1946 when he staged Much Ado Abo
Nothing with himself as Benedick. H
spirited rendering of the wordy warfa
with Beatrice was exemplary at a tim
when the speaking on the British stage w
much criticized. He gave another lesson
delivery when he joined the Old Vic con
pany in 1953 to play Becket in a produ
tion of T. S. Eliot's Murder in the Cathedr
Directed by (Sir) Robert Helpmann, th
was one of the most effective renderings
a play frequently revived. Donat was f
from being a player attached to one ty
of character. He was, however, seen at
best in parts which asked for splendo
of voice and dignity of bearing and
Becket was held by those who knew t
scope of his work to have a singu
beauty. Asceticism was a quality whi
came naturally to his delicacy of featu

but he had learned in his repertory years to be richly versatile. In naming his favourite roles he included the two gusty, outspoken Camerons of *A Sleeping Clergyman*. Here, and in *Murder in the Cathedral*, were perhaps the summits of his achievement on the living stage.

During the last five years of his life Donat was a constant invalid. He did not mind the seclusion since he was of a shy and retiring disposition and had never sought the bright lights of publicity. But the frustration was galling for an actor who was only just entering his fifties and should have been at the height of his powers. He died in London 9 June 1958.

In 1929 Donat married Ella Annesley Voysey, by whom he had two sons and one daughter, but the marriage was subsequently dissolved. In 1953 he married the actress Dorothy Renée Ascherson.

[J. C. Trewin, *Robert Donat*, 1968; private information; personal knowledge.]

IVOR BROWN.

DONNAN, FREDERICK GEORGE (1870–1956), physical chemist, was born in Colombo 6 September 1870, the second of the six children of William Donnan, a merchant of Belfast, and his wife, Jane Rose Turnley Liggate, also a native of Northern Ireland. All Donnan's early life was spent in Ulster whither he returned at the age of three, retaining no recollection of Ceylon. In 1879 an accident caused the loss of his left eye, a disability which did not prevent him from playing a quite remarkable game of lawn tennis; he was also a first-class swimmer and a notable high diver. He attended the Belfast Royal Academy where he acquired a good knowledge of English literature and history. His chief interest was mathematics and physical science; there being no laboratories in the Academy he did some practical work externally. At the Queen's College, Belfast, he was remarkably successful in his studies, made quite a good income from scholarships and fellowships, and obtained his B.A. (1892) and M.A. (1894) from the Royal University of Ireland.

He went next to the university of Leipzig where he did a year's chemistry under Wislicenus and then joined Ostwald to devote himself to the younger and rising discipline of physical chemistry. He obtained his Ph.D. *summa cum laude* in 1896. He finished his European tour with a year in the laboratory of J. H. van't Hoff in Berlin where he studied experimentally the hydrates of calcium sulphate and the vapour pressures of a number of saturated aqueous solutions of single and double salts occurring in van't Hoff's investigations on oceanic salt deposits.

In 1897 Donnan settled down quietly for a year's hard work at home 'to read more deeply in the literature of physical chemistry'. In 1898 he went to University College, London, as a senior research student in the laboratory of (Sir) William Ramsay (whose notice he subsequently contributed to this Dictionary). It was not until 1901 that he took his first paid post, as an assistant lecturer in Ramsay's laboratory; in 1902–3 he was assistant professor in University College; and in 1903–4 lecturer in organic chemistry in the Royal College of Science, Dublin. In 1904, however, a new chair of physical chemistry was founded in the university of Liverpool by Sir John Brunner and Donnan was invited to be its first occupant. He supervised the building of the Muspratt laboratory of physical chemistry and was its director from 1906 to 1913. He then succeeded Ramsay at University College, London, where he remained until his retirement in 1937.

In the war of 1914–18 Donnan was a member of a number of committees including those on chemical warfare and nitrogen products. He played an important part in the early stages of the research work at University College on synthetic ammonia and nitric acid and he assisted K. B. Quinan in the designs of plant for the fixation of nitrogen and for the production of mustard 'gas'. He was appointed C.B.E. in 1920. His connections with the chemical industry continued after the war: he was research consultant to Brunner Mond & Co. from 1920 to 1926 and a member of the research council of Imperial Chemical Industries from 1926 to 1939. He was particularly successful in raising money from industry and other sources to assist scientific research.

Although pre-eminently a teacher, Donnan was internationally known as a colloid chemist and in particular for his theory of membrane equilibrium. He was elected F.R.S. in 1911 and awarded the Davy medal in 1928. He received the Longstaff medal (1924) of the Chemical Society over which he presided in 1937–9, had no fewer than eleven honorary degrees, and was an honorary member of numerous academies and learned societies. His range of interests was extraordinarily wide; his early appreciation of the necessity of a united Europe led him to the study of artificial languages, whilst in his old age he was much preoccupied with cosmic problems.

Donnan was tall, good looking, well built and of great physical strength and endurance. Until he smiled his face in repose was often stern and rather sad. When he began to talk he radiated charm and sympathy. A tremendous worker, he kept odd hours: to retire at 1 a.m. was early for him and 2, 3, or even 4 a.m. were not infrequent. He was devoted to his friends and had his likes and dislikes. To accompany him abroad was to take part in a royal progress.

After his retirement Donnan remained in his home in Woburn Square until 1940 when he left only twelve hours before it was destroyed by a bomb. He went to live at Sittingbourne, and died at Canterbury 16 December 1956. He never married and owed much to two sisters who played an unobtrusive but important part in his life and both of whom died in the same year.

[F. A. Freeth in *Biographical Memoirs of Fellows of the Royal Society*, vol. iii, 1957; personal knowledge.]   F. A. FREETH.

DOUGLAS, CLIFFORD (HUGH) (1879–1952), originator of the theory of Social Credit, was born in Stockport, Cheshire, 20 January 1879, the youngest son of Hugh Douglas, draper, by his wife, Louisa Hordern. Educated at Stockport Grammar School, he entered on an engineering and managerial career which took him to India as chief engineer and manager of the British Westinghouse Company. In 1910 he spent two terms at Pembroke College, Cambridge. During the war of 1914–18, in which he reached the rank of major in the Royal Flying Corps and the Royal Air Force, he was sent to the Royal Aircraft Factory at Farnborough to reorganize production and cost accounting. He had already been reflecting on society's failure to utilize the full possibilities of modern technology; his work at Farnborough suggested an explanation of this, which in turn led to the theory of Social Credit. In every productive establishment the amount of money issued in a given period as wages, salaries, and dividends, which he took to be the amount available to purchase the goods produced in that period, was less than the collective price of those products. To remedy the supposed chronic deficiency of purchasing power he advocated the issuance of additional money to consumers, or of subsidies to producers to enable them to set prices below costs. By these devices, which came to be known as Social Credit, production was to be liberated from the price system, inaugurating an era of plenty, freedom, leisure, and human dignity, without altering the system of private ownership, profit, and enterprise.

Convinced that his analysis was the sole key to the understanding and remedying of the world's ills, Douglas devoted himself to developing its implications and pressing its claims. He found a platform in 1919 in the *New Age*, edited by A. R. Orage [q.v.], whose critique of society had anticipated Douglas's, and who became an enthusiastic convert to Douglas's economic theory, publishing Douglas's first book, *Economic Democracy* (1920), serially in the *New Age* (June–August 1919) and collaborating in his second, *Credit-Power and Democracy* (1920). In 1921 and 1922 Douglas's ideas attracted considerable public attention and earned the opposition of socialist writers and of the Labour Party, which formally rejected his doctrine in 1922. In 1923 Douglas was brought to Ottawa by some Canadian admirers to expound his views to the Canadian House of Commons committee on banking and commerce.

Public discussion of Social Credit declined in England after 1922, but with the depression of the thirties it revived in greater volume, supported now by the *New Age*, the *New English Weekly*, Douglas's own weekly *Social Credit*, and various pamphlets and books, some of which went through several editions. Douglas testified to the Macmillan committee on finance and industry (1930) and lectured as far afield as New Zealand and Canada in 1934.

By the late thirties the English Social Credit movement under Douglas's rather autocratic leadership had dwindled into an esoteric sect. But it had struck roots in Western Canada, where Douglas had had a following from the early twenties. When he visited Alberta in 1934 he won such wide support that the ageing United Farmers' government, in spite of their scepticism of Social Credit, appointed him (early in 1935) principal reconstruction adviser to the government of Alberta, with a two-year contract. However, they were swept out of office by the more zealous Social Credit League in the elections of August 1935. Relations between Douglas and the new government soon became strained. He resigned as adviser in 1936, publishing his account of the matter in *The Alberta Experiment* (1937). A back-benchers' revolt in 1937 compelled the government to ask Douglas's further help. He sent two of his staff, who prepared legislation which, when enacted, was invalidated by federal authorities. The provincial government remained Social Credit in name but virtually abandoned Douglas's principles.

Douglas's earlier writings were remarkable for their reasoned protest against the frustration of individuality by business civilization. But his economic theory never surmounted his initial fallacy of reasoning from one firm to the whole economy. And his social and political theory were vitiated by his engineering concepts. He was driven to attribute the thwarting of technology, and hence of human freedom, to a conspiracy of world Jewry, freemasonry, international finance, Bolshevism, and Nazism; and finally to denigrate democracy and denounce the secret ballot.

Douglas was married twice: first to Constance Mary, daughter of Edward Phillips, of Royston House, Hertfordshire; secondly to Edith Mary, daughter of George Desborough Dale, of the Indian Civil Service. He had one daughter by his second wife. He was a fisherman and yachtsman, and for a time ran a yacht-building shipyard at Swanwick, Southampton. He died in Dundee 29 September 1952. A painting by Augustus John was in the Royal Academy exhibition of 1934.

[C. B. Macpherson, *Democracy in Alberta*, 1953.]   C. B. MACPHERSON.

DOUGLAS, (GEORGE) NORMAN (1868–1952), writer, was born at Thüringen, Vorarlberg, 8 December 1868, the third son of John Sholto Douglass, and his wife, Vanda, daughter of Baron Ernst von Poelnitz. Her mother was a daughter of James Ochoncar, seventeenth Lord Forbes [q.v.]. Douglas's father managed some cotton mills in Vorarlberg for his father John Douglass, fourteenth laird of Tilquhillie, near Banchory. Douglas's first language was German and he lived at Thüringen until his sixth year. His father was killed in an accident in 1874; his mother soon married again; and the child was brought up by his relatives in Scotland and England.

In 1881 he was sent to Uppingham under Edward Thring [q.v.]. His reaction against this regime led to his being sent in 1883 to Karlsruhe Gymnasium where he remained until 1889. In addition to a thorough classical course, he learnt Italian, began Russian, and became an accomplished pianist. An early passion for natural history was further developed and in 1886 he made some contributions to the *Zoologist*. In 1888 during a tour of Italy he first visited Capri.

At twenty-one Douglas had a good income, lived a full social life, and prepared for the Foreign Office which he entered in 1893. A year later he was posted to St. Petersburg and in due course became third secretary. He resigned this post in 1896, bought a villa at Posilipo, and devoted himself to a wide range of studies and further travel. Until the end of his Russian period he had made more contributions to English and German zoological journals and written an official report on *The Pumice Stone Industry of the Lipari Islands* (1895) which he claimed later led to the abolition of child-labour there.

In 1898 Douglas married a cousin (connected through the Poelnitz family), Elizabeth (Elsa) Theobaldina, daughter of Augustus FitzGibbon. They lived at Posilipo, travelled in India and Tunisia (1902) and collaborated in *Unprofessional Tales* (1901) with the joint pseudonym of Normyx. The book made no mark, but Douglas used some of the contents in *Experiments* (1925) and *Nerinda* (1929). He obtained a divorce in 1904. He now moved to Capri, cultivated property there and wrote eight monographs on the island privately printed (limited ed. 1930). Hitherto he had signed his name 'G. Norman Douglass'. About 1908 he adopted 'Norman Douglas' for all purposes.

Substantial loss of income about 1907 compelled him to sell his property on Capri and turn to writing. An essay on Poe (1909) was his first serious contribution to literature. From 1910 to 1916 he was mainly in London and wrote a number of articles later embodied in his travel books, *Siren Land* (1911) about the Sorrentino peninsula, *Fountains in the Sand* (1912) about Tunisia, and *Old Calabria* (1915). Though not financially successful these books gained him recognition and from 1912 to 1915 he was assistant editor of the *English Review*. This post brought him acquaintance with D. H. Lawrence, Edward Thomas [qq.v.], and others. An older friend was Joseph Conrad [q.v.].

Douglas had been working for some time on *South Wind*. Meanwhile there appeared *London Street Games* (1916), 'a breathless catalogue' revealing an intimate knowledge of children. In the same year he left England, not to return for twenty-four years. He went first to Italy where he finished *South Wind* on Capri. From 1917 to 1918 he was in France, mainly in Paris, in a state of extreme poverty. *South Wind* was published in 1917 and was an immediate success, appealing, with its ironical treatment of conventional morality and its gay setting, to a war-weary generation. Nevertheless he was unable to continue his next novel, begun at St. Malo in 1918, for want of food. He finished it at Menton where he was 'feeling comfortable again'. This book was *They Went* (1920), and in the next three years he achieved the mellow quality of *Alone* (1921), his favourite book, and *Together* (1923), largely recollections of his childhood in Vorarlberg. By this time Douglas had settled in Florence where, with interludes of travel, he remained until 1937. This was the most serene epoch of his life. He was now famous and fairly well-off and much visited by post-war writers on whom his influence was great. Renewed acquaintance with D. H. Lawrence led to a literary quarrel, the fruit of which was the brilliant invective of *D. H. Lawrence and Maurice Magnus* (1924). Throughout these years his almost inseparable companion was Giuseppe (Pino) Orioli who also helped him to publish several limited editions most of which were later republished commercially in London. Meanwhile he had written *Looking Back* (1933), a discursive autobiography.

In 1937 Douglas left Florence and was chiefly in France until 1940 when he retreated to Lisbon, and finally returned to England. An *Almanac* (1945), a calendar of quotations, revealed the gnomic quality of his thought, and *Late Harvest* (1946) was a retrospective commentary with much autobiographical information. He returned to Capri in 1946 and remained there until his death, 9 February 1952.

While *South Wind* will remain the most popular and influential of Douglas's books, the three works on Southern Italy and Tunisia are generally recognized as his finest achievement. To them he brought a trained scientific mind, profound learning, and an intimate knowledge born of repeated visits. The same qualities appear in all his works together with his unique personality of which the keynote is anti-asceticism and a ruthless denunciation of 'crooked thinking'. His flexible style, equal to every mood, ranging over exuberant gaiety, sustained argument, and mellow retrospection, was carefully developed and often echoed his own voice.

Douglas was a tall man of distinguished presence in the care of which he wa scrupulous and even conventional, and th fine manners of his breeding never faile him. He was 'pagan to the core', ye though an epicurean he was no sybarite his habits were almost austerely method cal. He was, at different times of his life an ardent lover of both sexes. His adver tures involved exile and sudden depar tures, but he avoided serious trouble, an the evidence, such as it is, comes main] from his own writings. His great humanit made him a foe to all cruelty and stupidity and he won the friendship of the mos diverse types of people.

Douglas had two sons by his marriag the younger of whom, Robin Dougla was the author of *Well, Let's Eat* (1933 a guide to London restaurants, to whic his father contributed some comments.

A bust of Douglas by George Havar Thomas was exhibited at the Roya Academy in 1931 and is owned by h family. A drawing by Michael Ayrton is i the National Portrait Gallery.

[Douglas's own works, especially *Togethe 1923, *Looking Back*, 1933, and *Late Harves* 1946; Muriel Draper, *Music at Midnigh* 1929; G. Orioli, *Moving Along*, 1934; Joh Davenport in *The Twentieth Century*, Apr 1952, and Introduction to *Old Calabria*, 1955 H. M. Tomlinson, *Norman Douglas*, 1952 R. M. Dawkins, *Norman Douglas*, 1952; Co: stantine FitzGibbon, *Norman Douglas*, 195? Nancy Cunard, *Grand Man*, 1954; Cec Woolf, *A Bibliography of Norman Dougla* 1954; Robin Douglas in *The Cornhill*, Sun mer 1955; private information; person knowledge.]   D. M. Lov

DOUGLAS, SIR WILLIAM SCOT' (1890–1953), civil servant, was born i Edinburgh 20 August 1890, the elde child and only son of Daniel Dougla: solicitor, and his wife, Margaret Douga The Douglases were an old Edinburg family, burghers of the city. William Scot Douglas (1815–83, q.v.) was his grand father. Douglas went to George Heriot' School and Edinburgh University whe: he won the Lanfine bursary in economic (1911) and graduated with second cla: honours in history (1912). In 1914 h passed into the first division of the Civ Service in which his career was astonisl ingly varied. He had a natural talent fc administration and could turn his hand t any administrative task without becomin deeply involved with the subject. Wha fascinated him was negotiation and man agement, of both people and things; a these he was superbly good.

He started in the Customs and Excise department; but in 1920 he was appointed financial adviser to the Allenstein plebiscite commission which dealt with adjustments to the frontiers between East Prussia and Poland. There he attracted the notice of Sir John (later Lord) Bradbury [q.v.], principal British delegate to the Reparation Commission in Paris, whose private secretary Douglas became on first joining the delegation. Like many Scots he was completely at home in Paris, learning to speak French—and not only classical French—almost like a native. Gaiety was one of his especial characteristics and his six years in Paris were for him a time of great enjoyment. Customs and Excise, to which he returned in 1926, was never his spiritual home, but in those days civil servants were seldom consulted about their wishes. However, in 1929 he transferred to the Ministry of Labour to face the tremendous problem of unemployment, as divisional controller for the Midlands (1931–3), for Scotland (1933–5), and as an assistant secretary (1935–7). In 1937 he became secretary of the Department of Health for Scotland where he was a popular chief and did a great deal to bring the department into the administrative structure of the Service and to lay the foundations of its future.

In 1939 Douglas moved to the Treasury as third secretary in charge of the establishment division, succeeding the greatly loved Sir James (Jimmy) Rae who had done so much to make the Service one Service and so enable it to take the strain of war. Douglas was probably not at his happiest without his own machine to manage; the endless struggle to keep the fast-expanding departments amenable to some kind of financial discipline in pay and complements hardly suited his style. The story goes that he settled one battle with his old Scottish department by playing for it at golf; probably the Treasury came off best since he was a scratch performer. His major contribution in the Treasury lay in the planning and manning of the new departments needed for war; in starting the 'exchange and mart' by which the Treasury sought to place experienced men where they were most needed.

In 1942 Sir Andrew Duncan [q.v.] returned to the Ministry of Supply and picked Douglas to replace the permanent secretary who was in ill health. The two made an excellent team. Douglas was both adviser and friend to the minister and under the two of them the department worked both hard and effectively. It was a difficult Ministry with a number of prima donnas whom Douglas managed with an unfailing skill largely concealed by his charm.

In 1945 came Douglas's last and longest job, with his transfer to the Ministry of Health where Aneurin Bevan [q.v.] was setting up the National Health Service. There his gift for negotiation proved invaluable. It was not the detail, even the purpose, of the health service which absorbed him, but getting it across. It was an immense help that he got on extremely well with the, to him, new world of the medical profession and all its auxiliaries. Less personally involved than either the minister or the departmental officers who were closest to the operation, he could often smooth over difficulties or suggest a solution to an impasse. With his minister he had a happy and easy relationship founded on mutual respect although the two men could hardly have been more different. On the housing side he took a great interest in the production of non-traditional houses.

When in 1951 the housing and local government side of the Ministry joined with the Ministry of Town and Country Planning and the health side became a separate Ministry, Douglas stayed with the health work but retired later in the same year. He acquired several directorships and particularly enjoyed one at Slazengers, for golf was always a ruling passion. He was chairman of the Civil Service preparatory commission which investigated the form the public service should take under the proposed federation of Central Africa and his retirement promised to be as varied and active as his Civil Service career, but he died at Bishop's Stortford 17 February 1953. He was appointed C.B. (1938), K.C.B. (1943), G.C.B. (1950), and K.B.E. (1941).

In 1919 Douglas married Vera Paterson, daughter of George Macpherson Duffes, chief assistant keeper of the Sasines in Edinburgh, whom he had met while she was still at school. They had two daughters and took care that both should be born in Scotland: both went to St. Andrews.

[Private information; personal knowledge.]
                             SHARP.

DOWNEY, RICHARD JOSEPH (1881–1953), Roman Catholic archbishop, was born at Kilkenny, Ireland, 5 May 1881, the eldest of three children and only son of Thomas Downey, chemist, by his wife, Minnie Casey. Educated at Enniscorthy by the Irish Christian Brothers and, after the family moved to Liverpool, at Our Lady Immaculate elementary school, Everton, he entered St. Edward's College, the junior diocesan seminary, in 1894. In 1901 he went to St. Joseph's College, Upholland, near Wigan, for professional studies in philosophy and divinity, and was ordained priest in 1907. He failed by half a mark to achieve an all-time record by being top in every subject in the curriculum. Selected for postgraduate studies, he went to Rome and took a doctorate of divinity with distinction at the Gregorian University in 1911.

Returning to England, Downey joined the Catholic Missionary Society in London and for the next fifteen years was principally engaged in preaching and lecturing, frequently to non-Catholics and often from outdoor platforms, in all parts of the British Isles. He preached the Lenten course at Our Lady of Lourdes church, New York, in 1922 and the Advent course in 1925, on each occasion carrying out extensive lecture tours. He was co-founder and first editor of the *Catholic Gazette*, the monthly publication of the Missionary Society, and a regular contributor to contemporary theological and philosophical reviews. His scholarship earned for him membership of the British Psychological and Aristotelian societies and an honorary fellowship of the Philosophical Society. During his last six years in London Downey taught theology to the students of three religious orders and became professor of philosophy and psychology at the Sacred Heart College, Hammersmith. He was for some years external examiner in philosophy at the National University of Ireland. In 1926 he returned to St. Joseph's College, Upholland, as professor of dogmatic theology and dean of the departments of philosophy and theology, becoming vice-rector the following year.

The Holy See nominated Downey archbishop of Liverpool and metropolitan in 1928 and at forty-seven he became the youngest Roman Catholic archbishop in the world. He also provided the first instance since the Reformation of a priest in Britain being elevated to the archiepiscopal rank without previously holding some intermediate dignity. The consecration by the cardinal archbishop of Westminster took place at the Liverpool pro-cathedral of St. Nicholas on 21 September, and the

pallium was bestowed by Pope Pius XI in Rome on 17 December. At a great welcome-home demonstration in Liverpool shortly afterwards the archbishop announced his dual intention of completing the extension of the seminary then in progress and of building a cathedral worthy of the city and the archdiocese.

He set himself to these tasks with vigour and vision, and in 1930 saw the completion of the seminary at a cost of £250,000. In the same year he purchased the derelict Brownlow Hill workhouse and nine-acre site in the centre of Liverpool for £100,000, and shortly afterwards appointed Sir Edwin Lutyens [q.v.] as architect of the proposed cathedral. The foundation stone was laid at Whitsuntide 1933 in the presence of a papal legate. Only the crypt was finished when work came to a halt in 1941 and in post-war conditions the Lutyens design proved impracticable to complete.

Early in his episcopate the new archbishop established himself as a champion of the voluntary schools and although the youngest member of the bench of bishops was soon elected its spokesman on educational matters. In 1929, to celebrate the centenary of the Catholic Emancipation Act, no fewer than 400,000 people assembled at his invitation in the Liverpool suburban Thingwall Park, in what was described as the greatest gathering of Catholics in this country since the Pilgrimage of Grace. In the following year, when the Labour Government introduced education legislation unacceptable to Catholics, Downey called for a demonstration in the city, which drew 150,000 sympathizers and sealed the doom of the bill. He continued the struggle for denominational education and in 1937 proposed a £750,000 scheme for the reorganization of all Catholic schools in his archdiocese. The Liverpool Conservative council disapproved and for several months the Board of Education withdrew its educational grants to the city.

Downey was only five feet four inches in height and his natural obesity gave cause for alarm when he reached eighteen stone in weight in 1932. In August of that year by a system of dieting and exercise he reduced by four stone and continued his efforts until he had halved his weight to nine stone in 1939. He was inundated with letters from all parts of the world asking for the secret of his achievement.

Downey visited Australia in 1934–5 and Canada in 1951, but the war years of

1939–45 found him in his episcopal see denouncing Hitlerism, urging the war effort, and bringing solace to the afflicted. He saw the destruction of many of his churches, convents, and schools, and several times officiated at communal funerals and gave broadcast addresses.

His genial personality endeared him to all sections of the community and his natural wit and eloquence put him in great demand at all manner of sacred and secular functions. He was adamant on principle and those who attempted compromise found in him an accomplished controversialist. By appealing to the best instincts of the public at large no one did more to eradicate from Liverpool the religious strife which had besmirched its name in the first two decades of the century and lingered on into the thirties.

Downey's valued services as a member of the council of the university of Liverpool (1944–50) were acknowledged by the award of an honorary doctorate in 1953, but he died before the degree ceremony took place. Three other universities gave him honorary doctorates: the Gregorian, the National University of Ireland, and Toronto. The Royal Institute of British Architects elected him an honorary fellow (1946) and the Holy See appointed him as assistant at the pontifical throne in the silver jubilee year of his episcopate. He was elected a freeman of Kilkenny, Limerick, Sligo, Wexford, and Clonmel in his native Ireland, but he always described himself as 'a Lancashire lad from Kilkenny'.

The sixth to occupy the see of Liverpool since the restoration of the hierarchy in 1850, Downey was the first to have passed the age of seventy. He died in a nursing home in Woolton 16 June 1953, and was buried in the tomb designed by Lutyens twenty years before in the crypt of the future cathedral, after the largest funeral Liverpool had ever seen.

A portrait of Downey by Stanley Reed was hung in St. Joseph's College, Upholland, and belongs to the archdiocese of Liverpool.

[Private information; personal knowledge.]
CYRIL TAYLOR.

DREYER, SIR FREDERIC CHARLES (1878–1956), admiral, was born 8 January 1878 at Parsonstown, King's County, Ireland, the second son of John Louis Emil Dreyer, then astronomer with the fourth Earl of Rosse [q.v.], later director of Armagh Observatory (1882–1916), and

his wife, Katherine Hannah, daughter of John Tuthill, of Kilmore, county Limerick. His elder brother, John Tuthill Dreyer (1876–1959), entered the Royal Artillery and reached the rank of major-general. From the Royal School, Armagh, Dreyer entered the *Britannia* in 1891 where he gained maximum promotion time; he obtained first class certificates in all his sub-lieutenants' courses, and was promoted lieutenant in 1898. The following year he joined the *Excellent* gunnery school and passed the advance course with honours to become a fully qualified gunnery specialist. His first appointment as a gunnery lieutenant was to the instructional school at Sheerness.

In 1903 Dreyer became gunnery officer in the *Exmouth* which in the next year became flagship of Sir Arthur Wilson [q.v.], commander-in-chief of the Home, later Channel, Fleet. In the fleet competition for the best battleship in gunnery firing, the *Exmouth* was easily first. In January 1907 he was appointed for gunnery duties to the *Dreadnought*, the first all-big-gun battleship built for the navy. In April 1907 he was posted to the naval ordnance department in the Admiralty and in the same year he collaborated with Arthur Joseph Hungerford Pollen in the production of an aim corrector to improve the control of gunfire from ships. He was promoted commander at the end of the year, having been very highly recommended for early promotion by the admirals and captains of the ships in which he had served. By this time he was widely recognized in the navy as the most accomplished gunnery officer of his time.

At the end of 1909 he returned to sea in the *Vanguard*; then in December 1910 became flag commander to Sir John (later Earl) Jellicoe [q.v.], commander-in-chief Atlantic Fleet, in the *Prince of Wales*. Jellicoe was himself a notable gunnery officer and the two men became close friends. Dreyer had done brilliant work in improving the control of naval gunfire, not only with Pollen but also on his own account, being responsible for an improved method of rangefinding, the invention of a plotting table to provide automatic control of range and deflection in relation to the movement through the water of the firing ship and her target, and the design of a torpedo director for underwater firings. He was eventually awarded £5,000 in recognition of his various inventions. Jellicoe very strongly recomended Dreyer for promotion to captain, and this came in 1913 at the relatively early age of thirty-five. Dreyer was by then commanding the cruiser *Amphion*. Later that year he was appointed to the new battleship *Orion* as flag captain to Sir Robert Arbuthnot [q.v.].

Dreyer still held this appointment at the outbreak of war, but in 1915 Jellicoe obtained his transfer to the *Iron Duke*, flagship of the Grand Fleet, and he served as Jellicoe's flag captain until the end of 1916, when Jellicoe went to the Admiralty as first sea lord. Dreyer was present at the battle of Jutland (31 May 1916) and was highly praised by the commander-in-chief in his official dispatch. Dreyer, who had been awarded the C.B. (civil) in 1914 for his services to naval gunnery, was appointed C.B. (military).

The battle had indicated a failure on the part of British naval shells which broke up on oblique impact on armour instead of penetrating and bursting inside. Jellicoe formed several expert committees of serving officers in the fleet to inquire into the various shortcomings of British matériel, and Dreyer was a natural selection to head a gunnery inquiry. As a result, a new design of heavy armour-piercing shell with a new type of burster and a redesigned fuse was put into production.

Dreyer accompanied Jellicoe to the Admiralty to take over the duty of director of naval ordnance. He was thus able to oversee and press forward the manufacture of these new shells which, according to Jellicoe, certainly doubled the offensive power of heavy naval guns. Dreyer remained at the Admiralty until 1919—from 1918 as director of naval artillery and torpedoes—and was appointed C.B.E. in 1919.

In February of that year Dreyer was appointed commodore and chief of staff to Jellicoe for his mission to India and the dominions to advise on their naval requirements. He returned to the Admiralty in 1920 as director of the gunnery division and in 1922 was appointed to command the battle cruiser *Repulse*. He was promoted rear-admiral in December 1923 and in October 1924 was made a lord commissioner of the Admiralty and assistant chief of naval staff. He went to sea again in 1927 as rear-admiral commanding the battle cruiser squadron, flying his flag in the *Hood*, and was promoted vice-admiral in March 1929. He returned to the Admiralty in 1930 as deputy chief of naval staff and thus had to accept collec-

tive responsibility at the time of the Invergordon mutiny. From 1931 he served in addition as Admiralty representative on the League of Nations permanent advisory commission.

Dreyer was promoted admiral in 1932 and in the same year was promoted K.C.B. He was commander-in-chief of the China station in 1933–6 and promoted G.B.E. in 1937. He held a number of foreign decorations.

Dreyer was placed on the retired list in 1939 but on the outbreak of war was brought back into active service. He served as commodore of convoys in 1939 and 1940, and in 1941 was made inspector of merchant ship gunnery. He served also as chairman of the U-boat assessment committee and in 1942 was appointed chief of naval air services and, later deputy chief of naval air equipment. He reverted to the retired list in 1943.

Throughout his Service life Dreyer was a completely dedicated man, supremely efficient in all he undertook and sparing no pains to equip himself professionally to the highest pitch of knowledge and skill. He was an austere man in his personal life and a stern disciplinarian, with little sense of humour. He was the author of two books: *How to get a First Class in Seamanship* (1900) and *The Sea Heritage*, a study of maritime warfare (1955).

In 1901 Dreyer married Una Maria daughter of the Rev. John Thomas Hallett, vicar of Bishop's Tachbrook Leamington, and had three sons and two daughters. He died at Winchester 11 December 1956.

[Admiralty records; *The Times*, 12 December 1956; personal knowledge.]

P. K. KEMP

DRUMMOND, SIR JACK CECIL (1891–1952), nutritional biochemist, was born at Leicester 12 January 1891, the only child of John Drummond, a retired major of the Royal Horse Artillery who died the following June. He was brought up by his aunt and her husband, Captain George Spinks, a Crimean veteran and keen amateur gardener from whom Drummond probably derived his interest in wild flowers and birds. An early talent for drawing led him on to photography and thence to chemistry. After attending Roan School, Greenwich, and King's College School in the Strand, he entered East London (later Queen Mary) College and graduated in 1912 with first class honours in chemistry. In 1913 he became a research assistant in the department of physiology at King's College, London, a significant choice since the professor was W. D. Halliburton [q.v.] and his immediate supervisor Otto Rosenheim [q.v.], both of whom exerted a profound and lasting impression upon him. Halliburton was responsible for his appointment in March 1914 as assistant at the Cancer Hospital Research Institute where he joined Dr. Casimir Funk who had already coined the word 'vitamine'. Drummond's collaboration with Funk started his interest in nutrition.

In 1917 Halliburton, as a member of the food (war) committee of the Royal Society, invited Drummond to join him in experimental work on substitutes for butter and margarine which introduced Drummond to fat-soluble vitamins, one of his major fields of experimental work. More important, it led him to practical problems of human nutrition in which he took an immediate interest, as is shown by a paper on infant feeding published in the Lancet in 1918, the year in which he received the degree of D.Sc. of the university of London and succeeded Funk as biochemist at the Cancer Hospital. In the following year he was invited by E. H. Starling [q.v.] to University College, London, as research assistant in physiological chemistry. In 1920 he was appointed reader and in 1922, at the early age of thirty-one, to the newly created professorship of biochemistry.

His department was small and never autonomous, and inadequate financial resources were not helped by the negligible support of two successive secretaries of the Medical Research Council. A variety of lines of research was pursued, too various or errors to be avoided or major contributions made; Drummond's artistic temperament was better suited to the broad sweep of the canvas than to dull attention to detail. But his energy and enthusiasm inspired his colleagues and students, and his department was among the most important in the country for training biochemists; at the time of his death no fewer than nine of his colleagues or pupils were holding or had held chairs. The breadth of his interests and his approachability caused him to be much in demand as a lecturer and as a consultant to industry to which he devoted much time.

In the early thirties the need to apply the new knowledge of nutrition was becoming increasingly clear, largely from the work of Sir Robert McCarrison [q.v.] and Sir John (later Lord) Boyd Orr. This realization, together with Drummond's interest in gastronomy and in the pleasure of good wine and food, led him to study the dietary habits of the English over the previous 500 years. This unique survey, published in 1939 as *The Englishman's Food* (jointly with his secretary, Anne Wilbraham), would probably have been remembered as Drummond's most important contribution but for the important task which now lay ahead.

When war broke out Drummond was consulted by the Ministry of Food on gas contamination of food, and on 16 October 1939 he was appointed 'chief adviser on food contamination' to the Ministry. Once there he interested himself in its various scientific aspects and in December submitted a 'memorandum on co-ordination in investigation and development of new processes' in which he urged the creation of a co-ordinating unit in the Ministry with a scientific liaison officer in charge. When on 31 January 1940 a meeting was arranged by the parliamentary and scientific committee to discuss wartime bread, the Ministry of Health was represented by its nutritional expert, but Drummond stressed that he himself was speaking in a private capacity. The same day he submitted to his Ministry a memorandum 'on certain nutritional aspects of the food position'. Next day he was officially appointed scientific adviser to the Ministry of Food.

With the advent of Lord Woolton in April 1940 as minister of food, policy became a blend of scientific theory and practical possibilities, for the minister believed that his scientific experts should have a hand in framing policy. Lord Woolton, Drummond, and their colleague Sir Wilson Jameson in the Ministry of Health took the opportunity to combat nutritional ignorance and to improve—rather than merely to maintain—the nutriture of the population. The result was described by the Lasker Awards committee of the American Public Health Association as 'one of the greatest demonstrations in public health administration that the world has ever seen' and named Lord Woolton, Sir Jack Drummond, Sir Wilson Jameson, and Sir John Boyd Orr as 'the four great leaders in this historic enterprise'.

In 1944 Drummond became an adviser on nutrition to S.H.A.E.F. and the following year to the Control Commission for Germany and Austria (British element).

That year, 1945, he resigned his professorship on appointment as director of research to Boots Pure Drug Company, but he was seconded to the Ministry until 1946.

In 1915 Drummond had married a former fellow student, Mabel Helen, daughter of Philip Straw, schoolmaster. In 1939 this marriage was broken up and in the following year he married his co-author, Anne, daughter of Roger Wilbraham. On the evening of 4 August 1952 he, his wife, and their ten-year-old daughter were murdered, when camping in the French Alps. Two years later a 77-year-old farmer, Gaston Dominici, was convicted of the crime. The French newspapers, before identity was established, described Drummond's body as that of a man of forty, whereas he was sixty-one. He was small, neat, sprightly, and gay, abounding with energy and enjoying the company of others as well as the delights of good food and wine.

Drummond was knighted in 1944 and elected F.R.S. in the same year. He received the United States medal of freedom with silver palms, was a commander of the Order of Orange Nassau, and an honorary doctor of the university of Paris. Over £30,000 was contributed to a memorial fund for the foundation of a research fellowship in nutrition.

[F. G. Young in *Obituary Notices of Fellows of the Royal Society*, vol. ix, 1954; *British Journal of Nutrition*, vol. viii, 1954; *Journal of the Chemical Society*, 1953, vol. i; private information; personal knowledge.]

H. M. SINCLAIR.

DRUMMOND, JAMES ERIC, sixteenth EARL OF PERTH (1876–1951), first secretary-general of the League of Nations, was born in York 17 August 1876, the son of James David Drummond, later Viscount Strathallan, by his second wife, Margaret, daughter of William Smythe, of Methven Castle. He succeeded to the earldom on the death of his half-brother in 1937.

Educated at Eton, Drummond entered the Foreign Office in 1900. He was private secretary to the under-secretaries Lord Fitzmaurice (1906–8) and T. McKinnon Wood (1908–10), to the prime minister, Asquith (1912–15), and to the foreign secretaries Sir Edward Grey (later Viscount Grey of Fallodon) (1915–16) and Balfour (1916–18) [qq.v.]. He accompanied Balfour to the United States in 1917 and in 1918–19 was attached to the British delegation to the peace conference where his knowledge of procedure and grasp of detail, with a certain detachment and sincerity evident to all, won him a high reputation. It was recognized that the choice of the first secretary-general of the new League of Nations was of exceptional importance. After tentative proposals of political personalities such as M. Venizelos or Lord Robert Cecil (later Viscount Cecil of Chelwood, q.v.) had been dropped, Balfour suggested Drummond to Clemenceau and President Wilson and the appointment was agreed.

The new secretary-general needed qualities which would enable him to acquire the confidence of the ministers of the member States and be available to them for consultation and advice. He needed also to be exceptionally qualified for his primary task of building up and directing the new secretariat, conceived as an expert organization for drawing up objective statements on issues confronting the League. This responsibility was the more important because the major member States would have no resident representatives in Geneva and would only have direct control over the League's current activities through ministers meeting in the Council for a week three or four times a year and in the Assembly meeting annually for about a month. In the remaining ten months the task of securing the execution of policy decisions and preparing the presentation of issues for future decisions would fall primarily on the new secretariat, with such contact as might be necessary with the different Governments in their respective capitals.

In selecting and directing the members of the new secretariat Drummond had a rarely equalled opportunity. The war had discovered, developed, and tested special talent in many men in many countries. With the end of hostilities the ardent and general hopes in the new League of Nations made an appointment to its secretariat attractive. From a wide and promising field he chose carefully and personally, each being acceptable to the Government of his own country but not selected by it. His first team of principal officers was one in which all were soon proud to be serving. He was no less successful in making the best use of talent. He rode with a light rein, delegating generously to those he trusted. Within the secretariat he was the ultimate authority on the policy which must guide detailed executive action, and he was ready to intervene where controversial political issues were involved. But, subject to that he left the greatest possible initiative to the principal specialized heads of the various departments. He was always available for consultation and ready to give his guidance when sought, but he preferred to leave to them the primary responsibility of deciding whether his assent was required. This had the double advantage of bringing out the best in his officers and making his own influence more effective than if it had been imposed by more authoritative methods.

The secretariat was brought to its full development and established in its new headquarters in Geneva by 1920. The limits to the action of an inter-State (not supra-national) institution such as the League are, of course, set by the nature of its governing political authority. These limits were necessarily narrowed by the absence, throughout its existence, of the United States, and during its early period also of Germany and Russia. After a few years, however, the rather inimical abstention of post-war America was replaced, particularly while Mr. Stimson was secretary of state, by friendly consultation and a substantial measure of co-operation; and the membership was afterwards enlarged by the entry as full members of both Germany and Russia. With the later advent of Hitler, the gradual alienation of Italy after the Stresa period, and the League's inability, in the absence of the United States, to restrain Japan's aggression in China, followed by her resignation, the League became impotent to avert the second world war. Its ultimate failure should not, however, be allowed to obscure its achievements in its earlier period, especially in the later twenties when it had the requisite political authority for its European tasks. For several years the ministers at every Council meeting included the foreign ministers of Great Britain, France, and Germany; and Geneva during this period was the principal political centre for negotiations on European problems. The League was instrumental in settling some dangerous political conflicts. It quickly stopped a war between Bulgaria and Greece, reconstructed Austria and Hungary, re-established a mass of refugees in Greece and Bulgaria, directed the mandate system in former German colonies, and carried through a vast mass of technical tasks. That it was so far successful was in no small measure due to Drummond's guidance of this first great international institution of its kind. He acquired the

confidence of the many countries he served by the detachment and impartiality which he had shown in his work in Paris. At Geneva his real influence with the member States was the greater because he seemed always more concerned to help the Governments to find an agreed solution than to push any specific policy of his own.

In 1933 Drummond resigned from the League and became British ambassador in Rome. In spite of the gradually increasing alienation of Mussolini from the League and all that was associated with it, he established a good personal relationship both with him and with his foreign minister Grandi; and he was probably as successful as an ambassador could be in discerning and reporting the changing political attitude of Italy and in making his own Government's policy clear. The course of events, after the Stresa period of rapprochement had been followed by the Italian Abyssinia venture, was determined by developments outside the power of a British ambassador to influence.

Perth retired in 1939 and in 1941 entered the House of Lords as a representative peer of Scotland; in 1946 he became deputy leader of the Liberal Party there, and adequately discharged the not very exacting duties involved.

Of medium stature, Drummond had a presence and manner which reflected his personal qualities. With a wide acquaintance only rarely extending to intimacy, he took pleasure in such sociable relaxations as bridge and golf (as well as, more rarely in his active period, the less social sport of fishing). He had a pleasant sense of quiet humour, reflecting the general poise of his temperament. But he had no temptation to the dangers of the witty and memorable epigram. Nor had he the kind of uncompromising precision of thought and language which sometimes handicaps a chairman or a negotiator who is seeking a solution through compromise.

Himself a convert to the Roman Catholic faith, Drummond married in 1904 into a Catholic family, his wife being Angela Mary Constable Maxwell (died 1965), the youngest daughter of the eleventh Baron Herries. He had one son, John David (born 1907), who succeeded him in his titles when he died at Rogate, Sussex, 15 December 1951, and three daughters. Apart from his inherited titles he was appointed C.B. (1914), K.C.M.G. (1916), G.C.M.G. (1934), and was sworn of the

Privy Council in 1933. He was an honorary D.C.L. of Oxford and LL.D. of Liverpool, and was awarded the Wateler peace prize in 1931.

[Private information; personal knowledge.]
SALTER.

DUCKWORTH, WYNFRID LAURENCE HENRY (1870–1956), anatomist, was born at Toxteth Park, Liverpool, 5 June 1870, the eldest child of Henry Duckworth, J.P., F.R.G.S., by his wife, Mary J. Bennett. An uncle was Sir Dyce Duckworth [q.v.], a well-known consulting physician on the staff at St. Bartholomew's Hospital. A younger brother, F. R. G. Duckworth (1881–1964), became senior chief inspector at the Ministry of Education.

Educated at Birkenhead School and the école libre des Cordéliers in Dinan, Brittany, Duckworth became an exhibitioner of Jesus College, Cambridge, in 1889, was elected a scholar in 1890, and obtained a double first in the natural sciences tripos (1892–3). He was elected in 1893 into a college fellowship which he retained until his death; he was rarely out of office in the college, serving as its steward for over thirty years and as its bursar for some ten years. In the war years 1940–45 he was master of the college, and after superannuation from that post he continued to live in a fellow's set of rooms until his final illness.

Duckworth proceeded to his M.A. in 1896, completed his medical studies at St. Bartholomew's Hospital, took his M.D. in 1905 (winning the Raymond Horton Smith prize), and his Sc.D. in 1906. He was senior proctor (1904); university lecturer in physical anthropology (1898–1920); additional demonstrator in human anatomy (1898–1907); senior demonstrator of anatomy (1907–20); and reader in human anatomy (1920–40). He represented his university on the General Medical Council from 1923 to 1926. During the war of 1914–18 he was commissioned as a captain in the Royal Army Medical Corps; owing to severe injuries sustained in a riding accident, however, he never saw active service. He was president of the Anatomical Society of Great Britain and Ireland in 1941–3.

Duckworth's scientific interests covered a very wide field extending, as they did, far beyond the confines of human anatomy into those of many of the related disciplines. The breadth of his biological knowledge was reflected in his publications, which included a large number of contributions to physical anthropology, archaeology, primatology, embryology, teratology, and general natural history. He was a field as well as a laboratory anthropologist and in the furtherance of his investigations in archaeology and physical anthropology he travelled widely and studied peoples and prehistoric sites in the Balkans, Greece, Crete, and the Iberian peninsula. Much of Duckworth's earlier work was collected and published in 1904, by the Cambridge University Press, in a volume called Studies from the Anthropological Laboratory, Anatomy School. In the same year there appeared his Morphology and Anthropology, the aim and scope of which was to provide for students a combined presentation of physical anthropology and human anatomy. A second edition of this work was called for later, but only a part of it, as volume i, was published, in 1915. Although the field covered by Duckworth in this volume was largely limited to structural studies, the book has a distinct place in the history of preclinical education, for it was an early, albeit tentative attempt to present the medical student with a wider view of anatomy than the purely vocational; the volume was, in fact, an excursion into what has come to be called human biology. Another publication which had a wide sale and considerable popular success was his little volume published in 1912, in the Cambridge Manuals of Science and Literature series on Prehistoric Man.

A devoted student of the history of biology, Duckworth possessed a detailed and first-hand acquaintance with most of the major historical works on anatomy and embryology. A good classical scholar, he was widely read in the contributions to biological literature of the sixteenth and seventeenth centuries. Moreover, exploitation of his excellent knowledge of a number of modern European languages enabled him to be well orientated in the historical and critical studies relating to these contributions. An interest in plagiarism led him backwards to Galen, of whose works Duckworth became a most assiduous student. He devoted his Linacre lecture (1948) to aspects of Galen's anatomy, and after his death his rendering into English of Simon's German version of the Arabic translation of the later books of On Anatomical Procedures was published in 1962, edited by M. C. Lyons and I. Towers.

Duckworth always took his teaching duties, both in the Anatomy School and in college, very seriously. In his years of maturity his formal teaching was most impressive: a complete command of the facts; a finicky, indeed pedantic, precision in description; consummate, and ambidextrous, skill with chalk on blackboard; an elegance in manners which gave an eighteenth-century air to his presentation: these all combined to give an unforgettable character to his lectures. In more intimate teaching he was less successful, for his eager attempt to impart knowledge tended to swamp the recipients. His attention to his college students, however, was much appreciated; his affection for them was shown by his bequest, after a life interest, of a considerable fortune to forward medical studies in Jesus College.

Duckworth was an insatiable collector. The museum in the Cambridge Anatomy School owes much to him and to his world-wide contacts. Much of his anthropological collection is housed in the University Museum of Archaeology and Anthropology, in which the portion devoted to physical anthropology is named the Duckworth Laboratory.

In 1902 Duckworth married Eva Alice, widow of Charles Cheyne, Indian Staff Corps, and daughter of Frederick Wheeler; he predeceased him by exactly one year. There were no children of the marriage; a stepdaughter, Mariot Ysobel Cheyne, married the future Lord Ironside [q.v.]. Duckworth died at Cambridge 14 February 1956. Jesus College has a portrait of him by James Wood.

[Private information; personal knowledge.]
J. D. BOYD.

DU CROS, SIR ARTHUR PHILIP, first baronet (1871–1955), pioneer of the pneumatic tyre industry, was born in Dublin 6 January 1871, the third of seven sons of William Harvey du Cros by his first wife, Annie Jane, daughter of James Roy, a small landowner and farmer of Durrow, Queen's County, Ireland. The family was of Huguenot origin, an ancestor, Jean Peter du Cros, having settled in Dublin at the beginning of the eighteenth century as a refugee from religious persecution.

Du Cros was brought up in a home by no means affluent, for his father, at that time a book-keeper, had an income of only £170 a year, but the family was a happy one. Harvey du Cros was a man of great enthusiasm and energy, intolerant of injustice, and a champion of the underdog.

He was a noted athlete, and captain of the Bective Rangers Football Club, which he founded, and which won the Irish Rugby Championship. He was also president of the Irish Cyclists Association and it was this intimate connection with the sport which led him to appreciate the potentials of the pneumatic tyre. All the sons were brought up in a spartan manner to be keen athletes, particularly cyclists.

In 1888 John Boyd Dunlop [q.v.] obtained acceptance of his patent for pneumatic tyres. Later he made over his rights verbally to William Bowden, a Dublin cycle agent, who, with Dunlop's consent, brought in J. M. Gillies, manager of a leading Dublin newspaper, to share his responsibilities. Both men felt Harvey du Cros was the very man to organize and develop the pneumatic tyre. He agreed, with the stipulation that he should assume complete control. The company, originally called the Pneumatic Tyre and Booth's Cycle Agency (changed in 1893 to the Pneumatic Tyre Company) was thus founded in 1889 under Harvey du Cros's chairmanship.

In 1890 it was discovered that Dunlop's patent had been anticipated in 1845 by that of Robert William Thomson, which had remained largely undeveloped. However, the company were able to obtain patents for various subsidiary inventions and in 1891 purchased Charles Kingston Welch's patent of the year before for using endless wires for attaching the covers to the tyres. In the early years of difficulty and struggle Harvey du Cros showed complete faith in the future of the pneumatic tyre, imbued the shareholders with confidence in its ultimate success, and by his energy and ability converted this small modest company into an industry which was to revolutionize motor transport.

Meanwhile Arthur du Cros had attended a national school in Dublin and then, at the age of fifteen, entered the Civil Service in the lowest grade at 12s. 6d. per week. In 1892, however, he joined his father and brothers in the newly formed company, becoming general manager and in 1896 joint managing director. Du Cros laid the foundations of the industry in England at Coventry, while his five surviving brothers directed its development abroad: Alfred, Harvey, and George in America and Canada, and William and Frederick in Belgium and France.

In 1901 Arthur du Cros founded the Dunlop Rubber Company, subsequently developing the 400 acres at Fort Dunlop for the complete process of the manufacture of tyres. In 1912 he obtained the consent of the shareholders of the original company to the sale of all the goodwill and trading rights to the Dunlop Rubber Company, thus making the latter entirely independent. Following the founding of the Dunlop company du Cros devoted the next twenty-five years to its development. He became an expert on motor transport and continually pressed upon the Government its value to the army; in 1909, to demonstrate this, he assisted the Automobile Association in the successful transportation from London to Hastings in motor vehicles of a composite battalion of the Brigade of Guards.

In 1906 he had entered the political field, contesting unsuccessfully as a Conservative the Bow and Bromley constituency, for which his eldest brother Alfred was elected in 1910. In 1908, however, du Cros was elected member for Hastings in succession to his father. In 1909 he formed, and became honorary secretary of, the parliamentary aerial defence committee, to try to ensure the inclusion of funds for aeronautical development in the army. He and his father were strong advocates of the military uses of aviation and they jointly gave to the army its first airship.

During the war of 1914–18 du Cros worked in an honorary capacity for the Ministry of Munitions and he financed, at a cost of £50,000, three motor ambulance convoys, which he maintained at his own expense throughout the war. He also raised an infantry battalion and was for some years honorary colonel of the 8th battalion of the Warwickshire Regiment.

Du Cros was created a baronet in 1916. He continued to represent Hastings until 1918, but in that year he was elected as a Coalition Unionist for the Clapham division of Wandsworth, resigning four years later. He was a founder and the first chairman of the Junior Imperial League.

At one time du Cros was a man of great wealth, which he used with generous discretion, supporting many causes in which he was interested. Apart from his great public benefactions he was privately a very generous man. He is said to have lent Frances, Countess of Warwick [q.v.], who was in financial difficulties, over £60,000, a debt which he eventually agreed to overlook. When he learnt that she was considering the publication of intimate letters written to her by King Edward VII he

warned court officials of this possibility the latter promptly taking steps which prevented publication. In his publi benevolence he patronized particularl art and architecture and at Craigwei House, his home near Bognor (Regis), h had the rooms in which he displayed hi pictures designed to take advantage of th clean pure air of that part of the coast It was this house which he put at th disposal of King George V for his con valescence in 1929. He had a great love o beautiful things and, like his father, wh had been known as the best-dressed mai in the House of Commons, was alway immaculate in his personal appearance This is reflected in the character portrai of him by 'H. C. O.' which appeared i *Vanity Fair* in 1910.

Du Cros was a man of great foresigh and energy and this, combined with hi business acumen, his thoroughness fo detail and his hard work, was a majo contribution in bringing the name of Dun lop into world-wide renown. It was a sa misfortune for him personally that th Dunlop Rubber Company, of which he wa a founder and for many years chairma and managing director and later president failed to weather the economic storms o the late twenties, and much of his pei sonal fortune was involved in its failure Du Cros recorded the history of the pneu matic tyre industry in *Wheels of Fortune a Salute to Pioneers* (1938), a work he re garded as the discharge of a duty lai upon him by his father, who had died i 1918.

He married first, in 1895, Maude (die 1938), daughter of William Gooding, o Coventry, Warwickshire, by whom he ha two sons and two daughters. This mai riage was dissolved in 1923; he marrie secondly, in Paris in 1929, Florence Ma Walton, daughter of James Walton King of Walton, Buckinghamshire. She died i 1951 and he married later in that yea Mary Louise Joan (died 1956), daughte of Wilhelm Bühmann, a railway official o Hanover, Germany, who on her natural ization in 1934 assumed the surname o Beaumont. Du Cros died at his home a Oxhey, Hertfordshire, 28 October 195 His portrait by Sir William Orpen is in th possession of his elder son, Philip Harve (born 1898), who succeeded as secon baronet.

[*The Times*, 31 October 1955; Sir Arthur d Cros, *Wheels of Fortune*, 1938; Theo Lang, *M Darling Daisy*, 1966; private information.]
     G. K. S. HAMILTON-EDWARD

UFF, Sir LYMAN POORE (1865–
955), chief justice of Canada, was born
January 1865 at Meaford, Ontario, the
ounger son of the Rev. Charles Duff,
Congregationalist minister, by his wife,
abella, daughter of James Johnson. He
as educated at various village schools
Ontario and Nova Scotia and the
niversity of Toronto, where he was
tstanding in mathematics and philo-
phy. He obtained his B.A. *aegrotat*, with
onours, in 1887 and, two years later, his
L.B. with first class honours.

In order to finance his legal education,
th at university and at Osgoode Hall,
uff taught at Barrie Collegiate. He was
lled to the Ontario bar in 1893. After
actising briefly in Fergus, he went out to
ritish Columbia, where he was called to
e bar in 1895, to join a university friend,
ordon Hunter (later provincial chief
stice), in partnership at Victoria. The
xt year he became a partner of Ernest
. Bodwell, who had a thriving com-
ercial practice. Duff handled the firm's
igation and within a few years estab-
hed himself as one of the province's
ading counsel. He took silk in 1900.

Although he never ran for public office,
uff was an active Liberal and developed
close relationship with Senator William
empleman, the publisher of the *Victoria
imes*, who was in the Cabinet of Sir
ilfrid Laurier [q.v.] and responsible for
deral affairs in British Columbia. In
03 Duff was appointed junior counsel
r Canada at the Alaska boundary com-
ission hearing in London. The following
ar, at the age of thirty-nine, he was
ade a judge of the British Columbia
preme Court and, in 1906, when there
as a vacancy for a westerner on the
preme Court of Canada he received the
st.

Duff became Canada's most distin-
ished judge. Combining an exceptional
emory with tremendous intellectual
rce and a rare capacity for legal ana-
sis, he dominated the Supreme Court
roughout his thirty-eight-year term.
ch a striking impression was made by
m in Ottawa that the prime minister,
r Robert Borden [q.v.], when in diffi-
lty over conscription in 1917 and
inking of resigning in favour of some
n-partisan figure under whom a coali-
n would be possible, gave more serious
nsideration to Duff than to anyone else.
ter he finally decided to remain in
ice Borden asked Duff to enter his
binet and was extremely disappointed

when Duff declined. In 1933 R. B. (later
Viscount) Bennett [q.v.] appointed Duff
chief justice. He retired from the bench in
1944, his term having been twice extended
beyond the compulsory retirement age of
seventy-five by special Acts of Parliament.

Duff's contribution to Canadian jurisprudence was chiefly in the constitutional
field. Throughout his term of office the
Supreme Court carried on under the
shadow of the Privy Council and Duff
conceived it his duty strictly to follow
Privy Council views; nevertheless he
exerted a profound influence. The Judicial
Committee treated his judgements with
great respect and on several occasions
extensively quoted from them, one of the
last of these being in *A.-G. for Ontario* v.
A.-G. for Canada, [1947] A.C. 127, where
the Committee expressly approved Duff's
finding that a federal statute abolishing
appeals, both from federal and provincial
courts, to the Privy Council was valid.

Perhaps his most memorable judgement
was in the *Reference re Alberta Statutes*,
[1938] S.C.R. 100, where the Supreme
Court held *ultra vires* three Alberta Acts
which were an essential part of the Social
Credit scheme to bring about a new economic order. One of these statutes involved a substantial interference with the
press. Although property and civil rights
were a provincial matter, Duff took the
position that the Canadian constitution
contemplated a federal Parliament working under the influence of public opinion
and public discussion and that any attempt by a province to suppress the traditional forms of public debate would be
beyond its competence.

Duff engaged in considerable extra-
judicial work. In 1916, with Sir William
Meredith [q.v.], he was appointed to
investigate contracts for shells. He was the
central appeal judge under the Military
Service Act in 1917–18; chairman of the
1931–2 royal commission on transportation; and co-commissioner with Associate
Justice Van Devanter of the United States
in the 1935 inquiry into the sinking of
the Canadian rum-runner *I'm Alone* by an
American coastguard cutter. Finally, he
was the sole commissioner appointed by
the Government of W. L. Mackenzie King
[q.v.] to investigate the dispatch in
October 1941 of the Canadian expeditionary force to Hong Kong.

Duff acted as administrator of Canada
in the absence of governors-general and
twice opened sessions of Parliament, in

1931 and 1940, the first Canadian to perform this function.

In 1919 Duff became a member of the Judicial Committee of the Privy Council on which he served until 1946. He derived a great deal of satisfaction and pleasure from his transatlantic visits and his associations with such men as Birkenhead, Haldane, and Simon [qq.v.]. In 1924 he came to England for a special sitting of the Judicial Committee to advise on the constitutional position arising out of Ulster's refusal to appoint a boundary commissioner.

Nine universities conferred honorary degrees on Duff who was elected a bencher of Gray's Inn in 1924 and appointed G.C.M.G. in 1934 when Bennett revived the honours list.

In 1898 Duff married Elizabeth Eleanor (died 1926), daughter of Henry Bird, of Barrie, Ontario; they had no children. Duff died in Ottawa 26 April 1955. In the Supreme Court of Canada Building there is a portrait by Ernest Fosbery and a bust by Orson Wheeler.

[Winnipeg *Free Press*, 20 March 1933; Toronto *Globe and Mail*, 27 April 1955; *Canadian Bar Review*, vol. xxxiii, 1955; private information.]   RICHARD GOSSE.

DUKES, ASHLEY (1885–1959), dramatist, critic, and theatre manager, was born 29 May 1885 at Bridgwater, the son of the Rev. Edwin Joshua Dukes, Independent minister, and his wife, Edith Mary Pope. Educated at Silcoates School, he graduated in science at Manchester University in 1905 and went to London to lecture in science, though also (as he put it later) as 'an aspirant to the humanities'. In London he became interested in the modern drama. The naturalistic methods—the staging rather than the acting—of the famous Edwardian productions of Harley Granville-Barker [q.v.] at the Court Theatre dissatisfied him, and when in the early autumn of 1907 he had the opportunity of combining a postgraduate course at Munich University with private tutoring, he began eagerly to study the progressive German theatre on its own ground. He was abroad for two years, based first at Munich, then at Zürich.

On his return to England in 1909 he was glad to become a full-time professional writer, and to act as drama critic for A. R. Orage [q.v.] on the *New Age* (for this he received only ten shillings a week), with freedom—as he said—'to train the batteries of Continental criticism' upon such

writers as Barrie, Galsworthy [qq.v.], an Maugham. During 1910 the Stage Societ put on the first of his plays, a comedy *Civil War*; in 1911 he published his *Ne Age* essays on *Modern Dramatists*. I 1912–14 he was drama critic for *Vani Fair*; in 1913–14 for the *Star*; he als wrote short essays, known as 'turnovers for the *Globe*.

In 1914 he adapted for the Stag Society (Haymarket Theatre) Anato France's *Comedy of a Man Who Marrie A Dumb Wife*. Dukes was thorough cosmopolitan. He loved the Europea scene, and he read widely in German an French. These early days indicated future which was interrupted during th war of 1914–18 by western-front service the Machine Gun Corps from which he r tired with the rank of major, after holdin every rank—except that of sergeant— between private and company comma der. In 1918 he married the dancer Cyv Myriam Ramberg (Marie Rambert daughter of a Polish publisher. She ha studied with Dalcroze and later wit Diaghilev; after leaving his company sh came to London where she met Ashle Dukes.

During 1920–24 he wrote drama crit cism for the *Illustrated Sporting a Dramatic News* as well as contributing the *New Statesman* and other journal From the German he adapted Geo Kaiser's *From Morn to Midnight* (192 and Ernst Toller's *The Machine Wrecke* (1923). But it was his own *The Man Wi a Load of Mischief* which established h name. This, produced at the New Theat by the Stage Society in December 192 ran for 261 performances at the Ha market from June 1925, and in later yea had revivals at three London theatres. was a Regency fable by a man who ha always cared for the spoken word in th theatre, and whose poetic sense show in his prose rhythms. The play excite people whose ears had been dulled by th period's fashionably curt dialogue whi had reminded Mrs. Patrick Campb [q.v.] of typewriters tapping away in the night. If nothing much happened *The Man With a Load of Mischief*—an i where a valet, a Jacobin, wooed a lad and a lord was left in helpless anger what counted were the felicity of the pros Dukes's judgement and balance; his pla lighting candle after candle in the imag nation, was an enchantment from a tin hardly prodigal in them.

The success of this comedy gave Duk

his independence. He made many other adaptations and dramatizations, notably two for Matheson Lang [q.v.]—*Such Men Are Dangerous* (Duke of York's, 1928) from the German of Alfred Neumann's *Der Patriot*, and *Jew Süss* (Duke of York's, 1929) from Feuchtwanger's novel —and *Elizabeth of England*, from the German of Ferdinand Bruckner, in which Lang also appeared (with Phyllis Neilson-Terry) at the Cambridge Theatre in 1931. Further, he wrote a good deal of original work, including the 'heroic comedy' of *The Song of Drums*, or *Ulenspiegel*, performed at the Royal Flemish Theatre, Brussels, but not in London; *The Fountain-Head*, and *Matchmaker's Arms*.

His main task, however, was in his own theatre, the Mercury, which he opened to the public during 1933 in a converted church hall in Ladbroke Road, close to his Campden Hill home. He turned it eventually into a workshop for poets' drama and for his wife's Ballet Rambert, the senior English ballet company. There was much else to do. He travelled abroad; he acted as British delegate from the Critics' Circle at the International Congress of Critics in Paris (1926) and Salzburg (1927); he wrote on *Drama* (1926) for the Home University Library; he became one of the editors of the international *Theatre Arts Monthly*. But from the early thirties the Mercury Theatre preoccupied him, and its great day came in November 1935 when he brought T. S. Eliot's *Murder in the Cathedral* from the chapter-house at Canterbury for a run of 225 nights (it was transferred later to the west end). Various other poets' plays—among them *The Ascent of F.6* by W. H. Auden and Christopher Isherwood—followed on Dukes's small stage; and the Mercury, governed by its owner's taste and urbanity, moved safely into the history of the theatre. Simultaneously, Dukes still worked for the west end, as in *The Mask of Virtue* (Ambassadors, 1935), a very free rendering of Sternheim's *Die Marquise von Arcis*, in itself a dramatic version of a play by Diderot: it was this which brought Vivien Leigh to the west-end stage.

In 1945–9 Dukes held the kind of post for which no man was better fitted, despite its cumbrous title: theatre and music adviser, main headquarters Control Commission for Germany (British element). Later in London, though he had to pause in his work at the Mercury, he continued his series of adaptations. Sir Donald Wolfit toured during 1958 in Dukes's ver-

sions of two German plays, Kleist's *The Broken Jug* and Wedekind's *The Maestro*. Dukes died in London 4 May 1959; his wife (who was appointed D.B.E. in 1962) and two daughters survived him.

Ashley Dukes, a man of great charm and unobtrusive common sense, with the means to back his judgement, had much influence on the intellectual theatre of his time. Smilingly, he rejected any form of insularity: he was a European with a taste in wine as sure as his taste in the theatre and the fastidious cadences of his prose. *The Man With a Load of Mischief* and his one not very factual venture into autobiography, *The Scene is Changed* (1942), are likely to live when much else in the theatrical record of the period is lost.

A portrait of Ashley Dukes by Kostia (Constantine Irinski) became the property of Dame Marie Rambert.

[*The Times*, 5 May 1959; Ashley Dukes, *The Scene is Changed*, 1942; personal knowledge.]   J. C. TREWIN.

DULAC, EDMUND (1882–1953), artist, was born in Toulouse 22 October 1882, the son of Pierre Aristide Henri Dulac, a cloth merchant, and his wife, Marie Catherine Pauline Rieu. After graduation in science and philosophy at Toulouse University, three years' study at Toulouse Art School, and a short visit to Paris, he settled at the age of twenty-three in London where he soon had success with coloured illustrations for *The Arabian Nights* (1907), *The Tempest* (1908), *The Rubáiyát of Omar Khayyám* (1909), and books of fairy tales. He was naturalized in 1912.

During the war of 1914–18 his work included *Edmund Dulac's Picture-Book* for the French Red Cross (1915); masks worn by Henry Ainley [q.v.] and the Japanese actor Michio Ito in a private charity performance in April 1916 of *At the Hawk's Well* by W. B. Yeats [q.v.]; caricatures of personalities in the news, such as 'Lord Kitchener showing emotion at the breaking of a rare piece in his collection of Chinese porcelain' and 'Mr. Winston Churchill looking for more trouble by submitting a painting to the International Society of Sculptors, Painters and Gravers' (1915); *Edmund Dulac's Fairy-Book* (1916); and illustrations to Nathaniel Hawthorne's *Tanglewood Tales* (1918).

Between 1919 and 1929 Dulac designed costumes for very diverse theatrical productions including Robert Loraine's *Cyrano de Bergerac* (1919), a Beecham performance of Bach's *Phoebus and Pan*

(1919), and *Phi-Phi*, a revue at the London Pavilion (1922); he provided the *Outlook* with caricature cartoons, made witty caricature-dolls, e.g. George Moore (privately owned) and Sir Thomas Beecham (London Museum), and he painted some straight portraits such as that of Mrs. Wellington Koo (1921). He continued to produce his illustrated books; and from about 1926 he drew coloured decorative covers for the *American Weekly*, a profitable branch of his activities which lasted, with short intervals, for twenty-five years.

In the next decade he designed furniture and fittings for a Cathay smoking lounge in the *Empress of Britain* (1930–31) and costumes and scenery for the Camargo Society's ballet *Fête Polonaise*, first performed at the Savoy Theatre 13 June 1932, with Glinka's music arranged by Constant Lambert [q.v.]. He supplied the Mint with a model for the King's poetry prize medal (first awarded in 1935), and the Post Office with the unusual double-portrait coronation stamp (1937). He also modelled for the Post Office the King's profile which was used (within designs by Eric Gill [q.v.] for the lower values and within designs of his own for denominations above sixpence) on all stamps of George VI's reign.

During the war of 1939–45 Dulac left London for Dorset. There he designed the Free French colonial stamps (much sought after by philatelists), banknotes for the *Caisse Centrale de la France Libre*, and the first French liberation stamp, known in France as the *Marianne de Londres*. From 1946, in a new London studio, he was chiefly occupied with the illustration of three books for publication in the United States: Pushkin's *Golden Cockerel* (1950), Pater's version of *The Marriage of Cupid and Psyche* (1951), and Milton's *Comus* (1955).

Dulac died in London 25 May 1953; his Queen Elizabeth II coronation stamp appeared in June; and a memorial exhibition was arranged in December by the directors of the Leicester Galleries who had exhibited and sold the original drawings for all his early books.

Dulac was able to absorb the decorative character of any European or Oriental style and adapt it with delicate, meticulous, and infinitely patient craftsmanship to the task in hand. When engaged upon a design or composition he would draw and redraw the details on tracing paper until all were perfect by his standards; and if any flaw occurred in the final version of the Bristol board he always began again even though he had already worked on i for days. In his later book illustrations and contributions to the *American Weekly* h used clear, bright, opaque colours withou shadows; and the effect was often in the nature of those moments in the theatr when the rising curtain shows gaily cos tumed static figures radiant in limeligh and united in pattern with the sceni background—moments which vanish i the theatre when the figures begin t move and speak and thus become dis cordant three-dimensional humans in a two-dimensional cardboard world.

The variety of his professional outpu was matched by the variety of his relaxa tions. He was a student of Far Easter music, a collector of Japanese and Chines paintings, a first-class cook, and a cracl revolver shot. Everything in his studi was made from his designs; and a visito might find him constructing a bambo nose-flute, or binding a book, or cuttin an intricate stencil for a textile, or model ling a gesso rose within a tiny locket as present to a friend.

Dulac's first marriage, in 1903, to Alic May de Marini, was dissolved; his secon marriage, in 1911, to Elsa Arpalice Maria daughter of the late Pietro Bignardi, pro fessor of singing, ended in separation. H had no children.

[*The Times*, 28 May 1953; private informa tion; personal knowledge.]

R. H. WILENSK

DUNCAN, Sir ANDREW RAE (1884 1952), public servant, was born at Bowe Lodge, Waterside, Irvine, Ayrshire, 3 Jun 1884, the second of the three sons c George Duncan, a social worker, and h wife, Jessie Rae. There were also fiv daughters. He was educated at Irvin Royal Academy and Glasgow Universit where he graduated M.A. two month before reaching his nineteenth birthday He first taught English at Ayr Academ but having decided against teaching a a career, he entered the office of Biggar Lumsden & Co., solicitors of Glasgow, an studied law at the university, graduatin LL.B. in 1911. Before he was thirty he wa made a partner, specializing in the in dustrial side, and through his senio Thomas Biggart, honorary secretary of the Shipbuilding Employers' Federatio he was introduced to many of the prol lems and personalities of the shipbuildin and engineering industries.

The Shipbuilding Employers' Federation moved to London during the war of 1914–18: in becoming its full-time secretary Duncan took one of the decisive steps of his career. Soon afterwards (1916) he was appointed secretary of the merchant shipbuilding advisory committee by the shipping controller, Sir Joseph (later Lord) Maclay [q.v.], and later joint secretary of the Admiralty shipbuilding council by Sir Eric Geddes [q.v.], then first lord of the Admiralty. Lloyd George, Bonar Law, and Birkenhead all saw Duncan as a man of uncommon ability, and his career was hereafter assured although its pattern remained for some time in doubt, for after the war he twice unsuccessfully contested parliamentary elections in the Liberal interest, at Cathcart (1922) and Dundee (1924). In 1919 he was appointed coal controller charged with the task of supervising the return of the coal mines from public to private control. This task was completed in 1921 and in that year he was knighted.

From that point the pattern emerged with growing clearness. In the early twenties he built up a reputation as an arbitrator and chairman of commissions. But the next decisive step was his appointment in 1927 as chairman of the Central Electricity Board. The twofold task of organizing a large number of productive units on a national basis and of bringing about an interconnection between these units by the introduction of high voltage grid called for the drive, the experience of industrial affairs, and the diplomatic gifts which Duncan possessed to a high degree. This was the first large-scale piece of creative work through which he left a permanent mark on the industrial history of his times. Other offices and directorships (the Bank of England, 1929–40) came to him. But the next major step was the chairmanship, assumed in January 1935, of the British Iron and Steel Federation. He held this post until 1940, when he joined the Government, and again after the war when he returned to industry. Once more he was concerned with the efficient organization of a basic industry central to the economic development of the nation. His experience was further widened by his service on the boards of Imperial Chemical Industries, Dunlop Rubber, and the North British Locomotive Company.

The climax of Duncan's career was his contribution to the organization of the nation's industrial life in the war of 1939–45. He had taken an important part in the plans drawn up against the contingency of war. On its outbreak he became iron and steel controller. His liberal convictions, his natural combativeness, his love of his country all combined to make him throw himself wholeheartedly into the ministerial tasks he was given. In January 1940 he was made president of the Board of Trade by Neville Chamberlain; and shortly afterwards he was elected to Parliament as a member for the City of London. In October he became minister of supply under (Sir) Winston Churchill. The responsibilities of his new Ministry extended far beyond the familiar region of iron and steel: his jurisdiction included the manufacture of explosives, guns, tanks—the whole range of industrial supplies for Britain at war. All his previous experience had equipped him with the necessary skills, the knowledge of industry's ways and industry's leaders, the diplomacy and the power to persuade. After less than a year he was moved back to the Board of Trade. The work of that Ministry in the war—apart from its responsibility for coal production—seemed to Duncan more restrictive than creative, negative rather than positive, so it was with some sense of relief that he returned in 1942 to the Ministry of Supply. There he remained until the end of the war and the defeat of the Government in 1945 set him free to return to the British Iron and Steel Federation. He kept his seat in Parliament until 1950 and conducted a vigorous opposition to the nationalization of the iron and steel industry.

Had Duncan's convictions been other than they were he might have become a distinguished head of one of the nationalized industries. But although he was sympathetic to the idea of nationalized services he remained to the end unconvinced that the running of industries could be subject to political or Treasury control and yet be sufficiently flexible to answer the challenge of events at home or of competition from abroad. Thus he ended his career where he began, in the private sector. He was a pioneer in large-scale industrial management practised with professional responsibility. He wanted for himself, in the exercise of that responsibility, and for those who would follow him freedom from political or bureaucratic control on the one hand and from that of the shareholder on the other. Yet this was no mere wilful chafing against all restraint or accountability. He knew that the price of a proper measure of managerial freedom was, in the iron and steel industry, a willing adherence by the industry to a national economic policy nationally determined. Thus his efforts were directed to the twin aims of increasing the industry's efficiency and of guiding it towards acceptance of its social and national responsibilities. His suggestions for machinery to realize these aims were broadly accepted by the Conservative Government which came to power in 1951.

Duncan was an administrator of great distinction. His native Scottish thoroughness, the philosophical basis of his early studies, the rigour of his training in the law, his independent cast of mind combined to establish him as a professional in fields in which the conception of the amateur still had great influence. Whether as industrial executive or as minister he dominated the area of his jurisdiction by his mastery of its detail and by a breadth of view which embraced the inter-relation of its parts. Though he was not naturally at home in the Commons he won both its admiration and its ear by his complete knowledge of his subject and by his deep and manifest respect for the House itself.

Duncan presided in 1925 and in 1926 over two royal commissions in Canada. W. L. Mackenzie King [q.v.] paid a warm tribute to his work and he was given an honorary degree by Dalhousie University. In the United Kingdom he was a member in 1924 of the royal commission on national health insurance; in the same year he served on the dock strike inquiry. He was appointed G.B.E. (1938); sworn of the Privy Council (1940); was high sheriff of the county of London (1939–40); a lieutenant for the city of London; a bencher of Gray's Inn; and honorary LL.D. of Glasgow (1939).

He married in 1916 Annie, daughter of Andrew Jordan; they had two sons, of whom the elder was killed in action in 1940. Duncan died in London 30 March 1952.

A portrait, painted by Frank Eastman in 1954 from a photograph, belongs to the British Iron and Steel Federation.

[Private information; personal knowledge.]
FULTON.

DUNHILL, SIR THOMAS PEEL (1876–1957), surgeon, was born 3 December 1876, at Tragowel, Victoria, Australia, the elder of two sons of John Webster Dunhill, overseer on a cattle station, and his wife, Mary Elizabeth, daughter of George Peel, stonemason, of Inverleigh, Victoria. Dunhill's father died of typhoid fever at the age of twenty-six when the boy was only sixteen months old and before the birth of his brother at his mother's home at Inverleigh where the children grew up and went to school. When he was twelve his mother married again and the family moved to Daylesford, near Ballarat where his stepfather, William Laury, was manager of a gold mine, and where he completed his education at the grammar school. He was apprenticed to a chemist there and then opened a chemist's shop at Rochester in Northern Victoria. It was then that he decided to take up medicine and as soon as he had saved enough money he became a medical student at the university of Melbourne, where he won scholarship and obtained first class honours in several subjects. He took his M.B. in 1903, was appointed house physician to (Sir) Henry Maudsley at the Royal Melbourne Hospital, and obtained his M.D. in 1906. In 1908 he was appointed to the surgical staff of St. Vincent Hospital, Melbourne, and so was enabled to develop his special interest in exophthalmic goitre and the surgical treatment of thyroid disease, for which he established an international reputation.

While in Melbourne his contributions to surgery were twofold. By operating under local anaesthetic instead of chloroform and by removing sufficient of the thyroid gland by gentle dissection he was able to operate safely on the most severe cases of exophthalmic goitre, even those with heart failure, and restore them to useful active lives. At that time the mortality rate for cases treated without surgery was 25%; Dunhill recorded a post-operative mortality rate of 1·5% in contrast with rates of 4·5% and 8·1% claimed by famous surgeons in Europe and America. His other contribution was to stress the importance of the surgeon's gaining the confidence of the patient before operation especially if frightened and emotionally upset, by himself undertaking the pre operative treatment and control. The distinction which he attained was due not only to his surgical skill but to the thought time, and human sympathy expended on his care for each patient.

In 1914 he joined the Australian Army Medical Corps and served mainly in France, where he became known to and appreciated by his medical colleagues from the United Kingdom. He was three times mentioned in dispatches, became consulting surgeon to the British Expeditionary Force in 1918 with the rank of colonel, and was appointed C.M.G. in 1919. His return to Australia lasted a few months only, for in 1920 he accepted the invitation of George Gask [q.v.] to become assistant surgeon and assistant director of the newly formed surgical professorial unit at St. Bartholomew's Hospital medical college. He quickly impressed his colleagues in London by his skill and energy and his determination to overcome difficulties and neglect no precaution which could benefit his patients. He was essentially a modest, humble man, who never hesitated to seek advice from anyone who might be helpful. His reputation spread quickly and colleagues from all parts of Britain and from abroad visited him to see him operate and to study his methods. Although the surgical treatment of thyroid disease remained his special interest he was a general surgeon, with a large private practice.

He did not enjoy formal teaching and found difficulty in publishing his results, but by his example he had a powerful effect on the education of young surgeons and physicians in the inter-war period. His appointment as surgeon to the household of King George V in 1928 was warmly approved and followed by his promotion as surgeon to the King in 1930. In 1939 he became sergeant-surgeon; and in 1952 extra-surgeon. He was appointed K.C.V.O. in 1933 and G.C.V.O. in 1949.

At the Royal College of Surgeons of England he was Arris and Gale lecturer in 1931 when he chose as his subject carcinoma of the thyroid gland, and again in 1934 when he lectured on diaphragmatic hernia. In 1950 he was awarded the Cecil Joll prize and in 1951 he delivered the Cecil Joll memorial lecture on the recent history of the surgical treatment of xophthalmic goitre. In 1935 the university of Adelaide awarded him the honorary degree of M.D. and in 1939 the Royal College of Surgeons of England elected him an honorary fellow.

Dunhill was a short slim man who gave the impression of nervous tension and of mental and physical energy. An Australian colleague described him as made of 'stainless steel'. He had a charming smile, made friends easily, and saw quickly the good in each acquaintance, no matter of what social standing. For himself his standards were high and it was not only in his professional work that he sought expert advice wherever he could. Although a

keen and successful salmon and trout fisherman he took instruction in order to improve his style and methods; and his appreciation of antique furniture, of pictures, and of architecture was based on the best advice obtainable.

In 1914 he married Edith Florence (died 1942), daughter of James Affleck and widow of D. G. McKellar. They had no children. He bequeathed his portrait by (Sir) James Gunn to the Royal Australasian College of Surgeons in Melbourne of which he was an honorary fellow. He died in Hampstead 22 December 1957.

[*The Times*, 24 December 1957; *St. Bartholomew's Hospital Journal*, November 1960; *Medical Journal of Australia*, 22 March 1958; *British Medical Journal*, 4 January 1958; private information; personal knowledge.]

FRANCIS FRASER.

DUNSANY, eighteenth BARON OF (1878–1957), writer. [See PLUNKETT, EDWARD JOHN MORETON DRAX.]

EAST, SIR (WILLIAM) NORWOOD (1872–1953), criminal psychologist, was born in London 24 December 1872, the tenth in the family of twelve of William Quartermaine East and his wife, Charlotte Bateman. His father was proprietor of the Queen's Hotel, St. Martin-le-Grand, and was at one time sheriff of the City of London and deputy-lieutenant for London and Middlesex. The family home was at Epsom.

East was educated at King's College School and studied medicine at Guy's Hospital. He qualified in 1897, taking his M.R.C.S. and L.R.C.P.; and his M.B. (1898) and M.D. (1901) of London University. After various appointments on the house staff at Guy's and experience as a resident medical officer in mental hospitals, East joined the Prison Medical Service in 1899. He was posted to Portland as deputy medical officer, moving subsequently to Brixton, Liverpool, and Manchester prisons, finally returning to Brixton as senior medical officer. This involved many days spent in court prepared to give evidence if called upon; consequently much of the day-to-day work at the prison had to be done in the evening, and in this East never spared himself.

In 1924 East was appointed medical inspector of prisons and in 1930 a commissioner of prisons and director of convict prisons. He was also appointed inspector of retreats under the Inebriates

Acts. During his period of office at the Prison Commission he recommended the provision of an up-to-date operating theatre at Wormwood Scrubs so that major surgical operations could be carried out within the Prison Service. He also established a nursing service with state registered nurses to deal with women prisoners. Subsequently this scheme was extended to include certain men's prisons where there was a large hospital section.

With Dr. W. H. de B. Hubert, East carried out an investigation into the psychological treatment of criminals and in 1939 they recommended the establishment of a special institution under the Prison Commission to deal with psychiatric cases. It was to be a dual-purpose institution, primarily for research, but to include facilities for the treatment of suitable cases. Owing to the delay of the war years East did not live to see such an institution opened in 1962 at Grendon in Buckinghamshire. East was also one of the doctors appointed by the home secretary to inquire into the mental state of prisoners upon whom capital sentence had been passed, an exacting and responsible duty which he carried out until a few months before he died.

After his retirement in 1938 East continued with his lectures in forensic psychiatry at the Maudsley Hospital. He was an excellent and lucid speaker and his lectures were invaluable to those studying for the diploma in psychological medicine. He was the author of several books on his speciality: *An Introduction to Forensic Psychiatry in the Criminal Courts* (1927) and *Medical Aspects of Crime* (1936) were particularly useful. His last book, *Society and the Criminal*, in which he discussed many medico-sociological subjects, was published in 1949. He worked tremendously hard up to the end of his life. A great reader with a keen and retentive memory, East, with his wide experience in forensic psychiatry, was a formidable witness, well able to sustain any opinion he had formed about a case under the most rigorous cross-examination. He presided in turn over the Medico-Legal Society (1945–7), and the Society for the Study of Inebriety (1940–45), and was chairman of the psychiatric section of the Royal Society of Medicine in 1943.

Those who worked with East found him strict but fair and they learned much from him. It was not only his colleagues whom he helped; many prisoners were indebted to him, for he was blessed with a sympathetic understanding of their weaknesses and difficulties which he was able to help some of them to overcome. For relaxation his pursuits were contemplative rather than competitive. He enjoyed nothing more than fishing and after a day's work in Dartmoor, interrupted by only a sandwich lunch, if time and season allowed, would set off with the medical officer for a short spell with his rod and line. He was a keen gardener, and made a point of walking a few miles every day.

In 1900 East married Selina, only daughter of Alfred Triggs; they had one daughter. He was knighted in 1947 and died at his home at Crowthorne, Berkshire, 30 October 1953.

[*Lancet*, 7 November 1953; private information; personal knowledge.]

J. C. W. METHVEN

ECKERSLEY, THOMAS LYDWELL (1886–1959), theoretical physicist and engineer, was born in London 27 December 1886, the second son of William Alfred Eckersley, a civil engineer who built railway across Mexico. His mother was Rachel, a daughter of T. H. Huxley [q.v. in whose house Eckersley was born. He was educated at Bedales School between the ages of eleven and fifteen, after which he went, rather younger than most undergraduates, to University College, London where he obtained third class honours in engineering (1908). He then worked at the National Physical Laboratory until 1910 when he went to Trinity College, Cambridge, to read mathematics. In 1911 he was listed as being successful in part ii of the tripos, but as an 'advanced student' he was not eligible for the award of a class. In 1912 after the statutory lapse of one year he took his B.A. He then spent some time in the Cavendish Laboratory but after an unsuccessful attempt to gain Trinity fellowship, he left Cambridge and joined the Egyptian Government Survey as an inspector (1913–14). When war started he took a commission in the Royal Engineers and worked on problems of wireless telegraphy. By the time the war ended he had acquired a deep interest in problems of radio wave propagation and in 1919 he joined Marconi's Wireless Telegraph Company, Ltd., as a theoretical research engineer. The remainder of his career was spent with this company.

Although Eckersley studied engineering at London University and worked on experimental problems at the National Physical Laboratory and in the Cavendish

Laboratory, he came to realize that his real interest was in theoretical work, and this is where he found he could make original contributions, first during the war and later with the Marconi Company. While serving with the wireless intelligence branch of the Royal Engineers in Egypt and Salonika he was concerned with the problem of locating enemy radio stations by measuring the direction of arrival of the waves which they radiated. In this work he came to realize that waves reflected downwards from the Heaviside layer could interfere with the proper behaviour of the direction-finding equipment and he started to consider the mechanism of these reflections. It was problems of this kind which occupied most of his attention for the rest of his life.

He developed his ideas in a number of well-known papers mainly presented to the Institution of Electrical Engineers. In particular he showed how to evaluate the details of the reflection by a 'phase integral' method, and he emphasized the importance of waves scattered by irregularities in the ionosphere. He read widely in many branches of mathematical physics and much of his work on radio waves was closely parallel to similar work being done in a rapidly developing field. The title of one of his papers 'On the connection between the ray theory of electric waves and dynamics' shows how he drew on his wide knowledge of physical theory to discuss wave propagation in terms of other concepts.

Although Eckersley was predominantly theoretician, he led and inspired a small team of experimental workers and he was delighted to take part in observations with them at all times of day or night. If a line of research was not going well it was his habit to say 'Let's try a damn fool experiment' and he was frequently rewarded with some new insight into the mechanism of radio wave propagation.

Eckersley's ability was widely recognized. He was a much valued member of the Union Radio Scientifique Internationale and of the Comité Consultatif Internationale de Radio, whose assemblies he attended regularly. He was elected F.R.S. in 1938 and was awarded the Faraday medal of the Institution of Electrical Engineers in 1951. For each of his major papers in the *Proceedings* of the Institution he received a premium. His advice was of importance to the Marconi Company particularly in the development of their direction-finding apparatus and their

long-distance short-wave communication links.

Eckersley had such originality that he tended to see his theories in his own way and never troubled to relate them to other people's ways of thought. In this respect he was somewhat like Oliver Heaviside [q.v.]. If one looks back at Eckersley's work it is a matter of surprise that some of it, particularly that concerned with direction-finding errors and with the scattering of radio waves from the ionosphere, should have been so little appreciated when it was written. If he had taken more pains to make his work readable by others who were thinking about the same problems, it is probable that it would have been better appreciated during his lifetime.

In 1920 Eckersley married Eva Amelia, daughter of Barry Pain [q.v.]; they had one son and two daughters. When he retired from the Marconi Company in 1946 he was already suffering from multiple sclerosis and, although he continued to do theoretical work at home as a consultant to the company, the disease pursued its inevitable course and in his later years he was almost completely helpless. He died at Danbury, Essex, 15 February 1959. His elder brother, Roger Huxley Eckersley, who was director of programmes (1924–30), assistant controller (1930–39), and chief censor (1939–45) of the B.B.C., had died in 1955. His younger brother, Peter Pendleton Eckersley, who died in 1963, was chief engineer to the B.B.C. from 1923 to 1929.

[J. A. Ratcliffe in *Biographical Memoirs of Fellows of the Royal Society*, vol. v, 1959; *Nature*, 18 July 1959; private information; personal knowledge.]   J. A. RATCLIFFE.

EDMONDS, SIR JAMES EDWARD (1861–1956), military historian, was born in Baker Street, London, 25 December 1861, the son of James Edmonds, master jeweller, and his wife, Frances Amelia Bowler. He went as a day boy to King's College School, then still in the east wing of Somerset House, and astonished masters by the extent, maturity, and exactitude of his knowledge. He was wont to relate that he learnt languages at the breakfast table at home. In after life he could extract what he wanted from any European language and a number of Eastern, although he could not write an idiomatic letter in any language save German. He passed first into the Royal Military Academy, Woolwich, the most experienced examiners being unable to recall any year in which he would not have done so. As a matter of course he passed out first after winning the sword awarded for the best gentleman cadet, the Pollock medal, and other prizes. In 1881 he was gazetted to the Royal Engineers, specializing in submarine mining, then treated as a task which the Royal Navy could not be expected to undertake.

In 1885, after long anxiety about the possibility that Russia might walk into Hong Kong without warning, it was decided to reinforce the colony with two companies of engineers of which one, the 33rd, was Edmonds's. His criticism of the situation was blistering. The reinforcement of two companies reached the scene in one case eight strong, in the other about thirty. The non-starters were either sick, permanent invalids, or on attachment from which they had not been liberated in time to catch the boat. Edmonds found that the numerous rock pillars just below the surface in Hong Kong harbour were uncharted and consequently often grazed by ships, once in a while causing a serious accident. He set about demolition by trailing a rail between two longboats and lowering a diver to fix a gun-cotton necklace on the peak.

Three months' sick leave in Japan was followed by a leisurely return home in 1888 by way of the United States. In 1890 he became instructor in fortification at the Royal Military Academy, where he spent six happy years and made use of the long vacations to travel and learn more languages, including Russian. In 1895 he entered the Staff College, once again first. His conversation became more stimulating and impressive than ever. Among those who enjoyed it were Douglas (later Earl) Haig [q.v.], of whom he heard an instructor predict that he could become commander-in-chief, (Sir) Aylmer Haldane, and E. H. H. (later Viscount) Allenby [q.v.]. His verdict on Allenby was that it was impossible to hammer anything into his head, an error typical of Edmonds's worst side.

In 1899 Edmonds was appointed to the intelligence division under Sir John Ardagh [q.v.] with whom in 1901 he went to South Africa, at the request of the Foreign Office, to advise Lord Kitchener [q.v.] on questions of international law. Lord Milner [q.v.] next borrowed him (1902–4) in the task of establishing peace. Back at home in 1904, Edmonds resumed work at the War Office in the intelligence division and was put in charge of a sec-

tion formed to follow the Russo-Japanese war. He was promoted in 1907 to take charge of M.O.5 (counter-espionage, later known as M.I.5). It was Edmonds who in 1908 definitely convinced the secretary of state for war, R. B. (later Viscount Haldane [q.v.], of the size, efficiency and complexity of the German espionage network in Britain.

In 1911 Edmonds, who had reached the rank of colonel in 1909, was appointed G.S.O. 1 of the 4th division. His divisional commander, (Sir) Thomas Snow [q.v.] a formidable and irascible man, gave him his complete confidence and at an early stage said to him 'I provide the ginger and you provide the brains'. This was very much to Edmonds's taste, and if ever he spoke with excessive pride it was of his achievement in the training of the 4th division for the war, the summit of his career, although fatal to his personal ambitions. During the retreat from Mons he broke down from insufficient food, lack of sleep, and strain. The engineer-in-chief stretched out an arm to him from G.H.Q. where he remained for the rest of the war in the latter part of it as deputy engineer-in-chief. He was regularly consulted by Haig and regarded as a mentor on the general staff side and every branch of his own corps, which in its turn could afford him greater knowledge of transportation problems than those who had to undertake the tasks.

In 1919 Edmonds retired with the honorary rank of brigadier-general and was appointed director of the historical section, military branch, Committee of Imperial Defence. His task was to direct all narratives were to be written by historians; but finding the first choice unsatisfactory, Edmonds himself took over the main field, the western front, and sowed and reaped it to the end. He was altogether too patient with failures, although delighted to be able to say that he sacked three lieutenant-generals in quick succession. He has been blamed for tardiness in producing the history, but his resources were minimal by comparison with those accorded to the historians of the second world war. The first virtue of his style was compression, the second lucidity; but it was attractive to a minority only and came to be regarded as dull. A feature of the method, not new but brought to perfection, was the combination of material from British records with those of foes and allies with equal care, whereas many famous predecessors had left the second and third as pale as ghosts. He was allowed to establish liaison with his German opposite number and treated him with complete candour. He found Berlin equally reliable and disinclined to make propaganda; a practice which only began after Hitler's ascent to power. It may indeed be said that Edmonds revolutionized the very principles on which the history of campaigns and battles had hitherto been compiled in this country. His humour as chief was mordant, but when he denounced one man as a crook, another as a drunkard, and a third as utterly incompetent, he was nine-tenths of the time playing an elaborate game. Part of the vast stock of *boutades* took the form of letters which were treasured by recipients. Some turned up finally as evidence for theories which he would have repudiated: for instance, the belittlement of Haig.

Edmonds was gifted with a prodigious memory. He never forgot the sciences learnt in youth and kept up with them throughout his life. The originality of his reflections and his skill in engineering earned for him the sobriquet of 'Archimedes', which amused him and with which he frequently signed letters to the press. Between the two wars he made further contributions to knowledge in innumerable book reviews; and he wrote several notices for this Dictionary. A history of the American civil war (1905), in collaboration with his brother-in-law, W. B. Wood, ran through a number of editions and became an official textbook in the United States. He collaborated also with L. F. L. Oppenheim [q.v.] in the official manual *Land Warfare* (1912), an exposition of the laws and usages of war on land. After his retirement in 1949 he wrote *A Short History of World War I* 1951). Coming from an author almost ninety years of age it naturally showed signs of wear and tear, but it is none the less a highly useful and creditable vade-necum.

Edmonds was the happiest of men and never felt the slightest regret that he had not risen to a rank befitting his talents. As a soldier he was intellectually brilliant and in both theory and technical knowledge the outstanding figure of his generation; yet he could not be regarded as complete master of his profession or as having to reproach fortune for failure in attaining that status. He was over-sensitive, shy, inclined to be uncertain in emergency, and lacking in that sustained

energy, carried almost to the point of harshness and sometimes beyond it, which has marked great soldiers and without which powers of command are generally limited.

Edmonds was appointed C.B. in 1911, C.M.G. in 1916, and knighted in 1928. He received the honorary degree of D.Litt. from the university of Oxford in 1935. In 1895 he married Hilda Margaret Ion (died 1921), daughter of the Rev. Matthew Wood; they had one daughter. He died at Sherborne, Dorset, 2 August 1956.

[*Royal Engineers Journal*, December 1956; private information; personal knowledge.]

CYRIL FALLS.

EDRIDGE-GREEN, FREDERICK WILLIAM (1863–1953), authority on colour perception, was born in London 14 December 1863, the son of Thomas Allen Green, whose family were well known in the potteries as makers of Crown Staffordshire ware, and his wife, Maria Smith. After studying at St. Bartholomew's Hospital and at the university of Durham, he qualified L.R.C.P. in 1887 and in the same year obtained the M.B. (Durham) with first class honours. He was awarded the M.D. with gold medal two years later for a thesis which dealt with colour vision and contained his first criticism of the Holmgren wool test for colour defect. He passed the examination for fellowship of the Royal College of Surgeons of England in 1892. After serving as resident surgical assistant at Newcastle upon Tyne Infirmary, he became assistant medical officer of Northumberland House Asylum, and subsequently medical superintendent of Hendon Grove Asylum. The two dominant interests of his life thus asserted themselves early in his career.

Edridge-Green's professional work in mental disease in the earlier part of his life is reflected in his studies on memory on which he wrote whilst still a student and more extensively in a substantial volume, *Memory* (1888). *Memory and its Cultivation* appeared in the International Scientific Series in 1897. Phenomena of vision were, however, his main interest: his *Colour-blindness and Colour Perception* was first published in 1891 and had a second edition in 1909. His contention that the Holmgren wool test, based on matching coloured wools, ignored the factor of saturation and in practice did not pick up the dangerously colour-blind, attracted immediate attention but little support. even after he was appointed a member of the International Code of Signallers' committee. In 1892 a committee of the Royal Society unanimously recommended the continued use of the Holmgren test on railways and ships, but over the years an increasing number of observers, such as Doyne and Gotch at Oxford, recognized the validity of Edridge-Green's work. In his test for colour-blindness the examinee had to recognize and name a range of colours seen in normal conditions of lighting and through filters which produced anomalous conditions simulating low illumination, mist, or fog. After much controversy, and only after questions were asked in Parliament, the inadequate wool test was finally abandoned in 1915 by the Board of Trade and a lantern test, based on Edridge-Green's principles, adopted for testing pilots and other personnel. He was appointed ophthalmic adviser to the Board in 1920, the year in which he was appointed C.B.E. and published his *Physiology of Vision* which summarized in considerable detail his theoretical work on colour vision and other visual phenomena. A succinct statement of his mature views on colour vision was contained in his article for the *Encyclopædia Britannica* in 1922. The considerable opposition which his theoretical and practical work met is detailed in his booklet *Science and Pseudo-Science* (1933). In the later years of his life Edridge-Green devoted himself exclusively to ophthalmology, acting as adviser to the London Pensions Board and the Ministry of Transport as well as the Board of Trade. In the war of 1914–18 he had been chairman of the ophthalmic board of the Central London recruiting boards for national service.

Edridge-Green's colour perception lantern remained widely used, by the Royal Navy and British Railways amongst others, and his bead test by the national service boards. His practical tests have done much by eliminating the dangerously colour-blind from occupations where good colour vision is essential. They stimulated much work on the theoretical aspects of colour vision but his own academic contributions were unremarkable, being based less on laboratory investigations than on a pseudo-evolutionary theory of colour vision.

In 1893 Edridge-Green married Minnie Jane (died 1901), daughter of Henry Hicks, the geologist [q.v.]. There were two sons one of whom died in childhood and the other shortly after the end of the

war of 1914–18. Rather slight in build, Edridge-Green found relaxation in travelling, golfing, chess, and bridge; he was a member of the Savage Club. He died at Worthing 17 April 1953. A named memorial lecture at the Royal College of Surgeons was established under his bequest and is devoted to the physiology of vision. The College possesses an oil canvas by F. Walenn (1895) and a later caricature by George Belcher showing Edridge-Green in an excellent likeness rejecting a candidate at a test for colour vision.

[*British Medical Journal*, 2 May 1953; *Lancet*, 25 April 1953; personal knowledge.]

ARNOLD SORSBY.

EGERTON, SIR ALFRED CHARLES GLYN (1886–1959), scientist, was born 11 October 1886 at Glyn, Talsarnau, North Wales, the fourth son of (Sir) Alfred Mordaunt Egerton, comptroller to the Duke of Connaught [q.v.], and his wife, Mary Georgina Ormsby-Gore, elder daughter of the second Baron Harlech. His family traces its descent from Sir Thomas Egerton [q.v.] who was lord keeper to Queen Elizabeth and later lord chancellor to James I. Alfred Egerton was a direct descendant of a cadet of the family of the second Earl of Bridgewater. He was educated at Eton and University College London, where he worked under Sir William Ramsay [q.v.] and graduated in chemistry with first class honours in 1908. The following year he was appointed instructor at the Royal Military Academy Woolwich, where he stayed until 1913. After a short period of study in Nernst's laboratory in Berlin he returned to England on the outbreak of war and was soon directed to the department of explosives supply of the Ministry of Munitions. Later he took part in the design and erection of the great national explosives factories built to meet the munitions crisis of the mid-war years.

After the war Egerton accepted an invitation to work in the Clarendon Laboratory at Oxford and there he stayed for some seventeen years becoming reader in thermodynamics in 1921. He devoted himself largely to research and carried out an extensive investigation into the vapour pressures, latent heats of vaporization, and temperature coefficients of the specific heats of a number of metals and alloys. He also began the long series of researches into problems of combustion which constitute his main contribution to science. In 1936 he was appointed to the chair of chemical technology at the Imperial College of Science where he remained until 1952.

Egerton's principal contribution to science lay in the field of gaseous combustion and began with an extensive investigation into the causes of 'knock' in the internal combustion engine. This led him by logical steps to a more general study of the mechanism of hydrocarbon oxidation. As the result of this work he was able to establish the important role played by peroxides in the early stages of slow combustion. The advent of the turbo-jet engine in which large quantities of fuel have to be burnt completely and rapidly in as small a space as possible led Egerton to consider the possibility of using promoters or inhibitors to change the limits of inflammability of the fuel. He studied experimentally the propagation of flame in limit mixtures and developed a special type of burner by means of which a stationary plane flame front could be formed and its properties examined. He also carried out a detailed investigation into the oxidation of methane and was a pioneer in the use of liquid methane as a fuel in internal combustion engines.

In addition to his scientific researches and academic duties Egerton gave much of his time to public service. He was a member of the Advisory Council of the Department of Scientific and Industrial Research, of the Fuel Research Board, and the Water Pollution Board, and chairman of the scientific advisory council of the Ministry of Fuel and Power. During the war of 1939–45 he carried out much scientific work on behalf of the three Services, was a member of the War Cabinet scientific advisory committee, and in 1942 was given the task of reorganizing the British Central Scientific Office in Washington. He was knighted in 1943. Elected F.R.S. in 1926, he served on the council (1931–3), was physical secretary (1938–48), received the Rumford medal (1946), and was an *ex officio* member of innumerable committees connected with the work of the society. He served for many years on the governing bodies of Charterhouse and Winchester College, and in 1949–59 was director of the Salters' Institute of Industrial Chemistry.

Egerton was a man of wide and varied interests, a talented artist, a lover of music, a skilful and enthusiastic angler, and an experienced skier. He travelled widely and after his retirement visited many of the under-developed territories of the Commonwealth with a view to studying at first hand their problems and needs. But none of these interests diminished in any way his love of scientific research, and throughout a long life he was never happier than when working in his laboratory or discussing scientific matters with his colleagues and students. Among the many distinctions which he received were honorary degrees from the universities of Birmingham, Cairo, Nancy, and Helsinki and the fellowship of University College, London, the Imperial College of Science, and the City and Guilds College.

In 1912 Egerton married Ruth Julia, daughter of Sir C. A. Cripps, afterwards Lord Parmoor [q.v.]. They had no children but adopted a nephew. Egerton died at Mouans-Sartoux, France, 7 September 1959. A portrait by P. Annigoni is in the possession of the family.

[D. M. Newitt in *Biographical Memoirs of Fellows of the Royal Society*, vol. vi, 1960; personal knowledge.]   D. M. NEWITT.

ELKAN, BENNO (1877–1960), sculptor, was born at Dortmund, Westphalia, 2 December 1877, the son of Jewish parents, S. Elkan and his wife, Rosa Oppenheimer, and educated at the Dortmund Gymnasium, the Château du Rosey, Rolle, Lausanne, the Royal Academy, Munich, and at Karlsruhe. Thus far a painter, he reached Paris at the age of twenty-eight and at once fell under the influence of the sculptors Rodin and Bartholomé. Moving on to Rome he there married Hedwig Einstein (died 1959) in 1907. They had one son and one daughter.

Elkan caused something of a sensation in 1908 with his controversial polychrome 'Persephone' in Carrara marble, gold, bronze, jasper, and agate—the figure being partly draped with head bent over a posy of roses held in hands crossed on her breast, the dominating colours being violet, green, and yellow. This extremely elaborate *tour-de-force* certainly revealed an astonishing technical virtuosity, if no more.

In 1911 Elkan returned to Germany where he executed three bronze panels of 'The Sermon on the Mount', a 'Flute Player', and various plaques and medals, also a few public monuments in stone later destroyed by the Nazis. His granite figure of a sorrowing woman which he completed at such fever heat in 1913–14 that it sent him to hospital, exhibited at the Cologne exposition in that year with the prophetic title 'Germany Mourns Her Heroes', was erected as Frankfurt's memorial after the war of 1914–18. In 1933, however, it was damned by the Nazis and ceremoniously removed; but replaced in 1946.

It was in 1933 that Elkan came to England; in the next year he exhibited a bronze head of John D. Rockefeller at the Royal Academy where he was thereafter regularly represented by portrait heads and medals, mostly in bronze. His subjects included the King of Siam, Lords Beveridge, Lee of Fareham, Samuel, Keynes, Salisbury, also Prince Edward, Samuel Courtauld, James de Rothschild, Dr. Weizmann, John Spedan Lewis, Yehudi Menuhin, Toscanini, and Sir Winston Churchill. To Elkan is owed the first statue of Sir Walter Raleigh in Britain—a vigorous debonair figure bearing a sheaf of tobacco leaves which surmounts the portal of a factory which it greatly dignifies.

But Elkan will remain best known for his wonderful succession of great many-branched bronze candelabra intricately scrolled and foliated like stylized espalier trees supporting numbers of small but strongly detailed biblical or symbolic figures. The most impressive examples are in Westminster Abbey where, 7 feet high and 6 feet wide, each of the two candelabra carries 33 candles to illuminate some 30 figures. Lesser ones adorn Buckfast Abbey, Devon, King's College chapel, Cambridge, New College chapel, Oxford, and Israel's Parliament House—the last the gift of British members of Parliament and others. In these highly individual pieces, with Gothic as well as Renaissance references, and German as well as Italian influence, Elkan seemed to find the most apt expression of his own wide-ranging and complex creative urge.

Other works in this country include an orang-outang group for Edinburgh Zoo, a gold medal for the Hospital for Sick Children, Great Ormond Street, a silver-gilt fighting cock for the Arsenal Football Club, Mowgli's jungle friends, a plaque in lead on the memorial building for Rudyard Kipling [q.v.] at Windsor, and Abbot Vonier's tomb in Buckfast Abbey. Elkan is represented also in many museums in European countries where his works were shown at international exhibitions. Impressive as was anything from his hand these relatively small pieces seemed to promise still greater fulfilment in works on a heroic scale which, however, he was denied the chance to execute.

He had a rare faculty for translating sensitive allegory into vigorous plastic form, as in his great project for a 1914–18 national war memorial in Germany. It was to have taken the shape of a vast monolithic column with its surface enriched with scenes and figures emblematic of the *results* of war. Although the scheme had received official sanction and its cost had been guaranteed, the new regime came to power before it could be realized

In the man himself there was an earnest forcefulness, a prophetic intensity which, with his humane sincerity, deep voice and piercing eyes, made up an impressive personality not easily forgotten.

Elkan, who was naturalized in 1946 was appointed O.B.E. in 1957, and died in London 10 January 1960.

[*Country Life*, 26 November 1938; *The Times*, 12 January 1960; personal knowledge.
              CLOUGH WILLIAMS-ELLIS

ELLIOT, WALTER ELLIOT (1888–1958), politician, was born in Lanark 19 September 1888, the elder son of William Elliot and his wife, Ellen Elizabeth Shiels From his father, a prominent agriculturist and livestock auctioneer, he inherited a vivid personality and an unflagging capacity to express it. In appearance he was too rugged, not to say gawky, to be better than a *beau laid*, but his mind was a lovely thing, sensitive, attuned, and informed by a phenomenal memory Educated at Glasgow Academy and University he had his fair share of the gay brilliant life of pre-war undergraduates Among his friends were James Bridie (O. H. Mavor, q.v.), (Sir) John Boyd, (Sir Hector Hetherington, and James Maxton [q.v.]. The first class honours which he obtained in both science (1910) and medicine (1913) gave him his taste and capacity for research; non-academic activities, such as Union debates, gave him his grounding in politics which were his other love. In 1914–18 he served in France as medical officer to the Royal Scots Greys; his M.C and bar were no 'ration' decorations.

His political horizon in 1918 was still so wide that when he received a cable asking him to stand for Lanark he is said to have replied 'Yes, which side?' This story is certainly *ben trovato* for throughout his career, although far from uncombative or unzestful, he was at his best as an assessor of arguments and of men without regard to their labels. His happened to be 'Conservative', which was perhaps lucky for him and certainly lucky for the Conserva tive Party. He sat for Lanark until he was defeated in 1923; for Kelvingrove, Glasgow, the toughest of Clydeside seats, which only he could have held, from May 1924 until his defeat in 1945, and from 1950 until his death; and for the Scottish Universities from November 1946 until 1950.

On his election in 1918, the vast size of the coalition majority did not prevent his making his mark. He became private secretary to the under-secretary for health for Scotland in July 1919. Although he voted against the anti-Coalitionists at the Carlton Club meeting in October 1922 he was appointed under-secretary for health for Scotland in January 1923. He returned to the Scottish Office in November 1924 after the Labour interlude and remained there (as under-secretary of state from 1926) until 1929. As a member of the Empire Marketing Board from its inception in 1926 Elliot had an opportunity to further the kinds of speculative and often practical research which had been his delight.

For a time he himself had managed to combine politics with research, notably into nutritional problems, in alliance with John (later Lord) Boyd Orr and Professor T. B. Wood, at the Rowett Research Institute in Aberdeen. But soon the House of Commons was so firmly in his blood that politics were his pulse. After the Labour collapse in 1931 he became financial secretary to the Treasury and in 1932 he was sworn of the Privy Council and began four useful years at the Ministry of Agriculture. Few people then recognized that the economics of glut must differ from those of scarcity. But Elliot did, and his marketing boards enshrined an idea which has never been wholly dropped.

He seemed to be sailing straight for 10 Downing Street via the secretaryship of state for Scotland (1936–8) and the Ministry of Health (1938–40), his next posts in the Cabinet. But in 1938 he made his great tactical mistake. Nobody was more utterly instinct or conviction was more utterly opposed to the appeasement of Hitler. Yet he stayed in the Government, hoping, as so many have vainly hoped, to exercise more influence from within. When Chamberlain fell in 1940 Elliot was excluded from the forgiveness extended to many far more deluded by appeasement. He never held cabinet office again, although various minor posts were offered him, and the award of a C.H. in 1952 was perhaps one slight recognition of the injustice of his exclusion.

There were, of course, compensations. Loss of office enabled him, as he used to say, to 'wear the King's coat a second time' and become director of public relations at the War Office (1941–2). Later he became a brilliant freelance journalist and a highly popular broadcaster. In 1942–3 he was chairman of the public accounts committee of the House of Commons and in 1943–4 of a commission on higher education in West Africa which led to the establishment of separate University Colleges in Ghana, Sierra Leone, and Nigeria. He believed firmly in the future of the West African nations, and in the possibility of a multi-racial State in Central Africa. In 1956 he headed the parliamentary mission which presented a mace to the Nigerian parliament. Throughout his life he was one of the most resolute supporters of the State of Israel. With other members of Parliament of all parties he worked to establish better relationships with the Germans after the defeat of Nazism and also, through the establishment of a N.A.T.O. parliamentary conference, to forward the interests of the N.A.T.O. alliance. In politics he easily acquired the status of an 'elder statesman' to whom the House listens more attentively and often with more common consent than to ministers.

In Scotland Elliot was a beloved national figure, unchallenged in his lifetime. He was rector of the universities of Aberdeen (1933–6) and Glasgow (1947–50) and received honorary degrees from all four Scottish universities. He was made a freeman of Edinburgh in 1938 and in 1956 and 1957 was appointed lord high commissioner to the General Assembly of the Church of Scotland. He received honorary degrees also from Leeds, Manchester, and South Africa, and was elected F.R.S. in 1935 and F.R.C.P. in 1940.

In 1919 Elliot married Helen, daughter of Lieutenant-Colonel David Livingston Hamilton, R.A.M.C.T. Her death in a mountaineering accident on their honeymoon was a tragedy which saddened but never soured him. In 1934 he married Katharine, daughter, by his second wife, of Sir Charles Tennant [q.v.] and half-sister of Margot Asquith [q.v.]. Her steadfastness and loyalty greatly helped him to face unruffled both problems in, and frustrations out of, office. In 1958 she was created a life peeress as Baroness Elliot of Harwood. There were no children. Elliot died at Harwood, Bonchester Bridge, Hawick, 8 January 1958. A library has been endowed in his memory at Glasgow University.

[Sir Colin Coote, *A Companion of Honour*, 1965; private information; personal knowledge.]   COLIN COOTE.

ELVIN, SIR (JAMES) ARTHUR (1899–1957), founder of Wembley Stadium, was born in Norwich 5 July 1899, the son of John Elvin, a police officer who died while his son was still at school, and his wife, Charlotte Elizabeth Holley. Educated at a local elementary school, Elvin joined the Royal Flying Corps soon after the outbreak of war, became an observer, and was taken prisoner after being shot down. He escaped, possibly on two occasions, but was recaptured because he knew neither French nor German and could not swim. This, he said, gave him the determination to build a public swimming pool.

After the war he was employed by the concern which purchased the whole of the surplus war stores in northern France and this gave him a knowledge of metals by scratching them which later stood him in good stead. He returned to London at a time of depression and obtained a job which took him as a cigarette salesman to the British Empire exhibition at Wembley in 1924. Scratching the window frames of the cigarette kiosk he found to his surprise that they were real bronze; this encouraged him later to make an offer for the demolition of the buildings when offered to tender. Other contractors asked to be paid for the task; Elvin made an offer to pay, retaining the demolished materials, and got the contract.

While occupied in the demolition, Elvin became interested in greyhound racing, already successfully established at Manchester and the White City, and was advised by Sir Owen Williams that it would be possible to adapt the Wembley stadium which was then being used for football once a year and was consequently rapidly deteriorating. Elvin purchased the stadium, floated it as a private company, became managing director, and the first greyhound meeting was held in December 1927.

Elvin was not basically a money maker for himself, but he liked money because he liked to spend it, and he had moreover an ambition to make Wembley more than a racing track. Attached to the stadium was a considerable area of land and a lake and he first had ideas of a great amusement park, but finally decided to realize his early ambition and built the Empire Pool. Indoor swimming pools are not financially very successful so the bath was covered over with a removable floor in order to stage skating, ice hockey, ice spectacles, and boxing. This, together with greyhound racing and dirt-track cycle racing, involved Elvin in attending every day and night except Sundays. He was a great party giver and he had a restaurant for his parties on the balcony of the Empire Pool. Only too obviously this could only result in a great strain on his health for he was inclined to asthma and the smoky atmosphere of these entertainments was an aggravation.

During the war of 1939–45 he carried on as best he could at Wembley where he generously entertained Service men and women. The Pool was at this time occupied as a hostel for Gibraltarians. As far back as 1936 and earlier he yearned to have the Olympic Games in Wembley and he had visited the Games when they were opened in Berlin by Hitler. The war over, he returned to his ambition which he achieved in 1948, believed to be the only occasion when the Olympic Games, without a government subsidy, made a small surplus. This, of course, increased his entertaining and his work. He was hardly ever out of Wembley where he was a stern disciplinarian, sometimes almost to unkindness as people thought until they went sick or were in trouble, when he proved their greatest friend. His health deteriorated and he took a sea voyage to South Africa to recuperate but died and was buried at sea 4 February 1957. He was made an honorary freeman of the borough of Wembley in 1945, appointed M.B.E. in the same year, and knighted in 1946.

In 1925 Elvin married Jean, daughter of William Charles Harding and widow of William Heathcote Dolphin. It was a great sorrow to them that they had no children, who might have been a stabilizer in the hectic life in which they were involved. A bronze bust by A. J. Banks is at Wembley Stadium.

[Personal knowledge.]   OWEN WILLIAMS.

ENSOR, SIR ROBERT CHARLES KIRKWOOD (1877–1958), journalist and historian, was born 16 October 1877 at Milborne Port, Somerset, the third child and only son to survive infancy of Robert Henry Ensor and his wife, Olivia Priscilla, daughter of Charles Curme, banker, of Dorchester. A scholar of Winchester and of Balliol College, Oxford, he obtained firsts in classical moderations (1898) and *literae humaniores* (1900) and in 1899 the Chancellor's Latin verse prize and a Craven scholarship. He was elected president of the Union for Hilary term 1900 a few weeks before winning his Craven.

He was urged by his Oxford tutors and by M. J. Rendall [q.v.] of Winchester towards the bar and public life. 'You have too much vigour and force to be a don', Rendall wrote in August 1900, 'although I think you would make a good one.' This was perilous advice. As a result of disastrous speculation by his father some years earlier Ensor was short of money. His family was kept going by a finishing school which his mother and sisters ran in Brussels. He was not elected to the Oxford prize fellowships which would have given him some financial security. To overcome the drawback of poverty and succeed at the bar he would have needed a fine physique, patient devotion to the main chance, and acceptable views. He possessed none of these attributes. He was a small man, not notably robust, who blinked constantly. He was apt to disperse his energies: he might have had a fellowship of Merton or St. John's in September 1900 had he not been helping C. P. Scott [q.v.] in the election campaign at Leigh until just before the examination. He was not willing to wait indefinitely for an income: he married within five years of leaving Oxford. He had become an ardent socialist and was soon editing the collection of speeches and writings published in 1904 as *Modern Socialism*.

Ensor joined the *Manchester Guardian* at the end of 1901, succeeding L. T. Hobhouse [q.v.] as a leader-writer. Three years later he moved to London; and in 1905 he was called to the bar by the Inner Temple. He contributed to a number of journals at this time, notably the *Speaker*, the *Nation*, and the short-lived daily *Tribune*. He lived in Poplar and was soon active in Labour politics. In 1909 he served on the national administrative council of the Independent Labour Party. He was on the executive committee of the Fabian Society in 1907–11 and 1912–19 and a member of the London County Council from 1910 to 1913.

In 1909 Ensor abandoned the bar and became a leader-writer on the *Daily News*. He lost this post two years later when the paper was planning to amalgamate with the *Morning Leader*. In February 1912 he was appointed by (Sir) Robert Donald [q.v.] to a similar post on the *Daily Chronicle* and he remained there as chief leader-writer until the paper was amalgamated in 1930 with the *Daily News* to become the *News Chronicle*. During Ensor's early years on it the *Daily Chronicle* was a powerful paper. Most of its pronouncements came from his pen; and Liberal politicians treated them with respect. He wrote, for instance, the leader of 29 November 1916 which called for an improved prime minister's secretariat, and for a War Council reduced to four members and given 'the widest powers of prompt action'.

Although Ensor had moved in 1910 to High Wycombe where he was able to indulge his hobbies of gardening and bird watching, he remained for some years near the centre of affairs. He was the secretary of the foreign policy committee which a group of Liberals established early in 1912, in the hope of checking Sir Edward Grey (later Viscount Grey of Fallodon, q.v.) and promoting 'a friendly approach to the German government'. Ensor now became the leading Fabian authority on foreign policy. He was far more realistic about it than were most of his fellow socialists. He argued, for instance, that objections to Tsarist despotism should not affect British statesmen: there was 'a strong case for the entente with Russia' (*New Statesman*, 25 April 1914). He knew, according to his own later statements (*England, 1870–1914*), more about German war preparations than he was allowed to write in the *Daily Chronicle*.

None the less the German invasion of Belgium seems to have surprised him. He had long been at home in that country: the assault on it affected him deeply and drove him politically to the Right. On 1 August 1914 the *Daily Chronicle* was still taking the traditional Liberal view: a leader warned that Russia should not be supported 'so far as to win for her an unbalanced hegemony'. A leader by Ensor on 4 August announced a complete change; and to the *Chronicle* three days later the German invasion of Belgium represented 'a survival of immoral and barbarous forces which in the long run Europe must inevitably have had to subdue'. On 3 May 1915 Beatrice Webb [q.v.] recorded in her diary in a survey of Fabian views on the war: 'Ensor, one of the most accomplished of the middle-aged members, is complacently convinced of the imperative need not only of beating Germany but of dismembering the German Empire.'

Writing for the *Daily Chronicle* suited Ensor. He refused a proposal that he should become Berlin correspondent of *The Times*. But he suffered by the sale of the *Chronicle* to the Lloyd George group and by the Liberal decline in the twenties. When the amalgamation of 1930 brought his retirement he seemed a brilliant failure. He had attracted the attention, however, of (Sir) George Clark, the editor of the Oxford History of England; and in November 1930, although he had written nothing substantial except a short book on Belgium in the Home University Library (1915), he was chosen to write the most recent volume of the History. This bold choice proved to be inspired. Ensor's gifts and experience gave him a unique equipment as the historian of his own times. The range of his information was formidable and he had a wide acquaintance among public men. He was used to working quickly through masses of material. He had preserved in a career of journalism high standards of scholarship. He had himself published several volumes of verse and wrote with discernment on literature, music, and the other arts. *England, 1870-1914* appeared in 1936 and was acclaimed at once as a masterpiece. Authoritative and just in judgement, it was never heavy. A crisp style and delightful touches of idiosyncrasy made every chapter marvellously readable. His account of the events leading up to the outbreak of war in 1914 was particularly notable. He had already guessed when he wrote it that German policy would produce a crisis in 1938. In an article in the *Spectator* (7 October 1938) he explained that to someone who had studied *Mein Kampf* German methods, in both conscription and the purchase of raw materials, had pointed to this date.

Ensor had maintained his income meanwhile by freelance journalism and by some university work. He lectured at the London School of Economics in 1931-2 and was deputy for the Gladstone professor of political theory and institutions at Oxford in 1933. He even found time to write a comparison of the British, French, and German judicial systems (*Courts and Judges*, 1933). Once the History was published recognition from his university came quickly. He was a senior research fellow of Corpus Christi College, Oxford, from 1937 to 1946. He was made a faculty fellow of Nuffield College in 1939 and deputized again for the Gladstone professor from 1940 to 1944.

In Oxford as elsewhere he was handicapped by his inability ever to admit that he was wrong. But he became a renowned common-room conversationalist and an influential figure in the faculty of social studies where he joined in devising the degree of bachelor of philosophy. The first in his long series of 'Scrutator' articles in the *Sunday Times* appeared on 9 February 1941 and he contributed a number of notices to this Dictionary. He served on the royal commissions on population (1944-9) and the press (1947-9). He became an honorary fellow of Balliol and Corpus Christi colleges in 1953 and was knighted in 1955.

Ensor was happy in his private life. He married in 1906 Helen (died 1960), daughter of William Henry Fisher, of Manchester; they had two sons and three daughters. He died in Beaconsfield 4 December 1958.

[Ensor's papers in Corpus Christi College, Oxford; private information; personal knowledge.]   M. G. BROCK.

ENTWISTLE, WILLIAM JAMES (1895-1952), scholar, was born 7 December 1895 at Cheng Yang Kuan, the eldest of the four children of William Edmund Entwistle and his wife, Jessie Ann Buchan, both missionaries in China. Entwistle was taught by his father and at the China Inland Mission's school at Chefoo until 1910, and acquired a working knowledge of Chinese which he never lost. To the circumstances of his boyhood he must have owed something of his sobriety of taste and manner, and his marked inclination, as a scholar, to walk alone. After a year at Robert Gordon's College, Aberdeen, he entered the university with a bursary and in 1916 obtained a first class in classics, with distinctions in Greek history and comparative philology and was awarded the Simpson and Jenkyns prizes and the Seafield and the Town's gold medals. He then joined the Royal Field Artillery, later transferring to the Scottish Rifles, and was seriously wounded in 1917.

In the following year he was awarded the Fullerton classical scholarship at Aberdeen and an academic career in classics seemed the natural sequel. Already, however, the natural sweep of his mind, his voracious curiosity and his restless explorer's instinct urged him to seek less well-mapped territory, and he turned to Spanish. In 1920, with a Carnegie grant, he went for a year to Madrid. His prodigious assimilative powers enbled him, in that time, to acquaint himself with most aspects of the subject and also to accumulate a quantity of research material which kept him supplied or years. He learnt Spanish thoroughly, also Catalan and Portuguese, although he always spoke his languages with a pronounced Scots accent. Either then, or soon afterwards, he acquired some knowledge of Arabic and Basque. He formed no emotional attachment to Spain and his subsequent visits to the country were rare.

In 1921 Entwistle became lecturer in charge of Spanish at Manchester where he wrote his first book, *The Arthurian Legend in the Literatures of the Spanish Peninsula* (1925), a pioneer effort which showed his flair for ordering and relating a mass of facts, and some of those suggestive intuitions, at times bold to the point of rashness, which prevented his works from becoming mere tools for purveying erudition. In this year he became first Stevenson professor of Spanish at Glasgow, where, as always, he eagerly undertook whatever administrative duties came his way. He now embarked on the immense scholarly output which characterized his academic career. When in 1932 he became King Alfonso XIII professor of Spanish studies at Oxford, with a fellowship at Exeter College, at the early age of thirty-six he had two major works and thirty learned articles to his credit. His edition of the second part of the *Chronicle of John I of Portugal* was, however, never published. The proofs were deposited in the Taylor Institution.

Entwistle's previous experience and avowed belief in the professoriate as 'a sacred priesthood' did not make it easy for him to accept the marginal, undepartmentalized status of an Oxford arts professor, or many other Oxford attitudes to learning and teaching. For a time he seemed more anxious to introduce into Oxford the ways of the universities he knew than to adapt himself. There was in him, however, nothing intolerant or fanatical; while he always practised what he preached, he gradually reconciled himself with wry good humour to the fact that many of his opinions were not acceptable in Oxford. By dint of continuous pressure, he did succeed in getting an honour school of Portuguese established and himself became director of Portuguese studies (1933). He also succeeded in getting Catalan and Spanish-American literature put on the syllabus. Some felt this to be an empire-building gesture, but it would seem to have been justified by the increase in numbers reading Spanish to about a hundred by the end of his career.

Entwistle's first major work at Oxford was *The Spanish Language* (1936), a descriptive account of the languages of the Iberian peninsula which broke entirely new ground by the weight it gave to historical and social interpretations of linguistic fact. *European Balladry* (1939), his most important work on a literary subject, went for the first time beyond Iberian themes. He studied about a dozen more European languages, remarking apologetically in his preface that he had not read with his own eyes the Finnish and Esthonian ballads. The book marked an epoch in ballad criticism and despite the density of its material and the rigour of his method is humane and readable. In 1949 Entwistle published, in collaboration with W. A. Morison, *Russian and the Slavonic Languages* which he approached in the pioneer manner of his book on Spanish. Although he had only taken up Slavonic a few years previously, this book, and several articles, established him as an authority.

While preparing his major works Entwistle wrote, or collaborated in, various other books, including an attempt at a new assessment of Cervantes as a literary craftsman (1940) and a history of English literature (1943). His output of learned articles while at Oxford seems to have exceeded sixty, to say nothing of endless reviews. His articles deal with a great variety of Spanish, Portuguese, and South American literary, linguistic, and historical themes, with Slavonic language and literature, with Scandinavian material, with general linguistics, and much else besides. His attitude to his articles was peculiar. Whenever new ideas occurred to him, as they ceaselessly did, he at once worked them out in article form, but after they had been proof-corrected he often seemed to have no further interest in them. Sometimes they were so rapidly composed that his meaning is not easy to follow, but all contain a new point of view or a new contribution to knowledge. On the other hand, with his books he took endless pains, sometimes rewriting them as many as ten times before sending to the publishers a manuscript bare of any corrections.

His other activities were immense. He was joint-editor of the *Modern Language Review* (1934–48), general editor of the *Year's Work in Modern Language Studies*

(1931–7) and of the Great Languages Series (1940–52). He was also general editor of the linguistic contributions to the new edition of *Chambers's Encyclopædia*, to which he himself contributed an important article on Language. He served on several editorial boards including *Medium Ævum*, the *Bulletin of Hispanic Studies*, and the *Romanistisches Jahrbuch*. He was always ready to attend congresses or lecture abroad, visiting South America, Spain and Portugal, and Scandinavia. In 1942–3 he was educational director of the British Council. Outside Oxford, academic honours, which he received with an unexpected degree of satisfaction, were frequent. He was an honorary LL.D. of Aberdeen (1940) and Glasgow (1951), Litt.D. of Coimbra and Pennsylvania, as well as a corresponding member of the Spanish and Portuguese Academies of History, the Norwegian Academy, and other foreign learned societies. In 1950 he was elected F.B.A. and in 1952 he was president of the Modern Humanities Research Association.

A major operation, coupled with his extreme conscientiousness while visiting professor at Philadelphia and California in 1948–9, overstrained Entwistle beyond repair. Soon after his return home he was taken seriously ill and, until his death, which occurred suddenly at Oxford 13 June 1952, he was stricken but undaunted. His daemon seemed to drive him harder than ever. He began to write two new books. One, on Calderón, was never finished. The other, *Aspects of Language* (1953), a synthesis, is his greatest book and contains the fruits of his thinking based on a knowledge of many of the languages of the world. Its exploration of the non-Indo-European linguistic world is remarkable. Empirical, eschewing techniques and doctrines, and characterized by an optimism and dry humour difficult to associate with the circumstances in which it was written, it is largely free from the disconcerting whimsicalities of vocabulary and style which, in his determination not to be dull, he had sometimes used in earlier books.

The two men to whom Entwistle most wished to be compared were Wilhelm von Humboldt and Gaston Paris. The choice was characteristic, for he regarded much contemporary scholarship as narrow, and both arrogant and timid; his own work had the quality of genius. In private he was not formidable, conducting himself with a courtesy, loyalty, good humour,

and absence of showmanship which caused the sophisticated to underestimate him. On the surface it seemed he possessed a natural orderliness of habit and mind probably the result of the rigid disciplin ing of a naturally romantic temperament Even in his later work his emotions were so implacably controlled that only some o the warmth which was in the man emerged

In 1921 Entwistle married Jeanie Drysdale, daughter of John Buchanan, a Kirkcaldy business man, by whom he had one son, and who provided him with the happy unpretentious and secure home life which his highly strung temperamen needed. Although he had the speech and religion of Scotland, and his dark hair high cheek-bones, and slight physical un gainliness suggested a characteristic Scot type, his parents in fact came from Man chester and Sheffield. But his marriage completed the process of making him a Scot by adoption.

[A. Ewert in *Proceedings* of the British Academy, vol. xxxviii, 1952; private in formation; personal knowledge.]

P. E. RUSSELL

EPSTEIN, SIR JACOB (1880–1959) sculptor, was born 10 November 1880 in Hester Street, New York City, in the Jewish quarter near the Bowery, the third son of Max and Mary Salomon Epstein, a well-to-do merchant family of orthodox Jews, immigrants to America as a result o the persecutions and pogroms in Tsaris Russia and Poland. Epstein was interested in drawing as a boy and made many studies of life in the streets around hi home, crowded by Russians, Poles Italians, Greeks, and Chinese. Attracted in time to the practice of sculpture, h learned bronze casting in a foundry and studied modelling at evening classes fo professional sculptors' assistants con ducted by George Grey Barnard.

He continued to draw and was invited by Hutchins Hapgood to illustrate a book on the life of the East Side of New York called *The Spirit of the Ghetto*, which wa published in 1902. With the fees from thi work he paid for a passage to Paris in search of European influences and th inspirations he had failed to discover in the sculpture of America. He studied th sculpture in the Parisian museums and ar galleries; notably the early Greek work Cycladic carvings, the limestone bust o Akenaton, and also the primitive sculp ture at the Trocadero and the Chines collection at the Musée Cernuschi. H hared a studio with a New York friend, Bernard Gussow, in the rue Belloni behind the Gare Montparnasse. At the Beaux-Arts School he studied modelling from the nude ; but he left through the animosity of the French students when he refused to 'fag' for the entrants for the Prix de Rome concours, and transferred to the Julian Academy where he studied until he left Paris.

In 1905 he moved to London and took a studio in Camden Town. A visit as a steerage passenger to America failed to attract him to stay; he returned to London, settled in a studio in Fulham, and was naturalized in 1911. Meantime he met Francis Dodd, (Sir) Muirhead Bone [q.v.], Augustus John, and the artists of the New English Art Club circle; and studied at the British Museum: especially the Elgin Marbles and the other Greek sculpture, the Egyptian rooms, and the collections of Polynesian and African art. Francis Dodd introduced Epstein to Charles Holden [q.v.], the architect, who invited him to decorate his new British Medical Association building in the Strand. For this commission Epstein carved eighteen over-life-size nude figures symbolizing the stages of human life from birth to death, well proportioned and simple in movement. These very orthodox sculptures became a music-hall joke through philistine outcry against their nudity, started by a front-page article by an anonymous journalist in the *Evening Standard and St. James's Gazette* 19 June 1908. Correspondence in various journals, also petitions and parliamentary questions followed this essay. The statues were examined by a police officer who noted them as 'rude'. The bishop of Stepney, Cosmo Gordon Lang [q.v.], later archbishop of Canterbury, climbed the scaffolding to examine them and declared them innocent of any offence. They were also defended in the columns of *The Times*. Nevertheless the sculptor suffered the ordeal of a summons before a committee of the British Medical Association, reminiscent of the appearance of Veronese before the Inquisition in 1573. The officials of the Southern Rhodesian Government who later owned the building procured the mutilation and virtual destruction of the sculptures after twenty-nine years, against the protests of many of London's citizens. Epstein's sculpture drew further puritan attacks in later years; notably in 1912 over his carving for the tomb of Oscar Wilde [q.v.] in the Père Lachaise Cemetery

in Paris ; and also his first figure of Christ in bronze made during the war and exhibited at the Leicester Galleries, London, in 1920 (it was bought by Apsley Cherry-Garrard, q.v.) ; and his memorial to W. H. Hudson [q.v.], which was commissioned by the Royal Society for the Protection of Birds for a site in Hyde Park where it was unveiled by Stanley Baldwin in 1925. Epstein was particularly attacked by Roger Fry [q.v.], a critic who assailed many contemporary artists ; and also by John Galsworthy [q.v.]. His supporters in the different artistic crises were Muirhead Bone, Augustus John, Francis Dodd, and (Sir) Matthew Smith [q.v.]; Walter Sickert [q.v.] resigned from the Royal Academy in 1935 in protest at the Academy's equivocal attitude regarding the Strand statues.

An original member of the London Group, Epstein was rejected as a candidate for membership of the Royal Society of British Sculptors *circa* 1910, when proposed by Havard Thomas ; and later by the Royal Academy when proposed by Sir John Lavery [q.v.]. The National Portrait Gallery refused his original casting of his bust of Joseph Conrad (though a slightly damaged casting was later accepted). His Lucifer (1943–5) was refused as a gift by the Fitzwilliam Museum, Cambridge, and also by the Victoria and Albert Museum and the Tate Gallery. Several provincial art galleries requested it and it went to the Birmingham City Art Gallery.

Epstein's stone carving was more difficult for the public to assimilate than his modelled bronzes. Whilst the former were rooted in early or primitive sculpture, his modelling was in the baroque tradition deriving from the Renaissance or was at the earliest from the Byzantine, as with the Madonna and Child (1927).

Epstein's career falls into clearly marked phases. He was drawing and illustrating in New York until 1902 and studied in Paris from 1902 to 1905. His early struggles in London from 1905 to 1912, and his essays in cubism and the Vorticist movement from 1913 to 1915, were followed by a wide acceptance of him as a modeller of portrait bronzes from 1916 to 1929. During the latter period, however, his sitters were usually friends or professional models, and Rima (1925) was his only public commission between 1912 (the Wilde memorial) and 1929 (the London Underground Headquarters' building, again for Charles Holden). In 1938 he received an honorary LL.D. from

Aberdeen. Apart from this, his large stone carvings—Genesis (1931), Sun God (1933), Ecce Homo (1935), Consummatum Est (1937), and Adam (1939)—did not obtain for him the official recognition he desired.

During the war of 1939–45 he had several official war commissions for the Ministry of Information to make portrait bronzes of Service chiefs and also, just after the war, of (Sir) Winston Churchill. Although his next big venture Lazarus (1948) was not well received, it was officially invited to the Battersea Park exhibition for the Festival of Britain (1951); and in 1952 it was bought for New College, Oxford ('one of the happiest issues of my working life'). From this time onwards he received more important official commissions than he could execute for large sculptures in prominent public positions in London and elsewhere; including the Madonna and Child, for the Holy Child Convent, Cavendish Square; Liverpool Giant, for Lewis's of Liverpool; Christ in Majesty, for Llandaff Cathedral; the T.U.C. war memorial; Saint Michael and the Devil, for Coventry Cathedral; and the Bowater House Group.

In 1953 he received an honorary D.C.L. at Oxford and the following year was appointed K.B.E. The Royal College of Art, in 1954, placed a studio at his disposal in which he worked daily on the figure and bas reliefs for Lewis's building, Liverpool, and on the Christ for Llandaff Cathedral. In his autobiography Epstein expressed regret that he had never been asked to teach by any college.

Epstein possessed a gracious and courteous manner. His conversation was cultivated and, on the subject of art, very learned. He never lost his American accent. Despite his many frustrations and the attacks he had suffered he was of a kindly and compassionate disposition though impatient of anyone lacking humility concerning art. He might well have succeeded as a painter. His picture exhibitions were usually sold out: Paintings of Epping Forest (1933), Flower Paintings (1936 and 1940). As an illustrator he was less successful; neither his series of drawings for The Old Testament (1929–31) nor those for Baudelaire's Fleurs du Mal (1938) was well received. On 19 August 1959, although he was ill, he worked at his studio at Hyde Park Gate, London, on the Bowater Group, discussed the casting of it with his bronze moulder, and died the same night.

In 1906 Epstein married Margaret

Gilmour Dunlop (died 1947), by whom h had one son and one daughter. In 1955 h married Kathleen Esther, daughter of th late Walter Chancellor Garman, surgeon

The National Portrait Gallery has bronze of Epstein modelled by himself an drawings by Augustus John and Powy Evans.

[Bernard Van Dieren, Epstein, 1920; Jacc Epstein to Arnold Haskell, The Sculpt Speaks, 1931; Jacob Epstein, Let There I Sculpture, 1940, and Autobiography, 195: Richard Buckle, Jacob Epstein, Sculpto 1963; Epstein Drawings, 1962; Catalogue the Epstein retrospective exhibition at th Tate Gallery, 1952; Catalogue of the Epstei memorial exhibition at the Edinburgh Fest val, 1961; Catalogues of sixteen Epstei exhibitions at the Leicester Galleries, Londor private information.]   RICHARD SEDDO:

EVANS,   EDWARD   RATCLIFF GARTH   RUSSELL,   first   BARO MOUNTEVANS (1880–1957), admiral, w: born in London 28 October 1880, th second of the three sons and the thir child of Frank Evans, barrister, and h wife, Eliza Frances Garth. From the fir: he was of an adventurous disposition an more than once ran away from hom although not the eldest son, he was alwa the ringleader. He and his elder broth went in due course to Merchant Taylor School, whence they were soon expelle for repeatedly playing truant. Evans w: then sent to a school for 'troubleson boys' at Kenley where he was very happ He went on to Warwick House Schoc Maida Vale, whence he passed into th Worcester, mercantile marine trainin ship. Two years later he obtained a nav cadetship.

His first ship in the Royal Navy w: the Hawke, in the Mediterranean Fleet, good ship for one who loved 'clean, wel run ships and well-dressed, smart men-a arms', for she was famous for tho: qualities. He was later appointed to th training sloop Dolphin, where the e: perience of handling a ship under s: alone was later of inestimable value him. In 1900 he was promoted sul lieutenant and in 1902 he was selecte chiefly on account of his superb physic fitness, to be second officer of the Mornin the relief ship sent out by the Roy Geographical Society to the first Antarct expedition of R. F. Scott [q.v.]. T Morning located the Discovery fast the ice; but after revictualling her w: obliged to leave her there for a seco: winter. In January 1904 the Morning r urned, accompanied by the *Terra Nova*; he *Discovery* broke out of the ice in 'ebruary, and the three ships came home.

Evans, who had been promoted lieutenant in 1902, returned to naval duty and qualified as a navigating officer. In 1909 he was selected by Scott himself as second-n-command of his second expedition and aptain of the *Terra Nova* which left England in June 1910. He accompanied Scott in January 1912 to within 150 miles of the Pole where he turned back. Struck lown by scurvy he was saved only by the devotion of his two companions, Chief Stoker Lashley and Petty Officer Crean. After a brief period of convalescence in England, which he devoted to raising money for the expedition, he returned to take command of the *Terra Nova* in New Zealand and sailed south, only to find on arrival at Cape Evans in January 1913 that Scott had succumbed in an unparalleled period of bad weather while returning from the Pole in March of the previous year. After bringing home the expedition and clearing up its affairs Evans went on half pay and spent some time lecturing in Canada and the United States. He had been promoted commander in 1912.

In the summer of 1914 he resumed naval service in command of the *Mohawk*, destroyer, in the Dover Patrol. He went on to command various ships in the Patrol, the one for which he was best known being the *Broke*. In April 1917 the *Swift*, under Commander Ambrose Peck, and the *Broke* were sent out to counter-attack six German destroyers which had just bombarded Dover harbour. They met the enemy on opposite courses and at once fired torpedoes and turned to ram. The *Swift* was unsuccessful, passing through the enemy line, but the *Broke* rammed the G.42 and sustained forty casualties while the ships were locked together. There were no more German raids on Dover. This action struck the public imagination as the first in which ships came to close quarters in the old style, and he was always thereafter known as 'Evans of the *Broke*'. Peck and he were both appointed to the D.S.O. and promoted captain. He became chief of staff to the admiral of the Dover Patrol, Sir Reginald Bacon [q.v.]. When Roger (later Lord) Keyes [q.v.] took over the command Evans was eventually relieved, and until the end of the war, in the scout *Active*, was employed on escorting convoys to and from Gibraltar.

He paid off the *Active*, without orders, after the armistice, and following a period on half pay which he spent in Norway, he was for some months senior naval officer at Ostend, leaving only when all the mines had been swept up and the scars of war removed. He went next (1920–22) to the small cruiser *Carlisle* on the China station where he distinguished himself by swimming with a line to rescue the survivors on the steamer *Hong Moh*, ashore near Swatow, an exploit which again brought him before the public. After another leave in Norway he became in 1923 captain of the auxiliary patrol, later renamed the fishery and minesweeping flotilla, in the sloop *Harebell*. It was an appointment after his own heart, for he was his own master and was able to visit many out-of-the-way places, a rare privilege at that period. In 1926 he received one of the plums for a captain, the command of the battle cruiser *Repulse* which he held until shortly before his promotion to rear-admiral in February 1928.

His first flag command was the Australian squadron (1929), with his flag in the cruiser *Australia*. He was immensely popular in the Commonwealth, where his unconventional ways were fully appreciated. When he left in 1931, instead of inspecting each ship 'in all the dingle-dangle of braid', he entertained some 2,000 ratings and their wives at a cinema. He was promoted vice-admiral in 1932 and in the following year became commander-in-chief on the Africa station, where again he was immensely popular. But he was much criticized when acting in 1933 as high commissioner in the absence of Sir Herbert Stanley [q.v.], for his handling of the case of Tshekedi [q.v.], the regent of the Bamangwato tribe in Bechuanaland, who had ordered the flogging of a European accused of assault and known to be seducing African women in tribal territory. Evans travelled to Bechuanaland in state, accompanied by a strong force of armed sailors, suspended Tshekedi, and expelled the European. Tshekedi was recognized as, on the whole, an enlightened and capable chieftain and after a few weeks Evans reinstated him. It was thought that the case would have been better handled with less ostentation; but that was not Evans's way. While on the Africa station he attempted to renew his acquaintance with the Antarctic, shifting his flag in 1934 to the sloop *Milford* and visiting Bouvet Island to check its position on the charts; but he was unable to continue to the south as the *Milford*'s coal supply had been depleted by heavy weather.

Evans next served as commander-in-chief at the Nore (1935–9), an appointment which provided little scope for his special talents; but during his tenure he was promoted admiral (1936) and received the freedom of Dover (1938) and Chatham (1939), and many other distinctions. In the spring of 1939 he was made a regional commissioner for London under the civil defence scheme. After the German invasion of Norway in 1940 he was sent there to establish liaison with the King. On his return he was at first employed in organizing the defence of aircraft factories and only when that was completed did he resume his duties as regional commissioner. His energy and fearlessness through the blitz on London were an inspiration to all who served under him. He retired from the navy in 1941 but continued to hold his post in civil defence until the end of the war. In 1945 he was one of the seven selected for peerages, ostensibly to strengthen the Labour Party in the House of Lords, taking the title of Baron Mountevans. He had been appointed C.B. (civil, 1913, military, 1932) and K.C.B. (1935).

Evans was not a typical naval officer, except in his skill as a seaman. He revelled in publicity and was never happier than when in the public eye. That trait, which in a lesser man would have provoked severe criticism, was recognized as being part of his make-up and excused; for he was as universally popular with those brother officers who knew him personally as he was with the lower deck.

Evans was elected rector of Aberdeen University in 1936, a very unusual distinction for a serving officer; and he was re-elected in 1939. He wrote a number of books, one of the first being *South with Scott* (1921) which he wrote to beguile the tedium of his voyage to China to take command of the *Carlisle*. Exploration was the theme of most of his books, but he also had a flair for writing for boys. He was twice married: first, in 1904, to Hilda Beatrice (died 1913), daughter of Thomas Gregory Russell, barrister, of Christchurch, New Zealand. There were no children. Secondly, in 1916, to Elsa (died 1963), daughter of Richard Andvord, *statshauptman* of Oslo, by whom he had two sons.

Mountevans died at Golaa in his beloved Norway 20 August 1957, and was succeeded by his elder son, Richard Andvord (born 1918). There are two portraits of Mountevans in the possession of the family, by W. A. Bowring and Marie Grixoni; one by S. Morse Brown is in the National Museum of Wales, Cardiff.

[Lord Mountevans, *Adventurous Life*, 1946 and *Happy Adventurer*, 1951; Reginald Pound, *Evans of the Broke*, 1963; private information; personal knowledge.]

H. G. Thursfield

EVANS, MEREDITH GWYNNE (1904–1952), physical chemist, was born in Atherton, Lancashire, 2 December 1904 the son of Frederick George Evans, an elementary schoolmaster, and his wife Margaretta Eleanora Williams. From his father's school Evans won a county scholarship which enabled him to go to Leigh Grammar School, then to Manchester University. He evidently displayed an early interest in chemistry and both his younger brothers became scientists—one, A. G. Evans, professor of chemistry at University College, Cardiff, and the other, D. G. Evans, professor of bacteriology and immunology in the London School of Hygiene and Tropical Medicine. Evans's other interests in life included wide tastes in reading, and his residence in Manchester resulted in a interest in the Hallé Orchestra.

Evans graduated B.Sc. in 1926 with first class honours in chemistry. His academic ability was soon recognized and from 1926 until 1934 he was successively research scholar, assistant lecturer, and Sir Clement Royds scholar at Manchester. A turning-point in his researches came when he was awarded a Rockefeller fellowship in 1934 to work with Professor (Sir) Hugh S. Taylor at the Frick chemical laboratory in Princeton University. A year later he returned to a full lectureship at Manchester where he found Michael Polanyi installed as professor of physical chemistry. Similarity of chemical interest brought the two men closely together and led to a most fruitful period of collaboration which made a wide and profound influence on the development of the Manchester school of physical chemistry.

Evans's reputation grew quickly and in 1939 he was appointed professor of physical chemistry at Leeds. The outbreak of war interrupted his plans for academic research, but R. W. Whytlaw-Gray, the professor of chemistry, was engaged in researches in connection with chemical warfare problems particularly in the behaviour of smokes. Evans joined the team, turning his attention to matters new to him. University administration had to be attended to during a difficult period and his health suffered severely as a result of overwork. Fortunately he recovered and after the war was able to set about the development of the Leeds school with great effect. In January 1949 he returned to succeed Polanyi in the chair of physical chemistry at Manchester where he continued the work he started at Leeds. The school became one of the foremost centres of physical chemistry research in the country, combining theoretical and practical work in a most effective manner.

Evans was elected F.R.S. in 1947 and served for a period on the council. He was also a vice-president of the Faraday Society. He served the Ministry of Supply on its advisory council of research and development and the Government's advisory council on scientific policy. He paid numerous visits overseas as guest lecturer to many universities.

Evans's scientific work lay in the field of the mechanisms of chemical reactions that go to make up a complex reaction which overall is chemically very simple. His close collaboration with Polanyi on the theoretical side enabled him to begin to apply the principle of quantum mechanics to systems which could not be tackled rigorously. His skill lay in seeing how theory could bring some degree of rationality into the explanation of the absolute velocity and activation energy of the simpler gas and liquid phase reactions. At a later stage he turned his attention to polymerization reactions and brought the same penetrating methods of approach to this much more complex process.

In 1931 Evans married Millicent, daughter of Walter Trafford; they had one son and one daughter. He died in Manchester 25 December 1952.

[H. W. Melville in *Obituary Notices of Fellows of the Royal Society*, No. 22, November 1953; private information; personal knowledge.]   H. W. MELVILLE.

EVERSHED, JOHN (1864–1956), astronomer, was born at Gomshall, Surrey, 6 February 1864. He was the seventh of eight children (four boys and four girls) of John Evershed, a yeoman farmer, and his wife, Sophia Price. His brother Sydney (died 1939) invented electrical measuring instruments and was a founder of the firm of Evershed and Vignoles.

Evershed became interested in astronomy while still a pupil at a private school in Kenley, Surrey. His first employment was with a firm of chemical manufacturers whose products he analysed and tested. A friend gave him an 18-inch reflecting telescope and a small spectrohelioscope which he installed at Kenley, and with these, the latter of which he modified and greatly improved, he systematically observed solar prominences and obtained monochromatic photographs of the sun.

He was the first to demonstrate (in 1895) that the emission of the characteristic spectra of gases and vapours was caused by heat alone, in the absence of electrical and other influences which were thought at that time to be essential.

His employers granted him leave of absence to take part in solar eclipse expeditions. The first of these (to Varanger Fjord, Norway, 1896) was unfruitful owing to clouds; but it was there that he met Mary Acworth, daughter of Major Andrew Orr, R.A., whom he married in 1906 and who collaborated with him for many years. They observed other eclipses at Talni (India) in 1898, Maelma (Algeria) in 1900, Pineda de la Sierra (Spain) in 1905, Yorkshire in 1927, and a few miles south of Athens in 1936 from the deck of the P. & O. liner *Strathaird*.

In the eclipse of 1898 he obtained with his spectroheliograph the first observational verification of the Balmer continuum in the far ultraviolet and discovered a new coronal line at $\lambda3388$.

Evershed became a fellow of the Royal Astronomical Society in 1894. In 1906 he was appointed assistant director of Kodaikanal Observatory in India, and became director in 1911. He overhauled and greatly improved the instruments and constructed a large spectrograph with a diffraction grating made by A. A. Michelson. There he discovered the 'Evershed effect'—a radial circulation of gases in sun-spots, which flow outwards at a low level and inwards at a higher level. In recognition of this and other solar discoveries he was elected F.R.S. in 1915 and was awarded the gold medal of the Royal Astronomical Society in 1918.

When Evershed retired from Kodaikanal in 1923 he was appointed C.I.E. He returned to England and constructed a solar observatory at Ewhurst, Surrey, furnished with a coelostat and spectrographic equipment in an underground chamber. He used hollow box-like prisms filled with liquid having a very high dispersive power, together with an ingenious arrangement of plane mirrors which enabled him to pass the solar beam back and forth through the prisms as many as eight times. In this way very high dispersions were obtained. For example, the two sodium lines (λ5890 and λ5896) were as much as ¾ inch apart, corresponding to a length of about 35 feet for the whole visible spectrum.

For detecting and measuring Doppler shifts he devised an ingenious method consisting in superimposing a positive made from one negative spectrogram upon another negative taken in different conditions. For example an east-limb positive would be superimposed on a west-limb negative with the comparison-spectrum (iron-arc) lines in register. The relative displacement of the solar lines would be immediately apparent and could be measured directly, a micrometer screw enabling one spectrogram to be moved relative to the other to bring any pair of lines (positive and negative) into coincidence.

He also measured solar spectrograms made at Mount Wilson, California, by G. E. Hale, which were thought to show a general magnetic field, and he satisfied himself (and Hale) that they gave no evidence of such a field.

Evershed was the first to supply the explanation of the 'stationary' calcium lines in stellar spectra in which other lines showed large Doppler shifts. In a letter published in the *Observatory* (1924), he stated that this could only be due to calcium atoms in space.

He closed his observatory in 1953 and presented many of his instruments to the Royal Greenwich Observatory.

Evershed's first wife died in 1949; in 1950 he married Margaret Randall. He had no children. He died at Ewhurst 17 November 1956. A portrait by Victor Coverley-Price remained the property of the artist.

[Personal knowledge.] F. J. Hargreaves.

EWINS, ARTHUR JAMES (1882–1957), chemist, was born 3 February 1882, in Norwood, south-east London, the elder son of Joseph Ewins, a railway platelayer on what was then the South Eastern Railway, and his wife, Sophia Wickham. He won a scholarship to the Alleyn's School where he received a better grounding in the basic natural sciences than was then available to most schoolboys. In 1899,

with others of his standing from the same school, he entered the service of the Wellcome Physiological Research Laboratories as a research apprentice. These laboratories had recently been established by (Sir) Henry Wellcome [q.v.] whose aim was to ensure that the production of such remedies as the antitoxic sera could be associated with the researches necessary for their proper control and development and to provide opportunities for research in a wider range of the sciences contributory to a progressive therapeutics, including biochemistry and pharmacology.

Ewins worked in these Wellcome Laboratories as assistant to John Mellanby [q.v.], then, for a further and longer period, as assistant to George Barger [q.v.]. He thus had the opportunity of co-operating intimately in a wide variety of researches dealing with problems in biological, organic, and pharmaceutical chemistry. Most of the publications between 1905 and 1911 which bore the name of Ewins were made jointly with Barger; and their close association in this period extended to other researches, of which the results were published by Barger alone, or by Barger and (Sir) H. H. Dale who had joined the staff of the Wellcome Laboratories in 1904 and was later to become their director. When Barger left for an academic appointment in 1909 Ewins, who had graduated B.Sc. in 1909 at the university of London, was appointed to succeed to the charge of the chemical division; and thereafter his researches were largely associated with those of Dale and (Sir) P. P. Laidlaw [q.v.]. The work with Barger had been largely concerned with the activities and chemistry of that curious drug, ergot of rye—its specific alkaloids, and the series of putrefactive proteinogenous amines found in the conventional, pharmacopoeial, and other extracts from it. In co-operation with Laidlaw, Ewins found and synthesized another member of this series of amines, 3-β-aminoethylindole, from tryptophan —a close relative of the now widely investigated 'serotonine' (5-hydroxy-tryptamine). Then in 1914, from an extract of ergot in which a peculiar and intense activity had been observed, Ewins isolated the constituent responsible for this, and it was found to be acetylcholine—a substance which, in more recent years, has acquired a widely ranging physiological interest, through the recognition of its transmitter function, at a large proportion of the synaptic and neuro-effector junctions in the peripheral nervous system. Study of the distribution of the actions of acetylcholine furnished a further clue, which enabled Ewins to remove a long-standing puzzle from pharmacology, by showing that the so-called 'artificial muscarine', produced by the supposed oxidation of choline with strong nitric acid, was, in fact, a nitrous-acid ester of choline.

In 1914 Ewins moved with Dale from the Wellcome Laboratories as a member of the new staff of the National Institute for Medical Research. Almost immediately the outbreak of war diverted them from all normal research plans; Ewins thus became Dale's principal colleague in the creation and application of new standards for the safety and efficacy of the supplies of such essential remedies as salvarsan, as prepared on an emergency basis by manufacturers in Britain and allied countries, in replacement of those from Germany. This responsible work brought Ewins into contact with the directorate of Messrs. May and Baker who in 1917 offered him a research opportunity of such a kind that, even from the national point of view, it seemed proper for him to accept it.

The rest of Ewins's working life thus came to be spent in their service, as the director of their research department. Until his retirement in 1952 there were few scientific publications bearing his name, among those issued from the laboratories he directed. His own essential part, however, in the initiative and enterprise which they represented, was explicitly recognized by the members of his scientific staff, and was well known to the many others with whom he shared interests and retained friendly contacts. He never had the urge of the academic scientist to penetrate to the theoretical roots of a problem, or into essentially new territory. On the other hand he showed, in this major part of his career, a remarkable promptitude in recognizing and exploiting the practical possibilities of therapeutic developments, from discoveries which others had made. He and his team were the first, for example, to develop the chemotherapeutic possibilities of the diamidines, which Harold King and Warrington Yorke [qq.v.] had discovered. And when, from 1935 onwards, the anti-streptococcal action of 'Prontosil' had been discovered by Domagk, and that of its sulphanilamide moiety by Tréfouël, Bovet, and Nitti, and the possibilities of a more general and effective chemo-therapy of the bacterial infections had thus been brought into view, it was Ewins and his collaborators, again, who produced the first derivative with a more potent and specific action, in Sulphapyridine (first issued as 'M & B 693'), the agent which so radically improved the prospect of sufferers from the ordinary pneumococcal pneumonia—among them (Sir) Winston Churchill during the war. Ewins's most important service, indeed, to the progress of medicinal chemistry, in this country and in the world at large, was in the practical development of such researches on the chemotherapy of infections. He became a D.Sc. in the university of London (1914) and was elected F.R.S. in 1943.

Ewins married in 1905 Ada Amelia, daughter of James Webb, an inspector of weights and measures; they had one son and one daughter. He died in Bedford 24 December 1957.

[*Chemistry and Industry*, 22 February 1958; Sir Henry H. Dale in *Biographical Memoirs of Fellows of the Royal Society*, vol. iv, 1958; private information; personal knowledge.]

H. H. DALE.

FABER, OSCAR (1886–1956), consulting engineer, was born in London 5 July 1886, the eldest son of Harald Faber, Danish commissioner of agriculture in London, and his wife, Cecilie Sophie Bentzien. He was educated at St. Dunstan's College, Catford, and the Central Technical (later City and Guilds) College where he held the Clothworkers' scholarship, and of which, in 1906, he became an associate, and, in 1929, a fellow. After his graduation in 1907 he worked as an assistant engineer with the Associated Portland Cement Manufacturers, and in 1909 took up a similar position with the Indented Bar and Concrete Engineering Company. His great interest in structural engineering problems, and his realization of the potentialities of reinforced concrete at a time when its use in this country was limited, led him to carry out many theoretical and experimental investigations; and in 1915 he was awarded the degree of D.Sc. (London) for original research work on reinforced concrete beams in bending and shear. In 1912 he was appointed chief engineer of Trollope and Colls, and was responsible for the structural design of many large London buildings. During the war his department built factories for war work, and he himself advised the Admiralty on explosive anti-submarine devices made of reinforced concrete with non-ferrous reinforcement: for which in 1919 he was awarded the O.B.E.

In 1921 Faber set up in practice as a consulting engineer. He was one of the first to appreciate the growing importance of the mechanical and electrical services in large buildings, and almost from the beginning his office dealt with those services as well as with the foundations and structural design. He was responsible for the engineering of numerous large industrial and commercial projects, in the aesthetic problems of which he took a lively interest; and for many important buildings in London, above all the new Bank of England, burrowing deep beneath Soane's original wall (which Faber brilliantly underpinned) and rising symbolically solid above it. In other fields, his office was responsible for such widely differing projects as the installations for the Earl's Court exhibition buildings, and the underpinning of Durham Castle; for which, in 1935, he was awarded the honorary degree of D.C.L. by Durham University. In the course of his work he travelled very widely, visiting at different times all five continents and indeed most countries of the world. He yet found time to lecture to another generation of engineers at the City and Guilds College; to continue his researches, particularly into the long-term plastic yield of reinforced concrete under load, the results of which he published in 1936; and to take an active part in the affairs of the Institution of Structural Engineers which, as the Concrete Institute, he had joined in 1911 and of which he was president in 1935–6. He was also a member of the Institutions of Civil, Mechanical, and Electrical Engineers.

With the advent of war in 1939, his office was fully engaged on the design of munitions factories, ordnance depots, and other essential installations, and Faber himself flew to America to advise (Sir) Winston Churchill on aspects of the Mulberry harbour project, which he later helped to translate into its bold reality. The war was scarcely over when he was appointed consulting engineer for the rebuilding of the House of Commons, destroyed by German bombs in 1940, and ordained by Churchill to be rebuilt in the same style as it was before; but incorporating more accommodation and better facilities. Faber's brief covered the whole of the engineering work including the complicated services, and his approach to the problem of air-conditioning was typical: 'We shall never please six hundred members, so we will do it properly and please ourselves.' At the conclusion of the rebuilding, in 1951, he was appointed C.B.E.

In 1912 Faber put order and coherence into structural design with his book (with P. G. Bowie) *Reinforced Concrete Design*; and in 1936, with J. R. Kell, wrote *Heating and Air-Conditioning of Buildings*, which in succeeding editions became the standard work. He was also the author of *Reinforced Concrete Simply Explained* (1922) and *Constructional Steelwork Simply Explained* (1927), and of numerous papers to the engineering institutions, including the Institution of Heating and Ventilating Engineers, of which he was president during the difficult years 1944–5.

The post-war period saw the continued expansion of his already large practice. In 1948 he took into partnership five of his senior assistants, but far from taking the opportunity to transfer the burden he continued to work at full pressure until his death.

Notwithstanding his professional preoccupations Faber found time for relaxation in music and painting. He was an excellent water-colour artist, and would seldom return from even the most strenuous business trip abroad without a handful of paintings of great boldness and skill. He was passionately fond of music and a sympathetic player of the clarinet, the organ, and the piano, for which he composed several delightful works.

Faber was intensely interested in problems of every kind, and spared no trouble to arrive at a satisfying and elegant solution. His technical mastery of his subject was impeccable, but his approach was characteristically simple and direct, involving clear thinking supported but never obscured by technicalities. To his fellow engineers he was sometimes an enigma and always a challenge. To his staff he was a stimulating if exacting master; impatient of inexact thinking or tardy action; often critical of a proposal but always willing to spend much time in putting it right. To himself he was unsparing of physical as well as mental effort, and to everything he brought an apparently inexhaustible fund of energy. The distinction and success he achieved did not divert him from being himself, and while properly conscious of his own importance, he scorned the trappings and conventions of importance.

He married in 1913 Helen Joan, daughter of John Gordon Mainwaring, doctor, of London. They had two daughters and a son who became one of his partners. Faber died in Harpenden 7 May 1956. There is a bronze bust by Sir Charles Wheeler at the Bank of England.

[*Journal* of Institution of Heating and Ventilating Engineers, vol. xii, March 1944; *Structural Engineer*, August 1956; private information; personal knowledge.]

J. R. HARRISON.

FAIREY, SIR (CHARLES) RICHARD (1887–1956), aircraft manufacturer, was born in Hendon, London, 5 May 1887, the son of Richard Fairey, mercantile clerk, and his wife, Frances Jackson. His father died in 1898 leaving his family almost penniless. Both his mother and father could trace their histories back to Elizabethan times, and both families were famous as carriage builders in the old coaching days, rich in historical memories which made a deep impression on Richard Fairey. He was educated at Merchant Taylors' School and Finsbury Technical College, where he was trained under the great Silvanus Thompson [q.v.].

At the age of fifteen Fairey started working with an electric company in Holloway, while still being trained. At eighteen he had passed his examinations and progressed so well with his firm that he was placed in charge of the installing of electric lighting of the docks and warehouses at Heysham harbour. Shortly afterwards he was given a post in the power-station of the Finchley Council and added to his earnings by lecturing on engineering subjects.

From his schooldays he had designed and built aeroplane models, but it was not until 1910 that he was persuaded to enter an aeroplane model competition at the Crystal Palace, which he won easily. He was a great craftsman, skilled with his hands, and won not only the challenge up, but gold medals for steering, long distance, and stability, and a silver cup for the best model. Inadvertently he had infringed an early patent of J. W. Dunne, the pioneer of the stable aeroplane, which led to a meeting with Dunne in the following year. They joined forces and Fairey thus entered aviation. In 1913 he joined Short Brothers, the aircraft pioneers, and in 1915, at the age of twenty-eight, he formed his own aircraft company. Short Brothers gave him his first contract to build a dozen of their aeroplanes.

Fairey's ability quickly became known in the stress of war. Orders came in so fast that the firm was in the throes of constant expansion. Fairey learnt everything from aircraft design and construction to works organization, government contracts, and the business of selling the aircraft he designed. He was then more often than most managing directors in and out of the drawing and production offices, helping and planning.

For over forty years he played a leading and dominating part in all the affairs of his company. Over a hundred different types of aircraft were produced, largely inspired by Fairey, ranging from small single-seaters to four-engined flying bombers, from fast flying helicopters to supersonic aircraft. He played a vital part in negotiating their details of performance and their sales to the air forces of many countries. By 1925 more than half of all British military aircraft were Fairey types and Fairey himself became the leading aircraft designer who saw ahead, even of governments. In 1925 he had submitted a new design for a fighter bomber which was turned down by the Air Ministry. He built one at his own expense, known as the Fairey Fox, the fastest bomber of its time, an aeroplane which will always be remembered in any reference made to him. The Fox was demonstrated before the chief of the air staff, Sir Hugh (later Viscount) Trenchard [q.v.], at Andover, where No. 12 Bombing Squadron was stationed. It made a tremendous impression on the watchers and Trenchard immediately ordered a dozen of the machines for the squadron. Its aerodynamic design enabled it to fly fifty miles an hour faster than any other aeroplane of its type in the Royal Air Force. It was clear that the Fox had set a new standard. In 1931 Fairey founded the Avions Fairey Company in Belgium, which sold many aircraft deriving from the Fox on which the Belgian Air Force was based.

In the year 1928 came the first edition of the aeroplane known as the Long Range Monoplane which in 1933 flew the world's long-distance non-stop record of 5,309 miles, from Cranwell in England to Walvis Bay in South Africa. Later came the Swordfish, which fought throughout the war of 1939–45 and helped cripple the Italian fleet at Taranto.

Fairey had been overworking during those early years and in 1927, warned by his doctors to rest, he turned to yachting. He became a superb yachtsman, improving the design of racing yachts to such an extent in sails and hull that in the years 1931-3 he was top of the 12-metre class. He became the commodore of the Royal London Yacht Club in 1935, served on the council of the Royal Yachting Association, and began to make preparations to challenge the United States for the America's Cup, stopped by the outbreak of war.

Lord Beaverbrook, appointed to the Ministry of Aircraft Production, called in Fairey to help in the organization of the industry to increase the output of aircraft, both at home and abroad. Fairey was asked in 1940 to go to the United States to act as deputy to Sir Henry Self, director of the British air mission. Fairey was the ideal deputy, for he knew the American designers and the leaders of the aircraft industry, and was well aware of the tremendous help they could give. He visited the chief American factories and research centres and entered into technical discussions of vital importance. A powerful and appealing speaker at gatherings of the leaders and to the press, he proved to be a great ambassador for Anglo-American friendship and help. In 1942 he became the director of the British mission and in the same year he was knighted.

Following the end of the war the tremendous responsibility and unceasing work took its toll. In April 1945 he resigned from his mission in America and for the next three months he was in hospital in Boston. In 1947 the American Government awarded him the medal of freedom with silver palm for 'exceptional meritorious service in the field of scientific research and development'.

On his return to England he encouraged new ideas on research and turned his attention to the development of helicopters. In 1948 the Fairey Gyrodyne gained the international speed record for helicopters at 124 m.p.h. and work went ahead in the design of passenger-carrying helicopters. Fairey also pushed forward on problems of supersonic flight and the Fairey Delta, on 10 March 1956, flew at a speed of 1,132 m.p.h., the first plane officially to exceed 1,000 m.p.h.

In 1922 Fairey was elected chairman of the Society of British Aircraft Constructors, a position he held for two years. He was twice president of the Royal Aeronautical Society (1930-31, 1932-3). In 1931, at the suggestion of Lord Amulree [q.v.], secretary of state for air, he founded the British gold and silver medals of the Royal Aeronautical Society, for important achievements leading to advancement in aeronautics. Fairey himself was awarded the Wakefield gold medal of the society in 1936 for his design of the variable camber wing. He was a member of many important committees including the Aeronautical Research Committee (1923-6).

Fairey was a man of singular courage, of solid English stock, who was deeply interested in everything, from aeronautical research to chess; from sailing to shooting, in both of which he was highly skilled; and from the guidance of men who served him to the service he gave his country. Enthusiasm, concentration, independence, and originality were his, whatever he was doing. A pioneer in the early days he was a pioneer right to the end. There was nothing he touched which he did not adorn and embellish. Underneath his serious appearance he was basically shy, but he had the charm of the eternal boy.

In 1915 he married Queenie Henrietta Markey, by whom he had a son. The marriage was dissolved and in 1934 he married Esther Sarah, daughter of Francis Stephen Whitney, bank manager, by whom he had a son and a daughter. He died in London 30 September 1956. His elder son, Richard born in 1916, who also devoted himself to aviation, died in 1960. A portrait of Fairey by Cuthbert Orde belongs to the Royal Aeronautical Society.

[*Journal* of the Royal Aeronautical Society December 1956; private information; personal knowledge.] J. LAURENCE PRITCHARD

FARNOL, (JOHN) JEFFERY (1878-1952), novelist, was born in Aston Manor Birmingham, 10 February 1878, the eldest son of Henry John Farnol, brass founder and his wife, Katherine Jeffery. Ten years later the family moved to south London and from Lee and Blackheath the boy explored the unspoilt green fields and white roads of Kent which were to form the background of many of his romances He was educated privately; and his first job with a Birmingham firm of brass founders ended when he knocked down a works foreman for calling him a liar—showing a taste for fisticuffs which found its way into his books. He then attended the Westminster School of Art; and though he decided that he would never be a good artist, the training was useful when he found himself in New York where he went in 1902, and newly married he was able to earn a living painting scenery for the Astor Theatre. Meanwhile, he began to write and sell stories; and all his feeling for romance, all his homesickness for the fields and woods of England were poured into a long novel of the open road, *The Broad Highway*, set in Kent in the days of the Regency. American publishers found it much too long and 'too English'. After it had vainly gone the rounds it was sent home to England, whither Farnol followed it when it was eventually published in 1910. It was a great success, and was his freshest and probably his best book.

The hero, Peter Vibart, a scholarly young aristocrat who can use his fists, takes to the road, in the manner of Borrow, and has a great many adventures with other wayfarers, highwaymen, tinkers, and ladies in distress, before settling to earn his bread as a village blacksmith. To his woodland cottage comes a superb beauty named Charmian, in flight from a smoothly villainous baronet, who is the hero's cousin and counterpart; there is plenty of love and fighting before all ends well.

In Farnol's next most popular novel, *The Amateur Gentleman* (1913), he reversed the story: a hero from humble life inherits a fortune and cuts a figure in the fashionable world as a Regency buck, winning a spirited and lovely lady. The formula was established and varied little, whatever the period, in the romances which Farnol turned out regularly for the next forty years. The hero was brave and honourable, the heroine innocent and beautiful, the villain properly villainous: nor was the reader ever invited to sympathize with the base rather than with the honest characters. It was the stuff of dreams and archetypal romance: with enough magic in it to capture generations of young people, and do them no harm. Older readers would cherish their taste for these tales through all changes of fictional fashion, reread their favourites, and remember the days when every green wood or winding lane seemed to them likely to produce a gallant adventure or a glorious beauty.

There was thus an appreciative welcome over the years for all Jeffery Farnol's overlarge output, even though many of his later books were hurried and inferior. Among his best and most popular were *The Money Moon* (1911), *The Chronicles of the Imp* (1915), *Our Admirable Betty* (1918), *The Geste of Duke Jocelyn* (1919), *Black Bartlemy's Treasure* (1920), and *Peregrine's Progress* (1922).

As it must be one of the happier lots in life to give a great deal of pleasure to a great many people for a great many years, 'Jack' Farnol had a right to a happy disposition: and is recorded to have been exceptionally gentle, generous, and hospitable. His chief hobby was the collection of swords and armour belonging to the picturesque past of which he wrote.

He had one daughter by his first wife, Blanche, daughter of F. Hughson Hawley, of New York. This marriage was dissolved in 1938 in which year he married Phyllis Clarke. He died at Eastbourne 9 August 1952.

[*The Times*, 11 and 19 August 1952; private information.]   M. BELLASIS.

FAY, SIR SAM (1856–1953), railway general manager, was born at Hamble-le-Rice, Hampshire, 30 December 1856. Of Huguenot origin, Samuel Fay was the second son of Joshua Fay, farmer, and his wife, Ann Philpot. He was educated at Blenheim House School, Fareham, and entered the service of the London and South Western Railway in 1872 as a junior clerk at Itchen Abbas. After spells at Stockbridge and on the relief staff at various stations, he settled down at Kingston upon Thames. There, in 1881, in collaboration with two colleagues, Fay launched the *South Western Gazette*, the profits of which went to the L.S.W.R. Orphanage Fund. Two years later, thanks to a friendship formed with William Drewett, one-time editor of the *Surrey Comet*, he had published his first book, *A Royal Road*, a brief history of the L.S.W.R.

Fay's incursions into editorship and authorship brought him under the eyes of the management, besides giving him an early insight into the value and power of publicity. In 1884 he was appointed chief clerk to the traffic superintendent at Waterloo and in 1891 he became assistant storekeeper at Nine Elms. In the same year he was elected to the Kingston council, but his experience was short lived; early in 1892 he was appointed secretary and general manager of the Midland and South Western Junction Railway, then in receivership, and had to move his home to Cirencester. Fay restored his charge to solvency (a Cheltenham editor said he had made an empty sack stand upright), winning his spurs in parliamentary railway warfare on the Marlborough and Grafton Railway bill, and in 1899 he returned to Waterloo as superintendent of the line.

In 1902 Fay left the L.S.W.R. to become general manager of the Great Central which under his aegis became noted for its through services, its leadership in signalling, and as the birthplace of effective railway publicity. One of his greatest achievements was the development of Immingham dock, at the opening of which, 22 July 1912, he was knighted by King George V on the dockside. He was director of movements at the War Office from January 1917 to March 1918, then director-general of movements and railways, and a member of the Army Council until 1919, when he returned to the Great Central, remaining its general manager until it became part of the London and North Eastern Railway on 1 January 1923. Fay continued to lead a full and active life after leaving the hurly-burly of railway management. He became chairman of Beyer, Peacock & Co., Ltd., locomotive builders, a post which he held for ten years, and his directorships included the Buenos Aires Great Southern and Buenos Aires Western Railways. In 1937 he published his book *The War Office at War*.

One of the most characteristic illustrations of Fay was a cartoon published in *Vanity Fair*, 30 October 1907, when he was approaching the zenith of his railway career. This aptly portrays his distinguished and impeccable appearance, which gave one the impression that he had just stepped out of a bandbox. Added to this was his magnetic personality. Possessing great fertility of mind and pronounced literary tastes, he was decisive to the point of martinetcy, yet he was regarded with affection as 'Sam' by his staff of all ranks for his overall interest in their welfare.

In 1883 Fay married Frances Ann (died 1946), daughter of C. H. Farbrother, of Kingston upon Thames; they had two sons and four daughters. He died at Awbridge 30 May 1953, having outlived all his contemporary railway general managers.

[Great Central Railway records; private information; personal knowledge.]

GEORGE DOW.

FELLOWES, EDMUND HORACE (1870–1951), clergyman and musical scholar, was born in Paddington, London, 11 November 1870, the second son and fifth child of Horace Decimus Fellowes, of the family of Fellowes of Shotesham Park, Norfolk, assistant director of the Royal Army clothing depot, and his wife, Louisa

Emily, daughter of Captain Edmund Packe, Royal Horse Guards, of Prestwold Hall, Leicestershire. Fellowes showed musical gifts at an early age and in 1878 he received an offer from Joachim to be his pupil on the violin. Instead, he proceeded in due course to Winchester and Oriel College, Oxford, taking a fourth class in theology (1892) and becoming B.Mus. and M.A. in 1896. He was ordained deacon (1894) and priest (1895) and after a short curacy in Wandsworth became precentor of Bristol Cathedral in 1897. In 1900 he was appointed minor canon of St. George's chapel, Windsor Castle, where he remained until his death and where his rendering of the priest's part in the services was of exceptional dignity and beauty. From 1924 until 1927 he was in charge of the choir between the death of Sir Walter Parratt and the appointment of Sir Walford Davies [qq.v.]. In this capacity he toured Canada with the lay clerks in company with (Sir) Sydney Nicholson [q.v.] and boys from Westminster Abbey. As a minor canon of Windsor he was appointed M.V.O. in 1931; later he contributed five volumes to a series of historical monographs relating to the chapel.

While a young clergyman Fellowes acquired considerable knowledge of heraldry. But in 1911 his attention was drawn to the work of the English madrigal composers and this proved decisive. Thenceforward he applied himself to studying and editing English music of the period c. 1545–1640, on which he became the leading authority. Single-handed he edited 36 volumes of madrigals, 32 volumes of lute songs, and 20 volumes of Byrd's music; he was also the most pertinacious of the editors of *Tudor Church Music*. This work was supported by important biographical and critical writings, notably *The English Madrigal Composers* (1921) and *William Byrd* (1936), breaking much new ground. Meanwhile, as honorary librarian of St. Michael's College, Tenbury Wells, Worcestershire (1918–48), he arranged and catalogued the extensive musical library left by Sir Frederick Ouseley [q.v.].

By his investigation of original sources Fellowes shed fresh light on the idiom of this music and mapped out a considerable area, making it common property. For scholar though he was, he was a performing musician even more, and his aim was to be not only accurate and informative but comprehensive and practical. His editions were intended to get the music performed, not to rest on a scholar's desk but they were not to be mere selections. This conception was then a novelty; it has been amply justified by the natural familiarity of later generations with the field he tilled almost as a pioneer. When estimating his technical achievement as editor, as distinct from his range, discoveries, and fruitful practical impact, it must be remembered that in Fellowes's day there was no organized training for musical research in England. He had to find his own way, and thereby contributed largely to the standards by which he will be judged. On his critical writings, whose contributions to knowledge are plain for all to see, it is a just comment that he viewed his subject in too insular a light.

Parallel to his researches ran his lifelong efforts to improve church (and particularly cathedral) music. He was president of the Church Music Society (1946–51) in succession to Archbishop Lang [q.v.]. When president of the Musical Association (1942–7) he was instrumental in securing for that body the appellation 'Royal'.

Disappointed by failure to attain a canonry (though he was offered a non-tipendiary Wiccamical prebend of Chichester which he was precluded from accepting), Fellowes did not lack honours of another sort. He received the honorary doctorate in music from Dublin (1917), Oxford (1939), and Cambridge (1950), and was made an honorary fellow of Oriel in 937. In 1944 he was appointed C.H.

All his life he was an accomplished player of chamber music, and, in his earlier days, of tennis also. His interest in cricket led him to write a *History of Winchester Cricket* (1930). Rightly jealous for the things he had struggled for, Fellowes perhaps seemed forbidding to those who took things for granted; but he was the most loyal of men, kind to many a younger scholar. The essentials of his work and personality were thoroughness and tenacity.

In 1899 he married Lilian Louisa, youngest daughter of Admiral Sir Richard Vesey Hamilton [q.v.], by whom he had three sons and one daughter. He died at Windsor 21 December 1951.

[E. H. Fellowes, *Memoirs of an Amateur Musician*, 1946; *The Times*, 22 December 951; *Musical Times*, February 1952; personal knowledge.]   WATKINS SHAW.

FERGUSON, HARRY GEORGE (1884–960), engineer and inventor, was born 4 November 1884 at Growell, Hillsboro', County Down. He was the third son and fourth of eleven children born to James Ferguson, a farmer, and his wife, Mary Bell. He left his father's farm at the age of sixteen to start a garage business in Belfast with one of his brothers, financed by their father. He at once showed great aptitude in getting the most out of the crude motor-cars and motor-cycles then being made and, in common with Henry Ford, who was to become his great friend and partner, he raced successfully with machines whose engines he himself tuned. He then became interested in the infant aircraft industry and in 1909 became the first man to fly in Ireland, using a monoplane which he himself had designed and built. This aircraft was the first to have a tricycle under-carriage, used fifty years later by most big air-liners.

In 1913 Ferguson married Mary Adelaide, daughter of Adam Watson, of Dromore, and, after he had had several narrow escapes in flying accidents, she persuaded him to give up this venture. By this time his motor business, Harry Ferguson Motors, Ltd., of Belfast, had prospered and his own high reputation in mechanical matters had been established. In 1916 he was asked by the Government to take responsibility for farm machinery in the wartime 'Grow More Food' campaign in Ireland. Remembering from his childhood the time- and land-consuming burden of using horses for farm work, he quickly came to the conclusion that thorough mechanization was the only solution. He became known as 'that Ferguson fellow who has it in for horses'. In 1917 he met Charles E. Sorensen, of the Ford Motor Company, which was producing tractors for the allied war effort, and explained his ideas to him, including one of mounting the plough on the tractor, instead of trailing it behind. This was the first step in his eventual development of light manœuvrable tractors, cheap to buy and economical to run, which secured their necessary tractive power through transference of the weight of the plough and the suck of the soil to the tractor's rear wheels instead of from weight built into the tractor—'making natural forces work with you instead of against you'.

In 1919 Sorensen invited Ferguson to take his first rather primitive mounted plough to Dearborn to show it to Henry Ford. Ford looked at it and said to Sorensen 'hire him'; but Ferguson was not for hire. He returned to Ireland and for six years worked on improvements to his plough. He then went into business with

George and Ebor Sherman, Ford's largest distributors, in Evansville, Indiana, making ploughs for Ford tractors until production of these was stopped in 1928. Returning again to Belfast, he began to design his own tractor, a truly revolutionary machine, with which the mounted implements were integrated through a 3-point linkage, and their working depth was hydraulically controlled. This system has since been universally adopted. In 1935 the first prototype was built in Belfast and a year later he made an agreement with David Brown for manufacture, but he could not under this arrangement achieve the big volume and, therefore, the low price which he regarded as essential. So, in 1939, he again went to see Henry Ford and demonstrated to him 'The Ferguson System of complete Farm Mechanization'. This resulted at once in the famous 'handshake agreement' by which Ferguson became Ford's only partner, selling tractors made by the Ford Motor Company to his design, and implements, also to his design, manufactured by a number of suppliers. Between 1940 and mid-1947, in spite of steel rationing, which at times cut production to two-thirds of potential sales, 306,000 Ford–Ferguson tractors and 944,000 Ferguson implements were sold in the United States, for a total sum of $312 million.

In July 1947, Henry Ford and his son Edsel having both died and the Dearborn empire having passed to the grandson, Henry Ford II, the unwritten contract of partnership was repudiated by the Ford Motor Company. Deprived of a tractor manufacturing source and most of his distributors, Ferguson's earnings dropped from $59 million in the first half of the year to $11 million in the second half. His reaction was swift. He raised the finance to build his own plant on Ford's doorstep in Detroit and supplied his American customers, while it was being built, with tractors made for a new Ferguson company formed in Britain by the Standard Motor Company of Coventry. Within eighteen months his sales in the United States had jumped back to $33 million a year. In 1948 he filed a suit against Ford for conspiracy to ruin his business and non-payment of royalties on his inventions. One of the biggest civil lawsuits of all time, the case lasted over four years and cost $3 million. Ferguson himself answered 60,000 questions in the witness-box. Eventually, Ford agreed in 1952 to pay $9·25 million compensation—the largest amount ever won by a plaintiff in a patent action. Ferguson's comment was 'This is a victory for the small inventor. I didn't sue Ford and his colossal empire for the money but for the principle.' In 1953 he merged his companies with the Canadian Massey-Harris farm machinery concern, receiving $15 million in stock and becoming chairman of the new company. A year later, disagreeing with the costing procedures of his new associates and with engineering changes planned for the Ferguson line of products, he withdrew. Thereafter he devoted himself to a series of inventions designed to make road vehicles of all kinds a great deal safer by eliminating skidding due to spinning or locking of the driving wheels.

He died suddenly, 25 October 1960, at his home at Stow-on-the-Wold, Gloucestershire, leaving a widow and a married daughter, in the knowledge that his pioneer work had revolutionized farm mechanization and that his similar work for road vehicles was well advanced and with the financial provision which he had made for it to be carried on, would be completed.

Harry Ferguson, a small, spare, energetic, and neat man, considerably resembling Henry Ford I with his high forehead, lean face, and alert blue eyes was even more than Ford's description of him: 'an inventive genius whose name will go down in history with those of Alexander Graham Bell, the Wright Brothers, and Thomas Edison'; and much more than James Duncan's (former chairman of Massey-Harris): 'the most fantastic salesman I have ever seen'. He was a man with a vision and a mission based on a profound yet simple political-economic philosophy summed up in his statement to Franklin D. Roosevelt: 'The New Deal is economic nonsense; the right way to get rid of poverty and to raise the standard of living everywhere is not to spread more money about but to produce more real wealth by cost-reducing methods and so bring down prices.' For twenty years he exhorted every British prime minister to lead the country and the world with a policy of combined income restraint and price reduction to end the inflation which was robbing mankind of the rewards of scientific and technical advance. Although the policy for which he appealed was not to be accepted until after his death, and during his lifetime aroused no enthusiasm among politicians and economists, he inspired among those

who worked with him and knew him per-
onally profound respect for his judgement, strong admiration for his tenacity,
ervent enthusiasm for his philosophic
ision, and deep affection for him as
man. As one of his staff said: 'We were
ot employees: we were converts. Joining
he Ferguson organization was like joining
he Church.'

[Private information; personal knowledge.]
N. F. NEWSOME.

FERGUSSON, SIR CHARLES, seventh
aronet, of Kilkerran (1865–1951), soldier
nd administrator, was born in Edinburgh
7 January 1865, the elder son of Sir
ames Fergusson of Kilkerran, sixth
aronet [q.v.], by his first wife, Lady
dith Christian Ramsay, second daughter
f James, first Marquess of Dalhousie
q.v.]. His early childhood was spent in
outh Australia, where his mother died in
871, and in New Zealand of which his
ther was then governor. He was edu-
ated at Eton and the Royal Military
ollege, Sandhurst, where he passed out
ith honours, and was commissioned 7
ovember 1883 in the 1st battalion,
renadier Guards, becoming adjutant in
890.
In 1896 Fergusson joined the Egyptian
rmy and soon received command of the
Oth Sudanese battalion with which he
erved throughout the campaigns of 1896–
, being badly wounded at the battle of
osaires 26 December 1898. He then
aised and commanded the 15th Sudanese;
ceived a brevet of colonel in 1900; and
om 1901 to 1903 was adjutant-general of
he Egyptian Army.
Fergusson commanded the 3rd Grena-
ier Guards in 1904–7, served as brigadier-
eneral, general staff, Irish Command, in
907–8, and was promoted major-general
1908 although he had not been through
he Staff College. He succeeded to the
aronetcy in 1907 when his father was
lled in the Jamaica earthquake. In 1909
was appointed to the new post of
spector of infantry in which he remained
til December 1912. In February 1913
received command of the 5th division,
ationed in Ireland. A year later Fergus-
n succeeded by courageous and ener-
tic leadership—and no little diplomatic
ill—in holding its officers to their duty
rough the course of the 'Curragh inci-
nt'. His attitude, however, was not
preciated by everybody in the army.
He took the division to France in
gust 1914, was promoted lieutenant-

general, and led it through very hard
fighting in the battles of Mons, Le Cateau,
the Marne, and the Aisne. At Le Cateau
he held a vital position tenaciously and
extricated his command from it at the last
possible moment with great coolness and
skill. In October he was suddenly ordered
home. For two months he commanded
and trained the 9th division, then at the
end of the year returned to France to take
command of II Corps. In May 1916 he was
given XVII Corps which he commanded
until after the end of hostilities.
The XVII Corps' attack in the battle of
Arras (9 April 1917) Fergusson called his
'revenge for Le Cateau'. His three divisions
took 3,522 prisoners and 86 guns on that
day. Fergusson set himself to hold the
line reached and spent many months
strengthening it at Monchy-le-Preux
which commanded a superb field of observation. He was bitterly disappointed
when he had to withdraw without a fight
from Monchy on 22 March 1918 when the
neighbouring VI Corps was pressed back
by the German attack. He held his own
retracted front, although on 28 March he
had to commit to it every available man
'down to cyclists and details from wagon
lines'. This defence saved Arras and
formed the hinge of the British Army, on
which five months later it swung forward
to the final victorious advance. The XVII
Corps attacked on 26 August, penetrated
the Drocourt–Quéant switch, and on 2
September broke the main Hindenburg
Line at its strongest point. Fergusson's
plan of attack involved an audacious
change of direction. His casualties, however, were light, and he went on to capture
Cambrai, after further hard fighting, a
month later.
In December 1918 Fergusson was appointed military governor of Cologne. The
work was exacting and uncongenial, but
Fergusson succeeded in maintaining order
and minimizing industrial unrest. On
leaving in August 1919 he was warmly
thanked by Konrad Adenauer, then its
burgomaster, for his fairness and courtesy.
He had resigned after a disagreement with
Sir William Robertson [q.v.], commander-
in-chief of the Rhine Army. All home
commands were now filled and Fergusson
remained unemployed. He was promoted
full general in 1921 but when new appointments were announced in January 1922 he
was again passed over. He therefore sent
in his papers. He continued to devote himself to his family estate in Ayrshire and to
work for the Church of Scotland, of which

he was an elder, both in his own parish and presbytery and in the General Assembly.

In the general election of 1923 Fergusson stood for South Ayrshire in the Conservative interest but failed to unseat the Labour member. Before the next election he followed his father and father-in-law by accepting the post of governor-general of New Zealand and arrived in Wellington in December 1924. During over five years of office he and his wife visited every part of New Zealand and in 1926 its island dependencies. They were hosts to the Duke and Duchess of York (afterwards King George VI and Queen Elizabeth) who visited the dominion in 1927. Fergusson became a fluent and winning speaker, emphasizing in simple words the themes of loyalty and public service. He became a freemason and was grand master of New Zealand. His term of office ended in February 1930 and he returned to Great Britain, living until 1947 at Kilkerran, active even in old age in public and charitable work. At the end of 1932 he toured the West Indies as chairman of the closer union commission. He was for some years on Ayr County Council and was lord-lieutenant of Ayrshire in 1937–50. His last years were passed at Ladyburn, near Kilkerran, where he died 20 February 1951.

In person Fergusson was tall, erect, and handsome; robust and athletic, and a tireless walker. Portraits by F. M. Lutyens and Glyn Philpot are at Kilkerran and a drawing by Francis Dodd is in the Imperial War Museum. His character was strict and uncompromising, dominated by an unfailing sense of duty. He set both for himself and for others the highest possible standards but was never satisfied with his own performance. First and last he was a professional soldier and a Grenadier with, according to Lord Byng [q.v.], 'the highest ideals of soldiering'. He had considerable personal charm and got on well with French officers, whose language he spoke fluently, and with the Americans. Although never at ease with Haig and finding Allenby unsympathetic, he had close and cordial relations with Plumer, whom he greatly admired, and with Byng. His courage, based on a simple and deep religious faith, was serene. Both in defence and attack he was meticulous in preparation and attention to detail. He always insisted on an aggressive rather than defensive attitude in trench warfare; but, despite the boldness of his attack on the Hindenburg Line, he had a reputation for

caution which perhaps partly accounts f[or] his failure to reach higher command.

In 1901 Fergusson married Lady Ali[ce] Mary Boyle (died 1958), second daught[er] of the seventh Earl of Glasgow. They ha[d] three sons: James (born 1904), eight[h] baronet, author, and member of t[he] Queen's Bodyguard for Scotland an[d] keeper of the records of Scotland; Simo[n] who, having served in the Argyll an[d] Sutherland Highlanders, was ordained minister in 1957; and Sir Bernard Fergu[s]son who followed his father in his career [as] a successful soldier and also as governo[r] general of New Zealand (1962–7). The[re] was also a son who died in infancy and o[ne] daughter.

Fergusson was appointed C.B. (1911[)], K.C.B. (1915), and G.C.B. (1932[)] K.C.M.G. (1918) and G.C.M.G. (1924).

[Lord Ernest Hamilton, *The First Sev[en] Divisions*, 1916; Sir Horace Smith-Dorrie[n] *Memories of Forty-Eight Years' Service*, 192[5]; Sir J. E. Edmonds and others, (Official Histor[y]) *Military Operations, France and Belgium, 191*[4] 5 vols., 1935–47; Sir James Fergusson, *T[he] Curragh Incident*, 1964; private informatio[n] personal knowledge.]

JOHN WHEELER-BENNET[T]

FERMOR, SIR LEWIS LEIGH (188[0]– 1954), geologist, was born in London [1] September 1880, the eldest of six childre[n] of Lewis Fermor and his wife, Mar[y] James. Due to illness his father retire[d] prematurely from the London Joint Stoc[k] Bank, thereby involving his family [in] educational difficulties. From Goodri[c] Road board school Fermor went with [a] scholarship to Wilson's Grammar Schoo[l] Camberwell; thence with a nation[al] scholarship to the Royal School of Min[es] in 1898. He gained a first class in eac[h] year's course, won the Murchison med[al] for geology, and obtained an associateshi[p] in metallurgy. Not content, he worke[d] for the London University matriculatio[n] coming second out of 1,500 candidates an[d] winning an exhibition.

Fermor now applied for, and obtaine[d] a post as assistant superintendent und[er] (Sir) Thomas Holland (whose notice [he] later contributed to this Dictionary) in t[he] Geological Survey of India where [he] landed in October 1902. During his ver[y] distinguished service in India Fermor pu[b]lished numerous papers. His best know[n] was the *Manganese Memoir* (1909) whic[h] greatly advanced the scientific knowled[ge] of the world's manganese ores, and h[as] been a major contribution to the mineralogy and petrology. It has been most useful to miners, and it gave the Government of India a description of manganese deposits on which a rational policy for their extraction could be based. For his work he obtained the London B.Sc. (1907) and D.Sc. (1909).

His paper on the infraplutonic zone in the earth's crust (1913), which gained for him the Bigsby medal of the Geological Society, followed naturally from his field-work on the manganese deposits and his study of meteorites. In this he showed that at high pressures many rock-forming minerals are converted into garnet with a consequent reduction in volume of 20 per cent. Reasoning from this observation he built up a picture of the earth consisting of a series of shells of increasing density. His last scientific work in India consisted of memoirs covering all the Archaean rocks there. He described these in Mysore, Bihar and Orissa, and Bastar regarding them as one great sedimentary system. He also gave a detailed account of the cal-careous Sausar series which he considered an exceptional facies of the same system. Unfortunately he was never able to finish his series.

Fermor's mapping of the Sausar Tahsil, published after thirteen years of pains-taking field-work, displayed the Indian Archaeans in detail comparable to the classic researches in Canada, Finland, and Scotland. It also showed that the Deccan Trap had been both folded and faulted. This and his subsequent paper on the Bhusaval boring are of world-wide interest to geologists.

After manganese, Fermor's most im-portant economic work was done on coal. As the result of his map and report the formerly tiger-infested Korea State became a flourishing and important coal-field. He also mapped the Kargali coal-seam with 750 million tons of coal in an area of 10 square miles, and he was able to show that rocks mapped in Korea and Bokaro were in fact the burnt outcrops of coal-seams which were undamaged below water level.

During the war of 1914–18 Fermor worked first for the Indian Railway Board, then for the Munitions Board. He was appointed O.B.E. for his services. On his advice the Government of India passed very important legislation encouraging and stowing and reducing the unneces-ary use of scarce coking coal needed for iron smelting.

Fermor acted as curator of the geologi-cal galleries of the Indian Museum in 1905–7. In recognition of his work on manganese he was promoted superinten-dent in 1910. He officiated as director of the Geological Survey of India in 1921, 1925, and 1928, and finally served as director in 1930–35. During his director-ship he had the unpleasant task of defending his department against pro-posed cuts in the geological staff from thirty to eight and finally by his able advocacy succeeded in keeping twenty.

In 1934 Fermor was elected F.R.S. and in 1935 he was knighted. He retired from his directorship in that year but stayed in Calcutta working on his Archaean memoirs. After six months he visited Kenya, Natal, and South Africa, widening and enriching his geological experience. His last major report was written for the Colonial Office on the mining industry of Malaya. After investigating every aspect of mining there, he concluded that pros-pecting of all minerals should be pushed ahead both by Government and by private enterprise, and that a proportion of the revenue from mining should be put into a sinking fund for use when the more easily mined deposits were exhausted. War broke out before action on his recom-mendations could be taken. The Japanese printed a special edition of this report, indicating their high appreciation.

Later, as consulting geologist for various firms, Fermor visited Egypt, Rhodesia, Angola, Lisbon, India, and Malaya.

Fermor took an active part in many scientific societies. He represented the Government of India at four International Geological Congresses. He was a founder-member of the Mining and Geological Institute of India, contributing many papers to its transactions, one of which was awarded the Government prize and medal. For many years he was editor and honorary secretary, and in 1922 president. In 1906 he became a fellow of the Asiatic Society of Bengal, and was its president in 1933. By his patience and good temper he managed to restrain the rival factions threatening to wreck that ancient society. He took a leading part in founding the National Institute of Sciences in India which corresponds to the Royal Society in England, and became its first president in 1933, the year in which he presided over the Indian Science Congress. He gave his services also to many professional bodies in this country.

Fermor's interests were wide, and in-cluded philately, Persian rugs, and old

English glass, as well as all branches of natural history. He played no games, but he liked the races, and his tall straight figure might often be seen dancing in Calcutta.

In 1909 he married Muriel Aileen, daughter of Charles Ambler, of Dharhara, by whom he had a son and a daughter; the former, Patrick Leigh Fermor, became a well-known author. He married secondly, in 1933, Frances Mary, daughter of the late Edward Robert Case, of Fiddington, Somerset. Fermor died at his home near Woking 24 May 1954.

[H. Crookshank and J. B. Auden in *Biographical Memoirs of Fellows of the Royal Society*, vol. ii, 1956; private information; personal knowledge.]   H. Crookshank.

FERRIER, KATHLEEN MARY (1912-1953), singer, was born 22 April 1912 at Higher Walton, near Preston, Lancashire, the third surviving child of William Ferrier and his wife, Alice, daughter of James Murray. Her parents endowed her with a mixture of English, Welsh, Scottish, and Irish blood. Appointed headmaster of St. Paul's School, Blackburn, William Ferrier sent Kathleen to the high school which she left at fourteen to become a Post Office telephonist. Born into a musical family, she showed signs of ability on the piano at an early age and became a pupil of Miss Frances Walker when she was nine. At eighteen she had passed her A.R.C.M. and L.R.A.M. examinations for piano, had developed into a useful accompanist, and was winning prizes in local festivals. A move to Silloth near Carlisle after her marriage in 1935 brought a life of teaching the piano and many musical evenings with friends. As yet singing was for her own amusement. For a shilling wager she entered the Carlisle musical festival in 1937 for singing as well as pianoforte and won the Rose Bowl. Maurice Jacobson, the adjudicator, encouraged her to take singing lessons. From the autumn of 1939 until 1942 she studied with Dr. Hutchinson of Newcastle and gradually gained a solid local reputation which was extended when she was offered concerts with the Council for the Encouragement of Music and the Arts (C.E.M.A.) which became the Arts Council.

Valuable introductions followed. (Sir) Malcolm Sargent heard her sing and introduced her to John and Emmie Tillett, the London concert agents, who advised her to move to London. A flat was found in Hampstead into which she and her sister Winifred moved on Christmas Eve 1942 joined later by their widowed father. From February 1943 Kathleen Ferrier put herself in the hands of Roy Henderson with whom she had recently sung in *Elijah*. He became her 'Prof', an association which lasted for the rest of her life. Intensive training followed for the next three or four years, during which time she built up a national reputation, chiefly with choral societies. Joint recitals with her professor gave her experience in *Lieder* and art songs. Broadcasts and recording, chiefly for Decca, followed.

Benjamin Britten wrote the name part of his opera *The Rape of Lucretia* for her which she performed in 1946 at Glyndebourne where in the following year she made a profound impression in Gluck's *Orpheo*. The Glyndebourne manager Rudolf Bing, asked Bruno Walter to hear her; the result was world fame. Here was the ideal Mahler singer Walter was seeking. Concert tours, the operas *Lucretia* and *Orpheo*, and choral works followed in many European countries; Salzburg, Edinburgh and the English festivals, as well as tours in the United States and Canada. Bruno Walter accompanied her at a few recitals a rare mark of respect; but her favourite accompanist, who helped her throughout her career, was Gerald Moore who, in his turn, recorded that without her his life would have been 'immeasurably poorer' (*Am I too Loud?*, 1962).

Early in 1951 Kathleen Ferrier had a serious operation. Despite regular visits to hospital for deep X-ray treatment, she was singing as well as ever within three months. But the disease could not be arrested. Her last triumph was in 1953 at Covent Garden in *Orpheo* conducted by her great friend Sir John Barbirolli Although she was in great pain her glorious voice was in no way impaired. It was a superb end to a meteoric career. She died in London 8 October 1953, having been appointed C.B.E. and awarded the Royal Philharmonic Society's gold medal earlier in the year. The impact of her death on the musical world and her vast public was immense. Many were unable to obtain admission to the memorial service at a crowded Southwark Cathedral. Friends raised money for cancer research at University College Hospital where she had been a patient. The proceeds of a *Memoir* and choral societies provided money for Kathleen Ferrier scholarships for young singers.

The noble quality of Kathleen Ferrier's splendid voice, the great warmth of her heart, her gaiety, sense of humour, and the radiance of her personality, her fine musicianship, and above all her deep sincerity, all contributed to her success.

Her many hobbies included golf, photography, and, in later years, painting. It was, however, in her many friends that she found her greatest pleasure. To audiences and those who knew her best she was the most beloved singer of her time.

Her marriage in 1935 to Albert Wilson, bank clerk, was annulled in 1947. There were no children.

There are busts by Julian Allan at the Free Trade Hall, Manchester, and the Usher Hall, Edinburgh. Another, by A. J. Fleischmann, is in the Blackburn Art Gallery. A portrait by Maurice Codner is owned by Miss Winifred Ferrier.

[*Kathleen Ferrier, a Memoir*, ed. Neville Cardus, 1954; Winifred Ferrier, *The Life of Kathleen Ferrier*, 1955; personal knowledge.]
ROY HENDERSON.

FIFE, DUCHESS OF (1891–1959). [See ALEXANDRA VICTORIA ALBERTA EDWINA LOUISE DUFF, PRINCESS ARTHUR OF CONNAUGHT.]

FINZI, GERALD RAPHAEL (1901–1956), composer, was born in London 14 July 1901, the son of John Abraham Finzi, ship broker, and his wife, Eliza Emma Leverson. His general education was undertaken privately but from 1918 to 1922 he studied music under (Sir) Edward Bairstow [q.v.], organist of York Minster. Later, in 1925, he became a private pupil of R. O. Morris, a leading British authority on the aesthetics and technique of sixteenth-century polyphony, but this formal tuition lasted only a few months. For three years (1930–33) Finzi was a professor of composition at the Royal Academy of Music, but London was uncongenial to him and he held no other post save during the war of 1939–45 when he was employed in the Ministry of War Transport.

Finzi's art is rooted in English music, in English letters, and in the English countryside. As to music, composers so diverse as Parry, Elgar, and Vaughan Williams [qq.v.] all had a traceable influence on his thought. Finzi was, however, a wide reader and a real scholar. No composer so inveterately polyphonic as he could remain unaffected by the textures, and occasionally the forms, of J. S. Bach. Thus Finzi's counterpoint is often a concealed source of vitality and clarity in passages which, in clumsier hands, would have sounded thick and muddy. Its unobtrusiveness may be compared with those beautiful details of medieval architecture which do not show unless specially looked for.

He was devoted to English poetry for its own sake and his knowledge of the English masters was profound. It is in his settings of such intractable verses as those of Thomas Hardy [q.v.] that Finzi shows his special spark of genius. His ear for the music of words, alike as to sound and sense, was so acute that he was able, at his best, to create, within the orbit of pure melody and true musical inflexion, an integrated result akin to stylized or even idealized reading aloud; for him Voice and Verse were, in a special way, harmonious sisters. His love of the Wessex countryside and its history, his interest in rural pursuits such as apple-growing (at which he was expert), and not least his happy countrified family life all contributed to the personality which lay behind his music. He was musician first and foremost but his music was evoked and nourished by the wealth and warmth of his other enthusiasms.

Sir Donald Tovey [q.v.] said of Schubert that all his works were early works. In a sense this was true of Finzi who died in 1956 just when opportunity, largely through the West Country Festivals, was bringing him experience and confidence in the handling of big designs. He responded, notably in matters of dynamic energy, to the scale and scope of work on a broader canvas, but his style did not undergo a radical change. It is not that his imagination or his technique were unequal to the handling of large resources but rather that his very genius in lyric forms precluded mastery in those matters of sustained development which are of the essence of extended movements. His large choral works amply justify themselves on their own merits and they are highly individual. His *Intimations of Immortality* (Wordsworth), Op. 29 (1950), could not have been written by anybody else and his short Christmas Scene *In Terra Pax*, Op. 39 (1954), was surely a presage of things to come. In this, which in the event proved to be his last choral work, he had returned to Robert Bridges [q.v.], a poet with whom he was specially in sympathy and from whose verses he had already made 'Seven part-songs', Op. 17, in the thirties. Nevertheless it is doubtful whether Finzi's delicate art could ever have produced, in large forms, works more significant than the best of his songs with piano or his 'Dies Natalis' (Traherne), Op. 8 (1939), for solo voice and string orchestra. Indeed the short 'Intrada' to this work is among his most beautiful instrumental pieces.

Thus it is essentially as a composer of vocal music that Finzi has left his mark, and his finest writing is undoubtedly to be found in his songs for solo voice. There are three books of Hardy settings: Op. 14 (1933), Op. 15 (1936), and Op. 16 (1949). The collection of five Shakespeare songs Op. 18 (1942) called 'Let us garlands bring' is not a cycle but, in Finzi's words, 'put together as the only thing I can offer at present' (owing to his war work) as a greeting for Vaughan Williams on his seventieth birthday. It includes a specially sensitive setting of the Dirge from *Cymbeline* ('Fear no more') and in this song, for all its originality, he pays a subtle tribute to an earlier setting by Vaughan Williams himself.

Finzi's instrumental works are, however, by no means insignificant. Yet they derive from a vocal standpoint and from invention which is naturally melodic and declamatory. His orchestral output is comprised in five works including a Clarinet Concerto, Op. 31 (1949), and a Violoncello Concerto, Op. 40 (1956), with an especially beautiful slow movement. There are two chamber works, Op. 21 (1936), Op. 24 (1942), and a set of 'Bagatelles for Clarinet and Pianoforte', Op. 23 (1945).

The works which Finzi acknowledged are embodied in some thirty compositions or collections. His method of writing makes chronological reference a baffling business. He generally had several works 'on the stocks' at the same time and he allocated the opus numbers at the time of their inception. His meticulous criticism often meant that he withheld a work, already numbered, until after later ones had been completed and published. (Thus his Op. 5 and 21 are both of 1936, whereas Op. 9 is dated 1945.) It sometimes took years of intermittent sketching and patching before a piece reached what Finzi regarded as its definitive form. He did, in fact, withdraw altogether the early work ('A Severn Rhapsody', 1924) which had been published by the Carnegie Trust and which had first brought him to the notice of musicians. During the war his original work was in abeyance, but he founded a string orchestra at Newbury for which

he edited works of eighteenth-century composers, notably of John Stanley [q.v.]. Those which have been published show his practical musicianship as well as his careful scholarship.

Finzi made no bid for personal recognition, much less for popular appeal, but he was vigorous in bringing good music to the people around him. He kept his orchestra going after the war and took it about the countryside playing in churches and village halls. The pains he took over finding, preparing, and rehearsing this music is typical of his deep interest in all things old and odd. It also indicates the warmth of his feeling for friends and neighbours and not less his constant willingness to place his musical gifts at the service of the community. It is primarily owing to Finzi's sympathy, initiative, and persistence that the songs of Ivor Gurney have been preserved.

Finzi's music is of a restrained and contemplative order; sometimes withdrawn in its very eloquence, and often foreboding. Paradoxically, his most buoyant and least foreboding works were produced during his last few years when he knew his days were numbered; such is the nature of courage, and courage was of the essence of Finzi. He died in Oxford 27 September 1956.

In 1933 he had married Joyce Black; there were two sons.

[Private information; personal knowledge.]

HENRY HAVERGAL.

FIRTH, JOHN RUPERT (1890–1960), professor of general linguistics, was born 17 June 1890 at Keighley, Yorkshire, the elder son of William Firth, book-keeper, by his wife, Frances Elizabeth Waller. He was educated at Keighley Grammar School and the university of Leeds where he obtained first class honours in history (1911) and took his M.A. in 1913. After a brief appointment in the Leeds Training College he joined the Indian Education Service in 1915. In 1916–19 he saw military service in India, Afghanistan, and Africa. From 1919 to 1928 he was professor of English in the university of the Punjab at Lahore.

Firth enjoyed his time in India, a country for which he retained a great affection. But he was glad to return to England in 1928 to a senior lectureship in phonetics at University College, London which he held until 1938. He also had part time appointments elsewhere, as assistant in the sociology of languages at the Lon

lon School of Economics and Political
Science, as special lecturer in the phonetics
of Indian languages at the Indian Insti-
ute at Oxford, and as lecturer in linguistics
at the School of Oriental Studies in
London.

In 1937 Firth revisited India with a
Leverhulme fellowship and worked prin-
ipally on the Gujarati and Telugu
anguages. On his return in 1938 he became
a senior lecturer at what was by now the
School of Oriental and African Studies
and a full-time member of its staff until
his retirement in 1956. In 1940 the univer-
ity gave him the title of reader in
inguistics and Indian phonetics, and in
941 he succeeded A. Lloyd James [q.v.]
as head of the department of phonetics
and linguistics in the School. In 1944 he
was appointed to the newly created chair
of general linguistics in the university of
London, the first such chair in Great
Britain.

From 1941 to 1945 Firth's department was almost wholly occupied with
pecialized Service courses in Japanese,
asks in which he found great satisfaction
in applying his linguistic insight. He was
ppointed O.B.E. in 1946.

A member of the Scarbrough commis-
ion on the study of Oriental, Slavonic,
East European, and African languages
which reported in 1947, Firth played a
ull part in the expansion of the School
in the post-war years. He devoted all his
energies and authority to the development
of teaching and research in general
inguistics, both in the university of
London and in other universities in this
ountry where the subject had been
argely unknown.

In 1947 Firth spent three months as
isiting professor at the university in
Alexandria, and in 1948 he taught at
Michigan in the Linguistic Institute of the
Linguistic Society of America (of which
e was a member from that year). He
as active in attending international con-
resses on his subject and served on
nguistic committees of the Colonial
ocial Science Research Council and of the
British Council. He was a member of the
hilological Society of Great Britain from
933 and in 1954–7 was its president, an
onour he greatly appreciated.

On his retirement Firth became pro-
ssor emeritus and an honorary fellow of
he School of Oriental and African Studies.
With few hobbies or outside interests, he
as irked by retirement and despite in-
reasing ill health he gladly undertook

further appointments. In 1957 he visited
Pakistan to advise on the practical applications of linguistics; and in 1958 he much
enjoyed two terms as special lecturer in
the university of Edinburgh where he
received an honorary LL.D.

Firth had abundant energy and an
eager, original mind, almost wholly devoted to the furtherance of his subject,
general linguistics, as he saw it. In association with him one felt how deeply and
personally he involved himself in it. This,
combined with a certain irascibility and
Yorkshire bluntness (on which he prided
himself) and an occasional impatience of
criticism, made him at times difficult to
work with. But he was obviously a friendly
and loyal person, and he loved good company, in which he displayed his powers
as a conversationalist, being wonderfully
able to interest all comers with his subject
which he never allowed to become dry or
remote from daily life, however abstruse
his theorizing.

His most enduring achievement was the
establishment of general linguistics as a
recognized subject in British universities.
In the subject itself he is most remembered
for two developments: the contextual
theory of language and of linguistic analysis, and prosodic phonology. In his teaching, despite his innovations in theory, he
insisted, more than most of his contemporaries, on the recognition of the roots
that the subject had in the history of both
European and Indian scholarship.

Firth wrote many articles, the most important of which have been republished as
Papers in Linguistics 1934–1951 (1957).
His only two books, *Speech* (1930) and *The
Tongues of Men* (1937), were written as
deliberately popular works. In retirement
he planned but never completed a book
setting out his theoretical position in detail. A summary of his views may be
found in his 'Synopsis of Linguistic
Theory, 1930–55', a chapter in *Studies in
Linguistic Analysis* (Philological Society,
1957).

Firth's written style was distinctive,
readable, and compelling, always stimulating but often allusive and obscure in
places. This partly accounts for his failure
to reach a wider scholarly public through
his writings. He was best understood and
most influential in tutorials, seminars, and
private discussions. It was a source of
great pleasure to him to see his theories
and methods carried forward and applied
by several of his former postgraduate
pupils from different parts of the world,

over whom he exercised a strong and abiding influence.

In 1915 Firth married Annie Lister, daughter of William Clough, treasurer to Barrow-in-Furness local authority; they had one son and one daughter. He died at Lindfield, Sussex, 14 December 1960.

[*Language*, vol. xxxvii, No. 2, 1961; *Bulletin* of the School of Oriental and African Studies, vol. xxiv, part 2, 1961; *The Times*, 16 December 1960; private information; personal knowledge.]   R. H. ROBINS.

FIRTH, SIR WILLIAM JOHN (1881–1957), industrialist, was born in London 21 July 1881, the elder son of Richard Firth, sea captain, of Forest Gate, Essex, by his wife, Katie Ayton. He began work as an office boy earning ten shillings a week and soon became a salesman. In 1901 he entered the tinplate trade as an agent and merchant in London. Firth was closely associated with Henry Folland, who was appointed managing director of the Grovesend Steel and Tinplate Company in 1908, and by 1923 they had transformed this small and not very prosperous firm into the second-largest tinplate manufacturing business in the country.

Although highly individualistic, Firth was an advocate of central selling arrangements for tinplate, an industry of many small units mainly located in South Wales. In 1919 he proposed the setting up of a central selling agency, but the scheme made no progress owing to the non-co-operation of the largest tinplate manufacturer, Richard Thomas & Co., Grovesend's most powerful competitor. Firth persisted in his efforts for greater centralization in the tinplate business, and in 1923 he achieved the amalgamation of Grovesend and Richard Thomas, himself becoming a member of the Richard Thomas board. In the same year a tinplate selling agency was established. His energy and enterprise found increasing scope at the head of a great steel company now owning 6 steelworks, 159 tinplate mills, and 28 sheet mills. Richard Thomas's domination of the tinplate industry was now more marked than ever; they controlled one-third of its capacity. Firth became chairman of the company in 1931. He was knighted in 1932.

Firth became the centre of a major controversy in the steel industry through his determination to set up in Britain a continuous wide strip mill, of the kind already in successful operation for some years in the United States, to meet the growing demand for steel sheets, in pa[r]ticular for motor-cars. He received litt[le] encouragement for this project, and som[e] opposition from Baldwins, Ltd., th[e] other major South Wales producer [of] sheets and tinplates. Firth persisted, a[t] first considering the possibility of buildin[g] the new works at Redbourn, Scunthorp[e] near the source of East Midland ore, b[ut] later acquiring, in 1935, the Ebbw Va[le] Steel, Iron and Coal Company, with i[ts] site in an area of severe unemployment. I[t] has been argued that Ebbw Vale was, o[n] technical and economic grounds, a le[ss] suitable site than Redbourn for a con[tinuous hot-strip mill, but social an[d] political considerations helped, thoug[h] they did not entirely determine, the fin[al] decision in favour of Ebbw Vale. Th[e] difficulties of the site, rising prices, an[d] delays in deliveries of plant due to rearm[a]ment, led in 1938 to an arrangemen[t] whereby the Bank of England provide[d] new capital in return for the setting u[p] of a special controlling committee. Th[is] arrangement was always irksome to Firt[h] and led to a series of disputes, ending wit[h] his retirement from the chairmanship [of] Richard Thomas in 1940. By that tim[e] the value of the works in bringing abou[t] the industrial and social revival of Ebb[w] Vale had been demonstrated, and they wer[e] beginning to play their vital part in securin[g] supplies of sheet and tinplate in the war[.]

Objecting strongly to the cessation [of] his control over the works which his visio[n] and determination had brought into exis[t]ence, and still holding a very large shar[e] in Richard Thomas & Co., Firth frequentl[y] disagreed with the policy of the boar[d] after his retirement, and opposed th[e] amalgamation with Baldwins which too[k] place in 1945. In 1947 he went to Sout[h] Africa, where he died at his home [at] Kloof, Natal, 11 November 1957.

Firth was a man of driving energy, wit[h] a brilliant and very quick-moving min[d.] Although he had a somewhat exaggerate[d] reputation of being a difficult man to de[al] with, he had great charm and was muc[h] liked by his workpeople. In Ebbw Val[e] which he brought back to hope and pro[s]perity from the depths of poverty a[nd] depression, he is commemorated by th[e] town welfare ground, the memorial gat[es] of which were opened in 1959 by Aneur[in] Bevan [q.v.], whom Firth had first met [in] the early days of the project for the str[ip] mill.

Firth was vice-president of the Briti[sh] Iron and Steel Federation, chairman [of] the International Tinplate Cartel and of the Welsh Plate and Sheet Manufacturers' Association, and president of the Royal Metal Trades Benevolent Society.

In 1909 Firth married Helena Adelaide, eldest daughter of Joseph Garrett; they had two sons. A portrait by Howard Somerville was presented to Firth in 1931 and is in the possession of the family.

[*The Times, Manchester Guardian*, and *South Wales Evening Post*, 12 November 1957; *South Wales Argus*, 26 November 1957; *Ingot News* (newspaper of Richard Thomas and Baldwins, Ltd.), June 1959; J. C. Carr and W. Taplin, *History of the British Steel Industry*, 1962; private information.]

WALTER TAPLIN

FLEMING, SIR ALEXANDER (1881–1955), bacteriologist, was born 6 August 1881, the third of the four children of Hugh Fleming, farmer of Lochfield in Ayrshire, by his second marriage, to Grace Morton, the daughter of a neighbouring farmer. Hugh Fleming, whose ancestors probably came from the Low Countries, had four surviving children by his first marriage, was sixty at the time of his second marriage, and died when Alec was seven. Fleming was born at Lochfield, an upland sheep farm with some arable land, near Darvel. He had his early schooling in a small country school at Loudoun Moor, then at Darvel (four miles distant), and for eighteen months at Kilmarnock Academy. At fourteen he and his two brothers of the second marriage went to live with a doctor brother in London, where he continued his education for two years at the Polytechnic Institute in Regent Street. The next four years were spent as a clerk in a shipping office in the City, but on the advice of his brother and with the help of a small legacy Fleming, in 1901, became a student at St. Mary's Hospital medical school, where, besides the senior entrance scholarship in natural science, he won virtually every class prize and scholarship during his student career. He took the conjoint qualification in 1906 and the M.B., B.S. of London University in 1908 with honours in five subjects and a university gold medal. A year later he became F.R.C.S., having taken the primary examination as a student. As Sir Zachary Cope has said, 'Surgery might have gained what bacteriology would have lost. Yet surgery gained infinitely more, as things fell out.' Fleming had a very good memory and learning was never a burden to him. But he was no bookworm; both as undergraduate and as postgraduate he was an active and proficient member of the swimming, shooting, and golf clubs and even took some part in the students' theatrical entertainments.

Immediately after qualification Fleming began his association with (Sir) Almroth Wright [q.v.] as an assistant bacteriologist in the inoculation department at St. Mary's Hospital. He also held for some years the post of pathologist to the London Lock Hospital. He was appointed lecturer in bacteriology in St. Mary's medical school in 1920 and eight years later he was given the title of professor of bacteriology in the university of London. He retired from the chair with the title emeritus in 1948, but continued until the end of 1954 as principal of the Wright–Fleming Institute of Microbiology in which he had succeeded Almroth Wright in 1946.

During his early postgraduate years at St. Mary's medical school Fleming was to a considerable extent the apprentice of Almroth Wright, whose dominant character and fertile brain directed the general research of the inoculation department (later the Wright–Fleming Institute) for many years. But from the beginning of his career Fleming showed his ingenuity and originality in devising simple apparatus and techniques for tackling laboratory problems, for example, in his work on the opsonic index, recently introduced by Wright as a method for assessing the effect of vaccine therapy, and in a brilliant essay on 'Acute Bacterial Infections', published in *St. Mary's Hospital Gazette*, which won him the Cheadle gold medal. His capacity for original and accurate observation was also demonstrated in 1909 by a well-written article in the *Lancet* on the aetiology and treatment, with autogenous vaccines, of acne. About this time, Ehrlich had introduced salvarsan for the treatment of syphilis and Fleming made a typical contribution by devising a simple micro-method for the serological diagnosis of this disease.

Soon after the outbreak of war in 1914, Almroth Wright was invited by the Medical Research Committee to establish a research laboratory in Boulogne to study the treatment of war wounds. Fleming, who had joined the Royal Army Medical Corps as lieutenant (and later became captain), was a member of the team and although much of the work done during this period was published jointly with Wright and others, Fleming himself made some outstanding contributions to knowledge of the bacteriology and treatment of septic wounds. In a paper published in the *Lancet* a year after the outbreak of war, he noted the evil significance of *Streptococcus pyogenes*, which was also demonstrated in the blood of about a quarter of the more severe cases. He believed that the severity of wound infection was related to the presence of necrotic tissue in the wound and advocated early removal of this dead tissue at the same time as another Scotsman, Sir Henry Gray, had independently introduced surgical débridement to obtain healing by first intention. Later, with A. B. Porteous, Fleming showed that most streptococcal infections occurred *after* the patient was admitted to the base hospital, thus giving forewarning of the dangers of hospital cross-infection with this organism. He also made a significant contribution to knowledge of gas gangrene, and helped Almroth Wright in his advocacy of physiological principles rather than the use of antiseptics for the treatment of war wounds by devising numerous ingenious experiments.

In 1922 came the discovery of lysozyme, an anti-microbial substance produced by many tissues and secretions of the body, particularly in leucocytes, tears, saliva, mucus, and cartilage. Fleming probably regarded lysozyme, which he later called the body's natural antibiotic, as his most important discovery and, with V. D. Allison, he showed its wide distribution in nature, its enzymic quality and remarkable stability, and the interesting phenomenon of the development of bacterial resistance to its action. He also developed new techniques to demonstrate the diffusibility of lysozyme, techniques later to prove useful in his studies of penicillin.

In September 1928, Fleming made the world-famous observation which was to lead in time to the new antibiotic era. He was studying colony variation in the staphylococcus in relation to the chapter he was writing on that organism for the *System of Bacteriology*. This necessitated frequent examination of plate cultures of the organism over a period of days when 'It was noticed that around a large colony of a contaminating mould the staphylococcus colonies became transparent and were obviously undergoing lysis.'

As he himself often said, it was a chance observation which he followed up as a bacteriologist, and his previous experience with lysozyme which turned his alert mind

aside from study of the staphylococcus instead of 'casting out the contaminated culture with appropriate language'. Fleming in his original paper, published in the *British Journal of Experimental Pathology* (June 1929), described most of the properties of penicillin which became universally known. Some of the conclusions of that historic paper are worth quoting to illustrate the appreciation of the potentialities of this new 'antiseptic' by a man who had been an active antagonist of antiseptics generally. 'The active agent is readily filterable and the name "penicillin" has been given to filtrates of broth cultures of the mould.' 'The action is very marked on the pyogenic cocci and the diphtheria group of bacilli.' 'Penicillin is non-toxic to animals in enormous doses and is non-irritant. It does not interfere with leucocytic function to a greater degree than does ordinary broth.' 'It is suggested that it may be an effective antiseptic for application to, or injection into, areas infected with penicillin-sensitive microbes.'

Fleming noted particularly, as advantages over the known antiseptics, its diffusibility, its activity in dilutions up to 1 in 1,000 against the pyogenic cocci, and its complete absence of toxicity on phagocytes. He mentioned that 'Experiments in connection with its value in the treatment of pyogenic infections are in progress' and a few years later he noted that penicillin 'has been used in a number of indolent septic wounds and has certainly appeared to be superior to dressings containing potent chemicals'.

Fleming undoubtedly had some appreciation of the potentiality of penicillin as a systemic chemotherapeutic substance before the Oxford team demonstrated it, for he suggested its *injection* into infected areas and predicted that it could be used in the treatment of venereal diseases. Some attempt was made to concentrate penicillin, but as Fleming said in his Nobel lecture, 'We are bacteriologists—not chemists—and our relatively simple procedures were unavailing.' Besides, as Sir Henry Dale has written, 'neither the time when the discovery was made nor, perhaps, the scientific atmosphere of the laboratory in which he worked, was propitious to such further enterprise as its development would have needed'.

Meanwhile Fleming turned his attention to the new sulphonamides and having shown that these drugs were bacteriostatic and not bactericidal and were

nhibited by large numbers of living or
dead bacteria, he believed, prophetically,
hat they would not be effective in the
ocal treatment of septic wounds. Here
again and later when penicillin became
available for clinical use, he demonstrated
his technical skill and ingenuity in devising micro-methods for measuring the
oncentration of these drugs in the
patients' blood. Indeed, he was generally
acclaimed as the most skilled technician
among Almroth Wright's numerous colleagues and followers. He was his own
echnician to the end and it was always
a joy to watch his deft and neat handling
of glass slide and capillary pipette. But
echnical inventiveness is worth much
more to the research worker than technical skill and Fleming was equally well
ndowed with both. He was keenly
nterested in staining methods and when
ndia ink became unavailable after 1918
t was Fleming who introduced nigrosin as
a negative method of staining and showed
how it could be used for demonstrating
pores and capsules. He was probably the
first to grow bacteria and moulds on paper
or cellophane placed on top of nutrient
agar and he demonstrated the suitability
of paper for bringing out the pigment of
hromogenic bacteria. He left an interest-
ng collection of 'coloured pictures' composed entirely of bacterial cultures which
he was fond of showing to royalty and
other visitors to the Institute.

The catalogue of Fleming's published
work leaves little room for doubt that
he had to an unusual degree the almost
ntuitive faculty for original observation
coupled with a high degree of technical
nventiveness and skill. He had in fact
most of the qualities which make a great
scientist: an innate curiosity and perceptiveness regarding natural phenomena,
nsight into the heart of a problem,
echnical ingenuity, persistence in seeing
the job through, and that physical and
mental toughness which is essential to
he top-class investigator. He was a
natural biologist, keenly interested in and
very knowledgeable about birds, flowers,
nd trees. He appreciated the healthy
atmosphere of his early upbringing in the
ountry: tramping the upland moors and
earning the shorter catechism, he once
old a reporter, had been powerful in-
uences in shaping his life.

Physically, Fleming was short and
cockily built with powerful square
houlders and a deep chest, a fresh com-
lexioned face with a fine broad forehead,
intensely light-blue expressive eyes and
for many years a good crop of snowy
white hair. He had great powers of physical endurance and in the days when
burning the midnight oil was a regular
performance in the inoculation department, Fleming was always the first to
appear, fresh and fit, the following morning. Later he seemed to stand up astonishingly well to the heavy journeyings and
junketings he had to undergo, and he kept
his freshness and jaunty step to the end.
He was sensitive and sympathetic, enjoyed the simple things in life, and was
not impressed with the grandiose. A collection of schoolchildren's signatures or
a letter from a child or from some poor
person who had benefited from penicillin
gave him as much joy as the gold medals
and honorary degrees. But, like most
Scots, he had a 'guid conceit' of himself
and readily commanded respect from his
colleagues inside and outside the Institute.
He was essentially a humble, simple man
who to the end remained remarkably
unspoiled and unchanged despite all
the honours which were showered upon
him.

Fleming had a natural combativeness
and urge to win which was very apparent
in the games he played. This determination to succeed was evident in his tackling
of laboratory problems when he took
delight in using his technical skill and
inventiveness to overcome difficulties. On
the other hand, Fleming never took kindly
to administrative responsibility and shied
away from problems, preferring to 'wait
and see' rather than take immediate
decisions. He had tremendous constancy
and loyalty—to his friends and colleagues, to the inoculation department, to
St. Mary's and to its staff and students,
and this quality of steadfastness inspired
the confidence of his companions which
was never misplaced. He had a quiet
unruffled wisdom which made him a
shrewd judge of men, but tolerant of
weaknesses in his friends and colleagues.
He was not heard to speak ill of anyone
although he had decided likes and dislikes.
He was not an easy man to know well,
partly because of his natural reluctance to
talk and express his feelings. He was
not a conversationalist and awkward
silences were sometimes broken by awkward remarks: as one visitor put it—
talking with him was like playing tennis
with a man who, whenever you knocked
the ball over to his side, put it in his
pocket. But this was shyness, not

intentional rudeness, for he liked company and had many friends in various walks of life before he became famous. His association with the Chelsea Arts Club and some of its members gave him particular satisfaction and an outlet for his artistic sense, for he enjoyed beauty wherever he saw it.

Innumerable honours were conferred upon Fleming in the last ten years of his life. He was knighted in 1944, and was awarded the Nobel prize for medicine, jointly with Sir Howard (later Lord) Florey and (Sir) E. B. Chain, in 1945. He became a fellow of the Royal Society in 1943, of the Royal College of Physicians of London in 1944, of the Royal College of Physicians of Edinburgh in 1946, and an honorary fellow of the Royal Society of Edinburgh in 1947. Doctorates of medicine, science, and law were conferred on him by many British, European, and American universities. He was commander of the Legion of Honour in France, member of the Pontifical Academy of Sciences, fellow of important societies and academies in many countries, and the recipient of many medals and honorary lectureships. He was elected rector of the university of Edinburgh (1951-4), was a convocation member of the senate of the university of London from 1950, a member of the Medical Research Council (1945-9), and president of the Society for General Microbiology (1945-7). Besides becoming an honorary citizen of numerous cities in Europe, he was a freeman of the burgh of Darvel where he was born, of Chelsea where he lived, and of Paddington where his work was done.

There are several portraits of Fleming, of which perhaps the best known are those by T. C. Dugdale in the library of the Wright–Fleming Institute and by Anna Zinkeisen in the board-room of St. Mary's Hospital. The Imperial War Museum has one by Ethel Gabain. There is also a number of busts—those by E. R. Bevan and E. J. Clack are in the Wright–Fleming Institute, another by E. R. Bevan stands in the square of Darvel, Ayrshire, and one in bronze by F. Kovacs is in the Chelsea Town Hall. There is a memorial stone at Lochfield Farm, a plaque in the crypt of St. Paul's Cathedral and there are several monuments abroad. The Ministry of Health building at the Elephant and Castle is called Alexander Fleming House, and streets and squares in several countries have been named after him.

He died suddenly from a heart attack at his home, in Chelsea, London, 11 March

1955. He was buried in St. Paul's Cathe dral. Fleming was twice married: first, ii 1915, to Sarah (Sareen) Marion, daughte of a farmer, Bernard McElroy, count Mayo, Ireland, and herself a traine nurse, who died in 1949; secondly, in 195: to Amalia Voureka Coutsouris, daughte of a Greek doctor, and herself a medicall qualified bacteriologist. There was on son of the first marriage, who qualified i medicine and entered general practice.

[L. Colebrook in Biographical Memoirs (Fellows of the Royal Society, vol. ii, 1956 Robert Cruickshank in Journal of Patholog and Bacteriology, vol. lxxii, No. 2, Octobe 1956; British Medical Journal, 19 and 2 March 1955; André Maurois, The Life of S Alexander Fleming, 1959; personal know ledge.]　　　R. CRUICKSHANE

FLEMING, SIR ARTHUR PERC MORRIS (1881–1960), engineer, was bor 16 January 1881 in Newport, Isle of Wigh the youngest of the three sons of Fran Fleming and his wife, Fanny Morris, farming family of that locality. On con pletion of his education at the Portlan House Academy, Newport, Fleming er tered the Finsbury Technical Colleg London, as a student of electrical enginee ing. Following short periods with th London Electric Supply Corporation ar a firm of electrical instrument manufa turers, Elliott Brothers, he was selecte in 1900 by the newly established Britis Westinghouse Company (later Metr politan-Vickers) as one of the 'holy fort to undergo a course of training with th American firm at its East Pittsburg works. When he arrived at Manchest in 1902 he was engaged as a speciali on electrical insulation in the transform department of which he soon became chi engineer and, in 1913, superintendent.

Into his department Fleming soon bega to introduce arrangements for the furth education and systematic training of i schoolboy recruits. By 1908 he had e tended these arrangements throughout the company; in 1914 he established trade apprentice school; and in 1917 l became manager of the company's educa tion department. He used often to sa that the most important raw material industry is its young people, and he too steps to ensure that his own young peopl from the embryo craftsman to the unive sity graduate, were recognized and treate as such. They came not only from th schools and universities of Britain b from all over the world, for in the sphe of industrial training the name of Fleming and Metropolitan-Vickers became known internationally. Fleming's influence and inspiration penetrated widely into the electrical industry as a whole and the benefits have been profound.

His views on engineering education were matched by his realization of the need for research within industry, especially research not bounded by the short-term problems of existing products. His plans were delayed by the war of 1914–18 in which he and a few colleagues made important contributions to submarine detection, for which he was appointed C.B.E. in 1920. In that year the first buildings of his research department began to appear, and it was typical of his foresight and vigour that he arranged for these buildings to be used as the site for the transmitter and studios of the British Broadcasting Company's initial Manchester station—2 ZY—which began to broadcast within a day of the opening of 2 LO in London. By 1929 the department contained one of the largest high voltage laboratories in the world, and there were attracted to it a succession of men of ability who made many notable contributions to both pure and applied science. Particularly important was the development of demountable high-power thermionic valves which helped to make possible the installation just prior to the outbreak of war in 1939 of the first radar stations. In 1931 Fleming became the company's director of research and education and so continued until his retirement in 1954.

Fleming's achievement was due to an exceptional foresight, single-minded industry and tenacity, an extremely good memory, unlimited enthusiasm and vitality, and an ability to inspire and stimulate others. He was big enough to surround himself with men intellectually, perhaps, more gifted than himself, and to secure their willing co-operation and loyalty. He had the strength to ignore opposition as if it did not exist and to persevere until eventually, on many things, others came to think his way. He liked to quote with approval Drake's reflection that 'There must be a beginning of any great matter, but the continuing unto the end until it be thoroughly finished yields the true glory.'

Fleming's outside activities were manifold. He was a member of the council of the university of Manchester, of the governing body of the Imperial College of Science and Technology, of the delegacy of the City and Guilds of London Institute, of the Ministry of Education committee on the training of teachers and youth leaders, and of the War Cabinet engineering advisory committee; chairman of the electrical engineering committee of the central register of the Ministry of Labour, of the Athlone Fellowship committee, and of the Federation of British Industries overseas scholarships committee; and president of both the education (1939) and engineering (1949) sections of the British Association, and of the British Association for Commercial and Industrial Education. He also played an important part in the establishment of the Department of Scientific and Industrial Research and of the Electrical Research Association.

Within all these interests, the Institution of Electrical Engineers occupied a place of special importance; he became a member of its council (1932), a vice-president (1935), president (1938), an honorary member (1952), and was awarded the Faraday medal (1941). He received honorary degrees from Liverpool and Manchester and was awarded the Hawksley medal of the Institution of Mechanical Engineers. He was knighted in 1945.

Throughout his career Fleming lectured frequently, both at home and abroad, about industrial research and training, and wrote many papers, the value of which lay in the widespread practices they did so much to stimulate. He was joint-author of several books: *The Insulation and Design of Electrical Windings* (with R. Johnson, 1913); *Engineering as a Profession* (with R. W. Bailey, 1913); *The Principles of Apprentice Training* (with J. G. Pearce, 1916); *An Introduction to the Principles of Industrial Administration* (with H. J. Brocklehurst, 1922); *Research in Industry* (with J. G. Pearce, 1922); and *A History of Engineering* (with H. J. Brocklehurst, 1925).

In 1904 Fleming married Rose Mary (died 1948), daughter of William Ash, merchant, of Newport; they had two sons and one daughter. He died at his home at Bonchurch, Isle of Wight, 14 September 1960.

[Private information; personal knowledge.]
JACKSON OF BURNLEY.

FLETCHER, SIR BANISTER FLIGHT (1866–1953), architect and architectural historian, was born in Bloomsbury, London, 15 February 1866, the eldest son of

Fletcher, B. F.　　　D.N.B. 1951–1960

the architect Banister Fletcher [q.v.]. He was educated at the Norfolk County School, King's College and University College, London, and entered his father's office in 1884, studying architecture also at the Royal Academy Schools and the Architectural Association. He became an associate of the Royal Institute of British Architects in 1889 and a fellow in 1904. He was made a partner in his father's firm in 1889 and succeeded with his brother to the practice in 1899. In earlier life he may be regarded as one of the moderately original men of the 'early modern' movement; though little of his work was important, it did not lack character. It included buildings such as banks (as at Hythe); a church (at Stratford, E.); flats (in Harley and Wimpole streets); King's College School, Wimbledon Common (1899); shops, memorials, and houses; and an old building extended was Morden College, Blackheath (1933). The firm continued under the style of Banister Fletcher & Sons after the death in 1916 of his brother H. Phillips Fletcher. Two large works done in later years were the Roan School, Greenwich (with Percy B. Dannatt, c. 1926–8) and the Gillette factory, Osterley (c. 1936). Fletcher was for many years surveyor to the Worshipful Company of Carpenters, its master in 1936, and director of its Building Crafts Training School, St. Marylebone.

Fletcher was much better known, however, as the author (originally jointly with his father, 1896) of *A History of Architecture on the Comparative Method*; his wide travels provided material and his knowledge of London in particular was extensive. A definitive edition was the sixth (1921) with the text largely rewritten by Fletcher and his first wife and new plates brilliantly drawn by George G. Woodward and others; subsequently only minor revisions and enlargements were made until a major revision, within the old framework, was carried out by R. A. Cordingley for the seventeenth edition in 1961. The book was translated into several languages. An early book was the criticized *Andrea Palladio* (1902) and he wrote several slighter studies. With his brother he produced two handbooks: *Architectural Hygiene, or Sanitary Science as Applied to Building* (1899) and *Carpentry and Joinery* (1898) illustrated by his charming sketches. Other such sketches, in pencil and ink, are reproduced in the publication on his *Architectural Work* (1934).

Fletcher was president of the Royal Institute of British Architects (1929–31) and bore part of the cost of its library catalogue (2 vols., 1937–8). As a lecturer in his youth at King's College, following his father, and later on London University extension courses (1901–38), latterly given at the Central School of Arts and Crafts he did much to make the subject vivid and stimulating. Fletcher was called to the bar by the Inner Temple in 1908 and conducted arbitrations and advised on London Building Act disputes. He was for many years (1907–53) a common councillor of the City of London and the chairman at different times of the schools and library committees. In 1918–19 he was senior sheriff, receiving a knighthood in 1919 and various foreign honours.

Fletcher was a man of great intellectual ability in certain fields, with a capacity for hard work and organizing acumen, but he was happier in his more historical activities. An autocrat, and patronizing even to his peers, he expected much of his staff and scenes were common, but he had, beneath, a kindly concern for their physical welfare. The stress of the shrievalty campaign and the sheriff's duties seem to have affected his nerve and his impending encounters became a strain. In manner and appearance he was 'sometimes genial, sometimes austere, but always dignified'. A portrait by Glyn Philpot for his presidency hangs in the R.I.B.A. library. He bequeathed much of his property (slides, lecture diagrams, and so on) and money to the university of London and the R.I.B.A. library with the stipulation that the latter should be named the 'Sir Banister Fletcher Library'.

Fletcher married in 1914 Alice Maud Mary (died 1932), daughter of Edward Bretherton and widow of Sir John Bamford-Slack; secondly, in 1933, Mrs Howard Hazell (died 1949). There were no children. He died in London 17 August 1953.

[*Who's Who in Architecture*, 1926; J. A. Gotch, *Growth and Work of the Royal Institute of British Architects*, 1934; W. Hanneford Smith, *The Architectural Work of Sir Banister Fletcher*, 1934, 2nd ed. 1937; *Journal of the Royal Institute of British Architects*, September 1953; *Builder*, 28 August 1953; M. S Briggs, first Sir Banister Fletcher memorial lecture in *Journal* of the London Society, May 1954; personal knowledge.]

H. V. MOLESWORTH ROBERTS

FLETCHER, SIR FRANK (1870–1954), headmaster, was born 3 May 1870 at Atherton, near Manchester, the eldest son

366

of Ralph Fletcher and his wife, Fanny Smith. The family were colliery owners known for the care of their employees and among the first to install life-saving apparatus and pit-head baths. Frank was brought up to a simplicity of life and a sense of responsibility. At twelve he won a scholarship at Rossall School, then under H. A. James and afterwards C. C. Tancock. From Rossall (Sir) Henry Stuart-Jones and R. W. Lee [qq.v.] won scholarships at Balliol and Fletcher followed them in 1889. He became the pupil of W. R. Hardie [q.v.] and won first classes in classical moderations (1891) and *literae humaniores* (1893) as well as the Craven (1890), Ireland (1891), and Derby (1894) scholarships. In his last year he played in the university hockey team against Cambridge; trained on the sands of Rossall as an individualist he twice took the ball down the wing and scored a goal. He also acquired a passion for mountaineering, first in the Engadine and later in the southern Alps, becoming a member of the Alpine Club.

In Fletcher's day the classics were supreme in Oxford and with his record he might well have chosen to become a don. His interest lay, however, in the teaching of boys and after two terms tutoring at Balliol he accepted (1894) an offer from John Percival [q.v.] of a mastership at Rugby. There he taught the classical sixth, among whom were R. H. Tawney and later William Temple [q.v.], and also had the invaluable experience of teaching a low form.

Fletcher was ambitious and stood for several headmasterships before he was elected in 1903 to be master of Marlborough, the first lay headmaster of a great public school. He loved the place, his life, and his teaching. Plato, St. Paul, and Browning were his favourite subjects. He gained confidence in his capacity to rule. There were difficulties at first and no doubt mistakes; he was sometimes hasty, and rough places were not infrequently made plain by his wife's tact. But there was never ill will in his actions and the justice of his intentions was always afterwards recognized.

In 1911 a call came to him from Charterhouse which he felt bound to accept. It did not take him long to realize the problems or to start to deal with them and in consequence he was not at first popular. But masters and boys soon came to understand his aims and to recognize his fundamental kindliness and long before the end of his reign he was revered and loved. His chief visible contribution to Charterhouse was the war memorial chapel which added to the dignity of the whole life of the school. It was less tangible things which he most constantly gave. During his headmastership the academic successes and the general vigour of the school life were greatly increased. He chose his assistant masters wisely and let them develop on their own lines. He was himself a man of high ideals which he felt that he could reach. The result was a kind of unconscious conceit which deceived those who did not know him well. Beneath it was a true humility arising from a naturally religious life which showed itself in his sermons and speeches.

Fletcher took a keen interest in the concerns of the public schools in general and was many times chairman of the Headmasters' Conference. In 1924 he was made an honorary fellow of Balliol; and in 1937 he was knighted. In 1935 he retired and went to live near Dartmouth where he did great service on the Devonshire education committee and on the governing bodies of several schools. Returning to his classical interests he published an edition of the sixth book of the *Aeneid* (1941) and *Notes to the Agamemnon of Aeschylus* (1949), both admirable examples of the best sixth-form classical teaching. He was president of the Classical Association in 1946. In 1948 the Fletchers moved to Eashing near Godalming where they could revisit Charterhouse and their many friends. Fletcher died in a nursing-home at Hindhead 17 November 1954.

In 1902 he married Dorothy (died 1958), daughter of William Pope, of Crediton; there were no children.

A bust of Fletcher by Sir Jacob Epstein is at Charterhouse and a copy at Rossall School. Marlborough College has a portrait by George Harcourt.

[Sir Frank Fletcher, *After Many Days*, 1937; *The Times*, 18 November 1954; *The Carthusian*, March 1955; private information; personal knowledge.]   CYRIL BAILEY.

FOOT, ISAAC (1880–1960), politician, was born in Plymouth 23 February 1880, the fourth son of Isaac Foot, builder and undertaker, by his wife, Eliza Ryder. He was educated at the Plymouth Public School (where, he recorded, rather reluctantly he paid twopence a week for the privilege) and then at the Hoe Grammar School. Articled for five years to a Plymouth solicitor, Frederick Skardon, he was admitted as a solicitor in 1902 and shortly afterwards founded the enduring legal partnership of Foot and Bowden.

Foot entered politics as, and always remained, a Liberal. After two unsuccessful contests in ward elections in Plymouth he became a Liberal councillor for the Greenbank ward in 1907 and remained a member of the city council for some twenty years. The focus of his ambitions and the field of his talents was, however, to be the House of Commons. Remarkable about his Commons career was that it was all over in eight years, but in that short time he had won and preserved a national fame; one of the minor tragedies of English history between the wars was that Isaac Foot was not, except for these few years, in the Commons to shape it.

He fought the Totnes division in January 1910 and was beaten by the Conservative candidate, F. B. Mildmay (later Lord Mildmay of Flete). In December 1910 he fought the South-East Cornwall (Bodmin) division and was defeated by only 41 votes by Sir Reginald Pole Carew. In 1919 in the Sutton division of Plymouth he was beaten by Lady Astor—with whom thereafter he had a lifetime's fast friendship. He was first elected in 1922 for the Bodmin division at a by-election, was returned again in 1922 and 1923, but defeated in 1924 when the Labour Government fell. After a period in the wilderness he returned as member for the same division in 1929, was returned unopposed in the national crisis election of 1931, and defeated in 1935 when the division again returned a Conservative. He was subsequently defeated at St. Ives (1937) and Tavistock (1945).

On the formation of the 'national' Government in 1931, Foot was appointed parliamentary secretary for mines, where he made a great impression. But when he was faced with the Government's protection measures brought about by the Ottawa conference of 1932 he resigned instantly. The decision cost him the whole of his political future, as he must have known it would, but it was a decision which he made without hesitation and which he never regretted. He remained in the main stream of traditional Liberalism and refused to contemplate the prospects of continued office as a National or Simonite Liberal. He was sworn of the Privy Council in 1937.

Foot had been chosen as deputy mayor of Plymouth in 1920 and during his year of office he spent some time in the United States as Plymouth's representative at the *Mayflower* tercentenary. His gift for memorable oratory was by this time so well developed as to produce an indelible impression upon all those who heard him. In 1945 he was chosen by unanimous vote to be lord mayor of the city of Plymouth, an honour very rarely accorded to one not at the time a member of the city council. During his mayoralty his acute sense of history lent unusual distinction to the office. He made a point of visiting every school in the city in full robes to bring local history and civic pride to life in the minds of the children.

Out of office and out of the House of Commons, he devoted himself to the two other great enthusiasms of his life, the collection and reading of thousands of books and the study and practice of public speech. In 1904 he had married Eva (died 1946), daughter of Angus Mackintosh, M.D., a granddaughter of William Dingle, of Callington in Cornwall, and it was to that district that he later went to live. There they brought up a remarkable family in a house called Pencrebar some three miles out of Callington. There were two daughters, and five sons: Dingle, who became solicitor-general, with a knighthood, in the Labour Government of 1964; Hugh, who became Lord Caradon, and as Sir Hugh Foot was the last governor of Cyprus; Michael, the left-wing rebel, former editor of *Tribune*, and member of Parliament for Ebbw Vale in succession to his friend Aneurin Bevan [q.v.]; John (who received a life peerage in 1967); and Christopher who carried on the family law practice in Plymouth. His sons have all in their own way put on record their testimony to the fact that it was their father who had largely made them what they were. Another formative influence was undoubtedly the merciless cut and thrust of political and literary debate in that lively household.

In the manor house where these sons grew up under the eye of their father, there came into being also over the years a famous library of more than seventy thousand books which formed the basework of the remarkable photographic memory of Isaac Foot which so astounded his contemporaries and obliterated his opponents. He could remember for years not only the page but the location on the page of any one of thousands of passages, each to be called to mind and used with devastating precision on some exactly apposite occasion. All his life he was a

oracious reader, waking at five or earlier
very morning for the purpose. He taught
himself Greek at an advanced age in order
to read his New Testament in the original.
A fervent and convinced Methodist from
youth, he was a lifelong local preacher. His
sermons, like his speeches, were famous and
remembered for years by his hearers. They
were framed and composed with admirable
clarity and lapped round and incensed
with that rich Devon speech which he
never lost and which nobody in the west
country will ever forget. Fortunately for
posterity there exists in the archives of
the public library service in Plymouth the
tape-recording of three broadcast talks
Foot gave in 1951 about the west country
of his youth. In 1940 he broadcast about
Drake's Drum; and on the escape of the
Amethyst down the Yangtse, Foot was
the inevitable choice to put the event on
record. Of his oratorical gifts, his son
Hugh says in his book, *A Start in Freedom*,
that 'He was the finest speaker and
preacher I have ever heard.'

One of Oliver Cromwell's greatest disciples in this century, Isaac Foot was
president of the Cromwell Association for
many years until his death. Cromwell and
Lincoln were his great sources of inspiration. The Methodist Church made Foot its
vice-president in 1937–8, and the Liberal
Party its president in 1947. He held many
other presidencies in many different movements. Each office became charged with
further meaning and purpose by his
tenure, as all his successors have acknowledged. In 1959 he was given the honorary
degree of D.Litt. by Exeter University.

In 1945 Foot was appointed deputy
chairman of Cornwall quarter-sessions,
and in 1953 he was appointed chairman,
serving until 1955. The appointment of
a solicitor as chairman of such sessions is
very rare.

When Foot came to die at Callington,
13 December 1960, at the age of eighty his
powers had hardly begun to fade. In the
west country the Foot name has a magic
about it which is easily understood by
his countrymen but difficult to describe.
Isaac Foot was the last of the great
orators, and Lord Samuel said of him:
'He was a natural orator, drawing fresh
aspiration from Milton and Cromwell,
and many of his speeches in Parliament
and in his own county touched rare
heights of eloquence.' The *Western Morning News*, itself an old antagonist of Isaac
Foot, said of him: 'Each of his major
characteristics would have made a man

outstanding in his time. All of them
together combined to earn the respect or
even veneration of millions of many
nations.' This was a reference to his work
for India as a member of the Round Table
conference and the joint select committee
which earned for him the title of 'The
member for the Depressed Classes'.

Foot was survived by his second wife,
Catherine Elizabeth Taylor, whom he
married in 1951, and by his seven
children.

[Private information; personal knowledge.]
STANLEY GOODMAN.

FORBES, SIR CHARLES MORTON
(1880–1960), admiral of the fleet, was born
at Colombo 22 November 1880, the second
son of James Forbes, broker, and his wife,
Caroline Delmege. Educated at Dollar
Academy and Eastman's, Southsea, he
joined the Royal Navy as a cadet in the
Britannia in 1894. On passing out two years
later he obtained five first class certificates
and gained twelve months' seniority.
After serving in the flagships of the
Channel and Pacific fleets he was promoted lieutenant in 1901 and in the following year became a specialist in gunnery.
For the next eleven years he served as
gunnery officer in various cruisers and
battleships, and at the gunnery schools,
until his promotion to commander in 1912,
at which time he was serving as first
lieutenant and gunnery officer of the
battleship *Superb* in the Home Fleet.

Soon after the outbreak of war in 1914
Forbes was appointed to the newly commissioned battleship *Queen Elizabeth*
which bombarded the Gallipoli forts in the
initial attack on the Dardanelles in 1915.
Later in the same year he joined the staff
of Sir John (later Earl) Jellicoe [q.v.],
commander-in-chief of the Grand Fleet,
as flag commander in the *Iron Duke*. He
was present at the battle of Jutland and
was appointed to the D.S.O. After Sir
David (later Earl) Beatty [q.v.] succeeded
to the command of the fleet in 1916
Forbes was appointed to the staff of the
second-in-command, Sir Charles Madden
[q.v.], where he continued in the same
duties until his promotion to captain in
1917. He was then appointed to the command of the cruiser *Galatea*, in which he
was present at the surrender of the German High Seas Fleet in November 1918.
He thus served afloat throughout the
whole war and shortly before its end he
was awarded the Russian Order of St.
Stanislaus.

Thereafter, Forbes's Service life alternated between appointments at the Admiralty and Naval Staff College and in one of the two main fleets—Home or Mediterranean. His first Admiralty appointment was as naval member of the Ordnance Committee in 1919, to which duty he returned in 1925–8 as director of naval ordnance. On the staff side, he was deputy director of the Naval Staff College at Greenwich from 1921 to 1923. The remainder of his service in the rank of captain was spent in sea-going appointments, first as flag captain to the commander-in-chief, Atlantic Fleet, Sir John De Robeck [q.v.], in the *Queen Elizabeth*, and secondly as flag captain to the second-in-command, Mediterranean Fleet, (Sir) H. D. R. Watson, in the *Iron Duke*.

Forbes was promoted rear-admiral in 1928 and in 1930–31 commanded the destroyer flotillas of the Mediterranean Fleet. He then returned to the Admiralty as third sea lord and controller—an appointment generally recognized as one calling for exceptional qualities of technical knowledge and ability in committee. He was promoted vice-admiral in 1933.

In 1934 Forbes was again appointed to the Mediterranean, as vice-admiral commanding the first battle squadron, and second-in-command, Mediterranean Fleet; it was during this period of his service that the Abyssinian crisis occurred and a period of such strained relations with Italy that in preparation for hostilities the fleet transferred from Malta to Alexandria. In 1935 Forbes was appointed K.C.B. and in 1936 promoted admiral.

In April 1938 he was appointed commander-in-chief, Home Fleet, with his flag in *Nelson*, at a time of increasing international tension culminating in the outbreak of war in September 1939. The fleet was ready but the bases were not, and Forbes had the anxiety and responsibility of maintaining constant vigil and readiness for action with bases lacking anti-aircraft defence or anti-submarine protection. Their vulnerability was quickly demonstrated by a German air attack on Rosyth on 16 October, the sinking of the *Royal Oak* by a U-boat which penetrated Scapa Flow on 14 October, and the damage sustained by the flagship *Nelson* herself in December from a mine laid by a U-boat in Loch Ewe. Nevertheless, under Forbes's capable command, the fleet carried out its duty successfully during those testing months of 1939 and 1940 when the full effects of mass air power in

modern war were being learnt the har way. Opportunities for offensive actio were few, but they came with the Germa invasion of Norway in April 1940, ar with it the successful destroyer battles Narvik. But this campaign also include the ill-fated military expedition for tl defence of Norway, which started too la to be effective, and after only two mont! had to be withdrawn, after considerab loss. During these operations, Forbes temporary flagship, *Rodney*, was damage by air attack. The fleet suffered a numb of losses, the principal ones being the ai craft carrier *Glorious* and nine destroyer the German losses and damage were ver much greater. It was this fact whic rightly convinced Forbes that they wou not attempt a seaborne invasion England that year in the face of the ove whelming superiority of the Britis Fleet and the failure of the German a force to defeat the R.A.F.

In December 1940, seven months aft being promoted admiral of the fleet an G.C.B., Forbes was succeeded in the con mand of the Home Fleet by Sir John (lat Lord) Tovey, and in May 1941 he wa appointed commander-in-chief, Plymoutl which the enemy was then making a ta get for most savage air attacks. Neverth less, the operational work of the comman was prosecuted with vigour by the cruiser light forces, and coastal craft und Forbes's orders. Chief among these wei the many successful attacks in co-opera tion with Coastal Command on U-boa leaving and returning to their base Brest; the interception of enemy arme merchant vessel raiders trying to get bac to Germany; and raids on the enem destroyers and shipping passing along tl French coast. The gallant and successf attack on St. Nazaire was also mounted

During the final months of his con mand preparation for the reception an disposition of the American naval an military forces who would take part in tl invasion of France in 1944 was well a vanced, but Forbes's period of comman terminated before their arrival. His fla was hauled down for the last time 2 August 1943.

An officer of great experience of tl world and of men, Forbes was a maste of his profession and had the very gre: faculty of recognizing instantly all tl factors in any problem with which he w: faced, and in grappling competently wit all difficulties. No man ever saw hi rattled: he had full confidence in himse and he inspired it in those under him. His reserves of power, clear vision, sound judgement, and strong sense of proportion were a tower of strength to those who, working under him, shared his burdens though not his responsibilities. Modest and unassuming in demeanour, and with an attractive, dry sense of humour, he never feared to speak his mind, even though in conflict with the views of his superiors.

In his younger days he was fond of horses and hunting. He was also a keen golfer and played on several occasions in the 'Admirals v. Generals' match. He was most generous in his hospitality, and never failed to impress by the courtly grace and charm with which he habitually welcomed his guests.

After relinquishing his last appointment he returned to live at his home, Cawsand Place, Wentworth, Surrey. From 1946 until shortly before his death Forbes was a member of the councils of the Association of Retired Naval Officers and the National Association for the Employment of Regular Sailors, Soldiers, and Airmen, in whose work he was keenly interested. He died in London 28 August 1960.

He was twice married: first, in 1909, to Agnes Millicent (died 1915), younger daughter of J. A. Ewen, J.P., of Potters Bar, by whom he had one daughter and one son; and secondly, in 1921, to Marie Louise, daughter of Axel Berndtson, of Stockholm, by whom he had one daughter.

His portrait, by Sir Oswald Birley, is in the Greenwich Collection.

[*The Times*, 30 August 1960; private information; personal knowledge.]
CLIFFORD CASLON.

FOSS, HUBERT JAMES (1899–1953), musician and writer, was born at Croydon, Surrey, 2 May 1899, the thirteenth and youngest child of Frederick Foss, solicitor, mayor of Croydon (1892–3), and his wife, Anne Penny Bartrum. His grandfather was Edward Foss [q.v.]. An uncle, H. J. Foss, was bishop of Osaka, Japan; a first cousin was Brigadier C. C. Foss, V.C. (1885–1953). As a child Hubert Foss learnt to read exceptionally quickly and had a great feeling for words. Music attracted him intensely and obviously he possessed unusual talent. Soon he was put under Stanley Roper, sometime organist at the Chapel Royal, St. James's, who, impressed by his natural aptitudes and already marked talent for composition, undertook his musical education. This

influence ripened into a friendship which lasted until his death.

His father having died when the boy was nine, his mother sent him to St. Anselm's School, Croydon. From there he won a senior classical foundation scholarship to Bradfield College, where he remained until 1917, leaving with a Stevens senior classical scholarship. At Bradfield, F. H. Shera and B. Luard Selby exercised a beneficent and widening influence on Foss, who contributed much to the musical life of the school.

He then served in the 5th Middlesex Regiment as a second lieutenant and was discharged early in 1919. Later that year he took a post in a preparatory school, leaving to become assistant editor of *Land and Water*, whilst also contributing music and art criticism to many prominent journals.

In 1921 he joined the Oxford University Press as senior assistant to the educational manager in London. There his intense interest in music soon made itself evident. With youthful drive and vision Foss envisaged a new music department organized on music trade lines, as distinct from the book trade. This project was favourably received by (Sir) Humphrey Milford [q.v.], who appointed Foss its head and musical editor. Thus, at the age of twenty-five Foss began what was probably the most notable achievement of a brilliant but short life. Within a few years the Oxford University Press music department reached a world status second to none.

To the task of building up an international catalogue of music and books on music he brought an almost infallible instinct for what was vital and genuine in the work of young composers and writers. He published the first important works of (Sir) William Walton, from the famous *Façade* (1922) and *Belshazzar's Feast* (1931) to the later works. He also launched Constant Lambert [q.v.] whose vivid *The Rio Grande* achieved immediate success. Amongst other young composers Peter Warlock, E. J. Moeran [qq.v.], van Dieren, Rubbra, Rawsthorne, Britten, and John Gardner mostly owed their real start to Foss. The more established composers: Holst, Ethel Smythe [qq.v.], Ireland, Dyson, were glad to appear in the Oxford list. Above all Ralph Vaughan Williams [q.v.] became identified with the new department, and from 1925 onward many important works of his were issued under Foss's editorship.

A flow of important books on music was a natural development—amongst them the *Oxford Companion to Music* (1938) of Percy Scholes [q.v.]. And it was owing solely to Foss's patience and pertinacity that there appeared in permanent form as *Essays in Musical Analysis* (6 vols., 1935–9), the fruits of the encyclopedic learning of Sir Donald Tovey (whose notice, among others, Foss contributed to this Dictionary).

Towards the end of 1941, for personal reasons Foss felt impelled to resign his work, and when it was announced Vaughan Williams wrote: 'I did not know how much I counted on you. I know that I owe any success I have had more to you (except H. P. Allen) than to anyone else.' From 1942 a new phase began as freelance musician, author, and broadcaster. During the war he lectured for C.E.M.A. and for a period was music adviser to Eastern Command E.N.S.A. He was also an excellent and sympathetic broadcaster, and spoke on a wide variety of subjects on both the Home and Overseas services. In addition he wrote many excellent programme notes for the promenade concerts and others. As author and critic by *Music In My Time* (1933) he made his mark, and later came *Ralph Vaughan Williams—A Study* (1950). In 1947 he edited *The Music Lover* and in 1952 reissued Warlock's book of 1923 on Delius with additional valuable chapters from his own pen.

His early 'Seven Poems by Thomas Hardy' (1925) for baritone solo and male voice choir had revealed him as a sensitive composer, and much important music followed. And his acknowledged expertise as typographer and printer led to the founding of the Double Crown Club in conjunction with Oliver Simon [q.v.]. Thus he contributed notably to almost every form of musical and literary activity, and achieved in his fifty-four years more than many enjoying a far longer life.

Early in 1952 he underwent a major operation but continued his work for another year. Then his appointment as editor of the *Musical Times* was announced. But he did not live to take up this post for he died unexpectedly in London 27 May 1953.

Foss talked well, had a rare sense of humour, and could be an entertaining mimic. Certainly he had a genius for friendship, his friends coming from every walk of life, and he was loyal, generous, and considerate to them all. His humility in face of criticism and his ready acceptance of it ended by making his critics admire the totality of the man.

In 1920 Foss married Kate Frances, daughter of Charles Carter Page, seed merchant; there were two daughters. The marriage was dissolved. His second marriage in 1927 was to a gifted singer Dora Maria, daughter of Alfred Stevens, managing director; they had a son and a daughter.

[Private information; personal knowledge.]
NORMAN PETERKIN.

FOX, DAME EVELYN EMILY MARIAN (1874–1955), pioneer worker in the field of mental health, was born at Morges, Switzerland, 15 August 1874. She was one of four children, of whom two died in childhood, born to Richard Edward Fox, of Fox Hall, Edgeworthstown, county Longford (and related to Charles James Fox and Maria Edgeworth, qq.vv.), by his wife, Emily, daughter of Lieutenant-Colonel William Godley, H.E.I.C.S. After her father's death in 1885 Evelyn and her elder sister Adeline were brought up by their mother in Ireland and England and educated at the high school in Morges. At Somerville College, Oxford, she took second class honours in modern history in 1898. It was not until she was thirty-two that she decided to devote herself to the cause of the mentally handicapped. In the intervening years she qualified for her future career by training at the Women's University Settlement in Southwark and by undertaking work which brought her into personal touch with mentally defective children and their families.

In 1908 the royal commission on the care and control of the feebleminded issued a report which resulted in the Mental Deficiency Act of 1913. Evidence had been pouring in touching on the medical, social, educational, economic, eugenic and legal aspects. Public opinion had been roused and the time was ripe for action. Evelyn Fox was quick to realize the extent of the work which lay ahead. A voluntary co-ordinating body appeared to be the first need, to stimulate effort and to prepare the way, in co-operation with the new statutory authorities, for the implementation of the Act. The Central Association for the Mentally Defective was accordingly founded in 1913 under the chairmanship of (Sir) Leslie Scott [q.v.] with Evelyn Fox its honorary secretary and its material assets a borrowed typewriter and the promise of ten pounds. In response to widening demands and under her direct inspiration, the scope of the work grew rapidly and in 1922 the name of the Association was changed to the Central Association for Mental Welfare, later again (1946) in its turn to extend and, in amalgamation with other bodies, to form the National Association for Mental Health. By 1951 when Evelyn Fox retired the Association, as its title implied, had attained a national status, covering the whole field, administering some £100,000 yearly and employing a numerous paid staff including a medical director and a general secretary.

During these years of expansion Evelyn Fox was the guiding spirit. The uphill struggle, with set-backs including two world wars, called forth her fighting qualities; many pioneer schemes then initiated have since become an integral part of the national health services, for example community care, occupation centres, voluntary associations, and training courses for professional mental health workers. Although her work centred round the Association's London office, she had occasion to travel to all parts of the country, forming personal contacts and initiating local schemes. She took an active part also in wider movements of mental health; she became honorary secretary of the Child Guidance Council when it was first formed in England with the help of the Commonwealth Fund of America in 1927; she served on the Wood committee on mental deficiency which reported in 1929; and on the London County Council mental hospitals' committee from 1914 to 1924; she gave evidence before royal commissions and read papers at many conferences at home and abroad. In recognition of her services she was appointed C.B.E. in 1937 and D.B.E. in 1947.

Evelyn Fox's home life was full of human ties and many interests: art, music, books, young people, the garden, and her dog. She remained always a country woman at heart, facing a long daily journey to London from Aldbourne near Marlborough for the sake of the downs she loved. In 1945 she and her sister moved to Laughton in Sussex, accompanied by friends who looked after both sisters until they died. In appearance Evelyn Fox was short, round-faced, with rough, curly hair, white in later life. Her voice was strident, the result perhaps of her own and her sister's deafness. Her downright manner was tempered by the merriment and devilment in her eyes. She had a fundamental concern for humanity, clearness of vision and directness of aim, ceaseless and resilient energy, thoroughness, hatred of shams and sloppiness, and a very practical administrative ability. She died at her Sussex home 1 June 1955. A pastel portrait, executed by James Grant after her death, hangs in the council room of the National Association for Mental Health at 39 Queen Anne Street, London, W. 1.

[*Burke's Landed Gentry of Ireland*, 1912; private information; personal knowledge.]

RUTH REES THOMAS.

FOX-STRANGWAYS, GILES STEPHEN HOLLAND, sixth EARL OF ILCHESTER (1874–1959), landowner and historian, was born 31 May 1874 at his father's town house in Belgrave Square. The elder son of the fifth earl and his wife, Mary Eleanor Anne, daughter of the first Earl of Dartrey, he was descended from Stephen Fox, first Earl of Ilchester (1704–76), who added the name of Strangways and whose younger brother, Henry, first Baron Holland [q.v.], was the father of the statesman Charles James Fox [q.v.]. As a boy, the heir to considerable estates in the west country and to Holland House, Kensington, he combined personal charm, aristocratic bearing, and an addiction to outdoor activities with a wilfulness which prevented him from distinguishing himself in his studies at Eton and led to his leaving Christ Church, Oxford, without proceeding to a degree. His latent scholarly instincts came into play only after brief service as an officer in the Coldstream Guards, service which he resumed, as a king's messenger, in the war of 1914–18. He was awarded the Legion of Honour in 1918 and appointed O.B.E. in 1919. Meanwhile he had succeeded to the earldom in 1905.

The greater part of Ilchester's middle life, except during the war, was devoted to the management of his estates at Melbury and Abbotsbury, in Dorset, to breeding racehorses (he was a pillar of the Jockey Club) and other country pursuits, and to the study of the history of his family. The last of these interests culminated in the publication in 1937 of his two most important works, *The Home of the Hollands, 1605–1820* and *Chronicles of Holland House, 1820–1900*. Holland House, so named after Henry Rich, the weathercock first Earl of Holland and Baron Kensington [q.v.], had been acquired by

Henry Fox in the mid-eighteenth century and for a hundred years was a political, social, and literary focus of the Whig aristocracy. Ilchester's narrative of its fortunes, derived from extensive family archives, is in some measure also a narrative of those of the Whigs. With its fifty-four acres of park, Holland House was the last of the great country estates in London. The building was in large part destroyed in an air raid in 1940, but its valuable collection of documents, pictures, and *objets d'art* had been removed to safety. In 1951 the estate passed from the possession of the Fox family into that of the London County Council.

The other books written or edited by Lord Ilchester, the first two over his courtesy title of Baron Stavordale, were all also based on Holland House papers. They were (i) in collaboration with his mother, *The Life and Letters of Lady Sarah Lennox* (2 vols., 1901); (ii) *Further Memoirs of the Whig Party* by the third Lord Holland (1905); (iii) Elizabeth Lady Holland's *Journal* (2 vols., 1908) and her *Spanish Journal* (1910); (iv) *Letters to Henry Fox, Lord Holland* (Roxburghe Club, 1915); (v) *Henry Fox, first Lord Holland, his family and relations* (2 vols., 1920); (vi) *The Journal of Henry Edward Fox, fourth Lord Holland* (1923); (vii) in collaboration with Elizabeth Langford-Brooke, *Correspondence of Catherine the Great with Sir Charles Hanbury-Williams* and a life of Hanbury-Williams (1928); (viii) *Elizabeth Lady Holland to her Son* (1946); and (ix) *Lord Hervey and his Friends* (1950). Ilchester also did notable work for the Walpole Society on the notebooks of the eighteenth-century antiquary George Vertue [q.v.]. His distinction as an historian was recognized by his university with the conferment of an honorary doctorate of letters in 1949. He was promoted G.B.E. in 1950.

Only comparatively late in life did Ilchester become a public figure. He delayed his maiden speech in the House of Lords for more than a quarter of a century: speaking on behalf of the British Museum of which he had become a trustee in 1931, he moved for papers on the extermination of musk-rat and nutria. Most of his rare interventions in debates, all well informed and plainly argued, were inspired either by the museum or by the National Portrait Gallery (of which he was a trustee from 1922, chairman from 1940), or by bodies such as the British Field Sports Society: the subjects included the protection of wild birds (a matter of close concern to the owner of the swannery at Abbotsbury), the necessity for gin-traps ('I have lived all my life in a rabbit country'), and the pollution of the sea by waste oil. In his last speech in his eighty-fourth year he urged the appointment to the Portrait Gallery of elderly, rather than youthful, trustees.

Ilchester owed his position as a trustee of national institutions, and as chairman or president of the Royal Commission on Historical Monuments, Royal Literary Fund, London Library, Walpole Society, Roxburghe Club, and other bodies, in part to his unobtrusive scholarship, but also to integrity, assiduity, and tact. As a committeeman he could on occasion carry tenacity of principle to the point of obstinacy; but he earned the gratitude of the officers of the institutions over which he presided by the firmness with which he fought their battles, and he was noted for his courtesy to junior staff. The same courtesy, grave and somewhat aloof, marked his relations with his tenantry. He took an active interest in the local affairs of his county, of which he was a deputy-lieutenant, then vice-lieutenant. He is credited with having countered a move to grass over parts of the Cerne Giant with a proposal to form a society for the preservation of ancient erections. Over six-foot tall and of massive build, he was quiet in both movement and speech. Although reserved in manner in public, he was essentially clubbable and displayed an engaging frivolity among his chosen friends in the Society of Antiquaries.

He married in 1902 Helen Mary Theresa Vane-Tempest-Stewart (died 1956), daughter of the sixth Marquess of Londonderry [q.v.]. They had two sons and two daughters. He died in London 29 October 1959 and was succeeded by his elder son, Edward Henry Charles James (1905–64), who had lost both his sons during his father's lifetime. Ilchester's younger son died unmarried in 1961, and on the death of the elder the earldom passed to a cousin, Walter Angelo Fox-Strangways. A painting by Glyn Philpot and a drawing by Francis Dodd are in the possession of the family.

[*The Times*, 30 October and 3 and 16 November 1959; private information; personal knowledge.]   SIMON NOWELL-SMITH.

FRANKAU, GILBERT (1884–1952), novelist, was born 21 April 1884 in Gloucester Terrace, London, the eldest of three sons and one daughter of Arthur Frankau, a principal partner of the firm of J. Frankau & Co., wholesale cigar merchants, founded originally in 1837 to import leeches from France. His mother, Julia, daughter of Hyman Davis, wrote novels under the pen-name of 'Frank Danby' and achieved a considerable success as early as 1887 with *Dr. Phillips, a Maida Vale Idyll*; her best-known book was *Pigs in Clover* (1903). Her sister Mrs. Eliza Aria was also a writer and for many years contributed a weekly column to *Truth* entitled 'Mrs. A's diary'.

Frankau won a scholarship to Harrow, but did not take it, then another to Eton and went there, though not as a scholar. He took his first step towards becoming a writer while still a schoolboy when he launched and edited *The X* magazine, with Lord Turnour (later Earl Winterton) as his assistant editor. The magazine, too outspoken about the masters, was suppressed by the headmaster after only four numbers. Frankau immediately found a fresh outlet for his talent with a volume of satiric verse entitled *Eton Echoes* (1901).

He decided, however, to go into the family business and left school shortly afterwards to become a cigar merchant. He went to Hamburg to learn German. His aptitude for learning languages was remarkable; in time he had an equal fluency in French, Italian, and Spanish, then turned to learning Turkish. With concentrated application he quickly acquired a thorough knowledge of the cigar business and became managing director of the family firm at the age of twenty-one. His activities took him to Havana, then on a two-year world tour.

Writing was not altogether neglected. In 1912 he published *One of Us*, a novel in *ottava rima* as used by Byron in *Don Juan*, followed it up with a dramatic poem *Tid'apa* (1915) reprinted from the *English Review*, and two further books of poems—*The Guns* (1916) and *The City of Fear* 1917).

On the outbreak of war in 1914 he had joined up at once, was commissioned in the 9th battalion of the East Surrey Regiment in October, but transferred to the Royal Field Artillery five months later and served at Loos, Ypres, and the Somme. In October 1916 he was sent to Italy as a staff captain to undertake special duties to counter German propaganda against Britain. His activities involved a press and film campaign which he handled most effectively. But delayed symptoms of shell-shock led to his being invalided out of the army in February 1918. The family cigar business had already been disposed of and Frankau, with a wife and two daughters to provide for, decided to seek an income from writing. He embarked on his new career with the same concentration, zest, and efficiency which he had brought to the conduct of his business. Each book was planned with the utmost care, and regular hours were assigned to its writing. His study was his office and he would brook no interruption: no telephone calls were accepted, crises, no matter how grave and pressing, had to wait until he emerged. Strict routine now governed his whole life. Always something of an exhibitionist, he adopted an aristocratic air, engaged in hunting (although, as he admitted later, he was terrified of riding), joined the Cavalry Club where he played bridge, and took up fencing. Many found his arrogance insufferable, but he prided himself on being like the heroes in his books—dashing and tough: such was his outward pose, but to his more intimate friends he confessed that he was haunted by the doubt that underneath it all he was really a coward. Kindness he professed to regard as 'sloppy', but all through his life his deeds were far kinder than his words.

His first prose novel, *The Woman of the Horizon*, was published in 1917. With *Peter Jackson, Cigar Merchant* (1920) he attained both popular acclaim and prosperity. Doors instantly began to open: magazines begged for short stories, newspapers for articles; he was invited to make speeches at literary gatherings. Books now appeared with clockwork regularity: in 1921 *The Seeds of Enchantment*, in which he attacked indiscipline and proclaimed the superiority of the white above the black and yellow races; in 1922 *The Love-Story of Aliette Brunton* making a dramatic plea for divorce law reform. In 1924 his speeches took a political turn. His sympathies were with the extreme Right and one could not fail to discern the influence of Italian fascism.

A number of his novels were filmed, and in 1926, with the publication of *Masterson*, he undertook a long and strenuous tour of the United States, which he described vividly and entertainingly in *My Unsentimental Journey* (1926). An unhappy venture into journalism, his first since he was at Eton, came in 1928 when he launched and edited *Britannia*, a sixpenny weekly with a strongly emphasized imperialist note. It was not a success. The fees paid to contributors made even the recipients gasp. Advertisers held aloof and after ten issues Frankau returned to novel writing.

As a story-teller he had considerable talent. His narrative style was compelling, his characters often larger than life, his imagery inclined to be lavish; but, pains-taking in his research and meticulous in detail, he commanded a vast public both in Britain and in the United States. Of his later novels *Christopher Strong* (1932), *Three Englishmen* (1935), and *Son of Morning* (1949) may be singled out. His last book, considered by some as being among his best, was *Unborn Tomorrow* (1953), a vision of the future. Although aware that death was near, his iron resolve and self-discipline enabled him to finish it just before he died at his home at Hove 4 November 1952.

Frankau was thrice married: in 1905 to Dorothea Frances Markham, daughter of Charles Edward Drummond Black, by whom he had two daughters, one of whom, Pamela Frankau (died 1967), won fame as a novelist. The marriage ended in divorce and in 1922 Frankau married the actress Aimée, daughter of Robert de Burgh and formerly wife of Leon Quartermaine. This marriage also ended in divorce. In 1932 he married Susan Lorna, daughter of Walter Henry Harris. A portrait of Frankau by Flora Lion is in the possession of the family.

[*The Times*, 5 November 1952; Gilbert Frankau, *Self-Portrait*, 1939; Pamela Frankau, *Pen to Paper*, 1961; personal knowledge.]
R. J. MINNEY.

FREEDMAN, BARNETT (1901–1958), artist, was born in the east end of London 19 May 1901, the son of Jewish immigrants from Russia, Luis Friedman, journeyman tailor, and his wife, Reiza Ruk. Owing to persistent ill health, against which he fought intermittently throughout his life, the only formal education Freedman received was as a small child at an L.C.C. board school. From the age of nine until he was fourteen his time was spent in hospital where he read voraciously and also taught himself to draw and paint and play the violin. By the time he was fifteen his health had sufficiently improved to enable him to start work and for a short time he was an office boy. He then managed to secure employment as a draughtsman, first in the workshop of a monumental mason, then in an archi-tect's office. It was during this period that

he developed an interest in lettering which was to lead to his becoming one of the most distinguished letterers and typo-graphers of his era. For five years while he was thus employed he went to evening classes at St. Martin's School of Art. After three unsuccessful attempts to win an L.C.C. senior scholarship in art, he sought an interview with (Sir) William Rothenstein [q.v.], principal of the Royal College of Art, who was sufficiently im-pressed by the work Freedman showed him to use his influence in getting the L.C.C. to reconsider its decision, and in 1922 Freedman became a student at the Royal College.

He left the College in 1925 and spent the next few years in extreme poverty trying to earn his living as a painter, but with little success. Gradually, however his work became better known, largely through the private patronage of dis criminating collectors, and he began to expand his artistic activities, notably into the field of auto-lithography. Meanwhile he had returned to the Royal College as an instructor in still-life; a post he combined with teaching at the Ruskin School of Drawing at Oxford.

Although Freedman's ambition was to live by his painting, examples of which hang in numerous public collections, in cluding the Tate Gallery, the Victoria and Albert Museum, and the Fitzwilliam Museum at Cambridge, he was never quite as successful in this sphere as in that of commercial design, in which his output extended over a vast field of printed ephemera, ranging from cotton-reel label to the design for the silver jubilee postage stamp in 1935. Much of his best work wa in the form of book design and illustration and book jackets. Among the novels he illustrated with conspicuous success wer *War and Peace, Anna Karenina, Olive Twist, Jane Eyre,* and *Wuthering Heights.*

From 1941 to 1946 Freedman was an official war artist, first with the army in France, then with the Royal Navy in the battleship *Repulse,* on Arctic convoys t Russia, and in submarines. His painting of the beach at Arromanches on D-Day plus 20 (26 June 1944) and a number of other works, mainly water-colours, are in the Imperial War Museum.

Freedman's skill in lithography and hi immense knowledge of the craft did much to stimulate among other artists a revival of interest in this medium. He allowed n one but himself to put his designs on to the lithographic stone and personally super vised every move in the preparation of the designs for reproduction. It was this first-hand experience of the lithographic process which enabled him not only to perfect his technique, but to experiment with new forms and uses of lithography. Although his draughtsmanship was erratic, his skill and sensitivity as a craftsman were remarkable and it is upon these qualities rather than on his paintings that his reputation rests. His personality was that of a true original, showing marked independence of mind, coupled with a keen enjoyment of dialectic, eccentric humour, and a degree of intellectual curiosity and natural taste rarely found in someone emerging from such a background. It was one of the chief satisfactions of his life that he, a cockney from the east end, should have been elected in 1945 to membership of the Athenaeum Club. In 1946 he was appointed C.B.E. and in 1949 he received the Royal Society of Arts' highest award, that of a royal designer for industry.

In 1930 Freedman married Beatrice Claudia Guercio, a Sicilian, with whom he had been a student at the Royal College of Art. His portrait by Sir William Rothenstein is in the Tate Gallery. He died in London 4 January 1958, leaving one son.

[*The Times*, 6, 8, 9, 10, and 17 January 1958; Introduction by Sir Stephen Tallents to memorial exhibition at the Arts Council, 1958; Jonathan Mayne, *Barnett Freedman*, 1948; James Laver, 'Two Drawings' in *Signature*, March 1936; personal knowledge.]

NICOLAS BENTLEY.

FREEMAN, SIR WILFRID RHODES, first baronet (1888–1953), air chief marshal, was born in London 18 July 1888, the third son of William Robert Freeman, stone merchant, and his wife, Annie Farquharson Carr Dunn. Educated at Rugby and the Royal Military College, Sandhurst, he was gazetted to the Manchester Regiment in February 1908, in which he became captain and brevet-major. He learned to fly, privately, in France, and so was able in 1913 to obtain his licence as a pilot. In January 1914 he joined the Central Flying School and in April was transferred to the Royal Flying Corps to become one of the pioneers of military aviation.

On the outbreak of war in August 1914, Freeman proceeded to France with the first of the squadrons of the Royal Flying Corps to leave England: a pilot in No. 2 Squadron. Only a month later he barely

escaped capture by the Germans when his aircraft, a B.E.2, had to make a forced landing through structural failure behind the enemy positions. After two days of hiding and carefully working his way through what were later to become the front lines, he returned safely to his squadron. In this exploit alone he set an example right at the beginning of wartime flying which was to be followed by many thousands of other air crews.

Shortly afterwards Freeman became a flight commander in No. 2 Squadron, and for his flying during the battle of Neuve Chapelle in March 1915 he was awarded the M.C., one of the first of those awarded to the Royal Flying Corps. Even then he was showing a keen interest in the uses to which the air could be put in a more technical aspect than that of merely flying. His flight in No. 2 Squadron was equipped with some of the first of the wireless equipment used in the air on the western front. He was also beginning to make an impression on all those with whom he worked as a man who had a charm peculiarly his own. He was devoted to the new air service, and in it he found expression for the pointed and shrewd sense of humour for which he later became noted, a humour which could strike with vigour but which was never misused.

After a period as an instructor in England, Freeman was sent to the Middle East to command a squadron; but in December 1916 he returned to France and operations on the western front. As a lieutenant-colonel he was in command of the Tenth (Army) Wing during the battle of Arras in the early spring of 1917 and the third battle of Ypres later that year; and of the Ninth (H.Q.) Wing during the battle of Cambrai and the March retreat of 1918. At the end of the war in 1918 he was in command of No. 2 (Training) Group. He was appointed to the D.S.O. (1916), awarded the Legion of Honour, and thrice mentioned in dispatches. He was gazetted to the Royal Air Force on its formation on 1 April 1918 with the rank of lieutenant-colonel and was granted a permanent commission on 1 August 1919.

When the R.A.F. Staff College was established in 1922 Freeman was appointed an instructor with the rank of group captain, and later he became assistant commandant. In 1925–7 he was in command of the Central Flying School at Upavon, and in 1927 he became deputy director of operations and intelligence at the Air Ministry. In 1928–9 he was the commanding officer of the R.A.F. Training Base at Leuchars, after which he was chief staff officer, Inland Area (1929–30). In 1930 he went back to the Middle East as chief staff officer of the Iraq Command. For three years (1930–33) he was air officer commanding, Trans-Jordan and Palestine, after which he returned to England and from 1934 to 1936 was commandant of the R.A.F. Staff College.

In 1936 Freeman embarked upon what was to become the most successful period of his Service career, and during it he made a unique contribution to the history of the Royal Air Force and at the same time rendered the greatest service to his country. He became in that year, when the long-delayed expansion of the Royal Air Force finally got under way, the member of the Air Council responsible for research and development and from 1938 to 1940 for production. He was in office during the whole period when the Royal Air Force developed and brought into use radar and the eight-gun fighters which were to contribute so notably to the winning of the Battle of Britain. He was promoted to the rank of air chief marshal in 1940.

Of Freeman's contribution during those critical years, it was said by Marshal of the Royal Air Force Sir John Slessor that 'It was to him, more than any other man, that the nation and the R.A.F. owed the fact that the pilots of Fighter Command never ran short of those aircraft whose names—Hurricane and Spitfire—are now ... a part of British history ...'. From the manufacturers' point of view Lord Hives of Rolls-Royce recorded that 'It was the expansion which was carried out under Wilfrid's direction in 1937–9 which enabled the Battle of Britain to be won. Without that foresight and imagination, no efforts in 1940 would have yielded any results.'

In addition Freeman nursed along the early planning for the production of the four-engined bombers; and he was directly responsible for the acceptance by the Royal Air Force of the famous twin-engined Mosquito and the encouragement given to (Sir) Frank Whittle in the early stages of the production of his jet engine. Freeman was vice-chief of the air staff from 1940 to 1942, after which he retired from the Royal Air Force and became chief executive of the Ministry of Aircraft Production, in which office he served until the end of the war. Appointed C.B. in 1932, he was promoted K.C.B. in 1937 and

G.C.B. in 1942, and created a baronet in 1945. He was a fellow of the Royal Aeronautical Society.

To the public the name of Wilfrid Freeman was little known. Personal publicity he shunned like the plague. But in the annals of the Royal Air Force his name stands alongside those of Lord Trenchard [q.v.] and Lord Portal as one of the great men in British military aviation. He was a cultured, civilized man with a warm and human understanding leavened with a remarkably alert mind and an insistence upon quality in all endeavour.

He married in 1915 Gladys, daughter of John Mews, barrister, by whom he had a daughter and a son, John Keith Noel (born 1923), who succeeded his father. The marriage was dissolved and in 1935 Freeman married Elizabeth, daughter of Ernest Tatham Richmond, director of antiquities in Palestine (1927–37), by whom he had two daughters. He died in London 15 May 1953. A portrait by T. C. Dugdale is in the possession of the family.

[Private information; personal knowledge.]
DOUGLAS OF KIRTLESIDE.

FRENCH, EVANGELINE FRANCES (1869–1960), missionary, was born at Medea, Algeria, 27 May 1869; her younger sister FRANCESCA LAW FRENCH (1871–1960), missionary, was born at Bruges, Belgium, 12 December 1871. They were the daughters of first cousins, John Erington and Elizabeth French. Both girls were educated at the secondary school in Geneva. In 1893 after two years of training Evangeline French left for the mission field in China, where some years later, after the death of their mother, Francesca joined her. Henceforth their lives were inseparable from that of the third member of the trio, Mildred Cable, in whose notice in this volume will be found details of their joint career. Evangeline French died 8 July 1960 at Shaftesbury, Dorset, and Francesca French on 2 August 1960 in London. W. J. PLATT.

FRITSCH, FELIX EUGEN (1879–1954), algologist, was born 26 April 1879 in Camden Town, London, the second child of Ernst Theodor Hermann Fritsch, headmaster of a private school at 145 King Henry's Road, Hampstead, and his wife Josephine Guignon. He was educated at Warwick House School, Maida Vale, and graduated B.Sc. of London University in 1898. Immediately afterwards he went for health reasons to Munich where he became an assistant under Ludwig Radlkofer and obtained his D.Phil. (1899). He was much impressed by the change in outlook from the morphology and stelar anatomy dominating botanical thought in England to the awakening ecological and physiological interests on the Continent. Returning to this country in 1901 he worked for fifteen months in the Jodrell Laboratory at Kew where began an association with L. A. Boodle with whom he translated Solereder's *Systematic Anatomy of Dicotyledons* (1908). Towards the end of 1902 he was appointed to an assistant lectureship at University College, London, where F. W. Oliver and his assistant (Sir) A. G. Tansley [qq.v.] did much to further Fritsch's developing interest in ecology. As early as 1902 he began to publish on phytoplankton and periodicity problems which remained special interests in later years.

In 1905 Fritsch took up further lecturing work at Birkbeck College, obtained his London D.Sc., and began his long collaboration with Florence Rich. In 1906 he became assistant professor at University College and in the next year took charge also of the newly formed botany department at East London (later Queen Mary) College which he arduously equipped single-handed until 1911 when he obtained one assistant and gave up his work at University College.

The appointment of (Sir) Edward Salisbury as his assistant lecturer (1912–9) led to a collaboration which resulted in five widely used textbooks: *An Introduction to the Study of Plants* (1914), *Elementary Studies in Plant Life* (1915), *An Introduction to the Structure and Reproduction of Plants* (1920), *Botany for Medical Students* (1921), and *Plant Form and Function* (1928). In 1924 Fritsch received the title of university professor. In 1927 appeared his revised and rewritten edition of G. S. West's *Treatise of the British Freshwater Algae*. In the same year, as president of the botany section at the Leeds meeting of the British Association, he was first to emphasize the necessity for a British freshwater biological station. His vigorous campaign led to the formation of the Freshwater Biological Association (1929), of the council of which he was chairman until his death, and to the foundation of his greatest monument, the biological station at Wray Castle. He was elected F.R.S. in 1932, served on the council in 1938–9 and 1944–6, and received the Darwin medal in 1950. In 1932 he held a visit-

ing professorship to Stanford University, California; in 1938 he visited India and paid a second visit to Ceylon which he had first visited in 1903. The first volume of his monumental work *The Structure and Reproduction of the Algae* appeared in 1935; the second in 1945. On his retirement from his chair in 1948 he was elected a fellow of Queen Mary College and professor emeritus of the university, on the senate of which he served in 1944–8 and from which he received an honorary LL.D. in 1952.

Fritsch owed his enormous output, doubly astonishing in one of such small stature and frail constitution, to continuous industry applied with a perfectionist's sense of care and thoroughness and born of a conviction of the absolute value of knowledge and work. The complete clarity of his teaching arose also from perfect preparation and ponderously careful formulation. His personality was full of humour, lovable, genial, friendly, and unassuming and he gave its fruits liberally to all. In consequence of his genius for committee work and in particular for chairmanship much of his time was spent at meetings, where his grasp, sound judgement, fairness, unity of purpose, and perhaps above all his diplomacy were invaluable and unfailing.

Apart from walking and gardening, Fritsch's main recreation was music. His father a singer, his wife a pianist, his son a cellist, he was himself a violinist and experienced ensemble player; musical week-ends were a regular feature at his homes near Dorking before the outbreak of war in 1939. Thereafter he lived in Cambridge where after his retirement, as during the war years, he was given facilities for his work at the Botany School where he had initiated the national type culture collection of algae and protozoa. Here and on numerous committees in London and elsewhere he remained active and even contemplating further books and advanced lectures right up to his last illness. He was president of the Linnean Society in 1949–52, and of the International Association of Limnology and the Institute of Biology in 1953. In 1954 he was awarded the Linnean gold medal but died at his home in Cambridge 23 May, the day before the medal was to have been presented.

In 1905 he married Hedwig, daughter of Max Lasker, a German business man, and had one son.

A portrait by F. M. Haines is in the

possession of the botany department at Queen Mary College.

[Private information; personal knowledge.]
F. MERLIN HAINES.

FRY, CHARLES BURGESS (1872–1956), sportsman, was born at Croydon, Surrey, 25 April 1872, the eldest child of Lewis John Fry, a civil servant who became clerk of accounts at New Scotland Yard, and his wife, Constance Isabella White. He entered Repton School as an exhibitioner in September 1885 and in his six years there his remarkable endowment of body, mind, and personality dominated his generation. He was four years in the cricket eleven, being captain in his last two; he also captained the school in his third year in the football team, and twice won the individual athletic prize. Before he left Repton he had been selected to play for the Casuals in the F.A. Cup and in the August after leaving school in 1891 he played one match for Surrey. Yet there was never any question of games monopolizing his interest; he enjoyed the classics, worked hard, and had his reward in being placed first on the scholarship roll at Wadham College, Oxford, in December 1890, senior to F. E. Smith (later the Earl of Birkenhead, q.v.). At Oxford he more than fulfilled the promise of his Repton days; few men can more quickly or decisively have established themselves as an outstanding figure in university life. In his first term he won his blue for association football, and that winter gained a full international cap for England against a touring side from Canada. In April 1892 he won the long jump against Cambridge with 23 feet 5 inches, an English amateur record. Two centuries in trial games and another against Somerset secured him his third blue as a freshman.

For three more years he represented Oxford at cricket, football, and athletics, and was captain of all three in 1894 when he made a century against Cambridge. In 1893 he finished equal first in the hundred yards and won the long jump against Cambridge; earlier in the month he had tied the world's record long jump of C. S. Reber of America with 23 feet 6½ inches. In association football he continued for some years to be an automatic choice for the great Corinthian sides of that period and in 1901 he won another full international cap against Ireland. A year later he achieved the astonishing double of playing for Southampton in the final of the F.A. Cup on a Saturday and making

82 for London County against Surrey a the Oval on the following Monday. Onl an injury in the last trial fixture had pr vented him from gaining a fourth blue a a wing three-quarter in rugby football.

After obtaining a first class in classic honour moderations (1893) and a fourt class in *literae humaniores* (1895), Fry wa for a time (1896–8) on the staff at Charte house School. But he soon found in spor ing journalism a field in which he coul enjoy writing and at the same time hav more leisure to play first-class cricket. H first played for Sussex in 1894 but it wa not until he left Charterhouse that he wa able to play throughout the summe when he at once established himself a one of the most resolute and effecti batsmen in the country. In 1899 he wa picked to open the innings for Englan against the Australians at Nottingha two years later he had his greatest seaso with the bat, scoring 3,147 runs with a average of 78 and making 13 centuries, of them in succession. In four other yea he headed the English batting average the last time in 1912, when he was playin for Hampshire, to which county he ha migrated in 1909. His aggregate in firs class cricket was 30,886 runs with a average of over 50, and he made in a 94 centuries. Of these, two were in te matches: 144 against the Australians 1905; and 129 on a difficult, turnin wicket against the great South Africa googly bowlers in 1907. Perhaps the mo memorable of all his innings was his 23 not out, when in a wonderful partnershi with A. C. MacLaren [q.v.] he rescued t Gentlemen from an apparently hopele position against the Players at Lord's 1903. In 1912 he captained the Engli team which defeated both Austral and South Africa in the only triangul tournament which has ever been playe Even as late as 1921, when in his fiftie year, he was playing so well in occasion matches for Hampshire as to be invite again to represent England again Australia; but an injury to a finger pr vented his accepting. Nor was he ever ab to visit Australia as a cricketer.

In his school and university days F appeared a batsman of studied, eve slightly laboured, technique, althoug noteworthy already for his mastery back-play, rare among amateurs of th generation. By the turn of the centu he had reinforced his always vigilant a resourceful defence by an increasing repe toire of strokes, above all of the driv and had become a player of commanding personality and stature. The certainty of his driving, especially past or over the bowler and mid-on, was only equalled by its power; his concentration never relaxed, his physical stamina never weakened. He played always and rigorously within self-imposed limitations but these were wide enough to dominate or at least to defy the best of a great generation of bowlers. His great friend and partner in so many Sussex triumphs, Prince Ranjitsinhji [q.v.], gave it as his considered opinion that on all wickets he was the greatest batsman of his time. Certainly no better mind has ever or more assiduously applied itself to the game, and his studies of its technique in *Great Batsmen* (with George W. Beldam, 1905), *Great Bowlers and Fielders* (with George W. Beldam, 1906), and *Batsmanship* (1912) are still unrivalled in authoritative analysis. A fine out-fielder, he was in the nineties a good enough bowler to take wickets for the Gentlemen, although his action at times came under suspicion, and indeed censure. As a captain, he knew his own mind, was a shrewd tactician, and never left any doubt who was in command.

Fry was very much more than an exceptionally gifted all-round athlete. He was a great personality in his own right: handsome in an Olympian mould, with a well-stocked, active, and original mind, and the instinctive authority in any company of one who always knew where he was going and why it was worth while to go there. In all that he wrote, whether as a sporting journalist in the daily press, as athletic editor of the boys' monthly magazine the *Captain*, or in a wider field as editor and director of *Fry's Magazine*, the freshness of his approach and his lively style challenged attention.

In 1920 Fry went with Ranjitsinhji as a substitute delegate on the Indian delegation to the League of Nations at Geneva, and he later spent some months as a member of the prince's secretariat at Nawanagar. In 1928 he was in India again as assistant to Sir Leslie Scott [q.v.] who had been briefed for the Indian princes to prepare their case before the statutory commission. In the meantime he had stood three times (1921–4) without success as a Liberal candidate for Parliament. It was, however, as the director (1908–0) of the training-ship *Mercury* on the Hamble river that he found the central interest of his life and made his greatest contribution to the lives of others. There,

with the able and tireless help of his wife, he devoted himself to turning out generation after generation of boys destined for the Royal and Merchant navies; in recognition of this service he was made an honorary captain in the Royal Naval Reserve. His autobiography, *Life Worth Living* (1939), vividly reflects not only his own outlook on life and the values for which he stood, but assesses with authority the personalities and standards of the contemporary athletic world.

In 1898 Fry married Beatrice Holme (died 1946), daughter of Arthur Sumner; they had one son and two daughters. Fry died in London 7 September 1956. A lithograph by (Sir) William Rothenstein was reproduced in *Oxford Characters* (1896).

[C. B. Fry, *Life Worth Living*, 1939; *Wisden's Cricketers' Almanack*, 1957; A. Wallis Myers, *C. B. Fry*, 1912; Sir C. M. Bowra, *Memories*, 1966; private information; personal knowledge.]   H. S. Altham.

FRY, SARA MARGERY (1874–1958), reformer, eighth child and sixth daughter of (Sir) Edward Fry [q.v.] and his wife, Mariabella, daughter of John Hodgkin [q.v.], was born at Highgate 11 March 1874. Educated at home until she was seventeen, she then spent a year at Miss Lawrence's boarding school (later Roedean) at Brighton. In 1892 Fry retired from the bench and the family moved to Failand in Somerset. Encouraged by her brother, Roger Fry [q.v.], Margery hoped initially to go to Newnham, but her Quaker parents regarded Cambridge with suspicion as a breeding-ground of agnostics. (So, though she later came to accept an agnostic position, she reached it by another route.) Eventually she succeeded in obtaining permission to sit the entrance examination for Somerville College, Oxford, and went up to read mathematics in 1894, staying until 1897, but taking no examinations. Somerville friendships, with Eleanor Rathbone [q.v.] and Dorothea Scott among others, remained important through her life. For the next eighteen months she returned to the duties of a daughter at home. The opportunity for an active and independent life came with the unexpected offer of the librarianship at Somerville. There she spent five years from 1899, combining the development and re-housing of the college library with that understanding concern for the young and their problems which remained one of her outstanding qualities.

Her next post gave her scope to extend this interest in a new setting. Birmingham University had been granted its charter in 1900, and in 1904 she was appointed to the wardenship of a hall of residence for women students in Hagley Road, Edgbaston. Her functions were 'the superintendence of housekeeping and the maintenance of discipline': the latter she interpreted with her customary liberalism, reducing rules to a minimum and allowing students to invite their men friends to dances. In 1908 the hostel moved into new quarters at University House, for which she had worked hard, and where she used all the resources available to her—pictures, furnishings, music, play-acting, wit, and friendship—to create a living community. On the initiative of Charles Beale, the vice-chancellor, she was made a member of the university council. During this period the range of causes in which she was interested, and of committees on which she served, became increasingly wide—the Staffordshire education committee, the county insurance committee (set up under the National Insurance Act), the county sub-committee on mental deficiency. Practical experience of the problems of social reform sharpened her tendency towards radicalism. 'Brummagem', she wrote, 'is making a first-rate democrat of me.' Shortly before the outbreak of war in 1914 she became financially independent through a legacy from her uncle, Joseph Storrs Fry [q.v.], and in the summer of 1914 she resigned her post. Her Quaker background and conscience combined with her experience of social work made it natural that early in the war she should be drawn, with her younger sister Ruth, into work with the Friends' War Victims Relief Committee, first in the Marne and Meuse area, later in the whole of France. From early 1915 until the end of 1917 she remained based on Sermaize, with periodic journeys to other parts of France, dealing with the whole range of problems of those whose lives had been disrupted by the war, from the reconstruction of agriculture to the teaching of embroidery.

Back in England in 1918 Margery Fry was in some uncertainty where her next work should lie, although with a sense of continuing commitment to education in the widest sense. Three events particularly determined the subsequent direction of her life and activities. At the beginning of 1919 she moved to London and set up house at 7 Dalmeny Avenue, overlooking Holloway Prison, with her brother Roger and his children. She thus became more deeply involved in his world, his relationships with artists and writers in particular. In May 1919 she was invited to become a member of the newly established University Grants Committee, on which she continued to serve until 1948, devoting much of her time and energies to visiting universities and gaining first-hand knowledge of their problems. At the end of 1918 she had been persuaded by Stephen and Rosa Hobhouse to accept the secretaryship of the Penal Reform League which in 1921 amalgamated with the Howard Association to form the Howard League for Penal Reform, housed at this period in the Frys' front sitting-room. From then on the Howard League, which she served as secretary until 1926 and later as chairman and vice-chairman, remained the most important focus of her work. Her understanding of the problems of penal reform was increased by her appointment in 1921 as one of the first women magistrates and in 1922 as the first education adviser to Holloway. In her efforts to improve prison conditions one of the many developments which she initiated was to bring Marion Richardson in to teach painting to young prisoners. In practice her two main preoccupations became closely related: visits to universities were combined with visits to prisons; it was sometimes difficult to remember, she once remarked, whether students were in for crimes or prisoners in for examinations.

In 1926, on the retirement of (Dame) Emily Penrose [q.v.], Margery Fry somewhat reluctantly accepted the principalship of Somerville. In spite of her strong continuing affection for the college, on whose council she had served since 1904 she was genuinely doubtful about her suitability, as a 'non-academic' woman for the post and the limitations on her independence which it would involve. But though finding Oxford in many ways uncongenial and obscurantist, she enjoyed this new opportunity for exercising her remarkable talent for understanding, and unobtrusively advising, the young and opening their minds to her whole wide range of interests, from penal reform to birdwatching. Although never deeply involved in university politics, she made occasional notable incursions which left their mark, as when in 1927 she spoke in Congregation with Cyril Bailey [q.v.] in an unsuccessful effort to resist the imposition of a *numerus clausus* on the women' colleges. Students who came in contact with her were especially impressed by the fact that 'she knew so much about wickedness, and yet could make one believe and work for happy and rational solutions of the most tangled moral and political problems'. She continued to work on these problems—as a member of the Street Offences Committee (concerned with prostitution and soliciting, but doomed by its composition) and the Young Offenders' Committee through which she tried to secure an adequate probation service and to get probation extended to cover a much wider range of offences. But above all she was deeply involved, in association with Roy Calvert, D. N. Pritt, and others, in the campaign for the abolition of capital punishment, presenting evidence on behalf of the Howard League to the abortive select committee set up by J. R. Clynes [q.v.] as home secretary in 1929.

Margery Fry had never intended to spend more than about five years at Somerville. Soon after her retirement in 1931 she established a new base in London, at 48 Clarendon Road, Holland Park, 'absolutely on the borderline of slum and respectability', and filled it with paintings and objects of beauty collected over the years. For the remainder of her life this was her home, and a home for the homeless and wanderers of many countries, as well as a meeting-place for radicals and reformers with different interests and shades of opinion. In the thirties the worsening world situation and her own growing international reputation involved her in a new range of activities, supplementing but not displacing the old. In 1933, shortly after the Japanese invasion of Manchuria, the Universities China Committee invited her to make a lecture tour of Chinese universities. Her interest in the great transformations taking place in Chinese society, as well as in its ancient civilization, remained intense, expressed both through her friendships with Chinese teachers and students and her work with the China Campaign Committee, for which she lectured and spoke at meetings throughout Britain. Her understanding of Chinese politics made her particularly concerned to ensure that aid from Britain reached the Chinese Communists and was not directed solely to the Kuomintang Government. During this period also she became increasingly occupied with the problems of penal reform in an international setting, particularly in societies where conditions were worst and factual information

most defective. She visited Geneva in 1935 to try to induce the League of Nations to adopt a Convention which would lay down minimum standard rules for the treatment of prisoners. In 1936 she became a member of the Colonial Office's newly established advisory committee on penal reform, and in 1937 she took part in a Howard League mission to study the prisons and penal systems of South-Eastern Europe. In Britain during the late thirties her political sympathies were with those of the non-Communist Left who were working for some form of Popular Front. She consequently resigned her membership of the Labour Party (which she had joined in 1918) when early in 1939 its executive expelled Sir Stafford Cripps [q.v.] for advocating such a policy. One specific contribution which she made at this time to the effort to increase the effectiveness of radical intellectuals was her sponsorship of the serious but short-lived organization, For Intellectual Liberty.

When war began in 1939 Margery Fry was already sixty-five, no longer able, as in 1914, to move into some entirely different field of work. She carried on with her existing activities as far as practicable, and took on new commitments where this seemed likely to be useful. She continued to serve as a magistrate; worked on her Clarke Hall lecture, *The Ancestral Child* (never delivered, but published in 1940); visited France early in 1940 to investigate the problem of intellectual refugees; experienced the blitz; took part in a study of evacuation and evacuees; served, unwillingly, on the government committee on non-enemy interned aliens (those imprisoned under '18B'); wrote with Champion B. Russell an 'A.B.C. for Juvenile Magistrates' (published in 1942 as *A Note Book for the Children's Court*), regarding 'rational occupation', for herself as for prisoners, as the best remedy for misery. During the thirties she had discovered that she enjoyed broadcasting and was good at it, and had served for a time as a governor of the B.B.C. She took part in the earliest series of 'Any Questions?' and in 1942 became a member of the Brains Trust. Although much distressed by the prospect of leaving her sisters for so long a period, she spent the year 1942–3 in the United States, speaking on penal questions, visiting universities and prisons.

During the dozen years of life which remained after the war Margery Fry retained a vigorous interest in the causes with which she had become identified, withdrawing somewhat from active campaigning, but continuing to talk, write, and educate with all her old wit and understanding. Her central ideas on penal reform were set out in the pamphlet, *The Future Treatment of the Adult Offender* (1944). These were further developed in her one full-length book, *Arms of the Law* (1951), in which she put together the material which she had collected over the years on the development of crime and punishment in human society and her proposals for future advance. Some of the many objectives for which she had worked, notably the abolition of the death penalty, were partially realized in her lifetime. But half-measures, where she knew what ought to be done, left her unsatisfied. And at eighty she still had the freshness of mind to move into new fields and confront new problems: the importance of developing criminology and penology as academic studies; the need to work out a national scheme of compensation for the victims of violence; the problems of the aged, discussed in her address, 'Old Age Looks at Itself' (1955), to the International Association of Gerontology. But, though any account of Margery Fry's life is bound to pay attention to causes, persons mattered a great deal more to her than causes— or rather, causes were important because they were ways of trying to increase the happiness and diminish the misery of individual people. Deeply disliking all forms of dogmatism, in ethics and politics as well as religion, she believed in working for a world in which the sort of pleasures she valued most—playing the flute, painting pictures, walking in the woods of Provence, enjoying the conversation of friends—could be made as widely available as possible. She died at her home in Clarendon Road, where she could watch the birds in the trees at the back, 21 April 1958.

A portrait by Roger Fry is at Somerville College, Oxford.

[Enid Huws Jones, *Margery Fry*, 1966; *The Times*, 22, 23, 24, 25, 26, and 30 April 1958; private information; personal knowledge.]

THOMAS HODGKIN.

FURSE, DAME KATHARINE (1875– 1952), pioneer Service woman, was born at Clifton, Bristol, 23 November 1875, the fourth daughter of John Addington Symonds [q.v.] and his wife, Janet Catherine, sister of Marianne North [q.v.]

and daughter of Frederick North, squire of Rougham, Norfolk, and Liberal member of Parliament for Hastings. Owing to her father's ill health Katharine spent most of her youth at Davos, Switzerland, with frequent visits to Italy. She grew up the youngest of a loving and gifted family, in surroundings ideally suited to her enterprising and energetic nature, and in close contact with many famous literary and artistic figures. Her father's sister had married T. H. Green [q.v.], the Henry Sidgwicks and Benjamin Jowett [qq.v.] were regular summer visitors, and her two surviving sisters were later to marry Walter Leaf and W. W. Vaughan [qq.v.]. Educated by governesses, with somewhat spasmodic additions by her father, she owed to her mother her intimate knowledge of flowers and she developed natural artistic gifts in various forms of handicraft, including exquisite embroidery and wood carving. Her dynamic character was evident even from babyhood and she grew tall and strong, with a beauty of the Venus de Milo type. While still a child she was winning 'Ladies' tobogganing events in competition with adults.

An inherited tradition of social service showed itself early and she was a frequent visitor of the sick in Davos. A few months at a school in Lausanne, abruptly terminated by the death of her father, gave her lessons in first aid and home nursing which she afterwards followed up by studying massage in London. She had decided to train as a hospital nurse when she met C. W. Furse [q.v.], the painter. They were married in 1900 but he died four years later, leaving her with two sons, both of whom entered the navy.

Soon after the first Red Cross Voluntary Aid Detachments attached to the Territorial Army were formed in 1909 Katharine Furse enrolled, and she joined enthusiastically in training, camps, and studies. In September 1914 she was sent to France by (Sir) Arthur Stanley [q.v.] with other representatives for preliminary discussions, and the following month she headed the first official V.A.D. unit (twenty in number) to be sent abroad. They were instructed to install rest stations on the lines of communication, first at Boulogne. Many thousands of wounded men were ministered to before the end of 1914 when Katharine Furse was recalled to London to start a V.A.D. Department. The organization was gradually built up into an enormous service whose members were nvaluable assistants in hospitals at home and abroad. In 1916 Katharine Furse was decorated with the Royal Red Cross; a joint committee was set up to co-ordinate the V.A.D. work of the British Red Cross Society and the Order of St. John of Jerusalem and Katharine Furse was appointed commandant-in-chief, becoming a lady of grace of the Order. In 1917 she was one of five women appointed Dame Grand Cross in the newly created Order of the British Empire.

But Dame Katharine had not for some time been happy in her work. She had not the power to institute various reforms which she felt necessary, both in administration and in conditions of work. In November 1917 she and a number of her colleagues resigned. Several posts were immediately offered to her, and in the same month she became director, with the equivalent rank of rear-admiral, of a new organization, the Women's Royal Naval Service. Although the new Service saw only one year of war and never exceeded some seven thousand in number her creation earned a fine reputation and before it was disbanded had established a tradition—of which the officers' tricorn hat was not the least important detail—for the vast Service which was to be formed twenty years later.

After the war Dame Katharine joined the travel agency of Sir Henry Lunn [q.v.], working mainly in Switzerland where in winter she was a ski-ing representative of the Ski Club of Great Britain. Although in her youth she had been one of the first to experiment with ski, in company with Sir Arthur Conan Doyle [q.v.], it was not until after the war that she took it up seriously. She was the second British woman to be awarded the gold badge for passing the first-class ski-running test and the second president of the Ladies' Ski Club. She also took up Girl Guide work and at her suggestion the Association of Wrens, of which she was president, affiliated to the Girl Guides Association, Dame Katharine becoming head of the Sea Guides, later known as Sea Rangers. She was also for ten years director of the World Association of Girl Guides and Girl Scouts. She died in London 25 November 1952. A portrait by her husband, 'Diana of the Uplands', is in the Tate Gallery. A portrait in W.R.N.S. uniform by Marcelle Morley hangs in Furse House, W.R.N.S. quarters in London; another by Glyn Philpot is in the Imperial War Museum.

[*The Times*, 26 November 1952; Dame Katharine Furse, *Hearts and Pomegranates*, 1940; Dame Vera Laughton Mathews, *Blue Tapestry*, 1948; *British Ski Year Book*, 1953; personal knowledge.]

VERA LAUGHTON MATHEWS.

FYFE, HENRY HAMILTON (1869–1951), writer, was born in London 28 September 1869, the eldest son of James Hamilton Fyfe, barrister, by his wife, Mary Elizabeth Jonas. His father had at one time been parliamentary correspondent of *The Times*, and after education at Fettes Hamilton Fyfe followed his father on its staff. From reporting he passed to sub-editing, and in due course was made secretary to the editor, G. E. Buckle [q.v.]. In 1902 he moved to the *Morning Advertiser*, the old-established journal of the Licensed Victuallers' Association, with the task of editing and refashioning the paper.

Alfred Harmsworth [q.v.], later to become Lord Northcliffe, was so much impressed by Fyfe's innovations that he invited him to join his staff. From 1903 to 1907 Fyfe edited the *Daily Mirror*; then moved as special correspondent (1907–18) to the *Daily Mail*, where he became one of a very able group. He reported Blériot's Channel flight in 1909 and the exciting air race from London to Manchester between Claude Grahame-White [q.v.] and Louis Paulhan in 1910. He covered the events of 1911 in Russia, and in 1913 went out to Mexico for *The Times* (then under Northcliffe's control), to report the Carranza revolution. Meanwhile trouble was brewing in Ulster and Fyfe moved there direct from Mexico, then straight out to France on the outbreak of war in August 1914. His telegram to the *Daily Mail*, reprinted in *The Times* alongside a dispatch from their own correspondent (30 August 1914), on the retreat from Mons was a high point in journalistic history. There had been a good deal of undue optimism, with loose talk about the war being over by Christmas. Here, with brutal frankness, was the plain truth of a terrible and bitter setback, of bad leadership, shortage of men and shells, and of tragic horror.

In 1915 Fyfe was transferred to Russia, moving down from Petrograd, through Galicia, to Bucharest. Back in Russia in 1916 he was able to retail the career and murder of Rasputin. In 1917 he was sent, successively, to Spain, Portugal, and Italy; then to the United States as honorary attaché to Northcliffe's British

Fyfe

war mission. In 1918 he played a notable part in Northcliffe's organization at Crewe House for propaganda in enemy countries.

Fyfe's political affiliations had always tended towards the Left and in 1922 Arthur Henderson [q.v.] offered him the editorship of the *Daily Herald*. In four years he achieved a sizeable increase in circulation; but there was always difficulty in reconciling the aims of a national newspaper with those of the Trades Union Congress editorial board which then controlled it, and in 1926 Fyfe resigned. He moved to the Liberal *Daily Chronicle* but left it on its amalgamation with the *Daily News* in 1930. From then onward he did valuable work for *Reynolds' News* but became increasingly devoted to independent authorship and to political work in the Labour cause. He stood unsuccessfully for Parliament at Sevenoaks in 1929 and at Yeovil in 1931, both hopeless constituencies for a socialist candidate.

Fyfe was a versatile miscellaneous writer, whose output included novels, plays, biographies, and sociological and topographical works. He wrote, among other biographies, lives of Northcliffe (1930) and of T. P. O'Connor (1934), and the notices of Lord Rothermere and others for this Dictionary. His play, *A Modern Aspasia*, produced by the Stage Society in 1909 and later in Prague, was praised by G. B. Shaw [q.v.] and other good judges.

In a long career Hamilton Fyfe developed high skill in many editorial tasks. He had a very keen and critical sense of news values; his work on numerous special assignments was well informed, fearless, frank, and thoughtful, and much of it may rank as raw material of history. He was an even-tempered man, though he could be roused to impatience by inefficiency and pomposity. So deep was his dislike of this that he insisted on being 'Harry' rather than 'Henry' which he found pretentious. In his period of political activity he resigned from various 'protest' societies he had joined, on the same grounds. After his association with Northcliffe (whom he liked personally but deplored as a phenomenon) he became more and more inimical to established authority and looked upon himself as a rebel on the left fringe of Labour.

Fyfe had a passion for gardening and his enthusiasm for garden design even led him to move house several times for the sheer pleasure of making a fresh start on new territory. With his youngest brother, Sir William Hamilton Fyfe, principal and vice-chancellor of the university of Aberdeen (1936-48), he was a warm friend, and the two spent many continental holidays together in youth.

In 1907 Fyfe married Eleanor, daughter of William Kelly, of the War Office; they had no children. He died at Eastbourne 15 June 1951.

[*The Times*, 19 June 1951; private information.] HERBERT B. GRIMSDITCH

FYLEMAN, ROSE AMY (1877-1957), writer for children, was born at Basford on the outskirts of Nottingham 6 March 1877, the third child of John Feilmann, by his wife, Emilie Loewenstein who was of Russian extraction. Her father was in the lace trade, and the family were free-thinking Jews who had come from Jever in Oldenburg some seventeen years previously. She was educated at a private school, and first got into print at the age of nine when one of her school compositions was published in a local paper. She entered University College, Nottingham but failed in the Intermediate, thus frustrating her ambition to become a schoolteacher. She had, however, a fine voice, and her paternal aunt gave her £200 to study singing. She studied in Paris, then in Berlin under Etelka Gerster and finished at the Royal College of Music in London where she took her diploma as A.R.C.M. She received encouragement from (Sir) Henry Wood [q.v.] and made her first public appearance in London at the Queen's Hall in 1903. Subsequently she returned to Nottingham, teaching, singing and helping in her sister's school. With other members of her family she anglicized her name at the outbreak of war in 1914.

She was forty when it was suggested to her that she send some of the verse she had been writing to *Punch*. Her first contribution 'There are fairies at the bottom of our garden!' appeared 23 May 1917. This evoked immediate response and five publishers wrote to her within a week. It was followed by 'The best game the fairies play' (13 June) and a succession of other fairy poems. Readers of *Punch* were soon looking for the initials 'R.F.', and she became a regular contributor. Her verses enjoyed a similar success in book form, the first collection *Fairies and Chimneys* (1918) being reprinted more than twenty times during the next ten years. It was followed by *The Fairy Green* (1919), *The Fairy Flute* (1921), and *Fairies and Friends* (1925). These verses were eventually gathered together in *A Garland of Rose's* (1928). During the twenties and early thirties she held a firm place in nursery affection throughout the English-speaking world, and she kept her name alive with a flow of new publications of which *Forty Good-Night Tales* (1923) and *Twenty Teatime Tales* (1929) were particularly successful. She founded (1923), and for two years edited, a children's magazine *The Merry-Go-Round*, and as time went on devoted an increasing amount of attention to juvenile drama, writing amongst others *Eight Little Plays for Children* (1924), *Nine New Plays for Children* (1934), and *Six Longer Plays for Children* (1936). She had a Christmas play produced at the Old Vic in 1926, and with Thomas Dunhill [q.v.] a children's opera at Guildford in November 1933. She was also a linguist who translated books from French, German, and Italian; and an inveterate traveller visiting most European countries, and making two lecture tours in the United States, 1929–30 and 1931–2. She never married, and died in London 1 August 1957.

Like other successful writers for children, Rose Fyleman had not much time for them. Of medium height, with dark hair, large brown eyes, and strong features, she was outwardly a somewhat formidable character, and not the type of person likely 'to see fairies everywhere'. In fact she admitted that she did not believe in them. She was none the less a kindly person who could arouse affection, a cultivated and amusing conversationalist, and one who had a professional attitude to her work and was vitally interested in her craft. Her verse has a clear lyrical quality which makes each of her poems memorable, and ideal for recitation. Although she maintained herself with her pen for forty years, and lived to hear lines of her poetry become proverbial, she had to contend with the knowledge that her best work was her first, and that it was becoming dated. She rarely repeated the simple magic of her early fairy poetry.

[*Twentieth Century Authors*, 1942, and references there quoted; *The Times*, 2 August 1957; private information.]   IONA OPIE.

GARBETT, CYRIL FORSTER (1875–1955), archbishop of York, was born 6 February 1875 at Tongham, Surrey, the son of the vicar, the Rev. Charles Garbett, who was a brother of Edward and James Garbett [qq.v.]. His mother, Susan Charlotte Bowes, daughter of Lieutenant-General Bowes Forster and granddaughter of Sir Peregrine Maitland [q.v.], was Charles Garbett's second wife, and thirty years younger than her husband. In an ideally happy marriage she bore him five children, four boys and a girl, of whom the future archbishop was the eldest. Tongham was a small village, and his early life there gave Garbett a deep sympathy and understanding of village life and of the loneliness and other problems of the country clergy, which was to stand him in good stead in his years of episcopal ministry at Winchester and York. He was educated as a day boy at Farnham Grammar School, then as a boarder from the age of eleven at Portsmouth Grammar School. In 1895 he entered Keble College, Oxford, with a Gomm close scholarship for which he was eligible on account of his distant descent from the fourth Marquess of Lothian [q.v.]. While Garbett was at Oxford his father died suddenly and it was only by the sacrificial contrivance of his mother that he was able to remain and take a second in modern history (1898). His educational career had been entirely undistinguished, but his steady and already well-informed interest in social questions, and his sedulous practising of the arts of public speech, carried him into the president's chair at the Union (1898); and in achieving this ambition he won the self-confidence which had hitherto eluded him.

He had learned too to form his own judgements and to walk in his own paths, and this self-mastery he exhibited when he went to Cuddesdon, where he took what he wanted of the regime and the curriculum, and withdrew himself with quiet firmness from the rest. Cuddesdon was never to him the 'holy mount' that it was to his predecessor, Cosmo Gordon Lang [q.v.], but he formed there his lifelong habits of fidelity to a rule of life in which the times for prayer, theological reading, correspondence, interviews, newspaper study, and recreation were all laid down with a precise rigidity which left very little room for the pleasant indulgence of a friendly gossip; it did much to knock the element of spontaneity out of his life for many years.

Garbett was ordained deacon in 1899 and priest in 1901. Both at St. Mary's, Portsea, where he was curate (1899–1909) and vicar (1909–19), and in his first diocese of Southwark, he made the reputation he was never to lose of a firm, even an alarming, disciplinarian. The disciplines, always awe-inspiring and sometimes ruthless, to which he subjected his curates at Portsea and his clergy at Southwark were silken as compared with the iron bands with which he bound himself. St. Mary's was a parish with great traditions, particularly for the faithful work of its clergy. This tradition he strengthened by the zeal which both he and his curates brought to it. He carried the burden of that vast naval parish through the dark days of the war of 1914–18; but perhaps a greater contribution in those years was to furnish the Church with a copious stream of young curates, all of whom were very highly trained to know their job through and through, and had learned the art and cost of self-discipline. By the time they left Garbett most of them were ready for positions of considerable importance.

In 1919 Garbett became bishop of Southwark, notoriously the most exacting of all English dioceses. He was then forty-four and he stayed there for thirteen years, working from early morning until late at night. As well as all the normal routines of a diocesan bishop, he had many other tasks. South London had to cope with a sudden and dramatic influx of population. In every part of the diocese vast new housing estates were appearing for most of which there were no churches. When he had been in Southwark for six full years Garbett complained that he had yet to consecrate a new church, and he therefore launched an appeal for £100,000 to build twenty-five churches. Thanks largely to his own efforts, this sum was given in less than three years. It was an immense achievement and, quite apart from providing the necessary churches, gave the diocese a pride in itself which it urgently needed. It is primarily for this that his Southwark episcopate will be remembered; but his incessant visiting of clergy and people in those weary acres of mean streets gave him much else which was to be of great value to the Church. Always interested in social problems, at Portsea he had experienced them at close quarters; but it was at Southwark that the wretched dilemmas of the poor began to press daily upon him as a sore burden. He knew that many lived on the edges of despair caused by bad housing and malnutrition, subjects in which he made the time to become expert. He set himself to gather all the relevant information, since neither then nor at any time was it his way to speak publicly on any subject on which he was ill informed. In the rural section of his diocese he made pilgrimages on foot, carrying his pastoral staff in the shape of a shepherd's crook, a form of visitation which brought him considerable publicity in the press. To all this work at Southwark he added the chairmanship (1923–45) of the new religious advisory committee of the British Broadcasting Corporation.

Whereas Garbett himself did not at the time feel the strain of the pace which he set himself at Southwark, others saw signs of it; the authorities of Church and State were hoping that in due course he would succeed A. F. Winnington-Ingram [q.v.] on his retirement from the diocese of London which they mistakenly supposed could not be long delayed. They therefore judged the time had come to transfer Garbett for a while to a less exacting see. In 1932 he was offered Winchester which, although by no means the 'bishopric of ease' which the authorities and indeed Garbett himself supposed, was less wearing than Southwark. At first he refused, but when the archbishop of Canterbury let him know it was intended to be but an interlude of comparative rest, he agreed. He was enthroned on 21 June 1932 in the cathedral in which he had been ordained deacon by Randall Davidson [q.v.].

Living now in the house he loved best of all, the surviving wing of Wren's palace of Wolvesey with its beautiful but manageable garden, Garbett found real peace for perhaps the first and certainly the last period in his long life. He revelled in the countryside of Hampshire, and for the Channel Islands he developed a deep affection. A new mellowness of spirit came to him, and at Winchester he was seldom regarded as the formidable disciplinarian, but much more as the inwardly affectionate father-in-God who was always struggling to find the way to allow his affection to break down the barriers caused by his almost paralysing shyness and fear of emotion. Nevertheless, to the end of his days there, it was never possible to talk to him without first being involved in the struggle to break the ice of his reserve. Among all his clergy and even his suffragan bishops, only his domestic chaplains, whom he treated as his sons, knew his full mind. They shared all his life, and with them he was completely at his ease and fully himself. From the first who served him at Southwark to the last of the notable succession at York, all of them loved him as deeply as they admired him, and they alone among human beings saw what was really there.

His peace of mind at Winchester stayed with him until the war involved him deeply in the two great agonies through which the diocese passed in those years: the occupation of the Channel Islands and the bombing of Southampton. His conduct in these two crises showed that there were occasions when he could put away all reserves, comfort the afflicted, strengthen the weary hands, and weep with those who mourn. His personal diary, which his biographer, Canon Charles Smyth, used with such skill and discretion, revealed, rather to the surprise of those who knew him at the time, that in the first two winters of the war he passed through a very weary period of unhappiness and frustration which showed itself in prolonged periods of insomnia.

Deliverance was soon to come unexpectedly. In January 1942 Archbishop Lang announced his resignation from Canterbury and in February Archbishop Temple [q.v.] was chosen to succeed him. Garbett knew it was very likely and dreaded that he would be asked to take Temple's place at York, but after a short but grim struggle of conscience he accepted the charge. Thereafter, until his last illness, no more is heard in his biography of his insomnia, or of the note of self-distrust or the conviction of failure.

He was enthroned in York Minster on 11 June 1942. He was to serve there for thirteen years—exactly the same period he had given to Southwark—and to make it one of the most notable ministries in the long history of the Palace of Bishopthorpe. Its special distinction lay not in his serving of his own diocese, faithful, painstaking, and exact though that was, but in what he made of the function of an archbishop, as distinct from that of a diocesan bishop with which in England it has to be combined. The care of his diocese was familiar ground, but the care of his province was a novelty which at first made him uneasy. There seems to be no written trace left of his attempt to think out what his work as archbishop must be. Very soon after his enthronement, however, a recognizable pattern began to evolve. Presently it was complete and consistent, and it so exactly expressed all his native strengths that it is impos-

sible not to believe that he thought out a function for his unique office, then deliberately set himself to achieve it.

Here was a man of the highest distinction, whose love for and loyalty to the Church of England was beyond all question, a senior member of the House of Lords and an assiduous attender of its debates, whose feet were known (as it was suspected Temple's were not) to be planted firmly on this solid earth, and who had laboriously amassed a fund of wide knowledge of most of the problems with which his fellow countrymen were struggling. He was known to be the personification of common sense tempered by sanctity; all kinds of people who, though admiring Temple's mind and entranced by his personality, were yet distrustful of his judgement, felt that with Garbett they were safe, and that his opinions and judgements were their own. He knew the layman's mind, and he could always guess what the average layman was thinking about the problems of the day. His insight was hardly ever at fault. He spoke to the laity in their own language, giving back to them their own thoughts. Thus he was better known to, and more fully trusted by, the laity than any other ecclesiastic of his time. As archbishop of York he had a large, respectful audience, yet he enjoyed a greater degree of freedom of speech than his brother of Canterbury. Both Ebor and Cantuar may say the same thing on the same issue, but Cantuar cannot help but speak for the Church, whereas up to a point Ebor can speak for himself. To this may be added that Garbett was a synthesist of much talent who could weave into a pattern all sorts of unrelated facts and ideas which he had gathered from his exceedingly catholic reading. He had and needed no originality. One of his deepest admirers said of him, 'Garbett never had a single original idea in his life.' This he himself knew, making this very lack a primary condition of the new and creative task he set himself. His purpose was to use his office to build a bridge between the sacred and secular views of life which had become dangerously sundered. If he was to do this successfully he must interpret the English Church to the English people, and to Christians of other Churches in the British Isles and overseas. He therefore set himself to practise more fully than before the ministries of print and of travel.

He had already written several small books and pamphlets. In 1947 he turned to something bigger and more ambitious, with *The Claims of the Church of England.* Partly autobiographical, partly historical, partly descriptive, it is by common consent the best book he ever wrote: a practical, personal statement of what the Church of England stands for, with what special gifts God has equipped it, and a description of its work in the past and present, and its function in the future. In it is a particularly good section on 'The Work and Office of a Bishop' which did much to lay to rest the parochial clergy's deep suspicion for the episcopate which was then a sad feature in the life of the Church of England.

In *Church and State in England* (1950) Garbett put forward his arguments for 'some readjustment in the existing relationship between Church and State'. He was convinced that the State in England, as elsewhere, was moving in the totalitarian direction, and that its course could not be stayed. He wanted therefore to see the Church shaken loose from it, but without disestablishment. His thesis was persuasively argued, but it did not convince, and much to his disappointment the book in a reforming sense was stillborn.

Having described the Church of his baptism and its possible reform he then turned to the world in which he must live and work and published *In an Age of Revolution* (1952). Writing in the conviction that the world was passing through the greatest crisis in history, he set himself to give a Christian explanation of its meaning. The current secular remedies for man's unsatisfied spiritual hunger had catastrophically failed, but there were the Christian remedies which would become operative in proportion as the world learned how to apply Christian principles to the regulation of man's daily life and work. The book was a very comprehensive and exceptionally widely documented survey of the world crisis as seen by an experienced observer. These three books inevitably exhibited a personal portrait of their author, showing his depth of loyalty to the Church of England in which he served as a convinced catholic and a definite high churchman, who yet valued and even reverenced the more evangelical traditions which are embedded in its life.

The writing of such books constituted an impressive literary testimony, for by the time the third was published Garbett had passed his seventy-fifth year. Moreover he found writing slow and painful: it never came naturally to him. Most of it was done very late at night. Of the ministry of print, however, he had made the fullest proof possible to him, but he realized that books were not nearly enough to interpret the Church to the nation, the nation to itself, and the sacred to the secular. He whose natural shyness made him shrink from all publicity seemed suddenly, from his first days at York, to court it. Realizing that he could not fulfil his purpose without the full help of the press, he set himself to learn how to use both it, and the newer art of broadcasting. More successfully than any other ecclesiastic of the day he used the press to the full without ever allowing it to use him; handicapped as he was from ever entering this difficult field at all, his success was not short of a triumph. There came to be a vast audience for every pronouncement of his on the issues of the day. Many indeed were painfully obvious. He often said no more than almost all men of goodwill must think, but to have their thoughts reflected by a man of Garbett's eminence and sound judgement fortified them. He was not always obvious. One of the best and most courageous speeches of his life was made in the House of Lords on the day when, after tremendous searching of heart and conscience, he gave his reluctant support to the manufacture of atomic weapons of war on the ground that he believed them to be essential to the keeping of such peace as there was.

At the same time Garbett made himself a great ecclesiastical travelling ambassador. He was tireless in planning his journeys, but desperately fatigued when he came to the end of each one of them. Yet his pleasure in them was childlike. Riding the world in aeroplanes always thrilled him, and it never staled. The first great journey was in 1943 when he went to Moscow, flying by way of Tehran. The Metropolitan of Moscow had asked that a delegation from the Church of England should visit the Russian Orthodox Church. Garbett eagerly volunteered, and set out with two chaplains. He arrived in Moscow on 19 September and left on the 28th, reaching home again on 9 October after a week in Cairo. Within those three weeks he fulfilled a list of engagements which would have exhausted any man, yet it had all been more than worth while, for he had done much to create good relations between the separated Churches. He went also to the United States and Canada, to Greece and the Near East, to Malaya, Australia, and the Pacific Islands, to many

European countries, and last of all, made a final visit to the Holy Land. All this he accomplished between 1943 and 1955, between his sixty-eighth and eightieth years. He interpreted the Church wherever he went, and he strengthened every church to which he came, giving its hard pressed and often lonely priests and people new encouragement and new heart.

Garbett's life was already long, but the excessive rigours of the last journey to Palestine undoubtedly shortened it. On his return to York he was immediately taken ill and after a severe operation no serious work was any longer possible for him. Yet he hoped against hope that it might be, and it was only after a tremendous struggle that he was at last able to bring himself to the decision to resign his archbishopric. But he was allowed to die while still in harness as he had always wished, for the end came quietly and quickly, at Bishopthorpe 31 December 1955. No man had ever worked harder, and but few more effectively. He was buried at York 4 January 1956. He had been sworn of the Privy Council in 1942 and was to have been created a baron in the New Year honours. His portrait by David Jagger hangs at Bishopthorpe.

[Charles Smyth, *Cyril Forster Garbett*, 1959; personal knowledge.] ROGER LLOYD.

GARNER, WILLIAM EDWARD (1889–1960), chemist, was born at Hugglescote, Leicestershire, 12 May 1889, the eldest son of William Garner, baker, and his wife, Ann Gadsby. Sir Harry Garner and Professor F. H. Garner were younger brothers. He was educated at Market Bosworth Grammar School and the university of Birmingham where he studied under P. F. Frankland (whose notice he subsequently contributed to this Dictionary) and obtained honours in chemistry in 1912. He was awarded an 1851 Exhibition in 1913 to work with Gustav Tammann at the university of Göttingen and returned to England only just before the outbreak of war in the following year. He joined the scientific staff of Woolwich Arsenal (1915–8) where he carried out some outstanding research work with (Sir) Robert Robertson [q.v.] on the calorimetry of high explosives.

In January 1919 Garner was appointed assistant lecturer at Birmingham but in October moved to University College, London, where he enjoyed a close and happy association with F. G. Donnan [q.v.] and a fruitful period of research; he

became reader in physical chemistry in 1924. Three years later he was appointed to the Leverhulme chair of physical and inorganic chemistry at Bristol and until his retirement in 1954, except for the war period, carried out a series of experimental studies of far-reaching practical and theoretical importance. In particular he made a systematic study of the kinetics of solid reactions and of heterogeneous catalysis and the mechanism of interface reactions and nucleation processes; as with much of his other work on the solid state he was a pioneer in applying the newer ideas of quantum physics.

On the outbreak of war in 1939 Garner established an extra-mural research team in the university of Bristol to assist the government ordnance factories in explosives and munitions research. Although never losing contact with the work of this group, he moved to Fort Halstead in Kent in 1943 to become superintendent of chemical and explosives research for the Ministry of Supply; he later became deputy chief, then chief superintendent of armament research. His enthusiasm, wise guidance, and inspiration were of paramount importance. He served on many high-level committees and was associated with notable developments in new armaments and munitions. He was appointed C.B.E. in 1946.

On the cessation of hostilities Garner returned to his university work, although until his retirement he was actively engaged in the work of the scientific advisory council of the Ministry of Supply with which he had been associated since its inception. During this period he built around him in Bristol one of the strongest research groups in the country. He continued with increasing vigour his studies of heterogeneous catalysis. After his retirement he organized a symposium on *Chemisorption* at the university college of North Staffordshire which was published by the Chemical Society (1957), and edited a large volume on the *Chemistry of the Solid State* (1955).

Garner was a man of charm and kindness who won the affectionate admiration of all who came into contact with him. He was quiet, unobtrusive, and entirely devoid of personal ambition; devoted to his work whether in the laboratory or the councils of the university. These qualities did not obscure the greatness of the man. He was an enthusiastic and inspiring leader of research, conscientious in the discharge of his duties, and an adherent of the best traditions of science. His interests were wide; he was a collector of paintings and china; had a critical appreciation of art; and was an enthusiastic gardener. He was a man of great tenacity and courage. This characterized his scientific work and everything else he tackled; no problem ever daunted him. He was a well-known figure at scientific gatherings and scientific societies and government committees made great calls upon his time. He served on the council of the Royal Society, having been elected F.R.S. in 1937, and of the Faraday Society over which he presided in 1945–7. He was senior scientific adviser for civil defence in the south-west region; and in 1948 a member of the joint Services mission to the United States and Canada. He was a fellow of University College, London, an honorary member of the Polish Chemical Society, and a correspondent councillor of the Patronato 'Alfonso el Sabio', Madrid (1959). He died unmarried at Bristol 4 March 1960. A chalk drawing of Garner by (Sir) W. T. Monnington belongs to the university of Bristol.

[*Proceedings* of the Chemical Society, June 1960; C. E. H. Bawn in *Biographical Memoirs of Fellows of the Royal Society*, vol. vii, 1961; private information; personal knowledge.]

C. E. H. BAWN.

GARNETT, JAMES CLERK MAXWELL (1880–1958), educationist and secretary of the League of Nations Union, was born in Cambridge 13 October 1880, the eldest son of William Garnett, first demonstrator of physics in the Cavendish Laboratory under James Clerk Maxwell [q.v.], and later educational adviser to the London County Council, and his wife, Rebecca, daughter of John Samways, of Southsea. Maxwell Garnett was a scholar of St. Paul's School and of Trinity College, Cambridge, where in 1902 he was sixteenth, and his younger brother Stuart ninth, wrangler. He went on to take a first in part ii of the mathematical tripos (1903), was a Smith's prizeman (1904), and a fellow of his college (1905). He rowed in the university trial eight. From 1904 to 1912 he was an examiner at the Board of Education and he was called to the bar by the Inner Temple in 1908. In 1912 he became principal of the College of Technology, Manchester, where his concern was with the expansion of work at university level. In 1920 he resigned as a result of a difference of opinion with the education committee over the number of

degree students to be admitted to the college.

In the same year he was appointed secretary of the League of Nations Union, to which he devoted the best years of his life. The Union's object was to organize and educate public opinion in favour of the League of Nations. Working closely with Lord Cecil of Chelwood and later with Gilbert Murray [qq.v.] who succeeded Cecil as chairman of the executive committee, Garnett collected round him an able staff and was instrumental in enlisting many of the best minds in the country to serve on the Union's numerous committees and to speak on its platforms. Largely owing to his efforts the Union grew in membership and influence.

Garnett, who was a tall commanding figure, was a devout Christian, and saw in his advocacy of a new way of life for the nations of the world a means of giving practical expression to his religious beliefs. He belonged to a generation so many of whom were killed in the war of 1914–18, including his rowing blue brother, Kenneth, his brother Stuart who founded the Sea Scouts, and his Oxford rugger blue brother-in-law Ronald Poulton-Palmer. Garnett's consciousness of the debt to the fallen, as well as his own strong sense of Christian service, supplied much of the driving power for his championship of the League's cause.

His resignation from the secretaryship of the Union in 1938 was a sad affair. In the turbulent years immediately preceding the second war political passions in the international field were running high. In a letter to Lord Lytton [q.v.], the chairman of the executive committee, Garnett wrote that he believed he had 'come to be regarded by some . . . as the principal obstacle to the Union's being used as an instrument of political propaganda'. To this use of the Union he could not agree. Whatever the rights and wrongs of the argument, there is no doubt that Garnett, always something of a controversial figure, had become increasingly so with the passing of the years.

Like many prophets and idealists he was not free from the disadvantages of his own strong qualities. He was not an easy man to work with. His singleness of purpose sometimes prevented him from making the kind of allowances which less high-principled men are usually capable of making for the vagaries and weaknesses of human nature; nor did he appreciate to the full the subtleties and deviousness which so often characterize human action in the sphere of international and domestic politics. His approach to the problems of the day was greatly conditioned by his academic background, and his method of expounding his views would, some felt, have been more effective if less didactic. His strength, on the other hand, lay in his breadth of vision, in the need he saw for developing a sense of loyalty beyond mere national feeling, and in his profound conviction that with God's help the Kingdom of Heaven could be established on earth. That Maxwell Garnett rendered conspicuous service to a great cause few who knew him would dispute.

In addition to papers on mathematical and physical subjects, which appeared in transactions and proceedings of the Royal Society and elsewhere, his publications included: *Education and World Citizenship* (1921); *World Loyalty* (1928); *The Dawn of World-Order* (with N. C. Smith, 1932); *Knowledge and Character* (1939); *A Lasting Peace* (1940); and *The World We Mean to Make* (1943).

Garnett was a keen climber, and he enjoyed sailing at Seaview, Isle of Wight, where he died 19 March 1958. In 1910 he married Margaret Lucy, second daughter of (Sir) Edward Poulton [q.v.], by whom he had three sons and three daughters, the eldest of whom married Douglas Jay, president of the Board of Trade, 1964–7. Garnett was appointed C.B.E. in 1919.

[Personal knowledge.]   ALAN THOMAS.

GARRARD, APSLEY GEORGE BENET CHERRY- (1886–1959), polar explorer. [See CHERRY-GARRARD.]

GARROD, HEATHCOTE WILLIAM (1878–1960), scholar, was born at Wells 21 January 1878, the fifth of six children of Charles William Garrod, solicitor, and his wife, Louisa Ashby. From Bath College he went with an exhibition to Balliol College, Oxford, where in 1899 he gained a first class in honour moderations and won the Hertford and a Craven scholarship; in 1900 he won a Gaisford prize and in 1901 a first class in *literae humaniores*, the Newdigate prize, and a prize fellowship at Merton. He did some classical teaching at Corpus Christi College (1902–4) until he was elected to a tutorial fellowship at Merton. With a few short breaks he lived in Merton from 1904 until his death. Until 1922 he concerned himself in the main with classical scholarship. He pub-

lished an edition of Statius (1906) and of the second book of Manilius' *Astronomicon* (1911), and the *Oxford Book of Latin Verse* (1912), together with many contributions to learned periodicals. During the war he served with distinction, first in the Ministry of Munitions (1915–18), then for the last few months in the Ministry of Reconstruction, where this exact classical scholar, described by his superiors in the Civil Service as 'a man of quite exceptional ability and of more than academic distinction', dealt with 'the general economic problems created by a world shortage of capital, supply, tonnage, etc. . . .'. He was appointed C.B.E. in 1918.

On his return to Merton, although he continued his teaching for classical honour moderations, he became more and more interested in English literature and in 1925 resigned his tutorship for a research fellowship in English. His *Wordsworth: Lectures and Essays* (1923) won him much esteem in wider circles and led directly to his election to the professorship of poetry (1923–8) which fell vacant on the death of W. P. Ker [q.v.]. Thereafter he published several critical studies and collections of essays and lectures on various English authors—*The Profession of Poetry* (1929, lectures delivered during his Oxford professorship); *Poetry and the Criticism of Life* (1931, lectures delivered at Harvard while he was Charles Eliot Norton professor); *Keats—A Critical Appreciation* (1926); and *Collins* (1928). His chief contribution to English scholarship came in 1939 with the publication of his edition of Keats in the Oxford English Texts; the second edition of this work in 1958 remains an indispensable book for Keats scholars.

Apart from this critical output is his original work—*Oxford Poems* (1912); *Worms and Epitaphs* (1919); *Poems from the French* (1925); *Epigrams* (1946); and in 1950 a slim volume of belles-lettres entitled *Genius Loci*. His learned interest in Renaissance scholarship enabled him to do valuable work on the muniments, the library regulations, and the ancient painted glass of Merton. It culminated in his completion, with Mrs. Allen, of the edition of the *Letters of Erasmus* of P. S. Allen (whose notice Garrod contributed to this Dictionary). The three volumes, ix, x, and xi, for which Garrod was mainly responsible, appeared in 1938, 1941, and 1947.

In his early years Garrod delighted in daring and ingenious emendations of classical texts which did not always win acceptance. The solid worth of his scholarship shows itself in his editions of Statius and Manilius, the latter of which was severely criticized by A. E. Housman [q.v.] in volume v of his own edition of Manilius in 1930. The *Oxford Book of Latin Verse* brought Garrod wide acclaim. His subsequent editing of the *Letters of Erasmus* brought into play his qualities of sustained scholarship and his profound learning and in the opinion of good judges is likely to last longer than his classical work.

Garrod, who remained through his life a devoted disciple of Wordsworth and Matthew Arnold, brought to his literary criticism a high seriousness of judgement. He could not be deceived by the artificial and the pretentious; and poetry which made no claims on the deepest human feelings had no appeal for him. Yet the strong moral influence of Wordsworth and Arnold, which runs through all his work, is tempered by an irresistible tendency to mischief and impish witticisms. The consequence is that Garrod is never dull. His style, which perhaps owes something to Hazlitt, a critic whom he held in high esteem, is lively and alert. It is full of idiosyncrasies and tricks, inversions, daring colloquialisms, obtrusive parentheses, but it is never flat. His chief passion is good poetry and he likes to praise it, but his admiration always has what he called 'bone and gristle'. It never sprawls. He can moreover aim critical shafts of original force at work which seems to him to be based on falseness of feeling or shallowness of thought. A notable example of this is his lecture on A. E. Housman, included in *The Profession of Poetry*, where he effectively points a finger of scorn at what he calls 'the false pastoralism' of the *Shropshire Lad*. In his own poetry there is the same mixture of moods; his epigrams are neat and witty; his lyrics romantic and emotional; in both he achieved considerable technical skill. The variety of his learning and the liveliness of his manner are well illustrated in a collection of essays brought together after his death by John Jones and published in 1963 under the title *The Study of Good Letters*. In this judicious selection the severity of Garrod's scholarship is tempered by his wit and humanity, while beneath the bantering cleverness of his lighthearted essays are persistent undertones of his moral sensibility.

The differing elements in Garrod's personality, the cleverness, the caustic wit,

the profoundly romantic and moral feeling, the respect for exact scholarship—sometimes it seemed at war with each other—achieved a true harmony in his edition of Keats. Here all his powers are at work together; the scholarship is exact; the depth of feeling for his subject informs the whole work. The style of the introduction and notes is as lively as ever but it is firm and authoritative; the mannerisms of some of his earlier writing have been left behind.

For more than fifty years Garrod lived the life of an unmarried Oxford don and was never long away from Merton. But he took great delight in holidays with his Merton friends, young and old, mainly in the Lakes, in Devonshire, and in Dorset. In Oxford, the meadows saw him on most days exercising a succession of muchloved and much-spoiled dogs. Otherwise he rarely moved farther than Blackwell's bookshop where his figure was well known —standing firm upon small pointed feet, of medium stature, a slight tendency to obesity, his impressive head crowned with a trilby hat worn back to front, cigar held between the first two fingers of his right hand, intent upon a book. Yet more than most Oxford dons he seemed at home in any kind of company and understood what went on in the world. In his own college he was a presiding genius, and in friendship he was generous and unselfish, asking nothing in return. Other dons, undergraduates, Merton men of all generations, and friends from wider circles were drawn irresistibly to his rooms as to the centre of the college. They sought his company, sometimes for the fun of it, the lighthearted bridge, the chess, and other more trivial games, all played to the high quavering accompaniment of his provocative wit and deliberate absurdities, and sometimes to console themselves with his ready sympathy in some private perplexity, and at other times, if he were in the mood, to sit at his feet, to draw upon his stores of learning, to profit from his fine exacting taste and to treasure his wise and witty *obiter dicta*. 'In the back of my mind', he once wrote, 'there lies always the suspicion that the love of literature, like that of virtue, is probably best taught in asides'; certainly in that way one learnt a lot from Garrod. He was one of those rich, uncommon personalities who have added an imperishable part to the Oxford heritage. In words which he himself used about Sir Walter Raleigh [q.v.]— 'Their advent is rare and their sojourn brief, but the memory of them is sweet in the dust.'

Garrod received an honorary D.Litt. from Durham (1930) and an honorary LL.D. from Edinburgh (1953). He was elected F.B.A. in 1931 and an honorary fellow of Merton in 1955. He died in Oxford 25 December 1960. A portrait painted for his seventieth birthday by Rodrigo Moynihan is in the senior common-room at Merton and he figures in Sir Muirhead Bone's painting of the interior of Blackwell's.

[*The Times*, 28 December 1960; *List of the Writings of H. W. Garrod*, 1947; G. R. G. Mure in *Postmaster*, 1961; John Jones in *Proceedings* of the British Academy, vol. xlviii, 1962; private information; personal knowledge.]   GEORGE MALLABY.

GARSTANG, JOHN (1876–1956), archaeologist, was born in Blackburn 5 May 1876, the sixth child of Walter Garstang, consulting physician, and his wife, Matilda Mary Wardley. His eldest brother, Walter, was from 1907 to 1933 professor of zoology at Leeds. Educated at Blackburn Grammar School, Garstang's early interests lay in the classics and in astronomy; but circumstances forced him to specialize in mathematics in which in 1895 he obtained a scholarship at Jesus College, Oxford. While at school he often paid nocturnal visits to the observatory at Stonyhurst College, and as he passed the ruins of the Roman camp, Bremetennacum, at Ribchester, his interest in archaeology was aroused. He conducted excavations there, publishing the results in 1898. This came to the notice of F. J. Haverfield [q.v.] who encouraged Garstang to take up archaeology. He devoted his vacations as an undergraduate to excavating, first at Melandra in Derbyshire, then near by at Brough, and lastly at Richborough on the south coast of England.

After taking a third class in mathematics (1899), Garstang joined (Sir) Flinders Petrie [q.v.] at Abydos in Egypt. Here he had leisure to explore the vicinity, and having discovered the great tomb at Beyt Khallaf, he was provided with funds for its excavation. A visit from A. H. Sayce [q.v.] was the beginning of a lifelong friendship.

Appointed reader in Egyptian archaeology at Liverpool in 1902, Garstang led expeditions during the next few years to the Egyptian sites of Negadeh, Hierakonpolis, Esneh, and Beni Hassan.

Through his friendship with Sayce he became interested in the Hittites, and in 1904 he undertook a journey of archaeological exploration in Asia Minor. In 1907 a permit was secured for the excavation of the Hittite capital of Boghaz-Keui by a British expedition under Garstang's leadership; but on arrival at Constantinople he was disappointed to learn that the permit had been transferred to Hugo Winckler at the personal request of the German Emperor. He therefore made a second exploratory journey through Asia Minor, visiting Winckler at Boghaz-Keui, and in the following year he selected the late Hittite site of Sakje-Geuzi for excavation, while in the winter months he continued his explorations of the tombs at Abydos. He published a valuable topographical study of the Hittite monuments in 1910 under the title *The Land of the Hittites*.

In 1907 he was appointed to the newly founded professorship of the methods and practice of archaeology at Liverpool, a post which he held until 1941. There he took a leading part in organizing the Institute of Archaeology and a new journal, the *Annals of Archaeology and Anthropology*.

Largely at the instigation of Sayce, Garstang transferred his activities in 1909 to Meroë in the Sudan, and there conducted excavations every winter until the outbreak of war in 1914. The finds included a bronze head of Augustus, now in the British Museum. Of particular interest to Garstang was a graffito showing a primitive astronomical apparatus.

After serving during 1914–18 with the Red Cross in France, Garstang took charge of the newly created School of Archaeology in Jerusalem (1919–26); and as director (1920–26) also of the Department of Antiquities in Palestine found time for much archaeological exploration of the country. His discovery of the site of Hazor was a notable achievement. Subsequent research on the topography of Palestine resulted in the publication of *Joshua Judges* (1931) and *The Heritage of Solomon* (1934). His most important archaeological work in Palestine, however, was the excavation of Jericho where, under the patronage of Sir Charles Marston, he worked from 1930 until 1936 when political conditions obliged him to transfer his activities to another country.

It was to Turkey that he returned in the autumn of 1936 with an expedition sponsored by Francis Neilson. After a survey and soundings in the Cilician plain he selected Yümük Tepe near Mersin for a full-scale excavation; but only two winter seasons were possible before war broke out. In the early months of the war, however, he was again in Turkey in charge of the administration of earthquake relief. Returning in 1946, Garstang completed his interrupted work at Yümük Tepe and the results were published in *Prehistoric Mersin* (1953). While at Mersin he conceived the idea of a British Institute of Archaeology at Ankara, and in 1948, with the full support of the Turkish Government, the Institute was formally opened, with Garstang as its first director; he retired the following year, to assume the presidency of the Institute.

Garstang was appointed a chevalier of the Legion of Honour (1920), received the honorary degree of LL.D. from Aberdeen (1931), was made a corresponding member of the Institut de France (1947), and C.B.E. (1949). His death occurred on a cruise, at Beirut, 12 September 1956. His study of the geography of the Hittite Empire, on which he had spent many of the later years of his life, was published posthumously in 1959.

With his trim beard, his deep musical voice, slow speech, and air of abstraction, Garstang, especially after middle age, gave an impression of great learning. Yet his effective training was as a field archaeologist, and it is in this essentially practical field, as well as in that of organization for which he had a natural gift, that his permanent achievements are to be found. He was a sensitive, lovable character, with a boyish enthusiasm which never failed to infect those who worked with him.

He married in 1907 Marie Louise (died 1949), daughter of Étienne Bergès, of Toulouse; they had one son and one daughter. A portrait by G. Hall Neale (1906) is at Blackburn Grammar School; a bust (c. 1950) by Howard E. D. Bate is in the possession of the family.

[Reports of excavations; A. H. Sayce, *Reminiscences*, 1923; personal knowledge.]
O. R. GURNEY.

GASK, GEORGE ERNEST (1875–1951), surgeon, was descended from a family of Lincolnshire smallholders. His father Henry walked to London to seek his fortune, in which he and his brother succeeded by establishing a drapery business in Oxford Street. Henry married Elizabeth Styles and settled in Dulwich where

George, the youngest of four sons, was born 1 August 1875. He went to Dulwich College and also studied at Lausanne, Freiburg, and Baden before entering the medical school of St. Bartholomew's Hospital in 1893; he thus gained a working knowledge of German and French, some experience of continental methods of education, and a realization of the benefits of foreign travel which had a lasting effect upon his subsequent career.

He qualified L.R.C.P. and M.R.C.S. in 1898 and became house-surgeon to John Langton, proceeding to the fellowship of the Royal College of Surgeons of England in 1901. A period of training as a demonstrator of pathology and as surgical registrar led to his appointment in 1907 as assistant surgeon to (Sir) D'Arcy Power [q.v.], whose researches into the history of medicine were at once a stimulus and an example to Gask who ultimately became expert in the history of military surgery. He thus embarked on the life of a surgical consultant and teacher, and for five years was warden of the Bart's residential college.

In 1912 the younger surgeons at St. Bartholomew's formed a study group which they called the Paget Club, and in the light of subsequent events it is significant that at their second meeting Gask read a paper on the methods of teaching surgery in England, Germany, and America. In the previous year he had visited several of the university medical schools in the United States and advocated the incorporation of certain features of the foreign systems into British schools, but concluded that such innovations were hindered by the burden of routine work in the hospitals. Clearly he had the advantages of 'whole-time' academic units in mind, but had to wait until after the war of 1914–18 for a chance to translate his ideas into practice. During the war he distinguished himself in the surgery of chest wounds, being appointed to the D.S.O. in 1917 and C.M.G. in 1919 for his services as consulting surgeon to the Fourth Army.

As soon as he returned from France Gask set about forming the surgical professorial unit at St. Bartholomew's, manifesting from the outset an important attribute of a professor, good judgement in the choice of his assistants. He brought (Sir) Thomas Dunhill [q.v.] from Melbourne as his deputy. The unit gradually gained the confidence of the rest of the hospital staff who appreciated Gask's unselfish idealism and trusted him not to interfere with their work. A further evidence of his good judgement was his selection of subjects for research, and in due course significant contributions were made to thyroid surgery, to the use of radium for breast cancer, and to the surgery of the sympathetic nervous system. Gask was quick to appreciate the help he could obtain from his scientific colleagues, and the collaboration of Hopwood in physics, Woollard in anatomy, and Mervyn Gordon [q.v.] in virology was invaluable. He was a model director, providing the ideas and encouraging younger men to do the work. Even when teaching he tried to make the students find out things for themselves instead of telling them the answers; the undiscerning thought 'Uncle George' was merely lazy. Although not a brilliant operator his technique was gentle and based on sound principles. He organized the Pilgrim Surgeons who travelled widely to see the great masters at work, and he also arranged that in alternate years a leading surgeon should become temporary director of the surgical unit.

Gask, who retired in 1935, was called upon to serve on several bodies outside his own medical school. At the Royal College of Surgeons he was on the council from 1923 until 1939, he gave the Vicary and Bradshaw lectures, and was twice a Hunterian professor. He was an original member of the Radium Trust, and served on the Medical Research Council from 1937 to 1941. He took a leading part in planning the Postgraduate Medical School at Hammersmith and was an active member of its governing body. He succeeded Lord Moynihan [q.v.] as chairman of the editorial committee of the *British Journal of Surgery*. His own writings included a pioneer study of *The Surgery of the Sympathetic Nervous System* (with J. Paterson Ross, 1934) and *Essays in the History of Medicine* (1950). During the war of 1939-45 he acted as a temporary surgeon to the Radcliffe Infirmary, and greatly appreciated the consequent associations with the university of Oxford and the medical services in the Oxford Region.

In 1913 Gask married Ada Alexandra, daughter of Lieutenant-Colonel Alexander Crombie, of the Indian Medical Service; they had one son.

A likeable and even-tempered person of fine physique, in his younger days a distinguished mountaineer, Gask suffered

latterly from coronary disease and died at his home near Henley 16 January 1951. There are two portraits; one, a study for the group of the council of the Royal College of Surgeons painted in 1928 by Moussa Ayoub, is in the possession of his son, John, a medical graduate of Oxford who settled in practice at Market Drayton.

[Private information; personal knowledge.]
J. PATERSON ROSS.

GATENBY, JAMES BRONTË (1892-1960), zoologist, was born at Wanganui, New Zealand, 10 October 1892, the younger son of Robert McKenzie Gatenby, pharmacist, by his wife, Catherine Jane Brontë, a granddaughter of John Brontë, of county Down. He was educated at Wanganui Collegiate School, St. Patrick's College, Wellington, New Zealand, and Jesus College, Oxford, of which he was an exhibitioner. He graduated with first class honours in zoology (1916), was demonstrator in forest zoology and human embryology (1916-19), lecturer in histology (1917), and senior demy of Magdalen (1918). At University College, London, he was senior assistant in zoology and comparative anatomy (1919) and lecturer in cytology (1920); and at Trinity College, Dublin, professor of zoology and comparative anatomy (1921-59), and professor of cytology, a research chair specially created (1959-60). He was M.A., Ph.D. (Dublin), D.Phil. (Oxford), and D.Sc. (London).

As a boy Gatenby was fascinated by insects and collected butterflies. As a research worker he soon became interested in the structure of cells. The germ-cells and early development of parasitic hymenopterans attracted him first and subsequently he reverted at intervals to the study of insectan cytology. He was a cytologist in the classical descriptive style and his technique was superlative. He concentrated on the Golgi bodies, mitochondria and other cytoplasmic structures, and studied these in many animals, from protozoans to man. His description of the processes involved in fertilization of sponges is a classic, and so is his joint work with J. P. Hill on the corpus luteum of the platypus. Always distrustful of the newer cytochemical techniques until they were proven, he was outspoken in his criticism and was involved in many controversies which, nevertheless, served to focus interest on the cytoplasm. Much of his work on the structure of the germ-cells, using classical methods, has proved, in the light of modern findings with phase-contrast and with electron microscopy to be nearer the mark than that of some of his rivals. Yet he was never slow to avail himself of modern methods when opportunity offered and he was convinced of their value, as witnessed by the enthusiasm with which he turned to the electron microscope in his later years.

Gatenby took over a department in Dublin which was moribund. He laboured to build it up, but it was only after the war of 1939-45 that even the essentials of staff and equipment were forthcoming. As a teacher he had the supreme gift of inspiring interest, enthusiasm, and the ardour of exploration; the knowledge he could impart was limited by his facilities but the inspiration was lasting. Several of his pupils occupied university chairs of zoology, among them his successor in Trinity College.

Generous and warm-hearted, an original and witty conversationalist with decided views on many subjects, he loved social contacts and was a delightful companion at home or in the field. As a friend he was loyal almost to a fault and vigorous in defence of those whom he liked. He was apt to like, or dislike, a person almost at first sight, and liking soon developed into warm and lasting friendship. Unsparing in his denunciation of what he considered to be insincerity or unfairness, he was sometimes inclined to attribute to imagined intrigue honest actions of which he did not approve. He enjoyed travel; was visiting professor at Alexandria and visiting lecturer at Louvain; and went twice to the United States: as Theresa Seessel fellow of Yale (1930-31) and as visiting research fellow to the Argonne National Laboratory (1958). Shortly before his death he visited both his daughters, the one in Australia and the other in New Zealand, and seized the occasion to resume his studies of some New Zealand insects. But long residence had made Gatenby as Irish in outlook as any native and he was glad to return to fly-fishing its rivers and lakes, in which art he was skilled. He was an honorary fellow of the Royal Microscopical Society and of the Academy of Zoology of India and an honorary member of the Royal Society of New Zealand and of the International Society for Cell Biology.

Gatenby married in 1922 Enid Kathleen Mary (Molly) (died 1950), daughter of C. H. B. Meade, barrister, of Dublin. They had two daughters and two sons, of whom the elder, Dr. P. B. B. Gatenby became professor of clinical medicine at Trinity College. He married secondly, in 1951, Constance Harris, daughter of Captain W. W. Rossiter, of county Wicklow. He died while on a fishing holiday in Galway, 20 July 1960. A portrait by H. W. Addison is at Trinity College.

[*The Times* and *Irish Times*, 22 July 1960 *Nature*, 17 September 1960; *Trinity*, No. 12 Michaelmas, 1960; *Journal* of the Royal Microscopical Society, vol. lxxx, Part I, 1961 private information; personal knowledge.]

F. W. ROGERS BRAMBELL

GEDDES, AUCKLAND CAMPBELL, first BARON GEDDES (1879-1954), public servant, was born in London 21 June 1879, the second son of Auckland (originally Acland) Campbell Geddes, civil engineer, and his wife, Christina Helen Macleod Anderson. His two brothers were Sir Eric Campbell Geddes [q.v.] and Irvine Campbell Geddes, for many years chairman of the Orient Steam Navigation Company. One of his two sisters who survived infancy, Dr. Mona Chalmers Watson, was the first woman awarded an M.D. by Edinburgh University. Sir Alan Anderson [q.v.] was a first cousin.

Geddes was educated at George Watson's College, Edinburgh, where he shared with his contemporaries a great ambition to serve his country: five of them were in the Cabinet at the end of 1919. Meantime Geddes studied medicine at and played rugby football for Edinburgh University In 1898 he joined the University Rifle Volunteers, thereby beginning a lifelong interest in military matters. Defective eyesight delayed but did not prevent his enlisting as a second lieutenant in the 3rd battalion of the Highland Infantry with which he saw active service in South Africa in 1901-2.

On returning home he resumed his medical training and qualified in 1903 proceeding to his M.D. with gold medal in 1908. Shortly afterwards he was elected F.R.S.E. In 1906 he married Isabella Gamble (died 1962), daughter of W. A Ross, originally of Belfast, who had established himself in New York; there were four sons and one daughter. After marriage, whilst a university assistant in anatomy at Edinburgh, Geddes continued his voluntary military service, an interest which flourished through contact with a distant relative, R. B. (later Viscount) Haldane [q.v.], the minister for war. Geddes contributed some original thought to the development of the Territorial Army and sketched plans for national service in time of war.

The Scottish climate did not suit his wife and in 1909 Geddes was appointed professor of anatomy at the Royal College of Surgeons in Dublin; in 1913 he moved to the chair of anatomy at McGill University, Montreal, where he organized the expansion of the Officers' Training Corps. On the outbreak of war in 1914 he was called up and posted as a major to the 17th Northumberland Fusiliers in Hull where he sustained severe injuries in a riding accident. He was next posted to the staff of G.H.Q. in France where he became assistant adjutant-general until early in 1916 when he was appointed director of recruiting at the War Office with the rank of brigadier-general. He entirely reorganized the procedure for recruitment, divided the country into regions, and rearranged out-stations for recruiting purposes. For the handling of recruits on such a scale there were no precedents. Geddes was appointed C.B. and K.C.B. and sworn of the Privy Council in 1917. By the spring of that year it was decided that an independent Ministry should be responsible for the total allocation of labour for all purposes and Geddes, taking over from Neville Chamberlain an embryo national service organization, was in August appointed director-general and minister of national service. He resumed civilian status and sat in the House of Commons until 1920 as member for the Basingstoke division.

In November 1918 Geddes became in addition president of the Local Government Board as the preliminary to the establishment of a new Ministry of Health. But the post of first minister of health went to Dr. Christopher (later Viscount) Addison [q.v.] because Lloyd George had proposed to make Geddes chancellor of the Exchequer after the election of 1918. Ill health frustrated this project, and after recovering Geddes spent a few months winding up the Ministries of Reconstruction and National Service before being appointed president of the Board of Trade in May 1919. He joined the Cabinet in October and held office until March 1920. It was during this period that the foundations were laid for the system of export credit guarantees which was later to be greatly developed.

In February 1919 Geddes was elected principal of McGill University, a post

which he intended to take up in 1920. But Lloyd George prevailed upon him to become instead British ambassador in Washington. The high point in his public career came when he joined A. J. Balfour and Lord Lee of Fareham [qq.v.] as delegate to the Washington conference on the limitation of naval armaments in 1921. Geddes was much concerned with the negotiations for the dismantling, whilst still on the stocks, of the large American fleet which had been ordered at the end of the war. He later took part in the successful negotiations in 1922–3 for the settlement of the British war debt to America. He was appointed G.C.M.G. in 1922.

Owing to an accident leading to the loss of sight in one eye, Geddes resigned in 1924 and on returning to England was appointed chairman of the royal commission on food prices. Later he became chairman of the Rio Tinto Company, a position which he held for twenty-two years, and was the founding chairman of the Rhokana Corporation. The great development of the Northern Rhodesian copper-belt under British control owed much to his efforts.

From 1939 to 1941 Geddes was commissioner for civil defence in the south-eastern region (Kent, Sussex, and Surrey), above which the greater part of the Battle of Britain was fought. In 1941–2 he was commissioner for the north-western region. He was created a baron in the New Year honours of 1942 and from this date he had recurrent trouble with his vision resulting in his going totally blind in 1947. Whilst blind he wrote and dictated the book *The Forging of a Family* (1952) which describes many phases of his family history and personal activities.

Geddes had both an impressive grasp of facts and a wide ranging mind. He was very knowledgeable in the natural sciences and his powerful imagination enabled him vividly to illuminate any subject which held his attention. He was consequently an exceptional teacher and it was in that role that his charm and power lay. Like many Victorians he had a deep interest in death and extra-sensory perception. Some of his thoughts he expressed in plays, and he financed the production of one in which he had collaborated. His appreciation of art and music was conservative but he wrote the music for a score or so of student and military songs, some of which retained a place in popular esteem.

In politics Geddes was a perceptive

supporter of the Commonwealth. When a delegate at the Washington naval conference he was aware, as few then were, that this was an act marking the peak and that the dissolution of the British Empire was already beginning. This he accepted as desirable provided it was properly timed.

Geddes died in Chichester 8 January 1954 and was succeeded by his eldest son, Ross Campbell (born 1907). A bust of Geddes by P. Bryant Baker is in the possession of the family.

[Private information; personal knowledge.]
DAVID GEDDES.
SIDNEY G. DAVIS.

GEORGE VI (1895–1952), King of Great Britain, Ireland, and the British Dominions beyond the seas, was born at York Cottage, Sandringham, 14 December 1895, the second of the five sons of the Duke and Duchess of York, afterwards King George V and Queen Mary. A notice of the latter appears in this Supplement. His birth on the anniversary of the deaths of the Prince Consort (1861) and Princess Alice (1878) was an occasion for apprehensive apology, but Queen Victoria was gratified to become the child's godmother and presented him with a bust of the Prince Consort as a christening present. He was baptized at Sandringham 17 February 1896, receiving the names Albert Frederick Arthur George, and was known thereafter to the family as Bertie.

A shy and sensitive child, Prince Albert tended to be overshadowed by his elder brother, Prince Edward, and his younger sister Princess Mary. A stammer, developed in his seventh or eighth year, inhibited him still further, and of all the children it was probably he who found it least easy to withstand his father's bluff chaffing or irascibility. The boy withdrew into himself, compensating with outbursts of high spirits or weeping.

Nevertheless life passed evenly enough in the 'glum little villa' of York Cottage and in the other residences to which the migrations of the court took them, interrupted by such events as the funeral of Queen Victoria or the coronation of King Edward VII. By 1902 Prince Albert and his elder brother had graduated to the schoolroom under the care of Henry Peter Hansell, an Oxford graduate, formerly tutor to Prince Arthur of Connaught [q.v.]. Although he gained the affection of his pupils, Hansell was not the man to inspire small boys with a desire for

learning. He himself thought they should have been at school; but his earnest attempt to create the illusion that they were was not convincing. In the spring of 1907 Prince Edward departed for Osborne and Prince Albert, now 'head boy' with Prince Henry in second place, was left to struggle with the mathematics which seemed likely to prevent him from following suit. But here he showed that ability to face up to and overcome difficulties which was to be the marked characteristic of his career. When he passed into Osborne his oral French, despite his stammer, was almost perfect, and his mathematics 'very fair indeed'.

At Osborne and Dartmouth (1909–12), years which saw his father's accession to the throne, Prince Albert was never very far from the bottom of the class; but he was popular as a 'trier' and a good comrade, and there was a steady development of both character and ability. He was confirmed at Sandringham on 18 April 1912, a day he remembered as one on which he 'took a great step in life'.

After a training cruise in the *Cumberland*, during which he visited the West Indies and Canada, Prince Albert was posted in September 1913 as a midshipman to the *Collingwood* in the Home Fleet. To his great satisfaction he was able to see active service in her as a sub-lieutenant at the battle of Jutland, 31 May 1916. But the war years were in the main frustrating. Always a poor sailor, he was now suffering almost continuously from gastric trouble. An operation for appendicitis, performed in Aberdeen 9 September 1914, brought only temporary relief and there followed three years of misery before on 29 November 1917 an operation for duodenal ulcer proved more successful. The subsequent great improvement in the Prince's health was marked in 1920 by his winning the Royal Air Force tennis doubles with his comptroller, who had long been his mentor and friend, (Sir) Louis Greig. That he lost to Greig in the semi-finals of the singles did not surprise him.

Meantime the Prince had been forced to admit that life at sea was too much for him and in November 1917 he transferred to the Royal Naval Air Service and on 1 April 1918 was gazetted flight lieutenant in the new Royal Air Force. It was now that his interest in physical fitness was aroused through his work in the training of boys and cadets. He was in France when the war ended and was asked by his father to represent him when the King of the Belgians made his official entry into Brussels on 22 November: the first state occasion on which he acted for the King.

Returning to England in the following February, Prince Albert, disregarding his dislike of flying, became a fully qualified pilot, 31 July 1919, and received his commission as a squadron leader on the following day. But the time had come for him to leave Service life and take his share of the burden of public duties which falls to a royal family. As further preparation, in company with Prince Henry, he spent a year at Trinity College, Cambridge, which might have been more fruitful had they lived in college. He studied history, economics, and civics, and in particular the development of the Constitution; and tackled an increasing number of public engagements, each one an ordeal by reason of the stammer for which he had so far found no cure. He became president of the Industrial Welfare Society and thereafter until he came to the throne made it his special interest to visit industrial areas and seek to make contact with the people as informally as possible. His own personal contribution towards better relations between management and workers took the form of what became the famous Duke of York's camps for boys from public schools and industry which were held annually, with one exception, from 1921 until 1939. He remained keenly interested in them to the end and delighted in the informality of his visits to the camps when he always joined vigorously in singing the camp song 'Under the Spreading Chestnut Tree'.

In the birthday honours of June 1920 the King created his second son Baron Killarney, Earl of Inverness, and Duke of York. He had already conferred the Garter upon him in 1916 on the occasion of his twenty-first birthday and was to confer the Order of the Thistle on him on his wedding day. The Duke went on his father's behalf to Brussels in 1921 and twice in 1922 to the Balkans where his bearing during elaborate state occasions earned the highest praise.

On 26 April 1923 in Westminster Abbey the Duke married Lady Elizabeth Angela Marguerite Bowes-Lyon, youngest daughter of the fourteenth Earl of Strathmore and Kinghorne [q.v.], and together they entered upon that path of domestic happiness and devotion to public duty which was to earn them the nation's gratitude. They made their home first at White Lodge in Richmond Park which had been Queen Mary's childhood home; then from 1927 at 145 Piccadilly, with, later, the Royal Lodge, Windsor Great Park, as their country residence. Two daughters were born to them: Princess Elizabeth Alexandra Mary (21 April 1926) and Princess Margaret Rose (21 August 1930).

Official visits to the Balkans (1923) and Northern Ireland (1924) and many public engagements at home were followed by a tour of East Africa and the Sudan in the winter of 1924-5 which gave the Duke and Duchess a welcome holiday and the opportunity for big-game hunting. On his return the Duke presided over the second year of the British Empire exhibition at Wembley. Public speaking was still an ordeal for him but in 1926 he first consulted the speech therapist, Lionel Logue, who over the years was able to help him to overcome his stammer so that speech came much more easily to him and the listener was aware of little more than an occasional hesitation. It was therefore with a lighter heart that he left with the Duchess in 1927 for a strenuous tour of New Zealand and Australia, the highlight of which was the opening on 9 May of the first meeting of Parliament at the new capital city of Canberra. The natural sincerity of the Duke and the radiance of the Duchess evoked an enthusiastic response throughout the tour. On their return to London they were met at Victoria Station by the King and Queen, the Duke having been forewarned by his father: 'We will not embrace at the station before so many people. When you kiss Mama take yr. hat off': attention to detail inherited by the Duke who was in many ways his father's son.

During the King's illness of 1928-9 the Duke, who had been introduced into the Privy Council in 1925, was one of the counsellors of State. In May 1929 he was lord high commissioner to the General Assembly of the Church of Scotland, and, as his father was not sufficiently recovered to visit Scotland, he returned to Edinburgh in October to represent the King as lord high commissioner of the historic first Assembly of the two reunited Scottish Churches.

These were quiet years of home-making and of public duties faithfully performed, overshadowed perhaps by the King's failing health but with no realization of what was to come. With the death of King George V on 20 January 1936 and the abdication of his successor in the following

December all this was changed. The Duke and his elder brother had always been on good terms, but after the latter's accession the Duke found himself increasingly excluded from the new King's confidence. It was with the utmost reluctance that he finally brought himself to accept the fact that the King was determined to marry Mrs. Simpson even at the cost of the throne. Of this resolve the King informed him on 17 November. The days which followed were filled with 'the awful & ghastly suspense of waiting' until on 7 December the King told the Duke of his decision to abdicate. Two days later the Duke had a long talk with his brother but could do nothing to alter his decision and so informing his mother later in the day 'broke down & sobbed like a child'. On 12 December 1936 he was proclaimed King, choosing George VI as his style and title. His brother he created H.R.H. the Duke of Windsor.

Thus there came to the throne a man who had 'never even seen a State Paper', at a time when the monarchy had suffered the successive blows of death and abdication. 'I am new to the job', the King wrote to Stanley Baldwin at the end of the year, 'but I hope that time will be allowed to me to make amends for what has happened.' To this task he brought his own innate good sense and courage in adversity, disciplined by his naval training and sustained by the strength which he drew from his marriage, the sterling qualities of his mother, and the goodwill of the nation. The King had the same simple religious faith as his father and the coronation which took place in Westminster Abbey on 12 May 1937 was a genuine act of dedication on the part of the new King and Queen. It was shared by millions of their people, for the service was broadcast by the B.B.C., an arrangement which had the full support of the King against considerable opposition.

The brilliance of a state visit to France in July 1938 brought a momentary gleam of light in a darkening international situation. The King had full confidence in his prime minister and like Neville Chamberlain believed that every effort must be made to avoid a war. Final disillusionment came in March 1939 when the Munich agreement was swept aside and the Germans finally destroyed Czechoslovakia. Shortly after the return visit to Great Britain by President and Mme Lebrun later in the month there was announced the Anglo-French guarantee of

Polish independence against aggression. Two months later came the first occasion on which a reigning British monarch had entered the United States. The visit of the King and Queen to North America in May–June 1939 was a resounding success and gave them an increase of confidence. In Canada the King addressed the members of the Senate and the House of Commons and gave the royal assent to bills passed by the Canadian Parliament. At Hyde Park he was able to discuss with President Roosevelt the help which might be expected from the United States in the event of a European war. The warm regard which the two men felt for one another was thereafter maintained by correspondence. Nevertheless the King chafed in these years at his inability to influence the course of events. His successive suggestions of personal communications to Hitler, to King Victor Emmanuel to the Emperor of Japan, were felt to be inadvisable by a Government which did not share his belief in communications between heads of State.

When, inevitably, war with Germany came, the King broadcast to the Empire on the evening of Sunday, 3 September 1939, a simple call to his people to fight for the freedom of the world. Of the issue he was never in doubt and it was no small part of his contribution in the years to come that he was able to transmit this unclouded confidence to more complex and fearful minds.

In October the King visited the Fleet at Invergordon and Scapa Flow and in December he spent some days with the British Expeditionary Force in France. At Christmas he resumed his father's tradition of broadcasting a personal message to the Empire, a custom maintained for the rest of his life despite his dislike of the microphone. When Chamberlain resigned the premiership in May 1940 the King was distressed to see him go and would have liked Lord Halifax [q.v.] to succeed him. But Chamberlain informed him that Halifax, being in the Lords, was 'not enthusiastic' and the King accordingly accepted the advice to send for (Sir Winston Churchill. By September formal audiences had given way to a weekly informal luncheon and a somewhat guarded relationship had warmed into genuine friendship.

Throughout the war the King and Queen remained in London, sleeping at Windsor during the bombing. Buckingham Palace was hit nine times: in September 1940 it was bombed twice within three days. On the second occasion six bombs were dropped over the Palace by day and the King and Queen had a narrow escape—even the prime minister was not told how narrow. 'A magnificent piece of bombing', remarked a police constable to the Queen; but a tactical error. Prompt and indefatigable in their visits to bombed areas throughout the country the royal pair knew that it was realized that they too had suffered; it was now that they entered into the hearts of their people in a very personal way. It was the King's idea in 1940 to create the George Cross and Medal, primarily for civilian gallantry; and his idea two years later to award the Cross to Malta for heroism under siege. In that year of successive disasters to the Allies the tragedy of war touched the King more closely when his younger brother the Duke of Kent [q.v.] was killed on 25 August 1942 in a flying accident while on active service.

By 1943 the tide of the war had turned and in June the King visited his troops in North Africa where the Axis forces had surrendered. In two weeks he covered some 6,700 miles and although it involved some risk the tour included a visit to Malta, on which he was determined in recognition of the island's gallantry. After the surrender of Italy in September 1943 the King shared with J. C. Smuts [q.v.] some doubts about the wisdom of opening up a second front in France; they communicated their misgivings to Churchill who made it clear, however, that it was too late to change plans which were already well advanced. On 15 May 1944 the King attended the conference at St. Paul's School at which the preparations for invasion were expounded. Before D-Day (6 June) he had visited all the forces bound for Normandy. Both he and Churchill wanted to witness the assault from one of the ships taking part. The King, on reflection, was able with his usual common sense to see the unwisdom of this course; it was not without difficulty that he prevailed upon Churchill to abandon the idea on his own count. Only ten days after D-Day the King had the satisfaction of visiting General Montgomery's headquarters in Normandy. For eleven days in July–August he was with his armies in Italy, and in October he again visited the 21st Army Group. When the European war ended on 8 May 1945, Londoners crowded towards Buckingham Palace in their rejoicing as they had done

on 11 November 1918. In the evening the King broadcast a call to thanksgiving and to work towards a better world. There followed an exhausting fortnight of celebration which left the popularity of the monarchy in no doubt. There were state drives through London and services of thanksgiving at St. Paul's Cathedral (13 May) and at St. Giles' Cathedral, Edinburgh (16 May). On the 17th the King received addresses from both Houses of Parliament in the Great Hall of Westminster. Labour having withdrawn from the coalition, Churchill formed his 'caretaker' government and in July came the first general election of the King's reign. It proved a victory for Labour and, accepting Churchill's resignation, the King invited C. R. (later Earl) Attlee to form a government. When Attlee replied to the King's inquiry that he was thinking of Hugh (later Lord) Dalton as foreign secretary the King suggested that Ernest Bevin [q.v.] might be a better choice. This had indeed been Attlee's first thought but he had allowed himself to be influenced by Bevin's own desire for the Treasury. In the event it was Bevin who went to the Foreign Office.

The King opened Parliament on 15 August 1945, the day of the Japanese surrender, and ten days later he and the Queen left for Balmoral for a much needed rest. On his return to London in October he found that the advent of peace had done little to lighten his, or the nation's, burden. Great Britain, although still beset by austerity, was moving forward into the welfare State; the British Empire was evolving into the British Commonwealth of Nations; and Russian imperialism was on the march. Some of the new ministers lacked experience; while not out of sympathy with Labour there were occasions when the King felt that they were going ahead too fast and that he should exercise the right of the monarch to advise and even to warn. This he was able to do the more easily in that he now had a width of experience and a maturity of judgement which made it natural for people to turn to him for guidance.

In 1947 the King and Queen and the two princesses paid an extensive visit to Southern Africa where the King opened Parliament at Cape Town 21 February, and in Salisbury, Southern Rhodesia, 7 April, and where, also at Cape Town, the Princess Elizabeth celebrated her twenty-first birthday. It was always a matter of regret to the King that he was never able to visit India. The dissolution of the Indian Empire and the emergence of India as a sovereign independent republic within the British Commonwealth brought problems in the relation of the Sovereign to the Commonwealth in which he took great interest; but the necessary legislation had not been completed before he died.

On 20 November 1947 the Princess Elizabeth married Lieutenant Philip Mountbatten, R.N., son of the late Prince Andrew of Greece, whose elevation to the peerage as Duke of Edinburgh was announced on that day. Five months later, 26 April 1948, the King and Queen celebrated their silver wedding and drove in state to St. Paul's Cathedral for a service of thanksgiving. In the following October, for the first time since the war, the King opened Parliament in full state. He had, as usual, a heavy programme of engagements which included a visit to Australia and New Zealand in the spring of 1949. But symptoms of early arteriosclerosis had been apparent for some time and it now seemed that his right leg might have to be amputated. The first announcement of his condition was made on 23 November 1948 when the Australian tour was cancelled. A right lumbar sympathectomy operation was performed at Buckingham Palace 12 March 1949, from which the King made a good recovery although he was not restored to complete activity.

At the general election of February 1950 Labour was returned with but a narrow majority, and to anxiety at home over the uncertainty of government and a precarious economic situation was added anxiety over the outbreak of the Korean war. Both continued into the following year and even the Festival of Britain, opened by the King from the steps of St. Paul's on 3 May 1951, could not dispel the gloom. Towards the end of the month the King succumbed to influenza. There followed convalescence at Sandringham and Balmoral; but he was found to have a malignant growth and on 23 September underwent an operation for the removal of his left lung. Attlee had already asked for a dissolution of Parliament and on 5 October the King was able to give his approval to the act of dissolution. With the return of the Conservatives with a small majority Churchill once more became his prime minister. From the list of government appointments the post of

deputy prime minister, which had crept in during the war, was deleted on the King's instructions as being unconstitutional. As he did not fail to observe, it would have restricted his freedom of choice in the event of the death or resignation of the prime minister.

A day of national thanksgiving for the King's recovery was observed on 2 December and there followed a family Christmas at his beloved Sandringham. On the last day of January 1952 the King went to London Airport to see the Princess Elizabeth and the Duke of Edinburgh off on a visit to East Africa, Australia, and New Zealand. But their tour was perforce curtailed for after a happy day's shooting the King died in his sleep at Sandringham early on the morning of 6 February 1952. After lying in state in Westminster Hall he was buried on the 15th in St. George's Chapel, Windsor, where a memorial chapel was built and dedicated in 1969.

Trained to service, although not to the throne, the King had served to the limits of his strength and of the confines of monarchy. Scrupulous in observing his constitutional position, he was nevertheless determined to exercise the role of monarch to the full in the service of his people. It was always an underlying frustration that he could not do more; and a mark of his modest diffidence that he failed to appreciate how much he did by being what he was. The whole of his reign was overshadowed by war and the fears and changes brought about by war. At such a time a nation needs not only the warrior leader which it found in Churchill but also the image of the way of life for which it fights, and this it found in the King. Lithe and handsome, good at sports, an excellent shot and a skilled horseman, he was the country squire, the racehorse owner, the freemason, and above all the family man. His approach to life was one of common sense and humour. He made no claims to brilliance of intellect yet had a questing mind for which the twentieth century held no fears; his keenness of observation and determination to get to the heart of the matter could open up new lines of thought in others. He had few hobbies but was well versed in all that concerned his *métier* as monarch. He was the King *malgré lui* whom the nation had watched grow into kingship with a steadfast courage which had earned him their respect, their gratitude, and their affection.

The King was painted by many of the leading artists of the day, the state portrait of him in his coronation robes being by Sir Gerald Kelly in 1938. There was, in addition, the statue in the Mall by William McMillan which was unveiled by the Queen on 21 October 1955.

[John W. Wheeler-Bennett, *King George VI*, 1958.]   HELEN M. PALMER.

GERE, CHARLES MARCH (1869–1957), artist, was born 5 June 1869 in Gloucester. His father, Edward Williams Gere, a member of an American family long settled in Massachusetts, was a partner in the firm of Hayden, Gere & Co., brassfounders of Haydensville. After the death of his first wife he sold his share of the business and came to England where in 1868 he married Emma March, of Gloucester. Charles was their only child.

Educated at a school in Windsor, Gere received his first artistic training at the Gloucester School of Arts and Crafts. He continued his training at the Birmingham School of Art and taught there under E. R. Taylor, who kept the arts and crafts movement very much alive. Gere practised portrait painting, designing for stained glass, and embroidery. He went to Italy to study tempera painting and learnt to speak Italian fluently. For a time associated with William Morris [q.v.], among the books he illustrated for the Kelmscott Press were the *Fioretti* of St. Francis, Dante, and the *Morte d'Arthur*. Later he worked with St. John Hornby [q.v.] at the Ashendene Press.

At his studio at Bridge End, Warwick, Gere gradually became known as a painter of landscapes with figures in oil, tempera, and water-colour. He was a member of both the New English Art Club and the Royal Water Colour Society. He also exhibited with the Royal Academy. In 1904, with his half-sister Margeret Gere, herself a distinguished artist, he settled at Painswick, then a quiet village in the unspoilt Cotswolds between Stroud and Gloucester. He became a member of the Cheltenham Group of Artists and was its president in 1945; and a member of the Gloucester diocesan advisory committee. He was elected A.R.A. in 1934 and R.A. in 1939. In 1941 he exhibited at the Academy a striking battle scene 'The last stand at Calais'.

His early figure paintings were in the manner of the early Italian painters. An extraordinarily accurate and careful draughtsman, he trained his memory for landscape by making methodical notes of the subject on the spot, afterwards completing the work in the studio in oil or tempera on silk or thin canvas.

The best period of his art was when the Cotswold countryside inspired him. The small landscapes he then painted show that he was deeply conscious of the charm of the simple life and the sacramental significance of everyday actions; his holidays in Northern Italy and Wales provided him with rich and glowing subjects. These have a freshness of colour, and innocence of feeling and vein of lyricism, which, though gentler and more subdued, stand in the direct line of descent from the ecstatic poetic landscapes of Calvert and Palmer. His productions of landscapes in oil on a larger scale for the Academy were not always so successful. Although the structure of the hilly escarpments and broad sketches of the Severn Valley bathed in sunlight were realized with great fidelity, as in 'Tidal Severn' and 'Mouth of Severn', his pictures were in fact open windows with the subject cut by the frame, instead of being composed in relation to it. His paintings are to be seen at the Walker Art Gallery, Liverpool, the Birmingham Art Gallery, and in the Tate Gallery. Throughout his long life he painted exquisite water-colour portraits of children.

He was a man of great personal charm and urbanity, whose New England ancestry gave an austerity to his personality which strengthened the weight of his opinions. His level-headed kindliness of manner made him an excellent committee man and his advice was often sought by students and his many friends. He died, unmarried, in Gloucester 3 August 1957. There is a self-portrait in Cheltenham Art Gallery.

[Personal knowledge.]
     EDWARD R. PAYNE.

GIBB, SIR ALEXANDER (1872–1958), engineer, was born at Broughty Ferry 12 February 1872, the eldest son and fourth of the eleven children of Alexander Easton Gibb and his wife, Hope Brown Paton. For four generations his forebears had been civil engineers: his great-great-grandfather, William Gibb, was a contemporary of James Brindley and John Smeaton [qq.v.]; his great-grandfather, John Gibb [q.v.], an apprentice of John Rennie [q.v.], became a deputy to Thomas Telford [q.v.] and a founder-member of the Institution of Civil

Engineers; his grandfather, Alexander, was a pupil of Telford; and his father founded the contracting firm which became Easton Gibb & Son.

Gibb was educated at Rugby School and after a year at University College, London, was articled to (Sir) John Wolfe-Barry [q.v.] and Henry Marc Brunel. Two years in their office were followed by works experience on the Caledonian Railway and the new Barry dock. His pupilage completed, Gibb became Barry's resident engineer on the Metropolitan Railway extension between Whitechapel and Bow, but after two years he joined his father who was building the King Edward VII bridge at Kew. For sixteen years he remained with Easton Gibb & Son, his greatest and last contract being the construction of Rosyth naval base, which his energetic acceleration of the original programme brought into use during the war.

In 1916 Gibb was appointed chief engineer, ports construction, to the British armies in France with responsibility for organizing the reconstruction of Belgian ports and railway junctions which it was expected the Germans would demolish in their retreat before a British offensive. In 1918 he became civil engineer-in-chief to the Admiralty where to counter the submarine menace he developed the 'mystery towers' to be sunk in the English Channel, but the war ended before they could be used. In 1919 he became director-general of civil engineering in the newly created Ministry of Transport where the two projects which particularly engaged his attention were the Channel Tunnel and the Severn Barrage. He always maintained that the latter, a scheme for harnessing the tidal rise and fall of the river to produce electric power, would ultimately be built.

In 1921 Gibb left government service and entered upon a career as a consulting engineer, establishing in 1922 the firm of Sir Alexander Gibb & Partners at Queen Anne's Lodge, Westminster. During the first few months the firm undertook the design and erection of the aquarium for the Zoological Society and the first designs for Barking power-station. Gibb had great faith in the future of hydro-electric development and in collaboration with C. H. Merz [q.v.] and William McLellan was responsible for the Galloway scheme, which, completed in 1936, was the first major work of this kind. Among his other notable achievements were the Kincardine bridge, the Guinness brewery at Park

Royal, the Captain Cook graving dock at Sydney, the Singapore naval base, and, in wartime collaboration, the designs for Mulberry harbour and an underground factory for aeroplane engines at Corsham. Resolved to make his firm the largest of its kind in the country, Gibb was interested in projects all over the world and by 1939 had travelled 280,000 miles and visited sixty countries.

Of particular interest was the study Gibb made of the port of Rangoon. From 1910 the navigable channel to the port had been progressively obstructed by a silt bar about 7 miles long forming at the mouth of Rangoon River. Gibb was consulted in 1929; in 1931, when the depth of the channel had become seriously reduced, he decided to build a hydraulic model to elucidate the problem. This model, installed at University College, London, reproduced a year's tidal movements in fifteen hours. The river and sea beds were initially moulded to represent conditions as they existed in 1875 and the model was then run continuously to bring its state to 1932. The agreement between the observed conditions at Rangoon and those given by the model was good; the model was then used to predict probable future conditions. The indications were that after a few more years the bar would begin to disappear and Gibb therefore recommended that no expensive remedial works were necessary. In 1936 the silting reached its maximum and thereafter conditions steadily improved.

Gibb was appointed C.B. and K.B.E. in 1918 and G.B.E. in 1920. For his services to Belgium in the war of 1914–18 he was made a commander of the Order of the Crown of Belgium. He was elected F.R.S. in 1936, was president of the Institution of Civil Engineers (1936–7) and of numerous other professional bodies, received an honorary LL.D. from Edinburgh University, and was a member of the Queen's Bodyguard for Scotland (Royal Company of Archers) and of the Royal Fine Art Commission.

Gibb delighted in his work and in outdoor activities; shooting and fishing were his recreations. In 1937 his health began to fail but this interfered little with his work until 1940. From then onwards he was obliged to ease off, but until 1945 he paid at least two weekly visits to his office. He died at Hartley Wintney 21 January 1958.

In 1900 he married Norah Isobel (died 1940), daughter of Fleet-Surgeon John Lowry Monteith, R.N., and had three sons. The eldest, Alistair, succeeded as head of the firm after the war of 1939–45 but died after an accident in 1955.

Two portraits of Gibb by L. Campbell Taylor, one of them in full-length academic dress, are at Queen Anne's Lodge; a third, by Sir William Rothenstein, is in the collection of presidential portraits at the Institution of Civil Engineers.

[G. P. Harrison and A. J. S. Pippard in *Biographical Memoirs of Fellows of the Royal Society*, vol. v, 1959; Godfrey Harrison, *Alexander Gibb*, 1950; private information; personal knowledge.]

A. J. SUTTON PIPPARD.

GIBB, SIR CLAUDE DIXON (1898–1959), engineer, was born at Alberton, South Australia, 29 June 1898, the third child of John Gilbert Gibb, carrier, of Port Adelaide, and his wife, Caroline Elizabeth Dixon. He went to Alberton Primary School and Lefevre High School and thence by scholarship to the South Australian School of Mines where he studied mechanical and electrical engineering. He joined the Adelaide Cement Company as an electrician and in 1917–19 was a pilot in the Australian Flying Corps, serving in France.

After the war Gibb obtained a post as senior research assistant to (Sir) Robert Chapman at the university of Adelaide where he took his degree in engineering and the diploma in applied science in 1923 and in 1924 won an Angas engineering research scholarship. Deciding to get experience in England he joined Messrs. C. A. Parsons in 1924 as a student apprentice. He progressed to the drawing office and thence to the outside erection staff where his work attracted the attention of Sir Charles Parsons (whose notice he subsequently contributed to this Dictionary) who made him manager first of the steam test house and later of the design and drawing offices at the Heaton works. In 1929 he became a director and chief engineer; in 1937 general manager; and in 1943 joint managing director.

The firm's work for the navy brought Gibb into touch with Engineer Vice-Admiral Sir Harold Brown who became director-general of munitions production at the Ministry of Supply and who in October 1940 asked Gibb to join him as his assistant. Gibb became director-general of weapons and instruments production (1941) and his engineering common sense, organizing ability, firmness, and decisiveness won him a great reputation. In 1943

he became director-general of armoured fighting vehicles and in 1944 chairman of the Tank Board, still in the Ministry of Supply. At that time British tanks were in trouble: design was dispersed in the offices of a number of manufacturers without effective co-ordination and output was unsatisfactory. Gibb immediately decided that his department would take full responsibility for design and re-organized production. The Centurion and all the special tank developments for infantry support were the result.

At the end of the war, despite offers from various large engineering concerns, Gibb returned to Parsons where he became chairman and managing director in September 1945. His pride in the Parsons organization was unbounded and he wished for nothing more than to make the firm outstanding. In this he succeeded. Surmounting post-war difficulties of licences and priorities he re-equipped first the machine shops, then the foundry and erecting shops at Heaton; his vision in forecasting the post-war trend of size and design in turbo-alternators enabled Parsons successfully to expand their output. Gibb was also chairman of Grubb, Parsons & Co., and took a close interest in their specialized optical work. In 1944 he joined the Reyrolle board, becoming deputy chairman in 1945 and chairman in 1949–58. During this period Reyrolles expanded at a greater rate than ever before and largely re-equipped their factory.

Alone among the heads of the great British electrical firms, Gibb realized the importance of the new developments in atomic energy and in 1947–8 he collaborated with Risley in preparing the first designs for a graphite-moderated gas-cooled nuclear power plant. Although the scheme evolved was clumsy it proved the conception to be practical and formed the foundation for the design study at Harwell in 1952, which in turn provided the framework for the Calder Hall design. Gibb's engineers formed part of the Harwell team and later of the Calder Hall team at Risley. The turbo-alternators and the gas circulating blowers at Calder Hall were supplied by C. A. Parsons.

When it was decided that the responsibility for the design and construction of nuclear power plants should be given to industrial engineering firms, Parsons were one of the four electrical firms which were asked to form consortia. Gibb brought together eight companies already skilled in nuclear engineering and formed them into the Nuclear Power Plant Company which received one of the first two orders for industrial nuclear power plants. He also formed a joint company with the Great Lakes Carbon Corporation of America and built a factory in Newcastle for the manufacture of graphite for use in nuclear reactors.

Gibb was elected F.R.S. in 1946, was a member of the council in 1955–7, and vice-president in 1956–7. He was vice-president of the Institution of Mechanical Engineers (1945–51) and received its Hawksley medal (twice), the Parsons memorial medal, and the James Watt medal. He was president of the engineering section of the British Association in 1951; chairman of the council of the International Electrical Association, of the Athlone Fellowship committee, and of the committee on the organization and control of government research expenditure; and member of the Ridley committee on the use of coal, gas, and electricity, of the Board of Trade's informal advisory group on exports, and of the council of King's College, Newcastle upon Tyne. He received honorary degrees from London and Durham, was knighted in 1945, and appointed K.B.E. in 1956.

Gibb loved speed both in business and in movement. He was a good lecturer and speaker who never hesitated to state his opinions quite regardless of whether they would be unpalatable to his hearers or embarrassing to other people. As an organizer he was clear, firm, and methodical, but like many men who are full of energy and supremely confident he found it difficult, until his last years, to delegate responsibility. As a business man he was astute and far-sighted. He was an engineer of a type which is unfortunately rare: at home in the design office, proud to use workshop tools and machines as a craftsman, yet having a thorough grasp of the scientific theory on which the art of engineering rests. Although at times he could be quite infuriating to his friends, he won not merely respect but also deep affection from all those who worked for or with him.

In 1925 Gibb married Margaret Bate (died 1969), daughter of William Harris, of Totnes; they had no children. In 1948 he made a complete recovery from a severe coronary thrombosis, as he did five years later from a second and a third; but he collapsed and died at Newark, New Jersey, airport, 15 January 1959.

[Sir Christopher Hinton in *Biographical*

Memoirs of Fellows of the Royal Society, vol. ▪ 1959; private information; personal know ledge.]   HINTON OF BANKSIDI

GIBBINGS, ROBERT JOHN (1889 1958), wood-engraver, author, and boo designer, born in Cork 23 March 1889, wa the second son of the Rev. Edward Gibt ings, later canon of Cork Cathedral, an his wife, Caroline Rouvière, daughter c Robert Day, a business man of Corl He was educated at local schools and a eighteen matriculated at University Co lege, Cork, where for two years he studie medicine. In 1911 he went to London t study art at the Slade School. In 1912 h attended the Central School of Arts an Crafts where he was taught the techniqu of wood-engraving by Noel Rooke.

In August 1914 Gibbings was com missioned in the 4th Royal Munste Fusiliers. In 1915 he served in Gallipol where he was shot through the throat. I March 1918 he was invalided out of th army with the rank of captain. He the helped to form the Society of Woo Engravers, of which he was the firs honorary secretary. To the first exhibitio of this society, in 1920, Gibbings contr buted twelve prints. As a result he wa commissioned to engrave a number c designs for advertisements. In 1921 h produced his first book, *Twelve Woo Engravings*. He exhibited eight engraving in the second exhibition (1921), five in th third (1922), and six in the fourth (1923 In 1923 he was commissioned to illustrat Samuel Butler's *Erewhon*, and the nex year, by Harold Taylor, the founder of th Golden Cockerel Press, to illustrate Brar tôme's *Lives of Gallant Ladies*. Whils Gibbings was working on these block Taylor fell ill, and the Golden Cocker Press would have closed down if Gibbing had not been enabled to buy it by financia support from a friend.

The Press was at Waltham S Lawrence, in Berkshire. With Gibbings a its director and book designer it produce 72 books between 1924 and 1933, of whic 19 were illustrated by Gibbings himse Forty-eight of its productions were illu trated with wood-engravings. Among th engravers whom Gibbings employed— giving several of them their first commis sions—were John Nash, David Jone Eric Ravilious [q.v.], Blair Hughe Stanton, John Farleigh, and, mo notably, Eric Gill [q.v.], whose editior of the *Canterbury Tales* (1929–31) and th *Four Gospels* (1931) were probably th most significant achievements of the Press. For several years it enjoyed commercial success, but it was severely hit by the international slump and in 1933 Gibbings sold his financial interest in it.

He had, in the previous years, undertaken a few commissions for other publishers, including illustrations for *The Charm of Birds* (1927) by Lord Grey of Fallodon [q.v.]. In 1929 he had spent four months in Tahiti, having been commissioned to illustrate a book that James Norman Hall was to write. Instead of this, his visit resulted in two books, *The Seventh Man* (1930) and *Iorana* (1932), both written and illustrated by himself. He now illustrated books for several British publishers. For the Limited Editions Club of New York he illustrated *Le Morte d'Arthur* (1936). In that year he was appointed lecturer in book production in the university of Reading, a post which he held until 1942. He visited the West Indies and the Red Sea to make underwater drawings of fish and coral for his book *Blue Angels and Whales* (1938). In 1938 the National University of Ireland conferred an honorary M.A. upon him.

In 1939 Gibbings undertook a book about his exploration of the River Thames in a punt, and this enjoyed a great success when published as *Sweet Thames Run Softly* (1940). It was the first of a series combining topographical impressions, personal anecdote, and observations of nature, illustrated with the author's engravings. For many months in 1941 he lived in a remote cottage at Llangurig, close to Plynlimmon, writing and illustrating *Coming Down the Wye* (1942). He then returned to Ireland to produce *Lovely is the Lee* (1945) which became a Book-of-the-Month choice in the United States. *Over the Reefs* (1948) was the fruit of a long visit to the South Seas, and *Sweet Cork of Thee* (1951) celebrated another return to Ireland. *Coming Down the Seine* (1953) and *Trumpets from Montparnasse* (1955) recorded visits to France and Italy, during the second of which he resumed the painting in oils which he had abandoned after his student days. On his return to England he bought a cottage at Long Wittenham in Berkshire. Prophetically entitled *Till I End My Song*, his last book, again about the Thames, was completed there despite increasing ill health. He died in Oxford, 19 January 1958, three months after its publication.

A tall, massively built man, with twinkling eyes, aquiline features, and a beard, Gibbings had great natural charm, a fund of Irish humour, and an exceptional store of miscellaneous knowledge of birds, fishes, plants, geology, and archaeology.

His work as a book designer at the Golden Cockerel Press was rivalled only by that of Francis Meynell at the Nonesuch Press. As a wood-engraver he was one of the leaders of the revival of this art. His own work was at first characterized by bold contrasts and organization of masses, with a skilful use of the 'vanishing line'. Later his technique became more subtle, with greater emphasis on gradation of texture. The eight 'river books', containing altogether nearly 500 engravings, all closely integrated with his own text, represent a remarkable combination of the talents of author, illustrator, and book designer.

Gibbings married twice: first, Mary, daughter of Colonel Edward G. Pennefather, by whom he had three sons and a daughter; and secondly, Elisabeth, daughter of Arthur Herbert Empson, by whom he had one son and two daughters. A head by Marshall C. Hutson was exhibited at the Royal Academy in 1948.

[Thomas Balston, *The Wood-Engravings of Robert Gibbings*, 1949; *The Wood Engravings of Robert Gibbings, with Some Recollections by the Artist*, ed. Patience Empson, 1959; A. Mary Kirkus, Patience Empson, and John Harris, *Robert Gibbings, a Bibliography*, 1962; personal knowledge.]   J. C. H. HADFIELD.

GIBSON, WILLIAM PETTIGREW (1902–1960), keeper of the National Gallery, was born in Glasgow 3 January 1902, the elder son of Edwin Arthur Gibson, Scottish physician, by his wife, Ellen Shaw Pettigrew. He was educated at Wilkinson's in Orme Square, at Westminster, and at Christ Church, Oxford; at all three he was the exact contemporary and close friend of Humfry Payne [q.v.], later to become director of the British School at Athens, and his future career certainly owed something to the influence of Payne's artistic interests. He read medicine, and took a second in physiology at Oxford in 1924; but soon after he went down he abandoned his medical studies, much to his father's disappointment and at considerable sacrifice to himself, and devoted himself to the history of art. In 1927, after two difficult years during which he worked with great determination to fit himself for a new career, he was appointed to the staff of the Wallace Collection as lecturer and assistant keeper, and remained there until 1936, when he became reader in the history of art in the university of London and deputy director of the Courtauld Institute of Art. In 1939 he was appointed keeper of the National Gallery under Sir Kenneth Clark (later a life peer) and he remained in that appointment for the rest of his life. He married in 1940 Christina, youngest daughter of Francis Ogilvy, whose eldest sister had married (Sir) Philip Hendy, Gibson's contemporary at Westminster and Christ Church, his predecessor at the Wallace Collection, and afterwards his director at the National Gallery. The Gibsons settled soon after the war at Wyddiall Hall in North Hertfordshire, where Gibson, though brought up as a Londoner, came to take great interest in country pursuits, farming, and riding in company with his charming and talented wife. They had no children.

Gibson was a sympathetic lecturer in his days at the Wallace Collection, and three of his lectures on French painting were published in 1930. Apart from these, however, he published only an occasional article, usually on French art, in the learned art periodicals. For this reason, perhaps, he was less well known to the art world in general than were some of his colleagues; but his abilities were sincerely respected by a long succession of trustees of the Gallery during the twenty-one years of his keepership. Throughout the war he spent longer periods on duty, day and night, than any other member of the staff; and it was largely due to his devotion and imperturbability that the buildings did not suffer more from incendiary bombs. In later years, under a new director, his experience was equally valuable; he was conscientious and exact in keeping before the board the rules of the Gallery and the terms of the trusteeship, and his good manners, independence of judgement, and robust common sense lent weight to his advice. On what he considered a matter of principle he was determined, and could be obstinate.

Gibson was a tall, bulky man, of distinguished appearance, not athletic but physically very strong, having been an oarsman at Westminster and Christ Church. In personal relationships he was uncompromising, but most loyal to those who enjoyed his confidence and affection. When Sir Charles Prescott, one of his greatest friends, died in 1955, Gibson

collaborated with others in producing a memoir of him, which was privately printed; and the essay which he himself contributed to that book not only affords a good example of his elegant style as a writer, but also reveals something of his affectionate nature and of his own characteristic tastes. A devout member of the Roman Catholic Church, he died in London 22 April 1960.

[Private information; personal knowledge.

J. Byam Shaw

GILLIATT, Sir WILLIAM (1884-1956) obstetrician, was born 7 June 1884 at Boston, Lincolnshire. His father, also William Gilliatt, came of farming stock married Alice Rose, and later abandoned the land in favour of a chemist shop which he owned and administered in Boston. William, fourth in a family of five, was educated at Kirton village school and Wellingborough College. His headmaster, impressed by his ability persuaded him to give up his original idea of farming in favour of medicine. In 1902 he entered University College Hospital but after a year transferred to the Middlesex, where he had a distinguished career winning a number of scholarships. After qualifying in the London M.B., B.S. in 1908, he was awarded the Lyell gold medal in 1909 and went on to hold various resident house appointments, taking the London M.D. in 1910 and winning the gold medal in obstetrics and gynaecology. Two years later he took the F.R.C.S. (England) and the M.S. (London) while still holding the post of registrar and tutor in obstetrics and gynaecology at the Middlesex Hospital. In 1912 he was appointed first assistant resident medical officer at Queen Charlotte's Maternity Hospital, and later pathologist and registrar.

In 1916 Gilliatt was appointed to the honorary staff of King's College Hospital as assistant obstetric and gynaecological surgeon and lecturer in the medical school. In the same year he was elected physician to outpatients at Queen Charlotte's Hospital and in 1919 obstetric surgeon to inpatients. But in 1920 he resigned from Queen Charlotte's because he felt it impossible properly to fulfil the responsibilities of working in two large obstetrical departments at the same time He was thereby able to give more time and attention to the obstetric department at King's College Hospital, where his teaching abilities were given every opportunity and where he was senior obstetric

nd gynaecological surgeon from 1925 to
946. In 1926 Gilliatt was appointed to the
onorary staff of the Samaritan Hospital
or Women. His association with this
ospital continued without interruption
ntil 1946. Other hospitals where he
vorked as an honorary member of the
taff were Bromley, the Maudsley, and
St. Saviour's.

In his professional and academic life
Gilliatt will be remembered as a notable
eacher with a clear and concise method.
He was a skilful and dexterous obstetri-
ian, a painstaking but not spectacular
urgeon. Above all, he excelled as an
astute diagnostician and as a clinician
vith a remarkably good judgement and
ommon sense. He wrote relatively little,
out made valuable contributions on the
ubject of maternal mortality and mor-
idity. He contributed to the *Historical
Review of British Obstetrics and Gynaecology*
oublished in 1954 and was a regular con-
ributor to successive editions of the 'Ten
Teachers' series in obstetrics and gynae-
ology.

When the British (later Royal) College
of Obstetricians and Gynaecologists was
ounded in 1929, Gilliatt, as a member of
a teaching hospital staff, automatically
ecame a foundation fellow. From the
very earliest days of the College he played
an important role, being elected to the
ouncil in 1932, serving as president
1946-9), and remaining almost without
nterruption active in College affairs until
he day of his death. Gilliatt's capacity for
lear and logical thought and argument
made him an ideal committee man, and he
excelled as chairman of many committees
ooth in the College and at King's College
Hospital.

In spite of a very full academic pro-
essional life, Gilliatt developed a con-
iderable private practice especially in
obstetrics. Although devoted to his
oatients, he never allowed his private
oractice to become numerically large
enough to interfere with his other re-
ponsibilities. He attended Princess
Marina, Duchess of Kent, when all her
hildren were born and he also attended
Princess Elizabeth when Prince Charles
and Princess Anne were born in 1948
and 1950. After Princess Elizabeth
ucceeded to the throne Gilliatt was
appointed surgeon-gynaecologist to the
Queen. He was appointed C.V.O. in
936, knighted in 1948, and promoted
K.C.V.O. in 1949. In 1947 he was elected
R.C.P. and in 1953 was made an

honorary master of midwifery of the
Society of Apothecaries. In 1954–6 he was
president of the Royal Society of Medicine.

In his younger days Gilliatt played football for the Casuals, and later became
a keen and very good golfer. In later years,
however, his main recreation was on the
racecourse, for he was a member of many
racing clubs including Ascot and Kempton
Park, where he was a very regular visitor.
Although not a great clubman, he was
a keen freemason. Essentially of a shy disposition, Gilliatt built his success on the
foundation-stone of a strong character
combined with an inbred sense of duty
and responsibility. He was possessed of
a stern self-discipline and a single-minded
determination which at times gave the
impression of austerity and even ruthlessness. He thought carefully before speaking
and did not waste words, but was always
approachable and willing to give advice
and encouragement to the younger man.
As a public speaker he did not excel, but
his quiet dignity, courtesy, and sincerity
more than compensated. In his later years
he became a very successful elder statesman, guiding the affairs of those institutions which had absorbed the best years
of his life. There is a portrait in the Royal
College of Obstetricians and Gynaecologists, painted during his lifetime by
David Alison; and another painted from
a photograph after his death by Edward
I. Halliday hangs in the Royal Society of
Medicine.

In 1914 Gilliatt married Anne Louise
Jane, daughter of John Kann, stockbroker. She herself was a doctor and practised for several years as an anaesthetist.
They had one daughter, and a son, Roger
William, who became professor of neurology at the National Hospital for Nervous
Diseases. Gilliatt died in a motor accident
at Chertsey 27 September 1956.

[Private information; personal knowledge.]
JOHN PEEL.

GILLIES, SIR HAROLD DELF (1882–
1960), plastic surgeon, was born in Dunedin, New Zealand, 17 June 1882, the
youngest of the six sons of Robert Gillies,
a contractor and a noted amateur
astronomer, and his wife, Emily Street.
His great-uncle was Edward Lear [q.v.],
author of the *Book of Nonsense*. He was
educated at Wanganui College where he
was captain of cricket, and at Gonville and
Caius College, Cambridge, where he played
golf (1903–5) and rowed (1904) for the
university and obtained a second class in

part i of the natural sciences tripos in 1904. From Cambridge he moved for his clinical studies to St. Bartholomew's Hospital, qualifying in 1908 and obtaining his F.R.C.S. in 1910. After a minimal experience of general surgery he became interested in otorhinolaryngology and worked with (Sir) Milsom Rees.

Gillies's great opportunity came with the war of 1914–18. He joined the Royal Army Medical Corps in 1915, went to France, and was enormously impressed by the work of French and German surgeons in the field of reconstructive surgery in facial injuries. Such was his enthusiasm that a centre for the treatment of these patients was started at Aldershot later in the same year, and he was placed in charge of it under Sir Arbuthnot Lane [q.v.]. In 1918 the centre moved to Queen Mary's Hospital, Sidcup, and eventually was administered by the Ministry of Pensions to which Gillies became honorary consultant. The experiences gained in the reconstruction of facial wounds were rapidly expanded to cover the whole field of reconstructive surgery: burns, limb injuries, congenital malformations, and so on.

Many of the surgeons trained by Gillies returned after the war to their native lands. (Sir) William Kelsey Fry remained at Guy's Hospital to continue as the great dental collaborator and (Sir) Ivan Magill at the Westminster Hospital as the pioneer of intra-tracheal anaesthesia. Gillies found himself alone, with T. P. Kilner, who had joined him in 1918, as his assistant, and took the plunge into private practice as a specialist in plastic surgery. Things were difficult at first, but improved. Gillies became plastic surgeon to St. Bartholomew's and other hospitals, to the London County Council, and to the Royal Air Force. In 1924 he treated a number of Danish casualties in Copenhagen following the premature explosion of a phosphorous bomb and was subsequently made a commander of the Order of Dannebrog. He had been appointed C.B.E. in 1920 and was knighted in 1930.

When war broke out in 1939 most of Gillies's trainees were abroad. There were in the United Kingdom only four plastic surgeons of experience. His cousin, (Sir) Archibald McIndoe [q.v.], and another New Zealander, Rainsford Mowlem, were in partnership with him; Kilner was now working independently. It fell to these four men to train a multiplicity of surgeons in the field of plastic surgery,

whilst dealing with the many thousands o patients pouring into their units. Gillies team worked in Rooksdown House, nea Basingstoke, and the centre became famous one in plastic surgery, althoug not receiving the publicity which perhaț it deserved.

In 1946 Gillies became the first pres dent of the newly formed British Associ tion of Plastic Surgeons and in 1948 l was awarded the honorary fellowship the American College of Surgeons. In 195 he was elected the first president of tl International Plastic Society at Stocl holm. In 1948 he was made a commande of the Order of St. Olaf for trainin Norwegian surgeons during the war. H received honorary degrees from Ljubljar (1957) and Colombia (1959), and in 196 the special honorary citation of the Amer can Society of Plastic and Reconstructiv Surgery. In their journal (January 196 Dr. Jerome P. Webster wrote: 'He wa a giant pre-eminent in his chosen field endeavor. The ideas engendered by h fertile brain have spread and are bein spread afar, and generations of plast surgeons will be affected by what he ga\ forth to the world. His memory may peris but his influence is immortal.'

An indefatigable worker, Gillies wrot many papers and was in great deman as a lecturer. He published two notab books: *Plastic Surgery of the Face* (1920 which recorded his experiences in tl war, and *The Principles and Art of Plast Surgery* (with D. Ralph Millard, 2 vols 1957) which will remain a classic.

In versatility Gillies was a Renaissanc figure. He was a noted athlete in h younger days, an excellent artist, and or of the best dry fly fishermen in Englan He played golf for England against Sco land in 1908, 1925, and 1926, and won tl St. George's Grand Challenge Cup in 191 He thoroughly and unashamedly enjoye being in the limelight and his famous hig golf tee was typical. Finally he was re quested not to use it by the St. Andrew Golf Club but it afforded him enormot pleasure and not a little publicity as a eccentric. Until the end of his days l retained a 'Peter Pan' streak, enjoye practical joking, and could on occasior such as formal dinners behave in suc a way as to upset the more dignified an often much younger members of his pro fession. His zest for painting and h proficiency in oils were exemplified in 195 by a second one-man show at Foyles 132 paintings of which at least a thir

vere sold. His first exhibition was in 1947
nd a posthumous one was held at
Valker's Galleries in 1961.

In 1911 Gillies married Kathleen
Margaret (died 1957), daughter of Josiah
Jackson, a brick manufacturer; they had
two sons and two daughters. In 1957 he
married Marjorie, daughter of John T.
Clayton, a jeweller; she had worked with
him in the operating theatre for many
years.

Gillies died in London 10 September
1960. A portrait by Bernard Adams,
'Fishing the Test', is in the possession of
the family and another by the same artist
is in Queen Mary's Hospital, Roehampton.
A third portrait, by Howard Barron, was
presented in 1963 by the British Association of Plastic Surgeons to the Royal
College of Surgeons.

[Reginald Pound, *Gillies, Surgeon Extraordinary*, 1964; private information; personal
knowledge.]   RICHARD BATTLE.

GINNER, ISAAC CHARLES (1878–
1952), artist, was born 4 March 1878 in
Cannes, the second son of Isaac Benjamin
Ginner who kept a chemist shop there and
had married a Miss Wightman, a woman
of Scottish descent. Of his two brothers
one died in infancy and one became a
doctor; his sister became an actress who
concentrated on reviving Greek dancing.
Perhaps the most important member of
the family, and certainly the most useful,
was a Charles Harrison, the husband of his
mother's sister, who appears to have been
a financial prop to the Ginners in general
and, in emergencies, to Charles in particular.

Ginner left the Collège Stanislas at
sixteen after a serious illness and sailed in
a tramp steamer belonging to his uncle
which plied around the Mediterranean and
in the south Atlantic. His health restored,
he returned to Cannes and was employed
for a short time and without enthusiasm in
an engineer's office. His growing interest in
art met with family opposition but after
his father's death he was allowed to go
to Paris, and at the age of twenty-one
entered an architect's office where he
remained for some years.

In 1904, his family recognizing the
futility of further argument about art,
reconciled themselves to his studying
painting at the Académie Vitti. His master
was Gervais who disliked Ginner's brilliant palette so much that his pupil was
more or less forced to leave. He went to
the École des Beaux-Arts but returned to
the Vitti when Gervais left. He was, however, again unlucky in finding a master
partially unsympathetic to his ideas since
he ridiculed the artists Ginner admired.
Anglada y Camarasa who taught him had
no opinion at all of Van Gogh, who had
by this time become the most powerful
influence on Ginner and one who was to
inspire him throughout his painting career.
This sharp split of opinion decided Ginner
to leave the Vitti and work on his own.
There is no record of any sales during this
period in Paris, but in 1908 he sent work
to be exhibited at the Allied Artists' first
show in London and in 1909 he held a one-
man exhibition in Buenos Aires.

The year 1910 in which Roger Fry [q.v.]
organized the first Post-Impressionist
exhibition in London marked the moment
of revolution in England against Impressionism which was being carried to the
point of pastiche. Of the English artists
potentially distinguished at this period
few were more than dimly aware of the
new movements in art on the Continent.
The importance of Ginner was that with
his knowledge of France, and after his
discovery in London of a group with whom
he was instantly *en rapport*, he was able to
introduce to this country the ideals of Van
Gogh, Cézanne, Gauguin, Matisse, and so
on. Until then, only W. R. Sickert [q.v.]
(who always remained faithful to Impressionism), Spencer Gore, who annually
visited Dieppe, and Robert Bevan, who
had worked at Pont Aven with Gauguin,
had any first-hand knowledge of the
fundamental change taking place in
French painting. In this same year Ginner
settled in London in Chesterfield Street,
King's Cross. He attended regularly
Sickert's 'Saturdays' in Fitzroy Street,
and helped in the formation of the Camden Town Group in 1911, showing at all
the group's exhibitions at the Carfax Gallery. Later he became a founder-member
of the Cumberland Market Group and
exhibited with the London Group which
rose out of the ashes of the Camden Town.

In 1916 he was called up and joined
as a private the Ordnance Corps, being
transferred later as a sergeant in the
Intelligence Corps and stationed at Marseilles. He was recalled to England and
worked for the Canadian War Records as
lieutenant making drawings of a munitions
factory in Hereford. Of his war paintings
perhaps the most notable is 'Roberts 8,
East Leeds 1916' which was in the possession of Edward Le Bas who owned also a
self-portrait. In the years after the war

Ginner became a member of the New English Art Club. He lived variously in Hampstead, Claverton Street, and in the country. He became an A.R.A. in 1942 and was appointed C.B.E. in 1950. His main explanation in print of his beliefs as a painter was published under the title 'Neo-Realism' in the *New Age* (1 January 1914), in which he maintained that his aim in painting was a direct and complete transposition of nature and that this could only be achieved by working *en plein air* and never in the studio. The excess of detail and impasto in some of his landscapes or of Hampstead streets resulted occasionally in canvases like embossed wallpaper. But at his best his craftsmanship, control, and sensitive tonality set him so far apart from his contemporaries that he is instantly recognizable in any mixed exhibition. His influence on succeeding generations of artists was small. He died, unmarried, in London 6 January 1952. His work is to be found in a number of public collections including the Victoria and Albert Museum, and the Tate Gallery where a retrospective exhibition was held in 1954.

[Private information.]   J. WOOD PALMER.

GODLEY, SIR ALEXANDER JOHN (1867–1957), general, the eldest of the three sons of Colonel William Alexander Godley, 56th Essex Regiment, and his wife, Laura, daughter of the Rev. Godfrey Bird, rector of Great Wigborough, Essex, was born 4 February 1867. His autobiography opens in characteristic vein: 'The year Hermit won the Derby in a snowstorm, 1867, was that in which I saw the light—at Chatham, where my father was Superintendent of Gymnasia.' J. R. Godley [q.v.] was his uncle and A. D. Godley and Lord Kilbracken [qq.v.] first cousins. Godley went first to the Royal Naval School at New Cross, but family tradition in favour of the army resulted in his going to Haileybury. On his father's death straitened circumstances meant his transfer to the United Services College, whence he secured entry to the Royal Military College, Sandhurst. In 1886 he was gazetted lieutenant in the Royal Dublin Fusiliers and joined the 1st battalion at Mullingar. During 'seven delightful years of soldiering in Ireland' he developed his taste for riding, hunting, polo, and horse-racing. After a tour of duty at Sheffield and a Mounted Infantry course, he became in 1895 adjutant of the Mounted Infantry at Aldershot and was

promoted captain. In 1896 he went in the same capacity with a special service unit to South Africa, saw his first active service in the Mashonaland campaign, and was awarded his brevet majority. Back in England in June 1897 he had command of a battalion of Mounted Infantry before entering the Staff College, Camberley whence he proceeded to South Africa when war became imminent. After service as adjutant of a mounted regiment, a commander of the western defences in the siege of Mafeking, and as a staff officer to Baden-Powell and Plumer [qq.v.], Godley commanded a Rhodesian brigade with the brevet rank of lieutenant-colonel. After transfer to the Irish Guards in 1900 he returned to England in the next year. Following a term on the staff at Aldershot, he was commandant of the Mounted Infantry School at Longmoor Camp from 1903 to 1906. In that year he became G.S.O. 1 of the 2nd division at Aldershot. Visits to India and South America widened his experience and helped to prepare him for his appointment in 1910 as general officer commanding the New Zealand Military Forces with the temporary rank of major-general.

In New Zealand the Defence Act, 1909 provided for the introduction of compulsory military service in 1911. Acting on advice given by Lord Kitchener [q.v.] who had visited New Zealand in 1910, Godley arranged for the organization of a mounted brigade and an infantry brigade in each military district. He himself toured the country and stimulated a fiercely competitive spirit in the brigade camps which were held in 1913. The new territorial units, based on earlier volunteer battalions, had reached a high standard of efficiency and training by early 1914 when inspected by Sir Ian Hamilton [q.v.] inspector-general of overseas forces. Much of the credit was due to Godley who was appointed K.C.M.G. in that year.

On the outbreak of war in 1914 New Zealand offered to send an expeditionary force of all arms, and Godley was appointed to the command which he retained throughout the war. In the Gallipoli campaign he commanded the New Zealand and Australian division and in June 1916 he went to France as commander of I Anzac Corps. Until 1919 he retained command of this corps which in 1918, after the collection of all the Australian division into an Australian Corps, became the XXII Corps, retaining the New Zealand division. He was promoted temporary lieutenant-general in November 1915 and at Messines in 1917 had under his command about 120,000 men, 'twice as many as Wellington commanded at Waterloo'. He was appointed K.C.B. in 1916 and received eleven mentions in dispatches.

From 1920 until 1922 Godley was military secretary to (Sir) Winston Churchill, secretary of state for war. He was commander-in-chief of the British Army of the Rhine in 1922-4 and then (1924-8) held the appointment of G.O.C. Southern Command, England. From 1928 to 1933 he was governor of Gibraltar where he did much to stimulate interest in its past history. He was promoted general in 1923 and G.C.B. in 1928. For fifteen years he was colonel of the Royal Ulster Rifles in which capacity he visited the two regular battalions of that regiment in England, Ireland, Germany, Palestine, and Hong Kong.

'Alick' Godley was tall and handsome. Striking in appearance, he was very proud of his military bearing and turn-out. He exerted every effort to make the forces under him as efficient as possible. Naturally strict and somewhat aloof, he was not a popular commander, and many stories were told against him by the New Zealanders. Nevertheless, by his own dedicated service, he undoubtedly laid the foundations for the New Zealand division's successes and as a corps commander in France he won a very high reputation. When selecting supporters for his coat of arms he chose, dexter, an Irish Mounted Infantry soldier and, sinister, a New Zealand infantry soldier.

In 1898 Godley married Louisa Marion died 1939), eldest daughter of Robert Fowler, of Rahinston, county Meath, reputed to be 'the best woman across country' in all Ireland. She was mentioned in dispatches for her social and welfare work for New Zealand soldiers. There were no children. Godley died in Oxford 6 March 1957.

The Imperial War Museum has a charcoal and water-colour portrait by Francis Dodd and an oil by Sir Walter Russell.

[Sir Alexander Godley, *Life of an Irish Soldier*, 1939; H. Stewart, (Official History) *The New Zealand Division 1916-1919*, 1921.]

ANGUS ROSS.

GOGARTY, OLIVER JOSEPH ST. JOHN (1878-1957), surgeon, man of letters, and wit, was born in Dublin 17 August 1878, the eldest child and elder son of Henry Gogarty, a physician and

son and grandson of physicians, who died when Oliver was still a boy, and his wife, Margaret Oliver, of a family of millers in Galway. Educated first at Stonyhurst, Gogarty spent his last year at Clongowes Wood, the Jesuit college in Kildare. In England he had played professional football; at Clongowes he exhibited a precocious talent for Rabelaisian verse. He studied medicine for two years at the Royal University, then at Trinity College, Dublin, and qualified in 1907. Sir Robert Woods, the leading nose and throat surgeon of his time in Dublin, secured Gogarty's succession to him in the Richmond Hospital; later he was attached to the Meath Hospital, and he built up a large practice in his speciality.

Often distracted from his medical studies by literary pursuits, bicycle-racing, at which he was of championship class, politics and conviviality, Gogarty had made many important friendships. From James Joyce [q.v.] he was for a space of two years almost inseparable. They continued to correspond but Gogarty resented his portrait in *Ulysses* as 'stately plump Buck Mulligan' and complained that 'James Joyce was not a gentleman'. Gogarty's mocking irreverent manner, enthusiasm for the classics, with quotations always on his lips, his quips, parodies, and talent for occasional (and improper) verse, endeared him to some of the fellows in Trinity who encouraged and were amused by him: (Sir) J. P. Mahaffy, R. Y. Tyrrell, Edward Dowden [qq.v.], and H. S. Macran. Twice, successively, Dowden awarded him the vice-chancellor's prize for English verse. With the desire to emulate Oscar Wilde [q.v.], Gogarty contrived to go for two terms to Worcester College, Oxford, to compete for the Newdigate prize. In this he was unsuccessful, being defeated by a friend, G. K. A. Bell [q.v.], afterwards bishop of Chichester. Gogarty had the success accorded to witty Irishmen at Oxford but suffered some diminution in popularity by an ill-timed irreverence.

Back in Dublin, Gogarty forwarded a chance acquaintance with Arthur Griffith [q.v.] and spoke on 28 November 1905 at the first convention of Sinn Fein. Griffith, George Russell (AE) [q.v.], and Tom Kettle were the only three of Gogarty's friends against whom he never directed his wit. He formed one of the coterie which met in the Bailey restaurant, in a room specially provided, over which Griffith silently presided. (Sir) William

Orpen [q.v.], the painter, Seumas O'Sullivan, the poet, James Montgomery, wit, and afterwards film censor, were among the habitués of Dublin's equivalent to the Café Royal. There the legend of Gogarty's wit was established and the connections which, with the coming of the Free State, launched him on a political career. Gogarty was nominated to the first Senate and took a prominent part in the early days of the Free State, organizing the Tailteann Games. At the first of these he was awarded a gold medal for his book of verse, *An Offering of Swans* (1923). The title was suggested by a pair of swans he had vowed to present to the River Liffey when swimming for safety after eluding his Republican captors during the civil war. He removed for a while in 1923–4 to London where he continued to practise as a nose and throat specialist. He returned there in 1937 but after the outbreak of war in 1939 moved to America where he wrote and lectured between occasional trips to Dublin and where he remained until his death.

The occasion of Gogarty's final departure from Dublin was a successful action taken against him by Henry Morris Sinclair for libel in *As I was Going Down Sackville Street*, a book of reminiscences published in 1937. But it may be assumed that chagrin on this account was only the proximate reason for his departure. He had become increasingly a literary and political personality with inevitable repercussions in his medical practice. His house at Renvyle in county Galway, burned down in the civil war, had been rebuilt as an hotel to which he liked to invite Augustus John and other friends. W. B. Yeats [q.v.] had become an admirer and described him as 'one of the great lyric poets of our age' in his preface to his *Oxford Book of Modern Verse* (1936) in which he included seventeen of his poems. Yeats did not, however, succeed in setting a fashion for Gogarty's poetry and in subsequent anthologies he does not appear. His fame rests on his reputation as one of the great Irish wits in the tradition of John Philpot Curran [q.v.]. The vigour and spontaneity which was so much of his attraction may have militated against his success as an artist. He did not labour. Kindly and unaffected, he yet cultivated to excess the Dublin talent for denigration. Too much of his wit was directed at persons, and his loathing for Eamon de Valera became an obsession. A capacity for detecting flaws without a compensating restraint in

publishing them made Gogarty a formidable opponent and an unnerving friend. His athletic prowess and physical courage —he was a pioneer aviator in Dublin— were the admiration of his sedentary literary friends as much as his unabashed showmanship—fur coat and yellow Rolls-Royce—were looked at askance by the conservative professional classes of Dublin. He was out of place in a bourgeois community indifferent to his talent; but he never lacked admirers. He published further volumes of reminiscence: *Tumbling in the Hay* (1939) and *It Isn't This Time of Year at All* (1954), several novels, and his *Collected Poems* (1951). He contributed to this Dictionary the notices of Stephen Gwynn and James Stephens.

About five feet nine inches in height, brown haired, pale faced, with dark blue eyes under pince-nez, Gogarty altered very little in appearance. He walked briskly, head up, lips pursed, with laughter in his eyes. Orpen painted his portrait once and John twice.

In 1906 Gogarty married Martha, daughter of Bernard Duane, of Moyard, county Galway; they had two sons and one daughter. Gogarty died in New York 22 September 1957.

[Ulick O'Connor, *Oliver St. John Gogarty*, 1963; personal knowledge.]

TERENCE DE VERE WHITE.

GOLD, Sir HARCOURT GILBEY (1876–1952), oarsman, was born at Wooburn Green, Buckinghamshire, 3 May 1876, the ninth and youngest child of Henry Gold, of Hedsor, Buckinghamshire, and his wife, Charlotte Anne, daughter of Henry Gilbey, of Bishop's Stortford, Hertfordshire. He went to Eton where his genius as an oarsman first became evident in 1893 when he stroked Eton to victory in the Ladies' Plate at Henley Regatta; a triumph he was to repeat in 1894 and 1895. In the autumn of that year he went up to Magdalen College, Oxford, and with such a record behind him it was not surprising that he was picked as a freshman to stroke the Oxford crew of 1896. This race turned out to be one of the classic struggles, proving beyond doubt that his earlier Henley successes were founded on an innate and mature racing sense which in no way depended on any juvenile precocity. Cambridge, starting at three to one on favourites, led at one time by as much as a length and a half. With the station conditions against him, Gold bided his time, nursing his crew to Barnes bridge where, in calmer water, he made a dashing and spectacular spurt, gaining a hard-fought victory by the narrow margin of two-fifths of a length. With Gold at stroke, Oxford won the next two boat races. In 1897 they produced what was probably the fastest Oxford crew up to that time, winning as they liked in a time only two seconds outside the existing record. In the following year Gold was elected president of the O.U.B.C.

During his time at Oxford, Gold on three occasions stroked Leander to victory in the Grand Challenge Cup, whilst in 1898 and 1899 he recorded wins in Stewards' Fours, once for Leander and once for Magdalen. This latter year was the last season Gold enjoyed as an active oarsman, although he went on to prove himself an extremely successful finishing coach to a number of Oxford crews as well as to the two victorious Olympic eight oars of 1908 and 1912.

Gold became a steward of Henley Regatta in 1909 and a member of the committee of management in 1919. It was at this time that the stewards' enclosure came into being. This was his, both in conception and design, and proved the means of putting the regatta on a sound financial basis, relieving it of its recurrent financial strains of the Edwardian era. He was made chairman of the committee in 1945 and its first president in 1952. For many years he had represented the O.U.B.C. on the committee of the Amateur Rowing Association of which he was chairman from 1948. In 1949 he was knighted for his services to rowing.

'Tarka', as he was invariably known to his friends, was a man of medium build, immaculate attire and charming manner. Blessed with a buoyancy of spirit and a light and carefree wit, he was one of the most lovable and endearing of companions. With a genuine interest in his fellow men his conversation hinged on their enthusiasms, their hopes, and their fears rather than on his own. Particularly was this so in his contacts with the young who invariably responded wholeheartedly to his youthful and lively approach. His zest for life was infectious. An excellent shot with an extensive knowledge born of first-hand experience of all that pertained to game birds, many of his happier days were spent in the coverts of the south or on the grouse moors of the north. He had no use for the specialized one-sport mentality, and whether it was in the hunting field, on the tennis court, or golf course,

his supreme enjoyment of so many and varied pursuits made the doing of them so much more worth while to all those who were lucky enough to share them. He would give as much care and attention to the arrangements for a day's shooting, or the organization of a local point-to-point, as he would to the myriad details and complications connected with the smooth running of his beloved Henley Regatta.

In the war of 1914–18 Gold served with the Royal Flying Corps and Royal Air Force and was appointed O.B.E. in 1918. He married in 1902 Helen Beatrice, daughter of Dr. Thomas John Maclagan, of Cadogan Place, London, and had one son and two daughters. He died in London 27 July 1952. A cartoon by 'Spy' appeared in *Vanity Fair* 23 March 1899.

[Private information; personal knowledge.]
G. O. NICKALLS.

GOODEN, STEPHEN FREDERICK (1892–1955), engraver, was born 9 October 1892 in Tulse Hill, the only son of Stephen Thomas Gooden, publisher, and his wife, Edith Camille Elizabeth Epps. He was educated at Rugby and the Slade School of Art. During the war of 1914–18 he served in the 19th Hussars and later as a sapper. He began engraving in 1923 at a time when burin work was less regarded than etching, and soon proved that line-engraving, based on the technique of the great seventeenth- and eighteenth-century craftsmen, was still capable of exquisite refinement and expressiveness.

He made a series of illustrations in line-engraving, chiefly for the Nonesuch Press. The Nonesuch *Bible* (5 vols., 1925–7) was perhaps his masterpiece, but he also illustrated books for Heinemann and Harrap. His work may be seen at the British Museum, the Victoria and Albert Museum, the Fitzwilliam Museum, Cambridge, and the Ashmolean Museum, Oxford.

He was elected A.R.A. in 1937 and R.A. in 1946. In 1942 he was appointed C.B.E. In 1925 he married Mona, daughter of George Price, LL.D., of the Board of Public Works, Dublin. He died at Chesham Bois 21 September 1955.

[James Laver, 'The Line-engravings of Stephen Gooden', *Colophon*, part 2, 1930; *An Iconography of the Engravings of Stephen Gooden*, preface and introduction by Campbell Dodgson, 1944; personal knowledge.]
JAMES LAVER.

GOODENOUGH, SIR WILLIAM MACNAMARA, first baronet (1899–

1951), banker, was born in London 10 March 1899, the eldest son of Frederick Craufurd Goodenough [q.v.] by his wife, Maive, fifth daughter of Nottidge Charles Macnamara, F.R.C.S., of Calcutta and London. He was educated at Wellington College, where he was captain of cricket and rackets and head of the school. In January 1918 he obtained a commission in the Coldstream Guards with whom he saw active service with the 2nd battalion. After demobilization he went as a history scholar to Christ Church, Oxford, where he obtained a second class in the final honour school in 1922. In his last year at Oxford he was master of the Christ Church beagles, and further developed an already great interest in hounds, their breeding and their work, which remained with him throughout his life. In later years he became a joint master of the Vale of White Horse (Cricklade) Hunt.

Immediately on going down from Oxford he joined the staff of Barclays Bank, Ltd., of which his father had been chairman since 1917. After a short period in London he was appointed in 1923 a local director at Oxford; in 1929 he became a director of the Bank, in 1934 a vice-chairman, and in 1936 deputy chairman.

In 1925 his father had brought into being the great enterprise of Barclays Bank D.C.O., the overseas complement of the parent bank. Of this bank Goodenough became a director in 1933, a year before his father's death. In 1937 he became deputy chairman and in 1943 was elected to the chair. About this time he also became chairman of the Export Guarantees Advisory Council and of the executive committee of the Export Credit Guarantee Department.

In 1947, on the death of Edwin Fisher, he was elected chairman of the board of Barclays Bank, Ltd., and relinquished his post as chairman of Barclays D.C.O. In 1951, however, ill health forced him to retire, thereby bringing prematurely to an end a career which had already been one of fulfilment judged by any standard. But although the Bank in all its diverse activities was always Goodenough's first concern, as it had been with his father, his considerable powers for administration, coupled with an exceptional gift for leadership, particularly in handling teams with widely divergent views, led him into activities in many other fields.

The years at the Bank in Oxford from 1923 to 1934 in which latter year he moved to London, gave Goodenough ample scope to develop his powers not only as a banker but also in other lines. In 1927 he wa elected to the Oxfordshire County Coun cil, and in 1934, at the early age of thirty five, he became chairman. His greates achievements, however, came from hi association with the finances of the uni versity of Oxford, which at that time wa in the throes of administrative reform prompted partly by the report in 1922 o the royal commission but mainly by pres sures from within. In 1931 Lord Grey o Fallodon [q.v.], chancellor of the univer sity, appointed Goodenough a curator o the University Chest, where he brough his powerful influence to bear on the sid of reform, particularly in the financia administration, including investmen policy. But he also looked outward an was one of the moving spirits in th foundation of the Oxford Society, a pro ject which might well have foundere without him.

It was this quality of outward looking in addition to his financial skill, whic made Lord Nuffield see in 'Will' Good enough an ideal chairman for the trust which he founded to widen the scope o the Oxford medical school, and in 193 to establish Nuffield College. There wa a congruity in the purposes of thes foundations in that they were both in tended to promote the interaction of th academic and the practical. The medica bias of many of these undertakings an the ability with which Goodenough ha played his part caused him to be invited i 1942 to be chairman of the inter-depart mental committee on medical schools, th report of which, published in 1944, prove a landmark in medical education. He wa also appointed chairman of the Nuffiel Provincial Hospitals Trust which exer cised a strong influence on the eventua reorganization of the national hospita service. Yet another important connec tion with the Nuffield benefactions was hi chairmanship of the Nuffield Fund for th Forces of the Crown. In 1943 the associa tion of Nuffield and Goodenough reache its ultimate fulfilment in the formation o the Nuffield Foundation of which Good enough became the first chairman.

In 1930 Goodenough's father founde the Dominion Students' Hall Trus responsible for a hall of residence for post graduate male students in London from the dominions and colonies and known a London House; this work Goodenoug carried on as chairman of the governors Following the war he also founded a siste trust designed to provide similar facilities for women and married students, including students from the United States. The new hall of residence was named William Goodenough House.

With all these preoccupations with matters and undertakings of far-reaching importance, Goodenough remained primarily a countryman and his love of the land was never far from his mind. His interest in his own extensive and successful farming operations at his home at Filkins in Oxfordshire and his close association with the National Farmers' Union represented, perhaps, his happiest hours. He served as a member of the departmental committee on post-war agricultural education set up in 1941 by the Ministry of Agriculture and Fisheries.

Goodenough had a particular flair for choosing those who were to carry out his plans, and it was this quality which enabled him to surround himself with teams of loyal and eager workers. It was one of his greatest talents that, in his many positions as chairman, his sudden flashes of humour would frequently turn a difficult situation into one of good-humoured agreement.

Goodenough was created a baronet in 1943, and his work for the university of Oxford was recognized by the offer of an honorary D.C.L. which his untimely death prevented him from receiving. He had been elected an honorary student of Christ Church in 1947, was for many years a governor of Wellington, and received an honorary LL.D. from Manchester in 1949.

He married in 1924 Dorothea Louisa, eldest daughter of Ven. the Hon. Kenneth Francis Gibbs, archdeacon of St. Alban's, by whom he had four sons, of whom one died in infancy, and one daughter. Goodenough died at his home at Filkins Hall, Oxfordshire, 23 May 1951, and was succeeded by his eldest son, Richard Edmund (born 1925).

A portrait of Goodenough by (Sir) James Gunn is in the board-room of Barclays Bank D.C.O.; copies are at Barclays Bank, Ltd., and at London House, and another portrait by the same artist is at Filkins.

[Private information; personal knowledge.]
DOUGLAS VEALE.
CUTHBERT FITZHERBERT.

GOODEY, TOM (1885–1953), nematologist, the ninth and last child of Thomas Goodey, boot manufacturer, and his wife, Hannah Clayson, was born 28 July 1885, at Wellingborough, Northamp-

tonshire. He won a scholarship to the Northampton Grammar School, which he left in 1904 to become a pupil teacher. He did not enjoy school teaching and at the teachers' training college of Birmingham University he studied botany and zoology, in which he took the B.Sc. degree with honours in 1908. In the final examination, he was bracketed top with two other students; two scholarships each of £50 were shared between the three of them, and Goodey began his career as a scientist with a year's income of £33. 6s. 8d. A discovery about the gastric pouches of the jellyfish, made while he was still an undergraduate, provided his first research problem, and he next studied the anatomy of the frilled shark. He obtained the M.Sc. degree in 1909 and gained a further research scholarship of £50 for one year, with which he went in 1910 to Rothamsted Experimental Station, where he was soon awarded the Mackinnon studentship of the Royal Society of £150 a year.

The move to Rothamsted also meant changing to a subject new to him and to one full of controversy: whether soil contains protozoa that limit bacterial populations. Goodey showed that *Colpoda cucullus*, then assumed to be the chief protozoan in soil, was normally encysted and inactive there, and he doubted that protozoa were important predators of bacteria, but could not settle the controversy for his studentship expired before he could study other species. He returned to the zoology department at Birmingham University, where he worked on protozoa from various sources, and during the war of 1914–18 was protozoologist at the 2nd Southern General Hospital at Birmingham.

A return to Rothamsted in 1920 started Goodey on the work with helminths which was to occupy him for the rest of his life. He began with a study of clover stem eelworm, but this spell as a plant helminthologist was brief for in 1921 he joined the London School of Tropical Medicine and for the next five years worked mainly on parasites of vertebrates. When the Institute of Agricultural Parasitology was set up at St. Albans, Goodey became the senior member of staff there, a post he held until the Institute closed in 1947. There he specialized in studying plant-parasitic and free-living eelworms, the subject which came to be known as nematology and in which he was the acknowledged authority. He published many taxonomic papers in the *Journal of Helminthology* and in 1933 his first textbook *Plant Parasitic Nematodes and the Diseases they Cause*, which became the standard work. So, too, did his second textbook, *Soil and Freshwater Nematodes*, published in 1951, which described the morphology, biology, and behaviour of 190 genera, and was revised by his son Basil in 1963. When the book appeared, Goodey was again at Rothamsted, for when the Institute at St. Albans closed the members of its staff engaged in studying plant nematodes became the department of nematology of Rothamsted, with Goodey as its head. He retired from this post in 1952, but was still actively engaged in research when he died.

Goodey had an excellent voice and was also a skilled actor. Until 1916, when he was the paid tenor soloist in a performance of the *Messiah* at Dudley, he sang only as an amateur, but as his family responsibilities grew he increasingly accepted professional engagements, in oratorio, opera, and in the concert hall where as in many broadcast recitals he specialized in *Lieder* by Schubert and Hugo Wolf and in English songs. He was for long associated with the music of Rutland Boughton [q.v.] and the part of Angus in *The Ever Young* was written mainly for him. As the publicity from his performances embarrassed him as a scientist, from 1927 he used the stage name of Roger Clayson. His association on equal terms with the principal vocalists of the time did not detract from his willingness to sing with amateurs in modest surroundings or to mix fooling with his fine singing, as he did so memorably in many Christmas parties at Rothamsted.

A man of high ideals and standards, scrupulous in all his dealings, Goodey found a spiritual home in the Society of Friends, which he joined in 1933, following the lead set by his wife. His ability to speak powerfully and lucidly contributed to the prominence he gained in the Society, and he served as clerk of the Bedfordshire Quarterly Meeting from 1942 to 1946 and was an elder at the time of his death. Although deeply religious, he was no prude; indeed, his great sense of fun, youthful enthusiasm, and unfailing liveliness made him excellent company.

Goodey had many successes, both as scientist and artist, and these brought him great pleasure, especially his election as a fellow of the Royal Society in 1947. He was appointed O.B.E. in 1950 and was president of the Association of Applied Biologists in 1935–6.

In 1912 he married Constance, daughter of William Henry Lewis, a representative of a colour merchant, whom he had met while both were students at Birmingham. They had one son and four daughters. Goodey died in Harpenden, Hertfordshire, 7 July 1953, while walking home from a meeting of the Society of Friends.

[F. C. Bawden in *Obituary Notices of Fellows of the Royal Society*, vol. ix, 1954; private information; personal knowledge.]

F. C. BAWDEN.

GOODHART-RENDEL, HARRY STUART (1887–1959), architect, was born in Cambridge 29 May 1887, the only child of Harry Chester Goodhart, a lecturer in classics in the university, and his wife, Rose Ellen, daughter of Stuart (later Lord) Rendel, brother of Sir A. M. and G. W. Rendel [qq.v.]. In 1890 his father became professor of humanity at Edinburgh but he died in 1895, whereupon his widow went south with her son and, as Goodhart-Rendel expressed it later, 'shut herself up with her grief and me'. The boy had by then shown marked signs of musical talent, inherited from the Goodharts, and a strong aptitude for construction, inherited no less evidently from the Rendels. In 1899 his mother took Chinthurst Hill, near Guildford, a house recently completed by (Sir) Edwin Lutyens [q.v.] which, with its artful whimsicality, appealed to young Goodhart as 'a symbol of life and adventure'. After less than a year at Eton he was brought home with a badly poisoned foot and did not return. At home he cultivated music and architecture in his own way, discovering Gibbs and Hawksmoor (a lasting loyalty) and reading, among modern authors, (Sir) Reginald Blomfield [q.v.] and Heathcote Statham. Lessons from Claude Hayes at this time were the only instruction in drawing he ever received. He went next to Mulgrave Castle, Yorkshire, a school conducted by the Rev. Lord Normanby in whose library he discovered the works of Chambers and Soane. In 1902 his mother married Wilbraham Cooper, who had been Goodhart's tutor at Chinthurst. She remained, however, an important factor in her son's development and his subsequent life. Between 1902 and 1905 he spent much time with her not only at Chinthurst but also at Cannes (where Lord Rendel had a villa) and at Valescure where he became the francophil Englishman which he always remained. In 1902, at Lord Rendel's instance, he added the name of Rendel to his own.

With unlimited leisure to develop his abilities in the spheres which fascinated him—music and architecture—Goodhart-Rendel composed music in the manner of Delibes and Messager, and at the same time devoured the pages of the *Builder* and the *Building News*. Of his two pursuits, music seemed the more promising and it was arranged for him to study with (Sir) Donald Tovey [q.v.]. There was, however, a hopeless antagonism of tastes, Goodhart-Rendel's love of French light opera seeming to Tovey as incomprehensible as did Tovey's obsession with Brahms to Goodhart-Rendel. 'It was Tovey's efforts to make me a good musician that determined me to become an architect instead.'

In 1905 Goodhart-Rendel went up to Trinity College, Cambridge, graduating Mus.B. in 1909. While at Cambridge he provided designs for a commercial building in Calcutta and from 1909 onwards began to engage in architectural practice, his most important work from this period being 'The Pantiles', Englefield Green, Surrey (1911), for Miss Sophie Weisse and Donald Tovey, a house reflecting—partly through the clients' influence—the progressive German ideas of the period.

In 1913 Lord Rendel died, leaving his grandson a life interest in the bulk of his fortune, including the estate of Hatchlands, Surrey. In 1915 Goodhart-Rendel was commissioned in the Special Reserve, Grenadier Guards. This precipitated and in due course resolved an emotional crisis with his mother and at the same time brought him into a world of rigorous discipline and action where he soon came to believe what he had already suspected, that soldiering was his true vocation. Although ill health prevented his reaching the front (though he spent four months in France in 1917) this was probably the happiest time of his life. A company drill primer of which he was the author was issued in about 1917.

Demobilized, much against his inclination, in 1919, he resumed architectural practice at the office he had designed for himself (1912–13) at 60 Tufton Street, London, and in the course of the next twenty years became one of the most prominent and interesting figures in the profession. This was due less to his buildings, which were not, as a rule, kindly received by critics or by the profession at large, than to his personality, his scholarship, his eloquence, his wit, and his willingness to devote himself

assiduously and sympathetically to professional affairs. He was president of the Architectural Association in 1924–5, and of the Royal Institute of British Architects in 1937–9 when he aroused some controversy by his strictures on the quality of 'official' architecture at a time when the salaried element in the profession was in a sensitive mood. In 1933–6 he was Slade professor of fine art in Oxford. In 1936 he accepted the directorship of the Architectural Association school of architecture, but failed to attract the loyalty of the 'left-wing' youth of the thirties and resigned in 1938.

In the war of 1939–45 Goodhart-Rendel rejoined his regiment, returning afterwards to active practice with H. Lewis Curtis, his partner since 1930, and F. G. Broadbent who joined the partnership in 1945. He was president of the Design and Industries Association in 1948–50. In 1955 he was appointed C.B.E. for services to architectural criticism.

Goodhart-Rendel's architecture was a vigorous and original development of certain late Victorian tendencies. In his early years he was much influenced by Sir Charles Nicholson [q.v.], A. Beresford Pite, and Halsey Ricardo, the eclectic outlook of the last two being strongly reflected in his own work. His most important buildings between the wars were Broad Oak End, Bramfield, Herts. (for R. Abel Smith, 1921–3), influenced by Lutyens; additions to Tetton House, Taunton (for the Hon. Mervyn Herbert, 1924–6), somewhat in the style of Soane; Hay's Wharf (1929–31), a challenging attempt to interpret the modern movement in the 'rational' spirit of Viollet-le-Duc; St. Wilfrid's, Elm Grove, Brighton (1932–4), a modern church with a hard vigour recalling Butterfield; and Prince's House, North Street, Brighton (1934–5), introducing a novel decorative treatment for a frame building. He also built several villas in the south of France.

After 1945 Goodhart-Rendel was concerned mainly with churches, in some of which he was able to develop the ideas originated at St. Wilfrid's, Brighton. He built St. John the Evangelist, St. Leonards (1946–58), Our Lady of the Seven Sorrows, Liverpool (1951–4), and the Sacred Heart, Cobham, Surrey (1955–8). Holy Trinity, Dockhead, and Our Lady of the Rosary, Marylebone, were in progress at the time of his death. The Household Brigade war memorial cloister, Wellington Barracks

(1954–5), is a study in Roman Doric. A very large and detailed project for the Benedictine Abbey of Prinknash, in a modern equivalent of Romanesque, occupied much of his last years. Some foundations were laid and the architect is buried there. His designs, however, have been laid aside.

Although not in any strict sense an historian, Goodhart-Rendel possessed the most complete and detailed knowledge of English nineteenth-century architecture of anyone of his time and his annotated card-index of English churches (of which the master-copy is in the National Buildings Record) is a work of great authority. His familiarity with Victorian architects and their works, at a time when such things had begun to arouse an amused interest, gave him material for lectures of a peculiarly brilliant and entertaining kind. On broader architectural issues he spoke with insight and charm but without making any significant contribution. Nearly all his writing was in the form of essays, intended to be read as lectures. *Vitruvian Nights* (1932) and *English Architecture since the Regency* (1953) are collections of such essays. Of essays or lectures published singly the sensitive appreciation of *Nicholas Hawksmoor* (1924) is the most memorable.

In early life a devout Anglican, Goodhart-Rendel entered the Roman Church in middle age, his faith thereafter becoming the core and mainstay of his life. He never married. Music remained important to him. He was a pianist with a somewhat brittle touch and a phenomenal capacity for accurate sight-reading. As a composer he was not lacking in invention. Two of his piano pieces were published. He was vice-president of the Royal Academy of Music from 1953 (honorary F.R.A.M., 1958) and a governor of Sadler's Wells from 1934.

In appearance Goodhart-Rendel was tall, dark, and spare, with a narrow head, prominent nose, and olive complexion. He is well characterized in Augustus John's portrait at the R.I.B.A., where there is also a head by Dora Gordine. In society and in the committee-room he was distinguished by a patrician elegance, an ironic and slightly plaintive manner of speech, and by the sparkle of a wit issuing from a combination of logical thought and a profound love of paradox.

He died in London 21 June 1959.

[Private information; personal knowledge.]

JOHN SUMMERSON.

GORDON, MERVYN HENRY (1872–1953), medical bacteriologist, was born at Harting, Sussex, 22 June 1872, the sixth of ten children of the vicar, the Rev. Henry Doddridge Gordon. His mother was Elizabeth Oke, daughter of William Buckland [q.v.], the first professor of mineralogy and of geology at Oxford and later dean of Westminster. He was educated at Marlborough and Keble College, Oxford, where he obtained a second class in physiology (1894), proceeding thence to St. Bartholomew's Hospital, London, to study clinical medicine. After obtaining his B.M., Oxford, in 1898 (B.Sc., 1901, D.M., 1903), he began work in the pathology department at St. Bartholomew's under Emmanuel Klein, whose long-standing friendship with the Gordon family may have accounted for the choice both of the hospital and of the department in which Gordon was to spend the whole of his working life.

He remained on the regular staff of this department until 1923, and during this time engaged in three major research projects for which his name will be best remembered. One was a study with (Sir) F. W. Andrewes and T. J. (later Lord) Horder [qq.v.] of the characters of streptococci, leading to a classification into three species which gained universal recognition. An extension of this work was an attempt which he made much later to subdivide one of these species (*Streptococcus pyogenes*, or the haemolytic streptococcus) which had long been suspected of heterogeneity, because of the great variety and varying severity of the infections caused by it. Although he and Andrewes both made some progress in this direction, the final subdivision of this species into over thirty types by F. Griffith, using the same methods, was not to be achieved until over ten years later.

His second main interest was in the transmission of bacteria through the air. At a time when Flügge had recently shown that coughing, sneezing, and even speaking cause the expulsion into the atmosphere of 'droplets' of secretion from the mouth and throat, Gordon was given a remarkable opportunity of studying this phenomenon in no less a place than the House of Commons. Members had complained of the ventilation, and the Office of Works entrusted Gordon among others with an inquiry into it. He used bacteria as indicators both of pollution and of air movement, studying the distribution of streptococci from the mouths of speakers during sittings of the House, and of a characteristic harmless organism introduced into his own mouth when he had the debating chamber to himself, and was able to recite passages from Shakespeare in a loud voice from the Treasury bench to an audience of culture plates. The results of this work were published in a blue book of 212 pages in 1906: a landmark in the study of this subject, which was not to be advanced much farther until the discovery of the 'droplet nucleus' twenty years later, and proof of immense industry and ingenuity.

Gordon's third and perhaps greatest achievement was his study of cerebrospinal fever (meningococcal meningitis) during the war of 1914–18 when he was commissioned in the Royal Army Medical Corps, worked at the headquarters of the Corps at Millbank, and was given executive authority in all matters connected with the diagnosis and treatment of this disease. He was largely responsible for showing that it results from a rise in the carrier-rate in overcrowded and ill-ventilated quarters—a fact which accounts for its frequent occurrence in army barracks in war conditions. He showed that the meningococcus is divisible into four serological types, studied methods for producing more effective therapeutic serum, organized the treatment of carriers, and defined methods for better bacteriological diagnosis. He was certainly the leading authority on the disease in this country, and possibly in the world.

In 1923 Gordon resigned his position on the staff of St. Bartholomew's, but remained there as an external member of the staff of the Medical Research Council, and determined to devote himself entirely to the study of filtrable viruses. His early systematic studies of the viruses of variola and vaccinia are classical, and he made some observations also on mumps and psittacosis. An opportunity then occurred for engaging a team of workers to study lymphadenoma (Hodgkin's disease): Gordon undertook the direction of this team, and after discarding other hypotheses, reached the conclusion that this too was a virus disease. He devised a new animal test for its diagnosis, the basis of which was called in question, and even an immunological method for its treatment which other workers found even more difficult to accept. In his later years he was much inclined to attribute a virus origin to other diseases, including rheumatism and cancer, on grounds unacceptable

to those who were then advancing the study of virology by more modern methods.

Gordon was an original member (1909) of the Army Pathology Advisory Committee, and for many years thereafter consulting bacteriologist to the army. He was appointed C.M.G. in 1917 and C.B.E. in 1919. He was elected F.R.S. in 1924 and received the honorary LL.D. of Edinburgh in 1936. He never sought fame and was almost completely absorbed in his work, his only other interest known to his friends being in archaeology. A passion for research and a delight in any original discovery, even if unimportant, were his outstanding characteristics. His enthusiasm for his own work extended to that of his colleagues, however junior, and the encouragement he gave them by his interest, praise, and unstinted help was an important factor in many careers.

He married in 1916 Mildred Olive (died 1953), daughter of Sir William Power [q.v.]. She continued her work as an inspector for the Local Government Board; they had no children. He died at his home at Molesey 26 July 1953.

[L. P. Garrod in *Obituary Notices of Fellows of the Royal Society*, vol. ix, 1954; private information; personal knowledge.]

LAWRENCE P. GARROD.

GORDON-TAYLOR, SIR GORDON (1878–1960), surgeon, was born at Streatham Hill, London, 18 March 1878, the elder of two children of John Taylor, wine merchant, and his wife, Alice Miller, daughter of William Gordon, stockbroker, of Aberdeen. In 1885 John Taylor died and his widow moved with her son and daughter to Aberdeen where Gordon Taylor gained a scholarship at Robert Gordon's College. He was happy at school, a hard worker, fond of walking and climbing, and played a good deal of cricket; summer holidays were spent at Ballater on Deeside. He was brought up in the Presbyterian Church.

William Gordon Taylor, his name until he changed it in 1920 to Gordon Gordon-Taylor, held a bursary at Aberdeen University where in 1898 he obtained third class honours in classics; his constant pocket book through life was a volume of Horace. He entered the Middlesex Hospital with a scholarship and qualified in 1903. An intensive course of anatomical study was rewarded with first class honours (1904) in the newly instituted B.Sc. in anatomy of the university of

London. He obtained his F.R.C.S. in 1906 and a year later at the early age of twenty-nine was appointed assistant surgeon to the Middlesex Hospital. He was consulting surgeon to the Fourth Army in France during the war of 1914–18, after making a name for himself as a casualty clearing surgeon. He became full surgeon to the Middlesex Hospital in 1920 and in the next twenty years built up a great reputation for skill and courage in tackling new surgical problems, with unwearying ardour to prolong life and effect complete cure. A fine operator and an excellent clinician he became the doyen of British surgery. He was consultant to the Royal Navy in the war of 1939–45 with the rank of surgeon rear-admiral, travelling to Russia, America, and India in the course of his duties. He was appointed C.B. in 1942, K.B.E. in 1946, and was a commander of the United States Legion of Merit.

At the Royal College of Surgeons of England he served on the council (1932–48) and was vice-president (1941–3). He was a Hunterian professor on several occasions; delivered the Bradshaw lecture in 1942 on the abdominal injuries of modern warfare, and twice gave the Thomas Vicary lecture. In this he demonstrated both his knowledge of surgical history and his abiding Scottish patriotism, speaking in 1945 about the medical and surgical aspects of the 1745 rising, and recounting in 1954 the life and work of the great London-Scottish surgeon and anatomist, Sir Charles Bell [q.v.]. He enlarged the lecture on Bell into a full-length biography (1958, with E. W. Walls).

Gordon-Taylor played a leading part in the affairs of many societies and colleges; was an honorary fellow of the Irish, Australasian, Canadian, and American Colleges of Surgeons; an honorary foreign member of the Académie de Chirurgie in Paris; and received honorary degrees from Cambridge, Toronto, Melbourne, and Athens. He was president of the Association of Surgeons of Great Britain and Ireland, of the Medical Society of London (1941–2), and of the Royal Society of Medicine (1944–6), which also awarded him in 1956 its coveted and rarely bestowed gold medal. Among the many ceremonial addresses which he was invited to deliver were the Moseley lecture, Toronto 1938, the first Moynihan lecture, Leeds 1940, the Syme oration, Melbourne 1947, the Sheen memorial lecture, Cardiff 1949, and the John Fraser memorial lecture, Edinburgh 1957. He was a frequent contributor to medical and surgical journals and published a book on *The Dramatic in Surgery* (1930) and another on *The Abdominal Injuries of Warfare* (1939).

Gordon-Taylor married in 1920 Florence Mary (died 1949), daughter of John Pegrume; there were no children. He died in London, 3 September 1960, as the result of a road accident. He left his fortune, after the cessation of his sister's life interest and legacies to certain societies between the Royal College of Surgeons for its library and the Middlesex Hospital for its nurses.

His portrait by Anna Zinkeisen was reproduced in the special number of the *British Journal of Surgery* dedicated to him on his eightieth birthday in 1958. The original hangs in the board-room at the Middlesex Hospital in London. A portrait by (Sir) James Gunn is in the Royal Australasian College of Surgeons in Melbourne and a sketch in oils by the same artist is at the Royal College of Surgeons in London.

[*The Times*, 5 September 1960; *British Journal of Surgery*, vol. xlviii, November 1960; *Gordon-Taylor In Memoriam*, by his colleagues at the Middlesex Hospital, with a bibliography of his writings, 1961; private information; personal knowledge.]

CECIL WAKELEY

GOWER, SIR HENRY DUDLEY GRESHAM LEVESON (1873–1954), cricketer, was born 8 May 1873 at Titsey Place, Limpsfield, Surrey, the seventh of the twelve sons of Granville William Gresham Leveson Gower and his wife Sophia, daughter of Chandos, first Baron Leigh [q.v.] and sister of Sir Edward Chandos Leigh, Q.C., who was president of the Marylebone Cricket Club in 1887. Leveson Gower was educated at Winchester where he was in the eleven for three years and captain in the last (1892). Playing against Eton in that year he and J. R. Mason together dominated the match with both bat and ball and easily won for the second year in succession.

So successful was Leveson Gower that on going up to Magdalen College he was awarded his blue as a freshman. He played for Oxford for four years and in his last year was elected captain. The match against Cambridge in this year (1896) was perhaps his greatest triumph. Cambridge again adopted tactics, which afterward gave rise to some controversy, to avoid a compulsory follow-on (by Oxford) which the laws of cricket then stipulated in cer tain circumstances. Nevertheless Oxford reversed their defeat of the previous year, although they were set to make 330 to win in the last innings. By obtaining these with four wickets to spare, largely through a splendid 132 by G. O. Smith, the last choice, and a sturdy 41 by Leveson Gower, they performed a feat never before approached in the university match.

Leveson Gower, who became a stock-broker by profession, played for Surrey, which he captained from 1908 to 1910, but thereafter played little county cricket. He was one of the team taken by Lord Hawke [q.v.] to the West Indies in 1897 and later in the year went with (Sir) Pelham Warner to North America. In the winter of 1909–10 he captained the M.C.C. team in South Africa, a country which he had already visited with the team of 1905–6. Later he took teams to Malta (1929), Gibraltar (1932), and Portugal (1934). At home he devoted much energy to organizing teams such as those to meet Oxford and Cambridge at Eastbourne, and he was associated for over fifty years with the Scarborough Cricket Festival, receiving the freedom of the borough in 1930. For many years he served on the M.C.C. committee and from 1929 to 1940 he was president of the Surrey County Cricket Club. He was a frequent test match selector and several times chairman. His love for Oxford cricket was enduring and he retained a lifelong connection with the Harlequins and the Authentics, over both of which he presided in later years.

Leveson Gower was small, almost impish in his humorous ways, and full of vitality. He was known for the rest of his life by his apt schoolboy nickname 'Shrimp'. It was his energy and willingness to field anywhere which made him welcome as a member of a side; as a batsman, he was by no means classic, but rather an efficient run-getter who could improvise with such strokes as 'the cut'. A man of kindliness and humour, he had an exceptional number of friends to whom he gave a loyalty only equalled by that which he gave to cricket. He was knighted in 1953 for his services to the game.

In 1908 Leveson Gower married Enid Mary, daughter of the late R. S. B. Hammond-Chambers, K.C.; they had no children. He died in London 1 February 1954.

[*The Times*, 2 February, 1954; *Wisden's Cricketers' Almanack*, 1955; Sir Henry Leveson Gower, *Off and On the Field*, 1953; personal knowledge.]   R. H. HILL.

GOWRIE, first EARL OF (1872–1955), soldier and governor-general of Australia. [See HORE-RUTHVEN, ALEXANDER GORE ARKWRIGHT.]

GRAHAME-WHITE, CLAUDE (1879–1959), pioneer aviator and aircraft manufacturer, was born at Bursledon Towers, Bursledon, Hampshire, 21 August 1879, second son and youngest of the three children of John White, a man of independent means and a keen yachtsman, and his wife, Ada Beatrice, daughter of the late Frederick Chinnock, property agent of London and Dinorbin Court, Hampshire. He was educated at Bedford Grammar School and subsequently apprenticed to an engineering firm in the town. His first job in life was with an uncle, Francis Willey, later Lord Barnby, a Yorkshire wool magnate. Wool itself did not interest him, but the engineering side of the business did, and he introduced motor lorries to replace the horse vans. His first independent venture was to start a motor vehicle service at Bradford in competition with the steam trams. From Yorkshire he moved to Sussex where he spent three years as agent of a large estate. Then, after a lengthy visit to South Africa and a big-game hunting trip up the Zambezi, he set up as a dealer in motor-cars in London.

Blériot's Channel flight and a meeting with Wilbur Wright in 1909 very strongly impressed Grahame-White with the possibilities of aviation. He spent a highly instructive two months in Blériot's Paris factory, watching the construction of a machine for his use, and when it was ready he flew it solo without instruction. On 4 January 1910 he became the first Englishman to receive the pilot's certificate of the French Aero Club. He started a British flying school at Pau and himself did much flying. In the same year he made two attempts to win the *Daily Mail* prize of £10,000 for a flight from London to Manchester but was beaten by Louis Paulhan. His gallant fight and his persistence in covering part of the distance in darkness brought his name into worldwide renown. This year, 1910, was crowded with events and triumphs; he won valuable prizes at Wolverhampton and Bournemouth; flew over the Fleet at Penzance and the tower at Blackpool; and staged a demonstration of the military use of aircraft in carrying dispatches. In September he continued his triumphant career in the United States. After winning

£2,000 for a 33-mile flight round the Boston Light, and a number of other contests, he made a landing in Executive Avenue, Washington, and in New York won the international Gordon Bennett Cup and, after prolonged dispute, the Aero Club of America's £2,000 prize for a flight round the Statue of Liberty. He returned to England in December and was presented by Lord Roberts [q.v.] with a special gold medal of the Aerial League of the British Empire. In August of the following year he again carried all before him in America.

Early in 1911 Grahame-White set up the London Aerodrome at Hendon, and founded there the Grahame-White Aviation Company which trained many pilots. In September of that year he organized the first English official delivery of mail by air, from Hendon to Windsor. This astute observer and strong believer in the future of flying quickly sensed great possibilities for the military use of aircraft. He gave a demonstration for the parliamentary aerial defence committee at Hendon on 12 May 1911; and on the formation of the Royal Flying Corps in 1912 he wired to Lord Haldane [q.v.] offering his services in any capacity. In April he inaugurated weekly flying meetings at Hendon and at these carried hundreds of passengers without mishap. The aerial Derbys held there in 1912–14 aroused great public interest; moreover, the meetings were made to pay. In the workshops ceaseless improvement and experimentation produced sundry prize-winning models.

On the outbreak of war Grahame-White was commissioned as a flight commander in the Royal Naval Air Service. In 1915 he came down in the sea off Belgium and was rescued by a minesweeper. But discipline and routine irked him; the Government came to feel that he had a more valuable contribution to make in design and manufacture. He therefore resigned from the Service in August 1915 and for the rest of the war worked on construction at Hendon. After the war he was unable to regain possession of his aerodrome which after prolonged controversy was purchased by the Government with all the company's factories. Grahame-White had now reached the end of his effective career, but he continued to watch with keen interest the development of aviation. An extremely prescient man, he had been talking as far back as 1919 of speeds from 200 to 300 miles an hour and earlier still had foreseen the development of the aircraft

passenger carrier. His genius as a designer and his valour and skill as an aviator place him among the greatest names in the history of flight. He himself wrote many books on flying, a number of them in collaboration with Harry Harper, air correspondent of the *Daily Mail*. Grahame-White died 19 August 1959 in hospital at Nice.

He married first, in 1912, Dorothy, daughter of Bertrand Le Roy Taylor, of New York; the marriage was dissolved in 1916, in which year he married Ethel (Grace) Levey, an actress; this marriage was dissolved in 1939 and in that year he married Phoebe Lee. He had no children.

[*Aeronautics*, 16 October 1919; Graham Wallace, *Claude Grahame-White*, 1960; *The Times*, 20 August 1959; private information.

HERBERT B. GRIMSDITCH

GREEN, FREDERICK WILLIAM EDRIDGE- (1863–1953), authority on colour perception. [See EDRIDGE-GREEN.

GREEN, WILLIAM CURTIS (1875–1960), architect, was born at Alton, Hampshire, 16 July 1875, the second son of Frederic Green, barrister, by his wife Maria Heath Curtis. Educated at Newton College, he was articled to John Belcher [q.v.] and trained at the Royal Academy Schools under Phené Spiers [q.v.] where he learned a sure grip of the orders and a superb architectural draughtsmanship. He first made his name as a draughtsman in pen-and-ink, in which he showed an unerring hand and a grasp of perspective. For some years he contributed illustrations to the *Builder* in the days when photographic reproduction was not what it later became. For this purpose he travelled far, at home and abroad, and the fruits of these and later journeys are embodied in a book, published in 1949, which places his skill on permanent record.

Curtis Green commenced practice in 1898 and mastered the design of the small house. He was elected F.R.I.B.A. in 1909. When (Sir) Edwin Lutyens [q.v.] first went to New Delhi, he asked Green to take charge of his office while he was away. This greatly influenced him and enlarged his understanding of monumental work in the grand manner. Opportunity came to him when in 1912 he was taken into partnership by Dunn and Watson who had a large city practice, and soon he was left in sole charge of a going concern. As a result of this he made a lasting mark on Piccalilly. From 1919 to 1927 he practised on his own and then took into happy partnership his son, Christopher, and his son-in-law, Antony Lloyd.

Curtis Green's first large building was Wolseley House, later Barclays Bank, in Piccadilly, which made a great impact in its day and in 1922 received the first R.I.B.A. medal for the best building of the preceding three years. This was followed by the Westminster Bank on the other side of Piccadilly, not quite so successful; and later Stratton House next to Devonshire House, with a fine elevation. Six Duke Street, adjacent to Piccadilly, and the London Life Association building in King William Street belong to the same group of buildings of similar character. The sometimes austere, but finely detailed, masonry of his banks and insurance offices, with, in the earlier phase, a use of the classical orders that is a little overdone, is often relieved by the rich flow of his beautifully designed wrought-iron-work, in grilles and balconies, and by the scarlet, gold, and black of his colour schemes, particularly in the interior of Wolseley House. In one of his latest works, the charming little Barclays Bank, 61 New Bond Street, there is a gay 'chinoiserie'. His last phase, in which he had the association of his son-in-law and son, shows a quiet maturity, with elimination of the orders that was in keeping with the times.

The new building for Scotland Yard on the Embankment, and the exterior of the Equity and Law Life Assurance Society, in Lincoln's Inn Fields, have serene Portland stone elevations, with fine fenestration and a sense of scale that is urbane and satisfying. The small building for the Cambridge University Press, in the Euston Road, has similar qualities.

The Dorchester Hotel in Park Lane is perhaps Green's most familiar building. It is not his happiest creation, but he came to design it in unusual and difficult circumstances. Sir Owen Williams and three architects in succession had worked on the scheme and brought it up to ground level. The sponsors then asked Curtis Green to take it on. His hand was tied with existing foundations and a defined outline, but with energy and skill he tackled this complex problem, and the hotel was opened on the advertised date, thirteen months later: including the architectural design, intricate plan requirements, complex construction, décor, and furnishing. The builder told how in this hectic twelve months,

Green never lost his patience, unflagging enthusiasm, and sense of humour. The Queen's Hotel at Leeds, in collaboration with his partners and W. H. Hamlyn, also shows his skill in hotel planning.

Of his large amount of domestic work, most of which was small in scale, special mention should be made of Stockgrove Park near Leighton Buzzard, Bedfordshire. It was one of the largest houses built between the two wars, and in addition to the mansion, on its commanding site, with covered swimming bath, rackets court, and gardens, there is a detached stable court, with a water tower, a guest house, an agent's house, entrance lodges, gates, and cottages, and a delightful thatched boathouse on the lake. The main house is planned round a forecourt, and expresses a sumptuous way of life now past. It is a fine example of the second phase of Georgian architecture, humane, English, and satisfying, with its multi-coloured brickwork, its white sash windows, its green shutters and tiled roofs. House and garden are in excellent harmony. It was completed in 1939. Stanmore village, Winchester, and the housing estate at Chepstow, in collaboration with William Dunn, show his skill in planning layout and designing the small house.

His churches (the Good Shepherd, Dockenfield, Surrey; St. Christopher, Cove; St. George's, Waddon; St. Francis, Rough Close, Stoke-on-Trent; and All Saints', Shirley, Croydon) are quiet and satisfying examples. Curtis Green should be judged by the standards of his generation; and by that standard of scholarly, personal design, fine building, and good craftsmanship he stands high. His work has a lasting English quality, for he paid no heed to ephemeral fashions. In his long working life his never-failing enthusiasm and artistic integrity produced a remarkable output, and he was equally happy in town and country.

From his days as a student at the Schools, Curtis Green was a staunch supporter of the Royal Academy, to which he was elected as an associate in 1923, becoming a full academician ten years later. He was a Royal gold medallist of the R.I.B.A. in 1942 and was chairman of its board of architectural education. He was president of the Architectural Association, a member of the Royal Fine Art Commission, and officier d'Académie Française. For thirty-eight years he gave devoted service to the Artists' General Benevolent Institution, as honorary secretary, chairman of council, and vice-president.

Curtis Green was twice married: first, in 1899, to Cicely Dillworth (died 1934), daughter of Francis Henry Lloyd; and secondly, in 1935, to Laura Gwenllian (died 1952), widow of the third Lord Northbourne and daughter of Admiral Sir Ernest Rice. By his first marriage he had one son and four daughters. He died in London 26 March 1960.

[*The Times*, 28 March 1960; *Journal* of the Royal Institute of British Architects, June 1960; *The Drawings of W. Curtis Green, R.A.*, 1949; private information; personal knowledge.]   HUBERT WORTHINGTON.

GREENE, WILFRID ARTHUR, BARON GREENE (1883–1952), judge, was born in Beckenham 30 December 1883, son of Arthur Weguelin Greene, a solicitor, by his wife, Kathleen Agnes, daughter of Octavius Fooke. Although a Roman Catholic, he was educated at Westminster School and Christ Church, Oxford, where he was a scholar. He won the Craven scholarship in 1903 and the Hertford scholarship in 1904. In the same year he took a first in classical moderations. He won the Chancellor's prize for Latin verse in 1905, taking as his subject *Artes Magiciae*. He took a first in *literae humaniores* in 1906 and was elected a fellow of All Souls in 1907. He won the Vinerian scholarship in 1908. He was called to the bar by the Inner Temple in 1908, winning a studentship in the same year, and he went into the chambers of Philip Stokes, one of the busiest and most esteemed equity practitioners. Two years later he moved to the chambers of F. H. (later Viscount) Maugham [q.v.]. He had already created a profound impression as a junior, when war broke out in 1914. Within six weeks he was gazetted a second lieutenant in the Oxfordshire and Buckinghamshire Light Infantry in which he rose to be captain. He served in France, Flanders, and Italy, and with the rank of major was successively employed as G.S.O. 3 on the staff of the Fifth Army, G.S.O. 2 on the G.H.Q. staff in Italy, and G.S.O. 2 on the British Supreme War Council. His services were recognized by the award of the O.B.E., the M.C., the croix de guerre of France, and the Order of the Crown of Italy.

In 1919 Greene returned to the bar, taking silk in 1922, and in 1925 became a bencher of his inn. While carrying on one of the largest Chancery practices of

his day, he found time to perform a grea deal of unpaid public work. In 1925 h was chairman of the committee on com pany law, which laid the foundation of th Companies Act, 1929. In 1930 he becam chairman of the committee on trade prac tices. In 1931 he was chairman of th advisory committee to inquire into th position of Imperial and Internationa Communications, Ltd., in connectio with a cable merger. In 1934 he was chai man of the committee on the beet suga industry. Towards the end of his career a the bar he confined himself to appearin in the House of Lords and the Judicia Committee of the Privy Council but, eve so, by 1935 he was utterly exhausted b a practice of legendary proportions an after arguing a case in the Judicial Com mittee in July, he confessed that he wa 'really done'. Though he had extra ordinary mental stamina, his small, sligh build did not suggest a robust constitu tion.

The time had come for him to leave th bar and in October 1935, when Maugha became a lord of appeal in ordinary Greene succeeded him in the Court c Appeal, was knighted, and sworn of th Privy Council. In 1937 Greene was ap pointed master of the Rolls. He wa created a baron in 1941. By virtue of hi new office Greene also became head of th Record Office and to the duties which th imposed he devoted much energy. He wa chairman of the Royal Commission o Historical Manuscripts and president c the British Records Association from 193 During the war his zealous initiativ saved from destruction innumerable docu ments of historic importance, especiall local records. He worked with enthusias and energy as chairman of the Nationa Buildings Record Office (1941–5), forme at the start of the war in 1939 to preserv by drawings and photographs the detai of buildings imperilled by the hostilitie In June 1942 Greene also served as chai man of the board of investigation of th coalminers' wages claim.

The tenure of the office of master the Rolls for any considerable time notoriously exhausting. Greene held it fi twelve years and at the end he wa visibly worn out. When, in 1949, he wa appointed a lord of appeal in ordinary was hoped that less exacting duties woul restore him, but the hope was vain and May the following year he resigned on th ground of ill health. On 16 April 1952 died in Dorking. His home had been fi many years at Holmbury St. Mary, near Guildford.

Greene was a man of singular charm, sensitiveness, and modesty who brought to the practice of the law the mind of a scholar, as well as the highest sense of honour. To a natural lucidity of thought, he joined felicity and elegance of expression and, on occasion, a whimsical wit, which lent his arguments at the bar a quality all their own. It was written of him that 'he was great without pride, a genius without arrogance, one aureoled with success yet never world-hardened, never inviting or incurring either enmity or envy, a man who walked through life clothed with courtesy, consideration and amenity.'

In a speech which he delivered in 1947 as president of the Classical Association he affirmed his faith that the humanities alone 'can deepen the spirit of a man and teach him the eternal worth of beauty, of honest thought, and provide him with eyes to see the innumerable interests that surround him'. For him the legacy of Greece and Rome was 'integrity of mind, . . accuracy of thought and expression, and the impulse to reject what is slovenly or superficial; distrust of the catchword . . the habit and method of reasoned criticism which forbids us to accept or reject a proposition merely because it is pleasant to do so, or because it saves the trouble of thought; the power to recognise and enjoy beauty in all its forms'. All these were certainly characteristics of Greene himself.

Greene received a number of honorary degrees including the D.C.L. of Oxford, of which he was standing counsel in 1926-35. He was an honorary student of Christ Church, an honorary F.R.I.B.A., a trustee of the Pilgrim Trust, the British Museum, and the Chantrey Bequest, and principal, 1936-44, of the Working Men's College, St. Pancras.

In 1909 Greene married Nancy, eldest daughter of Francis Wright, of Allerton, Yorkshire; there were no children. The fine portrait of him in the Inner Temple by Miss H. Gluck, is a remarkably accurate likeness.

[*Law Times* and *Law Journal*, 25 April 1952; *The Times*, 18 April and 1 May 1952.]

F. H. Cowper.

GREENWOOD, ARTHUR (1880-1954), politician, was born at Hunslet, Leeds, 8 February 1880, the eldest son of William Greenwood, painter and decorator, by his wife, Margaret Nunns, of Dewsbury. From a board school he won a scholarship to Bewerley Street higher grade school. As the only means of continuing his studies, he became a pupil teacher and won a scholarship to the Yorkshire College, then a constituent of Victoria (and later to become Leeds) University. He obtained his B.Sc. (1905) and his Board of Education certificate, remaining another year to read economics and history. After a few years' teaching in various schools he became head of the department of economics and law at Huddersfield Technical College, and in 1913 lecturer in economics at the university of Leeds. He was active in the Workers' Educational Association, helped to create the Yorkshire (North) District of which he remained chairman until 1945, and devoted all his spare time to adult education and to work for the local Labour Party. Shortly before the outbreak of war in 1914 he went to London as general secretary of the Council for the Study of International Relations. By 1916 he had written many articles and extended pamphlets on child labour and juvenile unemployment, and on international problems. Prophecies of an output as prolific as that of Sidney and Beatrice Webb [qq.v.], of whom he was a protégé, and of a successful academic career were, however, belied.

In 1916 he became a wartime civil servant in Lloyd George's 'secretariat'. At first as assistant secretary to the Reconstruction Committee, then from 1917 to 1919 at the Ministry of Reconstruction, Greenwood impressed his minister, Christopher (later Viscount) Addison [q.v.], with his mastery of detail, his capacity to suggest general deductions, and his energy. He played a large part, with R. H. Tawney, in producing the report on adult education, and in the setting-up of Whitley Councils. When he unsuccessfully fought Southport in 1918 as Labour candidate he was reappointed to the Civil Service the day after his defeat. He was, however, already in touch with a group under the guidance of the Webbs and G. D. H. Cole [q.v.] which was seeking to formulate policy for the Labour Party. In 1920 Greenwood became secretary of the Labour Party research department and there he remained until 1943. Although only four Labour Party pamphlets during this period were attributed to him by name, his contribution to the drafting of all of them, to the formulation of policy and to the preparation of legislative proposals, was immense. Much of the credit for constructive thought in the party after 1931 was due to Arthur Greenwood. In those days, his post might be held in conjunction with membership of the House of Commons and in 1922 he was elected for Nelson and Colne, which he represented until 1931. In the following year he won at Wakefield by a majority of just over 300 in a poll of nearly 27,000, and he continued to represent the city until his death.

Although many, including Beatrice Webb, expected Greenwood to have a Ministry in the Labour Government of 1924, he modestly accepted the post of parliamentary secretary to the Ministry of Health. But in 1929 he became minister of health, a post which, with his combination of economic training and human sympathy, was ideal for him. Major measures for which he was responsible included the Widows', Orphans' and Old Age Contributory Pensions Act, 1929; the Housing Act, 1930; the town and country planning bill which was accepted with little change by his successor. But he disliked the frustration of minority government and in one way felt relief when Ramsay MacDonald's ministry fell. He unfalteringly opposed the prime minister's policy as the ministry came to an end, refused to accept a means test or cuts in benefit for the unemployed, and was among the defeated ex-ministers in 1931.

From 1932, when he returned to the House, until 1939, he played a prominent part not only in domestic affairs—Neville Chamberlain paid tribute to his contributions to long and complicated debates on rating and local government—but also in attacking the Government's foreign policy on Manchuria, Abyssinia, and Spain. In 1938 he earned the tribute of a personal onslaught by Hitler in his speech at Weimar. Many thought of him as successor to George Lansbury [q.v.] as early as 1932. When, in fact, C. R. (later Earl) Attlee succeeded to the leadership in 1935, Greenwood, who was unanimously elected deputy leader, gave him 'most loyal support and good counsel'. He spoke for the Labour Party during Attlee's illness in the critical days of 1939 and achieved his 'finest hour' in the House of Commons on Saturday, 2 September. Urged to 'speak for England', quietly and without rhetorical flourish but with firmness and sincerity, Greenwood insisted on England's duty to resist aggression.

In May 1940 he entered the War Cabinet as minister without portfolio in charge of economic affairs. In January 1941, however, changes to meet criticism of weakness in organization brought him into control of reconstruction. Before his retirement from the Cabinet in February 1942 he was responsible for the memorable appointment of the Beveridge committee. Thereafter until the end of the war he devoted himself to maintaining Labour support for the war effort while at the same time preparing his party for electoral battle whenever peace came.

After the general election in 1945 he became lord privy seal and chairman of various cabinet committees, and from July 1946 to March 1947 paymaster general as well. In April 1947 he became minister without portfolio. Within six months he was dropped from the Government. Despite the rather thin excuse that younger members had to be given their chance, and the hints that he might retire from politics, Greenwood showed no rancour. Although frequently incapacitated by ill health he continued to work faithfully and without stint for his party. He had been elected treasurer in 1943 and became chairman of the national executive in 1952. Although frail and tired, he was regarded, not inaccurately, as a powerful force for unity when factional dispute raged in the party. Relief was great when in 1953 Herbert Morrison (later Lord Morrison of Lambeth) withdrew his challenge for the treasurership. Greenwood remained a member of the national executive until his death.

During the Leeds municipal strike in 1913, Greenwood had annoyed both the university authorities and the city fathers by his outspoken support for the strikers. Yet in 1930 his university conferred upon him the honorary degree of LL.D., and he became an honoured freeman of the city. He was sworn of the Privy Council in 1929, and made a C.H. in 1945, but refused a viscountcy on his retirement from office.

Greenwood, or 'A.G.' as he was popularly known to his friends, had the happy knack of being able to understand and to keep together both wings of the Labour Party. His education, if not his origin, made him an 'intellectual'. He was an early Fabian and a founder of the University Labour Federation whose president he remained until 1940. Yet it was Arthur Henderson [q.v.] who gave him his chance and prophesied his success. The National

Union of Railwaymen used him as propagandist during the 1919 strike; the miners asked him to give evidence before the Sankey commission on the coal mines; the Trades Union Congress made him a spokesman before the Blanesburgh committee on unemployment insurance; trade-union support made him deputy leader. Loyalty to his party dominated his life and he had little use for rebels. His love of humanity, his gift for friendship, his sincerity, and his high standards of public service won for him the respect of all who knew him. To his contemporaries who worked with him, to younger men who learned much of their socialism from him, he was 'the best-loved man in the Labour Party'. When he returned after a long illness he was cheered as though he were the 'father of the House'. (Sir) Winston Churchill described him as 'a wise counsellor of high courage and a good and helpful friend'. Yet Greenwood never fulfilled the highest hopes of those who in the early days foresaw a future of unlimited possibilities. He was not made of stuff quite stern enough to reach the highest position. Sometimes his very strength became a source of weakness, as in his infinite sociability and his inability to relax from too much conviviality. But he made a very real contribution to British political life: one of the first generation of pioneers, he was also one of those who created a party not merely of opposition but of office.

In 1904 Greenwood married Catherine Ainsworth, daughter of John James Brown, clerk, of Leeds. They had one daughter and one son, Anthony Greenwood, who entered Parliament as a Labour member in 1946, was chairman of the national executive (1963-4), and held a succession of offices after Labour came into power in 1964. Arthur Greenwood died at his home in London 9 June 1954.

[*The Times* and *Manchester Guardian*, 10 June 1954; private information; personal knowledge.]   H. V. WISEMAN.

GREG, SIR WALTER WILSON (1875-1959), scholar and bibliographer, was born 9 July 1875 at Park Lodge, Wimbledon Common, the only son of William Rathbone Greg [q.v.] by his second wife, Julia, second daughter of James Wilson [q.v.]. He was named after his grandfather and after Walter Bagehot [q.v.] who married Wilson's eldest daughter. *The Economist*, founded by Wilson and bril-

liantly edited by Bagehot, was a family paper, and from infancy W. W. Greg was intended some day to be its editor. His father died in 1881, and with his mother he spent some years travelling in Europe, acquiring a knowledge of French and German and a passion for mountains and mountaineering. He did not distinguish himself at Harrow, and at Trinity College, Cambridge, his work for the modern and medieval languages tripos was so desultory that he was allowed only the pass degree (1897). But at Trinity he met R. B. McKerrow (whose notice he contributed to this Dictionary), who was by far the most formative influence on his life. All thoughts of a career in financial journalism were soon abandoned, and when he should have been writing essays on monetary theory he was collecting material for a bibliography of the English drama and discussing with McKerrow projects for editing Elizabethan drama and the textual methods to be used. In 1898 he joined the Bibliographical Society, a momentous year for him and for the society, and so began a forty years' friendship with its secretary, A. W. Pollard (whose notice he also contributed to this Dictionary). His first publication of importance was a finding-list of English plays written before 1643 and published before 1700 (1900). It was the beginning of that descriptive bibliography of the English drama of which the first volume was published in 1939 and the fourth and last in 1959. He had been 'sixty years on the job'.

He was fortunate in being able to follow his bent without the distraction of earning a living. From his Wimbledon home he was a constant visitor to the British Museum and in almost daily touch with Pollard and McKerrow. Near by was the publishing house of A. H. Bullen [q.v.], and it was Bullen who suggested and published McKerrow's great edition of Thomas Nashe and Greg's edition of the Henslowe *Diary* and *Papers* (1904-8). Greg's work on this edition laid the foundations of his expert knowledge of Elizabethan theatrical companies and Elizabethan handwriting. Bullen also published his one book on literary history, *Pastoral Poetry and Pastoral Drama* (1906), still the best survey of the theme down to 1650. At the same time in numerous articles he was establishing new standards of bibliographical and textual criticism in relation to Elizabethan texts. Almost as influential as his books and articles in raising the standards of English scholarship were his reviews, for he wrote more than two hundred and never one that did not contribute something to the subject in hand. He could be extremely severe, as in his review in the *Modern Language Review* for April 1906 of the edition of Robert Greene by Churton Collins [q.v.], but even so he was constructive while being destructive. His most brilliant work in these early years, and one which called widespread attention to the usefulness of the bibliographical tools which he and his friends Pollard and McKerrow were using, was the proof that ten early quartos of Shakespearian interest purporting to be published at varying dates from 1600 to 1619 were all printed by William Jaggard in 1619.

From 1907 until his resignation in 1913 Greg was librarian of Trinity College, Cambridge, his one salaried academic post. The treasures of that library might have led him to become a medievalist, and he published much work on medieval manuscripts of dramatic interest: but he was already committed to his dramatic bibliography and to the Malone Society. Of this society, founded at Pollard's suggestion for the exact reproduction of English plays and dramatic documents before 1640, Greg was the Atlas, and during his general editorship (1906–39) and presidency (1939–59) there were very few of its hundred-odd volumes which did not profit from his scrutiny. For many he was solely responsible. Pollard had insisted that the bibliographer must have continually in his mind's eye the actual material manuscript from which the compositor was working, and both Greg and McKerrow realized that before this was possible they must know much more than was known to older scholars like Sir Sidney Lee [q.v.]: more about the relations between publishers, printers, and booksellers; about the practices of Elizabethan printers in matters like casting-off and proof correction; about dramatic companies and their relations with dramatists and censors; about the different types of dramatic manuscripts and the handwritings of dramatists and playhouse scriveners. More than any man Greg made this evidence available, whether in the publications of the Malone Society or elsewhere. His editions and studies of Greene's *Orlando Furioso* and Peele's *Battle of Alcazar*, two 'bad quartos' marred by memorial transmission, put the problem of the origins of quartos like *Romeo and Juliet* (1597) and *Hamlet* (1603) in a new light. His great gifts as a textual

critic and palaeographer found most scope in his editions of manuscript plays, and of these the most famous was *Sir Thomas More* (1911), three pages of which are believed to be in Shakespeare's hand. Other valuable works are his *Dramatic Documents from the Elizabethan Playhouses* (1931) with facsimiles and discussion of surviving theatrical and dramatic documents and *English Literary Autographs, 1550–1650* (1925–32) which gives facsimiles and transcription with comment on the hands of dramatists and other writers. Thanks in part to these works, attempts to identify hands of dramatists and playhouse scriveners have met with striking successes.

On the function of bibliography and its relations to textual criticism he had much to say, and although he hardly ever produced an edition with established text and commentary he profoundly altered editorial procedure. Like McKerrow he maintained that bibliography is the study of books, irrespective of their contents, with the purpose of ascertaining the exact circumstances and conditions in which they were produced; but unlike McKerrow he extended its boundaries by insisting that manuscripts and the investigation of textual transmission fell within its province. The duty of the editor of a printed text was not only to establish the relationship between the different editions of a work but to attempt to discover what sort of copy a printer worked from and how far he may have departed from his copy-text. The boundary between bibliography and textual criticism may have become a little obscure sometimes, but thanks mainly to Greg's writings it came to be recognized that analytical bibliography was an essential preliminary to textual criticism. A corollary of his view was that no emendation ought to be considered *in vacuo* without reference to what we know or may surmise of the history of the text. At the same time he was far from supposing that textual criticism could be reduced to a set of mechanical rules or that the critic could be relieved of the responsibility of individual judgement. The finest practical example of his doctrine is his edition of the two substantive texts of Marlowe's *'Doctor Faustus' 1604~1616* (1950). Attacking the problem without *parti pris* he combined a minute vision for significant detail with a power of erecting hypotheses which fit and interpret the available evidence. In whatever he did he was by no means timid, but his daring never passed into temerity.

After the outbreak of war in 1939 Greg sold his Wimbledon house and settled at River in Sussex. There he spent the happiest and most fruitful years of his life. There he saw through the press his great bibliography and his *Doctor Faustus*, and in works like *The Editorial Problem in Shakespeare* (3rd ed. 1954), *The Shakespeare First Folio: Its Bibliographical and Textual History* (1955), and his Lyell lectures on *Some Aspects and Problems of London Publishing 1550–1650* (1956) the old master gave his ripest thoughts on matters he had long studied. In youth he was unusually handsome and in old age still an impressive figure. Redoubtable in print he was sometimes so in person if angered by pretence or arrogance or slipshod writing. But he had many friends, old and young, and he took extraordinary pains to help younger generations. He never crossed the Atlantic, much to the regret of American scholars, but he was accessible at his hospitable house and always a punctual correspondent. Books and letters alike were written in a hand which was beautifully neat and elegant. In style he aimed at exactness and lucidity, but in the prose of criticism as in mathematics held that there should be a quality of elegance beyond mere comprehensibility and correctness. All his life he loved the theatre, live if possible, but failing that the radio. He had no dogmatic views on religion but thought of this life as a time of service. He died at River 4 March 1959.

In 1913 Greg married his cousin Elizabeth Gaskell, youngest daughter of Walter Greg, of Lee Hall, Prestbury, Cheshire; they had two sons and one daughter. Greg's many honours included the honorary D.Litt., Oxford (1932), and LL.D., Edinburgh (1945), a fellowship of the British Academy (1928), and foreign membership of the American Philosophical Society (1945). He became gold medallist of the Bibliographical Society in 1935 and (the honour which pleased him most) honorary fellow of Trinity in 1941. In 1950 he was knighted 'for services to the study of English literature'.

A chronological list of Greg's writings down to June 1945 by F. C. Francis is printed in the *Library* of that date in a number presented to Greg on his seventieth birthday. A supplement in the *Library* for March 1960 completes the tale of his works except for his biographical index to *Licensers for the Press, &c. to 1640* (Oxford Bibliographical Society, 1961) and his *Companion to Arber* (2 vols., 1967) edited by C. P. Blagden and I. G. Philip. His *Collected Papers*, edited by J. C. Maxwell, were published in 1966.

[W. W. Greg, *Biographical Notes 1877–1947*, privately printed, 1960; *Library*, September 1959; F. P. Wilson in *Proceedings* of the British Academy, vol. xlv, 1959; private papers; personal knowledge.] F. P. WILSON.

GREGORY, SIR RICHARD ARMAN, baronet (1864–1952), author, scientific journalist, and editor of *Nature*, was born in Bristol 29 January 1864, the son of John Gregory, the poet cobbler, an active and devoted Wesleyan and social reformer, by his wife, Ann, daughter of Richard Arman, farm overseer, of Chiseldon. Gregory was educated first at a Wesleyan day school, then for a short time at Queen Elizabeth's Hospital School where his interest in science began, finally at an elementary school. At the age of twelve he began life—like Faraday—as a newspaper boy. In 1879 he was apprenticed to a boot and shoe factory as a clicker, to cut out the uppers. Unhappy in his work, he spent his spare time at evening classes at the Bristol Trade and Mining Schools (later the Merchant Venturers' College), where he won a prize for Latin. He was encouraged by J. M. Wilson [q.v.], the headmaster of Clifton, who offered him the post of laboratory assistant which included the care of an 8-inch telescope. He was then seventeen. Three years later he won a student-teacher scholarship at the Normal School of Science, South Kensington, where he was a fellow student of H. G. Wells [q.v.] who became his lifelong friend and associate.

In place of formal instruction Gregory and another student helped (Sir) C. V. Boys [q.v.] in his experiments with fine wires and fibres and their 'Note on the Tenacity of Spun Glass' was communicated by Boys to the Physical Society and praised by him. In 1887 Gregory gained first classes in astronomy and physics and for the next two years was science demonstrator at Portsmouth dockyard school. He returned to South Kensington in 1889 as computor to the Solar Physics Committee and assistant to (Sir) Norman Lockyer [q.v.]. His work was of a routine nature: measuring the areas and positions of sunspots, comparison of solar spectrum lines with those of the elements, and the photography of flame spectra. Lockyer's work on the orientation of temples in Greece and Egypt appealed to Gregory and started his lifelong interest in the relations of astronomy and religion.

Soon after he joined Lockyer, Gregory's articles and reviews on astronomical subjects began to appear in *Nature* and in 1890 he became an Oxford university extension lecturer in astronomy and physics. Two years later he left South Kensington to become a freelance lecturer and journalist. His first book, *Elementary Physical and Astronomical Geography*, was published in 1891. In 1893 came his *Honours Physiography* with H. G. Wells as joint-author and in the same year *The Vault of Heaven* and next year *The Planet Earth*. In 1893 Lockyer made him assistant editor of *Nature*, which brought him into touch with its publishers, Macmillans, who in 1905 made him their scientific editor, a position which he held until 1939. Under his editorship over 200 textbooks were published, many of which he had inspired, and of some of which he was a co-author.

Gregory remained a university extension lecturer until 1895 and from 1898 to 1917 he was professor of astronomy at Queen's College, Harley Street. In 1899 he was joint-founder of the *School World* which was incorporated in the *Journal of Education* in 1918. He remained joint-editor until 1939. He was keenly interested in the technique of teaching and in securing the proper place for science in the school curriculum. He took an active part in the formation in 1901 of Section L of the British Association, dealing with educational science. He was its first secretary, later its recorder, and its president in 1922 when it came of age. In his presidential address he maintained that the purpose of school science teaching was not 'to prepare for vocations, but to equip pupils for life as it is and as it soon may be'. Science had become 'a kingdom potent with possibilities for good or evil—an inheritance which cannot be renounced'. In his book *Discovery or the Spirit and Service of Science*, he gave a vivid picture of the different aspects of the advance of knowledge. First published in 1916 it ran through many editions until in 1949 Gregory revised and shortened it for Penguin Books. He had in his mind the whole story of discovery through the ages, he knew the personalities of the great men and their writings: writing with freshness and vitality and carrying his learning

lightly with the touch of the journalist at his best, he produced the most lasting of all his works.

Possessed of lucid style, a gift of phrase wide interests, and a sense of the significant, Gregory was the greatest scientific journalist of his day. More and more work fell to him as assistant editor of *Nature* and he was virtually the editor for at least twelve years before Lockyer resigned the office to him in 1919. Gregory had his own ideas and many new features were introduced. *Nature* became an institution in both the international and the national field, for he made it a clearing-house for new ideas. A letter to *Nature* became the accepted channel of rapid communication to the scientific world of a preliminary note of some new technique or discovery. But this was only one of its functions. Under Gregory's skilful editorship *Nature* kept pace with developments all over the world despite the rapid growth of specialization, the increasing complexity of the problems, and the extension of industrial research. He was always interested in the international contacts of science and gave generous space to such activities. One of the new features of *Nature* was the leading article, the first of which appeared in October 1915, on 'Science in National Affairs'. From November 1919 when he became editor they appeared every week, many from his own pen, emphasizing the importance of scientific developments in national policy.

By this time Gregory had become the moving spirit of the British Science Guild and many articles were in support of its objects. It had been founded in 1905 by Lockyer after he had failed to persuade the British Association to take a more active part in arousing awareness of the danger of neglecting science and in bringing to the notice of Parliament the scientific aspects of matters affecting national welfare. Gregory was at first doubtful of the breakaway from the Association, but he soon saw the advantages of the Guild as an agency for propaganda backed by men of influence like Lord Haldane and Lord Melchett [qq.v.] The Guild did in fact make a major contribution to a number of important developments such as the establishment of the National Physical Laboratory Gregory organized the exhibitions of British scientific products in 1918 and 1919, for which he received the recognition of a knighthood (1919). In 1922 he became chairman of the executive com mittee of the Guild and he was largely responsible for merging the Guild with the British Association in 1936 when its main work had been done.

After 1919 Gregory became steadily more and more a public figure. With his boundless energy and curiosity and his optimism about new causes he was a member of seventy organizations and served as president of twenty-five. In December 1938, just as he was leaving the editorial chair of *Nature*, he was invited to give a series of lectures at Harvard, Johns Hopkins, the Carnegie Institution, and elsewhere. The tour was a great success. Gregory in his seventy-fifth year was at his peak as an eloquent exponent of the doctrine of science. His addresses were a declaration of faith in what science could contribute to a disordered world if it were not perverted to destructive uses by the lust for power. On his return he embodied the materials for his lectures in his *Religion in Science and Civilization* (1940). Most of the copies were destroyed in an air raid and he recast it with the title *Gods and Men* (1949).

Of the many attachments Gregory formed during his life the longest and most intimate was his membership of the British Association which he joined in 1896. He threw himself into the work of the Association with energy and devotion, not only in Section L but on endless committees and as a member of council for many years. He took an active part in the formation of the new Division for the Social and International Relations of Science in 1938 after the merger with the British Science Guild. It was given powers to hold meetings apart from the annual meeting of the Association. Gregory was elected president of the British Association at Dundee in 1939 the day before war broke out and it fell to him to keep the Association in action during the war by a series of conferences to discuss post-war problems. In July 1946 he delivered his presidential address at the first short post-war meeting. His subject was 'Civilization and the Pursuit of Knowledge', and in it he recurred to his favourite topic, the gradual emergence of civilization. Love of science and an imaginative sense of the part it was destined to play in human affairs were the mainsprings of Gregory's life. He had, too, shrewdness and practical judgement, which had been sharpened by his early struggles and adversity. He was no specialist nor, in that sense, a profound thinker. He saw the broad picture and its

human bearings for he was essentially a humanist. He was elected into the Royal Society in 1933 under a special section of the statutes for 'conspicuous services to the cause of science'. He was created a baronet in 1931; and received honorary degrees from Bristol, Leeds, and St. Andrews.

He married first, in 1888, Kate Florence (died 1926), daughter of Charles Napier Pearn and widow of Frederick George Dugan; secondly, in 1931, Dorothy Mary, daughter of William Page [q.v.]. He had one son and one daughter by the first marriage, both of whom predeceased him. The baronetcy became extinct when he died at Middleton-on-Sea 15 September 1952. A portrait by Raeburn Dobson is in the possession of the family.

[*The Times*, 16 September 1952; *Nature*, 27 September 1952; F. J. M. Stratton in *Obituary Notices of Fellows of the Royal Society*, No. 22, November 1953; *The Advancement of Science*, vol. x, No. 39, December 1953; W. H. G. Armytage, *Sir Richard Gregory*, 1957; private information; personal knowledge.]

HAROLD HARTLEY.

GREY, CHARLES GREY (1875–1953), writer on aviation, was born in Sussex Place, Regent's Park, London, 13 March 1875, the third son of Charles Grey Grey, of Dilston Hall, Northumberland, and his wife, Emily Mary Bolton. He was a grandson of John Grey and nephew of Josephine Butler [qq.v.]. His father was a member of the Irish Land Commission and thus it came about that the thoroughly English Charles Grey was educated at the Erasmus Smith School in Dublin and acquired a deep and humorous insight into the Irish character. He went next to the Crystal Palace School of Engineering and later became a draughtsman with the Swift Cycle Company in Coventry at thirty shillings a week. By 1904, C.G.G., as he became known in the aviation world, had moved to journalism and joined the *Cycle & Motor Trades Review*. A year later he transferred to another paper owned by E. M. (later Lord) Iliffe [q.v.], the *Autocar*, and began to specialize on powered flight. He reported the first Paris aero show in December 1908. As a result he was made joint-editor of a new penny weekly named the *Aero* and attended the first international aviation meeting at Reims which marked the first real start to European flying.

In 1911 Grey started his own paper, the *Aeroplane*, backed by (Sir) Victor Sassoon with £1,000. Three years later the paper was paying its way and beginning to be a power in aeronautical affairs. During the war of 1914–18 the *Aeroplane* grew, with the air services, to substantial size. Grey battled on behalf of better equipment for the Royal Flying Corps, and against the government-run Royal Aircraft Factory at Farnborough. He made many friends—and enemies. He built up a lasting friendship with the future Marshal of the Royal Air Force Lord Trenchard [q.v.], with whom he campaigned strenuously for the preservation of an independent Air Force when, after the war, the two senior Services plotted its break-up. For a time the *Aeroplane* was banned from the wardrooms of ships of the Royal Navy.

In the early post-war years C.G.G. fought wordy battles with invective and ardour on behalf of the small British aircraft industry and against 'bumbledom' in every form. He also conducted an enormous correspondence with people interested in aviation all over the world, often sitting at a dictaphone long into the night. His writings built up the *Aeroplane* on a solid basis during the lean times between the wars. He forged a climate of opinion which was extensive and effective in the small world of aviation. Not only did he support Trenchard in the stabilizing of the Royal Air Force, but he also backed G. E. Woods Humphery's efforts to build Imperial Airways, Sir Sefton Brancker [q.v.] and (Sir) Geoffrey de Havilland in the promotion of British light aviation, and (Sir) Richard Fairey [q.v.] in introducing new ideas from the United States which Grey visited in 1923. His influential friends included Sir Samuel Hoare (later Viscount Templewood) and Lord Londonderry [qq.v.], air ministers in their day. Among those he attacked consistently were Lloyd George, (Sir) Winston Churchill, and all things from Farnborough.

Unfortunately Grey became susceptible to flattery, especially flattery from abroad. He was made much of in Italy and Germany during visits to aeronautical events in those countries and the result was a gradual build-up of bias in the *Aeroplane* in favour of Italian and German ways of life. As war loomed nearer his views became increasingly unpopular. He retired from his editorship in June 1939, five years after he had disposed of his interest in the paper to the Temple Press. Thereafter he wrote as air correspondent for northern newspapers.

The *Aeroplane*, indeed, reached its zenith of influence and popularity around the year 1935, when Grey, with his ardent team—Leonard Bridgman, Mrs. McAlery, Thurstan James, F. D. Bradbrooke, and Geoffrey Dorman—were at the peak of their dedication to things aeronautical and before international right-wing politics had seriously crept into the paper. Supported by this team—especially Leonard Bridgman—Grey also edited until 1941 Jane's *All the World's Aircraft* which he took over when Fred Jane died in 1916.

Grey was one of the half-dozen writers on aviation who left a significant impression upon the first generation of powered flight. He was a character—a 'card' in the terms of his heyday—and the most controversial figure in aeronautical journalism in the early years of aviation. He was a crusader who sometimes wrote unfairly, often inaccurately, but never dully. He could infuriate, but he never bored. He made the *Aeroplane* the most widely read and the most quoted aviation newspaper in the narrow circle of aeronautical intelligentsia during the quarter-century between 1912 and 1937. He boasted that for some twenty years he never missed a leader on 'Matters of Moment' in which he commented pungently on all aspects of aeronautical affairs—from the beginnings of air power and air transport, through aircraft manufacture and private flying, to all aspects of the political and economic scene. He contributed much to the existence of the Royal Air Force; gave zest to aeronautical thinking during and after the war of 1914–18; came near to ruining a fine reputation before the second war by his absorption of foreign right-wing propaganda; but regained all his old popularity among the aviation fraternity during the last mellow years before his death, when he again contributed periodic articles to his old paper.

He died 9 December 1953 in a way which would have given him sardonic amusement—in the arms of an Air Marshal in a cloakroom, at the Admiralty where he had gone for a press reception.

In 1899 Grey married Beatrice Lilla, daughter of Richard Thorneloe, watchmaker, of Coventry. The marriage was dissolved and in 1929 he married Margaret Sumner, daughter of John Sumner Marriner, solicitor. They had a son and a daughter. The Royal Aero Club has a portrait by Frank Eastman.

[*Aeroplane*, 18 December 1953; private information; personal knowledge.]

PETER G. MASEFIELD.

GRIERSON, Sir HERBERT JOHN CLIFFORD (1866–1960), scholar, was born 16 January 1866 in Lerwick, Shetland, the second son of Andrew John Grierson and his wife, Alice Geraldine Clifford. The Griersons had been lairds in Shetland since the mid-eighteenth century, owning the estate of Quendale, consisting of the south-west corner of the mainland, where Herbert Grierson spent his childhood summers. He was educated for a short period at the Anderson Institute, Lerwick, then spent two years at a school in Cheltenham run by two of his mother's sisters. In 1877 he went to the Gymnasium at Aberdeen (a school on the German model) and in 1883 entered King's College, Aberdeen, to take the standard arts degree which involved the study of Latin, Greek, mathematics, and physics, with some logic, rhetoric, and metaphysics. At the prompting of a friend, Grierson tried for the optional 'philosophy honours', which involved reading Plato and Kant on his own. In 1886 he obtained a temporary position as second housemaster at the Gymnasium, but this left him time to continue with his university work and he graduated in 1887 with the Bain gold medal in philosophy and the Seafield medal in English.

Two unsettled years followed, during which he taught for a while at a girls' school, tutored, and marked essays for William Minto [q.v.], professor of logic at Aberdeen. Learning that the Holford exhibition at Christ Church, generally confined to candidates from Charterhouse, would be open *pro hac vice*, Grierson went to Oxford and won it on the strength of an essay on 'Fanaticism' which greatly impressed D. B. Monro [q.v.]. At Oxford, where he made a greater reputation as a talker than as a scholar among his contemporaries, he got a second in classical moderations (1891) and a first in *literae humaniores* (1893). Just at this time changes in the structure of Scottish universities had introduced English language and literature as a full degree subject. John Gray Chalmers had given money to establish a chair of English at Aberdeen and the university proposed to appoint a lecturer until the ordinance founding the chair had been passed. With influential backing from Sidgwick in Oxford and Principal Sir W. D. Geddes [q.v.] of Aberdeen University, Grierson obtained the lectureship. He had at this time no professional qualifications in English, though he was fairly well read in English

poetry, which had always been a passion with him.

Grierson spent a year as lecturer, developing a course in rhetoric and reading hard in order to work up an historical course on English literature from Anglo-Saxon times. In 1894, with the support of local members of Parliament and of some influential Oxford voices, he became the first professor of English at Aberdeen. He set himself with great energy to master the whole field of English literature in order to justify not only his appointment but the full-dress academic study of English. George Saintsbury [q.v.] enlisted him to write a book on the seventeenth century in the series 'Periods of European Literature' which he was editing, and to do this Grierson learned Dutch so that he could do justice to the important Dutch literature of the period. *The First Half of the Seventeenth Century* (vol. vii of the series) appeared in 1906. A friendship formed with William Macneile Dixon, professor of English at Glasgow, resulted in the publication in 1909, under their joint editorship, of *The English Parnassus, an Anthology of Longer Poems*. Meanwhile Grierson had become engaged in a serious study of John Donne, as a result of his work on the seventeenth century. This led to his being asked to write the chapter on Donne in the *Cambridge History of English Literature*, which in turn led to his monumental two-volume edition of Donne's poems for the Clarendon Press (1912). His task in this great edition was not only to settle the text and the canon but also to provide a detailed explanatory commentary on this notoriously difficult poet. In 1921 he followed this up with an important and influential anthology of *Metaphysical Lyrics and Poems of the Seventeenth Century*; and in 1934 with G. Bullough he edited *The Oxford Book of Seventeenth Century Verse*.

Having established English studies at Aberdeen on a sound footing Grierson succeeded Saintsbury in the regius chair of rhetoric and English literature at Edinburgh in 1915 and held this position until his retirement in 1935. There he performed with great distinction the usual duties of a Scottish professor, giving to the first ordinary class the magisterial survey of English literature from its beginnings as well as lecturing on more detailed aspects of English literature to the honours students. He was now established as one of the major academic literary figures in the country. Among the many books and articles he wrote during his tenure of the Edinburgh chair were 'Milton' (article in the *Encyclopædia of Religion and Ethics*), *The Background of English Literature and Other Collected Essays and Addresses* (1925), *Lyrical Poetry from Blake to Hardy* (1928), and, one of his finest works, *Cross Currents in English Literature of the XVII Century* (the Messenger lectures delivered at Cornell University, 1926–7, published in 1929). He also edited the poems of Byron (1923) and Milton (1925) and produced a one-volume version of his edition of Donne with a new introduction and new and shorter notes. He had begun working on Sir Walter Scott about 1930, and between 1932 and 1937, in collaboration with Davidson Cook, W. M. Parker, and others, produced a great twelve-volume edition of Scott's letters. The new knowledge he thus gained about Scott led to his publishing in 1938 *Sir Walter Scott, Bart.*, a biography which supplemented and corrected Lockhart. He was elected rector by the students of Edinburgh University in 1936 and served until 1939. He was knighted in 1936.

Grierson lectured abroad many times, visiting America on a number of occasions, and giving a course of lectures at Heidelberg in 1929. He received honorary degrees from twelve universities and was elected F.B.A. in 1923.

In 1896 he married Mary Letitia (died 1937), daughter of (Sir) Alexander Ogston, professor of surgery at Aberdeen; they had five daughters. In his later years Grierson became increasingly crippled by arthritis and moved to Cambridge, where a daughter was married to Professor Bruce Dickins. He died there 19 February 1960. Edinburgh University has portraits of Grierson by Kenneth Green and David Foggie.

[David Daiches in *Proceedings* of the British Academy, vol. xlvi, 1960; *Seventeenth Century Studies*, presented to Sir Herbert Grierson, 1938, contains a full bibliography, 1906–37; personal knowledge.]   DAVID DAICHES.

GRIFFIN, BERNARD WILLIAM (1899–1956), cardinal, was born in Birmingham 21 February 1899, the twin son of William Bernard Griffin, a cycle manufacturer's manager, by his wife, Helen Swadkins. One of five children, he was brought up in the happy atmosphere of Catholic family life, his parents being active in the civic affairs of Birmingham and the pillars around which the new

parish of Sparkhill was formed. Encouraged by his parish priest, Bernard Griffin began his studies for the priesthood at Cotton College, Staffordshire, in 1913, shortly after his twin brother, Walter (who died in 1963), had entered the Benedictine order at Douai.

In 1917 their studies came to a halt when both brothers joined the Royal Naval Air Service from which they ultimately transferred to the Royal Air Force. Bernard Griffin's military service was distinguished only by his contracting rheumatic fever but this proved a considerable factor in his later illness. With characteristic determination, he refused medical discharge lest it should jeopardize his vocation. After demobilization in 1919 he entered Oscott College, Birmingham, where the rector, Monsignor Parkinson, did much to inspire in his pupil an abiding interest in social justice. In 1921 he was sent to the Venerable English College in Rome, the rector this time being Monsignor Hinsley [q.v.], later Griffin's predecessor at Westminster.

Ordained on 1 November 1924, Griffin remained in Rome until 1927, adding to his doctorate in theology one in canon law. When he returned to his native Birmingham he was appointed to curial duties, serving as secretary to two successive archbishops, the second being Dr. Thomas Williams, a courageous and forthright man who played a great part in the development of Griffin's character. Ten years later Griffin was made parish priest of Coleshill and administrator of the children's homes there. In 1938 he was appointed auxiliary to Archbishop Williams. At the time of his consecration he was the youngest bishop in the country and the energy and efficiency which he brought to his multiple duties rapidly won him a reputation throughout the Midlands. He became vicar-general of the diocese, organized the youth movement and other social welfare works, built a church at Coleshill, and even found time to serve as an air-raid warden. Nevertheless he was comparatively unknown to the nation as a whole when, in December 1943, he was appointed to Westminster as successor to Cardinal Hinsley.

The new archbishop rapidly won widespread renown by his public utterances and personal endeavours for international peace. At first he was subject to some criticism for his warnings about Soviet intentions in Eastern Europe, particularly in Poland, but subsequent events proved him correct. He was a great believer in strengthening by personal contact the bonds of understanding between nations and, as soon as the war was over, he visited Italy, Germany, and the occupied countries to re-establish contact with the bishops. Later he was to undertake immense journeys throughout Europe and North America. His emphasis on the universal nature of the Catholic Church was made at the direct request of Pope Pius XII who created him a cardinal on his forty-seventh birthday: his 'beloved Benjamin of the Sacred College'.

At home, the post-war legislation of the Labour Government called forth the archbishop's expert knowledge of social justice. Although opposed to the suppression of the voluntary spirit, he sought wherever possible to secure for his Church a place within the social systems of the welfare State. Several of the amendments he suggested were incorporated in subsequent legislation, but he remained an opponent of the Education Act of 1944, claiming that it placed an intolerable financial burden on his people. He also persuaded Aneurin Bevan [q.v.] to disclaim Catholic hospitals from the National Health Service. It was a tribute to his personality and negotiating skill that he enjoyed the abiding friendship of both Labour and Conservative leaders.

The cardinal attached much importance to the role of the layman in the Church. Encouraging Catholics to enter public life, he fostered the development of vocational guilds to fit them for their professional tasks. He championed the cause of the persecuted and of refugees from Communist countries and showed special concern for the welfare of the Irish immigrants. During his archiepiscopate the Catholic population of England and Wales increased by over one-third and in spite of building restrictions he succeeded in opening many new churches and schools. He was papal legate to the hierarchy centenary congress in 1950.

Behind this bare record of achievement lies a story of great courage in the face of ill health. Largely as a result of prolonged overwork, the cardinal suffered a severe illness in 1949 which left him partially paralysed. Unable to resign his office, he continued to carry out his duties sparing himself not at all and exercising the full measure of his jurisdiction. He suffered a series of heart attacks from which he eventually died at Polzeath in Cornwall on the feast of his patron, Saint Bernard,

20 August 1956. His body was buried in the crypt of Westminster Cathedral.

In the intervening years, Cardinal Griffin had won the deep affection of his priests and people for his cheerful courage and smiling simplicity. A great patriot, yet with an international outlook, in him was blended the learning of his high estate with the humble approachability of a father deeply concerned with the care of his spiritual children. He attached great importance to family life, his pastoral letters often dealing with such matters as the care of old people, housing, and child welfare, and he himself was always radiantly happy when he was with children. He made his own the teaching of Saint Thérèse of Lisieux for whom he had a great devotion, emphasizing the equality of human creatures in the eyes of God. Of him, Monsignor Knox [q.v.] wrote: 'He never failed in the performance of his pastoral duties. Undeterred by ill-health, he went on ruling his diocese, as if he were determined to throw away his life rather than fail in his duties to others.' A portrait by Allan Gwynne-Jones is at Archbishop's House where there is also a bronze by Miss Fiore de Henriques.

[*The Times*, 21 August 1956; Michael de la Bedoyere, *Cardinal Bernard Griffin*, 1955; *Tribute to Cardinal Griffin*, a symposium, 1956; personal knowledge.]

DEREK WORLOCK.

GRIGG, EDWARD WILLIAM MAC-LEAY, first BARON ALTRINCHAM (1879–1955), administrator and politician, was born 8 September 1879 in Madras, the only son of Henry Bidewell Grigg, of the Indian Civil Service, by his wife, Elizabeth Louisa, eldest daughter of Sir Edward Deas Thomson [q.v.], colonial secretary of New South Wales (1837–56). A scholar of both Winchester and New College, Oxford, he obtained a second class in classical moderations (1900) and a third in *literae humaniores* (1902). In 1902 he won the Gaisford Greek verse prize.

Journalism was his first calling. In 1903 he joined the staff of *The Times* as secretary to G. E. Buckle [q.v.], the editor; then moved to the *Outlook* as assistant editor (1905–6) to J. L. Garvin [q.v.]. In 1908, after two years of widespread and intensive travel, he returned to *The Times* as head of its colonial department. His family background, his personal knowledge of imperial affairs, and his reverence for Joseph Chamberlain and Lord Milner [qq.v.] well fitted him for this post. At no time in its history, he was later proud to recall, did that newspaper exercise a more salutary and decisive influence upon national policy than in the years immediately before the war. He resigned in 1913 to become joint-editor of the *Round Table*.

Grigg was thirty-four at the outbreak of war in 1914. Scorning the posts of dignified safety which could have been his for the asking, he joined the Grenadier Guards as an ensign and was sent out to the 2nd battalion in France. 'The Scribe', as he was affectionately called in the Brigade, showed outstanding qualities of gallantry and leadership throughout the heavy fighting in which the Guards division was engaged. (Sir) Winston Churchill, then a major in the Oxfordshire Yeomanry, was for a short time attached to his company to gain experience of trench warfare. Early in 1916 Grigg was transferred to the staff. By the end of the war he had risen to be a lieutenant-colonel and G.S.O. 1 of the Guards division. He was awarded the M.C. in 1917, appointed to the D.S.O. in 1918, C.M.G. in 1919, and mentioned in dispatches.

It was during his years in the Grenadiers that Grigg first met the Prince of Wales, whom he accompanied on tours of Canada in 1919 and of Australia and New Zealand in 1920 as military secretary and special adviser. For these services, not always free from anxiety, he was appointed successively C.V.O. (1919) and K.C.V.O. (1920). On his return he joined the staff of the prime minister, Lloyd George, as a private secretary. To the traditional loyalties of the post he added an intense personal admiration for his mercurial chief which blinded him to all criticism, however well founded. He served his master with memorable fidelity throughout some difficult political situations. At Cannes in January 1922 he took part in the historic game of golf which caused the downfall of M. Briand. When the prime minister himself fell from power later that year Grigg was offered a choice of senior appointments in the Civil Service. He preferred instead to enter the House of Commons for Oldham (1922–5) as a Lloyd George Liberal. As secretary to the Rhodes Trust (1923–5) he was also able to maintain a close interest in imperial affairs.

In 1925 Grigg was appointed governor of Kenya. Two years before, he had married Joan Alice Katherine Dickson-Poynder, only child of Lord Islington (whose notice he was later to contribute

to this Dictionary). Her instinctive sympathy for all races, expressed particularly in her patronage of nursing and maternity services, enhanced the distinction of her husband's administration. The task with which Grigg had been charged was to unite the three East African territories of Kenya, Uganda, and Tanganyika. Largely owing to the opposition of Sir Donald Cameron [q.v.], governor of Tanganyika, and to lukewarm support from the home Government, this mission failed. But there was much else in his programme which brought lasting economic benefit to the colony and created stable conditions most likely to attract European capital. Agriculture and forestry, communications and schools, town planning and security of land tenure were all improved during his energetic and sometimes exacting rule. Believing that the civilization of an age is reflected in its buildings, he dignified Kenya with two splendid Government Houses, at Nairobi and Mombasa, designed by Sir Herbert Baker [q.v.], but was unable to realize an ambitious project for central government offices. He was appointed K.C.M.G. in 1928.

Appreciation of his governorship has since been tempered by belittlement of his trust in tribal self-government and provincial autonomy. Grigg rejected the later fashion of thought that Kenya should progress through the multi-racial state towards a common citizenship. This, he believed, could lead only to the ultimate extinction of the white settler and to an overwhelming African ascendancy: a prospect he deplored, not because he felt that Africans as such were unfitted to govern themselves, but because he feared that they would be required to administer an alien system of western government without the necessary education and experience. To the end of his days he set his face against so abrupt an abdication of what he held to be Great Britain's imperial mission.

On returning to England in 1930 Grigg was offered a choice of Indian governorships. Neither he nor his wife, however, was in robust health and he refused them all. It was the fatal turning-point of his life. Whatever his opinion of African incapacity for self-rule, it did not extend to the peoples of India. As a boy he had seen his parents' house thronged with Indian visitors and developed a sympathetic understanding of their aspirations. He might have been one of the greatest of Indian administrators; instead he determined to remain at home and to plunge once more into the world of politics. Without the instincts of political manœuvre and self-advancement, and further handicapped by his known allegiance to Lloyd George, his venture was doomed to fail.

In the general election of 1931, although already adopted as Conservative candidate for Leeds Central, he stood down with characteristic unselfishness in favour of the former Labour member who proposed to stand as a 'national' candidate. Two years later, having in the meantime served as chairman of the milk reorganization commission, he returned to the House of Commons as member for Altrincham. It is to his credit that he recognized the menace of Nazi Germany before most of his colleagues. In two eloquent works, *The Faith of an Englishman* (1936) and *Britain Looks at Germany* (1938), he pleaded for a stern policy of defence. Yet he continued to believe that such a course of action was not incompatible with wholehearted support for the administrations of Stanley Baldwin and Neville Chamberlain. Too loyal to be a rebel, he would plead with his leaders in private but recoiled from criticizing them in public. His name is not to be found among those who voted against 'Munich'.

Denied office until the outbreak of war, he was appointed parliamentary secretary to the Ministry of Information in its opening days. In April 1940 he became financial secretary, and in May joint parliamentary under-secretary, at the War Office. He held the latter post until March 1942, having earlier refused Churchill's offer of promotion as first commissioner of works since it depended upon his acceptance of a peerage. Thereafter he was inadequately employed for a man of his talents, but in November 1944 returned to office as minister resident in the Middle East in succession to Lord Moyne [q.v.] and was sworn of the Privy Council. The defeat of the Churchill government in July 1945 put an end to both his political ambitions and his active political life, although he was to assume the editorship of the *National Review* in 1948. He was created Baron Altrincham in 1945 and died at Tormarton, his house in Gloucestershire, 1 December 1955, after a long illness. His last reserves of strength were drained in the completion of *Kenya's Opportunity* (1955), a final tribute to the land which was so much a part of his life. He had one daughter and two sons, the elder of whom, John Edward Poynder (born 1924), succeeded to the title, but disclaimed it in 1963.

'Ned' Grigg was a handsome man, well above middle height and with the complexion of a countryman. Yet his soldierly bearing concealed a nervous system ill suited to the hubbub of politics. Opposition to his impulsive enthusiasms evoked bursts of impatience, even of rage. Then the clouds would lift: in his family circle or when entertaining a few close friends drawn mostly from the Milner 'kindergarten' he would both show and inspire deep affection. He was half a poet. Few other colonial governors would have written: 'The very thought of Kenya is like sunlight to me, sunlight crisp as mountain air in the high places of the earth.' He found perennial solace in the plays of Shakespeare and in listening to music.

There is a pencil drawing of him by Ray Nestor at Tormarton.

[Grigg's own writings; *National and English Review*, January 1956; private information; personal knowledge.]   KENNETH ROSE.

GRIMBLE, SIR ARTHUR FRANCIS (1888–1956), colonial administrator, broadcaster, and writer, was born in Hong Kong 11 June 1888, the son of Frank Grimble who had business interests there, and his wife, Blanche Ann Arthur. He went to Chigwell School, Magdalene College, Cambridge, and continued his education in France and Germany. In 1914 he entered the Colonial Service as a cadet in the administration of the Gilbert and Ellice Islands, reaching the Central Pacific three months before the outbreak of war. Less than nine months after his arrival he was officer in charge of Ocean Island. After holding posts as lands commissioner and district officer he was appointed resident commissioner of the colony in 1926. In 1933 he transferred to St. Vincent in the Windward Islands as administrator and colonial secretary and in 1936 to the Seychelles as governor and commander-in-chief where he remained until 1942. In that year, a firm believer in West Indian federation, he was appointed back to the Windward Islands as governor and commander-in-chief. He retired in 1948.

From early in his career Grimble had published occasional verse for periodicals and serious ethnological papers for the *Journals* of the Royal Anthropological Institute and the Polynesian Society— 'From Birth to Death in the Gilbert

Islands' (*J.R.A.I.*, 1921), 'Canoes in the Gilbert Islands' (*J.R.A.I.*, 1924), 'Gilbertese Astronomy and Astronomical Observances' (*J.P.S.*, 1931), and 'Migrations of a Pandanus People' (*J.P.S.*, 1933). At ease with languages, Grimble was a Gilbertese scholar and his published papers reflect an insight into the people unbarred by language. They represent also original research in a field scarcely touched upon. Of first-class anthropological importance, their sphere is necessarily limited. Yet shortly after his retirement Grimble was to become almost a household name in Britain. Submitting some of his Pacific experiences in random form to the British Broadcasting Corporation he was surprised not that they were accepted but that he was invited to recount them himself. The classic and, of course, somewhat exaggerated octopus story was bound to be a success by reason of its content, but the manner of telling and the timbre of voice made him the envy of professionals and guaranteed wide popularity for the series.

In 1952 Grimble polished up the stories for publication under the title *A Pattern of Islands*. Immediately acclaimed, the book has since been published in many languages. Its charm lies in an apparently effortless simplicity of style, an uncoy modesty, and an endearing impression of life in a part of the Pacific not previously described except by R. L. Stevenson [q.v.] in a quite different manner. Writing of the minutest specks of coral twelve thousand miles away and of a period (1914–20) as long ago as almost forty years, Grimble brought to his war-weary readers the ultimate in escapism. It was pardonable for a degree of hyperbole to tinge the tales. To this was added less consciously a Gulliver-in-Lilliput aura: Grimble was a lean giant among the square stocky islanders. The tales are of uneven quality and are at their best when dealing with human frailties and peccadilloes, not least those of the author. The misfortunes and accidents of his earliest days, when he was acclimatizing himself to the customs of the kindly but critical Micronesians of the Gilbert Islands or the Polynesians of the Ellice Islands, are described with warmth, delicacy, and wit, and with that absence of embarrassment which a successful career assures. It is mostly comedy of a rich order. The fascination which Micronesian mythology held for him is evident from its domination of some of the stories, but it is less successfully transmitted than his affection for cricket and fishing. Part of the charm of the book, as of the broadcast tales, was that, however local, simple, and narrow the setting and theme, there was a cultivated, almost cosmopolitan air to the style of narrative. A slender work, it is neatly fined down. Nor did Grimble's elegance of writing flow smoothly from his pen. That he should produce the stories at all was the result of the utmost persuasion upon him, for he set himself high standards of taking pains and doubted whether he could supply the intense concentration without which he would not offer his work publicly. Consequently *A Pattern of Islands*, which was filmed in 1956 under the title *Pacific Destiny*, was virtually an isolated success. *Return to the Islands*, posthumously produced in 1957, covers the period 1921 to 1932; perhaps because it deals with periods of office in more senior and responsible posts it lacks much of the appeal of its forerunner. The stories have not the same *joie de vivre*; but they give the same impression of benevolence, justice, omniscience, and never-failing good temper—a commentary perhaps on the careers of proconsuls in the imperial twilight.

Grimble was appointed C.M.G. in 1930 and K.C.M.G. in 1938. Governed throughout his successes by modesty, he knew his limitations, and avoided public speaking appearances.

In 1914 Grimble married Olivia Mary, daughter of Lewis Jarvis, of Sharnbrook, Bedfordshire; they had four daughters. He died in London 12 December 1956.

[Private information; personal knowledge.]
PHILIP SNOW.

GURNEY, SIR HENRY LOVELL GOLDSWORTHY (1898–1951), colonial civil servant, was born at Poughill, Bude, Cornwall, 27 June 1898, the only son of Gregory Goldsworthy Henry Gurney, solicitor, and his wife, Florence Mary Lovell, daughter of Edwin Francis Chamier. From Winchester he was commissioned in 1917 in the King's Royal Rifle Corps and was wounded shortly before the armistice. He then went as a scholar to University College, Oxford, where he played golf for the university against Cambridge. In 1921 he was appointed an assistant district commissioner in Kenya where, showing no particular flair for native administration in the different districts in which he served, he was to find his *métier* in the secretariat.

There he did well, and in 1935 he was promoted to Jamaica as assistant colonial secretary, but resigned after a few months. After a spell in the Colonial Office he returned to Kenya in 1936 and two years later was appointed secretary to the East African Governors Conference and secretary to the high commissioner for transport. After Italy's entry into the war in 1940 the Governors Conference became an instrument of considerable importance in co-ordinating the defence and supply problems of the territories; the governor of Kenya became its permanent chairman; and in 1941 in recognition of his increased responsibilities Gurney's post was upgraded to that of chief secretary: a post calling for tact, administrative ability, and sound judgement of a high order. Despite the sometimes conflicting demands from the governments and military authorities concerned, Gurney usually obtained his objectives without loss of goodwill and with an imperturbability which his somewhat diffident and unimpressive demeanour belied. He relieved the chairman of detail, and thanks to his excellent relations with the military authorities had the knack of settling many problems with his opposite numbers without recourse to higher authority. His recreation was golf and through it he had his own circle of friends. In social activities he played no important part. He was appointed C.M.G. in 1942.

In 1944 Gurney was promoted to be colonial secretary of the Gold Coast where during his short service he won the confidence of the local population and was interested in the development of a ministerial system. Sir Alan Burns was very sorry to lose a wise counsellor when in 1946 Gurney received further promotion to the exacting post of chief secretary to the Palestine Government. He arrived here in the final days of the mandate, when terrorist outrages were increasing and passions at boiling-point. The role of both the civil and military authorities in maintaining law and order was the subject of much emotional criticism by the supporters of Jews or Arabs alike, both at home and abroad. In 1947 Gurney was knighted and when Sir Alan Cunningham, the high commissioner, went to London for consultation Gurney was left in charge of the administration. Thereafter in the difficult months which followed he and the other members of the civil administration worked untiringly in face of much calumny and imputations of par-

tiality in support of the policy of maintaining British impartiality between Jew and Arab, even when Jewish outrages on British troops raised clamour for reprisals. Sir Alan Cunningham, a general himself, although not in command of the troops in Palestine, paid tribute to the manner in which Gurney always remained on the best of terms with the general officers commanding the army, despite the necessity at times of restraining them from taking military reprisals for terrorist outrages. Whatever his personal feelings Gurney never allowed them to sway his judgement and he gave the high commissioner his loyal and unwavering support in carrying out what must have been at times a most distasteful and thankless task. He won the loyalty and confidence of his subordinates by his approachability and clear and firm decisions once his mind was made up; his imperturbability was proverbial in moments of recurring crises, which was one of the reasons why he earned the hatred of some of the Jews.

On the termination of the British mandate in May 1948, C. R. (later Earl) Attlee sent Sir Alan Cunningham and the Palestine administration a message of gratitude for the way in which they had carried out their duties. The manner in which Gurney had acquitted himself resulted in his selection to succeed Sir Edward Gent whose death in an aeroplane accident had left Malaya without a high commissioner at a time when the terrorist threats to internal security were creating a critical situation. He accepted the appointment only after some hesitation since he was attracted by the prospect of returning to Oxford to superintend courses for colonial service probationers. It was arguable even at that stage that the local situation would be better handled by a military rather than a civilian high commissioner. Lord Chandos in his *Memoirs* (1962) has trenchantly recorded his impressions of the administrative tangle which confronted him on his arrival after Gurney's death, when the situation had still further deteriorated. Its roots were deep-seated in past history, but its offshoots derived in part at least from the complicated terms of the federal constitution which contained many features making it an ineffective instrument for dealing with the emergency. Gurney inherited this constitution when he was appointed high commissioner in September 1948 and promoted K.C.M.G. Despite the tangles and the ill-defined boundaries between civil and military responsibilities he and General Sir Harold Briggs worked in the closest co-operation on what came to be called the Briggs Plan for concentrating the scattered Chinese population into defended villages. On the political side, by the grouping of departments Gurney strove to enlist the support of Malays, Chinese, and Tamils in fighting banditry. How far and how soon his efforts would have been successful it is idle to speculate for on 6 October 1951 he was ambushed and shot down in a gallant attempt to protect his wife who was with him; nevertheless he and Briggs had set the pattern and won local support for the pursuit of a more determined policy which was able to set Malaya on its feet again.

In 1924 Gurney married Isabel Lowther, daughter of T. Hamilton Weir, of Bude; they had two sons. A portrait by Harold Speed was hung in the Legislative Council Chamber at Kuala Lumpur and a copy is in the possession of the family.

[Private information; personal knowledge.]
                                    HENRY MOORE.

GUTTERIDGE, HAROLD COOKE (1876–1953), barrister and professor, was born at Naples 16 July 1876, the second son of Michael Gutteridge, a pioneer of departmental stores in Southern Italy, by his wife, Ada, daughter of Samuel Cooke, of Liversedge, Yorkshire. Until the age of twelve he was at a Swiss school in Naples where, in addition to Italian which was almost one of his native languages, he acquired much French and German. He then went to the Leys School and to King's College, Cambridge, where he took first class honours in the historical (1898) and law (part i, 1899) triposes. He was called to the bar in 1900 by the Middle Temple (ultimately becoming a bencher) and took silk in 1930. He practised mainly in commercial matters until the outbreak of war in 1914 when he joined the Territorial Force. He served in the Army Ordnance Corps with the British Salonika Force from 1916 to 1919, was mentioned in dispatches, and retired with the rank of captain.

In 1919 he was elected Sir Ernest Cassel professor of industrial and commercial law in the university of London. This post he held for eleven years (while maintaining a consultant practice) and played a very considerable part in developing the faculty of law from a body of part-

time teachers into a mainly full-tim faculty.

Although he was typically English i most respects, Gutteridge's knowledge (languages made him very popular wit foreign colleagues and pupils. Possessin this equipment and the large knowledge (commercial and maritime law which h had acquired both in practice and a a teacher, he found his interests becomin more and more directed towards conflic of laws and comparative law. In 1930 th university of Cambridge created for hi a readership in comparative law, whic enabled him to concentrate upon hi chosen field. It was later converted int a chair, which he held until 1941. He wa a fellow of Trinity Hall. His reputatio attracted many foreign research student to Cambridge, and in some wester European countries he was regarded a 'the apostle of the common law'.

He was a member of many governmen commissions and committees—the roya commission on the manufacture of an traffic in arms, the Law Revision Con mittee, the Enforcement of Foreig Judgments Committee, the Legal Educa tion Committee (1932), the Shippin Claims Tribunal, the Geneva conferenc on the unification of the law of bills c exchange and cheques, and the Hagu conference on private international law He was doctor of laws in the universitie of London and Cambridge and receive honorary doctorates from the universitie of Lyon, Grenoble, Paris, and Salonika.

Gutteridge's principal publications wer a notable thirteenth edition of *Smith' Mercantile Law* (1931), *Bankers' Con mercial Credits* (1932, a book on a subjec little known outside the circle of mer chants and bankers and their lega advisers), and *Comparative Law* publishe in 1946, followed by a second edition i 1949 and editions in French, Japanes and Spanish. A bibliography of his pub lications, comprising more than fift contributions to periodicals and join works, was compiled by his successor a Cambridge, Professor C. J. Hamso and printed in the July 1954 issue c the *International and Comparative La Quarterly*, together with three obituar notices. His first book was *Nelson an the Neapolitan Jacobins* (Navy Record Society, 1903) which is marked by 'hi great admiration of Nelson and his endur ing affection for Naples' and for the sea.

Although comparative law had alread occupied the attention of some dis inguished lawyers in Great Britain and he Society of Comparative Legislation nd its *Journal* had existed for half a century, Gutteridge's *Comparative Law* was he first systematic attempt to state the ase for the recognition of what was lmost a new subject in this country both s a branch of legal studies and as a practial instrument of legal progress. Moreover, t is clear throughout the book that he egarded one of the main functions of omparative law to be the promotion of a reciprocal basis of understanding mongst lawyers practising or teaching in videly differing legal systems, particularly the common law and the modern ivil law of continental Europe. His chievement in this respect needed more han sound learning and good judgement; c was largely due to the influence of his ersonality and to his evident intellectual ntegrity.

In appearance Gutteridge was short, ortly and rubicund, suggesting, perhaps, distinguished naval officer rather than scholar. He had a most lovable character vhich won for him a host of friends.

In 1905 he married Mary Louisa, aughter of Joseph Jackson. There were hree children: Joyce Ada Cooke Gutteridge, who became one of the legal dvisers to the Foreign Office; Michael, eutenant in the Royal Tank Corps who ied in India in 1935; and Richard, a chapin in the Royal Air Force.

Gutteridge died in Cambridge 30 December 1953.

[*International and Comparative Law Quarrly*, 1954; *Revue Internationale de Droit omparé*, 1954; *Cambridge Law Journal*, 954; *American Journal of Comparative Law*, 954; personal knowledge.]   McNAIR.

UY, SIR HENRY LEWIS (1887–1956), hartered mechanical engineer, was born t Penarth 15 June 1887, the second son f Richard Guy, wholesale meat supplier, nd his wife, Letitia Lewis. Railways ntrigued him, and after education at the ounty (later Grammar) School, Penarth, e became a pupil to the Taff Vale Railvay. He studied at the University Colege, South Wales, gaining in 1909 the ollege diploma in both mechanical and lectrical engineering, winning the Bayliss rize of the Institution of Civil Engineers, national scholarship, and a Whitworth xhibition. He then joined the British Vestinghouse Company and in 1915 ecame centrifugal pump and turboompressor engineer. Appointment as chief

engineer of the mechanical department of the Metropolitan-Vickers Electrical Company followed in 1918, a post which he retained until 1941, when he resigned to become secretary of the Institution of Mechanical Engineers, of which he was then a vice-president. He retired from professional work in 1951.

During his years in industry Guy was responsible for inventions and researches directed to the improvement of steam power plant and he regularly published the results of his work, mostly in the proceedings of the Institution of Mechanical Engineers. Among them was his paper on 'The Economic Value of Increased Steam Pressure' which gained the Hawksley gold medal in 1927; in 1939 he delivered the Parsons memorial lecture and was awarded the Parsons memorial medal.

His ten years' work as secretary of the Institution of Mechanical Engineers was pursued with characteristic vigour through the difficult war and post-war years. During this period the Institution not only increased considerably in size but in national and international prestige. He made significant contributions to the formation of the Royal Corps of Electrical and Mechanical Engineers, and also to the method of distribution of Institution *Proceedings*, by selection, to a materially increasing membership. After his retirement the honorary membership of the Institution was conferred upon him.

Elected a fellow of the Royal Society in 1936, Guy served on its council in 1938–9, was appointed chairman of the engineering sciences sectional committee in 1940, and in 1941 joined the executive committee of the National Physical Laboratory. Later he became chairman of the committee of the British Electrical and Allied Industries Research Association which organized the research work on the properties of steam, subsequently being appointed chairman of its power plant section, and member and chairman of several committees of the British Standards Institution.

Guy was a member of the scientific advisory council of the Ministry of Supply from 1939 and during the war was chairman of various committees dealing with such national issues as gun design, armament development, static detonation, the work and staffing of the Royal Aircraft Establishment, the organization of aircraft armament research and development, and the technical organization of the army; and in 1945–7 of the armaments development board. He served also from 1944 on the Advisory Council of the Department of Scientific and Industrial Research, was chairman from 1947 of the Department's mechanical engineering research board, and served also on its fuel research board and scientific grants committee. He was a member from 1942 of the mechanical engineering advisory committee of the Ministry of Labour and a trustee (1946-8) of the Imperial War Museum.

Guy received in 1939 the honorary D.Sc. of Wales and the honorary associateship of the Manchester College of Technology. He was appointed C.B.E. in 1943 and knighted in 1949.

Broad-shouldered and stocky, Guy was endowed with great physical strength. A tireless personal worker, he quested unceasingly for plans which would enhance the future of engineering and of engineers. He could not suffer fools gladly but took endless care to explain the details of his plans to those who were prepared to help. He had forthright respect for straight dealing, was completely unmoved by officialdom, and would tenaciously pursue a decided course even in the face of enlightened opposition. Unfortunately he overtaxed himself in later life by maintaining the pace and drive of his youth, and would have accomplished more, with less personal strain, had he learned to make full use of the initiative of those around him. He was devoted to graphs as aids to deductive planning. Once when a colleague asked him if he even graphed the trends of his household expenses, he smiled and said revealingly, 'No, that would take all the fun out of it.' In 1914 he married Margaret Paton, daughter of Samuel Benion Williams, coal merchant, of Holyhead. They had two daughters, both of whom married chartered mechanical engineers. When ill health forced Guy to retire he moved to Canford Cliffs, Dorset, spending much time painting in oils and listening to good music. He died there 20 July 1956.

[*Journal* of the Institution of Mechanical Engineers, February 1951; private information; personal knowledge.]

BRIAN G. ROBBINS.

GWYER, SIR MAURICE LINFORD (1878-1952), lawyer and civil servant, was born in London 25 April 1878, the eldest son of John Edward Gwyer, public auditor and secretary of the Provident Clerks' Life Assurance Association, and his wife,

Edith Linford. His sister, Barbara Elizabeth Gwyer, was principal of St. Hugh's College, Oxford, 1924-46. Educated a Highgate and Westminster, and electe to a Westminster exhibition at Chris Church, Oxford, after a first in classica moderations (1899) and a second in *litera humaniores* (1901), Gwyer took the B.C.L having in the meantime become in 190 a fellow of All Souls. Although only on fellowship had been offered, he and Ray mond Asquith so distinguished themselve that both were elected. Called to the bar i 1903 by the Inner Temple after a first i bar finals and the prizes of the Council c Legal Education for constitutional an criminal law, evidence and procedure Gwyer entered the chambers of (Sir Frank MacKinnon [q.v.]. To supplemen his income, in 1910 he took off the hand of Sir William Anson [q.v.] the late editions of the *Law of Contract*, and afte Anson's death in 1914 he emerged as th natural editor of his *Law and Custom of th Constitution*.

In 1912 (Sir) Warren Fisher [q.v.], afte an intensive search for the right ma invited Gwyer to join the legal staff of th National Health Insurance Commissio From 1913 to 1915 Gwyer was also lec turer in private international law a Oxford. In 1917 he was transferred to th Ministry of Shipping. After the war h returned to the bar, but in 1919, with som reluctance and mainly to ensure th financial security of his family (his wif had become an invalid), he accepte appointment as legal adviser and solicito to the Ministry of Health. He served und five different ministers (one of the twice) and dealt with a stream of conter tious legislation which covered the am bitious but ill-starred housing schem of Christopher (later Viscount) Addiso [q.v.] and the remedial measures of suc ceeding ministers, rent restriction, ratin and valuation, and contributory pension as well as three consolidation Acts an some highly technical routine Act Although Gwyer made little visible im pact on policy, his clear reasoning an drafting skill had a notable effect upon i presentation. He was also at work on th revision of Anson's *Law and Custom* (5t ed. vol. i only, 1922).

In 1926 Gwyer became Treasury solic tor and King's proctor and in 1929 he w a British representative at the conferen on the operation of dominion legislatio which drafted what became the Statute Westminster, a title which he suggeste

The conference described the proposed legislation in words characteristic of Gwyer as an 'association of constitutional conventions with law . . . [which] has provided a means of harmonizing relations where a purely legal solution of practical problems was impossible, would have impaired free development, or would have failed to catch the spirit which gives life to institutions'.

Gwyer took silk in 1930 and in 1934 became first parliamentary counsel to the Treasury. Almost at once he had to apply his accumulated experience to the drafting of the government of India bill to establish responsible government for both the provinces and the All-India Federation. The constitutions thus imposed did not furnish the freedom given to the existing dominions to legislate in terms repugnant to Acts of Parliament of the United Kingdom. Hence the need for a court to interpret the constitution in justiciable disputes between governments within the new federation. Gwyer's appointment in 1937 as chief justice of India, although he had had little forensic and no judicial experience, provoked no adverse comment, despite the prima-facie objection to a draftsman's becoming the judicial interpreter of his own draft. In the first twenty months of its existence his court dealt with three appeals only, although before his retirement in 1943 it had come to examine thirty-five more cases. Some of his judgements have been thought to have been unduly influenced by Gwyer's recollection of what the Act had been intended to mean.

Having at first little judicial work the chief justice was encouraged by the viceroy to take in hand the reform of the university of Delhi of which Gwyer was appointed vice-chancellor in 1938. Despite ill health he continued in that office until 1950. Almost from the first his house in Delhi became a place of meeting for British officials and political Indians. He also travelled widely and some of his visits to native States with which the Government was having difficulties caused embarrassment.

Gwyer, it was remarked as early as 1914, 'had something of the big man in him'; yet his was no originating mind. What he excelled in was polish: in manners as in craftsmanship. He wrote for his own amusement admirable translations of Catullus but no original poetry; he edited Anson but wrote no book of his own; he rescued the university of Delhi from neg-

lect and obscurity but was at pains that it should be run on conventional lines.

Gwyer was dark, sallow, very tall, and slow in his movements. He dressed well and looked distinguished in any company. Good living he enjoyed—and good company; Maurice Gwyer would have been at ease in Dr. Johnson's circle. He was by nature tolerant, ready to see redeeming features, but drawing a rigid line between frailty and vice. As King's proctor he welcomed the reduction of the vote which ended the routine rummaging into squalid details of undefended divorce suits. In 1928, with Sir Warren Fisher and Sir Malcolm Ramsay, he was called upon to investigate complaints about gambling in 'francs' by certain civil servants. The report (Cmd. 3037), mainly Gwyer's work, was uncompromising: 'Practical rules for the guidance of social conduct depend as much upon the instinct and perception of the individual as upon cast-iron formulas . . . and a standard . . . not only inflexible but fastidious.' The high value which he set upon honourable conduct made him generous to and therefore popular with subordinates.

Gwyer was appointed C.B. (1921), K.C.B. (1928), K.C.S.I. (1935), and G.C.I.E. (1948). He became an honorary student of Christ Church (1937), an honorary D.C.L. of Oxford (1939), LL.D. of Travancore (1943) and Patna (1944), and D.Litt. of Delhi (1950).

In 1906 he married Alsina Helen Marion, daughter of Sir Henry Burdett; they had one son and two daughters. Gwyer died at Eastbourne 12 October 1952.

[Private information; personal knowledge.]
DOUGLAS VEALE.

HADLEY, WILLIAM WAITE (1866–1960), editor of the *Sunday Times*, was born at East Haddon, Northamptonshire, 18 January 1866, one of the ten children of Joseph Hadley and his wife, Elizabeth Waite. Joseph Hadley, a head gardener, was a great reader and a stalwart Congregationalist, and as a boy his son also read widely, while attending the village school. Early in his teens he began to work for a career in journalism: he went to night school in Northampton and a part-time master at Rugby School taught him shorthand, essential to a reporter in the days of verbatim note-taking and long printed reports. At the age of fifteen he was apprenticed to the *Northampton Mercury*, where he learnt the craft of journalism from the lowest rungs of the ladder. Soon, however, his reporting assignments became more responsible and took him all over the county. Charles Bradlaugh and Henry Labouchere [qq.v.] were then members of Parliament for Northampton, a Radical borough, and in later life Hadley used often to recount how as a junior reporter he was present at the hustings at the famous by-elections caused by Bradlaugh's refusal to take the oath.

In 1887 Hadley joined the editorial staff of the *Rochdale Observer*, and in 1893 became its editor, returning to Rochdale after an eight-months' editorship of the *Merthyr Times*—an interlude which, brief as it was, had a crucial effect upon his later career; it was in Merthyr Tydfil that he made friends with the family of John Mathias Berry, two of whose sons were destined to become national newspaper proprietors, one of them, William, later Viscount Camrose [q.v.], being given by Hadley his first employment on the local paper.

After editing the *Rochdale Observer* for fifteen years, while taking an active part in local government and education, and in Liberal politics in Yorkshire, Hadley returned in 1908 to Northampton as managing editor of the *Mercury* group of papers, of which he soon became a director. Now a highly respected provincial newspaper editor and leader of his native community, he might have been thought to have fulfilled his main career; but in 1923 he was pressed by Liberal Party leaders to go to London, and in January 1924 he became parliamentary correspondent of the *Daily Chronicle*. When in 1930 the *Chronicle* was merged with the *Daily News*, he found himself at large, at the age of sixty-four, competing with much younger men who had spent most of their lives in Fleet Street. However, Lord Camrose, then chairman and editor-in-chief of the *Sunday Times*, offered him the assistant editorship, which he took up in 1931. A year later, in 1932, the editor, Leonard Rees, died, and Hadley was his natural successor. He remained editor of the *Sunday Times* (of which Lord Kemsley became chairman and editor-in-chief after he and his brother divided their press interests in 1937) until his retirement in 1950 at the age of eighty-four. He believed strongly in the close partnership of editor and proprietor in the conduct of a newspaper, and while Lord Kemsley greatly respected his wisdom and experience Hadley for his part admired and accepted Lord Kemsley's strong control of commercial and general policy.

Hadley's political guidance of an independent but Conservative newspaper was steady and moderate rather than dynamic. He became a friend and supporter of Neville Chamberlain, whose international policies he defended in his book, *Munich: Before and After*, published in 1944. The decline of the Liberal Party and his dislike of socialist ideas eased his political transition to the Right. Although, however, until his last few years as editor he was his own chief leader-writer, his greatest editorial contribution to the growing success of the *Sunday Times* was not in political persuasion but in his calm and wise guidance of a small but devoted editorial staff and his handling of a gifted team of regular contributors, including Ernest Newman, James Agate, (Sir) Desmond MacCarthy, (Sir) R. C. K. Ensor [qq.v.] and others. An essentially modest and friendly man, he was as unruffled by problems of personal relations as he was by sudden shifts in the news or by the difficulties of maintaining the character of the paper and the goodwill of its writers when wartime exigencies drastically cut its size.

In 1920 Hadley had written a short history of the *Northampton Mercury* to mark its bicentenary, and even in his last years he never lost touch with his native county, contributing articles in 1957, 1958, and 1959 to the journal of the Northamptonshire Record Society.

In 1889 he married Emma (died 1952) daughter of Joseph Chater, shoe manufacturer, of Northampton; they had three daughters. He died at Hindhead 16 December 1960.

[*The Times*, 17 December 1960; *Sunday Times*, 18 December 1960; *Haslemere Herald* 23 December 1960; *Northamptonshire Past and Present* (Journal of the Northamptonshire Record Society), vol. iii, No. 2, 1961; private information; personal knowledge.]

H. V. HODSON

HALCROW, SIR WILLIAM THOMSON (1883–1958), civil engineer, was born 4 July 1883 in Sunderland, the only son of John Andrew Halcrow, master seaman in the Merchant Service, and his wife, Jane Halcrow. After education at George Watson's College, Edinburgh, and Edinburgh University, he began his engineering career as a pupil to P. W. Meik, the senior partner of Thomas Meik & Sons, a leading firm of consulting engineers in London

Early in his training he became an assistant on the Kinlochleven hydro-electric works, thus beginning his connection with a branch of the engineering profession to which he was destined to make considerable contributions. In 1905 he became resident engineer at Pozzuoli, Italy, for the reconstruction in reinforced concrete of a deep-water pier, following which he was engaged as an assistant engineer on the construction of the Loch Leven water-power works, Scotland, before gaining further experience abroad in Italy, Portugal, and the Argentine.

In 1910 Halcrow became chief engineer to the contracting firm of Topham, Jones, and Railton, his major work being the construction of the King George V graving dock at Singapore, and in 1913 survey work for the dredging of the approach channel to the Rosyth dockyard then under construction. During the war he was engaged on several Admiralty projects in the Orkneys and Shetlands. Afterwards he worked on the construction of the Johore Causeway which joined Singapore Island to the mainland of Malaya, and on the design and construction of the Port of Beira. In 1921 he resumed his connection with consultant engineering, becoming a partner with C. S. Meik in the firm known as C. S. Meik and Halcrow until 1944 when after his knighthood the firm was renamed Sir William Halcrow & Partners.

Throughout his career as a consultant, Halcrow's work was widespread. He was joint consulting engineer with Sir Harley Dalrymple-Hay [q.v.] for the London Passenger Transport Board's tube railways, and he carried out the extensions of the Bakerloo Line to Finchley Road and the Northern Line as far as East Finchley. As a consultant under the Reservoirs (Safety Provisions) Act he inspected many dams for water-power companies and advised on canal reservoirs for the Railways and Birmingham Canal Navigations. During the war of 1939–45 he designed and constructed deep-level tunnel shelters in London for the Ministry of Home Security. He also acted as head of a group of consulting engineers who designed and constructed ordnance factories and storage depots. He was associated with the War Office also, on the design and construction of the 'Phoenix' units which formed part of Mulberry harbours for the invasion of Europe. In 1944 he was chairman of a panel of engineers appointed to report on the Severn Barrage tidal power scheme. In 1950 he advised the New Zealand Govern-

ment on traffic problems in the city of Auckland. In 1951 he was chairman of a panel of engineers reporting on the Kariba Gorge and Kafue River hydro-electric projects in Rhodesia.

He was president of the engineering section of the British Association in 1947 ; president of the Smeatonian Society (1953) ; vice-president of the commission on large dams of the World Power Conference (1955). He held many other appointments, amongst which were colonel-commandant (Engineer and Railway Staff Corps) Royal Engineers (T.A.) ; member of the Advisory Council of the Department of Scientific and Industrial Research ; chairman of the Hydraulics Research Board ; and member of the executive of the National Physical Laboratory and of the Royal Fine Art Commission. He contributed a notice of Sir Clement Hindley to this Dictionary.

Halcrow became a member of council of the Institution of Civil Engineers in 1934, a vice-president in 1943, and was president in 1946–7 ; in 1930 he received the Telford gold medal for his paper on the Lochaber (water-power) scheme. In 1937–9 he was president of the British section of the Société Ingénieurs Civils de France, whose gold medal he was awarded in 1939. He was a chevalier of the Legion of Honour and an officer of the Order of the Black Star.

In 1921 he married Phoebe Mary, daughter of Alfred Henry Roberts, civil engineer, by whom he had one son. He died at his home in Folkestone 31 August 1958. His portrait by (Sir) James Gunn is at the Institution of Civil Engineers.

[Private information ; personal knowledge.]
F. A. WHITAKER.

HALFORD, FRANK BERNARD (1894–1955), aircraft engine designer, was born in Nottingham 7 March 1894, the son of Harry Baker Halford, estate agent and surveyor, and his wife, Ethel Grundy. He was educated at Felsted School and Nottingham University College, but secured no academic qualifications. Yet for forty years he was one of the world's great aircraft engine designers. At the age of nineteen he learnt to fly at Brooklands and became an instructor at the Bristol School of Flying. In 1914 he entered the aeronautical inspection directorate of the War Office as an engine examiner where he was able to study aero engines, which became his lifelong interest.

Joining the Royal Flying Corps on the

Halford

outbreak of war in 1914 he was recalled from France to redesign the Beardmore Company's Austro-Daimler engine to give greater power. It was used extensively in the D.H.4 aeroplane, one of the outstanding bombers of the time. Later, in production form known as the Puma, it became a significant contribution to engine progress by a young man still in his early twenties.

In 1916 he met (Sir) Harry Ricardo, a brilliant engine designer, from whom Halford gained much experience. At the close of the war he joined Ricardo and spent two and a half years in the United States negotiating the licensing agreements for Ricardo's patents, returning to England to help in the development of the Ricardo-Triumph motor-cycle engine, which won many racing records in 1921–2. He designed the Halford engine which raced at Brooklands about this time, at 108 m.p.h. Halford also raced in the Isle of Man, riding his own machine.

In 1923 Halford became his own designer with one assistant, J. L. P. Brodie, who was to remain with him all Halford's life. In 1924–7 Halford worked for the Aircraft Disposal Company to modernize the large number of wartime aero engines. Halford's foresight was quite exceptional. From the company's engine, the Airdisco, he produced the Cirrus engine for the de Havilland light aeroplane, the Moth. Flown in February 1925, the Moth was the first practical private aeroplane, and in various forms proved to be a turning-point in Halford's career and a memorable date in British aircraft and engine progress. Halford had seized his opportunities brilliantly, making full use of obsolete war material. It was rightly declared that he had a feeling for engines comparable with that of a stock farmer for animals, bringing to his aid an intuitive talent which years of engineering training might not have provided. The Cirrus engine was remarkable for its silence; it was one of the quietest aircraft in flight. Both the engine and the plane heralded a revolution in flying, and became in demand all over the world. Halford had that genius for basic engine design which enabled increasing power to be obtained with little modification.

In 1928 he produced the Gipsy engine, following the demand for still more power for light aircraft; in various modifications it reached such power that light aeroplanes made aeronautical history on the long air routes: England to Australia, to South Africa, and the crossing of the North and South Atlantic, remarkable tributes to the reliability of the Halford engines. In its inverted form the Gipsy powered the de Havilland Comet aeroplane in 1934 to win the England–Australia race, for which, in the following year, Halford was awarded the silver medal of the Royal Aeronautical Society. A Gipsy engine energized a fifty-foot diameter alternator coil which was fitted under the fuselage of the Wellington bomber to destroy the magnetic bombs sown round the British coasts by Germany in the war of 1939–45. The Gipsy was still in use in the sixties and the Cirrus in the fifties.

Halford became responsible for the designs of the Rapier and Sabre series of engines for the Napier Company. The Rapier, a 16-cylinder engine of 400 horsepower, was fitted to a number of aircraft including the Mayo Composite, the first aeroplane to fly the Atlantic from east to west carrying a commercial load. The Sabre, with 24 cylinders, at the time the most powerful piston engine in operation in the air, developing 3,000 horsepower, was fitted to the Hawker aeroplane.

In 1941, at the request of the British Government, Halford entered the field of jet propulsion. He followed closely (Sir) Frank Whittle's pioneer work and designed the Goblin, with a 3,000-lb. thrust, for the Gloster Meteor aeroplane, the first British jet propulsion aircraft to fly. A more powerful version of the Goblin, the Ghost, was designed in 1945 and fitted to the Vampire aeroplane to fly at the then record height of 59,446 feet in 1948. From 1941 Halford also served on the then highly secret committee advising the ministers of aircraft production on engine, aircraft, and other aviation problems.

In 1935 Halford had become the technical director of the Napier engine company, a position he relinquished in 1944 to become the technical director of the newly formed de Havilland Engine Company. In the following year he was appointed a director of the de Havilland Aircraft Company.

The end of the war saw Halford leading a powerful engine design team. He never hesitated to give those he led full credit for their share in engine developments and his team led the way in developing the ever-increasing jet propulsion power. In 1953 appeared the Gyron, giving a thrust of 15,000 lb., doubled a few years later. Much of the development carried out after his death was due to his guidance for supersonic aircraft flight. The Sprite rocket motor and the larger Spectre only became known a few days after his death, when the veil of secrecy was raised.

In 1927 Halford was elected a fellow of the Royal Aeronautical Society; he was its president in 1951–2, and in addition to its silver medal, received its gold medal in 1950. In 1946 he read a paper on jet propulsion before the Royal Society of Arts, for which he was awarded its silver medal. In 1948 he was appointed C.B.E.

In 1920 he married Monica Bevan, of Hove, by whom he had a daughter. The marriage was dissolved in 1932. In 1939 he married Marjorie Moore. He died 16 April 1955 at his home at Northwood, Middlesex.

[*Journal* of the Royal Aeronautical Society, April 1959; private information; personal knowledge.]   J. LAURENCE PRITCHARD.

HALIFAX, first EARL OF (1881–1959), statesman. [See WOOD, EDWARD FREDERICK LINDLEY.]

HALL, SIR ARTHUR JOHN (1866–1951), physician, was born in Sheffield 27 July 1866, the second son and youngest of the three children of John Hall, a well-known medical practitioner in Sheffield, who had married his cousin, Elizabeth Hall. From Rugby, Hall was first sent to the Sheffield Medical School which was then a primitive place where some unpaid practitioners in their spare time gave dull and formal instruction in anatomy to a few students apprenticed to doctors in the town. Fortunately Hall's father was persuaded to send him to Caius College, Cambridge, and St. Bartholomew's. After qualifying in 1889 Hall spent a year assisting his father, but the practice was small and exclusive and finding himself inadequately employed he decided on a career as a physician. In 1890 therefore he became assistant physician to the Sheffield Royal Hospital (then called the Public Hospital and Dispensary) on the staff of which he spent the rest of his professional life.

Meanwhile the Medical School, having surprisingly survived its worst period, had been transferred to new premises close to Firth College and the Technical School. Hall was appointed assistant demonstrator in physiology there in 1889 and from that time onwards his great resources of energy, intellect, personality, and tact were largely devoted to building up the School, first so that it was a worthy place

to amalgamate with Firth College and the Technical School into what became in 1897 the University College of Sheffield, and later so that it might grow into the faculty of medicine in the university of Sheffield on its formation in 1905. Fifteen years later the faculty was to be regarded as one of the most advanced in Britain.

Although it is unquestionably right to look upon Hall as the very creator of the modern school of medicine in Sheffield, he had from the first the wisdom to realize that this was not a job for one man working single-handed, and it was his great endeavour to bring to Sheffield some of the most talented men he could find: among the first was Christopher (later Viscount) Addison [q.v.]; a later appointment was (Sir) Edward Mellanby [q.v.].

For a time Hall himself was responsible for the teaching in physiology, first as demonstrator and later as professor, in a part-time capacity, but as soon as the school was ready and able to finance a full-time chair Hall resigned to allow such an appointment to be made. He then turned his interests to pathology where he was first demonstrator and curator of the museum (which was largely of his own creation) and later professor in 1899, resigning in 1905 when a full-time chair of pathology was established.

Until his retirement in 1931, Hall was in consulting practice as a physician, on the medical staff of the Sheffield Royal Hospital, and actively teaching clinical medicine in the wards. He was dean of the medical faculty from 1911 to 1916 and professor of medicine from 1915 to 1931. Physicians and teachers of medicine of his day were not expected to make their name in research, but Hall's careful and meticulous observations of the two epidemics of encephalitis lethargica which visited Sheffield in 1917–18 and in 1924 contributed very greatly to knowledge of this disease in which he became an authority of international standing. His book on the subject was published in 1924.

Hall was of commanding appearance and personality, a man to whom one would listen in any company, who took himself seriously but was saved from being pompous by a brilliant wit and a delightful sense of humour. Although he had his critics he nevertheless had the talent of bringing men together and getting them to work smoothly with one another. He was a good physician and a good teacher at a time when both were rare, but his great talent was in administration. To his students he was friendly and approachable, but his nickname of 'Lord Arthur' showed that he had their respect as well as their affection and that, although approachable, he was not to be treated as an equal. As a young man he had considerable gifts as an actor and traces of this remained discernible throughout his life; but his main interest outside the medical school was music. He was a talented cellist who regularly played chamber music and it was one of his great regrets that after his retirement, when he would have had more time, he was unable to enjoy it because of increasing deafness.

Hall was elected F.R.C.P. in 1904 and served the College as examiner, councillor, Lumleian lecturer, and finally as senior censor. He was examiner in medicine to Oxford and Cambridge and several other universities and was a member of the Radium Commission and of the Industrial Health Research Board. During the war of 1914-18 he was in charge of the medical division of the 3rd Northern General Hospital. He received an honorary D.Sc. from Sheffield in 1928, was president of the Association of Physicians of Great Britain and Ireland in 1931, and was knighted in 1935. His portrait by Ernest Moore hangs in the Firth Hall of Sheffield University, with a copy at the Sheffield Royal Hospital.

In 1900 Hall married Hilda Mary (died 1945), daughter of Charles E. Vickers, solicitor, of Sheffield; they had two sons and one daughter. He died in Sheffield 3 January 1951.

[*Lancet*, 13 January 1951; *British Medical Journal*, 20 January 1951; Sheffield University records; personal knowledge.]   PLATT.

HAMBOURG, MARK (1879-1960), pianist, was born in Boguchar, Southern Russia, 31 May 1879, the eldest son of Michael Hambourg, a professor of music and head of the conservatoire at Voronezh, by his wife, Catherine Herzovna, a professional singer. Two younger sons were musical: Jan, a violinist, and Boris, a cellist. Mark received his first piano lessons from a devoted aunt; when on his fifth birthday he played some of Czerny's exercises his father was so delighted he decided that the boy's musical education should begin in a systematic way. A public appearance at the age of seven so impressed his father that he felt his son should have the best tuition available; he therefore obtained an appointment as a professor at Moscow Conservatoire,

uprooting himself and his family from the provincial surroundings of Voronezh. Mark proved such a remarkable pupil that he learned the whole of Bach's Forty-eight Preludes and Fugues before the age of eight and almost immediately after, in 1888, he appeared with the Philharmonic Society of Moscow in the Hall of the Great Nobles and at another concert before the Grand Duke Constantine.

Persuaded to try his fortunes in England, and being by nature an adventurer, Professor Hambourg arrived in London with Mark in 1889. Unable to speak a word of English, father and son had some initial struggles, but eventually a Russian friend introduced them to Daniel Mayer, a concert agent who had just presented Paderewski to the British public. Paderewski was so eulogistic of Mark's playing that Mayer decided to present him as an infant prodigy. His début persuaded another agent, Nathaniel Vert, to offer him a three-year contract. After the first of his recitals, at the age of eleven, he was booked to appear in almost every provincial concert hall. The professor now sent for his family to join him in London and as he had established himself as a teacher of the piano it was Mark's mother who chaperoned her son on his tours. Mark played to many famous people at this time, including Hans Richter who was particularly impressed. Eventually with the generous financial help of Paderewski and Felix Moscheles, a son of Ignatz Moscheles, a celebrated pianist, Mark was sent to Vienna at the age of twelve and a half, for a three years' period of study under Professor Leschetizky. One of Mark's fellow students was Artur Schnabel, who said that it was always Mark whom the master selected to demonstrate to the class in the weekly exhibitions. Schnabel envied him as the master's favourite pupil but admitted his rival's precocity.

At the age of fifteen Hambourg played at a Berlin Philharmonic concert conducted by Weingartner. In 1894 he received his first paid engagement in Vienna and won the Liszt scholarship of five hundred marks; in 1895 he made his début as a full-grown pianist at the Vienna Philharmonic Symphony Concert under the conductorship of Richter, who had continued to be a great friend. Other engagements followed and he returned to London to embark, at the age of sixteen, on the first of his many world tours. He made his American début with the Boston

Symphony Orchestra and then toured the United States to California. When Hambourg, who had been naturalized in 1896, arrived back in England the South African war was at its height and the musical world somewhat disorganized. He deputized for Busoni, with whom he was on terms of intimate friendship; he gave a series of concerts with Ysaye; and played pianoforte concertos at the newly organized Queen's Hall promenade concerts with (Sir) Henry Wood [q.v.] then at the outset of his career.

Tour after tour followed: the United States, Australia, New Zealand, South Africa, the Middle East, Poland, Russia, engagements in Brussels, Berlin, and Salzburg, where he played with Jacques Thibaud. Hambourg's concert activities easily out-distanced in number those of any of his contemporary colleagues.

In 1909 Hambourg made the first of a long series of gramophone records for the Gramophone Company, Ltd. (H.M.V.). The *Moonlight Sonata* was the first title issued and might almost be called his signature tune since it was a best-seller and usually found a place in the hundreds of recitals he gave up and down the country. This and a certain likeness to the Beethoven of our imagination, coupled with a platform manner which endeared him to the masses, made him one of England's most popular recitalists.

Although Mark Hambourg had a life-long love of chamber music, which he played with his brothers in his earlier days, and in middle age was a concerto player of authority and distinction, he will be remembered chiefly as a recitalist, and in that capacity he appealed to a wider section of the public than did anyone of his own day and age. Short in height, with a leonine head, a powerful frame, a phenomenal technique, and a genial personality, he commanded the attention of any audience. As a pianist he had the power to astonish; as a man his dynamic and lovable personality won for him the admiration of a wide section of the general public. He was the last of a long line of virtuoso pianists who might not so readily have pleased the pundits of a later age more concerned with the literal treatment of music than with its individual and personal artistic conception. He played for the last time in public on 2 March 1955 for a Henry Wood birthday memorial concert at the Royal Albert Hall, when he performed Tchaikowsky's Piano Concerto No. 1. His highly individualistic playing

in the grand virtuoso manner was both a thrilling and an affectionate memory.

Hambourg's musical publications include 'Variations on a Theme by Paganini', 'Volkslied', and 'Espièglerie'.

In 1907 he married Dorothea Frances, daughter of Sir K. A. (later Lord) Muir Mackenzie, by whom he had four daughters, one of whom, Michal, became an accomplished pianist. Mark Hambourg died in Cambridge 26 August 1960.

A portrait by Sir Oswald Birley is in the possession of the family.

[Mark Hambourg, *From Piano to Forte*, 1931, and *The Eighth Octave*, 1951; F. W. Gaisberg, *Music on Record*, 1946; personal knowledge.]   GEORGE BAKER.

HAMIDULLAH, NAWAB OF BHOPAL (1894–1960). [See BHOPAL.]

HARDIE, MARTIN (1875–1952), artist and museum official, was born in London 15 December 1875, the son of James Hardie, of East Linton, near Dunbar, by his wife, Marion Pettie. There was a strong artistic tradition in the family: two of his uncles were professional artists: Charles Martin Hardie and John Pettie [q.v.], and a great-uncle was Robert Frier, the well-known Edinburgh drawing master. James Hardie was the founder and headmaster of Linton House, a private preparatory school in London, whence his son passed first to St. Paul's School as a foundationer, then as an exhibitioner to Trinity College, Cambridge. He obtained a second class in part i of the classical tripos in 1898 and was successful in obtaining a post in the library of the Victoria and Albert Museum; in which institution he remained until his retirement in 1935.

Housed in the same building was the Royal College of Art, and at the head of the engraving department was (Sir) Frank Short (whose notice Hardie subsequently contributed to this Dictionary). Studying under Short in his spare time, Hardie acquired the art of etching and soon became an accomplished craftsman. He also perfected his technique of water-colour painting, and these two modes of expression were practised by him with enormous assiduity and increasing success for the rest of his life. He began to exhibit at the Royal Academy in 1908 and continued to do so regularly. His work was also seen at the Royal Society of Painter-Etchers and at the Royal Institute of Painters in Water Colours. Both these bodies elected him a member. He became

A.R.E. in 1907 and R.E. and member of council in 1920. He was also for many years its active honorary secretary as well as honorary secretary of its subsidiary body the Print Collectors' Club.

After war service in which he reached the rank of captain, Hardie returned to the museum and was put in charge, as keeper from 1921, of the newly created department of engraving, illustration, and design, and soon began to expand its scope to include subjects like the art of the theatre. By the end of his keepership it had become one of the most important collections of prints and drawings in the world. Hardie was also in charge of the department of paintings.

His main interest, however, was in water-colour and etching and his own skill in both gave him a special advantage in writing about the work of other artists in these media. In addition to editing many museum and other publications he catalogued the work of W. Lee-Hankey, James McBey [q.v.], and Short, and published works on these artists as well as on John Pettie (1908), Frederick Goulding (1910), Samuel Palmer (1928), Peter De Wint (1929), J. S. Sargent (1930), and Charles Méryon (1931). Perhaps his major achievement was the rediscovery of Samuel Palmer [q.v.], an exhibition of whose work was staged in Hardie's department and did much to start the enthusiasm for Palmer which was later taken for granted.

Meanwhile Hardie continued his own work as an artist, publishing in all 189 prints. He painted in many parts of western Europe and in Morocco in the best tradition of the British School but with wide varieties of style; but his real preference was for quiet water-meadows and estuaries, the becalmed vessel, evanescent effects of weather, and the fleeting shapes of clouds. A number of one-man shows were held in his lifetime and his work is represented in many public collections, notably that of the Ashmolean Museum at Oxford, which possesses almost all his prints and twenty-five of his sketch-books.

Among Hardie's other publications were *English Coloured Books* (1906); *Engraving and Etching* (translated from the German of Dr. Lippmann, 1906); *Boulogne: A Base in France* (1918); *Our Italian Front* (with text by H. Warner Allen, 1920); *War Posters* (with A. K. Sabin, 1920); and *The British School of Etching* (1921). His *magnum opus*, almost

completed at the time of his death, was a history of British water-colour painting of which the three volumes were published in 1966–8.

On his retirement Hardie was appointed C.B.E. He was active in the local affairs of Tonbridge and served as an air-raid warden in the war of 1939–45. He became honorary R.W.S. in 1943 and vice-president of the Artists' General Benevolent Institution in 1946, having previously served as secretary and treasurer. He was also vice-president of the Imperial Arts League.

Hardie married in 1903 Agnes Madeline, daughter of Admiral John Robert Ebenezer Pattisson, and had three sons. He died at Tonbridge 20 January 1952.

Hardie's portrait was both painted and etched by James McBey; the portrait is in Aberdeen Art Gallery. He is also depicted in a cartoon by Sir Max Beerbohm, together with Gordon Craig and his son, now in the Victoria and Albert Museum.

[*The Times*, 22 January 1952; private information; personal knowledge.]

JAMES LAVER.

HARDING, SIR EDWARD JOHN (1880–1954), civil servant, was born in St. Osyth, Clacton-on-Sea, 22 March 1880, the son of the Rev. John Harding, rector of Weeley, Essex, and his wife, Laura, daughter of William Hewlett. He was educated at Dulwich College and at Hertford College, Oxford, of which he was a scholar and, later, an honorary fellow. He took a prominent part in the life of the college, rowed in the college eight, and gained a first in honour moderations (1901) and a second in *literae humaniores* (1903). He took a high place in the Civil Service examination of 1903 and entered the Board of Trade, transferring to the Colonial Office in 1904 where he quickly made his mark. In 1912 he became assistant private secretary to Lewis (later Viscount) Harcourt [q.v.], then secretary of state. In the same year he was called to the bar by Lincoln's Inn. From 1912 to 1917 Harding was secretary of the dominions royal commission which was established as a result of a resolution of the Imperial Conference of 1911 to investigate the resources of the Empire. The commission produced a voluminous final report in the drafting of which Harding took his full share, and the first-hand knowledge which he gained in visiting the various dominions later stood him in good stead. He was appointed C.M.G. in 1917 and made a junior assistant secretary of the Imperial War Conference; he held a similar position in the succeeding conference of 1918. After this conference he was given permission to enlist and obtained a commission in the Royal Garrison Artillery. In 1916 he had been promoted to the rank of first class clerk; in 1920 he was appointed a principal; and in 1921 an assistant secretary.

After the war Harding was engaged almost entirely on political and constitutional work. He was deputy secretary to the Imperial Conference of 1923 and to the historic Imperial Conference of 1926. In 1925 he had been appointed assistant under-secretary of state in the newly constituted Dominions Office and with this appointment he held that of registrar of the Order of St. Michael and St. George. Throughout the conference of 1926 he was the right-hand man of L. S. Amery [q.v.], then secretary of state, and was closely concerned with all the discussions leading to the famous Balfour declaration on dominion status. He was appointed C.B. in 1926 and in 1928 promoted K.C.M.G.

In 1930 Harding became permanent under-secretary of state for dominion affairs. His ten-year tenure of this office was perhaps the most distinguished period of his career. As the trusted adviser of successive secretaries of state he took a vital part in the discussions culminating in the Statute of Westminster of 1931 and in the important consultations with the dominions on foreign affairs and economic issues during the troublous years which preceded the war. His aim and purpose, indeed his inspiration, was the attainment of the unity of the Commonwealth combined with recognition of the independent and international status of the dominions. No state servant played a greater part in bringing about these epoch-making and far-reaching developments which proved an essential contribution to achieving Commonwealth unity and co-operation in the war which followed. He was appointed K.C.B. in 1935 and G.C.M.G. in 1939.

In January 1940 Harding became high commissioner for the United Kingdom in South Africa. His tenure of office covered some of the darkest days of the war when Britain's resources were strained to the utmost. It was a difficult time politically in South Africa, and the close relations which Harding was able to establish with J. C. Smuts [q.v.], the prime minister, and with his ministers were of the utmost value

in furthering co-operative measures. As high commissioner also for Basutoland, the Bechuanaland Protectorate,and Swaziland he closely supervised the affairs of these territories and it was in his term of office that the recruitment there of the Pioneer Corps for service in the field was successfully undertaken.

Towards the end of 1940 Harding had a severe breakdown in health which compelled him to retire from the Service in February of the following year. In 1942 he was sufficiently recovered to be able to represent the high commissioner in Cape Town when the latter was resident in Pretoria. This temporary service concluded in 1944.

As a civil servant Harding combined tenacity of purpose with a quiet and effective manner. He never spared himself and was something of a perfectionist in the great importance which he attached to the quality of the work which passed through his hands and to accuracy and clarity in thought and expression. Though ruled by his head, he had a generous and kindly side to his character which he showed by many acts of personal kindness.

In addition to his official appointments he was for some years a governor of Dulwich College, a member of the Royal Commission for the 1851 Exhibition, and a member of the council of the Royal College of Music.

In 1929 Harding married Marjorie, daughter of the late Henry Huxley, of Boar's Hill, Oxford; they had no children. She was an ideal wife and helpmate and her sudden death in 1950 was a terrible blow to him. He died at Guildford 4 October 1954.

[*The Times*, 5 October 1954; private information; personal knowledge.]
ERIC MACHTIG.

HARDING, GILBERT CHARLES (1907–1960), broadcasting and television star, was born at Hereford 5 June 1907. His parents, Gilbert and May Harding, were workhouse officials, and he used to boast that he was born in a workhouse. He was educated at the Royal Orphanage, Wolverhampton, and Queens' College, Cambridge, where he obtained third classes in both parts of the historical tripos (1927–8). A man of very deep religious feeling he became a strong Anglo-Catholic at Cambridge and went to Mirfield to train for the Anglican priesthood. He left when in 1929 he became a convert to, and a devoted member of, the Roman

Harding, G. C. D.N.B. 1951–1960

Church, but he remained sympathetic to Anglicanism from the emotional point of view and never spoke of Mirfield with anything but the warmest affection and admiration. After some years as a schoolmaster, and a professorship in English at St. Francis Xavier University, Antigonish, in Nova Scotia, he joined the Bradford city police. An accident forced his retirement and he returned to teaching in Cyprus where he also acted as *The Times* correspondent. He took a very strong dislike to British rule in Cyprus and was regarded with a great deal of hostility by the administration. Returning to London, he read for the bar at Gray's Inn, but when war broke out in 1939 he joined the B.B.C. monitoring service. His health prevented him from serving actively in a war to which he was very much dedicated because of his detestation of fascism. After two years in the outside broadcasting department he was sent in 1944 to Canada where he carried out extremely useful propaganda work. Back once more in London in 1947 he got his first personal show in broadcasting as quiz master in 'Round Britain Quiz'.

From that point on, in radio programmes such as the Brains Trust and 'Twenty Questions', and the television 'What's My Line?', Harding became a great popular figure, especially of television in which he was probably the best-known performer in the country. He was a man under great emotional pressure. He disliked 'the Establishment' and continually involved himself in rows with authority. He was often the victim of alleged martyrs, many of whom were bogus. The apparent rudeness, which brought him much notoriety, was not an act, as was widely believed; he never suffered fools gladly, and he 'loved justice and hated iniquity' in no uncertain terms. 'I just behave as I am and talk as I think, which for some reason appears to be remarkably novel', was his comment. It was for this refreshing novelty and his genuine humanity that the public loved him; yet he thought it quite absurd that he should be so highly paid for being himself and, being fully aware of his difficulties of character and temperament, wanted desperately to be somebody different and better. His public performances often concealed the fact that he was in many ways a learned man. He had a wonderful memory for English poetry, which he loved. He was frustrated, amongst other things, by what he felt to

be the waste of his talents, and looked upon himself as a don *manqué*. In this he was almost certainly deceived but quite sincere. Despite the frustrations, he was candidly enough capable of enjoying, somewhat to excess, the luxuries which his large income made possible. He had known very hard times and did not pretend not to enjoy the easier times. He was lavishly generous of time and money, and the people who knew him best liked him most. His political views were always very much to the Left, and he continued in his prosperity to believe in the Labour Party and in the need for more equal distribution of wealth.

For most of his adult life Harding was in bad health, above all from asthma. He expected death to come at any moment and in fact dropped dead in Portland Place, 16 November 1960, as he was leaving the studio after a performance in 'Round Britain Quiz'. 'But I do wish that the future were over', had been the concluding words of his autobiography *Along My Line* (1953), a book which does not do justice to his remarkable intelligence and warmth of character. He never married. The Requiem Mass in Westminster Cathedral, at which Cardinal Godfrey presided, was crowded.

A portrait by Michael Noakes was acquired by Hereford Art Gallery.

[*The Times*, 17 November 1960; *Guardian*, 18 November 1960; personal knowledge.]
D. W. BROGAN.

HARDINGE, ALEXANDER HENRY LOUIS, second BARON HARDINGE OF PENSHURST (1894–1960), private secretary to King Edward VIII and King George VI, was born in Paris 17 May 1894, the younger son of Charles Hardinge, later first Baron Hardinge of Penshurst [q.v.]. He was educated at Harrow and Trinity College, Cambridge, and in 1915–16 was aide-de-camp to his father, then viceroy of India, who had recently sustained the loss of both his wife and his elder son. He served in France and Belgium in 1916–18 with the Grenadier Guards, was wounded and awarded the M.C., and in 1919–20 was adjutant of his regiment.

In 1920 Hardinge became assistant private secretary to King George V, being trained in his duties by Lord Stamfordham and Clive (later Lord) Wigram [qq.v.]. In 1935 he became in addition assistant keeper of the privy purse. In May 1936 King Edward VIII appointed him principal private secretary. At no

456

time did the new King take him into his confidence over his personal dilemma arising from his wish to marry Mrs. Simpson, but as early as August Hardinge began to warn him, as was his duty, of the constitutional difficulties he was likely to encounter. When Mrs. Simpson's divorce proceedings became imminent in October, Hardinge urged Stanley Baldwin, the prime minister, to see the King; and later himself saw to it that the King was aware of the open expression of opinion coming in from overseas whilst the press in this country still kept silent.

Finally, on 13 November 1936, after Baldwin had informed Hardinge that he had arranged a meeting of senior ministers to discuss the matter, Hardinge warned the King by letter that the silence might break at any moment; informed him of the meeting which was to take place; and advised him that in the event of the Government's resigning it was 'hardly within the bounds of possibility' that anyone else would be found capable of forming a government; the alternative would be a general election 'in which Your Majesty's personal affairs would be the chief issue—and I cannot help feeling that even those who would sympathize with Your Majesty as an individual would deeply resent the damage which would inevitably be done to the Crown . . .'. He ended by begging the King to consider the desirability of Mrs. Simpson's leaving the country without delay.

To a man of Hardinge's courage and integrity and with his wide knowledge and balanced judgement of men and affairs there could be no doubt where his duty lay in warning the King of the gravity of the situation. Nor did the King deny this (although he later claimed to having been 'shocked and angry'); but while continuing to conduct normal business with Hardinge, thereafter he made no reference to the subject and no use of him in the negotiations which culminated in the abdication.

On 29 November 1955 Hardinge included the text of his letter to the King in an article in *The Times* in which he refuted allegations that there had been a conspiracy to bring about the abdication and recalled that 'the one thing that everybody was trying to do was to keep the King on the throne'. Before dispatching his letter, he recorded, he had shown it to Geoffrey Dawson [q.v.], feeling that he 'desperately needed an outside opinion as to the general wisdom and propriety' of his letter; and he had shown it to a member of Baldwin's staff so that the prime minister might be aware of its contents. But 'both in conception and execution the idea was entirely my own'.

Exhausted by the strain, Hardinge went on three months' sick leave from which he returned to serve King George VI with unassuming devotion and efficiency through the difficult early years of his reign, then of the war, until in 1943 ill health compelled his resignation. In the following year he succeeded his father as second baron. He had been appointed M.V.O. (1925), C.V.O. (1931), C.B. (1934), G.C.V.O. and K.C.B. (1937), and G.C.B. (1943), and was sworn of the Privy Council in 1936. He was a governor of St. Bartholomew's Hospital and of the King's School, Canterbury, where his genuine and lively interest in the boys made him many friends.

In 1921 Hardinge married Helen Mary, only daughter of the late Lord Edward Cecil and his wife, who in that year became the Viscountess Milner [qq.v.]. They had two daughters and one son, George Edward Charles (born 1921), who succeeded as third baron when Hardinge died at Penshurst 29 May 1960.

[John W. Wheeler-Bennett, *King George VI*, 1958; Helen Hardinge, *Loyal to Three Kings*, 1967; *The Times*, 29 November 1955 and 30 May 1960; private information.]

HELEN M. PALMER.

HARRIS, (HENRY) WILSON (1883–1955), journalist and author, was born 21 September 1883 in Plymouth, the elder son of Henry Vigurs Harris, who carried on a family business as a house-decorator, and his wife, Fanny Wilson. The theologian James Rendel Harris [q.v.] was his uncle. Harris's parents being devout Quakers, their son was brought up in that persuasion. He was educated at Plymouth College and St. John's College, Cambridge, where he was a foundation scholar. In 1905 he was elected president of the Union and obtained a second class in part i of the classical tripos. After leaving Cambridge he contemplated being called to the bar, and also thought of making teaching his career; but in 1908 his literary gift and his sympathy for Liberal principles brought him to the staff of the *Daily News*, edited by A. G. Gardiner [q.v.]. He served on that paper successively as news editor, leader-writer, and diplomatic correspondent, his work in the last capacity establishing his reputation as a writer of trust.

On behalf of the *Daily News*, Harris

attended many international gatherings from the peace conference in 1919 onwards, acquiring a considerable knowledge of foreign affairs. He made his name as an author with *President Wilson: His Problems and His Policy* (1917) and *The Peace in the Making* (1919). From the start he was a convinced supporter of the League of Nations movement and soon decided to devote himself to the cause of peace and international friendship. In 1923 he joined the staff of the League of Nations Union, editing its journal *Headway*, and speaking at meetings up and down the country. His eager advocacy and his book *What the League of Nations Is* (1925) did much to clarify public understanding of the aims of the League.

Harris was, however, always a journalist at heart—and for him journalism was a serious calling. His staunch patriotism, active curiosity, and remarkable, if somewhat restless, energy were allied to a Quaker 'concern' to find Christian solutions for the world's political and social problems. It is not surprising that when in 1932 Sir Evelyn Wrench offered him the editorship of the *Spectator* he should have accepted with alacrity. For the next twenty-one years he devoted himself to that paper with unsparing diligence. A selection of his articles published under the title *Ninety-Nine Gower Street* (1943) indicates the high standard which he set himself; his reasoned and moderate approach and his talent for writing lucid character sketches of the public men of his time may alike have their relevance for future historians. Harris found an ideal outlet for his abilities in the conduct of a weekly review. Politically of the 'Left Centre', moving to the Right as time went on, he was able with his firm Nonconformist principles to give the *Spectator* a moral authority which was admired even by those of different opinions. The paper reflected his personality to an unusual degree: his hand could be detected not only in editorial comment but also in book reviews, while he made his pseudonym 'Janus' well known as that of a witty and incisive commentator on public affairs.

During the war years of 1939–45 Harris found time to return to authorship and published an informative little book on *The Daily Press* (1943), a sensible survey of the *Problems of the Peace* (1944), and useful biographies of Caroline Fox (1944) and J. A. Spender (1946). In 1945 he accepted an invitation to stand as an independent parliamentary candidate for Cambridge University and was elected after a close contest with J. B. Priestley for the second seat. No honour could have pleased him more. He rose to his opportunity and, being an excellent speaker, proved an acquisition to the debating strength of the House of Commons, where his independent views were always heard with respect. The abolition of the university seats brought his parliamentary career to a close in 1950; his editorship of the *Spectator* came to an end in 1953. Harris regretted the curtailment of his activities, as he showed in a characteristic autobiography *Life So Far* (1954). In the last two years of his life he wrote under his pseudonym 'Janus' in the columns of *Time and Tide*.

Tall, upright, spare of figure, with clear-cut features, genial and brisk in manner, Harris worked rapidly, and in his leisure hours was a voracious reader and a keen traveller and motorist. The reputation and the circulation of the *Spectator* were both enhanced during his long editorship. If the counterpart of his many great qualities was a certain stubbornness and narrowness of outlook, he deserves to be remembered as a journalist of deep integrity active for the common good, as an understanding colleague, and as a loyal friend. He was a member of the council of the Royal Institute of International Affairs, a governor of the Leys School, and in 1953 received the honorary degree of LL.D. from the university of St. Andrews.

In 1910 Harris married Florence, daughter of Alfred Midgley Cash, medical practitioner, of Torquay; they had one daughter. He died in a nursing-home at Hove 11 January 1955.

[Wilson Harris, *Life so Far*, 1954; *The Times*, 13 January 1955; private information; personal knowledge.]   DEREK HUDSON.

HARRIS, SIR PERCY ALFRED, first baronet (1876–1952), politician, was born in London 6 March 1876, the younger son of Wolf Harris by his wife, Elizabeth, daughter of David Nathan, general dealer, of Auckland, New Zealand. He was educated at Harrow (where (Sir) Winston Churchill was a slightly older contemporary) and at Trinity Hall, Cambridge, where he obtained a third class in the historical tripos in 1897. Two years later he was called to the bar by the Middle Temple, but never practised. He was then for some years engaged in the prosperous wholesale and manufacturing firm of Bing, Harris, which his father had founded in

New Zealand. Harris first helped to look after the London office, then spent three years in New Zealand. His lifelong interest in that country found expression in his book *New Zealand and its Politics* (1909).

Harris returned to England in 1903. Thenceforward his main interest was in politics, where he took his stand firmly on the Liberal side. These were the years leading up to the great Liberal triumph of 1906 when Harris contested Ashford; but this was a Conservative stronghold and he was narrowly defeated. In 1907 he was elected a Progressive (Liberal) member of the London County Council for South-West Bethnal Green, thus beginning a close association with the borough which lasted until the end of his life. His success coincided with his party's loss of the control over London's government which it had held since the Council's establishment in 1889 but was never to enjoy again. Nevertheless he played an important part in the work of the Council, becoming chief Progressive whip in 1912 and deputy chairman in 1915–16. His book *London and its Government* (1913, rewritten 1931) was considered a standard work of its kind. His special interest and knowledge was in those matters which particularly concerned his constituents, although some of these problems, such as education, housing, and unemployment, were of nation-wide as well as local significance.

After a predictable defeat at Harrow in January 1910 Harris entered Parliament at a by-election at Market Harborough in 1916. His main work in the short remainder of the wartime Parliament was as a member of the select committee on national expenditure. In the election which followed the armistice in 1918 he suffered for his loyalty to Asquith, and the refusal of the 'coupon' by the coalition leaders was sufficient to ensure his defeat.

In 1922 Harris returned to Parliament as member for South-West Bethnal Green. Amid the rising and more often falling hopes of a Liberal revival he won affection and respect as an industrious, knowledgeable, and independent-minded member. He was created a baronet in 1932; was chief Liberal whip in 1935–45; and in 1940, on Churchill's recommendation, was sworn of the Privy Council. Perhaps his most remarkable feat was to hold Bethnal Green against all comers in six successive general elections; for years his constituency was the only Liberal seat in or within a hundred miles of London.

His defeat in 1945 was not the end of his association with Bethnal Green, for in the next year he won back the seat on the London County Council which he had lost in 1934. In 1949 he was the only Liberal returned to that body in an election which resulted in the two main parties having an equal number of supporters. (Sir) David Low produced a cartoon depicting him as the dictator of London, but any hopes or fears in this respect were quickly dissipated when the allocation of aldermanic seats took place.

Percy Harris was a big, rubicund, extroverted man, who seemed to meet most people and situations with a beaming smile. It could not be claimed that he was either an orator or an original political thinker. The guiding principles of his career were an unfailing sympathy for the oppressed and the unlucky, and an inflexible loyalty to the Liberal cause. During his party's long decline many members of its radical wing found their way into the Labour camp, but he showed no inclination to follow. He remained a sturdy individualist valuing his independence more than anything else which politics could offer him, and deploring the growing power of the party caucus, especially in local government.

In 1901 Harris married Marguerite Frieda (died 1962), younger daughter of John Astley Bloxam, a well-known London surgeon. She was an artist of merit. They had two sons, the elder of whom, Jack Wolfred Ashford (born 1906), succeeded Harris when he died in London 28 June 1952.

[Sir Percy Harris, *Forty Years In and Out of Parliament*, 1947; private information; personal knowledge.]   FRANK MILTON.

HARRISON, HENRY (1867–1954), Irish nationalist and writer, was born at Holywood, county Down, 17 December 1867, the son of Henry Harrison, J.P., D.L., by his wife, Letitia Tennent, who afterwards married Hartley Withers [q.v.]. Harrison was educated at Westminster School of which he became a Queen's scholar, and at Balliol College, Oxford, where he obtained a third class in classical honour moderations (1888) and captained the cricket and football elevens. While still an undergraduate he developed what was to be a lifelong interest in Irish politics. He was secretary of the Oxford University Home Rule group, and in 1889, while witnessing a Donegal eviction, had the first of several clashes with the police. 'The stripling', as he was immediately nicknamed—a curious misnomer for a very large and powerful young man who generally gave as good as he got—became a nationalist celebrity overnight and the next year was elected to Parliament as member for mid-Tipperary.

He joined the Irish parliamentary party just as it was about to be torn asunder by the petition of W. H. O'Shea [q.v.] for a divorce from his wife on the grounds of her adultery with the Irish leader C. S. Parnell [q.v.]. In the famous 'split' Harrison was a devoted and uncompromising Parnellite, partly because of his instinctive faith in Parnell's honour as a gentleman and partly because he genuinely believed that for Irish nationalists to throw over their leader under pressure from Gladstone and the British Liberal Party was both disloyal and imprudent. After the party broke in two in December 1890, he campaigned with his chief in Ireland, constituting himself a bodyguard and aide-de-camp until Parnell's death in October 1891. Harrison, young though he was, hastened to Brighton to put his services at the disposal of Parnell's widow, and it was then that he heard from her a very different account from that given in the divorce court. This indicated that O'Shea's evidence in court had been completely untrustworthy, that he had apparently connived for a long period at Parnell's relations with his wife from whom he himself had virtually separated, and that his motives had been a mixture of political ambition and financial greed.

Harrison felt unable to publish this story until those most likely to be affected were dead, and he himself, having lost his seat in 1892, disappeared into obscurity. He re-emerged on the outbreak of war in 1914 and, although nearly fifty years of age, was commissioned in the Royal Irish Regiment in 1915. He fought with conspicuous gallantry and dash and was awarded the M.C. and bar and the O.B.E.

When the war was over 'Captain Harrison', as he was always to be known thereafter, threw himself eagerly into the affairs of the newly established Irish Free State. For a short period (1920–21) he was secretary of the Irish Dominion League and was closely associated with Sir Horace Plunkett [q.v.]. Then, from 1922 to 1927 he was Irish correspondent of *The Economist*, combining this between 1924 and 1927 with the editorship of a Dublin weekly, *Irish Truth*.

He next turned to what was to be the major work of his life—the rehabilitation of his beloved Parnell. In 1931 he published *Parnell Vindicated: the Lifting of the Veil*, which not only embodied the account Mrs. Parnell had given to him, but was also based on intensive and original research. It may fairly be said that, although not all of Harrison's conclusions are accepted by scholars, his work deeply and permanently changed the attitude of historians towards the *cause célèbre*. A notable exception was J. L. Garvin [q.v.], the early volumes of whose biography of Joseph Chamberlain [q.v.] ignored Harrison's findings. Harrison retaliated with a second book, *Parnell, Joseph Chamberlain and Mr. Garvin* (1938), which had the double aim of exposing the deficiencies of Garvin's biography and of implicating Chamberlain in a 'conspiracy' to bring about Parnell's downfall. The first object was easily enough achieved, but Chamberlain's complicity, despite some plausible evidence, was never conclusively proved. Harrison continued his defence of Parnell's reputation to the end of his life, for when in 1947 the third volume of the *History of 'The Times'* appeared, giving a distorted account of the Richard Pigott [q.v.] forgeries which had involved that newspaper with Parnell in 1887–9, Harrison at once challenged *The Times*, gained access to its records, and five years later had his reward when the fourth volume of the *History* acknowledged his intervention and included an appendix of *corrigenda* supplied by Harrison himself. Characteristically, he celebrated his victory with a pamphlet, *Parnell, Joseph Chamberlain and 'The Times'* (1953).

In that same year he made his last public appearance when he received an honorary LL.D. from Dublin University. A few months later he died in Dublin 20 February 1954, leaving to those who knew him the recollection of a warm and vital personality, an acute intelligence, vigorous and uninhibited conversation, and a memory for long past events so copious and exact as to make the man himself almost as valuable an historical source as his books. In addition to the works already mentioned his principal publications were: *Ireland and the British Empire, 1937, conflict or collaboration?* (1937); *Ulster and the British Empire, 1939, help or hindrance?* (1939); *The Neutrality of Ireland* (1942).

In 1895 he married Maie, daughter of J. C. Byrne, of New York. Their only child, a son, was seriously wounded at Gallipoli and died soon after the war.

The National Gallery of Ireland has a portrait by S. C. Harrison.

[*The Times*, 22, 23, and 25 February 1954; Henry Harrison, *Parnell Vindicated*, 1931; private information; personal knowledge.]

F. S. L. LYONS.

HART, SIR RAYMUND GEORGE (1899–1960), air marshal, was born 28 February 1899, at Merton, Surrey, the son of Ernest Joseph Hart, commercial traveller, and his wife, Emily Caroline Simmons. He was educated at the Simon Langton School, Canterbury, and enlisting in the Royal Flying Corps in 1916 was commissioned in 1917 and posted to a flying training unit. He had a short but distinguished period of service in France, being awarded the M.C. for his part in an historic air battle in which his R.E.8-type two-seater army co-operation aircraft destroyed three out of four attacking German aircraft. Hart was wounded and returned to England; on recovery he joined the school of technical training and was demobilized early in 1919.

Hart then joined the Imperial College of Science and obtained his A.R.C.S. with a second class in physics in 1921. In 1924 he was appointed a flying officer in the Royal Air Force on the reserve and in 1926 transferred to the active list. He qualified as a flying instructor and as a signals officer and with another British officer was sent to study at the École Supérieur d'Électricité in Paris where the pair of them passed out at the head of their group. Hart was a qualified French interpreter.

Between 1929 and 1933 Hart served on signals and flying duties at home and in India, being promoted flight lieutenant in 1930. After qualifying at the Royal Air Force Staff College he served in Nos. 9 and 12 Squadrons on flying duties until 1935. In 1936 he was promoted squadron leader and posted to Fighter Command for staff signals duties. He was attached to the team of scientists engaged on the development of what became known as radar to ensure the incorporation of Service requirements in the systems. He worked in close co-operation with Sir Henry Tizard [q.v.] and (Sir) Robert Watson-Watt in the establishment set up at Bawdsey for the purpose of applying the radar potential to the air defence of Great Britain. Hart continued in this work until the outbreak of war in 1939 and his contribution played a large part in ensuring that the defence system based on the radar

development was by then available to the Royal Air Force. Shortly after the outbreak of war Hart was posted for special duties to Fighter Command headquarters, where he organized the systems for the operational use of the information obtained by radar. He was promoted wing commander in 1940.

In 1941 Hart was posted to the Ministry air staff as deputy director of signals and later deputy director of radar; in this capacity he played a leading part in the development of airborne radar, then a vital requirement for the defence against the enemy night bomber offensive.

In 1943 Hart was appointed chief signals officer at Fighter Command headquarters and later that year to the same appointment on the headquarters of the Allied Expeditionary Air Force. He went to France with that headquarters in 1944 and remained until the end of the war. He served in Germany as chief signals officer, British Air Force, until early 1946, when he was appointed air officer commanding No. 27 Group in the United Kingdom. In 1947 he served in the Air Ministry as head of technical service plans; in 1949 he was appointed air officer commanding No. 90 (Signals) Group. In 1951 he returned to the Air Ministry as director-general of engineering. In 1955 he served as air officer commanding No. 41 Group and in 1956 he returned to the Air Ministry as controller of engineering and equipment until January 1959. He was gazetted air vice-marshal in 1953, air marshal in 1957, and placed on the retired list in 1960. In the meantime, in February 1959 he had been appointed director of the Radio Industry Council where he applied himself to co-ordinating the work of the industry to develop internationally accepted standards.

Hart was technically and operationally qualified by his early training, as an engineer and an experienced pilot, to contribute a major part in the development and application of radar to the needs of the Royal Air Force, first in the air defence of this country and later in the bombing of Germany and the anti-submarine offensive. His knowledge of the practical requirements of the Royal Air Force was understood by the scientists developing radar and they were spurred on by his enthusiasm and encouragement. His approach to the many problems was blunt and direct but his friendly personality enabled him to obtain the results he was striving for without undue friction.

Hart was appointed O.B.E. in 1940, C.B.E. in 1944, K.B.E. in 1957, and C.B. in 1946. He was thrice mentioned in dispatches and was a commander of the United States Legion of Merit and a chevalier of the French Legion of Honour.

In 1927 he married Katherine Gwenllian, daughter of Charles Penman Wiltshier, of Canterbury; they had one son.

Hart died 16 July 1960 as the result of an accident while using an electric lawnmower at his home at Aston Rowant, Oxfordshire.

[Private information; personal knowledge.]
VICTOR TAIT.

HARTLEY, ARTHUR CLIFFORD (1889–1960), engineer and inventor, was born at Springbank, Hull, 7 January 1889, the elder son of George Thomas Hartley, surgeon, and his wife, Elizabeth Briggs. From Hymers College, Hull, and after a brief period of engineering studies at Hull Technical College, Hartley went to the City and Guilds College, the engineering school of the Imperial College of Science and Technology at South Kensington. He passed out in 1910 with the college diploma and a B.Sc. (Eng.), London, with third class honours. Then came practical work, first as a pupil at Hull docks; then as assistant engineer with a Hull firm, and on to a London firm as works superintendent, following the usual pattern of postgraduate engineer training. In the war of 1914–18 Hartley was commissioned in the Royal Flying Corps, qualified as a pilot, earned the O.B.E. (1918) and the substantive rank of major. His forte, however, was invention and particularly the practical development of engineering concepts and he joined the armaments section of the Air Board where he worked under Bertram Hopkinson [q.v.]. Hartley was responsible for the development of the Constantinescu gear which enabled a Vickers machine-gun to be synchronized so that the pilot could fire straight ahead through the propeller blades.

After the war Hartley spent five years as a partner of a firm of consulting engineers until in 1924 he joined the Anglo-Persian Oil Company as assistant manager of its rapidly expanding engineering division, becoming chief engineer in 1934. During his twenty-seven years with the company he was a contemporary of G. M. Lees [q.v.], Hartley ultimately heading the engineering and Lees the geological division.

At the outbreak of war in 1939 Hartley was lent by the company to the Ministry of Aircraft Production to develop *inter alia* the stabilized automatic bomb sight which Bomber Command used to sink the *Tirpitz*. Next came FIDO (Fog Investigation Dispersal Operations). Air Marshal Sir Arthur Harris, in September 1942, demanded fog-clear airfield runways of 1,000 yards long by 100 feet high to reduce the devastating losses by bomber squadrons returning from raids to fog-bound England. The problem went to Hartley who was by then technical director of the petroleum warfare department. With A. O. Rankine, E. G. Walker, and a team of experts, he produced and installed fog dispersal equipment on fifteen airfields in the United Kingdom, as well as one in France and two in the United States. More than 2,500 aircraft made Fido-assisted landings in fog and mist. Hartley also helped in the development of flame weapons; but his most significant contribution was his idea which led to the construction of PLUTO (Pipeline under the Ocean). Admiral Mountbatten in April 1942 proposed the problem of laying across the Channel, sufficiently fast and secretly to avoid destruction by the enemy, pipelines to provide vital supplies of petrol after the allied landings. Conventional methods were doomed to failure in war conditions. Hartley's idea was to leave the copper out of a submarine electric cable and turn it into a high-pressure petrol pipeline. There were countless difficulties and many to say the idea was impossible, but Hartley's genius was to be the leader of the team which overcame the difficulties. Several hundred miles of HAIS (Hartley, Anglo-Iranian, Siemens) were made for PLUTO as well as HAMEL (Hammick, Ellis) pipe. Two HAIS and two HAMEL pipelines were laid from the Isle of Wight to Cherbourg, followed by nineteen HAIS submarine pipelines from Dungeness to Calais from October 1944 onwards, as well as land lines to the advancing armies through Ghent and Antwerp and across the Rhine to Eindhoven. Petrol was pumped through this system at the rate of a million gallons per day during the advance of the allied armies into Germany. In 1944 Hartley was appointed C.B.E. and in 1946 he received the United States medal of freedom for his war services.

When Hartley retired from the Anglo-Iranian Oil Company in 1951 it was to devote himself to further engineering problems as a consultant in private practice. His inventive capacity was with him to the end and his most notable achievement at this time was the Hartley hoister, a device for loading into tankers where no berthing facilities were available and where oil pipelines on the sea bed running from the installation ashore had to be connected to a tanker half a mile or more off-shore. The Hartley hoister raised its head like a sea monster from the sea bed and returned to the depths when the tanker was loaded. The first hoister was installed by the Kuwait Oil Company at Mina-al-Ahmadi and successfully loaded the 32,000-ton *British Courage* in January 1959. A further hoister began operating successfully in Bataan in the Philippines at the beginning of 1963.

In 1951 Hartley became president of the Institution of Mechanical Engineers. He was always prepared to give his time to such voluntary but onerous work. He had been president of the Old Centralians (former students of the City and Guilds College) in 1948. He was an honorary fellow of the City and Guilds Institute and of the Imperial College and in 1959 received the Redwood medal of the Institute of Petroleum. He served as a member of council of the Royal Society of Arts and was a manager of the Royal Institution. He was elected president of the Institution of Civil Engineers (where there is a portrait by John Codner) in 1959 but died in London, 28 January 1960, less than three months afterwards.

In 1920 Hartley married Dorothy Elizabeth (died 1923), daughter of Gavin Wallace, marine engineer, of Shanghai, by whom he had two sons. In 1927 he married, secondly, Florence Nina, daughter of William Egerton Hodgson, merchant, of Doncaster, by whom he also had two sons.

[*The Central*, vol. xliii, No. 97, June 1948; *Proceedings* of the Institution of Civil Engineers, vol. xv, April 1960; *The Civil Engineer in War*, I.C.E., 1948; personal knowledge.] A. C. VIVIAN.

HARTREE, DOUGLAS RAYNER (1897–1958), scientist, was born 27 March 1897 in Cambridge where his father William Hartree, a grandson of Samuel Smiles [q.v.], was a member of the teaching staff of the engineering laboratory; he retired in 1913, but thereafter continued to do scientific work, much of it as assistant to his own son. Hartree's mother, Eva Rayner, was the daughter of a prominent Stockport physician, and sister of E. H. Rayner who for many years was superintendent of the electricity division of the National Physical Laboratory. She was herself active in public affairs, serving as president of the National Council of Women and as mayor of Cambridge.

Douglas Hartree was the eldest of three sons, but alone survived to manhood. He was educated at Bedales School where the excellent teaching of mathematics gave the trend for his chief interests in later life. In 1915 he entered St. John's College, Cambridge, as a scholar, but after a year abandoned his studies for work in a team developing the new science of anti-aircraft gunnery. After the war he completed his university courses and was awarded a Ph.D. in 1926. He was elected fellow of St. John's (1924–7) and of Christ's (1928–9). He was next appointed to the chair of applied mathematics (1929–37) and of theoretical physics (1937–45) in the university of Manchester. In 1946 he became Plummer professor of mathematical physics at Cambridge, a chair which he held until his death, and was again a fellow of Christ's. He was elected F.R.S. in 1932.

The main scope of Hartree's work was largely determined by his early experiences in anti-aircraft gunnery. The calculation of trajectories involves much numerical work with pencil and paper, a type of mathematics in which he became expert; already at the age of twenty he introduced outstanding improvements into the calculation of trajectories. He continued to develop this kind of work all through his life, and he came to be regarded as one of the world's chief leaders in the science of computation, called in as consultant in many countries.

In the twenties Hartree applied his methods to the solution of problems associated with the new theories of the structure of the atom. In this field his most conspicuous work was the invention of the method of the 'self-consistent field'. This made possible the practical solution of a problem which, if exactly treated, would have a quite impossible degree of complexity. Ten years later numerical methods were much improved by the invention of the differential analyser by Vannevar Bush in America. Hartree visited him to study it and on return to Manchester himself made an analyser which came to be very widely used. He had intended its main purpose to be for the solution of atomic problems but with characteristic generosity gave its services for many other uses. In particular he thus became a leader in developing methods of automatic control for many complicated processes of manufacture. He could claim to be one of the fathers of the new techniques of automation.

Yet another revolution occurred in 1945 with the invention of the electronic digital computing machines. The first successful one was designed for anti-aircraft trajectories in America. Hartree's advice was sought and it was largely he who showed how its extreme rapidity of action could be exploited. A process which previously took a team of workers several days could now, by his ingenuity, be done in thirty seconds.

Hartree's distinction as a scientist was not so much in the depth of his researches as in their breadth. With the new methods it became possible to attack many problems in a great variety of subjects which had before been insoluble, and it was he who largely led the way in this new attack. His book, *Numerical Analysis* (1952), became a classic of the subject. He was a good lecturer and brilliant at clarifying a subject by an intuitive knowledge of the level of understanding of his listener.

From boyhood Hartree had a strong interest in railways and their signalling methods, and in later life this proved useful to the railway companies in relation to their complicated traffic problems. He served on a committee of the British Transport Commission and showed how to use the high-speed computing machines to solve traffic problems which had previously taken months of calculation. Music was among his other interests; he played the piano and other instruments and also conducted an amateur orchestra.

In 1923 Hartree married Elaine, daughter of Eustace Charlton, of Keswick. They had one daughter and two sons, all of whom inherited their father's scientific tastes. He died in Cambridge 12 February 1958.

[Sir Charles Darwin in *Biographical Memoirs of Fellows of the Royal Society*, vol. iv, 1958; personal knowledge.]   C. G. DARWIN.

HASLETT, DAME CAROLINE HARRIET (1895-1957), electrical engineer, was born at Worth, Sussex, 17 August 1895, the eldest daughter of Robert Haslett, a railway signal fitter and a pioneer of the Co-operative movement, and his wife, Caroline Sarah Holmes. She was educated at Haywards Heath High School and then took a post as secretary with the Cochran Boiler Company. Clerical work did not particularly attract her and she asked to be transferred to the works where she qualified in general and later in electrical engineering. For a period she was associated with Sir Charles Parsons [q.v.], the inventor of the Parsons turbine, and his wife, in the promotion of a journal devoted especially to women in the engineering industry. She was the first secretary of the Women's Engineering Society established in 1919 of which Lady Parsons was the founder, and was later for two years its president. She was also for many years the editor of the society's journal the *Woman Engineer*. She was never an ardent feminist but perceived the possibilities of engineering to raise the whole social status of women. She did valuable work in persuading engineering institutes to admit women to their examinations and not least in inducing employers to engage female labour. She founded the Electrical Association for Women in 1924 and remained its director until 1956 when she withdrew owing to ill health but continued as an honorary adviser. Through this organization she exercised a powerful influence on the development of the domestic use of electricity and with the encouragement of progressively minded people in the electrical industry achieved a remarkable measure of co-operation. A strong personality, she yet had the capacity for self-elimination at public functions, almost invariably preferring to delegate to other women such activities as would bring them into prominence. She aroused enthusiasm amongst her intimate colleagues who became devoted to her and to their work in the Electrical Association for Women.

Ever an ardent champion of the causes she advocated, Dame Caroline spoke and wrote frequently on the subjects which she had at heart, and the pages of the *Electrical Age*, the organ of the Electrical Association for Women, which she also edited, reflect her tireless energy in securing the development of electricity for domestic purposes. At the time of her withdrawal from active work the E.A.W. had 14,000 members, most of them housewives, domestic science teachers, and educationists, organized in 160 branches. Her solicitude for the well-being of women in their homes was only rivalled by her enthusiasm for the development of electricity as an agent in reducing domestic chores. She early realized the need for ensuring the safety of these devices and devoted much of her attention to promoting this in association with the manufacturers.

Dame Caroline was the first and only woman to be appointed a member of the British Electricity Authority on its inception in 1947 and to serve on its successors until the time of her death. Her keen mind and refreshing zest were a valuable asset to the newly integrated industry. Her practical wisdom and lively sense of humour did much to lessen the stresses and tensions of the early years when organization and human problems of some complexity had to be resolved. A motor vessel, of the Authority's collier fleet, was named *Dame Caroline Haslett*; and the E.A.W. founded the Caroline Haslett Trust to provide scholarships and travelling fellowships and exhibitions for its members.

Dame Caroline served on numerous public bodies including the British Institute of Management, the Industrial Welfare Society, the National Industrial Alliance, the British Electrical Development Association, the Royal Society of Arts, Bedford College for Women, the London School of Economics, Queen Elizabeth College, the Administrative Staff College, and King's College of Household and Social Science, and the Crawley Development Corporation. She travelled widely, and on government missions to the United States, Canada, Sweden, and Finland. She attended the World Power Conference several times as a British delegate and was the author of papers on home management to international Scientific Management Congresses in Europe. In 1950 she became the president of the International Federation of Business and Professional Women. After the war of 1939–45 she took a leading part in conferences organized for women in Germany by the British and American authorities and at the invitation of the United States Government visited the American zone of Germany to address conferences there.

Appointed C.B.E. in 1931 and D.B.E. in 1947, Caroline Haslett was a justice of the peace for the county of London and in 1932 was made a companion member of the Institution of Electrical Engineers. She never swerved from her high purpose of raising the social status of women, and her flair for organization and administration, her integrity of mind, healthy common sense, and love of simple things endeared her to those who had the good fortune to work with her.

She died 4 January 1957 at Bungay, Suffolk. A portrait by Sir Gerald Kelly belongs to the Royal Society of Arts and another by Dorothy Vicaji to the Electrical Association for Women. The Imperial War Museum has a lithograph by Ethel Gabain.

[*The Times*, 5 January 1957; *Woman Engineer*, Spring 1957; personal knowledge.]

CITRINE.

HASTINGS, SIR PATRICK GARDINER (1880–1952), lawyer, was born in London 17 March 1880 and was consequently given the name of Ireland's patron saint, there being Irish blood on both sides of the family. He was the younger son of Alfred Gardiner Hastings and his wife, Kate Comyns Carr, a pre-Raphaelite painter of some ability. The elder Hastings, although originally a solicitor, can hardly have been long in practice and seems to have been an unreliable parent. His son's early memories were of alternating penury and affluence. 'Bankruptcy in my family', he wrote, 'was not a misfortune, it was a habit.' His recollections of childhood included hours spent in his mother's studio where he was allowed to play with the paints on her palette, and of late nights spent in company with his father and his father's 'business friends', which frequently ended with himself falling asleep across the table. At the age of ten he was sent to a preparatory boarding-school which he hated, and the two years spent at Charterhouse were no improvement. He resented both the discipline and the classical regimen which taught him, he claimed, none of the practical things he required to know. He left Charterhouse at sixteen, undistinguished in work or games and a victim of chronic asthma.

Family fortunes at this time were at a low ebb and after eighteen months of precarious living in Corsica, France, and Belgium with his mother and elder brother, Hastings took a subordinate post as a mining engineer in North Wales. The mine proved unproductive and with his brother he joined the Suffolk Imperial Yeomanry and saw two years of active service in the South African war. On his return he found his parents in no position to help him towards a career. From quite early years, however, he had wanted to be a barrister and with scarcely a penny in his pocket he was admitted as a student to the Middle Temple where he did all his reading since he could not afford to buy books. From Putney where living was cheap he walked to work each day, went

without lunch, but treated himself to
dinner at a Soho restaurant for the price of
1s. 6d. He earned a few pounds weekly
by writing theatre reviews and gossip for
several newspapers. With no dress clothes
for attending the theatre, he wore a great-
coat tactically fastened over a white shirt
and white tie. By such expedients he
saved £100 to pay for his call in 1904.

He contrived almost immediately to
obtain some devilling work from (Sir)
Charles Gill, a busy lawyer with a large
criminal practice; some two years later
he found a seat in the chambers of (Sir)
Horace Avory [q.v.]. When Avory went
to the bench Hastings boldly took on the
chambers. He always declared that his
debt to Avory was enormous. From him
he learned never to make notes but to
read a brief thoroughly and commit it to
memory; then, as soon as the case was
over, dismiss the whole thing from his
mind.

In 1906 Hastings married Mary
Ellenore, daughter of Lieutenant-Colonel
Frederick Leigh Grundy; they had two
sons and three daughters. At the time of
his marriage he and his wife possessed no
more than £20 between them; but this
state of affairs was not to obtain for long,
for during the next few years he became
one of the busiest juniors at the common
law bar. When in 1919 he took silk, having
been rejected during the war as medically
unfit for service, his reputation as an
advocate was firmly established.

He was no less successful as a silk and
at the age of forty found himself with 'all
the cases that I wanted and perhaps more
than I could do'. Politically his interests
were always to the Left, although his
opinions mellowed in later years. In 1922
he was elected member of Parliament for
Wallsend. Experienced lawyers were rare
in the Labour ranks and Hastings was the
natural choice for attorney-general when
Ramsay MacDonald formed his government in January 1924; the post carried
with it the traditional knighthood. The fall
of the Government later in the year was
precipitated by the so-called Campbell
case. Hastings skilfully defended his action
in withdrawing the prosecution for sedition when he learned that Campbell was a
man with an excellent war record who was
only acting as a temporary substitute for
the Communist editor of the Workers'
Weekly; many members of all parties
thought Hastings's treatment by the
prime minister less than generous, a view
substantiated by the publication of the

Whitehall Diary of Thomas Jones [q.v.] i
1969. In the subsequent election Hasting
was again returned for Wallsend; but h
found the combination of parliamentar
work with a heavy law practice too muc
for his health and he resigned his seat i
1926.

From this date began his rapid clim
to leadership of the common law bar, a
eminence which he shared for many yea
with his friend and frequent opponen
Norman (later Lord) Birkett. Spectacula
cases, such as that of the 'Talking Mor
goose', the actions between Dr. Stopes an
Dr. Sutherland [qq.v.], and the Savidg
tribunal, brought him much publicity, bu
most of what became a very large incom
inevitably derived from less excitin
commercial work. He had a great gift fo
simplification and could make a com
mercial case so easy to follow that wha
might otherwise have taken weeks wa
completed in a few days. Although h
often appeared in the criminal courts, h
had a deep dislike of murder cases. Bu
his closing speech in defence of Mrs
Barney (1932), charged with the murde
of her lover, was described by Mr. Justic
Humphreys [q.v.] as 'one of the fines
speeches I have ever heard at the bar'.

In the war of 1939–45 Hastings serve
for a time as an intelligence officer a
Fighter Command headquarters, but hi
health proved unequal to the strain an
he returned to a law practice in whic
most cases were heard without a jury an
the importance of an advocate's role ha
greatly diminished. The death in action o
his younger son, David, hit him hard. Hi
last great success, in 1946, the defenc
against an action for libel brought by
H. J. Laski [q.v.], took a heavy toll from
him; in 1948 he decided to retire
He occupied himself by writing, an
achieved considerable success with hi
Autobiography (1948), Cases in Cour
(1949), and Famous and Infamous Case
(1950), and a play about the law courts
The Blind Goddess, which was also mad
into a film. The theatrical sense was very
strong in him and he tried his hand at hal
a dozen plays, of which only The Rive
(1925), Scotch Mist (1926), and The Blin
Goddess (1947) achieved any real success
He had not the temper of an intellectua
and his reading was largely confined to
law reports and thrillers such as those o
his friend Edgar Wallace [q.v.]. He was
a devoted husband and father, enjoying
nothing better than an open-air country
life spent with his family and intimate

friends. He was a good horseman, a first-class shot, and a passionately keen fisher-man. Tall, thin, dark-haired, with blue eyes and a very straight carriage, his personality was forceful and somewhat intolerant; he was a master of simple, unadorned language. Above all, he was a man of tremendous enthusiasms and great courage. His stature as an advocate was the result primarily of his brilliance in cross-examination. He neither bullied nor abused, but had learned from one of his early mentors, Sir Edward (later Lord) Carson [q.v.], the art of getting under a witness's skin with the first question. He was a dangerous, but always honourable, opponent, at his best when speaking directly to a jury. He earned headlines with his wit, not with histrionics. For the thundering emotional appeals which used to be the fashion he substituted an incisive appeal to intelligence. He is said by his family to have been incapable of dissimula-tion, but Birkett watching him in court was fascinated by the play of expressions on his face—'anger, surprise, incredulity, disdain . . . They were meant for the jury and were indeed more eloquent than words.'

In 1950 Hastings visited his son Nicho-las who was farming in Kenya and there suffered a slight stroke from which he never fully recovered. He died in his London home 26 February 1952. The National Portrait Gallery has a drawing by Nicolas Bentley.

[Hastings's own writings; H. Montgomery Hyde, *Sir Patrick Hastings, His Life and Cases*, 1960; Patricia Hastings, *The Life of Patrick Hastings*, 1959; *The Times*, 27 Feb-ruary 1952; private information.]

ANTHONY LEJEUNE.

HAWTHORN, JOHN MICHAEL (1929–1959), racing motorist, was born in Mexborough, Yorkshire, 10 April 1929, the only son of Leslie Hawthorn, motor engineer and racing motor-cyclist, by his wife, Winifred Mary Symonds. Educated at Ardingly, he achieved no great success as a sportsman, being 'indolent by nature'. His parents moved to Farnham in Surrey when his father became involved in motor-cycle racing at Brooklands, and when 'Mike' left school in 1946 he was apprenticed to Dennis Brothers, the commercial vehicle builders, in Guildford. Following the wish to join his father in business and become an automobile engineer, he went on from his apprentice-ship to Kingston Technical College and

then the College of Automobile Engineer-ing at Chelsea. The result of his efforts in this direction only made him certain that he would find his *métier* in the driving-seat rather than at the drawing-board.

Not unnaturally, his first interest as a young man was motor-cycles and it was in the field of motor-cycle sport that the name of Mike Hawthorn first came to the public notice—it was always 'Mike', a diminutive which fitted his character absolutely; but despite his modest success as a motor-cyclist, his parents were natur-ally anxious to get him on to four wheels, and as soon as was practicable his father provided him with a small car.

For a young man to break into motor-racing—as a professional—has always been difficult and the least easily satisfied of dreams, but Mike had a great ally in his father who was not only willing to see him do it, but anxious to help him toward this end. During 1951 he had his first racing season and achieved some success in a number of club races with a pre-war Riley. His first big chance came early in 1952 when an old friend of the family purchased one of the new Cooper-Bristols with a view to entering it in international races. He invited Hawthorn to be the driver. Hawthorn's first appearance with this car was at Goodwood on Easter Monday 1952, when, in a series of short races in which many world-famous drivers were competing, he did so well that before sundown his reputation was made and a new name was upon everyone's lips. No one seemed more surprised than the Hawthorns. His continued success in that year was rewarded by an invitation from Enzo Ferrari to drive for him in the fol-lowing season. It was during 1953, while he was still a comparatively new boy, that he won the French Grand Prix from Fangio, the then reigning champion, by a matter of seconds only. The sheer dash and courage he displayed on this occasion endeared him to everyone for, despite his debonair nature, he was certainly not without knowledge of fear. At the end of the race, perhaps his greatest moment of triumph, he found his lower lip seriously injured—he had bitten very nearly through it. At the end of the year he found his successes had brought him the coveted gold star of the British Racing Drivers' Club.

The year 1954 was an ill-fated one for him. He was the centre of a most unfor-tunate controversy over his call-up for national service. He next crashed in the

Syracuse Grand Prix and was very badly burned, and would probably have lost his legs but for the devoted nursing of some nuns in Sicily. He was moved to hospital in Rome, where he was to remain for some time, and where his condition so severely shocked his mother that she herself became ill. When he had recovered and was on the way to Le Mans to take part in the 24-hour race, he learned that his father had had a serious motor accident, but when he telephoned home to say that he hoped to arrive that night he was told that his father had died. Nevertheless he ended the year by winning the Spanish Grand Prix.

In 1955 he drove briefly for Tony Vandervell, but there were temperamental difficulties and he won the Le Mans race that year for Jaguar, beating Fangio in a Mercedes-Benz and setting up a fantastic lap record of 122 miles an hour. This was the race in which some eighty spectators were killed by a German car, and once more Hawthorn was the centre of controversy. Despite his normally happy disposition he was unfortunately capable of reacting very badly to press comment, particularly when he felt it to be uninformed, and in these circumstances he was usually his own worst enemy. For a man leading so sophisticated a life he was in some ways quite naïve, and deeply hurt when he thought, to use his own words, that he was 'being got at'. Nevertheless, he brought to motor sport a sense of chivalry and good fun, and his close friendship with Peter Collins and their constant references to each other as 'mon ami, mate' gave even those outside the sport some insight into his ebullient nature.

He had a reasonably successful season in 1956 and returned in 1957 to Ferrari, showing that he had lost none of his early ability and gained much in experience and determination. In 1958 he again won the French Grand Prix and at Casablanca on 19 October he achieved his highest honour and became the first British driver to be world champion.

He was awarded the British Automobile Racing Club's gold medal and two months later he confirmed that he was to retire from motor racing. It was common knowledge that he had hoped to get married, to settle down to build up the business he had taken over on his father's death, and to care for his mother in her declining years. It is an irony of fate that on his way to London from his home in Surrey he was killed 22 January 1959 in a motor accident on a public road near Guildford, in circumstances not so very different from those in which his father had died.

[*The Times*, 23 January 1959; Mike Hawthorn, *Challenge Me the Race*, 1958, and *Champion Year*, 1959; private information; personal knowledge.]   MICHAEL FROSTICK.

HAY, IAN (pseudonym), writer. [See BEITH, JOHN HAY.]

HEAL, SIR AMBROSE (1872–1959), furniture designer and dealer, was born at Crouch End, London, 3 September 1872, the eldest son of Ambrose Heal, furnisher, by his wife, Emily Maria, daughter of Thomas Stephenson, of Finchley. He was the great-grandson of John Harris Heal, who in 1810 had started business as a feather dresser at Rathbone Place, Oxford Street, London. In 1840 the business was moved to Tottenham Court Road. It became known chiefly as a provider of bedding; bedsteads were added in 1850; eventually the firm's interests were enlarged to include general furniture, a wide expansion taking place after 1875.

Educated at Marlborough, Heal spent some time recuperating from a football injury in the house of a private tutor, where he met his cousin, Cecil Brewer, who was in similar case. The boys became fast friends. They had common interests in the arts of design, and Brewer was soon to show great promise in architecture, only to be cut off by his early death in 1918. Leaving school in 1887 Heal was sent by his father to France for six months and then apprenticed to a cabinet-maker at Warwick, starting at the bench and afterwards spending some time in the drawing-office. When he joined the family firm in 1893 he had the root of the matter in him. At that time furniture styles tended to a vulgar over-elaboration, but salutary influences were at work, including William Morris [q.v.] and the Art Workers' Guild. Through Brewer, Heal met men like W. R. Lethaby, Selwyn Image, and C. F. Annesley Voysey [qq.v.]. The aesthetic climate in which he moved was thus a healthy one. He had developed a real appreciation of wood as a medium, and from the first revolted against the current fussiness of design and ornament. His furniture combined functional utility with a simplicity of line which left the chief aesthetic impact to be made by the marking and texture of the wood. It was a hard task to introduce what then seemed revolutionary ideas. Heal's salesmen asked how they could be expected to sell 'prison furniture', and the very cabinet-makers were in revolt. But Heal persisted; he won a silver medal at the Paris Exhibition of 1900 for a bedroom suite in oak, inlaid with ebony and pewter. The number of enlightened patrons gradually increased. He was a co-founder of the Design and Industries Association in 1915.

Meanwhile in 1913, following his father's death, he had become chairman of Heal & Son. Before long he greatly broadened the basis of the business and added general and office furniture and even kitchen and bathroom furnishings. He chose his buyers with care, but by no means gave them *carte blanche*. Heal was not only a craftsman but a business man with an eye for profit and he insisted on concerning himself closely with all the lines of goods it was proposed to sell.

Although for many years beds remained the mainstay of the business (a fourposter was still the trademark in the second half of the twentieth century), the scope of Heal's was progressively widened. An antique furniture department was followed by the pottery, carpets, textiles, and curtains sections, each and all notable for the originality and quiet good taste displayed. In the thirties the Mansard art gallery was added at the top of the buildings. In the war of 1939–45 mattresses were produced for the Services and the building survived hits by incendiary bombs. In 1941 a subsidiary wholesale and export department was formed; in 1944 a small building company was acquired; these were the first of a number of offshoots dealing with all aspects of the home. In January 1953 Heal resigned the chairmanship to his elder son but remained a director for life.

Heal was knighted in 1933. In 1939 he was appointed a royal designer for industry; in 1954 he was awarded the Albert medal by the Royal Society of Arts for services to industrial design. He will be remembered as one of the major craftsmen of his day. His most important service to furniture-making was to get rid of otiose decoration and to produce chastely designed and comfortable pieces which were an adornment to the home and not so expensive as to be obtainable only by the wealthy. Although fundamentally a pleasant character, Heal was rather a terrifying figure to his staff. He was a Victorian by temperament and preserved a certain aloofness even from his fellow directors. His private interests included the trade cards, billheads, and signboards of London shops, the work of the London goldsmiths and furniture makers, and calligraphy, subjects in which he made valuable collections and on which he himself wrote a number of works. His book *The English Writing-Masters and their Copy-Books, 1570–1800* (1931) is authoritative. He was a fellow of the Society of Antiquaries and a member of the advisory council of the Victoria and Albert Museum.

In 1895 Heal married Alice Rose (died 1901), daughter of Alexander Rippingille. They had one son who died at the age of nineteen. In 1904 he married Edith Florence Digby (died 1946), daughter of Dr. John Todhunter. They had a daughter and two sons, the elder of whom took over the business and the younger followed his father as a designer. Heal died at Beaconsfield 15 November 1959. There is a portrait of him by Edward I. Halliday in the board-room of the firm.

[*The Times*, 17 November 1959; *The History of Heal's* (leaflet), 1962; private information.]   HERBERT B. GRIMSDITCH.

HEILBRON, SIR IAN MORRIS (1886–1959), chemist, was born 6 November 1886 in Glasgow, the younger son of David Heilbron, wine merchant, and his wife, Fanny Jessel. Originally named Isidor, he eventually adopted the name of Ian by which he had been known for many years. He was educated at Glasgow High School, the Royal Technical College, Glasgow, and the university of Leipzig. Having come under the influence of G. G. Henderson [q.v.] and A. Hantzsch with particular respect to chemical research, Heilbron became a lecturer at the Royal Technical College, Glasgow, in 1909. After an interruption due to the war and a brief period with the newly formed British Dyestuffs Corporation, he became professor of organic chemistry there in 1919–20. He subsequently held the chairs of organic chemistry in Liverpool (1920–33), Manchester (1933–5, in 1935–8 Sir Samuel Hall professor of chemistry), and the Imperial College of Science and Technology, London (1938–49). He vacated the last chair to become director in 1949 of the newly formed Brewing Industry Research Foundation, Nutfield, Surrey, where he was mainly responsible for creating a centre of fundamental research into fermentation chemistry and biology. He retired in 1958.

Heilbron

Heilbron gained a world-wide reputation for his organizational skill and for his imagination in designing laboratories specifically fashioned to take advantage of new, especially physical, techniques in organic chemical research. He was himself largely responsible for the general introduction of many of these into research work in Britain, notably the use of various forms of spectrometry, molecular distillation, microanalysis, and chromatography. He was a most inspiring teacher and a remarkable number of his students achieved eminence in either the academic or the industrial spheres at home or abroad. Especially in his later years he was widely sought as a consultant of scientific industrial problems.

Heilbron's scientific work began with a few years devoted mostly to questions of the detailed structures of various synthetic coloured substances. From 1919 onwards he was increasingly interested in miscellaneous naturally occurring materials, especially ones of pronounced biological activity. He thus pioneered investigations on vitamins A and D as well as related carotenoid pigments and steroids, and over approximately thirty years became recognized as a world authority on the chemistry of these fields. This interest led to his opening up the broad topic of the general chemistry of acetylenic derivatives of diverse types to provide the foundation of much industrial development. Heilbron was in turn concerned with numerous other substances of actual or potential therapeutic interest and made important contributions to the chemistry of the penicillins, particularly during the war of 1939–45 when the subject was of major national importance but one of probably unsurpassed practical difficulty. He wrote extensively in the scientific field as the author or part-author of about 300 publications dealing with original work. He also brought into being the *Dictionary of Organic Compounds* associated with his name and played an important part as chairman of the editorial board responsible at one time for Thorpe's *Dictionary of Pure and Applied Chemistry*—the main reference work of its kind in English.

Heilbron received many academic honours including the fellowship (1931) and the Davy (1943) and Royal (1951) medals of the Royal Society, honorary degrees from Glasgow and Edinburgh, and membership and lectureships of the Chemical Society of London of which he was president (1948–50), the American Chemical Society, the French Chemical Society, and the Royal Netherlands Academy of Sciences.

He saw active service in the first war as lieutenant, later lieutenant-colonel, in the Army Service Corps, as assistant director of supplies in Salonika, and was appointed to the D.S.O. He was a scientific adviser successively to the Ministries of Supply (1939–42) and Production (1942–5) and played a forceful part in the introduction of D.D.T. as an insecticide which mitigated the difficulties of the war, especially in the South European and Far East regions. Both before and after the war he was active in other departments of public service, for over eventually fifty years his experience of the growth of science and its increasing penetration into industry and the public service was probably unrivalled. Thus he took over many years a leading part, especially after 1945, in the organization of the International Union of Pure and Applied Chemistry and acted as chairman of various government committees and of the advisory councils of the Department of Scientific and Industrial Research (1950–54) and the Royal Military College of Science (1953–5). He was knighted in 1946.

In a private capacity he was a man of fastidious taste, meticulous precision, and wide artistic interests. He died in London, 14 September 1959, five years after the death of his wife, Elda Marguerite, daughter of Herbert J. Davis, of Liverpool, whom he married in 1924. They had two sons.

[A. H. Cook in *Biographical Memoirs of Fellows of the Royal Society*, vol. vi, 1960; private information; personal knowledge.]

A. H. COOK.

HENDERSON, SIR HUBERT DOUGLAS (1890–1952), economist, was born at Beckenham, Kent, 20 October 1890, the third son and sixth and youngest child of John Henderson, then London manager of the Clydesdale Bank, by his wife, Sarah, daughter of William Thomson, of an Edinburgh shipping family. The Hendersons soon moved to Aberdeen where John Henderson was manager of the North of Scotland Bank, and later to Kelvinside, in Glasgow, where he was general manager of the Clydesdale Bank, and lived in prosperous circumstances.

Hubert Henderson was educated at Aberdeen Grammar School, at Rugby School and at Emmanuel College, Cam-ridge, to which he went in October 1909 with a mathematical exhibition. An exceptional teacher at Aberdeen Grammar School had aroused his interest in mathematics. At Cambridge this first enthusiasm was on the wane—he secured only a third in the first part of the mathematical tripos (1910)—being supplanted by a more enduring interest in debate. Debate led to politics, and politics, in the heyday of Liberal reform, to economics. He obtained a first in the second part of the economics tripos in 1912, in which year he was also president of the Union. He acquired Liberal and reforming views, at variance with those in which he had been reared; and he came under the influence of (Sir) Norman Angell.

While reading for the bar, his intended career, he supported himself by taking economics pupils for his college which gave him a small bursary. When war broke out his friend Walter (later Lord) Layton took him into a statistical section of the Board of Trade. He volunteered for military service but was rejected on medical grounds; and in 1917 he was sent to Manchester as secretary of the Cotton Control Board which he has described in a volume of the Carnegie Endowment's economic and social history of the war (1922).

After the war, although offered an established position at the Board of Trade, and although his father was willing to support his family—he had married in 1915—while he resumed his career at the bar, he accepted a fellowship at Clare College, Cambridge, and a university lectureship in economics. He wrote his book *Supply and Demand* in the long vacation of 1922; it was the first and one of the most successful of the Cambridge Economic Handbooks. Clear and down to earth, it is notably sceptical about the influence of price on the total supply of factors of production.

In 1923 J. M. (later Lord) Keynes [q.v.] and some friends bought the *Nation and Athenaeum*, a weekly, as a mouthpiece for the Liberals who had organized the summer school of 1922. Keynes persuaded Henderson, once his pupil, now a sympathetic colleague, to become editor. A newcomer to journalism Henderson made the *Nation* a formidable and respected organ of reformist opinion. He opposed the return to gold in 1925, supported a programme of national development, supported in 1924 and opposed in 1930 the repeal of the McKenna duties on

imported motors, noticed in 1926 the contrasting fortunes of the depressed north and west and the expanding industries of south-east England, opposed proportional representation, but hoped none the less that the Labour Party would share political power with the Liberals.

Henderson contributed both in discussion and with his pen to the preparation of *Britain's Industrial Future* in which the same group of Liberals set out their programme in 1928. For the 1929 election he and Keynes together prepared a pamphlet *Can Lloyd George Do It?* supporting the Liberal leader's claim that he could conquer unemployment. Henderson stood as a Liberal candidate for Cambridge University, but was unsuccessful.

In January 1930 Ramsay MacDonald set up the Economic Advisory Council consisting of ministers and eminent individuals with academic and practical knowledge of economics. Henderson, leaving the *Nation*, became, first, the council's assistant secretary, and, when Thomas Jones [q.v.] retired, its joint secretary until 1934. Whitehall and the great depression brought a sobering awareness of practical and political difficulties; but the optimism of his *Nation* days occasionally found an outlet, as when in 1932 he made an abortive proposal for an international note issue.

In 1934 Henderson left Whitehall Gardens for Oxford, on being appointed to a research fellowship at All Souls. Interested in population he traced a possible connection between a declining birth-rate and a lack of adaptability to economic change. Interviews with business men, conducted by a group of Oxford economists, under his chairmanship and at his instigation, led him and others to rather sceptical conclusions on the efficacy of the price mechanism and on accepted theories of the *modus operandi* of interest rates. He took an active part in the establishment of the Oxford Institute of Statistics. A stage in his own development is marked by his separation from Keynes's intellectual influence—although not his friendship. In 1936 he read a very critical paper on Keynes's *General Theory of Employment, Interest and Money* to the Marshall Society at Cambridge.

Henderson continued to play a part in public affairs. He remained an active member of the committee on economic information, all of the Economic Advisory Council that survived the change of government in 1931. He took part in an inquiry organized by Lord Astor and B. Seebohm Rowntree [qq.v.] into agricultural policy and wrote the report, 'The Agricultural Dilemma' (1935), which describes its conclusions. In 1938–9 he was a member of the royal commission on the West Indies and enjoyed the visit the commission and its chairman Lord Moyne [q.v.] paid to those islands.

Returning to England not long before the outbreak of war, with (Sir) Henry Clay [q.v.] he assisted in the survey of economic and financial plans for war Lord Stamp [q.v.] had been called upon to make. This little committee continued in existence until Stamp died in an air raid in 1941, and during its vigorous early days Henderson dealt comprehensively with many of the practical issues raised in the conversion of a peaceful economy to a war footing. By the summer of 1940 he was already dividing his time between the survey and the Treasury where he acted in a vaguely defined advisory capacity to successive chancellors of the Exchequer and their permanent officials. His critical powers, which were acute, found material in the projects for post-war Utopias which then absorbed the energies of many able men on either side of the Atlantic. Especially he opposed acquiescence in American proposals to implement our Lend-Lease agreement to liberalize world trade, which seemed to him to underestimate our task in making ends meet after the war. For this purpose he completed a controversial survey of international economic history between the wars which he had begun at All Souls before the war. He had had a coronary thrombosis in 1942 from which he recovered rapidly, but he had to end his work at the Treasury in December 1944.

Chosen in 1944 Drummond professor of political economy at Oxford, a chair attached to All Souls, he began his duties in October 1945. Appointed to the royal commission on population in 1944, he succeeded Lord Simon [q.v.] as its chairman in 1946. From 1945 to 1948 he was chairman of the statutory committee on unemployment insurance; at Oxford he became chairman of the Institute of Statistics, a member and for some time chairman of the board of the faculty of social studies, and a delegate of the University Press. Knighted in 1942, elected F.B.A. in 1948 when he was also president of the economic section of the British Association, he was elected president of the Royal Economic Society in 1950.

Although he took seriously the dutie these appointments involved, Henderso could still make characteristic contribu tions to controversies of the day. His Red lecture (1947) deals severely with som aspects of planning; his address to th British Association on the price syster is equally severe on the proponents c laissez-faire. Perhaps his most substantia article at this time was that on 'Th Function of Exchange Rates' (Oxfor Economic Papers, vol. i, January 194 where he restated an earlier conclusio that international financial equilibriur cannot be painlessly achieved by exchang rate variations.

In 1951 his college of All Souls did hir the rare honour of electing him, a Cam bridge man, as its warden. He lived only short time to enjoy a position to which hi talents and temperament were admirabl adapted. Towards the end of that year h had a third coronary thrombosis and h died in Oxford 22 February 1952.

After Henderson's death a selection c his papers made by Sir Henry Clay wa published under the title The Inter-Wa Years (1955). Approaching economics i the spirit of a public man seeking answer to practical questions, Henderson was im patient of the building of formal system and of the over-refinement of theoretica analysis. He stretched the boundaries c his subject to touch the political condi tions which limit the actions of statesmen on which his judgement was alway acute. His contemporary influence wa very considerable, and that of the writte word was supplemented by indefatigabl attendance at meetings of such bodies a the Tuesday Club, the Political Econom Club, and Chatham House, where hi interventions could be relied on to produc an effect.

He married in 1915 a student of econo mics, Faith, daughter of Philip H. Bagenal a political editor, of Dublin. They had tw daughters and one son and a singularl happy family life.

[Supplement to Oxford Economic Paper vol. v, 1953; Sir Dennis Robertson in Eco nomic Journal, December 1953; Sir Henr Clay's introduction to The Inter-War Year 1955; private information; personal know ledge.]   PIERS DEBENHAM

HENSON, LESLIE LINCOLN (1891 1957), actor-manager, was born in Nottin Hill, London, 3 August 1891, the eldest c the three children of Joseph Lincoln Hen son, tallow chandler, of Smithfield, and hi wife, Alice Mary, daughter of William Squire, of Glastonbury. He was educated at Cliftonville College and Emanuel School, Wandsworth. His parents, realizing where his talents lay, wisely swallowed their disappointment at his reluctance to stay in the family business and sent him to study acting under Cairns James. Beginning his professional career in 1910 as a member of a concert party called 'The Tatlers', he continued for the next five years to be engaged in concert-party work, alternating this with touring in musical comedy. He made his first London success at the Gaiety Theatre, 28 April 1915, as Henry in *To-Night's the Night*. It was appropriate that his success, which was instantaneous, should have been made at a theatre so closely identified with the reputations of many famous comedians.

All actors reflect, with varying degrees of distortion, the times in which they live. Henson was no exception. His cockney alertness, his bubbling humour, and his india-rubber face which never ceased to underline or embroider the lines he was speaking, exploded like a catherine wheel, in a theatre grown accustomed to the heavier humours of Edmund Payne and his contemporaries. Here was a different, a livelier talent.

Henson's emergence as a star of musical comedy was put into temporary eclipse by the war of 1914–18. Before joining the army, he flung himself into the work of entertaining the troops. Early in 1916 he appeared in a revue of his own contriving in the new garrison theatre at Park Hall Camp, Oswestry, one of the first of the new hutted camps soon to be dotted over the countryside. The building of this theatre out of the soldiers' regimental funds was the genesis of the system of government-sponsored entertainment in wartime which reached its full development in the war of 1939–45 under the aegis of E.N.S.A. The company, which included Melville Gideon, Stanley Holloway, and Davy Burnaby, and six girls from the Gaiety chorus, all of them destined to achieve success in one direction or another, left the Gaiety Theatre after the Saturday night performance, wrote the revue on the night mail to Chester, rehearsed it on the garrison theatre stage on the Sunday morning, and performed it twice that same evening: the kind of gay, chaotic improvisation in which Henson delighted. Later, he joined the Royal Flying Corps, was sent to France, commissioned, and put to work organizing

entertainment for the Fifth Army. The little company of actors which he gathered round him, some professional, some amateur, soon became famous as The Gaieties, making their headquarters at the municipal theatre in Lille.

Following demobilization Henson achieved a series of outstanding successes in musical comedy at the Winter Garden, of which *Sally* (1921) and *Kid Boots* (1926), both American importations, were best remembered. In 1935 he returned to the Gaiety to appear in a series of musical plays containing parts specially written for him, and to share in the management. He was also associated in management with Tom Walls [q.v.]. Together they were responsible for the production of the farce *Tons of Money* (1922), followed by the series of plays known as the Aldwych farces, a generic title acquired from the theatre in which they were presented. Henson also made a number of films. His star was now at its zenith and he was fully occupied until the outbreak of war in 1939.

Henson's sense of obligation towards the audiences who had welcomed him with such acclaim found its full expression in his untiring efforts throughout the war, when he worked almost continually for E.N.S.A., first in France, and later in North Africa, the Middle East, Italy, and India. Welcomed in every mess and canteen, raising uproarious laughter like clouds of desert dust wherever he went, this was Leslie Henson at his most fulfilled. He was a droll, a cockney clown, of unmistakable genius. Representing the art of the ridiculous in the theatre, he was at his best when pursuing the golden thread of absurdity through a maze of commonplace situations. His humour was as characteristic of the years in which he flourished as many of the gritty jokes of the television artists reflect the nervous hilarity of a later day. One of the best ways of remembering him is by the widely published photograph of King George VI roaring with laughter at a Henson joke during a performance for the Fleet at Scapa Flow.

The time came, after the war and coinciding with the natural decline in his own powers, when his brand of humour began to stale. The last production in which he may be said to have appeared in a characteristic part, largely of his own fashioning, was *Bob's Your Uncle*, at the Saville Theatre in 1948. Thereafter, he was forced to abandon the musical-comedy eccentricities in which he had made his name and to appear in plays where his inability to create a part otherwise than in terms of his own drollery became a serious handicap. His performances in the revivals of such plays as *1066 and All That* (1947), in *Harvey* (1950), and in the musical play about Samuel Pepys called *And So To Bed* (1951) had only equivocal success.

Like all great comic actors Henson took his work seriously, and he cheerfully accepted the responsibilities which success brought him. He was president of the Royal General Theatrical Fund from 1938 and remained to the last indefatigable in charitable causes.

Henson married in 1919 Madge Saunders, actress; the marriage was dissolved in 1925. His subsequent marriage to Gladys Gunn was also dissolved; and in 1944 he married Mrs. Harriet Martha Day, by whom he had two sons. He died at Harrow Weald 2 December 1957. A portrait by Frank O. Salisbury is in the possession of the family, and one of the actor as Mr. Pepys by Maurice Codner is in the hands of the artist's son.

[*The Times*, 3 and 9 December 1957; Leslie Henson, *My Laugh Story*, 1926, and *Yours Faithfully*, 1948; personal knowledge.]

BASIL DEAN.

HICKS, GEORGE ERNEST (1879–1954), trade-unionist, was born at Vernham Dean, Hampshire, 13 May 1879, the fourth of the nine children of William Hicks, bricklayer, and his wife, Laura Beckingham Clarke. Hicks attended the village school but left at the age of eleven to work with his father. He went to London in 1896 and joined the Pimlico branch of the Operative Bricklayers' Society. Appointed national organizer in 1912, he succeeded in recruiting many new members for his union which elected him general secretary in 1919, in which year he also became president of the newly formed National Federation of Building Trades Operatives. Hicks now took up proposals long delayed by apathy and prejudice to amalgamate the building trade unions. Adopting the slogan 'More unity and fewer unions' he succeeded in uniting the bricklayers' two unions and the Operative Stonemasons' Society in the Amalgamated Union of Building Trade Workers of which he was first general secretary from 1921 to 1940. Over the same period he sat upon the General Council of the Trades Union Congress. As a young man Hicks had been attracted to industrial unionism, akin to syndicalism,

and he continued to hold militant left-wing views; but in his capacity of chairman of the Trades Union Congress in 1926–7, after the failure of the general strike, he spoke with restraint of the need to maintain industrial peace.

A ready and humorous speaker for whom his own early struggles provided a background of conviction and experience, Hicks was an effective propagandist for trade-unionism and for his party which made much use of him on the platform and over a wide field of committee work, international delegation, and working-class education. He was elected Labour member of Parliament for East Woolwich in 1931 and retained his seat until his retirement in 1950. He was parliamentary secretary to the Ministry of Works from November 1940 until May 1945. He was not invited to serve in the Labour administration formed in July 1945. He was appointed C.B.E. in 1946, having declined in 1945 the prime minister's offer to submit his name for a knighthood.

There was a Rabelaisian flavour about Hicks: fat and red-faced in middle age, he indulged, not always wisely, a fondness for eating and drinking and the broad joke. He was twice married: first, in 1897, to Kate Louisa (died 1934), daughter of William Bennett, carpenter, by whom he had one son and two daughters; secondly, in 1938, to Emma Ellen, daughter of James William Arden, stevedore, and widow of Alfred Ellis. He died at Surbiton 19 July 1954. A portrait by Marck Zulauski became the possession of the Amalgamated Union of Building Trade Workers.

[R. W. Postgate, *The Builders' History*, 1923; private information; personal knowledge.]

E. DE NORMANN.

HILL, SIR LEONARD ERSKINE (1866–1952), physiologist, third son of G. B. N. Hill [q.v.], editor of Boswell, was born in Tottenham 2 June 1866. His two elder brothers were Sir Maurice Hill, the judge [q.v.], and Sir Arthur Norman Hill, an authority on shipping problems. His great-grandfather was T. W. Hill [q.v.] and great-uncles were Sir Rowland and Matthew Davenport Hill [qq.v.]. Hill was educated at Haileybury, where his studies were centred on the classics and general literature, with little in mathematics and nothing in experimental science; but he appears to have had some success at rugby football.

Leonard's own wish was to be a farmer; but he accepted his parents' choice of medicine, entering University College, London, for the preliminary science stage of its curriculum. Zoology gave him stimulating contact there with (Sir) Ray Lankester [q.v.]; but he thought that, even then, he was given too little physics and chemistry for his later needs as a physiologist. He duly qualified in medicine in 1889, became M.B. (London) in 1890, and was house-surgeon for a year at University College Hospital. Then he decided in favour of an academic career in physiology, and returned with a Sharpey scholarship to University College, where (Sir) E. A. (Sharpey-) Schafer [q.v.] was then professor. Hill found co-operative opportunity there, with such investigators as (Sir) John Rose Bradford and (Sir) William Bayliss [qq.v.]. His own initiative led to important studies of intra-cranial pressure, blood flow in the brain, and the effects of gravity on the general circulation. Hill began these at University College, partly with Bayliss, and continued them with H. L. Barnard and others at the London Hospital, where he was appointed lecturer on physiology in 1895, and was to become professor when the chair was instituted, but not until 1912. These researches on problems of the circulation provided the theme of his book on *The Physiology and Pathology of the Cerebral Circulation* (1896), based on his Hunterian lectures; and in 1900 he contributed the section on the circulation of the blood to a comprehensive *Text Book of Physiology*, edited by Schafer.

In the early 1900s Hill became engaged, with J. J. R. Macleod [q.v.] and M. Greenwood, in an investigation of the measures required for the safe decompression of deep divers and others who had been exposed to high air-pressures. Another study of the same problem was being undertaken for the Admiralty by J. S. Haldane [q.v.], with J. G. Priestley at Oxford and A. E. Boycott [q.v.] at the Lister Institute. There was agreement in confirming the earlier suggestion of Paul Bert, who had attributed the dangerous symptoms of sudden or rapid decompression to the release of bubbles of nitrogen in the blood-vessels and the tissues. A rather long controversy ensued, however, concerning the best method of avoiding this—the slow, continuous decompression favoured by Hill's team, or the less tedious, stage-wise procedure of Haldane and his associates. The principle of Haldane's method proved, in the end, to be the better; but its application was improved

in important detail by data provided by Hill and his team.

Hill accepted in 1914 the offer of appointment as head of a department of applied physiology, in the then projected National Institute for Medical Research; and he took office early in July of that year. The aims of such a department were obviously congenial to one who combined such ability in the design of simple but adequate methods for obtaining sound physiological data with so conspicuous an interest in the application of these to medical uses, and especially to the maintenance of the conditions of normal health. The almost immediate outbreak of war gave an unusual scope and direction to research enterprises of this kind. After the war, until his retirement in 1930, Hill and his department were engaged in a range of researches, largely designed to determine the significance and the modes of action of fresh air and sunshine in promoting the general health of mankind. His 'Katathermometer' embodied a characteristically simple but effective device for measuring efficiency of ventilation; and his colleague, T. A. Webster, made an important contribution to the discovery, then in progress at the Institute, of the vitamin D, as a product of the ultraviolet irradiation of ergosterol. In general, this final period, of sixteen years, gave Hill the opportunity of designing, advocating, and supervising practical applications of knowledge which he had gathered and interpreted during the preceding twenty-two years of active experimental research, largely concerned with the physiology of the circulatory and respiratory systems.

Hill's interests and abilities extended to more than one of the arts. He wrote two story-books for children which were published and well received; and, among those who knew them, his paintings in oils, water-colour and pastel, including landscapes, portraits, and studies of animals, were highly esteemed and were shown at a private exhibition. For some reason they were specially admired by Japanese visitors, who came to know them through his friendship with a Japanese artist; with the result that there were three successful exhibitions of his paintings in Japan. In Britain he became the first president of a Medical Art Society.

Hill was elected F.R.S. in 1900 and was knighted in 1930. He was an honorary LL.D. of Aberdeen, a fellow of University College, London, and an honorary

A.R.I.B.A. He received the gold medal of the Institution of Mining Engineers, in recognition of the value of his work for the ventilation of mines, the Harben medal of the Royal Institute of Public Health and Hygiene, and the Sidey medal of the Royal Society of New Zealand for his work on the significance of solar radiation for human health and comfort. He acted as an adviser to the medical organizations of all three armed services.

In 1891 Hill married Janet (died 1956), daughter of Frederick Alexander, a banker; they had four sons and two daughters. The third son, Sir Austin Bradford Hill, F.R.S., became honorary director of the statistical research unit of the Medical Research Council and professor of medical statistics in the university of London. The younger daughter, Nannette, married Dr. W. A. R. Thomson, editor of the *Practitioner*. Hill died at Corton, near Lowestoft, 30 March 1952.

[C. G. Douglas in *Obituary Notices of Fellows of the Royal Society*, No. 22, November 1953; personal knowledge.]   H. H. DALE.

HILL, SIR RODERIC MAXWELL (1894–1954), air chief marshal, was born in Hampstead 1 March 1894, the eldest of the three children of Micaiah John Muller Hill, professor of mathematics at University College, London, and his wife, Minna, daughter of Marriot Ogle Tarbotton, borough engineer of Nottingham. Sir George Francis Hill [q.v.] was his uncle. His obvious scientific and artistic talent was encouraged from an early age. From Bradfield College he went in 1912 to the fine arts department of University College, London, with the intention of becoming an architect. From 1909 onwards, however, he and his younger brother Geoffrey were becoming increasingly absorbed in flying. With money earned by Roderic from drawings published in the *Sphere* they built during 1913, and successfully flew, a glider of their own design. The following year, two months after the outbreak of war, Hill enlisted in the ranks.

Commissioned in the 12th Northumberland Fusiliers in December 1914, Hill was in France by the second half of 1915 and first saw intensive action in the battle of Loos, where he earned a mention in dispatches and suffered a wound in the side. While recovering, he successfully applied to join the Royal Flying Corps. By July 1916 he had earned his wings, shown sufficient ability to be put on the tricky Moranes, and joined No. 60 Squadron, at that time co-operating in the Somme offensive. Hill quickly made his mark as a skilled airman: from repeated patrol and engagements over the German lines he returned unharmed, including 'the first big air battle in history' of 9 November 1916. Shortly after this he was again mentioned in dispatches, and awarded the M.C. In December 1916 he became flight commander of No. 60 Squadron and was promoted captain. His growing reputation as a highly intelligent pilot capable of every aerobatic manœuvre then led to his posting in February 1917 to take over the experimental flying department of the Royal Aircraft Factory (later Establishment) at Farnborough. There his energy, enthusiasm, and skill and calculated daring as a pilot made a deep impression and his test-flying contributed greatly to the eventual success of such aircraft as the S.E.5, the R.E.8, and the D.H.9 with Napier Lion engine. In 1918 he became a squadron leader on the formation of the Royal Air Force, and in the same year was awarded the A.F.C. after flying into a balloon cable to test the efficacy of a newly invented protective device.

Hill remained at Farnborough until 1923, concerned among other matters with test-flying the new larger machines and the development of aids such as wireless direction finding. He was awarded a bar to his A.F.C., the R. M. Groves aeronautical research prize (1922), and elected a fellow of University College, London (1924). After attending the R.A.F. Staff College at Andover, Hill was sent out to command No. 45 (Bomber) Squadron at Hinaidi (1924–6) where he played an important part in the running of the new Baghdad–Cairo air mail and the preservation of the internal and external security of Iraq. He went next to the technical staff of R.A.F. Middle East headquarters at Cairo, but in 1927 was recalled to England to join the directing staff of the R.A.F. Staff College. In 1930–32 he was chief instructor to the Oxford University Air Squadron, receiving an M.A. by decree in 1931. Posted in 1932 to the Air Ministry as head of the newly formed deputy directorate of repair and maintenance, with the rank of group captain, he did much to improve the rudimentary aircraft repair facilities of the time, although his proposal for big civil repair centres to deal with work beyond the capacity of the Service depots was not adopted until later

In 1936 Hill received his first senior command: as air officer commanding

Palestine and Trans-Jordan. His two years there were marked by the great Arab strike of 1936 and by repeated disturbances and Hill co-operated closely and cordially with the army under Generals Dill and Wavell [qq.v.] successively, in the task of maintaining order. He was twice mentioned in dispatches. Back in England by 1938, Hill was appointed to the newly formed directorate of technical development within the Air Ministry; it was typical of him that although by 1939 an air vice-marshal he soon created an opportunity to fly the new advanced fighters: the Hurricane and the Spitfire. On the outbreak of war he was sent to Canada and the United States as the R.A.F. representative on the British Purchasing Mission, but by December 1939 he was back in the Air Ministry. In May 1940 his department transferred to the newly created Ministry of Aircraft Production. Although in temperament and character he had little in common with Lord Beaverbrook, he was able to remain on terms with his exacting chief, and later in 1940 he became director-general of research and development with the acting rank of air marshal. Among other valuable decisions in this post he insisted, against his chief's opinion, on persevering with cannon as the weapon to supersede machine-guns in Spitfires, and finally saw the initial problems of mounting and jamming successfully overcome.

In 1941 Hill was selected, to his disappointment, to be controller of technical services with the British Air Commission in the United States. He found, however, that he greatly enjoyed his American contacts and he did much useful work in ensuring that American aircraft arrived in Britain with equipment consonant to R.A.F. requirements. He was also an ideal vehicle for the exchange of technical information over a wide field, and among his achievements must be counted his part in persuading the Americans to make far greater provision for armament, including gun-turrets, in their heavy bombers than they had originally intended. He was appointed C.B. in 1941, and when the problems of the commission greatly eased after America's entry into the war, Hill asked to return home. He reluctantly accepted the post of commandant of the R.A.F. Staff College (1942–3), for which he was an ideal choice. But he was now clearly moving far away from the senior operational command he greatly desired. Retirement, indeed, was suggested to him; but such powerful personalities as Sir Guy Garrod and Sir Trafford Leigh-Mallory [q.v.] intervened. Although he had no direct experience of wartime operations, and was generally regarded as perhaps too quiet, too unaggressive, and too long habituated to technical posts to make an outstanding commander, Hill was given his chance with the command of No. 12 (Fighter) Group covering the eastern counties and the Midlands (July 1943).

So successful was he that only four months later he became air marshal commanding, Air Defence of Great Britain, with the main task of defending Britain from German air attack whilst the allied invasion of the continent was being prepared and launched. During the preparatory period he was entirely successful: the only sustained German air attack by night, the 'little blitz' on London in January–March 1944, achieved negligible results and German reconnaissance by day was consistently restricted. Meantime attack by flying bombs had been foreseen for some months and in December 1943 Hill had submitted a plan which basically envisaged defence in three successive zones: by the British fighters in the coastal areas, by the anti-aircraft guns in the folds of the North Downs (where their radar would be reasonably immune from jamming), and by a balloon barrage behind the guns. There would also, however, be guns at some vital points on the coast, and the fighters could enter the gun-belt either in good weather (when they would have priority) or when in actual pursuit of a bomb.

The first flying bombs were launched on 13 June 1944 and within a few days Hill's forces were deployed. Although results were not discreditable, far too many flying bombs were getting through. Only Hill's most modern fighters were fast enough to overtake the bombs; and misunderstandings were frequent between the guns and the fighters, with the result that the latter were sometimes coming under British fire. On 16 July Hill took a most courageous decision. Convinced by his own leading staff officers and by Sir Robert Watson-Watt, he ordered, without reference to the Air Ministry or to his superior, Leigh-Mallory, who was in France, a complete redeployment and segregation of the defences: the guns would take over the coastal belt, and the fighters operate in advance of them out to sea and behind them in the North Downs

area. A few hours later, some 23,000 men and women were on the move, just before they had become so firmly rooted in the original dispositions as to make such a switch impracticable. The move, which gave much greater freedom of action to the guns and enabled them to take full advantage of the new proximity fuses, was of course very acceptable to Sir Frederick Pile, the commander-in-chief Anti-Aircraft Command; but the Air Ministry disapproved and intimated to Hill that he had exceeded his powers and that his professional reputation would stand or fall by the outcome. For a few days, as the move proceeded, the casualties inflicted on the enemy declined; but thereafter they mounted steadily, with the guns beginning to claim the lion's share, and by 6 September it was clear that the main threat was defeated, even if individual flying bombs continued to get through. On that day the Air Council sent Hill their warm congratulations on the 'imaginative deployment of the defences to meet each phase of the attack as it developed'. The redeployment, one of the most dramatic and effective moves of the war, and one which saved London from a far worse bombardment than it received, was not Hill's own idea; but it was his decision, undertaken on his responsibility, and its successful outcome was accordingly his victory. He was appointed K.C.B. in 1944.

Throughout 1944 Hill was much concerned with plans for setting up the new Central Fighter Establishment. Towards the end of the year his command reverted to its old name of Fighter Command and Hill remained in charge until the final surrender of Germany. In May 1945 he became Air Council member for training, and the following year was appointed principal air aide-de-camp to the King. Meantime he was also acting as chairman of a committee on the future of the Technical Branch of the R.A.F. Among its recommendations, accepted in 1946, was the establishment of an expanded and distinctive Technical Branch as part of a three-pronged organization on the same footing as the existing Operational and Administrative branches. The new branch was to be headed and represented on the Air Council by an air member for technical services and this position Hill, though he was not and never had been a technical officer, was pressed to accept so strongly that he could hardly refuse. He took up this new post in January 1947 with the

rank of air chief marshal and retained it until July 1948 when he retired from the Service to become rector of the Imperial College of Science and Technology. To the last he had continued to fly—he had opened fire on a flying bomb from his Tempest—and the final entries in his pilot's log-book reveal that his appetite for flying was still as ardent as ever.

Although Hill was not a scientist and had never occupied an academic post, his links with distinguished scientists were close and he brought to his new post a determination to understand the problems of every department of the College and the desire to serve it to the full. His open-mindedness and intelligence made him an immediate success and he was able to give powerful help to the College in at least two directions—in its expansion and in a fruitful scheme to widen the interests of the students by the provision of lunch-hour concerts, illustrated lectures on the arts, and week-end study groups. In 1955 he was nominated vice-chancellor of London University, but ill health obliged him to resign in the following year before he had completed his term of office. He died in London 6 October 1954.

In 1917 Hill married Mabel Helen Catherine, daughter of Lieutenant-Colonel Edward Ross Morton, Indian Army; they had a son, killed in action in 1944, and two daughters. As a personality Hill was notable for his modesty, his rather shy and self-conscious air, and his quiet charm. He was above medium height, spare and very active. His alertness of mind, breadth of knowledge, interests and sympathy, and absence of any kind of pompousness or 'side' made an immediately favourable impression on nearly everyone who met him.

A portrait by Rodrigo Moynihan is in the Imperial War Museum.

[Sir Walter Raleigh and H. A. Jones, (Official History) *The War in the Air*, 6 vols., 1922–37; Denis Richards and Hilary St. George Saunders, *Royal Air Force 1939–45*, 3 vols., 1953–4; Basil Collier, (Official) *History of the Second World War. The Defence of the United Kingdom*, 1957; Prudence Hill, *To Know the Sky*, 1962; private information; personal knowledge.]   DENIS RICHARDS.

HILTON, JAMES (1900–1954), novelist, the only child of John Hilton and his wife, Elizabeth Burch, was born 9 September 1900 at Leigh, Lancashire, where his mother, before her marriage, had been a schoolmistress. John Hilton was at that time assistant master at the Forest Road elementary school, Walthamstow, and in 1902 became the first headmaster of the Chapel End elementary school, Walthamstow, where he remained until he retired at the age of sixty. He died in 1955. James Hilton was educated in Walthamstow at the Maynard Road elementary school and the Sir George Monoux Grammar School. He went on to the Leys School and Christ's College, Cambridge, where he obtained a second class in part i of the history tripos (1920) and a first class in the English tripos (1921).

While still at Cambridge he distinguished himself by publishing his first novel, *Catherine Herself* (1920), and by occasional contributions to the *Manchester Guardian*. Fortified by these achievements he spent the ten years after his graduation at home, turning out with great industry a number of novels which do not now survive in print and which he did not acknowledge when he came to fame. Nevertheless, they served as a whetstone to the mechanics of his writing, and two of the novels of this period, *Contango* (1932) and *Knight Without Armour* (1933), repay rereading.

Lost Horizon, James Hilton's first world-wide success, was published in 1933, and in the following year was awarded the Hawthornden prize. Its success led indirectly to his second great triumph. Commissioned by the *British Weekly* in 1933 to write a story for their Christmas number, he wrote in the short space of four days the 18,000 words of *Good-Bye Mr. Chips*. Its success when it was published in book form in 1934 was immediate. In this 'old-boy's-eye-view' of masters and boys at an English school the tender portrait of his father which he paints is not more exact than the reflection which he unconsciously gives of himself. This peculiarly English story might be thought to have had a limited appeal in the United States where it was published in the same year, but that would be to overlook the vein of sentiment, wholly admirable, which informs the story, and the wholeheartedness always of American response to this vein. Alexander Woollcott, then of great influence as a critic, eulogized the book, and soon America was devouring it.

James Hilton's talent—so amply demonstrated in *Good-Bye Mr. Chips*, though observable in Chang in *Lost Horizon*, and elsewhere—a talent for evoking the finer feelings in his readers,

for making people feel better about other people, for underscoring the praiseworthy virtues, was not overlooked in Hollywood. He was invited there to assist in the filming of his own books; he remained to write other scenarios; and when he was awarded the Hollywood Motion Picture Academy writing award for his script of *Mrs. Miniver*, he was said to be the highest-paid scenario writer in Hollywood.

Although actively engaged in this and radio work, he continued to publish novels at regular intervals, among them *Random Harvest* (1941), *The Story of Dr. Wassell* (1944), *So Well Remembered* (1947), *Nothing So Strange* (1948), *Morning Journey* (1951), and *Time and Time Again* (1953). While excellent by the standards of contemporary fiction, they showed in increasing degree the result of too close a contact with Hollywood, and too long an absence from England, which was the background of every story except one. They were suited to the popular taste and had an immense success on both sides of the Atlantic; but of his work only *Lost Horizon*, which has given the word Shangri-La to the English language, and *Good-Bye Mr. Chips* are likely to remain of interest.

James Hilton was a good-looking man with dark intelligent eyes, a warm, pleasant voice, and a charm of manner which won him considerable success in the last years of his life in a weekly programme on the American radio. He married twice; both marriages were dissolved; and he had no children. He died at Long Beach, California, 20 December 1954.

[Private information; personal knowledge.]
LOVAT DICKSON.

HIND, ARTHUR MAYGER (1880–1957), historian of engraving, was born at Horninglow, Burton-on-Trent, 26 August 1880, the second son of Henry Robert Hind, schoolmaster, by his wife, Sarah Mayger. He was educated at the City of London School and Emmanuel College, Cambridge, where he obtained first class honours in part i of the classical tripos of 1902. In the following year, after studying at Dresden under Max Lehrs, the distinguished authority on early German engraving, he entered the department of prints and drawings of the British Museum as an assistant, the equivalent of the later assistant keeper. His first important employment there was to help (Sir) Sidney Colvin [q.v.] in the preparation of a volume on native and foreign line-engravers in England from the time of Henry VIII to the Commonwealth, to which he contributed the lists of the works of the engravers. This was published by the trustees of the British Museum in 1905. Of greater intrinsic importance was the *Catalogue of Early Italian Engravings in the British Museum* issued in 1910 under the editorship of Colvin, but virtually the work of Hind. Many years later he returned to this subject to compile a complete illustrated corpus of all existing Italian engravings of the fifteenth century, which is certain to endure as the standard work in this field. The first part appeared in 1938 in four massive and finely produced volumes, but the second part (3 vols., 1948) was delayed by the war.

Although this corpus of Italian engraving was Hind's most impressive contribution to the material for the study of art, it was by no means the only one. Already by 1908 he had produced the useful *Short History of Engraving and Etching*, which went into a third edition (1923). He also compiled what on the whole remains the most satisfactory catalogue of Rembrandt's etchings. This first appeared in 1912 and was revised and reissued in 1923. His *Introduction to a History of Woodcut*, originally intended as a companion volume to the *History of Engraving and Etching*, did not appear until 1935 and then in two bulky volumes covered only the fifteenth century.

In the meantime Hind had turned his attention to the study of drawings and had projected a complete catalogue of the extensive series of those by Dutch and Flemish artists in the British Museum. The first volume dealt with the drawings of Rembrandt and his school and appeared in 1915. There followed a second on Rubens and his school in 1923 and finally in 1926 and 1931 two volumes of the Dutch drawings of the seventeenth century arranged in an alphabetical sequence. Although many of the conclusions reached in these volumes have been modified, they formed the basis and provided the data for such modifications. Indeed, it was characteristic of Hind that he was content to provide the material for further research and never resented, indeed welcomed, the rectification of any errors he might have committed. He was also a pioneer in the study of the drawings of Claude Lorrain, producing an admirable official handlist of the incomparable series of his drawings in the

British Museum (1926) and a book of plates a year earlier.

In 1933 he succeeded Laurence Binyon [q.v.] as keeper of the department of prints and drawings and retired in 1945. Realizing after his retirement that opportunities for travel and research would be lacking, Hind decided to devote his time to a more elaborate study of early English engraving. With undiminished energy he accordingly embarked on *Engraving in England in the Sixteenth and Seventeenth Centuries*, the first volume of which appeared in 1952, a second in 1955, while a third which had not been completed at his death in 1957 was published in 1964. This laborious undertaking, useful as it is, is valuable rather to the historian and bibliographer than to the student of art history.

Hind served from 1915 to 1918 in the Army Service Corps, being three times mentioned in dispatches, reaching the rank of major, and being appointed O.B.E. in 1918. He was an honorary LL.D. of Glasgow (1945), Slade professor of fine art at Oxford (1921–7), Charles Eliot Norton professor at Harvard (1930–31), and a Leverhulme research fellow (1945). His Harvard lectures on landscape design with special reference to Rembrandt, expanded into a book under the title of *Rembrandt*, were published in 1932, and contained in the final chapter a statement of his own artistic beliefs. In spite of his numerous accomplishments Hind was aware of his own limitations. He never professed to be infallible, even on the subject of early Italian engraving, and was always ready, perhaps too ready, to rely on the judgement of other 'experts' which may have been less sound than his own.

Two enthusiasms engrossed Hind's leisure, drawing and music. It was in fact uncertain at the beginning of his career whether he should devote himself professionally to the latter; and he liked to describe himself as a landscape painter rather than as a museum official. Competent, delicate, and sensitive as was much of his work as a landscape draughtsman, it lacked that spark of inspiration and originality which could raise it above the level of gifted amateurism. As a musician he was an extremely accomplished performer on the viola and violin. The concerts which he and his wife and daughters were in the habit of giving in their home were a source of great pleasure to himself and satisfaction to his audience.

He married in 1912 Dorothy Alice

Pakington, third daughter of the third Lord Hampton, by whom he had three daughters, all of whom became professional musicians. He died at Henley-on-Thames 22 May 1957.

A portrait drawing by Francis Dodd is in the print room of the British Museum and one by Leonid Pasternak is in the possession of the family.

[*The Times*, 23 May 1957; *Burlington Magazine*, vol. xcix, July 1957; private information; personal knowledge.] A. E. POPHAM

HIRST, FRANCIS WRIGLEY (1873–1953), economist and Liberal writer, was born 10 June 1873 at Huddersfield, the third child in a family of five born to a prosperous wool-stapler, Alfred Hirst, and his wife, Mary Wrigley. He was brought up in one of those rectory-style houses, with the appurtenances of glebe and livestock, which were in those days freely sprinkled among the industrial towns of the north. Through his mother he was a second cousin of H. H. Asquith. He was proud of his Yorkshire origins, and through life he showed the world the intellectual justification for the sturdy Yorkshire quality of thrift. He was educated at Clifton, when J. M. Wilson [q.v.] was headmaster, and was sent to the house of W. W. Asquith, elder brother of the future prime minister. The teaching of classics at the school was at that time deservedly renowned, and in 1891 Hirst was awarded an open scholarship in classics to Wadham College, Oxford. He took firsts in honour moderations (1894) and *literae humaniores* (1896) and in the latter year was elected president of the Union. He was awarded the Cobden prize in 1899. With C. B. Fry, J. A. (later Viscount) Simon, and F. E. Smith (later the Earl of Birkenhead) [qq.v.], Hirst made a quaternity varied in accomplishments but uniform in distinction which stood out the more clearly from the comparative smallness of Wadham.

In 1896 Hirst entered the London School of Economics and in 1899 he was called to the bar by the Inner Temple. He did not prosper and perhaps his essentially reflective mind, which in private life enjoyed refining issues and conceding points to those with whom he disputed, was not the true weapon for the courts. More certain and conspicuous was his talent for writing. He was fond of saying that as a writer he was only an amateur but that he had been enormously helped by his constant companions—the great writers of Greece and Rome. He was no

doubt also helped by a dictum of Lord Morley [q.v.] which he was fond of quoting—'The first business of a writer is to make his meaning plain. Style without lucidity is an offence.' He had himself a brisk and lively style of writing, was endowed with a great inquisitiveness about a great variety of subjects, and consequently had curious pockets of information. He wisely decided not to neglect these talents for the long drudgery and an uncertain career at the bar.

At the end of his time at Oxford Hirst had contributed the chapter 'Liberalism and Wealth' to *Essays in Liberalism* by Six Oxford Men (1897) of which he was also joint-editor. The book was noticed by the Liberal leaders, and partly for that reason and partly because Hirst had contributed to a popular life of Gladstone, he was asked by Morley, who was just starting the official biography of Gladstone, to help him in going through the papers at Hawarden. Perhaps the most important aspect of this task was that it brought him under the influence of Morley, whom he understood and intensely admired. He was a faithful disciple of that enigmatic character all his life, and, like him, showed the same unswerving attachment to principles fashioned in youth but fortified by reason. Some words which he himself once used of Morley could certainly be used of Hirst: 'Beneath a fine tolerance and affability in the society of friends from whom he differed, lay a stern fidelity to unfashionable principles, a grim loyalty to desperate causes.'

The outbreak of the South African war and the anti-imperial feelings which accompanied it gave Hirst a fair wind favourable to his opinions. He took an active part in forming the League against Imperialism and Militarism. At the same time he wrote regularly for the *Speaker* which, with the august approval of Morley in the background and with J. L. Hammond [q.v.] as editor, enjoyed remarkable influence though not complete solvency. The youthful editor and Hirst delighted in pricking the sensitive skins of such diverse supporters of the war as Milner, Rosebery, Beatrice Webb, and G. B. Shaw [qq.v.]. When Hammond gave up the editorship in 1907 the company owning the paper went into liquidation, but from its ashes emerged the *Nation* under the editorship of H. W. Massingham [q.v.], and in these negotiations Hirst played some part. He was always a welcome guest at those luncheons held in the National Liberal

Club where radical opinions were launched to sail far beyond the shining walls of that club. The controversies of the war had no sooner died down than the emergence of tariff reform gave Hirst another topic uppermost in political minds which he was peculiarly equipped to meet. He was largely responsible for *Fact versus Fiction* (1904) which was the answer of the Cobden Club to the 'raging, tearing campaign' of Joseph Chamberlain [q.v.]. In 1904 Hirst contributed a biography of Adam Smith to the 'English Men of Letters' series, and appropriately it was the last volume under the editorship of Morley. In 1906 he published anonymously *Arbiter in Council*, an analysis of the follies of war principally from the economic aspect; this was in dialogue form and perhaps owed a little to Landor's *Imaginary Conversations*. His book on the Stock Exchange in the Home University Library was published in 1911.

In 1907 Hirst was appointed editor of *The Economist*. When he succeeded to the chair a great part of the writing of the paper was done by divers hands outside. He made the decision to write all the policy leaders himself, and on foreign affairs these were highly critical of Sir Edward Grey (later Viscount Grey of Fallodon, q.v.), as was perhaps only to be expected from such a doughty opponent of the Liberal League. He also recruited a competent staff, and among others he gathered round him were Hilton Young (later Lord Kennet, q.v.), Mary Agnes Hamilton, Walter (later Lord) Layton, Joseph Redlich (afterwards the Austrian minister of education), Luigi Einaudi (afterwards president of the Italian Republic), and Dudley Ward. The influence of the paper decidedly increased under his editorship, but in a changing world he allowed no deviation from the traditional principles of peace, economy, and individual liberty. Adherence to such views made his tenure of office difficult after 1914, and he resigned in the summer of 1916. Hirst seems to have believed—and he was probably right—that some pressure from outside brought about the end of his editorship. His valedictory leading article said: 'Since the war began, the function of an editor who believes that truth and patriotism ought to be reconciled has been difficult and even hazardous.' His fall in 1916 has tended to obscure his important reforms and innovations in the conduct of the paper. Moreover his resignation marks the close of what the world—with a charac-

teristic surface judgement—might call hi success. For the remainder of his life h was a critic not a performer, a cautionar voice crying in the political wilderness But the bitterness which tends to afflic mankind in this position he never showed he was always good-humoured, alway unruffled.

In this period Hirst wrote severa books; the most successful were a bio graphy of Thomas Jefferson (1926), th *Early Life and Letters of John Morle* (2 vols., 1927) and the introduction t Morley's *Memorandum on Resignation* published in 1928, *Gladstone as Financie and Economist* (1931), *Wall Street and Lom bard Street* (1931), *Liberty and Tyrann* (1935), and *Economic Freedom and Privat Property* (1935). He also maintained remarkable output of articles includin many effective letters to *The Times*; h was a governor of the London School o Economics; he paid a number of visits t the United States where his writings wer always read with respect and where hi sister Beatrice was professor of classic in Barnard College, Columbia University His views were of course completely a variance with the then fashionable schoo of economists emerging from Cambridg under J. M. (later Lord) Keynes [q.v.] Sir Roy Harrod, espousing, perhaps a littl brusquely, the cause of those attacked b Hirst, has said that Hirst's criticisms wer quite shallow although delightfully pre sented. No doubt that should be state and was the opinion of several of th younger men. But Hirst was not disturbe by being thought outmoded.

In January 1910 he had stood for Sout Suffolk and in 1929 he stood for Shipley polling the sizeable vote for a Liberal o 11,712. But after 1929 he moved awa from the official leadership of the part and sharpened his difference by support ing the Munich agreement. Later he use to refer to the welfare State as th Beveridge hoax. He was for a period con nected with Sir Ernest Benn [q.v.] an the Individualists, but he found this bod more conservative than he had suppose and withdrew to his old position of isola tion towards the end of the war of 1939 45. With a character which was in som particulars old-fashioned but was dis played by a personality of great originalit Hirst, in maturity, won the respect o younger generations. He was made a honorary fellow of his old college, unde the genial sway of Sir Maurice Bowra after the second war, and delighted th common-room on one occasion by interrupting an anecdote of Lord Simon with the remark 'Oh yes, he was the man who kept his secretary in a grandfather clock.' On another occasion he brought a discussion of Morley's wife to an end with the information that 'she was a good walker'. He was a keen, if unorthodox, fisherman using his own fly, known as Hirst's fancy. His personal affinities with the great days of Liberalism were strong as he married Cobden's great-niece, Helena Cobden, in 1903, and latterly lived in Cobden's old home, Dunford House, in Sussex. He had no children.

Although Hirst's career may seem somewhat disappointing—a falling off from the spirited start—he had the compensations which consistency can give and the knowledge that he possessed the warm attachment of a wide circle of friends and admirers. He was a delightful companion —attentive to what was said to him and in return generally arresting and always sympathetic. His friend, E. C. Bentley [q.v.], said that in youth Hirst 'looked like a very able, good-humoured, hardheaded man of about thirty'. He looked exactly the same almost all his life. He died at Singleton in Sussex 22 February 1953.

[*F. W. Hirst, By His Friends*, 1958; F. W. Hirst, *In the Golden Days*, 1947; *The Economist 1843–1943, A Centenary Volume*, 1943; J. W. Robertson Scott, *Life and Death of a Newspaper*, 1952; E. C. Bentley, *Those Days*, 1940; Sir C. M. Bowra, *Memories*, 1966; private information.]   ROGER FULFORD.

HIRST, GEORGE HERBERT (1871–1954), cricketer, was born at Kirkheaton, near Huddersfield, 7 September 1871, the son of Mary Elizabeth Woolhouse. He left school at the age of ten and worked first as a hand-loom weaver and then at a neighbouring dye-works. By the time he was fifteen he was in the village eleven and frequently winning the prizes offered by a Sunday newspaper for outstanding feats in local cricket.

His subsequent performances for stronger clubs like Elland, Mirfield, and Huddersfield came to official notice and he had his first trial for the county in 1889. After a few games in 1892 he established himself in the Yorkshire side in 1893 by taking 99 wickets for 14·39, an average he bettered only once in his long career. So far he had been a tail-end batsman notable for defiance in a crisis, but in 1894 he made his first century, 115 not out against Gloucestershire, and with 98 wickets was again unlucky to miss the bowler's 'century' by a small margin. Next year he made sure of it with 150 wickets, and in 1896 he achieved the 'double' of over 1,000 runs and 100 wickets for the first time.

A stocky, powerfully-built man, Hirst bowled left-arm at above medium pace. At this time he was a useful rather than a great bowler, and with an average of only 60 wickets a season between 1898 and 1900, his bowling seemed to be declining as his batting steadily advanced. But while practising for the 1901 season he discovered the swerve which made him in English conditions one of the most dangerous bowlers in the game's history. He was able to make the ball dip into the batsman so sharply that one of his victims felt that 'it came at you like a hard throw from cover'. Many times he broke the back of an innings by removing the opening batsmen almost before they reached the crease, and H. S. Altham has written that his bowling had 'a resiliency, vigour, and optimism which from the very outset claimed from the batsmen the moral supremacy; and with all his pace and peculiarity of flight, his length was singularly accurate'.

He batted right-handed, and was so quick of foot and eye that it was difficult to find a length to inhibit his favourite strokes, the hook and the pull. Naturally pugnacious, he revelled in crisis; and when for a time he was obliged by the gravity of an occasion to restrain his aggressive instincts, he would finally break loose into a frenzy of hitting which rapidly turned an unpromising into a winning position.

The hard facts of his career tell a remarkable story of all-round accomplishment. Altogether he made 36,203 runs for an average of 34·05 and took 2,727 wickets for 18·77. He also made 601 catches, mostly at mid-off; and he probably caught more catches in front of the wicket than any other player.

He did the 'double' 14 times, a figure beaten only by his Yorkshire colleague Wilfred Rhodes (16). He made 1,000 runs 19 times, including totals of over 2,000 in consecutive seasons, 1904–6; he scored 60 centuries, of which the highest was 341 against Leicestershire in 1905 (it contained a six and 53 fours and is still a Yorkshire record); he played three other innings of over 200, and apart from his centuries had two hundred other scores over 50; against Somerset in 1906 he made a century in each innings and also took eleven wickets in the match.

As a bowler he had nine wickets in an innings on four occasions, the best being 9–23 (eight bowled) against Lancashire in 1910. His two hat-tricks were both against Leicestershire (1895 and 1907), against whom he took 12–66 in 1906 and 15–63 (his largest total) in 1907.

Hirst's supreme achievement was in 1906, when he made 2,385 runs (average 45·86) and took 208 wickets for 16·50. This has never been, and in an age of increasing specialization it is unlikely that it ever will be, equalled. When asked himself whether he thought that his record would be surpassed, Hirst replied: 'I don't know, but whoever does it will be very tired.' During a summer in which he reached his thirty-fifth birthday he had played 58 innings and bowled 7,837 balls.

For such a remarkable county cricketer Hirst's performance in test cricket was surprisingly modest. He toured Australia in 1897–8 and again in 1903–4, and although he played in nine tests he achieved little. The conditions did not suit his bowling and on Australian pitches his fondness for the hook was often his undoing. At home he played in each series between 1899 and 1909, and his two best performances were against J. Darling's 1902 team. At Birmingham he took 3–15 when Australia were dismissed for 36, their lowest score against England (and in their next match, at Leeds, Yorkshire put them out for 23, Hirst taking 5–9). He was omitted at Manchester, where Australia won the match and the rubber by 3 runs, but he was restored at the Oval, where the finish was equally dramatic. His first innings of 43 helped to save the follow-on, and then after an astonishing innings of 104 by G. L. Jessop [q.v.] he made 58 not out to win the match by one wicket. When his Yorkshire partner Rhodes came in at number eleven, 15 runs were needed. Legend has it that Hirst said, 'Wilfred, we'll get them in ones': as, after a hair-raising 45 minutes, they did.

When cricket was resumed after the war Hirst was nearly forty-eight, but in 1919 he made the first century of the season at Lord's: 180 not out after M.C.C. had led Yorkshire by 368. He followed this with 80 against Cambridge University and 120 off both Essex and Warwickshire, but he could not sustain this prolific rate of scoring and he was no longer an effective bowler. During the summer he accepted an invitation to become chief coach at Eton. He continued to play for Yorkshire during his vacations in 1920–21, but on his fiftieth birthday he retired from first-class cricket (apart from an ill-advised appearance during the Scarborough Festival in 1929) after leading the Players to victory against the Gentlemen. In acknowledging a warm-hearted ovation he merely hoped that those who followed him in the game would get as much pleasure from it as he had; adding that if they were all-rounders they would enjoy themselves twice as much.

During his eighteen years at Eton the school was never defeated at Lord's; and during the holidays he also coached the up-and-coming players of his old county. All the captains under whom he served regarded Hirst as the ideal professional cricketer, disciplined, good-tempered, and unfailingly loyal. The public's regard for him was shown at his benefit match in 1904, from which he received £3,703 a very large sum in the money values of the time, and it was exceeded only once before 1947. When in 1949 twenty-six former professionals were nominated to honorary membership of the M.C.C., Hirst was deservedly of their number.

In 1896 Hirst married Emma, daughter of George Kilner, a miner; they had one son and two daughters. He died at his home in Huddersfield 10 May 1954.

[*Wisden's Cricketers' Almanack*, 1955; A. A. Thomson, *Hirst and Rhodes*, 1959; Roy Webber, *Cricket Records*, 1961; H. S. Altham, *A History of Cricket*, vol. i, 1962.]

M. M. REESE

HITCHCOCK, SIR ELDRED FREDERICK (1887–1959), man of business, was born in Islington, London, 9 December, 1887, the eldest, with his twin sister Effie, of seven children of Eldred Hitchcock, superintendent of Dr. Barnardo's Home, Epsom, by his wife Louisa Naomi Orchard. He was educated at Burford Grammar School and in 1910 obtained a diploma in economics from the university of Oxford. He had become attracted to Fabian socialism and shortly afterwards became secretary of Toynbee Hall, being appointed warden in 1917. During the war of 1914–18 he served as a government wool statistician in the War Office and became deputy director of wool textile production. In the course of this work he had to visit a number of countries including Russia, and received from the Tsarist Government the Order of St. Stanislas. He was appointed C.B.E. in 1920.

In 1919 Hitchcock resigned the wardenship of Toynbee Hall and went into business on his own account, engaging (with varying degrees of success) in a multiplicity of activities, including a travel agency which brought him to the brink of disaster. In 1926 he acquired a block of shares in the sisal company which later became known as Bird & Co (Africa), Ltd. This gradually became his major interest, and after a few years he was elected to the board. He went to Tanganyika in 1937, and in 1939 took over the managing directorship of the company's sisal estates there, becoming also chairman of the company in 1950. He was appointed chairman of the Tanganyika Sisal Growers Association in 1946, and from that year until his death he was never out of office, either as chairman or vice-chairman; he was throughout this period unquestionably the most dominating personality in the industry. Late in life he turned his attention also to tea, and started a tea estate 3,000 feet up in the Usambara Mountains; this could not be counted among the more successful of his ventures.

During most of the war of 1939–45 and the early post-war period ending in 1948, when all Tanganyika sisal was bought by the British Government, Hitchcock acted as negotiator on behalf of the sisal industry with the various government departments concerned (the Treasury, Board of Trade, and Colonial Office); and by using all his qualities of skill in marshalling statistical data and argument, and by his pertinacity, he undoubtedly secured a much better deal for the sisal growers than would otherwise have fallen to their lot. In 1949 he established the voluntary selling organization known as the Tanganyika Sisal Marketing Association, which at the time of his death was marketing a little over half the sisal production of Tanganyika. Many of the smaller estates enrolled in it, and it has served them well.

Always an important figure in public affairs in Tanganyika, with the advent of Sir Edward (later Lord) Twining as governor, Hitchcock placed himself wholeheartedly behind the new policy of political evolution based on racial parity. In 1955 he accepted nomination to membership of the legislative council; but he was neither happy nor effective in that capacity and took the first opportunity of resigning.

Hitchcock was short in stature, pugnacious and rather aggressive by disposition, and he had a highly dynamic personality; when roused to anger he was often outrageously rude. In a number of ways he was a strange mixture. He could be extremely ruthless in achieving his ends; and there was a streak of vulgarity in his make-up which was apt to alienate those who did not know him well. On the other hand, he was conspicuously loyal to his friends and subordinates, and most warmhearted and generous; on many occasions in the course of his life he came to the rescue of persons who had suffered injustice or unmerited misfortune. He took great pains after 1945 to track down Dr. Richard Hindorff, a German who had introduced *agave sisalana* into Tanganyika in 1892, whom he found eventually, living in Berlin in dire poverty; he arranged for him to receive a pension for his remaining years from the Tanganyika Sisal Growers Association.

Hitchcock had a deep instinctive feeling for the visual arts, and his collection of medieval Islamic pottery was probably the best in private hands. He took an especial interest in the archaeology of Tanganyika; and it was owing to his influence that a department of antiquities was established and that the interest of leading authorities such as Sir Mortimer Wheeler was aroused. His election as a fellow of the Society of Antiquaries in 1957 was an honour which gave him immense pleasure.

Amongst his other activities Hitchcock founded a business called Sculptures and Memorials, not primarily for profit, but in order to raise the standard of memorials in English churchyards, partly by replacing Italian marble by English stones and by improving the lettering. A further motive was the desire (which proved successful) to secure more commissions for British sculptors, amongst whom he had some close friends, notably Eric Gill and Gilbert Ledward [qq.v.].

Hitchcock was knighted in 1955. He married in 1915 Ethel May ('Pat') Cooper (died 1956), daughter of Adolphus Frederick William Lorie, a New Zealand sheep farmer, and had a daughter and a son. He died in Tanga 6 April 1959 and his ashes were strewn in the churchyard of Burford church in which at his own expense he had a chapel admirably restored.

A portrait of Hitchcock by Harold Knight remained in Tanganyika.

[*The Times*, 7 April 1959; personal knowledge.]   C. W. GUILLEBAUD.

Hoare, R. H.

HOARE, SIR REGINALD HERVEY
(1882–1954), diplomatist, the fourth and
youngest son of Charles Hoare, senior
partner of Hoare's Bank, and his wife,
Katharine Patience Georgiana, daughter
of Lord Arthur Hervey, bishop of Bath and
Wells [q.v.], was born at Minley Manor,
Hampshire, 19 July 1882. He was educated
at Eton where he was in the eleven in 1901,
and entered the diplomatic service in 1905.

Between 1909 and 1918 he served
successively in Rome, Peking, and
Petrograd, returning to Russia in 1918
as secretary to the special mission to
Archangel headed by (Sir) Francis Lindley
[q.v.]. After short spells of service in the
Foreign Office, Warsaw, and Peking, he
was in 1924 appointed counsellor to the
embassy in Turkey where he remained
for four years. The period was one of
turmoil and crisis in Turkish interior
affairs as Mustapha Kemal consolidated
his authority in the opening years of the
republic, but in foreign relations the years
1924–8 were ones of relative calm, with
the exception of the Mosul crisis. Following
the Kurdish revolt of 1925, the Turkish
Government asserted its claim to this
former Ottoman possession. The dispute
was referred to the League of Nations
which in December 1925 upheld the
British contention that the Mosul province
should form part of Iraq, a decision in
which Mustapha Kemal acquiesced in
June 1926. To Hoare, who frequently
acted as chargé d'affaires, some of the
credit for this is due; he was appointed
C.M.G. in the same year.

After three years in Egypt where he
served under Lord Lloyd [q.v.] and Sir
Percy Loraine, Hoare was appointed
minister to Tehran in 1931. He came to a
difficult task. During the war of 1914–18
and especially after the Russian revolution British influence in Persia had increased, by force of circumstances, to an
extent which was resented by the Persians
and wholly unwelcome to successive
British Governments. The British aim was
to be in treaty relations with a self-reliant
and friendly Persia which would safeguard
the rapidly expanding interests of the
Anglo-Persian Oil Company. No privilege
was asked beyond a guarantee of the
company's contract and the right of ships
of the Royal Navy to call at the Gulf
port of Bushire. Hoare's predecessors had
already abdicated the major part of the
quasi-imperial British position, but in
spite of the strong British support given
at the time of his rise to power to the

maker of modern Persia, Reza Shah
Pahlevi, the latter and his Government
remained suspicious of British intentions.
No treaty had been signed when Hoare
arrived in Tehran and he made it quite
plain that he was in no hurry. His aim was
to restore calm to a situation which had
grown feverish. In 1932 the Persian
Government attempted a final show-down
with the British and cancelled the oil
concession. Hoare, influenced perhaps by
his Turkish experiences, advised his
Government to refer the matter immediately to the League of Nations. This was
done, resulting in a new contract between
the company and the Persian Government
being signed the next year. To the chagrin
of the extremists the show-down ended
quietly, without a breach in relations or
serious loss. The treaty, however, remained
unsigned. In 1933 Hoare was promoted
to K.C.M.G. and in February 1935 he was
transferred to Bucharest.

In Romania Hoare's task was to encourage the 'Little *Entente*' interest, but
after the defeat of all Romania's continental allies between 1938 and 1940,
pro-German elements inevitably gained
control. The German army began to move
in during early 1941. During this period
and often on his own initiative, Hoare
maintained protest against the atrocities
of the Nazi-style regime which had
followed King Carol's abdication in
September 1940. In February 1941 the
British Government decided to extend
economic warfare to Romania, and Hoare's
mission was withdrawn on the 10th. The
evacuation of the British community,
consulates, and legation was supervised
by Hoare with his accustomed calm, earning him much personal gratitude. In 1942
he retired from the service, with great
reluctance, but remained in government
employ until 1944. He then joined the
family bank in Fleet Street as a managing
partner. He died 12 August 1954 in
London after a short illness.

Hoare was a remarkably talented
diplomat whose abilities were easily
underestimated since at the height of his
career they were used in holding operations and not in posts where their effects
could be positive and spectacular. He
was aware of misfortune in this respect
but was incapable of embitterment.
He was of genial temper, with a strong and
somewhat fantastical sense of humour,
enjoying wide private interests from sport
to economics of which he was a gifted
student.

In 1922 Hoare married Lucy Joan, daughter of William George Frederick Cavendish Bentinck, J.P.; they had one son. A portrait of Hoare by Simon Elwes is in the possession of the family.

[*The Times*, 13 August 1954; personal knowledge.]   CHRISTOPHER SYKES.

HOARE, SIR SAMUEL JOHN GURNEY, second baronet, and VISCOUNT TEMPLEWOOD (1880–1959), statesman, was born in London 24 February 1880, the elder son of (Sir) Samuel Hoare, later first baronet, member of Parliament for Norwich (1886–1906), of Sidestrand Hall, Norfolk, by his wife, Katharin Louisa Hart, daughter of Richard Vaughan Davis, commissioner of audit. Educated at Harrow and New College, Oxford, he obtained first classes in classical honour moderations (1901) and modern history (1903) and represented the university at rackets and lawn tennis. A member of an old Norfolk banking family he unsuccessfully contested Ipswich in 1906 and first entered Parliament as Conservative member for Chelsea in January 1910, retaining the constituency until 1944. He was assistant private secretary to Alfred Lyttelton [q.v.], colonial secretary, in 1905; served on the London County Council from 1907 to 1910; and succeeded to the baronetcy in 1915.

During the war of 1914–18 Hoare served as a general staff officer with the rank of lieutenant-colonel in the military mission to Russia, 1916–17, and later in Italy, 1917–18. He was mentioned in dispatches and appointed C.M.G. in 1917. In *The Fourth Seal* (1930) he gave an account of his experiences in Russia.

Hoare was prominent amongst the group of Conservative members who brought about the break-up of the Lloyd George coalition in October 1922 and he became secretary of state for air in Bonar Law's Conservative administration, a post he was to hold no fewer than four times in the course of his political career. He was sworn of the Privy Council in November 1922. It fell to him, therefore, between 1922 and 1929, with the exception of the Labour interlude of 1924, to build up a new Service department in Whitehall and to shape the pattern of the Royal Air Force in the post-war period. His close association in this task with that formidable protagonist of an independent air force, Sir Hugh (later Viscount) Trenchard [q.v.], is fully told in Hoare's book *Empire of the Air* (1957). Hoare saw very clearly

the immense possibilities of air communications within the Empire, for both civilian and military purposes. He did much to persuade the public to be air-minded and was the first secretary of state for air to use aircraft as a normal method of travel. His arrival by air at Gothenburg in 1923 to attend the first International Aero Exhibition was considered to be something of an innovation. On Boxing Day 1926 he and his wife set off in an Imperial Airways de Havilland aeroplane on the first civil air flight to India, arriving in Delhi on 8 January 1927. In February his wife was appointed D.B.E. and in June he was appointed G.B.E. He published a short account of the flight, *India by Air* (1927).

With the formation of the 'national' Government in 1931 Hoare, who had been a member of the first Round Table conference, became secretary of state for India. He made a real effort during the second Round Table conference to find common ground with M. K. Gandhi [q.v.]. This met with a degree of reciprocity on Gandhi's part but the result fell a good deal short of what was needed for agreement on policy. For the next four years Hoare was occupied in the immense task of preparing the new Indian constitution. In 1933 a joint select committee of both Houses was set up to consider the white paper published as a result of the Round Table conference's proposals. It sat from April 1933 to November 1934, holding 159 meetings during which over 120 witnesses were examined; Hoare himself, as one of the principal witnesses, answered more than 10,000 questions in the course of his evidence in cross-examination. Lord Halifax [q.v.] recalled in his *Fulness of Days* that this was done 'with a grasp of his subject that in comparable circumstances can never have been surpassed and seldom equalled by any previous minister of the Crown'. There was a dramatic interlude in April 1934 when Churchill alleged that Hoare as secretary of state had exercised undue influence in persuading the Manchester Chamber of Commerce to alter its original evidence tendered to the joint select committee in respect of the Indian tariff duty on Lancashire cotton goods, which was thought likely to be increased in the context of the proposed new constitution for India. Churchill further alleged that the incident, which gave rise to his accusation of breach of parliamentary privilege, occurred at a dinner given by

Lord Derby [q.v.], himself a member of the joint select committee, to members of the Manchester Chamber of Commerce, at which Hoare was present. The committee of privileges, however, arrived at the unanimous verdict that there had been no breach of privilege.

The government of India bill which eventually received the royal assent in August 1935 contained 478 clauses and 16 schedules and was piloted through the House of Commons by Hoare in the face of bitter opposition from Churchill and the right wing of the Conservative Party. Hoare himself made a substantial proportion of the speeches which were over 1,900 in number. In 1934 he was appointed G.C.S.I.

When Baldwin succeeded MacDonald as prime minister in June 1935 he was in two minds whether to make Hoare viceroy of India or foreign secretary. Hoare expressed his preference for the former, but Baldwin finally decided to send him to the Foreign Office where he succeeded Sir John (later Viscount) Simon [q.v.] at a difficult period. Britain's defence forces had been cut to the bone by successive chancellors of the Exchequer and disarmament discussions at Geneva dominated the League of Nations. Meantime Germany, Italy, and Japan were flouting the Covenant and beginning to form a hostile and threatening bloc. The Manchurian crisis of 1931 had demonstrated that there was no military help forthcoming from the United States. In Britain the pacifist movement was at its height. Collective security, the popular panacea, in practice depended upon collective action by Britain and France. Since Britain was clearly too weak to risk becoming involved simultaneously with Germany and Japan, Hoare's policy was based upon gaining time to build up Britain's military strength and on keeping Italy isolated from Germany. His first step was to sign the Anglo-German naval agreement, designed to limit the German fleet to a ratio of 35 per cent of Britain's. His next problem was the Abyssinian crisis. The French repeatedly made it clear that they would not contemplate military action against Italy over Abyssinia. In a speech at the League Assembly on 11 September 1935 Hoare attempted to rally the League by emphasizing that collective security to be effective must be comprehensive. 'If the burden is to be borne, it must be borne collectively. If risks for peace are to be run, they must

be run by all.' He gave a pledge that Britain would be 'second to none to fulfil her obligations and he repeated again that the League and Britain with it stood for 'the collective maintenance of the Covenant'.

Although similar phrases used previously both in the House of Commons and outside had made no particular impression, this speech stirred the audience at Geneva and achieved wide publicity on the Continent and elsewhere. The effect, however, was short-lived, for Britain alone had taken any military precautions and it became abundantly clear that any temporary enthusiasm for further 'collective action' by other members of the League was confined to words. Later in September 'the committee of five' appointed by the League to mediate put forward proposals which were rejected by Mussolini who in October finally embarked upon the invasion of Abyssinia. After limited sanctions had been imposed against Italy by the League, the British and French Governments were deputed to seek some basis of agreement acceptable to both Italy and Abyssinia. (Sir) Maurice Peterson [q.v.] was sent to Paris where officials from both Foreign Offices set to work upon a plan. It was clear that any such agreement would have to be negotiated, not dictated, unless the League which for all practical purposes meant Great Britain and France, were prepared to go to war with Italy. The French Government again reaffirmed that they would not take military action and Laval himself expressed the view that an oil embargo, if imposed, might well drive Mussolini to an act of war. It was understood that the two Governments were acting on behalf of the League to which any plan produced would be referred for approval. In December 1935 Hoare who had been ill, was persuaded to break his journey in Paris on his way to Switzerland for a short holiday, in order to put the finishing touches to proposals which had been worked out. The ill-fated Hoare-Laval plan, as it subsequently became known, provided—first an effective outlet to the sea, with full sovereign rights for Abyssinia; secondly, the concession to Italy of some, but not all, of the territory in Tigre occupied by Italian forces together with other minor frontier rectifications; thirdly, a large zone in the south and south-west in which Italy acting under the League, would have the monopoly of economic development fourthly, the maintenance of Abyssinian sovereignty over all but the districts actually ceded to Italy; fifthly, the reference of the plan to the League for approval, or otherwise.

These proposals were considerably less than Mussolini's earlier demands. Hoare recommended them to the Cabinet for submission to the League and began his Swiss holiday. The plan 'leaked' into the French press on the following morning and when the details became known the reactions of the British press and of the rank and file of the Conservative Party were very violent, since the plan was considered to be a complete *volte-face* from the Geneva speech. The British Cabinet, having first agreed to accept the proposals, had second thoughts when they doubted the capacity of the Government to ride the storm. Baldwin asked Hoare to withdraw his approval of the plan but Hoare refused to do so and resigned. He held strongly that unless Britain was prepared without French support to declare war on Italy unilaterally, nothing short of these proposals would prevent the Italian occupation of the whole of Abyssinia, or satisfy Mussolini.

This was the turning-point of Hoare's political career. His reputation was much damaged in the eyes of the British public, who expected their foreign secretary to stop Mussolini in Abyssinia without involving Britain in the slightest risk of war, although no other member of the League of Nations was prepared to lift a finger against Italy, least of all France which was far more concerned with the growing menace of Germany.

Baldwin took Hoare back into the Government as first lord of the Admiralty in June 1936 and in the following May Hoare succeeded Simon as home secretary under Neville Chamberlain. Penal reform had been a tradition in his family since Samuel Hoare, his great-grandfather, and Elizabeth Fry [q.v.], his great-great-aunt, together formed the first committee for supporting it. He took immense pains in preparing the criminal justice bill which obtained its second reading in December 1938. The bill introduced two new types of prison sentence: corrective training and preventive detention; it dealt with alternative punishment for juvenile offenders; and abolished judicial flogging. Its final stages were almost completed when the outbreak of war in September 1939 intervened. Nine years were to elapse

before another home secretary piloted an essentially similar bill through the House of Commons.

As one of Chamberlain's senior cabinet ministers and closest associates Hoare was invited by Chamberlain to join an inner group of four ministers in September 1938 during the events which led to the Munich agreement. Throughout all the contemporary and subsequent controversy, Hoare stoutly defended the agreement, holding that without support from the French or from the Commonwealth, and with the Labour Party and public opinion at home bitterly opposed to military action over the Sudetenland, Britain was not in a position to declare war on her own against Germany until further progress had been made with rearmament. At the Home Office in the meantime he was recruiting for the A.R.P. services and for the W.V.S., an organization which owed much to his inspiration.

On the outbreak of war in September 1939 Hoare left the Home Office to become lord privy seal and a member of the War Cabinet. He was appointed for the fourth time secretary of state for air in April 1940. It was his last ministerial post and when Chamberlain resigned in May 1940 it was the end of Hoare's parliamentary career as a minister of the Crown but not the end of his career of public service. In the same month he was appointed ambassador to Spain, a post which he filled until December 1944, in critical circumstances in which he showed considerable skill and subtlety in dealing with the Spanish Government. Madrid was a great centre of both allied and enemy activity and Hoare and his staff succeeded in establishing a good enough relationship with the authorities to secure the release from Spanish prisons of some 30,000 allied prisoners of war and refugees from across the frontier.

Some months before his retirement Hoare was created Viscount Templewood. His Spanish mission marked the end of an exceptionally varied career, during which he had held more high offices of state than any other contemporary minister, with the exception of Churchill. He retired altogether from public life and, apart from making a few speeches in the House of Lords, lived quietly on his Norfolk estate. He had sold Sidestrand Hall a few years before the outbreak of war but retained the rest of the property. He built Templewood, a small classical villa in the Palladian style, on a beautiful site surrounded by his woods, three miles inland from the coast, to the design of his architect nephew, Paul Paget, a temple in a wood. It was typical of his tidiness of mind that the avenues were laid out and flowering shrubs planted long before work on the house itself was begun. All his life he had been a first-class shot and he continued to shoot with astonishing accuracy until a year before his death. He was immensely proud of his woods and shrubs of which he had a great knowledge. He was no mean naturalist. In his retirement he was a prolific writer. *Ambassador on Special Mission* (1946) described his time in Spain. *The Unbroken Thread* (1949) told family history of his forebears against a setting of sport and the Norfolk countryside. In *The Shadow of the Gallows* (1951) he set out his objections to capital punishment. *Nine Troubled Years* (1954) comprised his political memoirs between 1931 and 1940.

Hoare was chairman of the council of the Magistrates' Association, 1947–52; president of the Howard League for Penal Reform from 1947 until his death; president of the Lawn Tennis Association, 1932–56; and an elder brother of Trinity House. He received honorary degrees from Oxford, Cambridge, Reading, and Nottingham, and was chancellor of Reading University from 1937 until his death. He received a number of foreign decorations, was deputy-lieutenant and J.P. for Norfolk; and was awarded the silver medal for skating. His precise manner of speech, his extreme neatness of appearance, and his meticulous care for detail sometimes conveyed the impression of a certain lack of warmth and humour to those who did not know him well. In fact they were no more than superficial trappings which covered a kindness and understanding born of deep religious convictions. Although of Quaker ancestry he was brought up and remained in the Anglo-Catholic tradition. Throughout fifty years of happy married life he was sustained and encouraged by his wife, Lady Maud Lygon (died 1962), fifth daughter of the sixth Earl Beauchamp [q.v.], whom he married in 1909. There were no children and, his younger brother having predeceased him, both the viscountcy and the baronetcy became extinct when Templewood died in London 7 May 1959.

A portrait of him in the uniform of an elder brother of Trinity House by A. C. Davidson-Houston was presented to him in 1956 by the Lawn Tennis Association and hangs at Templewood.

[Lord Templewood's own writings; private information; personal knowledge.]

CHARLES MOTT-RADCLYFFE.

HOBART, SIR PERCY CLEGHORN STANLEY (1885–1957), major-general, was born at Naini Tal, India, 14 June 1885, the third son of Robert Thomson Hobart, Indian Civil Service, of Dungannon, county Tyrone, and his wife, Janetta, daughter of C. Stanley, of Roughan Park, Tyrone. His sister married the future Viscount Montgomery of Alamein. A scholar of Clifton College, he was in the first fifteen. At the Royal Military Academy, Woolwich, he captained the second fifteen and passed out in 1904 high enough to gain one of the few vacancies in the Royal Engineers. In 1906 he was posted to the 1st (later King George V's Own) Sappers and Miners in India and two years later saw his first active service in the Mohmand campaign. While serving on the Delhi durbar military staff (1911–12) his initiative and courage in dealing with a fire earned him the personal thanks of the King and official thanks of the Government of India. His recreations at this time were typical of his boundless energy—polo, pigsticking, and shooting.

In January 1915 Hobart (pronounced Hubbert) went to France with the first Indian Expeditionary Force. He won the M.C. at Neuve Chapelle and in September was appointed to the general staff of the 3rd (Lahore) division with which he went to Mesopotamia in January 1916. By now he had obtained a special qualification in aerial reconnaissance and in that role he was wounded in April 1916 and appointed to the D.S.O. He was soon back on active service in Mesopotamia as brigade-major of an infantry brigade, an appointment of which he was relieved when he not only refused to make a last-minute change in orders for a battle but by retaining physical possession of the field telephone prevented anyone else from doing so. The battle was won, but not for the last time Hobart sacrificed his job rather than carry out orders he was certain were wrong. He ended the war in Egypt, having received six mentions in dispatches, and was appointed O.B.E. in 1919.

After passing through the Staff College, Camberley, and a short spell at the War Office, Hobart returned in 1921 to active service on the Indian North-West frontier here he again distinguished himself. In 1922 he was posted as G.S.O. 2 at headquarters, Eastern Command, then at Jaini Tal, where he entered into the life of an Indian hill station with characteristic zest. A brilliant conversationalist, he could speak interestingly on a wide range of subjects. His views were always interesting or provocative but could not be ignored. He remarked one day that the next war would be won by the tank and in 1923 he joined the Royal Tank Corps.

In 1923–7 Hobart was an instructor at the Staff College, Quetta, where he showed that his ability as a trainer was on a level with the brilliance of his war record. He received brevets of lieutenant-colonel (1922) and colonel (1928). He was second-in-command of the 4th battalion of the Tank Corps at Catterick (1927–30) and commanding officer of the 2nd battalion at Farnborough (1931–3). In 1933 he became inspector, the head of the Corps, and in addition from 1934 he raised and commanded the 1st Tank Brigade. In his four years of command he evolved new tactical methods based on the fundamental principles of mobility, flexibility, and speed, and new techniques of command and control; developments far-reaching in their consequences. Training was relentless, for he was a stern taskmaster, but 'Old Hobo's' enthusiasm and imagination were the inspiration of a keen and happy formation.

In 1937 Hobart became deputy director of staff duties at the War Office for a very short spell before being promoted major-general and appointed director of military training. In 1938 he was sent to Egypt in the kind of role to which he had long aspired, to raise what was to become the 7th armoured division, much of the subsequent fame of which was undoubtedly due to his initial training and vision. But his advanced views on the employment of armour independently of the close support of unarmoured troops were not acceptable and from 1939 he was unemployed until recalled to active duty in 1941 by (Sir) Winston Churchill who in the following year wrote to the secretary of state for war: 'General Hobart bears a very high reputation, not only in the service, but in wide circles outside. He is a man of quite exceptional mental attainments, with great strength of character, and although he does not work easily with others it is a great pity we have not more of his like in the Service. I have been shocked at the persecution

to which he has been subjected. I am quite sure that if, when I had him transferred from a corporal in the Home Guard to the command of one of the new armoured divisions, I had instead insisted upon his controlling the whole of the tank developments, with a seat on the Army Council, many of the grievous errors from which we have suffered would not have been committed.'

Command of the 11th Armoured division (1941–2) in England was followed by that of the specialized 79th Armoured division which Hobart, perceiving the lessons of Dieppe, organized and trained for the invasion of the continent. In his diary on 27 January 1944 Sir Alan Brooke (later Viscount Alanbrooke) wrote: 'Hobart ... showed us his models and his proposed assault organization. We then went on to see various exhibits such as the Sherman tank for destroying tank mines with chains on a drum driven by the engine, various methods of climbing walls with tanks, blowing up of minefields and walls, flame-throwing Churchill tanks, wall-destroying engineer parties, floating tanks, teaching men how to escape from sunken tanks, etc. A most interesting day, and one which Eisenhower seemed to enjoy thoroughly. Hobart has been doing wonders in his present job and I am delighted we put him into it.'

The 79th division, with Hobart in charge, went on to play a vital part in the Normandy landings in 21st Army Group which his brother-in-law was commanding and to become 'the tactical key to victory' in the final stages of the war.

Hobart was appointed C.B. in 1939 and K.B.E. in 1943. He retired in 1946; was lieutenant-governor of the Royal Hospital, Chelsea (1948–53); and died at Farnham, Surrey, 19 February 1957. He was a commander of the United States Legion of Merit and colonel commandant of the Royal Tank Regiment.

In 1928 Hobart married Dorothea Florence, daughter of Colonel Cyril Field, Royal Marines, and former wife of Major A. F. Chater, R.E. He had one daughter.

A pastel by Eric Kennington is at Royal Tank Regiment headquarters and another is in the possession of the family.

[The Times, 21, 25, 28 February, and 4 March 1957; Winston S. Churchill, The Hinge of Fate, 1951; Sir Arthur Bryant, Triumph in the West, 1959; Kenneth Macksey, Armoured Crusader, 1967; The Tank, March 1957; History of the 79th Armoured Division, Hamburg, 1945.]   M. R. ROBERTS.

HODGSON, SIR ROBERT MacLEOD (1874–1956), diplomatist, was born in West Bromwich 25 February 1874, the eldest son of the Rev. Robert Hodgson, vicar of Christ Church, a founder of the West Bromwich Albion football club, later prebendary of Lichfield and arch-deacon of Stafford, by his first wife, Katharine Gamlen. He was educated at Radley and Trinity College, Oxford, where he captained the university hockey team (1896) and graduated in 1897. He began his connection with the Foreign Office by working in a subordinate position in the consulate-general at Algiers and later (1901–6) at Marseilles where he became a paid vice-consul in 1904. He had always taken a great interest in the commercial work of these posts and in 1906 he was sent by the Foreign Office to Vladivostok as commercial agent, being given the rank of vice-consul in 1908 and of consul in 1911. He remained there until 1919, acquiring that knowledge of the Russian language and character which was to determine the course of so much of his future career. During that strange and unhappy chapter of British diplo-matic history when, after the Bolshevik revolution, the Allies intervened in Russia, he was moved as acting high commissioner to Omsk where an anti-Bolshevik government had been set up. When Omsk was evacuated by the Allies in November 1919 he was appointed commercial counsellor in Russia.

After the signature of an Anglo-Russian trade agreement in 1921 Hodgson was appointed official agent on the British commercial mission to Russia. His posi-tion was a difficult one, in view of the two governments' attitude of mutual suspicion, but Hodgson was a man of transparent integrity, and so far as it was possible for any British representative at that time to do so he gained the goodwill of the Russians with whom he carried out a succession of prolonged and tedious negotiations. His clear and objective reports helped a not always receptive British Government to an understanding of the motives underlying the workings of the official Russian mind. With the diplomatic recognition of Russia by the Labour Government in 1924 Hodgson became chargé d'affaires; he remained in Moscow until 1927 when the diplomatic mission was recalled and the trade agree-ment ended.

In 1928 his appointment as minister to Albania was a disappointment to Hodgson

after his successful and arduous time i Russia, especially as he had been led t expect promotion to a more importar post. But he was the last man to nurs a grievance and threw himself with h wonted vigour into his new work an could soon boast with every justificatic that nothing of interest to the Britis Government could happen in Albani without his knowing of it. He retired i August 1936, having been kept on fc more than two years beyond the norms age. In December 1937 he was brougl back as British agent to General Franco administration in Burgos. In Februar 1939 he was accredited as chargé d'affair to the Spanish Government and it was surprise to many that he was not chose as ambassador in April on the establisl ment of full diplomatic relations wit General Franco. In 1944–5 he agai emerged from retirement to serve in tl Foreign Office as adviser to the censorshi

Hodgson was a man of dynamic energ His speech matched his mental process in speed and his powerful frame, like h mind, rebelled against inactivity. Retir ment was for him an irksome experienc For some years he was chairman of tl council of the School of Slavonic Studi and in 1953 he turned to authorship wit *Spain Resurgent*. Carpentry, which ha always been one of his hobbies, occupie much of his spare time, but he alway wanted more to do.

Lovable and of strong sensibilitie Hodgson had a multitude of friends an was deeply affected by the purges in Russ when so many of the people he had know were liquidated, often apparently for r other reason than having been his visito at the embassy. His skill in negotiation w; remarkable. It derived from clarity vision, tenacity, and an unmistakab uprightness and generosity of mind whi won the confidence and respect of h opponent. Possessing so varied ar formidable a diplomatic armoury he migl ordinarily have been expected to hav been chosen to fill posts of great responsibility, but he inevitably suffere from not having started his career in tl regular diplomatic service. He was appoi ted C.M.G. (1920), K.C.M.G. (1939), ar K.B.E. (1925).

In 1920 Hodgson married a Russia Olga, daughter of Paul Bellavin; they ha one son. Hodgson died in London October 1956.

[Private information; personal knowledg
DAVID SCOT

HOLDEN, CHARLES HENRY (1875–1960), architect, was born 12 May 1875 at Great Lever, Bolton, Lancashire, the youngest of five children of Joseph Holden and his wife, Ellen Bolton. Following bankruptcy of his drapery business his father left home to seek work elsewhere. His mother died soon afterwards when Charles was eight and his eldest sister, then a girl of eighteen, opened a shop and managed to provide for the family. Charles attended the village school until his father found regular work in St. Helens where he remarried. Charles then rejoined him and after attending local schools he found work first as a clerk in the railway stores, then as a laboratory assistant in a chemical works before returning to Bolton to help his brother-in-law, Frederick Green, a land surveyor who also drew plans for speculative builders. Green arranged for the boy to be apprenticed to E. W. Leeson, a Manchester architect, and he attended classes at the School of Art and Manchester Technical College. There he made rapid progress and after gaining first place in the honours examination in construction and design, he was put in charge of the class on this subject. At the same time, working at night, he prepared a regular entry under the *nom de plume* of 'The Owl', for the monthly student competitions organized by the *Building News*, until in one year he had an unbroken record of first and second places.

Joseph Knight, an art student with whom he travelled daily to Manchester, lent him a copy of *Leaves of Grass*, and learning that J. W. Wallace, a personal friend of Walt Whitman, lived in Bolton, Holden made his acquaintance. Wallace drew his attention to Whitman's cryptic 'Laws for Creations' and to the works of Thoreau and Edward Carpenter [q.v.]. Greatly impressed, Holden began to think of similar ideas in architectural terms. Knight introduced him to the painter Francis Dodd [q.v.] whose sister, Gertrude, was engaged to (Sir) Muirhead Bone [q.v.]; the two brothers, James and Muirhead Bone, became Holden's closest and lifelong friends.

Leaving Manchester, he worked for a short time with Jonathan Simpson in Bolton before going to London at the age of twenty-two to work with C. R. Ashbee [q.v.]. The aesthetic atmosphere of Ashbee's studio did not accord with his views and after a short break in Devonshire he joined Percy Adams in 1899 as chief assistant. A brilliant planner with competitive spirit, Adams had just won the Newcastle Infirmary competition. He gave his young assistant full scope and a series of buildings justifying this confidence followed in rapid succession, among them Belgrave Hospital, Kennington; the Law Society in Chancery Lane; the Seamen's Hospital, Constantinople; the Women's Hospital, Soho; Tunbridge Wells Hospital; and the King Edward VII Sanatorium at Midhurst. The Bristol Public Library (1906) was the outcome of a competition won with a set of drawings prepared in a fortnight by Holden in his spare time. Its happy relationship with the cathedral and the adjoining eleventh-century gateway, its dramatically simple rear elevation, and its freedom from any structural defect over a period of sixty years were remarkable achievements for one so young.

In 1907 he entered into partnership with Adams and among the works which followed were the British Medical Association (later Rhodesia House), the Bristol Royal Infirmary, the Institution of Electrical Engineers, and the Royal Northern Hospital. Lionel Pearson became a partner in 1913 and after the war, when Holden was one of the four chief architects of the Imperial War Graves Commission, the practice increased to such an extent that the responsibilities had to be divided between the partners.

Uncommitted to a particular style, Holden had used Gothic or classic forms with equal facility and understanding. In his design for the Law Society with its splendid library he acknowledged being influenced by Alfred Stevens [q.v.]. King's College for Women, Campden Hill (which became Queen Elizabeth College), shows his love for Wren. Belgrave Hospital, Sutton Valence School, and Midhurst Sanatorium might be personal tributes to Philip Webb [q.v.] and C. R. Ashbee. With an unerring sense of composition based on tradition and natural form, a sympathy for material, and an instinctive sense of construction, he continued to simplify his work until it achieved the clearest expression of purpose. He said, in character: 'When in doubt, leave it out.'

His powers were noted at meetings of the Design and Industries Association by Frank Pick [q.v.] who commissioned Holden to design the façade of Bond

Street tube station (1924). This was the beginning of fifteen years of happy collaboration with Pick during which Holden's influence extended into every part of the London Transport system: street signs, bus shelters, platforms, train sheds, cable posts, lamp standards. Everything he touched he improved. Designing more than fifty stations, free of all stylistic features, he established unsurpassed standards of transport architecture. This work was crowned by 55 Broadway where the difficulties of a diamond-shaped site were brilliantly overcome with a cruciform plan and a sculptural form which he described as 'a man on horseback with panniers'. For this steel-framed building which rises with easier grace than any of its contemporaries he was awarded the London Architecture medal (1929).

Commissioned in 1931 to design the new buildings for the university of London, Holden discarded the quadrangular plan in favour of a spine with ribs or, in his own words, 'a lion with cubs'. Based on a strictly rational assessment of his programme, the building has an elemental quality which expresses the austerity and simplicity to which his life was dedicated. His personal account of it is recorded in the *Journal* of the Royal Institute of British Architects of 9 May 1938. The building still lacks the sculpture for which he made provision in his design and which he regarded as a necessary complement to his abstract architectural composition.

His buildings display the work of many notable sculptors including Eric Gill [q.v.] and Henry Moore, but he is chiefly associated with the controversial figure of Sir Jacob Epstein [q.v.], early collaboration with whom convinced him of Epstein's artistic integrity and ability to infuse his work with life. Despite the reluctance of clients and public outcry following his sculptures for the British Medical Association, he continued to provide him with opportunities. Opening an exhibition of Epstein's work in Bolton in 1954, Holden said: 'Today we have his Virgin and Child in Cavendish Square in cast lead but floating in the air like a heavenly vision. How proud I would have been to see such a work on the base of my university tower in London.'

During the war of 1939–45 Holden turned his attention to town planning, advising the dean and chapter of St. Paul's, the university of Edinburgh, and the London County Council. He prepared a plan for Canterbury and with (Sir William (later Lord) Holford the plan for the City of London which was incorporated in the *County of London Development Plan* (1951). It may be true that this modest and retiring man left a more enduring mark on London than any architect of his generation.

Elected A.R.I.B.A. in 1906, winning the Godwin bursary in 1913, he became F.R.I.B.A. in 1921, vice-president in 1935–7, and in 1936 was awarded the Royal gold medal for architecture He was a member of the faculty of royal designers for industry and served on the Royal Fine Art Commission from 1933 to 1937. The universities of London and Manchester conferred honorary doctorates upon him.

Holden had an endearing sense of humour and a gentle manner which belied the incisiveness of his views Children loved him and he kept tit-bits in his pockets for the wild birds in his garden which came at his call. Playing the cello and later the piano, he loved music, finding affinities to architecture in the works of Bach. Clarity and economy characteristic of his designs, are also to be found in his superb drawings, in his correspondence, and his rare public addresses. Generous to weakness in others, he was a man of great strength of character who found much happiness in exercising his skill on the tasks entrusted to him.

For fifty years his life was shared with Margaret, daughter of J. C. Macdonald After her death in 1954 he gradually withdrew from active practice to live quietly at his home at Harmer Green where he died 1 May 1960.

A portrait of him as a young man by Francis Dodd hangs in the hall of the Art Workers' Guild of which he was a member. An etching also by Dodd and a study for it are in the National Portrait Gallery. A portrait medallion by Paul Vincze is in the Bristol Public Library.

[*The Times* and *Guardian*, 2 May 1960 private information; personal knowledge.]
CHARLES HUTTON

HOLMES, SIR VALENTINE (1888–1956), lawyer, was born in Blackrock county Dublin, 24 July 1888, the third son of Hugh Holmes, who was successively solicitor and attorney-general, judge, lord justice and privy counsellor, all in

Ireland, and who died in 1916, by his wife, Olivia Moule. Holmes's early years were mainly spent at the family home in Dublin. He was educated at Charterhouse and Trinity College, Dublin, where he obtained a senior moderatorship in classics with gold medal in 1911. After a pupillage with A. Neilson of the common law bar Holmes was called to the bar by the Inner Temple in 1913 and then devilled for (Sir) Leslie Scott [q.v.]. During the war Holmes served as an officer in the Royal Artillery and then returned to Scott's chambers. Solicitors who briefed Scott, perceiving the quality of Holmes's work, soon began to bring junior work to him and, being well content, to recommend him to others. When Scott relinquished his law officer-ship and returned to private practice it was natural that he should lead Holmes in some of the heavier cases which were by then coming Holmes's way. Perhaps the heaviest was in 1926 when the Graigola Merthyr Company sought to establish that the Swansea Corporation's reservoir endangered their colliery. Scott and Holmes were for the defendants and won after a fifty-six day hearing. Holmes was also associated with Scott during this period as adviser to certain of the Indian princes in connection with the consti-tutional changes then taking place in India.

In 1929 Holmes moved to chambers of his own with Frank Connett as head clerk and this partnership (and friend-ship) continued until the end. It was about this time that Holmes gained his repute in the law of libel and it was rare for there to be any important libel case in which he did not appear. His general practice also grew and from 1935 until he took silk in 1945 he had the largest junior practice at the bar. He was elected a bencher of his Inn early in 1935 and later that year was appointed 'Treasury devil': junior counsel to the Treasury in common law matters. The work of this office was not at that time so exacting as it had been during and immediately after the war but was heavy enough. Holmes was, however, a tremendous worker and discharged the additional work without any abatement of his private practice. The second war presented a further challenge since there was a great increase in government work without any corresponding diminution in his private practice and both his devils departed for war service. He met the challenge by working even harder. By tradition the labours of the 'Treasury devil' are rewarded by elevation to the bench after some five years' service, but Holmes's inclinations did not lie in that direction and he felt compelled to decline the offer. He relinquished his post in the spring of 1945 after serving twice the normal period. He was appointed K.C. immediately and was knighted in 1946 at the same time as his brother, Hugh Oliver Holmes (1886–1955), who was procurator-general of the Mixed Court of Appeal in Egypt (1929–49).

There was no period of waiting for Holmes—he stepped overnight from being the leading junior to being one of the two or three leading silks. He continued to appear in libel cases, many of which attracted considerable attention, and was a member of the committee whose report led to the passage of the Defamation Act, 1952. He was also in great demand in heavy commercial and common law actions both in the lower courts and in the House of Lords and Privy Council. He was for instance one of the counsel for the Australian banks in their success-ful appeal to the Privy Council on the issue that the legislation providing for their nationalization was unconstitutional. By 1949, however, nearly thirty years of overwork began to take their toll and Holmes decided to retire whilst still at the apex of his career. In the following year he was appointed consultant in legal matters to the Shell Oil group. He quickly won the confidence of directors and colleagues and continued to serve in this capacity until his death in London 19 November 1956. Until his fatal illness began earlier that year this was a period of great happiness.

Holmes had all the attributes necessary to success as a junior: these included the capacity to extract the essentials from the most voluminous set of papers in a short time, a great facility for expressing himself briefly but clearly on paper, and an amazing industry. Prior to the second war he would work from 9 a.m. one morning until 1 a.m. the next; during and after the second war the process was reversed and he would work from 3 a.m. until 6 or 7 p.m., save on fire-watching nights when it is doubtful if he slept at all. He had a wide knowledge of the law and the analytical mind necessary to apply it to the facts of the case in hand. His greatest gift was, however, his sound judgement which made him so valued as a counsellor. His opinions (all written in his own hand) may have been hard to decipher but long or short they were rarely wrong. One of his most courageous was of thirteen words—'The judgment of the Court of Appeal is wrong and will be reversed'—and it was. As an advocate Holmes had a slightly hesitant manner which at first went with an actual diffidence. However, as pressure of work grew the diffidence went and the hesitance of manner merely seemed to accentuate the force of his submissions and he became as successful an advocate in court as he had been with his paper work in chambers.

In his early years Holmes shot and played a good game of golf; but after 1935 he had little opportunities for these although he retained an interest in racing and shared with his clerk a fondness for 'the dogs'.

Holmes married in 1915 Gwen, daughter of Andrew Armstrong, of Dublin; they had one son and one daughter.

[Private information; personal knowledge.]
T. G. ROCHE.

HOLMYARD, ERIC JOHN (1891–1959), teacher, historian, and interpreter of science, was born at Midsomer Norton, Somerset, 11 July 1891, the son of Isaac Berrow Holmyard, a national schoolmaster, by his wife, Alice Cheshire. His early life was spent in Somerset—a county for which he had a deep affection and to which he returned in his retirement—and he was educated at Sexey's School, Bruton. From there he went to Sidney Sussex College, Cambridge, reading history and science, for both of which he had displayed an aptitude at an early age and which were to remain his lifelong interests. He obtained a first class in both parts of the natural sciences tripos (1910–12) and a second in part ii of the history tripos (1911).

He next spent a year at Rothamsted Experimental Station, where he was one of the Board of Agriculture's first research scholars. He quickly decided, however, that his real vocation was teaching and after a brief appointment at Bristol Grammar School and at Marlborough (1918–19) he became head of the science department at Clifton College in 1919, in which post he remained for some twenty years. Under his guidance Clifton established a reputation for science teaching probably unequalled, and certainly not surpassed, by any other British school. In 1926 he was chairman of the Science Masters Association. His influence extended far beyond Clifton, for during his time there he wrote a series of school textbooks, especially of chemistry, which were widely used throughout the English-speaking world. An important factor in the success of these books was that through them he gave expression to his profound knowledge of the history of science, especially of alchemy. In order to be able to read original Islamic manuscripts, from which much alchemical lore derives, he taught himself Arabic; he also had a fair knowledge of Hebrew. He edited several Arabic alchemical texts, including (1928) Richard Russell's translation (1678) of the works of Geber (Jabir ibn Hayyan). In 1928 his important contributions to this field of scholarship were recognized by Bristol University by the award of the D.Litt. Subsequently he held office as chairman of the Society for the Study of Alchemy and Early Chemistry and was a corresponding member of the Académie Internationale d'Histoire des Sciences. His *Alchemy* (1957) is recognized as an important addition to the literature.

The outbreak of war in 1939 launched Holmyard on a new career. The severe air raids on Bristol compelled Clifton to evacuate to Bude in 1940. Preferring not to move, Holmyard resigned just at the time when Imperial Chemical Industries conceived the idea of *Endeavour* as a new multilingual journal which would tell the story of Britain's contribution to the progress of science. He became the first editor, and established its reputation so firmly that when the war ended it was decided to continue its publication indefinitely; Holmyard remained as editor until 1954. Meanwhile, however, Imperial Chemical Industries had given him further opportunity to contribute to international scholarship. In 1950 the company undertook to sponsor the preparation of a comprehensive *History of Technology*, to be published by the Clarendon Press, Oxford, under the joint editorship of Holmyard and Charles Singer [q.v.]. The first volume appeared in 1954 and the fifth and final volume of this work, to which some 150 scholars of international reputation contributed, in 1958, only a year before Holmyard's death. The success of the venture owed much to his meticulously careful editorial work and his remarkably far-ranging historical knowledge.

Despite his gifts, Holmyard was of an unassuming and retiring disposition and his influence on the world of learning was made far more through his extensive writing than through personal contact. Although he rarely sought the company of his fellow men, those who came to him for information or advice unfailingly received it in full measure. Throughout his life, his greatest joy was in the simple pleasures of the countryside; in particular he was fond of horses and was a good judge of them and was a founder, and member of council, of the Somerset Horse Association. Gardening and walking were among his other leisure pursuits.

In 1916 Holmyard married Ethel Elizabeth Britten, a schoolmistress, by whom he had two sons. She died in 1941. No portrait of Holmyard exists, but a good photograph of him hangs in the room he formerly occupied in the Science School at Clifton College. He died at Clevedon, Somerset, 13 October 1959.

[*The Times*, 15 and 23 October 1959; *Endeavour*, January 1960; *Nature*, 31 October 1959; *Chemistry and Industry*, 2 January 1960; *I.C.I. Magazine*, December 1959; private information; personal knowledge.]
T. I. WILLIAMS.

HONE, EVIE (1894–1955), artist, was born in Dublin 22 April 1894, the daughter of Joseph Hone, maltster, and his wife, Eva Robinson. The Hone family is the most continuously distinguished in the history of Irish art in modern times. Evie Hone was a direct descendant of the brother of Nathaniel Hone [q.v.], a foundation member of the Royal Academy, and was always dedicated to the idea of being an artist. She was a deeply religious woman and once entered a convent with the idea of becoming a nun. Later she joined the Roman Catholic faith to which she belonged at the time of her death. Her lifelong friend and fellow artist, Mainie Jellett, although not a Catholic, considered this an absolutely essential step, since Evie Hone's warm and passionate nature demanded the mysticism which Catholicism provided. The second factor which played a large part in her life was her continued ill health due to early infantile paralysis. In her youth she could not travel or move about without a maid but later because of the devotion of Mainie Jellett and her own indomitable courage she was able to overcome her physical disability and live abroad.

In 1915 she studied at the Byam Shaw School of Art in London. In 1918 she attended the Westminster School of Art where she worked under Walter Bayes and the Central School under Bernard Meninsky. In 1920 she and Mainie Jellett became pupils of André Lhote in his studio in Paris. During the following year the two artists persuaded Albert Gleizes to accept them as his first pupils and until 1931 they worked for a period with him each year. They were elected to the group Abstraction-Création and their work was published in the journals of that society. Their work was also accepted in the exhibitions in Paris of the Indépendants, the Sur-Indépendants, and the Salon d'Automne.

Her first exhibition was a joint affair with Mainie Jellett at the Dublin Painters' Gallery in 1924 and she subsequently exhibited there and at the Contemporary Painters Gallery. From 1944 onwards her work was exhibited in various one-man shows at the Dawson Gallery, Dublin. Her style was closely allied to that of Gleizes and she liked to take the forms of nature or of existing Old Masters and to translate them into basic patterns of colour in order to exemplify an essential harmony without depending on the exact relationship of the recognizable or visible object. Thus her work while totally abstract was nevertheless carefully related to the rhythms of life. Later she indulged herself in figurative or naturalistic scenes but she was invariably more concerned with the underlying rhythm than with description.

She had become more and more interested in stained glass, largely perhaps through her intense interest in the work of Rouault and in 1933 she produced her first window, three small panels in the Church of Ireland church in Dundrum. Her stained-glass work was soon recognized as being unique and original and during the remaining years of her life she carried out some 66 commissions for churches and public places. This work can be divided into three main phases. The first was that inspired by the rich colours and expressionist technique of Rouault culminating in the large 'My Four Green Fields' of 1939 (C.I.E. office, Dublin). The second phase was that in which her approach to the human figure was bolder, the colour more splendidly contrasted, and the sense of dependence on her cubist painting less obvious. This period ended with the series for the Jesuit Fathers, Tullabeg, one of the unique shrines of stained glass in which no light enters the chapel except through her five windows. Her last phase was that in which the large window (504 x 360 feet) for Eton College was the central feature. This work depicts the Crucifixion and the Last Supper as main subjects and reflects the broad treatment of glass she adopted in her last years. By painting each interior piece of glass with loving care she sought to make it glow and give out the richness of colour which attracted her so much. As a result her last windows were not only moving designs in themselves but were enhanced by her reverence for the nature of glass as a medium quite separate from its descriptive aspects.

Evie Hone also produced over 150 small stained-glass panels for domestic use and continued to paint oils, gouaches, and water-colours and even ventured into such fields as tapestry and appliqué. She was so totally absorbed by her occupation as an artist that she hardly seemed aware of the fact that she was burning up her waning strength. She died in Dublin 13 March 1955. A head in bronze by Oisin Kelly remained in the collection of the artist.

[Mainie Jellett, *The Artist's Vision*, ed. Eileen MacCarvill, 1958; James White and Michael Wynne, *Irish Stained Glass*, 1963; personal knowledge.]   JAMES WHITE.

HOPE, VICTOR ALEXANDER JOHN, second MARQUESS OF LINLITHGOW (1887–1952), viceroy of India, was born at Hopetoun House, South Queensferry, West Lothian, 24 September 1887, the elder son of the seventh Earl of Hopetoun, afterwards first Marquess of Linlithgow and first governor-general of Australia [q.v.]. He was educated at Eton and succeeded his father as second marquess in 1908. An active Territorial, he served throughout the war of 1914–18, ending with the rank of colonel, with the Lothians and Border Horse, and in command of a battalion of the Royal Scots. After the war he became civil lord of the Admiralty in the Conservative Government (1922–4); deputy chairman of the Unionist Party Organization (1924–6); and president of the Navy League (1924–31). He was chairman of the Medical Research Council and of the governing body of the Imperial College of Science and Technology (1934–6). Closely interested in agriculture, he was chairman of the committee on the distribution and prices of agricultural produce (1923); president of the Edinburgh and East of Scotland College of Agriculture (1924–33); and chairman (1926–8) of the royal commission on agriculture in India, which completed a masterly survey in 1928. Already a K.T. (1928), he was appointed G.C.I.E. in 1929.

Although Linlithgow had in 1924 refused the governorship of Madras, his interest in India remained keen; and during his very important chairmanship (1933–4) of the joint select committee on Indian constitutional reform, on whose report was based the Government of India Act of 1935, he acquired a profound and specialized knowledge of India's political problems. His wide general experience and sound judgement made him an obvious successor to Lord Willingdon [q.v.] as viceroy in 1936. Sworn of the Privy Council in 1935, he was now appointed G.C.S.I.

Linlithgow's viceroyalty, the longest since 1856, covered a period of exceptional stress and difficulty. It fell to him, under the Act of 1935, to introduce provincial autonomy; to prepare for a federation of India; to superintend the separation of Burma from India; and to be the first crown representative in dealing with the Indian princely States. It was largely his personal reassurances which led the Congress Party in July 1937 to accept office in the six provinces in which it had a majority. In August 1937 he established personal contact with M. K. Gandhi [q.v.] and he was throughout in close touch with M. A. Jinnah [q.v.], with the leaders of the small minorities, and with the princes.

When war broke out in 1939 plans for federation were suspended and Linlithgow made an earnest appeal for unity and support of the war effort. Congress, however, refused to be associated with the war save on its own terms, and soon afterwards withdrew its ministries in the provinces. The Moslem League complained of Congress oppression in the provinces and demanded that no declaration on the future of India should be made without its approval and consent. There followed a period of intense activity, in which Linlithgow sought to induce the various political groups to sink their differences and to join his Council for the prosecution of the war. In a series of statements between 1939 and 1943, issued with the approval of the home Government, he outlined the steps by which India might attain full dominion status after the war under an agreed constitution. All were of no avail. In 1940 Congress initiated a civil disobedience movement directed against the war effort; the Moslem League advanced the doctrine of Pakistan, destined ultimately to lead to the division of India.

The rejection in 1942 by Congress, followed in varying degrees by the other parties, of far-reaching constitutional proposals brought to India by Sir Stafford Cripps [q.v.] on the War Cabinet's behalf vividly emphasized how intractable was the constitutional problem. Congress opposition to the war effort thereafter intensified and in August 1942 led to the arrest of Gandhi and the Congress Working Committee which continued under restraint until near the end of the war.

Linlithgow's term of office was marked by the expansion, during the war, of the governor-general's Council from a predominantly official and European body of seven into a body of fifteen, of whom, excluding the viceroy and the commander-in-chief, ten were Indians, and three Europeans, only two of them officials; and by an enhancement of India's international stature consequent on her representation at the War Cabinet, in Washington, Chungking, and on the Middle East Council in Cairo.

Outside the constitutional field, Linlithgow's great work was in organizing India to play her full part in the war. At the outset of his term, in 1936, he had urged on the defence authorities the importance of India's north-eastern frontier, and the case for an overland reinforcement route to Burma in emergency; but without carrying conviction. Equally he was throughout insistent on the importance of the area west of the McMahon line. Major and successful military operations on the north-west frontier (1936–8), engaging the largest forces ever employed there, helped India to reach a position of equilibrium on this frontier before war broke out.

Although Congress refused support for the war effort, the rest of the Hindu community, the Moslems, the Sikhs, the other minorities, and the princes gave generously in men, money, and supplies. After Dunkirk, it was clear that India must face East rather than West, and must co-operate with the other Commonwealth territories east of Suez in meeting both civil and military needs. Linlithgow established and rapidly expanded the India department of supply, and his

initiative in calling a regional conference which founded the Eastern Group Supply Council made a major contribution to the general war effort. In October 1941 a National Defence Council was set up which brought together British India and the princes; by the end of his term over two million men had been recruited for the army alone. His close and cordial relations with successive commanders-in-chief greatly contributed to the smooth working of the machine.

It was an outstanding achievement to maintain public morale from 1939 to 1943 in the face of Congress hostility and acute internal political difficulties; of an unbroken series of military reverses approaching ever nearer to the sub-continent; and, in the concluding months of his term, of a disastrous famine in Eastern India. Linlithgow carried a heavier burden than any of his predecessors. The viceroy at all times represented the sovereign and was also the working head of the administration. But from 1937, under the Act of 1935, Linlithgow in addition became personally responsible for supervising all provincial governors in the discharge of their special responsibilities and, after the Congress ministries resigned in 1939, for guiding the governors in running their provinces under the Act's emergency provisions.

In domestic and foreign affairs alike, Linlithgow was faced with the need for some decisions of unique perplexity and urgency. The former included his refusal to be deflected by Gandhi's fast of February 1943; the latter, the question of sending troops to Iraq in 1941, in which he played an important part. Throughout, Linlithgow showed a rocklike stability, a cool judgement, and a resolution, unshaken by adverse fortunes, the tonic effect of which on all who came in touch with him, and on morale, was great, particularly in wartime. He handed over to his successor a country organized for war and a political situation which, if uneasy, was under control.

In the civil field Linlithgow took a closer interest than any viceroy since Lord Curzon [q.v.] in internal administration in all its aspects: among innumerable other issues, rural uplift, the problems of the district officer, archaeology, the improvement of the imperial capital, and publicity.

On his retirement in October 1943 Linlithgow was appointed K.G. In 1944 he accepted the chairmanship of the

Midland Bank which he held until his death, in addition to other important business appointments. A sincere Presbyterian, he was lord high commissioner of the Church of Scotland in 1944 and 1945; chancellor of Edinburgh University from 1944 until his death; and chairman (1944-52) of the board of trustees of the National Gallery of Scotland.

Dignified and imposing, Linlithgow was an impressive figure in ceremonial and public appearances as viceroy. In private life, and in personal contacts with Indians and Europeans, he was interested, easy, with a sense of humour of his own, always prepared to recognize the sincerity of those who differed from him. His kindness, courtesy, and consideration, his capacity for hard work; his courage, fairness, readiness to take decisions, and skill in handling difficult political situations, early earned and kept for him the respect admiration, and liking of those who came in close touch with him. A keen sportsman, a bird shot of unusual skill, and a good golfer, he was a prominent figure in Scottish life, had been vice-lieutenant of West Lothian from 1927 and lord-lieutenant from 1929, and took an active interest in the development of his extensive estates in the Lowlands. He died suddenly, 5 January 1952, while out shooting at Hopetoun.

In 1911 Linlithgow married Doreen Maud, daughter of Sir Frederick George Milner, seventh baronet. They had twin sons and three daughters. The elder twin, Charles William Frederick (born 1912), succeeded to the family honours. The younger, Lord John Hope, became a Conservative member of Parliament in 1945, was minister of works in 1959-62, and was created Baron Glendevon in 1964. Linlithgow was survived by his widow who had throughout given him unfailing help. She received the C.I. and the Kaisar-i-Hind gold medal and will long be remembered in India for her interest in women's education and more especially for her campaign against tuberculosis. She died after a car accident in 1965. A portrait of Linlithgow by Sir Oswald Birley hangs in the former viceroy's house, now Rashtrapati Bhawan, in New Delhi; there is a copy at Hopetoun.

[V. P. Menon, *The Transfer of Power in India*, 1957; John Connell, *Auchinleck*, 1959; personal knowledge.] GILBERT LAITHWAITE.

HOPKINS, SIR RICHARD VALENTINE NIND (1880-1955), civil servant, was born in Edgbaston 13 February 1880, the son of Alfred Nind Hopkins, a business man, and his wife, Eliza Mary Castle. He was educated at King Edward's School, Birmingham, and at Emmanuel College, Cambridge, where he was a scholar, played rugby and cricket, and obtained a first class in part i of the classical tripos (1901) and in part ii of the history tripos (1902). At all times it was the classics which supported him, for he considered that they had summed up the world as it was.

He entered the Inland Revenue Department as a first division clerk in 1902 and in that relatively restful period in public finance gave his leisure to the Bermondsey Mission. He worked on Lloyd George's land values duties (which were repealed in 1920); and after war broke out in 1914 he and Josiah (later Lord) Stamp [q.v.] carried out and worked the excess profits duty. Hopkins became a member of the Board in 1916 and chairman in 1922, having been appointed C.B. in 1919 and K.C.B. in 1920. He gave valuable evidence before the royal commission on the income-tax (1919-20); was chairman of a departmental committee asked to devise a scheme for a levy on war wealth which, in the event, as a matter of policy, was not imposed; and advised on methods of dealing with the avoidance of super-tax.

In 1927 'Hoppy' transferred to the Treasury where the two branches of finance and supply services were combined under his control. He became second secretary in 1932 and permanent secretary in 1942. He was thus the chief Treasury adviser during a period which covered negotiations on reparations and war debts, the financial crisis of the early thirties, rearmament, and finally a second war; a period in which the scale of national finances and their attribution largely changed. The chancellors of the Exchequer whom he served, although differing widely in their politics and their personalities, each in their individual turn listened to Hopkins who, like the great Elizabethan servants of the State, inclined to his master's views, but held him clearly to the basic national traditions. His work at the Board of Inland Revenue had taught him that taxation was not a fantasy but a practical affair and he knew the two great secrets of his old department: what could be managed, and how far the taxpayers could be pushed. A great wealth of experience combined with his marked intellectual capacity and integrity to make him a counsellor whose opinion was rarely set aside. With Montagu (later Lord) Norman [q.v.], the governor of the Bank of England, Hopkins worked closely and as friends. Together they hammered out policies on foreign exchange and unemployment; and it became a feature of London life to see the governor's car outside the Treasury shortly before six o'clock each evening.

The Treasury in these years of financial difficulties could not avoid publicity and Hopkins as an official witness gained a reputation as one who was honest and loyal to his Government; mild and clear in his statements. When he saw a chancellor or a commission able to swallow a text but not to absorb it, he would go away, by himself, and seek out the full meaning until it was soluble. He came most notably—and, as always, reluctantly— before the public eye in 1931 while giving evidence before the royal commission on unemployment and insurance. Rather less publicity had attached to the meetings of the Macmillan committee on finance and industry in 1930 when Hopkins became locked in battle with J. M. (later Lord) Keynes [q.v.] who was challenging the precepts of Treasury finance. The issue of this conflict was characterized by Lord Macmillan [q.v.] as 'a drawn battle'. Although their views were at this time widely divergent, Keynes was wont to exclude Hopkins from his comminations, admitting that he did really understand public finance. The respect was mutual and after the outbreak of war Hopkins provided Keynes with a room at the Treasury where Keynes would exert himself to ensure that his point was properly put so that he might win Hopkins to his views.

Neither politician, banker, nor economist himself, Hopkins was able to work in harmony with all three, and he skilfully led the Treasury through eighteen years of changing problems and personalities. In his last three years he did not manage the Civil Service as his predecessors, Sir Warren Fisher [q.v.] and Sir Horace Wilson, had done. In the atmosphere of controversy which had marked their tenure he had had no share. Nor was it in his unassuming, friendly nature to dictate. Wise in his subject, humble and kind to his subordinates, who were in fact his colleagues, gifted with a quiet humour, he created a great warmth around him and impressed the stamp of his own personality upon the office of permanent secretary. He retired in 1945 and was sworn of the Privy Council; he had been promoted G.C.B. in 1941.

After his retirement Hopkins quietly indicated that he would like to serve the Church of England and was appointed to the central board of finance of which, in June 1947, he became chairman. He was seen going with delight to its conferences, and said: 'I have guided or tried to guide eighteen budgets in my time, but this afternoon I shall introduce my own budget.' He was also a crown member of the court of the university of London, a member of the Port of London Authority, of the Imperial War Graves Commission, and of a number of government committees, and a director of several companies. He was elected an honorary fellow of Emmanuel College, Cambridge, in 1946 and was Alfred Marshall lecturer in 1946–7.

Hopkins married in 1923 Lucy Davis, M.B., Ch.B. (died 1960), daughter of the late Francis Cripps; they had one son. Hopkins died in London 30 March 1955.

[*Public Administration*, vol. xxxiv, Summer 1956; R. F. Harrod, *The Life of J. M. Keynes*, 1951; private information; personal knowledge.]　　　　WILFRID EADY.

HORDER, THOMAS JEEVES, first BARON HORDER (1871–1955), physician, was born 7 January 1871, in Shaftesbury, Dorset, the fourth and youngest child of Albert Horder, a successful draper and business man who had married one of his own assistants, Ellen Jeeves. Two years after his birth the family moved to Swindon where he was educated at the high school and quickly showed himself an exceptional pupil. At the age of fifteen he was thought to have chest trouble and spent two years working on his uncles' farms among the Wiltshire downs. Returning home, he passed the matriculation examination of London University. He had still no idea what he wanted to do in life, except that he did not wish to enter the drapery business, and it was the family doctor who suggested medicine.

Horder took a correspondence course in biology with a tutorial college in Red Lion Square where his papers were corrected by H. G. Wells [q.v.], who is said to have noted on them that Horder was not cut out for research. Wells was later to be one of his patients. In 1891 Horder obtained an entrance scholarship to St. Bartholomew's Hospital, and he was awarded the junior and senior scholarships in anatomy and physiology in 1892 and 1893. He graduated B.Sc., London, in 1893 with second class honours in physiology and qualified in medicine in 1896. He obtained the degree of M.B., B.S. (London) with first class honours and gold medals in medicine, midwifery, and forensic medicine in 1898 and the M.D. in 1899. He became a member of the Royal College of Physicians of London in 1899 and a fellow in 1906.

His resident hospital experience began with his appointment as a house-physician to Samuel Gee [q.v.] at St. Bartholomew's Hospital. Gee was a gifted physician whose teaching was founded on observation and deduction at the bedside and regular attendance at the post-mortem room. He made a great impression on Horder who published a collection of 'Clinical Aphorisms from Dr. Gee's Wards (1895–6)' in *St. Bartholomew's Hospital Reports* in 1896. Up to this time Horder had been uncertain whether his future lay in biology, physiology, or medicine, and it was from Gee that he learned the fascination of the art of medical diagnosis which was to be the mainspring of his career. Horder subsequently held a number of junior appointments at St. Bartholomew's Hospital and the Hospital for Sick Children, Great Ormond Street; was demonstrator of practical pathology at Bart's in 1903 and medical registrar and demonstrator of morbid anatomy in 1904–11; he also became a member of the staff of the Royal Northern Hospital.

In later life he said that the three great advances of medicine in his lifetime were the integration of morbid anatomy with clinical medicine, the development of laboratory methods bringing about the birth of clinical pathology, and the arrival of X-rays. The combination of observation at the bedside with special investigations in the laboratory was the foundation of Horder's success. When accused of forsaking the bench for the bedside, he replied: 'No, I took the bench *to* the bedside.' This was true, and people soon began to talk about Horder's box, with its syringes and needles for venous and lumbar puncture, its tubes of broth and agar for preparing cultures at the bedside, its stains, cover-glasses, and folding microscope. In much of his work he was closely associated with Mervyn Gordon [q.v.] who was a brilliant pathologist and scientist; and while Horder himself never became a research worker, they together

greatly advanced knowledge of cerebrospinal fever, acute rheumatism, and infective endocarditis.

Horder began making a name for himself in the early years of the twentieth century and while still a registrar at Bart's he was able to afford a Rolls-Royce which he discreetly parked a few streets away from the hospital. His success was not altogether palatable to some of his senior colleagues who did not like his background or his new outlook on medicine and at times writhed under his criticism. His chance came when he was called in consultation to see King Edward VII and by a brilliant bit of observation was able to make the correct diagnosis. 'They can hardly fail to take me now', he said to a friend. In 1912 he was appointed assistant physician to St. Bartholomew's Hospital. He became a senior physician in 1921 and retired under the age limit in 1936. He was made honorary consultant physician to the Ministry of Pensions (1939) and medical adviser to London Transport (1940–55). He was the outstanding clinician of his time and one of the personalities in medicine best known to the British public. His patients included King George V, King George VI, Queen Elizabeth II, Bonar Law, and Ramsay MacDonald.

Horder was short and compact in build and his chief qualities have been described as sagacity, audacity, and humanity. The impression he gave in consultation or in committee was of organized common sense. He had the faculty of seeing the relevant facts in a clinical situation, arranging them in perspective, and comparing them with the previous data in his well-stored memory so as to arrive at the correct diagnosis. His help was much sought in committee work and he was chairman of the Ministry of Health advisory committee (1935–9), chairman of the committee on the use of public air-raid shelters (1940), and medical adviser to Lord Woolton at the Ministry of Food (1941). He was chairman of the scientific advisory committee of the British Empire Cancer Campaign for approximately thirty years and chairman of its grand council (1950–55). He was chairman of the Empire Rheumatism Council from its beginning in 1936 until 1953. Others of his numerous interests were the Noise Abatement League, the Family Planning Association, the Cremation Society, and the National Book League.

In his teaching he emphasized observation, precision, and logic. He used to say that the best book to read in medicine was the *Primer of Logic* by W. S. Jevons [q.v.]. Most of what he wrote was the current coin of medical literature but his book *Fifty Years of Medicine* (1953), which was an expanded version of his Harben lectures delivered in 1952, may still be read with pleasure, as may his occasional addresses, *Health and a Day* (1937). Horder was a rationalist who believed in the possibility of solving human problems by science, education, and reform and was not afraid to do battle for his beliefs. Characteristically, the subject he chose for his Conway memorial lecture in 1938 was 'Obscurantism'. He was an individualist who disliked many of the features of the National Health Service and he organized the Fellowship for Freedom in Medicine, becoming its first chairman in 1948. His main interests outside medicine and public life were literature and gardening.

Horder was knighted in 1918, created a baronet in 1923, and a baron in 1933. He was appointed K.C.V.O. in 1925 and G.C.V.O. in 1938; among his honorary degrees were the D.C.L. of Durham and the M.D. of Melbourne and Adelaide. He married in 1902 Geraldine Rose (died 1954), only daughter of Arthur Doggett, of Newnham Manor, Baldock, Hertfordshire. They had two daughters and one son, Thomas Mervyn (born 1910), who succeeded him when he died suddenly at Ashford Chase, Petersfield, 13 August 1955, having been blessed with abundant health and vitality to the end. A portrait by Sir William Nicholson hangs in the Great Hall at St. Bartholomew's Hospital and there is a bust by Olaff de Wet in the Royal College of Physicians, London. A bust by Donald Gilbert was exhibited at the Royal Academy in 1941 and a painting by Bernard Adams at the Royal Society of Portrait Painters in 1942.

[*The Times*, 15 August 1955; *British Medical Journal* and *Lancet*, 20 August 1955; Mervyn Horder, *The Little Genius*, 1966; private information; personal knowledge.]

L. J. WITTS.

HORE-BELISHA, (ISAAC) LESLIE, BARON HORE-BELISHA (1893–1957), politician, was born in London 7 September 1893, the only son of Jacob Isaac Belisha, an insurance company manager, and his wife, Elizabeth Miriam, daughter of John Leslie Miers. His father's family were Sephardic Jews who were driven out of Spain under the Inquisition and eventually settled in Manchester where they built up a cotton import firm. His grandfather, David Belisha, was one of the leading backers of the Ship Canal project, using up most of his fortune before it was finally carried through.

His father died when Hore-Belisha was less than a year old, and in 1912 his mother married (Sir) (Charles Fraser) Adair Hore who later became permanent secretary to the Ministry of Pensions. At his mother's desire he coupled his stepfather's surname to his own. She had devoted her life to him (long refusing to remarry for that reason) and continued to have a profound influence on him throughout his career. She made sacrifices in order to send him to Clifton College, for short periods to the Sorbonne and Heidelberg, and then to St. John's College, Oxford. At Clifton he made a mark in school debates, wrote vivid essays and also political verse which gained acceptance by the London press, attended the law courts in the holidays, and dreamed of becoming another Disraeli. At Oxford he quickly distinguished himself in Union debates, speaking on the Liberal side and as a Radical supporter of Lloyd George's social reforms. At the end of his first year war broke out. Enlisting in the Public Schools battalion of the Royal Fusiliers he soon gained a commission, in the Army Service Corps, and went to France early in November 1914, being attached to an infantry brigade in the 5th division. The skill and energy which he showed in developing local sources of supply led a year later to his appointment to the staff of the Third Army for that purpose and subsequently, with the rank of major, to army headquarters in Salonika. Early in 1918 he was invalided home with malaria.

Returning to Oxford he became a prominent figure and the first post-war president of the Union. On going down he read law, gaining the means to do so by a brilliantly quick success in journalism. Besides being a leader-writer on the *Daily Express*, he became a social and political diarist on the *Sunday Express*, starting 'The Londoner's Log' and then, under the signature 'Cross-Bencher', the commentary on 'Politics and Politicians'. He also wrote for the *Evening Standard* and the *Weekly Review*. Having made enough money for his purpose, he gave up journalism for a while to concentrate on his law studies. He was called to the bar by the Inner Temple in 1923. In the meantime he had been adopted as

Liberal candidate for the Devonport division of Plymouth and in the general election in the autumn of 1922 had made a promisingly strong challenge to the Conservative member. In 1923 he won the seat, which he held until 1945. To meet his expenses he found it necessary to return to journalism and also, with less successful results, to accept directorships in sundry companies. He had too little time to study their affairs and was only interested in money as a means to greater ends. Their failure was remembered against him later in his career.

In contrast, he made an intensive study of the many aspects of national life which came under discussion in Parliament, and frequently took a different line from the majority of his party. In particular he argued against cuts in social and defence expenditure. When the general election of 1924 swept away most of the Liberal Party, he was the only member in the south of England who survived, and in 1929 he was returned by a much increased margin. During these years he advocated bold measures of reform, particularly in the relief of unemployment. He criticized the second Labour Government for doing too little rather than too much and his own leaders for giving it continued support. At a party conference in the spring of 1931 he led an unsuccessful revolt and when the financial crisis came he quickly took the lead in organizing a new Liberal National Party to support the 'national' Government formed by Ramsay MacDonald and Baldwin. After the general election, in which he trebled his majority, Hore-Belisha was made parliamentary secretary to the Board of Trade; he succeeded so well that in 1932 he was appointed financial secretary to the Treasury at the special request of Neville Chamberlain who had found him of great help in working out tariff arrangements and now wanted his closer co-operation in steering the Ottawa agreements through the Commons. Hore-Belisha's grasp of the matter and his skill in debate and at subsequent international conferences rapidly increased his reputation for successfully tackling tough problems.

In 1934 when the road traffic bill had passed its third reading Hore-Belisha moved to the Ministry of Transport where he developed its provisions in fresh and impressive ways towards checking the rising toll of accidents. He extended the use of pedestrian crossings and introduced the illuminated amber globes mounted on black and white posts which were promptly christened 'Belisha beacons'. He put into force the provision for driving tests for new motorists; a revised highway code was brought out; and by these and other measures, and not least by the publicity which they received, he brought about a notable reduction in accidents. Looking to the future he sponsored extensive plans of new arterial road building, and as a preliminary transferred the care of the existing trunk roads from the county councils to the State. In 1935 he was sworn of the Privy Council and in 1936 raised to cabinet rank. In May 1937 Chamberlain, on becoming prime minister, transferred him to the War Office 'on the express ground', says his biographer, 'that he wished to see "drastic changes", writing "the obstinacy of some of the Army heads in sticking to obsolete methods is incredible"'.

Within a few months Hore-Belisha embarked on an extensive programme of reforms. He stimulated recruiting by increasing rates of pay and allowances, raising the standard of catering, modernizing barracks and building better ones, abolishing outworn restrictions upon the soldiers' freedom off duty, shortening the extent of service abroad, and providing more opportunity of training for a civilian trade. For officers up to the rank of major inclusive a time-scale was introduced which brought quicker promotion; the half-pay system was abolished; and the age limit of retirement for generals and colonels lowered. The cadet colleges were amalgamated, new tactical schools and courses provided, and facilities for staff training increased. Other reforms included the simplification of infantry drill, the introduction of battledress, and the fusion of the Cavalry and Royal Tank Corps in the Royal Armoured Corps. Much was done also to raise the status and standard of the Territorial Army.

At the same time Hore-Belisha sought to hasten the re-equipment and mechanization of the army and its tactical reorganization, and to develop its capacity for defence against air attack. The roles of the army were for the first time defined in order of priority, and the principle was adopted of regional strategic reserves in the Middle and Far East. Both the Middle East force and the larger strategic reserve maintained at home for the expeditionary force were intended to be primarily of a mobile armoured type likely to be more effective than infantry in a desert campaign and a more potent aid to European allies. These measures were not carried out as fast as Hore-Belisha desired or the situation demanded. After six months in office he sought, with Chamberlain's backing, to quicken the pace by appointing younger generals to the Army Council. The new men proved helpful in carrying out the lesser reforms which most soldiers had long desired; but they had been trained in the old school and when Hore-Belisha pressed measures of wider scope he soon found their hesitant acquiescence as frustrating as the direct resistance of their predecessors. Friction developed between him and his chosen official advisers who in their resentment at being pressed took little account of the frequent concessions to their point of view which he made, sometimes to the impairment of his plans. Nor were they mollified by his bigger change of course in April 1939 when he urged the Cabinet to introduce conscription in order to provide, as his official advisers and the French desired, a large army on the 1914–18 lines instead of the mechanized expeditionary force of high quality but smaller scale which had originally been envisaged.

Appreciation of his concessions was submerged by accumulated irritation over the way he prodded the generals, summoned them to meetings at short notice and inconvenient times, kept them waiting, expected them to be ready with detailed information and advice, and sometimes took quick decisions or made public announcements which committed them to steps for which they were not prepared. Such was the substance of their complaints, aggravated by dislike of forms of appeal to the public which they considered showmanship and self-advertisement. The habit of deference to superior authority prevented them from making their sentiments plain to Hore-Belisha, but their complaints were expressed very freely to influential circles outside the War Office and received a ready hearing among his political critics and rivals. Like most vivid personalities Hore-Belisha could arouse strong feelings.

By the time war came Lord Gort [q.v.], Hore-Belisha's own choice as chief of the imperial general staff, had reached a state of acute irritation which was but temporarily allayed when he went to France as commander-in-chief of the Expeditionary Force. Even during the first month of war moves were being made for the ejection of the war minister, and the conflict was brought nearer the surface in November by Gort's explosive reaction to some critical remarks of Hore-Belisha's about the slow progress of the defences in France, following similar but sharper criticisms which the Cabinet had received from two war-experienced dominion ministers, R. G. (later Lord) Casey of Australia and Deneys Reitz [q.v.] of South Africa, who had visited the front. Gort's complaints were taken up with the prime minister by the King and other very influential persons at home, while the French commander-in-chief signified his solidarity with Gort over the defences. Chamberlain asked Hore-Belisha whether he wished to change the commander-in-chief or the chief of the imperial general staff. Hore-Belisha, however, did not wish to take advantage of this opportunity and hoped that relations would improve. The prime minister himself went to France in an attempt to allay friction; but the storm did not abate and eventually, in the interest of harmony, he reluctantly decided to transfer Hore-Belisha. On 4 January 1940, telling him that 'there existed a strong prejudice against him for which I could not hold him altogether blameless', Chamberlain offered him the Board of Trade. Hore-Belisha preferred to resign, and in a letter to Chamberlain that evening wrote: 'you have been categorically assured that there is no reason whatever for anxiety about a German break-through. Yet my visits to France have convinced me that unless we utilize the time that is still available to us with far more vision and energy, the Germans will attack us on our weak spot somewhere in the gap between the Maginot Line and the sea.' (Sir) Winston Churchill records in his memoirs that Hore-Belisha had on several occasions drawn the attention of the Cabinet to the weakness of the Ardennes sector south of the British line where the Germans in fact pierced the front four months later. Hore-Belisha ended '. . . if I explain, as is usual with retiring Ministers, the reason for my departure, I shall be giving to the enemy information about the weakness of our defences and, if I do not, I lay the reason open to conjecture and perhaps to mis-representation . . . this will be the real measure of the sacrifice which I am called on to make.'

The news of his resignation came as a shock to the nation and it became very evident that most of the press and many of the public were strongly in favour of Hore-Belisha who was considered to have been one of the ablest members of Chamberlain's administration; but by abstaining from explanation he gave them no grounds upon which to support him. He resigned in March from the chairmanship of the National Liberal parliamentary party which he had held since its inception, and it was not until 1945 that he returned to office, when Churchill included him in his 'caretaker' Government as minister of national insurance, in an effort to provide an alternative to the Labour Party's social policy. But Labour won the election and Hore-Belisha himself lost his seat. He was then persuaded to join the Conservative Party, but nothing was done to provide him with a likely seat, and although he fought Coventry South in 1950 he was not successful. The prolonged absence from the House was fatal to his political prospects. In 1954 he accepted a peerage, and began to exert a renewed influence by his speeches in the House of Lords and chairmanship of committees, but this was cut short by his sudden death at Reims, 16 February 1957, when leading a parliamentary delegation on a visit to France.

Hore-Belisha's career reached its peak when he was only forty-three and virtually ended when he was forty-six. Its untimely end was due more to 'natural causes' than to the faults attributed to him. Urgent action was essential in 1937 in view of the impending danger of war. But it was natural that each particular change was repugnant to some section of military opinion, even though welcome to most, and the cumulative effect tended to produce an atmosphere of hostility. It was increased by the pace at which the changes had to be pushed through. Chamberlain recorded that he sent him to the War Office because he had 'very exceptional qualities of courage, imagination, and drive ... he has done more for the Army than anyone since Haldane'. But he added: 'Unfortunately, he has the defects of his qualities—partly from his impatience and eagerness, partly from a self-centredness which makes him careless of other people's feelings.' Anyone who worked closely with Hore-Belisha often felt exasperation, but there were those who found that with deepening associa-

tion it gave way to a growing blend of admiration and affection. The lack of patience and understanding shown by Gort and his fellows was the more regrettable since it is clear that more overdue and beneficial reforms were achieved in Hore-Belisha's years of office than in the previous twenty years.

Hore-Belisha married in 1944 Cynthia, daughter of the late Gilbert Elliot, of Hull Place, Sholden, Kent. There were no children and the peerage became extinct.

A portrait by Clarence White was exhibited at the Royal Academy in 1936.

[Keith Feiling, *The Life of Neville Chamberlain*, 1946; Sir Francis de Guingand, *Operation Victory*, 1947; Sir John Kennedy, *The Business of War*, ed. Bernard Fergusson, 1957; John W. Wheeler-Bennett, *King George VI*, 1958; R. J. Minney, *The Private Papers of Hore-Belisha*, 1960; private information; personal knowledge.]   B. H. LIDDELL HART.

HORE-RUTHVEN, ALEXANDER GORE ARKWRIGHT, first EARL OF GOWRIE (1872–1955), soldier and governor-general of Australia, was born at Windsor 6 July 1872, the second son of Walter James Hore-Ruthven, eighth Baron Ruthven in the peerage of Scotland and later first baron in the peerage of the United Kingdom, and his wife, Lady Caroline Annesley Gore, daughter of the fourth Earl of Arran. After education at Eton he joined the militia and served in the Nile expeditions of 1898 and 1899, winning the V.C. for rescuing a wounded officer in the face of fire from advancing dervishes. He was commissioned in the Cameron Highlanders in 1899 but until 1903 was employed with the Egyptian Army. In 1903–4 he took part in operations in Somaliland and from 1905 to 1908 he was military secretary and aide-de-camp to Lord Dudley [q.v.] and his successor as lord-lieutenant of Ireland. In 1908 he married Zara Eileen, daughter of John Pollok, of Lismany, county Galway, and achieved his substantive captaincy in the 1st (King's) Dragoon Guards. His friendship with Dudley resulted in the latter's choosing him for his military secretary, and incidentally providing a honeymoon journey, when Dudley was appointed governor-general of the Commonwealth of Australia. He held the post until 1910 and also served on the staff of Lord Kitchener [q.v.] during his investigation of Australian defences in 1909–10.

During the war Hore-Ruthven served as a brigade-major in France; was

G.S.O. 2 in the Welsh Guards at Gallipoli
in 1915 and was severely wounded;
became G.S.O. 1 to the 62nd division,
1916–17, and to the Guards' division,
September–December 1917; was brigadier-
general on the general staff of the 7th
Army Corps until July 1918 when he took
command of an infantry brigade. He was
appointed to the D.S.O., with bar, C.B.
and C.M.G., and was five times mentioned
in dispatches. He commanded the Welsh
Guards from 1920 to 1924 and the 1st
infantry brigade at Aldershot from 1924
to 1928.

In 1928 he was appointed K.C.M.G.,
retired from the army, and assumed
office as governor of South Australia.
The state was then prospering under the
Conservative leadership of (Sir) R. L.
Butler, but almost immediately entered
the world depression, and at a general
election in 1930 a Labour Party government was returned under L. L. Hill.
The Labour Party soon split in South
Australia, as in most parts of Australia,
on questions of depression policy, but
Hill struggled on as premier, supported
largely by the Opposition, until 1933 when
a general election again returned Butler
to power. Through these anxious times the
governor was drawn into some controversy and expressed views more congenial
to the political centre and Right than to
the socialist Left, which gave additional
force to current demands on the Left
for the abolition of the governorship.
Probably if the Left had won in 1933 the
governor's position would have become
impossible. However, he had throughout
excellent personal relations with the
parliamentary Labour Party leaders as
well as with the non-Labour parliamentarians, and the popularity of both himself
and his wife steadily increased because
of their active work on behalf of the poor
and unemployed. Hence the extension of
his term of office to 1934 was generally
applauded, and on his departure an
Adelaide crowd estimated at 100,000
bade him farewell.

Almost immediately he accepted the
governorship of New South Wales, whose
political history through the depression
years had been even more violent than
that of South Australia. The appointment
indicated a confidence that he could now
handle with the requisite tact and firmness
any Australian political situation. However, no such need arose, because after
holding the Sydney post from 21 February
1935 until 22 January 1936, a period of

political calm, he was appointed governor-
general at the urgent request of the
prime minister, J. A. Lyons [q.v.], and
took up a residence in Canberra which
lasted until 1944. He had been advanced to G.C.M.G. and created a
baron (as Lord Gowrie) in 1935 and was
sworn of the Privy Council in 1937. Five
prime ministers served under him, and
he was concerned with the abdication
problems in 1936, the war administration
from 1939, the political instability of the
Menzies and Fadden governments in 1941,
the formation of the Curtin Labour Party
administration in that year, and the
imminent peril of Japanese invasion.
His term of office was repeatedly extended
because he and his wife were widely
popular, his political and military experience was highly valued by the leaders of
all parties, and when arrangements for
his replacement—which for health reasons
he several times desired—broke down
he was prevailed on to continue. He
owed his record term of office to his
imperturbable good will, his common-
sense approach to political problems, his
dignity, and the energy and enthusiasm
which Lady Gowrie brought to a variety
of good works. Together they shared the
life of the Australian people, from the
sorrows of the war in which they lost
their only surviving child, Captain
Patrick Hore-Ruthven, to the growth
of the Australian national capital at
Canberra in whose planning Lady Gowrie
took a close interest. Their personal
relations with John Curtin [q.v.] were
particularly warm; governor-general and
prime minister met more frequently and
on more intimate terms than is known
to have occurred in any other case.

The Gowrie name will live long in
Australia, both because of its association
with a critical period in national history
and because that name now graces
several Australian institutions and places.
In 1938 Lady Gowrie persuaded the
Commonwealth Department of Health
to accept responsibility for co-ordinating
work throughout Australia on the health
and education of pre-school children,
previously a purely state matter, and as a
result there is now a Lady Gowrie Pre-
School Child Centre in each capital city.
When Gowrie's retirement was first
contemplated in 1943, the chief justice,
Sir John Latham, and others, organized
a Gowrie Scholarship Trust Fund, to
which the public subscribed nearly
£150,000, as a memorial to his Australian

services; the income is used to provide scholarships at secondary, university, and postgraduate levels for ex-Service personnel and their children. One of the largest government hostels in Canberra is called Gowrie House.

On relinquishing office Gowrie was created an earl and in 1945 was appointed deputy constable and lieutenant-governor of Windsor Castle, a position he retained until final retirement from public life in 1953; during that time he and Lady Gowrie entertained thousands of Australian visitors. He also became president of the Marylebone Cricket Club (1948), and was often host to Australian test teams. He died at his home in Gloucestershire 2 May 1955, his titles descending to his grandson, Alexander Patric Greysteil (born 1939). Lady Gowrie survived until 1965.

A portrait by (Sir) Charles Wheeler is in King's Hall, Parliament House, Canberra.

[*The Times*, 4 May 1955 and 30 July 1965; *Sydney Morning Herald*, 18 January 1945 and 4 May 1955; *Commonwealth Parliamentary Debates*, 3 May 1955; private information.]

GEOFFREY SAWER.

HORTON, SIR MAX KENNEDY (1883–1951), admiral, was born at the Maelog Lake Hotel, Anglesey, 29 November 1883, the second son of the family of four of Robert Joseph Angel Horton, a member of the London Stock Exchange, and his wife Esther Maud, daughter of William Goldsmid, also a stockbroker. In 1898 Max Horton joined the training ship *Britannia* where he played for the first eleven at football and won the middle-weight boxing prize. The technical side of the navy appealed to him strongly and while a senior midshipman his thoughts turned to the new submarine branch, where in addition to the attraction of intricate machinery there would be plenty of adventure and scope for initiative. At the age of twenty-two he was given command of A.1, a submarine of 200 tons used for experimental work. He later commanded C.8, and in 1910 returned to general service for two years in the cruiser *Duke of Edinburgh* where he was awarded the Board of Trade silver medal for heroism in saving life when the P. & O. liner *Delhi* was wrecked in a gale off Cape Spartel.

In the manœuvres of 1912 Horton, while in command of D.6, penetrated the Firth of Forth at periscope depth and

torpedoed two 'hostile' warships whi were above the bridge, an operation whi placed him in the front rank of submari commanders. On the outbreak of war 1914 he was in command of E.9, a ne ocean-going submarine; he took her in the fortified harbour of Heligoland; nex while on patrol outside the entrance, sank the cruiser *Hela*, the first enem warship to be destroyed by a Briti submarine, and then the destroyer S.1 a few miles from her own coast. For the achievements in the first two months war he was appointed to the D.S.O. a recommended for early promotion.

In October 1914 Horton, who w promoted commander at the end of t year, took E.9 into the dangerous wate of the Baltic where he sank two destroye torpedoed a large German cruiser, a with other British submarines disrupte the Swedish iron ore supplies to German In December 1915, although the Briti ambassador to Russia asked specifical that he might remain in the Baltic, was recalled to England to command J. a new submarine of 1,200 tons. For h services to Russia he was awarded t Order of St. Vladimir with swords, t Order of St. Ann with swords an diamonds, and the Order of St. Georg The French Government made him chevalier of the Legion of Honour and 1917 he was given a bar to his D.S.C Always prominent in matters of desig and experiment, Horton was in 19 given command of M.1, a large submarir carrying a twelve-inch gun. Her tria were successful and she was used oper tionally, but never fully tested in war.

In the spring of 1920, after another yea in the Baltic, this time in command of submarine flotilla with the delicate tas of assisting the small States agains Bolshevik aggression, he received second bar to his D.S.O. and in June wa promoted to captain at the age of thirty six. As a young submarine commande Horton had the reputation of being 'a b of a pirate' and also a gambler who playe high hands at bridge and poker, but h now seemed to withdraw from h companions. He loved power and used mercilessly, although he was toleran when people were prepared to admit thei mistakes as he admitted his own. Influence possibly by what he had seen in Russi he feared that industrial unrest migh spread to the navy and, since the in centive of war had gone, he demande the highest standard of discipline fror officers and men. In 1922 he was appointed to command a flotilla of large, fast, steam-driven submarines of the K class. They were clumsy and dangerous, and great skill was required when diving under a screen of destroyers to attack battleships moving at high speed. Horton, having no sympathy with the idea that wartime risks were not justified in peace, constantly practised his flotilla in this form of attack, impressing upon his commanders that sheer efficiency was the true safeguard against accidents, and that tolerance of inefficiency was dangerous.' In submarines', he said, 'there is no margin for mistakes, you are either alive or dead.'

After four years of shore service, at the Admiralty as assistant director of mobilization and at Portsmouth as chief of staff to Sir Roger (later Lord) Keyes [q.v.], he went to the Mediterranean for two years in command of the battleship *Resolution*. In October 1932 he was promoted rear-admiral and he flew his flag in the battleship *Barham* (1934–5) as second-in-command of the Home Fleet where his duties were mainly administrative. He was appointed C.B. in 1934 and in 1935 returned to the Mediterranean in command of the first cruiser squadron, a powerful force of eight fast heavily armed cruisers. In a period which included the Abyssinian crisis and the outbreak of the Spanish civil war he brought his squadron to a high standard of efficiency, but his ruthlessness and blunt manner alienated him from some senior officers who maintained that equally good results could have been obtained by less rigorous methods.

Horton was promoted vice-admiral in 1936 but when in the following year he was appointed to command the Reserve Fleet many people thought that it would be his last appointment. Horton was in no way disappointed: the responsibility for bringing this heterogeneous collection of 140 ships to a state of readiness for war strongly appealed to him and by mid-summer 1939 the whole fleet was ready to sail. He had been promoted K.C.B. in the New Year honours and on the outbreak of war took command of the Northern Patrol, responsible for intercepting merchant ships of all descriptions between Iceland and Scotland, thus enforcing a distant blockade of Germany. This dull routine was quite unsuited to a man of Horton's energy and temperament and in January 1940 he took up with alacrity the post of flag officer submarines,

establishing his headquarters at Swiss Cottage where he could be in close touch with the Admiralty and also the headquarters of Coastal Command. At the end of March Horton was convinced, contrary to official opinion, that the Germans were about to invade Norway. He concentrated all his submarines in the southern approaches to the Norwegian coast with orders to sink at sight. A week later, when the invading forces appeared, his dispositions proved so effective that twenty-one enemy transports and supply ships were sent to the bottom. His submarines also sank two cruisers and severely damaged a pocket battleship. The battle cruiser *Gneisenau* was put out of action in June when it was badly needed for the invasion of England and at the end of the year the Admiralty wrote to Horton that 'The high percentage of successful submarine attacks, and the low number of material failures, contributed a remarkable achievement.' In October 1940 Horton refused the command of the Home Fleet mainly because he would not have control of the various types of aircraft which he considered necessary. He knew that he was throwing away his chances of becoming an admiral of the fleet, but felt that he should use to the full his experience of submarine warfare. Later in the Mediterranean the submarines which he had trained and administered helped to bring Rommel's army to a standstill by wrecking transports and disrupting seaborne supplies. He also encouraged the development of midget submarines and human torpedoes.

As a submariner, Horton believed that German U-boats would be used ruthlessly in large numbers to prevent supplies coming across the Atlantic, and so reduce the army and air force to a state of impotence. He urged strongly that the Royal Air Force should share with the navy the responsibility for anti-submarine defence and both Services be trained to co-operate in the use of the latest weapons. In November 1942 when the Atlantic lifeline was stretched to its limit and the U-boats were increasing their stranglehold, Horton was appointed commander-in-chief of the Western Approaches with responsibility for ensuring not only that the people of Britain should be fed, but also that a constant flow of troops and military supplies should be maintained in safety. Although 700,000 tons of shipping had been sunk by U-boats in November, Horton was not dismayed.

The German submarine commander-in-chief, Admiral Doenitz, had found the soft spots in the allied defence; Horton knew where to look for them in the U-boat attack. Over a hundred U-boats were working in packs in mid-Atlantic where they hoped to be out of range of allied aircraft. He told the Admiralty that the best way to defend the convoys was to reinforce their escorts with highly trained and speedy Support Groups working in co-operation with very long-range aircraft, and free to take the offensive against the U-boats. As a result of his representations sixteen warships were released from close escort duty; and, after being augmented by a destroyer flotilla from the Home Fleet in March 1943, all were formed into five Support Groups. Meanwhile, seven squadrons of very long-range and long-range aircraft had been allocated to Coastal Command for use against the U-boats, and in addition aircraft carriers (converted merchant ships), joined Horton's command. He refused to rush his forces into action until they had been fully trained to work together, and in addition to other measures established a school of sea–air co-operation in Northern Ireland. In April 1943 the combined plan took shape: a main offensive by naval and air striking forces to destroy the U-boats in mid-Atlantic, and a subsidiary offensive by shore-based air forces to destroy U-boats near their bases in the Bay of Biscay. Surprise was achieved and success was complete. The brunt of the battle was borne by British and Canadian sea and air forces under Horton's command, the destruction of U-boats being shared equally by warships and aircraft. The spirit of the enemy was broken, and at the end of May Doenitz withdrew his U-boats from mid-Atlantic. From then onwards, Horton successfully countered all attempts by the enemy to resume the offensive. Acknowledging his request to retire at the end of the war in order to facilitate promotion, the Admiralty wrote to Horton: 'Never has this country endured so dangerous a threat to its existence, and with the overcoming of that danger your name and that of the Western Approaches Command will ever be associated.'

A great admiral in the tradition of St. Vincent rather than of Nelson, Horton had a technical knowledge and genius for detail which never obscured his eye for the main issues: he could see the wood *and*

the trees, and his driving force saw to it that the policies he initiated were always carried through. He said himself that he could be as obstinate as two mules when he knew that he was right. Many were thankful that some of his energies were used up on the golf course to which he repaired every afternoon, returning to fight the Battle of the Atlantic at night. Ruthless and intolerant of inefficiency he yet possessed an understanding and kindness of heart not always realized. He was famous for the accuracy of his hunches, not altogether attributable to knowledge and experience even at the service of a brilliant mind. He admitted that he prayed every night for guidance and foresight, and for the safe-keeping of his ships. Part Jewish, he was a deeply religious man who had leanings towards, but did not join, the Roman Catholic Church. He was a perfectionist, completely repudiating half-measures, and this perhaps explains a great devotion to Saint Thérèse of Lisieux which would have surprised his shipmates had they known of it. It was typical of Horton that they did not. He was an individualist who liked to keep sentiment away from his work and his social life apart from the navy. He passionately loved all that was beautiful, travelled as often as he could in Europe, was a devotee of opera, and had many friends in the theatrical world. His character was unusually complex and earned for him more admiration and criticism than falls to the lot of lesser men.

In June 1945 Horton was promoted G.C.B. and in 1946 appointed Bath King of Arms. The United States, France, Holland, and Norway conferred upon him their highest honours and he received the honorary degree of LL.D. from the Queen's University, Belfast (1947). But apart from the freedom of Liverpool (1946) where he had had the headquarters of his command, no other British honour came to him. He died in London 30 July 1951, having suffered from ill health brought on by the strain of the war and undergone five major operations. He was accorded a state funeral in Liverpool Cathedral, where a memorial to him was unveiled in 1957.

A portrait by John Worsley is at Fort Blockhouse, Gosport; another by Sir Oswald Birley is in the Greenwich Collection.

[W. S. Chalmers, *Max Horton and the Western Approaches*, 1954; Admiralty records; *His Majesty's Submarines*, H.M.S.O. 1945;

The Battle of the Atlantic, H.M.S.O., 1946;
private information; personal knowledge.]
                    W. S. CHALMERS.

HOULDSWORTH, SIR HUBERT
STANLEY, first baronet (1889–1956),
chairman of the National Coal Board,
was born at Heckmondwike 20 April
1889, the only child of Albert Edward
Houldsworth, drysalter, by his wife,
Susannah Buckley. He was educated at
Heckmondwike Grammar School and at
Leeds University where he obtained his
B.Sc. with first class honours in physics
in 1911, proceeding M.Sc. (1912) and D.Sc.
(1925), and joined the staff in 1916. In the
meantime he was fulfilling a boyhood ambition by reading for the bar and was called
by Lincoln's Inn in 1926. He was an able
advocate with a strong sense of humour,
and his practice on the North-Eastern
circuit steadily increased. After 1931 he
was occupied mainly with his brief as
standing counsel for the Midland District
executive board of colliery owners which,
under the Act of 1930, fixed a standard
tonnage for each colliery. If an owner were
aggrieved at the output decided upon for
his colliery he could appeal to independent
arbitration. Most owners did.

Control of selling was introduced
in 1935 and from 1936 until 1942
Houldsworth, who took silk in 1937, was
independent chairman of the committee
of the Midland scheme which administered these selling provisions. On the
outbreak of war he was appointed joint
coal supplies officer for the Midland
(Amalgamated) District and unobtrusively
exercised great influence on the national
administration of the government scheme
of control of coal supplies. In 1942 he
became regional controller for South and
West Yorkshire and in 1944 controller-
general of the Ministry of Fuel and Power.

In 1945 Houldsworth returned to the
bar but on the nationalization of the
mines in the following year he became
chairman of the East Midland division
of the National Coal Board, covering
the coalfields of Nottinghamshire, Derby,
and Leicester, relatively low-cost areas
with good labour relations. He knew the
division intimately and threw himself
with energy and skill into building up
its organization and securing increased
productivity and lower costs. He soon
realized the need for increased mechanization. Successful though he was in the
division, he resented the control exercised by the National Coal Board. He

accepted a measure of overall financial
control; but it was his view, openly
expressed, that in other respects the
divisional boards should be autonomous.

In 1951 Houldsworth became chairman
of the National Coal Board. His predecessor, Lord Hyndley, had built up an
organization for the nationalized industry;
a national plan for the reconstruction of
the collieries had been prepared. It was
Houldsworth's task, tackled with his
customary zeal, to secure the rapid
modernization of the industry. He urged
on the divisions the urgent need for more
and more mechanization; he appreciated
the need for improved management;
he strove for better labour relations. But
he still believed in divisional autonomy
and on 22 October 1953 a general directive
was issued to divisional chairmen and
heads of headquarters departments firmly
laying down the policy of *primus inter pares*.

Public comment on the need to review
the organization of the National Coal
Board caused the formation of an independent advisory committee in December
1953 under Alexander (later Lord) Fleck.
In its report published in February 1955
the committee approved the main structure of the Board's organization but
considered that it was too half-hearted
in seeing that the divisions carried out
the policies it laid down. It recommended
that the general directive of October
1953 be withdrawn and reissued emphasizing the authority of the Board.

Most of the committee's recommendations were adopted but its report was a
blow to Houldsworth, criticizing, as it did
so strongly, the policy he had consistently
advocated. Nevertheless, his dedication to
the industry was unimpaired. He continued
his travels throughout the length and
breadth of the coalfields. He ignored the
warning of a slight heart attack in 1955,
and died suddenly in his London flat
1 February 1956.

Houldsworth was knighted in 1944
and created a baronet in January 1956.
From 1949 until his death he was pro-
chancellor of Leeds University where
there is a portrait by Sir Gerald Kelly.
He received an honorary LL.D. from
Leeds (1951) and from Nottingham (1953).

In 1919 he married Hilda Frances,
daughter of Joseph Clegg, of Heckmondwike. They had one child, (Harold)
Basil (born 1922), who succeeded as
second baronet.

[Private information; personal knowledge.]
                    R. J. MOFFAT.

HOUSE, (ARTHUR) HUMPHRY (1908–
1955), scholar, was born at Sevenoaks
22 May 1908, the second son of William
Harold House, solicitor, and his wife,
Eleanor Clara Neve. A scholar of Repton
and Hertford College, Oxford, he took a
first in *literae humaniores* in 1929 and
in 1930 a second in modern history.
After a year of teaching at Repton, he
was ordained deacon in the Church of
England in 1931 and elected fellow,
lecturer in English, and chaplain at
Wadham College, Oxford; but during 1932
he felt unable to take priest's orders, so
resigned his fellowship and retired into
lay life. From October 1933 he spent two
years as assistant lecturer in classics and
English at University College, Exeter,
and then sailed for Calcutta, where he was
first professor of English at the Presidency
College and then lecturer in English at the
university.

In 1938 House returned to England and
in 1940 was elected a William Noble
fellow in the university of Liverpool, but
before long he was called up as a trooper
in the Royal Armoured Corps and served
in the army until 1945, when he was
invalided out with the rank of major. He
always said that he had begun to learn how
to organize paper, not in any university,
but at the Staff College at Camberley.

From 1947 to 1949 he was director of
English studies at Peterhouse, Cambridge,
and during those years he gave many
talks on the Third Programme of the
B.B.C. In 1948 he was appointed
university lecturer in English literature
at Oxford, and in 1950 was elected to
a senior research fellowship at Wadham.

From early years House concentrated on
the English nineteenth century—not only
its literature, but its history, economics,
manners, and particularly its religion—
believing that only in a synthesis of all
these could the truth be found. His
method was to analyse a work of literature minutely, as a classical scholar
would, but always to interpret it in the light
of the larger context. Despite the subtlety
of his approach he was never afraid to be
simple and direct. The first published
fruits of his method, and of the breadth of
his learning, appeared in his edition of
*The Note-Books and Papers of Gerard
Manley Hopkins* (1937), which, with its
massive organization and wide-ranging
notes, was immediately recognized as an
indispensable source for the study of that
poet and his work.

House then turned his attention to

Dickens, whose fame had hitherto been
supported mainly by enthusiastic amateurs. Three was no adequate biography or
collection of letters, no satisfactory edition
of the novels, and few critical studies
based on a thorough knowledge of the
period. House set about changing all that:
his book *The Dickens World* (1941) was
the first serious attempt to examine the
novels in the light of the times in which
they were written; he later began to
collect, date, and annotate every Dickens
letter that could be traced; and he
helped in launching the first critically
annotated edition of the novels. The two
last projects were to be completed by
others, but House was a prime mover.

In 1953 he published *Coleridge*, an
expanded version of the Clark lectures,
given at Cambridge in 1951–2. Here
his power of precise detail, biographical
and literary, combined with humanity
and vision to analyse those aspects
of Coleridge's genius which made him
inescapably the poet he was. In this book
House was able to make effective use of
quotations from Coleridge's notebooks
which had not before been printed. After
his death two posthumous books appeared:
All in Due Time (1955), a collection of
his essays, reviews, and broadcast talks;
and *Aristotle's Poetics* (1956), a course of
Oxford lectures, revised and introduced
by Colin Hardie, which had had a revolutionary success in the English school
when first given in 1952.

House's pupils—schoolboys, undergraduates, and graduates—thought him
the most inspiring teacher they had ever
known, and it is as a teacher-critic-
scholar that he would have liked to be
remembered. Of all his teaching he gained
most satisfaction from the lectures on the
nineteenth century which he gave to
graduate students during his final years at
Oxford—the culmination and reward, he
felt, of twenty years of work and reading.

Like Matthew Arnold, House knew a
great deal about schools and universities,
language and literature, and from this
solid base his critical and creative perception took wing. For him scholarship
involved discovering a writer's intention,
which inevitably led to a minute study of
the writer's life and personality and of
the society in which he lived. House had
an unusual sense of the past, of its remoteness, and at the same time of its
relevance to the present. His work contained no waste-matter, and his criticism
had an absolute directness and serious-

ness which brought it close to its living subject. He was the most imaginative of pedants, the most flexible of perfectionists.

At the time of his sudden death in Cambridge, 14 February 1955, House was deeply engaged in the editing of Dickens's letters, and his notes on them might well have proved his greatest monument, for his gift as a writer was to apply the severity of his scholarship to himself and to distil it into deceptively simple annotations.

No one could be long in House's presence without becoming aware of his intellectual stature and deep integrity. To strangers he might at first seem formidable—as in one sense he was—but closer knowledge soon disclosed his warmth, humour, kindliness, and generosity.

In 1933 House married Madeline Edith, daughter of Henry Pitman Church, company director; they had two daughters and one son.

[*The Times*, 17 February 1955; private information; personal knowledge.]

RUPERT HART-DAVIS.

HOUSMAN, LAURENCE (1865–1959), writer, was born 18 July 1865 at Perry Hall, Bromsgrove. His father, Edward Housman, a solicitor practising in Bromsgrove, was a whimsical character, not entirely successful as a solicitor, and a strong Tory who liked to say that he had been born in 1832, the year of England's greatest disaster. Housman's mother, Sarah Jane Williams, died when he was six, and he became much attached to the lady whom his father subsequently married. She won the affection of all her stepchildren (five sons and two daughters), the eldest of whom was A. E. Housman [q.v.]; Laurence was the youngest but one. He was educated at Bromsgrove School, but possibly owing to the somewhat drifting fortune of his father, he did not go on to the university. Narrow origins, confined within Worcestershire, may have circumscribed his outlook; he was perhaps more self-assertive than he would have been had he mixed in youth in a wider circle.

At eighteen he moved to London and studied art in Kennington and at the Lambeth School of Art, and later at South Kensington. During his early years he was greatly impoverished and was able to manage only by sharing, first lodgings, then a small house, with his favourite sister Clemence, an author and wood-

engraver who died in 1955. Her books were *The Were-Wolf* (1896), *The Unknown Sea* (1898), and *Sir Aglovale de Galis* (1905). Through A. W. Pollard [q.v.] Housman was introduced to Harry Quilter [q.v.] for whose flamboyant if short-lived *Universal Review* he both wrote and drew. Pollard also introduced him to Kegan Paul [q.v.], a man after Housman's own heart who had thrown up a conventional Church of England incumbency on account of curious religious opinions and of extreme political views, and led a rather precarious publishing existence in London. Kegan Paul encouraged him to write and in 1893 published his edition of a selection from William Blake.

In 1900 Housman published anonymously *An Englishwoman's Love-Letters* —to an extent a psychological study, innocuous enough by later standards but at that time regarded as somewhat daring. Variously attributed to Mrs. Meynell, Marie Corelli, and Oscar Wilde, the *Love-Letters* sold extremely well. Housman made £2,000 out of them: 'a mighty windfall from the worst book I ever wrote'. In 1895 Housman had become art critic on the *Manchester Guardian* and he used to say that the journal unwittingly saved him from Roman Catholicism by sending him on a foreign assignment which opened his eyes to the tawdriness of European Catholicism. A colleague, James Bone, testified to the force and wit with which Housman handled the many art controversies which developed while he was on the paper, notably the Chantrey Bequest inquiry and the dispute over the statues by (Sir) Jacob Epstein [q.v.] on the British Medical Association building. Housman's attachment on the *Manchester Guardian*, which lasted for sixteen years, marks the end of the first stage of his literary career. His work, especially some of his poems such as *Green Arras* (1896) and *Spikenard* (1898), carried (as was noticed in his obituary in *The Times*) 'introspective glimpses of his own soul of a disturbing oddity'. If, in his concern with these matters, he was something of a revolutionary, nevertheless, as was noticed by Grant Richards at the time, he represented much that was best in the literary work of his generation.

Coincident with his work for the *Manchester Guardian* he began a career as playwright, never completely successful but always pursued with determination. He elected to write on subjects

Housman

which, in the conventional feeling then prevailing and tightly held in the lord chamberlain's office, were bound to involve him with the censor. His first play *Bethlehem* was banned for many years although it was privately produced by Gordon Craig in 1902 at a financial loss to the author. His play *Pains and Penalties* (1911), about Queen Caroline, was deplorable history. On the grounds that it dealt with a sad historical episode of comparatively recent date it too was banned by the lord chamberlain for many years and was then released on the excision of one sentence and the single word 'adultery'. In 1906, in collaboration with Harley Granville-Barker [q.v.], he wrote *Prunella, or Love in a Dutch Garden* —a pierrot play—which was tolerably successful and escaped the wrath of the censor.

In the meantime Housman's political sympathies, deriving in part from his antipathy to the Toryism of his Bromsgrove home and in part from the discontent with established things which marked his literary associates at the turn of the century, led him to take up with vigour the cause of woman's suffrage. In June 1909 he was the centre of a disturbance in the central lobby of the House of Commons. He was a member of the men's section of the extremist Women's Social and Political Union, leaving them in 1912 only when, as he put it, militancy became violent rather than symbolic. His sister Clemence suffered brief imprisonment for refusing to pay taxes. In the course of the war of 1914–18 he gradually became a convinced pacifist. He was a courageous supporter of the ideals of a League of Nations and in 1916 crossed to the United States to proclaim his views in a series of lectures.

At the end of the war he published *Sheepfold* (1918), a novel based to some extent on the life of Mrs. Girling [q.v.]. Although this book was favourably noticed, Housman's most popular success lay ahead, in *The Little Plays of St. Francis* which were published in 1922 and had genuine charm. The year before he had published *Angels and Ministers*, scenes from the court of Queen Victoria, which in part caught the gentle mockery of the Queen prevailing in intellectual circles. It was true of so much of Housman's work that he successfully launched his often rather frail barque on the flood tide of fashionable views. During the

twenties he attempted two satirical novels: *The Life of H.R.H. the Duke of Flamborough* (1928) was based on George, Duke of Cambridge [q.v.]; *Trimblerigg* (1924) attacked a target which was more worth while and, in the thin disguise of a Nonconformist minister, focused attention on the embittered feelings about Lloyd George felt on the Left. Beatrice Webb [q.v.], always easily shocked by true feeling, called it 'savage'. Housman more correctly said that it was 'as useful and truthful a book as I have ever written'.

In the early thirties Housman published further selections of plays about Queen Victoria which, with *Angels and Ministers*, were collected in 1934 under the title *Victoria Regina* with illustrations by E. H. Shepard. Although in historical accuracy they showed no improvement they successfully caught the romantic charm of the Queen and Prince Albert. They were performed in 1935 at the Gate Theatre, and gained greatly from the superb and realistic acting of Pamela Stanley as the Queen which was repeated when the censor's ban was lifted (thanks in part to King Edward VIII) and the play opened at the Lyric Theatre on 21 June in the coronation summer of 1937. It was an enormous, deserved, and immediate success. After his long years of frustration with the censor, Housman had this one piece of crowning good fortune that the ban was lifted at the moment when public interest in the royal family was at its peak. He is believed to have made some £15,000 out of this success. With characteristic courage and indiscretion he spoke on the opening night of his gratitude to the Duke of Windsor.

Housman published an entertaining autobiography, *The Unexpected Years*, in 1937. He lived so long, was friendly with so many of the leaders of thought in the critical decades of his middle life, and was connected with such a diversity of 'progressive' causes that his writings will always remain a valuable reflection of opinion and feeling when the twentieth century banished the nineteenth. He never achieved the substantial work of which he was perhaps capable and, inspired partly by causes and partly by the necessity to maintain himself, wrote a great deal which was ephemeral. He noticed in the obituary of himself which he wrote for the old *Manchester Guardian* that he was charged with being 'too versatile'. Also for his permanent reputation he was too impetuous, too insensitive to entrenched opinion, and too eager to hack out what he thought dead. He was fortunate perhaps that the times were moving with him, and as a pioneer feminist, pacifist, and socialist he lived to see if not the triumph at least the general acceptance of those ideals which he had certainly encouraged by his talents. Although many of Housman's political and social opinions seemed somewhat silly and muddled, and not only to those who disapproved them, they never obscured the width of his interest, his taste, and the persuasive charm with which his opinions were held.

The relations between Housman and his renowned brother were somewhat formal although his admiration for A.E. was deep and unmixed with jealousy. Each enjoyed recounting how the works of one had been confused with those of the other, although A.E.'s enjoyment did not conceal a certain irony. Laurence Housman attempted a biography of his brother after his death, *A.E.H.* (1937), but some of his efforts to analyse A.E.'s feelings were superficial suggestions, better dealt with fully or left severely alone. His handling of his brother's poetical notebooks was not judicious: having asked (although he did not follow) the advice of three Cambridge friends of his brother about the notebooks, he was distressed at the end of his life by the use made of this material.

From 1924 Housman, who never married, lived at Street in Somerset with his sister. He used to attend the Friends meetings for many years and he became a Quaker in 1952. He died 20 February 1959 in hospital in Glastonbury.

A drawing by (Sir) William Rothenstein is reproduced in his *Liber Juniorum*.

[Laurence Housman, *The Unexpected Years*, 1937; *The Times* and *Manchester Guardian*, 21 February 1959; private information.]
ROGER FULFORD.

HOWE, CLARENCE DECATUR (1886–1960), Canadian minister, was born in Waltham, Massachusetts, United States, 15 January 1886, the elder child and only son of William Clarence Howe, a builder, and his wife, Mary Emma Hastings. Both parents were of sturdy New England stock and Howe inherited a builder's temperament; constructive in all his activities, his mind was competent, direct, unemotional, and pragmatic. After graduating in civil engineering from the

Massachusetts Institute of Technology in 1906 he spent the years 1908–13 on the staff of Dalhousie University, Canada. In 1913 he became a Canadian citizen and was appointed chief engineer of the newly formed Board of Grain Commissioners for Canada, in charge of design and construction of internal storage elevators. From 1916 to 1935 he built up a lucrative private engineering firm at Port Arthur, Ontario, specializing in grain elevators.

In 1935 W. L. Mackenzie King [q.v.] persuaded Howe to enter politics and when the Liberals returned to office in that year Howe, as member for Port Arthur, but with no previous political experience, became minister of railways and canals and minister of marine. His first task was to consolidate these two departments into one: the Department of Transport. In 1936, during his first session in the House, Howe introduced three important and controversial bills. One revised the capital structure of the Canadian National Railways, replacing the board of trustees by normal corporate management. Another established the Canadian Broadcasting Corporation in place of the Canadian Radio Commission. The third replaced numerous local harbour commissions by a three-man National Harbours Board in Ottawa. In 1937 he introduced a bill to set up Trans-Canada Airlines as a public corporation after it proved impossible to do so under joint railway ownership. An avowed proponent of private enterprise, Howe paradoxically brought into being more publicly controlled enterprises than has any other Canadian minister, but always for pragmatic reasons.

Howe's war work was an extension of this method of operating quasi-commercial and industrial government institutions under efficient business methods. As minister of munitions (1940–46) he mobilized Canada's entire industrial and economic facilities, turning the country into a highly industrialized State. He set up twenty-eight crown corporations; many of the most successful were disbanded at the end of the war; others were retained to serve particular needs. During the war Howe administered the war supplies agreement with the United States under the 1941 Hyde Park declaration and was the Canadian member of the Combined Production and Resources Board set up in June 1942 to integrate the requirements and supply of munitions of the United States, United Kingdom, and Canada. In October 1944 Howe also became minister of reconstruction; in January 1946 his two departments merged as the Department of Reconstruction and Supply. Howe thus remained in charge of the country's economy through the period of liquidation of war programmes, termination of contracts, disposal of war surpluses, re-employment of war service personnel, and restoration of peacetime economy. This difficult, unglamorous job was completed efficiently and with a minimum of dislocation and criticism.

In January 1948 Howe became minister of trade and commerce. After the Korean war broke out he was again called on to head a Department of Defence Production (1951–7) but the Department of Trade and Commerce continued to claim his major energies. His final year in office was the stormiest of his career. In 1956 he promoted the idea of a pipeline to bring natural gas from Alberta to the industrial areas of the East. He believed this would be of lasting economic advantage to Canada and provide an immediate stimulus to a lagging economy. He also believed he could use the same type of authoritarian and industrial approach which had been so successful in war. In this he was wrong; alleged abuse of closure and affront to parliamentary rights, not economics, became the issue. The immediate battle was won in Parliament but in the general election of 1957 the Liberal Party went down to defeat and Howe lost his seat.

This rejection after twenty-two years of almost superhuman performance did not embitter him. He withdrew from political life to become active in finance and industry and at the time of his death was a director of eleven industrial companies and seven financial institutions. In 1957 he became chancellor of Dalhousie University and later a member of 'The Corporation' of the Massachusetts Institute of Technology. In his last years he found these associations with the universities of his youth the most rewarding of all his multifold activities.

Howe was a doer not a philosopher. He was not a natural 'House of Commons man'. Procedural matters bored him; he believed in action not words. Essentially a gregarious and friendly man, he could be ruthless when crossed in what he thought was the proper course. A superb administrator, he delegated authority and trusted his staff. At his best in emergencies, he was resourceful, fearless but never reckless. He was not a bookish

person, his interests were men and their actions. He wasted few hours but mixed short periods of relaxation with his work and took a yearly fishing trip. He was a casual but competent bridge player and golf was a continuing pleasure throughout his life.

He was nominated to the Privy Council in 1946 and received the American medal for merit in 1947. He was awarded honorary doctorates by fifteen universities in Canada and elsewhere, was an honorary member of many national professional engineering societies, and was awarded the Hoover medal of the American Society of Civil Engineers (1952) and the Daniel Guggenheim medal and certificate (1954).

In 1916 Howe married Alice Martha, daughter of Joseph Ruggles Worcester, a successful consulting engineer in Boston with whom he had worked in 1905–8. They had two sons and three daughters. Howe died in Montreal 31 December 1960. A portrait by Robin Watt is the property of Dalhousie University.

[Private information; personal knowledge.]
C. J. MACKENZIE.

HUDSON, ROBERT SPEAR, first VISCOUNT HUDSON (1886–1957), politician, was born in London 15 December 1886, the eldest son of Robert William Hudson, who had sold the family business of soap manufacture as soon as he succeeded to it, and his first wife, Gerda Frances Marion Bushell Johnson, of Liverpool. Educated at Eton and Magdalen College, Oxford, where he obtained a second class in modern history in 1909, Hudson entered the diplomatic service in 1911 and was posted successively to St. Petersburg, Washington, Athens, and Paris. He became a first secretary in 1920 and resigned in 1923 to contest the Whitehaven division of Cumberland as Conservative candidate. He was unsuccessful in this first attempt, but was elected the following year and represented the constituency until 1929. In 1931 he again entered Parliament as member for Southport, a seat which he retained until his elevation to a viscountcy in 1952. In recognition of his services, Southport conferred on him the honorary freedom of the borough.

From 1931 to 1935 Hudson was parliamentary secretary to the Ministry of Labour, from 1935 to 1936 minister of pensions, and from 1936 to 1937 parliamentary secretary to the Ministry of Health. Then followed nearly four years

(1937–40) as secretary of the Department of Overseas Trade and a brief spell (April–May 1940) as minister of shipping. In these offices he established a reputation for competence and hard work; in particular he threw himself wholeheartedly into the organization of the British Industries Fair and other activities for the promotion of British overseas trade—activities which at that time were not always considered sympathetic to the claims of home agriculture for remunerative prices.

It was with some apprehension therefore that the agricultural world received the news of Hudson's appointment in 1940 by (Sir) Winston Churchill as minister of agriculture and fisheries, particularly as he was taking the place of Sir Reginald Dorman-Smith, who was a popular past-president of the National Farmers' Union, with first-hand knowledge of farming problems.

The choice, however, turned out to be ideal. Coming to his task with a fresh and fearless mind, Hudson quickly mastered the intricate problems involved in reviving a depressed industry and injecting into it the necessary finance and confidence. He then proceeded to drive it relentlessly through all the obstacles and difficulties of war to ever-increasing production and efficiency. The acreage in England and Wales of wheat, for example, was by 1944 increased by 82%, potatoes by 116%, sugar-beet by 24%, and the total area under tillage by nearly 4¾ million acres (69%). He achieved, in fact, an agricultural revolution, not only in cropping, but in the attitude of the farming community towards the changes necessary to increase the output of essential foods and thus save valuable shipping space. To support his demands he introduced a bold legislative programme based on guaranteed prices and markets which gave the farming community a stability which it had not enjoyed for a century. Moreover, he awoke the nation to the importance of home agriculture as a balancing factor to industrial development and a permanent safeguard in the national economy.

These spectacular results Hudson achieved largely by his own untiring efforts, working closely with the permanent secretary, Sir Donald Fergusson. The countrywide organization of county and district committees with their representatives in every parish, in all some five thousand voluntary workers recruited from within the industry itself—these were the spearhead of his drive. In a determined policy of decentralization they were given wide powers. It was a bold experiment in guiding and policing an industry not by officials but from within its own ranks. In war conditions it succeeded, for both those who gave orders and those who received them were engaged in the same task and filled with the same desire to contribute to the war effort. Probably no minister of the Crown has ever spent so much of his time in personal contact with the rank and file of the section of the community with which he was particularly concerned as did Hudson. Every day he could spare from Whitehall, including many Sundays, was spent in visiting the committees or in addressing mass meetings of farmers. At these meetings Hudson never minced his words, and at first his blunt approach sometimes caused dismay. He would brook no excuse or delay; objections were swept aside. He was too anxious to get things done to allow himself to accept any compromise or to waste time on conciliation. He deliberately set high and sometimes impossible targets of achievement. 'Don't you know', was one of his sayings, 'that what is difficult must be started tomorrow, but what is impossible to-day?'

His sincerity, ability, and leadership soon won a wide response from the agricultural community which learnt to respect his forthrightness and his readiness to take decisions and to back up any committee or individual, regardless of precedent or red-tape, when he thought that the right course was being followed. His gifts exactly matched the times and the difficulties he had to face; he proved a great administrator and was without doubt a great wartime minister of agriculture. He was sworn of the Privy Council in 1938, made a C.H. in 1944, and remained in office until Labour came into power in 1945. In the meantime he had become keenly interested in the practical problems of agriculture and purchased a farm in Wiltshire where he established a successful Friesian herd. In 1954–5 he was president of the British Friesian Society, and he also served on the council of the Royal Agricultural Society.

Hudson married in 1918 Hannah (died 1969), daughter of Philip Synge Physick Randolph, of Philadelphia, and had one son, Robert William (1924–63), who succeeded him. In his later years Hudson became chairman of the board of governors of the Imperial Institute and Britain's representative on the United Nations trusteeship committee. He also embarked on farming in Southern Rhodesia and it was during a visit there that he died, 2 February 1957.

[*The Times*, 4 February 1957; *Farmers Weekly*, 8 February 1957; *Lessons of the British War Economy*, ed. D. N. Chester, 1951; Sir Keith A. H. Murray, *Agriculture* (History of the Second World War. Civil Series), 1955; personal knowledge.]

WILLIAM GAVIN.

HUGHES, WILLIAM MORRIS (1862–1952), Australian prime minister, was born in London 25 September 1862, of Welsh parents; his father, William Hughes, was a carpenter of North Welsh artisan stock, and his mother, born Jane Morris, from a Montgomeryshire farming family. The mother died in 1869, and until 1874 the child lived with an aunt at Llandudno, where he attended the grammar school; he was then admitted to St. Stephen's School, Westminster, where he remained first as pupil then as pupil teacher until 1884, when he migrated to Queensland. For two years he wandered the back country taking odd jobs, until employment on a coastal ship brought him in 1886 to Sydney. After further casual employment, including that of a stage extra in *Henry V*, Hughes married in 1886 Elizabeth Cutts, said to have been his landlady's daughter, and settled in a small shop with residence in Balmain, a dockside slum area.

He now became active in the growing Labour movement, was employed in 1893 as an organizer for the newly created political organization of trade unions and Labour electoral leagues, and advocated the subjection of parliamentary Labour representatives to control by the annual conference, the central executive, and a majority in the parliamentary caucus: ironical having regard to his later quarrel with the Labour 'machine'. In 1894 he was elected as Labour Party member for the Lang electorate in Sydney, which included his dockside home, and rapidly rose to prominence in Parliament and in the outside Labour organizations; he held Lang with increasing majorities at elections in 1895 and 1898. In Parliament he was especially prominent in pushing through measures for 6 p.m. closing of shops and for old age pensions.

Hughes was disappointed when Labour failed to obtain election of any of its representatives to the decisive federal conventions of 1897–8, and his opposition to the federal scheme hardened when in 1899 (Sir) G. H. Reid [q.v.] failed to obtain the degree of modification of the draft constitution which Labour wanted, especially on the question of the powers of the Senate. Hughes accordingly became one of the main public opponents of federalism at the plebiscite of 1899, but the required majority for bringing New South Wales into federation was eventually obtained. Hughes then transferred to the federal sphere; at the first election for the Commonwealth House of Representatives in 1901 he was elected for West Sydney, which included his old state electorate.

The Hughes who now emerged on the federal stage, and soon became and long remained a dominating influence there, had already moved far in personal life and political views from the poverty-stricken doctrinaire whom we glimpse in the scanty records of his life from 1884 to 1893. Payment of members was adopted in New South Wales in 1888 and written into the federal constitution, and although the costs of being a member, and the demands of a rapidly increasing family, left little over, he never again suffered the grinding poverty and insecurity of earlier years. He was short, slightly built, stooped, with an engagingly ugly face and big ears, a gift to cartoonists but correspondingly soon familiar to the nation as 'Billy'. Ill health which had contributed to his migration from England had been made chronic by his early hardships in Australia; dyspepsia, and bad hearing necessitating the use of hearing aids, plagued the rest of his life, although he soon learned to use the deaf-aid as a weapon to avoid inconvenient questions or obtain time for a reply. Immense energy and drive largely overcame these handicaps, although ill health contributed to the surprising lapses in political judgement which marred his career after 1915. Throughout the nineties he both studied and practised public speaking, read for the bar (to which he was admitted in 1903), and developed a capacity for fluent writing as well as speaking. At his best, Hughes was a superb orator, using by turns a rollicking humour, satire, scathing invective, and emotional rhetoric, but with great clarity and directness where these were required.

His small figure became transformed by flailing arms and stamping legs into the embodiment of persuasion or domination.

The lessons in political realism learned in the New South Wales Parliament were reinforced by his experience of industrial warfare. In 1899 he reorganized and became secretary of the Sydney Wharf Labourers' Union, and held this position until 1915. In 1902 he created an Australia-wide Waterside Workers' Federation, became its first president and later procured its first award in the newly created Commonwealth Court of Conciliation and Arbitration. Hughes fought vigorously for the interests of this and other trade unions, but did so increasingly from the point of view of a tactician out to secure optimum gains in wages and conditions for a minimum loss through strikes and the antagonizing of public and even employer opinion.

Until Alfred Deakin [q.v.] formed a fusion of the non-Labour parties in 1909, Labour held the balance of power, and for two short periods itself held office; Hughes was minister for external affairs in the government of J. C. Watson [q.v.] in 1904 and attorney-general in the first government of Andrew Fisher [q.v.] in 1908–9. He became a principal Labour speaker on most subjects, and delivered masterpieces of invective against those who incurred his party's wrath, notably in the 1909 debates on Deakin's final decision to remove the Fisher government and join the Conservatives. Hughes's main constructive activities in this period concerned maritime legislation and defence. In 1904 he became chairman of a royal commission investigating a proposed federal code of navigation law, and in 1907 he visited England for a conference on the relation of such legislation to the imperial Merchant Shipping Acts; legislation based on his recommendations was ultimately passed in 1913. He adopted, and persuaded first his party and then the Deakin government of 1909 to adopt, the principle of compulsory military training for male citizens, with obligation to serve only within Australia, as the foundation of Australian military defence policy.

Labour swept the polls in 1910 and Hughes was attorney-general in the second Fisher government which held office until 1913. Besides his heavy involvement in the legal and constitutional aspects of government, including unsuccessful attempts at procuring consti-

tutional amendment by referendum in 1911 and 1913, he became main government spokesman on nearly all matters of difficulty. The constructive achievements with which he was associated included the creation of a Commonwealth Bank and a Commonwealth note issue, the extension of Commonwealth social services, and the introduction of a federal land tax.

The Fisher government was defeated at the election of 1913 but so narrowly that its opponents soon obtained a 'deadlock' double dissolution. War broke out immediately before polling day, and Hughes vied with Fisher in pledging the complete support of the Labour Party for the British war effort. Hughes had formed and led organizations interested in Australian defence from 1905 on, and during his 1907 visit to England had attracted attention by his vehement support for a strong defence policy. Without the authority of his party, he now proposed that the election be postponed and a political truce proclaimed for the duration of the war so that all effort should be concentrated on its conduct. Constitutional difficulties prevented this, but Hughes's attitude began the break between himself and the left wing of the Labour movement. At the election, Labour was returned with large majorities in both houses, and Hughes again became attorney-general under Fisher. Fisher retired from politics in October 1915 and Hughes succeeded him as party leader and prime minister, and remained attorney-general. While not wholly inattentive to Labour's social aims, he concentrated throughout this period on war problems, particularly the dissolution of German economic interests and influences in Australia and the vesting of the relevant enterprises in Australian concerns.

In March 1916 he arrived in England to consult with the Asquith administration on military and economic policy and attracted widespread attention in vigorous, patriotic speeches advocating a total war effort and a war aim of completely crushing the Central Powers, militarily and economically. Asquith was compelled to make him a delegate to the Paris economic conference in June, where his fire-eating policy pleased Clemenceau. He visited the Australian troops, and acquired the sobriquet of 'the little Digger'. He also negotiated contracts for the sale of Australia's wheat, wool, and other primary products and to ensure their shipment founded the Australian Commonwealth Shipping Line by purchasing fifteen cargo vessels. Attempts were made to induce him to remain in England, with suggestions that he should be given a Commons and a cabinet seat, but he returned to Australia in July.

Hughes was now convinced that voluntary recruitment was insufficient and conscription for overseas service, already mooted by leaders of the opposition Liberal Party, had become necessary. However, he knew that resistance to such a policy was widespread in the Labour movement, and accordingly on his return to Australia he toured the capitals, making patriotic public speeches on the one hand and on the other endeavouring in private to persuade Labour Party and trade-union leaders to back his judgement about conscription. The Labour Party's parliamentary caucus in Melbourne by majority approved a compromise proposal for putting the conscription issue to the electors at a plebiscite, but even the legislation for this was opposed in Parliament by a Labour minority and caused the resignation of a senior minister, and further resignations occurred when Hughes attempted to employ the plebiscite as a means of checking on 'draft-dodgers' under a home service call-up. The plebiscite held in October resulted in a narrow majority against conscription, and in November the caucus rebelled against the leadership of Hughes; anticipating a vote against him, Hughes on 14 November led twenty-four followers out of the Labour Party and formed a government from their number depending upon the benevolent support of the Liberals.

Hughes wished to create a 'National Labour' party to support him, but it became evident that the task of organizing a mass basis for a new party was beyond his resources, and the Liberal Party leaders were not prepared indefinitely to support a rump government, so the National Labour group merged with the Liberals to form the Nationalist Party, with Hughes as prime minister and attorney-general. At a general election in 1917 Hughes led the Nationalists to an overwhelming victory in both Houses, and continued as prime minister until 1923. He himself was returned for the Bendigo seat in Victoria. In November 1917 Hughes pledged himself to resign if conscription were not approved, and did so when a second plebiscite failed by a larger majority, but when it became obvious that no other leader could form a government, he again became prime minister and was able to concentrate on the war and its aftermath.

He went to England in June 1918 and remained until August 1919, pressing Australia's claims in the peace settlement. He was a member of the British delegation to the Paris conference in 1919, and was influential, with Sir Robert Borden and J. C. Smuts [qq.v.], in procuring the separate recognition of the dominions in the form of the peace treaty and their separate membership of the League of Nations. Hughes had no confidence in Wilson, or his 14 Points, or in the League; he favoured a harsh peace and wanted outright annexation of German territories near Australian shores, and heavy reparations. He settled for the C-class mandate system and the rejection of Japanese attempts to write a racial equality clause into the League covenant. On his return, Hughes received a thunderous popular welcome and the Nationalist Party scored another triumph at the 1919 elections. He again visited England in 1921 for the imperial conference and favoured renewal of the Anglo-Japanese Treaty, but accepted the United States proposals which led to the Washington naval conference.

From 1920 on Hughes's position in the Nationalist Party became increasingly precarious because the powerful conservative wing of the party and the newly created Country Party distrusted him. While Hughes had come to seem a conservative to his former Labour colleagues, he still seemed a dangerous socialist to many of his new political colleagues. He regarded government enterprise and intervention in economic affairs as natural and proper if undertaken in the national interest, and he had become increasingly overbearing and secretive, and in the opinion of many Nationalists inefficient in the way in which he conducted such affairs. He also continued to favour—and did throughout his life—expansion of federal power. The farmers objected to his handling of primary produce marketing, because he sought to stabilize food prices by government controls when in the post-war inflation a free market would have brought them higher returns, and there was a strong state-right element among his followers. The opposition to him reached a climax when after the election of December 1922 the Nationalist majority was reduced to a point which compelled them to seek a coalition with the Country Party; that party, in particular its leader (Sir) Earle Page, declined to support a government led by Hughes and accordingly he was induced to resign the prime minister-ship and the Nationalist leadership in favour of S. M. Bruce (later Viscount Bruce of Melbourne), who became prime minister on 9 February 1923.

At the 1922 election, Hughes again moved his constituency, from Bendigo to North Sydney. In 1920 admirers had presented him with £25,000 in recognition of his war services, and from now until 1928 he led a relatively quiet back-bencher's existence, but through 1928–9 became increasingly critical of the Bruce–Page government, particularly its handling of industrial disputes. In 1929 he and three other Nationalists voted with the Labour Party to defeat the Government on its proposal to remove the Commonwealth from the greater part of the field of in-dustrial arbitration. Thus was Hughes re-venged for the shabby treatment accorded him in 1923.

Hughes tried to form a new party called the Australian Party for the ensuing general election, but his efforts failed. The Labour Party obtained a majority in the Representatives, but, between its own dissensions and a hostile Senate, it achieved little and in 1931 split into three, one group combining with the Nationalists to form the United Australia Party. Hughes played only a minor part in the disputes about depres-sion financial policy which were the main cause of these crises. In 1931 he joined the United Australia Party, which under J. A. Lyons [q.v.] scored a decisive electoral victory; right-wing antagonism to Hughes because of his destructive activities in 1929 prevented his immediate appointment as a minister, but in 1932 he represented Australia at a League of Nations Assembly and in 1934 he became minister for repatriation and health in the Lyons government.

From 1934 until 1943 Hughes played a leading part in the United Australia Party, and was a minister almost con-tinuously until 1941. In 1939 (Sir) R. G. Menzies narrowly defeated him for the succession to the U.A.P. leadership on the death of Lyons; he was deputy leader until October 1941, when Menzies resigned from leadership and Hughes succeeded him, but their roles were again reversed in 1943. In 1944 Menzies trans-formed the U.A.P. into the Liberal Party, of which Hughes became a back-bench member. He was minister for health and repatriation from 1934 until 1937, with a brief break in 1935–6 when he was compelled to resign for a few months because he published a book, *Australia and War Today*, which con-tained views on the Italo-Abyssinian dis-pute at odds with the policy of the Lyons government. From 1937 until 1939 he was minister for external affairs, and from 1939 until 1941 attorney-general, and minister for industry (1939–40) and navy (1940–41). Under the Labour Govern-ment of John Curtin [q.v.] from 1941 until 1944 he was a member of the War Advisory Council. Throughout these years Hughes's experience was highly valued by Governments, and his manner of imparting it much mellowed. However, he adhered uncompromisingly to his dis-trust of international organization and his belief in a strong, independent Australian defence force. His vigorous exposition of these views grated somewhat on all the major parties in the period after 1935 when the public and Govern-ments were against rapid rearmament and hoped that appeasement policies would succeed, but his insistence con-tributed to the important defence measures which were begun, especially after 1938. As attorney-general after 1939 he was responsible for ferreting out enemy agencies, and banned the Communist Party in its anti-war phase, but he in-curred little of the distrust with which he had been regarded on the political Left in the first war.

After 1944 Hughes receded into the political background. At the redistri-bution in 1949 he chose the Bradfield division, part of his former seat. He had now become a legend in his own lifetime, much sought after as a raconteur and public speaker, and cheered by the marchers on each Anzac Day as he stood in Martin Place, Sydney, as he had done since 1920. He died at Lindfield 28 October 1952; still an M.H.R. and the last sitting survivor from the first Commonwealth Parliament. One hundred thousand people attended his state funeral in Sydney.

Hughes had seven children by his first marriage, of whom three sons and three daughters survived him; none achieved special eminence. His first wife died in 1906; in 1911 he married Mary Ethel, daughter of Thomas Campbell, a grazier of Burrandong, New South Wales. She was appointed G.B.E. in 1922. The one daughter of his second marriage predeceased him.

Hughes had a prose style almost as lively as his speaking style and his two volumes of memoirs, *Crusts and Crusades* (1947) and *Policies and Potentates* (1950), while unreliable in detail, convey excellently the atmosphere of many episodes in his earlier career. He also published *The Case for Labor* (1910), a selection from articles under that title which appeared in the Sydney *Daily Telegraph*, *The Splendid Adventure* (1929), and *The Price of Peace* (1934). He was sworn of both the Canadian and United Kingdom Privy Councils in 1916, took silk in 1919, and was made a C.H. in 1941.

A portrait by George Lambert and bronze bust by F. Derwent Wood are in King's Hall, Parliament House, Canberra; there is a portrait plaque in St. Paul's crypt, London; and cartoons in *The Billy Book* by (Sir) David Low (1918).

[L. F. Fitzhardinge, *William Morris Hughes*, 1964; W. F. Whyte, *William Morris Hughes*, 1957; F. C. Browne, *They Called Him Billy*, 1946; G. Sawer, *Australian Federal Politics and Law, 1901–1949*, 2 vols., 1956–63; private information.] GEOFFREY SAWER.

HUMPHREY, HERBERT ALFRED (1868–1951), engineer, was born at Hope Cottage, Gospel Oak, London, 2 December 1868, the son of John Charles Humphrey, accountant to the Metropolitan Board of Works, and his wife, Louise Frost. He was the third son and fifth child of a family of seven. He was educated at Cowper Street Middle Class School before attending Finsbury Technical Institute under John Perry and W. E. Ayrton [q.v.]. From there he went in 1885 to the City and Guilds Central Institution in South Kensington, where he was one of the five original students. There he had the advantage of coming into close personal contact with those great teachers W. C. Unwin [q.v.], Ayrton, H. E. Armstrong [q.v.], and Henrici. At the end of his college career he took a position with Heenan and Froude of Manchester and Birmingham, before joining Brunner Mond & Co., Ltd., in 1890, where the founder of the firm, Ludwig Mond [q.v.], immediately realized that he had found an engineer whose ability and freshness of outlook could be of the greatest use to the chemical industry in developing its many new processes. For the next eleven years

Humphrey worked at Winnington in connection with Mond Gas Producers.

In 1901 he went to London where he set up as a consulting engineer and was extremely successful. The experience he had gained with Mond Power Gas and with large gas engines helped to give him a world-wide reputation and he acquired a large number of clients and friends. It was during this period that he invented the Humphrey gas pump, of which four were installed at the Chingford reservoir by the Metropolitan Water Board. The patent rights of the pump were sold to the United States for the sum of £100,000.

When war broke out in 1914 Humphrey's wide experience and knowledge were put at the service of his country and he became technical adviser to the department of explosives supply which was part of the Ministry of Munitions. There he worked with Lord Moulton [q.v.] in ensuring the supply of ammonium nitrate for the making of explosives. Later with the munitions inventions department his task was to investigate the various known processes for the fixation of nitrogen. This led to the department of explosives beginning to plan the construction of a factory at Billingham-on-Tees where the German Haber process should be used. The end of the war came before work could be started and in April 1919 a British chemical commission was sent out to Oppau to see the Synthetic Ammonia Works there and Humphrey was one of the five. The commission met with a determined resistance from the start. The Germans were not co-operative and the fact that the works were in the French zone of occupation did not help. The Badische Gemeinschaft, which worked the process, did all they could to obstruct. They painted the front of gauges, took down lower rungs of ladders, disconnected pipes, and chipped off maker's names from machines. As soon as the commission entered the building all work stopped. However, they were not beaten and every night for five weeks went into conference and finally evolved a fairly accurate layout of the works. When they returned home in June, driving back to France, Humphrey's luggage containing their report followed by rail in a wagon under armed guard. But they had underestimated the enemy: the bottom of the wagon was removed and the luggage stolen. Fortunately the commission had all their notes and sketches and were able to rewrite their report.

Later in 1919 the Billingham site was acquired by Brunner Mond & Co., Ltd., who formed a company—Synthetic Ammonia and Nitrates, Ltd.—to develop the Oppau process. It followed naturally that Humphrey should be offered the posts of consulting engineer and director of the new firm. It was here that his great experience of engineers and their training was of value to the company. He was a very good engineer. Up to 1920 no other exceptional engineer had been employed in the chemical industry and he was able almost immediately to find others to train. Within a few years British chemical engineering surpassed that of Germany and America.

For this a great deal of credit must go to Humphrey. He was almost the ideal consulting engineer—learned, versatile, meticulous, hardworking, and quick to size up a situation and find out how to deal with it. In 1926 Imperial Chemical Industries was formed and he became consulting engineer to the whole of the combined company, which position he held until his retirement in 1931. One of the most important projects with which he dealt during his latter years with I.C.I. was the construction of the 40,000 kW. electric power-station at Billingham. It was probably his greatest achievement for it was well in advance of central station design at the time and began to supply power within twelve months of the first sod being cut.

Humphrey was a member of the Institutions of Civil, Mechanical, and Electrical Engineers and a fellow and vice-president of the Institute of Fuel. He was elected the first fellow of the City and Guilds Institute and also a fellow of the Imperial College. He read many papers on large gas engines and gas producer plants before learned societies which gained for him the Willans, the Telford, the Watt, and the Constantine gold medals. In 1930 a joint paper with J. W. Bansall and D. M. Buist describing the Billingham power plant was awarded the Paris premium of the Institution of Electrical Engineers and in 1939 he was given the Melchett medal of the Institute of Fuel for his lecture on the 'Supply of Explosives during the War and the Early History of Billingham'.

After the end of the war of 1939–45 Humphrey visited South Africa and decided to settle at Hermanus, C.P.

There he had no difficulty in acquiring a new life and a new circle of devoted friends. He died there 9 March 1951. He was married to Mary Elizabeth, daughter of Frederick Thomas Horniblow, coal factor, of Reading, and had three sons and two daughters. The eldest son, John Herbert Humphrey, F.R.S., became deputy director of the National Institute for Medical Research in 1961.

[V. E. Parke, Billingham: The First Ten Years, 1957; Proceedings of the Institution of Mechanical Engineers, vol. clxiv, 1951; personal knowledge.]　　　R. E. SLADE.

HUMPHREYS, SIR (RICHARD SOMERS) TRAVERS (CHRISTMAS) (1867–1956), judge, was born in Bloomsbury, London, 4 August 1867, the fourth son and sixth child of Charles Octavius Humphreys, a solicitor specializing in criminal cases, by his wife, Harriet Ann Grain, sister of the entertainer, R. Corney Grain [q.v.]. His father's half-sister was the first wife of the Earl of Halsbury [q.v.]. He was educated at Shrewsbury School and Trinity Hall, Cambridge, where he stroked a trial university eight. He was called to the bar by the Inner Temple in 1889 and, joining (Sir) Archibald Bodkin [q.v.] in the chambers of E. T. E. Besley, soon concentrated on practice in the criminal courts. He was appointed counsel for the Crown at the Middlesex and North London sessions in 1905, junior counsel for the Crown at the Central Criminal Court in 1908, and a senior counsel in 1916. As a prosecutor it was said of him that 'He's so damned fair that he leaves nothing for the defence to say.' He was recorder of Chichester from 1921 to 1926 when he became recorder of Cambridge. He was elected a bencher of his Inn in 1922 and knighted in 1925. There were at this time few judges who were specialists in criminal law and in 1928 Humphreys was appointed to the King's Bench division to redress the balance. In 1946 he was sworn of the Privy Council and when he retired in 1951 he was the senior and oldest King's Bench judge.

The story of Humphreys's life is the story of the criminal law of his time. He first came into prominence in 1895 when, led by Sir Edward Clarke and (Sir) Charles Mathews [qq.v.], he appeared as junior counsel in the cases linked with the downfall of Oscar Wilde [q.v.]. In 1910 he was junior counsel in the prosecution of H. H. Crippen for the murder of his wife.

Humphreys

He afterwards wrote that he never regarded Crippen as a great criminal; he considered that he was rightly convicted, but in another country would have been given the benefit of 'extenuating circumstances'. In 1912 he was junior counsel in the prosecution of F. H. Seddon for poisoning Eliza Barrow with arsenic. He always regarded the quality of Seddon's guilt as a conclusive justification for the retention of capital punishment for murder. In 1915 he appeared with Bodkin for the prosecution at the trial of G. J. Smith, the perpetrator of the 'Brides in the Bath' murders. In 1916 he was one of the brilliant team who prosecuted Sir Roger Casement [q.v.] for treason. At the Central Criminal Court in 1922 the calm skill of his cross-examination secured the conviction of Horatio Bottomley [q.v.] for fraudulent conversion. In the same year he was junior to the solicitor-general in the prosecution of Frederick Bywaters and Edith Thompson for the murder of her husband. In 1925 he led for the Crown in the prosecution of W. C. Hobbs, the blackmailer of Sir Hari Singh.

As a judge he tried many criminal cases which attracted much public attention. In 1932 he presided at the trial of Mrs. Barney, a society woman charged with the murder of her lover but acquitted at the Central Criminal Court. In the following year he tried Leopold Harris and fifteen other persons on charges arising out of systematic arson to defraud insurance companies. The case lasted thirty-three days and his summing-up to the jury took thirteen hours. In 1935 he tried Mrs. Rattenbury and her young lover, George Stoner, for the murder of her husband. The man was convicted, but did not hang; the woman was acquitted but committed suicide. At the Lewes assizes in 1949 Humphreys presided at the trial of J. G. Haigh, the acid bath murderer. The defence of insanity, as presented, made the case particularly difficult, but, although eighty-two years old, the judge handled it with conspicuous efficiency and impeccable fairness.

By the end of his life Humphreys had become in the public mind the embodiment of English criminal justice. He was vigorous, spare of figure, and dry in manner, and on the bench he was quietly efficient, without either vanity or display. Although without deep learning, he was an acknowledged master of the criminal law.

He was also a master of the art of summing up and approached every case with a coo good sense and knowledge of the world unimpressed by drama, romance, or 'glamour'. He was sociable and good company, but his keen sense of humour was always kept rigorously under control. This was characteristic of the habit of discipline inherited from the late Victorian middle class from which he sprang. His views on crime and its consequences were strict and traditional without sadism. He simply believed that punishment, including capital and corporal punishment, helped to diminish crime and that too much emphasis on the comfort of prisoners encouraged it. He also had a firm faith in the jury system and said that 'a jury, rightly directed, is always right'.

In 1946 Humphreys published a book of reminiscences under the title Criminal Days, which included a vivid account of his early background and of the courts during his first years at the bar. In 1953 he published A Book of Trials. He was a popular member of the Garrick Club and also an enthusiastic yachtsman. He died in London 20 February 1956. His portrait by Harold Knight is at the Hall of the Saddlers' Company of which he was prime warden in 1918.

In 1896 Humphreys married Zoe Marguerite (died 1953), daughter of Henri Philippe Neumans, the artist, of Antwerp. They had two sons, the elder of whom was killed in France in 1917. The younger (Travers) Christmas Humphreys, Q.C. who contributes to this Supplement, was himself in his turn senior counsel for the Crown at the Central Criminal Court for many years and appeared before his father in several of his famous cases; he was appointed an additional judge of the Central Criminal Court in 1968.

[The Times, 21 February 1956; Law Times 2 March 1956; Bechhofer Roberts, Sir Travers Humphreys. His Career and Cases 1936; Stanley Jackson, The Life and Cases of Mr. Justice Humphreys, 1952; Douglas G Browne, Sir Travers Humphreys, 1960.]

F. H. COWPER

HUNTER, PHILIP VASSAR (1883-1956), electrical engineer, was born in the Norfolk village of Emneth Hungate 3 August 1883, the eldest son of Josiah Hunter, a farmer, and his wife Sarah daughter of Philip Vassar, a neighbouring farmer. He was educated at Wisbech Grammar School and determined at an early age, despite his father's misgivings, to follow his boyhood idol, Sebastian de Ferranti [q.v.], in the new and exciting career of an electrical engineer. From school he went direct to Faraday House where in 1903 he gained his diploma with first class honours and, after a brief period of practical training under Robert Hammond, a well-known consulting engineer, joined in 1904 the staff of C. H. Merz [q.v.] and William McLellan in Newcastle. Here he made rapid progress and in 1909 became head of the electrical department, specializing in high-voltage systems and inventing new types of system protection such as the Merz–Hunter and split-conductor methods.

In 1915 he was lent to the Admiralty, as the engineering director in a special team of three formed within the anti-submarine division under the eventual leadership of (Sir) William W. Fisher [q.v.]. Their work culminated in the evolution of the ASDIC system of submarine detection, and for his part in this development Hunter was in 1920 appointed C.B.E.

In 1919 he joined Callender's Cable & Construction Company where, as chief engineer and joint manager, and later as a director, he devoted his energies to the development of high-voltage power cables. The scope of his work during this period ranged from preoccupation, in 1920, with improving the design of 33,000-volt cables to the invention of the buoyant cable used for sweeping magnetic mines, and to sponsoring in 1943 the world's first three-core cable for 132,000 volts. In 1934 he initiated the company's research laboratories at Wood Lane, and maintained the keenest interest in their work until his death. In 1946, on the merging of the company with British Insulated Cables, Ltd., he became engineer-in-chief of British Insulated Callender's Cables, and from 1947 to 1952 was joint deputy chairman of the new company. He was also chairman of nine, and director of many other, electrical companies.

As a sportsman he was in his younger days a keen skater and curler; and in 1935, after some years as secretary and treasurer, became president of the British Ice Hockey Association. He was well known as an enthusiastic golfer, and was chairman of Addington Golf Club of which he was for some years captain.

Hunter had a high reputation, both in his own country and internationally, not least for his ability to select the vital

and essential facts from a complex situation; and having done so, to put forward a solution with clarity and decisiveness. This gift of his was almost legendary, and many a harassed committee was grateful for it.

He possessed in the highest degree the quality of leadership, selecting his lieutenants with care and judgement, trusting them with a large measure of individual responsibility and helping them, not only with wise advice but with unfailing support. Although he was a man of compelling personality, he would never use it to beat down opposition. Indeed, one of his greatest pleasures was to stimulate discussion; and his junior engineers gratefully recognized that their opinions would always be received with courtesy and understanding, so long as they were to the point and honestly held. Quick to detect promise in his younger staff, he took every opportunity of fostering their ability and helping them to greater responsibility in their profession.

His imperturbability was one of his notable characteristics. He steadfastly refused to be diverted from the work in hand, whether by present danger or by apprehension about the future, and those who remember him in the dark days of 1940 recall with gratitude the steadying influence he exerted on all who worked with him then. This attitude of mind informed all that he did. He was a man of astonishingly equable temper; courteous, tolerant, and disdainful of provocation and malice. Few ever saw him angry.

He was president (1933-4) of the Institution of Electrical Engineers, and in 1951 achieved the ultimate distinction of honorary membership. He was chairman of many professional committees and a fellow of the American Institute of Electrical Engineers.

He was the author, in collaboration with J. Temple Hazell, of a comprehensive history of *The Development of Power Cables* (1956). Much of the subject matter was derived from a collection which he and Hazell had built up, over a period of some twenty years, illustrating the development of cable-making from 1882 onwards; and this was eventually presented to the Science Museum, where it is displayed as the Hunter–Hazell collection.

Hunter had three daughters—two by his first wife, Helen Maud, daughter of Charles Golder, whom he married in 1904, and one by his second marriage after the death of his first wife, in 1947, to Ruby Phyllis Hudson, of Herne Bay. He died at Addington, Surrey, 22 October 1956.

[Private information; personal knowledge.]
J. TEMPLE HAZELL.

HUTCHISON, SIR ROBERT, first baronet, of Thurle (1871–1960), physician and paediatrician, was born at Carlowrie House, Kirkliston, West Lothian, 28 October 1871, the youngest of seven children. His father, Robert Hutchison, was a partner in the family wine business in Leith but in later life played the part of a minor country gentleman with a keen interest in forestry on which he was an acknowledged expert and the author of a number of papers. His mother was Mary Jemima, daughter of the Rev. Adam Duncan Tait, minister of Kirkliston. His eldest brother, Sir Thomas Hutchison, first baronet, of Hardiston, was lord provost of Edinburgh in 1921–3.

Although his parents were far from poor Hutchison's early life was by no means pampered. He was educated at the Collegiate School and at the university of Edinburgh where he qualified with his basic medical degrees with the highest honours in 1893. Of his subsequent resident hospital appointments the most significant was at the Sick Children's Hospital in Edinburgh. After this he paid visits to Strasbourg and Paris, and was appointed to a junior post in the department of chemical pathology in Edinburgh. He obtained his M.D. in 1896 and in the same year moved to London when he began as a junior resident at the Hospital for Sick Children, Great Ormond Street. An appointment to the department of physiology at the London Hospital medical school was an interlude before 1900 when he was appointed to the visiting staff of Great Ormond Street Hospital and assistant physician to the London Hospital where he looked after both adults and children. He was elected F.R.C.P. in 1903.

Hutchison early showed a talent for teaching, both verbally and by the written word. His *Clinical Methods* (1897, with H. Rainy) was long a standard work, and in 1900, the year of his senior hospital appointments, he published his famous *Food and the Principles of Dietetics*. In 1904 he showed where his main interest lay when he published his *Lectures on Diseases of Children*. His prowess as a teacher and writer grew. At the time of a celebratory issue of the *Archives of Disease in Childhood* on the occasion of his eightieth birthday in 1951 there was a list of 276 references to books, articles, lectures, and letters to the press. He developed a busy consultant practice in London and received many distinctions including honorary degrees from Edinburgh, Oxford, Birmingham, and Melbourne. He was president of the Royal Society of Medicine (1934–5) and of the Royal College of Physicians of London (1938–41) and Harveian orator in 1931.

Those who worked for Hutchison developed a devotion and admiration just short of idolatry. His tall, slim figure, his retained Scottish accent, his scathing tongue, all created a distinctive personality. His academic and scientific position for his period was clearly paramount. Even before the reason for its value was clear, Hutchison was giving cod-liver-oil to poorly nourished children. He taught well and interestingly; his judgements and advice were sound, kindly, and helpful. He gave up his hospital appointments in 1934 and was created a baronet in 1939. After retirement to Berkshire in 1940 he held court for his previous pupils and successors. As a doting grandfather he belied much of what his attitude to parents and children had suggested in earlier days. His warm heart was sheltered behind a keen intellect and defensive manner. His pupils all over the world readily acknowledged his influence and untold numbers of children owed much to his skill.

In 1905 Hutchison married a qualified practitioner, Laetitia Nora (died 1964), daughter of the (Very) Rev. William Moore Ede, dean of Worcester in 1908–34. They had five children of whom one died at birth and a son died from an infection sustained during his anatomical studies as a medical student at Oxford. Two sons and one daughter survived; the eldest son, Peter (born 1907), succeeded his father when he died at Thurle Grange, Streatley-on-Thames, 12 February 1960.

A portrait by (Sir) James Gunn was presented to the Royal College of Physicians by Lady Hutchison in 1960.

[*The Times*, 13 February 1960; *British Medical Journal* and *Lancet*, 20 February 1960; *Journal of Pediatrics*, January 1961 private information; personal knowledge.]
ALAN MONCRIEFF

ILCHESTER, sixth EARL OF (1874–1959), landowner and historian. [See FOX-STRANGWAYS, GILES STEPHEN HOLLAND.]

ILIFFE, EDWARD MAUGER, first BARON ILIFFE (1877–1960), newspaper and periodical proprietor, was born in Coventry 17 May 1877, the younger son of William Isaac Iliffe, printer and stationer, and his wife, Annette, daughter of James Coker, of Guernsey. The elder Iliffe turned his attention to the production of periodicals and newspapers. He had the foresight to see a future for the new forms of mechanical transport, cycling, motoring, and aviation, and the three journals which he founded to cover these subjects remained authoritative and well considered: *Cycling* (1891), the *Autocar* (1895), and *Flight* (1909). Iliffe also founded the *Coventry Evening Telegraph* in 1891 and it was on this daily journal that his son was first employed at the age of seventeen. He proved an able lieutenant, and as the firm of Iliffe & Sons expanded, especially on the technical side, took an ever greater part in the management. On his father's death the periodical business was moved to London, where it continued to prosper and expand.

Early in the twenties Iliffe became associated with two brothers from Merthyr Tydfil, William and Gomer Berry, better known as Lords Camrose [q.v.] and Kemsley, who were moving on from success to success as periodical proprietors. In 1924 they formed Allied Newspapers, Ltd., to take over from Lord Rothermere [q.v.] a group of Manchester and London newspapers which he had acquired from the first Sir Edward Hulton [q.v.] the year before. The group, with which Iliffe was associated, also owned the *Sunday Times*. In 1927 the three associated owners had perhaps their most resounding success, in the shape of an offer by Lord Burnham [q.v.] for them to take over the *Daily Telegraph*. The change of proprietorship took place on 1 January 1928. The character of the paper remained unaltered, but when on 1 December 1930 the price of 2*d.* was halved, the sale, in Lord Camrose's words, 'practically doubled itself in one day'. After nine years of working together the three peers decided, in January 1937, to split their holdings, and Iliffe took over the valuable property of Kelly's Directories. In the provinces he acquired in 1943 the *Birmingham Post* and the *Birmingham Mail*.

Iliffe had sundry interests outside the journalistic field. In 1917–18 he served as controller of the machine tool department of the Ministry of Munitions. He sat in Parliament as a Conservative for Tamworth from 1923 to 1929. He was master of three City livery companies: the Stationers and Newspaper Makers, the Coachmakers and Coach Harness Makers, and the Clockmakers. He was president of the Association of British Chambers of Commerce in 1932–3 and of the Periodical Proprietors' Association in 1935–8. He had a considerable stake in insurance, being a member of Lloyd's, chairman of the Guildhall Insurance Company, and a director of the London Assurance.

In 1926 Iliffe acquired the estate of Yattendon, in Berkshire, which he eventually greatly expanded. He was appointed C.B.E. in 1918, knighted in 1922, raised to the peerage in 1933, and appointed G.B.E. in 1946. In the war of 1939–45 he was chairman of the Duke of Gloucester's Red Cross and St. John Fund which raised over £50 million. He showed cultural interests by benefactions to Coventry City School and Sherborne School, and he served as president of the trustees of the Shakespeare Memorial Theatre (1933–58). As a young man he excelled at lawn tennis and he continued to follow the game in later life. He was president of the International Lawn Tennis Club of Great Britain from 1945 to 1959.

In 1902 Iliffe married Charlotte, daughter of Henry Gilding, J.P., of Gateacre, Liverpool. They had one daughter and two sons, the elder of whom, Edward Langton (born 1908), succeeded to the title when Iliffe died in London 25 July 1960. A portrait by Frank O. Salisbury is in the possession of the family.

[*The Times*, 26 July 1960; Bernard Falk, *Five Years Dead*, 1937; Viscount Camrose, *British Newspapers and their Controllers*, 1947; *Report* of the Royal Commission on the Press, 1947–9, 1949; private information.]

HERBERT B. GRIMSDITCH.

INCE, SIR GODFREY HERBERT (1891–1960), civil servant, the eldest son of George Alfred Reynolds Ince, solicitor's clerk, and his wife, Emma Budgen, was born at Redhill 25 September 1891. From Reigate Grammar School he went with a county major scholarship to University College, London, where he had a brilliant career, graduating B.Sc. in 1913 with first class honours in mathematics, and in successive years was senior mathematics and senior physics prizeman. He was a keen and proficient games player and excelled at association football. He organized and captained the first university of London team and, as he never tired of recalling in his later life, took it to Moscow, returning triumphant.

In the war of 1914-18 Ince held commissioned rank in the East Lancashire brigade of the Royal Field Artillery and was wounded in action while attached to the Royal Engineers. In February 1919 he became a first class clerk in the Ministry of Labour which was to be his official home and the centre of his activities until his retirement in 1956. His early years were spent in what was later known as the industrial relations department, and he acted as secretary to a number of courts of inquiry, notably that on dock labour (1920) under the chairmanship of Lord Shaw (later Lord Craigmyle, q.v.). In 1928 Ince was transferred to the employment and insurance department where his phenomenal memory and mathematical brain enabled him to become quickly an expert on unemployment insurance. Two years later he was appointed principal private secretary to the minister, Margaret Bondfield [q.v.], and acted in a similar capacity to her immediate successors. In 1933 he was appointed chief insurance officer with the rank of assistant secretary.

In 1936-7 Ince was loaned to the Commonwealth Government of Australia to advise on national unemployment insurance. He made a thorough examination of the conditions in the different states and produced a comprehensive report. This was the type of work in which, with his powers of concentration and his delight in analytical tables, he was completely at home. His efforts were rewarded with an honorarium of £400 as a mark of the gratitude of the Australian Government.

After his return to England Ince was promoted principal assistant secretary (1938) and in May 1939 was put in charge of the military recruiting department, where it fell to him to make arrangements for implementing the Military Training Act. Registrations were to take place at the local offices of the Ministry of Labour, which thus assumed national service functions which it continued to exercise in the succeeding years. At the outbreak of war the Military Training Act was superseded by the National Service (Armed Forces) Act, and Ince, who was promoted to be an under-secretary in January 1940, became closely associated with the arrangements for call-up. This was work for which by temperament he was admirably suited. A strong-willed man of action, in times of crisis he was imperturbable and indefatigable. Of natural administrative gifts himself, he did not make the mistake of trying to keep everything in his own hands, but delegated authority to his staff with particular care that they understood clearly what they had to do. The success with which he handled this exacting task was recognized by Ernest Bevin [q.v.] who in June 1941 appointed him director-general of manpower. This new post was designed to bring under a single control the national service, military recruiting, and labour supply departments with their related problems. Under the permanent secretary the director was made immediately responsible to the minister for all matters affecting the call-up to the forces and the supply of civilian labour. Ince, who continued to hold this office until nearly the end of the war, was in close sympathy with the aims and ideas of his minister, nor was he afraid to criticize his schemes when they appeared to be inopportune or impracticable. Bevin on his side valued Ince's judgement and found it easy to work with a man whose advice was plain and direct and not hedged about with debating subtleties. There thus grew up between the two men a sense of mutual confidence, and the fruit of their co-operative thinking was the successful mobilization of the manpower of the country.

In these three years of constant strain and ever-expanding responsibilities Ince's exceptional gifts found their highest fulfilment. With a great devotion to his Ministry he welcomed its transformation into a major department of state and the consequent increasing authority which it was able to exercise in the determination of national policy. It would not be unfair to add that with an innate streak of vanity and personal ambition he enjoyed the power which fell into his own hands and the wide appreciation of his achievements. Convinced of the soundness of his own judgements he was not always an easy person with whom to negotiate. He was at times unwilling, or perhaps unable, to admit the honesty of opinions running counter to his own, and the strident tones in which he tried to dominate a conference tended to exacerbate, when a little persuasiveness might well have reconciled, his opponents. But these defects, if

)etraying a lack of mental flexibility, reflected the fearless determination which was the essence of his character.

In November 1944 Ince was chosen to succeed Sir Thomas Phillips as permanent secretary of the Ministry, and this post he held until his retirement on 1 February 1956. The plan ultimately approved for the demobilization of the forces owed much to his methodical and practical approach and to his insistence upon a procedure which would be simple, equitable, and intelligible. He was much involved in plans for the resettlement of men and women from the Services in civilian life, and he was chairman of a number of committees on this problem. Another of his major interests was the young, and in particular the importance of helping boys and girls on leaving school to choose and train for worthwhile jobs and careers. He presided over a committee of educationists and industrialists set up to inquire into the working of the Juvenile Employment Service. This report, which bears his name, was issued in 1945 and has become the foundation on which the Youth Employment Service has been developed, with vocational guidance its most distinctive feature.

As wartime controls with which the Ministry of Labour was concerned were gradually relaxed or removed, it was not surprising that there were calls for reductions in its large staff. Ince did not take kindly to these suggestions. He had built up a departmental empire and he was loath to accept any diminution of its powers. There was another and more commendable reason for his intransigence. He was always deeply interested in the welfare of his staff and encouraged social gatherings and athletic contests, in which he liked to take part. He was therefore anxious to ensure that as far as possible they should continue in post until reaching the normal age of retirement. Ironically enough this human regard for his staff met with little apparent response. Apart from his work and sport Ince had few, if any, outside interests, and he had no small talk. He was shy and taciturn, he neither drank nor smoked, and he was a little intimidating to a stranger or a junior. His fairly frequent visits to local offices tended to frighten rather than stimulate.

On his retirement, until his death in Wimbledon 20 December 1960, Ince was chairman of Cable and Wireless and its associated overseas telecommunication companies. He enjoyed the travelling which his duties made possible, especially on one occasion when his arrival in Australia coincided with the opening of the Olympic Games. This insatiable appetite for watching sporting events— he was a familiar figure at White Hart Lane and the Oval—made him in 1957 an obvious choice for membership of the Wolfenden committee on sport.

Ince was appointed C.B. (1941), K.B.E. (1943), K.C.B. (1946), and G.C.B. (1951). His old college elected him to a fellowship in 1946 and in 1951 he received an honorary LL.D. from the university of London.

In 1918 Ince married Ethel Doris, daughter of Charles Maude, of Northallerton, by whom he had three daughters.

A portrait by Harold Knight is in the possession of the family.

[H. M. D. Parker, *Manpower* (History of the Second World War. Civil Series), 1957; private information; personal knowledge.]

H. M. D. PARKER.

INGE, WILLIAM RALPH (1860–1954), dean of St. Paul's, was born 6 June 1860 at Crayke, Yorkshire, the elder son of William Inge, then curate of Crayke and later provost of Worcester College, Oxford, and his wife, Susanna Mary, daughter of Edward Churton [q.v.], archdeacon of Cleveland. His childhood was spent in Crayke, then an isolated parish in the North Riding. He was educated by his parents at home and, in later life, regarded this as a great advantage. 'No children', he wrote in *Vale* (1934), 'now have such a good education as we had, for both our parents, who were scholarly, and admirable teachers, gave up a great part of every day to their family, instead of sending them off to school.' He was brought up in the Tractarian tradition of Anglican piety and, although he afterwards became acutely critical of the theology of that school, he owed, no doubt, not a little of the bent of his mind towards mysticism to the training in devotion which he received in his early years.

In 1874 he was elected, second on the list, to an Eton scholarship. At Eton he worked hard—as he came to believe later, too hard—and in 1879 went up to Cambridge as a scholar of King's College. He described his academic career as 'mainly a record of scholarships and prizes'. Among them were the Bell, Porson, and Craven scholarships. He took a first class in both parts of the classical tripos (1882–3) and was senior Chancellor's medallist (1883). In 1885 he was Hare prizeman. After leaving Cambridge, he was for four years a master at Eton, but did not find the work of a schoolmaster congenial, and indeed he was not suited in temperament. In 1888 he was elected fellow and tutor of Hertford College, Oxford, being concerned mainly with classical teaching. In the same year he was ordained deacon, but did not present himself for priest's orders until four years later. There seems to be little doubt that this delay was due to some uncertainty about his vocation which probably arose mainly from intellectual difficulties. He has left on record the fact that his interest in philosophy did not begin until his Oxford period and that he was seeking, at that time, for a 'sound intellectual basis' for his religious belief. The years during which he was a fellow of Hertford were the time when he thought out his fundamental ideas.

From his childhood up to his marriage, Inge was subject to recurrent fits of melancholia and, from a comparatively early age, was afflicted by deafness, which grew worse in later years. These two disabilities affected his outlook on life to some extent and, perhaps, were partly responsible for a certain aloofness and detachment which characterized both his thought and his personality. Inge was inclined to attribute his melancholy fits to overwork while he was at school and in Cambridge, but it appears that this could not have been more than a contributory cause.

In 1899 he was Bampton lecturer and it is illuminating to learn from one who was his pupil at Hertford that Inge's appointment surprised the undergraduates as 'he had not previously been thought to be at all interested in theological speculations'. The subject of his lectures was 'Christian Mysticism' and Inge chose it because he had become convinced of two propositions: first, that the nature of religious experience was the most important problem for theology at that time; and, secondly, that in mysticism we have religious experience in its most concentrated and undiluted form. *Christian Mysticism* (1899) was widely read and Inge soon became known as one of the foremost writers on religion of the day. The book was, in fact, important in that it opened up new ground and had a considerable influence on theological thinking. Interest in mysticism, and study of

the mystics, increased and other authors, such as von Hügel and Evelyn Underhill [qq.v.], followed him with notable contributions to the subject.

In 1905 Inge became vicar of All Saints', Ennismore Gardens, and in the same year married Mary Catharine, daughter of Henry Maxwell Spooner, archdeacon of Maidstone, and niece of W. A. Spooner [q.v.], warden of New College. Inge always regarded his marriage as the most fortunate event of his life— and with justice, for it was the beginning of a partnership which brought him the peace of an affectionate home life and also the cessation of his moods of depression. Inge's brief experience of the life of a parish priest ended in 1907, when he was elected Lady Margaret's professor of divinity at Cambridge and fellow of Jesus College. He resumed his studies of mysticism and of Platonism in Christian theology. Plotinus had already attracted his attention and he now began the collection of material for a work on that philosopher. The most significant books published in this period were *Personal Idealism and Mysticism* (1907) and *Faith and its Psychology* (1909). The latter, although it did not approach some of his other writings in popularity, was always regarded by Inge as one of his best books. In 1911 *Speculum Animae*, four addresses to university teachers and schoolmasters, revealed something of Inge's personal religion.

In the same year he was appointed dean of St. Paul's. The choice of the Crown came as a surprise to the general public and to Inge himself. He had looked forward to an academic career and accepted the nomination to St. Paul's with hesitation. He brought distinction to an office which had been held by many eminent scholars and he reflected that 'by tradition the Deanery of St. Paul's is the most literary appointment in the Church of England'. His tenure of that office was not without difficulties and disagreements. The Chapter was not in sympathy with his liberal type of theology, and he found it hard to get co-operation from the canons. Towards the end of his time at St. Paul's he was in a happier position, but by then his interests had become largely directed on other matters and much of his energy was absorbed in writing. He was, however, a diligent attendant at the cathedral services and loved Wren's great church. He remained in the deanery throughout the war of 1914–18 and took part in the raising of funds for the preservation of St. Paul's when, after the war, it was found that the dome was in danger of collapsing. His chief service to the cathedral was his preaching which attracted increasing congregations up to the date of his retirement. He preached as he had lectured with no oratorical art and with his eyes fixed upon his manuscript. His power lay in the impression of his personality, his originality of thought, and his gift of startling epigram. Men recognized that he was a preacher who was always thinking for himself and speaking the truth that he had found.

Inge became a great popular figure with a nickname—'the gloomy dean'—largely because of his journalistic activity. His weekly articles in the *Evening Standard* (1921–46) were one of the best-known features of the periodical press and were widely discussed. He attacked what he believed to be superstitions of the day, among them the optimism of those who thought that the 'war to end war' had really succeeded in doing so and the conception of 'progress' as an inevitable process; nor did he conceal his contempt for 'democracy'. The title, 'gloomy dean', arose no doubt chiefly from his criticism of popular illusions. When war broke out in 1939 he remarked that he had not foretold anything as bad as what actually happened. Two volumes, entitled *Outspoken Essays* (1919–22), which had a great success with the educated public, presented clearly and forcibly his views on theological and political problems and included in the second volume a 'Confessio Fidei' which is the most succinct statement in existence of his fundamental religious convictions.

In 1917–18 he delivered the Gifford lectures on 'The Philosophy of Plotinus' in the university of St. Andrews. Inge regarded this (published in two volumes, 1918) as his *magnum opus*, and with reason. He had long been preparing for this opportunity and, in the fulfilment of the task, he displayed his sound classical scholarship, his philosophical acuteness, and his knowledge of mystical devotion. He was criticized by some theologians as being more Platonist than Christian, but he, like St. Augustine, was careful to point out where Plotinus fell short of the Christian doctrines of God, the Incarnation, and immortality. At the same time, he did not hide the fact that he held the philosophy of Plotinus to be the most congenial to him of all the great systems.

A small book, *Personal Religion and the Life of Devotion* (1924), had a considerable influence and is specially remarkable for a moving chapter on 'Bereavement', in which he commemorated his daughter, Margaret Paula, who died in childhood. The book was prefaced by a touching Latin poem, '*In memoriam Filiolae Dilectissimae*'. *Christian Ethics and Modern Problems* (1930) was called forth by Inge's feeling that one of the most menacing challenges to Christian faith came from modern developments of moral ideas and conduct. *God and the Astronomers* (1933) dealt with scientific cosmologies and their relation to theology and is probably the most comprehensive and systematic presentation of his metaphysical theories. This was the essence of the matter as Inge saw it: 'Our citizenship is in heaven, that is to say, in a spaceless and timeless world in which all the intrinsic or absolute values are both actual and active. In this higher world we find God and our own eternity. It is the only completely real world.'

Inge was probably the last dean of St. Paul's to be able to make full use of the opportunities for hospitality offered by the beautiful but very large house assigned to the office. He and his wife made it the centre of a cultivated social life.

Inge was for some years president of the Modern Churchmen's Union until he ceased to be dean of St. Paul's. After his retirement in 1934 he continued to write, for the most part books of a popular character, although he reviewed learned books on Platonism and allied subjects. Among his later writings, *The Diary of a Dean* (1949), *A Rustic Moralist* (1937), and *Talks in a Free Country* (1942) may be mentioned. The outbreak of war in 1939 found Inge in much the same position as he had held in 1914—both wars were, in his opinion, unnecessary and could have been avoided by wiser statesmanship. He was not averse from 'doing a deal with Hitler'. The death of his wife in 1949 was a heavy blow to him, but he continued to preach and lecture almost to the end of his life. Almost his last public lecture was on the theology of Origen. This was appropriate for, like the Christian Platonist of Alexandria, Inge believed that there is a *philosophia perennis* which is in harmony with the Christian faith properly understood and his constant endeavour was to elucidate the indestructible truth in Christianity behind the partial truths of popular religion. His last public lecture was on the faith of St. Paul in Westminster Abbey (1951). When Inge died at his home, Brightwell Manor, Wallingford, 26 February 1954, he had to a large extent outlived his popular reputation. The journalist and controversial figure were forgotten, but his solid contributions to religious thought remain.

Inge was appointed C.V.O. in 1918 and K.C.V.O. in 1930. He proceeded B.D. and D.D. at Cambridge in 1909, was the recipient of a number of honorary degrees, was an honorary fellow of Hertford College, Oxford, and of Jesus and King's colleges, Cambridge, and a lecturer on many endowments. He was elected F.B.A. in 1921, presided over the Aristotelian Society in 1920-21 and over the Classical Association in 1933.

He had three sons and two daughters. The youngest son, Richard Wycliffe Spooner, relinquished his curacy in order to join the Royal Air Force and was killed on active service in 1941. A portrait of Inge by his wife's cousin, Catharine Dodgson, is at King's College, Cambridge, by Arthur Norris in the National Portrait Gallery, and by P. A. de László at Brightwell Manor; a cartoon drawn for *Punch* by Sir Bernard Partridge is at Eton College; of three red chalk drawings by Catharine Dodgson, one is at Monkton Combe School, one at Brightwell Manor, and the third became the possession of Sir John Sheppard, sometime provost of King's College, Cambridge.

[W. R. Inge, *Vale*, 1934; private information; personal knowledge.]

W. R. MATTHEWS.

INGLIS, SIR CHARLES EDWARD (1875-1952), professor of engineering, was born at Worcester 31 July 1875, the second surviving son of Alexander Monro Inglis, M.D., of Auchindinny and Redhall, by his first wife, Florence, the second daughter of John Frederick Feeney, proprietor of the *Birmingham Daily Post*. His father moved from Worcester to Cheltenham and Inglis was educated at Cheltenham College, of which he became senior prefect and was, for more than twenty years before his death, a member of the College council. In 1894 he went up to Cambridge with a scholarship at King's College. He nearly achieved his blue for long-distance running but pulled a muscle and had to retire. In 1897 he was classed as 22nd wrangler in the mathematical

tripos and in the following year gained first class honours in part i of the mechanical sciences tripos. He went next as a pupil of Sir John Wolfe-Barry [q.v.] and Partners, consulting engineers. After a few months in the drawing office he was transferred to the staff of (Sir) Alexander Gibb [q.v.], Wolfe-Barry's resident engineer for the new extension to the Metropolitan Railway between Whitechapel and Bow. Inglis was engaged in particular on the design and supervision of the nine bridges crossing the railway, an experience which was of great value to him later in life when he became particularly interested in the behaviour of bridges. At this time, however, he also began a study, which lasted throughout his life, on the subject of mechanical vibration, and when in 1901 he was made a fellow of King's College, Cambridge, the subject of his thesis was 'The balancing of engines'. In this year he returned to Cambridge as assistant to (Sir) Alfred Ewing [q.v.]. After two years Ewing left to become the first director of naval education and was succeeded by Bertram Hopkinson [q.v.] who held the chair of mechanism and applied mechanics, as it was then called, until his death in a flying accident in 1918. Under Hopkinson, Inglis was appointed to a lectureship in engineering (1908) and continued his work on vibrations.

Inglis's interests were by no means confined to vibrations. In 1913 he published a paper on the stresses in a plate due to the presence of cracks and sharp corners. This may well be Inglis's most far-reaching contribution, since A. A. Griffith's classic explanation of the discrepancy between observed and calculated strengths of amorphous substances, such as glass and silica fibres, was based on it.

On the outbreak of war in 1914, Inglis was commissioned in the Royal Engineers. Earlier he had designed a light tubular bridge, readily transportable and easy to erect, which the War Office adopted. From 1916 to 1918 he was in charge of the department responsible for the design and supply of military bridges; for this work he was appointed O.B.E. His bridge came to the fore when the army was faced in 1917-18 with the tank bridging problem. His designs were very little used in the war of 1939-45, a neglect which he felt keenly.

In 1918 Inglis returned to Cambridge, and was elected in 1919 to the chair of mechanical sciences and head of the department of engineering, in succession to Hopkinson, a post which he held until his retirement in 1943. Before the war the number of undergraduates reading engineering at Cambridge had risen to the two hundred and fifty level, taxing to their utmost the laboratories in Free School Lane. In 1919 Inglis was met by an overwhelming entry of eight hundred and it became essential to move the department to an entirely new area. The four-acre Scroope House site in Trumpington Street was acquired. There, between 1920 and 1923, a single-storey laboratory building covering about fifty-thousand square feet was erected. Although, after 1945, large workshops and a five-storey building were added, more than quadrupling the floor area available, the Inglis Building was so well planned that it accommodated the main teaching laboratories of the department until the end of 1964.

Between the wars the department became the largest in the university and one of the most important engineering schools in the world. Having spent seventeen years as a lecturer, during which time he must have played a prominent part in the development of the school, it is not surprising that Inglis, on his return, made no striking innovations. He was strongly opposed to premature specialization; about the teaching of mathematics and the need for the subject to occupy a prominent position in any university engineering course he held strong views. Later in life he advocated the study of aesthetics for engineers as much for its cultural value as for its direct influence on their designs.

On the position research should occupy in a university engineering department he did not seem so clear. He was critical of the Cambridge Ph.D. course, since he felt that team work was an essential introduction for a beginner. Perhaps because of this he did not, unfortunately, found or lead a research team at Cambridge. However, his own research continued to be distinguished. He played a most prominent part in the work of the bridge stress committee, set up in 1923 to determine the behaviour of railway bridges under moving loads. Throughout the whole investigation he was indefatigable, providing all the mathematics and much of the drive which kept the experimental work going over the years. He contributed papers to the Institution

of Civil Engineers describing this research and also published a book *A Mathematical Treatise on Vibrations in Railway Bridges* (1934).

He served on the councils of the Institutions of Naval Architects and of Civil, of Structural, and of Water Engineers. He was president of the Institution of Civil Engineers in 1941-2; received the Telford and Parsons medals; and was an honorary member of the Institution of Mechanical Engineers. He received an honorary LL.D. from Edinburgh (1929), was elected F.R.S. (1930), and was knighted in 1945. From 1943 to 1946 he was vice-provost of King's College. Though he made no secret of his enjoyment of these honours, of his interest in research and other engineering activities, his overwhelming interest and pleasure was in teaching work at Cambridge. The last year of his life was almost as active as any that had gone before. He had the satisfaction of seeing the publication of his book, *Applied Mechanics for Engineers* (1951), and of spending three months in South Africa as a visiting lecturer continuing, what he did so superlatively well and loved so much, the teaching and inspiration of the young engineer.

In 1901 Inglis married Eleanor Mary, younger daughter of Lieutenant-Colonel Herbert Belasyse Moffat, South Wales Borderers. In 1904 they built Balls Grove, Grantchester, where they lived until 1925 and where their two daughters were born. Inglis died at Southwold only eighteen days after his wife, 19 April 1952.

There are portraits by Henry Lamb in the Institution of Civil Engineers and in King's College, Cambridge, and a third by D. Gordon Shields in the possession of the Engineering Department, Cambridge.

[J. F. Baker in *Obituary Notices of Fellows of the Royal Society*, No. 22, November 1953; personal knowledge.] J. F. BAKER.

INVERCHAPEL, BARON (1882-1951), diplomatist. [See CLARK KERR, ARCHIBALD JOHN KERR.]

INVERFORTH, first BARON (1865-1955), shipowner. [See WEIR, ANDREW.]

IRONSIDE, WILLIAM EDMUND, first BARON IRONSIDE (1880-1959), field-marshal, was born in Edinburgh 6 May 1880, the second child of Surgeon-Major William Ironside of Ironside, Royal Horse Artillery, by his wife, Emma Maria, daughter of William Haggett Richards, of

Stapleton House, Martock, Somerset. His father died in January of the following year and his mother, left badly off, frequently took him and his sister to the Continent where living was cheaper. These excursions bore fruit, for Ironside subsequently became a qualified army interpreter in seven languages. Educated at a preparatory school at St. Andrews, Tonbridge School, and the Royal Military Academy, Woolwich, Ironside was commissioned into the Royal Artillery in 1899. He served in the South African war and in 1902 escorted J. C. Smuts [q.v.] to the peace conference at Vereeniging. Then, disguised as a Boer transport driver, he accompanied the German military expedition to South West Africa where his adventures as an intelligence agent suggested the character of Richard Hannay to John Buchan (later Lord Tweedsmuir, q.v.).

After service in I (Bull's Troop) and Y batteries of the Royal Horse Artillery, Ironside was promoted captain in 1908 and appointed to cavalry and infantry brigade staffs in South Africa. He entered the Staff College in 1913 and in 1914 was sent to Boulogne as staff captain. When the 6th division arrived in France in October, he joined its 'G' staff and was promoted major. He became G.S.O. 1 of the 4th Canadian division in 1916 as a brevet lieutenant-colonel, and in 1917 took part in the battles of Vimy Ridge and Passchendaele. In 1918 he was appointed commandant of the Machine Gun Corps school at Camiers with the rank of temporary colonel. When the Germans broke through on the Somme in March he was sent with all its guns to fill the gap and forming a line beat off several attacks. He was then given command of the 99th Infantry brigade in Haldane's 2nd division, and directed its attacks at Albert and Bapaume.

In September 1918 Ironside went to North Russia as chief of the general staff of the allied forces, and soon took command with the temporary rank of major-general. He moulded a heterogeneous army of many nationalities into an efficient fighting force, and in the following March he became general officer commanding-in-chief of Archangel. Disaffection in Russian units and increasing menace from the Bolshevik forces led to the withdrawal of the expedition in the autumn of 1919. For his services he was promoted substantive major-general. His account of these operations was published in *Archangel 1918-1919* (1953).

In 1920 Ironside went to Hungary as chief of the military mission to Admiral Horthy's government; he was subsequently given command of the Ismid and North Persian forces against possible Turkish and Bolshevik incursions. In 1921, summoned to a conference at Cairo under (Sir) Winston Churchill, Ironside recommended that the Royal Air Force should be made responsible for the defence of Iraq. Flying there to arrange the handover he crashed, broke both legs, and was invalided home. In 1922 he was appointed commandant of the Staff College at Camberley, and in 1926 commander of the 2nd division at Aldershot. In 1928 he went to India to command the Meerut District where his training and tactical doctrine much impressed Sir Philip (later Lord) Chetwode [q.v.]. In 1931 he was promoted lieutenant-general, left India, went on half pay, and was appointed lieutenant of the Tower of London. In 1933 he returned to India as quartermaster-general and in 1935 was promoted general.

Returning to England in 1936, Ironside took over the Eastern Command. Units pitifully under strength, obsolete equipment, and the lack of government policy and tactical doctrine perturbed him. In 1937 he attended the German army manœuvres and met Hitler, Goering, Mussolini, and Badoglio. General Reichenau drank a whisky toast to 'brotherhood with England', adding drunkenly 'but only for two years'. Ironside, like Churchill, was sure that war would come in two or three years, but he was unable to convince the prime minister, Neville Chamberlain, or the secretary of state for war, Leslie (later Lord) Hore-Belisha [q.v.].

In the autumn of 1938 Ironside was appointed commander-in-chief designate of the Middle East and governor of Gibraltar where he greatly strengthened the fortress. By now he had 'little hope of any active command'. In May 1939 he was appointed inspector-general of overseas forces and made responsible for the higher training of the army and liaison with the dominions and India. But he was not allowed home until July, when Lord Gort [q.v.], the chief of the imperial general staff, told him that he was to be commander-in-chief of the British expeditionary force. In the meantime he was sent to Warsaw to discover Poland's plans to resist the imminent German invasion. On 3 September Hore-Belisha asked Ironside to become chief of the imperial general staff. Ironside had never served in the War Office in any capacity but felt it his duty to accept. 'I am bitterly disappointed,' ran his diary, 'that I am not to command the Army in the field.... I am not suited in temperament to such a job as C.I.G.S., nor have I prepared myself to be such.'

He found a singular lack of preparation: there was no 'imperial' plan; the only plan was to send four divisions to France. The Government, sheltering behind the Maginot line and the French Army, expected a stalemate on the western front, thought the war could be won by bombing and blockade, and saw little need for an expeditionary force. Ironside, on the contrary, maintained that Hitler would use his army and air force in co-operation to force a decision, and that the war would not be won until Hitler was defeated on land. He accordingly planned for armies of twenty divisions in France, twelve in the Middle East, and an imperial reserve of eighteen divisions at home. It would take three years to equip them. The Services worked on separate charters and there was little co-operation between them. Ironside was burdened by many committees; the machinery of government was incapable of quick decisions or even rapid improvisation; moreover his task was aggravated by a minister for war whom he found difficult. Ironside paid several visits to the B.E.F. and the Maginot line and attended conferences with the supreme commander, General Gamelin. The latter was convinced that the decisive battle would be fought on the plains of Belgium; Ironside forecast, correctly, that the German thrust would come through the Ardennes. Both agreed that the allied left wing should advance into Belgium, Ironside with the idea of attacking the German penetration in flank.

When Russia invaded Finland in November 1939 Ironside wanted to send a small force to help the Finns and a larger force to seize the iron-ore field at Gällivare. His plan was delayed by Norwegian and Swedish objections and was cancelled when Finland fell. In April 1940 the Allies decided to seize Narvik, but the Germans got there first. When the convoy dispatched to take Narvik from the Germans was at sea the Government changed the main objective to Trondheim, and Churchill, in spite of Ironside's protests, ordered the rear half to be diverted to Namsos. Both projects failed and the result was an improvised, hasty, but successful evacuation.

In May 1940 the German armoured columns broke through the Ardennes and cut the allied army in two. Ironside hoped to save the B.E.F. by thrusting southwards through the gap between the armour and its supporting columns, and he did his best to persuade the French to co-operate. They failed to attack and Gort's army was evacuated from Dunkirk. At the end of May, Ironside proposed, and the Government agreed, that he should become commander-in-chief of the home forces to prepare against invasion. Once again he had to build from scratch. In July he was succeeded by Sir Alan Brooke (later Viscount Alanbrooke), promoted field-marshal, and in 1941 raised to the peerage. He retired in silence and dignity to his home at Hingham in Norfolk where he devoted himself to his garden and the affairs of the neighbourhood. He became president of the South African Veterans and the Old Contemptibles. Simple, modest, and forthright, his kindness and friendliness made him universally liked and respected.

'Tiny' Ironside was 6 feet 4 inches tall, broad and deep-chested. Forceful, fearless, and outspoken sometimes to the point of indiscretion, he was an intelligent, imaginative, and unconventional soldier, a strong advocate of air co-operation and tank warfare, and essentially a commander. He never intrigued and never refused a job. He played rugby football for Scotland, was an excellent shot, 'plus two' at golf, and a keen follower to hounds. He was appointed C.M.G. (1918), K.C.B. (1919), and G.C.B. (1938), was appointed to the D.S.O. in 1915, and invested with the grand cross of the Legion of Honour in 1940. He received an honorary LL.D. from Aberdeen in 1936.

In 1915 Ironside married Mariot Ysobel, daughter of Charles Cheyne, of the Indian Staff Corps, by whom he had a daughter and a son, Edmund Oslac (born 1924), who succeeded him when he died in London 22 September 1959. Of six portraits, one by Eric Kennington is in the possession of the family; another by Kenneth Hauff is at Tonbridge School, and a third, by C. Corfield, is in the Royal Artillery Mess, Woolwich. The Imperial War Museum has a pastel by Eric Kennington.

[*The Ironside Diaries, 1937–1940*, ed. R. Macleod and D. Kelly, 1962; private information; personal knowledge.]   R. MACLEOD.

IRVINE, SIR JAMES COLQUHOUN (1877–1952), chemist and educationist, was born in Glasgow 9 May 1877, the younger son of John Irvine who came of yeoman farmer stock but was himself a manufacturer of light iron castings, and his wife, Mary Paton Colquhoun, of Highland descent, whose forebears had followed the sea, a love of which Irvine inherited and transmitted to his son; from his father, a close friend of Henry Drummond [q.v.], author of *Natural Law in the Spiritual World,* came his interest in science. He won an open scholarship tenable at Allan Glen's School, Glasgow, and at the age of sixteen entered the Royal Technical College, becoming a pupil of G. G. Henderson (whose notice he later contributed to this Dictionary). In 1895 he went to the university of St. Andrews as a lecture assistant to Thomas Purdie, became a matriculated student, and graduated B.Sc. in 1898 with special distinction in chemistry and natural science. His career in research began even before his graduation; in 1899 he was awarded an 1851 Exhibition scholarship and went to work in Leipzig with Wislicenus, studying also under Ostwald and attending lectures by Bechmann, Stobbe, and Pfeffer. In 1901 his thesis 'Ueber einige Derivate des Orthomethoxy Benzaldehydes' gained him a Ph.D. *summa cum laude.*

He returned to St. Andrews in 1901 as a junior lecturer and to work with Purdie on investigations of the carbohydrates, in which subject he made his major contributions to scientific discovery. He obtained his D.Sc. in 1903, becoming professor of chemistry in 1909 and dean of the faculty of science in 1912, posts which he held until he was appointed principal of St. Andrews in 1921.

While still working in Leipzig, Irvine had the idea of applying Purdie's alkylation technique of hydroxyl groups with silver oxide and alkyl iodide to structural work in all branches of sugar chemistry and thus elucidate the structure of the monosaccharides and polysaccharides. His work with his colleagues at St. Andrews included studies of the chemistry of inulin, of cellulose, and of starch. During the war of 1914–18 academic research on the carbohydrates was interrupted but the experience gained enabled the St. Andrews laboratories to make a significant contribution to the war effort. This included the production of bacteriological sugars and related substances for the army and navy medical services. Production of dulcitol, inulin, fructose, and mannitol was followed by the preparation of novocain and orthoform. In addition many research problems were undertaken at the request of the chemical warfare department and the department of propellant supplies, among them a search for large-scale methods of preparing mustard gas.

As a teacher Irvine was outstanding, his eloquent presentation of his subject commanding the attention of all his students and inspiring many to follow chemistry as a career in both the academic and industrial fields. He was a fine experimentalist and manipulator, laying considerable emphasis on the practical side of his subject, and he preserved to the end of his life his sureness and delicacy of technique. He worked long hours and expected the same of his staff and students. A strict disciplinarian, he was yet easy to approach and always encouraging and helpful if the case was good. Like Bishop James Kennedy [q.v.], the founder of St. Salvator's College, he 'believed in the master-disciple relationship as the most effective method of inculcating knowledge and of transmitting knowledge into wisdom'. He was noted for his eloquence as a student and became internationally famous for it as a principal.

The welfare of his students was Irvine's prime concern and he succeeded in making St. Andrews largely a residential university as it had been in the past. He revived old customs and traditions, improved many buildings, found donors for a graduation hall and for the renovation of St. Salvator's chapel and the restoration of St. Leonard's chapel. He widened the field of recruitment of students and raised the numbers to an economic level. In Dundee the schools of medicine, engineering, and chemistry were expanded and he devised methods of improving the college finances. The hostility which arose between the two parts of the university in St. Andrews and Dundee, resulting in a royal commission (1951–2), was most unfortunate. Irvine held strong opinions and so on occasion inevitably had to face opposition and criticism. The word autocratic was applied to him; but his was always benevolent autocracy and even his greatest enemies could not deny his unsparing devotion to his university.

Irvine travelled extensively in the interests of education. He went to India as chairman of the viceroy's committee on he Indian Institute of Science in 1936; to the West Indies as chairman of the committee on higher education in 1944 and in subsequent years as the prime mover in founding the University College of the West Indies. He was chairman of the Inter-University Council for Higher Education in the Colonies from its formation in 1946 until 1951. The Carnegie Trust, the Scottish Universities Entrance Board, and the prime minister's committee on the training of biologists (1933) were among the educational bodies on which he served. He was always warmly received in America where he had many friends, among them Edward Harkness who sought his advice on the formation of the Pilgrim Trust on which he served, as on the committee of the Commonwealth Fund. Irvine impressed such men by his penetrating judgement and clarity of expression; practical in outlook, in action he was level headed.

Irvine had a short, slim, athletic figure with a tanned skin and dark, bright eyes. In youth he was a good athlete, a versatile runner (his speciality the 100 yards), and a strong swimmer. Until late in life he played a good game of golf and tennis and maintained an interest in athletics and sport which was encouraging to the students. He was a most engaging companion, of catholic tastes and with a wide range of experience, backed by an astonishing memory for people and incidents. To scholarship he added wit, to knowledge wisdom, to sympathy discernment. Dignified in bearing, he compelled attention. When he was installed as principal the university was small and its financial resources had dwindled. By his skill, enthusiasm, and tact Irvine found the generous donors required to carry out his schemes for the improvement and expansion of the university.

Many honours came to Irvine who was elected F.R.S. in 1918, knighted in 1925, appointed C.B.E. in 1920 and K.B.E. in 1948. He received a number of medals from learned societies and honorary degrees from many universities, and his services to Polish and Norwegian forces in Scotland during the war of 1939–45 were recognized by decorations from their countries.

In 1905 Irvine married Mabel Violet, daughter of John Williams, of Dunmurry House, county Antrim, who was studying music in Leipzig when he was working under Wislicenus. She was a gifted musician and did much for music in the university. Their marriage was a never-failing source of happiness and inspiration. They had two daughters and a son who was accidentally drowned in Ceylon in 1944 when serving as a lieutenant in the R.N.V.R. Irvine died in St. Andrews 12 June 1952. The university has portraits by Sir Oswald Birley and Keith Henderson.

[*Alumnus Chronicle* of the University of St. Andrews, January 1953; John Read in *Obituary Notices of Fellows of the Royal Society*, No. 22, November 1953; private information; personal knowledge.]   DAVID TRAILL.

ISMAIL, SIR MIRZA MOHAMMAD (1883–1959), Indian administrator and statesman, was born in Bangalore, Mysore, 23 October 1883, the son of Aga Jan, honorary A.D.C. to Maharaja Chamarajendra Wadiyar. He was of Persian descent, his grandfather, Ali Asker Shirazi, having left Shiraz in 1824 and settled as an importer of horses in Bangalore where he prospered exceedingly. Mirza grew up with the young Maharaja of Mysore [q.v.], Krishnaraja Wadiyar, who was about the same age and who succeeded after the death of his father in 1894. Mirza was educated entirely in Bangalore, first at mission schools, then for five years in the Maharaja's special class under the tutorship of Sir Stuart Fraser of the Indian Civil Service, finally at the Central College, graduating in 1905 at the Madras University.

His first post was in the Mysore Police but he was quickly transferred to the Mysore Civil Service. He soon joined the Maharaja's own staff and became assistant secretary, Huzur secretary (1913), private secretary (1923, the first Indian to hold that post), and finally in 1926 dewan. There followed the happiest and most constructive period of his life and he remained in office until 1941, a year after the Maharaja's death. Mysore was his first and last love. As an administrator he was outstanding and made Mysore one of the best administered states in India. A lover of beauty, he created the gardens of Brindavan and Bangalore; and thousands from all parts of India still visit the illuminated gardens planned by him at the Krishnaraj Sagar Dam. He believed it obligatory for the administration to enable the poorer classes to enjoy themselves without expense. A born townplanner, he made Mysore and Bangalore famous for their ordered beauty. It was an experience to be with him on one of his weekly morning tours of Bangalore. He made them in a large car, accompanied by the municipal executive officers. Nothing escaped his attention: a road alignment, an uncovered rubbish bin, or an ungainly corner in a wall. Anything unsightly which offended his highly developed sense of beauty was dealt with on the spot. But Mirza's ideal was to make Mysore not only beautiful, but also a 'truly Socialist State'. He started several state industries, in the face of considerable opposition from the Government of India. He believed that in a backward country some state socialism was essential if industrialization was to make any substantial or rapid progress. In this, as in so many other matters, he was a pioneer, and by the middle of the twentieth century Mysore had a wide range of industries, some sponsored by the state, and others by the Government of India or by private enterprise.

In all these activities Mirza owed everything to the constant support and encouragement of the Maharaja between whom and his dewan there was a perfect partnership, rare in Indian states. The Maharaja was the wisest and most distinguished ruler Mysore had ever known and when he died in 1940 Mirza wrote to a friend that 'life without him can never be the same'. From 1942 to 1946 he was prime minister of Jaipur, one of the Rajput states, where he made his enlightened mark on the feudal administrative structure which he found. In 1946 he became president of the Nizam of Hyderabad's executive council, but his tenure of office was a failure and he resigned after only ten months. His policies of moderation and compromise were thwarted by extremists within and without the state and he was therefore a helpless witness of the final tragedy, and the end of an ancient dynasty. In 1950 he was appointed representative of the United Nations technical assistance for Indonesia but he found the environment uncongenial and after nearly a year was glad to return to his beloved home in Mysore. The remainder of his life was spent in Bangalore, carrying on a considerable correspondence with his many friends and associates in India and abroad and writing his memoirs, published in 1954 as *My Public Life*.

Mirza was of medium height, slim, erect, and always most carefully dressed. He had an aloof dignity and bearing which compelled respect, if not affection. His Persian origin, which showed itself clearly in his profile and complexion, gave him a de-

tached outlook on human affairs in general and on Indian politics in particular. A devout and broadminded Moslem, the dewan of a predominantly Hindu state, the servant and friend of an orthodox Hindu ruler, he was a living example of communal moderation and harmony. He belonged to and represented no political or communal party or group and he believed in the essential unity of the Indian continent. For these reasons his counsel had little influence on the extreme and rapid developments which led to the final creation of the two independent states of India and Pakistan. He had represented Mysore, and for part of the time the South Indian States, and Jodhpur and Jaipur, at the Round Table conferences in London in 1930–32 and attended the meetings of the subsequent joint parliamentary select committee. In 1937 he led the Indian delegation to the conference of Far Eastern countries on hygiene in Indonesia. He was appointed O.B.E. (1923), C.I.E. (1924), K.C.I.E. (1936), and knighted in 1930.

In 1906 he married Zeebeenda Begum, daughter of Mohammad Mirza Shiraza, by whom he had one son and two daughters. He died in Bangalore 5 January 1959.

[*The Times* and *Times of India*, 6 January 1959; Sir Mirza Ismail, *My Public Life*, 1954; private information; personal knowledge.]

FREDERICK JAMES.

JACKS, LAWRENCE PEARSALL (1860–1955), Unitarian divine, was born at Nottingham 9 October 1860, the second son of Jabez Jacks, an ironmonger, by his wife, Anne Steere. His father died when he was thirteen and the headmaster of University School, Nottingham, generously kept him on without fee. Desiring no longer to be a burden to his mother, a courageous woman, he left school before he was seventeen and taught in a number of private schools, most of which he found intolerable. Working in his spare time for an external London degree he incurred a breakdown in health, but was able to spend his convalescence learning German at Göttingen during part of 1881. A keen sermon-taster, he was attracted by Richard Armstrong at Nottingham and Stopford Brooke [q.v.], who had recently renounced his Anglican orders, in London, and decided to become a preacher himself. Still uncertain whether he was an Anglican or a Nonconformist, in 1882 he entered Manchester New College, which in theory at least was completely undenominational; the college was then in London with James Martineau [q.v.] as principal. There he took his London B.A. in 1883 and his M.A. three years later.

On leaving college in 1886 he proceeded as Hibbert scholar to spend a year at Harvard, at the end of which he was appointed assistant to Stopford Brooke at Bedford chapel, Bloomsbury. He returned to England in the same boat as some of Brooke's family and in the course of the voyage became unofficially engaged to the fourth daughter, Olive Cecilia (died 1948), whom he married in 1889, and by whom he eventually had five sons and a daughter.

The year at Bedford chapel was a somewhat humiliating experience; a large proportion of the fashionable congregation would walk out when they saw that it was only the assistant who was to preach. Jacks was also giving university extension lectures on political economy, and the strain almost led to another breakdown. He found himself, however, by way of compensation, in contact with a brilliant group including Burne-Jones, Oscar Wilde, G. B. Shaw, and the Webbs [qq.v.].

In 1888 at a remarkably young age, Jacks, now a Unitarian minister, was appointed to Renshaw Street chapel, Liverpool, and six years later moved to Birmingham as minister of the church of the Messiah. In 1902 he was appointed first editor of the *Hibbert Journal* and the success of this venture showed the need for a periodical giving scope for the free debate of all manner of religious and kindred subjects. It made demands upon its editor which could hardly be reconciled with the claims of a busy ministry and he was glad in the following year to accept the post of lecturer in philosophy at Manchester College, by now in Oxford. In 1915 he became principal, succeeding J. Estlin Carpenter [q.v.], to whose unfailing friendship he had owed much since student days. Glasgow, McGill, and Rochester conferred on him the honorary LL.D., Liverpool the D.Litt., and Harvard the D.D. He retired in 1931. Two years later he accepted an invitation to give three addresses at evening services in Liverpool Cathedral, the result being a storm which ended in the Convocation of York rebuking the cathedral authorities for offering the pulpit to a Unitarian.

Jacks's literary output was prodigious: many of his books were published lectures, delivered in Britain and in America which he visited several times, but they included *The Alchemy of Thought* (1910); full-scale lives of Stopford Brooke and Charles Hargrove; the *Smokeover* series of allegorical stories; and translations of the New Testament writings of Loisy. In his later years at the college he turned more and more away from institutional religion towards education as the hope for the future, and this gave some offence to both students and governing body; typical of his outlook was *The Education of the Whole Man*, published in 1931. He wrote a charming and candid autobiography, *The Confession of an Octogenarian*, in 1942, and ten years later a final testament, *Near the Brink*. In 1917 he was president of the Society for Psychical Research, a subject in which he was keenly interested. As a philosopher he was a disciple of Bergson, never greatly in sympathy with the prevailing trends of academic philosophy in Britain. His chief memorial is the *Hibbert Journal* which he conducted brilliantly until 1947. Perhaps he is best thought of as the last of the Victorian prophets in the line of Thomas Carlyle [q.v.], whom he greatly venerated.

Jacks died in Oxford 17 February 1955. There is a portrait by George Harcourt in Manchester College, Oxford. Of his sons, Graham Vernon was director of the Commonwealth Bureau of Soils (1946–66), Hector Beaumont headmaster of Bedales School (1946–62), and Maurice Leonard director of the department of education, Oxford University (1938–57).

[Private information; personal knowledge.]
L. A. GARRARD.

JAMES, ALEXANDER WILSON (1901–1953), footballer, was born at Mossend, Bellshill, Lanarkshire, 14 September 1901, the son of Charles James, railway yardsman, and his wife, Jane Ann Barrie Wilson. On leaving school he joined Bellshill Crusaders, a Glasgow junior team, and he later played for Ashfield before signing for Raith Rovers, a Scottish League club, during the season of 1922–3. He was with Raith for a couple of seasons, scoring 23 goals, and then he crossed the border to Preston North End. Preston, a club of proud traditions, had just been relegated from the first division, and James was signed to help them regain their former status. In this he was unsuccessful, and his four seasons with the club were spent in the second division. But his personal reputation as an inside-forward advanced rapidly. While he was a Preston player he was capped four times for Scotland, and in

1928 he scored two of the goals when Scotland's 'blue devils' beat England at Wembley by 5–1. But at Preston he was unfortunate in his colleagues. The team was described as 'Alex James and ten others'. He was frustrated and discontented and in 1929 he was put on the transfer-list.

Many well-known clubs wanted to sign him, and Herbert Chapman brought him to Arsenal at a fee of £9,000, then the second-highest sum ever paid for a footballer. Chapman had been manager of Arsenal for four years and he had not yet realized his ambition to put them on top of the football world. The signing of James as a midfield forager and schemer proved to be the turning-point.

James was with Arsenal for eight seasons, during which he received four more Scottish caps and the club won the League four times and the Cup twice. On the field James was the mainspring of this achievement, but it took him some time to fit into the Arsenal pattern. At Preston he had been an individualist and a striker, scoring some 60 goals. At Arsenal, Chapman required him to adapt his creativeness to a common purpose and fashion goals for other people. At first he slowed down the attack by holding the ball too long and by Christmas he had lost his place in the team. But when the Cup-ties came Arsenal were suddenly a different side. James recovered his form and confidence, carried the club into the final and at Wembley scored an early goal in the 2–0 defeat of Huddersfield Town.

In 1930–31 Arsenal, fourteenth the previous season, won the League with 66 points out of 84, a record which stood for 30 years. A year later they came close to achieving the 'double' of League and Cup, but an injury to James at Easter ultimately robbed them of both. He could not play in the final, when they lost to Newcastle United by a goal which the photographers later proved was not a goal at all. In the League they were second to Everton.

Three successive championships followed in the next three seasons, and in 1936 Arsenal again won the Cup. James played in the final against Sheffield United, but at the end of the 1936–7 season, in which he played only 19 League games, he retired. His delicate skill had always made him the object of rough tactics and he could no longer recover from injury as quickly as a younger man. Arsenal won the League again in the

season after his retirement, but it was not the emphatic, runaway victory of earlie years, and after that there was a definite decline. James was irreplaceable. The clu could not find another inside-forward wit his tactical flair. He was the team's uni fying force, the supreme organizer of vic tory. With his baggy shorts and flappin sleeves he stamped his personality o every game in which he played.

Scoring goals was not his job, and in 23 games for Arsenal he scored only 26. So i 1935 Sheffield Wednesday came to High bury with the idea that if they left Jame with the ball and marked everyone else Arsenal's attacking system would be dis rupted. James quickly found the answe to that: he held the ball and went throug to score himself. Arsenal won 3–0 an James had them all. It was characteristi of the panache and improvising geniu that made him the outstanding footballe of his time.

In the war of 1939–45 James served i the Maritime AA Regiment. After th war he was an Arsenal coach until hi health broke down, and he died in Londo 1 June 1953 after a long illness. He lef a widow, two sons, and a daughter.

[Bernard Joy, *Forward, Arsenal!, a Histor of the Arsenal Football Club*, 1952.]

M. M. REESI

JAMES, ROLFE ARNOLD SCOTT (1878–1959), journalist, editor, and literar critic. [See SCOTT-JAMES.]

JARDINE, DOUGLAS ROBERT (1900 1958), cricketer, was born at Bombay 2 October 1900, the only son of Malcolm Robert Jardine and his wife, Alison daughter of Robert Moir, M.D. His father who practised at the Bombay bar, ha himself played for Oxford and for Middle sex. Jardine went to Horris Hill, a pre paratory school renowned as a cradle o cricketers, and thence to Winchester where he was in the eleven from 1917 t 1919. Captain in his last year, he made 99 runs in 16 innings and played in the schools' representative games at Lord's.

At New College, Oxford, he gained hi blue as a freshman, but in four inning against Cambridge his highest score was 3 in Oxford's overwhelming victory in 192 In 1922 a damaged knee not only kep him out of the side but by hampering hi footwork retarded his development a a batsman. At Oxford he played severa fine innings, notably his 96 not out agains the all-conquering Australians in 192 ut he did not quite fulfil the exceptional promise of his schooldays. He also played tennis for the university in 1921 and he obtained a fourth in modern history in 1922.

Jardine qualified as a solicitor in 1926 and his professional commitments never allowed him to play first-class cricket regularly. But when he could spare the time he was always sure of his place in Surrey's already powerful batting side, and his unusual power of concentration enabled him to make consistently large scores even when he was short of practice. More than six feet tall, he had a boldly upright stance, and, apart from a certain restriction in his off-side play, he embodied the classical principles of amateur batsmanship: men who had played before 1914 took him to their hearts as one of themselves. What raised him above his own amateur contemporaries was the strength of his back-play, in which he was the equal of the best professionals. His technical gifts were reinforced by a combative determination to succeed, and as he matured he became one of the outstanding players of the era between the wars.

In 1927, although playing only 14 innings, he made 1002 runs, including five centuries, and headed the English averages with 91·09. Next year he averaged 87·15 in 17 innings and was again top of the averages. He made 193 for the Gentlemen against the Players at the Oval and played in two test matches against the West Indies, scoring 83 at Manchester. Invited to go to Australia with A. P. F. Chapman's side in 1928–9, he was one of the successes of the tour. He made centuries in three consecutive matches against state sides and played in all five tests, four of which were won. At Adelaide he scored 98 and his partnership of 262 with W. R. Hammond set up a new record for England's third wicket against Australia.

In the next two seasons Jardine was unable to give much time to cricket and so he did not play against the Australian side which recovered the Ashes in 1930. But in 1931 he was appointed captain in the three tests against New Zealand, and next year, after captaining England in the first representative match against India, he was invited to lead the side which visited Australia in 1932–3.

Thus began the most bitterly controversial series that has ever taken place between the two countries. The phenomenal batting of (Sir) D. G. Bradman had introduced a new and almost super-human element into the ancient rivalry, and in planning his strategy for the tour Jardine knew that he must contain Bradman if he was to win the rubber. Bradman was thought to be unhappy against genuinely fast bowling, and the type of attack which came to be known as 'body line' was born of the English team's determination to reduce him to mortal stature.

England won the first test at Sydney, lost the second at Melbourne, and went on to win the remaining three. With the bat Jardine had only a moderate tour, but he was the architect of England's victory, such as it was. Certainly no victory has had such bitter fruits. Jardine had never been personally popular with Australian crowds: on his previous visit they has found him dour and unresponsive, lacking the common touch, and they had resented his attachment to his Oxford Harlequin cap, which he even wore in test matches. On his second tour they accused him of winning the rubber by calculated intimidation, and his every appearance was greeted with barracking and execration of quite frightening intensity.

Jardine made no secret of the fact that as a tactical variation he would sometimes instruct his bowlers to direct their attack on the leg stump, so that a cluster of short legs might snap up the unwary stroke. This was conventional 'leg theory', with nothing new about it. It had been used before, by the Australian W. W. Armstrong among others, but it had never flourished because it was regarded as dull and ineffective. It simply inhibited stroke play and spoiled the game as a spectacle. But the difference now was that Jardine had at his command two Nottinghamshire bowlers, H. Larwood and W. Voce, of exceptional pace and accuracy. When they attacked the leg stump, they were fast enough to put the batsman in some physical danger. There can be little doubt that at times wickets were lost in defence of the person rather than the stumps.

For this type of bowling the Australians coined the term 'body line'. The injuries suffered by two Australian batsmen at Adelaide were not caused by leg theory, but in the heat of the moment the Australian Board of Control sent a cable to the M.C.C. accusing the English team of 'unsportsmanlike' methods which were 'making protection of the body by the batsmen the main consideration'. The M.C.C. replied that if things were as bad as that, perhaps the rest of the tour should be cancelled; and this threat to the game's finances caused the Australian authorities to frame their objections more carefully. The exchange of cables continued, and after an inquiry held at the end of the tour the M.C.C. were able to set the dispute in a clearer perspective. They agreed that a deliberate assault on the batsman would be contrary to the spirit of the game, but they did not believe that any English bowler had been guilty of it. They considered that 'the term "body-line" bowling is misleading and improper. It has led to much inaccuracy of thought by confusing the short bumping ball, whether directed on the off, middle, or leg stump, with what is known as "leg-theory"'.

It is significant that throughout a difficult and unhappy situation Jardine retained the loyalty and confidence of his team, and even his opponents admired his personal courage and tenacity of purpose. In a book about the series he repeated that leg theory was an accepted and legitimate tactic and he denied that the English bowlers had ever aimed deliberately to hit the batsman. At home in 1933 he gave a practical demonstration of his belief that leg theory, however fast, could be subdued by a batsman with the skill and nerve to meet it. At Manchester he made 127—his only century in a test—against West Indian fast bowlers who had the avowed object of giving him a taste of his own medicine.

But at the age of thirty-three, when he should have been in his prime, Jardine had come to the end of his active cricket career. Partly for business reasons he gave up the captaincy of Surrey, which he had held for only two seasons; and although he led the M.C.C. team to India in 1933–4, when the Australians came in the following summer they found him in the press-box instead of on the field. Voce and Larwood did not play either, and Bradman's average in the tests was 94·75.

Jardine's few subsequent appearances were in non-competitive cricket, although he retained his interest in the game through occasional journalism and from 1955 to 1957 he was president of the Oxford University Cricket Club. Altogether he made 14,821 runs, with an average of 46·90, the highest of his 35 centuries being 214 not out against Tasmania in 1928–9. He three times captained the Gentlemen against the Players at Lord's, and in his 22 tests, 15 as England's captain, he made 1,296 runs

with an average of 48. In his test career ▮ was only twice on the losing side.

Jardine was chairman of the New Sout▮ Wales Land Agency and a director of t▮ Scottish Australian Company. In the w▮ of 1939–45 he enlisted in the Roy▮ Berkshire Regiment and served in Franc▮ Belgium, and India.

In 1934 he married Irene Margare▮ daughter of Sir William Henry Peat; th▮ had a son and three daughters. He died ▮ Switzerland, 18 June 1958, followin▮ a fever contracted in Southern Rhodes▮ the previous year. A portrait by Herbe▮ A. Olivier is at Lord's.

[D. R. Jardine, *In Quest of the Ashes*, 193▮ and *Cricket*, 1936; *Wisden's Cricketer Almanack*, 1959; Roy Webber, *The Book Cricket Records*, 1961; H. S. Altham ar▮ E. W. Swanton, *A History of Cricket*, 1938.]

                                    M. M. REES

JARVIS, CLAUDE SCUDAMOR▮ (1879–1953), soldier, administrator, ar▮ orientalist, born at Forest Gate, Londo▮ 20 July 1879, was the son of John Bra▮ ford Jarvis, an insurance clerk, and h▮ wife, Mary Harvey. He does not seem t▮ have been educated with any profession i▮ mind, and at the age of seventeen h▮ joined the Merchant Navy as an appre▮ tice, sailing from Shadwell to Sydney an▮ back by way of Cape Horn. But on th▮ outbreak of the South African war in 189▮ he enlisted in the Imperial Yeomanry ▮ a trooper, and on his return to England i▮ 1902 was gazetted to the 3rd battalion, th▮ Dorsetshire Regiment (Special Reserve▮ In the war of 1914–18 he served in Franc▮ Egypt, and Palestine, reached the rank ▮ major, and acquired a good knowledge ▮ Arabic. Egypt was then a British pr▮ tectorate, and its desert borders had b▮ come of considerable military importanc▮ on the east as the main theatre of oper▮ tions against Turkey, and on the we▮ through Turkish subversion of the Senus▮ tribesmen. It was against the latter tha▮ a disproportionate number of troops wer▮ employed against what proved to b▮ a largely mythical enemy. It was to reduc▮ this commitment that the British hig▮ commissioner, Sir Reginald Wingat▮ [q.v.], succeeded in persuading the Egy▮ tian Government to establish a Frontie▮ Administration, and Jarvis was amongs▮ the first selected for this service, subse▮ quently to be described by him as 'brough▮ into the world by British influence an▮ afterwards treated with studied neglect b▮ Egypt'.

Nevertheless it was in this unpromising atmosphere that Jarvis achieved remarkable success, gaining not only the confidence of the tribal Arabs whom he governed but that of the Egyptian Government who, if they were niggardly in their financial aid, trusted him and gave him support. His first appointment was to the Western Desert, followed by the governorship of the oases of the Libyan Desert, but he was then transferred in 1922 to the Eastern Desert as governor of Sinai where he remained until he retired voluntarily in 1936, when he was appointed C.M.G.

Unfettered by bureaucratic control, and with what seemed to be a hopelessly inadequate budget, Jarvis became a legendary figure. His knowledge of Arabic, and of Bedouin customs and law, enabled him to settle tribal feuds, not only amongst the tribes under his official control, but their feuds with the neighbouring tribes in Trans-Jordania and Saudi Arabia. He virtually obliterated banditry, and contributed effectively to Egypt's efforts to suppress the drug traffic by the desert routes. He made a special study of the wanderings of the Israelites in the Exodus, and traced the remains of what, before the Arab conquest, must have been a flourishing Roman and later Byzantine settlement in the north of Sinai. There, by damming the Wadi Gedeirat (Kadesh Barnea of the Bible), and restoring the old stone channels, he transformed a small swampy waterhole into several hundred acres of olive and fruit trees. He was a botanist and naturalist of considerable skill, in addition to being a practical agriculturist and a water-colourist of some merit. He was among the last of the Englishmen in the great tradition of the early members of the Indian Civil Service whose usually single-handed contribution to the then isolated areas under their charge will probably, on the spot, not readily be forgotten.

Jarvis's retirement opened the final phase in his career. He joined the staff of *Country Life* where his 'A Countryman's Notes', with their knowledge of agriculture and wild life and their delightful anecdotes, gained a wide and appreciative readership for fourteen years until his death. He lectured frequently, and the Royal Central Asian Society awarded him the Lawrence memorial medal in 1938. He was a prolific author, writing not only on his experiences in Sinai and its history, but on Arab customs and agriculture, and sometimes in a lighter and satirical vein on the British in the Middle East. His best-known works were: *Yesterday and Today in Sinai* (1931), *Three Deserts* (1936), *Deserts and Delta* (1938), *Arab Command* (1942), *Heresies and Humours* (1943), and his autobiography, *Half a Life* (1943).

He was small in stature, but with great charm and wit both in speaking and writing, which enabled him to invest the animals, birds, and fishes which he knew so well with almost human characteristics. He died at his home in Ringwood 8 December 1953. He had married in 1903 Mabel Jane, daughter of Charles Hodson of the American Embassy, London; there was one daughter.

[*The Times*, 10 December 1953; *Country Life*, 17 December 1953; private information; personal knowledge.]   RONALD WINGATE.

JEFFERY, GEORGE BARKER (1891–1957), mathematician and educationist, was born in Lambeth, London, 9 May 1891, the son of George Jeffery, corresponding clerk, and his wife, Elizabeth McDonald McKenzie. He was educated at Strand School, King's College, London, and Wilson's Grammar School, Camberwell. In 1909 he entered University College, London, for a two years' course, followed by a year at the London Day Training College. He then returned to University College as a research student and assistant to L. N. G. Filon (whose notice he subsequently contributed to this Dictionary) and obtained his B.Sc. in 1912. In the same year his first research paper was communicated to the Royal Society. In 1914 Filon went away on war service and Jeffery, aged twenty-three, was left in charge of the department. Jeffery was a Quaker and in 1916 spent a short time in prison as a conscientious objector but was later allowed to do work of 'national importance'. In 1919 he returned to the college, again as an assistant to Filon.

During this time he published a series of papers on the mathematical functions which occur in the solution of Laplace's equation and on the theory of viscous flow. He was particularly interested in the general solution of Laplace's equation given by (Sir) E. T. Whittaker [q.v.] in 1902. He used this formula as a means of obtaining relations between spherical harmonics, cylindrical harmonics, and other such functions which occur in the solution of Laplace's equation. In fluid motion his object was to obtain exact solutions of the Navier-Stokes equation, and he discovered a number of new and interesting types of flow. His point of view was very practical. He was looking for exact solutions of definite physical problems, and often gave at the end of his papers a little table of numerical results.

In 1921 Jeffery became university reader in mathematics and in 1922 professor of mathematics at King's College, London, but in 1924 he returned to University College as Astor professor of pure mathematics. His researches at this time were mainly inspired by Einstein's theory of relativity, and he published a small book *Relativity for Physics Students* (1924). He was elected F.R.S. in 1926. In the years following the war he published a series of original papers in rapid succession. They were entirely in the field of applied mathematics in which his real scientific interest lay. He made no further original contribution to pure mathematics. He was becoming increasingly absorbed in the problems of college and university administration and even in applied mathematics his original work came to an early end. In all he published twenty-one original papers, the last in 1929.

Jeffery had many activities outside the work of his own department. He was Swarthmore lecturer to the Society of Friends (1934); president of the London Mathematical Society (1935–7), of the London Society for the Study of Religion (1937–8), of the Mathematical Association (1947); and a vice-president of the Royal Society (1938–40). He became a member of the senate of London University in 1935 and in 1939 chairman of the matriculation and school examination council of the university. In 1948 he became chairman of the South-West Middlesex Hospital management committee.

In 1939 a section of University College, London, moved to Bangor where Jeffery acted as pro-provost. When the war was over the college returned to London. Soon afterwards he resigned his chair to become director of the Institute of Education and entered upon what was in some ways the most successful period of his life. In 1945 London University accepted responsibility for the training of teachers in more than thirty colleges, many in the London area, but others scattered over the south-east of England. The shaping of the scheme for the whole area was almost entirely due to Jeffery who produced a plan in two days of concentrated work; it has needed no substantial alteration.

Through its colonial department the Institute of Education had strong overseas interests, especially among West African students, and Jeffery became interested in the problems of West African education. In December 1949 he visited West Africa to report upon a proposal for an examination council, spending eight weeks in Nigeria, the Gold Coast, Sierra Leone, and the Gambia. In his report (March 1950) he recommended the foundation of a West African examination council to control all the examinations in the area. In the next year Jeffery led a study group which visited West Africa for six months, at the same time as another group was visiting East and Central Africa. Presumably the West African section of the report *African Education, a Study of Educational Policy and Practice in British Tropical Africa* (1953) was largely Jeffery's work. Subsequently he paid an annual visit to West Africa to keep in touch with the work of the Examinations Council of which he was the founder. He also visited Russia with a study group and contributed to a report on the country's schools and training of teachers.

Jeffery was also much interested in craftsmanship. He was descended from a family of wheelwrights and was himself an expert cabinet maker: several tables in the staff common-room at University College were made by him. Late in life he took up silversmithing and registered his own hall-mark with the Goldsmiths' Company. From 1952 he was dean of the College of Handicraft. It was while driving home from the annual conference of this college, on 27 April 1957, that he died from a sudden seizure at Woolmer Green, Hertfordshire.

In 1915 Jeffery married Elizabeth Schofield; they had one son and two daughters.

[Private information; personal knowledge.]

E. C. TITCHMARSH.

JESSOP, GILBERT LAIRD (1874–1955), cricketer, was born in Cheltenham 19 May 1874, the son of Henry Edward Jessop, surgeon, and his wife, Susannah Radford Hughes. At the age of eleven he went to the local grammar school, of which his father was a governor, and in his second summer won his place in the first eleven as a hard-working long stop. But his father's sudden death when he was fifteen obliged him to leave school and earn his living; for the next six years he was an apprentice teacher at various schools. Masters were often allowed to play in the school team in club matches, and for Beccles College in 1895 Jessop scored 1,058 runs with an average of 132 and in 168 overs took 100 wickets for 2·5 each. By this time he had already played for Gloucestershire, making his first appearance at Manchester in July 1894, and in the following season he was in the team at Lord's when W. G. Grace [q.v.] completed his 1,000 runs in May.

Jessop went to Christ's College, Cambridge, in the Easter term of 1896 and played for the university for four years, being captain in 1899. Against Oxford he achieved little with the bat, making only two scores over 40, but he twice took six wickets in an innings. In 1897, however, he hit his first century, 140 for Cambridge against the Philadelphians, and later made three more for his county, including 101 (out of 118) in 40 minutes against Yorkshire. He played for the Gentlemen against the Players at Lord's, and altogether the season brought him 1,219 runs and 116 wickets.

He made his first appearance for England two years later, and in 1900, after Grace's long association with Gloucestershire had ended in a quarrel, Jessop took over the captaincy of the county. He held the post for thirteen years, during which they were never higher than seventh in the championship, their bowling being too weak to disturb the stronger teams. But Jessop's presence was a guarantee that their cricket was never lacking in colour and excitement.

He stood only 5 feet 7 inches, and his huddled posture at wicket earned him the nickname of 'the Croucher'. But he was exceptionally strong in the shoulders and arms, and once he had sighted the ball there was no bowler in the world to contain him. H. S. Altham has said that as a hitter he 'stands absolutely alone': others might have driven the ball harder and higher but 'no cricketer that has ever lived hit it so often, so fast, and with such a bewildering variety of strokes'. Length had no meaning for him. With his remarkable speed of foot he could run to meet even the fastest bowler and drive him over his head. Alternatively he would drop on the right knee and sweep the ball round to leg with an almost horizontal bat; and for variety's sake he possessed a 'wind and water' stroke with which he

cut past third man after he had begun by jumping out to drive.

His most astonishing feat of sustained scoring was at Hastings in 1907, against the Professionals of the South. He reached 50 in 24 minutes, 100 in 42, 150 in 63; and altogether he made 191, out of 234, in an hour and a half. Five times he played innings of over 200, and the largest of them, 286 (out of 355) against Sussex in 1903, occupied only 175 minutes. He reached 200 in two hours, the quickest double century on record.

In 1900, in a match not regarded as first class, he made 157 against the West Indies in an hour. Against Somerset in 1904 he reached 50 in twelve minutes, and other remarkable innings were 66 out of 66 against Sussex in 1901, 63 out of 65 against Yorkshire in 1895, and 171 not out in an innings total of 246 against Yorkshire in 1899. Four times he made a century in each innings of a match, although on no occasion did this enable Gloucestershire to gain a victory.

It has to be remembered that it was not until 1910 that it became a general rule for a stroke to count six when the ball was hit out of the playing area. Before this alteration to the laws it usually had to be hit out of the ground. Nearly all Jessop's big innings were played before this amendment, or his scores would have been even more startling.

In his career he made 26,058 runs for an average of 32·60. He scored over 1,000 runs in fourteen seasons, his highest totals being 2,210 in 1900 (when he also took 104 wickets) and 2,323 the following year. Altogether he made 53 centuries, six of them in less than an hour.

As a fast bowler he was good enough to be selected for England on at least one occasion in that capacity alone. On account of injury he did little bowling after 1900, but four times in his career he took eight wickets in an innings, his best performance being 8–29 against Essex in 1900. His complete figures were 851 wickets for 22·91. He was, moreover, a brilliant fieldsman at extra cover and deep mid-off, with a swift and deadly throw that brought many an innings to a premature end.

Jessop played in eighteen test matches and is best remembered for his match-winning innings at the Oval in 1902. He played in the first three games in the series, and his omission at Manchester was one of several blunders which helped Australia to win the match and the rubber by three runs. Brought back at the Oval, he went in when England, who needed to make 263 on a rain-damaged wicket, were 48–5. Jessop began uncertainly, giving a couple of early chances, but then he completely turned the game with an explosive innings of 104, out of 139, in 75 minutes. When he departed 76 were still needed, but the bowlers had lost their grip on the game and England won by one wicket. Against South Africa at Lord's in 1907 he hit their formidable array of spin bowlers for 93 runs off the 63 balls sent down to him. He was also a member of the teams which visited Philadelphia in 1897 and 1899, but the opposition was too weak to stimulate his highest effort.

Jessop was not only a cricketer. At Cambridge he was invited to play against Oxford as a hockey goalkeeper but missed his blue because he was taken ill. He would also have opposed Oxford at billiards had he not been gated for falling short in his attendances at chapel. He came near to getting a blue for football and later played for the Casuals, and at rugby he played wing three-quarter for Gloucester. He ran the 100 yards in little short of even time and he was also a scratch golfer, serving for some years as secretary of the Cricketers' Golfing Society.

Although in 1914 he was forty years of age, Jessop enlisted in the Manchester Regiment and was a captain when he was invalided out with a damaged heart four years later.

In *A Cricketer's Log* (1922) he wrote engagingly of his career in the game but with a modesty which prevented him from indicating how much he had himself contributed to it. He also wrote some schoolboy fiction and a manual, *Cricket and How to Play It* (1925).

He married in 1902 Millicent Osborne (died 1953), of New South Wales, whom he met while touring Australia with A. C. MacLaren [q.v.]. They had one son, the Rev. G. L. O. Jessop, who appeared in two matches for Hampshire in 1933 and later played with some success for Dorset, whose bowling averages he headed in 1939. It was at his vicarage at Fordington, near Dorchester, that Jessop died, 11 May 1955.

[G. L. Jessop, *A Cricketer's Log*, 1922; C. J. Britton, *G. L. Jessop*, 1935; *Wisden's Cricketers' Almanack*, 1956; Roy Webber, *Cricket Records*, 1961; H. S. Altham, *A History of Cricket*, vol. i, 1962.]   M. M. REESE.

JOAD, CYRIL EDWIN MITCHINSON (1891–1953), writer and teacher, was born 12 August 1891 at Durham, the only child of Edwin Joad by his wife, Mary Smith. At the time of his son's birth, Edwin Joad had just completed an eight-year fellowship at the university of Durham, later becoming an inspector of schools and residing at Southampton.

Joad was educated at the Dragon School, Oxford, Blundell's School, Tiverton, and Balliol College, Oxford, which he entered as a Blundell scholar in 1910. In 1914 he was awarded the John Locke scholarship in mental philosophy and obtained a first class in *literae humaniores*. On coming down from Oxford he joined the staff of the labour exchanges department of the Board of Trade which afterwards became part of the new Ministry of Labour. Like other civil servants, Joad took to writing, and in the following years a stream of books flowed from his pen, mainly on political and philosophical subjects. In 1930 he left the Ministry of Labour and became head of the department of philosophy at Birkbeck College, university of London, an appointment which he held until his death. He became D.Lit. in 1936 and was appointed reader in philosophy in the university in 1945.

Joad filled his life with an immense variety of activities. In the early days he took classes for the Workers' Educational Association, acted as guide in rambling and climbing clubs, spoke for the Fabian Society, and worked for many societies having as their object the preservation and increased enjoyment of the English countryside. He rode, played hockey and tennis, derived much pleasure from music, entertained lavishly and enjoyed quiet evenings of chess and discussion with his friends. During the war of 1939–45 he helped organize and took part in a series of open lunch-time lectures held at Birkbeck College, speaking mainly of his two great loves, Plato and Aristotle. He also made a name as a broadcaster, imparting much of the liveliness and sparkle to the first Brains Trust. The *Punch* cartoon which depicted him saying to a waiter 'It all depends what you mean by (a) thick and (b) clear' commemorated a characteristic phrase to which the listening public grew accustomed. Many men and women were led to a serious interest in philosophy by hearing his talks, either as adult students or as members of his audiences. But his reputation suffered when he was convicted in 1948 of travelling on the railway without a ticket.

The genius of Joad lay largely in his stimulating influence as a teacher. As an expositor he was admirable. His introductions to the various branches of philosophy and his expositions of the writings of the great thinkers of the past were remarkable for their lucidity and critical insight. By ruthless and persistent criticism he succeeded in imparting these qualities to his students and many of the young men and women who passed through his hands were made incapable of loose or vague thinking and expression.

As a philosopher, Joad suffered from being out of sympathy with the current methods of philosophizing. He admired the ingenuity and acumen of his younger contemporaries, but could not feel that they were working along profitable lines. He fought valiantly for the losing causes of his day: the objectivity of value in morals and art, the fruitfulness of metaphysical speculation, and the legitimate employment of reason upon the objects of religious knowledge. In *Decadence* (1948) Joad traced the evil of his times to what he called 'the dropping of the object', in theory of knowledge, aesthetics, ethics, and political philosophy, with the resulting emphasis upon states of mind in place of that upon which they are directed. In his philosophical life, he was thus forced continually into polemics and was hindered in the peaceful development of his own philosophical position.

In his later years, Joad divided his time between town and country, and to see him arrive in London after a long week-end of work on his Hampshire farm was to see abounding energy personified. Rosy-cheeked, bright-eyed, with neat white beard, his short stocky figure in shapeless tweed overcoat with hat to match, he would arrive carrying a great leather bag, in which would be his lecture notes, his latest manuscript, several books for review, and his evening suit. In the last he would array himself after lectures were over for the evening, and go off to dinners at which he would be a sparkling and entertaining guest, setting himself next morning as usual to write his daily quota. He pursued all sorts of experiences with zest, entering sympathetically into those of other people, interested to find out what it 'felt like' to be blind, how the handicaps might be overcome, and what were the compensations. He passed through change and development of his views, from pacifism to the belief that some evils must be combated by force,

from agnosticism to Christianity. The constant element through these changes was his absolute abhorrence of cruelty and his feeling for the suffering of fellow creatures. He traced carefully and completely the stages in the development of his beliefs, both for his own satisfaction and for the benefit of people struggling with similar problems. *The Recovery of Belief* (1952), the last of his autobiographical works, was published when he was already suffering from the disease from which he died at his home in Hampstead 9 April 1953.

Joad married in 1915 Mary, daughter of Richard William White, artist, by whom he had one son and two daughters. A portrait by Patricia Angadi remained in the possession of the artist.

[Private information; personal knowledge.]
Ruth L. Saw.

JOHN, Sir WILLIAM GOSCOMBE (1860–1952), sculptor and medallist, was born in Cardiff 21 February 1860, the elder son of Thomas John and his wife, Elizabeth Smith. He assumed the name Goscombe when a young man from a Gloucestershire village near his mother's old home. His father was a woodcarver employed in the workshops set up by Lord Bute [q.v.] for the restoration of Cardiff Castle. John was trained in Cardiff, and later in London with Thomas Nicholls (1881–6) and C. B. Birch [q.v.] (1886–7), at the City and Guilds School in Kennington, and, from 1884, at the Royal Academy Schools. With the help of money subscribed by supporters in Cardiff, he was able to visit Italy and France in 1888, and Greece, Constantinople, and Cairo in 1889. The award in 1889 of the Royal Academy's gold medal and travelling scholarship, for a group 'Parting' (cast in bronze for (Sir) Lawrence Alma-Tadema, q.v.), enabled him to extend his travels the next year to Sicily, North Africa, and Spain, and to take a studio in Paris for a year.

John returned to London in 1891 and settled in 1892 in St. John's Wood, in which district he remained for the rest of his life. He had first exhibited at the Academy in 1886. He was elected an associate in 1899 and an academician in 1909. He was knighted at Bangor in 1911.

When living in Paris, John had watched Rodin at work, and his nude 'Morpheus', which received an honourable mention in the Salon of 1892, shows clearly the influence of the latter's 'Age d'Airain'. In

England his teachers and contemporaries included Lord Leighton, Sir Thomas Brock, and Sir Alfred Gilbert [qq.v.]. Gilbert's brilliance, as revealed in his 'sentiment', particularly impressed John. 'Morpheus' was followed, during the next ten years, by other academic nudes: 'Girl binding her hair' (1893); St. John the Baptist, a half-clothed figure cast in block tin for Lord Bute (1894); 'Boy at Play' (1895); 'The Elf' (1898), John's diploma work; and 'Joyance' (1899). These are all characterized by complete anatomical mastery and suave rhythm, nor are they lacking in sentiment, which in the St. John is raised to a restrained eloquence of some distinction. This figure was awarded a gold medal at the Paris International Exhibition of 1900. 'Boy at Play' was purchased in 1896 by the Chantrey trustees. In 1916 John contributed a marble figure of 'St. David Blessing the People' to a group of ten figures commissioned by Lord Rhondda [q.v.] for Cardiff City Hall. This was the most important subject of the group, and by far the most successful.

John's numerous public statues included those of the seventh Duke of Devonshire, at Eastbourne (awarded a gold medal in the Paris Salon of 1901); equestrian statues of King Edward VII (Cape Town, 1904), Lord Tredegar (Cardiff, 1909), Lord Minto (Calcutta, 1913), and Sir Stanley Maude (Baghdad, 1921); the Salisbury tomb in Westminster Abbey (1908), and war memorials in Liverpool, Newcastle, and many other places. His portrait busts included men of such diverse eminence as Carnegie, Edmund Gosse, and Kitchener. He designed the regalia used at the investiture of the Prince of Wales at Caernarvon in 1911 and the commemorative medal, the Jubilee medal of King George V (1935), and the Great Seal of King Edward VIII (1936).

John's art may be described as a compound of realism and romanticism: it is illustrative, but inspired by fancy rather than by imagination. His style underwent little change throughout his long life, apart from a broadening in the treatment of portrait busts. Most of these were in bronze, but in bronze and marble alike he was a convincing portrayer of character and showed notable ability to render the soft surfaces of skin and hair.

He was an academic sculptor first and last: quite out of sympathy with what he termed the 'Easter Island' style of modern sculpture, which appeared when he was in his prime. Critical opinion consequently left him behind. Official honours, however, were not lacking, in France and Belgium as well as at home, and in 1942 he was awarded the gold medal of the Royal Society of British Sculptors. He exhibited annually at the Academy until 1948, a period of sixty-three years, and died in London 15 December 1952. There is a large collection of his work at the National Museum of Wales, described in a special catalogue issued by the museum in 1948. It includes a self-portrait.

John was a courteous and affable man, proud of his Welsh nationality and of his own success, but somewhat reserved. He married in 1890 Marthe (died 1923), daughter of Paul Weiss, of Neuchâtel. His only child, a daughter, married the son of Sir Luke Fildes [q.v.].

[*The Times*, 16 and 18 December 1952; National Museum of Wales archives; personal knowledge.]   R. L. CHARLES.

JOHNSON, ALFRED EDWARD WEBB-, BARON WEBB-JOHNSON (1880–1958), surgeon. [See WEBB-JOHNSON.]

JOHNSON, JOHN DE MONINS (1882–1956), printer and scholar, was born 17 May 1882 at Kirmington, Lincolnshire, the second son and third child of the vicar, the Rev. John Henry Johnson, and his wife, Anna Braithwaite Savory. He was educated at Magdalen College School, Oxford, and in 1900 won an open scholarship at Exeter College. He obtained a first class in classical moderations (1902) and a second class in *literae humaniores* (1904), remaining in residence an extra year reading Arabic in preparation for an appointment in the Egyptian Civil Service which he entered in 1905 and left in 1907.

From 1908 to 1911 Johnson was a senior demy of Magdalen and during this period and later, while a pupil of A. S. Hunt [q.v.], he was engaged in editing papyri: Johnson was chiefly responsible for volume ii of the *Catalogue of the Greek Papyri in the John Rylands Library* which was published in 1915. In 1911, and again in 1913–14, he was in Egypt conducting explorations on behalf of the Graeco-Roman branch of the Egypt Exploration Fund. During his second expedition he found at Antinoë the earliest known manuscript of Theocritus. It was edited by Hunt and Johnson together, but publication was delayed until 1930 when Johnson's name, unusually duplicated, appeared both on the title-page and in the printer's colophon at the end.

In 1915 he was appointed acting assistant secretary to the delegates of the Oxford University Press, and later assistant secretary. He was discerning in the selection of manuscripts, enterprising and persuasive in his search for authors, and, when there was opportunity, a brilliant innovator in illustration. For this, he went back to contemporary sources, and the archaeologist in him had an unerring instinct for what would most aptly illustrate a text.

In 1925 the delegates appointed Johnson to be printer to the university, a daring choice, for he had no practical knowledge of either printing or factory management. Nevertheless he possessed other significant qualifications: he was in his prime, his capacity proved; he was on terms with the delegates and apprised of policy; and known to the university and familiar with its governmental machinery.

He was immediately plunged into the less agreeable excitement of industrial management, for within a year he experienced, successively, a sectional strike, and the general strike of 1926, events which made a deep impression on him. He then faced the necessary unpleasantness of disturbing some members of his well-entrenched staff, and the introduction of replacements. In the factory he found on the one hand a modern bindery, on the other a department in which a hundred compositors still worked by candlelight. And as he moved among his intimates who were also publishers and printers he learned that the reputation of Oxford printing had fallen very low. The urgent need for planned re-equipment and development was recognized and the delegates gave Johnson a free hand in his spending.

For the next few years Johnson devoted those resources, and all his time, to the restoration of Oxford printing; but the slump of the early thirties arrested expansion, and the outbreak of war in 1939 ended it. Eventually ninety per cent of the Press's output was employed by the Government in the war effort. Johnson was appointed C.B.E. in 1945 and retired in the following year. He had been elected an honorary fellow of Exeter in 1936.

Many great and beautiful books were produced under the direction of Johnson who was in the van of those responsible for the renaissance of book printing in the twenties. In 1928 he completed the printing of the *Oxford English Dictionary* and

received from the university the honorary degree of D.Litt. Other works were the lectern Bible designed by Bruce Rogers and completed in 1935; the handsome *Survey of Persian Art* (1938–9) in six folio volumes; and the two-volume *Old Spain* (1936) printed for Macmillan with illustrations by (Sir) Muirhead Bone [q.v.] in colour collotype.

Johnson was quick to appreciate the importance of and assiduous in adding to the unique collection of printing material preserved at the Press where the typographical museum illustrates the history of Oxford printing. He also duplicated for the Press the collection, now at Princeton, which Falconer Madan had assembled when writing his *Oxford Books* (3 vols., 1895–1931). With his friend Strickland Gibson, Johnson edited *The First Minute Book of the Delegates of the Oxford University Press* (1943) and together they wrote *Print and Privilege at Oxford to the Year 1700* (1946).

His most notable monument, however, may prove to be the vast collection of printed ephemera which he gathered together and sorted throughout the years. The germ of the collection consists of proposals and prospectuses for books, starting early in the seventeenth century. To this have been added title-pages, specimen pages, material illustrating the history of printing, including copyright, spelling, and design, and there are specialized collections of banknotes, postage stamps, political pamphlets, Christmas cards, valentines, and cigarette cards: the richest collection of jobbing printing in existence. It has been named the Constance Meade collection after a friend of Johnson's who made over to him a mass of valuable material she had inherited. Housed originally at the Press the collection was moved in 1968 to the Bodleian Library.

There is a drawing of Johnson at the Press by Sir William Rothenstein (1940); a water-colour by H. A. Freeth (1956) and a drawing by Miss E. Plachte (1938) are at the Bodleian. Johnson was a tall man and well proportioned, slow and deliberate in his movements. His nose, large and pointed, was his most striking feature: his hair, thin and combed over his brow, completed an arresting head which was likened to that of the bust of Julius Caesar in the British Museum. Indeed, he turned a stern countenance to the world, and showed an explosive temper to those who displeased him; but he was a delightful conversationalist and a brilliant and voluminous correspondent. Ever a busy controversialist, he was fearless in a quarrel but not always wise in the causes he espoused or in his choice of opponent. Yet he was always ready to champion the weak and many were warmed by his kindness or helped by his charity. He devoted much time and energy to committees and public work, some of which he performed with almost possessive enthusiasm. In his later years he withdrew from all these activities save the Oxford Preservation Trust, spending most of his time in his museum at the Press.

In 1918 Johnson married Margaret Dorothea, daughter of Charles Cannan [q.v.], secretary to the delegates. They had one daughter, and one son, Charles Cannan Johnson, who became manager of the Canadian branch of the Press but who died in 1963. Johnson died in Oxford 15 September 1956.

[Private information; personal knowledge.]
CHARLES BATEY.

JOHNSON, SIR NELSON KING (1892–1954), meteorologist, was born 11 March 1892 at Barton Mill House, Canterbury, the second son of John Gilbert Johnson, master miller, and his wife, Emily Alice Williams. From the Simon Langton School, Canterbury, he obtained a scholarship to the Royal College of Science, South Kensington, where he took his B.Sc. (1913) and A.R.C.S., becoming an assistant demonstrator in spectroscopy in 1913. A year later he began the life of a professional astronomer by joining Sir Norman Lockyer [q.v.] at Sidmouth Observatory, but this career was terminated by the war and in 1915 he joined the Royal Flying Corps. His experiences as a pilot undoubtedly influenced his decision to join the Meteorological Office in 1919.

In 1921 Johnson was put in charge of the meteorological section of the Chemical Warfare Experimental Station at Porton, Wiltshire, a post he held until 1928. During these seven years he did the scientific work for which he is best remembered. He was charged with investigating the physics of the atmosphere very close to the ground, especially in relation to diffusion, a subject now known as micrometeorology. When he began, relatively little was known about these matters and few reliable systematic observations were available, but within a remarkably short space of time he and his team had not only

devised apparatus for the routine recording of the surface temperature and wind fields and their variations with height to an accuracy hitherto unapproached, but also laid the foundations, both experimental and theoretical, of the study of the diffusion of gases and suspended matter by the turbulence of the natural wind. For reasons of national security much of this work was withheld from open publication until after the war of 1939–45, but the claim may be fairly advanced that Johnson truly laid the foundations of micrometeorology, and his contributions were recognized by the award of the D.Sc. by the university of London in 1939.

Johnson became director of experiments at Porton in 1928 and afterwards chief superintendent of the chemical defence research department, War Office. In 1938 he succeeded Sir George Simpson as director of the Meteorological Office. Within a year he was faced with the reorganization of the service for war, when the staff rose from fewer than 1,000 to over 6,000. During this period he undoubtedly overworked and damaged his health. Apart from the successful organization of the wartime service he also, during this period, began organized research within the Office and founded the Meteorological Research Committee. In 1943 he was appointed K.C.B. After the war he turned his attention to re-creating international links and in 1946 became president of the International Meteorological Organization. In this capacity he did much to bring into being the World Meteorological Organization, acting as president for the first congress of the Organization in 1951. He retired from the Meteorological Office in 1953.

Johnson was a far-seeing, but not particularly forceful administrator, a characteristic dictated by his natural modesty and tendency to self-effacement. As an individual scientist his gifts inclined more to the experimental than the theoretical side and his work in atmospheric turbulence was distinguished chiefly by the excellence of the basic measurements which he made with simple but usually ingenious instruments. But for the intervention of the war he would undoubtedly have turned the Meteorological Office into a very effective research institution as well as a public service; but this had to wait for more favourable circumstances.

In 1927 Johnson married Margaret, daughter of J. Taylor, of Blackburn; they had one son and one daughter. He was a keen mountaineer, but during his later years contracted Parkinson's disease and this must have played a part in hastening his death, by his own hand, in London, 23 March 1954. A portrait in oils, made from a photograph, is in the possession of the World Meteorological Organization in Geneva.

[*The Times*, 24 March 1954; *Quarterly Journal* of the Royal Meteorological Society, vol. lxxx, 1954; *Journal of Atmospheric and Terrestrial Physics*, vol. v, 1954; private information; personal knowledge.]

O. G. SUTTON.

JOLOWICZ, HERBERT FELIX (1890–1954), academic lawyer, was born in London 16 July 1890, the third child and second son of Jewish parents, his father being Hermann Jolowicz, silk merchant, and his mother Marie Litthauer. His sister Marguerite married Martin Wolff [q.v.]. He was educated at St. Paul's School, from which he won a classical scholarship to Trinity College, Cambridge. He was placed in the first class of part i of the classical tripos in 1911 and in the first class of part i of the law tripos in 1913, a curious combination which committed him to Roman law and for the time being cut him off from almost all the more practical parts of English law. He then spent a year in Germany, sitting at the feet of two of the greatest Roman lawyers of modern times, Ludwig Mitteis at Leipzig and Otto Lenel at Freiburg. He escaped from Germany in 1914 with three days to spare and served throughout the war, for most of the time as an officer in the Bedfordshire Regiment, and was in Gallipoli, Egypt, and France.

Called to the bar by the Inner Temple in 1919, Jolowicz was first a pupil, then a member of the chambers, of (Sir) Henry Slesser. His name appears in the Law Reports as counsel in the leading case of *Chester* v. *Bateson* (1920). His wide linguistic gifts, however, made him an obvious choice as a teacher of Roman law and in 1920 he became non-resident All Souls reader in Roman law at Oxford. From 1924 he combined that post with a lectureship, later readership, in Roman law and jurisprudence at University College, London. When in 1931 he became professor of Roman law at University College, he relinquished his readership at Oxford. During his London career he took his full share of tutorial work, in addition to lecturing, and occupied several administrative posts in the college, thus acquiring an intimate knowledge of the students. He was also dean of the faculty of law in the university in 1937–8. He retained a close connection with University College until his death and was from 1947 until his death chairman of the library sub-committee of the Institute of Advanced Legal Studies, a part of the university.

During the Nazi persecutions he gave much unobtrusive help to refugees; on the outbreak of war in 1939 he rejoined the army and served as an officer in the Intelligence Corps until 1945. In 1948 he became regius professor of civil law at Oxford. During the autumn of 1953 he was visiting professor at the Tulane University of Louisiana (which conferred on him the honorary degree of D.C.L.) and travelled extensively in the United States, lecturing at such universities as Yale, Columbia, and Chicago.

Jolowicz published a number of articles and reviews, but only two books, one of which, his *Historical Introduction to Roman Law* (1932, 2nd ed. 1952), is an essential tool for both the student and the advanced worker and made his reputation abroad. It is a wonderfully well-balanced and soberly written work. The other book was a translation, with descriptive introduction and commentary, of a singularly intractable title of the Digest dealing with theft (*Digest XLVII. 2 (De Furtis)*, 1940). Both books covered, almost surreptitiously, much more ground than their titles promised. He would have written more had he not, as he said himself, been started off on a wrong track. The current search for interpolations in the Digest did not suit him, but, although he soon did independent work on very early Roman law, he took some time to develop his main interest, in the medieval and modern history of Roman law, especially in England. He left behind him a considerable fragment which was published in 1957 under the title *Roman Foundations of Modern Law*, covering the Sources, the Law of Persons, and Family Law (with the exception of Guardianship). The other main field of study which may be singled out from his almost universal interest in law was jurisprudence. He did not publish himself his University College *Lectures on Jurisprudence*, doubtless because, as they stood, they did not come up to his very exacting standard, but they were later edited by his elder son, J. A. Jolowicz, fellow of Trinity College, Cambridge, and appeared in 1963.

Jolowicz was, indeed, first and foremost a lecturer. He loved lecturing, and perhaps especially to young and immature students. He took immense pains over his lectures, getting them into the most perfect form before he delivered them. With all his breadth of interests he believed in and exercised the most accurate scholarship. He expressed a profound scepticism where broad intellectual constructions were in question, though he could use them as servants to hold an immense amount of knowledge in his capacious mind. He had great natural sagacity, which he was always ready to put at the disposal of his friends and of any institution he was connected with. He was an enthusiastic member of the Society of Public Teachers of Law, of which he was president in 1936–7. His greatest service to the Society and indeed one of the greatest services he performed to law in England was his editorship of the Society's *Journal* from its first number in 1924 to the day of his death. He did more than anyone else to set the character and tone of the *Journal*, which is indeed his monument.

In spite of many trials Jolowicz preserved a gay spirit and a puckish humour. He made his house a centre of hospitality and left his friends with the recollection of a very lovable man when he died in Oxford 19 December 1954. A bibliography of his writings is to be found in the H. F. Jolowicz memorial number of *Butterworth's South African Law Review*, 1956.

In 1924 Jolowicz married Ruby, daughter of Joseph Wagner, by whom he had two sons and one daughter.

[*Journal* of the Society of Public Teachers of Law, June 1955; private information; personal knowledge.]   F. H. LAWSON.

JONES, (ALFRED) ERNEST (1879–1958), physician and psycho-analyst, was born at Gowerton, Glamorgan, 1 January 1879, the eldest child and only son of Thomas Jones, then a colliery manager, by his wife, Mary Ann Lewis. He was educated at Swansea Grammar School and Llandovery College, then at University College, Cardiff; he completed his undergraduate medical studies at University College Hospital, London, where he qualified in 1900. In the examination for the London M.B. in 1901 he obtained first class honours in medicine and obstetrics, with gold medals in each and a university scholarship in obstetrics. In 1903 he obtained the degree of M.D. with gold

medal, and in 1904 his M.R.C.P. House posts in medicine and surgery at University College Hospital were followed by posts at the Brompton Chest Hospital and at the North-Eastern (later Queen's) Hospital for Children. Jones's hitherto brilliantly successful career was interrupted by a series of undeserved misfortunes in the next few years which prevented his obtaining appointments in London of the kind that a man of his attainments had the right to expect, and so in 1908 he secured an appointment as director of the psychiatric clinic in Toronto; a year or two later he was appointed associate professor of psychiatry there and remained until 1912.

Jones first read one of Freud's writings in 1905, and at the end of 1906 began practising psycho-analysis himself. In 1907 he met Jung and with him organized the first psycho-analytical congress, held in Salzburg in 1908, where he met Freud, and read his first psycho-analytical paper, on 'Rationalization' (an original concept and word). His active interest and pioneering work in spreading the knowledge of psycho-analysis continued in Canada and extended into the United States, where he was responsible for the foundation of the American Psycho-Pathological Association in 1910 and the American Psycho-Analytical Association in 1911. He also wrote a great deal during this period, including his well-known works *On the Nightmare* (English publication 1931) and on *Hamlet* (English publication 1947). His *Papers on Psycho-Analysis* was published in 1913 and reached a fifth edition in 1948.

Jones returned to London in 1913 and set up in psycho-analytic and consulting practice; he immediately founded the London Psycho-Analytical Society, which was dissolved and replaced by him in 1919 by the foundation of the British Psycho-Analytical Society, whose president he remained until his retirement in 1944. In 1920 Jones founded the *International Journal of Psycho-Analysis* as an official organ of the International Psycho-Analytical Association (founded 1910) and he remained its editor until 1939. Of the Association he was president in 1920–24 and 1932–49, was present at all but one of its congresses, and presided over seven of them. In 1924 he set up the Institute of Psycho-Analysis; one of its initial functions was the publication (with the Hogarth Press) of the International Psycho-Analytical Library, which remained under Jones's editorship up to the appearance of its fiftieth volume. The London Clinic of Psycho-Analysis was started in 1926, again largely on his initiative. In the same year, at the invitation and with the active encouragement of Jones, Melanie Klein [q.v.] came to London from Berlin and began her very influential teaching, which had far-reaching effects on the development of psycho-analysis in England. Jones played the leading part in presenting the case for psycho-analysis at a committee set up by the British Medical Association, whose report in 1929 established the principle that 'the term psycho-analysis can legitimately be applied only to the method evolved by Freud and to the theories derived from the use of this method'; this official pronouncement has done much to discourage the misuse of the term.

As Germany became increasingly dominated by the Nazis from 1933 onwards Jones worked hard in helping displaced German analysts to resettle in England and elsewhere. When the Nazis occupied Austria in 1938 it was Jones's personal and fearless intervention in Vienna which led to the release of Freud and his family and their safe transfer to England, where Freud died in the following year. To Jones is also due the main credit for securing the release of most of the other Viennese analysts, many of whom settled in England or the United States.

In 1944, Jones retired from the office of president of the British Psycho-Analytical Society, and thereafter devoted much of his time to the preparation of his three-volume biography, *Sigmund Freud, Life and Work* (1953–7); the last volume was published shortly before his death. This has been widely acclaimed as a masterpiece of biography; it is extremely well documented and scholarly, and by many is regarded as the supreme achievement of Jones's career. As the title indicates, it is not only a life-history, but also comprehends a masterly summary and assessment of Freud's extensive literary works.

Jones's main characteristics were his incisive and brilliant intellect, his moral courage, his incredible capacity for hard work of the highest standard, and his ability to combine an unswerving devotion to Freud's work with an independent and critical spirit. In his hobbies, too, he was remarkable; he was a good chess player, and a proficient figure skater and author of a standard textbook on the

subject. He published twelve books and three hundred papers on neurology, psychology, anthropology, etc. He was elected F.R.C.P. in 1942 and was also a fellow of the Royal Society of Medicine, the Royal Society of Arts, and the Royal Anthropological Institute, honorary president of the International and American Psycho-Analytical Associations and of the British Psycho-Analytical Society, and honorary member of numerous psychoanalytical societies throughout the world. He received an honorary D.Sc. from the university of Wales (1954).

In 1917 Jones married Morfydd Owen (died 1918), a Welsh musician. In 1919 he married Katharina Jokl, of Vienna, by whom he had two sons and two daughters, the elder of whom died in childhood. Mervyn Jones, the elder son, has made his name as a writer. Jones died in London 11 February 1958. His portrait, painted by Rodrigo Moynihan, and presented to him in 1946, hangs in the house of the British Psycho-Analytical Society in London.

[*International Journal of Psycho-Analysis*, vol. xxxix, 1958; *British Medical Journal* and *Lancet*, 22 February 1958; Ernest Jones, *Free Associations*, 1959; personal knowledge.]

W. H. GILLESPIE.

JONES, BERNARD MOUAT (1882–1953), chemist, principal of the Manchester College of Technology, and vice-chancellor of Leeds University, was born in Streatham 27 November 1882, the fourth son of Alexander Mouat Jones, wine merchant, and his wife, Martha Eleanor Brinjes. He was educated at Dulwich College and won a Brackenbury scholarship at Balliol College, Oxford. In 1904 he gained first class honours in chemistry, mineralogy, and crystallography, and was for a year research assistant in mineralogical chemistry at the Imperial Institute until in 1906 he became professor of chemistry at Government College, Lahore. Seven years later he returned to England as assistant professor at the Imperial College of Science and Technology. He went to France as a private in the London Scottish in 1914 and immediately after the first German gas attack in 1915 he joined the staff of the central laboratory, G.H.Q., formed to organize defensive measures. Most of the problems were chemical, and Mouat Jones's sagacity and sound judgement were of the utmost value to the chemical advisers with the armies. He developed an almost uncanny skill in identifying quickly any new gas used by the enemy and was the first to identify the chemical in mustard gas. For his services he was appointed to the D.S.O. in 1917, was three times mentioned in dispatches, and in 1918 became director of the laboratory with the rank of lieutenant-colonel.

In 1919 Mouat Jones returned to civil life as professor of chemistry and director of the Edward Davies laboratory in the University College of Wales, Aberystwyth. Facing the post-war bulge of students with very scanty resources, he soon had a most lively department thanks to his witty and stimulating lectures and his energetic action to secure equipment. Two years later he became principal of the Manchester College of Technology where he remained for seventeen years. It was not an easy post to fill for most of the day work of the college constituted the faculty of technology in the university, whereas the general administration and finances of the college came under the Manchester education committee and the city council. There was obviously the possibility of friction and misunderstanding; Mouat Jones, by securing the trust and confidence of both sides, reduced it to a negligible minimum. No doubt he was fortunate in that Sir Henry Miers [q.v.], under whom he had worked as an undergraduate, was vice-chancellor of the university until 1926.

Although the faculty of technology was sixteen years old when he went there, tradition dies hard, and to many people the college was still the 'night school'. By sheer force of personality and character Mouat Jones brought about a much wider appreciation of the true status of the college; he won the interest and co-operation of industry which took tangible shape in the form of scholarships and prizes. They were years of continuous development in which the influence of Mouat Jones was seen in many ways: the degree course in chemical engineering; the conferring of honorary associateship on distinguished scientists and technologists; the new lecture hall, the Reynolds Hall, which served as a home for the scientific societies of the district and brought them into closer touch with the college. Within the college he built up a wonderful spirit by bringing together the staff and students through the athletic clubs and various social activities. At the same time he took an active part in developing technical education in the district. He was president of a number of bodies including (1930) the

Manchester Literary and Philosophical Society.

In 1938 Mouat Jones became the fourth vice-chancellor of the university of Leeds and the first scientist to hold that office. Within a year the normal work of the university was interrupted by the outbreak of war and for six months in 1941 the vice-chancellor was once again directing research in chemical warfare, at Porton. During the years of reconstruction after the war the university owed much to his wise leadership. There was nothing despotic or quixotic about him, either personally or as an administrator. His outlook was essentially empirical; he was more interested in meeting immediate needs than in probing the function and purpose of a civic university in mid-twentieth-century England. The relations between town and gown had not been of the happiest and this Mouat Jones speedily remedied; the three years 1945-8 brought a number of endowments from industry. Under his imperturbable chairmanship of the senate and the council and his good personal relations with the faculty, the university gained a sense of self-confidence and tranquillity. When he retired in 1948 he left it a happy society. Once again his customary devotion to the interests of the students was seen—in new halls of residence and the completion of the Union. The testimonial fund raised on his retirement he gave as an endowment for bursaries for the foreign travel which he considered an essential part of a student's education.

Both at Manchester and at Leeds part of Mouat Jones's success came from his brilliance as a speaker and raconteur. He had a remarkable flair for graceful compliment and witty turns of phrase. He could delight every type of audience and by his ready wit could point a lesson where a homily would have failed. For his services to education he received honorary degrees from the universities of Durham, Leeds, and Wales. His early experience in India made him a valuable member of a number of government committees, among them the advisory committee on education in the colonies, the Makerere–Khartoum education commission (1937), and the commission on higher education in West Africa (1944-5).

After his retirement Mouat Jones lived at Farnham where he died 11 September 1953. He was unmarried and after a number of bequests he left the residue of his estate equally between Balliol College and

Leeds University. There is a portrait by Henry Carr at Leeds.

[*The Times*, 15 September 1953; *Manchester Guardian*, 16 September 1953; private information; personal knowledge.]
HAROLD HARTLEY.

JONES, (FREDERIC) WOOD (1879–1954), anatomist, was born 23 January 1879 at West Hackney, Middlesex, the youngest of the three children of Charles Henry Jones, an architect of Welsh descent, and his wife, Lucy Allin. Wood Jones entered the London Hospital in 1897 as a medical student and qualified M.B., B.S. in 1904. Even while a student he had contributed short articles to the *Journal of Anatomy and Physiology*, and he also won a succession of prizes in anatomy, physiology, and clinical medicine. He was throughout life a man of active and restless temperament, ever a seeker after knowledge in new fields, so that he did not retain any of his eminent academic posts for more than a few years. This adventurous spirit was shown at the very beginning of his career when in 1905 he took up an appointment as medical officer to the Eastern Extension Telegraph Company in the Cocos-Keeling Islands. He stayed for just over a year and in that short time made an intimate and important study of reef-building corals, the results of which appeared in a book entitled *Coral and Atolls* (1910). In 1907 he returned to England but soon afterwards left for Egypt to undertake field anthropological studies on behalf of the Egyptian Government Archaeological Survey of Nubia. He returned to England once again in 1909 on being appointed lecturer in anatomy at Manchester University, and a year later went to St. Thomas's Hospital medical school as senior demonstrator in anatomy. In this year also, he was awarded the D.Sc. degree of London University. In 1912 he transferred to the London School of Medicine for Women as professor of anatomy. In 1915 he delivered the Arris and Gale lectures at the Royal College of Surgeons on 'The influence of the arboreal habit in the evolution of the reproductive system', and it was on this occasion that he first came to public notice as a lecturer of unusual ability, with an original approach to the evidence of comparative anatomy in the problem of human evolution. He amplified his lectures in a book *Arboreal Man* (1916). Later, he expounded the view that there is no close relationship

between man on the one hand, and apes and monkeys on the other, but that the segregation of the evolutionary line leading to man occurred very early in geological time—as far back as the Eocene period. This thesis met with considerable criticism from other comparative anatomists.

During the war of 1914–18 Wood Jones was a captain in the Royal Army Medical Corps, stationed at the Military Orthopaedic Hospital at Shepherd's Bush. He made some useful observations on the effects of partial paralysis of limb movements in gunshot wounds, and in 1920 published one of his best, and most widely read, books *The Principles of Anatomy as Seen in the Hand*; a second edition appeared in 1941.

In 1919 Wood Jones went to Australia as professor of anatomy at Adelaide University where he remained for eight years, and engaged largely in field studies, taking part in several expeditions in South Australia. On these expeditions extensive zoological, botanical, and anthropological collections were made, some of which led to the discovery of new marsupial species as well as many new species of invertebrates. The results were published in the *Records of the South Australia Museum* and the *Transactions of the Royal Society of South Australia*. Between 1923 and 1925 he published a systematic catalogue of the mammals of South Australia—probably his most important work on comparative anatomy. A notable feature of this catalogue is the excellent series of 311 illustrations, all drawn by the author himself.

In 1927 Wood Jones accepted an invitation to fill the Rockefeller chair of anthropology in the university of Hawaii where he remained for two years. During this time he published a general systematic account of the comparative anatomy of the Primates in *Man's Place among the Mammals* (1929), and here he expounded in more detail his unorthodox attitude towards the commonly accepted view of man's relationship to the higher Primates. In 1930 he returned once more to Australia, this time to occupy the chair of anatomy at Melbourne University, and during the next few years took part in further zoological and anthropological expeditions, also finding time to complete a number of papers on strictly anatomical subjects. At the end of 1937 he left Australia for England where he accepted the professorship of anatomy at

Manchester University, and during the next few years continued to publish a series of papers on a variety of anatomical subjects, as well as editing the seventh edition of Buchanan's *Manual of Anatomy* (1946). In 1944 appeared his stimulating book *Structure and Function as Seen in the Foot*, a work of considerable value for orthopaedic surgeons. About this time also he wrote a number of books of biological essays, *Design and Purpose* (1942), *Habit and Heritage* (1943), and *Trends of Life* (1953), and in these he affirmed his adherence to a somewhat modified Lamarckian interpretation of evolution and at the same time expressed strongly anti-Darwinian views.

In 1945 Wood Jones assumed his last academic office, that of the Sir William H. Collins professor of human and comparative anatomy at the Royal College of Surgeons, which he held until 1952. He had been elected to the fellowship of the College in 1930. He died in London 29 September 1954, leaving behind him an abiding tradition of his vigorous personality. He was distinguished not only for his strictly scientific contributions but also for the healthy stimulus he gave to controversy by the occasional unorthodoxy of his opinions. His reputation as a lecturer brought him many requests to deliver memorial lectures and orations. He was elected F.R.S. in 1925 and received the honorary degree of D.Sc. from Adelaide (1920) and Melbourne (1934).

In 1910 Wood Jones married Gertrude, daughter of George Clunies-Ross [q.v.], owner of the Cocos-Keeling Islands. He left no issue. A portrait by W. S. McInnes is with the Australian College of Surgeons in Melbourne; a posthumous oil-painting by A. Egerton Cooper hangs in the Royal College of Surgeons of England.

[Sir W. E. Le Gros Clark in *Biographical Memoirs of Fellows of the Royal Society*, vol. i, 1955; private information; personal knowledge.]   W. E. LE GROS CLARK.

JONES, SIR HAROLD SPENCER (1890–1960), astronomer, was born in Kensington 29 March 1890, the third child and elder son of Henry Charles Jones, an accountant with the Great Western Railway Company, and his wife, Sarah Ryland, a former schoolmistress. Although without formal training in mathematics, his father acquired a considerable working knowledge of several branches of the subject, and gave active encouragement to his son, who early showed exceptional ability which was fostered at Latymer Upper School, Hammersmith, under the tutelage of G. M. Grace. He won a scholarship to Jesus College, Cambridge, where after a first in both parts of the mathematical tripos (1909–11) he took a first in physics in part ii of the natural sciences tripos (1912). He was elected Isaac Newton student in 1912 and in 1913 was second Smith's prizeman and elected to a research fellowship at his college.

In the same year the astronomer royal, (Sir) Frank Dyson (whose notice he subsequently contributed to this Dictionary), appointed him to Greenwich in place of (Sir) Arthur Eddington [q.v.] who had been elected to the Plumian professorship of astronomy in Cambridge. In spite of his work during the war on optical instrument design for the Ministry of Munitions, Spencer Jones found time to do original research on many diverse branches of astronomy, and to prepare the text for his comprehensive book *General Astronomy* which was published in 1922. It was during this active period of research that he whetted his appetite for what was to become his major research contribution to astronomy—the rotation of the earth and the so-called system of astronomical constants. In 1923 he was appointed astronomer at the Royal Observatory at the Cape of Good Hope, South Africa, to succeed S. S. Hough who had died in office.

His years at the Cape were prodigiously productive—in original research, in the prosecution and inauguration of observational programmes, in leadership and administration, in literary output, and in social life. He left behind him a united and vigorous staff fully engaged on observational programmes of the foremost importance; just as he himself had, in the great tradition, completed the programmes initiated by Sir David Gill [q.v.], these programmes have been brought to a triumphant conclusion by his successors.

In 1933 Spencer Jones was recalled to Greenwich to assume the office of tenth astronomer royal in succession to Dyson. He was rapidly immersed in many administrative and public duties, with the direction of the departmental work of the Observatory, with the putting into service of two new instruments (the 36-inch reflecting telescope presented by W. J. Yapp, and the new reversible transit circle to replace the 80-year-old instrument designed by Sir George Airy, q.v.), and with the serious problems arising from the rapidly increasing difficulties of conducting astronomical observations at Greenwich.

He continued to make significant contributions to many branches of astronomy, two of which, both involving the meticulous discussion of many thousands of observations, will always be associated with his name. His epoch-making paper 'The rotation of the Earth and the secular accelerations of the Sun, Moon and planets', published in 1939, demonstrated conclusively that the observed fluctuations were due to irregularities in the rate of rotation of the earth. It stands now as an unassailable landmark in the subject, leading directly as it did to the adoption, in 1950, of the concept of Ephemeris Time. In 1928 he had been appointed president of Commission 34 (on the solar parallax) of the International Astronomical Union, with the gigantic task of organizing a world-wide programme for the observation of the minor planet Eros at its favourable opposition in 1930–31; the object of this work was to determine the value of the 'solar parallax', equivalent to the 'astronomical unit of distance' from the earth to the sun. With typical thoroughness he not only made the major contribution to the observations from the Royal Observatory at the Cape, but personally undertook the collection, reduction, and discussion of all the observations. This work, which took nearly ten years to complete, culminated in a discussion, published in 1941, of extraordinary thoroughness and depth. For this work in 1943 he was awarded the gold medal of the Royal Astronomical Society and a Royal medal of the Royal Society of which he had been elected a fellow in 1930. That the value of the solar parallax (8″·790) resulting from this discussion has now been shown, as a result of direct measurements of distance by radar techniques, to have been affected by some systematic errors, probably in the observations, in no way diminishes the greatness of the accomplishment.

During this period Spencer Jones was faced with making the decision to recommend the removal of the Royal Observatory from its historic site at Greenwich, where it was established in 1675. The observing conditions were rapidly worsening and expansion was impossible. Spencer Jones sought and obtained approval in principle for removal to a more favourable site but it was not until after the war, in 1945, that it could be undertaken.

In a relatively short time he was able publicly to announce that 'The Royal Greenwich Observatory' would be established at Herstmonceux Castle in Sussex; but the actual move was necessarily slow and was not finally completed until after his retirement on 31 December 1955. Astronomy in this country will always be indebted to his great administrative achievement.

Spencer Jones also played a leading part in the negotiations leading to the initial approval for the 98-inch Isaac Newton Telescope to be erected at Herstmonceux; he presented the case for the provision of a large telescope in this country, originally drawn up by the councils of the Royal Astronomical Society and the Royal Society for a 74-inch telescope, so forcibly that the chancellor of the Exchequer was advised that provision should be made for a telescope of 100-inches aperture.

Spencer Jones's scientific activities covered a wide field. In particular he made notable scientific and administrative contributions to time-measurement and horology, and was responsible for the great expansion of the watch-repair services and watch-manufacturing industries. He was president of the British Horological Institute from 1939 and received its gold medal, and played a leading part in founding the National College of Horology. He also made many contributions to geomagnetism, both to the theory and to the practical application to navigation; he was inaugural president of the Institute of Navigation in 1947.

In later years, and especially after his retirement, he played a large part in the organization of international science. He was president of the International Astronomical Union from 1945 to 1948 and, as such, began his long service to the International Council of Scientific Unions (I.C.S.U.) as a member of the executive board. He was secretary-general from 1956 to 1958 and was one of the most enthusiastic organizers and active supporters of the International Geophysical Year; he edited the *Annals of the I.G.Y.* and became director of the I.C.S.U. Publication Office. He also represented the I.C.S.U. at meetings of UNESCO and contributed much to the weight that is given to the part of the UNESCO programme devoted to pure science.

Spencer Jones was awarded his Sc.D. from Cambridge in 1925 and made an honorary fellow of Jesus College in 1933.

He received, among others, the Janssen, Bruce, Lorimer, and Rittenhouse medals. He was knighted in 1943 and appointed K.B.E. in 1955. He was a foreign member of the principal academies of science and received honorary doctorates from some ten British and foreign universities.

Personally, Spencer Jones was a tall, upright, dignified figure who brought an air of distinction to any gathering. He had a fine presence, with a clear delivery and a ready command of language; he was certainly, in appearance, the most dignified astronomer of his era. But he was essentially a simple and kindly man, with high ideals and complete integrity of purpose, which he brought to all his many activities. He preferred logical and temperate argument to passionate advocacy; his beliefs were pursued, and generally achieved, with a quiet unspectacular persistence and with a fitting dignity. He also had a rare gift for finding the right way to lead, and for choosing the right phrase, or the right compromise, to obtain agreement. His capacity was enormous; he was able to assimilate the sense of long and complicated papers with apparently no more than a quick glance, and to express himself in writing—he rarely dictated—with a remarkable speed, legibility, and fluency. Although deeply immersed in so many activities, he was never hurried and treated all with kindness, consideration, and unfailing courtesy.

In 1918 Spencer Jones married Gladys Mary, daughter of Albert Edward Owers, a civil engineer; there were two sons. He died at his home in Kensington 3 November 1960.

[R. v. d. R. Woolley in *Biographical Memoirs of Fellows of the Royal Society*, vol. vii, 1961; *Quarterly Journal* of the Royal Astronomical Society, vol. iv, 1963; personal knowledge.]   D. H. SADLER.

JONES, SIR JOHN EDWARD LENNARD- (1894–1954), scientist and administrator. [See LENNARD-JONES.]

JONES, THOMAS (1870–1955), civil servant, administrator, and author, was born 27 September 1870 at Rhymney, a border mining village in Monmouthshire, the eldest of the nine children of David Benjamin Jones, who worked in the truck shop of the Rhymney Iron Company, and his wife, Mary Ann, daughter of Enoch Jones, a Rhymney storekeeper. His father was a Cardiganshire man, his mother was half Cardiganshire and half Somersetshire.

After his early education at Rhymney board-school and the Lewis School, Pengam, Jones began work as a timekeeper-clerk with the Rhymney Iron Company. His passion for reading had been roused by one of his teachers and it was nurtured by Rhymney's active Welsh literary life. This was centred in its churches and chapels, in his case Brynhyfryd Welsh Calvinistic Methodist chapel. He was Scripture gold-medallist and a promising preacher when in 1890 he entered the University College of Wales, Aberystwyth, where he became outstanding in its cultural and social life. He achieved London matriculation with difficulty but repeatedly failed in mathematics at the Intermediate level. In 1895 he migrated to Glasgow University, where the professor of moral philosophy, (Sir) Henry Jones [q.v.], rated him 'the best student I have ever had amongst my pupils'. In 1900 'Tom' Jones graduated, was elected Clark scholar, awarded a Bertrand Russell studentship at the London School of Economics and Political Science, and began examining in economics at the university of St. Andrews. He was placed in the first class in the honour school of economic science at Glasgow in 1901.

By this time Jones had given up preaching, partly under the influence of Henry Jones, but mainly because evangelicalism had lost its appeal and the prospects of an exclusively ecclesiastical career repelled him. In 1895 he joined the Independent Labour Party and the Fabian Society and became a close student of the problems of poverty. For some time he lived and worked in social settlements in Glasgow and Cardiff. This interest in social work became lifelong, but his family and not a few Nonconformists regretted the loss of an outstanding preacher.

In 1899 William Smart, the professor of political economy at Glasgow, made Jones a part-time assistant. In the following year he became a university assistant in political economy and so remained until 1909. He was Barrington visiting lecturer in Ireland (1904–5) and a special investigator for the royal commission on the Poor Law (1906–9). He became professor of economics in the Queen's University, Belfast, in 1909, but on the invitation of David (later Lord) Davies [q.v.] he returned to Wales in 1910 to become the secretary of the Welsh campaign against tuberculosis later known as the King Edward VII Welsh National Memorial Association. Two years later he became the first secretary of the National Health Insurance Commission (Wales).

Davies and his sisters, Gwendoline and Margaret, had great wealth, which they used with a high sense of social responsibility. They found in their fellow Calvinist a trusted adviser. In the case of the two sisters this developed into a close friendship which was immensely profitable to the cultural life of Wales. Jones helped to start the *Welsh Outlook* and edited it from its beginning in 1914 until 1916. During these years he was a treasurer of the Welsh district of the Workers' Educational Association and a governor of the University College of Wales, Aberystwyth, the National Library of Wales, and the National Museum of Wales.

His work in the National Health Insurance Commission brought him to the notice of Lloyd George who, when he became prime minister in December 1916, made Jones first assistant secretary (later deputy secretary) of the Cabinet. He held this office until 1930. He was a member of the cabinet reconstruction committee in 1917. In the Irish troubles his services as an official negotiator were acceptable to both sides, and with Lionel Curtis [q.v.] he was secretary to the British delegation at the conference on Ireland, 11 October–6 December 1921. Throughout the industrial unrest and economic depression of the twenties, and during the general strike, he exercised great influence behind the scenes. His experience, academic training, and wide range of personal acquaintances made him one of the best-informed civil servants of his day. His integrity, insight, and judgement made him the trusted counsellor of three of the four prime ministers whom he served—Lloyd George, Bonar Law, and Stanley Baldwin; his relations with Ramsay MacDonald were less happy.

Jones refreshed himself from the burdens of a busy official life with a round of good works spontaneously undertaken. His friendship with Lord Astor [q.v.] and Lady Astor introduced him to the company of eminent and distinguished leaders in many walks of life; some accepted him as a guide to philanthropy who was ready to ease opulent consciences. In the days of post-war reconstruction he was alert to the interests of the university of Wales and other cultural institutions in the principality. He helped to establish the Gregynog Press which between 1923 and 1940 published 42 limited editions of finely printed books. He was the principal founder (1927), chairman, and later president of Coleg Harlech (the residential college for adult education at Harlech). From 1921 to 1955 he was a commissioner for the Royal Commission for the Exhibition of 1851.

In 1930 Jones became the first secretary of the Pilgrim Trust, serving until 1945, and thereafter until 1952 was a trustee, and (1952–4) chairman. He was chairman of the South Wales coalfield distress committee, and a member (1934–40) of the Unemployment Assistance Board. In 1933 he was a member of the unemployment committee of the National Council of Social Service which was largely subsidized from public funds to undertake recreational and rehabilitation work in the depressed areas. Hundreds of clubs were organized in these areas and several social settlements, which usefully survived into happier days, were founded. His leadership of various voluntary movements in the attack upon the demoralizing effects of unemployment was positive, humane, and for a host of people redeeming. He was chairman of the York Trust (1934–40) and of the Elphin Lloyd Jones Trust (1933–45).

In May 1936 Jones was invited to pay a visit to Germany where he had an interview with Hitler. He tried to bring about a meeting between Baldwin and Hitler, and accompanied Lloyd George on his visit in September. In 1939 he was the prime mover in the establishment of the Council for the Encouragement of Music and the Arts (which became the Arts Council of Great Britain) and was its first deputy chairman (1939–42). He was chairman of the Royal Commission on Ancient Monuments in Wales (1944–8). When the *Observer* Trust was founded in 1946 he became a founder-trustee.

In October 1944 Jones was elected president of the University College of Wales, Aberystwyth, and from 1945 to 1954 he lived in Aberystwyth. He strove to develop the college as a centre of advanced learning and of Celtic studies. After resigning from the presidency he moved to Manor End, St. Nicholas-at-Wade, near Birchington, Kent, a place dear to him because he had built a cottage there in the early twenties. He continued to correspond with a wide circle of friends and busied himself with his literary reliquiae. His literary output was considerable: some of his occasional addresses appeared in pamphlet form; and he edited a volume of Mazzini's essays for the

Everyman's Library (1907), William Smart's *Second Thoughts of an Economist* (1916), and Sir Henry Jones's *Old Memories* (1922). His other works included *A Theme with Variations* (1933), the mainly autobiographical *Rhymney Memories* (1938), *Cerrig Milltir* (1942), *Leeks and Daffodils* (1942), *Welsh Broth* (1951), and *A Diary with Letters, 1931–1950* (1954). In 1951 he published his biography of Lloyd George, the notice of whom he also wrote for this Dictionary as well as those of Bonar Law and Baldwin. His political diaries (1916–30) were edited by Keith Middlemas and published in two volumes under the title *Whitehall Diary* in 1969, to be followed by a third volume dealing with Irish affairs.

Jones was appointed C.H. in 1929 and was elected a member of the Athenaeum in 1931. His native village of Rhymney honoured him with a public testimonial (1939) and he received honorary degrees from the universities of Glasgow (1922), Wales (1928), St. Andrews (1947), and Birmingham (1955). He was awarded the medal of the Honourable Society of Cymmrodorion in 1945, and in 1950, on the occasion of his eightieth birthday, an impressive company gathered in the dining-room of the House of Lords to do him honour.

In appearance Jones was firmly built, of medium height, with a quick, alert gait. In youth his hair was brown but it turned white somewhat prematurely. His eyes were large, lively, and grey-blue in colour. He was awkward with his hands and played no games. He was careless about his appearance but fastidious in his personal habits. He had a musical, light baritone voice which was pleasant to the ear. In his later years he avoided much public speaking. His style was conversational, crisp, and whimsical; his addresses were prepared with nervous care. His industry was immense, his use of time remorseless. His reading was serious and consistent—it ranged widely and was garnered into notebooks for ready reference. His Welsh upbringing never left him. His early Calvinism rooted him in Christian morality; his philosophy made the pursuit of the good, the beautiful, and the true the accepted ends of life; his knowledge of economics gave them a context in his day and generation. He was always on the lookout for promising persons and he helped them regardless of social distinctions. No conversation or person was safe from his disinterested

exploitation. He turned many friendly gatherings into committees of ways and means. He acted swiftly and took short cuts. Occasionally he opened his ears to the wrong people; he consistently cultivated the right ones. His range of friends and acquaintances was exceptionally wide —to them he was known as 'T.J.' Throughout his life he was a diligent letter-writer. To his friends everywhere, notably in Rhymney and in the United States which he visited several times, he sent innumerable messages. Their quality may be seen in *A Diary with Letters* in which he candidly admitted that he had enjoyed 'the plutocratic embrace'.

In 1902 Jones married Eirene Theodora (died 1935), daughter of Richard John Lloyd, D.Lit., reader in phonetics at Liverpool. There were three children: a daughter and two sons. The daughter, Mrs. Eirene Lloyd White, became Labour M.P. for East Flint in 1950, minister of state for foreign affairs (1966), for the Welsh Office (1967). The elder son, Tristan Lloyd Jones, became manager of the *Observer*. The younger son, Elphin Lloyd Jones, was killed in a motoring accident in 1928. In June 1955 Jones himself fell indoors at his home and was seriously injured. He died in London 15 October 1955; his remains were cremated.

The National Museum of Wales has drawings of Jones by Paul Artot (1914) and S. Morse Brown (1938), and a portrait by Ivor Williams (1939). The National Library of Wales has a bust by L. S. Merrifield (1929) and the Newport (Mon.) Museum and Art Gallery has one by Siegfried Charoux (1939). The University College of Wales, Aberystwyth, has a portrait by E. Perry (1951); Coleg Harlech has one by Murray Urquhart (1944). Mrs. Eirene White has a drawing by (Sir) William Rothenstein (1923) and a portrait by R. O. Dunlop (1929). Mr. Tristan Lloyd Jones has a portrait by John Merton (1937).

[Thomas Jones's own writings; private information; personal knowledge.]

B. B. Thomas.

JORDAN, (HEINRICH ERNST) KARL (1861–1959), entomologist, was born at Almstedt near Hildesheim in Hanover, 7 December 1861, the youngest of the seven children of a farmer, Wilhelm Jordan, and his wife, Johanne Vosshage. He was educated at Hildesheim high school and the university of Göttingen where he obtained his degree in botany and

zoology, *summa cum laude*, and a diploma
in teaching. In 1888 he was appointed
a master at Münden grammar school but
in 1893 he came to England to Tring
to take up the post of entomologist at
the zoological museum which was being
created by L. W. (later Lord) Rothschild
whose notice Jordan contributed to this
Dictionary). He found already accumu-
ated a vast collection of beetles, butter-
lies, and moths, all in the utmost confusion. By working far into the night,
a habit he never lost, these were reduced
to order in an incredibly short space of
time, and as a result Jordan found himself
confronted by just such an array of
material as he needed for the study of
variation, evolution, and their causes
which was his objective throughout his
career. He succeeded E. J. O. Hartert as
director of the Tring Museum (1930–39),
was president of the Royal Entomological
Society of London (1929–30), and was
elected F.R.S. in 1932.

Over the years, the product of much
research in entomology by amateur and
professional alike had been lost to science
through lack of publication. No charge of
failure in this respect lies against Jordan.
By the end of 1903 he had published,
either alone or jointly with Rothschild,
profusely illustrated papers running to
over 2,500 pages. The best known were
the *Revision of the Papilios of the Eastern
Hemisphere*, the *Monograph of Charaxes*,
and the *Revision of the Sphingidae*, all of
which remain standard works of reference. Side by side with these major
works and numerous descriptive papers
on the systematics of Coleoptera and
Lepidoptera, Jordan found time to publish several papers of a more philosophical
nature on such subjects as mechanical
selection and mimicry, and a critique of
the theory of orthogenesis as applied to
Papilionidae by Eimer. A remarkable
paper was one on reproductive divergence
which, as early as 1898 and before much
was known of the laws of heredity, he
showed not to be a factor in the evolution
of species. All this was but the result of his
first ten years' work at Tring. Between
1903 and 1958 he published a further 420
papers which, though mainly systematic,
were frequently interspersed with pointed
reflections upon their bearing on the problem of evolution. He deplored the amount
of time which had to be devoted to
descriptions of new genera and species,
a drudgery which was nevertheless in-
escapable if a sound classificatory basis

was to be provided for the study of
evolution.

About 1900 he took up the study of
fleas and in collaboration with Charles
Rothschild began to publish on the
systematics of this much neglected order.
Their work on the plague fleas of the genus
Xenopsylla provides a perfect example of
the importance of precise taxonomic work.
Gradually between them they built up the
immensely valuable collection of fleas
which now belongs to the British Museum
and provided, through their writings, the
fund of knowledge of these insects which
has proved of such great value to medical
entomologists throughout the world. The
'only truly satisfactory classification of
fleas' is said to be that published by Jordan when he was nearly ninety.

One other group of insects claimed
a large share of Jordan's interest—the
beetles, which had been his 'first love'. In
particular, especially in later life, he was
fascinated by the Anthribidae. In spite
of describing 150 new genera and nearly
two-thirds of the known species he never
completely extricated himself from the
drudgery phase. He would discuss their
infinitely bewildering variety by the hour;
but he never achieved, in this group, a
system of classification which satisfied him.

In science Jordan was an internationalist. To him national rivalries in
this field, like personal rivalries, were
abhorrent, and he deliberately ignored
them. To help break down the isolation of
entomologists of different nationalities,
and even of different interests in the same
field, he founded in 1910 the International
Congress of Entomology, remaining permanent secretary until 1948 when he was
elected honorary life president. In the
field of zoological nomenclature Jordan
unobtrusively rendered great service.
Confusion and bitter argument reigned
supreme until at the congress at Monaco
in 1913 he succeeded in reaching a compromise which has subsequently proved of
the greatest benefit. He served until 1950
as a member of the Commission on
Zoological Nomenclature, holding office as
president for nineteen years.

Many of Jordan's major contributions to zoological thought appeared in
scientific publications little consulted by
zoologists not primarily concerned with
entomology. His introductory note to the
revision of the oriental swallowtails (1895)
sets out clearly the taxonomic concepts
and general principles which guided all his
work. How sound were his concepts and

how modern, has been well shown by the authors who paid tribute to him in the series of essays published on the occasion of his ninety-fourth birthday (*Transactions of the Royal Entomological Society*, vol. cvii, 1955).

A naturally rather shy man, Jordan was inevitably somewhat overshadowed by the panoply of his surroundings at Tring. To meet him there, however, meant quick recognition of his friendliness, helpfulness, humour, and complete disinterestedness in everything but the pursuit of truth and the advancement of knowledge. His most incisive criticism never hurt.

In 1891 Jordan married Minna Brünig (died 1925), a childhood friend, by whom he had two daughters. He was naturalized in 1911 and died in Hemel Hempstead 12 January 1959.

[N. D. Riley in *Biographical Memoirs of Fellows of the Royal Society*, vol. vi, 1960; personal knowledge.]   N. D. RILEY.

JOWITT, WILLIAM ALLEN, EARL JOWITT (1885–1957), lord chancellor, was born 15 April 1885 at Stevenage rectory, the only son of the rector, the Rev. William Jowitt, by his wife, Louisa Margaret, third daughter of John Allen, of Oldfield Hall, Altrincham. He was educated at Marlborough and New College, Oxford, where in 1906 he took a first in jurisprudence. Three years later (1909) he was called to the bar by the Middle Temple and rapidly established himself in the best class of commercial work, besides acquiring an all-round practice. When he took silk in 1922 he had a high reputation as a jury advocate and within four years he was recognized as one of the leading King's counsel at the common law bar.

He entered politics in 1922 when he was elected Liberal member of Parliament for the Hartlepools. In 1924 he was one of the few Liberals who supported the Labour Party in the division lobby on the occasion of the defeat of the Labour Government over the 'Campbell case'. In the ensuing general election he lost his seat. In 1924–6 he was a member of the royal commission on lunacy and mental disorder. After the general election of 1929 the second Labour Government took office with a notable lack of forensic talent which made it hard for Ramsay MacDonald to fill the legal offices. Jowitt's acknowledged distinction at the bar, together with his fluent, forcible eloquence, marked him as well qualified, and although he had just been returned to Parliament as Liberal member for Preston, MacDonald invited him to join the Labour Party and become attorney-general. Without any apparent hesitation, Jowitt accepted, at the same time offering to resign his seat and stand again in his constituency as Labour candidate. His change of politics only a few days after the election was the subject of bitter controversy. Indignation at the bar was particularly strong and all but one of the men in Jowitt's chambers in the Temple abandoned them. Jowitt was knighted and on 31 July 1929 was returned as Labour member for Preston with a majority of 6,440. Thenceforward his political career was characterized by a see-saw of alternating allegiances. When the financial crisis of 1931 brought about the formation of the 'national' Government he rallied to its support, retaining the office of attorney-general. In consequence he was expelled from the Labour Party. At the general election in October he stood as National Labour candidate for the Combined English Universities (although he had previously advocated the abolition of the university franchise), but he was defeated. In January 1932 he resigned his office as attorney-general and, remaining out of Parliament for seven years, resumed his practice at the bar.

In 1930, as attorney-general, Jowitt prosecuted Clarence Hatry for fraud and in the following year he prosecuted Lord Kylsant [q.v.], a director of the Royal Mail Steam Packet Company, for publishing a prospectus which he knew to be false in a material particular. Jowitt's skilful handling of this case was considered a masterpiece of forensic ability. In 1934 he appeared for the defence in Princess Yousoupoff's famous libel action against Metro-Goldwyn-Mayer Pictures, Ltd.

In 1936 he was readmitted to the Labour Party and in October 1939 he was returned to Parliament unopposed as member for Ashton-under-Lyne. In (Sir) Winston Churchill's coalition Government in 1940 he served as solicitor-general under his former pupil Sir Donald Somervell (later Lord Somervell of Harrow, q.v.), who became attorney-general. In 1942 he succeeded Lord Hankey as paymaster-general, usually an unpaid sinecure, but for which he received a salary of £5,000 in respect of work in preparation for post-war reconstruction. In January 1943 he became minister without portfolio. In 1944 he was appointed minister of national insurance. The government white paper on this subject was put to test in the House of Commons on 2 November 1944 when Jowitt sought support for it in one of his admirably lucid speeches. However, before legislation could be framed, the general election of 1945 resulted in the formation of the third Labour Government with Jowitt as lord chancellor, with the title Baron Jowitt, of Stevenage. In his first year of office he presided at the dramatic hearing of the appeal to the House of Lords of William Joyce, convicted of treason. In 1947 a viscountcy was conferred on him. During this year two complex and important bills were debated in the Lords and Jowitt was mainly instrumental in securing their safe passage into law. One was the much-needed Companies Act and the other the revolutionary Town and Country Planning Act in which there were some 400 amendments.

In 1948 Jowitt moved the second reading of the criminal justice bill. Although he had declared himself opposed to the suspension of the death penalty, he acted in accordance with the free vote taken in the House of Commons and advised that the experiment of suspension should be tried. During his term of office as lord chancellor he bore the full burden of an overwhelming weight of legislation and he handled the affairs of the House with businesslike dispatch. It was said after his death that he was the most overworked lord chancellor in history. In 1951 he inaugurated in person the new Supreme Court of Appeal for East Africa which included Aden, the Seychelles, and Somaliland, enhancing the impressiveness of the occasion by all the traditional splendour associated with his office. After the general election of 1951 a Conservative Government was returned and on relinquishing the office of lord chancellor Jowitt was created an earl. However, he remained an active and spirited leader of the Opposition in the House of Lords from 1952 to November 1955. His hold upon his fellow peers never weakened for he never lost his clarity of exposition and adroitness in parliamentary procedure. Even after his retirement at the age of seventy he continued to give valuable service when occasionally he returned to speak in the House of Lords or preside over the Appellate Committee.

Lord Jowitt was always the embodiment of judicial dignity and in his splendid black and gold robes he looked every inch the lord chancellor. In voice, deportment, and person he had most of the qualifica-

tions for the discharge of his high office, yet it is chiefly as an advocate that he will be remembered. Alternately commanding and persuasive, his richly expressive voice was once compared to a violoncello. He was tall and gracefully athletic with steely-blue eyes and thin lips set in classical features. He was outstandingly handsome and his carriage was gravely dignified. He had great charm and wit, combined with an easy nonchalant manner which at times disarmed even his most scathing critics. Probably his greatest attribute at the bar was his exceptional ability to reduce the most complex problems to simple clear-cut terms by easy lucid exposition. His speeches in debate, like his rare platform utterances, were moderate and calm, delivered with skill and often with brilliance.

Jowitt travelled extensively after 1945 and was very popular abroad, for he was an accomplished lecturer and had a gift for making speeches which were both short and witty. He was a member of the Athenaeum and was the author of two books, *The Strange Case of Alger Hiss* (1953) and *Some Were Spies* (1954).

Despite the many public services he rendered Jowitt remained an equivocal and controversial character. He had a well-cultivated mind, was acutely intelligent, and his fine dignified presence was calculated to create a profound impression. Nevertheless, he may have lacked profound convictions. He was primarily an advocate and probably for this reason he failed to grasp the impression his political inconsistencies would make on others. To him the step from the left of the Liberal Party to the right of the Labour Party was a short one. Many squibs were written in comment on his change of politics but none so ironical as the motto he took for his coat of arms when he was raised to the peerage: 'Tenax et fidelis'.

In 1913 he married Lesley (died 1970), daughter of James Patrick McIntyre; they had one daughter. He died during the night of 15–16 August 1957 at his home at Bradfield St. George, near Bury St. Edmunds.

Although in his lifetime it had been generally assumed that Jowitt was not a rich man, his estate amounted to over £100,000. A portrait by Sir Gerald Kelly is in the Middle Temple and one by Ambrose McEvoy in the Tate Gallery.

[*Law Times* and *Law Journal*, 23 August 1957; *The Times*, 17 August 1957.]

MOLINA FULLMAN.

KEEBLE, Sir FREDERICK WILLIAM (1870–1952), botanist, civil servant, and industrial adviser, was born in London 2 March 1870, the second son of Francis Henry Keeble, cabinet maker, by his wife, Annie Eliza Gamble. Frederick was educated at Alleyn's School, Dulwich, and as a scholar of Caius College, Cambridge. He obtained a first class in part i of the natural sciences tripos in 1891 and a second in part ii in 1893, being appointed Frank Smart student in the same year. He spent a year on plant physiological research in Ceylon and in 1897–8 was an assistant lecturer in botany at Manchester. In 1902 he was appointed lecturer in botany and director of the horticultural department at Reading where he became professor in 1907, and was dean of the faculty of science for the sessions 1907–8 and 1908–9. During his years at Reading his scientific publications were mainly in two series of papers. The first in collaboration with F. W. Gamble, the zoologist, was on certain plant-animal symbioses and the second with E. F. Armstrong and others on the formation and inheritance of floral pigments. Together with two papers on the integration of plant behaviour published in 1929–30, also in collaboration, these completed his original contributions to science.

In 1914 Keeble left Reading to become director of the Royal Horticultural Society's gardens at Wisley, but almost at once, on the outbreak of war, he was transferred to the Board of Agriculture. He became controller of horticulture (1917–19) in the food production department, and eventually, in 1919, an assistant secretary to the Board. In this position he was able to facilitate the setting up of the East Malling Research Station as an independent institute for horticultural research. For his services in the war he was appointed C.B.E. in 1917.

Keeble returned to academic life in 1920 as Sherardian professor of botany at Oxford. In 1915 his first wife, Mathilde Marie Cecile, daughter of Henri Maréchal, of Paris, whom he married in 1898, died suddenly, leaving one daughter, Keeble's only child; in 1920 he married Lillah McCarthy [q.v.], the actress. Together they created the beautiful house and gardens at Hammels on Boar's Hill where they entertained extensively. Among their guests was Sir Alfred Mond (later Lord Melchett, q.v.), head of the firm which had developed the process for producing nitrogenous fertilizers from the

nitrogen of the air. He persuaded Keeble to relinquish his chair in 1927 to become agricultural adviser to Imperial Chemical Industries which had taken over the process. Keeble entered with enthusiasm into the task of organizing research upon the use of nitrogenous fertilizers. A station was set up at Jealott's Hill near Bracknell in Berkshire and a staff assembled. The programme was based on the belief that greatly increased use of fertilizers could with proper management lead to greatly increased yields both on arable and on grasslands. The station exists, much enlarged, at the present time as a centre of research and demonstration and, with the solution of the original problems, has passed on to others. When Keeble's association with it ended in 1932 its reputation, as a centre of research, had been established. After an interval Keeble took up his final appointment as Fullerian professor of the Royal Institution (1938–41).

His interest in the application of scientific botany to practical ends was recognized by his service as editor (1908–19) and thereafter as scientific adviser of the *Gardeners' Chronicle*, to which he contributed over a long period. He had also the unusual distinction of being successively president of the botany section (1912) and of the agricultural section (1920) of the British Association. He was elected F.R.S. in 1913 and knighted in 1922.

Besides his technical papers, Keeble published several books. The first, prepared with the help of Miss M. M. C. Rayner while he was at Reading, is notable for a lengthy preface, almost in the manner of his later acquaintance, G. B. Shaw [q.v.]. It assesses with percipience the value of its subject, *Practical Plant Physiology* (1911), as an instrument of education. The book itself was less successful. *The Life of Plants* (1926) was a short and readable account of its subject and *Science Lends a Hand in the Garden* (1939) an assembly of his more notable contributions to the *Gardeners' Chronicle*. All his writing exhibits a command of clear and felicitous English which he was apparently prepared to take great pains to achieve. *The Life of Plants*, the publishers complained, was rewritten in proof. In his sixties he wrote *Polly and Freddie* (1936) which has been described as an 'imaginative autobiography' including tales of biology told to his grandchildren. For some readers, at least, it possesses great charm. At this time he was a striking figure, well, if a shade flamboyantly, groomed and with an easy bearing devoid of aggressiveness.

In Keeble the training of a scientist was imposed upon the temperament of an artist, and sometimes the two seem to have warred with one another. He appears to have convinced himself that biology could afford to dispense with the rigour of scientific discipline for the niceties of which he seems to have had inadequate patience. It may be for this reason that his own work has left little mark on the development of scientific botany. His part was that of stimulant and irritant to others, and of his Oxford staff and students there were still those who spoke warmly of his skill in encouragement. He was a noted and witty conversationalist, and if in pursuit of his fancy he inflicted wounds his friends regarded him to the last as essentially warm hearted.

After his retirement he and Lady Keeble lived for a while at Fowey in Cornwall; but they returned eventually to London where he died 19 October 1952.

[*Nature*, 10 January 1953; V. H. Blackman in *Obituary Notices of Fellows of the Royal Society*, No. 22, November 1953; private information.]   W. O. JAMES.

KEEBLE, LILLAH, LADY (1875–1960), actress. [See McCARTHY, LILLAH.]

KEITH, SIR ARTHUR (1866–1955), conservator of the Hunterian Museum of the Royal College of Surgeons, was born 5 February 1866 at Old Machar, Aberdeenshire, the sixth of the ten children of John Keith, a farmer, and his wife, Jessie Macpherson. To prepare for a medical education he went to Gordon's College, Aberdeen, for a grounding in Latin and Greek, and in 1884 entered Marischal College. It was here that he came under the influence of James Trail the botanist and (Sir) John Struthers [q.v.], the anatomist, both of whom inspired him with the resolve ultimately to seek an academic career. He qualified with highest honours in 1888 and in the next year accepted a post as medical officer to a mining company in Siam, mainly with the intention of collecting botanical specimens; his collection was later used by H. N. Ridley [q.v.] in his comprehensive work on the *Flora of the Malay Peninsula*. But Keith himself became more interested in field and anatomical studies of the local monkeys and gibbons, and it was these activities which first began to focus his

attention on the comparative anatomy of the Primates, the evolution of man, and physical anthropology in general.

After three years in Siam, Keith returned home and in 1894 was awarded the degree of M.D. of Aberdeen University for a thesis on the myology of catarrhine monkeys, and in the same year passed the examination for the fellowship of the Royal College of Surgeons. In the following year he was appointed senior demonstrator in anatomy at the London Hospital medical school, subsequently becoming lecturer. In 1902 there appeared his well-known book *Human Embryology and Morphology* which reached a sixth edition in 1948. Of his earlier research work, that dealing with the anatomy of the heart won him the greatest distinction, and in seeking for one of the basic causes of cardiac arrhythmia, he discovered (with his colleague Martin Flack) the 'sino-auricular node' of the heart, a small condensation of specialized tissue of immense importance for the initiation and control of the normal rhythmic contraction of the heart.

In 1908 Keith was elected to the conservatorship of the Royal College of Surgeons, and under his inspired direction the Hunterian Museum of the College came to be recognized as one of the finest records of the structure and history of the human body, with particular reference to the anatomical and embryological basis of the surgical disabilities and disorders which may affect it. One of Keith's main duties at the College was to conduct courses of lectures, and he rapidly acquired a high reputation as a gifted lecturer. Soon after assuming his new office, he began to give his attention much more actively to problems of human evolution and the diversification of the modern races of mankind. There followed a number of palaeo-anthropological studies as a result of which Keith claimed a much higher antiquity for *Homo sapiens* than had hitherto been accepted. His conclusions have proved to be partly correct—but not entirely, for some of the fossil skeletons on which he relied for his evidence were later demonstrated by modern techniques of dating to be more recent than he had supposed.

The publication of the alleged discovery of the Piltdown skull in 1912 led Keith into serious controversy with those who claimed that the skull (as well as the jaw) displayed remarkable simian characters, and he was able to show that, if properly reconstructed, the skull was in fact quite like that of *Homo sapiens*. Nevertheless, though he expressed doubts as to the interpretation of this 'fossil' (now known to have been fraudulently fabricated), Keith thought that Piltdown man was indeed akin to a very early ancestor of modern man.

In 1915 *The Antiquity of Man* was published—a widely read book reviewing all the fossil remains of man at that time known. It was brought up to date in 1931 by a supplementary volume, *New Discoveries Relating to the Antiquity of Man*. During the war of 1914–18 Keith was occupied with problems of surgical anatomy related to war injuries, and published a number of lectures on the anatomical and physiological principles underlying the treatment of wounds involving muscles, bones, and joints. Some of his wartime lectures appeared in book form as *Menders of the Maimed* (1919). In 1913 he was elected to the presidency of the Royal Anthropological Institute, a position which he held for four years, and in 1916 he was invited to give the Christmas juvenile lectures at the Royal Institution; these were later published in a book entitled *The Engines of the Human Body* (1919), a second edition of which appeared in 1925.

During the years following the war, Keith's interests turned more to general themes of medical history and to somewhat speculative considerations of evolutionary processes in relation to the origin of man; at the same time he was always busy revising some of his books for new editions. He was elected F.R.S. as early as 1913, in 1921 he was knighted, and from 1918 to 1923 he occupied the position of Fullerian professor of physiology at the Royal Institution. He was then at the height of his distinguished career, and his election to the presidency of the British Association for 1927 came as no surprise to his colleagues. His presidential address, 'Darwin's theory of man's descent as it stands today', presented an affirmation of Darwin's general conclusions on the evolutionary derivation of the Hominidae from an ancestry in common with the anthropoid apes, amplified by references to the accumulation of comparative anatomical and palaeontological evidence since Darwin's time. One result of this meeting of the British Association was the immediate response to Keith's appeal for the preservation of Darwin's home at Downe in Kent.

In 1930 Keith was elected rector of Aberdeen University and in his rectorial address he developed the thesis that the spirit of nationalism is a potent factor in the evolutionary differentiation of human races. This thesis, later expanded in a book entitled *A New Theory of Human Evolution* (1948), met with some criticism. In 1933, after a severe illness, he retired from the Royal College of Surgeons and went to live at the Buckston Browne Research Institute in Downe. A year later he suffered the loss of his wife Cecilia Caroline (daughter of Tom Gray the artist) whom he had married in 1899. They had no children.

Except for his *Autobiography* (1950) which he published at the age of eighty-four, Keith's last work of importance was a comprehensive study of the skeletal remains of palaeolithic man found in the caves of Mount Carmel. The results of this work appeared in the treatise on *The Stone Age of Mount Carmel* (1939, with T. D. McCown).

Keith died suddenly at Downe 7 January 1955. Apart from his claims to distinction as a scientist, he was a much-loved man, kindly and gentle in manner, friendly and unassuming, and of a somewhat retiring disposition. It seemed entirely fitting that this devoted student of human evolution should himself spend the latter part of his long life in the countryside where his great predecessor Charles Darwin had once lived. Keith received honorary degrees from Aberdeen, Durham, Manchester, Birmingham, and Oxford. He was an honorary fellow of the Royal Societies of Edinburgh and New Zealand, and honorary member of the United States National Academy of Sciences and the New York Academy of Sciences. At the Royal College of Surgeons he is commemorated in an oil-painting by W. W. Ouless, and in a bronze bust by Kathleen Parbury. The National Portrait Gallery has two drawings, one by Sir William Rothenstein and the other by Juliet Pannett.

[Sir W. E. Le Gros Clark in *Biographical Memoirs of Fellows of the Royal Society*, vol. i, 1955; private information; personal knowledge.]   W. E. LE GROS CLARK.

KELLAWAY, CHARLES HALLILEY (1889–1952), scientist, was born 16 January 1889, in Melbourne, Australia, the son of the Rev. Alfred Charles Kellaway, curate to the dean of the pro-cathedral church of St. James, and his wife, Anne Carrick, daughter of Richard Roberts, who had married Frances Halliley, and who had been a North of England manufacturer, interested in chemistry, and a friend of the great John Dalton [q.v.].

Charles Kellaway was the eldest son and second child in a family of three sons and two daughters. He attended the Caulfield Grammar School and then, with a scholarship, the Melbourne Church of England Grammar School, passing the senior public examination with first class honours in physics and chemistry, and winning a scholarship to the university, which he attended as a home-boarder, supplementing his resources by coaching; he passed all his examinations with high honours, to qualify as M.B., B.S. in 1911. After resident appointments at the Royal Melbourne Hospital, he was acting as tutor in physiology at Trinity College when war came in 1914. He left Australia in 1915 as a captain, A.A.M.C., to serve in Gallipoli and then, in 1916, at the laboratory of the Third Australian General Hospital at Cairo. This gave him his first experience of research, in pathology and bacteriology, under the stimulating guidance of (Sir) Charles Martin [q.v.]. Kellaway went with Australian forces to the western front in Europe, was awarded the M.C. in 1917, and later in that year was rendered unfit for further active service, and acquired a permanent liability to bronchitis, through encountering a gas attack (phosgene). He was sent to London early in 1918, on duty which gave him free time for research on the physiological effects of anoxaemia, then of new interest in connection with high-altitude aviation.

During a return to Australia, Kellaway in 1920 was appointed Foulerton research student of the Royal Society and returned to London to engage in research there, first with (Sir) H. H. Dale at the National Institute for Medical Research, mainly on the nature of anaphylaxis, and then in T. R. Elliott's medical unit at University College Hospital, where his chief work, with S. J. Cowell, was on the resistance maintained by the suprarenal cortex to the effects of histamine and other toxic products of tissue injury.

In 1923 Kellaway received his main research opportunity, through his appointment as director of the Walter and Eliza Hall Institute for Pathological Research, in Melbourne. He was to hold this position for twenty-one years, during which, through his effective appeals for national support and private generosity, the Institute was to be greatly enlarged, while its scientific output won for it a leading position in Australia, and high rank among world centres of medical research. Kellaway's own researches in this period, with his immediate collaborators, included important series on the physiological analysis of the effects of the venoms of Australian snakes and other indigenous fauna, and of those of the toxins of pathogenic bacteria. In both these series, apart from more specific actions, evidence was found of the release of histamine from tissues injured by different poisons, and a link with the earlier studies of anaphylaxis was thus provided.

When war broke out again in 1939, Kellaway, with the rank of colonel, became director of pathology to the Australian Army Medical Service, organizing his Institute to meet the war's special demands. In 1941 he toured the United States on his way to London to establish scientific liaisons. News of the Japanese attack on Pearl Harbour in December 1941 hurried him from London back to Australia, which was to become a principal medical base for the allied armies in the Pacific. With the rank of brigadier-general, he served as scientific liaison officer to the director-general of the A.A.M.S. Two years later, in 1944, his friend and colleague (Sir) F. Macfarlane Burnet succeeded to his directorship of the Hall Institute, which had by then been greatly enlarged and rebuilt on a new site. Kellaway was then free to accept the position, in London, of director-in-chief to the research enterprises of the Wellcome Foundation, Ltd.; and he made distinguished use of this further opportunity for organizing researches in a wide medical range until he died in London 13 December 1952. He had made important contributions to medical knowledge by his own researches, and an even greater one by the energy and special ability which he devoted to the organization of research opportunities for others. He was elected F.R.C.P. in 1929 and F.R.S. in 1940. He married in 1919 Eileen Ethel Scantlebury, by whom he had three sons.

[Sir Henry H. Dale in *Obituary Notices of Fellows of the Royal Society*, No. 22, November 1953; private information; personal knowledge.]   H. H. DALE.

KELLY, SIR DAVID VICTOR (1891–1959), diplomatist, was born 14 September 1891 in Adelaide, South Australia, where his father, David Frederick Kelly, had recently settled as professor of classics in the university. His father's family were Londonderry landowners. His mother, Sophie Armstrong, daughter of the late Rev. Ignatius George d'Arenberg, was descended from a member of the Rhenish ducal house of that name who emigrated to Ireland after the Napoleonic wars. On his father's death his mother returned to Ireland, thence to England where Kelly went to St. Paul's School in time for the last year of the headmastership of F. W. Walker [q.v.], then to Magdalen College, Oxford. At St. Paul's, Kelly came to know Richard Johnson Walker, the high master's son and assistant master (later Kelly's stepfather), a brilliant scholar and a man of wide but wayward genius who, from being an agnostic, became an Anglican clergyman and later joined the Church of Rome. From him Kelly acquired an enthusiasm for the traditions and achievements of European culture and a lifelong passion for travel. As a demy of Magdalen he read history, fenced for the university, and settled down to an appreciation of the *douceur de vivre* of the pre-war era and to a gentle scepticism based on 'the limitations of humanity and the essential conservatism and passivity and gullibility of the mass of mankind'.

Kelly obtained first class honours in 1913 and on the advice of Sir Herbert Warren [q.v.] entered for the diplomatic service. His nomination was accepted just before the outbreak of war, but he volunteered and was commissioned in the Leicester Regiment. In 1914 he finally accepted Christianity and became a devoted Roman Catholic. He spent the war years from 1915 in France, chiefly as intelligence officer to the 110th Infantry brigade, and in 1917 he was awarded the M.C. He later published a record of his wartime experiences in *39 Months* (1930), partly in protest against the distortions of much post-war writing about life at the front.

In 1919 Kelly was at last free to begin his diplomatic career which centred mainly round Latin America (twice in Argentina and briefly, 1925–7, in Mexico), the Levant (Egypt and Turkey), and Russia. He was first posted to Buenos Aires (1919–21), where in 1920 he married his first wife, Isabella Adela, daughter of the late Henry Maynard Mills, who died in 1927, leaving a son and daughter. Later (1942–6) he returned to Argentina as ambassador; and he twice (1922–3, 1931–4)

served in the American department of the Foreign Office, where he was one of the architects of the Anglo-Argentine trade agreement of 1933. In handling Latin-American affairs, both in London and overseas, Kelly developed two of his main professional convictions, less widely accepted then than later: the need for close co-ordination between foreign policy and financial and economic policy and the need to cultivate not only governments and ministers in office but the financial, industrial, political, and social leaders who wield power and form opinion behind the scenes. He realized that the rule of the great Argentine landlords was ending and that new forces were emerging. His years as ambassador covered the difficult period of American endeavours to dominate Argentina politically and economically and Perón's rise to power. His attempts to arrange an Anglo-Argentine condominium for the British-owned railways were largely thwarted by British shortsightedness.

Kelly served in Egypt as counsellor, acting high commissioner, and chargé d'affaires in Cairo between 1934 and 1938, and as head of the Egyptian department in the Foreign Office in 1938–9. These years covered the last phase of King Fuad's duel with the Wafd, his illness and death, the treaty negotiations for a settlement of Anglo-Egyptian relations, and the threat from Italy culminating in the Abyssinian war. Kelly was a keen supporter of a treaty settlement and among the first to advocate the removal of the British garrison from Cairo to the Canal Zone.

Except for Switzerland and Russia, Kelly's European postings (Lisbon, 1923–5, Brussels, 1927–9, Stockholm, 1929–31) were less important; but his years in Belgium included his marriage in 1929 to Marie-Noële Renée Ghislaine de Jourda de Vaux, a member of the old Brussels aristocracy, who shared both his shrewd diplomatic sense and his delight in travel. As a hostess and as a writer and lecturer she gave added brilliance to his later career. There were two sons of the marriage.

In 1940–42 Kelly was minister at Berne, a post of central importance in war time as a source of intelligence and one requiring extreme diplomatic tact. It was to him that the peace overtures of Prince Hohenlohe were addressed. Appointed C.M.G. in 1935, Kelly was advanced to K.C.M.G. in 1942 on his transfer to Buenos Aires as ambassador; from his embassy in Argenina, already noted, he was transferred in 1946 to Turkey. With the promulgation of the 'Truman doctrine' in 1947 Britain ceased to bear the major responsibility for reinforcing the Turkish economy and Turkish defence. Thanks in no small degree to Kelly's influence Britain nevertheless remained a trusted adviser at a critical time when Turkey was trying to evolve a two-party parliamentary system. He was able to gain the confidence of the Turkish leaders and by extensive journeys throughout the country to form a first-hand opinion of its political, social, and economic problems. It was a congenial task and, apart from the professional advancement, he much regretted his transfer, in 1949, to Russia, where the scope for travel and for personal contact with leading men was very restricted. He had known Tsarist Russia from two visits as a young man and they had left him fascinated and appalled. In the wintry climate of Stalin's last years there seemed little a British ambassador could effect, but Kelly applied his analytic mind to the philosophy and practice of Soviet government and even in the sphere of travel he and his wife managed to secure unusual concessions. In 1950 he was promoted G.C.M.G. and in 1951 he retired. During his embassy Anglo-Russian relations were strained by the Korean war and irritated by the Russian peace campaign; the moral which Kelly himself drew from his Russian experiences was that only a policy combining rearmament and conciliation could maintain Western security and the general peace.

An important sequel to Kelly's last embassy was his work, after retirement, as a public commentator on Soviet affairs (1951–4) mainly in the *Sunday Times*. At a time when Russia was the subject of much emotion, conjecture, and misapprehension, Kelly's clear, comprehensive, and factual account was a valuable corrective. He was one of the first to describe the rise of the Russian managerial society and its tendency to follow the American pattern. In 1954 his articles were republished as a book, *Beyond the Iron Curtain*.

In his autobiography *The Ruling Few* (1952, German translation, 1963) Kelly defined the diplomatist's three main duties as stating the case for his own Government, attempting to influence in his own country's interest whatever social group forms the governing class of his country of residence, and keeping his own Government informed of leading personalities and trends in that country and of the probable course of events. His own career was highly successful; his strength lay in his quick, fact-loving mind, his lucid reporting, and his ability to win confidence as an experienced, discreet, and friendly observer. Temperamentally conservative in outlook and aim, he was readily experimental in method, and his last book, *The Hungry Sheep* (1955, German translation, 1959), might be described as a survey of the mid-twentieth-century scene by an acute eighteenth-century mind.

After retirement Kelly was chairman of the Anglo-Turkish Society and also of the British Atlantic Committee. In 1955 he became a director of the National Bank and chairman of the British Council and remained in office until his sudden death four years later, 27 March 1959, at his home in county Wexford, following a visit for the Council to India. To his chairmanship of the Council he brought not only wide experience and contacts and a delight in absorbing problems on the spot, but a conviction of the importance of national publicity in general and a determination to maintain British cultural connections with Europe beside the necessary expansion of work in other continents.

In appearance Kelly was a tall, bigboned man, with something of the scholar's stoop and, in manner, something of the scholar's reserve combined with the watchful affability of the diplomatist. He enjoyed entertaining and was a genial host and a kindly chief. His photograph in *The Ruling Few* shows him in later life—the asymmetrical Irish features, the narrowed, slanting, Elizabethan eyes, the decided, gently depressed line of the mouth. A bronze bust by J. R. Renard-Goulet is in the possession of the family.

[*The Times*, 28 March 1959; *Sunday Times*, 29 March 1959; Kelly's own writings; private information; personal knowledge.]

KENNETH JOHNSTONE.

KENNARD, SIR HOWARD WILLIAM (1878–1955), diplomatist, was born at Hove 22 March 1878, the younger son of Arthur Challis Kennard, landowner, of 17 Eaton Place, London, S.W., and his wife, Ann Homan, daughter of Thomas Homan Mulock. He was educated at Eton which he left in 1896 and entered the diplomatic service in 1901. In 1902 he was appointed attaché and in 1903 third secretary at the British embassy in Rome. He was transferred to Tehran in December 1904 and by July 1905 had already been granted an allowance for knowledge of Persian. He was moved to Washington in 1907 where he met and, in 1908, married Harriet (died 1950), daughter of Jonathan Norris, of New York. She was his constant companion in all his service and greatly appreciated by those who served under him for her kindness and generosity. They had one son.

After a short period in 1911 in charge of the British legation in Havana, Kennard was moved in the same year to Tangier, then an important post in view of the rivalry between Germany and the *Entente* powers for control of North Africa and its Atlantic ports. Kennard always spoke of his service there with great delight. He passed an examination in Arabic only a year after his arrival and found time also for hunting and shooting forays in the hinterland. He was promoted first secretary in 1914 and transferred to the Foreign Office in 1916.

In 1919 Kennard went back as counsellor to Rome where his piercing intellect and quick understanding of people and situations, as well as his personal charm, linguistic ability, and cultural background, made him particularly appreciated. He was appointed C.M.G. and C.V.O. in 1923.

In 1925 he became envoy extraordinary and minister plenipotentiary in Belgrade. The spirit of Rupert of Hentzau was always just over the hill outside the town or even in the parliament building. The kingdom of the Serbs, Croats, and Slovenes, torn by ancient feuds and rivalries, was with difficulty being amalgamated into Yugoslavia, while territorial disputes continued with Italy, Hungary, and especially Bulgaria. The British ministers in the various capitals were ever trying to prevent dangerous complications arising and used to assess and advocate the claims and complaints of their respective countries with a rival eloquence and intellectual ability into which Kennard plunged with his usual verve and vivacity. He also built up a reputation in these years for insisting on his staff's preserving full British standards in all circumstances, even if it required severity. He was appointed K.C.M.G. in 1929 and in the same year made minister in Stockholm, transferring to Berne in 1931. He became a devotee of skiing, until an accident gave him phlebitis which troubled him intermittently for years.

In 1935 Kennard was appointed ambassador in Warsaw where the Foreign Office needed one of its best diplomats since it was already evident that Poland was probably the area where the next war might begin. There was a clear German claim to the so-called 'Polish corridor' which cut off East Prussia from the rest of Germany. There had been constant incidents on the Polish frontiers with Germany, East Prussia, and the Free City of Danzig, which the British, as League of Nations rapporteur for such questions, had a certain responsibility for settling. Colonel Beck, the Polish foreign minister, had temporarily settled the trouble in 1934 by making an agreement with Hitler for which he was considered by the French and others in the West to have 'betrayed Europe'.

To this situation Kennard brought his penetrating, original, and objective mind. He showed some understanding of Beck's agreement with Hitler since the Poles had previously been blamed as disturbers of the peace. But he insisted that the Polish Government must not associate itself with Hitler's territorial expansionism or racial policies. Beck often remembered the interview in which Kennard came to protest about the Polish seizure of Teschen (Cieszyn) in Czechoslovakia at the time of Munich in 1938. After all the political and intellectual arguments were finished, Kennard said: 'And finally we think it is abominable to hit a man when he is down.' The conclusion of the British alliance with Poland in the following spring after Hitler's final rape of Czechoslovakia shows with what diplomatic ability Kennard had been able to redress the situation in Anglo-Polish relations. His telegrams and dispatches to the Foreign Office at this time are important historical documents, and show the overwhelming responsibility of Nazi Germany for the deterioration in German-Polish relations until the final aggression on 1 September 1939. He had been promoted G.C.M.G. in 1938 before the Czechoslovak crisis.

Kennard was famous for the rather sardonic humour which he could display in many languages and which greatly enhanced his popularity with his colleagues. When the French ambassador had shown him round the new French embassy building in Warsaw and when they had commiserated over the mixture of styles, the French ambassador said 'And shortly we will ask you to our housewarming—pour pendre la crémaillère.' To which Kennard

s said to have replied: 'Et j'espère que
ous allez aussi pendre l'architecte.'

In concert with his colleagues in other
European capitals, Kennard took every
onceivable action to delay and prevent
he outbreak of war. When Hitler invaded
Poland he followed the Polish Government into Romania and was later ac-
redited to the Polish Government in
xile at Angers and in London. He retired
n 1941 to live in Somerset and died at
Bath 12 November 1955.

[Private information; personal knowledge.]
HANKEY.

KENNAWAY, SIR ERNEST LAUR-
ENCE (1881–1958), experimental and
hemical pathologist, was born in Exeter
23 May 1881, the youngest of the five
hildren of Laurence James Kennaway,
colonial farmer, and his wife, Mary Louisa
Galton. His grandfather William Kennaway had twice been mayor of Exeter and
had played a leading part in combating
he cholera epidemic in that city in 1832.

Although Kennaway was somewhat
delicate as a boy, he soon evinced a remarkable interest in natural history, and
early revealed those acute powers of perception which were to mark his later
career. His scientific training started at
University College, London, in 1898,
whence he proceeded in the following
year to New College, Oxford, with an
open scholarship in natural science. He
graduated B.A. in 1903, obtaining a first
lass in the final honour school in physio-
ogy; and qualified in medicine in 1907,
after spending three years at the Middle-
ex Hospital where he held a university
cholarship. In 1909 he was Hulme student
n Brasenose College, Oxford, and during
he following year studied in Heidelberg
and Munich as Radcliffe travelling fellow.
He proceeded D.M. Oxford in 1911 and
D.Sc. London (in physiological chemistry)
n 1915.

Kennaway held relatively few appointments in his long and active life. Demon-
trator in physiology at Guy's Hospital
1909–14) and chemical pathologist to the
Bland-Sutton Institute of the Middlesex
Hospital (1914–21), in 1921 he transferred
o the Research Institute of the Cancer
Hospital (Free), (now the Chester Beatty
Research Institute, Institute of Cancer
Research: Royal Cancer Hospital). Ten
years later he succeeded Archibald Leitch
as director, and was elected professor of
experimental pathology in the university
of London. It was at the Cancer Hospital

that he was to perform his greatest work.
He retired in 1946, became professor
emeritus, and thereafter continued his
researches in the pathological laboratories
at St. Bartholomew's Hospital. He died in
London on New Year's Day 1958.

Kennaway's early investigations lay in
many fields of physiological chemistry,
especially relating to the purines, and here
he collaborated at different times with
Cathcart, Leathes, Kossel, Browning, and
J. S. and J. B. S. Haldane. When Kennaway began work at the Cancer Hospital,
great interest was being taken in the
cancer-producing qualities of coal tar.
From the occurrence of cancer of the skin
as a hazard in many occupations and
industries involving exposure to soot,
coal tar, pitch, shale oil, and mineral oil,
it had long been evident that these complex mixtures must contain an agent or
agents capable of inducing the disease. Yet
progress towards the chemical identification of such agents had earlier been
limited through inability to reproduce
cancer under experimental conditions at
will. After many failures, this essential
step was achieved when Yamagiwa and
Ichikawa in Tokyo in 1915 succeeded in
evoking cancer by the protracted application of coal tar to the skin of the rabbit
ear. Tsutsui (1918) later showed the
mouse to be peculiarly susceptible, and
these two discoveries soon provided an
immense stimulus to cancer research the
world over.

In the early twenties there had been
suggestions, from the work of Bloch and
his collaborators in Zürich, that the carci-
nogen in coal tar might well be a cyclic
hydrocarbon. Kennaway very rapidly
produced virtual proof by different
methods—e.g. by the artificial fabrication
of carcinogenic tars which could contain
only compounds of carbon and hydrogen,
from the pyrolysis of many natural products such as skin, hair, and yeast, or from
passing the simple hydrocarbons acety-
lene or isoprene with hydrogen through
heated tubes. A further vital clue came
from the property of carcinogenic tars to
show brilliant fluorescence in ultraviolet
light. W. V. Mayneord, also at the Cancer
Hospital, recognized the characteristic
features of the fluorescence spectrum, and
this proved to be, in Kennaway's words,
the single thread that led all through the
labyrinth in his search for the carcinogenic
molecule. I. Hieger detected the characteristic spectrum in the known hydrocarbon
1:2-benzanthracene, and very soon (1929)

Kennaway demonstrated pronounced cancer-producing activity in the related 1:2:5:6-dibenzanthracene—the first chemical individual to be recognized as endowed with this biological property. With the assistance of (Sir) J. W. Cook, C. L. Hewett, Frank Goulden, and others, Kennaway then directed an extensive synthetic programme which, among other things, soon led to the identification of 3:4-benzopyrene as the active substance of carcinogenic pitch and to the discovery of a great range of polycyclic aromatic carcinogenic hydrocarbons, methylcholanthrene being among the most powerful. Much of this work was embodied in a classical series of papers which appeared in the *Proceedings* of the Royal Society between 1932 and 1942. From the researches which Kennaway alone inspired over some thirty years, there emerged an elegant and satisfying series of relationships between chemical constitution and biological action. And altogether, apart from their fundamental significance, they had a vast practical impact on cancer research in almost every country, and so led to further advances. Kennaway's contribution was by no means limited to these fields, and he was a pioneer in the statistics and epidemiology of cancer, especially for example of the larynx and the lung.

From his personal qualities Kennaway was a born and devoted researcher and observer, solely concerned with the establishment of fact and not at all with speculation. His services to cancer research can hardly be over-estimated, and he was its doyen. He combined great mental and physical courage, as was seen by his resistance to the Parkinson's disease from which he suffered for many years. A profound and perhaps intolerant sceptic, in his later days he set forth his position in *Some Religious Illusions in Art, Literature and Experience* (1953).

Kennaway was the recipient of many honours which he carried lightly: he was William Julius Mickle fellow of the university of London (1922), fellow of the Royal College of Physicians and Baly medallist (1937), Anna Fuller prizeman (with others, 1939), honorary fellow of New College, Oxford (1942), Walker prizeman of the Royal College of Surgeons and Garton medallist of the British Empire Cancer Campaign (1946), honorary member of the American Association for Cancer Research (1947), honorary fellow of the New York Academy of Medicine and the Royal Society of Medicine, and honorary foreign member (1954) of the Académie royale de Médecine de Belgique; and Osler memorial medallist (Oxford, 1950) for his services to the science, the art and the literature of medicine. He was elected F.R.S. in 1934 and awarded a Royal medal in 1941. He was knighted in 1947.

In 1920 Kennaway married Nina Mario (died 1969), daughter of William Derry, bank manager, of Edgbaston; there were no children. His wife was not only his help, meet and support, but played a special part in assisting his scientific work throughout the whole of their married life.

[*The Times*, 2 and 13 January 1958; J. W. Cook in *Biographical Memoirs of Fellows of the Royal Society*, vol. iv, 1958; *British Medical Journal*, 24 September 1955 and 11 January 1958; *Lancet*, 11 January 1958; *Nature*, 1 February 1958; *Journal of Pathology and Bacteriology*, October 1959; *Monthly Record* (South Place Ethical Society), vol. lxiv, 1959; private information; personal knowledge.]   A. HADDOW

KENNET, first BARON (1879–1960), politician and writer. [See YOUNG, EDWARD HILTON.]

KENNEY, ANNIE (1879–1953), suffragette, was born 13 September 1879 at Springhead, Yorkshire, the fifth of the twelve children of Horatio Nelson Kenney, cotton operative, and his wife, Ann Wood. A younger brother, Rowland Kenney (1882–1961), after a career in journalism which included the editorship of the *Daily Herald*, entered the Foreign Office in 1920. He was press attaché in Oslo (1939–40) and from 1941 until the end of the war adviser to the Norwegian Government in London. At the age of ten Annie Kenney began part-time work in the mills and at thirteen became a full-time card and blowing-room operative. In 1905 she met and became the lifelong disciple of (Dame) Christabel Pankhurst and her mother Emmeline Pankhurst [qq.v.], then living in Nelson Street, Manchester. Her vague aspirations inspired by the writings of Robert Blatchford [q.v.] crystallized, she was at once persuaded of the urgency of obtaining parliamentary votes for women, and in the meantime became the first woman in the textile unions to be elected to her district committee.

On 13 October 1905 Annie Kenney and Christabel Pankhurst at a Liberal rally in the Free Trade Hall, Manchester, asked

Sir Edward Grey (later Viscount Grey of Fallodon, q.v.) and the Liberal candidate (Sir) Winston Churchill if they would make woman suffrage a government measure'. Receiving no answer they stood up on their seats, called out 'Answer our question' and unfurled banners inscribed 'Votes for Women'. Hustled out by stewards they held a meeting in the street until arrested for obstruction. On refusing to pay their fines Annie Kenney was senenced to three days' imprisonment and Christabel Pankhurst to seven: the first of many sentences in the long campaign for women's suffrage.

Two months later Annie Kenney interrupted the prime minister, Campbell-Bannerman, at a Liberal rally in the Royal Albert Hall and was again ejected. She next helped Keir Hardie in his election campaign and was then sent by the Pankhursts 'to rouse London' where she was befriended by Keir Hardie, W. T. Stead [qq.v.], and the Pethick-Lawrences and other supporters of the Women's Social and Political Union. In 1906 she spent two months in Holloway Prison for trying to force Asquith to receive a deputation and by 1912 she had been several times in gaol. When Mrs. Pankhurst and the Pethick-Lawrences went to prison in that year Annie Kenney took over the organization of the union. She was closely directed by Christabel Pankhurst who had taken refuge in France. A campaign of extreme militancy was decided upon which lost the union the support of the Pethick-Lawrences. In June 1913 Annie Kenney was sentenced to eighteen months' imprisonment, went on hunger strike and was released, but under the 'Cat and Mouse Act' was liable to rearrest. She adopted various disguises to avoid detection and was once smuggled into a meeting at the London Pavilion in a hamper marked 'Marie Lloyd'. She was several times imprisoned and released, until in the autumn she became seriously ill as a result of the hunger and thirst strikes she had undertaken. She had not long recovered when Christabel Pankhurst instructed her to claim the right of sanctuary in Lambeth Palace which she did on 22 May 1914 and there urged the archbishop, Randall Davidson [q.v.], that the Church should support her cause. Removed to Holloway she went on a thirst and hunger strike which secured her release a few days later, whereupon she returned to lie down outside Lambeth Palace until she was removed. Soon afterwards the outbreak of war brought an end to the militant movement. Annie Kenney helped the Pankhursts in their war work and retired from public life after the granting of votes to women in February 1918.

With her fair hair and blazing blue eyes, Annie Kenney made a vital and moving figure on all platforms. Her eloquence and her robust sense of humour, as well as her intimate knowledge of working-class life and her experiences in prison, made her a most effective speaker. Her strength lay in her complete surrender to her cause and its leader. Her unquestioning obedience and her forgetfulness of self endowed her with a reckless courage which made her remarkable even in a movement based upon such qualities.

In 1920 Annie Kenney married James Taylor, a civil servant; they had one son. She died in Hitchin 9 July 1953.

[*The Times*, 11 July 1953; Annie Kenney, *Memories of a Militant*, 1924; E. Sylvia Pankhurst, *The Suffragette Movement*, 1931; Emmeline Pethick-Lawrence, *My Part in a Changing World*, 1938; Roger Fulford, *Votes for Women*, 1957.]   H. BURTON.

KENNINGTON, ERIC HENRI (1888–1960), artist, was born in Chelsea 12 March 1888, the younger son of Thomas Benjamin Kennington, artist, by his Swedish wife, Elise Nilla Steveni. It seemed inevitable that he should follow the calling of his father who was a portrait painter and a painter of genre subjects, an original member and first secretary of the New English Art Club. Kennington attended St. Paul's School but failed to gain distinction in any subject other than drawing; he chiefly occupied his time carving and drawing figures of navvies and costers. Art seeming his one talent, his parents sent him to the Lambeth School of Art and to the City and Guilds School, Kennington. But his first attempts to earn a living as an illustrator came to nothing and he turned to portraiture. In this he achieved a fair amount of success and even carried out some commissions in Russia which he was persuaded to visit by some relatives who lived in St. Petersburg.

He first attracted attention by his paintings of cockney types and London scenes, in a style which owed much to the influence of the Italian primitives and of Botticelli. From 1908 he exhibited at the Royal Academy and the Leicester Galleries. 'Costermongers', painted in 1913, was one of the best-known examples of his work of this period. It was purchased by

(Sir) William Nicholson [q.v.] and presented to the Musée de Luxembourg, Paris.

When war broke out in 1914 Kennington enlisted in the 13th London Regiment, the Kensingtons. He served as a private in France and Flanders but in June 1915 he was invalided out of the army. 'The Kensingtons at Levantie', one of the most outstanding paintings developed from his war experiences, was exhibited at the Goupil Gallery in 1916. It depicts ten exhausted soldiers in a battered village and, in spite of its almost immaculate realism, something of the feeling of war's drained energies is conveyed in the portraits of the individual men which include Kennington himself. Like many of his child portraits this was painted on glass. Kennington returned to the front as an official war artist and among his drawings and paintings were some of the Canadian Scottish, of the Arras–Bapaume road, Havrincourt, La Neuville, Menin Gate, the 'Victims' and the 'Victors'.

In 1920, when Kennington's war pictures were exhibited at the Alpine Club Gallery, T. E. Lawrence [q.v.] and the artist became acquainted and a friendship began which was to continue until Lawrence's death in 1935. They planned to visit the scenes of the campaigns in the Near East together, but in the event Kennington went alone. He returned with a collection of striking portraits of the Arab leaders and exhibited them at the Leicester Galleries in 1921. Some were also used to illustrate the 1926 edition of Lawrence's *Seven Pillars of Wisdom* of which Kennington was art editor.

Kennington took up sculpture almost by accident. His old division, the 24th, asked him to recommend a sculptor for a war memorial and he decided to attempt the commission himself. It resulted in the stone carving of three infantrymen erected in Battersea Park. Kennington worked on it for two years and while its composition restricts its effectiveness to one particular aspect it was better than the many trite idealizations of men in uniform executed at the time. This memorial set Kennington on his path as a sculptor. He created the massive British memorial at Soissons, France, in 1927–8 from 22 tons of stone; the carvings in the School of Hygiene and Tropical Medicine, Gower Street; the bronze memorial head of Thomas Hardy at Dorchester (1929); and the unique carved decorations on the brick façade of the Shakespeare Memorial

Theatre, Stratford on Avon (1930), the latter representing 'Love', 'Jollity' 'Treachery', 'War', and 'Life and Death' Kennington's friendship with Lawrence produced many portraits in drawings and sculpture. In 1939 he made the recumbent effigy of Lawrence for St. Martin's Wareham, of which the Tate Gallery and the Aberdeen Art Gallery later acquired versions in ciment fondu. Also in the Tate is a bronze head of Lawrence modelled partly from life and partly from drawings another cast is in the crypt of St. Paul's Cathedral.

In 1940–45 Kennington was again an official war artist. His favourite medium was now pastel and he made scores of portraits of generals and ordinary soldiers of the line, the Home Guard, the Royal Navy, and the Royal Air Force. Swiftness and strong likeness were the keynote of these drawings which reproduced very well in his books: *Drawing the R.A.F.* (1942) and *Tanks and Tank Folk* (1943) and his illustrations for John Brophy's *Britain's Home Guard* (1945).

Tall, broad-shouldered, with a cheerful friendly manner, Kennington had a far from Bohemian outlook. His love of sculpting out of doors helped to give him the healthy appearance of a gentleman farmer. His work reflects uncomplicated euphoria coupled with an idealistic viewpoint which served to interpret twentieth-century men and themes in the anachronistic idiom of the *quattrocento*. He had the constant wish to see sculpture incorporated into architecture as decoration and ornament even in modern materials.

Kennington was elected A.R.A. in 1951 and R.A. in 1959. Other works of his in the Tate Gallery include a relief carving 'Earth Child' of about 1936 (his daughter was the model) and several drawings. The Imperial War Museum has a large collection of his work.

In 1922 he married Edith Celandine, daughter of Lord Francis Cecil, naval officer; they had a son and a daughter. He died in Reading 13 April 1960. He lived at Ipsden, Oxfordshire, and was buried at Checkendon by the lovely Norman church to which he gave much time and work in restoration.

A drawing of Kennington by Sir William Rothenstein is in the Manchester City Art Gallery.

[*The Times*, 16 and 21 April 1960; *Studio*, September 1927 and August 1936; private information.]   G. S. WHITTET.

KENNY, ELIZABETH (1880–1952), nurse, was born at Kellys Gully, near Warialda, New South Wales, 20 September 1880, the fifth child of Michael Kenny, a farmer, and his wife, Mary Moore. When she was eleven the family moved to Nobby, Queensland, where she attended primary school. There is no record of her undergoing a regular course in nursing. In 1912 she established a small cottage hospital at Clifton and in 1915 enlisted in the Australian Army Nursing Service. Most of her time was spent in the Sea Transport Service and it was on the voyages back to Australia with troops suffering from encephalitis that she became interested in the treatment of paralysis. She spent many hours in passively moving the paralysed limbs.

After discharge from the army in 1919 Sister Kenny continued private nursing. It was during this time that she nursed her first case of poliomyelitis; the patient recovered completely. In 1933, with the aid of voluntary subscriptions, she opened a clinic at Townsville for the treatment of patients suffering from the various types of paralysis, most giving a history of long-standing poliomyelitis. The treatment of many of these had been neglected and Sister Kenny, by carrying out active treatment, obtained movement in muscles which she thought were paralysed but which in fact were only apparently so, due to disuse. Publicity was given to her claims that she had 'cured' these patients and public pressure forced the Government in 1934 to take over her Townsville clinic and to open clinics in three other Queensland country centres. Clinics were opened at Carshalton, England, in 1937, and Minneapolis, United States, in 1940. She demonstrated her technique in many countries, including Russia, Czechoslovakia, and Spain.

In September 1935, at the request of Sister Kenny, the Queensland Government appointed a committee which a month later was given the status of a royal commission to investigate the 'Kenny treatment'. Two of its members were orthopaedic surgeons of the so-called orthodox or traditional school. The basic differences between the two methods were that the orthodox school rigidly splinted their patients and did not commence movement until four to eight weeks after the onset of the disease, whereas Sister Kenny employed non-rigid splinting, such as the use of sandbags, and movement was commenced in the first week.

The commission condemned the Kenny method because it thought muscle injury and deformity would result, but admitted that this did not occur as frequently as expected. Other observers stated that the method was not productive of deformities. Sister Kenny's fighting spirit was aroused by statements like 'the Kenny method of treating poliomyelitis differs very little at present from orthodox treatment' and the faint praise of 'she has drawn attention to the plight of the crippled child' and 'provoked a critical and in several respects beneficial review of poliomyelitis in general'. She used the press, politicians, and the public to have her treatment accepted. Today the treatment of poliomyelitis, if not strictly Kenny, is basically Kenny. The result is that stiffness of limbs is no longer seen, thus allowing maximum muscle power recovery. Expected deformities have not materialized, the nutrition of the skin and muscles is better, and patients are much more comfortable, cheerful, and easy to nurse in the acute stage of the disease. The Kenny treatment is not a cure for poliomyelitis. That its results were better than those of orthodox methods was never acknowledged by the medical profession.

Sister Kenny always claimed she would only treat patients in association with the patient's doctor, but her aggressive manner made it nearly impossible for a doctor to work with her; yet she sincerely wanted to co-operate with the medical profession. It was to her credit that she never received payment for treating a patient. All she wanted was recognition of the fact that she had introduced a new form of treatment which would produce maximum muscle recovery and that it should be acceptable to the medical profession.

Sister Kenny received honorary degrees from Rutgers University, New Jersey, New York University, and the university of Rochester, New York, as well as many awards from various organizations. A special Act of Congress was passed in 1950 to allow her entry and exit of the United States without a visa and she had a motion picture made of her life during her lifetime. In the American Institute of Public Opinion's 1951 survey to determine which woman, living in any part of the world, was held in highest esteem by the American public, Sister Kenny headed the poll, with Mrs. Eleanor Roosevelt second. Despite all the honours she received in the United States she always refused to consider becoming an American citizen.

She returned to Queensland in 1952 suffering from an incurable illness, died at Toowoomba, 30 November 1952, and was buried at Nobby.

[*Report* of the royal commission on the investigation of infantile paralysis, 1937; W. R. Forster and E. E. Price, *Report* on an investigation of 23 cases of poliomyelitis treated by the 'Kenny System', 1938; Kenneth W. Starr, A *Report* to the Minister for Health, N.S.W., on Sister Kenny's method of the treatment of infantile paralysis, 1939; Elizabeth Kenny, *And They Shall Walk*, 1951; private information; personal knowledge.]   A. FRYBERG.

KENT, ALBERT FRANK STANLEY (1863–1958), scientist, was born 26 March 1863 at Stratford Tony, Wiltshire, the sixth son of the rector, the Rev. George Davies Kent, and his wife, Anne, daughter of William Rudgard, of Newland House, Lincoln. He was educated at Magdalen College School and Magdalen College, Oxford, where he obtained a second in physiology in 1886 and proceeded to his D.Sc. in 1915. He was elected a member of the Physiological Society in 1887 and lived to be its senior member. After demonstrating in physiology at Manchester (1887–9), Oxford (1889–91), and St. Thomas's Hospital (1891–5), he became professor of physiology at Bristol in 1899.

At St. Thomas's Hospital, Kent, who was an early worker on X-rays, helped to develop the radiological department; but it was in Bristol that he found full scope for his enthusiastic energies and organizing ability. He founded and for some eight years carried on a clinical and bacteriological research laboratory which later became the city's public health laboratory and he was for a time bacteriologist to the Royal Infirmary. He was a leading spirit in the movement which led to the formation of the university of Bristol in 1909 and he designed the university's new department of physiology.

In the war of 1914–18 Kent became interested in problems of industrial fatigue and was responsible for several government publications on the subject. He became editor-in-chief in Great Britain of the *Journal of Industrial Hygiene* and in 1918 he edited a translation of Jules Amar's *Physiology of Industrial Organization*. In that year he resigned his chair in order to organize and direct a department of industrial administration in the Manchester Municipal College of Technology.

After his retirement in 1922 Kent returned to the west country and converting one room in his house into a laboratory continued his work on cardiac physiology which he had begun at Oxford and for which he is best known. In a series of communications to the Physiological Society (1892–3) he reported his investigation of the atrioventricular bundle and its properties which forms the basis of our knowledge of the normal conduction of the heart beat and of the functional dissociation of ventricles from atria which occurs in heart-block. He retained his interest in physiological matters until ill health overtook him a year or so before he died in Bath, 30 March 1958, and he left several thousands of sections representing the work of many years.

Kent was a man of slight build who worked to high standards and drove himself hard. This produced an atmosphere of great intensity which made him appear on first acquaintance as a rather austere man, but to those who came to know him well he was very friendly. He gave the impression of enjoying himself most when in the company of one or two friends with whom he could converse freely on some topic of mutual interest. In his school and college days he was active in rowing and rifle-shooting and he became a keen photographer. He enjoyed foreign travel and frequently took his holidays on the Continent.

In 1904 Kent married Theodora (died 1957), daughter of William Henry Hobson, of Great Berkhampstead and Upper Berkeley Street, London. They had a daughter who died in childhood.

[*Nature*, 3 May 1958; personal knowledge.]
R. J. BROCKLEHURST.

KENYON, SIR FREDERIC GEORGE (1863–1952), scholar and administrator, the seventh son of John Robert Kenyon, grandson of the first Baron Kenyon [q.v.], of Pradoe, Shropshire, fellow of All Souls and Vinerian professor of law at Oxford, and his wife, Mary Eliza, daughter of Edward Hawkins, F.R.S. [q.v.], keeper of antiquities in the British Museum, was born 15 January 1863 at his maternal grandfather's house, 6 Lower Berkeley Street, London, but from the age of six was brought up at Pradoe. From his preparatory school he went as a scholar to Winchester, thence, again as a scholar, to New College, Oxford, where he obtained first classes in both classical moderations

(1883) and *literae humaniores* (1886). From schooldays he had shown an interest in biblical study, winning prizes at each school; and at Oxford, besides the Chancellor's English essay (1889), he won the Hall-Houghton junior Greek Testament prize (1885) for a study of St. Matthew's gospel.

Kenyon obtained a fellowship at Magdalen in 1888 and in the next year entered the British Museum as an assistant in the department of manuscripts. Shortly afterwards he began to catalogue its collection of Greek papyri, and while he was thus engaged the museum made the remarkable acquisition of papyri which included Aristotle's treatise on the Athenian constitution, the mimes of Herodas, part of the speech of Hyperides against Philippides, a grammatical work by Tryphon, and a long medical treatise by an unknown author, besides known works of Demosthenes, Isocrates, and Homer. Kenyon's publication of the Aristotle (1891, 3rd and revised ed. 1892) brought him honorary doctorates at Durham and Halle and his election in 1900 as corresponding member of the Berlin Academy. In 1891 he published an English translation, and he edited the Greek text for the Berlin Academy's *Supplementum Aristotelicum* (1903) and for the Oxford Classical Texts (1920). The translation appeared in the Oxford translation of Aristotle's works (1920). The other literary papyri, except the medical treatise (copied by Kenyon, edited by Diels), were published or collated in *Classical Texts from Papyri in the British Museum* (1891). In 1896 the museum acquired the lost epinician odes and dithyrambs of Bacchylides, which Kenyon edited in 1897. An essay which won him the Conington prize at Oxford in 1897 was expanded into a volume, *The Palæography of Greek Papyri* (1899). His work on documentary papyri produced volumes i (1893) and ii (1898) of *Greek Papyri in the British Museum*; in volume iii (1907) he was assisted by a junior colleague. For the Oxford Classical Texts he edited all the extant works of Hyperides (1907).

Meanwhile he did much other work, official and private, including the cataloguing of the Hardwicke papers and many manuscripts of the Stowe and Royal collections. In 1895 appeared *Our Bible and the Ancient Manuscripts*, a valuable handbook which ran into several editions. This led the firm of Macmillan to commission his *Handbook to the Textual Criticism*

of the New Testament (1901). His *Facsimiles of Biblical Manuscripts in the British Museum* appeared officially in 1900. An interest in the Brownings dating from schooldays inspired several volumes, beginning with *The Brownings for the Young* (1896). In 1897 appeared his editions of Mrs. Browning's letters in two volumes and her poetical works in a companion volume to the two-volume edition of Browning's poems (1896) in which he had written brief notes to *The Ring and the Book*. Other work on the Brownings included the article in the *Times Literary Supplement* for the centenary of their marriage in 1946.

In 1898 Kenyon was promoted assistant keeper of manuscripts and in 1909 succeeded Sir Edward Maunde Thompson (whose notice he contributed to this Dictionary) as director of the museum, an office he held until 1930. He certainly ranks among the greatest directors. He was at once a scholar and an able administrator, possessing a legal mind which gave him a remarkable grasp of essentials and a judicial temper immune to personal bias; and, scholar though he was, he realized fully the need, in a national institution, to cater for a less instructed public. The antithesis of the pedantic specialist, he did much, including the introduction of guide lecturers and picture postcards, to stimulate popular interest in the collections. His wide interests made him an ideal head of what is both a library and a museum.

Official duties left little time for scholarly work, but this did not wholly cease, and he was active in many spheres. Not among the original fellows, he had a hand in the foundation of the British Academy in 1901 and became a fellow in 1903, a member of council in 1906, president, 1917–21, and in 1930 succeeded Sir Israel Gollancz [q.v.] as secretary, retiring in 1949; he was honorary treasurer, 1940–50, and an honorary fellow, 1950. After retiring he wrote *The British Academy: The First Fifty Years* (1952). He was an active member of the Territorial Army, joining in 1899 the Inns of Court Corps, in which he received a commission in 1906 (captain 1912, lieutenant-colonel 1917); he went to France in 1914 but was recalled at the request of the trustees. From 1917 he served on the Imperial War Graves Commission, visiting cemeteries in France and the Near East. He served on the Council for Humanistic Studies, was vice-president of the Hellenic Society (president 1919–24), vice-president of the Roman Society, and in 1913 president of the Classical Association. After the war he was a member of the University Grants Committee, and was closely associated from its foundation with the National Central Library. He was a fellow of Winchester College from 1904, and warden 1925–30. In 1926 he was nominated a fellow, *honoris causa*, of the Society of Antiquaries and was president, 1934–9.

His retirement in 1930 enabled Kenyon to return full time to scholarly work, and the opportune acquisition by (Sir) Chester Beatty of a valuable collection of biblical papyri, which Kenyon was asked to edit, provided the material. Hence arose also several other volumes, including *Books and Readers in Ancient Greece and Rome* (1932), *Recent Developments in the Textual Criticism of the Greek Bible* (1933), and *The Text of the Greek Bible: A Student's Handbook* (1937).

Kenyon married in 1891 Amy (died 1938), daughter of Rowland Hunt, of Boreatton Park, Shropshire. By her he had two daughters, the elder of whom, Kathleen Mary, became a well-known archaeologist, and principal of St. Hugh's College, Oxford, in 1962. Kenyon was often criticized as cold and remote from human contacts, but this was only in part true. His reserved manner, due partly to a certain shyness in personal matters, partly to a legal temperament which would have made him an ideal Chancery judge, hid much genuine kindness, never forgotten by those who benefited by it, and, despite his reserve, he could expand on occasion. He never allowed personal feeling to influence his official conduct or to interfere with his austere sense of duty, and his judicial temper and discriminating judgement made him an admirable chairman of committees. A corresponding member of many foreign academies and the recipient of numerous honorary degrees, he was appointed C.B. in 1911, K.C.B. in 1912 and in 1925 G.B.E.; in 1918 he was appointed gentleman usher of the purple rod in the latter order. He was an honorary fellow of both Magdalen and New College. He died 23 August 1952 at Oxted. The British Academy has a pencil drawing by Augustus John; a bronze bust by J. A. Stevenson stands in the board-room of the British Museum.

[A manuscript memoir, *Autobiographica*; Sir H. I. Bell in *Proceedings* of the British Academy, vol. xxxviii, 1952; personal knowledge.]   H. I. BELL.

KERR, ARCHIBALD JOHN KERR CLARK, BARON INVERCHAPEL (1882–1951), diplomatist. [See CLARK KERR.]

KERR, SIR JOHN GRAHAM (1869–1957), zoologist, born at Rowley Lodge Arkley, Barnet, 18 September 1869, was the only son of James Kerr, a former principal of Hoogly College, Calcutta, and his wife, Sybella Graham, of Hollows Dumfriesshire. He was third in a family of four but two of his sisters died in infancy. Graham Kerr, as he was generally known, went to the Royal High School Edinburgh, and subsequently to the university of Edinburgh. He first studied mathematics and philosophy but later joined the medical faculty. Whilst still a medical student he interrupted his studies to join an Argentine expedition for the survey of the Pilcomayo from the Paraná to the frontiers of Bolivia, under Captain Juan Page. The account of this famous expedition (1889–91), *A Naturalist in the Gran Chaco*, was not published until 1950. During this expedition he was engaged in the study of general natural history and especially ornithology, and many new species were collected, but as the result of an accident most of the collections were lost. His field notes showed that even at this early age he was not only an observer and naturalist of exceptional ability, but also a man of resource, courage, and endurance above the ordinary.

Returning to England in 1891 he entered Christ's College, Cambridge, and obtained first class honours in both parts of the natural sciences tripos (1894–6). At the same time he was making preparations for a second expedition to Paraguay with the main object of studying and collecting the lung-fish, *Lepidosiren*. He was accompanied on this second expedition (1896–7) by J. S. Budgett and their collections and also those of three subsequent expeditions to the Chaco region are preserved at the university of Glasgow. On his return Graham Kerr was appointed demonstrator in animal morphology (1897–1902) at Cambridge and was a fellow of Christ's (1898–1904). In 1902 he was appointed regius professor of zoology at Glasgow where he remained until 1935. Throughout his professorship he was specially interested in the teaching of medical students and his lectures were famous. The approach was largely morphological and embryological and is embodied in his *Zoology for Medical Students* (1921); *Evolution* (1926); and *An Introduction to*

Zoology (1929). Apart from his heavy teaching and administrative duties he carried on with research and a whole series of papers on Dipnoan embryology and other subjects was published from his department. He also wrote volume ii, *Vertebrata*, of the *Textbook of Embryology with the Exception of Mammalia* (1919).

In university affairs Graham Kerr took a very active part and was a member of the court from 1913 to 1921, and served on the governing bodies of various other institutions. He was particularly interested in marine biology and was mainly responsible for the foundation of the temporary marine station at Rothesay. He was president of the Scottish Marine Biological Association (1942-9) and devoted much time to the development of Millport. He was a member of the advisory committee on fishery research from its foundation in 1919 and chairman in 1942-9.

He was also concerned in the development of general scientific activities and especially natural history in Scotland. He was elected F.R.S. in 1909 and served on the council of the Society (1920-22, 1936-8), and was vice-president (1937-8). He was also president of the Royal Physical Society of Edinburgh (1906-9); of the Royal Philosophical Society of Glasgow (1925-8); and vice-president and Neill prizewinner (1904) of the Royal Society of Edinburgh. He served for many years on the council of the British Association and was president of the zoology section at the Oxford meeting in 1926. He was knighted in 1939 and other recognitions included the honorary LL.D. of Edinburgh (1935) and St. Andrews (1950); honorary fellowship of Christ's College, Cambridge (1935); the Linnean gold medal (1955); and associate membership of the Royal Academy of Belgium (1946).

Graham Kerr's research work was determined mainly by the general atmosphere of the Cambridge school of zoology which at that time was predominantly morphological. Apart from earlier taxonomic work he started with a study of the anatomy of *Nautilus* which was of importance in assessing the relations of the Cephalopoda to other Mollusca. His later work on the lower vertebrates and especially *Lepidosiren* and other Dipnoi led him to abandon the generally accepted view that the legs of land vertebrates had evolved out of the paired fins of fishes. He considered that the methods of movement of vertebrates supported the theory that the simple styliform limb diverged along two lines, one leading to the development of paired fins, the other to the development of jointed limbs. One subject in which he took a special interest was the application of correct biological principles in working out a system of camouflage and on the outbreak of war in 1914 he wrote to the Admiralty advocating the use of obliterative shading and disruption to render ships less conspicuous. This suggestion was eventually adopted and more than 5,000 ships treated in this way; it was used almost universally during the war of 1939-45.

Graham Kerr had a high sense of public duty and was a strong advocate of the value of a biological training. He gradually took a more active interest in politics and in 1935 was elected member of Parliament for the Scottish Universities. He then resigned his chair and went to live at Barley, near Royston in Hertfordshire, where he spent the remainder of his life. He was a very regular attender at the House of Commons, served on various committees and for a time was chairman of the parliamentary scientific committee. He remained a member until 1950 when university seats were abolished. He died at Barley 21 April 1957.

Graham Kerr was almost the last survivor of the famous zoologists of the nineteenth century, for the most part widely travelled, good naturalists, with an almost encyclopedic knowledge of their subject. His output of zoological work was very considerable but in later years his many public duties restricted his scientific activities.

He married first, in 1903, Elizabeth Mary (died 1934), a first cousin, daughter of Thomas Kerr, writer to the signet, by whom he had two sons and one daughter; secondly, in 1936, Isobel, daughter of A. Dunn Macindoe and widow of Alan Clapperton, solicitor.

A posthumous portrait by Bernard Adams and a charcoal drawing by Laura Anning Bell are in the possession of the family. There is an anonymous oil portrait in the department of zoology, university of Glasgow.

[Edward Hindle in *Biographical Memoirs of Fellows of the Royal Society*, vol. iv, 1958; private information; personal knowledge.]

EDWARD HINDLE.

KERR, (JOHN MARTIN) MUNRO (1868-1960), obstetrician and gynaecologist, was born in Glasgow 5 December 1868, the son of George Munro Kerr, a ship and insurance broker, and his wife, Jessie Elizabeth Martin. His education was at Glasgow Academy and University where he graduated in 1890, obtaining the degrees of M.B., C.M. and (in 1909) M.D. He later studied in Berlin, Jena, and Dublin, and on his return in 1894 was appointed assistant to the regius professor of midwifery and diseases of women in the university of Glasgow. In 1910 he was elected to a professorship in the Andersonian College of Medicine, and the following year was appointed to the Muirhead chair of obstetrics and gynaecology in the university of Glasgow. Later (1927) he was translated to the regius chair in those subjects, in which he continued until his retirement in 1934. During this period he held many important positions in Glasgow hospitals and was for a time a member of the board of governors of the Glasgow Samaritan Hospital.

Munro Kerr was a foundation fellow and vice-president of the British (later Royal) College of Obstetricians and Gynaecologists. Amongst other important positions he was a one-time president of the Faculty of Physicians and Surgeons of Glasgow, and president of the section of obstetrics and gynaecology of the Royal Society of Medicine. Among honours bestowed on him was the honorary LL.D. of Glasgow (1935) and the first Blair-Bell medal to be awarded by the Royal Society of Medicine (1950). Many medical societies in this and other countries, including the American Gynaecological Society, elected him to their honorary fellowship.

Munro Kerr's early training gave him fluency in many languages, and throughout his long life he acquired an almost encyclopedic knowledge of medical literature. His natural charm of manner combined with strength of character made him a most persuasive teacher; and his easy, conversational style gave his written words added interest and force. Chief among his many publications were *Operative Midwifery* (1908); *Clinical and Operative Gynaecology* (1922); *Maternal Mortality and Morbidity* (1933); and, with colleagues in Glasgow and Edinburgh, the *Combined Textbook of Obstetrics and Gynaecology* (1923). He was an acknowledged leader of British obstetrics during the first half of this century, bridging the days when obstetrical practice was relatively primitive to more modern times with a maternal mortality rate reduced to less than one-tenth of its previous figure. He initiated or sponsored many of the

innovations during this period; in particular, his name is associated with certain improvements in the technique of Caesarean section whereby that operation became decidedly safer; in the United States it is often referred to as the Kerr operation.

In 1899 he married Emelia Andrewina Elizabeth (died 1957), daughter of August Johanson of Gothenburg, by whom he had one son and three daughters. He died in Canterbury 7 October 1960. An excellent portrait by Simon Elwes hangs in the Royal College of Obstetricians and Gynaecologists in London.

[*Journal of Obstetrics and Gynaecology of the British Commonwealth*, vol. lxviii, 1961; private information; personal knowledge.]

CHASSAR MOIR.

KETÈLBEY, ALBERT WILLIAM (1875–1959), composer, was born 9 August 1875 in Aston Manor, Birmingham, the son of George Henry Ketèlbey, engraver, and his wife, Sarah Ann Aston. As a young boy he showed a remarkable talent for music and proficiency on the piano. At the age of eleven he composed a piano sonata which he performed publicly at the Worcester town hall and which earned in later years the praise of Sir Edward Elgar [q.v.]. Realizing the boy's promise his parents allowed him, after preliminary study in Birmingham, to compete for a scholarship at Trinity College, London. He came out many marks above the other entrants and at the age of thirteen was installed at the college as Queen Victoria scholar for composition. At the age of sixteen he was appointed organist of St. John's church, Wimbledon, and while there continued his composition studies.

After four years of organist's work, carried on mostly while still a student, Ketèlbey went on tour as conductor of a light opera company and at the age of twenty-two he was appointed musical director of the Vaudeville Theatre in the Strand. Although Ketèlbey's most notable work was in the sphere of light music, he also composed some serious music, including a quintet for wood-wind and piano, which won the Sir Michael Costa prize; a string quartet; an overture for full orchestra; a suite for orchestra; and a Concertstück for solo piano and orchestra; all of which had London performances.

But it was with the publication of pieces like 'Phantom Melody' (which won a prize offered by Van Biene), 'In a Monastery Garden', 'In a Persian Market', 'Sanctuary of the Heart', that Ketèlbey came into his own during the twenties as foremost British light composer of his day. To his music he brought the capacity to invent popular melodies with a character of their own. He was well equipped to write for the orchestra (he could play the cello, clarinet, oboe, and horn) and his orchestrations are colourful and well balanced. In Ketèlbey's day light music tended to be picturesque and romantic and it was performed principally in the palm courts of luxury hotels, in cafés and liners, and in the silent cinema. Most of his pieces have a programme-synopsis.

He was particularly successful as a composer of 'atmospheric' music specially written to accompany silent films, a highly profitable source of income in the days when every cinema of pretension employed a 'live' orchestra. His pieces appeared in the 'Loose Leaf Film Play Music Series' and included such titles as 'Dramatic Agitato', 'Amaryllis' (is suitable for use in dainty, fickle scenes), 'Mystery' (greatly in favour for uncanny and weird picturizations), 'Agitato Furioso' (famous for its excellence in playing to riots, storms, wars, etc.).

Other works by Ketèlbey were the concert pieces: 'Suite Romantique', 'Cockney Suite', and 'Chal Romano' overture; a comic opera, *The Wonder Worker*; and in lighter vein 'Gallantry', 'Wedgwood Blue', 'In the Moonlight', and 'Souvenir de Tendresse'.

His highly successful compositions enabled Ketèlbey, one of whose pseudonyms was Anton Vodorinski, to spend most of his later years in retirement in the Isle of Wight. He died at Cowes 26 November 1959.

After the death of his first wife, Charlotte Curzon, Ketèlbey married, in 1948, Mabel Maud, widow of L. S. Pritchett. He had no children.

[Private information; personal knowledge.]
MARK H. LUBBOCK.

KHAN SAHIB (1883–1958), Indian politician, was born in 1883 in the village of Utmanzai in the Peshawar district where his father, Khan Bahram Khan, was an influential Muhammadzai landowner. With his younger brother, Khan Abdul Ghaffar Khan, who later became known as 'the Frontier Gandhi', he was educated at the Peshawar government high school and mission college; with a very promising academic record he proceeded to Britain to study medicine. He qualified in 1917; worked for a time at St. Thomas's Hospital; married as his second wife an English lady; then sat successfully for the Indian Medical Service and returned to India. In 1920 he resigned, with the rank of captain, and set up in private practice in Nowshera.

The exclusion of the North-West Frontier Province from the benefits of the constitutional reforms of 1920 saw a new birth of political consciousness among the Pathans. Abdul Ghaffar Khan, who had kept to the traditional ways of the Pathan tribesman and had become the most outstanding personality in the province, became the leader of the Khudai Khidmatgar 'Servants of God' organization, better known as the Red Shirts. It was not long before Khan Sahib, who had made friends with Jawaharlal Nehru in London and through him had come under the influence of M. K. Gandhi [q.v.], decided to abandon medicine and join his brother. The alliance between the fanatically Moslem Pathans and the Hindu-dominated Congress Party was a development of the greatest political importance which only the Khan brothers could have brought about.

Frequent clashes between the Red Shirts and the Government led to the organization's being declared illegal in 1931 and to the arrest and imprisonment of both brothers. They were then externed from the province for some years. A considerable part of his exile was spent by Khan Sahib at Gandhi's headquarters in the Central Provinces. The agitation for political advance in the North-West Frontier was, however, successful and in 1932 it was raised to the status of a governor's province. It was not until 1937 that Congress agreed to accept office and in that year Khan Sahib became chief minister. His first term of office was marked by some useful measures for the economic development of the Frontier, but also by controversial legislation which alienated the sympathies of the large landowners and other conservative elements. Nevertheless his worth as an incorruptible and conscientious administrator was proved beyond question.

On the approach of war in 1939 Khan Sahib resigned office and was again placed under detention, with his brother. The resignation was against his own inclination, but was dictated by Congress. He himself was so intellectually and emotionally committed against Hitlerism and all it stood for that he would have wished to do everything in his power to further the war effort; indeed even out of office his influence with the Pathans was so powerful that the province gave little trouble to the Government during the war.

Khan Sahib returned to power as chief minister in 1945 after the Frontier Congress Party had obtained a clear electoral majority over the Moslem League. He remained in office until the transfer of power in 1947. At this period, however, he misjudged the political trend. The end to his hopes of maintaining the Congress alliance and the indivisibility of India came with the referendum of 1947, when the Pathans opted for Pakistan and Khan Sahib and his brother were swept from power. They were regarded as hostile to Pakistan and were arrested by the new Government of M. A. Jinnah [q.v.] in 1948. Abdul Ghaffar went to gaol for a considerable period while Khan Sahib remained under strict surveillance for three years. He was, however, a big enough man to realize that he had made a mistake. While his brother remained irreconcilable, he himself recognized that Pakistan had come to stay and that the cause of Pathan advancement would best be served by co-operation. Even so the Moslem League leaders were slow to forgive him and it was not until 1954 that he emerged from obscurity. In that year he was appointed minister of communications in a new coalition Government at the centre and in the following year he became chief minister of the newly integrated West Pakistan. The split with his brother, who bitterly opposed the merger, was now complete.

In the years of political turmoil which were to lead to the revolution which put President Ayub into power at the end of 1958 Khan Sahib's stature steadily grew. When the Moslem League leaders, some of whom remained inveterate in their hostility to him, defected from his coalition, he formed a new Republican Party which retained a majority, albeit a shaky one, until president's rule was imposed in West Pakistan in March 1957. In December he formed an anti-Moslem League group in the Central Assembly, and it was a measure of the general respect in which he was held that the members of all parties in this group, which outnumbered the League, pledged their support of the premiership of any person nominated by him.

In Lahore on 9 May 1958 Khan Sahib was assassinated by a petty official with a grievance. The event had no political significance but was a tragedy for Pakistan. Khan Sahib was a man of exceptional qualities. Quiet, patient, and courteous in manner, incorruptible and of deep sincerity, he had the stature of a statesman. He was loved for his warm-heartedness and integrity by his people and indeed by persons of all races with whom he came into contact.

He had two sons by his first wife, the elder of whom made some mark in politics and was for a short time a minister of the West Pakistan Government, and a son and a daughter by his English wife.

[C. F. Andrews, *The Challenge of the North-West Frontier*, 1937; Sir William Barton, *India's North-West Frontier*, 1939; private information; personal knowledge.]

F. M. INNES.

KIGGELL, SIR LAUNCELOT EDWARD (1862–1954), lieutenant-general, was born at Wilton House, Ballingarry, county Limerick, 2 October 1862, the son of Launcelot John Kiggell, of Cahara, Glin, who became a justice of the peace and a major in the South Cork Light Infantry Militia, and his wife, Meliora Emily, daughter of Edward Brown. His background and education were that of an Anglo-Irish family of modest means and he did not go to an English public school. From the Royal Military College, Sandhurst, he joined the Royal Warwickshire Regiment in 1882 and was adjutant of the 2nd battalion from 1886 to 1890. At a time when wealth and connection dominated, Kiggell diligently made his way as a career soldier in a line regiment. He passed out from the Staff College in 1894 and from 1895 to 1897 was an instructor at Sandhurst. He gained his first staff experience as deputy-assistant-adjutant-general to South-Eastern District in 1897–9 and thereafter his career lay entirely in staff appointments.

Kiggell served in South Africa throughout the Boer War, first on the staff of Sir Redvers Buller [q.v.], then for six months on the staff of headquarters at Pretoria, finally as assistant-adjutant-general, Harrismith District. After the war he held the same post in Natal. He was mentioned in dispatches and made a brevet lieutenant-colonel.

For three years from 1904 Kiggell was deputy-assistant-adjutant-general at the staff College. It was the beginning of a long association with military education at the key period when R. B. (later Viscount) Haldane [q.v.] was turning the British Army into a modern force with a brain in its new general staff. Kiggell now displayed the temper of his mind and personality: his military ideas were orthodox and plodding. In 1905 he read a paper to the Aldershot Military Society on the future shape of battle in which his prognostications were all based on distant historical examples from the Napoleonic wars or the Franco-Prussian war. He saw the battles of the next war as local affairs, with reserves within a few hours' march ready for the counter-stroke. He rested all his arguments on the examples and precepts of great commanders of the past, ignoring the lessons of the war in which he had just served or of the Russo-Japanese war then in progress. He was criticized by his audience in this sense and also for underrating the effects of modern firepower.

Further staff appointments followed: G.S.O. 1, army headquarters, 1907–9; brigadier-general in charge of administration, Scottish Command, March–October 1909; director of staff duties, War Office, 1909–13. In 1913–14 he was commandant of the Staff College. He revised *Operations of War* by Sir Edward Hamley [q.v.] for a sixth edition. In 1914 he was promoted major-general.

In the first two years of the war Kiggell was at the War Office, as director of military training, then director of home defence, finally, in November 1915, assistant to the chief of the imperial general staff. In December 1915 he became chief of the general staff to Sir Douglas (later Earl) Haig [q.v.], commander-in-chief of the British armies in France. Although Kiggell was his second choice for the post Haig recorded that he had 'the greatest confidence in him as a soldier also as a gentleman'.

Kiggell, however, had no experience of large-scale modern war in the field and his career and the tenor of his thought made him orthodox and doctrinaire. Throughout the campaigns of 1916 and 1917 it was in the intellectual climate of Kiggell's acquiescence and the optimism of John Charteris, director of military intelligence, that Haig lived. It was Kiggell who, in a fatal moment of independence, persuaded Haig to adopt the tactics of attack by successive waves on 1 July 1916 instead of by small groups as used by the Germans at Verdun. At the end of August 1917 Kiggell's hopes that the British Army could still clear the Belgian coast were even higher than Haig's. It was Kiggell who on 6 August 1917 persuaded Haig not to launch a tank offensive at Cambrai on 20 September, on the invincibly orthodox grounds that it would divide the British effort at the expense of the Passchendaele campaign. The Cambrai attack was therefore delayed until 20 November when it took place in a strategic vacuum. It was Kiggell who in October 1917 was in favour of the British pushing on to Passchendaele despite the weather and the exhaustion of the troops.

Remote from the reality of modern war Kiggell made war on paper with unimpeachable orthodoxy and lack of imagination. That he was far below the requirements of his post was well realized by Haig's army commanders. Sir Henry (later Lord) Rawlinson [q.v.] had remarked that Kiggell was 'new to the country' with 'a good deal to pick up'. Sir Hubert Gough, many years later, said that Kiggell was a yes-man, 'without initiative or decision', 'a clerk, not an executive instrument'.

After the failure of the Passchendaele campaign to produce the results hoped for in the summer of 1917 there was great political pressure on Haig to part with Kiggell and Charteris. Kiggell himself seems to have been strongly affected by a belated realization of the gulf between his paper work and the reality of the Passchendaele battlefield. Two doctors reported that he was suffering from 'nervous exhaustion owing to the very exacting nature of the work he has had to perform'. He went home at the beginning of 1918. Haig's opinion of him was as warm as ever: 'I am very loth to part with Kigg's help and sound advice . . . No one could possibly have discharged the duties of C.G.S. during the past two years of great difficulty better than Kiggell has.' To Lord Derby [q.v.] he wrote that Kiggell 'has a fine brain, very sound and practical as a soldier, very farseeing and absolutely honest and straightforward'.

Kiggell, who had been promoted lieutenant-general in 1917, was now given the post of general officer commanding and lieutenant-governor of Guernsey. He retired in 1920. For some time he helped in the compilation of the official history of the war but had to give it up owing to poor health.

583

Kiggell was appointed C.B. (1908), K.C.B. (1916), and K.C.M.G. (1918). In 1888 he married Eleanor Rose (died 1948), daughter of Colonel Spencer Field; there were three sons. He died in Felixstowe 23 February 1954.

[The Private Papers of Douglas Haig 1914–1919, ed. Robert Blake, 1952; Duff Cooper, Haig, 2 vols., 1935–6; John Terraine, Douglas Haig, the Educated Soldier, 1963; Sir Frederick Maurice, The Life of General Lord Rawlinson of Trent, 1928; B. H. Liddell Hart, Memoirs, vol. i, 1965; Transactions of the Aldershot Military Society, 1905; David Lloyd George, War Memoirs, 6 vols., 1933–6; The Times, 25 February 1954.]   CORRELLI BARNETT.

KIMMINS, DAME GRACE THYRZA (1870–1954), pioneer in work for crippled children, was born at Lewes, Sussex, 6 May 1870, the eldest of the family of four of James Hannam, cloth merchant, by his wife, Thyrza Rogers. Endowed with a powerful urge to serve the poor and suffering she started to work in the east end of London soon after leaving Wilton House School, Reading, and rapidly discovered that her special interest lay with the crippled and the handicapped. Under the influence of the famous book The Story of a Short Life by Mrs. Ewing [q.v.], and assisted by a distinguished band of helpers, she formed in 1894 the Guild of the Brave Poor Things with the motto Laetus Sorte Mea. The halt and the lame were made welcome once a week, first at the West London Mission, later at the Bermondsey Settlement, finally at the chapter house of Southwark Cathedral.

In 1897 she married Charles William Kimmins (died 1948), a scientist, and chief inspector of the education department of the London County Council (1904–23), to whom she was constantly to turn for help and advice. She realized that to improve the health of crippled children and give them the opportunity of growing into useful and happy citizens, part of the work must move to the country. Accordingly, in close collaboration with her lifelong friend, Alice Rennie, she founded a home at Chailey, Sussex, in 1903, while the Guild continued in London and spread to other parts of England. Accommodation at Chailey was unsuitable both for the seven boys who first went there and for the few girls who followed later, but for Grace Kimmins the dedicated work of a lifetime had been launched. From such a slender beginning, as yet unrecognized and with no financial support, the great idea was born of a public school of crippledom for

boys and girls at which the best of medical treatment in a healthy atmosphere, combined with education and specialized training, would bring them happiness and ensure their ability to earn a living.

Appeals for money brought generous response and willing helpers. Under the patronage of Princess Louise, Duchess of Argyll, and the presidency of A. F. Winnington-Ingram, bishop of London [qq.v.], the Heritage Craft Schools became established and by 1914 modern buildings had been built for both boys and girls, as well as the school chapel of St. Martin.

At no time in her life was Grace Kimmins's inspired vision and gift for organization more apparent than during the war of 1914–18. Realizing that a heavy demand would be made on all hospital accommodation, she moved the boys into temporary quarters and placed the main buildings at the disposal of the Government. Before long a stream of wounded men arrived, many of them shattered at the thought of future life without a limb. With great psychological insight she placed a crippled boy with a similar disability as orderly to each of them. The result was effective and immediate. A legless or armless soldier gained hope and courage within a matter of days from the sight of the cheerful youngsters around him. During the same period some six hundred raid-shocked children were housed and cared for.

By 1919 the Heritage Craft Schools were recognized as a national asset and crippled children were admitted from all parts of the United Kingdom. With tireless energy and determination Grace Kimmins appealed widely and successfully for more funds. In 1922 an extension to the surgical wing enabled the full range of orthopaedic surgery to be performed on the spot. In 1924 a school and hospital were opened at Tidemills, near Newhaven, for crippled boys who would benefit from sea air and sea-water, and flourished until the dangers of invasion in 1940 closed them. Until the outbreak of war in 1939 the Heritage Craft Schools were visited by several members of the royal family and their fame had spread to generous supporters all over the world, particularly in America. Further buildings were erected for both boys and girls and a new block was opened for the admission of small babies and toddlers. During the war special arrangements were again made for the reception of wounded men and blitzed children.

After the war conditions returned to normal and the Heritage Craft Schools by 1946 had reached their zenith. The number of children in residence had risen from seven to over five hundred and her ambition had been realized. The brilliant mind, the drive, and the vision never faded, but by now Grace Kimmins was too frail to continue as commandant and in 1948 her great work was handed over to the National Health Service. She continued to live at the Heritage and died at Haywards Heath 3 March 1954. There is a portrait of her at Chailey by Helen Gluck. She was appointed C.B.E. in 1927 and D.B.E. in 1950, and was also a dame of grace of the Order of St. John of Jerusalem. She had two sons: Lieutenant-General Sir Brian Kimmins, K.B.E., C.B., and Captain Anthony Kimmins, O.B.E., R.N., playwright, who died in 1964.　　　　　　　　　BRIAN KIMMINS.

KINDERSLEY, ROBERT MOLESWORTH, first BARON KINDERSLEY (1871–1954), banker and president of the National Savings Committee, was born at Wanstead 20 November 1871, the second son of Captain Edward Nassau Molesworth Kindersley of the 19th Regiment of Foot, and his wife, Ada Good, daughter of John Murray, solicitor, of London. Sir Richard Torin Kindersley [q.v.] was his great-uncle. He was educated at Repton School but left in 1887 when his father could no longer afford to keep him there and started work with A. F. Hills [q.v.] at the Thames Ironworks at the early age of fifteen. He became a member of the Stock Exchange in 1901 and a partner in the firm of David A. Bevan & Co. in the following year. In 1906 he joined the London branch of the international banking house of Lazard Brothers & Co. to which, either as a partner when it was a private firm, or as its chairman when in 1919 it became a limited company, he devoted the rest of his working life until he retired in 1953. He was a member of the Court of the Bank of England from 1914 until 1946 and governor of the Hudson's Bay Company from 1916 until 1925. He served as chairman of the Trade Facilities Act advisory committee (1921–5), as a member of the bankers' committee on German finance in 1922, and was senior British representative on the Dawes committee in 1924. For many years he produced and published in the *Economic Journal* an annual estimate of the oversea investments of this country which was the forerunner of official statistics on the subject. In 1946 the task was taken over by the Bank of England.

In 1916 Kindersley became first chairman of the War Savings Committee and from 1920 until 1946 he presided over the National Savings Committee. The remarkable success of the movement in these years, and most notably during the war of 1939–45 when the country saved over nine thousand million pounds, was due largely to his efforts. He had a strong and forceful character, combined with a penetrating and constructive mind and great charm. His power of work and his imaginative and creative approach to it made him a born leader. No one ever took to him a stubborn problem without finding a new light shed upon it. He had a great love for family life and liked nothing more than to have his house full of young people. The loyalty and devotion of his staff both in his office and in the National Savings Movement were the reflection of his own spirit and a solid proof of his unfailing courtesy and his great qualities of leadership at all times and in all spheres.

Kindersley was appointed K.B.E. in 1917, advanced to G.B.E. in 1920, and in 1941 created a baron in recognition of his work for national savings. He also received a number of foreign decorations and in 1928–9 was high sheriff of Sussex.

In 1896 Kindersley married Gladys Margaret (died 1968), daughter of Major-General James Pattle Beadle, R.E.; there were four sons and two daughters of the marriage. The eldest son, Lionel Nassau, was killed in action in 1917. When Kindersley died in hospital at East Grinstead, Sussex, 20 July 1954, he was succeeded by his second son, Hugh Kenyon Molesworth (born 1899), who served in the Scots Guards in both wars and followed his father as chairman of Lazard Brothers and as a member of the Court of the Bank of England. Sir William Orpen painted two portraits of Kindersley, one of which belongs to the Hudson's Bay Company, the other to the National Savings Association.

[Private information; personal knowledge.]
　　　　　　　　　BRAND.

KING, HAROLD (1887–1956), organic chemist, was born 24 February 1887 at Llanengan, Caernarvonshire, the eldest of the four children of Herbert King, and his wife, Ellen Elizabeth Hill. Both parents came from Lancashire farming families and were school teachers by profession; in

1891 they moved to Bangor where Harold King received his education, first in St. James's church school where his parents were head teachers, then in Friar's Grammar School, finally in the University College, where he had the good fortune to be a pupil of K. J. P. Orton who exercised a powerful and lasting influence, inspiring King with the love of chemistry which determined his choice of career.

After graduating with first class honours in 1908 and a period of research, King had a brief experience of analytical work with the Gas Light and Coke Company at Beckton (1911–12) as the holder of an industrial bursary awarded by the Royal Commission for the Exhibition of 1851; thence he moved in 1912 to the Wellcome Physiological Research Laboratories. This appointment, although of short duration, was of vital importance to his development, since it brought him into contact with (Sir) H. H. Dale and George Barger [q.v.] and taught him how fruitful true collaboration between biologists and chemists could be in furthering medical research. After only six months King moved again, to the Wellcome Chemical Works at Dartford where he remained until 1919. Here he received further training in organic chemical research under F. L. Pyman and also made several important contributions to problems of pharmaceutical chemistry which arose as matter of emergency during the war.

In 1919 King was appointed chemist on the staff of the Medical Research Council with special responsibility for the study of drugs. This post was tenable at the National Institute for Medical Research, Hampstead, and thus brought King again under Dale's direction. He served the Medical Research Council until his retirement in 1950, and during this period built himself an international reputation as a research worker in organic chemistry, particularly in its applications to therapy. Apart from his own experimental work he did much to keep the subject of chemotherapy in the forefront of scientific investigation.

When King began research in chemotherapy the only chemotherapeutic agent really established in medical practice was salvarsan; it was natural therefore that he should direct his first effort to the attempt to find other arsenical drugs with useful therapeutic properties; in this he had no direct success; however, he found out much about the mode of action of these compounds and his observations

were a direct pointer to the later discovery by others of British Antilewisite (BAL), the most successful known antidote to arsenical and heavy metal poisoning. He also attempted to produce more effective antimalarial drugs by modifications of the structure of the cinchona alkaloids; here again no immediate success was forthcoming but once more the work bore fruit later in the influence exercised on the vast programme of antimalarial research undertaken in the United States during the war of 1939–45. A third chemotherapeutic research, resulting in the discovery of antitrypanosomal activity in several series of diamidines and related compounds led to the development by A. J. Ewins [q.v.] in an industrial laboratory of stilbamidine, the most effective drug for the treatment of kala-azar.

If King had his full share of the disappointments which are only too common in chemotherapeutic research, he derived great satisfaction from work which led to the discovery of the methonium drugs, which themselves provided the first effective drug treatment of hypertension and which have led to further therapeutic advances of great importance. This work was a model of medical research; it began with King's classical study of tube curare from which he isolated the active principle (the alkaloid tubocurarine) and determined its constitution; from this he deduced the chemical features responsible for its muscle-relaxing properties and planned the synthesis of a series of simple compounds likely to possess similar activity; he then enlisted the collaboration of his physiological colleagues, who confirmed his prediction and in addition discovered the unexpected properties of some members of the series that gave them their value in the treatment of hypertension.

Although King was essentially an experimentalist it may well be that his name will be best remembered for a purely theoretical contribution: the revision by himself and Otto Rosenheim [q.v.] of the formulation of cholesterol and related compounds which had long been accepted on the authority of eminent German chemists. This brought clearer understanding of the chemistry of many biologically important compounds including sex hormones, adrenocortical hormones, and heart poisons, and was a scientific achievement of the first magnitude.

As a member of the staff of a research institute King was a valuable man. Quiet and retiring in disposition, and unashamedly insular in general outlook, he enjoyed the sheltered environment which such an institute can offer and in which he could spend his days almost uninterruptedly at the laboratory bench; he had no interest in teaching or administration. By nature cool and reserved in personal relationships, he was nevertheless always ready to help a colleague from his own store of knowledge; he in turn drew inspiration from his contacts with others and from his keen and knowledgeable interest in their researches, even in fields far removed from his own.

King retired before he needed to, going to live near Wimborne where he spent the last years of his life happily absorbed in his scientific hobby of amateur entomology. He died there 20 February 1956, being survived by his wife, Elsie Maud, daughter of Joseph Croft, master tailor, whom he had married in 1923, and their only child, a son.

King was elected F.R.S. in 1933 and was awarded the Hanbury medal of the Pharmaceutical Society (1941) and the Addingham gold medal of the William Hoffman Wood Trust (1952); he was appointed C.B.E. in 1950.

[Sir Charles Harington in *Biographical Memoirs of Fellows of the Royal Society*, vol. ii, 1956; personal knowledge.]

C. R. HARINGTON.

KINGDON-WARD, FRANCIS (FRANK) (1885–1958), plant collector, explorer, and author, younger child and only son of Harry Marshall Ward [q.v.], botanist, was born 6 November 1885 in Manchester where his father was lecturer in botany at the Owens College. His mother was Selina Mary Kingdon. He received his early education at St. Paul's School, went up to Christ's College, Cambridge, as a scholar, and graduated with second class honours in part i of the natural sciences tripos in 1906. In the following year he took a short-term appointment as teacher at the Shanghai Public School and in 1909 made his first exploratory journey into the interior of China. He was accompanied by an American zoologist, Malcolm P. Anderson, and they travelled to Tatsienlu in Szechwan and also reached Kansu. Kingdon-Ward made a small collection of botanical specimens on this expedition and this experience so appealed to his restless and inquiring

nature that it determined the future course of his life. He became a professional plant collector and was first commissioned in 1911 on behalf of Bees of Liverpool.

Apart from the periods of the two world wars he was constantly engaged over nearly fifty years on botanical exploration under various auspices and for various patrons. Before his second marriage in 1947 he preferred to travel alone and his financial resources were usually such that he had to live frugally and austerely on the local food. His prolonged journeys, always amongst mountains where communications were poor, were only possible because of his immense energy and endurance. He returned again and again to remote areas and undertook some twenty-five expeditions to the unexplored mountain regions where India, China, and Burma meet. Here and in the neighbouring countries he amassed huge collections and introduced to cultivation in Great Britain and America numerous attractive plants. The area is excessively rich in desirable species for gardens and Kingdon-Ward selected numbers of Rhododendrons, Primulas, Meconopsis, Gentians, and Lilies, many of which are now established in Britain and elsewhere. In the field he took great trouble to select only the best forms and by marking these while in flower he was able later in the season to collect seeds. Probably his best-known introduction is the blue poppy, *Meconopsis betonicifolia*, which is now one of the most prized garden plants. He had an excellent working knowledge of several plant groups and in the intervals between his expeditions he identified his specimens and, alone or in collaboration with specialists, described a number of new species especially of Rhododendron and Primula. His fully documented material, which is represented in the national herbaria of Britain and also in institutions overseas, revealed his keen observation of botanical detail and his understanding of plant ecology.

The problems of plant distribution posed by his field experience intrigued Kingdon-Ward and his published contributions to the study of plant geography were noteworthy. Despite objections from geologists and geographers he was firmly convinced that the axis of the Himalayan range extended eastwards from the loop of the Tsangpo across the tremendous gorge country into South-West China. This opinion was based on the observations made over many years of travel in the region, that the rain screen formed by the main range does not end at the Tsangpo Gorge but is traceable across the terrific longitudinal mountain ranges into North-West Yunnan. By this theory the rain screen acted as a barrier for north-ward or southward dispersal of plants but allowed western or eastern parallel extensions north and south of the screen. Thus a plausible explanation may be given to the striking similarities in the flora and fauna of the Himalayas and South-West China.

Kingdon-Ward was a prolific writer and contributed many articles to magazines, periodicals, and scientific journals. He wrote some twenty-five books, mostly descriptive of his expeditions and their botanical results, of which the most significant were: *The Land of the Blue Poppy* (1913), *In Farthest Burma* (1921), *The Mystery Rivers of Tibet* (1923), *The Romance of Plant Hunting* (1924), *From China to Hkamti Long* (1924), *The Riddle of the Tsangpo Gorges* (1926), *Plant Hunting on the Edge of the World* (1930), *Plant Hunting in the Wilds* (1931), *A Plant Hunter in Tibet* (1934), *The Romance of Gardening* (1935), *Plant Hunter's Paradise* (1937), *Assam Adventure* (1941), *Burma's Icy Mountains* (1949), *Plant Hunter in Manipur* (1952), *Return to the Irrawaddy* (1956). His notable expeditions which contributed so much to the geographical and botanical understanding of the regions he visited were as follows: West China, 1909-10, 1911, 1913, 1921-3; North Burma, 1914, 1919, 1926, 1930-31, 1937, 1938-9, 1942, 1953; South-East Tibet, 1924, 1933, 1935; Assam, 1927-8, 1935, 1938, 1946, 1948, 1949; French Indo-China, 1929; Thailand, 1941; East Manipur, 1948; Assam-Tibet frontier, 1950; Mount Victoria, West Burma, 1956.

Kingdon-Ward received many honours. The Royal Horticultural Society awarded him the Victoria medal of honour in 1932 and in 1934 the Veitch memorial medal for his explorations and introduction of new plants. From the Royal Geographical Society in 1930 he received its highest honour, the Founder's medal, and in 1916 and 1924 the society also awarded him the Cuthbert Peek grant. The Massachusetts Horticultural Society presented him with the George Robert White memorial medal in 1934. The Royal Scottish Geographical Society recognized his achievements with the award of the Livingstone medal in 1936. In 1952 for his services to horti-culture he received the O.B.E.

In 1923 Kingdon-Ward married Florinda Norman-Thompson, daughter of a landed proprietor in Ireland; there were two daughters of the marriage which was dissolved in 1937. In 1947 he married Jean, daughter of Sir Albert Sortain Romer Macklin, formerly puisne judge High Court, Bombay. Kingdon-Ward died in London 8 April 1958. A portrait by Miss E. M. Gregson is in the possession of the family.

[*The Times*, 10 April 1958; *Nature*, 31 May 1958; *Journal* of the Royal Horticultural Society, May 1959; E. H. M. Cox, *Plant Hunting in China*, 1945; Frank Kingdon-Ward, *Pilgrimage for Plants*, 1960; personal knowledge.]

                            G. TAYLOR.

KINNEAR, SIR NORMAN BOYD (1882-1957), ornithologist, was born in Edin-burgh 11 August 1882, the younger son of Charles George Hood Kinnear, of Drum, architect, and colonel of the Midlothian Volunteer Artillery, by his wife, Jessie Jane, daughter of Wellwood Herries Maxwell, of Munches, formerly M.P. for the stewartry of Kirkcudbright, and a grand-daughter of Sir William Jardine [q.v.]. He was educated at the Edinburgh Academy and Trinity College, Glenalmond, and subsequently went to the Duke of Rich-mond and Gordon's estate office as a pupil, and later acted as assistant in an estate office in Lanarkshire. Having since childhood been devoted to the study of natural history, particularly birds and mammals, in 1905 he became a voluntary assistant at the Royal Scottish Museum under W. Eagle Clarke where he was engaged in identifying the skin collections of birds. He accompanied Clarke on his expeditions to Fair Isle to assist in making observations on bird migration. In the spring of 1907 he made a voyage on a whaler to Greenland seas and collected natural history specimens, chiefly birds, which he presented to the Royal Scottish Museum.

In November 1907 Kinnear was ap-pointed officer-in-charge of the museum of the Bombay Natural History Society and shortly after became one of the editors of its journal. In 1911 he organized and directed a systematic survey of the mam-mals of India, Burma, and Ceylon, to provide material for a comprehensive study of the status, variation, and distribu-tion of the mammals of the 'India region'. Kinnear personally selected the areas in which the collectors should work and also assembled the large collections obtained

and provisionally identified and catalogued them before dispatch to the British
Museum in London.

On the outbreak of war Kinnear made
several attempts to join the Indian Army
in order to go on active service, but was
not permitted to do so; but he served
in the Bombay Volunteer Rifles and, in
addition, in 1915–19 acted as intelligence
officer for the Bombay Defended Port.
He was twice mentioned in dispatches.

In 1920 Kinnear returned to Britain to
become an assistant in the department of
zoology of the British Museum (Natural
History); he was appointed assistant
keeper in 1928, deputy keeper in charge
of birds in 1936, and keeper of zoology in
1945. In 1947, on the day after he had
reached the age of retirement, it was announced that he had been appointed
director of the museum, an exceptional
step, and one which was a great tribute to
his personal qualities. He was the first
ornithologist to assume this position
which he held for three years. He was
appointed C.B. in 1948 and knighted in
1950.

Kinnear joined the British Ornithologists' Union at the age of twenty and
for fifty-five years rendered notable service both to ornithology in general and
to the Union in particular. He was its
president in 1943–8 and after the war did
much to re-establish cordial relations with
ornithologists in other countries. He was
editor of the *Bulletin* of the British
Ornithologists' Club from 1925 to 1930.
He was also much interested in bird protection and was appointed a member of
the British section of the International
Council for Bird Preservation in 1935,
becoming chairman in 1947, a position
which he held until his death. He also
served on the Home Office advisory committee which drew up the proposals for the
Protection of Birds Act, 1954.

An active supporter of the National
Trust, Kinnear joined its estates committee in 1935 and the executive committee in
1942, remaining a member of both until
his death. He was a vice-president of the
Society for the Promotion of Nature
Reserves and took part in the work of the
investigation committees organized by
the society which led to the formation of
the Nature Conservancy. He was appointed
a member of the Conservancy on its
establishment in 1949 and served his full
term of office until 1955 and also served on
a number of its committees. He was a fellow of the Zoological Society of London,

for many years served on its council, and
was elected a vice-president. He was also
a fellow of the Linnean Society of London.

Most of Kinnear's published work,
which appeared chiefly in the *Ibis* and the
Journal of the Bombay Natural History
Society, dealt with birds, especially the
avifauna of the East, including central
and south Arabia, Indo-China, north-east
Burma, and south-east Tibet. He described a number of new forms in the
Bulletin of the British Ornithologists'
Club and was responsible for the zoological notes in the publications of the
Hakluyt Society. He was particularly
interested in the early ornithologists and
did much work on Cook's voyages and the
records made by his naturalists.

Kinnear's memory was phenomenal and
he could quote statements and references
with the greatest accuracy and detail, no
matter if they dated back thirty years or
more. He also made copious notes, mostly
on small pieces of paper, but writing did
not come easily to him and he was far
more inclined to place his knowledge at
the disposal of others and to help their
work to reach publication. He always took
infinite trouble and showed great courtesy
to anyone who asked his help, no matter
how young or unimportant. His retiring
nature sometimes resulted in an apparent
gruffness; he did not care for committees
and certainly disliked taking the chair,
but his great sense of duty impelled him to
undertake these tasks where his wide
knowledge and experience were only
equalled by his tact, understanding, and
ability to smooth down ruffled feelings.
Although specializing in birds, Kinnear
was a good general naturalist and was
equally interested in mammals, insects,
and plants. He enjoyed shooting and
fishing, but gardening was his greatest
hobby.

In 1913 Kinnear married Gwendolin
Beatrice Langford, daughter of William
Wright Millard, a medical practitioner in
Edinburgh, and had two daughters. He
died at his home in Wimbledon on his
seventy-fifth birthday, 11 August 1957.

[*Journal* of the Bombay Natural History
Society, December 1957; private information;
personal knowledge.]   P. BARCLAY-SMITH.

KIRK, KENNETH ESCOTT (1886–
1954), bishop of Oxford, was born 21
February 1886 in Sheffield, the eldest
child of Frank Herbert Kirk, secretary
and director of Samuel Osborn & Co. of
the Clyde Steel and Iron Works, Sheffield,

and his wife, Edith Escott. His grandfather, John Kirk, was a well-known Wesleyan Methodist minister in the neighbourhood and Kirk was baptized at the Wesley chapel, Fulwood Road, Sheffield. When he was about twelve years old his family joined the Church of England and he was subsequently brought up as an Anglican.

Kirk was educated at the Royal Grammar School, Sheffield, and St. John's College, Oxford, where he was a Casberd scholar. He took first classes in honour moderations (1906) and in *literae humaniores* (1908). In 1909 he was appointed secretary of the Student Union's organization for looking after oriental students in London. From 1910 to 1912 he was warden of the University College Hall at Ealing, and assistant to the professor of philosophy at University College, London. He was ordained deacon in 1912 and priest in 1913 and was curate of Denaby Main, Yorkshire, from 1912 to 1914. In 1913 he was awarded the senior Denyer and Johnson scholarship and in the following year made tutor of Keble College, Oxford, although the outbreak of war prevented him from coming into residence until 1919. During the war he served as a chaplain to the forces in France and Flanders, and his experiences led to the publication of his first book, *A Study of Silent Minds*, in 1918 and directed his thoughts to the subject of moral theology.

After the war he returned to Oxford, and in 1919 was elected a prize fellow of Magdalen, which office he held, together with his tutorship at Keble, until he was appointed fellow and chaplain of Trinity in 1922. In 1920 he published *Some Principles of Moral Theology*, to be followed in 1925 and 1927 by its two sequels, *Ignorance, Faith and Conformity*, and *Conscience and its Problems*. The study of moral theology which had flourished in England in the seventeenth century had in the two succeeding centuries been much neglected, and Kirk's three books were pioneer works which have done much to revive interest in the subject in the Church of England. He became reader in moral theology in 1927 and was the obvious successor to R. L. Ottley as regius professor of moral and pastoral theology and canon of Christ Church, to which he was appointed in 1933.

In 1928 Kirk delivered the Bampton lectures which were published in 1931 under the title *The Vision of God*. This is generally considered his greatest book and

is a work of immensely wide learning and insight. He also contributed essays on subjects of dogmatic theology to the volumes *Essays Catholic and Critical* (1926) and *Essays on the Trinity and the Incarnation* (1928), and in 1935 published a volume of highly characteristic sermons under the title of *The Fourth River*. He took the degrees of B.D. in 1922 and D.D. in 1926.

In addition to his academic distinctions Kirk was an active and influential tutor and college chaplain, and also played an important part in university administration. In 1921 he was appointed controller of lodgings in the university and in the course of the next few years he built up this office into a system of supervising and licensing lodgings which was of great benefit to the undergraduates.

Kirk's distinction and many-sided abilities made him an obvious candidate for a bishopric, and on the resignation of T. B. Strong [q.v.] in 1937 he was appointed bishop of Oxford. He was consecrated in St. Paul's Cathedral on 30 November and enthroned at Christ Church on 8 December. The exceptionally large diocese taxed his powers of administration to the full. He decided that it ought to be worked on the basis of the three counties of Oxfordshire, Buckinghamshire, and Berkshire which composed it. Each of these counties already constituted an archdeaconry, and the archdeacon of Buckingham was bishop suffragan of Buckingham, while the archdeacon of Oxford was also in episcopal orders. So that permanent episcopal care might be provided for each of the three counties Kirk secured the revival of the suffragan bishopric of Reading for Berkshire and the creation of a new suffragan see of Dorchester for Oxfordshire. Kirk had inherited to the full his father's business ability and he gave particular attention to the finances of the diocese. He transferred the whole administration of the diocese to Oxford from Cuddesdon and never himself took up residence there.

As bishop of Oxford he managed to retain a much closer touch with the life of the university than had any of his recent predecessors. He was a delegate of the University Press, honorary fellow of St. John's and Trinity colleges, president of the Oxford University Church Union and a much sought-after preacher in the university church, college chapels, and other churches frequented by undergraduates. During the latter part of his episcopate he held every term a simple and informal confirmation service for members of the university, at which his characteristically original and carefully thought out addresses always made a deep impression. Shortly before becoming a bishop he published a valuable *Commentary on the Epistle to the Romans* (1937); in 1939 he edited and contributed to the volume called *The Study of Theology*; and in 1946 he published a small book on the *Church Dedications of the Oxford Diocese*.

As well as being an administrator and a figure in academic life Kirk was very much a pastoral bishop. He had a singular gift for adapting his style of preaching to widely differing congregations; at parochial gatherings he made a point of speaking individually to as many as he could, and all to whom he spoke felt that he was interested in them as persons. He liked to attend clerical gatherings not as bishop of Oxford but as Dr. Kirk who had come to discuss common problems with fellow priests. No bishop was more free of pompousness and yet he was never without great personal dignity. Throughout the whole diocese he inspired a deep affection which manifested itself to a remarkable degree after his death.

In the Church at large Kirk's episcopate was remarkable in a number of ways. In 1938 he became chairman of the Advisory Council on Religious Communities in the Church of England which had been set up a few years before to help the bishops and the communities in a variety of problems which arose in their relationships. In addition he was visitor of thirteen communities and gained an intimate knowledge of their life. He was trusted by the communities as probably no bishop before him, and he was able to perform a unique work of quietly integrating them into the general life of the Church of England. The *Directory of the Religious Life* which was first published in 1943 was compiled under his immediate supervision.

Kirk's connection with the Woodard Schools dated from 1924, and he had shown his usefulness to such an extent that early in 1937, before his nomination as bishop of Oxford, he was elected provost of the southern division. He felt obliged, on account of other work, to resign this office in 1944, but two years later he became the first president of the entire Woodard Corporation (the Corporation of SS. Mary and Nicholas). His knowledge of the schools was close and intimate and he did much to place the finances of the corporation on a sound basis. In 1937 he wrote *The Story of the Woodard Schools* (new ed. 1952).

Theologically Kirk had always been associated with the Anglo-Catholic wing of the Church and, although his administration of the diocese was wholly free from partisanship and he was trusted and served by Anglo-Catholics and Evangelicals alike, it was inevitable that in the Church at large he should be regarded by high churchmen as their natural leader. Current schemes of reunion (particularly the South India scheme) led him into the position of spokesman for Anglo-Catholics in Convocation and at the 1948 Lambeth Conference. The volume *The Apostolic Ministry* edited and contributed to by him in 1946 was concerned very much with this subject. He took a strict view in matters relating to divorce and his position was expounded in a book *Marriage and Divorce* originally published in 1933 but completely revised in 1948 in the light of developments in Church and State and of his own experience as a bishop.

In 1921 Kirk married Beatrice Caynton Yonge (died 1934), daughter of Francis Reynolds Yonge Radcliffe, county court judge of the Oxfordshire circuit. They had three daughters and two sons. The elder son, Peter Michael, was first elected a Conservative member of Parliament in 1955.

Kirk died in Oxford 8 June 1954. A portrait by Harold Knight is in the Diocesan Church House, North Hinksey.

[E. W. Kemp, *The Life and Letters of Kenneth Escott Kirk*, 1959; private information; personal knowledge.]   ERIC KEMP.

KIRKWOOD, DAVID, first BARON KIRKWOOD (1872–1955), politician, was born at Parkhead, then a suburb of the city of Glasgow, 8 July 1872, the only surviving son of John Kirkwood and his wife, Jean, daughter of William Brown. His father was a labourer who rose to be winding-master in a weaving mill at a wage of 28s. a week and was a descendant of a family of farm workers who had migrated a century earlier from the hamlet of Gartmore in Perthshire on the ancestral estate of R. B. Cunninghame Graham [q.v.]. Kirkwood was compelled through straitened family circumstances to leave school (where his only noteworthy prize was one for Bible knowledge) at the age of twelve and take employment as a message boy at a weekly wage of 3s. 6d. From his first post he was speedily dismissed when a visiting factory inspector discovered his age, but he continued in similar employment until at the age of fourteen he was apprenticed as an engineer, working from 6 a.m. to 5.30 p.m. for a weekly wage of 5s. At twenty he became a member of the Amalgamated Society of Engineers. Three years later, when working at Parkhead Forge, controlled by William Beardmore (later Lord Invernairn, q.v.), he took part in a strike against what was claimed to be a dilution of labour when unskilled men, paid at labourers' rates, were put on to skilled engineers' work. At the conclusion of the strike, when the engineers were defeated, Kirkwood and one other were informed that they would never again be allowed inside the work gates. Nevertheless he returned there in 1910, having in the meantime worked at John Brown's on Clydebank, at the Mount Vernon Steel Works where he became engineer foreman, and elsewhere. In his spare time he had attended evening classes, temperance society meetings, and had read omnivorously in romantic Scots history and ballad literature. By 1910 he was taking a prominent part in trade-union affairs, and it was not long before he became convener of shop stewards at Parkhead Forge. He joined the Socialist Labour Party but at the outbreak of the war of 1914–18 he left it for the Independent Labour Party and the Union of Democratic Control, coming decisively under the influence of Ramsay MacDonald and John Wheatley [qq.v.].

In 1915 Kirkwood led an agitation to get the Clyde engineers an increase of 2d. per hour on the weekly wage of 38s. 3d., although he worked hard to avoid the ensuing strike on the ground that the nation was at war and that their brothers were in the trenches and short of guns and at once accepted an offer of 1d. an hour. But it was his outspoken antagonism to the Munitions Act, which outraged his sense of personal freedom, that brought him into national prominence. Lloyd George went to Glasgow to charm Kirkwood and his associates, without avail. About that time fuel was being added to the fire of the engineers' discontent by a widespread raising of house rents; property owners were taking advantage of the competition for accommodation for munition workers, and there were dramatic instances of soldiers' wives being evicted for inability to pay the increased rents. Kirkwood threw himself into the storm of protest. He always denied that he

had ever urged a strike of munition workers, but the Government used its powers under the Defence of the Realm Act and in March 1916 deported him to Edinburgh as a trouble maker; there for fourteen months he remained, persistently and indignantly refusing to sign any document promising 'good behaviour' as a condition of his return to the Clyde. Finally the order was revoked without Kirkwood's signing any document, and through the intervention of (Sir) Winston Churchill Kirkwood was employed as a manager at Beardmore's Mile-End shell factory. There he operated a bonus for production system: and doubled the output of his department.

At the general election of 1918 he stood for the Dumbarton Burghs constituency (Dumbarton and Clydebank) but was defeated. On 31 January 1919 there was a massed demonstration in front of the municipal buildings which culminated in a riot. Kirkwood left the buildings to appeal for order and restraint but in the mêlée he was struck by a police baton and rendered unconscious; a press photograph of the incident ensured his acquittal of complicity in a subsequent trial for sedition. Later in the year he entered Glasgow corporation as a representative of the Mile-End ward, having a majority of over 3,000 on a poll of 7,300. In the corporation he distinguished himself chiefly in housing problems and was a keen advocate of municipal housing financed by interest-free capital lent by the national Treasury.

In 1922, with a majority of 7,380, Kirkwood was elected member of Parliament for Dumbarton Burghs, a constituency which he represented until an electoral area rearrangement in 1950, when he represented East Dunbartonshire. He was perhaps the most vehement of all the Clydesiders in Parliament and twice he was suspended; in March 1925, when his suspension was clearly due to a misunderstanding on the part of the chairman of committees, the entire Opposition, led by Ramsay MacDonald, walked out in protest; and a few days later the suspension was withdrawn on the motion of Stanley Baldwin. In November 1937 Kirkwood asked a question about allowances for the unemployed, and being somewhat curtly referred to previous replies he lost his temper, and in the ensuing turmoil insulted the Speaker. He was a keen member of the Empire Parliamentary Association and in 1928 was a member of its delegation which toured

Canada. He promoted a bill in July 1924 to have the Stone of Destiny restored to Scotland, getting a first reading, after a division, for his bill, but that was the end of it.

Always the sentimental and romantic Scot, ready with quotations from the Bible, Robert Burns, and Scots proverbs, and with a great sense of humour, he toured the country as a propagandist for socialism. A sturdy fighter, he yet made friends in all the political parties, and the supreme achievement of his public career came when, almost unaided, he secured a resumption of work on the Cunarder, the *Queen Mary*, which had stood half-finished on the stocks, a gaunt reminder of the great depression on Clydeside. He was sworn of the Privy Council in 1948, was given the freedom of Clydebank in 1951, and in the same year was created a baron. In the House of Lords he made one forceful and noteworthy plea (7 May 1952) that the working people should be given 'wise, enthusiastic leadership and, above all, unselfish example' by their employers.

In 1899 Kirkwood married Elizabeth (died 1956), daughter of Robert Smith, of Parkhead; they had four sons and two daughters. He died in Glasgow 16 April 1955 and was succeeded in his title by his third and elder surviving son, David (1903–1970).

[David Kirkwood, *My Life of Revolt*, 1935; *Glasgow Herald*, 18 April 1955; personal knowledge.]   THOMAS JOHNSTON.

KLEIN, MELANIE (1882–1960), psychoanalyst, was born 30 March 1882, in Vienna, the youngest of four children. Her father, Moritz Reizes, doctor of medicine, Jewish scholar, and linguist, came from a rigidly orthodox family of Polish nationality. Her mother, Libusa Deutsch, of Deutsch-Kreuz in the province of Burgenland (then in Hungary), came of a more liberal-minded background; her maternal grandfather was a rabbi known for his tolerance and his progressive views.

She determined to study medicine while still at the lycée, and in spite of straitened circumstances managed to transfer to the gymnasium where her aptitude for learning and her capacity for enjoying life and friendship found full scope. But her studies were cut short, partly by financial difficulties, but chiefly because of her early marriage to a second cousin, Arthur Stephan Klein, a chemical engineer, of Ruzomberok (then in Slo-

vakia). His father, Jacob Klein, owned a paper mill and a small bank.

They had a daughter (later Melitta Schmideberg, an analyst) and two sons. By the time her younger son was born they were living in Budapest where they stayed until 1919. Her husband's work took them abroad, and for a short time she adopted Swedish nationality. In 1923 their marriage ended in divorce.

While in Budapest, Melanie Klein, through reading Freud's work, became interested in psycho-analysis and was herself analysed by Sandor Ferenczi, who was the first to bring out her gift for child analysis, then an almost untried field. She helped him in his children's clinic; and in 1919 she read her first paper to the Hungarian Psycho-Analytical Society, 'The Development of a Child' (*International Journal of Psycho-Analysis*, 1921, *Contributions to Psycho-Analysis*, 1948), on the strength of which she was made a full member. (In those early days there was no official training for psycho-analysts.)

At the suggestion of Karl Abraham, from whom she had more analysis, and who was the chief influence in her work, she went to Berlin in 1921 and began to practise in the Berlin Psycho-Analytical Society. Although some work had been done on children over the age of six, almost nothing was known about the mental life of younger children: Freud's conclusions were drawn from the analysis of adults. Her first patient was under three years old. She had to evolve a technique which would give her access to the deeper layers of the child mind, which she did by providing her patients with small toys and interpreting their free play and spontaneous associations in the same way that verbal associations are interpreted in adult analysis. Her play-technique, in a modified form, is still standard practice in a number of child guidance clinics. Her experience with children was of great use to her when she began analysing adults.

In 1925, at the invitation of Ernest Jones [q.v.], she gave six lectures on child development to the British Psycho-Analytical Society; and in 1926 she returned with her younger son to London, where she spent the rest of her long, hard-working, and immensely productive life. She was naturalized in 1934.

Both her methods and her findings aroused intense opposition and, among her colleagues, equally strong support. Controversy, arising in the Viennese

Society but soon spreading throughout the psycho-analytic world, centred round her unmodified application of Freudian techniques to child analysis—she would give neither advice, reassurance, nor any educational guidance; also her findings were found shocking, and therefore unbelievable, even by those who had come to accept Freud's views on child sexuality. Many analysts consider that she attributed to the infant mind complicated processes for which there is insufficient evidence. The debate still continues, although without the degree of personal bitterness with which it was carried on during her lifetime.

Her detailed knowledge of early development enabled her to confirm directly what Freud had inferred from adult material; she extended his work to cover infant development, and pushed back her own observations and theories to the first weeks of life. Prior to her work there was no clinical evidence of the extent to which feelings such as rage, satisfaction, fear, grief, and loss are present almost from birth, together with the beginnings of guilt, concern, and love which form the basis of all later patterns of behaviour. Her researches into the infant mind led her to the study of the manic-depressive and paranoid-schizoid groups of mental disorder and their roots in infancy, which made possible the treatment of patients hitherto considered beyond the reach of psychotherapy. In addition to her influence on theory and technique, she was to see before her death a fundamentally changed social attitude towards the care and education of children (for instance, the realization that lasting harm can be caused by emotional as well as physical deprivation), which can be traced to the pervasive influence of her work.

To the end of her life, Melanie Klein was endowed with an extraordinary vitality and a mobile, delicate beauty. She enjoyed meeting people, good talk, parties, and was an enthusiastic theatre-goer. Her devotion to and identification with her work made her intolerant of attacks and misconceptions; those who criticized her theories could find in her a passionate and often fierce adversary. But her direct and open understanding, expressed with an unassuming, rather astringent humour, made her the most stimulating companion; and her circle of friends, among them painters, writers, philosophers, and musicians, continued to grow almost up to the time of her death in London

22 September 1960. A painting of her by Mme Szekely-Kovacs is in the possession of her son, Eric Clyne. A drawing by Feliks Topolski belongs to the Melanie Klein Trust, and there are a number of copies in existence. The Trust was formed in 1955 to further her work and that of her colleagues through the publication of books, the provision of scholarships for the training of analysts, etc.

Among the most important of her books are: *The Psycho-Analysis of Children* (1932), *Contributions to Psycho-Analysis* (1948), *Envy and Gratitude* (1957), and *Narrative of a Child Analysis* (1961). For a full bibliography of her books and papers see the *International Journal of Psycho-Analysis* (vol. xlii, 1961). *New Directions* (1955), a collection of papers presented to her on her seventieth birthday, shows the extent to which Kleinian theory and practice had revolutionized psycho-analysis in applied as well as clinical fields.

[*The Times* and *Guardian*, 23 September 1960; Melanie Klein, *Contributions to Psycho-Analysis*, introduction by Ernest Jones, 1948; Ernest Jones, *Sigmund Freud*, vol. iii, 1957; Hanna Segal, *Introduction to the Work of Melanie Klein*, 1964; private information; personal knowledge.]   JEAN MACGIBBON.

KNOX, SIR GEOFFREY GEORGE (1884–1958), diplomatist, was born in Double Bay, New South Wales, Australia, 11 March 1884, the fourth child of George Knox, barrister, of Sydney, and his wife, Jane de Brixton Price. He was a grandson of (Sir) Edward Knox, one of the great Australian pioneers who had gone to Sydney from Denmark in 1839. Brought to England as a boy and educated at Malvern College, Knox maintained only the most tenuous connections with Australia throughout the rest of his life. A natural linguist, he passed the searching examination for the old Levant consular service in 1906 and after two years (1906–8) at Trinity College, Cambridge, where, with other successful candidates for the Levant service, he studied oriental languages, he started his career in Persia, which was at that time, owing to Russian intrigue, a danger spot in British foreign affairs. Here his knowledge of the language and his ability to mix on familiar terms with the Persians, the finer aspects of whose civilization greatly attracted him, made him a valuable observer and reporter to the legation in Tehran. From Persia he was transferred to Cairo in 1912 and was in Egypt at the outbreak of war.

In 1915, when British forces were sent to Salonika, Knox was moved there to help in the consulate-general whose work had been vastly increased by the demands of the military. As operations in that area developed Knox was employed on special service and, much to his amusement, for nobody was less like a naval officer, given an honorary commission as lieutenant R.N.V.R. (1917), receiving eventually a mention in dispatches.

Shortly before war ended Knox was recalled to the Levant consular service and sent in May 1919 to Bucharest. In 1920 he was one of the few consular officers transferred to the diplomatic service and was posted to Constantinople as second secretary and later (1923) first secretary. In 1923 he was moved to Berlin where he served for two fruitful years under the redoubtable but inspiring Lord D'Abernon [q.v.]. From Berlin he returned to Constantinople in 1926 with the acting rank of counsellor and remained there until 1928.

Knox's health had been affected by his service in the Middle East and for some time he was unemployed, but in 1931 he went to Madrid as counsellor. In 1932 he was selected to be chairman of the international Saar governing commission with the rank of minister. The post was a difficult one, demanding the exercise of great tact and firmness; and at the end of the three years allotted Knox had the satisfaction of bringing his work, unmarred by any unfortunate incident, to a successful conclusion, having coped with notable vigour, efficiency, and characteristic independence of judgement with the entirely novel set of problems confronting him as head of a mixed international governing organization.

In October 1935 Knox was promoted minister and sent to Budapest. After three and a half years his health again broke down but by the end of 1939 he had recovered sufficiently to be able to go as ambassador to Rio de Janeiro, where he remained until his retirement in 1942. He then went to live in California and died in Tobago 6 April 1958. He was unmarried. He had been appointed C.M.G. in 1929 and K.C.M.G. in 1935.

In 1942 Knox published *The Last Peace and the Next*, a searing and well-documented indictment of Prussian militarism with suggestions for avoiding the mistakes which had led to the war then in progress, but in the turmoil of events at home it passed almost unnoticed.

Knox, who will best be remembered for his work in the Saar, was a man of strong views, tenaciously held, and a pronounced realist. He had great intellectual powers which he exercised somewhat fitfully. With jutting chin and choleric, even pugnacious, aspect, he was no compromiser where his own affairs were concerned, and, fully conscious of his capabilities, took little pains to endear himself to his superiors. But for his friends he had a warm smile and an infectious laugh; was happy in his relations with his foreign diplomatic colleagues and highly skilful in his professional activities. He was fond of the good things of this world and had the means to ensure their enjoyment. As a result he sometimes incurred, though generally unjustly, for he had a great sense of duty, accusations of neglecting those less agreeable tasks which fall to be performed by British representatives overseas. It is a measure alike of his professional abilities and his powers of persistence that, in spite of considerable opposition in the Foreign Office, he succeeded in making for himself such a successful career and avoided being sent not only to posts ruled out by his frail health but also to those which his fastidious temperament regarded as uncongenial or unworthy.

[Private information; personal knowledge.]
DAVID SCOTT.

KNOX, RONALD ARBUTHNOTT (1888–1957), Roman Catholic priest and translator of the Bible, was born 17 February 1888 at Kibworth, Leicestershire, the youngest of six children of the rector, the Rev. Edmund Arbuthnott Knox [q.v.], later Anglican bishop of Manchester, and his first wife, Ellen Penelope, daughter of Thomas Valpy French [q.v.], bishop of Lahore. His eldest brother was E. V. Knox (Evoe), editor of *Punch* (1932–49). He was educated at Summer Fields, Oxford, and at Eton, where he entered college as the senior scholar of his year and became captain of the school. By his wit and felicity in the composition of verses, alike in English, Latin, and Greek, which he published under the title of *Signa Severa* (1906), he gained a nationwide reputation such as can rarely have been attained by anyone still in his schooldays. He carried that reputation with him up to Balliol College, Oxford, whither he went as a scholar. Although he unexpectedly failed to get a first in classical moderations owing to his neglect to read the prescribed books, he won the Hertford (1907), Ireland (1908), and Craven (1908) scholarships and the Gaisford Greek verse (1908) and Chancellor's Latin verse (1910) prizes. He was elected to the presidency of the Union (1909), took his first in *literae humaniores* (1910), and by epigram and paradox fully maintained his reputation for brilliance. Countless satirical verses and limericks were, not always correctly, ascribed to him.

Although his father was a leader of the Low Church party in the Church of England, Ronald Knox had from his schooldays taken an extreme Anglo-Catholic position. He was ordained deacon (1911) and priest (1912) and appointed a fellow (1910) and chaplain (1912) of Trinity College, Oxford. In the few years which remained before the outbreak of war he played a leading part in Anglican controversies of the times, championing the claim of the Church of England to be a branch of the Catholic Church and vigorously combating modernist trends. In *Some Loose Stones* (1913) he accused those of that school of thought of substituting for the authority of the Church as the test of truth the question 'How much will Jones swallow?' He wrote two works of great brilliance in support of his position—*Absolute and Abitofhell* (1913) in parody of Dryden to criticize the alleged disruptionary theology of some of his fellow chaplains as displayed in their publication *Foundations*, and *Reunion All Round* (1914) in parody of Swift and in satire on those who thought that religious unity could be built upon other than a dogmatic foundation.

With the outbreak of war, life at Oxford was disrupted and Knox taught for a time at Shrewsbury School, then worked at the War Office (1916-18). He had by this time become increasingly dissatisfied with his position in the Anglican Church and in 1917 was received into the Roman Catholic Church at Farnborough Abbey, publishing *A Spiritual Aeneid* in 1918 to explain his action. He received Roman Catholic orders in 1919 and taught at St. Edmund's College, Ware, from 1918 until 1926 when he was appointed chaplain to the Roman Catholic undergraduates at Oxford, where he remained until a few months before the outbreak of war in 1939. Throughout these years he maintained a literary output of books of various sorts from detective stories to works of apologetics and during the university vacations

gave retreats and sermons in different parts of the country many of which have been republished in book form. He perhaps made himself most notorious by a broadcast parody in January 1926 of an announcement on the B.B.C. of a pretended outbreak of revolutionary rioting in London which was taken seriously by some simple-minded listeners.

Increasingly Knox found that his duties at Oxford were a distraction which prevented him from the serious literary work which he felt to be his main vocation. He had formed the ambition to give to his co-religionists a new English version of the Bible, more true to the original and in a more contemporary idiom than the Douay version. The bishops encouraged him in the hope that this would be accepted as an official version. He therefore resigned the Oxford chaplaincy, proposing to devote himself entirely to his biblical work. In his last months at Oxford he published *Let Dons Delight* (1939), artistically perhaps the most triumphant of his books. It consists of a series of conversations in an imaginary Oxford common-room at intervals of fifty years from the time of Elizabeth I to 1938. In each conversation the senior fellow is the junior fellow, and the only survivor, of the previous conversation. With humour and subtlety Knox brings out the gradual erosion of a common culture, so that the dons, who in the early years all shared substantially the same interests, by the later years are hardly able to find a common language.

On leaving Oxford, Knox had arranged to live at Aldenham in Shropshire, the home of Lord and Lady Acton, where he looked forward to a life wholly free from distraction. No sooner was he installed, however, than war broke out, and a girls' school was evacuated there from London to which Knox was compelled to undertake the duties of chaplain. Nevertheless at Aldenham during the war years, and afterwards at Mells in Somerset where he went to live, he persevered with his task in spite of the difficulties until it was completed in 1955.

After the Bible his next great work was his *Enthusiasm* (1950). Knox had always been interested in the phenomenon of enthusiasm, in the technical theological sense—the claim of those who assert that they hold God within them and that they are possessed of a special revelation of His will. Convinced as he was of the divine and necessary authority of the Church, he was naturally unsympathetic to such individualistic claims and believed that they had wrought much havoc in the Christian world, particularly in the seventeenth and eighteenth centuries. Had the work, which he had to some extent carried in his mind throughout all his adult years, appeared in print when he was still a young man, it might well have been deeply controversial, for he was in those years full of a young man's zest for controversy. In middle age that zest had notably abated and he came greatly to dislike religious argument and to doubt whether it ever did very much good. As a result his *Enthusiasm* when it appeared, while maintaining his full religious position, was yet much more a work of objective record than of controversy. As such it is the most considerable of his original works. In the last years of his life he completed a translation of the *Autobiography* of Saint Thérèse of Lisieux (1958); his translation of the *Imitation of Christ* was finished by another hand, and the major work of apologetics which he was planning was never written.

In 1936 Knox was created a monsignor; in 1951 Pope Pius XII made him a protonotary apostolic; and in 1956 he was elected to the Pontifical Academy. He was made an honorary fellow of Trinity (1941) and Balliol (1953) and was invited to deliver the Romanes lecture at Oxford in 1957. The subject which he chose was 'English Translation' and he was able to fulfil this engagement in the university to which he had given so many years of his life, although it was known not only to himself but also to his audience that the hand of death was upon him. The lecture was a brilliant success and a poignant occasion for all who heard it. It was his last public appearance. He died at Mells 24 August 1957. A requiem Mass was said for him in Westminster Cathedral at which the panegyric was preached by Father Martin D'Arcy, S.J., one of his most intimate friends, and he was buried in the churchyard at Mells.

Ronald Knox was a small man, of frail drooping figure with a prominent nose, heavy underlip, unobtrusive chin, and large eyes. In his younger days his wit gained for him a certain reputation for flippancy, but none who knew him ever doubted at any time in his life the deep sincerity of his religious faith, and in later life, while wit could never wholly be suppressed, he came increasingly in his writing to shy away from the merely light-

hearted to the extent that some almost found him sometimes melancholy. Devotion to religion was overwhelmingly the main influence on his life. Shy and retiring, he seemed to some almost unduly diffident and there were those who thought that he shunned too much the rough and tumble of life, but he won and retained a host of friends such as few can command. The tributes at his death showed that he had established for himself a national position to an extent which he himself in his unaffected modesty had never guessed and there were many who said that the Roman Catholic Church had lost in England her most distinguished convert since Newman.

At the Manor House at Mells there is a terracotta by Arthur Pollen. A bronze cast of this head is at Trinity College, Oxford. A portrait of him by Simon Elwes hangs at the Catholic Chaplaincy at Oxford. The National Portrait Gallery has a drawing by Powys Evans.

[Evelyn Waugh, *Ronald Knox*, 1959; private information; personal knowledge.]

CHRISTOPHER HOLLIS.

KOMISARJEVSKY, THEODORE (1882–1954), theatrical producer and designer, born in Venice 23 May 1882, was the son of Theodore Komisarjevsky (who was first tenor of the St. Petersburg Opera and taught Stanislavsky) and his wife, the Princess Kourzevich. Vera Komisarjevskaya, the actress, was his sister.

Educated at a military academy and the Imperial Institute of Architecture in St. Petersburg, Komisarjevsky directed his first production in his sister's theatre in 1907. In 1910, the year of her death, he founded his own school of acting in Moscow, to which in 1914 he added a studio-theatre in her memory. From 1910 to 1913 he was producer at the Nezlobin Theatre in Moscow, and after an interlude with the Imperial Grand Opera House he became producer at Ziminne's Opera House, with which he remained when it became the Soviet Opera House. After the revolution he was also appointed director of the Moscow State Theatre of Opera and Ballet (previously the Imperial Grand Opera) and he was allowed to continue to direct his own small theatre. In 1919, believing that he was about to be arrested by the Cheka, he fled to Paris, where Diaghilev advised him to go to England. Within four weeks of his arrival he was entrusted by Sir Thomas Beecham with a production of *Prince Igor* at Covent

Garden, which immediately led to further opera productions in Paris and New York. On his return to London he began, at a time when the English theatre was inclined to insularity, a series of productions of plays by Russian authors including Chekhov, Gogol, Andreyev, Tolstoy, and Dostoevsky.

In 1925 he converted a small cinema at Barnes into a theatre with its own company which included (Sir) John Gielgud, Charles Laughton, Jean Forbes-Robertson, Jeanne de Casalis, and Martita Hunt. The standard of production in the English theatre (to quote from *The Times* of that day) was 'sloppy and slovenly'; there was little attempt at ensemble playing and the settings and lighting were dull and unimaginative. Komisarjevsky's productions at Barnes (1925-6) had an immediate effect on the English theatre by making the critics aware of its deficiencies. At a time when English acting had a glossy veneer which concealed its shallowness, Komisarjevsky demanded from his actors a new intensity of feeling and a deeper understanding of the characters they were playing. He introduced a method of acting based on the theories of Stanislavsky, although he never accepted them unconditionally and to some of them he was strongly opposed.

In 1932 Komisarjevsky became a British subject. It was the year of the first of his productions at Stratford on Avon; productions which were unorthodox and provocative, sometimes brilliant, sometimes merely wayward; all of them valuable as a means of making critics and audiences realize how conventional and humdrum had been the routine Stratford productions of Shakespeare. As a Shakespearian producer Komisarjevsky's weakness was that he had little respect for the text and small appreciation of the rhythms of the verse.

Komisarjevsky saw little to attract him to the ordinary west-end theatre, although Sir C. B. Cochran [q.v.] managed to persuade him to produce three plays there. He preferred to spend his time producing an extraordinary variety of plays in London, in the provinces, and on the Continent for any theatre or society (such as the Stage Society) which was leading rather than following theatrical tastes. His productions included *The Pretenders*, in Welsh, in a gigantic marquee at Holyhead; two productions at Oxford for the O.U.D.S.; *The Cherry Orchard* at the Leeds Civic Playhouse; *The Wild Duck* in

Riga; *Peer Gynt* in New York; *The Dover Road* (in English) in Paris; and *Cymbeline* in an open-air theatre in Montreal.

Besides being a great producer, Komisarjevsky was also a brilliant stage designer. Almost invariably he designed his own sets and costumes. He had nothing in common with the photographically realistic English designers. His settings reduced factual realism to a minimum, stressing mood rather than detail. The effectiveness of his settings was enormously enhanced by the skill and subtlety of his lighting which made dramatic use of highlights, shadows, and halftones to give emphasis to his beautifully composed groupings.

Komisarjevsky was a small man with a completely bald head, a beak nose, inscrutable brown eyes set in a pale face which seemed all the paler because of the small bright red scarf which he invariably wore around his throat at rehearsals. His rather melancholy air concealed a mischievous sense of humour which had a streak of cruelty in it. At work he was the quietest of producers. He would seldom give an actor an intonation or say how a line should be spoken. He preferred to discuss what a character was thinking or feeling, and leave it to the actor to work it out. Unfortunately, if he decided that an actor had no particular talent he would take no trouble over his performance but concentrate all his attention on the better actors, with the result that under his direction good actors usually surpassed themselves while dull actors seemed duller than ever.

In 1939, when war broke out, he was working in the United States. He felt that as he had become a British subject he should return to England, so he offered his services to E.N.S.A. But he was unable to get back and spent the rest of his life in America, devoting his time mainly to lecturing and teaching. He died at Darien, Connecticut, 17 April 1954.

In the twenty years during which he worked in the English theatre he had a greater influence than any other producer on methods of direction, acting, setting, and lighting. On his death, Sir John Gielgud described him in a letter to *The Times* as 'a great *metteur en scène*, an inspiring teacher, and a master of theatrical orchestration . . .'.

Komisarjevsky was three times married: first, to Elfriede de Jarosy; secondly, in 1934, to (Dame) Peggy Ashcroft; thirdly, to Ernestine Stodelle. The first

wo marriages were dissolved. He had two
ons and one daughter.

[*The Times*, 19 April 1954; Theodore
Komisarjevsky, *Myself and the Theatre*, 1929;
ersonal knowledge.]   NORMAN MARSHALL.

KORDA, SIR ALEXANDER (1893–
956), film producer, whose original name
vas Alexander Laszlo Kellner, was born
6 September 1893, at Pusztaturpaszto,
Hungary. He was the eldest of the three
ons of Henry Kellner, land agent to
. large estate, and his wife, Ernestine
Veisz. He was educated at Protestant
gymnasiums in Nagykoros and Kecskemet
and at a commercial school in Budapest.
His father died when he was thirteen and
o augment the family income he gave
essons in the evenings. Leaving school at
seventeen, he became a proof-reader and
newspaper reporter in Budapest and pub-
ished a novel under the name of Alexan-
ler Korda. In 1911 he went to Paris
vhere he became proficient in French but
could find no work. Back in Budapest he
had his first introduction to the infant
film world by translating sub-titles from
French into Hungarian. In 1912 he
founded a film magazine, the first of its
kind to appear in Budapest, and in 1913
with some friends he started to write and
lirect short film comedies.

Owing to his eyesight which was always
weak Korda was not called up after the
outbreak of war and was able to continue
as a film director. In 1915, with the
lirector of the Kolozsvar National Theatre
in Transylvania, he formed a plan to
make films with that company, using their
actors, scenery, and costumes. The course
of the war enforced a return to Budapest
where he took over the company and
built a studio, the Corvin. His first full-
length film, *The Man of Gold* (1918), taken
from M. Jokai's novel, was highly successful.

In 1919 there was unrest in Hungary
and Korda, together with many other
citizens, was arrested; by a fortunate
chance he shortly obtained his release,
and on returning home he took a bath,
changed his clothes, and departed from
Hungary for ever. In Vienna he joined the
Sascha studios which at that time were
making advanced films, and there he
matured his film-craft. Among his films of
this period were *The Prince and the Pauper*
(1920) and *Samson and Delilah* (1922). In
1923 he moved to Berlin and in 1926 to
Hollywood where amongst the films he
made was *The Private Life of Helen of*

Troy (1927) in which his wife, Maria
Corda, played the title role.

Returning to Europe in 1930 Korda
found work in Paris with the Paramount
Film Company, for whom he made the
classic film *Marius* (1931) from the play
by Marcel Pagnol, in which Raimu played
the leading part. In 1931 he went for
Paramount to London to direct *Service for
Ladies* which was an outstanding success
and proved the turning-point in Korda's
career, for he settled in London, formed
his own company, London Film Productions, with Big Ben as trademark, and
built the Denham studios and laboratories
which when completed in 1937 were the
most advanced in Europe. In the meantime Korda had become one of the most
notable personalities of the film world
with a series of pictures which obtained
world-wide fame. They included *The
Private Life of Henry VIII* (1933), *The
Private Life of Don Juan* (with a script
by Frederick Lonsdale, q.v., 1934), *The
Ghost Goes West* (1935, directed by René
Clair and starring Robert Donat, q.v.),
The Scarlet Pimpernel (1935, starring
Leslie Howard, q.v.), *Things to Come* and
The Man Who Could Work Miracles
(scripts by H. G. Wells, q.v., 1936),
Rembrandt (1936), *Knight Without Armour*
(1936), *Elephant Boy* (1936–7), *Fire Over
England* (Vivien Leigh's first film, 1937),
and *The Four Feathers* (1939).

No one in this country before or since
Korda has equalled his range and brilliance of faculties for film-making. Building studios and making pictures need
large sums of money and Korda seemed at
this period to conjure them out of the air.
His sense of romance and gift of story-
telling produced excellent scripts; his
knowledge, direction, and camera-work
brought to his service the finest technicians, among whom were his two
younger brothers, Zoltan and Vincent.
His tact and talent, together with his
generosity and personal magnetism, drew
to him the best actors in the world.

With the worsening international situation financial backing was gradually withdrawn and in 1939 Korda had to give up
the Denham studios. But he continued his
film-making with *The Thief of Baghdad*
(1939–40) and, immediately after the outbreak of war, the documentary *The Lion
has Wings*. During the war years he
moved between London and Hollywood
where he directed *Lady Hamilton* (1941)
and with his brother Zoltan produced
Jungle Book (1941); in Britain he made

Perfect Strangers (1944). After the war he
revived London Films as an independent
company, built studios at Shepperton,
and once again under his management
there came forth fine films, including *An
Ideal Husband* (1947), *The Fallen Idol*
(1948), *The Third Man* (1949), *The Wooden
Horse* (1950), *Sound Barrier* (1952), and
Richard III (1955). Working to the last,
Korda died in London 23 January 1956.

In 1921 Korda married Maria Farkas,
who acted under the name of Maria
Corda, by whom he had one son, Peter.
The marriage was dissolved in 1931. His
second marriage (1939), to Merle Oberon,
was dissolved in 1945. In 1953 he married
a Canadian, Alexandra Irene Boycun
(died 1966). Korda was naturalized in
1936 and knighted in 1942. He was made
an officer of the Legion of Honour in 1950.

[Paul Tabori, *Alexander Korda*, 1959;
private information; personal knowledge.]
                              RALPH RICHARDSON.

LAMB, HENRY TAYLOR (1883–1960),
painter, was born in Adelaide, Australia,
21 June 1883, the third son and fifth of
the seven children of (Sir) Horace Lamb
[q.v.], the mathematician and physicist.
Lamb's eldest sister, Helen, became a don
at Newnham College, Cambridge; his
eldest brother, Ernest, a professor of
engineering, Queen Mary College, London;
and his next eldest brother, (Sir) Walter,
was secretary of the Royal Academy.
Brought up in Manchester where his
father was professor of mathematics at the
university, Lamb spent 'eight years of
misery' at Manchester Grammar School
and, destined for medicine, four years at
Manchester University medical school,
obtaining a graduate scholarship in 1904.
Despite this success he abandoned medicine for painting and settled in London,
having already received training and
encouragement from Joseph Knight, art
master at Manchester Grammar School,
and from Francis Dodd [q.v.]. Lamb
studied at the art school run by Augustus
John and (Sir) William Orpen [q.v.] in
Flood Street, Chelsea, supplementing
a small allowance from a patron with
occasional commissions from the *Manchester Guardian* for drawings of famous
London buildings. He continued his
studies at La Palette, Paris, under J.-E.
Blanche in 1907–8. After returning to
London he took a studio at 8 Fitzroy
Street (1909–11), while the summers of
1910 and 1911 were spent in Brittany,
followed by some months in Ireland

(1912–13). He had first exhibited at the
New English Art Club in 1909, and his
allegiance to the progressives in English
art soon showed itself when he became
a founder-member of the Camden Town
Group in 1911 and of the London Group in
1913. On the outbreak of war he returned
to medicine and qualified at Guy's Hospital in 1916. Gazetted captain, he served as
battalion medical officer with the 5th
Inniskilling Fusiliers in Macedonia, Palestine, and France, was gassed and invalided
home. He was awarded the M.C. in 1918.

Lamb's early style was strongly influenced by the work of Augustus John
and his fine drawings of Dorelia John and
of Nina Euphemia Lamb (his first wife
daughter of Arthur Forrest, whom he
married in 1906 and from whom he
separated a few years later) executed
between 1907–10 equal John's in their
firm brilliance. Lamb's distinctive artistic
personality first flowered in a series of
paintings of Breton subjects, such as
'Death of a Peasant' (1911) and 'Lamenta-
tion' (1911, both Tate Gallery, London).
Here, austere realism, a restrained palette,
and striking, deceptively simple composition are qualities characteristic also of
much of his later work. With the exception of 'Phantasy' (1912, Tate Gallery),
a group of male nude equestrians perhaps
inspired by the circus scenes of Picasso's
'Pink period', Lamb seems to have been
almost impervious to the revolutionary
movements in contemporary French art.
This may account for the antipathy of
Roger Fry [q.v.] towards his painting; nor
did Lamb share the pacifist beliefs of some
of the Bloomsbury group. Yet it was the
large portrait of Lytton Strachey [q.v.]
completed in 1914 (Tate Gallery) which
brought him public notice and featured in
his first one-man exhibition at the Alpine
Club Gallery in 1922. Other writers who
sat to him were Evelyn Waugh (1930) and
Lord David Cecil (1935). Strachey, whom
he first painted in 1912, is shown seated
against a large window in Lamb's Vale of
Health studio, Hampstead, and though
avoiding caricature, Lamb has relished
emphasizing Strachey's gaunt, ungainly
figure, and the air of resigned intellectual
superiority with which he surveys the
world from that incredible slab-like head.
The trees in the vista seen through the
window are painted in a rhythmic, decorative manner which suggests that Lamb had
taken from the innovations of the Nabis
and Matisse what seemed consistent with
his own essentially academic approach.

Browns, violets, and greens here predominate, colours which were subtly woven into many later compositions making his work easily distinguishable in mixed exhibitions.

Lamb's wartime experiences inspired two large paintings, 'Palestinian War Picture' (1919, Imperial War Museum) and 'Salonika War Picture' (1920, Manchester City Art Gallery), the earlier of which is a remarkably vivid bird's-eye view of moving wounded from an outpost under fire. During the early twenties he painted several portrait groups of distinction, such as that of the architect 'George Kennedy and Family' (1921, J. L. Behrend), some details of which relate to the work of (Sir) Stanley Spencer [q.v.], whom he had given a room in his house at Poole after the war. The roof tops, warehouses, and narrow streets of the town delighted him and inspired many carefully observed compositions at this period. While good at official portraits, he was particularly happy at catching children's likenesses and the son and two daughters of his second marriage (in 1928, to Lady Margaret Pansy Felicia Pakenham, eldest daughter of the fifth Earl of Longford) appear in many family portraits of the thirties and forties. During the war of 1939–45 he was an official war artist, attached to the army, and painted portraits of Service men and foreign military attachés.

Failing health towards the end of his life forced him to abandon landscape, to concentrate on still life, and latterly to rework earlier themes of Breton and Irish life. He had lived at Coombe Bissett, Salisbury, after 1928 and died there 8 October 1960.

Of medium height, slightly built, and agile, Lamb was fond of riding and sailing, although his constitution was permanently weakened after the war of 1914–18. He had wide intellectual interests, was an accomplished performer on the piano and clavicord of the music of Mozart, Beethoven, and Bach, and was impatient of convention. Elected A.R.A. in 1940, he became R.A. in 1949. He was a trustee of the Tate Gallery (1944–51), and of the National Portrait Gallery (1942–60) which owns two self-portrait drawings of 1950–51 and an earlier oil self-portrait, and a drawing by Powys Evans. The Manchester City Art Gallery has a portrait by Francis Dodd. A memorial exhibition was held at the Leicester Galleries in December 1961. Portraits by him are in many British universities, and he is widely represented in the Tate Gallery and in provincial museums.

[G. L. K[ennedy], *Henry Lamb*, 1924; *The Times*, 10 October 1960; private information.]   DENNIS FARR.

LAMBE, SIR CHARLES EDWARD (1900–1960), admiral of the fleet, was born at Stalbridge 20 December 1900, the only son of Henry Edward Lambe, of Grove House, Stalbridge, and his wife, Lilian, daughter of John Bramwell, of Edinburgh. He was descended from Rear-Admiral Sir Thomas Louis [q.v.] who fought at the battle of the Nile and served with distinction in the Napoleonic wars. Joining *Osborne* as a naval cadet in 1914, he was a midshipman in the battleship *Emperor of India* from 1917 until the end of the war. After serving at home and overseas he joined the *Vernon* at Portsmouth in 1925 to qualify as a torpedo specialist. A good horseman, a keen shot, and skilful amateur pilot, he showed also much professional promise.

After service in the Mediterranean and qualifying at the Naval Staff College he joined the East Indies flagship, the cruiser *Hawkins*, in 1932, being promoted to commander in 1933. He next served on the staff of the Rear-Admiral A. B. Cunningham (afterwards Viscount Cunningham of Hyndhope) commanding all Mediterranean destroyer flotillas. Cunningham soon recognized Lambe's exceptional talents at handling men and affairs. Returning to England in 1935 Lambe became the commander of the *Vernon*, and was later appointed equerry to King Edward VIII and later to King George VI.

Promoted to captain in December 1937, shortly after his thirty-seventh birthday, he commanded the cruiser *Dunedin* for the first year of the war until in October 1940 he joined the joint planning staff in Whitehall as naval assistant director of plans. He soon became deputy director and then director of plans, serving as such until April 1944. This covered the period when virtually all the major strategic decisions of the war were taken. The agonizing military alternatives which faced the Government in the early part of this period together with the tremendous problems arising from the Russian, Japanese, and American entries into the war were the principal concern of the joint planning staff, who advised the chiefs of staff, and who in their turn were presided over by (Sir) Winston Churchill.

Lambe's influence was far reaching with his Service colleagues, and with the chiefs of staff. His judgement, his serenity of outlook, his ability to explain, persuade, and listen to all sides, and above all his imagination and ability to see the heart of a problem proved of exceptional value to his country.

On leaving Whitehall he commanded the aircraft carrier *Illustrious* in the Indian and Pacific oceans. Hit once by a Japanese suicide aircraft *Illustrious* took part in many operations. Soon after the end of the Japanese war he returned to the Admiralty as assistant chief of staff (Air) as an acting rear-admiral and went on to appointments where his knowledge of air problems both human and technical were of special value: flag officer Flying Training (1947–9), admiral commanding third aircraft carrier squadron (1949–51), and flag officer (Air) Home (1951–3). He became commander-in-chief Far East station in 1953 and served there with particular success in the difficult time following the Korean war. Later, in 1955 as second sea lord his sympathy for the less fortunate was of much value when heavy reductions were being made in naval personnel. Finally after being commander-in-chief Mediterranean (1957–9) he became first sea lord in 1959 to the delight of the navy, who were much saddened by his illness which led to his retirement in May, and his death on 29 August, 1960, at his home in Newport, Fife.

Promoted to vice-admiral in 1950, admiral in 1954, and admiral of the fleet in 1960, he was appointed C.V.O. in 1938, C.B. in 1944, K.C.B. in 1953, G.C.B. in 1957.

Lambe did many things so well and often so much better than other men, but there was something elusive about him. Endowed with much personal charm and greatly liked, he had a first-rate intellect which never tolerated insincerity—yet there was perhaps an inner sanctum in him which few penetrated but many sensed. His clear well-ordered mind saw through most problems, and also the most practical ways of solving them. His tastes were catholic and his enthusiasm infectious. Added to a love of outdoor pursuits he had a deep appreciation and understanding of many artistic things. He was a pianist quite out of the ordinary in performance, an accomplished watercolour painter, a lifelong member of the Bach Choir, and had an abiding appreciation of Shakespeare and Andrew Marvell's

sonnets which he enjoyed quoting. Yet for all this, his love of the navy and sense of service took priority over all else.

He married in 1940 Lesbia Rachel, daughter of Sir Walter Orlando Corbet, fourth baronet, formerly wife of V. I. H. Mylius, and had one son and one daughter. There is a portrait by Edward I. Halliday in the *Vernon* at Portsmouth.

[Personal knowledge.]   WILLIAM DAVIS.

LAMBERT, CONSTANT (1905–1951), musician, was born in London 23 August 1905, the younger son of the Australian painter George Washington Lambert, A.R.A., and his wife, Amelia Beatrice Absell. He was the brother of the sculptor Maurice Lambert. He was educated at Christ's Hospital and the Royal College of Music, where he studied with Ralph Vaughan Williams [q.v.] and R. O. Morris. He was introduced by Edmund Dulac [q.v.] to Diaghilev who commissioned him to write the ballet *Romeo and Juliet*. At this time Lambert was still a student and he was the first English composer to be commissioned by Diaghilev. The ballet which consists of thirteen short movements in classical forms was first performed in 1926 at Monte Carlo, with choreography by Nijinska.

Earlier Lambert had become acquainted with the Sitwells and he shared brilliantly with (Dame) Edith Sitwell the speaking part in the 1922 and 1923 performances of *Façade*, the entertainment with poems by Edith Sitwell and music by (Sir) William Walton. His second ballet, *Pomona*, was written at the Sitwell family home at Renishaw in Yorkshire in 1926; the story concerns the successful wooing of Pomona, the goddess of fruit, by the god Vertumnus. The ballet was first produced in Buenos Aires in 1927, again with choreography by Nijinska. Later in 1926 he set eight poems by the Chinese writer Li-Po for voice and piano, and afterwards made an arrangement of them for voice and a small combination of instruments. In 1927 came *Music for Orchestra*, a brilliant orchestral work which showed a masterly command of the medium. An 'Elegiac Blues' in memory of the negro singer Florence Mills showed Lambert's interest in jazz music, and this was shown even more strikingly in *The Rio Grande*, a setting of (Sir) Sacheverell Sitwell's poem for piano, chorus, and orchestra, which contains a number of jazz effects. This was first performed on 12 December 1929 in

Manchester by the Hallé Orchestra conducted by the composer; the orchestra's regular conductor, Sir Hamilton Harty [q.v.], played the difficult solo piano part. This performance was repeated on the following day at the Queen's Hall, London, and *The Rio Grande* remained Lambert's most popular work during his lifetime.

Between 1928 and 1931 Lambert wrote two works in classical forms, but also showing some influences of jazz: these are the Piano Sonata and the Concerto for piano and nine instruments (Lambert was an expert pianist himself). The Concerto was dedicated to the memory of Lambert's close friend Philip Heseltine (q.v., Peter Warlock) and ends with an elegiac slow movement.

In 1930 Lambert became conductor of the Camargo Society, and he conducted Vaughan Williams's ballet *Job* in his own version for theatre orchestra at the 1931 festival of the International Society for Contemporary Music in Oxford. From the Camargo Society grew the Vic–Wells Ballet (later the Sadler's Wells Ballet), of which Lambert became the first musical director, holding this post until 1947, after which he remained its artistic adviser. He was awarded the Collard fellowship of the Musicians' Company in 1934 and this enabled him to complete his largest work, the choral masque *Summer's Last Will and Testament*, to poems of Thomas Nashe [q.v.]. This was first performed in January 1936 at the Queen's Hall, with the composer conducting. Although Lambert here again makes use of classical forms, the work is not in the least archaistic, and shows a brilliant command of voices and instruments in combination.

Lambert's next ballet, *Horoscope*, was first performed at Sadler's Wells in 1938, with choreography by (Sir) Frederick Ashton; the story concerns the love of a man born with the sun in Leo and the moon in Gemini and a woman born with the sun in Virgo and the moon in Gemini. Lambert's own birthday was on the cusp between Leo and Virgo.) The ballet begins with an extraordinary palindrome, unique in Lambert's work, which the composer believed to have been dictated to him by his friend and colleague Bernard van Dieren, who had died shortly before.

Later works of Lambert include a setting for male voices and strings of the Dirge from Shakespeare's *Cymbeline* (1940) which is one of his most moving works; it

is dedicated to Patrick Hadley, Lambert's fellow student and later professor of music at Cambridge. In 1940 Lambert was with the Sadler's Wells Ballet in Holland and narrowly escaped capture at the time of the German invasion. This experience was reflected in the *Aubade Héroïque* for orchestra (1942) in which pastoral and warlike elements are strikingly combined; Lambert dedicated this work to his teacher Vaughan Williams on his seventieth birthday. His last ballet, *Tiresias*, was given at Covent Garden in 1951, shortly before his death, again with choreography by (Sir) Frederick Ashton and décor by his wife Isabel Lambert. The composer conducted the initial performances.

While director of the Sadler's Wells Ballet Lambert made many arrangements for them, including music of Meyerbeer (*Les Patineurs*), Purcell (*Comus*), Auber (*Les Rendezvous*), and Boyce (*The Prospect Before Us*). He also chose the late Liszt piano pieces used in *Apparitions*, and orchestrated Liszt's Dante Sonata for the company. Other transcriptions include works by Boyce, Handel, and Thomas Roseingrave, an Irish pupil of Domenico Scarlatti. Lambert did a great deal of conducting, at the promenade concerts, where he was associate conductor (1945–6), on the B.B.C. Third Programme, where he was always willing to perform unusual but interesting works, and at Covent Garden, where among other works he gave memorable performances of Purcell's *Fairy Queen* and Puccini's *Manon Lescaut* and *Turandot*. His book on the music of the twenties, *Music Ho!* (1934), subtitled 'A Study of Music in Decline', was brilliantly written and showed a wide and erudite knowledge of the arts and of life in general, if some of its conclusions have subsequently been questioned. Lambert also wrote musical criticism for the *New Statesman*, *Figaro*, the *Sunday Referee*, and other papers, and he contributed a number of extremely witty articles on non-musical subjects to *Lilliput* and other magazines. Apart from his brilliance as a composer and conductor, he was a warm and generous personality, a brilliant conversationalist, and a man of enormous knowledge who made a unique contribution to English music during the last twenty-five years of his short life.

Lambert married in 1931 Florence Chuter and had one son; the marriage was dissolved and in 1947 he married Isabel

Delmer. He died in London 21 August 1951.

A portrait by Michael Ayrton is in the Tate Gallery. Of two by Christopher Wood, one is at Covent Garden and the other in the National Portrait Gallery. The family owns a sculptured head by Maurice Lambert and a pencil drawing by his father. A portrait of him as a boy at Christ's Hospital by his father is at Christ's Hospital.

[*Grove's Dictionary of Music and Musicians*; personal knowledge.]   HUMPHREY SEARLE.

LAMBERT, GEORGE, first VISCOUNT LAMBERT (1866–1958), yeoman farmer and member of Parliament, was born at South Tawton in the county of Devon 25 June 1866 and lived at Spreyton near by. He was the eldest son of George Lambert of Spreyton by his wife, Grace, daughter of Thomas Howard, of South Tawton. Like his forebears for many generations he was a small landowner and yeoman. He was educated at the local grammar school and at the age of nineteen he was farming 800 acres of his own land. Public service began to attract him and in 1889, at the age of twenty-three, he became a county councillor; he was made an alderman in 1912 and did not retire until 1952.

In 1891, aged twenty-five, he won a notable victory as a Gladstonian Liberal at a by-election in South Molton which he represented in 1891–1924 and 1929–45. In all he fought fourteen elections, was four times unopposed, and only once beaten (1924) due to the over-confidence of his supporters. He was civil lord of the Admiralty from 1905 to 1915 and made lasting friendships with (Sir) Winston Churchill and Admiral Lord Fisher [q.v.]. His feelings for Fisher were akin to hero worship and on the latter's death Lambert became his literary executor. He was sworn of the Privy Council in 1912 and after 1915 he was twice invited to join the Government, by Asquith and Lloyd George respectively, but he preferred to remain a back-bencher.

Lambert was fond of recounting how he moved the Address in 1893 and had twice been called to Gladstone's room for consultation. At the customary eve-of-session dinner given by the prime minister to his colleagues Lambert sat next to Gladstone who resisted three attempts by the butler to remove his spoon, which he needed to call the diners to silence before the saying of grace—'a good old custom, Mr. Lambert', said Gladstone,

'which I will never forsake while breat remains in my body'. Next day in Parlia ment while Lambert was waiting to mov the Address the Irish members create such a disturbance during the prelimin aries that the Speaker 'adjourned th House to eat his chop'. Returning earl from dinner he called on Lambert to mov the Address when the only member present were Gladstone, Balfour, and th seconder of the Address.

In subsequent sessions Lambert's know ledge of farming and of the needs of rura life stood him in good stead and he mad a reputation as an expert. He early pro moted a private bill by which the farme would get fair compensation for dis turbance and could grow what he chose provided that he maintained the fertilit of the soil. The bill lapsed with the genera election of 1895. He was, however, success ful in putting on the statute book an Ac by which parish council elections were t be held every three years instead o annually.

Lambert served on the royal commissio on agriculture appointed in 1893. I general he was an economist of the old school—state action, he would argue involving controls, protective dutie subsidies, doles, and such perniciou socialist nostrums, paralysed those ster ling qualities of individual self-help an initiative which were the mainspring o Britain's greatness in the past. He onc likened the socialist State to Dartmoo prison—planned lives, equality main tained, up and to bed at the same times no unemployment, and no waiting list— an ideal socialist institution. He wa resolutely opposed to Lloyd George's lan policy formulated in 1924 and even con templated leaving the Liberal Party o account of it. In 1919–21 he had bee chairman of the parliamentary Libera Party and he used his influence to promot Liberal unity.

During 1931 when the Liberal Party le by Lloyd George kept a Labour Govern ment under Ramsay MacDonald i office, Lambert grew increasingly restiv and was among the first to make over tures for the 'national' Government whic was formed in August 1931 and supporte by the majority of Liberals in Parliamen who constituted the newly forme National Liberal Party. Lambert wa a man of strong convictions, who kne his own mind and spoke it. He was no given to subtlety of speech or opinion bu he was downright, steadfast, and incor uptible: a force to be reckoned with by party leaders. When he retired in 1945 he was created a viscount.

Lambert's name in Devonshire among the farmers and labourers was one to conjure with and 'Devonshire Jarge' never lost the support of the farming community. Through his friendship with C. H. Seale-Hayne [q.v.], whose executor he became, he was able to devote substantial sums for the building of the Seale-Hayne Agricultural College at Newton Abbot of which he became the foundation chairman.

Lambert was a good sportsman, a good shot, and a steady golfer. At the age of sixty-seven, on a handicap of fourteen, he won the parliamentary golf handicap in a 36-holes final at Coombe Hill, beating the Prince of Wales by five and four.

He married in 1904 Barbara (died 1963), daughter of George Stavers, shipowner, of Morpeth. They had two sons and two daughters. George, the elder son (born 1909), who succeeded to the title, followed his father as M.P. for South Molton, a constituency which became Torrington after 1950. Lambert's younger daughter Margaret was from 1951 editor-in-chief for the Foreign Office of the German documents captured in 1945.

Lambert died at Spreyton 17 February 1958 at the age of ninety-one.

There are two portraits: one by Arthur Hacker (1913) in possession of the family and the other by R. G. Eves (1934) at the Seale-Hayne College.

[*The Times*, 18 February 1958; private information; personal knowledge.]

GEOFFREY SHAKESPEARE.

LANE, LUPINO (1892–1959), actor and theatre-manager, was a member of a family of acrobats, dancers, and clowns whose record goes back to the eighteenth century. He was the elder son of Harry Lupino and his wife, Charlotte Sarah Robinson. So many of his cousins were already on the stage under the family surname that there was a danger that Henry William George Lupino might go unremarked. The 'Lane' half of his stage name was assumed in honour of his maternal great-aunt, Sarah Lane, whose management of the Britannia Theatre, Hoxton, had brought her wide fame and a great fortune.

Born in London 16 June 1892, the future Lupino Lane was bred to the stage as a matter of course, and made his first public appearance at the age of four, in a benefit performance for Vesta Tilley

[q.v.] at the Prince of Wales's Theatre, Birmingham. This was no more than a preliminary canter; but by 1903 he was far enough on in his profession to make his London début, under the name of 'Nipper' Lane, at the London Pavilion. From then onwards he proved a worthy upholder of his family tradition, and the various skills which he learned so thoroughly in those early days were invaluable to him when, with the years, he began to show himself a comedian with an endearing personality of his own.

The name 'Nipper' had suggested a creature small, quick, and neat; and small, quick, and neat he remained throughout his career. He was the very embodiment of cockneydom (it is the characteristic of the Lupinos that, although their name betokens a foreign origin, they became Londoners in grain). He had the true clown's gift of pathos, while the brilliantly executed struggles in which he could involve himself with inanimate objects—for instance, the peer's robe in which he fell from the stage into the orchestra in *Me and My Girl*—were a tribute both to his clown's instinct and his acrobat's immaculate sense of timing.

His progress towards a leading position in the world of revue and pantomime was not at first spectacular, but it was steady. In 1915 he appeared at the Empire in a successful *Watch Your Step*, and he remained there for the next two productions, and from then onwards he was seldom out of an engagement, playing 'funny man' parts of increasing importance in London, in New York, or in Manchester and the other principal cities in the then well-established touring network. Gradually the versatility of his talent became more clearly manifest. He tried his hand here at management or direction, there at authorship. He made a successful New York appearance as Ko-Ko in *The Mikado* in 1925. By the time he was forty he was well established as a leading comedian on both sides of the Atlantic.

It was not, however, until the part of the cheerful little cockney character, Bill Snibson, was written for him that his years of triumphant progress began. Snibson made his first appearance in *Twenty to One*, a musical farce by L. Arthur Rose and Frank Eyton, with music by Billy Mayerl, which opened at the London Coliseum on 12 November 1935, presented jointly by Lupino Lane and Sir Oswald Stoll [q.v.]. Lane as Snibson took the public fancy at once, and the piece ran for nearly a year and subsequently went on a long tour. This was success on a considerable scale, and turned Lane into a star performer as well as into a manager of substance; but it was swiftly put in the shade by the second Snibson play, *Me and My Girl*, in which L. Arthur Rose had Douglas Furber as collaborator and the music was composed by Noel Gay.

This piece, directed as well as presented by Lane, opened at the Victoria Palace 16 December 1937 and had the phenomenal run of 1,646 performances, for the first 1,550 of which Snibson, now raised to the peerage but still an irrepressible cockney, was played by Lane. Nor was this the end of it. The play was several times revived; and in 1942 the first Snibson play, *Twenty to One*, was revived at the Victoria Palace with Lane again in the part, and had a longer run than at first.

At the heart of the triumph of *Me and My Girl* lay, undoubtedly, the dance which swept the world—'The Lambeth Walk'. It was created by Lane to a happy little tune by Gay, and was the distilled essence of the cockney spirit. When the play was filmed (Lane yet once again playing Snibson), 'The Lambeth Walk' was chosen as title.

The result of all this was to make Lane a very rich man and a power in the world of the theatre. He was never again to enjoy success on the stage on the grand, or even on a noteworthy, scale; but he came spectacularly into the public eye in 1946 when he bought for £200,000 the Gaiety Theatre, with which his family had been connected for a hundred years. He failed, however, to find the financial backing necessary to reopen the theatre, and he resold the property in 1950.

In 1917 Lupino Lane married an actress, Violet, daughter of John Propert Blyth, sea captain; they had one son. Lane died in London 10 November 1959.

[James Dillon White, *Born to Star*, 1957; *The Times*, 11 November 1959; *Who's Who in the Theatre*; personal knowledge.]

W. A. DARLINGTON.

LANG, WILLIAM HENRY (1874–1960), botanist, was born in Groombridge, near Tunbridge Wells, 12 May 1874, the son of Thomas Bisland Lang, medical practitioner, and his wife, Emily Smith. From Dennistoun public school, Glasgow, he entered the university, obtaining his B.Sc. with honours in botany and zoology in 1894 and qualifying in medicine, with high commendation, in 1895. But he never

became an active practitioner; innate interest and the enthusiasm inspired by his teacher, F. O. Bower (whose notice he contributed to this Dictionary), led him into professional botany. His first researches were understandably concerned with development and structure in the ferns, on which, like his teacher, he became an authority. Further impetus to these interests was given by a period of work in the Jodrell laboratory at Kew where Lang began his classical observations on the enigmatic phenomena of apogamy and apospory in ferns. He made the discovery of sporangia on the prothallus of a fern (*Philosophical Transactions* of the Royal Society, 1898) which was of particular contemporary interest for biologists who were then exploring the manifestations of alternation of generations in plants and animals. All his life Lang seemed to have the knack of 'getting on to' interesting things. During the next thirty years he made further contributions to the same general theme, and he was usually to the fore when the topic of 'alternation', with its many vicissitudes, was under discussion.

At Kew, Lang came under the inspiration of D. H. Scott [q.v.], a leading exponent of fossil botany. Rumination on the nature of plant life in far-off Devonian and Carboniferous times, the cautious assessment of such incomplete fossil fragments as had been preserved, and, not least, the critical evaluation of the views of others on such materials, were occupations highly congenial to Lang. He had not only a scholarly and philosophic mind but unusual skill and patience in making the most of scanty and imperfectly preserved materials. To these were added an almost excessive caution and restraint in the eventual written interpretation of his findings, an attitude of mind which he was later to impress, perhaps with some over emphasis, on his students and colleagues.

In 1900 Lang and (Sir) A. G. Tansley [q.v.] paid a collecting visit to Ceylon and Malaya which led to subsequent publications on pteridophytes and bryophytes. In 1902 he returned as a lecturer in botany to the staff at Glasgow where he had as a colleague D. T. Gwynne-Vaughan, a plant anatomist whose research was characterized by exceptional practical skill and elegance of presentation. Bower, Gwynne-Vaughan, and Lang worked together in great harmony for some twelve years, making a famous trio—they were widely known as the Triumvirate—of whom many good stories are told. Bower, a somewhat stern disciplinarian, firmly decreed that, as students were forbidden to smoke, members of the staff must also refrain within official working hours, i.e. up till 5 p.m. Daily, as that hour approached, Lang and Gwynne-Vaughan, two sorely deprived men, were to be seen, seated in the room which they shared, each with a charged pipe in his left hand, while in the right a match was poised. As the great university bell began to toll, the soles of two left boots were simultaneously raised, two right hands swooped down in a synchronized movement to strike the matches, and two pipes in harmony began to discharge their consoling, aromatic fragrance.

During this period the Glasgow department was frequently visited by Robert Kidston of Stirling, a notable investigator of the Palaeozoic flora. Gwynne-Vaughan and he collaborated in the production of a notable series of memoirs on 'The Fossil Osmundaceae' (1907–10) and later, on the death of Gwynne-Vaughan, Lang joined with Kidston in investigating the now famous Rhynie Chert from Aberdeenshire. This was undoubtedly a landmark not only in the history of fossil botany but of botany. The silicified plant remains were in an excellent state of preservation and the two experienced investigators did not fail to make the most of them. Their observations, published in detail in the *Transactions* of the Royal Society of Edinburgh (vol. lii, 1917–21), provided quite remarkable demonstrations of the form and structure of a group of simple leafless and rootless vascular plants of early Devonian times—now known as the Psilophytales. *Psilophyton*, it is true, had been known since 1858, but it had been rather neglected and its structural features were imperfectly known. The precision with which Kidston and Lang were able to describe and portray essential morphological features and phylogenetic aspects of the new genera and species of the 'Rhynie fossils' gave great impetus and new direction to the whole of this branch of botany. These memoirs make a unique, factual contribution to evolutionary theory. At the time of their publication they had a very special interest for the many botanists who were then actively interested in the establishment of the original flora of the land in early geological times. Other neglected fossil materials, of the same general period and affinity and often of the most tenuous and fragmentary character, were subsequently

investigated by Lang. Later, in collaboration with Dr. Isabel C. Cookson, Lang was able to show, in a study of materials from the Australian Silurian, that primitive vascular plants, not unlike a lycopod in their general configuration, had flourished in geological times much earlier than the Devonian. Other ancient materials investigated by Kidston and Lang (e.g. *Sporocarpon, Transactions* of the Royal Society of Edinburgh, vol. liii, 1925) provoked new interest because they were made at a time when students of phylogeny were eagerly searching for evidence of possible connecting links between the algae and the first primitive land plants.

In 1900 Lang was awarded the D.Sc. degree of Glasgow and when the Barker chair of cryptogamic botany was established in the university of Manchester, he was the evident first choice. He took up his duties in 1909, and though tempted and urged by some of his friends to apply for professorships elsewhere, he refused to give up the freedom of what was virtually a research chair. When he retired in 1940 he had already been father of the senate and elder statesman for many years; his work for the university and his personal pre-eminence were recognized by an honorary LL.D. in 1942. He was elected F.R.S. in 1911 and awarded a Royal medal in 1931. In 1932 he received an honorary LL.D. from Glasgow. He was a foreign member of the Swedish Royal Academy of Science and in 1956 received the gold medal of the Linnean Society of London.

Lang was of tall stature, a keen walker, with the air of one who enjoyed good health. He was a distinguished professorial figure, for from his student days he had cultivated a noble dark beard. An amiable and stimulating conversationalist, with an agreeable, cynical pawkiness and jollity of delivery, the words fairly fizzed out of him, enjoyed no less by himself than his hearers. But he was essentially a quiet and modest man, with wide scholarly and artistic interests and a deep feeling for philosophy, especially for the caution and restraint which it could exercise on the facile and often superficial theorizing from which contemporary botany was by no means free. This attitude of mind pervaded his memorable presidential address to the botany section of the British Association in 1915. His discourse on 'Phyletic and Causal Morphology' was not only remarkable for its practical and philosophic insight into major problems of causation in plant development and evolution, reflecting as it did the best that had been thought and said by Hofmeister, Sachs, and Goebel, and by Lang himself, but also for his refreshingly critical attitude to the prevailing comparative morphology of the post-Darwinian period.

Lang married his cousin, Elsa Valentine, of Dublin, in 1910, but they had no family. On his retirement from Manchester his friends and associates hoped that there was still much more to come from his pen. But this was only to be fulfilled in a small measure, largely because of his wife's ill health. They moved to Milnthorpe in Westmorland where, after some years, she died, to be followed on 29 August 1960 by Lang himself.

A complete set of his published work is preserved in the university of Manchester where a fund perpetuates his memory.

[Private information; personal knowledge.]
C. W. WARDLAW.

LARKE, SIR WILLIAM JAMES (1875–1959), first director of the British Iron and Steel Federation, was born at Ladywell, Kent, 26 April 1875, the eldest son of William James Larke, builder, by his wife, Rosa Barton. He was educated at Colfe's School, Lewisham, and trained as an engineer with H. F. Joel & Co., Finsbury, and Siemens Brothers, Woolwich. In 1898 he joined the British Thomson-Houston Company, becoming engineer and manager of its power and mining department in 1899 and executive engineer in 1912.

He joined the newly established Ministry of Munitions in 1915 where he was mainly concerned with organizational and administrative matters, becoming director-general of raw materials in 1919. The administrative skill which he showed at the Ministry, added to his industrial experience as an engineer, provided the combination of qualities which he further exercised in the national organization of the steel industry after the war. Also linking his war experience with his later career was his service as secretary of the sub-committee of post-war iron and steel requirements of the Ministry of Munitions council committee on demobilization and reconstruction. The chairman of this group was Walter (later Lord) Layton, the first director of the National Federation of Iron and Steel Manufacturers, whom Larke succeeded in that office in 1922.

Taking over at a time of acute industrial depression, Larke steadily advanced the arguments for control of imports and a measure of protection for the British iron and steel industry. This policy was finally accepted by the Government and embodied in the Import Duties Act of 1932. As a result of the Act, and of recommendations from the Import Duties Advisory Council, which it set up, for a stronger central organization for the iron and steel industry, the British Iron and Steel Federation came into existence in 1934 and the National Federation was dissolved. Larke, who had played an important part in the transition, continued as director of the new and more powerful organization, under its chairman, Sir Andrew Rae Duncan [q.v.], until his retirement in 1946.

In 1939 Larke was made chairman of the advisory committee of non-ferrous minerals at the Ministry of Supply and in 1942 he became controller of non-ferrous mineral development, a post he held until the end of the war.

Larke was continuously active in promoting research and co-operation directed to technological efficiency within the iron and steel industry. Combining scientific knowledge, thorough experience of industrial affairs, and a genial personality, he fitted naturally into leading positions in a large number of industrial and professional bodies. In 1924, early in his association with the National Federation of Iron and Steel Manufacturers, the Federation undertook the organization of co-operative research. This work was transferred in 1929 to the Iron and Steel Industrial Research Council, of which Larke was chairman from 1938 to 1945. He was elected vice-president of the Iron and Steel Institute in 1934, became honorary vice-president in 1946, and was awarded the Institute's Bessemer medal in 1947. He was also in his time president of the Junior Institution of Engineers, of the Institute of Fuel, of the Institute of Welding, and of the British Standards Institution.

He was appointed O.B.E. in 1917, C.B.E. in 1920, and K.B.E. in 1921. He received the honorary degree of D.Sc. from the university of Durham in 1945. He married in 1900 Louisa Jane (died 1959), daughter of James Taylor Milton, chief engineer surveyor of Lloyd's Register of Shipping, of Blackheath; they had one daughter and a son, W. M. Larke, who became general manager of Stewart and Lloyds, Ltd., Bilston, Staffordshire. Larke died 29 April 1959 at his home at Sidcup, Kent.

[*The Times*, 1 May 1959; *Engineer*, 8 May 1959; J. C. Carr and W. Taplin, *History of the British Steel Industry*, 1962; private information.]   WALTER TAPLIN.

LAST, HUGH MACILWAIN (1894–1957), Roman historian and principal of Brasenose College, Oxford, was born at Putney 3 December 1894, the son of William Isaac Last, a civil engineer who became director of the Science Museum, South Kensington, by his wife, Anna Maria Quare, daughter of the medical writer George Macilwain [q.v.]. At St. Paul's School, of which he was a scholar, Last came particularly under the influence of T. Rice Holmes [q.v.] who turned his attention towards the world of Rome. In 1914 he passed with an open scholarship into Lincoln College, Oxford, where he remained a solitary undergraduate throughout the war, his heart having been affected by attacks of bronchitis. He obtained first classes in honour moderations (1916) and *literae humaniores* (1918), and established a very close relationship with his tutor W. Warde Fowler [q.v.] who revealed to him not only a comprehensive conception of Republican Rome but also that world of international scholarship which later formed the background of his life. Last had begun his Oxford career late, and undisturbed by the normal preoccupations of undergraduate life he matured intellectually at an early age. He was able to read deeply and widely in those branches of ancient history, notably the history of the ancient Orient, which were not part of the normal curriculum. This wide reading bore valuable fruit in a sympathetic understanding of the needs of such subjects, particularly Egyptology, which Last took practical steps to promote within and without the university. It also led to a close friendship with many leading figures in these subjects, notably H. R. H. Hall [q.v.]. Throughout his life Last formed his closest friendships with men considerably older than himself.

When in 1919 Last was elected to an official fellowship in ancient history at St. John's, his future as a Roman historian was already clear. He quickly made his mark in the college: as a teacher who, notwithstanding his confident mastery of his subject and Olympian manner, took endless pains with the second and third class men and won his pupils' affection, and in other walks of college life. He played an active part on the governing body and

soon stood out as an able man of affairs with a particular interest in the agricultural and financial policy of the college. In the wider field of university affairs Last was also making a mark: he was a trenchant, if slightly ponderous, debater and his frequently contemptuous dismissal of his opponents made him many enemies. A colleague recalls 'how he killed a proposal for an honour school of anthropology with the remark that "an acquaintance with the habits of savages is not an education" '. He was already consciously building the image of himself which he presented to the world: the international scholar who was also a man of affairs. To this image Last imparted a suitable outward appearance: tall, dark, and heavily built, with a deliberate gait, and always dressed with the greatest care, his Homburg hat, his pipe, his walking stick, and the grey woollen scarf thrown back over his shoulder. There is an admirable likeness of him in Sir Muirhead Bone's interior of Blackwell's of which he is the central figure.

Last's reputation as a Roman historian was firmly established by his contributions to the *Cambridge Ancient History* for which, with (Sir) Henry Stuart-Jones [q.v.], he was chosen to write on the earliest history of Rome in the seventh volume (1928). One of his only two sustained pieces of writing, these chapters reveal his historical position more clearly than his later account of Republican history from the Gracchi to Sulla which appeared in the ninth volume (1932). His account of early Rome shows an unusual combination of solid erudition, developed powers of close reasoning, admirable judgement, and a certain solemn eloquence, which (in spite of some unexpected heterodoxies) gives that work a lasting value and sets it at the head of his writings. Throughout this reconstruction he showed his close kinship with the two great historians Gaetano De Sanctis and Theodor Mommsen. These greatly influenced Last's notions of the social and political development of Rome. His admiration for Mommsen was an important factor in the development of that truly astonishing capacity for constitutional detail which later provided him, as Camden professor, with the raw material for his weighty and almost oracular lectures on the Roman Republican constitution. On the other hand, Last's reverence for the achievements of the nineteenth-century German historians led to some atrophy of his own wider interests (for instance in the ancient history of the Near East) and to his adoption of a rather negative attitude towards the discovery of new forms of investigation within the field of Roman history. To the end he was always captivated by the fascination of new evidence, but he remained unimpressed by many of the new approaches to the existing body of knowledge. While wholly familiar with inscriptions, papyri, and coins, these were for him simply historical material for his task of interpreting to the common man, and above all to the undergraduate, the spirit quickening Rome's history, and he rarely attempted direct technical work on them.

While developing into an authoritative and influential figure in the university and in the national field of Roman studies (he was president of the Roman Society in 1934–7), Last, who never married, still found time for other pursuits: his main recreations were nightly bridge in college with Stuart-Jones and others, golf, and occasional shooting at Bagley Wood, while in vacation he returned regularly to relax at his family home at Harlow in Essex. Of travel as an aid to the study of ancient history, he was frankly sceptical; apart from frequent visits to Italy (which gained him a facetious reputation as an admirer of Mussolini) he travelled little.

In 1936 Last, who had been university lecturer in Roman history since 1927, was appointed Camden professor and migrated to Brasenose. His influence in the sub-faculty was perhaps not much greater than it had been when he was a fellow of St. John's, even if he now became less critical of academic policy. But his influence as a teacher increased: he was free to lecture both on the subject always nearest to his heart, the Roman constitution, traditionally a lecture of the Camden professor, and on some more peripheral subjects. He was able to confirm and extend his influence on young graduates beginning the advanced study of Roman history; and he used his weighty authority in public debate, both in and out of the university, in the defence of classical studies. It was undoubtedly as a supervisor of young graduates that Last scored his greatest success; he possessed unusual patience and skill in determining suitable subjects of research, and remained a constant, if not infrequently sardonic, adviser as the work developed. The influence which he exercised over young historians

extended far beyond Oxford, and was acknowledged wherever Roman studies were prosecuted: he received honorary degrees from Edinburgh (1938) and Trinity College, Dublin (1948), and was elected a honorary fellow of Lincoln (1939).

Great though his professional achievement was, the passage of time brought no major work from Last's pen. With his main contributions to the *Cambridge Ancient History*, the last of which was published in 1936, his original work was largely over. Certainly he wrote much (although always with difficulty, and in an involved and unattractive style), but his published work took increasingly the form of learned and often elaborate reviews of the works of others. The intervention of the war (during much of which he was employed on government intelligence work) may have been partly responsible for this, but in fact the trend was already clear. Last had lost the most important qualities of an historian—a lively historical imagination and a lasting creative vein—and his hyper-developed critical sense made this defect only more marked. Nevertheless, while in these years he did not write the book which many hoped for on the Roman constitution, his interests were developing in another field, largely through the influence of N. H. Baynes. Last, as if conscious of his own deficiency, always had the greatest respect for those who possessed the gift of imaginative writing; nobody excited his admiration and affection as much as Baynes, whose profound learning and dramatic eloquence had done much to stimulate the study of the Christian Empire, and in these years Last's thoughts turned continually to the problems connected with the early history of Christianity. Another aspect of Roman civilization which increasingly occupied his attention was the Roman legal system; he sought to bring home in his later years the realities of the civil law to the historical student, and devoted several courses of advanced lectures to various aspects of this general problem.

In 1948 on the sudden death of W. T. S. Stallybrass [q.v.] Last was offered the principalship of Brasenose which he accepted against medical advice. In the years between the wars the college had been an affluent and convivial society but now the main task which faced Last was the restoration of its financial stability. In the few years available to him he notably improved the financial position of the college and left his mark upon its intellectual standards by his full encouragement of all aspects of college life. In 1956 ill health compelled him to resign and he was elected an emeritus fellow. He died at Harlow 25 October 1957.

[*The Times*, 30 October 1957; *Manchester Guardian*, 1 November 1957; *The Brazen Nose*, vol. xi, Winter 1957–8; *Journal of Roman Studies*, vol. xlvii, 1957 (volume of papers presented to Last, with bibliography); private information; personal knowledge.]

P. M. FRASER.

LATHAM, PETER WALKER (1865–1953), rackets and tennis champion, was born in Manchester 10 May 1865, the only child of William Latham, engine fitter, and his wife, Sarah Jane Hewitt. Latham was not a strong boy when, at the age of eleven, he started his ball-game life in the Manchester Rackets Club. However, he developed well in body and in the art of playing rackets until, in 1887, when not quite twenty-two, he challenged Joseph Gray of Rugby for the world's championship and won by 7 games to 4. In 1888 he was engaged as head professional of rackets at the Queen's Club, West Kensington, where, and at Charterhouse, he was successful in defending his title against Walter Gray of Charterhouse by 6 games to 3. During the next eight years, except for a professional championship in 1891 when Latham beat George Standing, professional to Prince's Club, Knightsbridge, by 5 games to 0, he was not challenged, and this gave him a good opportunity to devote his attention to real tennis. This game came easily to him, so that in 1895 he challenged Charles Saunders, who had for long held an impregnable position, and at Brighton won the British title by 7 sets to 2.

Latham was at his best at rackets in 1897 when he was challenged for the world's championship by George Standing who by this time had gone to America. In London Latham won by 4 games to 1, but in America he played what was probably the hardest and greatest match of his career, at one time coming within an ace of losing, but finally winning by 4 games to 3.

In the next year (1898) Latham was at his best at tennis when he played Tom Pettitt of Boston and for the first time met the 'railroad' service which he was only able to counter by his knowledge of rackets. Nevertheless he defeated Pettitt decisively by 7 sets to 0. For several years Latham remained supreme in both games.

In 1902 he retained the world's championship of rackets when challenged by Gilbert Browne of Prince's whom he easily defeated by 5 games to 0. He then resigned his title, although until 1909 he was rated scratch in the professional handicap competitions.

In the meantime he had become tennis professional to (Sir) Charles Rose who in 1901 built a tennis court at Newmarket. In 1904 he was challenged at tennis by C. (Punch) Fairs of Prince's and won at Brighton by 7 sets to 5. In the next year he lost the title to Fairs by 5 sets to 1—his only defeat in a championship match—but regained it two years later at the age of forty-two when he defeated Fairs by 7 sets to 3. He then retired from championship play and for some years played exhibition matches in America and on the Continent.

In 1916 Latham returned to the Queen's Club, where he did much to revive tennis after the war and was greatly sought after as a teacher. He was blessed with many exceptional qualities, which were not fully apparent to the spectator but were quickly discovered by his opponents. His service may not have looked remarkable but it was delivered to prevent his opponent from making his favourite return and to obtain the attack and put his adversary on the defensive. Always well balanced, he was very quick to move at the critical moment, so that it appeared as though the ball was always being hit towards him. In the words of an amateur who had played with Latham at his best in both games: 'He was an artist ever seeking perfection. For him it was not enough that a stroke should be a winner. It had to be that and more, the more being that even he could not improve it.'

Latham married in 1888 Annie Sarah Carpenter, daughter of Stephen Whetham, flax cleaner for rope making, of Bridport. They had one daughter and four sons, one of whom, Emil, became a tennis professional at Queen's Club. Latham died in his home at Chiswick, 22 November 1953. He appears in the painting 'In the Dedans at Queen's Club' by Mrs. Jean Clark which became the possession of Mr. P. M. Luttman-Johnson.

[Private information; personal knowledge.]

ABERDARE.

LAUTERPACHT, SIR HERSCH (1897–1960), international lawyer, was born 16 August 1897 at Zolkiew, a village near Lemberg (Lwow) in Eastern Galicia. His father was Aaron Lauterpacht, a timber merchant of fluctuating fortune. His mother was Deborah Turkenkopf. There were three children of the marriage, he being the younger son of a family deeply Jewish in sentiment and sympathy. The entire family in Poland, excepting only his sister's daughter who found refuge in a convent, was massacred during the war of 1939–45.

In 1910 the family moved to Lemberg to enable Hersch Lauterpacht to receive a better secondary education. On the outbreak of war, as an Austrian subject, he was mobilized into the Austrian army but was required to serve in his father's timber factory, which was requisitioned and in a territory occupied and reoccupied by the Russian and Austrian armed forces. After the war, because of academic difficulties at Lwow, he went to the university of Vienna where he obtained his doctorate in law in 1921 and, as a student of Hans Kelsen, a doctorate in political science in 1922.

Both at Lemberg and in Vienna, he took a very prominent part in Jewish and Zionist affairs, organizing schoolchildren and students not least in order to make provision for their desperate human needs. It was this early experience which moulded his intellectual and emotional interest in human rights and their international protection. He was a founder and president of a World Federation of Jewish Students.

In the spring of 1923 Lauterpacht came to England, and although he could barely speak English he entered the London School of Economics as a research student under the direction of A. D. (later Lord) McNair, for whom he always retained the deepest respect and affection, regarding him as the great formative influence in his life. He obtained his LL.D. in 1925 with a dissertation entitled 'Private Law Sources and Analogies of International Law' (published in 1927), which has been described as a 'seminal work of contemporary international law', and in 1927 he was appointed an assistant lecturer at the London School of Economics. At that point he decided to attach himself permanently to this country, and he was naturalized a British subject in 1931.

His career in his adopted country was truly remarkable. He became reader in public international law in the university of London in 1935. In 1938–55 he held the Whewell chair of international law in the university of Cambridge, in succession to McNair. In 1946 he became a fellow of

Trinity College and in 1948 of the British Academy. In 1936 he was called to the bar by Gray's Inn and he took silk in 1949. He did much advisory work at the bar, and was specially associated with the 'Continental Shelf' arbitrations, appearing for the Petroleum Development Company in the great *Abu Dhabi* case. During the war of 1939–45, in the critical period of American neutrality, he was able when visiting the United States to render very valuable service to the United Kingdom. He was a member of the British War Crimes Executive in 1945–6 and attended the Nuremberg trials. He was of counsel for the United Kingdom in the *Corfu Channel* and the *Anglo-Iranian Oil Company* (Interim measures) cases before the International Court of Justice at The Hague; he advised in other cases and was entrusted with the revision of the *Manual of Military Law*, eventually published by the War Office in 1958. He was a member of the Institute of International Law (associate in 1947 and titular in 1952); and he was elected to the United Nations' International Law Commission in 1951, discharging his heavy duties there with great conscientiousness during four years, two of them as special rapporteur on the law of treaties. He accepted visiting professorships at many universities, particularly at Geneva and in the United States, and he delivered courses of lectures at the Hague Academy of International Law in 1930, 1934, 1937, and 1947.

His lectures at Geneva were published in 1934 under the title *The Development of International Law by the Permanent Court of International Justice* (2nd and expanded ed. 1958).

Among his numerous other books and articles—there is a convenient account of them by Dr. C. W. Jenks—four require special mention: *The Function of Law in the International Community* (1933), *Recognition in International Law* (1947), and *International Law and Human Rights* (1950): the first being his most important contribution to the understanding and development of international law, the second his most comprehensive treatment of a topic of enduring and ever-increasing practical importance, the third the consecration of a lifelong interest and preoccupation. The fourth is his long anniversary article (vol. xxiii, *British Year Book of International Law*, 1946) entitled 'The Grotian tradition in International Law' which is a typical illustration of his own thinking and methods.

Concurrently he was fully occupied with his other academic duties. He took great pains with the standard course of lectures which he delivered as Whewell professor in Cambridge. The clarity of his presentation, the width of his learning, the skill of his exposition, and his own total commitment made an almost prophetical impression upon a succession of audiences. The success of his lectures was an important factor in the development of international studies at Cambridge. His reputation at home and abroad gathered round him a large number of research students who have claimed it as a special distinction that they were trained under his rigorous supervision.

His capacity for work was formidable, for in addition to the occupations already mentioned, he was concerned continuously with three major tasks—the editing, amplifying, and renovating of the standard two-volume textbook by L. F. L. Oppenheim [q.v.] on International Law (now 'Oppenheim–Lauterpacht') ; the editing of the *British Year Book of International Law*, of exceptional authority in this field, which was under his exclusive direction between 1944 and 1954 ; and the truly monumental *Annual Digest of Public International Cases* (now the *International Law Reports*) with which he was connected from its outset and for which he had sole responsibility for the twenty-eight years 1929–56.

His career culminated in his election in 1954 to a judgeship of the International Court of Justice, whereupon he was elected a bencher of his Inn in 1955 and was knighted in 1956. It was universally expected that during his tenure of the nine-year office (and its probable renewals) he would add to his achievements an epoch-making series of judgements. His contributions as a judge were indeed not negligible—they have been analysed in detail by Sir Gerald Fitzmaurice—but he suffered a severe heart attack in 1959 and on 8 May 1960 he died in London as the result of an operation, at the judicially almost immature age of sixty-two, to the great and untimely loss of international legal science.

In his personal life, he was most simple and modest and quiet—it was very hard to believe that he had once been an active Zionist. He was exceptionally good-humoured and good-natured, dedicated indeed and devoted to his work and to his students but without solemnity, of high but straightforward moral principles, deeply attached to his wife and son and

profoundly appreciative of the happiness of his home, kindly and friendly and cheerful. He had married in 1923 Rachel, the third daughter of Michael Steinberg, resident in Palestine. Their only child, Elihu, himself attained distinction in the international legal world.

There is a bust by Madeleine Winiarska-Cotowika in the possession of the family, and a memorial room in the Squire Law Library, Cambridge.

[Lord McNair in *Proceedings* of the British Academy, vol. xlvii, 1961 ; Dr. C. W. Jenks in vol. xxxvi *British Year Book of International Law*, 1960 ; Sir Gerald Fitzmaurice in vols. xxxvii–xxxix *British Year Book of International Law*, 1961–3 ; *Studies . . . in memory of Sir H. L.* published by the Faculty of Law of the Hebrew University of Jerusalem, ed. N. Feinberg, with bibliography, 1961 ; private information ; personal knowledge.]

C. J. HAMSON.

LAWRENCE, GERTRUDE (1898–1952), actress, was born in London 4 July 1898. Her real name was Gertrud Alexandra Dagma Lawrence Klasen, her father, Arthur Lawrence Klasen, a music-hall singer, being Danish, while her mother, Alice Louise Banks, was English. The child's parents were divorced while she was still in infancy, and she lived first with her mother, a small-part actress, then later with her father. She was thus brought up in a theatrical atmosphere from her earliest years.

She made her first stage appearance in a pantomime at Brixton in 1910. In his autobiography, (Sir) Noël Coward tells how he met her as a child-performer in the year 1913 : 'Her face was far from pretty, but tremendously alive. She was very *mondaine*, carried a handbag with a powder-puff and frequently dabbed her generously turned-up nose. She confided to me that her name was Gertrude Lawrence, but that I was to call her Gert because everybody did . . . I loved her from then onwards.' She became the foremost of all Coward's leading ladies, a perennial feather in his brilliant cap.

In her early days Gertrude Lawrence was solely a revue and cabaret artist. Her first manager was André Charlot [q.v.] and her first really big success was in *London Calling* in 1923, a revue written by Noël Coward. The best of his musical plays, *Bitter Sweet* (1929), was written with her in mind, but it was finally decided that her voice was too light for so heavy a singing part as that of Sari. So he wrote *Private Lives* (1930) in which

they played together. The play's success
was immediate in both London and New
York. Thereafter New York would never
willingly allow Gertrude Lawrence to
return to her native London. James
Agate [q.v.], seeing her in a musical
comedy, had already called her a very
considerable artist who could neither
dance nor sing but had an astonishing
power of mimicry and sense of fun, adding
that she gave a brilliant edge to everything she said and did. George Jean
Nathan in New York—another critic with
few favourites—spent the subsequent
twenty-five years praising her glitter and
effervescence in plays which included
Lady in the Dark and *Pygmalion*, and
finally the excellent and evocative musical
play, *The King and I*, in which Gertrude
Lawrence was triumphantly appearing on
Broadway when her fatal illness overtook
her.

Noël Coward knew and understood her
better than her critics or her public. In
the last pages of his *Present Indicative*
he records her personal qualities of
'quick humour, insane generosity, and a
loving heart', and recalls her performance
in *Private Lives*: 'the witty quick-silver
delivery of lines; the romantic quality,
tender and alluring; the swift, brittle
rages; even the white Molyneux dress'.
She was an actress of high vitality, keen
wit, and undoubted style—a fine flaunt-
ing player—with a strange gift of muta-
bility, of altering her appearance for
each part she played or even within the
same part.

Gertrude Lawrence was twice married:
first, in 1917, to Francis Xavier Howley,
playwright and producer, by whom she
had a daughter. The marriage was
dissolved. In 1940 she married Richard
Stoddard Aldrich, an American. She
published her own racy reminiscences,
A Star Danced, in 1945. But she comes
more vividly and touchingly to life
in Noël Coward's *Present Indicative* (1937)
and *Future Indefinite* (1954); her art,
charm, and elegance are best epitomized
in the recording she made with him of
scenes from his *Private Lives* culminating
in the haunting song, 'Some day I'll find
you'.

She died in New York 6 September 1952.
A film of her life, entitled *Star!*, was
made in 1968 with Julie Andrews playing
Gertrude Lawrence.

[Gertrude Lawrence, *A Star Danced*, 1945;
R. S. Aldrich, *Gertrude Lawrence as Mrs. A.*,
1957; private information.]   ALAN DENT.

LAWRENCE, SIR PAUL OGDEN (1861–
1952), judge, was born in Wimbledon,
Surrey, 8 September 1861, the second son
of Philip Henry Lawrence, solicitor, by
his wife, Margaret Davies. His father
conducted the heavy litigation which
resulted in the preservation for the
public enjoyment of the commons in the
vicinity of London. He was subsequently
solicitor to the Board of Works, was called
to the bar by Lincoln's Inn in 1872, and
died in 1895.

Lawrence was educated at Malvern
College and abroad and was called to the
bar by Lincoln's Inn in 1882. He joined
the Northern circuit and started practice
in the Liverpool chambers of (Sir) Ralph
Neville, subsequently a Chancery judge.
He practised in the Palatine Court until
1896 when, on taking silk, he removed to
London, attaching himself to the court
of Mr. Justice Kekewich [q.v.] in the
Chancery division. On that judge's death
in 1907 he attached himself to the court of
Mr. Justice Eve [q.v.]. He acquired a
considerable Chancery practice and often
appeared in the House of Lords and the
Judicial Committee of the Privy Council.
He was frequently engaged in Indian
appeals; and in 1918, towards the close of
his career at the bar, he appeared in the
special reference to the Judicial Committee of the claims to the ownership
of the unalienated lands in Southern
Rhodesia, representing the elected members of the legislative council. (See *In re
Southern Rhodesia*, [1919] A.C. 211.) At
the bar his exact knowledge, incisive and
lucid argument, and attractive advocacy
made him a formidable, but always fair
and courteous, opponent.

On the death of Neville, Lawrence was
appointed to succeed him in 1918 as a
Chancery judge and was knighted (1919).
He brought to the judicial office the
qualities of an eminently practical man of
the world and a scholarly lawyer, shrewd,
cautious, and strong. In 1926 he went to
the Court of Appeal (and was sworn of
the Privy Council) where he sat for the
last time on 21 December 1933. He died
at Wimbledon 26 December 1952.

In 1885 three of Lawrence's sisters,
Penelope, Dorothy, and Millicent, enlisted
his financial help in the foundation of
Roedean School, and he maintained a
close connection with it throughout his
life. In important decisions concerning
its development his advice was always
sought. For many years he was chairman
of the governing body, and generations of

upils knew him as 'Uncle Paul'. His portrait, by Hugh Riviere, hangs in the main hall at Roedean.

Lawrence became a conservator of Wimbledon Common in 1901. He was chairman of the General Council of the Bar from 1913 to 1918 and chairman of the Incorporated Council of Law Reporting from 1917 to 1919. He served as treasurer of Lincoln's Inn in 1925.

In 1887 Lawrence married Maude Mary (died 1947), daughter of John Turner, of Oaklands, Wimbledon Park; there were no children.

[*Law Times*, 9 January 1953; *The Times*, 29 December 1952.]   F. H. COWPER.

LEDWARD, GILBERT (1888–1960), sculptor, was born in Chelsea 23 January 1888, the third child of Richard Arthur Ledward, the sculptor [q.v.], and his wife, Mary Jane Wood, descendent of a long line of Staffordshire master potters and figure makers. He went to school at St. Mark's College, Chelsea, leaving in 1901 because his widowed mother had decided to take her five children to live in Germany. He returned to England alone after a year, lived with relatives and started full-time training as a sculptor at the Royal College of Art, under the tutelage of Edouard Lantéri. His early instruction was almost entirely in the art of modelling, the general practice of British sculptors at this period being to employ skilled professional carvers, who were mostly Italian, to do their stone-carving for them. In 1907 he went on to the Royal Academy School. In 1913 he completed his first important commission, a stone Calvary at Bourton-on-the-Water, Gloucestershire. In the same year he won the double honour of the Academy travelling studentship and gold medal and the first Rome scholarship in sculpture. He spent valuable months closely studying Italian art, making innumerable sketches and copious notes.

The outbreak of war brought his travels to an end, but 1917 found him back in Italy, on the front, serving as a lieutenant with the Royal Garrison Artillery. He was called home in May 1918 and seconded to the Ministry of Information as an official war artist. In this capacity he produced reliefs for the Imperial War Museum, work which gave full scope both to his power of composition and to his dramatic vision of the brutality and heroism of war. The demand for memorials brought commissions in Stockport,

Abergavenny, London, and many other places. Of these the best known is probably the Guards Memorial in London. In 1926–9 he was professor of sculpture at the Royal College of Art and in each of these three years one of his students won the Rome scholarship.

Never afraid to learn from his students it was during this time that Ledward began to make bold experiments in his own work. Hitherto he had been primarily a maker of modelled monuments in bronze but now he began to awake to the exciting possibilities inherent in direct stone carving. During the next few years he exhibited several groups at Burlington House which were recognized to be original and exciting examples of direct carving. Among these were 'Earth Rests', a life-size reclining figure in Roman stone, in the diploma gallery collection at Burlington House; 'The Sunflower', a life-size mother and child, in the Kelvingrove collection, Glasgow; and 'Monolith', purchased for the Tate Gallery under the Chantrey Bequest. Another enterprise of this period was the initiation of a movement for improving the design and carving of memorials and headstones in English churchyards and for encouraging the use of local stones.

In 1932 he was elected A.R.A. and in 1937 became R.A. He was always unfailingly loyal to the aims and values of Burlington House and outspoken in his defence of Academic traditions although he was always alert to praise the best in modern experimental work. Able to adapt himself to a wide variety of forms, he obtained commissions as varied as they were numerous. Among his many portrait busts those of Bishop de Labilliere (1944), Rachel Gurney (1945), and Admiral Sir Martin Dunbar-Nasmith, V.C. (1948) were especially praised. Other works that excited considerable interest were his memorial to the Submarine Service, Commandos, and Airborne Forces (1948) in the cloister of Westminster Abbey, the bronze groups for the Hospital for Sick Children, Great Ormond Street (1952), the Sloane Square fountain (1953), and the Great Seal of the Realm (1953). His last work, finished just before his death, was a great stone frieze above the entrance to Barclays D.C.O. Bank in Old Broad Street, E.C.2. Before starting this carving he toured Africa extensively, filling many sketch books with studies and using these drawings to give the work reality and strength.

In 1954–6 Ledward was president of the Royal Society of British Sculptors, in 1956–7 a trustee of the Royal Academy. In 1956 he was appointed O.B.E. He always maintained that of all the arts sculpture was the most permanent and the surest guide to the health of a nation —a barometer of civilization—and he never spared himself in his efforts to produce the best of which he was capable: a truly dedicated artist. He believed that sculpture, to be seen at its best, must stand in the open air and it is fitting that an early bronze figure, 'Awakening', considered by many to be his most inspired work, should grace a small garden on the Chelsea Embankment, very near to the house where he was born.

In 1911 Ledward married Margery Beatrix Cheesman (died 1960); they had two daughters and one son. He died in London 21 June 1960. A drawing of Ledward as a boy by Frederick Marriott is in the possession of the family.

[Private information; personal knowledge.]
CHARLES WHEELER.

LEE, ROBERT WARDEN (1868–1958), lawyer, was born at Hanmer 14 December 1868, the third son of the vicar, the Rev. Matthew Henry Lee, later canon of St. Asaph, and his wife, Louisa, daughter of Robert Warden. A scholar of Rossall School and Balliol College, Oxford, he obtained a double first in classics (1889–91). He spent the years 1891–4 in the Ceylon Civil Service, where his experience as a magistrate and commissioner of requests awoke in him an interest in Roman-Dutch law, the common law of Ceylon. He resigned for reasons of health and returned to England, where he was called to the bar by Gray's Inn (1896), obtained the degree of B.C.L. (1898), practised before the Privy Council, mainly in appeals from Ceylon, and taught law both at Worcester College, Oxford, of which he became a fellow in 1903, and at London University, where he held the chair of Roman-Dutch law from 1906. In 1914 he went to Montreal as dean of the law faculty of McGill University, but in 1921 Oxford called him back as its first and only professor of Roman-Dutch law. He occupied the chair, in conjunction with a fellowship of All Souls, for thirty-six years, and only retired in 1956 at the age of eighty-seven after a serious operation.

Most of Lee's writing was done while he held the Oxford chair, but his most famous work, the Introduction to Roman Dutch Law, of which five editions had appeared by 1953, came out in 1915. Admirably clear, attractive, and well proportioned, its concise and allusive language is designed, as he himself emphasized, to whet the appetite. Several generations of South African and Ceylon lawyers were brought up on it and as a laconic and ironical introductory work in the civil law tradition it can stand comparison with the Institutes of Gaius. Lee's two-volume work on Grotius' Introduction to the Jurisprudence of Holland (1926–36) is now of value chiefly for the English translation and commentary. His Elements of Roman Law (1944), published in his seventies, has been very successful with students.

Lee was a firm protagonist of codification and attached great importance to his part in producing the Digest of English Civil Law edited by Edward Jenks (whose notice Lee contributed to this Dictionary) and two similar volumes on the law of South Africa (1950–54) which he edited in collaboration with A. M. Honoré, although they did not give the impetus he hoped to the movement for codification.

Lee was a fine teacher, whose pupils included at least half a dozen judges. All his pupils, distinguished or not, could implicitly rely on his painstaking care and loyal support of their interests. His loyalties were also engaged by All Souls College and by the Inns of Court, where he was for long reader in Roman and Roman-Dutch law to the Council of Legal Education. He received many honours, for he was, inter alia, a K.C. of the Quebec bar (1920), a fellow of the British Academy (1933), a bencher of Gray's Inn (1934), an honorary doctor of the universities of Lyon, the Witwatersrand, and Ceylon, president of the Society of Public Teachers of Law, and vice-president of the International Academy of Comparative Law.

Although Lee devoted a good part of his life to the study of Roman-Dutch law, he looked upon it with detachment. Himself a classical scholar who delighted in composing Latin verses—his Series Episcoporum Romanae Ecclesiae (1935) is an elegant example—he was impatient of the historical bent of some South African lawyers and was apt to say, with a twinkle, that the old authorities should be burned. This has not happened, but the modern legal systems of South Africa and Ceylon have now come to be regarded as distinct from the Roman-Dutch law of renaissance Holland, and it has been said with some truth that this sturdy Victorian individualist was the last Roman-Dutch lawyer.

In 1914 Lee married Amice, daughter of Sir John Macdonell, the jurist, whose notice Lee contributed to this Dictionary. They had one daughter. Lee died in London 6 January 1958. A charcoal drawing by I. Plaente and a pastel by K. Lloyd are in the possession of the family.

[H. G. Hanbury in *Proceedings* of the British Academy, vol. xliv, 1958; *American Journal of Comparative Law*, vol. vii, Autumn 1958; *The Times*, 7 January 1958; personal knowledge.]   A. M. HONORÉ.

LEES, GEORGE MARTIN (1898-1955), geologist, born at Dundalk, county Louth, Ireland, 16 April 1898, was the third child of George Murray Lees, civil engineer, of Edinburgh, and his wife, Mary Martin. From St. Andrew's College, Dublin, he went to the Royal Military Academy at Woolwich. Commissioned at seventeen in the Royal Artillery he served in France but soon transferred to the Royal Flying Corps in which he won the M.C. After a tour of duty as flying instructor in Egypt he went to Mesopotamia for further active service, winning the D.F.C. in air operations. He took part in the capture of Kirkuk from the Turks, making a forced landing behind the Turkish lines in what is now the Kirkuk oilfield, regaining the British lines on foot by following geological outcrops seen from the air.

After the war Lees joined the civil administration in Iraq (1919-21), serving as assistant political officer in the mountainous Halabja district close to the Persian frontier. At the time of the insurrection he had an exciting escape, but later returned to Kurdistan. He resigned from the Iraq administration in April 1921 and began to study geology, in which he had become interested in Kurdistan. After a few months at the Royal School of Mines he joined the Anglo-Persian Oil Company (later the British Petroleum Company, Ltd.) in October 1921, as assistant geologist, without formal academic qualifications. The wisdom of this appointment was soon revealed by the excellence of his geological work and his appointment in 1930 as chief geologist of his company at the early age of thirty-two, a post held with distinction until 1953.

In 1922-5 Lees was in the Middle East

on geological surveys. In the winter of 1924-5 he accompanied an eminent Hungarian geologist, Hugo de Böckh, on a geological reconnaissance of south-west Persia, an experience which played an important part in his further geological education. In 1925-6 he made, with K. Washington Gray, a geological reconnaissance of Oman. During subsequent study leave in Vienna (1926-8) he attended lectures by F. E. Suess and L. Kober, both eminent geologists with world-wide interests, and was awarded a Ph.D. for a thesis on his Oman work, subsequently published by the Geological Society of London. In following years Lees examined oil prospects and oil company geological methods in many countries, including the United States, Canada, Egypt, Germany, and Australia. Under his geological direction his company in the Middle East discovered more oil for fewer wells drilled than the world had yet seen. Over 100,000 square miles of mountainous Persia were also geologically surveyed at appropriate scales. In 1933 he initiated a new programme of oil search in England and Scotland which resulted in the discovery of the East Midland oilfields in 1939: these explorations added much new information to British geology, discovering the Yorkshire potash deposits as a by-product. During the war of 1939-45 Lees was seconded for a period to the petroleum division of the Ministry of Fuel and Power and also carried out a special mission for the prime minister in the Far East. Other successful explorations which he helped to initiate and which came to fruition in post-war years were those in Nigeria, Libya, and Abu Dhabi (Trucial Coast).

In 1943 Lees was awarded the Bigsby medal of the Geological Society of London 'for his important geological work in Persia and Oman, and for his share in the discovery of oil in England'. In 1948 he was elected F.R.S. During subsequent years he was appointed a member of the Geological Survey Board and served on the councils of the Geological Society and Royal Society and on other committees. For the two years 1951-2-3 he was president of the Geological Society, the first geologist practising his profession in industry to achieve this distinction. His two presidential addresses, on 'Foreland Folding' and 'The Evolution of a Shrinking Earth', aroused considerable interest. In 1954 he was awarded the Sidney Powers memorial medal of the American Association of Petroleum Geologists, their highest distinction, never previously given to a non-American, for service to Middle East geology. Lees's publications, mostly on the Middle East, number about forty.

Lees had all the characteristics of a leader—outstanding personality; quickness of apprehension; capacity for constructive thinking; abundant common sense; skill in exposition; good humour; reasonableness; in discussion he was a catalyst and a listener rather than a talker. His geological career coincided with the discovery and development on scientific lines of the world's largest oilfields, to which his contribution was unique. He died in London 25 January 1955, after two years' illness following a life of vigour and good health.

In 1931 Lees married Hilda Frances, writer and musicologist, daughter of Francis Baugh Andrews, architect and antiquary; they had one son.

[W. J. Arkell in *Biographical Memoirs of Fellows of the Royal Society*, vol. i, 1955; *Proceedings* of the Geological Society of London, 9 March and 20 September 1955; *Journal* of the Central Asian Society, vol. xv, part 3, 1928; private information; personal knowledge.]   N. L. FALCON.

LEESON, SPENCER STOTTESBERY GWATKIN (1892–1956), schoolmaster and bishop, was born in Twickenham 9 October 1892, the son of John Rudd Leeson, a surgeon who had worked with Lister, who later became first mayor of the new borough of Twickenham; a man of unbounded vigour and a free-thinker whose independent views contrasted strongly with the piety of his wife, Caroline, daughter of Frederick Gwatkin, solicitor, of Lincoln's Inn. Both parents had been married before (Leeson had eight half-brothers and sisters) and both influenced him deeply. He grew up with a respect for middle-class integrity and a sympathy for the man in the street which gave him a sureness of touch later to prove one of his most considerable assets.

Leeson went from the Dragon School, Oxford, as a scholar to Winchester where, although not a notable figure, he was deeply affected by the life which he later described in *College 1901–1911* (1955). Never reckoning himself an arbiter of taste, he was peculiarly impressionable; the buildings of Winchester, with their atmosphere of intellectual activity, were an inspiration, as Chartres later. He was similarly affected at both Winchester and Oxford by music in which again, with no

pretence of catholic or critical appreciation, he allowed himself to be 'overwhelmed'. Already there was to be observed the religious inspiration which derived from his mother.

He went up to Oxford with a New College scholarship and in 1913 secured his first in classical honour moderations, on the strength of which he was awarded a 'war degree' in 1916. His contemporaries remember him as a man who seemed to have the 'gift of universal friendliness'. His characteristic greeting had a zest and wholehearted attention which won him devoted followers. He developed an eloquence which, interrupted by a slight stammer which did not embarrass him, was used to great effect. He would apologize for speaking from notes and for not producing a paper. The notes were three words on half an envelope, but the address would have a masterly coherence as well as a striking extempore quality which made him on occasion one of the most effective speakers of his day. The interests of Lionel Curtis and L. S. Amery [qq.v.] in imperial questions attracted him, as did Christian Socialism preached by Scott Holland [q.v.] and John Carter at Pusey House.

In August 1914 Leeson enlisted, was commissioned, and sent to Gibraltar. Thence he went to Flanders in March 1915, but was soon invalided home as a result of a severe bout of influenza affecting his heart. In September he joined naval intelligence in which he worked until the war ended. His marriage in 1918 to Mary Cecil, daughter of Dr. Montagu Lomax, gave him not only an unusually happy family life (they had one son and three daughters) but also a 'business manager'. Able administrator though he was, he could never be bothered with his own affairs and left them to his wife.

In 1919 he joined the Board of Education where he found a cause on which he could lavish that passionate interest in social conditions which he had developed at Oxford. Colleagues were impressed as well as amused by his seriousness about education—a seriousness at which Leeson could always laugh himself. In his five years at the Board he came under influences which affected him permanently, in particular that of Sir Amherst Selby-Bigge whom he served as private secretary. In 1922 he was called to the bar by the Inner Temple.

When he was offered a post at Winchester in 1924 it was clear that the choice

ould hardly have been better both for the
school and for Leeson himself. He had an
enthusiasm and abandon which, with his
ability, made him the ideal teacher for
clever boys. In later years when he
expected similar success in teaching,
despite an exceptionally heavy programme
of outside engagements, he was to some
extent disappointed. But at Winchester
and in his early years at Merchant Taylors'
he was one of the most successful teachers
of his generation. He went to Merchant
Taylors' as headmaster in 1927. The
school had become somewhat dim in spite
of his predecessor's scholarly distinction;
but particularly as a social problem the
post appealed to Leeson. He understood
the background of boys and governors.
His personal energies were poured out:
in teaching, in the inspiring of his staff, in
securing the confidence of governors and
parents. When he decided to move the
school from the grim and restricted buildings in Charterhouse Square loyal support
was assured him. He had chosen at Sandy
Lodge a spacious site on the outskirts
of north-west London, and the task of
planning and bringing into life what was
virtually a new school gave a new outlet
for his energies.

His task achieved, Leeson succeeded
A. T. P. Williams at Winchester where he
remained eleven years (1935–46). There
perhaps he expected almost too much:
when Wykehamists proved that they
would also be boys, they were falling short of his sacred ideal for them.
Nevertheless it was a remarkable headmastership, and the younger members of
his staff, in particular those who left
Winchester, as Leeson had done, to look
after great day schools, owed him a
special debt. Some of his most important work was done as chairman of the
Headmasters' Conference (1939–45, an
exceptionally long tenure); Winchester
colleagues who criticized him for absenteeism had little notion of what he was
doing for other schools. Ordained deacon
(1939) and priest (1940), his influence in
the Conference from the first had been
exercised to try to make school religion a
reality. War may have made his task
easier. He certainly inspired the Conference with his own conception of the
teacher's vocation, and persuaded it of
the importance of religion and religious
observance as the mainspring of education
in every school; of the importance also
of opening the doors to children from less
privileged families.

In 1946 Leeson stepped aside serenely
to become rector of Southampton,
characteristically seeking a job in what
he called 'the Church's front line'. His
gift for getting on with parishioners and
for making his small staff feel that they
were doing great service, his interest in
Sunday schools and in the reconstruction
of the bombed church, and his contact
with the university, all contributed to his
success. As at Winchester he was increasingly claimed by national causes; he would
have thought it wrong ever to refuse the
chairmanship of an educational body.
In 1949 he was consecrated bishop of
Peterborough. There the same themes
were repeated: devotion to every educational cause; determination to know every
parish priest in his diocese; readiness
to undertake any job of preaching or
speaking in which he reckoned he could
do God's work. During the last fifteen
years of his life he drove himself too hard
for there to be enough time for thought.
His speeches and sermons were in consequence less effective, although he could
still rise to a great occasion. But his
complete devotion to his work won the
deep affection of his clergy. A breakdown
in 1952 should have proved a warning; by
1955 it was apparent that the appalling
accumulation of tasks eagerly accepted
could not be sustained. He died in a
London hospital 27 January 1956.

Leeson published a number of books,
the most ambitious being his Bampton
lectures, *Christian Education*, published
in 1947. These surveyed the history of
Christian education—education with a
specifically Christian content, not simply
education in a nominally Christian society
—and sketched his own optimistic policy
for the Church in relation to the Education
Act of 1944 and the need for co-operation
with other denominations. His *Study of
the Gospel of Christ* (1941) expressed the
simple truths in which he believed with
characteristic fervour. There is a small
devotional book on *The Holy Communion*
(1943) and a number of essays and
leaflets on educational topics, and on the
welfare State which he accepted with
wholehearted enthusiasm. His writings
were by no means so important as his life
and the spoken word of his early addresses
which made him for years a dominating
figure in English education.

Leeson's portrait was painted by
(Sir) Oswald Birley for Merchant Taylors'
more sympathetically than it was by
Rodrigo Moynihan, who in his portrait

for Winchester gave the impression of a scheming prelate. Nobody disliked more heartily the trappings of power. But it is in photographs (such as those reproduced in *Spencer Leeson, a Memoir*, 1958) that the characteristic looks of puzzled seriousness or unaffected delight may be seen.

[Private information; personal knowledge.]

W. F. OAKESHOTT.

LEMON, SIR ERNEST JOHN HUTCHINGS (1884-1954), mechanical and railway engineer, was born 10 December 1884 at Okeford Fitzpaine in Dorset, the son of Edward Lemon, agricultural labourer and craftsman, and his wife, Martha Mary Rose. He was educated in the local primary school and sang in the choir where he attracted the notice of the rector, who soon recognized his promise. One of the rector's daughters married the younger brother of Arthur Pillans Laurie, principal of the Heriot-Watt College, Edinburgh (1900-28), who befriended him and arranged for his apprenticeship to the North British Locomotive Company in Glasgow, where Lemon attended the Glasgow Technical College. Lemon often spoke with gratitude for his start in life. In 1905 he worked for a time in the drawing office of Brown Brothers & Co. in Edinburgh and attended the Heriot-Watt College to obtain his professional status as a mechanical engineer. Later he worked for two years in the running department of the Highland Railway, and in 1907 joined Hurst, Nelson & Co. where he was employed in negotiating payments by the railways for damage in transit to privately owned wagons. The Midland Railway was impressed by his efficiency and in 1911 appointed him chief wagon inspector. Later Lemon was transferred to the Derby carriage and wagon works where his flair for production found its opportunity and in 1917 he became works superintendent. During the war he was responsible for building ambulance trains and in 1918 he received the O.B.E.

When the railways were amalgamated in 1923 Lemon became divisional superintendent with responsibility for the L.M.S. railway carriage and wagon works at Derby, Earlstown, and Newton Heath, where he soon installed mechanized construction of rolling stock. In 1927 he became carriage and wagon superintendent to the L.M.S. Railway and in 1930 he went with his vice-president and a group of railway engineers to the United States to study the working of their railways. On his return he was chairman of a committee, called the 'lightning committee', because of its quick report, which foreshadowed many of the changes introduced into the L.M.S. during the thirties under Lemon's vigorous leadership. In 1931 he became chief mechanical engineer and in the following year operating and commercial vice-president. This new position gave Lemon's fertile imagination full scope and the net revenue of the company benefited thereby. He reorganized the motive power depots to get better use of the locomotives, with a reduction in their number and in the staff. At the same time he accelerated the train services. Freight services were improved by his schemes for the modernization and mechanization of goods stations on novel lines. Lemon took a special interest in the recruitment and training of staffs and the appointment of traffic apprentices, including men from the universities. The building of the School of Transport at Derby and the making of a travelling instruction film were also due to his initiative.

In all this Lemon owed much to the backing and encouragement of Lord Stamp [q.v.] and his wise discrimination between Lemon's many schemes. It was a most happy combination of two minds, poles apart in outlook and experience, but with mutual trust and confidence.

As the result of the reputation Lemon had made as a planner of production, in 1938 he went to the Air Ministry as director-general of aircraft production, with a seat on the Air Council. He was closely associated with Sir Wilfrid Freeman [q.v.] who soon assimilated the secrets of Lemon's planning techniques. The Air Ministry had only a small production section which Lemon quickly enlarged, adding some half-dozen directorates to organize the work. He also reorientated the central planning section which became so important in the complex tasks ahead of it which Lemon had foreseen. In all this he had Freeman's wholehearted support and the organization remained unaltered after its transfer to the Ministry of Aircraft Production. Lemon also succeeded in persuading the aircraft industry to adopt the procedure of widespread subcontracting of component parts, whilst his wide contacts with the engineering industry were a great help in the rapid increase in production. His vision, drive, and creative resourcefulness provided the transformation vital for the unprecedented expansion of aircraft supply during the early critical war years.

In 1940 Lemon returned to the railway, and in 1941 he was knighted in recognition of his great contribution to the Royal Air Force. Stamp's death later in the year was a great blow to him and he was never quite the same man afterwards. He resigned from the L.M.S. in 1943, after a short spell of secondment to the Ministry of Production, and was then made chairman of a commission to consider the post-war planning of the railways. In 1948 he was chairman of a committee set up by the Ministry of Supply to consider the standardization of engineering products and for a time a member of the committee on the organization of the British Standards Institution.

Lemon had a fertile imaginative brain always seeking to find fresh and more efficient ways of doing things. He had also the gift of inspiring his colleagues with his own drive and sense of urgency. He was a pioneer of mechanized production and one of the early presidents of the Institution of Production Engineers.

In 1912 Lemon married Amy, daughter of the late Thomas Clayton, farmer; they had two sons. Lemon died in Epsom 15 December 1954.

[*The Times*, 17 and 23 December 1954 and 3 and 17 January 1955; *Engineer*, 24 December 1954; private information; personal knowledge.]   HAROLD HARTLEY.

LENNARD-JONES, SIR JOHN EDWARD (1894–1954), scientist and administrator, was born in Leigh, Lancashire, 27 October 1894, the eldest son of Hugh Jones, retail furnisher, by his wife, Mary Ellen Rigby. He was educated at Leigh Grammar School where he specialized in classics and at Manchester University where he changed to mathematics in which he took first class honours in 1915. He then joined the Royal Flying Corps, obtained his wings, saw service in France, and later took part in some research on aerodynamics. In 1919 he returned to university teaching and research, first in Manchester, then in Cambridge where he held a senior 1851 Exhibition at Trinity College, and then in Bristol where he went as a reader in 1925 and in 1927 was elected professor of theoretical physics.

At Cambridge, under the influence of (Sir) R. H. Fowler [q.v.], Lennard-Jones studied the forces between atoms and molecules and the possibility of deducing them from the properties of gases. He introduced an empirical form for the potential energy of two molecules when they are at a distance r from each other,

$$A/r^n - B/r^m$$

a form known by his name and still frequently used, and made use of all available experimental evidence to evaluate the constants in this formula.

Then came the discovery of quantum mechanics; Lennard-Jones studied this subject during 1929 at Göttingen. He was mainly responsible for introducing the new theories to the group of physicists at Bristol which A. M. Tyndall was gathering together in the newly built H. H. Wills physics laboratory. It was in this period that he began his well-known work on the theory of molecular orbitals in theoretical chemistry, of which he was one of the founders. In 1929 he used the theory in a paper entitled 'The electronic structure of diatomic molecules' to give the first explanation of the paramagnetism of the oxygen molecule, the starting-point of many later developments carried through in the United States and elsewhere.

In 1932 he was elected to the Plummer chair of theoretical chemistry in the university of Cambridge, the first chair of this subject in this country. He built up a very successful school by applying quantum mechanics to the properties of molecules and of liquids and many of his pupils became leaders in this subject.

Soon after the outbreak of war in 1939 the university mathematical laboratory became closely allied to the external ballistics department of the Ordnance Board and Lennard-Jones worked with his staff on problems of ballistics. In 1942 he was appointed chief superintendent of armament research, and undertook charge of the old research department at Woolwich in its new role as the armament research department at Fort Halstead in Kent. His major contribution to the war effort was made at this department, particularly in the changes he made in its administrative machinery, and his encouragement of personal responsibility for scientific work.

Unlike many of his academic colleagues, he stayed in government service for some time after the war; he was occupied with the reorganization of the department for peacetime conditions and became director-general of scientific research (defence) in the Ministry of Supply in August 1945. In spite of the offer of several positions in government service, however, he decided to return to academic life in the autumn of 1946, although he kept his connection with government science. In the post-war years he threw himself into the task of building up again his school of theoretical chemistry at Cambridge and seldom had fewer than fifteen research students working under his direction. His main work during this period was on 'molecular orbitals', and on the theory of liquids. He was also active in university policy-making. With the great expansion of the number of research students, many of them with only slight connections with existing colleges, he strongly advocated the foundation of a graduate college. He was also most concerned to form within the university a body competent to speak on matters of scientific policy, such as the desirable numbers of undergraduates and research students in scientific subjects and the organization of those branches of research which are less closely related to teaching.

Lennard-Jones was elected F.R.S. in 1933. In 1946 he was appointed K.B.E. and in the same year he was awarded the degree of Sc.D. by the university of Cambridge. In 1948–50 he was president of the Faraday Society and in 1953 he was awarded the Davy medal of the Royal Society and the Hopkins prize of the Cambridge Philosophical Society. From 1947 to 1954 he was a member of the research panel of the National Gallery. In 1954 he received an honorary D.Sc. from the university of Oxford.

Lennard-Jones had not intended to leave Cambridge but when he was invited to succeed Lord Lindsay of Birker [q.v.] as principal of the University College of North Staffordshire the educational experiment aroused his enthusiasm and after some months of hesitation he took up office in October 1953. Of his work at Keele, cut short after no more than a year, it is probably true that he had three things mainly in mind: the non-specialist teaching course which is the basis of the education there; the financial position of the college; and its relations with the outside world. He was responsible for setting up a special committee for improving the lecture content of the foundation year and at his suggestion two weekly discussion groups under the chairmanship of tutors of the college were started for students attending the course. He also felt that one of the problems facing a new college was to make itself known and by

speeches, by broadcasting, and by written articles, he did what was possible to bring the work and aims of the college to the public notice.

In 1925 Jones married Kathleen Mary, daughter of Samuel Lennard, boot and shoe manufacturer of Leicester, and took the name of Lennard-Jones. They had a son and a daughter. Lennard-Jones died at Stoke-on-Trent 1 November 1954.

[N. F. Mott in *Biographical Memoirs of Fellows of the Royal Society*, vol. i, 1955; personal knowledge.]   N. F. MOTT.

LENOX-CONYNGHAM, SIR GERALD PONSONBY (1866–1956), geodesist, was born 21 August 1866 at Springhill, Moneymore, Ireland, the seventh of eleven children of (Sir) William Fitzwilliam Lenox-Conyngham and his wife, Laura Calvert, daughter of George Arbuthnot, founder of the firm of Arbuthnot & Co. of Madras, India. When Lenox-Conyngham was ten years old the family moved to Edinburgh, where he attended the Edinburgh Academy. At seventeen he gained admission to the Royal Military Academy at Woolwich, and in 1885 passed out first in his batch with the sword of honour and the Pollock medal. As a lieutenant in the Royal Engineers he spent two years at the school of military engineering at Chatham before being posted to India. In 1889 he applied for a transfer to the Survey of India and joined the trigonometrical branch, where he entered on a career as a surveyor and geodesist, the main occupation and scientific interest of his long life.

The observations of the Survey included an extensive series of measurements of longitude along parallels of latitude intended to determine the curvature of the geoid in a direction perpendicular to that given by the older observations of latitude. These longitudes though determined with great care showed puzzling discrepancies. In 1889 (Sir) Sidney Burrard set out to find the cause of the discrepancies. Lenox-Conyngham was appointed his assistant, so beginning the long collaboration and friendship which was one of the main influences of Lenox-Conyngham's scientific interests. An explanation was found for the discrepancies and satisfactory measurements obtained.

In 1894 Burrard and Lenox-Conyngham undertook a redetermination of the longitude of Karachi relative to Greenwich by using the land telegraph line across Europe and Persia. The results were most satisfactory: a redetermination thirty years later using wireless signals gave a longitude differing by only 0·02 sec. from that which Burrard and Lenox-Conyngham had found.

Burrard next began a scrutiny of the substantial collection of observations of latitude acquired by the Survey over nearly a century. He concluded that the deflections in North India were arranged systematically in zones parallel to the mountains. He ascribed them to the attraction of a hidden range to the south of the Gangetic plain. The most direct method of locating such a hidden mass is by measurement of acceleration due to gravity. This had previously been done using the Royal Society's pendulum. New methods of eliminating the error due to the effects of sway of the support of the pendulums had been devised at the Prussian Geodetic Institute at Potsdam. Burrard and Lenox-Conyngham purchased an apparatus with four half-second pendulums and had it modified at Potsdam, and the constants determined both there and in London at the National Physical Laboratory. So from 1903 to 1908 Lenox-Conyngham was engaged in a series of gravity measurements in India which was perhaps his most important contribution to science.

In 1931 Lenox-Conyngham wrote: 'The pendulums do not reveal any great excess of mass where the hidden range was supposed to be, but they show that there is a great defect of' mass all along the foot of the Himalayas and for some distance from them.' This strip of negative gravity anomalies and deficient density is thought to be the first example of a phenomenon which has subsequently been shown to be of widespread occurrence particularly on the outer edges of island arcs. The work of Burrard and Lenox-Conyngham on the deflection of the vertical and the gravity anomalies in India revived interest in this branch of geodesy by showing that its results have a wider interest than the mere study and reduction of errors in surveying. The instruments used may now be seen in the Science Museum, London.

In 1912 Lenox-Conyngham became superintendent of the trigonometrical survey and in 1914 a colonel. In 1918 he was elected F.R.S. and in 1919 he was knighted.

He left India in 1920 and a few months after his return to England was asked to join a committee to consider the promo-tion of the study of geodesy in Cambridge. The university could provide no funds, but Trinity College offered a praelectorship in geodesy. This was offered to Lenox-Conyngham who took up residence in Cambridge and in 1921 was made a fellow of Trinity. In the following year the university created a readership in geodesy for him. With almost no financial support from the university he started to teach the basics of geodesy to a small group of undergraduates and later also to officers sent to Cambridge from many colonial survey departments. With the support of Sir Horace Darwin [q.v.] of the Cambridge Instrument Company he constructed a pendulum apparatus as an improvement on the one used in India. This new instrument with two invar pendulums swinging in opposite phase was entirely successful and is still in use for the most precise long-distance gravity connections. Lenox-Conyngham's one-man school of geodesy eventually became the department of geodesy and geophysics. The department expanded and its work extended into fields of seismology and geothermal measurements where Lenox-Conyngham had little previous knowledge. But his interest was keen and his encouragement indefatigable. He used his influence extensively in procuring funds and apparatus. He also travelled widely visiting scientific conferences all over the world. During the war he continued his lectures to rather depleted audiences although the experimental work in the department ceased. After the war when the department reopened great advantage was taken of the new techniques, in which Lenox-Conyngham took a keen interest even after his retirement in 1947.

Few men can have lived so full and useful a life as Lenox-Conyngham who had two complete and successful careers, one in India, the other in Cambridge. At a party to celebrate Lenox-Conyngham's eightieth birthday, the master of Trinity, G. M. Trevelyan, said: 'He is a scholar, a soldier, and a great public servant, and he looks all three.' He had a commanding presence and as he grew older became even more dignified and impressive. He had a rigid attitude to matters of the conventions in which he had been brought up, combined with an extraordinary openness of mind in matters of science. He was always delighted to see new methods of physics and engineering applied to the problems on which he had worked many years before. He never pretended to understand details of modern equipment but liked to be shown how it worked and was never lacking in his encouragement and support. This combination of genuine interest, friendliness, and lack of pretence, enabled him to be remarkably successful as head of a department in which most of the staff were forty years his junior.

In 1890 he married Elsie Margaret, daughter of Surgeon-General (Sir) Alexander Frederick Bradshaw who became head of the army medical services in India. They had one daughter. Lenox-Conyngham died in Cambridge 27 October 1956 not long after his ninetieth birthday. There is a chalk drawing by Henry Lamb (1947) at Trinity College, Cambridge.

[Sir Edward Bullard in *Biographical Memoirs of Fellows of the Royal Society*, vol. iii, 1957; *The Times*, 29 October 1956.]

MARY MUNRO.

LESTER, SEAN (JOHN ERNEST) (1888–1959), secretary-general of the League of Nations, was born in Woodburn, Carrickfergus, county Antrim, 27 September 1888, the son of Robert John Lester, a business man, by his wife, Henriette Mary Ritchie. He was educated at the Methodist College, Belfast, and began his career at the age of seventeen as a journalist on the *North Down Herald*. At about the same time, although a Protestant, he became active in the movement for national independence. After further journalistic experience in Dublin he became news editor on the *Freeman's Journal*, then in 1922 publicity officer in the Department of External Affairs. In 1929 he was appointed his Government's representative in Geneva and after the Irish Free State obtained a seat on the Council he took an active part in League affairs. His chairmanship of a committee which ultimately secured the settlement of a dispute between Peru and Colombia attracted attention, and in 1934 he became the League's high commissioner in Danzig where it was his duty to watch over the democratic operation of the constitution.

When the Nazis obtained a majority in the Danzig parliament they embarked on a brutal persecution of the minority and particularly of its Jewish element. Lester made vigorous protests and efforts were made to intimidate him but his complete disregard of his own safety in the face of anti-League demonstrations seriously worried the Nazi leaders who feared that it might not suit the Führer's book if the League's high commissioner were physically assaulted in the streets. Their discomfiture was a personal victory for Lester but it did nothing to alter the fact that the foundation of the League's position had disappeared, and since he had no longer any real function to fulfil he accepted the post of deputy secretary-general of the League and returned to Geneva early in 1937.

It was not long before he found himself in direct conflict with Joseph Avenol, the secretary-general. In Lester's view any compromise between Nazi doctrines and the principles of the League was unthinkable. He was therefore horrified to discover that, after the collapse of France, Avenol, convinced that England must suffer the same fate, was contemplating that the palace of the League in Geneva with its small remaining staff might become the co-ordinating centre of the New Europe which he believed was emerging. With a complete disregard of his obligations as secretary-general he wrote to the Vichy government putting himself at its disposal; he endeavoured to get complete personal control of the League's funds; and he made every effort to secure Lester's resignation. The deadlock was resolved by the arrival in Geneva of Adolfo Costa du Rels, the president of the League Council, who sided with Lester; Avenol resigned and Costa du Rels installed Lester as acting secretary-general.

From this time (August 1940) until the end of the war Lester's position was even less enviable than it had been in Danzig. The economic section of the secretariat had taken refuge in the United States where it continued its work in Princeton without any official status, and the small staff remaining in Geneva could do little more than preserve the League's records. Moreover Lester found that he was completely isolated. Accompanied by the president of the Hague Court of International Justice he attempted to attend a meeting of the League's supervisory commission in Lisbon, but the party was stopped at the Spanish frontier and after two days of fruitless telephoning to Madrid had to return to Geneva. Conditions there became increasingly uncomfortable. German irritation at the presence of the League headquarters on Swiss soil led to the vote for Switzerland's contribution to the League budget being defeated in the parliament at Berne.

The victory of the Allies came as a

welcome relief but it was followed by a painful disillusionment. The meeting in 1945 at San Francisco to lay the foundations of the new world order deliberately ignored the League. Russia had never forgiven her expulsion as an aggressor, and the United States felt no obligation to defend an institution of which she had never been a member. The adoption of the Charter of the United Nations sounded the death knell of the League, and it then became Lester's melancholy duty to arrange for its dissolution and the disposal of its assets. This task completed, he retired in 1947 to the west of Ireland where he could enjoy his favourite pastimes of fishing and gardening. The value of his achievement in setting a memorable standard of courage and integrity in international service was recognized by the title of secretary-general of the League conferred on him at the final meeting of the Assembly, by honorary doctorates from Trinity College, Dublin, and the National University of Ireland, by the Woodrow Wilson award, and by his appointment as president of the Permanent Norwegian-Swiss Conciliation Committee.

He married in 1920 Elizabeth Ruth Tyrrell, by whom he had three daughters. He died in Galway 13 June 1959. A portrait by the Irish artist James Sleator hangs in the library of the Palais des Nations, Geneva.

[Private information; personal knowledge.]
EDWARD PHELAN.

LEVESON GOWER, SIR HENRY DUDLEY GRESHAM (1873–1954), cricketer. [See GOWER.]

LEVICK, GEORGE MURRAY (1876–1956), surgeon and explorer, was born at Newcastle upon Tyne 3 July 1876, the son of George Levick, a civil engineer, and his wife, Jane Sowerby. He was educated at St. Paul's School where he developed that concern for physical fitness and interest in outdoor activities which remained with him throughout his life and which, combined with a very real interest in his fellow men, became the dominant factor in his life. He went on to St. Bartholomew's Hospital where he qualified M.R.C.S., L.R.C.P. in 1902 and in the same year he was commissioned as a doctor in the Royal Navy where he found himself at once at home. He was a keen rugby player, a good oar, and a magnificent gymnast, and was founder and secretary of the Navy Rugby Union.

In 1910 Levick was selected by Captain R. F. Scott [q.v.] as surgeon and zoologist on his second and last expedition to the Antarctic. His chief, Dr. E. A. Wilson [q.v.], veteran of Scott's earlier expedition and close personal friend of his leader, was the obvious choice for the medical care of the main party, and Levick was assigned to what became the northern party, six men who, through Roald Amundsen's pre-emption of their proposed field of action—King Edward VII Land—were destined to put in two years exploring the Victoria Land coast and, incidentally, to spend a whole winter existing on what they could pick up locally while living in a hole dug out from a snowdrift seven feet thick; an experience which in its severity and happy outcome is still an outstanding example of survival in the Antarctic. During that long-drawn-out trial, when all were extended to the uttermost, physically and psychologically, Levick was a tower of strength. Throughout the two years he played an invaluable part: as a doctor he was adequate though, on the whole, under-employed; he was a keen observer and made a thorough study of the Adélie penguin; as a photographer he kept a magnificent pictorial record which added significantly to the value of the expedition's scientific results; he was a chief contributor to the cultural life; confidant of the rank and file seamen; loyal and wise adviser of Lieutenant Victor Campbell his leader and friend.

On his return Levick served in the war in the Grand Fleet, the North Sea, and at Gallipoli where he was in the last party to leave; he was promoted surgeon-commander in 1915 and retired in 1917.

Concentrating upon his first and continuing interest, the fostering of physical fitness in his fellow men, Levick was at various times electrologist and medical officer in charge at St. Thomas's Hospital; consultant physiotherapist at the Victoria Hospital for Children; and a member of the London University advisory committee on physical education. In 1919 he was approached by the National Institute for the Blind about the feasibility of teaching blind students of massage some form of electrical treatment; through his untiring advocacy blind students were ultimately admitted to the examinations of the Chartered Society of Physiotherapy and a clinic was opened for and staffed by them. He was for thirty years medical director of the Heritage Craft School for Crippled Children founded by Dame Grace Kimmins [q.v.].

His best known and, in some ways, his most rewarding and nationally important work stemmed directly from his experiences with the Scott expedition. In 1932 he was personally responsible for the foundation of the Public Schools Exploring Society, later named, as its scope broadened, the British Schools Exploring Society. For the remainder of his life he was the society's head, at first chairman and later president; and was honorary chief leader of the first nine expeditions to some of the wilder parts of the world. The society's main objective has been to send boys to trackless country to teach them to fend for themselves; to foster in them the spirit of adventure; to test their endurance and help them acquire physical fitness; and to give them a taste for, and elementary training in, exploration and field research. Levick's personal influence in this particular field was well summarized by Major C. F. Spooner who was assistant leader of the 1947 expedition and thereafter led several further expeditions. 'What fun that expedition was. Looking back on it the actual enjoyment of it for me came almost directly from being with Murray himself. He was always so full of life and enthusiasm and he made everything such enormous fun; even a setback became the cause of greater enjoyment with him, as it simply offered a greater challenge. Coupled with this buoyant love of life was a quiet dogged persistence and a shrewd judgement which gave one great confidence. I cannot remember ever seeing him nonplussed and he was always the same whatever the circumstances, considerate and kindly to us all—one of those people whose gentleness emanates from their own great strength.' In 1942 the Royal Geographical Society recognized his services to exploration by the award of the Back grant.

During the war of 1939-45 Levick was recalled to the Royal Navy to assist in the training of commandos. In spite of all these activities he found time for writing. His medical publications were many and varied and his reports on the Adélie penguin were major contributions in their day.

In 1918 Levick married Audrey, second daughter of (Sir) Mayson M. Beeton; they had one son. Levick died at Budleigh Salterton 30 May 1956.

[*The Times*, 1 June 1956; private information; personal knowledge.]

RAYMOND PRIESTLEY.

LEWIS, PERCY WYNDHAM (1882–1957), writer and artist, was born 1 November 1882 on his father's yacht ot Amherst, Nova Scotia. His father, Captain Charles Edward Lewis, came of a prosperous merchant and legal family settled in New York State; after a year at West Point, he served under Sheridan in the Civil War and later wrote his war memoirs His mother was Anne Stuart, a British girl of Scottish and Irish descent. About 1893 his parents separated and he came with his mother to England where they existed precariously in the London suburbs. He was educated at a succession of private schools followed by two years (1897–8) at Rugby. He went next to the Slade School of Art which he left in 1901 In the following eight years he was for some time in Munich, visited Spain and Holland, but was most often in Brittany or Paris, where he was associated with the extreme right wing of Action Française and attended Bergson's lectures. His early letters, mostly to his mother, are filled with his own affairs: his bowels, his pocket, and his loves. 'Never destroy a single *written* page of mine', he wrote; later he kept drafts of his letters which survive as source material.

Lewis returned to England in 1909 and in the same year had three stories accepted by the *English Review* and was welcomed into the literary circle of its editor, Ford Madox Hueffer (later Ford, q.v.). In 1911 he exhibited drawings with the Camden Town Group and in 1912 at the Post-Impressionist exhibition organized by Roger Fry [q.v.] whose Omega workshop he joined in July 1913. By October he had publicly broken with Fry. In the same month he exhibited with Frank Rutter's Post-Impressionist and Futurist exhibition and in December with the new London Group. In the following spring he became director of the Rebel Art Centre, 'the seat of the Great London Vortex', and in June 1914 and July 1915 published the only two issues of *Blast*, the Vorticist review mostly written by himself. His principal associates were William Roberts, Edward Wadsworth [q.v.], Gaudier-Brzeska, Richard Aldington, and Ezra Pound. Pound had supplied the word Vortex which he described as that 'from which, and through which, and into which, ideas are consistently rushing'. But this was not exactly Lewis's idea. His Vortex appears rather as the still centre of the whirlwind, the arrest of flux. In his reaction against

Bergson he became the enemy of Time and of the cult of action. That is why he repudiated Futurism and, in later years, attacked James Joyce, Virginia Woolf [qq.v.], Hemingway, and Proust. In 1915 he organized the first and only English Vorticist exhibition, at the Doré Galleries. Twenty years later he described 'all this organized disturbance' as 'Art behaving as if it were politics'.

In March 1916 Lewis enlisted in the Garrison Artillery; by August he was a bombardier and by Christmas an officer. He served in France from early June 1917, first as a gunner and later as an official war artist. His first novel, *Tarr*, was published serially in that year and as a book in 1918. In February 1919 he held his first one-man show at the Goupil Gallery and later in the year he tried to revive Vorticism under the name of X Group. This held one exhibition (Mansard Gallery, 1920) and then died of Lewis's quarrelsomeness. It was his last connection with any group and in the next ten years or so he was hitting out in all directions, not least at his oldest supporters, T. S. Eliot and Pound; and he continually attacked Joyce, a later friend, with particular virulence.

There are few events to record during the inter-war years except his secret marriage in 1929 to Gladys Anne Hoskyns, an art student with a German mother and 'a good British farmer' for father. There were occasional visits to France, Italy, Germany, and the Pyrenees, and, in 1931, to North Africa, where he and his wife rode 'all over the Atlas' mountains on mules. But in spite of persistent illness and poverty these were frantically productive years. He held several exhibitions, published some twenty books and many articles, and edited the two issues of the *Tyro* (1921–2) and the three of the *Enemy* (1927–9).

On his visits to Germany in 1930 and 1931 Lewis discovered the Nazis as an 'aristocracy of intellect', Hitler as 'a man of peace', and 'the Hitlerist dream . . . as full of an imminent classical serenity'. He paraded this nonsense in a series of articles in *Time and Tide*, reprinted as *Hitler* (1931); his subsequent recantation in *The Hitler Cult* (1939) failed to wipe out the hostility he had aroused. In the meantime the rejection of his portrait of Eliot by the Royal Academy in 1938 brought him a great deal of publicity and provoked the resignation of Augustus John.

On the day before war was declared, Lewis and his wife left England. They spent the war years in the United States and Canada, where Lewis barely survived on pot-boiling portraits and occasional articles and lectures. He loathed both countries and ceaselessly abused them in his letters, although he found individual Americans kind and intelligent. His only break was an appointment, in 1943–4, to the faculty of Assumption College, Windsor, Ontario, where he was happy and found 'how good the religious disciplines are for people'. He was perhaps always aware how good they could have been for him. This is generally revealed in his tolerance of and interest in the Roman Catholic Church and particularly in his friendship with Father Martin D'Arcy, S.J., and in the tone of chapter xxxii in *Self Condemned*. His wife became a Catholic after his death.

By September 1945 Lewis was back in England and was soon re-established. In 1946 he was appointed art critic to the *Listener*; in 1949 he was given a retrospective exhibition at the Redfern Gallery, in 1951 a Civil List pension, and in 1952 an honorary Litt.D. by Leeds. In 1951 the B.B.C. presented his *Childermass* (1928) and subsidized its sequences, *Monstre Gai* and *Malign Fiesta*. The whole was broadcast and then published as *The Human Age* (1955–6). In 1956 the Tate Gallery held a large retrospective exhibition called 'Wyndham Lewis and Vorticism'.

Lewis's reputation was now restored but this was little consolation for the darkness of his last years. His eyes had first troubled him in 1941. In May 1951 he wrote his valediction in the *Listener*: 'my articles on contemporary art exhibitions necessarily end, for I can no longer see a picture.' By 1954 he was totally blind. He died in London 7 March 1957.

Michael Ayrton drew him several times in these last years and also described him: 'His eyes, no longer concentrated in their regard, were shaded by a green plastic peak. . . . The forehead . . . designed for striking blows, was now bisected but armed with a green obsidian cutting edge from beneath which the nose reared like a secret weapon; an armed head indeed.' (*Golden Sections*, 1957.) This is the revelation of a personality which the sitter so often proclaimed as The Enemy, armed with his 'Lewis gun'. Lewis admitted that the hero of *Tarr* was a 'caricatural self-portrait . . . of the merely physical attributes': his tallness, his 'steady, un-amiable, impatient expression', his 'grima-cing tumultuous mask for the face he had to cover'. But these descriptions and the drawing by Augustus John (1903), the self-portraits, and the numerous photo-graphs do not make a consistent image: his appearance is almost as elusive as his character.

In spite of long, although often inter-rupted, friendships and his kind patience to young writers and painters in his later years, the most obvious marks of Lewis's character were quarrelsomeness and a towering egotism: 'I will side and identify myself with the powerfullest Me, and in its interests I will work.' He could write of his 'friends, fiancées, "colleagues" ' as 'livestock' and of most people as simply 'things', as 'hallucinated automata'; his satires were based on the conviction that 'the root of the Comic is . . . in the sensations resulting from the observations of a *thing* behaving like a person'.

Lewis persistently and properly insisted that he was an artist and whatever his character and opinions an estimate of his value must be based on his works of art. These, in literature, are his major novels: *Tarr*, *The Childermass* and its sequels, *The Apes of God* (1930), *The Revenge for Love* (1937), and *Self Condemned* (1954). He must be ranked high among his contemporaries although we may hesitate to accept Eliot's estimate of him in 1955 as 'the most distinguished living novelist'. His only of book verse was *One-Way Song* (1933), difficult to accept as poetry. *Tarr* and *Self Condemned* are partly auto-biographical; *Blasting and Bombardiering* (1937) and *Rude Assignment* (1950) are overtly so. His critical books, which include *Men Without Art* (1934) and *The Writer and the Absolute* (1952), are neither judicious nor balanced; but they flash with sudden insights and passages of good writing. Lewis never achieved sus-tained greatness in any work: he was a master of the sentence, the paragraph, even the scene; but never of a whole book. He could rarely resist the temptation to crash through his creative fabric with long, repetitious, and noisy assertions of whatever opinion he was holding at the moment.

This lack of discipline is most obvious in his speculative, political, and polemical writings. They display no coherent or systematic development of thought and constantly degenerate into a display of prejudices and generalizations unsup-ported by evidence but often brilliantly witty, occasionally profound, and rarely dull for long. His excursions into politic were particularly unfortunate because they laid him open to a reasonable charge of fascism. But, although he contributed to Sir Oswald Mosley's journal, he did not join his party. He was far too much of an individualist to toe any line for long. He could write: 'Politically I stand nowhere and also: 'it is impossible to be non partisan'. Perhaps his political position is best described in his own statement in 1931: 'partly communist and partly fascist, with a distinct streak of monarchism in my marxism, but at bottom anarchist, with a healthy passion for order'. However, he had his more or less permanent and respectable enmities: he hated war, managerial and mass values, the mass media, vested interests, pseudo-revolu-tionaries, the 'millionaire Bohemia' of Bloomsbury, and professional politicians.

Fundamentally, all Lewis's stresses and strains, all his pursuits of hares, were due to a profound and unsolved inner conflict. He was utterly subjective while always claiming to be objective. His paeans to rationality were the emotional substitute for his own lack of it. His attacks on romantic intolerance were his most violent displays of intolerance. He was a man in a mask: ' "Bombardier" was after all a romantic incognito.' His greatest enemy was himself: 'It is chiefly myself I am castigating.'

This mask, in its metallic, tense rigidity, is fully evident in his drawings. He was above all a draughtsman, even when he painted. He defined the object, the thing seen, with the apparent detachment of a Mantegna. 'Deadness', he wrote, 'is the first condition of art . . . good art must have no inside'; and again: 'I am for the *Great Without*, for the method of *external* approach, for the wisdom of the eye.' At one time he proclaimed that 'the act of creation is always an act of will' but later that 'it seems very likely that the artist uses and manipulates a supernatural power'. In his Vorticist period he exalted abstract art, but by 1950 he could say: 'No-one but an idiot—or a Dutchman, like Mondrian—would pass his life in that vacuum.' He had by then long given himself to a representational art: portraits are among his most notable works.

Lewis's drawings can be most easily studied in his three publications, *Timon of Athens* (1914), *Fifteen Drawings* (1920), and *Thirty Personalities and a Self-Portrait*

(1932); and, with his paintings, in many galleries including in London the Tate, Victoria and Albert, British Museum, National Portrait Gallery, and Imperial War Museum. His most notable paintings are 'Surrender of Barcelona' (1934–7) and his portraits of Pound (1939) and (Dame) Edith Sitwell (1923–35), all in the Tate Gallery; 'A Battery Shelled' (Imperial War Museum, 1918); and his portraits of Eliot (1938, Durban Art Gallery, and 1949, Magdalene College, Cambridge) and of his wife (1937, Glasgow Art Gallery and Museum).

The Tate Gallery has a painting by William Roberts of the Vorticists celebrating at the Restaurant de la Tour Eiffel in which Lewis is the central figure.

[H. G. Porteus, *Wyndham Lewis: A Discursive Exposition*, 1932; Charles Handley-Read and Eric Newton, *The Art of Wyndham Lewis*, 1951; Geoffrey Grigson, *A Master of Our Time: A Study of Wyndham Lewis*, 1951; H. Kenner, *Wyndham Lewis*, 1954; E. W. F. Tomlin, *Wyndham Lewis*, 1955; Geoffrey Wagner, *Wyndham Lewis: A Portrait of the Artist as the Enemy*, with an extensive bibliography, 1957; *The Letters of Wyndham Lewis*, ed. W. K. Rose, 1963.] ANTHONY BERTRAM.

LEWIS, ROSA (1867–1952), hotel owner, was born 26 September 1867 at Leyton, Essex, the fifth of the nine children of William Edwin Ovenden, watchmaker and later undertaker, by his wife, Eliza, daughter of John Cannon, jeweller, and great-niece of Richard Cannon [q.v.]. Rosa left the Leyton board-school at the age of twelve to become a general servant for a shilling a week and her keep. At sixteen a fortunate recommendation took her to Sheen House, Mortlake, home of the exiled Comte de Paris. No apprenticeship could have been more valuable. She worked her way up to head kitchenmaid; was lent to the Duc d'Aumale at Chantilly; and took charge of the kitchen of the Duc d'Orleans at Sandhurst.

In 1887 she started going out to cook in private houses. Her cooking was basically French, as learnt in her royal French houses, but it was liked because of its simplicity: even her quails stuffed with *foie gras* were light compared with the interminable stodgy courses of the Mrs. Beeton school. First to employ her was Lady Randolph Churchill; then followed the Saviles, the Asquiths, and Captain Charles Duff, a prominent member of the Marlborough House set.

In gossip, spoken and written, her name has often been associated with King Edward VII. He first saw her at Sheen House when the dinner so pleased him that he asked his host to send for the chef: he was no less pleased with Rosa whose cockney wit amused him. For the next twenty years tactful hostesses entertaining him engaged the services of Rosa, whose cooking he liked best and who was careful to study his tastes.

In 1893 Rosa married—without any signs of enthusiasm—Excelsior Tyrel Chiney Lewis, a butler. They set up house —or as some said were set up in a house— in Eaton Terrace where they were to take in lodgers. Little is known of what went on there except that Lewis had little to do but drink. In 1903 she divorced him.

In 1899 she briefly and not very successfully took on the catering at White's Club, but her popularity in private houses grew. She now took a team of cooks with her but she was always prepared to do anything herself which needed doing— even scrubbing the steps—to ensure that all was as it should be. She did the marketing and prepared much of the food beforehand. She also gave lessons at half a guinea a time to people such as W. W. Astor's cook.

In 1902 Rosa Lewis bought the Cavendish in Jermyn Street, already a fashionable private hotel. Such was her energy that this added responsibility did not restrict her outside cooking activities but merely gave scope to her flair for furnishing and decoration. A tall and elegant hostess, she made the Cavendish so much like a private house that there seemed nothing odd about her favourite rebuke: 'You treat my house like an hotel.' Lord Ribblesdale had a permanent suite; Sir William Eden lived there for many years. In addition to distinguished English families—she preferred them distinguished—she welcomed presentable American millionaires.

Until the war of 1914–18 it was the height of chic for London hostesses to have Rosa to cook for them; and no hotel was more *comme il faut* than the Cavendish for those who lived in the country. With the war private entertaining on a grand scale ceased and Rosa had only the Cavendish to occupy her. Her immense good nature caused her to bring in impoverished young officers. They were never allowed to pay and Rosa embarked on the Robin Hood tactics of robbing the rich to pay for the poor which she continued until her death.

Rosa's tolerance of the behaviour of

others, her uninhibited language, the raffishness of some of the parties at the Cavendish, and the great names with which hers has been linked gave her in later life a reputation which she had not earned. She accepted the legend with a chuckle rather than a denial. As Evelyn Waugh, who portrayed her in *Vile Bodies* (1930), put it, she was 'a warm hearted, comic, and totally original woman' whose beauty was still discernible even in old age. She maintained throughout her life an affectionate if intermittent connection with the Church of England and was confirmed shortly before her death at the Cavendish 29 November 1952. Her sister's son, in whom she took great pride, Hugh Hamshaw Thomas, the palaeobotanist and F.R.S., has contributed to this Supplement.

A portrait of Rosa Lewis painted in the twenties by Chile Guevara is privately owned.

[Michael Harrison, *Rosa*, 1962; Daphne Fielding, *The Duchess of Jermyn Street*, 1964; personal knowledge.]   ROBIN McDOUALL.

LEWIS, WILLIAM CUDMORE McCULLAGH (1885–1956), physical chemist, was born in Belfast 29 June 1885, the only son in a family of five children, of Edward Lewis, linen merchant, and his wife, Frances Welsh, daughter of the Rev. William Cudmore McCullagh of Ballysillan Presbyterian Church, Belfast. Lewis was educated at Bangor Grammar School, county Down, and at the Royal University of Ireland which he entered as a medical student. Developing an interest in the physical sciences he changed his course and proceeded to obtain first class honours in experimental science (1905). In 1906 he was awarded the M.A. degree and a university studentship in experimental science. After acting as demonstrator in chemistry at the university for a year he left Northern Ireland to continue research at the university of Liverpool under F. G. Donnan [q.v.]—himself an Ulsterman and a first cousin of Lewis's father. After completing, with Donnan, a highly successful experimental examination of William Gibbs's theory of surface concentration, Lewis was awarded a scholarship which took him to Heidelberg to work for a year with the distinguished colloid chemist Bredig. In 1909 he returned to England and was appointed by Sir William Ramsay [q.v.] to a demonstratorship and later a lectureship at University College, London. Lewis's contributions to

physical chemistry had attracted considerable attention and in 1913 he succeeded Donnan in the chair of physical chemistry in Liverpool, a position he held until his retirement owing to ill health in 1948. He was elected F.R.S. in 1926.

Lewis was a pioneer in research and made notable contributions to physical chemistry. He will best be remembered for his studies in the theory of chemical change and colloid science. During his long association with the university of Liverpool he directed one of the outstanding schools of chemistry in this country. He was a friendly professor, always ready to give advice, to listen sympathetically to the difficulties of his students and colleagues and to help them on the way to a successful solution of their problems. He was a man of wide learning and considerable breadth of outlook; an ardent student of Samuel Johnson and also interested in, and knowledgeable about, early English architecture. Lewis was extremely retiring and hated publicity. He was sincere and kindly, had a keen sense of humour, and was devoted to university ideals and especially to research. Brought up in the Presbyterian tradition, he remained throughout his life a loyal churchman.

Although he always felt that his work was hampered by insufficient mathematical training, much of Lewis's best work was of a theoretical nature and his early studies on the nature of chemical mechanism and catalysis pointed the way to the use of methods of statistical mechanics in chemistry. In 1918 he proposed a theory of chemical change which was to form the basis of subsequent development in this subject. To physical chemists Lewis was widely known as the author of *A System of Physical Chemistry*, first published in two volumes in 1916, and in three volumes in 1918–19. The first original work in the English language to be devoted to physical chemistry for senior students, it was the standard work for students for two decades and went into four editions in ten years. Written at a time when the subject of physical chemistry was growing rapidly, it exerted a wide and lasting influence on the subject in this country. The task of preparing it was prodigious and revealed a breadth of outlook possible only in a man who had the widest grasp of the many developments occurring at that period.

In the years immediately following the

var of 1914–18 Lewis collaborated in the work of the Liverpool Cancer Research Organization. This body had been formed by Professor W. Blair-Bell who enlisted the services of many heads of departments in the university who were prepared to apply their expert knowledge to various aspects of this problem. These investigations influenced Lewis's future work and he transferred his research interests to the study of biological and physiological problems. He was interested in the physico-chemical processes which might underlie malignancy and he studied such properties as the electrical conductivity and ionic permeability of malignant tissue. He measured the pH variation of the blood of normal and diseased persons in the hope that significant differences might be observed, but none was found. From a survey of the literature he concluded that glycolysis was enhanced in cancerous cells and this led him to a study of the mechanism of glycolysis and in particular the acid and enzymatic hydrolysis of a number of glucosides. This phase of his work was rounded off by a physico-chemical study of the properties of' proteins, especially denaturation and electrophoretic behaviour.

Much of this work was brilliantly conceived and, although not always successful, it may be said that some of the projects were undertaken in advance of their time and before techniques had been developed for their successful prosecution.

Lewis married in 1914 Jeanie Waterston Darroch, of a Scottish family who had settled in London; they had one son, Ian, who became lecturer in physics at Liverpool University before joining the Atomic Energy Research Establishment at Harwell. Lewis died at Malvern 11 February 1956.

[C. E. H. Bawn in *Biographical Memoirs of Fellows of the Royal Society*, vol. iv, 1958; *Nature*, 31 March 1956; personal knowledge.]
C. E. H. BAWN.

LEYEL, HILDA WINIFRED IVY (MRS. C. F. LEYEL) (1880–1957), herbalist, was born in London 6 December 1880, the daughter of Edward Brenton Wauton, from 1881 an assistant master at Uppingham School, and his wife, Elizabeth Anne Drewitt. At Uppingham she developed a precocious interest in flowers and herbs and on leaving school she studied medicine. She then worked for a while with (Sir) Frank Benson [q.v.] and in 1900 married Carl Frederick Leyel

(died 1925), a theatrical manager of Swedish descent who later worked with Oscar Asche [q.v.]. They had two sons. As a young society hostess in her Charles II flat in Lincoln's Inn, she proved herself a connoisseur of food and wine, and made a number of influential friends who rallied round her when in 1922 she was prosecuted for running the Golden Ballot which raised a large sum for the benefit of ex-servicemen and various hospitals. Her acquittal helped to establish the legality of such ballots. She was elected a life governor of St. Mary's, the West London, and the Royal National Orthopaedic hospitals.

Soon, however, Mrs. Leyel began to concentrate on the nearly forgotten craft of herbalism. Although she lacked a scientific training in botany, she acquired a profound and detailed knowledge of the work of the herbalist Nicholas Culpeper [q.v.] and his predecessors, and re-presented this vast knowledge of herbs, culinary, cosmetic, and healing, for use in the modern world. In 1926 she wrote *The Magic of Herbs* and in 1927 she opened Culpeper House in Baker Street, a shop full of herbal medicines, foods, and cosmetics, designed especially to appeal to women. Her imaginative and practical talents ensured the success of this and similar shops, which were decorated by Basil Ionides. Encouraged to apply her knowledge of herbs and their healing properties to the needs of patients dissatisfied with the drugs of orthodox medicine, she founded the Society of Herbalists, a non-profit-making organization for the study and application of the herbal art, and made available her own magnificent library, the nucleus of which is now housed with the society. In 1941 the society's life was imperilled by the pharmacy and medicines bill which, as drafted, would have destroyed the work of the herbalist in England. Again powerful friends rallied to her support and the bill was sufficiently modified to enable patients to obtain treatment on joining the society.

As a herbal practitioner Mrs. Leyel stressed to her patients the profound difference between the effect of drugs and herbs on the body; the former tending to remove symptoms but to mask causes, the latter, working far more slowly, removing in time the actual causes of the disease. Herbs, she found, treat the whole man, on the physical and mental planes, and on those between. They are natural to the body and produce no reaction which may itself need treatment. Used whole, as nature intended, they include the factor which assists their digestion, yet they can be pinpointed in application, even to a small part of a single organ. Holding these views Mrs. Leyel co-operated with Sir Albert Howard in his campaign for compost versus artificial manure; and with those working for pure water and pure food of every kind.

In 1931 Mrs. Leyel edited Mrs. M. Grieve's *A Modern Herbal* in two volumes; she herself wrote a long series of works on herbs, perhaps the most complete extant; they include *Herbal Delights* (1937), *Compassionate Herbs* (1946), *Elixirs of Life* (1948), *Hearts-Ease* (1949), *Green Medicine* (1952), and *Cinquefoil* (1957); as well as others on cooking. She was honoured with the palme académique of France in 1924. She died in London 15 April 1957.

[Mrs. C. F. Leyel, *The Truth About Herbs*, 1943; private information; personal knowledge.]   CHRISTMAS HUMPHREYS.

LIAQAT ALI KHAN (1895–1951), first prime minister of Pakistan, was born 1 October 1895 at Karnal in the East Punjab, the second son of Ruknuddaulah Shamsher Jang Nawab Rustam Ali Khan, who claimed descent from King Nausherwan of Iran. The family had for some generations been settled in the United Provinces, where they had received grants of land from the Mogul emperors. After graduating from the Muhammad Anglo-Oriental College in 1918, Liaqat Ali Khan went to Exeter College, Oxford, where he took the shortened honours course in jurisprudence in 1921; he was called to the bar by the Inner Temple in 1922. On his return to India in that year he at once began to play an active part in politics, and in 1926 he became a member of the legislative council of the United Provinces. His pleasing personality and lucidity of expression soon brought him into prominence and in 1931 he became deputy president of the council. He quickly became of importance in the Moslem League and in 1936 was elected general secretary of the All-India Moslem League.

In the same year he was appointed to the League's parliamentary board, the body charged with the supervision of the League's legislative activities, both at the centre and in the provinces, and with the choice of candidates for election.

These activities brought him into close touch with M. A. Jinnah [q.v.] who had become permanent president of the League in 1934. The ties between these two Moslem leaders grew ever closer and from this time until the death of Jinnah unqualified loyalty to his leader was the keynote of Liaqat's life. Jinnah must often have been a difficult chief and on one occasion early in his tenure of office Liaqat resigned from the parliamentary board as a result of a disagreement with his president. This, however, was the only hitch and thereafter Liaqat's self-effacing modesty and his cool temperament made him an ideal second-in-command.

In 1940 Liaqat was elected to the central Legislative Assembly and became the deputy leader of the Moslem League Party. He soon made his mark and unlike Jinnah, the Quaid-e-Azam, was a regular attender, taking part in most important debates. He was a hard hitter and his closely reasoned speeches often embarrassed the Government of India. The excellent teamwork of Jinnah and Liaqat was an important factor in building up the Moslem League to a position of such strength that it was able to speak with authority at the time of the mission under Sir Stafford Cripps [q.v.] in 1942. In 1945, when the formation of an interim government pending the final constitutional settlement was discussed, the talks between Liaqat and Bhulabhai Desai, the leader of the Congress Party in the Legislative Assembly, as to the proportion of seats in the Cabinet to be held by Hindus and Moslems, came as near to success as was possible in the prevailing atmosphere. In the same year Liaqat was perhaps the principal organizer of the overwhelming Moslem League victory, on a partition ticket, in the elections for the Moslem reserved seats in the central legislature. The result left no room for doubt that the Moslems were solidly behind the demand for partition.

In 1946 Liaqat became finance minister in the interim government formed with Jawaharlal Nehru as prime minister. The Congress and the Moslem League—the two main elements in the Cabinet—were poles apart, and in 1947 the finance minister's budget proposals, which included a wealth tax, a capital gains tax, and an increase in general taxation, were openly opposed by his Congress fellow ministers. The awkward situation which resulted was terminated only by the partition of India in August 1947.

On the inauguration of Pakistan, Jinnah became governor-general with Liaqat as prime minister. On the generally accepted constitutional theory, the governor-general would normally act on the advice of his ministers, but as long as Jinnah was alive it was clear that he would completely dominate the situation. On his death in September 1948 the situation was completely changed. Khwaja Nazimuddin became governor-general, while Liaqat remained prime minister, but it was Liaqat who held the reins of power, while Nazimuddin became the constitutional governor-general of the textbooks.

Liaqat grew rapidly in stature and though he never acquired the dominating position of Jinnah, for a time he was able to provide the cohesive force which Pakistan so badly needed. He had grown up with the Moslem League and the mantle of the Quaid-e-Azam had fallen naturally on him; he became universally known in Pakistan as Quaid-e-Millat, leader of the people. In 1949–50 when relations between India and Pakistan were at their worst, and wild men in both countries talked of war, it was Liaqat Ali Khan in Pakistan and Nehru in India who pulled their countries back from the precipice. It was in the same spirit that the prime ministers of the two countries made a pact in 1950 on the treatment of minorities.

A more difficult task confronted Liaqat when consideration was given to the future constitution of Pakistan. He had to reconcile the democracy in which he firmly believed with the view of the Ulema that an Islamic constitution could not be fully democratic; the practical-minded Liaqat must have been very sorely harassed by the disputes of the theorists as to the validity of man-made law. Had he lived, his basic common sense might have helped Pakistan to avoid some of the pitfalls lying ahead, but on 16 October 1951 he was assassinated at Rawalpindi by one Said Akbar, for whose action it proved impossible to ascertain a motive.

Before he first went to England Liaqat Ali Khan married a cousin, Nawabzadi Jehangir Begum, by whom he had a son. In 1933 he married Rana Irene Pant, of Almorah, of Hindu descent, whose family had become Christians, and who had been educated at Lucknow University. She became converted to Islam on her marriage. They had two sons.

[Private information; personal knowledge.]
P. J. GRIFFITHS.

LIDGETT, JOHN SCOTT (1854–1953), theologian and educationist, was born in Lewisham 10 August 1854 of Methodist ancestry. His father, John Jacob Lidgett, who died when his son was fourteen, was a successful City business man, and his mother, Maria Elizabeth Scott, helped to found what became known as the 'Women's Work' of the Methodist Missionary Society. Her father, John Scott, was twice president of the Methodist Conference, first principal of Westminster Training College, and a powerful influence in his grandson's early days. After leaving Blackheath Proprietary School Lidgett went into a firm of insurance and shipping brokers but two years later entered University College, London, where he graduated B.A. in 1874 and M.A. in logic and philosophy in 1875. In the following year he was accepted for the ministry of the Wesleyan Methodist Church and for fifteen years served in a succession of circuits in Tunstall, Southport, Cardiff, Wolverhampton, and Cambridge.

During his Cambridge ministry, set in surroundings so well attuned to his personal interests, Lidgett became acutely mindful of the gulf between rich and poor, and of the evils of poverty, bad housing, and unemployment in different parts of the country. Stimulated by the encouragement of W. F. Moulton [q.v.] he resolved to establish in one of the most neglected districts of London a centre, evangelical in spirit and therefore, as he held, committed to ever-widening social and educational aims: a meeting-place for all classes of society, to provide facilities for the study of literature, science, art, to encourage participation in local administration and philanthropy, and to be inspired throughout by non-sectarian motives.

In 1891 the Bermondsey Settlement was founded, with Lidgett as warden and a group of permanent residents who mainly worked in London during the day. Lidgett remained in Bermondsey until 1949, by which time many of his early dreams had been fulfilled. The educational institute, the Alice Barlow House (the headquarters of a working women's society), the Beatrice Club for girls, the Rydal Club for boys, and other activities bear witness to the social work of the settlement, while workers were furnished to the School Board, the London County Council, the Bermondsey borough council, and the Board of Guardians. Classes for Sunday school teachers and teachers in apologetics were provided, and for a number of years two Wesleyan Methodist churches were maintained in Rotherhithe.

As early as 1897 Lidgett was elected a member of the London School Board and he represented the Free Churches in the controversy provoked by the education bill of 1902. His attitude to the bill was somewhat divided, for he welcomed the impetus it gave to the cause of higher education while strongly criticizing the provisions which seemed to deny justice to Nonconformists, although he declined to support the passive resistance movement. It is of interest that in 1941 he led the Nonconformists in the deputation of Anglicans and Nonconformists which waited on the president of the Board of Education and in which the cordial spirit was in marked contrast to the religious bitterness associated with the 1902 Act and the withdrawal of the proposed Birrell bill of 1906. He played an important part in the correlation of the powers given to the borough councils by the 1902 Act which resulted in the passing of a separate Act for London in 1903, giving full control to the London County Council.

Lidgett was an alderman of the L.C.C. in 1905–10 and 1922–8 and represented Rotherhithe in 1910–22. In 1918 he was elected leader of the Progressives and although they were then losing ground he succeeded in keeping the dwindling party together for ten years, a task which would have broken the spirit of a less courageous man. His paramount interest on the L.C.C. was Christian education. He was a member (1905–28) and deputy chairman (1917–19) of the education committee.

Lidgett served London University with unremitting loyalty and affection. In 1922 he was elected a member of the senate, becoming deputy vice-chancellor in 1929 and vice-chancellor in 1930–32. He continued to represent the arts graduates until he retired in 1946 at the age of ninety-two. He served on a large number of committees and governing bodies including those of women's colleges which could always count on his enthusiastic support. He was a member of the council for external students (1922–46) and of the university extension and tutorial classes council (1929–45), and he was chairman of the Universities' China Committee (1933–6).

In the affairs of his own Church, the Free Churches, and the ecumenical movement Lidgett took a leading part.

In 1908 he was president of the Wesleyan Methodist Conference and also chairman of the London South District of the Church. He took a prominent part in all the negotiations leading to the union of the Wesleyan, Primitive, and United Methodist Churches and was elected the first president of the united Church in 1932. In 1906 he was president of the National Council of Evangelical Free Churches and in 1923–5 moderator of the Federal Council of the Evangelical Free Churches. He was concerned that in this country the Free Churches should advance towards full unity, but he also longed for unity with the Church of England and for the visible unity of the Church of Christ which he believed to be one in its essential nature. He was a member of the joint committee set up by the Free Church Federal Council in 1920 to prepare a reply to the Lambeth Conference 'Appeal to all Christian People', and a leading member of the committee of bishops and Free Churchmen which met at Lambeth in 1922–5. Those conferences were resumed in 1930 and continued until 1938 with Lidgett still playing a decisive role. He advocated the formation of a Council of Churches in Great Britain and was one of the founder-members of the British Council of Churches which came into being in 1942. He was the trusted friend of Randall Davidson [q.v.] and laboured until his death for the unity of English Christendom. While he was sometimes regarded by Free Churchmen as an uncertain quantity in Anglican–Free Church conversations, Lidgett never ceased to affirm the reality of Free Church ministries and sacraments and the fundamental principles of Reformed theology.

His own most significant contribution to theological thought was his first work, *The Spiritual Principle of the Atonement* (1897), in which he contends that the fatherhood of God is the highest as well as the universal relationship in which God stands to mankind, the divine fatherhood being pre-eminently manifested in the unique obedience of Christ who by the filial satisfaction offered to God reconstitutes the human race of which he is the head into a new unity. In *The Fatherhood of God* (1902) Lidgett attempts to show that from the Middle Ages onwards the centrality of the doctrine of the fatherhood of God as found in the Bible has been supplanted by the concept of sovereignty. *The Christian Religion, its Meaning and Proof* (1907) was in its day n impressive contribution to Christian pologetics. *God in Christ Jesus* (1915) is profound exposition of the Epistle to he Ephesians which unfolds the relation etween the Father, the Son, and the life of Christians in the Church and Society. The loctrines upon which the Epistle hinges onstituted the unchanging foundation of Lidgett's high churchmanship. *Sonship md Salvation* (1921) is a further exposiion of the fatherhood of God in the light of the sonship of Jesus as set forth in the Epistle to the Hebrews. The invitation to leliver the Maurice lectures (*The Victorian Transformation of Theology*, 1934) gave aim the opportunity of expressing his appreciation of F. D. Maurice [q.v.] whom ne regarded as the most significant personality of the previous century. Lidgett's theological sympathies were closely akin to those of Maurice in whose writings he found a combination of prophetic witness, systematic thought, and creative endeavour. He wrote smaller books including *Apostolic Ministry* (1909), *God, Christ and the Church* (1927), *God and he World* (1943), and *The Idea of God and Social Ideals* (1938) in which he showed the relation of his theology to his public work.

Lidgett was editor of the *Methodist Times* (1907–18) and joint-editor, from the death of his uncle Sir Percy Bunting [q.v.] in 1911, of the *Contemporary Review*, although for the last twenty years of his life his responsibilities were largely nominal.

He had a rare combination of gifts— a massive yet singularly alert mind, an unusual facility of speech in conversation, preaching, and on the platform, an easy command as chairman of the most complicated agenda, and a mastery of the art of summing-up a discussion. He was in many respects an austere and exacting man with few intimate friends. But there were human touches and he evoked admiration and respect even among those who could not always follow his leadership. Of his sanctity, which was inseparable from devotion to human need, there is no dispute. In 1950, when he was ninety-six, he virtually completed the painful process of official retirement from his various offices. He ended his days in Epsom where he had accepted the chairmanship of the Quarry Centre of Psychotherapy for which he secured a substantial grant from the Pilgrim Trust a year before his death, which took place at Epsom 16 June 1953.

Lidgett received honorary degrees from the universities of Aberdeen, Oxford, and London; was made a freeman of the borough of Bermondsey (1952); and in 1933 became a Companion of Honour.

In 1884 he married Emmeline Martha (died 1934), daughter of Andrew Davies, physician, of Newport, Monmouthshire; they had one son and one daughter.

A portrait of Lidgett by Francis Dodd was exhibited at the Royal Academy in 1948; another, by Andrew Burton, is at the Bermondsey Settlement.

[J. Scott Lidgett, *Reminiscences*, 1928, and *My Guided Life*, 1936; *John Scott Lidgett*, a symposium, ed. Rupert E. Davies, 1957; personal knowledge.]   HAROLD ROBERTS.

LINDEMANN, FREDERICK ALEXANDER, VISCOUNT CHERWELL (1886–1957), scientist and politician, was born 5 April 1886 at Baden Baden where his mother was taking the cure. He resented all his life the accident of his birthplace being in Germany. He was the second of three sons of Adolphus Frederick Lindemann whose family was of Catholic (not, as was often stated, Jewish) French Alsatian origin, and his wife, Olga Noble, American daughter of a successful British-born engineer and widow of a rich banker called Davidson. She was a Protestant and insisted on her four children being brought up as Anglicans. Lindemann's father, born in 1846, emigrated to Britain in his twenties and later became naturalized. He was a wealthy man, and the combined income of him and his wife was about £20,000 a year. He was also a scientist and astronomer of distinction, and built a private laboratory at his home near Sidmouth.

Lindemann and his elder brother, Charles, were educated at Blair Lodge, Polmont, in Scotland, a school now extinct, and from 1902 first at the Real-Gymnasium then the Hochschule in Darmstadt. They both distinguished themselves sufficiently in science to be accepted as Ph.D. students by Professor Nernst, the celebrated head of the Physikalisch-Chemisches Institut in Berlin. Lindemann gained his doctorate, although oddly not with the highest honours, in 1910. He must have been an unusual student. His comfortable allowance of £600 a year enabled him to live in the luxury of the Adlon Hotel. Somewhat incongruously he was a vegetarian—a temporary fad of his mother having left a permanent influence on him. Moreover all his life he neither smoked nor drank alcohol except upon the rare occasions when at (Sir) Winston Churchill's insistence he would take a carefully measured glass of brandy. He was fond of music and an excellent pianist, but he was indifferent to the visual arts and to the end of his days had a 'low brow' taste in literature. The two brothers were first-class tennis players, winning many prizes. Later Lindemann achieved the probably unique distinction of competing at Wimbledon after he had become a professor.

Lindemann's most important personal contributions in the field of physics were made between 1910 and 1924. His first papers under Nernst's influence were concerned with low temperature physics, and his doctoral thesis on the law of Dulong and Petit was a criticism of Einstein's formula for explaining the startling decrease in the specific heat of diamond at the temperature of liquid hydrogen. He and Nernst devised a formula which gave a better explanation, but it was later caught up and replaced by the Debye formula whose superiority Lindemann at once recognized. At the same time he was working on the connection between the characteristic frequency and the melting-point of a solid, and produced a theory relating melting to the amplitude of oscillation of atoms. He was exceedingly versatile while in Berlin. He invented, along with his brother, a glass transparent to X-rays which he patented. He endeavoured to improve the electronic theory of metallic conduction. He contributed to the theory of solids and was probably the first person to notice the paradox that their breaking stress is nothing like as great as theoretical considerations would suggest. He wrote papers on astronomical problems including one in conjunction with his father on the use of photo-electric cells in astronomical photometry. In the same paper he gave the first account of his 'Lindemann fibre electrometer' which, with modification, became a standard instrument and was his main contribution to experimental techniques. In 1919 he collaborated with F. W. Aston [q.v.] in a paper on the possibility of separating isotopes. He did some valuable work on certain geophysical problems and in 1923 with G. M. B. Dobson produced a paper which, although some of its suggestions are not now accepted, was the beginning of the modern theory of meteorites. In 1920 and 1922 he made important contributions to the

theory of the mechanism of chemical reactions.

Lindemann's strength as a physicist rested on his remarkable capacity for simplification of problems and in his very wide range. His relative weakness was in mathematics and this was reflected in the limitations of his *Physical Significance of the Quantum Theory* (1932). He was a man of intuition and flair in widely diverse fields, but he never pursued any one subject long enough to become its complete master. Much of his brilliance was shown in discussion at scientific conferences and has not survived in published form. For this reason later generations have not found it easy to understand the high esteem in which he was held by such persons as Einstein, Planck, Born, Rutherford [q.v.], and Poincaré. He was elected F.R.S. in 1920.

Lindemann was playing tennis in Germany just before war broke out in 1914, but departed in time to avoid being interned. In March 1915, after vainly seeking a commission, he joined the Royal Aircraft Factory at Farnborough, the chief centre of experimental aviation in England. His most notable contribution was his solution to the problem of 'spin' in aircraft. According to official records he learned to fly in the autumn of 1916, invariably—to the surprise of his colleagues—appearing at the station with the bowler hat, black Melton coat, and furled umbrella which was to be his characteristic uniform all his life. During June and July 1917 he tested empirically the theory that he had worked out to explain the nature of a spin and the way to get out of it. He was not the first person to extricate himself from a spin but he was the first to establish the correct scientific principle—an achievement which not only entailed great courage, but the remarkable power of memorizing in nerve-wracking conditions no fewer that eight different sets of simultaneous instrument readings. The theory has been advanced that he performed this feat in June or July of the previous year, but the weight of the evidence is against it.

In 1919, thanks partly to (Sir) Henry Tizard [q.v.] who was a colleague of his Berlin days, Lindemann was elected Dr. Lee's professor of experimental philosophy (i.e. physics) in the university of Oxford. The chair was attached to Wadham College where he remained a fellow until his retirement. But in 1921

Lindemann was also elected, as was legally possible in those days, to a 'studentship not on the governing body' at Christ Church, which had provided the endowment for the chair. This entitled him to rooms more spacious than Wadham could provide, and from 1922 for the rest of his life he lived in Christ Church.

The chair gave him the headship of the Clarendon Laboratory whose prestige had sunk to a very low ebb. It had no research staff, and no mains electricity. Its principal contents were packing cases full of unused optical instruments. Although Lindemann's career is in many respects controversial, no one has disputed his massive achievement in turning this museum piece into a great laboratory. He was adept at extracting money from the university and from outside sources. Long before he retired, the new Clarendon which he had persuaded the university to build was one of the foremost physics departments in Britain. Lindemann did not concentrate on any one line, although there was a slight bias towards the nucleus. Among the earlier research workers whom he picked were (Sir) T. R. Merton, (Sir) A. C. G. Egerton [q.v.], G. M. B. Dobson, and Derek Jackson. In the thirties he was active in recruiting to posts in Oxford Jewish refugee scientists from Hitler's Germany. The most prominent of these was (Sir) Francis Simon [q.v.] who became one of Lindemann's closest friends and in 1956 succeeded him as Dr. Lee's professor.

Lindemann's academic career was not without friction and he had more than one clash with the university authorities. He was apt to make wounding and sarcastic remarks. He was both prickly and aggressive in the cause of science which he regarded with some justice as a slighted subject in Oxford. He did not readily suffer fools. His wealth—his father who died in 1927 had handed on a large sum to each of his sons—allowed him to move in circles very different from those of the academic middle class. He preferred ducal houses to North Oxford. In 1919 he was introduced by (Sir) J. C. Masterman to Lord Birkenhead [q.v.]—tennis being the link—and it was at Birkenhead's house that he received the nickname of 'the Prof' by which he came to be almost universally known. In 1921 through the Duke of Westminster he met Churchill— the beginning of a lifelong friendship.

Lindemann's political views were well to the Right. He was an out-and-out inequalitarian who believed in hierarchy, order, a ruling class, inherited wealth, hereditary titles, and white supremacy (the passing of which he regarded as the most significant change in the twentieth century). It was fully in keeping with this attitude that he should have mobilized some of the personnel (not wholly willing) of the Clarendon to assist the production of Churchill's *British Gazette* during the general strike of 1926. Exceptionally for a person of these views, Lindemann was one of the first to recognize the danger of Hitler. His pre-war sojourn in Germany had given him an acute awareness of that country's formidable strength and aggressive potentiality. Filled with these apprehensions he became gravely perturbed at the inadequacy of British air defence, and the seeming fatalism of the Government.

In 1934, both independently and through Churchill, he pressed for the creation of a high-level committee to consider the problem urgently. In fact the Air Ministry had decided towards the end of the year to set up a departmental committee of its own, the committee for the scientific survey of air defence under Tizard's chairmanship, with Dr. A. V. Hill, H. E. Wimperis [q.v.], and P. M. S. (later Lord) Blackett as members. The Tizard committee was to be responsible for one of the most important achievements in British defence—the effective application of radar to the interception of enemy bombers. But Churchill and Lindemann were convinced that a mere advisory departmental committee would not carry enough weight. In the spring of 1935 the Government partly gave way and agreed to set up the air defence research subcommittee of the Committee of Imperial Defence, with Sir Philip Cunliffe-Lister (later the Earl of Swinton) as chairman. Both Tizard and Churchill were members, but its functions were limited and in practice it seems to have been regarded as little more than a sop to Churchill. There was, however, one important by-product. Churchill insisted that Lindemann should be put on the Tizard committee.

Lindemann, who joined it at the end of June 1935, treated his colleagues from the start in a spirit of criticism bordering upon hostility. Relations between him and Tizard, which had previously seemed friendly enough, anyway on the surface, deteriorated rapidly to the consternation of their many mutual friends, and the breach was never healed. A year later the committee broke up with the resignation of Hill, Blackett, and Tizard in protest at Lindemann's tactics. It was promptly reconstituted in October, but without Lindemann.

The conflict has been wrongly presented by Lord Snow and others as a dispute about the priority to be given to radar. The evidence of its inventor, Sir Robert Watson-Watt, is conclusive that Lindemann very strongly backed radar, although he was more apprehensive than the others about the possibility of enemy jamming. It is true too that Lindemann favoured the simultaneous exploration of various other defence devices which turned out to be impracticable, such as aerial mines. But the real conflict was over the status of the committee. Lindemann with his grand social and political contacts was prepared to go to almost any lengths, including publicity and political lobbying, to obtain real executive powers for it. His objective was sound, but his methods difficult to defend, and Tizard and his colleagues found it intolerable that Lindemann should report behind their backs to Churchill on the air defence research committee. With their Service background and orthodox approach, they considered that it was not for them to try to change the terms of reference laid down by the Air Ministry.

Their doubts about Lindemann cannot have been allayed by his efforts to enter Parliament for Oxford University on a programme of revitalizing British air defence. He failed to secure the second Conservative nomination at the general election of 1935, being defeated by C. R. M. F. Cruttwell [q.v.], principal of Hertford College, who to Lindemann's glee subsequently lost his deposit. In 1937 there was a by-election. Lindemann resolved to fight with or without the official nomination which in the event went to Sir Farquhar Buzzard [q.v.]. They were both easily beaten by Sir Arthur (later Lord) Salter standing as an independent.

The next few years were a period of frustration for Lindemann, but with the outbreak of war in 1939 he moved at once to the centre of affairs as personal assistant to Churchill at the Admiralty and head of his statistical section. He continued the same work when Churchill became prime minister in May 1940.

Lindemann was made a peer in 1941 with the title of Baron Cherwell, of Oxford.

In 1942 he became paymaster-general in 1943 a privy counsellor. Although never a member of the War Cabinet he frequently attended its meetings. His loyalty to Churchill was absolute, his influence on him profound.

Cherwell was a master at the art of lucidly presenting highly complicated matters with the greatest economy of words. He wrote about 2,000 minutes to Churchill during the war on a vast range of topics. The prime minister greatly admired this gift, and would often pass on bloated memoranda from other departments with the request, 'Prof. 10 lines please'. Cherwell's advice was by no means only scientific. He had a staff of economists, headed by (Sir) Donald MacDougall, one of whose tasks was to produce charts and graphs for Churchill so that he could visualize changes in weapon production, food imports, shipping losses, etc. Another—and very unpopular one—was the critical scrutiny of departmental statistics. For example, Lindemann correctly discovered that the German front-line strength in bombers in 1940 was grossly exaggerated, and after an inquiry by a high court judge into the rival statistics Lindemann's became the basis of policy. He also came to the less agreeable—but no less correct—conclusion that British night bombing at that time was less than one-third as accurate as the Air Ministry claimed. Navigational aids were at once improved. Another result of his quantitative analysis was to cut by a factor of more than two the ships going to the Middle East and America in the summer of 1942.

Lindemann was active in the support of experiments in new weapons of every sort. Hollow charge bombs and proximity fuses were among those whose development he pressed. One of his major contributions was the 'bending' of the wireless beam on which in 1940 German night bombers were relying for finding their targets. R. V. Jones, a former pupil then employed at the Air Ministry, was the first to suspect that the Germans possessed this device. Tizard appears to have been sceptical. If Lindemann had not pressed for counter-measures with all his weight, the consequences might have been disastrous. Cherwell also strongly backed the researches of his old pupil, Derek Jackson, into microwave radar. One of many important results was the invention of H_2S, the name of the device which gave a radar picture of the country to the navigators of the Pathfinder night bombers. It is probably fair to say that what Tizard did for Fighter Command Cherwell did for Bomber Command.

His judgement, like that of most persons in high places during the war, sometimes went astray. He greatly overestimated the damage that could be done by the massive area bombing of German towns, and was rightly criticized by Tizard and Blackett. But it seems unlikely that his famous minute in 1942 to Churchill on this theme was the determining factor in a decision which had its roots far back in recommendations of the chiefs of staff in 1940. He was wrong, too, to advise postponing for nearly a year the use of 'Window', the technique of confusing enemy radar by dropping strips of tinfoil. Although he had encouraged its development he feared lest the enemy would be alerted to use it too, and it should be said in justice to him that many radar experts took the same view. Another error was his excessive scepticism about the German rocket bomb or V2. He was right in ridiculing the danger of its possessing a ten-ton warhead, but he was characteristically extremist in maintaining that it did not exist at all. But when all criticisms have been made, the value of his war work must be regarded as immense. Churchill, and through Churchill the whole country, owed him a great debt of gratitude.

With the fall of the Churchill administration in 1945 Cherwell returned to Oxford and the Clarendon. He was at the same time a member of the shadow Cabinet, and principal Opposition spokesman in the House of Lords on economic affairs. He was also prominent in discussion of the atomic bomb and had nothing but contempt for the arguments of those who wished to ban tests. In October 1951 he reluctantly joined Churchill's Cabinet, again as paymaster-general. His main achievements were to defeat the Treasury proposals to bring in immediate sterling convertibility together with a floating rate of exchange and to prize the control of atomic energy out of the Ministry of Supply and into the hands of an independent authority. He had a great dislike of Whitehall 'bureaucracy', though happy relations with many individual civil servants.

In 1953 his leave of absence from Oxford ran out and he resigned his government post. He was made a C.H., and three years later was created a viscount.

Although he possessed life tenure of his chair, he retired in 1956. But he was allowed to reside in college, for, whatever friction there might have been in the past, he was now regarded as the most interesting and entertaining of companions. His last important speech in the House of Lords was an acid analysis of the United Nations in December 1956. For some time his heart had been giving him trouble, and he died in his sleep in Oxford on the morning of 3 July 1957. His will was proved at nearly a quarter of a million pounds. After various bequests and interests he left the residue as to two-thirds to Christ Church and one-third to Wadham. He never married and his titles became extinct.

Lindemann was on any view a remarkable person. The combination of his scientific expertise, his clarity of mind, and his personal friendship with one of the greatest statesmen in British history enabled him to exercise more influence in public life than any scientist before him. He had a brilliant mind—'one of the cleverest men I ever met, as clever as Rutherford', to quote Tizard's generous judgement. He was a man of extremes, passionate loyalty to friends, implacable detestation of enemies. And he inspired correspondingly extreme sentiments, deep devotion on the one hand and something near to hatred on the other. There were curious apparent contradictions about him. He was an ascetic who deeply distrusted asceticism in others. It came as a surprise to many to learn how vigorously he campaigned in the war for the plain man against austerity and meagre rations. Yet he knew singularly little about how the vast majority of his fellow countrymen lived—even the middle classes, let alone the masses. He believed that most people were stupid and needed to be governed for their own good by an élite. He was a most amusing, indeed fascinating, controversialist, but he could utter sentiments so cynical and sardonic as to shock his hearers, especially the young. Yet he was kind-hearted and secretly most generous to those in need. The sinister picture of him drawn by Hochhuth in his play, *The Soldiers*, was to anyone who knew Cherwell an absurd travesty.

Lindemann's voice was curiously frail, and his rather mumbling mode of delivery somewhat marred his lectures and speeches which read better than they sounded. In appearance he was a big man with broad shoulders, and an aquiline countenance. He dressed conventionally and immaculately, but he was a striking figure in any company. Few who met him ever forgot him.

A portrait by Henry Carr is in the Imperial War Museum.

[Sir George Thomson in *Biographical Memoirs of Fellows of the Royal Society*, vol. iv, 1958; Sir Roy Harrod, *The Prof*, 1959; C. P. Snow, *Science and Government*, 1961, and *A Postscript to Science and Government*, 1962; The Earl of Birkenhead, *The Prof in Two Worlds : the Official Life of Viscount Cherwell*, 1961; R. V. Jones in *Oxford Magazine*, 9 May 1963; R. W. Clark, *Tizard*, 1965; Sir C. M. Bowra, *Memories*, 1966; Lord Moran, *Winston Churchill : The Struggle for Survival, 1940–65*, 1966; personal knowledge.] ROBERT BLAKE.

LINDRUM, WALTER ALBERT (1898–1960), billiards player, was born at Bourke, near Kalgoorlie, the Western Australian gold mining centre, 29 August 1898, the son of Frederick William Lindrum and his wife, Harriett Atkins. Both Lindrum's father and grandfather had been champions and the former took over a hotel billiard-room when Walter was seven years old and set him to practising intensively. As a youngster, an accident with a mangle placed his career in jeopardy, half his index finger having to be amputated; his father was in despair, but the mishap proved a blessing in disguise as it enabled him to make a better bridge. After a thorough apprenticeship he made a 500-break. Fred Lindrum junior, born in 1889, was a highly skilled player and won the championship in 1912. Walter, however, gradually overhauled him and defeated him in 1914, with breaks of 363, 309, and 248, his first serious try-out, and a feat which earned for him the title of 'the fifteen-year-old phenomenon'. Expert opinion adjudged him the 'most skilled player of his age the world had known'. Meanwhile, in England, a young Australian red-ball specialist had created a sensation by making 23 thousand breaks by the red-ball route.

The young Lindrum's achievements continued to astonish the billiards world, and in 1922 H. W. Stevenson, the famous English ex-champion, visited Australia, but Lindrum defeated him with ease and made a great break of 1,417. He was now twenty-three and his fame had penetrated overseas, but English opinion was somewhat sceptical and he was regarded as a billiards freak who would soon be found out. After his defeat of Stevenson, a visit to England was broached but his father considered the proposal premature. However, in 1924 a great English player Claude Falkiner, toured Australia and after games with Lindrum, wrote: 'I had read of his prowess and expected to find the picture overcoloured but I was mistaken. He is a truly wonderful player he can play nursery cannons as well as anyone, has nothing to learn about the top-of-the-table game, and, on the red can be as prolific as George Gray: he scores at a tremendous pace.' A break of 1,879 against Falkiner added greatly to Lindrum's fame and in 1929 came his greatest test when Willie Smith of England, who had made a wonderful break of 2,743, without a single nursery cannon, and was scoring prolifically in England, visited Australia. Three matches with Lindrum took place and the Australian won two of them. This confirmed his genius.

Lindrum was prevailed upon by Smith, who termed him 'the most deadly opponent' he had ever met, to embark on an English tour, and accordingly, with Clark McConachy, a great New Zealand player, he set out for England, where they arrived in October 1929. 'Walter Lindrum in England at last!' was an English newspaper headline. Lindrum beat McConachy by 3,000 points in his first match and in the third of his seven matches against Smith he had a winning margin of 21,285, an all-time record. He won ten of his fourteen matches and, against Smith, made a magnificent break of 3,262, a world record apart from breaks made predominantly by exploitation of one type of stroke. He made 67 thousand-odd breaks during his tour and created 17 world records. In his second tour in England (1930–31) he again made 67 breaks of a thousand-odd and this time made a great break of 3,905, a record. Such had been his superiority over his rivals in his first tour that he now gave starts of 6,000 and more. In February 1931 he was invited by King George V to Buckingham Palace for an exhibition of the game. He was to make two further visits to England (1931–2 and 1932–3) and in the third he eclipsed all his previous feats by making a break of 4,137 which took 2 hours and 55 minutes to compile: it remains the world record. It was made against Joe Davis at Thurston's Hall on 19 and 20 January 1932. He made his final visit in October 1932 and in 1933 left England never to return.

During his career Lindrum broke all billiards records, including the following: a run of 529 nursery cannons; a session average of 2,664; a session average of 262 for a fortnight's match; an aggregate of 36,256 for a fortnight's game; eleven breaks of a thousand-odd in one match; 3,530 points in three consecutive visits. He entered twice for the world championship and beat Joe Davis on each occasion (1933, 1934). During his career as a whole he made one break of 4,000-odd, 6 of 3,000-odd, 29 of 2,000-odd, and 711 of 1,000-odd.

It was a matter of surmise why he never returned to England—his second championship win, in 1934, against Joe Davis, nearest to him in billiards genius, was in Australia—and the general impression was that he had no further fields to conquer. He made breaks of 3,000-odd four times against his brother (1941, 1944), and retired at the age of fifty. Thenceforward he devoted his activities to charitable work in the course of which he raised over a million pounds. He was appointed M.B.E. in 1951 and O.B.E. in 1958.

In 1929 Lindrum married Rose, daughter of Frederick Coates, ganger. After her death he married in England in 1933 Alicia, daughter of the late Thomas George Hoskin, farmer. The marriage was dissolved and in 1956 he married, thirdly, Beryl Elaine Russell. He had no children. He died while on holiday at Surfers' Paradise, near Brisbane, 30 July 1960.

[Private information.]   RICHARD HOLT.

LINDSAY, ALEXANDER DUNLOP, first BARON LINDSAY OF BIRKER (1879–1952), educationist, was born in Glasgow 14 May 1879, the eldest of the three sons of the Rev. Thomas Martin Lindsay [q.v.], historian of the Reformation, and nephew of W. M. Lindsay the classical scholar [q.v.]. One of his two sisters married (Sir) Frederick Maurice Powicke, the historian. Brought up in a liberal Calvinist family with strong social awareness, Lindsay was educated at Glasgow University, where he obtained a second in classics (1899). He failed to win a scholarship at Balliol College, Oxford, but was successful at University College. He obtained firsts in classical moderations (1900) and *literae humaniores* (1902) and in the latter year was president of the Union. From 1902 to 1904 he was Clark philosophy fellow at Glasgow University and from 1904 to 1909 Shaw philosophy fellow at Edinburgh. He was also, in 1904–6,

assistant to Samuel Alexander [q.v.], professor of philosophy at Manchester. In 1906 Lindsay was elected fellow and classical tutor at Balliol where he remained until 1922.

In this period Lindsay earned a great reputation as a tutor who forced even the most reluctant to think for themselves. His lectures lacked polish and formal structure, but they were impressive demonstrations of an acute mind thinking aloud, meeting objections as they arose. In 1907 he published a translation of Plato's *Republic*; in 1911 a book on *The Philosophy of Bergson*. But his interests were already turning outwards from Oxford. Like R. H. Tawney and other dedicated spirits of his generation he was an enthusiastic lecturer for the Workers' Educational Association. He was also a resolute popularizer. In 1913 he published a small volume on *The Philosophy of Immanuel Kant* for the People's Books; his introduction to Hobbes's *Leviathan* (Everyman's Library, 1914) is an excellent example of his vigorous, clear-cut, stimulating manner. His own translation of Plato was published in the same series in 1935.

During the war of 1914–18 Lindsay served with labour battalions, rising to be deputy controller of labour in France (1917–19), with the rank of lieutenant-colonel. He was several times mentioned in dispatches and was appointed C.B.E. After a brief period as professor of moral philosophy at Glasgow (1922–4), he returned to Balliol as master and in the next twenty-five years became a national figure, more by virtue of his moral fervour and wide-ranging interests than by his contributions to scholarship.

His election as master was not uncontroversial. He had known left-wing views, had not himself been an undergraduate at the college, and several fellows older than himself and senior to him in college standing were passed over in his favour. In 1926 he won some notoriety as one of the few Oxford teachers who supported the appeal by Archbishop Davidson [q.v.] for a negotiated settlement of the general strike. But it was not long before Lindsay impressed his personality on the college, and, although he never lacked enemies, he was held in considerable respect and indeed awe. He insisted on taking part in the educational activities of the college and was an outstanding tutor who, notwithstanding his own strong views, was always open to fresh ideas. He had a quite exceptional human sympathy which made him always ready to help a colleague or undergraduate in trouble. This loyalty could be abused: he was not good at detecting plausible rogues. But there was something grand and, some felt, even saintly about his imaginative sympathy. Oxford was ceasing to be the preserve of the rich and was being opened to wider social classes: 'Sandy' Lindsay approved the change, more perhaps than did most leading Oxford figures, and helped to get it accepted. His social and economic interests, and his feeling for the underdog, also made him a great influence on the socially conscious generation of undergraduates of the thirties. 'The place exists', he wrote in his last letter to Balliol men, in 1949, 'and I hope always will exist, for the young men.'

Lindsay's outside interests extended in many directions: the Oxford tutorial classes committee, W.E.A. and university extension lectures. He was chairman of the National Council of Social Service and connected with many unemployed clubs, including the South Wales settlement at Maes-yr-haf. He was the trusted adviser of the Labour Party and the Trades Union Congress on educational matters; and for five years Oxford correspondent for the *Manchester Guardian*. In 1930 he spent four months in India as chairman of a mixed East-West commission set up by the International Missionary Council to survey the work of Protestant colleges in India; and he played a large part in drafting its report. He struck up a friendship with M. K. Gandhi [q.v.] who came to stay with him in Balliol during his visit to England for the second Round Table conference.

From 1935 to 1938 Lindsay was vice-chancellor of the university of Oxford. By general agreement he was a great vice-chancellor, who did much to stabilize Oxford's finances and to adjust the administrative structure of the university to the needs of the twentieth century. He sponsored an appeal for funds and piloted through a number of schemes for the expansion of the science departments— the new Clarendon Laboratory and the conversion of the old one into the Department of Geology, the Physical Chemistry Laboratory, the reorganization of the Forestry Department, the absorption of Lord Nuffield's large benefactions for the Institute for Medical Research and for Nuffield College. In the creation of this

last, the first of Oxford's graduate college for men and women, Lindsay played a large part.

Meanwhile he had become increasingly concerned about the economic and political events of the time. Under his influence Balliol gave a home to a number of distinguished German and Austrian academic refugees. In October 1938 a by-election occurred in the city of Oxford just after the Munich agreement, which Lindsay abhorred. He was persuaded to stand on an anti-Munich platform against the Conservative candidate, Quintin Hogg. The Labour and Liberal candidates stood down in Lindsay's favour but he was not elected although his reduction of the Conservative majority from 6,645 to 3,434 was regarded as a significant political gesture. When war broke out in 1939 Lindsay became chairman of the Joint Recruiting Board, with the task of allocating conscientious objectors to work of national importance other than military service. In 1940 he took the lead in organizing education for the armed forces. After the war he accepted a peerage from the Labour Government and spoke from time to time on educational matters in the House of Lords. In 1948 he was chairman of a commission on the reform of universities in the British-occupied zone of Germany which produced an interesting but ineffective report.

Lindsay's interests were turning increasingly towards North Staffordshire, where Oxford had established the first of the original tutorial classes. For over twenty years he played a big part in adult education there. After the war this work culminated in negotiations with the University Grants Committee for the establishment of a university college in North Staffordshire which finally opened in 1949. Lindsay, who had ceased to be master of Balliol in that year on reaching the age of seventy, was at once appointed first principal. Balliol made him an honorary fellow; he was also an honorary LL.D. of Glasgow, St. Andrews, and Princeton.

The University College at Keele was a significant new academic experiment and in one sense the crowning achievement of Lindsay's career. Its curriculum marked a decisive break with tradition. Work for the first degree lasted for four years, the first of which was spent on foundation studies whose object was to acquaint future arts and science students with each other's disciplines and to impress

Lindsay, A. D.

upon them the unity of knowledge. The three-year course covered not less than four subjects, two at a considerable level of specialization. This was a logical extension of the Modern Greats school (philosophy, politics, and economics) which Lindsay had taken the lead in establishing in Oxford in 1922, and of the Science Greats (combining philosophy with the principles of natural science) for which he had failed to win acceptance. Keele's object was to break down what Lindsay regarded as the excessive specialization of the older universities. He sometimes expressed this hatred of narrow specialization as a dislike of research which he regarded as a form of self-indulgence tolerable only if subordinated to the requirements of teaching. He always hated pedantry and negative, merely destructive, criticism. Keele ran into many difficulties after Lindsay's death and its achievement fell short of his hopes. Some of its ideas were taken over by universities founded later in more propitious circumstances. But Keele opened the doors, by breaking away from much of the machinery of external control hitherto imposed on new colleges, and by using this freedom to devise a new style of academic curriculum. It was a portent and a turning-point in English educational history.

Lindsay was an academic politician rather than a philosopher. His reputation and influence were far greater than can be explained by his published work. His philosophy was completely out of touch with fashionable attitudes in Oxford and Cambridge in the thirties and forties. His most ambitious philosophical work, *Kant* (1934), is little read; although *The Essentials of Democracy* (1929) and *The Modern Democratic State* (of which only the first volume was published, 1943) were widely read, they are unsystematic and incomplete. Lindsay never fully stated his own philosophical position. There are hints of an historical theory which would relate moral standards, at once objective and improvable, to social development: Lindsay described himself as a 'sociologically minded person'. But these are no more than fragments, and Lindsay too often evaded difficulties by falling back on Christian commonplaces. He owed to his father a deeply religious outlook on life. As master of Balliol he preached once a term in the college chapel. He was a close friend of Archbishop William Temple [q.v.] who

shared his social outlook. Lindsay's democratic theories were the outcome of his Christian beliefs, his respect for ordinary people. Goodness, like democracy, he thought, was learned in the self-government of small communities, especially religious congregations. He referred again and again in his writings to the Putney debates in Cromwell's army in 1647 and to the practice of the Society of Friends. 'As though there were any point in freedom', he said, 'if we do not use it to serve other people, as though any decent man ever wanted to be free except to be able to do his job.' (*Religion, Science, and Society in the Modern World*, 1943.)

Lindsay's democratic theories were closely related to his educational theory. In 1928 he spoke to the students of Cardiff of 'the great democratic commonwealth of learning, which transcends division of class, religion, and nationality, which takes the co-operation of all for granted, and which has worked out a wonderful technique of co-operative thinking'. This was the conviction which underlay the Keele experiment.

At Oxford, Lindsay was always too much of a radical to be completely happy. For all his achievements, he was continually having to compromise, to make concessions to the politically possible: to the extent even of sometimes convincing himself that the politically possible was also theoretically desirable. There is something pathetic in his last letter to Balliol men. Jowett's Balliol, he wrote, 'prepared the governing class to play its part in a classless society' by purging them of the aristocratic vices. Keele was not a classless society either, but it was far more like it than Balliol or Oxford had been. Lindsay was more at home in Keele, with his utter freedom from affectation and self-importance, his profound sense of the dignity and equality of all human beings, or at least of all human beings who had the root of the matter in them.

Lindsay was a powerful personality who could be ruthless with those who opposed what he believed to be right. He did not suffer gladly either the intellectually pretentious or those whose orthodoxy was conventional and not thought out. His idea of democracy was a vigorous, hard-hitting debate: he expected no more quarter than he gave. He could not believe that it was possible for a man to have convictions on which he did not act. As he grew older, stories collected about his authoritarianism, his determination to get his own way. He could be as wily and circumspect politically as his hero Oliver Cromwell: and as hypocritical, his enemies would have added. But he drove no one so hard as he drove himself. His influence on students between the two world wars was incalculable, and time and time again he gave a lead where few others in university circles did—in attempting reconciliation during the general strike, in doing something for the unemployed during the depression, in opposing Nazism earlier than was fashionable, helping German refugees and taking a public stand against Munich, in modernizing and democratizing Oxford, in the Keele experiment. In all these ways his influence prepared for the welfare State, if not the classless society.

In 1907 Lindsay married Erica Violet (died 1962), daughter of Francis Storr. They had a daughter and two sons, the elder of whom, Michael Francis Morris (born 1909), specialist in Chinese economics, succeeded to the title when Lindsay died at Keele 18 March 1952.

At Balliol there is a portrait by Lawrence Gowing and a bust by (Sir) Jacob Epstein in the Lindsay room. At Keele there is a copy of Gowing's portrait, made by the artist; and another portrait painted after Lindsay's death by Robin Goodwin.

[W. B. Gallie, *A New University: A. D. Lindsay and the Keele Experiment*, 1960; H. W. C. Davis, *A History of Balliol College*, revised by R. H. C. Davis and Richard Hunt, 1963; Sir C. M. Bowra, *Memories*, 1966; private information; personal knowledge.]

CHRISTOPHER HILL.

LINDSAY, GEORGE MACKINTOSH (1880–1956), major-general, was born in Cardiff 3 July 1880, the fifth son of Lieutenant-Colonel Henry Gore Lindsay, of Glasnevin House, Dublin, and his wife, Ellen Sarah, daughter of the first Baron Tredegar. He was educated at Sandroyd and Radley. Shortly before his eighteenth birthday he received a militia commission in the Royal Monmouthshire Royal Engineers, and in 1900 a regular commission in the Rifle Brigade, during the South African war—where he served in Natal and the Transvaal, earning a mention in dispatches.

In 1906 he became adjutant of a Volunteer regiment, and on the formation of the Territorial Army he became adjutant (1908–11) of the 17th (County of London) battalion of the London Regi-

ment. In 1913 he was appointed instructor at the School of Musketry, Hythe, but went to France in 1915 as a machine-gun officer. He was selected as instructor at the newly formed G.H.Q. Machine-Gun School, and later in the year was brought back to England as G.S.O. 2 of the Machine-Gun Corps training centre at Grantham. Returning to France in June 1916, he was brigade-major of the 99th brigade, with which he took part in the battles of the Somme and Arras. He was appointed to the D.S.O. in 1917. In March 1918 he became machine-gun officer at the headquarters of the First Army, with the rank of colonel.

After the war he passed through the Staff College and was then given command, in June 1921, of No. 1 Armoured Car Group of the Tank Corps, stationed in Iraq, where he carried out experiments in the use of a mechanized force in combination with aircraft, and maintained entirely by air supply.

It was George Lindsay's unique distinction that he played a leading part in the development of two of the most important instruments in modern warfare, the machine-gun and the tank, and of the corps which handled them. An ardent advocate of the machine-gun before 1914, when few soldiers recognized its potentialities, he became the moving spirit in the formation of the Machine-Gun Corps, and the formulation of its tactical technique, in the war of 1914–18. Then he turned, with even more far-reaching vision, from the instrument which had paralysed tactical mobility to one which would revive it, and became one of the foremost advocates of mobile armoured warfare.

When tanks were definitely accepted as a permanent part of the army, and constituted in 1923 as the Royal Tank Corps, Lindsay came back to England to guide its training as chief instructor at the Royal Tank Corps Centre for two years, then as inspector of the Corps from 1925 to 1929. Those years were of far-reaching importance, not only for the future of the Corps but also for the future of warfare. The history of armoured forces, not only in the land of their birth, is a record of checks imposed, and confusion caused, by the way the higher authorities repeatedly selected for the key posts in this field officers who had no previous experience of it, in preference to those who had both knowledge and enthusiasm. Lindsay's appointment at this juncture was a happy exception.

During Lindsay's two years at the Central Schools the system of instruction was improved, and a number of changes made in the courses at both the Driving and Maintenance School at Bovington and the Gunnery School at Lulworth. But the most significant change was the increased emphasis on the tactical side of the instruction. At the same time increased use was made of the Schools for experiment with and report on machines and weapons.

The primary task of those who had grasped the new idea was to spread it. Within the Centre Lindsay was the chief instructor; outside he became the chief evangelist. His charter to visit other places gave him frequent opportunities of 'preaching the gospel', and they multiplied when he became inspector. He was a good lecturer and a good talker, with a knack of arousing interest and a manner which disarmed opposition, and he was able to influence the minds of many soldiers who were not accustomed to read military books and journals. In that way he very effectively reinforced the prophets who used the printed word to propagate the idea. A lecture on 'Fire-power' which he had given to many audiences in his Machine-Gun Corps days was developed into one which coupled 'fire-power and mobility'. He used to begin by reciting the story of David and Goliath, as an allegory of 'a new idea' defeating 'brainless brute force', and rubbed it in with aptly chosen examples from subsequent military history, of which he was a keen student. As a teacher he knew the value of constant repetition of the essential points, and of keeping them unbefogged, while varying the exposition so far as to ensure that his theme did not grow stale.

In 1929 Lindsay became brigadier general staff in Egypt, where he repeatedly urged the importance of creating an armoured force such as eventually proved the decisive instrument in repelling the Axis invasion of Egypt and, later, in throwing the enemy out of Africa.

In 1932 he returned home, on being appointed to command the 7th Infantry brigade at Tidworth, one of the two experimental motorized brigades. In the final exercise of the 1934 training season he was given an opportunity of commanding an improvised armoured division, but was so hampered by the directing staff that the opportunity of showing what such a division could achieve was largely

spoiled, and the trial was not renewed until three more years had passed.

Meanwhile Lindsay, following his promotion to major-general in 1934, had gone to Calcutta in 1935 as commander of the Presidency and Assam District, where he remained until his retirement in 1939. That he had no further opportunity in the field of mechanized warfare was a deplorable loss in the crucial years before 1939.

As a leader he was lacking in toughness, and almost too kindly, but he did much to increase efficiency by infecting officers and men with his own enthusiasm. He was the most sympathetic of reformers, with a geniality rare in dynamic men. The response it evoked was exemplified in the way all who came in contact with 'George Lindsay' found it hard to use his surname without the affectionate coupling of his Christian name.

On the outbreak of war in 1939 he was recalled to command the 9th Highland division, and in 1940 he was appointed deputy regional commissioner for civil defence in the south-west of England, where he showed untiring activity during the many air raids. In 1944 he was appointed commissioner of the British Red Cross and Order of St. John in North-West Europe, and held that post for two years. He was colonel-commandant of the Royal Tank Regiment from 1938 to 1947. In 1942 he gave the Lees Knowles lectures on military history at Cambridge.

Lindsay was appointed C.M.G. (1919), C.B. (1936), and C.B.E. (1946). In 1907 he married Constance, daughter of George Stewart Hamilton, by whom he had two daughters, one of whom died at birth. He died in Epsom 28 November 1956.

[B. H. Liddell Hart, *The Tanks*, vol. i, 1959; personal knowledge.]

B. H. LIDDELL HART.

LINLITHGOW, second MARQUESS OF (1887-1952), viceroy of India. [See HOPE, VICTOR ALEXANDER JOHN.]

LIPSON, EPHRAIM (1888-1960), economic historian, born in Sheffield 1 September 1888, was the son of Hyman Lipson, furniture dealer, and his wife, Eve, daughter of Michael Jacobs. His elder brother, D. L. Lipson, was independent member of Parliament for Cheltenham from 1937 until 1950. A childhood accident left Ephraim Lipson grievously deformed and his health was never robust. Scholarships carried him through Sheffield Royal Grammar School and Trinity

College, Cambridge. He obtained first class honours in both parts of the historical tripos (1909–10) but since Cambridge offered no opportunity for remunerative work he migrated to Oxford and became a private tutor.

At that time economic history was advancing rapidly in academic and popular appeal. The first generation, represented by Ashley and Cunningham, was giving place to the second, with (Sir) J. H. Clapham [q.v.], Lilian Knowles, W. R. Scott, and George Unwin as notable teachers and a growing company of younger scholars entering the field. The universities, in collaboration with the Workers' Educational Association, were providing evening classes in which 'industrial history' was a favourite subject. Meanwhile, the rapidly growing library of published national and local records was rendering existing surveys of English economic history out of date. Lipson therefore resolved to produce a new survey based on 'both the older sources of evidence and the new material'. The first fruits of this herculean task, *An Introduction to the Economic History of England: I. The Middle Ages*, appeared in 1915, when he was in his twenty-seventh year. Its welcome was enthusiastic. Reviewers lauded its 'mastery of pretty well all the abundant new material, primary and secondary', its 'precision and critical acumen', and its solid worth in enriching the pictures of the guilds, the woollen industry, and other topics on which the new sources threw the strongest light. The book was conservative in its concept of the content and questions of economic history; it fitted the new facts into the old frame, wrestled with ancient controversies, but started no new ones. Yet its merits outweighed these defects and Lipson's reputation rose so high that in 1922 he was appointed reader in economic history at Oxford and fellow of New College.

There followed a decade of intense many-sided activity. His lectures became so popular and his work with research students so well known that it could be said 'Lipson was economic history at Oxford'. He served as external examiner at other universities, including Cambridge. More than any other individual he was the creator in 1926 of the Economic History Society and of the *Economic History Review* which first appeared in 1927. He had sponsored the proposal to found the journal; induced his own publishers to

produce it; planned its form and content and for eight years bore the main burden of editorship. He secured articles from virtually all the veteran distinguished scholars, as well as from many who later stepped into their shoes, in Europe and North America; he provided lists of new publications in many countries; and wrote dozens of short reviews himself.

Meanwhile he worked steadily on the next instalment of his *Economic History of England*. By late 1930 he had finished volumes ii and iii, ranging from the Elizabethan Age to the eve of the Industrial Revolution and sub-titled 'The Age of Mercantilism'. On learning that Oxford intended to establish a Chichele professorship in economic history he urged his publishers to get the volumes out before the electors met in June 1931. Copies were in the electors' hands by early May. But when the selection was made it did not fall on Lipson.

With this hard blow, Lipson's formal academic career—and his home life—ended. Hurt and angry he left Oxford, rarely to return; sold his house and disposed of his library. Invitations to deliver the Lowell lectures in Boston (Mass.), then to lecture in a number of North American universities, led to a leisurely tour round the world in 1932–4. Thereafter his life was divided between summer lodgings at the National Liberal Club in London and escape from bronchial troubles by wintering abroad in warmer climates. The war drove him out of London and restrictions on travel limited his range of refuge to south-west England.

In such circumstances the old life of sustained research and writing was no longer possible. There could be no volume iv, but since the other three were the only current substantial survey, an attempt had to be made to keep them up to date. Volume i was revised and enlarged in 1937. Volumes ii and iii were expanded in the third edition (1943) by appending a hundred pages of new material and adding a long introduction in which Lipson reiterated the theme that had run throughout the first edition: 'There is no hiatus in economic development, but always a constant tide of progress and change in which the old is blended almost imperceptibly with the new.' In particular his study of organization and ideas before 1750 had convinced him there was no 'Industrial Revolution', no violent breach with the past, in the eighteenth century—or in any other. To that central motif he added another conviction that the tide of human affairs was governed by the law of ebb and flow, with pendulum-like or cyclical alternating periods of co-operative or corporate control and of free enterprise. Medieval society was co-operative and corporate; after a full turn of the wheel, mercantilism emerged as 'England's first Planned Economy'; and by the 1940s the wheel was again coming full circle 'to the spirit of an older régime based on co-operation' and social control.

It was easier to philosophize than to keep up with the rapid advances on the research frontier. Two minor works, published in 1950 and 1953 respectively, made no attempt to do so; they belonged to 'the economic history of yester-year'. Lipson died in London 22 April 1960. He had never married.

[Private information; personal knowledge.]
HERBERT HEATON.

LITHGOW, SIR JAMES, first baronet, of Ormsary (1883–1952), shipbuilder and industrialist, was born at Port Glasgow, Renfrewshire, 27 January 1883, the elder son of William Todd Lithgow, shipbuilder, of Drums, Langbank, Renfrewshire, and of Ormsary, Argyllshire, by his wife, Agnes, daughter of Henry Birkmyre, of Springbank, Port Glasgow, partner in the Gourock Ropework Company, the borough's main and oldest industrial works.

Lithgow on his father's side came of a family which was strongly Presbyterian and church-going and of a covenanting tradition. He was educated at Glasgow Academy and in Paris. On reaching the age of sixteen he was offered by his father three possibilities: to live comfortably as a country gentleman; to go to a university and enter some profession; or to serve an apprenticeship in the family shipyard. This choice was later put to Lithgow's younger brother Henry; both sons chose to enter the shipyard. Lithgow took his apprenticeship seriously and yardsmen recalled for many years the red-haired long-legged apprentice who did jobs twice as quickly as other people, and earned the nickname 'the Scarlet Runner'. His particular interest was in plumbing and many years afterwards, during the war of 1939–45, when on leave at Ormsary from his work as controller of merchant shipbuilding, he surprised a naval guest by meeting him with a bag of tools and apologizing for his inability to join him at the shoot until he had mended a burst pipe.

In 1906 he became a partner of Russell & Co. of Port Glasgow, the shipbuilding firm of which his father was a co-founder, which later became Lithgows, Ltd., and won a world-wide reputation in the shipping world. In 1908 his father died a millionaire and left Lithgow and his brother with the heavy responsibility of the management of a great industry. Their capability soon became apparent. In 1912 Lithgow, while still under thirty, was elected president of the Clyde Shipbuilders' Association.

As a Territorial he was embodied on the outbreak of war in 1914, and commanded in France a heavy battery of the Royal Garrison Artillery largely made up of men from his shipyard. He was wounded, received the M.C. and a brevet lieutenant-colonelcy. His brother remained behind in charge of the shipyard and its vital war work. In 1917 Lithgow was himself brought back from France to become director of merchant shipbuilding at the Admiralty.

During the years of depression following the war Lithgow played an important part in stimulating industrial revival in Scotland and in rationalizing shipbuilding after its abnormal expansion during the war. This was effected by the industry itself, in contrast, for instance, to that carried out in the cotton industry after the war of 1939–45 at considerable expense to the public. Lithgow's efforts in helping to salvage Scottish industry were disinterested and self-sacrificing. In 1936 he was elected chairman, at the time of its worst crisis, of the great Scottish steel and armaments firm of William Beardmore & Co. He rescued it from its difficulties at some sacrifice to his own business and to his health. He did the same for the Fairfield Shipbuilding & Engineering Company, the Lithgow brothers taking over a majority of the firm's ordinary shares and meeting the dishonoured bills on which the firm seemed likely to founder.

His skill in handling industrial problems and manpower led him to a number of influential appointments. In 1920 he was elected president of the Shipbuilding Employers' Federation. From 1922 to 1925 and from 1933 to 1935 he was the British employers' delegate to the International Labour Organization at Geneva. In 1924 he was president of the National Confederation of Employers' Organizations and from 1930 to 1932 president of the Federation of British Industries.

In 1930 the National Shipbuilders'

Security, Ltd., was established, with Lithgow as its first chairman, to help rescue those shipyards unable to weather the economic storms of the time by buying them out at terms more favourable than they could have got in the open market; yards thus taken over were guaranteed not to be used for shipbuilding for forty years. Lithgow had a thankless and unpopular task but his efforts helped to tide over the adverse times in the shipyards and avoid the financial collapse of the whole industry.

Lithgow was in advance of current thought in many of his ideas and this, combined with his practical ability, enabled him to establish methods for organized co-operation in industry. As an enthusiast for the use of electricity he strongly supported in 1927 the formation of the Central Electricity Board and Sir Andrew Duncan [q.v.], its first chairman, insisted on Lithgow's being a member of the board. Lithgow's work as chairman of the executive committee of the Scottish National Development Council, a non-political body formed in 1931 to work for the economic revival of Scotland, was particularly marked. It was part of Lithgow's philosophy that 'those who made their money in Scotland have an obligation to keep it there and to use their best endeavours to develop and keep healthy the industry to which they owe their own prosperity'.

During the war of 1939-45 he was almost immediately appointed controller of merchant shipbuilding and repairs and was a member of the Board of Admiralty from 1940 to 1946. His expert handling of this key post, particularly in the spring crisis of 1941, was a considerable factor in the successful prosecution of the war, as was his successful drive in tank production, the output of which in this same period was dangerously low. Lithgow was persuaded by (Sir) Winston Churchill and Sir Andrew Duncan to become temporary chairman of the Tank Board and head of the tank division of the Ministry of Supply. When the pressure of his task in the early war years diminished a little, Lithgow took over the presidency of the Iron and Steel Federation (1943-5) and concerned himself mainly in plans for the industry after the war.

For his services to his country and to industry Lithgow was created a baronet in 1925 and in 1945 appointed G.B.E.; in 1947 he was appointed C.B. for his work as chairman of the County of Renfrew

Territorial and Auxiliary Forces Association. In 1946 Glasgow University conferred on him an honorary LL.D. and from 1943 until his death he was vice-lieutenant of Renfrewshire. But probably the honour he most appreciated was being made, on 7 November 1951, the first honorary freeman of his home town of Port Glasgow, the 'dirty wee port' for which in later years he shyly confessed his deep affection. He was already by then a sick man and the provost and councillors had to bring the casket containing his burgess ticket to his home at Gleddoch House. It was there that he died 23 February 1952.

Lithgow was a man of great determination and energy, with an analytical and penetrating insight into problems, outspoken to a degree which usually stimulated, sometimes shocked, and occasionally provoked hostility. His partnership with his brother (who died in 1948) was a well-balanced one, for Henry Lithgow's quieter, more deliberate nature counterbalanced his elder brother's more dynamic and impulsive personality. Lithgow was an exceedingly generous man, usually anonymously. He gave liberally to the Church of Scotland and also to the Iona Community, telling Sir George MacLeod (later Lord MacLeod of Fuinary) that he disagreed with, but respected, his pacifist views. He was a man more at home with country than with city men and probably among his happiest hours were those spent shooting at Ormsary or deer-stalking on his estate at Jura, when his lifelong boyish spirit and humour were most manifest.

He married in 1924 Gwendolyn Amy, who succeeded him as chairman of Lithgows, only daughter of John Robinson Harrison, shipowner, of Scalesceugh, Cumberland. By her he had a son and two daughters. The son, William James (born 1934), succeeded as second baronet and, in 1958, as chairman of Lithgows.

Lithgow's portrait, with his favourite dog Dazzle, by (Sir) Oswald Birley, is in the family's possession.

[*The Times*, 25 February and 15 March 1952; J. M. Reid, *James Lithgow, Master of Work*, 1964; H. C. Whitley, *Laughter in Heaven*, 1962; private information.]

G. K. S. HAMILTON-EDWARDS.

LIVINGSTONE, SIR RICHARD WINN (1880-1960), educationist, was born in Liverpool 23 January 1880, the son of the Rev. Richard John Livingstone, vicar of Aigburth and later honorary canon of

Liverpool, and his Irish wife, Millicent Julia Allanson-Winn, daughter of the third Baron Headley. A scholar of Winchester and New College, Oxford, Livingstone was Hertford scholar (1900), obtained first classes in honour moderations (1901) and *literae humaniores* (1903), and won the Chancellor's Latin verse (1901) and the Arnold historical essay (1905) prizes. He became fellow, tutor, and librarian of Corpus Christi College where he remained until 1924, interrupted by a year (1917–18) as an assistant master at Eton. He made a deep and lasting impression on many able pupils, for he had a power to charm and a genuine interest which brought out the best in others. Beneath a somewhat dreamy manner lay a certainty of purpose which developed with the years. As a young tutor at Oxford he was eager to improve the teaching and active with William Temple, H. W. Garrod [qq.v.], and others in a pressure for reform which was to bear fruit in the royal commission which reported in 1922. Livingstone himself was a member of the prime minister's committee on the classics in 1920, the year in which he became joint-editor of the *Classical Review*, a position which he held until 1922.

Livingstone's first publication, *The Greek Genius and its Meaning to Us* (1912), showed that he had learned well from the example of Gilbert Murray [q.v.] 'to look on Greek thought as a living thing'. His scholarship was graced by the elegance with which he wrote or translated and illuminated with 'the habitual vision of greatness' of which he loved to speak. The humanism of the Greeks he saw as complementary to Judaism: 'And so when Christianity comes she finds the world in a sense prepared for her.' In *A Defence of Classical Education* (1916) he maintained that 'We study Ancient Greece as containing, with Rome, the history of our origins, and explaining much in our literature, language and ideals'; Greek was 'an introduction to modern problems: in history, thought and politics'. He pursued this theme as editor successively of *The Legacy* (1921), *The Pageant* (1923), and *The Mission* (1928) of Greece.

Meantime he had moved in 1924 to Belfast where as vice-chancellor of Queen's University he was persuasive in arousing throughout the six counties a pride in the university and a sense of responsibility towards it which brought valuable financial support. He was knighted in 1931.

Returning to Oxford in 1933 as president of Corpus, Livingstone was able to exert a wider influence, his interests now extending to the whole field of the aims and methods of education. He was president of the educational section of the British Association in 1936; Rede lecturer at Cambridge in 1944 when he spoke on 'Plato and Modern Education'. In 1937 and 1938 he was an originator of summer schools at Oxford for colonial administrators. 'Adult education for the educated' was a subject later developed in *The Future in Education* (1941), a book which included his views on part-time continued education instead of a general raising of the school age and a suggestion for residential colleges for adults on the Danish system which aroused much interest. In 1948 he had the satisfaction of opening Denman College, the Women's Institute residential college at Marcham named after Lady Denman [q.v.] which owed much to his inspiration. He is commemorated there by a lecture-room which bears his name and in the garden by a life-size bust of him lecturing, executed by Kathleen Parbury.

Over his own college (where there is a portrait by Eric Kennington) Livingstone presided with dignity and shrewdness. It was perhaps unfortunate that he served as vice-chancellor of Oxford at a difficult time (1944–7) to which his particular talents were not best suited. He failed to gain the full confidence of the university.

In 1950 Livingstone retired but he continued much in demand as a lecturer, especially in the United States where his reputation was greater than it was at home. He was a lucid and skilful speaker, and popular as a broadcaster. He had remained active in his own field: as president of the Hellenic Society in 1938 and of the Classical Association in 1940–41. His translation of Plato, *Portrait of Socrates*, appeared in 1938 and his edition of a translation of Thucydides on the Peloponnesian War in 1943. He was also the originator and general editor of the Clarendon Greek and Latin Series of texts issued partly in the original and partly in translation, with introductions, notes, and vocabularies. He never ceased to emphasize his belief in the value of a classical education. The complete education, he maintained, must give man a philosophy of life and 'Greece and Christianity are the two supreme masters of the ethical, the spiritual life'. In *The Rainbow Bridge*

(1959), a collection of essays and addresses, he was still calling for university reform: towards a more liberal education which would include some study of religion or philosophy, or both.

Livingstone received honorary degrees from ten universities and was awarded the King Haakon VII Liberty Cross. He was a commander of the Legion of Honour and was made a knight commander of the Order of King George I of Greece shortly before his death, which took place in Oxford 26 December 1960. He married in 1913 Cécile Stephanie Louise, daughter of George Maryon-Wilson, of Searles, Fletching, Sussex. He had two daughters and two sons, one of whom was killed in action in 1944.

[*The Times*, 28 December 1960; *Oxford Magazine*, 16 February 1961.]

HELEN M. PALMER.

LLEWELLIN, JOHN JESTYN, BARON LLEWELLIN (1893–1957), politician and first governor-general of the Federation of the Rhodesias and Nyasaland, was born at Chevening, near Sevenoaks, 6 February 1893, the younger son of William Llewellin, later of Upton House, Poole, by his first wife, Frances Mary, daughter of Lewis Davis Wigan, of Oakwood, Maidstone. He was educated at Eton and University College, Oxford (later being elected to an honorary fellowship there). In September 1914 he was commissioned into the Dorset Royal Garrison Artillery and served in France (1915–19), winning the M.C. in 1917 and achieving the rank of major. On his return to England he read for the bar and was called by the Inner Temple in 1921. His real interests, however, lay in the field of politics. In 1929 he gained the Uxbridge division of Middlesex for the Conservatives and very soon made his mark in the House. He was parliamentary private secretary to the postmaster-general (Sept.–Oct. 1931) and to the first commissioner of works (1931–5); assistant government whip (1935–7); and civil lord of the Admiralty (1937–9).

In July 1939 he became parliamentary secretary at the Ministry of Supply, a key department which had recently inherited from the Board of Trade responsibility for the whole of the Government's supplies organization, and was thus engaged in quietly making preparation against a war. In May 1940 he went as parliamentary secretary to the Ministry of Aircraft Production for which he was spokesman in the House of Commons, Lord Beaverbrook

being in the Upper House. Everything which could be done to produce the quality and quantity of aircraft needed to hold and defeat the Luftwaffe was done under Lord Beaverbrook's dynamic driving power, and in this historic endeavour Llewellin ably assisted him.

In May 1941 Llewellin became parliamentary secretary to the Ministry of Transport and was sworn of the Privy Council. He was spokesman in the House for the departments of both shipping and transport which were in the process of being amalgamated as the Ministry of War Transport of which he became joint-parliamentary secretary in June. In February 1942 he attained cabinet rank as president of the Board of Trade, but in the same month was transferred back to his old department as minister of aircraft production. The need was as urgent then as it had been before and it was a great moment and a tribute to his own endeavours when in May he was able in a broadcast speech to assure the Commonwealth that our aircraft had improved 'out of all recognition' and were superior to anything which the enemy could put in the air. In November 1942 he was appointed to Washington to fill the new post of minister resident for supply, for which his recent ministerial experience particularly suited him and which he greatly enjoyed. At the end of 1943 he returned to England to succeed Lord Woolton as minister of food at a time when food problems were becoming increasingly difficult. Here he remained until July 1945 and again a difficult job was well done.

In the general election of 1945 Llewellin lost his seat and in the resignation honours was created a baron. For a few years he was able to enjoy a somewhat more leisured life, although he was a regular attendant at the House of Lords and active outside Parliament in his various capacities as deputy-lieutenant for Dorset, chairman of Dorset quarter-sessions, president of the Royal Society for the Prevention of Accidents, president of the Chambers of Commerce of the British Empire, a member of the B.B.C. general advisory council, and in many other interests such as freemasonry and the British Legion.

In September 1953 he took up his appointment as first governor-general of the newly created Federation of the Rhodesias and Nyasaland in Central Africa. This was an office calling for the greatest tact and skill. He had not only to

advise the federal prime minister on political matters, but also to help establish
relations between the federal government
and the territorial governments, in particular the governors of the two colonial
territories of Northern Rhodesia and
Nyasaland who were answerable to the
Colonial Office. The first federal elections
were held in December and resulted in
a sweeping victory for the Federal Party
led by Sir Godfrey Huggins (later Viscount
Malvern). Then followed the difficult
tasks of forming a federal administration
and civil service, an operation which
afforded plenty of play for the part of
mediator. White Rhodesians called for
'improved status' and discussions over the
federal franchise occupied the political
stage in Salisbury. In this Llewellin's intimate knowledge of the political temperature in Britain was of especial value.

'Jay' Llewellin as he was generally
called was a warm and genial Englishman
(his name was pronounced accordingly)
who enjoyed wide interests and activities.
A keen sportsman, he was in 'upper boats'
at Eton where he also went in for athletics
and football, and later rowed for the
University College boat which ended up
head of the river in 1914. He was a
countryman at heart and an enthusiastic
gardener, and always went to Upton
whenever he could, even at the busiest
time of his career. When tied to London he
used to enjoy quick visits to Hurlingham.
His sister ran Upton for him and acted as
hostess there and at the governor-
general's house in Rhodesia where his
facility for informal entertainment was of
particular value. Perhaps because he was
a bachelor he was a strong opponent of
women in public life, particularly in
politics. 'They are always inclined to be so
bossy', he used to say, 'and the ladies in
the House of Commons have a tremendous
amount of bees in their bonnets.' He
strongly opposed the admission of women
into the House of Lords.

He was appointed C.B.E. in 1939 and
G.B.E. in 1953. He died in Salisbury 24
January 1957. One of his last public acts
was to open the arts wing, which was
named after him, of the then new University College of Rhodesia and Nyasaland. A portrait by C. J. McCall was
hung in the Federal Assembly building in
Salisbury.

[*Manchester Guardian* and *The Times*, 25
January 1957; *Dorset Year Book*, 1957–8;
Gil Thomas, *Llewellin*, 1961; personal know-
ledge.]   JONATHAN LEWIS.

LONSDALE, FREDERICK (1881–1954),
playwright, whose original name was
Lionel Frederick Leonard, was born in St.
Helier, Jersey, 5 February 1881, the third
and youngest son of John Henry Leonard,
seaman, and his wife, Susan, daughter of
James Belford, a tobacconist. Lonsdale
was educated locally and joined the army
as a private. There is a story, probably
apocryphal, that he first came to the
attention of Frank Curzon, the producer,
while acting in an army amateur performance, which he himself had written.
He was discharged from the army on
medical grounds and was employed for
a time as a railway clerk in St. Helier.
He worked his passage to Canada as a
steward on a liner and when he returned
to England his occupations included
various odd jobs on the Southampton
docks.

By this time he had already begun to
write plays under the name of Lonsdale
which he adopted by deed poll in 1908.
A Lonsdale play is always distinguished
by its notable conversational quality and
brilliance of dialogue, but particularly by
its intimate knowledge of the manners and
behaviour and jargon of a class from which
Lonsdale did not spring, but which almost
immediately received him with interest
and enthusiasm. He was an attractive and
entertaining talker, verging occasionally
on the outrageous, and with growing success and self-confidence his inborn dislike
of the self-important might have led him,
were it not for his roguish sense of fun,
into occasional conflict. Because he himself was the friend of friends, the devotion
of his many friends easily and often protected him.

Frank Curzon produced his first play,
The King of Cadonia, a musical comedy
with lyrics by Adrian Ross and music by
Sidney Jones [qq.v.], at the Prince of
Wales's Theatre in 1908, and a farce, *The
Early Worm*, at Wyndham's in the same
year. With Curzon's production of *The
Best People* at Wyndham's the following
year, and *The Balkan Princess*, a musical
play, in 1910 at the Prince of Wales's,
Lonsdale's reputation was established.
The truly astonishing skill which enabled
him to produce a new play almost every
year seemed to come in cycles. Thus it was
not until 1915 that he produced his next
batch of successes, namely *Betty* (a musical play, Daly's, 1915), *High Jinks*
(a musical comedy adaptation, Adelphi,
1916), and *The Maid of the Mountains*
(a musical play with music by Harold

Fraser-Simson and J. W. Tate, Daly's, 1917]. This last was a tremendous success and ran for 1,352 performances. It was produced by Oscar Asche [q.v.] with José Collins [q.v.] as Teresa. *Monsieur Beaucaire*, a romantic opera (Prince's Theatre), came in 1919 and *The Lady of the Rose*, a musical play adaptation at Daly's, in 1922.

The comedy *Aren't We All?* which Lonsdale and his great following considered to be his best play was produced at the Globe Theatre in 1923. Then *Madame Pompadour* (musical play adaptation with Harry Graham, Daly's, 1923), *The Fake* (Apollo, 1924), *The Street Singer* (musical play, music by Fraser-Simson, Lyric, 1924), *Spring Cleaning* (Eltinge Theatre, New York, 1923, St. Martin's Theatre, London, 1925), *Katja the Dancer* (musical play adaptation with Harry Graham, Gaiety, 1925). In 1925 was also produced *The Last of Mrs. Cheyney* at the St. James's Theatre with the leading roles played by (Dame) Gladys Cooper, Ellis Jeffreys, Ronald Squire, and Sir Gerald du Maurier [q.v.]. This famous play ran for 514 performances and is generally recognized as his best-known play. The third act was written by Lonsdale while the piece was being rehearsed and in consequence it has something of the quality of a one-act play. His inability to finish a play was a curious weakness of Lonsdale's which often landed him in difficulties.

Tom Walls [q.v.] produced *On Approval* at the Fortune Theatre in 1927 and also *The High Road* at the Shaftesbury Theatre in the same year. *Lady Mary*, a musical comedy with John Hastings Turner, at Daly's, followed in 1928; *Canaries Sometimes Sing* (Globe, 1929); *Never Come Back* (Phoenix, 1932); *Once is Enough* (Henry Miller Theatre, New York, 1938); *Foreigners* (one of his few failures, it only ran for a week, Belasco Theatre, New York, 1939); *Another Love Story* (Fulton Theatre, New York, 1943, Phoenix Theatre, London, 1944); *But for the Grace of God* (St. James's, 1946); and finally, *The Way Things Go* (Phoenix, 1950).

Since Lonsdale's plays dealt always with the activities of the worldly and the well-bred they seemed to become dated and the last few plays he wrote did not enjoy the success to which he was accustomed. The taste of playgoers was modified by war and its ensuing psychological turbulence, and the theatre-going audiences were no longer so willing to be titillated by the drawing-room comedy and the problems of the rich. Towards the end of his life Lonsdale became acutely aware of and much distressed by this rather dismal trend, which carried none of the variety and colour of the life which he had enjoyed. He wrote scripts for two films for M.G.M., *The Devil to Pay* (1930) and *Lovers Courageous* (1932); and for (Sir) Alexander Korda [q.v.] the scenario for *The Private Life of Don Juan* (1934).

In 1938 Lonsdale decided to settle in America and remained there throughout the war. After the war he returned, occasionally, rather sadly to England, and after 1950 lived mostly in France. On his last visit to London he died, 4 April 1954, as he was walking home after he had dined in his usual merry fashion.

Freddy Lonsdale was as naturally entertaining as anyone could be. He had that amusing attribute of laughing through his speech, which was infectious and attractive, and was helped by his puckish foxy face. He was gay, mischievous, perceptive, and funny, never anecdotal, and his appearance anywhere—white socks, white muffler, his hat on the back of his head—was always a herald of delight.

In 1904 Lonsdale married Leslie Brook, daughter of Lieutenant-Colonel William Brook Hoggan, R.A.; there were three daughters of the marriage, the eldest of whom, Mrs. John Donaldson, wrote an admirable biography of her father. Of two portraits of Lonsdale by Simon Elwes one became her property.

[Frances Donaldson, *Freddy Lonsdale*, 1957; private information; personal knowledge.]   SIMON ELWES.

LORAINE, VIOLET MARY (1886–1956), actress, was born in Kentish Town, London, 26 July 1886, the daughter of Henry Edmund Tipton, commercial clerk, and his wife, Mary Ann Eliza Garrod. She was educated at Trevelyan House, Brighton, and went on the stage at the age of sixteen, as a chorus girl. Although her status was humble her surroundings were not, for her first job was in the Drury Lane pantomime of 1902, *Mother Goose*. Small parts in musical plays followed at once and carried her through to 1905, in which year she had her first taste of straight acting (in a revival of the old farce, *Our Flat*, at the Comedy Theatre) and of the variety stage, when she appeared in revue at the Palace. By now well launched, she toured for George Edwardes in *The Spring Chicken* and *The Girls of Gottenburg*; made her first venture on to the 'halls' as a single turn at the old Oxford Theatre; became a popular principal boy in provincial pantomimes; and in 1911 returned with glory to her starting-point, playing lead in the Drury Lane pantomime *Hop o' My Thumb.*

When war broke out in 1914 she was already a well-known performer. In 1914 and 1915 she found a place in a series of productions at the London Hippodrome: *Hullo, Tango!, Business as Usual,* and *Push and Go.* Her big chance came in April 1916 when *The Bing Boys are Here* was put on at the Alhambra in Leicester Square and she was given the leading female part, Emma, with (Sir) George Robey [q.v.] playing Lucius Bing. This entertainment caught the special taste of the troops on leave and, with its two sequels, the not altogether successful *The Bing Girls are There* (1917) and the immensely popular *The Bing Boys on Broadway* (1918), made the Alhambra a rallying-place for uniforms until long after the fighting was over.

Violet Loraine became a figure of national importance. With her warm, friendly personality, her gaiety, her rich humour, and the sincerity she could bring to such basically sentimental songs as 'If you were the only girl in the world' or 'Let the great big world keep turning', she was a symbol of delight. The public, armed forces and civilians alike, took her to its heart and was inconsolable when, at the very peak of her success, she married into the Northumbrian squirearchy and left the stage. As often happens when a stage artist makes a popular hit, the magnitude of Violet Loraine's success was due to the chance that she was on a particular spot with particular talents at a particular time. There was a public need, and she was there to supply it. The success itself, however, she had earned for herself by hard work. After the war she appeared in *Eastwood Ho!* at the Alhambra (1919), *The Whirligig* at the Palace (1920), and *London, Paris and New York* at the London Pavilion (1921).

In September 1921 she announced her retirement from the stage on her marriage to Edward Raylton Joicey (died 1955), son of Colonel Edward Joicey, of Blenkinsopp Hall, Haltwhistle, Northumberland. There were two sons of the marriage.

In May 1928 Violet Loraine took part in a charity performance of *The Scarlet Pimpernel* at the Palace and later that year she made a return to the professional stage, playing the name part in *Clara*

Gibbings. This was not the kind of venture to appeal to her old public and it seemed—like other returns which she made in 1932 and 1934—to be evidence of a passing desire for a glimpse of her old world of the theatre rather than a serious intention to win back her former place in it. She died in Newcastle upon Tyne 18 July 1956.

[*Who's Who in the Theatre*; *Burke's Landed Gentry*; *The Times*, 20 July 1956; private information.]　　　　W. A. DARLINGTON.

LOWE, EVELINE MARY (1869–1956), first woman chairman of the London County Council, was born 29 November 1869 in Rotherhithe, the daughter of the Rev. John Farren, a Congregational minister, and his wife, Sarah Saint Giles. She was educated at Milton Mount College and trained as a teacher at Homerton College where she became a lecturer in 1893 and vice-principal in the following year, when the college removed from London to Cambridge. She retired in 1903 on her marriage to George Carter Lowe, a veterinary surgeon in Bermondsey who qualified as a doctor in 1911 and went into partnership with Alfred Salter who was later to sit for many years as Labour member of Parliament for West Bermondsey. Dr. Lowe was a quiet and modest man, greatly respected by all who knew him; his death in 1919 was deeply felt by his widow. There were no children.

Early in her married life Mrs. Lowe was elected to the Bermondsey Board of Guardians and entered upon a career of public service in the borough in the course of which she acquired a really informed and personal knowledge of conditions in the London home. She loved Bermondsey and lived among its people as a patently sincere person in whom everyone could confide on terms of friendship. For many years she went among the members of the Bermondsey Independent Labour Party collecting subscriptions, delivering notices, and selling copies of the Bermondsey Labour magazine. At election times she took her share in door-to-door canvassing. In 1919 she was co-opted a member of the education committee of the London County Council on the nomination of C. G. (later Lord) Ammon; three years later she was elected to the Council as a Labour member for West Bermondsey, a constituency which she represented until 1946, when the borough showed its appreciation of her services by making her a freeman.

The Labour Party in 1922 was in

a minority on the Council and Mrs. Lowe became leader of the opposition on the education committee. Although she took part in other work at County Hall she specialized on the work of the education department and when the Labour Party won its majority in 1934 it was with every confidence that Herbert Morrison recommended that Mrs. Lowe should be the chairman of the education committee. She held this heavy post of great responsibility until 1937. Mrs. Lowe knew about education; moreover she had a keen and incisive mind coupled with a rare patience and kindliness; she was wise in her recommendations as to the chairmen and vice-chairmen of sub-committees; she handled her Labour colleagues well and was courteous to the Conservative opposition, commanding their respect, if not their agreement, at all times. She was not a keen party politician; she thought more of the children and their education than she did of party strategy. Nor was she happy with newspapermen: she was polite but distant, rather cold, and obviously doubtful of them. Nevertheless, when she took the chair at a press conference called to launch a three-year education plan, in the preparation of which she had played a leading part, Mrs. Lowe came through the gruelling task of answering the reporters' questions with flying colours.

In 1929–30 Mrs. Lowe served as deputy chairman of the Council and ten years later she was elected the first woman chairman. She discharged the responsibilities of this high office with dignity, impartiality, and competence. It was the Council's jubilee year and as its chairman Mrs. Lowe attended many public functions and ceremonies, winning praise from all parties for her charm, intelligence, and sincerity. The outbreak of war brought sterner duties and new responsibilities which she met with her usual courage and calm resourcefulness. In all her public work Mrs. Lowe was a woman of great integrity. She never sought personal publicity or political kudos; she was not a careerist and resisted all pressure to enter Parliament. Her biggest mission in life was to improve and promote London education and the mental and physical well-being not only of London's children but of the adolescents who attended the polytechnics and evening institutes, the young people whom the Council helped to get a university education, and the teaching staff. In the course of her lifetime public education ceased to be regarded as a concession and came to be

accepted as the birthright of every child in a welfare State; it was her life work to help to bring about this change in the climate of public opinion.

After her retirement from the Council in 1946 Mrs. Lowe was co-opted for a further three years as a member of the education committee, on which she thus served in all for thirty years. She was at different times a member of twelve other of the Council's committees and chairman of three of them. She represented the Council on the Burnham Committee, the Child Guidance Council and the London (Central) Advisory Committee for Juvenile Employment. She was also closely connected with the university of London, representing the Council on the court and on the councils of Bedford College (of which she was a governor) and the Institute of Education, and on the training colleges delegacy. In 1950 the university conferred upon her the honorary degree of LL.D. She died in Dulwich 30 May 1956. A portrait by A. K. Lawrence is in the Ayes Lobby at County Hall. A primary school of advanced design in the Old Kent Road district of Southwark has been named after her.

[Private information; personal knowledge.]
MORRISON OF LAMBETH.

LOWKE, WENMAN JOSEPH BASSETT- (1877–1953), model maker. [See BASSETT-LOWKE.]

LOWRY, CLARENCE MALCOLM (1909–1957), author, was born at Liscard, Cheshire, 28 July 1909, the youngest son of Arthur Osborne Lowry, cotton broker, by his wife, Evelyn Boden, both Methodist teetotallers.

He was educated at Caldicote preparatory school, Hitchin, and the Leys School, Cambridge. He won the Junior Public Schools Golf Championship, played the ukelele, wrote jazz music and poems. Before going up to St. Catharine's College, Cambridge, he persuaded his father to send him to sea as 'the quickest way out of Liverpool'. A voyage to the China Seas (May–October 1927) provided material for his first novel *Ultramarine*. There followed a year at the English School in Bonn and a visit to the poet Conrad Aiken in Cambridge, Massachusetts, before he went to St. Catharine's. Aiken and Nordahl Grieg the novelist whom he visited in Norway as an undergraduate became his lifelong literary fathers. He left Cambridge in 1932 with an undistinguished third class in the English tripos and a fabulous reputation as a writer and drinker of enormous capacity.

Recognizing both, his father throughout his lifetime made an allowance, generous enough, he hoped, to allow him to write and insufficient for him to drink himself to death.

In 1933, after many rewritings and a characteristic loss of the manuscript, Lowry published *Ultramarine*, distinguished from other 'before the mast' novels by its subjectivity and symbolic undertones.

In December 1933 Lowry married, in Paris, a young New York writer, Jan Gabrial, whom Aiken had introduced in the hope that she would solve Lowry's alcoholic problem. The marriage was turbulent and in 1935 Lowry went to New York ahead of her, seeking new material for his autobiographical myth. After an alcoholic fugue, he was given brief treatment in Bellevue Hospital. Out of this experience he wrote *Lunar Caustic*, a novella frequently revised, but only posthumously published: in *Paris Review* (No. 29) in 1963 and in book form in 1968.

Joined by Jan, Lowry drifted first to Los Angeles, then to Mexico, where they rented a villa in Cuernavaca in 1936. Attracted by the Mexican awareness of death, Lowry wrote a short story about the roadside death of an Indian. This became the central episode of *Under the Volcano*. But before this was published much had to happen.

After a period of sobriety, Lowry started drinking again. When his wife left him and went to Los Angeles in December 1937 he plunged into the alcoholic abyss, seeking there his literary subject. He was gaoled in Oaxaca and in July 1938 deported. He followed Jan to Los Angeles but she refused to see him and demanded a divorce. He met Margerie Bonner, another American aspirant writer, and after his divorce married her in December 1940 in Canada where he lived, with intermissions, until 1954.

Working for the most part in a seashore shack at Dollarton, British Columbia, Lowry wrote and rewrote *Under the Volcano*, descriptive of the Day of the Dead in Mexico, 1938, the last day in the life of the drunken consul Geoffrey Firmin and his wife Yvonne. Lowry was aided by Margerie, a simple life, and wartime scarcity of hard liquor and by June 1945 the fourth and final version was finished and dispatched.

In the summer of 1944 the Dollarton shack burnt down and the Lowrys tried to rebuild it themselves. It was not completed by the winter of 1945 and in December Lowry took his second wife to Mexico to show her places and people described in *Under the Volcano*, hoping incidentally to find material for a new novel. Although their visit was cut short by the Mexican authorities, he found material for two novels, never finished. *Dark as the Grave Wherein my Friend is Laid*, edited by Professor Douglas Day and Margerie Bonner Lowry from Lowry's notes and drafts, appeared in 1968. *La Mordida* awaited similar editing.

While in Mexico in 1946 Lowry learnt of the acceptance of *Under the Volcano* by Reynal and Hitchcock in the United States and of the interest of Jonathan Cape [q.v.] provided the book was drastically revised. In rebuttal of Cape's arguments, Lowry wrote an astonishing 15,000-word letter explaining the plan and purpose of his masterpiece 'so designed, counterdesigned and interwelded that it could be read an indefinite number of times and still not have yielded all its meanings or its drama or its poetry'. No author has ever written so brilliant a defence and exposition of his work. The achievement is the more astonishing since Lowry was drinking heavily throughout and at one point attempted suicide.

A work of genius, *Under the Volcano* has glaring faults. Lowry partially distributed elements of his personality and experience among the main male characters, but the wife Yvonne begins as Jan Gabrial and ends as Margerie Bonner without ever attaining substance. Its success after publication in 1947 was immediate in the United States and Canada, not long delayed in France, but slower in Great Britain. American students of Eng. Lit. found it a treasury of Ph.D. theses, as rich in literary allusions and cross-references as *Ulysses*, if not *Finnegans Wake*. Lovers of literature cherish it for the robustness of its humour, the beauty of its description, the resonance of its imagery, the intricacy of its mosaic pattern, the preservation of sanity within insanity, and the Faustian sense of the spiritual damnation in attempting through alcohol to take a short cut to mystical illumination.

Lowry intended all his work to be part of a vast corpus called *The Voyage That Never Ends*, of which *Under the Volcano* was the central novel. Perhaps for that reason the work on the rest never ended in

Lowry

D.N.B. 1951–1960

the lifetime which was cut short, after several attempted suicides, by his death 'by misadventure', 27 June 1957, at Ripe, Sussex, where he and his wife had been living since 1955. *Hear Us O Lord From Heaven Thy Dwelling Place*, a collection of short stories and occasional pieces (1962), *Selected Poems* (1962), *Lunar Caustic*, and *Dark as the Grave*, like the undergraduate novel *Ultramarine*, are all unmistakably by the author of *Under the Volcano*. But though they have individual passages of beauty, wit, power, and strangeness, their main importance is that they provide the foothills by which the more easily to scale the eminence of Lowry's masterpiece. Leaving aside the as yet unpublished *La Mordida*, the most important aid to *Under the Volcano* (apart from the letter to Cape printed in *The Selected Letters*, 1967), is *Dark as the Grave* which rehearses, though with deliberate changes of fact, the events which went towards the composition of *Under the Volcano*. The second Mexican excursion was a deliberate reliving of the first, in the conscious hope of finding a happier end and the unconscious desire by venturing once more into Hell to discover a self-fulfilment (or self-annihilation) which had not been found in the Paradise of Dollarton.

[*The Selected Letters of Malcolm Lowry*, ed. Harvey Breit and Margerie Bonner Lowry, 1967; 'Portrait of Malcolm Lowry', especially Professor Douglas Day, B.B.C. Third Programme, 1967; Conrad Knickerbocker, 'Malcolm Lowry in England', *Paris Review*, No. 38, 1966 (an untrustworthy source); personal knowledge.]   ARTHUR CALDER-MARSHALL.

LYLE, CHARLES ERNEST LEONARD, first BARON LYLE OF WESTBOURNE (1882–1954), industrialist and politician, was born at Highgate, London, 22 July 1882, the only son of Charles Lyle and his wife, Margaret Brown. He was educated at Harrow, Trinity Hall, Cambridge, and Kahlsruhe University, from which he joined the family sugar refining firm of Abram Lyle & Sons.

Lyle was always a fine athlete with a catholic taste in games. He represented England at lawn tennis and was a well-known figure at Wimbledon and was thus particularly suited to be chairman of the Lawn Tennis Association in 1932 and later an honorary life vice-president. He was the first chairman of the International Lawn Tennis Club from 1924 to 1927. His remarkable eye also enabled him to hit a long ball on the golf course, but he was never a championship player and he mainly owed his tenure of the presidency of the Professional Golfers' Association from 1952 to 1954 to qualities of good fellowship. He was also a keen yachtsman and was elected a member of the Royal Yacht Squadron in 1952.

Lyle's political career started when in 1918 he became the Coalition Unionist member of Parliament for the Stratford division of West Ham, a part of London which he knew well and with which he remained closely associated as chairman for many years of Queen Mary's Hospital, the maternity wing of which, named after his mother, owed much to his personal efforts for its endowment. He was defeated in the 1922 general election and did not stand for Stratford again. In 1923 he was elected Conservative member for Epping which he represented for only a year, after which he stood down to be succeeded by (Sir) Winston Churchill. Lyle did not stand again for Parliament until 1940 when he was elected Conservative member for Bournemouth where he had gone to live. He stood again in 1945 when he obtained the largest Conservative majority of that election, and shortly afterwards went to the House of Lords. He had been knighted in 1923 and created a baronet in 1932.

Lyle was an active and influential backbencher who took a special interest in Commonwealth affairs and the preservation of the rights of the individual. These interests led him to become the chairman of the Empire Industries Association, for which he spoke fearlessly and powerfully. Later he became president of the Aims of Industry, an organization devoted to the promotion of free enterprise.

His interest in the West Indies, and particularly in Jamaica, was far warmer than one would have expected merely from the fact that he was chairman of Tate & Lyle's subsidiary company there. He contrived to reach out across what might have been formidable barriers of misunderstanding and form a deep personal friendship with (Sir) Alexander Bustamante who, in addition to being then chief minister, was also leader of the trade union with the largest following in the sugar industry. So far from regarding Lyle as a wicked 'Sugar Baron', Bustamante never ceased to express his affection and admiration for him long after Lyle had died.

Lyle's industrial interests were almost exclusively concerned with his family firm of Abram Lyle & Sons which amalga-

656

nated in 1921 with Henry Tate & Sons to
orm Tate & Lyle. He was a member of
he boards of other companies, but these
never absorbed his full attention. He became the chairman of Tate & Lyle at the
early age of forty and continued in this
office until he became president of the
company in 1937. He will be best remembered for his outspoken opposition to
he nationalization of the sugar-refining
industry as proposed by the Labour
administrations of 1945–50 and 1950–51.
He employed robust but never undignified methods to put his case against
nationalization before what he called 'the
tribunal of the great British public'. He
was deliberately provocative and to be so
employed the device of an animated and
slightly grotesque cartoon figure known as
Mr. Cube', which became the symbol of
anti-nationalization. Lyle's forceful statements were always his own. They were
uttered in a characteristic yet somehow
unexpectedly gentle voice, which in no
way robbed them of their pungency.

Lyle, who acted with the authority of
an overwhelming majority of his company's shareholders, endured with great
good humour many personal clashes with
Labour spokesmen. But in spite of much
hard hitting, there was never malice, and
he died as he had lived, a man who was
popular with all his acquaintances and
loved by his intimates. Even in his
seventies he gave the appearance of someone who had only recently ceased to be
an active sportsman, and this no doubt
helped him to overcome occasional bouts
of ill health, and to stand the strain of the
major political campaign which he initiated, dominated, and won for his company late in life.

In 1904 Lyle married Edith Louise (died
1942), daughter of John Levy. They had
two daughters and one son, Charles John
Leonard (born 1905), who succeeded him
when he died in Bournemouth 6 March
1954. A posthumous portrait by Bernard
Dunstan hangs in the board-room of
Tate & Lyle.

[Private information; personal knowledge.]
PETER RUNGE.

LYNSKEY, Sir GEORGE JUSTIN
(1888–1957), judge, was born at West
Derby, Liverpool, 5 February 1888, the
son of George Jeremy Lynskey, a prominent solicitor in the city, and his wife,
Honora Mary Kearney. He was educated
at St. Francis Xavier's College and the
university of Liverpool where he graduated

LL.B. (1907), LL.M. (1908), and was later
proud to receive the honorary degree of
LL.D. (1951). Entering his father's firm he
qualified as a solicitor and was awarded
the Rupert Bremner gold medal of the
Law Society in 1910. In 1920 he was called
to the bar by the Inner Temple, joined the
Northern circuit, and quickly acquired one
of the largest practices known at the
junior bar in the present century which
enabled him to take silk in 1930. As
a leader his practice continued to grow so
that between 1930 and the outbreak of
war in 1939 there were but few cases at
the Liverpool and Manchester assizes in
which he was not briefed to appear.

His calm, reasoned, and untheatrical
style of advocacy caused Lynskey to
become respected as a formidable opponent; the extent and quality of his
work soon made him well known also in
London and it became obvious that he was
destined to join the long line of Northern
circuit advocates to receive judicial preferment. His first experience of the bench
came in 1937 when he was appointed to be
the judge of the Salford Hundred Court of
Record, a position which he filled with
distinction and held (in the early years of
the war concurrently with the chairmanship of the North-West Region advisory
committee on aliens) until 1944 when he
was elevated to the King's Bench division
with the customary knighthood.

Meanwhile in 1938 he had been elected
a bencher of the Inner Temple where his
kindly convivial and genial nature won
him many friends as it had done already
among the circuiteers in the north. As
a judge he rapidly and fully justified the
golden opinions which the legal profession
had formed of him at the bar. In 1948 he
enhanced an already great reputation by
his chairmanship of the long judicial
inquiry into allegations concerning activities connected with the Board of Trade.

Lynskey was regarded by his contemporaries as possessing an immensely wide
knowledge of the practice of the law which
he was at all times ready to put at the
disposal of the many who were accustomed
to seek advice which invariably he seemed
able to give with the authority of one who
had encountered and dealt with the precise question involved. His clear and
quick mind and wide experience of the
practice of the law, coupled with a quiet
manner, always courteous and patient,
caused confident expectation of his
judicial advancement, but he declined
promotion to the Court of Appeal when it

was proposed to him by Lord Jowitt [q.v.]. He died 21 December 1957 while presiding as the assize judge at Manchester on the Northern circuit which he loved so well; it was said of him at that time (*Law Times*, 3 January 1958) that 'by many competent to make the assessment he was reckoned the soundest of the puisne judges, with an especial talent for finding a short way to torpedo ingenious but bad points'.

Lynskey was a devout Roman Catholic whose religion and home life formed the basis of his work. In 1913 he married Eileen, daughter of John Edward Prendwille, of Liverpool; they had two daughters.

[Private information; personal knowledge.]
FRED E. PRITCHARD.

MACALISTER, SIR (GEORGE) IAN (1878–1957), secretary of the Royal Institute of British Architects, was born in Liverpool 1 April 1878, the younger son of (Sir) John Young Walker MacAlister, librarian, later secretary of the Royal Society of Medicine, by his wife, Elizabeth Batley. He was a nephew of Sir Donald MacAlister [q.v.], chancellor of Glasgow University. He was educated at St. Paul's School, where he was a foundation scholar, and as an exhibitioner of Merton College, Oxford, where he obtained second classes in honour moderations (1899) and *literae humaniores* (1901). In 1902–4 he was aide-de-camp and secretary to the Earl of Dundonald [q.v.], general officer commanding the Canadian Army. After leaving Canada and before going to the Royal Institute of British Architects in 1908 MacAlister was a freelance journalist particularly interested in the Commonwealth and in naval and military history as well as history and politics in general. In the war of 1914–18 he was a lieutenant in the Royal Defence Corps.

MacAlister's long tenure of office until his retirement in 1943 saw remarkable changes in the Royal Institute of British Architects for which he was in a large measure responsible. Until the early part of the century the Institute was very much a London society; its members in the provinces and overseas had very little influence in its government. MacAlister was determined to alter this; he encouraged and helped to organize the foundation of Allied Societies in the provinces and the Commonwealth; in 1908 there were 18 at home and 1 abroad; in 1939, 73 and 34. He was particularly keen on ensuring closer links with the members in the dominions and the Allied Societies overseas. Similarly he was anxious to secure friendly relations with the American Institute of Architects of which he was elected an honorary member in 1930. Visitors from the Commonwealth and America always received a warm and friendly welcome.

The membership of the Institute increased greatly during MacAlister's secretaryship; at the same time standards of qualification were raised. He worked enthusiastically for architectural education especially in the expansion of the Board of Architectural Education which was responsible for maintaining standards and encouraging the growth of the recognized schools of architecture. Perhaps his greatest triumph was in securing the passing of the Architects Registration Acts of 1931 and 1938. He bore a particularly heavy burden in advising his council on the policy to be followed when it was made clear by the Government that they would not agree to the Institute's being made the registering authority. He had to ensure that standards would not suffer even although the Institute was not in complete control. There were many hard struggles but in the end he was signally successful in achieving the aims and objects which he and the council had so much at heart—the greater unity of the profession and the competence of its members.

In 1934, the centenary year of the Institute, and the year in which he was knighted, MacAlister organized its move from its old home in Conduit Street to its new headquarters in Portland Place.

MacAlister had an attractive personality. He was good-looking with blue eyes, a high colour, an expressive mouth, and a winning smile which added charm to the warmth of his greeting. He was also a persuasive speaker with a scholarly choice of phrase. His letters, and he was a tireless writer of letters and memoranda on a wide variety of subjects, professional and otherwise, were full of shrewd and witty comments. He always preferred to write these and used the services of a stenographer only for routine correspondence. He had a wholly admirable passion for clear concise English and detested sloppiness and the use of commercial jargon.

Shortly after his retirement MacAlister was knocked down by a motor-cyclist dispatch rider in the City and after many months in hospital remained a seminvalid for the rest of his life. He moved from Hampstead to Tonbridge where he enjoyed coaching some of the senior boys at Tonbridge School and when his health allowed was a regular spectator at the school cricket and rugby matches.

MacAlister married in 1909 Frances Dorothy, elder daughter of Robert Cooper Seaton, barrister, and later classical master at St. Paul's School. He had four daughters and three sons of whom the two elder lost their lives while serving with the Royal Air Force in the early part of the war of 1939–45. He died at Tonbridge 10 June 1957. A portrait by Harold Knight is in the possession of the Royal Institute of British Architects.

[*The Times*, 11 June 1957; *Journal* of the Royal Institute of British Architects, July 1957; private information; personal knowledge.]   CYRIL D. SPRAGG.

MACAULAY, DAME (EMILIE) ROSE (1881–1958), author, was born at Rugby 1 August 1881, the second of the seven children of George Campbell Macaulay, then assistant master at Rugby School, by his wife, Grace Mary, daughter of the Rev. William John Conybeare [q.v.]. Among her Macaulay antecedents was the historian, Lord Macaulay [q.v.], a first cousin of her paternal grandfather. For eight years of her childhood her family lived at Varazze near Genoa—a time of great happiness for her—and her early education was mostly from her parents. Then, after the Macaulays returned to England in 1894, she and two of her sisters attended the Oxford High School. In 1900, thanks to the generosity of her uncle and godfather, R. H. Macaulay, she went to Somerville College, where she read history and acquired a lasting affection for the seventeenth century. She was awarded an *aegrotat* in 1903. University life stimulated her independence and she lost the intense shyness from which she had suffered since leaving Italy.

Her earliest published writings were poems entered for competitions in the *Westminster Gazette*, and her first novel, *Abbots Verney*, appeared in 1906. By 1914 she had written six more novels; one of them, *The Lee Shore*, was awarded first prize in a Hodder and Stoughton novel competition in 1912. These early novels showed much promise, but her satire was still embryonic, taking the form of an earnest, sometimes naïve, questioning of the more unreasonable aspects of contemporary society. Her books of poems,

The Two Blind Countries (1914) and *Three Days* (1919), belong to this early period. Many of them reveal a sensitivity to beauty in nature and an apprehension of disquieting unseen influences.

During her early years as a writer Rose Macaulay was living at home with her family, first in Wales and then after 1906 at Great Shelford near Cambridge, where her father had become a university lecturer in English. Increasingly she gravitated towards London and before long acquired a flat of her own there— again thanks to her wealthy godfather— eventually making her permanent home in Marylebone. She entered eagerly into the literary world, which in the years immediately before the war she found both dazzling and entrancing. After 1914 she took part in various kinds of war work, but this did not prevent her from writing more novels; *What Not* (1918) was the first with a newly satirical flavour.

It was in the twenties, the middle period of her fiction, that Rose Macaulay's talent as a novelist flowered. Her gentle irony, effervescent wit, fastidious turn of phrase, and lightness of touch in exposing the absurdities of the day won for her a large, varied, and enthusiastic public. *Potterism* (1920) was the first of her novels in that decade; then followed *Dangerous Ages* (1921), which was awarded the Femina Vie Heureuse prize. Her popularity continued with *Told by an Idiot* (1923), *Orphan Island* (1924), *Crewe Train* (1926), and *Keeping up Appearances* (1928), all written in a vein of detached amusement at the follies of the human race. She was also, at this time, writing many lively articles for the daily press, as well as books of essays with a more learned flavour: *A Casual Commentary* (1925) was followed by *Catchwords and Claptrap* (1926) which reflected the pleasure she derived from the English language and her insistence on verbal precision.

They Were Defeated (1932), her only historical novel, centring upon Robert Herrick, was her own favourite among her books. This novel and her brief, scholarly study *Some Religious Elements in English Literature* (1931) initiated a new stage in her writing, with a decidedly more serious emphasis. Her short biography of Milton and her anthology *The Minor Pleasures of Life* were published in 1934, as well as her novel *Going Abroad*. In 1935 she began writing the weekly column 'Marginal Comments' for the *Spectator* and also published her best volume of essays, *Personal Pleasures*; later came her book of literary criticism *The Writings of E. M. Forster* (1938).

During the war of 1939-45 Rose Macaulay wrote little. For nearly three years she served as a voluntary part-time ambulance driver in London and her life was disrupted by bereavements, illness, and the loss of all her belongings when her flat was bombed. Her next two books, *They Went to Portugal* (1946) and *Fabled Shore* (1949), established her as a writer on travel and travel history, a field she continued to explore in *Pleasure of Ruins* (1953). Throughout her life she delighted in foreign parts, and was especially fond of the Mediterranean countries. She returned to fiction after ten years with *The World my Wilderness* (1950) which showed that new depths of pity had transmuted her satirical approach. A revivified understanding of the human heart was even more evident in her final novel *The Towers of Trebizond* (1956) which was awarded the James Tait Black memorial prize. During her last years she also wrote prolifically for periodicals such as the *Times Literary Supplement*, the *Spectator*, the *New Statesman*, the *Observer*, and the *Listener*.

In 1951 Cambridge University conferred an honorary Litt.D. upon her and in 1958 she was appointed D.B.E. She died suddenly at her home in London 30 October 1958.

Three volumes of her letters were published posthumously. The first two, *Letters to a Friend* (1961, with a bibliography of her major works and a genealogy) and *Last Letters to a Friend* (1962), contain letters written to a distant cousin, the Rev. J. H. C. Johnson, S.S.J.E., during the last eight years of her life, when she returned to the Anglican Church after a long estrangement. *Letters to a Sister* (1964) is a selection of letters to her sister Jean, accompanied by a fragment of *Venice Besieged*, the novel she was working on when she died.

As a writer Rose Macaulay's especial gift was the ability to blend irony and sympathy, to express fluently the thinking which owed as much to an affectionate nature as to a sparkling wit. She possessed a scholar's learning and integrity at the same time as the flair of a journalist: the erudition of her more serious works was matched by the brilliant choice of topical targets in her many novels (she wrote twenty-three in all). Her character

was paradoxical. A gay and spirited conversationalist, she was usually reticent about her inmost feelings and beliefs. She was beloved by an exceptional number and variety of friends: her kindness and interest in human beings were remarkable. Yet she could sometimes be acid, even alarming. Tolerant in the extreme where mere frailty was concerned, she was severely intolerant of anything which seemed to her stupid or vulgar. In physique she was wiry and long-limbed, with an appearance of fragility that belied her remarkable stamina—she delighted in strenuous activities such as swimming. She also joined in an unceasing social round, and habitually overworked herself, continuing to lavish her energy upon literary journalism when she had no financial need. By preference she lived austerely, although she was very comfortably off towards the end of her life. Seemingly ageless, she never lost her eagerness for life, which gave her a special affinity with the young.

[Private information; personal knowledge.]
CONSTANCE BABINGTON SMITH.

McBEY, JAMES (1883-1959), etcher and painter, was born at Newmill, Foveran, near Aberdeen, 23 December 1883, the son of James McBey, farmer, and Annie Gillespie, a blacksmith's daughter. He was educated at the school in the fishing village of Newburgh, leaving at the age of fifteen to become a clerk in the Aberdeen branch of the North of Scotland Bank. His interest in etching was aroused by an article in the *Boy's Own Paper*, and in the Aberdeen Public Library he found a copy of Maxime Lalanne's *Traité de la Gravure à l'Eau-Forte*, translated by S. R. Koehler, and from this learned the rudiments of etching. In 1926 he presented the library with a new copy, having worn out the old one. At the age of seventeen, with no more than the book-learning thus acquired, he began his own experiments with etching, using zinc plates instead of copper because they were cheaper. His first plate of any note, 'Boys Fishing', etched in 1902, already showed a hint of his later masterly handling of line and tone. Two years later he was transferred to the Edinburgh branch of the bank and etched 'The Dean Bridge' and other local subjects. Back in Aberdeen he devoted his leisure for two years to drawing and painting, but etching still remained his principal interest and most natural form of expression.

In 1910 he took the drastic step of giving up the bank. He went to Holland, determined to see through his own eyes the scenes which Rembrandt, the greatest etcher of all time, had depicted with so much mastery. He was no servile imitator of the Dutch master but he certainly learned from him that economy of line which became one of the most striking characteristics of his own work. In that summer he produced twenty-one plates. After a brief period in Aberdeen in 1911 he visited Wales and Spain and had his first exhibition at the Goupil Gallery in London. Malcolm Salaman, the accepted etching critic of the day, immediately saw the value of the young Scotsman's work. So did Martin Hardie [q.v.] who was himself an etcher as well as an official of the Victoria and Albert Museum. The result of their praise was that all available prints were sold, and the publication of McBey's future work was taken up by Gutekunst in London and Davidson in Glasgow. McBey had now enough money to set out once more on his travels. He visited Holland again and then went to Morocco, but in 1911–14 he also produced etchings of Cornish scenes, Sandwich, and London's Thames-side. It was the last which gave him the subjects for two of his most successful early plates, 'The Lion Brewery' and 'The Pool'. Here he was treading in the footsteps of J. A. McN. Whistler [q.v.] whom McBey recognized as his second master after Rembrandt.

In 1916 he went to France and while attached to the Army Printing and Stationery Service in Boulogne and Rouen made some drawings of the battlefields; in the following year he was appointed official artist to the Egyptian Expeditionary Force. He remained in the Near East until 1919. He painted General Allenby, the Emir Feisal, and Lawrence of Arabia and made hundreds of water-colours. Much of his finest work there, including one of his finest plates, 'Dawn. Camel Patrol Setting Out', is now in the Imperial War Museum. After the war he revisited Holland and went to Venice where he strove to emulate Whistler in his later, looser manner, and if his etchings of Venice do not quite reach Whistler's standard of delicacy they are none the less very fine prints.

McBey was fortunate in finding himself at the height of his powers during the 'etching boom' of the twenties. In 1925 Martin Hardie brought out a *catalogue*

raisonné of his etchings and prints and in 1929 Malcolm Salaman, who in 1924 had included him in the Studio series 'Modern Masters of Etching', published a well-illustrated account of his life and work. Some of McBey's plates were sold at very high prices, at that time the highest ever realized by the work of a living etcher. In 1937 he had an exhibition of his oil-paintings at Colnaghi's. Examples of his work are preserved in the British Museum, the Victoria and Albert Museum, the Maritime Museum at Greenwich, the Luxembourg Gallery in Paris, and all the principal print rooms of Great Britain and America. There is a James McBey Room and Art Library in the Aberdeen Art Gallery, where there is a comprehensive collection of his working drawings, water-colours, trial proofs, and etchings (given by an American collector, H. H. Kynett). A similar collection is at the Boston Public Library in Massachusetts (given by Albert Wiggin) and one at the National Gallery in Washington (given by Lessing Rosenwald). McBey received an honorary LL.D. from Aberdeen University in 1934.

In 1931 McBey married Marguerite Huntsberry, daughter of Adolf Loeb, of Philadelphia, and in 1942 he himself became an American citizen. His last years were spent mostly in Tangier and he died there 1 December 1959. He was buried in a large parkland he owned overlooking the Straits of Gibraltar. There is a self-portrait in the Imperial War Museum, a pencil sketch by Martin Hardie in the National Portrait Gallery, and a water-colour by the same artist of McBey sketching in the Aberdeen Art Gallery. Gerald Brockhurst painted him for the Boston Public Library. He also made an etching. There is a fine bronze head by Benno Schotz. This is in the Aberdeen Art Gallery as well as in the Cummer Gallery of Art in Jacksonville, Florida, which houses another large collection of McBey's work.

[*The Times*, 3 December 1959; private information; personal knowledge.]

JAMES LAVER.

McCABE, JOSEPH MARTIN (1867–1955), rationalist, was born at Macclesfield 12 November 1867, the son of William McCabe, draper, and his wife, Harriet Kirk. His education began in a Roman Catholic elementary school in Gorton, Manchester, in which district he was later employed in a local warehouse. Gorton

McCabe

D.N.B. 1951–1960

was the scene of some of the worst features of the industrial revolution and some of his writings, such as *1825–1925: a Century of Stupendous Progress* (1925), reveal the impact of his environment upon his thought. The Franciscan fathers observed his exceptional ability and character and made it possible for him to enter their preparatory college in Manchester. At the end of May 1885 he went to the Franciscan Friary at Killarney as a novice, taking Antony as his name in religion. A year later, at the age of eighteen, he made his simple vows, followed three years afterwards by his solemn profession. In the meantime he had transferred to Forest Gate to study for the priesthood. He was ordained in 1890 and was professor of philosophy and ecclesiastical history at Forest Gate for the next five years, with the exception of a year at Louvain University where he studied philosophy and Semitic languages. In 1895 he was appointed rector of a new foundation, St. Bernadine's College, Buckingham; but from the time of his novitiate he had entertained doubts on the validity of the Christian faith he was professing, and he now found himself unable to continue. In February 1896 he left his order and the Roman Catholic Church and immediately plunged into a lecturing and writing campaign against all his earlier beliefs. *Twelve Years in a Monastery* (1897) was written with the encouragement of (Sir) Leslie Stephen [q.v.], and in the same year he wrote *Modern Rationalism* for a group which by 1899 had formed itself into the Rationalist Press Association, Ltd., with George Jacob Holyoake [q.v.] as chairman. McCabe was one of the original directors and remained actively associated with the Rationalist Press until a year or so before his death, when he resigned because he felt that the Association was not sufficiently militant. He was also closely associated with the National Secular Society and delivered many lectures under its auspices.

During his long life McCabe worked indefatigably for rationalism and free-thought. It is estimated that he wrote over two hundred books and pamphlets, many of which were first published in America. He translated over fifty scientific and free-thought publications, including Ernst Haeckel's *Riddle of the Universe*. His energy seemed inexhaustible and, in addition to his prolific literary output, he went on lecture tours in both hemispheres, taking part in numerous debates with popular contemporary figures. Because of his unorthodox views he made many enemies; in consequence he had to fight hard for a livelihood and the financial necessity of writing popular works meant that his considerable scholarship was at times obscured. But his persistent efforts gained him the attention of the public, mainly on account of his fascinating exposition of the many aspects of the theory of evolution.

McCabe was a regular lecturer at a number of ethical and progressive societies, including for many years the South Place Ethical Society and the South London Ethical Society. It was his wish that he should be known as an agnostic, although, as he stated in his *Biographical Dictionary of Modern Rationalists* (1920), he had no doubt that when man's knowledge was complete materialism would prove to be the correct theory of reality. He believed that the Church of Rome was an enemy of the people, science, and progress, and he denounced it with no uncertain voice. But he was a great humanist and believed profoundly in man and championed many unpopular causes designed to free man from the tyranny of Church, squire, and industrial magnate. In his *Life and Letters of George Jacob Holyoake* (2 vols., 1908), in his short biographies of Holyoake (1922) and Robert Owen (1920), and in his *Century of Stupendous Progress*, he showed his understanding of the social revolution through which Britain had passed. His facility for biography was evident in studies ranging from Augustine to Abelard, Goethe and Edward Clodd [q.v.], the last a devoted colleague and friend. Among other works may be mentioned *The Splendours of Moorish Spain* (1935), *The Golden Ages of History* (1940), and *The Testament of Christian Civilization* (1946), a piece of painstaking scholarship in which, in the role of *advocatus diaboli*, he reproduced, mainly in his own translation, extracts from documents reflecting unfavourably upon the value of Christianity to civilization.

In 1899 McCabe married Beatrice, daughter of William Lee, a foreman of works at Leicester, where McCabe spent a year as secretary to the Leicester Secular Society. They had two sons and two daughters. McCabe died in London 10 January 1955.

[J. M. McCabe, *Twelve Years in a Monastery*, 1897; private information; personal knowledge.]   JOSEPH REEVES.

McCARRISON, SIR ROBERT (1878–1960), medical scientist, was born in Portadown, Ulster, 15 March 1878. He was the second son of Robert McCarrison, of Lisburn, county Antrim, flax-buyer for the Island Spinning Company, and his wife, Agnes McCullagh. After qualifying with first class honours in medicine in 1900 at Queen's College, Belfast, and the Richmond Hospital, Dublin, he entered the Indian Medical Service the following year and sailed for India on his twenty-third birthday. He was a regimental officer in Chitral (1902–4) and later (1904–11) agency surgeon in Gilgit. Chitral is at the extreme north-western boundary of what was then the Indian Empire; and in this remote region (in his words) 'nature makes large-scale experiments upon man'. In the summer of 1903 his garrison was afflicted with an apparently new disease, a 'three-day fever', which after careful investigation he correctly concluded was transmitted by the sandfly (*Phlebotomus*); but before he could prove this he was posted to Gilgit.

At the foot of the Himalayas in Kashmir, Gilgit consisted of nine villages. There, as at Chitral, goitre was endemic, and was accompanied by cretinism, deaf-mutism, and idiocy. But McCarrison noticed that one of the villages was spared, and this had a water supply from a pure spring whereas the other eight used a polluted surface stream. By adding the suspended matter of the impure water to the pure spring water, McCarrison produced goitre in volunteers, including himself, and thus proved the presence of a goitrogenic substance which enhanced deficiency of iodine. In 1913 he was assigned for special study of goitre and cretinism in Kasauli. Although interrupted by the war of 1914–18, his researches spanned thirty years (1905–35) and received wide recognition. Selwyn Taylor, dean of the Postgraduate Medical School of London, wrote of McCarrison's work in 1953: 'I know of no one else alive today who has contributed so much that is new to so many varied aspects of the goitre problem.'

McCarrison's studies of the thyroid gland and its disorders included the effects of deficient food upon that organ, and hence he was led in 1913 to begin a wider investigation into the nature of deficiency diseases. But in October 1914 he went on active service, and these studies were delayed until March 1918, when he returned as lieutenant-colonel to India and was assigned an empty room in the Pasteur Institute at Coonor. There he set to work, his apparatus a microscope and a microtome, his staff a clerk borrowed from the post-office and his wife's cook who was released when a Sikh, Mula Singh, returned from the war. In January 1920 McCarrison was invalided to England and himself paid for Mula Singh to accompany him to the laboratory of (Sir) Charles Scott Sherrington [q.v.] in Oxford and be trained in histological methods. Upon McCarrison's return to India in 1922 he found his apparatus dispersed and his room again empty. He enlisted the support of another Indian assistant to study beri-beri, but the following year the Inchcape committee stopped his work for reasons of economy, and he resigned. His dogged persistence and Irish powers of persuasion stood him in good stead, and in 1925 he resumed his research. Lord Linlithgow [q.v.] was deeply impressed when in 1926, as chairman of the royal commission on agriculture, he insisted on seeing the work at Coonor; a member of his commission, the Rajah of Parlakimedi, upon hearing McCarrison's exposition immediately gave a lakh of rupees to assist his work. In 1929 McCarrison was appointed director of the Nutrition Research Laboratories at Coonor, and held this position until he retired from the I.M.S. as major-general in 1935. During this period, with encouragement from Linlithgow as viceroy, he built up one of the finest institutes for nutritional research in the world.

McCarrison then went to live in Oxford. In 1939–45 he was chairman of the local medical war committee, and deputy regional adviser in medicine to the Emergency Medical Service. From 1945 to 1955 he was the first director of postgraduate medical education at Oxford. On his seventy-fifth birthday, in 1953, he was presented with a *Festschrift*, entitled *The Work of Sir Robert McCarrison*, a volume which arose from the request of certain Indian scientists in particular to be able to have ready access to his important papers. These were reprinted, together with a complete bibliography and introductory assessments of the importance of his work by H. M. Sinclair, by W. R. Aykroyd (who succeeded him as director at Coonor), and by the great American biochemist E. V. McCollum. What gave him and his friends especial pleasure was a warm tribute sent by the Indian minister of health, Rajkumari

Amrit Kaur, who described the great debt owed to McCarrison by India and the whole world.

This debt was appreciated by world-wide recognition. As early as 1911 McCarrison had been awarded the first class Kaisar-i-Hind gold medal for public service in India, and in 1914 the Prix Amussat of the Academy of Medicine of Paris for his original researches on goitre and cretinism. He was appointed C.I.E. in 1923, honorary physician to the King (1928–35), and was knighted in 1933. When on leave in 1921 he made a lecture tour in the United States, giving the Mellon lecture at Pittsburgh, the Mary Scott Newbold lecture at Philadelphia, the Hanna lecture at Cleveland, the Mayo Foundation lecture at Rochester, and the De Lamar lecture at Johns Hopkins University, Baltimore. In Britain his lectures included the Milroy lectures before the Royal College of Physicians (1913), the Cantor lectures of the Royal Society of Arts (1936), the Lloyd-Roberts lecture at the Medical Society of London (1936), and the Sanderson-Wells lecture at the Middlesex Hospital medical school (1939). He received the honorary LL.D. of Belfast in 1919, was elected F.R.C.P. in 1914, and was awarded various academic prizes and medals. A McCarrison Society has been founded in London.

The great importance of McCarrison's work, not properly appreciated at the time (he was never elected to the Royal Society), lay in his combination of laboratory experimentation with observations in the field. The classical paper on vitamins of (Sir) F. G. Hopkins [q.v.] was published in 1912, and the following year McCarrison began his field work on vitamin deficiencies. While others were studying pure deficiencies of single nutrients in lower animals, McCarrison observed the different diseases of peoples subsisting on different diets, and reproduced these in lower animals by those diets: 'My own method, on the other hand, has been to observe the more general symptomatic and pathological effects of faulty food on the animal body as a whole, and thereby to ascertain what forms of human illness might reasonably be attributed to it.' Despite the great difficulties in his way (his advice to his successor was: 'Remember, things move slowly in the East'), he was a pioneer in a branch of medical science that has been shown to be abundantly fruitful.

McCarrison married in 1906 Helen Stella (died 1968), third daughter of Joh Leech Johnston, of the Indian Civil Se vice. A girl, the only child, was stillborn i Gilgit in 1910. McCarrison died in Oxfor 18 May 1960. A bust by Lady Kennet is i the possession of the family.

[*The Work of Sir Robert McCarrison*, ec H. M. Sinclair, 1953; personal knowledge.]

H. M. SINCLAIR

MacCARTHY, SIR (CHARLES OTTO DESMOND (1877–1952), literary an dramatic critic, the only son of Charle Desmond MacCarthy and his wife, Louis Joanne Wilhelmine von Chevallerie, wa born 20 May 1877 at Plymouth where hi father was sub-agent to the Bank o England. He was educated at Eton an Trinity College, Cambridge, where h graduated (*aegrotat*) in history in 1897 Desmond MacCarthy's mind develope early and he probably changed very littl in himself after his Cambridge days, fo his ability then to choose lifelong friend was as mature as his youthful criticisn proved to be years later: some of th early and intimate associations he mad at that time (he was an 'Apostle') wer with G. E. Moore [q.v.], G. M. Trevelyan and the children of (Sir) Leslie Stephe [q.v.] and their circle. His talent fo criticism, and above all for conversation led his friends to expect from him ar important creative work of his own: but this never materialized and he became what he himself described as a literary journalist. He began as a freelance and by 1903 he was writing reviews and dramatic criticism for the *Speaker*: he covered for that journal the Vedrenne–Barker seasons at the Royal Court Theatre where he saw many of the plays of G. B. Shaw [q.v.] for the first time, and his criticisms of these productions were included in his first publication *The Court Theatre 1904–1907* (1907). When the Shavian notices were republished in *Shaw* (1951), together with his criticisms of later productions of the same plays, although he had some new points to make, MacCarthy had no judgements to withdraw.

From 1907 to 1910 MacCarthy edited the *New Quarterly* and he wrote regularly for the *Eye-Witness* when it was started in 1911 and after it became the *New Witness* the following year. In 1913 he joined the staff of the newly formed *New Statesman*, as dramatic critic, under the editorship of Clifford Sharp, and he was later (1920–27) literary editor, reviewing regularly until 1929 over the pen-name 'Affable Hawk'. This was an apt self-description; he had a beak-like nose and friendly eyes: while he never allowed personal considerations to influence his judgements he did not enjoy inflicting pain, preferring to ignore a bad book unless he felt that an attack was demanded. (His review of a Tennyson anthology in the *Sunday Times* in 1946 is a good example of his bird-of-prey descent upon something which had earned his disapproval.) Soon after the outbreak of war in 1914 he joined the Red Cross and he served until 1915 with a section attached to the French Army: some of his impressions were later published in *Experience* (1935).

His full-time association with the *New Statesman* lasted until he succeeded Sir Edmund Gosse [q.v.] in 1928 as senior literary critic on the *Sunday Times* in which he continued to write weekly articles until he died. During this last period he also wrote occasional dramatic criticism for the *New Statesman*; and *Life and Letters* was founded in 1928 primarily to give MacCarthy a platform of his own. He was editor for five years but the experiment was not entirely successful: editing and the meticulous organization and time-keeping which it involved were not his forte. The *Sunday Times* gave him a larger public and the financial security and position which, as a man of the world, he greatly enjoyed. He was that rare type of critic who was read and appreciated alike by the ordinary reading public and by more intellectual and academic readers. Mac-Carthy believed that literary appreciation and judgement must always be based on wide reading and the widest possible general knowledge of the conditions in which books were written. This was his fast rule and if necessary he would visit the London Library to fill in any gap he felt he had in relation to a particular book. His article may sometimes not have been completed until the eleventh hour, but it was never written without full preparation and knowledge of the subject. There was always in his work the precise thought and element of philosophic interest which he had learned at Cambridge. When he gave the Leslie Stephen lecture there in 1937 he chose Stephen as his subject. Just as he measured new writing with the old and established, so he tended to measure his own work alongside Leslie Stephen's, and on one occasion he insisted on a collection of his own writings being

disbanded because it 'fell so far below the standard of *Hours in a Library*'. Desmond MacCarthy believed that 'criticism must be in great part a Natural History of Authors' and like Leslie Stephen he upheld that when it comes to judgement the test to be applied is the relation of a work to life, the extent to which it ministers, in one way or another, to all human good. He was 'most at home', Lord David Cecil wrote in his preface to *Humanities* (1953), 'with the writers who do not go in for spell-binding; with Tolstoy and Trollope, Ibsen and Chekhov. These last two particularly; for, when Desmond MacCarthy wrote about them, they were still relatively uncharted ground for the critic to work on, and he therefore got a chance to display his greatest gift, which was the capacity to understand and expound some new, fresh vision of reality.'

But it was MacCarthy's readableness which made him a popular success, and his easy colloquial style came into its own on the air. After the theatre, this was the work he enjoyed most: as one of the best conversationalists of his time, broadcasting was an art he excelled in and with which he felt completely at ease. His pleasure in a book he had enjoyed was infectious and it was increased in the following days if he heard that people had bought the book as a result of his review. 'I wanted to give that author a present', he would say.

As a young man he delighted in coming to know writers and famous people and his portraits of Samuel Butler, Meredith, Henry James, Shaw, Conrad, Ruskin, and Asquith are among his best pieces. He was always, he once said, a hero-worshipper in temperament, although not on paper, where a more detached being took the pen. Latterly his habit was to move less in purely literary circles. He had never in any case belonged to a 'set', even to the Bloomsbury group although its members were all his friends and he saw them frequently. But this detachment from professional writers did not prevent him from enjoying their company from time to time and helping them by drawing attention to their work and giving them encouragement. He also assisted young critics to master their craft, and Raymond Mortimer and Cyril Connolly have both acknowledged their indebtedness in prefaces to his first posthumous book of essays (*Memories*, 1953).

Although Desmond MacCarthy produced

no major work, seven volumes of his collected writings were published during his lifetime and of these probably *Portraits* (1931) and *Shaw* (1951) will best stand the test of time. During the two years following his death three more new volumes were published in England, and in America where he was hitherto virtually unknown, and his reputation grew rather than diminished. An honorary LL.D. of Aberdeen University (1932) and in 1945 elected president of P.E.N. in England, he was knighted in 1951. He died in Cambridge 7 June 1952, two days after the university had conferred on him the honorary degree of doctor of letters.

He married in 1906 Mary (died 1953), daughter of F. W. Warre-Cornish [q.v.], the vice-provost of Eton. There were two sons of the marriage and a daughter who married Lord David Cecil. Lady MacCarthy was herself a writer of ability —*A Nineteenth-Century Childhood* (1924) and her novel *A Pier and a Band* (1918) appeared in new editions many years after their first publication. MacCarthy was proud of his wife's talent and during a luncheon party at Garrick's Villa, Hampton, where they latterly lived, he turned to her with his infectious chuckle and said: 'Yes, Molly, you must go on writing! I have always wanted to be *Mister* Henry Wood!' A portrait of MacCarthy by Henry Lamb is in the National Museum of Wales; drawings by Duncan Grant and Robin Guthrie are in the National Portrait Gallery.

[*The Times*, 9 and 20 June 1952; private information; personal knowledge.]

JAMES MACGIBBON.

McCARTHY, LILLAH (1875–1960), actress, was born in Cheltenham 22 September 1875, the third daughter and seventh of the eight children of Jonadab McCarthy, furniture broker, and his wife, Emma Price. When she was eight her father, a handsome imaginative Irishman, whose interests ranged between furniture and astronomy (he was a fellow of the Royal Astronomical Society), decided to teach her himself. She studied with him at home until, on the advice of the young actor-manager (Sir) Frank Benson [q.v.] whose company had already begun to achieve its status as a 'touring university of the theatre', Jonadab McCarthy moved to London so that his daughter might be trained in elocution with Hermann Vezin [q.v.] and voice production with Emil Behnke. As an amateur she appeared

during May 1895 as Lady Macbeth in a Shakespeare Society production at St. George's Hall, the occasion on which she first used the stage name of Lillah, her real names being Lila Emma. G. B. Shaw [q.v.], who went to the play for the *Saturday Review* of which he had not long been dramatic critic, wrote of her: 'She is as handsome as Miss [Julia] Neilson; and she can hold an audience whilst she is doing everything wrongly . . . I venture on the responsibility of saying that her Lady Macbeth was a highly promising performance, and that some years of hard work would make her a valuable recruit to the London stage.'

She began at once the years of hard work by appearing in Shakespeare with the touring manager (Sir) P. Ben Greet [q.v.], and in playing Berenice in the London production of *The Sign of the Cross* (Lyric, 1896) for Wilson Barrett [q.v.], the melodramatic actor with whom she spent eight years, off and on, touring England, Australasia, and South Africa. Her parts included Mercia in *The Sign of the Cross*, Virginia in *Virginius*, Desdemona in *Othello*, and Ophelia in *Hamlet*. Barrett had intended to set her up in her own company, but died before he could do so. After working with (Sir) Herbert Beerbohm Tree [q.v.] in the theatrically sumptuous surroundings of His Majesty's (among her parts was Calpurnia in *Julius Caesar*), she called upon Shaw to tell him that the years of apprenticeship were up. In consequence she was cast presently as Nora in a revival of *John Bull's Other Island* (May 1905) and Ann Whitefield in the original production of *Man and Superman* (May 1905), each play produced at the Court Theatre by Harley Granville-Barker [q.v.] whom she had met while touring with Greet. She played through the Court season of 1906, succeeding Tita Brand as Gloria in *You Never Can Tell* and creating Jennifer Dubedat (whose Celtic quality she could suggest with ease) in *The Doctor's Dilemma*. By now this tall, statuesque young woman with the dark velvet voice was bringing to every part a sure theatrical instinct: her fault was a certain heaviness. In a preface to her autobiography Shaw wrote: 'Lillah McCarthy's secret was that she combined the executive art of the grand school with a natural impulse to murder the Victorian womanly woman; and this being just what I needed I blessed the day when I found her.'

In 1906 she married Granville-Barker.

she went on to use her tragic gift in the title-part of John Masefield's Gloucestershire *Nan* (Royalty, 1908). Later, in marked contrast, she created the drawling Lady Sybil in Barrie's *What Every Woman Knows* (Duke of York's, 1908); and she appeared at the same theatre during the repertory season of 1909 as Madge Thomas in Galsworthy's *Strife*. Lillah McCarthy needed sustained tragic intensity: hence her success (Court, 1911) as Anne Pedersdotter in *The Witch*, adapted by John Masefield from the Norwegian of H. Wiers-Jenssen. During her personal management of the Little Theatre in the Adelphi during 1911, she played, among other parts, Hilde in Ibsen's *The Master Builder*, and Margaret Knox in Shaw's *Fanny's First Play*, described as 'a strong, springy girl of eighteen, with large nostrils, an audacious chin, and a gaily resolute manner'. Greek tragedy, which became one of her passions, occupied her at the beginning of 1912: Jocasta in *Oedipus Rex*, presented by (Sir) John Martin-Harvey [q.v.] at Covent Garden in January, and Iphigenia in *Iphigenia in Tauris* at the Kingsway in March. It was almost immediately after this that she entered, with her husband, upon the management of the Savoy Theatre, and later of the St. James's, in a sequence of provocative and historic productions.

At the Savoy in the autumn and winter of 1912 she was Hermione in *The Winter's Tale* and Viola in *Twelfth Night*, revivals from which all stock Shakespearian business was eradicated. During 1913 her major part at the St. James's was Lavinia in Shaw's *Androcles and the Lion*; she returned to the Savoy in February 1914 as Helena in her husband's third Shakespeare production, *A Midsummer Night's Dream*. She was a beautiful and moving actress, but not an intellectual match for Barker, although she did much for him by finding backers. During 1915 she went with him to America, acting a few parts. Then in 1916—when she used her lesser gift of comedy as Maude in Somerset Maugham's *Caroline* (New)— she heard from Barker that he did not wish to return to her. It was a grave blow; but for a time, with the counsel and encouragement of Shaw, she went on working after the divorce in 1918. In April 1919, during a brief management of the Kingsway Theatre, she played Judith in Arnold Bennett's Apocrypha-based drama of that name, a second-rate work which she could not lift.

Lillah McCarthy did little more in the theatre after two showy parts with Matheson Lang [q.v.] at the New: Joanne in Temple Thurston's *The Wandering Jew* (1920) and Doña Sol in Tom Cushing's *Blood and Sand* (1921). Later, after her second—and intensely happy—marriage to (Sir) Frederick Keeble [q.v.] in 1920 she settled down near Oxford. During the thirties she undertook a number of recitals in various parts of the country (scenes, for example, from *Twelfth Night* and *Iphigenia in Tauris*) and her voice was the first to be heard on the stage of the second Shakespeare Memorial Theatre at Stratford on Avon on its opening afternoon, 23 April 1932: she spoke John Masefield's prologue, with its line, 'The acted passion beautiful and swift'. Her husband died in 1952 and she was living in London when she died 15 April 1960. She had no children.

Her autobiography, *Myself and My Friends* (in which Granville-Barker forbade any mention of his name), published in 1933, is the record of a warm-hearted woman and a potentially fine actress. Owing to the breaking of her first marriage, she never did what had been expected of her, although she won the loyalty of such diverse figures as Masefield and Shaw.

Two portraits of Lillah McCarthy by Charles Shannon are in the Cheltenham Art Gallery. These represent her as Doña Ana in the dream scene (sometimes detached as *Don Juan in Hell*) of Shaw's *Man and Superman*, and as the Dumb Wife in Anatole France's *The Man Who Married a Dumb Wife* which she acted in the Ashley Dukes [q.v.] version. Charles Ricketts added the butterfly on the veil of the high head-dress.

[*The Times*, 16 April 1960; Lillah McCarthy, *Myself and My Friends*, 1933; Desmond MacCarthy, *The Court Theatre 1904-1907*, 1907; C. B. Purdom, *Harley Granville Barker*, 1955; G. B. Shaw, *Our Theatres in the Nineties*, vol. i, 1932; personal knowledge.]

J. C. TREWIN.

MACDONALD, SIR MURDOCH (1866–1957), engineer, was born 6 May 1866 in Inverness, the seventh of the nine children of Roderick MacDonald, of Faillie, Strathnairn, carter, and his wife, Margaret Mackay, of Croy. He was educated at Dr. Bell's Institution, later known as Farraline Park School, Inverness. On leaving school he served as an articled clerk in the Highland Railway and then was apprenticed to the chief engineer. In 1891-4 he was resident engineer on the

Black Isle Railway in charge of its location and construction, and also designed and supervised various works in the district. Following this he worked in the engineering office, engaged on design and superintendence of extensions of the railway.

In 1898 he resigned from the Highland Railway, and almost immediately was appointed by Sir Benjamin Baker [q.v.], consulting engineer to the Egyptian Government, to a post of assistant engineer on the Aswan Dam construction. After the dam's completion he was retained in the Egyptian service as resident engineer for the regulation, and for the construction of protecting aprons down-stream, of the dam. Following this he supervised the heightening of the Aswan Dam and the building of the Esna Barrage. While this work was in progress there was a disaster at the Delta Barrage, where the regulator at the head of one of the three main canals of Lower Egypt collapsed in a few hours. MacDonald designed and built the new structure, all in a few months. For this work he was appointed C.M.G. (1910), and in 1912 he became under-secretary, and later adviser, to the Egyptian Ministry of Public Works. He then became responsible for developments in irrigation in Egypt and in particular for the work of drainage and reclamation of waste land in the north of the Delta. At the same time schemes were being prepared for the extension of cultivation, in the Sudan by means of the Sennar Dam on the Blue Nile, and in Egypt by the Gebel Aulia Dam on the White Nile. The war of 1914–18 held up progress on these schemes, and MacDonald, who had been advanced to K.C.M.G. in 1914, served as a colonel in the Royal Engineers to advise the commander-in-chief, Middle East, on various engineering matters connected with the defence of the Suez Canal and the water supply for the advance across the Sinai Desert. He was three times mentioned in dispatches and appointed C.B. in 1917.

About this time he was maliciously attacked on his Nile projects, with charges of incompetence and falsification of information. The charges were investigated by two commissions of eminent engineers and scientists, and finally by a prosecution in the British Supreme Court in Egypt. The result of each of these three inquiries was that the charges were proved to be entirely without foundation. In 1920 MacDonald published *Nile Control* (2 vols.) describin the projects, and in 1921 he retired fro the Egyptian Government service. A fe years later the Sennar and Gebel Auli Dams were built and have fully justifie themselves by their results. During h service he received six decorations, th highest being the Grand Cordon of th Nile; and on his retirement he was grante a substantial pension in recognition of h great services to Egypt.

In 1921 he founded the London firm MacDonald and MacCorquodale, consul ing engineers, afterwards Sir Murdoc MacDonald & Partners, of which h elder son became the senior partner afte his death. While MacDonald was workin the firm carried out the second heightenin of the Aswan Dam, designed a third dam and investigated five other proposa relating to Nile dams or barrages, which however, were later superseded by th High Aswan Dam scheme. The firm wa also employed on irrigation, drainage hydro-electric power, and harbour project in England, Scotland, Spain, Portugal Greece, Jordan, Iraq, and Pakistan.

MacDonald was elected member o Parliament for Inverness in 1922 as Liberal supporting Lloyd George. H retained his seat as a National Libera until 1950 when he did not seek re election. His political opinions wer always Liberal, but he never agreed wit extreme views. In all his elections he wa returned on his personality as a distin guished Highlander, and throughout hi political career his main interest was th welfare of the Highlands. His constituenc stretched right across Scotland and in cluded some of the isles, but even when h was the eldest member of the House h continued to make the long journeys in volved in touring his district, by which h had become personally known to practi cally all his constituents to whose needs h attended assiduously.

He was instrumental in getting the secretary of state for Scotland to issue an order protecting the Loch Ness monster. which someone had arranged to shoot, and which MacDonald claimed that he had once seen. He was very quick-witted and a good speaker. One of his professional characteristics was the ability to make rapid approximate calculations to test results found by more elaborate processes. He was slightly above the average height with a well-developed head and impressive manner. He played football and billiards well and was a good shot. In 1898 he was ice-president of the North of Scotland ootball Association.

He was president of the Institution of ivil Engineers (1932, and twice received he Telford gold medal); of the Junior istitution of Engineers (1927–8); and of he Smeatonian Society (1952). He was member of the Society of Engineers ɡold medallist); of the Royal Institution; ɛ the Royal Astronomical Society; and f the panel of consulting engineers to the Iorth of Scotland Hydro-Electric Board.

In 1899 MacDonald married Margaret lied 1956), daughter of Alexander Munro, ostmaster of Lochalsh, Wester Ross; hey had two sons. MacDonald died at Jairn 24 April 1957.

His portrait in oils by (Sir) James Gunn s in the Institution of Civil Engineers, nd a head in bronze by Mrs. Gladys Barron is in the Town Hall, Inverness. Ie was made a freeman of the royal burgh f Inverness in 1930, and was presented vith the official badge of the Inverness own council in 1956.

[*The Times*, 25 April 1957; Institution of ʼivil Engineers, *Proceedings*, September 1957; *:ngineer*, 3 May 1957; *Inverness Courier*, 6 April 1957; private information; personal nowledge.]   H. E. HURST.

IacFARLANE, SIR (FRANK) NOEL IASON- (1889–1953), lieutenant-general. See MASON-MACFARLANE.]

IcGRIGOR, SIR RHODERICK ?OBERT (1893–1959), admiral of the leet, was born in York 12 April 1893, the nly son of Major (later Brigadier-Ŧeneral) Charles Rhoderick Robert IcGrigor, of the King's Royal Rifles, and iis wife, Ada Rosamond, daughter of ?obert Hartley Bower, of Welham, Yorkshire. He was a great-grandson of 3ir James McGrigor [q.v.], chief of the nedical staff of Wellington's army in the ?eninsular War. Although he had no iaval connections, McGrigor from a very :arly age had set his heart on joining the iavy. He spent his childhood in South Africa and did not go to a preparatory ;chool in England until he was eleven. He missed two terms at Osborne and Dartmouth through illness but neverthe-less passed out top of his term.

In the war of 1914–18 he served in lestroyers in the Dardanelles campaign, ind in the *Malaya* in the Grand Fleet at the battle of Jutland. After the war he specialized in torpedoes. In addition to service on the East Indies station and in

the Admiralty he commanded destroyers in the Nyon patrol during the Spanish civil war.

The outbreak of war in 1939 found him as chief of staff to Sir Percy Noble [q.v.] on the China station, and there he remained until after the fall of France. Returning to England at the end of 1940 he became commanding officer of the *Renown*, where he served under Sir James Somerville [q.v.] in the *Bismarck* action and also at the bombardment of Genoa. His special selection for early promotion to rear-admiral reduced his time in command to only eight months. This was a disappointment since he was essentially a seaman and a wartime fighting leader who loved nothing better than being on his own bridge at sea. He joined the Board of Admiralty towards the end of 1941 as assistant chief of naval staff (weapons), a post in which he was able to make full use of his interest in, and unusual grasp of, technical matters, in dealing not only with the traditional weapons of the navy but also with the many new devices, including radar, which were being designed to meet the novel conditions of the war.

After eighteen months of desk life McGrigor was appointed a Force com-mander, first for the capture of Pantel-leria and shortly after for the assault of Sicily, where he was appointed to the D.S.O. In these conditions he was in his element, training crews of the many and varied kinds of landing craft to be used for the first time. He remained in Sicily for a few months as the flag officer in charge, and then moved to Taranto where he was the naval commander in Southern Italy, and chief naval liaison officer with the Italian Navy.

In March 1944 he returned home and took command of the first cruiser squadron in the Home Fleet based on Scapa Flow. There for the last fifteen months of the war in Europe he carried out many successful attacks against the enemy off the coast of Norway, and took a number of convoys to and from North Russia.

Shortly after V.J.-Day he became vice-chief of the naval staff. In this appointment, he had the depressing task under the first sea lord of putting the navy's fighting machine into reverse, transforming it into a much smaller peacetime force, and of closing down as rapidly as possible bases and establish-ments built up during the war, many of which had only just been completed.

In 1948, the year in which he was

promoted admiral, he became commander-in-chief of the Home Fleet, when, through a temporary shortage of personnel, most of his fleet was immobilized for his first six months. Nevertheless he did a great deal to maintain the standard of training and keep alive the traditions of the Service at a difficult time, and had the satisfaction of turning over to his successor an efficient and highly trained force.

In 1950 he was appointed commander-in-chief, Plymouth, where he served for eighteen months before he became first sea lord in December 1951 and achieved a lifelong ambition of reaching the highest office in his profession. This was at a time when the whole future of the Royal Navy was at stake and particularly that of the aircraft carriers. McGrigor fought hard for their retention and, though he was not to know it when he left in 1955, his work had done much to help the navy through one of its most critical peacetime periods.

He was appointed C.B. (1944), K.C.B. (1945), and G.C.B. (1951), first and principal aide-de-camp to the Queen in 1952, and in 1953 was promoted admiral of the fleet.

McGrigor was not a born chairman and was by temperament better at stating his case on paper than verbally. A man of boundless energy, he never moved slowly and because he did not tire easily he was never happy unless doing something. He always put everything he had into the job in hand. Modest almost to the point of shyness, McGrigor was essentially a kindly and homely man, affectionately known throughout the Royal Navy as 'The Wee-Mac'—an allusion to his stature.

He spent his last few years in his beloved Scotland, having been elected rector of Aberdeen University in 1954. He died quite suddenly after an operation in Aberdeen 3 December 1959. He married in 1931 Gwendoline, daughter of the late Colonel Geoffrey Glyn and widow of Major Charles Greville, Grenadier Guards. She survived him only a short time. They adopted twin boys both of whom joined the armed forces.

[Personal knowledge.]   G. B. TEALE.

McINDOE, SIR ARCHIBALD HECTOR (1900–1960), plastic surgeon, was born in Dunedin, New Zealand, 4 May 1900, the second of the four children of John McIndoe, printer, and his wife, Mabel Hill. He received his early education at Otago High School and University, qualifying M.B., Ch.B. in 1924 and winning the junior medicine and senior clinical surgery prizes. With the first New Zealand fellowship of the Mayo Foundation he left for the United States to continue his post graduate training. At the Mayo Clinic he had a brilliant career and was considered one of the most promising of the younger group. Lord Moynihan [q.v.] was so impressed with his surgical skill as to suggest a permanent career for him in England. With an M.S. (Rochester) added to his list of degrees, McIndoe arrived in London in the winter of 1930 to find to his consternation that there was no appointment and no remuneration available to him.

Fortunately his cousin, Sir Harold Gillies [q.v.], the plastic surgeon, came to his rescue. McIndoe had unusual skill as an abdominal surgeon and was already an authority on the surgery of the liver and biliary passages. He lost no time in the ensuing years in adapting himself to the meticulous plastic surgery practised by his cousin. He passed his F.R.C.S. (England) in 1932 and soon afterwards was appointed to the Hospital for Tropical Diseases as a general surgeon. In 1934 he obtained the fellowship of the American College of Surgeons.

By the outbreak of war in 1939 McIndoe was a plastic surgeon of great promise and had added to the literature of plastic surgery with a number of papers on general aspects of the work. In order to shed some of his responsibility, Gillies arranged for McIndoe to become the consultant in plastic surgery to the Royal Air Force. He also sent him down to East Grinstead to make arrangement for a centre which would serve the south-east of London and receive facial injuries and burns from air-raid casualties. McIndoe was a strong and determined man who had the knack of getting what he wanted, even if it meant treading on other people's toes. His advice to a colleague on receiving his fellowship was: 'Well, now you can put on your heaviest pair of boots and tread on anybody who gets in your way.' McIndoe did just that, and achieved the impossible. At the tiny Queen Victoria Hospital he built up a centre which rapidly became a model to the country and which by careful publicity on behalf of the Royal Air Force became widely known. He treated several hundred severely burned airmen, fought to get them better pay and conditions until they were rehabilitated, saw to their rehabilitation himself, and even lent them money to set them up in civilian life. He did this by never sparing himself or those around him and by very wisely refusing to be put into uniform, thus being able to talk directly to those at the top. It was a particularly able and enlightened air staff with which he had to deal and he met with few of the tribulations and vexations which other pioneers in organization, such as Florence Nightingale, had to suffer in their time. As a result of the combined efforts of McIndoe, the Air Council, and others, every airman going into action knew that behind him there was a first-class medical service to take care of him, however severely injured he might be. Those who did become patients at East Grinstead were so skilfully handled psychologically that they were not self-conscious about their mutilations; they founded their own club, 'McIndoe's Guinea Pigs', which continued to meet annually after the war to follow up the health and welfare of its members.

'Archie' McIndoe's success during the war can be attributed to the fact that for once the right man was in the right place. There were only three other experienced plastic surgeons available in 1939 and his personality and independent outlook, together with his American training, put him into a unique position. He was a first-class surgeon, a striking administrator, and a powerful personality; so powerful that there was no share of the limelight even for his immediate colleagues. But it was his personality which pulled the airmen through.

McIndoe was appointed C.B.E. in 1944, knighted in 1947, and received numerous foreign decorations. His last years were spent largely in the service of the Royal College of Surgeons on the council of which he served from 1948. As chairman of the finance committee he is reported to have raised over $2\frac{1}{2}$ million pounds for the College, of which he was vice-chairman in 1957–9. In the post-war years he also increased the facilities at East Grinstead and appointed a number of consultant staff who helped with the training of plastic surgeons from all over the world. He helped to found the British Association of Plastic Surgeons and was its third president (1949). He managed somehow to run an extremely busy and remunerative private practice and still find time to travel abroad and write articles on his own subject. He will not be remembered particularly for his writings or for original thinking in his speciality, although

he made contributions to the treatment of burns and on surgical technique which were accepted as authoritative. In 1953 he took part in the formation of the first Hand Club of Great Britain. Further recognition of his work came from abroad with a number of honorary doctorates and fellowships. He was very widely liked and admired in the United States where he was a frequent visitor, and he was given a second, honorary, fellowship of the American College in 1941.

In 1924 McIndoe married Adonia, daughter of Thomas Aitken, by whom he had two daughters. The marriage was dissolved after the war and in 1954 he married Mrs. Constance Belchem, daughter of John Hutton, a member of Lloyd's. McIndoe died in London 12 April 1960 and his ashes were buried in the Royal Air Force church of St. Clement Danes in the Strand, an honour unique to a civilian doctor from his combatant colleagues.

The Queen Victoria Hospital, East Grinstead, has a portrait by M. Easton and the Royal College of Surgeons one by Edward I. Halliday. In the possession of his elder daughter is one by Cathleen Mann; and his second wife has one painted by his mother who was a talented artist. The Imperial War Museum has a painting of him operating, by Anna Zinkeisen.

[Leonard Mosley, *Faces from the Fire*, 1962; Hugh McLeave, *McIndoe: Plastic Surgeon*, 1961; private information; personal knowledge.]   RICHARD BATTLE.

McKENZIE, ALEXANDER (1869–1951), professor of chemistry, was born at Dundee 6 December 1869, the eldest son of Peter Mitchell McKenzie, a Scottish dominie of the old type, and his wife, Isobel Buchanan, of farming stock, who came from Lochgoil. He received his early education in his father's schools at Dundee then at Tealing, where he was well grounded in the classics. In 1882 he entered the High School of Dundee and drove the four miles to school daily with a local farmer's son in a pony cart. In 1885 he was awarded the Edinburgh Angus Club medal in Latin. At the early age of fifteen he entered United College, St. Andrews, graduating M.A. four years later. He went on to take his B.Sc., specializing in chemistry and natural philosophy, in 1891. His interest in chemistry had already been stimulated at the High School by Frank Young and also, as he himself said, from an inherited interest from forebears alleged to have had an illicit still in Glen Shee. In 1891–3 he was chemistry lecture assistant to Thomas Purdie, thereby gaining much knowledge of the art of lecturing and of carrying out lecture bench demonstrations, the latter to become a great feature in his own later first-year courses. In 1893–8 he was a university assistant; and to further his chemical research work he next went to Berlin, where under the supervision of Marckwald he graduated Ph.D. *cum laude* in 1901. While in Berlin he attended lectures by such eminent scientists as Landolt, Emil Fischer, Van't Hoff, Gabriel, and Jacobson, visited art galleries and operas, and became a fluent speaker and writer of German.

With a research studentship (1901–2) of the Grocers' Company, McKenzie worked under (Sir) Arthur Harden [q.v.] at the Jenner (later Lister) Institute. In 1902 he became assistant lecturer in chemistry in the university of Birmingham and began his thirty-six years of academic teaching and research. In 1905 he returned to London as head of the chemistry department in Birkbeck College, where teaching duties were very heavy and he could mostly do his research work only by using what would normally have been his leisure hours. His final move was in 1914 to the chair of chemistry at Dundee. With smaller classes and no evening teaching and after completion of his wartime work of national importance he built up a vigorous organic research school.

His main topics of research lay in the stereochemical field and were mainly on the Walden Inversion, racemization, catalytic racemization, asymmetric synthesis, intramolecular rearrangements, and Grignard reactions. In all he published alone and with his co-workers 122 papers, most of which appeared in the *Journal* of the Chemical Society and the *Berichte* of the German Chemical Society.

During his professorship many honours came his way: he was elected F.R.S. in 1916 and was a fellow of the Chemical Society and of the Institute of Chemistry; member of the Deutsche Chemische Gesellschaft; a secretary of the chemistry section of the British Association (1908) and for several years a member of the council and of the publication committee of the Chemical Society. In 1932 he was elected to the Kaiserlich Deutsche Akademie der Naturforscher zu Halle, and in 1939 was given an honorary LL.D. by St. Andrews. He lectured in Berlin in 1931 at the invitation of the Kaiser Wilhelm-

Gesellschaft and later in the same year at the invitation of the university of Basle delivered a course of six lectures, all given by him in German. The young country lad o' pairts had developed into a man of wide interests, highly regarded by his colleagues, friends, and students as a man of great honesty in thought and action.

In the Grey City by the Sea, McKenzie learned to play the 'royal and ancient' game of golf. At one time a scratch player, he continued to play an excellent game until stopped by ill health. Although holding a life appointment, after developing asthma he retired from his chair in 1938 in the interests of his department. Until his death, 11 June 1951, at Barnhill, Angus, he continued to take an active interest in chemistry, reading the monthly journals and making notes for the use of his former colleagues and research students.

In 1906 McKenzie married Alice Helene Sand, a sister of Dr. Henry Sand, well known for his work and writings on electro-chemistry. They had one son who became an electrical engineer.

[J. Read in *Obituary Notices of Fellows of the Royal Society*, No. 21, November 1952; personal knowledge.]   ISOBEL A. SMITH.

MACLAGAN, SIR ERIC ROBERT DALRYMPLE (1879–1951), director of the Victoria and Albert Museum, was born in London 4 December 1879, the only son of William Dalrymple Maclagan [q.v.], bishop of Lichfield, later archbishop of York, by his second wife, Augusta Anne, daughter of the sixth Viscount Barrington. Educated at Winchester and Christ Church, Oxford, where he obtained a third class in honour moderations (1900) and a fourth in *literae humaniores* (1902), he joined the staff of the Victoria and Albert Museum in 1905 as assistant in the department of textiles. Maclagan's capacity for hard work and ready absorption of knowledge was revealed when, in 1907, he produced *A Guide to English Ecclesiastical Embroideries*, a forerunner of the many catalogues and handbooks, published under his aegis, which set a standard of scholarship and usefulness sedulously followed and developed. From textiles, Maclagan was transferred in 1909 to the department of architecture and sculpture, to which he was to bring great distinction, borne out in the publication, in 1924, of the *Catalogue of Italian Plaquettes*.

In 1916 Maclagan was transferred

temporarily to the Foreign Office and later to the Ministry of Information. He became head of the Ministry's bureau in Paris and its controller for France in 1918, a post for which his fluent French especially fitted him. In 1919 he was attached to the British peace delegation and was present at the signing of the treaty. Characteristically Maclagan found time to write a daily account of these events in his diary, expressed in stylish, yet economical, prose, and written in an impeccable hand. For his services in France, Maclagan was appointed C.B.E. in 1919.

On the retirement of Sir Cecil Harcourt-Smith [q.v.] in 1924, Maclagan was appointed director. During his twenty-one years in office, the museum further increased its reputation as a centre for research and learning, to which Maclagan's monumental *Catalogue of Italian Sculpture*, produced in 1932 in collaboration with Margaret Longhurst, then assistant keeper (later keeper) in the department, bears witness. But the director's scholarly approach did not deflect him from an awareness of the growing interest of the general public in the resources of the museum. Under his influence important advances towards the popularization of the museum were made, not only in the increase of inexpensive publications and the organization of public lectures, but also in various devices by which the vast collections could be made more accessible to people of general rather than specialized knowledge. A welcome innovation was the placing in the entrance hall each Monday of the 'Object of the Week'. In this connection it is, perhaps, significant that, among the number of the learned articles, catalogues, and other erudite material which he produced, he was the author of one best-seller: an essay on *The Bayeux Tapestry*, published as a King Penguin in 1943. Maclagan was the first to envisage the system of rearranging the museum according to primary and secondary collections, thereby making the task of obtaining some impression of the museum as a whole a less formidable proposition for the general visitor. This reorganization proved impracticable in the financial climate of the thirties and was not realized until Sir Leigh Ashton reassembled the collections after 1945, when a new field of opportunity was opened and a fresh emphasis was placed upon the whole question of museum display.

During Maclagan's term of office, fresh interest was focused on the museum either by the acquisitions or by the series of distinguished exhibitions which he personally organized. These reflected the fastidious precision of his scholarship and the wide range of his perceptions as a connoisseur. Among the most outstanding were the exhibitions of works of art belonging to the livery companies of the City of London (1926); of English medieval art (1930), a landmark in its time; the William Morris centenary exhibition (1934); and the exhibition of the Eumorfopoulos collection (1936). In 1933 Maclagan was knighted and in 1945 he was appointed K.C.V.O.

Maclagan had many outside interests and held important appointments both at home and abroad. In 1927–8 he was Charles Eliot Norton professor at Harvard, his lectures, published in 1935 as *Italian Sculpture of the Renaissance*, representing, perhaps, his most important general work. He was vice-president of the Society of Antiquaries (1932–6), president of the Museums Association (1935–6), and chairman of the National Buildings Record. He was also appointed to lectureships at Edinburgh, Belfast, Dublin, and Hull and was given honorary degrees at Birmingham (LL.D., 1944) and Oxford (D.Litt., 1945). As chairman of the fine arts committee of the British Council Maclagan organized many exhibitions and undertook many journeys to distant countries where he consolidated his reputation, not only as a scholar of deep and wide culture, but also as a polished speaker and entertaining conversationalist. Maclagan was a gifted lecturer and combined this talent with a flair for after-dinner speaking which he could undertake with fluency and wit in French as well as English. He was proficient in German and until the end of his life read Greek and Latin for pleasure. A familiar figure at the Athenaeum and, latterly, at the Beefsteak, his discriminating taste in food and wine made him a valued dining companion.

Maclagan's personal predilections were varied and extended well beyond the confines of his specialization in the field of Early Christian and Renaissance studies; he was sympathetic with the aims of many modern artists and had in his possession a bust of himself by Meštrović; he was one of the first private collectors to buy the work of Henry Moore and unveiled the painting of the

Crucifixion by Graham Sutherland in the church of St. Matthew at Northampton. A keen churchman and, after his retirement, a member of the Church Assembly, he took a prominent part in the affairs of the Anglo-Catholic movement; and he performed much public service on behalf of the Church through the Cathedrals Advisory Council and the Central Council for the Care of Churches, which then had its headquarters in the Victoria and Albert Museum. Maclagan's knowledge of literature, especially of poetry, was profound; he could quote extensively, and at times amusingly, from poets both good and bad. He made several translations of the work of French poets, especially of Rimbaud and Valéry and, whilst an undergraduate, in 1902 published a volume of poems, *Leaves in the Road*, for which he designed the jacket. He also made a special study of Blake's *Prophetic Books* and with A. G. B. Russell published editions of *Jerusalem* (1904) and *Milton* (1907). He took an interest in book production and was one of the first to recognize the genius of Edward Johnston [q.v.] on whose formal script he based his own handwriting. He designed several bookplates, including one for his friend Bernard Berenson.

Maclagan's overriding interest in beautiful things made him a passionate traveller. It was perhaps fitting that he should have died, suddenly, 14 September 1951, in Spain, when making the ascent to see the church of Santa Maria de Naranco.

In 1913 Maclagan married Helen Elizabeth (died 1942), daughter of Commander Frederick Lascelles, second son of the fourth Earl of Harewood. They had two sons, the younger of whom was killed in action in 1942. The elder, Michael, a fellow of Trinity College, Oxford, contributes to this Supplement.

[Private information; personal knowledge.]
TRENCHARD COX.

McLAREN, HENRY DUNCAN, second BARON ABERCONWAY (1879–1953), industrialist, was born in Barnes, Surrey, 16 April 1879, the eldest child of Charles Benjamin Bright McLaren, later first Baron Aberconway [q.v.], by his wife, Laura Elizabeth, daughter of Henry Davis Pochin, of Bodnant, Denbighshire. He was educated at Eton where he became captain of the Oppidans, a position which he was proud to see occupied in turn

by his three sons. At Balliol College, Oxford, he obtained a second in modern history (1902) and was captain of the college hockey team. He then travelled for a year or two and was called to the bar by Lincoln's Inn in 1905 although he never practised.

McLaren had inherited a strong Liberal background and from his maternal grandfather a talent for, and insight into industrial techniques despite his lack of a technical education. After he had acquired some business experience mainly in the enterprises in which his Pochin grandfather had concerned himself, he entered the House of Commons in 1906 as Liberal member for West Staffordshire. Until 1910 he was parliamentary private secretary to Lloyd George for whose intellect he formed and kept the liveliest admiration. Defeated in January 1910, in December he was elected for the Bosworth division of Leicestershire which he continued to represent until 1922 when he was again defeated and did not seek re-election. After he succeeded to the peerage on his father's death in 1934, he attended the House of Lords from time to time, but seldom spoke. His other interests left him too little time for politics, and while in the Commons he did not do justice to his abilities.

During the war of 1914–18 McLaren was director of area organization at the Ministry of Munitions. After the war his business interests increased and in due course he succeeded his father as chairman of John Brown & Co. and was also chairman of other companies including the Sheepbridge Coal & Iron Co., Yorkshire Amalgamated Collieries, and the Tredegar Iron & Coal Co. He was a director of the National Provincial Bank and the London Assurance. But the field of industry in which he was most knowledgeable was that of china clay, where from an early age he had closely concerned himself with a family company, H. D. Pochin & Co; in 1932 he brought about an amalgamation of several china clay companies, to form English Clays Lovering Pochin & Co., Ltd., of which he was chairman.

McLaren's political and business activities had to compete with his many other interests. He was an enthusiastic and splendid shot; he enjoyed travelling; he liked to drive himself in open Rolls-Royce cars of which he had a succession; he presided diligently over the local bench and was chairman of the Denbighshire quarter-sessions; he was a keen and knowledgeable collector of antique furniture, ornaments, and pictures. But before all these came plants and gardening which were his great love. At Bodnant, taking advantage of the site and the lie of the land, he laid out with great skill and taste a magnificent series of terraces, and fashioned a wonderful wild garden; he planted a wide range of rare shrubs, especially rhododendrons, in which genus he hybridized extensively. In 1949 he gave the garden to the National Trust. His imagination, drive, and business experience, combined with his presence and personality, made him a most distinguished president of the Royal Horticultural Society from 1931 until his death.

McLaren was a man of prodigious energy, who never felt tired; of considerable intellect who could see to the root of each problem and could expound irresistibly his views upon it; of remarkable ability to switch his mind from one subject to another, showing deep knowledge of each. Above all, he was a creator, in his work and in his hobbies; imaginative and forward looking, he was resolute that his companies and interests should be in the forefront of technical progress.

In 1910 McLaren married Christabel Mary Melville, daughter of Sir Melville Leslie Macnaghten, chief of the Criminal Investigation Department. His marriage was exceptionally happy. His gifted wife shared his artistic interests and he depended greatly upon her companionship and judgement. They had two daughters and three sons, the eldest of whom, Charles Melville (born 1913), succeeded to the title when he died at Bodnant 23 May 1953.

A portrait by P. A. de László is at Bodnant. The Royal Horticultural Society and John Brown's own portraits by Sir Oswald Birley.

[Personal knowledge.]   ABERCONWAY.

MACLAY, JOSEPH PATON, first BARON MACLAY (1857–1951), shipowner and shipping controller, was born in Glasgow 6 September 1857, the third son of Ebenezer Maclay, master upholsterer, and his wife, Janet, daughter of Joseph Paton, of Paisley. Maclay, whose ancestors had for several generations been natives of Glasgow, was educated there as a boy and began business as a clerk. In 1885 with Thomas Walker McIntyre (father of Lord Sorn) he established the trampship firm of Maclay and McIntyre, which became one of the largest shipping concerns on the Clyde. He served on the Clyde Trust and the Glasgow town council, and as a magistrate. A Liberal in politics, he was a strong advocate of temperance and was active in the evangelical and philanthropic life of Scotland; and for his services he was created a baronet in 1914.

It was with the formation of the Lloyd George administration of December 1916 that Maclay emerged from the life of a wealthy and public-spirited Glasgow shipowner on to the national stage. The new prime minister 'felt that our shipping had become the most vital and vulnerable point in the issue of victory or defeat'. He at once invited Maclay, not previously known to him but suggested by Bonar Law, to be shipping controller and head of a new Ministry of Shipping; and under their combined pressure Maclay reluctantly accepted. He faced a heavy responsibility. The organization to deal with the submarine attack on shipping and its consequences was dispersed and inadequate. The Admiralty was failing to give effective protection and, at that time, had no belief in the convoy system which in the following year gave the answer to the even more formidable submarine campaign which had by then developed. The Board of Trade, the department mainly concerned with shipping in peacetime, was now on the side lines with a minor and diminishing role in war control. All the great war departments were competing for the inadequate shipping available, and there was no authority powerful enough to control their demands and adjudicate between them. The responsibility for allotting ships fell on the transport department of the Admiralty, in peacetime a small branch of the larger office with modest duties and status, but now a pivotal department in the whole of the war supply system. It had recruited the best brains in the shipping world and by 1916 had acquired the requisite ability and experience and internal organization. What it chiefly lacked was the authority to impose decisions upon interests and departments more powerful than itself. The new shipping controller was well qualified to supply this authority alike by his personality, his standing in the shipping world, and the circumstances of his appointment. A spare form, above medium height; a head of light red hair; blue eyes with a glint of steel; a straight slit of a mouth; a slightly jutting chin—constituted an unmistakable Scots figure which would have been a good subject for Raeburn, and at once suggested self-discipline, a strong will, and an inner life. A certain hesitancy in speech and a natural courtesy sometimes veiled, but did not long disguise, a confident judgement of men and things which did not easily yield to either pressure or persuasion. He was inclined to regard the orderly marshalling of the pros and cons of a case as a Whitehall game bearing little relation to the process by which decisions are, or should be, reached. In seeking cabinet approval he stated what he wanted starkly, with as little explanatory information as possible for 'those 10 Downing Street fellows'. He never entered Parliament himself and had indeed no high regard for politicians as a class, or even for ministers as such; and in dealing with the Cabinet he preferred to deal with Bonar Law, whom he trusted, and through him with the prime minister.

The year and a half which followed Maclay's appointment comprised the decisive stages in the shipping struggle. Requisition was extended over all British shipping; with this as the pivot, a strict system of control of all imported supplies was built up; on America's entry into the war the shipping effort of the two countries was co-ordinated; the convoy system was successfully introduced; the British control of shipping and supplies was expanded into an allied organization comprising also America, France, and Italy. Shipbuilding had been increased, and supplemented by a vast American programme. Long before the end of the war the shortage of shipping had ceased to be a limiting factor to the general war effort. This success was due partly to the success of the convoys and partly to greater efficiency in the use of ships and the materials they carried. The credit must be shared among many; but on any list of honour the shipping controller must stand high.

Maclay was sworn of the Privy Council in 1916 and created a baron in the resignation honours of 1922. He was a man of simple piety, and it is characteristic that his one publication, in 1918, was *The Starting Place of the Day*, a book of prayers for family worship which he compiled and edited.

In 1889 he married Martha (died 1929), daughter of William Strang, muslin manufacturer, of Glasgow, by whom he had five sons and two daughters. Two sons were killed in the war of 1914–18 and in their memory Maclay and his wife, in 1921, presented to the university of Glasgow (of which he had been made an honorary LL.D. in 1919) a student hostel, Maclay Hall. Of his other sons, Sir Joseph Maclay, K.B.E. (1899–1969), who succeeded him when he died at his home, Duchal, Kilmacolm, Renfrewshire, 24 April 1951, had been a Liberal member of Parliament from 1931 to 1945, and president of the Chamber of Shipping in 1946–7; and John Scott Maclay, secretary of state for Scotland in 1957–62, was created Viscount Muirshiel in 1964.

[*Glasgow Herald* and *The Times*, *passim*; David Lloyd George, *War Memoirs*, vol. iii, 1934; personal knowledge.]   SALTER.

McLINTOCK, WILLIAM FRANCIS PORTER (1887–1960), geologist, was born in Edinburgh 2 February 1887, the third child and elder son of Peter Buchanan McLintock, cashier, by his wife, Jane Porter. He was educated at George Heriot's School and Edinburgh University, graduating B.Sc. with special distinction in botany in 1907. In the summer of that year he was the successful candidate in a written and practical examination in crystallography, mineralogy, and chemistry for the post of assistant curator in the Museum of Practical Geology, London. There he worked on the mineral and gemstone collections, producing studies of datolite (1910) and beryl (1912), and a short guide to the gemstone collection (1912) remarkable for its introduction which in thirty-four pages was an early handbook to the scientific study and identification of gemstones and their imitations. In 1911 McLintock became curator of geology in the Royal Scottish Museum, Edinburgh, where he carried out a brilliant research on the zeolites of the Tertiary lavas of Mull which he successfully offered as a thesis for the D.Sc. degree of Edinburgh University in 1915. While in Edinburgh he lectured in geology as part of his duties in the museum and to evening classes in the Heriot-Watt College.

In 1914–18 McLintock found scope for his skill in precision instrumentation in the devising, preparation, and testing of gauges for use in munition factories. He returned to the Museum of Practical Geology in London as curator early in 1921 and, although becoming more and more occupied by administrative and committee work, published research on the Strathmore meteorite (1922) and on the rare mineral petalite first identified by him as a British species (1923) from Okehampton, Devon. He travelled to Persia in 1926 as the senior of two representatives of the Geological Survey invited by the Anglo-Iranian Oil Company to study the geophysical surveying there in progress. Geophysical survey towards elucidation of concealed geological structure was then in its infancy and little of scientific consequence had been published on its geological potentialities. On his return test surveys were undertaken by the Geological Survey under McLintock's charge over the years 1927 to 1930 and impartial reports on the relation of the gravity anomalies to known geological structures were presented for assessment by geologists.

In the early thirties McLintock's most urgent and momentous duty was the planning of the new Geological Museum at South Kensington and the transfer of the library and collections from the dilapidated building in Jermyn Street. Alive to opportunity and after a tour of European museums having learned, as he said, what to avoid, McLintock developed revolutionary ideas towards popular exposition of a science largely unknown and without apparent appeal to the general public. Enthusiastically supported by a modern outlook in the Ministry of Works and firm in his conviction that it was necessary to attract as well as instruct, he withstood attack from scoffing and outraged authorities of scientific tradition. The new museum was opened on 3 July 1935. Laid out as McLintock had conceived it, the gemstone collection forming the centrepiece supported by illuminated dioramas of practical geological interest, the exhibition was immediately and progressively successful. When war came in 1939 McLintock, as deputy director since 1937, became responsible for the administrative side of the war effort of the Survey and Museum. He initiated the organizations dealing with strategic materials, underground storage, and geological issues in military and economic warfare. Appointed director in succession to Sir Edward Bailey in 1945 he restored the museum from the chaos of wartime occupation as Civil Defence headquarters and reorganized the Survey to peacetime activities greatly expanded by official recognition of the need for geological advice on underground water,

nationalized coal, hydro-electric schemes, discovery of new sources of the raw materials of atomic energy, and research on their mineralogy and evaluation. His museum was the first of the national museums to reopen, in 1947. His programme for the post-war development of the Survey—logically, clearly, concisely, forcefully, and promptly presented, as were all his official papers—was accepted and forthwith he conjoined the extending geological activities with those of the appropriate Ministries and Boards, at once preserving the integrity of the Survey as the organ of official geology and ensuring these bodies of the most experienced and balanced advice.

Entirely loyal to his service and to the just interests of his staff McLintock was ready to battle with highest authority for the resources and conditions he considered necessary for the efficiency and welfare of his organization. His long experience in official negotiations, a prodigious memory, acute logical intellect, and capacity for clear presentation combined with a gift for discerning and tenacious argument usually brought him success. Towards his own preferment he was not indifferent but not solicitous. After resigning his appointment as director in 1950 he was appointed C.B. (1951).

Outwith his official service McLintock was vice-president of the eighteenth International Geological Congress, to which he offered the hospitality of the museum headquarters in 1948. He led the British delegation to the United Nations conference on the conservation of mineral resources at Lake Success in 1949 and served for many years on the Board of Overseas Geological Surveys, the geological advisory panel of British Petroleum, Ltd., and the Iron and Steel Board.

Tall, spare, and of distinguished appearance McLintock was always elegantly dressed in town. A keen golfer and trout-fisher, he enjoyed also riding and shooting. He was a ready, illuminating, and witty conversationalist and an evening's argument, in which he was ready to take any side to draw an opponent, was a spice to life. To his family he was a responsibly loyal son and brother. In 1939 McLintock married Maude Alice, widow of J. M. Marshall and daughter of Major-General W. L. Dalrymple. Some years after retirement to their home at Rosemount, Perthshire, he suffered a serious heart attack from which under his wife's care he apparently recovered, but on a visit to

Edinburgh he collapsed and died, 21 February 1960.

[*The Times* and *Scotsman*, 23 February 1960 ; *Year Book* of the Royal Society of Edinburgh, 1961 ; *Proceedings* of the Geological Society of London, 1960 ; Sir John S. Flett, *The Geological Survey 1835–1935*, 1937 ; private information ; personal knowledge.]   JAMES PHEMISTER.

MACMILLAN, HUGH PATTISON, BARON MACMILLAN (1873–1952), judge, was born in Glasgow 20 February 1873, the only son among the six children of the Rev. Hugh Macmillan [q.v.] by his wife, Jane, daughter of William Patison, of Edinburgh. He was educated at the Collegiate School, Greenock, at Edinburgh University, where he graduated in 1893 with first class honours in philosophy, and Glasgow University where he obtained his LL.B. in 1896, becoming Cunninghame scholar. He passed advocate in 1897 after devilling to C. J. (later Lord) Guthrie. While building up his practice at the Scots bar he acted as reporter for the *Scots Law Times*, as an examiner in law at Glasgow University, and as editor of the *Juridical Review*. Macmillan had no influence to bring him work, but the care and assiduity with which he conducted his cases soon brought his name to the attention of solicitors. He took silk in 1912 and his practice thereafter continued to grow until he became one of the busiest seniors at the Scots bar. He was in great demand in cases which involved municipalities and public bodies and was senior legal assessor to Edinburgh Corporation (1920–24) and standing counsel to the Convention of Royal Burghs (1923–30). In 1918 he spent some months as an assistant director of intelligence at the Ministry of Information.

In 1924 the Labour Party, in office for the first time, had no member with sufficient legal qualifications to become lord advocate. Macmillan was neither a member of Parliament nor a Socialist, and had indeed earlier been adopted as a Unionist candidate. But he accepted from Ramsay MacDonald the office of lord advocate, having as solicitor-general Sir John Fenton, also a non-political appointment. The experiment worked well enough although it has never been repeated. Macmillan was sworn of the Privy Council and made an honorary bencher of the Inner Temple. When the Labour Government fell Macmillan returned to the bar, establishing himself in chambers in London, where he enjoyed a varied practice in the House of Lords, the Privy Council, and before parliamentary committees. He was appointed standing counsel for Canada (1928) and for Australia (1929). One of his most distinguished appearances was in 1928 on behalf of the railway companies in the road transport bills in which they obtained power to provide road services in face of the increasing competition of bus companies and road hauliers.

In 1930 Macmillan was made a lord of appeal in ordinary with a life peerage. After a period (1939–40) as minister of information, he returned to the House of Lords as a lord of appeal in 1941, until his resignation in 1947. Shortly after his appointment he sat in the case of *Donoghue* v. *Stevenson*, [1932] A.C. 562, known as the case of the snail in the ginger beer bottle. He delivered a careful judgement justifying the result that the manufacturers were liable in negligence to the consumer. 'The law takes no cognizance of carelessness in the abstract . . . The grounds of action may be as various and manifold as human errancy . . . The categories of negligence are never closed' are passages which are often quoted. During the war he was a party to the decision in *Blyth* v. *Lord Advocate*, [1945] A.C. 32, which established that a company commander in the Home Guard was a 'common soldier' within the meaning of the Finance Act and that his estate was exempt from estate duty. Other well-known cases in which he delivered judgements were *Woods* v. *Duncan*, [1946] A.C. 401 (the *Thetis* disaster), and *Joyce* v. *Director of Public Prosecutions*, [1946] A.C. 347 ('Lord Haw-Haw'). After Macmillan's death Viscount Simonds wrote : 'His judgments have a clarity and precision which will lead students of the law to turn to them for guidance and they have too an elegance and felicity which would delight the adventurous layman who strayed into that field of literature . . . Courteous and patient, even long-suffering his less patient colleagues might think, . . . he was to me the model of what a member of an appellate tribunal should be.'

Macmillan's wit, urbanity, and charm were accompanied by an underlying seriousness of purpose which increasingly found expression in public service as his talents for chairmanship were recognized. He had an astonishing versatility and could give his mind to any problem with a lucidity tending towards solution rather than perplexity. He is perhaps best known for his chairmanship of the Treasury committee on finance and industry (1929–31), which surveyed the nation's financial system in relation to industry. Its report became known by his name although much of it was written by J. M. (later Lord) Keynes [q.v.]. Macmillan was chairman also of the royal commission on lunacy (1924–6); of the court of inquiry into the coal mining industry dispute (1925); of the sub-committee on the *British Pharmacopoeia* (1926–8); of the Home Office committee on street offences (1927–8); of the shipbuilding industry conferences (1928–30); of the Treasury committee on income-tax law codifications (1932–6); of the royal commission on Canadian banking and currency (1933); and of the committee on the preservation of works of art in enemy hands (1944–7). He was a member of the Political Honours Committee from 1929 and chairman from 1935. An original trustee of the Pilgrim Trust he was chairman from 1935 until his death. He was chairman of the court of London University (1929–43) and of the lord chancellor's committee on an institute of advanced legal studies which was inaugurated in 1948. He was chairman also of the Great Ormond Street Hospital for Sick Children (1928–34); of the King George V memorial fund; of the general committee of the Athenaeum (1935–45); and of the B.B.C. advisory council (1936–46). Other bodies on which he served were the British Museum, the Soane Museum, the Carnegie Trust for Scottish Universities, the National Trust, King George's Jubilee Trust, and the Society for the Promotion of Nature Reserves. He was president of the Scottish Text Society and instrumental in founding the Stair Society in 1934. It was largely due to his efforts that the Advocates Library was taken over as the National Library of Scotland in 1925. He himself possessed a library of outstanding quality and at his wish part has been placed in the House of Lords library and part in the Advocates Library at Parliament House, Edinburgh, where closely adjacent there is a commemorative plaque.

A collection of Macmillan's essays and addresses was published in 1937 under the title *Law and Other Things* and his autobiography, *A Man of Law's Tale*, appeared in 1952 shortly after his death. He was a regular contributor to this Dictionary.

Macmillan received honorary degrees from thirteen universities. He was made an honorary burgess of Edinburgh in 1938 and appointed G.C.V.O. in 1937.

He married in 1901 Elizabeth Katharine Grace (died 1967), daughter of William Johnstone Marshall, M.D., of Greenock; they had no children. He died at Ewhurst, Surrey, 5 September 1952. A portrait by L. Campbell Taylor is in the Senate House of London University and a drawing by Sir William Rothenstein belongs to the Athenaeum.

[*The Times*, 6, 11, 12, and 16 September 1952; *Law Times*, 12 September 1952; personal knowledge.]   GUEST.

McNEIL, HECTOR (1907–1955), journalist and politician, was born at the Temperance Hotel, Garelochhead, Dumbartonshire, 10 March 1907, the second of seven children of Donald McNeill, journeyman shipwright, and his wife, Margaret McPherson Russell. His father's family originated in the island of Barra and his mother's in Islay. When the family moved to Glasgow, McNeil attended secondary schools and the university. At first he studied for the ministry, but after touring Canada and the United States in 1931–2 as a member of the British universities' debating team he decided to devote himself to journalism and politics. After a period as a freelance he joined the staff of the *Scottish Daily Express* as a reporter, later becoming a sub-editor, night news editor, and finally leader-writer. In 1938 he was transferred for a time to London but subsequently returned to Glasgow as assistant to the editor. He was active in local politics, served on the Glasgow town council (1933–6, 1937–8), and was river bailie (1937–8).

In the meantime he had stood unsuccessfully as a Labour candidate in Galloway at the general elections of 1929 and 1931. In the general election of 1935 he failed by only 149 votes to defeat Walter Elliot [q.v.], the sitting member for Kelvingrove, Glasgow; and in February 1936 he nearly doubled the previous Labour vote in a by-election contest against Malcolm MacDonald in Ross and Cromarty. Finally, as a result of the wartime electoral truce between the parties, he was returned unopposed in July 1941 for the burgh of Greenock, a constituency which he succeeded in retaining at four subsequent elections and which he represented until his death.

In 1942–5 McNeil was parliamentary private secretary to Philip Noel-Baker, parliamentary secretary to the Ministry of

War Transport. After the election of 1945 C. R. (later Earl) Attlee appointed him parliamentary under-secretary of state at the Foreign Office under Ernest Bevin [q.v.]. In the following year he was sworn of the Privy Council on his promotion to be minister of state for foreign affairs, in which office he remained until Parliament was dissolved in February 1950. It was this period at the Foreign Office which gave McNeil most satisfaction and brought him most prominently before the public. He became the recognized spokesman of the Government at the annual General Assemblies of the United Nations, where the propaganda contest between the Soviet Union and the western powers was then reaching its height. McNeil had always been a debater of unusual force, and he more than held his own in this forum, becoming even better known in the United States than he was at home. Among his many other activities were his participation in the Paris peace conference of 1946, and in negotiations leading up to the Brussels Treaty in 1948. He also took part in some of the more specialized work of the United Nations, in particular in the formation of the International Refugee Organization, a subject for which he felt a special sympathy and concern.

Following the election of 1950 McNeil became secretary of state for Scotland, with a seat in the Cabinet, until the defeat of the Labour Party at the polls in October 1951. During this brief period he showed a keen interest in the breeding of Highland cattle; and scored a personal success in arranging that facilities in Switzerland for the treatment of tuberculosis should be available to the British health services. He was also able to use his own international connections to attract new industries to Clydeside. After his party went into opposition he gave part of his time to private business, becoming managing-director and chairman of the British company producing the *Encyclopædia Britannica*. He also became very popular on radio and television. While travelling to the United States on business he suffered a haemorrhage and died in New York 11 October 1955. His early death cut short a career which had seemed to ensure for him an important place for many years to come.

In 1939 McNeil married Sheila, daughter of Dr. James Craig, of Glasgow; they had one son.

[Public records; private information; personal knowledge.]   KENNETH YOUNGER.

MACQUEEN-POPE, WALTER JAMES (1888–1960), theatre manager, publicist, and historian, was born in Farnham, Surrey, 11 April 1888, the elder son of Walter George Pope, hop factor, and his wife, Frederika Macqueen. He was proud of his theatrical connections, a great-aunt several times removed having been the celebrated Mrs. Elizabeth Pope [q.v.], the original Mrs. Candour in *The School for Scandal*. 'Popie', as he was universally known in his long career as manager and as press-agent, could further trace his theatrical ancestry back to Morgan Pope, owner of the Bear Garden, Bankside, and to Thomas Pope, one of Burbage's actors and shareholder of the Globe Theatre, Bankside, in the late sixteenth century.

'Popie' was educated at Tollington School and began his working life as a shipping clerk, but transferred to the theatre world as soon as possible, acting for several years as secretary to the impresario, Sir George Dance, and then becoming business-manager for Sir Alfred Butt at the Queen's, St. James's, the Lyric, and other theatres. For three years (1922–5), he was manager of the Alexandra Palace. But this was not the inner heart of the theatre for Pope. After 1925 he worked in a managerial capacity successively at the Duke of York's Theatre (1927–9), the new Whitehall Theatre (1929–32, in Walter Hackett's highly successful seasons), at the Aldwych Theatre (in the heyday of the Walls–Lynn farces), and then as press representative for Drury Lane (1935–56) and many other managements.

For the first four years of the war he worked for E.N.S.A. as public relations officer, with his headquarters at Drury Lane Theatre. He was a marvellous personal guide to this theatre and would particularly dwell there on stories of the building's reasonably well-authenticated ghost in the upper circle.

In his last fifteen years Pope turned author and produced an astonishing number of big volumes, at least one a year, about particular theatres and their history (among them Drury Lane, St. James's, the Haymarket, and the Gaiety), about pantomime and the music-hall, about London's pleasure gardens, and about 'the good old times' generally. These volumes were enthusiastic and accurate rather than brilliantly descriptive or informative.

From 1955 until his death 'Popie' was also in demand as a lecturer on the theatrical subjects he loved, and he appeared often in the same capacity on radio and on television. Vivian Ellis sketches a vivid picture of him in his book, *I'm on a See-Saw* (1953): 'Somewhere in a series of offices, in the upper circles of darkened theatres or high above the roar of the London traffic, Macqueen-Pope has always sat, rather like an extinct bird in its lofty eyrie. There he broods, surrounded with bound volumes of old plays and prints, typing, smoking, and saying how tired he is of it all, but never too tired to share a laugh, a sorrow, or his own unrivalled knowledge of our contemporary, as well as non-contemporary, stage.'

Two notices by Macqueen-Pope appear in this Supplement, but he died, in London, 27 June 1960, before he could complete all that he had undertaken.

He married in 1912 Stella Suzanne Schumann, by whom he had one daughter.

[Private information; personal knowledge.]
ALAN DENT.

MALAN, DANIEL FRANÇOIS (1874–1959), South African prime minister, was born 22 May 1874 in the Western Cape Colony on the farm Allesverloren, near Riebeek West. J. C. Smuts [q.v.] had been born on a neighbouring farm four years earlier. Malan was the eldest son of Daniel François Malan, a wine farmer of Huguenot descent, and his wife, Anna Magdalena du Toit. With Smuts, a boyhood friend and for a time his Sunday-school teacher, Malan had his early schooling in Riebeek West. He was a serious-minded but not outstanding scholar. Suffering from weak eyesight, he took little part in sport but preferred social problems upon which he could bring to bear a kind of idealistic discontent. In his twenty-seventh year, after obtaining an M.A. in philosophy at Stellenbosch, he went on to the university of Utrecht where he obtained his doctorate in divinity with a thesis on 'The Idealism of Berkeley'.

On his return to South Africa he began as a teacher but soon exchanged the schoolroom for the Church. In 1906 he went to Montagu in the Cape Colony where from his Dutch Reformed Church pulpit he preached strict temperance, if not prohibition, to the wine farmers. Admiring his courage, they hardly appreciated his views and in 1912 he migrated to Graaf-Reinet, a town in a sheep-farming area of the Cape Midlands, where the different agricultural interests provided a more congenial atmosphere for local veto and kindred subjects.

It was soon clear that the pulpit was too confined and academic for Malan who had already shown himself a great force in the promotion of the Afrikaans language and now began to take an interest in politics. His career as a predikant came to a close in 1915 when the Nationalist Party decided to launch its own newspaper in Cape Town. Malan was persuaded to accept the editorship and on 26 July 1915 he produced the first issue of *Die Burger*. His declared mission was to raise the tone of polemics and foster a spirit of unity among the people. For many years, however, he brought not peace, but a political sword. His editorials breathed the race-exclusiveness of the Old Testament. He turned his wrath upon General Botha [q.v.] as a Judas of the Afrikaner race when he was leading South African troops in German South West Africa on the side of the Allies; Botha and Smuts were accused of having involved South Africa in a foreign war in which she had no interest, an indictment of Smuts which Malan repeated in 1939. Secession and republicanism were the constant theme, Malan insisting that only independence from the British Empire could ensure the future inviolability of South Africa. He remained editor of *Die Burger* for nearly nine years and until his death he retained a close bond with the newspaper which grew to wield immense influence in South African politics.

Malan's entry into politics coincided with his first association with *Die Burger*. He took a lead in the somewhat protracted formalities of launching the Cape Nationalist Party; and in September 1915 presided over its first congress at Middelburg. He remained the party's leader in the Cape until 1953. He was defeated in the general election of 1915 at Cradock and again, by only sixteen votes, in a by-election at Victoria West in 1917. In 1919 W. P. Louw, who many years later became his father-in-law, resigned to enable Malan to take over his Calvinia seat. This he retained until 1938 when, scenting danger, he transferred to Piketberg which he held with overwhelming majorities until his retirement from politics.

Malan's first visit to England was in 1919 when he was one of the freedom deputation whose representations in favour of secession met with a brusque refusal. In 1924 J. B. M. Hertzog [q.v.] entered into an election pact with the Labour Party. Malan, who had earlier vehemently opposed any idea of coalition, gave his blessing to the arrangement which defeated Smuts and resulted in a Pact government. By this time Malan had also modified his secessionist and anti-English tone. He drew subtle distinctions between 'sovereign independence' and 'republican independence', averring that the Nationalists had never contemplated the abolition of the common monarchy. On the eve of the election he had publicly repudiated a leading article in *Die Burger* which merely reiterated his own pre-Pact sentiments. He resigned his editorship and was given the portfolios of interior, public health, and education in Hertzog's Cabinet. He soon revealed the qualities of an able administrator and, once again, the zeal of the reformer. He reformed the language settlement in the South Africa Act by substituting Afrikaans for Dutch as the second official language of the Union. He reformed the Senate. He reformed the conduct of elections and introduced voting by post. He reformed the Civil Service. And he attempted to reform the press. He gave South Africa its own flag after days of bitter controversy. He also attempted a settlement of the problem of Indians in South Africa by concluding the Cape Town round table agreement in 1927 which aimed at a reduction in their numbers through repatriation, although this subsequently proved impracticable. While openly advocating the principle that, all things being equal, Civil Service posts should be given to Nationalists, he refused to indulge in witch hunts and there were fewer complaints of political bias in his departments than in any other.

When Hertzog and Smuts formed a coalition government in 1933 Malan gave it nominal support but refused office. In 1934 he resisted the fusion of their parties into the United Party and with a small group of diehard republican Nationalists crossed the floor to the opposition benches, where he became the leader of the group calling themselves the 'Purified' Nationalists. He was branded a schismatic, a traitor to his leader, and a racialist. Hertzog now became the target of Malan's contumely, and a period of bitter verbal conflict followed. But departure from the gold standard (December 1932) led to a spectacular economic revival and little thought was given, outside political ranks, to Malan's fulminations. The general election of 1938 increased the strength of his group from 19 to 27 in a House of 154 members.

The split between Smuts and Hertzog on the outbreak of war in 1939 brought about a temporary reunion between Hertzog and Malan who had sent a letter to Hertzog pledging support for neutrality which Hertzog had failed to disclose to his colleagues. The new-found unity, however, did not last long. An internal crisis in the reunited National Party came to a head at a Free State congress in November 1940 which adopted a programme which Hertzog declared ignored the rights of the English-speaking people of the Union. He and N. C. Havenga, the former minister of finance, left the congress hall and the field clear to Malan.

At the general election in 1943 Malan gained only forty-three seats but his confidence was increased by the fact that all the various dissenting Nationalist movements were rejected by the electorate; with a limited following in Parliament he pursued his pressure on Smuts.

In 1946 the Government received copies of papers found in the German Foreign Office in which there was a reference to communications which Hans Denk, a Nazi formerly residing in South West Africa, was alleged to have had in 1940 with Malan through Mrs. Denk who entered the Union from Portuguese East Africa. A select committee appointed by Parliament exonerated Malan and accepted that although he had had an interview with Mrs. Denk there was no connection between this and a Nationalist peace resolution tabled in the House three days later.

In March 1947 Malan reached an election agreement with Havenga, the sequel of which was Malan's victory on a policy of apartheid in May 1948 by a majority of five members over the United Party. For Smuts a lifelong struggle with Malan had ended in defeat and with the aid of Havenga Malan emerged from the political wilderness at the age of seventy-four to become the fourth prime minister of the Union. The formation of an exclusively Afrikaner and republican Government followed.

There were those who thought that his narrow victory would soon be reversed. Malan, however, resolutely set about entrenching himself in power and paving the way for a republic. The South West Africa constitution was amended to give the mandated territory six seats in the Assembly and four in the Senate, all of which went to the National Party. Dual citizenship for immigrants from the Commonwealth and the right of appeal to the Privy Council were abolished. Malan was the author of apartheid, a policy which brought South Africa in conflict with world opinion. Under his guidance there were introduced the Group Areas Act, the Mixed Marriages Act, and the Immorality Act which made intercourse between white and non-white a criminal offence. Apartheid was insisted upon in railway stations, suburban trains, post offices, and many other places. Malan's efforts to remove Cape Coloured voters from the common roll, a right they had enjoyed for a century, were frustrated by decisions of the Court of Appeal. Nevertheless Malan gained a decisive victory at the 1953 election. As prime minister he went to London to attend the coronation of Queen Elizabeth. At the 1949 Commonwealth prime ministers' conference he had concurred in the decision to allow India, although an independent republic, to remain in the Commonwealth. Malan subsequently defined his attitude to the Commonwealth by saying that, whatever differences might exist about a republic, it was his wish to remain within it. His views had mellowed considerably and during the period of his premiership he revealed a less exclusive attitude towards English-speaking South Africans.

Malan resigned as Cape leader in 1953 and as prime minister in November 1954. His decision to leave the political scene at the height of his success and before his leadership was affected by his diminishing physical strength showed his objectivity towards himself. He tried unsuccessfully to designate Havenga as his successor. Thereafter he lived in seclusion at his home Morewag at Stellenbosch where he settled down to write his memoirs which dealt with the restoration of the unity of Afrikanerdom. He died at Stellenbosch 7 February 1959.

Malan's first marriage, in 1926, was to a widow, Mrs. Van Tonder, formerly Martha Margaretha Elizabeth Zandberg, who died in 1930. They had two sons. In 1937 Malan married Maria Ann Sophia, daughter of W. P. Louw. They adopted a German orphan girl in 1948. In 1955 the airport at Cape Town was named after Malan and a portrait by Geoffrey Wylde was presented to the South African Parliament.

[D. F. Malan, *Afrikaner-Volkseenheid en my Ervarings op die Pad Daarheen*, 1959; Eric Robins, *This Man Malan*, 1953; L. E. Neame, *Some South African Politicians*, 1929; private information; personal knowledge.]   HARRY LAWRENCE.

MALCOLM, SIR DOUGAL ORME (1877–1955), scholar and imperialist, was a cadet of the house of Malcolm of Poltalloch, belonging to a branch of which his cousin and brother-in-law Sir Neill Malcolm was the head. He was the younger son of William Rolle Malcolm, senior partner of Coutts's bank, and his first wife, Georgina Wellesley, sister of the fourth Duke of Wellington, and was born in Epsom 6 August 1877. Although his career lay wholly in England and the Empire oversea, he was tenacious of his Scottish patriotism. He was educated at Eton and New College, Oxford, where he graduated with a double first in the classical schools of honour moderations (1897) and *literae humaniores* (1899). While his fine scholarship, which was a great part of the man, was literary rather than philosophical, the Greats teaching had developed in him an exceptionally keen logical faculty. In 1899 he was elected, like his father before him, a fellow of All Souls, a rare family 'double' since the abolition of the privileges of founder's kin; later he was joined there by his schoolfellow and lifelong intimate Robert (later Lord) Brand.

In 1900 Malcolm entered the Colonial Office, where he acted as private secretary to Sir Alfred (later Viscount) Milner [q.v.], high commissioner in South Africa, during Milner's visits to headquarters in London. Like many of his New College contemporaries he fell under Milner's spell and desired to enlist under his leadership. Brand had already obtained an appointment as assistant town clerk of Johannesburg which enrolled him in the band of young Oxford men, nearly all from New College, afterwards nicknamed 'Milner's kindergarten'; but Malcolm's chance did not come until 1905, when he went out to Cape Town as private secretary to Lord Selborne [q.v.] who had been appointed to succeed Milner and carry on his work of reconstructing the four colonies of South Africa after the South African war.

Malcolm was immediately accepted into the brotherhood of the kindergarten. He fell also under the influence of the ideas of Cecil Rhodes [q.v.] for imperial development north of the Limpopo, mediated through (Sir) Leander Starr Jameson [q.v.], for Rhodes himself had died in 1902. The immediate task of the kindergarten, however, was to work for the achievement of Milner's project of uniting the four colonies into a single state. This project eventually took shape in the document which was adopted by the high commissioner and became known as the Selborne memorandum. While the text of the memorandum was from the pen of Lionel Curtis [q.v.], in the long debates in the kindergarten out of which it emerged, it was largely Malcolm's critical analysis which translated Curtis's enthusiasm into practical politics.

After the Union of South Africa in 1909, the kindergarten began to break up. Curtis, Brand, and others transferred themselves to London, where they embarked on study of schemes for applying the principles of the union of the four colonies on the larger scale of the British Empire. They founded the quarterly review, the *Round Table*, as an organ for discussion of the imperial problem. Malcolm remained in South Africa until Selborne's term of office ended in 1910, but kept in touch with them by post and continued to criticize the drafts of the work eventually published under Curtis's name as *The Problem of the Commonwealth* (1916). Then, after a few months as private secretary to Lord Grey [q.v.], governor-general of Canada, he was transferred in 1912 to the Treasury and later in the year appointed secretary to the dominions royal commission.

At the end of the year, however, Malcolm retired from the Civil Service, having been nominated a director of the British South Africa Company on the departure of the vice-president, James Rochfort Maguire (whose notice he subsequently contributed to this Dictionary), to take charge of the company's affairs in Rhodesia. This was Rhodes's chartered company, founded in 1889, and still administering the territories of Matabeleland and Mashonaland, where the founders had obtained concessions of mining and other rights from Lobengula. The management of this great enterprise was Malcolm's main professional occupation for the remainder of his life, although as the years passed he accepted places on the boards of many other companies, including another chartered company, that of British North Borneo, of which he became vice-president. In 1923 the British South Africa Company surrendered its political functions to the colonial governments of Southern and Northern Rhodesia, so that Malcolm, when he became president in 1937, succeeded only to the control of a powerful commercial corporation, the principal assets of which

were the mineral rights and the major share in the ownership of the railways. In due course the movement toward self-government, which always had Malcolm's warm sympathy, became jealous of this privileged position. It fell to him, therefore, to conduct the prolonged negotiations which led, first to the sale of the railways, on profitable terms, to the Government in 1947, and to a new agreement for the mining rights in 1950. By this the company agreed to surrender its rights in 1986, meanwhile paying one fifth of its net revenue from mining to the Northern Rhodesian Government, the amount to be regarded as an expense for the purpose of the colony's income-tax. In return the Government agreed that no special tax should be imposed on mining royalties as such. For the remaining years of his life Malcolm continued to take a close consultative interest in the progress of the two Rhodesias towards independence; but he was strongly opposed to the creation of the Federation of the two colonies and Nyasaland, holding that they could prosper only under a unitary government. He maintained also that the attempts to give special constitutional protection to native interests must be illusory, there being no aspect of Rhodesian politics in which the race question was not involved.

Public work undertaken during the last thirty years of Malcolm's life included the chairmanship of the 1820 Settlers Memorial Association, through which he did much to encourage migration to South Africa; the chairmanship from 1925 of the inter-departmental committee on education and industry which reported in 1926 and 1928; and membership of the British economic mission which visited Australia in 1928. Although his staunchly Conservative and imperialist principles had nothing in common with the trend of thought popularly associated with the London School of Economics, he served that institution faithfully as vice-chairman of the court of governors. He was particularly assiduous in his attention to the editorial affairs of the *Round Table*, co-operating with his old friends of the kindergarten and the younger men who were brought in to fill the gaps that mortality from time to time created, and occasionally contributing an anonymous article himself, generally on some Rhodesian topic.

Busy as were Malcolm's days in his many board-rooms or at Charter House,

Salisbury, he was the most gregarious of men and lived for civilized social intercourse. He was a fascinating conversationalist, drawing upon an astonishing memory for four great literatures, Greek, Latin, English, and French. He was most at home in the kind of coteries where these delights are appreciated. One was the Literary Society in London, whose dinners he could seldom be persuaded to forgo, even when the severe asthma which afflicted his old age made it medically undesirable. Another was the Beefsteak Club. But above all he belonged to the intimate brotherhood of All Souls where he spent every week-end in term that was physically possible. By a dispensation made in 1922 to cover the missing age-group due to the wartime casualties and suspension of elections, the college made it possible for him and one or two contemporaries to be re-elected periodically all their lives, in spite of marriage which was conventionally a bar for non-residents. This was Malcolm's spiritual home. When in 1928 his close friend Cosmo Lang [q.v.] vacated his fellowship on becoming archbishop of Canterbury and visitor *ex officio*, Malcolm succeeded to the dignity of Lord Mallard, which is not mentioned in the statutes but conveys an informal presidency of the convivial side of college life. At the 'mallard table' in the common-room the younger fellows, and some seniors who had retained the youthful spirit, gathered eagerly round Malcolm on Saturday and Sunday nights. It was also remarked that more than one academic dignitary, in and out of the college, whose duties required the delivery of an occasional Latin oration, contrived to do so with an elegance equally suggestive of Marcus Cicero and Dougal Malcolm. One of his lifelong intimates, the first Earl of Halifax [q.v.], chancellor of the university, made no secret of his reliance on this source of inspiration. This was Malcolm in exclusively male environments; but his handsome features and courtly manners gave him also great popularity among women, especially young women, hosts of whom adopted him as a sort of honorary uncle and later brought their daughters to him, from the schoolroom or even at the font. In his old age he was a figure of infinite benignity, almost too great a Christian, wrote his oldest friend, Lord Brand, because he could not be brought to think ill of even the most obviously malicious adversary.

Malcolm was appointed K.C.M.G. in 1938 and in 1950, in recognition of his services to good relations between the Rhodesias and Portuguese Africa, was awarded the grand cross of the Order of Christ.

Malcolm left no issue. He married in 1910 Dora Claire, daughter of John Montagu Stopford; she died in 1920. In 1923 he married Lady Evelyn Farquhar, daughter of the fifth Earl of Donoughmore and widow of Colonel Francis Farquhar who had been killed in action. Malcolm died in London 30 August 1955; his widow died in 1962.

He wrote *The British South Africa Company 1889-1939*, a short commemorative volume published for the anniversary in the latter year; and *Nuces Relictae* (1926) which includes a selection of his epigrams in Greek and Latin elegiacs.

A portrait, in Highland dress, was painted for his wife by Sir Oswald Birley; a replica of the upper part of the figure is at All Souls.

[*The Times*, 31 August and 2 September 1955; *Round Table* papers; Curtis papers; personal knowledge.]   DERMOT MORRAH.

MANECKJI BYRAMJI DADABHOY, SIR (1865-1953), Indian lawyer, industrialist, and parliamentarian. [See DADABHOY.]

MANN, CATHLEEN SABINE (1896-1959), painter, was born in Newcastle upon Tyne 31 December 1896, the second of the three daughters of Harrington Mann, a gifted Scottish portrait painter, and his first wife, Florence Sabine Pasley. She showed artistic skill early, though her first ambitions were towards the stage. Having found her vocation, she studied in her father's studio in London and at the Slade School. Through her father she came to know (Dame) Ethel Walker [q.v.] who gave her a rare degree of encouragement and private lessons. Her influence is often happily discernible in Cathleen Mann's best portraiture and flower pictures.

Her development was interrupted by ambulance service during the war of 1914-18, but as early as 1924 Cathleen Mann had two portraits in the Royal Academy where she became a regular exhibitor after 1930, as also at the Royal Society of Portrait Painters. In 1926 she married the tenth Marquess of Queensberry. Artistically this had the unfortunate effect of giving her a meretricious reputation as a 'painting peeress' which obscured her genuine merit and which she bitterly resented, not least when financial embarrassment obliged her to exploit it.

In the war of 1939-45, after completing a series of commissions in America, Cathleen Mann was appointed an official war artist, working chiefly as a portraitist, her models including Sir Adrian Carton de Wiart. The post-war years were ones of great distress. Her marriage to Lord Queensberry was dissolved in 1946 and she married as her second husband John Robert Follett. His death in 1953 was followed in the next year by that of her first husband for whom she had never lost her affection. The impact of these events nearly caused a complete nervous breakdown from which she was saved only with difficulty and by the devotion of friends. Yet it was during this unhappy period that her painting took on new energy, through the influence of Sir Matthew Smith [q.v.]. Her best and most interesting work belonged to her last ten years and included a portrait of Smith (National Portrait Gallery), some remarkable child studies, and landscapes which often drew Smith's warm approbation. She also did a number of interesting drawings of nude models and with her ceaseless love of experiment made some vigorous essays in abstract painting and sculpture. Generous in her praise of other artists, she remained dissatisfied with her own achievement. She was fully aware of the handicap of her own excessive facility which could certainly lead her astray, especially in her fashionable years, and she often underestimated the originality of her later work. A study of a group of boys by the Serpentine, completed within a few days of her death, is among the best things she ever did.

Of diminutive stature and infectious vitality, Cathleen Mann appeared to enjoy limitless energy. She worked hard, often starting at dawn and continuing until last light. To this she added a full social life and numerous charitable works little known to her friends. But throughout life her high spirits had to be paid for in periods of nervous exhaustion which in later years became frequent and dangerous. It was during one of them that she took her own life, 8 September 1959, in her London studio. She had one son, the eleventh Marquess of Queensberry, and a daughter. In the possession of the Queensberry family there are portraits of

her by Harrington Mann (as a child and as a young woman) and by Sir Matthew Smith.

[*The Times*, 10 September 1959; personal knowledge.]   CHRISTOPHER SYKES.

MANSBRIDGE, ALBERT (1876-1952), founder of the Workers' Educational Association, was born at Gloucester 10 January 1876, the fourth son of Thomas Mansbridge, carpenter, and his wife, Frances Thomas. Educated at board schools and at Battersea Grammar School, of which he was a scholar, he ended his primary education when he was fourteen, owing to narrow home circumstances. During the next ten years he was occupied in clerical work, being a boy copyist in the Department of Inland Revenue and in the Committee of the Privy Council on Education (ultimately the Ministry of Education) and later a clerk in the Goldsmiths' and Silversmiths' Company and then in the Co-operative Wholesale Society, becoming, in 1901, cashier of the Co-operative Permanent Building Society. During these years he had continued his education by attending university extension lectures and classes at King's College, London; later, he himself became a teacher, under the London School Board, of evening classes in industrial history, typewriting, and economics. Always keenly interested in the Church of England, he was an active worker in its service and was admitted as a lay reader at the age of eighteen. It was at this time that he first met Charles Gore [q.v.], then a canon of Westminster, who remained his friend and counsellor for the rest of his life.

From his experiences of evening classes, both as a student and as a teacher, Mansbridge came to the conclusion that the time was ripe for a great development in adult education. The university extension movement, founded in 1873, which had made some appeal to the working classes, particularly in the north, had been discovered by the leisured classes, and by the end of the century had become mainly a middle-class movement. Mansbridge visualized a new organization, under which the demand for further education, however inarticulate and ill-defined it might appear, should come from the workers themselves, the function of the universities being to meet it. In other words, the demand was to create the supply rather than supply the demand, thus putting the initiative and the organization upon the workers themselves. On this assumption, he had contributed an article in January 1903 to the *University Extension Journal*, followed by two more (in March and May) in which he outlined a scheme for placing adult education on a new footing. In the same year he formed an Association to Promote the Higher Education of Working Men, a title afterwards changed to the Workers' Educational Association, and thus began the great work of his life. In August, the Association was placed on a permanent basis, with Mansbridge as its honorary secretary. In 1905 he resigned his post in the Co-operative Permanent Building Society, to become general secretary of the W.E.A. The first branch had been formed at Reading in October 1904, and for the next ten years Mansbridge was occupied in starting other branches all over the country, organizing them in districts and conducting ceaseless propaganda to win the support of working-class and academic opinion. William Temple [q.v.] became president of the Association in 1908 and it received recognition from most of the English universities.

Mansbridge considered that the outstanding creation of the W.E.A. in its early years was the university tutorial class. He had never ceased to regret that circumstances had denied him a university education, and the idea behind this further development of adult education was that those wishing to study the subjects of university extension lectures as completely as possible should pledge themselves to attend courses regularly for three years, to write essays and to read as widely as they could, under the direction of highly qualified university tutors. Backed by Mansbridge's unrivalled combination of moral earnestness and practical sense, the proposal quickly won its way in quarters which a less persuasive advocate might well have left unmoved. Canon S. A. Barnett and R. D. Roberts [qq.v.] had already contemplated continuous class study in connection with the university extension movement, and at Rochdale, with its strong educational tradition, as well as at several other centres, it had been the practice for the university extension lectures to be followed by a class. In 1906 a conference was held at the university of London, which resulted in a proposal to start a tutorial class, and in 1907 a class similar in some respects to those afterwards established under the same name met in Battersea under (Sir)

Patrick Geddes [q.v.]. A deputation of working men from Rochdale convinced T. B. Strong [q.v.], then chairman of the Oxford University Extension Delegacy, that there was a real demand, and (Sir) Robert Morant [q.v.], fired by the idea, did everything possible to secure the support of the Board of Education. As a result of a conference of working-class and educational organizations held at Oxford in 1907 under the auspices of the Workers' Educational Association, a committee was appointed consisting of seven persons nominated by the vice-chancellor and seven persons nominated by the Workers' Educational Association, which issued a report recommending that Oxford should promote the establishment of tutorial classes. In 1908, before the report appeared, classes of some thirty students at Rochdale and Longton pledged themselves to attend for three years and to write essays, and R. H. Tawney, then an assistant in political economy at Glasgow, undertook to be their tutor. The demand for classes spread rapidly, and by 1914 there were 145 in England and Wales, with 3,234 students attending them, undertaking work of university standard under tutors provided by every university in the country.

In 1913 Mansbridge visited Australia, on the invitation of the university of Melbourne, where he organized the foundation of the W.E.A. in each state of the Commonwealth. Briefer visits to New Zealand and Canada, on his way home, enabled him to arouse interest in the movement in these countries also. On his return to England, however, in 1914, he was stricken with cerebro-spinal meningitis, and after a long and grave illness he was compelled to retire from the secretaryship of the Association. In 1910 he had become a director of the Co-operative Permanent Building Society, and this, together with a Civil List pension and assistance from an educational trust fund formed by some of his friends, enabled him to continue his work for the promotion of adult education in various directions. Thus, in 1916, he saw the realization of his work for the foundation of a students' library, the Central Library for Students, afterwards renamed the National Central Library. Lack of access to the books necessary for advanced or specialized study by students unconnected with academic institutions, particularly with the increase in university tutorial classes, had induced an imperative need for an efficient central library containing many duplicates of essential books. Local libraries, public and otherwise, could have recourse to it for books not on their own shelves required by students, and, particularly, by groups of students attending advanced classes. Financial support was forthcoming from the beginning from the Carnegie United Kingdom Trust, and in due course a Treasury grant was approved conditional upon adequate contributions being made by public library authorities. Thus, in some dozen years, the organization of adult education, as Mansbridge had conceived it, was complete—in the W.E.A., the tutorial classes, and the National Central Library.

Although Mansbridge's health was never robust after his illness, he continued for the rest of his life, through writing, lecturing, organizing, and serving on numerous public bodies and commissions, to work for the cause of adult education. In 1918 he founded the World Association for Adult Education, in 1919 the Seafarers' Educational Service, and in 1921 the British Institute of Adult Education. He was a member of the adult education committee of the Ministry of Reconstruction, which reported in 1919, and of the royal commission on the universities of Oxford and Cambridge, which reported in 1922, and became a member of the statutory commission on Oxford in 1923. He delivered a course of lectures on the Lowell foundation, Boston, United States, in 1922 on 'The Older Universities of England', and in 1934 on 'An English Gallery'; and in 1926 on the Earle foundation in the university of California on 'The Spiritual Basis of Adult Education'. A selection of his essays and addresses, *The Kingdom of the Mind*, was published in 1944; his other published works included a life of Margaret McMillan (1932), whose notice he also contributed to this Dictionary, and *Brick upon Brick* (1934), an account of the Co-operative Permanent Building Society. He was made an honorary M.A. of Oxford in 1912, an honorary LL.D. of Manchester (1922), Cambridge (1923), Pittsburgh (1927), and Mount Allison (1938). In 1931 he was appointed a Companion of Honour.

Mansbridge married in 1900 Frances Jane, daughter of John Pringle, of Dublin. Their only child, John Mansbridge, the painter, was born in 1901. A portrait of Mansbridge, painted by his son, hangs in the board-room of the National

Central Library, another is in the National Portrait Gallery. He died at Torquay 22 August 1952.

[*The Times*, 25 and 30 August 1952; Albert Mansbridge, *An Adventure in Working-Class Education*, 1920, and *The Trodden Road*, 1940; T. W. Price, *The Story of the Workers' Educational Association, 1903–1924*, 1924; personal knowledge.]   C. S. ORWIN.

MANSON, THOMAS WALTER (1893–1958), biblical scholar, was born at North Shields, Northumberland, 22 July 1893, the only son of Thomas Francis Manson, schoolmaster in his own private school, and his wife, Joan, daughter of Walter Johnston, of Cunningsburgh, Shetland. The eldest child, he was followed by eight sisters. He was educated by his father, then at Tynemouth Municipal High School and Glasgow University where he took his M.A. with honours in logic and moral philosophy (1917), his course being interrupted by war service in the Royal Field Artillery during which he was wounded in France. In 1919 he was awarded the Clark scholarship by Glasgow and the Ferguson scholarship in philosophy open to all four Scottish universities. At Westminster College, Cambridge, he prepared for the ministry of the Presbyterian Church of England, and also entered Christ's College, gaining a first class in part ii of the oriental languages tripos, in Hebrew and Aramaic, in 1923. At Westminster College he was awarded the Crichton-Munro scholarship and the Williams and Elmslie open scholarships; Christ's College made him a research scholar and he won the Tyrwhitt Hebrew scholarship (1924) and the Burney (1923) and Mason (1924) prizes.

After a short period as tutor in Westminster College, Manson was ordained in 1925 at Howard Street church, North Shields, and served for a year in the Jewish Mission Institute in Bethnal Green. In 1926 he married and took charge of the church at Falstone, Northumberland. There he produced his first book, *The Teaching of Jesus* (1931), for which Glasgow awarded him a D.Litt. in 1932. His specialized work in Cambridge had been in Hebrew and Semitic studies in which he retained a lifelong interest and might readily have attained distinction; but with the publication of this book his eminence as a New Testament scholar was immediately recognized; thenceforth, his work lay principally in this field. It was enriched by his expert knowledge of the Old Testament and his access to rabbinical Hebrew and Syriac. Already he had taken a particular interest in the Septuagint, and this led to his developing interest in the Apocryphal and Pseudepigraphical literature. Later he acquired Coptic, making his linguistic equipment for New Testament work exceptionally strong; the breadth of his learning gave a richness to all his work which was widely recognized.

In 1932 Manson was appointed to the Yates chair of New Testament Greek in Mansfield College, Oxford, in succession to C. H. Dodd, and in 1936 he again succeeded Dodd, in the Rylands chair of biblical criticism at Manchester where he remained, despite attractive opportunities elsewhere, until his death. For many years he served as dean of the faculty of theology, and for four years as pro-vice-chancellor. He was also a governor of the John Rylands Library and a feoffee of Chetham's Library. In the war of 1939–45 he was an operations officer in the room which controlled civil defence operations in the north-west from Chester to Carlisle during the period of heavy bombing. He also took charge of St. Aidan's Presbyterian church, Didsbury.

Many honours came to him including the honorary degrees of D.D. from Glasgow (1937), Durham (1938), Cambridge (1951), Pine Hill (Halifax, Nova Scotia, 1953), and Trinity College, Dublin (1956), and of D.Theol., Strasbourg (1946). He was elected F.B.A. in 1945 and was awarded the Academy's Burkitt medal in 1950. He took a leading part in the formation of the *Studiorum Novi Testamenti Societas* and was its president in 1949–50. He lectured in universities in several foreign countries, was an honorary member of the American Society of Biblical Literature and Exegesis and of the Göttingen Akademie der Wissenschaften, and for many years delivered an annual lecture in the John Rylands Library. These were published in the library's *Bulletin* and a number reissued in a volume edited by Matthew Black, *Studies in the Gospels and Epistles* (1962).

Manson's books were not numerous, but were always important. Among them may be mentioned *The Sayings of Jesus* (Part II of *The Mission and Message of Jesus*, in collaboration, 1937; published separately, 1949); *The Church's Ministry* (1948); and *The Servant-Messiah* (1953). He was a member of the New Testament and Apocrypha panels for the preparation of the New English Bible. He accepted the editorship of the Cambridge Larger Septuagint (he had been Grinfield lecturer at Oxford, 1943–5) and had hoped to devote his retirement to the continuation of this great task.

With all his academic work Manson never lost his interest in the work of the Church. As a preacher he was welcomed in the pulpits of his own and other denominations. He was not gifted with a strong voice, but he could arrest and hold the interest of his congregation with a word which was always addressed to both mind and heart. For ten years he was president of the Manchester, Salford, and District Free Church Council, and in 1953 he was moderator of the General Assembly of the Presbyterian Church of England. He had great administrative gifts, which Manchester University fully exploited. His gentleness of spirit was combined with a strong conviction, and he could speak with much force and fire. He was a good raconteur, and his admirable wit showed to most advantage when he presented honorary graduands in the university (he was presenter for twenty years). He was a brilliant teacher, commanding the admiration and the affection of his students, for whom he would never spare himself. Every subject he touched he illuminated. Whatever he did he did well, and there were few things relevant to the career he chose which he did not do with supreme distinction.

In 1926 Manson married Nora, daughter of James Robert Wilkinson Wallace, master butcher, of North Shields; they had no children. Some time before his death, failing health caused him to move to Milnthorpe, Westmorland, near waters in which he had long delighted to fish. He died there, 1 May 1958. His colleagues and friends planned to present him with a *Festschrift* for his sixty-fifth birthday, but it became a memorial volume, *New Testament Essays* (ed. A. J. B. Higgins, 1959). The wide esteem in which he was held was shown by a memorial service held in Manchester Cathedral at which the bishop of Manchester gave the address.

[M. Black in *Proceedings* of the British Academy, vol. xliv, 1958; H. H. Rowley, foreword to *Studies in the Gospels and Epistles*, 1962; private information; personal knowledge.]

H. H. ROWLEY.

MARIE LOUISE, PRINCESS, whose full names were FRANZISKA JOSEPHA LOUISE AUGUSTA MARIE CHRISTIANA HELENA (1872–1956), was born at Cumberland

Lodge, Windsor, 12 August 1872, the youngest child of Prince Christian of Schleswig-Holstein and his wife, Princess Helena Augusta Victoria, Queen Victoria's third daughter. Her conventional education at home was relieved by holidays with relations in Germany, during one of which visits she met Prince Aribert of Anhalt. With the encouragement of her cousin the Emperor William II she married him in St. George's chapel, Windsor, 6 July 1891. He proved an unsatisfactory husband. After nine distressing years the childless marriage was annulled by Prince Aribert's father, exercising his medieval right as a sovereign prince. The Princess, a devout churchwoman, believed her wedding vows to be binding and never remarried.

Returning to her family in England, she devoted more than half a century of her life to furthering charitable causes and social services. Nursing, the care of lepers, youth clubs, the relief of poverty, and organizations for international understanding particularly touched her imagination. She became a familiar figure at balls and bazaars, committees and receptions, commemorative services and picture exhibitions. Standing above average height and with imposing features, she brought to all formal occasions an air of dignity softened by kindliness. Her neat and pointed speeches always refreshed and sometimes surprised her audience. There was charm, too, in her conversation. She was a tireless traveller, and few corners of the world had escaped her curiosity or failed to stimulate her talents for humour and mimicry.

Princess Marie Louise's patronage of the arts enabled her to acquire a wider circle of friends than usually surrounds royal personages. She moved at ease in the society of writers, actors, and musicians, and at one time in her life lived contentedly in a bedsitting-room at a ladies' club. Her happiest years were spent between the wars at Schomberg House, Pall Mall, which she shared with her sister Princess Helena Victoria [q.v.]. Together they gave memorable parties which became a valued institution among London music lovers. From her mother Princess Marie Louise had inherited a passion for Bach, to which was added a later appreciation of Wagner. She visited Bayreuth more than once, attended Covent Garden regularly, and was the friend of Lauritz Melchior, the tenor.

Among the Princess's recreations was the delicate art of enamelling in precious metals. Her work in this medium includes the clasp on the cope worn by the prelate of the Order of St. Michael and St. George. She was also an assiduous collector of Napoleonic relics, though free from the megalomania which often accompanies such a pursuit. A self-imposed task which gave her pleasure was the planning of an elaborate doll's house, now at Windsor Castle, for presentation to Queen Mary. To secure contributions to this record of twentieth-century craftsmanship she wrote two thousand letters in her own masterful but barely legible hand.

Throughout her long life the Princess was a voracious reader, particularly of history, biography, and detective fiction. In November 1956 she published a volume of her own reminiscences. *My Memories of Six Reigns*, of which 40,000 copies were sold within a few months, is a penetrating portrait of a vanished age. In a style of confiding intimacy, the Princess mingled a playful disrespect for the etiquette of German courts with a loving reverence for her grandmother Queen Victoria. Although in visibly failing health she insisted on attending a luncheon to mark the publication of the book, but was unable personally to deliver the message of greeting she had composed for all who shared her delight in writing.

She died a few days later, 8 December 1956, at her grace-and-favour residence in Fitzmaurice Place. The funeral was at Windsor on 14 December, that most melancholy of dates in Victorian memory, exactly ninety-five years after the death of her grandfather the Prince Consort. The congregation in St. George's chapel included three 'pearly queens' and a 'pearly king' who, in the gay colours of their calling, had come from Finsbury to pay a farewell tribute to their friend and patron. The remains of the Princess were later transferred to the private cemetery at Frogmore.

Princess Marie Louise, the last British princess to bear the style of Highness, was also one of the last surviving members of the Royal Order of Victoria and Albert. She was appointed a lady of the Imperial Order of the Crown of India by Queen Victoria (1893), G.B.E. by King George V (1919), and G.C.V.O. by Queen Elizabeth II (1953). There is a portrait by Harrington Mann in the Forum Club, Belgrave Square.

[H. H. Princess Marie Louise, *My Memories of Six Reigns*, 1956; private information; personal knowledge.]   KENNETH ROSE.

MARILLIER, HENRY CURRIE (1865–1951), journalist and expert on tapestries, was born at Grahamstown, South Africa, 2 July 1865, the eldest child and only son of Captain Charles Henry Marillier of the Cape Mounted Rifles and formerly fellow of King's College, Cambridge. His mother, Margaret, daughter of Alexander Braithwaite Morgan, surgeon to the 57th Regiment of Foot, had been brought up in Grahamstown by her uncle Sir Walter Currie who was Marillier's godfather. In 1870 Marillier's father became aide-de-camp to his brother-in-law Major-General (Sir) John Jarvis Bisset at Gibraltar and died there suddenly in 1875.

Instead of going to Eton, Marillier was entered at Christ's Hospital, leaving with a scholarship for Peterhouse, Cambridge, where, helped by friendship with his father's contemporaries at King's, he was able to make the most of his social opportunities. He was a member of the Shelley Society, interested in the performance of the *Eumenides* and entertained Oscar Wilde [q.v.]. He took a second class (division 2) in part i of the classical tripos in 1887, and having previously failed to obtain a Royal Engineers' commission in the Indian Army, he travelled to Egypt as private secretary to F. A. Yeo, M.P. He then worked at Hinchinbrooke on the papers of the fourth Earl of Sandwich [q.v.], discovering letters from Lady Mary Fitzgerald, a selection from which he later quoted in a paper read in 1897 (published 1910) before the Sette of Odd Volumes to which he was knyght-erraunt. In the following year he read another paper on 'University Magazines and their Makers' which was published in 1899.

In search of experience Marillier meanwhile entered the turbine works of (Sir) Charles Parsons [q.v.] at Heaton as a labourer's apprentice, and after two years became the outside manager, supervising the electrical tests of Chilean gunboats at Laird's, Birkenhead. Before his marriage in 1893 he went to London to study with the idea of becoming a consulting engineer, but instead accepted the editorship of *Lighting*, a new electrical weekly. In the golden age of freelance journalism, Marillier began to contribute occasional verse to the *Pall Mall Gazette*, and after his articles in October 1893 showing up Harness's 'electropathic belt' joined the editorial staff of H. J. C. Cust [q.v.] as scientific correspondent. This led to his reporting on the Nobel patents

case, investigating the growing of opium, a flight in the steam-driven aeroplane of (Sir) Hiram Maxim [q.v.] and later in the first Zeppelin.

Becoming interested in book illustration, Marillier wrote the biographies to go with the outstandingly good photogravure and half-tone reproductions of *Men and Women of the Century* (1896) portrayed by Rudolf Lehmann [q.v.], and after Cust left the *Pall Mall Gazette*, Marillier joined Cameron Swan, his wife's cousin, in the Swan Electric Engraving Company. His circle of friends in the world of art widened, he wrote the preface to the *Early Works of Aubrey Beardsley* printed by the Swan Company (1899) and then a memoir of D. G. Rossetti (1899) with a chronological list of paintings. George Rae of Birkenhead who owned a number of Rossetti's paintings next encouraged Marillier to write *The Liverpool School of Painters 1810–67* (1904) which has remained a standard work. In the meantime Marillier had joined W. A. S. Benson's art metal business, but the vogue for beaten copperwork was already passing.

Although he had rented Kelmscott House, Hammersmith, from Mrs. Morris since 1897, Marillier did not enter the Morris company until 1905. There again he found a decline, but as the demand for Morris textiles fell, he wisely developed the craft of repairing tapestries. In the war of 1914–18, during which Marillier was an anti-aircraft gunner in London, the Merton Abbey Tapestry Works profitably manufactured aeroplane propellers; but the post-war deterioration of materials, especially of dyes, led to further loss of business. In 1940 Marillier wound up the company, having written the history of its tapestries in 1927. Many of the original designs passed into the hands of museums, but all the records of the firm were destroyed.

During the last thirty years of his life Marillier's most important work was the compilation of a huge subject-index and illustrated catalogue of the tapestries of Europe. On behalf of the Morris company he visited most of the larger private houses in the United Kingdom; he collected photographs on the Continent, and advised collectors of tapestries, dealers, and auctioneers. When in 1945 the material was finally given to the department of textiles in the Victoria and Albert Museum, it extended to fifty volumes of script and photographs. Marillier wrote occasional articles on tapestries, including those at Hampton Court (1912), but only published two sections of his researches, *English Tapestries of the Eighteenth Century* (1930) and a *Handbook to the Teniers Tapestries* (1932).

Marillier left Kelmscott House soon after his second marriage and lived in St. John's Wood until 1940, when he and his wife joined Sir Ernest Pooley at Westbrook House near Petworth. After the war he continued to act as a tapestry consultant. He died 27 July 1951 at his home and was buried in Brighton cemetery.

Marillier was a sociable man, musical, keen on travel, fishing, and shooting. He belonged to the Bath Club and finally to the Athenaeum where he found congenial company. He was twice married: first, in 1893, to Katherine Isabella (died 1901), daughter of John Pattinson, public analyst of Newcastle upon Tyne. They had two daughters. In 1906 Marillier married Winifred Christabel, daughter of Arthur Hopkins, artist, by whom he had one son.

[*The Times*, 28 July 1951; unpublished autobiographical notes; private information; personal knowledge.]   J. L. NEVINSON.

MARKHAM, VIOLET ROSA (1872–1959), public servant, was born at Brimington Hall, near Chesterfield, Derbyshire, 3 October 1872, the younger daughter and fifth child of Charles Markham, colliery owner, and his wife, Rosa, daughter of Sir Joseph Paxton [q.v.], designer of the Crystal Palace. A few months later the family moved to Tapton House, once the home of George Stephenson [q.v.], on a hill a mile outside Chesterfield.

Violet Markham went to no university. At West Heath, Ham Common, she learned a great deal; but she always declared that she received most of her education from her mother. She grew up in a house where mining problems were daily discussed although the living conditions of the miners were seldom touched upon. She herself early turned her mind to the study of the slum conditions in which they lived with no recreational facilities. In 1902 she started a settlement in Chesterfield where she met with opposition, incredulity, and even ridicule, but she persisted in her project and for many years to come her settlement was a centre for a wide variety of activities.

In 1901 she had received a legacy from an old friend of her father which made her independent and she set up house at Gower Street, London, which soon became a meeting-place for many people who counted in the worlds of politics, the arts and personal social service. In the war of 1914–18, through the influence of Sir Robert Morant [q.v.], she joined the executive committee of the National Relief Fund; and in 1917 she was deputy director under her friend May Tennant (whose notice she contributed to this Dictionary) of the women's section of Neville Chamberlain's department of national service.

In common with many other members of the Liberal Party, Violet Markham was opposed to women's suffrage, although she never ceased to declare that women should take part in local government and herself sat on the committees of many and varied public bodies. In the course of the war she changed her views and in 1918 she stood for the Mansfield division of Nottinghamshire which was a supposedly safe Liberal seat and had been represented by her brother Sir Arthur Markham from 1900 until his death in 1916. She was handsomely beaten by the Labour candidate and never again stood for Parliament. Her rejection was unfortunate, for she would have made her mark in the House. She was an admirable debater, her speeches in both form and content were on a high level of excellence; and she had formidable powers of hard work. These she now devoted to a very heavy programme of public service. She had been a member since its inception in 1914, and was for many years chairman, of the Central Committee on Women's Training and Employment which in its first twenty years trained nearly 100,000 women, principally for domestic service. She was especially interested in this side of the committee's work for what she had seen of the conditions of domestic service made her wish to raise its status. In 1919 she was appointed a member of the Industrial Court and she was an early member of the lord chancellor's advisory committee for women justices. In 1934 she entered upon what was probably the most important work of her life when she joined the new Assistance Board of which she was deputy chairman in 1937–46.

In addition to her work in London and in Chesterfield (where she was town councillor (1924), mayor (1927), and vice-chairman of the education committee),

Violet Markham was interested in the overseas dominions, especially Canada and South Africa, countries which she visited more than once. She kept in regular touch with W. L. Mackenzie King [q.v.] of whom she wrote an admirable character sketch in her book *Friendship's Harvest* (1956). In 1923 she represented the Canadian Government on the governing body of the International Labour Office in Geneva.

After the outbreak of war in 1939, while continuing with her work on the Assistance Board, she started and largely financed and ran a canteen in south London. When the canteen was bombed she started it again in other premises. She also sat on the appeal tribunal on the internment of aliens and others under the defence of the realm regulations, and on an advisory committee on air-raid shelters. In 1942 when there were highly coloured rumours of immorality in the women's Services she was chairman of a committee of investigation whose report to a great extent dissipated the rumours and paid strong tribute to the work and courage of the members of the women's Services. She coined the phrase 'virtue has no gossip value'. In 1945 she and (Dame) Florence Hancock turned their minds to post-war organization of private domestic employment. Their report published in June of that year attracted much interest. She also lectured for the British Council in France and elsewhere.

Violet Markham was a woman of middle height who wore appropriate and well-chosen clothes. She had small features and dark expressive eyes. Her movements expressed a controlled force and energy. She talked well, throwing out ideas and showing great fairness when discussing controversial matters with companions who disagreed with her. Her house in the country, Moon Green, near Wittersham in Kent, was a converted oasthouse to which she had added a library and other rooms. It stood in a pleasant garden and orchards and was a place of welcome and cheerfulness. She had a succession of Labrador dogs to which she was devoted. She enjoyed good wine, good food, warmth and comfort, and she saw to it that as many people as possible enjoyed these good things with her. Many who spend much of their time sitting on committees tend to regard people as 'cases' and to legislate for them in the mass. Violet Markham had the rare gift of seeing everyone with whom she came in contact as an individual and however busy she was she entered with zest into their joys and sorrows and difficulties. Her generosity with her time was amazing and her financial help to those in need prompt, useful, and anonymous.

In 1915 she married Lieutenant-Colonel James Carruthers, D.S.O., M.V.O., younger son of Peter Carruthers of Portrack, Dumfriesshire. She continued for the convenience of her public life to be known (except to her friends) by her maiden name. After the war she accompanied her husband to Cologne where he had a command and in 1921 she published *A Woman's Watch on the Rhine* in which she packed a great deal of shrewd observation. Her marriage surprised her friends for Colonel Carruthers was a racehorse owner whose interests were not primarily intellectual. But she added an interest in racing to her own widely different ones and she grieved deeply when her husband died suddenly in 1936. They had no children.

In her last years Violet Markham had to fight against blindness, but sustained by the deep religious faith to which she came through the influence of Hensley Henson [q.v.], she neither grumbled nor complained but carried on with her work. Her books include *Paxton and the Bachelor Duke* (1935) which treats of her grandfather's work at Chatsworth; her autobiography *Return Passage* (1953); and *Friendship's Harvest* in which she gives recollections of her friends, among them Lord Haldane, Sir Robert Morant, Thomas Jones, and John Buchan [qq.v.]. She wrote discursively but with vividness and sincerity. Her autobiography gives a picture of her upbringing in a rich mine owner's household. Her innate sense of fairness made her show the best of those days as well as the darker and less fortunate lives of many people at that time. She was equally fair in describing what she felt to be the gains and also the losses sustained by her own country in the latter days in which she wrote.

Violet Markham was appointed C.H. in 1917; received the honorary degrees of Litt.D. (Sheffield, 1936) and LL.D. (Edinburgh, 1938), and the freedom of Chesterfield (1952). She was a fellow of the Royal Historical Society and the Royal Geographical Society. She died at Moon Green 2 February 1959.

[*The Times*, 3 February 1959; Violet Markham, *Return Passage*, 1953; personal knowledge.]   SUSAN TWEEDSMUIR.

MARSH, SIR EDWARD HOWARD (1872–1953), civil servant, scholar, and patron of the arts, was born in London 18 November 1872, the second child and only son of Frederick Howard Marsh, by his first wife, Jane, daughter of Spencer Perceval, Irvingite angel to Italy and eldest son of Spencer Perceval [q.v.], the prime minister who was assassinated in 1812 in the lobby of the House of Commons. Jane Perceval had become a nurse and had founded in Queen Street the Alexandra Hospital for Children with Hip Disease where she had met her husband, a surgeon who later became professor of surgery at Cambridge and (1907–15) master of Downing College. Their elder daughter died in infancy; the younger married Sir Frederick Maurice [q.v.]. As a result of mumps and German measles in early adolescence Marsh was destined never to marry. He was educated at Westminster, studying Greek under W. Gunion Rutherford [q.v.], and at Trinity College, Cambridge, where he continued his classical studies, specializing in the emendation of texts under A. W. Verrall [q.v.]. This grounding in pure scholarship prepared 'Eddie' Marsh for the work which occupied his leisure in the latter part of his life. He obtained first classes in both parts of the classical tripos (1893–5) and in the latter year was awarded the senior Chancellor's medal. At Cambridge his view of life was influenced by his close friendship with his fellow 'Apostles' G. E. Moore [q.v.] and Bertrand (later Earl) Russell; whilst through Maurice Baring [q.v.] he was brought to the notice of (Sir) Edmund Gosse [q.v.] who admitted him to his literary circle in London. His association with Oswald Sickert, editor of the short-lived *Cambridge Observer*, gave him the opportunity for his first essays in criticism, and through his ardent championship of Ibsen, whose work was then making its first appearance on the English stage, Marsh attracted considerable attention before ever he was launched upon a professional career.

In 1896 he was appointed a junior clerk in the Australian department of the Colonial Office under Joseph Chamberlain and subsequently Alfred Lyttelton [qq.v.]. By December 1905 he had become a first class clerk and was at work in the West African department when (Sir) Winston Churchill became parliamentary under-secretary for the colonies and invited Marsh to become his private secretary.

For the next twenty-three years Marsh was at Churchill's right hand whenever he was in office. He toured British East Africa, Uganda, and Egypt with him in 1907–8; followed him to the Board of Trade (1908–10) and to the Home Office (1910–11), being present with him at the Sidney Street siege. In 1911 he moved with him to the Admiralty where he saw the pre-war reconstitution of the fleet, the foundation of the Royal Naval Air Service, and the early vicissitudes of war culminating in the failure to force the Dardanelles. From May to November 1915 Churchill was chancellor of the Duchy of Lancaster; on his departure on active service in the army Marsh became an assistant private secretary to the prime minister, his especial responsibility being the Civil List pensions, in which capacity he was able to be of assistance to James Joyce [q.v.] and others. After Asquith's fall in December 1916 Marsh was virtually unemployed until Churchill was appointed minister of munitions (July 1917) and subsequently (1919–21) secretary of state for war. Marsh went with him in 1921 to the Colonial Office where he played a more than normally active part in negotiations over the Irish treaty. He remained at the Colonial Office as secretary to the Duke of Devonshire (1922–4) and (1924) to J. H. Thomas [qq.v.] and then served for the last time under Churchill, at the Treasury (1924–9). When Labour came into power in 1929 he returned to J. H. Thomas, moving with him to the Dominions Office in 1930. There he remained until his retirement in February 1937, serving from November 1935 as secretary to Malcolm MacDonald.

While still at Cambridge Marsh had made the acquaintance of W. R. Sickert [q.v.] through the latter's brother Oswald, but it was not until 1896 when he met Neville (later the Earl of) Lytton, then an art student in Paris, that Marsh began to cultivate the eye of an art connoisseur and started collecting pictures. With Lytton's guidance he specialized at first in the English water-colourists, in particular Girtin, Sandby, Cotman, and the two Cozens [qq.v.], and in 1904, through the good offices of Robert Ross, acquired the Horne collection of drawings, so that almost overnight he became one of the most important private collectors in the country. The turning-point came in December 1911, when his purchase of a painting by Duncan Grant, contrary to

Lytton's advice, led him to launch out on his own as a patron of contemporary British painting, and he gathered around him several of the young men from the Slade, chief among them John Currie and Mark Gertler [q.v.]. Turning his back on the past he also took under his wing the brothers John and Paul Nash [q.v.] and (Sir) Stanley Spencer [q.v.], and by 1914 had brought together the nucleus of what was to be one of the most valuable collections of modern work in private hands.

Meanwhile he had been no less active in the field of literature and his apartments at 5 Raymond Buildings, Gray's Inn, had become the rendezvous of poets as well as painters. Early in 1912 his critical appreciation of the poems of Rupert Brooke (whose notice he was to write for this Dictionary) in the *Poetry Review* brought him the acquaintance of Harold Monro [q.v.] and established his friendship with Brooke on a new footing. A casual remark of Brooke's led to the scheme of an anthology of modern verse which Marsh undertook to edit under the title *Georgian Poetry*. With Monro's Poetry Bookshop as the publishing house the anthology appeared in December 1912 and eventually developed into a series of five volumes published over a period of ten years. During those years Marsh introduced to the general reader almost three generations of poets. Among the original 'Georgians' were Brooke, J. E. Flecker, Lascelles Abercrombie, Gordon Bottomley, W. H. Davies, Walter de la Mare, and D. H. Lawrence [qq.v.]. In 1917 a new group appeared, characterized by the powerful 'realistic' war poetry of Siegfried Sassoon, Robert Nichols [q.v.], and Robert Graves. The fourth volume (1919) revealed a certain limitation of theme and a pervading mannerism of style, and although the fifth volume of the series (1922) introduced Edmund Blunden, yet another new poet of high promise, it was clear that the movement had played itself out, yielding place to a less traditional conception of poetry derived from the pre-war work of T. E. Hulme and Ezra Pound.

By instituting a royalty system instead of outright payment Marsh was able to make the anthologies of considerable benefit to his contributors over the years, and through undertaking to do the accounting himself he not only kept himself in regular touch with his poetical 'family' but was often able to eke out their portion with a small gift wherever there was hardship. For this Marsh used what he called his 'murder money', a source of income which he had inherited on the death of an uncle in 1903, being one-sixth of what remained of the compensation granted to the Perceval family in 1812. This fund, now reserved for the patronage of the arts, was augmented by the royalties from Marsh's memoir of Rupert Brooke, a biographical essay attached as introduction to the *Collected Poems* which he edited and brought out in 1918. From the poet's death in 1915 until 1934 he was indefatigable as literary executor, editing Brooke's posthumous prose and verse, thereby laying the basis of Brooke's reputation.

By the end of the Georgian enterprise a new interest had entered Marsh's life when he began translating the Fables of La Fontaine. These came out in two small volumes, followed by a complete edition in two volumes in 1931. Thereafter he published translations of the *Odes of Horace* (1941), Fromentin's *Dominique* (1948), and two works by the Princess Marthe Bibesco, *The Sphinx of Bagatelle* (1951) and *Proust's Oriane* (1952). In 1939 he published a book of reminiscences entitled *A Number of People*, and in 1952 the Fables were reissued in Everyman's Library. A scholarly form of hobby which proved of considerable benefit to English letters was the correcting of proofs for other authors which in Marsh's practice was an elaborate process involving the composition of numerous notes on syntax, literary style, matters of fact, and conduct of the writer's argument. His first major operation of this kind was Churchill's *Marlborough* (4 vols., 1933–8), which was followed by all Churchill's subsequent literary productions up to the first volume of the *History of the English-Speaking Peoples* (1956). In 1934 Marsh was invited by Somerset Maugham to do likewise for his *Don Fernando* (1935) and the next fifteen of that author's productions were submitted to Marsh's painstaking scrutiny.

On his retirement from the Civil Service Marsh was appointed a trustee of the Tate Gallery and a governor of the Old Vic, having for several years served on the committee of the Contemporary Art Society (of which he was chairman, 1936–52) and the council of the Royal Society of Literature. His taste in contemporary painting advanced with the times with easier adaptability than his appreciation of verse, yet he remained loyal to the principles of representational art as against the various 'abstract' manifestations which won favour in his time. His thorough grounding in the Greek and Roman classics, and his friendship with Robert Bridges [q.v.] which began in boyhood, determined his predilection for verse in the central tradition. In spite of an abnormally acute aesthetic sensibility, his temperament was essentially methodical and rational, so that the one side of his nature was nicely balanced by the other, checking him from ever erring to an extreme on either side, except at the theatre where, by his own admission, he enjoyed the play like a child, and showed it. Through his friendship with Ivor Novello [q.v.] he developed an ardent enthusiasm for first nights.

In appearance Marsh was fair-haired, a little over middle height, broad-shouldered, erect in carriage, groomed to a nicety, and invariably composed in manner. He used a monocle to point his discourse, but was most easily distinguished from the throng by his tufted eyebrows swept up at their outer extremities lending this genial and softly-spoken scholar a curiously mephistophelian air. Although correct in the presentation of himself, almost to the point of dandyism, his physical make-up was of exceptional toughness; he set high store by the creature comforts of food and drink in society, but his life at home was plain and on occasion almost Spartan. He was eminently sociable, though at first his somewhat stiff demeanour could be forbidding to a stranger. Always anxious to please in social intercourse, which was his favourite pastime, for he was a master of anecdote, nevertheless he could be ruthlessly uncompromising whenever one of his cherished principles of scholarship was at stake. He was agnostic in religion and in the literal sense conservative in politics. His was an eighteenth-century cast of mind, and his humorous observation of men and manners was brilliantly served by an easy gift for gossiping on paper with wit and elegance, so that the reader of his letters is inevitably reminded of Horace Walpole [q.v.]. Asked what he would say if told that he would die next day, he replied without hesitation 'Thanks for the party'. In him the late Victorian educational system with its aristocratic tradition produced what was perhaps its most highly evolved and representative figure. He died, 13 January 1953, in the Knightsbridge flat which had been his post-war home.

Marsh was appointed K.C.V.O. on his retirement in 1937. There are portraits by Sir Oswald Birley in the National Portrait Gallery and by Neville Lewis in the possession of the Royal Society of Literature. He featured in a conversation piece by Anthony Devas which remained the property of the painter. A drawing by Violet, Duchess of Rutland, became the property of Mr. Wilfrid Gibson. There are also portraits by Leonard Applebee, Neville Lytton, and (Sir) Winston Churchill, a pencil drawing by Joan Hassall, and a portrait bust by Frank Dobson. Marsh featured with Churchill in two caricatures by Sir Max Beerbohm.

[Sir Edward Marsh, *A Number of People*, 1939; *Eddie Marsh, Sketches for a Composite Literary Portrait*, ed. Christopher Hassall and Denis Mathews, 1953; Christopher Hassall, *Edward Marsh, A Biography*, 1959; personal knowledge.]   CHRISTOPHER HASSALL.

MARSHALL, SIR GUY ANSTRUTHER KNOX (1871–1959), entomologist, was born in Amritsar, Punjab, 20 December 1871, the only son of (Colonel) Charles Henry Tilson Marshall, Bengal Staff Corps, and his wife, Laura Frances, daughter of Sir Jonathan Frederick Pollock, first baronet [q.v.]. His uncle was Major-General George Frederick Leycester Marshall, R.E. Both these distinguished officers were keen naturalists, Marshall's father being joint author with A. O. Hume [q.v.] of *The Game Birds of India, Burmah and Ceylon* (3 vols., 1879–81), whilst his uncle wrote on *Birds' Nesting in India* (1877) and on the butterflies of India, Burma, and Ceylon.

Marshall was sent at an early age to a preparatory school at Margate, where his interest in natural history was further stimulated by his headmaster. At Charterhouse (on the governing body of which he was later to serve) he transferred his attentions from butterflies to beetles, considered a less eccentric hobby. He failed the Indian Civil Service examinations to his father's disappointment but perhaps not greatly to his own. His father's reaction was to pack him off at the age of nineteen to a sheep farmer in Natal; for the next fifteen years he had a most varied career, leaving the sheep farm to become a cattle man and later to join a firm of mining engineers in Salisbury, Rhodesia. Finally he became co-manager of the Salisbury Building and Estates Company.

Despite these activities Marshall maintained the keenest interest in entomology.

By 1896 he was in touch with (Sir) Edward Poulton [q.v.], Hope professor of zoology at Oxford, who encouraged him to carry out a considerable series of experiments on mimicry and protective resemblance, the results of which appeared under their joint authorship in the *Transactions* of the Entomological Society of London in 1902. It was presumably through Poulton's influence that Marshall was appointed curator of the Sarawak Museum in 1906, but on his way there he was taken ill in London with a complaint contracted in Africa and had to relinquish the post.

In 1909 Marshall was appointed scientific secretary to the Entomological Research Committee (Tropical Africa) by the secretary of state for the colonies. It was from this committee that there evolved in 1913 the Imperial Bureau (later the Commonwealth Institute) of Entomology of which Marshall was director until he retired in 1942. Soon after the Bureau came into being, war broke out and Marshall's energy, foresight, and guidance helped it to survive this critical period; his accurate assessment of the needs of overseas entomologists, from his own personal experience, enabled him to lay down the sound lines on which its future development was based. The function of the Bureau was to act as a centre of information on all matters relating to insect pests and so successfully was this carried out that the Bureau formed the model for the creation subsequently of two new institutes and ten bureaux covering all branches of agricultural science. All these information services were brought together in 1933 under an organization later known as the Commonwealth Agricultural Bureaux.

Marshall played an important role as adviser on entomological matters to the Colonial Office between the two world wars and in advising on specific problems, thus exerting a direct influence on the development of economic entomology in the colonies; he was always ready to welcome entomologists from the colonies and to hear about their work and problems, and he never ceased to stimulate, inspire, and help them. His reputation was such that he was well known personally or by repute to entomologists throughout the world irrespective of nationality. These contacts throughout the years enabled him to amass an encyclopedic knowledge of world entomology and entomologists.

Marshall's career was remarkable in that he had never attended a university or received any formal education in science. Moreover he did not take up entomology as a profession until the age of thirty-eight, but his family background coupled with his enthusiastic amateur spare-time work stood him in good stead. Consequently he was not unduly impressed by academic degrees despite the fact that the university of Oxford conferred an honorary D.Sc. on him in 1915. His outlook was also unorthodox in that he did not allow his choice of staff to be hampered by nationalistic considerations and at various times he appointed a Russian, a Swiss, a Dutchman, and Canadians. He was a firm believer in commercial companies and insecticide manufacturers employing their own entomologists and his influence in the latter direction did much to raise the standard of insecticide products. In later years he developed an interest in commercial entomology and founded one of the first companies for pest control which occupied him for some years after his retirement.

After he left Africa in 1906 Marshall's personal research work was almost exclusively taxonomic. Through his identification work in the early days at the Bureau he developed a wide knowledge of all groups of insects but he came to specialize on the beetles of the family Curculionidae. His choice of this particular field was determined by the curious accident that when he returned to England on leave in 1896 the greater part of his beetle collection was lost in transit and there survived only the Curculionidae which happened to have been packed separately, so that he was able to study this weevil material at the British Museum during his leave. Altogether he published some 200 papers on the Curculionidae, including several major works, and he described some 2,300 species new to science. He was an acknowledged authority on the family on which he continued to work at the Natural History Museum until a very few weeks before his death in London 8 April 1959.

Marshall was a very able administrator who believed in delegating responsibility and seldom interfered unless it became necessary or his advice was sought; he was most approachable. He was of medium height, compact build, and distinguished appearance; he never sought publicity and was by nature of a retiring disposition. He consistently refused to accept the presidency of the Royal Entomological Society of London. He was elected F.R.S.

in 1923 and was an honorary member of many overseas societies. He was appointed C.M.G. in 1920, knighted in 1930, advanced to K.C.M.G. in 1942, and received the Belgian Order of the Crown.

In 1933 he married Hilda Margaret (died 1964), daughter of the late David Alexander Maxwell and widow of James Ffolliott Darling. They had no children.

[*The Annals and Magazine of Natural History*, 13th Series, vol. i, 1958–9; *Nature*, 16 May 1959; W. R. Thompson in *Biographical Memoirs of Fellows of the Royal Society*, vol. vi, 1960; personal knowledge.]

W. J. HALL.

MARSHALL, SIR JOHN HUBERT (1876–1958), archaeologist, was born at Chester 19 March 1876, the youngest son of Frederic Marshall, who took silk in 1893, by his first wife, Annie, daughter of J. B. Evans, of Wanfield Hall, Staffordshire. He was educated at Dulwich College and King's College, Cambridge, where he took first classes in the classical tripos (1898–1900), was Porson prizeman (1898), Prendergast Greek student (1900), and Craven student (1901). From 1898 to 1901 he was at the British School at Athens and took part in the excavations then beginning in Crete. In 1902, in spite of his youth and inexperience, he was appointed to the director-generalship of archaeology in India, a post which, after a long period of neglect, had just been revived and greatly enlarged by the viceroy, Lord Curzon [q.v.].

The task which awaited Marshall in India was immense. Throughout the land age-long indifference had imperilled ancient structures, sculptures, and painting, often of great beauty and importance. No methodical effort had been made to explore the buried history and prehistory of the sub-continent. There was no antiquities law on a modern pattern. Marshall, improvising as he went along, resurrected the Archaeological Survey of India on an adequate scale and turned it first to the clearance and conservation of upstanding structures. Alongside this urgent work of salvage he began to survey and dig, and in 1913 inaugurated the systematic exploration of the ancient Taxila, near Rawalpindi, a project which was to occupy some part of his attention for more than twenty years. The results, published in 1951, justified his persistence. For a thousand years (500 B.C.–A.D. 500) Taxila had been both a local capital and a trading station on an arterial route into India; with it were associated the names of Alexander the Great, the Buddhist king Asoka, King Gondofares, St. Thomas and Kanishka. Its periodical removal from site to site in the same general locality helped incidentally to provide an automatic substitute for archaeological stratification, which Marshall never adequately understood. Even more important in a wider view was his development, in and after 1922, of discoveries made by members of his staff in the Indus valley of the Punjab and Sind. His announcement in 1924 that he had there found a new civilization of the third millennium marked an epoch in modern discovery; the so-called Indus Valley Civilization is now recognized as the most extensive civilization of the pre-classical world. Parallel with these enterprises he directed a large number of projects which partook rather of conservation than of excavation: notably on the great Buddhist site of Sanchi in central India, where his restorations gave a new meaning and security to a remarkable group of buildings and carvings mostly of the last two centuries B.C.

Marshall's methods were often summary, and have been criticized; and it is true that, preoccupied from an early age and largely in isolation with a task of gigantic proportions, he was insufficiently aware of developing standards and modes in the West. But alike at Taxila and in his exploration of the Indus Valley Civilization at Mohenjo-daro, his wholesale and speedy methods revealed expressive, if synthetic, pictures of great cities in a measure which more scientific and necessarily slower techniques would have failed to approach. His mass-excavation of large areas at Mohenjo-daro, for example, published in 1931, showed a great city, dating from before and after 2000 B.C., planned and drained on a vast scale and in a regimented fashion, with wide thoroughfares and closely built houses and shops. Detail, and often important detail, was recklessly lost; but, like Schliemann before him, Marshall got to the heart of the matter and gave what was needed first in the current state of knowledge, namely the general shape, the sketch, of a thitherto unknown civilization. He was a pioneer of a high order.

His two major excavations, at Taxila and at Mohenjo-daro, are his outstanding contributions. Nevertheless, they represent but a fraction of his actual achieve-nent. There is scarcely a part of India, or Pakistan, or indeed of Burma, which also came within his province, where his care and zeal, particularly in conservation, are not manifest in one form or another. Behind all this lay the tedious negotiation and persuasion constantly necessitated by a Government and people which, apart from Curzon's initial stimulus, were not yet ready to appreciate the value of the country's immense heritage. As an administrator in these circumstances Marshall was personally brilliant; f he failed at any point, it was in the training of his colleagues in individual responsibility and in technical practice, with the result that his retirement from the director-generalship to take up special duties in 1928 (from which he finally retired in 1934) was followed by a sharp decline in standards. It has been said of him, with some truth, that he was 'a tree under which nothing grew'; but there are no two opinions about the splendour of the tree.

In the course of his work Marshall prepared a comprehensive Antiquities Law on the lines of those which had already been tried out by British authorities in western Asia and Europe. In modified form this law has remained in force and is a testimony to its draftsman. In this and in other ways he gradually brought under firm central control the monuments and ancient sites of 'British' India, and, by example and advice, those of the Indian states where his writ did not run. His successful work as conservator of ancient buildings aided this process; he began to create an appreciative if still uninstructed public opinion. He took especial delight in the restoration of the gardens which, particularly in Mogul India, had formed an essential feature of tombs and palaces but which had been allowed to decay or even to revert to jungle. Good taste lies at the core of good conservation and Marshall's taste was nearly impeccable. Thus it was that the consolidation of ancient structures in general accompanied by the re-creation of their ancient amenities and the recapture of much of their original beauty and significance. His work has remained as an accepted pattern and challenge to his successors.

During his active period of office Marshall produced a substantial *Annual Report* which is a permanent source. Otherwise his principal published works are *Mohenjo-Daro and the Indus Civili-*

zation (3 vols., 1931); *The Monuments of Sanchi* (with A. Foucher, 3 vols., Calcutta, 1940); and *Taxila* (3 vols., 1951).

Marshall was appointed C.I.E. in 1910 and knighted in 1914. He was elected an honorary fellow of King's College, Cambridge, in 1927 and F.B.A. in 1936. On the eve of sailing for India in 1902 he married Florence, daughter of Sir Henry Bell Longhurst, surgeon-dentist. They had one son and one daughter. Marshall died at Guildford 17 August 1958.

[Private information; personal knowledge.]
MORTIMER WHEELER.

MARTEL, SIR GIFFARD LE QUESNE (1889–1958), lieutenant-general, was born in Millbrook, Southampton, 10 October 1889, the only son of (Sir) Charles Philip Martel, later chief superintendent of ordnance factories, and his wife, Lilian Mary, daughter of W. H. Mackintosh, M.D. He was educated at Wellington College, where he won the Wellesley scholarship awarded annually to the top boy on the modern side, and represented the school in gymnastics. In 1908 he entered the Royal Military Academy, Woolwich, and the next year was commissioned in the Royal Engineers. In 1912 and 1913 he won the welterweight championship not only of the army but of the combined Services; after the war he won the army championship (1920) and the imperial Services championship (1921 and 1922).

In August 1914 Martel went to France where for two years he carried out the normal duties of a field company officer, attaining command of his unit in the second year. In the summer of 1916 he was sent home temporarily to design a practice battlefield, based on the trench-front in France, in the secret area at Thetford, in Norfolk, where the crews for the newly produced tanks were being trained. This had a far-reaching effect on his career: early in October, three weeks after the tanks had made their début on the battlefield in France, he was chosen for the key appointment of brigade-major in the small headquarters of the new arm at Bermicourt. There were only three other members, apart from the commander, (Sir) Hugh Elles [q.v.]; but in the following May, as the result of enlargements, Martel became G.S.O. 2 and was promoted from captain to major.

In November 1916 Martel wrote a paper entitled 'A Tank Army' (reprinted in *Our Armoured Forces*, 1945) which showed his long-range vision at a time when the tank was generally regarded as no more than a limited aid to the infantry assault, and when no tank could move at more than four miles an hour. His paper forecast the creation of 'tank armies' and their domination of future great wars. He proposed that they should be organized and operate like fleets at sea, with 'destroyer', 'battle', and 'torpedo' tanks, carrying with them in 'supply' tanks their requirements for an extensive operation. His forecast overlooked some basic differences between the conditions of sea and land warfare, and was only fulfilled in part, but it was of great value in lifting thought out of the rut of trench warfare. The extent to which Martel overshot the mark of potentiality was less than that by which the general run of military thought fell short.

In a more immediate way he contributed much to the performance of the Tank Corps in 1917-18 by his activity and boldness in reconnaissance. He was continually up at the front and lived up there with unit representatives during the preparatory period before offensives were launched. There is a vivid pen portrait of him in a private record written by Sir Evan Charteris. He described 'Q' Martel as a man:

Of a desperate bravery, who was, however, supposed to have an exact instinct for the falling place of shells and to be a very safe guide. He was a small, loose-limbed man, a natural bruiser, and winner of the army boxing, with a deep hoarse laugh which ... had a most peculiar note of good-humoured ferocity in it. Tales which made the ordinary mortal's flesh creep produced from him regular salvos of this notable laughter ... On leave, his idea of recreation was to shut himself up in a mobile workshop of his own and work at a lathe. At the front, his idea of pleasure was to get into a shelled area and dodge about to avoid the bursts.

After the war, during which he was appointed to the D.S.O. and awarded the M.C., Martel returned to duty with the Royal Engineers, and remained with them when the Royal Tank Corps was formed on a permanent basis in 1923, a choice for which he was later criticized by some of his comrades in the wartime Tank Corps and by others who joined it after its creation. But he continued to take a very active interest in the development of tanks and armoured warfare, writing much on the subject as well as conducting experimental work—initially in the prob-

lems of tank-bridging. Shortly before the armistice in November 1918 he had been sent home to command a tank bridging battalion of the Royal Engineers which had been formed at Christchurch in Hampshire, and after the war this was converted into an experimental establishment. One product of this period was the Martel box girder bridge, which became the standard girder bridge of the army in place of the more expensive and less adaptable tubular girder bridge.

In 1921 Martel went to the Staff College and after graduating was appointed in 1923 to the directorate of fortifications and works at the War Office, where he remained until the summer of 1926. Meanwhile he had become convinced of the need for small and inconspicuous armoured and tracked vehicles to aid and operate with, the infantry. Finding little official encouragement, he designed and built such a machine in the garage of his own house at Camberley, which he completed and demonstrated in 1925. At first called the 'one-man tank' and then the tankette, a small number were ordered for the original Experimental Mechanized Force of 1927. It became the prototype both of the light tank and also of the machine-gun carrier.

In 1926 Martel himself was given command of the first field company R.E. to be mechanized, and with it took part in the trials of the Experimental Force during the next two years. In this period he devised a 'stepping-stone' bridge, made up of timber crates spaced at short intervals, which a tank pressed down into the bed of the stream as it ran across them—a device of which the Russians made use during their 1943 advance and later. He also devised a 'mat bridge' composed of a chain of timber panels, or rafts, which were pushed across the stream and over which vehicles could cross so long as they kept moving—an idea which was revived in the Normandy landings of 1944.

His numerous articles in the military journals during the twenties made a wide impression, especially abroad. Guderian, the creator of the German armoured forces, refers to Martel in his memoirs as one of the three men who 'principally' excited his interest in such forces and describes Martel as one of those three 'who became the pioneers of a new type of warfare on the largest scale'. In 1929 Martel went out to India where in 1930 he became an instructor at the Quetta

Staff College, remaining until 1933. There followed in 1935 a year's course at the Imperial Defence College. In 1931 he published a book entitled *In the Wake of the Tank*, and an enlarged edition in 1935, but he did not otherwise write so much in this decade as in the previous one.

Much of his technical inventive work had been done at his own expense and with little or no aid from official quarters. He was not given an opportunity to take a hand in directing tank development and production until 1936, by which time Britain had lost her former lead in this field. Then, as assistant director of mechanization, and from January 1938 as deputy director, he strove vigorously to make up the lost years. In the autumn of 1937 the new secretary of state for war, Leslie (later Lord) Hore-Belisha [q.v.], considered making him master-general of the ordnance, although he was still only a colonel. Martel's own diffidence about such a big jump over the heads of his seniors was one of the factors which led to a different decision. At the beginning of 1939 he left the War Office on promotion to command a motorized division—the 50th Northumbrian, of the Territorial Army.

After the German break-through on the Meuse in May 1940 which was followed by the Panzer forces' drive to the Channel, Martel's division, which had been in France since January, was rushed to the scene. He was put in charge of the improvised counter-attack delivered at Arras on 21 May by two of his battalions and all the serviceable tanks of the 1st Army Tank brigade. This stroke hit the flank of Rommel's Panzer division, causing disorder, and the news so alarmed the German higher command that their drive was nearly suspended. The shock effect, out of all proportion to the small size of the force, enhanced Martel's reputation, but his conduct of the operation and its faulty co-ordination led to much sharp criticism from the tank officers taking part, who felt that his powers as a commander and tactician did not match his gifts as a technician.

After the fall of France there was growing pressure for the appointment of a single chief of the armoured forces in Britain. (Sir) Winston Churchill himself supported the proposal and wished to see the post given to (Sir) Percy Hobart [q.v.]. Although the Army Council reluctantly agreed to the appointment of a single head of the armoured forces, they were unwilling to meet Hobart's condi-tions and felt that of the few armoured experts available Martel was likely to be the most amenable: in December 1940 he was appointed commander of the Royal Armoured Corps, under the commander-in-chief Home Forces.

This soon brought Martel into conflict with Hobart, and the tension between these two old friends became severe. It was sharpened when Churchill created what he called a 'tank parliament' where the various armoured division commanders and other experts could meet and express their differing points of view. Martel disliked the arrangement as interfering with his authority and showing a lack of confidence in himself. Moreover, like many champion boxers he was basically a gentle and conciliatory man, anxious to please as well as to avoid trouble, and in his over-tactful efforts to reconcile differing views and interests, particularly of cavalrymen and tankmen, he eventually lost the confidence of both.

In September 1942 he went to India and Burma on a lengthy tour and while he was away his post was abolished. On return he was sent to Moscow as head of the military mission: another frustrating post. He returned to London in February 1944 and a fortnight later lost an eye in the bombing of the Army and Navy Club. He was placed on retired pay in 1945. In the general election of that year he stood unsuccessfully as a Conservative candidate for the Barnard Castle division of Durham. In the same year he published *Our Armoured Forces* which aroused wide interest, but also considerable criticism. In subsequent years he wrote several more books, dealing with his experiences in Russia and expressing a strongly anti-Communist view; his writings always received more attention, and circulation, in Russia than they did at home. Although his career ended in a series of disappointments, Martel deserves recognition for the mark he made on the development of modern warfare. He was appointed C.B. (1940), K.B.E. (1943), and K.C.B. (1944). He had been promoted lieutenant-general in 1942.

In 1922 he married Maud, daughter of Donald Fraser MacKenzie, of Collingwood Grange, Camberley, by whom he had a son and a daughter, the latter killed tragically in 1941 in a riding accident. Martel died in Camberley 3 September 1958.

[Sir Giffard Martel, *An Outspoken Soldier*, 1949; private information; personal knowledge.]   B. H. LIDDELL HART.

MARTIN, Sir CHARLES JAMES (1866–1955), physiologist and pathologist, was born at Hackney 9 January 1866, the twelfth child and youngest son of Josiah Martin, actuary in the British Life (later merged with the Prudential) Assurance Company, by his second wife, Elizabeth Mary Lewis who also had been married before. In his own words 'the family was a Nonconformist middle class one characteristic of the period, with a fading flavour of piety and a small revenue ... the boys had to start earning their living at 15 years of age'. Charles Martin was nominated for Christ's Hospital, then in the City of London, but being a delicate child went instead to a boarding-school at Hastings. When fifteen he became a junior clerk in his father's actuarial department, but against his family's wishes he decided to become a doctor. By home study and evening classes at Birkbeck College and King's College, he matriculated and entered St. Thomas's Hospital where he concentrated on physiology. In 1886 he took his B.Sc., gaining the gold medal in physiology and a university scholarship which took him to Leipzig to work under Karl Ludwig. After six months he returned to London as demonstrator in biology and physiology and lecturer in comparative anatomy at King's College (1887–91). He continued his medical studies at St. Thomas's and qualified M.R.C.S., L.S.A. in 1889 and M.B. London in 1890.

In 1891 Martin went to Australia as demonstrator in physiology at the university of Sydney; six years later he moved to Melbourne where he later occupied the chair of physiology (1901–3). While in Australia he made his classic study on the venom of certain native snakes, and cleared up the confusion about the variable nature of their action. He was skilful with his hands and a master of apparatus. His gelatin ultra-filter, which figured subsequently in much research, enabled him to demonstrate two separate poisons in black snake (*Notechis pseudechis*) venom; one, a neurotoxin, passed through the filter; the other, a blood-clotting enzyme with a larger molecule, did not. Martin investigated also the metabolism and internal heat regulation of the Australian monotremes, primitive half-mammals, intermediate between cold-blooded reptiles and true warm-blooded mammals. His Australian researches revealed him as an outstanding investigator and he was elected F.R.S. in 1901.

He was no less successful as a teacher and his vivid method of imparting knowledge made a profound impression on Australian medical education, then in its formative years. His lasting influence was recognized in 1951 by the foundation by the National Health and Medical Research Council of Australia of the Sir Charles James Martin fellowships in medical science to give young graduates experience overseas.

In 1903 Martin returned to England to become director of the Lister Institute of Preventive Medicine, the first establishment in Britain devoted to medical research. Under his guidance the Institute expanded in many directions. Very little of the original work published from the Institute bore his name, but little was done without his help and inspiration; he was an unselfish director caring little where the credit went as long as the work was well done. At times he could be impatient and harshly critical but he was also sympathetic and appreciative of any good work, including that performed by 'lab boys' and charwomen. His personal investigations were important. The work on bubonic plague in Bombay between 1905 and 1908, by which the Indian rat flea was proved to be responsible for its spread, owed much to the plans laid at the start when Martin spent several months with the team drawn from the Institute's staff and the Indian Medical Service.

Work on the internal heat regulation of man and animals, made in experiments largely on himself, was summarized in the Croonian lectures of the Royal College of Physicians delivered in 1930 and in the presidential address to the hygiene section of the Pan Pacific Congress meeting in Sydney in 1923, when the use of white labour in tropical conditions was under discussion. Other of his investigations included the mechanics of the disinfection process, heat coagulation of proteins, virus of rabbit myxomatosis, vitamins and deficiency diseases, and nutritional value of proteins. In all his work he used precise and quantitative methods, a practice unusual at the time in biological studies. In 1912 he was appointed professor of experimental pathology in London.

In 1915 Martin joined the Australian forces with the rank of lieutenant-colonel as pathologist to the Third Australian General Hospital on the island of Lemnos. There he improvised an efficient pathological laboratory serving 10,000 hospital beds. He found that the

cause of the prevalent enteric fever was
not the typhoid bacillus against which the
men had been vaccinated, but the related
organisms of paratyphoid A and B.
Vaccination against those microbes was
therefore added to the existing routine
vaccination, a measure adopted later by
the British Army medical service. While
in Lemnos, Martin diagnosed as beriberi a
disease among the soldiers which had
baffled the physicians; he realized that the
Australian soldiers' ration of white bread
and tinned meat had the same vitamin
deficiency as that of polished rice which
caused epidemics of beriberi in Asia.
He therefore caused experimental work on
soldiers' rations to be started immediately
at the Lister Institute. In consequence a
vitamin 'soup cube' was devised for use
by the troops in the Middle East, and a
division of nutrition which was active for
the next thirty years was created at the
Institute.

After retirement in 1930 under the age
limit, Martin in the next year accepted
the invitation of the Australian Council
of Scientific and Industrial Research to
become director of its division of nutrition
at the university of Adelaide where he
was made professor of biochemistry and
general physiology. Research was centred
on protein and mineral requirements of
sheep, in view of the deficiencies in certain
Australian pastures.

He stayed three years and then settled
at Roebuck House, Chesterton, Cambridge, but again retirement was but
nominal. At the request of the Australian
authorities he made an experimental
study of the virus of myxomatosis and its
method of spread among rabbits. The
work was carried out at the Cambridge
University department of experimental
pathology and on the rabbit-infested
island of Skokholm in Pembrokeshire; it
was published in 1936. In collaboration
with colleagues at the Lister Institute
pellagra was produced experimentally
at Cambridge in pigs fed largely on maize.
The disease followed the pattern of human
pellagra as seen among populations having
maize as their staple food.

At the outbreak of war in 1939 Martin
offered space at his home to the division
of nutrition evacuated from the Lister
Institute. He contributed much to its
research, concerned perforce with wartime food problems. Work on the vitamin
and protein value of different portions of
the wheat grain enabled the authorities
to decide which fractions should be

included in the flour to make the
most nutritious and economical national
loaf.

Martin was a lover of the country and of
many open-air activities; as a young man
he spent vacations in camping and canoe-
ing. He was a good swimmer, fond of
playing tennis, and among the early
owner-drivers of a motor-car.

Martin's honours included: fellowships
of King's College, London (1899), of the
Royal College of Physicians (1913), and
of the Royal Society (1901) from which he
received a Royal medal in 1923; honorary
degrees from the universities of Sheffield, Dublin, Edinburgh, Durham, and
Cambridge. He was appointed C.M.G.
in 1919 for his war service and twice
mentioned in dispatches. He was knighted
in 1927.

In 1891 Martin married Edith Harriette
(died 1954), daughter of Alfred Cross,
architect, of Hastings; they had one
daughter. He died at Chesterton 15
February 1955. A portrait by M. Lewis is
in the possession of the family; there is
also a drawing by A. J. Murch. Copies of
both are in the Lister Institute.

[The Times, 17 February 1955; Dame
Harriette Chick in Biographical Memoirs of
Fellows of the Royal Society, vol. ii, 1956;
British Journal of Nutrition, vol. x, No. 1,
1956; Journal of Pathology and Bacteriology,
vol. lxxi, No. 2, April 1956; Lancet, 26 February 1955; Nature, 2 April 1955; personal
knowledge.]   HARRIETTE CHICK.

MARTIN, HERBERT HENRY (1881–
1954), secretary of the Lord's Day
Observance Society, was born 4 December
1881 in Norwich, the fourth of the five
children of James William Martin, boot
and shoe manufacturer, by his wife, Mary
Ann Blyth. He was educated at Alderman
Norman's Endowed School, Norwich, a
school founded for the education of
Alderman Norman's male descendants
among whom Martin was included through
his mother.

Martin was apprenticed to his
father's trade but, having experienced
conversion to Christ at the age of fourteen,
he felt the urge to enter whole-time
Christian service. His principals released
him from his indentures and at the early
age of sixteen he became the first of the
'Wycliffe preachers' of the Protestant
Truth Society founded by John Kensit
[q.v.]. His first public address in that
capacity was delivered 17 August 1898 on
the beach at Great Yarmouth. For the

next twenty-five years Martin threw all his energy and religious zeal into this society's work of protest against the doctrines and practices of the Roman Catholic Church and the Romeward movement in the Church of England—a task involving self-sacrifice, hardship, and some personal danger. In 1902 Martin preached on Thornbury Plain, Bristol; refusing to desist he was fined 1s.; declining payment he was imprisoned for three days in Horfield jail, an experience he was fond of citing as an important landmark of his life-work.

During these years of travelling throughout Britain, the need for arresting the ever-growing disregard for Sunday as the divinely appointed day for rest and worship impressed itself increasingly upon Martin until it became the conviction which shaped the remainder of his career. He took up whole-time work in this cause when he joined the staff of the Imperial Alliance for the Defence of Sunday in 1923. Finding insufficient outlet there for his boundless energy and evangelistic fervour he welcomed the invitation which came in 1925 to become secretary of the Lord's Day Observance Society which from its foundation in 1831 had always been the foremost instrument for the preservation of Sunday. Martin found the society in dire straits financially and in a state of ineffectiveness. By dint of his great organizing capacity, his unique flair for advertising and publicity, his infectious enthusiasm, and, above all, his deep spiritual conviction, he put this old society on the map and made it a power to be reckoned with in the national life. He soon gathered around him a loyal and steadily increasing staff by means of whom every part of the country was reached in the campaign to defend Sunday from secular encroachment. He revolutionized the publications of the society which, in some years, ran into millions of copies; and exploited to the full such national occasions as the silver jubilee of King George V and the coronation of King George VI for the issue of special propaganda inculcating not only the observance of Sunday but also the reading of the Bible and acceptance of its teaching.

Fearing the introduction of the continental Sunday into Britain, Martin paid several visits to Paris and other European cities in order to study the subject closely, following which he wrote many articles on the theme. He travelled to Geneva in 1931 and spoke against calendar reform proposals before a League of Nations committee. In the same year he organized nation-wide opposition to the legalization of the Sunday opening of cinemas. He was more successful in 1941 when his vigorous endeavours helped to bring about the rejection by the House of Commons of the Sunday opening of theatres.

A convinced churchman, Martin enjoyed fellowship with those Christians of other persuasions who shared his evangelical principles. The very nature of his activities brought upon him much unpopularity, misunderstanding, and even abuse, but his radiant buoyancy surmounted it all. Even his adversaries admired him as a clean fighter, and those who journalistically dubbed him 'Misery Martin' knew and loved his happy jubilant personality. In 1951 he retired; his powers thereafter failed rapidly and he died 30 March 1954 at Tunbridge Wells.

Martin married in 1903 Gertrude Elizabeth Eugene (died 1939), daughter of John Farley, by whom he had one son. In 1942 he married Elsie Lilian, daughter of John Verdon, builder, of Kilburn.

[Records of the Lord's Day Observance Society; private information; personal knowledge.]   H. J. W. LEGERTON.

MARTINDALE, HILDA (1875–1952), civil servant, was born in Leytonstone, London, 12 March 1875, the third daughter of William Martindale, City merchant, by his second wife, Louisa, daughter of James Spicer of a great Liberal-Nonconformist family whose business was paper manufacture. Her father and one sister died before she was born and Hilda and her elder sister Louisa (who became one of the first women surgeons) were brought up by their mother, a woman of remarkable personality. She was tirelessly energetic in the Liberal cause, the women's suffrage movement, and many other social, political, and religious activities. To Margaret Bondfield [q.v.] as to many others, she was 'a most vivid influence in my life', and she early decided that her youngest daughter's vocation was to social service. Hilda Martindale was educated in Germany, at the Brighton High School, the Royal Holloway College, and at Bedford College where she studied hygiene and sanitary sciences. On the advice of Graham Wallas [q.v.] she next spent some months visiting poor-law schools and other institutions and then for eight months helped with a boarding-out plan for infants sent to the homes of Dr. Barnardo [q.v.]. In 1900 she went with her mother and sister on a world tour. Her interest then, as throughout her life, lay mainly with children, and she was indefatigable in studying what was being done for them in the countries which she visited. On her return she addressed the State Children's Association on the subject, whereupon (Dame) Adelaide Anderson, principal lady inspector of factories at the Home Office, who was in the audience, offered Hilda a temporary post as an inspector (1901).

Hilda Martindale began by visiting west-end dressmakers where women and girls over fourteen were allowed by law to work twelve hours a day but were all too often kept longer and over the week-end. Their fear of dismissal made it difficult to obtain evidence and to prosecute offending employers; but so extensive was the abuse that Hilda Martindale felt it a waste of time to go to court unless she had summoned three or four firms to appear on the same day. She next reported on conditions in the brickfields of England, Wales, and Scotland, the dust-yards of London, on the breeze banks of South Staffordshire, and in home industries in the Midlands. In 1903 she was stationed in the Potteries where many women and children were the victims of lead poisoning despite the efforts of the Women's Trade Union League, and in particular of Gertrude Tuckwell [q.v.], to draw public attention to the danger.

In 1905 Hilda Martindale was sent to Ireland where she travelled the whole country visiting factories, workshops, laundries, cottages—wherever women and children worked. It was a hard life spent in hotels, with no office or clerk, visiting late at night and very early in the morning, meeting acute poverty among the people and sometimes shameful maltreatment of labour. Nor from an Irish bench was it always possible to get a conviction for even the most blatant offence. But she never lost heart and the steady stream of her reports (written in her early days at marble wash-stands in hotel bedrooms) contributed much, in time, to the improvement of labour regulations. In 1908 she was made a senior lady inspector and established an office in Belfast but in 1912 she moved to Birmingham as senior lady inspector of factories for the Midlands.

The substitution of men by women during the war added to her duties but she was encouraged by the improvement which it brought in wages and conditions. Other tasks which fell to her included the investigation with (Dame) Ellen Pinsent [q.v.] of excessive drinking by the young girls working in Birmingham. In 1918 she was appointed O.B.E. and moved to London as deputy principal lady inspector and later senior lady inspector for the South-Eastern Division. Her unquestionable success in her work and the affection and respect which she inspired both among her colleagues and among her many contacts in the industrial world contributed much to the gradual acceptance of equality of opportunity for women: in 1921 the men's and women's sides of the inspectorate were amalgamated and she became a superintending inspector and in 1925 a deputy chief inspector. In this year she was deputed to help in creating the Home Office Industrial Museum under the inspiration of Sir Malcolm Delevingne (whose notice she contributed to this Dictionary). Much of her time was henceforth to be spent in committee work, on selection boards, and as technical adviser to the British Government delegation at International Labour Conferences.

In 1933 Hilda Martindale was appointed director of women establishments at the Treasury and in 1935 she was promoted C.B.E. A position which was confined to women's problems was not altogether congenial to her for she was always a convinced, and indeed dogmatic, believer in equal opportunity for women in the Civil Service. Although herself a quiet and even diffident person, she fought obstinately for this principle throughout her career and particularly after some misgivings which she had felt about the ability of women to share the work of men in the factory inspectorate had proved unfounded; gentle and reserved, she was seldom roused, but she could be very persistent. She made herself a useful and most acceptable member of the Treasury and in so doing continued the process of breaking down the fear of women in high position. She retired in 1937 at her own request so that her post might be absorbed into the ordinary grade and she had the satisfaction of seeing a woman appointed an assistant secretary responsible for men and women alike. When some years later a woman became principal assistant secretary in charge of all Treasury general establishment work, she wrote: 'Now indeed my desire was fulfilled.'

In her retirement Hilda Martindale found many opportunities for public service and wrote a history of *Women Servants of the State* (1938), *Some Victorian Portraits and Others* (1948), and memoirs of her mother, her sister, and herself in *From One Generation to Another* (1944) which gives a drily vivid description of industrial conditions as she found them in the first quarter of the century. She died, unmarried, in London 18 April 1952.

[Personal knowledge.]   SHARP.

MARY, (VICTORIA MARY AUGUSTA LOUISE OLGA PAULINE CLAUDINE AGNES) (1867–1953), queen consort of King George V, was born 26 May 1867 at Kensington Palace in the room in which Queen Victoria was born. She was the eldest child and only daughter of Francis, Prince (after 1871 Duke of) Teck and his wife, Princess Mary Adelaide. The Prince was the only son of Duke Alexander of Wurtemberg by his morganatic marriage with Claudine, Countess Rhédey, of an illustrious Protestant Hungarian house. Her ancestor, Samu Aba, married a sister of St. Stephen and was King of Hungary (1041–5). The Prince was brought up in Vienna and in due course served the Emperor with considerable military promise in the 7th Imperial Hussars. At the invitation of the Prince of Wales he first paid a visit to England in 1864, but it was not until 1866 that he met Princess Mary Adelaide. His wooing was of the briefest. Queen Mary's mother was the younger daughter of Adolphus, Duke of Cambridge (q.v., seventh son of George III), and therefore a first cousin of Queen Victoria. Three sons in due course followed the Princess: Princes Adolphus (afterwards created Marquess of Cambridge, died 1927), Francis (died 1910), and Alexander (afterwards the Earl of Athlone, q.v., died 1957) for whom his sister always felt a special devotion, perhaps tinged with envy for his successes in public life in fields open only to men. The Princess was popularly known as Princess May until her marriage although she used the official 'Victoria Mary' as her signature.

Early influences in the formation of Princess May's character are not to be lightly dismissed. The Tecks were a devoted if tempestuous couple and remarkably different in character. He was tall and good-looking, orderly and neat in dress and habits, often quick-tempered, extremely conservative especially on the question of women's spheres of usefulness and a stickler for etiquette. He had some artistic tastes and hobbies, but outside his family his life perhaps was not made as happy as his modest ambitions may have expected. He may have suffered some of the handicaps which early faced the Prince Consort. The Duchess was liberal-minded, expansive, cheerful, warm-hearted, a garrulous but very intelligent conversationalist, a good mixer, catholic in her choice of friends—her devoted admirers came from every class—typically English if rather bohemian, a bad manager, and incurably unpunctual; indeed her unpunctuality was heinous in a royalty; but she delighted in and deserved her popularity. The Duke had no private fortune. The Duchess's parliamentary grant, eked out by graces and favours from the Queen, was insufficient to meet the costs of moderate 'State' in the rooms allotted at Kensington Palace and at the large and graceful White Lodge in Richmond Park, and generous gifts to charity.

Princess May in her childhood was constantly with her popular mother and learned from her to understand and sympathize in the lives and aspirations of all classes, and to comprehend the relative values of money in the income groups. For the Duchess had an understanding far ahead of her times of what 'the poor' really needed, as her Village Homes at Addlestone and her Holiday Homes proved. Princess May was clearly often overshadowed by her mother's popularity and no doubt by reaction she acquired the virtue of punctuality; she had few opportunities of practising small talk in her mother's company. Her parents had no ambition for her education beyond the normal drawing-room accomplishments of her kind in her day. It was her own determination, later reinforced by her Alsatian governess, Hélène Bricka, a very strong-minded, well-educated, politically liberal companion, to pursue it beyond that range. Accordingly when in 1883–5 the family spent eighteen months in Italy by the need for retrenchment, although the Princess was at first intensely homesick, her interest in art and history, later to be enlarged among the royal collections, quickly expanded. When she returned to England, to enter the social round of London society, she continued for several hours a day to improve her own education without parental encouragement, and she became proficient in French and German and in European history. By the time she became Queen, she had gained a wide knowledge of political and social life in the German principalities.

She had from childhood seen something of the children of the Prince of Wales, the first cousins being all too young to share their interests, and she and her brothers had sometimes found the rough manners and boisterous fun of their second cousins rather trying. In 1887 she began to know them well. From the first Queen Victoria, who was fond of the Duchess, had taken an interest in the daughter and henceforth watched her closely and began to see in her a worthy choice for the Prince of Wales's eldest son, the Duke of Clarence. She had all the qualifications, lacking only the self-confidence which is required of a social leader. In later life Queen Mary sometimes questioned the verdict that she was very shy. She certainly never shared Queen Alexandra's taste for ragging nor perhaps Queen Victoria's liking for an occasional robust laugh, although among her intimates she could reveal her own sense of fun. She argued that a love of serious conversation and of relevance could be described as shyness and suggested that people who were themselves natural and truth-loving had no need to be shy in her presence. Yet the attribution that she was shy and shy-making survived and it cannot be said that in her twenties the Prince of Wales's family helped her to cure it. Nevertheless, Princess May enjoyed her dancing years in London with her brothers, now coming to man's estate and all destined for the army, and amid the rural charms of White Lodge and in the pre-Edwardian circle of the Prince.

There was a certain inevitability in the announcement of her engagement to the Duke of Clarence at the end of 1891 when Princess May was approaching twenty-five. She was the only available English Princess not descended from the Queen. In that sense, it was an 'alliance'. The test of whether it would prove a love match was eliminated by the Duke's sudden death in January 1892. Prince George, becoming heir to the throne next after his father, was created Duke of York and the public's anxiety for the succession was transferred to him. In May 1893 his engagement to Princess May was announced to the intense satisfaction of the Queen. The Prince of Wales approved it, if the Princess's enthusiasm was modified by the recent memory of her elder son's

death. The marriage was solemnized 6 July 1893 in the chapel of St. James's Palace. Once more no doubt it was argued that this was a 'marriage of convenience'. The Duke of York's private diary and contemporary letters to his friends make it quite clear that it was soon very much a love match, and in the first years of marriage, largely spent at York Cottage at Sandringham, his home for much of his life, his happiness grew and broadened into a placid contentment with his lot. They were quiet years. Children were born—the eldest (subsequently the Duke of Windsor) at White Lodge, 23 June 1894, the second (subsequently King George VI, a notice of whom appears in this Supplement) at York Cottage 14 December 1895; on 25 April 1897 a daughter (subsequently the Princess Royal); and on 31 March 1900 a third son (subsequently the Duke of Gloucester). The Duke's diary is proof positive that for him life was an idyll whether at York House, St. James's, or at the ugly, inconvenient cottage at beloved Sandringham.

For the Duchess, as her family increased, the idyll was sometimes marred by the benevolent tyranny exercised from the Big House. The Duke himself was aware of it. To his mother he remained to the last the second son. She always addressed her letters to him as 'King George', never 'The King'. In a letter to the writer (25 July 1939) Queen Mary commented that for King George V his reign was the most interesting part of his life 'but a good deal of the early times helped him to understand the human point of view. The rough and tumble of former days was very good for us both.' Those early years had an influence on the Duchess's character. She was living on an estate which drew its inspiration wholly from the Prince and Princess of Wales and she had married into a family which was certainly a closely guarded clique and was not far short of a mutual-admiration society. It was a family little given to intellectual pursuits, not easily to be converted to any other manner of life than that which they had found all-sufficing. The Duchess was intellectually on a higher plane, and constantly seeking to increase her store of knowledge in many fields beyond the range of the Princess of Wales and Princess Victoria. Their recreations were not hers. She needed outlets and wider horizons; sometimes her intellectual life may have been starved and her energies atrophied.

It was for her no training in self-confidence. Her husband was very conservative, not easy to convert or remould. Sandringham ways were perfect in his eyes. His admiration for his father was boundless and tinged with awe. Yet soon enough the Duchess began to improve his taste and education. Late in her life, in conversation with an intimate and in her valiance for the truth, Queen Mary remarked: 'It is always supposed that my mother-in-law had no influence whatever over my father-in-law and that I have strong influence over my husband. The truth happens to be the exact opposite in each case.' Some influence over the Duke must, however, be conceded her in those early times. But all her life she was afraid of taking too much upon herself, in her reverence for 'The Sovereign'. Indeed, in many ways she was timid.

Shortly after the diamond jubilee the Duke and Duchess paid a most successful visit to Ireland. With the death of Queen Victoria and the coronation of Edward VII they began to assume (but modestly) some of the duties of the heir to the throne. Before mourning for the Queen was over the *Ophir* tour gave them an opportunity to test their own qualities and to find their feet in an Empire which knew little of them and in a society which regarded them as too little go-ahead for Edwardian brilliance and initiative. They travelled as Duke and Duchess of Cornwall (to which title the Duke succeeded) and York. The prime purpose was to open the first federal Parliament of the new Commonwealth of Australia, but the tour embraced the greater part of the Empire and lasted more than seven months. Of the two, the Duchess was better equipped to meet the tests. Once or twice, when the Duke was overstrained, she stepped into the breach and did his part. Her own embraced the interests of the women of the Empire and for both of them it was a successful education and graduation under the careful coaching of Sir Arthur Bigge (afterwards Lord Stamfordham, q.v.). The bitter parting from their young family was forgotten in the happy reunion and the warm approval of the people and of the King who now created the Duke Prince of Wales. In a speech in the City the Prince jolted the public out of its complacent views on the Empire and revealed that he had gained a good deal of self-confidence during his tour.

The new Prince and Princess of Wales began to take a larger share of ceremonial and of the responsibilities of the heir to the throne. They resisted, with mild criticism from some quarters, going with the Edwardian stream. Nevertheless, they entertained constantly and carried out a number of engagements during and after the coronation, a few months after which on 20 December 1902 the Princess gave birth to her fourth son, Prince George (subsequently the Duke of Kent, q.v.). In the next year they moved into Marlborough House. On 12 July 1905 the youngest child, Prince John, was born; he died 18 January 1919. Never robust, he was very dear to his family who treasured his quaint sayings.

In the winter of 1905–6 the Prince and Princess of Wales had another opportunity to extend their knowledge of the Empire and increase their self-confidence when they made a highly successful tour of India. Their coach and guide on this occasion was Sir Walter Lawrence [q.v.] and before and during the arduous tour they both went through the most complete and detailed preparation. The Princess's interest, assiduity, and energy in mastering and executing her special functions among the women of India were highly praised. The tour covered India from end to end, and all her life Queen Mary's love of India was graven on her heart. She would sometimes compare her sense of loss, when the Indian Empire ceased, to another Queen Mary's feelings over the loss of Calais.

In May 1906 they went to Madrid for the marriage of Princess Ena of Battenberg to the King of Spain and were unhurt when a bomb was thrown at the wedding procession. In June they were in Norway for the coronation of the King and Queen. Thenceforward to the end of the reign of King Edward their lives continued on a fixed and not too arduous pattern. No shadow of jealousy marred the relations between the King and his heir. King Edward died 6 May 1910 and the new Queen became known as Queen Mary. She and the King faced some early criticism of a pin-pricking sort. There were lampoons ('The King is duller than the Queen' and vice versa, ran a refrain) whispered among the old set which feared (with reason) that the 'great days' and the brilliance were gone from court and society, and some scandalous imputations against the King were soon exploded. In the face of these small discouragements (not unfamiliar at the accession of British sovereigns), the King and Queen soon began to strike out a line of their own and once again proved that the changing times had found appropriate leadership from the throne. After the exhausting funeral ceremonies, followed in 1911 by the unveiling of Queen Victoria's memorial in the Kaiser's presence and by the coronation, made specially remarkable by the grace and dignity of the new Queen, they paid their second visit to India for the durbar. Neither ever forgot the splendours and the strain of this tour (1911–12) throughout which the energy and sustained interest of the Queen were universally remarked and praised.

State visits to Berlin (1913) and Paris (1914) further impressed on the nation the worth and the dignity of the new sovereigns. There were also tours of industrial areas. There Queen Mary was in her element. Margaret Bondfield [q.v.] once remarked that Queen Mary would have made a good factory inspector. She could comprehend poverty, her sympathy was genuine, her clear mind, her curiosity and skill in detail enabled her to enter with remarkable understanding into the problems of the small house and the family budget. Not for her the dazzling smile, the apt and gracious word in a non-stop progress. Her visits were exhaustively and exhaustingly carried out, and they created a new model of a sovereign's functions. She was genuinely interested and never taken in by surface appearances.

In their private life the King and Queen continued to live very simply and sought to accord to their children a sensible and, as far as possible, democratic upbringing. From the earliest years, and even as her official and self-imposed functions increased, Queen Mary usually found time for 'the children's hour'. She superintended their religious grounding, and gave them practical rather than sentimental attention. The maternal instincts were never strong in her, although she had an understanding of children, a sympathy too, unless they were spoilt and tiresome. She always backed up the justified discipline meted out by tutors, governesses, and servants, but was always ready to contest any over-harsh discipline by their father. She would reason her eldest son out of his natural revolts, insisting on the obligations of his unique position. For already with her and her husband loyalty to the monarchy transcended all other loyalties. Soon enough it was to her the children turned for sympathy and advice, for their father's methods inspired in them an awe and unease which in time (until their marriages, and always with the eldest) grew into a major and almost national tragedy. Her influence over them grew. It was a pity that her influence over her husband on such matters did not keep pace. With her children she was not austere. No doubt Prince George was her favourite son because he most keenly shared her intellectual tastes. She joined occasionally in their jokes, even practical jokes, and taught them hobbies; and since she disliked yachting, although she usually attended Cowes week, and was bored by grouse shooting, she would have the children to herself in August and September at Frogmore or Abergeldie, when she did not go abroad. Gradually life consolidated into an unchanging routine, as the boys moved on from Osborne, Dartmouth, or private schools to Oxford or into the Services. The King and Queen set a new pattern in the face of criticism which soon enough turned to approval and admiration. And so they came to the test of world war.

Queen Mary's part between 1914 and 1918 was arduous and invaluable. She turned her Needlework Guild into a world-wide collecting and distributing organization. There was at first some fear, which Mary Macarthur [q.v.] did not hesitate to express to the Queen, that this voluntary work might increase the already serious problem of unemployment among women. The Queen at once insisted that the problem should be tackled. The Central Committee on Women's Employment was set up with Mary Macarthur as honorary secretary and The Queen's Work for Women Fund was administered by the committee. This brought Queen Mary into close touch with the leading women in the Labour movement such as Gertrude Tuckwell [q.v.]. Queen Mary was indefatigable in visiting hospitals and largely responsible for founding the workshops at Roehampton and a number of hospitals for troops in and round London. When the reputation of the Women's Army Auxiliary Corps stood low Queen Mary gave it her patronage. She directed the austerity of the royal household and her example and unwearying energy were everywhere acknowledged. The King's duties were heavy at home and in his visits to the troops and navy. In the summer of 1917 the Queen accompanied him to France where her visits to the hospitals established a legend of her tirelessness and practical sympathy. And through it all, a very personal anxiety for their sons and other relations and friends played a heavy part in the strain and stress of war. When it ended, both had triumphantly passed their supreme tests.

The war had marked them both, and the King, who was never the same man after an accident in France, showed it clearly. The armistice and the celebrations of their silver wedding in 1918 gave them further proofs of public respect and affection and led the way to an abnormal amount of state ceremonial in the years which followed. There were state visits from allied sovereigns and leaders, the great Wembley Exhibition, and more personal and private events to occupy them in the marriages of Princess Mary (1922) and the Duke of York (1923). The post-war years passed in a social revolution which affected all classes and called for the highest examples of restraint, dignity, and tact, and to these duties the King and Queen gave constant attention. Their concern for the convenience of the first Labour Government did much to remove socialist misconception about the monarchy. For the King they were years of almost ceaseless difficulty and anxiety which he was physically ill-fitted to endure. When in 1928 he became desperately ill, Queen Mary proved, first to the doctors and to her family, and gradually to the whole nation, the strength of her character. The King's doctors acknowledged her great share in the miracle of his recovery. The Duke of York, meeting the Prince of Wales on his arrival from East Africa, remarked: 'Through all the anxiety she has never once revealed her feelings to any of us. She is really far too reserved . . . I fear a breakdown if anything awful happens. She has been wonderful.' There was no breakdown. In the period of convalescence, in the years which remained to the King, she knew the truth: she carried the anxiety and maintained before the world a serenity and calm and dignity, half comprehended and wholly admired. Henceforward, the King was physically unfit for half the duties of his office and he was not an easy man to deflect from duty or habituated routine. She was constantly at his side in his public engagements. In the celebrations of their jubilee in 1935 the full realization of the nation's respect and affection for them came to both, and King George's personal reference to her, spoken

in deep emotion in Westminster Hall, acknowledged his own debt to her lifelong service to himself and the nation. Eight months later the King died at Sandringham on 20 January 1936, in the presence of his family, soon after the last council at his bedside. At once the Queen kissed the hand of her eldest son. Her self-command in those anxious hours was noted by all who saw her. She completed the last entry in King George's diary with a touching note and spoke in a message to the nation her heartfelt gratitude for the affection shown to them.

After the King's death, Queen Mary moved into Marlborough House which had stood empty since the death of Queen Alexandra. It had been to some extent renovated and, when Queen Mary's taste had had full play in the arrangement of her own collections, gradually assumed a dignity and even charm which it had never known. But the normal period of mourning held for her the tremendous stress and strain of the abdication crisis. She met it with the calmness, sympathy, tact, restraint, and dignity of which she was a mistress and was guided in her course by the chief loyalty of her life—to the monarchy—in the best interest of the nation. But that crisis might well have marked and aged a woman less physically and mentally strong. It was not in her character to accept retirement or the hitherto conventional lifelong privacy of Queen Mothers. She began to resume her public engagements and created a precedent in attending the coronation of her son King George VI. Her interest in works of art continued to develop and she made her own a large variety of cultural and industrial projects. She was already famous for her interest (and endurance) at the British Industries Fair (it was calculated that from first to last she walked a hundred miles round the Fairs); and she became a regular visitor to the Wimbledon tennis championships.

In May 1939 Queen Mary had a car accident which severely shook her and permanently injured her eyesight. With the outbreak of war she reluctantly accepted the necessity for her removal from London and she established herself at Badminton, the home of her nephew-by-marriage, the Duke of Beaufort. Her activities varied but did not lessen: she worked and planned in the woods, visited the neighbouring towns, would stop to give lifts to servicemen, and got through a great deal of tapestry work at which she was an acknowledged expert. Some of it—a great carpet in particular—was exhibited and sold overseas and earned praise and dollars for worthy objects. She was at Badminton when she received the news of the death of the Duke of Kent in a Service flying accident 25 August 1942. She went at once to her daughter-in-law and attended the funeral at Windsor. She refused to surrender to the shock and bitter grief. She returned to London when the war with Germany was over and resumed her public engagements right up to and indeed beyond the death of King George VI in 1952. She never failed to receive important visitors such as J. C. Smuts [q.v.] and General Eisenhower and many social workers from the dominions. In 1947 she celebrated her eightieth birthday, an occasion saddened by the death of her son-in-law the Earl of Harewood [q.v.]. Her own death took place after a short illness, 24 March 1953, at Marlborough House, in her eighty-sixth year, and she was buried beside King George V in St. George's chapel, Windsor. Her effigy, later set over the tomb beside that of King George, had been made simultaneously by Sir William Reid Dick. Her death and funeral evoked remarkable tributes of public respect and affection. (Sir) Winston Churchill in a broadcast spoke of the long range of her experience; but Queen Mary, he said, did not cling to the past. She moved easily in the swiftly changing scenes. New ideas had no terrors for her. Dispassionate in judgement, practical in all things, she was far too much interested in the present to be unduly prejudiced by the past. Above all, she died in the knowledge that the Crown was far more broadly based on the people's love and on the nation's will than in the sedate days of her youth.

She was a great queen-consort. It was her destiny during many troubled years of war and social revolution to serve as an example at the head of the State, through times of bitterness and disillusion when ethical standards and conventions were being questioned or abandoned and a looser morality gained ground in society; and the chief quality with which she performed her function was perhaps a golden sense of what was fitting, not alone for a queen, a court, or a monarchy, but for men and women in every rank of life. She was elastic for change, rigid for conduct, resolute for the dignity of the Crown and of human life. She possessed few of the graces and the dazzling charms of her mother-in-law. Indeed, she was formidable and could appear austere. But she had the charm of incisive judgement tempered by great kindness. Nothing could hide her practical human sympathy or chill the warmth of her heart. Simple, straightforward, forthright, blazingly truthful, she could feel sympathy for the delinquent when she visited the juvenile courts in East London, but none for the liar, while to the end her spirit scorned the laggard and the fainthearted. Only her remarkable physical strength and extraordinary self-discipline and mental vigour could have enabled her to do the public work she did in anxiety, sorrow, and old age.

'Genius' in the usual sense cannot justly be applied in any field to Queen Mary. Her genius lay in her intense loyalty and selfless service to the monarchy, in her tact and most particularly in her political tact, for she never discussed politics (taking a lesson from Queen Adelaide's failing), in her safety as a recipient of confidences, in her rigid upholding of all that was of good report, in her self-discipline in controlling inherent timidity and shyness.

But genius in the accepted sense of rare intellectual powers she would not have claimed. Her mind, essentially urban, was factual rather than analytical. Of country matters she knew little. Life at Balmoral was not to her taste; she preferred Sandringham which was less remote. Diligent always, she absorbed information and stored it in a strong and orderly memory. Thus, her collection of art treasures was guided less by intuition and taste than by accepted doctrine. The monarchy being her first interest, her preference in paintings spread outward from the basic subject of English royal portraiture and, although this led her into wider fields, she never acquired a taste for gallery pictures outside the historical. This did not prevent her lending continuous encouragement to museums and galleries, and often she impressed the staffs by her memory. The latter years of her life were chiefly devoted to adding to her collection of bibelots, and perhaps the quality of the whole would have profited had she paid more for less. Her reading she pursued steadily to the end, usually in the field of serious memoirs, historical and contemporary, English and foreign. She read some current fiction, but when in her last years her ladies read to her, she usually chose classic novels. Her brief and factual diary throws little light on her private thoughts and inner life, and is devoid of criticism of political events or of personalities. She cared intensely, to the minutest detail, for any subject great or small which she set out to master, or for any object to achieve, however trivial, even to the choice of a birthday present (she was the first Queen to visit the shops) or some practically thoughtful action to a humble dependant who had served her well.

It was this capacity, allied to that refusal to be prejudiced by the past, which enabled her with her husband King George V to create a new conception of constitutional monarchy and its responsibilities. It was durable and remained a pattern for succeeding reigns because it was based on the human virtues of duty and integrity, simplicity and sympathy, loyalty and love.

In appearance Queen Mary was above the average height of women. Her intimates among women considered that she looked her best in black, a colour she detested. Her own favourites were pale pastel shades, preferably blue. She always wore a toque, except occasionally in the garden when she would wear a hat, and on suitable occasions she carried a long umbrella or parasol. She appeared often, owing to her dress and carriage, to tower over King George, although she was exactly the same height. This gave her in the public view the appearance of moral ascendancy also. It was an illusion. The King was very much master in his house and she, even to the subduing of an innate gaiety of heart, known only to her intimates, was a submissive partner in her loyalty to the monarchy.

Queen Mary sat to many artists during her life. (Sir) William Llewellyn painted the state portrait (1911–12), remarkable for its dignity, which is now at Buckingham Palace. (Sir) John Lavery's group (1913) of the King and Queen with the Prince of Wales and Princess Mary is in the National Portrait Gallery where there is also a bronze by Sir William Reid Dick. There are several more portraits at Windsor Castle or the Palace. A. T. Nowell produced the best likeness. Tyrell, von Angeli, G. Koberwein, and E. Hughes painted her before 1900; (Sir) Oswald Birley, David Jagger, and Simon Elwes painted her in the thirties or later. She was a good and constant subject for photographers.

[H.R.H. The Duke of Windsor, *A King's Story*, 1951; John Gore, *King George V*, 1941; James Pope-Hennessy, *Queen Mary*, 1959; Queen Mary's private diaries; private information.]
JOHN GORE

MASON-MacFARLANE, SIR (FRANK NOEL (1889–1953), lieutenant-general, was born 23 October 1889 in Maidenhead, the elder son of Dr. David James Mason, a Scotsman who later changed his name to Mason-MacFarlane, and his wife, Mary Blanche Anstey. He was educated at Rugby and the Royal Military Academy, Woolwich, and was gazetted to the Royal Artillery in 1909. War service in France, Belgium, and Mesopotamia gained him a Military Cross with two bars, two mentions in dispatches, and a croix de guerre. He took part in the Afghan war of 1919 and in 1920 went to the Staff College at Quetta. In 1931 he became military attaché in Vienna with responsibility also in Budapest and Berne. He graduated from the Imperial Defence College in 1935, and two years later became military attaché in Berlin, with responsibility also in Copenhagen. He acquired an unrivalled knowledge of the German Army and twice observed it in action: on its entries into Austria and Czechoslovakia. Concluding that Hitler's word was not to be trusted and that Germany was bent on unlimited expansion by military aggression, he believed that to attempt to negotiate with the Nazis was futile and dangerous. Since war appeared to him inevitable he argued further that Hitler should not be allowed to choose his own time but should be driven into aggression when circumstances were unfavourable to him. These views brought Mason-MacFarlane into conflict with authority.

As director of military intelligence, with the rank of major-general, with the British Expeditionary Force in France in 1939, Mason-MacFarlane's knowledge of Germany and the German Army was invaluable. When the Germans broke the Ninth French Army front he improvised and commanded a scratch force to protect the British right and immediate rear. 'MacForce' was behind the First French Army, whose front never actually broke, was afterwards withdrawn to prepare the defence of Cassel, and was then disbanded. Mason-MacFarlane and other key officers were ordered back to Britain. For his work in France he was appointed to the D.S.O.

In June 1940 he was sent as deputy governor to Gibraltar where his energy, character, and leadership, in extremely difficult circumstances, performed miracles in reorganizing the defences and maintaining morale. After a brief but treasured interlude commanding a division in Kent, Mason-MacFarlane was sent to Moscow in 1941 as head of the British military mission, with the task of maximizing the effectiveness of allied aid to Russia. Once more he came up against authority by deprecating over-optimistic promises and opposing aid without conditions. In June 1942 he returned to Gibraltar, this time as governor and commander-in-chief. He now had the invidious task of continuing preparations for defence, and maintaining morale while the risks of attack decreased. He accommodated General Eisenhower's headquarters for the invasion of North Africa and gave valuable support to these operations. In 1943 he was promoted K.C.B.; he had been appointed C.B. in 1939.

Italy surrendered on 3 September 1943 and Mason-MacFarlane headed a military mission to Brindisi on the 13th. Then, and later as head of the Allied Control Commission from January 1944, he set about converting an enemy into a co-belligerent. The King and Marshal Badoglio had at first to be supported because it was they who had agreed to fight the Germans, and were, indeed, the only government available. But they lacked popular support. The King was persuaded to resign and Mason-MacFarlane was charged to form a democratic government on the liberation of Rome, where liberal political leaders were gathered. These refused to serve under Badoglio, but agreed to form a government under Bonomi. Hesitation, or the continuance of Badoglio in power, might have resulted in the emergence of a rival government, or even governments, and Mason-MacFarlane accepted Bonomi and his Cabinet. But Whitehall wanted Badoglio because it was he who had bound himself to bring the Italian forces on to the allied side, and withheld recognition. (Sir) Winston Churchill made his displeasure clear. Eventually the Bonomi government was accepted; but Mason-MacFarlane, already a grievously sick man, resigned.

As a schoolboy he had broken his neck. Later a fall, pigsticking, injured his back, and a motor accident broke a number of ribs close to the spine. From about 1940, as a result, presumably, of these injuries, he suffered increasing paralysis. By 1944 he was in constant pain. The rest of his life was a tragic tale of operations and increasing disability. Nevertheless, in the general election of 1945, moved by a long-standing lack of sympathy with the ruling party, he stood for Parliament in the Labour interest and from his wheelchair won the constituency of North Paddington from Brendan (later Viscount) Bracken [q.v.]. He was mentioned as a possible secretary of state for war, but his health forced him to give up in 1946. He died 12 August 1953 at his home at Twyford, Berkshire.

Mason-MacFarlane has been described by one who served under him (and later became a field-marshal) as a near-genius. Basically, he was a very fine fighting soldier. He had an acute brain, a realistic understanding of people and events, and a gift of lucid exposition. He was a fine linguist, speaking excellent French and German, and some Spanish, Hungarian, and Russian. He was an outstanding athlete. To his staff he was a most inspiring leader. He had the panache and idiosyncracy which focus, but also the common touch which retains, the loyalty of troops. He was impetuous to espouse causes which were lost, or nearly so. Less well liked by contemporaries and those under whom he served, he was too often right, and there was a sarcastic edge to his tongue. He had, too, a full share of personal ambition. In the last resort, there was, perhaps, some lack of judgement. But of his dynamism, will-power, and courage there was never any doubt.

In 1918 he married Islay (died 1947), daughter of Frederick Islay Pitman, stockbroker; they had one son and one daughter.

There are two portraits of Mason-MacFarlane by R. G. Eves in the Imperial War Museum.

[L. F. Ellis, (Official History) *The War in France and Flanders 1939–40*, 1953; C. R. S. Harris, (Official History) *Allied Military Administration of Italy, 1943–45*, 1957; private information.]   F. S. V. DONNISON.

MASSINGHAM, HAROLD JOHN (1888–1952), author and journalist, was born in London 25 March 1888, the eldest of the six children of Henry William Massingham [q.v.] by his first wife, Emma Jane Snowdon. Educated at Westminster School and the Queen's College, Oxford, where owing to illness he did not graduate, he began his career on the editorial staffs of the *Morning Leader*, where he survived for only three weeks, and the National

Press Agency. Articles in the *New Age* brought him into touch with a remarkable group of writers and artists, including W. H. Davies [q.v.] and Ralph Hodgson, although no one influenced him more than his friend W. H. Hudson [q.v.].

Between 1916 and 1924 Massingham was a regular contributor on literary and natural history topics to the *Nation* and the *Athenaeum*, and for a time he served on their editorial staffs. It was Ralph Hodgson, in a poem burning with rage and pity, who inspired him to launch a small society called the Plumage Group. On the successful completion of its campaign against the trade in the feathers of birds, he joined the Board of Trade committee formed to implement the Importation of Plumage (Prohibition) Act of 1921.

Soon after publishing his successful *Treasury of Seventeenth Century Verse* (1919), Massingham embarked on those long treks across comparatively untrodden corners of the English countryside which resulted in his admirable *Wold Without End* (1932), *English Downland* (1936), *Cotswold Country* (1937), and many other books. They portrayed the English scene through the eyes of a warm and vigorous character who was both naturalist and archaeologist as well as an authority on country crafts. For a time he explored the upland homes of prehistoric man as a member of the anthropological staff of (Sir) Grafton Elliot Smith [q.v.] at University College, London, and *Downland Man* (1926) reveals his skill in bringing the buried past to life. Yet he was always the enthusiastic and self-taught amateur, quick to observe how attractively the Cotswold villages were clustered on the hills or dispersed along the valleys, delighting in the way the winds and sheep of Sussex made midgets of the downland flora, pausing in wonder and gratitude before the skill of native craftsmen whose work reflected the traditions of the region. During these walks with his faithful sheep-dog, or between weeks preparing *The Great Victorians* (1932) which he edited with his brother Hugh Massingham, he liked nothing better than to converse with the country craftsmen he chanced to encounter, just as Langland or Cobbett might have done. Indeed, Massingham and Cobbett had much in common—the same deep love for the land and its peasantry, a keen appreciation of the virtues of smallness, a habit of expressing forceful opinions on matters on which they were not always well informed,

a rare sense of the organic unity of the countryside.

Massingham wrote regularly for the *Field* from 1938 to 1951 (and then for the *Spectator*) without 'one single word of complaint from the editor', and he was a brisk and conscientious correspondent. He and Esther Meynell wrote to each other week after week for many years, although they never met, nor possessed any strong desire to do so. Nothing, unless it was his Nonesuch edition in two volumes of *The Writings of Gilbert White of Selborne* (1938), gave him more pleasure than his garden on the western slopes of the Chilterns, where he planted a few score trees, kept two geese and a pig, and regretted that his days could not be shared between the pen and the plough. It was when cutting ivy from an ash in the Upper Windrush valley, one evening in 1937, that he tripped over a hidden feeding trough, rusty from disuse, an accident which was to cost him a leg and a foot and which nearly ended his life. He attributed his survival through 1940, when struggling to find the strength to edit *England and the Farmer* (1941), largely to the skill of his surgeon and the courage of his wife.

He celebrated his recovery with the publication of perhaps his best work, *The English Countryman* (1942), a vivid study of the peasant and parson, yeoman and squire, and other rural types. If he wrote too much—more than forty books and many articles and reviews in some thirty years—it was because he was a man with a mission, the ex-townsman who longed to save the English countryside from decay, the youthful free-thinker turned Roman Catholic who wanted the post-Christian age to rediscover the ancient links between worship, work, and recreation. It was typical of the man that shortly before his death he presented his treasured collection of some 250 bygones to the new Museum of English Rural Life at the university of Reading. He died at his home at Long Crendon, Buckinghamshire, 22 August 1952.

In 1914 he married Gertrude Speedwell, daughter of Arthur Black, of Brighton. The marriage was dissolved and in 1933 he married Anne Penelope, daughter of the late A. J. Webbe. There were no children of either marriage. Always as self-effacing as he was charming, Massingham was never the subject of a portrait, apart from a crayon drawing by Powys Evans which has been lost.

[H. J. Massingham, *Remembrance, an*

Autobiography, 1942; *The Times*, 25 August 1952; private information; personal knowledge.]   GARTH CHRISTIAN.

MATHEWS, BASIL JOSEPH (1879–1951), writer and teacher on the missionary and ecumenical movement, was born at Oxford 28 August 1879, the eldest son of Angelo Alfred Hankins Mathews, insurance broker, and his wife, Emma Colegrove. The Mathews line has been traced to Sir David Mathew who was standard bearer to Edward IV at the battle of Towton and whose tomb is in Llandaff Cathedral. The name acquired its final 's' in the lifetime of William Mathew of Bristol (1746–1830), author, and publisher to John Wesley and Hannah More.

Mathews's formal schooling, which was begun at the Oxford High School, ended through family misfortunes at the age of fourteen. After working in the Bodleian and Oxford Public libraries Mathews became private secretary to A. M. Fairbairn [q.v.], principal of Mansfield College. Contact with Fairbairn strengthened a natural aptitude for study and hard work and while still in his employ Mathews entered the university through what was then the non-collegiate delegacy. In 1904 he took second class honours in modern history. With journalism in view he joined the staff of the *Christian World* and in 1910 attended as a reporter the World Missionary Conference at Edinburgh, a turning-point in the modern history of the ecumenical movement. This experience kindled in Mathews a lifelong enthusiasm for Christian missions and in the same year he became editor of the London Missionary Society's publications. It was quickly apparent that missionary propaganda under Mathews's pen was entering a new phase. To the skill of a professional journalist he joined natural teaching gifts, a fine understanding of a great field of Christian thought and action, and the persuasiveness of a man who believed what he wrote and wrote what he believed. One of his earliest books, *Livingstone the Pathfinder* (1912), won speedy and widespread popularity and set the pattern for a successful series of missionary biographies.

The war of 1914–18 brought Mathews into a fresh field of activity. He joined the staff of the Ministry of Information and became chairman and secretary of its literature committee. After the war his widening range of interests included work with the opium commission of the League of Nations in 1923. In the meantime he had in 1919 left the London Missionary Society to become editor of the Far and Near Publications Company, a task which included the editorship of a short-lived but valiant monthly journal, *Outward Bound*. From 1920 to 1924, as head of the Press Bureau of the Conference of British Missionary Societies, he served all the British missions and was active in the affairs of the United Council for Missionary Education and its counterpart in the United States, the Missionary Education Movement. From 1924 until 1929 he was literary secretary to the World's Committee of Young Men's Christian Associations in Geneva. In addition to his editorial work he was in growing demand as a public speaker, especially to student audiences. In these years he travelled widely in the Near East, West Africa, and India, and in 1931 paid his first visit to the United States. From 1932 to 1944 he was first visiting lecturer and then resident professor of Christian world-relations in the school of theology of Boston University and at the Andover-Newton Theological Seminary, Massachusetts. From 1944 to 1949 he held a similar professorship at Union College, university of British Columbia, from which he received the honorary degree of LL.D. in 1949.

Mathews was a prolific writer. In addition to editorial work and a constant stream of articles, he published over forty books, many of which appeared in translations. Among the best known, apart from his biography of Livingstone, were those on John R. Mott (1934) and Booker T. Washington (1949) and his presentation of racial and ethnic problems in *The Clash of Colour* (1924) and *The Jew and the World Ferment* (1934). Much of his writing was topical, but behind a vivid popular style there lay great industry and a power of discernment which made his work more than transient. Students remembered him as an inspiring teacher and men and women of many nationalities took delight in his friendship. He endured a long illness, in which he knew that he was under sentence of death, with fortitude and grace. To the end his pen was busy and he still conversed with zest on the great causes to which he had dedicated uncommon gifts. In the history of the ecumenical movement during the twentieth century Mathews represents, in his writing and standpoint, a significant period; it was one in which, primarily through practical co-operation in the missionary enterprise, the course was being set towards the Churches' deeper understanding of their unity and mission.

Mathews married first, in 1905, Harriett Anne (died 1939), daughter of William Henry Passmore, farmer; secondly, in 1940, Winifred Grace, daughter of John Wilson, chemist. There were no children of either marriage. He died 29 March 1951 in Oxford.

[*The Times*, 31 March and 3 April 1951; private information.]   NORMAN GOODALL.

MATHEWS, DAME VERA (ELVIRA SIBYL MARIA) LAUGHTON (1888–1959), director of the Women's Royal Naval Service, was born in London 25 September 1888, daughter of (Sir) John Knox Laughton [q.v.], naval historian, notable contributor to this Dictionary, and founder of the Navy Records Society, of which he was secretary for twenty years. A child of his second marriage, with Maria Josefa, daughter of Eugenio di Alberti, of Cadiz, she inherited from her father her great love for the sea.

She was educated at convents of the Religious of St. Andrew in Streatham and Tournai and at King's College, London. Shortly before 1914 she became deeply interested in the women's suffrage movement, being at one time sub-editor of *Suffragette*. Immediately on the outbreak of war she volunteered for service at the Admiralty, but was told that no women were—or would be—employed. She turned to journalism, but on learning in November 1917 that the Admiralty proposed to form a Women's Royal Naval Service for shore duties she immediately gave up her post as sub-editor of the *Ladies' Field* in order to apply.

After taking the first officers' course she was sent to the R.N.V.R. depot at the Crystal Palace to recruit and train Wrens. She was appointed M.B.E. for her services but in 1919 the Wrens were completely disbanded.

In 1920 Vera Laughton helped to found the Association of Wrens, while continuing her career as a journalist, becoming the first editor of *Time and Tide*. She became a commissioner of the Girl Guides and, under Dame Katharine Furse (whose notice she has contributed to this Supplement), founded the Sea Guides, later called the Sea Rangers.

In 1924 she married Gordon Dewar Mathews (died 1943), an engineer, with whom she spent several years in Japan,

and by whom she had two sons and a daughter. On her return to England she once again interested herself in the Sea Rangers, local politics, and women's movements, becoming chairman of St. Joan's Social and Political Alliance in 1932 and representing this body at the League of Nations Assembly in 1935.

Late in 1938 the Admiralty started discussions on a women's auxiliary service and shortly afterwards called for 1,500 volunteers. It received over 15,000 replies. In February 1939 Mrs. Mathews was summoned to the Admiralty and in April appointed director of the Women's Royal Naval Service, about to be reformed.

For the next eight years her story was largely that of the Service which she formed, organized, and led with signal ability. Her declared aim was that 'whatever the Navy demands of the Wrens shall be fulfilled'. This, to a remarkable degree, she achieved, thanks to a strong, friendly and unselfconscious personality, excellent organizing ability and, above all, insistence that only the best was good enough—either *for* the Wrens or *by* the Wrens. Progressively through the war years Wrens took over more and more jobs previously thought of as beyond their skill or strength, or as 'unsuitable' for a number of reasons, none of which proved valid: visual signalling and W/T, heavy transport, armament maintenance, naval control of shipping (including boarding officer's duties), and many more. In 1942 the first Wren officer qualified as a signal officer—passing out top of her course. The introduction of the 'boat's crew' category gave scope to those who 'really wanted to go to sea'. Thanks to her insistence and encouragement, the Wren crews became an integral and highly efficient part of the base organization. On the subject of categories and their popularity, she once commented: 'It's difficult to recruit stewards to clean rooms, but put them in dungarees to swab a deck, call them "Maintenance" and there's a queue.'

In 1946 the Admiralty announced that the W.R.N.S. would continue as a permanent Service. Shortly afterwards, in November 1946, Dame Vera retired from the post which she had held throughout the hostilities—a unique distinction among the women's Services in the second world war. Over a hundred thousand women had served in the W.R.N.S. during her years as director. She had been appointed C.B.E. in 1942 and D.B.E. in 1945 and had also received the Cross of Orange Nassau for her work in connection with the training of MARVA, the Netherlands counterpart of the Service. Her history of the W.R.N.S., entitled *Blue Tapestry*, was published in 1948.

After her retirement Dame Vera became chairman of the Domestic Coal Consumers' Council and a member of the South Eastern Gas Board, also holding the appointment of adviser on women's affairs to the Gas Council. She was president of the Smoke Abatement Society. She died in London 25 September 1959, on her seventy-first birthday. There is a memorial alcove in the north aisle of Westminster Cathedral in which St. Christopher is seen holding a boat with a wren perched on an anchor. A portrait by Anthony Devas is in the Imperial War Museum and a copy is at the W.R.N.S. establishment at Burghfield, Reading.

[Private information.]   J. M. PALMER.

MATTHEWS, ALFRED EDWARD (1869–1960), actor, was born at Bridlington, Yorkshire, 22 November 1869, the son of William Matthews and his wife, Alice Mary Long. His father was one of the Matthews brothers of the original Christy Minstrels and his great-uncle was the famous clown, Thomas Matthews [q.v.], who had been a pupil of Grimaldi [q.v.]. He was educated at Stamford, Lincolnshire. Thereafter, according to his own story (of which he had plenty), he proceeded to an office-boy's desk in London on which were carved the initials 'J.H.B.' which he was told were those of (Sir) Henry Irving [q.v.] whose original name was Brodribb. Inspired by this coincidence he got himself a job as a call-boy. He soon rose, via stage management and understudy, to touring actor and, in 1889, he toured South Africa with Lionel Brough [q.v.]. In 1893–6 he toured Australia and then returned to the west end of London in a long list of plays. In 1910 he made his first trip to New York and played Algernon Moncrieffe in *The Importance of being Earnest*. By then 'Matty' was in great demand at home and overseas, among his authors being Pinero, Galsworthy, and Barrie [qq.v.].

After the war one finds him taking over from such players as (Sir) Gerald du Maurier [q.v.] (in *Bulldog Drummond*, 1921, New York and London), Owen Nares, or Ronald Squire. Yet, at all times, like other actors in his constellation who employed initials rather than their Christian names, his star, though minor, was truefixed and constant, only waiting for the opportunity to show it had no fellow in its chosen firmament. It had to wait another twenty years. Meanwhile, however, in the twenty-five years after 1918, he was in a further thirty different plays.

In 1947, in his seventy-eighth year, Matty at last became a great star in his own right, in the line of Sir Charles Hawtrey [q.v.] and du Maurier—the part the Earl of Lister, the play *The Chiltern Hundreds*, the theatre the Vaudeville where he had once been call-boy. In 1949 he went to New York in the same play (renamed *Yes, M'Lord*) and then returned to make the film at Pinewood in his eightieth year. He was appointed O.B.E. in 1951, published *Matty*, his autobiography, in 1952, repeated his success as Lord Lister in a sequel to *The Chiltern Hundreds* in 1954, and went on acting in both films and plays. Aged ninety, indomitable to the last and working still, 'How do I do it?' he echoed an inquiring reporter, 'Easy! I look in the obituary column of *The Times* at breakfast and, if my name's not in it, I go off to the studio.'

Matty was a playwright's dream—the grand old man of the theatre without being remotely grand—the oldest actor acting with the youngest mind—the best-dressed member of the Garrick Club, even though he would travel by underground on a wet day in a deerstalker hat and a pyjama coat over his tweed suit and gumboots. He knew more about the technique of light comedy acting than any of his colleagues, yet, such was his spontaneity, he succeeded in giving the impression that he knew nothing at all. He was as selfish as any actor ever was but he was kindness personified. He was crochety but he had a heart of gold. He was unpredictable, easily bored, perhaps a shade close with the drinks, but he had as much charm as any man in any other walk of life and he loved beauty in women and animals and he encouraged youth.

He married first, in 1909, Caroline May, divorced wife of Richard Cave Chinn and daughter of James Blackwell. They had twin sons and a daughter. The marriage was dissolved and in 1940 he married Patricia Lilian, the divorced wife of William Robson Davies and daughter of Jeremiah O'Herlihy, solicitor.

Matthews died as Bushey Heath 25 July 1960.

[Private information; personal knowledge.]
WILLIAM DOUGLAS-HOME.

MAUGHAM, FREDERIC HERBERT, first VISCOUNT MAUGHAM (1866–1958), lord chancellor, was born in Paris 20 October 1866, the second of the four sons of Robert Ormond Maugham and his wife, Edith Mary, daughter of Major Charles Snell who had died in India in 1841. The youngest son was the writer William Somerset Maugham. His grandfather was the eminent solicitor Robert Maugham [q.v.]; his father was also a solicitor, with a large practice in Paris where he was legal adviser to the British Embassy. One of Maugham's earliest memories was the flight to England as the German army approached the city, and it was not until the Franco-Prussian war had ended and order had been restored that they returned to Paris. There he was educated first by English governesses, then for a short time at a *lycée*, until with his two brothers he was sent to Dover College. Before he had left school both his parents had died and it was only by winning a leaving school scholarship and a senior mathematical scholarship at Trinity Hall that he was able to go to Cambridge where, as he wrote, he had very little money and no one to assist or encourage him in making a success in his chosen profession of the bar. In the mathematical tripos of 1888 he was a senior optime. His success might have been greater had he not given himself wholeheartedly first to rugby football, then to rowing. He rowed No. 7 in the victorious Cambridge boats of 1888 and 1889 and was regarded as an outstanding oar of his generation. For his future career he prepared himself by speaking at the Union of which he became president in 1889.

In 1890 Maugham was called to the bar by Lincoln's Inn. His choice of inn was determined by his friendship formed in his first days at Trinity Hall with Mark (later Lord) Romer, son of Sir Robert Romer [qq.v.]. Apart from his valuable connection with the Romer family, cemented by his marriage in 1896 to Romer's sister Helen, Maugham had no friends in the law. His progress was slow: 'I shall never forget those unhappy days', he wrote. But to such ability as his, success could not for ever be denied. In 1913 he took silk, attaching himself to the court of Mr. Justice Eve [q.v.], and

by 1928, when he was appointed a judge in the Chancery division of the High Court (with the customary knighthood), he had acquired one of the largest practices at the bar. As an advocate he was forceful and lucid, courteous, and scrupulously fair, and his wide knowledge of the law and careful study of the facts of the particular case made him as formidable an opponent as any member of the bar.

In 1934 Maugham was promoted to the Court of Appeal and sworn of the Privy Council; in the next year he was appointed a lord of appeal in ordinary, with a life peerage. As a judge in the Chancery division and in the appellate courts Maugham deserved and won a high reputation. The qualities which gave him pre-eminence at the bar did not leave him on the bench. The same thoroughness and courtesy, joined with a conspicuous determination to do justice, made him an ideal judge. It may be true that the practitioner will seldom turn to one of his judgements as the *locus classicus* upon any branch of the law, but it is beyond dispute that he made a solid contribution to the corpus of English law, particularly in relation to such difficult subjects as patents and trademarks. Examples of his thoroughness and power of lucid exposition may be found in such cases as *Crofter Hand Woven Harris Tweed Co.* v. *Veitch*, [1942] A.C. 435, in which it was held that, if the predominant purpose of combination is the legitimate interest of the persons combining and the means employed are not criminal or tortious in themselves, the combination is not unlawful; or the much-debated case of *Liversidge* v. *Anderson*, [1942] A.C. 206, in which in a discussion of Regulation 18B of the Defence General Regulations 1939 it was held that a court of law could not question the statement of a secretary of state that he had reasonable cause for belief in certain facts; or again in *Wolstanton Ltd.* v. *Newcastle-under-Lyme Corporation*, [1940] A.C. 860, where an alleged custom for the lord of a manor to get minerals beneath the surface of copyhold or customary freehold lands without making compensation for subsidence or damage to buildings was held to be invalid. In *Sammut* v. *Strickland*, [1938] A.C. 678, delivering the judgement of the Judicial Committee of the Privy Council, Maugham made a valuable contribution to constitutional law in his discussion of the prerogative right of the Crown to legislate for a ceded colony by letters patent or order in Council.

In March 1938 Maugham was invited to become lord chancellor in place of Lord Hailsham [q.v.] who was in failing health. He accepted with reluctance; although in 1922 Bonar Law had suggested that he might become solicitor-general, he had been unable to find a seat; he had consequently no political experience and was of an age at which the new duties of a very onerous office might appear insupportable. He was, however, persuaded to undertake them upon the understanding that in the troublesome state of affairs then prevailing he might be asked to resign before the end of the Government, when he would, if there were a vacancy, return to his former office. On the outbreak of war in September 1939 he willingly and gracefully gave way to Lord Caldecote [q.v.]; was created a viscount; and shortly afterwards was reappointed a lord of appeal in ordinary, from which office he finally resigned in 1941.

Although Maugham did not for long occupy the Woolsack he was able to take a leading part in the passing of several important bills, notably the Coal Act, in which 117 amendments, mostly drafted by him, were made in the House of Lords, and the Law of Evidence Act which he had introduced shortly before he became lord chancellor. Upon his resignation the leader of the Labour Party in the House of Lords, Lord Snell [q.v.], expressed appreciation of his courtesy and helpfulness to them in their work.

While still at the bar Maugham wrote *The Case of Jean Calas* (1928), the story of a celebrated French judicial error in 1761–2 which Voltaire had long before exposed. This involved much research in the libraries of France during vacations. In 1936 he published *The Tichborne Case*, an elaborate review, upon which he had long been engaged, of the trial of the Tichborne claimant. To many people it may have seemed that with this book the last word had been said on the subject and that the claim of Arthur Orton [q.v.] had for ever been exploded. If so, they have been disappointed. After his retirement Maugham wrote a short book called *The Truth About the Munich Crisis* (1944), in which he vigorously refuted what he deemed to have been unfair attacks upon Neville Chamberlain. Later, in *U.N.O. and War Crimes* (1951), he was moved to challenge the theory that the Charter of

Nuremberg was justified by any rule of international law. It appeared to him, as to Lord Hankey, who wrote a postscript to the book, that although the judgements of the Nuremberg tribunal might be regarded as lawful in Germany during her occupation by the allied forces, it was a misnomer and a dangerous precedent to treat them as justified by international law, the whole basis of which rests on the previous agreement of the nations concerned.

Finally, in 1954 Maugham published a discursive book called *At the End of the Day* in which he not only reviewed the events of his own life but also commented at large on public affairs in general whether or not he had played any part in them. The legal profession would have preferred a larger share to have been given to his own life story.

During his professional vacations Maugham travelled widely both in Europe and farther afield. He was an earnest and competent golfer and a fair shot, although he had little opportunity of indulging in this sport. In 1896 he married Helen Mary (died 1950), daughter of Sir Robert Romer. They had one son, Robert Cecil Romer (born 1916), who succeeded as second viscount and who as Robin Maugham is known as a writer; and three daughters, all of whom have distinguished themselves in literature or art: Kate Bruce and Diana Marr-Johnson as writers and Honor Earl as a portrait painter. Maugham died in London 23 March 1958, in his ninety-second year. There are portraits of him by R. G. Eves in Lincoln's Inn (of which he was a bencher) and by Sir Gerald Kelly in Trinity Hall (of which he became an honorary fellow in 1928). A charcoal drawing by Honor Earl is in the possession of the family.

[Viscount Maugham, *At the End of the Day*, 1954; Robin Maugham, *Somerset and all the Maughams*, 1966; *The Times*, 24 March 1958; private information; personal knowledge.]

SIMONDS.

MAURICE, SIR FREDERICK BARTON (1871–1951), major-general, was born in Dublin 19 January 1871, the eldest son of (Major-General Sir) John Frederick Maurice [q.v.], and grandson of Frederick Denison Maurice [q.v.]. He was educated at St. Paul's School and the Royal Military College, Sandhurst, from which he was commissioned in 1892 in the Derbyshire Regiment (later renamed the

Sherwood Foresters). While a subaltern he served as aide-de-camp to his father and with his battalion in the Tirah campaign of 1897–8. He took part in the South African war as special service officer and as D.A.A.G., and was mentioned in dispatches and promoted brevet major at the age of twenty-nine. On his return to England he graduated at the Staff College and held a number of staff appointments including service at the War Office in the directorate of staff duties under Sir Douglas (later Earl) Haig [q.v.].

In 1913 Maurice went as instructor to the Staff College where his father had been professor of military history over twenty years earlier. For the first nine months Sir William Robertson [q.v.] was commandant, and a close friendship began which had a marked influence on Maurice's subsequent career. When war broke out in 1914 he went to France with the headquarters of the 3rd division, and during the retreat from Mons was promoted to be head of the general staff of the division. Officers who were serving with him have recorded his coolness in action and the clarity and speed with which he dictated orders.

At the end of January 1915 Robertson became chief of the general staff, British Expeditionary Force, and a few months later he selected Maurice to take charge of the operations section at G.H.Q. Maurice thoroughly understood his chief's method of work and served him admirably throughout 1915. He was appointed C.B. and promoted to brevet colonel. When Robertson became chief of the imperial general staff in December 1915 he took Maurice with him to the War Office as director of military operations with the rank of major-general, and they continued in the complete accord which had marked their association in France. For his services Maurice was appointed K.C.M.G. in January 1918. In February Robertson relinquished his appointment and Maurice did the same on 21 April.

Shortly afterwards Maurice brought his military career to an abrupt end by writing a letter to the London newspapers in which he accused Lloyd George's government of deceiving Parliament and the country about the strength of the British Army on the western front, the extension of the British line there, and other matters. Robertson and Maurice had for long been at loggerheads with the prime minister whom they distrusted both as a man and as an amateur strategist.

They consistently maintained that the western front was the decisive theatre but Lloyd George, shocked by the terrible casualties in Haig's battles, was ever seeking some more effective and less costly strategy and was strongly attracted by the eastern policy of defeating Germany by 'knocking away the props'. He had no confidence in his military advisers and he would gladly have dismissed Haig had he felt strong enough to do so.

The Cabinet had underrated Robertson's warnings of the impending German attack in the west, and had not acted upon his recommendations for reinforcing Haig and raising more men for the army. When the Germans broke through our lines in March and drove us back almost to the Channel ports, the Government was charged with having contributed to these disasters by failing to strengthen the army in France with drafts which were available at home. Lloyd George defended himself and his ministers by stating on 9 April 1918 that on 1 January 1918 Haig's army was 'considerably stronger' than it had been on 1 January 1917. Maurice's letter, published on 7 May, gave the direct lie to this and other statements made by the Government.

The military reverses in France had alarmed the whole nation and this indictment came at a time when the general direction of the war had, for some months, been under severe criticism in Parliament and the press. Formidable forces existed which were ready to combine against Lloyd George, and, as he himself recorded, the controversy which ensued threatened the life of his Government. The debate on the Maurice letter took place on 9 May and in it Lloyd George defended himself successfully and by a majority of almost three to one defeated the Opposition motion which amounted to a vote of censure. He reaffirmed his statement of 9 April and a further statement made by J. I. Macpherson (later Lord Strathcarron, q.v.), the undersecretary for war, on 18 April with regard to the strength of Haig's army. These, he said, were based upon figures supplied to him by the War Office, which indeed was true.

The figures on which Lloyd George had based his statement of 9 April were his own analysis of a War Office statistical return. Maurice considered that Lloyd George had deceived the House of Commons both by misuse of the statistics of the non-combatants as distinguished from the combatant strength of the army and by implying that there had been no diminution between January and March 1918. This was the foundation of the main charge of his letter. On 18 April Maurice's department provided material for the answer by Macpherson to a question in the House on the point of combatant as distinct from non-combatant forces. But in these figures the strength of the army in Italy was inadvertently included in that of the army in France. A return from the adjutant-general's department of 7 May showed a decrease in the fighting forces in France in January 1918 as compared with the position in 1917 of some 95,000, of which some 70,000 were infantry. It now seems certain that these figures were known to Lloyd George before the debate of 9 May, but that he chose to ignore them. A copy of the return was sent by the War Office to 10 Downing Street where on the morning of 9 May Philip Kerr (later the Marquess of Lothian, q.v.), the prime minister's secretary, on noting the discrepancy, made inquiries of the deputy director of military operations. Only then was it that the mistake in the figures provided on 18 April was discovered. Kerr was informed before luncheon on the 9th. Nevertheless in that afternoon's debate Lloyd George relied upon the incorrect figures. After the debate he was officially informed by Macpherson and Lord Milner [q.v.] of the mistake, of which he already knew, but he took no action to correct it, saying that he could not be held responsible for an error made by General Maurice's department.

Although Maurice was still technically in charge of his department on 18 April his successor was already in the War Office and Maurice himself knew nothing of the question and answer until Lloyd George repeated the inaccurate figures during the debate of 9 May. He knew that the prime minister, although informed of the mistake after the debate, took no action to put the matter right. It was not apparently until December 1919 that he learned that correct figures had been supplied to the prime minister before the debate. Many years later, after both Lloyd George and Maurice were dead, Lord Beaverbrook published an extract from a diary kept by Miss Frances Stevenson, later Lloyd George's second wife, which recorded the burning by (Sir) J. T. Davies of a paper from the D.M.O. found forgotten in a dispatch box. Much

publicity was given to the 'burnt paper' and it was supposed Lloyd George had never received the revised figures; but further evidence suggests that this was another copy of the adjutant-general's return which had been sent to the secretary of the War Cabinet.

Whether Maurice hoped to bring the Government down when he wrote his letter must remain one of the enigmas of history. Beyond a shadow of doubt he was not a party to any intrigue, military or political, to oust Lloyd George. Whether he was right or wrong in what he did, there can be no difference of opinion regarding his supreme moral courage and sense of duty. His action was instigated by a sincere belief confirmed by a visit to France that the morale of the troops was in danger of being undermined by attempts to shift responsibility for the March disaster on to the shoulders of the military leaders and by the conviction that a plot was being hatched to remove Haig. To the end of his life Maurice believed that he had saved Haig, whose only reaction at the time was a characteristic disapproval of conduct which he regarded as mistaken and improper.

Before Maurice's letter appeared in the press, he wrote to his daughter Nancy, who was then seventeen, telling her with moving sincerity that he fully realized what the consequences might be for himself and his family. He ended: 'I am persuaded that I am doing what is right, and once that is so, nothing else matters to a man. That is I believe what Christ meant when he told us to forsake father and mother and children for his sake.'

The Maurice debate had a lasting importance in political history, far transcending the immediate issue. It marked a turning-point in Lloyd George's career, for his triumph left him in a position of undisputed authority. But in the sequel the debate had, as Lloyd George put it, 'a disruptive effect upon the fortunes of the Liberal Party', by bringing about the emphatic cleavage between his followers and those of Asquith.

In writing the letter Maurice had committed a grave breach of discipline which could not be condoned or overlooked by the Army Council however much the members may have appreciated his motives. He was at once retired from the army, and was refused a court martial or inquiry.

He tackled the problem of earning his living with courage and enterprise. He turned to teaching and writing and in both he achieved considerable success. From 1922 to 1933 he was principal of the Working Men's College, which his grandfather had helped to found in 1854. In 1927 he was appointed professor of military studies at London University, and a year later he became chairman of the adult education committee of the Board of Education. He became D.Lit., London, in 1930. From 1933 to 1944 he was principal of the East London College (later Queen Mary College), university of London, where he was not only highly successful in maintaining the academic standards but also made a great contribution to the development of the social life of both staff and students. He became a fellow of Queen Mary College in 1946 and was a member of the university senate. He was made an honorary LL.D. of Cambridge in 1926, was Lees Knowles lecturer at Trinity College in 1925–6, and was elected an honorary fellow of King's College in 1944 in recognition of the good relations he established between the colleges when Queen Mary College was moved to Cambridge in the war.

Maurice published a number of admirable historical studies including books on the *Russo-Turkish War 1877* (1905) and Robert E. Lee (1925). He wrote a life of his father, and collaborated with Sir George Arthur in a biography of Lord Wolseley (1924). He also wrote biographies of Lord Haldane (2 vols. 1937–9) and Lord Rawlinson (1928). Among his other books are *Governments and War* (1926), *British Strategy* (1929, based on a series of lectures), *The 16th Foot* (1931), a *History of the Scots Guards* (2 vols., 1934), and *The Armistices of 1918* (1943). *Forty Days in 1914* (1919) is a particularly good study of the B.E.F. in the opening campaign of the war; *The Last Four Months* (1919) is hardly on the same level. He was for a time military correspondent to the *Daily Chronicle* and the *Daily News*, and was a contributor to many magazines and reviews and also to the *Cambridge Modern History*. His contributions to this Dictionary include the notices of Haig, Robertson, and Rawlinson.

Maurice took a deep interest in the British Legion and was indefatigable in his work for the welfare of ex-servicemen. He became its honorary treasurer in 1930 and was president in 1932–47. In September 1938 he flew to Berlin and offered the services of the Legion to Hitler for duty in the plebiscite areas of Czecho-slovakia, with the result that a contingent of 1,200 ex-servicemen was assembled before the plebiscite was called off. A year later, three days before Great Britain entered the war, he broadcast to the soldiers of the German Army on behalf of the Legion, appealing to them not to bring about another fight with England by attacking Poland. He was colonel of his regiment from 1935 to 1941; was a commander of the Legion of Honour and of the Order of the Crown of Belgium, and had the Russian Order of St. Stanislas and the French croix de guerre.

In appearance Maurice was tall and fair, a little bent, with a round face and a boxer's flattened-out nose. He had a rather abrupt manner and he spoke and wrote with great clarity and conciseness. Those with whom he served were impressed by his efficiency, loyalty, and capacity for friendship. He loved poetry and when he was incapacitated by illness in his last years he would recite aloud favourite passages from Tennyson, Wordsworth, and Kipling. As a soldier his talents were those of a staff officer rather than a commander. He inherited a family tradition of high idealism and readiness to sacrifice personal interests to the cause of truth, and the letter which ended his military career was in that tradition.

He married in 1899 Helen Margaret (died 1942), daughter of Frederick Howard Marsh, later professor of surgery at Cambridge and master of Downing College, and sister of (Sir) Edward Marsh [q.v.]. They had one son and four daughters, one of whom, Joan Violet Robinson, became professor of economics at Cambridge in 1965. Maurice died at his home in Cambridge 19 May 1951. A portrait by Henry Lamb is in Queen Mary College.

[*The Times*, 21 May 1951; *Westminster Gazette*, passim, 1922; *Spectator*, 2, 16, 23 November and 7 December 1956; Sir Frederick Maurice, *Intrigues of the War* (preface by the Marquess of Crewe), 1922; David Lloyd George, *War Memoirs*, vol. v, 1936; Sir Edward Spears, *Prelude to Victory*, 1939; Lord Beaverbrook, *Men and Power*, 1956; S. W. Roskill, *Hankey, Man of Secrets*, vol. i, 1970; private information; personal knowledge.]

JOHN KENNEDY.

MAVOR, OSBORNE HENRY (1888–1951), better known as the playwright JAMES BRIDIE, was born in Glasgow 3 January 1888, the eldest son of Henry Alexander Mavor, a man of many gifts who made a comfortable living as an engineer, and his wife, Janet Osborne.

The houses in which the Mavors lived had an atmosphere of dignity and good manners and a smell of old books and ink.' So wrote O. H. Mavor in *One Way of Living* 1939), an autobiography which refuses, with charm and gaiety, to endow its subject with the importance he deserved. Educated at Glasgow Academy, he took advantage of the solid comfort in which he had grown up to spend nine or ten years at Glasgow University, ostensibly as a medical student, but more remarkably as a source of high spirits, light verse, ingenious ragging, and talkative and persistent friendships: one of his fellow students, and a friend until death, was Walter Elliot [q.v.].

Having qualified in 1913 Mavor, like Elliot, joined the Royal Army Medical Corps and the war of 1914 with an enthusiasm typical of his generation. This enthusiasm somehow survived service in Flanders, was depressed in Mesopotamia, but revived in the romantic circumstances of the expedition which Major-General Dunsterville led from northern Persia to the Caspian shore of Russia. Some twenty years later, at the age of fifty-one, Mavor returned to the R.A.M.C. and a second war, and saw brief service in Norway. Although by then he had found his true vocation, it was not so exclusive as to despise a latent romanticism or reject an old-fashioned call to duty.

As a practitioner and teacher his medical career was respectable: he was a consulting physician to the Victoria Infirmary and for some time professor of medicine in the Anderson College of Glasgow. But the work for which he is known began, or had its public beginnings, in 1928, when he wrote a play called *The Sunlight Sonata* which bewildered a Glasgow audience and included in its *dramatis personae* Beelzebub, some ebullient Deadly Sins, and three starchy redeeming Graces. This was a romping prologue to the vigorous, imaginative, and wonderfully diversified *œuvre* of the next twenty years.

He wrote in all some forty plays, under the pseudonym James Bridie, and entered the great world of the theatre under the auspices of Sir Barry Jackson, who presented *The Switchback* in Birmingham in 1929 and at the Malvern Festival in 1931. *The Anatomist*, with Henry Ainley [q.v.] in the leading part, had a London production in the latter year, and Bridie was involved in an argument which was to becloud his reputation for the rest of his life. It was said—by James Agate [q.v.]

the first time—and endlessly repeated, that he could not construct a last act. The accusation may not be logically maintained, for his last acts were always logical, but what may readily be admitted is that they did not always meet the expectation of critics or of an audience anticipating a conventional gesture of conclusion. The eponym of *The Anatomist* was Dr. Knox, the teacher of anatomy whose cadavers were supplied by Burke and Hare. In 1933 Bridie again found a subject for drama in his familiar medical world and wrote one of his best plays, *A Sleeping Clergyman*, in which, declaring that 'to make for righteousness is a biological necessity', he admitted his sanguine temperament and the stubborn remnant of a faith which his Calvinist forebears had bred in him. It was one of his private jokes to pretend that he kept the Calvinist belief; more certainly, an invaluable part of his heritage was his profound knowledge of the Bible.

His biblical plays—*Tobias and the Angel* (1930), *Jonah and the Whale* (1932), *Susannah and the Elders* (1937)—are the most delightful of his writings, instinct with wit, insight into character, and essential common sense; or, perhaps, uncommon understanding. They are, moreover, written with a gracious and fluent command of language, and his dialogue demonstrates to perfection how phrases may be carpentered to reveal the precise and necessary meaning of their words. He was a master of polite English, he was at home on the borderland of poetry, and he could make his Scotch characters talk as convincingly as did Sir Walter at his best.

As popular successes, *Mr. Bolfry* (1943), a brilliant and immensely comic sermon with Alastair Sim in the pulpit, and *Daphne Laureola* (1949), in which Dame Edith Evans played with entrancing virtuosity, were outstanding. A good play, *The Queen's Comedy*, was insufficiently rewarded at the Edinburgh Festival in 1950; *The Baikie Charivari* (1952), his last work, is admittedly difficult, and, unique in his *œuvre*, darkened by pessimism and anger; but Walter Elliot declared it to be Scotland's *Peer Gynt*.

Of Bridie's importance to Scotland, as well as to the Scottish theatre—which, indeed, hardly existed before his time, and has shown no great liveliness since his death—there is no doubt whatever. He was an innovator, and a creator of more than words and dramatic scenes: he

created an *ambiance* of confidence, gaiety,
and affection, and while he might describe his fellow man as 'a droll wee
slug wi' the shifty e'e', he loved all
life and welcomed all sorts and kinds
of his fellow men for their comical
and unexpected contributions to it.
Although fundamentally serious, passionately devoted to the Citizens' Theatre
which he established in Glasgow in 1943,
and most patiently concerned with the
improvement of young writers whom his
work had inspired, Bridie never let
solemnity darken his utterance or magnify
his personality. He thought well of his
work, but preferred to live in the relaxed
and easy temper which his natural geniality prompted. Without protestation of
virtue or inhibition of his fine talent for
invective, he was essentially a good man,
and the clarity, the fine manners, and the
fun which pervade his writings were all
reflections of his intrinsic charity.

Bridie himself was a man of no great
physical attraction, but his appearance in
maturity acquired a ponderous, craggy,
and magnificent benignity. In compensation for his own plainness, he married in
1923 Rona Bremner, a girl of notable
beauty, who had loved him all her life.
They had two sons, one of whom, serving
with the Lothians and Border Horse, was
killed in France in 1944; the other, having
qualified and practised in medicine, chose
to exemplify the proverb *Bon chien chasse
de race* by taking to the theatre and
dramatic criticism.

Bridie was appointed C.B.E. in 1946
and died in Edinburgh 29 January 1951.
In 1939 he received the honorary degree
of LL.D. from Glasgow University where
there is a bronze bust of him by Loris
Rey. A water-colour self-portrait is in the
possession of Mrs. Bannister; a terracotta
by Benno Schotz belongs to the Arts
Council, Scottish committee; an oil painting by Stanley Cursiter, showing Bridie
in conversation with other Scottish
authors (Edwin Muir, q.v., Neil Gunn, Eric
Linklater) is in the Glasgow City Art
Gallery.

[James Bridie, *Some Talk of Alexander*,
1926, and *One Way of Living*, 1939; Winifred
Bannister, *James Bridie and his Theatre*,
1955; personal knowledge.] ERIC LINKLATER.

MAWSON, SIR DOUGLAS (1882–1958),
scientist and explorer, was born at Shipley,
near Bradford in Yorkshire, 5 May 1882,
the son of Robert Ellis Mawson, who came
from sturdy yeoman stock, and his wife,

Margaret Ann Moore, of the Isle of Man
His colouring and striking physiqu
seemed to indicate Viking blood. Durin
Mawson's childhood the family moved t
Australia; he was educated at the famou
Fort Street School and the university c
Sydney where in 1902 he obtained hi
B.E. in mining and a demonstratorshi
in chemistry, and in 1905 his B.Sc
During this period he came under th
influence of Professor A. Liversidge, wh
interested him in chemical geology, an
of his lifelong friend (Sir) Edgeworth Davi
(whose notice he subsequently contri
buted to this Dictionary).

In the New Hebrides in 1903 Mawso
carried out geological investigations i
dangerous jungles infested by hostil
natives upon which he subsequentl
reported. In 1905 he went as a lecture
in mineralogy and petrology to Adelaid
where he took his D.Sc. in 1909 an
served as first professor of geology an
mineralogy from 1920 until 1952.

On David's recommendation Mawso
was invited to join the 1907 expedition o
(Sir) Ernest Shackleton [q.v.] as a physicist. Sailing to Ross Sea in *Nimroa*
Mawson was chiefly concerned with
geomagnetic and auroral studies, but he
opened his outstanding contribution to
Antarctic exploration by two notable
achievements with David: the ascent and
geological examination of the active volcanic cone of Mount Erebus (1908) and the
attainment of the south magnetic pole
(1909), a success which demanded a
pioneer ascent of the high and bitter
Antarctic plateaux and the man-hauling
of sledges for some 1,300 miles. Captain
R. F. Scott [q.v.] asked Mawson to join
his last and fatal expedition to the Pole,
but the scientific and mechanical age of
Antarctic exploration was succeeding the
'heroic period' and Mawson preferred to
concentrate on the scientific appraisal of
the coastlands of what was to become the
Australian sector. He organized and led
the noted Australasian Antarctic Expedition of 1911–14. Sailing in the *Aurora*
(Captain J. K. Davis) Mawson left a wireless station at Macquarie Island under
G. F. Ainsworth and in the continent
established his own main base at Cape
Denison in what was later to become
George V Land and that of J. R. F. Wild
[q.v.] on the Shackleton Ice Shelf in Queen
Mary Land farther west. Davis and the
land parties explored nearly 2,000 miles
of coastline while sledge parties traversed
some 4,000 miles in the coastlands and

interlands gaining scientific information of great value. In George V Land the explorers encountered one of the most stormy and crevasse-imperilled regions of the world; on one inland sledging expedition Mawson lost both his companions, Xavier Mertz and B. E. S. Ninnis, and only survived himself by the exercise of iron determination, superb physique, and the unfailing courage evident in all his expeditions. His return to base was so delayed that the party was obliged to stay another winter before they could be relieved.

The outbreak of war in 1914 naturally submerged the achievements of the expedition and delayed the publication of the valuable scientific information it had secured. Later, however, the reports on geography, oceanography, glaciology, biology, terrestrial magnetism, and other scientific subjects proved of major importance. In the meantime Mawson enlisted for war service; was promoted major; carried out important work with explosives and supervised the supply of munitions to various countries, including Russia, which he visited.

After the war international rivalry developed in the Antarctic, due mainly to the growth of the whaling industry based on improved methods of locating and killing the mammals and on huge diesel-engined factory ships. In 1923 Britain established the Ross Dependency under New Zealand to preserve her whaling rights and licence fees; the Australian Government secretly, and Mawson openly, urged the annexation of Antarctica from the Ross Dependency to Enderby Land, mainly on account of the eastward advance of the Norwegian whaling fleets. Britain reached a secret agreement with Norway under which that country would respect the lands discovered by Britons in this sector in return for British recognition of the Norwegian annexation of Peter I and Bouvet islands, which had been discovered by the Russians and the French. This arrangement, however, did not protect the unknown coast between Wild's area of operations in Queen Mary Land and Enderby and Kemp Lands. Britain refused to annex the region without the dispatch of a further exploring expedition which was organized by Mawson with the help of private supporters and the Governments of Britain, Australia, and New Zealand, and was known as Banzare (1929–31).

Lars Christensen, the great Norwegian

scientific whaler, and Mawson, in Scott's old steam vessel *Discovery*, now both had expeditions at sea, nominally with scientific but also with territorial objectives. In an almost romantic climax Mawson, after conducting scientific work on Kerguelen, possibly sighted Princess Elizabeth Land in December 1929; certainly discovered MacRobertson Land, which he named after his principal financial supporter (Sir) MacPherson Robertson, and landing at Proclamation Island in Enderby Land, annexed what became the western end of the Australian sector. The Norwegian explorer, Riiser Larsen in *Norvegia*, now arrived from the west where he had been coaling after reaching and proclaiming the annexation of Enderby Land, an action which the Norwegians repudiated. The rival explorers agreed to work westwards and eastwards respectively; the Norwegian turned and steamed westward to conduct explorations which helped to give his country the vast territory of Queen Maud Land.

In the following year Mawson landed at the scene of his earlier explorations in George V Land, which he annexed. *Discovery* and her aircraft then made a sporadic examination of the coastline right around to Princess Elizabeth Land, and to the Mackenzie Sea coast of MacRobertson Land which the party discovered only two days before the Norwegians. Landing at Scullin Monolith in East, and at Cape Bruce in West, MacRobertson Land, Mawson proclaimed further annexations.

The expedition had now fulfilled the requirements of the British Government which in 1933 annexed, with the exception of Adélie Land, the vast territory of nearly two and a half million square miles between the Ross Dependency and Enderby Land, and handed it to Australia. Although the United States and Russia refused to recognize any annexation of Antarctic territory unless accompanied by occupation, it may be fairly said that Mawson staked for the Commonwealth a legal and widely admitted claim to the Australian Antarctic.

The Banzare expedition also gained notable scientific results although publication was again delayed by the worldwide economic depression and the outbreak of war in 1939. Later, however, the federal Government provided the means to issue the reports which Mawson himself edited until he died.

Despite his lifelong interest in Antarctic affairs Mawson gave notable services also to South Australian geology, reports on which comprise the larger part of the 123 books and articles which he published. He travelled over much of the difficult and arid regions of this state of 380,000 square miles, usually taking parties of students with him. Very early in his career he was attracted by the arc of Pre-Cambrian and highly mineralized rocks which runs eastwards from the Mount Lofty and Flinders ranges to New South Wales and contains the noted Broken Hill silver lead deposits. Mawson postulated that these rocks should be grouped into an older 'Willyama' and a younger 'Torrowangee' series, a supposition which isotopic age determination has proved correct, as also his belief that the older series is Archaean and the younger Proterozoic. In 1906 Mawson identified some specimens as uranium minerals which were in consequence developed at Radium Hill near Olary. There, too, he discovered a new radioactive mineral which he named Davidite. Subsequent discoveries of uranium and other minerals at Mount Painter were also of importance.

Mawson's work in the Antarctic gave him an intense interest in glaciology. Proterozoic sediments and glacial beds had been found in the gorge of the Sturt river near Adelaide and Mawson showed the existence of similar beds of extraordinary extent, thickness, and importance. Indeed, he made the remarkable discovery that these glacial formations, in some places tillite but generally glaciomarine, extend for a thousand miles in the interior of South Australia and indicate that glacial conditions existed intermittently in the Proterozoic over an immense period of time.

Mawson was knighted in 1914; appointed O.B.E. in 1920; received the King's Polar medal with three bars, and awards from many British and foreign learned societies, including the Antarctic (1909) and Founder's (1915) medals of the Royal Geographical Society. The university of Adelaide established in 1961 the Mawson Institute of Antarctic Research where most of Mawson's papers are deposited. Nevertheless, although Mawson's Antarctic nomenclature was very generous, not only to his supporters and colleagues but also to his foreign rivals, his own name was not adequately recognized in Antarctica until his death. At that time the Russians in particular proclaimed him as the outstanding scientific explorer of the Antarctic and the

Australian Government named, in his honour, a Mawson coast. The region selected in MacRobertson Land was most appropriate as it was discovered by Mawson, is the site of the Mawson scientific station, and adjoins the coast named after his great Norwegian rival Lars Christensen.

For his services to geology Mawson received medals from a number of geological societies including the Bigsby medal of the Geological Society of London. He was elected F.R.S. in 1923 the Australian and New Zealand Association for the Advancement of Science awarded him the Mueller memorial medal in 1930 and elected him to its presidency in 1935-7. The new laboratories in the school of geology at Adelaide were named after him.

Mawson married in 1914 Francisca Adriana (Paquita), daughter of Guillaume Daniel Delprat, the leading founder of the Broken Hill Proprietary. They had two daughters, the elder of whom, Patricia Marietje Thomas, of the university of Adelaide, continued her father's work as general editor of the Banzare publications. Humble-minded and almost retiring as Mawson was, unless he was fighting with iron determination in a worthwhile issue, he and Lady Mawson, who received the O.B.E. for her services to infant welfare, made an important contribution to the life and development of South Australia. When Mawson died in Adelaide, 14 October 1958, he was accorded the honour of a state funeral. The Mawson Institute for Antarctic Research has a portrait of Mawson (1933) by H. J. Haley. A portrait (1957) by Ivor Hele is in the Bonython Hall of the university of Adelaide and another (1959) by the same artist belongs to the Royal Geographical Society of London.

[Sir Douglas Mawson, 'Geographical Narrative and Cartography', *AAE Scientific Reports*, series A, vol. i, Sydney, 1942; *The Home of the Blizzard*, 2 vols., 1915; 'The B.A.N.Z. Antarctic Research Expedition, 1929-31' in *Geographical Journal*, August 1932; A. Grenfell Price, 'Geographical Narrative', *Banzare Scientific Reports*, series 1, vol. i, 1962; A. R. Alderman and C. E. Tilley in *Biographical Memoirs of Fellows of the Royal Society*, vol. v, 1959; E. M. Suzyumov, *A Life given to the Antarctic—the Antarctic Explorer, Sir Douglas Mawson*, Moscow, 1960; R. A. Swan, *Australia in the Antarctic*, Melbourne, 1961; *Sir Douglas Mawson Anniversary Volume*, Adelaide, 1952; private information; personal knowledge.]   A. GRENFELL PRICE.

MAXSE, SIR (FREDERICK) IVOR (1862–1958), general, was born in London 2 December 1862, the elder son of Admiral Frederick Augustus Maxse [q.v.] and his wife, Cecilia, daughter of Colonel James Steel, Indian Army. His father was a friend of George Meredith [q.v.] who portrayed his character in *Beauchamp's Career*. Leo Maxse [q.v.], his younger brother, became editor of the *National Review*. His sister Violet, of whom there is a notice in this Supplement, married first Lord Edward Cecil [q.v.], and secondly Lord Milner [q.v.].

Maxse was educated at Rugby and the Royal Military College, Sandhurst, and was commissioned in the 7th Royal Fusiliers in 1882. With family encouragement he transferred to the Coldstream Guards in 1891 with the rank of captain. In 1893 and 1894 he was aide-de-camp to Sir A. J. Lyon Fremantle in command first of Scottish District, then of Malta, but finding Malta too far from the social and cultural life of London Maxse resigned. Active soldiering interested him more than the Staff College and in 1897 he went instead to Cairo where he was seconded to the Egyptian Army and saw service as a staff officer; he was a brigade-major at the battles of Atbara and Khartoum in 1898, being appointed to the D.S.O., and was a battalion commander in the final defeat of the Khalifa in 1899. On the recommendation of Lord Kitchener [q.v.] he was sent straight on to South Africa as a brevet lieutenant-colonel. He was a transport officer on the staff of Lord Roberts [q.v.] as a deputy-assistant-adjutant-general. After the capture of Pretoria he became commander of its police.

Back in England the pattern of the fashionable officer once more unfolded: brevet colonel in 1905 and command of a battalion of the Coldstream. Yet he possessed an extremely quick and curious mind and his experiences of war had awakened him to the dangers threatening the world of Edwardian London. In 1905 he published a biography of Seymour Vandeleur, some chapters of which had already appeared in the *National Review*, in which he made penetrating criticisms of the English public school, its ethos, and its education, as inadequate in a competitive world.

When war broke out in 1914 Maxse had been brigadier-general in command of the 1st Guards brigade since 1910. He was promoted major-general and took the brigade to France and led it through the campaigns of Mons, the Marne, and the Aisne, but only saw serious action at the Aisne (14 September). He was sent home to command and train the 18th division, one of Kitchener's New Army formations, which went to France in July 1915 and took part in the tragically misconceived grand assault of 1 July 1916 which opened the battle of the Somme. Maxse was fortunate: his division was on the right of the British line, in XIII Corps which profited from the heavier and denser artillery bombardment of the neighbouring French Army and the rapid advance of the experienced French infantry. Maxse's division captured its allotted objectives. On 14 July his division took part in the successful surprise dawn attack on the Bazentins and Longueval which marked an abandonment of the earlier rigid linear tactics. In September 1916 the 18th division took part in the successful attack on the powerfully fortified Thiepval ridge and captured the Schwaben Redoubt, and in October Maxse's troops were involved in the battle of the Ancre.

At the beginning of 1917 Maxse was promoted temporary lieutenant-general and given the XVIII Corps. In this command he took part in the Passchendaele campaign of July–November 1917 and in the spring of 1918 formed part of the Fifth Army under Sir Hubert Gough during the great German offensive. Although in the end swamped by German weight and numbers his defence was as successful as any in Gough's army; during the retreat he handled his corps with energy and decision, despite some confusion of understanding with Gough which led to the premature retreat of the XVIII Corps to the line of the Somme.

The operations of Maxse's corps had been marked by the thoroughness and excellence of his preliminary training; and training, thorough, professional, and based on open-minded evaluation of the lessons of battle, was henceforth the keynote of his career. He was a member of the board of inquiry into the local collapse of the British defence at Cambrai and contributed a note on the needs and methods of training troops. He was among the first British commanders to accept the new German concepts of attack by infiltration and defence in greater depth. In April 1918 he was appointed inspector-general of training in France, a post in which he was able to do much to amend the rigidity and orthodoxy of the British tactics and command methods: the results were seen in the offensive battles of August–October 1918.

In 1919 Maxse went to Northern Command in the United Kingdom where he remained until 1923. There he had a marked but regrettably not long-lasting influence on the post-war training, organization, and tactics of the British Army. It was Maxse's interest and patronage which launched the career as a military thinker of (Sir) B. H. Liddell Hart. At his request Liddell Hart was transferred to Northern Command headquarters to collaborate in rewriting the *War* volume of *Infantry Training*. Despite Maxse's encouragement the novelties of idea and presentation were well watered down by the War Office before publication. Maxse also superseded the Cardwell system by drafting direct from the depots.

In 1923 Maxse was promoted full general and in 1926 he retired to enter upon a successful career of commercial fruit growing. He was appointed C.B. (1900), C.V.O. (1907), and K.C.B. (1917); and was elected a fellow of the Royal Geographical Society for exploration on the River Sobat, Upper Nile.

A formidable personality, Maxse has been described by Liddell Hart as 'short and dark, with a sallow complexion, small deep-set eyes, and a long drooping moustache, which gave him the look of a Tartar chief—all the more because the descriptive term "a Tartar" so aptly fitted his manner in dealing with lazy or inefficient seniors and subordinates. . . . His fierce manner concealed a very warm heart, and he particularly liked people who showed that they were not afraid of him.'

In 1899 Maxse married Mary Caroline Wyndham (died 1944), eldest daughter of the second Baron Leconfield; they had two sons and one daughter. He died at Midhurst 28 January 1958.

Maxse was painted by Sir Oswald Birley and Sir John Lavery and there is a charcoal and water-colour drawing by Francis Dodd in the Imperial War Museum.

[The Maxse papers in the Imperial War Museum; B. H. Liddell Hart, *Memoirs*, vol. i, 1965; Sir Hubert Gough, *The Fifth Army*, 1931; *The Times*, 29 January, 5 and 14 February 1958.]   CORRELLI BARNETT.

MEGHNAD SAHA (1893–1956), scientist, was born 6 October 1893 in the village of Seoratali in the district of Dacca, later in East Pakistan. He was the fifth child in the family of five sons and three daughters of Jagannath Saha, shopkeeper, and his wife, Bhubaneswari Devi. A precocious student, he was equally good in mathematics and languages; in 1905 he received a government scholarship which enabled him to join the Government Collegiate School in Dacca but which he soon had to forfeit for his part in the boycott of a visit by the governor of the Bengal Presidency. In 1911 he passed the intermediate science examination from Dacca College. He then moved to the Presidency College, Calcutta, where he obtained his B.Sc. with honours in 1913 and the M.Sc. degree in applied mathematics in 1915. In the next year he was appointed lecturer in mathematics in the newly established postgraduate University College of Science in Calcutta. About a year later (Sir) C. V. Raman, who in 1928 discovered the effect known by his name, joined the college as Palit professor of physics.

Saha became especially interested in the quantum theory of the atom then being developed by Niels Bohr. It was fortunate that at about the same time he came across the popular books of Agnes Clerke [q.v.] on the sun and stars which gave him some idea of the outstanding problems in astrophysics. This background, in a sense, paved the way for his theory of temperature ionization which marked the first effective step in linking the atoms and the stars together. In 1919 he obtained the equation of temperature ionization which goes by his name. His classic paper on the physical theory of stellar spectra appeared in 1921. Much of the later work in stellar spectroscopy has been dominated by Saha's theory and ideas. The theory has all the simplicity and inevitableness which characterize an epochal contribution. It is a direct consequence of the recognition that the laws of classical thermodynamics and kinetic theory of gases can be extended to a gas of free electrons. Apart from astrophysics, the theory has found numerous other applications, as in the study of ionosphere, conductivity of flames, electric arcs, explosive phenomena, and shock waves.

Saha was awarded the Premchand Roychand scholarship of Calcutta University and spent two years travelling in Europe. He worked for some time in London in the laboratory of the great spectroscopist, Alfred Fowler [q.v.], and spent about a year in W. Nernst's laboratory in Berlin. On returning to

India, Saha joined the university of Calcutta as Khaira professor of physics, but in 1923 accepted the professorship at the Allahabad University. A most conscientious and inspiring teacher, he completely reorganized the teaching in the department and developed a vigorous school of research in theoretical astrophysics and experimental spectroscopy.

In 1938 Saha left Allahabad to take up the Palit professorship at Calcutta in succession to Raman. There he developed an extensive programme of work in nuclear physics. It was due to him that the Institute of Nuclear Physics was established at Calcutta in 1948; after his death it was named after him. Saha took an active interest in the Indian Association for the Cultivation of Science and was largely responsible for its new laboratories.

Saha's scientific work may be divided under three periods: 1918–25 when he was largely occupied with astrophysics; 1925–38 devoted mostly to spectroscopic and ionospheric studies; and 1939–55 when he was mainly concerned with nuclear physics. The most creative years belong to the first period, when he devoted himself almost completely to scientific work. Later his interests became more widespread. He was deeply involved in problems of national planning and the impact of science and technology on economic growth. He was an active member of the National Planning Commission (1939–41); and at the time of his death he was an elected independent member of the Indian legislature.

Saha was the general president of the Indian Science Congress Association in 1934. In his presidential address he drew pointed attention to the problem of recurring floods in Indian rivers. It was due to his pioneering efforts that the multi-purpose Damodar River Valley Project was established, on the lines of the Tennessee Valley Authority in the United States. It served as the forerunner of several other multi-purpose river projects in India. As a member of the governing body of the Indian Council of Scientific and Industrial Research he played an active role in the establishment of several national laboratories; and he was a member of the Indian Education Commission appointed by the Government of India in 1948 under the chairmanship of Dr. S. Radhakrishnan.

In 1927 Saha was elected F.R.S. He was president of the National Institute of Sciences of India and of the National Academy of Sciences (Allahabad). He published about a hundred scientific papers in Indian and foreign journals and wrote extensively on scientific policy and national affairs in the journal *Science and Culture* which he founded. He also published, in 1931 (with B. N. Srivastava), an internationally famous textbook on heat which has gone into several editions.

The life of Saha was an integral part of the scientific renaissance in India. He was fearless in his criticism of men and things; extremely simple in his habits and completely dedicated to his chosen vocation to the total disregard of his personal comforts. A detailed account of his work and life is given in the commemoration volume brought out by the Indian Association for the Cultivation of Science for Saha's sixtieth birthday.

In 1918 Saha married Shrimati Radha Rani Saha; they had three sons and three daughters. Saha died in Delhi 16 February 1956.

[Private information; personal knowledge.]
D. S. KOTHARI.

MEIGHEN, ARTHUR (1874–1960), Canadian statesman, was born at Anderson, Perth County, Ontario, 16 June 1874, the second child and eldest son of Joseph Meighen, farmer, and his wife, Mary Jane, daughter of Henry Bell, farmer. He attended rural public schools, the St. Mary's Collegiate Institute, and the university of Toronto, from which he graduated in 1896 with first class honours in mathematics. He then enrolled in the Ontario College of Pedagogy but after one year as a high-school teacher moved to Winnipeg and began studying law as an articled clerk. Upon being admitted to the Manitoba bar in 1903 he established his own practice in the town of Portage la Prairie.

In his first bid for public office Meighen was elected to the House of Commons in 1908 as a Conservative, representing the Portage la Prairie riding, and was re-elected in 1911 and 1917. He soon distinguished himself in Parliament by his remarkable industriousness, brilliance of mind, political courage, and forensic power. In 1913 he entered the ministry of (Sir) Robert Borden [q.v.] as solicitor-general and was promoted to cabinet rank two years later. Occupying successively the positions of secretary of state (1917) and minister of the interior (1917–20) he became one of the leading figures in the wartime Government, not because of the importance of the portfolios he held, but because of his prominence in the framing of contentious measures and in their passage through Parliament. These included the Military Service Act, imposing a system of selective conscription, the Wartime Elections Act, drastically altering the franchise for the general election of 1917, and numerous enactments bringing under public ownership various railways later combined in the Canadian national railway system.

His close connection with such widely unpopular policies, coupled with his earlier prominence in introducing closure into the rules of the House to overcome Opposition obstruction, and his activity in suppressing the Winnipeg general strike of 1919, won him much enmity. So did his pre-eminence as a parliamentarian. Although his exceptional ability earned him the respect of all, his skill and self-assurance in debate, along with his caustic wit and at times arrogant manner, aroused on many occasions the fury of his opponents. The cold, analytical brilliance of his mind seemed suited to his slight, frail-looking body and to the ascetic quality of his countenance, with its pronounced cheek bones and brooding, deepset blue eyes. There was an austerity about him as a public man, both in appearance and demeanour, which hid the warmer side of his nature: his capacity for affection, his love of droll stories, his gift of mimicry, and detestation of snobbery and affectation. In his public capacity he was a controversialist to the manner born who asked and gave no quarter. It was in part the knowledge that he had made many enemies, and especially that policies with which he was closely identified, like conscription and the public ownership of railways, were particularly repugnant to the province of Quebec, that caused powerful elements in the Government to oppose his selection as successor to Borden when the latter retired as prime minister in 1920. However, there was also strong support for Meighen, who was thought to have earned advancement, and in the event he received and accepted a commission to form an administration.

The regime of which he now took command was disintegrating. The coalition of Conservatives and Liberal conscriptionists, formed in 1917, began to break apart with the end of the war which had called it into being. Quebec had been alienated from the Conservative Part' and among the farmers of the prairie and Ontario there was developing a power ful movement of agrarian protest, in th' shape of the National Progressive Party against the policies of both Liberals and Conservatives and in some measure again' the party system itself. There now began a long, bitter struggle for power between Meighen and the Liberal leader W. L. Mackenzie King [q.v.]. The latter's ob jective was to assimilate the Progres sive movement into the Liberal Party with the claim that the two were not separated by any real difference of policy or principle. Meighen sought to counter this strategy and to re-establish the Conservatives in Quebec, the province which was King's main bulwark, with the argument that King would seriously impair the protective tariff system in order to obtain Progressive support

King won the first round. The general election of 1921 installed him in power and reduced Conservative strength in the 235-seat House of Commons to fifty members. During the next few years, however, the Conservatives made a remarkable recovery and in the 1925 election gained a plurality, though not a majority, of the seats. Despite this reverse King was able to hold precariously to office with the help of various minor groups in the House. Late in June 1926, threatened with defeat in the Commons as the result of a scandal in the Department of Customs and Excise, King advised the governor-general, Lord Byng [q.v.], to dissolve Parliament before a motion censuring his Government was voted on. When Byng rejected this advice King resigned. Meighen was asked to form an administration and did so. In short order his Government met defeat in the House and Byng accepted Meighen's advice to dissolve. Mackenzie King fought the ensuing campaign mainly on the alleged 'constitutional issue' arising from Byng's refusal to accept his advice. Although the issue probably had less influence on the outcome of the 1926 election than has generally been believed, King was returned to office and Meighen, having failed as Conservative leader in three general elections to gain a secure hold on power, retired from politics, joining an investment banking firm in Toronto in a senior executive capacity.

In 1932 he returned to public life as government leader in the Senate and minister without portfolio in the Cabinet of R. B. (later Viscount) Bennett [q.v.]. Late in 1941 he reluctantly resumed the leadership of the Conservative Party and resigned from the Senate in order to re-enter the House of Commons. His effort to do so, in a by-election in the riding of South York, Ontario, failed and he re-signed as leader at the end of 1942, retiring once more from public life, this time permanently.

In 1904 Meighen married Isabel, daughter of Charles Cox, of Granby, Quebec; they had two sons and one daughter. He died in Toronto 5 August 1960 and was buried at St. Mary's, Ontario, near his birthplace. A portrait by Ernest Fosbery hangs in the House of Commons, Ottawa.

[Eugene Forsey, *The Royal Power of Dis-solution of Parliament in the British Common-wealth*, 1943; Roger Graham, *Arthur Meighen, a Biography*, 3 vols: *The Door of Opportunity*, 1960, *And Fortune Fled*, 1963, *No Surrender*, 1964; Arthur Meighen, *Unrevised and Un-repented: Debating Speeches and Others*, 1949.]

ROGER GRAHAM.

MELLANBY, SIR EDWARD (1884-1955), medical scientist and administra-tor, was born at West Hartlepool, county Durham, 8 April 1884, the youngest of the four sons and six children of John Mellanby, manager of the shipyard of the Furness-Withy Company, and his wife, Mary Isabella Lawson. Elder brothers were John Mellanby [q.v.], the physiologist, and Alexander Lawson Mellanby (1871-1951), who became professor of civil and mechanical engineering at the Royal Technical College, Glasgow. From Barnard Castle School, where he was head boy and captain of cricket and football, Mellanby gained an exhibition to Emmanuel College, Cambridge. Having been placed in the second class in part i of the natural sciences tripos (1904) and the first class with physiology as his special study in part ii (1905), he obtained a research studentship at Emmanuel, which he held until 1907, working under the guidance of (Sir) Frederick Gowland Hopkins [q.v.], his former tutor, whose influence largely determined the rest of his career. He completed his medical studies at St. Thomas's Hospital, London, where in 1909-11 he was a demonstrator in physiology and in 1910-12 held a Beit memorial fellowship for medical research. In 1913 he became a lecturer in and later professor of physiology at King's College for Women, London, where he remained until 1920. He maintained a highly distinguished association with Cambridge where he proceeded M.D. in 1915 and was awarded the Walsingham medal (1907) and the Gedge (1908) and Raymond Horton-Smith (1915) prizes.

In 1914 Mellanby married May, eldest daughter of George Tweedy, of London, who had been a fellow student at Cambridge, was by this time engaged in physiological research at Bedford College, London, and was to be his lifelong colleague; they had no children.

Mellanby was appointed in 1920 to the newly founded chair of pharmacology at the university of Sheffield and honorary physician to the Royal Infirmary. This double appointment he held until, in 1933, he succeeded Sir Walter Fletcher [q.v.] as secretary of the Medical Research Council. Prior to taking this office, he was a member of the Council for two years, and shortly after his appointment he accepted the Fullerian professorship of the Royal Institution (1936-7). He retired from the Council's service in 1949, the year before there was opened at Mill Hill the new Institute for Medical Research, with the planning of which he had been closely concerned.

The research work for which Mellanby was perhaps best known was his investi-gation on rickets, begun in 1914 at the request of the Medical Research Commit-tee. His first major publication on the subject was in 1919: he established that the main cause of the disease was defi-ciency of a fat-soluble vitamin, which came to be known as vitamin D. At a later stage he demonstrated the rachitogenic action of certain cereals. His researches, however, extended over a wide range and he was recognized as an outstanding expert in the biochemical and physiological field. He continued his work until the end of his life: it was in 1946 that he drew attention to the toxic effect of agenized flour.

While Mellanby was in Sheffield he was appointed chairman of an international conference for the standardization of vitamins in 1931; further conferences took place in 1934 and 1949. He was also chair-man of the international technical com-mission on nutrition in 1934, and was part author of an influential report on the rela-tionship of human nutrition to agriculture. Before and during the war of 1939-45 he was involved in schemes concerning war-time diet as well as the welfare of Service personnel and civilians, and was chairman

of the Royal Naval and the Flying personnel research committees, a member of a
similar committee relating to the army,
a member of the Scientific Advisory
Committee of the Cabinet, and chairman
of the Colonial Medical Research Committee. The Medical Research Council,
under Mellanby's direction, and the Ministry of Health were jointly responsible in
1939 for the setting up of an Emergency
Public Health Service, which after the
war became the Public Health Laboratory
Service.

Mellanby was appointed K.C.B. in 1937
and G.B.E. in 1948 and received a number
of foreign decorations. From 1937 to 1941
he was an honorary physician to King
George VI. He was elected F.R.S. in
1925, F.R.C.P. in 1928, and honorary
F.R.C.S.Ed. in 1946. In 1935 he and
his wife were jointly awarded the Charles
Mickle fellowship of Toronto University.

Among other awards were the Royal and
Buchanan medals from the Royal Society
and the Bissett-Hawkins, Moxon, and
Baly medals from the Royal College of
Physicians, the Halley-Stewart prize for
medical research from the British Medical
Association, and the Cameron prize from
Edinburgh University. He was elected an
honorary fellow of Emmanuel College,
Cambridge (1946), and received honorary
degrees from a number of universities.
He gave many special lectures on medical
and scientific subjects, including the
Croonian lecture of the Royal Society, the
Oliver Sharpey and Croonian lectures and
the Harveian oration of the Royal College
of Physicians, the Linacre and Rede
lectures of Cambridge University, the
Ludwig Mond lecture (Manchester University), a special bicentenary lecture
at the Royal College of Surgeons, and
the Robert Boyle, Stephen Paget, and
Hopkins memorial lectures. In 1947 he
held the Abraham Flexner lectureship
at Vanderbilt University, Nashville,
Tennessee, which involved a period of
three months' residence in Nashville.

During the last year or two of his
secretaryship of the Medical Research
Council, Mellanby attended meetings
abroad on behalf of the British Government and the Colonial Office and at the
invitation of the South African Council of
Scientific and Industrial Research. After
his retirement he undertook two further
advisory missions, the first to India
(where he played a significant part in the
establishment of the Central Drug Research Institute at Lucknow and was its

first director for a few months in 1950–51
and the second to Australia and New
Zealand. For the most part, however, he
spent his retirement at work in his
laboratory at Mill Hill and it was there
that death came to him, quietly and
unexpectedly, 30 January 1955.

Mellanby was tall and handsome,
friendly and unaffected, with a great
sense of fun and a certain boyishness
which was one of his most lovable
characteristics. To those who did not
know him well, his more endearing
personal qualities were sometimes masked
by his rather brusque, forthright manner
which made him say what he thought
apparently without consideration for the
feelings or position of the person to whom
he was speaking; generally, however, this
was really due to a wish to stimulate
argument and, if his help was being
sought, to find out what was in the mind
of his inquirer, so that he could advise to
the best of his knowledge and ability.
As one of his friends wrote after his death,
'what a listener thought about him
temporarily did not matter, so long as
medical science was advanced or a new
scientist born'. He had a rare gift for
recognizing the possibilities in both
people and research and spared no pains
to see that the necessary facilities were
provided.

There is a portrait of Mellanby by
(Sir) James Gunn in the possession of the
family and a chalk drawing by H. A.
Freeth in the Imperial War Museum.

[Sir Henry Dale in *Biographical Memoirs of
Fellows of the Royal Society*, vol. i, 1955;
British Medical Journal, 5 and 12 February
1955; Prefatory chapter, *Annual Review of
Biochemistry*, vol, xxv, 1956; private informa-
tion; personal knowledge.]   B. S. PLATT.

MENDELSOHN, ERIC (1887–1953),
architect, was born in Allenstein, East
Prussia, 21 March 1887, of German-Jewish
parents; he was the fifth of the six children of David Mendelsohn, who kept a
store in the town, and his wife, Emma
Jaruslawsky. Among the important influences of his childhood was his mother's
enthusiasm for music (she was a gifted
musician) and for plants and flowers, which
she imparted to her son. Mendelsohn was
educated at the Gymnasium in Allenstein and early entertained an ambition to be an architect; but by his father's
wish he was apprenticed to a Berlin firm
of merchants. This he detested and
abandoned. He then studied architecture

or four years, first at the Technische Hochschule in Berlin-Charlottenburg, then at Munich where he graduated in architecture in 1912. At the outset of his career he was engaged in stage designing and during this period he became interested in the German Expressionist movement. Shortly after the outbreak of war in 1914 he enlisted with the Engineers and served first on the Russian, later on the western, front.

In 1919, at Paul Cassirer's galleries in Berlin, Mendelsohn held an exhibition of his sketch designs which he called 'Architecture in Steel and Reinforced Concrete' and which represented the work of several years, a large number having been made while he was on military service. They are projects for a wide variety of buildings in which steel and concrete partly determine the character of the buildings, and where purpose is partly expressed by symbolic forms, thus showing the influence of Expressionism. The most famous of Mendelsohn's early buildings is the Einstein Observatory at Potsdam (1920) which, although conceived in reinforced concrete, was built mainly in brick owing to the shortages of materials. The rounded shapes which compose the buildings are expressive of optical instruments, and these forms, together with the deep window recesses on the curved surfaces, allow a dramatic play of light and shadow, and convey a sense of mystery particularly appropriate to the purpose of the building. After the Einstein Observatory Mendelsohn built up a very extensive practice; he was the architect of a large number of buildings, among them a hat factory at Luckenwalde; the Herpich Fur Store, Berlin; the Petersdorff store at Breslau and the Schocken stores at Stuttgart and Chemnitz; and in Berlin a group of buildings adjoining the Kurfurstendamm which included houses, a block of flats, a cinema and a cabaret theatre, and Columbus House in the Potsdamerplatz, a large block of offices with shops below. In all these buildings the newer materials of steel and concrete are used expressively, and the designs of the façades show a strong horizontal emphasis with large alternating bands of fenestration and opaque panelling. In the Schocken store at Chemnitz and in Columbus House an effect of lightness is achieved by a cantilevering which thrusts the walls forward beyond the structural supports.

After the advent of Hitler in 1933

Mendelsohn moved to London where he began practice in partnership with Serge Chermayeff. Their first work in England was a house at Chalfont St. Giles in 1933. Early in the next year they won the competition for a municipal social centre at Bexhill which was named the De La Warr Pavilion and opened by the Duke of York. The long low mass of this building in steel and concrete with horizontal emphasis accords well with its position by the sea, and the glass wall terminating in the semi-circular glass projection of the stairway is reminiscent of a similar feature in the famous Schocken store at Stuttgart. Another work in England was a house in Church Street, Chelsea, while the partners were responsible also for several projects: a large scheme for flats and exhibition centre at the White City, and large hotels at Southsea and Blackpool.

Mendelsohn's original permit to stay in England for five weeks was extended to five years as a result of the representations of the Royal Institute of British Architects which elected him a fellow in February 1939 after his naturalization in the previous year. In the meantime the partnership with Chermayeff, which was not a happy one, had been dissolved in 1936. Thereafter Mendelsohn's principal work was in Palestine to which he made long and frequent visits. He became the architect for houses for Chaim Weizmann [q.v.] and Salman Schocken, the Hadassah University Medical Centre on Mount Scopus, Jerusalem, the Anglo-Palestine Bank, Jerusalem, and the Research Laboratories and Agricultural College at Rehoboth.

In June 1939 Mendelsohn finally left England, and after two years in Palestine, and unsuccessful attempts to join the British Army, he went to America. In 1945 he started afresh in San Francisco and such was his reputation that he quickly built up a considerable practice. He was the architect of the Maimonides Hospital in San Francisco and of a series of large combined synagogues and community centres. Those completed during his life were at St. Louis, Missouri; at Cleveland, Ohio, which includes a dome 100 feet in diameter; at Grand Rapids, Michigan; and at St. Paul, Minnesota. He was also the architect of laboratories for the Atomic Energy Commission in California. Among his projects was an impressive design for a memorial in New York to the six million Jews killed by the Nazis.

Mendelsohn's architecture was characterized by an expression of purpose partly by means of symbolic forms. He was one of the first to realize the architectural potentialities of steel, concrete, and glass, which he used expressively. His designs were always actuated by the principles of organic structure so that each part by its character denotes its relation to the whole, and he always aimed at the integration of the building with the site and the surroundings. In his work the laws which govern natural forms were applied to architectural design, and his great achievement was that in most of his buildings there is this feeling of organic rhythm and unity combined with expression of purpose in terms of steel, concrete, and glass. His work has been one of the vital architectural influences of the century. In the period of austere building in England after the war of 1939–45 his reputation suffered something of an eclipse but about the year 1958 there came a revival of interest with a renewed appreciation of the value of architectural expression of a more positive and symbolic character.

Mendelsohn was a man of wide cultural interests. Probably his chief enthusiasm after architecture was music, and he had a particular fondness for Bach whose music he liked to hear while he worked. He often said that music gave him ideas for designs, and many of his sketch projects bear the titles of musical compositions. Physically he was a man of medium height, rather thickset. His was a dynamic personality. He was a tireless worker and rarely took a holiday. He had a remarkable intuitive faculty of quickly grasping the essential significance of relationships and situations, revealed in his masterly analysis of the relation of the Jews to modern society in a pamphlet which he wrote in 1933 on the political, economic, and social conditions of the world.

In 1915 Mendelsohn married Luise Maas, a cellist, daughter of Ernst Maas, a tobacco merchant in Baden; they had one daughter. Mendelsohn died in San Francisco 15 September 1953.

[Oskar Beyer, *Eric Mendelsohn. Briefe eines Architekten*, Munich, 1961; Wolf Von Eckardt, *Eric Mendelsohn*, 1960; Mario Federico Roggero, *Il Contributo di Mendelsohn alla evoluzione dell'architettura moderna*, Milan, 1952; Arnold Whittick, *Eric Mendelsohn*, 2nd ed. 1956; private information; personal knowledge.]

ARNOLD WHITTICK.

MENDL, Sir CHARLES FERDINAND (1871–1958), press attaché, was born in London 14 December 1871, the second son of Ferdinand Mendl and his wife Jeannette Rachel Hyam. His elder brother was Sir S. F. Mendl who became distinguished in the City. Their father had been born at Tarbor in Bohemia and sent to London as a youth to work on the Baltic Exchange; he had subsequently formed a small family grain firm and become a British subject. Mendl, on leaving Harrow, entered the family firm and later started a branch in Buenos Aires. He next migrated to Paris and went into another business. On the outbreak of war he volunteered, but was seriously injured in an accident whilst an interpreter with the 25th Infantry brigade and invalided out in 1915. After working in Paris on intelligence for the Admiralty in 1918, he was attached to the British embassy during the peace conference and in 1920 appointed Paris representative of the Foreign Office news department. Knighted in 1924, he was press attaché at the embassy from 1926 until 1940.

Mendl quickly established friendly relations with the Paris press, whether correspondents, editors, or proprietors. His relationship with the British correspondents was equally friendly. Press attachés were then a new institution and journalists readily responded to the appointment of a man who was always available to them. Mendl was ever ready to produce information as far as he was authorized and to arrange meetings with appropriate officials. But it was always a two-way traffic. Mendl proved no less effective as a news-gatherer for the embassy and this came to be almost his most important function. His genial social qualities, which blossomed in these surroundings, made him a first-class mixer and brought him wide contacts with the political and social world. A generous and hospitable man, an excellent judge of wine, he loved to entertain. To small intimate parties at his flat in the Avenue Montaigne, he would invite carefully selected guests two or three times a week: it might be journalists one day, politicians another, business people, or a skilfully chosen mixture, not excluding the social world. Without profundity himself, he had the knack of evoking those witty and salty discussions which Frenchmen enjoy. He would always have at his table one or two members of the embassy, often a senior whom his guests wanted to meet; and he was especially kind in providing new arrivals on the staff with contacts. A lover of music and a former pupil of Jean de Reszke, he had a fine baritone voice and would delight his friends by his singing of German *Lieder*.

As time went on Mendl became an institution. He was essentially a contact man, able to adapt himself and make himself agreeable to anybody. Shrewd, if without great political judgement, he absorbed information and passed it on to his chiefs for their assessment. He produced the talk of the town with his own comments, but he was not, as legend had it, a sort of *éminence grise*. Loving France as he did, he was yet a robust upholder of Britain and served his five successive ambassadors faithfully and stoutly, being particularly close to Lord Tyrrell and Sir Eric Phipps [qq.v.]. His reports may sometimes have aroused indignation, as when he foresaw that the French would not fight in 1939, but he was unfortunately correct. He had a particularly close friendship with the famous Pertinax of the *Echo de Paris*. A generous, genial and kindly man, Mendl was a typical figure of Paris between the wars, sharing its standards and its frivolities. He went everywhere, knew everyone, and entertained everyone. He was a man of his period which ended fittingly with his resignation in May 1940.

In 1926 Mendl married Elsie Anderson, daughter of Stephen de Wolfe, doctor. She was an American who had made a fortune in New York as a fashionable decorator and during the war had nursed in Paris. She rented the Villa Trianon at Versailles where both before and after her marriage she entertained lavishly the international world of Paris. Although Mendl always attended her Sunday gatherings, he himself continued to live and entertain his own friends at the Avenue Montaigne, whose society was more congenial to him. On the collapse of France the Mendls left for Lisbon and the United States where they settled in Beverly Hills. After the war they returned to France, but the days of the Avenue Montaigne were gone. Paris was a new world, run by new people too young to have known Charles Mendl in his heyday. He continued to entertain his old friends to little parties, now in the Avenue d'Iena, where he resided, whilst his wife, who was considerably older, lived at the Villa Trianon until she died in 1950. In 1951 Mendl married a talented Belgian lady,

Yvonne Marie Marguerite Isabelle, daughter of Jules Hector Henri Victor Steinbach of Brussels and divorced wife of Baron de Heckeren, but she died of a lingering disease in 1956. Mendl himself died in Paris 14 February 1958. There were no children.

[*The Times*, 15 February 1958; private information; personal knowledge.]

HARVEY OF TASBURGH.

MERCER, CECIL WILLIAM (1885–1960), novelist under the name of DORNFORD YATES, was born at Wellesley House, Upper Walmer, Kent, 7 August 1885, the only son of Cecil John Mercer, solicitor, of King's Bench Walk, and his wife, Helen Wall. He was a first cousin of 'Saki' (H. H. Munro, q.v.). He was educated at Harrow and University College, Oxford, where he obtained a third in jurisprudence (1907) and was president of the O.U.D.S. (1906–7). He was called to the bar by the Inner Temple in 1909 and in the following year made a dramatic beginning by assisting (Sir) Travers Humphreys [q.v.] throughout the Crippen case. In the war of 1914–18 he was commissioned in the 3rd County of London Yeomanry and saw service in Egypt and Salonica. It left him with the rank of captain and extremely painful chronic rheumatism. After the war he therefore began to spend his winters in the south of France and settled at Pau with the American wife whom he married in 1919—Bettine, daughter of Robert Ewing Edwards, of Philadelphia. Later, when he had earned a comfortable fortune, he was to build a house there, exactly to his wishes, which he described in *The House that Berry Built* (1945).

In some stories in the pre-war *Windsor Magazine*, writing under the name of Dornford Yates, he had already created a group of characters who were to become increasingly popular with the publication of *The Brother of Daphne* (1914), *The Courts of Idleness* (1920), *Berry and Co.* (1921), *Jonah and Co.* (1922), and their successors, written to meet an eager demand. 'Berry' Pleydell and his relatives —'of White Ladies, in the county of Hampshire'—were all handsome, well-born, rich, and witty; they took part in romantic comedies narrated by 'Boy' Pleydell, and one of the group, Jonah Mansel, a strong silent bachelor with a taste for adventure, was the chief protagonist in the romantic thrillers, such as

She Fell Among Thieves (1925), narrated by William Chandos.

Dornford Yates readily acknowledged his debt to Ruritania: setting these adventures in such parts of Europe as might provide mountain castles with dungeons, splendid or villainous nobility, and unpoliced spots suitable for the burial of slain caitiffs. One book, *The Stolen March* (1926), acknowledged itself the stuff of dreams by turning into an actual fairy-tale; but this was a mere frolic; his general purpose was to introduce high romance into an increasingly drab, democratic, and mechanized world. As romance is a timeless human need, his readers were accordingly grateful; and never suffered any of his books to go out of print, but bought more than two million copies of them, excluding large American sales. With one feature of the mechanical age Dornford Yates made friends: since his chivalrous paladins and their faithful henchmen could not go adventuring on horseback, they were equipped from the start with the noblest of cars—the Rolls-Royce. A Rolls of the twenties, sumptuous, silent, powerful, and big enough to live in, takes a leading part in *Blood Royal* (1929). Even in later books, when the characters are allowed a few money troubles and White Ladies has been handed over to the nation, they are seldom reduced to their last Rolls-Royce.

In 1933 Mercer's first marriage, by which he had one son, was dissolved; in 1934 he married Elizabeth, daughter of David Mather Bowie. In 1939 his fine house at Eaux Bonnes was completed; but during the next year it had to be vacated before the German advance. Escaping through Spain they went to South Africa where Mercer volunteered for service first at imperial headquarters, then with the Southern Rhodesia forces with the rank of major. His health, however, did not permit him to serve for long. Upon returning to Europe at the end of the war, he found living conditions difficult and his once cherished home shabby and neglected; he therefore designed and built another such house at Umtali, Southern Rhodesia, where he settled down to write several more books. These included *As Berry and I Were Saying* (1952) and *B-Berry and I Look Back* (1958) in which he identified himself as 'Boy' and recounted and discussed his experiences and opinions with his other not altogether fictional characters. He died at Umtali 5 March 1960.

[*The Times*, 7 March 1960; Richard Usborne, *Clubland Heroes*, 1953.]

M. BELLASIS

MICHELL, ANTHONY GEORGE MALDON (1870–1959), engineer, was born 21 June 1870 in Islington, London, the younger son of John Michell and his wife, Grace Rowse. Of Cornish and perhaps Huguenot extraction, his parents were reared near Tavistock in Devon. Energetic and adventurous people, unscholastic but serious minded, they emigrated to Australia about 1855 and settled in the small gold-mining community of Maldon, north-west from Melbourne. To further the education of their sons, the younger of whom had been born during a visit to England, they removed first to Melbourne; then to Cambridge. George Michell completed his schooling at the Perse School, while his elder brother, John Henry Michell, F.R.S. (1863–1940), was becoming successively senior wrangler, Smith's prizeman, and fellow of Trinity. About 1890 the family returned to permanent residence in Melbourne, where Michell took up, simultaneously, the courses in civil and mining engineering at the university. After completing his studies with great distinction (B.C.E. 1895, M.C.E. 1899), he became pupil assistant and later partner with Bernhard Alexander Smith in his engineering practice.

In 1903 Michell commenced an independent practice, centred on hydraulic engineering; this involved extensive travel in Victoria and Tasmania. *Inter alia* he was consultant to the Mount Lyell Copper Mining Company which made one of the first hydro-electric installations in Australia; designer of the pumping machinery for the Murray Valley irrigation works; and investigator (1919) for the Victorian Government of the hydro-electric possibilities later developed on the Kiewa River. Along with this activity he pursued his ideas for mechanical inventions, which probably had begun to germinate before 1900. Amongst engineers and shipbuilders his name (properly pronounced Mitchell) became famous through his invention of the Michell thrust-block, a device for supporting a rotating propeller- or turbine-shaft against a large longitudinal force externally applied to it. This invention, patented in 1905, was based on theoretical investigations regarding fluid motion and the principles of lubrication. It was in every way superior to those previously in use—dissipating less energy, more reliable and compact, and easier to adjust; it made possible much of the modern development of steam and water turbines and of large fast ships. Of his other inventions the most striking and potentially revolutionary was the 'Michell crankless engine', which was patented in or before 1922. In an endeavour to arrange for the manufacture of these engines Michell gave up his Victorian practice in 1925 and spent some years travelling in Britain, Europe, and the United States. He returned permanently to Melbourne about 1933.

In 1934 Michell was elected F.R.S.; in 1938 he was awarded the Kernot memorial medal of the university of Melbourne; and in 1942 the James Watt international medal of the Institution of Mechanical Engineers, London. In publication he was sparing; the most accessible are his book *Lubrication: its principles and practice* (1950) and three theoretical papers reprinted in 1964 along with those of his brother. Many of his results in theoretical and experimental mechanics were published only in the specifications of his patented inventions, which numbered a dozen or more.

Michell's achievements rested on the rare combination of mathematical and theoretical power with mechanical flair and inventiveness, all of which he had in high degree; his own assessment of their relative importance is shown on the title-page of his book on lubrication, where he quoted Leonardo da Vinci's 'theory is the captain, practice the soldiers'. But his achievements rested equally on his character, in the formation of which family influence was very strong. In work and conduct he adhered firmly to the highest standards; he found refreshment from contact with nature and simple country life which to him was 'essential to his mental health and comfort'. Hence came his ideal, 'that the products of mechanical art should be truly serviceable and durable, and hence of necessity simple in construction, however recondite in theory'. A reticent man, who sought only a small circle of friends, Michell displayed always a direct quiet manner and genuine courtesy and modesty. His conversation was (in his latter years at any rate) rather deliberate, underpinned by wide knowledge and keen intelligence, with sometimes a flash of dry humour.

Michell, who never married, died at Melbourne 17 February 1959.

[T. M. Cherry in *Biographical Memoirs of Fellows of the Royal Society*, vol. viii, 1962; personal knowledge.]   T. M. CHERRY.

MILFORD, SIR HUMPHREY SUMNER (1877–1952), publisher, was born at East Knoyle, Wiltshire, 8 February 1877, the youngest of the ten children of the rector, (Canon) Robert Newman Milford, by his wife, Emily Sarah Frances, daughter of Charles Richard Sumner, bishop of Winchester [q.v.]. He was a scholar of Winchester and of New College, and obtained first classes in classical moderations (1898) and *literae humaniores* (1900). He was then appointed assistant to Charles Cannan [q.v.], the secretary to the delegates of the Oxford University Press, and six years later was transferred to the London office, where he was to spend the rest of his working life. In 1913 he succeeded Henry Frowde [q.v.] as manager of the London business and publisher to the university of Oxford.

The range and scale of the output of the University Press during Milford's forty-five years in its service grew almost beyond recognition. When he joined in 1900 it had long been known for its learned books and had acquired a more recent reputation for school textbooks. Outside academic circles, however, to the general reader and in the book trade, almost the only well-known Oxford books were the Bibles and prayer books published *cum privilegio*. By 1945 when Milford retired the Press had become one of the three or four largest publishing houses in the country, with more branches overseas than any other. In this transformation Milford played an indispensable part. The Bible warehouse set up in London in the eighteenth century had grown, under Frowde, into the headquarters for the trade distribution of all Oxford books. Cannan determined to make the Oxford Press 'what it ought to be: the first Press in the world'. He discerned the possibilities of a great extension of its usefulness by encouraging the London office to enter active publishing on its own account. Milford was the chosen instrument. It was not long before 'Humphrey Milford, Oxford University Press, London' became a well-known imprint on books in many fields, distinguishing the 'London' books from the 'Clarendon Press' books produced under the direct supervision of the delegates in Oxford. Oxford Medical Publications were launched in 1907 (the year after Milford became Frowde's

Milford

assistant) with the advice and assistance of (Sir) William Osler [q.v.], himself a delegate, and grew into a notable series of books for practitioners. In the same year a new department was set up for the production of children's books, for the schoolroom and the nursery. A thriving family of hymn books (including the *English Hymnal* and *Songs of Praise*) stemmed from the prayer book privilege; and Milford's lifelong interest in music led to his most striking enterprise, the Oxford music department, started in 1923 under the energetic direction of Hubert Foss [q.v.]. Its first modest group of publications was cautiously classified in the general catalogue as 'general literature'.

Milford's main preoccupation was in fact literature. He was specially devoted to the poets, novelists, and letter-writers of the nineteenth century, a preference perhaps drawing its strength from the country rectory of his childhood—the rectory where Sir Christopher Wren was born—and reflected in the inclusion of the bulk of Trollope's novels in the World's Classics, and in Milford's own scholarly editions of Leigh Hunt, Browning, and others. But he was an omnivorous, and very rapid, reader, devouring great quantities of history, biography, and letters, snapping up detective stories by the dozen, and working with hard-won enjoyment at modern poetry. He was the originator of the *Oxford Dictionary of Quotations* and editor of the *Oxford Book of English Verse of the Romantic Period*.

Milford was of middle height and slightly built, nimble and athletic, but clumsy with his fingers. He was a first-class lawn tennis player, difficult to beat even at Wimbledon; but he could not mend a fuse. His handwriting was, in his middle and later years, strikingly illegible, but his communications were very brief. His personality was strongly marked but elusive. What he said or did was seen to be characteristic, yet could not easily be predicted, and he inspired a lively but wary devotion in his staff. He was a leading figure in the publishing world, and from 1919 to 1921 president of the Publishers' Association. On the completion of the *Oxford English Dictionary* in 1928 he received the honorary degree of D.Litt. from his university. He was knighted in 1936.

He married first, in 1902, Marion Louisa (died 1940), daughter of Horace Smith, metropolitan police magistrate, and secondly, in 1947, Rose Caroline (died 1966), widow of Sir Arnold Wilson [q.v.]. There were two sons and one daughter of the first marriage. The elder son, Robin, a composer of note, died in 1959; the younger, David, a schoolmaster, was many times amateur rackets champion of England. A portrait of Milford by (Sir) William Coldstream is in the possession of his niece, Anne Ridler, the poet (Mrs. Vivian Ridler). Milford died in Oxford 6 September 1952.

[Personal knowledge.]

A. L. P. NORRINGTON

MILLAR, GERTIE (1879–1952), actress, was born at Bradford 21 February 1879 of humble and obscure parentage. When still under fourteen she had an instantaneous success on her first public appearance in a Manchester pantomime, and thereafter she never looked back. Slender, tall, and remarkably graceful, Gertie made no pretence at rivalling the more massive and handsome beauties of the lyric stage. But her small and winning face sparkled with fun and her smile was enchanting and infectious. Her singing voice had a delicious squeak to it, and it was this combined with the champagne-like effect of her personality which led an Edwardian wag to bestow on her the nickname 'Bubble and Squeak'. Her histrionic ability did not range very widely beyond the sparkling (as in *Our Miss Gibbs*) and the demure (as in *The Quaker Girl*). These two musical comedies (1909–10) belong to her heyday, and both had lilting music by Lionel Monckton whom she married in 1902.

It was a halcyon time when ladies wore feather-boas and huge hats with osprey feathers, and when a dashing new game called diabolo was all the rage, and the world seemed to revolve in three-four time to the irresistible tunes of composers like Monckton and Ivan Caryll and Paul Rubens, or Leo Fall and Franz Lehar. *The Toreador* (1901) at the Gaiety (with music by Monckton and Caryll) began Gertie Millar's triumphant series, and the revival of *A Country Girl* at Daly's Theatre (the music wholly by Monckton) concluded it in the darkling autumn of 1914. She made some intermittent appearances thereafter in less successful plays and in variety. Most often her manager was the great George Edwardes; usually, although by no means always, the theatre was the Gaiety, and throughout he first half of the century she was egarded as the Gaiety Girl *par excellence*. Long afterwards ancient playgoers were till to be met who could hum her avourite ditties in *Our Miss Gibbs*: We never do that in Yorkshire' and 'I'm uch a silly when the moon comes out'. n other of the shows she had an unfailing ppeal when being sung to by the young nen of the chorus in top hats, addressing her gallantly as 'Elsie from Chelsea', or Sweet Katie Connor—I dote upon her', or even, at the beginning of the war, as Sister Susie sewing shirts for soldiers'.

After Monckton's death in 1924, she married the second Earl of Dudley [q.v.], a second happy marriage which lasted until his death in 1932. To the end of her ife she was a keen first-nighter, and her appearance always caused a stir of acclaim in the crowd outside as well as in the foyer. In her last few years she might be supported by two walking-sticks or even be wheeled into the theatre in a chair. But she was enthusiastic for the theatre to the end of her charmed and charming life. She wrote no autobiography nor any books or articles of reminiscence.

Gertie Millar died at Chiddingfold in Surrey 25 April 1952. She had no children.

[Private information.] ALAN DENT.

MILLS, WILLIAM HOBSON (1873–1959), organic chemist, was born in London 6 July 1873, the eldest of the five children of William Henry Mills, a Lincolnshire architect, by his wife, Emily Wiles Quincey, daughter of William Hobson, of Spalding, Lincolnshire. Mills's parents returned to Spalding in the autumn of 1873, so that he became a Lincolnshire man in every respect other than that of his birthplace.

Mills was educated at Spalding Grammar School and Uppingham. He entered Jesus College, Cambridge, in October 1892, but spent the academic year 1893–4 at home recovering from a foot injury received at school. He obtained a first class in part i of the natural sciences tripos in 1896 and in part ii (chemistry) in 1897, being elected a fellow of Jesus in 1899. In this year he went to Tübingen to work for two very interesting and happy years under Hans von Pechmann. His interest arose from his chemical work and his novel and congenial environment; his happiness was due largely to an early meeting in the Tübingen laboratory with N. V. Sidgwick [q.v.] who became his lifelong friend. The two men shared a deep interest in both chemistry and natural history; in later years they occupied very similar positions, Sidgwick at Oxford as a chemist interested primarily in matters of structure, Mills at Cambridge as an organic chemist.

In 1902 Mills became head of the chemical department of the Northern Polytechnic Institute in London. In 1912 he returned to Cambridge to occupy the demonstratorship to the Jacksonian professor of natural philosophy, Sir James Dewar [q.v.], and was elected a fellow and lecturer of Jesus College. He was appointed a university lecturer in organic chemistry in 1919, and reader in stereochemistry in 1931, an appointment from which he retired in 1938. In 1940–48 he was president of Jesus.

Mills's chemical work can be divided almost entirely into two main groups, stereochemistry and the cyanine dyes, in each of which he attained an outstanding position. The most important stereochemical investigations of Mills and his co-workers were: (*a*) the first experimental confirmation of the Hantzsch–Werner theory of the isomerism of the oximes; (*b*) the first optical resolution of a spirocyclic compound and of an allene compound; (*c*) the confirmation of the tetrahedral configuration of the ammonium ion and of the planar configuration of the platinous complex; (*d*) the 'obstacle' theory, involving restricted rotation, to explain the optical activity of certain substituted diphenic acids. He synthesized and resolved several novel types of compounds, the optical activity of which was dependent on restricted rotation.

His work on cyanine dyes arose early in the war of 1914–18. German photographic reconnaissance was carried out using plates which, by the addition of minute quantities of certain highly coloured compounds, had been 'sensitized' throughout the violet-blue-red regions, whereas the Allies were initially using untreated plates which were not sensitive in the red region and thus gave particularly poor results in the red sky of early morning. (Sir) William Pope [q.v.] and Mills investigated the preparation and chemistry of these 'photographic sensitizers', with the result that nearly all the sensitizing dyestuffs used by the Allies in the manufacture of panchromatic plates were produced in the Cambridge laboratory. Mills subsequently extended widely our knowledge of the structure and chemical range of these compounds.

Mills was elected F.R.S. in 1923 and

received its Davy medal in 1933. The Chemical Society of which he was president in 1941–4 awarded him the Longstaff medal in 1930. He was president of the chemistry section at the British Association meeting in 1932.

After his retirement Mills devoted his leisure to the study of the sub-species of British bramble which he collected, classified, and finally preserved in the botany department of the university. His collection of examples of 320 of the 389 'micro-species' of Rubus fruticosus consists of about 2,400 sheets, of which 2,200 were meticulously mounted and arranged in systematic order.

In 1903 Mills married Mildred May, daughter of George James Gostling, a dental surgeon and pharmaceutical chemist; they had one son and three daughters. Mills died in Cambridge 22 February 1959. A pencil sketch by Randolph Schwabe (1945) is at Jesus College.

[The Times, 23 February 1959; Nature, 4 April 1959; F. G. Mann in Biographical Memoirs of Fellows of the Royal Society, vol. vi, 1960; Proceedings of the Chemical Society, 1960; personal knowledge.] F. G. MANN.

MILNE, ALAN ALEXANDER (1882–1956), author, was born 18 January 1882 at Henley House in Kilburn. He was the youngest of a family of three sons, a fact which seems to have suggested to him as he grew up the romantic approach to life of a fairy-tale. His father, John Vine Milne, a Scotsman of Aberdonian descent, had married, at Buxton, Sarah Maria, daughter of Peter Heginbotham, a manufacturer. Both parents at the time conducted private schools. While the mother is remembered chiefly as an embodiment of all the domestic virtues, his father was an educational enthusiast, hero and mentor to his sons. H. G. Wells [q.v.] was for a time a science master at Henley House and remained always a family friend.

A. A. Milne obtained a Westminster scholarship at the age of eleven, an unprecedented achievement, and proceeded to Trinity College, Cambridge, where he disappointed his tutor by accepting the editorship of the Granta and preferring journalism to the mathematical tripos, in which he gained a third class (1903). It was not only his ambition to write, but to write exactly as he pleased, and returning to London he became in 1906, after various less successful ventures, assistant editor of Punch under (Sir)

Owen Seaman [q.v.]. In this capacity he showed a remarkable gift for light and witty dialogue and a sense of dramatic form, which soon attracted the attention and admiration of a large circle of readers.

The war interrupted his literary career. He served as a signalling officer in the Royal Warwickshire Regiment in England and overseas, but he was able in 1917 to stage his first fantasy, Wurzel-Flummery, which was followed in 1920 by the far more considerable comedy, Mr. Pim Passes By.

Leaving the staff of Punch in 1919 Milne thereafter devoted the greater part of his time to stage comedy. Clearly the success of Sir J. M. Barrie [q.v.] was a guiding influence: the paradoxical situation, the mingling of much laughter with a little pathos, and, if need be, the fairy wand. But Milne had a fancy and a style which were all his own, and if his dream world was not so wistful as Barrie's, it was whimsical enough and his characters could sustain ingenious and airy conversations which never failed to amuse.

His first successes were followed by a long series of plays in which the attempt to create genuine characters became more marked. The most notable of these were The Truth About Blayds (1921), the story of a poetical imposter, which provided an excellent part, as the unmarried daughter, for (Dame) Irene Vanbrugh [q.v.]; The Dover Road (1922), a light-hearted homily on divorce, in which Henry Ainley [q.v.] appeared; and The Great Broxopp (1923), in which the role of a romantic advertising agent was assumed by Edmund Gwenn. Later came To Have the Honour (1924); The Fourth Wall (1928), a cleverly contrived murder mystery; Michael and Mary (1930); and Other People's Lives (1932). Toad of Toad Hall, his dramatization of The Wind in the Willows by Kenneth Grahame [q.v.], was first staged in 1929.

Milne also wrote The Red House Mystery, a detective story (1922); two novels: Two People (1931) and Chloe Marr (1946); and many essays in various moods, some of them an expression of his serious views on world politics and peace. But he had found a new and wider public as early as 1924 when he published When We Were Very Young, a series of verses for children dedicated to his son, Christopher Robin, who was born in 1920. Now We Are Six followed in 1927. In the same genre, but in prose, he produced Winnie-the-Pooh (1926) and The House at Pooh Corner

(1928), which bring to life the unforgettable character of a child's nursery
toys, a thought suggested to him by his
wife. On both sides of the Atlantic and
in other languages, including Japanese
and Bulgarian, these enchanting stories
with their attractive illustrations by
E. H. Shepard acquired a popularity
which seemed almost likely to rival an
earlier Wonderland.

Milne married in 1913 Dorothy (Daphne),
daughter of Martin de Sélincourt, a City
merchant. He died at his home at
Hartfield, Sussex, 31 January 1956. The
National Portrait Gallery has a drawing
by Powys Evans.

[*The Times*, 1 February 1956; A. A. Milne,
It's Too Late Now, 1939; private information;
personal knowledge.]   E. V. KNOX.

MILNER, VIOLET GEORGINA,
VISCOUNTESS MILNER (1872–1958), editor
of the *National Review*, was born
1 February 1872 at 38 Rutland Gate,
London, the youngest of the five children
of Admiral Frederick Augustus Maxse
[q.v.] and his wife, Cecilia, daughter of
Colonel James Steel, Indian Army. Her
parents suffered from incompatibility
and separated; but she derived something
from both of them and improved upon it.
From her father came courage and a
better version of the restlessness which
caused him to move through a succession
of dwelling-houses. In her it became a
determination to get to the bottom of
every incident and issue which she came
across; and she had the vivid intelligence
necessary to do so. From her mother came
her passionate devotion to the arts, which
in her early days meant all things French.
Her addiction to France owed something
also to her father who became a lifelong
friend of Clemenceau. After education
by governesses, she spent over two years
with her father in Paris where she studied
painting.

Although the Maxse family was connected with the peerage through the
barony of Berkeley into which her grandfather had married, she did not really
enter the highest echelons of society and
politics until her marriage in 1894 to Lord
Edward Cecil [q.v.], son of the third
Marquess of Salisbury [q.v.]. Her husband
was a distinguished soldier who was appointed to the D.S.O. in the Sudan in 1898
at the same time as her brother (Sir) Ivor
Maxse [q.v.]. She accompanied her husband to South Africa during the Boer war
and it was there that she first met Sir

Alfred (later Viscount) Milner [q.v.] whom
she married in 1921 after the death of her
first husband in December 1918. It is
generally supposed that she was responsible for the publication in 1921 of Lord
Edward's book *The Leisure of an Egyptian
Official*, a witty skit on Cairene personalities which was not popular on the Nile.

Her only son George was killed in
action in September 1914 and she had
perhaps never quite the same delight in
life thereafter, although the child of her
only daughter Helen, the third Lord
Hardinge of Penshurst, replaced him in
name and in her affections. She had
always declared the Germans to be bent
on war before 1914 and she repeated these
warnings before 1939 with all the more
force because she was wielding an instrument of her own. This was the *National
Review* which she took over as a labour
of love, and at a moment's notice, after
the sudden illness and death in 1932 of
her brother Leo Maxse (a notice of whom
she contributed to this Dictionary). She
found it one of the most original, independent, and forthright periodicals of all
time, renowned for its line on the Dreyfus
case and the pre-1914 German menace;
this prestige she enhanced.

The general tone of the paper caused her
to be suspected of being on the extreme
Right. But many right- as well as left-
wing swans appeared geese to her and the
gaggle included not only the League of
Nations, the Socialists, Lloyd George,
the Front Populaire, and Hitler, but also
Dr. Malan [q.v.], Neville Chamberlain, and
even on occasion Stanley Baldwin and
(Sir) Winston Churchill. One reason why
Milner attracted her was probably that he
also was a curious political mixture, and
he too, having been largely brought up in
Germany, had a similar assessment of the
Germans. In any case, the marriage gave
Milner a golden evening and left his widow
with a mass of documents, the historical
importance of which she well understood.
She gave Milner's papers about the
Doullens meeting in 1918, when Foch was
appointed generalissimo, to the Public
Record Office, and most of the other
Milner papers to New College, Oxford.
To the King's School, Canterbury, she
gave the lovely Jacobean house Sturry
Court which became the junior school.

It is as much for what she was as for
what she did that Lady Milner is remembered. The glow of a lively, incisive, and
sometimes fierce mind shone in a face
framed in an aureole of curly hair. Until

the accident which brought her editorship of the *National Review* to an end in 1948 she was as lithe and active in body as in mind. To the very last her mind never lost its full powers. She had read and remembered all the chief treasures of English and French literature. A brilliant raconteuse, there poured from her a spate of stories about the famous: Clemenceau, Rhodes, Queen Victoria, Meredith, Kipling. Her only volume of autobiography, *My Picture Gallery 1886–1901* (1951), was not a success, perhaps because it was not so vivid as her conversation. She would not have minded much. What she liked was not material success but meeting people, liking and sometimes loathing them, encouraging the young, consoling the old, probing, perfecting, prophesying. Every epoch has its grains of gold and she was one of them. Her talents made her one of that small band which raised the whole status and sphere of her sex during the latter half of the Victorian age and the subsequent generation. She died, 10 October 1958, in the lovely home she had made for herself at Great Wigsell in Kent.

A portrait by Noëmi Guillaume and a sketch by Sickert are reproduced in her autobiography.

[Private information; personal knowledge.]
COLIN COOTE.

MINETT, FRANCIS COLIN (1890–1953), veterinary pathologist, was born in Acton Turville, Gloucestershire, 16 September 1890, the son of Francis Minett, farmer, and his wife, Elizabeth Louisa Birch. He attended King Edward's School, Bath, and the Royal Veterinary College, London, becoming M.R.C.V.S. in 1911. In 1912 he obtained the degree of B.Sc. (veterinary science) of the university of London, and was awarded a research scholarship by the Board of Agriculture. He continued his studies in Paris at the Institut Pasteur, and, returning to the Royal Veterinary College, came under the influence of Sir John McFadyean who, with A. L. Sheather, was studying contagious abortion, tuberculosis, and other diseases of the domesticated animals.

On the outbreak of war Minett joined the Royal Army Veterinary Corps with which he served for ten years in France, Egypt, and England, attaining the rank of captain, and was awarded the M.B.E. During his period of service he studied and wrote on the pathology and control of equine infections, especially ulcerative lymphangitis, a disturbing disease among the horses in France during the war. Some of Minett's observations were of interest to comparative pathologists, for he demonstrated the presence of diphtheria bacilli, presumably of human origin, in some of the lesions on the limbs of horses. It is now recognized that diphtheria bacilli may be involved in skin wounds in man, horses, and elephants.

Returning to civilian life in 1924, Minett worked on foot and mouth disease as a research officer at the Ministry of Agriculture's veterinary laboratory at Weybridge. In 1927 he was appointed director of the research institute in animal pathology at the Royal Veterinary College, which at that time was separate from the teaching activities of the college. In the same year he obtained the D.Sc. degree of the university of London. With his colleagues, A. W. Stableforth and S. J. Edwards, he made a survey of the bacterial causes of bovine mastitis, a disease which had not previously been studied extensively in this country. Minett and his colleagues were responsible not only for drawing attention to its economic significance, but for distinguishing the different bacteria which cause the disease in this country, paying special attention to the types of streptococci involved. Minett also extended his investigations to include problems involving staphylococci, *Brucella*, and other organisms. Some of these bacteria are pathogenic for man and conveyed by cows' milk; he thereupon collaborated with many who were interested primarily in human health.

In 1933 there was some reorganization in the Royal Veterinary College and Minett combined his duties as director of the institute with those of professor of pathology. He himself undertook the teaching of the morbid-anatomical aspects of the pathology of animal diseases and of those diseases caused by viruses. He held this dual post until 1939 when he resigned to become director of the Imperial Veterinary Research Institute at Mukteswar in India. He was appointed C.I.E. in 1945 but in 1947 left Mukteswar, which was within the Indian part of the sub-continent, and accepted the post of animal husbandry commissioner with the Government of Pakistan. He remained for about two more years and was back in England by 1950.

In the same year he joined the Animal Health Trust as director of their farm livestock research station; shortly after accepting this post, however, he was released to advise the Turkish Government on some of their difficulties connected with diseases of animals. He returned to England in 1952 to resume the direction of the station, where he continued his work on Johne's disease in which he had been interested for many years, and also investigated the diseases of young pigs.

Minett was a curious individual, not easy to know. He was meticulous in everything he did; this was demonstrable in his technique at the laboratory bench and in his attention to detail in the writing of reports. These were his characteristics, but there were times when he was unable to see broader issues because he was surrounded with such a mass of detail. His energy and enthusiasm coloured his outlook, and it was some time before one realized that a sensitive nature lay beneath a rather brusque exterior.

In 1919 Minett married Iza, daughter of Robert Stitt, of Belfast; they had one son. Minett died at Hartley, near Dartford, Kent, 26 December 1953.

[*Veterinary Record*, 13 February 1954; personal knowledge.]   R. LOVELL.

MINTON, FRANCIS JOHN (1917–1957), artist, was born at Great Shelford, Cambridgeshire, 25 December 1917, the second of three sons of Francis Minton, solicitor, then of East Sheen, and his wife, Kate Key Webb. He received his education between 1925 and 1935 at Northcliffe House, Bognor Regis, and at Reading School. Thereafter he studied for a time under P. F. Millard at the now defunct St. John's Wood Art School. It was there that he met Michael Ayrton who, though his junior by several years, greatly affected his development by introducing him to James Thrall Soby's *After Picasso*. Minton's response to the work of the Parisian neo-romantics described therein was only increased by eight months spent in Paris and les Baux de Provence immediately prior to the outbreak of war. The influence of Eugène Berman, Tchelitchew, and the early de Chirico was plainly evident in the crepuscular street scenes which formed the core of his work until about 1942. He collaborated with Ayrton on costumes and décor for (Sir) John Gielgud's production of *Macbeth* (1942); in the same year he shared an exhibition with Ayrton at the Leicester Galleries.

Having withdrawn an earlier expressed conscientious objection to the war, Minton

was called into the Pioneer Corps in the autumn of 1941, was commissioned in 1943, but released on medical grounds in the summer of that year. On his return to London he shared a studio until 1946 with the Scottish painters Robert Colquhoun and Robert MacBryde; thereafter for some years with Keith Vaughan. It was now that his mature style was formed: a compound of urban romanticism learned from Berman and rural intricacy learned from Samuel Palmer [q.v.]; of the metallic formalizations employed by Wyndham Lewis [q.v.] and the rich colour employed by Colquhoun and MacBryde. These diverse influences were completely digested, however, and Minton quickly gained recognition as a leading figure in that generation of young romantics which dominated English painting during the first post-war years.

His activities were manifold and his capacity for work exceptional. He taught in turn at three distinguished schools— Camberwell, the Central School of Arts and Crafts, and the Royal College of Art. He undertook very many decorations and illustrations for books, magazines, and advertising—notably a travel book on Corsica (*Time Was Away*, 1948) with Alan Ross and an English translation of Alain-Fournier's *Le Grand Meaulnes* (1947). He made occasional sorties into almost every field of design, from wallpaper to the Chelsea Arts Ball, and returned to the theatre—to which his gifts were peculiarly suited—with settings for *Don Juan in Hell* at the Royal Court Theatre (1956). All this time paintings, drawings, and water-colours poured forth in a steady stream, many reflecting his travels in Spain (1948 and 1954), the West Indies (1950), and Morocco (1952). Between 1945 and 1956 he held no fewer than seven one-man shows at the Lefevre Gallery, as well as contributing to many mixed exhibitions. From 1949 he showed regularly at the Royal Academy's summer exhibitions and in the same year he was elected a member of the London Group. His work is to be found in the Tate Gallery and in many public and private collections at home and abroad.

His natural facility for picture-making was great. An exceptional sense of decoration and colour was combined with precision of draughtsmanship—seen clearly in his many admirable portraits of friends—and with an unfailing feeling for his medium. He made for himself a place in the English topographical tradition; in the elegiac undertones of his best work, he added a sharp sense of the poignant evanescence of physical beauty that was entirely personal.

Increasingly, after 1950, Minton felt himself out of contact with international fashion. This was possibly one factor, among others springing from the ambiguities of his own nature, which added an increasingly febrile note to his way of life. He lived in the moment, impelled urgently by a need for company and change. These he found in full measure in the pubs and clubs of Soho. Ranged always on the side of the 'have-nots', generous to a degree, 'Johnny' Minton was an exuberant companion beloved by his very many friends for the sweetness of his character, for his gaiety, and for the intelligence which underlay his defensive clowning.

In appearance he was striking, with a shock of jet-black hair surmounting a lantern face, of extraordinary gravity in repose but totally transformed by mirth. His hands were long and lean. From his gangling presence came a ceaseless crackle of nervous energy. He died in London, by an overdose of drugs, in his fortieth year, 20 January 1957, predeceased by his parents and both his brothers.

A number of portraits and self-portraits exist, the latter including a head (1953) in the possession of the Leicestershire Education Committee.

[Personal knowledge.]

MICHAEL MIDDLETON.

MIRZA MOHAMMAD ISMAIL, SIR (1883–1959), Indian administrator and statesman. [See ISMAIL.]

MOLLISON, JAMES ALLAN (1905–1959), airman, was born in Glasgow 19 April 1905, the son of Hector Alexander Mollison, consultant engineer, and his wife, Thomasina Macnee Addie. He was educated at the Glasgow and Edinburgh academies and received a short-service commission in the Royal Air Force in 1923 on the nomination of the lord provost of Glasgow. He learnt to fly at Duxford, was posted to India in 1925, and after returning to England took the Central Flying School course at Wittering and went on as an instructor to the Flying Training School at Sealand. On transferring to the reserve in 1928 he went to Australia where he was first a bathing beach attendant, next an instructor at the Adelaide branch of the Australian Aero Club, then an airline pilot.

Lord Wakefield [q.v.], who helped so many ambitious pilots, gave Mollison the initial impetus in his meteoric career of record-breaking flights by providing him with a Gipsy Moth. Seeking to establish a new record for the solo flight in a light aeroplane from Australia to England Mollison wrecked his heavily loaded machine on taking off from Darwin. Wakefield gave him another Moth, a D.H.60 Gipsy 2, in which Mollison took off from Wyndham on 30 July 1931, and set course for England, making Pevensey Bay in just over 8 days 19 hours. As in most of his record-breaking flights he pressed himself and his aircraft to the limits of endurance.

His flight from England to the Cape in 1932 again revealed those qualities which were to make him famous. After leaving on 24 March in a Puss Moth with Gipsy 3 engine, he took only just over 4 days 17 hours for the flight and arrived over Cape Town aerodrome in the evening in such a state of physical fatigue that double vision caused him to land on an adjacent beach and overturn his machine into the sea.

A solo flight east to west across the North Atlantic, not previously attempted and fraught with risk because of prevailing adverse winds, attracted intense public interest, enhanced by his marriage in July 1932 to Amy Johnson [q.v.]. The flight was made in the de Havilland Puss Moth G–ABXY with 120 horse-power Gipsy 3 engine and an extra 160-gallon fuel tank in the cabin. It was named the 'Heart's Content' after a town in Newfoundland. He took off 18 August 1932 from Portmarnock Strand in Ireland; 19 hours 5 minutes afterwards he crossed the Newfoundland coast only 20 miles north of the landfall he had planned. Finally he landed in a field at Pennfield Ridge, New Brunswick, after 31 hours 20 minutes flying. It was the longest duration flight in a light aircraft, the first crossing of the Atlantic in such a machine, and the fastest east–west crossing.

On 6 February 1933 Mollison set out from Lympne to fly the South Atlantic solo from east to west in the 'Heart's Content'. He flew by way of Casablanca, Agadir, Villa Cisneros, and Thies in French West Africa, to Port Natal, Brazil, making the 2,000-mile ocean crossing in the record time of 17 hours 40 minutes. With Amy Johnson on 22–3 July 1933 he flew from Britain to the United States in a de Havilland Dragon. After a flight of

19 hours 42 minutes they ran short of fuel, landed in the dark at Bridgeport, overturned their machine in a swamp, and were lightly injured. In October 1934 in a de Havilland Comet they set a record of 22 hours for the stage from England to India in the England to Melbourne race. In October 1936 in a Bellanca aeroplane Mollison made the first flight from New York to London in 17 hours, crossing the North Atlantic in 13½ hours. In November and December 1936 he flew from England to the Cape by the eastern route in 3 days 6 hours.

In 1933 Mollison was awarded the Britannia Trophy for his flight from England to South America. He was also awarded the Johnston memorial air navigation trophy and the Argentine gold medal for aeronautics. He was twice awarded the gold medal of the City of New York and received the freedom of Atlantic City.

In 1946 Mollison was appointed M.B.E. for his work with Air Transport Auxiliary and with 'Atfero' which assisted with ferrying American machines across the Atlantic. He undertook many difficult ferrying missions and delivered a vast number of machines for the Royal Air Force. He earned a high reputation both as a pilot and as an especially gifted navigator. His determination not to take things too seriously was indicated by his oft-repeated claim that in an emergency he would rather jettison a navigational instrument than his bottle of brandy. He faced danger with an ironical smile and to the hazardous flights he undertook he always contrived to give his own characteristic faintly humorous flourish.

His marriage to Amy Johnson was dissolved in 1938 and he married, secondly, in the same year Phyllis Louis Verley Hussey. This marriage was dissolved in 1948 and he married, thirdly, in 1949, Maria Clasina Eva Kamphuis. He had no children.

A film based on some of the flights by Mollison and Amy Johnson called *They Flew Alone* was made with Robert Newton and Anna Neagle. Mollison published *Death Cometh Soon or Late* (1932), in which is reproduced a portrait by Margaret Lindsay Williams, and *Playboy of the Air* (1937). He died at Roehampton 30 October 1959.

[C. Collinson and F. McDermott, *Through Atlantic Clouds*, 1934; *Who's Who in British Aviation*, 1935; *Royal Aero Club Gazette*, November 1963; *The Times*, 2 and 6 November 1959; private information; personal knowledge.]   OLIVER STEWART.

MONTAGU-DOUGLAS-SCOTT, LORD FRANCIS GEORGE (1879–1952), soldier, Kenya farmer and political leader. [See SCOTT.]

MOORE, GEORGE EDWARD (1873–1958), philosopher, was born in the London suburb of Upper Norwood, 4 November 1873, the third son and fifth of the eight children of Daniel Moore, M.D., and his wife, Henrietta Sturge. George Moore (1803–80, q.v.) was his grandfather; his eldest brother was T. Sturge Moore, the poet. He was educated at Dulwich College where for the last two years he was captain of the school and at Trinity College, Cambridge, where he held a major scholarship. He was placed in the first class of part i of the classical tripos (1894), won the Craven scholarship (1895), obtained a second class in part ii of the classical tripos and a first in part ii of the moral sciences tripos (1896), and in 1898 was elected by his college into a fellowship which he held for six years. From 1904 to 1911 he lived, first in Edinburgh, then in Richmond, Surrey, having sufficient private means to work at philosophy without an academic appointment. Returning to Cambridge he was university lecturer in moral science (1911–25) and professor of philosophy (1925–39). From 1921 to 1947 he was editor of *Mind*.

Among Moore's friends at Cambridge was Bertrand (later Earl) Russell, philosopher and mathematician, and it was due to his advice and encouragement that Moore began to study philosophy. The reciprocal influence of Moore and Russell upon each other was very great and of immense importance for the development of their thought. Each published his first major, and probably his greatest, work in 1903, Russell *The Principles of Mathematics* and Moore *Principia Ethica*. In the preface to his book Russell wrote:

'On fundamental questions of philosophy my position, in all its chief features, is derived from Mr. G. E. Moore. I have accepted from him the non-existential nature of propositions (except such as happen to assert existence) and their independence of any knowing mind; also the pluralism which regards the world, both that of existents and that of entities, as composed of an infinite number of mutually independent entities, with relations which are ultimate, and not reducible to adjectives of their terms or of the whole which these compose. Before learning these views from him, I found myself completely unable to construct any philosophy of arithmetic, whereas their acceptance brought about an immediate liberation from a large number of difficulties which I believe to be otherwise insuperable.'

In a short 'Autobiography' which he contributed to an American book, *The Philosophy of G. E. Moore* (1942), Moore remarked that this passage had caused many people to believe that he was older than Russell and that Russell had been his pupil, whereas he was two years junior to Russell. In the ten years before the publication of their major works in 1903 they met frequently in Cambridge and were in the habit of discussing philosophical questions, and it was thus that Moore developed the philosophy which had so profound an effect upon Russell. But owing to these discussions their influence was reciprocal, and Moore wrote of Russell that although 'I have not agreed and do not agree with nearly everything in his philosophy', yet 'I should say that I certainly have been more influenced by him than by any other single philosopher'.

When Moore began to study philosophy, the most influential teacher of the subject in Cambridge was J. M. E. M'Taggart [q.v.], fellow of Trinity, who was a Hegelian. Russell and Moore were personal friends of his and it was due to his influence that they both began their philosophical careers as adherents of the school of idealism and Hegelianism. It was Moore who first revolted; 'he found the Hegelian philosophy inapplicable to chairs and tables', wrote Russell many years afterwards, 'and I found it inapplicable to mathematics; so with his help I climbed out of it, and back to common sense tempered by mathematical logic . . . With a sense of escaping from prison, we allowed ourselves to think that grass is green, that the sun and stars would exist if no one was aware of them.'

The key words in Russell's statement— and indeed in Moore's philosophy—are 'back to common sense'. Moore himself once said that with him the main stimulus to philosophize had always been, not the world or the sciences, but things which other philosophers had said about the world and the sciences, and he had been interested in two sorts of problems.

The first was 'what on earth a given philosopher *meant* by something which he said', and the second was the problem of discovering what reasons there are for believing that what he meant was true or false. In dealing with these two problems his philosophical method was twofold. In order to discover the philosopher's meaning he subjected his statements to intensive analysis; having established the meaning, he subjected the statement, in order to establish its truth or falsehood, mainly to the test of experience and common sense. His personal statement contributed to *Contemporary British Philosophy* (vol. ii, 1925), was entitled 'A Defence of Common Sense'.

Moore's most important philosophical work was in ethics and epistemology. From the first he was concerned with these two branches of philosophy. In 1896 when he decided to compete for a Trinity fellowship, he chose Kant's Ethics as the subject of his dissertation. His first attempt was unsuccessful, but in 1898 he successfully resubmitted the dissertation with the addition of a new section in which he dealt with Kant's term 'reason' and the nature of 'truth' and 'ideas'. In the next few years he worked intensively on the subject of ethics, first in preparing two courses of lectures in London, secondly in writing *Principia Ethica*. The book contained the essence of his philosophy and nearly all the important, fundamental ideas through which he had a profound influence upon other thinkers in the years which followed.

Moore began by asking two questions: first, what things ought to exist for their own sakes, or in other words are good in themselves, have intrinsic value ? secondly, what kinds of actions ought we to perform ? But the formulation of these two questions leads directly to a third question: what is the nature of the evidence by which an ethical proposition can be proved or disproved, i.e. what kind of reasons are relevant as arguments for proving or disproving any particular answer to the first two questions ? Practically all the most original and important contributions of Moore to philosophy he made in the process of formulating and answering these three questions.

It was in the process of formulating the questions that Moore made his major contribution to epistemology and became a leading figure in the twentieth-century revolution in philosophy. He insisted that, if we want to know the truth about an thical question, we must first determine xactly what the question means, and urther that, as soon as we see the exact neaning of the first two ethical questions osed by him, the nature of the evidence which can prove or disprove them becomes lain. Here is the bald description and ustification of Moore's analytic method of hilosophical investigation, and it was hrough this method that he had the most nportant connection with and influence n contemporary schools of philosophy. From the original logical positivism of he Vienna Circle, through the logical tomism of Russell and Ludwig Wittgentein [q.v.], to the later logical positivsm when the school was translated o or reborn in Britain and America, nodern philosophers have concentrated heir attention more and more upon the analysis of ideas, statements, words, and questions as a means to the understanding of reality and the nature of vidence by which propositions can be roved or disproved. Moore himself was never a member of any school of hilosophy, but he influenced them all: it is', wrote Professor Gilbert Ryle, 'no reak of history that the example and the reputation of Moore's analytic method of philosophizing proved so influential; since here was a philosopher practising a specific method of investigation, with obviously high standards of strictness'.

Another important attribute of Moore's thought is immediately obvious in Principia Ethica: his attitude to common sense. He insisted that philosophy should stick closely to common sense. For instance, he points out that, when he asks the main question of ethics: What is good? he is concerned with the idea which the word 'good' is generally used to stand for, i.e. the common sense meaning of the word. But he went farther than this. He refused to accept philosophical, particularly metaphysical, propositions which seemed to him to contradict common sense. His attitude is admirably shown in an anecdote which he related about himself. When a young man at Cambridge, he heard M'Taggart 'express his well-known view that Time is unreal. This must have seemed to me then (as it still does)', wrote Moore fifty years later, 'a perfectly monstrous proposition.'

The basis of Moore's ethics was his distinction between what is good as an end or intrinsically good and what is good as a means, and his assertion that good in itself cannot be defined. This ethical doctrine was attacked from many different sides, as also was one of his central epistemological doctrines, the view, namely, that what we are directly aware of in sense perception are 'sense-data'. As regards his original propositions about good as an end, he admitted, with his usual simplicity and directness, towards the end of his life, that he could not make up his mind whether they were true or false.

Moore was an unprolific writer, for he wrote slowly and unwillingly. After Principia Ethica he published only three books: Ethics (1912), a small book in the Home University Library; Philosophical Studies (1922), a volume of collected essays; and Some Main Problems of Philosophy (1953), consisting of lectures delivered at Morley College in 1910–11. His literary style was an exact reflection of his character and his conversation, remarkable for its simplicity, remorseless clarity, unadorned sincerity. Beneath the simple, sometimes almost naïve, surface, Moore had extraordinary passion, primarily for truth; but he played the piano and sang, played games or shook his head when he disapproved of a statement with the same kind of passion. It was the combination of a powerful mind with this profound simplicity and passion which, quite apart from his books, gave him great influence over many generations of Cambridge young men, which included, for instance, Lytton Strachey and Lord Keynes [qq.v.]. He was an outstanding teacher and lecturer. 'Moore was, I think', wrote G. A. Paul, 'at his very best in his class at Cambridge. It is not easy to imagine how lecturing could be done better than he did it.' In the classroom he seemed, not to be delivering a prepared lecture, but to be working out again the problems which he had come to discuss, and the audience soon felt that they were not mere spectators or listeners, but were themselves taking an active part in Moore's passionate search for truth.

Moore had a shy retiring disposition and was the last man to seek publicity or honours. It was therefore remarkable that in 1951 he consented to be appointed to the Order of Merit. He was elected F.B.A. and received an honorary degree from St. Andrews in 1918.

In 1916 he married Dorothy Mildred, daughter of George Herbert Ely, of Croydon; they had two sons. From 1940 to 1944 he was in the United States as visiting professor in various colleges and universities. Thereafter he lived in Cambridge where he died 24 October 1958. There is a drawing by Percy Horton in the National Portrait Gallery and another by H. A. Freeth in the Fitzwilliam Museum, Cambridge.

[*The Philosophy of G. E. Moore*, ed. P. A. Schilpp, 1942; *The Revolution in Philosophy*, with introduction by Gilbert Ryle, 1956; *The Autobiography of Bertrand Russell, 1872–1914*, 1967; private information; personal knowledge.]   LEONARD WOOLF.

MORGAN, CHARLES LANGBRIDGE (1894–1958), novelist, critic, and playwright, was born at Bromley, Kent, 22 January 1894, the younger son of (Sir) Charles Langbridge Morgan, civil engineer, president of the Institution of Civil Engineers in 1923–4, and his wife, Mary, daughter of William Watkins. Both parents were of Welsh origin: their forebears had migrated to Australia to take part in the construction of railways, whence Charles Morgan senior returned to make his career in England.

Charles Morgan, youngest of his four children, entered the Royal Navy in 1907 and served in the Atlantic Fleet and China station. Although he was always proud of his naval training, it proved a false start for an acutely sensitive boy already ambitious to become a writer. The ill treatment which he and his fellow midshipmen suffered in the *Good Hope* became the theme of his first novel *The Gunroom* (1919). In 1913, encouraged by (Commander) Christopher Arnold-Forster whom he encountered in the *Monmouth* and who became a lifelong friend, Morgan resigned from the navy. He was entered at Brasenose College, Oxford, but with the outbreak of war in 1914 immediately rejoined the Service and took part in the disastrous Antwerp expedition with the Naval Brigade of the R.N.V.R. After the fall of Antwerp, part of the Naval Brigade crossed the frontier into Holland, where Morgan remained interned until 1917. This period was of the greatest importance in his development as a writer, since he had the good fortune to be put on parole and to live almost as a guest of the de Pallandt family on their estate of Rosendaal in Guelderland. There he received an education in the culture and languages of Europe, acquired especially an enduring love of French thought, and learned to believe that literature has no frontiers. Later, in *The Fountain* (1932), he used the background

of Rosendaal Castle (but not the family o Baron de Pallandt) for one of his mos successful novels. Meanwhile in Hollan he had written *The Gunroom*, and re written it after a German mine had sun the ship in which he was returning t England, with all his baggage, includin the manuscript of his novel.

The year 1919 brought Morgan to th long-desired goal of Oxford, where h read history and became president o the Oxford University Dramatic Society A meeting with A. B. Walkley [q.v. dramatic critic of *The Times*, led to hi joining the paper's editorial staff in 1921 and on Walkley's death in 1926 he suc ceeded him as principal dramatic critic a post which he held until 1939.

A second novel, *My Name is Legion* was published in 1925. Morgan late regarded his first two books as juvenilia not until 1929 did he achieve an ac complished mastery of the novelist' craft with *Portrait in a Mirror*, whicl brought him recognition and the Femin Vie Heureuse prize (1930). Turgenev' influence is apparent in the form of th book. On the nature of inspiration, where the artist's joy is described as receptiv rather than creative, there is a debt tc Keats and a key to much of Morgan' thought. *The Fountain* (1932), winner o the following year's Hawthornden prize to the author's surprise was an immediat best-seller in England, on the Continent and in America. The amalgam of a passion ate love story, set in 1915, with echoes o the poetry and quietism of seventeenth century mystics, told with great lucidity technical skill, and beauty of diction proved to the taste of critics and publi alike.

Epitaph on George Moore (1935), a brilliant essay in place of the full biography which Moore had wished Morgan to under take, was followed by *Sparkenbroke* in 1936. It is the longest and most inward looking of his novels, set partly in Italy, with the triple theme of 'art, love, and death'. Two years later, Morgan turned playwright with *The Flashing Stream*, produced in London, September 1938, with (Sir) Godfrey Tearle [q.v.] and Margaret Rawlings in the leading parts. The play prospered, but the author considered it 'a swerve' from his novels and returned gladly to *The Voyage* (1940), a story warm with his love of France, placed in the country of the Charente and the Paris music-halls, which won the James Tait Black memorial prize.

During the war of 1939–45 Morgan served with the Admiralty, with an interval for a lecture tour in the United States on behalf of the Institute of International Education. A short novel, *The Empty Room*, appeared in 1941. The following year, while still working for naval intelligence, he began a series of weekly articles for *The Times Literary Supplement* under the title of 'Menander's Mirror', republished in the two volumes of *Reflections in a Mirror* (1944–6). Their purpose—a reconsidering of values in life and literature—showed the range of his ideas and his quality as an essayist.

Among Frenchmen exiled in England in these years, and with Resistance workers abroad, the name of Charles Morgan was potent. Articles from his pen circulated secretly through Occupied France. For Morgan the permanence of French genius was freedom of thought. Regimentation of ideas, in his opinion, as shown constantly in his writing, was the greatest danger threatening humanity. When the liberation of Paris came in August 1944, he was among the first English civilians to enter the city. A month later an 'Ode to France' from his pen was read aloud at the reopening of the Comédie Française.

This passionate belief in a man's right to think for himself can be found in the next novel, *The Judge's Story* (1947), a conflict between good and evil which reflects Morgan's innate puritanism. A lecture tour of French universities in the following year became a triumphal journey among delighted students. France was the partial scene of his next book, *The River Line* (1949), later turned into a play (1952). It is a tale of enemy occupation: the study of a spiritually minded man against a background of movement and violence.

At this period Morgan was obsessed by a sombre vision of the human lot if science were allowed to outstrip man's moral nature. In another book of essays, *Liberties of the Mind* (1951), he predicted the overthrow of human personality, threatened by possessive control and 'barren materialism'. The same grave warning was the theme of his last play, *The Burning Glass*, produced in 1953; yet in the preface to the printed edition he wrote, 'To doubt that there is a way out is to acquiesce in chaos and to doubt God's mercy.' For some years Morgan had been working on an immense novel dealing with this same problem. It was never finished, but for a time he abandoned it

and wrote a youthful love story, *A Breeze of Morning* (1951), which returned happily to the spirit of his master, Turgenev, and to his own *Portrait in a Mirror*. The last of his novels, *Challenge to Venus*, with an Italian setting, was published in 1957.

Charles Morgan was a romantic, a philosophic idealist, and something of a mystic. The strong appeal which he made to his English public in the thirties and early forties had ebbed by the time he reached middle age, so that he grew isolated from the young intellectuals of the day, not then concerned with Morgan's attentiveness to an inner world, his message of renewal, or the loftiness of his standards. The highest integrity, with extreme care and polish, marked everything he touched, from the urbane essays of his ripe years to the smallest piece of anonymous dramatic criticism. His books were translated into nineteen languages, and readers on the Continent continued to hold him in the greatest esteem as a novelist.

Although good-looking and distinguished in appearance, Morgan was often suspected of being cold and aloof. He was neither, being a man of deep friendships, a kind, witty, and even gay companion. His presidency of International P.E.N. from 1953 to 1956 was a notable success. He received many honours, including honorary degrees at Scottish and French universities and was an officer of the Legion of Honour. Nothing gave him keener pleasure than when, in 1949, he was made a member of the Institute of France, to which no other English novelist, except Rudyard Kipling [q.v.], had been elected.

In 1923 Morgan married the novelist, Hilda Vaughan, daughter of Hugh Vaughan Vaughan of Builth, Breconshire, a solicitor, descended from the family of Henry Vaughan [q.v.], the seventeenth-century poet. They had one son and a daughter who married the seventh Marquess of Anglesey in 1948. Morgan died in London 6 February 1958.

A drawing of Morgan by Augustus John is in the National Portrait Gallery. There are other portraits in the possession of the family.

[Personal knowledge; private information, and the editing of Charles Morgan's letters published in 1967.]   EILUNED LEWIS.

MORGAN, JOHN HARTMAN (1876–1955), lawyer, the son of the Rev. David Morgan, Congregational minister of Ystradfellte, Glamorgan, and his wife,

Morgan, J. H.

Julia, daughter of Felix Wethli, of Zürich, was born on 20 March 1876. From Caterham School he went with a scholarship to the University College of South Wales where he obtained his London M.A. in 1896, and with another scholarship to Balliol College, Oxford, where in 1900 he was placed in the second class of the honour school of modern history. He made his mark at the Union, and also as a serious scholar of modern history, especially diplomatic history. Accordingly, although on leaving Oxford he joined the Inner Temple, and began to read for the bar (to which he was called in 1915), at the same time joining the literary staff of the *Daily Chronicle* (1901–3), he continued his postgraduate studies at the London School of Economics under W. A. S. Hewins [q.v.]. He gained a research studentship with which he studied for a time at the university of Berlin. Shortly after his return to England he became a leader-writer for the *Manchester Guardian* (1904–5). In addition, he had political ambitions, standing unsuccessfully in 1910 as a Liberal candidate for the Edgbaston division of Birmingham in January and West Edinburgh in December.

At the outbreak of war in 1914, Morgan volunteered for combatant service, but his special qualifications were responsible for his appointment to the adjutant-general's staff as Home Office representative with the British Expeditionary Force, to inquire into the conduct of the Germans in the field. His report was published by the Parliamentary Recruiting Committee. In 1919 he attended the peace conference as assistant adjutant-general, and was later sent to Cologne to report on the British occupation of the Rhineland, becoming British military representative on the Prisoners of War Commission. Later still, he was for some years in Germany as a member of the Inter-Allied Council of the Control Commission for the disarmament of Germany, finally retiring from the army in 1923 with the rank of brigadier-general. Morgan was convinced from the outset of his work with the Control Commission that Germany had no intention of disarming, and after his return he attempted by letters and articles to show that Germany was preparing for another war. But his efforts evoked little response, until, at the conclusion of the war of 1939–45, his book, *Assize of Arms* (1945), gathered together the record of his experiences into a formidable indictment.

In 1916 Morgan appeared as counsel for the defence in the trial of Sir Roger Casement [q.v.] and it was at Morgan's suggestion that, on appeal, it was strenuously argued on Casement's behalf that seeking to seduce troops from their allegiance whilst prisoners of war in Germany was not within the Statute of Treason of 1351. Morgan had given some lectures on constitutional law as early as 1908, and in 1915 had been appointed professor of constitutional law at University College, London. During his absence, Dr. Thomas Baty deputized for him, but in 1923 Morgan returned to active teaching and until his retirement in 1941 his lectures, with their forceful expression of clear-cut opinions upon constitutional developments, never failed to attract large audiences. In addition, in 1926–30 he was reader in constitutional law to the Inns of Court. He took silk in 1926 and his authority in the field of constitutional law was recognized by his appointment, first to advise the Indian Chamber of Princes on constitutional changes in India from 1934 to 1937, then to advise Western Australia at hearing before Parliament of the secession petition of that state in 1935.

To the end of his life Morgan remained actively opposed to German rearmament, and he appeared in person at Nuremberg at the trial of the major war criminals, most of whom he had himself interrogated, and his last official duty was to act as legal adviser to the American War Crimes Commission from 1947 to 1949.

Morgan wrote freely, and with the same force which he displayed in court and in lecturing, and he enjoyed controversy. Among his principal publications were *The House of Lords and the Constitution* (1910); a translation of *The German War Book* (1915); *War, its Conduct and Legal Results* (with T. Baty, 1915); *Leaves from a Field Note-Book* (1916); *Gentlemen at Arms* (1918); *The Present State of Germany* (1924); *Viscount Morley, an Appreciation* (1924); *Remedies against the Crown* (1925); *The Great Assize* (1948); and many contributions to legal and other periodicals.

Morgan died at Wootton Bassett 8 April 1955. His marriage in 1905 to Clara Maud, daughter of Henry Antony Hertz (the actress Margaret Halstan, died 1967), did not last.

[Personal knowledge.]

GEORGE W. KEETON.

MORSHEAD, Sir LESLIE JAMES (1889–1959), lieutenant-general, was born 18 September 1889 at Ballarat, Victoria, Australia, the fourth son and fifth child of William Morshead, miner, and his wife, Mary Eliza Rennison. He was educated at Mount Pleasant state school, Ballarat, and the Teachers' Training College, Melbourne. When war broke out in 1914 Morshead was a master at the Melbourne Church of England Grammar School, having previously been on the teaching staff of the Armidale School in New South Wales. Commissioned in the 2nd battalion, First Australian Imperial Force, in September 1914, he landed at Anzac on 25 April 1915 as a captain and second-in-command of a company. He was promoted major in June 1915 but in October he contracted enteric fever and was invalided to Australia. On recovery he was promoted lieutenant-colonel and given command of the newly formed 33rd battalion (3rd division), which he trained in Australia and England and took to France in September 1916. He remained in command of the battalion until the conclusion of hostilities, leading it with rare distinction at Armentières, Messines, Passchendaele, Villers-Bretonneux, and along the Somme in the final offensives. By the end of the war he had been wounded twice, mentioned in dispatches six times, and had been appointed to the D.S.O., and received the C.M.G. and the French Legion of Honour.

After demobilization, Morshead tried his hand at sheep farming near Merriwa, New South Wales, but soon joined the staff of the Orient Steam Navigation Company. In 1948 he became the company's general manager in Australia.

Between the wars Morshead combined success in business with continued interest in the Citizen Military Forces. From 1920 to 1931 he commanded Citizen Force battalions, and in 1933 he was promoted colonel and given command of an infantry brigade. When war broke out in 1939 he was selected to command 18th brigade, one of the first formations to be raised for overseas service with the Second Australian Imperial Force. In February 1941 he was promoted major-general and given command of the newly formed 9th Australian division.

Before it was fully equipped and trained, Morshead's division was sent to Cyrenaica to relieve the more experienced formations withdrawn for service in Greece. When the British forces in Cyrenaica were driven back into Tobruk by the sudden onslaught of the German Africa Corps, Morshead became the fortress commander. His resolute leadership quickly welded his motley collection of troops into an effective fighting force which defied all Rommel's efforts to capture the bastion.

The division was relieved in October 1941 and was recuperating in Syria when the remainder of the Australian Corps was transferred from the Middle East to the Pacific early in 1942. Morshead was promoted lieutenant-general and became general officer commanding the Australian Imperial Force in the Middle East. He led his division with distinction at the battle of El Alamein, and then took it to the South West Pacific Area. After a short period in command of New Guinea Force he became general officer commanding 1st Australian Corps and directed the complicated amphibious operations which resulted in the recapture of Borneo.

Morshead was one of the finest products of the Australian Citizen Force system of military service. Slight of build, he had a mild facial expression which masked a strong personality, the impact of which, even on first acquaintance, was quickly felt. He was unsparing and outspoken in criticism, yet quick to commend and praise when the occasion demanded. First nicknamed 'Ming the Merciless' by his troops, he became just 'Ming' as they learned to appreciate the quality of his leadership, particularly his talents as a battle commander. He was appointed K.B.E. and K.C.B. in 1942 and received a number of foreign decorations.

After the war Morshead returned to business pursuits and occupied many important appointments in Australian commerce and industry.

In 1921 Morshead married Myrtle, daughter of the late William Woodside, of Melbourne; they had one daughter. He died in Sydney 26 September 1959. A portrait by Ivor Hele is in the Australian War Memorial.

[Australian War Memorial records; *Australia in the War of 1939–45*, Series 1 (Army), vols i–vii, ed. Gavin Long, 1952–63; private information; personal knowledge.]

E. G. KEOGH.

MOUNTBATTEN, EDWINA CYNTHIA ANNETTE, Countess Mountbatten of Burma (1901–1960), was born in London 28 November 1901, the elder daughter of Colonel W. W. Ashley, P.C., M.P., later Baron Mount Temple [q.v.], of Broadlands, Romsey, and Classiebawn Castle, county Sligo (both inherited from Palmerston), and his first wife, Amalia Mary Maud, only child of Sir Ernest Cassel [q.v.]. On her father's side she was the great-granddaughter of the seventh Earl of Shaftesbury [q.v.], the social reformer. King Edward VII was her godfather.

She was nearly twenty when Cassel died and left between her and her younger sister the income from an immense fortune. In 1922 she married, at St. Margaret's, Westminster, Lieutenant Lord Louis Mountbatten, Royal Navy, younger son of Admiral of the Fleet the Marquess of Milford Haven, formerly Prince Louis of Battenberg [q.v.], and his wife, Victoria, a granddaughter of Queen Victoria. As the wife of Lord Louis, who was pursuing a highly successful career in the navy, she had a very full social life, but her energy and inquiring mind led her to undertake world-wide tours and numerous charitable activities on her own account.

The outbreak of war in 1939 provided the real outlet for her talents and aspirations for social welfare work and marked the beginning of a distinguished career of service with the Order of St. John. After undertaking numerous duties for the Order, including work in the east end of London at the time of the intensive raids, she was appointed superintendent-in-chief of the St. John Ambulance Brigade in July 1942. The scope of her operations, involving extensive tours of inspection, widened with the course of the war and her husband's rapid military promotion. When he was appointed chief of Combined Operations in 1942 she organized the Command's welfare branch. But it was after he had become supreme allied commander South East Asia in 1943, and in the wake of the Japanese surrender in 1945, that she was able to make perhaps her greatest contribution to the allied cause. In a gigantic rescue operation covering effectively the whole of South East Asia she inaugurated desperately needed welfare services for the returned allied prisoners of war and internees.

No sooner had this task been completed than another historic role awaited her. She was to be at her husband's side for the decisive period (March 1947 to June 1948) when he was the last viceroy and the first governor-general of independent India.

The implementation of his policy fo rapid transfer of power involved man, acts of social as well as political concilia tion in which Lady Mountbatten's insigh and initiative were of primary importanc, in strengthening the ties of friendship be tween the British and Indian peoples.

Independence, however, brought in it, train grave massacres and the migration, of whole populations in the Punjab t, which she responded with prodigiou, efforts to stem the tide of human suffering Under her chairmanship the Unite, Council for Relief and Welfare wa, formed which included all the major voluntary organizations and co-ordinated their activities.

On their return from India, Lord Mountbatten's resumption of his Service career meant no diminution of Lady Mountbatten's welfare work. In 1948 she became chairman of the St. John and Red Cross Services Hospitals welfare department and in 1950 superintendent-in-chief of the St. John Ambulance Brigade Overseas, making further long-range tours of inspection and severely taxing her strength in the process. It was on one of these exhausting missions to the Far East on behalf of the Order of St. John that she died in her sleep at Jesselton, North Borneo, on the night of 20–21 February 1960. Her body was flown back to England and buried at sea off Portsmouth with naval honours.

She was actively and officially associated with some hundred organizations. In addition to the St. John Ambulance Brigade she took a special interest in the Save the Children Fund of which she was president, and the Royal College of Nursing, of which she was a vice-president. To enable her work for these three particular causes to be perpetuated the Edwina Mountbatten Trust was formed.

Many dignities and decorations were conferred on the Mountbattens. He was created successively viscount (1946) and earl (1947) for his services in South East Asia and India. She was appointed C.I. (1947), G.B.E. (1947), D.C.V.O. (1946), and G.C.St.J. (1945).

She had two daughters, Patricia, born in 1924, who married the seventh Baron Brabourne in 1946, and Pamela, born in 1929, who married David Hicks in January 1960.

Lady Mountbatten was not content to rest on her inheritance of beauty, wealth, and privilege but made her mark on the history of her times as an emancipator, a tough and relentless fighter against poverty and suffering. She had an abundance of charm and compassion which reinforced her powers of leadership. In support of her husband in South East Asia and India her social conscience played a significant part in mitigating the consequences of the political and military crises with which her husband was grappling. She had, as India's prime minister, Jawaharlal Nehru, said of her, 'the healer's touch'.

There are portraits of her by P. A. de László and Salvador Dali (at Broadlands) and by Edward I. Halliday (in New Delhi).

[Private information; personal knowledge.]
      ALAN CAMPBELL-JOHNSON.

MOUNTEVANS, first BARON (1880–1957), admiral. [See EVANS, EDWARD RATCLIFFE GARTH RUSSELL.]

MUIR, EDWIN (1887–1959), writer, was born at the Folly in Deerness on the Orkney mainland 15 May 1887, the youngest of the six children of James Muir, farmer, and his wife, Elizabeth, daughter of Edwin Cormack. Two years later the family moved to the Bu, a hundred-acre farm on the small island of Wyre, where there was a strong sense of community among its few families. The child had also a sense of a larger unity—between the human community and the animals and the natural surroundings. In the home the arts were a natural part of life, and the evenings were filled with story-telling and singing. When he was eight the family moved to Garth, another hundred-acre farm, four miles from Kirkwall on the mainland. He went irregularly to the grammar school and began to read avidly. The farm did not prosper and when he was fourteen the family moved to Glasgow—a sudden transition from a pre-industrial community into the modern world. Within five years his father and mother and, after slow painful illnesses, two of his brothers were dead. Muir worked as office-boy and clerk in Glasgow and Greenock. As a boy he had experienced two emotional conversions at revivalist meetings, but his early religious faith was undermined by what he saw in the slums and by the deaths of his brothers, and was replaced by faith in socialism and later in Nietzscheanism, two philosophies which he desperately tried to reconcile. He was a member of the Clarion Scouts,

of the Independent Labour Party, and of the Guild Socialist movement. From 1913 he contributed to the *New Age* propagandist verses of little merit and later aphorisms in the manner of Nietzsche which were collected in *We Moderns* (1918). He volunteered for the army but was rejected as physically unfit.

In 1919 he married Wilhelmina (Willa) Johnstone, daughter of Peter Anderson, draper, of Montrose, Angus, left Glasgow for London, and became assistant to A. R. Orage [q.v.] on the *New Age*. The unhappiness of the Glasgow years had brought him close to nervous breakdown and he underwent a course of psychoanalysis. This, and more congenial work, but especially his wife helped him in the quiet years which followed, in Prague, Germany, Italy, and Austria (1921–4), to recover inner peace; his imagination woke, and he began to write poetry.

In Buckinghamshire (1924–5), France (1925–7), Surrey (1927–8), Sussex (1928–32), Hampstead (1932–5), and St. Andrews (1935–42), Muir made his living by voluminous work as critic and, with his wife, translator; wrote three novels, a life of John Knox (1929), and *Scottish Journey* (1935), and gradually improved in skill as a poet. With his wife, a better linguist who did most of the work, he produced some forty volumes of translations, mostly from German, making the works of Kafka and of Hermann Broch available to English readers, as well as Feuchtwanger's *Jew Süss*. His criticism is contained in about a thousand reviews; in numerous articles (some collected in *Latitudes* (1924), *Transition* (1926), and *Essays on Literature and Society* (1949)); in broadcast talks; and in *The Structure of the Novel* (1928), *Scott and Scotland* (1936), *The Present Age* (1939), and *The Estate of Poetry* (1962); it is marked by scrupulous fairness and independence of judgement. T. S. Eliot thought his 'the best criticism of our time'. Fiction was not his *métier*, but his novels are of interest for their poetic quality. His finest prose work is *An Autobiography* (1954) in which visionary radiance is combined with the realism to be expected in a farmer's child. His mature prose reflects his character—quiet, lucid, witty without striving after effect. But his poetry is his great achievement.

Coming to poetry late, Muir went on maturing to the end, and wrote his best poems when over fifty. He used traditional metres and made no startling innovations in technique, being concerned only to convey his vision clearly and honestly. Beneath the story of his life he saw the fable of man—Eden, the Fall, the journey through the labyrinth of time. He made much use of his dreams and of myths, for in them the fable is most clearly seen; but in his later poems he was able to relate a widening range of temporal experiences —the war, the Communist victory in Prague, fears of atomic war, his marriage— to his perception of an underlying timeless reality. He experienced to the full the doubts and fears characteristic of his century, and his honest facing of them makes the more impressive his vision of 'boundless union and freedom'. He came to see the Incarnation as the answer to the problems of time and eternity, necessity and freedom; but his poetry embodied vision rather than belief. Immortality was to him a state of being, something immediately experienced. His apparently simple words carry a great weight of meaning. His poems are mostly short; but they are not fragments—all are related to his central vision of the mystery of our common humanity. His collected poems were published in 1960.

From 1942 to 1945 Muir worked for the British Council in Edinburgh and was then director of its Institutes in Prague (1945–8) and Rome (1949–50), and warden of Newbattle Abbey, an adult education college near Edinburgh (1950–55). After a year as Charles Eliot Norton professor at Harvard (1955–6), he settled at Swaffham Prior near Cambridge. He was appointed C.B.E. in 1953 and received honorary degrees from Prague (1947), Edinburgh (1947), Rennes (1949), Leeds (1955), and Cambridge (1958). He died in Cambridge 3 January 1959. He had one son. Willa Muir died in 1970.

Muir was a man of complete integrity; gentle, unassuming, and vulnerable, but with firm tenacity of purpose; sometimes abstracted, but strongly affectionate and quick in sympathy. He spoke in a soft lilting voice and sang almost in tune.

In a picture by Stanley Cursiter in the Glasgow City Art Gallery, Muir is portrayed with O. H. Mavor [q.v.], Eric Linklater, and Neil Gunn. There is a bust by Marek Szwarc owned by the Saltire Society, Edinburgh.

[Edwin Muir, *An Autobiography*, 1954; P. H. Butter, *Edwin Muir: Man and Poet*, 1966; Willa Muir, *Belonging: a Memoir*, 1968; personal knowledge.]   P. H. Butter.

MUIR, Sir ROBERT (1864–1959), pathologist, was born at Balfron, Stirlingshire, 5 July 1864, the second child and only son of the Rev. Robert Muir, a Presbyterian minister of saintly character and decidedly liberal outlook, and his wife, Susan Cameron, daughter of William Duncan, a Dundee merchant. One of his four sisters wrote short stories, another was a classical scholar of Edinburgh University, and the youngest, Anne Davidson Muir, acquired fame in Scotland as a painter in water-colours, especially of flowers. In later life Muir, who never married, lived with two of his sisters.

Following a brilliant career at Hawick High School and Teviot Grove Academy, Muir entered the university of Edinburgh with the Sir Walter Scott bursary in classics and mathematics. He graduated M.A. in 1884 and M.B., C.M. with first class honours in 1888, after obtaining the Grierson bursary and the much-coveted Vans Dunlop research scholarship. Most of this time he carried a heavy burden of coaching, for his father's death in 1882 faced him with considerable family responsibilities. Nevertheless he chose the rather precarious career of pathology, largely through the influence of William Smith Greenfield, Edinburgh's unrivalled pathologist and clinician. Muir acquired valuable experience as a clinician, bacteriologist, and what is now called haematologist as assistant to Greenfield (1892–8) and lecturer on pathological bacteriology (1894–8). He examined at the university and at the Royal Colleges of Physicians and Surgeons of Edinburgh and fostered closer personal contacts between staff and students with whom he was a universal favourite. With James Ritchie, lecturer in pathology at Oxford, he wrote the *Manual of Bacteriology* (1897) which has passed through eleven editions.

In 1898 Muir was called to the new chair of pathology at St. Andrews, held in Dundee, where his reputation as an original researcher and far-seeing administrator led to the offer of the chair of pathology at Glasgow which he held from 1899 until 1936. There he gained world fame as a teacher, investigator, and writer, for in 1924 his *Textbook of Pathology* became a substantial success and has maintained its place among the leaders. Muir's pupils, too, have included many men whose contributions to pathology are well-nigh inestimable, while his integrity and sound judgement brought many calls from university and public

life. He served on the university court at
Glasgow, the Medical Research Council
(1928–32), the councils of the Imperial
Cancer Research Fund and the British
Empire Cancer Campaign, and on committees for investigation of foot and
mouth disease. During the war of 1914–18
he held the rank of lieutenant-colonel and
was in charge of the pathological and
bacteriological routine of the 3rd and
4th Scottish General Hospitals, and also
acted as inspector of laboratories in
Scotland. Elected F.R.S. in 1911, he
served on the council (1926–7) and was
awarded a Royal medal for his work on
immunity in 1929. He was knighted in
1934; received honorary degrees from the
universities of Bristol, Dublin, Durham,
Edinburgh, Glasgow, and Leeds; was an
honorary fellow of the Royal Colleges of
Physicians of London and Edinburgh, of
the Royal Faculty of Physicians and
Surgeons of Glasgow, and of the Royal
Society of Medicine, and an honorary
member of the Pathological Society.
He was awarded the Lister medal for
1936.

Muir's discoveries fit so well into the
mosaic of progress in pathology that it is
difficult to realize now how fresh and
original they seemed at the time of their
announcement. His papers are still worth
reading for they teem with unusual
observations and offer many admirable
lessons in planning and explaining experiments for the young pathologist. Three
major fields of medical endeavour Muir
made his own. He was an unrivalled
exponent on diseases of the blood cells,
largely because he had realized that much
of their puzzling behaviour reflects the
closely geared relationship between the
bone marrow, where the red corpuscles and
many of the white corpuscles are formed,
and the sites of cell destruction. From these
studies came fundamental knowledge about
the meaning of the leucocytosis of infection
and pus formation. Red cell destruction
was linked up with iron metabolism,
since these corpuscles are important iron
carriers, and in this way came an explanation of some of the anomalies of anaemia.
Such studies brought Muir face to
face with the vigorous science of immunology and he joined the ranks of
Ehrlich, Bordet, and Landsteiner with
whom he bears comparison. Thus he
added many new facts about the nature
and mode of action of immune body and
complement, from which emerged improvements in techniques, especially of

the Wassermann reaction for syphilis,
which gave a strong impetus to clinical
serology. Muir played no small part in
earning for the United Kingdom a high
place in world immunology. Finally, in
his latter years, he returned in earnest
to the problems of cancer and in a
brilliant series of papers devoted to
cancer of the breast he clarified the
relationship which exists between duct
papillomas, cystic hyperplasia, and intra-
duct cancer. His microscopical study of
Paget's disease of the nipple is unsurpassed and has left no doubt about
the serious nature of this misleading
disease.

Muir was a shy, aloof man who gave
praise rarely, never shirked an unpleasant
duty, yet seldom made an enemy. Only
his most intimate friends knew of the
warm heart which was carefully concealed
by a deliberately cultivated austerity.
He knew instinctively when young people
needed help and made it his business to
see that it was forthcoming. His habit of
absent-mindedly pocketing other people's
matches, his fanatical devotion to golf,
and his ill-concealed delight in deflating
pompous colleagues endeared him to his
juniors. Many good stories are told of
him, some no doubt invented, for his
Olympian reserve was fair game for
boisterous Scottish students. They were
devoted to the one and only 'Bobby' and
he in turn loved them all.

He retired in 1936 and spent the
remainder of his life in Edinburgh
where he quietly pursued his interest in
botany and geology, fished a stream, or
played his favourite golf and bridge. He
flew to Australia to see his eldest sister
when he was close upon ninety; and
died peacefully in Edinburgh 30 March
1959.

Muir's portrait, painted in 1931 by
G. Fiddes Watt, hangs in the university
of Glasgow; a bust by G. H. Paulin is in
the Pathological Institute of the university. A pencil sketch by his sister Anne has
been widely reproduced.

[Sir Roy Cameron in *Biographical Memoirs
of Fellows of the Royal Society*, vol. v, 1959;
Journal of Pathology and Bacteriology, vol.
lxxxi, No. 1, January 1961; private information; personal knowledge.] ROY CAMERON.

MUNNINGS, SIR ALFRED JAMES
(1878–1959), painter, was born 8 October
1878 at Mendham Mill on the Waveney,
Suffolk, the second of the four sons of
the miller, John Munnings, and his wife,

Ellen, daughter of William Ringer, a farmer. His mother gave him greater encouragement and sympathy than his father who was often short-tempered, though he captivated his family by reading aloud in the evenings, usually from Dickens. Munnings himself became famous for his spirited recitations from Surtees, Shakespeare, and other favourites, though he sometimes caused embarrassment.

Educated at the village school, at the small grammar school at Redenhall, and for four unhappy terms at Framlingham College, Munnings left school at fourteen. He was apprenticed to Page Brothers, lithographers at Norwich, where for six years he worked with enthusiasm for ten hours a day at tasks which were almost entirely commercial, and then rushed off for a couple of hours at the Norwich School of Art. Lithography permits no mistakes and through his strict training Munnings acquired an enviable facility and assurance in drawing. He was fortunate in finding encouragement from Norwich art dealers, from Walter Scott, the head of the Art School, from James Reeve, curator and connoisseur of Crome and Cotman, who bought one of his earliest paintings for £85, and from Shaw Tomkins, manager of Caley's chocolate factory, who took the boy with him on trips abroad which enabled him to see fine art galleries. Munnings designed posters for the firm's chocolates and crackers and continued to do so, when hard up, after he had left Pages.

Although fortunate too in the robust health he inherited from his East Anglian forebears, Munnings had the misfortune to lose the sight of his right eye in 1898 when it was accidentally pierced by a thorn. From the age of thirty he also suffered from painful attacks of gout to which was sometimes attributed his explosive and lurid language.

There was never any doubt about Munnings's vocation. He loved the countryside; he loved painting; he loved all animals; in particular he idolized horses which he rode untiringly and of which he made thousands of sketches and paintings. He was not moved by nature's mystery but by the visual beauty of skies, trees, meadows, and especially of flowing water. He was never in a studio if he could be in the open air. At first he painted landscapes, gipsies and their horses in Norfolk; but about 1911 he moved to Cornwall where he was warmly welcomed by the Newlyn group around Stanhope

Forbes [q.v.] which included Harold and (Dame) Laura Knight and Lamorna Birch.

Refused by the army because of his disability, Munnings eventually got himself accepted in 1917 to look after the welfare of horses. He was next attached, without military rank, to the Canadian Cavalry Brigade as an official war artist. He went to France, fitted comfortably into army life, was popular with everybody, and worked tremendously hard making sketches and paintings in oils and water-colours. His fine portrait (now in the National Art Gallery at Ottawa) of General J. E. B. Seely (later Lord Mottistone, q.v.) on his horse Warrior was his first sensational success. It started a vogue and for the next forty years he produced a great many equestrian portraits in the same style, such as Lord Mildmay [q.v.] on Davy Jones, Lord Harewood [q.v.] with the Princess Royal, and Lord Birkenhead [q.v.], 'about my best portrait of a man on horseback'.

At Epsom races Munnings was always surrounded by members of the gipsy families he had painted on visits to Alton before the war, and it was his studies of them, both new and old, which first brought him fame and financial success. The sale of a great number of sketches and paintings to James Connell & Sons of Old Bond Street set Munnings up for life by giving him an initial capital. In 1919 he took his first studio in London, in Glebe Place, and entered boisterously into London's social life, first at the Chelsea Arts Club, then at the Café Royal, the Arts Club in Piccadilly, and the Garrick Club. He was a robust and delightful companion, vital, warm-hearted, gay, impulsive and totally unaffected. He took little interest in politics or in current affairs, but he was absorbed in his work as a painter, read widely, especially the work of sporting writers, and had a lifelong passion for poetry about the English countryside. Later he had a spacious studio built in Chelsea Park Gardens and was able to fulfil a dream by the purchase of a Georgian house, Castle House, in Dedham, near Colchester.

Between the wars Munnings's vogue was tremendous, and he stayed at many great houses in order to draw horses and hounds. He was considered the finest painter of the epoch of animals and of the English country scene. During the war of 1939–45 he developed a voracious appetite for painting on Exmoor where he frequented the grazing grounds of herds of wild ponies and would be out painting them all day.

In 1924 at the invitation of the director of the Carnegie Institute at Pittsburgh, Munnings had paid his first visit to America in order to be a judge at a Pittsburgh international exhibition of pictures. But he allowed himself to become worn out by accepting too many portrait commissions from enthusiastic Americans. In 1926 he went to Spain where he saw pictures by Velazquez, El Greco, and Goya, but despite the impression made upon him by the Prado and his visits to Toledo, Seville, Granada, and Ronda, the memory which haunted him ever afterwards was the misery of the horses in the country and particularly in the bullring.

Munnings had been elected A.R.A. in 1919 and R.A. in 1925, and was elected president of the Royal Academy in 1944 when he received twenty-four votes to Augustus John's eleven. He had no administrative gifts, no patience with meetings, agenda or minutes, and no interest in the financial position of the Academy, although he appreciated its amenities and privileges and felt pride in it as an institution. He took no part in the arrangement of the exhibition of the royal collection in the winter of 1946-7; but his was the excellent idea for the Chantrey Bequest exhibition in 1949; and he showed enthusiasm for many of the nineteenth-century pictures which had become unfashionable. Also in 1949 it was his idea, and his alone, that (Sir) Winston Churchill, who was devoted to painting and who had practised it for years, should be made honorary academician extraordinary; and it was at Churchill's suggestion that Munnings restored the famous annual dinner, suspended by the war. Unfortunately he chose the occasion to make a prejudiced, indiscreet speech in which he spoke ill of artists of whom he disapproved and of modern art in general. His hostility towards the whole modern movement made him unable to believe that any sincere artist could think differently from himself.

Munnings was knighted in 1944 and received an honorary LL.D. from Sheffield in 1946. In 1947 he was appointed K.C.V.O., received the freedom of Norwich, and an exhibition of his work at the Leicester Galleries under the title 'The English Scene' brought in £20,788, a record for a living artist. In 1951-2 he gave two unexpectedly splendid lectures on Stubbs and Constable at the Royal Institution; and in 1956 an enthusiastic public flocked to a one-man exhibition of his work in the diploma gallery of the Royal Academy, the presidency of which he had resigned at the end of 1949.

Munnings published a discursive autobiography, richly illustrated, in three volumes: *An Artist's Life* (1950), *The Second Burst* (1951), and *The Finish* (1952). When speaking in public or writing he was unwilling and unable to keep to his subject, a characteristic which often added to the charm of what he had to say. By his gay exuberance and love of life, Munnings attracted friends throughout his long life, although they were exasperated by his headstrong follies and unreasonable temper.

In 1912 Munnings married Florence Carter-Wood who died in 1914. In 1920 he married a young widow, and accomplished rider, Violet McBride, daughter of Frank Golby Haines, an Edgware riding master. She proved an ideal wife. He gave her his power of attorney and she took complete control of the business and domestic sides of his life, leaving him free to devote himself to his painting. Yet she it was who said: 'He was never such a good artist after he married me . . . It meant painting for money.' He earned enormous sums from the rich, though these canvases are not his best; his best are close to the poetry he loved and to the country as he loved it; his good pictures (and there are many of them) will probably outlast much art as it is now practised. In 1969 his painting 'The Whip' sold for 17,000 guineas. He was among the best painters of a horse who have ever lived and immortalized many famous horses, among them Humorist, Radium, Hyperion, and Brown Jack, whose statuette is on view at Ascot when the Brown Jack stakes are run.

Munnings, who had no children, died at Castle House, 17 July 1959, and his ashes were buried in the crypt of St. Paul's Cathedral. The National Portrait Gallery has a drawing of Munnings by himself; and he figures in his fine portrait of his wife on horseback.

[Sir A. J. Munnings's own writings; *A. J. Munnings, R.A., Pictures of Horses and English Life*, with an appreciation by Lionel Lindsay, 1927; Reginald Pound, *The Englishman*, 1962; private information; personal knowledge.]

GERALD KELLY.

MURRAY, GEORGE GILBERT AIMÉ (1866-1957), classical scholar and internationalist, was born in Sydney 2 January

1866. His father, (Sir) Terence Murray, and his brother, (Sir) Hubert Murray [qq.v.], early awoke his love of books and of aboriginal peoples. The family, of Irish descent and military tradition, had been expropriated after the battle of the Boyne. 'We tended to be "agin the Government" ', he writes; ' "Pity is a rebel passion" and we were . . . passionately on the side of those likely to be oppressed.' His misery at the torture of animals and his fights with bullies remained sharp memories of the little school in the bush where he began Greek.

He left for London at the age of eleven with his widowed mother, whose cousin (Sir) W. S. Gilbert [q.v.], the origin of his name Gilbert, was then at work on *H.M.S. Pinafore*. At Merchant Taylors' Murray got a first-rate classical training, a little Hebrew, and leisure to read English poetry, J. S. Mill, and Comte. In his first year at St. John's College, Oxford, he won the Hertford and Ireland scholarships (1885) and made 40 runs in the Freshmen's match; then came a full bag of academic honours including a first in *literae humaniores* and a fellowship of New College (1888). He had already foreshadowed his international activities in a motion at the Oxford Union calling the free nations to unite against German and Russian militarism; and in his concern for peace, characteristically, he joined the Volunteers. He had made many friends, notably Charles Gore and H. A. L. Fisher [qq.v.]. To senior scholars the Australian seemed a model of English classical education.

Yet English classical education dissatisfied him, like many others of his day, by its narrow insistence on the arts in which he excelled: Greek and Latin composition. His excellence—still unrivalled in Greek—came of a power to make the language his own by intensely imaginative reading of the literature; and this recipe he always prescribed. But some tutors were treating the literature as a stock of serviceable tags for pupils' exercises; its remote and difficult beauty, without rekindling interpretation, seemed to many minds cold beside the living poets—Browning, Tennyson, Swinburne. At Oxford the consummate learning of Ingram Bywater [q.v.] was expounded too drily to inspire most young men. Of Murray's tutors Arthur Sidgwick had the live spark, but Sidgwick was no savant; indeed, the range

of erudition expected of a Hellenist was so limited that even Sir Richard Jebb [q.v.] could describe the twenty-three-year-old Murray as 'the most accomplished Greek scholar of the day'. Murray himself was eager for an expansion of Greek studies into fresh fields of research; and if, as Derby scholar in 1889, he had taken his projected road to Göttingen, he would have gained this enrichment under Wilamowitz, whose wide and exact learning overcame Murray with longing for such guidance.

But in 1889 Murray was in love with the beautiful and ardent Lady Mary Howard; the chair of Greek at Glasgow offered him a marriageable income; and the work among poorer students appealed strongly to the liberal idealism of the pair. In his inaugural lecture, and ever after, Murray took another road to the expansion of classical studies. Their monopoly was broken; the claim of new disciplines was just; Greek, too stiff for the masses but too precious for a class's preserve, must compete in a free market on its merits, without the subsidy of vested interests or other forms of what Murray often called *paracharaxis*—stamping a false value on a coin. For this experiment Glasgow, poor in social privilege and rich in brains, was a promising field, and Murray a masterly director. He taught by the strictest standards, but never snubbed ignorance or spared himself pains. His power of communicating the life of a subject is attested even by those who disputed some of his judgements. He had a natural presence, an actor's gift of staging and rendering, great beauty of voice and language, a proved telepathic faculty; but it was his inner experience of Greek poetry which convinced critical spirits—John Buchan, H. N. Brailsford [qq.v.], Janet Spens. His lectures (another pupil wrote) 'for some of us changed the whole outlook of our world'.

The problem of students wanting Greece on inadequate Greek forced Murray into translation. He had written plays; his *Carlyon Sahib* was produced (1899) in London by Mrs. Patrick Campbell [q.v.] but was found too grim for the public taste. His versions of Greek drama began as lecturing devices, and Glasgow men received them with Scottish stampedes of applause, but he published none until 1902, on a peremptory request from G. B. Shaw [q.v.]. They 'came into our dramatic literature' (Shaw wrote in 1905) 'with all the impulsive power of an original work'; to shouts of 'Author!' Murray had to reply that the author was dead. The translations filled a cockney music-hall as full as west-end theatres, and drew poets and scholars, miners and villagers, over the English-speaking world. By the mid-century their idiom seemed alien, even repellent. For all its faults, Murray was faithful to the Greek in choosing a poetic diction, removed from prose and common speech, unafraid of archaisms, sharply contrasting the metre of rhetoric with the lyric chorus, and rendering both in formal verse which contemporary actors enjoyed. He knew, besides, that action on the stage is more than diction in the arm-chair. It is true that both in his versions and in his book *Euripides and his Age* (1913) Murray often made the ideas of Euripides too like his own. Yet, above all ideas, Euripides was a playwright; and this was what Murray demonstrated to a generation who could not believe that the *Troades* would act. They were converted by his theatrical sense and his effort to obey his own precept: 'so understand as to relive'.

For a generous teacher Glasgow was hard work, and in 1899 exhaustion was mistaken for a fatal disease. He retired from his chair to Churt in Surrey. In 1905 he returned to New College as a fellow; he was elected F.B.A. in 1910. In these years he edited Euripides for the Oxford Classical Texts (3 vols., 1901–9). His edition, still the best after sixty years, shows his keen intellect and sensitive tact of the Greek language; but as an editor he had faults of method, and some waywardness in emendation or choice of readings was immediately rebuked by his friend A. E. Housman [q.v.], who generally approved his edition and his translations. Not every scholar had applauded his youthful *Ancient Greek Literature* (1897; republished 1956); in the margin of the preface Henry Jackson [q.v.] scribbled 'Insolent puppy'. He had misgivings of his own; in 1908, just before his appointment as regius professor at Oxford, he wrote to his wife: 'In the watches of the night it has become clear to me that I am not fit for the Chair of Greek. I am not learned or industrious enough to organize the study; I am too diverse in my interests.' Housman soon proposed to visit him, with the words: 'I have chosen a dry subject for my paper, as I have no doubt that scholarship at Oxford is taking an excessively literary

tinge under the influence of the new Professor of Greek.' But Murray as candidly disapproved Housman's dichotomy between scholarship and literature. He admired, but lacked, Housman's ambition to leave an enduring monument; he chose the ephemeral work of a teacher and interpreter. In its day his impact was extraordinary. His *Rise of the Greek Epic* (1907) has been republished since his death, though scientifically out of date, for its vivid poetic feeling and its style of eloquent speech directly attuned to listeners, which made his voice famous as a broadcaster. His *Four Stages of Greek Religion* (1912; extended in 1925 to *Five Stages*) is his most typical book. It reflects the temper of an agnostic able to apprehend religious experience outside his personal belief. His anthropological curiosity, enlarged by the work of Sir James Frazer and Jane Harrison [qq.v.], quickened his awareness of the savage and irrational elements behind Greek civilization. In Murray's conception of these elements and of the mature canons of Hellenism much is now obsolete, but his chapters on the later Pagans displayed a vision far beyond the classical conventions of the time, and prophetic of later explorations.

After Glasgow, the other turning-point was 1914. Murray's *Foreign Policy of Sir Edward Grey* (1915) temporarily estranged him from such close friends as Brailsford and Bertrand (later Earl) Russell. In 1900 he had denounced nationalism with ferocity ('National Ideals' reprinted in *Essays & Addresses*, 1921). Now he argued that Germany's desire for power after power had to be met with force after conciliation had failed. The corollary duty was to prevent more wars by international action, and from 1919 until his death it ate up his leisure. He was a founder (and chairman of the executive council, 1923–38) of the League of Nations Union, with the Council for Education in World Citizenship; and after the war of 1939–45 joint president (1945–7, 1949–57) and sole president (1947–9) of the United Nations Association. To his ninetieth year he travelled indefatigably lecturing in these causes. Much of his time between the wars was spent at Geneva as a delegate for South Africa (1921–3) and from 1922 as a member (for eight years chairman) of the Committee on Intellectual Co-operation—'a subject which bores me stiff', he wrote at first, but he soon warmed to the work with

Einstein, Mme Curie, and Paul Valéry as colleagues.

In 1923 the vice-chancellor of Oxford asked him whether he ought to pursue these activities while retaining his chair. He was teaching to the full, but he had not time for the sustained research and bibliographical digestion expected of a professor. His *Classical Tradition in Poetry* (1927, Harvard lectures) and *Aristophanes* (1933) are books of a scholar but not of scholarship; his text of Aeschylus (1937) was poor, though later improved (1955); his translations (except those of Menander) grew tired, a hobby for odd moments. Some regretted the dispersal of his phenomenal energies in the uncertain cause of peace. Murray was surprised and angry. To decline public service for one's privately preferred studies was a reversal of his classical and Victorian principles. He replied (with indubitable truth): 'I care far more for teaching Greek than for any other pursuit in life'; and he taught it, financing a research studentship from his salary for full measure, until he retired from his chair in 1936. As it happened, his most permanent service to pure scholarship was given in these latter years—not by his own research but by his personal exertions, backed by all his international influence, for the reception of refugee scholars in British universities. Murray's academic standards were never provincial, and he saw it not only as a humanitarian concern but as a fertilization of humane studies through that widened erudition which he himself had not fetched from Göttingen to Glasgow and Oxford.

He still regarded classics as an education for others besides specialists, and Hellenism (like a Greek play) as something to be understood by reliving. The magnanimous ideal sometimes touched his picture of Hellenism with anachronistic colours; his thought, though lucid and trenchant, was unhistorical. He had rare sincerity of mind and feeling without Housman's rare passion for exactitude. Not that he tolerated woolliness; his Greek composition kept its brilliance and resource, and his curiosity its alertness; all the week before his last illness he was absorbed in new Aeschylean labours and in his first reading of Etienne de la Boëtie. Yet he had blind spots—Tacitus, the Psalms, music. Liberal in politics (he thrice stood unsuccessfully for Oxford University) and in ideas, he saw both sides of a question, but he was obstinate in his underlying beliefs. Rationalism he defined not as the sufficiency of reason but as its limitation to frontiers facing unknown worlds; the child of a mixed marriage, he maintained a reverent aloofness from institutional religion. An episode near his death, when Roman Catholic sacraments were administered according to his own and his father's baptism, was later publicized; a responsible comment appeared in the *Tablet*, 29 June 1957.

Murray's personality had a striking coherence, which made him (in Auden's phrase) a mythopoeic character. The public perceived clear outlines and endowed him with virtues or absurdities which he did not possess. Shaw's portrait in *Major Barbara* catches the paradox in 'the life-long struggle of a benevolent temperament and a high conscience against impulses of inhuman ridicule and fierce impatience', from which his noted serenity, gentleness, and balance emerged. He was agile and footsure, a capable boxer in youth, a fearless glacier-walker in his sixties. Many were surprised by his irrepressible sense of the thrill in war and his buoyancy at its outbreak in 1939. Working with incessant hope for humanity, he saw human nature as 'the carnivorous ape ... a vain mischievous cruel licentious beast'. Devoted to international concord, he was none too fond of foreign travel, and harboured some insular distrust of 'small dark nations'. The teetotaller and vegetarian was at home in any good-humoured society, a versatile host at Yatscombe, near Oxford, a born mimic and parodist (his Ramsay MacDonald speech ended: 'I shall not shrink from hesitating to refuse'). In that house the duty of response to present demands was paramount, and he was too busy to take much thought for posterity's opinion of his work ('none of it is great or solid achievement' was his own, written to his wife). Yet he was pleased by public honour, proud of the Order of Merit (1941) and the proffered freedom of the City of London. His place in Westminster Abbey was a congenial tribute to a high mind and an illuminating spirit in his generation.

By his marriage in 1889 to Lady Mary Henrietta Howard (died 1956), eldest daughter of the ninth Earl of Carlisle, he had three sons and two daughters. He died at his home on Boar's Hill 20 May 1957. The National Portrait Gallery has a drawing by Augustus John and a painting by Murray's grandson Lawrence Toynbee.

A drawing by Francis Dodd is in St. John's College, Oxford.

[The Gilbert Murray papers (Bodleian Library); *An Unfinished Autobiography*, with essays by friends, 1960; J. A. K. Thomson in *Proceedings* of the British Academy, vol. xliii, 1959; E. R. Dodds in *Gnomon*, 1957; Sir C. M. Bowra, *Memories*, 1966; personal knowledge.]   M. I. HENDERSON.

MURRY, JOHN MIDDLETON (1889–1957), author, was born at Peckham, London, 6 August 1889, the elder of two sons of John Murry, a clerk in the Inland Revenue Department, and his wife, Emily Wheeler. Murry's father had taught himself to read and write and had begun as a boy messenger; the family was poor and it was through scholarships that Murry obtained his education at Christ's Hospital and Brasenose College, Oxford, where he obtained a first class in honour moderations (1910) and a second in *literae humaniores* (1912). He wrote for the *Westminster Gazette* (1912–13), then for the *Times Literary Supplement*, and worked in the political intelligence department of the War Office from 1916, being appointed chief censor in 1919 and O.B.E. in 1920. In *Between Two Worlds* (1935) he has described his early life up to and including his marriage in 1918 to Katherine Mansfield [q.v.] with whom he had lived since 1912. His second marriage (1924) was to Violet, daughter of Charles le Maistre, general secretary of the International Electrotechnical Commission. After her death in 1931 he married Elizabeth Ada, daughter of Joseph Cockbayne, farmer; and on her death in 1954, fourthly, Mary, daughter of Henry Gilbert Gamble, architect, with whom he had lived since 1941.

Murry had been forced to overwork as a child and for the greater part of his life he worked, at first from financial necessity and later, perhaps, partly from habit, at abnormally high pressure. It is therefore all the more remarkable that so much of his prodigious output of both literary and social criticism should be of value. When he was appointed editor of the *Athenaeum* in 1919, at the age of thirty, he was a key figure, and perhaps then the leading figure, of the post-war literary generation which included T. S. Eliot, Aldous Huxley, and D. H. Lawrence [q.v.] with whom his relations were particularly intimate and stormy. Murry's literary popularity was short-lived and he came to be described by a friendly critic

as 'the best-hated man of letters in the country'. Although it had been brilliantly successful intellectually, the *Athenaeum* had lost money and in 1921 it was merged with the *Nation*, when Murry resigned, mainly on account of Katherine Mansfield's serious illness. After her death in 1923 Murry founded the *Adelphi*, which he controlled until 1948. At first it was a sensational success, but the success was of a kind to alienate some of his most discriminating readers. Although this was partly due to their own impercipience, it is nevertheless true that in the *Adelphi* Murry did at times exhibit an emotionalism which was the flaw in the element of mysticism which had been latent in his work from the beginning and became more manifest after Katherine Mansfield's death. At its best this mystical element was responsible for the extraordinary penetration of Murry's criticism, which is evident in his first critical study, *Dostoevsky* (1916), and in all his more important works. It was, however, completely at odds with the prevailing literary trends.

For many years after Katherine Mansfield's death, Murry lived a strenuous and tormented life which was divided into what appeared to be three almost watertight compartments: first, his literary work, which included books on Keats, D. H. Lawrence, Blake, and Shakespeare; second, his political and social activities, which included lecturing and the organization of a farm community, but which also produced books on his religious thought, on Communism, and on pacifism; third, his home life, which was almost continuously painful. His second wife, by whom he had a son and a daughter, died, like his first, of consumption. There were also a son and a daughter of his third marriage which was unhappy; it was only with his fourth wife that he at last achieved a life of peaceful happiness. With his *Jonathan Swift* (1954), *Unprofessional Essays* (1956), and *Love, Freedom and Society* (1957) he began to regain some of his former reputation as a literary critic. Yet *Love, Freedom and Society*, which was based upon a comparative study of Albert Schweitzer and D. H. Lawrence, was in reality a masterly synthesis of his own literary, religious, and social thought, and its favourable reception might suggest that readers were beginning to catch up with Murry's method. In the long run, however, he will probably be best remembered for

his studies of Shakespeare, Keats, and
D. H. Lawrence, and perhaps even more
for his adherence, in an age of academic
sterility, to the humane tradition of
culture. In the words of his biographer,
F. A. Lea, he owed 'his unique understanding of the Romantics and his total
neglect by the academics to the persistence
of his quest for "the good life"—a quest
that carried him, as it did Coleridge and
Arnold, ever farther away from literature in the direction of philosophy and
sociology' (*A Defence of Philosophy*, 1962).

Murry died at Bury St. Edmunds,
Suffolk, 13 March 1957. There is an
interesting drawing of him in his youth
in (Sir) William Rothenstein's *Twenty-
Four Portraits* (2nd series, 1923).

[J. M. Murry, *Between Two Worlds*, 1935,
and other works, *passim*; F. A. Lea, *Life of
John Middleton Murry*, 1959; private information; personal knowledge.]   RICHARD REES.

MYRES, SIR JOHN LINTON (1869–
1954), archaeologist and historian, was
born 3 July 1869 at Preston, Lancashire,
the only son of the Rev. William Miles
Myres, vicar of St. Paul's, Preston, and his
first wife, Jane, daughter of the Rev.
Henry Linton. He won scholarships to
Winchester, thence to New College,
Oxford, where he took first classes in
honour moderations (1890) and *literae
humaniores* (1892). He had already shown
a lively interest in antiquities and local
history as an undergraduate, publishing
articles, digging at Alchester, and organizing the local history museum at Aylesbury.
As a fellow of Magdalen (1892–5) and
Craven fellow (1892) he was able to visit
the Mediterranean, travelling in the
Greek islands, exploring Caria and the
Dodecanese, and working with (Sir)
Arthur Evans (whose notice he later
contributed to this Dictionary). He
travelled widely in Crete, collecting minor
antiquities and copying inscriptions. These
were the early days of excavation in the
island and of the discovery of Minoan
civilization, although Knossos itself had
yet to be dug. By comparing Cretan
vases with some vase fragments found by
(Sir) Flinders Petrie [q.v.] in Egypt, at
Kahun, he found the first important link
and correlation to be observed between
the two ancient civilizations. He did not
join Evans in the excavations at Knossos,
but dug with the British School at
Palaikastro, and, notably, at the hill-
top shrine of Petsofa, the finds from which
he soon published.

It was to Cyprus and to Cypriot antiquities that much of his archaeological
work was at first devoted, and he several
times returned to the problems of its
archaeology in his writings. He had conducted excavations in the island in 1894,
at Kition; he wrote a catalogue of the
Cyprus Museum (1899, with M. Ohnefalsch-
Richter); and in 1914 published an
exemplary catalogue of the rich Cesnola
collection in New York. In these years he
had been a student of Christ Church
(1895–1907) and university lecturer in
classical archaeology, and he went to
Liverpool as professor of Greek and
lecturer in ancient geography (1907–10).
In his early teaching and writing his
knowledge of the geography of the
Aegean was put to good account and he
had the happy gift of being able to elucidate problems of antiquity by modern
analogies. Quite apart from his Greek
studies he wrote a schools' *History of Rome*
which was published in 1902.

The creation of the new Wykeham
professorship in ancient history brought
Myres back to Oxford in 1910 and he held
this chair until his retirement in 1939.
The title of his inaugural lecture—'Greek
Lands and the Greek People'—set the
theme of his future interests and these
years saw the publication of several
books on the various aspects of ancient
history which his wide experience could
control. *The Dawn of History* (1911) was
a semi-popular exposition of fundamental
principles about the study of early civilizations and approach to ancient history.
It displayed already the easy style of
writing which informed all his work.
To the *Cambridge Ancient History* he
contributed several chapters. *Who were
the Greeks?* (1930) was his most brilliant and
provocative work, based on the Sather
lectures which he had been again invited
to deliver in California in 1927 (the first
time had been in 1914). On Sir Arthur
Evans's death in 1941 he took on the
task of editing the Linear B tablets from
Knossos which, half a century after their
discovery, were finally published (as
Scripta Minoa II) in 1952, and he lived to
applaud the decipherment by Michael
Ventris [q.v.] of their language as Greek.
Myres continued writing until his death—
a vivid and highly personal account of
Herodotus, Father of History (1953) and
essays on *Homer and his Critics*, edited
after his death by Miss D. H. F. Gray
in 1958. To his collection of essays,
Geographical History in Greek Lands (1953),

e appended a select bibliography of his writings. The most valuable aspect of his work was probably not so much the new material or solutions which he presented—although these were numerous —but the challenging approach to the more conventional problems of ancient history which a scholar versed in geography, anthropology, and the classics could take. His services to scholarship were recognized by honorary degrees from Wales, Manchester, Witwatersrand, and Athens, and the Victoria medal of the Royal Geographical Society (1953). He was elected F.B.A. in 1923 and knighted in 1943.

Myres's interests were not confined to any narrow field of research in antiquity. When he went to Greece in 1892 one of his awards was the Burdett-Coutts geological scholarship. As an anthropologist he served the Royal Anthropological Institute as its honorary secretary, then president (1928–31); and in 1901 he had inaugurated its new monthly periodical *Man* which he edited in 1901–3, and again in 1931–46, and to which he regularly contributed on subjects often far removed from classical studies. As a Hellenist and archaeologist he was vice-president of the Society of Antiquaries (1924–9) and its gold medallist in 1942; president of the Hellenic Society (1935–8); chairman of the British School at Athens (1934–47), and organizer of its jubilee exhibition in Burlington House in 1936. He was librarian of New College up to 1946. He was general secretary of the British Association from 1919 to 1932, following its conferences to many parts of the world. His range in scholarship was matched by the variety and vigour of his other activities. As well as his concern for the administration and welfare of the various societies which he served he was active in Oxford politics, in the establishment of new graduate degrees, and the promotion of new subjects, notably geography and anthropology. In the war of 1914–18 he commanded small craft in raiding operations on the Turkish coast on the tug *Syra* and then the former royal yacht *Aulis*. In this his ingenuity and buccaneering spirit served him no less than his detailed knowledge of the geography and people of the Asia Minor coast. He ended the war as acting commander R.N.V.R. and was awarded the O.B.E. and the Greek Order of George I. In the war of 1939–45 he used his great experience of the geography of Greece in editing handbooks for naval intelligence.

Through most of his life Myres was troubled by his eyesight and at the end, although still writing, was quite blind. In appearance he was a handsome man, bearded and blue-eyed. Drawings of him, by Albert Rutherston, hang in New College senior common-room and the Oxford School of Geography. In his dealings with younger scholars he was generous and kindly, and his work must be judged not only by what he wrote but also by what he inspired in others, by example or casual precept. He founded no school. In his lifetime he saw classical archaeology grow from a dilettante study to a discipline which has much to contribute to all departments of classical scholarship. His part in this development was to show how historian, archaeologist, anthropologist, and geographer should combine their skills in the study of antiquity.

In 1895 Myres married Sophia Florence (died 1960), daughter of Charles Ballance, by whom he had two sons and one daughter. The younger son, John Nowell Linton Myres, was Bodley's librarian at Oxford, 1948–65. Myres died in Oxford 6 March 1954.

[T. J. Dunbabin in *Proceedings* of the British Academy, vol. xli, 1955; private information.]   J. Boardman.

NAMIER, Sir LEWIS BERNSTEIN (1888–1960), historian, was born 27 June 1888 at Wola Okrzejska, to the east of Warsaw, the only son of Joseph Bernstein (originally Niemirowski), advocate and landowner, by his wife, Ann, daughter of Maurice Theodor Sommerstein. Both parents were Polonized Jews who no longer adhered to the Jewish religion. Ludwik Bernstein was educated privately, and after brief periods at Lwow and Lausanne universities came to England, where he spent a year at the London School of Economics and entered Balliol College, Oxford, in 1908. He took a first in modern history in 1911 and was awarded a share in the Beit prize in 1913. Throughout his life Oxford, and especially Balliol, had a high place in his affections. He took British nationality in 1913 and changed his name by deed poll.

In 1913 Namier went to the United States to take up a post with one of his father's business associates. There he began research on eighteenth-century parliamentary history, and he returned to England in 1914 with the intention of writing a book on the British Parliament during the American revolution. On the outbreak of war he joined the army and served as a private in the Royal Fusiliers, but his knowledge of east European affairs led to his transfer to the Foreign Office where he worked from 1915 to 1920, first in the propaganda, then in the political intelligence, department. He was much concerned with the settlement of Polish affairs at the Paris peace conference.

Namier spent 1920 and 1921 as a tutor at Balliol. He had hoped to resume his historical work but found teaching occupied too much of his time, and in 1921 he again entered business in order to amass a competence. He became the European representative of a firm of Manchester cotton manufacturers, with his headquarters in Czechoslovakia, and a correspondent of the *Manchester Guardian*. From 1924 to 1929 he was occupied fully with historical research. He had no private income, and when his capital ran out he lived on his earnings from journalism, loans from friends, and two grants from the Rhodes Trustees. The results of his labours, *The Structure of Politics at the Accession of George III* (1929) and *England in the Age of the American Revolution* (1930), were immediately recognized as epoch-making for the study of the eighteenth century and established him in the front rank of British historians. Yet they represented only the first instalment of what was intended to be a multi-volumed study of Parliament during the period of the American revolution—a project which Namier did not resume until over twenty years later.

While rejecting the Jewish religion Namier had early become a Jewish nationalist, and his sympathy with Zionism increased during the post-war period. In 1929 he became political secretary to the Jewish Agency for Palestine, but his position was ambiguous and in 1931 he left to take up the chair of modern history in the university of Manchester. This he retained until his retirement in 1953. From 1931 to the outbreak of war his historical work took the form largely of essays and lectures, notably the Ford's lectures in 1933–4 on 'King, Cabinet and Parliament in the Early Years of George III'. What time he could spare from university teaching was spent in helping Jewish refugees from Germany. In 1939 he was adviser to Chaim Weizmann [q.v.] at the Palestine conference, and from 1940 to 1945 he was again engaged on full-time political work with the Jewish

Agency. The events of the war reawakened his old interest in European history, and in 1946 he published *1848: The Revolution of the Intellectuals*, an expanded version of the Raleigh lecture delivered to the British Academy in 1944, the year of his election as a fellow. This masterly study of the revolutions in eastern Europe was followed by one on the German revolution of 1848, delivered as a series of lectures at Magdalen College, Oxford.

Namier had been a determined opponent of the policy of appeasement, and during the war of 1939–45 he settled down to study the diplomatic origins of the conflict. Although the principal documents were not then available, he was able to talk with men who had taken part in the events he narrated and much of *Diplomatic Prelude* (1948) was based on their recollections and notes. This was followed by two further volumes of essays on pre-war diplomatic history (*Europe in Decay*, 1950, and *In the Nazi Era*, 1952), and in 1951 Namier returned to what he described as his chosen field of British parliamentary history. He had been a member of the Treasury committee set up in 1929 to consider plans for writing a history of Parliament, and when the scheme was revived in 1951 he was appointed to the editorial board and given responsibility for the period 1754–90. The last nine years of his life were devoted almost entirely to this task, despite the handicaps of increasing deafness and a paralysed right hand which made writing almost impossible. He lived to see the biographies and constituency histories almost completed, but the introductory survey, in which he had planned to sum up the results of a lifetime's research, was hardly begun, when he died suddenly in London 19 August 1960. The work was completed by his chief assistant John Brooke and published in three volumes in 1964.

Namier was both a stimulating and a controversial figure. His foreign birth and his experience in business and politics gave him an attitude towards history which was not shared by most of his academic contemporaries, and with scholars he was ill at ease. An historical sense, he once remarked, is 'an intuitive understanding of how things do not happen'. He had vast learning and creative imagination of a high order, but was unable to discipline either, so that his published work represents but a fragment of what he had intended to do. Two problems in history particularly interested him: the composition and working of legislative assemblies (particularly the British Parliament) and the growth of nationalism in modern Europe. But *England in the Age of the American Revolution* stops short before the American revolution has even begun, while instead of the history of Europe during the nineteenth century which he had planned to write he left only detached essays on isolated subjects. Many of Namier's profoundest observations on history and historical problems are scattered in essays which he wrote as *pièces d'occasion* or in the guise of book reviews and afterwards republished in book form (in particular, *Avenues of History*, 1952, *Personalities and Powers*, 1955, *Vanished Supremacies*, 1958, and *Crossroads of Power*, 1962). In part Namier's failure to achieve his aims was due to his meticulous concern for accuracy and an exact prose style, but in part also it was due to his inability to correlate ends to means. Although he believed that 'what matters in history is the great outline and the significant detail', he could never resist the temptation to wander down some fascinating by-path of his story, regardless of his main theme, and his books are spoilt for the general reader by the proliferation and over-elaboration of his footnotes.

Despite these defects in his work, Namier exerted a greater influence over historians than perhaps any other scholar of his generation. Although strongly criticized, especially in his later years, his view of eighteenth-century political history has been generally accepted, and it is impossible to write on this period in terms of the pre-Namier era. It is in the field of his method and technique that his critics have gained most ground. He believed that in order to understand an institution or a society it must be broken up into its component parts, and these studied in isolation and then in relation to the whole. When he began work on *The Structure of Politics* he tried to find out all he could about every member who sat in the Parliament of 1761 and then to study 'how they consorted together' (in the words of a quotation from Aeschylus which he took as the motto for the book). Critics have pointed out, not always unfairly, that he was more interested in the parts than the whole, and that his method of structural analysis ignored the importance of ideas in history. What in fact Namier did was to bring to the study of history the post-Freudian conception of the mind: the belief that the reasons men give for their actions are rationalizations designed to cloak their deeper purposes. This led him to distrust political ideas as the explanations of historical movements and to stress the determinism underlying history.

It would be more correct to say that Namier paid insufficient attention to culture, of which ideas are but a part. Although a tireless searcher after historical material, he was little acquainted with the art, music, literature, or science of the period he studied. As a result he placed a low value on human achievements. His mind was powerful but his interests were narrow, and while for those of similar tastes he could be a fascinating companion he lacked the ability to make himself generally agreeable. A Conservative in politics in the tradition of Burke and a Calvinist in religion, he had also great sympathy for human distress and weakness. The dominating passion in his historical work was the search for truth: he would take immense pains to check the most insignificant details; and he dealt harshly and not always wisely with the errors of others. Yet he could also accept criticism or correction of his own work, and would praise a research student who had discovered a mistake in one of his books. He could win loyalty, and his assistants on the *History of Parliament* were devoted to him.

Namier was a tall, heavily built man, with a serious if not grim expression, lightened by vivacious eyes. Although a master of written English, he habitually spoke with a foreign accent; and he had a wide command of languages. In later years he mellowed considerably, under the influence of his second marriage and the general recognition of his work. He was knighted in 1952; was an honorary D.Litt. of Durham (1952), Oxford (1955), and Rome (1956); honorary Litt.D. of Cambridge (1957); and honorary D.C.L. of Oxford (1960). Perhaps he derived most pleasure, however, from his election to an honorary fellowship of Balliol in 1948 and from the invitation to deliver the Romanes lecture at Oxford in 1952.

In 1917 Namier married Clara Sophie Edeleff, a widow, and daughter of the late Alexander Poniatowski, doctor of medicine. She died in 1945. He married secondly, in 1947, Iulia, daughter of the late Mikhail Kazarin, barrister at the Russian Law Court, and widow of

Nicholas de Beausobre. There were no children.

[Lucy S. Sutherland in *Proceedings* of the British Academy, vol. xlviii, 1962; Sir Isaiah Berlin, 'Lewis Namier: A Personal Impression', in *A Century of Conflict, Essays for A. J. P. Taylor*, ed. Martin Gilbert, 1966; Arnold J. Toynbee, *Acquaintances*, 1967; private information; personal knowledge.]

JOHN BROOKE.

NEILSON, JULIA EMILIE (1868–1957), actress, was born in the Tottenham Court Road, London, 12 June 1868, the only child of Alexander Ritchie Neilson, silversmith, and his wife, Emilie Davis. The latter, a Jewess, *en secondes noces* became the wife of an eminent solicitor, William Morris, who had been previously married to Florence, sister of Fred Terry [q.v.] who in 1891 became Julia Neilson's husband.

Julia Neilson's career began with her eyes fixed on the concert platform rather than the stage. At the age of fifteen, after several years at school in Wiesbaden, she began her studies at the Royal Academy of Music, where she won several prizes, and studied elocution under Walter Lacy [q.v.]. She was still a student when she made her first professional appearance at the St. James's Hall on 1 April 1887, when she sang as a mezzo-soprano. Influenced, however, by the friendly counsel of (Sir) W. S. Gilbert [q.v.], she abandoned music for the theatre, and made her first stage appearance at the Lyceum Theatre on 21 March 1888 as Cynisca in *Pygmalion and Galatea* with Mary Anderson, and later in the same play as Galatea at the Savoy with Lewis Waller [q.v.]. Engagements followed with Rutland Barrington [q.v.] for a season at the St. James's, and with (Sir) Herbert Beerbohm Tree [q.v.] at the Haymarket, where she stayed for five years—a period which included Hester Worsley in *A Woman of No Importance* (1893) and Lady Chiltern in *An Ideal Husband* (1895). In December 1895 she went with (Sir) John Hare [q.v.] to the United States, making her first appearance in New York at Abbey's Theatre in *The Notorious Mrs. Ebbsmith*. On her return to England she joined (Sir) George Alexander [q.v.] at the St. James's to play Princess Flavia in the immortal *Prisoner of Zenda* (1896) and remained there until 1898 playing, among other parts, Rosalind in *As You Like It* and Beatrice in *Much Ado About Nothing*. This was followed by a return to Tree for whom she played Constance in *King John* (1899) and Oberon in *A Midsummer Night's Dream* (1900).

The turning-point of her career came in 1900 when, following a tour of *As You Like It* with William Mollison, she entered on London management for the first time with her husband, Fred Terry, the youngest of the famous acting family. Their first venture, *Sweet Nell of Old Drury*, with Julia Neilson in the part of Nell Gwyn, opened at the Haymarket on 30 August. This initiated not only a management but an acting partnership which continued until 1930. Some people lamented that talents which had been seen to advantage in the plays of Pinero, Wilde, and Shakespeare should have been—comparatively speaking—squandered with such generosity in the field of romantic-costume-fustian; just as they complained that Fred Terry, who might well have been the supreme Falstaff of all time, was wasted as Sir Percy Blakeney or Henry of Navarre. The fantastically large and touchingly faithful audiences, which in London, America, and especially on tours throughout the United Kingdom took the couple, complete with cloaks, swords, and all the paraphernalia of romance, to their hearts, would not have agreed for a moment. Histrionic romance was mingled agreeably with a suggestion of an idealized domesticity.

The Scarlet Pimpernel, perennial and most famous of plays associated with the Neilson–Terry partnership, made its bow at the New Theatre 5 January 1905. This piece, together with *Sweet Nell of Old Drury* and *Henry of Navarre*, formed the backbone of the material for the seasons of touring, and they came to be welcomed regularly as old friends. Dorothy Vernon in *Dorothy o' the Hall*, Margaret Goodman in *Mistress Wilful*, Queen Mary in *The Borderer*, Sarah, Duchess of Marlborough in *The Marlboroughs*, and Katherine in *The Wooing of Katherine Parr* never quite reached the triumphant successes of Lady Blakeney, Nell Gwyn, and Marguerite de Valois.

Julia Neilson's acting talent is remarkably difficult to appraise. Perhaps she owed her first successes rather to her face and voice than to her acting *pur sang*. And most of the material of the great years of partnership was hardly testing from the point of view of the highest standards. But she possessed that personality so essential to success for English players, to the degree of 'star quality'. Nothing that she did could lack significance. Her record was that of a genuine trouper and she unquestionably gave immense pleasure to thousands who saw her over the years. She may not have been a great actress, but she was accomplished, vital, and much loved in her profession. She was one of the acknowledged beauties of an era famous for feminine beauty. Hers was a loveliness essentially dignified, designed to grow with the years into the elegant and almost majestic *grande dame.* Yet the few people who knew her intimately were aware of a remarkable sense of fun; usually hidden, but when released almost diabolic in its lack of inhibition. She lived, as she acted, on the grand scale: a splendid vitality against a background of outsize furniture. She was a vigorous and spirited conversationalist. And she had the warmest and most generous of hearts.

After Fred Terry's death in 1933 Julia Neilson appeared at Daly's in *Vintage Wine* in 1934; was the guest of honour at a testimonial luncheon given in honour of her jubilee on the stage in 1938; and acted for the last time in 1944 at the Q Theatre in *The Widow of Forty.* She died in London 27 May 1957. Both her son, Dennis Neilson-Terry (died 1932), and her daughter, Phyllis Neilson-Terry, made for themselves distinguished theatrical careers.

[Julia Neilson, *This for Remembrance*, 1940; *Who's Who in the Theatre*; private information; personal knowledge.]   VAL GIELGUD.

NEWMAN, ERNEST (1868–1959), musical critic, whose real name was William Roberts, was born 30 November 1868 in Everton, Lancashire, the only child of Seth Roberts, a tailor, and his second wife, Harriet Spark, whose first married name was Jones. Both parents also had families by their first spouses. William Roberts was educated at Liverpool College and University College, Liverpool. He was intended for the Indian Civil Service, but illness prevented him from taking the examination and he became a clerk in the Bank of Liverpool (1889–1903), meantime contributing to a number of progressive journals articles not only on music but on literature, religion, and philosophical subjects. He published his first book, *Gluck and the Opera*, in 1895, as Ernest Newman. The pseudonym was intended to signify his outlook, but it corresponded to some psychological need, since he thereafter adopted it in private as well as public life, although he

never legally ratified the change. In 1897 he published *Pseudo-Philosophy at the End of the Nineteenth Century*, a criticism from the point of view of aggressive rationalism of writings by Benjamin Kidd, Henry Drummond, and A. J. Balfour [qq.v.], under the name Hugh Mortimer Cecil, but he did not use this name again.

In a series of articles contributed to *Cassell's Weekly* from March 1923 Newman described how he contrived to find time for an immense amount of reading and for self-education in music during his time at the bank. He had only one half-hour lesson in harmony, which was enough to convince him that he could do better for and by himself than by formal instruction, but he worked at composition for five years and at playing the piano, and made himself an expert score-reader.

His first musical journalism was written for (Sir) Granville Bantock [q.v.] in his *New Quarterly Musical Review.* He also owed to Bantock commissions to write programme-notes for his concerts at New Brighton, and later (1903) when Bantock was principal of the Birmingham and Midland Institute school of music, an invitation to join the staff. In 1905 Newman published his *Musical Studies* and left Birmingham to become music critic of the *Manchester Guardian*, in which his trenchant pen and independence of view sometimes upset the Hallé committee and Hans Richter but established his critical reputation. So much so that in 1906 the *Birmingham Daily Post* recalled him to Birmingham where he remained until 1919.

During these years Newman wrote studies of Wagner (1899 and 1904), Strauss (1908), Elgar (1906), and Hugo Wolf (1907). This last book remained for thirty years the best monograph on its subject and was translated into German. In 1914 came *Wagner as Man and Artist* which showed Newman's analytical powers, his independence—it was critical of *Mein Leben* and consequently not well received at Bayreuth —his appreciation of the Wagnerian music-drama, and his extreme care over documentation and detail. It led him on to his *magnum opus, The Life of Richard Wagner* in four volumes published in 1933, 1937, 1945, and 1947, which itself gave rise as a by-product to a study of *The Man Liszt* (1934). Newman had no illusions about Wagner's moral character and no doubts about his unique genius. Such was the clarity of his mind in the small things as well as the great that the biography, which involved a stupefying mass of material, is likely to remain definitive, unless Bayreuth improbably yields up further material of some wholly unexpected importance.

When he went to London in 1919 Newman began to write regularly for the *Observer*, but in the following year he joined the *Sunday Times* and thereafter, until 1958, he was its music critic, writing a weekly article and noticing the more important events in London music. His critical aim was objectivity—not for him the adventures of the soul among masterpieces—although he professed no interest in anything but the best, at any rate not until the second-rate had acquired historical interest. Although he could not turn criticism into a science, as he would have liked to do, he set out his critical creed in *A Musical Critic's Holiday* (1925), and in *The Unconscious Beethoven* (1927) a method of what soon came to be known as style criticism. A collection of his articles was published in 1919 entitled *A Musical Motley*; and from the *Sunday Times* two other selections were culled by Felix Aprahamian in 1956 and 1958. These served to show Newman's great range, which was sometimes overlooked because of his undoubted predilection for the nineteenth century and for opera, on which he published *Opera Nights* (1943), *Wagner Nights* (1949), and *More Opera Nights* (1954). He had translated most of Wagner's opera texts by 1912 and he was also responsible for translations of Weingartner's *On Conducting* (1906) and Schweitzer's *J. S. Bach* (1911).

Newman rigidly refused all honours until in extreme old age he no longer had the energy to decline them: Finland conferred on him the Order of the White Rose in 1956; Germany the Grosse Dienstkreuz in 1958; and the university of Exeter the D.Litt. in 1959. In 1955 he was presented with a *Festschrift*, a collection of essays by colleagues and admirers, *Fanfare for Ernest Newman*, edited by Herbert van Thal who later (1962) edited a further selection of Newman's essays and papers in *Testament of Music*.

In conversation Newman was as witty and kindly as he was witty and formidable in writing. In both and behind his amused smile was to be detected an underlying pessimism. In extreme age Beethoven's late quartets became his bible, for though he affected boredom with listening to music and was a rationalist by creed his

values were determined by the big things in music. In appearance he was slight in build and after an illness in early middle life totally bald.

Newman was twice married: first, in 1894, to Kate Eleanor (died 1918), daughter of Henry Woollett, an artist descended from the engraver William Woollett [q.v.]; secondly, in 1919, to Vera, daughter of Arthur Hands, a Birmingham jeweller. There were no children of either marriage. He died at Tadworth, Surrey, 7 July 1959.

[Vera Newman, *Ernest Newman*, 1963; private information; personal knowledge.]

FRANK HOWES.

NICHOLSON, CHARLES ERNEST (1868–1954), yacht designer, was born at Gosport 12 May 1868, the second son in the family of three boys and five girls of Benjamin Nicholson, naval architect, and his wife, Sarah Watson. Educated at Mill Hill School he joined the family firm of Camper and Nicholsons, Ltd., in 1886 and at the age of twenty-one became the firm's chief designer, a post which he filled until his death. Later, he was chairman and managing-director, to the age of seventy-two.

Nicholson rapidly made his presence felt in the firm and soon sailing yachts of all kinds from his board were challenging those of G. L. Watson [q.v.], the acknowledged master of the time. Nicholson, a rare combination of artist, technical genius, and business man, was undoubtedly one of the greatest and most versatile yacht architects of all time. His skill as a helmsman contributed in no small measure to his success. He built up the greatest yacht yard in this country at Gosport and later a second at Southampton. Both had difficulty in keeping pace with the designs of yachts of all conceivable kinds which flowed in a steady torrent from his imaginative brain.

He designed sailing craft of all sizes from a 12-ft. dinghy for his grandchildren to J-class America's Cup challengers of which he built four, notably *Shamrock IV* in 1914 and *Endeavour* in 1934, both potential winners; that they failed to win the cup was due to extraneous circumstances and no fault of Nicholson's. In 1939, which marked the end of the pageant of big-class yacht racing, the 12-metre fleet was almost entirely of Nicholson's design and construction. By the mid-thirties ocean racing was becoming popular and inevitably Nicholson was commissioned

:o design and build a suitable vessel. Not imited by cost, he produced the cutter *Foxhound* in 1935, 45-ft. on the waterline, about the same size as a 12-metre. Nothing comparable had been built in this country. She was followed by the yawl *Bloodhound* and *Stiarna*, a cutter, of similar design. These yachts were highly successful and throughout long careers stood up to the hard punishment of offshore racing; and, in the sixties, were still in commission, *Bloodhound* being then owned until 1969 by Queen Elizabeth II and the Duke of Edinburgh. Nicholson designed cruising yachts of all kinds from 5-tons up to such vessels as the 699-ton schooner *Creole* (1927).

Nicholson was always a jump ahead. He was the first yacht designer to see the possibilities of Bermuda rig and, in 1921, re-rigged the 23-metre *Nyria*, which he had designed and built in 1906, with a jib-headed mainsail. This brought a storm of derision characteristically and rightly ignored by Nicholson. She proved a great success and revolutionized the rig of all modern yachts.

In between the sailing vessels came steam and motor yachts, enough of them alone to constitute a man's life-work. In about 1911 he produced two beautiful traditional clipper-stem steam yachts *Marynthea* (900 tons) and *Miranda*. He then turned his attention to diesel yachts, the first being *Pioneer* (400 tons), and, in 1937, *Philante* (1,612 tons), the largest motor yacht until then built in Britain. She later became the Norwegian royal yacht. These fine vessels were of a type quite different from the traditional steam yacht. Entirely 'Nicholson' in conception, they were excellent sea boats, with fine accommodation and a wide radius of action.

In the war of 1914–18, as a separate venture, Nicholson designed and built flying-boat hulls in wood. In the same period he formed, as a separate firm, the Laminated Wood Ship Company, to design and build wooden cargo vessels of 1,000 tons dead weight to help the urgent need for tonnage to replace losses due to enemy submarine action. The method of construction was original, based on a longitudinal system of framing with multi-skin planking and deck, and planned to use home-grown timbers such as oak, fir, and larch. Some of these ships were still in commission many years after the war. As a further example of his versatility, Nicholson designed a training ship *Sebastian de Elcano*, 3,000 tons, for the Spanish Government. She was a fore-and-aft four-masted schooner. The drawings included the minutest detail so that she could be built in Spain.

Nicholson's vast output was due not only to his tremendous capacity for concentrated thought and work but also to his ability and judgement in gathering to work under him a team of men each an expert in his own sphere. Unfortunately for students of Nicholson's work most of his drawings and plans were burned in a fire at the works in 1910 and again in 1941 when the yard at Gosport was virtually destroyed by enemy action. Fortunately Beken's matchless photographs are still available.

Nicholson was the technical brain of the Yacht Racing Association from 1910 until the outbreak of war in 1939. He was also a member of the Royal Institution of Naval Architects. In 1944 he was awarded the diploma of royal designer for industry and in 1949 he was appointed O.B.E. Throughout his life he devoted much time to the Gosport War Memorial Hospital of which he became chairman in 1934; in that year he was made the first honorary freeman of the borough of Gosport.

In 1895 Nicholson married Lucy Ella (died 1937), daughter of William Edmonds, a solicitor. They had two daughters and three sons, the second of whom, John, followed his father in the firm and became chairman in 1940. He owns a portrait of his father by Percy Beer. Nicholson died at his home at Hill Head, Hampshire, 27 February 1954.

[*Yachting World*, April–July 1954; private information; personal knowledge.]

E. F. HAYLOCK.

NOBLE, SIR PERCY LOCKHART HARNAM (1880–1955), admiral, son of Charles Simeon and Annie Georgina Noble, was born 16 January 1880 in India where his father was a major in the Bengal Staff Corps. He entered the *Britannia* in 1894 and spent his midshipman's time in the *Immortalité* on the China station. In view of his subsequent career it seems strange that his captain should notice him in his report as lazy and dull. During his sub-lieutenant's courses Noble was detailed for the naval guard of honour mounted at Windsor for the funeral of Queen Victoria. When the horses which were to draw the gun-carriage bearing the coffin became restive, and later unmanageable, Noble suggested that they be unhitched and the gun carriage drawn by the naval guard of honour, a precedent followed in every subsequent royal funeral. He was appointed M.V.O.

After service in the battleships *Hannibal* in the Channel squadron and *Russell* in the Mediterranean, Noble was appointed flag lieutenant to (Sir) A. L. Winsloe, commanding destroyer flotillas at home. He commanded the destroyer *Ribble* from 1907 to 1908, when he joined the signal school at Portsmouth and qualified as a signal specialist. A brief appointment to the royal yacht *Victoria and Albert* for King Edward's visit to Copenhagen was followed by a commission in China as flag lieutenant to Winsloe, and on completion of that duty he returned to the royal yacht as first lieutenant, being promoted commander when he completed the appointment in 1913. In December he joined the *Achilles*, in the second cruiser squadron, Home Fleet, as executive officer, and three years later was transferred, still as executive officer, to the large cruiser *Courageous*, flagship of the light cruiser force, Grand Fleet. His promotion to captain came in June 1918 and in October of that year he was made flag captain to Sir Allan Everett in the *Calliope*, transferring to the *Calcutta* in 1919. In 1922 he was appointed to the *Barham* in command and as flag captain to Sir Edwyn Alexander-Sinclair [q.v.], then commanding first battle squadron, Atlantic Fleet. He was promoted C.V.O. in 1920.

His next command (1925) was the *Ganges*, the boys' training establishment at Shotley, and his experience in this post led to his selection two years later (1927) as the first commanding officer of the *St. Vincent*, a new boys' training establishment being set up at Gosport. This was followed by an appointment as director of the operations division on the naval staff, 1928–9, and his promotion to rear-admiral (1929).

In 1931 he became director of naval equipment in the Admiralty and at the end of the following year was selected to command the second cruiser squadron in the Home Fleet, flying his flag in the *Dorsetshire*, then in the *Leander*. In 1935 he was brought back to the Admiralty as fourth sea lord where he was successful in obtaining marriage allowances for naval officers. He was promoted vice-admiral while holding this appointment and in 1937 was chosen to command the China station. He was appointed C.B. in 1932 and K.C.B. in 1936.

Noble's qualities of tact and restraint were continuously called into play during this difficult period in the Far East. The Japanese were engaged in their war with China and frequently made threatening advances to the borders of the British settlements at Hong Kong and Shanghai. Noble managed to prevent any of these threats from developing into outright hostilities, and the skill with which he handled all such incidents brought him many expressions of the Admiralty's appreciation.

In 1939 Noble was promoted admiral, relinquished his command in July 1940, and in February 1941 was appointed commander-in-chief Western Approaches. It was this command which bore the responsibility for the war against German U-boats, which by that time had established a definite ascendancy in the Atlantic. Setting up his headquarters in Liverpool, Noble set about his task with his usual thoroughness. He realized that special training in anti-submarine warfare was the key to ultimate victory in this campaign, and although he was continuously hampered by a shortage of anti-submarine forces, he laid down the principles of training and also established the group organization of escort forces which was later to pay a high dividend in the Atlantic war. He himself went to sea and flew with Coastal Command so that the crews knew that he understood their problems and there were forged 'links of mutual confidence of inestimable value'. By the time he left the command, the British anti-submarine forces had reached a degree of organization and training which left his successor Sir Max Horton [q.v.] a firm and lasting foundation on which to wage successful warfare.

On leaving Liverpool in the autumn of 1942 Noble was sent to Washington as head of the British Admiralty delegation. He saw the switch from the defensive to the offensive in the naval war, and much of the credit for the smooth co-operation both in planning and in operations between the British and American navies was owed to Noble for the qualities of firmness, tact, and sound sense which he brought to the deliberations of the combined chiefs of staff. For his services in Washington he was appointed G.B.E. in 1944 and was made a commander of the U.S. Legion of Merit in 1946.

In 1943 Noble was appointed first and principal naval aide-de-camp to King

George VI. He retired from the navy on 16 January 1945 and was made rear-admiral of the United Kingdom. He received the grand cross of the royal Order of St. Olaf for his services to the Royal Norwegian Navy. He died in London 25 July 1955.

Noble was twice married: first, in 1907, to Diamantina Isabella (died 1909), daughter of Allan Campbell. Their son, Commander Sir Allan Noble, on retiring from the navy entered Parliament and was minister of state for foreign affairs in 1956-9. In 1913 Noble married, secondly, Celia Emily (died 1967), daughter of Robert Kirkman Hodgson; there was one son.

A portrait by Sir Oswald Birley is in the Greenwich Collection and a pen-and-ink drawing by Jan Rosciwewski is in the Imperial War Museum.

[Admiralty records; *The Times*, 26 July 1955; S. W. Roskill, (Official) *History of the Second World War. The War at Sea*, vol. ii, 1956; personal knowledge.]   P. K. KEMP.

NORTON, EDWARD FELIX (1884–1954), lieutenant-general, was born 21 February 1884 at San Isidro, Argentina, the second son of Edward Norton, a director of the Royal Mail and Union Castle lines, and his wife, Edith Sarah, daughter of Sir Alfred Wills, judge of the Queen's Bench division. Norton's father established the Estancia la Ventura on wild pampa some 300 miles south of Buenos Aires, but Norton was brought back to England as an infant. He was educated at Charterhouse and the Royal Military Academy, Woolwich, and was commissioned in 1902. In 1907 he was posted to the Royal Horse Artillery at Meerut and during this period was aide-de-camp to the viceroy. In 1914 he went to France with D battery, Royal Horse Artillery, and later served as staff officer, Royal Artillery, to the Canadian Corps. He was three times mentioned in dispatches, was appointed to the D.S.O. and awarded the M.C. After the war he commanded D battery in India and later served on the staff at Chanak at a time when British relations with the Turks called for much diplomacy and tact. He attended the Staff College and later the Imperial Defence College before returning to India as senior instructor at the Staff College at Quetta (1929–32). He then became commander, Royal Artillery, to the 1st division at Aldershot, and subsequently chief of staff to the Aldershot Command. He was appointed aide-de-camp to King George VI in 1937. In 1938 he commanded the Madras District and was appointed C.B. in the following year. He was acting governor and commander-in-chief, Hong Kong (1940–41), where he had a serious accident from which he never quite recovered and which forced him to retire in 1942, while holding command of the Western Independent District, India. He was granted the honorary rank of lieutenant-general, and in 1947 he was appointed colonel commandant of the Royal Horse Artillery.

Norton began alpine climbing at the 'Eagle's Nest' above Sixt, in Savoy, originally built by his grandfather, Sir Alfred Wills, who was a founder and third president of the Alpine Club. There, with his brother, he successfully stalked chamois over ground which was so bad that the local men kept off it, although the shooting was not preserved. He also visited the Patagonian Andes and climbed wherever opportunity offered during his service abroad. In 1922 he was selected for the second Mount Everest expedition. With George Leigh Mallory [q.v.] and Dr. T. H. Somervell he reached the then record height of 26,985 feet. They were the first to pass the critical level of 8,000 metres; and this without oxygen. For the third Everest expedition, in 1924, he was selected as second-in-command to C. G. Bruce [q.v.] who developed malaria in Tibet and had to be evacuated, so that Norton became leader. After many difficulties and hazards, due to bad weather, he led the first serious assault. At 28,000 feet his companion, Somervell, had to fall out with severe throat trouble and Norton continued alone to a height of 28,126 feet: a new altitude record, again without oxygen, which was possibly not surpassed until the successful ascent of Mount Everest twenty-nine years later. The second assault was undertaken by Mallory and A. C. Irvine, but they never returned.

In 1922 Norton was elected to the Alpine Club of which in later years he twice refused the presidency. In 1926 he was awarded the Founder's medal by the Royal Geographical Society.

Norton was a fine horseman, a hunting man and pig-sticker, and runner-up for the Kadir Cup in 1922. Although a keen big-game shot and an enthusiastic fisherman, he was just as interested in natural history as in sport. He was fondest of birds and flowers and during the two Mount Everest expeditions made collections of both for the Natural History

Museum. He took a deep interest in pictures and himself had considerable artistic skill. A man of many interests he was widely read and well informed upon many subjects. Integrity was the essence of his character. He was a charming companion and a born leader. In the army he was very popular with all ranks; he understood and got on well with Indians and with the Gurkhas, Sherpas, and Bhotias on Everest. When leading the Everest expedition he would make up his own mind about the best line to pursue and then call in the whole team for discussion: they invariably accepted his advice.

In 1925 Norton married Isabel Joyce, daughter of William Pasteur, C.B., C.M.G., physician, by whom he had three sons. He died at Morestead Grove, Winchester, 3 November 1954.

[Private information; personal knowledge.]
T. G. LONGSTAFF.

NORWAY, NEVIL SHUTE (1899–1960), novelist under the name of NEVIL SHUTE and aeronautical engineer, was born in Ealing 17 January 1899, the younger son of a Cornishman, Arthur Hamilton Norway, who became an assistant secretary of the General Post Office, and his wife, Mary Louisa Gadsden. At the age of eleven Norway played truant from his first preparatory school in Hammersmith, spending days among the model aircraft at the Science Museum examining wing control on the Blériot and trying to puzzle out how the engine of the Antoinette ran without a carburettor. On being detected in these precocious studies he was sent to the Dragon School, Oxford, and thence to Shrewsbury. He was on holiday in Dublin, where his father was then secretary to the Post Office in Ireland, at the time of the Easter rising of 1916 and acted as a stretcher-bearer, winning commendation for gallant conduct. He passed into the Royal Military Academy with the aim of being commissioned into the Royal Flying Corps; but a bad stammer led to his being failed at his final medical examination and returned to civil life. The last few months of the war (in which his brother had been killed) were spent on home service as a private in the Suffolk Regiment.

In 1919 Norway went up to Balliol College, Oxford, where he took third class honours in engineering science in 1922 and rowed in the college second eight. During the vacations he worked, unpaid, for the Aircraft Manufacturing Company at Hendon, then for (Sir) Geoffrey de Havilland's own firm, which he joined as an employee on coming down from Oxford. He now fulfilled his thwarted wartime ambition of learning to fly and gained experience as a test observer. During the evenings he diligently wrote novels and short stories, unperturbed by rejection slips from publishers.

In 1924 Norway took the post of chief calculator to the Airship Guarantee Company, a subsidiary of Vickers, Ltd., to work on the construction of the R.100. In 1929 he became deputy chief engineer under (Sir) Barnes Wallis and in the following year he flew to and from Canada in the R.100. He had a passionate belief in the future of airships but his hopes foundered in the crash of its government rival, the R.101, wrecked with the loss of Lord Thomson [q.v.], the minister of aviation, and most of those on board. He had watched with mounting horror what he regarded as the criminal inefficiency with which the R.101 was being constructed. His experience in this phase of his career left a lasting bitterness; it bred in him almost pathological distrust of politicians and civil servants.

Recognizing that airship development was a lost cause, he founded in 1931 Airspeed, Ltd., aeroplane constructors, in an old garage and remained joint managing-director until 1938. The pioneering atmosphere of aircraft construction in those years suited his temperament. He revelled in individual enterprise and doing things by improvisation on a financial shoestring. When the business grew and was becoming one of humdrum routine, producing aircraft to government orders, he decided to get out of the rut and live by writing. He had by 1938 enjoyed some success as a novelist and had sold the film rights of *Lonely Road* (1932) and *Ruined City* (1938).

On the outbreak of war in 1939 Norway joined the Royal Naval Volunteer Reserve as a sub-lieutenant in the miscellaneous weapons department. Rising to lieutenant-commander he found experimenting with secret weapons a job after his own heart. But his growing celebrity as a writer caused him to be in the Normandy landings on 6 June 1944, for the Ministry of Information, and to be sent to Burma as a correspondent in 1945. He entered Rangoon with the 15th Corps from Arakan. Soon after demobilization in 1945 he emigrated to Australia and made his home in Langwarrin, Victoria. High taxation and what he felt to be the decadence of Britain, with the spirit of personal independence and freedom dying, led him to leave the old country.

His output of novels, which began with *Marazan* (1926), continued to the end. Writing under his Christian names, Nevil Shute, he had an unaffectedly popular touch which made him a best-seller throughout the Commonwealth and the United States. The secret of his success lay in the skill with which he combined loving familiarity with technicalities and a straightforward sense of human relationships and values. He conveyed to the readers his own zest for making and flying aircraft. The hazards and rewards of backroom boys have never been more sympathetically portrayed nor with closer inside knowledge. His natural gift for creating briskly moving plots did not extend to the delineation of character in anything more than conventional terms. He retained to the last the outlook of a decent, average public-school boy of his generation. Although he lived into the James Bond era he never made the slightest concessions to the fast-growing appetite in the mass fiction market for sadism and violence.

No Highway (1948), dealing with the drama of structural fatigue in aircraft, set in human terms of those responsible for a competitive passenger service, gave full scope to both sides of his talent. Machines and men and women share in shaping the drama. *A Town Like Alice* (1950), describing the grim Odyssey of white women and children in Japanese-occupied Malaya, captured the cinema audiences as completely as it did the reading public. *Round the Bend* (1951) was thought by Norway himself to be his most enduring book. It told of the aircraft engineer of mixed eastern and western stock who taught his men to worship God through work conscientiously and prayerfully performed and came to be regarded as divine by people of many creeds. *On the Beach* (1957) expressed Norway's sensitive appreciation of the frightful possibilities of global warfare and annihilation by radio-active dust.

Other novels, several of them filmed, were *What Happened to the Corbetts* (1939), *An Old Captivity* (1940), *Landfall* (1940), *Pied Piper* (1942), *Pastoral* (1944), *In the Wet* (1953), and *Requiem for a Wren* (1955).

In *Slide Rule* (1954), sub-titled 'the autobiography of an engineer', he told, candidly and racily, of his life up to 1938 when he left the aircraft industry.

The stammer, which was as much a stimulus as a handicap, did not prevent Norway from being good company, always welcome at social gatherings of his many friends. An enthusiastic yachtsman and fisherman as well as an air pilot, he delighted in outdoor life, and his gaiety was not dimmed by the heart attacks from which he suffered.

In 1931 Norway married Frances Mary Heaton, by whom he had two daughters. He died in Melbourne 12 January 1960.

[Norway's own writings; personal knowledge.]   A. P. RYAN.

NORWICH, first VISCOUNT (1890–1954), politician, diplomatist, and author. [See COOPER, ALFRED DUFF.]

NORWOOD, SIR CYRIL (1875–1956), educationist, was born 15 September 1875 at Whalley in Lancashire, the only child by his second marriage, to Elizabeth Emma Sparks, of the Rev. Samuel Norwood, headmaster of the local grammar school which was closed in 1886, when the family moved to Leytonstone. He never spoke of his early years in a home which was darkened and impoverished by his father's intemperance: the lasting impression they made was later shown in Norwood's deep reserve, his teetotalism, special sympathy with early hardship, and the resolve that his own children should have a happy home. His education was won by his own effort; and hard work at school and university, to qualify himself to support his mother and make his own home, deprived him of much normal social enjoyment. He entered Merchant Taylors' School in 1888 and left as head of the school and scholar of St. John's College, Oxford, where he won first classes in classical moderations (1896) and *literae humaniores* (1898). In 1899 he headed the list for entry to the Civil Service and was posted to the Admiralty.

As a junior civil servant Norwood found small scope for initiative and in 1901 he left the service and went as sixth-form master to Leeds Grammar School. Before the end of the year he married the lady to whom he had long been engaged, Catherine Margaret, daughter of Walter John Kilner, a medical practitioner, of Kensington. She bore him three daughters. His marriage and the discovery of his true vocation gave Norwood lasting content and happy release of energy. In 1906 he was appointed headmaster of Bristol Grammar School and so started the career of command which made his name. This post, already declined by two selected applicants, was a bold undertaking. The school was in poor condition, with falling numbers and a general loss of confidence; but Norwood brought it fresh vigour and new esteem in the city of Bristol. Within ten years he had almost tripled the number of boys and attracted generous local benefaction to enlarge and improve their accommodation. Academic and other success multiplied and the school throve in every way. Bristol University recognized his achievement by an honorary doctorate, and Norwood became known as 'second founder' of the school.

Late in 1916 he was made master of Marlborough College, an appointment which was at first criticized on the ground that he knew nothing of boarding-schools; but it was soon amply justified. The school had lost momentum under war conditions and nine months of interregnum, but it quickly felt Norwood's strong and wise direction. He was the first among public school headmasters to adapt the curriculum to the system of external school examinations, and he gave new emphasis and scope to the study of natural science. After the war there ensued a period of striking academic success and great well-being at Marlborough, and the school's reputation rose high. Norwood and his family were nowhere happier than in their Wiltshire home, and his public status was established by his appointment in 1921 as chairman of the Secondary Schools Examination Council, an office which he held until 1946.

In 1925 the headmastership of Harrow School fell vacant and strong pressure from the chairman of governors and the archbishop of Canterbury persuaded Norwood to leave Marlborough for the Hill (January 1926). His mandate was to raise the standard of work and discipline and he started, as at Marlborough, by himself devising a new timetable of work throughout the school. On the side of discipline, his problem was to make his authority generally felt and especially above that of certain senior masters. He waited patiently for clear opportunity to remove those whose support he could not win. Some of the changes Norwood made in life at Harrow were not wholly welcome at first, but it became obvious that the school was growing stronger and healthier under his control, and when he said good-bye to them in 1934 the boys expressed their loyalty and admiration in a remarkable ovation.

On leaving Harrow, Norwood started his twelve years' presidency of St. John's

College, Oxford, to which he had been elected. Although accustomed to a head-master's autocracy, he never sought to dominate his college but was content to give careful service there and in the university. He lacked, however, the social adaptability which counts for much in university life and, especially during years of war, public and other outside claims filled much of his time. As a result, his presidency was not so memorable as his headmasterships had been.

Norwood gave important service as governor of schools, notably to a group of recent foundations, including Stowe, Canford, and Westonbirt, which were re-organized in 1934 as the Allied Schools under a central council of which he was chairman for many years. His constructive courage and financial acumen were decisive in saving these schools from premature collapse. But his interest and influence in school education spread far beyond the independent schools, and he was a leading speaker and writer on education: his best-known book, *The English Tradition of Education*, was published in 1929. His advice was often sought by the Board of Education and in 1938 he was knighted for his public service. This culminated in the report, made in 1943 and known as the Norwood report, of a special committee under his chairmanship on curriculum and examinations in secondary schools. Many of the recommendations of this report, including the provision of secondary education for all children, were embodied in the Education Act of 1944, introduced by R. A. Butler (later Lord Butler of Saffron Walden), who had first known Norwood as his headmaster at Marlborough.

When he left Oxford in 1946 for Iwerne Minster in Dorset, Norwood was a tired man, but the countryside and village life refreshed him and, free from office, he enjoyed local society and endeared himself to many neighbours. But soon his happiness was clouded by his wife's failing health, and her death in 1951 ended a close companionship of almost fifty years. He died in hospital in Oxford 13 March 1956.

Norwood was a man of impressive stature, physical, intellectual, and moral. High courage, strategic foresight, and tactical skill might have made him a great soldier; and his measured utterance from pulpit or platform commanded the allegiance of all but his most critical hearers. His greatest happiness was found in his home and with close friends, to whom he discovered a gay humour and warmth of spirit which few who knew him less intimately suspected. Throughout his life he was guided by firm Christian conviction, uncomplicated by theological or ecclesiastical dogmatism (he was for ten years president of the Modern Churchmen's Union), and he had always a vivid sense of over-ruling Providence. More than any of his contemporaries, Norwood was in the tradition of the great Victorian headmasters, and the rapid spread of English education gave him a wider stage than theirs on which to play his part.

There are portraits by Sir Oswald Birley at St. John's College, Oxford; George Harcourt at Marlborough College, with copies at Bristol Grammar School and Harrow; and R. G. Eves at Marlborough. A drawing by H. A. Freeth is in the London board-room of the Allied Schools.

[Private information; personal knowledge.]
G. C. TURNER.

NOVELLO, IVOR (1893–1951), actor-manager, dramatist, and composer, whose real name was David Ivor Davies, but who took the name of Ivor Novello by deed poll in 1927, was born in Cardiff 15 January 1893. He was the only son of David Davies, a rate collector for the municipality of Cardiff, and his wife, Clara Novello Davies, a well-known musician and teacher of music and singing, who won many international awards with her Welsh Ladies' Choir. Brought up in an atmosphere of music, he showed an early aptitude both as musician and singer. He was educated privately in Cardiff and Gloucester and then won a scholarship at Magdalen College School, Oxford, in the celebrated choir of which he became prominent as soloist; but after his voice broke he had no mature singing voice at all. He soon began to compose and evinced a great love for the theatre. In his early teens his first song was published. Called 'Spring of the Year' it was sung at the Royal Albert Hall with Novello as accompanist and attracted no attention whatever, but when in 1910 his song 'The Little Damozel' was sung there it scored a considerable success.

For a time Novello taught the piano in Cardiff but soon he joined his mother in London, spending all the time he could at the theatres, especially Daly's and the Gaiety, watching the musical productions of George Edwardes by which he afterwards set his standards. He would wait at stage doors for the autographs of players many of whom were later to appear under his own management. He wanted to go on the stage, but his mother disapproved and managed to prevent him from joining the chorus at Daly's. He continued to compose and Ada Crossley sang his setting of 'Oh God Our Help in Ages Past' at the Crystal Palace. Novello wrote some music for a Festival of Empire there and when this went to Canada and the United States he went with it. He spent some time in New York and there wrote and composed his first musical play, *The Fickle Jade*, which was never produced, although he used much of the music from it in subsequent successes. His mother now moved into a flat on the roof of the Strand Theatre—No.11, Aldwych—which remained his home until he died there. Later he bought his beloved country house, 'Redroofs', at Littlewick Green, near Maidenhead.

When war broke out in 1914 Novello was twenty-one. In competition with his mother, he wrote a patriotic song, 'Keep the Homes Fires Burning', which was an immediate success when sung at a National Sunday League concert. It swept the country, made him a fortune, and rocketed him into fame. He had songs in revues and musical comedies, such as *See-Saw*, *Arlette*, and *Tabs*, and had his first chance to write a full score in 1916 for *Theodore and Co.* which was a big success at the Gaiety Theatre. In the meantime he had joined the Royal Naval Air Service, but he was no good as an airman and after two bad crashes was put on to clerical work at the Air Ministry. Demobilized in 1919 he again visited America. On the ship returning home he received a cable offering him, on the strength of a photograph, a part in the film *The Call of the Blood*. Almost at once this dark, handsome young man with the wonderful smile and exceptional profile became a star of the silent, as later of the talking, films. He made many, but his heart was firmly in the theatre. He had music in *Who's Hooper?* (1919), *A to Z* (1921), and other shows, and was successful with his second full-length score, *The Golden Moth*, at the Adelphi in 1921.

Novello's chance to appear on the stage came in the same year when he played a small part in *Deburau* at the Ambassadors' Theatre. The play failed, but he never looked back. Very soon crowds of admirers began to wait at the stage door for Ivor, as everybody called him, and nobody, with the possible exception of Lewis Waller [q.v.] in his prime, ever had such a tremendous or so devoted a following of fans.

He made many more pictures and at the end of 1922 went to Hollywood for D. W. Griffith, the great film director; but he was using the films as a means to becoming an actor-manager. He achieved that ambition in 1924 when with Constance Collier he wrote *The Rat*, staged it himself at the Prince of Wales's Theatre, London, and played the lead. It was an immense success and they followed it with *Down Hill* at the Queen's Theatre in 1926. Novello also made acting successes in 1925 in revivals of *Old Heidelberg* at the Garrick Theatre and *Iris* at the Adelphi. He was now an established actor as well as dramatist. Between 1928 and his death in 1951 he wrote thirteen comedies, only four of which were not successful, and he played in the greater number of them himself. They included *The Truth Game*, *A Symphony in Two Flats*, *Fresh Fields*, *Proscenium*, *Murder in Mayfair*, *Full House*, *Comedienne*, and *We Proudly Present*. In 1936 he presented a very beautiful version of *The Happy Hypocrite* by (Sir) Max Beerbohm [q.v.], dramatized by Clemence Dane, in which he played Lord George Hell.

In 1935 Novello undertook to supply the book and music for a musical play at the Theatre Royal, Drury Lane. He had not an idea when he accepted the offer, but the result was *Glamorous Night* which brought that famous theatre back into success and prestige. He wrote, devised, composed, and played in three more successes at Drury Lane: *Careless Rapture* (1936), *Crest of the Wave* (1937), and *The Dancing Years* (1939). He also played *Henry V* there (1938), composing the incidental music. He wrote and composed *Arc de Triomphe* produced at the Phoenix Theatre in 1943, but this was less successful than his other musical plays, chiefly because he did not appear in it himself. His plays, straight or musical, were always successes when he was in them.

The Dancing Years, brought back to the Adelphi Theatre in 1942, was the outstanding success of the war of 1939–45 and Novello's own popularity in it was undiminished after a month's absence in 1944 whilst he served a prison sentence for evading the petrol restrictions. Before the end of the war he had written and composed—and played in—*Perchance to Dream* which ran for over a thousand performances at the London Hippodrome. He followed this in 1949 with *King's Rhapsody* at the Palace Theatre which was in many ways his best work and in which he gave his best performance. Whilst it was

running he wrote and composed *Gay's The Word* which proved a big success at the Saville Theatre. It was whilst playing in *King's Rhapsody* that early in the morning of 6 March 1951 he died very suddenly of thrombosis. He was unmarried.

Novello was a good and improving although never a great, actor, and his complete understanding of the art of the theatre made him one of the notable figures of the British stage. He was a completely happy man and never happier than when working in the theatre which he loved so much. His success never turned his head or made him conceited; he took infinite pains to achieve it and was always grateful for it. He set himself a high standard and never fell below it. He was much beloved in and out of the theatre and tens of thousands of people attended his funeral, as a tribute to the man who had given them so much pleasure. As a composer he will always be remembered, for his works are in the national repertory of theatre music.

A bust of Novello by Clemence Dane stands in the Theatre Royal, Drury Lane.

[Peter Noble, *Ivor Novello*, 1951; W. Macqueen-Pope, *Ivor*, 1951; personal knowledge.]   W. MACQUEEN-POPE.

NOYES, ALFRED (1880–1958), poet, was born in Wolverhampton 16 September 1880, the eldest of the three sons of Alfred Noyes, a grocer who later became a teacher, and his wife, Amelia Adams Rowley, who became an invalid after the birth of the youngest child. Educated on the classics at schools in Aberystwyth amid the mountains and sea-coast of Wales, which inspired his early gift for verse, Noyes went in 1898 to Oxford and rowed for three years for Exeter College, collecting two oars, with one of which he rowed at Henley. He missed his degree, for which Oxford forgave him, through keeping an appointment which obtained publication of his first book of verse, *The Loom of Years* (1902). He owned Ernest de Selincourt [q.v.] as his teacher and influence and henceforth all his life wrote poetry in a strain of old-fashioned metre and Victorian romance. *The Flower of Old Japan* (1903) was followed by a collection of *Poems* (1904) which included 'The Barrel-Organ' with its well-known refrain 'Come down to Kew in lilac-time'. His epic on *Drake* (2 vols., 1906–8) which was serialized in *Blackwood's Magazine* made his name widely known and he learnt to his pleasure that a copy accompanied Admiral

Beatty [q.v.] into the combats of the war of 1914–18. In the meantime *Forty Singing Seamen* had appeared in 1907.

In 1913 Noyes gave the Lowell lectures at Boston on 'The Sea in English Poetry' and in 1914–23 he held the chair of modern English literature at Princeton. During the war of 1914–18 he was an effective advocate of the British cause in the United States; but returned for a time to work at the Foreign Office and in France, writing several books on the war at sea. He was appointed C.B.E. in 1918.

Although Noyes wrote novels and poetic plays, it was by lyric, ballad, and epic that he won his public. In *The Torch-Bearers*, an epic in three volumes (1922–30), he sought to harmonize the great scientists with the Christian faith. This led him to move to the religious Right and to his reception into the Roman Catholic Church in 1927 when he was at the top of his career. There followed his two most important books: *The Unknown God* (1934), a work of apologetics directed primarily to the agnostics; and *Voltaire* (1936), designed to show that in his deism Voltaire was nearer to the Christians than to the agnostics. This caused a tremor in Catholic circles but the matter was tactfully dealt with by Cardinal Hinsley [q.v.]. More than a tremor was caused by Noyes's attack on the authenticity of the diaries of Roger Casement [q.v.] which he had become convinced bore the mark of the forger. This was after W. B. Yeats [q.v.] had bitterly attacked Noyes as an official traducer.

Noyes was fond of controversy which he carried on with gay determination. He would not allow the Victorian classics to be mocked and in consequence took a considerable amount of mockery himself. His teaching place in English letters will be marked by the steady and satiric campaign which he, with such as G. K. Chesterton and Lord Dunsany [qq.v.], maintained against the eccentricities of modern poetry. Of those who defied the moral code in the name of art he was an implacable enemy. He attacked the works of James Joyce [q.v.] so far as to stop the public auction of a copy of *Ulysses* in the catalogue of the first Earl of Birkenhead [q.v.] and he once ordered Sir Hugh Walpole [q.v.] to leave his house for recommending the book to a young girl.

After 1929 Noyes made his home in the Isle of Wight where he became friends with his neighbour Admiral Jellicoe [q.v.] and composed the noblest wreath crowning his funeral. During the war of 1939–45 he took his children to Canada and remained to lecture there and in the United States, once more proving himself an able interpreter of British war aims. By this time his sight was failing and an operation in California resulted in serious damage. Thereafter he could not read a book and became slowly blind. Hence his continual interest in the blind and his poignant poem 'Look down on us gently who journey by night' which became a widespread anthem for the sightless. He met his disaster with perfect courage, blaming no one, but falling back upon the stores which his mind had already gathered from the English and Latin poets, as well as from the English classics, among whom he set challengingly first Johnson, Dickens, and Tennyson. In their company he continued his gallant journey from twilight to the darkening end. He was practically blind when he appeared at a heartening reception which friends of all manner of letters and beliefs offered him on his seventieth birthday.

In 1949 he had returned to his home in the Isle of Wight and there he wrote his autobiography *Two Worlds for Memory* (1953) in which he described contacts with fellow poets like Hardy, Meredith, and Swinburne whose adoration of the sea he shared, and showed a genius for humorous anecdote which could only be equalled by his friend Sir Edmund Gosse [q.v.]. He died in hospital in the Isle of Wight, 28 June 1958, and was buried near Farringdon, as he wished, for he had ever knelt at the shrine of Tennyson.

Noyes was president of the Dickens Fellowship and the Johnson Society and received honorary degrees from Yale, Glasgow, Syracuse, and Berkeley (California). At Oxford, Exeter College added his name to her worthies in a commemorative window in her Hall.

Noyes's family life was always happy. He married first, in 1907, Garnet, daughter of Colonel B. G. Daniels, of the United States Army. She died in 1926 and in the next year he married Mary Angela, widow of Richard Shirburne Weld-Blundell and granddaughter of Sir Frederick Weld [q.v.]. They had one son and two daughters. His best likeness is a bronze relief, owned by the family, by William King which shows the inspiration and strength underlying his blindness. A marble replica is in the Newport asylum for the blind.

His collected poems appeared first in two volumes in 1910. A final collection, edited and introduced by his son Hugh, was published in 1963.

[Walter Jerrold, *Alfred Noyes*, 1930; Alfred Noyes, *Two Worlds for Memory*, 1953; *Tablet*, 5 July 1958; private information; personal knowledge.]   SHANE LESLIE.

OGDEN, CHARLES KAY (1889–1957), linguistic psychologist and the originator of Basic English, was born 1 June 1889 at Rossall School, Fleetwood, the elder son of a housemaster, Charles Burdett Ogden, and his wife, Fanny Hart. He was educated at a preparatory school in Buxton by his uncle, Thomas Jones Ogden, then at Rossall. He was a good athlete, with school colours for fives, until a serious attack of rheumatic fever when he was sixteen. Turning to intensive study he won a scholarship to Magdalene College, Cambridge, where he obtained a first class in part i of the classical tripos in 1910 and played billiards for the university. During the year 1913 he visited schools and universities in Italy, Germany, Switzerland, and India, investigating methods of language teaching. On his return in 1914 he published, with R. H. Best, *The Problem of the Continuation School* and also translated Dr. Kerschensteiner's *Grundfragen der Schulorganisation* as *The Schools and the Nation* (1914).

In 1912 Ogden founded the weekly *Cambridge Magazine* which, selling at a penny, was astonishingly successful. In 1916 he converted it into an organ of international opinion and comment on politics and the war, digesting and translating from 200 periodicals weekly for a regular survey of the foreign press which in 1917 and 1918 filled more than half of each issue. The circulation rapidly rose to over 20,000. Poems by Siegfried Sassoon and John Masefield, contributions from Hardy, Shaw, Bennett [qq.v.] and other well-known authors were another unusual feature of this university magazine. Throughout this period Ogden was also very busy as president of the Heretics Society which he had founded in 1911 together with H. F. Jolowicz [q.v.], P. Sargant Florence, and F. P. Ramsey. The Heretics too became a publishing outlet and papers read before the society by Jane Harrison, Shaw, Chesterton, F. M. Cornford [qq.v.], and G. M. Trevelyan were published between 1911 and 1914.

During a discussion with I. A. Richards on 11 November 1918 Ogden outlined a work to correlate his earlier linguistic studies with his wartime experience of 'the power of Word-Magic' and the part played by language in contemporary thought. Ogden converted the *Cambridge Magazine* into a quarterly in which he and Richards published a series of articles as a first draft of the book which appeared in 1923 as *The Meaning of Meaning*. This concrete approach to theoretical confusion about language, setting forth principles for the understanding of the function of language, rapidly became one of the important books of the decade. A special study at the same time of the linguistics factor in aesthetics, with I. A. Richards and the artist James Wood, appeared as *The Foundations of Aesthetics* in 1922.

The year 1922 saw the end of the *Cambridge Magazine* and to a great extent the end of Ogden's Cambridge period. He took over the editorship of the international psychological journal *Psyche* as a vehicle for publishing research in international language problems and continuing the work of the post-war *Cambridge Magazine*. Also in 1922 he accepted the planning and editing of two major series: 'The History of Civilisation' and 'The International Library of Psychology, Philosophy and Scientific Method'. The latter series produced a hundred volumes in its first decade, many of them stimulated and initiated by Ogden. With the help of F. P. Ramsey he translated for this series the *Logisch-Philosophische Abhandlung* of Ludwig Wittgenstein [q.v.] whom he introduced to English readers in *Tractatus Logico-Philosophicus* as early as 1922.

Throughout this busy period his linguistic researches gathered pace and momentum. From his earlier studies of the writings of Horne Tooke and Bishop Wilkins [qq.v.] he moved to the neglected contributions to linguistics of Jeremy Bentham [q.v.]. Basic English first took shape between 1925 and 1927, as 'an auxiliary international language comprising 850 words arranged in a system in which everything may be said for all the purposes of everyday existence. Its distinctive features are the selection of words so that they cover the field, the restriction of the vocabulary, and the elimination of verbs except for the sixteen verb-forms which deal with the fundamental operations ("put", "take", "get", etc.) and their replacement by the names of operations and directions ("go in", "put in", etc.).' Ogden established the Orthological Institute in 1927 and completed the Basic vocabulary in 1928, revised and published it for copyright purposes in 1929, and in rapid succession published the first four essential books: *Basic English* (1930), *The Basic Vocabulary* (1930), *Debabelization* (1931), and *The Basic Words* (1932). After a detailed study of Bentham's writing both published and unpublished Ogden wrote several articles in *Psyche*, edited editions of Bentham's *Theory of Legislation* (1931) and *Theory of Fictions* (1932), and published his Bentham centenary lecture entitled *Jeremy Bentham, 1832–2032* (1932).

Basic English developed rapidly, setting up agencies in thirty countries and at the outbreak of war in 1939 Ogden had produced in *Psyche*, 'Psyche Monographs', and 'Psyche Miniatures' and other series some 200 titles in print in or about Basic English. In 1943 (Sir) Winston Churchill set up a cabinet committee on Basic English under the chairmanship of L. S. Amery [q.v.] and made a statement to the House of Commons on its report on 9 March 1944. He outlined the steps which the Government would take to develop Basic English as an auxiliary international and administrative language through the British Council, the B.B.C., and other bodies. A Basic English version of this statement and of the Atlantic Charter, side by side with the original texts, was published as a white paper (Cmd. 6511) later in the month. Thereafter Ogden, as he tersely recorded in *Who's Who*, was 'bedevilled by officials, 1944–6'. He was requested to assign his copyright to the Crown which he did in June 1946 and was compensated by £23,000, a sum selected because it was the compensation paid to Bentham for his expenditure on the Panopticon or reformed prison. The Basic English Foundation was established with a grant from the Ministry of Education in 1947.

Throughout his life Ogden was a voracious collector of books, amassing complete houses-full of thousands of volumes. In 1953 University College, London, bought his manuscripts, incunabula, early printed books, and his collection on Bentham and Brougham which included almost 60,000 letters to Lord Brougham [q.v.]. The 100,000 books he left when he died in London 20 March 1957 were bought by the university of California at Los Angeles.

Ogden never married. The best known drawing of him by his friend James Wood is privately owned.

[I. A. Richards, 'Some Recollections of C. K. Ogden' in *Encounter*, September 1957; private information; personal knowledge.]

                       J. W. Scott.

OLIVER, FRANCIS WALL (1864–1951), palaeobotanist and ecologist, was born 10 May 1864 at Richmond, Surrey, where his parents lived prior to his father's appointment as keeper of the herbarium at Kew. His mother was Hannah, daughter of James Wall, of Sheffield, and his father Daniel Oliver, F.R.S., a distinguished systematist who exhibited a great flair for plant affinities and was the author of the first three volumes of the *Flora of Tropical Africa*. He was a member of the Society of Friends and sent his son at the age of nine to the Friends' School at Kendal where he developed a passion and skill for mountaineering which persisted; in later years he climbed the Alps with J. Norman Collie [q.v.] and E. J. Garwood. He went next to Bootham School, York, where he was given charge of their $4\frac{1}{2}$-inch telescope and might have adopted astronomy as a career but for an enthusiast who developed in him a predilection for botany. After a year at University College, London, he went to Trinity College, Cambridge, where he obtained a foundation scholarship and first class honours in both parts of the natural sciences tripos (1885–6). Vacations were occupied in study at Bonn and Tübingen, where he met many of the leading botanists of the day.

In 1888 Oliver took his father's place at University College, London, first as lecturer, then in 1890 as Quain professor of botany, a chair which he held until 1929. In 1894–5, with the help of others, he translated the *Pflanzenleben* of Kerner von Marilaun, under the title of *The Natural History of Plants*, which was a great success financially and doubtless stimulated in Oliver's mind the ecological bias which had been aroused by his contacts at Bonn and which he in turn imparted with good effect to (Sir) A. G. Tansley [q.v.] and others.

At the Jodrell laboratory at Kew, Oliver became associated with D. H. Scott [q.v.] and induced him to give the famous lectures on fossil plants at University College. Soon afterwards Oliver began his fruitful researches, which might be described as meticulous palaeobotanical detection, on fossil seeds, and led to the recognition of *Lagenostoma Lomaxi* as the seed of a woody, fern-like plant, the well-known fossil, *Lyginopteris Oldhamia*

(*Phil. Trans. Roy. Soc. (B)* 1905). Oliver thus established the existence of a group, the Pteridosperms, with fern-like habits but bearing seeds, as an important feature of the Coal-Measure vegetation. Apart from this, his chief contributions to the subject were a detailed account of a primitive type *Physostoma elegans* (*Ann. Bot.* 1909), of *Stephanospermum* (*Trans. Linn. Soc.* 1904) and, with (Sir) E. J. Salisbury, an account of the seeds of the genus *Conostoma* (*Ann. Bot.* 1911). For his contributions to palaeobotany Oliver was elected F.R.S. in 1905.

From 1904 to 1908 Oliver organized September visits to the Brittany coast to study salt-marsh vegetation, and after 1910 he annually took his honours students for a fortnight to Blakeney Point, Norfolk, to study plant life in relation to habitat conditions and raised the funds to erect the field laboratory there. In his later years Oliver turned his attention increasingly towards the dynamic aspects of ecology, studying in particular the physiography of shingle beaches and salt-marsh development in relation to their vegetation. As an outcome he became interested in the value of Cord Grass (*Spartina townsendii*) as a reclaimer of mud flats and subsequently in collaboration with a marine engineer, A. E. Carey, published a book on *Tidal Lands* (1918) which emphasized the role which plants could play in coastal conservation. Oliver's earliest papers were mostly of a physiological character and mention should be made of his pioneer investigations of the effect of fog on vegetation at the time when 'London particulars' could turn daylight into darkness (*Journal R.H.S.* 1891).

On retiring from University College, Oliver became professor at the Cairo University until 1935, when he went to live on the edge of the desert and studied the changing aspects of its vegetation. He returned finally to England only a year before he died. Robust physically, with a strikingly well-cut physiognomy, Oliver had only one serious illness. He was fundamentally shy and reserved, with a marked capacity for silence, but he evoked the affection of his close associates.

Oliver married in 1896 Mildred Alice (died 1932), daughter of Charles Robert Thompson, surgeon, of Westerham, whom he encountered when climbing in the Alps. They had one daughter and two sons both of whom attained distinction in the navy. Oliver died at Limpsfield, Surrey,

14 September 1951. A drawing by Miss F. A. de Biden Footner is at University College, London.

[Sir Edward Salisbury in *Obituary Notices of Fellows of the Royal Society*, No. 21, November 1952; personal knowledge.]
E. J. SALISBURY.

OPPÉ, ADOLPH PAUL (1878–1957), art historian and collector, was born in London 22 September 1878, the third son of Siegmund Armin Oppé, a silk merchant, by his wife, Pauline Jaffé. He was educated at Charterhouse, St. Andrews University, and New College, Oxford, where he was an exhibitioner and took first classes in classical moderations (1899) and *literae humaniores* (1901). In 1902 Oppé was appointed assistant to the professor of Greek and then lecturer at St. Andrews, and in 1904 lecturer in ancient history at Edinburgh University. In 1905 he entered the Board of Education, where he remained, with three years (1910–13) as deputy director of the Victoria and Albert Museum, until his retirement in 1938, after serving as head of the branch dealing with the training of teachers. He was appointed C.B. in 1937.

Apart from essays on classical subjects published while he was at St. Andrews and Edinburgh, Oppé's first writings were studies in Italian art: *Raphael* (1909) and *Botticelli* (1911). After these, he wrote almost entirely on English subjects. He had collected drawings, both English and foreign, since 1904, starting with a beautiful early Cotman [q.v.], and his interest had soon been caught by the then almost unstudied English water-colours of the eighteenth and early nineteenth centuries, and the discoveries he made among them.

In 1910 he made the most remarkable of these discoveries: acquiring for twenty-five shillings a lot of seventeen drawings by Francis Towne [q.v.], including the artist's two masterpieces of the *Source of the Arveyron*. At that time they could be related only to a practically unseen collection at the British Museum; but some years later a chance remark led Oppé to the Devon home of the Merivales who still owned the mass of Towne's drawings, which the artist himself had left to them. These and some Merivale papers enabled Oppé in 1920 to establish this forgotten artist's position with an article in a Walpole Society volume.

The year before (1919), in the *Burlington Magazine*, Oppé had demolished the legend that Alexander Cozens [q.v.] was the son of Peter the Great. Under his iconoclastic pen many similar legends about English artists were to be shattered. It was typical of his painstaking quest for finality that he did not publish any book on Alexander Cozens until 1952 when his *Alexander & John Robert Cozens* embodied the researches of over forty years. In this, as in all his books, his criticism was constantly enriched by his extensive knowledge of the art of other countries and by his classical scholarship.

As well as these works, Oppé published books on: *Rowlandson* (1923); *Cotman* (1923); *Turner, Cox and de Wint* (1925); the *Sandby Drawings at Windsor Castle* (1947); *Hogarth* (1948); and the *English Drawings at Windsor Castle* (1950). He also wrote the section on 'Art' in *Early Victorian England* (1934), edited by G. M. Young [q.v.]. In all these publications the same exacting and uncompromising scholarship prevailed. The chiselled precision of his prose owed a great deal to his classical attainments. His style was terse but never dull, for he succeeded in combining in all he wrote the scholar's love of truth with the aesthete's love of beauty.

Paul Oppé was a born collector. With a very perceptive eye, he bought regardless of fashion at a time when drawings were still relatively cheap. His collection included, besides its English treasures, drawings by such masters as Fra Bartolomeo, Giovanni da Udine, Barocci, Veronese, Poussin, and Claude. Oppé's judgement of drawings was widely respected and for the last twenty years of his life he acted as adviser to the department of drawings of the National Gallery of Canada.

The critical faculties which distinguished Oppé as a scholar were reflected in his temperament. He was quickly irritated by false attributions, careless assumptions, and slovenly writing, and the culprits were liable to be castigated by his caustic wit. It was reserved for his friends to appreciate what one of them has described as 'the humour, humanity and generous width of sympathy which were the complement to his rigorous intellect'.

Oppé was elected F.B.A. in 1952 and made an honorary LL.D. of Glasgow in 1953. He died in London 29 March 1957. A life-size bronze bust of Oppé, modelled by Uli Nimptsch in 1949, was presented by his friends to the print room of the British Museum as a memorial to one whose influence had done so much to establish the study of English drawings on a sound and scholarly basis. Oppé married in 1909 Valentine (died 1951), daughter of the late Rev. Ralph William Lyonel Tollemache-Tollemache. They had a son and a daughter.

[*The Times*, 1, 3, and 12 April 1957; *Burlington Magazine*, June 1957; Royal Academy *Catalogue of the Paul Oppé Collection*, 1958, which contains a list of his principal publications and articles and a foreword by Sir Kenneth Clark; personal knowledge.]

BRINSLEY FORD.

OPPENHEIMER, SIR ERNEST (1880–1957), South African financier, was born in Friedberg, Germany, 22 May 1880, the fifth son and eighth in a family of ten children born to Eduard Oppenheimer, a cigar merchant, and his wife, Fanny Hirschhorn. He was educated at the Augustinerschule in Friedberg and began his career in 1896 when he became a junior clerk in the London firm of Dunkelsbuhler & Co., a member of the Diamond Syndicate with important affiliations with Rand gold mining interests. Two older brothers, (Sir) Bernhard and Louis, were successively connected with the firm, Louis until the final dissolution of the business. Ernest Oppenheimer was naturalized in 1901 and in 1902 went to represent his firm at Kimberley where he entered municipal politics and was mayor in 1912–15.

Moving to London for a while he entered into close relations with the Consolidated Mines Selection Company, one of the two linked Rand mining concerns with which Dunkelsbuhlers were closely related, the other being the Rand Selection Company. The area of expansion in gold mining at that time was the Far East Rand, where the C.M.S. Company was represented. It was on the basis of this contact and with this area in view that Oppenheimer decided to form his own mining house. With the aid of W. L. Honnold, he got in touch with Herbert Hoover, a distinguished mining engineer and later president of the United States, and through him with American interests, J. P. Morgan & Co. and the Newmont Corporation. This association of American finance with South African mining enterprise was a new and dramatic feature. The Anglo American Corporation of South Africa, Ltd., was formed in 1917 and its first activities were concerned with the Far East Rand.

It was not long, however, before

Oppenheimer extended the interests of the new corporation. When he first went to South Africa the De Beers Company dominated the world output of diamonds, whilst the market was managed by the Diamond Syndicate. The output of diamonds outside the Union (and it was in the main alluvial output which mattered) was now to expand, first by the discovery of the South West African fields, and gradually to include Angola, the Belgian Congo, West and East Africa. By acquiring control of the South West African production in 1920 and creating a single unit there in the Consolidated Diamond Mines of South West Africa, Ltd.; by obtaining control over the new Lichtenburg field, and of the diamonds found in Namaqualand; by sales agreements with, and participation in stock-ownership in, other African producers; by associating his corporation with the Diamond Syndicate and subsequently reorganizing it, he gradually acquired bargaining power sufficient to force his full acceptance by De Beers, of which he became chairman in 1929. In this position he succeeded in bringing about a much greater degree of integration among South African producers. The difficulties caused by the depression of the thirties enabled him in the end to replace the Syndicate by the Diamond Corporation (1930); to create a new unifying agency between all South African producers (which now included the Union Government) in the shape of the Diamond Producers' Association (1934); and finally, by arranging that the control of the Diamond Corporation should pass to South African producers whilst it maintained sales relations with the outsiders, he unified the diamond industry throughout Africa on a scale hitherto deemed impossible.

The courage and skill required to bring all this to pass served him in good stead in the second great enterprise of his career: copper mining in Northern Rhodesia. His first step was to get his firm to act as consulting engineers to the new 'concession companies' floated as a result of the British South Africa Company's 'forward' policy in Northern Rhodesia; this gradually led to financial participation in mining and to the creation of a subsidiary, Rhodesian Anglo American, Ltd. (1928). A competing group, created earlier in the year, the Rhodesian Selection Trust, led by (Sir) A. Chester Beatty, was strongly representative of American interests. These interests were invited to assist in the

further financing of copper production, which would have meant the control of the Copperbelt by American mining houses. Strongly resisted by Oppenheimer and his group 'for imperial and financial reasons', this move was in the end defeated. American participation continued, but the balance of power shifted decisively to the British side.

Oppenheimer's third great enterprise was the opening up of the Orange Free State goldfield. The devaluation of the South African pound, following the British, in 1931, stimulated prospecting activity, first on the Far West Rand and the Klerksdorp areas, a little later on the area south of the Vaal River. In the end, the area round Odendaalsrust, hitherto an obscure little 'dorp' to the south, proved to be the centre of activity. By a series of bold financial coups, Oppenheimer acquired control of the most promising 'prospects', taking over the interests of Sir Abe Bailey [q.v.] (Western Townships) and obtaining the ownership of Lewis and Marks. Consequently when production began the dominating name was the Anglo American Corporation and its subsidiary, the Orange Free State Investment Trust (1944).

From 1924 until 1938 Oppenheimer, who was knighted in 1921, represented Kimberley in the Union Parliament as a supporter of J. C. Smuts [q.v.]. He was a man of great charm, great modesty, infinite kindness, and a passionate believer in the Commonwealth and in African advancement. His influence above all was responsible for the loan made by the mining houses of three million pounds to the municipality of Johannesburg for the creation of adequate housing for the Bantu population. His own benefactions included a considerable grant towards the establishment of Queen Elizabeth House at Oxford; towards medical research in South Africa; and towards scientific research at Leeds University and elsewhere. He was a benefactor of and honoured by the leading South African universities and received an honorary D.C.L. from Oxford in 1952. His benefactions were continued after his death by the Ernest Oppenheimer Memorial Trust to which his son and sole heir to his personal estate of £3,600,000 gave a million pounds.

Oppenheimer married first, in 1906, May Lina (died 1934), daughter of Joseph Pollak, a London stockbroker. Her sister married his brother Louis. Oppenheimer had two sons, the elder of whom succeeded him as head of the Anglo American Corporation; the younger died as the result of an accident in 1935. Oppenheimer married secondly, in 1935, Caroline Magdalen, widow of his nephew, Sir Michael Oppenheimer.

When Oppenheimer died in Johannesburg, 25 November 1957, there was national mourning and flags were flown at half-mast on all government buildings throughout South Africa.

There are portraits by: W. Bartis (1913) in the possession of the municipality of Kimberley; T. Epstein (1936) and R. Tollast (1957) belonging to the Anglo American Corporation; T. Cuneo (1954) in the possession of the family. A posthumous pastel by G. A. Campbell belongs to the Anglo American Corporation and is based on a portrait by the same artist which was presented by H. F. Oppenheimer to the South African Institute of International Affairs in 1960.

[*Cape Times*, 26 November 1957; *The Times*, 26 and 29 November 1957; Sir Theodore Gregory, *Ernest Oppenheimer and the Economic Development of Southern Africa*, 1962; private information; personal knowledge.]

THEODORE GREGORY.

ORWIN, CHARLES STEWART (1876–1955), agricultural economist, was born 26 September 1876 at Horsham, Sussex, into a medical family with a reputation for independent, radical thinking. He was the only son of Frederick James Orwin, gentleman, by his wife, Elizabeth, daughter of Robert Campbell Stewart, of Blackheath, and niece of George Gawler [q.v.], governor of South Australia (1838–41). From his earliest days Orwin wanted to be a farmer and, on leaving Dulwich College, he obtained a county scholarship and entered the South Eastern Agricultural College at Wye. There he established a lasting friendship with the principal, (Sir) (A.) Daniel Hall (whose notice he later contributed to this Dictionary), which enriched his whole life. He left Wye with a college diploma, another from Cambridge—there was no degree in agriculture in those days—and an associateship of the Surveyors' Institution.

Since there was not enough money in the family to start him in farming, Orwin decided on a career as land agent and joined a west-end house agent; a year later, when the firm opened a country office, he found himself in charge of it. In 1903 he accepted a lectureship at his old college at Wye, of which he later became an honorary fellow. In 1906 he was recommended as agent to Christopher Turnor (whose notice Orwin later contributed to this Dictionary). Turnor had recently inherited nearly 25,000 acres in Lincolnshire. Orwin accepted a job which was to enable him to use to the full his already remarkably comprehensive knowledge of the country and to develop his latent talent as a far-sighted administrator. The property, although large, was not wealthy; and he had to work hard and quickly, assisted by only one clerk. He was also active in local government and, then and later, in the affairs of the Church. This did not prevent him from finding time to work out a system of cost accounting which would give the farmer much the same control over his affairs as the industrialist had over his factory and would also provide a reliable basis for sound agricultural policy, a contribution soon to be given an added significance by war.

When (Sir) Daniel Hall, representing the Development Commission, persuaded the university of Oxford to sponsor a research institute in agricultural economics, Orwin became its first director (1913). Hitherto the subject had not been recognized as one for academic study; it fell to Orwin to be the architect in this new field, to introduce the subject to a rather suspicious public, to attract promising young men to study it, and to lead the way with his own lively and penetrating researches. He was the first to use extensively surveys, first by county, then by topic, in the study of agricultural economics. When he retired in 1945 nearly every university in England, Scotland, and Wales had a department of agricultural economics, and the Ministry of Agriculture its economics branch; most of these were led or staffed by men who had had their initial training at the Oxford Institute for Research in Agricultural Economics. Orwin's energy and capacity for original thinking appealed to young men, whom he went out of his way to encourage.

Early in his career at Oxford he became connected with Balliol, of which he was a fellow (1922), estates bursar (1926–46), and honorary fellow (1946). In 1939 he became the first D.Litt. in the Oxford school of social studies. As a research worker in land problems, he did not lose sight of practical issues. He served on the council of the Land Agents' Society and of the Royal Institution of Chartered

Surveyors; as editor of the *Journal* of the Royal Agricultural Society (1912–27) he was in touch with the more prominent landowners and farmers in England; and he was a member of the first Agricultural Wages Board (1917–21). He was also president of the agricultural section of the British Association (1921) and assessor to the Agricultural Tribunal of Investigation (1922–4).

Orwin had remarkable talents as an advocate of original views derived from experience and prolonged study. He contended that many farms were too small in acreage to take advantage of the economies offered by modern techniques, and that this could not be rectified without drastic changes in the system of land tenure. In later years the need dominated his thinking. No one can now give serious thought to land reform without incurring a heavy debt to the author of such books as *The Tenure of Agricultural Land* (with W. R. Peel, 1925), *The Future of Farming* (1930), *Speed the Plough* (1942) and *Problems of the Countryside* (1945), and to the editor of *Country Planning* (1944). His mastery of English prose, grasp of logic, and avoidance of provocation enabled him to write books and articles which were as enjoyable as they were persuasive. He also brought to bear on present-day problems a strong sense of history. In addition to books on farming as a business, among them *Farm Accounts* (1914), *The Determination of Farming Costs* (1917), and *Estate Accounts* (with H. W. Kersey, 1926), he wrote *The Reclamation of Exmoor Forest* (1929) during the time he had his home in Minehead, *A History of English Farming* (1949), and, with his second wife, *The Open Fields* (1938, 2nd ed. 1954, his most enduring work), and *Farms & Fields* (1944).

Charles Orwin was very tall, his appearance most impressive, his face handsome and leonine. Generous in his affections and opinions, he could be easily hurt, for he was a deeply sensitive man. He gave short shrift to the sillinesses of cleverer men, as Balliol anecdotes testify, but to the young he reached out with an especial and characteristic courtesy.

In 1902 Orwin married Elise Cécile (died 1929), daughter of Edouard Renault, of Cognac, France; they had three sons and three daughters. In 1931 he married, secondly, Christabel Susan, daughter of the late Charles Lowry, headmaster of Tonbridge School (1907–22). Orwin died

at Blewbury, Berkshire, 30 June 1955. There is a portrait by Richard Murray at the Institute for Research in Agricultural Economics, Oxford.

[*Countryman*, Autumn and Winter 1946, Autumn 1955; private information; personal knowledge.]   JOHN CRIPPS.

PAGE, SIR LEO FRANCIS (1890–1951), magistrate, was born at Hobart, Tasmania, 2 April 1890, the youngest of six sons, only two of whom survived childhood, of William Humphrey Page, of the Indian Civil Service, and his wife, Alice, daughter of Richard Pope. His father had become a Roman Catholic in early manhood and Leo was educated at Beaumont College. At the wish of his father he entered the Royal Military Academy, Woolwich, and after a year transferred to the 16th Lancers. But he was not suited to the army and withdrawing he entered University College, Oxford, where he obtained second class honours in jurisprudence in 1914. On the outbreak of war he joined the Royal Flying Corps, but after a serious accident while bringing home a plane from France he was invalided out in 1916, having attained the rank of flight commander. In that year he married Edith Violet, daughter of Captain Frederick Cleave Loder-Symonds, R.A., of Hinton Manor, Faringdon, Berkshire, by whom he had two sons and a daughter.

Page became a member of the Inner Temple and was called to the bar in 1918. He practised for several years and had reason to anticipate success, but he was never robust and tuberculosis developed. Enjoying a secure private income, he abandoned practice and settled with his family at Faringdon. There in 1925 he became a justice of the peace for Berkshire and a member of the bench at Faringdon where his father-in-law had earlier been chairman for many years. In 1946 he was elected chairman, an office which he held until his death. He also served as chairman of the local juvenile court and for a period as chairman of the appeals committee at the Berkshire quarter-sessions.

In all this work Page took more than the ordinary interest. While doing his full share of the court work, he made a deep study of the problems of local justice. Not content with his limited experience in a rural court, he visited many other courts in different parts of the country. This qualified him to write several books about the work of magistrates on which he became a leading authority. The most influential were *Justice of the Peace* (1936) and *Crime and the Community* (1937). In court, while always merciful, Page was a realist and more open to appeals to reason than to sentiment.

Although he was known primarily as a leading justice of the peace, Page also gave much time and enthusiasm to helping prisoners and ex-prisoners, and this became his main interest in his later years. From 1939 for many years afterwards he was chairman of the visiting magistrates at Oxford prison; he also became chairman of its Discharged Prisoners' Aid Society. He took a keen interest in many individual cases and kept in touch with some of them after their release. No case which Page considered deserving was too much trouble for him, although he had a quick eye for those who sought to impose on him without adequate effort to make good.

From 1940 to 1945 Page served in the lord chancellor's department as secretary of commissions of the peace. He had a freer hand than was usual since Lord Simon [q.v.] was much occupied with wartime problems outside his office. Page was considerably shocked by much of what he saw. Many of those recommended for appointment as justices of the peace in local areas were, in his own words, 'older than was desirable', and selected in recognition of some other form of public service. It was 'rare to find anyone wholly without political connection'. Page did all he could to improve matters. The reforms which took place after the war were not yet being planned, but when they came Page's influence was apparent. It was he who influenced the lord chancellor to secure the passing into law of an Act in 1941 which empowered him to prevent elderly and infirm lay justices from sitting in court.

Page was essentially a conservative reformer. Keen and successful though he was in bringing about many reforms within the existing system, he was apparently not aware that demands were being made for radical changes in the system itself. To some extent his mind widened as his experience increased. In 1937 Page was nominated by his bench as its representative on the council of the Magistrates' Association, many of whose members, without being in any way extremists, had ideas for reform beyond what Page then considered reasonable. To such members

Page seemed unwilling to pursue his ideas to their logical conclusions. For instance, while he profoundly believed that criminal courts should be better informed about the offenders whom they convicted, he was at first satisfied with the existing method whereby such social inquiries as were made about offenders took place before trial and thus before guilt was established. A substantial majority took the view that most serious cases should be adjourned after conviction for full inquiries to be made before sentence was passed. Page resigned in protest in 1940 and took no further part in the Association's work. This was mainly due to the claims of his official work, but when this ceased he did not return to the Association although he later accepted the idea that serious cases should be adjourned for inquiries after conviction.

In 1946 a strong royal commission was set up under Lord du Parcq [q.v.] to inquire into the work of justices of the peace. Page's evidence was printed as an appendix to its minutes of evidence. The report of this commission (1948) greatly influenced the preparation of the post-war reforms and reflected many of the ideas which Page had laid before it. Valuable as the new code was, the reforms were all within the existing system and on some points were less drastic than Page himself had hoped.

The usefulness of psychiatry was gradually realized by Page who wrote 'Medical men who have specialised in this branch of research have a very definite and valuable contribution to make to the treatment of delinquency' (*Quarterly Review*, April 1940). But in his view the help of such experts applied only to abnormal cases and should be limited to examining and reporting on offenders. He was not in sympathy with the suggestion that psychiatrists should share the responsibility of selecting appropriate sentences, a task which Page considered those on the bench were competent to perform, although he urged that they should be better informed about the various methods of dealing with offenders. Thus in 1948 he wrote in his book *The Sentence of the Court* that all those on the bench, including professional lawyers, should receive instruction which would fit them to pass sentence. But he put forward no plan whereby lawyers appointed in mid-life to the criminal bench could receive such instruction.

Page was high sheriff for his county in

1937. In 1948 he received a knighthood, but he was already in severe ill health although continuing bravely with as much work as he could undertake. His consistent love for suffering humanity and his humility were the qualities most valued by his friends; to the end his sense of humour never left him. He died at his home at Faringdon 31 August 1951.

[Private information; personal knowledge.]
CLAUD MULLINS.

PAGET, SIR RICHARD ARTHUR SURTEES, second baronet, of Cranmore (1869–1955), barrister and physicist, the eldest son of (Sir) Richard Horner Paget, M.P., later first baronet, by his wife, Caroline Isabel, daughter of Henry Edward Surtees, of Redworth Hall, county Durham, was born at Cranmore Hall, Somerset, 13 January 1869. He was educated at Eton and Magdalen College, Oxford, where he obtained a third class in chemistry in 1891; was called to the bar by the Inner Temple in 1895; and succeeded his father in 1908.

Paget's legal and scientific background, together with his engaging personal qualities, fitted him admirably for negotiatory tasks such as those of secretary successively to the patent law committee (1900), the court of arbitration dealing with the Grimsby fishing dispute (1900), the court of arbitration under the Metropolitan Water Act (1902), the University College transfer commission (1905), and the submarine and electrical section of the Admiralty board of inventions (1915–18).

Possessed of intellectual gifts and potentialities of an unusually high order, coupled with originality and inventiveness of mind, Paget was obviously marked out for distinction in whatever field he cared to cultivate. As it happened, it was not necessary for him to become a narrow scientific specialist; instead, he made contributions of significance to many varied departments of knowledge, both scientific and artistic, such as acoustics, music, architecture, town-planning, agriculture, anthropology, and human speech, besides cultivating practical music and artistic crafts such as pottery and drawing. The versatility and boldness of his achievements surprised as much by their novelty and unexpectedness as by their shrewd perspicacity. His penetrating foresight into the innate possibilities of ideas prompted the remark that he was always 'forty years ahead of his time'; this was certainly true with regard to the streamline car he designed in 1910 also of some aspects of speech. His book *Human Speech*, first published in 1930 was reissued in 1964 because of it connection with modern developments in communication engineering.

Undoubtedly, Paget's most important original investigations were those connected with language, not only in regard to phonetics and the technique of vocalization, or linguistics and vocabulary—to all of which he added new conceptions—but in the most fundamental processes and means through which individuals can transfer ideas from one to another. His famous theory of pantomimic action of the tongue and lips explained lucidly how language arises at all and related it directly to the senses and affections. From this followed naturally his special interest in the communication problems of the deaf and dumb. The models he designed for illustrating the action of the human speech organs were deposited in the Royal Institution.

Paget was singularly well equipped for work in language and speech for he possessed an abnormally remarkable musical aural sensitivity which was no doubt responsible for that instinctive harmonic creative ability ascribed to him by all those who heard his improvisatory musical performances; in addition, he had a passionate interest in his fellow men, being genial, deeply sympathetic, not without humour, and capable of great affection for young and old alike; hence his efforts on behalf of those deprived of the powers of speech and hearing. He laid down the principles for an entirely new approach in communication with deaf and dumb people by means of a systematic sign language, the further development of which was continued after his death.

Paget was frequently described as an amateur scientist: a term of both admiration and honour. He was one of the rare number of distinguished individual workers who pursued scientific investigation privately and did so much to promote discovery and invention before the age of organized science and the professional scientists. Greatly esteemed as a lecturer and research worker, he was an active member of several learned societies: fellow of the Institute of Physics, of the Physical Society, and of the Royal Anthropological Institute, honorary associate of the Royal Institute of British

Architects, honorary associate member of the Town Planning Institute, and member and sometime manager of the Royal Institution.

By his first wife, whom he married in 1897, Lady Muriel Paget [q.v.], he had two sons (one of whom died in infancy) and three daughters. His second wife, whom he married in 1939, was Grace Hartley, only daughter of Walter Herbert Glover, of Birkdale and Grasmere. Paget died in London 23 October 1955 and was succeeded by his surviving son, John Starr (born 1914).

There is a portrait in the book *Portrait Drawings* (1949) by Peter Scott of which the original is in the possession of the family.

[*The Times*, 24 and 28 October 1955; *Year Book* of the Physical Society, 1956; *Nature*, 31 December 1955; *Motor*, 29 August 1956; personal knowledge.]   H. LOWERY.

PAINE, CHARLES HUBERT SCOTT-(1891–1954), pioneer of aviation and of high-speed motor-boats. [See SCOTT-PAINE.]

PALAIRET, SIR (CHARLES) MICHAEL (1882–1956), diplomatist, was born 29 September 1882 at Berkeley, Gloucestershire, the youngest of the three sons of Charles Harvey Palairet, captain in the 9th Lancers, and his wife, Emily Henry. He was descended from a French family called Palayret who settled in Holland after the revocation of the Edict of Nantes. John and Elias Palairet [qq.v.] settled in England where subsequent members of the family usually resided. In Palairet's lifetime the family name was notable for the cricketing prowess of his older cousins, L. C. H. and R. C. N. Palairet. On his mother's side he was a great-grandson of Thomas Allan, the mineralogist [q.v.].

Educated at Eton, he went next to Touraine to perfect his French and to Weimar for German. He was nominated for the diplomatic service in 1905 and sent in the following year to Rome where in 1907 he was appointed third secretary. He served successively in Vienna, Paris, where he and his wife were received into the Roman Catholic Church in 1916, and Athens. He returned to Paris on the staff of the British delegation to the peace conference (1918–19) and later in the embassy (1920–22). As counsellor in Tokyo (1922–5) he took charge during the absence of the ambassador, Sir Charles

Eliot [q.v.], and narrowly escaped injury in the disastrous earthquake of 1923 when the embassy buildings collapsed. He and his wife became friends of Paul Claudel who was then the French ambassador.

In 1928 Palairet went as counsellor to Rome but in December 1929 was promoted to be minister in Bucharest where their charm and hospitality and keen interest in Romanian culture won the Palairets a wide circle of friends. Prince Carol, who returned from exile and became king in 1930, showed no grudge at having been requested to leave England in 1928 because of his alleged involvement in a plot to place him on the Romanian throne. Good Anglo-Romanian relations, both political and commercial, were established, but before Palairet's transfer to Stockholm in February 1935 German economic and political penetration had become menacing.

Transferred to Vienna in 1937, Palairet found German National Socialism ruthless and aggressive. He keenly realized the dangers to which Nazi control of Austria would lead and had little patience with those in Great Britain and France who were complacent or defeatist over the problem. Palairet admired, though he thought it risky, Dr. Schuschnigg's bold challenge to Hitler by announcing a plebiscite. Early in the morning of 11 March 1938 Palairet reported the closing of the Austrian frontier with Germany, the prelude to the Nazi invasion of Austria, after which he was recalled and the legation closed. In June of the same year he was appointed K.C.M.G. and in September–December he took charge of the British legation in Bucharest during the illness of Sir Reginald Hoare [q.v.].

In June 1939 Palairet went as minister to Athens, a welcome appointment but soon overshadowed by war. In October 1940 the Italians invaded Greece but met with such effective resistance that in the following April German forces were sent to their assistance. Despite British intervention which Palairet had advocated with notable pertinacity it proved impossible to prevent the German occupation of the mainland and the abandonment of Crete, to which the Greek king, accompanied by Palairet, had withdrawn on 23 April. A month later they were taken off Crete and eventually arrived in London in September. Palairet remained accredited to the Greek monarch and in May 1942 his status was raised to ambassador. He retired in April

1943, but returned to the Foreign Office as a temporary assistant under-secretary of state, dealing with matters concerning prisoners of war, until July 1945.

Palairet was tall, slim, distinguished in appearance; scrupulous and tolerant, with a wide, cultivated taste. His integrity and steadfastness of character sprang from a deep religious faith, which never wavered even in the most frustrating and dangerous crises of his career. In his retirement one of his occupations was the translation of German religious books. He died 5 August 1956 at his home at Allerford, Minehead, Somerset.

In 1915 Palairet married Mary de Vere, daughter of Colonel (later Brigadier-General) Herbert William Studd, of the Coldstream Guards. They had one son, and a daughter who married the second Earl of Oxford and Asquith.

[Private information; personal knowledge.]
ALEC RANDALL.

PANETH, FRIEDRICH ADOLF (1887–1958), scientist, was born in Vienna 31 August 1887, the second of the three sons of Joseph Paneth, a distinguished physiologist, and his wife, Sophie Schwab, the daughter of a leading industrialist. Living in a highly cultured milieu, Paneth was educated at the Schotten Gymnasium and the university of Vienna. He then studied for a year under Adolph von Baeyer in Munich before returning to Vienna to obtain his Ph.D. in 1910. In 1912 he became an assistant in the Radium Research Institute attached to the Vienna Academy of Science; in 1917 he joined the Prague Institute of Technology; but two years later he went as assistant professor to the university of Hamburg. In 1922 he became head of the inorganic department of the chemical institute of the university of Berlin and in 1929 head of the chemical institute of the university of Königsberg, an unusual distinction for an inorganic chemist. When Hitler came into power in 1933 Paneth happened to be in London and remained there as a guest of the Imperial College of Science and Technology where in 1938 he became reader in atomic chemistry. In 1939 he was invited to the chair of chemistry at Durham. In 1943–5 he was in charge of the chemistry division of the joint British–Canadian atomic energy team in Montreal. After the war he returned to Durham where he established the Londonderry Laboratory for radiochemistry and resumed his former researches. After his

retirement in 1953 he accepted an invitation to become a director of the Max-Planck Institute of Chemistry in Mainz where the last five years of his life were spent in building up an active research school.

One of Paneth's first pieces of research was an attempt to separate radium D from radiolead. George Hevesy was engaged in a similar attempt in Manchester and the results of their investigations were published in a joint paper in 1913. Early in January of that year the first joint investigation with radioactive tracers was carried out in the study of the solubility of lead sulphide and lead chromate; and labelled lead and bismuth were used in electrochemical studies. In the ensuing years Paneth carried out several important studies applying radium D and E and thorium B as tracers. One of these was the study of adsorption of ThB, ThC, and Ra on such compounds as titanium, chromium and manganese oxides, barium sulphate and chromate, and the silver halides. Adsorption was strong when the radioelements formed an insoluble compound with the electronegative component of the adsorbing material.

Before he left the Radium Research Institute Paneth discovered the existence of a volatile polonium hydride. This led to the discovery of a volatile bismuth hydride and later of a volatile lead hydride. After he left Vienna he discovered a volatile hydride of tin and much enlarged the knowledge of an already known germanium hydride. These studies led to the recognition that all elements with atomic numbers which have one to four units less than a rare gas are capable of forming gaseous hydrides. Through these investigations Paneth became the greatest authority of his time on volatile hydrides.

At Hamburg Paneth continued his important studies on the surface adsorption and worked out a method which enabled him to determine the surface area of powders by using radioactive indicators.

Possibly Paneth's most important work, the demonstration of the existence of free radicals, was to a large extent carried out whilst he was at Königsberg. The preparation of free methyl had been attempted by Kolbe in 1849 and from that time the concept of an organic radical was prominent in many theories of organic reactions, although direct proof was lacking. Paneth and his co-workers succeeded in showing that free methyl radicals produced in the gas phase could persist for a small but measureable time before recombining to form methane. Free ethyl was similarly produced from lead tetraethyl and shown to react with zinc, cadmium, antimony, and lead. He also succeeded in estimating the mean half-life of radicals.

In the spring of 1913 Paneth had spent a few months with Frederick Soddy [q.v.] at Glasgow where he became interested in gas analytical methods which he later developed to a most remarkable extent and applied to the study of the isolation and measurement of minute amounts of helium and other gases of the atmosphere. He then applied these methods of helium analysis to the determination of the age of meteorites. He arrived at very high values for the age of some meteorites but the discovery of the production of helium by cosmic rays led him in 1952 to re-examine some of his conclusions. He arrived at the result that a substantial part of the helium present in iron meteorites was composed of He3 and the age of the meteorites correspondingly less. According to his paper published in 1954 the age of most meteorites is between 100 and 200 million years and some very much less. He investigated numerous meteorites and bequeathed to the Radium Research Institute in Vienna his collection of over a hundred specimens together with literature on the subject. His studies of meteorites led him on to the problem of the formation of the elements and the universe. Always a most fascinating lecturer, he was especially stimulating on these topics.

The methods of separating and measuring very small quantities of helium and other rare gases were used in other ways by Paneth. The first recorded measurement of a microscopic product in a nuclear reaction involving neutrons was made by him when he succeeded in measuring the helium formed in the neutron irradiation of methyl borate. He also made numerous contributions to the study of the stratosphere.

The energy with which Paneth pursued his professional activities did not prevent him from developing his early cultural interests which in later years focused mainly on history, especially the history of science. He was an eminent connoisseur of the history of alchemy and made a special study of the works of Robert Boyle [q.v.]. When he went to Durham he was astonished to find that hardly anyone there was familiar with the name of Thomas Wright [q.v.] who first discerned the nature of the Milky Way, or knew that the round stone tower at Westerton near Durham had been Wright's observatory. Paneth succeeded in arousing public interest with the result that a memorial plaque was affixed to the tower and the two hundredth anniversary of the publication of Wright's *Original Theory* duly celebrated in 1950.

Paneth was naturalized in 1939 and while conserving his feelings of gratitude towards his native country became thoroughly steeped in the British way of life. He was a member of the Athenaeum and was elected F.R.S. in 1947. In 1913 he married Else Hartmann, a doctor of medicine of Vienna and later of Edinburgh. She was the daughter of the distinguished historian Ludo Moritz Hartmann, Austrian ambassador in Berlin after the war of 1914–18. Paneth had a son and a daughter. He died in Vienna 17 September 1958 and is buried in the suburban churchyard of Döbling, where by his wish the inscription on his grave bears no more than his name followed by the letters F.R.S.

[H. J. Eméleus in *Biographical Memoirs of Fellows of the Royal Society*, vol. vi, 1960; personal knowledge.]   G. HEVESY.

PANKHURST, DAME CHRISTABEL HARRIETTE (1880–1958), suffragette, was born at Manchester 22 September 1880, the eldest child of Richard Marsden Pankhurst, a lawyer of advanced political opinions, and his wife, Emmeline Pankhurst [q.v.]. Although Richard Pankhurst in public life was an austere character, he was an indulgent family man. He chose Christabel for the name of his first child because of the lines in Coleridge's poem:

> The lovely lady, Christabel,
> Whom her father loves so well.

Although intellectually exciting the Pankhurst home was not prosperous. After a few years the family migrated to London and lived in Russell Square, Mrs. Pankhurst opening a shop in Bloomsbury where she sold silks, pottery, lampshades, and the like, while Richard Pankhurst divided his time between chambers in Manchester and London. They returned eventually to Manchester where Richard Pankhurst died prematurely in 1898. In an age when poverty was regarded as something of a disgrace the Pankhursts comforted themselves with the knowledge that they were only poor because they were idealists: they preferred causes to comfort. Although after her husband's death Mrs. Pankhurst was compelled to work, she devoted her spare time and distinctive talents to the two causes with which he had been most closely associated—the Independent Labour Party and women's suffrage.

From the first she formed the highest opinion of the talents and capacity of her eldest daughter, and it was decided that she should follow in her father's footsteps and read law at Manchester. She was refused admission to Lincoln's Inn, of which her father had been a member, because she was a woman. At this time she met two remarkable women, Esther Roper and Eva Gore-Booth (sister to the Countess Markievicz who was the first woman elected to the House of Commons); they had come to the north to organize women workers in the mills for economic and political purposes. The three young women were much influenced by the spirit of revolt against the depressed position of women which was then making itself felt among independent and intelligent youth. Mrs. Pankhurst was working to form what she had almost decided to call the Women's Labour Representation Committee, on the precedent of the Labour Representation Committee. Christabel Pankhurst then intervened with the suggestion that the body should be called the Women's Social and Political Union. This was formed in 1903, and, in its abbreviated form of W.S.P.U., was to attract the loyalty of countless women and to introduce militant action into the calm of British politics.

Christabel Pankhurst had grown into an attractive young woman—essentially feminine, with a lovely complexion and a beautiful speaking voice, but where the women's cause was concerned there was in her character that streak of iron which had marked her father. A close friend of the family observed that both Christabel and her next sister, Sylvia, had a hardening influence on the personality of their mother. Certainly from the time of the organization of the W.S.P.U. Mrs. Pankhurst deferred to the zeal and markedly martial qualities of her eldest daughter. For two years after 1903 they devoted themselves to propaganda in Lancashire, attracting to them a valuable recruit in Annie Kenney [q.v.] to whom Christabel Pankhurst became warmly attached. In 1905 came the first act of militancy.

On 13 October, with Annie Kenney, Christabel Pankhurst attended a Liberal meeting in the Free Trade Hall, Manchester, held in support of (Sir) Winston Churchill's candidature for north-west Manchester. The principal speaker was Sir Edward Grey (later Viscount Grey of Fallodon, q.v.), and ironically enough both men were supporters of women's franchise. Annie Kenney asked whether the Liberals, if they came to power, would make women's suffrage a government measure. When no reply was given, Christabel Pankhurst rose and held up a banner on which was written 'Votes for Women'. The two girls were then somewhat roughly expelled from the meeting, and on attempting to make a speech outside were arrested and subsequently fined a few shillings with the alternative of prison, which they chose. This episode is commemorated in the Free Trade Hall by a plaque which was put up in 1960. As soon as the girls were set free they were welcomed by a mass demonstration at the Free Trade Hall, organized by the Independent Labour Party with Keir Hardie [q.v.] as principal speaker; the wit and accomplished oratory of Christabel captured the audience.

When the general election of 1906 was over Christabel Pankhurst concentrated on working for her degree at Manchester and in that year, with one other, obtained a first class with honours in the final LL.B. examination. She then went to join her family in London where the headquarters of W.S.P.U. were established in Clement's Inn. After an internal convulsion (which was not to be the last), the Union was reformed in the autumn of 1907 and Christabel Pankhurst was appointed its organizing secretary. Her organizing genius was remarkable and it was backed by authority which was absolute. She took little direct part in the militant demonstrations, her work as organizer being too useful to risk the interruptions of imprisonment. On 21 June 1908 the Union, supported by all shades of opinion favouring the women's vote, was responsible for a gigantic rally in Hyde Park, at which half a million people were calculated to be present. Christabel Pankhurst, speaking from a farm-cart, made a speech which was long remembered.

Later in the same year she and her mother were arrested for appealing to the public to help the suffragettes rush the House of Commons. The case came up at

Bow Street on 21 October 1908. Christabel Pankhurst subpoenaed and cross-examined the home secretary, H. J. (later Viscount) Gladstone [q.v.] and the chancellor of the Exchequer, Lloyd George. (Sir) Max Beerbohm [q.v.] was in court and has left this impression of Miss Pankhurst:

She has all the qualities which an actress needs, and of which so few actresses have any. Her whole body is alive with her every meaning. As she stood there with a rustling sheaf of notes in one hand, the other hand did the work of twenty average hands. . . . As she stood there with her head inclined merrily to one side, trilling her questions to the Chancellor of the Exchequer, she was like nothing so much as a little singing bird born in captivity.

In the result she was sent to prison for ten weeks but was released in time for Christmas.

Innumerable plots and ruses sprang from Christabel Pankhurst's fertile brain during the militant campaign, which gathered momentum from 1908 onwards. When the methods of the suffragettes progressed from clashes with the police to attacks on property and arson, the Government decided to arrest the leaders of the Union on a charge of conspiracy (1912). In order to continue the work of organization Christabel Pankhurst escaped to Paris, where she remained in 'hiding' until the outbreak of war. In 1912 there was a second split in the Union which resulted in the removal of its journal *Votes for Women*. To fill this gap Christabel Pankhurst edited a new paper, *The Suffragette*, from Paris. This was conducted with vigour and even ferocity and indulged in many rather wanton diatribes against the male sex.

With the outbreak of war in August 1914 Christabel Pankhurst returned to England to put her talents at the service of the State; she spoke at many recruiting meetings. In 1918 she stood as coalition candidate for Smethwick; although she was unsuccessful she polled a remarkable vote, 8,614, the largest for any woman at that election, the first in which they could take part. In 1919 she became candidate for the Abbey division of Westminster but did not contest an election. With the return of peace there was some discussion whether W.S.P.U. should be continued, not so much for political and militant purposes, but as a rallying force for women in national life. Mrs. Pankhurst and her daughter decided

against this, with the result that both of them became somewhat withdrawn from public notice. Mrs. Pankhurst went to Canada where she was joined by Christabel who subsequently lived much in the United States, proclaiming her belief in the Second Advent. She was appointed D.B.E. in 1936; finally settled in the United States in 1940; and died at Los Angeles 13 February 1958. Her younger sister, Estelle Sylvia, who was born in Manchester in 1882, worked for the suffrage cause in the east end of London: she was imprisoned many times and also forcibly fed. But her violent opposition to the war caused her to be publicly repudiated by her mother. She enthusiastically embraced the Russian revolution and in later years took up the cause of Abyssinian independence, dying in Addis Ababa 27 September 1960.

The youngest sister, Adela Constantia Mary, was born in 1885 and was perhaps the most extreme of the family. She worked for a short time with her mother for the Women's Social and Political Union. When she was in her early twenties she emigrated to Australia where she organized the Women's Party and later the Australian Socialist Party. She published *Put up the Sword* in the first, and was interned in the second, war. She married Tom Walsh, sometime president and secretary of the Australian Seamen's Union, and had one son and three daughters. She died in Australia 23 May 1961.

While the value of militancy in speeding the women's vote is a matter of opinion, the courage and resourcefulness shown by Christabel Pankhurst, at a time when women were still excluded from whole regions of the national life, made forcibly plain to all the world that this exclusion could no longer be maintained. In 1959 a bronze medallion of Christabel by Peter Hills was added to the memorial statue of Emmeline Pankhurst in Victoria Tower Gardens. There is an oil-painting by Ethel Wright in the possession of Mrs. Victor Duval; the National Portrait Gallery has a drawing by Jessie Holliday.

[E. Sylvia Pankhurst, *The Suffragette Movement*, 1931; Dame Christabel Pankhurst, *Unshackled*, ed. Lord Pethick-Lawrence, 1959; Roger Fulford, *Votes for Women*, 1957.]

ROGER FULFORD.

PARKER, ERIC (FREDERICK MOORE SEARLE) (1870–1955), author and journalist, was born at East Barnet, Hertfordshire, 9 October 1870, the eldest son of Frederick Searle Parker, a solicitor of Bedford Row, by his wife, Elisabeth, daughter of William Wilkieson, of Woodbury Hall, Bedfordshire. As a King's scholar at Eton, fishing was already his passion and, with no encouragement, he was a keen naturalist. He went as a postmaster to Merton College, Oxford, where he obtained a second class in classical moderations (1891) and a fourth in *literae humaniores* (1893). Then came a few years of schoolmastering until in 1900, at the age of thirty, he entered journalism as a junior assistant editor on the *St. James's Gazette*, at first under (Sir) Theodore Cook. He soon started to write also for St. Loe Strachey [q.v.] in the *Spectator*, to which he was a regular contributor for twelve years. In 1902 Strachey bought the *County Gentleman*, a sporting weekly devoted mainly to horses, and, with Parker as editor, set about widening its appeal. Meanwhile *Macmillan's Magazine* had serialized Parker's first novel, *The Sinner and the Problem*, published as a book in October 1901 and twice reprinted within three months.

When Strachey's ownership and his editorship of the *County Gentleman* came to an end in 1907, Parker devoted himself with his customary thoroughness to the Surrey volume (1908) in Macmillan's 'Highways and Byways' series, exploring on foot every nook and cranny of the county where much of his life was to be spent; few came to know it better or loved it more. For two years (1908–10) he edited the monthly *Gamekeeper*; and it was then, in *A Book of the Zoo* (1909), that he foresaw that the grey squirrel might 'become a country problem', a couple of decades before it was officially recognized as such. In 1910 Parker was in the running for the post of editor-in-chief of the *Field*; but the trustees regarded him as 'too much of a poet' and appointed the same Theodore Cook with whom he had started his journalistic career. Cook invited Parker to help him and a year later appointed him shooting editor, a post he was to fill with distinction for over twenty years (1911–32). At this time he was writing regularly for the *Field*, *Spectator*, and *Cornhill Magazine*, but he found time to finish a novel of child life, *Promise of Arden* (1912), to prepare with William Hyde *A West Surrey Sketch-book* (1913), and to undertake at the request of Reginald J. Smith [q.v.] a book of reminiscences, *Eton in the 'Eighties* (1914).

In November 1914 Parker was gazetted to a captaincy in the 5th battalion of the Queen's Royal West Surrey Regiment, in which he served until June 1918, when he was sent to the War Office. During the war years he wrote *Shooting Days* (1918) and began *Playing Fields* (1922), the story of life at a prep. school and at Eton as seen through the eyes of a schoolboy; it has been described as the best school story ever written. Between the wars not a year passed without the appearance of at least one book written, compiled, or edited by him. A few titles must suffice to indicate their range: *Elements of Shooting* (1924), *Between the Wickets* (1926), *Field, River and Hill* (1927), *English Wild Life* (1929), *Ethics of Egg-Collecting* (1935), *The Gardener's England* (1936), and the autobiographical *Memory Looks Forward* (1937).

In 1928 Parker became editor of 'The Lonsdale Library of Sports, Games & Pastimes'. Then, in December 1929, came Sir Leicester Harmsworth's offer of the post of editor-in-chief of the *Field*. In the eight years which followed he put new life into the weekly, widening its interest and appeal. His most noteworthy achievement was the devastating exposure of the trapping and caging of linnets, goldfinches, and other small birds which was largely responsible for the passage of the Protection of Birds Act, 1933. He also campaigned against the docking of horses, which was later made illegal. At the end of 1937 Parker gave up his post with the *Field*, so that he might have more time for writing and broadcasting, and accepted a seat on the board.

His literary output was maintained, although with less emphasis on field sports and more on cricket, dogs, natural history, and gardens. He contributed the volume on Surrey (1947) to Hale's 'County Books' series and added to the Lonsdale Library *The History of Cricket* (1950). The last of his fifty-odd books, *Surrey Gardens* (1954), was published shortly before his death at his home at Hambledon, Surrey, 13 February 1955.

In his bearing, talk, kindness, honesty of mind and purpose, outlook on life, and general character Parker was outstandingly an English country gentleman. He had a fund of humour, was a keen observer, and wrote with ease and sureness. He enabled readers to see about them things which had hitherto passed unobserved, and shared with them delightfully his appreciation of beauty in the countryside.

Parker married in 1902 Ruth Margaret (died 1933), daughter of Ludwig Messel, of Nymans, Handcross, Sussex. They had four sons, two of whom were killed in the war of 1939–45, and two daughters.

[Eric Parker, *Memory Looks Forward*, 1937; *The Times*, 14 February 1955; private information; personal knowledge.]

JOHN CRIPPS.

PARKER, JOHN (1875–1952), founder and editor of *Who's Who in the Theatre*, was born Jacob Solomons, in New York City 28 July 1875, the only child of David Solomons and his wife, Florence Joel. His father, a sailor, was a native of Warsaw, but all family links with Poland were lost after his death by drowning in 1881. The widow, who had been born in Cardiff, decided to return to the United Kingdom where some of her family still lived; choosing to keep both her son and her independence, she took the post of caretaker at Clarence Chambers, King William Street, in the City of London, and enrolled her son at the Whitechapel Foundation School where he was a fellow pupil of Herman Finck.

After a short period as an office boy, he accepted the offer of a commercial acquaintance to return to the United States to improve his prospects, but within a few months he found himself stranded and obliged to work his passage back to England. It was about this time that he decided, on the advice of his mother, to adopt the name of John Parker, which he legalized in 1917. There is evidence that between the years 1892 and 1903, while employed in various capacities, Parker had made a start in journalism; he soon became sufficiently well informed on theatrical matters to be able to write to the eminent critic, Clement Scott [q.v.], of the *Daily Telegraph* and point out errors of fact where they occurred in his columns. This enthusiasm and passion for accuracy appealed to Scott who allowed the boy the pleasure of carrying his copy to the newspaper office, encouraged his talent for research, and from 1900 published regular contributions from him in his weekly paper the *Free Lance*. In 1903 Parker was appointed London manager, critic, and correspondent of the *New York Dramatic News*, a post which he held for seventeen years, and in the same year he was made the London correspondent of the *New York Dramatic Mirror*. From 1901 until his death, Parker managed to divide his time between his business as a shipping agent and his work for the theatre which was his first love.

During the nineteenth century several reference works of dramatic biography appeared, but none of these was to reach more than two issues. For the 1907 edition of the *Green Room Book* Parker was invited to provide additional information for the biographies and to contribute the entire section on the American theatre. He then succeeded as editor but was able to bring out only two more editions (1908 and 1909) before it came to an end with the death of the publisher.

Parker's reputation as a theatre historian had by this time become well established, and in 1912 Sir Isaac Pitman & Sons, Ltd., published his new venture *Who's Who in the Theatre*. The success of the very first edition brought from Sir Herbert Beerbohm Tree [q.v.] the commendation 'As a monument of industry, *Who's Who in the Theatre* seems to me to be absolutely pyramidal.... It is a work which assuredly deserves the gratitude of everyone connected with the theatre.' Over a period of forty years, until his death, and surviving the publishing hazards of two world wars, Parker compiled eleven editions of his *Who's Who* almost single-handed, an astonishing achievement in view of the ever-expanding spheres of the theatre with the growth of the cinema and television. His success as an editor lay in the accuracy and balance of his records. The motto which headed his editorial stationery 'Sine timore, aut favore' indicated his inflexible rule, a rule which made him a number of enemies in the profession, principally by his refusal to allow his subjects to falsify their ages. It is conceivable that the unsolved mystery of the burglary of his study in September 1928 was the work of some aggrieved actor. All Parker's notes and all the copy for his sixth edition, then ready for press, were stolen. After his first shock had subsided, he rewrote in his own hand all the new material, including more than 450 new biographies.

Parker was a regular contributor to this Dictionary. He also found time to give active support to the Critics' Circle, of which he was a founder-member, honorary secretary (1924–52), and in one year president. In 1937 he represented the Circle as British delegate at the International Congress of Critics in Paris. He was also the honorary editor of the *Critics' Circular*.

With little time to spare for the more

conventional recreations, Parker had one passing 'hobby' and one sport, albeit as a spectator. He was an accomplished illuminator, and spent many a Sunday morning, during 1905 and 1906, in night-shirt, silk dressing-gown, and smoking cap, designing and carrying out, in all their elaborate colour and gold leaf, two 'vellums' for presentation to Lionel Brough [q.v.] and (Dame) Ellen Terry [q.v.], respectively, on the celebration of their stage jubilees. His enthusiasm for cricket—he was a member of the Surrey County Cricket Club—was lifelong, but chiefly as a spectator.

Parker was fastidious in both dress and speech. At one time he took lessons in elocution and delighted in imparting what he had learned to his family. In 1899 he married Edith Maud (died 1942), daughter of his schoolmaster, Montague Belfield Pizey, by whom he had a daughter, and a son who produced a twelfth edition of *Who's Who in the Theatre* in 1957. In 1944 Parker married, secondly, Doris Mary, daughter of George Sinclair. He died in Twickenham 18 November 1952.

[*The Times*, 20 November 1952; *Green Room Book*, 1909; private information.]

FREDA GAYE.

PARSONS, SIR JOHN HERBERT (1868–1957), ophthalmologist and physiologist, was born in Bristol 3 September 1868, the youngest of the five children of Isaac Jabez Parsons, grocer, and his wife, Mary Goodhind Webb. He was educated at Thomas Turner's private school, Bristol Grammar School, and University College, Bristol, where he studied arts, science, and medicine. His entry into the college was aided by his gaining a Gilchrist scholarship and his medical studies by a Stewart scholarship and the first entrance scholarship to Bristol Royal Infirmary. Leaving Bristol in 1889 he pursued his medical studies at University College, London, where he graduated B.Sc. with honours in physiology (1890) and completed his medical course in St. Bartholomew's Hospital, graduating M.B. in 1892. He thereupon returned to University College as Sharpey scholar and assistant and demonstrator to (Sir) E. A. (Sharpey-) Schafer [q.v.] in physiology. After a short period in general practice in Finchley Parsons found himself compelled to return to his initial interest in physiology and through this took up ophthalmology, becoming a clinical assistant at Moorfields Eye Hospital. Acquiring his F.R.C.S. in

1900, he was elected pathological curator and librarian at Moorfields Hospital and in 1904 was elected to the consulting surgical staff of that hospital and University College Hospital, both of which he served throughout his working life; he was also for a time consulting surgeon to the Hospital for Sick Children, Great Ormond Street. At the same time he conducted a large ophthalmic practice at a house in Queen Anne Street.

Parsons's interest, however, did not lie essentially in hospital work or private practice; to explore the working of the eye and its behaviour in health and disease was his main object in life, first by himself and later by the encouragement of others for the same end. His first book was a small manual, *Elementary Ophthalmic Optics* (1901), an attempt to impress on the student that it was wrong to test a patient's vision or examine him clinically without a thorough understanding of the optics of the methods he was using. Simultaneously he undertook research work on the physiology of the eye in the department of physiology of University College. The innervation of the pupil and the lacrimal gland claimed his attention initially and his fundamental work on the control of the intra-ocular pressure was summarized in his second book, *The Ocular Circulation* (1903). For these researches he obtained the degree of D.Sc. (London, 1904). Thereafter he turned his attention seriously to ocular pathology and from his laboratory at Moorfields there emanated a series of original papers, while the whole subject was correlated and integrated for the first time in his first classical treatise, *The Pathology of the Eye*, which appeared in four volumes (1904–8). With its appearance Parsons became a world authority and his hospital clinics a Mecca for students from abroad. At the same time his maturing clinical experience was reflected in the appearance of a comprehensive and yet concise clinical textbook, *Diseases of the Eye*, which, soon after its appearance in 1907, became the most popular of its type; the tenth edition appeared in 1942 and was reprinted in 1944, whereafter he transferred the authorship to other hands.

After this preliminary phase which by itself could well be said to constitute a life-work, Parsons's interests diverted to the psychology of vision and perception; in this vast field his main thesis was that perceptive phenomena could be analysed only on a factual basis, that the only safe approach to their understanding was a materialistic one through physiological experimentation, and that introspective psychology divorced from biology was dangerous. Endowed with untiring energy, unusually wide knowledge and critical ability as well as great scientific honesty, he attained a unique place in the scientific world by the publication of four books on this wide subject, two of them classical, *An Introduction to the Study of Colour Vision* (1915) and *An Introduction to the Theory of Perception* (1927), and two of them small and incidental, *Mind and the Nation: A Précis of Applied Psychology* (1918) and *The Springs of Conduct* (1950), the latter a summary of his neuropsychological creed written when he was eighty-two.

Parsons had wide interests in public, professional, and cultural life. He served on several government commissions, his greatest contribution in this respect being in the adequate lighting of factories, a subject gravely neglected at the time. During the thirty-one years of the activities of the departmental committee set up by the Home Office on factory lighting he played a prominent part; and he was one of the founder-members of the Illuminating Engineering Society of which he was the first chairman of council, its president in 1924, and honorary member (1943). In professional societies he participated wholeheartedly. To the Ophthalmological Society of the United Kingdom, which he joined in 1900, he made some 140 contributions and was its president in 1925. He was president of the Royal Society of Medicine (1936–8) and honorary fellow (1942). In international ophthalmology he took a prominent part, directing his influence towards the resumption of friendly relations between ophthalmologists throughout the world after the war of 1914–18; he was one of the moving spirits in creating the International Council of Ophthalmology (1927) and in arranging for the very successful 13th International Congress of Ophthalmology in Amsterdam (1929). In addition he acted as chairman of the editorial committee of the *British Journal of Ophthalmology* from its foundation in 1917 to 1948. He was one of the founder-members of the British Council of Ophthalmologists and was largely responsible for its substitution by the Faculty of Ophthalmologists to serve as the co-ordinating and academic custodian of the speciality. Of the greatest importance was his association with the Medical Research Council on which he served in 1929–32; to his influence was largely due its efforts to maintain an interest in research in visual problems in the period between the two wars. In the first of these he served initially with the rank of captain as ophthalmic surgeon to the 3rd London General Hospital (1916–17) and then with the rank of colonel as ophthalmic consultant to the Home Forces (1917–18), and thereafter served in an advisory capacity to the Army, the Navy, and the Royal Air Force. In 1919 he was appointed C.B.E.

The Royal College of Surgeons invited Parsons to give the Arris and Gale lectures (1903–4); from the British Medical Association he received the Middlemore prize in 1904 and again in 1914. From the Ophthalmological Society he received the Nettleship gold medal (1907) and the Bowman lectureship (1925); from the Oxford Ophthalmological Congress the Doyne medal (1919); and from the American Ophthalmological Society the Howe medal (1936). He was given the honorary degree of D.Sc. from his own university of Bristol (1925) and an LL.D. from Edinburgh (1927). In 1921 he was elected F.R.S., serving on its council (1926–7 and 1941–3) and becoming a vice-president (1941–2). In 1922 he was knighted. On his eightieth birthday he was presented with his portrait, painted by John Gilroy, by the Faculty of Ophthalmologists and the Ophthalmological Society; and the same occasion was marked by the appearance of a special number of the *British Journal of Ophthalmology* consisting of contributions made by his scientific and clinical pupils and associates.

Parsons's life was full of work, but he also enjoyed leisure. He appreciated good company and was a delightful host, particularly to the young, on whom he lavished much kindness, assisting them freely in their work and professional troubles. He had a great appreciation of music and used to go to the opera armed with a score. His knowledge of languages was wide and Persian literature and art interested him greatly. Golf was an absorbing hobby most of his life and even in advanced age he frequently found refreshment and rest in periodic holiday cruises.

At the outbreak of war in 1939 Parsons left London and retired from practice, lending his London house to the French Red Cross, and went to live in Leeds with long-standing friends, but visited London frequently. In his later years progressive deafness, an annoying tremor, and cardiac troubles, disabilities exasperating to a nature so forceful and active, gradually curtailed his activities. He died in London 7 October 1957. His wife, Jane Roberta, daughter of John Hendrie, of Uddingston, near Glasgow, whom he married in 1894, died in 1911, and he left a son and a daughter. His portrait hangs in the board-room of the Institute of Ophthalmology, university of London.

[Personal knowledge.]

STEWART DUKE-ELDER.

PATERSON, SIR WILLIAM (1874-1956), mechanical engineer, was born at Roslin, Midlothian, 5 August 1874, the fifth (and youngest) son of James Paterson, director and manager of Stewart and Widnall, Ltd., by his wife, Anne Hall. He was educated in Edinburgh at the Heriot-Watt College, afterwards serving six years' apprenticeship in the drawing office and workshops of a firm of paper mill engineers. From his earliest days he realized the importance of water treatment developments and filed patents in 1898-1902 covering processes and equipment in this field. In the latter year he formed in Edinburgh a company concerned particularly with the purification of water for industrial purposes and public drinking supplies. In 1904 he transferred his offices to London and for some years shared lodgings with two other Scotsmen also destined to attain eminence in their professions—John Anderson (later Viscount Waverley, q.v.) and (Sir) Alexander Gray, both of whom were present at the celebration in 1952 of the jubilee of the founding of William Paterson's company.

In the earlier years of his company he was particularly concerned in developing and patenting improved means for treating water for industrial use, a matter of great importance with the growing development of large manufacturing organizations, but within ten years he had directed his attention to the need for improved methods for purifying public drinking-water supplies. Amongst early installations in this field was one for the Weardale & Consett Water Company for the pre-treatment of two and a half million gallons of water per day to improve its condition before passing through slow sand filters then in general use. This pre-treatment greatly prolonged the runs of the slow filters and obviated large and costly extensions. In 1910 he designed and installed a plant for the complete purification of four million gallons daily pumped from the river Severn for the drinking supply of Cheltenham, and this was the first plant in Britain using chlorine for the routine sterilization of a water supply to eliminate pathological bacteria. He was always interested in the prevention of water-borne diseases, and had extensive researches carried out on the use of chlorine gas for this purpose, either alone or in connection with ammonia to form chloramine. This led to important improvements in the manner of and equipment for applying these reagents for water sterilization, and also in the use of ozone (O_3) for the same purpose.

In 1913 Paterson was asked by the Indian Army medical authorities to visit their headquarters in Poona to advise on the most suitable means of purifying the polluted water supplies in general use in India, where widespread outbreaks of dysentery and other water-borne diseases were common. A successful demonstration plant built at Poona led to the adoption of this process throughout India and eventually to the formation of a Paterson company in that country.

The war of 1939-45 presented problems in the supply of drinking water to troops in the field, and a mobile filtration and sterilizing unit was designed which combined light weight and compactness with high capacity and great efficiency. This type of filter was adopted widely by the British, American, and colonial forces, and was responsible to a large degree for the extremely low incidence of fatal outbreaks of water-borne diseases.

Many important new developments in water treatment were the result of Paterson's activities including the excess lime process of water softening and sterilization for public supplies in which he collaborated with Sir Alexander Houston (then director of water examination of the Metropolitan Water Board) and the use of chlorine gas for inhibiting algal accumulations in power-station condenser systems, a method adopted on a world-wide scale, with consequent important fuel economies.

Paterson was a man of singular directness of thought, with the power of simplifying problems and mechanical designs by the elimination of all non-essential or adscititious features.

As a result of his lifelong association with John Anderson he was asked by him in 1938 to devise a form of shelter suitable for economical construction and simple and rapid erection in individual homes for protection against blast from bombing attacks. A simple shelter (known as the Anderson shelter) was designed and patented by Paterson and Oscar C. Kerrison, this patent (taken out to prevent commercial exploitation) being presented to the nation. The extensive adoption of this shelter (of which over three million were supplied to the public) was responsible for the saving of many lives.

In 1944 Paterson was knighted. In 1948 he was elected an honorary member of the Institution of Water Engineers, and in the subsequent year an honorary member of the Royal Sanitary Institute. He was the donor to the Institution of Water Engineers of the Whitaker medal and the Alexander Houston medal to be awarded for outstanding papers on the treatment of water supplies.

In January 1955 he retired from active participation in the affairs of the numerous companies comprising the Paterson group. He died in London 9 August 1956. After his death Lady Paterson presented to the Heriot-Watt College a portrait (attributed to Raeburn) of his great hero James Watt.

Paterson married in 1910 Dorothy Isabel, daughter of Herbert Frank Steedman, accountant, of Bournemouth; they had one daughter.

His portrait by Philip Kaufmann is in the possession of the family.

[Private information; personal knowledge.]
O. C. KERRISON.

PEAKE, SIR CHARLES BRINSLEY PEMBERTON (1897–1958), diplomatist, was born 2 January 1897 in Leicester, the third child and only son of William Pemberton Peake, surgeon and medical officer, and his wife, Alice Ambrosing Bucknell. From Wyggeston School, Leicester, he joined the army in 1914, serving throughout the war as an officer in the Leicestershire Regiment. He was mentioned in dispatches and awarded the M.C. He was badly wounded in the leg and suffered from the wound, often severely, throughout his life.

After the war Peake went to Magdalen College, Oxford, where he took his degree in French in 1921. He entered the diplomatic service in 1922. After serving at various posts abroad, he was transferred to the news department of the Foreign Office in 1936 and became its head in 1939. When Lord Halifax [q.v.]

was appointed ambassador in Washington in 1941 Peake accompanied him as a personal assistant and became his intimate and devoted friend. In 1942-3 Peake had the difficult assignment of British representative to the French National Committee; and in 1943-5 he was political adviser to the supreme commander, Allied Expeditionary Force. In 1945 he was appointed to Tangier as consul-general; in 1946 he went as ambassador to Belgrade and in 1951 to Athens. He retired from the Foreign Service in 1957 and acted for a time as special adviser to the Colonial Office on Cyprus.

Peake's principal aptitude was with people. His talents were employed most conspicuously in Yugoslavia, where his term as ambassador covered the period during which Marshal Tito broke with the Cominform (1948). By that time Peake had gained some influence with the Yugoslav leaders and a good understanding of their mentality. He was thus able to play an important part in the delicate task of re-establishing good relations between the western powers and Yugoslavia after a period of considerable bitterness. Most of his time at Athens was overshadowed by the dispute with Greece over Cyprus, which could hardly be mitigated by personal diplomacy.

Peake devoted fully to his work the resources of a colourful and many-sided personality. He was a notable raconteur, whose conversation displayed an often flamboyant command of English and a keen sense both of the dramatic and of the nonsensical. Together with his wife, he was most generous in hospitality and friendship, the reflection of a profoundly and openly religious nature. In 1926 he had married Catherine Marie, daughter of George Wiliam Knight, of the Indian Educational Service; they had four sons. Peake was appointed C.M.G. (1941), K.C.M.G. (1948), and G.C.M.G. (1956). He died in London 10 April 1958.

[The Times, 11 and 17 April 1958; private information; personal knowledge.]
DUNCAN WILSON.

PEARCE, SIR GEORGE FOSTER (1870–1952), Australian statesman, was born at Mount Barker, South Australia, 14 January 1870, the fourth son in the family of ten children of James Pearce, a blacksmith who had emigrated from Cornwall, and his wife, Jane Foster, of London. He was educated at a government school in Redhill until the age of eleven and at fifteen, after some years as a farm labourer, became an apprentice carpenter. On completing his time he moved to Adelaide where he was caught up in the turmoil of the maritime strike and the economic recession. Continuous unemployment induced him to migrate in 1892 to Western Australia where he immediately became associated with the embryonic Labour movement. For the next nine years he worked untiringly organizing unions and agitating for democratic and social reforms. He also did his utmost to interest conservative craft unionists in political action, a frustrating task which fully tested his patience and perseverance. By 1900 he had become the best known and most popular labour leader in the colony.

In 1901 Pearce was elected to the first federal Senate. He retained his seat for thirty-seven years and held ministerial and cabinet rank for twenty-five: as minister for defence in 1908–9, 1910–13, 1914–21, and 1931–4; minister for home and territories, 1921–6; vice-president of the executive council, 1926–9; and minister for external affairs, 1934–7. In the defence department he was responsible for putting into operation the scheme for compulsory military training recommended by Lord Kitchener [q.v.] and in 1913 he established a military aviation school at Point Cook which proved to be the origin of the Royal Australian Air Force. During the war of 1914–18 he arranged and supervised the transportation and provisioning of the Australian troops and in 1919 he came to Britain to take control of their demobilization. On Australia's behalf he signed the peace treaty with Austria at St. Germain. He represented his country also at the Washington conference of 1921–2 and led the Australian delegation to the League of Nations Assembly in Geneva in 1927. At home in the twenties the development schemes showed many signs of his influence, particularly in the efforts made to apply science to industry; and in 1935 he reorganized the Department of External Affairs along lines which substantially endured. He was an exemplary administrator, attentive to detail, willing to take advice but equally willing to take decisions. His counsel was much valued by the prime ministers under whom he served.

In 1916 the Australian Labour movement split irreparably on the question of conscription for overseas military service.

Pearce, W. M. Hughes [q.v.], and a number of other prominent Labour politicians supported conscription, were consequently expelled from the federal Labour Party, and formed a minority Government of their own, soon to be amalgamated in 1917 with the Liberal Party to form a national Government. Hitherto Pearce had been held in high regard by Labour. But the conscription dispute engendered such bitterness that past services were forgotten and for years he was mercilessly harried, his offence heightened by his continual occupancy of ministerial posts in non-Labour Governments. He became increasingly involved in controversy. From 1922 onwards, as Western Australia's only federal minister, he was held accountable for the evils, real and imaginary, which federation had imposed on the state. Although he fought hard for his state's interests Pearce was never a parochial politician and he refused to support irresponsible state rights claims. He strongly opposed the Western Australian secession movement which gathered strength in the early thirties. At the elections of 1937 the 'Put Pearce last' campaign of the leading secessionist body, 'The Dominion League', brought about his defeat.

Pearce made no attempt to re-enter Parliament, but further demands were made upon his great experience. He served on the Commonwealth Grants Commission in 1939–44 and made a considerable contribution during the war of 1939–45 as a member of the Defence Board of Business Administration of which he was chairman from 1940 until it was disbanded in 1947.

Neither outgoing nor convivial, Pearce was a serious-minded man and a teetotaller who lacked the gift, though not a sense, of humour. He was uncommunicative to all but his closest friends and kept his feelings well under control. His political ideas were never extremist. He was an empirical reformer, his political creed stemming from a keen sense of fair play. He often claimed that he sought a 'fair and reasonable' deal for the working class. He was not a socialist yet he possessed the Labour man's traditional fear of monopolies and favoured the nationalization of certain industries. Even in the nineties he was reckoned a moderate among Labour men and it was not long before the movement accepted his ideas as basic policy. He ended his political career opposed to militant trade-union leaders and supporting conservative schemes for Australia's recovery from the world-wide economic collapse. The reforms which most interested him were implemented by the Labour Government of 1910–13 and its Liberal predecessor. Thereafter he had little to offer in the way of new social legislation and he was quite unable to sympathize with the radical socialists who became increasingly influential in Australia.

In 1897 Pearce married Eliza Maude (died 1947), daughter of Richard Barrett, a french polisher, of Perth, Western Australia; they had two sons and two daughters. Pearce was sworn of the Privy Council in 1921 and appointed K.C.V.O. in 1927. He died at his home at Elwood 24 June 1952. He had no firm religious beliefs although towards the end of his life he regularly attended Presbyterian services. A portrait by W. A. Dargie hangs in the library of the Commonwealth Parliament at Canberra.

[Sir G. F. Pearce, *Carpenter to Cabinet*, 1951; Ernest Scott, *Australia During the War*, vol. xi of the *Official History of Australia in the War of 1914–18*, 1936; *West Australian*, 25 June 1952; *Argus*, 1 July 1938.]

JOHN MERRITT.

PEASE, EDWARD REYNOLDS (1857–1955), founder-member and secretary of the Fabian Society, was born 23 December 1857 at Henbury Hill, near Bristol. He was the eldest son by his third marriage of Thomas Pease, a well-to-do retired woolcomber; his mother was Susanna Ann Fry of the Quaker family of cocoa manufacturers. Thomas Pease was himself a Quaker, a cousin of the more famous Peases of Darlington [qq.v.]. Edward Pease was educated at home, until at the age of seventeen he went up to London to become a clerk in a firm of textile merchants run by his brother-in-law (Sir) Thomas Hanbury. Six years later he went into partnership with a stockbroker; but his heart was not in the City, and when in 1884 his father died and left him £3,000 he made all haste to leave it.

Meantime his future for his long life had, in effect, been settled. Through his cousin Emily Ford who was an ardent spiritualist he had made the acquaintance of another spiritualist, Frank Podmore [q.v.], the biographer of Robert Owen [q.v.]; and as a result of long talks, conducted sometimes while waiting for spirits to materialize, Podmore induced

Pease to join an earnest body called the Fellowship of the New Life, founded by the wandering scholar Thomas Davidson. The objects of the Fellowship were all-embracing, including 'the attainment of a perfect character by all and each'; and not long after joining, Pease and Podmore, with several others, decided to form a rather less ambitious body, the socialist Fabian Society, which was officially founded in January 1884 and was almost immediately joined by Bernard Shaw and later by Sidney Webb [qq.v.]. Its early meetings were held in Pease's rooms at Osnaburgh Street, St. Pancras.

Pease, like many other socialists of his day, had been much influenced by William Morris [q.v.], and after his father's death he decided that he ought to become a working craftsman. He trained himself as a cabinet-maker and in 1886, having failed to secure employment in Morris's firm, he moved to Newcastle, where he worked as a cabinet-maker for three years and in 1889 married Mary Gammell (Marjory), daughter of the Rev. George Smyttan Davidson, minister of the parish of Kinfauns. Sydney (later Lord) Olivier [q.v.] took over the secretaryship of the Fabian Society; but Pease kept in close touch. Following the great success of *Fabian Essays in Socialism* (1889), the Fabian Society decided to venture upon employing paid staff. Pease was taken on in 1890 as part-time secretary at £1 a week; and earned a similar sum nominally as secretary to Sidney Webb, but really on Fabian duties. (A year previously, Webb and Pease had gone together on a tour of the New World.) After a year, the appointment was made full-time, and Pease held it until 1913. In that year he inherited a capital sum from his uncle, Joseph Storrs Fry [q.v.], which enabled him to retire from paid work. The parting gift of the society was a set of the *Encyclopædia Britannica*, exactly appropriate, Shaw remarked, since Pease was now to be deprived of daily access to Sidney Webb. His post at the Fabian Society was taken by W. Stephen Sanders while he himself became honorary secretary (acting as general secretary from 1915 to 1918 while Sanders was in the army), and retained that position and his seat on the executive committee until the reconstruction of the society in 1939.

Pease's secretaryship coincided almost exactly with all the excitements of the first thirty years of the Fabian Society. He was a founder; he became its paid servant just when its influence was beginning to make itself felt in politics—the Newcastle programme of the Liberal Party, which was largely a Fabian draft, was carried in 1891, and in the London County Council elections of the following year the Progressives, including Webb, came home to victory on a Fabian policy; Pease took part in the formation of the Labour Representation Committee which became the Labour Party and sat as Fabian representative on its executive for fourteen years; and he was the faithful watchdog of the Fabian executive through its recurrent political excitements, from the quarrel about the South African war to the famous battle of Shaw and Webb with H. G. Wells [q.v.] recalled in the pages of *The New Machiavelli* (1911), and the later Guild Socialist attack led by G. D. H. Cole [q.v.] and William Mellor. In Pease, as Wells remarked, the executive had a man who 'did the work of a cabinet minister for the salary of a clerk'; and they invested well. In all the disputes, Pease was firmly on the side of the strict collectivist faith of the leaders; he admired Sidney Webb more than any other man in the world and was convinced of his rightness on every occasion, and of the foolishness of his opponents. After the outbreak of war the storms died away; during the long period of quiescence there was little for Pease to do, and he turned more and more to local political work—and gardening—at his home in Limpsfield in Surrey, where he had a number of distinguished and like-minded friends; when the society revived he was too old and too deaf to take part. He wrote its official *History* in 1916 (revised ed. 1925), several Fabian Tracts, as well as reviews and articles, and a book on *The Case for Municipal Drink Trade* (1904); but his main work was administrative.

Pease was a shy man whose rather gruff manner and dislike of all ceremony sometimes obscured at first sight his natural kindliness, which was none the less considerable. He was a man of his own pleasures, including Norse sagas; and he was a completely disinterested servant of the cause he had made his own. His wife, herself a magistrate and local councillor, died in 1950; two sons survived him when he died at Limpsfield 5 January 1955.

[E. R. Pease, *History of the Fabian Society*, revised ed. 1925, and unpublished reminiscences; Beatrice Webb, *Our Partnership*, ed. Barbara Drake and Margaret Cole, 1948;

Fabian Society records; *Fabian Journal* March 1955; private information; personal knowledge.]   Margaret Cole.

PEERS, Sir CHARLES REED (1868–1952), antiquary, was born at Westerham, Kent, 22 September 1868, the eldest son of the Rev. William Henry Peers, then curate at Westerham, and later vicar of Harrow Weald and lord of the manor of Chiselhampton, Oxfordshire, and his wife, Dora Patience, daughter of William Carr, of Dene Park, Tonbridge. Peers was educated at Charterhouse and at King's College, Cambridge, where he obtained a second class in both parts of the classical tripos (1890–91). He then studied at Dresden and Berlin and in 1893 entered the office of the distinguished architect (Sir) Thomas Jackson [q.v.] who encouraged his pupil's early interest in medieval architecture. A season in Egypt as a colleague of Somers Clarke at El Kab and elsewhere was followed by six years' work as a practising architect; but in 1902 he returned to Egypt for another season, and thereafter devoted himself exclusively to the historical and archaeological aspects of his profession. In 1903 he was appointed architectural editor to the *Victoria County Histories of England*, and the high reputation acquired by these *Histories* as an architectural record was in considerable measure his creation.

When in 1910 he was appointed inspector of ancient monuments in the Office of Works, a wide administrative field was opened to him. His first task was to advise on the reform of the Ancient Monuments Act which, as formulated in 1882, had long fallen behind the growing sense of responsibility for the well-being of ancient sites and buildings. The new Act of 1913 enlarged the powers of the commissioners of works to conserve ancient structures and to prevent or at any rate delay damage to listed 'monuments'. To cope with these new charges, the inspectorate was increased; Peers became chief inspector of ancient monuments, with inspectors for England, Scotland, and Wales. The Act was further strengthened in 1931, still under Peers's guidance. He retired in 1933 on reaching the age of sixty-five.

During the twenty-four years in which Peers thus controlled the Ancient Monuments Department, he laid down the principles which have governed architectural conservation in the United Kingdom and have served as a model in other parts of the world. His cardinal principle was to retain but not to restore the surviving remains of an ancient structure; and in this respect he departed emphatically from the tradition of Viollet-le-Duc and his successors in France and Italy, where exuberant restoration frequently obscured the evidence upon which it was based. The stern puritanism with which Peers stripped abbeys and castles of their 'romantic' but destructive weeds found compensation in the smooth lawns and clean masonry which became a sort of sign-manual of our national monuments under his direction. Above all, his sound scholarship ensured that the historical evidence implicit in these structures was preserved and displayed, both by clearance on the ground and by the publication of succinct guides, many of them written by himself. If the process of clearance was sometimes carried through with less than the meticulous supervision demanded by modern standards, the immensity of Peers's pioneer task is at least a partial excuse. In matters of excavation, which lay outside his personal experience, he was always ready to listen to criticism and to accept advice if proffered from authoritative quarters. But he never suffered fools gladly.

In his retirement his experience was put to active use in other ways. In 1935 he became surveyor of Westminster Abbey, where his ashes were eventually buried in the Islip chapel. He was consulting architect to York Minster and Durham Cathedral, and at Durham supervised the difficult enterprise of pinning the Bishop's Castle to the steep rock from which it was slipping. He was also seneschal of Canterbury Cathedral, and at Oxford he sat on the diocesan advisory committee and carried out architectural work within the university. Alongside all these preoccupations he was throughout his life employed, often anonymously, in a great variety of ways. From its establishment in 1908, he was closely associated with the Royal Commission on Historical Monuments (England) and in 1921 became a commissioner. To the preparation of the Commission's reports he gave much time and thought, and regularly found opportunity to collaborate with the Commission's staff in the field. From 1900 until 1903 he was honorary editor of the *Archaeological Journal*, the publication of the Royal Archaeological Institute; and in 1901 his election to a fellowship of the Society of

Antiquaries began a long and fruitful association with that senior body. In 1908 he became its secretary, and occupied the office until 1921 when he was elected director. From 1929 to 1934 he held the five-year tenure of the presidency, and to the end he was closely identified with the society's interests. In 1938 he received its gold medal. Other honours came to him: the C.B.E in 1924; knighthood in 1931; the Order of knight commander of St. Olaf when he went in 1936 to Oslo as the retiring president of the Congress of Prehistoric and Protohistoric Sciences; honorary doctorates of Leeds (1933) and London (1936); the Royal gold medal of the Royal Institute of British Architects (1933). He was an honorary fellow of King's College, Cambridge, and a governor of Charterhouse. He was a trustee of the British Museum from 1929 and of the London Museum from 1930, and he was antiquary to the Royal Academy of Arts. He was also a fellow of the British Academy (1926).

In his early days Peers had sought a post in the British Museum. His successful competitor, (Sir) George Hill [q.v.], later director of the museum, became his lifelong friend, and it was in the company of chosen companions such as Hill that Peers shone as a conversationalist, with the quick wit and wide learning that sometimes suggested another age. His was in the fullest sense a cultivated mind, sympathetic to the listener but sharpened by idiosyncrasy. As a companion he was an unceasing stimulus, with an ardour which, in the field, stretched the endurance of his associates. With the younger generation in particular he was always at home, and many of his successors owed more to his restless and comprehensive intelligence than they themselves perhaps fully realized. In 1924 he returned to live in the family Georgian manor house at Chiselhampton, where he entertained his friends in a singularly appropriate setting. His spare time was devoted to his garden and his farms under increasingly difficult economic conditions.

In 1899 Peers married Gertrude Katherine (died 1953), daughter of the late Rev. Frederick Shepherd, vicar of Stoke-sub-Hamdon, Somerset, by whom he had three sons. He died at Coulsdon, Surrey, 16 November 1952.

[C. A. Ralegh Radford in *Proceedings* of the British Academy, vol. xxxix, 1953; private information; personal knowledge.]
MORTIMER WHEELER.

PEERS, EDGAR ALLISON (1891-1952), Hispanic scholar and educationist, was born at Leighton Buzzard 7 May 1891, the only son and elder child of John Thomas Peers, civil servant, by his wife, Jessie Dale, daughter of Charles Allison. From Dartford Grammar School and study abroad he proceeded to Christ's College, Cambridge, of which he was a scholar and prizeman, his first interests being English and French literature. In 1910 he obtained his B.A., London, with second class honours in English and French, and in 1912 at Cambridge a first class in the medieval and modern languages tripos. He shared the Winchester reading prize (1912), and won the Harness (1913) and the Members' English essay (1914) prizes. From 1913 to 1919 he taught successively at Mill Hill, Felsted, and Wellington as modern languages master. His first publications still concerned English and French literature (*Elizabethan Drama and its Mad Folk*, 1914; *The Origins of French Romanticism*, with M. B. Finch, 1920), but already he was becoming attracted to Spain, and in 1920 he was appointed to the Gilmour chair of Spanish at Liverpool, where he remained thereafter.

Peers was among the first to realize the importance and the potentialities of Spanish studies in Great Britain after the war of 1914-18. Through lectures, visits to schools, teachers' conferences, vacation courses in England and in Spain, and the editing of a steady stream of textbooks, anthologies, and study aids (notably *Spain, A Companion to Spanish Studies*, 1929; *A Handbook to the Study and Teaching of Spanish*, 1938; *A Critical Anthology of Spanish Verse*, 1948) he laboured indefatigably and with great effect to further them at both school and university level. Always keenly interested in the methods and aims not merely of modern language teaching but of higher studies in general, he wrote under the pseudonym of Bruce Truscot two books, *Redbrick University* (1943) and *Redbrick and These Vital Days* (1945), which made a major contribution, from the standpoint of the modern civic university, to the discussion of university problems and policies at the close of the war of 1939-45. To his talent for organizing he gave expression in a number of directions. He founded in 1918, and was for eleven years honorary secretary of, the Modern Humanities Research Association, and its president in 1931-2; founded in 1923 and

edited until his death the quarterly *Bulletin of Spanish* (from 1949 *Hispanic*) *Studies*; founded in 1934 at Liverpool the Institute of Hispanic Studies; and was educational director from 1943 to 1946 of the Hispanic Council.

These manifold activities threw into the higher relief a record in scholarship impressive both in its scope and in its originality. Two fields in Spanish letters, nineteenth-century romanticism and the sixteenth-century mystics, he made particularly his own while they were still comparatively little known and studied even in Spain. Much penetrating spade-work and genuine research, fructifying in both cases in a number of preliminary volumes, underlay his great *History of the Romantic Movement in Spain* (2 vols., 1940) and his *Studies of the Spanish Mystics* (2 vols., 1927-30). The latter, along with the masterly translations of the complete works of St. John of the Cross (3 vols., 1934-5) and of St. Teresa (3 vols., 1946, and her *Letters*, 2 vols., 1951), caused Spanish mysticism to be known and appreciated by English readers as never before. His achievement here, which received the *imprimatur* of the Catholic Church, was the more remarkable in one who was neither a Roman Catholic by persuasion nor a theologian by training. A number of his critical works in both these fields were republished in Spanish translation in Spain. Peers's other great enthusiasm was Catalonia and its medieval splendours: of Ramon Lull he translated much, including *Blanquerna* (1926), and wrote a full-scale biography (1929), while in *Catalonia Infelix* (1937) he traced a sympathetic picture of the Catalan people and its history.

Peers's interest in Spain was always warm and personal. Over many years he spent there some four months out of every twelve and a number of travel volumes, chief among them *Spain, A Companion to Spanish Travel* (1930) and *The Pyrenees, French and Spanish* (1932), bear witness to his feelings for and gift in describing the Spanish scene. A close student no less of contemporary events, he analysed these for close on a quarter of a century in 'Spain Week by Week', a regular feature of the *Bulletin of Spanish Studies*. The outbreak of the Spanish civil war in July 1936 thus found him admirably equipped to interpret to the English-speaking world its underlying causes. This he did in *The Spanish Tragedy* which, written with striking prescience, appeared within three months of the outbreak of the conflict and was many times reprinted. *The Spanish Dilemma* (1940) and *Spain in Eclipse* (1943) provided a similarly penetrating guide to its aftermath. Himself an Anglican of deep religious conviction, he wrote in *Spain, the Church and the Orders* (1939) a warm defence of the record of the Catholic Church in Spain.

Peers received the honorary degree of LL.D. from Glasgow University in 1947. Foreign distinctions included visiting professorships of English literature at Madrid University (1928 and 1929), of modern comparative literature at Columbia University (1929–30), and of Spanish at the universities of New Mexico and California (1930). He was Rede lecturer at Cambridge (1932), Centennial lecturer at New York University (1932), and Taylorian lecturer at Oxford (1939), and was a member and medallist of the Hispanic Society of America, and honorary member of the American Academy of Arts and Sciences, and of the Institut d'Estudis Catalans.

Peers lived single-mindedly for his subject, and accomplished so much in part through meticulous planning and use of his time, down to the shortest train journey. Apart from a keen delight in music he confessed to no recreations, and was of somewhat brusque exterior and approach, although affable and given to the exercise of a keen sense of mimicry in the company of intimate friends. He married in 1924 Marion, daughter of James Frederic Young, director of education for Devon; there were no children. He died at Liverpool 21 December 1952.

[*Bulletin of Hispanic Studies*, No. 117, January–March 1953 (memorial number with selective bibliography); private information; personal knowledge.]

WILLIAM C. ATKINSON.

PEPLER, SIR GEORGE LIONEL (1882–1959), town planner, was born at Croydon, Surrey, 24 February 1882, the third child and second son of George Henry Pepler, brewer, and his wife, Emma Florence Mills. Educated at Bootham School, York, and the Leys School, Cambridge, and articled to Walter Hooker, surveyor, of Croydon, he carried on a practice in surveying and the then emerging vocation of town planning from 1905 until 1914 in partnership with Ernest G. Allen. They were awarded three gold medals at housing exhibitions in 1908 and 1910 and were among the first to specialize in laying out new villages and housing estates for landowners: among others at Fallings Park near Wolverhampton and at Knebworth, Hertfordshire. During that period Pepler became a member of the Garden City (later Town and Country Planning) Association, and was active in the advocacy of the garden city concept and of the operation by local authorities of their permissive planning powers under the first Town Planning Act, of 1909. In 1914 John Burns [q.v.], the 'father' of the Act, called Pepler into the planning administration of the Local Government Board where he succeeded Thomas Adams as chief technical planning officer, a position which he retained, through several changes of his designation and that of the department, until 1946.

Pepler's qualities proved admirably suited to the task of inducing local authorities to adopt town planning powers and guiding them in putting these into practice. Having a passionate belief in the necessity of planning, as well as persuasiveness, patience, and tact, he was allowed by successive ministers, or perhaps quietly assumed, exceptional freedom and scope in what was essentially propaganda. He was a major influence in the conversion of public and official opinion to acceptance of a new, contentious, and difficult governmental process. The experience and authority which he gained in this key position enabled him, just before his retirement, to make a weighty contribution to the formulation of the Town and Country Planning Act of 1947 which established the planning of all land as a normal function of central and local government.

His work and influence in planning extended far outside his official position. He was one of the founders in 1913 of the Town Planning Institute; its honorary secretary and treasurer until his death; twice president (1919–20, 1949–50); and first gold medallist (1953). Keenly interested in the training of planners, he was unfailingly helpful in encouragement and advice to students and young members of the profession, and was chairman (1930–59) of the Town Planning Joint Examination Board. He attended regularly the annual sessions of the Town and Country Planning Summer School from its foundation in 1933, and was its president in 1943–59.

Realizing the importance and value of exchanges of experience, Pepler was active in the work of the International Federation for Housing and Town Planning of which he was president (1935–8, 1947–52) and thereafter honorary president for life. The survival of the Federation from the disruption of the war of 1939–45 was due mainly to his devotion and that of his second wife (as honorary secretary) during the war years.

Pepler was a member of the regional survey committee for South Wales (1920), of the unhealthy areas committee over which Neville Chamberlain presided (1921), and of the royal commission on common land (1955–8); chairman of the Institution of Professional Civil Servants (1937–42), of the inter-allied committee for physical planning and reconstruction (1942–5), and for many years an active influence in the Council for the Preservation of Rural England and the National Playing Fields Association. With P. W. Macfarlane he prepared the outline plan for the north-east development area (1949) and in 1950–54 he was planning adviser to Singapore.

His interests extended into all the wide range of issues with which planning is interconnected. By his official work and by incessant effort in the education of specialist and general opinion through lectures, conference papers, and articles in learned journals, he made a massive, indeed unique, contribution to progress in his field. His success in this was due to consistency of purpose and thought, with a tactical elasticity of course when obstacles were encountered and a resilient resumption as they were overcome. Always calm and unruffled, he never seemed to seek to dominate opponents, but waited patiently until they saw for themselves the force of his suggestions. He was much aided in this by his sense of humour and gentle wit, which made him highly popular with colleagues and an admirable chairman of committees and conferences. Perhaps his most notable attribute, however, was the disciplined energy with which he carried out any responsibility he undertook. He scarcely ever missed a meeting of any body of which he was a member, or failed to produce punctually any report, article, review, or memorandum he had promised. He was appointed C.B. in 1944, knighted in 1948, and elected an honorary associate of the Royal Institute of British Architects in 1937.

His recreations were mainly out of doors and included golf and other games,

swimming, gardening, and bonfires. He had a cottage in a much-loved countryside at Lulworth, Dorset, where, with his family, for nearly fifty years he spent happy holidays by the sea. In 1960 the headland previously known as East Point, Lulworth Cove, was renamed 'Pepler's Point'.

Pepler married first, in 1903, Edith Amy (died 1942), daughter of Alfred E. Bobbett, solicitor, of Bristol, by whom he had two daughters and one son; secondly, in 1947, Elizabeth, daughter of Eldred Halton, of London, merchant in China; she was deputy chairman of the London County Council in 1956–7. Pepler died at Weymouth 13 April 1959. A posthumous portrait in oils by (Sir) Robin Darwin was presented in 1959 to the Town Planning Institute.

[*Journal* of the Town Planning Institute, June 1959; private information; personal knowledge.]   FREDERIC J. OSBORN.

PERCY, EUSTACE SUTHERLAND CAMPBELL, BARON PERCY OF NEWCASTLE (1887–1958), politician and educationist, was born in London 21 March 1887, the seventh son of Henry George Percy, then Earl Percy and subsequently seventh Duke of Northumberland, by his wife, Lady Edith Campbell, eldest daughter of the eighth Duke of Argyll [q.v.]. He grew up in a household which even in that day was somewhat old-fashioned, dominated by evangelical Christianity, an austere tradition of public service, and a contempt for opulent idleness. He was educated at Eton and at Christ Church, Oxford, where in 1907 he was awarded the Stanhope historical essay prize and placed in the first class of the honour school of modern history. In 1909 he entered the diplomatic service. From 1910 to 1914 he served in the Washington embassy, finding an exuberant interest in many aspects of American life. The Foreign Office, where, apart from another year in Washington, he spent the years 1914–18, was less to his taste, and although he attended the peace conference in 1919 as assistant to Lord Robert Cecil (later Viscount Cecil of Chelwood, q.v.) he resigned from the service in that year. It was his grief then, and more acutely afterwards, that neither the war nor the peace had provided a basis for future Anglo-American co-operation: the social demands of a European embassy or legation would have bored and repelled him.

ιord Eustace Percy stood, unsuccess-
y, as a Conservative candidate for
ιtral Hull in 1919 but in 1921 was
:ted for Hastings, a seat which he held
hout difficulty until he left politics in
;7. His rise, at first, was rapid and,
ετ holding minor office, he was ap-
nted president of the Board of Edu-
ion with a seat in the Cabinet, and was
ιrn of the Privy Council, in November
:4. It was not a time when spectacular
νances could be made. Percy was
ptical about raising the school-leaving
:, deeply interested in the development
technical education, and assiduous in
:ouraging by personal contact the hard-
:ssed men and women on whom the
rden of teaching and administration
. But he was not proving himself
good House of Commons man'. He was
npered by lack of partisanship, by a
» obvious distrust of political pro-
ιncements unrelated to administrative
ιerience, and perhaps by the gradual
.lization of a conclusion which he was
express in 1935, that 'many of the
ιatest crimes and greatest failures of
tory have been due to the attempt to
ιlize the highest human ideals through
litical authority'.
The defeat of the Conservatives in 1929
ιnoved a possibility which had much
racted him, that of going as ambassador
Washington, and his exclusion from
ιce between 1931 and 1935 was fatal
his political career. These were not,
ιwever, idle or wasted years. They saw
ε publication of his *Democracy on Trial*
»31), *Government in Transition* (1934),
.ε *Study of History* (1935), and the
iting of *John Knox*, published in 1937.
s interest in active participation in
litics, though declining, was not yet
tinct. He played some small part in
ιrming, and a prominent part in defend-
ς, the Government's India policy; and
would probably have accepted the
ιcretaryship for war had it been offered
him in 1935. Instead, in June of that
ιar he became minister without portfolio.
.terwards he described his acceptance of
ιt office, with undefined duties and no
ιff, as 'suicidal'. His resignation in
ιrch 1936, during the crisis caused by
ε German re-militarization of the Rhine-
ιd, was not, explicitly, a protest against
ε lack of effective British reaction:
was, rather, the result of a sense of
ιtional, governmental, and personal
ιdequacy.
After a short term as chairman of the

British Council, Percy in 1937 accepted
the rectorship of King's College, Newcastle upon Tyne, into which the College
of Medicine and Armstrong College had
recently been amalgamated. He thus
became head of the Newcastle division
of the university of Durham and vice-
chancellor of the university in rotation
with the warden of the Durham colleges.
Later he came to believe that the federal
structure of the university was a drag
upon the progress of both divisions,
particularly on that of Newcastle, which
he wanted to see established as an independent university. In this he proved to be
a dozen years ahead of events. There were
other things with which he was impatient:
pedantry masquerading as scholarship;
the concept of universities as 'ivory
towers' whose inhabitants, relieved of
public responsibilities, were to pursue
individual excellence in increasingly narrow fields; the failure, on the national
level, to find a solution to the problems of
technological education. In 1944 he was
chairman of a departmental committee on
higher technological education. Yet his
was, for the most part, a genial impatience,
the product of a selfless devotion to his
duties, a fertile imagination, and a determination to translate policy into action.
The speed with which King's College was
able to begin its programme of building
after the war was largely due to the plans
Percy had made in anticipation of new
requirements. But it would be mistaken
to regard him as concerned merely or
chiefly with physical expansion and
administrative efficiency. His greater
contributions to the college and the university lay in the high standard of intellectual and moral integrity which he stood
for and the inspiration of a leadership
which, though occasionally impetuous,
was never harsh or insensitive.
Weakening health determined Percy's
resignation in October 1952 and in the years
of his retirement he wrote *The Heresy of
Democracy* (1954) and *Some Memories*
(1958), a sensitive and perhaps unduly
self-critical piece of autobiography. In
1954–7 he was chairman of the royal commission whose recommendations were
embodied in the Mental Health Act,
1959.
A portrait by Lawrence Gowing, in the
possession of the university of Newcastle,
gives a just impression of Percy's strength
and thoughtfulness. He was not a simple,
but he was an uncomplicated, man, with
depths of serenity and humility beneath

an agile intelligence and a briskness of purpose. In the tradition of his family he was a member of the Catholic Apostolic Church as well as of the Church of England. In his youth it seemed that no great office of state was beyond his reach: it was wholly consistent with his deep religious convictions and his acute sense of public duty that in his last years he should serve as churchwarden and lay-reader at Etchingham in Sussex where he settled after his retirement, and where he took much pleasure in gardening. He had never shown much sympathy for the preoccupations, still less for the opinions, of the sporting aristocrat, but in his youth he shot and hunted a good deal.

In 1918 he married Stella Katherine, daughter of Major-General Laurence George Drummond. It was a marriage of rare and manifest felicity. Lady Percy and their two daughters survived him when he died at Etchingham 3 April 1958. He had been created Baron Percy of New-castle in 1953 and the title became extinct upon his death.

[*The Times*, 5 April 1958; Eustace Percy, *Some Memories*, 1958; *Durham University Journal*, new series, vol. xx, No. 3, June 1959; private information; personal knowledge.]

W. L. Burn.

PERKINS, ROBERT CYRIL LAYTON (1866–1955), entomologist, was born 15 November 1866 at Badminton, the second of the five children of the Rev. Charles Mathew Perkins and his wife, Agnes Martha Beach, daughter of the Rev. Percy Thomas. His grandfather, father, and uncle were all interested in natural history in which Perkins himself showed an interest at a very early age. He was educated at Merchant Taylors' School and Jesus College, Oxford, where after two years, due to the good offices of (Sir) E. B. Poulton [q.v.], he changed from classics to science in which he obtained a fourth class in 1889. His first great interest in entomology was Lepidoptera, but in his last years at school he got in touch with Edward Saunders [q.v.] who fostered his developing interest in Aculeate Hymenoptera which remained a prime interest throughout his life.

Perkins's first employment was as a private tutor at Dartmouth, but in 1891 he was selected by the 'Sandwich Islands committee' (set up by the British Association and the Royal Society) to go as collector to the Hawaiian Islands. There he spent the greater part of the next ten

years, collecting all groups of terrest animals, returning to England perio ally to aid in working out the resu His expeditions into the mountain fore were almost always made alone si native porters refused to stay in the fore Each trip lasted about six weeks, for was unable to carry equipment for longer stay, and being short and spare stature required great stamina for work. In 1895 he met Albert Koebele, a in the next few years helped him at tin with the liberation of insect parasi which Koebele was sending to Honol for the control of pests. In 1897 th visited Mexico and from observations the *Lantana* weed there they started successful use of insects in controlli its spread in the Hawaiian Islands.

In 1902–4 Perkins worked for the boa of agriculture of the Territory of Hawa his concern the inspection of import plants in order to prevent the int duction of pests. In 1904 the Hawaii Sugar Planters' Association added to experimental station a division of ent mology with Perkins as director. T most urgent problem was to preve the havoc being caused in the cane fie by the sugar-cane leaf-hopper. No suitab means could be found of applying insec cides in cane fields. Perkins and Koebe therefore went for six months to Austra to collect the parasites of leaf-hoppers in t cane fields there, where the hoppers a peared to cause little damage. The stocks parasites thus obtained were increased the laboratory for liberation and dispers in the Hawaiian fields where their intr duction proved of great benefit. This wo occupied Perkins throughout the day. night he spent long hours studying t classification of these insects of whi little was known. In several groups was able to correlate various biologic observations with taxonomy, particular in the Dryinidae. The results of this wo were published by the Hawaiian Sug Planters' Association in a series Bulletins.

Perkins retired from his post in 19 on account of ill health and returni to England settled in Devon, but w retained on the staff as a consultir entomologist. Henceforth his work Hawaiian insects was concerned main with taxonomy. He also resumed h study of the British Aculeate Hymeno tera which led to a series of papers on t species of the larger and more difficu genera, greatly simplifying their reco

ion. Associated with this work, he
died the *Stylops* parasites of British
es. He had a large correspondence and
s most prompt in his replies, determin-
: much material for other workers and
particular helping young students of
menoptera. This encouraged a con-
ued interest in the group which was con-
quently one of the best worked of the
ler in Britain, both systematically and
logically. In the early twenties Perkins
ned his attention to the British
wflies in order to aid the Rev. F. D.
rice in his contemplated revision of the
up. This led to preliminary revisions
some of the critical genera.

In addition to his entomological work,
rkins had wide interests in terrestrial
ology and the information which he
pplied on the Hawaiian birds, many of
ich are now extinct, was of con-
lerable importance. He had most acute
sion and a remarkable visual memory.
is greatly aided his flair for both field
d taxonomic work. In the latter he had
faculty for observing and selecting
aracters which vary little within a
ecies and thus making identification
npler.

Although not robust Perkins had a
eat interest in sport. In his young days
enjoyed skating and while working at
artmouth he used to run with the beagles.
bove all else he preferred trout fishing
hich he continued until his eyesight
gan to fail. He retained his great
terest in classics throughout his life.

In 1906 Perkins was awarded an Oxford
Sc. and in 1912 he received the gold
edal of the Linnean Society of London.
e was elected F.R.S. in 1920.

In 1901 Perkins married Zoë Lucy
errard Alatau (died 1940), daughter of
. T. Atkinson, sometime superintendent
' public schools in the Hawaiian Islands,
d granddaughter of Thomas Witlam
tkinson [q.v.]. Of the four sons, one died
infancy. In 1942 Perkins married Mrs.
lara M. J. Senior who died in 1949. In
s last days Perkins went blind; he died
Bovey Tracey 29 September 1955.

[Hugh Scott in *Biographical Memoirs of
ellows of the Royal Society*, vol. ii, 1956;
rsonal knowledge.]   J. F. PERKINS.

ERRING, WILLIAM GEORGE
RTHUR (1898–1951), director of the
oyal Aircraft Establishment, was born
; December 1898 at Gillingham, Kent,
e eldest son of John Richard Brooking
erring, a shipwright, and his wife, Alice

Johns. Educated locally, it seemed natural
that he should start his career by becoming apprenticed at the Royal Naval
Dockyard, Chatham, in 1913. This gave
him very wide experience in all branches
of ship work, both design and construction. With a scholarship from the
Worshipful Company of Shipwrights he
took the three-year course at the Royal
Naval College, Greenwich, where in 1922
in the final examination he gained a first
class professional certificate in naval
architecture. He was next awarded an
1851 Royal Commission postgraduate
research scholarship with which he
worked for two years in the Froude ship
tank at the National Physical Laboratory,
Teddington. During this time he became
an associate member of both the Institution of Naval Architects and the North-
East Coast Institution of Engineers and
Shipbuilders, and won a prize for a paper
on 'The Stability of Ships'. Another
paper on 'The Influence of the Type of
Engine on the Running Costs of Ships'
was significant in revealing that he was
not only well qualified in the more scientific aspects of ship propulsion (he made a
study of the application of airscrew vortex
theory to the performance of ships' propellers), but had also a wide appreciation
of the many factors affecting the overall
economy of ships' operation. This breadth
of approach was later of profound
importance in a different field.

Perring next sought to join one of the
leading shipbuilding firms, but owing to
the onset of the industrial depression they
were not recruiting. Finally, he applied
in 1925 for a modest post in the Royal
Aircraft Establishment at Farnborough,
thus changing his professional field from
ship design to aeronautics—a change
not very violent, but fortunate for
aeronautics and one which gave him at
that time much better opportunity.
He spent several years on wind tunnels at
Farnborough, working on a wide variety
of tests, and was then sent for six months
to Felixstowe to gain experience in marine
aircraft before returning to Farnborough to help construct and operate
an entirely new flying-boat test tank. In
1937 he was promoted to take charge of
the design and construction of the new
high-speed tunnel at Farnborough, the
most novel and difficult design problem
of its kind in England. Besides being a
most able design engineer, Perring was
a first-class research scientist capable not
only of good experimentation but also

of dealing with the mathematics of his subject. These abilities, coupled with a prodigious appetite for work, marked him as a leader in his field. He was not modest in the sense of being too retiring; he knew his own value and, without bombast, claimed his deserts. He could champion his staff and his Establishment fiercely if necessary, but as a personality and a leader he was always considerate and kind.

Appointed superintendent of scientific research in 1940, Perring served from 1941 as deputy to the director at the Royal Aircraft Establishment; his vast experience as a scientific worker, coupled with his gifts as a leader, made him, when the director's post fell vacant in 1946, the natural successor. The war years saw him busy with the commissioning of his high-speed tunnel and by 1943 he was already looking forward to the post-war national need for new aeronautical research facilities. The planning of Bedford National Aeronautical Establishment was largely his personal work, including the design of the new tunnels and their novel driving plant. In the last year of the war he assembled overnight a small team which achieved remarkable success in investigating the characteristics of the German V.2 weapon from fragments sent over to England. He wisely found time to keep in touch with trends in the United States where he paid several visits and where he was welcomed as a highly expert colleague. As deputy director and later as director he welded together the various specialist departments in the Royal Aircraft Establishment so that he was able to bring to bear on any aeronautical problem a fully integrated team able to explore it in all its aspects. As a result the effectiveness of the Establishment was enormously enhanced.

Perring was a member of the Aeronautical Research Council, a member of the council of the Royal Aeronautical Society (whose gold medal he received), and he was appointed C.B. in 1949.

He married in 1926 Joyce Carver, by whom he had one son, who died in 1939, and two daughters. His wife died in 1933 and in 1942 he married May Elizabeth Willstrop, widow of an old friend of his college days. He died suddenly at his home in Camberley 8 April 1951. A portrait in oils by H. J. Proctor hangs in the Perring memorial room at the Royal Aircraft Establishment.

[Personal knowledge; private information.]

J. E. SERBY.

PERRINS, CHARLES WILLIA DYSON (1864–1958), collector and be factor, was born in the parish of Clain near Worcester, 25 May 1864, the or son of James Dyson Perrins by his wi Frances Sarah, daughter of Char Perrins. His father was one of t original partners in the firm of Lea a Perrins, makers of Worcester sauce, fr which the family derived its weal Educated at Charterhouse and the Quee College, Oxford, he served from 1888 the 4th battalion of the Highland Lig Infantry, but retired in 1892 with the ra of captain and began to devote hims to the family business and to pub service. He was mayor of Worcester the jubilee year 1897, and high sher of Worcestershire two years later. I benefactions went hand in hand with services to public life and to educatio after twenty-six years as a member of t governing body of the Worcester Roy Grammar School, in 1916 he became chairman for the next thirty-four yea and built for the school the Perrins Ha in memory of his father who had be a governor before him, and a scien laboratory. He maintained a continui interest in education as a life governor Birmingham University and a member the council of Malvern College. To Malver where he lived, he presented Rose Ba house and gardens on his retirement 1918 from the chairmanship of the urb district council, and also gave the tow its hospital (himself providing the sit buildings, and equipment) and its pub library, in conjunction with the Carneg Trust. His own university received fro him a large gift of money to foster t study of organic chemistry, and a furth sum for the construction of the laborato named in his honour, which was opene in 1916 and for which Oxford expresse its gratitude in 1919 by making him honorary D.C.L.

Meanwhile his name had begun become familiar in the world of the ar and of book-collecting. His father ha collected pictures—among them t great painting of 'Palestrina' from t middle period of J. M. W. Turne [q.v.] which Dyson Perrins was bequeath to the National Gallery—but h own tastes were as wide as were his mea to gratify them, while his choice was sure as his generosity was public-spirite in buying treasures and presenting the to appropriate national institution Always a discriminating benefactor, h

e or bequeathed objects of the highest
stic value and historic interest to, for
mple, the Victoria and Albert Museum,
National Gallery, the Ashmolean at
ord, and the British Museum, which
ived by bequest two of his most
ndid manuscripts, to which his heir
wed a further eight to be added by
chase at a specially reduced price.
main period of his book-collecting
in the two decades from 1900 to 1920,
n he boldly took opportunities, the
of which will hardly recur, to acquire
nuscripts and printed books of the
st quality from a series of great auction
es such as those of the libraries of
d Amherst, Bishop Gott, and A. H.
th [qq.v.]. He was no less inspired in
purchases by private treaty: in 1906
bought 33 manuscripts from Charles
rfax Murray, and in the same year
uired *en bloc*, on the eve of its dis-
sal by public auction, the great col-
tion of early woodcut books formed by
hard Fisher of Midhurst.

Iis prowess as a collector was recog-
ed in 1908 by his election to the
xburghe Club, and though he wrote
hing himself his patronage and his
lections led to the publication of a
able series of volumes written by
olars who enjoyed his friendship.
st among these was the monograph on
Gorleston Psalter, published in 1907
(Sir) Sydney Cockerell, on whose
vice Dyson Perrins had bought the
nuscript in 1904, under the very nose
his friend and rival Henry Yates
ompson [q.v.]. His own presentation
ume to the Roxburghe Club followed
1910, the *Epistole et Evangelii . . . in
gua Toscana*, reproducing over 500
rentine woodcuts from an all but
ique 1495 edition which he owned.
is was edited by A. W. Pollard [q.v.],
o went on to publish in 1914 *Italian
ok-illustrations and Early Printing.
catalogue of early Italian books in the
rary of C. W. Dyson Perrins*, which
nains a prime work of reference. In 1916
Roxburghe Club members jointly
ued *Topographical Study in Rome in
81*, edited by Thomas Ashby [q.v.]
m a manuscript in Dyson Perrins's
rary. Four years later came the
nptuous *Descriptive Catalogue* of his
minated manuscripts, the work of
George Warner [q.v.], in two volumes,
scribing in detail what has proved to be
most the last, and certainly one of the
est, gatherings of illuminated manu-

scripts formed by a single individual of
the golden age of private collecting. The
end of the series inspired by the Dyson
Perrins collections came with a volume
published in 1927 devoted to another
single manuscript, the *Apocalypse in
Latin*, described by M. R. James [q.v.].

Only a few additions were made after the
issue of the 1920 catalogue of his manuscripts, but one such purchase, made from
a Yates Thompson sale, was the finest of
the three surviving mid-twelfth-century
bindings executed at Winchester; this
he later presented, with characteristic
generosity, to Winchester Cathedral
Library. In 1946 Dyson Perrins decided to
sell his printed books, in order to spend the
proceeds on what had always been one of
his special interests, the Royal Worcester
Porcelain Factory. His own collection of
Worcester china, probably the best in
existence, and as strong in everyday
pieces as in special ones, he eventually
presented to the china works, which he
had so long befriended and supported.
After the first world war, when the factory
was in economic difficulties and closure
would have added to local unemployment
as well as ending an historic enterprise,
Dyson Perrins himself had for a time taken
over the management and kept the china
works in operation at his own expense.
After the second war he determined to re-
equip the factory to resume production
up to the highest standard of the past,
and the money raised by the auction of
his printed books at four sales during
1946–7, which totalled £147,627, was
earmarked for this purpose. After his
death, 29 January 1958, in Malvern in his
ninety-fourth year, his illuminated manuscripts, with a few outstanding printed
books, were dispersed in three auction
sales during 1958–60, at which foreign
national libraries competed with booksellers from all over the world to pay a
record sum for only 154 lots. Including the
earlier printed book sales and the British
Museum's private purchases, the Dyson
Perrins library brought nearly £1,100,000,
the largest amount ever fetched by one
man's collection.

Despite the fame of his possessions and
the publicity attendant on his numerous
benefactions, Dyson Perrins was personally extremely modest and deliberately
shunned the limelight. Besides his various
fields of collecting he enjoyed pursuits
such as photography, and was a keen
sportsman, for whom an estate in Ross-
shire provided the stalking, fishing, and

shooting in which he delighted. He married twice: first, in 1889, Catherine Christina, daughter of Alexander Allan Gregory, corn merchant, of Inverness; she died in 1922 and in 1923 he married Frieda, younger daughter of John Milne, of Belmont, Cheadle. By his first marriage he had two sons and two daughters, one of whom predeceased him. A portrait of Perrins by Arthur Hacker hangs in the Perrins Hall in the Worcester Royal Grammar School.

[*The Times*, 30 January 1958 and 9 January 1959; *Berrow's Worcester Journal*, 31 January 1958; *Times Literary Supplement*, 1946–7, 1958–61; *The Book Collector*, 1958–61.]
DAVID ROGERS.

PERTH, sixteenth EARL OF (1876–1951), first secretary-general of the League of Nations. [See DRUMMOND, JAMES ERIC.]

PETERSON, SIR MAURICE DRUMMOND (1889–1952), diplomatist, was born in Dundee 10 March 1889, the younger son of the classical scholar and university administrator, (Sir) William Peterson [q.v.], and his wife, Lisa Ross.

Taken to Montreal at the age of six, when his father became principal of McGill University, he spent eight happy years in Canada (for which, as for North America as a whole, he cherished a lasting affection), before being sent to Rugby and Magdalen College, Oxford, where he took a first in modern history in 1911. In December 1913 he qualified by examination for a Foreign Office clerkship and was posted to the parliamentary department, where he came under the wing of Miles Lampson (later Lord Killearn), whose path his was again to meet, on Egyptian affairs twenty years later. The Baghdad Railway negotiations and the revolutionary troubles in Mexico engaged his attention until the outbreak of war (in which he was rejected for military service because of an eye defect). After passing the customary Foreign Office examination in international law, he moved in 1916 to the newly created foreign trade department, later the Ministry of Blockade. There his duties twice took him across the Atlantic, first after the publication of the British black list, and then again, after the entry of the United States into the war, as a member of the Balfour mission to Washington. Immediately after the armistice he moved to the Eastern department of the Foreign Office, and into a somewhat

chastening contact with Lord Cur [q.v.] whom he greatly admired a foreign secretary, much as he resented bullying.

At the end of January 1920, as a m ber of the reorganized diplomatic serv Peterson was sent as second secretary Washington, where, in October 192 few months after his promotion to secretary, he was detached from embassy staff to serve as private secret to A. J. Balfour, then head of the Brit Empire delegation to the naval armament conference. He worked with Balfour, and this helped to estab his reputation as an 'all-rounder', wh led, after a further period in the Fore Office, to his appointment in the sum of 1923 as first secretary at Prague (wh he deemed it a great privilege to m Thomas Masaryk), and then, in Decem 1924, to his transfer in a similar capac to Tokyo. During his two and a quar years in Japan he took pains to beco proficient in the language and he liked country; but the 'singularly childlike a undeveloped' personality of his amb sador, Sir Charles Eliot [q.v.], irk him, as did later similar characteristics another diplomat of the same school, George Grahame, under whom he was serve as counsellor in Madrid from 1929 1931. But the late twenties were not wi out their compensations. In 1927 contracted a singularly happy marria with Eleanor Angel, the second daught of the Rev. Henry William Leyces O'Rorke, of North Litchfield Man Hampshire, by whom he had three so Shortly after his marriage he was sent counsellor of the residency in Cairo und Lord Lloyd [q.v.], whose resolute b complex character and methods made lasting if not completely favourab impression upon him. He became e tremely fond of Egypt, and was happy return there temporarily as acting hi commissioner in the summer and autun of 1934.

In October 1936, having served for few months as head of the new departme set up to deal with Abyssinia, an having been intimately concerned with th negotiation of the abortive Hoare–Lav proposals (which he believed to be fa better than the alternatives posed by the rejection), Peterson received his fir independent mission as minister t Bulgaria. Eighteen happy months followe before he was promoted and sent east c Suez again as ambassador to Baghda

re he managed to establish good
tions first with Jamil Madfai, then
h Nuri Said, and to keep to a minimum
harm done to British interests by King
azi's instability and the growing un-
in Iraq. He believed himself to be
erving well of his country, and it was
h regret that he learned early in 1939
t he was to be transferred to San
·astian as first British ambassador to
nco Spain which the Chamberlain
vernment had recently recognized. His
ipathies having inclined towards the
tionalists in the civil war, he now did
best to establish harmonious relations
h the new Spanish regime, if only to
.igate the hardships to which British
·jects living under its jurisdiction found
mselves exposed and also to keep Spain
itral after the outbreak of the second
·ld war. Confident that he was suc-
.ding in both these objectives, and
·ing been personally congratulated by
·d Halifax [q.v.] upon his success, he
s dumbfounded to receive on 12 May
.0 a letter from the Foreign Office
nplaining of his alleged failure to
:ain 'hoped-for results' or to safeguard
itish interests in the manner expected,
l stating that he was to be replaced
mediately. The news that his successor
s to be the ex-foreign secretary, Sir
muel Hoare (later Viscount Temple-
od, q.v.), did nothing to soften the
·w to his pride, from which he never
npletely recovered.

Returning home, Peterson found em-
·yment, first as controller of foreign
blicity at the Ministry of Information
·40–41), and then, after a few months
disponibilité, as under-secretary super-
ending the Eastern, Far Eastern,
.yptian, and Refugee departments of
e Foreign Office, before again, in
ptember 1944, receiving an appoint-
·nt much to his liking, as ambassador
Turkey. During the next two years he
.s to make many new and close friends,
t least the Turkish president, Ismet
onu, and the prime minister, Sukri
rajoglu.

In May 1946 Peterson was chosen by
nest Bevin [q.v.] to be ambassador to
·scow in what was to be his last and in
ne ways least agreeable post. While he
ver ceased—as he later emphasized in
tirement—to believe that Anglo-Soviet
.derstanding could and should be
hieved, he found this aim unattainable
the face of Stalin's growing suspicion
, and hostility towards, the West, and

of Molotov's 'obstructive', 'evasive and
insincere' tactics. Life in Moscow, with the
restrictions which the Russians imposed
upon western diplomats, began to pall,
and, to add to his other difficulties, his
health now failed, necessitating his recall
in 1948 and his retirement in the following
year. Joining the board of the Midland
Bank shortly afterwards, he found time
before he died at his home at Kintbury in
Berkshire, 15 March 1952, both to record
with great acumen the lessons of his
diplomatic career and to ventilate his
accumulated and pent-up resentments in
an elegantly written volume of memoirs,
Both Sides of the Curtain (1950).

Peterson, who was appointed C.M.G. in
1933, K.C.M.G. in 1938, and G.C.M.G. in
1947, was one of the ablest, although not
the most successful, of the Foreign Office
clerks who passed into the new diplomatic service with the reforms of 1920.
He had a quick mind and an impatient
temper, which was roughened by his disappointments; beneath this the warmth
of his nature showed warily. When amused,
he could giggle rather unexpectedly;
and his friendship and trust, when given,
were warming. It was unfortunate that
he should have become embittered;
he was a man who was respected,
if perhaps relatively few, in his later
years at any rate, penetrated beneath the
shyness and reserve sufficiently to like
him.

[Sir Maurice Peterson, *Both Sides of the
Curtain*, 1950; Foreign Office records; personal knowledge.]   CLIFTON J. CHILD.
                                      ROGER ALLEN.

PHILBY, HARRY ST. JOHN
BRIDGER (1885–1960), explorer and
orientalist, born at St. John's, Badula,
Ceylon, 3 April 1885, was the second son
of Henry Montague Philby, tea planter,
and through his mother, May Beatrice, a
grandson of General John Duncan who
had commanded the troops in Ceylon
and later the Bombay Army. A scholar
of Westminster and head boy, he went
with a scholarship to Trinity College,
Cambridge, where with visits to Europe
he early showed his bent for languages.
After a second class in part i of the classical tripos (1906) he achieved a first class
in the modern languages tripos and passed
high into the Indian Civil Service in 1907.
He was posted to the Punjab where his
trop de zèle in one of his early appointments caused a temporary setback in his
career, and turned his attention again to

languages in which he gained the highest honours in Urdu and Persian, and the appointment in 1915, owing to a wartime vacancy, of secretary to the board of examiners in Calcutta. The demand for linguists with the forces in Mesopotamia was now high, and after a few months he found himself an assistant political officer, Mesopotamian Expeditionary Force, and was at Basra, and later Baghdad, from 1915 until 1917, being appointed C.I.E. (1917). His relations with his superiors and with the army were not entirely happy and in the autumn of 1917 the opportunity was taken of attaching him to a mission to Abdul Aziz ibn Saud (later King of Saudi Arabia) at his capital of Riyadh, whose help the Government was anxious to secure against the Turks. The mission was successful and Philby, instead of returning to Basra to report, sent his report by messenger and set off with transport provided by Ibn Saud for Jedda, achieving in forty-four days the first east–west crossing of Arabia from sea to sea.

This journey and contacts with the Sharifian regime in the Hejaz convinced him of the unsuitability of the Sharif Hussain (King Hussain of the Hejaz), at that time the favoured candidate of the British Government for ruler of liberated Arabia, and of the inevitability of the eventual success of Ibn Saud. Philby was posted again to Riyadh whence he undertook a remarkable journey to the Wadi Duwasir. He was in England when, after the Arab rebellion of 1920 in Mesopotamia (Iraq), he was asked by Sir Percy Cox [q.v.] to accompany him as one of his staff on his recall to Baghdad. The nomination of Faisal, son of the Sharif Hussain of the Hejaz, as King of Iraq by the British Government, which he held to be a contravention of the promise of free elections made to the people of Iraq, led to Philby's resignation. He became (1921) chief British representative in Trans-Jordania in succession to T. E. Lawrence [q.v.] but resigned in 1924; there followed an abortive attempt in a private capacity to act as an intermediary between the forces of Ibn Saud surrounding Jedda and the beleaguered Sharif Ali, which caused some embarrassment in official circles; his resignation from the Indian Civil Service took effect in 1925.

His fortunes were now bound to Arabia, and his friend to whom he was loyally devoted, King Abdul Aziz ibn Saud. He set up business as Sharqieh Ltd. in

Jedda, and acted as an unofficial coun[s]lor of the king's. In 1930 he embraced Moslem faith. A great portion of his ti[me] he devoted to exploration, with the h[elp] and finance of the king and if, to t[he] extent, his lot as an explorer was eas[ier] than some of his great predecessors in [the] Arabian field, this in no way detra[cted] from the outstanding quality of his wo[rk] He was a skilled cartographer, natural[ist] and botanist, and his contribution in [the] field of archaeology to knowledge [of] early Thamudic inscriptions in Arabia w[as] of considerable importance.

In 1939 during a stay in Engla[nd] Philby was attracted to politics and unsuccessfully fought a by-election [at] Hythe as the anti-war candidate of [the] British People's Party. He then return[ed] to Arabia, and his strong advocacy o[f a] policy of 'non-involvement' for Sa[udi] Arabia and his general anti-war attitu[de] resulted in his arrest in 1940 in India o[n his] journey to America, and his incarce[ra]tion in England under Section 18B of t[he] Defence Regulations. Some five mont[hs] later a committee charged with t[he] examination of his case complet[ely] exonerated him. After a brief flirtati[on] with the short-lived Commonweal[th] Party he returned to Arabia in 1945.

By 1952 his growing criticism of t[he] extravagance and inefficiency of t[he] Saudi regime following on the vast[ly] increased oil revenues found expression [in] his book Arabian Jubilee. In Novemb[er] 1953 the old king died. In 1955 Phil[by] was exiled from Saudi Arabia and to[ok] up his residence in Beirut. A reconcili[a]tion was effected with the new king a ye[ar] later, but Philby's remaining years we[re] spent in Beirut in literary studies a[nd] completing his memoirs. He died the[re] 30 September 1960.

Philby was a prolific author and [his] Heart of Arabia (2 vols., 1922), Sheb[a's] Daughters (1939), and Arabian Highlan[ds] (1952) give an illuminating and valuab[le] account of his journeys in hitherto u[n]known portions of the Arabian peninsu[la.] He also wrote on Islam and Arabia[n] history and numerous papers to the Roy[al] Geographical Society, of which he w[as] awarded the Founder's gold medal in 192[0] and other societies. He received the fir[st] Sir Richard Burton memorial medal of t[he] Royal Asiatic Society in 1925.

Although his work as an explorer a[nd] as an adviser to King Ibn Saud w[as] praised and received recognition, it w[as] perhaps inevitable that Philby's ou[t]

okenness and at times anti-British atti-
de aroused considerable criticism in
ngland. It is doubtful if this was justi-
d. He firmly believed that friendship
tween British and Arabs was essential
: the security and progress of the Middle
nst, but that the open political support
Whitehall, which entailed, in his view,
volvement in policies dangerous and
elevant to Arabia and the Arabs, was
tal for an Arab ruler. The disturbed
nes in which he lived, and the fluctuations
British Middle-East policy undoubtedly
nforced these views. He was throughout
s life a strong individualist, who found
scipline and even collaboration difficult.
et it is mainly to him that the world
ves its present knowledge of Central
rabia.

In 1910 Philby married Dora (died
57), daughter of Adrian Hope Johnston,
the Indian Public Works Department,
d granddaughter of Alexander Johnston,
e painter [q.v.]. They had three daugh-
rs and one son, Harold (Kim) Philby,
no after service as a diplomat became a
urnalist in the Middle East and sub-
quently took up residence in the
.S.S.R., whose agent he had been while
rving in British intelligence.

A drawing by Elisabeth Ada Mont-
mery is reproduced in Philby's auto-
ography *Arabian Days* (1948).

[Philby's own works; Sir Arnold Wilson,
yalties, 1930; *The Times*, 3 October 1960;
ivate information; personal knowledge.]

               RONALD WINGATE.

HILLPOTTS, EDEN (1862–1960),
riter, was born at Mount Aboo, Raj-
utana, India, 4 November 1862, the son
' Henry Phillpotts, an officer in the
dian Army and political agent in two
dian states, who died when his wife
as only twenty-one. She was Adelaide
atilda Sophia, daughter of George
enkins Waters, of the Madras Civil
ervice, and on the death of her husband
ne returned to England with her three
ons of whom Eden, the eldest, in his
outh gave no indication that he was to
ecome a writer. He was educated at
annamead School (later incorporated
ith Plymouth College), and at seventeen
ent to London where he earned his
ving for ten years as a clerk in the Sun
ire office. His mother hoped he would
nter the Church, but his own ambition
as to be an actor, and after office hours
e studied at a school of dramatic art,
nly to realize that he was unfitted for

acting. His two years' training, however,
came in useful when he turned to writing,
to which he devoted his evenings. Before
long he was earning £400 a year in his
leisure by writing novels and short stories,
and also one-act plays, sometimes in
association with Arnold Bennett [q.v.]
who became his friend. Eventually leaving the insurance business he became
assistant editor to a weekly periodical,
Black and White, for three days of his
writing week.

Lying Prophets (1897), Phillpotts's
first important work of fiction, was commended by James Payn [q.v.]; his next,
Children of the Mist (1898), won him wider
welcome and was praised by R. D.
Blackmore [q.v.], author of *Lorna Doone*,
whose memorial Phillpotts was to unveil
in Exeter Cathedral six years later.
Mostly with Dartmoor as the background,
a flood of novels followed. Year after year,
indeed for more than half a century, an
average of three or four books came
regularly—poetry, short stories, plays
and essays, mystery fiction, and retold
legends from the classics.

Phillpotts commenced playwright in
1895 when he collaborated with Jerome
K. Jerome [q.v.] in a comedy, *The Prude's
Progress*. When success eventually rewarded his writing for the theatre, it
was with *The Farmer's Wife*, entirely
his own work. Theatre-managers looked
doubtfully at this comedy of rustic
life, and more than a dozen rejections preceded its presentation at the
Birmingham Repertory Theatre in 1916.
The eventual London production in
1924 was phenomenally popular. It ran
for three years, bringing to the playhouse a reminder that the rural atmosphere and country dialogue which had
been a characteristic of English drama in
Shakespeare's time could well be exploited
anew. There followed other plays in the
same genre, notably *Yellow Sands* (1926,
with his daughter Adelaide).

Only one setback marred these successes. A peasant tragedy, *The Shadow* (1913),
written prior to *The Farmer's Wife*, had
given a hint of what was possible to
Phillpotts in the theatre, and *The
Secret Woman*, originally a novel (1905),
was recast for the stage seven years later.
It was banned by the censor because the
author refused on principle to delete two
sentences 'that mattered nothing to the
play and involved no sacrifice of art',
he afterwards recalled. A protest was
widely signed by his fellow writers,

including G. B. Shaw and Henry James [qq.v.]. Nevertheless, looking back, Phillpotts felt that he should have done what was directed 'without demur'.

As a novel *The Secret Woman* stands high, not only among Phillpotts's writings, but in English regional fiction. The granite of central Devon and Dartmoor's 'unchanging vastness' brood like an ageless world in the mind of the generations who have lived and died there. The opening pages of the localized stories are devoted to the 'unchanging vastness' as a prelude to and in preparation of the human scene. Not only the Dartmoor novels have 'these chaotic wastes of earth and stone' for background, but the poetry of Eden Phillpotts—ten volumes in all, beginning with *Wild Fruit* (1910)—and the essays, first collected in *My Devon Year* (1904), have the flavour of a rich ancestral speech. The artist's use of dialect led him, as he matured, from word distortion to rhythmic suggestion and Phillpotts's creative prose had as a consequence something of the easeful power of his exemplars, Thomas Hardy and Henry Fielding [qq.v.]. His rationalist philosophy, genial and manly, but less oppressed by such fatalism as Hardy's, was steadfast. *My Devon Year* and *From the Angle of 88* (1952) could not conceivably have come from any other mind and spirit, although half a century separated the two.

In 1892 Phillpotts married Emily (died 1928), daughter of Robert Topham. They had a daughter who became an author under her father's tutelage and a son on whose future the novelist may have allowed imagination to play as well as memory of his own early growth, so that when he turned to his 'holiday task', as he called it, he wrote humorous stories of boyhood, among them *The Human Boy* (1899) and *The Human Boy Again* (1908). Phillpotts married secondly, in 1929, Lucy Robina Joyce, daughter of Dr. Fortescue Webb. He died at his home at Broad Clyst, Exeter, 29 December 1960. There is a portrait of him in the possession of the family by Beryl Trist.

[Eden Phillpotts, *From the Angle of 88*, 1952; Percival Hinton, *Eden Phillpotts, a bibliography of first editions*, 1931; *Eden Phillpotts, An Assessment and a Tribute*, ed. Waveney Girvan, 1953; private information; personal knowledge.]   THOMAS MOULT.

PIGOU, ARTHUR CECIL (1877–1959), economist, was born 18 November 1877 at Ryde, Isle of Wight, the son of Clare[n]ce George Scott Pigou and his wife, No[ra] second daughter of Sir John Le[e]. Clarence Pigou was a retired army offi[cer] of little distinction, but descended from [a] Huguenot family which had long co[n]nections with China and India, first [as] traders, then as members of the Indi[an] Civil Service. The Lees were equally [if] distinguished in that generation, [but] again descended from a family wh[o] acquired distinction and wealth in Ir[ish] administration. Pigou went, like [his] father, to Harrow where his natu[ral] abilities won him an entrance scholarsh[ip]. He was athlete enough to win appro[val] in the sphere then more importa[nt,] scholar enough to win a number of priz[es]. He was the first boy on the modern si[de] to be head of the school.

At King's College, Cambridge, Pig[ou] first read history under Oscar Browni[ng] [q.v.], became a scholar in 1898, a[nd] obtained a first class in the history trip[os] of 1899. It was in the Union Society th[at] he first made his mark in a generation [of] brilliant debaters, becoming president [in] 1900. It was in that year that he obtain[ed] a first in part ii of the moral scien[ce] tripos and thus came to economics as p[art] of the tripos. That introduction w[as] important in the shaping of Pigou's su[b]sequent thinking. He came to economi[cs] first by way of history, then by way [of] philosophy and ethics, and only lat[er] acquired the mathematical techniqu[e] which he used in the writings of his mo[re] mature years. When he began to tea[ch] economics he was scarcely regarded as [a] specialist in the subject in an age in whi[ch] specialism was less regarded and less nec[es]sary. Indeed, he had won the Chancello[r's] medal for English verse in 1899, t[he] Burney prize in 1900, and submitted as [his] first, and unsuccessful, attempt for [a] fellowship at King's a thesis on 'Browni[ng] as a Religious Teacher'.

Pigou began to lecture on economics [in] 1901, before his election to a King's fello[w]ship in 1902 at his second attempt, a[nd] was made Girdler's lecturer in the summ[er] of 1904. He lectured in those early yea[rs] on a variety of subjects which would see[m] uncongenial to those who knew him [in] later life. But already in 1901–2 he ha[d] begun to give the course on advance[d] economics to second-year students whi[ch] formed the basis of the education [of] countless Cambridge economists over t[he] next thirty years. In 1908 he was elect[ed] at the remarkable age, in Edwardia[n]

mbridge, of thirty, to the chair of
itical economy, to the delight of
red Marshall [q.v.] whom he succeeded,
t to the chagrin of some of the older
eration, and especially H. S. Foxwell
v.], who had believed their claims to be
ater. He held the professorship until
13 when he reached the age of retire-
nt and continued to live in King's
til his death 7 March 1959. He was
cted F.B.A. in 1927.

Pigou was throughout his life a devo-
1—some would say a too devoted and
critical—pupil of Alfred Marshall.
gou's course of lectures became the
ncipal channel through which the oral
dition of Marshall's economics was
ssed down. Marshall himself had never
en a systematic lecturer. Pigou, until
1ess in later years impaired his vigour,
s a brilliantly lucid and systematic
positor, maintaining the traditions the
1ool of moral sciences had inherited from
nry Sidgwick [q.v.], whose lectures
had attended, and giving Marshall's
as a clarity and architecture they had
ked in Marshall's own lecturing. Pigou
1s uncritical, however, in the sense that
was he, more than any other, who
ought up a generation of Cambridge
onomists in the conviction that (in his
t-repeated words) 'it's all in Marshall'.
the thirties he found his loyalties to
arshall too constraining when first Piero
affa and later J. M. (later Lord) Keynes
.v.], both in his own college, challenged
me of the orthodoxies of Marshallian
onomics. But it was Pigou who, as
arshall had rightly foreseen, provided
1at was essential in the Cambridge
1ool of economics. Keynes gave those
nerations of students their enthusiasms,
eir sense of the importance of discover-
g solutions to the economic problems
the world. Pigou gave them their
1ining in the disciplines and tech-
ques of economic reasoning. Clarity of
1alysis and a willingness to follow an
gument through to the end were the
sence of his own exposition and
what he demanded in others.

Pigou's first book, *Principles and
1ethods of Industrial Peace* (1905), was an
xpansion of an essay which had won
m the Adam Smith prize in 1903 and
so, in modified form, his fellowship
the second attempt. Its later interest
s largely in the method of writing of the
oung Pigou—so different from that of
s more mature years. He uses the
ethod of the philosopher, clarifying the

issues, dissecting them and analysing
them, trying to see how far varied assumptions will lead to varied results—the
analytical method applied with great
precision. But he uses scarcely any statistical argument and no mathematics. The
book reflects throughout his own upbringing in the moral sciences.

It was in 1912 that Pigou published the
first edition of the book by which his
ultimate standing as an economist will
almost certainly be judged—*Wealth and
Welfare* as it was originally called, *The
Economics of Welfare* as it became in the
later editions in which it grew vastly in
size. This book created the branch of
economics which has subsequently come
to be known as the theory of welfare.
Pigou started from two existing ideas,
both to be found in the Cambridge tradition of Marshall and Sidgwick. Marshall had discussed (as had Bastiat before
him) the concept of maximum satisfaction
and the conditions in which it might be
achieved. Sidgwick, in a much less rigorous
discussion of the same problem, had made
use of the idea of divergence between utility
to the individual and utility to society as a
whole. Pigou's treatment was both more
ambitious and more rigorous. He set out
to examine the full conditions for maximum
satisfaction, the conditions in which private
and social net product (as he called them)
might diverge, and the measures which
could be taken to bring them into equality
and maximize satisfaction.

It was not to be expected that Pigou's
work in the years before 1912 would survive unchallenged by subsequent generations. Challenge was, perhaps, the more
likely because he argued that more equal
distribution of income was likely to
increase economic welfare. This led,
inevitably, to vigorous discussion of the
legitimacy of making comparisons of the
welfare of different individuals, or of
attaching meaning to an aggregate of
welfare of many individuals. Most of the
subsequent argument has been about these
issues. The challenges came principally
in the fifties when Pigou had retired from
his chair and was no longer as vigorous as
in early years. He was himself never
convinced by his critics, and in his
seventy-fourth year wrote an eloquent
and moving defence of his position,
arguing that satisfactions are not in
principle incomparable, even if they are
not directly measurable, that there was a
sufficient body of evidence that people
were on average much alike in many

characteristics and that, for large groups of people, it was not unreasonable to treat them as such. In the views which stimulated this controversy some of Pigou's own personal characteristics were evident. He was a passionate believer in justice. He insisted through life in protecting the under-dog. To him it was just and proper to treat all men as equals and to treat the poor as if they were equal in value and capacity to the rich. If one sought to invent exceptions, to one of his Victorian uprightness they seemed to savour of special pleading.

Pigou's strong principles created problems for him when war came in 1914. Although he was still young, he was not prepared to undertake military service to the extent of accepting an obligation to destroy a human life. He remained in Cambridge, but devoted all his vacations to driving an ambulance at the front for the Friends' Ambulance Unit, and no doubt at the instigation of the same conscience insisted on undertaking jobs of particular danger. Towards the end of the war he was persuaded to accept a post in the Board of Trade, but showed little aptitude for the type of work in which others of his Cambridge colleagues and pupils were making names for themselves. In the years soon after the war he accepted rather reluctantly the obligation to serve on the Cunliffe committee of 1918–19 and the Chamberlain committee of 1924–5, where he was one of those who recommended an early return to the gold standard—a recommendation severely attacked by Keynes in his *Economic Consequences of Mr. Churchill*. It became evident to Pigou that this was not a field in which he could make his best contributions to economics and in later years he withdrew from national affairs, save for the occasional letter to *The Times*, and devoted himself almost completely to more academic economics.

Through the remaining years Pigou gradually retreated into the ordered life of a recluse. In term time he lived in his rooms in King's, emerging to give lectures, to take his afternoon walk to Coton, to dine in the college Hall. In vacations, he removed to his beloved cottage in Buttermere, or in the earlier years to climb the Alps. The lectures cost him little effort. He worked incessantly and regularly at his books. He read widely in economics, but rather to find the pertinent example or quotation for his own work than to learn from the

thinking of others. Within this priv world there were a few privileged a devoted friends. They were chosen usua because they shared his love of mountains. He was a competent but supremely great climber; he introdu to climbing several who, like Wilf Noyce, became far greater climbers. T mountains were his love, and they serv to illustrate one problem after anoth in his lectures and writings. Into t private world few women were admitt And as the years went on Pigou tended become more isolated, more eccentr and in more sartorial disarray. All this v accentuated by an illness affecting heart which, from the beginning of t thirties, curtailed his climbing, impai his vigour, and left him intermitten through the rest of his life in phases debility. And with this, something w lost both from the liveliness of lecturing and the vigour of his writing.

Through the years after 1918 he w prolific as a writer. *The Economics Welfare* went through four main editio and numerous reprintings and consum much of his time. Apart from a number smaller books and papers in the journa he wrote five major books during the years: *Industrial Fluctuations* (192 *A Study in Public Finance* (1928); *T Theory of Unemployment* (1933); *T Economics of Stationary States* (193 *Employment and Equilibrium* (1941). these were important in their generatio Most of them have been overtaken other work and have left less permane impress on the body of economics than d *The Economics of Welfare*.

When Keynes published his *Gener Theory* in 1936, it affected Pigou doubl Keynes had dared to attack Marsha and had used Pigou's *Theory of U employment* as a stalking horse, quoti widely from Pigou as a representative the classical theories he was seeking demolish. Pigou retaliated, more Marshall's account than on his own, wi a severe review of Keynes's book *Economica*. But shortly before the end his life he came to see more clearly t essentials of Keynes's arguments an asking permission to give a public lectu he said with great generosity that he h come with the passage of time to feel th he had failed earlier to appreciate some the important things that Keynes w trying to say. It was the very noble a of a man who put truth beyond vanity ar another's reputation beyond his ow

gou and Keynes had a great mutual re-
rd and affection for each other, and their
rsonal friendship was never seriously
opardized by their intellectual differences.
It is not easy to place Pigou in the
eogony of economists. Since his death
e has probably been more underrated
an any economist of first distinction,
ainly because writers have tended to
efine their own views in terms of their
ifferences from Pigou. As teacher and
uilder of the Cambridge school of
onomics in the Marshallian tradition and
n the basis of Marshall's economics tripos
e set a pattern for Cambridge economists
r a generation and saw his pupils
lling the chairs of economics around
e world. But his innate and notorious
yness, increasing as the years went
y, cut him off from close personal
fluence on the development of econo-
ics apart from his writings. He was, it
ight truly be said, the last of the great
lassical school of economists, who sur-
ived into a generation which had lost
omething of its reverence for them.

There are two portraits of Pigou, both
y E. H. Nelson. One hangs in the Hall of
King's College, the other is in the Marshall
Library of Economics in Cambridge.

[Private information; personal knowledge.]
E. A. G. ROBINSON.

PIROW, OSWALD (1890–1959), South
African lawyer and politician, born at
Aberdeen, Cape Province, 14 August
890, was the eldest of three children.
His German parents, Carl Bernhard
Ferdinand Pirow and his wife, Henrietta
Comby, went to South Africa in 1888.
Pirow's schooling began at Potchefstroom,
Transvaal, where his father practised
medicine. For further study, Pirow
proceeded to the Itzehoe Gymnasium in
Germany, then to London to read law,
being called to the bar by the Middle
Temple in 1913. After returning to South
Africa he practised as an attorney, and
in 1915 transferred to the Pretoria bar.
His effectiveness as an advocate soon won
wide recognition, and in 1925 he took silk.

As one of the Afrikaner 'Young Turks'
of the Transvaal under Tielman Roos,
Pirow had meanwhile entered politics.
He supported J. B. M. Hertzog [q.v.]
and his National Party. After three unsuccessful attempts, dating from 1915,
Pirow entered Parliament in 1924 as the
member for Zoutpansberg. At the next
general election in 1929 he unsuccessfully
opposed J. C. Smuts [q.v.] in Standerton.

After Roos's resignation from the
Cabinet later in 1929, Hertzog invited
Pirow to take his place as minister of
justice. Having consulted Roos himself,
Pirow agreed. Following a spell as a
nominated senator, Pirow, in a by-
election in October 1929, was returned to
the Assembly for Gezina, the constituency
which he continued to represent until 1943.

His friendship with Roos notwithstanding, Pirow supported Hertzog in
negotiating the coalition with Smuts in
1933 which spelt ruin to Roos who had
returned to politics during the gold
standard crisis. Pirow also approved the
fusion of the National and South African
parties in 1934. In the new Government
Pirow held the portfolios of defence and of
railways and harbours. With Smuts and
N. C. Havenga he was also a member of
Hertzog's 'inner Cabinet'. Recognizing
Pirow's parliamentary skills, Hertzog
delegated to him the piloting of several
important measures, notably the Status
Act of 1934. An able administrator of his
departments, Pirow, who was a keen
amateur flyer, encouraged the formation
of South African Airways in 1934.
Although he was discredited after the
outbreak of war in 1939 by Smuts's
mockery of his notorious 'bush carts',
Pirow's stewardship of the Defence Ministry had not earlier been attacked.

In October 1938 Pirow began a tour of
western Europe. At Smuts's suggestion,
Chamberlain evidently utilized Pirow,
who was in England on defence
business, as an informal mediator with
Hitler. Pirow subsequently claimed that
at Berchtesgaden in November he sounded
Hitler on an offer of a free hand in eastern
Europe in return for an undertaking to
allow the German Jews to emigrate.
Pirow's tour, during which he also met
Mussolini, Salazar, and Franco, profoundly
affected his outlook. Already an admirer
of Hitler's domestic policies, he returned
to South Africa convinced that in the
approaching war the forces of National
Socialism, to which he was shortly to
announce his conversion, would triumph.

With the outbreak of war Pirow supported Hertzog after his defeat in
Parliament and resignation on the neutrality issue and in his later reunion, in the
Herenigde Nasionale Party, with the
'purified' Nationalists of D. F. Malan [q.v.]
who had declined to enter fusion in 1934.
At the end of 1940, when Hertzog and
Havenga broke with the H.N.P., Pirow
remained in the party and in Parliament.

At this point he launched his New Order for South Africa, a movement based on the Nazi ideology of race and on a rejection of parliamentary democracy. For a time Pirow tried to keep his group within the H.N.P. on the basis of a common republicanism; but the condemnation of a national socialism by Malan and J. G. Strijdom [q.v.] forced him and his followers to quit the H.N.P. caucus in January 1942. In the general election of 1943 supporters of the New Order were eliminated, while Pirow himself declined to stand for re-election. He continued to propagate his views in his newsletter until 1958, but his political influence had disappeared long before.

After leaving Parliament, Pirow resumed his practice in Pretoria. He retired in 1957, but re-emerged later in the year when he was briefed by the Crown in the Pretoria treason trial—a tribute as much to his consistent advocacy of uncompromising white supremacy as to his legal skills. The trial was still in progress at the time of his sudden death in Pretoria 11 October 1959.

At the height of his career in the thirties, Pirow's ability and energy had marked him out as Hertzog's lieutenant and likely successor. Turbulent in spirit, brusque, dynamic, and combative, Pirow was a vigorous personality. A notable athlete in youth and a keen hunter, he was also a prolific writer, his most serious work being his biography of Hertzog (1958). After the early promise, Pirow's political eclipse, with its note of wasted talent, reflected not only his misjudgement of the course of world events and of Afrikaner political proclivities in a crisis, but also a streak of undisciplined opportunism in his own character.

In 1919 Pirow married Else, daughter of Albert Piel, the founder of a cold storage concern; there were two sons and two daughters.

[O. Pirow, *J. B. M. Hertzog*, 1958; *Die Burger*, 13 and 21 October 1959; *Star* (Johannesburg), 12 October 1959; *The Times*, 12 October 1959; private information.]

N. G. GARSON.

PLIMMER, ROBERT HENRY ADERS (1877–1955), biochemist, was born at Elberfeld, Germany, 25 April 1877, the eldest son of Alfred Aders, a Manchester business man, and his German wife and first cousin, Bertha Helena Aders. The child was brought to England when a few months old and soon afterwards the

Aders settled in Surrey on the southe outskirts of London. Alfred Aders died 1885 and in 1887 his widow marri Henry George Plimmer, F.R.S., who lat became professor of comparative path logy at Imperial College. By example a advice Plimmer greatly influenced t lives and characters of the Aders childre especially the eldest son who lat acknowledged his indebtedness by adop ing the surname of Plimmer by the wi of his stepfather.

Educated at Dulwich College ar University College, London, where studied chemistry under (Sir) Willia Ramsay [q.v.], Plimmer graduated B.S in 1899, then, on his stepfather's advic turned his attention to the chemistr of living organisms. A year at Genev University was followed by two years Berlin under Emil Fischer, where bega his lifelong interest in the chemistry proteins. He obtained a Ph.D. (Berlin) an D.Sc. (London) in 1902, and was awarde a Grocers' Company research studentshi which enabled him to work for two yea at the Lister Institute of Preventiv Medicine.

In 1904 Plimmer returned to Universit College as an assistant in the departmen of physiology under (Sir) W. M. Baylis and E. H. Starling [qq.v.]. His dutie were to teach physiological chemistry an to engage in research. He soon became we known in both spheres. Practical notes fo his students developed into a textboo of *Organic and Bio-Chemistry* (1915) an his contributions to scientific journa drew attention to his researches into th chemistry of proteins. With (Sir) Frederic Gowland Hopkins [q.v.] he was co-edito of an extremely valuable series of mono graphs on biochemistry to which he himsel contributed 'The Chemical Constitution o the Proteins' (1908). He also wrote a account of the work of Emil Fischer an his school.

Plimmer was elected a fellow o University College in 1906, assistan professor of physiological chemistry ir 1907, and university reader in 1912 Biochemists of his generation remembere him with affection for the part he playe in the founding of the Biochemical Societ and in nursing it through the early difficult years. He and his friend J. A. Gardner are regarded as the co-founders in 1911 of the Biochemical Club which became the Society in 1913. The first meeting was held in Plimmer's department, and the annual general meetings

ntinue to be held at University College.
immer was the first secretary (1911–19),
s made an honorary member (1943),
d wrote the *History of the Biochemical
ciety* (1949). He lived to see the society
urish beyond all expectations of the
nders, the original membership of
ty growing into thousands.

During the war of 1914–18, Plimmer,
th the rank of captain, was attached to
e directorate of hygiene, War Office, and
alysed common foodstuffs, the results
ing published in 1921 as *Analyses and
nergy Values of Foods*. This work
imulated his interest in nutrition, and
1919 he left University College to
come biochemist at the Rowett Instite for Research in Animal Nutrition,
berdeen, where he was able to take part
feeding experiments on a large scale.
ut in 1922 he returned to London as
ofessor of chemistry at St. Thomas's
ospital medical school, a position which
filled with great distinction for twenty-
e years. He continued his research work
ith great vigour, and a steady stream of
pers appeared in various journals. In
dition to his teaching duties, examiner-
ips, and service on numerous university
ards and committees he found time to
ve public lectures on diet, vitamins,
c., and with his wife to write popular
oks on nutrition, balanced diets, vita-
ins, and the choice of foods.

Plimmer reached retiring age in 1942
hen he was made honorary consulting
emist to the hospital; in 1944 the title
f professor emeritus of chemistry was
onferred upon him by the university of
ondon. In January 1943 he joined the
aff of the Postgraduate Medical School,
ammersmith, to assist Professor E. J.
ing in the biochemistry department.
t was intended to be a temporary ap-
ointment during a staff shortage but
sted for more than twelve useful years.

A tall, lean figure, with strong, deeply
ned face and kindly eyes beneath bushy
yebrows, Plimmer had a very friendly
isposition and loved entertaining his
any friends. He enjoyed good music,
rt, literature, theatre, cricket, and
notoring. He was especially kind and
elpful to younger colleagues.

In 1912 Plimmer married Violet
eraldine (died 1949), daughter of
rederick Sheffield, solicitor; they had
ne son and three daughters. He died
n London 18 June 1955.

[*The Times*, 21 June 1955; *British Medical
ournal*, 2 July 1955; *Nature*, 13 August
1955; *St. Thomas's Hospital Gazette*, October
1955; *Biochemical Journal*, vol. lxii, 1956;
private information; personal knowledge.]

JOHN LOWNDES.

PLUNKETT, EDWARD JOHN
MORETON DRAX, eighteenth BARON
OF DUNSANY (1878–1957), writer, was born
in London 24 July 1878 in the house of
his grandfather, Admiral Lord Dunsany.
He was the eldest son of John William
Plunkett, wit, amateur scientist, and
member of Parliament (1886–92) for
South Gloucestershire. His mother, Ernle
Elizabeth Louisa Maria Grosvenor, daughter of Colonel Francis Augustus Plunkett
Burton, Coldstream Guards, was very tall,
an heiress, and a beauty. She was a
relative of the Dunsany family and of Sir
Richard Burton [q.v.], the translator of
the *Arabian Nights*, and said to be of
Romany descent. The Plunketts are an
old Norman family; the title is a fifteenth-
century Irish one.

The boy's early years were passed at
Dunstall Priory, a small but attractive
property in Kent belonging to his mother;
and after his father had succeeded to the
title in 1889 he spent some of his holidays
at the family seat, Dunsany Castle,
county Meath. By birth and upbringing
he may truly be called an Anglo-Irishman;
an intermediate position which was very
noticeable throughout his life. He went to
Eton where he was not industrious. Sport
meant more to him than learning, although
he always felt an interest in writing and,
like his father, in amateur science. His
father removed him and sent him to
crammers to enable him eventually to
enter Sandhurst. He joined the Coldstream
Guards in 1899, the year in which he succeeded to the title, and served as a second
lieutenant throughout most of the South
African war. The continent influenced
him profoundly and African themes were
to appear much in his writing. For a short
time his uncle (Sir) Horace Plunkett [q.v.]
was his guardian, but they were not very
sympathetic to each other. After the war
he settled at Dunsany, where he started
a pack of harriers and devoted himself to
various sports, shooting, hunting, and
cricket. He went big-game shooting in
Africa and Dunsany Castle was adorned
with many trophies. He was a superb shot
with a rifle and also a first-class chessplayer.

Meanwhile Dunsany had begun to
write short stories and poems and in 1905
published his first book of stories, *The Gods
of Pegana*. In 1906 he stood unsuccessfully for Parliament in Wiltshire. Although

he held strong Conservative views, he was not particularly suited for politics and thenceforth he devoted himself increasingly to literature. Originally a man of some wealth, changing circumstances made him partly dependent on his pen for support, although he continued to figure as landlord, sportsman, and soldier. His natural bent was for lyric poetry, short stories, and short plays. He became associated with the Irish literary renaissance and his first play, *The Glittering Gate*, was produced at the Abbey Theatre, Dublin, in 1909. He did not find it easy to agree with those controlling the theatre and afterwards had little to do with the movement. He was not in any case a man who fitted into movements. He took no part in Irish politics and in a half-passionate half-humorous way was utterly opposed to Irish nationalism, although he loved the country and retained many Irish literary friends, notably Oliver St. John Gogarty and George Russell [qq.v.].

In 1911 his short play *The Gods of the Mountain* was produced in London. He wrote a number of other plays, often dealing with imaginary countries, unhistoric periods, and fantastic religions. Irish themes he avoided at this time. In the war of 1914–18 he was a captain in the Royal Inniskilling Fusiliers. Becoming involved in the suppression of the Easter week rebellion in Dublin in 1916 he was wounded and taken prisoner by the rebels. He also saw service in France.

From 1916 Dunsany's short plays became enormously popular in the United States where they were presented in Little Theatres and colleges all over the country. On his first American lecture tour (1919–20) he was welcomed as an international literary celebrity. He visited America five times in all. In England he also became famous although only one full-length play, *If* (1921), reached the west end. Believing the market for short stories to be limited, he now attempted the novel with *The Chronicles of Rodriguez* (1922), *The Blessing of Pan* (1927), and others. But he did not desert the short story. Further visits to Africa in search of big game inspired the Jorkens stories, perhaps his best, purporting to be the tales of an outrageous drink-cadging liar, who claimed among other things to have married the mermaid at Aden. Short stories, novels, and verse flowed easily from his quill, and he was successful as a writer of plays and stories for broadcasting. He also wrote three autobiographical

works: *Patches of Sunlight* (1938), *Wh* the Sirens Slept (1944), and *The Sire Wake* (1945); a book on Ireland, *M Ireland* (1937); and some novels on Iri themes such as *The Curse of the W Woman* (1933) and *Rory and Bran* (193 After 1939 he served for a time in t Home Guard in Kent and then wer to Athens as Byron professor of Engli literature, visiting Turkey en route. Th arrival of the Germans forced him escape under aerial attack. His travels ar experiences at this time he treated in narrative poem, *A Journey* (1943), h finest and most sustained work in verse.

Dunsany was a striking figure, very tal athletic, handsome, and in later yea bearded. He was unconventional in dre and manner. He expressed his opinion freely and strongly. He objected to man features of modern life, especially adve tising and patent foods. Although h outspokenness sometimes made enemie he was the kindest of men, particular to the young, and he delighted to assis literary aspirants. He was devotedl interested in animals, and a great observe of nature, in particular of facts whic others fail to observe. He painted a littl and, although not a performer, love music. He also attempted pottery. As writer he was above all original an outspoken, following the lights of poetr and humour wherever they might lea him. His handwriting was beautiful: h usually wrote with a goose-quill an never blotted a line. He was amazingl prolific and, as might be expected, uneven He followed no fashion; founded n school; and had no use for selfconsciousl modern writing. His work, althoug occasionally influenced by his period, i above all his own. He was a popula lecturer and broadcaster and was an honorary Litt.D. of Dublin (1940).

In 1904 Dunsany married Lady Beatric Child-Villiers (died 1970), daughter of the seventh Earl of Jersey [q.v.]. They had on son, Randal Arthur Henry (born 1906) to whom Dunsany handed over Dunsan Castle after 1945 and who succeeded hin in the title when he died in Dublin 25 October 1957.

At Dunsany there is a portrait by A Jonniaux and a bust by A. Power; at Dunstall a portrait by E. March, a bust by Strobl, and a water-colour by G. Brockhurst.

[Lord Dunsany's own writings; private information; personal knowledge.]

LONGFORD.

OLE, Sir FELIX JOHN CLEWETT (1877–1956), railway general manager and industrialist, was born at Little Bedwyn, Wiltshire, 1 February 1877, the second son of Edward Robert Pole, schoolmaster, and his wife, Emma, daughter of Charles Clewett, of Wincanton, Somerset. With a village school education, agreeable manner, quick comprehension, retentive memory, and healthy ambition, at the age of fourteen he joined the Great Western Railway as a telegraph clerk at Swindon. After two years he was promoted to Paddington, serving in the offices of the telegraph superintendent, chief engineer, and (from 1904) general manager. He revived the moribund staff magazine, and edited it for several years with conspicuous success, undertaking literary work for the railway press in his spare time. He also became a fluent speaker and conversationalist, and, from close association with the earliest staff conciliation schemes, a skilled negotiator. He was rejected for military service in the war of 1914–18 owing to poor eyesight. His abilities brought him rapid promotion. By 1919 he was assistant general manager, and in 1921, when forty-four, he became general manager, the highest executive officer.

Two pressing tasks confronted Pole: to restore financial stability after wartime government control; and to weld together the seven constituent and twenty-six subsidiary companies which, under the Railways Act of 1921, were now to form the enlarged Great Western Railway. He accomplished the first by firmer control of departmental expenditure, with fixed targets, streamlining the organization, more intensive use of rolling stock, and a 'drive' for increased traffic. Net revenue was increased and dividends improved. The second was completed with the minimum of friction and delay by skilful reconciliation of differing practices and personalities. His innate friendliness and honesty of purpose gave him a remarkable ability to handle men. He strove for keenness and efficiency, fostering the family spirit amongst all ranks, whether at official meetings or staff functions, and won their confidence. He could also be firm when necessary, as instanced by his energetic and resourceful action, when chairman of the railway general managers' conference, in helping to break the general strike of 1926. He encouraged good customer relations and frequently addressed chambers of commerce, Rotary clubs, and civic functions.

Receptive to new ideas, he pursued an imaginative progressive policy, endorsed by his board. Strengthening of track and bridges enabled the most powerful ('King' class) locomotives in the country to be designed to haul heavier, high-speed trains; higher capacity wagons were adopted, reducing track occupation; safety techniques lowered the staff accident rate; propaganda and publicity received a new look; housing schemes were established.

In 1923–4 Pole visited the Sudan, investigated the operation of the government railways and steamships, and effected improved organization and accounting. In 1931 he again reviewed the expenditure, also visiting Egypt and Palestine, advising on railway policy and development.

In 1929 Pole became chairman of a newly formed group of electrical companies (British Thomson-Houston, Metropolitan Vickers, Edison Swan, Ferguson Pailin, and others) known as Associated Electrical Industries, the largest group in the country, but was retained by the Great Western Railway for special consultation. His first concern was the integration of these large electrical undertakings, with conflicting traditions, practices, and capital structures, in one case largely American-owned. Initially, the goodwill and individuality of the separate companies were maintained, with central direction. Serious trade depression in the early thirties made inter-company co-operation extremely difficult, delaying co-ordination of manufacturing and marketing effort, but a start was soon made by combining British and American interests in Australia, establishing A.E.I. (India), Ltd., and concentrating the manufacture of electric motors, traction equipment, lamps, etc. By frequent consultation with the principal executive officers and staff at all levels, he won their co-operation, and inculcated the team spirit. Staff welfare was improved, and a pension scheme introduced. Trade revived, the efficiency and morale of the new giant was at a high level and A.E.I. achieved world-wide reputation. Pole travelled extensively in its interests, and in ten years visited most European countries, as well as Russia, Turkey, Iraq, Syria, Southern Rhodesia, South Africa, India, Ceylon, Brazil, the United States, and Canada. The contribution to the war effort of 1939–45 by A.E.I. was massive, and the Trafford Park works, Manchester, materially assisted in winning the Battle of Britain by producing radar.

Pole resigned the chairmanship in 1945 owing to blindness, but remained a director. He learnt Braille and continued many former activities, including the chairmanship of the *Reading Standard* and his lifelong recreations, natural history and fishing. Friends all over the world, high and low, still corresponded with him and visited his home. Selected for the office of high sheriff of Berkshire in 1947, he renounced the honour owing to his blindness. His affection for the G.W.R. never waned, and in 1956 an express 'Castle' engine was renamed 'Sir Felix Pole' in his memory. He had served on numerous government committees.

He married in 1899 Ethel Maud (died 1966), daughter of Horace Flack, a west-end shoemaker, and had one son and two daughters, He was knighted in 1924 and died in Reading 15 January 1956.

[*Felix J. C. Pole, His Book*, privately printed, 1954; personal knowledge.]

K. W. C. GRAND.

POLLITT, HARRY (1890–1960), general secretary and subsequently chairman of the British Communist Party, was born in Droylsden, Lancashire, 22 November 1890, the second of the six children of Samuel Pollitt, blacksmith's striker, and his wife, Mary Louisa Charlesworth. His mother, who came of a Yorkshire family, was a foundation member of the Independent Labour Party and the British Communist Party, a Co-operator, and a member of the Ashton and District Weavers' Association until she died. She was her son's original political mentor and ideal representative of the working class for whom he worked all his life. He went to his local elementary school and at the age of twelve became a half-timer in the local weaving mill. At thirteen he became a full-time worker. At this period he was taken by his mother to his first socialist lecture, by Philip (later Viscount) Snowden [q.v.] whose claim that 'Only when capitalism has been abolished will it be possible to abolish poverty, unemployment and war' stuck in Pollitt's memory, for it confirmed his own observations of conditions in Lancashire.

At fifteen Pollitt was apprenticed to Gorton Tank, the locomotive-building plant of the Great Central Railway; he attended night classes in mathematics, machine-drawing, shorthand, and econ-

omics, reading political writings voraciously; in 1912 he became a first-class member of the Boilermakers' Society. He had joined the Independent Labour Party in 1909 and his first leaflet, on 'Reform v Revolution', was published by the Openshaw Socialist Society. He had also begun to earn a reputation as a political speaker and between 1911 and 1914 he addressed socialist meetings all over Lancashire and Yorkshire. In 1911 and 1912, as a member of the British Socialist Party, he worked for them against the less radical Labour Party in Manchester city council elections.

During the war Pollitt opposed British participation and in 1915 as a trade unionist he organized a strike against dilution in Thornycroft's Southampton shipyard. He was elected secretary of the London district of the Boilermakers Society in 1919 and later in the year national organizer of the 'Hands Off Russia' movement which, although it failed to achieve immediate industrial action against the supply of arms to the counter-revolutionary forces, encouraged the London dockers to strike in 1920 and so prevented the *Jolly George* from sailing with ammunition for Poland.

Pollitt was a foundation member of the British Communist Party when it was formed in 1920, and in the following year he attended the third congress of the Communist International in Moscow where he met Lenin. From then on he was always at the centre of political militancy In 1924 he became secretary of the National Minority Movement which aimed to bring the trade unions under Communist control. The fall of the first Labour Government in that year drove the British Communists to even greater activity and in 1925 Pollitt was one of the twelve leading members tried at the Old Bailey for publishing seditious libels and incitement to mutiny. He was sentenced to twelve months' imprisonment and so missed the general strike.

But it was from 1936, at the time of the Spanish civil war and the Popular Front movement, that Pollitt's gifts as an agitator, orator, and a warm-hearted personality were at their height. This short, strongly built man of shining honesty and twinkling humour could work and express hate against political reaction most effectively, but it is doubtful if he could feel personal animosity against any individual. He was the epitome of the British revolutionary movement in the rst half of the twentieth century; and, espite his extremism, one of the most ved figures of his time in radical olitics.

In 1929, when Pollitt became general ecretary of the British Communist Party, was a small, sectarian organization, out f the mainstream of the Labour movement. Under his leadership it developed to a significant (if still very small) political force which exerted an influence out of ll proportion to its size. He himself stood everal times, unsuccessfully, in parliamentary elections. When England declared var on Hitler's Germany, Pollitt was robably the happiest man in the country: e immediately wrote a pamphlet, *How to Vin the War*. Although he loyally stood by his party's switch against the war nly a few days later, the decision ertainly saddened as much as it embarrassed him. For some two years he eased to lead his party, but when Russia oined the Allies he was reinstated; in 956 he became chairman and so remained until his death, 27 June 1960, on oard the liner *Orion* on his way home rom Australia.

In 1925 Pollitt married Marjory Edna Brewer who stood as a Communist parliamentary candidate in 1950. They ad a daughter and a son, Brian, who vas president of the Cambridge Union in 1962.

[Harry Pollitt, *Serving My Time*, 1940, and *Selected Articles and Speeches*, 2 vols., 1953–4; *The Times*, 28 and 30 June 1960; private information; personal knowledge.]

JAMES MACGIBBON.

PONSONBY, VERE BRABAZON, in the peerage of Ireland ninth and in the peerage of the United Kingdom first EARL OF BESSBOROUGH (1880–1956), governor-general of Canada, was born in London 27 October 1880, the eldest son of Edward Ponsonby, later eighth Earl of Bessborough, by his wife, Blanche Vere, daughter of Sir Josiah John Guest [q.v.] and his wife, Lady Charlotte Guest (later Schreiber, q.v.). He went to Harrow in the family tradition, then to Trinity College, Cambridge, and after taking his degree in 1901 was called to the bar by the Inner Temple in 1903. Bessborough, county Kilkenny, still remained the family home, and there his father, who succeeded to the title in 1906, established a pack of hounds to hunt the neighbouring country, and Duncannon, as he then became, carried the horn.

He held a commission in the Bucks Hussars and in 1906 stood for Parliament unsuccessfully at Carmarthen. During these years, he might well have been spoilt in the role of an eligible and good-looking *parti* in the Edwardian Vanity Fair. But he was level-headed and industrious and, after failing for Parliament, he put in three useful years (1907–10) representing Marylebone East on the London County Council. In January 1910 he was returned to Parliament for Cheltenham but lost his seat in the election of December. In 1912 he made the happiest of marriages with Roberte, only daughter of Baron de Neuflize, banker, of Paris, and next year was returned to Parliament for Dover, which he continued to represent until his father's death in 1920.

In the war of 1914–18 he served in Gallipoli as G.S.O. 3 and later and longer in France under Sir Henry Wilson [q.v.] on the staff. He was appointed C.M.G. in 1919. After the war he went into the City and became chairman of the San Paulo Railway, deputy chairman of De Beers, and chairman of the Margarine Union until its merger in 1929 into Unilever of which he became a joint chairman with (Sir) D'Arcy Cooper [q.v.].

In 1923 the family home in Ireland was burned down in the troubles. Earlier, prudence had decided that pictures and other treasures should gradually be removed to England, and thus a number of them were saved. Bessborough spent a year or so looking round for another home and settled on Stansted Park, Rowland's Castle, on the Hampshire border of Sussex, a fine Queen Anne replica in a wide and classic setting, and possessing a 400-year-old chapel, with literary and historic associations, which he restored. Inheriting also the family flair for acting, he built a theatre, and soon enough performances of a high order were annually given before the neighbourhood. He encouraged cricket and maintained an excellent shoot. But before all these matters were completed, he accepted in 1931 the post of governor-general of Canada. If at first the appointment caused surprise in some quarters, he could offer many qualifications: his service on the L.C.C. and in Parliament, his business experience, an innate dignity, proved thoroughness and industry, and, perhaps not least, the fact that he and his wife, who though French had a Protestant background, were bilingual, and her beauty and ability and charm outstanding. He was sworn of the Privy Council and advanced to G.C.M.G. in 1931 and remained in Canada until 1935, years in which he was not called on to deal with constitutional problems of the gravity which had faced his predecessors. Throughout his term, he proved a valuable cultural influence all over Canada, encouraging drama and the arts generally. His monthly 'duty' letters to the sovereign were well written, full, and lucid, and received the King's careful attention, and he conducted the office with great dignity after he had adapted himself to the manners and customs of a new world with which he was unfamiliar. In 1937 his Irish earldom was raised to an earldom of the United Kingdom for his services.

On his return to England in 1935 Bessborough resumed many of his City interests and became in 1936 president of the Council of Foreign Bondholders and director (he was later chairman) of the Rio Tinto Company. Among his voluntary activities he was chairman of the board of governors of Cheltenham Ladies' College and president and chairman of the council of the British Hotels and Restaurants Association. He found time, too, to edit some of the family archives, and in *Lady Bessborough and her Family Circle* (1940) he presented with considerable literary skill the first authentic portrait of his great-grandmother, Henrietta, and disposed of some of the inaccuracies which malice and gossip had piled up round her and her daughter Caroline Lamb [q.v.]. He also edited (1950–52) two volumes of diaries and papers of his grandmother, Lady Charlotte Schreiber.

With the influx into Britain of refugees and the Resistance after the outbreak of war in 1939 Bessborough was an obvious choice to organize at the Foreign Office in 1940–45 a department to co-ordinate all activities concerned with the welfare of the French in Great Britain. This he did very well, and it was a cause for which he worked until his death with constant interest and remarkable tact and ability, to which Lord Silkin paid high tribute in the House of Lords. Among other foreign decorations, Bessborough received the grand cross of the Legion of Honour.

As he grew old, his activities became no less, but more local. He was instrumental in the foundation of both the Regency exhibitions in the Brighton Pavilion and the Regency Society. In the diocese of Chichester he was for years chairman ⟨ the board of finance and did a great de of more general work for the Church i Sussex and in the Empire, to which h friend and bishop, G. K. A. Bell [q.v. paid unqualified tribute after his death.

He was an excellent landlord, knowin the family details of his tenants an neighbours and taking a deep interest i their affairs. He and his wife suffered tw separated and grievous tragedies in th deaths by accidents of their two younge sons; that of his youngest in 1951 wa a blow which must have shortene Bessborough's life. Yet he never su rendered to grief and continued his activ ties to the end. Nor did his own tragedie ever reduce the interest he felt and th sympathy he showed to the children ⟨ others. He died 10 March 1956 at Stan sted and was succeeded by his eldest an surviving son, Frederick Edward Neufliz (born 1913). There was also one daughter Portraits of him by P. A. de László (1914 and by Alphonse Jongers (in the uniform of governor-general, 1935), and a grou picture of the opening of Parliament i Ottawa in 1932, by Richard Jack, han at Stansted.

[Private information; personal knowledge.
JOHN GORE

POPE, WALTER JAMES MACQUEEN (1888–1960), theatre manager, publicist and historian. [See MACQUEEN-POPE.]

POPHAM, SIR **(HENRY) ROBERT (MOORE) BROOKE-** (1878–1953), ai chief marshal. [See BROOKE-POPHAM.]

PORTER, SAMUEL LOWRY, BARON PORTER (1877–1956), judge, was born ir Headingley, Leeds, 7 February 1877, the son of Hugh Porter, warehouse manager, and his wife, Mary Ellen Lowry. He was educated at the Perse School and Emmanuel College, Cambridge, of which he eventually became an honorary fellow (1937), for which he always retained a deep affection, and where he frequently resided. He obtained a third class in part i of the classical tripos (1899) and a second in part ii of the law tripos (1900). He was called to the bar by the Inner Temple in 1905, and, having first worked up a good general practice, later specialized in the Commercial Court. His practice was interrupted by the war of 1914–18, when he served as a captain on the general list. He took silk in 1925, was recorder of Newcastle-under-Lyme, 1928–32, and

alsall, 1932–4. In 1934 he was appointed
udge of the King's Bench division and
ighted, and in 1938 a lord of appeal in
linary (when he received a life peerage
d was sworn of the Privy Council),
thout passing through the Court of
peal.

Porter's judgements in the King's
nch division were always very sound.
ey were not spectacular, as he aimed at
nciseness, and avoided the utterance of
unnecessary word. The two most
table are perhaps *Mutual Finance,*
d. v. *John Wetton & Sons Ltd.*, [1937]
K.B. 389, and *Lloyds Bank, Ltd.* v.
nk of America etc. Association, [1937]
K.B. 631. The former is a valuable
ntribution to the doctrine of undue
fluence, and lays down that a trans-
tion can be avoided if it has been
ocured by a threat to prosecute any
rson whose safety, for whatever reason,
as desired by the promisor, such desire
ing known to the promisee. The latter,
hich was affirmed by the Court of Appeal
1938] 2. K.B. 147), concerns agency, as
exponent of which Porter attained the
nk of Ellenborough. It enunciates the
roposition that where B pledges docu-
ents relating to merchandise to A, and A
ands them back, to enable B, in con-
rmity with a course of dealing pursued
etween the parties over several years,
sell the merchandise as trustee for A,
ut B, instead, pledges the documents
ith C, who takes them in good faith,
cannot recover them from C.

Although Porter never courted publi-
ty, as a lord of appeal he inevitably
chieved it by the very high standard of
is speeches. The two by which he should
erhaps be best remembered are speeches
f dissent: in *Joyce* v. *Director of Public
'rosecutions*, [1946] A.C. 347, and *National
nti-Vivisection Society* v. *I.R.C.*, [1948]
.C. 31. In the former, a treason trial, the
rown based its case on the very dubious
round that the mere renewal by Joyce
f his British passport on 24 August 1939,
or the customary period of one year,
ecessarily imposed on him, although an
lien resident outside the realm, the duty
f allegiance to the Crown. The trial judge
eft to the jury simply the question
whether Joyce, in delivering his broad-
asts from Germany during the war, had
r had not adhered to the King's enemies,
question which could clearly be answered
nly in one way. The Court of Criminal
Appeal, and the majority of the House of
Lords, regarded this as an adequate

direction, but Lord Porter unhesitatingly
pointed out the error, which lay in the
placing of the onus of proof. It should, in
his view, be incumbent on the Crown to
prove, not only the renewal of the passport, but also its retention and use on and
after 18 September 1939, when Joyce was
first employed by the German radio company of Berlin as broadcaster to Great
Britain. His speech concluded with a
serious warning that, especially in a case
of treason, the jury should never, even in
war time, unless under statutory authority,
be ousted from a function that is rightly
its own.

The other case is one of the most important authorities on the law of charitable trusts. Here again, Porter was the
sole dissentient. The majority held that
the objects of the Anti-Vivisection Society
could not be charitable because (*a*) they
contemplated legislation, and therefore
were of a political character, which necessarily excluded them from the charitable
field, (*b*) they were not beneficial to the
community, because any benefit to public
morals obtained by their success would be
outweighed by the detriment which would
inevitably be suffered by medical science.
Porter dissented on both grounds. On (*a*)
he would exclude from the charitable
definition only those trusts whose objects
could be attained by no other means than
by legislation. On (*b*) his view may be summarized as suggesting that a judge need
not take upon himself the burden of weighing against one another the possible advantages and disadvantages which may
accrue from the success of the objects of
a trust, which, if it once satisfies the definition of charitable, does not cease to satisfy
it merely because it may bring harm as
well as benefit to the community.

He delivered the leading speech in
Reading v. *A.-G.*, [1951] A.C. 507, a
unanimous and bold decision, in that it
extended the scope of the action for money
had and received, by allowing the Crown
to claim sums obtained illegally and cor-
ruptly, and quite outside his employment,
by an army sergeant. Here, as in many
other cases, Porter showed himself a
really learned lawyer, who could turn his
mind with equal facility to any branch of
the law. But he came more into prominence
in a quasi-judicial capacity, as chairman
of the tribunal appointed to inquire into
the budget leakage of 1936 which resulted
in the resignation of J. H. Thomas [q.v.].
He was much interested in international
law, and did much valuable work for the

International Law Association. He was chairman of the committee on the law of defamation which reported in 1948, and for some years until his death chairman of the national reference tribunal of the coal-mining industry. He received the honorary degree of LL.D. from Birmingham (1940) and Cambridge (1947), and was appointed G.B.E. in 1951. He retired in 1954 and died, unmarried, in London 13 February 1956.

[Private information; personal knowledge.]
H. G. HANBURY.

POWER, SIR ARTHUR JOHN (1889–1960), admiral of the fleet, was born in London 12 April 1889, the son of Edward John Power, corn merchant, by his wife, Harriet Maud Windeler. He entered the *Britannia* in 1904 and won the King's gold medal for the best cadet of the year. In his sub-lieutenant's courses he gained first class certificates in each subject and in 1910 he was promoted lieutenant. In 1913 he was appointed to the *Excellent* to specialize in gunnery. His service in the war included appointments as gunnery officer of the battleship *Magnificent*, the cruiser *Royal Arthur*, the monitor *Raglan* in which he took part in the Dardanelles operations, and the battle cruiser *Princess Royal* in the Grand Fleet.

Power was promoted commander in 1922 and served for two years in the Admiralty as assistant to the director of naval ordnance. He was selected for a Staff College course in 1924 and, after passing, joined the battle cruiser *Hood* as executive officer. From 1927 to 1929 he was on the instructional staff of the Naval Staff College at Greenwich, and after promotion to captain in 1929 became naval member of the Ordnance Committee. He commanded the cruiser *Dorsetshire* from 1931 to 1933 as flag captain and chief staff officer to E. A. Astley-Rushton, rear-admiral commanding second cruiser squadron, and to his successor (Sir) Percy Noble [q.v.]. He was appointed to the Imperial Defence College as naval member of the directing staff in 1933, and from 1935 to 1937 commanded the naval gunnery school *Excellent*. He was in charge of the naval party which drew the gun carriage at the funeral of King George V in January 1936 and was appointed C.V.O.

In January 1938 Power was appointed to command the new aircraft carrier *Ark Royal* and was still holding this appointment at the outbreak of war in

1939. The target for many attacks by t German air force and her sinking ma times claimed, she was torpedoed Gibraltar in November 1941. Meantir Power was called to the Admiral in May 1940 as assistant chief of nav staff (Home) and was promoted re admiral one month later.

In August 1942 Power returned to sea fly his flag in the *Cleopatra* as flag offic commanding fifteenth cruiser squadro but early in 1943 was appointed flag offic Malta as acting vice-admiral, a post particular importance at that time sin it was in Malta that the planning a organization of the invasions of Sicily a Italy were being prepared. Power's ke brain and his gifts of quick decision a high organizing ability did much to ensu the rapid success of both invasions wi remarkably few casualties. After the su render of Italy he went to sea again command of the naval force occupyi Taranto and was appointed as head the allied military mission for admin stration to the Italian Governmen His promotion to vice-admiral was date 4 August 1943, and for a brief peri he acted as second-in-command of th Mediterranean Fleet.

In January 1944 Power arrived in Cey lon as second-in-command of the Easter Fleet. Many of the bombardments an naval air strikes carried out against th Japanese positions in the East Indies wer under his active leadership. On the forma tion of the British Pacific Fleet i November 1944 Power became com mander-in-chief, East Indies, initiatin many of the naval strikes and assault which brought the Japanese to defeat i Borneo and Malaya. Flying his flag in th *Cleopatra* he entered Singapore on 3 Sep tember 1945, the first ship of the Roya Navy to do so since 1942.

Power returned to England in 1946 an for the next two years was a lord com missioner of the Admiralty and secon sea lord, an appointment in which he wa in charge of the complicated run-down o the personnel of the navy to its peace time strength. He was promoted admira in 1946 and in 1948 took command of th Mediterranean Fleet. In 1950–52 he wa commander-in-chief at Portsmouth an while holding this post was promote admiral of the fleet (1952). He was als in that year allied commander-in-chie Channel and Southern North Sea. The previous year he had been made first an principal naval aide-de-camp to the King

For his war services he was appointed C.B. (1941), K.C.B. (1944), and G.B.E. (1946). He was promoted G.C.B. in 1950 and held a number of foreign decorations. Power was twice married: in 1918 to Amy Isabel (died 1945), daughter of Colonel D. A. Bingham, by whom he had three sons; secondly, in 1947, to Margaret Joyce, a second officer in the W.R.N.S., daughter of A. H. St. C. Watson, of Hendon. Power died at the naval hospital at Haslar 28 January 1960. A portrait by Sir Oswald Birley is in the Greenwich Collection.

[Admiralty records; The Times, 29 January 1960; personal knowledge.]   P. K. Kemp.

PRESTAGE, EDGAR (1869–1951), historian and professor of Portuguese, was born in Manchester 20 July 1869, the only surviving child of John Edward Prestage and his wife, Elizabeth Rose, of High Wycombe. His interest in Portugal arose from the reading of stories of adventure, particularly Vasco da Gama's voyage to India, and while still at school at Radley he began to study Portuguese with a shilling grammar. He was converted to Roman Catholicism with his mother in 1886 and in 1891 he first visited Portugal where the kindness of his reception, at a time when Lord Salisbury's ultimatum had caused much distress to the ancient ally, gave him a permanent bond with the Portuguese. Religion, he said, proved a closer tie than nationality. His lecture on 'Portugal: a Pioneer of Christianity' (1933) was perhaps the fruit of this early approach.

Prestage graduated at Balliol College, Oxford, with a second class in modern history in 1891, was admitted in 1896 and practised as a solicitor in his father's firm, Allen, Prestage & Whitfield, at Manchester, until 1907. His first published work (1893) was a translation from the French of the celebrated Letters of a Portuguese Nun ('Marianne Alcoforado'), now usually considered a literary fabrication. Prestage himself became convinced of this and refused to allow further editions after the third. He also translated for the Hakluyt Society the chronicler Azurara in collaboration with (Sir) C. R. Beazley (2 vols., 1896–9). Between 1891 and 1906 he often visited Lisbon, mainly for historical research, and made friends with a number of prominent Portuguese scholars. Already in the nineties he was elected to the Portuguese Royal Academy of Sciences. He was introduced in Lisbon to the salon of Dona Maria Amália Vaz de

Carvalho, herself a distinguished writer and widow of the Brazilian poet Gonçalves Crespo. In 1907 Prestage married her only daughter Maria Christina. His mother, who had a strong influence over him, opposed his intention of settling in Portugal, but his wife was unhappy in Southport and they soon returned to Lisbon and occupied the flat over Dona Maria Amália's in the Travessa Santa Catarina overlooking the Tagus and the Arrábida mountains.

During the following years Prestage worked continuously at his researches in the Portuguese state and private libraries. A traditionalist by temperament, he was much attached to the monarchy, and never reconciled himself to the republican regime until the advent of Dr. Salazar. He published numerous articles in Portuguese historical reviews, completed his long biography, in Portuguese, of the great writer D. Francisco Manuel de Mello (Coimbra, 1914), and published various of the Lisbon parish registers. From 1917 to 1918 he was press officer at the British legation in Lisbon. In the latter year his wife died by her own hand.

In 1923 Prestage was appointed to the Camoens professorship of Portuguese at King's College, London. It involved little teaching and he was able to devote most of his time to research, arranging periodical public lectures on Portuguese themes. In 1924 he married Victoria, daughter of Charles Davison Cobb, who had family connections with Oporto, and they settled down at her Queen Anne house at 16 Holland Street, Kensington, visiting Lisbon frequently in the spring.

At this time Prestage's main publications were connected with the period of the Portuguese Restoration of 1640. He printed much of the relevant diplomatic correspondence including (in collaboration) that of João F. Barreto, Relação da Embaixada a França em 1641 (Coimbra, 1918), and F. de Sousa Coutinho, Correspondência Diplomática (Coimbra, vol. i, 1920, vol. ii, 1926, vol. iii unpublished). His account of the Diplomatic Relations of Portugal with France, England and Holland from 1640 to 1668 was published at Watford in 1925 and in Coimbra in 1928. It is a valuable survey of the whole subject, skilfully reduced to readable proportions, but like much of Prestage's work somewhat deficient in human values. In 1929 he published an account of Afonso de Albuquerque which was followed by a general survey of the Portuguese

discoveries, *The Portuguese Pioneers*
(1933), which has been translated into various languages. He delivered the Norman
MacColl lectures at Cambridge in 1933,
and his short and necessarily incomplete
account of the Anglo-Portuguese Alliance
was presented as a lecture to the Royal
Historical Society and included in the
society's *Transactions* for 1934. After this
he wrote no major work, for in his later
years he was more concerned with spiritual
matters than with his life-work, although
he contributed chapters to several publications, and compiled a bibliography on
Portugal and the War of the Spanish
Succession. He remained professor until
two years after the usual retiring age and
died in London 10 March 1951.

Prestage was a devoted and meticulous
scholar, many of whose works have permanent value for reference. He was
elected F.B.A. in 1940, was a grand
officer of the Order of São Tiago, a
corresponding member of the Lisbon
Academy of Sciences, the Portuguese
Academy of History, and the Lisbon
Geographical Society.

[H. V. Livermore and W. J. Entwistle,
Portugal and Brazil, 1953, dedicated to Prestage and A. F. Bell as the pioneers of Portuguese studies in the United Kingdom, contains
an autobiographical memoir by Prestage;
personal knowledge.]   H. V. LIVERMORE.

PUGH, SIR ARTHUR (1870-1955), trade-
union official, was born at Ross-on-Wye
19 January 1870, the fourth son and fifth
and youngest child of William Thomas
Valentine Pugh, a native of Neath and a
civil engineer, who was at one time engaged on the construction of the Ross
to Monmouth railway, and his wife,
Amelia Rose Adlington, of Malvern Link,
Worcestershire. He had an elementary
education and at an early age was apprenticed to a farmer and butcher. When
he was twenty-four he migrated to South
Wales and secured employment at the
Cwmavon Steel Works. In his 600-page
book, *Men of Steel* (1951), a chronicle of
eighty-eight years of trade-unionism in
the British iron and steel industry, he
gives a vivid description of the job in
which he was first employed: the hours
were long, the heat intense, and the wages
4s. 6d. a shift of twelve hours.

Later Pugh went to work as a steel
smelter at the Frodingham Iron and Steel
Company in Lincolnshire. At the age of
twenty-eight he joined the British Steel
Smelters' Association and soon became
an active trade-unionist, becoming assistant secretary of his union in 1906. He
laboured assiduously for the amalgamation of the several unions then existing
and, largely as a result of his efforts, a
highly centralized organization, the Iron
and Steel Trades Confederation, was
formed in 1917, Pugh becoming the general
secretary.

In the early days of the Confederation,
its largest constituent organization was
the British Iron, Steel and Kindred
Trades Association, which formed an
essential element in the process of amalgamating the unions and of which Pugh was
also secretary. His administrative ability
attracted attention in the wider trade-
union movement and in 1920 he was elected
to the Parliamentary Committee of the
Trades Union Congress, and, on that
body's being replaced by the General
Council, he remained a member until his
retirement at the end of 1936.

Pugh was a born conciliator and did
much to promote the good relations
which existed between the workers and
the trade unions in the iron and steel
industry and the employers. In September
1925 he became chairman of the Trades
Union Congress. In the summer of that
year important discussions had taken
place between the T.U.C., the miners, and
the Government, in respect of the threatened lockout of miners by the owners to
enforce a severe reduction in wages. The
outcome of this was that for twelve months
the Government granted a subsidy of
some £20 million in the aid of wages in the
industry. In the interim, a royal commission under the chairmanship of Sir Herbert
(later Viscount) Samuel was actively at
work considering means to reorganize the
industry. Pugh took no direct part in these
discussions but as chairman of the T.U.C.
industrial committee was intimately
concerned with the negotiations with the
Government which ensued in the first
half of 1926 following the Samuel report
in March. At this time, he was about
fifty-six and at the height of his powers
as a negotiator. Throughout the exhausting discussions, sometimes lasting well
after midnight, Pugh never showed signs
of the severe strain under which he was
labouring. A man of temperate habits,
medium height, and wiry build, of fresh
complexion, with greying hair and moustache, and a high bald forehead, he looked
what he was, a kindly but resolute and
energetic man, of equable temperament
and balanced judgement.

Distressed as he was when the negotia-
ons were broken off by the Government
the early hours of 3 May 1926, he
mained throughout his calm, courteous
lf. The national strike which followed
volved nearly three million workers
d lasted nine days, during which
e T.U.C., under Pugh's chairmanship,
et daily in an almost continuously
nse atmosphere. Discussions also went
with Samuel on the memorandum
iich he eventually presented to the
overnment as a basis for settling the
spute. It became apparent that there
as no hope of a settlement satisfactory
the miners, and in a final meeting with
e Miners' Executive Pugh made an
rnest appeal for them to join with the
eneral Council in accepting the principles
the Samuel memorandum and to end
e strike. Suspicion and bitterness
ustrated this, and Pugh clearly saw that
decision of the T.U.C. alone to terminate
e strike would lead to recriminations.
evertheless he courageously faced this
sue with his colleagues, and after nine
ys the national strike was ended. The
ckout of the miners continued for nearly
x months, and when the position was
viewed, at a special conference of all
e unions, the action of the T.U.C. was
ndicated.

Until his retirement from the General
ouncil in 1936, Pugh continued to serve
e movement with diligence and capacity.
e was an ardent educationist, and, as
aairman of the Workers' Educational
id T.U.C. committee, gave unstinted
rvice to this cause.

He was not an orator, but his speeches
ere fluent, factual, and constructive.
nlike the vast majority of trade-union
fficials of his day, he read most of the
eeches he made in conference or in public
eetings. This habit militated somewhat
gainst his success as a platform speaker,
e absence of any emotional appeal being
haracteristic of Pugh's method of advo-
acy. He was appointed C.B.E. in 1930 and
nighted in 1935.

In 1901 he married Elisabeth (died
939), daughter of David Morris, of Port
'albot; they had one son and three
aughters. Pugh died in Bedford 2
ugust 1955.

[Personal knowledge.]   CITRINE.

'YE, SIR DAVID RANDALL (1886–
960), engineer and administrator, was
orn 29 April 1886 in Hampstead, London,
he sixth of the seven children of William

Arthur Pye, wine merchant, and his wife,
Margaret Thompson, daughter of James
Burns Kidston, writer to the signet, of
Glasgow. A scholar of Tonbridge School
and Trinity College, Cambridge, he was
placed in the first class of the mechanical
sciences tripos in 1908; he also won his
half blue for rifle shooting. In 1909 he was
invited by C. F. Jenkin [q.v.], who had
just been appointed the first professor of
engineering science at Oxford, to join him
in laying the foundations of the Oxford
engineering school. He was elected a
fellow of New College in 1911.

During the war of 1914–18 Pye taught
at Winchester (1915–16), then worked as
an experimental officer in the Royal Flying Corps on design and testing and learned
to fly as a pilot. In 1919 he returned to
Cambridge as a lecturer, and became a
fellow of Trinity. There he met (Sir)
Henry Tizard [q.v.] and (Sir) Harry
Ricardo, his association with whom led to
important pioneer work on the internal
combustion engine. His outstanding expositions on *The Internal Combustion
Engine* (2 vols., 1931–4) were published in
the Oxford Engineering Science series, of
which he became an editor. In 1925 he
was appointed deputy director of scientific research at the Air Ministry under
H. E. Wimperis [q.v.]. He succeeded him
as director in 1937 and in the same year
was appointed C.B. and elected F.R.S.
During the early war years he became
closely associated with the development
of the new jet propulsion aircraft engine
which he did much to encourage.

Pye was a man of many interests besides science and engineering and the fact
that he devoted so much of his earlier
life to military aircraft engines was perhaps the result of the two wars which
made demands upon his services which he
could hardly decline. It was no surprise
when in 1943 he accepted the provostship
of University College, London. He entered
upon his new duties with enthusiasm and
determination to make a real contribution
to the college and to post-war education.
Before serious illness caused his resignation in 1951, he had seen the college
through an extremely difficult period of
rebuilding, following war damage, and of
reorganization: probably the greatest
achievement of his career. He was knighted
in 1952 and in the same year became president of the Institution of Mechanical
Engineers, to which he gave a memorable
presidential address on the higher education of engineers.

Pye was fastidious and had the charm of a man of taste and intelligence who preferred to convince others by persuasion rather than by asserting the superiority of his own ideas. Believing in the highest standards, he was never arrogant or certain that he was right. Partly perhaps because he appeared to have no ambitions to leadership he was trusted and followed by his many colleagues in all his working life.

An enthusiastic climber, Pye led the first ascent of the severe Crack of Doom in Skye; in 1922 he was elected to the Alpine Club of which he became vice-president in 1956. He was a friend of G. L. Mallory (whose notice he contributed to this Dictionary) and in writing of his loss on Everest, with his companion A. C. Irvine, Pye perhaps best revealed his own character and sensitivity: 'Those two black specks, scarcely visible among the vast eccentricities of nature, but moving up slowly, intelligently, into regions of unknown striving, remain for us a symbol of the invincibility of the human spirit.'

In 1926 Pye married Virginia Frances, daughter of Charles Moore Kennedy, barrister. She became a well-known writer of books for children under the name of Virginia Pye and was a younger sister of the writer Margaret Kennedy. Pye had two sons and a daughter. He died in Godalming 20 February 1960.

[O. A. Saunders in *Biographical Memoirs of Fellows of the Royal Society*, vol. vii, 1961; *Alpine Journal*, 1960; personal knowledge.]

O. A. SAUNDERS.

QUICKSWOOD, BARON (1869–1956), politician and provost of Eton. [See CECIL, HUGH RICHARD HEATHCOTE GASCOYNE-.]

QUILTER, ROGER CUTHBERT (1877–1953), composer, born in Brighton 1 November 1877, was the third son of (Sir) Cuthbert Quilter, who became the first baronet [q.v.], and his wife, Mary Ann Bevington. He learnt from his parents, to whom he was devoted, to cultivate kindness and restraint and his artistic impulses were fostered in particular by his mother. He was educated at Eton and then went to Frankfurt where he studied music with Iwan Knorr. There he belonged to a circle of young British musicians which also included Balfour Gardiner [q.v.], Percy Grainger, Norman O'Neill,

and Cyril Scott; their individuality w encouraged but their training w thorough. A marked feature of Quilte subsequent work was his fastidiousness technical matters amid the warmth a glow of his essentially romantic muse.

The music of Quilter reflects with co siderable accuracy the relationship b tween his native temperament, h upbringing, and his particular artist bent. His quiet, sympathetic natu ripened in a cultivated and spacious hom He learnt to appreciate and enjoy thin of beauty and among them the treasu of the best lyric poetry in the Engli language. His gentleness was, howeve seasoned with a puckish humour whi often saved the day when his roman cism might have degenerated into sen mentality. Although unmarried he w devoted to children and his music parties seem often to have developed in a good romp in which the children we by no means the only participants.

Quilter was under no compulsion to ea a living. He never took pupils or held an appointment and, with his talent for eas flowing melody, he might well have b come a mere dilettante but for his eclect taste and his searching self-criticism. H would not have recognized the moder line dividing the professional from th amateur. Much of his music-making w with amateurs but there is nothing am teurish about his compositions. His ve as a composer was a small one, almost– although not entirely—limited to the fiel of English song. He chose only first-rat texts and his earliest success was wit 'Three Shakespeare Songs' (1905) whic are still firmly in the repertoire. Beside much else of Shakespeare he set man texts of Herrick, Shelley, Keats, R. I Stevenson, and others.

Quilter was long interested in the theatr and from 1911, when (Sir) Charles Hawtre [q.v.] commissioned him to write the musi for the children's play *Where the Rainbo Ends*, to 1936 when his own opera *Juli* was produced, he wrote much incidenta music of delicate charm. His best know orchestral work, *A Children's Overtur* (1914) incorporating tunes from *Th Baby's Opera*, a favourite nursery picture book by Walter Crane [q.v.], conceal beneath its ingenuous appeal his usua technical adroitness.

In 1934 a 'Pageant of Parliament' wa produced by Walter Creighton to whom Quilter had dedicated his first 'Shakespear Songs'. Quilter contributed a fine, broa

ral setting of 'Non nobis, Domine'
ich has been popular at musical festi-
ls ever since.

It may well be that Quilter's continued
d on public affection—and scarcely less
the respect of discerning musicians—is
e to the fact that he never buried his lyric
ent beneath the weight of sterile essays
symphonic forms. The significance of
share in the renaissance of the English
song lay in his ability to write, with
e purity of style, songs which were yet
eptable to audiences accustomed to the
nalities of the Victorian ballad. He did
t cultivate the continental tradition of
musical education or explore the new
ths of his contemporaries. His work
ows no trace of the influence of the
k-song revival. He speaks, without
accent, in a voice inveterately English
d in a tone of voice unmistakably his
rn.

Most of the leading singers of his day,
nong them Plunket Greene [q.v.] and
hn Coates, were glad to sing Quilter's
ngs, but the predominant influence on
s work and its reputation was his friend-
ip with Gervase Elwes [q.v.] in whom he
und an ideal interpreter. 'He inspired me
much', wrote Quilter, 'that I could
ver have written in quite the same way
I had not known Gervase.' Both were
en of cultivated background, and of
fined tastes. Both were acutely sensi-
ve to the nuances of verbal inflexion.
e sincerity and integrity of Elwes made
ery song the better for his singing and
e eloquence of his interpretations con-
yed Quilter in the best possible light, not
ast in assimilating the weaker musical
oments into the unity of the whole. For
any years the sound of Quilter's songs
as inseparable from the memory of the
ice of Gervase Elwes.

Quilter was no musical philosopher.
ore poet than prophet he did not seek
plumb the depths or argue the im-
ensities through his art. He sought to
chant rather than to edify, to persuade
ther than to perplex. But, by the time
his death in London, 21 September
)53, he had decorated a page of English
usical history with a distinctly indivi-
ual mark.

The National Portrait Gallery has a
ortrait by W. G. de Glehn.

[Private information; personal knowledge.]
HENRY HAVERGAL.

AIKES, HUMPHREY RIVAZ (1891–
)55), chemist, and principal and vice-

chancellor of the university of the
Witwatersrand, Johannesburg, was born
14 July 1891 at Ide Hill, Kent, the third
son of the vicar, (Canon) Walter Allan
Raikes, by his wife, Catherine Amelia,
daughter of William Cotton Oswell [q.v.],
the great African hunter. Raikes was
first at Tonbridge, then at Dulwich, where
he learnt to use tools and machines on
the engineering side. He was a Williams
exhibitioner at Balliol College, Oxford,
in 1910, Abbott scholar in 1911, and took
a first class in the final honour school of
chemistry in 1914. He was a keen soldier
and while an undergraduate held a
special reserve commission with the Buffs
with whom he went to France in the
autumn of 1914. After recovering from a
severe wound in May 1915 he transferred
to the Royal Flying Corps for experimental work and took a leading part in
the development of the early bombing
techniques. In January 1918 he became
chief experimental officer, Royal Flying
Corps, and later was a member of the
Royal Air Force mission to the United
States. He was awarded the A.F.C. in
1918.

Returning to Oxford in 1919 Raikes
was elected to a tutorial fellowship at
Exeter College where he became sub-
rector in 1924 (and in 1946 an honorary
fellow). He was a most stimulating
teacher, his main interest being electro-
chemistry, and his colleagues in the
growing school of physical chemistry
owed much to his skilful administration
of the Balliol and Trinity laboratories
where much of the teaching and research
in this subject were then done. In 1925
he rejoined the Royal Air Force as chief
instructor to the Oxford University Air
Squadron with the rank of wing
commander.

Raikes's striking personality and
breadth of interests had marked him out
for action in a wider sphere and in 1927
he was appointed principal of the university of the Witwatersrand, Johannesburg,
of which he became in addition vice-
chancellor in 1948. He had inherited an
interest in the African continent from his
grandfather whose sketch-map of his
journeys used to hang in his study. Those
who had the perspicacity to appoint
Raikes could not have made a wiser choice.
The university with 1,500 students had
just moved to an almost empty site at
Milner Park, and the medical school at
Hospital Hill was housed in the unfinished fragment of the final building.

Raikes's constructive mind, care for detail, aesthetic sense of fitness, determination, and untiring energy found expression in the fine group of buildings which the university and medical school enjoy. When he retired in 1954 the number of students had trebled. The destruction of the university library by fire in 1931 gave him the opportunity to build a new and finer library, for which his appeal (in which he was helped by William Cullen, q.v.) brought contributions of books from universities in many countries.

Raikes never lost his love for scientific work and he did much to encourage the development of postgraduate studies in pure and applied sciences. For some years after he went to Johannesburg he took an active part in the teaching of chemistry and one of his first tasks was to reorganize the university laboratories. When war came in 1939 he advised the older men to finish their courses and the younger to join up at once. He served as commanding officer of the Rand University Training Corps and his work as chairman of the Aptitude Tests Board, which was responsible for the methods of personnel selection for the South African Air Force, was the major influence in establishing the National Institute for Personnel Research under the South African Council for Scientific and Industrial Research. After the war he did his best by skilful improvisation to ensure that those who could profit by a university education should not suffer for their devotion to duty. Nearly 3,000 ex-servicemen entered the university and its numbers rose from three to five thousand.

In his final charge to his students Raikes spoke of 'the divine gift of statesmanship'. It was this quality, together with his modesty, which won the respect and confidence of those whom he did not hesitate to criticize if he felt it necessary. He held decided views on the relationship of white and black in South Africa, urging that the white race could not prevent but should encourage the advance of the other races. He approved the inclusion of all races in the university and felt that this was of special value to the training of medical students. When he first went to South Africa, he quickly decided that the university should assist the development of the Afrikaans-medium university of Pretoria in every way possible, and he took infinite pains in

understanding the Afrikaans point view and in addressing meetings in t language so far as he was able.

He took a broad progressive view of place of a university in modern life a under his guidance Witwatersrand veloped on lines which enabled it to m the varied needs of commerce a industry as well as to strengthen position as a centre of academic stud and research. His services were recogniz by honorary degrees from the univ sities of Bristol, Cambridge, Cape Tow and Toronto, and finally of the Witwate rand only a fortnight before his sudd death in Johannesburg 13 April 1955.

Raikes married first, in 1931, Jos daughter of Charles Mylne Mulla Indian Civil Service; the marriage w dissolved and he married secondly, 1936, Alice Joan, daughter of Willia Arthur Hardy, accountant, of Norwic There was no issue of either marriag A portrait by R. Broadley hangs in t senate room at Johannesburg.

[*The Times*, 22 April 1955; *Journal* the Chemical Society, June 1956; person knowledge.]   HAROLD HARTLE

RAM, SIR (LUCIUS ABEL JOH GRANVILLE (1885–1952), parliamenta draftsman, was born in Chester Squar London, 24 June 1885, the only survivi son of Abel John Ram, barrister, wh became a distinguished leader of t parliamentary bar, and his wife, Ma Grace O'Brien, daughter of the thirteent Lord Inchiquin. He was educated at Eto and Exeter College, Oxford, and called the bar by the Inner Temple in 191 being a pupil of (Sir) H. A. McCard [q.v.]. In the war of 1914–18 he served Egypt, Gallipoli, and France with t Hertfordshire Yeomanry, in which attained the rank of captain, and w later adjutant of the South Irish Horse.

After the war he did not return practise at the bar, although he possesse the qualities for success, but embarked c a career in the public service, as assistar solicitor, and from 1923 solicitor, to th Ministry of Labour. In 1925 he was ap pointed third parliamentary counsel t the Treasury and for the remainder of h life was a leading figure in the field government legislation. He became secon parliamentary counsel in 1929, was firs parliamentary counsel from 1937 to 194 and thereafter took charge of the consolida tion branch of the parliamentary counsel office until his death. He was appointe

B. in 1931, K.C.B. in 1938, and took
lk in 1943.

Ram believed that the draftsman had a
art to play in working out the policy as
ell as shaping the form of a bill and that
s interests and experience outside his
ecialist's field could be of value. His
wn work certainly bore this out. Thus, in
afting the big Unemployment Act of
934 his earlier experience at the Ministry
: Labour was very useful. His deputy
airmanship and subsequent chairman-
ip of the Hertfordshire quarter-sessions
ave him a special interest in the adminis-
ation of justice and penal reform, and
is was the background of his work on
e Administration of Justice Acts of
933 and 1938 and (in its initial stages)
e important measure which became the
riminal Justice Act of 1948. Perhaps the
est example was the notable Education
ct of 1944, when he worked in unusually
lose association with R. A. Butler (later
ord Butler of Saffron Walden), the
inister of education. Ram was again in
is element for he had much knowledge
f and interest in education, was a
ember of the Association of Governing
odies of Public Schools, and himself a
overnor of a number of schools.

Ram was not a lawyer of an academic
tamp and he relied a good deal on the
esearches of his assistants. He was in-
lined to be impatient when the niceties
f the law or the details of administration
ot in the way of his conception of the
orm a bill should take. His strength lay
n his creative approach, his refusal to be
lefeated by difficulties, and his resource in
inding solutions which were politically
cceptable. When he was convinced that
he course he favoured was the right one
e could deploy a formidable advocacy
nd tenacity of purpose.

During the decade before the war he
vas mainly responsible for building up the
trength of the office of the parliamentary
ounsel by recruiting a number of excep-
ionally able men, he also did much
hen and later to improve its status and
alary structure. The result was that when
he spate of legislation broke after the war
he office was equal to it. Ram himself
vas a very good head of the office, with
a sure touch in matters of administration and a readiness to stand up for his
olleagues in times of difficulty and
stress.

When he retired in 1947 from the post of
irst parliamentary counsel he took charge
of the new consolidation branch of the
office. The reform of the statute book was a
project dear to his heart and perhaps he
had too rosy a vision of a tidy and systematic arrangement of the law. If so, he
carried the lord chancellor with him in his
enthusiasm, for Lord Jowitt [q.v.] wrote
after his death: 'To no man was it given to
make a more profound alteration to the
form of our legislation. No man ever did
more to produce order out of chaos.' The
phrase 'profound alteration' was putting
it too high, but 'order out of chaos' was
nearer the mark. Ram's combination of
idealism and ability to get things done
succeeded where many had failed before
him, and the steady stream of consolidation Acts, proceeding under the aegis of a
revitalized Statute Law Committee, has
made a big difference to the availability
and manageability of the ever-growing
body of statute law.

In 1924 Ram married Elizabeth,
youngest daughter of Edward Alfred
Mitchell-Innes, K.C. They had three sons
and two daughters and their family life at
Berkhamsted Place was a full and happy
one. In spite of the demands upon his
time Ram was never too busy to enjoy
the company of his family and friends and
was always ready to advise and help
others in their troubles. It was this interest in people and human affairs which
gave depth and purpose to his public
work. He died in London 23 December
1952.

[*The Times*, 27 December 1952 and 8
January 1953; Burke's *Landed Gentry of
Ireland*, 1958; private information; personal
knowledge.]   H. S. KENT.

RAU, SIR BENEGAL NARSING (1887–
1953), Indian judge and diplomatist, was
born at Karkala in South India 26
February 1887, the second of four sons of
Benegal Raghavendra Rao, a doctor in the
service of the Madras government, and
his wife, Radha Bai. A younger brother
was Sir Benegal Rama Rau. Rau stood
first in every examination of the Madras
University for which he sat and then went
up to Trinity College, Cambridge. He was
ninth wrangler in 1909; and in the same
year he passed the Indian Civil Service
examination.

Rau was posted to Bengal in 1910 and
served as a magistrate in various districts,
transferring to Assam in 1920 in the same
capacity. In 1925 he became secretary
to the legislative department and legal
adviser. In 1933 he went to London to
present the case of Assam before the joint

select committee of Parliament on constitutional reforms. He also, at the request of that committee, prepared a scheme for a federal upper chamber under the new constitution. He was appointed C.I.E. in 1934.

On his return to India, Rau was offered a judgeship in the Calcutta high court but opted for the less remunerative but to him more rewarding post of draftsman in the law department of the Government of India. He revised the central and provincial statutes to bring them into line with the Government of India Act of 1935. Sir Maurice Gwyer [q.v.], the first chief justice of the federal court, was anxious to have Rau as a colleague; but as Rau could not be considered until he had served for at least five years as a judge of a high court, Gwyer persuaded Rau to return to Calcutta as a judge in 1938, the year in which he was knighted. Even in that capacity Rau's services were sought by the Government of India. He arbitrated in a dispute between the Government and a railway company, served as chairman of a committee to suggest revision of the civil laws pertaining to Hindus, and presided over a commission to consider the distribution of the waters of the Indus River.

These demands on Rau's time robbed him of the appointment to the federal court and in 1944 he retired from the Civil Service and accepted the prime-ministership of Kashmir State. The intrigues of an Indian court were, however, distasteful to him; and in addition he found himself in disagreement with the Maharaja on fundamental issues of policy. So in June 1945 he resigned and secured re-employment in the reforms office of the Government of India.

His work at Delhi brought Rau into contact with the Indian nationalist leaders, who were now out of jail; and, although an official in British service, his objectivity and silent patriotism commanded their respect. He assisted, from behind the scenes, in the defence of the members of the Indian National Army who were tried for treason in 1945. The next year he was appointed, with the approval of all concerned, constitutional adviser to the Constituent Assembly. It was testimony to the general regard for Rau that his advice was sought by the Government, the representatives of the Congress, and by the president of the Moslem League, M. A. Jinnah [q.v.]. Some of Rau's memoranda on the constitution have been published since his death (*India's Consti-*

tution in the Making, 1960). He also assisted the Government of Burma in drafting its constitution.

After the attainment of independence, the prime minister, Jawaharlal Nehru, was anxious to utilize Rau's services in implementing India's foreign policy. Rau was a member of the Indian delegation to the United Nations General Assembly in 1948, and represented India on the Security Council during 1950–51. He was president in June 1950 when the Council recommended intervention to help South Korea, was active in the discussions for a peaceful settlement, and was one of the three members of the cease-fire commission. His name gained wide support for the post of secretary-general but he accepted election in December 1951 as a judge of the International Court of Justice at The Hague. He had little time to make his mark there before his death in Zürich 29 November 1953.

Rau was one of the outstanding Indian members of the Indian Civil Service, whose integrity and legal acumen won worldwide recognition. He was a man of small build with a soft voice and refined features, crowned, in later years, with silver hair. He was an excellent player of bridge, golf, billiards, and in particular tennis.

[*The Times*, 1 December 1953; private information; personal knowledge.]

S. GOPAL

RAVERAT, GWENDOLEN MARY (1885–1957), artist, daughter of (Sir) George Howard Darwin [q.v.] and his wife Maud du Puy, of Philadelphia, was born 26 August 1885 in Cambridge where her childhood was spent, with periodic visits to Down House in Kent, the home of her grandfather, Charles Darwin [q.v.]. Her father was professor of astronomy and she had two uncles at Cambridge, while her mother's uncle by marriage was Sir Richard Jebb [q.v.], professor of Greek.

By the age of ten she was already drawing continuously from life and strongly wished to become an artist, and in 1908 went to the Slade School then under Frederick Brown and Henry Tonks [qq.v.]. At Cambridge before the war she found herself a member of a group of clever young men and women of whom the most prominent was Rupert Brooke [q.v.]. She fell in love with Jacques Pierre Raverat, a young French mathematical student from the Sorbonne who was continuing his studies at Emmanuel College and persuaded him to become a painter

d join her at the Slade. They were
rried in 1911.

At the outbreak of war they were
ing in Cambridgeshire but in 1915 they
nt to Le Havre to be near her husband's
nily. Raverat, by then suffering from
sseminated sclerosis, tried to join the
ench Army as an interpreter. Failing
er this, they returned to England and
ed at Weston, near Baldock, where
eir two daughters were born. In 1920
ey went again to France and lived at
nce where Jacques Raverat died in
25. Gwen Raverat then returned to
gland to live at the Old Rectory at
arlton near Cambridge until 1941 when
e moved into rooms in Cambridge and
ally took the Old Granary at the end
the garden of Newnham Grange where
e had been born.

Everything that Gwen Raverat under-
ok was done with intelligence and skill:
r graphic work for naval intelligence in
e second war as well as her theatre
signs and paintings and drawings; but
was through wood-engraving that she
as able to communicate her vision most
lly. In her engraving she did not aim at
coration or use a strong decorative line,
ke her friend Eric Gill [q.v.], or experi-
ent with new textures; nor was she a
aturalist interested in the rendering of a
rd's plumage or an animal's fur like
homas Bewick [q.v.]. Rather, she was a
aster of chiaroscuro and her simple
chnique was completely adequate for its
rpose. By her handling of light and by
od drawing she was able to turn the
ackness which the uncut block repre-
nts into a mirror of something she had
en or imagined.

Apart from illustrating Spring Morning
915), a little paper-bound book of early
oems by her lifelong friend and cousin
rances Cornford [q.v.], her work until
e thirties consisted of single prints.
hese gave her a standing among fellow
rtists and collectors and she was a
ounder-member of the Society of Wood
ngravers in 1920. But after 1932, when
e Cambridge University Press published
er engravings for a second edition of
he Cambridge Book of Poetry for Children,
elected by Kenneth Grahame [q.v.], her
ork was in continual demand from pub-
shers. Her illustration, including a few in
olour, has the seriousness and vividness
f the best Victorian work and often a
harp sense of humour. Her last important
ork was the writing of her altogether
elightful Period Piece (1952), an account,

mainly, of her childhood. She had contributed art criticism to Time and Tide
between 1928 and 1939 but had never
thought of herself as a writer and was
amazed to find her book a best-seller on
both sides of the Atlantic.

After a stroke in 1951 she could no
longer engrave but she continued to paint.
In her last years she looked like one of
her own engravings of an ancient. 'You
are an old monolith', Virginia Woolf
[q.v.] once said to her. She enjoyed the
company of the young who gave her their
respect and affection and were delighted
to sit at her feet. She died in Cambridge
11 February 1957. A self-portrait became
the property of Sir Geoffrey and Lady
Keynes.

[The Wood Engravings of Gwen Raverat,
selected with an introduction by Reynolds
Stone, 1959; Cambridge Review, 23 January
1960.]   REYNOLDS STONE.

READ, GRANTLY DICK- (1890–1959),
obstetrician and advocate of natural childbirth. [See DICK-READ.]

REDMAYNE, SIR RICHARD AUGUS-
TINE STUDDERT (1865–1955), mining
engineer, was born at South Dene, Low
Fell, county Durham, 22 July 1865,
the fourth son of John Marriner Redmayne, alkali manufacturer, by his wife,
Jane Anna Fitzgerald Studdert. He was
educated privately and at the College of
Physical Science, Newcastle upon Tyne.
An articled apprentice of William Armstrong, a prominent north-country mining
engineer, he was trained at Hetton
Collieries, county Durham. There he rose
to be an under-manager, before leaving
for South Africa in 1891 to develop a
coal property in Natal. Two years later he
returned to England and, in 1894, became
the resident manager at Seaton Delaval
Collieries, Northumberland.

In 1902 he was appointed professor of
mining in the newly created university of
Birmingham. His first task was to design
and equip a new department and prepare
a scheme of instruction. The mining
industry at that time laid little stress on
university education for its engineers,
dependence being mainly placed on
articled apprenticeship, or practical experience as a mine workman and minor
official, supplemented by education obtained at local technical colleges. With
only two British mining schools approaching university standard, Redmayne studied at first hand the methods followed by

advanced mining schools in the United States and Canada. There he found systems based on simulating in the laboratory, classroom, and field, the conditions in which the student had to work in the practice of his profession. With these in mind, Redmayne drafted his syllabus and designed his department which, for the first time in this country, included an ore-dressing laboratory and a model underground coal mine where problems associated with the practical working of a mine could be studied and explained. His pioneer work in this field stimulated new thought about higher education and training for mining engineers, and greatly encouraged its extension.

Redmayne was much at home on committee work and official inquiries. In 1906 he was a member of a committee which inquired into the probable economic effect of a limit of eight hours to the working day of coal miners—the first time any British government had essayed to fix by law the length of the daily period of employment of workers in that industry. In 1908 he became chairman of a committee to study the causes and means of prevention of accidents in mines arising from falls of ground, underground transport, and in shafts. The voluminous report of this committee—written by Redmayne—was probably the best piece of work of his career. He rejoiced that all its conclusions were subsequently incorporated in legislation. The year 1908 also saw his appointment as commissioner to inquire into a disaster at Hamstead Colliery, the first of many such appointments. Between 1908 and 1913 he conducted inquiries into disasters at Maypole, West Stanley, Wellington, Hulton, Cadeby, and Senghenydd collieries—disasters which caused a loss of 1,250 lives.

In 1908 Redmayne resigned his professorship to join the Home Office as the first chief inspector of mines in Britain, with duties which included supervising the work of district inspectors of mines, advising the secretary of state on important mining matters, conducting inquiries into accidents in mines, and editing the annual report on mines and quarries. Since he was not a civil servant this appointment met with considerable criticism, but Redmayne easily weathered the storm. From 1914 he undertook additional duties, including that of chief technical adviser (1917–19) to the controller of coal mines. In 1919 he acted as assessor to Sir John (later Viscount) Sankey [q.v.],

chairman of the royal commission coal mines. Of Redmayne's twelve yea as chief inspector, perhaps the yea 1910–11 were the most strenuous, devot as they were to framing a comprehensi Coal Mines Act, 1911. The Act—oft called the miner's safety charter—was regulate the conditions of work in Briti mines for over forty years. Altogeth his was a memorable period of servi saddened by many serious colliery d asters, but relieved by the beneficial effe of the Act of 1911, which, with its a tendant regulations, greatly helped ensure those higher standards of safe in mines which Redmayne and his co league (Sir) Malcolm Delevingne [q.v.] ha done so much to promote.

He resigned in 1919 to devote himse to the work of the Imperial Miner Resources Bureau (amalgamated in 19 with the Imperial Institute), of which was chairman from 1918 until 1935, a to practise as a consulting enginee Chairman of the Board for Mini Examinations from its inception in 19 until 1950, he also became, in 1922, t first president of the Institution Professional Civil Servants, an office which he was re-elected annually un his death. For several years he w chairman of the Road Haulage Wag Board. He played an active part in t work of professional engineering instit tions, by some of which he was honoure being elected honorary member of t Institution of Mining Engineers in 190 president of the Institution of Mining an Metallurgy in 1916, and president of t Institution of Civil Engineers in 1934– He was appointed C.B. in 1912 and K.C. in 1914. He was a companion of the Ord of St. John of Jerusalem and a chevali of the Legion of Honour.

An able administrator and speaker, man of fine presence, tact, and charm, h was a good mixer. He enjoyed the conf dence of the miners. Possessing a kee sense of humour he was a superb teller stories in the Tyneside dialect. He enjoye walking, fishing, and natural history.

Redmayne made numerous contribu tions to professional and technical journal and was the author of several book The best known are: Colliery Workin and Management (5th ed. 1951); Moder Practice in Mining (5 vols., 1908–32 and Men, Mines and Memories (1942), a autobiography written in fine style whic throws interesting sidelights on some little known aspects of British industrial life.

In 1898 he married Edith Rose (died
42), daughter of Thomas Picton
ichards, shipowner, of Swansea; they
d one son and two daughters. He died at
ttle Hadham 27 December 1955. His
rtrait, by Dorothy Vicaji, hangs in the
stitution of Civil Engineers.

[Sir Richard A. S. Redmayne, *Men, Mines
d Memories*, 1942; personal knowledge.]
ANDREW BRYAN.

EED, AUSTIN LEONARD (1873–
54), men's outfitter, was born at
ewbury, Berkshire, 6 September 1873,
e eldest son of William Bilkey Reed,
sier and hatter in Reading, and his
ife, Emily Florence Bowler. After educa-
on at Reading School, Reed joined his
ther's business in 1888. Within a few
ears he went to the United States to
udy American business methods, work-
g with Wanamaker's in Philadelphia
d Chicago, and returned with the am-
tion of founding a store which could
ovide a man, within a few hours, with
erything necessary for any occasion,
om an investiture to a tour of service in
e tropics. At the age of twenty-seven he
ked his father to lend him a thousand
ounds with which to start a business in
e City of London. With a further
ousand from the bank this was forth-
ming, and on 2 July 1900 Reed opened
s first shop, in Fenchurch Street.

From the beginning he worked on clear
inciples. Good merchandise was to be
esented without extravagant eulogy;
ices were to be plainly marked; and com-
laints met in a civil and generous spirit.
uch attention was devoted to originality
window display and from the first
dvertising played an important part in the
xpansion of the business. By 1908 there
ere three shops in the City and in 1911
ame the first west-end branch, in Regent
treet. In 1913 Reed made his first
xcursion into the provinces, in Birming-
am. Manchester followed the next year
nd by 1930 most of the largest cities in
ngland were served, as well as Glasgow
nd Belfast. In 1929 a shop was opened
board the liner *Aquitania*. Two each
ere later placed in the *Queen Mary* and
he first *Queen Elizabeth*.

In 1910 the concern had become a
rivate company; in 1920 Austin Reed,
td., offered their shares to the public on
he Stock Exchange. It was in 1920 also
hat Reed implemented his plan to pro-
ide what he called 'a Savile Row suit for
he middle-class man' at a price he could

afford. He deplored the decline in British
taste and especially deprecated the habit
of going hatless: to Reed 'man's crowning
glory is his hat!' A worthy setting for his
ideas was the new Regent Street shop
opened in 1926. Nash's Regent Street was
in process of demolition and Reed was
lucky to obtain a place in the admirable
Quadrant at the lower end designed by
Sir Reginald Blomfield [q.v.]. There the
firm was able to provide every facility,
including bathrooms and changing-rooms
where men could exchange office clothes
for evening dress. 'Austin Reed of
Regent Street' became the slogan. Reed
was a founder-member of the Regent
Street Association and its chairman in
1927. He was also a founder-member of
the National Association of Outfitters,
a president of the City of London Trade
Association, a council member of the
Multiple Shops Federation, and master of
the Glovers' Company.

Austin Reed was not only a highly
skilled business man, but won wide regard and friendship by his ideals of simplicity, sincerity, and a service devoted to
good distribution with fair dealing and
avoidance of exploitation. He was an
active Congregationalist and was deeply
influenced by Frank Buchman, founder of
the Moral Rearmament movement, whom
he met in 1933.

In 1902 Reed married Emily (died 1953),
daughter of Alfred Wilson, a Reading
butcher; they had two sons and four
daughters. The younger son was killed as
a fighter pilot in North Africa during the
war. The elder, Douglas, became vice-
chairman of the firm when his father retired as advisory director in 1953. Reed
died at Gerrard's Cross 5 May 1954.
A portrait by (Sir) James Gunn is in
the possession of the family and there
is a replica in the firm's board-room.

[*Fine and Fifty* (jubilee booklet), 1950;
The Times and *Daily Telegraph*, 6 May 1954;
Berkshire Chronicle, 7 May 1954; private
information.] HERBERT B. GRIMSDITCH.

RENDEL, HARRY STUART
GOODHART- (1887–1959), architect.
[See GOODHART-RENDEL.]

RHONDDA, VISCOUNTESS (1883–1958),
founder and editor of *Time and Tide*.
[See THOMAS, MARGARET HAIG.]

RICHARDSON, LEWIS FRY (1881–
1953), physicist and meteorologist, was
born at Newcastle upon Tyne 11 October

1881, the youngest of the seven children of David Richardson, a Quaker and a tanner in an old family business, and his wife, Catherine Fry, of a family of corn merchants in Devon. Sir Ralph Richardson, who contributes to this Supplement, is his nephew. Richardson left Bootham School in 1898 with the conviction 'that science ought to be subordinate to morals', spent two years at Durham College, entered King's College, Cambridge, in 1900 and, obtained a first class in part i of the natural sciences tripos in 1903. After a number of appointments including one with the National Peat Industries, Ltd., he entered the Meteorological Office in 1913 as superintendent of Eskdalemuir Observatory, to begin his fruitful association with (Sir) Napier Shaw [q.v.]. In 1916–19 he served in the Friends' Ambulance Unit with the French Army. In 1920 he took charge of the physics department of Westminster Training College and in 1929 he became principal of Paisley Technical College and School of Art, retiring in 1940 to do research on the causes of war and on eddy diffusion.

It was the practical problem of the flow of water in peat which led Richardson to devise his method for the approximate solution of the intractable differential equations of this and similar problems in physics and engineering. He demonstrated how the appropriate use of finite differences should and could secure a degree of accuracy far surpassing that previously obtainable. It was natural that in the Meteorological Office he should use this knowledge to construct 'a scheme of weather prediction which resembles the process by which the *Nautical Almanac* is produced in so far as it is founded upon the differential equations and not upon the partial recurrence of phenomena in their ensemble'. Richardson's achievement was to set out the dynamics and thermodynamics of the atmosphere in the light of the recently acquired knowledge of the upper air and the roles of radiation and eddy diffusion and to show how the resulting equations could be solved with the accuracy permitted by the basic data, the actual meteorological observations. The result was published in 1922 in his classical work *Weather Prediction by Numerical Process*. Application of the method proved conclusively that the required degree of accuracy and promptness in producing the prediction could not be achieved with the means of observation

and computation then available. Eddi various-sized parcels of air in circulato motion of which the atmosphere is cons tuted, collectively represent its turbulen Richardson showed that a suitable c terion for increase or decrease of turb lence was the ratio between the opposi effects of wind and temperature. There a ancillary effects but the ratio, now call the Richardson number, Ri, ranks atmospheric turbulence with the Reyno number, R, the criterion for turbulen due to molecular viscosity. A furth method of treating eddy diffusic introduced by Richardson in 1926, l dormant for twenty years until it w rediscovered.

Richardson was also a pioneer in t mathematical investigation of the caus of war, first publishing a paper on t mathematical psychology of war in 191 The relations between nations can expressed by mathematical symbol equations, readily soluble if the differe elements can be given numerical values, recognized difficulty, practically insupe able for the imponderables. Neverthele useful conclusions may be drawn fro the symbolic equations themselves. A arresting example is that unilateral di armament cannot be permanent. He e panded his early paper in a book *Arms a Insecurity* and added a second book *Stat tics of Deadly Quarrels* in which he tabul ted all the wars between 1820 and 194 classified according to their magnitu and their origins, adding ten chapters comment and explanation. The tw books were published in 1960 throug the efforts of American scientists an publicists who, recognizing the value Richardson's work, raised the necessar funds.

Richardson's character and his ex perimental ability and gift for th improvisation of apparatus stood him i good stead at Westminster and Paisle Problems in practical physics whic troubled his staff were soon solved b consultation with the principal. He wa a clear lecturer but regarded adminis trative work though rather dreary as task to be performed with diligence an foresight but with none of the thrill c research. Nevertheless it was by the fu exercise of such diligence and foresight tha he succeeded in obtaining an extension o the laboratories at Paisley during a perio of general retrenchment.

Research for Richardson was th inevitable consequence of the tendenc

his mental machine to run almost, but
t quite, of itself. So he was a bad
tener, distracted by his thoughts, and
bad driver, seeing his dream instead of
e traffic. The same tendency explains
ly he sometimes appeared abrupt in
anner, otherwise inexplicable in one of
s character. In the motor convoy in
ance he evoked the affection of all and
monstrated the dignity of service by the
nplicity with which he performed the
ost menial tasks; that character of
ndness and service was maintained at
estminster and Paisley.

Richardson married in 1909 Dorothy,
ughter of William Garnett, after whom
rnett Technical Training College was
med. They had no children but adopted
o sons and a daughter. Richardson
us elected F.R.S. in 1926 and died at
s home at Kilmun, Argyllshire, 30
ptember 1953.

[E. Gold in *Obituary Notices of Fellows of
: Royal Society*, vol. ix, 1954; private
:ormation; personal knowledge.]

E. GOLD.

[CHARDSON, SIR OWEN WILLANS
379–1959), physicist, was born 26 April
79 in Dewsbury, Yorkshire, the eldest
the three children of Joshua Henry
ichardson, woollen manufacturer, and
s wife, Charlotte Maria Willans. From
. John's church day school, Dewsbury,
ichardson won a scholarship to Batley
rammar School. Another scholarship took
m to Trinity College, Cambridge, where
: gained a first class in part i of the
itural sciences tripos (with distinction in
iysics, chemistry and botany, 1899) and
oceeded in physics and chemistry to
first in part ii (1900). He was elected a
llow of Trinity in 1902, became Clerk
axwell scholar in 1904, and was awarded
e London D.Sc. in the same year.

By this time Richardson was absorbed
research among the illustrious company
spired by (Sir) J. J. Thomson [q.v.] at
e Cavendish Laboratory. One of his
st investigations (c. 1901) concerned the
aximum electron current (i) which could
: drawn by an electric field from a hot
atinum filament (temperature T) con-
ined in a vacuum tube. He formulated
general theory of the process wherein
ectrons in the metal, responsible for its
ectrical conductivity, were regarded as
aporating through a potential barrier
its surface. The classical kinetic theory
gases was applied to a postulated elec-
on 'gas' inside the metal. His measure-

ments fitted his formula $i = A_1 T^{\frac{1}{2}} e^{-\phi/kT}$
where A_1 and k are constants and ϕ (the
'work function') is the energy needed to get
the electrons over the barrier. However,
difficulties in other fields of physics led
to reconsideration of the theory from
less specific thermodynamical approaches.
Richardson, Harold Albert Wilson, and
several others gradually improved the
derivation of the emission formula obtaining $i = A_2 T^2 e^{-\phi/kT}$ which has become
known as Richardson's law, familiar to
physicists and electronic engineers. A_2
is a constant different from A_1. Experimentally the formulae are difficult to
distinguish because of the overwhelming
control by the exponential term. The
second formula has withstood the test of
experiment and time; nevertheless almost
a quarter of a century elapsed after its
original derivation about 1903, whilst
radical changes in the electron 'gas'
concept occurred, before the theory was
hammered into something like its present
form. The basic, evaporation--potential
barrier, idea is retained. Richardson's
contribution in this field was recognized
by the award of the Nobel prize in physics
in 1928. He coined the word thermion,
hence thermionics referring to the emission
of electricity—negative or positive—by
hot bodies.

The difficulties encountered raised other
questions. Mathematical studies of ionic
recombination contributed to understanding of what was going on in the imperfect
vacuum outside the emitting surface. Experimental and theoretical investigations
of diffusion problems, e.g. of hydrogen
through palladium and platinum, contributed to ideas on what was going on inside
metals. These seem to have been guiding
principles for Richardson's further Cambridge researches in physics, but an element of indecision regarding his future
course is evident from other investigations
in physical chemistry and from a record
of an application for a chair of physical
chemistry at Liverpool.

In 1906 Richardson was appointed to
the chair of physics at Princeton. His
researches soon covered most phenomena
directly relatable to thermionic emission:
cooling and heating effects accompanying
thermionic emission and absorption,
energy distribution and properties of
thermions, reflexion of slow electrons
from metallic surfaces, theory of contact
e.m.f. and thermo-electricity, the photo-
electric effect and the emission of positive
ions from heated salts. With K. T.

Compton he played an important part in the verification of the Einstein photo-electric law. His acquisition of a powerful X-ray machine probably enabled A. H. Compton to discover the Compton effect. These and other of Richardson's Princeton students later became outstanding figures of American science. Richardson intro-duced the technique of screening electro-meter leads in dry metal tubes and so enabled work in the humid summer months.

In broader fields of electron physics Richardson speculated on the possibility of explaining gravitation in terms of electron theory and predicted (1908) a rotational reaction on magnetization of iron. He failed to detect this effect, but it was observed by Einstein and de Haas in 1919 and has been called the Richardson –Einstein–de Haas effect. The converse phenomenon, observed by S. J. Barnett (1914), has been termed the Richardson–Barnett effect. These 'gyromagnetic' and 'magneto-mechanical' phenomena were more fully explained after the electron 'spin' concept had been introduced by Uhlenbeck and Goudsmit (1925).

In 1914 Richardson returned to England to assume the Wheatstone chair of phy-sics at King's College, London. His splendid book, *The Electron Theory of Matter* (1914), based on his Princeton lectures, was followed by *The Emission of Electricity from Hot Bodies* (1916). At King's College, under the impact of the quantum theory and the stimulus of Bohr's explanation of the hydrogen spectrum, he began a protracted series of spectroscopic researches, although therm-ionics, the photoelectric effect, metallic conduction, reflexion of slow electrons from metals, emission of electrons in chemical reactions, and problems of theoretical physics continued to occupy him. He was elected F.R.S. in 1913 and appointed Yarrow research professor in 1924, being thereby relieved of teaching duties.

Richardson will always be remembered for his basic contributions to the analysis of the molecular hydrogen spectrum. His book *Molecular Hydrogen and its Spectrum* (1934) is based on his Silliman memorial lectures at Yale in 1932. He acquired a magnificent reflexion echelon for which he devised a bold and stimulating programme mainly to test what have proved key-stones of physics: theories of the spectra of atomic hydrogen and its isotopes. By far the most accurate wave number

measurements of hydrogen spectrum lin hitherto made were obtained with th instrument (1940) but a flaw in the analy of the fine structure components (probab occasioned by disruption of work due the imminence of war) most regrettab obscured a vital feature only cleared in 1947 by Lamb and Retherfor Richardson's greatest project, to use th instrument for measurements on t Lyman α-line, was abandoned because the war, but before the evacuation King's College in 1940 and the destructi of his laboratory by enemy action, son measurements were obtained on fi structures in the molecular hydrog spectrum which beautifully confirme his previous work. He continued scienti work long after retiring from his Yarro professorship in 1944 and between 19 and 1953 published, with his collaborator over 130 scientific papers.

He received honorary degrees fro Leeds, St. Andrews, and London; was fellow of King's College, London (192 and an honorary fellow of Trini College, Cambridge (1941). From the Roy Society he received the Hughes med (1920) and a Royal medal (1930). He w knighted in 1939. He was president of th Physical Society in 1926–8 and its hono ary foreign secretary from 1928 to 1945.

Richardson married in 1906 Lilia Maude (died 1945), daughter of Albe William Wilson, goods manager to th North Eastern Railway Company Darlington, and sister of his friend H. Wilson. The Richardsons had two sons an a daughter. The elder son became profess of physics at Bedford College, Londo and the younger a psychiatrist. In 194 Richardson married Henrietta Mari Rupp, family friend for many years an former wife of Professor E. Rupp Berlin-Reinickendorf. Richardson's sister married distinguished Americans, th physicist C. J. Davisson, and the mathe matician Otto Veblen.

Richardson was short, wiry, and shar featured, in contrast with his first and i common with his second wife. In h younger days he was fond of fell an mountain walking, sometimes alone, an could cover forty miles in one day. H had been known to take a sleeper to For William, climb Ben Nevis, and return b the next sleeper.

The Richardsons had a home of extra ordinary beauty containing the fines English period furniture and a wonderfu collection of paintings by Dutch and othe

d masters. They kept a large and
eautiful garden. Richardson had a fund of
umorous after-dinner stories, sometimes
ld in the West Riding dialect, which he
ould speak perfectly. He had a hesitant
it precise manner of speech. He kept a
ood table and a well-stocked cellar (where-
whisky was drawn from the wood). He
ise late but seldom retired before 3 a.m.;
is he said left it too late for burglars to
art operations and he could work well
the early hours of the morning. He was
kindly man with much sympathy for
fugees from totalitarian countries whose
isdirection of science he detested. He
ice remarked that he held practically
) absolute conviction about anything
xcept that science should be free. His
ork had practical applications in radio
id other fields but he declined himself
) be sidetracked from fundamental
vestigations.

In 1939 Richardson moved from Hamp-
ead to Alton, Hampshire. Partly as a
ar effort he bought a large farm at
edstead, near by, which he supervised
osely for several years. He was president
' the North-East Hampshire Agricultural
ssociation in 1948–9. He died at Alton
5 February 1959.

[*The Times*, 16 and 21 February 1959;
. T. Flint in *Yearbook* of the Physical
iciety, 1959; William Wilson in *Biographical*
lemoirs of Fellows of the Royal Society, vol. v,
59; *Nature*, 4 April 1959; private informa-
on; personal knowledge.]　　E. W. FOSTER.

IDLEY, HENRY NICHOLAS (1855–
156), plant-geographer and economic
otanist, was born 10 December 1855 at
Vest Harling Hall, Norfolk, the third
iild of the Rev. Oliver Matthew Ridley
nd his wife, Louisa Pole, daughter of
Villiam Stuart, of Aldenham Abbey.
 great-great-grandfather was John
tuart, Earl of Bute [q.v.], who also
:hieved botanical distinction and acted
s scientific adviser to Princess Augusta
hen she was initiating the botanical
ardens in her private domain at Kew. At
Iaileybury, Ridley's biological predilec-
ions received encouragement. At Exeter
ollege, Oxford, where he obtained a
econd class in natural science in 1878, his
iterests were centred more on geology and
oology than on botany; in 1880 he was
warded the Burdett-Coutts scholarship
a geology. Nevertheless the necessity of
btaining a remunerative post led him in
880 to apply for a position in the botani-
al department of the British Museum at

South Kensington, where he began to
develop his lifelong interest in the geographical distribution of plants. Seven
years later he was selected to accompany
the Edinburgh zoologist, G. A. Ramage,
on an expedition to Brazil which was
sponsored by the Royal Society.

This tropical experience led to his selection, in 1888, as director of the gardens
at Singapore. Part of his duties there was
the making of a preliminary forest survey
and the expeditions he carried out in this
connection and his extensive exploration
in the adjacent territories provided much
of the material and information which
resulted in his *Flora of the Malay Peninsula* (5 vols., 1922–5). In addition to
his travels within the Malay peninsula
Ridley also visited Borneo and Sumatra
(1897) and the Christmas and Keeling
Islands (1890–91). He was in Sarawak
four times between 1903 and 1915. In 1911
he was in southern Siam and in the following year in Burma, India, and Egypt. In
1915 he was in Java and a year later in
Jamaica. From all these areas he brought
back material which enriched the collections at Kew and one genus *Ranalisma*
is known only from the specimens which
Ridley collected.

On his appointment to Singapore
Ridley found there seedlings of the Para
rubber tree which had been sent from
Kew through the enterprise of Sir
Clements Markham and Sir Joseph Hooker
[qq.v.]. But it was Ridley's faith in the
value of the Para rubber as a plantation
crop in Malaya which led him to persuade
planters to experiment with the new crop
and to surmount the initial difficulties.
His services in establishing the rubber
plantation industry were recognized by
the award of the gold medal of the Rubber
Planters' Association in 1914 and fourteen
years later by the award of the American
Frank Meyer medal. His active interest
in the applied aspects of botany was
further demonstrated by his initiation of
the *Agricultural Bulletin of the Malay
States* which contained many papers contributed by himself, and by his book on
Spices (1912).

Ridley was always keenly interested
in problems of dispersal, especially by
animals and wind. This finally found
expression in his book, *The Dispersal of
Plants Throughout the World* (1930),
which he wrote after his retirement from
Singapore in 1911, when he returned to
England to live until he died in the
Cumberland Road, Kew.

Ridley was a versatile and entertaining conversationalist who, almost to the end of his days, enjoyed imparting his reminiscences to others. He was elected F.R.S. in 1907, appointed C.M.G. in 1911, and awarded the gold medal of the Linnean Society in 1950. On his hundredth birthday he received numerous tributes from home and overseas amongst which was an appreciation from the president and council of the Royal Society. He was a prolific writer. On botanical subjects alone his papers comprised some 270 items, over fifty others dealt with zoological topics; about ninety more were on agricultural and applied botanical subjects and some forty on a variety of topics, geological, medical, ethnological, and biographical. Until he became bedridden he was a never-failing observer of the birds in Kew Gardens. Ridley was short in stature and in later years distinctly rotund, but his appearance was not undistinguished because of the keen observant eyes.

In 1941 Ridley married his housekeeper Lily Eliza, daughter of the late Charles Doran, builder. He died 24 October 1956 less than two months before his 101st birthday. He was the last surviving founder-member of the Society for Psychical Research.

[Sir Edward Salisbury in *Biographical Memoirs of Fellows of the Royal Society*, vol. iii, 1957; personal knowledge.]

E. J. SALISBURY.

RIVERDALE, first BARON (1873–1957), industrialist. [See BALFOUR, ARTHUR.]

ROBEY, SIR GEORGE EDWARD (1869–1954), comedian, whose original name was George Edward Wade, was the elder son of George Wade, civil engineer, and his wife, Elizabeth Mary Keene. He was born at 334 Kennington Road, London, 20 September 1869. Since his father's profession involved moving from one constructional task to another, Robey spent his boyhood and youth in a variety of addresses and at several schools. The family moved at various times from London to Hoylake, back to London, and then to Germany, where his father was engaged on tramway work. At the age of eleven, Robey was at an academy in Dresden, where he learned to speak excellent German and did well in classics. He then moved to Leipzig University where he studied science for a year and a half and was wounded in

a duel which might have proved fatal to both parties.

When his father's contract was concluded the Wades returned to England and Robey found a post in his father's profession, beginning on the clerical side in connection with tramway work in Birmingham. His recreations were football, painting, and music: he soon developed a talent for singing, was a favourite amateur performer at concerts, with voice and mandolin, and then discovered his capacity as a comedian. He returned to his family at Brixton Hill in London and there he continued his amateur appearances with increasing success: soon he found that he could earn small but welcome fees. Since there was some domestic dismay that he should be earning money in this way, he took the stage-name of Roby, later Robey. This was the name of a builder's business in Birmingham, and it appealed, for stage purposes, as simple, robust, and easily pronounced. He adopted it later by deed poll.

His first success came by co-operation with a hypnotist, 'Professor' Kennedy who staged a popular act at the Royal Aquarium in Westminster. This hall had largely abandoned the display of fish and was exploiting a variety entertainment. Young Robey's miming of a hypnotized singer was so effective that he attracted professional and managerial notice and was engaged to make his first music-hall appearance at the Oxford in June 1891 at the age of twenty-one. He was billed only as 'an extra', but his popularity was immediate and his name was soon exhibited on the posters and proved an attraction. He rapidly established not only a name but an aspect, the aspect by which the public knew and richly enjoyed his turn for much of the rest of his long life. Part of the aspect was conventional: the 'red nosed comedian' was a fact as well as a phrase and so, accepting the tradition, he applied the scarlet. But to this he added strongly blackened eyebrows and he chose as a contrast to the bibulous colour scheme, a long black frock-coat and top hat. (Later this was abandoned and a squashed bowler took its place.) This almost funereal solemnity was countered by the total absence of any collar and by the carrying of a masher's cane. So the total effect was that of a debauched piety and of a respectability at once tattered raffish, and gay, half Bardolph, half Stiggins, wholly Robey.

His career in 'the halls' was one of great ~~si~~dustry—often he played several 'houses' ~~a~~ night—and of continuously mounting ~~sys~~teem. He possessed the qualities essen~~ti~~al to capturing the huge and often ~~re~~stless audience of the old 'palaces of ~~va~~riety': quenchless vitality and an im~~m~~ense power of attack. He was billed later ~~on~~ as 'The Prime Minister of Mirth', but ~~pr~~ime ministers are the dominant figures ~~in~~ democracies, ruling by persuasion. ~~R~~obey could more accurately have been ~~ca~~lled the dictator of laughter, so firmly ~~di~~d he grip and subdue his audiences. ~~T~~he immediate assault upon the centre of ~~th~~e stage, the beetling brows, the abrupt ~~an~~d shattering defiance of any unruly ~~la~~ughter, the swift plunge into song and ~~p~~atter, the absolute sureness of command ~~—~~these were the signs and proofs of ~~so~~vereign power.

There were occasional alterations from ~~th~~e customary Robey uniform. He ran~~sa~~cked history for a series of famous or ~~in~~famous characters; and in pantomime, ~~w~~here he was a constant favourite, he ~~u~~sually played the dame, bonneted and ~~st~~ridling, at once grotesque and genial, ~~cr~~eating out of a termagant's tantrums a ~~fo~~untain of hilarity. The leading dramatic ~~cr~~itics made a point of seeing Robey ~~w~~hen they could and he evoked notices ~~fr~~om the most distinguished pens. C. E. ~~M~~ontague [q.v.] wrote of Robey's work in ~~h~~is *Dramatic Values* (1911) that, while ~~th~~e range of characterization was small, ~~t~~he study is diabolically intimate, and the ~~ex~~ecution edged and finished like a cut ~~je~~wel. . . . You may call the topics out~~w~~orn and trivial, the mere words insig~~n~~ificant, the humour metallic, rasping, ~~o~~r worse, but the art, within its limits, is ~~n~~ot to be surpassed in its gleaming, ~~el~~liptical terseness, the volumes it speaks ~~i~~n some instants, its suddenness, fire, and ~~z~~est.'

When the 'single turn' began to go out ~~o~~f fashion, Robey appeared frequently as ~~th~~e comedian of large-scale revues. One ~~o~~f his most notable appearances in this ~~k~~ind of revue was during the war of 1914– ~~1~~8. With Alfred Lester and Violet Loraine ~~[q~~.v.] he made *The Bing Boys are Here* at ~~th~~e Alhambra one of the greatest of war~~ti~~me consolations for men on leave. Its ~~m~~ost popular number was the straight ~~d~~uet, 'If you were the only girl in the ~~w~~orld . . . ', which he sang with Violet ~~L~~oraine.

He left revue for operetta in 1932 ~~w~~hen he played Menelaus in (Sir) A. P.

Herbert's version of Offenbach's *La Belle Hélène* with Max Reinhardt as producer and (Sir) C. B. Cochran [q.v.] as manager. The weak husband was an odd part for Robey, to whose comedy trucul- ence was natural. In such a situation he had to tone down the vigour of his usual bravura comicality and he accepted the discipline so well that James Agate [q.v.] described his performance as 'a miracle of accommodation like that of a trombone- player obliging with a pianissimo'.

In 1935 came a Shakespearian interlude. Robey was persuaded to play Falstaff in a revival of *Henry IV, Part I* at His Majesty's Theatre. He took this risk with natural trepidation and, although on the first night he had not completely mastered his lines, he triumphantly mastered his audience, including the critics. It was agreed that the man from the music-halls could play the classic character as well as the classic buffoon, with communicable relish of Shakespeare's wit and with a well-controlled ability to make the most of the fat knight's ebullience and humilia- tions. When a colour film of *Henry V* was produced by (Sir) Laurence Olivier nine years later, the death-scene of Falstaff, only described in the text, was inserted pictorially, with Robey briefly appearing as the knight in his last moments.

At all times, and especially during two wars, his services to charity were un- grudging: he was at the head of an always generous profession and he led the appro- priate response to all calls on its good will. Honours were now coming to the theatre and he had been offered a knighthood after the first war, but he modestly thought that this was too much for a comedian and in 1919 accepted a C.B.E. instead. Knight- hood did come to him in the late evening of his life, in 1954.

Robey's recreations, when beyond the years of field-sports, were the collection of stamps, china, and porcelain, painting, and the making of violins. Thus he relieved the leisure moments of a long and industrious as well as an illustrious life, during which he won a full meed of friendships far and wide as well as of honours from the State. An athletic youth, prudent living, and great natural vigour sustained him to his ripe maturity, and great knowledge of the comedian's craft promoted him at length from the broader to the finer drol- lery. That he could hold his own in a Shakespearian company of many talents showed the measure of his art and his adaptability. But it was as Robey of the abbreviated bowler-hat and the suit of solemn black, rubicund and raffish, that his contemporaries would most gratefully remember a radiant and uproarious presence.

His first marriage, in 1898, to a musical-comedy actress, Ethel, daughter of Thomas Haydon, of Melbourne, was dissolved in 1938; his second wife, whom he married in that year, was Blanche, daughter of F. R. Littler, an active member of a family highly placed in theatrical management. By his first marriage he had a son, Edward George Robey, who practised at the bar and in 1954 became a metropolitan magistrate, and a daughter, Eileen Robey, a portrait painter. Robey died at Saltdean, Sussex, 29 November 1954. Drawings of himself are at the National Portrait Gallery.

[George Robey, *My Life Up Till Now*, 1908, and *Looking Back on Life*, 1933; A. E. Wilson, *Prime Minister of Mirth*, 1956; private information; personal knowledge.]

IVOR BROWN.

ROBINSON, (ESMÉ STUART) LENNOX (1886–1958), Irish dramatist and theatre director, was born in Douglas, county Cork, 4 October 1886, the youngest of the seven children of Andrew Craig Robinson, stockbroker, and his wife, Emily Jones. His father took orders in 1892 and served as curate of Kinsale until 1900 when he became rector of Ballymoney. Robinson was educated at home and at Bandon Grammar School. His first dramatic work, a one-act play, *The Clancy Name*, based on a story by his sister, was staged at the Abbey Theatre, Dublin, in 1908. The theatre was soon to absorb almost all his activity, although he also worked (1915–25) as organizing librarian for the Carnegie Trust in Ireland.

This was a time of change in the Irish theatre. The work of J. M. Synge [q.v.] was almost finished and the Abbey was still suffering from that lack of public enthusiasm not quite amounting to a boycott which followed the hostile reception of *The Playboy of the Western World* (1907). There was need for some more popular appeal and the trend seemed to be away from romanticism. *The Clancy Name*, although inclined in this direction, was rather melodramatic, telling of a family saved from disgrace over giving help to a murderer by the accidental death of John Clancy while trying to save a child from a runaway horse. In 1909 Robinson tried a problem play, *The Cross*

Roads, more akin to the later 'Manchester School'. His third play, *Harvest* (1910) was didactic but showed him as a man well started on the way to a dramatic career. At this time W. B. Yeats [q.v.] wrote of him that he 'does not argue like the imitators of Ibsen though his expression of life is as logical, hence his grasp of active passion' and 'He is a serious intellect and may grow to be a great dramatist'. He did not become great in the sense that Synge or Sean O'Casey did, but the Abbey Theatre was deeply in his debt for furnishing a steady flow of good plays during thirty years—plays which were typical of the modern Irish drama as any of those by dramatists with more resounding reputations. Among them may be mentioned *Patriots* (1912); *The Dreamers* (1915); *The Whiteheaded Boy* (1916); *The Lost Leader* (1918); *Crabbed Youth and Age* (1922); *The Round Table* (1922); *Never the Time and the Place* (1924); *Portrait* (1925); *The White Blackbird* (1925); *The Big House* (1926); *The Far Off Hills* (1928); *Ever the Twain* (1929); *Drama at Inish* (1933); *Church Street* (1934); *Killycreggs in Twilight* (1937); and *Bird's Nest* (1938).

From the first Robinson applied himself particularly to the technical problems of building plays which could be acted in the limitations of a small theatre with a small cast and not much money. On these foundations he developed into a craftsman of the theatre whose work was an example to younger dramatists who thought plays were something to be easily and quickly thrown together. Many other Irish dramatists owed a lot to Robinson for advice on what to do with the intractable play. The care with which he built up his characters and the situations he put them in is typified by one of his beliefs that even when dealing with imaginary people 'there must always remain the country on the dark side of the moon, unknown to the audiences but as vivid to the playwright as the side that shines on the stage'.

Robinson was appointed manager of the Abbey Theatre in 1910 and almost at once ran into trouble. His was the only theatre in the then United Kingdom to remain open on the night after King Edward VII's death. He had telegraphed for instruction to Lady Gregory [q.v.] whose advice to close 'through courtesy' arrived too late. The theatre remained open. Robinson was treated almost as a hero by the nationalists, but there were rious consequences for the theatre. The accident brought to a head disagreements between the directors and Miss . E. F. Horniman [q.v.] who was then subsidizing the theatre but shortly afterwards severed all connection with it.

Robinson's first period of management 1910–14) was a difficult one financially or, without the Horniman money, the theatre had little, sometimes nothing, in reserve. His second period (1919–23) was still more difficult owing to the Anglo-Irish war. In 1923 he became a director of the theatre which in the next year became the first state-subsidized theatre in any English-speaking country. The same year (1924) saw the production of *Juno and the Paycock* by Sean O'Casey whose qualities Robinson was among the first to realize. More perceptively he backed O'Casey's change of style which began to show in *The Silver Tassie* (1929) with the remark that he was glad to see him groping towards a new manner since he could not go on writing slum plays for ever.

A vigorous and authoritative lecturer, Lennox Robinson paid a number of visits to the United States. His two main excursions into journalism were in 1924 when he contributed to the *Observer* for a year, and in the fifties when he became a regular essayist for the *Irish Press*. The circumstances in which he lost this post were in character. He was not a strongly politically minded man and believed firmly that politics were better kept out of cultural matters (except possibly in the case of plays by Sean O'Casey). Therefore he saw no wrong in accepting an invitation to visit China as a representative Irish intellectual. Nobody could have had less inclination towards Communism, but his journey compromised him. *I Sometimes Think* (Dublin, 1956) is a selection from the essays written at this period. His many other publications included other essays, a novel, short stories, anthologies of verse, and two volumes of autobiography: *Three Homes* (with his brother and sister, 1938) and *Curtain Up* (1942). He edited *Further Letters of J. B. Yeats* (1920) and *Lady Gregory's Journals* (1946). In 1951 he published *Ireland's Abbey Theatre*, the best collection of facts so far made about the first half-century of the modern Irish theatre, but not in itself a complete guide to all that happened in the period. He received the honorary degree of D.Litt. from Trinity College, Dublin, in 1948.

In 1931 Robinson married Dorothy Travers Smith, of Dublin; there were no children. He died at Monkstown, county Dublin, 14 October 1958, and was buried in St. Patrick's Cathedral, Dublin. He was a tall, fragile-looking man with a faraway look in his eye, but entirely down to earth when looking after the business of the Abbey Theatre, where there is a portrait by James Sleator. A drawing by (Sir) William Rothenstein is reproduced in *Twenty-four Portraits*, second series, 1923.

[Private information; personal knowledge.]

GERARD FAY.

ROBINSON, ROY LISTER, BARON ROBINSON (1883–1952), forester, was born 8 March 1883 in the village of Macclesfield, near Adelaide, South Australia, the eldest son of William Robinson, a mechanical engineer, and his wife, Annie Lowe. He was educated at St. Peter's College, and at the university, Adelaide, where he graduated B.Sc. in 1903 and obtained his diploma in applied science (mining engineering) in 1904. A brilliant scholar and also an athlete, he was selected as the second Rhodes scholar from the state of South Australia, and went up to Magdalen College, Oxford, in 1905. He obtained a first class in natural science (geology) in 1907 and was awarded the Burdett-Coutts scholarship. He then obtained his diploma in forestry which he studied under Sir William Schlich [q.v.] who on more than one subsequent occasion acclaimed Robinson as his most brilliant student. His athletic prowess was equally remarkable for he represented his university at lacrosse (1906–9), athletics (1907–9), and cricket (1908–9). He continued to play cricket until middle life, when he changed to golf but retained his cricket stance.

He decided to stay in Britain and in 1909 he was appointed an assistant inspector in the Board of Agriculture and Fisheries, and was rapidly promoted inspector and superintendent. By intensive surveys in Wales and the north of England he laid the foundations of his wide knowledge of the growth of trees in Britain. In 1915 he was seconded to the Ministry of Munitions but in the next year he became secretary to the forestry sub-committee of the Reconstruction Committee, and helped to frame its final report which became the basis of forest policy for the next twenty years. Robinson was appointed O.B.E. in 1918 and became technical commissioner in the Forestry Commission which was set up in the following year. He became vice-chairman in 1929 and was chairman from 1932 until his death. On the post-war reorganization of the department he was also director-general (1945-7).

For over thirty years Robinson laboured to build up the forests of this country. The task was full of difficulties, political, economic, and technical. War and its consequences had been responsible for the birth of the Commission, and again from 1939 war called for even greater contributions from the woodlands. After a year as deputy controller in the Ministry of Supply's timber control, Robinson returned to forestry. He took a leading part in the preparation of the forestry commissioners' report on 'Post-War Forest Policy' (Cmd. 6447, 1943) which became the basis of government policy and in the supplementary report on private woodlands (Cmd. 6500, 1944). In both wars most of the timber had come from private woodlands and to restock them a scheme known as the 'Dedication of Woodlands' was devised as a means of co-operation between the State and the private owner.

Robinson's work was not limited to the United Kingdom. He was the only man to attend each of the first six Commonwealth Forestry Conferences held after 1918 to review and discuss forestry problems in all parts of the Empire. At each successive conference he played an increasingly important part in shaping its deliberations. He returned to Australia in 1928 for the third conference of which he was a vice-chairman, and he was chairman of the fourth conference held in 1935 in South Africa and of the fifth held in 1947 in Britain. It was while attending the sixth conference in Canada that he died, 5 September 1952, in Ottawa. His ashes were brought home and scattered in Kielder Forest, Northumberland, the largest State forest in Britain.

To the task of creating these forests Robinson brought a combination of distinctive qualities: he had a first-class brain, a forceful personality, and an impressive physique which gave him a natural authority. Success in a long-term enterprise calls for tenacity of purpose and this was one of his chief attributes, while he was always cautious when faced with difficult technical problems. Although much of his work was administrative, he went continually into the woods and remained an observant and practical forester until the end.

Robinson was knighted in 1931 and raised to the peerage in 1947, the first Rhodes scholar to receive either distintion. He took the title of Baron Robinso of Kielder Forest and of Adelaide. I was the first recipient (1947) of the med of the Society of Foresters of Great Brita of which he had been first preside (1926-8), and he received the honorar degree of LL.D. from the university Aberdeen (1951). He was a member the Forest Products Research Board, governor of the Imperial Forestry Inst tute, Oxford, from its inception in 192 until 1934, an honorary member of th American Society of Foresters and of th Institute of Foresters of Australia, and corresponding member of the Agricultur Academy of France. In the last year Robinson's life the forestry commissione and their staff commissioned T. C. Dugda to paint a portrait which is in the posse sion of the family.

In 1910 Robinson married Charlott Marion Cust, daughter of Henry Cus Bradshaw. They had two daughters an one son, a wing commander who was kille in action in 1942. The peerage therefo became extinct when Robinson died. On of the daughters married J. J. B. Hunt wh became first civil service commissioner i 1968.

[*The Times*, 6 and 11 September 1952 *Empire Forestry Review*, vol. xxxi, No. 1952; *Forestry*, vol. xxvi, No. 1, 1953; *Natur 4 October 1952; *Scottish Forestry*, vol. v No. 4, 1952; *Quarterly Journal of Forestr vol. xlvii, No. 1, 1953; private information personal knowledge.]   H. M. STEVE

ROCHE, ALEXANDER ADAIR, BARO ROCHE (1871-1956), judge, was born 2 July 1871, the second son of Willian Roche by his wife, Mary, daughter William Fraser. Roche's father and grand father were doctors in Ipswich (the grand father having come from county Cork The Frasers were of Highland extractio but established as merchants in Ipswich Roche was born there and went to Ipswic Grammar School whence he won a classi cal scholarship to Wadham College Oxford, where he was a contemporary o two future lord chancellors (Birkenhea and Simon, qq.v.). He took a first i honour moderations in 1892 and i *literae humaniores* in 1894. He became a honorary fellow of his college in 1917.

On leaving Oxford, Roche worked fo a time in the office of his uncle, a solicito specializing in maritime matters. Thi experience was to shape his futur career. After reading as a pupil with Scot

ox of the North-Eastern circuit he was
alled to the bar by the Inner Temple in
396. He was elected a bencher of his Inn
1 1917 and served as treasurer in 1939.

At first Roche's practice was almost ex-
usively on the North-Eastern circuit and
cluded both criminal and civil work but
1e former soon gave place to commercial
ases. At that time the British merchant
eet dominated the seas and no small
art of it was built and owned on the
orth-east coast. Individual fleets were
naller, merchants more numerous, the
w less settled, and the mercantile com-
aunity more litigious than in later times
nd as a result seaborne trade gave rise to
substantial volume of litigation. To deal
ith this class of case the Commercial
ourt was established in London in 1895.
or some years, however, a substantial
olume of commercial work continued to
e tried at Newcastle, Durham, and Leeds
ssizes and there were small Admiralty
ases in county courts. Roche was soon
ell established in both these classes of
rork on circuit and early in the new
entury began to get corresponding work
London. At first the work came from
lients on the north-east coast but the
eld soon widened to give him an exten-
ve practice in the Commercial Court
nd a substantial one in the Admiralty
ourt.

After taking silk in 1912 Roche con-
entrated almost entirely on commercial
ases and arbitrations in London and for
period just short of five years held one
f the largest leading practices in this
eld. Of the 182 cases reported in the
'ommercial Reports for this period Roche
vas counsel in 88. These figures probably
eflect correctly enough both his share of
he business and the high esteem in which
is services were held by the maritime
ommunity who still formed the bulk—
hough by no means the whole—of his
lients. The outbreak of war in 1914
rought business to the Prize Court
which had last sat in the Crimean War)
nd Roche appeared as counsel in several
mportant cases both before the judge and
n appeal to the Privy Council.

In 1917 he was appointed a judge of the
King's Bench division and knighted. He
ook his regular turn in the Commercial
ourt but when not so required he had a
trong preference for circuit work. This
vas due in part to his belief in the value
f the circuit system and his pride in its
raditions and in part to the facilities it
rovided for sport on non-sitting days.

In 1934 he was appointed a lord justice
and sworn of the Privy Council. In 1935
he became a lord of appeal in ordinary
with a life peerage. On both occasions the
promotion was to succeed a judge trained
in the same school of commercial law as
himself: Lord Justice Scrutton [q.v.] and
Lord Wright. After so many years as
master in his own court Roche found life
in, and the slower pace of, the then Court of
Appeal somewhat irksome, but he found
no such difficulties in either the House of
Lords or the Judicial Committee and very
much enjoyed the work. He retired in
1938 to have more time to devote to
country pursuits but continued to sit
occasionally in commercial and Admiralty appeals for a further nine years.

As an advocate Roche was clear and
concise, but was best remembered, even
forty years later, for his vigour. As a
judge he was intensely interested in the
due administration both of criminal and
of commercial law. In criminal matters
he was a sound judge and devoted much
thought to the difficult task of sentencing.
In the commercial field his wide knowledge
of the relevant law, his firm grasp of the
principles involved, and his long experience of the ways of the sea and of
commerce enabled him to proceed with
considerable expedition. Outside these
fields his interest was practical rather than
theoretic and his judgements explored the
law no farther than was strictly necessary
for the matter in hand.

Apart from the law Roche's main interests were in sport and country life. As a
boy he drove his father long distances in
a dog cart on his country rounds and he
never lost his eye for and love of horses.
He was a fearless man to hounds and after
he went to live in Oxfordshire in 1920 was
well known in the Heythrop country.
As late as 1930 he 'went' the North-
Eastern circuit accompanied by four
hunters and he rode to hounds until he
was eighty. He was a competent shot
but the sport he loved above all others
was fly fishing. Roche was, however,
willing to accept the duties as well
as the pleasures of country life. He was
chairman of the Agricultural Wages
Board (1940–43) and of the county
quarter-sessions, and after his retirement
took part in many local activities. He was
a stalwart member of the Church of
England. He married in 1902 Elfreda
(died 1955), daughter of John Fenwick,
of Wimbledon; they had two sons and
a daughter. Roche died at Chadlington,

Oxfordshire, 22 December 1956. Wadham College has a portrait by (Sir) James Gunn.
[Personal knowledge.]   TOM ROCHE.

ROE, SIR (EDWIN) ALLIOTT VERDON VERDON- (1877–1958), aircraft designer and constructor. [See VERDON-ROE.]

ROSENHEIM, (SIGMUND) OTTO (1871–1955), organic chemist and biochemist, was born at Würzburg, Germany, 29 November 1871, the second son of Meier Rosenheim and his wife, Adelheid Rosenheim. He studied in Würzburg for his Ph.D., being examined on his thesis by Hantzsch, and also spent some time in Bonn where he attended lectures by that pioneer of organic chemistry, Kekulé. Thus he was linked with the 'classical' period of development of structural organic chemistry, and when his interests turned to physiology his natural inclination brought him into the main stream of contemporary ideas in which the task was to elucidate by the methods of organic chemistry those specific chemical structures associated with specific physiological activities. In a more personal sense his student days were decisive. Once, when it was rather naïvely remarked that Bonn must have been a pleasant place in which to be a student, Rosenheim replied 'Not when one was a Jew!' In the days of Hitler's persecution he said that he had 'seen this coming thirty-five years ago'.

After his military service, in the horse artillery and, because of his race, in the ranks, Rosenheim went to Geneva to work with Graebe. Thence, having been accepted by W. H. Perkin [q.v.] as a research student for the session 1894–5 at Manchester University, he came to England. Here he made his career, was naturalized in 1900, married an Englishwoman, and acquired a grammatical and scholarly style in writing English although his speech retained a marked accent. He was not happy to be reminded of his German origin and, perhaps as a result of his early experiences, was extremely reticent about his personal affairs.

In 1896 he joined Philip Schidrowitz in a practice as analytical and consulting chemists in London. Schidrowitz described him as greatly interested in the scientific side of his work and as a remarkable craftsman, excelling in glassblowing, photography, and manipulative procedures. He became interested in biological chemistry and his true life's work began in 1901 when he was appointed

research student of pharmacological chemistry at King's College in the Strand. In 1904 he was appointed lecturer in chemical physiology and in 1915 the title of reader in biochemistry was conferred on him. Having financial independence, he resigned from this position with its teaching duties in 1920 so that he might undertake research free from interruption and at his own pace. In 1923 he and his wife went to work at the National Institute for Medical Research where they were associated with H. W. Dudley in the chemical laboratory. The atmosphere was congenial and there followed perhaps the most productive period of his career, until in 1932 he again decided to retire. He took with him a scientific problem which would not let him rest, and within six weeks he was back in the laboratory to discuss with Harold King [q.v.] the structure of the ring system of sterols and bile acids. The joint publication which resulted was a major event in this field of the chemistry of natural products.

Rosenheim's first scientific publications were with Schidrowitz and with F. W. Tunnicliffe of King's College. With F. S. Locke he collaborated in a classical investigation of the effect of sugars on the isolated mammalian heart and on the quantitative disappearance of dextrose when perfused through such a heart. With Miss Tebb, whom he subsequently married, he worked on protagon and other compounds from brain, a task in which his great manipulative skill was fully used. His interest in spermine brought him into contact with Dudley; then, pursuing another trail of his own, he was led to the discovery, with T. A. Webster, that ergosterol was a parent substance of vitamin D, the antirachitic vitamin. His individualism kept him from collaboration with the team which subsequently took up this investigation in competition with continental laboratories. Rosenheim was at his best with a single partner in a research which proceeded at a deliberate pace.

He continued work in the Hampstead laboratory with several collaborators until his final retirement in 1942. The last of his 133 scientific publications was in 1945, jointly with the pioneers of paper chromatography, on 'The non-identity of Thudichum's glycoleucine and norleucine'. It reflected a lively interest of some years standing in the pioneer work of Thudichum on the chemistry of brain, reinforced by his discovery of many of Thudichum's original specimens, and also his continued intellectual activity and awareness of applicability and importance of new hniques.

Rosenheim was affectionately remem-ed by many at the Institute as the erly and dumpy but dignified figure ich came into the laboratory in the ter part of the morning wearing in his el, whenever possible, a flower from rock garden. After this had been ad-red he would inquire what his assistant d been doing and his own day's work gan. They also remembered the kind d fatherly interest he took in junior leagues and their work, giving advice d criticism and suggesting subjects ich 'might be interesting to play with'. Rosenheim was one of the original mbers of the Biochemical Society rmed in 1911 as the Biochemical Club), ving on its committee from 1916 to 20. He was elected F.R.S. in 1927, was a low of the Linnean Society, and served e Medical Research Council as a member the accessory food factors committee. 1910 he married his collaborator, Mary ristine (died 1953), daughter of William bb, of Rede Hall, Burstow. They had children. He died at his home in ampstead Garden Suburb 7 May 1955.

[H. King in *Biographical Memoirs of llows of the Royal Society*, vol. ii, 1956; rsonal knowledge.]　　　R. K. CALLOW.

OSS, SIR IAN CLUNIES (1899–1959), eterinary scientist and scientific adminis-ator, was born 22 February 1899 at athurst, New South Wales, the youngest four sons of William John Clunies Ross, hool teacher and amateur natural scien-st. His father had been born in London midst 'a confusion of Clunies Ross and oss-Clunies relatives', some of whom ollowed vague but picturesque occupa-ons in Siam or Singapore or the Cocos slands'. The Clunies-Ross 'dynasty' of he Keeling–Cocos Islands came from he same stock. His mother, Hannah lizabeth Tilley, was born in Australia, he daughter of an English Nonconformist issionary.

When Clunies Ross was four years of ge the family moved to Sydney where e was educated at Newington College nd the university, graduating B.V.Sc. vith honours in 1921. A Walter and Eliza Iall research fellowship (1922–4) took im to England for postgraduate studies t the London School of Tropical Medicine nd the Molteno Institute, Cambridge. Ie returned to Sydney as lecturer in

veterinary parasitology in 1925. In the following year the Council for Scien-tific and Industrial Research (C.S.I.R.) was established by the Commonwealth Government and Clunies Ross was ap-pointed veterinary parasitologist. There followed a period of intensive laboratory research with tick paralysis and hydatid disease as the two central topics. For this work he received his D.V.Sc., Sydney, in 1928.

It was by now evident that Clunies Ross had qualities which would take him into wider fields, and in the decade before 1939 the general pattern of his subsequent career became evident. His interest in international affairs was kindled by a two years' visit to Japan (1929–30) where he carried out research at the Institute of Infectious Diseases in Tokyo, learned to speak Japanese, and developed an abiding interest in Asia. In 1931 he was appointed officer-in-charge of the McMaster Lab-oratory which had been built for research in animal health by C.S.I.R. in the grounds of the university of Sydney veterinary school. At this time Clunies Ross's primary interest was in the internal parasites of sheep; a textbook on the subject, written in collaboration with H. M. Gordon (Sydney, 1936), remained a standard work. It was natural, however, that his interests should expand to cover the whole biology of the sheep and even-tually the pastoral industry in all its aspects. For the rest of his life Clunies Ross was concerned with Australia's wool and all that this entailed at scientific, pastoral, financial, and political levels. In 1935–6 he studied sheep and wool production in North-East Asia and in 1937 he became Australian representative on, and chairman of, the International Wool Secretariat in London. After war broke out, he returned in 1940 as professor of veterinary science to Sydney, but was immediately seconded to the Common-wealth Government for tasks concerned with scientific manpower and the war organization of the pastoral industry.

In 1946 Clunies Ross joined C.S.I.R. as executive officer and in 1949, following the retirement of Sir David Rivett, he became first chairman of the renamed and reorganized Commonwealth Scientific and Industrial Research Organization (C.S.I.R.O.). In this position, which he held up to the time of his death, he was brilliantly successful. He saw the Organi-zation's activities enlarge enormously and its repute increase amongst both the scientists of the world and the people and the politicians of Australia. His early scientific work was competent and opened up an immensely important approach to the improvement of sheep husbandry in Australia; but its real significance lay in the background it provided to his work as a scientific administrator. His main interest was in people; he was utterly remote from the ivory tower of academic science, but he could understand and appreciate the academic as well as the politician or the pastoralist. He liked people and could make them like him. He was strikingly good-looking in a dark, well-groomed, slightly Mephistophelian style, youthful-looking even in his fifties. He was an excellent conversationalist, humorous and eager to open up whomever he was talking to, whether the driver of his car or a visiting dignitary from Asia. He had an extraordinary memory for people and events, but seemed never quite able to immerse himself comfortably in the world as it was. He looked on things a little from outside, being always something of an actor with slightly exaggerated courtesies and some characteristic mannerisms of mobile lips and eyebrows, or the stylized manipulation of a long cigarette-holder. It was all part of a vivid and charming personality which helped very greatly in building up enthusiasm for C.S.I.R.O. amongst the pastoralists and industrialists whose prosperity was the objective of his Organization, and equally amongst its scientific employees. He had the loyalty and liking of his colleagues and was on excellent terms with his political masters. C.S.I.R. had been built up and made a going concern by Rivett, in many ways a greater man than Clunies Ross, but it needed the human qualities of the younger man to bring the Organization to its full usefulness.

Amongst a wide range of ancillary activities it may be mentioned that Clunies Ross was Australian delegate to the League of Nations (1938–9); first chairman of International House, a residential hall for Asian and other overseas students, Melbourne University (1958); member of the Murray commission on Australian universities (1957); and deputy chancellor of Melbourne University (1958–9). He was appointed C.M.G. in 1954 and knighted later in the same year. He received honorary degrees from Melbourne, New England, and Adelaide universities and the gold medal of the Royal Agricultural Society of England. He was a fellow of

the Australian Academy of Science ; received the James Cook medal of Royal Society of New South Wales.

In 1927 Clunies Ross married Ja Leslie, daughter of H. B. L. Carter; t had three sons and an adopted daugh He died in Melbourne 20 June 1959. T only portrait painted during his life by Norman Carter and remained in possession of the artist. Of two po humous portraits, one by Judy Cas is in the McMaster Laboratory, Sydn and the other by Harley Griffiths in t C.S.I.R.O. head office in Melbourne.

[*Ian Clunies Ross, Memoirs and Pap* ed. F. Eyre, Melbourne, 1961; *Nature*, July 1959; personal knowledge.]

F. M. BURN

ROWLANDS, SIR ARCHIBALD (189 1953), civil servant, fourth son of Dav Rowlands, grocer, and his wife, Sar Thomas, was born at Twyn-ny-rody Glamorgan, 26 December 1892. Educat at Penarth County School, the Universi College of Wales, where he obtained fi class honours in modern languages 1914, and as a Welsh scholar of Jes College, Oxford, Rowlands's universi career was interrupted by three yea service in the war. He reached the ra of captain, was appointed M.B.E., a mentioned in dispatches. Appointed 1920 to the War Office on entering t administrative Civil Service, Rowlan was promoted principal in 1923 a assistant secretary in 1936. His exception qualities had already attracted notice, n only as private secretary to three co secutive secretaries of state, but for t breadth of his approach and his person contribution towards breaking down t traditional barrier between military an civilian functions in a department with single purpose.

Seconded to the Government of Indi as defence finance adviser in 1937, afte a year at the Imperial Defence Colleg Rowlands brought a similarly constructiv and energetic personality to bear o building up India's defences at the tim of the Chatfield inquiry. His assignmen was one of wide and substantially inde pendent financial responsibility, for, i collaboration with the commander-in chief, subject only to the control of th finance member and Executive Counci he had virtually full powers over th employment of the funds allocate annually to defence which then absorbe over half India's central revenues.

Rowlands emerged with a widely hanced reputation for farsighted defence nking and his abilities carried him idly to high responsibilities once war gan. Recalled to London in 1939 as puty under-secretary, Air Ministry, he s appointed in May 1940 first permant secretary of the Ministry of Aircraft oduction, newly created to push through unparalleled output of military aircraft. orthodox, even privateering, methods re initially invoked to requisition emises and plant, and to compete for our. The department itself was a pidly assembled concentration of powerl figures drawn largely from outside, any accustomed to wielding indepennt authority. If results were to be both ickly achieved and soundly based, a -ordinated departmental machine had iftly to be forged to encourage, harness, d control the energies of so many pable if mettlesome personalities. Indistably, Rowlands stood out as principal chitect in forming, from a partially ndom amalgam of officials, technogists, and industrialists, an uncharacristic government department, with a tal strength ultimately exceeding 50,000, organize the activities of nearly two illion people eventually employed on rcraft work. Rowlands regarded himlf throughout as managing director of an mense industrial enterprise, rather than nventional senior official. Difficulties countered with his first minister, Lord eaverbrook, whose abundant vitality imulated, but whose idiosyncratic methls sometimes confused, direction of the isk, were composed in terms of mutual d enduring respect. The output of rcraft, 8,000 in 1939, quintupled in umbers by 1944, and by a far greater ultiple in all-up weight.

Meanwhile, by late 1943, India was eing prepared as a base for offensive gainst Japan. There was a great influx f Commonwealth and United States rces; the Indian armed forces, which ad expanded tenfold to over two million, ere fighting in virtually all theatres of ar with complex logistic cross-currents of pplies moving into and out of the subontinent. By agreement between (Sir) Vinston Churchill and Lord Wavell [q.v.], owlands was appointed adviser to the iceroy on war administration, with the nction of co-ordinating and mitigating he impact of all these pressures on the orts, transport system, resources, and od supplies of a country which, although increasing in industrial potential, was still essentially a primitive peasant economy. Rowlands approached this task of creating understanding between India and her military guests not merely with administrative acumen and vigour, but with a wide human interest in Indian affairs nurtured by deep reading and many friendships deriving from his earlier sojourn. In 1944–5, following public disorder consequent upon famine in Bengal, Rowlands presided over an inquiry which reported in comprehensive, clearsighted, and far-thinking terms on Bengal's administration. The war ending, Rowlands was appointed in 1945 finance member of the viceroy's Executive Council to initiate the process of post-war reconstruction and social development with independence already in view, and through a budget which his Indian successor would carry out.

Save for a three months' assignment in 1947 as special adviser to M. A. Jinnah [q.v.] on the administrative structure of Pakistan after partition, Rowlands, returning to London in mid-1946, spent the remainder of his career, until retirement early in 1953, as permanent secretary of the Ministry of Supply in work of rehabilitation and development at a time of post-war economic change and experiment. Following amalgamation with the Ministry of Aircraft Production, the Ministry was confronted by intimidating responsibilities: the future size and shape of the aircraft industry; atomic energy; the highly controversial nationalization, and subsequent denationalization, of the steel industry; the manufacture in government factories of goods for the civil market; facilitating the transition to peacetime export objectives of the entire engineering industry; rearmament for the Korean war. For seven years, energies unabated, Rowlands presided over a leviathan of a department, still employing over 100,000 people, which had constantly to adapt itself to the stresses of the times.

Rowlands brought to this varied career a formidably effective administrative personality, in which prodigious powers of application were compounded with characteristic Welsh vivacity, shrewdness, and a catholic human sympathy and sensibility. Clear thinking and unambiguous; forceful and determined in action yet quiet spoken and imperturbable; impatient but often disarming of opposition; attracting and sustaining devoted subordinates, intellectually stimulating, he dominated his official environment, sometimes treading on toes, making few enemies. Combining in his make-up the training and technique of an official with a clubbable masculine outlook and the robust habits of a man of the world, he met the varied world on its own terms of social exchange and did business with it. Industrialists responded to him; so did Indians. He was a conspicuous example of the senior civil servant equipped and eager to travel beyond Whitehall into more uncharted areas of administration. He was appointed K.C.B. in 1941 and promoted G.C.B. in 1947.

In 1920 Rowlands married Constance May, daughter of P. W. Phillips, general manager of the Swansea Harbour Trust; they had no children. He died at Henley-on-Thames 18 August 1953.

[J. D. Scott and R. Hughes, (Official History) *The Administration of War Production*, 1955; B. H. Liddell Hart, *Memoirs*, vol. ii, 1965; private information; personal knowledge.]

HOWARD HOOPER.

ROWNTREE, BENJAMIN SEEBOHM (1871–1954), sociologist, was born in York 7 July 1871, the second son of Joseph Rowntree [q.v.] and his second wife, Emma Antoinette, daughter of Wilhelm Seebohm. He followed his father to Bootham School, York, then read for five terms at the Owens College, Manchester, where his studies included chemistry. He joined the family firm of H. I. Rowntree & Co. in 1889, becoming a director when it was converted into a limited liability company in 1897, and chairman in 1923–41. His father took the view that his employees should 'never merely be regarded as cogs in an industrial machine, but rather as fellow workers in a great industry', and applying his Quaker beliefs to capitalist enterprise endeavoured to develop his business as a trust. He translated this conception into practical and legal form by creating charitable, social service, and village trusts, with which Seebohm Rowntree was closely associated. His father's influence on his life and thoughts was decisive; it has been said that the relationship was 'a process of cross-fertilization, and no one now can tell how many of Seebohm's theories he ,owed to his father, or how many of Joseph's projects grew out of discussions with his sons'. In the twentieth century the firm became a leader in the field of scientific management and industrial welfare. Seebohm Rowntree was its first

labour director; the eight-hour day w introduced in 1896, a pension scheme 1906; a works doctor was appointed 1904. To deal with the problems of e ploying large numbers of women, 'soc helpers' were recruited as early as 189 under Seebohm's direction they ultimate became members of a full-fledged labo department. Works councils were set in 1919 and in the same year a 44-ho five-day week was introduced; prof sharing was introduced in 1923; a psych logical department was set up in 192

Until he retired from his executi directorship in 1936, labour manageme was one of Seebohm Rowntree's ch interests, but he did not allow this restrict a steadily growing awareness and responsibility for the solution problems of industrial management general. He was, as Beatrice Webb [q.v put it, 'more a philanthropist than capitalist'. His study of the problem unemployment which he published 1911 with Bruno Lasker showed th welfare had become a dominant intere in his life, and this is true also of much the other work which he produced at th time. During the war he was director the welfare department of the Ministr of Munitions (1915–18) and a member the Reconstruction Committeee in 191' This provided the background to h *Human Factor in Business* (1921), re garded at the time as complementary t his *Human Needs of Labour* (1918, revise ed. 1937). Turning from the examinatio of the needs of the individual as a con sumer he studied his equally importan requirements, as an employee, for reason able comfort at work, and the provisio of the kind of industrial conditions whic promote efficiency. This interest lay out side the field of philanthropy as it i usually thought of, and ultimately le Rowntree to play an active part in th study and practice of industrial manage ment. He participated in the Liberal in dustrial inquiry which published *Britain' Industrial Future* in 1928 and assisted i the foundation of the Industrial Welfar Society in 1918 and of the Nationa Institute of Industrial Psychology in 1921 remaining a member of its executive com mittee until 1949 and serving as chairma in 1940–47. He was responsible for th foundation of the Oxford conferences o employers, managers, and foremen in 192(and of the Management Research Groups (1927). In 1952 he was presented with ar honorary fellowship of the British Insti-

e of Management in recognition of the
ɔt which the management movement
ed to him.

Ihe most formative incident in Rown-
e's life was, perhaps, his visit to the
ɪms of Newcastle upon Tyne in 1895,
ɪch sharpened his Quaker sense of
ligation to the downtrodden to such an
tent that he may be said to have, spent
ɛ rest of his life in an endeavour to
charge it. The work of Charles Booth
v.] in London made a great impression
his mind, giving him a clearer sense of
ɛection and purpose. He determined to
d out whether the state of the poor in his
ɪn city of York was as bad as Booth had
ɪnd it to be in London. Rowntree spent
ɪst of 1897 and 1898 away from the fac-
ɾy, pursuing the necessary investiga-
ɪns, and in 1901 was able to publish
verty, a Study of Town Life, which soon
came one of the classic texts of the
ɛial sciences. With Booth before him and
ɪr) Arthur Bowley [q.v.] afterwards, he
lped to create a methodology, the
portance of which for British empirical
ɛiology is hard to exaggerate. Poverty
ɪs clearly written, and its conclusions
ɪre accepted as supporting Booth's. Its
luence on the public mind and on the
velopment of social policy was great.
ɔm the point of view of the social
ences it was an advance on Booth's
ɪrk, in so far as it was based on data
llected from an entire population,
ther than a selected group; Rowntree's
finition of 'poverty' was more precise,
king into consideration 'physical effi-
ɪncy' alone, and he employed his own
ɪff to obtain information, rather than
lying on 'indirect interviewing' as
ɪoth had done. In some respects he
ught for more precision than was
ɪssible. On the one hand he was later
ɪmpelled to admit that his distinction
tween 'primary' and 'secondary' poverty
ɪe latter arising if earnings sufficient for
ɪysical efficiency were spent on some
ɪher object) could not be maintained.
ɪ the other, his desire to exclude any
ɪggeration in his estimate of the number
the poor led him to a very strict defini-
ɪn of poverty which assumed that the
ɪallest amounts of the cheapest food
ɪuld be bought, and his work was used
terwards by Bowley and others to
termine the lowest wage on which a
ɪmber of the working classes could meet
s responsibilities. Harsh rigour of this
ɪd had little bearing on social realities,
ɪwever, and unintentionally on his part

Rowntree's desire to produce a firm estimate of poverty created trouble later on
with the labour movement.

The Second York Survey, carried out
in 1936, which was published under the
title Poverty and Progress in 1941, displayed more sophistication in the analysis
of the data; to establish the poverty line
use was made of material included in The
Human Needs of Labour. The Second
Survey also dealt with housing, religion,
and leisure-time activities. Finally, in
collaboration with G. R. Lavers, Rowntree produced in 1951 Poverty and the
Welfare State, the report of the Third
Survey of York, which was restricted to
an examination of the extent to which
poverty in York had been reduced by the
operation of the various social services,
and English Life and Leisure which was
unfavourably compared with his earlier
work, on the ground that it contained
too much moralizing, and that the case
studies in it could not be held to be
representative of any social group or class.
Even so, the case studies themselves were
valued for their vividness, and the irony
of the comments embodied in them.

As a sociologist, Rowntree shared with
Booth an interest aroused by conscience,
a distaste for a priori reasoning, and a desire to ascertain 'actual facts'. He avoided
sweeping generalizations, and possessed
an ability to ask really significant questions, ranging from the frequency of
poverty in 1901 to the nature of 'mass
culture' fifty years later. It was perhaps
because of this more than anything else
that his work was highly esteemed by
contemporaries, such as R. H. Tawney.
In his best writing he gave a precise
picture of the life of the people with
whom he was concerned; this was especially true of Poverty and of How the Labourer Lives, a small book published in 1913
in collaboration with May Kendall which
dealt with the way of life of the agricultural labourer. An earlier publication,
Land and Labour, Lessons from Belgium
(1910), had led to his appointment by
Lloyd George to the land inquiry committee of 1912–14.

Rowntree was never prominent in political life although he was intimate with
Lloyd George, especially between 1926
and 1935 when he advised him on questions of unemployment, housing, and
agriculture. He collaborated with Lord
Astor [q.v.] in a series of studies of British
agriculture, in the hope that farming
could be made to contribute to the relief

of unemployment and the development of the economy, but he was speedily disillusioned. The first report, *The Agricultural Dilemma*, was published in 1935; it challenged Lloyd George's optimistic estimate of the number of persons who could be settled on the land, and this ended Rowntree's friendship with him. Rowntree's collaboration with Astor continued, however, until 1946.

Rowntree was never able to make close relations with the Labour Party, and this restricted the extent to which he was able to participate in politics. He was an independent and successful, if unacknowledged, conciliator in the railway strike of 1919; he attempted to mediate in the coal dispute in 1926 when he was highly critical of the intervention of the Churches' committee. But he had neither the necessary temperament nor the desire to play a leading role; he was not the kind of man to lead movements or to exercise power. In Beatrice Webb's opinion he was even 'too modest and hesitating in opinion to lead a committee'. He was rather, as Sir Patrick Abercrombie [q.v.] put it, 'one of those who combine imaginative outlook with the most exact study'. His poverty surveys were his most scholarly achievements and his most effective contributions to social policy, though the part he played in the development of a more humane understanding of problems of industrial welfare, which he combined with a very practical approach to business administration, also contributed perhaps as much to his reputation. He was a trustee of the Nuffield Fund for distressed areas from 1936, president of the Outward Bound Trust, and in 1944–6 chairman of the Nuffield committee on old age. He received an honorary LL.D. from Manchester in 1942. He was appointed C.H. in 1931, but he rejected those distinctions which, he thought, might put a barrier between him and his fellow men. Although not fully recognized in this way, his influence was considerable, especially in the United States, where he had many friends and was widely consulted both in business and in the universities.

In 1897 Rowntree married Lydia (died 1944), daughter of Edwin Potter, of Middlesbrough; there were four sons and one daughter. He died at his home in a wing of Disraeli's old house at Hughenden, High Wycombe, 7 October 1954.

[Asa Briggs, *Seebohm Rowntree*, 1961; private information; personal knowledge.]   SIMEY.

ROXBURGH, JOHN FERGUSS((1888–1954), first headmaster of Sto School, was born in Edinburgh 5 May 18 the second son of Archibald Roxbur, foreign merchant, of Valparaiso a Liverpool, by his wife, Janet Brig daughter of John Cathcart, of Edinbur; At Charterhouse he won several pri including the Thackeray prize for Engl literature three years in succession. I he was not wholly happy and it was s: at Stowe that he meant there to enj vicariously the happy schooldays he h missed. An exhibitioner of Trinity C lege, Cambridge, he was placed in t third division of the first class in part i the classical tripos in 1910. He obtain his L. ès L. of the university of Paris a in 1911–22 was sixth-form master Lancing College, where his pupils membered him as liking to wear his S(bonne gown, which went well with his : of being a great actor whose audien must never suffer a dull moment. I loved to recite French, Latin, and Engl poetry, resonantly thumping the metr into his pupils' heads. He was fond saying that 'a classroom in which t master is talking is a classroom in whi no education is going on', but when himself was teaching his voice could heard six classrooms away; he was : outstanding teacher of oral French.

After the war, during which he serv for a time in France with the Corps Signals and was mentioned in dispatche Roxburgh returned to Lancing whe he was Sandersons housemaster until December 1922 he was appointed fir headmaster of Stowe before it opened : May 1923 with 99 boys. He took with hi some Lancing boys as prefects; and two the early masters had also been educate at Lancing. By September 1930 there wei 500 boys at Stowe and the intervenir years had seen a steady programme development of the school, yet withou greatly changing the character of tl former palace of the Dukes of Buckingha; which housed it. In 1924, 160 old Etoniar subscribed to purchase the Great Avenu for the school, and the same year saw th opening of laboratories, a gymnasiun and squash courts. In 1927 Queen Mar laid the foundation stone of the chap(which was opened two years later by Princ George. The first university scholarship were won in 1927 (two at Oxford and one a Cambridge) and in 1930 one old Stoic wa president of the Oxford Union and anothe won the sword of honour at Sandhurst.

The school was very much Roxburgh's personal creation. Although he could not manage work to economize energy, his guts thoroughness and industry made his administration sufficiently successful. He made no major changes in the conventional public school curriculum, beyond introducing regular teaching in geography, but he was an unusual headmaster in maintaining a very close personal relationship with all the boys in the school and with old boys. Every Stowe boy killed in the war of 1939–45 was a personal tragedy for him. His correspondence, largely in his own hand, with boys, old boys, parents, and past masters, was so vast as to seem incredible to anyone who did not know him. His manners were so charming that parents often thought they had themselves charmed him, but when after retiring he taught in a prep. school he made the condition 'no contact with parents'. To his masters he was at home every weekday from 10 p.m. onwards. It was once said that when the door closed behind the last master the room was left empty. This criticism, though unjust, was understandable, for he had developed an ability to be interested in every individual whom he felt to be socially on his own level. But his undue sensitiveness to social levels narrowed the range of his response to individuals as human beings and often concealed his real virtues from those whose good opinion would have been well worth having.

A master once asked Roxburgh why he had originally appointed him and was told that at the interview he had ignored some questions and answered all the others wrongly, but that Roxburgh had felt that he 'had a dynamo inside'. Sometimes in giving way to such impulses Roxburgh chose unsuccessfully; he then felt very guilty and would support the inadequate master with unshakeable loyalty. Although this attitude caused occasional difficulties, it gave his staff the confidence of being trusted and on balance was good for the school. So also was his curious habit, rare in anyone so circumspect as a headmaster must be, of occasionally speaking the exact truth as he saw it, without warning. A boy asked to go to the test match. 'No, you may not.' 'Why not, sir?' 'Because your parents and your housemaster would disapprove.' 'If I get leave from my parents and my housemaster, may I go, sir?' 'No, you may not.' 'Why not, sir?' 'I can't think why not at the moment, but I'm sure there must be a reason.'

Roxburgh published two books: *The Poetic Procession* (1921) and *Eleutheros* (1930). His feeling for the arts was never generalized but always attached to particular works. He kept a gramophone in his study solely to play Beethoven's Kreutzer Sonata. An intense desire that his own words should be well chosen and should give pleasure made his sermons—never more than once a term—immensely attractive. The masters were the only group of regular voluntary attenders, and the fullness of their stalls when 'J.F.' was preaching was very striking. The actual content of his sermons was not memorable; what was attractive was the charm and grace of his words, vitalized by the sympathy for individual people which shone behind them. His capacity for personal affection for a very large number of individuals, particularly boys who had been at Stowe, was generally recognized for the extremely unusual virtue it was, and notably demonstrated one way of being a great headmaster.

Roxburgh, who never married, retired in 1949 and died at Great Brickhill, Bletchley, 6 May 1954. There is a portrait by (Sir) James Gunn at Stowe.

[*Some Notes on the Early History of Stowe*, by a Member of the Sixth Form, 1932; Lord Annan, *Roxburgh of Stowe*, 1965; private information; personal knowledge.]

HUGH HECKSTALL-SMITH.

ROYDEN, (AGNES) MAUDE (1876–1956), preacher, was born 23 November 1876 at Mossley Hill near Liverpool, the sister of Thomas (later Lord) Royden [q.v.] and youngest daughter of (Sir) Thomas Bland Royden, shipowner and later first baronet, and his wife, Alice Elizabeth, daughter of Thomas Dowdall, stockbroker, of Liverpool. She was educated at Cheltenham Ladies' College and Lady Margaret Hall, Oxford, where she obtained a second class in modern history in 1899. After three years at the Victoria Women's Settlement, Liverpool, she became parish worker at South Luffenham, county Rutland, whose incumbent was the Rev. George William Hudson Shaw. As a lecturer in English literature to the Oxford University extension delegacy she discovered her gift for public speaking, which from 1908 to 1914 was mainly devoted to women's suffrage; during the last two years of this period she edited the *Common Cause*. The religious and ethical, rather than the strictly political, aspects of the women's movement were those which most strongly appealed to her, although she did not then foresee that the pulpit rather than the platform was to become her *métier*.

In 1917 she accepted Dr. Fort Newton's invitation to become assistant preacher at the City Temple, Anglican pulpits not being open to women. There she soon established her reputation as a preacher. Throughout her life she remained a devoted member of the Church of England and described herself as 'a soul naturally Anglican' (*I Believe in God*, preface, 1927), although after going down from Oxford she had for a time been attracted by Roman Catholicism. It was the misfortune of the Church of her adherence that her official connection with Nonconformity at the City Temple (1917–20) synchronized with the beginnings of the Life and Liberty Movement in the Church of England, for it was that connection which lost to the council of the Movement one whom F. A. Iremonger, in his life of Archbishop William Temple [q.v.], described as 'one of the strongest and most influential personalities of all the religious leaders and teachers of the day'.

In 1920 Maude Royden acquired an interdenominational pulpit through the 'Fellowship Services' which started at Kensington town hall but were soon transferred to the Guildhouse in Eccleston Square. There she found a work after her own heart in which she was ably assisted by Percy Dearmer [q.v.] and Martin Shaw. Her sermons, delivered without notes and effectively phrased, in which she drew upon her extensive knowledge of theology, literature, and social history, covered a wide range of subjects, including current international and political issues. She was a demanding and persuasive preacher, her constant theme being the application of Christian principles to all moral, social, and political problems. What she called 'hard thinking' was to her a Christian duty and the 'after-meetings' for discussion were an important part of the Guildhouse programme. Among visiting preachers there was Albert Schweitzer, for whom she acted as interpreter. Thanks to the generosity of her congregation Schweitzer was able to add to his hospital at Lambaréné a ward for mental patients.

Her preaching tours included the United States, Australia, New Zealand, India, and China. A student at Oberlin College described, thirty years later, an address which she gave in the chapel as the turning-point in the lives of many young

men who were then 'reaching for fait In the pulpit and on the radio Mau Royden had the advantage of a voice unusual charm and distinctiveness; b all her life she suffered from lameness d to dislocated hips, a physical disabili which must have demanded consta courage on the part of one who work so hard, travelled so far, and was temperament athletic. In her young days she was a keen swimmer. Her coura of conviction, which enabled her champion unpopular causes, was nev more clearly exemplified than by h public renunciation, during the war 1939–45, of her former pacifism. In 19 she had resigned her pastorate of t Guildhouse in order to devote herself the cause of world peace.

In October 1944 she married, tw months before his death, the Rev. Huds Shaw, whom she had known and love and whose work she had shared, for fort three years.

In 1930 Maude Royden was appoint a Companion of Honour. In 1931 Glasgo University conferred on her an honora D.D., and in 1935 she became an honora LL.D. of Liverpool. She died at her hom in London 30 July 1956. A portrait k P. A. de László is at Lady Margaret Ha Oxford.

[*The Times*, 31 July 1956; Maude Royde *A Threefold Cord*, 1947; personal knowledg
PERCY MARYON-WILSO

RUFFSIDE, VISCOUNT (1879–1958 Speaker of the House of Common [See BROWN, DOUGLAS CLIFTON.]

RUSSELL, EDWARD STUART (1887 1954), biologist, was born at Port Glasgo Renfrewshire, 25 March 1887, the eight and last living child in his family. H father, John Naismith Russell, who second Christian name indicates a relatio ship with the famous engineer and th well-known artist, was a minister of th Free Church of Scotland. His mothe Helen Cockburn Young, was the daught of a blacksmith of East Lothian. Russe was educated at Greenock Academy an Glasgow University where he obtaine his M.A. in 1907. He worked for a whil at Aberdeen where contact with (Sir) Arthur Thomson and through him wit (Sir) Patrick Geddes [q.v.] helped to colou the philosophy of his zoological thinkin For some years work on the morpholog and general biology of coelenterate an molluscan species occupied his attentio

d resulted in a number of original
pers. Later his studies of animals
rned towards their behaviour and he
gan to formulate an underlying zoolo-
al faith which was well expressed in
series of essays on current biological
emes. Papers in *Scientia* with such
les as 'The transmission of acquired
aracters', 'Vitalism', and 'Évolution ou
igénèse' are examples. They culmin-
ed in his masterpiece *Form and Function*
16), a deep and scholarly summary of
e various biological theories of the
igin and development of form. It led
n to the conclusion that the most
warding study of the living organism
s in the concept of the dynamic en-
ety of the individual. Materialist and
echanistic explanations were rejected
d contrary to prevailing opinions he
ve general support to Lamarckian
ews. Other books developing this main
eme, or parts of it, were *The Study of
ving Things* (1924), *The Interpretation
Development and Heredity* (1930), *The
haviour of Animals* (1934), *The Direc-
eness of Organic Activities* (1945) and,
blished since his death, *The Diversity
Animals* (1962).

In 1909 Russell was appointed to the
ard of Agriculture and Fisheries.
uring the short period before the out-
eak of war in 1914, when the Board had
cently taken over fisheries research
om the Marine Biological Association,
e began to examine and make good sense
the mass of catch statistics, fish
easurements, and condition analyses
hich were being collected. The war years
ere spent as a fishery inspector on the
uth coast where he combined an under-
anding friendliness towards the fisher-
en, to whom he had to interpret wartime
gulations, with a clear conception of
ow to wield his administrative powers.
1 1921 he became director of fishery
vestigations for England and Wales, a
ost which he held until 1945 when he
ecame fisheries scientific adviser until
e retired in 1947.

Russell's career in fisheries research was
ng and luminous and may be said to
onstitute another life than that of Russell
e philosopher, scholar, and student of
nimal behaviour. From the start he had
n eye for the essentials of sea fishery
anagement. This was well shown by his
rganization of the collection of statistics
y small square areas and the taking of
atch as well as fishing effort figures each
onth for trawl-caught fish of the North

Sea. As theories of fishing and yield
calculation developed this method proved
essential and was adopted by most of the
nations of North-West Europe. Between
the two wars he did much to foster fishery
conservation methods by the institution of
mesh selection experiments. Much of this
work was done in the setting of the programme of the International Council for
the Exploration of the Sea, a body in
which Russell did a great deal to bring the
United Kingdom into a position of leadership. As its first editor (1926–40) he set
a high standard for the *Journal du Conseil*
and from 1938 to 1946 he was chairman of
the Council's consultative committee. In
a classic paper in the *Journal* in 1931 he
set out in simple English and even simpler
arithmetic a statement of the chief factors
which affected the state of the stocks
subject to fishing. It is largely from this
paper that the more efficient dynamic
formulations of the state of fish stocks
have been derived and used as bases for
many international conservation measures.
In 1942 he summarized what was then
known about fishing theory in *The
Overfishing Problem*, a small book based
on his De Lamar lectures given at
Johns Hopkins University in the spring
of 1939.

The atmosphere necessary for good
research work can be difficult to maintain
in a government department but Russell
managed to provide for his staff at the
fisheries laboratories a complete shield
from the vexations which might otherwise
have come to them. This he achieved by
stationing himself in London where in a
small attic at 43 Parliament Street he
handled all the administrative relationships with great skill. The main laboratory
at Lowestoft saw its director about once
a fortnight, when he usually managed to
wander around the building in a quiet
and unobtrusive manner and have a few
words with everyone. His remarks were
short, sometimes facetious or even cynical,
but he managed to convey an underlying
sympathy. Everyone knew that he had a
very complete idea of what was going on
and his apparently casual suggestions to
naturalists were treated with great respect. While his views and opinions had not
the contagion of fire, they penetrated and
prevailed like oil; and they were rarely
wrong. He possessed a quality of humility
and comradeship with his associates,
particularly with the ordinary people,
and was widely known as 'Bill'. He disliked pomp, had little desire for marks of

preferment, and took up the office of director with reluctance. Nevertheless he would accept positions of distinction when they lay in the path of his scientific interest. He was president of the zoology section of the British Association in 1934 and president of the Linnean Society in 1940–42. He was appointed O.B.E. in 1930. Intellectually in his later years he turned towards the nihilistic philosophy of Schopenhauer—'nothing mattered'—but the pursuit of truth and knowledge in the Aristotelian sense mattered a lot to him, and he showed a tender care for his fellow men.

In 1911 he married Jeanne Amelia, daughter of Charles Owen Minchin, who had been a chief clerk in the estate duty office of the Inland Revenue. He died at St. Leonards-on-Sea 24 August 1954.

[Private information; personal knowledge.]
R. S. WIMPENNY.

RUSSELL PASHA, SIR THOMAS WENTWORTH (1879–1954), Egyptian civil servant, was born 22 November 1879 at Wollaton Rectory, fourth child and third son of the Rev. Henry Charles Russell, grandson of the sixth Duke of Bedford [q.v.], by his wife, Leila Louisa Millicent Willoughby, daughter of the eighth Baron Middleton, whose Nottinghamshire property comprised Wollaton with eight hundred acres of deer-park. From the rector, who combined the functions of parson and squire, Russell learned, in an atmosphere of religious assurance and sporting affluence, to box, shoot, hunt, and fish until, like his father, 'there was nothing he could not catch'. He was educated at Cheam, Haileybury, and Trinity College, Cambridge, contriving throughout to gratify his passion for field sports. His choice of career was settled when, on vacation at Applecross in Ross-shire, another Willoughby 'paradise' with eighty thousand acres reserved for sport, he was invited to visit Cairo by Percy Machell, a distant cousin, then adviser to the Egyptian minister of the interior. He came home to graduate, entering Egyptian service in October 1902.

After apprenticeship with the Alexandria coastguards he was appointed provincial sub-inspector in January 1903 and served, later as inspector, in every Egyptian province, thus acquiring unrivalled knowledge of local officials, while directing police activities which ranged from coping with the consequences of

Nile floods and plague epidemics to pitch battles against bedouin brigands; th depredations were virtually elimina by the police camel corps formed Russell's initiative in 1906. In 1911 was appointed assistant-commandant police in Alexandria where he enjoyed foretaste of dealing with city demonst tions, 'sporting evenings' raiding gamblir dens, and an interlude in command western desert anti-contraband operatio He was transferred to Cairo as assista commandant in 1913; in 1917, following line of British notables, he was appoint commandant of the Cairo city poli with rank of Lewa (major-general) a title of Pasha. By then Egypt was British protectorate; under war stre British power, far from withering awa was everywhere in irritating evidenc smouldering Egyptian resentment, ful comprehensible to Russell, flared in violence in March 1919; a clash betwe hysterical mobs determined to demo strate and British troops committed enforce a ban, seemed inevitable; bu thanks to Russell's inspired interventio the demonstrations were converted int orderly processions which he led throug Cairo streets, standing in an open car on foot, with a pause for brandy-and-soc at the Turf Club.

After Egyptian independence in 192 Russell served under twenty-nine diffe ent ministers of interior; oppositio leaders were government quarry, bu by adroit manœuvre combined with pe sonal charm, he mitigated the violence internecine political warfare, notably i 1932 when, reducing crisis to comedy, h avoided using force against an entir Wafdist shadow Cabinet. While retainin the esteem of most politicians, he de plored their quarrels, which seemed, i his perhaps over-simplified view, t hamper the real progress of a nation h loved. His own talents were increasingl diverted to the scourge of growing drug addiction. He pressed evidence on th prime minister; in 1929 the Egyptia Central Narcotics Intelligence Burea was formed; as director, operating wit small capital resources and hereditar enthusiasm, he hunted the sources o supply; tracks led to Switzerland, France Bulgaria, Turkey, and Greece. At Genev he bluntly presented his findings. Mora pressure, backed by incontrovertibl evidence, was so effective that by 1939 when he was elected vice-president of th League of Nations advisory committee o

ium traffic, most European bases of
ply were destroyed. In 1940 Cairo
ain became the pivot of British military
erations. Egyptian police discipline,
ttressed by Russell's presence, held
n under strain; co-operation with the
iting army was close, surviving even the
e of British tanks to compel King
rouk to change his ministers in Feb-
ary 1942, a controversial expedient
ich pained and surprised Russell. In
46, still popular, he retired, the last
itish officer in Egyptian service.

Amid the conflict of Egyptian national-
n, British exigencies, and European
inority pretensions, Russell remained
impartial guardian of law and order,
stly renowned for professional expertise.
though political assassinations were all
prevalent, the murderers rarely con-
ved to escape. He was a remarkable
d solicitous police chief, a link in the
st British tradition with Egypt, and,
his campaign to suppress drug traffic,
pioneer in an important international
use.

Tall and commanding, a sportsman, a
ndy, a horseman who made history by
ding his camel over fences, as much at
se in his wife's salon as in any desert
mpany, ready for any discomfort on an
ex trail but a *bon-viveur* in town, finding
mour in everything and friends every-
here, Russell was a legend in his life-
ne. Some of the flavour was happily
eserved in his own published reminis-
nces.

He died in London 10 April 1954,
rvived by his wife, Evelyn Dorothea
mple (died 1968), daughter of Francis
oore, stock-jobber. They were married
1911 and had one son, Sir John
riothesley Russell, who became am-
ssador to Spain in 1969, and one
ughter, Camilla Georgiana, married to
ristopher Sykes who contributes to
is Supplement. Russell Pasha was apinted O.B.E. in 1920, C.M.G. in 1926,
d K.B.E. in 1938. He also held numer-
s foreign decorations. There is a post-
mous portrait at Haileybury painted by
hn Ward.

[Sir Thomas Russell Pasha, *Egyptian Ser-
ce*, 1949; private information; personal
owledge.]   P. J. V. ROLO.

ADLEIR, MICHAEL THOMAS
ARVEY (1888–1957), writer and pub-
sher, was born in Oxford 25 December
888, the only child of (Sir) Michael
rnest Sadler [q.v.]. He adopted an early

variant of the family name, Sadleir, as a
nom de plume to distinguish himself from
his father, whom he called 'my best and
wisest friend' and whose biography (1949)
he wrote with affectionate understanding.
Sadleir was educated at Rugby and
Balliol College, Oxford, where he took
second class honours in history in 1912
and won the Stanhope prize for an essay
on Sheridan. In the same year he entered
the publishing firm of Constable, of which
he became a director in 1920 and chairman
in 1954. He served in the war trade
intelligence department (1915–18), was
a member of the British delegation to the
peace conference in 1919, and for a brief
period in the following year of the secretariat of the League of Nations.

Sadleir was an all-round man of letters
who notably distinguished himself in each
department of his activity; he may be
described, however, as the most accomplished book-collector of his time.
His achievement as a collector not only
laid the foundation of his success as a
novelist and biographer, but also affected
his policy as a publisher. He began to
collect books as an undergraduate,
specializing for some years in first editions
of contemporary poets and novelists, of
certain authors of the nineties, and of the
French symbolists and decadents. About
1918 he reverted to an early enthusiasm
for the novels of Anthony Trollope which
led him, in turn, to form an unrivalled
collection of Victorian fiction of the three-
decker period. This was developed into a
sort of bibliographical museum illustrating
the history of the novel during the nineteenth century, including cheap editions,
among them the famous 'yellow backs',
and a variety of material on Victorian
night-life. He also collected the Gothic
romances of the period of about 1780 to
1820, and this collection found its way in
due course to Charlottesville, Virginia,
just as his Trollopes eventually went to
Princeton, and his great collection of
nineteenth-century fiction, over 10,000
volumes, to the university of California
at Los Angeles.

The first work which showed that
Sadleir was destined to revolutionize the
bibliographical approach to books of the
machine-printed and edition-bound era
was his *Excursions in Victorian Bibliography* (1922); this was followed by two
books which pioneered the revival of
interest in Trollope's novels: the admirable *Trollope: A Commentary* (1927), which
has become the standard biography, and

the masterly *Trollope: A Bibliography* (1928). His *Evolution of Publishers' Binding Styles, 1770–1900* (1930) was another fertile and influential book. Sadleir's study of Victorian author–publisher relationships, distribution methods, and reading habits culminated in his two-volume *XIX Century Fiction: A Bibliographical Record* (1951). He was Sandars reader in bibliography at Cambridge University, 1937, and president of the Bibliographical Society, 1944–6.

In his introduction to *XIX Century Fiction* Sadleir confessed: 'I have never undertaken the intensive collection of any author or movement without the intention of ultimately writing the material collected into biography, bibliography or fiction.' Sadleir's avowed practice, most strikingly exemplified in the case of Trollope, was continued in biography with *Bulwer: A Panorama* (1931), later renamed *Bulwer and His Wife, 1803–1836*, and its successor *Blessington–d'Orsay: A Masquerade* (1933). Both these books were sparkling original studies in the morals and taste of the early nineteenth century. As a biographer Sadleir combined a fluent and graceful style with an unusually discriminating sense of period.

While Sadleir's narrative gift imparted zest to his serious historical writing, his work as a novelist brought him popular fame. In his novels his understanding of period was markedly stronger than his imaginative impulse. *Privilege* (1921) chronicled the collapse of the old order which was accelerated by the war of 1914–18, and *The Noblest Frailty* (1925) had as its theme the decay in the ruling stock of mid-Victorian times. Meanwhile *Desolate Splendour* (1923) had emphasized Sadleir's weakness for melodrama and his absorption in the seamy side of nineteenth-century life, which he investigated with a sociological passion worthy of Henry Mayhew [q.v.]. He returned to fiction in 1937 with *These Foolish Things*, described by himself as 'a first-person experiment in emotional intimacy'. *Fanny by Gaslight* (1940), his most successful novel, sold 150,000 copies at its original price in five years, was made into a film, and was widely translated. Both this novel and *Forlorn Sunset* (1947) depicted the vicious underworld of the London of the 1870s in authentic detail, but while the scrupulous finish of *Fanny by Gaslight* enabled Sadleir to carry off the element of artificial melodrama so often found in his plots, *Forlorn Sunset*, no less highly

coloured, proved a more rambling ε consequently less convincing book.

Although he spent much of his life London, Sadleir lived for many years Gloucestershire and latterly at Oak Green near Windsor. Tall, distinguish in appearance, alert in movement, he ν by nature retiring but, overcoming shyness, could dispense hospitality w great personal charm. It was not oɪ through his own writings that he fluenced the literary life and taste of time. When his advice was sought, trouble was too much for him, and ma were the authors who benefited from encouragement and enthusiasm, not leɪ those whose nineteenth-century stud were published by his firm. The rare co bination in his work of original reseaɪ and creative exposition made Sadleir figure of unique authority in his chos sphere.

Sadleir married in 1914 Edith, daugh of Albert Darell Tupper-Carey, canon the Church of England. They had o daughter and two sons, of whom the elɪ was killed in action while serving with t Royal Navy during the war of 1939– Sadleir died in London 13 December 19ξ

[*The Times*, 16 and 20 December 19ξ private information; personal knowledge.]
DEREK HUDSC

SAHA, MEGHNAD (1893–195ɪ scientist. [See MEGHNAD SAHA.]

SALAMAN, REDCLIFFE NATHA (1874–1955), authority on the potato, w born in London 12 September 1874, tʜ ninth of a family of fifteen, of who seven boys and seven girls survived adults. The family home was at that tiɪ in Redcliffe Gardens and this was tɪ reason for what was originally Salamaɪ second forename. His father was Mʏ Salaman, an ostrich feather merchaɪ his mother was Sarah Soloman.

Salaman was an exhibitioner at S Paul's School and a scholar of Triniɪ Hall, Cambridge, where he was placed the first class of part i of the natuɪ sciences tripos in 1896. He qualified medicine from the London Hospital 1900, and obtained his M.D. in 1904. ʌ this date he developed tuberculosis of tɪ lung and had to give up all his medic work, spending six months in Switzerlaɪ and about two years in the country makiɪ a recovery. He then bought a fine hous 'Homestall', in Barley, near Roysto

rtfordshire, his home for the rest of his
.
Perhaps largely through his friendship
th William Bateson [q.v.], Salaman
nd his interests turning to the study of
netics but he was uncertain of a suitable
bject for study. 'No one, so I thought',
recorded, 'had tackled the genetics of
y of our common vegetables; why
buld I not have a try? In the summer
1905 I declared my intentions to my
rdener, a man of stately mien who,
bking down on me from his 6ft. 2 ins.,
id that if a gentleman in my position
ust use his spare time playing about with
getables, he would advise the Potato,
cause he himself knew more about the
ot than any man in England.'
All Salaman's genetical work was car-
d out privately in his garden at Barley.
ere, also, was discovered in 1908 the
netic resistance to potato blight,
hytophthora infestans; this was repeated
1914, and the work was enlarged and
tended at Cambridge.
The results of Salaman's work at
irley were published in 1926 in a book
otato Varieties. In 1926 also he interested
s friend Sir Daniel Hall [q.v.] and the
inistry of Agriculture in the foundation
an institute at Cambridge for the
vestigation of plant virus diseases with
pecial reference to the potato. This was
nown as the Potato Virus Research
istitute, directed by Salaman until 1939,
d was the forerunner of the virus
esearch unit of the Agricultural Research
Duncil.
Salaman's interest however, was more
the potato than in viruses; throughout
s fifty years of preoccupation with it
nere ran one continuous thread which had
othing to do with genetics, virus diseases,
pathology, but was the study of the
otato from a sociological and economic
oint of view. For many years he methodi-
lly collected material bearing on the
rogress of the potato as a food of the
eople, and finally incorporated his
udies in The History and Social Influence
the Potato (1949).
A man of culture and wide interests
alaman had many local activities; he
as vice-president of the Royston and
istrict Hospital and a magistrate for
orty-three years, being chairman of the
ench for twenty-three before he retired
1950. He was deeply interested in the
ebrew University of Jerusalem and did
uch to help it in its earlier years. His
ther great interest was the Society for

the Protection of Science and Learning
and he worked hard to give new opportunities to displaced scientists and
scholars and personally helped many to
start again.

Salaman was elected F.R.S. in 1935,
of all his honours the one he valued
most. In 1955 his election as an honorary
fellow of Trinity Hall gave him great
pleasure but came too late for him to
enjoy it.

In 1901 Salaman married Nina (died
1925), daughter of Arthur Davis, by whom
he had four sons and two daughters;
in 1926 he married Gertrude, daughter of
Ernest D. Lowy. Salaman died at his
home in Barley 12 June 1955. A portrait
by 'Chattie' Salaman is in the National
Institute of Agricultural Botany.

[Kenneth M. Smith in Biographical Memoirs of Fellows of the Royal Society, vol. i, 1955;
personal knowledge.]   KENNETH M. SMITH.

SALTER, HERBERT EDWARD (1863–
1951), Oxford historian, the second son
of a Harley Street doctor, Henry Hyde
Salter, F.R.S., and younger brother of
(Sir) Arthur Clavell Salter [q.v.], was born
in London 6 February 1863. His father
died when he was only eight years old, and
his mother, Henrietta Laura, daughter of
the Rev. Edward Powlett Blunt, took him
to live with her family at Spetisbury in
Dorset. He attended Wimborne Grammar
School. From it he won, in 1876, a scholarship at Winchester, where he became
eventually prefect of hall. From Winchester he went, again with a scholarship,
to New College, Oxford. He took a second
class in classical moderations in 1883, a
first in literae humaniores in 1886, and a
first in theology in 1887. He then went to
Cuddesdon College, was ordained in 1888
and took priest's orders in 1889. After
serving as curate at Sandhurst (1888–91)
he was appointed vice-principal of Leeds
Clergy School. He left Leeds in 1893
when he married and became vicar, first
of Mattingley in Hampshire, and then,
in 1899, of Shirburn in South Oxfordshire.

It was during the ten years which he
spent at Shirburn, and when he was
nearing forty, that Salter first began
historical work by collecting material
for the history of his parish. In 1904 he
offered to edit the Eynsham Cartulary for
the Oxford Historical Society. This was
the first of thirty-four volumes which
he brought out for that society, and
he paid for the cost of producing eleven
of them. The Eynsham Cartulary was

straightforward editing and in that respect differed from the *Cartulary of the Hospital of St. John the Baptist* (1914–16) and the yet more elaborate six-volume edition of the *Oseney Cartulary* (1929, 1931, 1934–6) both of which were based primarily upon the original deeds. In them and in other works—*Oxford Balliol Deeds* (1913), *Oxford City Properties* (1926), and *Oriel College Records* (1926)—he adopted the plan of arranging his documents under parishes and, within the parish, under tenements, and of carrying down the history of each tenement through subsequent leases to the nineteenth century. The abundance of his sources enabled him to construct a detailed history of house-sites in a manner which had not been attempted for any other English city. The results are recorded in an unpublished 'Survey of Oxford', the typescript of which is on the open shelves of the Bodleian Library. He observed the principle that 'whatever is written about Oxford ought to be thorough so far as it goes, so that the work need not be done again': so his *Mediaeval Archives of the University of Oxford* (1917, 1919) completed the publication of all surviving university archives before 1485, and his *Munimenta Civitatis Oxonie* (1917) contained the transcripts by Brian Twyne [q.v.] of the lost city deeds.

Salter did more than edit. He contributed articles on ecclesiastical history and on religious houses to volume ii of the *Victoria County History of Oxfordshire* (1907) and in 1933 was appointed to edit, and planned, a further volume on the history of the university and city. His *Medieval Oxford* (1936) was a publication of the Ford's lectures which he gave in 1934. His *Early History of St. John's College* (1939) was compiled from materials left by his friend, W. H. Stevenson [q.v.]. And although he disclaimed having studied history of any kind except the medieval history of Oxford, he edited for the Canterbury and York Society (1922) the *Chapters of the Augustinian Canons* and collaborated with G. J. Turner in the publication, for the British Academy, of the *Register of St. Augustine's Abbey, Canterbury* (1915, 1924).

His rich store of transcripts, largely from Oxford college muniment rooms, contained in nearly a hundred notebooks, along with many copies of plans of property in Oxford, is in the Bodleian Library. Transcribing made him expert in diplomatic, as may be seen from the fine volume of *Facsimiles of Early Charters in Oxford Muniment Rooms* which printed privately in 1929. He was led to a special study of the royal charters Henry I, Stephen, and Henry II, lend liberally from his collections both H. W. C. Davis [q.v.] and to Leopold Delisle, and contributing short articles the *English Historical Review*.

He came to be recognized as the leading authority on Oxford history sin Anthony Wood [q.v.]. Magdalen Colle elected him to a research fellowship 1918, and this he held until 1939, voting his stipend to the cost of pub cations. He was made a fellow of the British Academy in 1930 and, in the same year, an honorary freeman of the city Oxford. In 1933 he received from his university the honorary degree of doct of letters.

He was twice married: first, in 1893, Beatrice Eva (died 1932), daughter of the Rev. James Steuart Ruddach, by who he had a son and three daughters. The son died when still a boy at Wincheste He married secondly, in 1933, Glad Nina, daughter of Douglas Dewar, wh survived him. Giving up parochial duti in 1909, he went to live nearer to Oxfo at Dry Sandford, and later at Frilford; b in 1942 he returned to Dorset, the count in which he had spent his boyhoo and died there, 23 April 1951, at Broa Oak, Sturminster Newton. He was happ in the countryside; was given to th keeping of bees and ferrets, to th growing of fruit and vegetables, and, u to the last year of his life, to felling tree and sawing logs. Physically active, he wa a good walker; when he was at Shirburn h used to cycle the fifteen miles into Oxfo two or three times a week to work i Oxford libraries, and he still went ou with the beagles when he was seventy five. He had an excellent memory, alik for the personnel of medieval Oxford an for the details of cricket matches playe seventy years before. He shared to th full the qualities of industry and accurac with which he credited an earlier Oxfor antiquary, Thomas Hearne [q.v.]. To grea modesty he united shrewd common sens and, though full of a quiet reserve, he wa kindly and liberal in the help he gav to younger students of medieval history a number of whom united to publish i his honour in 1934 a volume of *Oxfor Essays in Medieval History*. The wor contains a good photograph of Salter and list of his published writings up to 1933.

[*The Times*, 2 May 1951; W. A. Pantin i

ceedings of the British Academy, vol. xl,
4; private information; personal know-
ge.]   EDMUND CRASTER.

RKAR, SIR JADUNATH (1870–1958),
lian historian, third son of Raj Kumar
·kar and Hari Sundari, was born 10
cember 1870 at Karachmaria in the
jshahi district of Bengal. His father
onged to a Kayastha *zamindari* family.
ucated at the Rajshahi and Calcutta
legiate schools and the Presidency
llege, Calcutta, in 1892 he stood first
the first class in the university of
lcutta's M.A. examination in English.
om 1893 to 1896 he taught English at
pon College before serving as professor
English at the Vidyasagar College.
inning the Prem Roychand scholar-
p in December 1897, Sarkar entered
e provincial educational service in June
98. After a year at the Presidency Col-
·e he was transferred in 1899 to Patna
llege where he served as professor of
iglish and then as professor of history
til retirement from government service
1926, with, however, an interval (1917–
) as head of the department of history
the new Hindu University of Banaras
d as professor of history and English
erature at Ravenshaw College, Cuttack
919–23). In 1918 he was promoted to
e Indian Educational Service.
From 1926 to 1928 Sarkar was vice-
ancellor of Calcutta University. From
29 to 1932 he served as a nominated
ember of the Bengal legislative council.
ppointed C.I.E. in 1926, he was knighted
1929. He was a founder-member of the
idian Historical Records Commission
919), an honorary member of the Royal
siatic Society (1923), Campbell gold
edallist and honorary fellow of the
ombay branch of the Royal Asiatic
ociety (1926), and a corresponding mem-
er of the Royal Historical Society (1935).
As an historian, Sarkar found the study
' the history of the later Moguls un-
ertainly dependent on European travel-
rs' accounts and late Persian histories
challengeable English translations. He
ft it resting firmly upon rich resources of
ontemporary letters, news reports, offi-
al documents, and histories in Persian,
larathi, French, and Portuguese. Holding
nat Indian historiography at the be-
inning of the twentieth century stood
here European historiography had stood
t the beginning of the nineteenth, Sarkar
as indefatigable in search of material
idden away in libraries and private col-

lections in India. He drew attention to
the Jaipur archives and had a large share
in the publication of the Poona residency
correspondence. As president of the
Indian Historical Records Commission
Sarkar inspired, led, and directed a
generation of Indian archivists and historians in the salvaging of historical evidence. Sarkar himself was ever most
generous in granting access to his own
fine collection of manuscripts, particularly to young and humble scholars.

In his own work on Aurangzib and his
successors (*History of Aurangzib*, 5 vols.,
1912–24, *Fall of the Mughal Empire*,
4 vols., 1932–50, and his edition and continuation of W. Irvine [q.v.] in *Later
Mughals*, 2 vols., 1922), Sarkar narrated
meticulously the fortunes and misfortunes of the Mogul dynasty. Although
he recognized the importance of economic,
social, and cultural history, he felt that,
for his lifetime, the establishment of a
detailed and accurate political chronology
must be given priority. But in his choice
of subject and in its treatment within the
framework of general history, Sarkar was
very much the child of his time. Proud of
the Bengali renaissance of the nineteenth century which he attributed largely
to the stimulus and protection afforded
by British rule, Sarkar wrote from the
premiss that in the late seventeenth and
eighteenth centuries the history of India
was moving in the right direction and that
the passing of Moslem rule was not to be
regretted as under it India had lain inert.
Believing that 'history when rightly read
is a justification of Providence a revelation of a great purpose in time', Sarkar did
not always avoid anachronistic judgements and a certain lack of sympathetic
awareness of the dilemmas facing the
peoples of India in the eighteenth century.
He regretted that they failed to form and
the Moguls failed to foster 'a compact
nation with equal rights and opportunities
for all'.

Sarkar's study of Aurangzib led him on
to Maratha history and to more than
fifty years of friendship and co-operation
with the doyen of Maratha history, Dr.
G. S. Sardesai. The outcome, e.g. his
Shivaji and his Times (1919) and *House of
Shivaji* (1940), did not altogether please
Maratha sentiment since Sarkar was critical of what he regarded as the mercenary
shortsightedness of eighteenth-century
Maratha leadership.

Sarkar's acquisition of Persian, Sanskrit,
Portuguese, Hindi, Urdu, Marathi, and

French did not prevent him from venturing into general history as his *Chaitanya, Pilgrimages and Teachings* (1913), *India through the Ages* (1928), and *Military History of India* (1960) bear witness. Sarkar was moreover a voluminous writer in Bengali, popularizing the findings of his scholarly work in his mother tongue. In numerous articles for the *Modern Review* and other English language periodicals and newspapers he often drew contemporary morals for India from her past history. He was a severe critic of Indian education, calling for the establishment of higher academic standards and for reforms of the examination system.

Sarkar was a stern Victorian moralist, a staunch patriot, but critical of the generation which brought India to independence and partition. He himself practised what he preached—habits of regularity, frugality, punctuality, self-discipline, and devotion to his calling. Reserved and taciturn, sharp and outspoken, not a clubbable man, Sarkar lived up to his own conceptions, expressed in his *Economics of British India* (1919, 1st ed. 1909), of the Englishmen of his earlier days as 'methodical, cool-headed, strenuous and thorough in all they undertake, self-confident and filled with a divine discontent with things as they are'.

In 1893 Sarkar married Kadambini, daughter of Madhu-sudan Chaudhuri; they had two sons and three daughters. He died in Calcutta 15 May 1958.

[*Life and Letters of Sir Jadunath Sarkar*, ed. Hari Ram Gupta, Hoshiarpur, 1957; *The Times*, 21 May 1958; private information.]
P. HARDY.

SAYERS, DOROTHY LEIGH (1893–1957), writer, was born in Oxford 13 June 1893, the only child of the Rev. Henry Sayers, headmaster of Christ Church Choir School and later rector of Bluntisham in Huntingdonshire. Her mother, Helen Mary Leigh, was a great-niece of Percival Leigh [q.v.], one of the earliest members of the staff of *Punch*. She was educated at the Godolphin School, Salisbury, and went as a Gilchrist scholar to Somerville College, Oxford, where in 1915 she took first class honours in modern languages. After teaching for a year at Hull High School she became an advertiser's copy-writer with S. H. Benson, Ltd., an employment which she retained until 1931.

Her earliest publications were in verse: *Op. 1* (1916) and *Catholic Tales* (1918).

Shortly after 1920 she appears to h formed a plan for earning a livelihood writing detective stories, and she ceeded, characteristically, to master mechanics of the craft by making a cl analytical study of the best models. was a period at which the 'classical' m tery story had already become an est lished genre and was understood to be favourite reading of intelligent and cu vated persons. Dorothy Sayers fores the success which might attend upo more specific appeal to such readers wh approval would establish a reputati and since the books need not be diffic —except in the teasing sense—a wi public might quickly be educated up them. There were already many ingeni writers, but most of them either wrote a pedestrian style, with little concern anything except a puzzle, or rashly corporated out of traditional fiction ments over which they had no comma Dorothy Sayers was not always to kn in advance what she could bring off. E her academic training enabled her to lea quickly. She mastered the art of givin, pleasant literary flavour to her stor while at the same time keeping within own imaginative range.

Perhaps no writer of detective nov has yet succeeded in fusing the attra tions of the kind with the values of serio fiction. But no writer since Wilkie Colli [q.v.] has come nearer to it than Dorot Sayers. That her mysteries all fall with little more than a decade, and that in t remaining twenty years of her life s chose to contribute only to entirely diffe ent fields, must suggest that it was wi impatience that she came finally to reali the necessary limits of the twentiet century version of the sensation nov But although she was to write oth things with success, her detective stori are likely to constitute her best memori As with Sir Arthur Conan Doyle [q.v before her, she remains the prisoner of h own felicity in a literary form of which sl came to speak without much respect.

Whose Body? (1923), the first fruit her study, introduced Lord Peter Wimse a private detective equipped with learne and artistic interests, nonchalant manner an insatiable interest in crime, and reliable manservant named Bunter. The attributes in themselves would not hav taken him out of the ruck; but Dorothy Sayers developed extraordinary ski in contriving for him the illusion penetrating intelligence and outstandin

vers of logical inference. Within nine
ars he had appeared in eight further
oks: *Clouds of Witness* (1926); *Un-
ural Death* (1927); *Lord Peter Views
Body* (1928); *The Unpleasantness at the
lona Club* (1928); *Strong Poison* (1930);
e Documents in the Case* (with Robert
stace, 1930); *The Five Red Herrings
31); and *Have his Carcase* (1932).
e constant but varied excellence of
se was the product of a mind always on
alert for seminal ideas.

Monsignor Ronald Knox [q.v.], him-
f a writer of detective novels, told
story illustrating this. A group of
iters was discussing a proposed colla-
ation in a play for broadcasting, and
e was in favour of beginning with
iver of blood flowing from under a
tain and surrounding a group of intent
dge players. Another declared that
od would not behave in such a way,
less it were from a haemophiliac', and
idea was abandoned. Dorothy Sayers
l not contribute to the discussion at
s point, but was observed to make an
try in a notebook. From this she evolved
e of her cleverest novels.

In her last few years as a mystery
iter she made some interesting attempts
extend her range. In *Murder Must
lvertise* (1933), *The Nine Tailors* (1934),
d *Gaudy Night* (1935) she allowed in-
ased scope to her powers as an atmo-
heric writer and a writer of social
medy. And there was another develop-
nt. In *Strong Poison* Lord Peter had
ared of a charge of murder, and fallen
love with, a woman writer of detective
ries. The relationship was continued
Gaudy Night and again in *Busman's
neymoon* (1937), which was sub-titled
love story with detective inter-
ptions'. Dorothy Sayers rang down the
rtain on Lord Peter at this point
terally so, since *Busman's Honeymoon
is successfully dramatized in collabora-
n with M. St. Clare Byrne). It seems
obable that the writer had come to share
th her readers a sense that her hero was
tting a little out of hand. She had pro-
led him with an entry for *Who's Who
d with ancestors whose histories and
nography she elaborated in the course
private literary diversions among her
ends. Although she was not without
onouncedly masculine characteristics
r temperament was essentially feminine;
ving Lord Peter, she contrived for him
ese little gifts of Tudor portraiture and
teenth-century manuscripts.

The death of the detective novelist
was the birth of the Christian apologist.
With *The Zeal of Thy House* (1937) and
The Devil to Pay (1939), plays written for
the Canterbury Festival, she established
a second reputation which was subsequently much extended by a radio drama,
The Man Born to be King (broadcast at
monthly intervals between December
1941 and October 1942), and by several
similar pieces. From 1940 onwards she
published a number of volumes containing studies, essays, and speeches on
critical, theological, and political topics.
She had already shown an interest in the
problems of verse translation by producing *Tristan in Brittany* in 1929; in 1949
she published a translation of Dante's
Inferno and in 1955 of the *Purgatorio*,
each with a commentary. She was at work
upon the *Paradiso* at the time of her
death, which took place at Witham,
Essex, 17 December 1957.

In 1926 Dorothy Sayers married
Captain Oswald Atherton Fleming, well
known as a war correspondent, who died in
1950. She had no children, but adopted
a son. In 1950 she received an honorary
D.Litt. from Durham University.

[Private information; personal knowledge.]
J. I. M. STEWART.

SCHOLES, PERCY ALFRED (1877–
1958), musical writer and encyclopedist,
was born at Headingley, Leeds, 24 July
1877, the third child of Thomas Scholes,
commercial agent, and his wife, Katharine Elizabeth Pugh. Ill health limited
his attendance at school (he was a lifelong
sufferer from severe bronchitis), but he
gave much time to miscellaneous reading
and the assiduous study of the elements of
music. After a couple of years earning
10s. a week as assistant librarian of the
Yorkshire College (later the university
of Leeds), he taught music at Kent College,
Canterbury (1901), and Kingswood College,
Grahamstown, South Africa (1904). On his
return to England at the age of twenty-
eight his career began to take a more definite direction. He became an extension
lecturer to the university of Manchester on
what was coming to be known as 'musical
appreciation', and continued in this way
very successfully for the next six years.
Meanwhile he took his A.R.C.M. diploma
and (after a false start at Durham)
entered St. Edmund Hall, Oxford, gaining his B.Mus. in 1908.

In 1907, following a series of lectures
for the Co-operative Holidays Association,

he formed the Home Music Study Union, whose organ, *The Music Student* (in later years *The Music Teacher*), he edited from its foundation in 1908 until 1921. He married in 1908 and in 1912 made the decisive step of moving to London, his only guaranteed income being £40 a year as assistant to J. S. Shedlock, music critic of the *Queen*. With the support of such men as H. C. Colles [q.v.] and (Sir) Percy Buck, he was soon making his mark as a journalist and as an extension lecturer for the universities of Oxford, Cambridge, and London. From 1913 to 1920 he was music critic of the *Evening Standard*.

When war broke out in 1914 he was on a lecture tour of colleges in the United States and Canada. On his return he headed, until 1919, the 'music for the troops' section of the Y.M.C.A. in France, further developing his twin gifts of detailed organization and the ability to hold the attention of the unpractised listener. From this work came his very successful *Listener's Guide to Music* (1919).

Early in 1920 he became music critic of the *Observer*, following the abrupt departure of Ernest Newman [q.v.] who had accepted a substantial offer from the rival *Sunday Times*. For the next five years Scholes filled the position with notable success. His style, always fluent and readable, gained distinction. He continued to regard his role as primarily that of an educator, and was undoubtedly among the first to see the educational potentialities of broadcasting, the gramophone, and the player-piano. He gave a weekly radio talk commenting on the previous week's broadcasts: from 1926 to 1928 he was musical editor of the *Radio Times*. He was usually at work on several books at once. His home was a busy office with as many as six or more typists and co-workers, including his devoted wife.

A contract to provide pianola roll annotations for the Aeolian Company provided him with the means to detach himself from journalism. In 1928 he moved to Switzerland, and thenceforward lived in the neighbourhood of Montreux. The following year he organized an 'Anglo-American Music Educators' Conference' at Lausanne, which was repeated in 1931. He made four further lecture tours of the United States. He was now able to give time to more solid scholarship and his thesis on 'The Puritans and Music' gained him in 1934 his D.ès L. from Lausanne University.

For some time Scholes had planned

a more comprehensive work, tentativ called 'Everyone's Musical Encycloped for the great new body of listeners brou, into being by radio and the gramopho The book finally appeared as the *Oxf Companion to Music* in the autumn 1938. Scholes's varied experience teacher, lecturer, journalist, critic, a scholar was at last drawn together one accomplishment—'the most ext ordinary range of musical knowled ingeniously "self-indexed", ever writt and assembled between two covers one man' (*Grove*).

In 1940 he made his way to Engla just before the fall of France; his warti homes were first at Aberystwyth, then Oxford, where he was elected to t board of the faculty of music. He co pleted a monumental biography of I Charles Burney (2 vols., 1948, Jan Tait Black memorial prize), a model humane scholarship, and continued l lexicographical labours with his *Conc Oxford Dictionary of Music* (1952) a *Oxford Junior Companion to Music* (195 After the war he returned to Switzerlan and built a house at Clarens. In 19 the devaluation of the pound drove h back to Oxford, where he spent t next six years losing inch by inch l battle against the complications in l lifelong bronchitis brought on by a vancing age and an inimical clima Every winter he returned to Switzerlan and there, at Vevey, he died, 31 July 19 He was survived by his wife, Do Wingate, daughter of Richard Lean, ci engineer. There were no children.

Scholes was of middle height, and though not robust, an active walke He worked long hours with great conce tration, with methodical interruptions f exercise. His conscience was strong protestant, totally divorced from ar conventional religious expression. He w warmly humanitarian; a long-standi and articulate vegetarian and oppone of blood sports. There were those for who his clarity of thought, total absence of hui bug and affectation, and ironic humo made him seem something of a philistir He was charitable in good causes, war and generous in personal dealings, at tl same time disinclined to give ground business matters. Traces of his nati Yorkshire speech remained with him the end. In a letter to his publisher l once wrote, 'the epitaph I should desi for myself, were it not already appli to another and a greater man, wou

"The common people heard him
.dly".'

Scholes valued his well-earned academic
distinctions which in addition to those
.eady mentioned included: from Oxford
: honorary degree of D.Mus. (1943),
A. (by decree, 1944), and D.Litt.
'50), and from Leeds an honorary
.t.D. (1953). He was an honorary fellow
.d trustee of St. Edmund Hall, Oxford;
officer of the Star of Romania (1930),
5.A. (1938), and O.B.E. (1957). His
.narkable library, one of the largest of
kind in private hands, was acquired by
: National Library of Canada, Ottawa.
'rivate information; personal knowledge.]
              JOHN OWEN WARD.

'HUSTER, CLAUD, BARON SCHUSTER
369–1956), civil servant, was born in
.nchester 22 August 1869, the only
.n of Frederick Leo Schuster, merchant,
. his wife, Sophia Ellen, daughter of
.-Colonel Herbert William Wood,
.dras Army. Schuster was a second
.usin of Sir Arthur Schuster and Sir
.lix Schuster [qq.v.]. Schuster's father
.d uncles were born in England, their
.ther, Samuel Schuster, having come
.m Frankfurt in 1824. One of the
.cles, the Rev. William Percy Schuster,
.came curate at Corfe Castle and later
.ar of Lulworth. As a boy Schuster used
. stay with him and so acquired such a
.ve of Dorset that in later life he made
.s country home there. Schuster was
.ucated at Winchester and New College,
.xford, where he obtained a second class
. history (1892), was called to the bar
. the Inner Temple (1895) and joined
.e Northern circuit. His father having
.st his money, Schuster had to earn his
.vn living. He doubted whether he would
.cceed quickly at the bar and went as
.cretary to the London Government
.ct Commission from 1899 to 1902.

There he caught the eye of (Sir) Robert
.orant [q.v.] in the Board of Education
.d became his legal assistant (1903),
.gal adviser (1907), and principal assistant
.cretary (1911). His experience under
.orant was invaluable. He confirmed
.s grasp of the importance and the work-
.g of local government; he was in close
.uch with Sir Arthur Thring on the
.afting of education bills under two
.overnments with widely differing poli-
.es on Church schools; and he was
.tively concerned in the consequent
.tigation.

In 1911 Morant, on his transfer to

national insurance, insisted on taking
Schuster with him. The change taught
Schuster new lessons. The education
office had been highly specialized. Under
Lloyd George's complicated scheme of
insurance Schuster became one of the able
team of commissioners who used the
whole Civil Service as a single instrument
of policy to bring the Act into operation
within six months and thereafter to
administer it. Schuster served in various
capacities, but most usefully as legal
adviser.

In 1915 the offices of clerk of the Crown
in Chancery and permanent secretary in
the lord chancellor's office were due to
fall vacant by the retirement of Lord
Muir Mackenzie. Lord Haldane [q.v.]
with good reason chose Schuster, a
lawyer with twelve years' experience of
constructive administration and with the
machinery of government at his fingertips. Haldane regarded the office of chancellor as an intolerable burden for one
minister to carry. His mind was moving
towards a division of the duties between
the chancellor and a minister of justice to
be appointed after the war; Schuster, he
thought, would be the very man to create
the new Ministry when the time came.

By the time Schuster took up his post
on 1 July 1915, however, Haldane had
ceased to be lord chancellor and his
proposals were later rejected by Lord
Birkenhead, the first chancellor to be appointed after the war (and whose notice
Schuster contributed to this Dictionary).
The lord chancellor continued therefore
to bear an exceedingly heavy burden and
his staff had to make it possible for him
to sustain it. Schuster, until his retirement in 1944, enabled ten successive
chancellors to perform their amazingly
multifarious duties.

For this task Schuster had natural
advantages. He was a quick reader and
thinker, fluent on paper and lucid in
stating a case. He was, on principle, as
anxious as Haldane himself to see that the
right men were put in the right places
with the best possible conditions of service
in both the public interest and their own.
He had to adapt his technique of a higher
civil servant to a new environment in
which judges receive with circumspection
any advice from an emissary of the executive. A chancellor, although head of
the judiciary, does not command judges,
but seeks their advice. Schuster's role
was often to suggest who should be asked
to advise, what should be referred to

a committee, who should be invited to serve, and what should be done with the report. He saw to it that action swiftly followed; and the judges, the bar, the Law Society, and members of both Houses were the more ready to give the chancellor their help when they found that it yielded practical results.

The chancellors' reforms during Schuster's tenure of office were many and technical. They included the Law of Property Act, 1922, and the Acts of 1925 which replaced and superseded it. The most fruitful committees which he suggested and on which he sat were the Swift committee of 1919 which led to much greater efficiency in the county court system, the Law Revision Committee of 1934 from which sprang the first series of Acts reforming defects in the common law, and the Rushcliffe committee of 1944 which gave birth to legal aid. But executive action is not all initiative. It is also the response to what happens; and the chancellor being a kind of universal joint between Cabinet, judiciary, and Parliament, there was hardly a public event which did not call for action of some sort on his behalf. Schuster was always alert, his reaction to the news immediate, his course of action soundly planned and quickly put in train. The benefit to the chancellor was that whenever he had an administrative decision to make, Schuster presented the facts so clearly and above all so fairly, that the chancellor could give a decision which was truly his own in the brief time available to him for departmental business.

With the conspicuous exception of Lord Hewart [q.v.], the author of *The New Despotism* (1929), who had a deep-rooted antipathy to administrators and feared them *et dona ferentes*, Schuster, as the years went by, obtained more and more co-operation between the judges and the chancellor. When he retired, the bench and both branches of the legal profession had come to regard the chancellor's office as itself a Ministry which could serve them well, and through them the cause of justice.

The independence of the judiciary can be more surely defended by a chancellor than by any other minister. By stilling the movement for a Ministry of Justice during his tenure of office Schuster enabled chancellors to retain for a generation the duty of choosing judges, a function on which the liberties of the

nation largely depend; and if some of t other duties of the chancellor have to transferred to another minister, Schuste development of the chancellor's off will have smoothed the way for t transfer.

From 1944 to 1946 Schuster was he of the legal branch of the Allied Cont Commission (British zone) in Austria. was over seventy-five and tackled t unexpected with the zest of a young ma After his return he initiated a debate the House of Lords on Austria (January 1947) and wrote a technical lively article on military government Austria in the *Journal* of the Society Public Teachers of Law for 1947. In t same year he did good work as treasu of the Inner Temple in its reconstructi after the bombing of the war. His mi never lost its vigour, and he died on June 1956 while attending an old Wyk hamist dinner.

As a young man Schuster had bla hair, piercing blue eyes, and the ne spare figure which he kept all his li He climbed in the Alps from the age seventeen and took to ski in 1921. He w the first man to be president both of t Ski Club of Great Britain (1932-4) and the Alpine Club (1938-40). At the age sixty-four he took to hunting agai which he had not done since he was a b in Cheshire. His love of natural beau and his sensitive appreciation of liter ture are both reflected in the style a matter of his *Peaks and Pleasant Pastur* (1911) and *Postscript to Adventure* (195

His friendships were lasting and fine description of Lord Sterndale [q. in *Men, Women and Mountains* (193 shows the kind of man he admired mos He had many of the prejudices comm amongst Englishmen of his class, and often gave pungent expression to h dislikes. This was occasionally undipl matic in official life, but for his friends added spice to friendship.

Schuster was knighted in 1913, appoi ted C.V.O. in 1918, K.C. in 1919, K.C. in 1920, and G.C.B. in 1927. He serve as high sheriff of Dorset in 1941 and w raised to the peerage in 1944. He was a honorary fellow of St. Catharine's Colleg Cambridge.

He married in 1896 Mabel Elizabet (died 1936), daughter of W. W. Men [q.v.], rector of Lincoln College, Oxfor They had one son, who was killed o active service in France in 1918, and on daughter.

An oil-painting of Schuster by Harry Ellison is in the possession of the family.

[*The Times*, 29 June, 4 and 11 July 1956; *w Times*, 6 July 1956; *Alpine Journal*, 56; *British Ski Year Book*, 1957; private information; personal knowledge.]

ALBERT NAPIER.

SCOTT, LORD FRANCIS GEORGE MONTAGU-DOUGLAS- (1879–1952), soldier, Kenya farmer and political leader, was born at Dalkeith 1 November 1879, the sixth and youngest son of William Henry Walter Montagu-Douglas-Scott, Earl of Dalkeith and later sixth Duke of Buccleuch and eighth Duke of Queensberry, by his wife, Louisa Jane Hamilton, third daughter of the first Duke of Abercorn [q.v.]. Francis Scott was educated at Eton and Christ Church, Oxford, but did not graduate as he abandoned his studies for the Grenadier Guards and the South African war. From 1905 to 1910 he was aide-de-camp to the Earl of Minto [q.v.], viceroy of India, whose daughter, Eileen Nina Evelyn Sibell Elliot (died 1938), he married in 1915 and by whom he had two daughters. His recreations were cricket and pigsticking but all this was ended by the outbreak of war in 1914. Severely wounded in the leg at the battle of Mons with the Grenadier Guards he was appointed to the D.S.O. and mentioned in dispatches. He served the rest of the war in command of the depot battalion of his regiment at Wellington Barracks. Many men later to be distinguished or famous in the military and political world, including Lords Gort [q.v.], Alexander of Tunis, and Chandos, and Harold Macmillan, experienced the measure of his sense of duty and integrity during this period.

After the war Lord Francis Scott retired with the rank of lieutenant-colonel and emigrated to Kenya where in 1920 he bought 3,500 acres of land at Rongai from the third Lord Delamere [q.v.] and built his home, a rather severe patrician stone house with sweeping lawns and tall dark glossy-leaved green-heart trees. He soon, in 1924, entered politics in his new country as a substitute for Delamere and in 1925 was elected in his own right for the Ukamba constituency. In 1931 he was chosen by his colleagues to lead the settlers' delegation to give evidence on closer union before the joint select committee of both Houses of Parliament presided over by Lord Stanley of Alderley. His moderation and realistic assessment of the Kenya opposition to closer union impressed the committee and his colleagues. On Delamere's death in November of the same year he succeeded him as leader of the European elected members and represented the Rift Valley constituency, the heart of the colony's agriculture and politics. He was a member of the governor's executive council in 1932–6 and again in 1937–44 and was appointed K.C.M.G. in 1937, an unusual distinction for an unofficial representative in those restricted days of colonial officialdom.

In the war of 1939–45 Scott was again mentioned in dispatches and his intimate knowledge of everyone and everything in the colony served him well as military secretary to the commander-in-chief, East African Forces, from 1943. His constituents, however, did not appreciate his long and exhausting hours of work in Nairobi, often more than a hundred miles away from their own troubles, over difficult and sometimes impassable roads. In 1944, as a result of increasing criticism, he resigned from his constituency and devoted himself solely to his military work until the termination of his appointment in 1946. The next year was spent in England but in 1948 on his return to Kenya his many old supporters pressed him to contest once again the Rift Valley seat. In a three-cornered contest he was opposed and defeated by 86 votes by a younger farmer, (Sir) Michael Blundell, who had returned from the war and was to follow Scott in the Rift Valley for the next fifteen years. In a momentary wave of bitterness Scott, after twenty years of great influence in the life of the colony, retired to Deloraine. Subsequently he felt, however, that the long election campaign had done much to mould Blundell's political thinking and as a result the two men became great friends and Scott was able to put his knowledge and experience freely at the service of the younger man to whom it was invaluable.

Scott's political views were not always popular. He was far in advance of his constituents in his appreciation of the future position of the African people. By the European voters, the day for African responsibility was not even dreamed of, but in 1939 Scott wrote a memorandum in which he foresaw the advent of African political leaders with responsibilities as ministers of the Crown.

He was critical of Colonial Office handling of educated African leaders and felt that more positions of responsibility should be open to men like Mbiu Koinange (later one of Jomo Kenyatta's strongest nationalist supporters). He was also heir to the full tradition of opposition to the colonial Government which was the standard political doctrine of the day. Perhaps he was too optimistic but he felt that a Government formed from his fellow settlers would deal with the problems of the country and understand the Africans much more realistically than the remote arbiters of the country's fate in Whitehall. Above all he never ceased to attack the Government in the pursuit of economies in the cost of administration. As he would exclaim: 'The people's money is best in the people's pocket.' He had one bitter disillusionment. True to his beliefs and his age he strongly opposed the imposition of income-tax. He finally agreed—much to the anger of his constituents—on the understanding that it would be a temporary measure. Subsequently, when the Government insisted that the system was intended to become a permanent feature of the taxation structure he felt strongly, like the leaders of the European community before and after him in other matters, that the British Government had been dishonest and had misled him. These may seem small problems and small upsets in the formative years of an African country but to him they were real and important issues of principle. Spare of figure, with a pronounced limp, an attractive decisive voice, he was the embodiment of a simple sense of duty and desire to serve his country. He did not suffer fools gladly, indeed was rather short-tempered, but the charitable dismissed this with an explanation of the constant pain arising from his leg which was amputated in 1933 as a result of his war wound.

Death came to him, 26 July 1952, in a manner which fitted his life and his traditions. He died peacefully after a heart attack as he waited in his railway carriage at Paddington on his way to meet Queen Elizabeth at Windsor on the occasion of the presentation of new colours to the Blues.

An excellent portrait of him by Sir Oswald Birley, the property of the Government of Kenya, is hung at Deloraine on loan to his elder daughter.

[Personal knowledge.]

MICHAEL BLUNDELL.

SCOTT, SIR GILES GILBERT (188 1960), architect, was born in Church Ro Hampstead, 9 November 1880, the son George Gilbert Scott, a noted expone of the Gothic revival in Britain, and l wife, Ellen King-Sampson. He was grandson of Sir George Gilbert Sc [q.v.], chiefly remembered for th courageous work, the Albert Memori: He was educated at Beaumont Colleg then became, in 1898, a pupil of t architect Temple Moore [q.v.] in who office, probably, he saw the possibility designing in Gothic, without reproduci all its detail. There too, by working night, he went in for and won the co petition for the new Liverpool Anglic: cathedral. This remarkable feat emba rassed the selection committee when discovered the winner to be a young m: of twenty-two, of no experience, a furthermore a Roman Catholic. Sco himself was surprised. Nevertheless was appointed architect for the cathedr: with G. F. Bodley [q.v.], once a pupil Sir Gilbert Scott, as collaborator. Th imposition was removed when the pla were finally drawn up and the first co tract placed in 1903.

This great undertaking covered an ar almost twice that of St. Paul's. Sco made all the drawings and only one maj revision: he abandoned the twin towers his winning design in favour of a muc larger central tower. Looking at th whole exterior sixty years later one struck by the dependence on mass rath than intricacy, and on well-proportione stone surfaces, deftly pierced by window betraying no more than a Gothic ancestr The cathedral shows both a knowledge structure and a belief in its anatomy the chief factors in architectural design.

Naturally such an early triump launched Giles Scott on an evenly suc cessful career. The other churches he wa asked to design in the ensuing years a had a quality traceable to the paren building at Liverpool: the same relianc on mass for effect; a look of strengt always; together with an imaginativ and wise handling of detail. He neve repeated himself; but, when he was abl to incorporate it, he preferred a stron square tower at the west end. An excep tion to this is St. Alban's at Golde Green, where a very squat central towe draws together happily the sloping tile roofs grouped round it. Another is th chapel for Charterhouse School. This no more than a long, narrow, and loft

fice, almost in the class of industrial
hitecture; but admirably proportioned
1 lit by tall narrow windows with deep
eals. More interesting is the large chapel
Ampleforth Abbey in Yorkshire,
ich took over twenty years to build.
e is impressed again here by the
ssive piling up of the exterior; and,
ernally, by the roughly plastered sures between the piers and arches. Scott
s inspired by the narrowness of the site
wed to the chapel to form a crypt
der the south half of the slope of the
und, which provides space for side
pels and is reached most attractively
a wide stone staircase taking up much
the south transept. Moreover, the high
ar, standing roughly in the centre, is a
ble one facing east and west. A strong
ly designed stone baldachino rises
kly to a great height above it.

)ther churches which must be
ntioned are St. Michael's, Ashford,
ddlesex; St. Francis, Terriers, Buck-
hamshire; St. Andrew's, Luton; and
Maughold's, Ramsey, Isle of Man. The
t two have west end towers. The church
tt built in Oldfield Lane, Bath, differs
m those four in that it achieves unusual
rm from its great simplicity inside.
e aisles are divided from the nave by
y short fat round columns, joined by
ck semi-circular arches, which spring
m sculptured capitals reminiscent of
th-century work in the Vosges. Then
re is Oban cathedral, built for the
man Catholic diocese of Argyll and the
es; a late work, and not very well
wn; but finished in time for Scott
see it. All his churches with west end
vers are crowned by this instance: the
ssive square feature, built in roughly
wn granite—grey with a touch of pink—
nds very dominantly almost on the
ge of the sea, facing the Atlantic blasts.
is anchored there by twin porches at its
se, rising unusually high but effectively
egral with the tower itself. Although a
all cathedral, it looks large inside, due
rtly to the absence of subdivisions in
length and partly to the extreme
plicity—almost innocence—of the
atment. The nave piers are very tall
d very plain; and a rugged look is
en by the roof, seemingly constructed
old ships' timbers. The high altar,
ain, richly outshines all the other
nishings. Oban cathedral is a notable
ample of a design most suitable to its
e and, in every way, to its purpose. It
s Scott's power to grasp clearly the

practical object of a building and design
it on that basis. Appearance followed
from the expression of this more than
from a preconceived idea of beauty.

The University Library which Scott
built for Cambridge is little more than
a towering bookstack. Fortunately it is
not overwhelmingly too near the ancient
colleges. But the large addition to the
Bodleian at Oxford had of necessity to be
in the centre of the city to provide storage
for millions of books within easy reach of
the ancient reading-rooms. An immense
stack on a corner site in Broad Street
would have been impossible. Hence the
new structure, deeply sunk into the earth
and screened by two elevations no higher
than its neighbours. In an attempt to be
polite to these—which vary from late
Gothic to Victorian Tudor—Scott produced a not very impressive neo-Jacobean
design. If this is compared to the addition
he made to Clare College, Cambridge, the
Bodleian extension loses interest. For the
former is the straight provision of two
blocks of rooms in a simple Georgian
idiom, linked by a memorial arch of great
beauty. The unexpected value of this lies
in its showing that Scott could design in
the spirit of the late eighteenth century
with a facility equalling his handling of
Gothic.

Scott was appointed architect for the
new Waterloo Bridge in 1932; and it was
opened to traffic in 1945. This is an
engineering work married to architecture
most properly and in sharp contrast to
the fanciful liaison of Tower Bridge. The
clean sweep of the five unadorned arches
reflects admirably the invisible steel
anatomy. One feels and enjoys the
tension expressed in the form. The great
spans bounding across the Thames testify
to the purpose of the structure—the rapid
conveyance of traffic. And again, the right
collaboration between engineer and architect can be appreciated in the great Battersea power-station. Its high walls of plain
good brickwork seem as if they encased big
machinery; while the huge chimneys—as
pleasant to look at as many campaniles—
hint, in the strength and delicacy of their
design, at the puffing of smoke in tall
clouds.

Some restoration of buildings damaged
or destroyed by enemy bombing in the
war of 1939–45 fell to his lot. The mid-
Victorian Gothic-revival Carmelite church
in Kensington, popular but of little charm,
with a number of altars in the sugary
fourteenth-century style much favoured

871

at that time, was practically obliterated. Scott made no attempt to reproduce it; as the church was hemmed in closely by narrow streets at each side, he made the new building follow the plan of the old but lit it with top lights inserted in the curve of the roof. His restoration of the Guildhall consisted chiefly of saving what remained and strengthening the roof with steel, inserted above the old timbers. In what amounted to a rebuilding of the House of Commons, Scott was instructed by the select committee to re-state the Chamber in its original form, but to eliminate much of the ecclesiastical Gothic detail and ornament. The foundation stone was laid in 1948 and the new Chamber first used in October 1950.

Scott was elected an associate of the Royal Academy in 1918 and a full academician in 1922. He was knighted in 1924 and appointed to the Order of Merit in 1944. He was an honorary D.C.L. of Oxford (1933) and LL.D. of Liverpool (1925) and of Cambridge (1955). He received the Royal gold medal of the Royal Institute of British Architects (of which he became a fellow in 1912) in 1925; in 1933–5 he was president of the Institute which celebrated its centenary in 1934. When in 1949 Princess Elizabeth presented him with the Albert medal of the Royal Society of Arts she hailed him as 'the builder of a lasting heritage for Britain'.

This excellent architect was a man of medium height and, at first sight, not unduly impressive, in view of his high distinction. He was very modest and approachable, with a charming sense of humour. Golf was his great recreation. He married in 1914 Louisa Wallbank Hughes who died in 1949, leaving two sons. Scott himself died in London 8 February 1960. The National Portrait Gallery possesses drawings of him by Robin Guthrie and Powys Evans and a painting by R. G. Eves.

[Private information.]   A. S. G. BUTLER.

SCOTT-JAMES, ROLFE ARNOLD (1878–1959), journalist, editor, and literary critic, was born at Stratford on Avon 21 December 1878, the son of the Rev. John Scott James, a Congregational minister, by his wife, Elizabeth Barnard. He was the youngest but one of eight children, six of them girls. They were an enterprising family whose active careers took them to many parts of the world. Scott-James was educated at Mill Hill School and

won a scholarship to Brasenose Colle Oxford. After obtaining a third class *literae humaniores* (1901) he worked at ᴧ Canning Town Settlement and at Toynᴸ Hall before joining the staff of the *Da News* in 1902. He was appointed literaᴦ editor at the early age of twenty-sev and occupied this post with notaᴸ success for the next six years, duriᴧ which he also became a leader-writer ᴣ the paper, his assistant editor at this ti being the essayist Robert Lynd (whᴇ notice he subsequently contributed this Dictionary).

The *Daily News* was a journal rooᴛ in the Liberal and humanitarian traᴅ tion—Dickens had been its first editoᴦ and Scott-James himself possessed strongly developed social conscienᴇ this manifested itself at many differᴇ points in his career in activities whiᴄ if distinct from his literary gifts, at ᴛ same time enriched them. He travelled Macedonia shortly before the first Balk war and served for many years on ᴛ Balkan Committee; and immediatᴇ after the loss of the *Titanic* he sailed America in her sister-ship to investigᴀ the case of the five hundred firemen w had struck in protest against conditioᴇ revealed by the sinking of the liner. ᴌ was also one of the earliest advocates the National Theatre, championed ᴛ idea in the *Daily News,* and remained member of the committee until the eᴅ of his life. These experiences sharpen his awareness of the potentialities of prᴇ comment, and in 1913 he published *T Influence of the Press,* a study of new papers as a factor in moulding pubᴸ opinion. He was a lifelong supporter the Liberal Party and frequently wrᴄ political commentaries for the *Daily Neᴥ* In 1924 he contributed a report ᴏ 'Housing Conditions in Mining Areas' Lloyd George's survey of *Coal and Poᴥ* and in 1932, the year of Roosevelt's fiᴦ election as president, he accompaniᴇ Lloyd George's tour of the United Stat as correspondent for the *Daily Chronic* During his years with the *Daily Neᴥ* Scott-James became acquainted wi many of the principal figures of tᴈ Edwardian literary world, and amoᴧ the younger generation he was a clo friend of Wyndham Lewis [q.v.]. ᴵ March 1914 he became the first editor the *New Weekly,* one of the most vigᴄ ous journals of a period which aboundᴇ in new and meteoric literary enterprisᴇ Within four months its contributoᴦ

luded Agate, Belloc, Bennett, Chester-
n, W. H. Davies, de la Mare, Ford
adox Hueffer (later Ford), Forster,
alsworthy, Gosse, Cunninghame Gra-
m, Edward Thomas, Tomlinson, Wells,
eats, and the French critic Valéry
arbaud. The *New Weekly* quickly earned
high prestige, but it could not survive
e outbreak of war. At the age of thirty-
ven Scott-James enlisted and was com-
issioned in the Royal Garrison Artillery.
e served in France, rose to the rank of
ptain, and in 1918 was awarded the
.C.
In the following year he returned to
urnalism: he worked from 1919 to 1930
leader-writer for the *Daily Chronicle*,
om 1933 to 1935 and throughout the war
1939–45 as leader-writer and assistant
litor of the *Spectator*, and he was well
nown to the readers of the *Christian
ience Monitor* as a leader-writer on
reign news. In 1940 he became editor
the British Council monthly journal
ritain To-day, an appointment which he
ld until 1954, when he was appointed
.B.E. Apart from his versatility in
aily journalism, his more permanent
hievements undoubtedly lay in literary
iticism and in editorship, where he
ombined an intellectual integrity with
warmth of personality which greatly
adeared him to his colleagues.
In 1934 Scott-James succeeded Sir John
quire [q.v.] as editor of the *London
Iercury*. In the first editorial Squire had
aimed a wider scope than that of any
revious English literary magazine, and
ae journal published poetry, fiction, and
elles-lettres besides reviewing literature
nd the arts. Scott-James proved himself
oth an exacting and a receptive editor:
e restored the originally high standard
f visual presentation and continued to
roaden the range of contributors. If the
Iercury did not attain the critical power
f the *Criterion* or *Scrutiny*, nevertheless
performed the important function of
ringing together the new and the estab-
shed, and its last issue in April 1939
ttingly contained one of its finest contri-
utions, W. H. Auden's 'In Memory of
V. B. Yeats'.
Of Scott-James's critical writings *The
Iaking of Literature* (1928) remains a
emarkably perceptive survey of the de-
elopment not only of criticism but of the
terary aesthetic from the Periclean age
o the twentieth century. If the approach
s a little academic compared with that of
he critical pioneers of the inter-war years,

the book admirably illustrates the breadth
of its author's classical scholarship, his
inquiring cast of mind, and his recognition of an underlying unity in the creative
processes of literature. His *Fifty Years
of English Literature 1900–1950* (1951)
reveals the catholicity of his taste and
his capacity to communicate his enjoyment of the imaginative writing of his
lifetime. His other publications include
Modernism and Romance (1908), *Personality in Literature* (1913), and short studies
of Thomas Hardy (1951) and Lytton
Strachey (1955).

Scott-James married in 1905 Violet
Eleanor (died 1942), daughter of Captain
Arthur Brooks; there were a son and two
daughters of the marriage: Marie, a
literary critic (died 1956), and Anne, well
known as a journalist. His second marriage, to Paule Honorine Jeanne, daughter
of P. E. Lagarde (barrister, Paris Court of
Appeal) and head of the department of
French at the London School of Economics, took place in 1947.

Scott-James died in London 3 November 1959.

[Private information; personal knowledge.]
                              I. SCOTT-KILVERT.

SCOTT-PAINE, CHARLES HUBERT
(1891–1954), pioneer of aviation and of
high-speed motor-boats, was born at New
Shoreham, Sussex, 11 March 1891, one of
three sons of Henry Paine, an ironmonger, by his wife, Roseanna Scott.
From his earliest youth Paine (he and his
brothers later added their mother's family
name to their own) had a passion for the
sea and ships. In the best tradition, he is
said to have run away to sea from school.
However, in 1910 he had a short flight in
an aeroplane and this was the start of an
equal enthusiasm for the air. In 1912 he
met Noel Pemberton Billing who was
already active in aviation and in the
following year Scott-Paine joined Pemberton Billing, Ltd., on its formation to
manufacture seaplanes at Woolston,
Southampton. This company, which later
became Supermarine, concentrated from
the beginning on flying boats: seaplanes
with hulls which performed the dual
functions of accommodation and flotation.
The first Supermarine product, an advanced but unsuccessful flying boat with
circular-section hull, was displayed at
the fifth Aero Show held at Olympia in
1914. Following the outbreak of war the
prototype of a landplane scout was
designed and built in the remarkably

short time of eight days. This was followed by a number of other experimental aircraft of unusual design.

When Pemberton Billing joined the Royal Naval Air Service in 1914 Scott-Paine became the firm's general manager. In 1916 Pemberton Billing entered Parliament and sold his interest in Supermarine, transferring some of his shares to Scott-Paine who became managing director. For the rest of the war, under government control, Supermarine manufactured in quantity a successful series of flying boats. It also produced several experimental seaplanes to Admiralty designs. In 1919, 1922, and 1923 Scott-Paine entered Supermarine seaplanes for the international Schneider Trophy races. Victory in 1922 and three successive Supermarine victories some years later were finally to win the contest outright for Britain in 1931 with (Sir) John Boothman [q.v.] as pilot.

In 1919 Scott-Paine opened a flying-boat airline service to the Isle of Wight, and, in the following year, one between Southampton and Le Havre. These experimental services did not long survive but in 1923 Scott-Paine and (Sir) James Bird [q.v.], who had joined Supermarine in 1919, founded the British Marine Air Navigation Co., Ltd. This pioneer airline operated regular services from Southampton to the Channel Islands with Supermarine flying boats and became one of the four constituent companies in the national 'chosen-instrument' airline, Imperial Airways, Ltd., formed in 1924. Scott-Paine remained on the board of Imperial Airways until it was itself absorbed into British Overseas Airways Corporation after the latter's formation in 1939.

In 1922 outside interests, represented on the board by Bird, took shares in Supermarine and acquired complete control in 1923, when Scott-Paine left the company. He and a colleague then bought the boat-yard of May, Harden and May at Hythe near Southampton, and there in 1927 founded the British Power Boat Co., Ltd., of which he remained chairman for the rest of his life. His enthusiasm for the sea was given greater scope in the new company, and he was able to concentrate entirely on the fascinations of producing and racing high-speed motor-boats. A skilful boat driver, he won many races and made records himself.

The most famous of his boats, 'Miss Britain III' (now in the National Mari-

time Museum), was the first really successful all-metal motor-boat and the first to be powered with an aero-engine. From this boat were developed the Royal Navy M.T.B.s and motor gunboats and the R.A.F.'s rescue launches which rendered notable service during the war of 1939–45. Shortly before the war started Scott-Paine took one of his boats to the United States and the Electric Boat Company of Bayonne, N.Y., undertook the manufacture of similar craft for the U.S. Navy. Scott-Paine then settled in Greenwich, Connecticut, and formed the Marine Design and Engineering Development Corporation and the Canadian Power Boat Co., Ltd. After the war he was associated with the Sea Beaver Corporation at Greenwich which successfully marketed fast pleasure boats and later became a supplier of PT boats to the U.S. Navy.

Scott-Paine was a burly, good-natured, exceptionally energetic man, with a will to get things done. His far-sightedness stimulated the early development of marine aircraft and their later application to air transport. He made a significant contribution to the inauguration of the airline industry and was one of the most important figures in the development of the modern high-speed motor-boat, by initiating the hard-chine boat of high power-to-weight ratio which owed much to aircraft design and construction techniques. His sound engineering common sense and, particularly, his practical eye for good hull design contributed to the success of the early Supermarine aircraft and later to that of his motor-boats. It also helped him to make full use of engineers like R. J. Mitchell [q.v.] who joined Supermarine as Scott-Paine's personal assistant in 1916, became chief engineer in 1919, and later designed the Spitfire and other outstanding aircraft. Scott-Paine was a born salesman and this quality almost as much as their intrinsic merit was perhaps responsible for the success of his boats.

Scott-Paine was first married between the wars but was later separated from his wife. He married a second time in 1946, to Margaret Dinkeldein, and had a son and three daughters. He died 14 April 1954 at his home, Smythe House, Greenwich, Connecticut.

[Aeroplane, 9 October 1953 and 30 April 1954; Flight, 18 April 1940, 2 October 1953, 29 January 1954, and 30 April 1954; C. G. Grey, British Fighter Planes, 1941, and Sea *rs*, 1942; *Jane's All the World's Aircraft*, 13-23; private information.]

PETER W. BROOKS.

NANAYAKE, DON STEPHEN (1884– 52), first prime minister of Ceylon, was rn in Ceylon 20 October 1884, the unger son of Mudaliyar Don Spater d Elizabeth Catherine Senanayake. His ther, a devout Buddhist, none the less it his elder son to an English university d the younger to St. Thomas's College, lombo. There he made his mark, not as scholar but as a keen sportsman and dent cricketer. He remained a loyal pporter of his old school and became member of its governing body. After short period as a clerk in the surveyor-neral's office he left to manage the mily coconut and rubber estates and eir interests in plumbago mines. His ergy in jungle clearing earned him the ckname 'Jungle John'.

In 1912 his brother, F. R. Senanayake, as active in organizing a temperance mpaign in which D. S. Senanayake made s first appearance as a public speaker. e is reported as having no great com-and of either Sinhalese or English at at time. In the riots of 1915 he was der arrest for a few weeks. The after-ath of the riots led to the formation 1917 of the Ceylon Reform League hich in 1919 was merged in the Ceylon ational Congress of which Senanayake as a founder-member. Pressure for con-itutional reform in 1924 culminated in e grant of an unofficial majority in the gislative council and in that year nanayake was returned unopposed as e of three members representing the 'estern Province. As secretary to the official members he gained much prac-cal experience of the working of the vernment machine. In 1928 the report the constitutional commission under ord Donoughmore [q.v.] received a very ixed reception in Ceylon. Sir Herbert tanley [q.v.], the governor, was luke-arm; the professional politicians were dignant. Many of them had been to nglish universities and were looking for onstitutional advance on the West-inster model. Instead they felt they were eing fobbed off with a London County ouncil form of administration. They lso felt that the introduction of universal ffrage, sponsored by (Sir) Drummond hiels [q.v.], would lead to gross abuses. enanayake with his shrewd common nse and much courage took the line that

half a loaf was better than no bread. At the end of 1929 the legislative council accepted the report by a majority of only two, Senanayake and (Sir) Baron Jayati-lake voting for it. In 1931 Senanayake was elected unopposed as member for Minuwangoda, unanimously elected chair-man of the executive committee of agriculture, and appointed minister. He was thus in a position to give practical proof of his determination to raise the standard of living of the Ceylon peasant whose interests he had passionately at heart. He had big ideas and was in a hurry to carry them out. He was apt to be suspicious of criticism of his schemes; but once he was satisfied that it was intended to be constructive and not ob-structive it left no abiding rancour. He was no respecter of persons; but the civil servant who won his confidence could count on his support. The Land Development Act and the irrigation schemes which he revived or initiated are a lasting tribute to his achievements.

A clash in 1940 between the governor and the board of ministers over the action of the inspector-general of police in chal-lenging the orders of Jayatilake, home minister, resulted in the ministers, led by Senanayake, resigning office. Although the breach was subsequently healed, the entry of Japan into the war in December 1941 brought Ceylon within the danger zone. In these circumstances Admiral Sir Geoffrey Layton was appointed com-mander-in-chief with responsibility for defence, while Sir Andrew Caldecott [q.v.] remained titular governor in charge of the civil administration. A war council was established under the presidency of the commander-in-chief, of which the governor, all the ministers, and the civil defence commissioner, (Sir) Oliver Goone-tilleke, were members. Jayatilake became Ceylon representative in India and was succeeded in the leadership of the State Council (1942) by the more forceful Sena-nayake.

The demand for dominion status con-tinued unabated, and in 1943 the British Government issued a statement that the post-war re-examination of the consti-tution would be 'directed towards the grant to Ceylon of full responsible govern-ment under the Crown in all matters of internal civil administration'. This declar-ation, while it was regarded as a personal triumph for Senanayake, became the sub-ject of much controversy, but on the strength of it the ministers, with the

assistance of (Sir) Ivor Jennings, prepared a draft order in Council and submitted it to the British Government in
February 1944, urging that it should be
considered at once and not await the end
of the war. The Government appointed
another commission under Lord Soulbury;
but the ministers decided officially to
boycott it and withdraw their own draft.
Thanks to the wisdom of Senanayake
and the wiles of Sir Oliver Goonetilleke,
however, the commission was cour-
teously received and enabled to obtain a
reasonable cross-section of local opinion.
Senanayake was then invited to London
to discuss the commission's report. His
position was delicate. He had co-operated
with the commission in Ceylon, but as its
recommendations fell short of full dominion status he knew that they would be
bitterly attacked by his political opponents, and might even lose him the
support of some of his own party. He
therefore continued to press officially
for dominion status, while being personally
prepared to accept something less if he
could satisfy his critics that he had done
his best. This was reflected in the terms of
the motion which he moved in the Council
in November 1945. It accepted the Soulbury report by 51 votes to 3. But the
motion was very nearly never tabled at all,
for in London Senanayake had gained the
impression, rightly or wrongly, that the
new Labour Government was prepared
to grant full dominion status. He felt he
had been duped and returned to Ceylon
a very angry man.

When at the end of 1946 Burma was
offered independence within or without
the Commonwealth, Senanayake returned
to the attack. In the light of the new
situation the governor, Sir Henry Moore,
gave his wholehearted support. Sir
Oliver Goonetilleke was deputed to press
Ceylon's claims in London and eventually
the British Government bowed to the
inevitable and on 4 February 1948 Ceylon
became independent, with Senanayake as
prime minister and minister of defence
and external affairs. He was sworn of the
Privy Council in 1950, but died in
Colombo as the result of a fall from his
horse 22 March 1952.

Senanayake inspired popular confidence
by his personal integrity and powers of
leadership. He was a big man both
physically and in his approach to the problems which confronted him. Although a
devout Buddhist he was tolerant of the
religious susceptibilities of others. No one

suggested that he coveted power for
own personal aggrandizement. He want
it for the accomplishment of the schen
which were so near his heart. He hop
to build up the United Party as rep
sentative of a Ceylonese nationho
working for the improvement of lo
conditions regardless of caste, creed,
race. Although he could castigate
opponents in debate, they bore him
ill will, as he would meet them on the me
friendly terms outside the Chamber a
was always ready to listen to complain
Perhaps one of the best tributes to
memory was made by one of his me
implacable political opponents: 'I ha
differed from him bitterly and ev
violently on most political issues. B
never once had I an occasion to falter
my regard and respect for him. He w
indeed a political foe worthy of our stee

In 1909 Senanayake married Emi
Maud Dunuwille (died 1964). They ha
two sons, the elder of whom, Dudl
Shelton, after serving under his fath
as minister of agriculture, succeeded hi
for a short time as prime minister (195
3), and returned to office again in Marcl
April 1960 and in 1965.

[Sir Ivor Jennings, *The Constitution
Ceylon*, 1949; Sir Charles Jeffries, *Ceylon—T
Path to Independence*, 1962; private inform
tion; personal knowledge.] HENRY MOOR

SERVICE, ROBERT WILLIAM (187
1958), versifier, was born 16 January 187
in Preston, Lancashire, the eldest in
family of seven boys and three girls
Robert Service, a Scottish bank teller, ar
his wife, Emily Parker, daughter of a
English owner of Lancashire cotton mill
Between the ages of six and twenty-o
Service lived in Glasgow, where he wa
educated at Hillhead High School, attende
a few university classes, read books whic
kindled his wanderlust, and worked in th
Commercial Bank of Scotland. In 1895 h
emigrated, crossed the Atlantic in a tram
steamer, and proceeded to British Colun
bia, where he enjoyed the freedom of
backwoods ranch in a rough, but not law
less, part of the 'wild' west. Then h
turned again to wandering; he worked h
way up and down the Pacific coast o
the United States, becoming, as he said
'half a hobo'.

The other 'half' of Service was a sens
tive Scot, an observer rather than a whole
hearted participant. He had an ear fo
popular speech, and he strove to 'feel an
know' life in its raw-exotic aspects whil

e guarded his moral detachment, akin
) artistic objectivity. A steady position,
aken when he was twenty-nine, happily
d to his most romantic adventure. The
anadian Bank of Commerce moved him
arough branches at Victoria and Kam-
•ops in British Columbia to Whitehorse
nd Dawson in the Yukon, almost in the
anadian Arctic. From 1904 until 1912, as
bank clerk and then as a freelance writer,
e watched the decline of the Klondike
old rush, which had reached its height in
898. Rhyming was easier than digging:
e made his fortune with 'The Shooting of
•an McGrew' and 'The Cremation of Sam
IcGee'.

These and other verses were published
1 1907 in Toronto as Songs of a Sourdough
nd in New York as The Spell of the Yukon.
. sequel, Ballads of a Cheechako, appeared
1 1909. 'Sourdough' and 'cheechako'
ecame household words for 'prospector'
nd 'newcomer'. Fresh frontier realism,
omantic motifs, and rollicking measures
lade the Yukon a legendary land. Be-
ause Service was in this rough life, but
ot of it, he could follow up his casual suc-
ess by deliberate literary exploitation.
'he Trail of '98, a novel (1910), was weak
nd rhetorical, but his readers again felt
hat they shared his gay eloquence and
is virility in Rhymes of a Rolling Stone
1912). Service left Canada in that year to
eport the Balkan war for the Toronto
'tar.

As long as he lived after 1913, Service
lad homes in France but remained a
3ritish subject. During the war he served
vith the American ambulance unit and
vith Canadian army intelligence; his ex-
•eriences yielded a very popular book,
lhymes of a Red-Cross Man (1916). When
he war was over, he resumed his life in the
.atin quarter (see The Pretender, a novel,
914), adopted a monocle, travelled to
Iollywood (1921-2), indulged in a trip to
'ahiti, and returned to explore the Pari-
ian slums.

Moving pictures of the 'magic land of
nake believe' encouraged him to write
nore negligible melodramatic romances,
'he Poisoned Paradise (1922), The Rough-
ieck (1923), The Master of the Microbe
1926), and The House of Fear (1927). In
hese years his avowed programme for a
good life took shape: to enjoy in health and
eisure the huge income he had gained
intil he was a hundred years old (see Why
Not Grow Young?, 1928). Few readers
vould have recognized this quiet, hand-
iome, rosy-hued gentleman as the 'rough-

neck poet'. 'I was not my type', he said,
while he wrote what his public liked,
Ballads of a Bohemian (1921) and Bar-
Room Ballads (1940).

When another war began, shortly after
Service's return from a second trip to
Russia, he and his family found refuge in
Hollywood. In 1945 he went back to Brit-
tany and Nice, and purchased a villa in
Monte Carlo. More books appeared: Songs
of a Sun-Lover (1949), Rhymes of a Rough-
neck (1950), Lyrics of a Lowbrow (1951),
Rhymes of a Rebel (1952), Songs for my
Supper (1953), Carols of an Old Codger
(1954), and Rhymes for My Rags (1956).
Two volumes of Service's collected verse
contain more than 1,700 pages; to the
last he wanted only the title of a popular
poet. He died 11 September 1958 at
'Dream Haven', Lancieux, Brittany.

In 1913 Service married Germaine,
daughter of Constant Bourgoin, owner of
a distillery at Brie-contre-Robert, near
Paris; they had one daughter.

[Robert Service, Ploughman of the Moon,
1945, and Harper of Heaven, 1948; private
information.] CARL F. KLINCK.

SETON-WATSON, ROBERT WILLIAM
(1879-1951), historian, was born in London 20 August 1879, the only child of
William Livingston Watson, a well-to-do
Scottish merchant in Calcutta and London
and a landowner in Scotland, and his wife,
Elizabeth Lindsay, daughter of the Scottish genealogist George Seton [q.v.]. His
mother was an invalid and his upbringing
was entrusted to a female relative whose
strict discipline may have accounted in
part for an apparent diffidence of manner
which he never quite overcame. Behind
this manner lay passionate devotion to
what he felt to be right and true, and a
temperament in which his father's cautious shrewdness and his mother's idealism were curiously blended. Winchester,
under a famous headmaster, and New
College, Oxford, where H. A. L. Fisher
[q.v.] was his tutor, set their stamp on him
and encouraged him to follow his bent for
exact historical research. Before taking
his degree with a first class in modern
history in 1902 he revealed his talent by
winning the Stanhope historical essay
prize in 1901. He next spent a winter at
Berlin University, a year at the Sorbonne,
and roamed through the cities of Italy,
half-disposed to undertake a history of
Bologna.

In 1905 Seton-Watson arrived in Vienna
with the intention of writing a history of

Austria since Maria Theresa. The conflict between the Crown and a majority of the Hungarian Chamber over the constitutional right of the Crown not to permit the substitution of Magyar for German as the language of command in the Hungarian regiments of the joint regular Army was at its height and rekindled Seton-Watson's Scottish Liberal sympathies for Hungary as 'a nation rightly struggling to be free'. He had already written occasionally to the *Spectator* over the signature 'Scotus Viator' and he resolved to use this channel to correct what he thought the unfairness to Hungary of British newspaper reports from Vienna. With characteristic thoroughness he went to Hungary in the spring of 1906 to spend three months studying the situation before writing upon it. His appetite for facts was keen, and he felt sure they would give him full proof that his cherished convictions were well founded. Within six weeks he returned to Vienna, filled with wrath. The Magyars, he explained, had 'lied' to him. Exactly how they had disillusioned him was not quite clear. His apparent timidity, abundant good faith, and eager simplicity may have tempted them to overload his mind with assurances which would not bear investigation. The trouble was that he did investigate them. He found it hard to believe that Slovaks, Rumanes, and other non-Magyars were really Magyars of slightly different kinds; nor could he reconcile his faith in Hungarian parliamentary democracy with the discovery that the non-Magyar half of the population held fewer than 40 seats in a Chamber of 415. In short, he caught a glimpse of the reality which lay behind the imposing frontage presented by Hungary to western Europe—a shattering experience for so earnest a seeker after truth.

Not less important than the change it wrought in his view of Hungary was the effect of this experience upon Seton-Watson's respect for the Dual System fashioned by the constitutional settlement of 1867. The Magyars, he felt, were abusing the power it gave them to oppress the non-Magyars; but was the Dual System otherwise sound and workable ? He saw in the Habsburg dominions a wide field for research and inquiry which British writers had left almost wholly unsurveyed. He resolved to study it thoroughly, never dreaming that he himself, by writing upon it, would become a feature of it. He could hardly foresee that knowledge of what he was telling the outer world about them

would put heart into the Slovaks and R.. manes of Hungary, or that 'Scotus Viato.. would presently be impersonated in a Cr.. atian election as a British observer sent t.. see fair play. Yet so it was; and Magya.. denunciations of his 'corrupt' and pe.. nicious activities served only to enhanc.. his reputation.

His conscientious diligence was exempl.. lary. To his proficiency in German, Frenc.. and Italian he added a working knowledg.. of Magyar, Serbo-Croatian, and Czech. If hi.. first work in permanent form, *The Futur..* *of Austria-Hungary* (1907), was partly .. reprint of immature *Spectator* articles, hi.. *Racial Problems in Hungary* (1908), *Politi.. cal Persecution in Hungary* (1908), *Cor.. ruption and Reform in Hungary* (1911).. *Absolutism in Croatia* (1912), and espe.. cially *The Southern Slav Question and th..* *Habsburg Monarchy* (1911), with an en.. larged, German, edition (1913), wer.. painstaking records of facts and docu.. ments almost unknown to British readers.. His work on the Southern Slav (or Yugo.. slav) question was remarkable for its scop.. and erudition. It remains an indispens.. able record of the movement for Yugosla.. unity and of the inner history of Austro.. Hungarian failure to deal constructivel.. with an issue decisive for the survival of th.. Habsburg monarchy itself. So impresse.. was Seton-Watson by the importance o.. the problem that he dedicated his book t.. 'that Austrian statesman who shall pos.. sess the genius and the courage necessary.. to solve it; but he also expressed his fore.. bodings. He was deeply distressed by th.. administrative and judicial unmorality.. not to say the downright wickedness, h.. had seen in the notorious 'high treason.. trial of Habsburg Serbs at Zagreb in th.. summer of 1909 and by the proof tha.. forgeries had been officially used agains.. the Yugoslav leaders in the Croatian Die.. which was furnished by the still mor.. notorious Friedjung trial in the followin.. December.

Disillusioned about Hungary, Seton.. Watson had clung to a belief that savin.. grace might be found in Austria and, in.. the case of the Southern Slavs, that th.. heir apparent would somehow manage t.. bring about the replacement of Dualisn.. by a Triple System, or 'Trialism', in whicl.. a union of Habsburg Yugoslavs woul.. offset Hungarian preponderance. This be.. lief was sorely shaken by the Friedjung.. trial and totally dispelled by Thoma.. Masaryk's subsequent revelations that th.. anti-Yugoslav forgeries had been fabri..

ated in the Austro-Hungarian legation at Belgrade. As a Scottish Puritan, for whom might was right and wrong was wrong, Seton-Watson concluded mournfully that a polity so unethical as he now recognized the Habsburg monarchy to be was self-doomed to disaster. Nor was he alone in his conclusion. Masaryk shared it for other and more comprehensive reasons. Indeed, when the two men first met in 1910, after the Friedjung trial, Masaryk doubted the soundness of Seton-Watson's ideas. Not till they met again, at Rotterdam in October 1914, were the foundations of their enduring friendship, and of Seton-Watson's later academic career, unwittingly laid. His little work, *Masaryk in England* (1943), tells too modestly the story of their relations at that time, and of the part Seton-Watson played in obtaining for Masaryk in 1915 a lectureship in the new School of Slavonic Studies at King's College, London. It was therefore peculiarly fitting that he should become in 1922 Masaryk professor of Central European history at King's College after having been for some years an honorary lecturer in East European history. With Sir Bernard Pares [q.v.] he founded and edited the *Slavonic Review* and helped the eventual establishment of the School as a central activity' of the university.

Between 1915 and 1922 Seton-Watson's activities were many and varied. He was honorary secretary of the Serbian Relief Fund (1914–21) and in 1916 he and Masaryk founded and, for a while, edited jointly an excellent weekly review, the *New Europe*, which Seton-Watson financed. Soon it gained noteworthy influence upon serious opinion, not least because his own contributions to it were free from the insistent documentation which was apt to encumber his historical works. In quarters where its frankness was resented an attempt was made to silence it, and him, by calling him up for military service; and, since he was physically unfit for active soldiering, he was drafted in 1917 into the Royal Army Medical Corps, and employed in scrubbing hospital floors. Only after the War Cabinet had twice ordered his release was he seconded for work in the Cabinet's intelligence bureau until, early in 1918, he was entrusted with the Austrian section of the Crewe House enemy propaganda department. As a member of that department's mission to Italy he helped to prepare a basis for the successful Rome congress of subject Habsburg nationalities in April 1918; and he also wrote, at the Italian front, a guide to the racial composition of the Austro-Hungarian army for the British commander, Lord Cavan [q.v.]. At the Paris peace conference, as a private observer, his advice was sought upon the delimitation of' Italo-Austrian and Italo-Yugoslav frontiers, but he grew increasingly indignant about the inadequacies of 'the pygmies at Paris'. Meantime his literary output continued; one of his best works, *The Rise of Nationality in the Balkans*, had appeared in 1917. There followed *Europe in the Melting-Pot* (1919), *The New Slovakia* (1924), *Sarajevo* (1926), and other books of which the most notable were *A History of the Roumanians* (1934), *Disraeli, Gladstone, and the Eastern Question* (1935), and especially *Britain in Europe 1789–1914* (1937). From current problems he had turned gradually to a study of the history of the countries in which he was interested and of British diplomacy.

Many honours were bestowed on him, not less as retrospective tributes to 'Scotus Viator' than in recognition of his academic standing. The universities of Prague (1919), Zagreb (1920), Bratislava (1928), Belgrade (1928), Cluj (1930) gave him honorary degrees as well as Birmingham (1946), and he was an honorary citizen of Cluj (Transylvania) and Turciansky Sv. Martin (Slovakia). In Romania in 1920 the chamber of deputies suspended its sitting to acclaim him when he appeared in the gallery. In 1928 he was Creighton lecturer in the university of' London, and for 1931 Raleigh lecturer to the British Academy of which he became a fellow in 1932. In 1939 he delivered the Montague Burton lecture at University College, Nottingham. In 1945 he became president of the Royal Historical Society and was appointed first professor of Czechoslovak studies in Oxford. If, as a lecturer, he never quite shook off' the semi-apologetic shyness which usually marked his bearing on public occasions, the depth and range of' his learning, and his personal kindliness, won him the admiration and often the affection of students who found in him a teacher and guide untiring in his efforts to lead them, as an elderly comrade, in search of knowledge and truth. For university business he found no time; he was unpunctual, untidy, and too preoccupied with more important matters.

At no period of his life was Seton-Watson more clear-sighted or more insistent in a conscientious endeavour to enlighten public opinion than during the years immediately before and after the sacrifice of Czechoslovakia to Hitler at Munich in September 1938. In closer touch it seemed with the realities of the European situation than any member of the Government, he published in May 1938 *Britain and the Dictators* as a massive warning against a foreign policy neglectful of moral values. An equally outspoken though smaller work, *Munich and the Dictators* (March 1939), dealt perspicaciously with 'the crisis that culminated, or at least seemed to culminate, in the settlement of Munich'. It closed with the prediction '*Nondum est finis*'. On the outbreak of war he joined the foreign research and press service and in 1940 the political intelligence department of the Foreign Office, serving as a personal link with his friend Dr. Benes, then head of the provisional Czechoslovak Government in London.

The last of Seton-Watson's major works, *A History of the Czechs and Slovaks*, appeared late in 1943 avowedly with the aim of depriving future politicians of any pretext for saying that the Czechoslovaks were 'people of whom we know nothing'. It was an exhaustive and somewhat exhausting account of Czech and Slovak history in a volume of 250,000 words. Containing all the ascertained facts, it tended to become an historical catalogue with rare excursions into luminous generalization; and for these excursions, grateful though readers might be for them, he felt bound to plead extenuating circumstances; Seton-Watson's passion for facts once more overcame his care for literary artistry. Yet, like his other major works, it remains a volume indispensable to any true understanding of its subject.

The satisfaction he had felt in 1945 at the restoration of Czechoslovak independence, within the pre-Munich frontiers, waned as the ascendancy of Communist Russia became more evident. His end was undoubtedly hastened by grief at the tragic death of his intimate friend Jan Masaryk in March, and that of Benes, again ex-president, in September, 1948. If his faith in 'the indwelling righteousness of things' was too deeply rooted for despair to prevail over his conviction that his life-work had been done to the best of his ability and with total honesty of purpose, his sorrow told upon a physique that had never been robust. Yet it was in keeping with his undeniable greatness of spirit that no word of complaint should have escaped him. He was a dear soul, tender and sensi-

tive, tenacious and righteous, prudent and brave. On relinquishing his chair at Oxford in 1949 he was elected an honorary fellow of both New College and Brasenose and retired to his country home Kyle House in the Isle of Skye—where in happier days he could indulge a modest taste for yachting and sea fishing—until he died there 25 July 1951.

In 1911 Seton-Watson married Marion Esther, daughter of Edward Stack, of the Bengal Civil Service, to whose understanding companionship and devoted helpfulness his achievements were in large measure due. They had one daughter and two sons, both of whom attained academic distinction, the elder, George Hugh Nicholas, becoming professor of Russian history in the School of Slavonic Studies, the younger, Christopher Ivan William, fellow of Oriel College, Oxford.

A bronze by Ivan Mestrovic is part of a memorial tablet to Seton-Watson in the School of Slavonic and East European Studies.

[*The Times*, 28 July 1951; G. H. Bolsover in *Proceedings* of the British Academy vol. xxxvii, 1951; private information, personal knowledge.]   WICKHAM STEED

SHEPHERD, GEORGE ROBERT, first BARON SHEPHERD (1881–1954), Labour Party national agent, was born in Spalding, Lincolnshire, 19 August 1881, the son of George Robert Shepherd, tailor, and his wife, Helena Sophia Hensman. Educated at a board-school he was required at an early age to support a large family on the death of his father. Starting work as a shoe shop assistant, he continued his studies by reading extensively, a practice which he followed throughout his life. In 1901 he joined the Shop Assistants' Union and the Independent Labour Party and in 1908 became an organizer for the Midland division of the latter. In 1909–11 he was agent for Alex Wilkie, Labour member for Dundee, and then went to Blackburn as agent for Philip (later Viscount) Snowden [q.v.].

In 1924 Shepherd was appointed assistant national agent for the Labour Party and in 1929 became national agent. He soon gained a reputation of sagacity and resourcefulness as an organizer and strategist. The stresses of the inter-war years showed the strength of the organization he had created. Leaders might come and go; the rank and file remained steadfast. Those who knew him then were impressed most of all by the combinaon of justice and mercy with which he administered party discipline. At times, under the instructions of the national executive, he had to take fundamental steps to maintain order but no one could doubt his reluctance to enforce the full rigour of the party laws if gentleness and patience offered an alternative solution. He more than anyone ensured that the party was ready for the general election 1945 which swept Labour into office.

Shepherd then retired from his post and 1946 entered the House of Lords where he was soon appointed a whip, and became chief whip in 1949. His political knowledge and his capacity for clear reasoning in debate impressed friend and foe alike. He seemed to come into his own in quite a new way and played a large part in giving the Labour Party a new image in the upper House—radical, resolute for change, but always good-tempered and dignified and British through and through. His experience as a party organizer was an important factor in his work on the Representation of the People Act of 1948 and the measures dealing with electoral laws. He was sworn of the Privy Council in 1951.

In 1915 Shepherd married an early trade-union worker, Ada, daughter of Alfred Newton, jobbing gardener. They had a son and a daughter. Shepherd died in London 4 December 1954 and was succeeded by his son, Malcolm Newton born 1918), who, after making his mark in the army in the war (his father in 1914–18 had been a conscientious objector) and in business, became Opposition chief whip in 1963 and followed his father as chief government whip (1964–7) when the Labour Party came into office.

[*The Times*, 6 December 1954; private information; personal knowledge.]

LONGFORD.

SHERRINGTON, SIR CHARLES SCOTT (1857–1952), physiologist, was born 27 November 1857 in Islington, London, the son of James Norton and Anne Brookes Sherrington, of Great Yarmouth. Sherrington and his two younger brothers went to Ipswich Grammer School where Charles was deeply influenced by one of the masters, Thomas Ashe [q.v.], a poet of some note. Sherrington was rather small in stature but sturdy and full of fire. He was good at his studies and excellent on the soccer field. Later he played rugger for St. Thomas's and Caius and also rowed for his college.

At Cambridge, where Sherrington be-

came a scholar of Gonville and Caius College (1881–4), (Sir) Michael Foster [q.v.] had a way of selecting promising students to carry out research in his laboratory and here Sherrington worked in a stimulating atmosphere with Balfour, Gaskell, Langley, and others. His first publication in 1884, written with J. N. Langley (whose notice Sherrington subsequently contributed to this Dictionary), was read to the Royal Society while he was still a student. It was an anatomical study of the nervous system of a famous dog presented before the International Medical Congress in 1881 by Professor F. Goltz of Germany. The dog had moved about in a placid manner for months after surgical excision of the forebrain.

Sherrington obtained first classes in both parts of the natural sciences tripos (1881–3) and completing his studies at St. Thomas's Hospital in London obtained his M.R.C.S. (1884) and L.R.C.P. (1886) and his Cambridge M.B. (1885), M.D. (1892), and Sc.D. (1904). After his M.B. he spent much of the next two years upon graduate work in Germany and France. At considerable risk to himself he made a study of cholera in Spain and later Italy, carrying out autopsies when possible. In 1887 he returned to Cambridge as a fellow of his college and also became a lecturer in systematic physiology at St. Thomas's. He now turned from pathology to physiology. In 1891 he moved to London as professor-superintendent of the Brown Animal Sanatory Institution. Sherrington was never the narrow-minded specialist in science. Before he left Cambridge he was already a book-collector. In time off he was a skier in Switzerland, an ardent sailor, an interested traveller, a lover of art and music and drama. He was a brilliant conversationalist in any social gathering. He always seemed more enthusiastic about the work of others than about his own. He lectured as though his researches were no more than a series of questions asked and answered.

The Spanish anatomist, Ramón y Cajal, was his guest at his house in London when on the way to Cambridge for an honorary degree. Cajal had established the neurone theory showing that nerve cells were separate units connected to each other by conducting expansions. 'This', Sherrington wrote, 'was something so much clearer and so other than it had been as to be a system almost new, and one immensely more intelligible.'

In 1895 Sherrington moved to Liverpool

as Holt professor of physiology. The following sixteen years were happy ones, a time of solid achievement. He set out to explain the reflexes and reactions of Goltz's dog. Making acute decerebrate preparations of his own, he studied 'decerebrate rigidity'. He worked out the neurone connections, in the spinal cord and brain-stem, that subserve the normal maintenance of muscle tone and the maintenance postures or reflex-movements in the limbs as in walking. He explained the reciprocal innervation that relaxes the antagonistic muscles automatically while the muscles, which cause the limb to move, contract. Passing on from the spinal cord and brain-stem to the forebrain of cat and anthropoid ape, he mapped out the motor key-board of the cerebral cortex and showed that the response to electrical stimulation at any cortical point was subject to facilitation and augmentation or even reversal by means of immediately preceding applications of the electrode.

In 1904 Sherrington gave the Silliman lectures at Yale, published in 1906 under the title of *The Integrative Action of the Nervous System*. In 1947 the Physiological Society reprinted the book without alteration so that it might be read by 'all students of physiology and reread by their teachers'. As Lord Adrian was later to remark, Sherrington's researches had 'opened up an entirely new chapter in the physiology of the central nervous system'.

In 1913 Sherrington was offered the Waynflete chair of physiology at Oxford, with a fellowship at Magdalen. He was fifty-six: there was no stated age of retirement, or promise of a pension. But intrigued by Oxford life Sherrington accepted. A pleasant house was found at 9 Chadlington Road: near the laboratory and also near the Cherwell where he and his wife delighted to spend pleasant hours in punt or canoe. He sometimes wrote his scientific papers on the river. Oxford society he found 'a trifle rigid' but in the home of the regius professor of medicine, Sir William Osler [q.v.], there was 'refreshing and stimulating refuge from formality'. In May 1913 British physiologists accepted an invitation to St. Petersburg and Sherrington dined privately with the famous physiologist, Ivan Pavlov. Entertained by the Tsar, who asked for news of his cousin, Sherrington had to reply that he had not seen much of the King of England lately.

So little was the value which Sherrington

put on his own work that during the war wrote to a friend that feeling it to be mote 'from the great practical effort n in hand' he had undertaken unskilled w₍ in a munitions factory. He was in f₍ studying industrial fatigue for the W Office, and he became chairman of t Industrial Fatigue Research Board. ₁ served also on committees on lockjaw ₍ on alcohol and was Fullerian professor physiology at the Royal Institution 1914–17.

In 1920–25 Sherrington was preside of the Royal Society of which he had be elected a fellow in 1893. In 1922 he w president of the British Association me₍ ing at Hull and in that year he w appointed G.B.E. In 1924 he was admitt₍ to the Order of Merit. In the next year, the surprise of even his most intim₍ friends, he published a slender book *T Assaying of Brabantius and Other Ver₍* In 1932 he shared with E. D. (later Lor₍ Adrian the Nobel prize for medicine. Oth honours and awards came to 'the phil sopher of the nervous system' from ₍ over the world and were received wit₍ modest surprise that they should not ha₍ gone to others more deserving.

After retiring from his chair at Oxfor at the end of 1935 Sherrington, wit₍ regret, left his Magdalen friends. It ha₍ been 'a busy and fruitful autumn ₍ scientific endeavour in which much of h₍ earlier work came to full harvest'. In 193 and 1938 he gave the Gifford lectures ₍ Edinburgh and published them in 194 under the title *Man on his Nature*. Th book was widely read and went into a₍ exceedingly popular paperback edition Thus the physiologist turned to man an₍ to philosophy. In 1946 he published a₍ excellent biography of an early Frenc physiologist, *The Endeavour of Jea₍ Fernel*.

In 1950 at a special meeting of th₍ Soviet Academy of Science Sherringto₍ was referred to as the world's leader i₍ regard to the dualist point of view amon₍ physiologists. But Sherrington had con cluded only this: 'We have to regard th₍ relation of mind to brain as still not merel₍ unsolved but still devoid of a basis for it₍ very beginning.' (*The Brain and It₍ Mechanism*, Rede lecture, Cambridge 1933).

In 1891 Sherrington married Ethel Mar₍ (died 1933), daughter of John Ely Wright, of Preston Manor, Suffolk. She was a₍ musician, a good linguist which made her an excellent comrade on many trip₍

abroad, and one who loved the out of doors. She made their home in Oxford a centre of hospitality and laughter and much kindness. They had one son who became a railway economist.

Sherrington died at Eastbourne 4 March 1952. In 1948 the Sherrington lectures had been founded in his honour in the university of Liverpool where the University Club has a portrait by Augustus John. Portraits by R. G. Eves are in the possession of the Royal Society and the National Portrait Gallery.

[Lord Cohen of Birkenhead, *Sherrington*, 1958; E. G. T. Liddell, *The Discovery of Reflexes*, 1960; *Selected Writings of Sir Charles Scott Sherrington*, ed. D. Denny-Brown, 1939; C. E. R. Sherrington, *Memories*, 1957; personal knowledge.]   WILDER PENFIELD.

SHIELS, SIR (THOMAS) DRUMMOND (1881-1953), physician and politician, was born in Edinburgh 7 August 1881, the second of the eight children of James Drummond Shiels, lithographic printer, and his wife, Agnes Campbell. After an elementary school education in Glasgow where his family lived for a time, Shiels entered the employment of a firm of photographers at the age of twelve and continued his education at night schools. Later he joined his father and a brother in setting up a photographic studio in Lauriston Place, Edinburgh.

In the war of 1914-18 Shiels served with the 9th (Scottish) division, reaching the rank of captain and being awarded the M.C., the Belgian croix [de guerre, and a mention in dispatches. On returning to the family business his growing urge towards social service impelled him, in his spare time, to study medicine at Edinburgh University where in 1924 he qualified M.B., B.Ch. He had already been elected Labour member of the town council and had taken part in various political and local government activities and was invited to stand for Parliament as Labour candidate for Edinburgh (East). He won the seat in 1924 and held it until he was defeated at the general election of 1931.

During these seven parliamentary years Shiels developed what was to be a lifelong interest in Commonwealth and Empire affairs. In 1927-8 he was a member of the commission on the constitution of Ceylon, the report of which led to the introduction of democratic self-government based upon universal adult suffrage. On the formation of the Labour administration of 1929 Shiels became under-secretary of state for

India and later in the year transferred to the corresponding post at the Colonial Office. After 1931 he became a medical school inspector under the London County Council and medical secretary to the British Social Hygiene Council. In 1940 he was appointed deputy and later acting secretary of the Empire Parliamentary Association; from 1946 to 1949 he served as public relations officer in the Post Office; and in 1950 he was appointed secretary to the Inter-Parliamentary Union (British Group), a post which he held until his death.

Shiels was continuously active in writing, speaking, and in editorial work in connection with many social and political subjects, especially those concerning Commonwealth relations and the advancement of the colonial territories. His energy and influence contributed much to the awakening in the Parliament and public of the United Kingdom of a sense of responsibility for the progress and welfare of the colonial peoples, and helped to create the new climate of opinion which found expression in the Colonial Development and Welfare Acts of 1940 onwards. His prominence in this sphere was recognized by his appointment as an original member of the Colonial Economic and Development Council in 1946. He had refused a peerage when under-secretary but accepted a knighthood in 1939.

Shiels was a man of warm-hearted and indeed, sometimes, undiscriminating generosity in both public and private affairs. The deep impression made upon him by his family's early struggle with poverty left him without bitterness but possessed by a passionate desire to champion the cause of the less fortunate, first in his own country and then, as his experience broadened, in the oversea territories for which the United Kingdom was responsible. A powerful advocate of radical reform, he desired always that it should be brought about by peaceable persuasion and constitutional methods. He was indifferent to personal success or financial profit. Much of his time and energy was given ungrudgingly to the work of voluntary organizations and institutions serving the causes to which he was devoted, especially the Royal Empire Society, the Royal African Society, the East India Association, the Anti-Slavery and Aborigines Protection Society, the Royal Society of Medicine, and the Royal Society for the Prevention of Cruelty to Animals. If earnestness and a single-minded tenacity of purpose were amongst his chief traits, they were balanced by simplicity, sincerity, and general friendliness, allied to the saving grace of·a pawky humour.

In 1904 Shiels married Christian Blair (died 1948), daughter of Alexander Young, of Gilmerton, Edinburgh, by whom he had one daughter; secondly, in 1950, he married Gladys Louise (died 1968), daughter of John James Buhler. Shiels died in London 1 January 1953.

[*The Times*, 3 January 1953; private information; personal knowledge.]

CHARLES JEFFRIES.

SHUCKBURGH, SIR JOHN EVELYN (1877–1953), civil servant, was born at Eton 18 March 1877, the eldest son of Evelyn Shirley Shuckburgh [q.v.], an assistant master. A scholar of Eton and King's College, Cambridge, he took his degree with first class honours in the classical tripos in 1899. He passed the first division examination of the Civil Service and in 1900 entered the India Office, where he spent twenty-one years, the last four as secretary of the political department. He was appointed C.B. in 1918. In 1921 he was·selected by (Sir) Winston Churchill, the colonial secretary, to be the first assistant under-secretary of state in charge of the new Middle East department formed to administer and set up civil government in those parts of the Turkish Empire (Mesopotamia, Palestine, and Trans-Jordan) which were then under British military administration as occupied enemy territories.

The task was an unusual one, and Shuckburgh, with his long experience of dealing with Indian native states, was probably the man best qualified for it. The team which was given him to help was also, to put it no higher, unusual. An Indian political officer, (Sir) Hubert Young [q.v.], who had spent most of the war and post-war period in various military appointments, mainly in the field of occupied enemy territory administration in the Middle East, became assistant secretary; one principal was transferred from the Foreign Office, and one principal and two assistant principals were supplied by the Colonial Office. The team was completed by three advisers—political, military, and financial. The four senior administrative officers were all Old Collegers, and five of the team had seen long active service in the territories which they were to administer. Between them the team had more 'man on the spot' knowledge of these territories, and probably less experience of the techniques of civil administration, than had ever been assembled in a department of the Colonial Office. It says much for Shuckburgh's ability and tact that he succeeded in converting them into an efficient administrative organization, although T. E. Lawrence [q.v.], the political adviser, left a few months later.

In Mesopotamia Sir Percy Cox [q.v.] was well qualified to place the Emir Feisal on the throne and hand over the reins of government to him, while still supplying a strong and efficient team of British advisers to help him to organize his kingdom. Nor did Trans-Jordan present great difficulties. The Emir Abdullah, once he had got over his initial chagrin at seeing his younger brother given a bigger and richer kingdom than himself, settled down happily to the congenial task of ruling a rather primitive country with the support of a competent team of British advisers and substantial grants in aid from the British Treasury. In Palestine the problems were infinitely more complex. The high commissioner, Sir Herbert (later Viscount) Samuel, had been a distinguished cabinet minister and so was much less amenable to guidance than an ordinary colonial governor, although neither he nor more than very few of his principal officers had any experience of·the particular kind of administration which they were called upon to organize. Furthermore, as a practising Jew, Samuel found it equally difficult to convince the Arabs that he was not favouring his co-religionists and the Jews that he was not showing undue favour to the Arabs, although he took infinite pains to treat them both alike. It required endless tact, patience, and firmness on Shuckburgh's part to convert the rough and ready do-it-yourself Palestine government by remote control into a normal and competent administration and curb the wilder eccentricities of its officers, one of whom had a habit of describing himself as a direct successor of Pontius Pilate.

As the immediate pressure of Middle East affairs diminished, Shuckburgh's responsibilities in the Colonial Office were gradually widened and more departments were placed under his supervision. He was appointed K.C.M.G. in 1922 and in 1931, as part of·a reorganization of the Office, the new post of deputy under-secretary of state was created with Shuckburgh as its first holder.

In 1939 when he had already passed the normal age of retirement, he agreed to

cceed Sir Bernard Bourdillon [q.v.] as
vernor of Nigeria, but in the event he
mained to help to see the Colonial Office
to the war. In 1942 on reaching the age
sixty-five he retired, but only to cross
e road to the Cabinet Office, where he
ent the next six years in the historical
ction, writing the history of the colonial
mpire in the war. It was during this
riod, in 1946, that he published a volume
f collected essays from the *Spectator* and
ther periodicals under the title *An Ideal
oyage*.

In 1906 Shuckburgh married Lilian
iolet, elder daughter of Arthur George
eskett, fellow of Magdalene College,
ambridge, by whom he had three sons
nd two daughters. His eldest son, (Sir)
Charles Arthur) Evelyn Shuckburgh,
ined the diplomatic service in 1933 and
as ambassador to Italy in 1966–9; his
oungest son was killed in action over
rance in 1941. Shuckburgh himself died
n London 8 February 1953.

[Private information; personal knowledge.]
                                    GERARD CLAUSON.

HUTE, NEVIL (pseudonym), novelist.
See NORWAY, NEVIL SHUTE.]

IDGWICK, NEVIL VINCENT (1873–
952), chemist, was born in Oxford 8 May
873, an only child, of intellectual stock
n both sides. His father, William Carr
idgwick, from whom he inherited his dia-
ectic skill, had been a classical fellow of
Merton and later became a lecturer at
Oriel. His uncles were Henry Sidgwick
q.v.], professor of moral philosophy in
Cambridge, and Arthur Sidgwick, reader in
Greek at Oxford. His mother, to whom he
owed his love of science, was descended
from a Swiss family called Perronet. She
was Sarah Isabella, daughter of John Vincent Thompson, serjeant at law, brother
of General Thomas Perronet Thompson
[q.v.]. Her sister married Sir Benjamin
Brodie, second baronet [q.v.]. Sidgwick was
educated at Summer Fields and Rugby,
where he was in both the classical and
science sixths. After failing to win a classical scholarship, in 1892 he was elected to
a scholarship in natural science at Christ
Church where his tutor, A. G. Vernon
Harcourt [q.v.], introduced him to the
new domain of physical chemistry. After
getting a first class in chemistry in 1895
Sidgwick decided to read *literae humaniores*
and got another first class in 1897, helped
by a brilliant *viva voce* in philosophy.

After this remarkable intellectual feat

he demonstrated in the Christ Church
laboratory for a year and then went to
Leipzig to work in Ostwald's laboratory
but fell ill and had to return home. In 1899
he went to Tübingen to work under von
Pechmann and in 1901 was awarded a
Sc.D., *summa cum laude*, for his thesis on
some new organic derivatives. He had
already been elected to a tutorial fellowship at Lincoln College which was to be
his home all his life as he never married.
For some years he taught at both Lincoln
and Magdalen and he continued to work
as a college tutor until 1948 when he was
made a supernumerary fellow of Lincoln.
Sidgwick taught by example rather than
by precept and he won the gratitude and
affection of many generations of pupils by
his stimulating intellect and his personal
interest in their lives. Among them were
Sir Henry Tizard [q.v.], Sir David Rivett,
D. Ll. Hammick, and L. E. Sutton.

In 1901 there was no school of chemical
research in Oxford so Sidgwick struck out
on his own line by examining the physico-
chemical properties of organic compounds,
their ionization, solubility, and colour.
With the exception of the discovery of one
anomaly which later paid a dividend, the
results were not striking. However, in
1910 Sidgwick published his first book
Organic Chemistry of Nitrogen which
immediately attracted attention by the
originality of its treatment. It displayed
Sidgwick's encyclopedic knowledge, his
lucid style, and his success in blending the
disciplines of organic and physical chemistry. During the war of 1914–18 he was
working on government projects which
made his ability known to a wider circle
outside Oxford.

The turning-point in Sidgwick's career
had already come in 1914 when he sailed
to Australia for a meeting of the British
Association in the same ship as Sir Ernest
(later Lord) Rutherford [q.v.], fresh from
the triumphs of his nuclear atom. Sidgwick
fell under Rutherford's spell and became
his lifelong admirer. It was at Rutherford's
suggestion that he determined to devote
himself to the electronic theory of atomic
structure and chemical constitution. With
this in mind his work was given a fresh
stimulus in 1919. It quickly gave results
leading to his election into the Royal
Society in 1922. In these years Sidgwick
was developing the ideas already suggested
by Kossell, G. N. Lewis, Langmuir, and
(Sir) G. T. Morgan [q.v.]. His immediate
objective was to elucidate the structure
of various types of complex compounds

which had not been satisfactorily explained. His ideas were confirmed by a remarkable series of experimental papers by his young assistants. Meanwhile his mind was moving in a wider orbit and in 1927 he published his second book *The Electronic Theory of Valency* which made him famous. He had recognized that to be valid a theory must be able to explain all known instances not merely a few selected tests. So he set himself the task of applying the theory of the Rutherford–Bohr atom to the whole range of chemical compounds without infringing the physical concepts on which it was based. This he succeeded in doing in a remarkable way thanks to his penetrating intellect, his orderly and critical mind, his prodigious memory, and dogged perseverance. His book had a widespread influence on the minds of chemists as for the first time the most diverse structural phenomena covering the whole field of chemistry were rationally systematized. Sidgwick was not a mathematician but he had the knack of expressing physical theory in clear lucid words.

The next development came from a suggestion from Debye, when he was staying with Sidgwick in 1928, that the investigation of dipole moments might help him over a difficulty. Sidgwick followed up this new route and the results appeared in the lectures he gave at Cornell University in 1931, which were published in 1933 under the title *Some Physical Properties of the Covalent Link in Chemistry*.

From then onwards Sidgwick's energy was mainly given to lectures and review articles and to writing the second volume of his *Electronic Theory of Valency* forecast in volume one. Gradually he realized the magnitude of the task he had undertaken which developed into two volumes of 750,000 words. He left the revision of his *Organic Chemistry of Nitrogen* to his younger collaborators after rewriting the first five chapters and devoted himself to collating the known facts relating to the occurrence, stability, and structure of the typical compounds of all the known elements. This involved the consultation of 10,000 papers. The great task occupied Sidgwick for nearly twenty years and he was seventy-seven when his final book, *The Chemical Elements and their Compounds* (2 vols., 1950) was published. The edge of his mind had not lost its keenness and this massive work of scholarship was distinguished by its clarity and by its astonishing freshness and liveliness.

Sidgwick's vigorous personality play[] an important part in the development the Oxford school of chemistry and h[] generous hospitality brought many en[] nent scientists to Oxford and helped give the school a sense of unity. His ou[] standing characteristics were his passio[] ate devotion to truth in all matters, h[] insatiable curiosity, his desire to go dee[] into things, and his loyalty to his friend[] He had a sharp tongue and pungent wi[] quickly roused by any loose or pretentio[] statement or by a sense of injustice, fro[] which few of his colleagues escaped at on[] time or another. He enjoyed the societ[] of young people and was gentle with them[] At Cornell in 1931 he lived in a fraternit[] house with undergraduates where h[] formed friendships which brought hi[] much happiness in later life. From the[] onwards he often returned to America[] where he had countless friends. In 1951 h[] underwent a serious operation in order t[] pay a final visit to Cornell. He had a strok[] on the boat coming home and after som[] months in a nursing-home died peacefull[] in Oxford 15 March 1952.

Sidgwick held the readership in chem[] istry of the university of Oxford in 1924[]45, with the title of professor from 1935 and he was for many years a delegate o[] the University Press. Among the man[] honours which fell to him were a Roya[] medal and the Bakerian lectureship of th[] Royal Society, the Longstaff medal an[] Liversidge lectureship of the Chemica[] Society, the presidency of the Chemical an[] Faraday societies and honorary member[] ship of the American Academy of Arts[] and Sciences. He was appointed C.B.E[] in 1935.

A portrait commissioned by some of his[] old pupils from John Merton is at Lincoln[] College, Oxford.

[Sir Henry Tizard in *Obituary Notices of Fellows of the Royal Society*, vol. ix, 1954; *Proceedings* of the Chemical Society, 1958; *The Times*, 17 March 1952; private information; personal knowledge.]

HAROLD HARTLEY.

SILBERRAD, OSWALD JOHN (1878–1960), scientist, was born at Buckhurst Hill, Essex, 2 April 1878, the third son of Arthur Pouchin du Toict Silberrad, 38th Baron (Franconian cr. 1002) of the house of Willigis (von der Silber-Rad), prince of the Holy Roman Empire, merchant, and his wife, Clarissa Lucy Savill, sister of Thomas Dixon Savill [q.v.]. His aunt Emma married Sir Charles Wyndham

v.]. His sister, Una Lucy, was an
thoress. He was educated at Dean Close
morial School, Cheltenham, the City
d Guilds Technical College, Finsbury,
d the university of Würzburg. In 1902
was appointed head of the experimental
tablishment at Woolwich of the War
fice explosives committee of which
rd Rayleigh [q.v.] was chairman.
either Silberrad nor the small staff of
chemists with which he was originally
ovided had prior acquaintance with
plosives, but under his brilliant leader-
ip and youthful urge fundamental re-
arches were put in hand which proved
inestimable value to the fighting
rvices. Most notable among the ex-
osives which he developed was trini-
ophenylmethyl nitroamine, orginally
dbbed Silberrad's Explosive S. 15, later
nown as Tetryl, which continues to find
important application in a wide variety
munitions. Through its agency he found
eans of detonating lyddite shell which
d failed lamentably to explode during
e South African war. Sir William
rookes [q.v.] was a frequent visitor to
e laboratories and impressed by the
ork in progress minuted the War Office
mphasizing the need for larger labora-
ries and additional staff. Of Silberrad
wrote that it was 'wrong to employ a
acehorse to cart bricks'. As a result
Iberrad was instructed to design new
uildings and to include provision for
etallurgical research. These when erec-
d were known as the chemical research
epartment and Silberrad was appointed
uperintendent of chemical research and a
ember of the explosives committee.

In 1906 this committee was disbanded
nd in the same year Silberrad resigned
become for the rest of his career a
onsulting research chemist and director
f the Silberrad Research Laboratories
rst at Buckhurst Hill, then at Loughton.
lthough primarily a chemist he had
icked up a valuable knowledge of metal-
urgy and in 1908 at the instigation of the
irector of naval construction he investi-
ated the cause of a form of erosion in
hips' propellers so severe that it looked
s if the application of the steam turbine
shipbuilding was doomed and that a
peed exceeding about 20–22 knots was
npracticable for surface craft. Silberrad
iscovered the cause of this erosion and
roduced a bronze which withstood it and
vith which the propellers were made
hroughout the navy. It was also used in
ther high-speed ships including the

world's great liners. In conjunction with
the firm of Hotchkiss he worked on erosion-
resisting gunsteel which rendered the
75-mm. gun a practical proposition in the
war of 1914–18.

In 1915 the scientific committees
advising the Ministry of Munitions had
insisted that lyddite could be made only
in earthenware, hence its manufacture
from dinitrochlorbenzene via dinitrophenol
which requires a high temperature was
impracticable. Silberrad showed how this
could be done in large charges in iron
vessels with perfect safety and many
thousands of tons were made by this
method in both world wars. He also developed a flashless propellent for use in
large howitzers. He discovered how to
make dyestuffs from a special type of
carbon and also from the residues from
T.N.T. manufacture. Among his many
other discoveries may be mentioned a new
chlorinating agent, a method for manufacturing isoprene, the artificial retting of
flax, a plastic explosive free from nitro-
glycerine, and a new method of blasting
petroleum wells. He was the author of
numerous scientific papers and of a
treatise on the chemical stability of
nitrocellulose. He was a fearless experi-
menter, on one occasion making a
kilogram of nitrogen iodide, an explosive
which when dry detonates on the slightest
touch. He had great personal charm and
was altogether a lovable man.

In 1922 he married Lilian Glendora,
daughter of Edward George, knight of the
Order of Militia Templi, of Ballinasloe and
Oxford; they had one son. Silberrad died
at his home, Dryads' Hall, Loughton,
Essex, 17 June 1960.

[*The Times*, 18 June 1960; *Nature*, 13
August 1960; private information; personal
knowledge.]   GODFREY ROTTER.

SIMON, ERNEST EMIL DARWIN, first
BARON SIMON OF WYTHENSHAWE (1879–
1960), industrialist and public servant,
was born in Didsbury, Manchester, 9
October 1879, the eldest son by his second
wife, Emily Stoehr, of Henry Gustav
Simon who had arrived in Manchester
from Germany in 1860. Like many liberal
Germans, Henry Simon found the political
climate of his native Prussia uncongenial.
He became a naturalized British citizen,
and founded two engineering firms:
Henry Simon, Ltd., which made flour-
milling machinery, and Simon Carves,
Ltd., which exploited a French patent for
a by-product coke oven. Both achieved

immediate success and in due course became the Simon Engineering Group, with world-wide commitments. Ernest Simon was destined to take command of both at an early stage owing to his father's death in 1899. Educated at Rugby and Pembroke College, Cambridge, where he obtained a first in part i of the mechanical sciences tripos in 1901, even before completing his engineering degree he was burdened with responsibility for both companies and for the destinies of a large family of younger brothers and sisters. It was under his leadership that the family business triumphantly survived the impact of two world wars and provided the ample resources which Ernest Simon required for the prosecution of his public work outside his business commitments.

It is possible that this early assumption of leadership, plus the enjoyment of comparative wealth, isolated him from the day-to-day experiences of common men and intensified a natural shyness which made him appear both impersonal and insensitive. He was in fact a dedicated and altruistic humanitarian with a sensitive and self-searching social conscience. Like Sidney and Beatrice Webb [qq.v.], whose work inspired his earliest commitment to social reform, and with whom he was associated in founding the *New Statesman*, he thought statistically rather than personally. Statistics of overcrowding, as later the measured mileage of devastation achievable by a hydrogen bomb, roused him to a fury of reforming zeal. This led him to a progressive delegation of business responsibility which caused him to be known to the public rather as a great social reformer than as the successful industrial tycoon which indeed he was.

By 1912 he had found time to become a member of the Manchester city council, an activity which led in 1921 to his election as lord mayor. During these years he became widely known as an expert on smoke abatement, housing, and the machinery of local administration—on all of which subjects he wrote and published books. Subsequent events rendered much of what he wrote out of date; but his book *A City Council from Within* (1926) remains an illuminating study of incentives and personal relations in municipal administration. In all this work he was supported by his wife, Dorothy Shena, daughter of John Wilson Potter, shipowner, of Westminster, whom he married in 1912. In many ways the working

partnership of the Simons resembled tl of the Webbs. Both Simon and We married beautiful and intelligent wom shared their public work and lived hap ever after. But for the Simons the inter of a family was added. Two sons, neitl of whom chose to enter the family busine provided in due course daughters-in-l and grandchildren. Their youngest chi a daughter of remarkable intelligence a charm, died at the age of twelve, leavi a shared sadness which the years did n dim.

From local government, Simon mov by stages into the sphere of national po tics. But Manchester remained his hom and an honorary LL.D. of its universi (1944) and the freedom of the city (195 probably caused him more satisfacti than the knighthood conferred in 1932 the peerage conferred in 1947. Neverth less experiences in municipal housing h; convinced him that local frustrations we conditioned by national legislation; at tl same time association with Manchest liberalism and C. P. Scott [q.v.] of tl *Manchester Guardian* brought him in touch with the intellectual élite of tl Liberal Party. He became a leading men ber of the Liberal summer schools whic starting from a small house-party of h own in 1920, developed into the period gatherings which in 1928 produce *Britain's Industrial Future* (better know as the *Yellow Book*), a programme social and economic reform with whic the Liberal Party faced the general elec tion of 1929. These political contac involved Simon in two brief spells House of Commons membership (1923-4 1929-31), during the Labour Party's tw experiences of minority office. Both, i spite of a fortnight's enjoyment of offic as parliamentary secretary to the Minis try of Health in Ramsay MacDonald' pre-election 'national' Government, lef him with tarnished faith in party politics He was neither a good party man nor : congenial House of Commons man. H could not suspend his critical faculties ii the interest of party policy and he foun the procedure of the House frustratin; and unbusinesslike. Its club life left hin cold.

The war of 1939-45 (like the first war found him busily engaged in the conduc of the Simon engineering firms, working at high pressure. But demands were also made on his business experience by various official bodies. From his point o view, the most significant of these was the entral Council for Works and Buildings. That he learned under its auspices of the ructure and potentialities of the building ıdustry served as the basis of his book *ebuilding Britain, a Twenty Year Plan* ıblished in the spring of 1945. It was ypical of him to start planning for peace hile his country was still at war.

In 1946 he joined the Labour Party, ıough remaining critical, in the light of ıis own business experience, of its generalıed commitment to the nationalization of ıdustry. It was now effectively in power; ınd he felt that working from within he ıould best serve the causes he had at ıeart: education, municipal ownership, ıown planning. His peerage enabled him ıo do this without again enduring the ıoredom of the House of Commons. The itle adopted was derived from Wythenıhawe Park and Hall, which he and his ıvife had bought and presented to the ıity of Manchester to form a central ıeature of the great municipal housing ıstate which both had worked hard to ıring into being. A second result of his ıew party affiliation was his appointment ıor a five years' term as chairman of the 3ritish Broadcasting Corporation (1947–ı2). This brought him into touch with an ınfamiliar sphere of human activity: the ıvorld of entertainment. He threw himself ınto its complexities with a zest which ın occasions bewildered the B.B.C. His ıreign coincided with the renewal of its ıharter. A journey to the United States ıonvinced him of the superiority of public ıervice over commercial broadcasting and ıe found himself in violent opposition to ıthe campaign waged by the commercial ınterests supported by the Conservative ıParty to secure the introduction of comımercial television in competition with the ıB.B.C. On this issue the close of his chairımanship brought disappointment and ıdefeat.

It was during these post-war years that Simon's attention was for the first time in his life diverted from local and national to world problems. It seemed to him that the whole future of humanity was menaced by two developments: overpopulation and nuclear armaments. To both subjects he devoted time, money, and deep study. His interest in the first involved an investigation on the spot of Barbadian economic resources in relation to population growth, and was perpetuated after his death by the endowment of a Simon Population Trust for research and education on population problems. The second

led him into active co-operation with the Campaign for Nuclear Disarmament. It was a campaign which involved more emotional drive and less opportunity for objective investigation than any he had yet undertaken. Nor was he wholly at ease with those of his fellow campaigners who advocated civil disobedience. But he was able to challenge government nuclear policy in the House of Lords, and finance the publication of an informative book on the subject by Wayland Young.

It was fortunate for Simon that throughout his working life his faith in human betterment was sustained by a belief in the saving grace of education. If political democracy was found wanting, it was because humanity was ill equipped to understand the operation of political and economic controls for the greatest happiness of the greatest number. It must be *made* to understand. In the thirties he initiated and financed a campaign for 'Education for Citizenship' in secondary schools. But already, as early as 1916, had begun an association with Manchester University which ended with the chairmanship of its council (1941–57) and involved the endowment by him of the Simon Fund for the provision of research fellowships. Outside his own university he used his membership of the House of Lords, which otherwise he seldom attended, to promote a series of debates on the inadequacy of government provision for university and technological education.

During the closing years of his life this was the main focus of his activities; and the last public act of his long and varied career was the introduction in the House of Lords on 11 May 1960 of a motion calling on the Government to 'appoint a committee to inquire and report on the extent and nature of the provisions of full-time education for those over the age of 18, whether in universities or in other educational institutions'. The reply on behalf of the Government was indecisive and Simon was disappointed. He need not have been; for on 20 December 1960 the Government announced the appointment of a committee under the chairmanship of Lord Robbins, granting all that Simon had asked. Simon's death in Manchester, 3 October 1960, robbed him of the satisfaction of knowing that his meticulously prepared campaign had initiated a stirring of educational waters destined to usher in a new era of expansion in universities, colleges of technology, and teacher training. The House of Lords

Simon, E. E. D.

debate on 11 May 1960 was his finest hour.

Simon was succeeded in his peerage by his elder son, Roger (born 1913), who preferred not to use the title.

A bust by Sir Jacob Epstein belongs to the Simon Engineering Group.

[Mary Stocks, *Ernest Simon of Manchester*, 1963; personal knowledge.]   STOCKS.

SIMON, SIR FRANCIS (FRANZ) EUGEN (1893–1956), physicist, was born 2 July 1893 in Berlin, the only son and second of the three children of Ernst Simon, a well-to-do real estate developer, and his wife, Anna, daughter of Philibert Mendelssohn, a surveyor and an able mathematician. An ancestor was the brother of Moses Mendelssohn, the eighteenth-century Jewish philosopher; two of Simon's cousins became scientists: Dr. K. Mendelssohn, F.R.S., reader in physics in the university of Oxford, and Dr. H. Mendelssohn, professor of zoology at the university of Tel Aviv.

At the Kaiser Friedrich Reform Gymnasium in Berlin, Franz Simon's talent for mathematics and physics soon showed itself. After overcoming strong family opposition—his father thought physics an insecure profession—he matriculated in 1912 at the university of Munich where he spent two semesters followed by one at Göttingen. His studies were interrupted first in 1913 by compulsory military service then by the war of 1914–18 in which he served in the Field Artillery, mainly on the western front. He became an officer, was twice wounded, and was one of the earliest poison gas casualties.

In the spring of 1919 he resumed his studies of physics and chemistry at the university of Berlin, where he came under the influence of Planck, von Laue, Haber, and in particular of Nernst, then director of the Physikalisch–Chemisches Institut of the university, under whom he did his thesis work on specific heats at low temperatures. He obtained his Dr. Phil. in December 1921 and spent the next ten years in the same laboratory, becoming in 1924 a *Privatdozent* and in 1927 an 'extraordinarius' (associate professor).

The Berlin period was a most fruitful one and established Simon's reputation as a great thermodynamician and the outstanding low-temperature physicist of his generation. Much of his work in Berlin was directly connected with the Nernst heat theorem, which in its fifteen years of existence had already proved its worth by

enabling the prediction of chemical equilibrium with the help of the postulate of vanishing entropy differences between condensed phases at the absolute zero of temperature. There were, however, a number of cases which seemed to contradict the Nernst heat theorem and in the ensuing controversy Simon took the line that these violations were only apparent and were due either to incorrect extrapolation of specific heats to absolute zero or to the fact that the system was not in internal equilibrium and hence thermodynamic arguments were not applicable. Many specific heat measurements were carried out in his laboratory to prove this view and it is largely thanks to Simon's work that the Nernst heat theorem has come to be regarded as the third law of thermodynamics equal in fundamental importance to the first and second laws.

It was in Berlin that Simon began his extensive researches on fluids at high pressures and low temperatures in what he called 'model' experiments. The basic idea was that by studying the melting pressures of substances with low boiling-points, i.e. weak intermolecular attractive forces, one could predict how other substances would behave under conditions difficult to realize in practice. Thus, his success in solidifying helium at 50 °K, that is ten times the critical temperature, enabled him to make hypotheses about the earth's core.

These and other experiments required liquid hydrogen and liquid helium, and the Berlin phase was notable for the development of many new low-temperature techniques. For the liquefaction of helium on a small but useful scale Simon developed the 'desorption' method and in 1927 his laboratory became the fourth institution in the world where experiments down to the temperature of liquid helium could be carried out.

Early in 1931 Simon succeeded A. Eucken as professor of physical chemistry at the Technische Hochschule of Breslau: an appointment of some piquancy in view of Simon's recent heated controversies with Eucken about the third law. The spring semester of 1932 was spent as visiting professor at the university of California at Berkeley, where Simon conceived and developed his idea of the so-called 'expansion' method for helium liquefaction and was thus the first person to liquefy helium in the United States. The simplicity and cheapness of the method made it for the next twenty years the mainstay of many

890

w-temperature laboratories; it was with e of the earliest Simon expansion lique-rs installed at the Clarendon Laboratory Oxford in 1933 that helium was first quefied in Britain.

When Hitler came to power Simon cided to leave Germany although as a ar veteran and holder of the Iron Cross st class he was exempt from the decree smissing Jews from university posts. He rrectly foresaw the trend of events and August 1933, at the invitation of F. A. indemann (later Viscount Cherwell, q.v.), e moved to the Clarendon Laboratory in xford on one of the research grants ovided by Imperial Chemical Industries r refugee scientists from Germany. He ecame reader in thermodynamics in)36; was accorded the title of professor id became a student of Christ Church in)45; in 1949 a chair of thermodynamics as specially created for him.

The Clarendon Laboratory when Simon ame to it was small and not too well quipped, but the period of 1933–9 was evertheless rich in achievements. The mag-etic cooling method to reach tempera-ures down to 0·001 °K proposed in 1926 by)ebye and by Giauque fascinated Simon ho had earlier carried out experiments to stimate the scope of the method and now evoted much of his energy to develop-ig it as a practical technique for experi-ienting in an entirely new temperature ange. This work, carried out with a small roup of collaborators, led to the discovery f new super-conductors and new magnetic henomena in paramagnetic substances nd included experiments on thermal con-uctivity and thermal relaxation. It was luring the same period that experiments vith helium II (the 'superfluid' low-emperature modification of liquid helium) ed Simon to postulate the existence of a mobile helium II film on all surfaces in ontact with the liquid.

The outbreak of war in 1939 brought his research work to an end. Simon, a iaturalized British subject since 1938, ried hard to contribute to the war effort iut there was reluctance to entrust secret vork to ex-enemy aliens. With other refu-gee scientists, notably (Sir) R. E. Peierls ind (Professor) O. R. Frisch, he became nterested in the possibility of an atomic iomb and began to work on the problem iefore it had become an official project: hence the paradoxical fact that in its early days the 'Tube Alloys' project was run mainly by foreign-born scientists. Simon was mainly concerned with the separation

of the uranium isotopes by the gaseous diffusion method and his report in late 1940 contained the first realistic proposal for a sizeable separation plant. He was also involved in many other aspects of atomic energy and his stimulating views played a part in Britain's atomic energy developments both during and after the war.

With the resumption of peacetime re-search at the Clarendon Laboratory, Simon, while continuing some of the earlier work, turned his attention to some new fields. With H. Halban he initiated work on nuclear orientation: the study of the anisotropy in the intensity of radiation emitted by preferentially oriented radio-active nuclei, a technique fruitful for both nuclear and solid state physics. Even more spectacular were the experiments on nuclear cooling, an extension of the mag-netic cooling method to nuclear magnetic moments, which resulted in temperature of about 1/1,000,000th of a degree absolute.

During the last ten years of his life Simon devoted much of his time to the wider social and political aspects of science and technology. His varied activities had one basic idea: an uncompromising dislike of waste in any form. He castigated the Government for its lack of an integrated power and fuel policy; he deplored the waste of fuel in open grates and the waste of scientific manpower through the lack of good technological education or through the ineffective use of the intellectual po-tential of the country. Many of his ideas found expression in his articles in the *Financial Times* of which he was scientific correspondent between 1948 and 1951. His immediate impact on public affairs was only slight, partly because the uncom-promising crusading fervour with which he propounded his many ideas tended to put people off. But through public dis-cussions, stimulated by his views, he did ultimately influence the country's think-ing.

Underlying Simon's whole work was a vivid appreciation of thermodynamics which to him was a living subject, drawing strength continuously from the interpre-tation of new phenomena. His career roughly coincided with the period during which low-temperature physics grew into a varied yet unified discipline and he was the outstanding figure of that era. It was largely thanks to him that the Clarendon Laboratory came to possess one of the world's largest and most renowned low-temperature schools. As chairman of the commission of very low temperatures of the International Union of Pure and Applied Physics, and as president of the first commission of the International Institute of Refrigeration, he played an important part in fostering the exchange of ideas and international collaboration in these fields. He was elected F.R.S. in 1941 and received the society's Rumford medal in 1948. He became an honorary foreign member of the American Academy of Arts and Sciences in 1952 and was awarded the Kamerlingh Onnes gold medal of the Dutch Institute of Refrigeration (1950) and the Linde medal of the German Refrigerating Association in 1952. He was appointed C.B.E. in 1946 and knighted in 1954.

On Cherwell's retirement in 1956 Simon succeeded him as Dr. Lee's professor of experimental philosophy and head of the Clarendon Laboratory; but within a month of taking up his new position he died in Oxford, 31 October 1956.

Simon's most notable quality was a profound and warm-hearted interest in people for their own sake. He was kindly and generous, devoid of all pomposity; he made friends easily and was particularly successful in gaining the confidence and devotion of young people. He was proud of his pupils—many of whom reached prominence in academic and industrial life—and tended to regard them as members of a large family. His influence as a teacher and as the founder and head of a great low-temperature school was mainly through personal contact; lecturing was not his strength. Although tolerant by nature he was uncompromising on matters of principle. To the end of his life he could neither forget nor forgive the record of Nazi Germany and remained convinced that the spirit which made Nazism possible was still alive in Germany. He was a scientist to the core. His scientific outlook permeated his whole life and coloured his judgements on public affairs and his relations with others. It was the blend of lovable subjective qualities with the disciplined objectivity of the physicist which gave Simon's personality its cachet.

In 1922 Simon married Charlotte, daughter of a successful Berlin business man, Sigismund Münchhausen; they had two daughters.

[N. Kurti in *Biographical Memoirs of Fellows of the Royal Society*, vol. iv, 1958; Nancy Arms, *A Prophet in Two Countries*, 1966; personal knowledge.]   N. KURTI.

SIMON, JOHN ALLSEBROOK, fi VISCOUNT SIMON (1873–1954), statesm and lord chancellor, was born in Manch ter 28 February 1873, the only son a elder child of the Rev. Edwin Simc Congregational minister, and his wi Fanny, daughter of William Pc Allsebrook, a farmer. To his mother wl claimed connection with Cardinal Pc [q.v.] he was devoted. His father was t son of a small farmer and mason Stackpole Elidor in Pembrokeshire. Aft a period at Bath Grammar School, Simc went with an entrance scholarship Fettes where he had a respectable ac demic and athletic career and was head the school. To the end Simon retained a interest in games and was a devoted u holder of the public school system. In 18 he went up to Wadham College, Oxfor as a classical scholar. After a second i mathematical (1893) and classical (189 moderations he obtained a first in *liter humaniores* and was president of the Unio in 1896 and in 1897 was elected a fello of All Souls. To the companionship of A Souls, as exacting intellectually as ur demanding emotionally, he owed much, an in an increasing degree, throughout his lif He also owed something to a group of me of remarkable abilities who were member of Wadham at the same time—F. E. Smit (later the Earl of Birkenhead, q.v.), C. R Hone, later bishop of Wakefield, C. B. Fr [q.v.], H. M. Giveen, A. A. (later Lord Roche [q.v.], and F. W. Hirst [q.v.].

In 1899 Simon was called to the bar b the Inner Temple. In the same year h married Ethel Mary, daughter of Gilber Venables. She died in 1902. A widowe while still under thirty Simon becam increasingly reserved. He himself, as we as his friends, ascribed his 'frigid and un responsive' manner to this tragedy, but hi nature had always been self-contained 'Shyness has always been my trouble though I have learned to conceal it.' A the bar Simon's career followed the patterr usual to the lives of successful advocates A pupil of (Sir) Reginald Acland, he earned 27 guineas in his first year but soor moved into the very highest class of civi practice, taking silk only nine years afte he had been called. Simon's qualities a an advocate were admirably summarized in his own description of Rufus Isaacs, Marquess of Reading [q.v.]. He 'had every accomplishment that goes to make a great advocate in the courts—an uncanny sense of the point that would impress the tri bunal, a manner that was authoritative thout being truculent, a fine presence, perfect temper, and a complete command every detail in the most complicated ief'. To this might be added Simon's own culiar ability to expound the most comicated matters in language of extreme nplicity. In later years this was to make m a leading authority on revenue law. Nevertheless he did not rate the law as e of the highest achievements of the uman mind; nor did he plan to devote s entire life to forensic disputes. He garded the bar as a stepping-stone to olitics. He was elected Liberal member ' Parliament for Walthamstow in 1906 nd held this seat until 1918, when, not olding Lloyd George's 'coupon', he was efeated at the general election of that ear. But in 1922 he was returned for pen Valley and retained the seat until lay 1940.

In 1910 Simon was appointed solicitor-eneral, with a knighthood, at the early ge of thirty-seven. He was sworn of the rivy Council in 1912 and in 1913 he ucceeded Rufus Isaacs as attorney-eneral with a seat in the Cabinet. In 1914 e at first supported those like Morley and Burns [qq.v.] who favoured neutrality ather than intervention, but in the end vithdrew his proposed resignation. In May 915 he refused the position of lord chanellor; had he accepted he would have een the youngest lord chancellor with the xception of Jeffreys in 1685. His refusal vas almost certainly due to his desire not o put a premature end to his political areer by going to the upper House: 'The ack rather than the Woolsack', he wrote. Instead he went to the Home Office, a position from which he resigned in January 1916 on the issue of conscription. He later realized that from all points of view this decision had been a mistake, but at the time he was able to produce some traditional Liberal arguments in support of t. Simon was now out of ministerial office for fifteen years. The intervening period was occupied partly by war service in the Royal Flying Corps and partly by steady devotion to his careers at the bar and in the House of Commons. In May 1926 he achieved what had hitherto eluded him— a major parliamentary success, when his speech on the illegality of the general strike indubitably had some effect in bringing it to an end.

In the spring of 1927 Simon gave up his practice at the bar in order to accept the chairmanship of the Indian statutory commission which was to investigate the development of the government of India since the Montagu–Chelmsford reforms of 1919 and to recommend on the degree of constitutional progress which would be suitable for the future. This vast task called out all that was best in Simon— his exceptional powers of analysis and exposition, his ability to master complex material, and his willingness to work hard in the public interest. It was a major disappointment when the Labour Government in October 1929 issued a statement to the effect that 'the natural issue of India's constitutional progress . . . is the attainment of dominion status' before the commission had reported on the matter. In India Simon was dealing with local politicians who were even more sensitive and unwilling to take responsibility than he was said to be, but he got the best out of them and secured a general assent to the proposals made by his commission in its report of 1930. Unfortunately events were in control and by 1935 the huge report with so much careful learning clearly set out was no more than a storehouse for historians. In 1930, after refusing a peerage, Simon returned to the bar. In the following year he formed and led the Liberal National Party (which later changed its name to National Liberals), whose object was to support the newly formed 'national' Government and the basis of whose policy was anti-socialism.

From 1931 to 1935 Simon was foreign secretary and had to deal with Germany, Italy, and Japan in general and disarmament in particular. It is probable that those who were responsible for the formation and execution of British foreign policy in those years would never have been entirely satisfied that justice had been done to them. But after all allowances have been made it must be recognized that Ramsay MacDonald had lost and Simon was lacking in the power to seize and take the initiative in matters of high policy. Simon was criticized especially for his failure to take a stronger line over Japanese aggression in Manchuria. Nor was his view that 'we must keep out of trouble in Central Europe at all costs' calculated to deflect Hitler and Mussolini from their designs; by the time Simon left office the aggressors were well away.

In 1935 Baldwin transferred Simon to the Home Office and in 1937 Chamberlain on his accession to the premiership moved him to the chancellorship of the Exchequer. Throughout this period Simon was part of the inner Cabinet concerned with the

Simon, J. A. D.N.B. 1951–1960

formation and execution of both domestic and foreign policy. He took a prominent part in such events as the abdication of King Edward VIII in 1936. His talents were those of the efficient chief of staff rather than of the inspiring commander-in-chief, and he was neither responsible for, nor even showed any desire to introduce, any major legislative reform. At the same time Simon's own personal popularity with the younger members of both parties in the House of Commons sank still farther. In part this may have been due to the traditional House of Commons belief that lawyers are lacking in conviction and willing to speak on either side of any issue. But Simon's self-contained manner had often caused deep offence, and also conveyed an unjustified impression of insincerity and deviousness. He seemed to be entirely lacking in any of those human failings which the British public likes its politicians to possess in a mild degree. His unpopularity became associated with that of the Government which was swept away in the Churchillian gale of May 1940. With Churchill personally Simon had been on friendly terms since the days when they both sat in Asquith's Cabinet, and he accepted the office of lord chancellor, with a viscountcy.

Although he had been for so long out of the practice of the law Simon had no difficulty in presiding on the Woolsack with exceptional distinction during a period when the other law lords were a team of unusual strength: Maugham, Wright, Porter, Atkin, Russell of Killowen, Romer, and Macmillan. These Simon was careful to consult at all stages about proposed judgements or law reforms—he introduced and carried through Parliament two important statutes, the Law Reform (Frustrated Contracts) Act, 1943, and the Law Reform (Contributory Negligence) Act, 1945. It is paradoxical that at the end of his long public career Simon should have been more successful as a lawyer than as a politician. (He was not a member of the War Cabinet, and had little contact with the direction of the war.) The Appeal Cases of these years contain numerous decisions of the highest importance in which his skill as a jurist is manifested to the full. He delivered judgements on torts, contracts, property, criminal law, revenue law, and evidence. In each of these different fields he moved with easy mastery. His judgements were soundly based on the authorities but contain no unnecessary parade of elaborate learning. Occasionally

he attempted to restate the law in th form of numbered propositions. These di played all his analytical skill and pow of exposition and although on occasic later courts have felt constrained t modify them he has an assured plac among the greatest jurists who have bee on the Woolsack.

In appearance Simon was a tall an well-built man with a fine head. He wa not exactly handsome or distinguishe but his manner, and still more his conve sation, at once displayed him as a perso of consequence. He was appointe K.C.V.O. in 1911, G.C.S.I. in 1930, an G.C.V.O. in 1937. He was proud to becom high steward of Oxford University i 1948. After 1945 Simon continued to tak an active part in the legal and politica business of the House of Lords. He showe few signs of advancing years: he coul still consult the London telephone direc tory without the aid of glasses. It wa noted that on his eightieth birthday h had many more friends than on his seven tieth. He died in London 11 January 195 and in accordance with his express in structions was cremated in his D.C.L gown without any religious ceremony.

By his first wife Simon had one son John Gilbert (born 1902), who succeeded him as second viscount (and who contri butes to this Supplement), and two daugh ters. There were no children by his second marriage (1917) to Kathleen (died 1955) widow of Thomas Manning and daughte of Francis Eugene Harvey, of Kyle county Wexford. She was devoted to many good causes, especially the emancipation of slaves, and in 1933 was appointed D.B.E. for her work.

There are portraits of Simon by Sir Oswald Birley (Inner Temple), P. A. de László (All Souls), and Frank O. Salisbury (Privy Council). A pencil drawing by Edward I. Halliday (1948) is an admirable likeness. A bust by Lady Kennet is in All Souls.

[Viscount Simon, *Retrospect*, 1952; *The Times*, 12 January 1954; *Oxford Magazine*, 11 March 1954; *Law Quarterly Review*, April 1954; private information; personal knowledge.]   R. F. V. HEUSTON.

SIMON, OLIVER JOSEPH (1895–1956), printer, was born 29 April 1895 at Sale, Cheshire, the eldest son of Louis Simon, cotton merchant, and his wife, Louisa, sister of (Sir) William Rothenstein [q.v.] and Albert Rutherston. He was educated at Charterhouse and Jena. In the war of

894

14–18 he served in Gallipoli, Egypt, and Palestine, countries which made a profound impression on him. Later he visited Palestine and his intense interest in the country led to the founding of the Aladin Club. The membership included Sir Ronald Storrs, Chaim Weizmann [q.v.], Lord Samuel, Malcolm Macdonald, and Norman Bentwich.

With no certain idea of what his future would be, Simon went to London in 1919. Seeing a collection of finely printed books, he realized with a flash of certainty that his life's work must be with printing. His uncles helped him with introductions and after a short time as a pupil with Charles T. Jacobi at the Chiswick Press, he met Harold S. Curwen who agreed to take him for a year's training at the Curwen Press. At the end of 1920 he persuaded Curwen to let him stay on and examine the prospects of adding book-printing to the Curwen activities, with the result that he remained with the Press for the rest of his life; in 1949 he became its chairman.

In 1923 Simon published the first volume of *The Fleuron*, a journal of typography, of which, in conjunction with Stanley Morison, seven numbers were produced, the last three being edited by Morison. It was characteristic that the first number contained no introduction with elaborate statement of aims and objects, and no promises for the future. Exquisitely produced, it made its own way.

Simon and Hubert Foss [q.v.] helped by two or three others founded in 1924 the Double Crown Club, a dining club for typographers, designers, artists, authors, and publishers. Its influence on the design and production of British books cannot be exactly measured, but it was certainly responsible for fostering and encouraging a sound contemporary style of printing in all its forms.

In November 1935 Simon brought out the first number of a periodical, *Signature*, which was to appear two or three times a year until 1954 with the exception of the war years, 1941–5. It contained articles on the arts of design, illustration, printing, and calligraphy, and provided a fitting monument to his own ideals of beautiful production. In 1945 he published an *Introduction to Typography* which was quickly accepted as a standard work.

Although he was recognized internationally as a typographical authority with an intimate knowledge of the importance and influence of the famous English private presses, Simon's aim was to do first-rate contemporary and commercial printing. Under his guidance, the Curwen Press played a major part in the improvement of printing in all its aspects after 1918. He encouraged many artists to use their talents in the direction of printing and book design, among them Eric Ravilious, Paul Nash, Barnett Freedman [qq.v.], Edward Ardizzone, Edward Bawden, Reynolds Stone, John Piper, and Graham Sutherland.

Printer and Playground (1956), Simon's autobiography, is the story of an idealist, a man dedicated to his calling, a typographical craftsman of uncompromising standards, but no pedant. He appears sociable but not gregarious, ever modest of his own accomplishments, affectionate, humorous, with an invincible courage and unflinching tenacity of purpose.

Simon was appointed O.B.E. in 1953 and died in London 18 March 1956. He married in 1926 Ruth, daughter of Christopher Henry Ware, of Herefordshire, and had one daughter and one son, who, in his turn, became a director of the Curwen Press. A drawing by Brian Robb is reproduced in *Printer and Playground*.

[*The Times*, 20 March 1956; private information; personal knowledge.]

G. Wren Howard.

SIMONSEN, Sir JOHN LIONEL (1884–1957), organic chemist, was born in Levenshulme, Manchester, 22 January 1884, the only son of naturalized British parents of Danish origin. His father, Lionel Michael Simonsen, was a velveteen merchant, of Jewish stock, and his mother, Anna Sophie Bing, had relatives in academic circles in Denmark and Sweden. Simonsen was educated at Manchester Grammar School where he was stimulated by Francis Jones, a distinguished pioneer in the teaching of the elements of chemistry. Fortunately some of his schoolmates had a definite predilection for science. Among them were C. S. Gibson, D. M. S. Watson, and K. Fisher. The last (who later became headmaster of Oundle), after working under Knorr at Jena, met Simonsen again in the laboratory of W. H. Perkin [q.v.] at Manchester University. Summer holidays were spent in the Copenhagen laboratory of an uncle by marriage, Professor V. Henriques, a physiologist. This and other contacts with his Danish scientific relatives doubtless determined the direction of Simonsen's interests. Forfeiting a scholarship in modern languages, he became a student in the school of chemistry of Manchester University, already a renowned and leading centre of research. He graduated with first class honours in 1904, obtained his D.Sc. in 1909 and from 1907 was assistant lecturer and demonstrator.

Even in those early days Simonsen was recognized as a brilliant experimentalist. His work was always neat and careful and so well described that it could be easily reproduced by other chemists. His main task was to find a synthesis of norpinic acid. This end-product of a degradation of pinene carried out by A. von Baeyer proved elusive but the syntheses incidentally effected gave fresh starting-points in unanticipated directions. Simonsen recorded new syntheses of terebic acid and two homologues and in collaboration with (Sir) Robert Robinson reinvestigated rhein and alo-emodin which were shown to be respectively dihydroxyanthraquinonecarboxylic acid and the related p-alcohol, $(HO)_2C_{14}H_5O_2 \cdot CO_2H$ and $(HO)_2C_{14}H_5O_2 \cdot CH_2OH$. This interest arose from a study of barbaloin which Simonsen resumed much later and then established facts which were fundamental for the final solution of the difficult problem.

In 1910 Simonsen went to Madras as professor of chemistry at the Presidency College. Almost at once he devoted himself to the improvement of Indian scientific work and education beyond the limits of his post. He took the initiative in 1914 in helping to found the Indian Science Congress Association of which he was general secretary until 1926 and which owed its success largely to his efforts. Indian science became much better known to and appreciated by Europeans, and many western scientists, most of them British, were enabled to visit India. Simonsen also assisted the Government in various ways: during the war of 1914-18 he was controller of oils and chemical adviser to the Indian Munitions Board. In 1919-25 he was chief chemist of the Forest Research Institute and College at Dehra Dun and in 1925-8 professor of organic chemistry at the Indian Institute of Science at Bangalore.

In 1928 Simonsen returned to England and worked for a time at the chemical laboratory of Guy's Hospital, but in 1930 he resumed academic work as professor of chemistry at the University College of North Wales, Bangor, where he remained until 1942. The main current of his mature original scientific work was concerned with

the chemistry of the terpenes and se quiterpenes. His name will always associated with the very interesting di covery of $\triangle^2$-carene in Indian turpentin This gave the clue to the reason for th apparent structural anomaly presented b sylvestrene and thus strengthened th belief that the 'head to tail' isopentar rule is valid. Some of his studies of sesqu terpenes were started in India (long folene, 1920) but the greater part of th important work was carried out i Bangor, partly in collaboration wit A. E. Bradfield and often with A. F Penfold, director of the Museum Applied Arts and Sciences in Sydney N.S.W. This long-distance arrangemen was very effective; Penfold isolated ne natural products and Simonsen devel oped their chemistry. Their fruitfu labours led to the establishment of th structure of the sesquiterpenoid ketone eremophilone, though not without stumble on the way. The final elucidation de pended on the recognition of an intra molecular migration of a methyl group a some stage in the biosynthesis from thes 'head to tail' isopentane units (farnesan type). This type of migration, first indi cated in the case of eremophilone, be came of great value in helping to an understanding of the biogenesis of the sterols.

Simonsen and his colleagues determined the molecular structure of α- and β-cyperones, discovered the *cyclo*butane element of the caryophyllene molecule and laid the foundations for the determination of the structure of longifolene. He made numerous further significant contributions to knowledge which are described in about 180 memoirs. In addition to his scientific papers Simonsen's literary output included a comprehensive account of the terpenes published in five volumes (1947-57, with L. N. Owen, D. H. R. Barton, and W. C. J. Ross) which constitute the standard work of reference in the field.

In 1943-52 Simonsen was director of research of the Colonial Products Research Council. He also worked on the insecticide panel and stored foods committee. He was appointed member of the Agricultural Research Council in 1945 and was British delegate to the Food and Agriculture Organization specialists committee in London in 1947. In all this work he displayed impressive energy and administrative ability. In 1944 with Sir Robert Robinson he visited the United States and he Caribbean. Results of this visit were he founding of the Microbiological Instite in Trinidad and the clearance of mosquitoes from the coastal strip of British Guiana. The infantile mortality ate was dramatically reduced, an adance which brought further problems in s wake. In 1946 with Sir Ian Heilbron q.v.] he visited East and South Africa. he necessity for a wider front than that mplied by 'colonial products research' ecame apparent and eventually the erm 'tropical products research' was dopted.

Simonsen's abilities as a scientist were lmost entirely on the experimental side; e had little interest in theory but his aboratory work was superb both in plan nd execution. He had many students and unior collaborators whose subsequent chievements bear testimony to his bility as a teacher. Simonsen was at the ame time exacting and generous; formal when occasion demanded it, but always varm-hearted. He would go to any possble lengths to help a younger man and his oyalty to his high ideals, his friends, and is country, had no limits.

Simonsen was elected F.R.S. in 1932 and warded the Davy medal in 1950. He was he first recipient of the American Chemial Society's Fritzsche award (1949) and received honorary degrees from the universities of Birmingham, Malaya, and St. Andrews. He was honorary secretary of the Chemical Society (1945–9) and was knighted in 1949.

In 1913 he married Jannet (Nettie) Dick (died 1960), daughter of Robert Hendrie, of Nairn. She had been a brilliant surgeon and at the time of her marriage was in charge of the Caste and Gosha Hospital at Madras. They had no children but adopted a daughter. Simonsen died in London 20 February 1957.

[Sir Robert Robinson in *Biographical Memoirs of Fellows of the Royal Society*, vol. v, 1959; personal knowledge.]

R. ROBINSON.

SINGER, CHARLES JOSEPH (1876–1960), historian of medicine and science, was born in Camberwell 2 November 1876, the fifth child and fourth son of the Rev. Simeon Singer and his wife, Charlotte Pyke. Three years later his father, a notable classical and Hebrew scholar, became rabbi of the New West End Synagogue. Singer went to the City of London School, then to a tutorial college to prepare for his matriculation. He began

the medical course at University College, London, did well in zoology and decided to read for a B.Sc. in zoology under W. F. R. Weldon [q.v.], to whom he became demonstrator. But he obtained an exhibition in zoology at Magdalen College, Oxford, where he read nothing but zoology. The subject remained a lifelong interest, and he was especially grateful for the assistance and friendship of E. S. Goodrich [q.v.]. Singer obtained second class honours—there were no firsts in zoology that year—in 1899, and circumstances now induced him to return to the study of medicine. He entered St. Mary's Hospital, Paddington, as a medical student and qualified M.R.C.S., L.R.C.P. in 1903. He had thus spent ten years over his university studies. Immediately on qualifying Singer was appointed medical officer to a small geographical expedition to Abyssinia where he spent nearly a year.

On his return Singer filled various posts in London, Brighton, and in Singapore (1908). During these years he graduated B.M. at Oxford (1906) and on his return he was admitted M.R.C.P. London (1909) and was appointed registrar to the Cancer Hospital and physician to the Dreadnought Hospital. At the former he did pathological research of some importance and at the latter he extended his already deep interest in tropical diseases. He retained these posts until he went to Oxford in 1914 and for a time he was concurrently in consulting practice in the west end of London.

In 1910 Singer married Dorothea Waley Cohen (1882–1964), second daughter of Nathaniel Louis Cohen and sister of (Sir) Robert Waley Cohen [q.v.]. Dorothea Singer devoted herself to many humanitarian and social activities, but she will be best remembered for her scholarly work in the history of science and medicine, notably her monumental catalogue of Greek, Latin, and vernacular alchemical manuscripts in the British Isles (1924–31), her unpublished extension of that work to cover all scientific subjects, deposited on cards in the British Museum, and her study of Giordano Bruno (1950). In 1911 Singer graduated D.M. at Oxford and in that year also, while he was actively pursuing his pathological researches, he was led by accident to write on an historical subject. The result was two papers on Benjamin Marten, a precursor of the germ-theory of disease, and within the next three years several other historical papers followed. A parting of the ways occurred in 1914 when Sir William Osler [q.v.] offered Singer a studentship in pathology—the duties of which were to be mainly historical—at Oxford. After their removal to Oxford the Singers threw themselves into the task of improving the facilities for the study of the history of science in the Radcliffe Camera. During most of the war Singer served as a pathologist, with the rank of captain, in the Royal Army Medical Corps, and he saw much service in Malta and at Salonika. While he was on military service he published some fifteen notable papers on medieval and renaissance medicine, and also his first major work, the first volume of his *Studies in the History and Method of Science* (1917).

On his return from the war Singer found that the Oxford which he had known had changed, and he was in 1920 induced to accept a lectureship in the history of medicine at University College, London. The mental stimulus provided by the staff of that college at that time proved very congenial to him, and the next twelve years were richly productive. In 1921 the second volume of his *Studies* appeared, and in the same year he contributed the chapters on biology and medicine to *The Legacy of Greece*. He wrote also for later volumes of the 'Legacy' series, and with E. R. Bevan [q.v.] he edited *The Legacy of Israel* (1927) to which both he and his wife contributed. In the first volume of the *Studies* Singer had included his important discussion of the visions of St. Hildegard of Bingen, and in 1922 the university of Oxford awarded him a D.Litt. for that and other historical essays. He had been elected F.R.C.P. in 1917 and in 1923-4 he gave the FitzPatrick lectures of that College. They were published in extended form in 1925 with the title *The Evolution of Anatomy*, the first serious study of that subject in English. In that and the following year there appeared his translations of significant medieval anatomical works. In 1927 he published his important paper on the herbal in antiquity, and in 1928 his well-known works *From Magic to Science* and a *Short History of Medicine*.

In 1930 Singer gave the first Noguchi lectures at Johns Hopkins University, Baltimore, and after a short time at the Huntington Library at Pasadena he spent three months as a visiting professor at the university of California at Berkeley. In 1931 he was invited to fill the chair of the history of medicine at Johns Hopkins, but this he refused after much considera-

tion as he had just had conferred on him the title of professor of the history of medicine in the university of London. From January 1932 he spent another year as visiting professor at Berkeley, and the results of the lectures given during these two extended visits appeared as his *Short History of Biology* (1931) and his *Short History of Science* (1941).

In 1934 the Singers removed to the fine house, 'Kilmarth', near Par, Cornwall, which for a quarter of a century was to be a focal point for scholars from many countries, and in which his magnificent library was adequately housed. In it during the war years he taught practical biology with great success to boys of the King's School, Canterbury, evacuated to Cornwall. In the pre-war years he was much engaged with the activities of the Society for the Protection of Science and Learning in helping scholars suffering from Nazi oppression.

The end of the war marked the beginning of Singer's Indian summer. In 1946 he published (with Chaim Rabin) a study of the Arabic sources in the *Tabulae anatomicae sex* of Vesalius; in 1948 a sumptuous book on the early history of the alum industry; in 1952 a translation and study of the writings of Vesalius on the human brain, and also (with J. H. G. Grattan) an important work on Anglo-Saxon magic and medicine, a subject which Singer had first explored in a British Academy lecture in 1920; and in 1956 an annotated translation of Galen's work *On Anatomical Procedures*. Meanwhile, from about 1950, he had been engaged on what may prove to be his most enduring work, the arrangements for the great *History of Technology* (5 vols., 1954-8), of which he was throughout editor-in-chief.

Singer was always very active in the international field, and he was president (1928-31) of the Académie Internationale d'Histoire des Sciences, and of the international congresses held in London in 1922 and in 1931. He was an original member and president (1920-22) of the history of medicine section of the Royal Society of Medicine, and founder-president of the British Society for the History of Science. In 1936 Oxford made him an honorary D.Sc., and he was thus probably the only man to hold the three Oxford doctorates in medicine, science, and letters. He was an honorary fellow of Magdalen College, Oxford, and of the Royal Society of Medicine, and a fellow of University

ollege, London. He was awarded the
sler medal by the university of Oxford,
ad he and Dorothea Singer jointly re-
ived the Sarton medal of the American
ociety for the History of Science. In
953 Singer was presented with a work in
vo volumes, *Science Medicine and History*
dited by E. A. Underwood), consisting
' essays written in his honour by scholars
om many countries; it contains a biblio-
aphy of Singer's published writings to
953.

Singer was sturdily built, but he took
ttle interest in sport, and his main out-
oor activities were walking and swim-
ing. His chief recreations were travel,
alking, reading, and, in later life, growing
acculent plants. He was a witty con-
ersationalist, and his talk was salted with
aecdote. To the end he kept up an
amense correspondence, and his in-
uence was felt even in fields remote from
is main subjects. He died at his home in
ornwall 10 June 1960.

[E. A. Underwood in *Science Medicine and
istory*, 1953; in *Medical History*, October
060; in *Proceedings* of the Royal Society
' Medicine, vol. lv, 1962; in *British Medical
ournal*, 18 June 1960; in *British Journal for
e History of Science*, June 1965; private
formation; personal knowledge.]

E. A. UNDERWOOD.

INGLETON, SIR JOHN EDWARD
885–1957), judge, was born at St.
lichael's on Wyre, Lancashire, 18 Jan-
ary 1885, the third son of George
ingleton, of Howick House, Preston, and
is wife, Eleanor Parkinson. He was
lucated at the Royal Grammar School,
ancaster, and Pembroke College, Cam-
ridge, where he obtained third classes in
oth parts of the law tripos (1904–5) and
ecame an honorary fellow in 1938. He
ead for the bar first in Lincoln's Inn,
fterwards in Liverpool, and was called
t the Inner Temple in 1906, when he
oined the Northern circuit. He quickly
uilt up a reputation as a junior before his
areer was interrupted by the war in which
e served in France and Belgium in the
.oyal Field Artillery, was mentioned in
ispatches, and rose to the rank of captain.
.eturning to his practice he soon acquired
large common law business based on
iverpool and was principally engaged
n the Northern circuit until in 1922 he
ook silk and accordingly moved to
ondon, although he never lost contact
ith, or wavered in his devotion to, his
ative county. In the same year (1922) he
fought the Lancaster division as a Conservative and defeated his Labour opponent, Fenner (later Lord) Brockway, by a
large majority; but in 1923 he lost his
seat to the Liberal candidate and never
afterwards returned to politics. His success in his profession continued and he
became a prominent leader of the common
law bar. He was a judge of appeal, Isle of
Man (1928–33), and recorder of Preston
(1928–34).

A keen, straightforward advocate,
devoted to his art and thoroughly competent, Singleton's standards were of the
highest. In two lectures given to students
at the instance of the Council of Legal
Education and published in book form as
Conduct at the Bar (1933) he set forth his
views on the true professional spirit and
the conduct required of a barrister. Since
then each student called by the Inner
Temple has been handed a copy of this
book which is consequently in the possession of many hundreds of barristers
throughout the Commonwealth; it is not
only a valuable work of instruction but a
memorial of the esteem in which Singleton
was held as an exemplar of the art of
advocacy in the courts.

Singleton was appointed a judge of the
King's Bench division (with a knighthood)
in 1934 and a lord justice of appeal (and
sworn of the Privy Council) in 1948, in
which office he served until his death,
becoming at the end of his career the
senior lord justice in the Court of Appeal.
In 1949 he received an honorary LL.D.
from the university of Liverpool. Soon
after he was appointed judge he was
called upon to try Dr. Buck Ruxton on a
charge of the murder of his wife, Isobella,
at Manchester assizes. This sensational
trial in which eminent counsel were engaged lasted no less than eleven days,
at the end of which the accused was
convicted.

As a judge Singleton will be remembered
as a man of stout Lancastrian common
sense, ready to apply the law as he understood it, if possible in the simplest manner,
without recourse to subtlety, and anxious
at all times to do justice. He may not
have had a profound interest in the law
as a science, but he was none the less
well equipped for his work, for his mind
never deviated from the purpose of doing
justice in the particular case with which
he had to deal. He was not concerned to
extend the law or to be remembered for
the grace of his judgements but rather to
perform that which he had to do, not so

much as a jurist or a craftsman, but as a just and workmanlike professional. He carried out the judicial task as well as in him lay and continued to find satisfaction in it until the end of his life. He would no doubt like to be remembered as a no-nonsense judge, ready to listen patiently to evidence and to argument, yet intolerant of waste of time or any lapse from the standard of conduct which he expected from the bar.

Singleton became a bencher of his Inn in 1929 and in due course treasurer in the year (1952) in which the Queen laid the foundation stone for the new buildings to replace those destroyed in the war. He was always devoted in his service to the Inn for which he had an enduring affection and in which he made his home during the last years of his life.

In the war of 1939–45 Singleton gave valuable service in connection with government inquiries into submarine services, the production of stabilized bomb sites, and the comparative strength of British and German air forces. In December 1945 he was appointed British chairman of the Anglo-American Palestine commission; this was perhaps the most important of his public services outside his judicial work.

Singleton never married. He was a sturdy and affectionate friend, full of fun, and popular within and without his profession. He enjoyed life in all its aspects, was a keen though indifferent golfer and a good shot, and during the shooting season spent as much time as he could on the Yorkshire moors. It was shortly after returning from a day's shooting on the moors near Pateley Bridge which he loved so well that he died, 6 January 1957.

[Private information; personal knowledge.]
                                    HODSON.

SMART, SIR MORTON WARRACK (1877–1956), manipulative surgeon, was born in Edinburgh 1 December 1877, the third son of John Smart, a landscape painter, by his wife, Agnes Purdie Main. He was educated in Edinburgh at George Watson's College, the university, and the Royal College of Surgeons, graduating M.B., Ch.B. in 1902 and proceeding M.D. in 1914. He served with the Black Watch in the South African war and in 1914–18 was a combatant with the Royal Naval Volunteer Reserve in many parts of the world. In 1914 he was chief of staff to the admiral in command of gunboats on the Belgian canals. In 1915 he was attached

to the First Army in France; in 1915–1 he commanded a gunboat flotilla in t Dardanelles; he was in command of a fl tilla of motor-launches which made t passage from England to Mudros in t Aegean and later at Salonika; reache the rank of commander, was mentioned dispatches, and appointed to the D.S. in 1917. In 1918–19 he was senior nav officer in Trinidad.

In his early days Smart was attached the medical staff of the Great Ormor Street Hospital for Sick Children charge of the electrical department. F became one of the leading exponents manipulative surgery and an authority physical medicine and rehabilitation. F founded and was for many years in charg of the London Clinic for Injuries Grosvenor Square. He was manipulativ surgeon to Kings George V, Edwan VIII, George VI, and Queen Elizabeth I He was appointed C.V.O. (1932), K.C.V.C (1933), and G.C.V.O. (1949), and receive a number of foreign decorations. He was member of the Central Medical War Con mittee and of the Empire Rheumatisr Council and a fellow of the Royal Societ of Medicine. In the war of 1939–45 h acted as consultant in physical medicine t the Royal Air Force at their rehabilitatio clinic in Regent's Park. He contribute many articles on muscle and joint injurie to medical journals and encyclopedias an in 1933 published *The Principles of Trea ment of Muscles and Joints by Graduate Muscular Contractions.*

Smart was a man of many facets, fo apart from being one of the pioneers c physical medicine and manipulative tech niques, he was a fearless sailor and a early exponent of motor-boat racing; great horticulturist, winning many prize for his gladioli in which he specialize and serving as president of the Britis Gladiolus Society; and he was a super raconteur of his experiences in the man spheres of his busy life.

In 1923 he married Lilian, daughter o William S. Gibson, J.P., of London, an widow of Major P. V. Lavarack, M.C They had no children. He died at his hom at Cooden Beach, Bexhill-on-Sea, 16 Marc 1956.

[*British Medical Journal*, 31 March 1956 personal knowledge.]   W. E. TUCKER

SMITH, SIR ERNEST WOODHOUSI (1884–1960), fuel technologist, was bor in Gorton, Manchester, 13 February 1884 son of the Rev. Harry Bodell Smith nitarian minister, and his wife, Mary iranda Woodhouse. He was educated at rnold School, Blackpool, and the uniersity of Manchester where his brilliance rought him eventually the award of the .Sc. (1918). In the meantime, after an lventurous year as chemist to the Gold redging Company in Saskatchewan, he ad become in 1908 the first research iemist to be appointed by the Institution f Gas Engineers to work at the university f Leeds: the start of a unique and unroken association between the university nd the gas industry of immense benefit ɔ both.

After distinguished service to the city f Birmingham gas department (1910–20), ɪrnest Smith went to London as techical director of the Woodall-Duckham ompanies, a position which he held until 944. During the war he was seconded in 942–3 as director-general of gas supply ɪ the Ministry of Fuel and Power. From 949 to 1956 he was technical adviser to istrict valuation boards of the coal ɪdustry (coke ovens division). He had iven outstanding service to the Woodall-Ɔuckham Companies but his decision to esign in 1944 to devote himself to the ʌroblems of fuel during the period of postvar reconstruction betokened both his trong sense of public duty and his avoidnce of self-interest.

As a pioneer in the field of fuel Smith ɪad contributed greatly to the technical ʌrogress of the gas industry and he was ne of the founders of the Gas Research 3oard. Among his many distinctions may ʌe mentioned his honorary membership ʌf the Institution of Gas Engineers and he presentation to him of its highest ɪward, the Birmingham medal. His long xperience, shrewdness and constructive ʌutlook, and his charm and friendliness ɪn particular inevitably brought him to nany high offices in fuel affairs: honorary .ecretary of the World Power Conference 1928); chairman of the Society of British ɪas Industries (1931–2) and president 1954); and chairman of the Industrial ʌoal Consumers' Council (1947–57). His ʌresidency of the Institute of Fuel from ⁘943 to 1945 reflected his long devotion ɔo the service of the Institute and the ʌrominent part he played in the petition ʌr a royal charter which was successful n 1946. He was continually active in the ʌause of smoke abatement, being honorary ɪreasurer and later president for two years ʌf the society which was to become the National Society for Clean Air. He was

appointed C.B.E. in 1930 and knighted in 1947.

In 1912 Smith married Beatrice (died 1955), daughter of George Arnfield, of Dolgelly; they had one son and one daughter. Smith died at Effingham, Surrey, 7 November 1960.

[Private information; personal knowledge.]
    A. L. ROBERTS.

SMITH, SIR MATTHEW ARNOLD BRACY (1879–1959), painter, was born in Halifax 22 October 1879, the second of three sons of Frederic Smith, wire manufacturer, and his wife, Frances Holroyd. He was educated at Halifax Grammar School and Giggleswick School. His childhood and youth were dominated by the commanding figure of his father, a strict Nonconformist who went to chapel twice every Sunday, ran his business with notable success, and in his spare time passed for a lover of the arts. Frederic Smith's collection of violins was well known to visiting virtuosi; he had published a book of Browningesque verses; and he had commissioned a painting called 'Stradivarius in his Studio' from Seymour Lucas.

Attempts to place his son in the business world were a failure and in the face of his father's intense disapproval Matthew Smith won permission to study applied design at the Manchester School of Art. His range of activity was severely restricted—'I was twenty-one', he said later, 'before I saw a good picture.' But an iron determination lay concealed within his frail body and apparently timorous nature and at the late age of twenty-six he was allowed to go to the Slade. In fact he was unhappy there for Henry Tonks [q.v.] often handled him roughly in front of the entire class, and on his doctor's advice he went to Pont Aven in Brittany in the late summer of 1908: a decision, he would often say, which marked the true beginning of his life.

The great days of Pont Aven as an artistic centre were over, but Smith fell in love with France and with French life, and thereafter never felt really at home anywhere else. Enough of the Gauguin tradition lingered in Pont Aven for him to learn the uses of pure colour, as distinct from the tyranny of 'pure drawing' maintained at the Slade. When he moved to Paris he was able to show, in 1911 and 1912, at the Salon des Indépendants in company with Matisse, Kandinsky, Léger, and Rouault. He was lucky enough, also, to glimpse Matisse and his methods at first hand through attendance at the school, soon to be disbanded, which Matisse had run since 1908; and if his personal contacts with Matisse were of the slightest the experience was revelatory in the highest degree.

Towards 1914 Smith's personal circumstances were radically altered by the death of his mother (1912) and of his father (1914), and by his marriage in 1912 to Gwendolen Salmond (died 1958), a fellow student of his at the Slade and a close friend both of Gwen John and of Ida Nettleship (the first Mrs. Augustus John). Her two brothers were Sir Geoffrey Salmond [q.v.] and Sir John Salmond.

Matthew Smith had yet to show a painting in his own country, but when the war forced him and his wife to interrupt their sojourns in France he took a studio in Fitzroy Street, where W. R. Sickert and (Sir) Jacob Epstein [qq.v.] were among his neighbours. There he painted the first of the pictures in which the lessons of France were truly digested, and in 1916 Epstein persuaded him to show a painting in the London Group exhibition. From 1916 to 1919 Smith was in the army—initially in the Artists' Rifles and later as an officer in the Labour Corps—and in 1918 he was wounded by shrapnel. After his demobilization he went with his wife and their two sons to Cornwall. At St. Columb Major he produced a series of landscapes in which the dark, saturated colour of Gauguin was happily combined with reminiscences of the spatial organization in certain Florentine predellas. With the two 'Fitzroy Street nudes' of 1916 these constitute Smith's first original contribution to English painting.

Smith had always been delicate, and there was throughout his life an apparent discrepancy between his aghast and tentative approach to the practical aspects of living and the imperious energy which went into his work. Early in the twenties the normal shortcomings of his health allied with the sense of something unfulfilled in his personal life to produce a serious breakdown; and it was not until he found in Vera Cuningham the ideal model for his art that he recovered and, indeed, redoubled his ability to work. He took a studio at 6bis Villa Brune, in Montparnasse, and was soon producing one after another the long series of female nudes which established him as one of the few English painters ever to master this most exacting of subjects. Of the 'Femme

de Cirque' (National Gallery of Moder Art, Edinburgh) Roger Fry [q.v.] wrot that 'It is a picture planned in the grea tradition of pictorial design, and carrie through without any failure of the in pulse.' From 1923 until 1940 Smith er joyed a period of unbroken creativity If Paris and the nude were predominar in the twenties, the thirties saw a shift t Provence, in geographical terms, and landscape as his preferred theme. Througl out these years his first responsibility wa owed to his work; and although he was devoted father he was inflexible in hi will to cut free from any entanglemen which might impair the freedom to wor which he had sought for so long and ha found only in his middle forties.

In June 1940 Smith had to be evacuate from France by the R.A.F., leaving man canvases behind him in Aix-en-Provence There followed a period of great private un happiness on more than one count; abov all, the loss of his two sons on activ service was a blow from which he took long time to recover. The petty vicis situdes of London life during and afte the war found in Smith a most consisten victim; he was troubled, also, by ai affliction of the eyes which later cause him to undergo a serious operation. I spite of all this his natural toughnes empowered him to go on working, and th still-lifes and large decorative subjects o the mid-fifties have a grandeur of spiri and an unforced amplitude which pu them very high in the canon of his work The year 1955 saw the onset of the illnes from which he eventually died; but eve when it was clear that life was with drawing its benefits one by one he wen on working as best he could. His las years saw a general realization that as master of paint he had had few rival among the English artists of this century He was appointed C.B.E. in 1949 an knighted in 1954. In 1953 a large retro spective exhibition of his work was held a the Tate Gallery, and in 1956 Londor University gave him an honorary D.Lit Equally precious was the affection anc respect in which he was held not only b friends and colleagues of a lifetime, lik Augustus John and Jacob Epstein, but b younger artists: Francis Bacon above all

Smith was most often talked of as colourist, but he did not altogether car for the appellation. 'They all praise the colour', he would say, 'but if the pictures hold together there must be something else, you know. There must be some-ing else.' Tenaciously, although with characteristic discretion, he had studied ngres, Courbet, Rembrandt, and Tintor-tto. His landscape-practice was based to surprising degree on the study of Rubens's ndscape-sketches. He read enormously a an unstudied way, and although he was ne last man to 'keep up with' his friends a conventional sense, few people have ad a securer hold on the affections of thers. He spoke, someone once said, ike a highly intelligent moth'; but, nce his confidence had been won, the igh seriousness implicit in two of his iven names (Matthew Arnold) was allied a his talk with an idiosyncratic and un-orgettable sense of fun.

Matthew Smith died in London 29 eptember 1959. A self-portrait and a ortrait by Cathleen Mann are in the ational Portrait Gallery and a portrait y Augustus John is in the Tate Gallery.

[Philip Hendy, *Matthew Smith*, 1944; *atalogue* of the memorial exhibition at the toyal Academy, 1960; Sir Philip Hendy, 'rancis Halliday, and John Russell, *Matthew mith*, 1962; personal knowledge.]

JOHN RUSSELL.

MITH, VIVIAN HUGH, first BARON 3ICESTER (1867–1956), banker, was born n London 9 December 1867, the eldest f six sons of Hugh Colin Smith, a descen-lant of the banking family which founded mith's Bank at Nottingham, eventually bsorbed into the National Provincial 3ank, and his wife, Constance Maria 'osepha, daughter of Henry John Adeane, f Babraham, Cambridge. Two of the six ons entered the Royal Navy and retired s admirals; the remaining four achieved onspicuous success in various spheres of ctivity in the City of London.

Educated at Eton and Trinity Hall, 'ambridge, without any particular aca-lemic success, Vivian Hugh Smith entered he firm of Hay's Wharf, wharfingers in he Pool of London, of which his father vas chairman, bringing to the business hat energy and vision which were notable hroughout his life. In his thirties he oined the merchant banking firm of Morgan Grenfell, & Co. where he was ssociated with his cousin Edward Gren-ell (later Lord St. Just, q.v.) and with he American partners of J. P. Morgan k Co. of New York. The two houses, s the bankers and buying agents of the 3ritish and French Governments during he early years of the war of 1914–18 before the United States came in, played an indispensable part in the war effort of the Allies. Vivian Smith became a director of many important companies but was most notable in the City for his term of no fewer than sixty years as a director and later as governor of the Royal Exchange Assurance which he built up to become one of the major insurance companies in the country. He was created a baron in 1938.

All his life Bicester loved horses; his time at Eton was marred by a painful episode for absenting himself to attend the Ascot Summer Meeting which resulted in the continuing restriction of the movement of Etonians at that time of year. Although he preferred to live in the country while working in London, it was only late in life that he acquired a property of his own, at Tusmore Park near Bicester where he was able to indulge at close quarters his passionate interest in horses. When owing to a hunting accident he was no longer able to ride much, he acquired a string of steeplechasers—he was not really interested in flat racing—which in the heyday of his racing career were second to none in the country. His ambition to win the Grand National failed but he achieved at one time or another all the other major steeplechases.

Unintellectual but with a good command of words and a fantastic memory shared with many of his family, Bicester found it difficult to express himself on paper: but his humour and quickness in repartee enabled him to mix well with all sorts of people. It was because of the confidence he inspired in people by his sense of justice and right behaviour that he became the confidant and adviser of many who brought their troubles to him whether or not he was personally concerned. If he was quick-tempered, he bore no malice because he liked helping people, especially the young, and he liked to be asked to help. In his prime between the wars he was one of the leading personalities in the City where he was looked upon with respect for all his qualities of leadership and fairmindedness. Politically he never played any public part in spite of being for many years chairman of the Conservative Party in the City. He was one of the last survivors of a generation of business men descended from business people: a man who will be remembered for his great contribution to all the ramifications of commerce and finance, but most of all as an Englishman whose first and foremost characteristic, behind all the conventional appearance of dress, habits, and standards, was that of justice, decency, and a deep appreciation of the point of view of the other man. He accepted in religious, artistic, and intellectual matters what he did not understand or care to pursue provided he personally had confidence in the men whom he recognized as leaders in their own fields. He was lord-lieutenant of the county of Oxford (1934-54) and received the freedom of Oxford City in 1955.

He married in 1897 Lady Sybil Mary McDonnell, the only daughter of the sixth Earl of Antrim, and had three sons and four daughters. He died at Tusmore Park 17 February 1956 and was succeeded by his eldest son, Randal Hugh Vivian (1898-1968).

There is a portrait by Sir William Orpen at the Royal Exchange Assurance and one by (Sir) James Gunn is owned by Morgan Grenfell, & Co. Another portrait of Bicester, on horseback in hunting pink, by Sir Alfred Munnings, is in the possession of the family.

[Personal knowledge.]   RENNELL.

SODDY, FREDERICK (1877-1956), chemist, was born at Eastbourne 2 September 1877, the seventh and youngest son of Benjamin Soddy, a London corn merchant, and his wife, Hannah Green, who died some eighteen months after he was born. At Eastbourne College he came under the influence of the science master, R. E. Hughes. They worked together in a striking way and in 1894 were joint authors of a paper in the *Chemical News* on the action of dried ammonia on dried carbon dioxide. This followed the pattern of the work of Brereton Baker [q.v.] on dried gases. From Eastbourne Soddy went for a period to University College, Aberystwyth, before going as a postmaster to Merton College, Oxford, where he obtained first class honours in chemistry in 1898. For the Oxford Junior Science Club he wrote a very fine paper on the life and work of Victor Meyer.

Learning that the chair of chemistry at Toronto University was vacant Soddy decided to apply for it and went there to further his application. He quickly decided that his prospects were non-existent, and before returning to England decided to call in at the chemistry department of McGill University, Montreal. There he was offered and accepted a position as a demonstrator at a salary of £100 per annum. Ernest (later Lord) Rutherford [q.v.] had recently been elected to junior professorship in physics and it was not long before the two came together to collaborate on radioactive investigation on thorium salts. This joint work resulted in the formulation of the theory of atomic disintegration, which has had such profound effect on scientific thought. The collaboration extended over some two and a half years and it can be said that the joint authors were truly equal contributors. Attempts on numerous occasions to discuss with Soddy their relative contributions always met with the same answer: fundamental concepts were supplied by both contributors and no distinction could be made as between the thinkers or the concepts produced.

In 1903 Soddy decided to return to London to investigate the position of helium in the context of radioactive disintegration. For this he worked with Sir William Ramsay [q.v.], and together they demonstrated the production of helium from radium.

Glasgow University was now taking an active interest in the newer aspects of physical chemistry and, before leaving for a lecturing tour in Western Australia, Soddy agreed to go there as lecturer in physical chemistry and radioactivity. He took up his duties at the beginning of the session 1904-5. Soddy's time at Glasgow was as he himself said his most productive period. He began his important measurements on the rate of production of radium from uranium. Under his guidance an important series of measurements were made on the uniformity of γ rays and he inspired and indeed supervised the work on the Displacement Law and all that that meant in the conception of isotopes. By the end of the Glasgow period that work was finished. In particular, the formulation of the Displacement Law was completed: (a) after the emission of the alpha particle, the remaining atom moved back two places in the periodic table, and (b) after the emission of the beta particle the remaining atom moved forward one place in the periodic table. All this work led to the conception of isotopes, i.e. elements of differing atomic weight which occupy the same place in the periodic table. Such elements have the same atomic number and have identical chemical properties.

In 1914 Soddy moved to the professorship of chemistry in Aberdeen where his work took on a new direction. Active chemical ideas were not so pronounced, but they were still there. This period cludes the initiation of the work which 1s basically carried out by J. A. Cranston 1 the parent of actinium and also saw e publication of the work (with H. yman) on the atomic weight of lead from ·ylon thorite. This was the first time it 1s demonstrated that lead from a parti- 1lar radioactive element had an atomic eight differing consistently from the omic weight of the international tables d this was because the lead was reason- ·ly believed to be derived from what was sentially a radioactive mineral. The raightforward work of scientific re- arch was much interrupted by the events the war and Soddy devoted much effort · ancillary war problems. For example, · worked on the recovery of olefines and nzene from town's gas. This and similar pes of work were carried out under the neral aegis of the Board of Inventions d Research.

Soddy moved in 1919 to Oxford as r. Lee's professor of chemistry and re- red in 1936. In many ways this was an happy period: he failed to capture the agination of his pupils; he found cause enter into fierce and frequently acri- onious discussions with his academic lleagues. It was perhaps not surprising erefore that he turned his attention to atters which had long interested him. fter Aberdeen he published practically research results but he was always very vigorous writer, often on matters t connected with science, although s publications included such notable orks as *The Interpretation of Radium* 909) and *The Interpretation of the Atom* 932). While his interests in science nged over a wide field he took a broad tlook on world affairs in general. omen's suffrage and the Irish question ere subjects which interested him tensely. As early as 1906 he lectured to e Electrical Engineers on the 'Internal nergy of Elements' and involved himself a discussion about the wisdom of using ld as a currency material. This led him be interested in all aspects of economic d monetary reform. Such papers as artesian Economics' (1921) and 'A hysical Theory of Money' (1934) he re- rded as of great importance, but they ere not so regarded by the economists.

Soddy's character was an immensely mplicated one. Personally he was nerous in his outlook and to his friends d collaborators no one could be more nd and considerate. Of physicists in neral, however, he took a very bitter

view and blamed them for being un- appreciative of the workings of the chemical mind. During his Aberdeen period he gave voice to views which on the surface seemed to indicate that he was becoming rather socialistic in outlook; but in fact he remained a rugged indi- vidualist to the end of his life. He was always willing to fight against what he conceived to be wrongful activities in any sphere of public service. Thus he did battle with the Carnegie Trustees because he thought they were not properly carrying out the terms of their trusteeship. Again 'Frederick Soddy calling all taxpayers' (1950) was a complaint against what he considered unjust methods used for tax purposes. His attitude on such matters was not negative; in 1926 he put forward a 'Reformed Scientific National Monetary System'.

Soddy married in 1908 Winifred Moller (died 1936), the only daughter of (Sir) George Beilby [q.v.]; there were no children. The marriage was a very happy one; they travelled extensively together, mainly in the Alps and other mountain- ous regions. She undertook research measurement work on various types of radioactive questions, and there are a number of papers published in their joint names.

Soddy was elected F.R.S. in 1910 and received the Nobel prize for chemistry in 1921. He died in Brighton 22 September 1956.

[Sir Alexander Fleck in *Biographical Memoirs of Fellows of the Royal Society*, vol. iii, 1957; Muriel Howorth, *Pioneer Research on the Atom*, 1958; private information; personal knowledge.]   FLECK.

SOMERVELL, DONALD BRADLEY, BARON SOMERVELL OF HARROW (1889– 1960), politician and judge, was born at Harrow 24 August 1889, the second son of Robert Somervell, master and bursar (1888–1919) of Harrow School, and his wife, Octavia Paulina, daughter of the Rev. John Churchill. He went himself to Harrow, going up to Oxford in 1907 with a demyship at Magdalen. He obtained first class honours in chemistry (1911), a choice of subject surprising in light of his subse- quent career, but typical of his exceptional mental energy and versatility. In 1912 he was elected a fellow of All Souls, an event which, like his first election to Parliament, he himself regarded as particularly memo- rable, since he was the first man who, having taken a degree in chemistry, was later elected to an All Souls fellowship. He joined the Inner Temple but his projected career was interrupted by the outbreak of war in which he served in India (1914–17) and Mesopotamia (1917–19), with the 1/9 Middlesex Regiment and as staff captain with the 53rd Infantry brigade; he was appointed O.B.E. in 1919.

Somervell had been called to the bar *in absentia* in 1916 and began practice in the chambers of W. A. (later Earl) Jowitt [q.v.] whose pupil he had been. Somervell's mental agility and temperament did not attract him to the ordinary run-of-the-mill common law practice; the art of cross-examination did not appeal to him, seeming indeed to his naturally kind heart apt to be unfair. His arguments were expressed briefly and lucidly, without any emotional or histrionic quality. He applied himself to the mentally exacting problems created by the commercial clauses of the Treaty of Versailles, gaining a considerable practice before the mixed arbitral tribunal established under the treaty.

He took silk in 1929 and soon began his political career. Politics had a special fascination for him since boyhood and his choice of profession was largely governed by his belief that the bar would provide a ready introduction to politics. At Oxford his friendship with Cyril, later Lord, Asquith of Bishopstone [q.v.], had much inclined him to the Liberals, but the serious decline of that party, his disapproval of the performance of the Labour Party, and above all his admiration for Stanley Baldwin, whom he particularly respected for his freedom from class bitterness, self-esteem, or ambition, converted Somervell to the Conservative cause. He was defeated at Crewe in 1929 but was successful in 1931 and again, by a narrow majority, in 1935 when he characteristically refused a safer seat, preferring to remain where he had made and valued many local contacts.

To Somervell the House of Commons was both a goal and a home. In his view it was a truly democratic institution in which the ministers were in a real sense subject to the influence of the elected representatives of the nation. He was an assiduous attender, particularly in committees, and he genuinely enjoyed the discussions on public affairs. 'Having got a seat he·sat in it.' His maiden speech was on the Statute of Westminster bill, when he found himself (as often, before 1940) in a measure of disagreement with (Sir) Winston Churchill.

In 1932 Somervell appeared as one of the leading counsel for the Bank of Portugal in the important case of *Waterlo & Sons* v. *Banco de Portugal* in the House of Lords. In the autumn of 1933 he succeeded Sir Boyd (later Lord) Merriman as solicitor-general and was knighted accordingly. Sir Thomas Inskip, later Viscount Caldecote [q.v.], was attorney-general. As attorney-general himself from 1936 he had under him first his old friend Sir Terence O'Connor who had greatly influenced and helped him early in his political career, then Jowitt; and later Sir David Maxwell Fyfe, afterwards the Earl of Kilmuir. Somervell was sworn of the Privy Council in 1938.

The functions of a law officer *vis-à-vis* the heads of the various Ministries, subject on which he addressed the Holdsworth Club in the university of Birmingham in 1946, gave exceptional scope to Somervell's qualities. His emphatic view was that, as a law officer, he should always be available to informal approach by the legal advisers of the various Ministries, a view which bore remarkable fruit during the war of 1939–45. Never afraid of quick decision, he was confident in his judgement which was undoubtedly sound and based on a robust common sense. He wished especially to avoid having to say 'if only you had told me of this before'. Nor was he a man ever to worry over hypothetical situations.

The exceptionally long period of his law officership included problems such as the budget leakage in 1936, the abdication of King Edward VIII, and the form of the Oath appropriate to the coronation of King George VI, a matter involving him in successful negotiations with the representatives of the Commonwealth countries. He also played an important part in debate on such measures as the incitement to disaffection bill and the government of India bill. He strongly supported the line taken by Neville Chamberlain at Munich. During the war his considerable energies were greatly called upon in connection with the very numerous statutory instruments which the exigencies of war demanded, with such legislation as the War Damage Act, and with the vexed problem of war crimes. In respect of all these exacting duties his lucidity, friendliness and above all his quickness of mind gained him the respect of members of all parties. He applied himself to his duties, in back bencher opinion, 'without publicity and with great ability and diligence'.

Somervell frequently began his day at the Law Courts at 8.30 a.m. and remained in the House until late risings, finding none the less time to prepare fully for his appearance in a complicated case next day. His remarkable energy was assisted by his capacity for decision without worry. But his intellectual capacities were not even exhausted by his pressing duties as a member of the bar, as a law officer, or later as a judge. He was an insatiable reader and found time to study diverse and complex subjects, upon which he would summarize his conclusions in papers prepared not for publication but for his own clarification, such as 'Christian Art 12th–15th Centuries', 'The Background to the New Testament', and 'Relativity'.

From 1940 to 1946 Somervell was recorder of Kingston upon Thames. His twelve years as a law officer ended with his appointment as home secretary in the caretaker Government of 1945. The defeat of the Conservative Party put an end to his political career but in 1946 he was appointed, on the recommendation of Jowitt, by now lord chancellor, a lord justice of appeal, a position which he held until 1954; for most of this time he presided over one of the divisions of the Court of Appeal. After the exertions of his ministerial work he felt judicial life to be relatively unexacting since he was able to reach clear conclusions rapidly and to deal speedily with the cases which came before his court. Frequently he would shorten the argument of counsel, not by putting questions critical of their arguments, but rather by summarizing them and then asking: 'That is your case, is it not?' or 'Do you see what I mean?' If Somervell's judgements were not always framed in careful literary style and were, in his own words, inclined to be slapdash, they were notable for lucidity and absence of prolixity. It was his strong view that our law suffered from too much verbal inflation, and of one of his colleagues he observed that 'he would never use one word when ten would do'. As in his political career, he earned the affection of his colleagues both in the court and at the bar.

In 1933 Somervell married Laelia Helen, daughter of Sir Archibald Buchan-Hepburn. They had no children. If 1933—the year of his marriage and his appointment as solicitor-general—had been a triumphant year for Somervell, 1945 was, by contrast, a bleak one. In that year the death of his wife after a long illness ended a perfect partnership and about the same time the defeat of the Conservative Party ended his career in politics which had been the principal focus of his mind and energies. Somervell tried to maintain as his home the Old Rectory at Ewelme in Oxfordshire which he had bought shortly after his marriage (and where he was buried) but in 1955 he felt compelled to abandon it. Thereafter he lived in chambers in the Inner Temple, paying frequent visits to All Souls. In 1953 he suffered a slight thrombosis. From this he recovered but in 1954 he assumed the less arduous work of a lord of appeal in ordinary, with a life peerage; he later became afflicted with a cancer which caused his judicial retirement in 1960 and his death in London 18 November of the same year. Meanwhile he had served in 1957 as treasurer of his Inn and in 1959 was made an honorary D.C.L. of Oxford; he had been elected an honorary fellow of Magdalen in 1946 and received an honorary LL.D. from St. Andrews in 1947. He had also been a governor of Harrow from 1944 to 1953 and for the last six years a most energetic and influential chairman of the governors.

Apart from reading Somervell derived great pleasure from music, especially the gramophone records of chamber music by the classical masters. He was for many years on the governing body of the Royal College of Music. He was also chairman of the reviewing committee on the export of works of art and from 1944–9 a trustee of the Tate Gallery. His pleasures throughout his life had never been the playing of games although at one time he was an enthusiastic if not greatly skilled horseman. For him the greatest enjoyment, whether alone or in company, lay in travel and the open countryside and its wild bird and animal life. He bore his last illness with extraordinary cheerfulness and courage, spending more and more of his time at All Souls, his love of which was demonstrated by his gift of the iron gate in the northwest corner of the Great Quadrangle which he did not live to see in place.

[Private information; personal knowledge.]
EVERSHED.

SORABJI, CORNELIA (1866–1954), Indian barrister and social reformer, was born at Nasik, in the Bombay presidency, 15 November 1866, the fifth daughter of the Rev. Sorabji Karsedji, a Christian convert from the Parsee community, and his wife, Franscina. Cornelia, her six sisters, and one surviving brother were brought up to respect all that was best in both the Indian and British ways of life. The whole family were encouraged to share their mother's interest in social service; and it was out of her concern at the injustices often suffered by Indian women who lived *purdah nasheen* (sitting behind the curtain), that Cornelia's later vocation arose. She resolved to fight the legal battles of wives, widows, and orphans who could not be expected to break from their customary seclusion. She was the first woman student admitted to the Deccan College, Poona. The first class degree she was awarded there in 1886 would, but for her sex, have entitled her to a scholarship at a British university. She taught instead at Gujerat College, Ahmedabad, and in 1888, through the help of friends, went to Somerville Hall, which had been opened at Oxford nine years earlier. At Oxford she enjoyed the friendship of Benjamin Jowett [q.v.] who introduced her to many people distinguished in politics, the law, social service, and literature. She met the aged Florence Nightingale [q.v.] and was presented at court. She read the B.C.L. course and in 1892 was given special permission to sit for the examination, the first woman ever to do so. She was placed in the third class and then continued to read law with a firm of solicitors at Lincoln's Inn. It was not possible until 1919 for women to become barristers; and she had to wait until 1922 before she actually received her B.C.L. degree. In that year she was admitted a member of Lincoln's Inn; and in the following year she was called to the bar.

All this took place, however, after she had already laboured on behalf of her *purdah-nasheens*, as she called them, for well over a quarter of a century. She had returned to India in 1894 and had undertaken educational work in Baroda. Then one day she appeared at the Poona sessions court as a private person speaking in defence of a woman accused of the murder of her husband. The woman was acquitted. Then followed a period during which Cornelia Sorabji appeared in a similarly private capacity in the agency courts of Kathiawar and Indore. Seeking to persuade the Indian legal world to grant her some professional standing, she sat for the LL.B. examination of the university of Bombay and a high court pleader's examination at Allahabad; but, in spite of passing both, she was still not allowed, because of her sex, to be registered as a practising lawyer.

During a second visit to Britain sh[e] suggested to the India Office that a[n] adviser might be attached to the court [of] wards in Bengal, Bihar, and Orissa t[o] deal with the problems connected wit[h] women and minors whose estates wer[e] being administered by that court, as [a] kind of liaison officer between women i[n] *purdah* and the outside world. In 190[?] Cornelia Sorabji was invited to return t[o] Calcutta to begin such work. Her ex[?]periences while so engaged may be found i[n] her autobiographical *India Calling* (193[?] and *India Recalled* (1936). Although she ha[d] no other status than that of adviser, som[e] six hundred wives, widows, orphans, an[d] minor heirs received the benefit of her help[.] In addition to her legal work, she was a[n] organizer of social service, infant welfare[,] and district nursing. She was awarded th[e] Kaisar-i-Hind gold medal in 1909, wit[h] the bar of the first class in 1922. At th[e] end of 1918 her eyesight gave troubl[e] but a temporary cure was effected. Whe[n] she came to London in 1922 to prepare fo[r] her call to the bar she also retired from her work for the court of wards. But i[n] 1924 she returned to India where she wa[s] at last able to practise as a barrister.

In 1929 she visited the United State[s] and while there her eyesight began seri[-]ously to fail. From then on she settled i[n] London, going to India only durin[g] winters. She had a great love for Britai[n] and scant sympathy with the movement i[n] India for independence. She turned mor[e] and more to writing and produced man[y] vivid, moving, or humorous sketche[s] arising out of her work, and also a bio[-]graphical account of her parents entitle[d] *Therefore* (1924) and *Susie Sorabji, A Memoir* (1932), the life of an educationis[t] sister who had died in 1931. Her las[t] literary work was to help in the editin[g] of *Queen Mary's Book for India* (1943), [a] small anthology on themes connected wit[h] India published in support of the India[n] Comforts Fund. By this time Corneli[a] Sorabji was approaching eighty and wa[s] almost blind. She died in London 6 Jul[y] 1954. A writer in the *Manchester Guardia[n]* (9 July 1954) described her as 'an arrest[-]ing figure with a superb profile, alway[s] perfectly dressed in the richly coloure[d] silk sari to which the modern Parse[e] woman has remained faithful. Her Englis[h] speech was distinguished. She talked and spoke in public with equal brilliance, and her gift of phrase remained with her to th[e] end.'

[Her own writings; *The Times*, 8 July 1954[.]

T. H. Mair, *Behind the Curtain*, Madras, 1961; private information.]

WILLIAM A. W. JARVIS.

SPARE, AUSTIN OSMAN (1886–1956), artist, was born in King Street in the City of London 30 December 1886, the son of Philip Newton Spare, a policeman, and his wife, Eliza Ann Osman. He left his elementary school at thirteen, and was afterwards self-educated. He had, however, some formal tuition in art at the Lambeth School of Art and the Royal College of Art. At the age of sixteen he was already exhibiting at the Royal Academy, but soon ceased to do so. His first one-man exhibition was at the Baillie Gallery in July 1914.

Spare was passionately interested in the occult and not without psychic gifts, some of his drawings being done apparently without the co-operation of the conscious mind. If these tended to be somewhat deficient in clear draughtsmanship this was certainly not true of his ordinary work which combined strength and delicacy.

From October 1922 to July 1924 he collaborated with Clifford Bax in the sumptuous quarterly the *Golden Hind* and reproduced in this periodical were some of his finest drawings.

During the war of 1939–45 he was injured by a bomb while fire watching and for a time lost the use of both arms. However he started painting again in 1946 in a cramped basement in Brixton and shortly afterwards was able to exhibit more than 150 pictures. He died in hospital in London 15 May 1956.

[*Book-Lover's Magazine*, vol. viii, 1909; *The Times*, 16 May 1956; personal knowledge.]

JAMES LAVER.

SPENCE, SIR JAMES CALVERT (1892–1954), paediatrician, was born at Amble, Northumberland, 19 March 1892, the fourth son and seventh child of David Magnus Spence, architect, and his wife, Isabella Turnbull, both of old Northumbrian stock. Spence was educated at Elmfield College, York, and entered the university of Durham College of Medicine, Newcastle upon Tyne, in 1909. His career as a medical student, though more particularly characterized by athletic prowess, was not undistinguished, and he graduated in 1914 with second class honours. On the outbreak of war in August, he joined the Royal Army Medical Corps with which he served continuously until early 1919 in various theatres of war, including Gallipoli, Egypt, France, and Belgium. He was awarded the M.C. as a field ambulance medical officer in 1917, and a bar thereto in 1918.

On his return to civil life, the course of his medical career was at first somewhat uncertain. He held a junior appointment at the Hospital for Sick Children, Great Ormond Street, and subsequently it looked as if he might be attracted to biochemistry, his first contributions to scientific literature, from St. Thomas's Hospital, being in that field. But his appointment as medical registrar and chemical pathologist brought him back in 1922 to his old teaching hospital, the Royal Victoria Infirmary, Newcastle upon Tyne, and enabled him to continue both his clinical and laboratory interests. In one capacity or another he was associated with the hospital for the rest of his life.

Shortly after his return to Newcastle, he resumed his interest in paediatrics by joining the medical staff of a day nursery which had been established for the benefit of wartime munition workers. Largely as a result of his energetic reorganization and reorientation this nursery later became the Newcastle Babies' Hospital. In this institution, Spence with the enthusiastic assistance of medical, nursing, and lay colleagues developed the practice of social paediatrics with which his name will always be associated. Together with his friend and later professorial colleague, A. F. Bernard Shaw, the pathologist, Spence spent the academic year 1926–7 as a Rockefeller fellow at Johns Hopkins Hospital, Baltimore, and laid the foundations of many of his American friendships.

On his return to Newcastle he was appointed in January 1928 assistant physician to the Royal Victoria Infirmary, with all the heavy responsibilities of hospital duties, teaching, research, and consultant practice which this involved. The next six years saw the publication of a number of his most important contributions to scientific medicine on such subjects as chronic nephritis in childhood, night blindness due to nutritional deficiencies, and benign tuberculosis in children. He also carried out, at the request of the Medical Research Council, one of the earliest controlled trials in the use of individual drugs. This was concerned with ascertaining the efficiency (which it did) of pure crystalline vitamin D in the treatment of rickets.

In 1933 Spence made his first major excursion into the field of communal and social paediatrics. Newcastle, like the whole of Tyneside, was suffering severely from the economic depression, and there had been press references to the great increase in poverty, sickness, and malnutrition amongst the poorest classes of the city. The Newcastle city health committee accordingly invited Spence to carry out a comparative study of 'The Health and Nutrition of Certain of the Children of Newcastle upon Tyne between the Ages of One and Five Years'. He showed that 36 per cent of the children from 'poor districts of the City . . . were unhealthy or physically unfit, and as a result . . . appeared malnourished'. The fact that he was unable to find this high incidence of malnutrition in the control group of children of better class families suggested that it was due to preventable causes.

Meanwhile at the Babies' Hospital, Spence was developing another aspect of social paediatrics, which at that time was unique in Great Britain. He began admitting mothers to the hospital with their sick children, so that they might nurse them. Spence described it as an advantage to the mother 'to have felt that she has been responsible for her own child's recovery', thereby establishing a new relationship with her child. Already Spence's reputation was growing, and he began to receive invitations to professorial chairs, none of which he accepted as they would have involved his leaving Newcastle and the work to which he felt himself dedicated. He was by now paediatric physician at the Newcastle General Hospital and honorary physician to the Royal Victoria Infirmary.

In 1942, however, the Nuffield Foundation decided to establish a chair of child health in Newcastle, for which Spence was the only possible choice. He accepted gladly, as it gave him greater facilities and opportunities for research, both scientific and sociological, for the organized teaching of paediatrics, and for the study of the field of medical education as a whole.

Although it was created in 1942, wartime conditions prevented the full functioning of the department of child health until 1945. This interval was not without its advantages for from 1940 onwards Spence had been called upon to undertake a number of medical and scientific committee activities for which his background and experience especially fitted him. He

was appointed chairman of the social medicine committee of the Royal College of Physicians (1941), and a member of the medical advisory committee of the Nuffield Provincial Hospitals Trust (1940), the University Grants Committee (1943), and the Medical Research Council (1944). He also gave evidence to the interdepartmental committee on medical schools under the chairmanship of Sir William Goodenough [q.v.], which had been appointed to advise the Government on the steps which should be taken to provide the increased number of doctors required by the proposed reorganization of the country's health services and which reported in 1944. When the National Health Service came into existence in 1948, Spence was one of the original members of the minister of health's general health services council, and its standing medical advisory committee. He was also appointed to the board of governors of his own teaching hospital.

With the completion of the staffing of the department of child health, Spence was able to create something new both in the training of the medical student in the social context of medicine, and in the inclusion of the home as well as the hospital in the medical care of the sick child. Throughout his teaching, account was taken both of the preventive and curative aspects of paediatrics. His many contributions to medical literature about this time included the Bradshaw and Charles West lectures at the Royal College of Physicians on 'The Nature of Disease in Infancy' and 'The Care of Children in Hospital'.

Spence's reputation as a combination of paediatrician, educationist, and philosopher brought many requests for his services as a lecturer and adviser. In this capacity, he visited Belgium, Czechoslovakia, Australia, New Zealand Canada, and the United States. In 1949 he delivered the Cutter lecture at Harvard, taking as his subject the most ambitious of the inquiries which he had inspired in the field of social medicine. The lecture was entitled 'Family Studies in Preventive Paediatrics', but it was essentially a preliminary report on 'A Thousand Families in Newcastle upon Tyne'. This was a long-term study carried out by the department of child health and the Newcastle city health department into the incidence and causation of disease amongst a thousand children born of Newcastle parents in May–June 1947. It ultimately extended ver fifteen years, and became a classic of ocial paediatrics.

In 1952 Spence was again invited to erve on the Medical Research Council. This was at a time when the respective oles of the universities and the medical esearch institutions as regards medical esearch were under review. Spence was ery apprehensive lest the universities play minor part, and at his last appearance at he Council, before his untimely death at Newcastle 26 May 1954, he had vigor-usly expressed himself in their support.

By his contemporaries, Spence was niversally accepted as a wise counsellor, noderate in the presentation of his views, ut nevertheless enthusiastic: a practical-ninded visionary. As a clinician he was n the highest class, and his sensitivity o the needs and fears of patients and arents made him a supremely under-tanding physician, with a whimsical harm which made him a most attractive ersonality. His scientific ability was erhaps overshadowed by his clinical nterests, but as a teacher and leader of ounger men he was exceptional. 'The rst aim of my department' he wrote 'is omradeship, not achievement.' But his chievements were in fact great, and his onstructive and far-sighted aims for British medicine and medical education vere recognized in 1950 by his knighthood.

Throughout his life Spence was a lover f the countryside, a hardy fell walker, nd an experienced mountaineer.

He married Kathleen, daughter of Robert Downie-Leslie in 1920; they had ne son and four daughters.

[*The Purpose and Practice of Medicine*, elected writings of Sir James Spence, with ibliography and memoir, 1960; *British Medical Journal* and *Lancet*, 5 June 1954; ersonal knowledge.]　　　J. A. CHARLES.

SPENCER, LEONARD JAMES (1870–1959), mineralogist and geologist, was born t Worcester 7 July 1870, the eldest son f James Spencer and his wife, Elizabeth Bonser. His father was a schoolmaster who ecame head of the day school department f Bradford Technical College, in which chool his sons were educated. At the ge of sixteen Spencer gained a Royal xhibition to the Royal College of Science, Dublin, where he obtained a first class in hemistry in 1889 and also read geology nder J. P. O'Reilly. Proceeding with a cholarship to Sidney Sussex College, Cambridge, he obtained first classes in oth parts of the natural sciences tripos

(1892–3) and won the Harkness scholar-ship for geology in 1893. At Cambridge he had added mineralogy to his other subjects and the occurrence of a vacancy in the department of mineralogy at the British Museum (Natural History) offered an opportunity which decided his future career. He was successful in the examina-tion for the post and after a few months at Munich studying mineralogy under Paul Groth and petrology under Ernst Weinschenk he took up his appointment on 1 January 1894 and devoted himself heart and soul to mineralogy for the re-mainder of his life.

During his forty-one years at the British Museum, Spencer wrote a great many papers on minerals and on meteorites and earned a high international reputation in those fields. He also translated Max Bauer's *Edelsteinkunde* (1904) and Rein-hard Brauns' *Das Mineralreich* (1908–12) and wrote two useful textbooks, *The World's Minerals* (1911) and *A Key to Precious Stones* (1936). The discovery of meteorite craters in South Australia in 1931 and by H. St. J. B. Philby [q.v.] in Arabia in the following year provided material then new to science, and it fell to Spencer to study it. He published several papers on meteorite craters giving evidence of the very high temperatures produced by the impact of very large meteorites and drawing comparisons between the few known meteorite craters on the earth and the craters on the moon.

Apart from his own publications Spencer made two other contributions to mineralogy. At the British Museum he established the present system of labelling and registering the vast collection of minerals, taking great pains over every detail of the registers, labels, and even the ink employed. At first he did a great part of this work himself and when he suc-ceeded G. T. Prior as keeper of minerals in 1927 his assistants continued on the lines he had laid down. When he retired in 1935 the collection was probably the largest and certainly the best documented collection of minerals in the world.

Spencer's other major contribution lay in the field of mineralogical literature and bibliography. He took over the editorship of the *Mineralogical Magazine* from (Sir) Henry Miers [q.v.] in 1900 and continued as editor for over fifty years, carrying out his duties with meticulous care. In 1920 he voluntarily undertook the preparation and editing of *Mineralogical Abstracts*, a new publication by the Mineralogical

Society. Spencer had already catalogued mineralogical literature for the Royal Society's *Catalogue of Scientific Papers*, 4th series (1884–1900) and for the mineralogy volumes of the *International Catalogue of Scientific Literature* (1901–14). *Mineralogical Abstracts* was intended to preserve continuity with the latter by covering the period from 1915 onwards. For many years Spencer contributed by far the greater part of the abstracts himself, devoting most of his spare time to the work, which he continued long after his retirement from the museum. He retired from the editorship of the *Mineralogical Magazine* and the *Abstracts* in 1955 at the age of eighty-five, but he continued to write occasional papers and to prepare abstracts, particularly on meteorites, almost until the day of his death.

In his early years at the museum Spencer did not travel extensively outside the British Isles, but attendance as a delegate to meetings of the British Association gave him opportunity to travel and collect minerals in the United States and Canada in 1924 and in South Africa, Southern Rhodesia, and South West Africa in 1929. In 1934, although then sixty-four, he took part in an expedition to the Libyan Desert to investigate the site where Colonel P. A. Clayton had discovered the mysterious Libyan Desert glass, a silica glass of unknown origin but thought to have some connection with meteorites.

From his Cambridge undergraduate days Spencer put his work before almost everything else. He worked extremely long hours and allowed himself little relaxation of any kind. Gardening was the only hobby on which he spent much time, and most of his vacations were given up to visiting mines and collecting minerals. His manner was at times brusque and he spoke his mind unhesitatingly but he had a saving sense of humour and a more generous and kindly character than he allowed to appear. He never sought company but he never missed a Mineralogical Society meeting. Visiting mineralogists were always welcome at his London home and to the end of his life he had many friends among mineralogists of many ages and many nations.

Spencer became Sc.D. of Cambridge in 1921. He was elected F.R.S. in 1925, appointed C.B.E. in 1934, awarded the Murchison medal of the Geological Society of London in 1937, and the Roebling medal of the American Mineralogical Society in

1941. He was president of the Mineralogical Society of Great Britain in 1936– and its foreign secretary in 1949–59.

In 1899 Spencer married Edith Mar (died 1954), daughter of Islip J. Close, Mortimer, Berkshire. They had one so and two daughters, the elder of who provided a fund in memory of her fathe to be used for travelling grants to student working in the department of mineralog and petrology at Cambridge and engage on research. Spencer died in Londo 14 April 1959.

[*The Times*, 16 April 1959; *Nature*, 6 Jur 1959; *Mineralogical Magazine*, December 195 March 1956, and September 1959; person knowledge.]　　　W. CAMPBELL SMITH

SPENCER, SIR STANLEY (1891–1959 artist, was born at Cookham-on-Thame Berkshire, 30 June 1891, the seventh so in a family of eleven children of Williar Spencer, an organist and music teache and his wife, Anna Caroline Slack. Hi brother Gilbert was born in the followin year. Spencer had no formal educatio attending only a class which met in corrugated iron building in the Spence garden and was presided over by his siste Annie, who, he said, despaired of him.

In 1907 Lady Boston, who had bee giving Spencer private drawing lesson sent him to the Technical School a Maidenhead. A year later she sent he protégé to the Slade School with intro ductions to Professors Tonks and Brow [qq.v.]. He was accepted but continue to live at home catching an evening trai back—a routine which nourished his gifts his already vivid imagination was roote in Cookham and its surroundings an inhabitants. The subject-matter of hi art was already clear and distinct in hi mind; the Slade developed his powers t express the vision. In 1912 he gained th Melville Nettleship prize (a scholarship and the composition prize for a paintin 'The Nativity'.

Spencer painted a series of memorabl canvases while still a Slade student: 'Tw Girls and a Beehive' (1910), 'John Donn arriving in Heaven' (1911), 'Joachin among the Shepherds' (1912), 'Appl Gatherers' (1912–13), the last of whicl was acquired by the Tate Gallery. In 1912 his last year at the Slade, he began on of his finest paintings, 'Zacharias anc Elizabeth' (1912–13).

Spencer had attained both technica and imaginative maturity while still student. In the introduction he contri

ted in 1955 to the catalogue of the
te Gallery retrospective exhibition of
s work, Spencer himself commented on
hat he considered the best period of his
interly life. He described the 'state of
reness' he was in before the war of
14–18, a state which after the war
ntinued to about 1922–3 'when I did
e Betrayal. At this time I did the series
drawings for the Burghclere Memo-
al and also the drawing for the 1927
esurrection. So that all the painting I
as to do from 1922 to 1932 was settled
nearly every detail: ten years of solid
liss were ahead of me. But I knew in
922–3 that I was changing or losing grip
something. I was, I feared, forsaking
e vision and I was filled with consterna-
on. All the ability I had was dependent
n that vision.'

The vision he lived with was a vision of
eaven in Cookham's streets and of the
cidents of Christ's life, with which the
mily Bible-readings had enkindled his
nagination, as enacted there; it was a
ision in which Cookham scenes and
iblical stories were simultaneously in
ocus and interpenetrated. This private
nd ecstatic way of seeing so engrossed
im that even in so large (and so vivid)
family circle he lived much within him-
elf, and when not painting his 'vision'
as walking alone along the river or
round the village seeing the everyday
hings in which he delighted all the more
harply for their irradiation in a light of
eaven.

These were the seminal years of
pencer's career. This trance-like life was
nterrupted by the war. He joined the
oyal Army Medical Corps in 1915 and
as sent to Macedonia in the summer of
916. In 1917 he volunteered for the
nfantry (the 17th Royal Berkshires), also
n the Macedonian theatre, and served
here until demobilization.

While still in Macedonia he had been
commissioned to do a war painting, and
this he carried out on his return home—
'Travoys arriving with Wounded' (Imperial War Museum). He also finished
'Swan Upping' (Tate Gallery), which he
had left two-thirds completed four years
earlier.

To the years 1919–23 belong either in
execution or in conception most of his
finest and also most mature works: paintings such as 'The Robing of Christ' and
'The Disrobing of Christ', of 1922 (Tate
Gallery); the drawings for the great 'Resurrection, Cookham' which he painted in

1923–7—the completed picture was exhibited in Spencer's first one-man exhibition
in 1927 and bought by Sir Joseph (later
Lord) Duveen [q.v.] and presented to the
Tate Gallery; and the drawings for one
of his 'chapels in the air', which subsequently became the Burghclere murals.
For in 1926–7 Mr. and Mrs. J. L. Behrend
built a war memorial chapel at Burghclere in Berkshire, in commemoration of
their relative Harry Willowby Sandham,
in order to make it possible for Spencer to
realize this cycle of drawings. The painting of these murals occupied him without
interruption from 1927 to 1932 and they
are his most impressive achievement.

In 1925 Spencer had married Hilda
Anne Carline. Two daughters were born:
in 1925 and 1930. The marriage was a
failure (his wife showed progressive
symptoms of mental ill health) and by
the time Spencer returned to Cookham in
1932 it had broken. But he continued to
see Hilda frequently until her death in
1950 and his love for her remained the one
enduring bond of his life. In the early
thirties he grew acquainted with Patricia
Preece, whom he married in 1937 after
divorce from Hilda.

This new emotional relationship in
his life was largely responsible for a
radical change in his painting. He now
had two women to provide for, in addition
to two daughters (one of whom was cared
for by relatives). Until this period in his
life he had been virtually maintained by
friends and patrons (from 1919 to 1923,
for example, he had lived in the houses of
friends), but now, back in Cookham, he
had to stand on his own feet and to earn
all the money he could: 'I was making
big demands on life at the time', he subsequently wrote, 'and had to paint far
more than I would have wished.' He
turned out what he called his 'pot-boilers',
landscapes and flower-pieces, at the rate
of one a week or every ten days. These
pictures, rendered in pre-Raphaelite exactitude, are often beautiful, sometimes
mechanical, but they afforded no joy of
creation to their maker.

Moreover, since (according to Spencer)
the relationship with Patricia had no
physical fulfilment, his sexuality sought
expression in erotic paintings and in
erotic writings in the form of a diary-
letter to Hilda. The paintings had little
appeal and were largely unsaleable.

The thirties were years of artistic
frustration for Spencer, although he painted some figure-pieces which brought him

further acclaim and were bought by many art galleries both in the provinces and in London. Among his best paintings of these years are 'Sarah Tubb and the Heavenly Visitors' (1933); 'Separating Fighting Swans' (1933) and 'Hilda, Unity and Dolls' (1937), both at the City Art Gallery, Leeds; 'St. Francis and the Birds' (1935); and 'The Cedar Tree, Cookham' (1934–5). Among the erotic paintings were a number of nudes of Patricia Preece, some of which were bought by W. A. Evill. 'Promenade of Women' (1937) and a series entitled 'The Beatitudes of Love' (1937–8) were among Spencer's own favourites of the period.

In 1935 he resigned from the Royal Academy, to which he had been elected as an associate member three years before, on its rejection of two of his pictures for the summer exhibition. He rejoined as a full R.A. in 1950. In 1938 twenty-two of his paintings were exhibited at the Venice Biennale, at which he had also been represented six years earlier.

Although he was prolific of landscapes and flower-pieces and also of portraits, and although they sold well, Spencer was sued by Hilda on a number of occasions during the thirties for arrears of maintenance. Even the tiny sum of fifty shillings a week for herself and their daughter Unity was not forthcoming. Spencer himself lived on about forty shillings a week or less. The shock of appearing in court together with years of over-work on his pot-boilers brought on, in 1938, a breakdown of several months' duration, during which he was quite unable to paint at all. At this time his dealer and friend, Dudley Tooth, however, agreed to take over the management of his finances, paying a weekly allowance to each of the dependants as well as a small sum to Spencer himself. He also paid off the many debts contracted in the thirties and the arrears of income-tax.

The tribulations of these years, when Spencer was also without a home and (as he said) felt himself a vagrant, were the inspiration for a series of small paintings of 'Christ in the Wilderness'; four of the series belong to 1939, two to 1940, one to 1942, while the eighth and last was painted in 1953. The first of them was made in lodgings in London, for in the autumn of 1938 Spencer left Cookham on account of personal unhappiness. He had never lived with his second wife.

In 1940 Spencer was commissioned by the war artists advisory committee to paint pictures of shipyards. He beg work at Port Glasgow, making visits the shipyards for studies for larger pain ings until the end of the war. While Port Glasgow the sight of a cemetery cemeteries were always powerful imagin tive stimulants for him—inspired him another series of resurrection canvase he painted eight in all. It had been h earnest wish that the complete cycle mig hang together, but the pictures we bought separately: 'Resurrection: Tid ing' (1945) by the City Art Galler Birmingham; 'Resurrection: Reunio (1945) by the Aberdeen Art Gallery 'Resurrection with Raising of Jairus Daughter' (1947) by the Southampto Art Gallery; 'Resurrection: the Hill Sion' (1946) by the Harris Museum an Art Gallery, Preston; 'Resurrection: Por Glasgow' (1947–50) by the Tate Gallery.

In 1945 Spencer returned to his nativ Cookham and remained there until hi death, devoting his time principally to a enormous cycle of about sixty drawings o 'Christ preaching at Cookham Regatta and later to the painting of it. He worke on these canvases until too weak to con tinue. Another huge painting of his las years, an altar-piece in praise of Hilda was also not completed by the time of hi death.

A retrospective exhibition of Spencer' work (68 paintings and 27 drawings) wa held at Temple Newsam House, Leeds, ir 1947, and another (83 paintings) at the Tate Gallery in 1955. He was appointed C.B.E. in 1950 and knighted in 1959. In 1958 the vicar of Cookham organized an exhibition of Spencer's paintings in Cookham church and vicarage; it drew large crowds and, set in his own beloved Cookham, gave particular gratification to Spencer himself. The following winter he fell ill and he died in hospital at Cliveden 14 December 1959 and is buried in Cookham churchyard.

Stanley Spencer was the outstanding— the most potent and fertile—imaginative painter of the English-speaking people in the first half of the twentieth century. As he himself often said and wrote, the quality of his imaginative work deteriorated after the twenties; after the completion of the Burghclere murals both the intensity and the focused and integrated unity of inspiration which animated his early works and fused into one his dual vision of the commonplace and of the divine consistently evaded him. How this came about has been suggested above,

t it may be added that Spencer was in
 sense strongly rooted in a religious
th nor had he any clear or reasoned
nvictions, so that in the pressures of life
s early poetic empathy with the New
stament faltered and waned and the
al vision was no longer possible. Cook-
m became no longer the suburbs of
aven but suburbs; the later Resurrec-
ns are just vast conversation-pieces
ammed with anecdote. His figure paint-
g, including much which was in intention
ligious, came to be an expression of
otesquerie and whimsy. The ordinary
ings and objects and events of life he
ved with passion, and in his painting he
anted to show them as being, in what
ey are, heavenly and somehow divine
-this is why his Resurrections are
sistently filled with incidents of trivial
ily life—but it was an aim which in
e second half of his life he could no
nger successfully achieve.

Spencer's early paintings were not only
rong in their draughtsmanship and
omposition; they were distinguished by
ainterly qualities as well. Later on,
owever, he came to take delight only in
e drawing and in the composition of his
ictures. With the painting of them he
as, he admitted, bored. His paintings,
erefore, came to be coloured drawings,
onceived as drawings, rather than paint-
gs conceived in terms of paint. It was
nother element in the fragmentation of
is imagination in consequence of which,
 place of a dominant and unifying in-
ensity, there is an evenly distributed
tensity over his themes, so that every-
hing is illumined but nothing is picked
ut and the whole is but the sum of its
arts.

It was Spencer's proud claim to be an
rdinary Cookham villager. 'My mother
vas just a little village biddy.' In appear-
nce, even to the end of his life, he was
ke a village urchin. So tiny was he that
is clothes were always too large, but as he
uite often wore his suit over his pyjamas,
vhich, even so, peered out at ankle and
vrist, this was an advantage.

His hair, unparted, hung in an unkempt
ringe over his eyes. His glasses he usually
ought at Woolworths. They did not fit
nd slid to the end of his nose, so that, to
eep them in balance, Spencer had a habit
f tilting his head slightly backwards.

In repose his features were without
istinction; his eyes looked tired and
leepy. When he was aroused, however, by
nthusiasm (over his own work or imagin-

ings) or by anger, the eyes widened and
glittered. His speech, which was ordinarily
a village diction uttered in a squeaky
nasal voice, would then become resonant
with language cast in biblical words and
phrases. On such occasions—and they were
very numerous—he was a fierce, prophet-
like presence, and a compelling speaker.

Spencer drew and painted innumerable
self-portraits. The first, painted in 1913,
hangs in the Tate Gallery. The central,
nude, figure in 'The Resurrection, Cookham', also in the Tate, is the painter
himself. The last self-portrait, and the
finest, was painted in 1959 and became the
property of Mrs. Dennis Smith.

[*Stanley Spencer, a Retrospective Exhibition*,
Tate Gallery, 1955; *Stanley Spencer: Resurrection Pictures (1945–1950)*, 1951; Gilbert
Spencer, *Stanley Spencer*, 1961; John Rothenstein, *Modern English Painters*, vol. ii, 1956;
Elizabeth Rothenstein, *Stanley Spencer*, 1962;
private information; personal knowledge.]

ELIZABETH ROTHENSTEIN.

SPRY, CONSTANCE (1886–1960), artist
in flower arrangement, was born in Derby
5 December 1886, the only daughter and
eldest of the six children of George
Fletcher, railway clerk, later assistant
secretary to the department of agriculture
and technical instruction in Ireland, and
his wife, Henrietta Maria Clark. She was
educated at Alexandra School and College,
Dublin, and in early life her natural talent
and rare skill with flowers were already
clearly evident. But in her teens her sympathy and enthusiasm were devoted to
helping Lady Aberdeen [q.v.] in her work
for the children in South Ireland, especially against tuberculosis. During the
war of 1914–18 she was head of women's
staff at the department of aircraft production of the Ministry of Munitions and later
she was principal of the London County
Council day continuation school in
Homerton.

If primarily a lecturer, her totally fresh
approach to the use of flowers, their leaves,
branches, and fruits, for decorative purposes, soon established her world-wide
reputation after she opened a shop in
London under the name of Constance
Spry. The artist in her was irrepressible,
so that for royal occasions and society
functions, when sheer beauty matched with
imagination and a break-away from the
ordinary were required, the name of
Constance Spry came uppermost. Her exquisite handling of flowers was seen at the
weddings of the Duke of Gloucester and
the Princess Elizabeth. For the latter's

coronation she was made adviser to the minister of works; did the flowers for the Abbey annexe and decorations on parts of the royal route; and in Parliament Square she and her staff actually planted all the plants sent over from various parts of the Commonwealth. For her services she was appointed O.B.E. (1953).

Prior to the war of 1939–45 Constance Spry had started a school of floristry and flower decoration. A suggestion from students that when it was reopened cookery should be added to the curriculum proved impracticable; but with her friend Rosemary Hume, a professional *cordon-bleu* cook and teacher, the Cordon Bleu Cookery School was started in London. Later, at Winkfield Place, near Windsor, a residential school was established for young people to learn all aspects of running a home efficiently.

Constance Spry wrote twelve books on flower arrangement, entertaining, and cookery; completed a correspondence course on flower arrangement; designed many flower vases; and for some years designed floral carpets. As a lecturer and demonstrator she was well known in Britain, the United States, and Australia. She had a singularly easy manner, a lively wit, and her enthusiasm for what she was saying and doing just bubbled over; her vitality was so contagious that those who heard her would not want to miss a word and right away would want to follow her example. She was eternally young in heart and mind and from this stemmed her exceptional capacity for inspiring and handling the younger generation. To her fingertips she was essentially a woman—of rare and original talent. At flower shows she was an exacting, fair, and stimulating judge. She did much to encourage the Flower Club movement, while her work for the Royal Gardeners' Orphan Fund raised considerable money for children in need. After her death, at Winkfield Place, 3 January 1960, this charity set up a special Constance Spry Fund to her memory. A pastel by M. Forestier-Walker is in the possession of the family.

[Private information; personal knowledge.]
JULIA CAIRNS.

SQUIRE, SIR JOHN COLLINGS (1884–1958), poet and man of letters, was born at Plymouth 2 April 1884, the only son of Jonas Squire, veterinary surgeon, and his wife, Elizabeth Rowe Collings. He was educated at Plymouth Corporation Grammar School, Blundell's School, Tiverton,

and was a scholar of St. John's Colleg Cambridge, where he obtained a second history (1905). He was prominent in t Fabian Society but his love of literatur especially of poetry, strove with his po tical ardour, although in later years stood unsuccessfully for Parliament, co testing Cambridge University for Labor in 1918 and Brentford and Chiswick 1924 for the Liberals. His first boo *Poems and Baudelaire Flowers* (1909 made little impression, but signalled h principal interest.

After working as a journalist in Pl mouth and London, Squire in 1913 be came literary editor of the newly founde *New Statesman*. His critical essays, whic he signed with humorous melanchol 'Solomon Eagle', became popular. Thre volumes of these papers, entitled *Books General* (1918–21), showed that few auth ors of importance had escaped him. H wrote for the common reader. Throughou his life he contributed regular causeries weekly journals and now and then collec ted them in such volumes as *Sunda Mornings* (1930) from the *Observer*. Hi liking for witty company perhaps helpe in his production of parodies, which als won him a name; generous as he was b nature, he could write them cuttingly referring nevertheless to 'a not wholl admirable art'. His *Collected Parodie* appeared in 1921.

A small book of poems by Squire calle *The Survival of the Fittest* (1916) was re printed several times, and calls for mentio as being perhaps the earliest poetic protes against the war to win much attention i England. It included the epigram, 'Go heard the embattled nations sing an shout', which was quoted by many wh did not know the name of the author. I 1917 the other side of Squire's poetica character was shown in a visionary poem still remarkable, in which 'the exotic struggles with the homely', entitled *Th Lily of Malud*.

On the return of peace, Squire in 191 set up a nobly printed monthly magazine with a title revived from the eighteent century: the *London Mercury*. Its contents were well varied, and the first volume opened, editorial greetings apart, with poems by Thomas Hardy [q.v.] and others and closed with an estimate of the collec ted scientific papers of an ingenious Vic torian, John Henry Poynting [q.v.]. The encouragement of the poets in the new magazine never failed. In the original series the *London Mercury* lasted unti

34 by which time Squire, despite his
tholicity and editorial vivacity, had
'ended many intellectuals, not least by
s unbusinesslike methods.

After the war Squire also founded a
icket club, 'The Invalids', whose mem-
rs were usually men concerned with
erature and many of whom were sur-
vors from the battlefield. This meant
ten a day in the country, and Jack
quire at his happiest. In the intervals of
e game he might touch on the desira-
lity of a minister of the fine arts, and the
ondon Mercury was part of his campaign
r a reunion in English life of the useful
id the beautiful. From 1922 to 1928 he
as chairman of the Architecture Club;
s distinctions included the F.S.A. and
ie honorary A.R.I.B.A.; such facts
iow his outlook. His zeal for the arts in
tion, for design and colour in our prac-
cal setting, was one of the makings of
is magazine. In another way his enthu-
iasm resulted in his many anthologies of
oetry old and new, serious and light-
earted. They were his own choice, of
ourse, yet they were intended for general
rculation; the most influential probably
as his series of selections from contem-
orary poets, ultimately in a single volume
1927). He also edited A Book of Women's
'erse for the Oxford University Press
1921) and the Cambridge Book of Lesser
'oets (1927). His labours were eased by
is exceptional memory; he had merely to
ead and like a poem once to have it in his
aind for life. He was also continually
diting or introducing volumes of prose or
erse by authors from the poet J. E.
Flecker [q.v.] onwards.

In 1926 his dramatization, with J. L.
Balderston, of The Sense of the Past by
Ienry James [q.v.] as a play in three acts
alled Berkeley Square, had a considerable
uccess. In the following year Squire took
part in the first broadcast running com-
nentary on the boat race. He was by now
a celebrity and in 1933 he was knighted.
After leaving the London Mercury he con-
inued as a reader for Macmillans and in
1937 became a reviewer for the Illustrated
London News. He presided over the later
additions to the English Men of Letters
series; and in 1937 stood forth as host in
a volume on cheeses, Cheddar Gorge, his
special topic therein being Stilton. His
professional and private life, however, had
become increasingly disorganized: he had
left home and was dependent on the care
of friends and the stimulus or sedative of
alcohol.

Still, Squire was naturally what he
modestly hoped to be accounted in years
to come: a poet with his own conceptions.
In the thirties he replied to the question
why did he not publish more: 'Oh,...the
world is too much with us.' But, so long as
his crowding avocations left him energy,
Squire was a poet of some power. It is
likely that 'The Rugger Match' was the
first noteworthy poem in English on football; 'Rivers', 'The Moon', 'The Birds',
were resourceful meditations. In American
Poems (1923) a long interpretation of
Chicago struck English readers. Later on,
quieter and shorter pieces still had a note
which may be called Squire's private tune.
His Collected Poems were published in 1959
with an introduction by (Sir) John
Betjeman.

Squire, eminent to the last among the
critics of current books week by week, became patriarchal in appearance, and the
cricket captain's romantic Devonian face
was disguised with a grey beard. The
utterances from that visage were more
fragmentary than of old, but decisive
and entertaining. He is affectionately portrayed by A. G. Macdonell in England their
England (1933) which includes a hilarious
account of the Invalids at cricket.

In 1908 Squire married Eileen Harriet
Anstruther, daughter of the Rev. Anthony
Anstruther Wilkinson; they had three
sons, the youngest of whom was killed on
active service in 1943, and one daughter.
He died at Rushlake Green, Sussex, 20
December 1958; his widow in 1970.

A portrait by John Mansbridge is in the
National Portrait Gallery and a drawing
by (Sir) William Rothenstein is reproduced
in Twenty-four Portraits, 2nd series, 1923.

[Patrick Howarth, Squire: Most Generous
of Men, 1963; private information; personal
knowledge.]   EDMUND BLUNDEN.

STACPOOLE, HENRY DE VERE
(1863–1951), novelist, was born at Kingstown, county Dublin, in April 1863, the
youngest son of the Rev. William Church
Stacpoole, who conducted Kingstown
School, and his wife, Charlotte Augusta
Mountjoy, of Sally Park, Tallaght. His
mother, like his father, was of Irish origin,
but she had been born and spent the first
twelve years of her life in Canada. Stacpoole travelled widely with his mother as
a boy and was then sent to Malvern
College. He subsequently studied medicine
at St. George's and St. Mary's hospitals,
London, and, after qualifying in 1891,
made several voyages as a ship's doctor,

during which he went all over the world and was able to indulge his great love of the sea and to accumulate experience which he later used in his novels.

Stacpoole first appeared in print with a poem in *Belgravia*, an outcome of his youthful friendship with Mrs. Pearl Craigie (q.v., John Oliver Hobbes). In the nineties he was friendly with many of the writers and artists of the *Yellow Book* period, including Aubrey Beardsley [q.v.]. His earliest novels, such as *The Intended* (1894), *Pierrot!* (1896), and *Death, the Knight and the Lady*, a ghost story (1897), reflect the preoccupations of that period. *The Doctor* (1899)—the first of his next group of novels which included *The Bourgeois* (1901) and *The Lady-Killer* (1902)—showed a considerable advance, and this portrait of an old-time practitioner remains an attractive social study. Stacpoole was not financially successful with these novels, however, or with some excursions into farce, but his perseverance was amply rewarded when he produced two novels with exotic and tropical settings, *The Crimson Azaleas* (1907), set in Japan, and *The Blue Lagoon* (1908).

A romantic story of two children shipwrecked on a Pacific island, *The Blue Lagoon* at once captured public attention and was reprinted twenty-three times in the next twelve years. It takes its place in an historical perspective along with *Peter Pan*, Maeterlinck's *The Blue Bird*, and certain tales of Algernon Blackwood [q.v.] as representative of an Edwardian vein of childhood fantasy and sentiment; but the novel was distinguished by genuine charm in the writing and a poet's delight in communicating the wonders of a tropical island. *The Blue Lagoon* was made into an episodic play produced at the Prince of Wales's Theatre, London, in 1920, and was also filmed. Stacpoole followed up its success in a long series of books of romantic tropical appeal, such words as blue, coral, pearls, reef, and beach appearing significantly in their titles; and as late as 1933 there was a market for *The Blue Lagoon Omnibus*.

It would be a mistake to think of Stacpoole as unduly obsessed by his best-selling tropical formula. *The Street of the Flute-Player* (1912) was set in Athens and *Monsieur de Rochefort* (1914) in eighteenth-century France. *Goblin Market* (1927) was a tender story of the Isle of Wight. He published several volumes of simple uncomplicated verse about England, the sea, and the countryside, which, though often

rather thin, had its effective moments; also translated Sappho and Villon, a produced a popular biography of Vill (1916).

Many of his fifty or so novels are hard to be taken seriously, but Stacpoole w a skilful and sensitive craftsman with real gift for describing natural scenery an an easy flow of humour at his comman His chatty discursive autobiographie *Men and Mice* (1942) and *More Men an Mice* (1945), do not show him at his be as a writer, but they give a good idea the man. Tall, broad, and handsome, had a happy disposition, typical Iris geniality mingling with an occasional das of hot temper. He found great joy flowers, and during his later years he zes fully took up the cause of the sea birds an the problem of the pollution of the se with oil.

In 1907 Stacpoole married Margare Ann, daughter of William Robson, Tynemouth. They lived for some years a Stebbing, Essex, where Stacpoole was justice of the peace, but later moved t Cliff Dene, Bonchurch, Isle of Wight. Afte his wife's death in 1934 he presented pond at the foot of his garden, a haunt c rare birds, to Ventnor as a memorial t her. In 1938 he married his first wife' sister, Florence, who survived him. Ther were no children of either marriage Stacpoole died in Shanklin 12 Apri 1951.

[*The Times*, 13 April 1951; private informa tion.]   DEREK HUDSON

STANLEY, SIR HERBERT JAMES (1872–1955), colonial administrator, wa born in Manchester 25 July 1872, the so of Sigismund Sonnenthal (later Stanley merchant, and his wife, Anna Rose Meyer He was educated at Eton, where he wor the Prince Consort's German prize and the English essay prize; and at Balliol College, Oxford, where he obtained a third class in classical honour moderations (1893) and graduated in 1897. He retained throughout his life a strong affection for his old school and college.

Stanley entered public life by holding a series of private secretaryships: to the British minister at Dresden (1897–1902); to the first lord of the Admiralty (1906–8); to the lord president of the Council (1908– 10); and, finally, to Lord Gladstone [q.v.], whom he accompanied to South Africa on his appointment as the first governor-general of the Union. In 1913 Stanley was ade official secretary to the governor-neral; and in 1915 he became resident mmissioner for Rhodesia.

In 1918 a new post of imperial secretary as created to help the governor-general his special responsibilities as high com-issioner for the British territories in uth Africa. Stanley was selected and rried out the duties with conspicuous ccess, earning a particularly warm mmendation from Prince Arthur of onnaught [q.v.] for his skill in negotiat-g the complex constitutional settlement y which the British Government took er from the British South Africa Com-any responsibility for the administration f Northern and Southern Rhodesia and stablished the two territories as, respec-vely, a British protectorate and a self-overning colony. The value of Stanley's ork and experience was fittingly recog-ized by his appointment as the first overnor of Northern Rhodesia in 1924.

Stanley was a less obvious choice for the overnorship of Ceylon when it became acant in 1927. Doubts were expressed in ome quarters as to the wisdom of sending o the 'premier colony' a governor whose xperience was confined to Southern frica and who was quite unacquainted ith the technique of administering an riental country. In fact, the historian nay well conclude that Stanley's four ears in Ceylon, although in a sense but n interlude in a career otherwise con-erned entirely with Africa, were decisive ot only for Ceylon but for the whole uture of the British colonial empire.

Ceylon had reached a stage of politi-al, social, and economic development at vhich the traditional system of crown olony administration had ceased to be cceptable, but no provision existed for urther constitutional advance. The British Government sent out an inter-party com-nission, under Lord Donoughmore [q.v.], o examine the problem, and in its report of 1928 the commission proposed a bold cheme for a new constitution giving the olony internal self-government based upon universal adult suffrage. The issue vas highly controversial: the political parties and racial and religious groups in the island all disagreed with various parts of the plan, but disagreed radically amongst themselves upon what amend-ments were desirable. Stanley had the extremely difficult and exacting task of carrying out long and patient discussions and negotiations with the numerous par-ties and factions, of evaluating the possi-bilities of the situation, of advising the British Government on the action to be taken, and of persuading the Ceylonese to accept that Government's decision when made. In the result, the Donoughmore scheme, with only minor modifications, was accepted by the Ceylon legislative council and remained the basis of the island's government until 1947. Under it the ground was prepared for indepen-dence; and, once Ceylon had established the principle that a British colony could become an independent State, it became inevitable that other territories would follow suit. Had Stanley's negotiations broken down, the outcome might have been very different.

In 1931 Stanley returned to South Africa as the first high commissioner for the United Kingdom. He combined the dip-lomatic functions of this post with ad-ministrative responsibility for the British high commission territories which had previously rested with the governor-general. In 1935 he moved to his last official post: the governorship of Southern Rhodesia. He was due to retire in 1937, but so greatly was he valued that his term of office was extended until 1941.

Stanley then settled in Cape Town and continued to take an active interest in South African affairs. He was chief com-missioner of Boy Scouts in South Africa, sub-prior of the Order of St. John, presi-dent of Toc H, and a director of De Beers Consolidated Mines, Ltd., and of the Anglo American Corporation of South Africa.

Dignified and impressive in person, Stanley was also sociable and a well-known figure at race meetings and other sporting events. He was immensely hard working and conscientious, and had a genuine con-cern for the welfare of the less privileged members of the community. Although of Jewish origin, he was himself a devout Anglican churchman.

In 1918 Stanley married Reniera, daughter of Henry Cloete, C.M.G., of Wynberg. She was appointed D.B.E. in 1941 and died in 1950. There were two sons and two daughters of the marriage.

Stanley was appointed C.M.G. in 1913, promoted K.C.M.G. in 1924, and G.C.M.G. in 1930. He died in Cape Town 5 June 1955. A portrait by a Ceylonese artist was added to the collection of governors' portraits at Queen's House, Colombo.

[*The Times*, 6 June 1955; private informa-tion; personal knowledge.]

CHARLES JEFFRIES.

STANSFELD, MARGARET (1860–1951), pioneer in physical training for women, was born in London 10 March 1860, the third of the six children of James Stansfeld (or Stansfield), baker, and his wife, Mary, daughter of James Fallon, a clerk. Their father died young and their education was guided and controlled chiefly by their mother. From a day school in Bloomsbury Margaret Stansfeld and her eldest sister went as pupil teachers with their head-mistress when she took charge of a large school under the School Board. Later the Board appointed as lecturer in physical education Miss Bergman (afterwards Mme Osterberg) whose pioneer college at Hampstead Margaret Stansfeld eventually joined. Her duties involved a good deal of travelling to schools outside London and in 1887 she began to teach at Bedford High School which had been founded five years earlier. The gymnasium was a shed with very little apparatus and games were played in the gravel playground until Margaret Stansfeld's immense enthusiasm brought about the acquisition of a proper playing field and the building of a fine gymnasium.

In 1903 Margaret Stansfeld, with six students resident in one house, founded the Bedford Physical Training College which by the time of her retirement had grown to twelve houses accommodating a hundred and fifty students. From the beginning the college was recognized as one of the principal centres of physical education in the country because of the thoroughness of the training, the good conditions for teaching practice, and the excellence of the staff. Physical education to Margaret Stansfeld meant a way of life, and the training was disciplined, varied, and sound. She was a woman of brilliant intellect, forceful personality, and immeasurable generosity who inculcated in her pupils her own wide outlook and regard for the deepest values. She believed that in education the child should take precedence over the subject taught, and health education and child psychology were important parts of the curriculum. She laid stress on an erect posture, control and precision, good balance and rhythm, for she sought a harmonious development of the whole body. Hitherto physical training had implied over-developed muscles, and gymnastics had been no more than 'physical jerks'. The college first introduced into this country modern 'educational dance' which is now widely taught in Britain.

Margaret Stansfeld was appointed O.B.E. in 1939. She was a founder member of the Ling Association of Teachers of Physical Education and its vice-president or president continuously from 1901 until 1920. She was also presented with the Swedish 'Grand-titre honorofique de la Fédération Internationale de Gymnastique Ling'. On her retirement in 194? she went to live at Berkhamsted. Two years later the sudden death of her successor brought her back to the college for several weeks. She died at Bedford 28 June 1951. The portrait of her which hangs in the college was painted by Arthur Mill? from a photograph.

[Private information; personal knowledge.]
                                    K. M. WESTAWAY

STANSGATE, first VISCOUNT (1877–1960), parliamentarian. [See BENN, WILLIAM WEDGWOOD.]

STAPLEDON, SIR (REGINALD) GEORGE (1882–1960), pioneer of grassland science, was born in Northam, Devon 22 September 1882. A member of a large family he was the youngest son of William Stapledon, a man with marine interests and his wife, Mary Clibbett. He was educated at the United Services College, Westward Ho!, and Emmanuel College, Cambridge, where he obtained a second class in part i of the natural sciences tripos in 1904. After two years in the Mediterranean as representative of the family business, Stapledon was invalided home, a turning-point in his career. He became interested in agriculture and spent another year at Cambridge devoting his time to the biological sciences and particularly the ecological aspects of herbage flora. In 1910 he joined the staff of the Royal Agricultural College, Cirencester, and during the dry summer of 1911 he made an intensive study of the spread of wild white clover on the Cotswolds. From that time onwards he became not only a scientist but also a philosopher, enthusiastically interested in the part which white clover could play in the improvement of pastures and still more in building up the fertility of the soil.

In 1912 Stapledon went to Aberystwyth as advisory officer in agricultural botany at the University College of Wales. During the war of 1914–18 he spent much time in London with the food production department of the Board of Agriculture, where his chief aim became the provision of better seed, free from weeds and of a reliable 'type'. This eventually led to the

ablishment of the Seed Testing Station
ich Stapledon himself directed during
initial temporary phase in London
fore it transferred to the National
stitute of Agricultural Botany in
mbridge.

Whilst this transfer was in progress
apledon in 1919 received another call
om Wales, to start an entirely new ven-
re in the form of the Welsh Plant Breed-
g Station at Aberystwyth, where he
mained until 1942. As director of this
ation and through his versatile pen,
apledon drew the attention of research
orkers, farmers, and politicians through-
it the Commonwealth to the tremendous
rt which grassland has to play in the
eding of the people. Through the efforts
his team of workers he gave farmers new
 d improved varieties of grasses, clovers,
d oats, all of which were designated as
e 'S' strains. Many of these became the
isic and standard varieties in use
roughout the temperate areas within
e Commonwealth, particularly in New
ealand.

Stapledon soon gained an international
putation as the greatest authority on
rassland development, and in 1937 the
rassland research workers from thirty-
ght countries paid him their tribute by
ecting him president of the Fourth
iternational Grassland Congress held that
ear in Britain with Aberystwyth as the
enue. In 1939 he was knighted and in the
me year elected F.R.S.

During the war of 1939-45 Stapledon
gain threw himself wholeheartedly into
ie problems of food supply and particu-
irly the improvement of hill pastures to
place the lowland areas turned over to
rable cropping. Accordingly in 1942 he
elinquished his position at Aberystwyth
o start another research station at
)rayton, Stratford on Avon, devoted ex-
lusively to the improvement of grassland,
specially in the most difficult areas of
3ritain. There he was able to put into
peration all the modern techniques result-
ng from his experimental work, a great
pportunity which he appreciated and
njoyed as director until he retired in 1946,
y which time he had impressed upon the
government the need for tackling grass-
and research on a totally different scale,
vith a far bigger station and improved
acilities. That dream materialized as the
Grassland Research Station at Hurley,
3erkshire, where it had been arranged for
he foundation stone to be laid by Staple-
lon in person. Unfortunately the break-

down in his health made this impossible
but the tribute remains, and through the
medium of his portrait, by Allan Gwynne-
Jones, which hangs in the main hall at
Hurley there will always be a reminder of
the true foundation to grassland science
laid by Stapledon.

The most notable feature of his personality was his enthusiasm for all he undertook. He was a great pioneer and his
success was due in large measure to the
infectious way he managed to make his
colleagues share in his enthusiasm. In the
formation of the British Grassland Society
Stapledon took a leading part and he became its first president in 1945.

In addition to many scientific papers
mainly dealing with ley farming, Stapledon
published several books including *A Tour
in Australia and New Zealand* (1928), *The
Land: Now and Tomorrow* (1935), *The
Plough-up Policy and Ley Farming* (1939),
The Way of the Land (1943), and *Disraeli
and the New Age* (1943). Among the
honours conferred upon him was the gold
medal of the Royal Agricultural Society
of England and an honorary life membership of the Royal Highland and Agricultural Society of Scotland.

Stapledon was a keen golfer, regularly
enjoying his round or two each week. In
this, as well as in all his travels, he was
accompanied by his devoted wife, Doris
Wood (died 1965), daughter of Thomas
Wood Bourne, whom he married in 1913.
They had no children. Stapledon died in
Bath 16 September 1960.

[Sir John Russell in *Biographical Memoirs
of Fellows of the Royal Society*, vol. vii, 1961;
Robert Waller, *Prophet of the New Age*, 1962;
personal knowledge.]   MARTIN JONES.

STEED, HENRY WICKHAM (1871-
1956), editor of *The Times*, was born at
Long Melford, Suffolk, 10 October 1871,
the son of Joshua George Steed, solicitor's
clerk, and his wife, Fanny Wickham. He
was educated at Sudbury Grammar School
and a cycling accident on the eve of the
examination prevented his entry into the
Civil Service. Instead he went into a City
office, but in 1891 he heard J. A. Spender
[q.v.] lecture at Toynbee Hall on old-age
pensions and submitted a report which
was published in the *Pall Mall Gazette*.
This turned his thoughts to journalism
and he decided to study economics and
sociology at German and French universities. From Berlin he sent reports to
Dalziel's news agency. In 1893 he moved
to Paris to study history at the Sorbonne

and in 1895 an interview with Millerand which he contributed to the *Westminster Gazette* brought from Joseph Pulitzer an invitation to act as his Paris correspondent. In one day he interviewed seven of the leading French economic authorities, monometallists and bimetallists, and his remarkable memory enabled him to write their statements without having taken a single note. This so impressed Pulitzer that he sent Steed back to Germany to obtain the opinion of German currency experts.

Steed became *Times* correspondent in Berlin in 1896 and made his mark by his detection of the authorship of an anonymous article in the *Hamburger Nachrichten* which revealed the secret treaty of re-insurance which until 1890 had existed between Germany and Russia and had been concluded behind the back of Germany's partners in the Triple Alliance. Steed was alone in Germany in immediately attributing the disclosure to Bismarck. In 1897 he was appointed *Times* correspondent in Rome and in 1902 transferred to Vienna. When he returned to London in 1913 he published his book *The Hapsburg Monarchy* based on the very wide knowledge which he had acquired during his time in Austria.

In January 1914 Steed was appointed head of the foreign department of *The Times* by Lord Northcliffe [q.v.] who declared that he would not be susceptible to the German propaganda which, according to Northcliffe, had gained considerable influence over the British Government and some sections of the press. Northcliffe and Steed were convinced that Berlin was striving to drive a wedge between England and France. After the assassination at Sarajevo at the end of June, Steed felt that the crime might be used by the military party in Vienna as an excuse for an attack on Serbia, and in a series of leading articles warned that this would end only with disaster to both the Central Powers. It fell to Steed, as foreign editor throughout the war, to advise his paper and also the responsible statesmen on problems of Austrian diplomacy. He opposed a separate peace with Austria, seeing more clearly than most her dependence upon Germany and the problem of the future of the non-Germanic and non-Magyar peoples of Central Europe. He was closely associated with Northcliffe in organizing propaganda in enemy countries and in 1918 undertook a successful mission at the Italian front.

When owing to personal differences between Northcliffe and Geoffrey Dawson [q.v.] the latter resigned in February 1919 the editorship was accepted by Steed, who outlined that it would be his policy in *The Times* to maintain its independence towards all parties, politicians, and governments; to work immediately for a settlement of the Irish question, both for its own sake and for the sake of stability in Anglo-American relations; to support the just claims of France and the other allies so that admonitions might be addressed to them when it should be necessary in the interests of Great Britain and of Europe; to advocate and support constructively and critically the League of Nations as the chief hope of avoiding future war; and to deal fairly with Labour demands and movements in Great Britain while resisting any Bolshevist tendency.

Steed had become profoundly distrustful of Lloyd George and *The Times* played no small part in the return of the Bonar Law government in 1922. But he had 'impressed his own personality so strongly on the paper's policy' that his editorship ended on 30 November 1922, little more than a month after *The Times* had been taken over by its new proprietors, Colonel John Astor (later Lord Astor of Hever) and John Walter. The *History of 'The Times'* remarks that 'Steed joined *The Times* as a junior foreign correspondent in 1896 at the age of twenty-five and was dismissed from the highest position on the paper at the age of fifty-one.' 'Steed's editorship was the shortest, most anxious, and most eventful in the whole history of *The Times*.' There were few more dramatic occasions than the editorial conference when Steed announced with quiet dignity that he was no longer the editor and the rest of the business was carried on with an empty editorial chair. When he left Printing House Square the circulation of *The Times* stood at 184,166, the highest figure it had attained since 1914 when the price was lowered to one penny.

The idea, entertained by some of the public men of his day, that Steed cared too little for his own country was utterly misleading. Those who came into contact with him in his daily work at Printing House Square knew that he was intensely interested in domestic affairs and no editor was ever more delighted to publish a well-written home news story. Many journalists treasured notes of congratulation from their chief for the manner in which a home news story had been presented to the reader.

After leaving *The Times* Steed's life mained a full one. He bought the *Review Reviews* which he edited from 1923 to 30; wrote his autobiography *Through hirty Years* (2 vols., 1924); lectured in ngland, France, Germany, and the nited States, and attended regularly the ssemblies of the League of Nations. He as lecturer at King's College, London, on entral European history from 1925 to 38; and from 1937 to 1947 was one of e chief broadcasters on world affairs for e empire and overseas services of the ritish Broadcasting Corporation.

In 1937 Steed married Violet Sybille, aughter of the late James Francis Mason, f Eynsham Hall, Witney. He died 13 anuary 1956 at Wootton-by-Woodstock.

A portrait in oils by Charles Shannon is a the possession of *The Times*.

[*The Times*, 14 January 1956; *History of 'he Times'*, vols. iii and iv, 1947–52; personal nowledge.]   A. P. ROBBINS.

TEWART, SIR (PERCY) MALCOLM, rst baronet, of Stewartby, county edford (1872–1951), industrialist, was orn at Hastings 9 May 1872, the second on of (Sir) Halley Stewart [q.v.], the ounder of the trust bearing his name. Ie inherited a robust constitution and a trong radical outlook from his father and randfather, Alexander Stewart, whose iary, when a prisoner in France during he Napoleonic wars, was one of his most reasured possessions. He was educated at he University School, Hastings, King's chool, Rochester, the Royal High School, :dinburgh, and in Germany. At the age of ineteen he joined a Thames lighterage irm and later his father's oil seed crushing usiness.

In 1900 his lifelong link with the brick ndustry was forged when his father ac-quired a financial interest in B. J. Forder & Son, Ltd., a company owning brick, ime, whiting, and cement works in Bed-ordshire. Malcolm Stewart became mana-ing director, a position he held for fifty ears, and after Forder's had absorbed ondon Brick Company in 1923, and fin-lly adopted its name, he was chairman or twenty-five years until his retirement n 1950 when he was elected president for ife. In 1900 the annual output of bricks vas seventeen millions; in 1950, in its ubilee year, it was seventeen hundred and ifty millions.

In 1912 Forder's cement, lime, and vhiting assets were sold to British Port-and Cement Manufacturers, of which

Stewart became a managing director, and thus began his long association with what was to become the 'Blue Circle' group. By 1924 he was chairman and a managing director of the Associated Portland Cement Manufacturers and British Portland Cement Manufacturers. This position he held until he retired from executive responsi-bility at the end of 1945 and became president. He was successively chairman and president of the Cement Makers' Fed-eration from 1918 until his death.

When Stewart joined the brick and cement companies, he found them engaged in cut-throat competition and in the throes of depression. Under his guidance each of them became the largest producer in the world in its own field. The secret of Stew-art's success was that he persuaded the makers of both bricks and cement to co-operate with their competitors and to end the rivalry between individual producers. Thus, planned production and stability of price were achieved. Furthermore, he was a generation ahead of his time in management–labour relations. Welfare and pension schemes, joint consultation, profit-sharing, holidays with pay, all these he introduced into the companies of which he became chairman, with the result that stoppages and strikes were almost un-known. His quick comprehension and foresight inspired confidence, and his con-sideration for those working for him and his understanding of their problems created in them a desire to give of their best and a feeling of partnership in a common adven-ture. He was fond of quoting 'Let him that laboureth be first partaker of the fruits', and this was the very kernel of his indus-trial philosophy. From 1919 onwards he was chairman for twenty-seven years of the cement industry's national joint in-dustrial council, for the formation of which he was largely responsible. He was also the first chairman of the national joint council for the Fletton brick industry.

Stewart took great pride in converting the drab hamlet of Wootton Pillinge in Bedfordshire into a garden village which bore the new name of Stewartby. There, beneath the shadow of towering brick chimneys grew a model village, architect-planned, with low-rented modern houses for employees, a united church, schools, sportsground, swimming bath, canteens, offices, research centre, and a memorial hall.

From 1917 to 1919 Stewart was director for the Ministry of Munitions of the gov-ernment rolling mills at Southampton;

but it is for his great contribution to the problem of alleviating unemployment that this clear-sighted industrialist will be remembered. As commissioner for the special areas in England and Wales from 1934 to 1936, he devised and operated schemes for bringing industry to trading estates in areas of high unemployment. In his report for 1936 he drew attention to the importance of the 'location of industry' which resulted in the appointment of a royal commission on the distribution of the industrial population (Barlow report, 1940); he is generally regarded as the father of the Greater London Plan of 1944.

Stewart inherited and made considerable fortunes, which he used for innumerable benefactions. He gave an estate of 540 acres at Potton, Bedfordshire, to settle unemployed men in smallholdings to make a living by market gardening. He was a generous supporter of the Royal Caledonian Schools and the National Council of Social Service (of both of which he was president), of the Industrial Co-partnership Association (of which he was a vice-president), and of Ruskin College. His presentations to the National Maritime Museum included Nelson's famous telescope.

Not only was Stewart chairman of his father's charitable trust, but in 1945 he founded and generously endowed a general charitable trust called after himself. This trust has promoted a scheme for providing homes, rent-free, and a community hall, for retired employees of London Brick Company. The plans and layout were designed by Sir Albert Richardson. Situated in a beautiful setting in the centre of Stewartby, the homes are a fitting tribute to Malcolm Stewart's memory.

Stewart was fond of swimming, shooting, stalking, and big-game hunting. He went on safari in Kenya the year before his death. His real passion was motoring: a fast but careful driver, he was never so happy as when driving at speed in his four-and-a-half litre Bentley.

In 1918 he was appointed O.B.E., and in 1937 created a baronet for his work as special commissioner. He was high sheriff of Bedfordshire in 1941, a justice of the peace, and a deputy-lieutenant for the county. He received the honorary degree of LL.D. from Manchester in 1937.

Stewart was twice married: first, in 1896, to Cordelia (died 1906), second daughter of Sir Joseph Compton Rickett, then Liberal member of Parliament for Scarborough, by whom he had two sons

and one daughter; secondly, in 1907, to Beatrice Maud (died 1960), second daughter of Joseph Bishop Pratt [q.v.], the mezzotint engraver, by whom he had one son and one daughter. He died at his home at Sandy in Bedfordshire, 27 February 1951, and was succeeded in the baronetcy by his second son, Ronald Compton (born 1903). There are two portraits by (Sir) James Gunn and Sir Oswald Birley respectively, and a bronze bust by Sir William Reid Dick, all in the possession of the Sir Malcolm Stewart General Charitable Trust to which, on the death of his widow, Stewart bequeathed the residue of his estate of over half a million pounds. The two portraits are in the custody of Sir Ronald Stewart at Maulden Grange, and the bust is loaned to the community hall, Stewartby. Most of his valuable pictures, tapestries, furniture, and *objets d'art*, however, he left to the National Trust, to be assembled as a collection in Montacute House, near Yeovil, Somerset.

[*Phorpres News* (magazine of London Brick Company), June 1950; private information, personal knowledge.]

GEOFFREY SHAKESPEARE

STEWART, SIR (SAMUEL) FINDLATER (1879–1960), civil servant, was born 22 December 1879, at Brisbane School House, Largs, one of the seven children of Alexander Stewart, a teacher, and his wife, Isabella Finlator, the original version of Stewart's second name. He entered Edinburgh University at fourteen, took his M.A. with honours in 1899, and spent the period before he was of age to compete for the Civil Service teaching astronomy and navigation in the training ship *Conway*.

Appointed after the examination of 1903 to the India Office, in which he spent most of his official career, he became joint secretary in the military department in 1920; assistant under-secretary of state, and clerk of the Council of India, in 1924; and permanent under-secretary of state for India in 1930.

Stewart was closely associated with the two major Indian inquiries which took place between the passing of the Government of India Acts of 1919 and 1935. In 1923 he was made joint secretary (with (Sir) Arthur Street, q.v.) of the royal commission on the superior civil services in India, which recommended a great and progressive Indianization, coupled with the encouragement of increased British recruitment in the years of transition.

e Government's acceptance of these
oposals held the Indian services to-
ther, and in good heart, over an anxious
riod. It also contributed materially to
uipping the future independent India
th a substantial and highly trained
dian nucleus in all services.

On the appointment in 1927 of the
atutory commission headed by Sir John
ter Viscount) Simon [q.v.] to in-
uire into Indian political advancement,
ewart was selected as its secretary.
s labours, over two years, complicated
they were by a Congress boycott and
e absence of Indian membership, were
eavy. Stewart's familiarity with India,
s knowledge and ability, his clear and
xcellent draftsmanship, his realistic
proach, and his capacity for selecting
e essential, made his contribution to its
port of real importance.

Stewart held office as permanent under-
cretary (1930–40) during a critical
eriod in India's history. It fell to him to
dvise successive secretaries of state
uring the three sessions (1930–33) of the
ndian Round Table conference; and
ereafter during the deliberations of the
int select committee of both Houses of
arliament, under the chairmanship of
ord Linlithgow [q.v.]. On the recom-
endations of the select committee were
ased the proposals for the future Govern-
ent of India, and for the separation of
urma from India, which, after lengthy
nd controversial debates in both Houses,
ere embodied in the Acts of 1935.

The labour involved was formidable.
ir Samuel Hoare (later Viscount Templewood, q.v.), who was secretary of state
or India from 1931 to 1935, paid tribute
n his *Nine Troubled Years* (1954) to the
ssistance he had from Stewart, who, he
aid, of all the civil servants who had
elped him in his various departments,
tood out 'pre-eminent as a dependable
ounsellor and friendly colleague'.

On the passing of the India and Burma
Acts of 1935, and the separation of Burma
rom India, Stewart became permanent
nder-secretary of state for Burma as
well as for India, and was closely associa-
ed with the earlier stages of constitutional advance in Burma.

In India, the Act provided for the institution in the British provinces of provincial autonomy, based on a much enlarged
franchise, and for a Federation, at the
centre, of British India and the Indian
princely states. Stewart saw the successful introduction in 1937, not without

initial difficulties, of provincial autonomy.
Arrangements for establishing the complicated structure of the proposed Federation of India had advanced materially by
the outbreak of war in 1939, but much
still remained to be done, particularly in
terms of the accession, and the terms of
accession, of the requisite minimum of
Indian princely states, and the outbreak
of war inevitably meant postponement.

Early in the war Stewart was for a few
weeks seconded from the India Office as
director-general of information. On the
fall of France in 1940 he left the India
Office, as it proved, for good, to hold a
series of posts of great importance to the
war effort. He was appointed chairman of
the Home Defence Executive and chief
civil staff officer (designate) to the
commander-in-chief, Home Forces. The
success he achieved in co-ordinating the
work of the civil departments with military requirements in the face of threatened
invasion led to a variety of tasks, as the
pattern of the war changed, in which
combined military and civil effort was
required. The techniques he formulated
have influenced subsequent organization
in the defence field.

With the entry of the United States into
the war, Stewart became chairman of the
Anglo-American co-ordinating committee
set up to deal with the logistic problems
of the establishment of the United
States forces in Britain. He played a
significant part during this period in
dealing with the problems of security;
and was particularly successful in dealing,
among other major questions, with the
wide variety of tasks—especially in respect of supply, accommodation, and
other provision for the United States
forces—arising out of the mounting of
the 'Overlord' operation. His excellent
relations with his American colleagues
were recognized at the end of the war by
the United States medal of freedom with
gold palm.

Retiring from the Civil Service at the
end of the war, Stewart entered the City
as first chairman of the new British and
French Bank, set up to promote Anglo-
French trade. He was also a director of
the Finance Corporation for Industry, and
he served too in a variety of governmental
capacities. They ranged widely from
membership of a selection jury at an
International Film Festival to inquiries
into Services' entertaining allowances,
and the work and organization of both
the British Council and the Security

Service, and an inquiry into matters affecting the Order of St. John of Jerusalem.

Stewart's sound practical judgement of men and things; his capacity to delegate; his economy of the written word; the confidence inspired in ministers by his pungent and concise advice; his gift for friendship, and his ability to command the respect and affection of his colleagues and subordinates, whether in the Civil Service or in business, all these were reflected in his distinguished and varied career.

After retirement he made his home near Blandford, where he died 11 April 1960. He married in 1910 Winifred, daughter of the late James Tomblin, by whom he had two daughters. She died in 1915 and he married secondly, in 1940, Mary Stephanie, only daughter of S. Whitmore Robinson. Stewart was appointed C.I.E. (1919), C.S.I. (1924), K.C.I.E. (1930), K.C.B. (1932), G.C.I.E. (1935), and G.C.B. (1939). In 1931 he was made a chevalier of the Legion of Honour. He had also from his own university (Edinburgh), and from Aberdeen, the honorary LL.D.

[Private information; personal knowledge.]
GILBERT LAITHWAITE.

STEWART-MURRAY, KATHARINE MARJORY, DUCHESS OF ATHOLL (1874–1960), public servant, was born in Edinburgh 6 November 1874, the eldest child of Sir James Ramsay [q.v.], tenth baronet, of Bamff, in East Perthshire, by his second wife, Charlotte Fanning, daughter of Major William Stewart, of Ardvorlich. Her father was an Oxford double first in classics and history, her mother a gifted singer. Her half-sister Agnata, who married H. M. Butler [q.v.], after winning a scholarship at Girton headed the Cambridge classical honours list in the first division of the first class. Katharine herself was both scholar and musician. She was educated at Wimbledon High School and the Royal College of Music, handing over the proceeds of a piano scholarship to a needy student, Samuel Coleridge-Taylor [q.v.]. It seemed at one time as though music would be her chosen career; public service associated with her husband, shared interest in his military life (she was the editor and main contributor to a *Military History of Perthshire*, 2 vols., 1908), and later a political career of her own diverted her. But it remained throughout her life a solace to herself and a delight to her friends. In 1899 she married John George Stewart-Murray, Marquess of Tullibardine, eldest surviving son of the seventh Duke of Atholl to whose title he succeeded in 1917.

Public service in many fields brought the Duchess of Atholl recognition in the form of a D.B.E. (1918) and in due course honorary doctorates from seven universities. Successive Governments found her a competent and hard-working member of innumerable official committees and commissions. She was a prominent figure in Scottish social service and local government, and an active supporter of the Conservative Party organization. Her election to the House of Commons in 1923 as member for Kinross and West Perthshire, and the first woman member from Scotland, seemed a logical outcome of these activities and brought her into national politics in time to make feminist history, though herself no feminist. Her party standing and intellectual calibre marked her for ministerial office. Margaret Bondfield [q.v.] had been first in the field as parliamentary secretary to the Ministry of Labour in the Labour Government; Katharine Atholl came second on her appointment in 1924–9 as parliamentary secretary to the Board of Education. She was clearly the right woman in the right job, for the educational world was her spiritual home.

To her contemporaries at this time Katharine Atholl presented the picture not so much of a duchess as of an inspired but somewhat humourless headmistress, slight, upright, and uncompromising. To many she appeared both highly conventional and socially reactionary, an impression confirmed by a book entitled *Women and Politics* which she published in 1931. In the same year labour conditions in Soviet Russia inspired her to write *The Conscription of a People*. But the fire which smouldered undetected in her small body had not in 1931 encountered the blast which was to fan it into a flame. When it did, the flame burned through party loyalties, social conventions, hereditary prejudices, and landed her in strange company.

This was because Katharine Atholl, behind a demure exterior, had a nerve peculiarly and undiscriminatingly sensitive to cruelty and oppression. From 1933 to the end of her life world events pressed relentlessly on this nerve and perpetually inflamed it. Many of those who reacted violently to the cruelties of the Russian

olution remained undisturbed during
e thirties by the rigours of Nazi rule.
ıny who crusaded against fascism turned
•lind eye to the darker aspects of Com-
ınism. Katharine Atholl knew no such
stinction. Cruelty was cruelty by whomever committed, and was an evil not to
tolerated. This, as time went on, under-
ned her influence as a reliable party
litician and involved her in extraneous
ıses. For instance, in 1929 she declared
ır on a cruel African custom known as
male circumcision', and conducted a
mpaign in association with the left-
ng independent member, Eleanor Rath-
ne [q.v.]. As she said many years later,
was not a very easy thing to do'. This
ıs an understatement; it was a difficult
ıd unpleasant but to her a wholly
cessary thing to do.

The Duchess supported (Sir) Winston
ıurchill in his opposition to the Govern-
ent's proposals for a new constitution
r India, and on this issue she gave up
e party whip. She returned to the fold
hen Mussolini declared war on Abyssinia
ıt the Spanish civil war brought her again
to conflict with her own Government
ıd finally lost her the party whip. She
as not convinced of the rightness of
eneral Franco's campaign, still less of
ıe methods by which he waged it. She
ade a close study of the Spanish situa-
on and herself visited Spain in company
ith Eleanor Rathbone and the socialist
llen Wilkinson [q.v.]. What she saw
volved her in active work for the care
' Spanish republican refugees as well as
ben criticism of the Conservative Govern-
ıent's toleration of fascist support for
ranco in violation of a non-intervention
act to which Great Britain was party.
ler Penguin *Searchlight on Spain* (1938)
as widely read.

Finally her opposition to the Chamber-
ain policy of appeasement in face of
ıcreasingly flagrant German aggression
ıused her in 1938 to resign her parlia-
ıentary seat and seek re-election in her
wn constituency as a supporter of
hurchill's policy of resistance to further
erman encroachments. There ensued in
December a campaign in which the
huchess's cause commanded the support
f a galaxy of political and literary talent
omprising members of all parties. That,
owever, did not save her seat, which she
bst by 1,313 votes to an official Con-
ervative candidate. She celebrated her
efeat by playing Beethoven's Waldstein
nd Appassionata sonatas, hoping, she

said, that she would now have more time
for her husband and for music.

This hope was frustrated by war activities, the illness and death in 1942 of her
husband, and the persistence of cruelty
in the world at large. Her autobiography,
published in 1958 under the title *Working
Partnership*, makes clear that the driving
force which in the thirties had caused her
to be pilloried as 'the Red Duchess' was
the same as that which in the fifties
earned her the designation of 'fascist
beast'. For now the cruelty and oppression
was coming mainly from the Left, and
resistance to it brought her into association with right-wing elements. The fate
of Poland, Czechoslovakia, Hungary, the
care of refugees from Communist tyranny,
the horrors of Stalinism, these causes
now focused her interest and inspired her
activities. She was from 1944 the moving
spirit and active chairman of a British
League for European Freedom, a body
which she served, though by now a rather
frail and lonely figure in the political
world, until her death in Edinburgh 21
October 1960. She had no children.

Portraits by George Henry (1903) and
Sir James Guthrie (1924) and a bronze
bust by Prince Serge Yourievitch are at
Blair Atholl.

[Duchess of Atholl, *Working Partnership*,
1958; personal knowledge.]   STOCKS.

STIRLING, WALTER FRANCIS (1880–
1958), lieutenant-colonel, was born in
Southsea 31 January 1880, the only son
and younger child of Captain Francis
Stirling, R.N., and his wife, Mary Caroline
Francis. He never knew his father, who
was commanding the training ship *Atalanta*
when it left Bermuda on a trial voyage in
January 1880 and was lost at sea. His
mother was offered apartments at Hampton Court, Stirling's home for many years.
He was educated at Kelly College, Tavistock, and the Royal Military College,
Sandhurst, being gazetted to the Royal
Dublin Fusiliers in 1899. This was the prelude to an astonishingly varied career in
which 'Michael' Stirling, as his wife and
many of his friends later called him,
stamped himself on all who met him as one
of the most vital and colourful characters
of his time.

Soon after being commissioned Stirling
went out to the South African war, and
after a short period with his regiment,
during which he took part in the relief of
Ladysmith, he transferred to the newly

formed Mounted Infantry of the 4th division. Subsequently he became adjutant of the 14th battalion M.I., serving in the action at Laing's Nek and the later operations in the Orange River Colony and the Transvaal, receiving a mention in dispatches and being appointed to the D.S.O. In 1906 he was seconded to the Egyptian Army and spent some five years with an Arab battalion patrolling the Eritrean and Abyssinian borders, in the course of which he acquired a fluent knowledge of Arabic. In 1912 he retired from the army and after spells of fruit farming in Canada and working with Shell in London he became secretary of the Sporting Club in Alexandria, then of the Gezira Sporting Club in Cairo.

After the outbreak of war in 1914 Stirling joined the Royal Flying Corps as an observer in Ismailia until he learned that his old regiment had lost almost all its officers in the Gallipoli landings, when he obtained leave to rejoin. After three months in Gallipoli he was invalided home. Returning to Egypt he served as G.S.O. 2 Intelligence, then Operations, in the Palestine campaign until in 1918 he was appointed chief staff officer to T. E. Lawrence [q.v.] whose close companion he became in the final phase of the war, the advance to Damascus. 'Stirling the imperturbable', as Lawrence called him, was awarded the M.C. and a bar to his D.S.O. He was promoted lieutenant-colonel in 1920.

After serving as adviser to Emir Feisal and as deputy chief political officer in Cairo (1919), Stirling in 1920 was appointed acting governor of Sinai and later in the year became governor of the Jaffa district in Palestine. He succeeded in gaining the trust of the Jews as well as the Arabs, his house becoming a meeting-place for both, before in 1923 a reorganization dispensed with his post. He then became adviser to the Albanian Government, under Ahmed Bey Zogu, who in 1928 became King Zog I: a very difficult task because both Italy and Yugoslavia were striving for control of the country. Stirling steered an impartial course, although politely threatened with assassination from both sides. In seeking to keep a balance he took a large part in establishing a force of *gendarmerie*.

After giving up this turbulent task in 1931 Stirling returned home to discover that employment was difficult to find. Eventually he joined the firm of Marks and Spencer, working his way up from assistant porter via floor walker to jun buyer. He left to collaborate with (S Alexander Korda [q.v.] on a film of *Se Pillars of Wisdom* which it proved i possible to finance.

When war broke out in 1939 Stirling h just returned from Romania where was representing a British firm of w merchants. For a time he worked in t continental telephone censorship but June 1940 the War Office sent him ba to the Balkans on intelligence work. Af the German invasion he moved to Jeru lem; then joined the Spears mission a became political officer for northern Syr In 1943 he was appointed military co mander of east Syria and in 1944 of t desert and frontier areas with hea quarters in Damascus. There he remain after the war, becoming local correspo dent for *The Times*. In 1949 three arm men broke into his house when he was dinner in an attempt to assassinate hi apparently from political motives; l cook and nightwatchman died and he hi self was left riddled with bullets. His stea courage was never more impressive th during the last eight years of his li that he survived so long was perhaps t most extraordinary feature of his extr ordinary career. He moved to Egyp but was expelled by the Government the in 1951 and settled in Tangier.

Stirling's autobiographical account his varied career, *Safety Last* (1953), w a challenge to the motto 'Safety Firs which he complained had been 'inscrib not only on every London omnibus but c the very hearts of the country's ruler thus denying us our Elizabethan birt right: the right to adventure in eve quarter of the globe'. Stirling amp lived up to his own, opposite, motto. H was a 'new Elizabethan' in actuality, n merely in aspiration. Yet for all tl variety and unconventionality of his care he was much more than a seeker of a venture. It was his diplomatic gifts an knack of handling widely different typ of men which most impressed Lawrenc who described him as 'a skilled sta officer, tactful and wise': qualities notab called for during his time in Palestine an Albania.

Stirling died in Tangier 22 Februar 1958. He was fortunate in that his wi had a courage matching his own. In 192 he had married Eileen Mary May (Mary gold), elder daughter of Lieutenant Colonel Mackenzie-Edwards of the Roya Berkshire Regiment. They had a son wh

ed a few months after birth and one
aughter.

A portrait by Joseph Oppenheimer is
produced in *Safety Last*.

[Lt.-Col. W. F. Stirling, *Safety Last*, 1953;
ivate information; personal knowledge.]

B. H. LIDDELL HART.

TOOP, ADRIAN DURA (1883–1957),
gby footballer, was born in London
March 1883, the elder son of Frederick
rnelius Stoop, stockbroker, and his
ife, Agnes Macfarlane Clark. His father
as of Dutch origin. Stoop was educated
Dover College, Rugby School, and
niversity College, Oxford, where he ob-
ined a third in law in 1905. He was
lled to the bar by the Inner Temple in
08 but had only one brief; it is doubtful
hether he really ever intended to prac-
se. His great interest was rugby football
d it was as a notable player of the game
at he became legendary. More than
nyone Stoop designed the game as it
me to be played. There have, of course,
een a few variations, but basically it
still what was developed by Stoop
nd other famous Harlequins—H. J .H.
ibree, R. W. Poulton-Palmer, J. G. G.
irkett, and D. Lambert.

Stoop's association with the Harlequins
egan in 1900 when he was invited to join
e club when still at Rugby. It was not
ntil 1902 that he played his first game
r the club: against Oxford University
here he was then an undergraduate.
n the same year he got his blue and in
904 he captained the university against
ambridge. While he was at Oxford his
ppearances with the Harlequins were
ecessarily limited but when he left the
niversity he threw himself whole-
eartedly into club activities. In 1905 he
as elected vice-captain and secretary.
hat was the real starting-point of the
Stoop era'. From 1906 to 1914 he was
aptain and secretary and the master mind
f the Harlequins whose methods were
uickly adopted by other leading clubs.

Stoop was not a big man but anything
e lacked in inches was more than made
p by courage. Between 1905 and 1912 he
vas capped for England fifteen times,
lthough, surprisingly, he was not inclu-
led in the English side in the years 1908
nd 1909. While he was a great individual
layer and a great individualist in his
deas he was, even more, a magnificent
eader who had a ready sense for spotting
promising player and deciding, nearly
always rightly, which was that player's

ideal position in the field. It was typical
that he switched Sibree from full-back to
scrum-half and those who saw Stoop and
Sibree as partners at half-back for Harlequins and England saw one of the great
partnerships of rugby football.

D. Lambert was another example of
Stoop's flair for picking the right man for
the right job. In a pre-season trial game
Lambert was playing forward. Coming
into personal contact with Lambert's
great speed Stoop at once made him into
a wing three-quarter in Harlequins' first
fifteen and in that position Lambert
played seven times for England. It is
remarkable that no fewer than six
Harlequin half-backs or three-quarters of
the great Stoop era were capped for
England: a tribute to Stoop's magnetic
influence on his club in particular and the
game in general.

It was always a strong argument in
Stoop's teaching that it was the three-
quarters generally who were to be the
scorers of tries. This, of course, had always
been a recognized feature of rugby football, but Stoop developed it. As a critic at
the time said, the Harlequins 'never miss
an opportunity of throwing the ball about
with a freedom bordering on recklessness,
but they have learnt the art not only of
passing, but of taking the ball on the run
with safe hands'. That summed up what the
Harlequins, guided by Stoop, were doing
for rugby football. It was not really new;
but Stoop had seen how the game, hitherto
much slower, with little in it that was unexpected, could be developed.

Stoop was an officer in the 5th battalion the Queen's Royal West Surrey
Regiment (Territorial Army). For his
soldiering as for his rugby football he had
intense enthusiasm and it was almost
inevitable that during the fighting in
Mesopotamia in the war of 1914–18 he
won the M.C.

When the Harlequins were re-formed
after the war Stoop at thirty-six was of an
age when most men are content to be
watchers. Not so Stoop, who as president
(1920–49) and until 1946 secretary once
again became the guiding spirit of the
fortunes of the club; he even played a
few times for the first fifteen and, as ever,
set a standard of perfection. He said once
that any player accepted for membership
should be able to win a blue if he were
at Oxford or Cambridge. It was an exaggerated idea but it showed the high
standard he expected. He had no use
for anything mediocre. When his own

playing days were finally ended he was still
a keen follower and outspoken critic of
the Harlequins, whether as a team or as
individuals. At one club meeting a certain
famous international was proposed as captain. Stoop's terse comment that although
X was a great player he would be a bad
captain was met by X's reply that as long
as Adrian was on the touch-line there
was no need for a captain on the field.
Both remarks underline Stoop's influence.
For several years he was an England
selector and in 1932–3 was president of the
Rugby Union.

One facet of Stoop's character was a
great interest in spiritual healing and he
himself developed considerable powers as
a healer. He was also an enthusiastic
beekeeper and a keen ornithologist.

In 1918 Stoop married Audrey, daughter of Frederick Needham, of East Bengal;
there were four sons.

He died at his home at Hartley Wintney
27 November 1957. There is a portrait of
Stoop by D. Q. Fildes.

[H. B. T. Wakelam, *Harlequin Story*, 1954;
private information; personal knowledge.]
                              CEDRIC VENABLES.

STOPES,   MARIE   CHARLOTTE
CARMICHAEL (1880–1958), scientist
and sex reformer, was born in Edinburgh
15 October 1880, the elder daughter of
Henry Stopes, a man of private means
whose passionate hobby was archaeology,
by his wife, Charlotte Carmichael, a
pioneer of women's university education
who had studied at Edinburgh University,
and who became well known for her
research on Shakespearian questions.
Marie Stopes sometimes called herself a
child of the British Association, for her
parents first met at one of its meetings,
and as a girl she attended them regularly.
When she was six weeks old her parents
moved to London. Her mother tried to
initiate her at the age of five into Latin
and Greek, but she showed no aptitude,
becoming far more interested in her
father's large collection of flint implements. She had little formal education
until at the age of twelve she went to
St. George's, Edinburgh, then two years
later to the North London Collegiate
School. At University College, London,
in 1902 she obtained at the same time
first class honours in botany and third
class honours in geology and physical
geography. After a year of research under
F. W. Oliver [q.v.], she went with a scholarship to Munich where she obtained her

Ph.D. for work on the cycad ovules whic
proved fundamental to the understandin
of the evolution of integumentary stru
tures. In the same year she was appointe
assistant lecturer and demonstrator i
botany at Manchester where she was th
first woman to join the science faculty
She obtained her D.Sc., London, in th
following year. In 1907–8 she spent som
eighteen months in Japan with a grant fo
research from the Royal Society. After
further period as lecturer in palaeobotan
in Manchester she settled in London afte
her marriage in 1911, and from 1913 t
1920 she was lecturer on the same subjec
at University College, London, of whic
she became a fellow in 1910.

In the same year she published an ele
mentary textbook *Ancient Plants*. He
main interest at this time was the Creta
ceous floras on which she was invited t
work by the British Museum: her *Cata
logue of the Cretaceous Flora* in the Britisl
Museum was published in two volume
(1913–15). Meantime the advent of war ha
turned her attention increasingly to coa
itself. She published a number of memoir
of fundamental importance, mainly witl
R. V. Wheeler, with whom she collabora
ted in a standard work, *The Constitutio*
of Coal (1918). A short paper which th
Royal Society published in 1919, *The Fou
Visible Ingredients in Banded Bituminou
Coal: Studies in the Composition of Coal*
changed the attitude of palaeontologist
and chemists to its structure, and he
later classification of coal ingredients (*Fue*
1935) was almost universally adopted.

It was, however, for her work for se
education and birth control that Marie
Stopes became widely known. He
concern was undoubtedly aroused by he
first marriage, to a Canadian botanist
Reginald Ruggles Gates, whom she met i
America and married in Montreal in 1911
The marriage was annulled in 1916 on he
suit of non-consummation. In 1918 sh
married Humphrey Verdon-Roe (die
1949), who had joined his brother, (Sir
Alliott Verdon-Roe [q.v.], in the manufacture of aircraft. He was already interested in birth control and the marriage
was initially a perfect union of common interests: together they founded the Mothers'
Clinic for Birth Control in London in 1921,
the first of its kind in England. Dr. Stopes,
who retained her maiden name in both
her marriages, relinquished her lectureship and henceforth her dominating
interest was family planning and sex
education for married people.

Her first book on the subject, *Married Love* (1918), had been drafted in 1914 to crystallize her own ideas. It became an immediate success and was eventually translated into thirteen languages, including Hindi. Its frank discussion of sexual relations for the ordinary public was, by the standards of the time, sensational, and it caused a furore. The book dealt scarcely at all with birth control but she received so many requests for instruction on the subject that she published later in 1918 a short book, *Wise Parenthood*, with a preface by Arnold Bennett [q.v.]. This too was an immediate success and quickly outstrode its predecessor: within nine years it had sold half a million copies in the original English edition alone. (Like other of her works it was banned in several states of America.) For some twenty years Dr. Stopes's books were leading popular works on their subject. She published some ten others of which *Radiant Motherhood* (1920) and *Enduring Passion* (1928) were, to judge by their sales, the most influential. By the time of her death their romantic presentation had become outmoded, but she was still regarded as the great pioneer fighter for the movement. And a fighter she was, for, especially in the early days, she was attacked sometimes to the point of persecution, notably during her prolonged libel action against Halliday Sutherland [q.v.] which she won on appeal but lost when the case went to the House of Lords.

Marie Stopes's great achievement was the transformation of the subject of birth control into one which was openly discussed. Her advocacy of birth control was based on her wish to see woman's lot become a happier one—a pursuit of a general happiness which she did not herself attain. Her elder son was stillborn, while both her younger son and her husband eventually became alienated from her. But this fearlessly dedicated woman, with a touch of the mystic, for all her arrogant argumentativeness and vanity which made co-operation so difficult, had very many loyal friends and supporters among leading churchmen, doctors, and writers as well as social workers. For a quarter of a century the personalities of the day corresponded with or visited her at Norbury Park, her fine eighteenth-century mansion near Dorking. Friendship with Dr. Stopes was a prickly, demanding, but always stimulating business. Her demonic advocacy of planned parenthood never waned; but towards the end of her life her interest in her own poetry and in literature generally occupied more of her time; in the forties she took an almost naïve pride in reading a paper on her friend, Lord Alfred Douglas [q.v.], to the Royal Society of Literature of which she was a fellow and to which she bequeathed Norbury Park and the residue of her estate. Almost all her publications after 1939 were volumes of verse, of which her long poem, *The Bathe* (1946), a sensuous and rather high-flown work, was typical.

Convinced until almost the end that she would live to be 120, Marie Stopes died at Norbury Park 2 October 1958. She left her portraits by Sir Gerald Kelly and Augustus John to the National Portrait Gallery and that by Gregorio Prieto to the National Gallery of Edinburgh.

[Aylmer Maude, *The Authorized Life of Marie C. Stopes*, 1924; Keith Briant, *Marie Stopes*, 1962; *The Times*, 3 and 8 October 1958; *Nature*, 1 November 1958; private information; personal knowledge.]

JAMES MACGIBBON.

STORRS, SIR RONALD HENRY AMHERST (1881–1955), Near Eastern expert and governor, was born at Bury St. Edmunds 19 November 1881, the eldest son of the Rev. John Storrs by his wife, Lucy Anna Maria Cust, sister of the fifth Baron Brownlow. His father, for thirty years the popular vicar of St. Peter's, Eaton Square, became dean of Rochester in 1913. Storrs went from Charterhouse with a classical scholarship to Pembroke College, Cambridge, taking a first class in the classical tripos in 1903. In the following year he entered the Egyptian Civil Service and was first posted in the Ministry of Finance. In this and other administrative departments he spent the next five years, but administration was never in his line. He was more interested in absorbing the *genius loci*, in perfecting himself in the study of Arabic and the manners and customs of the Egyptians, and in laying the foundation of the art collection later to be destroyed in unhappy circumstances. He did not really find his *métier* until 1909 when he was appointed oriental secretary at the British Agency in Cairo under Sir Eldon Gorst [q.v.].

Storrs was now in his element. For an Englishman without a drop of non-English blood he had a surprisingly cosmopolitan outlook on life, to which were added a discriminating taste, a Voltairian cynicism, a lucidity of thought recalling Anatole France, and a wide but critical and discerning appreciation of the good things of this life, whether in art, literature, cooking, conversation, or, may it be added, the company of those prominent socially and in the world of affairs. He was ready, indeed anxious, to mix with all and sundry, with Turks, Jews, heretics, and infidels, provided always that their company was worth while. He would derive amusement and pleasure from intercourse with an entertaining scoundrel; none from that with a socially orthodox bore. Beneath his little foibles and poses he was a deep lover of literature, classical and modern; and Dame Ethel Smyth [q.v.] described him as one 'who really loves music'. In his philosophy of life as in his dress he modelled himself on his brilliant uncle Harry Cust [q.v.].

Gorst's tenure of office in Egypt provided a sharp contrast with that of his predecessor Lord Cromer [q.v.] and was not altogether happy. But Storrs, with his quick and almost feminine perceptions, understood what Gorst was driving at and remained loyal to his memory. With Gorst's successor Lord Kitchener [q.v.] he found himself as oriental secretary even more closely *en rapport*. Both men understood, as few others have done, the devious methods and mentality no less than the cynical humour of oriental politicians, and enjoyed the interplay of wit with them; both were ardent collectors of *objets d'art* in the same field, and Storrs, while assisting his chief in forming his collection, was able simultaneously to develop his own. His taste was impeccable, his flair for discovering something good remarkable, and his command of colloquial Arabic, his aplomb, and a complete absence of self-consciousness combined to make him one of the few people able to defeat a Mouski dealer on his own ground.

After the outbreak of war in 1914 Storrs remained at the residency under Sir Henry McMahon [q.v.], being closely concerned with the negotiations which were initiated with Sherif Husain. T. E. Lawrence (whose notice Storrs later contributed to this Dictionary) has a good deal to say of Storrs's activities at this time in *Seven Pillars of Wisdom* (1935) and in its abridgement, *Revolt in the Desert* (1927), the first chapter of which is entitled 'Storrs goes to Jiddah' and illustrated with a clever portrait of him by Eric

Kennington [q.v.]. In 1917 Storrs was ass tant political officer to the Anglo-Fren political mission of the Egyptian Expe tionary Force and visited Baghdad on behalf. He was also for a short ti attached to the secretariat of the Briti War Cabinet in the autumn of 1917. the end of the year came his appointme to Jerusalem, as military governor fro 1917, as civil governor of Jerusalem a Judaea from 1920 with the beginning of t mandate. Storrs had no easy time, and wi his staff had constantly to be on the ale Lawrence describes him in Jerusalem as 't urbane and artful Governor of the plac The description is apt, but Storrs was mo than this. For the detail and drudgery official administration he had neith liking nor time and he left it to othe But the post was a new one, its pos bilities unfettered by precedent; an Storrs, with his imagination and ur to foster the things of the mind, promot musical societies, chess clubs, art exhib tions, and above all the Pro-Jerusale Society, guardian of the city's beauti and the only body in the Holy Lan which could bring together to its counci table the leaders of Jerusalem's diver and bitterly opposed communities. And h was the impetus in the revival of the ar of pottery, weaving, and glass-blowing.

In 1926 Storrs went as governor Cyprus where one of his first acts was t bring about the cancellation of the island share of the Turkish debt. For a time h enjoyed considerable popularity but th waned with the growth of the agitatio for union with Greece on the part of th Cypriot Greek politicians. Always bette at negotiating than in coping with vic lence, he refused to be provoked by th aggressiveness of the *Enosis* extremists in 1931 there was a sudden and unexpecte outburst in which the wooden Govern ment House, where Storrs was in resi dence, was burned down. Order wa restored within a fortnight by ships an troops promptly dispatched from Malt and Egypt; but utterly destroyed were th works of art and books whose acquisitio had been one of the main joys of his life.

At the end of 1932, on the expiry of hi normal term in Cyprus, Storrs was ap pointed governor of Northern Rhodesia where one of his first tasks was to organiz the transfer of the capital from Living stone to the more conveniently situate Lusaka. It was an uncongenial post for man of his background; he found th contrast 'almost overwhelmingly dis agreeable', and he did not repine unduly when ill health caused him to be invalided from the service in 1934. In a sense there could be 'no promotion after Jerusalem', as he remarked in his memoirs, *Orientations* (1937), a fascinating record, brilliantly told, which achieved, despite its length, an outstanding success. He had also a gift for conversation which he consciously developed into an art; and in his latter years was a sought-after professional lecturer on Dante, the Bible, Shakespeare, and T. E. Lawrence. He represented East Islington on the London County Council (1937–45), was chairman of the Lesser Eastern Churches committee of the Church of England Council on Foreign Relations, and gave his services to many other bodies, especially those concerned with music.

Storrs married in 1923 Louisa Lucy, daughter of Rear-Admiral the Hon. Algernon Charles Littleton and widow of Lieutenant-Colonel Henry Arthur Clowes. He was popular with the young who enjoyed his humorously chaffing way with them, but he had no children of his own; Lady Storrs had a family by her first husband. She died in 1970.

Storrs was appointed C.M.G. (1916), C.B.E. (1919), K.C.M.G. (1929); he had been knighted in 1924. He was a knight of justice of the Order of St. John of Jerusalem, held Italian and Greek decorations, and was an honorary LL.D. of Aberdeen and Dublin. He died in London 1 November 1955.

[Sir Ronald Storrs, *Orientations*, 1937; Sir George Hill, *A History of Cyprus*, vol. iv, 1952; Sir Harry Luke, *Cities and Men*, vol. ii, 1953; personal knowledge.]   HARRY LUKE.

STRADLING, SIR REGINALD EDWARD (1891–1952), civil engineer, was born in Bristol 12 May 1891, the second of three children and only surviving son of Edward John Stradling, forage merchant, and his wife, Sarah Mary Bennet. Educated at Bristol Grammar School, he was awarded in 1909 a Surveyors' Institution scholarship to the university of Bristol where he read civil engineering and graduated B.Sc. in 1912. After practical training with A. P. I. Cotterell, a consulting engineer of Bristol and Westminster, he worked successively with firms in Bolton and Birmingham.

At the outbreak of war in 1914 he volunteered for service with the Royal Engineers, was commissioned, and went to France with the 16th division in 1915.

By 1917, when he was invalided from the army, he was captain and adjutant, Divisional Engineers; had been twice mentioned in dispatches, and awarded the M.C. On his recovery he became a lecturer in civil engineering in Birmingham University and began research into the properties of building materials which led in turn to the award of the Ph.D. (Birmingham, 1922) and the D.Sc. (Bristol, 1925). In 1922 he accepted the headship of the civil engineering and building department of Bradford Technical College but two years later resigned it to become director of building research in the Department of Scientific and Industrial Research.

Stradling's work during the inter-war years was invaluable in establishing a department which was to assume during that period and afterwards a key position in the application of science to building. One of his memorable achievements was to set up the Steel Structures Research Committee under the chairmanship of Sir Clement Hindley [q.v.] with Stradling himself as executive officer and (Sir) John Baker (who contributes to this Supplement) as technical officer. The work of this committee has had far-reaching results, both directly and through the stimulus it provided to the search for a scientific and practical approach to the design of structural steelwork.

Stradling would have wished for nothing better than to continue his work in the department which owed so much to his initiative and in 1935–9 included also road research, but in 1937 the threat of war caused the Home Office to constitute an inter-departmental committee on Air Raid Precautions. The resources of the Building Research Station were placed at its disposal and research was at once directed to the problems connected with bomb damage from blast, splinters, etc. Stradling took a great personal interest in this work which soon became so exacting that in 1939 he had to relinquish his post as director of building research to become chief adviser to the Ministry of Home Security. When war began in 1939 the research and development department of this new Ministry, of which Stradling had already organized a nucleus, was transferred to the Forest Products Research Laboratory at Princes Risborough and with the help of the Civil Defence Research Committee, set up earlier that year under the chairmanship of (Sir) Edward Appleton, this became the centre of all civil defence scientific activity throughout the war. The work grew rapidly and ultimately embraced camouflage, smoke-screen protection, and operational research as well as the development of direct protection such as the Morrison and Anderson air-raid shelters.

After the war, housing was one of the most urgent questions facing the country and Stradling, chief scientific adviser to the Ministry of Works (1944-9) and adviser on civil defence to the Home Office (1945-8), assumed responsibility for the direction of research to increase the efficiency of post-war reconstruction. In 1947 he became a member of the Advisory Council on Scientific Policy under the chairmanship of Sir Henry Tizard [q.v.] and in the same year made an extensive tour, of some three months, of New Zealand and Australia, at the invitation of their respective Departments of Scientific Research, to advise them on building research.

In the following year his health failed and he relinquished his posts, but a partial recovery enabled him in 1949 to undertake half-time duty as dean of the Military College of Science, Shrivenham, and he found much satisfaction in a return to academic pursuits. He worked with his characteristic enthusiasm to the last and died suddenly at Shrivenham 26 January 1952.

Stradling was appointed C.B. in 1934, knighted in 1945, and awarded the American medal for merit in 1947. In 1943 he received the James Alfred Ewing medal for 1942 and was also elected F.R.S. He was an active member of the council of the Institution of Civil Engineers from 1939 until his death and had been nominated for the presidency in 1949 when illness forced him to withdraw.

In 1918 he married Inda, daughter of Alfred William Pippard, builder and contractor, of Yeovil, Somerset. They had one daughter and one son, Dr. Peter Stradling, who became physician in charge of the chest clinic of Hammersmith Hospital.

A portrait by Rodney Burn is in the Imperial War Museum.

[A. J. S. Pippard in *Obituary Notices of Fellows of the Royal Society*, vol. viii, No. 21, November 1952; private information; personal knowledge.]   A. J. S. PIPPARD.

STRANGWAYS, GILES STEPHEN HOLLAND FOX-, sixth EARL OF ILCHESTER (1874-1959), landowner and historian. [See FOX-STRANGWAYS.]

STRATTON, FREDERICK JOHN MARRIAN (1881-1960), astrophysicist, was born in Birmingham 16 October 1881, the eighth and youngest child of Stephen Samuel Stratton, professor of music, and his wife, Mary Jane Marrian. He was educated at King Edward's Grammar School, at Mason University College (afterwards the university of Birmingham), and at Gonville and Caius College, Cambridge. He was third wrangler in the mathematical tripos of 1904 (the senior wrangler was (Sir) A. S. Eddington, q.v.), Isaac Newton student in 1905, and a Smith's prizeman in 1906, the year in which he was elected a fellow of Caius College. Until 1914 he was a mathematics lecturer at his college and also assistant director of the Solar Physics Observatory under H. F. Newall [q.v.]. His early publications in astronomy covered a wide range, including celestial mechanics, but the outburst of the star Nova Geminorum (1912) focused his attention on novae, which proved to be a problem of lifelong interest.

A few years earlier he had organized a Signal Company in the Cambridge University Officers' Training Corps, to pioneer the military use of wireless telegraphy, then in its infancy. The group of young enthusiasts he collected at that time was also remarkable for a wide range of very distinguished careers in later life. On the outbreak of war in 1914 Stratton was with Newall in the Crimea, where they were preparing to observe the total solar eclipse of 21 August. Leaving immediately, he hurried back to England, and joined the Signal Service, R.E. He served in France, reaching the rank of brevet lieutenant-colonel and being appointed to the D.S.O. and awarded the Legion of Honour.

The war over, Stratton returned to Caius, first as tutor, then as senior tutor, to face what was a difficult time of readjustment for the university, as for Britain as a whole. It was a job for which his personality and experience admirably suited him and which he carried out with much success. He continued to give lectures on astronomy, among them one of the first general courses on astrophysics to be given in Britain, which later appeared in book form, *Astronomical Physics* (1925). He contributed an article on novae to the *Handbuch der Astrophysik* (1928). Somehow he also found time to go for the 1926 total solar eclipse to Sumatra, where with C. R. Davidson he

ade important observations of the spec-
um of the sun's chromosphere.

On Newall's retirement in 1928, Strat-
n was appointed professor of astro-
iysics and director of the Solar Physics
bservatory, relinquishing his tutorship
. Caius. He held this post until 1947,
though his tenure was interrupted,
·st by a serious illness in 1931, and later
uch more extensively by the war. He
ganized three more eclipse expeditions,
, Siam, Canada, and Japan, but was
·gged by bad luck with the weather.
nly in Japan in 1936 were results of
·y scientific value obtainable, and even
en success was only partial, the sun
·ing covered by a cloud almost at the
stant when totality commenced. How-
·er, members of his team made good
easurements of wavelengths in the
·ectrum from near the edge of the sun's
isc, settling a technical point then of
·me interest, and obtained photographs
f the chromospheric spectrum, study
i which stimulated a good deal of later
·ork.

In 1934 Nova Herculis appeared, one
f the most interesting stars of its kind,
nd despite the inadequate equipment of
·e observatory at Cambridge, Stratton
nd his staff during the next few months
·btained a remarkable record of the
hanges in its spectrum. Work on this
·bsorbed much of his energies for several
·ears, culminating in the production with
·. H. Manning of the *Atlas of Spectra of
·ova Herculis 1934* (1939), using material
·ade available from all over the world.
t is still one of the most complete records
f a nova outburst.

In 1939 Stratton was bitterly disappoin-
·d to be refused for active service at the
·ge of fifty-seven. Eventually he spent
·e war travelling extensively, in Canada,
·ustralia, India, and elsewhere, on duties
·r the Royal Corps of Signals. There-
·fter he had only two more years as
·rofessor of astrophysics, and in the
·isorganized post-war conditions he real-
·zed that he could do little. He did,
·owever, complete an interesting *History
f the Cambridge Observatories* (1949).
·fter his retirement he was deputy
·cientific adviser to the Army Council
·or two years and continued to serve on
·nnumerable committees. He was elected
·.R.S. in 1947.

To celebrate his seventieth birthday
·ome of his pupils undertook, with A. Beer
·s editor, to produce what was to have
·een a *Festschrift*, but which expanded,

as more and more of his friends came to
hear of it, into two large volumes, *Vistas
in Astronomy* (1955–6). The publication
quite outgrew its original purpose and
several later volumes were produced.

Stratton's official posts formed only a
part of his activities. In 1925–35 he was
general secretary of the International
Astronomical Union, and did much to
foster what was one of the earliest and
most successful of the international
scientific unions. He was also general
secretary of the International Council of
Scientific Unions from 1937 to 1952, and
general secretary of the British Association, 1930–35. He was president of the
Royal Astronomical Society (1933–5),
treasurer (1923–7), and its foreign secretary (1945–55). He helped to found the
Society for Visiting Scientists and was its
honorary secretary, 1948–55. He was
president of Caius College in 1946–8 and
at the time of his death the senior
fellow. He was president of the Society for
Psychical Research in 1953–5. For more
than fifty years he was chairman of the
Unitarian Church at Cambridge. He was
ever active on behalf of ex-servicemen's
societies and causes and in the early
thirties he gave much help to refugee
scientists from Central Europe.

To his many friends and acquaintances
he was variously known as Professor,
Colonel, Tubby, or Chubby. Short and
rotund, until his last years he lived life at
the double. He thought fast, talked fast
(so that even close friends sometimes had
difficulty in following him), decided fast,
and in his younger days moved fast. He
allowed himself fewer hours for sleep than
most. Despite his great sociableness and
much hospitality, few people knew him
really well, in part because he tended to
keep a life of wide interests and activities
in watertight compartments. His chief
contributions to science and learning were
through help and encouragement to
younger men, and not merely in Britain
alone. As president of I.A.U. Commission
38 his activities in this direction continued
until a few days before his death. A
bachelor, he was completely devoted to his
college, to his pupils, to astronomy and
especially to the International Astronomical Union, to his comrades of the first
world war, and to his duty wherever he
thought it to lie. Personal convenience,
comfort, or profit came very low indeed
on his scale of priorities. Accurately described as a man of tremendous principle,
he also bubbled with good humour and

was of outstanding generosity and modesty.

Stratton died in Cambridge 2 September 1960. A portrait by Sir Oswald Birley is at Caius College.

[*Vistas in Astronomy*, ed. A. Beer, vol. i, 1955; *Nature*, 5 November 1960; *Quarterly Journal* of the Royal Astronomical Society, March 1961; Sir James Chadwick in *Biographical Memoirs of Fellows of the Royal Society*, vol. vii, 1961; personal knowledge.]

R. O. REDMAN.

STREET, SIR ARTHUR WILLIAM (1892–1951), civil servant, was born 16 May 1892 at Cowes, Isle of Wight, the son of William Charles Street, a licensed victualler, by his wife, Minnie Clark. He was educated at the county school, Sandown. At the age of fifteen he went to London to start in the Civil Service as a boy clerk. Street was determined to improve his position by further study at King's College in the Strand and by 1914 had become an established second division clerk at the Board of Agriculture and Fisheries.

During the war of 1914–18 he served on various fronts—mainly in the Middle East —was wounded, mentioned in dispatches, awarded the M.C., and attained the rank of major.

On his return to his old department, Street became private secretary to Lord Lee of Fareham [q.v.], who was so impressed with Street's ability that he took him with him to the Admiralty. When Street returned in 1922 to the Ministry of Agriculture as a principal, a small marketing department was created in which he served and which issued reports on co-operative marketing in other countries and on the marketing in the United Kingdom of agricultural commodities. These reports bore fruit in agriculture marketing Acts in the thirties, affording some protection for the producers on condition that they organized themselves more efficiently, and creating new administrative machinery for these purposes in the form of marketing boards independent of the Government.

Throughout the thirties Street moved up rapidly in the Ministry of Agriculture and Fisheries, becoming second secretary in 1936–8. He was fast gaining a reputation in Whitehall and beyond as a leading civil servant, who combined an intense devotion to duty with an ability to formulate proposals on which ministers could make decisions on policy.

It was no surprise, therefore, when Street was transferred to the Air Ministry in 1938, becoming permanent under secretary of state and a member of the Air Council in 1939. This was a difficult change. The role of the permanent head of a Service department is less clear-cut than in a civil department. The Air Council in Street's day consisted of the minister, his parliamentary secretary, the leading Service officers, and one civil servant. Moreover, the Air Ministry was, perhaps, the most difficult of Service departments. A war was imminent which for the first time in history would be extensively fought in the air. The air marshals who formed the Air Council believed passionately in the importance of the Royal Air Force and they considered it Street's function to find the resources they deemed necessary for expansion. But Street, as accounting officer to the Air Ministry, was responsible for its expenditure and it was his duty, therefore, from time to time, to ask questions which the air marshals might dislike. Moreover, as a newcomer he had to work doubly hard to master the unfamiliar facts of a rapidly expanding department.

Street took to his task very carefully. By intensive hard work and with his remarkable ability for working with other people, he convinced his fellow members of the Air Council that he had the interest of the Air Force as much at heart as anyone. The air marshals found in Street an adviser and a friend to whom they could bring their problems with the full confidence that they would obtain guidance and inspiration.

Before the war broke out in 1939 Street completed one congenial task in the field of civil aviation: he took a leading part in the preparation of the British Overseas Airways Act in 1939.

During the war Street did not spare himself. He worked far into the night, and slept at his office. His influence on the department was profound: he always found time to attend to the personal problems of his staff. His own tragedy was the death of his youngest son, who was one of the fifty Air Force officers who were shot attempting to escape from Stalag Luft III.

At the end of the war Street took charge of a new Office to supervise the British Control Commissions in Germany and Austria. But in July 1946 he was called to his last great task—the deputy chairmanship of the National Coal Board which

January 1947 took over the coal-
ning industry of Great Britain.
Street's task at the Coal Board was
rculean: he had to create an organiza-
n to replace 800 colliery companies and
had to do it quickly. The nationaliza-
n Act of 1946 left the Board to devise
own organization. The coalmining
ustry was run down after the war:
l was in very short supply and in
bruary 1947 there was the worst fuel
sis in British history. There was the
ensely human and long-standing prob-
n of relations with the miners. Again
eet did not spare himself and gradually
organization took root. It should have
en no surprise that Street, worn out
th his incessant labours, died in London
February 1951. Had he lived he was
have succeeded Lord Hyndley as
airman.

Street had a commanding presence and
rsonality; his powers of persuasion
re legendary yet he rarely seemed to
gue. He was always good company, and
interest, enthusiasm, and capacity for
rk swept along all who met him. A man
great vision and a designer of large
licies, he could yet lavish tremendous,
newhat excessive, pains on matters of
tail. Among his wide circle of friends
re men of affairs and leaders of thought,
t only in this country but also abroad,
ecially in France and the dominions.
t the least of his achievements was his
erest in and influence on the group of
ung administrative officers in the Air
nistry, many of whom subsequently
se to high positions in other depart-
nts.

In 1924 Street was appointed C.I.E.
had been joint secretary with (Sir)
ndlater Stewart [q.v.] of the royal com-
ssion on superior civil services in India);
1933 he was appointed C.M.G. after the
tawa conference; in 1935 he was apinted C.B., in 1941 advanced to K.C.B.,
d in 1946 to G.C.B.; in 1938 he had been
pointed K.B.E. He was also a com-
ander of the Legion of Honour and held
her foreign decorations.

Street was first married, in 1915, to
nise, daughter of Jules Mantanus, a
lgian man of business. By her he had
ree sons and a daughter. In 1926, his
fe having died, Street married her sister,
gèle Eleanore Theodorine Mantanus.
A portrait by Henry Carr is in the
perial War Museum.

[*Public Administration*, Winter 1951;
vate information.]   R. KELF-COHEN.

STRIJDOM, JOHANNES GERHARDUS
(1893–1958), South African prime minister,
born 14 July 1893 near Willowmore,
Cape Province, was the second son in
the family of eleven children of Petrus
Gerhardus Strijdom, farmer, and his wife,
Ellen Elizabeth Nortje. After attending
the Fransch Hoek High School, Strijdom proceeded to Victoria College (later
Stellenbosch University), and in 1912
graduated B.A. Following a spell of
ostrich-farming, Strijdom moved to Pretoria, joining the public service in 1914.
After the outbreak of war, he served in
South West Africa, first as a trooper and
subsequently as a non-combatant. After
his discharge in August 1915, he joined a
firm of Pretoria attorneys, obtained his
LL.B., and in 1918 was admitted to the
bar.

Strijdom next moved to Nylstroom in
the northern Transvaal to practise as
an attorney. There he entered politics,
becoming secretary for the Waterberg
division of the National Party of J. B. M.
Hertzog [q.v.]. A part-time farmer,
Strijdom also served as secretary to the
Waterberg Agricultural Union (1923–9).
In the general election of 1929 Strijdom
was returned to Parliament as the member for Waterberg, the constituency which
he continued to represent until his death.

Although Strijdom, like D. F. Malan
[q.v.], the Cape Nationalist leader, stood
as a coalitionist in the general election of
1933, he joined Malan in the following
year in denouncing the fusion of parties,
led respectively by Hertzog and J. C.
Smuts [q.v.], as a betrayal of Nationalist
principles. Following the formation of the
'purified' National Party, Strijdom until
1938 was its only parliamentary representative from the Transvaal, and became
its leader in that province. As chairman of
the company publishing the Nationalist
newspaper, *Die Transvaler*, he was assisted in building up the party by its
editor, H. F. Verwoerd, subsequently his
successor as prime minister.

After Hertzog's defeat in Parliament
and resignation over the war issue,
Strijdom became joint leader in the Transvaal with General J. C. G. Kemp, of the
Herenigde (reunited) *Nasionale Party*,
formed in 1940. Opposing any compromise
over the republican aim, to which he had
long been committed, Strijdom believed
that a German victory might furnish an
opportunity to achieve it. He refused to
follow Hertzog in undertaking to guarantee English-speaking rights. Insistent

nevertheless that the republic should be achieved by constitutional means, Strijdom supported Malan in successfully resisting (as the general election of 1943 demonstrated) the claims of extra-parliamentary movements to challenge the H.N.P. as the political voice of the Afrikaner *volk*.

When the Nationalists came to power in 1948, Strijdom received the relatively minor portfolio of lands (and later also irrigation) in Malan's Cabinet. He tackled his departmental work with vigour and simultaneously succeeded in raising his prestige in the party as a whole. Malan, upon retiring in 1954, intended to advise the governor-general to invite N. C. Havenga, the minister of finance, to succeed him; but Strijdom's supporters, representing the radical element in the party and especially strong in the Transvaal, insisted that the parliamentary caucus elect the new party leader and prime minister. Strijdom's unanimous election was ensured by Havenga's withdrawal.

In the four years of his premiership Strijdom, who by now accepted that the republic could not be established by a simple majority in Parliament and that English-speaking rights must be respected, continued to pursue his republican goal. Legislation in 1957 secured that South Africa would have one national flag and anthem.

The most controversial issue of Strijdom's premiership derived from the struggle to remove the Cape Coloured voters from the common roll. Through the enlargement of the Senate Strijdom in 1956 obtained the necessary two-thirds majority of both Houses, and the Appeal Court upheld the Government by validating the Senate Act.

Strijdom, who suffered poor health throughout his premiership, became ill shortly before the general election of 1958. He recovered sufficiently to participate in the campaign, but afterwards his condition deteriorated. He died in Cape Town 24 August 1958.

As a *volksleier*, Strijdom commanded the almost unqualified devotion of many of his followers. His personal appeal and integrity, his accessibility and his active membership of the Dutch Reformed Church all played their part. To his opponents, however, his steadfastness and his blunt oratory typified the intransigent *Broederbonder*, pursuing a narrow and exclusive Afrikaner cause.

In 1931 Strijdom married Susa daughter of the Rev. W. J. de Klerk; th had a son and a daughter. An earli marriage to Margaretha van Hulste (the actress Marda Vanne), daughter Sir Willem van Hulsteyn, a form member of Parliament, had been d solved.

[G. Coetsee, *Hans Strijdom*, 1958; G. Carter, *The Politics of Inequality*, 195 J. M. Strydom, *J. G. Strijdom*, 1965.]

N. G. GARSO

STRONG, LEONARD ALFRE GEORGE (1896–1958), writer, was bo in Plymouth 8 March 1896, the elder chi and only son of Leonard Ernest Stron who worked for a firm of manufacture of artificial fertilizers and ultimate became a director of Fisons, by his wif Marion Jane, daughter of Alfred Monga a lawyer's clerk in Dublin. His father wa half-English, half-Irish; his mother wa wholly Irish. A delicate boy, Strong wc an open scholarship to Brighton Colleg and thence an open classical scholarshi to Wadham College, Oxford. Illne interrupted his schooling and kept hi from active service in the war. In 191 he became an assistant master at Summe Fields School, Oxford, returning to Wac ham in 1919 to take pass classics an English, graduating B.A. in 1920. He we back to Summer Fields and remained master there until 1930, when his i creasing reputation as a writer enable him to devote himself entirely to literar work.

Strong's early years influenced hi profoundly. His childhood Irish an Devon memories reappeared in his fictio which often had Ireland, Devonshire, c the Scottish Highlands as the backgroun The obscure spinal trouble from which h suffered kept him from sport, excep swimming, and may explain the emphasi in much of his writing on physical strengt not unmixed with brutality.

He began to send contributions t editors in 1915. At Oxford he wrote fo undergraduate journals, and in 1921 h settled down in earnest to freelanc writing, deriving many of his subject from schoolmastering. As an author h started with two books of poems, *Dubli Days* (1921) and *The Lowery Road* (1923 and he drew on these and later volumes o poetry for his collected poems *The Body' Imperfection* (1957). His achievement a a lyric poet of tenderness and wit, an often of epigrammatical conciseness, wa

rhaps not sufficiently appreciated in his
etime. Poetry undoubtedly lay at the
art of his talent as a novelist.
The great success of Strong's first pub-
hed novel *Dewer Rides* (1929), a story
Dartmoor, encouraged him to give
schoolmastering, and he followed it
th *The Jealous Ghost* (1930); *The
rden* (1931), which was largely auto-
ographical; *The Brothers* (1932), a
ory of Highland fishermen; *Sea Wall*
933), set chiefly in Dublin; and *Corporal
une* (1934). By this time he had become
established novelist with a regular
llowing of readers. Among his more
table later novels may be mentioned
he *Seven Arms* (1935), *The Open Sky*
939), *The Bay* (1941), *The Director*
944), full of perceptive Irish characteri-
tion, and *Deliverance* (1955). His
llections of short stories, *The English
ptain* (1929), *Travellers* (1945), which
as awarded the James Tait Black mem-
ial prize, and *Darling Tom* (1952),
owed him in turn as a master of comedy
d sentiment, of the macabre, the fear-
l, and the ironic.
Strong developed into an extremely
olific and versatile writer, increasingly
illing to turn his hand to anything that
me along. He became a zealous specta-
r and defender of boxing, on which he
rote in *Shake Hands and Come Out
ighting* (1938). He was the biographer
Thomas Moore (*The Minstrel Boy*, 1937),
John McCormack (1941), and of Thomas
over (*Dr. Quicksilver*, 1955). He com-
led anthologies and wrote one-act plays,
ooks for children, school books, detec-
ve stories, film scripts, radio and tele-
sion plays, and even *The Story of Sugar*
954). As a literary critic he is not to be
iderestimated, as his book on James
oyce, *The Sacred River* (1949), and his
ersonal Remarks* (1953), containing
emorable studies of Synge and Yeats,
oth showed. He turned his novel *The
irector* into a play which was put on at
e Gate Theatre, Dublin. A singer himlf, he had a passionate interest in the
rt. He was an impressive lecturer and
came an inspiring teacher of drama and
oice production, notably at the Central
hool of Speech and Drama; he was the
ithor of a book on the speaking of
nglish, *A Tongue in Your Head* (1945).
s an adjudicator in amateur dramatics
e travelled all over the country. Strong
as a member of the Irish Academy of
etters, a fellow of the Royal Society of
iterature, and for many years honorary

treasurer of the Society of Authors. In
1938 he became a director of Methuens,
the publishers.
Although Strong may be criticized as
something of a 'literary chameleon', and
although this attitude to writing, which he
did not deny, deprived him of a certain
single-mindedness even in his fiction, he
may be remembered by his early novels,
his short stories, and his poetry.
Strong was of medium height and pleasant in looks. Contradictory as he could
appear in his writings, he was personally
a man of most engaging modesty, charm,
and humour who would go to any length
to help a fellow writer. In 1926 Strong
married Dorothea Sylvia Tryce, younger
daughter of Hubert Brinton, assistant
master at Eton College; they had one
son. Strong died in Guildford, Surrey,
17 August 1958. He left a posthumous
autobiography of his early life, *Green
Memory* (1961), and there is considerable
autobiographical material, as well as
much practical advice, in his book *The
Writer's Trade* (1953). A drawing by
Wyndham Lewis and a caricature by (Sir)
David Low are in the possession of
the family.

[*The Times*, 19, 23, and 26 August 1958;
R. L. Mégroz, *Five Novelist Poets of Today*,
1933; private information; personal knowledge.]   DEREK HUDSON.

STUART, SIR JOHN THEODOSIUS
BURNETT- (1875–1958), general. [See
BURNETT-STUART.]

SUETER, SIR MURRAY FRAZER
(1872–1960), rear-admiral, was born in
Alverstoke, Gosport, 6 September 1872,
the son of fleet-paymaster John Thomas
Sueter and his wife, Ellen Feild Light-
bourn. He entered the *Britannia* in 1886,
served as a midshipman in the *Swiftsure*,
flagship on the Pacific station, was
promoted lieutenant in 1894, and appointed to the *Vernon* to qualify as a torpedo
specialist in 1896. He commanded the
destroyer *Fame* at the diamond jubilee
naval review of 1897, and after a further
two years' service on the staff of the
Vernon was appointed in 1800 to the
Jupiter for torpedo duties.
In 1902 Sueter received an appointment
to the gunboat *Hazard*, at the time
commanded by (Sir) Reginald Bacon
[q.v.] and recently commissioned as the
first parent ship for submarines, of which

the Holland boats were just entering for service as the navy's first submarines. While serving in the *Hazard*, Sueter distinguished himself by entering the battery compartment of the submarine A.1, after an explosion caused by a concentration of hydrogen, to assist in the rescue of injured men who would otherwise have been badly burned. This period of service with the early submarines led to a lifelong interest in these vessels, and in 1907 Sueter published one of the first books of real merit on this subject under the title *The Evolution of the Submarine Boat, Mine and Torpedo*.

Sueter was promoted commander in 1903 and appointed in 1904 to the Admiralty to serve as assistant to the director of naval ordnance. He returned to sea in 1906 to command the cruiser *Barham* in the Mediterranean, returning two years later to the naval ordnance department in the Admiralty. He was promoted captain in 1909.

The Admiralty at this time was considering the use of aircraft, especially airships, for reconnaissance duties with the fleet and in 1909 had placed contracts for the construction of a rigid airship to be named *Mayfly*. Sueter took a very keen interest in her construction and contributed many useful suggestions during her building. As a result he was appointed in 1910 to command the cruiser *Hermione* with the additional title of inspecting captain of airships. Unfortunately before her first flight the *Mayfly*'s back was broken while she was being manœuvred out of her hangar in a high wind in 1911, an accident which for a time put a stop to further airship development for the navy. In 1912 Sueter was brought back to the Admiralty to take over the new air department and much of the rapid development of the seaplane as a naval aircraft was due to his enthusiasm. Shortly before the outbreak of war in 1914, and largely on Sueter's suggestions, the naval wing broke away from its parent body, the Royal Flying Corps, to become the Royal Naval Air Service. For his work on the development of naval flying Sueter was appointed C.B. in 1914.

Sueter was promoted commodore 2nd class shortly after the outbreak of war and, still as director of the air department, was largely instrumental in the rapid build-up of the R.N.A.S. to a full war strength. In this he was encouraged by (Sir) Winston Churchill, the first lord, and by Lord Fisher [q.v.], recalled as first

sea lord in October 1914. Sueter, wl had continued with some success to pre for airship development, was very large responsible for the design and rap production of small non-rigid airshi designed to search out U-boats operati in British coastal waters. In all, some 2 of these were built and proved of gre value particularly when convoy w adopted later in the war. Sueter al interested himself in the development torpedo-carrying aircraft, and, worki with Lieutenant Douglas Hyde-Thomso it was he who initiated the design whi was adopted in the navy. An early succe when a Turkish supply ship was sunk an air-launched torpedo in the sea Marmara in 1915 not only vindicat Sueter's ingenuity and foresight b proved to be the first step in the develo ment of one of the navy's most powerf weapons.

In 1915 Sueter turned his inventi mind to new avenues of service for th R.N.A.S. and advanced the idea of pr viding armoured cars for the defence airfields established abroad. During tl early months these cars did useful wor in Flanders and northern France but the war settled into its static phase trench warfare their value declined. Tw squadrons of these armoured cars we sent abroad, one to Russia under Con mander Oliver Locker-Lampson and or to Egypt under the Duke of Westminste

Sueter's restless brain, not content wit the armoured car design, concentrate on means of giving it a cross-countr capability by fitting it with caterpilla tracks. From this advance it was a sho step to the development of the tank.

With the appointment of an officer flag rank in September 1915 as fifth se lord with responsibility for naval aviatio Sueter was made superintendent of ai craft construction with full responsibilit for the matériel side of all naval aircraf At the same time he was promote commodore 1st class. But in 1917, afte some differences of opinion with the Boar of Admiralty, he was sent to souther Italy to command the R.N.A.S. unit there. Later in the year Sueter wrote letter to King George V on the subject o recognition of his work, and that of tw other officers associated with him, i initiating the idea of tanks. This wa passed to the Admiralty in the norma manner and roused considerable resent ment. Sueter was informed that he ha incurred their lordships' severe displeasur

nd relieved of his command. He returned
> England in January 1918 and despite
is protests no further employment was
>und for him. He was placed on the
·tired list early in 1920 and shortly
fterwards the Admiralty obtained a
pecial order in Council to promote him
> rear-admiral.

Sueter was gifted with a restless brain
vhich he used skilfully and effectively to
uggest means of overcoming difficulties,
oth technical and professional. He was
lways outspoken, and intolerant of
fficial lethargy in any matter in which
e took an interest. It was this intolerance,
llied to a headstrong character, which
rought to an end a naval career of
onsiderable future promise.

After the war Sueter did much useful
vork in the development of the Empire
ir mail postal services, and he received
he thanks of three successive postmasters-
eneral for his assistance in organizing
hese services. In 1921 he was elected an
ndependent member of Parliament for
Iertford, remaining a member as a Con-
ervative until the general election of 1945.
Ie was knighted in 1934. In 1928 he
vrote *Airmen or Noahs*, largely auto-
iographical but also attacking current
oncepts of naval and military warfare
nd advocating the development of inde-
endent air power. It was followed in 1937
>y *The Evolution of the Tank*.

Sueter married in 1903 Elinor Mary de
Vinton (died 1948), only daughter of Sir
Andrew Clarke [q.v.], and had two daugh-
ers. He died at his home at Watlington,
)xfordshire, 3 February 1960. A portrait
>y (Sir) William Russell Flint was exhibi-
ed at the Royal Academy in 1928.

[Admiralty records; *The Times*, 5 February
1960.]   P. K. KEMP.

SULLIVAN, ALEXANDER MARTIN
1871–1959), barrister, was born at Bel-
ield, Drumcondra, Dublin, 14 January
1871, the second son of Alexander Martin
Sullivan [q.v.], one of the founders of the
Home Rule League and proprietor and
·ditor of the *Nation* after (Sir) Charles
Gavan Duffy [q.v.] had left for Australia.
He was educated at Ushaw, Belvedere,
nd Trinity College, Dublin, and in early
ife worked as a journalist on the Dublin
Evening News, contributing also to the
Nation and the *Weekly News*. He was
:alled to the Irish bar in 1892 and, having
oined the Middle Temple, to the English
bar in 1899, taking silk in Ireland in 1908
and in England in 1919. He was third

King's Serjeant in Ireland (1912), second
Serjeant (1913), and first Serjeant, the
last to hold office (1920); he continued to
use the title by courtesy after he left
Ireland and practised exclusively at the
English bar.

Sullivan's rise at the Irish bar was rapid;
since in Ireland there was little tendency
to specialize in common law or Chancery
work, he acquired familiarity with both,
although his style of advocacy was better
suited to the former. His professional
background and experiences in a system
free and easy in its personal contacts and
far less technically rigid than the English
are vividly recreated in his two books of
reminiscences *Old Ireland* (1927) and *The
Last Serjeant* (1952).

From childhood Sullivan, through his
father, family, and friends, had been
strongly attached to the Irish Nationalist
Party and its constitutional methods.
In the long crisis of violence which began
with the Easter Rising of 1916 he was
uncompromisingly opposed to the physical
force and terrorism of Sinn Fein, which he
regarded as no better than that of the
Black and Tans. As violence developed
he played an active and courageous part
in the courts in striving as he saw it to
maintain order through the established
forms of administration of justice. In
January 1920 an attempt was made on
his life near Tralee and later shots were
fired at a railway carriage in which he was
travelling.

After the establishment of the Free
State in 1922 Sullivan moved to England
where he was already well known for his
brave defence of Sir Roger Casement
[q.v.] in 1916, which he had undertaken
out of a sense of professional duty,
although he personally was strongly
opposed to the accused. He was warmly
received at the English bar, became a
bencher of the Middle Temple in 1925,
and served as treasurer in 1944, the year
in which the Queen was admitted as a
bencher. Tall and neatly bearded, Sullivan
was an impressive figure in the courts,
fiercely independent and zealous for his
clients' rights to the point of personal
recklessness. He was a profound and
learned lawyer with a superb memory,
and beneath a grave demeanour there ran
his own vein of ironical wit. Among his
best known cases was the libel action
brought by Marie Stopes [q.v.] against
Halliday Sutherland [q.v.], whom Sullivan, himself a devout Roman Catholic, successfully represented. His most notorious

client was W. C. Hobbs, the villain of the 'Mr. A' case, for whom he appeared in his libel actions against various newspapers. In these proceedings Sullivan quarrelled bitterly with Lord Chief Justice Hewart [q.v.].

After the Republic of Ireland Act of 1949 Sullivan considered himself an alien disqualified from practising at the English bar and retired to Dublin; but he retained his house at Beckenham, Kent, where he died 9 January 1959.

In 1900 Sullivan married Helen (died 1952), daughter of Major John D. Keiley, of Brooklyn, New York; they had five sons and seven daughters. One of the daughters, Mrs. Nora Ambrose, received the Queen's Commendation for bravery for tackling an armed robber in 1967.

Sullivan figures in a painting of the Casement trial by Sir John Lavery which is in the President's House in Phoenix Park.

[*The Times*, 10 January 1959; *Solicitors' Journal*, 16 January 1959; *Law Times*, 23 January 1959; *Irish Law Times*, 17 and 31 January 1920, 31 January 1959; private information; personal knowledge.]

F. H. COWPER.

SUMNER, BENEDICT HUMPHREY (1893–1951), historian, was born in London 8 August 1893, the second of the three sons, in a family of five children, of George Heywood Maunoir Sumner and his wife, Agnes Mary, daughter of William Benson, a sister of Lord Charnwood and Sir Frank Benson [qq.v.]. Heywood Sumner, a figure of patriarchal dignity and the son and grandson of bishops (his father was bishop of Guildford and his grandfather was C. R. Sumner [q.v.], bishop of Winchester), forsook the episcopal tradition for art. He was a disciple of William Morris [q.v.] and a painter who in later life became a distinguished archaeologist. Nevertheless the Barchester atmosphere lingered in the Sumner household, and Heywood's mother, the foundress of the Mothers' Union, made a deep impression on her five grandchildren. Sumner went up to Balliol, his grandfather's college, as a Brackenbury scholar from Winchester in 1912, but his career there was interrupted by the outbreak of war in 1914. After three gruelling years as an officer in the King's Royal Rifle Corps he was invalided home and transferred to the directorate of military intelligence at the War Office in 1917. Thence he passed to the peace conference, and from 1920 to 1922 served in the International Labour Office. In 1919 he had been elected to fellowship at All Souls, and from Geneva he returned to Balliol in 1922 to serve as fellow (1925) and tutor in modern history for the next twenty years.

In this difficult period Sumner was a tower of strength in the life of the college. The effects of the war upon Oxford were profound and to many disquieting. The numbers of the college rose steeply, accommodation, staffing, and finance became major problems, and new schools were altering the traditional balance between the humanities and the sciences. The teaching load, too, was very heavy, and in this Sumner, despite the efforts of his colleagues, carried always more than his proper share. His life as a tutor was of a piece with the whole man—a prodigious capacity for work, an almost over-developed conscientiousness, and an unusual ability for assimilating facts. In teaching he distrusted generalization and disliked epigram. His own range was immense, and if he set both himself and his pupils an unattainable standard, yet his teaching had always a wide horizon.

In scholarship, his personal interest ran to contemporary history, and he was closely concerned with the inception and development of the (Royal) Institute of International Affairs at Chatham House. He had already begun to learn Russian while at school, and characteristically published little until he had achieved a mastery unique in this country in his chosen subject. Then in 1937 he published a large book on *Russia and the Balkans*, a work of patient learning, which was to be his chief contribution to history. He followed this up in 1944 with his more popular *Survey of Russian History*, which went into two editions, and though no easy reading was soon recognized as the safest guide yet written to Russian history. In 1945 he was elected to the British Academy, and four years later he published *Peter the Great and the Ottoman Empire* (1949), a short but original work of complicated research; and in 1950 his last book, *Peter the Great and the Emergence of Russia*, which has been described as 'much the best short account of its subject in English, perhaps in any language'. The 'immense mass of ordered material' on which all his books, whether learned or popular, were based was gained the hard way, and he left behind him a large collection of notebooks in which with meticulous thoroughness, he had

itomized the most fundamental original
orks on Russian history of all periods.
The early years at Balliol were perhaps
e happiest of Sumner's life. Tall and wiry,
great pipe smoker and a keen walker,
e was the very centre of the teaching in
odern history and 'Modern Greats'. He
emed to have endless reserves of strength
d energy until, in the year 1931, a per-
rated appendix involved three major
erations. He made an excellent re-
overy, but between 1939 and 1943 in the
idst of a second world war, he came near
breaking down under the double strain
college work and a post with the foreign
esearch and press department, organized
y the Royal Institute of International
ffairs, which was then located in Balliol
ollege. There was another serious opera-
on, due to ulcer trouble; and although
e again made a good recovery, his health,
s it proved, was permanently impaired.
1944 he was induced to leave Balliol
r the less exacting position of professor of
istory at Edinburgh, but only to return
Oxford in the course of the next year
warden of All Souls.

Succeeding Dr. W. G. S. Adams on his
etirement, Sumner threw himself not
nly into the task of building up All
ouls after the war, but also of ensuring
s co-operation with the university. In
e period of reconstruction, he was
onstantly on the alert that the college by
s finance, by its elections, and not least
y its hospitality, should make its maxi-
um contribution, while retaining its dis-
nctive character as a place of liaison
etween public and academic life. His
fforts won general confidence, founded as
ey were upon the respect he enjoyed for
is farsighted and sober judgement; while
ithin the college itself his consideration
r each individual, and his private hospi-
lity in the Lodgings, which owed much
o his sister Beatrix, made a lasting im-
ession. But the work was very heavy,
nd he was drawn into endless committees,
f which not the least onerous was the
niversity Grants Committee. His health
egan to fail. He was often confined to bed
r weeks on end, and there was another
erious operation. For the last time he
ecovered: but a new illness required still
nother operation, faced with the same
nperturbability as the others, and he
ied in hospital in Oxford 25 April 1951.
e was unmarried.

It would be a great mistake to think
hat Sumner's last years, clouded though
hey were by ill health, were unhappy.
It was not for nothing that he had been
nicknamed 'the Emperor' in his early
days at All Souls, for he lived on a very
high plane and was above all that is
implied by ambition. Much more might
be added of his artistic and literary
interests; and more especially of his love
of Shakespeare and of Dante, on whom
he published two papers. He delighted
in parodies and in round games like demon
patience (at which he was a real expert),
and he was a valued accession at nursery
tea in the houses of his married friends.
Not unnaturally, as a student of Russia,
he took a prominent part in the affairs
of the British national committee of
the International Congress of Historical
Sciences, and he strove though without
success to be allowed to entertain Russian
historians in Oxford.

A scholar's life, spent largely in Oxford,
is naturally uneventful, and Sumner is
especially likely to be remembered more for
what he was than for what he did. Even
his scholarship, only fully appreciated
since his death, seemed then merely
incidental. His influence—and it was very
great—was essentially that of a commanding personality who struck all,
friends and pupils alike, as a good and
a great man. His impenetrable reserve,
although no bar to friendship, repelled
intimacy, and it was only on the rarest
occasions he showed by a sudden forthright judgement the strength of feeling
that underlay his iron restraint. Even his
friends were sometimes tempted to suppose hidden depths of repression behind
such invariable moderation; but it seems
more likely that he was a man moulded
by the traditional religious influence of his
childhood against which he never rebelled.
A loyal member of the Church of England,
he delighted in its liturgy, and as warden
the details of every special college service
engaged his attention. Here too he sometimes lifted the veil of his reserve, as
when he wrote to an old Balliol pupil:
'Sheer human friendliness: more and more,
I feel, that is what makes life deeply
worth while: that, and the ineffability of
God keep me going when I am most
despondent, or irritated and tired.'

An unfinished portrait by Augustus
John and a bronze bust by David Wynne
are at All Souls College.

[*The Times*, 26 April 1951; Sir Charles
Webster in *Proceedings* of the British Academy, vol. xxxvii, 1951; private information;
personal knowledge.]

V. H. GALBRAITH.

SUTHERLAND, HALLIDAY GIBSON (1882–1960), physician, author, and controversialist, was born in Glasgow 24 June 1882, the elder son of John Francis Sutherland, M.D., deputy commissioner for lunacy in Scotland, and his wife, Jane, daughter of John Mackay, a Free Church minister in Caithness. After the Glasgow High School and Merchiston Castle School, Edinburgh, he studied medicine at Edinburgh University, where he graduated M.B., Ch.B. in 1906 and M.D. with honours in 1908. As an undergraduate, Sutherland was a leading debater and prominent personality in Liberal politics, although in 1945 it was as a Labour candidate that he stood unsuccessfully for the Scottish Universities.

One of Sutherland's Highland relatives happened to be in medical practice at the Rio Tinto mines at Huelva in Spain where Sutherland spent some time learning many things, including the rudiments of bullfighting—knowledge which he later developed imaginatively in one of his books.

Soon after graduation, Sutherland came under the influence of (Sir) Robert William Philip, pioneer of modern anti-tuberculosis schemes, on whose model in 1911 he opened a tuberculosis dispensary in St. Marylebone, London. It included the original feature of an open-air school, conducted in the bandstand of Regent's Park. He also produced a cinema film on tuberculosis which was probably the first health education film in this country. In 1911 Sutherland edited a remarkable compilation of tributes to Philip's work from pupils all over the world. Brought to the attention of a prime minister's wife, the volume gained Philip a knighthood and secured official approval for his tuberculosis schemes in which Sutherland played a leading part.

War service in the Royal Navy and the Royal Air Force interrupted his career. He used the opportunity to write a textbook on *Pulmonary Tuberculosis* (1916). Although planned before the war, it was actually written near the equator when he was medical officer in the armed merchant cruiser *Empress of Britain*.

On returning to practise in London, Sutherland became physician to St. Marylebone (later St. Charles') Hospital, Ladbroke Grove, and assistant physician to the Royal Chest Hospital. Between 1920 and 1925 he was deputy commissioner (tuberculosis) for the south-west of England, and then joined the medical service of the London County Council.

Sutherland's many-sided personalit was now ripe for new expression. In 19: he had married and become a Roma Catholic. It happened that a book b Marie Stopes [q.v.] called *Married Lov* published in 1918, had made birth contr a lively public issue, and Sutherlan plunged into controversy, attacking th practice on sociological and religio grounds. The subject was new and shoc ing, and Sutherland became an uni hibited and pungent critic. He asserte in his book *Birth Control, a Statemer of Christian Doctrine* (1922) that it w truly amazing that this monstrous can paign of birth control should be tolerate by the home secretary, and that Charl Bradlaugh [q.v.] had been condemned jail for a less serious crime. Dr. Stope herself no mean controversialist, sue him for libel. After prolonged litigatio Sutherland's defence to this action wa upheld by the House of Lords (1924) an the case became a leading one in th English law of defamation. His opponen described Sutherland as 'the most cocksu man in the British Empire'. This sel confidence was both his strength and limitation. He never had any doubts. H could produce an impressive argumen but it did not always seem convincin In truth, he was more temperamentall fitted for law or politics than for medicin in which his reputation never maintaine the level of a brilliant beginning. In 194 he became deputy medical officer of healt for Coventry, and in 1943 started the Mas Radiography Centre in Birmingham whic he directed until 1951. He also spen periods of general medical practice i north London.

In the meantime he had made his nam as a writer, publishing in 1933 a ver readable volume of reminiscences, *Th Arches of the Years*, a title taken from 'Th Hound of Heaven' by Francis Thompso [q.v.]. Enormously successful, it ran t thirty-two English editions, and wa translated into eight languages. It wa followed by further anecdotal auto biographies—*A Time to Keep* (1934), *I My Path* (1936), *Lapland Journey* (1938) *Hebridean Journey* (1939), *Southwar Journey* (1942), *Spanish Journey* (1948) and *Irish Journey* (1956). Sutherland' great theme was himself. When describin his triumphs or misadventures, wit doctors, with bullfighters, or in the la courts, his style is terse, emphatic, an very sympathetic. He explored no ne pathways of human experience, but hi

liosyncrasies and pugnacious judgements
vere highly entertaining.

Sutherland had red hair and blue eyes.
Ie was thickset and not very tall. Touches
f humour came through his ceremonious
nd resonant tones of voice in which there
vere echoes of the pulpit. He was indeed
ifted with his mother's Highland tempera-
nent and his grandfather's Free Church
ervour. Courage and provocative wit
;ained him friends but also enemies.

In 1920 Sutherland married Muriel,
laughter of John Frederick Fitzpatrick,
he managing director of a City firm of
oriental importers. They had five sons
and one daughter. He was made a knight
commander of the Order of Isabel the
Catholic in 1954 and died in London 19
April 1960. There is in the possession of
the family an oil portrait by an Australian
artist.

[*The Times*, 20 April 1960; *British Medical
Journal* and *Lancet*, 30 April 1960; personal
knowledge.]   HARLEY WILLIAMS.

SWINBURNE, SIR JAMES, ninth baronet
(1858–1958), pioneer of electrical engineering and of plastics, was born in
Inverness 28 February 1858, the third of
the six sons of Lieutenant (later Captain)
Thomas Anthony Swinburne, R.N., and
his wife, Mary Anne, daughter of Captain
Edward Fraser of Gortuleg. A descendant
of the second baronet, Swinburne succeeded a kinsman in 1934. Much of his
childhood was spent in the lonely little
island of Eilean Shona in Loch Moidart,
where the servants and the children all
spoke Gaelic. He was educated at Clifton
College which was particularly strong on
the science side; then apprenticed to a
locomotive works in Manchester where he
developed his remarkable inherent skill
with his hands. Later he went to a
Tyneside engineering firm and became
interested in the rising electrical industry.
In 1881 (Sir) Joseph Swan [q.v.] engaged
him to establish a lamp factory in Paris
and in the next year he went to America
on a similar mission. For some three years
after 1885 he worked as technical assistant and later manager in the dynamo
works of R. E. B. Crompton [q.v.] and it
was during this time that he invented a
watt-hour meter and his well-known
hedgehog transformer. Then he set up as a
consultant, moving in 1894 to Victoria
Street where he had his own beautifully
equipped workshop and a chemical and
physical laboratory.

Swinburne's contribution to the early
development of electrical engineering
included work on the theories of dynamo
design, of armature reaction in direct current machines and in alternating current
dynamos and motors, and of alterna-
ting-current measuring instruments; he
worked also on Clark's standard cells;
investigated the action of various kinds
of secondary batteries with lead and
other electrodes; and questions of high
vacua and methods of measuring very
small pressures. It was he who coined
the words 'rotor' and 'stator'. He was
president of the Institution of Electrical
Engineers (1902–3) and of the Faraday
Society (1909–11), and was recognized as
one of the leading authorities of the
electrical industry. He was elected F.R.S.
in 1906.

Swinburne's professional interests were
not confined to electrical engineering. In
1904 he published a useful book on
*Entropy, or Thermodynamics from an
Engineer's Standpoint*. Much of his research work was intimately connected
with the application of physics and
chemistry to industrial purposes and he
was particularly susceptible to any suggestion for the development of new materials. It was he who suggested that lamp
filaments and artificial silk might be made
from viscose; he had a share in the syndicate manufacturing artificial silk which
not long afterwards was taken over by
Courtaulds. On seeing an interesting but
useless specimen of resin obtained from
the reaction between phenol and formal-
dehyde, he came to the conclusion that
something useful could be made, and
formed a syndicate to investigate the
process. When he sought to file his patent
in 1907 he found that he had been anticipated by the Belgian chemist, L. H.
Baekeland, working in the United States,
who thus swept the solid field. But Swinburne was successful in making a lacquer
and in 1910 established the Damard
Lacquer Company in Birmingham. Eventually Baekeland bought the Damard and
other companies and established Bakelite,
Ltd., in Great Britain (1926), making
Swinburne its first chairman, in which office
he continued until 1948, remaining on the
board until 1951 when he became honorary
life president. He was president of the
Plastics Institute in 1937–8.

On the occasion of Swinburne's hundredth birthday, Mr. Justice Lloyd-Jacob
in the Chancery division paid tribute to
the tremendous contribution which he had
made to patent jurisprudence. Over a

long period he was greatly in demand as an expert witness in fields which extended far beyond those of electrical engineering and included such diverse inventions as pneumatic tyres, soda syphons, and golf balls. Given with candour and humour, his evidence was unshakeable and completely honest. He himself filed 123 patents. His vigour was as remarkable as the range of his interests which included paper-bag machinery and naval gunnery; raising bullion from the *Egypt*, organ-building, and the work of the Royal Musical Association; sociology, and horology to which he returned as a hobby in the years of his retirement. A man of great integrity, Swinburne was quite unimpressed by himself and never alluded to his own achievements. He was usually laconic in speech but could be a good talker and was an excellent listener. His sense of humour was acute; he could be scathing but rarely was; seldom lost his temper, and gave the impression of complete imperturbability. He neither smoked nor drank and had a lifelong sympathy with poor people deriving from his apprentice days when he had little money. He was of medium height, very good looking, and had the courteous manners of a Victorian gentleman at his best.

In 1886 Swinburne married Ellen (died 1893), daughter of Robert Harrison Wilson, doctor, of Gateshead-upon-Tyne, by whom he had three sons, the second of whom, Spearman Charles (1893–1967, the survivor of twins), succeeded as tenth baronet. In 1898 he married Lilian Gilchrist (died 1964), daughter of (Sir) Thomas Godfrey Carey, bailiff of Guernsey (1895–1902), by whom he had two daughters. He died in Bournemouth 30 March 1958, the third fellow of the Royal Society to live to be over a hundred years old; the second was H. N. Ridley, also noticed in this volume.

There is a portrait by T. C. Dugdale in the possession of the family.

[F. A. Freeth in *Biographical Memoirs of Fellows of the Royal Society*, vol. v. 1959; *New Scientist*, 27 February 1958; *Journal of the Plastics Institute*, July 1958; *Journal of the Institution of Electrical Engineers*, May 1958; M.E.S. and K.R.S., *Sir Joseph Wilson Swan F.R.S.*, 1929; private information; personal knowledge.]   F. A. FREETH.

SWINTON, SIR ERNEST DUNLOP (1868–1951), major-general, was born in Bangalore, Mysore, 21 October 1868, the fourth son of Robert Blair Swinton, a judge in the Madras civil service, and h wife, Elizabeth Dorothy Rundall, daugh ter of a business man in India. He wa educated at University College Schoo Rugby, Cheltenham, and Blackheat Proprietary School before passing into th Royal Military Academy, Woolwich. I 1888 he was commissioned in the Roya Engineers and he spent five years in Indi before being appointed in 1896 assistan instructor in fortification at the schoo of military engineering, Chatham. Soo after the outbreak of the South Africa war he was sent out for bridging dutie on railways and became adjutant to an later commanded the 1st battalion Rail way Pioneer Regiment, an irregular unit He was appointed to the D.S.O. in 190 and remained on railway work throughou the war.

Swinton had a marked tactical bent combined with literary talent, and transmuted the results of his observation and reflection into a stimulating and amusing little treatise on minor tactics cast in fictional form, and reprinted in 1904 from the *United Service Magazine* under the title *The Defence of Duffer's Drift* and the pseudonym 'Backsight Forethought'. It soon came to be widely recommended to young officers as simple to read and easy to assimilate. It ran through many editions, was published in numerous countries, and was still much used during the war of 1939–45. Subsequently Swinton wrote a series of superb stories dealing with future warfare, particularly with its psychological aspects, published as *The Green Curve* (1909) under the pseudonym 'Ole Luk-Oie', a Danish term meaning, roughly, 'Shut-Eye'. It likewise had a wide and long circulation. A further volume of stories, *The Great Tab Dope*, was published in 1915.

Meanwhile, Swinton served on the engineer side of the War Office, was promoted major in 1906, and in 1907 became chief instructor in fortification and geometrical drawing at the Royal Military Academy, Woolwich. In 1910 he was posted to the historical section of the Committee of Imperial Defence and employed on the British official history of the Russo-Japanese war, for which he was awarded the Chesney gold medal of the Royal United Service Institution. In 1913 he was made assistant secretary of the Committee of Imperial Defence.

On the outbreak of war in 1914 Swinton was appointed deputy director of railway transport but was soon diverted, by choice

Lord Kitchener [q.v.], to be a kind of official war correspondent with the expeditionary force, reporting under the pen-name 'Eyewitness' when Joffre's ban on press correspondents in the war zone aroused growing public complaint about lack of information. While the official position was a handicap on frank comment, Swinton's reports were well enough written to appease public clamour for a time. Far more important, however, was the opportunity it provided for fresh thought based on close observation. He was quick to perceive the trench deadlock, even as it developed, from the growing defensive domination of the machine-gun in conjunction with trenches and wire entanglements.

In his book *Eyewitness* (1932) Swinton tells the story of how the solution of the problem came to him. The vague idea of an armoured vehicle crystallized into the more definite idea that it should be 'capable of destroying machine-guns, of crossing country and trenches, of breaking through entanglements, and of climbing earthworks'. Later in the book Swinton refers to 'The Land Ironclads', a prophetic story by H. G. Wells [q.v.] in 1903, but says: 'I had read this story when it first came out, but had looked upon it as a pure phantasy and had entirely forgotten it.' It is reasonable to surmise that the impression had remained in his subconscious mind—as it had in others.

Swinton's account relates that on 20 October 1914, during a brief visit to London, he went to see his erstwhile chief, Maurice (later Lord) Hankey, secretary of the Committee of Imperial Defence, described the stalemate on the western front, reminded him of the Holt caterpillar tractor, and suggested that some of these tractors might be converted into fighting machines. Although the prime minister was interested, the idea was rebuffed in high military quarters but was seized upon by (Sir) Winston Churchill, then first lord of the Admiralty, who had already ordered experiments with a trench-crossing machine to be carried out by the Royal Naval Air Service armoured car force. In February 1915 he set up a 'landships committee' under (Sir) Eustace Tennyson-d'Eyncourt [q.v.], but the machine envisaged was primarily for transporting troops forward.

The failure of the allied offensives in the spring of 1915 now gained more support for Swinton who had been fostering his suggestion at G.H.Q. At the beginning of June 1915 he defined his proposals in a memorandum which made a considerable impression despite the engineer-in-chief's caustic comment that 'before considering this proposal we should descend from the realms of imagination to solid facts'. Later that month Swinton submitted specific details of the conditions to be fulfilled including the ability to surmount a parapet 5 feet high and cross a trench up to 8 feet wide. He also provided a clear picture of how these armoured machine-gun destroyers should be used in battle.

A fresh threat to the project had been caused on the formation of a coalition Government by Churchill's departure from the Admiralty. But his successor, Arthur Balfour, took a sympathetic interest, preserving the experimental detachment which the sea lords wanted to disband, and it received powerful backing from Lloyd George in the new post of minister of munitions. Swinton's memoranda were forwarded by Sir John French (later the Earl of Ypres, q.v.) and with the newly gained support of G.H.Q. the landships committee was converted into a joint naval and military body. Fresh impetus came from its secretary, (Sir) Albert Stern, as well as continued efforts from (Sir) Murray Sueter [q.v.] the leading enthusiast on the naval side.

In July 1915 Swinton was brought back to London, at Hankey's instigation, to act as secretary to the Dardanelles committee of the Cabinet while Hankey went out to visit that theatre. Swinton was thus well placed to follow up his memoranda and co-ordinate activities. Before the end of the month a definite contract was placed, with Foster's of Lincoln, and early in September a prototype emerged from the workshop, designed by (Sir) William Tritton and Lieutenant (later Major) W. G. Wilson [qq.v.]. The first two trials of 'Little Willie' were disappointing but by the time of the second (19 September) Tritton and Wilson had produced a fresh design and mock-up of such obvious promise that it was promptly adopted: 'Big Willie' also came to be called 'Mother' and for camouflage it was given in December, at Swinton's suggestion, the generic name 'tank'. A demonstration for ministers and higher generals was held on 2 February 1916 which greatly impressed most of them although Kitchener dubbed it 'a pretty mechanical toy' which would quickly be knocked out by the enemy's artillery. G.H.Q. asked for forty machines; on Swinton's initiative the figure was raised to a hundred; Sueter thought the figure should be three thousand.

A start in providing personnel to man the tanks was made by appointing Swinton as commander, but it was made clear to him that he was only to train the new force and that once it reached France it would be placed under the local commanders. The force was initially entitled the Heavy Section, then Heavy Branch, Machine Gun Corps, and in July 1917 re-entitled the Tank Corps.

In February 1916 Swinton completed his lengthy 'Notes on the Employment of Tanks'. Unfortunately some of the keypoints were ignored in the planning of operations in France until the epoch-making Cambrai offensive of November 1917. In April 1916 Swinton saw Sir Douglas (later Earl) Haig [q.v.] in London who expressed agreement with the memorandum but then asked if he could have some tanks for the coming summer offensive on the Somme. Swinton swallowed his own inclination to protest against the premature use and consequent disclosure of the new secret weapon. Under further pressure, after the tragic opening failure of the offensive on 1 July, some fifty tanks were sent over to France in August with semi-trained crews, and used in the renewed attack of 15 September. In places they had a startling effect, but this was naturally limited by their small number and the shortness of training, while the enemy was alerted to the threat.

When Swinton went over to France early in October 1916 Haig showed more satisfaction with the results than did most of his subordinates. Swinton found that the detailed organization of the new arm was being drafted, without reference to him, and heard privately that he was to be superseded even at home. Shortly after his return to England he was 're-leased' to return to his former duties in the War Cabinet secretariat. Thus ended the connection between the new force and the man who had fathered it, until in 1934 he was chosen to be colonel-commandant of the Royal Tank Corps. By that time the significance of his early services had come to be better appreciated; above all in the Corps itself.

After the United States entered the war

Swinton accompanied Lord Reading [q.v] to that country in 1917 and again in 191 when he was given the temporary rank c major-general. At the request of the Stat Department he toured the country speak ing on behalf of the Third Liberty Loan He retired from the army in 1919 and unt 1921 was at the Air Ministry as controlle of information in the civil aviation depart ment. For the next three years he deville for Lloyd George who was preparing t write his war memoirs. He also, in 1922 became a director of the Citroen Company an appointment which he retained to th end of his life. In 1925 Swinton was electe Chichele professor of military history a Oxford and held the chair until 1939. H was popular in All Souls common-room where his humour was appreciated, and in the university generally, although he lef no deep mark on the teaching. He had been chosen in the hope that his lecturing gift and 'Ole Luk-Oie' style would arouse interest in the subject, but he felt, regret tably, that he must endeavour to be more academic and discourse upon Clausewitz. But he had made his own indelible mark on the history of warfare by his pioneering work in the origination of tanks and armoured forces. He was appointed C.B. in 1917 and K.B.E. in 1923.

In 1897 Swinton married Grace Louisa, second daughter of his second cousin Major (Sir) Edward Gilbert Clayton, secretary to the Prison Commission. They had two sons, and a daughter who was killed in a road accident during the war of 1939–45. Swinton died in Oxford 15 January 1951.

A portrait by Eric Kennington is in the Royal Tank Regiment's Officers' Club in London.

[Sir Ernest Swinton, *Over My Shoulder*, 1951; B. H. Liddell Hart, *The Tanks*, vol i, 1959; private information; personal knowledge.]   B. H. LIDDELL HART.

SYKES, SIR FREDERICK HUGH (1877–1954), chief of air staff and governor of Bombay, was born in Croydon, Surrey, 23 July 1877. His father, Henry Sykes, who died less than two years later, was a mechanical engineer; his mother, Margaret Sykes, was a distant cousin of her husband. Sykes had 'a somewhat chequered education': five years at a preparatory school on the south coast; then from the age of fifteen two years in Paris learning French in the hope of a diplomatic career. For a time he worked in a general store in order to save money.

On returning to London he entered a shipping firm; then spent some time working on tea plantations in Ceylon, eventually making a leisurely return to England via Burma, China, Japan, and the United States.

On the outbreak of the South African war, Sykes booked a passage to Cape Town and joined the Imperial Yeomanry Scouts as a trooper. He was taken prisoner by C. R. De Wet [q.v.] at Roodevaal but was soon released. He was next commissioned in the bodyguard of Lord Roberts [q.v.] and was wounded during a commando raid in 1901. Later in the year he joined the regular army and was gazetted second lieutenant in the 15th Hussars.

He served in India and West Africa, was promoted captain in 1908, and passed the Staff College in 1909. Very early on he was an enthusiast for ballooning. In 1910 he learned to fly and obtained his pilot's certificate (No. 96) in 1911. In 1912 he became commander of the Military Wing of the newly founded Royal Flying Corps. But on the outbreak of war in 1914 he was considered too junior to command the R.F.C. in action abroad, as still only an acting lieutenant-colonel. The command was given to Sir David Henderson [q.v.], previously director-general of military aeronautics, and Sykes served as his chief of staff. He was succeeded as commander of the Military Wing by Major Hugh (later Marshal of the R.A.F. Viscount) Trenchard [q.v.]. The two men were deeply antipathetic, and a bitter argument during the takeover set the keynote to their relationship for the rest of Sykes's military career.

Trenchard's hostility was soon displayed. In November 1914 Sykes was appointed to command the R.F.C. in place of Henderson who was promoted to command the 1st division. Meanwhile Trenchard had been posted to France to take charge of one of the new operational wings into which the R.F.C. had been divided. As soon as he found that he was to be under Sykes he requested to be transferred to his original regiment. Lord Kitchener [q.v.] intervened to insist upon Henderson and Sykes reverting to their previous posts: an episode not calculated to improve relations.

During the next few months Henderson was on sick leave and Sykes acted as his deputy. According to Trenchard, Henderson came to the conclusion that Sykes was intriguing to replace him.

Whatever the truth of it, the upshot was that Henderson developed a deep distrust of Sykes who was sent in May to Gallipoli to report on air requirements there and in July was given command of the Royal Naval Air Service in the Eastern Mediterranean when the Gallipoli campaign was at its height. He remained there until the end, carrying out his task with conspicuous success and being appointed C.M.G. in recognition.

In March 1916 Sykes was made assistant adjutant and quartermaster-general of the 4th Mounted division at Colchester. In June he became assistant adjutant-general at the War Office with the task of organizing the Machine Gun Corps. In February 1917 he was promoted temporary brigadier-general and deputy director of organization at the War Office. At the end of the year he joined the planning staff of the Supreme War Council under Sir Henry Wilson [q.v.]. Meanwhile the Government, on the recommendation of J. C. Smuts [q.v.], strongly backed by Henderson yet opposed by Trenchard, had decided to create an independent air force with its own Ministry. Nevertheless Trenchard became the first chief of air staff, under Lord Rothermere [q.v.], the first air minister; both were appointed on 3 January 1918. Henderson was made vice-president of the newly formed Air Council.

Trenchard and Rothermere soon quarrelled and Trenchard tendered his resignation on 19 March but was persuaded to defer it until after the official birth of the Royal Air Force on 1 April. On 13 April Sykes, promoted to major-general, succeeded him: a choice inevitably controversial in these circumstances; Henderson promptly resigned too. The confusion was increased by Rothermere's own resignation which took effect on the 25th. He paid a high tribute to Sykes in his resignation letter as 'this brilliant officer with his singularly luminous mind . . . an ideal Chief of Staff of the Royal Air Force'.

Rothermere was succeeded by Sir William (later Viscount) Weir [q.v.] who retained the post until the end of the war. Sykes was chief of staff throughout this significant period and as a convinced supporter of an independent air force did much to establish the new Service. His post-war plans, however, were regarded as too grandiose by Weir's successor, (Sir) Winston Churchill, who from January 1919 held the posts of both war and air minister. He preferred those of Trenchard whom he was consulting behind Sykes's back. In February 1919 Trenchard again became chief of air staff and Sykes was shunted into the post of controller of civil aviation. One of the conditions of this appointment was that he gave up his military commission and thus ended his career in the armed Services.

In 1920 he married Isabel (died 1969), elder daughter of Andrew Bonar Law [q.v.]; they had one son. Sykes resigned from the Air Ministry in April 1922, dissatisfied with the financial treatment of civil aviation. He was offered but refused the governorship of South Australia, and decided to enter politics. At the general election of 1922 he was elected Unionist member for the Hallam division of Sheffield. In May 1923 he conveyed to King George V his father-in-law's letter of resignation from the premiership. He retained his parliamentary seat until 1928 when he was appointed governor of Bombay.

His term of office in India covered a period of unprecedented financial difficulties and political and industrial unrest which Sykes faced with resolution and a patient determination to improve the lot of the common people. He would have wished for greater powers to deal more promptly and effectively with civil disobedience, but was loyal in conforming to the central Government's policy of conciliation. It was not until 1932 that emergency powers were granted; then, with civil disobedience on the decline, Sykes was able to give attention to the social and economic difficulties which he felt to be the real problem of India. When he left Bombay in 1933 he had the satisfaction of knowing that the outlook for the presidency was more hopeful than it had been five years earlier.

Sykes was again in Parliament from 1940 to 1945 as Conservative member for the Central division of Nottingham. He was chairman of government committees on meteorological services (1920-22), and broadcasting (1923), of the Broadcasting Board (1923-7), of the Miners' Welfare Commission (1934-46), of the Royal Empire Society (1938-41), and for many years honorary treasurer of the British Sailors' Society. He was also a director of various public companies. His autobiography, *From Many Angles*, was published in 1942. He died in London 30 September 1954.

Sykes was a person of high intelligence and much charm, although he did not thaw very easily. He was clearly a most capable administrator but his contribution to the formative period of the air force as an independent arm has been obscured by the hostility between him and some of his brother officers, Trenchard especially, whose opinions subsequently became gospel in the Royal Air Force, thereby conditioning much of the Service's historiography.

Sykes was appointed K.C.B. and G.B.E. in 1919, G.C.I.E. in 1928, and G.C.S.I. in 1934. He was sworn of the Privy Council in 1928. His portrait, painted by Sir William Orpen while he was chief of air staff, is at his home, Conock Manor, near Devizes. A bronze bust by L. F. Roslyn is in the Imperial War Museum.

[Sir Walter Raleigh and H. A. Jones, (Official History) *The War in the Air*, 6 vols., 1922-37; Sir F. Sykes, *From Many Angles*, 1942; Robert Blake, *The Unknown Prime Minister*, 1955; Lord Beaverbrook, *Men and Power*, 1956; Andrew Boyle, *Trenchard*, 1962; Sir Philip Joubert de la Ferte, *The Third Service*, 1955; W. J. Reader, *Architect of Air Power: the Life of the first Viscount Weir of Eastwood*, 1968; private information; personal knowledge.]

ROBERT BLAKE.

TALLENTS, SIR STEPHEN GEORGE (1884-1958), civil servant, was born in London 20 October 1884, the eldest son of George William Tallents, conveyancing barrister, and his wife, Mildred Sophia, daughter of the first Baron Ashcombe. He was descended from a brother of Francis Tallents [q.v.], a seventeenth-century fellow of Magdalene College, Cambridge, and through his mother from Thomas Cubitt [q.v.], who designed Osborne and the east front of Buckingham Palace for Queen Victoria, and died leaving over a million pounds and the longest will then on record.

Tallents was educated at Harrow where his father had been (as each of his two younger brothers was later) head of the school. At Balliol College, Oxford, he obtained a second class in both classical moderations (1905) and *literae humaniores* (1907). After a short time at Grenoble, then at Toynbee Hall, he entered the Civil Service in April 1909 and was posted to the marine department of the Board of Trade. In January 1911 he was transferred to the labour exchanges and unemployment insurance department, where he worked with William (afterwards Lord) Beveridge and Sir Hubert Llewellyn Smith [q.v.]. In January 1912 he was put in charge of staff. On the outbreak of war in 1914 he was employed with Humbert Wolfe [q.v.] in a continuous night and day shift for the rapid recruitment of dockyard labour.

From 1903 until 1912 Tallents had held a commission in the Surrey Yeomanry, but in 1914 it had a full complement of officers and in September he joined instead the reserve battalion of the Irish Guards. He was severely wounded at Festubert in May 1915, but not before he had written and sent home a 3,000-word pamphlet 'for the guidance of platoon commanders in the trenches', which was later adopted by the War Office. As soon as he had discarded his crutches in the autumn of 1915 he was brought by his old chiefs into the Ministry of Munitions, where Lloyd George was minister. He was concerned in the struggle with the War Office to secure exemption from military service for genuine munition workers; and in the course of this conflict on one occasion, although dressed only as a subaltern in the Irish Guards, he withstood Lord Kitchener [q.v.] himself. In August 1916 he was passed fit for military service, but was retained by the Civil Service and in December transferred to the Ministry of Food. At the climax of the food problem he was mainly instrumental, against departmental opposition, but finally with the approval of Lord Rhondda [q.v.], in doing away with food queues by a system of swift local rationing. In 1918 he was made chairman of a new Milk Control Board.

After the armistice Tallents at his own suggestion was appointed chief British delegate for the relief and supply of Poland, and later British commissioner in the Baltic provinces, with the acting rank of lieutenant-colonel. There, on a somewhat vague assignment, he had the help of three British officers, one of them the future Earl Alexander of Tunis, and the support of an occasional destroyer. Conditions in the Baltic states were chaotic, with German, Bolshevik, Latvian, Estonian, and Lithuanian troops under no unified command, and recognizing no common authority. While their fate was being settled at the peace conference, the day-to-day task of restoring peace and order fell on the commissioners of the allied powers. In conditions of great discomfort and personal risk, Tallents came to realize, he said, 'that there was no problem to which a British representative in the Baltic states must confess himself unequal'. In this spirit he accepted every sort of responsibility, drawing up the terms of an armistice between the Germans and the Estonians, acting for five days as governor of Riga whilst supervising the German evacuation, and delimiting the Latvian-Estonian frontier.

Replaced by a professional diplomat, Tallents served in 1921–2 as private secretary to Lord FitzAlan of Derwent [q.v.], the last lord-lieutenant of Ireland, and in 1922–6 was imperial secretary in Northern Ireland where he administered certain reserved services and acted as liaison officer with the Northern Ireland Parliament.

In 1926 he returned to England and was secretary to the cabinet committee which dealt with the general strike. His services were then obtained by L. S. Amery [q.v.] who had his eye on Tallents as the ideal man for what has been described as 'that gallant adventure, the Empire Marketing Board'. To this Tallents brought, said Amery, 'a completely open and receptive mind, unlimited fertility of imagination and contrivance and remarkable organizing power'. These years were the most prolific in Tallents's official career. In the next seven years the Board evolved a new technique in marketing, advertising, and research. It was on the last that 65 per cent of the Board's resources were spent, and Tallents put intense labour into that side of its work. It was through him that there were set up the eight inter-imperial bureaux which the Empire countries decided in 1927 to maintain in the United Kingdom for the scientific study of agricultural problems and for keeping each part of the Empire in touch with the most recent developments in those fields of research which most concerned it.

That was only part of his contribution to the national cause, although perhaps the part most likely to survive. His pamphlet The Projection of England (1932, reissued 1955) was a convincing plea for the projection by England upon the screen of world opinion of 'such a picture of herself as will create a belief in her ability to serve the world under the new order as she has served it under the old'. Projection to him meant more than mere publicity. When he popularized, perhaps even invented, the term 'public relations', he was thinking always of a two-way traffic. He was the first civil servant to make a study of publicity, and he owed much to the help of experts like Frank Pick [q.v.] of the London Underground and Sir William Crawford.

The effects of posters, exhibitions, Empire shops and shopping weeks were all studied and tried out. Later his appointment of John Grierson as film officer, and the formation of a film unit, led to the British documentary film. 'The influence of documentary film production all over the world to-day is . . . one of his monuments' (John Grierson in *The Times*, 23 September 1958).

In 1931 Tallents was appointed by C. R. (later Earl) Attlee to the Post Office telephone publicity committee, and when the Empire Marketing Board closed down in 1933, Sir Kingsley Wood [q.v.], as part of his adoption of commercial methods at the Post Office, appointed Tallents to the new post of public relations officer. Tallents saved the life of the film unit and library by getting permission to take them with him to the Post Office. In 1935 he was the first civil servant to win the cup of the Publicity Club of London, and his success in this more or less new field was marked when he retired from it in the same year by a comment in the *New Statesman* (13 July): 'If the Post Office is no longer criticised that is not only because long impending changes have actually matured under the energetic administration of Sir Kingsley Wood, but also because, for the first time, we have had a Government department properly advertised.'

In 1935 Tallents transferred to the British Broadcasting Corporation as controller of public relations until 1940, and of the Overseas Service from 1940 to 1941 when he resigned. He was also (1936–8) director-general-designate of an embryonic Ministry of Information. But he was disappointed at not succeeding Sir John (afterwards Lord) Reith as director-general of the B.B.C. in 1938. From 1943 to 1946 Tallents was principal assistant secretary to the Ministry of Town and Country Planning. His subsequent leisure was very fully occupied by public services and private interests. He was fellow and first president of the Institute of Public Relations (1948–9) and president again (1952–3). He was made an honorary A.R.I.B.A. in 1946 and honorary fellow of the Society of Industrial Artists in 1949; member of the council of the Royal Society of Arts (1953) and elected president of the Design and Industries Association (1954). He took an active part in various ventures, among them 'Cockade', an enterprise aimed at enlisting at every stage of production the services of the trained designer and the accomplished craftsman Group I Ltd., a consortium of civil engineering firms aimed at securing contracts for British industry; and a number of lesser enterprises.

Nobody without a combination of unusual qualities could have made a success of such a multiplicity of posts. Tallents combined a wide-ranging imagination with relentless attention to detail. But his imagination was always controlled by realism, and never ran away with him. The more people he met and the more things he noticed, the more ideas there were to work out and to translate into practical effect. He had a well-compartmented memory, and all through his career his numerous contacts with every sort of person resulted in striking examples of the cross-fertilization of ideas. He went through life with receptive eyes and ears, missing little and extracting full value from every experience. He was an early riser and never spent an idle hour. There was nobody quite like him, but of all his many qualities perhaps the one which endeared him most to his friends was his faithfulness to people, places, and things.

His more private interests chiefly centred round his home at St. John's Jerusalem, Dartford, which he gave to the National Trust in 1943. They included among others the growing of willows for cricket-bat blades, the collection of mole skins, the making of rat skins into light leather, the use of grey squirrels for food, the collection of thistledown for pillows, the testing of the combustion qualities of different timbers, the simplification of chimney sweeping, a medicinal herb garden, and a complete history of the science and art of scything. He also gave his services most generously as a lecturer all over the country on these and other favourite subjects.

Tallents's literary output by contrast was small. It began in 1918 with *The Starry Pool and Other Tales*, mostly short sketches written for the *Manchester Guardian*. This was followed by *The Dancer and Other Tales* (1922) inspired by his early married life and the nursery. In 1943 came his autobiography *Man and Boy*, adventurous and revealing, but unfortunately not extending past 1920. *Green Thoughts* (1952), the most attractive of all his books, contains his reflections on and researches into out-of-door things and country life. In 1950–55 he contributed fortnightly articles to the *Sunday Times*.

Tallents was appointed C.B. (1918),

.B.E. (1920), C.M.G. (1929), and
.C.M.G. (1932). He married in 1914
Bridget (died 1968), daughter of Major
Samuel Hugh Francklin Hole, of Caunton
Manor, Newark on Trent, son of Samuel
Reynolds Hole [q.v.]. He had two sons
and two daughters. He died in London
1 September 1958.

[Sir Stephen Tallents, *Man and Boy*, 1943;
The Times, 13, 17, 18, and 23 September 1958;
private information; personal knowledge.]
                                    A. L. F. SMITH.

TANSLEY, SIR ARTHUR GEORGE
1871-1955), plant ecologist, was born in
central London 15 August 1871, the only
son and younger child of George Tansley
and his wife, Amelia Lawrence. George
Tansley conducted a profitable London
business providing for society functions,
but his real interest was devoted to the
Working Men's College, where he studied,
then taught. Arthur admired his father
who was the primary source of his own
liberal outlook. From another instructor
at the college he received early encouragement in field botany. Finding Highgate
School 'farcically inadequate' in science,
he left and went to classes at University
College, London. In 1890 he entered
Trinity College, Cambridge. With a first
in part i of the natural sciences tripos
(1893), but part ii (1894, another first)
still to come, he returned to University
College, now a colleague instead of pupil
of F. W. Oliver [q.v.], the youthful professor of botany. Oliver's interest in fern-like
plants was echoed by Tansley's earliest
published investigations (in which one of
his student collaborators became his wife).

Oliver was also developing the study of
vegetation and its habitats—the newly
expanding subject of ecology. Tansley
never lost interest in the development of
botany as a whole and soon became influential through his single-handed launching in 1902 of a botanical journal, *The New
Phytologist*, which he edited for thirty
years. But ecology was becoming his chief
concern. In 1904 a dozen British botanists,
with Tansley at their centre, had constituted themselves as the 'British Vegetation Committee' in order to further the
description of British plant communities.
Their efforts led to the publication in 1911
of *Types of British Vegetation*, which
Tansley edited and largely wrote. In 1913
the ground was ready for the formation of
the British Ecological Society. Tansley
became the first president and, in 1917,
editor for twenty-one years of the *Journal*

of Ecology, a periodical which enhanced
the society's reputation and his own. From
1907 onwards he had been a lecturer in
botany at Cambridge, with a house at
Grantchester which always remained his
home.

In 1923 Tansley resigned his university
post. His interest, always inclined towards philosophy, had now become
preoccupied with psychology, particularly
as expounded by Freud. After writing
his successful book *The New Psychology
and its Relation to Life* (1920), he had
visited Freud in Vienna. In 1923-4 he
studied there as Freud's pupil. During
four years of uncertain prospect he
continued his botanical writing, which
included substantial additions made
jointly with his friend Stephen Adamson
to their hitherto separate studies of the
vegetation of the South Downs.

The uncertainty was ended by the
university of Oxford, where in 1927
Tansley was appointed Sherardian professor of botany. He raised the standing
of Oxford botany by his own teaching and
prestige and by gaining very able staff.
He never amassed a following of personally directed research students, but
many were helped by the trouble he
took in correspondence and editing.
His own research largely avoided experimentation and was devoted to description, comparison, and synthesis. In
the sphere of ecological theory his lucid
writing argued for realism and moderation.

Two years after his retirement from
Oxford appeared Tansley's largest,
celebrated book, *The British Islands
and their Vegetation* (1939). There was yet
to come what may be thought his greatest
work. Concerted planning began in 1941
for the post-war conservation of nature
in Britain as a government responsibility.
Tansley's energies were transferred wholeheartedly to this task, and he played
a guiding part in the work which led
to the foundation of the Nature Conservancy in 1949. Now aged seventy-
seven, he became the Conservancy's first
chairman and held office until 1953. His
knighthood came in 1950. He had been
a fellow of the Royal Society since
1915 and in 1944 was elected an honorary
fellow of Trinity College, Cambridge.

After middle age Tansley's silvering
hair, tallish, spare figure and somewhat
unathletic movements suited his unassuming distinction. On relaxed occasions he was jovial and humorous.
He overlooked faults in others, thinking

virtues more important. To his close friends, whether distinguished or not, 'A.G.' made it impartially clear that he valued their friendship.

He died at Grantchester 25 November 1955. His wife, whom he married in 1903, was Edith, daughter of Samuel Chick, lace merchant. They had three daughters, whose careers—respectively in physiology, architecture, and economics—were all distinguished. A vivid painting of Tansley by W. G. de Glehn and two crayon portraits by Mrs. de Glehn have remained with the family.

One of the first National Nature Reserves established was Kingley Vale on the Sussex Downs, a place beloved by Tansley. His name is inscribed there on a memorial stone.

[H. Godwin in *Biographical Memoirs of Fellows of the Royal Society*, vol. iii, 1957, and *Journal of Ecology*, vol. xlvi, 1958; private information; personal knowledge.]

J. F. HOPE-SIMPSON.

TARN, SIR WILLIAM WOODTHORPE (1869–1957), ancient historian, was born in London 26 February 1869, the elder son of William Tarn, silk merchant, of Fan Court, Surrey, and his wife, Frances Arthy. He was a King's scholar at Eton and captain of the school. Thence he entered Trinity College, Cambridge, as a pensioner, soon to be elected scholar. He was fortunate in his teachers, above all, Henry Jackson [q.v.], to whom he owed a lasting interest in Greek philosophy while he studied for part ii (1892) of the classical tripos, after taking a first in part i (1891). He might well have become a candidate for a fellowship, but his father had always wished him to go to the bar, and this he did. He studied at the Inner Temple in the chambers of a leading Chancery barrister, Spencer Perceval Butler, brother of the master of Trinity. On being called in 1894 he began what soon became a promising career.

In London, Tarn had many friends, and the practice of the law gave scope to his keen mind, shrewd judgement, and precise memory. Then a long dangerous illness of his wife, whom he tended with anxious care, and the stress of professional work undermined his strength. In 1905 a serious breakdown compelled him to retire to the country until, as his health returned, the intellectual interest he had found in the law revived in the leisurely study of Hellenistic culture and political history, in which field Tarn won and maintained for

forty years a pre-eminent position. His interest in Greek philosophy reappears in his first book, *Antigonos Gonatas* (1913) dedicated to Henry Jackson.

In 1914 Tarn was refused by the army because of his sight, but he spent the next four years in confidential work for the intelligence division of the War Office, in which his literary gifts were skilfully employed. The war ended he had no need to seek academic employment and no desire to limit his freedom by its claims. He published in learned journals work which revealed an especial interest in ancient geography and military and naval establishments and Greek warships. His most notable single contribution to the art of war was his Lees Knowles lectures at Trinity, published under the title *Hellenistic Military and Naval Developments* (1930). This small book was written *con amore* and with an easy command of the scattered evidence, more enlightening to the specialist than anything before on these matters.

Tarn's most productive period lay between the two wars. He wrote, first, nine chapters in volumes vi and vii of the *Cambridge Ancient History*, describing the rise of the Hellenistic world. Long study had made its personalities come alive to him, and he added to his narrative of war and diplomacy a just appreciation of the culture, the politics, and the economic forces of the time. The chapters on Alexander were infused with admiration amounting to hero-worship, also reflected in a doctrine very dear to him, that Alexander was the true begetter of the idea of the unity of mankind, which went beyond the fusion of Macedonians and Iranians under his kingship. In 1948 he added to these chapters a volume of studies on the sources for Alexander and on particular problems. This crowned an achievement unsurpassed by any other ancient historian of his day. He also completed a masterly work which justified its title *Hellenistic Civilisation* (1927). Tarn contributed to volume ix of the *Ancient History* a chapter on Parthia, in which he combined Chinese and Greek sources in a balanced survey. In volume x he wrote parts of the chapters between the death of Caesar and the death of Cleopatra, in which the figure of the last of the great Macedonian queens stands out with clarity and brilliance.

As he grew older, Tarn rarely met other

cholars, but his advice was often sought
nd never refused. He conducted a wide
orrespondence, as appears from the
material used in his *The Greeks in Bactria
nd India* (1938), a pioneer work in
which much evidence was marshalled and
ombined for the first time. Even so, it
emains an adventure in scholarship of
great range and lasting value. In 1928
Tarn was elected F.B.A. and in 1931 he
proceeded to the Cambridge degree of
Litt.D. He was a foreign member of the
Royal Netherlands Academy, the American Philosophical Society, and the German
Archaeological Institute. The university of
Edinburgh conferred upon him its honorary LL.D. (1933) and in 1939 he received
the distinction which he prized above
them all, an honorary fellowship of Trinity.
Finally, in 1952 he was knighted.

In 1896 Tarn to his great happiness
married Flora Macdonald, third daughter
of John Robertson, landowner, of Orbost
in the Isle of Skye. They had one child,
a daughter, for whom Tarn wrote a
fairy story, *The Treasure of the Isle of
Mist* (1919), which became a classic of
its kind. So long as his health allowed,
Tarn was devoted to the avocations of
a country gentleman, in which he was
skilled, being accounted among the six
best game shots in Great Britain. He
was also a good pianist and a student
of English literature. Until his wife
died in 1937 his house, Mountgerald, and
afterwards Muirtown, near Inverness,
was the centre of much hospitality to his
English friends and his Highland connections. With the approach of old age
he lost something of his zest for life.
But he had much affection to give and
receive, and, summer after summer, he
would travel to Skye and find a kind of
rejuvenation in his daughter's house
(where there is a portrait of him by Somer-
led Macdonald). He died at Muirtown
House, 7 November 1957.

[Sir Frank Adcock in *Proceedings* of the
British Academy, vol. xliv, 1958; private
information; personal knowledge.]

F. E. ADCOCK.

TATLOW, TISSINGTON (1876–1957),
general secretary of the Student Christian
Movement, was born in Crossdoney,
county Cavan, 11 January 1876, the
eldest son of Tissington W. G. Tatlow,
land agent to Lord Kingston's estate,
and his wife, Blanche, daughter of
Thomas Steuart Townsend who was
bishop of Meath in 1850–52. Tatlow

was educated at St. Columba's College,
Rathfarnham, and in the engineering
school of Trinity College, Dublin. He
decided to become a foreign missionary
and on graduating at the age of twenty-
one became travelling secretary of the
recently formed Student Volunteer Missionary Union. A year later he was
appointed secretary of its associated
body, the British College Christian Union,
soon renamed the Student Christian
Movement, which had been founded in
1893. In 1900 he returned to Trinity
College, this time to the divinity school,
and he was ordained deacon in 1902 and
priest in 1904. In 1902 he became curate
at St. Barnabas, Kensington, but in 1903
he was called back to the general secretaryship of the S.C.M., an office which he held
until 1929. Although not its founder, it
was owing to him more than to any other
one man that the Movement came to
exercise its great influence over the life of
the Church. Tatlow was the vital centre
of its committee and secretarial group, its
spiritual leader and brilliant organizer.
Not content to remain in his office chair
he travelled widely to visit the colleges and
universities not only of this country but
also of Europe and America, and took a
leading part in the life of the World's
Student Christian Federation. When Edinburgh University made him an honorary
D.D. in 1925, W. P. Paterson [q.v.]
deservedly hailed him as 'the apostle
of the student world'.

In 1926 Tatlow was appointed rector of
All Hallows, Lombard Street, and in 1937,
on the amalgamation of a number of City
parishes, rector of St. Edmund the King.
In addition to the normal work of a City
parish he made his church a centre for
students and teachers. He held the living
until his death. In 1926 he was appointed
honorary canon of Canterbury. He was
honorary fellow and treasurer of Sion
College and president in 1940–41.

Tatlow was a man of many interests.
In 1936 he launched the Institute of
Christian Education and as its honorary
director for over twenty years gave
outstanding leadership in its work of
promoting the cause of Christian education in this country and overseas.
His name soon became as well known
among the schools as it had been for years
in the universities. He was founder
in 1912 of the influential Anglican
Fellowship, its first secretary, and in
1913–17 its chairman. He was associated
with William Temple [q.v.] and others

in the gallant attempt to launch a new kind of Anglican weekly, the *Challenge*, and was chairman of its board (1915–22). Under his leadership the Student Christian Movement had a way of initiating other enterprises in such realms as religious education, foreign missions, literature, social responsibility, care for foreign students, theological education, and Christian unity, which after a while were deliberately detached from the Movement so that often they became unaware of the source of their initial impulse. He brought a most creative mind to the service of the whole Church and touched its life for good at many points. His achievement was not less because normally he was content to remain in the background, not caring who got the credit so long as the job was done.

Next to students and teachers, nearest to his heart was the cause of Christian unity. He had a large share in securing the success in 1910 of the World Missionary Conference at Edinburgh which was by common consent the starting-point of the modern ecumenical movement. The archbishops made him honorary secretary of their committee to prepare for the world conference on Faith and Order, in Lausanne (1927), and Tatlow became the European treasurer of the resulting Faith and Order Movement, which was to become a constituent part of the World Council of Churches. So closely was he associated with a number of the organizations involved that he must be reckoned one of the chief architects of the British Council of Churches and of the ecumenical movement as a whole. At a luncheon in Tatlow's honour on his eightieth birthday, Archbishop Fisher, who presided, paid tribute to his far-reaching influence, and spoke of the debt which he and his three immediate predecessors felt they owed him.

Perhaps Tatlow's most profound mark on the Church was made through his training of generations of S.C.M. secretaries. Many thousands of students came under his influence at the annual conferences and in other ways, but closely associated with him were young colleagues, twenty to thirty at a time, who served the Movement for two or three years before going on to their life work. Tatlow knew how to pick men and women and how to get the best out of them, and many who later occupied positions of leadership in different walks of life have testified to what they owed to his pastoral care and

inspiring guidance. A man who got thin[g] done with efficiency, 'T', as everybod[y] called him, was also a strong and sym[-] pathetic personality.

Tatlow married in 1903 Emily, daught[er] of Richard Scott, insurance manager, [of] Dublin, and had three daughters. He die[d] in London 3 October 1957. A portrait b[y] Delmar Banner is at S.C.M. headquarter[s] and a drawing by Alice M. Burton is i[n] the possession of the family.

[Tissington Tatlow, *The Story of the Stude[nt] Christian Movement*, 1933; private informa[-] tion; personal knowledge.]   HUGH MARTIN

TATTERSFIELD, FREDERICK (1881– 1959), chemist, was born at Kilpin Hil[l] near Dewsbury, Yorkshire, 23 April 1881 the third son of Frederick Tattersfield[,] woollen manufacturer, and his wife Frances Mary Walker. He was educate[d] at the Wheelwright Grammar School Dewsbury, and the university of Leeds taking first class honours in chemistry a[t] London University (1908) as an externa[l] student. He was awarded a D.Sc. in 1927. His first job was in association with the Leeds city analyst, where his work ranged over all the typica[l] activities in such a department, from food and drug analysis to post-mortems. In 1908 he joined the International Paint and Antifouling Co., Ltd., where for five years his work was chiefly concerned with research on anti-fouling paints. On the outbreak of war in 1914 he went to France as a founder-member of the Friends Ambulance Unit. In 1917 he was invalided back to England and early in 1918 went to the Rothamsted Experimental Station to work with A. W. Rymer Roberts on soil insecticides. He remained at Rothamsted for the rest of his working life. He originally had a temporary appointment in the chemistry department, but he soon founded the department of insecticides and fungicides of which he was the head for twenty-nine years.

His earliest work was concerned with the control of soil pests, and he carried out some work on the structure–toxicity relationships of chemicals to wireworms. He also studied the factors influencing the decomposition of naphthalene in the soil and the effect of different rates of decomposition on its insecticidal action. He then proceeded to study the effect of a wide range of chemicals on the insects which attack the aerial parts of the plant, again attempting, as far as ossible, to relate toxicity with structure in some systematic way. In the course of his work he discovered the outstanding vicidal properties of dinitro-*o*-cresol, a substance which has been used in winter washes for fruit trees ever since. At that time the chemical manufacturers had little confidence in the development of effective synthetic organic chemicals for pest control and the resources of laboratories financed from government or private sources were much too meagre for such a project, so Tattersfield in his search for highly biologically active chemicals for insect control turned his attention to plants as a source for these materials.

He examined a wide variety of plants for insecticidal activity, but his main work was done on the fish poison group, particularly *Derris* spp. and *Tephrosia* spp. and on pyrethrum. His contributions on the isolation of the active principles of these plant products, the assessment of their insecticidal activity and their chemical estimation were quite outstanding. He studied many phases of the production and assay of pyrethrum as an insecticide and played a large part in the founding of the Kenya pyrethrum industry which became of the greatest value to the economy of that country. Furthermore the Kenya pyrethrum industry proved a great asset in the war of 1939–45 when an accessible supply of pyrethrum greatly helped to safeguard health by controlling insect carriers of disease and food supplies by controlling insect pests of stored food. During the course of his work Tattersfield evolved precise methods of administering doses of chemicals to insects and introduced statistical procedures for the quantitative assessment of results.

A catalogue of Tattersfield's contributions to knowledge on insecticides, substantial though they were, gives a very inadequate idea of what the subject owes to his influence, which, fortunately, was widely felt owing to his high international reputation. When he started work on the subject the standard of research work was very low and seldom was any serious attempt made to obtain reproducible quantitative results of known significance. He insisted on the importance of precise quantitative data where the factors known to influence the results were standardized, so far as possible, and where both the design of the experiment and the results would satisfy accepted statistical criteria. In doing this he set standards which, over the course of years, have been accepted, to the inestimable benefit of the subject.

Tattersfield may legitimately be described as the founder of modern research on insecticides and he led the way for many years. He was always most anxious, however, that anyone who was associated with him should not be left out and would insist on the value of the help he received from Sir John Fryer, C. T. Gimingham, and R. A. Fisher, and later from his junior colleagues. Tattersfield was always a source of inspiration to his colleagues to whom he was unfailingly kind and helpful. His justly acquired reputation never changed his modest and unassuming manner, or affected the uncompromising integrity which was perhaps his most notable quality, combined with great gentleness and a delightful sense of fun. He retired in 1947 and was appointed O.B.E.

In his youth Tattersfield was a very good cricketer and he remained keenly interested throughout his life. He was also a man of wide cultural interests. He was at one time an active member of the Literary and Philosophical Society of Newcastle and he had a fine appreciation of poetry. He collected etchings, engravings, and mezzotints. He was keenly interested in archaeology and was a member of the Pre-Historical Society. A member of the Society of Friends, he became a much respected elder.

In 1931 Tattersfield married Janie, elder daughter of Archibald Campbell, farmer, of Ennerdale, Cumberland; they had one son. Tattersfield died in Harpenden 1 May 1959. A drawing by Herry Perry is in the possession of the family.

[*Nature*, 27 June 1959; private information; personal knowledge.]   C. POTTER.

TAYLOR, FRANK SHERWOOD (1897–1956), chemist, historian of science, and director of the Science Museum, South Kensington, was born at Bromley 26 November 1897, the son of Seaton Frank Taylor, solicitor, and his wife, Helen Sennerth Davidson. He was educated at Sherborne School and Lincoln College, Oxford, where he was elected to a classical scholarship. The war of 1914–18, in which he was severely wounded at Passchendaele in 1917, while serving in an infantry unit of the Honourable Artillery Company, deflected his more active interests from classics to chemistry. After graduating at Oxford in 1921, he taught chemistry at various public schools, including Gresham's and Repton, until 1933, when he was appointed assistant lecturer in inorganic chemistry at Queen Mary College, university of London, where he remained until 1938. After some experience with a firm of publishers and following the outbreak of war in 1939, he returned temporarily to teaching chemistry at Llandovery College, Carmarthenshire, until in 1940 he was appointed to the curatorship of the Science Museum, Oxford. In 1950 he became director of the Science Museum, South Kensington.

In the meantime Taylor's interest in chemistry had extended to the history of alchemy and in 1931 he had been awarded the degree of Ph.D. by the university of London, his thesis being entitled 'A Conspectus of Greek Alchemy', a notable research which was published in the *Journal of Hellenic Studies* (June 1930). This work was followed by an annotated translation (*Ambix*, December 1937 and June 1938) of the alchemical writings of Stephanos of Alexandria (seventh century A.D.) which, with his later study, *The Alchemists* (1949), revealed his deep understanding of a literature generally obscure and often mystical. During these years he wrote a number of textbooks of chemistry, which brought him a considerable reputation for their lucid exposition; his *Inorganic and Theoretical Chemistry* (1931) appeared in a ninth edition (1952) and his *Organic Chemistry* (1933) in a fifth edition (1953), while his *General Science for Schools* (1939) reached revised editions in 1952 and 1953; and there were many others.

Taylor, classic and chemist, disliked the widening gulf between the arts and the sciences, and *The World of Science* (1936, with revised editions and reprints), a large volume written for the general reader, was perhaps his greatest success, holding its place as an outstanding work of its kind thirty years after its first publication. He wrote also several books on the history of science: *Galileo and the Freedom of Thought* (1938); *A Short History of Science* (1939); *Science Past and Present* (1945 and 1949: an anthology of extracts from the classics of science with commentaries); *The Century of Science* (1941 and later editions); *British Inventions* (1950); and *An Illustrated History of Science* (1955). *A Century of British Chemistry* (1947) was written for the centenary of the Chemical Society of London

and *A History of Industrial Chemistr* (published posthumously in 1957) wa completed during his last illness. He wa active in the foundation of the Societ for the Study of Alchemy and Earl Chemistry and was honorary editor of th society's journal, *Ambix*, from its incep tion in 1937 until his death in 1956. H was similarly concerned in the foundatio of the British Society for the History o Science and served as the society's presi dent (1951–3).

During his later period in Oxford Taylor joined the Roman Catholic Church which was no surprise to his close friend who had always been aware of th religious and mystical element in hi thought. In *The Fourfold Vision* (1945) h pleaded with his usual sincerity for the re jection of materialism and the unificatio of science and religion. His other publica tions included papers on the history o science in *Ambix* and *Annals of Science*, and a chapter in Singer and Holmyard's *History of Technology*.

All Taylor's writings were marked by scholarship, clarity, and unity of purpose, and those on the history of science, especially of alchemy, have an enduring value; his reorganization of the Museum of the History of Science in Oxford was memorable; when director of the Science Museum in London, administration took too great a toll of his time for research, and he often longed for the different life of Oxford; the strain told, and he died at Crowthorne, Berkshire, 5 January 1956.

He was of middle height, dark-haired and pale, bearded in later life; when tired, he limped from his war wounds; he was an attentive listener, often shy and hesitant in discussion, disliking dissension and always anxious to understand the basis of a different opinion. He was an unswervingly loyal friend and much attracted to such mystics as Henry Vaughan the Silurist and his twin-brother Thomas, and William Blake.

[*The Times*, 7 and 11 January 1956; *Nature*, 28 April 1956; *Ambix*, October 1956; personal knowledge.]   DOUGLAS McKIE.

TAYLOR, SIR GORDON GORDON- (1878–1960), surgeon. [See GORDON- TAYLOR.]

TAYLOR, SIR THOMAS WESTON JOHNS (1895–1953), scientist and academic administrator, was born in Little Ilford, Essex, 2 October 1895, the only

n of Thomas George Taylor, account-
it, and his wife, Alice Bessie Aston
ohns. He was educated at the City of
ondon School and Brasenose College,
xford. From 1914 to 1918 he served
the Essex Regiment, in France and at
allipoli, and was twice wounded. He re-
irned to Oxford after the war, obtained a
rst in chemistry and was elected fellow of
is college in 1920, and became university
cturer in organic chemistry in 1927. In
931 he was a Rhodes travelling fellow.

Taylor was an able and versatile, if not a
emarkably original, scientist. He edited
new edition of *Organic Chemistry of
Nitrogen* by N. V. Sidgwick [q.v.] (with
V. Baker, 1937); and with A. F. Millidge
he second volume of Richter–Anschütz,
The Chemistry of the Carbon Compounds
1939). He contributed a number of papers
o the *Journal* of the Chemical Society,
nd served on its council from 1936 to
939. His greatest ability, however, lay in
eaching. He had a genius for communi-
ating enthusiasm as well as knowledge.
Ie greatly enjoyed teaching under-
raduates and his help was much sought
fter by research students, some of whom
hemselves subsequently achieved great
istinction. Sometimes in later life he
xpressed a mild regret that he had not
iimself reached the highest academic
ionours; but the range of his interests was
o wide that he would have found it hard
—even had he so wished—to maintain a
single-minded devotion over a long period
o a particular line of research. He was
nterested in too much: he was a capable
ield naturalist, with an encyclopedic
knowledge of the flora and fauna of many
parts of the world; he took part in two
mportant ecological investigations, in
Spitsbergen in 1936 and in the Galápagos
Islands in 1938–9, and on each occasion his
skill in improvising field techniques contributed much to the success of the expedition.
Outside the range of the natural sciences,
he was a competent amateur in water-
colours; a more than competent amateur
musician; a voracious reader, with an open
book on every flat surface in his home; and
an ardent francophil, steeped in the literature, archaeology, history, and natural
history of France, where, between the
wars, he spent most of his long vacations.

When war broke out in 1939 Taylor
joined the chemical branch of the Royal
Engineers. He served for three years
in the Middle East and was mentioned
in dispatches. In 1943 he was appointed
secretary, and a little later director,
of the British Central Scientific Office
in Washington, a post for which his
wide interests and out-of-the-way knowledge made him peculiarly well fitted.
The range of his concerns included
such unconnected topics as insecticides,
the design of paper parachutes for
dropping small packages, the prevention
of metal corrosion, and the composition
of shark repellents. In 1944, pursuing a
similarly wide range of problems, he
was transferred to South-East Asia
Command as head of the operational
research division, where he remained to
the end of the war. He was appointed
C.B.E. in 1946.

Taylor's war experience revealed in
him an unsuspected talent for organization, and gave him a taste for life in
the tropics. At that time the Government
was much concerned with the establishment of university institutions in a
number of tropical colonies and in
1946 Taylor was appointed principal of
the proposed University College (later
the University) of the West Indies,
which was to be sited in Jamaica but to
serve all the countries of the British
Caribbean. The difficulties of the task
included shortage of capital money in
a time of rapid inflation, the mutual
jealousies of the Caribbean governments,
and many local misconceptions of the
nature and purpose of a university.
Taylor assembled a gifted and—under his
leadership—closely united senior team. He
quickly infected not only these chosen
colleagues, but many of the leaders of
local opinion also, with his own energy and
enthusiasm. His prodigious capacity for
work and his talent for improvisation overcame, at least in part, financial stringency.
The university became a lasting success:
a sturdy, growing institution with high
academic standards in teaching and research and with a tradition of devoted
service to the peoples of the West Indies.
The physical aspect of the university
buildings is a standing memorial to
Taylor's sense of urgency and of good
design. He was knighted in 1952, the year
in which he left Jamaica to become principal of the University College of the South
West, later the university of Exeter. But
he died suddenly in the following year,
29 August 1953, while on holiday in Italy.

'T' was a slight, bird-like man, who
seemed to irradiate ideas and restless
energy. He had a quick, irreverent wit,
and was often impatient of people slower
than himself. With friends and colleagues

he was direct and plain in speech, sometimes to the point of rudeness; but any offence he might have given was quickly removed by his evident warmth and friendliness, and by a quick smile of singular sweetness and charm. His colleagues were devoted to him.

In 1922 Taylor married Rosamund Georgina, younger daughter of Colonel Thomas Edward John Lloyd, of Plâs Tregayan, Anglesey, who shared his wide interests and introduced him to some new ones, including painting and botany. They had no children. His portrait, painted by Hector Whistler in Jamaica, is in the University of the West Indies.

[Private information; personal knowledge.]

J. H. PARRY.

TEARLE, SIR GODFREY SEYMOUR (1884–1953), actor, was born in New York 12 October 1884, of theatrical stock on both sides. He was the elder son of Osmond Tearle [q.v.], by his second wife, Marianne Levy, widow and actress, daughter of F. B. Conway, the American actor and manager. Godfrey Tearle and his younger brother Malcolm who also became an actor were therefore familiar with the atmosphere of the playhouse from babyhood. He had his first speaking part when he was nine, in his father's touring Shakespearian company which was well known in the English provinces and a famous training ground for young actors. After 1899 he remained with it until his father's death in 1901 when he himself was nearly seventeen.

With such antecedents and training, and great natural gifts, Godfrey Tearle might well have been expected to make an early leap to the head of his profession. He had inherited from his father a notably fine voice, and had learnt from him how to use it to the best advantage. He trod the stage with a natural authority. Yet it seemed that in his early manhood he failed to make the impression that might have been expected either upon the public or upon the theatre managers, for he was kept year after year playing important but never quite leading parts.

The war of 1914–18 helped to retard his career and it was not until J. B. Fagan [q.v.] invited him to appear as Othello at the Royal Court Theatre in 1921 that London playgoers were given their first chance to see what he could do in one of the great classical parts. It was a performance of beauty and emotional power which fell only just short of greatness.

But here, too, he was unlucky. In that post war decade the classics were out of fashion. Although he now took rank as a leading London actor, his talents were wasted on run-of-the-mill comedies, and he was not given another chance to appear in Shakespeare until 1930, when he was cast as Horatio in an all-star special performance of *Hamlet* at the Haymarket. To many in the audience it seemed that here was an actor whose full quality had not been recognized. As a result he was invited to play Hamlet at the same theatre, which he did in 1931, but without notable success. He had to wait until 1946, when he acted Antony opposite Dame Edith Evans' Cleopatra at the Piccadilly, and until 1948 when he repeated his Othello at Stratford on Avon with the added authority of twenty-five years, before he could bring it truly home to critics and playgoers that he had the stuff of greatness in him.

It was said of Tearle by some among his multitude of friends that the only reason why he was not a great actor was that he was too nice a man; and although this was intended as a witticism it may well have been the truth. He lacked the core of hardness, the dedicated purpose, the ruthless ambition, which carries men to the top of the tree, and this streak of softness showed sometimes in the characters he played. It was impossible for Tearle to be convincingly cruel, as was seen when in 1950 he took over the part of the father in *The Heiress*. He went through all the motions of cruelty, but the character remained almost benign.

Nevertheless Tearle was a superbly well-endowed actor. It was remarked that he had an ability to suggest, as some actors of an older day had learned to suggest, magnificence borne in on the senses of an audience by his mere presence and sheer authority, so that he seemed a little larger than life. This made him an ideal hero of romance, and he was much in request for such parts when he returned to the stage after his three years in the army. Perhaps the most striking of these was Boris Androvsky in the spectacular and very popular stage version at Drury Lane in 1920 of the novel *The Garden of Allah* by Robert Hichens [q.v.].

After winning a prize in a sweepstake amounting to several thousand pounds, Tearle used the money to go into management at the Apollo; everybody wished him well for he was very popular, but

is first production failed outright and
is second, *The Fake* (1924) by Frederick
Lonsdale [q.v.], did only moderately,
and the money was lost. It was not in
his nature to repine. A chance to become
a prosperous actor-manager had been
missed, but engagements continued to
flow in. On stage or film, in England or
America, at headquarters or on tour, he
pursued his career, rising to opportunities for distinction when they came
his way, yet never going out of his way
to seek for them, except perhaps in 1938
when he made his second and more
successful appearance as actor-manager,
presenting at the Lyric *The Flashing
Stream*, the first play by Charles Morgan
[q.v.]. Though Tearle's career was not
that of an ambitious man, it was that of a
man of excellent gifts and a high sense of
professional integrity, and when it was
rewarded in 1951 with a knighthood there
was a general sense of satisfaction. He had
been the first president of Equity in 1932.

Tearle's first marriage, to Mary Malone,
actress, was dissolved. He married, secondly, in 1932, Stella Freeman, actress,
who died in 1936; his third marriage in
1937 to Barbara Mary Palmer, actress,
was also dissolved. He had no children.
He died in London 8 June 1953.

[*Who's Who in the Theatre*; *The Times*,
10 June 1953; private information; personal
knowledge.]   W. A. DARLINGTON.

TEMPLEWOOD, VISCOUNT (1880–1959),
statesman. [See HOARE, SIR SAMUEL JOHN
GURNEY, second baronet.]

TENNYSON-D'EYNCOURT, SIR
EUSTACE HENRY WILLIAM, first
baronet (1868–1951), naval architect, the
sixth and youngest child of Louis Charles
Tennyson-d'Eyncourt, metropolitan magistrate, and his wife, Sophia, daughter
of John Ashton Yates, of Dinglehead,
Lancashire, was born 1 April 1868 at
Hadley House by Barnet Green, Hertfordshire. His father was a cousin of Alfred
Tennyson [q.v.]; his grandfather Charles
Tennyson had added to his name that of
d'Eyncourt, the family through which he
was descended on the maternal side.

Leaving Charterhouse at eighteen
Tennyson-d'Eyncourt became an apprentice at the Elswick shipyard of Armstrong,
Whitworth & Co., and after two years
spent in going through the various
shops took as a private student the
naval architecture course at the Royal

Naval College, Greenwich. Returning to
Elswick, he was placed in the design
office under J. R. Perrett and remained
there on the permanent staff at the conclusion of his five years' apprenticeship.
At that time very many warships were
being built for the British and other
navies, the 'Elswick cruisers' having a
specially high reputation. This was
valuable experience, but it did not include
mercantile shipbuilding, and in 1898
he obtained a post as naval architect
with the Fairfield Shipbuilding and
Engineering Company, at Govan, Glasgow, where, in addition to naval vessels,
both passenger liners and cargo ships
were under construction.

In 1902, however, d'Eyncourt received
what he termed 'an irresistible opportunity to go back to the Tyne'. (Sir)
Philip Watts [q.v.] had left Elswick to
become director of naval construction;
Perrett had succeeded Watts at Elswick
and invited d'Eyncourt to take charge
of the design office. This post involved
many trips abroad to negotiate naval
contracts. In 1904, after handing over
the new cruiser *Hamidieh*, he was asked
by the Turkish Government to report
on the condition of its navy. In view
of the poor state of many of the ships,
this called for very tactful wording and
he was awarded a third class Medjidieh
for his efforts.

In 1912 d'Eyncourt was appointed
director of naval construction in succession to Watts, (Sir) Winston Churchill
having decided to bring to the Admiralty a relatively young man instead of
promoting a senior constructor who was
near the retiring age. During d'Eyncourt's
term of office 21 capital ships, 53 cruisers,
133 submarines of eleven different classes,
and numerous other vessels were added to
the Royal Navy. The battleships of the
Royal Sovereign class were the first capital
ship designs for which he was responsible.
In lieu of two of the class, the battle
cruisers *Renown* and *Repulse* were designed
and built in under twenty months. He
introduced the 'bulge' form of protection
against torpedo attack and no ship so
fitted was sunk in the war of 1914–18 by
torpedoes. In 1915 he was entrusted with
the design of rigid airships for the navy and
retained this responsibility until it was
transferred to an air department. In February of the same year Churchill had asked
him to undertake the design of a 'landship'. Material for the army was certainly
not normally his province, but d'Eyncourt

was keenly interested in the project and agreed to head a committee formed to design and produce landships or 'tanks' as they were later termed. The prototype was ready for trials early in 1916 and the first tanks saw action at the battle of the Somme. Although the original Admiralty landship committee was disbanded after the early and successful trials, d'Eyncourt was retained as chief technical adviser.

Among the many naval developments which took place during the war perhaps the most important were those in the design of aircraft carriers. Under d'Eyncourt's guidance there was rapid progress and a pattern of bridge and superstructure was set which has been followed by all other navies. His most impressive design was that of the battle cruiser *Hood*, the first capital ship to be fitted with small tube boilers, a type he had long advocated. In the post-war years, he had to contend with the difficult problems consequent on the Washington Treaty of 1922 and the *Nelson* and *Rodney* represented his solution for the most powerful battleship of less than 35,000 tons.

D'Eyncourt resigned from the Admiralty in 1924, but remained for some time a special adviser. From 1924 to 1928 he was a director of his old firm, Armstrong, Whitworth & Co. He then joined the board of Parsons Marine Steam Turbine Company until his retirement in 1948. During the inter-war years he designed numerous merchant ships including the very novel heavy lift 'Belships'. He was appointed K.C.B. in 1917 and in 1918 was made a commander of the Legion of Honour and also awarded the American D.S.M. He was elected F.R.S. in 1921, and received honorary degrees from Durham and Cambridge. In 1930 he was created a baronet and in 1937 he was elected foreign associate member of the French Académie de Marine in succession to Lord Jellicoe [q.v.].

D'Eyncourt was chairman of the advisory committee of the William Froude Laboratory for fifteen years and was a prominent and active member of many societies and institutions, including the Worshipful Company of Shipwrights, becoming a master in 1927. He read several important papers before the Royal Institution of Naval Architects and was elected a vice-president in 1916 and an honorary vice-president in 1935. He was president of the North-East Coast Institution of Engineers and Shipbuilders from 1925 to 1927.

In 1898 d'Eyncourt married Janet, daughter of Matthew Watson Finlay, of Langside, near Glasgow, and widow of John Burns, of Glasgow. She had two children by her first marriage and a son and a daughter by her second and died in 1909 when accompanying her husband on a business visit to the Argentine. D'Eyncourt died in London 1 February 1951 and was succeeded as second baronet by his son, Eustace Gervais (born 1902).

A portrait by Sir Oswald Birley was hung in the office of Brixton Estate, Ltd., a company d'Eyncourt had formed in conjunction with his son and son-in-law.

[Sir Charles Lillicrap in *Obituary Notices of Fellows of the Royal Society*, No. 20, November 1951; Sir Eustace Tennyson-d'Eyncourt, *A Shipbuilder's Yarn*, 1948; private information.]   K. C. BARNABY.

THOMAS, DYLAN MARLAIS (1914–1953), poet, was born in Swansea 27 October 1914, the only son and younger child of David John Thomas, English master at the Swansea Grammar School, by his wife, Florence Hannah Williams. 'Marlais', the name of a small stream in Carmarthenshire, links Thomas with his parents' native county. After the normal primary school education, Thomas entered the Swansea Grammar School, and its school magazine, of which he first became sub-editor then, in his final year, editor, bears ample testimony, in prose and verse, to the creative assiduity with which he applied himself to his editorial tasks. He left school with an undistinguished academic record in 1931 to join the *South Wales Daily Post* as a reporter but by the end of 1932 he had left the paper. This marked the beginning of his career as a professional poet.

In September 1933 the *Sunday Referee* printed his first poem to find publication in the London press, and in the next year he was awarded the paper's 'major prize' which led to the publication of his *18 Poems* (1934). These were marked by an impression of early maturity. The themes which were to sustain his poetic output to the end of his days are all found here: the 'Genesis' theme, the 'Adam' myth, and the creative 'Word'. These themes, continually developed throughout his career, and worked out with meticulous craftsmanship, justify his later claim that his poems were ritten for the love of Man and in aise of God'.

In November 1934 Thomas moved to ondon to work as a freelance and ere he laid the foundations of the gend of the beer-swilling, roystering ohemian, who behaved as some people 1agined a poet should. At intervals ∶ returned to Swansea where he spent ιe end of 1935 and the beginning of ·36 working on *Twenty-five Poems*, ιblished in the latter year. In these)ems he continues his probing into the ιture of man, his beginning and end, ιd his place in the economy of creation. is essentially religious nature informs ιese poems, and his perceptive glimpse ∶' the sacramental nature of the universe ι the beautifully turned lyric, 'This read I Break', presages the change hich was to be even more clearly iscerned in *The Map of Love*, published ι 1939. In the words of his close friend, ernon Watkins, 'Each [poem] is an xperience perceived and controlled by ιe religious sense, and each answers s own questions. He has pared his nagery without losing any of its force.'

In 1937 Dylan Thomas married Caitlin, ιughter of Francis Macnamara; they ad two sons and one daughter. At ιis time they settled in Laugharne. n 1939 *The World I Breathe* was pubshed in America. It contained selecons from *18 Poems*, *Twenty-five Poems*, 'he *Map of Love*, and additional new tories. In the following year, *Portrait f the Artist as a Young Dog* appeared—a hinly disguised autobiographical account f his boyhood in Swansea, Gower, and he Carmarthenshire countryside. In these tories we find the quintessence of 'homas's rich humour and sense of the omic, allied to a compassionate affection)r all sorts and conditions of men.

During the war Thomas lived in ,ondon, interrupted by frequent spells in ,augharne and Swansea. He returned o Carmarthenshire in 1944, and in the utumn of that year settled in New Quay, 'ardiganshire, moving back to London in ieptember 1945, where he remained until 4arch 1946 when he moved to Holy-rell Ford, Oxford. In 1947 he moved to outh Leigh and in 1949 returned to ,augharne. The war period was perhaps he most fruitful of Thomas's whole career. ιpart from his radio writing, collected)osthumously in *Quite Early One Morning* 1954), he began to be used extensively by he B.B.C. as an actor and reader of poetry.

His gifts as a reader were outstanding. At his best, he displayed a sensitivity which enabled him to ally himself, as it were, with the poet, in the very act of creating. There is little doubt that it was this gift for reading, which insinuated an ease of understanding into the most difficult of his own poems, that brought him his early fame and popularity. He confessed that his work for the B.B.C. and his public readings contributed towards that greater simplification and clarity which is displayed in his later work.

Apart from his work with the B.B.C., he was engaged in this period on script-writing for films—*Lidice*, *The Three Weird Sisters*, *These are the Men*, *Our Country*, *The Doctor and the Devils* (published 1953), *The Beach of Falesá* and *Twenty Years A-Growing* (the last two published posthumously). Among his posthumous publications is *Adventures in the Skin Trade* (1955), an unfinished novel describing the arrival of a young poet in London, which was begun at some time prior to 1941. It is, like many of his stories, richly comic, and is all of a piece with his other writing. It was never completed, perhaps because of the war and the changed vision of this city of fire-raids and holocausts.

It was *Deaths and Entrances*, published in 1946, which sealed his promise, and secured for him a place in the English poetic tradition—in the direct line of his Welsh predecessors Donne, Herbert, and Vaughan. Although this volume contains a number of poems which arise from the great tragedy and holocaust of the war, yet it succeeds in conveying an impression of light and illumination. Here are the great poems of the holy innocence of childhood. This movement into light is accompanied by a simplifying of style, and an attendant gain in lucidity. In these poems, Thomas is a ritualist, celebrating the glory of the material order and his imagery takes on a 'Catholic' flavour, no doubt under the influence of Gerard Manley Hopkins, a poet whose work he loved.

The first of Thomas's four visits to America was made in the spring of 1950. There is little doubt that these trips were undertaken 'to make some money' which he badly needed. He was completely incapable of ordering the material side of his life, and even the prospect of 'making money' bored him. His account of one of his marathon tours is described in the hilariously funny broadcast talk 'Visit to America' and is a healthy antidote to

Thomas, D. M.

D.N.B. 1951–1960

J. M. Brinnin's lurid but one-sided account in *Dylan Thomas in America*.

Collected Poems was put together at the suggestion of his publishers in 1952, and contained all that he wished to preserve. The following January he was presented with the William Foyle poetry prize. When the time comes to make a final assessment of his work, his stature will be determined, not so much upon the strength of a handful of random poems, nor even on *Deaths and Entrances*, but on the *Collected Poems* seen as a unity, the fruit of a life of dedication to his 'craft and sullen art'. The 'Author's Prologue', a poem written expressly as an introduction to the *Collected Poems*, was to be his last completed poem and his final declaration of the relevance of his art to the human condition.

In January 1952 he made his second visit to America, and in April 1953 his third. Then came the final visit in the autumn of the same year when he arrived a sick man. He was scheduled to take part in the first performance of his 'play for voices', *Under Milk Wood*, on 24 October at the Poetry Center, New York. (The first part of this play had already appeared in *Botteghe Oscure* in 1952 under the title *Llareggub*, but it seems that Thomas worked on it right to the end. The final version was broadcast in the Third Programme of the B.B.C. on 25 January 1954.)

The presentation in New York was agreed by critics to be the finest performance of *Under Milk Wood*. It was his last appearance. Within a few days, after bouts of excessive drinking of hard liquor, he succumbed to alcoholic poisoning and died in New York 9 November 1953. His body was brought back to Laugharne and was interred in the burial ground of the parish church of St. Martin.

Portraits by Augustus John and Alfred Janes and a bronze bust, from a death mask, by David Slivka and Ibram Lassaw, are in the National Museum of Wales. The National Portrait Gallery has portraits by G. T. Stuart and Rupert Shephard and drawings by Michael Ayrton and Mervyn Levy. The Tate Gallery has a head painted by Eileen Agar.

[*The Times*, 10 November 1953; Dylan Thomas, *Letters to Vernon Watkins*, 1957; J. M. Brinnin, *Dylan Thomas in America*, 1956; J. A. Rolph, *Dylan Thomas: A Bibliography*, 1956; Augustus John, *Finishing Touches*, 1964; Constantine FitzGibbon, *T[he] Life of Dylan Thomas*, 1965; *Poet in t[he] Making: The Notebooks of Dylan Thomas*, e[d.] Ralph Maud, 1968; personal knowledge.]

ANEIRIN TALFAN DAVIE[S]

THOMAS, FREDERICK WILLIA[M] (1867–1956), orientalist, was born a[t] Wilnecote, Tamworth, Staffordshire, 2[1] March 1867, the son of Frederick Thoma[s], colliery clerk, and his wife, France[s] Blainey. He was educated at Kin[g] Edward VI's High School, Birmingha[m], whence he gained a scholarship [at] Trinity College, Cambridge. He w[as] awarded a first class in part i (188[7]) and part ii (with distinction, 1889) [of] the classical tripos, followed by a fir[st] class in the Indian languages trip[os] (1890). He won medals for Greek epigra[m] (1887), Latin epigram (1888), and Gree[k] ode (1889), the Members' prize for Lati[n] essay (1888), and, twice, the Le Ba[s] essay prize (1890–91). Captain of his schoo[l] he practised many sports at Cambridg[e] and was capped for lacrosse. In 189[?] he was elected into a fellowship at Trinit[y] College, which he held *in absentia* whil[e] headmaster's assistant (1891–8) at hi[s] old school. In 1898 he was appointe[d] assistant librarian of the India Offic[e] under C. H. Tawney, whom he succeede[d] as librarian in 1903. This post he hel[d] until 1927, when he was elected Bode[n] professor of Sanskrit at Oxford. H[e] vacated his chair, and with it his fellow[-]ship at Balliol, in 1937.

As a classical scholar Thomas ha[d] specialized in philology, and it was a[s] a philologist that he contributed mos[t] to oriental studies. His first publication[s] the two Le Bas essays, were devoted t[o] the history of British education in Indi[a] and the mutual influence of Mohamme[-]dans and Hindus. He soon turned t[o] more austere topics and in 189[7] in collaboration with his teacher E. B[.] Cowell (whose notice he contribute[d] to this Dictionary), he produced th[e] standard translation of the *Harsa-carit[a]* of Bana. At the India Office he threw him[-]self with enthusiasm into the massiv[e] task of arranging and cataloguing th[e] large accumulations of oriental book[s] and manuscripts in many languages[.] When Sir Aurel Stein [q.v] discovere[d] the famous 'hidden library' near Tun[-] huang and all the documents in Tibeta[n] passed to the India Office library, Thoma[s] found a wonderful outlet for his lin[-] guistic gifts which occupied him for th[e]

964

st of his life. Among his many dis-
veries in this collection was a hitherto
nknown language of the Sino-Tibetan
orderland which he successfully deci-
hered and to which he gave the name
Nam'. His specialist interests, however,
anged far beyond pure philology. He
made important contributions to Buddh-
st studies, and was an authority on
ainism. His acute mind found delight
a expounding the intricacies of Indian
hilosophy and logic. He wrote important
apers on Tibetan mythology and folk-
re. In all he published 250 books and
rticles. True to the exact tradition of
ndian scholarship established by men
ke Jones, Wilkins, and Colebrooke,
e also inherited their universality in a
ime when the frontiers of Indian studies
vere widely extended to the north and
ast. He was a pioneer of the new school
f Asian philology and his influence has
roved to be far-reaching.

In 1937 to mark his seventieth birthday, ninety-nine colleagues in orientalism
f many lands signed a memorial in his
onour; two years later he received a
olume of studies to which forty-eight
cholars contributed and which contained
a bibliography of his writings down to
939. He was elected F.B.A. in 1927;
ppointed C.I.E. in 1928; received hono-
ary degrees from Munich, Allahabad,
nd Birmingham; and in 1941 was
awarded the triennial gold medal of the
Royal Asiatic Society.

To his last years Thomas retained
the lean and athletic figure of the strenuous sportsman. His manner was keen
and affable, and he enjoyed speaking in
earned company. He celebrated his
retirement by undertaking a tour of
India in 1938 which would have taxed
the strength and energies of the most
ntrepid traveller. He retained the full
scope of his great intellectual powers
to the end, although deafness at the last
diminished his social enjoyment. He
lied at Bodicote, Oxfordshire, 6 May
1956.

In 1908 Thomas married Eleanor
Grace, daughter of Walter John Hammond, engineer, of The Grange, Knock-
holt, Kent; they had one son and one
daughter.

[H. N. Randle in *Proceedings* of the British
Academy, vol. xliv, 1958 (bibliography,
1940–57); L. D. Barnett in *Journal* of the
Royal Asiatic Society, part 2, 1957; private
information; personal knowledge.]
A. J. ARBERRY.

THOMAS, SIR HENRY (1878–1952),
Hispanologist and bibliographer, was born
at Eynsham, near Oxford, 21 November
1878, the third child and second son of
Alfred Charles Thomas, minister of the
local Irvingite congregation, and his wife,
Hannah Friday. The family derived from
Coventry, where its members had long
been silk-weavers. His parents moving to
Birmingham, Thomas entered King Edward VI Grammar School, Aston, where
he soon distinguished himself and as head
boy matriculated at Mason College, later
the university of Birmingham. There he
did brilliantly in the classical languages,
French, and English philology, becoming
research scholar in classics and Constance
Naden memorial gold medallist. In October 1903 he entered the British Museum as
assistant in the department of printed
books. Soon after, he began to learn Spanish
and by 1910 he was already well known as
a Spanish scholar. Iberian studies remained his chief interest and brought him
many honours; he was an honorary councillor of the Spanish Higher Council for
Scientific Research, a member of the
Spanish and Luso-Brazilian Councils, and
president of the Anglo-Spanish Society
(1931–47). A monograph on *Spanish and
Portuguese Romances of Chivalry* (1920),
expanded from his Norman MacColl lectures at Cambridge in 1917, brought
Thomas the Bonsoms prize and gold medal
of the Institut d'Estudis Catalans in 1921,
and in 1922 he delivered the Taylorian
lecture at Oxford on 'Shakespeare and
Spain'. His *Spanish Sixteenth-Century
Printing* (1926) was translated into German (1928). For the Bibliographical
Society of London, of which he was president in 1936–8, he wrote a monograph,
*Early Spanish Bookbindings, XI–XV
Centuries*, with plates from photographs
of his own taking (1939), and a paper on
'Copperplate Engravings in Early Spanish
Books' (1940). He produced an edition
(1923) and a verse translation (1935) of the
anonymous drama *La Estrella de Sevilla*
(2nd eds. 1930 and 1950) and a verse
translation of J. E. Hartzenbusch's *Los
Amantes de Teruel* (1938, 2nd ed. 1950),
doing much translating in daily suburban
trains.

Thomas's vacations were usually passed
in Spain, where he had many friends.
Retracing on foot the medieval pilgrim
way to the shrine of Santiago de Com-
postela, he corrected certain errors in
the accepted itinerary, and he gave
a humorous account of a miracle story

current among the medieval pilgrims in *Monster and Miracle* (privately printed, 1935); a Catalan translation appeared in 1942 and he himself did a Spanish version in 1946. When after the Spanish civil war and the war of 1939-45 he was able to revisit Spain, Thomas earnestly set himself to counteract Anglo-Spanish misunderstandings. He broadcast several times in 'La Voz de Londres'. In 1947 he was the guest of the Spanish Government at the Cervantes quatercentenary celebrations.

At the British Museum, Thomas was responsible for the *Short-Title Catalogue of Books printed in Spain and of Spanish Books printed elsewhere in Europe before 1601 now in the British Museum* (1921). This volume sets out the bibliographical essentials concerning at least 2,500 books and Thomas worked out a very successful scheme for keeping the entries as succinct as was compatible with accuracy. He applied the same method, still within the compass of a single volume, to the museum's 12,000 French books printed before 1601 (1924) and later to the Portuguese (1940) and Spanish-American books (1944). When in 1936 the museum acquired the manuscript of an unknown Portuguese account of the discovery of Abyssinia, Thomas contributed to the officially published edition of this an introduction, an English translation, and notes (1938). Thomas became deputy keeper in the department of printed books in 1924 and principal keeper in 1943, when it fell to him to deal with the problems of post-war reconstruction. In these he was greatly interested and overtaxed his strength by his labours. In December 1944 he accompanied the director of the museum to the United States and Canada on a three-months' official visit for study of recent library design and organization. He retired in 1947 and immediately resumed the Spanish studies which other occupations had made him put aside, but his health, which had at all times given him trouble, was now manifestly failing and in the autumn of 1950 he had a seizure. Others followed and he died at Birmingham after great suffering, 21 July 1952.

Thomas was knighted in 1946. He was D.Litt. and honorary LL.D. of Birmingham University and D.Lit. of London University, and became a fellow of the British Academy in 1936. Numerous Spanish, Portuguese, and South American

learned societies elected him honorary or corresponding member.

Thomas had many subsidiary interests and held detached and moderate views He was a skilful photographer and resourceful motorist. He was long a member of the Oxford and Cambridge Musical Club and read a paper on 'Musical Settings of Horace's Lyric Poems' before the Musical Association in 1920.

Unconditional integrity and devotion to duty were the basis of Thomas's character and he could be severe on derelictions in these respects. A very quiet manner was the cover both for great kindness and generosity and for great determination, and he was the most loyal of friends. He had much dry humour and could on occasion be a great talker. He never married but was devoted to the family at Birmingham.

[V. Scholderer and S. Morison in *Proceedings* of the British Academy, vol. xl, 1954 private information; personal knowledge.]

VICTOR SCHOLDERER

THOMAS, JAMES PURDON LEWES, VISCOUNT CILCENNIN (1903-1960), politician, was born 13 October 1903 at Caeglas, Llandilo, Carmarthenshire, the only son of John Lewes Thomas, a justice of the peace, by his wife, Anne Louisa, daughter of Commander George Purdon R.N., of Tinarana, county Clare. He was educated at Rugby (becoming a governor in 1937 and chairman in 1958) and at Oriel College, Oxford, where he obtained an *aegrotat* degree in French in 1926.

From a minor post in the central office of the Conservative Party Thomas was in 1929 appointed an assistant private secretary to the prime minister Stanley Baldwin. In the same year he stood unsuccessfully as member of Parliament for Llanelly. He was elected in 1931 for Hereford, retaining the seat until created a peer in 1955.

Preferring the discreet business of political manœuvre to the open exercise of power, Thomas made an ideal parliamentary private secretary. His first master (1932-6) was his namesake J. H. Thomas [q.v.], secretary of state for the dominions and later for the colonies. Outwardly they were an ill-assorted pair, the defiant plebeian and the self-possessed patrician. Yet each took a humorous view of life which led many to underestimate their judgement. At no time was the younger man's affection and loyalty more movingly displayed than during his chief's resignation in 1936, the result of a leak of budget secrets. During the war, too, he was to place personal allegiance above cautious conformity by openly visiting Baldwin at the nadir of that statesman's fortunes.

Thomas gave the same unstinted devotion to Anthony Eden (later the Earl of Avon), secretary of state for foreign affairs, whose parliamentary private secretary he became in 1937. Less than a fortnight after his appointment, Thomas was approached by emissaries of the prime minister, Neville Chamberlain. Fearing that Eden's open mistrust of Hitler and Mussolini threatened Chamberlain's policy of appeasement, they begged Thomas 'to build a bridge between 10 Downing Street and the Foreign Office'. This he interpreted as an invitation to spy on his chief and he rejected their overtures with indignation. On Eden's resignation in 1938, Thomas unflinchingly followed him into what then seemed the political wilderness, and he abstained from voting in favour of the Munich agreement.

At the outbreak of war in 1939 he volunteered for military service, but was rejected because of a permanently injured knee, and instead joined Eden at the Dominions Office. From 1940 to 1943 he was a tactful and popular government whip in the Commons. Then he became financial secretary to the Admiralty, his first opportunity of showing that attachment to the Royal Navy which was the ruling passion of his life. An irresistible charm and a readiness to admit to ignorance of technical subjects ensured his success in solving labour problems in the dockyards—a necessary prelude to the invasion of Normandy.

After the general election of 1945, Thomas became the Opposition spokesman on naval affairs and deputy chairman of the Conservative Party. From Lord Woolton, the chairman, he accepted the task of preparing a list of parliamentary candidates for the guidance of constituencies. His ability to win the confidence of those he interviewed while shrewdly assessing their character enabled him to recruit much youthful talent. This was reflected in the return of his party to power at the general election of 1951.

Thomas had no illusions that he was fitted either by temperament or by reverence for party dogma to occupy the highest offices in the Cabinet. Since his wartime years at the Admiralty, however, he had pined to return to this department and his ambition was fulfilled when he became first lord in October 1951. He was sworn of the Privy Council in November. 'There is only one test of a first lord', he used to remark, 'Will he look well in a yachting cap when visiting the fleet?' Standing over six foot, with boldly cut features and a fresh complexion, Thomas was as much at ease on the lower deck as in the ward room. His popularity was immediate and lasting, his progress round any naval establishment a convivial occasion. During his five years at the Admiralty he accepted the controversial recommendation that no officer should be recruited under the age of eighteen, a measure subsequently endorsed by other first lords. He resisted pressure to abolish the Fleet Air Arm, considered by some to be unduly expensive in both men and money. Working with the first sea lord, Lord Mountbatten, he also set up a committee which achieved remarkable economies without substantially reducing naval strength.

In December 1955 Thomas was created Viscount Cilcennin, taking his title from the little river which runs through his family property in Carmarthenshire. Less than a year later, although only fifty-two, he decided with regret to retire from politics to his house at the foot of the Malvern hills. His instinct of hospitality and the splendour of his official residence, Admiralty House, had tempted him to spend more than he could afford. He also suffered increasing pain from arthritis of the hip, which he bore with stoicism. So that his links with the navy should not be snapped too abruptly, he was invited to join the royal yacht *Britannia* for the Duke of Edinburgh's tour of the Commonwealth in 1956–7.

Having represented Hereford in the Commons for nearly twenty-five years, he was no less delighted to be appointed lord-lieutenant of the county in 1957. His financial burden was eased by invitations to serve on the boards of several companies, and he proved an energetic and lively chairman of Television Wales and Western. In his leisure hours he wrote an attractive little volume on Admiralty House, the profits from which he characteristically decided should be given to a naval charity. He did not live to see its publication, but died in London 13 July 1960. He was unmarried.

Jim Thomas had a genius for friendship. He was an entertaining talker who radiated gaiety as he sat on into the early hours recounting those personal adventures which owed as much to a sense of poetry as to historical accuracy. He loved gossip but was utterly without malice. The malice of others he dismissed with chuckles and puffs of his pipe. He was quietly well read, a gardener, and a gourmet.

A portrait by Simon Elwes remained the possession of the artist. Others by Mary Rennell and John Ward belong to the family.

[Private information; personal knowledge.]
KENNETH ROSE.

THOMAS, MARGARET HAIG, VISCOUNTESS RHONDDA (1883–1958), founder and editor of *Time and Tide*, was born in London 12 June 1883, the only child of David Alfred Thomas, later Viscount Rhondda [q.v.], a coal owner and politician, of Llanwern, and his wife, Sybil Margaret, fourth daughter of George Augustus Haig, of Pen Ithon, Radnorshire, a member of the ancient family of Bemersyde to which Earl Haig [q.v.] belonged.

She was educated by governesses until she was thirteen and then as a day girl at Notting Hill High School. She edited a printed magazine called *The Shooting Star*, for the doubtful benefit, as both readers and contributors, of her family. Two years later, by her own wish, she went as a boarder to St. Leonards School where she was very happy. Afterwards she had three London seasons, which, being shy, she disliked, and spent a scarcely more fruitful year at Somerville College, Oxford. In 1908 she married (Sir) Humphrey Mackworth (died 1948), later the seventh baronet, of Caerleon-on-Usk. The marriage was not a success. Mackworth loved hunting, his wife loved books; she wanted children and had none. She divorced him in 1923, but always insisted that he was 'a very nice man'.

Because her husband was a Conservative, she joined the Conservative Party although she had been brought up as a Liberal; but only a few months after her marriage she detached herself from all party allegiance by joining the militant suffragettes in the Women's Social and Political Union. Searching for a rational basis to an emotional decision, she read widely and began to write articles on the suffrage question; later she looked back on this as the time of her real education. Her militant activities culminated in an attempt to destroy the letters in a pillar box with a chemical bomb. She was sent to Usk prison where she went on hunger strike and was released after five days.

Her father, whom she described as a liberal education in himself, took her still farther out of her husband's world by appointing her his personal assistant and proxy in many business interests. In 1915 they returned from a visit to America in the *Lusitania*. When the ship was torpedoed she went down with it and floated in a lifebelt for three hours before being picked up unconscious. Just a month before he died in 1918, Lord Rhondda, then a baron, was created a viscount with special remainder to his daughter. She inherited both his title and his many business interests. In a long legal dispute she claimed the right to sit in the House of Lords; an attempt which was finally defeated largely by the opposition of Lord Birkenhead [q.v.].

Much though she enjoyed business life, there was something else she wanted more: to run a weekly political review which should be influential because it reached influential people. In 1920 she founded *Time and Tide*, which she effectively controlled from the beginning although she did not assume the editorship until 1926. Under Mrs. Helen Archdale the paper was left-wing and aggressively feminist. By the time Lady Rhondda died, it was called right-wing and women were seldom mentioned in it. These changes were partly apparent, because the world had moved to the Left, partly real, because Lady Rhondda's political judgement had matured. She saw that her old principles, consistently applied, must be maintained against new opponents. She still believed in equal rights for women (although she said latterly that it had been wrong to lower the voting age to twenty-one) but realized that the fight was over and that her influence would be greater if she detached herself and the paper from it.

Time and Tide became one of the leading weeklies, impressed always with her own strong personality, shaped in every detail to her wishes, standing for the things in which she passionately believed: the infinite value of individuals, personal freedom, opposition to tyranny both at home and abroad. She wrote of Munich with relief that 'there will be no bombs tonight' but in the certainty that

: was a disastrous betrayal. After the war
he held that the new enemies of freedom
vere Communism abroad and socialism
t home.

She loved and knew good writing.
Iany of the distinguished authors of
he day contributed to *Time and Tide*:
:. B. Shaw (who would never accept pay-
nent), G. K. Chesterton, Charles Williams,
;ilbert Murray, G. M. Young [qq.v.],
Dame) Rebecca West, and many others.
Theodora Bosanquet (Lady Rhondda's
losest friend and companion), (Sir) John
Betjeman, and (Dame) C. V. Wedgwood
vere among those who worked on the
taff.

Except during the war years *Time and
Tide* always required a heavy subsidy.
3y 1958 Lady Rhondda's money was
iearly at an end. She had made desperate
attempts to obtain new backing or to
ind an acceptable purchaser, but to
ittle avail. At the last moment a fund
vas started among the paper's own readers
ind enough money was raised to enable
t to continue temporarily. Exhausted
oy the struggle Lady Rhondda died
suddenly in London 20 July 1958. Her
ashes were buried at Llanwern. It emerged
that she had spent some quarter of a
million pounds on *Time and Tide* and that
there was not enough left to meet even
the principal legacies in her will. For
thirty-eight years the paper had been her
whole life. People found her difficult
because she expected from them an
equally single-minded devotion to the
paper. She had deliberately discarded
all her other interests, except her love
of gardening and of the Welsh countryside.

Mill and Plato were two of her favourite
authors. She was a democrat but not an
egalitarian; a strong patriot; and in later
life a strong Christian. Many tributes were
paid to her political acumen and the
nobility of the causes she espoused, but
those who knew her best admired most
the indomitable courage which refused
to accept defeat.

In looks she was sturdily built with curly
hair and a very determined mouth and
jaw, softened by a hint of ready laughter.
A portrait of her in early middle age,
painted by S. J. Solomon, is at Pen Ithon;
another, painted in 1932 by Alice M.
Burton, was hung in the offices of *Time
and Tide*.

[Viscountess Rhondda, *This Was My World*,
1933; private information; personal knowledge.]　　　　　　　ANTHONY LEJEUNE.

THOMAS, SIR WILLIAM BEACH
(1868–1957), journalist and author, was
born at Godmanchester, Huntingdon,
22 May 1868, the second son of the Rev.
Daniel George Thomas, who became
rector of Hamerton, Huntingdonshire,
in 1872, by his wife, Rosa Beart. His
early years in his father's parish gave
him a deep love for the countryside.
He was educated at Shrewsbury, where he
was a member of the football and cricket
elevens and distinguished himself as a
runner, being appointed huntsman of the
Royal Shrewsbury School Hunt. In 1887
he went with a Careswell exhibition to
Christ Church, Oxford, winning a full
college scholarship in 1891 but obtaining
only a third class in classical moderations
(1889) and *literae humaniores* (1891). His
record as an athlete was, however, most
impressive. With his conspicuous height
and huge stride, he was magnificent in
action; for three years in succession he
represented the university, first in the
mile, then in the hundred yards, and in
the quarter-mile which he won in 1890.
In 1890–91 he was president of the
Athletics Club. He also played both
association and rugby football and cricket
for his college.

On leaving Oxford, Beach Thomas—he
used his second Christian name as a surname—taught at Bradfield (1891–6), then
at Dulwich (1897–8); but teaching proved
uncongenial and he turned to journalism
as one of the writers of the 'By the Way'
column in the *Globe*. J. L. Garvin [q.v.]
then invited him to write about the open
air for the *Outlook* which he was editing,
and Beach Thomas was thus happily
employed for nearly two years until the
Outlook changed hands. For some time
he was on the staff of the *Saturday
Review*, which he did not greatly enjoy,
and he contributed both prose and verse
to many other papers. He wrote the
volume on *Athletics* for the Isthmian
Library (1901), but the next milestone
in his career was an interview at the
Daily Mail office with Lord Northcliffe
[q.v.], whom he at once felt to be a 'chief'
'whom it was very pleasant and honourable
to serve'. Northcliffe engaged him as a
writer on country life, and to his joy
agreed that he should live in the country
and 'not come to London more than
twice a week'. He settled in a cottage
in the valley of the Mimram in Hertfordshire, and as early as 1908 published
a selection of his essays under the title
From a Hertfordshire Cottage, which well

displayed his powers of observation and his unusual gifts as a writer on natural and rural subjects. Beach Thomas's style was distinctive; it came from a deep love of words and a determination to present a picture and a personal feeling, not primarily to tabulate facts.

One of Beach Thomas's best works was also one of the earliest—the three distinguished volumes of *The English Year* (1913-14) which he wrote in collaboration with A. K. Collett. He spent most of the war as an outstandingly successful correspondent in France for the *Daily Mail*—he wrote *With the British on the Somme* (1917)—and in 1918 he was sent on an American tour, meeting Theodore Roosevelt, President Wilson, and Henry Ford, from which he returned in time to report the allied victories. He treasured a tribute to his vivid war reporting from an unknown correspondent who wrote: 'Without your despatches we could never have persuaded the men to work throughout the bank holiday.' Beach Thomas remained in Germany until May 1919 (and was back there for the occupation of the Ruhr in 1923). In 1922 he went on a tour of the world for the *Daily Mail* and *The Times*. Most of his later writing on country matters is to be found in the *Observer*, the paper in which, renewing his friendship with its editor J. L. Garvin, he became most at home and for which he wrote regularly until 1956. He also contributed the 'Country Life' column to the *Spectator* for many years, and wrote its centenary history, *The Story of the 'Spectator'* (1928).

Beach Thomas showed himself a prolific author in his sixties and seventies. Among other books, he produced *A Letter to my Dog* (1931), *The Yeoman's England* (1934), in which he took the reader month by month through the country calendar, *The Squirrel's Granary* (1936), *Hunting England* (1936), *The English Landscape* (1938), *The Poems of a Countryman* (1945), which displayed a sensitive writer of light verse with a taste for epigram, *A Countryman's Creed* (1946), *The Way of a Dog* (1948), and *Hertfordshire* (1950), a pleasantly discursive account of his own county.

He wrote two autobiographies: *A Traveller in News* (1925) and *The Way of a Countryman* (1944). The first is perhaps the more interesting, not only for his war experiences but also because it contains his vindication and warm appreciation of Lord Northcliffe, whose success

he attributed to a perception which wa 'almost uncanny'; the second condense some of the same material and empha sizes his delight in the country life.

Beach Thomas excelled in all the attri butes of a countryman and naturalist. I addition, he was a great bookman. Ta and lean, with thin weather-beaten feature and a moustache, he was a man of th utmost charm and humour. He died i the house he had built for himself, High Trees, Wheathampstead, Hertfordshire 12 May 1957. He was a chevalier o the Legion of Honour (1919), and wa appointed K.B.E. (1920) for his wor as a war correspondent.

Beach Thomas married in 1900 Hele Dorothea, daughter of Augustus Georg Vernon Harcourt [q.v.], F.R.S., chemist and tutor of Christ Church, Oxford. Ther were three sons and one daughter. Th second son, a lieutenant-commander i the navy, was killed in the war of 1939- 45. A chalk drawing of Beach Thomas by Sir Muirhead Bone is in the Imperial Wa Museum.

[*Spectator*, 15 September 1950; *The Times* 14 May 1957; private information.]

DEREK HUDSON

THOMPSON, ALEXANDER HAMIL TON (1873-1952), historian, the eldest child and elder son of the Rev. John Thompson, then vicar of St. Gabriel's, Bristol, and his wife, Annie Hastings. daughter of Canon David Cooper, was born 7 November 1873 at Clifton. He entered Clifton College as a scholar in 1883, leaving in 1890, and proceeding to St. John's College, Cambridge, in 1892, where he was placed in the third division of the second class in part i of the classical tripos three years later. Weak health at this time led him to take up tutoring on the Riviera for two years. In 1897 he was appointed extramural teacher by Cambridge University, and in the same year appeared his first published work, a popular guide to 'Cambridge and its Colleges'. For the next dozen years, however, his publications, although wide in scope, were comparatively small in number and at the end of the period only the shrewdest observer would have seen something of the shape of things to come. Inevitably Hamilton Thompson was mainly occupied with lecturing, and the constant travelling that now involved, together with conduct of examinations, constituted a serious drain on his time. But the extensive travel involved facilitated the acquisition of that enormous knowledge of English topography which was to be one of his major historical assets, and the work stimulated the humanity and developed the clarity which impregnated his studies. He lived at this time partly at Henbury and partly at Chichester and St. Albans. In 1903 he married Amy, daughter of Alfred Gosling, of Colchester, and soon after moved to Lincoln.

By this time he had made the acquaintance of two of the leading medieval archaeologists of the day, (Sir) William St. John Hope (whose notice he contributed to this Dictionary) and John Bilson, both of whom were to be his closest friends for the rest of their days. His own work in their field bore its first major fruits in the publication of his *Military Architecture in England during the Middle Ages* (1912); this, with the much slighter but valuable 'Ground Plan of the English Parish Church' (1911) and 'English Monasteries' (1913), showed a remarkable grasp of English medieval architecture and its problems. Hamilton Thompson never returned to general architectural surveys of this nature, for which he developed unparalleled qualifications. But a stream of monographs on particular buildings or localities continued almost unbroken until the end, including studies of Bolton Priory (1928) and Welbeck Abbey (1938).

But in these years a very large part of Hamilton Thompson's activities centred not on history but on literature. His second publication had been a *History of English Literature* (1901) founded on that of T. B. Shaw [q.v.] and this was quickly followed by school editions of various literary texts, chiefly of the English Romantics. In 1919 Hamilton Thompson was appointed lecturer in English at Armstrong College, Newcastle upon Tyne, where two years later a readership in medieval history and archaeology was instituted for him in recognition of his scholarship. Like his contemporary, G. G. Coulton [q.v.], Hamilton Thompson thus entered full academic teaching after and not before acquiring a reputation for scholarship. Almost immediately he moved to Leeds where he became reader in medieval history in 1922, professor in 1924, and head of the department in 1927, a post which he held until his retirement in 1939.

As time went on, Hamilton Thompson's main interest lay increasingly in the publication of original records of English medieval Church history. His first major venture was based on the registers of the medieval bishops of Lincoln and in 1914 appeared the first volume of his *Visitations of Religious Houses in the Diocese of Lincoln*. As Hamilton Thompson once remarked to the writer, no small fraction of his life had been passed in making transcripts in the Archbishop's Registry at York. In 1928 he completed for the Surtees Society Part II of the *Register of Archbishop Thomas Corbridge*, and followed this up by the publication of the *Register of Archbishop William Greenfield* in five volumes (1931, 1934, 1936–8). Meanwhile steadily he produced other texts which included *Northumberland Pleas from the Curia Regis and Assize Rolls* (1922), *Registers of the Archdeaconry of Richmond* (1919, 1930, 1935), *Liber Vitae Ecclesiae Dunelmensis* (1923), *A Calendar of Charters and other Documents belonging to the Hospital of William Wyggeston at Leicester* (1933). In the year before the latter appeared, he was made Ford's lecturer at Oxford and in 1933 Birkbeck lecturer at Trinity College, Cambridge. For both he took as his theme the English Church at the end of the Middle Ages, and the fruits of his labour here finally appeared in 1947 in *The English Clergy and their Organization in the later Middle Ages*, a massive and masterly consideration of 'ecclesiastical institutions in fifteenth century England'. The death of his wife in 1945 had ended a married life of singular felicity and to her Hamilton Thompson, in a touching dedication, inscribed this his greatest work of scholarship.

As a professor at Leeds he had a unique reputation. He had little interest in the generality of committees, although as chairman of the library committee he put the university not a little in his debt. His innate friendliness led him to entertain great and small in remarkable numbers at his little house at Adel and this, with his immense memory for detail, gave him an astounding knowledge of his pupils. He answered indefatigably and immaculately the hosts of historical and antiquarian queries which beset him unceasingly and equally unstintingly gave his services as a lecturer and guide to no small fraction of the local archaeological societies of England. By 1940 his output of published works totalled 373 items of one kind or another, but this did not prevent a considerable social activity or painstaking membership of the various official bodies to which he belonged; he was a member of the Cathedrals Commission (1925–8), a cathedral commissioner for England

(1932–42), a member of the Archbishops' Commission on Canon Law (1943–7), of the Royal Commission on Historical Monuments (1933–52), and of the Ancient Monuments Board for England (1935–52). So full a life was only made feasible by Hamilton Thompson's remarkable powers of work. Until shortly before his retirement it was usual enough for him to work daily into the early hours although he was almost invariably at work at the university by nine. In later life he never took exercise, but his health was unbroken until his final illness. He died in Exmouth 4 September 1952.

Recognition of his eminence had been widespread. He was elected F.B.A. in 1928, honorary A.R.I.B.A., an honorary fellow of St. John's College, Cambridge (1938), and president of the Royal Archaeological Institute (1939–45). He was awarded the C.B.E. in 1938 and given honorary doctorates by Durham, Leeds, and Oxford.

Vicarage bred, Hamilton Thompson remained steadfastly a devout son of the Church of England, exhibiting unfailing concern for its welfare, although, like most of his generation, not always at home in the social and economic problems of the post-war world. He had two daughters, the elder of whom, Beatrice Mary, was awarded the Ellerton theological essay prize at Oxford in 1931 and was librarian of St. Hugh's College (1931–6).

[An Address presented to Alexander Hamilton Thompson, with a Bibliography of his Writings, privately printed, 1948; private information; personal knowledge.]   J. C. DICKINSON.

THOMPSON, JAMES MATTHEW (1878–1956), scholar, was born 27 September 1878 at Iron Acton, Gloucestershire, the eldest son of the rector, the Rev. Henry Lewis Thompson, formerly student and censor of Christ Church, Oxford. From his beautiful and gifted mother, Catharine, elder daughter of Sir James Paget, first baronet [q.v.], the surgeon, Thompson probably inherited his remarkable energy, love of nature, and artistic skill. A sheltered and happy childhood in the country was followed, after his father had become warden of Radley College in 1887, by an invigorating early education at the Dragon School, Oxford, which Thompson left as head of the school and winner of the eleventh scholarship to Winchester. There he formed some of his lifelong friendships, matured his classical scholarship, and began to work out his

highly individual outlook on life. In 189' he went up to Christ Church, as ope scholar. He displayed little enthusiasm for honour classical moderations in which he took a second class in 1899, but this was redeemed by a first in *literae humani ores* in 1901 and by his election as Liddo student at the House. A year later he ob tained second class honours in theology Ordination in 1903 as deacon (following two terms at Cuddesdon theological college) and a brief curacy at St. Frideswide's Poplar, were the prelude to his election on taking priest's orders, as fellow of Magdalen College, Oxford, in 1904.

Thompson's career, which promised to be so outwardly untroubled, was first broken by his involvement in distressing theological controversy and then interrupted and diverted by the war, which also led him towards virtual agnosticism. From 1905, when he became full official fellow at Magdalen, to 1915 when he ceased to be dean of divinity at the college, Thompson was a vigorous protagonist of modernist theology at Oxford and an energetic promoter of university reform. After various forms of non-combatant service in France and at the Admiralty during the war and two years' teaching at Eton, he returned to Oxford where in 1920 he found a more congenial vocation as tutorial fellow in modern history at Magdalen.

Between the wars Thompson quickly made his mark by his published works on modern European history and, after his election in 1931 to a university lectureship in French history, by specialist studies in the history of the French revolution. He also gave unstinted service to his college both as a devoted and inspiring tutor and, between 1920 and 1927, as home bursar and, from 1935 to 1937, as vice-president. His retirement at the age of sixty in 1938 and the challenge of the second war gave him the stimulus to renewed activity as historian, occasional poet, and editor of the *Oxford Magazine* (1945–7) and to further voluntary public service as trustee and convener of the Oxford Preservation Trust.

By any standard Thompson's achievements and literary craftsmanship as an historian of revolutionary and Napoleonic France were outstanding. His record was all the more impressive since, in this field, he was virtually self-taught and since his professional career as an historian began when he was over forty. Yet it may well seem that his early career as a modernist theologian, blighted by episcopal disapproval and inhibition, was an unconscious and even fruitful preparation for his later historical studies. The non-miraculous view of Christianity which he had expounded in one of his theological treatises—*Miracles in the New Testament* (1911)—had been based not merely on the Catholic modernism of Loisy, but also on the methods of modern biblical criticism which were essentially historical. From first to last Thompson remained faithful to the personal approach to history and, with the exception of his general study of the French revolution published in 1943, all his major works were biographical in form. Although he continued, in retirement, to maintain his mastery over this medium, by biographies of Napoleon I (1951) and Napoleon III (1954), his most enduring achievement will probably prove to be his two-volume study of Robespierre (1935). His work gained him international recognition, election in 1944 to an honorary fellowship at Magdalen, and in 1947 to a fellowship of the British Academy.

Thompson married in 1913 Mari Meredyth, daughter of the Rev. David Jones, vicar of Penmaenmawr, and had one son. A gifted athlete, a sensitive artist in watercolours, and a fine contemporary poet, Thompson had a rationalist philosophy unshaken in its integrity and a reticent but charming personality. He died in Oxford 8 October 1956. Magdalen College has a pencil drawing of him by Randolph Schwabe.

[A. Goodwin in *Proceedings* of the British Academy, vol. xliii, 1957; J. M. Thompson, *My Apologia*, 1940, *Collected Verse (1939–46)*, 1947, 'Oxford Modernism, 1910–1914' in *Oxford Magazine*, 28 October 1948; private information; personal knowledge.]

A. GOODWIN.

TILLEY, VESTA (1864–1952), male impersonator, whose real name was Matilda Alice Powles, was born in Worcester 13 May 1864, the second child of the family of thirteen of William Henry Powles and his wife, Matilda Broughton. Her father was a painter on chinaware and also a clever entertainer and musician, playing the violin and piccolo. He found this more lucrative than his painting and became manager of a variety hall in Gloucester, to which city the family moved. He took the name of Harry Ball. Father and daughter were devoted to each other and when she was three years old little Matilda showed remarkable talent. Her father took her to the hall with him each evening and on returning home she would re-enact all that

she had seen. He arranged a medley of songs which she sang to friends and when he was given a benefit in Gloucester Matilda made her début at the ripe age of three and a half. She first wore boy's clothes on the stage at Birmingham when she was five and that determined her future. Touring with her father, she appeared all over the country and came to London in 1878. She was a great success and appeared at three or four music-halls each evening, billed as 'The Great Little Tilley'. Since audiences were puzzled whether she was a boy or a girl she eventually adopted the name of Vesta Tilley. As she grew up she represented the perfect pattern of the well-dressed man of the period. Her clothes, hats, gloves, shirts, everything she wore, were of superlative cut and quality.

She became a celebrated principal boy in provincial pantomimes and twice appeared at Drury Lane: in *Sindbad* in 1882 in a part specially written for her and in 1890 as principal boy in *Beauty and the Beast*. She also appeared in musical comedy, straight plays, and burlesque, and was as successful in the United States as in her own country. Her real fame was achieved on the music-halls which were then at the very peak of their popularity. Popularly known as 'the London Idol', in the eyes of her faithful public she could do no wrong. She never descended to vulgarity; no breath of scandal ever touched her; and she was a perfectionist in everything she undertook. This tiny woman with the trim figure, the piquant face, and the clear voice and diction and the most immaculate male clothing, had a succession of splendid songs and sang them in a manner all her own. Among them were 'Following in Father's Footsteps', 'Burlington Bertie', 'The Piccadilly Johnny with the little glass eye', 'The Midnight Son', 'Angels without wings', 'Oh! you Girls', 'The Tablet of Fame', 'For the sake of the dear little Girls', 'Daughters', and 'Sweetheart May'. She represented not only smart young men-about-town, but also judges, clergymen, and boys in Eton suits. Some of her biggest successes were sung in military uniform. She championed the soldier when most music-hall songs glorified the sailor. One such song, 'Jolly Good Luck to the Girl who Loves a Soldier', caused a boom in recruiting; another big hit was 'The Army of To-day's all right'. During the war of 1914–18 her soldier songs 'London in France', 'Six Days' Leave', and 'A Bit of a Blighty One' were a great aid to morale.

On 5 June 1920 she retired and said farewell from the stage of the London Coliseum. It was an occasion of great enthusiasm and very considerable emotion. The immense auditorium was packed from ceiling to floor. And as Vesta Tilley stood, in khaki uniform and half buried in bouquets, bowing to the wonderful ovation, (Dame) Ellen Terry [q.v.] made a charming speech and presented her with a set of handsomely bound volumes containing the signatures of nearly two million of her admirers.

In 1890 Vesta Tilley married (Sir) Walter de Frece (died 1935), a music-hall magnate who later entered politics and was a member of Parliament from 1920 to 1931. It was an ideally happy marriage. She greatly helped him in his political career and did much quiet unobtrusive work for charity. They had no children. She died in London 16 September 1952.

[Lady de Frece, *Recollections of Vesta Tilley*, 1934; private information; personal knowledge.]   W. MACQUEEN-POPE.

TIZARD, SIR HENRY THOMAS (1885–1959), scientist and administrator, was born at Gillingham, Kent, 23 August 1885, the only son among the five children of Thomas Henry Tizard [q.v.], navigator of the *Challenger* and later assistant hydrographer of the navy, and his wife, Mary Elizabeth Churchward. He came of stock distinguished in engineering and the fighting Services; a remote ancestor was Sir Paul Rycaut, F.R.S. [q.v.]. Unable to enter the navy because of defective eyesight, Tizard went first as an exhibitioner, later as a scholar, to Westminster where he studied science and mathematics and learnt to write good English. Elected to a science demyship at Magdalen College, Oxford, in 1903, he went up in 1904 and gained a first class in mathematical moderations (1905) and in chemistry (1908). His tutor was Nevil Sidgwick [q.v.], with whom he formed a lifelong friendship. After starting research with Sidgwick in Oxford, he spent a semester with Nernst in Berlin, when he met F. A. Lindemann (later Viscount Cherwell, q.v.). Ten years later Tizard's support was a major factor in Lindemann's election to lead the Clarendon Laboratory in Oxford. As neither of the projects chosen for him by Nernst showed any promise, Tizard returned to Oxford for the summer of 1909 and then spent a year at the Royal Institution, investigating the colour changes

of indicators. The papers he published revealed a clarity and elegance of approach which established Tizard's reputation as an investigator. His report in 1911 to the British Association on 'The Sensitiveness of Indicators' was published *in extenso* in the report of the Portsmouth meeting.

In 1911 Tizard returned to Oxford as a tutorial fellow at Oriel, and he also held a demonstratorship in the electrical laboratory, which led to several papers on the motion of ions in gases of which he was a part author. August 1914 found him on board a ship with Sir Ernest (later Lord) Rutherford (whose notice he later contributed to this Dictionary) bound for the meeting of the British Association in Australia. He came home at once and joined the Royal Garrison Artillery, where his unorthodox methods of training recruits were supported by higher authority. In June 1915 R. B. Bourdillon, who had just started experimental work on bomb-sights with G. M. B. Dobson at the Central Flying School at Upavon, secured Tizard's transfer to the Royal Flying Corps as an experimental equipment officer. Tizard, whose eyesight had improved, soon learned to fly, an indispensable qualification for understanding the airman's problems. From bomb-sights Tizard turned his attention to the testing of new aircraft and in 1917 Bertram Hopkinson [q.v.], who was responsible for research and development in aeronautics, put him in charge of the testing of aircraft at the experimental station at Martlesham. There Tizard developed a scientific system for investigating the performance of aircraft which he described in a paper published by the Aeronautical Society in 1917. Martlesham was the prototype of future experimental stations such as Boscombe Down. Tizard flew as one of his own test pilots, showing skill and imaginative foresight as well as courage. When Hopkinson went to the headquarters of the Ministry of Munitions at the end of 1917 Tizard went with him as his deputy with the rank of lieutenant-colonel and after Hopkinson's death in 1918 Tizard carried on in his place.

In the spring of 1919 Tizard returned to Oxford and early in 1920 he was made reader in chemical thermodynamics. Meanwhile he had been working in a new and important field. During the war when supplies of aviation fuel were short owing to loss of tankers, Tizard had suggested the addition of gasworks benzole which gave excellent results, apart from the freezing of the benzene at low temperatures. Toluene from Borneo petroleum proved to be equally good and did not freeze. This brought Tizard into contact with (Sir) Harry Ricardo who was investigating the performance of petrol engines. He invited Tizard and (Sir) David Pye [q.v.] to join him. Tizard agreed, on condition that the results of the work were published, to which (Sir) Robert Waley Cohen [q.v.], of Shell who were financing the work, agreed.

By the summer of 1919 Tizard and Pye had prepared an analysis of the physical and chemical properties of the range of fuels which were to be examined and Ricardo had built a new variable compression engine. Tizard's help was particularly valuable in devising ingenious tests and in his astuteness in analysing the results. As they expected, the incidence of detonation was found to be the most important single factor limiting the performance of the petrol engine. Tizard suggested the term 'toluene number' to express the detonation characteristics of each fuel. Toluene was the least prone to detonate of all the fuels they examined, and the 'toluene number' was the proportion of toluene that was added to heptane, the most prone to detonation, in order to match the performance of each fuel they examined. Several years later the Americans substituted the use of iso-octane for toluene and the expression 'octane number' became universal. The results of this classic investigation were published in a series of papers which were Tizard's major contribution to scientific literature. They marked a new era in the understanding of the internal combustion engine.

In 1920 Tizard accepted an invitation from Sir Frank Heath (whose notice he contributed to this Dictionary) to go to the Department of Scientific and Industrial Research as assistant secretary. He had realized that he was unlikely to do outstanding work in pure research and had seen the great opportunities offered in the application of science to practical problems, for which he felt himself to be better suited. He was first in charge of a new division created to implement a government decision charging the D.S.I.R. with the co-ordination of the scientific work of the defence and civil departments. Several co-ordinating research boards were set up which led to numerous cross-contacts at scientific working level between the departments, and this continued when the rather cumbrous machinery of the boards was abandoned. Meanwhile they gave Tizard a most valuable bird's-eye view of what was happening. In 1924 he saw the need to co-ordinate scientific research in the Air Force and suggested the appointment of a director with similar responsibilities to (Sir) Frank Smith, the director of scientific research in the Admiralty. Pressed to accept the post himself, Tizard declined and H. E. Wimperis [q.v.], the deputy director, was promoted to it in 1925.

In 1922 Tizard had become principal assistant secretary and in 1927 he succeeded Heath as permanent secretary. During these years he exercised an increasing influence on the policy of D.S.I.R. and was largely responsible for establishing the Chemical Research Laboratory at Teddington, renamed later the National Chemical Laboratory. He left the D.S.I.R. in 1929 when he became rector of the Imperial College, an office he held until 1942. Tizard's decision to go to Imperial College was influenced by his conviction of Britain's need for more scientists and engineers. He soon raised funds to complete the new Beit building and his great service to the College was his imaginative grasp of the site planning needed for its future expansion. He fought tooth and nail and with his customary opportunism to secure the use of the whole site north of Imperial Institute Road for education and to move all museums south of it. His foresight undoubtedly made the later development of the College possible. In many other ways the College benefited by his imaginative approach to its problems such as the introduction of an undergraduate course in chemical engineering, and a scheme for entrance scholarships for boys who had not specialized in science at school. He had the great gift of being able to talk on seemingly equal terms to people of all kinds and all ages and find out what they were thinking so that he kept his finger effectively on the pulse of the organization and inspired people with his own enthusiasm for getting things done.

Meantime Tizard was increasingly occupied with the problems of defence. He had been a member of the Aeronautical Research Committee since 1919 and in 1933 he became chairman. He was also chairman of the engine sub-committee. It was a period of revolutionary advances in aircraft and engines and Tizard, with his background of experience in the first war and his knack of selecting the significant factors, was an admirable choice. While he did not contribute much in the way of original ideas he was a most stimulating chairman and he gave great encouragement to those like (Sir) Frank Whittle, with his jet engine, who were endeavouring to break fresh ground. One important suggestion arising out of his work with Ricardo was that new engines should be tested at pressures higher than those reached with normal fuel so that they could use higher octane fuels when they became available. In 1938 at the end of his five-year term of office he was invited by the Air Council, who wished to retain his 'invaluable assistance', to serve for a second five years and he continued as chairman until 1943.

Baldwin's statement in November 1932 that 'the bomber will always get through', underlined by the air exercises in 1934, had the merit of concentrating attention on this issue. Lindemann in August 1934 wrote a letter to *The Times* calling for action. His papers show that on 15 November he met Tizard and told him of his plan for a sub-committee of the Committee of Imperial Defence, since it was too important to be dealt with by a departmental committee. He noted that Tizard promised his help if possible.

Meanwhile Wimperis at the Air Ministry a few days earlier had recommended the appointment of a small committee, with Tizard as chairman, Dr. A. V. Hill, P. M. S. (later Lord) Blackett, and himself as members, and Dr. A. P. Rowe as secretary, to consider how far recent advances in scientific and technical knowledge could be used to strengthen defence against hostile aircraft. His recommendation was accepted, and all three men agreed to serve.

In December Lindemann, unaware of these proceedings, wrote to the air minister pressing for a C.I.D. committee. When he was told of the existence of the Tizard committee he regarded it as a plot by the Air Ministry and Tizard to circumvent his own proposal. This was the start of the unfortunate quarrel between them which was to loom so large over the next five years. Both were convinced of the importance of science in future warfare and each anxious to play his part. With this common objective they might have worked together, but the trouble lay largely in their different avenues of approach. Tizard relied on his influence with the air staff and civil servants, whom he understood and whose confi-

dence he had won. Lindemann relied on the politicians which, in Tizard's mind implied intrigue and was anathema to him.

The Tizard committee met first on 28 January 1935 when Wimperis told them of (Sir) Robert Watson-Watt's view that it might be possible to detect the presence of aircraft by a radio beam. At the next meeting on 21 February they had a memorandum by Watson-Watt and, after a successful experiment to detect an aircraft in flight at Daventry on 26 February, Sir Hugh (later Lord) Dowding, air member for research and development, agreed to an expenditure of £10,000 to carry out experiments at Orfordness. By June, planes were detected at fifteen miles. The Tizard committee was only advisory, without executive functions, but Tizard kept the air staff in close touch with its proceedings so that they were actively concerned with its deliberations from the start.

Meanwhile Lindemann and (Sir) Winston Churchill combined to press for a C.I.D. committee to deal with the political and financial problems of air defence and in April such a committee held its first meeting under the chairmanship of Sir Philip Cunliffe-Lister (later the Earl of Swinton), soon to become air minister. The Tizard committee became its sub-committee, responsible for research. In June Churchill joined the C.I.D. committee, of which Tizard was a member, and Lindemann became a member of Tizard's committee.

From his first meeting Lindemann was at odds with his colleagues over both projects and priorities. The crisis came in June 1936 when Lindemann went behind the backs of his colleagues by arranging a meeting between Churchill and Watson-Watt, who said that he was dissatisfied with the rate of progress under the normal ministry machinery. This led to a stormy meeting of the Swinton committee when Churchill attacked Tizard. Shortly afterwards Lindemann announced his intention of standing for Parliament where he could raise the question of the country's air defences. Four days later A. V. Hill sent his resignation to Swinton; this was followed by Blackett's and Tizard's. In October Swinton reconstituted the committee, substituting (Sir) Edward Appleton for Lindemann, and in 1939 (Sir) T. R. Merton was added as a member.

In spite of these controversies, the

evelopment of radar had continued and when Tizard reported progress to the winton committee the large sums eeded for the work were always forthcoming. In September 1935 Watson-Vatt moved to Bawdsey and in December 935 sanction was given to build the first ive radar stations. In the summer of 1936 Tizard told the air staff that the time had ome for the Royal Air Force to learn how o use RDF, as it was called, in combat and to find out the ground organization which would be needed. On 4 August 1936 Tizard met the officers of the bombers and ighters who had been detailed to Biggin Hill for such trials and explained to them that they were to investigate the best way of intercepting a formation of enemy bombers, if they were given fifteen minutes' warning of its approach and its position and altitude at minute intervals. Hitherto the normal procedure was to put fighters up on patrol at suitable points in anticipation of attacks. The Biggin Hill trials were a classic instance of operational research. Methods were gradually evolved for tracking the bombers which gave their position by wireless, thus enabling the fighters to take off and secure an interception. Tizard took an active part in the trials and on one occasion simplified procedure by pointing out an easier means of determining the correct course of the fighter: this was generally adopted and known as the 'Tizzy angle'.

The trials having proved the practicability of this new method of interception, Fighter Command then took over the introduction of the new technique into the defence organization. This was a complex task and it had its difficulties, but Tizard kept in close touch with developments, ever ready with help and advice. He was largely responsible for the introduction of the 'filter room' by means of which the corrected courses of enemy aircraft were clearly presented to the controller in the operations room. When war broke out both the radar chain and the means of using the information it obtained were ready, thus providing a new system of air defence by day.

The Biggin Hill trials were only one of the practical steps which Tizard took to ensure the effective use of radar. In 1938 he persuaded (Sir) Mark Oliphant, then at Birmingham, to drop some of his nuclear research and concentrate on the development of an improved source of short-wave radiation. This led to the invention by (Sir) John Randall and Dr. H. A. H.

Boot of the cavity magnetron, a major advance in radar technique. Foreseeing the numbers of scientists that would be required to service the radar stations, Tizard early in 1938 told (Sir) John Cockcroft, then working in the Cavendish Laboratory, what was on foot and took him to one of the new radar stations. After a visit by Watson-Watt to Cambridge, scientists were enlisted and shown the stations. Large-scale trials were planned for 1 September 1939, so that when war broke out all the stations were manned for action.

The ground radar stations were not effective by night and much effort was directed to various means of night defence. Tizard realized that the solution lay in the development of airborne radar, and, thanks to his encouragement, the research team led by E. G. Bowen had produced in 1939 an airborne radar set, AI, which needed considerable development before it was suitable for operational use. Tizard gave it his full support in its early stages when doubt was cast on its operational value. Success depended on intimate co-operation between the radar observer and the pilot and gradually the difficult art of interception was learnt. The air-crews' confidence in AI owed much to Tizard's advice on his visits to the squadron. He was also responsible for the night interception committee, and the fighter interception unit for carrying out scientific trials of AI in combat, which paid a dividend in its later stages. Tizard's advocacy won the day and airborne radar played a decisive part in the air war by land and sea.

Intelligence was another field in which Tizard's initiative was to prove decisive. In 1939 we knew little or nothing of what Germany was doing in military research and in April Tizard persuaded Pye, Wimperis's successor, to ask for someone to be appointed in the Air Ministry to deal with scientific intelligence. (Professor) R. V. Jones, known to Tizard by his work on infra-red radiation, then in the Admiralty research laboratory, was selected for the appointment. He was not released by the Admiralty until 1 September, but from then on his flair for interpreting intelligence reports, backed by his shrewd scientific judgement, played a vital part in our defences.

During the first ten months of the war Tizard had advised the chief of the air staff on scientific matters in addition to continuing the chairmanship of the Defence and Offence committees which in

October 1939 amalgamated as the Committee for the Scientific Survey of Air Warfare. Its most important decision was to form the Maud committee under (Sir) George Thomson in March 1940 to investigate the feasibility of an atomic bomb after Oliphant had given Tizard the remarkable memorandum by (Professor) O. R. Frisch and (Sir) R. E. Peierls.

When Churchill went to the Admiralty in 1939 with Lindemann as his scientific adviser, and in 1940 became prime minister, Tizard's position gradually became more difficult and when Sir Archibald Sinclair (later Viscount Thurso) became air minister he also sought Lindemann's advice. This uncertainty as to his responsibility led to Tizard's resignation in June 1940 from all his Air Ministry commitments, with the exception of the Aeronautical Research Committee.

From the outbreak of war Tizard was seized with the importance of winning the sympathy and technical support of the United States of America. At his suggestion, A. V. Hill went to Washington in 1940 as 'supernumerary air attaché' to Lord Lothian [q.v.]. Hill's exploration of the position made it clear that the President would welcome a proposal from Britain to share all scientific knowledge of weapons and equipment. Lothian strongly supported the plan to send a British scientific mission and the mission, led by Tizard, went to America in August 1940. Very wisely he went first to Canada, taking details of Britain's war inventions and a list of problems in which Canada might help. This gave Canada her first start in war research and won for Tizard the regard and affection of all the Canadians he met. Subsequently he was frequently their guest and they attached great value to his advice on their military and scientific problems. When he left for Washington Tizard took with him Professor C. J. Mackenzie as Canada's representative on his mission. It was a stroke of genius on Tizard's part to take with him a mixed team of scientists and serving officers from the Army, Navy, and Air Force with battle experience. This gave him the entrée to the armed Services in Washington, not easy for civilians at that time, and within a few days Tizard, Cockcroft, and other civilians were lecturing to the military Services and establishing a confidence and co-operation which were maintained throughout the war. Tizard also took with him in his famous black box the prints of Britain's war devices such as radar and a specimen of Randall and Boot's 9·5 c.m. resonant cavity magnetron which gave the American work on radar a new stimulus. Tizard's brilliant leadership of the mission was one of his greatest services to Britain.

After his return from America in the autumn of 1940 Tizard became a semi-official adviser to successive ministers of aircraft production, sitting on the Aircraft Supply Committee and representing the Ministry on the Air Council from June 1941. He was particularly active in securing the flow of up-to-date information to Washington. In April 1941 after the jet engine had left the ground on a taxiing run, he sent a verbal message to Dr. Vannevar Bush, unintelligible to the bearer, but sufficient to keep Bush informed of progress. The development of (Sir) Barnes Wallis's dam-busting bomb owed much to Tizard's support. His influence was felt in the greater use of scientific evaluation of our military operations, such as (Sir) Solly Zuckerman's mission to North Africa, and in the expansion of operational research. When in March 1942 Cherwell recommended bombing built-up areas of Germany in order to break the spirit of the German populace, Tizard queried his estimate of the number of bombers available and the amount of damage to be expected, concluding that the policy would not be decisive and by concentrating bombers on the offensive might risk losing the war through inadequate defence. But by this time Cherwell's influence with the prime minister was much greater than Tizard's.

In 1942 Tizard felt that his whole-time service in the Ministry was no longer needed and he accepted the presidency of Magdalen College, Oxford, at a time when the college was preparing for the adjustments which would be needed in a post-war world. Tizard quickly acquired an admirable grasp of the rather complicated college statutes and he gave much thought to the financial fortunes of the college, incidentally reorganizing the bursary. He soon made up his mind about what he wanted the college to do and he gave a clear lead to those who worked closely with him in small committees. He was less successful in handling a large college meeting when he had to pilot controversial issues through a very varied and independent-minded body of fellows. Perhaps he had too authoritarian a background to fit easily into the democratic ways of a college.

During the years at Magdalen, Tizard's service was much in demand by the Service chiefs, both here and in the dominions. In 1943 he was preparing to lead a mission to Russia on the same lines as his mission to America, but eventually this was abandoned. He was then invited by the Australian Government to spend three months visiting defence establishments and advising them on scientific developments, particularly in relation to the Pacific war. Tizard's experiences of government machinery and his personal knowledge of people in key positions enabled him to help the Australians to clarify a number of war problems and to secure the co-ordination of their war research with developments at home.

In 1944 Tizard was chairman of a committee set up by the chiefs of staff to assess the probable effects of new weapons on defence policy. Soon after its report in 1945 the Labour Government turned to Tizard for advice on the place of science in post-war development. In September at a meeting of the chiefs of staff Tizard pressed for the formation of a scientific organization under a defence ministry to keep scientific development under continuous review. He developed this idea in October in a paper on 'The Central Direction of the Scientific Effort' advocating the appointment of a scientific adviser who would act as chairman of a deputy chiefs of staff committee and would also serve on a new body to consider science in relation to civilian needs. These recommendations were approved but a year elapsed before action was finally taken. Meanwhile in the spring of 1946 Tizard had acted as chairman of a Commonwealth conference on defence science at which he advocated the dispersal of scientific effort and the encouragement in the dominions of great centres of scientific education and research. In 1945 he had already made suggestions which led directly to the Woomera rocket range. In August 1946 Tizard was invited to undertake the chairmanship of the two committees he had suggested, involving his resignation of the presidency of Magdalen. He was divided in his mind and asked the advice of his colleagues, who suggested combining one chairmanship with the presidency. A large majority wished him to remain at Magdalen, but since it was not a unanimous decision he resigned.

So in January 1947 Tizard found himself again in Whitehall. Both positions, as chairman of the Defence Research Policy Committee and the Advisory Council on Scientific Policy, were fraught with difficulties. Tizard's instinct was always for action, but with the end of the war the motive of urgency had disappeared, people were tired, including Tizard, and needed time for recovery. Moreover, they were looking again to their own immediate interests and resented any encroachment of their authority. The authority of the Defence Ministry was as yet uncertain and the Services were inclined to stand on their own. The fact that the Defence Committee was debarred from discussing nuclear weapons did not help.

It was an uphill fight and some of Tizard's most effective work was done in the dominions, during visits to Canada and Australia. However, Tizard, in his position of authority as chairman of the Defence Research Policy Committee, succeeded in establishing the position that science had an extremely important part to play in framing the policies of the defence departments and the later organization evolved directly from his efforts.

On the civil side Tizard had a more difficult task, lacking the prestige and record of achievement with other scientific administrators that he had earned so fully with the Services. There was less belief amongst the interested parties that co-ordination of their activities towards the formation of a national scientific policy was necessary, let alone achievable. The bodies concerned, the Research Councils, under their own autonomy, had already achieved much success.

Nevertheless Tizard succeeded in laying some foundations. A small fact-finding staff was created and a forum for discussion provided, but the body was far less executive than was even its military counterpart, and Tizard undoubtedly felt frustration. But he had three important successes. He was able strongly to influence the need for a long-term plan for the training of scientists, particularly technologists. His influence in ensuring that scientific views were fed in at the policy-forming stage was pervasive and effective, and he succeeded in securing the appointment of a chief scientist, who had the necessary powers and appropriate access, in Ministries which lacked such senior scientific officers and needed them most.

The long strain had told on Tizard's health and in 1949 he had wished to retire. Finally in 1952 he left Whitehall for the last time. 'These last six years of his active life were in a real sense the fulfilment of his quarter-of-a-century-old belief in the importance to the life and prosperity of Great Britain of a close relationship between the administrative and scientific worlds . . .' (P. M. S. Blackett, Tizard memorial lecture to the Institute for Strategic Studies, 11 February 1960).

The rest of Tizard's life was directed partly to his educational interests as pro-chancellor of Southampton University and chairman of the Goldsmiths' education committee and partly to his services on the board of the National Research Development Corporation and of several chemical concerns. He took an active interest in their affairs, frequently visiting their plants and research laboratories where his presence gave encouragement to younger chemists and engineers. He foresaw the need for a large expansion of university education and his advice was eagerly sought on his visits to Southampton. He died of a cerebral haemorrhage at his home at Fareham 9 October 1959. His ashes were buried in the floor of the ante-chapel of Oriel College, Oxford.

Tizard had a quick, alert, well-stored mind, great moral and physical courage, and a high sense of integrity which was a handicap in political infighting. Without marked scientific originality, he was quick to see the practical issues raised by new discoveries and indeed to foresee the fields in which research was most needed. He could draw out the best from young scientists or engineers or Service officers. Wit and humour were his in abundance. On his own wide range of topics he was an excellent critic, reserving his more barbed shafts for his equals, superiors, or the scientifically arrogant. He was at his best when faced with a problem calling for a decisive answer as he saw so clearly the practical issues involved and could explain them in simple words. This made him the ideal interpreter between the Services and the scientists, having the confidence of both; it was in this respect that Britain had the advantage over Germany.

Tizard received many honours: an Air Force Cross in 1918, a C.B. in 1927, K.C.B. in 1937, and G.C.B. in 1949, and the American medal for merit in 1947. He was elected F.R.S. in 1926, was foreign secretary of the Royal Society in 1940–45, and vice-president (1940–41 and 1944–5). He was an honorary doctor of ten British and Commonwealth universities, an honorary fellow of Oriel and Magdalen at Oxford, and of the Imperial College and University

College in London. He was awarded the go medals of the Royal Society of Arts and th Franklin Institute, and the Messel med of the Society of Chemical Industr Many learned societies acclaimed him a an honorary member. In 1948 he wa president of the British Association; ar from 1937 until 1959 he served as trustee of the British Museum.

In 1915 Tizard married Kathlee Eleanor (died 1968), daughter of Arthu Prangley Wilson, mining engineer; the had three sons.

There is a portrait of Tizard by Bernar Hailstone in the Imperial War Museun one by Cuthbert Orde at the Imperia College; and a pastel by William Dring a Magdalen College, Oxford.

[Sir William Farren (and R. V. Jones) i *Biographical Memoirs of Fellows of the Roy Society*, vol. vii, 1961; R. W. Clark, *Tizar* 1965; R.V. Jones in *The Times*, 6, 7, and 8 Apr 1961 and *Oxford Magazine*, 9 May 1963 C. P. Snow, *Science and Government*, 1961 C. Webster and N. Frankland, (Official History *The Strategic Air Offensive Against German 1939–45*, vol. i, 1961; Sir Harold Hartley i *Proceedings* of the Chemical Society, May 1964 *Nature*, 5 March 1960 (P. M. S. Blackett Tizard memorial lecture); *Journal* of th Royal Aeronautical Society, August 196 (A. R. Collar, Tizard memorial lecture) private information; personal knowledge.]

HAROLD HARTLEY

TOMLINSON, GEORGE (1890–1952) politician, was born 21 March 1890 a Rishton, Lancashire, the fourth child o John Wesley Tomlinson, a weaver, an his wife, Alice Varley. Educated at Rishton Wesleyan School he began half-time work in the local cotton mill at the age of twelve and went on full time a yea later. For a while he attended evening classes and then studied for the ministry for which, however, he was not accepted. Turning his attention to trade-union matters he became president of the Rishton District Weavers' Association when only twenty-two and in 1914 was elected to the urban district council. In the same year he married a fellow worker, Ethel, daughter of Humphrey Pursell, a taper, by whom he had one daughter. Not long afterwards he moved to Farnworth to work with his brother-in-law who was a herbal brewer. He registered as a conscientious objector in 1916 and for three years was obliged to take agricultural work away from home.

In 1925 Tomlinson returned to public life as a member of the Farnworth urban

istrict council. He became chairman of
he education committee in 1928 and
efore long his special interest in educa-
on brought him on to the executive of
he Association of Education Committees
f which he was afterwards to be president
(1939 and 1940). In 1931 he was elected
ᴐ the Lancashire County Council where
gain education was one of his main
interests. In 1935 he left Farnworth to be-
ome secretary to the Rishton Weavers'
Association, but in 1938 he was returned
ᴐ Parliament for the Farnworth division
ᴐf Lancashire, a seat which he retained
until his death.

In February 1941 Tomlinson began his
first experience in office as joint parliamentary secretary to the Ministry of
Labour and National Service. Because
'George cares for people', Ernest Bevin
q.v.] put the Ministry's work for disabled
persons in his charge, and he was chairman
ᴐf the inter-departmental committee on
their rehabilitation and resettlement, the
eport of which was generally known as
the Tomlinson report. It was left to Tom-
inson to move the second reading of the
disabled persons (employment) bill which
was enacted in 1944 and for which he was
primarily responsible. He also did useful
work in transferring textile workers to
munitions. There followed an interval
during which he headed the British
delegation to the International Labour
Conference at Philadelphia (1944) where
his success was due in large measure to
the sincerity, good temper, and unfailing
humour which he brought to a difficult
task. He later took part in the inaugural
meeting of the United Nations at San
Francisco. Probably nobody was more
surprised than Tomlinson to find himself
one of a world assembly of statesmen; but
in after years his chief recollection was of
journeys through the American continent
so astonishing to one who had never
travelled abroad.

In the Labour Government of 1945
Tomlinson became minister of works and
was sworn of the Privy Council. It was
not the office he would have chosen
although he found sufficient scope for his
energies and his trade-union experience.
His work brought him into contact with
members of the royal family with some
of whom, and particularly with Queen
Mary who called him 'my minister', he was
privileged to enjoy a personal friendship.

On the death of Ellen Wilkinson [q.v.]
in February 1947, Tomlinson came into
his own as minister of education with a

seat in the Cabinet. It was a difficult time.
What was required of the minister was not
to negotiate a new legislative settlement
(that had already been achieved, in the
Education Act of 1944) but to complete
the new pattern of schools, colleges, and
administration and help to make it work.
Those (and they were not the educationists)
who felt misgivings that this task should
be entrusted to a man of elementary
school education proved wrong. Tomlinson knew his own limitations and was
determined that other people's children
should not suffer as he had done from
stunted education. Moreover, in dealing
with the particular task that faced him
as minister he had two great advantages:
first, his long experience of local government and his sympathy with local education authorities helped him to build up
a powerful partnership between local and
central government; secondly his endearing personal qualities made a firm ally
of the whole organized teaching profession. He was sometimes criticized, especially for accepting the recommendation
of the Secondary School Examinations
Council that a minimum age should be
fixed for taking the General Certificate of
Education. But his term of office (which
lasted until the defeat of Labour in 1951)
was not only longer than that of most of
his predecessors but at least as successful
as any in administrative achievement.
The raising of the school-leaving age to
fifteen and a spectacular rise in the birth-
rate combined with post-war housing
developments called for an immense
increase in school places at a time when
materials and labour were both scarce.
The architects and buildings branch which
Tomlinson established at the Ministry
brought together in a new working partnership all the various types of expert
concerned and created a new relationship
with the local authorities which not only
led to the building of a record number of
schools each year but won praise for
British school building from informed
opinion in many countries. Nor did he
allow his judgement on questions of
educational organization or theory to be
warped by party politics or denominational prejudice but courageously applied
it to the merits of each case. The chief
reason, however, for the remarkable
popularity of 'this capable, vigorous and
genial son of Lancashire' was his palpable
sincerity.

Tomlinson was a product of those twin
influences which did so much to shape

the Labour movement in its early days: trade-unionism and the Methodist Church. By upbringing and conviction he was a fervent Wesleyan and throughout his life he gave his services from time to time as a preacher at local chapels. He had been nourished on the finest models of English and throughout his life he spoke and wrote with a simplicity and vigour not unworthy of John Bunyan. In his public career his desire was to improve social conditions for the people and particularly to help those who by misfortune or injustice were prevented from leading a full life. Although he had suffered much himself from the hardships of a faulty educational and industrial system he never bore malice. He had little liking for party polemics and distinctions of class or wealth were of no importance to him. His attitude to persons or things was friendly and understanding and it was only rarely— when he found himself rebuffed or treated with condescension—that his good temper deserted him.

Tomlinson had an inexhaustible fund of stories which he told on all occasions. Most of them derived from Lancashire which came to have an almost mystical value for him. Occasionally he lapsed into sentimentality and startled a sophisticated gathering with some piece of childish whimsy but more often his native humour and simplicity made him a welcome and effective speaker. In his later years he was obliged to spend much of his time in London. He was perfectly content to sit in the House of Commons listening to the debates and going out from time to time to meet friends in the lobbies or tea rooms. Occasionally he went to the theatre and he was equally pleased by a play of Shakespeare or a musical show with plenty of healthy slapstick. He never missed an important football match on Saturday if he could help it and when a Lancashire side was playing it became a holiday of obligation. He had hoped to retire to a cottage near Blackpool among his friends but symptoms of serious illness appeared in 1951 and he died after an operation in London 22 September 1952. He received the honorary degree of LL.D. from the university of Liverpool in 1947.

[*The Times*, 23 September 1952; Fred Blackburn, *George Tomlinson*, 1954; personal knowledge.]   Griffith Williams.

TOMLINSON, HENRY MAJOR (1873–1958), writer, was born in Poplar 21 June 1873, the eldest in the family three sons and one daughter of Hen Tomlinson and his wife, Emily Majo daughter of a master gunner in the nav His father was a foreman at the We India Dock, and as a boy Tomlinso became familiar with ships and seame and the lure of the sea. After h father's death in 1886 he was taken fro school and placed in a City shippin office at a wage of six shillings a wee He knew poverty and remembered all his life; but with his mother's er couragement he soon began to rea widely, especially in the history of trav and navigation, and in time he turne to the study of geology, to which h added botany, zoology, and mineralog In 1894 he was considered as a possib geologist for the Jackson–Harmswort polar expedition, but, much to his di appointment, was advised that his healt would not stand the strain.

Tomlinson grew increasingly restive i his office occupation although his fre quent opportunities for visiting th ships and the docks were a source c inspiration for much of his future writing It was not until 1904, however, that after an office quarrel, he applied for job with the radical *Morning Leader* a paper to which he had already contri buted. He was engaged as a reporte and his love of the sea was soon turned t good account by his editor, Ernest Parke who sent him to live for several weeks in midwinter, with a fleet of trawler on the Dogger Bank. An assignmen to the naval manœuvres was a sequel Parke later made him still happier b sending him, ostensibly as ship's purser on a voyage to Brazil and two thousan miles up the Amazon and Madeira rivers in the first English steamer to make that passage. His first book, *The Sea and the Jungle*, followed in 1912. It was immediately hailed as a classic and subsequently appeared in many editions The beauty of the prose and the descriptive writing showed Tomlinson to be a new author of unusual quality. He was also at this time contributing to the *English Review* edited by Ford Madox Hueffer (later Ford, q.v.). When the *Morning Leader* was amalgamated with the *Daily News* in 1912 Tomlinson stayed on as a leader-writer; he became a war correspondent in Belgium and France in August 1914 and was official correspondent at British G.H.Q. in France in 1914–17. He was literary editor nder H. W. Massingham [q.v.] of the Nation from 1917 to 1923.

Thoreau and Emerson helped to mould Tomlinson's thought and a style which was never that of a fashionable author but won the deep admiration of fellow craftsmen. In the post-war years he travelled widely and established himself as a writer of poetic essays and stories in collections such as *Old Junk* (1918), *Waiting for Daylight* (1922), and *Gifts of Fortune* (1926). *London River* (1921) was a moving book of personal memories and self-communings on the theme nearest his heart, while *Tidemarks* (1924) took the reader to the islands and straits of the Dutch East Indies. His first novel, *Gallions Reach* (1927), which was awarded the Femina Vie Heureuse prize, was acclaimed as an important work on both sides of the Atlantic. Yet, although Tomlinson was a born descriptive writer, he was not a born novelist. His next book, *All Our Yesterdays* (1930), a story of the war of 1914–18, demonstrated that he was more of a poet, journalist, philosopher, and student of humanity, than an inventor of plot and fictional character.

Tomlinson continued to produce novels until the end of his life. His writings became increasingly permeated by a hatred of war—specifically proclaimed in *Mars His Idiot* (1935)—but they also showed a redeeming belief in the supreme value of individual personality. Although his later work was somewhat uneven, he still conveyed his old mastery as an essayist in collections such as *The Turn of the Tide* (1945), while *A Mingled Yarn* (1953), a series of autobiographical sketches, displays him at his characteristic best in reminiscence and description. Tomlinson's gifts as a writer can be well studied here, and in the selection from his work made by Kenneth Hopkins (1953). In his last book, *The Trumpet Shall Sound* (1957), the story of the impact of the blitz on an English family, Tomlinson put into memorable words what many of those who lived through the war of 1939–45 thought only in their hearts.

Tomlinson was short of stature and his deeply lined face reflected a thoughtful and contemplative disposition. He suffered from deafness caused by a football accident in early youth and aggravated by gunfire on the western front. This handicap led people to think of him as a shy man, but he was constantly sought after by his many friends, who appreciated his fine sense of humour and fondness for good conversation in a small company. A keen naturalist, Tomlinson loved walking, and even in his later years thought nothing of taking long walks through the unspoiled Dorset countryside where he spent each summer.

In 1899 he married Florence Margaret, daughter of Thomas Hammond, ship's chandler, by whom he had one son and two daughters. Tomlinson received the honorary degree of LL.D. from Aberdeen in 1949. He died in London 5 February 1958 and was buried in the churchyard at Abbotsbury, Dorset. A portrait by Richard Murry became the possession of Mrs. Mary Middleton Murry; pencil drawings by William A. Wildman and Colin Moss and a bronze head by Sava Botzvaris are in the possession of the family.

[*The Times*, 6 and 14 February 1958; H. M. Tomlinson, *A Mingled Yarn*, 1953; Frank Swinnerton, *The Georgian Literary Scene 1910–1935*, 1935, and *Figures in the Foreground*, 1963; private information.]

DEREK HUDSON.

TOWNSEND, SIR JOHN SEALY EDWARD (1868–1957), pioneer in physics of ionized gases, was born at Galway, Ireland, 7 June 1868, the second son of Edward Townsend, professor of civil engineering at Queen's College, Galway, by his wife, Judith, daughter of John Sealy Townsend, a Dublin barrister. He was educated at Corrig School and Trinity College, Dublin, where he read mathematics, mathematical physics, and experimental science. In 1888 he was elected to a foundation science scholarship in mathematics; in 1890 he obtained a double senior moderatorship, being placed first in mathematics, and graduated B.A. For the next four years he was a fellowship prizeman and engaged in teaching, especially mathematics. In 1895, at the age of twenty-seven, he became a member of Trinity College, Cambridge, and an advanced student of the university. He was one of the research students of (Sir) J. J. Thomson [q.v.] who worked in the Cavendish Laboratory together with Ernest (later Lord) Rutherford, (Sir) J. Larmor, C. T. R. Wilson [qq.v.], as well as Paul Langevin with whom he maintained a close friendship throughout his life. Already Townsend's earliest experimental work showed both originality in thought and tenacity in execution: he was elected in 1898 a Clerk Maxwell scholar and in 1899 a fellow of Trinity, coupled with an assistant demonstratorship in the Cavendish.

When in 1900 the Wykeham chair of experimental physics was founded in Oxford, Townsend was elected the first professor, with a fellowship at New College. At that time the physics department, the old Clarendon Laboratory, was directed by R. B. Clifton, the professor of experimental philosophy. Townsend's duties were chiefly to lecture and give instruction in electricity and magnetism, subjects which were apparently not Clifton's favourites. From 1902 Townsend occupied research rooms first at the Observatory, then in the department of physiology, and later in the University Museum, until 1910 when the new electrical laboratory was opened, a gift of the Drapers' Company to the university, where Townsend worked until his retirement in 1941.

In Cambridge Townsend had studied the electric properties of gases obtained by electrolysis of liquids and shown that the condensation of atmospheric clouds is due to electrification of gases. This was followed by the first measurement of the elementary ionic charge, an outstanding example of elegance and simplicity, using but a laboratory balance, an electrometer, and a photographic camera. Subsequently he studied secondary X-rays and also the diffusion of ions in gases which he found to be slower than that of neutral particles.

In Oxford, Townsend laid the foundation to the theory of multiplication of electrical charges in gases under the influence of an electric field. He assumed ionization to occur by electrons colliding with gas molecules, later including positive ions. He showed that the electron energy required to accomplish ionization was about an order of magnitude smaller than was thought. These theoretical and experimental studies led to a simple mathematical relation which will always be connected with Townsend's name.

Another new concept which he introduced was the 'electron gas'. He showed that electrons form an assembly of their own which may have a much higher average energy than the molecules of the gas in which they move. However, the 'hot' electron gas is not easily cooled by the cold neutral gas because of the large difference in mass between electrons and molecules.

Townsend contributed to the problem of electric breakdown of gases which results from multiplication of charges in the gas supported by secondary electrons released from the negative electrode as well as in the emission of light from electrically excited gases.

Another major contribution was the relation between the diffusion of ions and their mobility, showing Townsend's profound insight in kinetic theory of gases, by proving the equivalency of singly charged ions in gases and of monovalent ions of electrolytes. Finally, he discovered simultaneously with German workers that the mean free path of electrons depends on their energy; in particular he found that slow electrons can traverse argon gas without feeling its presence. This, the Ramsauer–Townsend effect, puzzled physicists until wave-mechanics provided the solution. Townsend showed early an interest in wireless and later in high frequency research, including the magnetron and the electrodeless discharge.

Townsend made the electrical laboratory the centre of research on ionized gases long after Cambridge had abandoned the field. He had usually only a few researchers around him at a time, many of them Rhodes scholars. Some of them became well known in the world of science: Moseley, Tizard, Bailey, Huxley, Focken, van de Graaff, Gill, Pidduck, and Llewellyn Jones, many in positions of responsibility. He rarely read scientific publications and was very sceptical of others' new ideas. He was always picking holes in Maxwell's theory and disliked the concept of displacement currents.

He was fond of walking and talking, a good shot, a huntsman and a keen rider. He liked sporting competitions and played a good game of tennis. His striking personality made many of his pupils and followers reason and work along the lines their master had laid down and some have continued to do so. As a true Irishman he loved arguments and was an excellent storyteller. His experimental skill, draughtsmanship, knowledge of workshop practice, and shrewdness in design of apparatus were remarkable. He seldom attended scientific gatherings, though there were exceptions, like his visit to the United States in 1924 when he was made a member of the Franklin Institute, and the reception at the first International Conference on Ionized Gases in Oxford in 1953.

Besides a large number of papers Townsend wrote a classic book, *Electricity in Gases* (1915), which followed an earlier small book, *The Theory of Ionization of Gases by Collision* (1910). After his retirement he published three smaller books: *Electricity and Radio Transmission* (1943), *Electrons in Gases* (1947), and *Electromagnetic Waves* (1951). He was elected F.R.S. in 1903, was an officer of the Legion of Honour and a corresponding member of the Institut de France (Académie des Sciences), received an honorary D.Sc. of Paris, and was elected an honorary fellow of New College. He was knighted in 1941.

Townsend married in 1911 Mary Georgiana, the daughter of Peter Fitzwalter Lambert, of Castle Ellen, county Galway. She became an active worker in municipal affairs, an alderman, twice mayor, and an honorary freeman of the city of Oxford. They had two sons. Townsend died in Oxford 16 February 1957.

[A. von Engel in *Biographical Memoirs of Fellows of the Royal Society*, vol. iii, 1957; *Year Book* of the Physical Society, 1957; private information; personal knowledge.]
A. VON ENGEL.

TRENCHARD, HUGH MONTAGUE, first VISCOUNT TRENCHARD (1873–1956), marshal of the Royal Air Force, was born at Taunton 3 February 1873, the second son and third of the six children of Henry Montague Trenchard, a provincial lawyer, and his wife, Georgiana Louisa Catherine Tower, daughter of John McDowall Skene, captain R.N. His father came of an ancient west-country family, among them Sir John Trenchard [q.v.], once considerable landowners, but latterly dependent on professional earnings. A happy early childhood, from which conventional learning was almost completely absent, ended when he went to a preparatory school and thence to a crammer's for entry to the Royal Navy. However, he failed the Dartmouth entrance, and so was sent to an army crammer, where his strong preference for sports and games, and the absence of any properly balanced studies, produced in him a certain philistinism which subsequently took many years to eradicate. At the age of sixteen, while still a boarder at this school, he learnt that his father's law practice had failed, and bankruptcy followed. This disgrace weighed heavily upon the boy. Maintained at school by the generosity of relatives, he reluctantly worked out a most unhappy period of his life, first failing the Woolwich entrance examination, then twice failing the examination for militia candidates. Finally, in 1893, he just passed, was gazetted as a second lieutenant in the 2nd battalion Royal Scots Fusiliers, and posted at once to his regiment in India.

These formative years had been almost wholly disastrous, and produced a man tense, taciturn, reserved, and half-educated. The five years' garrison and frontier duty he now served slowly eased some of this tension. Trenchard was a large man, tall and strong. He devoted himself to riding, and principally to polo, during most of his leisure hours, finding in the arrangement of teams and tournaments a natural gift for organization, and reading extensively to repair the gaps in his education.

Comparatively uneventful years in India ended with the outbreak of war in South Africa where Trenchard went to rejoin his battalion. He was promoted to the rank of captain, and given the task of raising and training a mounted company. By unorthodox methods, including the incorporation of Australian volunteers, he quickly assembled a small flying column. While commanding this unit he pursued a large Boer raiding party, cornering them at Dwarsvlei in Western Transvaal. During the engagement that followed he was hit in the chest by a bullet, narrowly escaping death. Half-paralysed, with his left lung permanently damaged, he was invalided back to England. Six months of violent self-cure, including winter sports and tennis, miraculously fitted him, in his own opinion at least, for further active service, and he returned to South Africa as a captain in the 12th Mounted Infantry. Until the end of the war he continued to serve with irregular mounted infantry units, gaining a high reputation for daring, initiative, and will-power.

On leave in England at the end of the war he was considering leaving the army when he was offered the post of assistant commandant of the Southern Nigeria Regiment as a brevet major. He accepted and sailed for Nigeria in 1903. For the next seven years he led the life of a soldier and administrator in an unknown country just opening to colonial law and organization. He was twice mentioned in dispatches, appointed to the D.S.O. in 1906, and in 1908 was promoted temporary lieutenant-colonel and became commandant of the regiment. Expeditions, surveys, patrolling, road-building, and occasional clashes with the Ibos of the interior passed the years until in 1910 he fell dangerously ill with an abscess of the liver and was once more invalided home. After a long convalescence, still unfit for tropical duty, he rejoined his old regiment, dropping in rank to major, and served in Ireland for the next two years.

In 1912 he was a thirty-nine-year-old bachelor, and still held the rank of major. Although he had many adventures behind him there was little in his military career or prospects to distinguish him from hundreds of other officers of his age. Once more he thought of retirement. It was then that Captain Eustace Loraine, an old colleague of his Nigeria service, wrote to tell him that he had taken up flying, and enthusiastically advised him to do the same. To Trenchard it seemed as good an idea as any. Obtaining three months' leave, he paid £75 for flying lessons at the Sopwith School at Brooklands. As he began his instruction he learnt that Loraine had been killed in a flying accident, but he passed his tests after two weeks, including one hour and four minutes flying time, and qualified for his pilot's certificate (R. Ae. C. No. 270) on 31 July 1912.

The Royal Flying Corps had formed on the previous 13 May. The new aviator was seconded to it, and posted to the Central Flying School at Upavon. Instead of a pupil's course, his age and military experience sent him at once to the staff, first as an instructor and later as assistant commandant. There he played a leading part in devising the so far unknown techniques of flying instruction, setting the standards of technical knowledge required of pupils while continuing his own training. His age and his fierce reticence made him a figure more respected than loved by the much younger pupils, and it was here that his large frame, ponderous manner, and loud voice first earned him his lifelong nickname of 'Boom'. He was out of his age-group but he had found his *métier*.

By the outbreak of war in 1914 Trenchard was a well-known figure in the Royal Flying Corps, and when senior aviation officers were so scarce he had high hopes of a flying command with the British Expeditionary Force. Instead he was posted as commandant of the

Military Wing at Farnborough, responsible for the organization backing the rapidly expanding front-line squadrons. Trenchard found himself called upon to improvise the complete groundwork of a considerable new fighting force. Hardly had he started when a reorganization of the Royal Flying Corps in France gave him command of No. Wing in the First Army Corps and the opportunity to pursue the war from the muddy airfields of the western front. The early months of 1915 found him strongly pressing for the equipment of his squadrons with airborne radio and cameras. The British spring offensive gave him his first opportunity to try out tactical bombing techniques. But his chief concern was always for the morale of his men and for inculcating in them an aggressive fighting spirit: his first rule of war.

In August 1915 he succeeded Sir David Henderson [q.v.] in command of the Royal Flying Corps in France with the temporary rank of brigadier-general. Sir Douglas (later Earl) Haig [q.v.] was his immediate superior; Maurice Baring [q.v.] his improbable but indispensable aide. The advent of the Fokker monoplane curbed his new tactical innovations and forced his squadrons on to the defensive, a state of war intensely distasteful to him. Regretfully restricting his scope, he instituted larger escorts and bigger formations, and so held on until in early 1916 the new British fighters arrived to redress the balance.

In the meantime in London, resolution of the responsibilities and claims of the army and navy in the field of aviation was becoming monthly more difficult, as the air arms grew in size. Trenchard continued to push, wheedle, and inspire his squadrons through the great land battles they supported from time to time, and the fight for air superiority they waged continually. His struggles in France were matched at home by an ever-increasing contest of the two fighting Services for complete control of the new air weapon.

Through the battles of the Somme, Arras, and Messines, third Ypres, and Cambrai, Trenchard's reputation grew with the size and effectiveness of his force. In these campaigns he was able to drive home his greatest precept, and his legacy to the modern Royal Air Force, that only by persistent attack can air mastery be obtained. This he made into an instinctive and a fundamental basis for all air doctrine, which was never questioned by anybody who came under his influence.

In London the Derby committee, the Bailhache committee, and the Air Board each wrestled ineffectively with the problem of controlling inter-Service air priorities. At last the committee under J. C. Smuts [q.v.] finally gained acceptance of its recommendations for an Air Ministry, and a third Service, the Royal Air Force. Although completely convinced of the rightness of this doctrine Trenchard did not want to execute it in the middle of the war. By the end of 1917 he had begun bombing Germany and his squadrons were heavily engaged throughout the length of the British front. He therefore heard with mixed feelings of his appointment, under Lord Rothermere [q.v.] as air minister, to be first chief of the new air staff, in January 1918, at which date he was also appointed K.C.B. Haig parted from him with the utmost reluctance, but it was not long before Trenchard was back in France. Before the day for the formation of the new Royal Air Force, 1 April 1918, could dawn, Trenchard and Rothermere had proved utterly incompatible. Extreme political pliability met unyielding principle, and the new chief of air staff's resignation took effect on 13 April, an event closely followed, under pressure from his own colleagues, by that of the air minister.

Trenchard returned to France in May 1918 at the head of a new concept, an independent bombing force, which after lengthy negotiation was confirmed in October as the Inter-Allied Independent Air Force, subordinate only to Marshal Foch the supreme allied commander, charged with the task of carrying the war directly to Germany by strategic bombing. Although the first squadrons assigned flew a large number of raids against the enemy homeland, the force was not designed to develop its full potential until mid-1919, and so was disbanded before it could show its power. It is sometimes stated, wrongly, that Trenchard was a fanatical advocate of the military value of this force. In fact he had some considerable doubts concerning its strategic worth at that time and place and compared with other war requirements, though none about the details of its training and employment.

For his war services Trenchard received a baronetcy (1919) and a grant of £10,000. Once again he thought of civilian life. But in 1919 (Sir) Winston Churchill became war and air minister and invited Trenchard to return to his briefly held post as chief of air staff. He took office on 15 February and kept it for more than ten years. He now embarked on two tasks, of a size which taxed even his immense energy and application. The first was to create a new permanent fighting Service out of the ruins left by the precipitate disarmament of 1919, and to build strongly and soundly for the future on the slender budgets allowed by the aftermath of world war. Everything was new, and he had to design everything, down to ranks, uniforms, and insignia. The second task was to guard this growing infant from the wicked uncles whose neglect had helped to create it—the two older Services. He was convinced, as of nothing else, that the air weapon could only develop its full potential in an independent Service, and with the war and its immediate dangers over nothing could hold him back from full insistence on this doctrine. If air power was to be shackled to fleets or armies, he declared with a new fluency, it would go down before any opponent who had grasped the lesson that the air was indivisible, and centrally controlled air power the spearhead of national defence.

Thus the chief of air staff of the new Royal Air Force divided his time between building up his young Service and fiercely protecting it from the attempts of the War Office and Admiralty to reabsorb it into the army and navy. These attempts were not long delayed, or easily disposed of, or very scrupulously conducted. First the War Office attacked, in a campaign lasting many months. A useful weapon in Trenchard's defence was his scheme for 'Air Control' of Iraq, whereby small numbers of R.A.F. aircraft and armoured cars kept the peace in an area which had previously needed three times as large a force of soldiers. The outstanding success of this scheme greatly improved his standing, and that of the Air Force, in the eyes of the politicians. By 1925 the army campaign died down, but in the meantime the navy, headed by the first sea lord, Admiral Beatty [q.v.], developed a continuous, virulent, and wearing assault. Trenchard fought off these and other attacks, simultaneously consolidating the

Royal Air Force by such important foundations as an Apprentice School, a Cadet College, and a Staff College. In all of these the importance of quality above quantity was persistently preached. He received some criticism for this policy from those who would have had all Air Force money devoted to the maximum number of first-line squadrons, but when in the middle thirties government policy permitted the introduction of a phased expansion of the Royal Air Force, this early doctrine ensured that the quality of the whole was un-matched, and able to absorb the further enormous expansions of the war of 1939-45.

His long period as chief of air staff transformed a high reputation into a legend. As a founding father with a long unbroken reign he knew everything there was to know of a force which never exceeded a total of some 30,000 men. His formidable appearance, strong voice, and decisive manner made him a source of affection, admiration, and apprehension to all who worked for him. He was promoted G.C.B. in 1924, became the first marshal of the Royal Air Force in 1927, and in 1930, after his retirement at the end of 1929, he was created a baron. It seemed impossible to imagine the Royal Air Force without him.

He had scarcely time to settle into civilian life before the Government asked him to take office as commissioner for the Metropolitan Police, whose morale and efficiency then gave grounds for concern. He accepted in November 1931, and plunged at once, with characteristic energy, into a programme of reforms and reorganizations. The most important of these were the creation of a Police College and Forensic Laboratory at Hendon and a ten-year engagement scheme for police officers, both designed to improve the qualifications of the higher ranks of the force. Once more his prime concern was for the creation of a high quality individual, by training, selection, and care of the human units of the organization. For this work he was appointed G.C.V.O. in 1935. Inevitably his actions aroused great controversy inside and outside the force, particularly among the more traditional officers. When he gave up the post in 1935 his major reforms were not pressed home by his successor, and many of them lapsed in 1939.

Created a viscount (1936), and once more released from government service Trenchard joined the board of the United Africa Company, whose Nigerian interests brought him back to ground familiar in his youth. He became chairman in 1936 and held that position until 1953. At the age of sixty-six, with the outbreak of war, he put on uniform again, once more to serve his country as a kind of roving ambassador of the Air Council, travelling far and wide among the units of the Service, informing, reporting, and inspiring. Completely without ceremony he moved about, greeted everywhere as a universal elder brother to the Royal Air Force. When the war was over, until the end of his life, he continued, in the House of Lords and elsewhere, to support the cause of air power. He was appointed to the Order of Merit in 1951. He was also an honorary LL.D. of Cambridge and D.C.L. of Oxford, an honorary major-general in the army, and colonel of the Royal Scots Fusiliers.

Although his work as police commissioner was memorable, and his early career by no means negligible, Trenchard's fame was established for all time on his work between 1912 and 1929. In these seventeen short years of his forties and fifties he built up and proved in action the principles of air operation; and then created an Air Force which, within his own lifetime, saved his country from certain disaster. He not only created and preserved the third fighting Service and hammered it out in his own image, but he also fathered the doctrine of air power as an independent force, the prerequisite of successful operations by land and sea. He had the supreme satisfaction of seeing all his prophecies completely, indeed lavishly, fulfilled before his eyes. Although he disliked the label 'Father of the Royal Air Force' he was in fact the progenitor of almost all independent air forces. His character: strong, stern, touched with eccentricity, but basically kind and humane, assured him the love of all who worked for him.

In 1920 Trenchard married Katherine Isabel Salvin (died 1960), daughter of the late Edward Salvin Bowlby, and widow of Captain the Hon. James Boyle. Her sister was the wife of Lord Keyes [q.v.]. There were two sons, of whom the elder was killed in action in North Africa in 1943. The younger,

Thomas (born 1923), succeeded his father when he died in London 10 February 1956. He was buried in Westminster Abbey.

There are portraits by Sir William Orpen and Francis Dodd in the Imperial War Museum; by A. R. Thomson at the Royal Air Force Staff College, Bracknell; by E. Verpilleux at Royal Air Force College, Cranwell; by Frank Beresford at H.Q. Fighter Command, Bentley Priory; and by Sir Oswald Birley at the Royal Air Force Club. A memorial bronze statue by William McMillan stands in Embankment Gardens, outside the Ministry of Defence.

[*The Times*, 11 February 1956; Andrew Boyle, *Trenchard*, 1962; Sir Walter Raleigh and H. A. Jones, (Official History) *The War in the Air*, 6 vols., 1922–37; private information.]

PETER WYKEHAM.

TREVELYAN, SIR CHARLES PHILIPS, third baronet, of Wallington (1870–1958), politician, was born 28 October 1870 in London, the eldest son of (Sir) George Otto Trevelyan [q.v], later second baronet, and his wife, Caroline, daughter of Robert Needham Philips, Liberal M.P. for Bury, Lancashire. He succeeded his father in 1928; his brothers were Robert Calverley Trevelyan, the writer, and George Macaulay Trevelyan, the historian. Trevelyan was educated at Harrow and Trinity College, Cambridge, where in 1892 he took a second class in the history tripos. After going down from Cambridge he lived with his parents on the family estate, Wallington, Cambo, Northumberland. He took much interest, along with his brothers, in walking and climbing, especially in the Lake District, where he initiated a game of hare and hounds over the mountains which has continued. His interests were more political than literary and in 1892–3 he was secretary to Lord Houghton (later the Marquess of Crewe, q.v.) when he was lord-lieutenant of Ireland; his first acquaintance with Ireland had been at the age of twelve when his father was made chief secretary after the Phoenix Park murders and he remembered not being allowed out of the grounds of the Lodge without detectives. His ambition led him to seek election to Parliament and in 1895 he unsuccessfully contested North Lambeth. In 1896–7 as a member of the London School Board he had his first experience of the administration of education in which he spent some of the most active years of his public life. His chance came in 1899 when he successfully contested as a Liberal the Elland division of Yorkshire which he retained until 1918, during which time he developed strong radical sympathies. He took part in a movement to open the mountains and moors to the public and introduced a private member's bill to bring this about; he did not succeed in getting it on the statute book but lived to see much of what he fought for in this respect carried out.

In 1906–8 Trevelyan was parliamentary charity commissioner; in 1908 he was appointed parliamentary secretary to the Board of Education where he was to some extent able to use his influence in favour of secular and undenominational teaching. His junior government appointment moreover did not prevent him from advocating a number of other causes he felt strongly about. He took part in the formation of the 'Russia committee' which exposed the persecution by the Tsar's government of those in Russia who had taken part in the revolution of 1904. He also took steps behind the scenes with others outside the Government to oppose Russian aggression in Persia. When, in 1913, it began to be known that Great Britain had, after a naval understanding with France, taken on a moral obligation to enter a war in her defence, he became active in a movement to oppose secret treaties. He was for some years before 1914 entirely out of sympathy with his Government's foreign policy; he thought that Sir Edward Grey (later Viscount Grey of Fallodon, q.v.) was committing Great Britain to support certain European powers in the interests of the 'balance of power' and not considering the merits of international issues as they arose.

When war came in August 1914, he resigned from the Government and became active in the creation of the Union of Democratic Control, along with E. D. Morel, Arthur Ponsonby (later Lord Ponsonby of Shulbrede, q.v.), Ramsay MacDonald, and others. He continued throughout the war to advocate 'peace by negotiation' and the end of secret treaties. These activities and his courageous idealism made him increasingly unpopular and at the general election in 1918 he lost his seat. Soon after this he joined the Labour Party and its ginger group, the I.L.P.

At the general election in 1922 Trevelyan was elected Labour member for the Central division of Newcastle; he became the spokesman of the party on education and when the first Labour Government was formed in 1924 he was appointed president of the Board of Education. He now had the opportunity he had long sought; he was undoubtedly a good administrator and knew the way about his department. His great ideal was to popularize education and let nothing stand in the way of giving every child a full opportunity for a career in life. He immediately withdrew Circular 1190 which had been issued by his predecessor to restrict expenditure; local education authorities were now encouraged to go ahead. His sincerity, however, often led him to be intolerant of other people's opinions and with a greater degree of tact he could probably have accomplished much of what he wanted; but that was not in his nature; on the other hand, nobody could question his idealism and sincerity. He had no great power of thinking out a problem but he relied on instinct, which was generally right.

After the fall of the Labour Government Trevelyan retained his seat at the election in the autumn of 1924. He now took up other subjects as well as education and was very active in support of the Soviet Union. His uncritical enthusiasm prevented him from seeing any fault in the Russian Communist system. But he was effective from the front Opposition bench in criticizing the education policy of the Conservative Government and what he considered its general lack of expansion and its shortsighted economy.

On the formation of the second Labour Government in 1929 Trevelyan again became president of the Board of Education. He introduced an education bill which was to raise the school-leaving age to fifteen and provide grants for parents in the lower income groups. Trouble arose over the denominational schools: Trevelyan strongly resisted development grants for these schools, but after the Scurr amendment, moved from his own side of the House, finally he agreed to some state support. The bill, however, was rejected by the House of Lords in February 1931 on the grounds

of expense in view of the grave economic situation. Trevelyan resigned from the Cabinet and Government in March because he distrusted some of his colleagues who, he thought, were proposing to cut public expenditure on projects on which he and a large part of the parliamentary Labour Party had set their hearts. At the general election following the formation of the 'national' Government he lost his seat in Newcastle and this ended his active political career. He had been appointed lord-lieutenant of Northumberland in 1930. In this capacity he took steps to reorganize the magistracy in the county and make it representative of all sections of the community. He was prime mover in the founding of the People's Theatre in Newcastle and gave steady encouragement to the Youth Hostels Association in the north.

In international affairs Trevelyan never developed a mature judgement on Russian Communism. He turned a blind eye on what he did not want to see. What interested him was the epic struggle of the Russian people to throw off the yoke of Tsarism. He had no doubts where the menace to civilization lay and when war came in 1939 he wholeheartedly supported it, even before Russia came in.

He was much attached to his family home and estate. His grouse moors were some of the best in Northumberland and he was a keen shot; he did something, however, to show that he felt it his duty to use his property for the public interest; thus he made over most of his grouse moors to the Forestry Commission and did extensive tree planting himself. He initiated children's allowances for his employees on the estate and did house building. He worked to keep his estate together by arranging that in 1941 the whole property should be made over to the National Trust in his lifetime, while he continued to reside at Wallington as tenant.

In 1904 Trevelyan married Mary Katharine (died 1966), youngest daughter of Sir Hugh Bell, half-sister of Gertrude Bell and granddaughter of Sir Isaac Lowthian Bell [qq.v.]. They had four daughters and three sons, the eldest of whom, George Lowthian (born 1906), succeeded to the title when he died at Wallington 24 January 1958. There is a bronze bust by Gertrude Hermes at Wallington.

[Private information; personal knowledge.]

M. PHILIPS PRICE.

TREVELYAN, HILDA (1877–1959), the stage name of Hilda Marie Antoinette Anna Blow, actress, was born at West Hackney, London, 4 February 1877, the daughter of John Joseph Tucker, farmer, and his wife, Helene Adolphine Marie Foulon. She was educated at an Ursuline convent and made her first stage appearance at the age of twelve as one of the schoolchildren in a revival of *The Silver King* (1889) at the Princess's Theatre, London. When she was sixteen she was touring in *A Gaiety Girl*, and it was not long before she established herself as a provincial leading lady, touring, for example, in a play called *Newmarket* in which she acted the heroine to the hero of (Sir) George Arliss [q.v.], then unknown. Her first serious London engagement, at the Court in 1898, was as understudy to Pattie Browne as Avonia Bunn, cheerful soubrette of the Sadnigge–Wells Theatre in *Trelawny of the 'Wells'*, the comedy by (Sir) A. W. Pinero [q.v.]. Hilda Trevelyan, who would play her many times in later life, had the personality for Avonia's affectionate exuberance. There were few actresses with her special way of gaining and holding the sympathy of an audience; she had no mannerisms but she took listeners into her confidence with a warmth to which they responded at once.

In 1899 she went out as Lady Babbie in a touring company of *The Little Minister* by (Sir) J. M. Barrie [q.v.], a dramatist who would mean so much to her career. The 'minister' himself was Sydney Blow (stage name of Luke Sydney Jellings Blow, died 1961) whom Hilda Trevelyan married in 1910; he became better known as a dramatist, particularly of light comedy and farce. After nearly 700 touring performances in *The Little Minister*, Hilda Trevelyan had a variety of London parts. She specialized in the appealing waif or the buoyant soubrette: her comedy and pathos were always very close to each other. She had also the range to succeed the comedienne Louie Freear as Fi-Fi in *A Chinese Honeymoon* at the Strand Theatre during 1903. It was in the following year that she had the kind of east-end part in which she would be unexampled: the cockney Amanda Afflick in *'Op o' Me Thumb*, a one-act play at the Court. She was so affecting in this that one critic, referring to T. F. Robson [q.v.], the Victorian actor of the comic-pathetic, called her 'a Robson

in petticoats'. Later that year she toured with (Sir) John Hare [q.v.] as Moira in one of Barrie's lesser-known comedies, *Little Mary*, a character described by the author himself as 'an old-fashioned little girl of twelve, very earnest and practical and quaint, and with all the airs of an experienced mother. She carries the baby with extraordinary rapture.' This was an exact description of Hilda Trevelyan's most telling style. It was not surprising that, later in the year, Barrie cast a player so suited to his work, physically and temperamentally, as Wendy in the Christmas fantasy of *Peter Pan*. It opened at the Duke of York's on 27 December 1904. Hilda Trevelyan would repeat this performance in many revivals and on more than 900 occasions. 'You are Wendy, and there will never be another to touch you', Barrie wrote to her in 1920.

After this she became, in public imagination, predominantly 'the Barrie actress'. She had the shade of quaintness and whimsicality that Barrie demanded. During her stage life which lasted for just half a century until retirement in 1939, she appeared in ten other Barrie parts, either new or in a variety of revivals. They included such creations as the resourcefully managing Maggie Wylie who knew that charm was 'a sort of bloom on a woman', in *What Every Woman Knows* (Duke of York's, 1908), and Miss Thing, the cockney maidservant who becomes her own version of Cinderella, in *A Kiss for Cinderella* (Wyndham's, 1916). She was also Tweeny in the 1908 revival of *The Admirable Crichton* at the Duke of York's, Mrs. Morland in the 1926 and 1929 Haymarket revivals of *Mary Rose*, and the maid Patty in *Quality Street* at the Haymarket in both 1921 and 1929. Besides Barrie's tribute to 'my incomparable Wendy', various critics called her 'almost magical' and 'unapproachable'. She played for Barrie, on one night only, 22 February 1908, the extra scene that he devised for *Peter Pan* as a gift to Charles Frohman, the American manager, who came to London for the last night of the 1907–8 run. In this brief episode that followed the ordinary performance of the play, the dramatist answered a question often asked: 'What happened to Wendy when she grew up?' Hilda Trevelyan played a Wendy now twenty years older, a real mother with a daughter Jane who had been the Baby Mermaid.

At curtain-fall Barrie slipped the manuscript into Hilda Trevelyan's hands, saying, 'Now you know my afterthought.'

Hilda Trevelyan had various other parts during her sustained career. Thus when she was twenty-eight she played Oliver Twist most winningly in the production by Sir Herbert Beerbohm Tree [q.v.] at His Majesty's (July 1905). She was Lily Wilson in Elizabeth Baker's study of suburban domesticity, *Chains* (1910), during the Frohman repertory season at the Duke of York's. She managed the Vaudeville Theatre for a very short time, with Edmund Gwenn, in the summer of 1912. She acted Wish Wynne's original part of Janet Cannot—another of the agreeably managing 'Maggie' characters she assumed so easily—in a revival of *The Great Adventure* by Arnold Bennett [q.v.] at the Haymarket in 1924; and at the Open Air Theatre, Regent's Park, in June 1936, a surprising place and personage for her, she was—very shrewdly and surely—the Old Lady, Anne Boleyn's confidante, in Robert Atkins's production of *Henry VIII*. After leaving the stage in 1939, she lived for twenty years in happy retirement, with her husband, at their country-house near Henley-on-Thames, where she died 10 November 1959. They had no children.

It might be said of Hilda Trevelyan that she played Wendy throughout life. She had no major ambitions and never went beyond the reach of her technique, venturing very seldom indeed into Shakespeare or the classics. A natural actress, she was fortunate enough to live in a period fruitful in the kind of work she could do best. Later generations, demanding a more astringent tone, would find many of the parts unacceptable, but Hilda Trevelyan managed them so sensitively that in her day she had no real rival. In private life she kept her stage charm; and when during 1910 P. P. Howe described her as 'the most reticent and sympathetic of stars', he captured an endearing player's quality.

[*The Times*, 11 November 1959; *Who's Who in the Theatre*; Sydney Blow, *The Ghost Walks on Fridays*, 1935; Denis Mackail, *The Story of J.M.B.*, 1941; J. M. Barrie, *When Wendy Grew Up: An Afterthought*, 1957; Roger Lancelyn Green, *Fifty Years of Peter Pan*, 1954; P. P. Howe, *The Repertory Theatre: A Record and a Criticism*, 1910; personal knowledge.]   J. C. TREWIN.

TRISTRAM, ERNEST WILLIA (1882–1952), painter and art historian, w. born 27 December 1882 at Carmarthe Wales, the fourth child in a family of fiv of Francis William Tristram, engine (permanent way inspector), by his wif Sarah Harverson.

After he had spent some years at th Grammar School, Carmarthen, where h early showed great promise and abilit in drawing, painting, and design, Tri tram obtained an exhibition at th Royal College of Art, South Kensingto as well as an exhibition in chemistr at the Royal College of Science. H elected to take up the College of A award and studied there mainly in th design school, from which he was awarde a travelling studentship which enable him to study early French and Italia painting, as well as examples of Englis medieval art, especially wall paintin and manuscripts, in which he ha early taken a particular interest. proved in the end to be his principa life's work, for the background of whic he was particularly well equipped a a practising member of the Roma Catholic Church into which he wa received in 1914. (His elder brothe Henry was a priest at the Birmingham Oratory, and author of several book on Cardinal Newman, and his younge brother a teacher.)

While still a student Tristram ha begun making the meticulous water colour copies of medieval wall and pane paintings which were to grow into very large and important collection representing almost the only approach to a national record of such things which this country possesses. Several hundreds of his sketches, copies, reconstructions, and other records are in the department of illustration and design at the Victoria and Albert Museum, and were acquired over a number of years. A further large collection was bequeathed at his death to Buckfast Abbey, Devonshire. He studied under and was much influenced by W. R. Lethaby [q.v.] who had published in 1906 his study of *Westminster Abbey and the King's Craftsmen*. Tristram thus acquired a peculiar feeling for the artists of the Westminster or Court school of painting, so well brought out in his copies and reconstructions of paintings in the chapter house, on the sedilia, tombs, and south transept in the Abbey, and in the fragments in St. Stephen's.

He returned to the Royal College of
rt as a member of the staff in 1906,
d after passing through various grades
became professor of design in 1925,
post he held until his retirement in
48, when he became professor emeritus.
queue of students could always be found
the corridor outside his room waiting
discuss their work; and in his room
ere generally examples of medieval work
his own copies. Although he was
somewhat unbusinesslike man and
ot always easy of approach, he was
ways generous of his advice to genuine
udents of interests similar to his own.
One of the earliest occasions on which
ny considerable assembly of Tristram's
csimiles was seen was in the exhibition
British Primitives at Burlington
ouse in 1923. The catalogue, published
a limited edition of 150 copies in 1924,
eproduced some twenty of these copies,
ith a general introduction by W. G.
onstable, with whom Tristram was
lso associated.

Tristram's own first important work
vas the *English Medieval Painting*,
ublished in 1927, jointly with Tancred
orenius, in which a high proportion
f the plates were reproductions of Tris-
ram's own drawings. Here Tristram, in
ddition to his now well-developed and
ensitive artistic technique as a recorder of
nglish medieval paintings, showed his
bility as an art historian, and demon-
trated his wide knowledge and feeling for
he whole background of the subject. His
leductions and interpretations were not
lways sound or accurate (the 'Christ
is Piers Plowman' is an example),
nd his dating was often based more on
stylistic grounds, intuition, and experience
than on reasoned argument and comparison. But this did not seriously detract
from his great knowledge and achievement.

There had been a paper in 1924 on
'English Methods of Wall Painting', and
a very important paper appeared in
Archaeologia (1926/7), jointly with M. R.
James [q.v.], on the wall paintings
in Croughton church, Northamptonshire, one of the earlier parish church
series with the uncovering, preservation,
and recording of which Tristram had
been concerned with his three assistants,
the Mobberleys, craftsmen in the village,
whom he had trained.

It may be said that Tristram handled
and recorded almost every well-known
wall painting, and many minor ones,
throughout the whole country, as well
as a number of monuments. These
examples included Westminster Abbey,
Canterbury, Norwich, Exeter, St. Alban's, and Winchester cathedrals, St.
George's (Windsor), Eton College, Christ
Church, Oxford, and innumerable lesser
places. He was also concerned with
the restoration of the pre-Raphaelite
paintings in the Oxford Union, and
the cleaning of the Thornhill paintings
in the dome of St. Paul's Cathedral.

Publications continued, in the journals
of almost every county archaeological
society where he had done work, notably
in Norfolk, Suffolk, Essex, and Buckinghamshire. But his greatest works were
to come. These were the monumental
volumes published with the aid of the
Pilgrim Trust in 1944 and 1950 on
English Medieval Wall Painting, the
twelfth and thirteenth century respectively, with elaborate discussions of iconography, technique, and subject-matter,
with indexes and catalogues, and almost
entirely illustrated by his own copies.
A third volume, on the fourteenth
century, was posthumously published
in 1955, edited by his second wife,
Eileen Tristram, with a catalogue by
Monica Bardswell.

In addition to his sensitive copying
of ancient examples, Tristram produced
some good original work, such as the
paintings to be seen in York Cathedral,
St. Elizabeth's church, Eastbourne, St.
Finbarre's Cathedral, Cork, and the
reredos in Kedington church, Suffolk,
where his second wife was his model
for the Virgin Mary.

In assessing the value of Tristram's
work (apart from his teaching) it may
be said to lie first in what he did by
publication and lecturing to record and
bring to public notice the importance,
value, and interest of English medieval
painting and the crying need for its
preservation; and secondly in the unsurpassed records he made by means
of a series of water-colour copies in which
not only the substance and texture, but
also the spirit and atmosphere, of the
originals were reproduced in a masterly
way. It must unhappily be said that
his technical methods of preservation
or treatment were in a great many cases
not merely unsound, but disastrous. The
wax which he often used as a fixative,
dissolved in turpentine and driven in
with heat, produces an impervious shiny
surface which blooms and collapses

when lime-impregnated damp in walls cannot get out. This can be put right, if tackled in time, by technicians, and should not be allowed to detract from the greatness of Tristram's achievement.

Tristram was twice married: first, in 1920, to Mary Esther Hedgecock, daughter of the Rev. Henry Colborn, vicar of St. Barnabas church, Gillingham, Kent. This marriage was annulled and there were no children. In 1934 he married Eileen Maude, a student at the Royal College of Art, daughter of the late Henry Churnside Beaumont Dann, a lieutenant-colonel in the Indian Army. They had two daughters.

Tristram's work was widely recognized. He received an honorary D.Litt. from Oxford (1931) and Birmingham (1946); he was an honorary A.R.I.B.A. (1935) and, for a time, a fellow of the Society of Antiquaries. He died at Newton Abbot 11 January 1952.

[Records of the Royal College of Art; private information; personal knowledge.]

E. CLIVE ROUSE.

TRUEMAN, SIR ARTHUR ELIJAH (1894–1956), geologist and administrator, was born in Nottingham 26 April 1894, the son of Elijah Trueman, journeyman lacemaker, and his wife, Thirza Newton Cottee. He was educated there at the High Pavement School and the University College, where he graduated in 1914 with first class honours in geology (London) under H. H. Swinnerton, with whom he researched until 1917, having been rejected on medical grounds for service in the war. He was awarded the D.Sc. degree (London) in 1918.

Trueman was appointed assistant lecturer at University College, Cardiff, in 1917 under (Sir) Franklin Sibly [q.v.]. Sibly became principal of University College, Swansea, and Trueman joined him as lecturer and head of the department of geology when the college was opened in 1920. He played an important part in the early development of the college, initiated two departments, geology and geography, and in 1930 was appointed professor of geology and head of the department of geography.

In 1933 Trueman was appointed professor of geology at Bristol and four years later to the chair of geology at Glasgow, where he remained until 1946. He continued active in teaching and research and as elsewhere took part in the general work of the university,

serving as deputy principal during his last two years at Glasgow. He had many other commitments, among them membership of the commission on higher education in West Africa under Walter Elliot [q.v.].

Trueman was appointed deputy chairman of the University Grants Committee in 1946, and three years later chairman, remaining in that office until he resigned because of ill health in 1953. He served in the critical years of the transition of the universities from war to peace conditions and the great expansion after the war. There was concern that the development of the universities should be adequate for the nation's needs, and there was increasing dependence of the universities upon public funds. He brought to these tasks academic distinction and experience in many universities, a logical mind and the highest integrity, which gained for him the respect and affection of his colleagues in the committee and in the universities.

Trueman was an outstanding teacher with his sense of humour, clarity of expression, and mastery of his subject he secured the devotion of his students Furthermore, he was interested in the popularization of geology, writing books appropriate for pupils in schools and for the layman. It was thus natural that he was a prominent member of scientific societies both local and national and his influence was widely felt in the general world of science.

Whilst at school he was interested in natural history and his earliest researches were concerned with the Liassic rocks and fossils of the Nottingham district, and in particular with ammonites; in this he owed a great deal to the guidance and stimulus of Swinnerton. His appointment at Cardiff provided an opportunity for the study of the Liassic rocks of South Wales; this was continued at Swansea and elsewhere; and it was natural that he should extend his researches across the Bristol Channel into the Mendips, throwing new light on the varied and complicated geological history of the South Wales–Mendip region in Liassic times.

He also continued his studies in palaeontology. He made, for example, a detailed study, using statistical methods, of the lamellibranch *Gryphaea* in the Liassic strata of the Vale of Glamorgan, showing that this represented a true

netic series. He worked on the syste-
atics and evolution of the ammonites.
e was interested in and made contri-
utions to the principles and concepts of
alaeontology. He also found time for
aluable studies on the physical and
conomic geography of South Wales.

Trueman's interest in the Jurassic rocks
nd fossils was maintained throughout
is life but whilst in South Wales he began
is studies, which will be especially remembered, on the stratigraphical palae-
ntology of the Coal Measures. As early as
923 he discussed the difficulties of classi-
ying and correlating the Coal Measures,
mphasizing the theoretical and practical
nportance of being able to identify hori-
ons in those rocks. He stated that the
vidence derived from the fossils associa-
ed with the coal seams was not only re-
able but permitted precise correlation;
nd he stressed the need for dividing the
oal Measures into zones each with a
haracteristic assemblage of fossils.

It had been thought that the species of
on-marine lamellibranchs found in the
Coal Measures were of little value in classi-
ication and correlation owing to their long
ertical range but in 1927 a classic paper
n collaboration with J. H. Davies on the
evision of these fossils in the South Wales
oalfield, based on a detailed examination,
using statistical methods, of several thou-
and shells of *Carbonicola*, *Anthracomya*,
nd *Naiadites* established a zonal classifi-
ation applicable over that coalfield, and
ater was shown to be applicable over other
oalfields in Britain. There followed many
publications, often in collaboration with
olleagues, on various coalfields; by 1933
Trueman had put forward a correlation of
the Coal Measures of England and Wales.
These and other investigations were
reviewed in two presidential addresses
to the Geological Society of London
dealing with stratigraphical problems in
Britain, Europe, and North America.
During the last years of his life, he edited
and contributed to an authoritative book
on the coalfields of Great Britain published
in 1954.

Trueman wrote many papers with
other workers; his friendliness and enthusiasm made him especially successful
as a collaborator in research. He was
also in close touch with the Geological
Survey of Great Britain, particularly
in work on the coalfields. He was a member of the Geological Survey Board
for sixteen years and for eleven years
its chairman (1943–54), during the war

and in the post-war years of reorganization and expansion.

Many honours were conferred upon
Trueman: the gold medal of the South
Wales Institute of Engineers; the Bigsby
and Wollaston medals of the Geological
Society of London; fellowship of the Royal
Societies of Edinburgh and London; the
honorary LL.D. of Rhodes, Glasgow,
Wales, and Leeds; and he was appointed
K.B.E. in 1951.

Trueman married in 1920 Florence
Kate Offler, who contributed greatly to
his many achievements; their son, Dr.
E. R. Trueman, became a zoologist on
the staff of Hull University. Trueman
died in London 5 January 1956.

[Sir William Pugh in *Biographical Memoirs
of Fellows of the Royal Society*, vol. iv, 1958;
private information; personal knowledge.]
W. J. Pugh.

TRUSCOT, BRUCE (pseudonym). [See
Peers, Edgar Allison.]

TSHEKEDI KHAMA (1905–1959), African leader, was born 17 September
1905 at Serowe in the Bechuanaland
Protectorate, the son of Khama, chief
of the Bamangwato, and of Semane,
his fourth wife. Tshekedi first went
to school at Serowe in 1912 and then in
1916 to Lovedale, the Church of Scotland institution in Cape Province. In
1923 he entered the South African
Native College at Fort Hare.

Khama died in 1923 and was succeeded by Tshekedi's half-brother Sekgoma, a son of one of Khama's earlier
marriages. Sekgoma died in 1925 whereupon Tshekedi was called to rule the
Bamangwato as regent for Sekgoma's son
Seretse, who was still a child.

Tshekedi's father Khama was one of
the most remarkable Africans of his
time. An early convert to Christianity
he was a zealous moral reformer and a
man of rigid principle. He was also a
masterful ruler, and his authoritarian
nature did not welcome opposition. While
he had many admirers he had also made
a number of enemies, especially among
his own relatives. Tshekedi thus became
heir to a series of family feuds, and the
early years of his rule were punctuated
by disputes and disturbances. These
included an attempt on his life, a conspiracy to oust him from the regency,
allegations of tyranny and oppression,
and a bitter quarrel with influential

Tshekedi Khama

kinsmen. The young regent fought back adroitly and with vigour, emerging successfully from trials which would have undone a weaker man.

In 1930 Tshekedi visited England to discuss with the secretary of state the mining concession which Khama had granted to the British South Africa Company in 1893. Tshekedi not only urged that the concession itself should be cancelled but also declared himself and the tribe opposed to any mining at all in their country. However, after complicated negotiations a new concession was evolved in 1932, which in the event the company abandoned in 1934.

In 1933 an incident occurred which aroused wide public interest. The regent was accused of causing a European to be flogged. The affair was much inflated and led to the visit to Serowe of the acting high commissioner, Admiral Evans (later Lord Mountevans, q.v.), with a strong naval escort. Tshekedi was deposed but was reinstated shortly afterwards.

In 1934 important changes were made in the protectorate system of native administration. The chiefs had hitherto adjudicated in their own courts according to native law and custom. It was now decided to regulate their administrative and judicial functions by law. Tshekedi and chief Bathoen of the Bangwaketse took exception to the draft legislation on the grounds that it infringed the chiefs' prerogative and was against the interests of the people. The proclamations were promulgated nevertheless and in 1936 Tshekedi and Bathoen brought an action against the high commissioner to test their validity. The suit was not successful.

Tshekedi played a loyal and effective part in the war of 1939–45, heartily sponsoring recruitment to the forces. In company with the resident commissioner he toured the Middle East, where he visited units in which Bechuana were serving.

Soon after the war Tshekedi started on a long-cherished project, that of building a secondary school at Moeng. Before this ambitious task was completed he heard in 1948 that Seretse, his nephew, whom he had sent to study at Oxford, was about to marry an Englishwoman.

Tshekedi's reaction to this news and the subsequent marriage was utter dismay. He found support for his opposition among the conservative element in the tribe. The occasion resuscitated dormant rancours, and Tshekedi removed himself and his adherents to the country of the Bakwena. At the same time he made it clear that his attitude was based on principle and was not inspired by any wish on his part to withhold the chiefship from the rightful heir. Eventually in 1950 the British Government debarred both Seretse and Tshekedi from residence in the Bamangwato country for reasons of security.

It soon became evident that Seretse had the support of the majority of the tribesmen, and a reconciliation took place between uncle and nephew. When in 1956 both were permitted to return to the country as private persons Tshekedi and Seretse lived henceforward in perfect amity. It was at this time that Tshekedi initiated negotiations with the Rhodesian Selection Trust which ended three years later in an agreement for mineral development in the Bamangwato country.

In 1959 Tshekedi was taken seriously ill and was flown to England for treatment. He died in London 10 June 1959 and his body was taken back to Bechuanaland to be buried near Khama at Serowe. Seretse Khama became first president of the republic of Botswana in 1966 and was appointed K.B.E. in that year.

Tshekedi, short and thick-set in stature, gave an impression of extraordinary mental and physical energy. He was a forceful speaker both in English and Sechuana, profoundly versed in the lore of his tribe, extremely well read, and intensely aware of broad political issues, European and African. Personally he was affable and courteous, a thoughtful host, and excellent company whether at home or by the camp fire. He was keenly interested in farming, stock breeding, and allied activities such as water conservation and grain storage. Though he was an almost fanatical advocate of African advancement, especially in the economic and educational fields, he was quite without racial bias and never lapsed into nationalist clichés. He was known and admired far outside the confines of Bechuanaland and in England he had a wide and distinguished circle of friends.

Tshekedi was not an easy man with whom to co-operate. Although free from personal vanity, he was extremely ensitive to criticism of his objects and methods and prone to suspect ill will in the most disinterested opposition. This led to conflicts with people who were also in their way unquestionably devoted to African welfare. But however profound such disagreements might be, no responsible person ever doubted Tshekedi's sincerity.

Tshekedi married in 1936 his cousin Bagakgametse, the daughter of Moloi. This marriage was of short duration and ended in divorce. In 1938 he married Ella Moshoela, by whom he had five children. A bust by Siegfried Charoux became the possession of the Hon. David Astor.

[Mary Benson, *Tshekedi Khama*, 1960; Lord Hailey, *Native Administration in the British African Territories, Part V*, H.M.S.O., 1953; Anthony Sillery, *The Bechuanaland Protectorate*, 1952; personal knowledge.]

ANTHONY SILLERY.

TUCKWELL, GERTRUDE MARY (1861-1951), philanthropic worker, was born in Oxford 25 April 1861, the second daughter of the Rev. William Tuckwell at that time master of New College School, and his wife, Rosa, daughter of Captain Henry Strong, of the East India Company. Educated at home largely by her father who was known as 'the Radical parson', she grew up from her earliest days in an atmosphere of left-wing thought, and was a supporter throughout her life of the Labour Party. Her father's views were reinforced by those of her maternal aunt, Mrs. Mark Pattison, subsequently Lady Dilke [q.v.], a remarkable woman equally gifted as an art critic and a pioneer of trade unions among women. In 1885 Gertrude Tuckwell became a teacher under the London School Board until in 1893 she succeeded May Abraham (later Mrs. H. J. Tennant, q.v.) as secretary to her aunt. In the household of Sir Charles Dilke [q.v.] she came in touch with the progressive thinkers of the day in and out of Parliament. As the honorary secretary, and after the death of her aunt as president, of the Women's Trade Union League, she was prominent among a little group of women, including Mrs. Tennant, Mary Macarthur [q.v.], Lucy Deane Streatfeild, and (Dame) Adelaide Anderson, who made a frontal attack on low wage rates, bad sanitation, and bad industrial conditions. She took a leading part in the formation of the Industrial Law Committee, in the campaign against

white lead poisoning, and in promoting the exhibition of sweated industries in 1906 which gave a powerful impetus to the passing of the Trade Boards Act in 1909.

In later years, as a recognized authority on industrial matters, she served on many public and official bodies including various committees of the Ministry of Reconstruction, the advisory committee to the Ministry of Health (1905-23), the Central Committee on Women's Training and Employment, and the royal commission on national health insurance (1924-6). She was president of the Women Public Health Officers' Association and chairman of the National Association of Probation Officers. As one of the first women justices of the peace she served on an advisory committee to assist the lord chancellor in appointing women justices; she took an active part in the development of probation to which she attached great importance, and was one of the founders of the Magistrates' Association. With Mrs. Tennant and others she established the maternal mortality committee in 1927. In 1930 she was appointed C.H.

Margaret Bondfield [q.v.], who had read Gertrude Tuckwell's book *The State and Its Children* (1894) some years before she met her, 'was astonished that so lovely a lady should know so much more than I did about the children of the poor'. Tall and beautiful, Gertrude Tuckwell was not only a highly cultured and distinguished woman but she had a rare and tender nature unswerving in its affection and loyalty. Passionately convinced that Sir Charles Dilke had been the victim of a miscarriage of justice she never ceased to work for the restoration of his good name. She was his literary executor and with Stephen Gwynn [q.v.] wrote a biography based on his memoirs and correspondence (2 vols., 1917). Like her aunt she combined love of the arts with generous fervour for the welfare of the poor. Her house was a meeting-place for friends of many varying views who found common ground in her single-minded enthusiasms. Failing health and eyesight never dimmed her spirit or her charm. She died at the age of ninety as the result of an accident, in hospital at Guildford, Surrey, 5 August 1951.

[*The Times*, 6 August 1951; *Labour Leader*, September 1951; *Magistrate*, October 1951; personal knowledge.] VIOLET MARKHAM.

TURING, ALAN MATHISON (1912–1954), mathematician, was born in London 23 June 1912, the younger son of Julius Mathison Turing, of the Indian Civil Service, and his wife, Ethel Sara, daughter of Edward Waller Stoney, chief engineer of the Madras and Southern Mahratta Railway. G. J. and G. G. Stoney [qq.v.] were collateral relations. He was educated at Sherborne School where he was able to fit in despite his independent unconventionality and was recognized as a boy of marked ability and character. He went as a mathematical scholar to King's College, Cambridge, where he obtained a second class in part i and a first in part ii of the mathematical tripos (1932–4). He was elected into a fellowship in 1935 with a thesis 'On the Gaussian Error Function' which in 1936 obtained for him a Smith's prize.

In the following year there appeared his best-known contribution to mathematics, a paper for the London Mathematical Society 'On Computable Numbers, with an Application to the Entscheidungsproblem': a proof that there are classes of mathematical problems which cannot be solved by any fixed and definite process, that is, by an automatic machine. His theoretical description of a 'universal' computing machine aroused much interest.

After two years (1936–8) at Princeton, Turing returned to King's where his fellowship was renewed. But his research was interrupted by the war during which he worked for the communications department of the Foreign Office; in 1946 he was appointed O.B.E. for his services.

The war over, he declined a lectureship at Cambridge, preferring to concentrate on computing machinery, and in the autumn of 1945 he became a senior principal scientific officer in the mathematics division of the National Physical Laboratory at Teddington. With a team of engineers and electronic experts he worked on his 'logical design' for the Automatic Computing Engine (ACE) of which a working pilot model was demonstrated in 1950 (it went eventually to the Science Museum). In the meantime Turing had resigned and in 1948 he accepted a readership at Manchester where he was assistant director of the Manchester Automatic Digital Machine (MADAM). He tackled the problems arising out of the use of this machine with a combination of powerful mathematical analysis and intuitive short cuts which showed him at heart more of an applied than a pure mathematician. In 'Computing Machinery and Intelligence' in *Mind* (October 1950) he made a brilliant examination of the arguments put forward against the view that machines might be said to think. He suggested that machines can learn and may eventually 'compete with men in all purely intellectual fields'. In 1951 he was elected F.R.S., one of his proposers being Bertrand (Earl) Russell.

The central problem of all Turing's investigations was the extent and limitations of mechanistic explanations of nature and in his last years he was working on a mathematical theory of the chemical basis of organic growth. But he had not fully developed this when he died at his home at Wilmslow 7 June 1954 as the result of taking poison. Although a verdict of suicide was returned it was possibly an accident, for there was always a Heath-Robinson element in the experiments to which he turned for relaxation: everything had to be done with materials available in the house. This self-sufficiency had been apparent from an early age; it was manifested in the freshness and independence of his mathematical work; and in his choice of long-distance running, not only for exercise but as a substitute for public transport. An original to the point of eccentricity, he had a complete disregard for appearances and his extreme shyness made him awkward. But he had an enthusiasm and a humour which made him a generous and lovable personality and won him many friends, not least among children. He was unmarried.

[M. H. A. Newman in *Biographical Memoirs of Fellows of the Royal Society*, vol. i, 1955; Sara Turing, *Alan M. Turing*, 1959; *The Times*, 16 June 1954.]

HELEN M. PALMER.

TURNBULL, HUBERT MAITLAND (1875–1955), pathologist, was born in Glasgow 3 March 1875, the fifth of the six children of Andrew Hugh Turnbull, actuary, who later became manager of the Scottish Widows Fund in Edinburgh, and his wife, Margaret Lothian, daughter of Adam Black [q.v.]. He was educated at Charterhouse and Magdalen College, Oxford, where he played association football for the university (1897), obtained a second in physiology (1898), and was awarded the Welsh memorial ize in anatomy (1899). In 1900, with the Price university entrance scholarship, he began his clinical studies at the London Hospital, taking the conjoint qualification (M.R.C.S., L.R.C.P.) and the degrees of B.M., B.Ch., and M.A. (Oxford) in 1902. His long career, up to retirement in 1946, was spent at the London Hospital with a brief interlude (1904–6) of study at Copenhagen and Dresden as Radcliffe travelling fellow. His experiences as voluntary assistant to Professor Georg Schmorl at Dresden determined his choice of pathology as his career. Schmorl was a vivid teacher and leading exponent of bone-pathology. His pupil carried his methods back to London where he developed that as a speciality.

In 1906 Turnbull accepted the appointment of director of the Institute of Pathology at the London Hospital, and held this until 1946, receiving the title of reader in morbid anatomy in London University (1915), professor (1919), and professor emeritus (1947). In 1906 he proceeded to the degree of D.M., Oxford, and in 1945 received an honorary D.Sc. He was elected a fellow of the Royal College of Physicians in 1929 and of the Royal Society in 1939. He was a founder-member of the Pathological Society of Great Britain and Ireland and was elected honorary member in 1948.

Turnbull's principal aim in pathology was to raise the study of morbid anatomy to a scientific level. To this end he introduced meticulous methods of observation and recording of biopsies and necropsies, building up a body of data unrivalled in this country as a source for research. His teaching was mainly based upon his own experience and dictated by passion for truth; it was often in advance of the current textbooks. Thus his reputation grew, and a steady stream of postgraduates, from home and abroad, came to study in the Institute. Inspired by their experience, they implanted Turnbull's methods widely in other centres.

Long hours spent in supervising his pupils meant that many of Turnbull's original observations were published under their names. His own reluctance to publish was attributable to extreme caution over controlled observation, and criticism of his own arguments. But he could speak and write with authority upon any tissue of the body, especially the skeleton. He is perhaps best known

as the first to identify post-vaccinal encephalomyelitis (1922–3).

In person Turnbull was tall and thin, with scholarly ascetic features. Lifelong suffering from migraine made him somewhat of a recluse, but his visitors' book proclaimed his international reputation. Within his department he was an exacting master, but severity masked great depths of altruism and understanding.

In 1916 he married Catherine Nairne Arnold (died 1933), daughter of Frederick Arnold Baker, solicitor; they had one daughter and three sons. The family home at Woking gave scope for bird-watching, the cultivation of rhododendrons, and golf. Other hobbies were fishing, geology, and water-colour sketching. Turnbull died in the London Hospital 29 September 1955.

A portrait by Wilhelm Kaufmann is in the Bernhard Baron Institute of Pathology; another, by Edmund Nelson, hangs in the Medical College, the London Hospital.

[Autobiographical notes prepared for the Royal Society; personal knowledge.]
                              DOROTHY S. RUSSELL.

TURNER, GEORGE GREY (1877–1951), surgeon, was born in Tynemouth 8 September 1877, the second son of James Grey Turner, a bank clerk, and his wife, Evelyn Grey. He was educated at a private school and at the Newcastle medical school of Durham University where he graduated M.B., B.S. with first class honours (1898), M.S. (1901), and was Heath scholar in 1910. He obtained his M.R.C.S. in 1899 and his F.R.C.S. in 1903. After holding resident surgical posts at Newcastle, Turner went to London and continued his postgraduate studies at King's College Hospital, then situated in Portugal Street, just behind the Royal College of Surgeons. He next visited the many different hospitals in Vienna. Returning to Newcastle he soon became an able clinical teacher and was appointed to the staff of the Royal Victoria Infirmary. He greatly admired Rutherford Morison who was professor of surgery at Newcastle and was delighted when Morison asked him to become his assistant.

In his early years as a surgeon Grey Turner not only operated at the Infirmary but in very many nursing-homes, houses, and cottages in the surrounding district. He was to be seen at his best operating on an improvised kitchen operating table, with an oil lamp as a source of light, and the assistance of a country practitioner. (Anaesthesia in those days was either ether or chloroform or a mixture of both.) He thoroughly enjoyed these all too common occurrences and the more difficult and urgent the operation the better he became. He was a sound, experienced surgeon and his methods and techniques soon became familiar to surgeons both at home and abroad. The Newcastle school of surgery owes much to such men as Morison and Turner.

On the outbreak of war in 1914 Turner was called up for service in the Royal Army Medical Corps which he had joined when the Territorial Force was formed, and after two years as consulting surgeon in the Middle East with the rank of colonel became consulting surgeon and specialist in chest surgery to the Northern Command in England. After the war he returned to his duties at the Royal Infirmary, Newcastle, and to the Tynemouth Infirmary, and was professor of surgery at Newcastle from 1927 until 1934. He then became the first director of surgery at the new British Postgraduate Medical School at Hammersmith where he remained until 1946. There he gathered around him postgraduate students from all over the world to hear his lectures and attend his operation sessions. He had always shown a great interest in cancer and devised many new techniques for the removal of cancer in different parts of the body, especially the gullet.

Besides his active academic duties Turner's other interest was the Royal College of Surgeons of England. He was elected to the council in 1926, and served three terms of eight years, retiring in 1950. He was Hunterian professor (1928 and 1944), Bradshaw lecturer (1935), and Hunterian orator (1945), and was elected trustee of the Hunterian Collection in 1951. He was particularly interested in the museum and the library and he had a very extensive knowledge of John Hunter [q.v.] and his writings and his museum which the government of the day in 1799 gave to the College. Turner's Hunterian oration—'The Hunterian Museum: yesterday and tomorrow'—formed the basis for the replanning of the museum after the war. Turner was also active at the Royal Society of Medicine and took part in many discussions at its meetings. He was president of the

sections of surgery and proctology a was president-elect of the clinical secti at the time of his death.

Turner travelled widely and visit America, Australia, Canada, Africa, a the main cities of Europe, particular Athens, Brussels, Rome, and Stockhol He was a prodigious writer and mar hundreds of his papers were published English and American surgical journal He was an honorary fellow of the Ame can (1918) and Royal Australasian (193 Colleges of Surgeons and received a honorary LL.D. from Glasgow (193 and D.Ch. from Durham (1935).

Turner was a short man who dresse shabbily and wore a very old bowl hat on the back of his large head. H wore heavy boots with thick soles; an in the winter months, his hands we encased in knitted mittens. His frienc were apt to chaff him on his appearanc and ask him 'if he had come to men the clock'. Turner took this in goo part, but it was like water off a duck' back for he never altered. His kindnes and courtesy were appreciated by a who knew him and he was dearly love by his colleagues and students. In 190 he married Alice (Elsie) Grey (died 1962 daughter of Frederick E. Schofield, J.P of Morpeth. There were three daughters and one son, Elston Grey Turner, M.R.C.S. who won the M.C. in Italy in 1944.

On moving to London in 1934 Gre Turner settled at Huntercombe Manor near Taplow, an historic house with beautiful garden and fine topiary hedges There he died 24 August 1951. Two goo likenesses of him can be seen in the Royal College of Surgeons of England in the portrait groups of the Colleg council by Moussa Ayoub (1929) anc Henry Carr (1947).

[*The Times*, 28 August 1951; *Britisl Journal of Surgery*, November 1951; *Britisl Medical Journal*, 1 September 1951; *New castle Medical Journal*, December 1951 private information; personal knowledge.]

CECIL WAKELEY.

TWYMAN, FRANK (1876–1959), designer of optical instruments, was born at Canterbury 17 November 1876, the seventh of nine children of George Edmund Twyman, ropemaker, by his wife, Jane Lefevre. He was educated at the Simon Langton School, Canterbury, and at Finsbury Technical College (under Silvanus Thompson, q.v., Perry, and Meldola) where he won the Siemens

holarship to the Central Technical
llege, South Kensington, which later
rmed part of the Imperial College.
e assisted W. E. Ayrton [q.v.] to the
triment of his own studies and claimed
at, until elected F.R.S. in 1924, his
ghest academic distinction had been
have failed in chemistry and biology
the Intermediate B.Sc. examination.

In 1897 he obtained a post with the
owler Waring Cables Company but,
ding the work uninteresting, he left
February 1898 to become assistant,
twenty-five shillings a week, to Otto
ilger, optical instrument maker, who
d followed his brother Adam Hilger
head of their business in Camden
own in 1897. When Otto Hilger died
1902 Twyman succeeded him. The
mpany was incorporated as Adam
ilger, Ltd., in 1904, with Twyman as
anaging director. He continued in that
ost until 1946; when the firm was amal-
amated in 1948 to form Hilger and Watts,
e became a director until 1952, and
rved thereafter until his death as
chnical adviser.

It was from Otto Hilger that Twyman
arned the fundamentals of optical
esign of which he himself later became
master. He worked at the bench,
d calculations, and tested, mostly
ectroscopes. Until 1910 he made de-
gns and working drawings and super-
tended the construction of all new
struments. One of these, the constant
eviation wavelength spectrometer
1902), considerably simplified spectro-
hemical analysis and made it a feasible
dustrial and research method. A second
tep in this development was the design
f a quartz spectrograph (1910) for work
n the ultraviolet part of the spectrum.
his was followed by a larger model in
912. These instruments were used in the
United States and the results attracted
onsiderable attention. Thenceforward
Hilgers developed their high reputation for
pectroscopic apparatus, and American
nd continental instrument makers were
ot slow to enter the field. In 1913 Twyman designed a spectrometer to work at
nfra-red wavelengths and, later, one for
very short wavelengths for which the
whole instrument needed to be evacuated
f air. He also made an instrument for
tudying X-ray spectra. The development
nd use of spectroscopes for analytical
urposes, now standard practice in
metallurgy, was described in detail in
Metal Spectroscopy (1951).

Twyman became an acknowledged
authority in the design of optical instruments of all kinds except microscopes
which did not seem to interest him;
he was also an authority on the means
of manufacture. He had introduced the
use of test or proof plates early in his
association with Hilger. Between 1918
and 1923 in collaboration with Alfred
Green, the foreman of the optical shop,
he modified the Michelson interferometer,
in the Twyman–Green interferometer, in
a form suitable for testing the profiles
of the surfaces of optical components.
The introduction of this instrument
into the technique of instrument testing
was a tremendous step forward and its
use became universal in optical practice.
Twyman was awarded the Duddell
medal of the Physical Society (1927)
and the John Price Wetherill
medal of the Franklin Institute (1926).
He was interested also in the materials
of optical instruments, particularly
in glass. During the war of 1914–18, in
collaboration with Chance Brothers, he
developed new techniques for studying
the annealing of glass, based on the
polarization of light, which ensured the
maintenance of vital supplies which had
hitherto all come from Germany. His book
Prism and Lens Making (1943) is a standard work of reference in this field.

Twyman was an approachable, friendly
man. He was very interested in young
people, especially in apprenticeship and
apprentices, and he delighted in fine
craftsmanship. Despite the expansion
of his business interests, he claimed to
have remained a scientist at heart and
demonstrated it by freely lending new
apparatus to young research workers
on terms sometimes too generous even
for his very tolerant business associates.
His hobby was music. He once said
that had he been allowed to choose
as a young man he would have wished
to become a musician. Later in life he
often shut himself in his office during
lunch hours and played his violin,
telling visitors privileged to intrude into
these sessions that he was on the way
to becoming a third class amateur instead
of a third class professional. He read
widely and was a keen gardener. He was
interested in the theatre, and loved
a good story. Those who knew him respected him for his kindness and helpfulness; but his influence on optical
design and optical manufacture is his
memorial. He was president of the

Optical Society (1930-31) and was a founder-member of the Institute of Physics. He received the gold medal of the Society of Applied Spectroscopists of the United States in 1956.

In 1906 Twyman married Elizabeth K. P. Hilger; they had three daughters and a son whose death in a motor-cycle accident while still an undergraduate was a grievous blow. Twyman died in London 6 March 1959.

[A. C. Menzies in *Biographical Memoirs of Fellows of the Royal Society*, vol. v, 1959; *Nature*, 25 April 1959; *The Times*, 10 March 1959; personal knowledge.]   C. B. ALLSOPP.

TYRWHITT, SIR REGINALD YORKE, first baronet (1870-1951), admiral of the fleet, was born in Oxford 10 May 1870, the fifth son of the Rev. Richard St. John Tyrwhitt [q.v.], vicar of St. Mary Magdalen, and the fourth by his second wife Caroline, daughter of John Yorke, of Bewerley Hall, Yorkshire. He entered the *Britannia* in 1883, served in the *Australia* and *Ajax* for the naval man-œuvres of 1889 and 1890 respectively, and in 1892 was promoted lieutenant and appointed to the light cruiser *Cleopatra* on the North America station.

In 1896 Tyrwhitt took over the command of the *Hart*, one of the very early destroyers in the navy, and thus began a long and distinguished association with this class of ship. Towards the end of the year he was appointed first lieu-tenant in the *Surprise*, the commander-in-chief's yacht in the Mediterranean, and followed that with a similar post in the *Indefatigable* on the North America station. He was promoted commander in 1903 and appointed to the *Aurora*, tender to the *Britannia* at Dartmouth. He commanded the destroyer *Waveney* (1904-5) and the scouts *Attentive* (1906) and *Skirmisher* (1907).

In June 1908 Tyrwhitt was promoted captain and, with a long record of destroyer command behind him, was selected in August to command the *Topaze* as captain (D) of the fourth destroyer flotilla at Portsmouth. After holding that command for two years he was made flag captain to Sir Douglas Gamble on the Mediterranean station, commanding successively the *Bacchante* and the *Good Hope*. In 1912 he returned home to command the *Bellona* as captain (D) of the second destroyer flotilla of the Home Fleet, and in 1914 was promoted commodore (T) being then in

charge of all destroyer flotillas in the fleet. In addition to his main interest in destroyer tactics, Tyrwhitt was a strong supporter of the introduction of flying in the navy and his encouragement was a considerable factor in the formation of the Royal Naval Air Service.

At the outbreak of war Tyrwhitt was at Harwich, flying his broad pennant in the light cruiser *Amethyst*, with the first and third destroyer flotillas in company. As commodore—and from 1917 rear-admiral—Harwich Force, he served throughout the whole war in that single appointment, an indication of the Admiralty's high appreciation of the skill and leadership with which he led the force throughout the strenuous operations in which it was engaged.

It was as a war leader that Tyrwhitt really blossomed. He had in abundance the four 'aces' which make the great commander: a gift for leadership, a fertile imagination and a creative brain, an eagerness to make full use of the brains and ideas of juniors, and an offensive spirit. His were the first ships to be in action in the war when they sank the German minelayer *Königin Luise* off the Thames estuary on 5 August 1914. Twenty-three days later the Harwich Force was engaged in the Heligoland Bight action, an operation jointly planned by Tyrwhitt and Roger (later Lord) Keyes [q.v.], commanding the British submarine flotillas. Three German cruisers were sunk in the engagement and although Tyrwhitt's ship, the *Arethusa*, was severely damaged in the action she returned safely to Sheerness where, Tyrwhitt recorded, (Sir) Winston Churchill 'fairly slobbered over me'. He was awarded the C.B.

There followed the German battle-cruiser raid on Scarborough and Hartlepool on 16 December 1914 when, although the sea was too rough for his destroyers, he was at sea with his light cruisers and only just failed to make contact with the enemy ships. He commanded the covering force in the Heligoland Bight for the naval seaplane raid on the Zeppelin sheds at Cuxhaven on Christmas Day 1914, and in January 1915 his Harwich Force played a notable part in conjunction with the battle cruisers of Sir David (later Earl) Beatty [q.v.] at the battle of the Dogger Bank.

On intercepting the 'enemy sighted' signal on 31 May 1916 which heralded the battle of Jutland, Tyrwhitt put to a with the Harwich Force only to be called by signal from the Admiralty. ventually he was permitted to sail, but rived on the scene too late to take any art in the action. In the German fleet eration of 19 August 1916, which was be a bombardment of Sunderland, e ships of the Harwich Force were e only British vessels to sight the erman fleet. Scheer, the German commander-in-chief, ordered a withdrawal efore the bombardment could take ace and it was as the enemy retired at Tyrwhitt sighted them. He was in ase until nightfall, but as his only ance of making an attack on them ould be after the moon had risen, he as forced to draw off before bringing em to action. In uninformed circles yrwhitt was later criticized for failing) press an attack home, but virtual icide was no part of his plan and his tion in withdrawing was upheld by oth Sir John (later Earl) Jellicoe [q.v.] nd the Admiralty.

In 1917 and 1918 the Harwich Force ngaged in several small-scale actions, ainly off the Dutch coast or in co-peration with the destroyers of the over Patrol, and as the covering rce for naval air attacks on enemy stallations. After the armistice it was 'yrwhitt's Harwich Force which accep-ed the surrender of the German U-boats.

Tyrwhitt was appointed to the D.S.O. 1 1916 and in 1917 promoted K.C.B. He was created a baronet in 1919 and ranted £10,000 by Parliament for his ervices during the war. He received any foreign decorations and an honorary).C.L. from Oxford (1919).

After the war Tyrwhitt was appointed enior officer at Gibraltar and in 1921 e returned to sea as flag officer com-anding third light cruiser squadron n the Mediterranean. He was command-ng officer Coast of Scotland and ad-iral superintendent Rosyth dockyard n 1923-5 and in 1925 was promoted ice-admiral. He was commander-in-hief China station from 1927 to 1929, erving there with great tact and dis-inction during the threat to the Inter-ational Settlement at Shanghai during he Chinese civil war. He was promoted dmiral on relinquishing command in China and was also promoted G.C.B. In 930-33 he was commander-in-chief at the Nore, becoming first and principal naval ide-de-camp to the King in 1932. In 934, being the senior admiral on the list,

he was promoted admiral of the fleet when a vacancy occurred. During the war of 1939-45, at the age of seventy, he joined the Home Guard in 1940 and for a short time commanded the 3rd Kent battalion.

Tyrwhitt married in 1903 Angela Mary (died 1953), daughter of Matthew Corbally, of Rathbeale Hall, Swords, county Dublin, and had one son and two daughters. He died at Sandhurst, Kent, 30 May 1951, and was succeeded by his son, St. John Reginald Joseph (1905-1961), who also entered the navy, becoming second sea lord in 1959. His elder daughter, Dame Mary Tyrwhitt, retired as director of the Women's Royal Army Corps in 1950.

Portraits of Tyrwhitt by Francis Dodd and Glyn Philpot are in the Imperial War Museum. Tyrwhitt also figures in Sir A. S. Cope's 'Some Sea Officers of the War of 1914-18' in the National Portrait Gallery.

[Admiralty records; *The Times*, 31 May 1951.]   P. K. KEMP.

VACHELL, HORACE ANNESLEY (1861-1955), novelist, was born at Sydenham 30 October 1861, the eldest of the three sons of Richard Tanfield Vachell, late of Coptfold Hall, Essex, and his wife, Georgina, daughter of Arthur Lyttelton Annesley, late of Arley Castle, Staffordshire. He was a distant kinsman of Edward and Alfred Lyttelton [qq.v.]. Part of his boyhood was spent at Hursley, near Winchester, and his frequent journeys to the city and its cathedral made a profound mark upon his spirit. He was educated at Harrow and at the Royal Military College, Sandhurst, where, in 1881, he won the half-mile race against Woolwich. Afterwards he served for a time as lieutenant in the Rifle Brigade; but he spent most of the eighties in California. There, in 1889, he married Lydie, daughter of C. H. Phillips, of San Luis Obispo, managing director of a land company, with whom Vachell went into partnership. Vachell had one son who became a captain in the Royal Flying Corps and died as a result of an aeroplane accident in 1915, and one daughter, whose birth in 1895 was followed by the death of her mother.

Before the end of the century Vachell had returned to England and settled down to his long career as a writer. Independent means were an undoubted help, but, as he himself admitted, success came easily. By the time he ceased work, he had written more than fifty novels and volumes of short stories; fourteen plays, several of them adapted from his novels; numerous collections of essays; and several autobiographical books, the last of them, *More from Methuselah* (1951), published when he was in his ninetieth year. Conspicuous among the novels are *John Charity* (1900), *Brothers* (1904), and his first great popular success, *The Hill* (1905), a school story with Harrow as its scene. Later came *Her Son* (1907), *The Fourth Dimension* (1920), and *The Fifth Commandment* (1932).

Vachell's most famous play, *Quinneys'* (1915), gave Henry Ainley [q.v.] a Yorkshire role which was probably his greatest success in a character part. It was followed in 1916 by the oddly titled *Fishpingle*. Of the essays, *Little Tyrannies* (1940) gives a characteristic sample: and the last autobiography but one, *Methuselah's Diary* (1949), showed Vachell's rambling, intimate kindly commentary still in full flower.

In any of his chosen media Vachell was not an important writer. He was too well satisfied with the world around him, and accepted too readily its values and conventions. To be 'out of the top drawer' was for him a virtue in itself. His place as a writer lies somewhere between John Galsworthy [q.v.] and such purveyors of popular entertainment as W. J. Locke [q.v] and E. Temple Thurston. He wrote honestly and carefully, and his work illumines, with shrewdness and good humour, the beliefs, customs, and circumstances of English upper-middle-class life over a long period. Many of the comments in his autobiographical books have pith in them, and all reveal a sunny, open nature. He was a fellow of the Royal Society of Literature.

Vachell had at all times a distinguished appearance, particularly in his later years, when his noble head and silvery hair gave him both dignity and panache. He affected a high stiff collar, stock, and morning coat, and his voice, musical and precise, with its clipped Edwardian diction, enhanced the charm of his talk. He was a generous and vivid raconteur: his stage reminiscences were exceptionally lively, covering a period of vigorous development and change in the English theatre. He kept to the end of his life an alert mind, and took a craftsman's interest in the practice of the new novelists and dramatists. He kept, too,

his delight in good food and good wi. His home, Widcombe Manor, near Ba an old house of great beauty, he e riched with books and pictures a fine furniture. The terraced gard was his particular pride, and in it w set a superb fountain brought from Ita. In his last years he moved, much to grief, into a smaller house at Sherbor He died 10 January 1955 at Widcom Bath.

[H. A. Vachell, *Distant Fields*, 1937; p sonal knowledge.]   L. A. G. STRON

VALLANCE,   GERALD   AYLME (1892-1955), journalist, was born Partick, Lanarkshire, 4 July 1892, t son of George Henry Vallance, a sha manufacturer, and his wife, Agn Felton. He was given the names Geor Alexander Gerald, but later in his li he changed to Gerald Aylmer. He w an open scholarship to Fettes, becan head of the school, won two Governor prizes and a Governors' exhibition, a an open classical scholarship to Ball College, Oxford, where he obtained a fir class in honour moderations in 1913.

At this point his career of brillia promise was interrupted by the outbre of war: in 1914 he was commission a second lieutenant in the Somers Light Infantry; he transferred to t Intelligence Corps in 1915; graduat from the Staff College in 1917; a ended the war as brigade-major of t 2nd Indian division.

Although his education had be classical, Vallance's interests now turn towards economics and administratic and from 1919 to 1928 he successful filled the post of general secretary the National Maritime Board. There h gifts attracted the attention of Walt (later Lord) Layton, then editor an director of *The Economist*, and in 1929 joined its editorial staff. His brilliance an his gifted personality increasingly earne the admiration of Layton and his journa istic colleagues and in 1933 the board the *Daily News*, Ltd., of which Layton ha become chairman, offered him the edito ship of the *News Chronicle*, vacant throug the resignation of Tom Clarke [q.v. Vallance made an immediate impact b the incisiveness of his judgement and h spirited enthusiasm, which much con mended themselves to his staff; and he s about collecting under him an able tea of young men, several of whom were t become renowned in journalism. Ur

appily his editorial reign was brief: to-
ards the end of 1935 he suddenly fell out
ith the proprietors on political and per-
nal grounds and at the beginning of 1936
e resigned.

This event proved a watershed: the
arly and dazzling success was not there-
fter sustained, although his intellectual
bilities and his ready pen continued to
e put to valuable creative purpose.
n 1937 he acccepted an invitation to
erve as assistant editor of the *New
Statesman* under Kingsley Martin, where
e remained for the rest of his life.
t was not a position in which he had
he same personal opportunities to shine
s in his previous posts, but the *New
Statesman* greatly benefited from his
rofessionalism and versatility.

In the war of 1939–45 Vallance served
n the general staff at the War Office—as
ight be expected in the field of intelli-
ence, where he did valuable liaison work
ith the press. He also wrote a number
f pamphlets for the Army Bureau of
urrent Affairs. In 1945 he returned to
he *New Statesman*, with which through-
ut the war he had never lost touch,
riting for it a good deal anonymously.

Aylmer Vallance made a vigorous
ontribution to journalism in a period
hich was one of intense political con-
roversy and upheaval. He came to hold
omewhat extreme political views on
ome issues; but while this may possibly
ave contributed to the fact that his
arlier promise was not completely ful-
illed, it never affected his loyalty or the
rofessional devotion he always brought
o the task in hand. Those who worked
ith and for him responded to his warmth
f personality, and found particular relish
n his quick, irreverent sense of humour.

Vallance wrote four books: *The Centre
of the World* (about the City of London,
1935); *Hire-Purchase* (1939); *Very Private Enterprise* (a study of famous
frauds, 1955); and *The Summer King*,
a biography of the King of Corsica,
published posthumously in 1956.

In 1928 Vallance married Phyllis
Taylor Birnstingl, a widow with two
daughters. The marriage was dissolved
and in 1940 he married Helen, divorced
wife of J. R. H. Chisholm and daughter
of Philip Gosse, medical practitioner;
they had one son and one daughter.
After the dissolution of this marriage
he married in 1950 Ute, daughter of
Max Ferdinand Fischinger, an officer
in the German Army.

Vallance died in London 24 November
1955.

[Private information; personal knowledge.]
GERALD BARRY.

VANSITTART, ROBERT GILBERT,
BARON VANSITTART (1881–1957), diplomatist, came of a long line of distinguished forebears, six of whom are
recorded in this Dictionary. He was
born at Wilton House, Farnham, 25
June 1881, the eldest of three sons among
the six children of Robert Arnold Vansittart, of Foots Cray Place, Kent,
a captain in the 7th Dragoon Guards,
and his wife, Susan (Alice), daughter
of Gilbert James Blane, of Foliejon
Park, Berkshire.

'Van' to his many friends, 'Bob Vansittart' to the fringe, and just Vansittart
to the rest, he spent a full seven years
at Eton, unusual at any time. He con-
fesses in his autobiography to a devotion
to, and a hope of success in, ball games
which was not wholly fulfilled; but he
won two school races and was in the
cricket Twenty-two. His forte was modern
languages and he won the rare, if not
unique, distinction of both the French
and German Prince Consort prizes in
the same year. He finished his career as
captain of the Oppidans and was, of course,
in Pop. He left regretfully and, as others
before and since, lingered on at the last
day, after the rest had gone home. This
was perhaps symbolic of his loyal attachment to all he held dear—places, family,
friends, and last but not least his country.

He next turned to serious work for
the diplomatic examination. A second
visit to Germany, less unpleasant than
an earlier one which was perhaps the
foundation for his subsequent attitude to
the Germans, was followed by a sojourn
in Paris. He entered the service as an
attaché and was posted to Paris (1903)
becoming a third secretary in 1905.
In 1907 he was transferred to Tehran
and in 1909 to Cairo where, as in Tehran, he qualified for an allowance for
knowledge of the local language. Two
years later he established himself in
the Foreign Office which was thenceforward his headquarters.

During the war of 1914–18 he was
joint head of the contraband department; then head of the prisoners of war
department under Lord Newton [q.v.].
He attended the peace conference in Paris
and emerged in 1920 as an assistant
secretary in the Foreign Office and in

1920–24 was private secretary to the secretary of state. In 1928 he became private secretary to the prime minister, Stanley Baldwin, and continued in the same post with Ramsay MacDonald until on 1 January 1930 he was appointed permanent under-secretary in the Foreign Office. Eight years later, after serving through some of the most critical years in modern times, he was removed to the specially created post of diplomatic adviser.

The story of this 'kick upstairs' is long and tortuous. It has been put in a nutshell by (Sir) Winston Churchill in *The Gathering Storm* (1948). It begins in 1935 with what Churchill rightly calls Vansittart's 'fortuitous connection with the Hoare–Laval pact' which at the time was regarded as a scuttle. His connection may only be judged, if at all, as that of a wise adviser; the ultimate decision lay with the Government, with whom must lie also responsibility for the country's weakened situation. As the policy of appeasement grew in strength the direction of foreign affairs passed from the Foreign Office to 10 Downing Street and Vansittart was blamed for his warnings against imminent German aggression and for hostility to Germany. He was removed from his direction of the Foreign Office to the unique post, created *ad hoc*, of 'chief diplomatic adviser to His Majesty's Government' which he held from 1938 until he retired in 1941. Whether his advice was ever taken is doubtful, but in any case it was by then too late for it to be effective. He continued his theme both publicly and in the House of Lords which he entered on his retirement; the vigour of his campaign against the Nazis was such that it was seriously asked whether he was not perhaps at heart a pro-German whose campaign was deliberately planned to produce the reaction of 'Don't let's be beastly to the Germans'. Nothing could have been farther from the truth.

The epilogue to Vansittart's autobiography, *The Mist Procession* (1958), one of the outstanding contemporary accounts of the time, begins with the words 'Mine is a story of failure'. But failure is an expression of various facets, and though he may have 'failed' to convince the Government at the climax of his career that he was right and they were wrong, no life can be called a failure which was enriched by so noble, affectionate, and loyal a character, by such wide experience, and such remarkable

ability. Vansittart's literary style, like his speech, was rapid, incisive, and idiomatic. It often needed an effort to keep up with his thoughts, but if you could 'take' the speed, you could 'take' the meaning. His writings were numerous and varied and included poems and plays. Perhaps his most original fea was to have a play in French run for four months in Paris when he was secretary at the embassy.

Vansittart's first marriage (1921) to Gladys, daughter of William C. Heppenheimer, of the United States Army happy in other respects, was clouded by the tragic death in an accident of he son by a former marriage; and she herself died in 1928. They had one daughter In 1931 Vansittart married Sarita Enriqueta, daughter of Herbert Ward of Paris, and widow of his late colleague Sir Colville Barclay. She sustained him through the years of frustration and enabled him to surmount with cheerfulness disappointments which he was perhaps too much inclined to take to heart, and the inevitable concomitants of advancing age which he bore without complaint He died at their beautiful home at Denham 14 February 1957. The peerage became extinct. A portrait by A. R Thomson remained in the possession of the artist.

Vansittart was appointed M.V.O (1906); C.B. (1927); K.C.B. (1929) G.C.B. (1938); C.M.G. (1920), G.C.M.G (1931); he was sworn of the Privy Council in 1940 and created a baron in 1941.

[*The Times*, 15 February 1957; Lord Vansittart, *The Mist Procession*, 1958; Ian Colvin, *Vansittart in Office*, 1965; personal knowledge.]   NEVILE BLAND.

VAUGHAN WILLIAMS, RALPH (1872–1958), composer, was born 12 October 1872 at Down Ampney, Gloucestershire, into a family of mixed Welsh and English descent whose members went chiefly into the law or the Church. Sir Edward Vaughan Williams [q.v.] was his grandfather, Sir Roland Vaughan Williams [q.v.] his uncle. He was the younger son of the vicar, the Rev. Arthur Vaughan Williams, and his wife, Margaret, daughter of the third Josiah Wedgwood, grandson of the potter, who had married his cousin, Caroline Darwin, niece of Charles Darwin [q.v.]. His parents' two families had come to live at Leith Hill in Surrey in the middle of the nineteenth century and Ralph

Vaughan Williams was to continue his association with the Leith Hill musical festival until the middle of the twentieth. He was brought up at Leith Hill Place because his father died when he was only two. There was music in both families but the child was no precocious genius. He wrote a little piece four bars long for piano when he was six, and by the time he was eleven he was playing the violin quite well, but, when he was an undergraduate at Cambridge his Darwin cousins thought he was wasting his time trying to be a composer, and he was thirty by the time he had found his real idiom. However, he relates in a musical autobiography contributed to *Ralph Vaughan Williams* (1950) by Hubert Foss [q.v] that while he was still at Charterhouse he organized a concert at which one of his own works was played. Before he went up to Trinity College, Cambridge, in 1892 he spent two years at the Royal College of Music studying composition with (Sir) Hubert Parry and (Sir) Charles Stanford [qq.v.] and he was able to take his Mus. Bac. in 1894 while still reading history in which he obtained a second in 1895. He then put in another year at the Royal College but he still had not found himself and went off to Berlin to work with Max Bruch. Years later he was still dissatisfied with his technique and in 1907–8 worked for some months at refining it with Ravel in Paris. But he had taken his Cambridge doctorate in 1901. Thereafter he was known to the world, since he declined a knighthood, as Dr. Vaughan Williams and later to younger generations as 'Uncle Ralph'.

Vaughan Williams was by creed and practice a nationalist, like those Slavonic, Latin, and Scandinavian musicians who in the nineteenth century turned against the long hegemony of German and Italian music to native sources of inspiration in order to secure emancipation for themselves and the ultimate enrichment of European music. Chief of these sources for Vaughan Williams was English folksong, but other influences were hymnody, including plainsong, to which he was led by his editorship of *The English Hymnal* (1906), Purcell, of whose works he edited a volume of the Welcome Odes for the Purcell Society (1904–6), and the Elizabethan madrigals to which he was devoted all his life both publicly and domestically. In him English music

secured independence of the continental dominance which had been exerted by the powerful figures of Handel and Mendelssohn for a century and a half. He was assisted in this movement by his friend Gustav Holst [q.v.], but he did not in the end establish a school, for the emancipation when it came was complete, and nationalism had spent most of its force in the early twentieth century.

Vaughan Williams had the integrity and independence of his middle-class origins, the lively conscience and streak of puritanism of his formal education, and an impressive physical presence. He belonged to that small class of Englishmen who are by temperament and upbringing radical traditionalists or conservative liberals; he could even be described as an agnostic Christian, in that while cherishing the main traditions of English life, its folksong, its hymnody, its ecclesiastical occasions, its liberal politics, its roots, he was forward-looking, outspoken, and quick to protest at official obscurantism, timidity, or intolerance, as when he publicly deprecated the banning of Communist musicians from access to the radio during the war of 1939–45. In the war of 1914–18 he enlisted as a private in the Royal Army Medical Corps and went to France and then to Salonica, but in 1917 he was transferred to the Royal Garrison Artillery and given a commission. He was sent again to France in March 1918 at the time of the great retreat. During his time in the army he had organized such music as was possible in recreation huts and after the armistice was made director of music, First Army, B.E.F., France, until he was demobilized.

His earliest music, apart from student and prentice work, consisted of songs, of which 'Linden Lea' (1902), the first published work, became and remained a classic. Another early song, 'Silent Noon' (1908), which was, however, one of a sequence of six settings of sonnets by Dante Gabriel Rossetti [q.v.], also achieved a wide and lasting currency. In retrospect Rossetti seems less suited to his robust imagination than R. L. Stevenson [q.v.] (*Songs of Travel*, 1904) or Walt Whitman (*Towards the Unknown Region*, 1907) who provided texts for more characteristic music. By the time the latter had been given at the Leeds Festival of 1907 and had proclaimed that a new voice was to be heard in English music, a crisis in style had been resolved by Vaughan Williams's discovery of English folksong. He had been attracted in youth by Christmas carols and such few folksongs as came his way —'Dives and Lazarus' was a favourite which years later was to give him the 'Five Variants of "Dives and Lazarus"' for harp and string orchestra (1939) —but in December 1903 he collected 'Bushes and Briars' in Essex, the first of several hundreds of authentic folksongs taken down from the lips of traditional country singers in the course of the next few years. The modal character of these tunes unlocked for him the idiom which had been struggling to erupt and the first-fruits of the emancipation were three orchestral 'Norfolk Rhapsodies' (1906–7) and the *Fantasia on Christmas Carols* (1912). The rhapsody and the fantasia were the forms found by all nationalist composers to be more suited to thematic material derived from national tunes than conventional sonata form, which is recalcitrant to extended melody. He continued to compose songs on and off throughout his life but in diminishing numbers after about 1930, although his last completed work was a set of 'Four Last Songs' (1958).

Vaughan Williams would not have been the traditionalist he was had he failed to contribute to the long tradition of English choral music. After the success of his Whitman cantata at Leeds in 1907 it was natural for him to provide something more substantial for the premier choral festival: the *Sea Symphony*, with words again by Whitman, for the festival of 1910. More than Beethoven's Ninth is this a true choral symphony since all its four movements are vocal and at the same time are cast in one or other of the symphonic forms. As Vaughan Williams's mind gradually turned towards the symphony, which was eventually to form the central corpus of his output, this large-scale cantata took its place as the first in the canon of his nine symphonies. There is only one oratorio actually so called among his choral works with biblical words, *Sancta Civitas* (1926), of which the words are derived from the Apocalypse and prefaced by a quotation from Plato. *Hodie* nearly thirty years on (1954), however, is, in fact if not in official nomenclature, a Christmas oratorio. Of the other choral works some are occasional pieces, *Benedicite* (1929), *Dona nobis pacem* (1936), *Flourish for a Coronation* (1937), *A Song*

of *Thanksgiving* (1944), and only *Fi[v]e Tudor Portraits* (1935) is of the dimen[sions] of a secular oratorio, althoug[h] *An Oxford Elegy* and *Fantasia on th[e] 'Old 104th'* (both 1949) employ a choru[s] the one with an obbligato for a speake[r] the other with an obbligato for pianc forte.

His first purely instrumental symphon[y] was the *London*, completed before th[e] war but revised before publication i[n] 1920. Two other of his nine symphonie[s] bear titles, No. 3, the *Pastoral* (1922) and No. 7, *Sinfonia Antartica* (1952) which was an overflow from the musi[c] he had composed for a film, *Scott of th[e] Antarctic*. Nos. 4 (1935) and 6 (1948) are so angry and disturbing that the[y] have also suggested a submerged pro gramme, which the composer himse[lf] firmly deprecated. No. 5 (1943) ha[s] an avowed connection with *The Pilgrim'[s] Progress*, on a setting of which the com poser was contemporaneously working Nos. 8 (1956) and 9 (1958) show a pre occupation with formal experiment an[d] tone colour. No. 9 was performed onl[y] four months before his death and whil[e] it showed no lack of vigour it did soun[d] a note of something like resignatio[n] not previously heard in his music. Th[e] range of experience covered is wide although the subjective emotions explore[d] by the German symphonists are not pro minent.

Vaughan Williams also composed [a] good deal of dramatic music, whic[h] includes incidental music to pageants masques, Shakespeare, Greek plays (o[f] which the overture and suite for *Th[e] Wasps* of Aristophanes, 1909, is the chie[f] and has an independent existence) film scores, ballets, and operas. These last are heterogeneous, ranging from the quasi-ballad opera to the text of Harold Child [q.v.], *Hugh the Drove[r]* (1924), to the full-length comedy *Si[r] John in Love* (1929); from the farcica[l] extravaganza *The Poisoned Kiss* (1936) to the word-for-word setting of the tragic *Riders to the Sea* (1937) and the 'morality' *The Pilgrim's Progress* (1951). In none of these is the dramatic touc[h] as certain as in the symphonies and choral works and they are not wholly proof against theatrical mischance, yet the work which is not only utterly charac teristic but reveals supreme mastery is a stage work, the ballet *Job* (1931).

Many of his most characteristic works are not classifiable in the normal cateories. Such are the *Serenade to Music* (1938) dedicated to Sir Henry Wood [q.v.], *Flos Campi* (1925) which is a suite scored for solo viola, small orchestra, and small chorus, and his most important chamber work is a song sequence 'On Wenlock Edge' (1909) with accompaniment for string quartet and piano. There is an element of cussedness in his attitude to the concerto: he wrote four so called, besides two 'Romances' and a suite, for instrumental solo with orchestra. Those for violin are not virtuoso works; that for piano the composer rearranged for two keyboards to make it more effective; on the other hand it was a particular performer's virtuosity which evoked the concerto-type works for viola, oboe, harmonica, and tuba.

There is no side of music which Vaughan Williams did not touch and enrich, although some of his compositions were primarily of occasional and local significance, and for piano and organ he wrote little. His settings and arrangements of folksongs, however, are a valuable parergon. He conducted the Bach Choir from 1921 to 1928 and taught composition at the Royal College of Music for twenty years. His literary output consisted mostly of pamphlets and lectures, which were reprinted in book form, the chief being *National Music* (1934) in which his aesthetic creed was formulated. He did his share of committee work, notably in connection with the English Folk Dance and Song Society, of which he became president in 1946. The honours which came to him, an honorary doctorate of music from Oxford (1919), an honorary fellowship of Trinity College, Cambridge (1935), and the Order of Merit (1935), were no doubt for his eminence as a composer, but they were also a recognition of the manifold services he rendered to English music. It was not until he was an old man that it was realized that there was no formal portrait of him. The Royal College of Music therefore commissioned one from Sir Gerald Kelly which hangs in the college. The Manchester City Art Gallery has a bronze by Epstein and the National Portrait Gallery drawings by Juliet Pannett and Joyce Finzi and a bronze by David McFall.

In 1897 Vaughan Williams married Adeline (died 1951), daughter of Herbert William Fisher and sister of H. A. L. and Sir W. W. Fisher [qq.v.]. In 1953 he married Ursula, daughter of Major-General Sir Robert Lock and widow of Lieutenant-Colonel J. M. J. Forrester Wood. He died in London 26 August 1958 and was buried in Westminster Abbey.

[Ursula Vaughan Williams, *R.V.W.: A Biography of Ralph Vaughan Williams*, 1964; Michael Kennedy, *The Works of Ralph Vaughan Williams*, 1964; personal knowledge.]

FRANK HOWES.

VENTRIS, MICHAEL GEORGE FRANCIS (1922–1956), architect and archaeologist, was born at Wheathampstead, Hertfordshire, 12 July 1922, the only child of Edward Francis Vereker Ventris, an officer in the Indian Army, by his wife, Dora Janasz, who was partly of Polish descent. He was educated at Stowe School, and went in 1940 to the Architectural Association school in London. He served as a navigator in the Royal Air Force during the war, and afterwards completed his training as an architect, taking his diploma with honours in 1948. He worked as a member of the Ministry of Education development group of schools branch, and together with his wife designed their own house in Hampstead. His work had already attracted notice, and a brilliant career as an architect had been predicted for him. In 1956 he was awarded the first research fellowship offered by the *Architects' Journal*.

His fame, however, was the product of his hobby. From childhood he had been keenly interested in languages and scripts—at preparatory school in Switzerland he ran a club called La Kaboule—and a lecture by Sir Arthur Evans [q.v.] turned his attention at the age of fourteen to the problem of the undeciphered Minoan scripts. These, called by Evans Linear A and Linear B, were written on clay tablets by the prehistoric inhabitants of Crete and mainland Greece. The Linear B script, which Ventris eventually deciphered, may be dated roughly between 1400 and 1200 B.C.

He began by proposing, when only eighteen, in an article published in the *American Journal of Archaeology* for 1940, that the language was related to Etruscan; and he clung to this mistaken idea until his work forced him to recognize the existence of Greek in the texts. Returning to the problem after the war, he corresponded with the chief scholars all over the world who were working in this field, and circulated month by month reports on his own work.

The publication in 1951 of the tablets found at Pylos in south-west Greece in 1939 provided him with a great increase of material, and his systematic analysis of this was the foundation of his success. The graphic system consists of about ninety syllabic signs, supplemented by numerals and rough pictograms, representing persons, objects, and commodities. Painstaking work combined with imaginative skill enabled him to establish connections between the syllabic signs, so that many of them could be linked as sharing the same vowel. In this way he built up a table, or 'grid' as he called it, showing the relationship of the signs before any had been given a phonetic value.

All that was then necessary was to find the values of a few signs, which would automatically determine the linked signs. This vital step was taken by means of some words which Ventris identified as Cretan place-names; and the substitution of these values in other words immediately suggested a Greek interpretation. The Greek solution was first tentatively suggested in a privately circulated note dated 1 June 1952, and repeated with more confidence and examples in a broadcast talk a month later. He at once sought the help of Greek scholars in developing his theory, which he published in the *Journal of Hellenic Studies* for 1953. The theory was at first treated with some scepticism, but within a year of the first announcement a new tablet was published which strikingly confirmed the values already proposed. This proof was accepted by the great majority of Greek scholars.

Ventris's only printed book was *Documents in Mycenaean Greek* which was on the point of publication at the time of his death. His achievement ranks not only with the great decipherments of the nineteenth century, with Grotefend, Rawlinson, and Champollion; but also with the archaeological discoveries of Schliemann and Evans, in opening up a new vista in Greek history. The demonstration that Greek was already spoken in Greece in the Mycenaean age was a satisfying confirmation of generally held views; but theories of the relationship of Crete and the mainland have had to be drastically revised. Knowledge of the Mycenaean dialect has thrown new light on the history of the Greek language; and the study of Mycenaean institutions as revealed by the tablets has provided much new material for comparison with Homer.

Ventris received the O.B.E. in 195? the university of Uppsala conferre upon him an honorary doctorate, an University College, London, made hi an honorary research associate. In spit of honours he remained modest an unassuming; gay, witty, and versatil he was never too busy to answer a re quest for help or to listen to a suggestion His charm and skill as a linguist mad him popular at international meetings.

He was killed in an accident nea Hatfield, while driving alone in hi car in the early hours of the mornin of 6 September 1956. A fund was opene to create a studentship in his memor to encourage his two chief interests architecture and Mycenaean civilization and he was posthumously awarded the Kenyon medal for classical studies by the British Academy. He married i 1942 Lois Elizabeth, daughter of Hugh William Knox-Niven, lieutenant-colonel, by whom he had a son and a daughter.

[*The Times*, 8, 10, and 17 September 1956; John Chadwick, *The Decipherment of Linear B*, 1958; private information; personal knowledge.]   JOHN CHADWICK.

VERDON-ROE, SIR (EDWIN) ALLIOTT VERDON (1877–1958), aircraft designer and constructor, was born at Patricroft, Manchester, 26 April 1877, son of Edwin Hodgson Roe, a doctor, and his wife, Sofia Verdon. He was the fourth of a family of three girls and four boys. He left St. Paul's at the age of fifteen and after a year in British Columbia in 1893 became an apprentice at the Lancashire and Yorkshire Railway Locomotive works, afterwards studying marine engineering at King's College, London. In 1899 he joined the British and South African Royal Mail Company. During his last voyage in 1902 as engineer he became fascinated by the way birds flew and made many flying models which determined him to take up the problem of mechanical flight. He took a job in the motor-car industry and spent all his spare time making and studying flying models.

In 1907 Roe entered a model aeroplane competition, defeating 200 competitors to win a £75 prize. With it he built a full-sized aeroplane, a copy of his winning model. He was grudgingly allowed to try out his experimental machines at Brooklands, then a motor track, but the authorities gave him no encouragement whatsoever. In May

1908 he fitted a more powerful engine to his machine. After a few trials he was forced to leave Brooklands, despite the fact that he had made a number of short flights. They were the first occasions when a British-designed and British-built aeroplane had risen from the ground under its own power, piloted by the designer and constructor.

He went next to his brother's coach-house in Putney and there built a triplane fitted with a 9 h.p. J.A.P. motor-cycle engine. The triplane made a number of flights in 1909 and is now preserved in the Science Museum, South Kensington. In January 1910 his brother, H. V. Roe, who was head of a manufacturing firm in Manchester, helped to found the Avro Company in Manchester. The new facilities brought dramatic results from Roe, who showed an astonishing instinct for the right proportion and shape of aeroplanes. In 1911 he designed the first enclosed cabin aeroplane, which flew in 1912 and was entered in the British military trials that year. In October 1912 it established a British flying record of seven and a half hours.

In the following year Roe designed and built the famous Avro 504 which in its improved form became the best-known military aeroplane of the war of 1914–18. It was revolutionary in its design and so successful that the greater part of the world's aircraft designers adopted the general layout of this tractor biplane. In its various forms and improvements it was in use until 1939. In 1917 it became the standard trainer and for a quarter of a century, with very little change except for increased engine power, it was renowned for a system of pilot training far ahead of any other method.

The Avro 504 was also used as a bomber by the Royal Navy: three naval pilots carried out a raid on the Zeppelin sheds at Friedrichshafen on 21 November 1914, the first air raid in the history of warfare.

In 1928 the controlling interest in the Avro Company was obtained by the Armstrong Siddeley Motor Company; Roe sold out and bought an interest in Saunders, Ltd., of Cowes, the boat builders. The name was changed to Saunders-Roe, and their flying boats became famous. He remained president of the company for the rest of his life.

On 8 June 1928, the twentieth anniversary of his first flight, the leading aeronautical bodies united to give Roe a dinner in recognition of his pioneer work for British aviation.

In June 1954, when Brooklands had ceased to be a race-track and testing-ground for motor-cars, and had become the centre of aircraft design and construction, a memorial plaque was placed there to 'the first of the long line of famous pioneers and pilots . . . on this flying field of Brooklands'.

In 1929 Roe was knighted although it was not until 1933 that he assumed the additional name of Verdon in honour of his mother. He died at his home, Long Meadows, Rowland's Castle, Hampshire, 4 January 1958. He married in 1910 Mildred Elizabeth (died 1965), daughter of Samuel Kirk, of Derby, by whom he had four sons and five daughters. Two of his sons were killed on operational flying duties in the war of 1939–45. To the last Roe believed that the conquest of mechanical flight would bring immense benefits to the world. He was full of ideas and clear in his vision of the future. More than thirty years before his death he had predicted that aircraft would be flying at over a thousand miles an hour at heights of over twelve miles, with passengers in warm, pressurized cabins. He believed firmly that speeds would increase with height above the earth and the times of long journeys be reduced to an astonishing degree.

Roe joined the Royal Aeronautical Society in 1909, only a year after he had designed, built, and flown the first British aeroplane; in 1948 he was elected an honorary fellow. Portraits by Frank Eastman are at Avro's, Manchester, the Royal Aero Club, and in the possession of the family.

[L. J. Ludovici, *The Challenging Sky*, 1956; private information; personal knowledge.]

J. LAURENCE PRITCHARD.

VICKERS, KENNETH HOTHAM (1881–1958), historian, and principal of University College, Southampton, was born 22 May 1881 at Naburn, near York, where his father, the Rev. Randall William Vickers, was then vicar. He was the youngest of a family of four, having a brother and two sisters. His mother, Emma Mary Davidson, was of Scottish descent. He was at school at Oundle until the age of fifteen, when, as a result of polio, he was left with a serious weakness in one arm and one leg, a disability he faced with great courage, to live a normal life full of activity. He had been a good cricketer at Oundle and retained a keen interest in the game. In spite of his leg he did much walking in Germany and Eastern Europe. He spoke German well and liked the German people.

With the aid of private tuition Vickers gained an open scholarship in history at Exeter College, Oxford, matriculating in October 1900. Among his fellow students were Herbert (later Lord) du Parcq [q.v.], (Bishop) Blunt, and Alfred Noyes [q.v.]. Then, as later, he was a friendly, good-natured man who 'used to sing'. He just missed a first in the final history school (1904), but was twice *proxime accessit* for the Stanhope prize essay, college prizeman (1903), and *proxime accessit* for the Arnold prize (1906).

For three years (1905-8) Vickers was lecturer in history at University College, Bristol; he was organizer and lecturer in London history for the London County Council (1907-9), then tutor to the university of London joint committee for tutorial classes (1908-13). Extramural work was developing rapidly and in this arduous work of popular education Vickers revealed himself as a teacher of great power and devotion. He attracted students to his voluntary classes and retained them year after year. Vickers also gained experience in the organization of academic teaching of great value to him later and did much work for the Historical Association and similar bodies. He became a fellow of the Royal Historical Society in 1909. Meanwhile his own studies were not neglected and the results were published in a biography of Humphrey, Duke of Gloucester (1907), *England in the Later Middle Ages* (1913), and *A Short History of London* (1914).

In 1913 Vickers was elected professor of modern history in the university of Durham at Armstrong College, later the university of Newcastle. There he spent the war years and in 1922 published volume xi of the *Northumberland County History*.

In 1922 he became principal of the University College of Southampton, and thereafter until his retirement in 1946 devoted himself to the task of developing the college to full university status. The provision of new buildings was a major need. When Vickers was appointed the college consisted of two wings of brickwork united by a corridor with an arched roof, which he once described as its most notable architectural feature, and a number of wooden huts. The huts, which continued in use to some extent throughout Vickers's time, were a legacy of war when the newly erected buildings, formally opened in June 1914, but not yet occupied, had been handed over for use as a hospital.

The new principal faced a heavy task: 'Throughout the twenty-four years during which I was responsible for the administration', he wrote, 'there was no time when lack of money did not prove a serious obstacle.' The long succession of financial difficulties, the critical situations which arose, the appeals for money, only partially successful, and the timely aid of generous benefactors have been set out in detail in the centenary history of *The University of Southampton* (1962) by A. Temple Patterson.

Deficits of two or three thousand pounds, mainly due to capital expenditure, in those days caused serious concern and even reduction of staff and equipment. As late as 1937, when a refectory and students union building was planned at the modest cost of £10,000, the University Grants Committee undertook to make a grant of £8,000 only on condition that the remaining £2,000 was obtained from private donors. Vickers fought on and held fast to the principles he considered essential to a university. He stressed the importance of residence and of tutorial supervision of students and their self-government in many activities, and particularly strove to ensure that the academic body should have a large share in all matters of policy.

Much had been achieved by 1939. A new library of some distinction linked the two wings, science departments had been partly rehoused, and work begun in some new and promising fields such as aeronautics. Halls of residence had been provided for men and women and further building was planned. Again the incidence of war suspended development and it was not until 1952, six years after Vickers retired, that his final aim was reached, when the university of Southampton was constituted by royal charter. In its rapid growth and expansion it retains much of Vickers's design, not least in its social and democratic quality. The university recognized its debt to him by conferring upon him an honorary LL.D. in 1953.

Vickers's career was characterized by

a humane and liberal outlook owing much to deep religious conviction. In some autobiographical papers which he left he recalled the religious atmosphere of his home leading him to fall naturally into the acceptance of religion as the foundation of life and the guide to conduct. Himself a churchman of High Anglican views he was at the same time singularly free from bigotry or intolerance. 'In my opinion true Christianity teaches men to look at the other man's point of view and to feel that in the grace of God one has the power and the duty to practise charity in the true sense of the word.' This ideal, his devotion to his difficult task, his shrewdness of judgement, and his courage in the face of all obstacles and physical handicaps enabled Vickers to carry his team with him through long years of effort, often of frustration and disappointment.

Vickers married in 1911 Alice Margretha (died 1948), daughter of Dr. Edward Crossman; they had two sons of whom one died in infancy. Vickers died 5 September 1958 at Southampton. There is a portrait by Alexander Stuart Hill in the University Library.

[Private information; personal knowledge.]
G. F. FORSEY.

VILLIERS, GEORGE HERBERT HYDE, sixth EARL OF CLARENDON (1877–1955), public servant, was born at the Grove, Watford, 7 June 1877, the only son of the fifth Earl of Clarendon of the second creation, by his first wife, Lady Caroline Elizabeth Agar, daughter of the third Earl of Normanton. His father was lord-in-waiting to Queen Victoria (1895–1901) and lord chamberlain to King Edward VII (1901–5). His ancestors included on his paternal side Edward Hyde and the Villiers family, who were close friends of the Stuart kings, and on his maternal side a daughter of Oliver Cromwell. Heredity thus produced in him a blend of Roundhead integrity with the gaiety and tolerance of the Cavaliers.

While at Eton he fell down a flight of stone stairs running for a fagmaster's call and broke his hip. He was in hospital for eighteen months. When the college chapel bell tolled for the death of the wife of the vice-provost, it was assumed that it was for the young Lord Hyde, who had the rare experience of reading a notice of his death in The Times of the following day. He was left with a perma-

nently stiff hip, and an athletic career of great promise was brought to an abrupt end. His father, who had pinned great hopes on him, was uncontrollably disappointed and immediately took his name off the list of candidates for the M.C.C., the Royal Horse Guards, and Oxford University.

On leaving school Lord Hyde lived at his father's house, the Grove, near Watford, an eighteenth-century mansion which, in the days of his grandfather, the fourth Earl of Clarendon [q.v.], had been a centre for Victorian Liberals such as Palmerston, Macaulay, and Lady Holland. There he spent his time in such country pursuits as he could indulge. His reputation as a shot and his skill at billiards and golf were indications of the games-player and sportsman he might have become.

In 1902 Lord Hyde went to Ireland as extra aide-de-camp to the lord-lieutenant, Lord Dudley [q.v.]. In 1905 he returned to marry Adeline Verena Ishbel (died 1963), daughter of Herbert Haldane Somers-Cocks, sister of the sixth Lord Somers [q.v.], a marriage which was ideally happy for over fifty years. His father insisted that the young couple live with him at the Grove and continued to treat his son with the austere discipline of a Victorian parent. In 1909 Lord Hyde became a deputy-lieutenant and justice of the peace for Hertfordshire. After six uncomfortable and frustrating years, Lord and Lady Hyde left England with Lord Somers and their uncle, Percy Somers-Cocks, to settle in Canada where they built their own farmhouse and ran a fruit farm in Ontario. On the outbreak of war and on the death of his father in 1914 they returned to England. Unfit for active service, Lord Clarendon nevertheless joined the Hertfordshire Volunteer Regiment, becoming temporary lieutenant-colonel and county commandant from 1916 to 1920.

The war over, he entered politics as a Conservative, and from 1919 to 1921 was chancellor of the Primrose League. In 1921 he was appointed a lord-in-waiting to King George V, and from 1922 to 1925 he was chief Conservative whip in the House of Lords and captain of the Honourable Corps of Gentlemen-at-Arms. From 1925 to 1927 he was parliamentary under-secretary for dominion affairs and chairman of the Overseas Settlement Committee, in which capacity he made a tour of Canada and reported on the great success of the group system of settlement. From 1927 to 1930 he was chairman of the British Broadcasting Corporation, of which Sir John (later Lord) Reith was then director-general. There Clarendon's tact and courtesy made him a popular head of a new and growing service.

In 1931 Clarendon succeeded Lord Athlone [q.v.] as governor-general of South Africa, and was sworn of the Privy Council. J. B. M. Hertzog [q.v.] had asked for Clarendon who became entirely acceptable to the Afrikaans-speaking population, as he naturally was to the British element. He was not only the first governor-general appointed on the direct recommendation of the prime minister of South Africa and the first to serve solely as the representative of the Crown, but also the last English-man to hold the appointment. At the Imperial Conference of 1926 he had impressed Hertzog by his frank and open manner, and by his tact and earnestness. He also had a gift for languages, and quickly acquired a working knowledge of Afrikaans which was useful when he visited the country districts and could discuss weather and crops with farmers. Clarendon's impartiality and straight-forwardness impressed itself on all sections of political opinion and his time as governor-general was not complicated by any outstanding political difficulties. The *rapprochement* between Hertzog and J. C. Smuts [q.v.], in which he played a personal part, was deeply satisfying to him. Even more so was the return of prosperity to South Africa due to the revival of the gold-mining industry after the strain of maintaining the gold standard. The happy tenure of his office was suddenly clouded (as the Athlones' had been) by the accidental death in 1935 of his elder son, Lord Hyde. He was immediately offered and accepted a two-year extension of his term of office.

On his return to London in 1937 Clarendon was appointed a knight of the Garter. In the following year he succeeded Lord Cromer [q.v.] as lord chamberlain of the household to King George VI and chancellor of the Royal Victorian Order. For the next fourteen years his dignity of manner, his friendliness, and his good judgement stood him in good stead as head of the royal household. For most of his time the ceremonial side of his work was severely restricted by the war and the years of economy which followed it. The King, however, held an abnormally large number of investitures at which it was the duty of the lord chamberlain to announce the names of recipients of awards or of the next-of-kin of those who had been killed. Clarendon had a resonant, sympathetic voice, and a remarkable linguistic capacity for pronouncing foreign names.

Another of his duties was to supervise the censorship of plays. His integrity, courtesy, and good manners, together with a gentle and tolerant understanding, made him many friends in the theatrical and literary professions. He possessed, how-ever, a quiet firmness and successfully intervened in 1940 with theatrical mana-gers to curb immodesty on the stage and in night clubs.

In the early years of the war, the King had made St. James's Palace, including the lord chamberlain's office, the headquarters of the British Red Cross and St. John's War Organization. Clarendon was appointed head of the department of services for British prisoners of war which in 1941 was responsible for the dispatch of no fewer than two million parcels. He then became successively vice-chairman and chair-man of the War Organization, which had the spending of over fifty million pounds. He found time too to serve as chairman of the council of the Royal Empire Society from 1943 to 1948. Other offices which he filled were the chancellorship (1938–46) of the Venerable Order of St. John of Jerusalem of which he was lord prior (1946–8), and the chancellor-ship of the Order of St. Michael and St. George (1942–55). He had also played his part earlier in life in his native Hert-fordshire, having been chairman of the incorporation committee of Watford borough and its charter mayor in 1922. He was subsequently made an honorary freeman of the borough.

On the death of the sovereign it is the duty of the lord chamberlain to break his wand of office over the coffin. This moving tradition Clarendon fulfilled on the death of King George VI in 1952. Six months later he resigned, being advised that, in view of his lameness, he should not undergo the long periods of standing which the coronation cere-monies of the new Queen would impose upon the lord chamberlain. He was invested with the Royal Victorian Chain and made a permanent lord-in-waiting. He had been appointed G.C.M.G. in 1930 and G.C.V.O. in 1939.

Clarendon died in London 13 December 1955. He had two sons and a daughter, and was succeeded as seventh earl by his grandson, George Frederick Laurence Hyde (born 1933).

A portrait by a Canadian artist, Molly Guion, is in the possession of the family, and another, by Sir Oswald Birley, is at Pretoria.

[*The Times*, 14 and 23 December 1955; personal knowledge; private information.]

EDWARD FORD.

VOIGT, FREDERICK AUGUSTUS (1892–1957), journalist, was born in Hampstead 9 May 1892, the youngest of the five children of Ludwig Reinhard Voigt, a wine merchant who, like his wife, Helene Mathilde Elizabeth Hoffmann, had been born in Germany. Voigt, who was originally called Fritz August, was educated at Haberdashers' Aske's School, Hampstead, and Birkbeck College, where he obtained first class honours in German in 1915. He was called up in the following year and served as a private in the Royal Garrison Artillery at home and on the western front. After the war he joined the staff of the *Manchester Guardian* where he worked at first in the advertising office. He was next transferred to reading the foreign press and reporting upon it to the editor, C. P. Scott [q.v.]. In February 1920 he was sent to report on Germany for the *Manchester Guardian* and thus was there at the time of the Kapp Putsch in March. During disturbances arising out of the Ruhr miners' strike he was sentenced to death by a group of Freikorps men but reprieved at the last moment; later he received an official apology from the German Foreign Office.

F. A. Voigt soon became one of the most famous foreign correspondents of the period, based on Berlin but reporting on all eastern Europe. In December 1926 he published an article which revealed that, in order to evade the disarmament clauses of the Treaty of Versailles, the German Army was collaborating with the Soviet military authorities in the training of airmen and the manufacture of poison gas on Russian territory. This long-term manœuvre was parallel with the policy exemplified by the Treaty of Rapallo. In bringing the matter up in the Reichstag, the Socialist deputy, Scheidemann, based himself upon Voigt's statements which have been fully justified by the evidence later made available. In 1930 he added to his fame by a merciless description of the 'Pacification of the Ukraine', the ruthless suppression by the Poles of the Ukrainian unrest in Eastern Galicia.

Voigt was one of the first foreign correspondents to draw public attention to the true nature of National Socialism which he examined on the spot in the provinces, Thuringia and Brunswick, where its representatives first gained local political power. Strangely enough he was transferred from Berlin to Paris just before Hitler became German chancellor in January 1933. Regarding his successor's accounts of the early days of National Socialism in power as too timid, Voigt persuaded the *Manchester Guardian* to send him back to Berlin as a special correspondent to cover the elections of March 1933. After this reportage it was impossible for him to stay in, or return to, Nazi Germany. He was appointed diplomatic correspondent of the *Manchester Guardian* in London: he remained in this position until after the outbreak of war when for a short time he held a government post concerned with propaganda against the enemy.

In 1938–46 Voigt edited *The Nineteenth Century and After* and in his remaining years he was absorbed in a more literary life. In his youth he had written a very early war book called *Combed Out* (1920). Later he had done a good deal of translation from the German, such as Bülow's *Memoirs* (with G. Dunlop, 1931–2) and E. F. Podach's book on *The Madness of Nietzsche* (1931). In 1938 he brought out a polemical book called *Unto Caesar* which he had finished writing just before Hitler annexed Austria. In 1949 he published *Pax Britannica* and *The Greek Sedition*.

In his heyday F. A. Voigt was an outstanding figure in Berlin, the confidant of a number of liberals and leftists in the Weimar Republic, the man who exposed the Reichswehr: he was a great journalist in an age of great journalism. He was absolutely fearless; a man of erudition to the point of pedantry; and a considerable eccentric. Stiff and prudish in manner, he was by contrast somewhat free in his behaviour and his conversation. There was a touch of the macabre and pessimistic about him which made him better able than most of his contemporaries to face the stark reality of Hitlerism. *Unto Caesar* was

characteristic of the later Voigt. Its
furious assertions against Hitler and
Lenin are fully supported by learned
footnotes. The Russia of the Stalinist
trials is condemned as the ultimate
wickedness. There are signs of the deeply
Christian feeling of the last years of his
life when he reversed nearly all his
earlier tenets.

Voigt married first, in 1926, Margaret
Lola, daughter of an American business
man, Bernard Goldsmith, and herself
a writer. She divorced him in 1935 and
he married in that year Janka, daughter
of Oskar Radnitz and formerly wife
of Johannes Heinrich Dransmann, by
whom he had one daughter. The marriage
was dissolved and in 1944 he married
Annie Rachel, daughter of the late Rev.
Hugh Frederic Bennett.

Voigt died in Guildford 7 January 1957.

[Private information; personal knowledge.]
ELIZABETH WISKEMANN.

WADSWORTH, ALFRED POWELL
(1891–1956), journalist and economic
historian, was born at Rochdale 26
May 1891, the elder son of John William
Wadsworth, master tailor, by his wife,
Jane Seeley. From Cronkeyshaw School
he won a scholarship to the higher grade
school in Fleece Street, later known
as the Central School. At the age of
fourteen he started as a copy holder in
the reading-room of the *Rochdale Observer*.
The editor, W. W. Hadley [q.v.], promoted him to junior reporter two years
later and trained him in accuracy and
newspaper ethics, lessons which remained
with him all his life. A zest for knowledge prompted Wadsworth to join as
its youngest member the first tutorial
class organized by the Workers' Educational Association, then a young venture
with a doubtful future. The class was
arranged at Rochdale under R. H.
Tawney. Wadsworth developed an eager
interest in the economic and social
features of our history. While taking
a full share of the routine duties of a
young reporter he began to specialize
in local industrial affairs, and in the
paper's monthly literary supplement
conducted a notes and queries department to save local antiquarian lore in
danger of being lost.

In 1917, already an accomplished
craftsman, he joined the staff of the
Manchester Guardian. He won distinction when in 1920 he went to Ireland
to report 'the troubles'. An investigation

of Black and Tan outrages earned him
the warm approval of his editor, C. P.
Scott [q.v.], who promoted him to be
labour correspondent. In this capacity
he wrote occasional leaders on industrial
and labour subjects. He held this post
for about sixteen years while organized
labour was growing in strength and
stature and sharpening some of its
methods. On the death of E. T. Scott,
C. P. Scott's son, in 1932 Wadsworth
became a general economic and political
leader-writer, but continued to attend
the annual conferences of the Labour
Party and Trades Union Congress until
1936. He became an assistant editor
in 1940 and in 1944 became editor in
succession to W. P. Crozier (whose notice
he contributed to this Dictionary). The
circumstances were not propitious. Owing
to shortage of staff under war conditions
Wadsworth had not been able to take
a night off (except on a Saturday) for
many months. He now had to write a
leader every night, and sometimes two,
while maintaining a minutely critical
oversight of the paper without the men
to help him he would have had in peaceful times. He worked with a speed and
sureness of judgement which impressed
all his colleagues.

The coming of peace was slow to facilitate the paper's expansion towards
its pre-war fullness. Like its rivals, it
continued to be cramped by newsprint
restrictions. It had among provincial
papers unrivalled authority as a national
and international influence. Wadsworth
chose to concentrate on this public
service rather than on spacious treatment of northern affairs. The policy was
found to be justified when the government restraint on newspaper sales ended
and the demand for the *Manchester
Guardian* rose significantly, the sales increasing each time the newsprint ration
was adjusted. Under Wadsworth's editorship they rose from 72,527 a day to 168,773.

Wadsworth made his political power
felt in the general election of 1945.
Although he admired (Sir) Winston
Churchill as the greatest living Englishman he held that 'nothing could be
worse than another House of Commons
in which the Tory party was all-power-
ful'. When Labour won its emphatic
victory he hailed it as 'The Silent Revolution'. In the following five years he
gave Labour discriminating support but
at times expressed disappointment with
its actions. Intellectually he had much in

ommon with Liberalism, for which the *Manchester Guardian* had done so much, but his long experience with the unions gave him a sympathetic understanding of the Labour Party, even when he was criticizing its faults. In the 1950 election he was accused of impartial ferocity towards all the party programmes. In 1951 his dissatisfaction with Labour increased. 'For the next few years at any rate', he wrote, 'a Churchill Government is, it seems to us, the lesser evil.' It was not that he began to be won over to Conservatism. He wanted the Left to find a settled philosophy again and to reconcile its idealism with the changed economic status of the country. In 1955 he hoped there would not be a big Conservative majority.

Besides being a vigilant and outspoken editor, in the C. P. Scott tradition, and creator of the post-war *Guardian*, Wadsworth made his name as an economic historian. Stimulated by Professor George Unwin he collaborated with Julia Mann (then principal of St. Hilda's College, Oxford) in *The Cotton Trade and Industrial Lancashire 1600–1790* (1931), a masterpiece of enlightening scholarship. With R. S. Fitton he wrote *The Strutts and the Arkwrights 1758–1830* (1958). Papers for such bodies as the Rochdale Literary and Scientific Society and the Manchester Statistical Society were the outcome of patient research.

The university of Manchester conferred upon Wadsworth the honorary degree of M.A. in 1933 and of LL.D. in 1955. He was a governor of the John Rylands Library, Manchester, a visiting fellow of Nuffield College, Oxford, and an enthusiastic member of the International Press Institute.

Wadsworth saw the life of his day with an historian's perspective. His writing was like the man—straightforward, quick in getting to the point, unpretentious. Though modest in demeanour—'a small, plump, soft-spoken, twinkling man'—he stood out as a strong personality in the sudden crises of a newspaper office, when his firm judgement gave confidence to all his colleagues.

He married in 1922 Alice Lillian (died 1955), daughter of Handel Ormerod, coal merchant, of Rochdale; they had one daughter. Wadsworth had a strong constitution and for most of his life worked twelve hours a day, six days of the week. But in 1955–6 he contracted what appeared to be an obscure virus disease which proved to be incurable,

and five days after his official retirement he died in Manchester 4 November 1956.

The originals of a drawing of Wadsworth by (Sir) David Low and a cartoon by him in which Wadsworth appears with other newspaper editors are in the family's possession.

[*Manchester Guardian*, 31 October and 5 November 1956; *The Times*, 5 November 1956; T. S. Matthews, *The Sugar Pill*, 1957; personal knowledge.]   LINTON ANDREWS.

WALKDEN, ALEXANDER GEORGE, BARON WALKDEN (1873–1951), railway trade-unionist, was born in Hornsey 11 May 1873, the second of the nine children of Charles Henry Scrivener Walkden, accountant, by his wife, Harriet Rogers. He was educated at the Merchant Taylors' School and in 1889 began as a clerk on the Great Northern Railway, subsequently becoming a freight representative at Nottingham, and finally achieving the position of goods agent at Fletton by 1906.

Very early in his career Walkden felt the urge to organize the black-coated railway employees into a body with sufficient power to improve their almost intolerable working conditions. The Railway Clerks' Association was founded in 1897 to this end and in 'Alec' Walkden it had a dedicated and enthusiastic servant. For some years the very existence of the union was in jeopardy and it was due to Walkden's indomitable spirit that it survived. The pioneers met with much to discourage them and at the end of eighteen months a proposal was made at the first annual conference to abandon plans for a separate union for railway clerks. The proposal was defeated, but by one vote only, and the great need for such an organization was ironically demonstrated by a decision to reduce union dues from 3*d*. per week to 6*d*. per month because members could not afford the former.

By 1906 very little progress in real organization had been made; funds were almost depleted, and morale low. Years of persuasion, of pleading a just cause, of fighting injustice had increased the membership from 7 branches with 297 members to 67 branches with 4,000 members, but the future was far from clear. Walkden was a member of the executive committee, and such was his faith in the rightness of the cause that he agreed to become the full-time secretary of the union.

This was not an easy decision to take.

Walkden

Walkden himself had good prospects on the railway, having become a goods agent at the early age of thirty-three; the work was congenial; the contacts interesting. He was married. On the other side, the prospects of the union were not encouraging. But for Walkden there could be but one decision, and to his new task he brought rare gifts in great abundance: a radiant and attractive personality, faith, courage, imagination, enthusiasm, and boundless energy. In full measure he poured them into his work, believing sincerely that railway clerks could and should become as good trade-unionists as any other workers without abandoning the greater responsibilities which might devolve upon them. In fact, under his shrewd guidance and wise counsel the union came to be recognized as one of the finest in the world.

For many years Walkden (widely known as 'AG') worked tremendously hard. He had to scorn delights, and live laborious days; most of his evenings, Saturday afternoons, and Sundays were given to union service. At first he had to do everything, including the humdrum tasks and irksome routine. He was inclined to be impetuous but he always treated his branch and divisional council workers with extreme tact and patience. He never forgot that they were voluntary workers and that without them the association could not succeed. Slowly he gathered around him a band of hand-picked dedicated men. So careful was he in his choice that they all achieved their own personal success in their separate ways and time.

It was not until February 1919 that Walkden's dearest wish was achieved and this only after the threat of a strike. Official recognition of the union as a negotiating body was conceded by the railway companies. During the war of 1914–18 membership had risen from 25,791 to 71,441 and with recognition the union went from strength to strength. Until that time each railway company had its own rates of pay and conditions of service for its salaried grades, but in 1919 negotiations were begun which resulted in the introduction of a national agreement with standard minimum conditions covering all railways. Collected together in one green-covered book, they represented the ultimate outcome of one man's dedicated faith. Walkden seldom referred to it as other than the 'Bible of the RCA'.

Walkden was an excellent speaker and writer, and although he knew that especially in negotiations and agreements it was necessary to be clear, exact, and precise, he disliked punctiliousness, pedantry, niggling, and hair-splitting. His cleverness showed through in debate and on occasion he would detract from the essential values of the subject by casting some doubts on his opponents' real wish to nurture such thoughts. He was at his rhetorical best when 'fighting back'. It was inevitable that such a man should have much demand made upon his time and ability, and the wider sphere of the trade-union and labour movement made its claims upon him. He sat as a very popular member of the General Council of the Trades Union Congress from 1921 until his retirement in 1936, serving as its president in 1932–3. His trade-union activities spread also to the international field through his membership of the International Transport Workers' Federation.

Walkden was elected Labour member of Parliament for Bristol South in 1929 and although he failed to secure re-election in 1931, he was successful in 1935 and retained the seat until 1945, when he was created a baron. Between 1943 and 1945 he served on the administrative committee of the parliamentary Labour Party. From 1945 to 1949 he was captain of the King's Bodyguard of the Yeomen of the Guard and government second whip in the House of Lords.

Walkden was a man of great personal charm with a twinkle in his eyes, but when he thought injustice was being done an iron will prevailed, and his eyes then flashed lightning. Small of physical stature, with a beard which particularly suited his features, he was in every other sense a big man. Deep of voice, his disarming throaty chuckle was at its best when deriding opposition. When the debate was tough he brought into play this tactic and it seldom failed. With his audience in a good humour he strode in with all his command of words.

Brought up in the country by a father who wrote on small-holdings for the socialist paper of William Morris [q.v.], 'AG' always remained a countryman at heart. He liked the theatre and the cinema, and was particularly fond of Gilbert and Sullivan and Garbo. He had a profound knowledge of trees, birds, and flowers. Although he did not care for sport, it was most appropriate that his dapper little man of the flashing ye, ready wit, and determined mind red as a hobby some of the best old English game-cocks in Britain.

On Walkden's retirement in 1936 testimonial moneys were collected throughout the Association; but with a typical AG' gesture he asked for them to be used to endow a men's ward at Manor House Hospital, Golders Green, and to provide books for the library of Ruskin College, Oxford. Although his beloved Railway Clerks' Association changed its title to Transport Salaried Staffs' Association, taking cognizance of the expanded interests of the union, its registered office has been named Walkden House and has his portrait in bronze by E. J. Clack.

In 1898 Walkden married Jenny (died 1934), daughter of Jesse Wilson, director of a brickworks at Market Rasen; there were three daughters. Walkden died in Great Bookham 25 April 1951.

[*Journal* and *Annual Reports* of the Transport Salaried Staffs' Association; private information; personal knowledge.]

AUBREY C. PING.

WALKER, DAME ETHEL (1861–1951), painter and sculptress, was born in Edinburgh 9 June 1861, the daughter of Arthur Abney Walker and his second wife, Isabella Robertson. Her father was a Yorkshireman, a member of the firm of iron founders which built Southwark Bridge. About 1870 he settled in Wimbledon where Ethel Walker attended a private school. In after-life Yorkshire and London shared her affections. She had a studio in Cheyne Walk, Chelsea, and a cottage at Robin Hood's Bay, where she painted in the summer, notably a series of pictures of the sea in all its moods. She does not seem to have been seriously interested in art until her late twenties when she went to Putney Art School. Later she attended the School of Art at Westminster where Frederick Brown [q.v.] was quick to recognize her talent. When, in 1892, he was appointed Slade professor at University College, she followed her teacher and remained at the Slade for two years. About this time she visited Spain with her friend, Claire Christian, and always said Velazquez made her a painter. Although it is difficult to see any direct influence on her work, she copied from his pictures and for her, as for many others, the experience made her realize for the first time what great painting could be. On her return she passed through Paris and met George Moore [q.v.] who introduced her to the Impressionists, and the impact of Velazquez was tempered by that of Manet. Ethel Walker and Claire Christian are referred to under the pseudonyms of 'Florence' and 'Stella' in George Moore's *Hail and Farewell*.

Her early painting owes a great deal to Brown and to the general ambience of the New English Art Club. She painted mainly figures in interiors where the emphasis is on drawing, tone, and atmosphere rather than colour. She confessed she learnt much from W. R. Sickert [q.v.]. Typical of her work at this time is 'Angela, 1899' (privately owned), which appears to have been her first exhibited work. The subject, a girl in a white dress, is clearly derived from J. A. McN. Whistler [q.v.] but painted in a more rugged and less precious manner. In the early 1900s she broke away from the New English tradition, and developed a new and individual style inspired by her study of Impressionism and her poetic vision of the golden age.

Although she painted good portraits of men and older women, notably Miss Buchanan (Tate Gallery), it was the freshness and sparkle of young girls which pleased her most, and it was these she painted most often. Her portraits are modelled in quick touches of bright colour, usually completed at one sitting. As in all her work, the decorative use of colours and shape was always evident in her portraits—sometimes, it must be confessed, at the expense of character. Flowers provided an admirable opportunity for exploiting her somewhat staccato style of painting, and her imaginative grouping would defeat the ingenuity of a most accomplished pupil of Constance Spry [q.v.].

Perhaps her most individual work was as a designer of decorative compositions inspired by her vision of a golden age, notably the 'Zone of Hate' and the 'Zone of Love' which she presented to the Tate Gallery in 1946. She was greatly interested in philosophical religion, more particularly theosophy, and these visionary decorations owed much to her speculation in this field. They were composed from drawings, the colour being suggested by a few bright objects in the studio. The picture surface is well organized, but whilst emphasis is laid on linear and colour rhythms, there is always a sense of space, and although essentially decorative they communicate her vivid imagination and sense of wonder. At her best her draughtsmanship was fine and she was an interesting sculptress, but it was colour and paint she loved, and she would remark somewhat disconcertingly when showing her work, 'Isn't it lovely?' Yet she was without conceit. She was a prolific worker, and the unevenness of her output somewhat detracted from her reputation.

Ethel Walker was a wide reader and a stimulating conversationalist. Her visionary world was in sharp contrast to her appearance and to the studio where she lived with her canvases around her, clearing a space for meals on a table strewn with papers, brushes, and paint. The small energetic figure dressed in a rough tweed suit was a familiar sight in Chelsea, striding in Battersea Park with her dogs who shared her studio.

During her lifetime she exhibited a great deal at the New English Art Club, of which she became a member in 1900, and at the Royal Academy (she was made an A.R.A. in 1940), and at many mixed exhibitions. She also had a number of 'one-man' shows. She was one of the most distinguished women artists of her day in England and was appointed C.B.E. in 1938 and D.B.E. in 1943. Her work is well represented in the Tate Gallery (where there is a self-portrait) and in many provincial museums. She died in London 2 March 1951.

[Private information; personal knowledge.]
MARY WOODALL.

WALKER, SIR GILBERT THOMAS (1868–1958), applied mathematician and meteorologist, was born in Rochdale, Lancashire, 14 June 1868, the fourth child in a family of seven of Thomas H. Walker, civil engineer, and his wife, Charlotte Haslehurst. His father moved to Croydon and Walker was educated at St. Paul's School from which he gained a mathematical scholarship to Trinity College, Cambridge. He was senior wrangler in 1889, obtained a first class in part ii of the tripos in 1890, was elected a fellow of Trinity in 1891, and became lecturer in mathematics in 1895. From 1892 onwards he published a series of papers on electromagnetism for one of which, 'Aberration and some other problems connected with the electromagnetic field', he was awarded an Adams prize in 1899. This interest appears to have come to a close with the

publication of his lectures on the *Theory of Electromagnetism* in 1910.

An equally early but more sustained interest was in the physics of projectiles, ball games, and flight. Here his work was both practical and theoretical, for he became expert in the design and use of 'primitive' projectiles, such as the boomerang and stone-age celt—he was known to his early Cambridge friends as 'Boomerang Walker'—and he contributed a fine article entitled 'Spiel und Sport' to the great *Enzyklopädie der Mathematischen Wissenschaften* in 1900. His interest in flight was later stimulated, in India, by the magnificent soaring and gliding of Himalayan birds whose actions in relation to their environment he did much to clarify. An article by him on natural flight in the *Encyclopædia Britannica* placed much of this work on permanent record. Later still this interest was extended to human gliding and soaring and he greatly encouraged the sport in England in its early days.

Walker left Cambridge for India in 1904 to become director-general of observatories, which post he retained until retiring age in 1924. His administration of the Indian state meteorological service was most enlightened and in particular he gave their heads to the notable young scientists, like (Sir) George Simpson and (Sir) Charles Normand, whom he collected round him. From the beginning of his appointment he became much concerned with the vital problem for India of the variability of monsoon rainfall—the great Indian famine of 1899–1900 was much in people's minds—and he set out to find sound methods of forecasting the incidence of the Indian monsoon. This was a highly intractable problem for there was practically no quantitative theory of the monsoon nor therefore of its changes from year to year. Walker was thus led to seek empirical relations between antecedent events in and outside India and the Indian monsoon itself. Such relations are not difficult to find from the meteorological records over any given span of years but their persistence into the future, when lacking any theoretical basis, is uncertain. (Any two series of random numbers may show quite high but chance correlations over some part of their course.) Walker was well aware of the pitfalls pertaining to the method and he adopted the most stringent statistical tests of his analysis. Useful results were achieved but in spite f his tremendous effort to break it the monsoon problem really remained unsolved at the end of his term of office.

On retirement from India Walker became professor of meteorology at the Imperial College of Science and Technology in London and he continued to explore the relations between weather in different parts of the world in a series of memoirs, entitled 'World Weather', to the Royal Meteorological Society. He also engaged with students on a series of laboratory researches on the forms of motion in shallow fluids when heated gently from below, (Bénard cells), and on the changes induced in these motions when a horizontal motion, varying with height, was imposed on the fluid. These experiments enabled Walker to identify the conditions of formation of many beautiful thin layer-clouds (alto-cumulus) which commonly occur in the middle troposphere. He retired from his chair to Cambridge in 1934 but remained active, scientifically and in music (he was responsible for improvements in the design of the flute), until well over eighty years of age.

Walker was president of the Royal Meteorological Society (1926–8), its Symons gold medallist (1934), and editor of its *Quarterly Journal* (1935–41). He was elected F.R.S. in 1904; appointed C.S.I. in 1911; and knighted in 1924. These and other honours he wore lightly and ever remained modest, kindly, liberal minded, wide of interest, and a very perfect gentleman.

In 1908 he married May Constance (died 1955), daughter of Charles Stephens Carter, gentleman farmer, and had one son and one daughter. He died at Coulsdon, Surrey, 4 November 1958.

[*Indian Journal of Meteorology and Geophysics*, January 1959; private information; personal knowledge.]   P. A. SHEPPARD.

WALTON, ARTHUR (1897–1959), physiologist, was born in London 16 March 1897, the second son of Edward Arthur Walton, of Renfrewshire, one of the Glasgow school of artists, and his wife, Helen Urie Henderson, also of Renfrewshire. His elder brother, John, became professor of botany at Glasgow (1930–62) and a sister married Sir W. O. Hutchison, president of the Royal Scottish Academy (1950–59). He was educated at Daniel Stewart's College and at Edinburgh University where he qualified B.Sc. (Agric.) in 1923. In Edinburgh, in the

newly created Animal Breeding Research Department, his early training in research took place under Professor F. A. E. Crew, and his interest in sperm physiology led to his first scientific paper, 'The Flocculation of Sperm Suspensions in Relation to Surface Charge', which was published in 1924. This interest took him to Cambridge to work with F. H. A. Marshall and (Sir) John Hammond, which led to a Ph.D. degree (1927) for research on the preservation of mammalian spermatozoa. He remained at Cambridge for the rest of his life, on the staff of the School of Agriculture and as a scientific member of staff of the Agricultural Research Council at its Animal Research Station, of which he became deputy director.

Walton's contribution to knowledge in the field of sperm physiology was sustained and fundamental. He demonstrated that the metabolic activity of ram and bull spermatozoa, particularly their respiration, is directly correlated with motility and that respiring spermatozoa produce under certain conditions hydrogen peroxide which, in turn, is responsible for a gradually inhibitory effect on respiration and a decline in motility. He also developed an ingenious method of maintaining sperm alive for long periods, in a perfusion apparatus where nutrient substrates are fed continuously to a sample of semen and the toxic metabolites removed at the same time. He was the first to arrange the long-distance transport of ram semen, properly collected and stored, to Poland where it was used successfully to inseminate ewes.

His agricultural training, linked with his main research interest, caused Walton to be a strong protagonist of the introduction to Great Britain of the application of the technique of artificial insemination to cattle breeding. He was joint-author of a memorandum to the Agricultural Improvement Council advocating this in 1941 and a founder-member of the Cambridge Cattle Breeding Society, a farmers' co-operative, in 1942. He lived to see the practice become national in scope, and in 1957 was awarded the Royal Agricultural Society of England medal 'for outstanding research in agriculture'.

Walton will be remembered by research workers in animal physiology throughout the world who came to Cambridge as research students and found in him a most humane, patient, and very thorough teacher. His interests in animal behaviour and in social medicine led him into a varied circle of activities, and at a time when the subject was not widely discussed he lectured extensively on sex education.

In 1939 he married Elsie Anne Sheldon; they adopted a son and a daughter. He died in Cambridge 6 April 1959. A portrait of him as a child, painted by his father, is in the possession of the family.

[Nature, 27 June 1959; private information; personal knowledge.]   JOSEPH EDWARDS.

WARD, FRANCIS (FRANK) KING-DON- (1885-1958), plant collector, explorer, and author. [See KINGDON-WARD.]

WARD, SIR LANCELOT EDWARD BARRINGTON- (1884-1953), surgeon. [See BARRINGTON-WARD.]

WARDLAW, WILLIAM (1892-1958), chemist and university teacher, was born 29 March 1892 at Newcastle upon Tyne, the elder son of William Wardlaw, a journeyman joiner, and his wife, Margaret Kirkup. He was educated at Rutherford College and then at Armstrong College (later King's College), university of Durham, where he obtained his B.Sc. in 1913. Early in his career he showed an aptitude for inorganic chemistry and in 1913, entering for the Freire–Marreco prize and medal in this subject, he was awarded an honourable mention and a special prize. He retained his interest in this branch of chemistry throughout his life.

Wardlaw volunteered for military service in the war, but was transferred to the army reserve and employed as a chemist by the Ministry of Munitions. His academic career began in 1915 on his appointment as assistant lecturer and demonstrator in chemistry in the university of Birmingham. He was promoted lecturer in 1921 and senior lecturer in 1929. There was an interruption in his twenty-two years' service in Birmingham when he contracted tuberculosis but treatment in a sanatorium led to a complete recovery. Promotion to the chair of physical chemistry tenable at Birkbeck College in the university of London came in 1937, and Wardlaw held this appointment until his retirement in 1957. On joining the college he found a department in which quality and enthusiasm had perforce to compensate for spaciousness of accommodation and fashionable equipment. With the aid

of a small staff he had to teach a large number of students in inadequate laboratories, and continue his research work in frustrating circumstances.

In addition to his academic duties Wardlaw undertook other work of national importance. In 1940 he accepted an appointment on the staff of the central register of the Ministry of Labour and National Service. Undoubtedly he had a flair for accurate judgement of character and ability, and as he was never actuated by self-interest, he was universally trusted. In 1944 he was invited to act in a part-time capacity as scientific adviser to the Technical and Scientific Register, and he held this post until his death. In 1941-5 he also served on behalf of the Ministry of Production as joint-secretary of the Scientific Advisory Committee of the War Cabinet. He was appointed C.B.E. in 1949.

Wardlaw held strongly the belief that scientists should contribute to the well-being of their subject and profession through membership of scientific societies and professional bodies. Throughout his career he gave unstinting service in this connection and achieved the rare distinction of being elected president of the Chemical Society (1954-6) and of the Royal Institute of Chemistry (1957 until his death).

Because he understood himself and knew his capabilities, Wardlaw was an effective man in everything he undertook. Although kindly and understanding, he was not sentimental and was not easily deceived. He could not bear slipshod work or slackness and both stung him to forthright censure. A man of much charm and unfailing courtesy who was gifted with a sense of humour, he made many friends who welcomed his companionship. In the opinion of many, Wardlaw did more for British science and scientists than most men of his generation.

Wardlaw married first, in 1921, Margaret Emily (died 1930), daughter of William Griffin, printer, of Knaresborough. He married secondly, in 1932, Doris, daughter of George Whitfield, who had been one of his pupils; they had one daughter. He died in London 19 December 1958.

[Private information; personal knowledge.]
                                W. G. OVEREND.

WARING, SIR HOLBURT JACOB, first baronet, of St. Bartholomew's in the City of London (1866–1953), surgeon, was born at Heskin, Chorley, Lancashire, 3 October 1866, the eldest son of Isaac Waring, schoolmaster, and his wife, Catherine Holburt. He was educated at the Owens College, Manchester, and entered St. Bartholomew's Hospital, London, as a scholar. He qualified M.R.C.S., L.R.C.P. in 1890 and obtained his F.R.C.S. in 1891. He took his B.Sc., London, in 1888 with second class honours in physiology, and proceeded M.B. (1890), B.S. (1891), and M.S. (1893).

Waring's whole career was centred on three institutions: St. Bartholomew's Hospital, the Royal College of Surgeons of England, and the university of London. At the hospital he held several teaching appointments and was appointed assistant surgeon to W. Harrison Cripps in 1902, becoming full surgeon in 1909. He ultimately became consulting surgeon and governor of the hospital, and had the distinction of having a ward named after him during his lifetime. He was also consultant surgeon to the Metropolitan Hospital, the Royal Dental Hospital, and the Ministry of Pensions. He was very interested in the subject of cancer and for many years was treasurer of the Imperial Cancer Research Fund (1933–52). He published in 1928 a book *Surgical Treatment of Malignant Disease.* His best-known work was *A Manual of Operative Surgery* (1898) which went through several editions and was an examination classic.

To the College of Surgeons Waring devoted a great deal of his time and energy. He was Jacksonian prizeman in 1894 for his essay on 'The diagnosis and surgical treatment of diseases of the liver, gall-bladder and biliary ducts'. He was Erasmus Wilson lecturer (1898), Bradshaw lecturer (1921), and Hunterian orator in 1928, the bicentenary of the birth of John Hunter [q.v.]. He served as vice-president (1923–5) and as president (1932–5). While on the College council he represented that body on the General Medical Council and was its treasurer (1917–32). He served on the court of examiners (1911–20); was a Hunterian trustee; and received the first past president's badge in 1951.

In the university of London, Waring was dean of the faculty of medicine (1920) and vice-chancellor (1922–4). He was governor of the Imperial College of Science (1930–47) and governor and almoner of Christ's Hospital for a number of years. He was president of the Medical Society of London (1925–6) and president of the section of surgery of the Royal Society of Medicine (1928–30). He served as chairman and treasurer to the London School of Hygiene. He promoted the connection of the medical schools with the university of London and was the first to develop postgraduate training and research at the Royal College of Surgeons. He did much to encourage Egyptian medical education and paid several visits to Cairo. In 1935 he opened the new Royal Australasian College of Surgeons (of which he was an honorary fellow) at Melbourne and was presented with a ceremonial gold key.

During the war of 1914–18 Waring served as colonel in the Royal Army Medical Corps and was consulting surgeon to the London Command in addition to his hospital work. He was appointed C.B.E. in 1919, knighted in 1925, and created a baronet in 1935. He was an officer of the Legion of Honour and received honorary degrees from Bristol, Durham, and Cairo.

He was a man of few words, inclined to be rude to his juniors, and always liked to have his own way. Of stern appearance, he seldom smiled. During the last ten years of his life he became interested in printing and this interest made him a very rich man. He did not get on well with his only son, and so he left his money to a potential grandson, and should he not materialize Waring's fortune, estimated to be in the region of a million pounds, was to go to St. Bartholomew's Hospital.

In 1900 Waring married Annie Cassandra (died 1948), daughter of Charles Johnston Hill. Their son, Alfred Harold (born 1902), a research engineer in the Imperial Chemical Industries, succeeded as second baronet when Waring died at Pen-Moel, Tidenham, Chepstow, Gloucestershire, 10 February 1953.

[*The Times*, 11 and 19 February 1953; *Annals of the Royal College of Surgeons of England*, vol. xii, 1953; *Royal College of Surgeons of England, A Record of the Years 1901–1950*, 1951; *St. Bartholomew's Hospital Journal*, May 1953; *Lancet* and *British Medical Journal*, 21 February 1953; private information; personal knowledge.]

CECIL WAKELEY.

WATSON, SIR MALCOLM (1873–1955), malariologist, was born at Cathcart, Scotland, 24 August 1873, the second son of George Watson, clothier, of Bridge of Allan, and his wife, Mary McFarlane, and a kinsman of (Sir) David Bruce [q.v.] of tsetse-fly fame. Educated at high school and Glasgow University he graduated in medicine with commendation in 1895 and proceeded in 1903 to the degree of doctor of medicine, again with commendation. He held resident posts at the Glasgow Royal Infirmary and in 1900, having taken the diploma in public health at Cambridge University and travelled as a ship's surgeon, he entered the Malayan medical service. The Malay States were then in a phase of rapid development with devastating epidemics of malaria an inevitable sequel. This was the situation in and around the township of Klang where in 1901 Watson took up his duties as district surgeon. Inspired by the work of (Sir) Ronald Ross [q.v.] on the transmission of malaria by mosquitoes, he embarked on a vigorous programme of mosquito control. His success was a landmark in preventive medicine. Thenceforth malaria and its prevention were his lifelong interests.

Working in a field where little was known, Watson set himself to study the carrier mosquitoes and the terrain in which they bred. The vector mosquitoes, he found, were of differing habit: one species bred in sunlit streams, another in shade, a third in the brackish water of the coastal plains, and from these and other differences he was led to realize that anti-mosquito measures must be attuned selectively to each of the vector species. Thus he introduced into malaria prevention the new and important concept of 'species sanitation'. Suiting his approach to the species and terrain, he developed methods of mosquito control—subsoil and other types of drainage, larvicidal oiling, the clearing of jungle or the promotion of shade, and other methods—which, tested and proved in the towns and on the rubber estates of Malaya, were woven into the pattern of malaria prevention throughout the world. He wrote the first accounts of the early sexual development in the blood of the malignant malaria parasites and of the renal complications of quartan malaria; and to industrial technology he contributed a patent process for tapping rubber trees and, with his wife, a device for controlling dust in mines.

In 1908 Watson left government service for general and consultant prac-

tice. Rubber planters and others saw the promise of his practical approach to malaria control—a factor in the early development of the great Malayan rubber industry—and in Malaya and elsewhere his guidance was eagerly sought. He was a founder-member of the Malayan Malaria Advisory Board and at various times an adviser on the prevention of malaria to governments or industries in the Malay States, Singapore, India, Nepal, Africa, the Balkans, and South America. In 1928 he left Malaya to serve at Ross's request as consultant to the newly created Ross Institute of Tropical Hygiene and from 1933 until his retirement in 1942 he was the director of the Institute and of branches he established in India and West Africa. There, and in the Rhodesian copper belt where he was medical adviser to a group of mining companies, he continued to promote the spread of preventive medicine with a special regard for the health problems of industry and the training of laymen.

For his work on the prevention of malaria Watson was knighted in 1924 and in the same year the university of Glasgow conferred on him the honorary degree of LL.D. He was an honorary fellow of the Incorporated Society of Planters, Malaya (1925), and of the Royal Faculty of Physicians and Surgeons of Glasgow (1933), and a fellow of the Geological Society of London (1943). Among his awards were the gold medal of the Rubber Growers Association (1914), the Stewart prize of the British Medical Association (1927), the Sir William Jones gold medal of the Asiatic Society of Bengal (1928), the Mary Kingsley medal of the Liverpool School of Tropical Medicine (1934), and the Albert medal of the Royal Society of Arts (1939). In 1948 at the age of seventy-five he delivered the Ronald Ross oration in Washington D.C. His writings include *The Prevention of Malaria in the Federated Malay States* (1911, 2nd ed. 1921), *Rural Sanitation in the Tropics* (1915), and *African Highway* (1953).

In 1900 he married Jean Alice, eldest daughter of David Gray, engineer, of Coatbridge, Lanarkshire. Herself a nurse, she assisted him in his early hospital work in Malaya. They had four sons. His wife died in 1935 and in 1938 he married Constance Evelyn, daughter of Lieutenant-Colonel Walter L. Loring, Royal Warwickshire Regiment, by whom he had one daughter. Watson died 28

December 1955 at his home in Peaslake, Surrey, where he had spent his declining years in active and rewarding retirement.

[*Lancet*, 7 January 1956; *Journal of Tropical Medicine and Hygiene*, vol. lix, No. 2, 1956; personal knowledge; private information.]
JOHN FIELD.

WATSON, ROBERT WILLIAM SETON- (1879–1951), historian. [See SETON-WATSON.]

WATT, GEORGE FIDDES (1873–1960), portrait painter, was born in Aberdeen 15 February 1873, the only son of George Watt, joiner and ship-wright, and his wife, Jean Frost, daughter of a North of England weaver working at an Aberdeen linen factory. Fiddes was the eldest of a family of five. His mother, a handsome woman of musical tastes, was the active force in bringing up the family and looking after their welfare. As a boy Fiddes Watt was handicapped by a stammer which he overcame later in life. On leaving school at fourteen, he was apprenticed, like so many artists, to a firm of lithographic printers, in Aberdeen. During these seven years he attended evening classes at Gray's School of Art where among his fellow students were Robert Brough and Douglas Strachan [qq.v.].

At the age of twenty-one Watt went to Edinburgh to study in the life class of the Royal Scottish Academy. For a time he found life hard, and a struggle to make ends meet, but through exhibiting his paintings he soon obtained small commissions. One of the earliest of his portraits to attract attention was that of Provost Smith of Peterhead. Another striking portrait painted about this time was of Provost Wallace of Tain; his spirited rendering of this bearded Highlander—seated with a walking stick in hand—was a fine achievement and laid the foundation of Watt's success.

In 1903 Watt married Jean Willox, art teacher in Peterhead Academy, and the daughter of a farmer in the Buchan area. They had three sons and a daughter. Shortly after his marriage Watt painted his wife and entitled it 'The Lady in White'. Shown at the Royal Scottish Academy exhibition it was acclaimed by artists and laymen alike. It was followed by several portraits of women, including the fine 'Mrs. Jas. A. Hood of Midfield', the attractive 'Lady with

Violin', and a portrait of his mother which was bought out of the Chantrey Bequest for the Tate Gallery. In the opinion of many Watt never did anything better than these paintings. His reputation, however, rests on his portraits of men. He was interested in strong character, expressed with vigour and freedom of handling. His most vital works were stimulated by men with the personality and type of Lord Haldane whom he painted for Lincoln's Inn. Watt believed 'that good portraits happen when the minds of sitters and artists "click", when some spark of sympathy temporarily unites them'.

When commissions continued to come in steadily, he felt justified in moving to London where he rented a large studio in the Cromwell Road. Among the numerous portraits of distinguished persons he painted are those at Balliol College, Oxford, of Asquith and Lord Loreburn. Other portraits are those of Lord Ullswater (House of Commons); the first Viscount Finlay (Middle Temple, replica at the Palace of Peace, The Hague); A. J. Balfour (Eton); H. F. Newall (Cambridge Solar Physics Observatory); and Cosmo Gordon Lang (All Souls, Oxford).

Throughout his career, Watt's painting did not change much. His work may be regarded as that of a sound practitioner in the well-tried Scottish tradition stemming from Raeburn, with its unaffected simplicity and robust directness of handling. Another early influence was that of Sir George Reid, a fellow Aberdonian, a painter whose work had a refinement of draughtsmanship and a largeness of design which attracted him. Watt was elected an associate (1910) and a full member (1924) of the Royal Scottish Academy. In 1955 the university of Aberdeen conferred on him the honorary degree of LL.D.

During the war of 1939–45, when the bombing of London became severe, Watt retired to his native Aberdeen. From then on he painted very little due to failing eyesight and late in life he was granted a Civil List pension. His wife died in 1956; all through their long married life she had been a steadying influence and her death was a severe blow to him. He was of a convivial disposition; possessing a good voice, he was fond of singing Scottish songs and ballads. In his later years, a well-known figure in Aberdeen, with his vandyke beard, deer-stalking cap, and carrying a long shepherd's crook, he attracted attention wherever he went. He died there 22 November 1960.

There is a bronze head of Fiddes Watt by T. Huxley Jones in the Aberdeen Art Gallery.

[*Press and Journal* (Aberdeen), 3 November 1932 and 28 January 1963; *People's Journal* (Dundee), 26 November 1960; Royal Scottish Academy *Annual Report*, 1960; private information; personal knowledge.]

D. M. SUTHERLAND.

WAVERLEY, first VISCOUNT (1882–1958), administrator and statesman. [See ANDERSON, JOHN.]

WEBB, CLEMENT CHARLES JULIAN (1865–1954), theologian, philosopher, and historian, was born in London 25 June 1865, the youngest child of Benjamin Webb [q.v.] and his wife, Maria Elphinstone, daughter of William Hodge Mill [q.v.]. Webb was much influenced by the interests and environment of his father and wrote about them in this Dictionary (1899) and, later, in the *Church Quarterly Review* (vol. lxxv, October 1912–January 1913, pp. 329–48). He liked to recall a conversation which he had with Mr. Gladstone during his memorable visit to Oxford in 1890. Being then a probationer fellow of Magdalen, Webb met Gladstone at a breakfast party, 'and he said to me that in knowledge of English churches my father came next after his (Gladstone's) own brother-in-law, Sir Stephen Glynne' (*Oxoniensia*, vol. vi, 1941, p. 91; *cf.* for Webb's recollections of Gladstone, *Church Quarterly Review*, vol. cliii, July–September 1952, pp. 320–34). Webb was educated at Westminster School, where he was captain of the school, whence he passed to Christ Church, Oxford, as a Westminster scholar. His devotion to Westminster was enduring. From 1905, when he became a governor of the school, he remained until his death in the closest contact with its affairs. In 1888 he graduated with first class honours in *literae humaniores*.

On 6 November 1889 Webb was elected a fellow, and, in the next year (12 March), he was appointed a tutor in philosophy in Magdalen College, Oxford. During the year 1889–90 he did some philosophical teaching at New College, where one of his pupils was

H. W. B. Joseph (whose notice he contributed to this Dictionary), later his brother-in-law. He attended his first college meeting at Magdalen on 10 December 1890. Webb was a fellow and tutor of Magdalen for thirty years during thirteen of which (1907–20) he also acted as tutor in philosophy in the Society of Non-Collegiate students. In 1905–6 he was senior proctor. Throughout his Oxford life he took a lively interest in academic affairs, with active periods of service on the hebdomadal council and other university bodies. From 1911 to 1914 he was Wilde lecturer on natural and comparative religion. In 1920 he became the first Oriel professor of the philosophy of the Christian religion. The new chair had been founded by C. F. Nolloth, whose name it now bears, with Webb's peculiar claims directly in view. Hence in 1922 he vacated his fellowship at Magdalen and became a fellow of Oriel. On reaching the retiring age in 1930 he entered upon the last, but no less active, period of his life. He died at Oxford 5 October 1954. In 1905 he had married Eleanor Theodora (died 1942), daughter of the Rev. Alexander Joseph, honorary canon of Rochester. There were no children. During their happy, busy, and hospitable life together, the Webbs lived first at Holywell Ford, close to Magdalen, then in Old Marston (where Webb was a churchwarden), and finally at the Old Rectory, Pitchcott, near Aylesbury.

Webb was by nature both determined and possessed of a spirit of inquiry. He responded to every call on his loyalty (for he seemed to be the embodiment of *pietas*) without loss to his independence. His mental curiosity constantly enriched an orderly intelligence which tried to take account of everything relevant to its purpose. Indeed, the rich experiences of a quiet life, at school, in Oxford, and in foreign travel, were related, to an unusual degree, to his literary output. Most of his theological and philosophical writings, for example, were first delivered as lectures; lectures which, in their turn, imparted the activity of a mind eager for fresh contacts with other minds and almost naïvely happy in discussion. On the other hand, beyond and more influential upon him than the more casual contacts with academic society and the literary world, a spiritual crisis, through which he passed in his first year as an undergraduate and which he vividly described forty years later, best explains the concentration of his learning and interests in the service of the philosophy of religion and, in more practical ways, of the Church of England. As he wrote in 1925 this experience left him 'with a profound conviction of the reality of God and of the duty of openmindedness and intellectual honesty; a belief that it was the first of religious duties to keep one's ears open to any voice, from whatever quarter, which might convey a message from God'. A 'sense of expectation of strange and wonderful things' strengthened his lifelong refusal to withdraw dogma based upon historical fact from the scrutiny and criticism of reason, to make a clear-cut distinction between what is historically mediated and what is revealed through a process of philosophical speculation, and to admit that 'within the knowledge of God, however we may have come by it', there is a portion guaranteed to be unmixed with error. Webb could recognize infallibility nowhere, in Pope, Church, or Bible. (See *Religious Experience*, a lecture of 19 May 1944, printed with a foreword by L. W. Grensted and a bibliography of Webb's published writings as presented to him in Oriel College on his eightieth birthday, 25 June 1945, pp. 41–5.) As he himself noted in 1925 he was acutely aware of the sense of insecurity which so easily besets the mind drawn to metaphysical reflection. It has been observed that he had little to contribute to the age-long discussion of the problem of immortality. (Grensted, in op. cit., p. 16.) He found relief from the sense of tension between time and eternity in his profound conviction in the reality of God, in his personal experience of God as a Person, and in the abiding impression made on him as an undergraduate by Kant's presentation of morality as a categorical imperative. Here he was strengthened by the companionship of his school and college friend, C. J. Shebbeare. Mental satisfaction he found in the teaching of John Cook Wilson [q.v.], 'a man to whom I owe more than to any other of my philosophical instructors', for, in Cook Wilson's realism he saw a realism 'for which spirit is no less real than matter, and the spiritual values of truth, goodness, and beauty no mere creations of finite minds' (ibid., p. 35).

Webb rejoiced in the meetings of the Aristotelian Society, which at first met in the rooms of Ingram Bywater [q.v.], and, perhaps still more, in the discussions of the anonymous philosophical club which had its centre in Cook Wilson. As boy and man he had always taken an effortless delight in the rich traditions of his surroundings. He made full use of the opportunities revealed to him by his contemporaries in Magdalen to train and indulge his historical curiosity. Indeed he became one of a very distinguished group of scholars at Magdalen. His closest friends in the college were H. A. Wilson, Cuthbert Turner [q.v.], and Paul Benecke, but probably he owed most to Reginald Lane Poole [q.v.], who was elected a fellow in 1898, when he was forty-one years of age and already recognized as one of the best historical scholars of his time. In his father's house Webb had lived in an ecclesiological world inspired by J. M. Neale [q.v]. At Westminster and Christ Church his sense of historical realities was strengthened. And now in Magdalen his intense philosophical interests were given an historical setting which, however strange it might seem to be to others, was very satisfying to himself. His scholarly editions of two important medieval texts, the *Policraticus* (1909) and the *Metalogicon* (1929) composed by John of Salisbury [q.v.] when he was in the service of Theobald [q.v.], archbishop of Canterbury (d. 1161), were as congenial and apposite to Webb's outlook as were the two series of his Gifford lectures, *God and Personality* (1918) and *Divine Personality and Human Life* (1920). In his work on John of Salisbury, work which in part was taken over from R. L. Poole, he paid tribute to one who, more than any other, is able to guide the student of public life and of the various schools of philosophy in the twelfth century. Webb realized, perhaps even more clearly than did his friend Hastings Rashdall (whose notice he contributed to this Dictionary), the permanent significance of the issues raised in the twelfth century for the student of the history and philosophy of religion. His mastery of historical technique and criticism, which is very remarkable, may well have come to him so easily because the object of his investigations gave him such pleasure. As the numerous essays, reviews, and notes mentioned in the bibliography of his writings show, medieval problems fascinated him to the end of his life. In one of his last papers, he returned to a theme, the dialogue of Gilbert Crispin [q.v.] between a Christian and a heathen (c. 1093–8), with which he had dealt forty years earlier in his *Studies in the History of Natural Theology* (1915), and he printed the dialogue for the first time (*Mediaeval and Renaissance Studies*, ed. R. W. Hunt and R. Klibansky, vol. iii, 1954, pp. 55–77).

Webb was alert to the practical bearing of movements of thought upon ecclesiastical activities and personal religion both throughout the centuries and in the world about him. His first review was a note on *Lux Mundi* (*Oxford Magazine*, 12 February 1890), his first articles were on Scotus Erigena and John of Salisbury (*Proceedings* of the Aristotelian Society, vol. ii, 1892, 1893). His first book, on the devotions of St. Anselm (1903), appeared soon after a long review by him of a big book on the philosophy of the Christian religion by A. M. Fairbairn [q.v.] (*Journal of Theological Studies*, January 1903). The publication of his edition of the *Policraticus* in 1909 was followed in 1910 by a report, 'Recent movements in Philosophy in relation to Theistic Belief'. And so he was engaged until his death. He wrote a short history of philosophy for the Home University Library (1915) and in 1932 put together what he knew and felt about John of Salisbury and his writings in another little book contributed to a series on great medieval churchmen. His wide range is best revealed in his fine Gifford lectures, notably in the second series in which he relates the many-sided experiences of human life, economic, aesthetic, political, moral, religious, to the fact (as he insisted it to be) of divine personality (1920). His concern with the 'problems in the relations of God and Man', the title of one of his books (1911, corrected ed. 1915), increased as he concentrated less on problems of 'natural and comparative religion' and more on the problems of 'philosophy and the Christian religion', the titles of his inaugural lectures as Wilde lecturer (1912) and Oriel professor (1920). Significant later books are *Religious Thought in the Oxford Movement* (1928), *Pascal's Philosophy of Religion* (1929), *Religion and the Thought of To-day* (the Riddell lectures, 1929), *A Study of Religious Thought in England from 1850* (1933, being the Olaus Petri lectures delivered in Uppsala in 1932). Webb's practical expression of these interests was shown between 1924 and

1938 when he was an active member of the Archbishops' Commission on Doctrine in the Church of England. His critical power in discussion was freed from any trace of offence by his modesty and exquisite courtesy. These traits in him were revealed very happily when in 1930–31 he delivered at Calcutta the Stephanos Nirmalendu Ghosh lectures on *The Contribution of Christianity to Ethics* (published 1932, and later, in Cairo, in an Arabic translation). Webb's interests seemed to know no limits, and he naturally formed many friendships, whose range may be seen in his memorial notices of Arthur Balfour, the Abbé Bremond, W. G. de Burgh, Charles Gore, Friedrich von Hügel, Henry Miers, C. F. Nolloth, R. L. Poole, Hastings Rashdall, and William Temple.

In 1927 Webb was elected F.B.A. and he proceeded to his Oxford D.Litt. in 1930. He was honorary LL.D. of St. Andrews (1921), D.Theol. of Uppsala (1932), and D.D. of Glasgow (1937). From about 1880 until his death he kept a diary now deposited in the Bodleian Library. An unpublished autobiographical sketch, in the possession of his executor, was used by Sir David Ross in his British Academy memoir.

A portrait of Webb painted in 1929 by Delmar Harmood Banner was presented after his death to Oriel College and hangs in the Provost's Lodging. A sepia drawing by Sir William Rothenstein, dated 1933, is at Magdalen College.

[Webb's article in *Contemporary British Philosophy*, *Personal Statements* (second series), 1925; *Religious Experience*, with a foreword by L. W. Grensted, printed with a bibliography of Webb's published writings, and presented to him in 1945 (*supra*); Sir David Ross in *Proceedings* of the British Academy, vol. xli, 1955; private information; personal knowledge.]

F. M. Powicke.

WEBB-JOHNSON, ALFRED EDWARD, Baron Webb-Johnson (1880–1958), surgeon, was born at Stoke-on-Trent 4 September 1880, the second son and third child in the family of eight of Samuel Johnson, medical officer of health for the town, by his wife, Julia Ann, daughter of James Webb, army agent. His esteem for his mother prompted him to add her surname to his own in 1915.

He was educated at Newcastle under Lyme High School and the Owens College, Manchester, where he graduated M.B., Ch.B. with honours in 1903, and won the Dumville surgical prize and the Tom Jones scholarship in surgery; he devoted this time to a study of ligature materials and developed a method of sterilization of catgut. He was appointed demonstrator of operative surgery in the university and became surgical registrar at the Manchester Royal Infirmary and assistant medical officer at the Children's Hospital. His surgical training in Manchester was greatly influenced by (Sir) William Thorburn. Gaining his F.R.C.S. in 1906 Johnson went to London in 1908 and successfully applied for the post of resident medical officer at the Middlesex Hospital in succession to (Sir) Gordon Gordon-Taylor [q.v.]. Only three years later he was elected to the honorary staff of the hospital as assistant surgeon. He also served as clinical assistant to St. Peter's Hospital where he developed his lifelong interest in urological surgery. He visited urological clinics in Berlin, Vienna, and Berne and was a pioneer of pyelography in Great Britain.

When war broke out in 1914 Johnson was called up for service in the Royal Army Medical Corps; became colonel A.M.S. and consulting surgeon to the expeditionary force; and at one time commanded the 14th General Hospital, Wimereux. He was appointed to the D.S.O. (1916), thrice mentioned in dispatches, and appointed C.B.E. (1919). His interest in army affairs continued throughout his life: he became consultant surgeon to the Queen Alexandra Military Hospital and to the Royal Hospital, Chelsea, and was chairman of the Army Medical Advisory Board (1946–57).

In 1919 Webb-Johnson was made dean of the Middlesex Hospital medical school and at once took steps to bring it up to university standards. He succeeded in enlisting the help of wealthy benefactors so that from 1920 there were university chairs of physics, chemistry, anatomy, physiology, pathology, and experimental pathology, all adequately endowed, shortly to be followed by a chair of biochemistry. At the same time the existing departments were enlarged or rehoused. The changes made in clinical teaching were influenced by a tour of North America in 1923. What he found worthy, Webb-Johnson imitated at Middlesex, but he considered there was too much laboratory work in the American system and too little clinical experience at the bedside. Consequently, rather than clinical professorships, the system of registrars was adopted at Middlesex. He saw the advantages of having properly developed special departments in a general hospital and he himself started the urological clinic at Middlesex.

He ended his term of office as dean in 1925, the year in which serious defects were discovered in the foundations of the old hospital. He became chairman of the plans committee and the chief moving spirit in the rebuilding. With the slogan 'The Middlesex Hospital is falling down' he was instrumental in raising a very large part of the million and a quarter pounds needed. On the completion of the building in 1935 the board took the unprecedented step of naming his own ward after him whilst he was still on the active staff. In 1946 he retired and was appointed consulting surgeon and vice-president.

From 1936 to 1953 Webb-Johnson was surgeon to Queen Mary who esteemed him highly. He was knighted in 1936; appointed K.C.V.O. (1942) and G.C.V.O. (1954); and created a baronet in 1945 and a baron in 1948.

Concurrently with his hospital activities, the affairs of the Royal College of Surgeons of England occupied an increasing amount of his time. He was a member of the court of examiners (1926–36) and of the council (1932–50). In 1940, as vice-president, he gave the Bradshaw lecture on 'Pride and Prejudice in the Treatment of Cancer'. In 1941 he was elected president, a position which he held for a record period of eight years and which he made a full-time job, rarely missing a day at the College. Only a few weeks before his election the College had been severely damaged in an air raid. Temporary repairs were quickly made so that essential work could continue. In planning the rebuilding he seized the opportunity to reorganize and expand the College, in a manner previously unconceived, as a centre of postgraduate education and research and a live headquarters of surgery in England and the Commonwealth. The primary examination for the fellowship was reorganized and reciprocity with other Colleges established. Tenure of office of members of the council and court was limited. The specialist associations were encouraged by providing them with a secretariat which would keep them within the orbit of general surgery; representatives of the major surgical specialities and of general practice were co-opted to serve on the council. A faculty of dental surgery was formed in 1947 and of anaesthetists in 1948; special examinations for the fellowship in ophthalmology and in otolaryngology were instituted in 1947; teaching in the basic sciences was assured by the appointment of professors in physiology, pathology, and anatomy for which he again succeeded in obtaining endowments from wealthy donors. The building of the Nuffield College of Surgical Sciences provided residential accommodation for the increasing number of postgraduate students coming from overseas; it enabled him to realize his dream of an 'All Souls of surgery'. Overseas ties were strengthened by the endowment in 1946 of the Sims Commonwealth travelling professorships and by the foundation in 1947 of the College's own monthly *Annals*, which obtained a world-wide circulation.

In 1939 Webb-Johnson visited Egypt to inspect medical schools and went on to Australia where he delivered the Syme oration to the Royal Australasian College of Surgeons on 'Surgery in England in the Making'. He received the honorary fellowship of the College, as also of those of America, Edinburgh, Glasgow, Ireland, and Canada, and of the faculties of dental surgery and anaesthetists in England. In 1949 an annual Webb-Johnson lecture was endowed by the faculty of dental surgery. He was made an honorary LL.D. of Liverpool and of Toronto; was awarded the honorary medal of the Royal College of Surgeons in 1950, and in 1956 was one of the first members of its newly formed court of patrons. After leaving the council of the College he was elected a trustee of the Hunterian Collection and took an active interest in the rebuilding of the museum up to the time of his death.

Throughout this period he found time to devote to other interests. He was president of the Royal Medical Benevolent Fund and in 1951 president of Epsom College for which he organized a successful appeal. He played a prominent part in the activities of the Order of St. John, becoming hospitaller (1946–54) and receiving the grand cross of the order in 1955. After the destruction of the Ophthalmic Hospital in Jerusalem in 1948 he planned a new hospital with a research centre for the prevention of eye diseases.

No truly great man can escape criticism; at the birth of the National Health Service Webb-Johnson adopted the role of mediator between the minister of health and the British Medical Association when tempers ran high. He was criticized for accepting a barony at this time but few of his critics knew that he had already twice declined that honour. His intervention in debate on a medical subject in the House of Lords was always to the point.

In 1950–52 Webb-Johnson was president of the Royal Society of Medicine and he was the inevitable chairman of the building committee when funds were forthcoming from the Wellcome trustees for an enlargement of the society's house which was completed in 1953.

His achievements as an administrator and organizer have tended to divert attention from the fact that Webb-Johnson was first and foremost a surgeon. His judgement was sound and his technique faultless; his opinion was frequently sought by his colleagues and he excelled in the management of a difficult case. His ready wit and unfailing good humour and sympathy made him loved by his patients. His lectures and ward rounds were always popular and he taught the students the essentials of surgery. His own special subject was urology and he liked to remember that he was born in 1880, the year when Henry Morris was the first to remove a stone from an otherwise healthy kidney. He was a most generous chief and gave his assistants ample opportunities to practise what he had taught them. Postgraduate surgical education in London owes much to his vision and foresight. He was a man of resolution, the whole pattern of whose life showed a consistent determination and ability to see what was wanted and get it done. The experience of one phase led naturally to the next so that whilst his career was one of constant preparation it was also one of constant achievement.

Personally he was a man of great charm, a generous host, and an entertaining after-dinner speaker. He was slow to show anger, but ready to give a reprimand whenever and wherever it was needed. His rebuke might be couched in terms of apparent jest but it was still to be taken seriously. He was always immaculate in dress and his cartoon in the hospital journal bore the title of 'The Groomy Dean'. A patron of the arts, he was at one time a director of the Savoy Theatre and was a frequent visitor to Covent Garden. His knowedge of silver was great and he was the recognized authority on the silver treasures of the College. He was a lover of Kipling and like his mentor Sir John Bland-Sutton [q.v.] had a deep knowledge of the Bible and of Shakespeare. His memory was good and he rarely used notes for a speech or a lecture. Although one of his ambitions, the establishment of an academy of medicine on the south side of Lincoln's Inn Fields, was never realized, he left behind many material reminders of his achievements when he died in London 28 May 1958.

He married in 1911 Cecilia Flora (died 1968), daughter of Douglas Gordon MacRae, the founder of the *Financial Times*. To commemorate her father and her husband she made the MacRae–Webb-Johnson gift in 1952 to the Hunterian trustees to maintain and improve the museum. There were no children and the peerage became extinct.

A portrait by Francis Hodge (1943) is in the Royal College of Surgeons; one by T. C. Dugdale (*c.* 1952) at the Royal Society of Medicine; another by Hodge (*c.* 1954) at the Middlesex Hospital, where a memorial window by Miss Howson was dedicated in the chapel in 1964.

[H. Campbell Thomson, *The Story of the Middlesex Hospital Medical School, 1835–1935*, 1935; Sir Zachary Cope, *The History of the Royal College of Surgeons of England*, 1959; Maurice Davidson, *The Royal Society of Medicine*, 1955; *The Times*, 29 May 1958; *Lancet* and *British Medical Journal*, 7 June 1958; private information; personal knowledge.]   ERIC RICHES.

WEDGWOOD, SIR RALPH LEWIS, first baronet (1874–1956), railway administrator, was born at Barlaston, north Staffordshire, 2 March 1874, the third surviving son of Clement Francis Wedgwood, master potter, and his wife, Emily Catherine, daughter of James Meadows Rendel [q.v.]. J.C., later first Baron, Wedgwood [q.v.] was a brother. The children grew up in home surroundings noted for the benevolent yet youthful attitude of their father, for the idyllic relationship which existed between their parents, and for the candour and liberal outlook which they inspired, alien to so many contemporary Victorian households. Wedgwood was educated at Clifton, where he was head of the school, and at Trinity College, Cambridge, where he obtained first classes in both parts of the moral sciences tripos (1895–6).

At the age of twenty-two Wedgwood entered the service of the North Eastern Railway, becoming district superintendent at Middlesbrough in 1902 and secretary of the company two years later. Shortly afterwards, at his own request, he returned to the traffic department; rapid promotion followed. He became northern divisional goods manager at Newcastle in 1905, assistant goods manager at York in 1911, and chief goods manager soon afterwards. He added the passenger department to his responsibilities in 1914. On the outbreak of war Wedgwood at once volunteered for service abroad and, with the rank of major, Royal Engineers, acted as deputy assistant director of railway transport in France. In July 1915 he was transferred to the Ministry of Munitions with the temporary rank of lieutenant-colonel. In October 1916 he was made director of docks in France with the temporary rank of brigadier-general. He was appointed C.M.G. in 1917, C.B. in 1918, received a number of foreign decorations, and was five times mentioned in dispatches.

Returning to the North Eastern as chief goods and passenger manager in June 1919 he added to this dual office, two months later, that of deputy general manager. At the beginning of 1922 he succeeded Sir A. Kaye Butterworth as general manager of the company. The destinies of more than 120 British railways were then in the melting-pot, with four big railway groups in process of formation. The second largest, the London and North Eastern, was to contain the North Eastern as its financially strongest component. When the L.N.E.R. began to operate on 1 January 1923 it was natural that Wedgwood should become chief general manager of a system which employed more than 220,000 staff, possessed 6,590 route miles of line, and was the largest dock-owning railway company in the world.

Sustained by a shrewd board and supported by a versatile band of senior aides, Wedgwood took his charge through the difficulties of trade depression, fluctuating traffics, ever-increasing road competition, and developing air services for sixteen eventful years. By the time he was approaching the calmer waters of retirement the L.N.E.R. was renowned for the thoroughness of its staff training and educational schemes, for its bold incursions into new signalling and marshalling-yard techniques and for the all-round excellence of its express passenger services. The latter included the longest non-stop and some of the fastest runs in the world, and Britain's first streamlined trains. Wedgwood, an imaginative and adventurous administrator, and Sir H. Nigel Gresley, his brilliant locomotive, carriage, and wagon designer, both of them much-travelled men, had kept the L.N.E.R. in the forefront of railway progress. Despite these preoccupations Wedgwood often acted as spokesman for the four railway groups and served outside bodies such as the Weir main line electrification committee (1930–31), the Central Electricity Board (1931–46), and the Chinese Government Purchasing Commission (1932–51). He was chairman of the Indian railways committee of inquiry in 1936–7.

In March 1939 Wedgwood retired, but returned in September on the outbreak of war as chairman of the railway executive committee and was thus in the thick of the intensive railway reorganization which took place in the early years of the war. He finally retired in August 1941.

'R.L.W.', as he was known in railway circles, was remembered for his tall, distinguished appearance, his brisk walk, and the infectious smile which would so often light up his intelligent countenance. Endowed with great clarity of mind, he was a recognized expert on the intricacies of rail and road freight rates. Yet with all his accomplishments he retained an innate modesty, preferred the velvet glove to the mailed fist, and never lost a childhood love for maps and the complexity of a railway timetable.

Wedgwood was knighted in 1924 and created a baronet in 1942 simultaneously with the elevation to a peerage of his brother Josiah. By mutual agreement the latter assumed 'of Barlaston' as his territorial designation and Ralph took 'of Etruria' as his, in remembrance of the original pottery works.

In 1906 he married Iris Veronica, daughter of Albert Henry Pawson, of Farnley, Leeds. They had one son, John Hamilton (born 1907), who succeeded to the baronetcy; and a daughter, Cicely Veronica, who has achieved distinction as an historian, influenced by her father's friendship with G. M. Trevelyan, and was appointed D.B.E. in 1968.

Wedgwood died at his home near Dorking 5 September 1956 and was buried at Barlaston. A bust by Arnold Machin is in the possession of the family.

[C. V. Wedgwood, *The Last of the Radicals* 1951; 'The London & North Eastern Railway 1923–38' by R. Bell in *Journal of Transport History*, May 1962; L.N.E.R. records; personal knowledge.]   GEORGE DOW.

WEEKS, RONALD MORCE, BARON WEEKS (1890–1960), industrialist and soldier, was the second son in the family of five children of Richard Llewellyn Weeks, mining engineer, and his wife, Susan Helen Walker McIntyre. He was born at Helmington Row, county Durham, 13 November 1890, and educated at Charterhouse and Caius College, Cambridge, where he obtained third class honours in part i of the natural sciences tripos in 1911 and captained the university association football team before joining Pilkington Brothers, Ltd., in 1912 as a technical trainee.

Commissioned into the Prince of Wales's Volunteers T.F. in 1913, Weeks on mobilization experienced active service from February 1915 until the end of the war. He displayed notable aptitude for the profession of arms, and in recommending him in 1917 for a regular commission as captain in the Rifle Brigade, the general commanding, Fourth Army, personally described him as a first-rate staff officer, with an exceptionally quick brain embodied in an effective, rounded personality. Attaining his brevet majority, Weeks was thrice mentioned in dispatches, awarded the M.C. (1917) with bar (1918), and the croix de guerre (1918), and was appointed to the D.S.O. (1918).

On returning to Pilkington's in 1919, Weeks's maturing capacities steadily established themselves on the basis of a far-seeing view of the wider commercial and financial implications of contemporary technical change in the glass industry. Promptly appointed in 1920 manager of the plate glass works, he was made a director in 1928 and eventually chairman of the executive directors in 1939 while still under fifty. Such advance demonstrated a catalytic contribution which Weeks's persistently persuasive energies were able to make in leading a family firm towards diversifying, modernizing, and extending its scope internationally as well as at home.

Nevertheless in 1934–8 Weeks had made time to command the 5th battalion of the South Lancashire Regiment, T.A. On the outbreak of war in 1939 he was first appointed G.S.O. 1 of the 66th division. Although amply endowed for command in the field, a combination of personal capacity and circumstances took him in fact to the top of a ladder of appointments responsible for equipping the army in war. He was first posted as brigadier general staff (staff duties) Home Forces headquarters in July 1940, concerned with the restricted field of Home Forces equipment; then in March 1941 he was given the comprehensive responsibilities of director-general of army equipment; next in June 1942 he was made deputy chief of the imperial general staff, with the rank of lieutenant-general and a seat on the Army Council, a unique position for a citizen soldier. This was a newly created post, acknowledging on the one hand the prospect that both chief and vice-chief of the imperial general staff must necessarily become more exclusively preoccupied with allied operations; and on the other, the need to concentrate at the centre responsibility for equipment and organization under an authority of outstanding capacity, percipiently qualified to appraise the ability of industry to provide what would be required. In clarity of mind, tireless industry, decisiveness, balanced approach, Weeks was strikingly equipped for the task of assembling the changing picture of a fighting army's needs, and negotiating through the Ministry of Supply the priorities for meeting them. This work completed in June 1945, Weeks spent two months as deputy military governor and chief of staff in the Control Commission in Germany before returning to civil life.

While retaining his seat on the Pilkington board, Weeks was invited to join Vickers in 1945 and made deputy chairman a year later, with the chairmanship ultimately in prospect. Attaining this office in 1949, Weeks saw his post as an essentially executive appointment for the purpose of co-ordinating in some depth the adjustments which would be called for in adapting to a fresh economic environment such a diversified industrial group embracing engineering, steel shipbuilding, aviation, and nuclear power. There again, his varied experience, personal vision, vitality, and familiarity with the working of the government machine were brought to constructive effect in successfully putting this major industrial organization on a soundly based footing.

Retiring from the chairmanship of Vickers in 1956, Weeks found his experience and energies in pressing demand, despite his indifferent health, for a wide range of activities bearing mainly on industrial affairs and development. He became treasurer of the Industrial Fund for the Development of Scientific Education in Schools which raised £3,500,000 for a purpose in which he felt close personal interest; he had been chairman (1948–56) of the National Advisory Council for Education in Industry and Commerce. He also became chairman of the Finance Corporation for Industry; vice-chairman of the King George's Jubilee Trust, a trustee of Churchill College, Cambridge, and a governor of Charterhouse. He was appointed government director of British Petroleum, Ltd., and served on the boards of various companies including Associated Electrical Industries, Royal Exchange Assurance, and the Hudson's Bay Company.

The contribution which Weeks made in three inter-related environments: industry, the army, and public service, reflected the personal qualities he was able to bring to it. In particular, he was prompt to recognize the revolutionary character of the evolving economic background. His mind was inquisitive, questioning of established practice, attuned to change. Hence his preoccupation with technical education, in school and industry. Supporting this vision were the characteristic attributes of managerial ability. Purposively energetic, Weeks was gifted with an acute capacity for penetrating through detail towards isolating the objective, and then delegating responsibility. Sociable, of handsome presence, and resolute personality, he identified himself with his assignments and expected his associates to be equally unsparing. Fairminded, tempering criticism with kindness, he remained accessible at all levels, with a retentive interest in people's personal affairs from shop floor to board-room. Informing these qualities was a catholic and imaginative acquaintance with the world at large and how it could be made to function.

Weeks was appointed C.B.E. in 1939 and K.C.B. in 1943, and made commander of the U.S. Legion of Merit. He was created a baron in 1956. He was elected honorary fellow of Caius College (1945); given honorary doctorates by the universities of Liverpool (1946), Sheffield (1951), and Leeds (1957); and accorded honorary recognition by the Colleges of Technology of Manchester and Birmingham.

Weeks died in London 19 August 1960, when the peerage became extinct. He married first, in 1922, Evelyn Elsie (died 1932), daughter of Henry Haynes, of Clifton, Nottinghamshire. The marriage was dissolved and in 1931 he married Cynthia Mary Cumming, daughter of John Wood Irvine, stockbroker, of Liverpool, by whom he had two daughters. His portrait by Sir Gerald Kelly is in the possession of the family.

[Private information.]   H. O. HOOPER.

WEIR, ANDREW, first BARON INVERFORTH (1865–1955), shipowner, was born at Kirkcaldy, Fifeshire, 24 April 1865, the eldest son of William Weir and his wife, Janet, daughter of Thomas Laing of the same place. Both his father and his maternal grandfather were cork merchants, and none of his immediate ancestors was connected with shipping.

After attending the high school at Kirkcaldy, Weir at an early age entered the Commercial Bank of Scotland, but this routine work gave little scope for his ambitions and interests and after a few years he forsook his cashier's desk and moved to Glasgow, where he served for a short time in a shipping office. On 5 May 1885, shortly after his twentieth birthday, he began his life as a merchant shipowner, buying a sailing ship, the barque *Willowbank*, which he employed in the coasting trade, renting a small room in Hope Street, Glasgow, as an office. His inborn optimism and opportunism were the seed from which grew the great shipping business of Andrew Weir & Co., which became managing owners of the Bank Line, Invertanker, Inver Transport and Trading Company, and several other shipping companies. The next year Weir began building sailing ships of modern design and within a few years had built up a fleet of fifty-two, the largest sailing ship fleet under one owner flying the red ensign.

In 1896, moving to London, Weir turned from sail to steam. At a later period he recognized the advantages of the marine internal combustion engine and converted the majority of his ships to diesel power. In all these developments he showed an innate skill and efficiency in management and ensured that the foundations of his company were on sound business lines.

During the war, when Lloyd George formed his Government in 1916, Weir was mentioned as a possible minister of shipping, but this appointment went to Sir J. P. (later Lord) Maclay [q.v.]

and Weir directed his talents into other wartime channels. In March 1917 Lord Derby [q.v.], then secretary of state for war, asked Weir to report on the commercial organization of the supply branches of the army. Weir recommended the appointment of a surveyor-general of supply, with a seat on the Army Council, to take over from the various War Office departments the work of supplying the army with all its stores and equipment other than munitions. His recommendations were accepted and he himself appointed to the post. At first that caused some resentment and opposition among certain senior civil servants, but his directness and sincerity of purpose, his natural friendly manner and approachability soon won their co-operation. Shortly after his appointment he made a tour of the battlefields on the Continent, accompanied by Sir John Cowans [q.v.] and (Sir) Crofton Atkins. As a consequence he drew up far-reaching schemes, which resulted in salvage of materials in the various war zones and the elimination of tremendous wastage.

His success in this field led to his appointment in January 1919 as minister of munitions, with the gigantic task of liquidating the enormous commitments of the war, entailing the examination of some hundreds of thousands of accounts and contracts and their subsequent disposal. He remained in this office until March 1921, when, until May, he took over the chairmanship of the Disposals and Liquidation Commission, which was responsible for selling the vast quantities of army stores throughout the various theatres of war and in the British Isles. Again his genius for organization and great business acumen converted what might have been worthless goods or liabilities into considerable assets. It was not without reason that he was termed 'the man who saved Britain millions'.

For his services in the war he was in 1919 sworn of the Privy Council, created a baron, and received the American D.S.M.

On returning to the world of commerce and business, Lord Inverforth, as he now was, devoted his energies particularly to communications. He interested himself in the Marconi group of companies, becoming president of the Radio Communication Company, the Marconi International Marine Communication Company, and Cable and Wireless (Holding). In other spheres he was chairman of the Anglo-

Burma Rice Company and of the Wilmer Grain Company, and was also on the board of Lloyds Bank. In 1945 he was elected president of all the associated enterprises of the communications group of companies.

Inverforth was also founder and first chairman of the United Baltic Corporation, which came into existence in 1919 largely through King George V's desire, after the war, that British shipping and trading should replace that of Germany in the Baltic and with Denmark. To this end the King consulted Inverforth, bringing also into the consultation H. N. Anderson, founder and chairman of the East Asiatic Company of Denmark. The corporation was unique in that exactly 50 per cent of its shares were held by British and 50 per cent by Danish shareholders, the chairman having the casting vote. It is a tribute to the good relations which, since its formation, have existed between the directors of the two countries, and also to the sagacious chairmanship of Inverforth and of his successor in the chair, the second Lord Inverforth, that a casting vote has never yet been necessary. In recognition of this work Inverforth received in 1937 the grand cross of the Order of Dannebrog of Denmark and in the following year the grand cross of the Grand Duke Gedinimas of Lithuania.

Inverforth continued his active life, attending his office in Bury Street four days a week, into his ninety-first year. On his ninetieth birthday he received many tributes of affection from his friends and staff. He died at his home in Hampstead 17 September 1955.

Because of his quiet modesty and dislike of publicity and limelight, Inverforth's great services to his country were not widely known. But those who knew him closely instinctively recognized his high qualities. He possessed great energy and enthusiasm and also that almost essential quality of leadership: the ability to select suitable subordinates and leave them to carry on without interference. His integrity, great driving force, and brilliant organizing ability made him a man of power and influence in the commercial world. His friends and employees, terms frequently synonymous, knew his unobtrusive generosity and kindness. He was particularly approachable: even the most junior employee, who had some suggestion towards the improvement or well-being of the firm, would be sure of a patient and appreciative hearing and would carry away the remembrance of a kindly twinkle in Inverforth's eye and a good-humoured quiet voice. In many ways he was a model employer, taking interest in the welfare of his staff and their families both during and after their service with him. For many years, until he was eighty, he was treasurer of the Royal Merchant Navy School and, even after he had handed over this office to his friend, Sir Leighton Seager (later Lord Leighton of St. Mellons), he continued to take a deep interest in the children.

Inverforth married in 1889 Tomania Anne, younger daughter of Thomas Kay Dowie, coach smith, of Kirkcaldy. The celebration of their golden wedding in 1939 was a particularly happy occasion and Lady Inverforth's death in 1941 was keenly felt by her husband. They had one son and five daughters. The son, Andrew Alexander Morton (born 1897), besides succeeding his father in the title and as chairman of the United Baltic Corporation, did so also as chairman of Andrew Weir & Co.

Four portraits by Frank O. Salisbury and one by R. G. Eves are in the possession of the family or of the family firms; a portrait by Frank O. Salisbury is in Glasgow City Art Gallery.

[*The Times*, 19 and 24 September 1955; *Manchester Guardian*, 19 September 1955; *Transactions* of the Institute of Marine Engineers, November 1955; *The Navy*, April 1965; private information.]

G. K. S. HAMILTON-EDWARDS.

WEIR, SIR CECIL McALPINE (1890–1960), industrialist and public servant, was born at Bridge of Weir, Renfrewshire, 5 July 1890, the youngest of four sons of Alexander Cunningham Weir and his wife, Isabella McLeish. He was educated at Morrison's Academy, Crieff, and in Switzerland and Germany. On his return, he spent two years in business training before joining the family firm, Schrader, Mitchell, and Weir, leather and hide merchants in Glasgow, of which he was a partner from 1910 until 1956. On his frequent business visits to the Continent his fluency in French and German was invaluable.

In the war of 1914–18 Weir served in the Cameronians, was wounded, and awarded the M.C. Settling afterwards in Helensburgh, he took a keen interest in church work, the Liberal Party, and other local activities, including tennis and golf, and was chairman of the company which administered St. Bride's School.

He became increasingly interested in public affairs and it was he who formulated the idea of holding an Empire Exhibition in Glasgow, for which he obtained wide support. He was chairman of the administrative committee and it was largely through his remarkable leadership that the exhibition of 1938 achieved a large measure of success despite the menacing international situation. He was appointed K.B.E. in 1938; was president of the Glasgow Chamber of Commerce in 1939–40; and a director of the Union Bank of Scotland from 1939 until 1947.

From August 1939 until March 1940 Weir was civil defence commissioner for the western district of Scotland and responsible for the operation of the civil defence organization serving sixty per cent of the population of Scotland. Early in 1940, however, he was called to London by Sir Andrew Duncan [q.v.] to become an executive member of the industrial and export council of the Board of Trade, on which he remained until 1946. In 1941–2 he was controller-general of factory and storage premises; and in 1942–6 director-general of equipment and stores, Ministry of Supply. In 1946 he became economic adviser, Control Commission for Germany, and on his return to the United Kingdom in 1949, full-time chairman of the Dollar Exports Board until 1951. In 1952 he became head of the United Kingdom delegation to the High Authority of the European Coal and Steel Community and served in that capacity for three years. He was appointed K.C.M.G. in 1952. In his latter years he was executive chairman of International Computers and Tabulators and a part-time member of the British Transport Commission.

Weir's capacity for organization was accompanied by great personal charm. He had a remarkable memory, seldom forgetting a face or a name, a good sense of humour, and a gift for getting the best out of those associated with him in any project.

In 1915 Weir married Jenny Paton, daughter of William Paton Maclay and a niece of the first Lord Maclay [q.v.]; her death in an air crash in Italy in 1958 was a tragic loss. They had a son and a daughter. Weir died in London 30 October 1960.

[Sir Cecil Weir, *Civilian Assignment*, 1953; personal knowledge.]   BILSLAND.

WEIR, WILLIAM DOUGLAS, first VISCOUNT WEIR (1877–1959), industrialist and public servant, descended from Robert Burns [q.v.] through his illegitimate daughter Elizabeth Paton, was born in Glasgow 12 May 1877, the eldest of three children of James Weir, engineer, and his wife, Mary, daughter of William Douglas, of Kilmarnock. He left Glasgow High School at sixteen and joined his father's firm G. & J. Weir, becoming managing director in 1902 and chairman by 1912. In July 1915 he became director of munitions for Scotland. His main task was to thrust dilution (chiefly the employment of women) into Clydeside engineering against every instinct of the industry. In the spring of 1916 commissioners appointed at Weir's suggestion broke a strike and deported the men's leaders; thereafter there was no more serious trouble. Restrictive practices had to go if the war was to be won; Weir was one of those chiefly responsible for getting rid of them. His impatience with the skilled craftsman's traditional outlook made him unpopular with the Left; it did not later prevent Labour ministers from seeking his advice.

In February 1917 Weir went to the Ministry of Munitions as controller of aeronautical supplies and member of the Air Board and in December he became director-general of aircraft production. He rationalized the production of airframes and engines in the teeth of the rivalry between the War Office and the Admiralty, each of which had its own system of aircraft supply. In April 1918, with strong backing from (Sir) Winston Churchill, Weir succeeded Lord Rothermere [q.v.] as air minister. He found Sir Hugh (later Viscount) Trenchard [q.v.] unemployed and distrustful of the recent decision to create a third fighting Service. By a direct exercise of authority Weir persuaded him unwillingly to take command of the independent air force then getting ready to bomb Germany, the post from which Trenchard went on to become the acknowledged father of the Royal Air Force. Weir's abrupt dismissal of the commandant (Miss Violet Douglas-Pennant) of the Women's Royal Air Force, although justifiable, was widely, loudly, and influentially held to be unjustified. Weir (with the support of Churchill) successfully asserted the right of a minister in wartime to dismiss without question any official whom he considered incapable.

Weir had no taste for ministerial office and resigned as soon as the war was over. He was chairman of the advisory committee on civil aviation in 1919 and a succession of other committees, and he remained one of a group of men, many Scots, mostly in business, whose advice was continually sought and sometimes acted on by Governments. He influenced many aspects of policy but between 1919 and 1934 his main achievements were three: first to help to fight off the assault by Admiral Beatty [q.v.] on the Royal Air Force in 1923; secondly, to preside over the committee which, reporting in 1925, devised the main principles of the national 'grid' for distributing electricity; thirdly, to bring about the Cunard–White Star merger (1934). Privately he attached great importance to his attempts to introduce factory-made houses (1923–7) which again brought him into conflict with traditionalists, and to the group of companies which he founded in the mid-twenties for processing sugar beet.

After 1933 Weir was drawn increasingly into preparing for war. With Sir Arthur Balfour (later Lord Riverdale) and Sir James Lithgow [qq.v.] he put forward the idea of 'shadow factories' which was fundamental to the organization of British war production. As a member of the prime minister's defence policy and requirements committee (1935–7) he influenced the determination of the widest questions of defence policy, always in the direction of the supremacy of air power expressed chiefly in the form of strategic bombing. At the Air Ministry (1935–8) as adviser to the air minister, Lord Swinton, he gave practical effect to his ideas by bringing officials, serving officers, business men, and scientists into partnership to lay the foundations of the wartime Royal Air Force, with a heavy emphasis on bombers. In 1937 he was defeated in an attempt to stop the Admiralty's take-over bid for the Fleet Air Arm, and then his influence began to decline, especially after Chamberlain replaced Baldwin as prime minister in May 1937. In May 1938, when Swinton was dismissed, Weir left the Air Ministry in sympathy, and the historically important part of his career, covering nearly twenty-five years, was over.

In 1939 Weir became director-general of explosives at the Ministry of Supply and deputy chairman of the Supply Council, but his old happy relationship with Churchill had perhaps been spoilt by his political associations just before the war. He left when Lord Beaverbrook became minister in June 1941, was chairman of the Tank Board in 1942, but took no

further significant part in the organization of supplies for war. He devoted himself largely to his own business and to his directorships of I.C.I., Shell, and especially International Nickel of Canada, all of which marked his continuing place at the centre of British industry. In 1953 he gave up the chair of Weirs and all his directorships except International Nickel, and retired generally from affairs. He died at his home at Giffnock, Renfrewshire, 2 July 1959.

Small in build, very sparing of words, 'Willy Weir' could nevertheless carry a point against the giants of his time: Trenchard, Beatty, Churchill among them. He did not thereby as a rule make enemies, although his speech might be blunt enough, and his gift for personal relationships was shown by the fact that he could be a close friend of Trenchard whilst Sir Frederick Sykes [q.v.], Trenchard's unsuccessful rival, could deplore Weir's passing from the Air Ministry after the first war as a national misfortune. The independent existence of the Royal Air Force in 1939 was in no small degree due to Weir's force of character many years before, and the excellence of British war production owed perhaps as much to Weir's technical knowledge, skill in negotiation, and grasp of complicated problems as it did to Beaverbrook's rumbustiousness.

Weir was knighted in 1917, sworn of the Privy Council in 1918, created a baron in the same year, advanced to viscount in 1938, and appointed G.C.B. in 1934. He received an honorary LL.D. from Glasgow in 1919.

In 1904 Weir married Alice Blanche (died 1959), daughter of John MacConnachie, solicitor, of Glasgow; they had a daughter and two sons, the elder of whom, James Kenneth (born 1905), succeeded his father.

A portrait by Dame Laura Knight is in the possession of the family; another by T. C. Dugdale is in the board-room at Holm Foundry, Cathcart, Glasgow; a third by Cuthbert Orde is at the premises of the Royal Aeronautical Society, London.

[Christopher Addison, *Politics from Within*, vol. ii, 1924; Sir Frederick Sykes, *From Many Angles*, 1942; Andrew Boyle, *Trenchard*, 1962; Robin Higham, *Britain's Imperial Air Routes*, 1960; N. Potter and J. Frost, *The Mary*, 1961; Lord Swinton, *I Remember*, 1948; Lord Swinton in collaboration with J. D. Margach, *Sixty Years of Power*, 1966; William Hornby, (Official History) *Factories and Plant*, 1958; J. D. Scott and R. Hughes,

Weir, W. D.   D.N.B. 1951–1960

(Official History) *The Administration of War Production*, 1955; W. J. Reader, *Architect of Air Power: the Life of the first Viscount Weir of Eastwood*, 1968; private information.]

W. J. READER.

WEIZMANN, CHAIM (1874–1952), Zionist leader and first president of the State of Israel, was born at Motol, near Pinsk (province of Grodno) in the Jewish Pale of Settlement in Russia, most probably on 27 November 1874, although certain early documents give the date as 12 November 1873. He was the third child of Ezer Weizmann, a struggling timber merchant, by his wife, Rachel Leah, daughter of Michael Tzchmerinsky, of Motol. After receiving an elementary education on traditional Jewish lines, Weizmann was sent to the high school in Pinsk, where one of his teachers encouraged him to specialize in chemistry. Jews were not welcome at Russian universities and accordingly he turned westwards and, with such help as his father could afford, supplemented by some meagre earnings from teaching, he pursued his scientific studies, with the emphasis on chemistry, at the Darmstadt and Charlottenburg polytechnics and, finally, at the Swiss university of Freiburg where, in 1899, he gained his doctorate *summa cum laude*. Soon afterwards he embarked on an academic career as a *Privatdozent* in chemistry attached to the university of Geneva.

In 1904, now thirty years of age, he decided that the time had come for him to seek larger scope for his talents. His choice fell upon England where, with a useful introduction from his Geneva professor to W. H. Perkin [q.v.], he soon found an opening at Manchester University, which gave him facilities for research, employed him, despite his halting English, as a lecturer, and in 1913 promoted him to a readership in biochemistry. Meanwhile he had become a British subject in 1910, but jealously preserving his identity as an unhyphenated Jew he never became, or wished to become, a member of the assimilated Anglo-Jewish community. Nevertheless he spoke, in his autobiography, of the profound admiration for England which influenced him in deciding where to make a fresh start, and a significant part of the background both to his successes and to his defeats as a Zionist leader lay in the strength of his attachment to the country which was for some forty years his home.

During his student years Weizmann,

like many others of the younger members of the Russian Jewish intelligentsia, had been attracted by the 'Back to Palestine' movement known by the Hebrew name of *Hibbath Zion* ('Love of Zion'). The response, in many parts of the Jewish world, to the lead given by Theodor Herzl in his tract 'The Jewish State' resulted in the setting up, in 1897, of the Zionist Organization and the supersession of the tentative gropings of *Hibbath Zion* by a more precise and more ambitious programme—the establishment in Palestine, under international guarantees, of a home for the Jewish people. Weizmann from the start identified himself wholeheartedly with the Zionist Movement and its objective, although, as time went on, he began to be openly critical of what he regarded as an excessive preoccupation with purely political activities, urging that more attention should be paid to stimulating the national consciousness of the Jewish masses. By the outbreak of war in 1914 he had become a prominent, though not yet a commanding, figure in the Zionist Organization, generally recognized as a coming man, but not holding any position entitling him to speak for the Movement as a whole in a representative capacity. This did not deter him from taking the initiative in grasping the opportunity which, as he at once perceived, was presented to the Zionists by the entry of Turkey into the war on the side of the Central Powers. It was clear that an allied victory would bring with it the dismemberment of the Turkish Asiatic empire, of which Palestine formed part. To Weizmann it seemed self-evident that a determined effort ought to be made to convince the British Government that, by sponsoring Zionist aspirations, Great Britain would not only be helping to give the Jews their rightful place in a new world order but would be fortifying her own political and strategic position in a region whose future could not be a matter of indifference to her.

Starting almost single-handed but inspired by his sense of mission, Weizmann had within a few weeks after the outbreak of war taken the first steps on the road which was to lead to the Balfour Declaration. By sheer force of personality, coupled with unwearying persistence, a sure instinct for the right approach, and an intuitive grasp of the significance of any new turn in the political situation, the biochemist from Manchester, endowed, as it turned out, with diplomatic gifts of the

1038

first order, found his way to the highest levels of public life, where he gradually built up an impressive body of support for his ideas about British relations with the Zionists. In this he was powerfully aided by Herbert (later Viscount) Samuel, whom he found, when introduced to him towards the end of 1914, to have been thinking independently about the future of Palestine on much the same lines as himself, and who, from within the Cabinet, and later from outside, but with all the weight of an ex-cabinet minister, pressed upon the Government the case for a pro-Zionist policy. Among other leading figures in public life whose active interest was engaged were Balfour and Lloyd George. Remembering how greatly he had been impressed by Weizmann's exposition of the Zionist case at an interview in Manchester during the general election of 1906, Balfour received him again towards the end of 1914, and showed himself warmly sympathetic. So did Lloyd George, to whom Weizmann got access early in the war through C. P. Scott [q.v.] of the *Manchester Guardian*. Soon afterwards he was brought closer to Lloyd George, then minister of munitions, by his successful application of his chemical researches in the field of fermentation to the overcoming of a serious shortage of acetone, a chemical product of vital importance in the manufacture of explosives required for the navy. Besides his work for the Ministry of Munitions, Weizmann was in the autumn of 1915 given an Admiralty appointment as adviser on acetone supplies, and by the end of that year, having been released from his university duties, he had left Manchester and established himself in London.

The tide began to flow more strongly in favour of the Zionists when at the end of 1916 Lloyd George became prime minister with Balfour as foreign secretary. In 1917 there were practical reasons for believing that British interests would be served by a public declaration of sympathy with Zionist aspirations. It was these considerations which turned the scale when the War Cabinet finally decided to authorize Balfour's assurance, in his letter to Lord Rothschild [q.v.] of 2 November 1917, that, subject to certain provisos, the Government would use their best endeavours to facilitate the establishment in Palestine of a national home for the Jewish people.

In 1918 Weizmann headed a Zionist Commission sent to Palestine, under the auspices of the British Government, to explore the ground. In February 1919 he took a leading part in the presentation of the case for a Jewish national home in Palestine when a Zionist delegation was given a hearing by the Council of Ten at the Paris peace conference. In the events which had by this time culminated in a firm understanding between Great Britain and the Zionists, Weizmann, having started with no formal credentials, had emerged with an unchallengeable ascendancy in the Movement, as was recognized by his election in 1920 as president of the World Zionist Organization.

Great Britain having accepted a mandate for Palestine, and the military regime having been replaced by a civil administration under Samuel, the time had now arrived for the implementation of the British assurances. But the road forward was found to be strewn with pitfalls, and Weizmann soon began to run into difficulties. Mounting signs of Arab unrest, growing dissatisfaction with what the Jews regarded as the unhelpful or even unfriendly attitude of some of the members of the British administration, the publication, in 1922, of a statement of British policy in Palestine interpreted by many Zionists as a serious whittling down of the Declaration of 1917—all this created an awkward dilemma for Weizmann who could not close his eyes to the Jewish grievances but, while protesting to the British authorities, was compelled to justify in the eyes of his disappointed followers his conviction that Zionist interests would best be served by patience, moderation, and restraint.

In 1929 Weizmann realized a long-cherished dream by his success in creating a Jewish Agency for Palestine with a governing body including, in addition to leading Zionists, Jews of high standing and reputation not identified with the Zionist Movement but now prepared to co-operate in the building up of the Jewish National Home. This was an impressive achievement, but it was almost immediately followed by anti-Jewish demonstrations, accompanied by acts of violence, on the part of the Palestine Arabs, and Weizmann found himself in a difficult position when, in 1930, the British Government published a fresh statement of policy, making, as the Zionists saw it, a long retreat even from the statement of 1922. With the support of powerful elements in British public life, the Zionists managed to extract what amounted to a partial retraction, but this did not suffice to restore Weizmann's shaken prestige. Neither the skill with which he had steered the Movement through turbulent waters nor his indefatigable personal exertions in propagandist campaigns designed to provide it with the large resources which had now become indispensable could save his leadership from being seriously challenged, and in 1931 the adoption by the Zionist Congress of a vote of no confidence led to his retirement from office. Before long it was realized that he was irreplaceable, and he was recalled to the presidency in 1935 a few months before the appointment of the royal commission on Palestine under Lord Peel [q.v.] which, in 1937, reported in favour of the termination of the British mandate and the partitioning of Palestine into Jewish and Arab States. Weizmann was from the start a wholehearted supporter of the partition scheme which, however, evaporated with the Government's decision in 1938 that it could not be proceeded with. One more attempt at an agreed settlement of the Palestine question failed with the collapse of the St. James's Palace conference early in 1939 and the publication, against the vehement protests of the Zionist delegates, headed by Weizmann, of a statement of policy even less acceptable to the Zionists than that of 1930.

Weizmann's contacts with British statesmen during the war encouraged him to hope that, when peace came, the situation might still be restored. The report of the Anglo-American commission of inquiry, before which he gave evidence early in 1946, showed how deeply it had been impressed by his plea for the recognition of the now desperate need of the Jews for a secure home in Palestine. The British response was chilling, but Weizmann still clung, hoping against hope, to his faith in the British connection. That faith was not shared by the majority of the first post-war Zionist Congress which, at the end of 1946, with the American delegation in the lead, declared in effect that it was not interested in further discussions with the British Government and, without appointing a successor, let Weizmann lay down his office, this time not to return.

Although no longer occupying any official position in the Movement, Weizmann remained its most impressive and, in the eyes of the outside world, its most

representative figure. It was to him that the Zionists turned when in 1947 they urgently needed American support for their views on the proposals then before the United Nations for the partition of Palestine. His personal intervention with President Truman helped materially to open the way for the adoption by the Assembly of a scheme assigning a viable area to the proposed Jewish State and again a few months later to bring about the immediate recognition of the State of Israel by the United States when its establishment was proclaimed, directly after the British withdrawal from Palestine in May 1948. Weizmann was at once invited to become president. Though now in his seventy-fourth year and in failing health, he had expected to be treated as an elder statesman and not, as happened, as little more than a figurehead. This deeply wounded him, but his frustrations were in some measure relieved by the solace of his beloved laboratories, where, in the closing years of his life, he returned to the scientific studies for which, for all the distractions of his public career, he had never lost his zest. Although it is as a Zionist leader that he will have his place in history, he also managed by some miracle of concentration to gain a considerable reputation in the scientific world of his day both on the academic plane and as an industrial chemist with important inventions to his credit. It was these which, after the end of the war of 1914–18, made him financially independent and free to devote himself to the service of the Zionist cause without anxiety for his future. Before he died, at Rehovoth, 9 November 1952, he had had the happiness of seeing both the seats of learning in Israel whose foundation he had inspired—the Hebrew University of Jerusalem and the Weizmann Institute of Science at Rehovoth—securely established and well on the way to justifying the high hopes he had reposed in them. Honorary degrees were conferred upon him by Manchester (1919), the Hebrew University (1947), and the Haifa Polytechnicum (1952).

With an unmistakably Jewish cast of features, but of a Russian-Jewish type bearing no resemblance to the conventional image of the Jew, Weizmann was a little above middle height, broad-shouldered and well proportioned, with a good figure and an erect and confident carriage. Sir Harold Nicolson, who was in frequent contact with him in the Balfour

Declaration period, has spoken of the respect—even awe—inspired by his commanding presence and dignified bearing: 'I sometimes wonder whether his fellow-Jews realise how deeply he impressed us gentiles by his heroic, his Maccabean quality.' As he grew surer of himself in his English environment, he developed social gifts which, combined with the elegance and *savoir-faire* of his wife, made him acceptable both as host and guest in circles to which no other Zionist leader had access. In his relations with the British statesmen and civil servants with whom he had to deal he showed diplomatic address of a high order, with a sensitive feeling for atmosphere and an intuitive grasp of the right approach to each individual. His charm, when he chose to exert it, served him well, but what made him incomparably the most effective advocate of the Zionist cause was his power to kindle the imagination of those who came under his spell and to impart to them some of his own mystical faith in the destiny of his people and the significance of its survival. If he not only captivated them but won their confidence, it was because—as one of them, Sir Charles Webster, has told us—'all those with whom he came into contact believed absolutely in his probity and sincerity and learnt to work with him as a partner in a great enterprise'.

By his marriage in 1906 to Vera (died 1966), daughter of Isaiah Chatzman, of Rostov-on-the-Don, he had two sons, the younger of whom was killed in 1942 while serving in the Royal Air Force.

A portrait of Weizmann by Sir Oswald Birley and busts by (Sir) Jacob Epstein and Benno Elkan are in the Weizmann House, Rehovoth.

[Chaim Weizmann, *Trial and Error*, 1949; *Chaim Weizmann*, ed. P. Goodman, 1945; Sir Isaiah Berlin, *Chaim Weizmann*, 1958; Leonard Stein, *The Balfour Declaration*, 1961; *Chaim Weizmann*, ed. M. W. Weisgal and J. Carmichael, 1962; *The Impossible Takes Longer*, memoirs of Vera Weizmann as told to David Tutaev, 1967.]

LEONARD STEIN.

WELLESLEY, DOROTHY VIOLET, DUCHESS OF WELLINGTON (1889–1956), poet, was born 30 July 1889 at Heywood Lodge, White Waltham, Berkshire, the only daughter of Robert Ashton, of Croughton, Cheshire, and his wife, Lucy Cecilia Dunn Gardner. After her father's death her mother married, in 1899, the tenth Earl of Scarbrough. In 1914

Dorothy married Lord Gerald Wellesley, who succeeded his nephew as seventh Duke of Wellington in 1943. They had one son, the Marquess Douro, and one daughter, Lady Elizabeth Clyde.

Dorothy Wellesley started writing poetry at a very early age. Slight of build, almost fragile, with blazing blue eyes, fair hair, transparently white skin, she was a natural rebel, rejecting all conventions and accepted ideas, loving to proclaim herself an agnostic, a fiery spirit with a passionate love for beauty in all forms, whether of flowers, landscape, or works of art. Her friend Sir George Goldie [q.v.], whose biography she wrote in 1934, after investigating her scalp when she was eleven years old, informed her that she had the three bumps of temper, pride, and combativeness more developed than anyone he had ever known. She was a born romantic by temperament, but the bad fairy at her christening had decreed that her intellectual power should never equal her gifts of imagination; consequently, the poems which she dashed off as fast as she could write them down never received the revision they demanded. 'Oh, I can't be bothered'—grammar and syntax bored her; impatiently she rejected the counsel of her friends. Unfortunately her education was carried out at home, mostly by foreign governesses, when the discipline of school and the intellectual stimulus of a university were what she really needed.

Fancying herself as something of a philosopher, with a sense of history and a smattering of archaeology, all somewhat amateurish, she often imposed upon her verse a weight it should never have been asked to carry. She felt; she saw; she interpreted. Her undoing, as a poet, sometimes, was that she thought she could think. She should have stuck to her very personal vision of Nature, and to what W. B. Yeats [q.v.] (who greatly admired her work and whose *Letters on Poetry* to her were published in 1940) called her 'passionate precision'. This precise, almost myopic observation of Nature, Tennysonian in its detail, might, under the floodlighting of her spacious imagination, have produced a far better poet than she ever troubled to become. Selections of her poems were published at intervals from 1913 onwards; *Early Light*, her collected poems, appeared in 1955.

Dorothy Wellesley loved entertaining her friends, both at Sherfield Court in Hampshire and subsequently at Penns in the Rocks, Withyham, Sussex, where she died 11 July 1956. No biographical sketch of her would be complete without a mention of the charm and gaiety she could display as a hostess. She never cared much for London, but was happy in the country with her garden, her books, her dogs, her friends, her children, her grandchildren, and her writing. Fortune, in the material sense, had been kind to her: she could indulge her taste for beautiful objects and all the amenities of a comfortable life, in which she was anxious that others should participate. Her autobiography, *Far Have I Travelled* (1952), was unfortunately written when her health, never very robust, had considerably deteriorated and only her natural courage kept her going.

Two pencil portraits by Sir William Rothenstein are in the possession of the family.

[Private information; personal knowledge.]
V. SACKVILLE-WEST.

WELLESLEY, SIR VICTOR ALEX-ANDER AUGUSTUS HENRY (1876-1954), diplomatist, was born at the British Embassy, St. Petersburg 1 March 1876, the only child of the military attaché, Colonel Frederick Arthur Wellesley, and his first wife, Emma Anne Caroline Bloomfield, daughter of Lord Augustus Loftus [q.v.], ambassador in Berlin and Vienna. His father was the son of Earl Cowley [q.v.], ambassador in Paris, and the grandson of the first Baron Cowley [q.v.], ambassador in Paris and Vienna, and youngest brother of the Iron Duke. Victor Wellesley who thus belonged by birth to the old diplomacy was to become an originator of the new diplomacy, based on economics. He was a page of honour to his godmother Queen Victoria (1887-92) and was educated for the most part in Germany, first at Wiesbaden, where his mother lived, and later at Heidelberg. He returned to England when he was about twenty and lived with his grandfather Loftus at Leatherhead where he studied by himself until he was of age and could raise the money for cramming at Scoones's. He passed into Sandhurst, but was rejected for his eyesight.

He was accepted, however, for the diplomatic service in 1899. After serving as second secretary at Rome (1905-6), he was secretary to the British delegates to the labour conference at Berne (1906); commercial attaché for Spain (1908-12); and controller of commercial and consular affairs at the Foreign Office (1916-

19), proceeding on a tour of inspection of missions and consulates in South and Central America in 1919-20. Thereafter he remained permanently in the Foreign Office—as counsellor in charge of the Far Eastern department (1920-24), as assistant under-secretary of state (1924-5), and as deputy under-secretary (1925-36). He was appointed C.B. in 1919 and K.C.M.G. in 1926.

Wellesley was thus virtually in charge of Far Eastern affairs from 1920 onwards, during the period of the termination of the Anglo-Japanese alliance, the Washington conference on the limitation of armament, the second Chinese revolution and the establishment and recognition of the Kuomintang Government, the dispatch of the British defence force to Shanghai, the Japanese invasion of Manchuria, and the commission under Lord Lytton [q.v.]. Wellesley was profoundly suspicious of Japanese ambitions and methods in China. He believed that the continuance of our alliance was disadvantageous to the development of our trade with China and an obstacle to friendship with the United States. He was one of the architects of the Washington agreements (1923).

More important was Wellesley's influence in the encouragement of the economic side of Foreign Office work, with which he was connected from 1908. He was Foreign Office representative on the committees which towards the end of the war of 1914-18 were appointed to examine the inadequacies of the existing machinery for the development of British trade abroad. As a result, his old commercial and consular department was remodelled and the new semi-independent Department of Overseas Trade was set up in 1917. This did not meet Wellesley's recorded view (1918) that the economic factor regulated the political atmosphere in all countries and dominated international relations. He considered it the defect of the Foreign Office that it was not constituted on lines best calculated to deal with the economic aspect of foreign affairs. His conception of diplomacy was ignored until the economic crisis of 1929-31. Then, backed by Arthur Henderson [q.v.], he again put forward arguments for an economic department in the Foreign Office. Henderson's approach displeased Ramsay MacDonald and the project was opposed by Sir Warren Fisher [q.v.] at the Treasury; but a small economic section crept into being which subsequently grew into one of the most active and effective branches of the Office.

With the advent of the 'national' Government in 1931 and Lord Reading [q.v.] as foreign secretary, Wellesley, in the absence of Sir Robert (later Lord) Vansittart [q.v.], was instructed to submit the views of the Foreign Office on the world situation. He drew special attention to German restlessness, the uncertainties of the Polish frontier, French fears for her security, the call for more explicit guarantees by Great Britain, and her opportunity to use economic and financial weight to effect a political settlement. Sir John (later Viscount) Simon [q.v.], succeeding to Lord Reading, had this memorandum submitted to the Cabinet but took no further steps to support it or to get it adequately considered before the Government took its plunge into successive conferences on disarmament, reparations, and on dominion and world economics in Ottawa and London. The Foreign Office programme did not suit the 'national' Government, it offended the Treasury and the Board of Trade which considered that the Foreign Office was trespassing on their ground. As it was, he lived in his retirement after 1936 to see his worst apprehensions realized. Before 1939 he had completed the greater part of the volume which embodies his reflections, *Diplomacy in Fetters* (1944), a book full of experience and observation, but devoid of the sensationalism which attracts readers. He published also *Conversations with Napoleon III* (with Robert Sencourt, 1934) and *Recollections of a Soldier-Diplomat* (1947), embodying his father's lively and amusing autobiography.

Wellesley had not the influence on policy of his more famous colleagues, Sir Eyre Crowe and Lord Tyrrell [qq.v.]. He had not the forcefulness of Crowe or the supple brilliance of Tyrrell. But he was a mandarin of the first class, in some respects in advance of his time, a Cassandra in the Office. The elephant might be taken as his symbolic beast—massive, ponderous and pondering, noble, patient, wise, gentle, loyal and lovable; yet aloof and very different from the other creatures.

In 1909 Wellesley married Alice Muriel, daughter of Oscar Leslie Stephen. She died in 1949 and they had lost their only child, a little daughter. He was a lonely man, after 1948 an invalid, and for the last two or three years of his life very nearly blind. This was a great affliction,

for he read extensively and his hobby all his life had been painting. He was a distinguished amateur painter of landscapes and portraits, and his pictures were frequently exhibited at the Royal Academy and elsewhere. He also had an extensive collection of autographs and documents which was dispersed after his death which took place in London 20 February 1954. A portrait by Louis Powles is privately owned.

[Private information; personal knowledge.]
F. ASHTON-GWATKIN.

WELLINGTON, DUCHESS OF (1889–1956), poet. [See WELLESLEY, DOROTHY VIOLET.]

WHETHAM, WILLIAM CECIL DAMPIER (1867–1952), scientist and agriculturist. [See DAMPIER.]

WHIPPLE, ROBERT STEWART (1871–1953), manufacturer and collector of scientific instruments and books, was born in Richmond, Surrey, 1 August 1871, the eldest son of George Mathews Whipple [q.v.], scientist and later superintendent of the Royal Observatory, Kew, and his wife, Elizabeth Martha, daughter of Robert Beckley, chief instrument mechanic at Kew. Whipple was educated at King's College School, Wimbledon. He entered Kew Observatory as an assistant in 1888, leaving eight years later to become assistant manager to L. P. Casella, a firm of instrument makers. In 1898 he was appointed private assistant to (Sir) Horace Darwin [q.v.], who had founded the Cambridge Scientific Instrument Company, of which Whipple became manager and secretary at the end of that year. In 1899 he matriculated at Trinity College, but did not proceed to a degree. In 1909 Whipple and C. C. Mason became joint managing directors of the firm, a post he held until his retirement from active management of the company in 1935. For ten years from 1939 he was chairman of the directors of the firm.

During the war of 1914–18 Whipple rendered important service to the Ministry of Munitions in connection with the supply of optical instruments and fine mechanisms for fuses; and early in the second war he was recalled from retirement to give further help with instrument production. Just after the end of the first war, the Government sought to assist industry with research and development by supporting conjoint research associations for each of a few carefully selected industries. The first of these was the British Optical Instrument Research Association, which later became the British Scientific Instrument Research Association. It was hardly surprising to his contemporaries that Whipple's infectious enthusiasm for scientific instruments made him one of the leaders of the industry which succeeded so early in establishing its own research association.

Whipple was a founder-fellow of the Institute of Physics and served on its board for no fewer than twenty-one years in five spells from 1920 to 1945. He was a fellow of the Physical Society, one of its vice-presidents (1914–16 and 1936–9), and honorary treasurer (1925–35). He was also a fellow of the Optical Society over which he presided in 1920–22; and was president of the mathematics and physics section of the British Association at its Dundee meeting in 1939. He was a member of the Institution of Electrical Engineers, serving on its council from 1929 to 1932. He published a number of papers in its *Journal*, for two of which, concerned with medical applications of instruments, he was awarded the Ayrton premium in 1919. In 1937 he gave the Institution's Faraday lecture on 'Electricity in the Hospital'. He was president (1926–8) of the British Optical Instrument Manufacturers' Association which later became the Scientific Instrument Manufacturers' Association of Great Britain, Ltd., of which he was president in 1932–7. Whipple was elected president of the Highgate Literary and Scientific Institution in north London in 1937 and was re-elected annually until his death. That this institution, founded in 1839, remained in existence was largely due to his leadership and generosity during the seventeen years he was president. Shortly before he died, in Highgate 13 December 1953, he founded a trust, bearing his name, for the promotion of the arts and science in north London, which was able to continue to help the institution.

Whipple was intensely interested in the history and development of scientific instruments and he amassed an important and valuable collection of specimens of historic interest dating from the sixteenth century; he also collected valuable original scientific books and his collection of some 1,500 included several important works such as those of Gilbert, Bacon, Galileo, Boyle, Hooke, and Newton. In a characteristically generous manner he presented these collections to the university of Cambridge in 1944, where they are displayed in the museum devoted to the history of science and known as the Whipple Museum. Whipple was a true Victorian gentleman, whose charm and grace made it a delight to be in his company. He was kindly and generous in supporting, often anonymously, the causes in which he believed. Many a young scientist and engineer owed much to his gentle help and encouragement.

In 1903 Whipple married Helen, daughter of the late Allan Muir, a teacher, of Glasgow. There were two daughters of the marriage and a son, George Allan Whipple, who followed his father in the scientific instrument industry. A bas-relief of Whipple was made by Mrs. Mary Gillick.

[Private information; personal knowledge.]
H. R. LANG.

WHITBY, SIR LIONEL ERNEST HOWARD (1895–1956), medical scientist and regius professor of physic in the university of Cambridge, was born in Yeovil 8 May 1895, the second of the three sons of Benjamin Whitby, glovemaker, and his wife, Jane Elizabeth Milborne. He was educated at King's College, Taunton, and Bromsgrove School (of which he later became a governor), and won a senior open scholarship for Downing College, Cambridge. At this point war broke out and he served with distinction as a machine-gunner in the Royal West Kent Regiment in Serbia, Gallipoli, and France. A severe wound in March 1918 resulted in the amputation of a leg, and he ended as a very young major with the M.C. and a lifelong disability.

Undeterred by this misfortune he went up to Cambridge in October of the same year to study medicine and completed his training at the Middlesex Hospital in London as a Freeman scholar and Hudson and Hetley prizeman. He qualified M.B., B.Ch., Cambridge (1923), took the diploma of public health (1924), and his M.D., Cambridge, and M.R.C.P. (1927).

In 1923 Whitby was appointed assistant pathologist in the Bland-Sutton Institute at the Middlesex Hospital where he began to develop the wide range of expert knowledge in pathology, bacteriology, and haematology which was eventually embodied in his three books: *The Laboratory in Surgical Practice* (1931, with

(Sir) Charles Dodds), *Medical Bacteriology* (1928, 6th ed. 1956), and *Disorders of the Blood* (with C. J. C. Britton, 1935, 7th ed. 1953). These books, like his lectures, showed a most effective combination of erudition, clarity, and common sense.

Whitby sprang into prominence when he was invited to join the team of doctors attending King George V in his illness of 1928–9. He was appointed C.V.O. During the next ten years he busied himself with medical research, largely on blood diseases, and with a growing practice in clinical pathology. One of his best known researches established the drug sulphapyridene, at first called 'M & B 693', after May and Baker, the firm in whose laboratories the drug, with hundreds of others, was first synthesized by A. J. Ewins [q.v.] and his colleagues. This work, which led to a vast improvement in the treatment of pneumonia, was summed up in Whitby's Bradshaw lecture to the Royal College of Physicians (1938) and won him the John Hunter medal and prize from the Royal College of Surgeons (1939).

On the outbreak of war in 1939 Whitby, who had stayed with the Territorial Army, held the rank of colonel. He was appointed the first officer in charge of the army blood-transfusion service. Understanding of the complexity of the blood-groups was still rudimentary, so that both basic research and continual improvements of technique were urgently necessary. Whitby's imperturbable and friendly competence lightened the exacting team-work of his assistants, in spite of the severe bombing of Bristol where he had his chief depot for the collection and processing of blood and for training transfusion units to work with the army at home and abroad. By the end of the war his service had become a model for future peacetime services in the larger medical centres, and he himself had been promoted a brigadier. The development of blood-transfusion for the wounded saved innumerable lives and continues to be one of the major medical and surgical advances of our time.

Whitby was often called into consultation when (Sir) Winston Churchill was ill and in 1944 went with him to the Quebec conference. He was knighted in 1945. In the same year he was appointed to the regius chair of physic at Cambridge where he inspired and helped the medical school to develop important new features, such as the organization of postgraduate studies, the health service for under-graduates, and a department of human ecology.

These years also proved him to be an ideal chairman of large medical conferences. Able at a moment's notice to compose a pithy introductory speech and to extract the essence from a medley of opinions, he acted as a most successful president of the British Medical Association (1948–9) and chairman of the Association's educational committee; and in 1953 he was equally effective as president of the first World Conference on Medical Education. He was president also of the International Society of Haematology (1950) and of the Association of Clinical Haematologists, and president of the Association of Clinical Pathologists and of the first International Congress in that subject (1951).

His election in 1947 to the mastership of Downing added further responsibilities. The college was enriched with a new chapel, a spacious court, and a hall restored and freshly adorned; and all branches of study found stimulation in his wide intellectual interests. Meanwhile his medical research continued and his books needed periodical revision. As chairman of the medical committee of Addenbroke's Hospital he played a leading part in planning improvements, in easing the take-over of the hospital by the Health Service, and in organizing the clinical instruction of medical graduates. In 1951–3 Whitby reached the peak of his academic career when he served as vice-chancellor of the university. His quickness of thought and steadiness of judgement, combined with a sympathetic understanding of diverse characters, ensured a distinguished term of office. His duties tied him closely to Cambridge, but before and after this period he travelled widely on medical and academic missions. He gave the Cutter lecture when he was visiting professor at Harvard in 1946; and was Sims Commonwealth travelling professor in 1956.

Whitby was elected F.R.C.P. in 1933; he received the gold medal of the Royal Society of Medicine (1945) and of the Society of Apothecaries (1948). He was a commander of the American Legion of Merit and a chevalier of the Legion of Honour; an honorary member of the American Association of Physicians and of the New York Academy of Medicine; an honorary fellow of Lincoln College, Oxford; and received honorary degrees from Glasgow, Toronto, and Louvain.

In 1922 Whitby married Ethel, daughter of James Murgatroyd, leather merchant, of Shelf, Yorkshire. She had been a fellow undergraduate, qualified in medicine, and served under him in the army blood transfusion service with the rank of major in the Royal Army Medical Corps. Highly gifted in physical, intellectual, and artistic qualities, she gave her husband invaluable help. They had a daughter and three sons, two of whom followed their father with distinction into the more scientific branches of medicine.

Two portraits of Whitby were painted by Waldron West, the second a replica of the first. One hangs in Bromsgrove School, the other in Downing College, Cambridge. Whitby died in London 24 November 1956.

[*British Medical Journal* and *Lancet*, 1 December 1956; *Nature*, 5 January 1957; private information; personal knowledge.]

A. D. GARDNER.

WHITE, CLAUDE GRAHAME- (1879–1959), pioneer aviator and aircraft manufacturer. [See GRAHAME-WHITE.]

WHITE, LEONARD CHARLES (1897–1955), general secretary of the Civil Service Clerical Association, was born at Cromer, Norfolk, 12 November 1897, the son of Charles Harold White, a postal clerk, and his wife, Lelita Beatrice Clayton. 'Len' White had part of his education at Paston Grammar School, North Walsham. Entering the Post Office as a learner in 1914, the following year he became a sorting clerk and telegraphist at Northampton. There he showed early interest in trade-union affairs.

In 1916 he enlisted in the Royal Naval Divisional Engineers as a sapper, but he was invalided out in 1917 and returned to his job in the Post Office. Finding that avenues of promotion from 'minor and manipulative' grades to the clerical class were closed for the duration, White threw up his permanent position in the Post Office to become a temporary clerk in the Admiralty. He was successful in a limited competition for clerical posts and was appointed to the Admiralty naval ordnance in 1920.

In the thick of union work again he was in turn elected secretary of the local branch, assistant secretary of the wider Admiralty section of the Civil Service Clerical Association, a member of the Admiralty departmental Whitley Council and, more significant still, to the national executive committee of the Civil Service Clerical Association, all within the four years to 1924. This rapid advance to the forefront of the association was remarked by the general secretary, W. J. Brown [q.v.], who noted that in the Admiralty he had a branch secretary of unusually high standard.

When strengthening the headquarters' staff in 1925, Brown urged White to apply for a post of clerical assistant. This was obviously an apprenticeship. It was followed by elevation to assistant secretary in 1928; to assistant general secretary in 1936; and to general secretary in 1942, on Brown's election to Parliament. Although Brown became 'parliamentary general secretary' and continued until 1949, White assumed full command of administration and negotiation and had complete authority as leader of the Civil Service Clerical Association from 1942. He was also associated with Brown as adviser to the Prison Officers' Association; and acted as secretary of the Civil Service Alliance (of the four clerical unions) for seventeen years.

The repeal of the Trade Disputes Act of 1927 by the Labour Government in 1946 enabled the Civil Service Clerical Association, along with other Civil Service organizations, to resume affiliation to the Trades Union Congress. Two attempts to secure White's election to the T.U.C. General Council failed. His first defeat in 1946 by the general secretary of the Union of Post Office Workers was not surprising. By the time a second seat on the General Council came to be allotted to the Civil Service associations in 1951, there was no doubt that White had become unacceptable to the powerful men on the General Council because of his known Communist sympathies and his membership of the board of the *Daily Worker*. They mobilized their large card votes against him and elected Douglas Houghton, M.P., of the Inland Revenue Staff Federation, by a six to one majority.

Neither in this defeat nor in other disappointments did White show any personal feeling of resentment. He was a good loser and a lovable man, a cheerful companion and a staunch friend.

As a platform speaker he was rational, moderate, and convincing. In committee he was businesslike and spoke to the point. In negotiation he was well informed, ably marshalled his facts, and presented his case in a persuasive manner and without over-statement or sabre-rattling.

White's great and lasting contribution to Civil Service staff unionism was his resolve to build up strong central government in the National Staff Side of the Civil Service Whitley Council. He condemned sectional attempts at 'leapfrogging' in pay claims. To White the authority of the National Staff Side was all important. He made the C.S.C.A. subordinate to it and called upon others to do the same.

In his last years he was for curbing intemperate policies and militant postures; he stood for honouring agreements, and for infusing the elements of statesmanship in the governance of the Association and the wider field of Civil Service affairs. His aim, his strength, and his achievements all lay in the opposite direction to those of his predecessor. On becoming general secretary of the C.S.C.A. he inherited a legacy of unilateral action and waywardness. The Civil Service staff movement had been seriously weakened. White knew this and was determined to repair the damage. This he did so successfully that when, in 1955, the National Staff Side were seeking a successor to Sir Albert Day, the choice fell unanimously on L. C. White. No higher tribute could have been paid to him: no greater confidence shown in his ability and integrity. White was ready to make the change but he died in London 11 May 1955, before the appointment could be made.

White's first marriage, to Ellen Ellis, was dissolved. He married secondly, in 1945, Roma Iris Clara, daughter of Harold Larmer, civil servant; they had one son.

[Private information; personal knowledge.]
DOUGLAS HOUGHTON.

WHITEHEAD, JOHN HENRY CONSTANTINE (1904–1960), mathematician, was born in Madras 11 November 1904, the only child of Henry Whitehead, bishop of Madras and sometime fellow of Trinity College, Oxford, and his wife, Isobel, daughter of the Rev. John Duncan, vicar of Calne, and an early mathematical student of Lady Margaret Hall. A. N. Whitehead [q.v.] was his uncle. He was educated at Eton, where he was a member of the Society, and at Balliol College, Oxford, where he was first a Williams exhibitioner, chosen it is said from far down the list by J. W. Nicholson, and then an honorary scholar and where he obtained

first classes in mathematical moderations (1924) and in the final honour school (1926), his work much influenced by H. O. Newboult of Merton. Whitehead played billiards and boxed as a welterweight for the university and was elected to the Authentics. He shared with G. H. Hardy [q.v.], whom he met at this time, a passion for cricket.

After eighteen months in the City under the guidance of O. T. Falk of Buckmaster and Moore, stockbrokers, Henry Whitehead returned to Balliol in 1928 for further work in mathematics and in the following year went with a Commonwealth Fund fellowship to Princeton to study under Oswald Veblen. Much of his work was done in differential geometry and in 1932, with Veblen, he published the classic Cambridge Tract on *The Foundations of Differential Geometry*.

In 1932 Whitehead became lecturer in mathematics, and in 1933 fellow and tutor, at Balliol in succession to Nicholson. During the war of 1939–45 he served in the Admiralty and the Foreign Office. Returning to Oxford he became Waynflete professor of pure mathematics in 1947 and thus migrated to Magdalen. Towards the end of his time at Princeton he had turned to the study of topology in which most of his remaining work was done and in which his contribution was both massive and fundamental. Some of his most original work was completed in the years before the war although its importance was not fully recognized until later. After the war he produced a large volume of work in combinatorial topology and then in the algebraic side of homotopy theory, returning in the last few years of his life to a more geometrical kind of topology. His reputation was international and research students came from many countries to work enjoyably with him. He was largely responsible for establishing the Mathematical Institute at Oxford; was a committee member of the British Mathematical Colloquium; and in 1953–5 presided over the London Mathematical Society. He was elected F.R.S. in 1944.

A sociable and inspiring teacher, Whitehead threw himself with rotund zest into college and university life. He would travel willing summer miles in his elderly motoring car, of which he was the most conversational of drivers, to play village and especially Barnacles cricket, at which he continued to wear his Eton Ramblers' cap which, as he and it grew older, made him come more and more to resemble Tweedledum, his stance at the crease and more notably in the field remaining imperially upright to the end. After and sometimes during the game he was an enthusiastic controversialist especially in country inns where he was eternally ready to engage in protracted discussions of social and athletic problems which he had just invented. He remained too a learned devotee both of the works of P. G. Wodehouse and of the game of poker the enjoyment of which he claimed to have learned at his mother's knee. Whatever he did was fun for him and for his companions. His friendships were wide in both range and age-group; and they were well repaired. 'It was in long mathematical conversations in which every detail had to be hammered out till he had it quite correct and secure that he most delighted and it is by these conversations, gay and informal, in which he contrived to make everyone his own equal' that his fellow mathematicians have recalled him most gratefully. Cosy to everyone, towards women he had an old-fashioned courtesy uniquely his own. He was very happily married. In 1934 he married a concert pianist, Barbara Sheila, daughter of Lieutenant-Colonel W. Carew Smyth, R.E., and they had two sons. The Whiteheads excelled in informal hospitality, first in North Oxford, then at their farm at Noke on Otmoor where they kept with great success the well-bred herd of cattle which Henry had inherited from his mother. Stories about him were legion; all were kindly; and the most convincing he probably made up himself. Nobody ever accused him of wisdom. An affectionate and lovable character, Henry Whitehead was a seminal mathematician and an ingenious and humane man.

Whitehead died 8 May 1960 while on sabbatical leave at the Institute for Advanced Study at Princeton. There is a portrait by Gilbert Spencer in the Mathematical Institute at Oxford where the library has been named after Whitehead.

[*Journal* of the London Mathematical Society, 1962; *Nature*, 18 June 1960; M. H. A. Newman in *Biographical Memoirs of Fellows of the Royal Society*, vol. vii, 1961; biographical note in *The Mathematical Works of J. H. C. Whitehead*, ed. I. M. James, vol. i, 1962; private information; personal knowledge.]

E. T. WILLIAMS.

WHITELEY, WILLIAM (1881-1955), politician, was born 3 October 1881 in the mining village of Littleburn near Durham, the fourth son of Samuel Whiteley, miner and checkweighman, and his wife, Ellen Bragan. A man of strong character, Samuel Whiteley was for many years a Methodist local preacher; William also held many Methodist offices. Leaving the Brandon Colliery school at the age of twelve, Whiteley worked in the pit until he was fifteen when he became a clerk in the offices of the Durham Miners' Association. He attended classes in shorthand, book-keeping and kindred subjects, gaining a first class certificate, and himself teaching evening classes. Strongly built, he was a good cricketer and played football for the Sunderland League side. He might have become a professional, had not his father, a strong teetotaller, finding that the team changed in public houses, burnt his son's football clothes and boots.

In early life a Liberal, and prominent in a local debating society, in 1906 Whiteley joined the Labour Party. He helped to found the Durham City Labour Party and became president of the Durham County Federation of Labour Parties. In 1912 he was appointed a miners' agent and from 1915 to 1922 served on the executive of the Miners' Federation of Great Britain. In 1918 he unsuccessfully contested the Blaydon division of Durham for Labour, but in 1922 he won the seat and, except for the years 1931-5, held it until his death. In the House of Commons he was soon recognized as a steady hard-working member. His speeches, generally on mining subjects, were well informed. Respected and trusted by his colleagues, he was elected a Labour whip in 1926 and in 1929-31 he served in the Labour Government as a junior lord of the Treasury. Losing his seat in the Labour rout of 1931 he earned his living by working in the public assistance department of the Durham County Council and by once again teaching evening classes.

Re-entering Parliament in 1935, Whiteley resumed his position in the whips' office, and on the formation of the coalition Government in 1940 he became comptroller of the household. Two years later he became joint parliamentary secretary to the Treasury and chief whip of the Labour Party in succession to Sir Charles Edwards; in the difficult conditions of a coalition he was successful in keeping the party united. He was sworn of the Privy Council in 1943.

During the whole period of the Labour

Government of 1945–51 Whiteley was parliamentary secretary to the Treasury, and he remained chief Labour whip until June 1955. By common consent he was considered one of the greatest of all chief whips. To a dignified presence he added a fine character. Absolutely just, he was firm yet conciliatory, earning the affection of his colleagues as well as their respect and that of their opponents. In wartime he worked harmoniously and loyally with his Conservative colleague. The task of maintaining discipline without cramping individual initiative is never easy, particularly in the Labour Party where there is always an impatient left wing, but Whiteley achieved this. He had the difficult task, during the second Parliament after the war, of sustaining a Government with a majority of only six; yet he was never defeated on a major issue. He inspired loyalty in his junior whips and in the rank and file. He sought no higher office, but was content to serve in the post for which he was specially fitted. His appointment as C.H. in 1948 was generally approved as a fitting recognition of his services. On his retirement a presentation was made to him at the annual party conference.

Whiteley was a deputy-lieutenant of his county. A well-read man himself, he took a keen interest in education. He was a member of the county education committee, governor of several schools, and honorary treasurer of the northern district of the Workers' Educational Association. His greatest interest, however, outside politics, was in the Durham Aged Miners' Homes Association of which he was president for over thirty years. He had a broad outlook and had widened his experience by much travel, including a visit to Spain during the civil war.

In 1901 Whiteley married Elizabeth Swordy, daughter of James Urwin Jackson, blacksmith at Littleburn Colliery; they had one son and one daughter. He died in Durham 3 November 1955.

[Private information; personal knowledge.]
ATTLEE.

WHITTAKER, SIR EDMUND TAYLOR (1873–1956), mathematician, astronomer, and philosopher, was born in Southport 24 October 1873, the only son of John Whittaker, gentleman, and his wife, Selina Septima, daughter of Edmund Taylor, M.D., who practised as a physician at Middleton near Manchester. In his earlier years his only teacher was

his mother; at the age of eleven he entered Manchester Grammar School on the classical side but on promotion to the upper school gladly escaped to specialize in mathematics. A scholar of Trinity College, Cambridge, he was bracketed second wrangler (1895); obtained a first class in part ii of the tripos, the Tyson medal, and was elected a fellow of Trinity (1896); and was awarded the first Smith's prize (1897).

In 1906 Whittaker was appointed professor of astronomy in the university of Dublin, with the title of royal astronomer of Ireland. The observatory at Dunsink was poorly equipped and it was tacitly understood that the chief function of the professor was to strengthen the school of mathematical physics in the university where Whittaker gave courses of advanced lectures. Some of his pupils were members of other academic foundations, among them Eamon de Valera.

In 1912 Whittaker was elected to the professorship of mathematics at Edinburgh where he taught until his retirement in 1946 and where his personal achievements included the institution in 1914 of what was probably the first university mathematical laboratory, the establishment of a flourishing research school, and the development of the Edinburgh Mathematical Society.

Whittaker made numerous and important contributions to mathematics and theoretical physics which had a profound effect by reason of their great range, depth, and fertility; but these are rivalled, if not surpassed, in interest, importance, and influence by his scientific books and monographs. In addition to these he wrote numerous philosophical and historical papers and books, which all bear the marks of his learning, literary powers, and critical judgement.

His contributions to pure mathematics were mainly to the theories of interpolation, of automorphic functions, of potential theory, and of special functions. His interest in the theory of interpolation arose from his association with the actuaries engaged in life assurance in Edinburgh, especially G. J. Lidstone. He succeeded in solving two fundamental questions and thus provided a logical basis for the Newton–Gauss formula and for the method of the graduation or adjustment of observations. In the theory of automorphic functions he solved the problem of the uniformization of algebraic functions of any genus by considering a special discontinuous subgroup of elliptic transformations each of period 2.

The most significant section of his researches, however, relates to the special functions of mathematical physics regarded as constituents of potential functions. He obtained a general solution of Laplace's equation which brought a new unity into potential theory by exhibiting all the usual special functions in the form of a 'Whittaker' integral, and he also introduced the important confluent hypergeometric functions. In theoretical physics he made substantial contributions to dynamics, to relativity and electromagnetic theory, and to quantum theory. In dynamics his discovery of the 'adelphic' integral provided the solution of the difficulties indicated by Poincaré's celebrated theorem relative to the convergence of the series solutions of celestial mechanics. In electromagnetic theory he gave a general solution of Maxwell's equations in terms of two real scalar wave functions, and gave a relativistic generalization of Faraday's theory of tubes of force. In general relativity he investigated the problem of giving an invariant definition of distance which should correspond to the actual procedure adopted by astronomers, and he obtained a generalization of Gauss's theorem on the Newtonian potential. In his researches on quantum theory he generalized Hamilton's 'principal functions', expressing them in terms of non-commutating variables and thus obtained a new foundation for Schrödinger's wave equation.

Three of Whittaker's scientific books have had a great influence. *A Course of Modern Analysis*, published in 1902, and in many subsequent editions with the collaboration of Professor G. N. Watson, F.R.S., was the first, and for many years almost the only, book in English to provide students with an account of the modern theory of functions. The great *Treatise on the Analytical Dynamics of Particles and Rigid Bodies* (1904) remains the standard work on this classical subject. *The Calculus of Observations* (1924, with G. Robinson) was a pioneer work which opened up a new field of mathematical exploration.

A fourth great work stands in a class apart: the monumental treatise on *A History of the Theories of Aether and Electricity*, first published in one volume in 1910 and subsequently in a greatly enlarged edition of which Whittaker lived to complete only two volumes (1951–3).

The *History* provides a complete, systematic, and critical account of the development of the physical theories of electromagnetism, atomic structure, and of the quantum theory from their remote beginnings up to the year 1926. It will remain an outstanding achievement by reason of the clarity of the exposition, the comprehension of its range, and the penetration of its criticism, which give it all the force and authority of an original investigation.

Whittaker, who was knighted in 1945, was elected F.R.S. in 1905, served on the council in 1911–12 and 1933–5 (vice-president 1934–5) and was awarded the Sylvester medal in 1931 and the Copley medal in 1954. With the Royal Society of Edinburgh he had continuous contact, being Gunning prizeman in 1929 and president in 1939–44. He was president of the Mathematical Association (1920–21), of the mathematical and physical section of the British Association (1927), and of the London Mathematical Society (1928–9), being awarded its De Morgan medal in 1935. He was an honorary member of a number of foreign learned societies, received honorary degrees from several universities, was an honorary fellow of Trinity College, Cambridge (1949), and was frequently invited to lecture on special foundations. At Cambridge in his Tarner lectures (1947) he lucidly traced the development of natural philosophy from Euclid to Eddington, and in 1951 he gave the Eddington memorial lecture on 'Eddington's Principle in the Philosophy of Science'. At Oxford he gave the Herbert Spencer lecture (1948) on 'The Modern Approach to Descartes' Problem'. He figured as a natural theologian in his Riddell memorial lectures (Durham, 1942) on 'The Beginning and End of the World' and in the Donnellan lectures (Dublin, 1946) on 'Space and Spirit' in which he restated the classical scholastic arguments for the existence of God in the light of current theories of scientific cosmogony. He was received into the Roman Catholic Church in 1930; was honorary president of the Newman Association (1943–5); was awarded the cross Pro Ecclesia et Pontifice in 1935; and appointed a member of the Pontifical Academy of Sciences in 1936.

Whittaker's death in Edinburgh, 24 March 1956, marked the end of an epoch, for he was almost the last polymath who took all mathematical knowledge for his province. His pervasive influence in mathematics is seen in his peculiar facility for coining names for analytical concepts and entities, many of which have obtained a wide currency in the language of mathematics. Such names as 'isometric circle', 'adelphic integral', 'cotabular functions', 'cardinal function', 'congruent hypergeometric function', 'Mathieu function', and 'calamoids' are examples of a vocabulary which ranges easily over a vast field of modern mathematical physics and forms a lasting tribute to Whittaker's influence. That influence was mainly the effect of his amazing intellectual powers—his rapidity of thought, his infallible memory, and his remarkably lucid style of exposition—but it was reinforced by his never-failing kindness to his students, the hospitality offered in his Edinburgh home, his slightly mischievous humour—and by the devotion and support of his wife.

In 1901 Whittaker married Mary Ferguson McNaghten, daughter of the Rev. Thomas Boyd, of Cambridge, Scottish secretary of the Religious Tract Society, and granddaughter of Sir Thomas Jamieson Boyd [q.v.]. They had three sons and two daughters. His second son, 'Jack', was professor of pure mathematics at Liverpool (1933–52) and vice-chancellor of the university of Sheffield (1952–65).

A bronze portrait head of Whittaker by Benno Schotz was subscribed for by the fellows of the Royal Society of Edinburgh and placed in the Society's House at the end of Whittaker's tenure of the presidency. The National Portrait Gallery has a painting by Trevor Haddon.

[G. Temple in *Biographical Memoirs of Fellows of the Royal Society*, vol. ii, 1956; *Journal* of the London Mathematical Society, vol. xxxii, April 1957; private information; personal knowledge.]　　　G. TEMPLE.

WHITWORTH, GEOFFREY ARUNDEL (1883–1951), founder of the British Drama League, was born in Kensington 7 April 1883, the youngest child of William Whitworth, barrister, by his wife, Phyllis Mary Draper; he had two brothers and two sisters. Owing to early developed spinal trouble which prevented him from going to school and which he met courageously, he was educated privately until he went up to New College, Oxford, where he obtained a third class in modern history in 1906. He next joined the staff of the *Burlington Magazine*, edited by (Sir) Charles Holmes [q.v.]; then, from the autumn of 1907, he worked for Chatto and Windus, the publishing firm. There, in the task of creating a list of contemporary books he was a colleague of Frank Swinnerton, the novelist, who remarked his 'eager adventurousness' and his 'indomitable good temper, a part of his nature and his faith'. Whitworth had a wide acquaintance among writers, established or new; it was through him that there ultimately came to the firm works by such authors as G. K. Chesterton, Lytton Strachey [qq.v.], and Clive Bell.

Whitworth's main love was the theatre. He enjoyed going to plays, and occasionally writing them; he had frequented the Court Theatre and was devoted to G. B. Shaw [q.v.]. But his first enthusiasm at that time was for the project of a national theatre, to be regarded as a Shakespeare memorial and (it was hoped) opened in time for the tercentenary in 1916 of Shakespeare's death. With all his preoccupations in publishing, and his own writing—for example, *A Book of Whimsies* (with Keith Henderson, 1909) and a study of *The Art of Nijinsky* (1913) —Whitworth never ceased to think of the national theatre. Although with the coming of war in 1914 these plans were shattered, Whitworth became in 1919 the honorary secretary of his own organization, the British Drama League, which he founded 'to assist the development of the art of the Theatre and to promote a right relation between Drama and the life of the community'. In the previous autumn he had been much impressed by an amateur rendering, half-reading, half-performance, of a one-act play in a hut attached to a factory at Crayford in Kent —something undertaken, he said, 'in the spirit of community enterprise . . . which had endowed the performance with a peculiar dignity'. He held that this dignity must be the mark of a national theatre, and that the theatre itself, 'for all its costly elaboration, for all its perfection or professional technique', must be 'nothing more and nothing less than a Community Theatre writ large'. For him the drama was *par excellence* the art of the people, and the theatre everybody's business'.

Hence the conception of the British Drama League, with Lord Howard de Walden [q.v.] as president, Harley Granville-Barker [q.v.] as chairman of council, and Whitworth as honorary secretary. It held its first annual conference in the summer of 1919 at Stratford on Avon, where one resolution pledged members to help the development of 'acting, the drama, and of the Theatre as forces in the life of the nation', and another called for 'a National Theatre policy adequate

Whitworth

to the needs of the people'. These phrases might speak for Whitworth's career: his constant and ardent advocacy of the theatre as a power in life. Rapidly the Drama League burgeoned. In 1928, when Whitworth at last left publishing to give his whole time to the League as a practical achievement, and to the national theatre as a hoped-for vision, he was able to see in the League's growth, its many affiliated societies, its hundred thousand actors and playgoers, its training department, its National Festival of Community Drama, and its library (eventually the largest in the world devoted solely to the theatre), a 'new and extraordinary outbreak of dramatic energy'. His steady insistence on the value of drama in education prepared the way for the appointment of full-time professional county drama advisers.

No man was better fitted than Whitworth, selfless, persuasive, and much-loved, to battle for causes he admired. As director of the League and as honorary secretary of the Shakespeare Memorial National Theatre Committee (1930–51), he used his talents as speaker and organizer. Before giving his entire time to these tasks, he acted as drama critic of *John o'London's Weekly* (1922) and the *Christian Science Monitor* (1923); in 1924–5 he organized the theatre section of the British Empire Exhibition at Wembley. From 1919 until 1948 he edited the League's magazine, *Drama*.

At a public tribute to him in 1934, the year before the League's move from Adelphi Terrace to Fitzroy Square, Shaw described Whitworth as 'one of the most important people in the theatre today'. When war again intervened, Whitworth did not cease from crusading. It was owing to his persistence and vision that the League's civic theatre scheme—first suggested in 1942—was approved, and that in 1948 the insertion of a clause (132) in the Local Government Act enabled municipal authorities to spend up to the value of a sixpenny rate on providing all kinds of entertainment, including the theatre. Whitworth had a final reward when the Queen laid the National Theatre foundation stone (later moved) upon the South Bank site in July 1951: it was just two months before his death at his Oxford home, 9 September 1951. He had retired from the directorship of the Drama League (a retirement he described as 'a sort of minor death') during 1948 and become instead chairman of the council.

Whitworth, a fellow of the Royal Society of Literature, translated *The Legend of Tyl Ulenspiegel* (1918); and wrote a novel, *The Bells of Paradise* (1918), and two notable plays, *Father Noah* (1918) and *Haunted Houses* (1934). He was also the author of works on his special subject, *The Theatre of My Heart* (1930; revised 1938) and *The Making of a National Theatre* (1951) as well as *The Civic Theatre Scheme* (1942). He served on the executive committee of governors of the Shakespeare Memorial Theatre and the committee of the Carnegie United Kingdom Trust. In 1947 he was appointed C.B.E.

In 1910 Whitworth married Phyllis Grace, fifth daughter and ninth of the ten children of the Rev. George Edward Bell, vicar of Henley-in-Arden, Warwickshire, from 1876 to 1914. They had a son, Robin, who became deputy chairman of the Drama League, and a daughter. During the first two years of their marriage Mrs. Whitworth did the secretarial work for a monthly literary magazine, the *Open Window*, which her husband published from their Chelsea home with Vivian Locke Ellis. Later she was tireless on behalf of the League. Mrs. Whitworth, who died in 1964, also directed, and managed between 1924 and 1931, the Three Hundred Club for staging plays of merit likely at first to have a limited public.

A portrait of Whitworth by Roger Fry, and two busts, by Oscar Nemon and James Butler, are at the headquarters of the British Drama League.

[*The Times*, 11 September 1951; *Drama*, Winter, 1951; Geoffrey Whitworth, *The Theatre of My Heart*, revised 1938; *A Mystic of the Theatre* (biography in MS.) by Robin Whitworth and Charles Tennyson, with chapters of autobiography by Geoffrey Whitworth; Frank Swinnerton, *Swinnerton: An Autobiography*, 1937; personal knowledge.]   J. C. TREWIN.

WIGRAM, CLIVE, first BARON WIGRAM (1873–1960), private secretary to King George V (1931–6), was born 5 July 1873 at Madras, the eldest son of Herbert Wigram, Madras Civil Service (of the family of Wigram, baronets of that name since 1805). His mother, Amy Augusta, was a daughter of Lieutenant-General John Wood Rideout, of the Indian Army. His two younger brothers had distinguished careers in the senior fighting Services, both dying unmarried before him. He was educated at Winchester where his prowess at ball games, notably cricket and rackets, became a legend. Later on, in India, he became a fine polo player and shone at cricket as an all-rounder. In due course, he was to inspire King George V with some of his enthusiasm for sporting events. In 1893 he was commissioned in the Royal Artillery and two years later was appointed aide-de-camp to Lord Elgin [q.v.], viceroy of India. In 1897 he exchanged into the 18th Bengal Lancers, serving in the Tirah and other campaigns on the North-West Frontier, and he was in South Africa with Kitchener's Horse in 1900. Lord Curzon [q.v.] on succeeding Elgin retained him as aide-de-camp until 1904. When Sir Walter Lawrence [q.v.] was invited in 1905 to act as chief of staff to the Prince of Wales on his first visit to India, he 'made it a condition' that Wigram should be his assistant. After the tour Wigram was appointed equerry to the Prince. In 1906 he received his brevet majority and in 1908 became military secretary to the commander-in-chief at Aldershot. He relinquished this post in 1910 when the Prince succeeded to the throne as King George V to become his assistant private secretary. In the view of his military contemporaries he thereby sacrificed an army career of great promise.

Four-fifths of Wigram's long service in the secretariat was spent as assistant to Arthur Bigge, Lord Stamfordham [q.v.], during which time he profited by the wisdom and experience of a great private secretary who steered the King through the major shoals of his reign. He learned to appreciate the ever-growing importance of the office, as a result of the gradual acceptance that a constitutional sovereign's prerogative is strictly limited to the right 'to be consulted, to encourage, and to warn' and in consequence of the far-reaching changes in dominion status. From Bigge's example he learned too, to be selfless and tireless, to be completely trusted by his sovereign, yet hardly less so by politicians of all parties from whom, as 'eyes and ears' of the King, he must seek the best sources of information. Above all, he learned that in matters trenching on the sovereign's prerogative, one false step in intervention might precipitate a constitutional crisis. When Stamfordham died in 1931 the King expressed himself as 'utterly lost' at the death of the man who 'taught me how to be a King'. But he wrote in his diary: 'His loss is irreparable. I shall

now make Wigram my Private Secretary.' Wigram, appointed K.C.V.O. in 1928, had long enjoyed the close friendship and trust of the King and Queen. If in the five years of his tenure of the office he never attained Bigge's mastery as a draftsman and précis writer, he proved that he had acquired many of the essentials. He was more approachable than Bigge, for his nature was genial and he was a man with many friends and possessed of a fund of practical sympathy for all sorts and conditions of men, young and old. Shrewd, but far from subtle, his success was due to the virtues of constant loyalty and honesty rather than to intellectual gifts. Indeed, he was very like the King he served, in his geniality, in his simple and direct nature and his hatred of shams and deceit. He knew the King's mind.

Within a few months of his appointment, he, too, was faced with a major problem when the 'national' Government was set up to meet the financial crisis of that year. In the subsequent five years several matters arose on which the King felt deeply, as trenching on his own 'prerogative' or threatening the integrity of the Commonwealth of which he was now the sole unifying symbol. They included the questions of the appointment of governors-general, of the royal title and of the removal of vestiges of subordination in dominion status, and the question of honours. Not less anxiously did the King follow the emergence of Indian nationalism and the Government of India Act.

Before these matters were all decided, the King's health rapidly declined and Wigram's responsibilities increased, while he added to his other duties the post of keeper of the privy purse. As the end approached, with Queen Mary's co-operation, he added the role of nurse and played his full part as trusted friend and counsellor to his dying master.

Six months after the King's death, he handed over to Alexander Hardinge (later Lord Hardinge of Penshurst, q.v.) and was appointed deputy constable and lieutenant-governor of Windsor Castle, living in the Norman Tower where he applied his mind to horticulture and gradually converted the moat garden into a botanical showplace. After the abdication he was briefly recalled by King George VI and appointed permanent lord-in-waiting. He finally left the secretariat in the latter half of 1937. In 1945, having reached the age limit, he resigned his remaining court appointments and went to live in London.

Wigram received a variety of honours. He had the rare distinction of gaining three brevets. He was appointed C.S.I. in 1911; between 1918 and 1933 he was advanced from C.B. to G.C.B.; and between 1903 and 1932 rose step by step in the grades of the Victorian Order to G.C.V.O., receiving the Victorian Chain in 1937. He was sworn of the Privy Council in 1932 and raised to the peerage in 1935. He held a number of foreign orders and was a fellow of the Royal Geographical, Horticultural, and Zoological societies. From 1932 to 1945 he was colonel of the 19th (K.G.O.) Lancers, Indian Army.

During and long after his tenure of the office of private secretary, Wigram was constantly active in the welfare and promotion of many educational and hospital institutions. He was at various times a fellow of Winchester and a governor of Wellington and of Haileybury. For a quarter of a century he worked inspiringly on behalf of the Westminster Hospital; he was a very active vice-president of King Edward VII's Sanatorium, on the council of Queen Mary's Hospital, Roehampton, vice-president of the National Association of Boys Clubs, and on the board of the Jubilee Trust and other youth organizations. He was for many years a director of the Midland Bank and of the L.M.S. Railway.

In appearance Wigram was good looking, nearly six feet tall, of athletic build and soldierly bearing, retaining his youthful appearance and vigour of speech to a remarkable degree until near the end of his long life.

Wigram married in 1912 Nora Mary, only daughter of Colonel Sir Neville Chamberlain, K.C.B. They had two sons, the younger of whom was killed in action in 1943, and a daughter. They were a devoted family. Lady Wigram died in 1956 and his daughter two years later. Thereafter Wigram's health declined and his mental powers began to fail. He died in London 3 September 1960 and was succeeded by his elder son, George Neville Clive (born 1915).

A not very successful picture by L. Calkin, painted in 1925, is in the possession of the family. There is a tablet to Wigram's memory in the north quire aisle of St. George's Chapel, Windsor.

[John Gore, *King George V*, 1941; Harold Nicolson, *King George V*, 1952; John W. Wheeler-Bennett, *King George VI*, 1958; *The Times*, 5 September 1960; private information; personal knowledge.]

JOHN GORE.

WILBRAHAM, SIR PHILIP WILBRAHAM BAKER, sixth baronet (1875–1957), ecclesiastical lawyer and administrator, was born at Rode Hall, Scholar Green, Cheshire, 17 September 1875, the younger and only surviving son of (Sir) George Barrington Baker, who took the additional surname of Wilbraham by royal licence in 1900, and his wife, Katharine Frances, only child of General Sir Richard Wilbraham. A descendant of Sir George Baker [q.v.], the physician who demonstrated the possibility of poisoning through the use of leaden vessels, notably in the manufacture of Devonshire cider, Wilbraham succeeded his father in the baronetcy in 1912. He was educated at Harrow, where he was a scholar and head of the school, and at Balliol College, Oxford, where he was an exhibitioner and obtained a first in classical moderations (1896) and second classes in *literae humaniores* (1898) and jurisprudence (1899). Standing as a candidate in law he was elected a fellow of All Souls in 1899 but having married in the meantime was unable to renew his fellowship when it expired in 1906; he retained a deep affection for All Souls throughout his life.

Entering the chambers of (Sir) Charles Sargant (whose notice he subsequently contributed to this Dictionary), Wilbraham was called to the bar by Lincoln's Inn in 1901 and practised, though not with the compulsion which lack of means might have supplied. Confining his interest to ecclesiastical matters, he was appointed chancellor of the diocese of Chester (1913), chancellor and vicar-general of York (1915), and chancellor of the dioceses of Truro (1923), Chelmsford (1928), and Durham (1929), offices which he held until his appointment in 1934 as dean of the Arches, master of the faculties, and vicar-general of the province of Canterbury, and auditor of the chancery court of York. These appointments he resigned in 1955 owing to failing health. As dean of the Arches Wilbraham's reputation is overshadowed among lawyers by that of his immediate predecessor Sir Lewis Dibdin [q.v.]. Few appeals came before him. Throughout the war the court was little used; a pre-war case (St. Hilary) was heard by deputy since Wilbraham himself had already been consulted as chancellor of the diocese of Truro; the three reported judgements of Wilbraham were Ogbourne St. George (1941), St. Saviour's Walthamstow (1950), and Lapford (1954).

Wilbraham was one of the original members of the Church Assembly and its first secretary (1920); he resigned the secretaryship in 1939 on accepting from the Crown the office of first Church estates commissioner, remaining, however, an active member of the Assembly. His influence on the Assembly during its formative years was very great. His co-operation with Lord Hugh Cecil (later Lord Quickswood, q.v.) produced the rules for conducting the Assembly's business, the one supplying the legal experience and the other knowledge of parliamentary procedure. As member and secretary of the Assembly he was also member and secretary of all the committees; he used the power thus given so constructively as to earn everybody's complete trust. It fell to him not only to prepare reports and the (at least first) drafts of measures, work he especially enjoyed, but also to expound often complicated clauses to the Assembly. This he did in short, careful sentences, impossible to misunderstand and entirely convincing by their reasoned impartiality. In the verbatim record his speeches stand out from others in the debates. His refusal to fight and his advocacy of acceptable compromises counteracted that divisive tendency, induced by suspicions between differing schools of churchmanship, which might have marred the Assembly's work.

To administration, as first Church estates commissioner, Wilbraham in 1939 came late. He expected to carry through amalgamation of the ecclesiastical commissioners and Queen Anne's bounty, plans for which had already been laid. He looked forward to visiting the estates. Instead came adaptation of curtailed activities to war conditions; evacuation of sections of the two offices to different parts of the country; estate visits impracticable; his London house given up. Case work and preparation for the future occupied him. Yet it was a period of greatest happiness; gradualness suited his inclination. He had time to grow into the work and to love it. When the delayed amalgamation matured after the war he was qualified as nobody else (and not even he earlier) to complete it. Trying negotiations were followed by legis-

lation which might easily have become dangerously controversial. The successful launching of the Church commissioners in 1948 and their harmonious development over the first five critical years testify to his skill and patience in leadership. He liked to carry everybody with him. The deliberately slower pace he preferred provided a firm foundation for greater advances to follow. Nevertheless, it was in his time that the commissioners' over-large agricultural holdings were reduced and their reinvestment of securities began. He put through the Assembly the measure (diocesan stipends funds, 1953) which freed large holdings of trustee stocks for profitable reinvestment. He retired in 1954 and was appointed K.B.E. in the same year.

By virtue of tenure of the Rode estate Wilbraham was high steward of Congleton from 1912; he was a J.P. for the county of Cheshire from 1919; he was appointed commissary by the dean and chapter of St. Paul's in 1942. Archbishop Lang [q.v.] conferred on him the Lambeth degree of D.C.L. in 1936 and he was elected a bencher of Lincoln's Inn in 1942.

In 1901 Wilbraham married Joyce Christabel (died 1958), daughter of Sir John Henry Kennaway, third baronet. They had three daughters and one son, Randle John Baker (born 1906), who succeeded Wilbraham in the baronetcy when he died at Rode 11 October 1957.

Tall, somewhat forbidding, Wilbraham exhibited the gravity of innate shyness covering natural friendliness. He lost his reserve in the Athenaeum billiard-room. At home at Rode with his wife, who was of the utmost help to him, he was a delightful host. That the Church formed the centre of his interests was no accident. He was in the best sense a good churchman, deeply religious, conducting family prayers each morning in the old tradition. A portrait by Sir Oswald Birley hangs in Church House, Westminster; a replica is at Rode.

[Private information; personal knowledge.]
JAMES BROWN.

WILKINS, SIR (GEORGE) HUBERT (1888–1958), polar explorer, climatologist, and naturalist, was born at Mount Bryan East, South Australia, 31 October 1888, the thirteenth and youngest child of Harry Wilkins, grazier, and his wife, Louisa Smith. Until 1903 he lived and worked on his parents' sheep station where outdoor activities, coupled with his early experience of the devastation caused by drought, laid the foundations for his lifelong interest and work in the natural sciences, climatology, and meteorology.

From 1903 to 1908, at the Adelaide School of Mines, he studied electrical and general engineering, extending his studies also to photography and cinematography. In 1908 he left Australia as a ship stowaway and commenced his career of adventure in Algiers. Later he worked in London as a newspaper reporter and cameraman with assignments in many countries, the most interesting being some months in 1912 spent filming the fighting between the Turks and the Bulgarians. Over this general period he found time also to take flying lessons and to experiment in aerial photography.

The year 1913 saw the beginning of his career as a polar explorer with his appointment as photographer to Vilhjalmur Stefansson's Canadian Arctic Expedition. Thereafter, until early 1916 when he returned to Australia to enlist, he acquired much experience in the techniques of living, travelling, and working in the Arctic region; added greatly to his knowledge of the natural sciences; became convinced that the aeroplane could be used to explore and map the polar regions; and developed a plan to set up a series of permanent weather stations in those regions as part of a world-wide scheme for systematic and co-ordinated weather forecasting.

With a commission in the Australian Flying Corps, Wilkins was sent to Europe where he was appointed assistant to the official photographer to the Australian forces, Captain Frank Hurley, of Antarctic fame. His subsequent work as a war photographer in France was of such quality that he rose to the rank of captain, received the M.C. with two bars, and was twice mentioned in dispatches. He was several times wounded and acquired a reputation for daring, courage, and leadership.

The war over, Wilkins gained further flying experience, first as navigator on an unsuccessful attempt to fly from England to Australia in late 1919, then in British airships. Later he was appointed photographer to a mission sent to the Dardanelles to reconstruct the Gallipoli campaign. On his discharge from the services, he immediately took steps to further his own plans for polar exploration. But his scheme for polar weather stations was rejected by the Royal Meteorological Society, while a proposal to fly an airship in the Arctic received no support in either England or Germany. Finally, in 1920–21 he had his first taste of work in the Antarctic as second-in-command of J. L. Cope's ill-fated expedition working in the Graham Land area. This was followed by service as naturalist with Sir Ernest Shackleton [q.v.] in his *Quest* expedition, and later by a period in Soviet Russia spent surveying and filming the effects of drought and famine—subjects close to his mind since they illustrated the need for an international weather forecasting service. Next came an expedition (1923–5) for the British Museum through Northern Australia, to carry out a biological survey and to collect specimens of the rarer mammals. His book *Undiscovered Australia* (1928) shows clearly the extent and high quality of his work, the collections made including plants, birds, insects, fish, minerals, fossils, and aboriginal artefacts, as well as mammals.

Plans for an Antarctic expedition failing through shortage of funds, Wilkins turned his attention to the Arctic where he successfully carried out a remarkable programme of pioneering air exploration which culminated in his historic flight with Carl Ben Eielson as pilot from Barrow in Alaska, eastward over the Arctic Ocean, to Spitsbergen, in April 1928. The purposes behind this work (as indicated in his book *Flying the Arctic*, 1928) were, first, to prove the value of the aeroplane for polar exploration, and then to further his cherished plan for polar meteorological stations.

Wilkins next revived his plans for aerial exploration in the Antarctic where, between 1928 and 1930, he led two expeditions, making, with Eielson, the first flight in that area on 16 November 1928, as well as numerous significant geographical observations and discoveries from the air. Wilkins's reputation as a pioneer of the air age in polar regions was by now firmly established.

In 1931 came his famous venture by submarine in Arctic waters made, as he explained in *Under the North Pole* (1931), with the twofold purpose of exploring the region from Spitsbergen westwards via the North Pole to the Siberian coast and experimenting with the craft as a weather station, both above and below the ice and in radio contact with the outside world. A series of mishaps and mechanical breakdowns caused the expedition of the

Nautilus to be abandoned, but not before it had been shown that a submarine could operate safely beneath the polar ice.

The thirties also saw Wilkins working with the American, Lincoln Ellsworth, on four expeditions to the Antarctic continent, using the ship *Wyatt Earp* and aeroplanes. During 1937 and 1938 he also played a major role in search operations for the Soviet aviator Sigismund Levanevsky lost over the Arctic Ocean, at the same time carrying out pioneering work in moonlight flying under winter conditions; a large programme of meteorological work; and constant studies of ice movements from the air.

When war broke out in 1939 Wilkins, who was in the United States, became involved, first in missions concerned with aircraft manufacture on behalf of the allied powers; and later in American government missions through the Office of Strategic Services, work which took him to the Middle and Far East. With the entry of America into the war he served from 1942 onwards as a geographer, climatologist, and Arctic adviser with the U.S. Quartermaster General's Corps, being particularly concerned with the development of efficient operational and survival techniques and equipment for the Arctic and sub-Arctic regions. After the war he served first with the U.S. Navy Office of Scientific Research (1946–7), then in an advisory capacity with the U.S. Weather Bureau, later with the Arctic Institute of North America. Finally in 1953 he was appointed geographer to the research and development command, specializing in studies and research connected with human activities in the polar regions.

Wilkins had the restless mind and outlook of the true pioneer. He possessed tremendous mental and physical drive— assets which, joined to a vivid imagination and a supreme faith in his purpose, enabled him to overcome all obstacles. He was continually on the move, being irresistibly drawn to new ideas and practical projects. He rarely concerned himself with the more obvious results, implications, and significance of an achievement and consequently the published records of his many projects and expeditions were unfortunately scanty. He was primarily a field explorer and trailblazer, working to a clear, if long-range plan, based upon his conviction of the necessity for a world-wide meteorological organization. He was convinced that a direct relationship existed between the meteorology of the polar regions and weather conditions elsewhere and that a full knowledge of polar geography would be required before his plan for polar weather stations could be realized. In these fields he was a pioneer, as he was in polar exploration by air and submarine.

As a person Wilkins was reticent, self-sufficient and infinitely adaptable. Interested in everything, he enjoyed the company of his fellows, yet found it easy to live and work among primitive peoples, if only because he shared their intense awareness of nature in all her moods. He had a strong religious background and was actively interested in such matters as telepathy and life after death. A solitary by nature and by no means the ordinary gregarious man, he was yet a good mixer and companion both on and off the job.

In 1929 he married a fellow Australian then working in New York as an actress, Suzanne Bennett (Bennett was a stage name), daughter of John Evans, a mining engineer of Victoria, Australia. They had no children. It was a happy marriage in which both parties by mutual agreement pursued their chosen careers.

Wilkins was knighted in 1928. He was a fellow of the Royal Meteorological Society and of the Royal Geographical Society which awarded him its Patron's medal. Among the many other medals which he received were the Samuel Finley Breese Morse medal from the American Geographical Society, the gold medal of the International League of Aviators, and the Norwegian Air Club's gold medal of honour. He was a companion of the Order of St. Maurice and St. Lazarus of Italy and in 1955 received the honorary degree of D.Sc. from the university of Alaska.

On 30 November 1958 Wilkins died suddenly in his hotel at Framingham, Massachusetts. He had often expressed a wish that his ashes might be scattered near the North Pole and this service was carried out by the nuclear-powered submarine *Skate*, breaking through the polar ice after a long voyage thereunder such as Wilkins himself had planned.

Five portraits of Wilkins are in the possession of his widow: two by Lady Wilkins, one by Vuk Vuchnich, one by Roland Hinton Perry, and one by James Peter Quinn. Another by Lady Wilkins is in the museum of the Marine Historical Association, Mystic, Conn., U.S.A.; one by Reynolds Mason hangs at the entrance to the Wilkins Arctic test chamber in the

U.S.A. Army Quartermaster Research and Engineering Center, Natick, Mass., U.S.A.

[Vilhjalmur Stefansson, *The Friendly Arctic*, 1921; Frank Wild, *Shackleton's Last Voyage*, 1923; J. Gordon Hayes, *The Conquest of the South Pole*, 1932; *National Geographical Magazine*, August 1938; C. E. W. Bean, *Gallipoli Mission*, 1948; E. W. Hunter Christie, *The Antarctic Problem*, 1951; John Grierson, *Sir Hubert Wilkins: Enigma of Exploration*, 1960; Lowell Thomas, *Sir Hubert Wilkins: His World of Adventure*, 1961; R. A. Swan, *Australia in the Antarctic: Interest, Activity and Endeavour*, 1961; C. E. W. Bean and others, *Official History of Australia in the First World War*, 12 vols., 1921–42; private information.] R. A. SWAN.

WILLIAMS, RALPH VAUGHAN (1872–1958), composer. [See VAUGHAN WILLIAMS.]

WILLIAMSON, JOHN THOBURN (1907–1958), geologist and diamond millionaire, was born at Montfort, Quebec, Canada, 10 February 1907, the second of four children and elder son of Bertie J. Williamson, manager of a timber company, and his wife, Rose C. Boyd. His parents, who were Canadian by birth but of Irish descent, moved to Montreal when he was twelve. From Macdonald High School at St. Anne de Bellevue Williamson entered McGill University where he was soon diverted from arts to geology in which he became so interested that he spent most of the night studying in the library. He also became well read in more general literature. Social life he despised but he liked outdoor activities and especially enjoyed fencing. He obtained his B.A. in 1928 with honours in geology, was awarded the Leroy memorial fellowship in geology in 1929, a bursary of the National Research Council of Canada in 1930–31, became a demonstrator in geology and minerology, and took his M.A. in 1930 and Ph.D. in 1933.

In the following year Williamson was sent as a geologist to Northern Rhodesia by the Anglo American Corporation of South Africa, but he moved in 1935 to Tanganyika where he spent the next two years prospecting for diamonds without much success for the Tanganyika Diamond and Gold Development Company, Ltd. When the company gave up this part of its activities in 1937 Williamson took out rights entitling him to prospect for diamonds in Tanganyika.

He prospected all over the Lake and the Western Province but found nothing worth while. He next took a sub-lease of the Mabuki diamond mine, the first to be discovered in Tanganyika, which had been worked since 1925 but yielded too few diamonds to be economic. He pegged two claims near by and another area at Kizumbi. By now he had found many diamondiferous areas and odd diamonds here and there in the course of his prospecting and had formed the theory that all these emanated from one source somewhere in Lake Province. In his search for this he lived rough, was often ill, and had very little money; but he had a determined faith in his theory which finally brought him to an area which became known as Mwadui. There he found a good gem and from the formation of the gravel came to the conclusion that Mwadui was the source he had been seeking. On 6 March 1940 he pegged some mining claims and an exclusive prospecting licence. In April he pegged further claims and another licence. Suddenly further prospecting in the country was forbidden and Williamson was unable to register all his claims. An Indian lawyer, I. C. Chopra, living at Mwanza, who was his legal adviser, became his partner.

Owing to the war and the threat of Italian invasion Williamson had to operate with the most primitive equipment and very little help. He himself started the men on their work early in the morning and supervised the digging, washing, and sorting of the gravel. Then he drove twelve miles to a river for water in a lorry which often got stuck or broke down. On his return he gave food to the men, then dealt meticulously with the paper work. Despite the difficulties Williamson spared no effort or expense in looking after his workmen of whom there were soon 2,500. Using mostly local materials he provided houses, a hospital, offices, and other buildings. But it was not until after 1947 that the mine could be properly developed.

Meantime in 1941 the Colonial Office had advised Williamson of the urgent need for industrial diamonds and he made every effort to produce as many as possible. The Germans who were in still greater need managed to get some parcels of stolen diamonds smuggled through to them before the Allies put an end to the traffic. The theft of diamonds from the mine, however, continued and by 1946 had reached such proportions that there were those who thought that the mine had petered out. Williamson knew better, but it was not until 1947 that the Government could provide police and not until some years later that the ringleaders were caught and given sentences so stiff that the theft of diamonds was suppressed.

After 1948 expansion was rapid. Many buildings were erected, a heavy media plant was ordered to be built, roads were constructed and planted with shady trees. Mwadui became a garden city, and the mine became a sanctuary for birds which came in hundreds to settle on the ponds. Williamson built two very large dams near the mine so that the country round about became cool and green and the increased rainfall brought many benefits. He was most averse from declaring any dividend of the profits of the mine. They were either ploughed back or utilized for contributing to the general good of the country. He provided a school at Shinyanga, financed higher education, and gave £50,000 to Makerere College, Uganda, for building science classrooms.

Intensely loyal to the Crown and Commonwealth, Williamson subscribed heavily to the War Loan, gave generously to wartime funds and the Red Cross, and in recognition of his war services transferred a quarter of the mine to his brother who had been seriously wounded in a commando raid. A pink diamond of rare beauty weighing 54½ carats was cut and polished and made into a brooch surrounded with over a hundred blue white diamonds of finest purity and presented to the Queen. Another magnificent brooch of blue white diamonds was presented to the Princess Margaret.

Williamson gave large sums to help mining ventures in East Africa and had he not died he would have contributed considerably to the building up of a newly independent East Africa and especially Tanzania. But symptoms of cancer of the throat became manifest and despite consultation and treatment in London and Canada he died and was buried at Mwadui 8 January 1958. There is a statue of him near the baobab tree where he first camped when he started prospecting at Mwadui. He received an honorary D.Sc. from McGill in 1956 but as a Canadian citizen had to refuse the offer of a knighthood.

Williamson seldom spent any money on himself and went about in khaki drill trousers and an open-necked shirt with short sleeves. He was a handsome man, nearly six feet tall, with dark brown hair, and was often mistaken for a well-known film actor. He was shy and retiring but had charming manners. He received dozens of letters a day from women all over the world offering marriage. But he died a bachelor. The mine became owned half by the Government of Tanganyika and the other half by De Beers Consolidated Mines, Ltd.; the production of diamonds in 1964 was worth over six million pounds.

[Montreal *Gazette*, 9 January 1958; personal knowledge.]   I. C. CHOPRA.

WILSON, CHARLES THOMSON REES (1869–1959), physicist, was born at Glencorse, Midlothian, 14 February 1869, the youngest son of John Wilson by his second wife, Annie Clark Harper, of Glasgow. His father, a progressive sheep farmer, who himself wrote on various experiments in farming, died when Wilson was four years old and the family moved to Manchester. Wilson was educated at the Owens College where he graduated B.Sc. in 1887. In 1888 he gained an entrance scholarship at Sidney Sussex College, Cambridge, where he obtained first classes in both parts of the natural sciences tripos (1890–92). He held the Clerk Maxwell scholarship from 1895 to 1898 and in 1900 was elected fellow of his college. He was university demonstrator (1900–1) and lecturer (1901–19) in experimental physics and reader in electrical meteorology (1919–25). In 1925 he was elected Jacksonian professor of natural philosophy, retiring from his chair in 1934 but remaining in Cambridge for two more years before returning to Scotland.

Wilson was accustomed to trace the main lines of his original work back to his experiences as a relief observer at the Ben Nevis observatory in September 1894, to the optical properties of clouds as he then saw them, and to the scale and magnitude of the electrical phenomena in storms. From 1895 to 1899 he carried out the experiments which established the main features of condensation of water droplets from a supersaturated dust-free gas, showing that at a definite supersaturation condensation took place only upon ions, and that there was, further, a difference of the limiting value for condensation on positive and negative ions. The abundant condensation, which ensues at a rather higher supersaturation, he identified as drop growth from small pure aggregates of water molecules. This work was notably to lead, ten years later, to the development of the cloud (track) chamber but immediately it led Wilson to speculate and experiment on the way in which ions are normally found to be present in clean air, and on the small but reproducible electrical conductivity exhibited by dust-free air. He devised a gold-leaf electroscope in which surface leakage from the charged leaf to the case of the instrument was not possible, thus excluding the essential source of uncertainty in observations of gaseous conductivity. He established that the conductivity of the gas of the electroscope was the same in daylight as in the dark, was independent of the sign of charge and, for a considerable range, of leaf potential, and that it was equivalent to that to be expected from the continuous release of about twenty pairs of ions per second in each cubic centimetre of gas. In 1901, commenting on these observations, Wilson wrote: 'Experiments were now carried out to test whether the production of ions in dust-free air could be explained as being due to radiation from sources outside our atmosphere. . . .' Then followed a description of what must be the first deliberate investigation of a cosmic radiation. The actual experiment, in which conductivity in the electroscope gas was found to be indistinguishable outside and inside a railway tunnel near Peebles, gave no further lead.

In the years 1903–10 Wilson's main interest was directed to the phenomena of atmospheric electricity and of thunderstorms, and this was to remain a major field of interest to him; his last scientific paper (1956) was on 'A theory of thunder-cloud electricity'. His contributions on this subject brought out to the full Wilson's extreme skill and insight for physical measurement. The work led through a study of the fine-weather potential gradient in the low atmosphere, and the associated earth current, to measurements of fields, currents, and field changes under discharge conditions. Such measurements allowed the altitude and magnitude of the region of charge separation to be deduced, while the rate of recovery after discharge drew attention to the magnitude of the system of charge separation which brought conditions to the discharge situation. In 1920 he suggested that the fields and currents

in fine-weather conditions were balanced by the currents and rain-carried charge in storms, a view which has come broadly to be accepted, and in later papers (1929, and again in 1956) he developed his views about the actual mechanism of charge separation. While his proposed mechanism, in which he considers the movement, polarization, and charge collection of water droplets of differing size in a vertical potential gradient, must certainly operate, it is probably inadequate to describe the full magnitude of charge separation which takes place in nature. His contribution to the study of atmospheric electricity rests not upon the success of any particular theory, but rather upon the stimulus which his exceptional insight and experimental skill gave to the whole mode of investigation.

In 1910, under the growing interest in, and understanding of, the radiations from radioactive substances, X-rays, and the mechanism of ionization, Wilson resumed condensation experiments with the intention of achieving conditions in which the track of a single ionizing particle might be made visible in the supersaturated gas of the chamber. He developed a chamber in the form of a short cylinder in which controlled supersaturation was attained by the mechanical withdrawal of one end of the cylinder (the piston) through a determined distance, while the condensation phenomena were viewed through the other end (front window), and in 1911 the first cloud chamber photographs were published. These preliminary results were quickly followed in 1912 by photographs with an improved chamber. Although through the years many developments of cloud chambers by very many workers have led to the application of the method over a greatly extended field, the quality of the photographs published in 1912 will bear comparison with that of all subsequent work.

The stimulus provided by these photographs among workers in atomic physics can hardly be overstated. Much of a picture which had hitherto been painfully pieced together from indirect observations was now to be seen, often in striking detail, as a whole. The photographs showed convincingly that ionization by X-rays was in fact that of secondary electrons, while the large angle scattering of alpha-particles, deduced scarcely a year earlier by E. (later Lord) Rutherford [q.v.] from counting experiments, was there for all to see. The cloud chamber was indeed, as Rutherford described it, 'the most original apparatus in the whole history of physics', and the beauty of fine track photographs was to fascinate nuclear physicists in the coming years. In spite of his recurring interest in atmospheric electricity, Wilson returned to cloud-chamber work in 1920, and published two notable papers in 1923 on the tracks of beta-particles and of the secondary electrons from X-rays, but the contribution to physical method which demanded his special skills and experience was accomplished in 1912.

Wilson had, in quite exceptional measure, a combination of great patience and determination, deep and seemingly intuitive physical understanding, and the ability to devise effective experimental arrangements of striking simplicity and elegance, although this often called for daunting skill of hand. These qualities are not only to be seen in his original work, where, none the less, the 1912 cloud chamber, the tilted gold-leaf electrometer, and his development and application of the Lippmann capillary electrometer in his work on atmospheric electricity are examples interesting in their variety. For many years he was in charge of the final year practical class at the Cavendish Laboratory. The simple but searching exercises which he was accustomed to set demanded skill which could often develop only from patient improvement of dexterity and made their contribution to the aptitude for experiment of many of those who worked through the most notable phase in the history of the Cavendish. As a lecturer Wilson was quite deficient in the normal qualities: hesitant in delivery, voice little above a whisper, and blackboard writing almost invisible. But beyond this barrier, his teaching exhibited the outstanding characteristics of the man and the physicist. The simplicity, penetration, and elegance of his approach, above all in the field of physical optics, have been acknowledged by those who themselves were to become lecturers of distinction.

In general estimation, Wilson's achievements reach a climax in the development of the cloud chamber. The essential simplicity of the device might well obscure the continuity of its development from the earlier condensation experiments. Moreover, it does not stand alone; the whole development of other, and in some ways more powerful, methods of trajectory recording has been guided and

built upon the successes of the cloud track method. This great field of experimentation, decisive in its impact on the development of almost all aspects of particle physics, is the direct growth from the intuition and skill of his work.

Wilson was elected F.R.S. in 1900 and received the Hughes medal (1911), a Royal medal (1922), and the Copley medal (1935). With the appearance of his last scientific work in 1956, sixty years after his first publication, for the first time in perhaps three hundred years the oldest living fellow communicated a paper to the Society. In 1927 jointly with A. H. Compton he was awarded the Nobel prize for physics, and in 1937 he was appointed C.H. He received the honorary Sc.D. from Cambridge in 1947 and held honorary degrees also from Aberdeen, Glasgow, Manchester, London, and Liverpool.

Among the most distinguished physicists of his time, Wilson stands out in his quiet kindliness and modesty. To those privileged to work with him, these qualities were the other, perhaps natural, aspect of his essentially simple, penetrating, and untiring application to the problems which through his long life attracted and held his thoughts. Below average height, and slightly built, Wilson was a man whose interests remained throughout those of the countryman. In conversation his keen and continuing interest in the field of physics in which he had worked was closely linked, through the deep impression which the phenomena of atmospheric physics made always upon him, with his enthusiasm for the mountains of Scotland and particularly of Arran. There, his activity, beyond his eightieth year, matched that of men a generation his junior, and when at the age of eighty-six he flew for the first time, in flights carried out for students of meteorology, his interest was torn between the atmospheric phenomena around him (once so rough as to demand a forced landing) and the interest provided by this new viewpoint over country which he had known so long from the ground.

In 1908 Wilson married Jessie Fraser (died 1967), daughter of the Rev. George Hill Dick, of Glasgow, and for half a century owed much to her sympathy and understanding. They had one son and two daughters. Some years after his retirement he settled in the village of Carlops near Edinburgh and no great distance from his birthplace. There, beside

the road to Edinburgh and with a green
path leading from his garden over a rocky
burn and then directly into the heart of
the Pentland hills, he spent the last
ten years of his life with his family. There
he died 15 November 1959.

A portrait by (Sir) James Gunn, delighting those who knew him well, is at
Sidney Sussex College, Cambridge.

[P. M. S. Blackett in *Biographical Memoirs
of Fellows of the Royal Society*, vol. vi, 1960;
The Times, 16 November 1959; private information; personal knowledge.]

JOHN G. WILSON.

WILSON, WALTER GORDON (1874–
1957), engineer, was born in Blackrock,
county Dublin, 21 April 1874, the fifth
son of George Orr Wilson, barrister, and
his wife, Annie Shaw. Wilson started his
career as a naval cadet in the *Britannia*.
In 1894 he entered King's College,
Cambridge, where he was elected to an
honorary exhibition in 1896, and in 1897
was placed in the first class in part i of the
mechanical sciences tripos.

The inventive genius which characterized the engineering achievements for
which Wilson later became known was
strikingly evidenced in his first engineering venture. Through Lord Braye,
Wilson was introduced to Percy Pilcher,
a lecturer in naval architecture and a
keen participant in the art of gliding.
Wilson observed Pilcher's gliding activities with a profound technical interest
and soon became enthused with the
possibilities of powered flight. In 1898
the three formed the firm of Wilson and
Pilcher with the primary objective of
building what might have been the
world's first internal combustion aero-
engine. One year later Wilson had designed a prototype engine which Pilcher
was to test, but before it was built
Pilcher was killed in a gliding accident
in 1899. The shock put an end to Wilson's
plans for powered flight and he was soon
turning his pioneering instincts to the
field of the 'horseless carriage'. In new
premises in Westminster he created the
Wilson–Pilcher motor-car embodying epicyclic gears and some remarkable new
features which in later years came to
be regarded as the hallmark of good
design in motor-cars of quality.

In 1904 he joined the firm of Armstrong Whitworth & Co., where he designed the Armstrong Whitworth car.
From 1908 to 1914 he worked with
J. & E. Hall of Dartford and designed

for them the Hallford lorry, which was
extensively used by the army in the war
of 1914–18.

When war broke out Wilson rejoined
the navy and served as a lieutenant with
armoured cars, which at that time were
used by that arm to defend naval air bases
on the coasts of France and Belgium.
Already well known as an engineer he
was soon engaged in the construction
of these vehicles. When (Sir) Winston
Churchill set up the landships committee
under (Sir) Eustace Tennyson-d'Eyncourt
[q.v.] at the Admiralty in early 1915 to
investigate the possibility of building
an armoured fighting vehicle capable of
resisting rifle and machine-gun fire, destroying barbed wire entanglements, and
crossing trenches, Squadron 20 of the
Royal Naval Armoured Car Division was
placed at the committee's disposal. Wilson
was posted to Squadron 20 and placed in
charge of the first experiments at Burton-
on-Trent. So he came to be concerned in
the birth of the tank.

In the designing of these vehicles he
was to play a part of the first importance.
Others contributed ideas, but it was
Wilson and his colleague in design, (Sir)
William Tritton [q.v.], who created a
machine capable of the tasks required
of it; and to the inventive genius and
engineering skill of these two men the
speedy success of the tank was chiefly
due. In August 1915 the design of the
'Tritton' machine, or 'Little Willie', was
already well advanced when fresh and
more stringent requirements were laid
down by the War Office. To meet them,
Tritton and Wilson concentrated on a new
design, on which they were already working, in which the tracks, at Wilson's suggestion, were carried all round the machine.
This design, known first as the 'Wilson',
then the 'Centipede', next 'Big Willie',
was ready for official trials early in 1916.
On 2 February in Lord Salisbury's park
at Hatfield, before a company which included Kitchener, Balfour, Lloyd George,
and General Robertson, it successfully
demonstrated its ability to fulfil not only
the official requirements but far more
exacting tests. Production orders were
placed immediately and 'Big Willie', now
named 'Mother', became the prototype of
the Mark I tank which went into action
on the Somme in September 1916. Other
designs followed, and Wilson's development of epicyclic transmissions for these
machines was an achievement of outstanding importance, culminating in 1937

with his design for a new epicyclic steering which provided a larger turning radius at high speeds than at low speeds.

Wilson transferred to the army in March 1916 with the rank of major in the Heavy Branch, Machine-Gun Corps, renamed in 1917 the Tank Corps. He served as chief of design in the mechanical warfare department of the War Office until the war ended. He was twice mentioned in dispatches and was appointed C.M.G. in 1917.

After the war he invented the well-known Wilson self-changing gearbox, used in many cars, and founded the firm of Self-Changing Gears, Ltd., of Coventry. He was an honorary member of the Institutions of Automobile and Mechanical Engineers and of the Junior Institution of Engineers and a member of the Institution of Civil Engineers. A man of strong character and shrewd judgement, he was a great lover of the countryside, a fine shot and an expert fly fisher.

Wilson married in 1904 Ethel Crommelin (died 1963), daughter of Samuel Octavius Gray, chief accountant to the Bank of England, and had three sons. He died at his home in Itchen Abbas, near Winchester, 30 June 1957. A portrait by Cecil Jameson is in the possession of the family.

[King's College, Cambridge, *Annual Report*, 1957; B. H. Liddell Hart, *The Tanks*, 2 vols., 1959; private information; personal knowledge.]   A. A. MILLER.

WIMPERIS, HARRY EGERTON (1876–1960), scientist, was born in London 27 August 1876, the only son of Joseph Price Wimperis, who was in the London office of a New Zealand merchant firm, and his wife, Jemima Wood-Samuel. His father having died when Wimperis was very young, his mother had a struggle to educate him. After an early but short apprenticeship as an engineer he resisted a strong attraction towards astronomy and entered the Royal College of Science (where he was a Tyndall prizeman) and subsequently went with a Whitworth scholarship to Gonville and Caius College, Cambridge, where he was a Salomons scholar and in 1899 took part ii of the mechanical sciences tripos as an advanced student. He had for financial reasons to decline a fellowship after graduating and went to Armstrong Whitworths, following which he was appointed engineering adviser to the crown agents for the colonies. During the war of 1914–18, he served

as an experimental scientist with the Royal Naval Air Service (he was a lieutenant-commander in the R.N.V.R.) and in 1918 was gazetted a major in the Royal Air Force aircraft production department. This brought to the fore his latent interest in aeronautics and his active and inventive mind found scope there in certain inventions, notably his course setting bombsight which the R.A.F. used until 1939. When the Air Ministry set up a scientific laboratory in the Imperial College in London, in the latter part of the first war, Wimperis was the first superintendent, and there a small team worked on bombing aids, aircraft engines, and a few vital tasks of that kind. As a result, when the Air Ministry decided to set up a more formal relationship with science and establish a directorate of scientific research, Wimperis was the 'sitting candidate' for the post of director. In spite of the showing he had made by directing the Air Ministry laboratory he was at first elected as deputy director while the Air Ministry sought elsewhere for a director, and it was not until a year later (1925) that he was appointed to the office itself. This was his first great opportunity. It lay in his hands to plan and then construct and mould the scientific research branch of Britain's youngest Service department. To this task he rose magnificently, novel though it was, as well as being strangely limited since both radio and armaments were specifically excluded. A man less temperate might have refused a task so ludicrously circumscribed, but fortunately Wimperis was not so short-sighted—trusting no doubt that as time went by he would be allowed a proper coverage of the whole scientific field: a circumstance not finally encompassed even in his time.

His new task was in any event a revolutionary one. It was one thing for senior military officers to recognize the importance of scientists and even commission them to do specific tasks, but to set up a whole nest of them within their Ministry and be expected to share work and secrets with them—that was an innovation indeed. Wimperis was probably ideal for this task. His scientific work in the navy had taught him how to 'live with the Service', he was eminently acceptable in personality, he was a close friend and colleague of many of the leading scientists of the country, and he learned to become a good administrator. For this task alone he would have deserved well of his country. He was to bring about one further achievement of far greater national importance. He caused to be set up the Committee for the Scientific Survey of Air Defence, known as the Tizard committee, which sponsored the development of radar, without which the outcome of the war of 1939–45 might have been very different. In 1934 a few thoughtful people realized that the state of air defence of Great Britain against bomber attack was deplorably weak, largely because there was no method of detecting the approach of aircraft which were more than a few miles way. Instead of setting up another departmental committee to study the problem, Wimperis persuaded the secretary of state for air to set up a committee mainly of 'independent' scientists. Headed by (Sir) Henry Tizard [q.v.], and comprising Dr. A. V. Hill, P. M. S. (later Lord) Blackett, and himself, with Dr. A. P. Rowe as secretary, he had assembled as powerful and competent a committee as this country has ever congregated and one which was to plan and progress radar for air defence in such a way and at such speed that England was ready with a warning system in 1939. This came about by chance. Wanting to dispose of the 'death ray' as an ogre, Wimperis wrote to (Sir) Robert Watson-Watt for his opinion. The reply made it clear that it was not feasible, but in the same letter Watson-Watt pointed out that radio detection of aircraft in the sky at some miles' range should be possible, if one used techniques which he and (Sir) Edward Appleton had already used for meteorology. With this foundation and with strong backing from the Tizard committee, a radio defence technique (radar) was developed in a surprisingly short time.

Wimperis was a member of many bodies, including the Aeronautical Research Council, the Royal Aeronautical Society (of which he was president in 1936–8), the executive committee of the National Physical Laboratory, the council of the Institution of Electrical Engineers, and he was a fellow of the American Institute of Aeronautical Sciences. He was president of the engineering section of the British Association in 1939 (council member, 1948–54); read the Wilbur Wright lecture to the Royal Aeronautical Society (1932); and the Hawkesley lecture to the Mechanical Engineers in 1944. Retiring in 1937, he was invited to visit Australia and advised the

Government there on the furthering of aeronautical research. As a result an Aeronautical Research Laboratory under the C.S.I.R.O. was set up at Melbourne and a chair of aeronautics at Sydney University.

As a leader Wimperis—to his junior staff—was stern and remote, but to his closer colleagues and to the younger ones who showed courage and endeavour (gifts pre-eminently his own) he was a good friend, with a high sense of truth, purpose, and intellectual integrity. As a civil servant who made it his life-work to build up a new branch he had perforce to fight for it and its needs, and his quiet perseverance and great strength of character served him well. From his father's side there was a strong hereditary bent towards craftsmanship (some of his cousins were prominent in water-colour painting and architecture) and this showed itself in his skill with delicate instruments. As well as being a most dutiful son to his mother, to whom he owed such a lot in his early struggles and whom he was proud to support as soon as he could, he was a devoted husband and father. His quiet whimsical humour delighted his close friends, including many in the Athenaeum, of which he was for long a member and staunch supporter. He married in 1907 Grace d'Avray, third daughter of (Sir) George Parkin [q.v.], who was for many years organizing secretary of the Rhodes Trust. Wimperis had three daughters. He was appointed O.B.E. (1918), C.B.E. (1928), and C.B. (1935). He died in Edinburgh 16 July 1960, his wife surviving him by only a few weeks. A portrait in oils by Cuthbert Orde hangs in the lecture hall of the Royal Aeronautical Society.

[Private information; personal knowledge.]
J. E. SERBY.

WINFIELD, SIR PERCY HENRY (1878–1953), lawyer and legal scholar, was born at Stoke Ferry, Norfolk, 16 September 1878, the fifth child and youngest son of Frederick Charles Winfield, corn merchant, and his wife, Mary Flatt. He was educated at King's Lynn Grammar School (later King Edward VII School) and at St. John's College, Cambridge, where in his first year he took a first class in the college examinations in law (1897) and was elected an exhibitioner and proper sizar. In 1898 he was senior in part i of the law tripos and was elected a foundation scholar, and in part ii (1899) was again at the head of the first class. In 1900 he was awarded a Whewell scholarship in international law and his college elected him to a McMahon scholarship founded for graduates intending to prepare themselves for the legal profession. Called to the bar by the Inner Temple in 1903, he joined the South-Eastern circuit; but he soon returned to Cambridge to teach, both privately and (from 1911) in lecture and problem classes recommended by the special board for law. After the war of 1914–18, during which he was commissioned in the Cambridgeshire Regiment (1915), was approved in absence for the LL.D. degree, and was wounded in action (August 1918), he lectured (Roman law, torts, criminal law) under the auspices of two colleges, Trinity and St. John's. St. John's soon elected him into an official fellowship (1921). In 1926 he became a university lecturer and in 1928 he was elected to the new Rouse Ball professorship of English law.

Winfield's lectures were well attended and appreciated. One recalls the elegant handwriting upon the blackboard before his lecture-hour began, the lecturer's spare athletic figure and lean judicial face, his flashes of dry humour, and the problem classes in which all in turn must act as counsel. His success as author and scholar owed much to his habit of thoroughly investigating the history of a legal topic before tackling its subtleties in the modern law. Early in 1914 the Law Quarterly Review published the first of his many legal articles, 'Some Bibliographical Difficulties of English Law', exposing the deficiencies which then handicapped that method of approach. Then followed two monographs, both published in 1921, upon the History and (largely post-war work) the Present Law of Abuse of Legal Procedure, in which that method was employed. Next, in 1925, his admirable Chief Sources of English Legal History (based upon a course of lectures he had delivered at Harvard) more than remedied the bibliographical deficiencies which his first legal article had deplored. Then his writings turned to the history and development of various aspects of the law of torts, which had now become his chief concern, and in 1931 he published his Province of the Law of Tort, examining its shadowy boundaries, past and present, and those of its neighbours, such as quasi-contract. The book, originally his Tagore lectures

in Calcutta (1930), did much to stimulate academic discussion—e.g. is there a general law of tort?—and enabled him to proceed to a detailed analysis of the modern law. This he did in his Textbook of the Law of Tort (1937). 'Intended primarily for students', the textbook rapidly attained an outstanding reputation both in the academic world and among practitioners and judges wherever our common law is known. A critical review of it (Law Quarterly Review, January 1938) foresaw this, emphasizing its infectious enthusiasm, unusual charm of style, and brilliant analysis of the more difficult problems. Before Winfield died it had reached its fifth edition. It has been a formative influence in our law.

Winfield's other publications included Salmond and Winfield on Contracts (1927), in which, punctiliously enclosing his own contributions within square brackets, he preserved and completed Sir John Salmond's unfinished work; three editions of Pollock on Contracts (1942–50); and a little book on the Foundations and Future of International Law (1941), the fruit of wartime lectures to groups of army officers. His Select Legal Essays (1952) contain fifteen of his numerous legal articles, reprinted from the learned journals of this country and overseas, including some of his later work on that arduous topic quasi-contract ('unjust enrichment') to which a chapter of his Province had already made notable contributions. He edited the Cambridge Law Journal for twenty years (1927–47).

As reader in common law to the Council of Legal Education (1938–49) Winfield lectured also at the Inns of Court. He was elected an honorary bencher of the Inner Temple (1938), served on the Lord Chancellor's Law Revision and Law Reporting committees, was for many years a borough magistrate and at one time a deputy county court judge. He took silk in 1943, the year in which his tenure of the Rouse Ball chair expired. He was elected F.B.A. in 1934, was an honorary LL.D. of Harvard (1929), Leeds (1944), and London (1949), and was president of the Society of Public Teachers of Law for 1929–30, and a vice-president of the Selden Society (1944–6). He was knighted in 1949.

Winfield had a great capacity for friendship and hospitality, delighting in the company of old and young alike and ever ready to spend time and trouble on their problems. His chief recreation was lawn tennis, in which he had gained college

Winfield

and 'Grasshopper' university colours and had captained the county (1912–14). He was also a keen supporter, latterly president, of the rugby football clubs of his college and university.

He married in 1909 Helena Chapman, daughter of William Thomas Scruby, estate agent, of Cambridge. He died at Cambridge 7 July 1953 and she, his devoted partner, in the following year. They had two sons and one daughter. A drawing of Winfield by John Hookham (1945) is in the library of St. John's College.

[S. J. Bailey in *Proceedings* of the British Academy, vol. xli, 1955; *Cambridge Law Journal*, 1954; private information; personal knowledge.]   S. J. BAILEY.

WINGATE, SIR (FRANCIS) REGINALD, first baronet (1861–1953), soldier and governor-general of the Sudan, was born at Port Glasgow in Renfrewshire 25 June 1861, the seventh son and youngest of the eleven children of Andrew Wingate, textile merchant, and his wife, Elizabeth, daughter of Richard Turner, of Hammersmith, county Dublin. He was a cousin of the father of Orde Wingate [q.v.]. In 1862 his father died and the family moved to Jersey where living was cheap.

Wingate went to St. James' Collegiate School where he showed 'determination and initiative', and in December 1878 entered the Royal Military Academy, Woolwich. He passed out tenth in 1880 and was gazetted as second lieutenant in the Royal Artillery. He was posted to India but soon after his arrival his battery was sent to Aden. There he studied Arabic, later becoming an expert. In June 1883 he joined the reorganized Egyptian Army.

Before General Gordon [q.v.] left Cairo for the last time in 1884 Wingate had been appointed aide-de-camp to Sir Evelyn Wood [q.v.], sirdar of the Egyptian Army. He assisted in the preparations for the Gordon relief expedition and took part in it with distinction; he was mentioned in dispatches and received three decorations. But Gordon's death and the consequent withdrawal of the troops put an end to Wingate's active service. He was appointed assistant military secretary to the sirdar; shortly afterwards assistant adjutant-general; then in 1889 director of military intelligence with responsibility for gathering information of every kind from the Sudan. His book *Mahdiism and the Egyptian*

Sudan (1891) and the accounts of Father Ohrwalder's and R. C. Slatin Pasha's experiences as prisoners of the Mahdi, which he translated and edited, bear witness to his profound knowledge of the Sudan.

His intelligence system was to prove its value when in 1895 the reoccupation of the Sudan was begun under Sir H. H. (later Earl) Kitchener [q.v.]. Dongola Province was occupied without difficulty in 1896 and the successful battles of the Atbara and Omdurman followed in 1898. The Khalifa's power was broken and a year later a force under Wingate brought him to battle and he was killed at Debeikerat.

In late 1899 Wingate succeeded Kitchener as governor-general of the Sudan and as sirdar and during the next seventeen years Wingate brought the country from anarchy to stable and progressive government. Slave raiding and trading were abolished; courts of justice and the rule of law were established; communications (railways, steamer services on the Nile, posts and telegraphs) were opened up and the various departments of a modern state were founded. An administrative machine was created, whereby a chain of authority ran from the governor-general to the district officers in the most remote parts of the country. Economic progress was encouraged and experiments in cotton growing led ultimately to the vast Gezira irrigation scheme. This project Wingate sponsored wholeheartedly and in 1913 he gained the support of Lloyd George, then chancellor of the Exchequer. Wingate presided over all this creative work and chose good subordinates in Slatin, (Sir) Edgar Bonham-Carter [q.v.], (Sir) James Currie [q.v.], and (Sir) Edgar Bernard. By constant touring and inspection he encouraged his officials, winning their sincere respect and the affectionate nickname of 'Master'. He laid the foundations of an administration which in later years won much praise for its efficiency, humanity, and progressive ideals.

When war came in 1914 it was doubtful whether the Sudan peoples would remain loyal to the British or side with Turkey as a Moslem power, but headed by their civil and religious leaders they remained unaffected, except for the Sultanate of Darfur, which Wingate occupied in 1916 after a short and well-planned operation. Lord Cromer [q.v.] wrote to Wingate to say, 'It is to my mind the most remarkable compliment that could possibly be paid to

British rule that the Sudan should have remained quiet: and this is mainly due to your wise government.'

The Arab revolt in the Hejaz gave Wingate other problems and he carefully fostered the strength of Sharif Hussain with money, food, and men in conditions of considerable difficulty and uncertainty; work he was able to continue when in January 1917 he became high commissioner in Egypt.

This was the most difficult and unhappy part of Wingate's career. As a British base, Egypt was full of British troops to whom the delicacy of the constitutional position was unknown; for the civil population supplies were short, and the requisitioning of animals and foodstuffs upset the peasant population; conscription was imposed to provide labour for the army and in spite of Wingate's efforts to ensure honest dealing, there was much discontent.

The Sultan and his ministers, like all Egyptians, wanted self-government, and were under some pressure from the extremists. Wingate foresaw and continually warned the British Government that when peace came relations between Britain and Egypt would deteriorate. The Anglo-French declaration, promising self-determination to the Arabs, who had been freed from Turkish rule, brought things to a head in November 1918.

The British Government were too occupied with Europe and the start of the peace conference to heed Wingate's warnings, and in January 1919 Wingate went to Paris and London to persuade the British ministers to receive an Egyptian delegation. Lord Curzon [q.v.], however, was adamant in refusing and his telegram to Cairo was followed by the immediate resignation of the Egyptian Government: agitation, disorder, and the death of Europeans and British officers resulted, and for a time law and order were completely overthrown. Although Wingate had given correct advice and this had been ignored, he clearly could no longer represent the British Government in Egypt, and he did not return. Lord Allenby [q.v.] was appointed in his place with instructions to carry out a conciliatory policy on the lines of Wingate's previous recommendations, and Wingate was allowed to bear the blame for the Government's failure to take his advice until forced to do so by bloodshed and disaster.

Wingate, who had reached the rank of general, was never again employed and henceforth occupied himself in other ways. A director of various companies, colonel commandant of the Royal Artillery, a governor of the Gordon College in Khartoum, and president of several local organizations at his home at Dunbar, he led a long and useful life. He married in 1888 Catherine Leslie Rundle, sister of a brother officer (Sir) (H. M.) Leslie Rundle [q.v.]. She was his devoted partner and helper and Wingate never recovered from her death in 1946. He died in his ninety-second year at Dunbar 28 January 1953. He had three sons and a daughter; the eldest son, Ronald Evelyn Leslie (born 1889), who contributes to this Supplement, succeeded his father, but the second died an infant and the third was killed in action in 1918.

Wingate was appointed K.C.M.G. (1898), K.C.B. (1900), G.C.V.O. (1912), G.C.B. (1914), G.B.E. (1918), and created a baronet in 1920. He was appointed to the D.S.O. in 1889.

A cartoon by 'Spy' was published in *Vanity Fair* in 1897; and a portrait by by W. W. Ouless was presented to the borough council of Dunbar.

[Sir Ronald Wingate, *Wingate of the Sudan*, 1955; personal knowledge.]

J. W. ROBERTSON.

WITT, SIR ROBERT CLERMONT (1872-1952), art collector, was born in London 16 January 1872, the eldest of the six children of Gustavus Andrew Witt, merchant, and his wife, Helene de Clermont. He was educated at Clifton and New College, Oxford, where he obtained a second in history in 1894; he subsequently became an honorary fellow. He served in the Matabele war in 1896 and acted as war correspondent with Cecil Rhodes [q.v.]. Returning to London he qualified as a solicitor and eventually became senior partner in the firm of Stephenson, Harwood and Tatham, making it one of the most prominent firms of solicitors in London.

Witt was a man of great energy who contrived to combine with his professional career a lifetime of intense activity in the cause of art which was his governing passion. He made no claim to be an authoritative critic, but as early as 1902 he published *How to Look at Pictures* which was several times reprinted during his lifetime and ranks as a minor classic in criticism. In 1903 he co-operated with Lord Balcarres (afterwards the Earl of

Crawford), (Sir) Claude Phillips, D. S. Mac-
Coll, and Roger Fry [qq.v.] in founding the
National Art-Collections Fund. He was the
first honorary secretary of the Fund (1903–
20), then chairman (1920–45), and saw it
grow into an organization of great national
importance. When he retired from the
chairmanship in 1945 he was made its first
president and in his honour a special exhibition of the principal acquisitions made
for the nation by the Fund was organized
at the National Gallery. Witt was also a
trustee of the National Gallery (1916–23,
1924–31, 1933–40); trustee of the Tate
Gallery (1916–31); and of the Watts Gallery, Compton. In 1932 he collaborated
with Samuel Courtauld and Lord Lee of
Fareham [qq.v.] in founding the Courtauld
Institute of Art and remained a member
of its committee of management until his
death.

When still undergraduates both Witt
and his future wife began collecting
photographs and reproductions, a hobby
which later led during their long married
life to the formation of the vast Witt
library of photographs numbering three-
quarters of a million. In 1944 Witt
executed a deed of gift making over this
library to the Courtauld Institute but
continued to administer it himself at his
home in Portman Square where he had
turned his spacious house into a reference library; all the walls in the rooms,
passages, and even the bedrooms were
crowded with shelves containing boxes
of photographs always readily available
to students and collectors. At Witt's death
the library was transferred to the premises
of the Institute which also benefited by
the bequest of his large collection (4,000)
of Old Master drawings planned as a
complement to the Library of Reproductions and making the whole 'an
incomparable weapon of scholarship'.
The collection has since been extensively
enlarged through a fund which came to
the Institute as his residuary legatee.

Witt published a catalogue of painters
and draughtsmen represented in his
library in 1920 and a supplement in 1925.
His conception was copied abroad,
notably in the United States where he
personally helped Miss Helen Frick to
create what is now the Frick Library of
Reproductions on the same lines, and in
Tokyo by Professor Yukio Yashiro.

In the course of forming his library
and collection Witt acquired an encyclopedic knowledge of art and of the where-
abouts of art treasures throughout the
world. This knowledge he placed freely
at the disposal of students and collectors,
the value of his contribution being enhanced by his quality as a speaker and
lecturer. An excellent talk on 'The Art of
Collecting' was reprinted and circulated
to the ten thousand members of the
National Art-Collections Fund. He was
an active controversialist on art subjects
and in the dispute over the pictures
of Sir Hugh Lane [q.v.] his solicitor's
training made him an outspoken defender
of the strictly legal interpretation of the
rival claims of London and Dublin. He
played a prominent part in the organization of the annual winter exhibitions
of foreign art at Burlington House in the
thirties, writing the introduction to the
souvenir catalogue of the Italian exhibition of 1930.

Witt found time to show himself a
devoted son of his school and college and
to serve as the vice-president of the
Institute of Industrial Psychology. A man
of spartan habits, he never wore an overcoat and uncomplainingly bore many
years of severe arthritis which compelled
him to use crutches. He loved young
people and in his old age and in great
pain would go swimming with them when
on holiday. He died in London 26 March
1952, retaining to the end his interest
and vigour. He was appointed C.B.E. in
1918 and knighted in 1922.

In the formation of his vast reference
library Witt had the enthusiastic help
of his wife, Mary Helena, daughter of
Charles Henry Marten, stockbroker, whom
he married in 1899, and who survived
him only a few months. Their only child,
a son, John, followed his father as senior
partner in his firm of solicitors and also
on the board of the trustees of the
National Gallery of which he was chairman when the arrangements were completed with the Irish Government for
the exhibition of the Hugh Lane pictures
in Dublin.

A presentation portrait of Witt by Sir
Oswald Birley is in the Witt Library at
the Courtauld Institute where there is
also a painting by T. C. Dugdale of
Witt sitting in his library when it was
in his home in Portman Square.

[Private information; personal knowledge.]
                                ALEC MARTIN.

WITTGENSTEIN, LUDWIG JOSEF
JOHANN (1889–1951), philosopher, was
born in Vienna 26 April 1889, the
youngest in a family of eight children.

The family was of Jewish origin. Wittgenstein's paternal grandfather had moved from Saxony to Austria; his father, Karl Wittgenstein, was prominent in the iron and steel industry of the Danubean monarchy. Wittgenstein was educated at home until his fourteenth year when he went to school at Linz in Upper Austria. After his matriculation in 1906 he took up mechanical engineering at the Technische Hochschule in Berlin-Charlottenburg. In 1908 he moved to England where for three years he was a research student in the department of engineering at the university of Manchester. His early interests were in aeronautics, and at Manchester he invented a jet reaction propeller for aircraft. It seems to have been the design of this propeller which stimulated his interest in mathematics. This in turn led him to study the philosophical foundations of mathematics. At this time he read Bertrand (later Earl) Russell's *Principles of Mathematics* (1903) and perhaps the works of Frege. Another influence on his philosophic development was Schopenhauer.

In 1911 Wittgenstein changed to philosophy. It may have been on Frege's advice that he decided to go to Cambridge to study with Russell. He certainly met Frege at about this time and had several discussions with him. Early in 1912 Wittgenstein was admitted to Trinity College, Cambridge, where he spent all three terms of 1912 and the first two terms of 1913. In October of that year he settled at Skjolden in Sogn, Norway, and corresponded with Russell about the progress of his work in logic.

After the outbreak of war in 1914 Wittgenstein entered the Austrian army as a volunteer. He fought on the eastern and southern fronts and was taken prisoner by the Italians in November 1918. On his release in August of the following year he returned to Vienna where he completed a course for teachers. During the war he had come under the influence of the ethical and religious writings of Tolstoy. He now gave away the great fortune which he had inherited from his father and henceforward his manner of life was characterized by great simplicity. Until 1926 he worked as a schoolmaster in various remote villages in Lower Austria, and from 1926 to 1928 as an architect in Vienna.

In 1918 Wittgenstein had finished his *Logisch-Philosophische Abhandlung*, the work which has become more widely known

under the title *Tractatus Logico-Philosophicus*. It first appeared in Ostwald's *Annalen der Naturphilosophie* in 1921 and was published in England in 1922, with a translation (by C. K. Ogden [q.v.] with the help of F. P. Ramsey) running parallel to the original text. Save for a short paper, 'Some Remarks on Logical Form', in the supplementary volume to the *Proceedings* of the Aristotelian Society for the year 1929, the *Tractatus* was the only work which Wittgenstein published in his lifetime. During his years as a schoolmaster and an architect, he did not actively engage in philosophical research. He had, however, some contact with F. P. Ramsey of Cambridge and with Moritz Schlick and Friedrich Waismann in Vienna. Through the two latter, Wittgenstein came to exercise a considerable influence on the so-called Vienna Circle, from which sprang the movement in contemporary thought known as logical positivism.

Early in 1929 Wittgenstein returned to Cambridge to take up research in philosophy. In June of the same year he obtained his Ph.D., submitting the *Tractatus* as a thesis. In 1930 he was made a fellow of Trinity College, under Title B, a singular honour. When the fellowship expired in 1936, Wittgenstein left Cambridge and withdrew for nearly a year to his hut near Skjolden in Norway. There he began writing his *Philosophical Investigations*. He returned to Cambridge in 1937 and two years later succeeded G. E. Moore [q.v.] in the chair of philosophy. He had been a probationary faculty lecturer from 1930 to 1933, an assistant faculty lecturer from 1933 to 1935, and had lectured without holding a staff appointment in 1936, 1938, and 1939. In the academic year 1933–4 he dictated, in the course of his lectures, the so-called 'Blue Book', which signalized a radical change in his thinking. The 'Brown Book', dictated in 1935, anticipates leading ideas of the *Philosophical Investigations*.

Wittgenstein's teaching was interrupted during part of the war of 1939–45 when he took up voluntary service, first as a porter in Guy's Hospital, and later as an assistant in a medical laboratory at Newcastle. In the Easter term of 1947 he gave his last lectures at Cambridge, and from the end of the year he resigned his professorship. He lived in Ireland until the spring of 1949 when he completed the second part of his *Philosophical*

Investigations. During the last two years of his life he was severely ill and he died at Cambridge 29 April 1951. He was unmarried.

Although Wittgenstein lived the major part of his adult life in England—he became a naturalized subject in 1938—he continued to write his thoughts in German. As a master of German prose he has few equals. His style bears a striking resemblance to some writers, such as Lichtenberg and Lessing, among the German humanists of the late eighteenth and early nineteenth centuries, the period most congenial to his own tastes in literature and the arts.

The *Philosophical Investigations* were published in 1953 and *Remarks on the Foundations of Mathematics* (written in 1938–44) in 1956, both translated by Miss G. E. M. Anscombe. Of considerable interest are some writings anterior to the 'Blue Book'. They show Wittgenstein's thoughts in a transitional stage between the early *Tractatus* and the later *Investigations.*

Wittgenstein's *Tractatus* grew out of problems of logic which had occupied Frege and Russell. The earliest of its leading ideas is that logical (formal, necessary) truths are *tautologies.* A tautology is a kind of *truth-function* which has the peculiar property that the function is a true proposition, independently of whether its arguments are true or false propositions. The theory of truth-functions forms the basis of much development in modern logic. Wittgenstein's contributions to this theory are considerable, and his use of it to clarify the notion of logical truth is, even if not conclusive, a milestone in the philosophy of logic.

The most consequential of Wittgenstein's earlier views is perhaps his picture-theory of language. According to it, any significant proposition can be analysed into parts which correspond to elements in reality. The simple parts of propositions he called 'names' and their counterparts in the world 'things'. The way in which the parts of the proposition are combined—the *structure* of the proposition—depicts a possible combination of elements in reality, a possible 'state of affairs'. The possibility of this combination Wittgenstein calls a *logical form.* Language thus has its logical form in common with reality.

The conception of language as a picture has as a consequence an interesting theory of the *limits* of linguistic expression. The logical form of a proposition cannot be pictured. Which form it is *shows* itself to the understanding but cannot be *said.* It is a further consequence of this distinction between saying and showing, that there are no propositions of philosophy. Philosophy, Wittgenstein contends, is an activity and not a doctrine. This activity consists in displaying the limits of the thinkable. The solution to the problems of philosophy is the insight that, in trying to articulate an answer to them, we make the self-frustrating effort to say the unsayable.

Wittgenstein's idea that all meaningful propositions are truth-functions of some elementary propositions which stand in a picturing relation to reality was interpreted by the logical positivists as asserting a dependence of meaning upon verifiability through sense-experience. (The Verificationist thesis). This interpretation has no ground in Wittgenstein's book. It is worth noticing that the positivists' *monistic* conception of the world as a logical unity of experiential data and constructions out of them is at explicit variance with Wittgenstein's view of the anumerical multiplicity of logical forms.

In his later writings Wittgenstein abandoned the picture-theory of language, the view that all meaningful propositions are truth-functions of elementary propositions, and the doctrine of the unsayable. But the problem of meaning, of the 'possibility of language', remains central to his later thinking too. And so also the view that philosophy is, in some sense, a clarification of thought through a critique of language and not a theory about the foundations of knowledge or the nature of reality.

Typical of the later Wittgenstein's thinking is the discussion of language in the *Philosophical Investigations.* Instead of raising the question of the nature and general form of propositions, as he did in the *Tractatus,* Wittgenstein considers simplified situations, *language-games,* in which the actual working of language is clearly displayed, perspicuous ('übersichtlich'). When a great variety of such language-games are presented, it becomes clear that these games have no features in common which characterize them as language; that there *is* no general form of proposition or 'essence' of symbolism. The mutual interrelatedness of various language-games, which make up all the variety of linguistic usage, is a *family-resemblance,* where any member of the family-tree resembles some other member, but where there is no *one* pervading feature (or combination of features) which marks them as members of the same family.

Thus the philosopher's quest for essences is an uneasiness of the mind which is brought to rest by a perspicuous presentation of the case. The method of philosophy is strictly *descriptive*. And the philosophic achievement is not an answer to a question, but the dropping of a question which rested on a misunderstanding of our ordinary use of words.

Wittgenstein's later thinking has exercised an influence on contemporary thought comparable to the influence of the *Tractatus* on the teaching of the logical positivists. Most of what is known under the names of 'analytic', 'linguistic', or 'semantic' philosophy is inspired, directly or indirectly, by Wittgenstein's teaching at Cambridge in the thirties and forties or by his published work. To what extent contemporary philosophical analysis can be regarded as illustrative of Wittgenstein's way of thinking is, however, uncertain. Wittgenstein tended to repudiate the results of his own influence and was probably justified in thinking that his ideas were usually misunderstood and distorted even by those who professed to be his disciples.

Wittgenstein was undoubtedly a philosopher of rare genius and originality. He questioned the nature of philosophy itself and drew a line of demarcation between philosophy and the sciences which constitutes a lasting clarification of the possibilities and limitations of both types of inquiry. He was a man of forceful and unusual personality, who could not fail to make an impression upon everyone who knew him. His life was an unending journey in search of truth. Doubt was the moving force within him, and discussion one of his chief means of travel. It was in the nature both of his character and of his philosophy to raise questions rather than to answer them. He seldom looked back on his earlier views, and when he did so it was usually to repudiate them.

[G. H. von Wright: 'Ludwig Wittgenstein, a Biographical Sketch', *Philosophical Review*, vol. lxiv, 1955; Norman Malcolm, *Ludwig Wittgenstein, a Memoir*, with a biographical sketch by G. H. von Wright, 1958.]

G. H. VON WRIGHT.

WOLFF, MARTIN (1872–1953), academic lawyer, was born in Berlin 26 September 1872, the elder child and only son of Wilhelm Wolff, banker, and his wife, Selma Ball. After studying under Heinrich Brunner and Otto Gierke, he became in 1900 a *Privatdozent* in the Berlin faculty of law and in 1903 an extraordinary professor; in 1914 he was called to Marburg as an ordinary professor; in 1918 to Bonn; and finally in 1922 back to Berlin, where he taught until 1935 when, as a Jew, he was ousted by the Nazis. In 1938, on the invitation of All Souls College, Oxford, he emigrated to England where he was naturalized in 1945.

Trained in the German universities at a period when the best energies of academic lawyers were bent towards the completion of the German Civil Code, it fell to Wolff more than anyone else to explain that part of the Code which enacted the law of property, to place it in its historical setting and to draw out its consequences. This he did in lectures which have become a legend among German lawyers and above all, in 1910–12, in the relevant parts of Enneccerus–Kipp–Wolff, *Lehrbuch des Bürgerlichen Rechts*, a book of the highest authority and influence which in his lifetime ran into nine editions and which the Nazis found no way of superseding. All German private law, indeed, fell within his province, and he wrote extensively on it, but more significant for his later career was his interest in private international law and comparative law, in both of which he acquired an audience extending far beyond Germany. He wrote a succinct but highly authoritative work on the former subject as applied in Germany and he was one of the most active participants in the work of the great Kaiser Wilhelm Institute for Comparative Law. He was one of the editors of the *Zeitschrift für ausländisches und internationales Privatrecht* and of the *Rechtsvergleichendes Handwörterbuch für das Zivil- und Handelsrecht*, the nearest thing that has yet appeared to a comprehensive encyclopedia of comparative private law. He also lectured regularly on French civil law.

In England Wolff was financially assisted by All Souls College in preparing a book on English *Private International Law*, which appeared in 1945 and rapidly established itself as an important authority. He made a special contribution to the subject by introducing a comparative element and used foreign experience to suggest the solution of problems which had not hitherto come before the courts; but so accurate was his exposition of English law and so complete his familiarity with the English point of view that reviewers disagreed with him as though he were one of themselves and not an intruder from abroad. A second edition appeared in 1950. He also found time in England to contribute a long account of French Private Law to the new edition of *Chambers's Encyclopaedia* and a brilliant summary of Commercial Law to the *Manual of German Law* published under the auspices of the Foreign Office. He saw appear at last, in 1950–52, a three-volume work to which he had made large contributions, the *Traité de droit comparé* by Arminjon, Nolde, and Wolff.

Wolff's greatest strength probably lay in his lecturing, which was characterized by extreme lucidity, a wonderful gift for making abstract principles live by an apt choice of examples, and a patently sincere pursuit of justice. In the largest hall of Berlin University, holding between one and two thousand students, this tiny man with his light but clear voice commanded absolute silence by the sheer force of his personality, except when some witticism dissolved his audience into laughter. Moreover, although he never sought to dominate his more intimate pupils but strove to make of them independent thinkers, most if not all of them remained immune from Nazi influence.

In Oxford Wolff gave only one lecture, a famous and classical one on 'The Nature of Legal Persons'; he did, however, attend regularly seminars on comparative law and so came into contact with quite a number of undergraduates, who learnt to know his power as a teacher. He enjoyed these opportunities of meeting young men until his health began to fail during the last year or two of his life. Since he made no attempt to put himself forward, in the unpropitious conditions of the war and the immediate post-war period he did not become so rapidly known to his fellow lawyers, although he occasionally acted as examiner of a thesis. But in the end he became well known and when he reached the age of eighty the university conferred on him the honorary degree, rarely given to academic lawyers, of D.C.L. Scholars from different countries combined to offer him a *Festschrift* which contains a full bibliography of his writings, and the Bundesrepublik conferred

on him the Grosser Verdienstkreuz. He held honorary doctorates from Marburg and Thessaloniki.

Wolff united a remarkably sweet and gentle disposition to a sharp and pungent wit and a clear insight into his own and other people's abilities and character. Those qualities, together with a wide range of interests, of which perhaps the most vital was in the theory and practice of music, made him excellent company. One of the greatest jurists of his age, he influenced deeply a whole generation of pupils and colleagues.

In 1906 Wolff married Marguerite, daughter of Hermann Jolowicz, silk merchant in London, and sister of H. F. Jolowicz [q.v.]. They had two sons. He died in London 20 July 1953.

[Private information; personal knowledge.]
F. H. LAWSON.

WOOD, EDWARD FREDERICK LINDLEY, first EARL OF HALIFAX (1881–1959), statesman, was born at Powderham Castle, Devon, the home of his maternal grandfather, 16 April 1881. He was the fourth son and youngest of the six children of Charles Lindley Wood, later second Viscount Halifax [q.v.], by his wife, Lady Agnes Elizabeth Courtenay, only daughter of the eleventh Earl of Devon [q.v.]. Born with an atrophied left arm which had no hand, he shrugged off his disability even as a child; the Christian belief which was the passion of his father's life and which permeated his own upbringing precluded self-pity. He quickly learned to shoot and ride to hounds, and as heir to great estates in Yorkshire, his three brothers having died young while he himself was between the ages of four and nine, was able to share without embarrassment the traditional pursuits of a countryman.

He was educated at Eton and Christ Church, Oxford, where in 1903 he took a first class in history followed by a fellowship at All Souls. He taught history, hunted twice a week, travelled round the world, and wrote a biography of John Keble (1909) reflecting the Anglo-Catholic faith he shared with his father. In 1909 his marriage to Lady Dorothy Evelyn Augusta Onslow, younger daughter of the fourth Earl of Onslow [q.v.], brought lasting happiness and a family of three sons, and twin daughters only one of whom survived. The loyalty which at his wedding burdened him with a solid gold cup nearly two feet high as a tribute from the tenantry helped to ensure his election in January 1910 as

Conservative member of Parliament for Ripon. He held the seat in December, and thereafter was returned unopposed until created a peer in 1925.

On the outbreak of war in 1914 Wood was serving as a yeomanry officer in the Yorkshire Dragoons. The failure of the allied armies to pierce the western front denied his regiment the mobile role of their hopes, confining them instead to a monotonous routine behind the lines. Wood was mentioned in dispatches in January 1917 and later that year returned to England at the invitation of Sir Auckland (later Lord) Geddes [q.v.] to serve for the rest of the war as an assistant secretary in the Ministry of National Service. In 1920, when not yet forty, he accepted the governor-generalship of South Africa but was obliged to withdraw when the Union expressed a preference for a man of cabinet rank or a member of the royal family. So he remained in the Commons where, although neither fluent nor brilliant, his thoughtful contributions to debate were heard with attention. His first ministerial office, as under-secretary for the colonies, began bleakly in April 1921. The secretary of state, (Sir) Winston Churchill, had wanted someone else and being much preoccupied with Middle Eastern problems made no time to receive him. The new under-secretary eventually forced his way into his chief's office, where a brisk exchange laid the foundations of co-operation. On a mission to the West Indies Wood studied the economics of sugar and demands for constitutional reform.

Wood felt an aloof distaste for the ways by which Lloyd George attempted to hold together his uneasy coalition. Characteristically, he had objected less to the activities of the 'Black and Tans' in Ireland than to the Government's evasiveness on the subject. He was also troubled by allegations that honours were being sold. He did not hesitate to vote for the downfall of Lloyd George in October 1922. In the new administration of Bonar Law he entered the Cabinet for the first time, as president of the Board of Education, and was sworn of the Privy Council. He found the work uncongenial, lacked interest in educational problems, and could not hope to inspire a department which was being financially starved; but he remained until the fall of Baldwin's government in January 1924. He was equally ineffective as minister of agriculture in Baldwin's second administration. However rooted his personal belief in the virtues of the land, he accepted an official policy that shrank from the expense of sustaining an enfeebled industry. He was released from frustration by his appointment in November 1925 as governor-general and viceroy of India, his name having been suggested to Baldwin by King George V.

For a man without overt ambition, Wood had risen swiftly to high office. Initially he owed it to family. His grandfather, the first Viscount Halifax [q.v.], was one of the earliest secretaries of state for India and author of the dispatch recognizing British responsibility for Indian education. Yet in his own right the new viceroy was hardly less well equipped than his predecessors. Immensely tall, with a fine domed head and the face of an ascetic, he bore himself as majestically as Lord Curzon [q.v.], and if intellectually he could not quite match that relentlessly energetic mind, he brought a calmer and more balanced temperament to the rule of 400 million people. Once only in five years, it was afterwards recalled, did he lose his temper—at the disappearance of a disreputable old hat to which he was much attached. Lord Irwin, as he was created in December 1925, landed at Bombay on Maundy Thursday, 1 April 1926. His aim, he told one of his staff in June, was 'to keep a contented India in the Commonwealth twenty-five years hence'. A few weeks later, on 17 July, speaking in Simla at the Chelmsford Club, one of the few open to both Europeans and Indians, he set the tone of his viceroyalty. In phrases of burning sincerity which accorded with the Indian mind he appealed in the name of religion for an end to communal strife between Hindu and Moslem: a theme to which he returned again and again. For as long as such hatreds persisted even the most sympathetic of viceroys would be reluctant to meet Indian demands for self-government.

The Act of 1919 which embodied the Montagu–Chelmsford reforms had provided for a statutory commission to report within ten years. Upon this Indian aspirations were fixed. Thus the announcement in November 1927 that the commission was to consist entirely of British members of Parliament affronted educated Indian opinion. Its chairman was Sir John (later Viscount) Simon [q.v.], and its members included C. R. (later Earl) Attlee, who as

prime minister in 1947 was to be responsible for granting independence to the sub-
continent. Such names in 1927 were of no
account among Indians and even those of
temperate views determined to boycott
an inquisition by foreigners into their
country's fitness for self-government.
Various attempts to associate Indians
with the commission proved unsuccessful.
Irwin afterwards admitted that he had
been wrong in advising the secretary of
state, Lord Birkenhead [q.v.], not to include Indians. He had reasoned that a
mixed body would fail to reach agreement;
that the Moslems could be persuaded to
co-operate with an all-British commission;
and that the Hindus would follow suit,
however reluctantly, rather than allow
their traditional opponents to be heard
unchallenged. For his part, Birkenhead
feared that an alliance between British
Labour and Indian members of a mixed
commission might produce dangerously
inconvenient majority conclusions. He
must share responsibility for the gravest
mistake of Irwin's viceroyalty.

As the Simon commission gathered its
evidence in an atmosphere of glacial hostility, the viceroy searched for a formula of
reconciliation. He acted as resolutely as
any predecessor against increasing outbreaks of violence but came to recognize
that only a generous gesture of friendship would break the sullen silence. The
imaginative scheme which he evolved was
in two parts—a Round Table conference
embracing all parties in the British Parliament, all parties and interests in British
India, and the Indian princes; and a formal declaration on dominion status. In
this, as in subsequent policy, his hand was
strengthened by a change of government
at home. The second Labour Government
of Ramsay MacDonald, which took office
in June 1929, shared the viceroy's view
that benevolent paternalism must give
way to partnership no less in India than
elsewhere throughout the Commonwealth.
In the talks held in London during his
leave that summer Irwin was to find in
Wedgwood Benn (later Viscount Stansgate, q.v.), the new secretary of state, a
more accommodating ally than Birkenhead. It was therefore with confidence that
in October the viceroy risked his reputation for statesmanship by publicly announcing a Round Table conference and
the British Government's view that the
natural issue of India's constitutional
progress was dominion status.

The result was tragically disappointing.

Among Indians, an initial restoration of
faith in the motives of British rule rapidly
gave way to mistrust and dismay at
reports of the scornful fury which the
viceroy's words had evoked in London.
Birkenhead and Churchill were predict-
ably vehement among Conservatives;
Lord Reading [q.v.] condemned him with
the authority of a popular ex-viceroy,
his juridical mind outraged by the impre-
cision of the term dominion status; Simon
was annoyed that Irwin had anticipated
the commission's report. Hoping to save
the situation by personal persuasion, the
viceroy invited Indian political leaders,
including M. K. Gandhi [q.v.], to meet
him in New Delhi. The conference was abortive. Disillusioned by unfriendly speeches
at Westminster and unable to extract
an early or exact date for the implementation of dominion status, Gandhi
and his associates withdrew to plan a
campaign of civil disobedience with complete independence as its ultimate goal.

Again India passed through the weary
cycle of resentment, rebellion, repression,
and reprieve. In the spring of 1930
Gandhi led a march to the sea to defy the
salt laws which imposed a tax minute
in its incidence but to the Indian imagination a symbol of oppression. Irwin,
whose compassion concealed a steely
regard for law and order, was reluctant
to add martyrdom to the other spiritual
qualities which elevated Gandhi above
all other Indian leaders. But when
defiance provoked violent and bloody
riots, the viceroy did not hesitate to authorize his arrest and the use of full emergency powers against unlawful gatherings
and a seditious press. So long as Gandhi
remained in prison there could be peace
of a sort but no progress. In January 1931,
combining magnanimity with political
shrewdness, Irwin ordered the release of
the one man who could speak for India.
They met eight times and after protracted
discussion came to an understanding
known as the Delhi Pact. Few proconsuls
other than Irwin could have demonstrated
a subtlety of mind to match that of
Gandhi or driven so hard a bargain clothed
in the language of friendship: there was to
be an end to civil disobedience and the
economic boycott of British goods; Congress was to be represented at future sessions of the Round Table conference to
discuss India's future in an All-India
Federation, Indian responsibility, and reservations or safeguards on such matters
as defence, external relations, the position

of minorities, and India's financial credit. Conservative opinion in England, which had begun to discern some good in a viceroy who refused to entertain criticisms of a much-tried police force or to commute death sentences for crimes of violence, reacted harshly both to the discussions and to their outcome. Irwin saw things differently. When asked whether Gandhi had not been tiresome he replied: 'Some people found Our Lord very tiresome.'

In a lifetime of public service, the viceroyalty must be accounted Irwin's most exacting task. But for all his vision, his sympathy and his administrative skill, he could not secure an immediate measure of constitutional progress or a calming of racial strife. Within a year of his sailing for England in April 1931 the second Round Table conference had ended inconclusively, civil disobedience was widespread, and Gandhi once more in prison. Irwin nevertheless printed on the Indian mind a remembrance of tact and patience and a courage which recognized neither political expediency nor physical fear. More than once his life was in danger, notably when his train was almost derailed by a terrorist bomb as he approached New Delhi to take up residence for the first time in the oriental Versailles created by Sir Edwin Lutyens and Sir Herbert Baker [qq.v.]. His own preference in the capital was for the Anglican church of the Redemption, enriched by his private raising of funds and consecrated in the last days of his rule. Appointed G.C.S.I. and G.C.I.E. in 1926, he was made K.G. in 1931, becoming chancellor of the order in 1943.

In the autumn of 1931 Irwin was invited to become foreign secretary in Ramsay MacDonald's 'national' Government. He declined, preferring to savour the renewed enjoyment of Garrowby, his estate near York, and to prolong his reunion with his father whom he had hardly dared hope to see again. He was also aware that he had become something of an embarrassment to right-wing members of his own party. Such tensions, he felt, unfitted him for an office which should be as far removed as possible from parliamentary strife. In the summer of 1932, however, he was persuaded to return to the Board of Education. He liked in later years to recall how the proconsul fresh from the rule of a sub-continent was refused a new pair of curtains for his office. The appointment he found as drably uncongenial and as economically restricted

as it had been earlier. He accepted it only when urged to place his knowledge of Indian affairs at the disposal of the Cabinet and assist Sir Samuel Hoare (later Viscount Templewood, q.v.), the secretary of state, in the drafting and parliamentary progress of an immense government of India bill which did not reach the statute book until 1935. Two pleasures sustained him during this gruelling task. In 1932 he became master of the Middleton foxhounds and in 1933 he was nominated unopposed as chancellor of Oxford University in succession to Lord Grey of Fallodon [q.v.]. Early in 1934 his father died in his ninety-fifth year at the other family estate of Hickleton, in Yorkshire. It was a bereavement which, although scarcely unexpected, left the son conscious of an acute loneliness after the shared intimacies of half a century. Five months as secretary of state for war in 1935 revealed to him the paucity of our defences but did not impress him with an urgent need for rearmament. After the general election in November, Halifax, as he now was, became lord privy seal and leader of the House of Lords and on Baldwin's retirement in 1937 he was appointed lord president of the Council in Chamberlain's administration. During his tenure of both these offices without departmental responsibilities he applied himself increasingly to foreign affairs.

With Anthony Eden (later the Earl of Avon), who became foreign secretary in December 1935, Halifax at once established a harmonious relationship. Both were disturbed by the growing belligerency of Nazi Germany; neither, aware of British and French military weakness, was prepared in March 1936 to contemplate resistance to Hitler's occupation of the Rhineland. Exposed to scorn and easy abuse in later years, their caution at the time accurately reflected the attitude of many of their countrymen. What began increasingly to separate the two ministers was their contrasting approach to the efficacy of negotiation. Halifax believed that the Nazis were reasonable men whose ambitions could be modified by patient and persuasive discussion; Eden feared that without substantial rearmament such exchanges would be mistaken for weakness and serve only to encourage aggression. The doubts of the foreign secretary were justified by the visit which Halifax made to Germany in November 1937.

Eden had reluctantly agreed that Halifax should meet Hitler in Berlin under guise of accepting an invitation, bizarrely addressed to him as master of the Middleton, to shoot foxes and to attend a hunting exhibition. By subsequently agreeing to journey to Berchtesgaden for his interview with Hitler, Halifax unwittingly cast himself in the role of eager supplicant; and by omitting to deliver an unambiguous warning against German designs on Austria and Czechoslovakia, as instructed by the foreign secretary, he deprived his mission of deterrent effect. 'He struck me as very sincere', Halifax recorded of his talk with the Führer. Other Nazi leaders he found likeable though slightly comic. The squire of Garrowby could well discern their social inadequacies; the Christian failed to detect their wickedness.

Eden resigned in February 1938: the essential issue was whether British foreign policy should emanate from the Foreign Office or from No. 10 Downing Street. In agreeing to succeed as foreign secretary Halifax implicitly accepted a more subordinate role than that of his predecessor, an understanding which weakened his tenure of the Foreign Office and delayed his conversion to robustness. He embarked on his duties assiduously but without enthusiasm. His knowledge of European history and thought was not profound and he never read *Mein Kampf*. He was nevertheless welcomed, even by Churchill, as a man whose desire for peace did not preclude a readiness to resist aggression. His attitude was soon put to the test. Three weeks after Halifax became foreign secretary, Hitler invaded Austria and incorporated it within the German Reich. Czechoslovakia now lay exposed to the same fate and German minorities on the Sudeten border were incited to demonstrate with increasing violence against the alleged oppression of the Czech Government. Three factors left Halifax little room for diplomatic manœuvre. The first was British military weakness, in spite of a slowly increasing preoccupation with rearmament. The second was a persistent and paralysing over-estimate of German military strength. The third was the geographical remoteness of Czechoslovakia. To guarantee the independence of Czechoslovakia in March 1938, either alone or in alliance with a debilitated France, was a risk Halifax dared not take. If his bluff had been

called and Britain had been drawn into a declaration of war on Germany, it would have been without hope of protecting either Czechoslovakia from German tanks or London from German bombs. So in courteous tones which aroused only the contempt of the Nazi leaders he begged them to moderate their claims in the interests of world peace; simultaneously he urged the Czechs not to be so disobligingly slow in bowing to German demands. In July he dispatched Lord Runciman [q.v.] to Czechoslovakia as a mediator.

Responsibility for that chapter of appeasement in British foreign policy belongs more to Chamberlain than to Halifax. The foreign secretary did not attend, or resent not attending, any of the three meetings held successively at Berchtesgaden, Godesberg, and Munich in September 1938 at which the prime minister reached agreement with Hitler on the dismemberment of Czechoslovakia. Nor did he consider Chamberlain's dependence in foreign affairs on an adviser such as Sir Horace Wilson, who was not a member of the Foreign Office, a matter on which he should protest, much less resign. At two moments during the crisis Halifax did show to some advantage. Stiffened by Sir Alexander Cadogan, permanent under-secretary at the Foreign Office and his mentor in the realities of international affairs, he insisted on Chamberlain's rejection of the terms proposed by Hitler at Godesberg for the immediate occupation of the Sudeten territories. His gesture of defiance, however, was too belated to earn the Czechs more than a ten-day reprieve from Germany for their Sudeten territories and an empty guarantee of what was left of their country from Britain and France. Halifax also felt he must intrude on the welcome given to Chamberlain on his return from Munich. As they drove together through cheering crowds from Heston airport to Downing Street, he warned the prime minister that he should resist the temptation to consolidate his position by calling for an immediate general election and that he should strengthen his Cabinet by bringing in not only Churchill and Eden but also members of the Labour Party if they could be persuaded. In the event there was no general election; but neither was there an attempt to construct a truly national government dedicated to rearmament. Halifax was the one member of Chamberlain's administration who, by threatening resignation, might have ensured it. His quiescence did not spring only from loyalty to a leader and a friend. His lifelong resort to regular and unhurried worship brought him consolation at times of stress, a serenity transcending the cares of statecraft, and a detachment from the evil realities of life which was of no service to a foreign secretary. A humble acceptance of Divine Will protected him from self-reproach, even from self-examination, on the consequences of his actions; and a belief in immortality made the sufferings of those enslaved by the Nazis seem less tragic than they were.

Hitler's occupation in March 1939 of the truncated and wholly Slav remains of Czechoslovakia which had been denied him five months before roused British public opinion and caused Halifax's attitude to harden more than that of the prime minister. Although there were still echoes of appeasement in his speeches in the House of Lords, he recognized that to remain inactive in the face of Hitler's mounting threats towards Poland would be merely to postpone an unavoidable war against an enemy who drew strength from each successive plunder. An expanding programme of British rearmament, even if still inadequate, also engendered a growing spirit of confidence in the Foreign Office. So within a few days of the German march into Prague it was announced that Britain had guaranteed the independence of Poland. In April Italy invaded Albania and the British Government gave firm assurances of support to Greece and Romania. A measure of military conscription was introduced, although opposed by both the Labour and Liberal parties. In May Halifax sent a representative to Moscow for tripartite talks with Russia and France; clouded by mistrust, they were stifled in August by the conclusion of a Russo-German pact for the partition of Poland. Some held Halifax responsible for the belatedness and hesitancy of the British approach to Moscow. But whatever slender prospect there may have been at that stage of securing Russia as an ally against Germany was doomed by Russia's insistence that Britain should recognize her right of military intervention in the Baltic states and that Poland should agree to the entry of Soviet troops into her territory in the event of war with Germany. On 1 Sep-tember German armies invaded Poland. There followed a day of confused exchanges with the French Government on the timing of an ultimatum before Britain was at war with Germany.

Halifax remained foreign secretary and directed his efforts to persuading the neutral nations to support the Allies or at least to withhold aid from Germany. In May 1940 a vote in the House of Commons reflected the disenchantment of all parties with Chamberlain's irresolute conduct of the war. Halifax escaped much of the odium, partly because he had been less personally identified than Chamberlain with Munich, partly because there was about him, as in India, an aura of disinterestedness and moral purpose which transcended the grievous consequences of British policy during his tenure of the Foreign Office. He was thus considered by many to be as suitable a successor as Churchill in the hours which immediately preceded Chamberlain's resignation as prime minister on 10 May. The prospect appalled him. He knew he did not possess those qualities of popular leadership and ruthlessness which the situation demanded; he realized how difficult if not impossible it would be for any prime minister to control the war effort from the remoteness of the House of Lords, with Churchill running defence. So it was with relief that he welcomed the choice of Churchill as leader of an all-party government. Among those who recorded initial disappointment on both public and private grounds was King George VI, whose friendship extended to granting Halifax the unusual privilege of walking through the garden of Buckingham Palace on his daily journey from Eaton Square to the Foreign Office. Halifax was invited by the new prime minister to remain at his old post and to continue as a member of the War Cabinet. After the German advance across the Low Countries and France and the escape of the British Expeditionary Force from Dunkirk, he flew with Churchill to Tours on 13 June for a fruitless meeting with Paul Reynaud, the French prime minister, five days before Marshal Pétain sued for peace.

In December Halifax's own fortunes took an unexpected turn when he was urged by Churchill to succeed Lord Lothian [q.v.] as British ambassador in Washington. In his sixtieth year he was justifiably reluctant to exchange an historic, influential, and by now familiar office of state for a 'high and perilous charge' among a people he barely knew. He was sensitive, too, to whispers that the prime minister would not be sorry to rid himself of a colleague whose long association with Chamberlain detracted from his usefulness at home. His sense of duty prevailed and in January 1941 he crossed the Atlantic in the newly commissioned battleship *King George V*. Although President Roosevelt paid Halifax the unusual compliment of greeting him personally in Chesapeake Bay, the welcome given to the ambassador elsewhere was discouraging. In spite of some sympathy for a nation under enemy fire, American public opinion was largely isolationist; and the initial difficulty of following so congenial an envoy as Lothian was aggravated by indiscretions from which Halifax's advisers failed to save him. He called on the chairman of the foreign affairs committee in the House of Representatives while lend-lease proposals for aid to Britain were being debated in Congress, thereby seeming to interfere in the decisions of the legislature; he accepted an invitation to hunt the fox, a sport suggestive of aristocratic leisure even more in the New World than in the Old; he made jokes about baseball. One humiliating incident, however, was turned neatly to advantage. Having been pelted with eggs in Detroit, he was widely, although incorrectly, reported as saying that the United States were fortunate to have eggs to throw, at a time when the ration in England was one a month. As the prospect of war with Japan loomed large, American critics of the supposedly belligerent and reactionary country he represented began to lose their influence. Halifax reinforced his growing popularity by extensive speaking tours, a burden made lighter both by the radiant sympathy of his wife and by the bonhomie of his cousin, friend, and stage-manager, Colonel Angus McDonnell. If most at his ease with landowners and mystics, Halifax soon learned to overcome his natural reserve among audiences which did not often include either. Nor, save in appearance, did he conform to the expected caricature of an English aristocrat. He reacted with good humour to intrusive curiosity and with deliberate charm to outspoken and sometimes ill-informed criticism of his country's alleged motives in India and elsewhere. Although he never quite achieved Lothian's ascen-

dancy, no ambassador more adroitly or more successfully adapted himself to a role for which at heart he had little relish. A speech in Canada, however, on 24 January 1944, about the future of the Commonwealth, made a far less acceptable impression there.

The Japanese attack on Pearl Harbour in December 1941 welded Britain and the United States into alliance against Japan, Germany, and Italy. The emphasis of Halifax's task shifted accordingly from public relations to the strengthening of links between the two governments. To this end the British missions, both civil and military, soon came to number 1,200 including no fewer than six fellows of All Souls. Halifax had already won the confidence of Cordell Hull, the secretary of state, with whom he transacted day-to-day diplomatic business. Even more fruitful was his intimacy with Harry Hopkins, the president's most trusted adviser, which won him unprecedented freedom of access to the White House. But however serviceable the easy relationship he established with Roosevelt, his personal influence in Washington was inevitably eclipsed by Churchill's periodic visits and his own exclusion from talks between president and prime minister. More than pre-war disagreements over India and the policy of appeasement, a fundamental difference in temperament separated them. One was accommodating, reflective, and cautious: the other resolute, impulsive, self-inspired. Thus the abassador's wary affection and admiration for the prime minister as a war leader was qualified by doubts about the clarity of his judgement; and understandable irritation at being kept ignorant of decisions reached in private by Churchill and Roosevelt was sharpened by lesser grievances. He was exhausted by his guest's apocalyptic table-talk which flowed into the early hours of the morning and he complained of the cigars which left the embassy 'stinking like a third class smoking carriage'. Deep personal sorrow was added to restiveness when, towards the end of 1942, the second of his three sons was killed in battle and the third gravely wounded. A few months later he confided to Eden, his successor as foreign secretary, that he would like to be relieved of his appointment and come home. But he was persuaded to remain in Washington for another three years, thus bridging both Truman's elevation to the presidency on Roosevelt's death in April 1945 and the defeat of the Churchill government which brought Attlee to power three months later. In July 1944 he was created an earl.

On the abrupt cancellation by America of the lend-lease agreement at the end of the Japanese war, Halifax helped Lord Keynes [q.v.] in the protracted negotiations for a loan of 3·75 billion dollars from the United States Government. The sum was smaller and more hedged about with conditions than the British team had hoped for, but it was enough to tide a near-bankrupt nation over the immediate crisis. Halifax also took part in the conference at Dumbarton Oaks in 1944 which began to shape the charter of the United Nations and in the meetings at San Francisco, where he took a strong stand against the Russian interpretation of the Yalta formula on the unanimity rule in the proposed Security Council, whilst persuading Commonwealth delegates reluctantly to concur in the procedure recommended. His perceptive description of Molotov, the Soviet foreign minister, as 'smiling granite' did not, however, extend to an appreciation of Stalin's ambitions in Europe, much less to the formidable nature of the Communist society. When Churchill drew public attention to these dangers in a speech at Fulton, Missouri, in March 1946, Halifax tried to persuade him to qualify his words in his next speech. In this Halifax was unsuccessful, for Churchill felt it would be 'like going to see Hitler just before the war'. In May he returned to England and later that year was admitted to the Order of Merit.

The last years of his life were spent increasingly in familiar places and among old friends. In 1946 he rejoined the governing body of Eton, having originally been elected a fellow in 1936, and drew much refreshment from liturgical disputes with the provost, Lord Quickswood [q.v.]. As chancellor of Oxford, he gave a more than formal attention to the university's problems and took every opportunity of renewing his links with All Souls, 'a second home for more than fifty years'. Two more honours came to him in 1947 when he was appointed chancellor of Sheffield University and high steward of Westminster. He liked pageantry and found the wearing of ceremonial robes and insignia no burden either as chancellor of the Order of the Garter or as grand master from 1957 of the Order of St. Michael and St. George. As president of

the Pilgrims he was able both to maintain his transatlantic friendships and to relive those evenings of sustained oratory which had never ceased to amaze him as ambassador. In 1947 he became chairman of the general advisory council of the B.B.C. He spoke from time to time in the House of Lords, enjoyed foreign travel, and wrote a gently evasive volume of memoirs, *Fulness of Days* (1957). But it was in taking up once more the threads of his family life in Yorkshire that he found true happiness and peace. He resumed the mastership of the Middleton hunt and immersed himself in farming, estate management, and local church affairs. A few weeks after celebrating his golden wedding he died at Garrowby 23 December 1959 and was buried at Kirby Underdale. He was succeeded by his eldest son, Charles Ingram Courtenay (born 1912). His youngest son, Richard Frederick, was minister of power (1959–63) and of pensions (1963–4), and his daughter, Anne, married the third Earl of Feversham.

Halifax's character was of baffling opaqueness. On some contemporary minds he left the imprint of statesmanship suffused by Christian faith; others suspected that his churchmanship concealed a strain of shrewd worldliness and expediency. Even the habitual ambiguity of his speeches might be variously interpreted either as a humble search for truth or as a form of verbal insurance against the unexpected. His rigid adherence to religious principles could make him seem heartless in his judgement of human frailty; thus he regarded divorce followed by remarriage, whatever the circumstances, as scarcely removed from bigamy. He loved family life and guarded his privacy well. But having been brought up by his father to think of racing as immoral and ballet as indecent, he observed with tolerant melancholy the addiction of his own sons to those pastimes. Among friends he was a lively talker with a smile of singular sweetness: his difficulty in pronouncing the letter 'r' added charm to a pleasant tenor voice. Those who saw him only on official occasions thought him aloof and consciously representative of an aristocracy whose continued and effortless lien on political power seemed anachronistic, even dangerous. Halifax sometimes doubted his fitness for a particular task yet believed in the ordered world into which he had been born and did not question his right to be called to high office. To his intimates he was a man of simple disposition; and the young, who are sensitive to pretentiousness, found him an enchanting companion.

There is a portrait of Halifax by Sir Oswald Birley at All Souls and another by Lawrence Gowing at Christ Church, Oxford. Lionel Edwards painted him with his father, then aged ninety-three, and his eldest son, at a meet of the Middleton hounds: the picture hangs at Garrowby.

[The Earl of Halifax, *Fulness of Days*, 1957; S. Gopal, *The Viceroyalty of Lord Irwin, 1926-31*, 1957; the Earl of Birkenhead, *Halifax*, 1965; private information; personal knowledge.]   KENNETH ROSE.

WOODS, HENRY (1868-1952), palaeontologist, was born in Cottenham, near Cambridge, 18 December 1868, the only child of Francis Woods, a farmer, and his second wife, Mary Ann, daughter of Thomas Granger, farmer, of Haddenham, Cambridgeshire. His father died when he was only two years old. He began his education at the local village school but in 1880 his mother moved with him to Cambridge where he was admitted to the higher grade school (later the Central School for Boys). He appears to have been a pupil of considerable promise and gained several prizes, but leaving school in 1883 took up local employment, continuing with his studies in his spare time. In October 1887 means were found for him to enter St. John's College, Cambridge, where he proved to be a brilliant student. In 1889 he gained a first class in part i of the natural sciences tripos and was made a scholar of his college; in the following year he obtained a first class in part ii of the tripos, taking geology as his subject. He was also awarded the Harkness scholarship for the best performance in the examination.

In 1892 as demonstrator in palaeobotany Woods joined the teaching staff of the Cambridge University department of geology with which he remained connected until almost the end of his life. In 1894 he also became demonstrator in palaeozoology; and from 1899 until 1934 he held the post of lecturer in palaeozoology. Although he then retired from teaching work, he continued to act as departmental librarian until over the age of eighty. Even prior to his first official appointment Woods had evidently been working on the extensive palaeontological collections of the department,

as his *Catalogue of Type Fossils in the Woodwardian Museum, Cambridge* appeared in 1891. From that period until it was recognized (in the twenties) that the services of a full-time curator were required he devoted much time to the care of the collections. He also became involved almost immediately in drawing up plans for a new university geological museum (the Sedgwick Museum), and when, after many years' discussion and delay, this was eventually completed in 1904, he played a leading part in the arrangement of the exhibits and study collections in their new home. The zeal with which he embarked upon his teaching duties was also noteworthy. His lecture notes were soon transformed into a textbook, *Palaeontology: Invertebrate*, a much-needed and very successful elementary systematic treatise which first appeared in 1893 and by 1946 had reached its eighth edition.

Woods's original contributions to science established him as one of the foremost invertebrate palaeontologists of his generation. His best-known work is his *Monograph of the Cretaceous Lamellibranchia of England* (1899-1913), published in two volumes of substantial size by the Palaeontographical Society. It has remained an indispensable work of reference for advanced students and amateur collectors of fossils alike. Equally thorough, but not so well known since it deals with a less abundant group, is his *Monograph of the Fossil Macrurous Crustacea of England* (1925-31), published by the same society. Among his other monographs are those dealing with Cretaceous Mollusca from South Africa, New Zealand, and Northern Nigeria, and with Tertiary Mollusca from Peru. His publications were embellished by the admirable illustrations of his lifelong friend, T. A. Brock, whose drawings of fossils have never been surpassed. All Woods's scientific work was characterized by its thoroughness and by the meticulous care with which he recorded his observations. Stress was placed throughout on pure morphology. He was generally reluctant to indulge in speculative hypothesis, although one of his earlier papers dealt with a supposed succession of evolutionary stages shown by species of the bivalve genus *Inoceramus* during the Cretaceous period.

Woods was tall and spare, with a quiet reserved manner. He was by no means a dynamic personality, but his teaching methods were thorough and conscientious and he instilled a love for fossils and their study in many of the students who attended his lectures. The Geological Society of London awarded him the Lyell fund (1898), the Lyell medal (1918), and the Wollaston medal (1940). He was elected F.R.S. in 1916, and also became an honorary member of the Royal Society of New Zealand and of the Yorkshire Philosophical Society.

In 1910 Woods married Ethel Gertrude (died 1939), daughter of W. W. Skeat [q.v.], professor of Anglo-Saxon at Cambridge. She was herself a palaeontologist who made useful contributions to the science. There were no children. Woods died 4 April 1952 at his home at Meldreth, near Royston, Hertfordshire, where he had lived since 1924.

[O. M. B. Bulman in *Obituary Notices of Fellows of the Royal Society*, No. 22, November 1953; personal knowledge.]   L. R. Cox.

WOOLLARD, FRANK GEORGE (1883–1957), pioneer of mass production in the motor industry, was born in Kensington 22 September 1883, the son of George Woollard, general steward to a firm of private bankers, and his wife, Emily Constance Powell. He was educated at the City of London School and at the Goldsmiths' and Birkbeck colleges in London. He served his apprenticeship with the London and South-Western Railway at Eastleigh and was involved in the design and development of the famous Clarkson steam omnibus. This led him to turn his attention to motor-car design and production. At the Birmingham works of E. G. Wrigley & Co., Ltd., Woollard was responsible for designing and producing, under sub-contract, the axles and gear boxes of the first Morris-Cowley motor-car to go into serial production. He was subsequently appointed to take charge of the engine factory of Hotchkiss et Cie at Coventry and, in 1923, general manager of the engines branch of Morris Motors, Ltd. It was there during the period 1923–5 that Woollard and his colleagues commissioned the first automatic transfer machines for engineering production, some twenty years ahead of similar developments in the United States, and nearly thirty years ahead of the general adoption of this form of automation elsewhere in the United Kingdom. Woollard was director of Morris Motors, Ltd. (1926–32), managing director of Rudge Whitworth, Ltd. (1932–6), and director

of the Birmingham Aluminium Casting (1903) Co., Ltd., and of the Midland Motor Cylinder Co., Ltd. (1936–53), after which he retired.

Woollard was an active member of the Institution of Mechanical Engineers and, especially, of the Institution of Automobile Engineers of which he was president in 1945–6. The successful merger of the two institutions in 1947 owed much to his organizing ability and to his flair for creating the right kind of atmosphere in committee negotiations. After the amalgamation he served on the Institution of Mechanical Engineers' council as chairman of its automobile division (1946–7), and did much to foster the activities of the Motor Industry Research Association of which he was a founder-member. He was a member also of the Institution of Production Engineers, chairman of the executive committee of the Aluminium Development Association (1949–52), chairman of the Zinc Alloy Die Casting Association (1952–6), and chairman of the industrial administration group of the Birmingham College of Technology (1951–7). He was a founder-member of the British Institute of Management and a member of the American Society of Automotive Engineers.

His extensive experience in production engineering and management was recorded in many contributions to technical journals and was summarized in his *Principles of Mass and Flow Production* (1954) which served as a basis for a regular series of lectures to postgraduate students of engineering production in the university of Birmingham and in the Birmingham College of Technology, which conferred on him an honorary associate-ship. Everyone knew him as 'a kindly personality, gifted and philosophical, to whom one could turn for advice and help. They will remember his humour, the apt turn of phrase, his twinkling eyes, the direct look and the sincere interest which he always showed for the welfare of his colleagues and his students.'

In 1911 Woollard married Catherine Elizabeth, daughter of Henry Richards, engraver; they had a son who died in infancy and a daughter Joan, who became known as a sculptor and painter. He was appointed M.B.E. in 1916, and died in Edgbaston, Birmingham, 23 December 1957.

Portraits of Woollard 'large in frame and distinctive in appearance' include one by his daughter and one by B. Fleetwood-Walker; both remained in the possession of the artists.

[*Journal* of the Institution of Production Engineers, vol. xxxvii, No. 6, 1958; private information; personal knowledge.]

N. A. DUDLEY.

WOOLLEY, SIR (CHARLES) LEONARD (1880–1960), archaeologist, son of the Rev. George Herbert Woolley, curate of St. Matthew, Upper Clapton, and his wife, Sarah Cathcart, was born in Upper Clapton 17 April 1880. He was a member of a large family and had to pay for his education through scholarships which he won for St. John's, Leatherhead, and subsequently for New College, Oxford, where he obtained a first class in *literae humaniores* in 1903 and a second in theology in 1904. It was W. A. Spooner [q.v.] who with a rare discernment told him that he must abandon his intention of becoming a schoolmaster and make archaeology his career. Much of his youth was spent in a poor parish in Bethnal Green and at an early age he acquired an interest in paintings, was a frequent visitor to the Whitechapel Art Gallery, and became familiar with the Old Masters. This taste remained with him all his life and in his retirement he collected begrimed paintings at country auctions, cleaned and repaired his acquisitions, some of which were of a high quality and found their way to important exhibitions and national art galleries. He was deft with his hands and many a delicate and fragile antiquity was salvaged in the course of his excavations by his imaginative methods combined with an exceptional dexterity.

After graduating from Oxford he went to France and Germany in order to study modern languages and in 1905 was appointed assistant to (Sir) Arthur Evans [q.v.], then keeper of the Ashmolean Museum, where he served a valuable apprenticeship before committing himself entirely to field archaeology. His work in the Near East began in 1907 when he excavated in Nubia in partnership with D. Randall-MacIver [q.v.] to whose precise methods he owed much and who, at that time, was field director of the Nubian expeditions of the University Museum of the university of Pennsylvania. At Karanog he dug the first big Meroïtic cemetery on record; but in spite of the rich finds which included inscribed and painted gravestones, bronze vessels of Greek workmanship, and painted pottery, he concluded that 'the whole

Meroïtic civilization was, but a backwater, remarkable as an isolated phenomenon in African history, but contributing nothing to the general stream of culture and of art'. Such discoveries did not satisfy his original and creative mind but he was all the time gaining experience in practical problems, in the control of workmen, and in fields of discovery which ranged from the Early Dynastic down to Roman times. A brief interlude in Italy, where he conducted a small dig in the ancient baths at Teano on a wooded hill-top in ancient Sabine territory, completed the formative stage of his training as a field archaeologist. In 1912 Woolley was appointed to succeed R. Campbell Thompson [q.v.] as leader of the British Museum expedition to Carchemish where he was accompanied by T. E. Lawrence [q.v.]. There he made a number of spectacular discoveries in the temples and palaces of the Neo-Hittite period. A series of orthostats with carvings of north Syrian gods and rulers, many contemporary hieroglyphic inscriptions, and the layout of the town defences were considerable contributions to knowledge at that time.

While he was employed in north Syria Woolley, together with Lawrence, took the opportunity during the off season from Carchemish to make an archaeological survey in Palestine of the country stretching northwards from Akaba towards the southern end of the Dead Sea. In the course of six weeks the two men obtained a general knowledge of an area which, except for the few centuries of settled Byzantine government, had changed little since the days of Moses. The account of this work under the names of Woolley and Lawrence was first published by the Palestine Exploration Fund as *The Wilderness of Zin* (1915).

The dig at Carchemish was interrupted by the war in which Woolley undertook intelligence work on the staff in Egypt. He was blown up at sea off the coast of south Asia Minor and in 1916–18 was in a Turkish prison camp, where his manual skill and inventiveness did much for the amenities.

In 1919 he concluded the dig at Carchemish under considerable difficulties, for he found that his camp was in a no-man's-land between the French army and Kurdish irregulars; both sides consulted him at intervals. Subsequently he moved to Egypt and did fruitful work, particularly in a house-quarter once occupied by ancient craftsmen on the site of Tel-el-Amarna, for the Egypt Exploration Society.

Fortified by much experience Woolley

began his major work at Ur in 1922 and dug there systematically at intervals for thirteen years. He began by concentrating on the Temenos or sacred area within which lay the principal temples and palaces. There he established a tremendous sequence of cities which began on water-logged soil, perhaps in the fifth millennium B.C. at what is known as the Al-'Ubaid period, and rose one over the other to form a mound some seventy feet in height, until the last occupation in the fourth century B.C. At Ur he exposed a complete range of town plans which revealed more fully than ever before the architectural achievements which had occurred in south Babylonia from Sumerian times onwards. In the revelation of Sumerian civilization Woolley did his richest and most productive work. The climax of the expedition was the discovery of the famous royal cemetery of Ur which yielded the incomparable treasures of Sumerian civilization, many of them deposited in shafts with multiple burials, before 2500 B.C.

The documents, which included some of the earliest literature known to mankind, were also of extraordinary archaeological interest because of the light they throw on all the buildings and small remains associated with them. The sculpture of these early periods, as well as the metallurgy, is of a very high order and Woolley's remarkable insight into the methods used by ancient craftsmen and builders was one of his most valuable contributions to knowledge. His understanding of ancient methods also enabled him to follow up clues in the ground with a penetration often denied to skilled diggers.

Woolley, however, found so much that he was handicapped in finding time to consult other authorities, and academically his work often suffered accordingly; in particular his chronology was often at variance with accepted criteria. There seems to be little doubt now that his dating of the royal cemetery was several centuries too early and similarly there are many who cannot accept his sequence dating for the sculpture at Carchemish. In judging works of art, too, a Victorian outlook was not acceptable to the critics, and his book on The Development of Sumerian Art (1935), while invaluable in all matters touching on craftsmanship, appears to be aesthetically defective. His books on The Sumerians (1928) and Abraham (1936) were out of touch with linguistic and literary problems and thus fell short of being authoritative.

For all these defects, however, there was ample compensation in the imaginative treatment throughout his writings of whatever he found. Gifted with an unusually fluent style, an enchanting lecturer, no one has better described the sequence of his discoveries, and many of his popular books have enthralled a very wide public. Digging up the Past (1930) ran into many editions, and even more successful was Ur of the Chaldees (1929, subsequently translated into many languages), which took the reader on a tour of the excavations and enabled him to feel at home among ancient Sumerian as well as Babylonian remains. To follow Woolley round the site at Ur and to hear him talk about the private houses was to feel oneself living among a vanished people. If his imagination sometimes outran the facts, that to him was preferable to allowing knowledge to lie dormant and inconclusive.

His industry was prodigious. While on the dig he slept little, rising with the sun and often still at work in his study or in the catalogue room until two or three o'clock in the morning. He could not have published so much had he not been exceptionally quick in composition, and he used to say that writing was an enjoyment to him. The large definitive publications of Ur came out in a steady stream from 1927 onwards. These volumes include Ur Excavations, vol. i, Al-'Ubaid, in collaboration with H. R. Hall (1927), mostly concerned with prehistoric and Early Dynastic remains; vol. ii, The Royal Cemetery (1934), contained in two parts some 600 pages of text and 274 plates, a magnum opus which no other living archaeologist could have produced in so short a time. Volume v, The Ziggurat and its Surroundings (1939), is a testimonial to his insight into ancient architecture. Volume iv, The Early Periods (1955), an invaluable summary of discoveries concerned with remains prior to 2000 B.C., could no longer keep pace with collateral evidence from elsewhere. He left two more completed volumes in manuscript. For the general reader his Excavations at Ur, A Record of Twelve Years' Work (1954) is a most readable summary account of these achievements. To have dug so much and left nothing unwritten was indeed a phenomenal record.

When he had completed his work at Ur Woolley went on to dig at Al Mina near Antioch in Syria, where he made many discoveries concerning the import and export trade between the Aegean and Syria. Even more remunerative were his

Woolley

discoveries at Atchana in the Hatay
(1937-9 and 1946-9), where the palaces,
temples, sculpture and pottery of the second
millennium B.C. were of a type hitherto
little known. Once again a rich find of
associated documents provided new concepts of the political history and everyday
life in the small kingdoms of the time.

The scientific account of this dig was
incorporated in a book entitled *Alalakh,
excavations at Tell Atchana* (1955), full of
original material and of controversial
matter; his early chronology is, however,
not generally accepted. The popular account appeared in a Pelican book entitled
A Forgotten Kingdom (1953).

In 1938, less than a year before the outbreak of war, Woolley accepted an invitation from the Government of India to
advise them about their programme of
archaeological work. He completed this
task in a remarkably short time with
considerable perceptiveness. Many of his
recommendations were carried out and the
subsequent fruitful developments in India
and also in Pakistan owed much to his
advice.

During the war he served with the rank
of lieutenant-colonel and devoted his
indefatigable energy to the safeguarding
of monuments, work of art, libraries, and
archives in Europe.

Woolley will be remembered as one of
the most successful diggers ever engaged in
field archaeology on account of his extraordinary flair not only for choosing a
potentially rich site but also for attacking
those parts of it which concealed the most
important remains. He was very good
company, a delightful raconteur, and had
a good understanding of his workmen in
the Orient. *Dead Towns and Living Men*
(1920) contains many reminiscences which
well illustrate his sense of humour, ingenuity, and an unaffected *joie de vivre*
which was one of the most charming
facets of his character. Between him and
his foreman Sheikh Hamoudi Ibn Ibrahim
there was a lifelong friendship. Hamoudi
was foreman on all his principal expeditions from the time he went to Carchemish
in 1912, and gave devoted service which
Woolley would always have wished to be
remembered.

Woolley was knighted in 1935; received
honorary degrees from the universities of
Dublin and St. Andrews; was an honorary
fellow of New College, Oxford, and of the
Turkish Historical Society; and was an
honorary A.R.I.B.A. (1926). He was
awarded the Lucy Wharton Drexel medal,

Museum of the university of Pennsylvania
(1955), the Flinders Petrie medal, university of London (1957), and in the last year
of his life was to have been presented with
the gold medal of the Royal Society of
Antiquaries, London.

In 1927 Woolley married Katharine
Elizabeth, widow of Lieutenant-Colonel
Francis Keeling. She took an active part
in his work and did much to attract financial support for his excavations. She died
in 1945 and Woolley died in London 20
February 1960.

[*The Times*, 22 February 1960; *Iraq*, vol.
xxii, 1960; personal knowledge.]
M. E. L. MALLOWAN.

WORKMAN, HERBERT BROOK (1862-
1951), Methodist divine and educationist,
was born in Peckham 2 November 1862, a
son of the Rev. John Sansom Workman,
a Wesleyan minister, and his wife, Mary
Brook. Educated at Kingswood School,
of which his younger brother, W. P. Workman, was later headmaster (1889-1918), he
took a London B.A. (1884) and M.A. (1885),
from the Owens College, Manchester,
and prepared at Didsbury College for the
Methodist ministry. He had a notable
spell of fifteen years as a circuit
minister before serving as principal of
Westminster Training College in 1903-30.
After the long regime of the redoubtable
J. H. Rigg [q.v.] the college needed a new,
tough broom. Workman brought to the
task not only his own growing reputation
as a scholar, with a flair for picking colleagues and pupils of coming eminence, but
great gifts of shrewdness and administrative prescience. He raised the college to a
new eminence, and his concentration on
training teachers at Westminster and at
the sister college of Southlands stood his
Church in valuable stead at a time of
crisis in its educational policy when numbers of Methodist day schools were closing.
From 1919 until his retirement in 1940 he
held the important office of secretary of
the Methodist Education Committee. The
most notable of his achievements was the
consolidation of a ring of Methodist residential schools, to which, through his
efforts, there were notable additions. He
was a member of the senate of the
university of London which awarded him
the degree of D.Lit. (1907).

Workman was the first distinguished
Church historian to come from the Methodist Church, and perhaps the first Protestant and Nonconformist scholar to show
sensitive sympathy with the medieval

Church. It is true that his first historical writings, begun as a circuit minister, treated the elements of dissent within medieval Christendom. The small volumes, *The Church of the West in the Middle Ages* (2 vols., 1898-1900) and *The Dawn of the Reformation* (2 vols., 1901-2), have little survival value, but they are remarkable for the care and accuracy with which their author had studied a great range of authorities, and sought the truth among the primary documents. These studies found their climax in the sympathetic portrayal of John Hus to which his *Letters of John Hus* (1904) formed a useful epilogue. There followed studies in the early Church, *Persecution in the Early Church* (1906) and *The Evolution of the Monastic Ideal* (1913), which show his flair for colourful and interesting narrative material, so that despite much that is dated in his approach these volumes are still in demand. His *Christian Thought to the Reformation* (1911) is in contrast disappointing and not very perceptive. His great work, however, was his massive study of *John Wyclif* (2 vols., 1926). Into it went many years of study and research, which called forth the best of his considerable abilities. Studies of medieval theology have subsequently advanced far and a whole generation of research into the theologies of Wyclif and Hus has modified and in parts much dated many of Workman's conclusions. But the volumes are still to be read with profit, and the reader may easily miss the painstaking diligence which went into the lucid writing. Workman was preparing a further volume to cover the history of later Lollardy but had not got farther than the preparation of a mass of beautifully arranged notes when he died. Probably his best single writing was his classic essay *The Place of Methodism in the Catholic Church* (1921), originally written for the *New History of Methodism* (2 vols., 1909) of which he was one of the editors. There his evangelical convictions and his wide catholic sympathies enabled him to set the evangelical revival against the long perspective of the Christian past. The worth of his studies was recognized by the university of Aberdeen which awarded him the degree of D.D. in 1914.

Workman married in 1891 Ethel Mary, daughter of Alban Gardner Buller, solicitor, of Birmingham; they had two sons and one daughter. He died in London 26 August 1951.

[Private information; personal knowledge.]

E. G. RUPP.

WYLIE, SIR FRANCIS JAMES (1865-1952), first warden of Rhodes House, Oxford, was born in Bromley, Kent, 18 October 1865, the second son of Richard Northcote Wylie and his wife, Charlotte Greenlaw. The Wylies had had a long connection with Russia. Wylie's father was a member of the Bourse in St. Petersburg, and his great-uncle, Sir James Wylie [q.v.], had been physician at the court of the Tsar. Wylie himself spent short periods in Russia during childhood, but had no special association with that country in later life.

He was educated at St. Edward's School, Oxford. At the suggestion of his uncle by marriage, Edward Caird [q.v.], (who was then professor of moral philosophy at Glasgow and was later to become master of Balliol), the promising young man went from school to pursue his classical studies at the university of Glasgow, from which he won a Snell exhibition to Balliol. He went up to Oxford in 1884 and soon showed himself a classical scholar of mark. He took a first class in honour moderations in 1886 and in *literae humaniores* in 1888. He was not, however, the 'mere bookworm' whom Cecil Rhodes [q.v.] deprecated; though of slight build he rowed in the Balliol eight and was elected to Vincent's Club and Leander. Throughout his long life he retained an alert and critical interest in rowing.

After taking his degree he spent a few months teaching at his old school and then engaged in private tutoring until, after being made a lecturer of the college in 1891, he was elected a fellow of Brasenose in 1892. There he proved himself a successful and assiduous tutor and when he died there still survived a few of his former pupils who remembered with gratitude his lectures on Aristotle's Logic. He was junior proctor in 1903-4, a year which was to prove a turning-point in his lifework. He cultivated a brisk diversity of interests, not the least of them in military service. It was characteristic of his dominant sense of duty that he was a zealous member of the Oxford University Volunteers. As a company commander in that corps he took part in the official obsequies of Queen Victoria. When, in the later chapter of his life, war broke out in 1914, he was too old for service in the field, but he threw himself with energy into the work of the Oxford University Training Corps and made a spirited contribution to its courses of instruction.

The will of Cecil Rhodes was made

public in April 1902, and the trustees appointed by it were soon busy making plans for the inauguration of the scholarships. One of the trustees was Lord Rosebery [q.v.], whom Wylie had come to know as private tutor to his two sons. (Sir) George Parkin [q.v.] had been appointed organizing secretary to the Rhodes Trust, and in February 1903 Wylie was invited, through Rosebery, to supervise the Oxford side of the system and to assume a general tutelage of the scholars in residence. It was not an easy decision to make. He had an established position in a college to which he was much attached; he was well known in the academic sphere and was about to become a proctor; he was now invited to occupy an office with no academic standing, since the Rhodes trustees were a body outside the university organism, and to assist in launching a scheme which at that time was highly experimental. The project of the Rhodes scholarships was not universally welcomed in Oxford; the university and colleges were far more inbred in 1903 than they have since become, and there was considerable scepticism about an influx of 'Colonials', Americans, and Germans, who, it was feared, might lower academic standards, especially in the classics, besides making undue demands on the limited room and resources of colleges. Wylie was under no illusions about the problems which would face him, and it was again a sense of duty which prompted him to accept the trustees' invitation. He had the opportunity, which he was amply to fulfil, of doing a notable service to imperial and Anglo-American relations, and he was never the man to shrink from responsibilities.

He was soon to receive invaluable aid in his task. In 1904 he married Kathleen, daughter of Edmond Kelly, an American lawyer in Paris, where much of her girlhood was spent. Wylie had met his future wife when she was a member of Lady Margaret Hall, Oxford. For the next twenty-eight years this was to prove an ideal partnership for developing and influencing Cecil Rhodes's 'great idea' in both its administrative and its personal aspects. Four sons and two daughters were born of the marriage, the eldest son dying in childhood. The fourth son, Shaun, was elected a fellow (mathematics) of Trinity Hall, Cambridge, in 1939. One of the daughters, Vere, married an Australian Rhodes scholar, Lewis Charles Wilcher, who became in 1956 the first warden of Queen Elizabeth House, Oxford.

The story of the growing-pains and adventurous adolescence of the Rhodes scholarships has been told vividly by Wylie himself in his contribution (pp. 59–125)—which he wrote almost at the end of his life—to the volume *The First Fifty Years of the Rhodes Trust and the Rhodes Scholarships* published by the Rhodes trustees in 1955. To him, probably more than to any other individual, belongs the credit for having woven a fabric which was to become an integral part of the whole Oxford design. There were vicissitudes at first; but Wylie and his wife enjoyed the reward of seeing hundreds of young men from many far countries derive from Oxford what their benefactor had intended for them and acquit themselves with distinction in their later careers. There was none of them who did not acknowledge his debt to the Wylie influence and guidance.

Responsibilities constantly increased with the expansion of the Rhodes network by additional scholarships which the trustees established in British areas overseas, until the number of Rhodes scholars at Oxford at any one time grew to nearly two hundred, composed about equally of British and American nationals, with a small group of Germans. After twenty-eight years of arduous service, Wylie retired in 1931, but not before he had had the satisfaction of seeing the completion of Oxford's permanent memorial to the founder, Rhodes House, of which he became the first warden. He was knighted in 1929, on the occasion of the reunion of Rhodes scholars at Oxford when Rhodes House was formally opened, and he was elected an honorary fellow of Brasenose in 1931. His portrait, painted by Edward I. Halliday in 1952, and an earlier pencil drawing by Miss F. A. de Biden Footner, done in 1935 and reproduced for presentation to all Rhodes scholars of his period, hang in Rhodes House.

Retirement, however, was by no means the end of Wylie's services to the Rhodes scholarships. For upwards of another twenty years he kept regular touch with his former charges. His worldwide correspondence with them was indefatigable and his personal memory and knowledge of them throughout the years were remarkable. Of the many Rhodes scholars who revisited Oxford from time to time few failed to make a pilgrimage to the Wylie home near Oxford, where perennial welcome awaited them, their kindred, and their friends. On Boar's Hill, with a panorama of the Berkshire downlands spread before him, Wylie's tranquil life and temperament made light of the burden of years. He had always been a man of simple tastes, and he found continual refreshment in the Matthew Arnold country, which he knew intimately, in birds and flowers, in parish work, and in country walks which to the end of his life lost nothing of their zest and vigour. His faculties seemed to be quite unimpaired when, without warning, he died in his sleep at his home 29 October 1952.

With his wife he made many journeys throughout the English-speaking world on embassies for the Rhodes trustees. Three universities in the United States—Union College, Schenectady (1932), Swarthmore College (1933), and Bowdoin College (1933) —conferred honorary degrees upon him. In 1945 the Rhodes trustees permanently commemorated his name in Oxford by the foundation of a Wylie prize for an essay on some aspect of the relations between the American colonies or the United States and any part of the British Empire or Commonwealth. Lady Wylie died in 1969.

[*The Times*, 30 October, 1, 15, 17, and 20 November 1952; *Oxford Magazine*, 29 January 1953; *United Empire*, November 1952; *New York Times*, 3 November 1952; *Bowdoin Alumnus*, November 1952; *The First Fifty Years of the Rhodes Trust and the Rhodes Scholarships, 1903–1953*, ed. Lord Elton, 1955; personal knowledge; private information.]   C. K. ALLEN.

YATES, DORNFORD (pseudonym), novelist. [See MERCER, CECIL WILLIAM.]

YEATS, JACK BUTLER (1871–1957), painter, was born 29 August 1871 at 23 Fitzroy Street, London, the youngest of the five children of Irish Protestant parents, John Butler Yeats, painter, and his wife, Susan Pellexfen. Although his eldest brother was the poet W. B. Yeats [q.v.], his father once announced that he would be remembered as the father of a painter. When he was only eight Jack B. Yeats joined his grandparents in county Sligo and for the next eight years he roamed in the countryside around and furnished his mind with all those images of circuses, fairdays, sailing boats and sailors, and the strange customs of the people which even fifty years later were still to be the subject matter of his pictures. Travelling players specially interested him and an early water-colour shows him standing

before a toy theatre which he had received as a present when he was only nine or ten. Later he wrote plays and stories and illustrated them himself. His concept of art, therefore, was clearly related to the heroic and imaginative achievement and he always seemed to measure life in terms of idealism and nobility.

In 1888 he attended the Westminster School of Art and later he made a living as a successful illustrator for such varied publications as *Boy's Own Paper*, *Judy*, and the *Vegetarian*. He also illustrated a large number of broadsheets and in 1912 published drawings and paintings of *Life in the West of Ireland*.

Between 1890 and 1900 he held a number of one-man shows in London but they were confined to drawings and water-colours and then he returned to Ireland where he remained for the rest of his life, short holidays apart. In the famous Armory exhibition of 1913 in New York he showed five oils and from then onwards was principally engaged as an oil painter. He returned again and again to his study of figures and places in water-colour and to the various sketch-books of drawings which he continued to fill on expeditions.

His oil paintings up to the early 1930s were comparatively direct transcriptions from life, with the human figure graphically treated but with the summary style of his water-colours. He had a most productive period following the 1916 Rising and some of his most moving pictures were inspired by this period, particularly 'Bachelors Walk, in Memory', 'Communicating with Prisoners', and 'The Funeral of Harry Boland'.

In the middle 1930s he began to depart from the illustrative phase and he commenced to use paint with a great deal more richness and sparkle and he seemed to avoid simulating natural tones. This was the period of 'The Scene Painters Rose' and other romantic works which preceded the war of 1939–45.

He had had a one-man show in Arthur Tooth & Sons, London, in 1926 and a number of exhibitions in Dublin and from 1943 onward Victor Waddington became his dealer. The relationship proved fruitful and the demand for his works and his prices rose steeply. Not only was he famous but he was also the centre of the *avant garde* movement for the younger generation although he was by then two generations ahead in years.

In 1942 Yeats had a retrospective

exhibition at the National Gallery, London, and in 1945 a national loan exhibition of almost a hundred pictures was held in Dublin. For the first time an Irish artist was regarded as a prophet in his own land. More important for himself, however, he was inspired by it to greater freedom and originality. His new pictures were filled with a splendour of colour and he invented imaginative, dreamlike places with titles of accompanying grandeur like 'A Race in Hy-Brazil', 'Tinkers' Encampment—The Blood of Abel', 'There is no Night', and 'Death for Only One'.

Jack B. Yeats died in Dublin 28 March 1957 but seemed thereafter to suffer no eclipse of reputation. Exhibitions in various parts of the world continued: due in part to the fact that he was an expressionist artist—a style which remained in fashion; but due also to his essential optimism and his belief in mystery, legend, and poetic allusion. He affirmed man's belief in himself and yet remained modern.

In 1894 Yeats married Mary Cottenham (died 1947), daughter of the late John Phillips White. The National Gallery of Ireland has a self-portrait in pencil and portraits by J. B. Yeats (as a boy) and Lilian Davidson.

[Thomas MacGreevy, *Jack B. Yeats*, 1945.]
JAMES WHITE.

YOUNG, EDWARD HILTON, first BARON KENNET (1879–1960), politician and writer, was born in London 20 March 1879, the fourth child and third son of Sir George Young, third baronet [q.v.]. His childhood was darkened by the death of a beloved sister, Eacy, and lightened by a family printing press on which his picaresque novel, *The Count*, was printed when he was nine.

After a brief period of ill health and emotional crisis at Marlborough, he went to Eton where he joined the army class, then the only way to study science, and became its captain. After a short time studying chemistry under (Sir) William Ramsay [q.v.] at University College, London, he went to Trinity College, Cambridge, whence he emerged in 1900 as president of the Union, editor of the *Cambridge Review*, and with a first in natural sciences. His friends were G. M. Trevelyan, E. M. Forster, and the circle which later became known as 'Bloomsbury'. It was to him that 'Bloomsbury' turned in 1914 for evidence that their pacifism antedated the war.

Leaving chemistry for law he was called by the Inner Temple in 1904. He held a few briefs, but it did not take. After a short period studying international law at the university of Freiburg he found a truer line of progress as a writer and journalist about finance and a Liberal Party worker. He was assistant editor of *The Economist* from 1908 to 1910, and organized Free Trade Unions in Yorkshire and the City of London. In 1910 he became City editor of the *Morning Post* and London correspondent of the *New York Times* financial supplement. In 1912 he published *Foreign Companies and Other Corporations*, and in 1915 *The System of National Finance* which, reissued in 1924 and 1936, remained the standard textbook until 1939.

He joined the Royal Naval Volunteer Reserve in 1914. His war service was varied, including spells with the Grand Fleet, with the naval mission to the Serbian Army on the Danube and its evacuation to Corfu, with light cruisers on the Harwich station, and with naval siege guns ashore on the Belgian beach at Nieuport les Bains. For this last he was awarded the D.S.C. and the croix de guerre. In 1918 he volunteered for the blocking of Zeebrugge and, serving in the *Vindictive*, commanded a gun turret while smoking a cigar until his right arm was shot away. From this battle he acquired a bar to his D.S.C., forty years of intermittent pain, and the beautiful half-uncial script he learned to write with his left hand. When he had recovered he volunteered for service in Russia where he found himself in command of an armoured train fighting a war of head-on confrontation with Bolshevik trains coming up from Vologda. For this he was appointed to the D.S.O. In 1920 he published a book of war memoirs *By Sea and Land*.

Twice before the war he had stood unsuccessfully for Parliament as a Liberal; in 1915 he had been returned unopposed in his absence at a by-election in Norwich. At the 1918 general election he was returned as a 'free Liberal' but soon threw in his lot with Lloyd George. He gained the ear of the House of Commons with speeches mainly on finance, and became financial secretary to the Treasury in 1921. After the election of 1922 he became chief whip of the Lloyd George Liberals, was sworn of the Privy Council, and regulated the disordered finances of his party. He lost his seat in 1923 but regained it in 1924.

Socialism he would not have, and when in 1926 Lloyd George propounded a land policy which he thought socialistic, Hilton Young left the Liberals and became an independent. At the time of the general strike, believing that socialism and 'direct action' could be effectively met only by a single party, and that this could never again be the ruined Liberal Party, he joined the Conservatives. By agreement with his constituents he kept his seat until the general election in 1929, and was then returned for the Sevenoaks division of Kent, which he held until 1935. He was appointed G.B.E. in 1927.

During the Labour Government of 1929–31 he attended the Conservative shadow Cabinet and attained a leading position in debate in the House. He was also general editor of a group of journals, of which the *Financial News* was the chief. In 1931 he became minister of health in Ramsay MacDonald's 'national' Government. His main job was slum clearance and rehousing. His policy was to confine subsidies to clearance, thereby encouraging local authorities to attack that vigorously, while stimulating private builders to provide new houses by releasing them from subsidized competition. The policy resulted in an unprecedented rate of progress with both clearing and building. But it was unpopular with the Left because of its emphasis on the private builder, and alienated important interests on the Right because it had no place for compensation to slum landlords. 'You do not', he wrote, 'compensate the butcher for selling fly-blown meat.'

He was responsible for the Town and Country Planning Act of 1932, the first to apply to all 'developable' land, and for a Housing Act (1935) which was the first to lay down standards of accommodation and provide for their enforcement.

When Ramsay MacDonald resigned in 1935, Hilton Young accepted a peerage as Lord Kennet of the Dene, and took no further part in politics. The name Kennet was taken from the river by which he had a cottage in Wiltshire.

The unusual breadth of his early training—science, law, finance, and journalism, as well as politics—had made him a valuable negotiator and committee chairman. He was British representative at the Hague conference on credits for the Soviet Union in 1922, and a member of the British delegation to the League of Nations Assemblies in 1926, 1927, 1928, and 1932. He headed a British mission to Poland (1923–5) which laid the foundation of a balanced budget and got the zloty through

some of its early difficulties. He did much the same for Iraq in 1925 and 1930, designing the Iraqi currency and remaining chairman of the Iraq Currency Board in London for many years. In 1925–6 he was chairman of the royal commission on Indian finance which stabilized the rupee and drew up the constitution of the Indian Reserve Bank. In 1928 he chaired a mission to East Africa which advised on the closer union of the British territories there, drawing up a plan which was partially adopted over the years.

At home he was chairman of the 1925 departmental committee on the constitution of the university of London, and the first lay member (for the Crown) of the General Medical Council (1926–31). Appointments which would have meant his leaving Parliament he refused.

During the war of 1939–45 he was chairman of the joint committees of the Treasury and the Ministry of Labour which administered the exemption from military service of civil servants, workers in financial institutions, and university teachers, and in 1939–59 he was chairman of the Capital Issues Committee, which administered the control of investment throughout the economy. For all this work he accepted no payment, public or private, and it was his practice to write his own reports.

At different times he was also chairman and director of many commercial and financial corporations, among them English Electric, Hudson's Bay, Denny Mott and Dickson, Union Discount, British Bank of the Middle East, and Equity and Law Life Assurance. After 1935 his working life was passed mainly in the City, where he was known as a specialist in reordering the finances of companies standing in need of it.

His varied presidencies included the Royal Statistical Society, the Association of Technical Institutions, the Poetry Society, the Gas Federation of Great Britain, the Association of Municipal Corporations, and the National Association of Youth Clubs.

His leisure interests were old books, which he collected—principally Venetian incunabula and first editions of the English philosophers—and birds, about which he published a book of essays *A Bird in the Bush* (1936) illustrated by his stepson Peter Scott. He also published a book of verse *A Muse at Sea* (1919) reprinted with additions as *Verses* in 1935. One became an anthology piece: 'A boy was born at

Bethlehem'. He was an enthusiastic small boat sailor until his sixtieth year, sailing single-handed in a stricter sense of the word than is usual, and a good swimmer and diver. He was a spirited draughtsman, usually for political or didactic purposes. All the special skills which were necessary to maintain an active physical life with one arm he carefully learned and maintained.

He was of compact build and average height, handsome in youth with curly dark hair and straight nose, alert and courteous in white-haired age. He was on affable terms with his eldest brother, Sir George Young, bart., the eccentric diplomat and historian of Turkish law, and on terms of intimate affection with his next brother, Geoffrey Winthrop Young, the mountaineer and writer, a notice of whom appears below. He was on the whole a man's man, and used to quote: 'A man of the world! Where's my hat?'

He was brought up in a rather rigid Broad Church family but, under the influence of G. E. Moore [q.v.] and Bertrand Russell at Cambridge, abandoned Christianity for an aesthetically flavoured humanism. Face to face with death in 1914 he felt the need for a stricter system, and studied Spinoza among shellbursts. He remained a Spinozan pantheist till his death. Towards the end of his life he wrote essays for private circulation, tracing this philosophical development, and examining the defects of democracy in general and the House of Commons in particular. He held that the chief threat to the welfare of a community comes from the excesses of extremists both left and right, and that it is the duty of rulers to counteract them by leaning right or left as the times require. Spinoza was his philosopher, 'Trimmer' Halifax [q.v.] his statesman.

He was at home in scholarship, in administration, and in debate, but never in party politics. These he held in contempt, and it showed. A reserved manner and a certain caustic and even farouche integrity prevented his achieving the highest political offices. He had a good measure of the brilliant contrariety characteristic of his family, but balanced it with a genial empiricism of his own. He called himself a jack of all trades: his admirers called him a *uomo universale*.

In 1922 he married Kathleen Scott [q.v.] the sculptor. Although entered into late in life the marriage was singularly successful, their temperaments being nicely complementary: hers passionate and intuitive;

his quizzical and rather reserved. He died at Lockeridge in Wiltshire, 11 July 1960, and was succeeded by his only child Wayland Hilton (born 1923). There exist portrait drawings of him by Sir William Rothenstein and Peter Scott, and a statuette by his wife. All are in the possession of his son.

WAYLAND YOUNG.

YOUNG, FRANCIS BRETT (1884–1954), novelist, was born 29 June 1884 at Halesowen, Worcestershire, the eldest son of Thomas Brett Young and his wife, Annie Elizabeth, daughter of John Jackson, a surgeon, of Somerby, Leicestershire. As the son of a doctor he was educated at Epsom College, where he won a prize for English literature, and then graduated M.B., Ch.B. at Birmingham University (1907). His experiences at school and university were the basis of his early novel *The Young Physician* (1919).

In 1908 Brett Young married a teacher of physical training who later became a concert singer, Jessica, daughter of John Hankinson, farmer, and settled in practice in Brixham, Devon, where 'in between epidemics' he wrote his earliest novels, *Deep Sea* (1914), *The Dark Tower* (1915), and *The Iron Age* (1916). Joining the Royal Army Medical Corps he served with the 2nd Rhodesian Regiment in Smuts's campaign in East Africa. *Marching on Tanga* (1917) was the fruit of his experiences, but the campaign took a heavy toll of his health. He wrote *The Crescent Moon* (1918) and *Poems 1916–1918* (1919) while still convalescent in Africa.

Even on his return to England Brett Young was not well enough to resume medical practice. His wife gave up her concert career and they settled in Anacapri. There, curiously enough, beneath Mediterranean skies, his first essentially West Midland stories, *The Black Diamond* (1921) and *Portrait of Clare* (1927), were conceived and written. The latter, a story of considerable length and of the type now generally associated with his name, was awarded the James Tait Black memorial prize and was his first real success. In spite of the exotic friendships of Capri, the couple longed for an English home which the sales of this novel and *My Brother Jonathan* (1928) made financially possible. They settled in the Lake District until in 1933 they purchased Craycombe House, standing on a hill overlooking the Avon valley above Evesham, in the very heart of what was already becoming known as 'the Brett Young country'. Until the outbreak of war in 1939 he published at least one book a year—among them *Mr. and Mrs. Pennington* (1931), *The House Under the Water* (1932), and a moving story of the life of a general practitioner, *Dr. Bradley Remembers* (1938), clearly based on the life of his own father. Most of them were set in his 'own country', but he wrote also two vast panoramic novels—he did not live to complete the trilogy—*They Seek a Country* (1937) and *The City of Gold* (1939) which set forth the story of the South African peoples from the days of the Great Trek to the Jameson raid.

The great drama of the Battle of Britain inspired Brett Young to undertake his most ambitious work, *The Island* (1944), in which he described in verse the conquests and vicissitudes in our island history from the earliest times until the final defeat of the German invader in the air. It left a strain upon his heart and health so heavy that on medical advice he settled near Cape Town, where he died 28 March 1954. There were no children. His widow brought his ashes to England and they were laid to rest in Worcester Cathedral which he greatly loved.

There is a portrait by Cathleen Mann, painted in 1922, in the library of the medical faculty in the university of Birmingham. Brett Young looked what in fact he was, a landowner and a physician, a man typical of his class. Nowhere was he more at home than amongst his fellow members of the committee of the Worcestershire County Cricket Club. It is from this background that his novels in the main derive. They have the charm of being typically English, written in a leisurely and accomplished manner which at times achieves a genuine lyrical quality. Brett Young received the honorary degree of D.Litt. from the university of Birmingham in 1950.

[E. G. Twitchett, *Francis Brett Young*, 1935; Jessica Brett Young, *Francis Brett Young*, 1962; personal knowledge.]

ARNOLD GYDE.

YOUNG, GEOFFREY WINTHROP (1876–1958), mountaineer, the second son of Sir George Young, third baronet [q.v.], was born in London 25 October 1876. A notice of his younger brother appears above. He was educated at Marlborough and Trinity College, Cambridge, where he was twice awarded the Chancellor's verse medal (1898–9), published anonymously 'The Roof-Climber's Guide to Trinity',

and graduated in 1898. After further study at Jena and Geneva universities he was an assistant master at Eton (1900–5), an inspector of secondary schools (1905–13), consultant for Europe to the Rockefeller Foundation (1925–33), and reader in comparative education in the university of London (1932–41). During the war of 1914–18 he commanded the Friends' Ambulance Unit in Belgium (1914–15) and the First British Ambulance Unit for Italy (1915–19). His leg was amputated above the knee as the result of wounds sustained in the battle of San Gabriele. He was mentioned in dispatches and received Belgian and Italian decorations.

Young was one of the greatest mountaineers that Britain has produced. No one in the twenty years before 1914 had a longer list of first ascents, among them a new route up the Weisshorn from Zinal, the Younggrat on the Zermatt Breithorn, the south face of the Täschhorn, the direct route up the Grépon from the Mer de Glace, and, his last great climb, the Rote Zähne ridge of the Gespaltenhorn. After his leg had been amputated he climbed the Wellenkuppe, the Weisshorn to within five hundred feet of the summit, the Matterhorn, Petits Charmoz, Requin, Grépon and Zinal Rothorn, and Monte Rosa. To have climbed one peak with an artificial leg would have been remarkable, but to continue climbing peak after peak with an artificial leg is proof of indomitable spirit. On most of these climbs Young, the greatest amateur of the period, was accompanied by the greatest of contemporary guides, Joseph Knubel.

In the word painting of mountain scenery Young is only surpassed by Sir Leslie Stephen and Lord Conway [qq.v.] and in the records of mountain adventure there is nothing more enthralling than Young's story of the Täschhorn climb in *On High Hills* (1927), and little more moving than his story of his one-leg climbs in *Mountains with a Difference* (1951). But he was often tempted to overwrite and over-embroider his descriptions, and the first versions of his story of two classic climbs, the north face of the Weisshorn and the south face of the Täschhorn, which appeared in the *Cornhill* are preferable to the final and revised versions in *On High Hills*. Young's *Mountain Craft* (1920) was recognized throughout the mountain world as the outstanding analysis of mountaineering technique. Young made a most important contribution to the history of mountaineering not only in the Alps, but also in Great Britain. His contribution to the *Alpine Journal* (November 1943) 'Mountain Prophets' was notable for his superb characterization of those of the pioneers whom he knew. He was proposed for the Alpine Club in 1900 by Sir Alfred Wills, from whose ascent of the Wetterhorn in 1854 it is customary to date the beginning of the golden age of mountaineering. Finally, although mountain beauty is the theme of many poems, Young is the outstanding poet of mountaineering. His *Collected Poems* were published in 1936. His literary ability did not decline with the years. Much of his best work was written in his eighties, such as his admirable contribution to the *Mountain World* (1955) in which he deplored the increasing tendency of mountain narratives to be written in the style of an engineer's report. He wrote nothing finer than the paper which he read before the Alpine Club, 10 December 1957, his last appearance before returning to the London hospital where he died 6 September 1958. As his musical voice lingered on the phrases which evoked the remembered loveliness of the hills, his hearers knew that from the valley of death he was lifting his eyes to the hills of memory whence help would assuredly come.

The influence which Young exerted through the written word was reinforced by his close contacts with successive generations of mountaineers. He lived for many years in Cambridge where he was accepted as a discerning authority not only on the technique but also on the traditions of mountaineering. He was president of the Alpine Club in 1941-4 and his great services to the club during that difficult period were recorded in *A Century of Mountaineering* (1957).

In 1918 Young married Eleanor, daughter of a great mountaineer, William Cecil Slingsby; she had an affectionate understanding of his endearing weaknesses and a discerning admiration for his great qualities as a man and as a writer. They had one son and one daughter.

[Personal knowledge.]   ARNOLD LUNN.

YOUNG, GEORGE MALCOLM (1882-1959), scholar, was born at Charlton, Kent, 29 April 1882, the only son of George Frederick Young, waterman, later a steamer master, of Greenhithe, and his wife, Rosetta Jane Elizabeth Ross. A scholar of St. Paul's, he became captain of the school. A scholar of Balliol, in the year (1900) in which William Temple [q.v.] was elected to an exhibition, Young gained a first in classical honour moderations (1902) and a second in *literae humaniores* (1904), having rowed in the second torpid. He was elected a fellow of All Souls in 1905 and became a tutor at St. John's (1906-8). In 1908 he joined the Board of Education, then under the sway of Sir Robert Morant [q.v.] to whom he remained devoted. Young became a junior examiner in the universities branch; then, in 1911, the first secretary of what was to burgeon into the University Grants Committee. In 1916 he joined the newly formed Cabinet Office. Appointed C.B. in 1917, he was chosen as joint secretary of the new and shortlived Ministry of Reconstruction. He accompanied Arthur Henderson [q.v.], then a member of the War Cabinet, as secretary on his notorious visit to Russia in 1917 where Young met (Sir) Francis Lindley [q.v.] at that time counsellor in the British Embassy. He went with Lindley to Archangel and later accompanied him to Vienna when Lindley went there as minister. In Vienna, Young was for a time a director of the newly founded Anglo-Austrian Bank: 'a curious anaemic-looking man' not mixing readily but already recognized by his younger British colleagues as 'a great scholar with a wide range of knowledge and a wonderful command of the English language'.

Abandoning the public service in the early post-war disillusion, Young decided to devote himself to writing, but nothing could remove that intense interest in education which shone throughout all his work. He was at heart a born teacher, thirsting to impart the results of his own sharp and constructive thoughts bred of a wide and deep reading in a formidable variety of subjects. Yet he was in no hurry. Although his essay on 'Victorian History' had caught discerning eyes in 1931, it was not until he was fifty that he published his first book, *Gibbon* (1932), a work of pietas but partly too of deliberation to impress upon the new biographers that neither Freud nor Marx had yet explained why there should be great men. And he was to note in Gibbon that 'sense of place' he was himself so compellingly to reveal. He made his home in Wiltshire where at the Old Oxyard at Oare near Marlborough he fell upon the antiquities of Wessex, not forgetting 'Pond Barrows', with far more knowledge and no less eagerness than did his favourite John Aubrey [q.v.]. He shared house with his lifelong friend Mona Wilson, authoress and sister of Sir Arnold Wilson [q.v.]; there she took charge of all those details of everyday life in which Young himself was oddly helpless and dependent. Surrounded in this neighbourhood by many cronies, including a bevy of ex-ambassadors, Young became, alongside Miss Wilson with her short fireside pipe, the centre of intellectual gossip and a dispenser of fascinating talk drawn from the resources of an astonishing memory. Urban in origin and urbane by disposition he was no less at home with countrymen and the railway workers of Swindon. He took pleasure in finding himself a Tory and 'no Tory of whatever rank or class ever thought of a merely moneyed man as his social equal'.

At the perceptive invitation of the Oxford University Press, no doubt at the instigation of (Sir) Humphrey Milford [q.v.], he edited the two volumes of *Early Victorian England* which appeared in 1934 and to which he himself contributed that final summary chapter which brought his especial quality to the attention of a wider and delighted public, an essay which he developed into *Victorian England, Portrait of an Age* (1936) by which he will be remembered. What was important in history was, in his view, 'not what happened, but what people felt about it when it was happening'. Young had the industry, the learning, the memory, and above all, the penetration to disentangle the main themes from the confused Victorian clamour. His advice to the historian was 'to go on reading until you can hear people talking'. He did not point out that it might still require an interpreter of his talent, erudition, and perception—or with the gifts of his revered F. W. Maitland [q.v.]; and embedded in Young's writing was more food for thought than the common reader had been accustomed to encounter. Nor was his aim objective; even in narrative he would not forgo comment, with an epithet, an adverb, a tone of voice. His Clio was a muse with a sting.

After *Charles I and Cromwell* (1935), an essay in detection published before his developed Victorian masterpiece, came *Daylight and Champaign* (1937), a collection of essays and reviews many of them reprinted from the literary periodicals such as the *Sunday Times* to which Young was by now a valued contributor. There, and in other reprints, which included addresses such as his Romanes lecture on Gladstone

in 1944, in his *Today and Yesterday* (1948) and in *Last Essays* (1950) he found elbow-room for good talk, addressed purposely to the middlebrow, about literature, persons, and manners. Unbuttoned, he might be colloquial, give full play to his humour, even show off a little since he was enjoying himself, yet literature remained a very serious matter for him, as were the duties of the clerisy and the continuity of civilization. He was deeply concerned with language as a means of communication; good speech he deemed 'the first political art'. A university he regarded as 'a place where young men and women educate one another by conversation, under the guidance of people a little older, and, more often than they might imagine, somewhat wiser than themselves'.

Young was a trustee of the National Portrait Gallery (from 1937) and of the British Museum (1947–57), a member of the Standing Commission on Museums and Galleries (from 1938), and of the Historical Manuscripts Commission (from 1948); all work lying very close to his being and, until his health began to fail, he gave it much attention and thought. His was a slight figure with a scholarly stoop; he had a longish, inquisitive nose, eyes twinkling well ahead of a coming quip, an unusual manner of clearing his throat, a voice warm and vibrant. He was a shy man and because sensitive, sometimes sharp: an intellectual who lived by his deep if hidden affections. Mona Wilson's death not long after the war, then the sale of the Oxyard were blows from which he never recovered, but he built himself a new existence on his re-election in 1948 to All Souls which provided him with a familiar and congenial refuge. He became a member of the royal commission on the press (1947–9) and he received honorary degrees from Durham (1950) and Cambridge (1953); and what he valued most, Balliol elected him to an honorary fellowship in 1953.

His last book, *Stanley Baldwin* (1952), had been undertaken reluctantly, at Baldwin's own request. As he grew closer to his subject Young was clearly somewhat taken aback by his discoveries and it is not a satisfying book; Young's touch had begun to fail him. In 1956 he published, in collaboration with W. D. Handcock, a volume of *English Historical Documents, 1833–74*, but Young's part in it, undertaken in 1947, was small. An invitation to lecture in Athens, which he had never visited, for a while renewed his flagging spirits, then a cloud descended on him and his death in a nursing-home near Oxford 18 November 1959 was a genuine release.

Young has been called a 'pantomath'; a comment not displeasing to him. If he was not quite that, it was well said of him that few writers have said so many good things upon so many subjects. He lived up to his own definition of the historian as 'one for whom the past keeps something of the familiar triviality of the present, and the present has already some of the shadowy magnificence of the past'. The National Portrait Gallery has a drawing by Henry Lamb.

[*The Times*, 19 and 24 November 1959; R. H. Bruce Lockhart, *Retreat from Glory*, 1934; W. D. Handcock, introduction to *Victorian Essays*, 1962; private information; personal knowledge.]   L. E. JONES.
                            E. T. WILLIAMS.

YOUNG, SIR ROBERT ARTHUR (1871–1959), physician, was born 6 November 1871 in the Norfolk village of Hilborough, the only son of William Young, labourer, and his wife, Hannah Elizabeth Ann Fairs who when registering the birth signed her name with a mark. After attending Westminster City School and King's College, London, he became a medical student at the Middlesex Hospital. He obtained his B.Sc. with a first class in physiology in 1891 and his M.B. in 1894, and became a licentiate of the Society of Apothecaries in a period when the quill pen was still used and the doctor carried his stethoscope in his silk hat. He was elected a member of the Royal College of Physicians of London in 1897 and fellow in 1905. After obtaining his M.D., London, with a gold medal (1895), and doing postgraduate work at Vienna, he settled in London as a consulting physician and was appointed to the Middlesex Hospital, the Brompton Hospital for Diseases of the Chest, and later the King Edward VII Sanatorium, Midhurst.

At the beginning of the century a chest specialist had to rely entirely upon observation and the patient's story, with only his five senses to help him. Of this personal technique Young became one of the greatest exponents medicine has ever known. He was incapable of superficiality and with extraordinary tenacity would relentlessly pursue each sign and symptom until he penetrated its meaning. Even when X-ray diagnosis became general, he never consulted the film until he had carried his personal methods as far as they would go.

In his large consulting room in Harley Street, over-furnished with cupboards and clocks, he sat at an overcrowded desk and inscrutably pursued his remorseless clinical routine. Nothing was allowed to come between him and the patient, and he never gave up until he had used every available method and discovered all he needed. His remarkable clinical sense was built upon memory and observation and he certainly understood that the physician's role includes giving not merely a diagnosis but some comfort and hope. He would take endless trouble with his patients. Medicine can never be an exact science or a perfect art, but in his hands it seemed both, and he fully deserved his remarkable success. By the time of the war of 1914–18 he was a rising chest consultant; but during the twenties and thirties he was supreme.

A man who had so perfected the orthodox clinical methods might have been expected to be hesitant about accepting the newer technical outlook, but Young was able to preserve the one and acquire the other, for his greatness as a physician included remarkable flexibility. He took up X-rays when the method became universal in the twenties. Artificial pneumothorax (for lung tuberculosis), mass radiography, and, greatest revolution of all, penicillin and streptomycin, each of these advances he mastered with his characteristic thoroughness. His Lumleian lecture (1929) put a physician's seal upon surgery in the treatment of lung diseases.

His practice continued to flourish long after he retired in 1936 from the Middlesex Hospital and even after the age of eighty he gave a sound opinion. Before King George VI underwent an operation for lung cancer in 1951 Young was the leader in a group of eminent clinicians summoned to advise.

Young was chairman of innumerable societies and committees, notably the National Association for the Prevention of Tuberculosis. He was an excellent leader, governing the proceedings with suavity and an extra sense of what was being thought round the table. He was an accomplished conciliator, adept in the formula which unites. Everyone looked to him for he had the knack of being right. He could express well the majority opinion because this was the way he felt himself. Large affairs did not attract him, and he did not mingle in medical controversies over the National Health Service.

A rather hieratic manner, sedulously cultivated as a young man, mellowed greatly in later life, although his speech kept a touch of unctuous sentiment belonging to an earlier period. He made a considerable fortune from practice in an age when this was the accepted measure of professional success. His private passion was collecting. Over the years a prodigious accumulation of china, glass, prints, clocks, and old instruments filled his rooms. He had not much artistic sense and preferred the quaint rather than the enduring. He cherished every object and nothing was ever allowed to go.

'R.A.' (as he was affectionately known) was of medium height with a large, impressive head, and eyes which seemed to penetrate to the depths, though they also flickered with kindly reassurance. He was essentially a kindly man, wrapped up in his grandchildren, his many friends, and favoured organizations. He never missed a medical banquet and kept up his committees, full of industrious goodwill, until a week before his death.

Young's prodigious industry and impressive personal qualities brought him wide recognition. He was Harveian orator (1939) of the Royal College of Physicians; both the Apothecaries and the Royal Society of Medicine gave him their gold medals. He was appointed C.B.E. in 1920 and knighted in 1947. He was one of those men whose contemporary eminence is seldom understood by the succeeding generation, for it was his quality to personify the best average of his time rather than to display a unique genius.

In 1912 Young married Fanny Caroline Phoebe (died 1944), daughter of Robert Muirhead Kennedy, of the Indian Civil Service, and had one son. Young died in London 22 August 1959.

[*The Times*, 24 and 26 August 1959; *British Medical Journal*, 29 August 1959; *Lancet*, 5 September 1959; private information; personal knowledge.]

HARLEY WILLIAMS.

YULE, GEORGE UDNY (1871–1951), statistician, was born at Morham, near Haddington, East Lothian, 18 February 1871, the youngest of the three children surviving infancy of Sir George Udny Yule [q.v.], Bengal Civil Service, and his wife, Henrietta Peach, daughter of Captain Robert Boileau Pemberton, of the Indian Army. Sir Henry Yule [q.v.] was his uncle.

Yule was educated at Winchester and intended for the Royal Engineers, but objecting, instead he studied civil engineering at University College, London, which he entered at the age of sixteen. As there was then no engineering degree he left after three years without graduating. He spent a year in a small engineering works, but in 1892 he went to study physics at Bonn University. While at University College he had become acquainted with Karl Pearson [q.v.], then professor of applied mathematics, and in 1893 Pearson offered him a job as demonstrator. He was promoted to assistant professor of applied mathematics in 1896. Pearson was at that time just beginning to work on statistics and this marked the beginning of Yule's interest in the subject.

In 1899 he married May Winifred, daughter of William Hayman Cummings, principal of the Guildhall School of Music, but the marriage was not a success and in 1912 it was annulled. There were no children. In consequence of his marriage he gave up his post in University College and took up more remunerative work as assistant to Sir Philip Magnus, superintendent of the department of technology, City and Guilds of London Institute. Yule was, however, able to keep up his statistical work in the evenings and in 1902 he was appointed Newmarch lecturer in statistics at University College, holding the two posts concurrently until 1909. This involved lecturing in the evenings to a small class, largely of civil servants. These lectures provided the foundation of his *Introduction to the Theory of Statistics* (1911), which became a standard textbook and by 1932 had run through ten editions; in revised form (Yule and Kendall) it remained widely used.

In 1912 Yule accepted the newly established university lectureship in statistics at Cambridge and concurrently became statistician to the School of Agriculture. He was made a member of St. John's College in 1913, elected a fellow in 1922, was college director of studies in natural sciences (1923–35), and resided in college for almost the whole of the rest of his life.

In the war of 1914–18 he was seconded as a statistician to the director of army contracts and later worked with the Ministry of Food, being appointed C.B.E. in 1918.

Yule had great influence on the early development of modern statistics. His main contributions in the theoretical field were concerned with regression and correlation, with association, particularly in 2×2 contingency tables, with time-series, with Mendelian inheritance, and with epidemiology. He was elected F.R.S. in 1921. He played a very active part in the affairs of various scientific societies, in particular the Royal Statistical Society, of which he was honorary secretary (1907–19) and president (1924–6), and was awarded the society's Guy medal in gold (1911).

Yule was never, nor did he regard himself as, a great mathematician, but he had a very clear idea of what could and could not be accomplished by mathematical analysis and never permitted himself to be led astray by mathematical reasoning. In his early years he was a good friend of Karl Pearson: they spent several holidays together—in Cumberland, Yorkshire, and Norway—and Yule found him always a delightful companion. Had Pearson been of a more accommodating temperament, they might have become an ideal team, for in many ways their abilities were complementary. Yule's caution, his much greater regard for the fundamentals of the phenomena underlying the data he was examining, and his more critical attitude to the conclusions reached by mathematical analysis, were just what Pearson lacked. But as Yule himself wrote in his obituary of Pearson (Royal Society, 1936): 'Those who left him and began to think for themselves were apt, as happened painfully in more instances than one, to find that after a divergence of opinion the maintenance of friendly relations became difficult, after express criticism impossible.'

Yule was a quiet and unassuming man, liked by all, the enemy of none. His wide knowledge and interests and his kindly and gentle nature made him an excellent companion. He was not ambitious, regarding freedom to pursue whatever inquiries took his fancy or seemed to him worth while as of more importance than name or fortune. He was a man of varied and surprising attainments. He had marked literary interests and composed humorous verses in both Latin and English. In his fifties he developed a keen interest in motoring, with a taste for fast driving. On his retirement from his university post, raised to a readership, in 1931, he took up flying, purchasing his own aeroplane because it was impossible to arrange insurance on a hired machine. He obtained his pilot's 'Certificate A' when nearly sixty-one. When nearing retirement he resumed the study of Latin with a view to reading in the original *De Imitatione Christi*, St.

Augustine's *Confessions*, and Boethius's *De Consolatione Philosophiae*. The first of these led to consideration of the authorship controversy and to other works of Thomas à Kempis. This suggested to him the idea of using statistical methods to provide evidence of authorship and in 1944 he published *The Statistical Study of Literary Vocabulary*.

After his retirement Yule continued to take an active part in college affairs; but in 1935 his heart gave serious trouble and thereafter he was compelled to be physically inactive. He died in Cambridge 26 June 1951. St. John's College has a drawing by Henry Lamb.

[F. Yates in *Obituary Notices of Fellows of the Royal Society*, No. 21, November 1952; *The Eagle*, vol. lv, 1952; personal knowledge.]

F. YATES.

ZIMMERN, SIR ALFRED ECKHARD (1879–1957), scholar and authority on international institutions, was born in Surbiton 26 January 1879, the only son of Adolf Zimmern, China and East India merchant, and his wife, Matilda Sophia Eckhard. His father was one of a Jewish family of liberal outlook who had migrated from Germany to England after the defeated revolution of 1848.

A scholar of Winchester and New College, Oxford, he obtained first classes in honour moderations (1900) and *literae humaniores* (1902) and was awarded the Stanhope historical essay prize (1902). He became a lecturer in ancient history and (1904–9) a fellow and tutor of his college. After an early study of Henry Grattan (1902) he wrote *The Greek Commonwealth* (1911) which quickly won a world-wide reputation and proved to have a more enduring quality than any of his later books. He seemed destined to a distinguished but essentially academic career, as scholar and historian, although he had some practical work in relation to working-class education and in 1912–15 was an inspector of the Board of Education.

The first great war and the problems confronting the world when it ended completely changed the centre of gravity of Zimmern's interests. During the war itself he joined the political intelligence department of the Foreign Office (1918–19) and, with memories doubtless of his own family history, became one of a circle of political thinkers who influenced policy towards the liberation of subject peoples and persecuted minorities. He was one of those who helped to found the (Royal)

Institute of International Affairs (Chatham House) and to guide and inspire its work during its early years. It was above all, however, the new League of Nations which became the focus of his interests and of his work as a teacher and lecturer. For two years (1919–21) he held the newly created Wilson professorship of international politics at Aberystwyth. In 1921 he married Lucie Anna (died 1963), daughter of Pastor Maurice Hirsch, previously the wife of a colleague there. But his, and her, hopes and interests were centred on what was happening in Geneva. There they soon went and not only studied the early development of the new institution but did their best to influence the inner circles of those who participated in the Council and Assembly, of the secretariat and of interested public supporters. His own convictions as to the desirable character of the League's organization and policy reflected now not only his previous experience and philosophy but also the influence of his wife, a forceful personality and ardent patriot. To his family traditions, his classical study of Athenian democracy, and his deep interest in British political history and the gradual transformation of the British Empire into an increasingly self-governing Commonwealth, was now added a continental, and in particular a French, point of view. In personal contacts, in successive books, and in lectures both elsewhere and in Geneva, where he was director of the School of International Studies (1925–39), he advocated with persuasive lucidity his transparently sincere political convictions. In 1926–30 he had official responsibility as deputy director of the Institute of Intellectual Co-operation in Paris. This, however, was only an interlude, and his essential role, as indeed his personal outlook, was not that of an administrator but of a student, teacher, and lecturer.

In 1930 Zimmern returned to Oxford as the first Montague Burton professor of international relations and occupied that chair until 1944. In the war of 1939–45 he served in the Foreign Office research department and for a brief period at the end of the war he was an executive director of Unesco. This again was only an interlude in his normal work as teacher and writer and in 1947–9 he was a visiting professor at Trinity College, Hartford, Connecticut. His work and the wide range of his reputation were reflected in honorary doctorates from that college and from Aberdeen,

Bristol, and Melbourne, and also by the knighthood which he received in 1936.

Short in stature, and in physical presence at first unimpressive, Zimmern's vitality, his rapid response in discussion, his persuasive lucidity in exposition or advocacy, the transparent sincerity of his exceptionally cosmopolitan outlook, remained a vivid memory with all who met him. The books he wrote, after the first war had diverted him from academic life, recall by their titles, but do not in themselves adequately express, his actual contribution. *Nationality and Government* (1918), *Europe in Convalescence* (1922), *The Third British Empire* (1926), *Solon and Croesus* (1928), *Prospects of Democracy* (1929), *The League of Nations and the Rule of Law* (1936), *Spiritual Values and World Affairs* (1939), and *The American Road to World Peace* (1953) are for the most part collected essays, written in relation to current problems and events. Neither these nor other extant records convey adequately the measure of his influence and authority in his prime, as they remained in the memory of his contemporaries and colleagues.

Zimmern's career and personal life reached their climax in the twenties, the decade of both political recovery and progress, marked by Locarno, the League's brief period of successful authority, the wide extension of parliamentary recovery, and for a time unprecedented prosperity—the temporary triumph of all the causes whose success he had ardently desired. The twenty years of his life that remained witnessed the collapse of what he had hoped for. He continued to work indefatigably, without visible decline of his powers, for many years, although inevitably with less personal influence than he had had in his prime. He died at Avon, Connecticut, 24 November 1957. He had no children.

[*The Times*, 25 November 1957; Arnold J. Toynbee, *Acquaintances*, 1967; private information; personal knowledge.] SALTER.

ZULUETA, FRANCIS DE (FRANCISCO MARIA JOSÉ) (1878–1958), academic lawyer, was born 12 September 1878 in the Spanish Embassy in London. His father, Don Pedro Juan de Zulueta, was a member of the Spanish diplomatic service; his mother, Laura Mary, daughter of Sir Justin Sheil [q.v.], at one time British minister in Persia. Although a Spaniard by birth, and a cousin of Cardinal Merry del Val, he was only one-quarter of Spanish blood: his father was on one side Scottish, descended in the female line from Brodie M'Ghie Willcox, one of the founders of the P. & O. Steam Navigation Company. The Zuluetas, a Basque family, settled in Cadiz in the eighteenth century, had left Spain on account of their Liberal opinions and later established a business in London where for much of the nineteenth century they served as the agents of the Spanish Government. Don Pedro felt himself so much at home that in order to remain permanently in London he resigned from the Spanish diplomatic service. His son regarded himself as British rather than Spanish.

He was educated at Beaumont and the Oratory School and went with an open scholarship to New College, Oxford, where he was placed in the first class in classical moderations (1899), *literae humaniores* (1901), and jurisprudence (1902). He was elected to a prize fellowship at Merton (1902), won the Vinerian law scholarship (1903), and was called to the bar by Lincoln's Inn (1904). In 1907 he returned to New College as a tutorial fellow and from 1912 to 1917 was All Souls reader in Roman law.

On the outbreak of war in 1914 he felt himself so closely identified with this country that he became naturalized, obtained a commission in the Worcestershire Regiment, and served in France. On his return to Oxford in 1919 he was appointed to the regius chair of civil law, which he held until 1948.

A first-rate classical scholar, Zulueta had also the good fortune to be one of the earliest members of the seminar of (Sir) Paul Vinogradoff [q.v.], the first to be established on continental lines in Oxford. He always admitted his deep indebtedness to Vinogradoff and the methods of research inculcated by him. The fruit of this work was an essay, contributed in 1909 to Vinogradoff's *Oxford Studies in Social and Legal History*, on 'Patronage in the later Empire'. Thereafter he published much less than his contemporaries desired and expected. He became in truth too learned to see opportunities for originality in a well-tilled field; and his scepticism in matters of legal scholarship not only led him to leave questions open which others might have answered, but to entertain a radical and very un-Catholic disbelief in natural law. He was out of tune with the dominant school of Romanistic research, then devoted to the search for interpolations in the Corpus Juris, which he regarded as piling hypothesis upon hypothesis and encouraging anyone who practised it not to admit the unsoundness of any theory he had once adopted. He is also reported to have said to a younger friend, 'Don't read, or you won't write'. It was characteristic that much of his most valuable work is to be found in his bibliographical contributions to the *Journal of Egyptian Archaeology*. One of his colleagues once likened him to a person with a big bunch of keys: he might not be able to tell you what you wanted to know but he would certainly be able to tell you where to find it. His relative unproductiveness was perhaps partly due to an unfortunate occasion, during his period of teaching at New College, when a number of undergraduates, finding their stock of combustible materials running out, burnt the papers he had prepared for a forthcoming book. This rankled, though in the end he came to think that the enforced rewriting had resulted in a much better book. However surprising it may have been to those who knew him later, he was at that time rather unpopular, being less able than subsequently to control a naturally quick temper.

In 1927 Zulueta edited for the Selden Society Vacarius's *Liber Pauperum*. But he will be best known to ordinary students by three most useful works: his little edition of the *Digest* titles on Ownership and Possession (1922) for use by B.C.L. candidates, his *Roman Law of Sale* (1945), and his edition of the *Institutes of Gaius*, of which the Text and Translation appeared in 1946 and the Commentary in 1953. In all these he displayed a conciseness of utterance which is often disconcerting, not only to the elementary student, but which on more diligent perusal discloses the products of his profound erudition.

In lecturing he believed in systematic exposition which did not perhaps show him at his best. Temperamentally he was better fitted to the more explosive method appropriate to informal instruction or to revision lectures in which he could assume a general knowledge of the subject and needed only to draw attention to interesting points which had probably been neglected.

A devout Roman Catholic, he actively supported the Oxford University Catholic Association and the local branch of the Society of St. Vincent de Paul. His religious convictions made him effective in helping Polish refugees during the war of 1939–45 although they were not so exclusive as to preclude his doing just as much for Jewish and other refugees. They prompted his intervention in Malta's constitutional controversy in the thirties and combined with his intense conservatism to make him an ardent supporter of General Franco in the Spanish civil war. As a young man he had taken a prominent part in games. Those who knew him later remember his handsome face and figure, the natural courtesy of his manners, perfect in his relations with all sorts of people and especially with children, and his great usefulness, with a knowledge of many languages, in dealing with foreign scholars. He was a loyal colleague whose sound legal instinct was displayed not only in his own special field and whose shrewdness and sagacity in discussions of policy and of ways and means were highly prized by his colleagues on the board of the faculty. His helpfulness to scholars of all ages even extended to the humble but exacting tasks of the editor and translator. He received many honours, including fellowship of the British Academy, an honorary fellowship of Merton, an honorary doctorate of Paris and of Aberdeen, and fellowship of the Accademia dei Lincei.

In 1915 he married Marie Louise (died 1970), daughter of the late Henry Alexander Lyne Stephens, of Grove House, Roehampton, and left one son, (Sir) Philip Francis de Zulueta.

Zulueta died in London 16 January 1958. A list of his publications is prefixed to *Studies in the Roman Law of Sale* (1959), dedicated to his memory and edited by David Daube.

[*The Times*, 18 January 1958; private information; personal knowledge.]

F. H. LAWSON.

CUMULATIVE INDEX

TO THE BIOGRAPHIES CONTAINED IN THE SUPPLEMENTS

OF THE DICTIONARY OF NATIONAL BIOGRAPHY

1901–1960

Abbey, Edwin Austin	1852–1911	Agnew, Sir William Gladstone	1898–1960
Abbott, Edwin Abbott	1838–1926	Aidé, Charles Hamilton	1826–1906
Abbott, Evelyn	1843–1901	Aikman, George	1830–1905
À Beckett, Arthur William	1844–1909	Ainger, Alfred	1837–1904
Abel, Sir Frederick Augustus	1827–1902	Ainley, Henry Hinchliffe	1879–1945
Aberconway, Baron. See Mc-Laren, Charles Benjamin Bright	1850–1934	Aird, Sir John	1833–1911
		Airedale, Baron. See Kitson, James	1835–1911
Aberconway, Baron. See Mc-Laren, Henry Duncan	1879–1953	Aitchison, Craigie Mason, Lord	1882–1941
Abercorn, Duke of. See Hamilton, James	1838–1913	Aitchison, George	1825–1910
		Akers, Sir Wallace Alan	1888–1954
Abercrombie, Lascelles	1881–1938	Akers-Douglas, Aretas, Viscount Chilston	1851–1926
Abercrombie, Sir (Leslie) Patrick	1879–1957		
Aberdare, Baron. See Bruce, Clarence Napier	1885–1957	Akers-Douglas, Aretas, Viscount Chilston	1876–1947
Aberdeen and Temair, Marquess of. See Gordon, John Campbell	1847–1934	Albani, Dame Marie Louise Cécilie Emma	1852–1930
		Alcock, Sir John William	1892–1919
Aberdeen and Temair, Marchioness of (1857–1939). See under Gordon, John Campbell		Aldenham, Baron. See Gibbs, Henry Hucks	1819–1907
		Alderson, Sir Edwin Alfred Hervey	1859–1927
Aberhart, William	1878–1943		
Abney, Sir William de Wiveleslie	1843–1920	Alderson, Henry James	1834–1909
Abraham, Charles John	1814–1903	Aldrich-Blake, Dame Louisa Brandreth	1865–1925
Abraham, William	1842–1922		
Abul Kalam Azad, Maulana. See Azad	1888–1958	Alexander, Mrs., pseudonym. See Hector, Annie French	1825–1902
		Alexander, Boyd	1873–1910
Acland, Sir Arthur Herbert Dyke	1847–1926	Alexander, Sir George	1858–1918
Acton, Sir Edward	1865–1945	Alexander, Samuel	1859–1938
Acton, John Adams-. See Adams-Acton	1830–1910	Alexander, William	1824–1911
		Alexander-Sinclair, Sir Edwyn Sinclair	1865–1945
Acton, Sir John Emerich Edward Dalberg, Baron	1834–1902	Alexandra, Queen	1844–1925
Acworth, Sir William Mitchell	1850–1925	Alexandra Victoria Alberta Edwina Louise Duff, Princess Arthur of Connaught, Duchess of Fife	1891–1959
Adam, James	1860–1907		
Adam Smith, Sir George. See Smith	1856–1942	Alger, John Goldworth	1836–1907
		Alington, Baron. See Sturt, Henry Gerard	1825–1904
Adami, John George	1862–1926		
Adams, James Williams	1839–1903	Alington, Cyril Argentine	1872–1955
Adams, Sir John	1857–1934	Alison, Sir Archibald	1826–1907
Adams, William Davenport	1851–1904	Allan, Sir William	1837–1903
Adams-Acton, John	1830–1910	Allbutt, Sir Thomas Clifford	1836–1925
Adamson, Sir John Ernest	1867–1950	Allen, George	1832–1907
Adamson, Robert	1852–1902	Allen, Sir Hugh Percy	1869–1946
Adderley, Charles Bowyer, Baron Norton	1814–1905	Allen, Sir James	1855–1942
		Allen, John Romilly	1847–1907
Addison, Christopher, Viscount	1869–1951	Allen, Percy Stafford	1869–1933
Adler, Hermann	1839–1911	Allen, Reginald Clifford, Baron Allen of Hurtwood	1889–1939
Adshead, Stanley Davenport	1868–1946		
AE, pseudonym. See Russell, George William	1867–1935	Allen, Robert Calder	1812–1903
		Allenby, Edmund Henry Hynman, Viscount Allenby of Megiddo	1861–1936
Aga Khan, Aga Sultan Sir Mohammed Shah	1877–1957		
Agate, James Evershed	1877–1947		
Agnew, Sir James Willson	1815–1901		
Agnew, Sir William	1825–1910		

Atholl, Duchess of. See Stewart-
Murray, Katharine Marjory 1874–1960
Atholstan, Baron. See Graham,
Hugh 1848–1938
Atkin, James Richard, Baron 1867–1944
Atkins, Sir Ivor Algernon 1869–1953
Atkinson, Sir Edward Hale
Tindal 1878–1957
Atkinson, John, Baron 1844–1932
Atkinson, Robert 1839–1908
Atthill, Lombe 1827–1910
Aubrey, Melbourn Evans 1885–1957
Aumonier, James 1832–1911
Austen, Henry Haversham God-
win-. See Godwin-Austen 1834–1923
Austen, Sir William Chandler
Roberts-. See Roberts-Austen 1843–1902
Austen Leigh, Augustus 1840–1905
Austin, Alfred 1835–1913
Austin, Herbert, Baron 1866–1941
Austin, John Langshaw 1911–1960
Avebury, Baron. See Lubbock,
Sir John 1834–1913
Avory, Sir Horace Edmund 1851–1935
Ayerst, William 1830–1904
Ayrton, William Edward 1847–1908
Azad, Maulana Abul Kalam 1888–1958
Azariah, Samuel Vedanayakam 1874–1945

Babington Smith, Sir Henry.
See Smith 1863–1923
Backhouse, Sir Edmund Tre-
lawny 1873–1944
Backhouse, Sir Roger Roland
Charles 1878–1939
Bacon, John Mackenzie 1846–1904
Bacon, Sir Reginald Hugh Spencer 1863–1947
Badcock, Sir Alexander Robert 1844–1907
Baddeley, Mountford John Byrde 1843–1906
Badeley, Henry John Fanshawe,
Baron 1874–1951
Baden-Powell, Robert Stephen-
son Smyth, Baron 1857–1941
Bailey, Sir Abe 1864–1940
Bailey, Cyril 1871–1957
Bailey, John Cann 1864–1931
Bailey, Mary, Lady 1890–1960
Bailey, Philip James 1816–1902
Bailhache, Sir Clement Meacher 1856–1924
Baillie, Charles Wallace Alex-
ander Napier Ross Cochrane-,
Baron Lamington 1860–1940
Baillie, Sir James Black 1872–1940
Bain, Alexander 1818–1903
Bain, Francis William 1863–1940
Bain, Sir Frederick William 1889–1950
Bain, Robert Nisbet 1854–1909
Bainbridge, Francis Arthur 1874–1921
Baines, Frederick Ebenezer 1832–1911
Baird, Andrew Wilson 1842–1908
Baird, John Logie 1888–1946
Bairnsfather, Charles Bruce 1888–1959
Bairstow, Sir Edward Cuthbert 1874–1946
Bajpai, Sir Girja Shankar 1891–1954
Baker, Sir Benjamin 1840–1907
Baker, Henry Frederick 1866–1956
Baker, Sir Herbert 1862–1946
Baker, Herbert Brereton 1862–1935

Baker, James Franklin Bethune-.
See Bethune-Baker 1861–1951
Baker, Shirley Waldemar 1835–1903
Baldwin, Stanley, Earl Baldwin
of Bewdley 1867–1947
Baldwin Brown, Gerard. See
Brown 1849–1932
Balfour, Sir Andrew 1873–1931
Balfour, Arthur, Baron River-
dale 1873–1957
Balfour, Arthur James, Earl of
Balfour 1848–1930
Balfour, Lady Frances 1858–1931
Balfour, George William 1823–1903
Balfour, Gerald William, Earl of
Balfour 1853–1945
Balfour, Henry 1863–1939
Balfour, Sir Isaac Bayley 1853–1922
Balfour, John Blair, Baron Kin-
ross 1837–1905
Balfour, Sir Thomas Graham 1858–1929
Balfour of Burleigh, Baron. See
Bruce, Alexander Hugh 1849–1921
Ball, Albert 1896–1917
Ball, Francis Elrington 1863–1928
Ball, John 1861–1940
Ball, Sir Robert Stawell 1840–1913
Ballance, Sir Charles Alfred 1856–1936
Banbury, Frederick George,
Baron Banbury of Southam 1850–1936
Bancroft, Marie Effie (formerly
Wilton), Lady (1839–1921). See
under Bancroft, Sir Squire
Bancroft
Bancroft, Sir Squire Bancroft 1841–1926
Bandaranaike, Solomon West
Ridgeway Dias 1899–1959
Bankes, Sir John Eldon 1854–1946
Banks, Sir John Thomas 1815?–1908
Banks, Leslie James 1890–1952
Banks, Sir William Mitchell 1842–1904
Bannerman, Sir Henry Campbell-.
See Campbell-Bannerman 1836–1908
Banting, Sir Frederick Grant 1891–1941
Bantock, Sir Granville Ransome 1868–1946
Barbellion, W. N. P., pseudonym.
See Cummings, Bruce Frederick 1889–1919
Barbour, Sir David Miller 1841–1928
Barcroft, Sir Joseph 1872–1947
Bardsley, John Wareing 1835–1904
Barger, George 1878–1939
Baring, Evelyn, Earl of Cromer 1841–1917
Baring, Maurice 1874–1945
Baring, Rowland Thomas, Earl of
Cromer 1877–1953
Baring, Thomas George, Earl of
Northbrook 1826–1904
Baring-Gould, Sabine 1834–1924
Barker, Sir Ernest 1874–1960
Barker, Harley Granville Gran-
ville-. See Granville-Barker 1877–1946
Barker, Sir Herbert Atkinson 1869–1950
Barker, Dame Lilian Charlotte 1874–1955
Barker, Thomas 1838–1907
Barkla, Charles Glover 1877–1944
Barling, Sir (Harry) Gilbert 1855–1940
Barlow, Sir Thomas 1845–1945
Barlow, William Hagger 1833–1908
Barlow, William Henry 1812–1902

Benson, Richard Meux	1824–1915	Birdwood, William Riddell,	
Benson, Robert Hugh	1871–1914	Baron	1865–1951
Benson, Stella. See Anderson	1892–1933	Birkenhead, Earl of. See Smith,	
Bent, Sir Thomas	1838–1909	Frederick Edwin	1872–1930
Bentley, Edmund Clerihew	1875–1956	Birley, Sir Oswald Hornby	
Bentley, John Francis	1839–1902	Joseph	1880–1952
Benton, Sir John	1850–1927	Birmingham, George A., pseud-	
Beresford, Lord Charles William		onym. See Hannay, James	
De La Poer, Baron	1846–1919	Owen	1865–1950
Bergne, Sir John Henry Gibbs	1842–1908	Birrell, Augustine	1850–1933
Berkeley, Sir George	1819–1905	Birrell, John	1836–1901
Berkeley, Randal Mowbray Tho-		Biscoe, Cecil Earle Tyndale-. See	
mas (Rawdon), Earl of Berkeley	1865–1942	Tyndale-Biscoe	1863–1949
Bernard, Sir Charles Edward	1837–1901	Bishop, Edmund	1846–1917
Bernard, John Henry	1860–1927	Bishop (formerly Bird), Isabella	
Bernard, Thomas Dehany	1815–1904	Lucy	1831–1904
Berners, Baron. See Tyrwhitt-		Blackburn, Helen	1842–1903
Wilson, Sir Gerald Hugh	1883–1950	Blackburne, Joseph Henry	1841–1924
Berry, Sir Graham	1822–1904	Blackett, Sir Basil Phillott	1882–1935
Berry, William Ewert, Viscount		Blackley, William Lewery	1830–1902
Camrose	1879–1954	Blackman, Frederick Frost	1866–1947
Bertie, Francis Leveson, Viscount		Blackwell, Elizabeth	1821–1910
Bertie of Thame	1844–1919	Blackwood, Algernon Henry	1869–1951
Besant, Annie	1847–1933	Blackwood, Frederick Temple	
Besant, Sir Walter	1836–1901	Hamilton-Temple, Marquess	
Bessborough, Earl of. See Pon-		of Dufferin and Ava	1826–1902
sonby, Vere Brabazon	1880–1956	Blair, Eric Arthur, 'George Or-	
Betham-Edwards, Matilda Bar-		well'	1903–1950
bara. See Edwards	1836–1919	Blake, Edward	1833–1912
Bethune-Baker, James Franklin	1861–1951	Blake, Dame Louisa Brandreth	
Betterton, Henry Bucknall,		Aldrich-. See Aldrich-Blake	1865–1925
Baron Rushcliffe	1872–1949	Blakiston, Herbert Edward	
Bevan, Aneurin	1897–1960	Douglas	1862–1942
Bevan, Anthony Ashley	1859–1933	Blamey, Sir Thomas Albert	1884–1951
Bevan, Edwyn Robert	1870–1943	Bland, Edith (E. Nesbit)	1858–1924
Bevan, William Latham	1821–1908	Bland, John Otway Percy	1863–1945
Bevin, Ernest	1881–1951	Bland-Sutton, Sir John. See	
Bewley, Sir Edmund Thomas	1837–1908	Sutton	1855–1936
Bhopal, Hamidullah, Nawab of	1894–1960	Blandford, George Fielding	1829–1911
Bhownaggree, Sir Mancherjee		Blanesburgh, Baron. See Young-	
Merwanjee	1851–1933	er, Robert	1861–1946
Bicester, Baron. See Smith,		Blaney, Thomas	1823–1903
Vivian Hugh	1867–1956	Blanford, William Thomas	1832–1905
Bickersteth, Edward Henry	1825–1906	Blatchford, Robert Peel Glan-	
Bidder, George Parker	1863–1953	ville	1851–1943
Biddulph, Sir Michael Anthony		Blaydes,Frederick Henry Marvell	1818–1908
Shrapnel	1823–1904	Bledisloe, Viscount. See Bathurst,	
Biddulph, Sir Robert	1835–1918	Charles	1867–1958
Bidwell, Shelford	1848–1909	Blennerhassett, Sir Rowland	1839–1909
Biffen, Sir Rowland Harry	1874–1949	Blind, Karl	1826–1907
Bigg, Charles	1840–1908	Blogg, Henry George	1876–1954
Bigge, Arthur John, Baron Stam-		Blomfield, Sir Reginald Theodore	1856–1942
fordham	1849–1931	Blood, Sir Bindon	1842–1940
Bigham, John Charles, Viscount		Bloomfield, Georgiana, Lady	1822–1905
Mersey	1840–1929	Blouet, Léon Paul, 'Max O'Rell'	1848–1903
Bikaner, Maharaja Shri Sir Ganga		Blount, Sir Edward Charles	1809–1905
Singh Bahadur, Maharaja of	1880–1943	Blumenfeld, Ralph David	1864–1948
Biles, Sir John Harvard	1854–1933	Blumenthal, Jacques (Jacob)	1829–1908
Binnie, Sir Alexander Richardson	1839–1917	Blunt, Lady Anne Isabella Noel	
Binnie, William James Eames	1867–1949	(1837–1917). See under Blunt,	
Binyon, (Robert) Laurence	1869–1943	Wilfrid Scawen	
Birch, George Henry	1842–1904	Blunt, Wilfrid Scawen	1840–1922
Birch, Sir (James Frederick) Noel	1865–1939	Blythswood, Baron. See Camp-	
Bird, Henry Edward	1830–1908	bell, Archibald Campbell	1835–1908
Bird, Isabella Lucy. See Bishop	1831–1904	Bodda Pyne, Louisa Fanny	1832–1904
Bird, Sir James	1883–1946	Bodington, Sir Nathan	1848–1911
Birdwood, Sir George Christo-		Bodkin, Sir Archibald Henry	1862–1957
pher Molesworth	1832–1917	Bodley, George Frederick	1827–1907
Birdwood, Herbert Mills	1837–1907	Body, George	1840–1911

Cardew, Philip	1851–1910
Carey, Rosa Nouchette	1840–1909
Carlile, Wilson	1847–1942
Carling, Sir Ernest Rock	1877–1960
Carlisle, Earl of. See Howard, George James	1843–1911
Carlisle, Countess of. See Howard, Rosalind Frances	1845–1921
Carlyle, Alexander James	1861–1943
Carlyle, Benjamin Fearnley, Dom Aelred	1874–1955
Carlyle, Sir Robert Warrand	1859–1934
Carman, William Bliss	1861–1929
Carmichael, Sir Thomas David Gibson-, Baron	1859–1926
Carnarvon, Earl of. See Herbert, George Edward Stanhope Molyneux	1866–1923
Carnegie, Andrew	1835–1919
Carnegie, James, Earl of Southesk	1827–1905
Carnock, Baron. See Nicolson, Sir Arthur	1849–1928
Caröe, William Douglas	1857–1938
Carpenter, Alfred Francis Blakeney	1881–1955
Carpenter, Edward	1844–1929
Carpenter, George Alfred	1859–1910
Carpenter, Sir (Henry Cort) Harold	1875–1940
Carpenter, Joseph Estlin	1844–1927
Carpenter, Robert	1830–1901
Carpenter, William Boyd	1841–1918
Carrington, Sir Frederick	1844–1913
Carson, Edward Henry, Baron	1854–1935
Carte, Richard D'Oyly	1844–1901
Carter, Sir Edgar Bonham-. See Bonham-Carter	1870–1956
Carter, Howard	1874–1939
Carter, Hugh	1837–1903
Carter, Thomas Thellusson	1808–1901
Carton, Richard Claude	1856–1928
Carver, Alfred James	1826–1909
Cary, Arthur Joyce Lunel	1888–1957
Case, Thomas	1844–1925
Casement, Roger David	1864–1916
Casey, William Francis	1884–1957
Cash, John Theodore	1854–1936
Cassel, Sir Ernest Joseph	1852–1921
Cassels, Sir Robert Archibald	1876–1959
Cassels, Walter Richard	1826–1907
Cates, Arthur	1829–1901
Cathcart, Edward Provan	1877–1954
Catto, Thomas Sivewright, Baron	1879–1959
Cavan, Earl of. See Lambart, Frederick Rudolph	1865–1946
Cave, George, Viscount	1856–1928
Cavell, Edith	1865–1915
Cavendish, Spencer Compton, Marquess of Hartington, afterwards Duke of Devonshire	1833–1908
Cavendish, Victor Christian William, Duke of Devonshire	1868–1938
Cawdor, Earl. See Campbell, Frederick Archibald Vaughan	1847–1911
Cecil, Edgar Algernon Robert Gascoyne-, Viscount Cecil of Chelwood	1864–1958
Cecil, Lord Edward Herbert Gascoyne-	1867–1918
Cecil, Hugh Richard Heathcote Gascoyne-, Baron Quickswood	1869–1956
Cecil, James Edward Hubert Gascoyne-, Marquess of Salisbury	1861–1947
Cecil, Robert Arthur Talbot Gascoyne-, Marquess of Salisbury	1830–1903
Chads, Sir Henry	1819–1906
Chadwick, Hector Munro	1870–1947
Chadwick, Roy	1893–1947
Chalmers, James	1841–1901
Chalmers, Sir Mackenzie Dalzell	1847–1927
Chalmers, Robert, Baron	1858–1938
Chamberlain, (Arthur) Neville	1869–1940
Chamberlain, Sir Crawford Trotter	1821–1902
Chamberlain, Houston Stewart	1855–1927
Chamberlain, Joseph	1836–1914
Chamberlain, Sir (Joseph) Austen	1863–1937
Chamberlain, Sir Neville Bowles	1820–1902
Chambers, Dorothea Katharine	1878–1960
Chambers, Sir Edmund Kerchever	1866–1954
Chambers, Raymond Wilson	1874–1942
Chamier, Stephen Henry Edward	1834–1910
Champneys, Basil	1842–1935
Champneys, Sir Francis Henry	1848–1930
Chance, Sir James Timmins	1814–1902
Chancellor, Sir John Robert	1870–1952
Channell, Sir Arthur Moseley	1838–1928
Channer, George Nicholas	1842–1905
Chaplin, Henry, Viscount	1840–1923
Chapman, David Leonard	1869–1958
Chapman, Edward John	1821–1904
Chapman, Robert William	1881–1960
Chapman, Sir Sydney John	1871–1951
Charles, James	1851–1906
Charles, Robert Henry	1855–1931
Charlesworth, Martin Percival	1895–1950
Charley, Sir William Thomas	1833–1904
Charlot, André Eugene Maurice	1882–1956
Charnwood, Baron. See Benson, Godfrey Rathbone	1864–1945
Charrington, Frederick Nicholas	1850–1936
Charteris, Archibald Hamilton	1835–1908
Chase, Drummond Percy	1820–1902
Chase, Frederic Henry	1853–1925
Chase, Marian Emma	1844–1905
Chase, William St. Lucian	1856–1908
Chatterjee, Sir Atul Chandra	1874–1955
Chauvel, Sir Henry George	1865–1945
Chavasse, Francis James	1846–1928
Cheadle, Walter Butler	1835–1910
Cheatle, Arthur Henry	1866–1929
Cheetham, Samuel	1827–1908
Chelmsford, Baron. See Thesiger, Frederic Augustus	1827–1905
Chelmsford, Viscount. See Thesiger, Frederic John Napier	1868–1933
Chermside, Sir Herbert Charles	1850–1929
Cherry-Garrard, Apsley George Benet	1886–1959
Cherwell, Viscount. See Lindemann, Frederick Alexander	1886–1957
Chesterton, Gilbert Keith	1874–1936
Chetwode, Sir Philip Walhouse, Baron	1869–1950
Chevalier, Albert	1861–1923

Collins, John Churton	1848–1908
Collins, Josephine (José)	1887–1958
Collins, Michael	1890–1922
Collins, Richard Henn, Baron	1842–1911
Collins, William Edward	1867–1911
Colnaghi, Martin Henry	1821–1908
Colomb, Sir John Charles Ready	1838–1909
Colton, Sir John	1823–1902
Colvile, Sir Henry Edward	1852–1907
Colville, David John, Baron Clydesmuir	1894–1954
Colville, Sir Stanley Cecil James	1861–1939
Colvin, Sir Auckland	1838–1908
Colvin, Ian Duncan	1877–1938
Colvin, Sir Sidney	1845–1927
Colvin, Sir Walter Mytton. See under Colvin, Sir Auckland	
Commerell, Sir John Edmund	1829–1901
Common, Andrew Ainslie	1841–1903
Comper, Sir (John) Ninian	1864–1960
Compton, Lord Alwyne Frederick	1825–1906
Comrie, Leslie John	1893–1950
Conder, Charles	1868–1909
Conder, Claude Reignier	1848–1910
Congreve, Sir Walter Norris	1862–1927
Coningham, Sir Arthur	1895–1948
Connard, Philip	1875–1958
Connaught and Strathearn, Duke of. See Arthur William Patrick Albert	1850–1942
Connemara, Baron. See Bourke, Robert	1827–1902
Connor, Ralph, pseudonym. See Gordon, Charles William	1860–1937
Conquest, George Augustus	1837–1901
Conrad, Joseph	1857–1924
Conway, Robert Seymour	1864–1933
Conway, William Martin, Baron Conway of Allington	1856–1937
Conybeare, Frederick Cornwallis	1856–1924
Conyngham, Sir Gerald Ponsonby Lenox-. See Lenox-Conyngham	1866–1956
Cook, Arthur Bernard	1868–1952
Cook, Arthur James	1883–1931
Cook, Sir Basil Alfred Kemball-. See Kemball-Cook	1876–1949
Cook, Sir Edward Tyas	1857–1919
Cook, Sir Francis	1817–1901
Cook, Sir Joseph	1860–1947
Cook, Stanley Arthur	1873–1949
Cooke, George Albert	1865–1939
Coolidge, William Augustus Brevoort	1850–1926
Cooper, Sir Alfred	1838–1908
Cooper, Alfred Duff, Viscount Norwich	1890–1954
Cooper, Sir Daniel	1821–1902
Cooper, Edward Herbert	1867–1910
Cooper, Sir (Francis) D'Arcy	1882–1941
Cooper, James	1846–1922
Cooper, James Davis	1823–1904
Cooper, Sir (Thomas) Edwin	1874–1942
Cooper, Thomas Mackay, Baron Cooper of Culross	1892–1955
Cooper, Thomas Sidney	1803–1902
Cooper, Thompson	1837–1904
Cope, Sir Alfred William	1877–1954
Copeland, Ralph	1837–1905
Copinger, Walter Arthur	1847–1910

Copisarow, Maurice	1889–1959
Coppard, Alfred Edgar	1878–1957
Coppin, George Selth	1819–1906
Coppinger, Richard William	1847–1910
Corbet, Matthew Ridley	1850–1902
Corbett, Edward James (Jim)	1875–1955
Corbett, John	1817–1901
Corbett, Sir Julian Stafford	1854–1922
Corbould, Edward Henry	1815–1905
Corelli, Marie, pseudonym. See Mackay, Mary	1855–1924
Corfield, William Henry	1843–1903
Cornford, Frances Crofts	1886–1960
Cornford, Francis Macdonald	1874–1943
Cornish, Charles John	1858–1906
Cornish, Francis Warre Warre-. See Warre-Cornish	1839–1916
Cornish, Vaughan	1862–1948
Cornwallis, Sir Kinahan	1883–1959
Cornwell, James	1812–1902
Corry, Montagu William Lowry, Baron Rowton	1838–1903
Cory, John	1828–1910
Coryndon, Sir Robert Thorne	1870–1925
Couch, Sir Arthur Thomas Quiller-, ('Q'). See Quiller-Couch	1863–1944
Couch, Sir Richard	1817–1905
Coulton, George Gordon	1858–1947
Couper, Sir George Ebenezer Wilson	1824–1908
Coupland, Sir Reginald	1884–1952
Courtauld, Augustine	1904–1959
Courtauld, Samuel	1876–1947
Courthope, William John	1842–1917
Courtney, Leonard Henry, Baron Courtney of Penwith	1832–1918
Courtney, William Leonard	1850–1928
Cousin, Anne Ross	1824–1906
Cowan, Sir Walter Henry	1871–1956
Cowans, Sir John Steven	1862–1921
Coward, Sir Henry	1849–1944
Cowdray, Viscount. See Pearson, Weetman Dickinson	1856–1927
Cowell, Edward Byles	1826–1903
Cowen, Sir Frederic Hymen	1852–1935
Cowie, William Garden	1831–1902
Cowley, Sir Arthur Ernest	1861–1931
Cowper, Francis Thomas de Grey, Earl	1834–1905
Cox, Alfred	1866–1954
Cox, George (called Sir George) William	1827–1902
Cox, Harold	1859–1936
Cox, Sir Percy Zachariah	1864–1937
Cozens-Hardy, Herbert Hardy, Baron	1838–1920
Craddock, Sir Reginald Henry	1864–1937
Cradock, Sir Christopher George Francis Maurice	1862–1914
Craig, Isa. See Knox	1831–1903
Craig, James, Viscount Craigavon	1871–1940
Craig, Sir John	1874–1957
Craig, William James	1843–1906
Craigavon, Viscount. See Craig, James	
Craigie, Pearl Mary Teresa, 'John Oliver Hobbes'	1867–1906
Craigie, Sir Robert Leslie	1883–1959
Craigie, Sir William Alexander	1867–1957

Davids, Thomas William Rhys	1843–1922	Harvey, Viscount Frankfort	
Davidson, Andrew Bruce	1831–1902	de Montmorency	1835–1902
Davidson, Charles	1824–1902	De Morgan, William Frend	1839–1917
Davidson, James Leigh Strachan-.		Denman, Gertrude Mary, Lady	1884–1954
See Strachan-Davidson	1843–1916	Denney, James	1856–1917
Davidson, John	1857–1909	Denniston, John Dewar	1887–1949
Davidson, Sir John Humphrey	1876–1954	Denny, Sir Archibald	1860–1936
Davidson, John Thain	1833–1904	Denny, Sir Maurice Edward	1886–1955
Davidson, Randall Thomas,		Dent, Edward Joseph	1876–1957
Baron Davidson of Lambeth	1848–1930	Dent, Joseph Malaby	1849–1926
Davie, Thomas Benjamin	1895–1955	Derby, Earl of. See Stanley, Ed-	
Davies, Charles Maurice	1828–1910	ward George Villiers	1865–1948
Davies, David, Baron	1880–1944	Derby, Earl of. See Stanley,	
Davies, Sir (Henry) Walford	1869–1941	Frederick Arthur	1841–1908
Davies, John Llewelyn	1826–1916	De Robeck, Sir John Michael	1862–1928
Davies, Robert	1816–1905	De Saulles, George William	1862–1903
Davies, (Sarah) Emily	1830–1921	Desborough, Baron. See Gren-	
Davies, William Henry	1871–1940	fell, William Henry	1855–1945
Davies, Sir William (Llewelyn)	1887–1952	De Selincourt, Ernest. See Selin-	
Davis, Charles Edward	1827–1902	court	1870–1943
Davis, Henry William Carless	1874–1928	Des Vœux, Sir (George) William	1834–1909
Davitt, Michael	1846–1906	Detmold, Charles Maurice	1883–1908
Dawber, Sir (Edward) Guy	1861–1938	De Vere, Aubrey Thomas	1814–1902
Dawkins, Richard McGillivray	1871–1955	De Vere, Sir Stephen Edward	1812–1904
Dawkins, Sir William Boyd	1837–1929	Deverell, Sir Cyril John	1874–1947
Dawson, Bertrand Edward, Vis-		De Villiers, John Henry, Baron	1842–1914
count Dawson of Penn	1864–1945	Devlin, Joseph	1871–1934
Dawson, (George) Geoffrey	1874–1944	Devonport, Viscount. See Kear-	
Dawson, George Mercer	1849–1901	ley, Hudson Ewbanke	1856–1934
Dawson, John	1827–1903	Devonshire, Duke of. See Caven-	
Day, Sir John Charles Frederic		dish, Spencer Compton	1833–1908
Sigismund	1826–1908	Devonshire, Duke of. See Caven-	
Day, Lewis Foreman	1845–1910	dish, Victor Christian William	1868–1938
Day, William Henry	1823–1908	Dewar, Sir James	1842–1923
Deacon, George Frederick	1843–1909	De Wet, Christiaan Rudolph	1854–1922
Deakin, Alfred	1856–1919	De Winton, Sir Francis Walter	1835–1901
Deakin, Arthur	1890–1955	De Worms, Henry, Baron Pir-	
Deane, Sir James Parker	1812–1902	bright	1840–1903
Dearmer, Percy	1867–1936	Dewrance, Sir John	1858–1937
De Bunsen, Sir Maurice William		D'Eyncourt, Sir Eustace Henry	
Ernest	1852–1932	William Tennyson-. See	
De Burgh, William George	1866–1943	Tennyson-d'Eyncourt	1868–1951
De Burgh Canning, Hubert		Dibbs, Sir George Richard	1834–1904
George, Marquess of Clanri-		Dibdin, Sir Lewis Tonna	1852–1938
carde. See Burgh Canning	1832–1916	Dicey, Albert Venn	1835–1922
De Chair, Sir Dudley Rawson		Dicey, Edward James Stephen	1832–1911
Stratford	1864–1958	Dick-Read, Grantly	1890–1959
Deedes, Sir Wyndham Henry	1883–1956	Dickinson, Goldsworthy Lowes	1862–1932
De Ferranti, Sebastian Ziani.		Dickinson, Henry Winram	1870–1952
See Ferranti	1864–1930	Dickinson, Hercules Henry	1827–1905
De Havilland, Geoffrey Raoul	1910–1946	Dickinson, Lowes (Cato)	1819–1908
Delafield, E. M., pseudonym. See		Dicksee, Sir Francis Bernard	
Dashwood, Edmée Elizabeth		(Frank)	1853–1928
Monica	1890–1943	Dickson, Sir Collingwood	1817–1904
De la Mare, Walter John	1873–1956	Dickson, William Purdie	1823–1901
Delamere, Baron. See Cholmon-		Dickson-Poynder, Sir John Poyn-	
deley, Hugh	1870–1931	der, Baron Islington. See	
De la Ramée, Marie Louise,		Poynder	1866–1936
'Ouida'	1839–1908	Digby, William	1849–1904
De la Rue, Sir Thomas Andros	1849–1911	Dilke, Sir Charles Wentworth	1843–1911
De László, Philip Alexius. See		Dilke, Emilia Frances, Lady	1840–1904
László de Lombos	1869–1937	Dill, Sir John Greer	1881–1944
Delevingne, Sir Malcolm	1868–1950	Dill, Sir Samuel	1844–1924
Delius, Frederick	1862–1934	Dillon, Emile Joseph	1854–1933
Dell, Ethel Mary. See Savage	1881–1939	Dillon, Frank	1823–1909
Deller, Sir Edwin	1883–1936	Dillon, Harold Arthur Lee-,	
De Montmorency, James Edward		Viscount Dillon	1844–1932
Geoffrey	1866–1934	Dillon, John	1851–1927
De Montmorency, Raymond		Dimock, Nathaniel	1825–1909

Dutton, Joseph Everett	1874–1905	
Duveen, Joseph, Baron	1869–1939	
Duveen, Sir Joseph Joel	1843–1908	
Dyer, Reginald Edward Harry	1864–1927	
Dyer, Sir William Turner Thiselton-. See Thiselton-Dyer	1843–1928	
Dyke, Sir William Hart	1837–1931	
Dyson, Sir Frank Watson	1868–1939	
Dyson, William Henry (Will)	1880–1938	
Eady, Charles Swinfen, Baron Swinfen	1851–1919	
Eardley-Wilmot, Sir Sainthill. See Wilmot	1852–1929	
Earle, John	1824–1903	
Earle, Sir Lionel	1866–1948	
East, Sir Alfred	1849–1913	
East, Sir Cecil James	1837–1908	
East, Sir (William) Norwood	1872–1953	
Eastlake, Charles Locke	1836–1906	
Eaton, Herbert Francis, Baron Cheylesmore	1848–1925	
Eaton, William Meriton, Baron Cheylesmore	1843–1902	
Ebsworth, Joseph Woodfall	1824–1908	
Eckersley, Thomas Lydwell	1886–1959	
Eddington, Sir Arthur Stanley	1882–1944	
Eddis, Eden Upton	1812–1901	
Edge, Sir John	1841–1926	
Edge, Selwyn Francis	1868–1940	
Edgeworth, Francis Ysidro	1845–1926	
Edmonds, Sir James Edward	1861–1956	
Edouin, Willie	1846–1908	
Edridge-Green, Frederick William	1863–1953	
Edward VII, King	1841–1910	
Edward of Saxe-Weimar, Prince	1823–1902	
Edwards, Alfred George	1848–1937	
Edwards, Sir Fleetwood Isham	1842–1910	
Edwards, Henry Sutherland	1828–1906	
Edwards, John Passmore	1823–1911	
Edwards, Matilda Barbara Betham-	1836–1919	
Edwards, Sir Owen Morgan	1858–1920	
Egerton, Sir Alfred Charles Glyn	1886–1959	
Egerton, Sir Charles Comyn	1848–1921	
Egerton, Hugh Edward	1855–1927	
Elgar, Sir Edward William	1857–1934	
Elgar, Francis	1845–1909	
Elgin, Earl of. See Bruce, Victor Alexander	1849–1917	
Elias, Julius Salter, Viscount Southwood	1873–1946	
Eliot, Sir Charles Norton Edgecumbe	1862–1931	
Eliot, Sir John	1839–1908	
Elkan, Benno	1877–1960	
Ellerman, Sir John Reeves	1862–1933	
Ellery, Robert Lewis John	1827–1908	
Elles, Sir Hugh Jamieson	1880–1945	
Ellicott, Charles John	1819–1905	
Elliot, Arthur Ralph Douglas	1846–1923	
Elliot, Sir George Augustus	1813–1901	
Elliot, Gilbert John Murray Kynynmond, Earl of Minto	1845–1914	
Elliot, Sir Henry George	1817–1907	
Elliot, Walter Elliot	1888–1958	
Elliott, Sir Charles Alfred	1835–1911	
Elliott, Edwin Bailey	1851–1937	

Ellis, Frederick Startridge	1830–1901	
Ellis, Henry Havelock	1859–1939	
Ellis, John Devonshire	1824–1906	
Ellis, Robinson	1834–1913	
Ellis, Thomas Evelyn Scott-, Baron Howard de Walden. See Scott-Ellis	1880–1946	
Ellis, Sir William Henry	1860–1945	
Elphinstone, Sir (George) Keith (Buller)	1865–1941	
Elsmie, George Robert	1838–1909	
Elton, Oliver	1861–1945	
Elvin, Sir (James) Arthur	1899–1957	
Elwes, Gervase Henry [Cary-]	1866–1921	
Elwes, Henry John	1846–1922	
Elworthy, Frederick Thomas	1830–1907	
Emery, William	1825–1910	
Emmott, Alfred, Baron	1858–1926	
Ensor, Sir Robert Charles Kirkwood	1877–1958	
Entwistle, William James	1895–1952	
Epstein, Sir Jacob	1880–1959	
Ernle, Baron. See Prothero, Rowland Edmund	1851–1937	
Esdaile, Katharine Ada	1881–1950	
Esher, Viscount. See Brett, Reginald Baliol	1852–1930	
Esmond, Henry Vernon	1869–1922	
Etheridge, Robert	1819–1903	
Euan-Smith, Sir Charles Bean	1842–1910	
Eumorfopoulos, George	1863–1939	
Eva, *pseudonym*. See under O'Doherty, Kevin Izod	1823–1905	
Evan-Thomas, Sir Hugh	1862–1928	
Evans, Sir Arthur John	1851–1941	
Evans, Daniel Silvan	1818–1903	
Evans, Edmund	1826–1905	
Evans, Edward Ratcliffe Garth Russell, Baron Mountevans	1880–1957	
Evans, Sir (Evan) Vincent	1851–1934	
Evans, George Essex	1863–1909	
Evans, Sir John	1823–1908	
Evans, John Gwenogvryn	1852–1930	
Evans, Meredith Gwynne	1904–1952	
Evans, Sir Samuel Thomas	1859–1918	
Evans, Sebastian	1830–1909	
Evans, Sir (Worthington) Laming Worthington-	1868–1931	
Eve, Sir Harry Trelawney	1856–1940	
Everard, Harry Stirling Crawford	1848–1909	
Everett, Joseph David	1831–1904	
Everett, Sir William	1844–1908	
Evershed, John	1864–1956	
Eversley, Baron. See Shaw-Lefevre, George John	1831–1928	
Eves, Reginald Grenville	1876–1941	
Ewart, Alfred James	1872–1937	
Ewart, Charles Brisbane	1827–1903	
Ewart, Sir John Alexander	1821–1904	
Ewart, Sir John Spencer	1861–1930	
Ewing, Sir (James) Alfred	1855–1935	
Ewins, Arthur James	1882–1957	
Eyre, Edward John	1815–1901	
Faber, Oscar	1886–1956	
Faed, John	1819–1902	
Fagan, James Bernard	1873–1933	
Fagan, Louis Alexander	1845–1903	

Forbes-Robertson, Sir Johnston.
  See Robertson   1853–1937
Ford, Edward Onslow   1852–1901
Ford, Ford Madox (formerly
  Ford Hermann Hueffer)   1873–1939
Ford, Patrick   1837–1913
Ford, William Justice   1853–1904
Fordham, Sir Herbert George   1854–1929
Forestier-Walker, Sir Frederick
  William Edward Forestier   1844–1910
Forman, Alfred William. See
  Forman, Henry Buxton
Forman, Henry Buxton   1842–1917
Forrest, Sir George William
  David Starck   1845–1926
Forrest, John, Baron   1847–1918
Forster, Hugh Oakeley Arnold-.
  See Arnold-Forster   1855–1909
Forster, Sir Martin Onslow   1872–1945
Forsyth, Andrew Russell   1858–1942
Fortescue, George Knottesford   1847–1912
Fortescue, Hugh, Earl   1818–1905
Fortescue, Sir John William   1859–1933
Foss, Hubert James   1899–1953
Foster, Sir Clement Le Neve   1841–1904
Foster, Sir George Eulas   1847–1931
Foster, Joseph   1844–1905
Foster, Sir Michael   1836–1907
Foster, Sir (Thomas) Gregory   1866–1931
Fotheringham, John Knight   1874–1936
Foulkes, Isaac   1836–1904
Fowle, Thomas Welbank   1835–1903
Fowler, Alfred   1868–1940
Fowler, Ellen Thorneycroft. See
  Felkin   1860–1929
Fowler, Henry Hartley, Viscount
  Wolverhampton   1830–1911
Fowler, Henry Watson   1858–1933
Fowler, Sir James Kingston   1852–1934
Fowler, Sir Ralph Howard   1889–1944
Fowler, Thomas   1832–1904
Fowler, William Warde   1847–1921
Fox, Dame Evelyn Emily Marian   1874–1955
Fox, Sir Francis   1844–1927
Fox, Samson   1838–1903
Fox Bourne, Henry Richard.
  See Bourne   1837–1909
Fox Strangways, Arthur Henry.
  See Strangways   1859–1948
Fox-Strangways, Giles Stephen
  Holland, Earl of Ilchester   1874–1959
Foxwell, Arthur   1853–1909
Foxwell, Herbert Somerton   1849–1936
Frampton, Sir George James   1860–1928
Frankau, Gilbert   1884–1952
Frankfort de Montmorency,
  Viscount. See de Montmo-
  rency, Raymond Harvey   1835–1902
Frankland, Percy Faraday   1858–1946
Fraser, Alexander Campbell   1819–1914
Fraser, Sir Andrew Henderson
  Leith   1848–1919
Fraser, Claud Lovat   1890–1921
Fraser, Donald   1870–1933
Fraser, Peter   1884–1950
Fraser, Simon Joseph, Baron
  Lovat   1871–1933
Fraser, Sir Thomas Richard   1841–1920
Frazer, Sir James George   1854–1941

Fream, William   1854–1906
Fréchette, Louis Honoré   1839–1908
Freedman, Barnett   1901–1958
Freeman, Gage Earle   1820–1903
Freeman, John   1880–1929
Freeman, John Peere Williams-.
  See Williams-Freeman   1858–1943
Freeman, Sir Ralph   1880–1950
Freeman, Sir Wilfrid Rhodes   1888–1953
Freeman-Mitford, Algernon Ber-
  tram, Baron Redesdale. See
  Mitford   1837–1916
Freeman-Thomas, Freeman, Mar-
  quess of Willingdon   1866–1941
Fremantle, Sir Edmund Robert   1836–1929
French, Evangeline Frances   1869–1960
French, Francesca Law   1871–1960
French, John Denton Pinkstone,
  Earl of Ypres   1852–1925
Frere, Mary Eliza Isabella   1845–1911
Frere, Walter Howard   1863–1938
Freshfield, Douglas William   1845–1934
Freyer, Sir Peter Johnston   1851–1921
Friese-Greene, William. See
  Greene   1855–1921
Frith, William Powell   1819–1909
Fritsch, Felix Eugen   1879–1954
Frowde, Henry   1841–1927
Fry, Charles Burgess   1872–1956
Fry, Danby Palmer   1818–1903
Fry, Sir Edward   1827–1918
Fry, Joseph Storrs   1826–1913
Fry, Roger Eliot   1866–1934
Fry, Sara Margery   1874–1958
Fry, Thomas Charles   1846–1930
Fryatt, Charles Algernon   1872–1916
Fuller, Sir Cyril Thomas Moulden   1874–1942
Fuller, Sir (Joseph) Bampfylde   1854–1935
Fuller, Sir Thomas Ekins   1831–1910
Fuller-Maitland, John Alexan-
  der. See Maitland   1856–1936
Fulleylove, John   1845–1908
Furneaux, William Mordaunt   1848–1928
Furness, Christopher, Baron   1852–1912
Furniss, Harry   1854–1925
Furniss, Henry Sanderson, Baron
  Sanderson   1868–1939
Furnivall, Frederick James   1825–1910
Furse, Charles Wellington   1868–1904
Furse, Dame Katharine   1875–1952
Fust, Herbert Jenner-. See
  Jenner-Fust   1806–1904
Fyfe, Henry Hamilton   1869–1951
Fyleman, Rose Amy   1877–1957

Gadsby, Henry Robert   1842–1907
Gainford, Baron. See Pease,
  Joseph Albert   1860–1943
Gairdner, James   1828–1912
Gairdner, Sir William Tennant   1824–1907
Gale, Frederick   1823–1904
Galloway, Sir William   1840–1927
Gallwey, Peter   1820–1906
Galsworthy, John   1867–1933
Galton, Sir Francis   1822–1911
Gamgee, Arthur   1841–1909
Gandhi, Mohandas Karamchand   1869–1948
Gann, Thomas William Francis   1867–1938
Garbett, Cyril Forster   1875–1955

Goldschmidt, Otto 1829–1907
Goldsmid, Sir Frederick John 1818–1908
Goldsmid-Montefiore, Claude Joseph. See Montefiore 1858–1938
Gollancz, Sir Hermann 1852–1930
Gollancz, Sir Israel 1863–1930
Goodall, Frederick 1822–1904
Goode, Sir William Athelstane Meredith 1875–1944
Gooden, Stephen Frederick 1892–1955
Goodenough, Frederick Craufurd 1866–1934
Goodenough, Sir William Edmund 1867–1945
Goodenough, Sir William Macnamara 1899–1951
Goodey, Tom 1885–1953
Goodhart-Rendel, Harry Stuart 1887–1959
Goodman (formerly Salaman), Julia 1812–1906
Goodrich, Edwin Stephen 1868–1946
Gordon, Arthur Charles Hamilton-, Baron Stanmore 1829–1912
Gordon, Charles William, 'Ralph Connor' 1860–1937
Gordon, George Stuart 1881–1942
Gordon (formerly Marjoribanks), Ishbel Maria, Marchioness of Aberdeen and Temair (1857–1939). See under Gordon, John Campbell
Gordon, James Frederick Skinner 1821–1904
Gordon, John Campbell, Marquess of Aberdeen and Temair 1847–1934
Gordon, Sir John James Hood 1832–1908
Gordon, Mervyn Henry 1872–1953
Gordon, Sir Thomas Edward 1832–1914
Gordon-Lennox, Charles Henry, Duke of Richmond and Gordon 1818–1903
Gordon-Taylor, Sir Gordon 1878–1960
Gore, Albert Augustus 1840–1901
Gore, Charles 1853–1932
Gore, George 1826–1908
Gore, John Ellard 1845–1910
Gorell, Baron. See Barnes, John Gorell 1848–1913
Gorst, Sir John Eldon 1835–1916
Gorst, Sir (John) Eldon 1861–1911
Gort, Viscount. See Vereker, John Standish Surtees Prendergast 1886–1946
Goschen, George Joachim, Viscount 1831–1907
Gosling, Harry 1861–1930
Gossage, Sir (Ernest) Leslie 1891–1949
Gosse, Sir Edmund William 1849–1928
Gosselin, Sir Martin le Marchant Hadsley 1847–1905
Gosset, William Sealy, 'Student' 1876–1937
Gotch, John Alfred 1852–1942
Gott, John 1830–1906
Gott, William Henry Ewart 1897–1942
Gough, Sir Charles John Stanley 1832–1912
Gough, Sir Hugh Henry 1833–1909
Gough, John Edmond 1871–1915
Gough-Calthorpe, Augustus Cholmondeley, Baron Calthorpe 1829–1910
Gough-Calthorpe, Sir Somerset Arthur. See Calthorpe 1864–1937
Gould, Sir Francis Carruthers 1844–1925

Gould, Nathaniel 1857–1919
Goulding, Frederick 1842–1909
Gower, (Edward) Frederick Leveson-. See Leveson-Gower 1819–1907
Gower, Sir Henry Dudley Gresham Leveson 1873–1954
Gowers, Sir William Richard 1845–1915
Gowrie, Earl of. See Hore-Ruthven, Alexander Gore Arkwright 1872–1955
Grace, Edward Mills 1841–1911
Grace, William Gilbert 1848–1915
Graham, Henry Grey 1842–1906
Graham, Hugh, Baron Atholstan 1848–1938
Graham, John Anderson 1861–1942
Graham, Robert Bontine Cunninghame 1852–1936
Graham, Sir Ronald William 1870–1949
Graham, Thomas Alexander Ferguson 1840–1906
Graham, William 1839–1911
Graham, William 1887–1932
Graham-Harrison, Sir William Montagu 1871–1949
Graham-Little, Sir Ernest Gordon Graham 1867–1950
Grahame, Kenneth 1859–1932
Grahame-White, Claude 1879–1959
Granet, Sir (William) Guy 1867–1943
Grant, Sir (Alfred) Hamilton 1872–1937
Grant, Sir Charles (1836–1903). See under Grant, Sir Robert
Grant, George Monro 1835–1902
Grant, Sir Robert 1837–1904
Grant Duff, Sir Mountstuart Elphinstone 1829–1906
Grantham, Sir William 1835–1911
Granville-Barker, Harley Granville 1877–1946
Graves, Alfred Perceval 1846–1931
Graves, George Windsor 1873?–1949
Gray, Benjamin Kirkman 1862–1907
Gray, George Buchanan 1865–1922
Gray, George Edward Kruger 1880–1943
Gray, Herbert Branston 1851–1929
Greaves, Walter 1846–1930
Green, Alice Sophia Amelia (Mrs. Stopford Green) 1847–1929
Green, Charles Alfred Howell 1864–1944
Green, Frederick William Edridge-. See Edridge-Green 1863–1953
Green, Samuel Gosnell 1822–1905
Green, William Curtis 1875–1960
Greenaway, Catherine (Kate) 1846–1901
Greene, Harry Plunket 1865–1936
Greene, Wilfrid Arthur, Baron 1883–1952
Greene, William Friese- 1855–1921
Greene, Sir (William) Graham 1857–1950
Greenidge, Abel Hendy Jones 1865–1906
Greenwell, William 1820–1918
Greenwood, Arthur 1880–1954
Greenwood, Frederick 1830–1909
Greenwood, Hamar, Viscount 1870–1948
Greenwood, Thomas 1851–1908
Greer, (Frederick) Arthur, Baron Fairfield 1863–1945
Greet, Sir Phillip Barling Ben 1857–1936
Greg, Sir Walter Wilson 1875–1959
Grego, Joseph 1843–1908

Hambourg, Mark | 1879–1960
Hamidullah, Nawab of Bhopal. See Bhopal | 1894–1960
Hamilton, David James | 1849–1909
Hamilton, Sir Edward Walter | 1847–1908
Hamilton, Eugene Jacob Lee-. See Lee-Hamilton | 1845–1907
Hamilton, Lord George Francis | 1845–1927
Hamilton, Sir Ian Standish Monteith | 1853–1947
Hamilton, James, Duke of Abercorn | 1838–1913
Hamilton, John Andrew, Viscount Sumner | 1859–1934
Hamilton, Sir Richard Vesey | 1829–1912
Hammond, John Lawrence Le Breton | 1872–1949
Hampden, Viscount. See Brand, Henry Robert | 1841–1906
Hanbury, Charlotte (1830–1900). See under Hanbury, Elizabeth
Hanbury, Elizabeth | 1793–1901
Hanbury, Sir James Arthur | 1832–1908
Hanbury, Robert William | 1845–1903
Handley, Thomas Reginald (Tommy) | 1892–1949
Hankin, St. John Emile Clavering | 1869–1909
Hanlan (properly Hanlon), Edward | 1855–1908
Hannay, James Owen, 'George A. Birmingham' | 1865–1950
Hannay, Robert Kerr | 1867–1940
Hanworth, Viscount. See Pollock, Ernest Murray | 1861–1936
Harben, Sir Henry | 1823–1911
Harcourt, Augustus George Vernon | 1834–1919
Harcourt, Leveson Francis Vernon-. See Vernon-Harcourt | 1839–1907
Harcourt, Lewis, Viscount | 1863–1922
Harcourt, Sir William George Granville Venables Vernon | 1827–1904
Harcourt-Smith, Sir Cecil | 1859–1944
Harden, Sir Arthur | 1865–1940
Hardie, James Keir | 1856–1915
Hardie, Martin | 1875–1952
Hardie, William Ross | 1862–1916
Hardiman, Alfred Frank | 1891–1949
Harding, Sir Edward John | 1880–1954
Harding, Gilbert Charles | 1907–1960
Hardinge, Alexander Henry Louis, Baron Hardinge of Penshurst | 1894–1960
Hardinge, Charles, Baron Hardinge of Penshurst | 1858–1944
Hardwicke, Earl of. See Yorke, Albert Edward Philip Henry | 1867–1904
Hardy, Frederic Daniel | 1827–1911
Hardy, Gathorne Gathorne-, Earl of Cranbrook. See Gathorne-Hardy | 1814–1906
Hardy, Godfrey Harold | 1877–1947
Hardy, Herbert Hardy Cozens-, Baron Cozens-Hardy. See Cozens-Hardy | 1838–1920
Hardy, Thomas | 1840–1928
Hardy, Sir William Bate | 1864–1934
Hare, Augustus John Cuthbert | 1834–1903
Hare, Sir John | 1844–1921

Harewood, Earl of. See Lascelles, Henry George Charles | 1882–1947
Harington, Sir Charles ('Tim') | 1872–1940
Harker, Alfred | 1859–1939
Harland, Henry | 1861–1905
Harley, Robert | 1828–1910
Harmsworth, Alfred Charles William, Viscount Northcliffe | 1865–1922
Harmsworth, Harold Sidney, Viscount Rothermere | 1868–1940
Harper, Sir George Montague | 1865–1922
Harraden, Beatrice | 1864–1936
Harrel, Sir David | 1841–1939
Harrington, Timothy Charles | 1851–1910
Harris, Frederick Leverton | 1864–1926
Harris, George Robert Canning, Baron | 1851–1932
Harris, (Henry) Wilson | 1883–1955
Harris, James Rendel | 1852–1941
Harris, James Thomas ('Frank') | 1856–1931
Harris, Sir Percy Alfred | 1876–1952
Harris, Thomas Lake | 1823–1906
Harrison, Frederic | 1831–1923
Harrison, Henry | 1867–1954
Harrison, Jane Ellen | 1850–1928
Harrison, Mary St. Leger, 'Lucas Malet' | 1852–1931
Harrison, Reginald | 1837–1908
Harrison, Sir William Montagu Graham-. See Graham-Harrison | 1871–1949
Hart, Sir Raymund George | 1899–1960
Hart, Sir Robert | 1835–1911
Hartington, Marquess of. See Cavendish, Spencer Compton | 1833–1908
Hartley, Arthur Clifford | 1889–1960
Hartley, Sir Charles Augustus | 1825–1915
Hartog, Sir Philip(pe) Joseph | 1864–1947
Hartree, Douglas Rayner | 1897–1958
Hartshorn, Vernon | 1872–1931
Hartshorne, Albert | 1839–1910
Harty, Sir (Herbert) Hamilton | 1879–1941
Harvey, Sir John Martin Martin-. See Martin-Harvey | 1863–1944
Harwood, Basil | 1859–1949
Harwood, Sir Henry Harwood | 1888–1950
Haslett, Dame Caroline Harriet | 1895–1957
Hassall, John | 1868–1948
Hastie, William | 1842–1903
Hastings, James | 1852–1922
Hastings, Sir Patrick Gardiner | 1880–1952
Hatton, Harold Heneage Finch-. See Finch-Hatton
Hatton, Joseph | 1841–1907
Havelock, Sir Arthur Elibank | 1844–1908
Haverfield, Francis John | 1860–1919
Haweis, Hugh Reginald | 1838–1901
Haweis, Mary (d. 1898). See under Haweis, Hugh Reginald
Hawke, Sir (John) Anthony | 1869–1941
Hawke, Martin Bladen, Baron Hawke of Towton | 1860–1938
Hawker, Mary Elizabeth, 'Lanoe Falconer' | 1848–1908
Hawkins, Sir Anthony Hope, 'Anthony Hope' | 1863–1933
Hawkins, Henry, Baron Brampton | 1817–1907
Haworth, Sir (Walter) Norman | 1883–1950
Hawthorn, John Michael | 1929–1959

Hipkins, Alfred James	1826–1903	Holmes, Timothy	1825–1907
Hirst, Francis Wrigley	1873–1953	Holmes, Sir Valentine	1888–1956
Hirst, George Herbert	1871–1954	Holmyard, Eric John	1891–1959
Hirst, Hugo, Baron	1863–1943	Holroyd, Sir Charles	1861–1917
Hitchcock, Sir Eldred Frederick	1887–1959	Holroyd, Henry North, Earl of	
Hoare, Joseph Charles	1851–1906	Sheffield	1832–1909
Hoare, Sir Reginald Hervey	1882–1954	Holst, Gustav Theodore	1874–1934
Hoare, Sir Samuel John Gurney,		Holyoake, George Jacob	1817–1906
Viscount Templewood	1880–1959	Hone, Evie	1894–1955
Hobart, Sir Percy Cleghorn		Hood, Arthur William Acland,	
Stanley	1885–1957	Baron	1824–1901
Hobbes, John Oliver, *pseudonym*.		Hood, Sir Horace Lambert Alex-	
See Craigie, Pearl Mary Teresa	1867–1906	ander	1870–1916
Hobday, Sir Frederick Thomas		Hook, James Clarke	1819–1907
George	1869–1939	Hooker, Sir Joseph Dalton	1817–1911
Hobhouse, Arthur, Baron	1819–1904	Hope, Anthony, *pseudonym*. See	
Hobhouse, Edmund	1817–1904	Hawkins, Sir Anthony Hope	1863–1933
Hobhouse, Henry	1854–1937	Hope, James Fitzalan, Baron	
Hobhouse, Leonard Trelawny	1864–1929	Rankeillour	1870–1949
Hobson, Ernest William	1856–1933	Hope, John Adrian Louis, Earl	
Hobson, Geoffrey Dudley	1882–1949	of Hopetoun and Marquess of	
Hobson, John Atkinson	1858–1940	Linlithgow	1860–1908
Hocking, Joseph (1860–1937).		Hope, Laurence, *pseudonym*. See	
See under Hocking, Silas Kitto		Nicolson, Adela Florence	1865–1904
Hocking, Silas Kitto	1850–1935	Hope, Victor Alexander John,	
Hodge, John	1855–1937	Marquess of Linlithgow	1887–1952
Hodgetts, James Frederick	1828–1906	Hope, Sir William Henry St. John	1854–1919
Hodgkin, Thomas	1831–1913	Hopetoun, Earl of. See Hope,	
Hodgkins, Frances Mary	1869–1947	John Adrian Louis	1860–1908
Hodgson, Richard Dacre. See		Hopkins, Edward John	1818–1901
Archer-Hind	1849–1910	Hopkins, Sir Frederick Gowland	1861–1947
Hodgson, Sir Robert MacLeod	1874–1956	Hopkins, Jane Ellice	1836–1904
Hodgson, Shadworth Hollway	1832–1912	Hopkins, Sir Richard Valentine	
Hodson (afterwards Labouchere),		Nind	1880–1955
Henrietta	1841–1910	Hopkinson, Sir Alfred	1851–1939
Hoey, Frances Sarah (Mrs.		Hopkinson, Bertram	1874–1918
Cashel Hoey)	1830–1908	Hopwood, Charles Henry	1829–1904
Hofmeyr, Jan Hendrik	1845–1909	Hopwood, Francis John Stephens,	
Hofmeyr, Jan Hendrik	1894–1948	Baron Southborough	1860–1947
Hogarth, David George	1862–1927	Horder, Percy (Richard) Morley	1870–1944
Hogg, Douglas McGarel, Vis-		Horder, Thomas Jeeves, Baron	1871–1955
count Hailsham	1872–1950	Hore-Belisha, (Isaac) Leslie,	
Hogg, Quintin	1845–1903	Baron	1893–1957
Holden, Charles Henry	1875–1960	Hore-Ruthven, Alexander Gore	
Holden, Luther	1815–1905	Arkwright, Earl of Gowrie	1872–1955
Holder, Sir Frederick William	1850–1909	Hornby, Charles Harry St. John	1867–1946
Holderness, Sir Thomas William	1849–1924	Hornby, James John	1826–1909
Holdich, Sir Thomas Hungerford	1843–1929	Horne, Henry Sinclair, Baron	1861–1929
Holdsworth, Sir William Searle	1871–1944	Horne, Robert Stevenson, Vis-	
Hole, Samuel Reynolds	1819–1904	count Horne of Slamannan	1871–1940
Holiday, Henry	1839–1927	Horniman, Annie Elizabeth	
Hollams, Sir John	1820–1910	Fredericka	1860–1937
Holland, Henry Scott	1847–1918	Horniman, Frederick John	1835–1906
Holland, Sir Henry Thurstan,		Horridge, Sir Thomas Gardner	1857–1938
Viscount Knutsford	1825–1914	Horsley, John Callcott	1817–1903
Holland, Sydney George, Viscount		Horsley, John William	1845–1921
Knutsford	1855–1931	Horsley, Sir Victor Alexander	
Holland, Sir Thomas Erskine	1835–1926	Haden	1857–1916
Holland, Sir Thomas Henry	1868–1947	Horton, Sir Max Kennedy	1883–1951
Hollingshead, John	1827–1904	Horton, Robert Forman	1855–1934
Hollowell, James Hirst	1851–1909	Hose, Charles	1863–1929
Holman Hunt, William. See		Hosie, Sir Alexander	1853–1925
Hunt	1827–1910	Hoskins, Sir Anthony Hiley	1828–1901
Holme, Charles	1848–1923	Hoskyns, Sir Edwyn Clement	1884–1937
Holmes, Augusta Mary Anne	1847–1903	Houghton, William Stanley	1881–1913
Holmes, Sir Charles John	1868–1936	Houldsworth, Sir Hubert Stanley	1889–1956
Holmes, Sir Richard Rivington	1835–1911	House, (Arthur) Humphry	1908–1955
Holmes, Thomas	1846–1918	Housman, Alfred Edward	1859–1936
Holmes, Thomas Rice Edward	1855–1933	Housman, Laurence	1865–1959

Ismay, Joseph Bruce	1862–1937
Iveagh, Earl of. See Guinness,	
Edward Cecil	1847–1927
Iwan-Müller, Ernest Bruce	1853–1910
Jacks, Lawrence Pearsall	1860–1955
Jacks, William	1841–1907
Jackson, Sir Cyril	1863–1924
Jackson, Sir (Francis) Stanley	1870–1947
Jackson, Frederick George	1860–1938
Jackson, Sir Frederick John	1860–1929
Jackson, Frederick John Foakes	1855–1941
Jackson, Henry	1839–1921
Jackson, Sir Henry Bradwardine	1855–1929
Jackson, Sir Herbert	1863–1936
Jackson, John	1833–1901
Jackson, John Hughlings	1835–1911
Jackson, Mason	1819–1903
Jackson, Samuel Phillips	1830–1904
Jackson, Sir Thomas Graham	1835–1924
Jackson, William Lawies, Baron	
Allerton	1840–1917
Jacob, Sir Claud William	1863–1948
Jacob, Edgar	1844–1920
Jacobs, William Wymark	1863–1943
Jagger, Charles Sargeant	1885–1934
James, Alexander Wilson	1901–1953
James, Arthur Lloyd	1884–1943
James, Henry, Baron James of	
Hereford	1828–1911
James, Henry	1843–1916
James, James	1832–1902
James, Montague Rhodes	1862–1936
James, Rolfe Arnold Scott-. See	
Scott-James	1878–1959
Jameson, Andrew, Lord Ardwall	1845–1911
Jameson, Sir Leander Starr	1853–1917
Japp, Alexander Hay, 'H. A.	
Page'	1837–1905
Jardine, Douglas Robert	1900–1958
Jardine, Sir Robert	1825–1905
Jarvis, Claude Scudamore	1879–1953
Jayne, Francis John	1845–1921
Jeaffreson, John Cordy	1831–1901
Jeans, Sir James Hopwood	1877–1946
Jebb, Eglantyne	1876–1928
Jebb, Sir Richard Claverhouse	1841–1905
Jeffery, George Barker	1891–1957
Jelf, George Edward	1834–1908
Jellicoe, (John) Basil (Lee)	1899–1935
Jellicoe, John Rushworth, Earl	1859–1935
Jenkin, Charles Frewen	1865–1940
Jenkins, Ebenezer Evans	1820–1905
Jenkins, John Edward	1838–1910
Jenkins, Sir Lawrence Hugh	1857–1928
Jenkinson, Francis John Henry	1853–1923
Jenks, Edward	1861–1939
Jenner-Fust, Herbert	1806–1904
Jephson, Arthur Jermy Mounte-	
ney	1858–1908
Jerome, Jerome Klapka	1859–1927
Jerram, Sir (Thomas Henry)	
Martyn	1858–1933
Jersey, Countess of. See Villiers,	
Margaret Elizabeth Child-	1849–1945
Jersey, Earl of. See Villiers,	
Victor Albert George Child-	1845–1915
Jessop, Gilbert Laird	1874–1955

Jessopp, Augustus	1823–1914
Jeune, Francis Henry, Baron St.	
Helier	1843–1905
Jex-Blake, Sophia Louisa	1840–1912
Jex-Blake, Thomas William	1832–1915
Jinnah, Mahomed Ali	1876–1948
Joachim, Harold Henry	1868–1938
Joad, Cyril Edwin Mitchinson	1891–1953
Joel, Jack Barnato (1862–1940).	
See under Joel, Solomon	
Barnato	
Joel, Solomon Barnato	1865–1931
John, Sir William Goscombe	1860–1952
Johns, Claude Hermann Walter	1857–1920
Johnson, Alfred Edward Webb-,	
Baron Webb-Johnson. See	
Webb-Johnson	1880–1958
Johnson, Amy	1903–1941
Johnson, John de Monins	1882–1956
Johnson, Lionel Pigot	1867–1902
Johnson, Sir Nelson King	1892–1954
Johnson, William Ernest	1858–1931
Johnson, William Percival	1854–1928
Johnston, Christopher Nicholson,	
Lord Sands	1857–1934
Johnston, Edward	1872–1944
Johnston, George Lawson, Baron	
Luke	1873–1943
Johnston, Sir Harry Hamilton	1858–1927
Johnston, Sir Reginald Fleming	1874–1938
Johnston, William	1829–1902
Joicey, James, Baron	1846–1936
Jolowicz, Herbert Felix	1890–1954
Joly, Charles Jasper	1864–1906
Joly, John	1857–1933
Joly de Lotbinière, Sir Henry	
Gustave	1829–1908
Jones, Adrian	1845–1938
Jones, (Alfred) Ernest	1879–1958
Jones, Sir Alfred Lewis	1845–1909
Jones, Bernard Mouat	1882–1953
Jones, (Frederic) Wood	1879–1954
Jones, Sir Harold Spencer	1890–1960
Jones, Sir Henry	1852–1922
Jones, Henry Arthur	1851–1929
Jones, Henry Cadman	1818–1902
Jones, Sir Henry Stuart-	1867–1939
Jones, (James) Sidney	1861–1946
Jones, John Daniel	1865–1942
Jones, Sir John Edward Lennard-.	
See Lennard-Jones	1894–1954
Jones, Sir John Morris-. See	
Morris-Jones	1864–1929
Jones, John Viriamu	1856–1901
Jones, Sir Robert	1857–1933
Jones, Sir Robert Armstrong-.	
See Armstrong-Jones	1857–1943
Jones, Thomas	1870–1955
Jones, Thomas Rupert	1819–1911
Jones, William West	1838–1908
Jordan, (Heinrich Ernst) Karl	1861–1959
Jordan, Sir John Newell	1852–1925
Jordan Lloyd, Dorothy. See	
Lloyd	1889–1946
Joseph, Horace William Brindley	1867–1943
Jourdain, Francis Charles Robert	1865–1940
Jowitt, William Allen, Earl	1885–1957
Joyce, James Augustine	1882–1941
Joyce, Sir Matthew Ingle	1839–1930

Milner, Violet Georgina, Vis-
countess | 1872–1958
Milnes, Robert Offley Ashburton
Crewe-, Marquess of Crewe.
See Crewe-Milnes | 1858–1945
Minett, Francis Colin | 1890–1953
Minto, Earl of. See Elliot, Gilbert
John Murray Kynynmond | 1845–1914
Minton, Francis John | 1917–1957
Mirza Mohammad Ismail, Sir
See Ismail | 1883–1959
Mitchell, Sir Arthur | 1826–1909
Mitchell, John Murray | 1815–1904
Mitchell, Sir Peter Chalmers | 1864–1945
Mitchell, Reginald Joseph | 1895–1937
Mitchell, Sir William Gore Suther-
land | 1888–1944
Mitford, Algernon Bertram
Freeman-, Baron Redesdale | 1837–1916
Moberly, Robert Campbell | 1845–1903
Mocatta, Frederic David | 1828–1905
Möens, William John Charles | 1833–1904
Moeran, Ernest John | 1894–1950
Moffatt, James | 1870–1944
Moir, Frank Lewis | 1852–1904
Mollison, Amy. See Johnson | 1903–1941
Mollison, James Allan | 1905–1959
Molloy, Gerald | 1834–1906
Molloy, James Lynam | 1837–1909
Molloy, Joseph FitzGerald | 1858–1908
Molony, Sir Thomas Francis | 1865–1949
Molyneux, Sir Robert Henry
More-. See More-Molyneux | 1838–1904
'Môn, Hwfa', pseudonym. See
Williams, Rowland | 1823–1905
Monash, Sir John | 1865–1931
Moncreiff, Henry James, Baron | 1840–1909
Moncrieff, Sir Alexander | 1829–1906
Mond, Alfred Moritz, Baron Mel-
chett | 1868–1930
Mond, Ludwig | 1839–1909
Mond, Sir Robert Ludwig | 1867–1938
Monkhouse, William Cosmo | 1840–1901
Monro, Sir Charles Carmichael | 1860–1929
Monro, Charles Henry | 1835–1908
Monro, David Binning | 1836–1905
Monro, Harold Edward | 1879–1932
Monro, Sir Horace Cecil | 1861–1949
Monson, Sir Edmund John | 1834–1909
Montagu of Beaulieu, Baron. See
Douglas-Scott-Montagu, John
Walter Edward | 1866–1929
Montagu, Edwin Samuel | 1879–1924
Montagu, Lord Robert | 1825–1902
Montagu, Samuel, Baron Swayth-
ling | 1832–1911
Montagu-Douglas-Scott, Lord
Charles Thomas. See Scott | 1839–1911
Montagu-Douglas-Scott, Lord
Francis George. See Scott | 1879–1952
Montague, Charles Edward | 1867–1928
Montague, Francis Charles | 1858–1935
Monteath, Sir James | 1847–1929
Montefiore, Claude Joseph
Goldsmid- | 1858–1938
Montgomerie, Robert Archibald
James | 1855–1908
Montgomery-Massingberd, Sir
Archibald Armar | 1871–1947

Montmorency, James Edward
Geoffrey de. See de Mont-
morency | 1866–1934
Montmorency, Raymond Harvey
de, Viscount Frankfort de
Montmorency. See de Mont-
morency | 1835–1902
Monypenny, William Flavelle | 1866–1912
Moody, Harold Arundel | 1882–1947
Moor, Sir Frederick Robert | 1853–1927
Moor, Sir Ralph Denham Ray-
ment | 1860–1909
Moore, Arthur William | 1853–1909
Moore, Edward | 1835–1916
Moore, George Augustus | 1852–1933
Moore, George Edward | 1873–1958
Moore, Mary. See Wyndham,
Mary, Lady | 1861–1931
Moore, Stuart Archibald | 1842–1907
Moore, Temple Lushington | 1856–1920
Moorhouse, James | 1826–1915
Moran, Patrick Francis | 1830–1911
Morant, Sir Robert Laurie | 1863–1920
More-Molyneux, Sir Robert Henry | 1838–1904
Moresby, John | 1830–1922
Morfill, William Richard | 1834–1909
Morgan, Charles Langbridge | 1894–1958
Morgan, Conwy Lloyd | 1852–1936
Morgan, Edward Delmar | 1840–1909
Morgan, Sir Gilbert Thomas | 1872–1940
Morgan, John Hartman | 1876–1955
Moriarty, Henry Augustus | 1815–1906
Morison, Sir Theodore | 1863–1936
Morland, Sir Thomas Lethbridge
Napier | 1865–1925
Morley, Earl of. See Parker,
Albert Edmund | 1843–1905
Morley, John, Viscount Morley
of Blackburn | 1838–1923
Morley Horder, Percy (Richard).
See Horder | 1870–1944
Morrell, Lady Ottoline Violet
Anne | 1873–1938
Morris, Edward Patrick, Baron | 1859–1935
Morris, Sir Lewis | 1833–1907
Morris, Michael, Baron Morris and
Killanin | 1826–1901
Morris, Philip Richard | 1836–1902
Morris, Tom | 1821–1908
Morris, William O'Connor | 1824–1904
Morris-Jones, Sir John | 1864–1929
Morrison, Walter | 1836–1921
Morshead, Sir Leslie James | 1889–1959
Moseley, Henry Gwyn Jeffreys | 1887–1915
Mott, Sir Basil | 1859–1938
Mott, Sir Frederick Walker | 1853–1926
Mottistone, Baron. See Seely,
John Edward Bernard | 1868–1947
Moule, George Evans | 1828–1912
Moule, Handley Carr Glyn | 1841–1920
Moulton, James Hope | 1863–1917
Moulton, John Fletcher, Baron | 1844–1921
Mount Stephen, Baron. See
Stephen, George | 1829–1921
Mount Temple, Baron. See Ash-
ley, Wilfrid William | 1867–1938
Mountbatten, Edwina Cynthia
Annette, Countess Mount-
batten of Burma | 1901–1960

Nightingale, Florence	1820–1910
Nixon, Sir John Eccles	1857–1921
Noble, Sir Andrew	1831–1915
Noble, Montagu Alfred	1873–1940
Noble, Sir Percy Lockhart Harnam	1880–1955
Nodal, John Howard	1831–1909
Noel-Buxton, Noel Edward, Baron	1869–1948
Norfolk, Duke of. See Howard, Henry FitzAlan-	1847–1917
Norgate, Kate	1853–1935
Norman, Conolly	1853–1908
Norman, Sir Francis Booth	1830–1901
Norman, Sir Henry Wylie	1826–1904
Norman, Montagu Collet, Baron	1871–1950
Norman-Neruda, Wilma Maria Francisca. See Hallé, Lady	1839–1911
Northbrook, Earl of. See Baring, Thomas George	1826–1904
Northcliffe, Viscount. See Harmsworth, Alfred Charles William	1865–1922
Northcote, Henry Stafford, Baron	1846–1911
Northcote, James Spencer	1821–1907
Northumberland, Duke of. See Percy, Alan Ian	1880–1930
Norton, Baron. See Adderley, Charles Bowyer	1814–1905
Norton, Edward Felix	1884–1954
Norton, John	1823–1904
Norton-Griffiths, Sir John	1871–1930
Norway, Nevil Shute, 'Nevil Shute'	1899–1960
Norwich, Viscount. See Cooper, Alfred Duff	1890–1954
Norwood, Sir Cyril	1875–1956
Novar, Viscount. See Ferguson, Ronald Crauford Munro-	1860–1934
Novello (afterwards Countess Gigliucci), Clara Anastasia	1818–1908
Novello, Ivor	1893–1951
Noyes, Alfred	1880–1958
Nunburnholme, Baron. See Wilson, Charles Henry	1833–1907
Nunn, Joshua Arthur	1853–1908
Nunn, Sir (Thomas) Percy	1870–1944
Nutt, Alfred Trübner	1856–1910
Nuttall, Enos	1842–1916
Nuttall, George Henry Falkiner	1862–1937
Oakeley, Sir Herbert Stanley	1830–1903
Oakley, Sir John Hubert	1867–1946
Oates, Lawrence Edward Grace	1880–1912
O'Brien, Charlotte Grace	1845–1909
O'Brien, Cornelius	1843–1906
O'Brien, Ignatius John, Baron Shandon	1857–1930
O'Brien, James Francis Xavier	1828–1905
O'Brien, Peter, Baron	1842–1914
O'Brien, William	1852–1928
O'Callaghan, Sir Francis Langford	1839–1909
O'Connor, Charles Yelverton	1843–1902
O'Connor, James	1836–1910
O'Connor, Thomas Power	1848–1929
O'Conor, Charles Owen ('O'Conor Don')	1838–1906
O'Conor, Sir Nicholas Roderick	1843–1908
O'Dohert y, Kevin Izod	1823–1905

O'Doherty (formerly Kelly), Mary Anne (1826–1910). See under O'Doherty, Kevin Izod	
O'Donnell, Patrick	1856–1927
O'Dwyer, Sir Michael Francis	1864–1940
Ogden, Charles Kay	1889–1957
Ogilvie, Sir Frederick Wolff	1893–1949
Ogle, John William	1824–1905
O'Hanlon, John	1821–1905
O'Higgins, Kevin Christopher	1892–1927
Oldham, Charles James (1843–1907). See under Oldham, Henry	
Oldham, Henry	1815–1902
O'Leary John	1830–1907
Oliver, David Thomas	1863–1947
Oliver, Francis Wall	1864–1951
Oliver, Frederick Scott	1864–1934
Oliver, Samuel Pasfield	1838–1907
Oliver, Sir Thomas	1853–1942
Olivier, Sydney Haldane, Baron	1859–1943
Olpherts, Sir William	1822–1902
Olsson, Julius	1864–1942
Oman, Sir Charles William Chadwick	1860–1946
Oman, John Wood	1860–1939
Ommanney, Sir Erasmus	1814–1904
Ommanney, George Druce Wynne	1819–1902
Onslow, William Hillier, Earl of Onslow	1853–1911
Oppé, Adolph Paul	1878–1957
Oppenheim, Edward Phillips	1866–1946
Oppenheim, Lassa Francis Lawrence	1858–1919
Oppenheimer, Sir Ernest	1880–1957
Orage, Alfred Richard	1873–1934
Oram, Sir Henry John	1858–1939
Orchardson, Sir William Quiller	1832–1910
Orczy, Emma Magdalena Rosalia Marie Josepha Barbara, Baroness	1865–1947
Ord, William Miller	1834–1902
O'Rell, Max, pseudonym. See Blouet, Léon Paul	1848–1903
Ormerod, Eleanor Anne	1828–1901
Orpen, Sir William Newenham Montague	1878–1931
Orr, Alexandra Sutherland	1828–1903
Orr, William McFadden	1866–1934
Orton, Charles William Previté-. See Previté-Orton	1877–1947
Orwell, George, pseudonym. See Blair, Eric Arthur	1903–1950
Orwin, Charles Stewart	1876–1955
Osborne, Walter Frederick	1859–1903
O'Shea, John Augustus	1839–1905
O'Shea, William Henry	1840–1905
Osler, Abraham Follett	1808–1903
Osler, Sir William	1849–1919
O'Sullivan, Cornelius	1841–1907
Otté, Elise	1818–1903
Ottley, Sir Charles Langdale	1858–1932
Ouida, pseudonym. See De la Ramée, Marie Louise	1839–1908
Ouless, Walter William	1848–1933
Overton, John Henry	1835–1903
Overtoun, Baron. See White, John Campbell	1843–1908
Owen, John	1854–1926
Owen, Robert	1820–1902

Rattigan, Sir William Henry	1842–1904
Rau, Sir Benegal Narsing	1887–1953
Raven, John James	1833–1906
Raven-Hill, Leonard	1867–1942
Raverat, Gwendolen Mary	1885–1957
Raverty, Henry George	1825–1906
Ravilious, Eric William	1903–1942
Rawling, Cecil Godfrey	1870–1917
Rawlinson, George	1812–1902
Rawlinson, Sir Henry Seymour, Baron	1864–1925
Rawlinson, William George	1840–1928
Rawson, Sir Harry Holdsworth	1843–1910
Rayleigh, Baron. See Strutt, John William	1842–1919
Rayleigh, Baron. See Strutt, Robert John	1875–1947
Read, Sir Charles Hercules	1857–1929
Read, Clare Sewell	1826–1905
Read, Grantly Dick-. See Dick-Read	1890–1959
Read, Sir Herbert James	1863–1949
Read, Walter William	1855–1907
Reade, Thomas Mellard	1832–1909
Reading, Marquess of. See Isaacs, Rufus Daniel	1860–1935
Reay, Baron. See Mackay, Donald James	1839–1921
Redesdale, Baron. See Mitford, Algernon Bertram Freeman-	1837–1916
Redmayne, Sir Richard Augustine Studdert	1865–1955
Redmond, John Edward	1856–1918
Redmond, William Hoey Kearney	1861–1917
Redpath, Henry Adeney	1848–1908
Reed, Austin Leonard	1873–1954
Reed, Sir Edward James	1830–1906
Reed, Edward Tennyson	1860–1933
Reeves, Sir William Conrad	1821–1902
Regan, Charles Tate	1878–1943
Reich, Emil	1854–1910
Reid, Archibald David	1844–1908
Reid, Forrest	1875–1947
Reid, Sir George Houstoun	1845–1918
Reid, James Smith	1846–1926
Reid, Sir John Watt	1823–1909
Reid, Sir Robert Gillespie	1842–1908
Reid, Robert Threshie, Earl Loreburn	1846–1923
Reid, Sir Thomas Wemyss	1842–1905
Reilly, Sir Charles Herbert	1874–1948
Reitz, Deneys	1882–1944
Rendall, Montague John	1862–1950
Rendel, Sir Alexander Meadows	1829–1918
Rendel, George Wightwick	1833–1902
Rendel, Harry Stuart Goodhart-. See Goodhart-Rendel	1887–1959
Rendle, Alfred Barton	1865–1938
Rennell, Baron. See Rodd, James Rennell	1858–1941
Repington, Charles à Court	1858–1925
Reynolds, James Emerson	1844–1920
Reynolds, Osborne	1842–1912
Rhodes, Cecil John	1853–1902
Rhodes, Francis William	1851–1905
Rhondda, Viscount. See Thomas, David Alfred	1856–1918
Rhondda, Viscountess. See Thomas, Margaret Haig	1883–1958

Rhys, Ernest Percival	1859–1946
Rhys, Sir John	1840–1915
Richards, Sir Frederick William	1833–1912
Richardson, Ethel Florence Lindesay, 'Henry Handel Richardson'	1870–1946
Richardson, Henry Handel. See Richardson, Ethel Florence Lindesay	1870–1946
Richardson, Lewis Fry	1881–1953
Richardson, Sir Owen Willans	1879–1959
Richmond, Sir Herbert William	1871–1946
Richmond, Sir William Blake	1842–1921
Richmond and Gordon, Duke of. See Gordon-Lennox, Charles Henry	1818–1903
Ricketts, Charles de Sousy	1866–1931
Riddell, Charles James Buchanan	1817–1903
Riddell, Charlotte Eliza Lawson (Mrs. J. H. Riddell), 'F. G. Trafford'	1832–1906
Riddell, George Allardice, Baron	1865–1934
Ridding, George	1828–1904
Ridgeway, Sir Joseph West	1844–1930
Ridgeway, Sir William	1853–1926
Ridley, Henry Nicholas	1855–1956
Ridley, Sir Matthew White, Viscount	1842–1904
Rieu, Charles Pierre Henri	1820–1902
Rigby, Sir John	1834–1903
Rigg, James Harrison	1821–1909
Rigg, James McMullen	1855–1926
Ringer, Sydney	1835–1910
Ripon, Marquess of. See Robinson, George Frederick Samuel	1827–1909
Risley, Sir Herbert Hope	1851–1911
Ritchie, Anne Isabella, Lady (1837–1919). See under Ritchie, Sir Richmond Thackeray Willoughby	
Ritchie, Charles Thomson, Baron Ritchie of Dundee	1838–1906
Ritchie, David George	1853–1903
Ritchie, Sir Richmond Thackeray Willoughby	1854–1912
Rivaz, Sir Charles Montgomery	1845–1926
Riverdale, Baron. See Balfour, Arthur	1873–1957
Riviere, Briton	1840–1920
Robeck, Sir John Michael De. See De Robeck	1862–1928
Roberts, Alexander	1826–1901
Roberts, Frederick Sleigh, Earl	1832–1914
Roberts, George Henry	1869–1928
Roberts, Isaac	1829–1904
Roberts, Robert Davies	1851–1911
Roberts-Austen, Sir William Chandler	1843–1902
Robertson, Archibald	1853–1931
Robertson, Sir Charles Grant	1869–1948
Robertson, Douglas Moray Cooper Lamb Argyll	1837–1909
Robertson, George Matthew	1864–1932
Robertson, Sir George Scott	1852–1916
Robertson, James Patrick Bannerman, Baron	1845–1909
Robertson, John Mackinnon	1856–1933
Robertson, Sir Johnston Forbes-	1853–1937
Robertson, Sir Robert	1869–1949

Rutherford, William Gunion	1853–1907
Rutland, Duke of. See Manners, (Lord) John James Robert	1818–1906
Ryder, Charles Henry Dudley	1868–1945
Rye, Maria Susan	1829–1903
Rye, William Brenchley	1818–1901
Ryle, Herbert Edward	1856–1925
Ryle, John Alfred	1889–1950
Ryrie, Sir Granville de Laune	1865–1937
Sackville-West, Lionel Sackville, Baron Sackville	1827–1908
Sadleir, Michael Thomas Harvey	1888–1957
Sadler, Sir Michael Ernest	1861–1943
Saha, Meghnad. See Meghnad Saha	1893–1956
St. Aldwyn, Earl. See Hicks Beach, Sir Michael Edward	1837–1916
St. Davids, Viscount. See Philipps, Sir John Wynford	1860–1938
St. Helier, Baron. See Jeune, Francis Henry	1843–1905
St. John, Sir Spenser Buckingham	1825–1910
St. John, Vane Ireton Shaftesbury (1839–1911). See under St. John, Sir Spenser Buckingham	
St. Just, Baron. See Grenfell, Edward Charles	1870–1941
Saintsbury, George Edward Bateman	1845–1933
Saklatvala, Shapurji	1874–1936
Saladin, pseudonym. See Ross, William Stewart	1844–1906
Salaman, Charles Kensington	1814–1901
Salaman, Julia. See Goodman	1812–1906
Salaman, Redcliffe Nathan	1874–1955
Salisbury, Marquess of. See Cecil, James Edward Hubert Gascoyne-	1861–1947
Salisbury, Marquess of. See Cecil, Robert Arthur Talbot Gascoyne-	1830–1903
Salmon, Sir Eric Cecil Heygate	1896–1946
Salmon, George	1819–1904
Salmond, Sir (William) Geoffrey (Hanson)	1878–1933
Salomons, Sir Julian Emanuel	1835–1909
Salter, Sir Arthur Clavell	1859–1928
Salter, Herbert Edward	1863–1951
Salting, George	1835–1909
Salvidge, Sir Archibald Tutton James	1863–1928
Salvin, Francis Henry	1817–1904
Sambourne, Edward Linley	1844–1910
Sampson, George	1873–1950
Sampson, John	1862–1931
Sampson, Ralph Allen	1866–1939
Samson, Charles Rumney	1883–1931
Samuel, Marcus, Viscount Bearsted	1853–1927
Samuelson, Sir Bernhard	1820–1905
Sanday, William	1843–1920
Sandberg, Samuel Louis Graham	1851–1905
Sanderson, Baron. See Furniss, Henry Sanderson	1868–1939
Sanderson, Edgar	1838–1907
Sanderson, Frederick William	1857–1922
Sanderson, Sir John Scott Burdon-. See Burdon-Sanderson	1828–1905
Sanderson, Thomas Henry, Baron	1841–1923
Sanderson, Thomas James Cobden-. See Cobden-Sanderson	1840–1922
Sandham, Henry	1842–1910
Sands, Lord. See Johnston, Christopher Nicholson	1857–1934
Sandys, Frederick	1829–1904
Sandys, Sir John Edwin	1844–1922
Sanford, George Edward Langham Somerset	1840–1901
Sanger, George ('Lord' George Sanger)	1825–1911
Sankaran Nair, Sir Chettur	1857–1934
Sankey, John, Viscount	1866–1948
Sankey, Sir Richard Hieram	1829–1908
Santley, Sir Charles	1834–1922
Sapper, pseudonym. See McNeile, (Herman) Cyril	1888–1937
Sargant, Sir Charles Henry	1856–1942
Sargeaunt, John	1857–1922
Sargent, John Singer	1856–1925
Sarkar, Sir Jadunath	1870–1958
Sassoon, Sir Philip Albert Gustave David	1888–1939
Sastri, Valangiman Sankaranarayana Srinivasa	1869–1946
Satow, Sir Ernest Mason	1843–1929
Saumarez, Thomas	1827–1903
Saunders, Edward	1848–1910
Saunders, Sir Edwin	1814–1901
Saunders, Howard	1835–1907
Saunderson, Edward James	1837–1906
Savage (formerly Dell), Ethel Mary	1881–1939
Savage-Armstrong, George Francis	1845–1906
Savill, Thomas Dixon	1855–1910
Saxe-Weimar, Prince Edward of. See Edward of Saxe-Weimar	1823–1902
Saxl, Friedrich ('Fritz')	1890–1948
Sayce, Archibald Henry	1845–1933
Sayers, Dorothy Leigh	1893–1957
Schafer, Sir Edward Albert Sharpey-	1850–1935
Scharlieb, Dame Mary Ann Dacomb	1845–1930
Schiller, Ferdinand Canning Scott	1864–1937
Schlich, Sir William	1840–1925
Scholes, Percy Alfred	1877–1958
Schreiner, Olive Emilie Albertina (1855–1920). See under Schreiner, William Philip	
Schreiner, William Philip	1857–1919
Schunck, Henry Edward	1820–1903
Schuster, Sir Arthur	1851–1934
Schuster, Claud, Baron	1869–1956
Schuster, Sir Felix Otto	1854–1936
Schwabe, Randolph	1885–1948
Scott, Archibald	1837–1909
Scott, Charles Prestwich	1846–1932
Scott, Lord Charles Thomas Montagu-Douglas-	1839–1911
Scott, Clement William	1841–1904
Scott, Dukinfield Henry	1854–1934
Scott, Lord Francis George Montagu-Douglas-	1879–1952
Scott, George Herbert	1888–1930

Trench, Frederic Herbert	1865–1923
Trenchard, Hugh Montague, Viscount	1873–1956
Trent, Baron. See Boot, Jesse	1850–1931
Trevelyan, Sir Charles Philips	1870–1958
Trevelyan, Sir George Otto	1838–1928
Trevelyan, Hilda	1877–1959
Treves, Sir Frederick	1853–1923
Trevethin, Baron. See Lawrence, Alfred Tristram	1843–1936
Trevor, William Spottiswoode	1831–1907
Tristram, Ernest William	1882–1952
Tristram, Henry Baker	1822–1906
Tritton, Sir William Ashbee	1875–1946
Trotter, Wilfred Batten Lewis	1872–1939
Troubridge, Sir Ernest Charles Thomas	1862–1926
Troubridge, Sir Thomas Hope	1895–1949
Troup, Robert Scott	1874–1939
Trueman, Sir Arthur Elijah	1894–1956
Truman, Edwin Thomas	1818–1905
Truscot, Bruce, *pseudonym*. See Peers, Edgar Allison	1891–1952
Tshekedi Khama	1905–1959
Tucker, Alfred Robert	1849–1914
Tucker, Sir Charles	1838–1935
Tucker, Henry William	1830–1902
Tuckwell, Gertrude Mary	1861–1951
Tuke, Henry Scott	1858–1929
Tupper, Sir Charles	1821–1915
Tupper, Sir Charles Lewis	1848–1910
Turing, Alan Mathison	1912–1954
Turnbull, Hubert Maitland	1875–1955
Turner, Sir Ben	1863–1942
Turner, Charles Edward	1831–1903
Turner, Cuthbert Hamilton	1860–1930
Turner, George Grey	1877–1951
Turner, Herbert Hall	1861–1930
Turner, James Smith	1832–1904
Turner, Walter James Redfern	1889–1946
Turner, Sir William	1832–1916
Turnor, Christopher Hatton	1873–1940
Turpin, Edmund Hart	1835–1907
Tutton, Alfred Edwin Howard	1864–1938
Tweed, John	1869–1933
Tweedmouth, Baron. See Marjoribanks, Edward	1849–1909
Tweedsmuir, Baron. See Buchan, John	1875–1940
Twyman, Frank	1876–1959
Tyabji, Badruddin	1844–1906
Tyler, Thomas	1826–1902
Tylor, Sir Edward Burnett	1832–1917
Tylor, Joseph John	1851–1901
Tynan, Katharine. See Hinkson	1861–1931
Tyndale-Biscoe, Cecil Earle	1863–1949
Tyrrell, George	1861–1909
Tyrrell, Robert Yelverton	1844–1914
Tyrrell, William George, Baron	1866–1947
Tyrwhitt, Sir Reginald Yorke	1870–1951
Tyrwhitt-Wilson, Sir Gerald Hugh, Baron Berners	1883–1950
Ullswater, Viscount. See Lowther, James William	1855–1949
Underhill, Edward Bean	1813–1901
Underhill, Evelyn (Mrs. Stuart Moore)	1875–1941
Unwin, Sir Raymond	1863–1940

Unwin, William Cawthorne	1838–1933
Ure, Alexander, Baron Strathclyde	1853–1928
Urwick, William	1826–1905
Uthwatt, Augustus Andrewes, Baron	1879–1949
Vachell, Horace Annesley	1861–1955
Vallance, Gerald Aylmer	1892–1955
Vallance, William Fleming	1827–1904
Vanbrugh, Dame Irene	1872–1949
Vanbrugh, Violet	1867–1942
Vandam, Albert Dresden	1843–1903
Vane-Tempest-Stewart, Charles Stewart, Marquess of Londonderry	1852–1915
Vane-Tempest-Stewart, Charles Stewart Henry, Marquess of Londonderry	1878–1949
Van Horne, Sir William Cornelius	1843–1915
Vansittart, Edward Westby	1818–1904
Vansittart, Robert Gilbert, Baron	1881–1957
Vaughan, Bernard John	1847–1922
Vaughan, David James	1825–1905
Vaughan, Herbert Alfred	1832–1903
Vaughan, Kate	1852?–1903
Vaughan, William Wyamar	1865–1938
Vaughan Williams, Ralph	1872–1958
Veitch, Sir Harry James	1840–1924
Veitch, James Herbert	1868–1907
Venn, John	1834–1923
Ventris, Michael George Francis	1922–1956
Verdon-Roe, Sir (Edwin) Alliott Verdon	1877–1958
Vereker, John Standish Surtees Prendergast, Viscount Gort	1886–1946
Verney, Margaret Maria, Lady	1844–1930
Vernon-Harcourt, Leveson Francis	1839–1907
Verrall, Arthur Woollgar	1851–1912
Vestey, William, Baron	1859–1940
Vezin, Hermann	1829–1910
Vezin (formerly Mrs. Charles Young), Jane Elizabeth	1827–1902
Vickers, Kenneth Hotham	1881–1958
Victoria Adelaide Mary Louise, Princess Royal of Great Britain and German Empress	1840–1901
Victoria Alexandra Olga Mary, princess of Great Britain	1868–1935
Villiers, George Herbert Hyde, Earl of Clarendon	1877–1955
Villiers, John Henry De, Baron. See De Villiers	1842–1914
Villiers, Margaret Elizabeth Child-, Countess of Jersey	1849–1945
Villiers, Victor Albert George Child-, Earl of Jersey	1845–1915
Vincent, Sir (Charles Edward) Howard	1849–1908
Vincent, Sir Edgar, Viscount D'Abernon	1857–1941
Vincent, James Edmund	1857–1909
Vines, Sydney Howard	1849–1934
Vinogradoff, Sir Paul Gavrilovitch	1854–1925
Voigt, Frederick Augustus	1892–1957
Von Hügel, Friedrich, Baron of the Holy Roman Empire	1852–1925

Watts, George Frederic	1817–1904
Watts, Henry Edward	1826–1904
Watts, John	1861–1902
Watts, Sir Philip	1846–1926
Watts-Dunton, Walter Theodore	1832–1914
Wauchope, Sir Arthur Grenfell	1874–1947
Waugh, Benjamin	1839–1908
Waugh, James	1831–1905
Wavell, Archibald Percival, Earl	1883–1950
Wavell, Arthur John Byng	1882–1916
Waverley, Viscount. See Anderson, John	1882–1958
Weaver, Sir Lawrence	1876–1930
Webb, Alfred John	1834–1908
Webb, Allan Becher	1839–1907
Webb, Sir Aston	1849–1930
Webb, Clement Charles Julian	1865–1954
Webb, Francis William	1836–1906
Webb, (Martha) Beatrice (1858–1943). See under Webb, Sidney James	
Webb, Mary Gladys	1881–1927
Webb, Philip Speakman	1831–1915
Webb, Sidney James, Baron Passfield	1859–1947
Webb, Thomas Ebenezer	1821–1903
Webb-Johnson, Alfred Edward, Baron	1880–1958
Webber, Charles Edmund	1838–1904
Webster, Benjamin	1864–1947
Webster, Dame Mary Louise (May) (1865–1948). See under Webster, Benjamin	
Webster, Richard Everard, Viscount Alverstone	1842–1915
Webster, Wentworth	1829–1907
Wedgwood, Josiah Clement, Baron	1872–1943
Wedgwood, Sir Ralph Lewis	1874–1956
Weeks, Ronald Morce, Baron	1890–1960
Weir, Andrew, Baron Inverforth	1865–1955
Weir, Sir Cecil McAlpine	1890–1960
Weir, Harrison William	1824–1906
Weir, William Douglas, Viscount	1877–1959
Weizmann, Chaim	1874–1952
Welby, Reginald Earle, Baron	1832–1915
Welch, Adam Cleghorn	1864–1943
Weldon, Walter Frank Raphael	1860–1906
Wellcome, Sir Henry Solomon	1853–1936
Welldon, James Edward Cowell	1854–1937
Wellesley, Dorothy Violet, Duchess of Wellington	1889–1956
Wellesley, Sir George Greville	1814–1901
Wellesley, Sir Victor Alexander Augustus Henry	1876–1954
Wellington, Duchess of. See Wellesley, Dorothy Violet	1889–1956
Wells, Henry Tanworth	1828–1903
Wells, Herbert George	1866–1946
Wemyss, Rosslyn Erskine, Baron Wester Wemyss	1864–1933
Wemyss-Charteris-Douglas, Francis, Earl of Wemyss	1818–1914
Wernher, Sir Julius Charles	1850–1912
West, Sir Algernon Edward	1832–1921
West, Edward William	1824–1905
West, Lionel Sackville-, Baron Sackville. See Sackville-West	1827–1908
West, Sir Raymond	1832–1912

Westall, William (Bury)	1834–1903
Westcott, Brooke Foss	1825–1901
Wester Wemyss, Baron. See Wemyss, Rosslyn Erskine	1864–1933
Westlake, John	1828–1913
Westland, Sir James	1842–1903
Weston, Dame Agnes Elizabeth	1840–1918
Weston, Sir Aylmer Gould Hunter-	1864–1940
Weston, Frank	1871–1924
Wet, Christiaan Rudolph De. See De Wet	1854–1922
Weyman, Stanley John	1855–1928
Weymouth, Richard Francis	1822–1902
Wharton, Sir William James Lloyd	1843–1905
Wheatley, John	1869–1930
Wheeler, Sir William Ireland de Courcy	1879–1943
Wheelhouse, Claudius Galen	1826–1909
Whetham, William Cecil Dampier. See Dampier	1867–1952
Whibley, Charles	1859–1930
Whibley, Leonard	1863–1941
Whipple, Robert Stewart	1871–1953
Whistler, James Abbott McNeill	1834–1903
Whistler, Reginald John (Rex)	1905–1944
Whitby, Sir Lionel Ernest Howard	1895–1956
White, Claude Grahame-. See Grahame-White	1879–1959
White, Sir (Cyril) Brudenell (Bingham)	1876–1940
White, Sir George Stuart	1835–1912
White, Henry Julian	1859–1934
White, John Campbell, Baron Overtoun	1843–1908
White, Leonard Charles	1897–1955
White, William Hale, 'Mark Rutherford'	1831–1913
White, Sir William Hale-. See Hale-White	1857–1949
White, Sir William Henry	1845–1913
Whitehead, Alfred North	1861–1947
Whitehead, John Henry Constantine	1904–1960
Whitehead, Robert	1823–1905
Whiteing, Richard	1840–1928
Whiteley, William	1831–1907
Whiteley, William	1881–1955
Whiteway, Sir William Vallance	1828–1908
Whitla, Sir William	1851–1933
Whitley, John Henry	1866–1935
Whitley, William Thomas	1858–1942
Whitman, Alfred Charles	1860–1910
Whitmore, Sir George Stoddart	1830–1903
Whitney, James Pounder	1857–1939
Whittaker, Sir Edmund Taylor	1873–1956
Whitten Brown, Sir Arthur. See Brown	1886–1948
Whitty, Dame Mary Louise (May) (1865–1948). See under Webster, Benjamin	1864–1947
Whitworth, Geoffrey Arundel	1883–1951
Whitworth, William Allen	1840–1905
Whymper, Edward	1840–1911
Whymper, Josiah Wood	1813–1903
Whyte, Alexander	1836–1921
Wickham, Edward Charles	1834–1910

PRINTED IN GREAT BRITAIN
AT THE UNIVERSITY PRESS, OXFORD
BY VIVIAN RIDLER
PRINTER TO THE UNIVERSITY